BUILD YOUR CROP PROTECTION LIBRARY
TO LEAD YOU INTO THE NEXT MILLENNIUM

"A New Century of Leadership"

All New!
FARM CHEMICALS
HANDBOOK 2000

Enhanced coverage of:
- Fertilizers
- Crop Protection
- Regulatory Compliance
- Sourcing

Special Offer: *Just $92.00*
Available in January 2000

Item # 1 **FARM CHEMICALS HANDBOOK 2000**
Item # 1A **ELECTRONIC PESTICIDE DICTIONARY**

"Weed Control Solutions for the New Millennium"

The All-Crop, Quick Reference
Weed Control MANUAL
Weed Control Solutions For The New Millennium
2000

- Enhanced Seed
- Traditional Weed Control
- Weed ID Color Photos
- Suppliers Directory
- Indexed by crop, weed, and product
- Use Recommendations

Price $59.95 each

Item # 2 **WEED CONTROL MANUAL 2000**
Item # 2A **WCM-ELECTRONIC**

"Current Solutions for Pest and Disease Control"

Insect and Disease Control Guide
Accurate, up-to-date answers for today's pest and disease problems
- Detailed product listings by crop
- Over 100 color photos
- Complete Worker Protection info
Introducing IDCG-E

- Contains Color ID Photos
- Complete worker Protection
- Indexed by crop, insect, and product
- Use recommendations

Price $54.00 each

Item # 3 **INSECT and DISEASE CONTROL GUIDE**
Item # 3A **IDCG-ELECTRONIC**

MEISTERPRO
reference guides

VEGETABLE INSECT MANAGEMENT
With emphasis on the Midwest

- Photos
- Charts
- Insects and IPM

Price $54.00 Hard Cover
$40.00 Soft Cover

Item # 4 **VEGETABLE INSECT MANAGEMENT - HARD**
Item # 4A **VEGETABLE INSECT MANAGEMENT - SOFT**

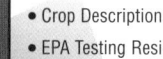

FOOD and FEED CROPS of the United States
Second Edition, Revised
A Descriptive List Classified According to Potentials for Pesticide Residues
A Regulatory Food Safety Focus
G.M. Markle, J.J. Baron and B.A. Schneider

- Crop Descriptions
- EPA Testing Residue Guidelines
- Crop Classifications
- Scientific and Common Crop Names

Price $34.95

Item # 5 **FOOD and FEED CROPS of the U.S.**

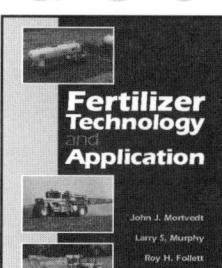

Fertilizer Technology and Application
John J. Mortvedt
Larry S. Murphy
Roy H. Follett

- Physical and Chemical Compositions
- Application Equipment and Technology
- More than 110 Illustrations
- Covers the Most Common Fertilizers

Price $32.00

Item # 6 **FERTILIZER TECHNOLOGY and APPLICATION**

IT'S EASY TO ORDER

Call: 440/942-2000 or 1-800-572-7740 (in U.S. only) • Fax: 440/942-0662
Email: fchb_circ@meisterpubl.com • Website: www.meisterpro.com
or fill out the order form below and mail to:
Meister Publishing Company, 37733 Euclid Ave, Willoughby, OH 44094, U.S.A

Name _____

Co. Name _____

Occupation and Title _____

Address _____

City _____ State _____ Zip _____

Country _____

Phone (_____) _____ Fax (_____) _____

E-Mail _____

☐ Check enclosed (Make checks payable to Meister Publishing Company. All International
☐ Bill Me   orders must be pre-paid. Check must be in U.S. funds, drawn on a U.S. bank)

WCM00

Charge my: ☐ VISA   ☐ Mastercard   ☐ AMEX   ☐ Discover

Account # _____ Exp. date _____/_____

Signature _____

THE MORE YOU BUY - THE MORE YOU SAVE
TAKE $5.00 OFF THE PRICE PER ITEM ORDERED UP TO $20.00

Item No.	Description	Qty.	Price

D1242538

MERCHANDISE TOTAL	
SHIPPING: (U.S. only) $8.00 for 1st item. $4.00 each additional item (All other countries) $35.00 airmail for 1st item. $15.00 each additional item	
DISCOUNT: Take $5.00 off the price per item ordered up to $20.00	
TAX: U.S. residents of CA, FL, IL, NY, OH, TN, WA add applicable sales tax Canadian residents add GST tax	
TOTAL AMOUNT DUE	

MEISTER**PRO**
reference guides

Visit Our Website
www.meisterpro.com

**FARM
CHEMICALS
HANDBOOK**

EPD

INSECT AND
**DISEASE
CONTROL
GUIDE**

IDCG-E

Communication and Information Center

for Worldwide Specialized Agriculture

**VEGETABLE
INSECT
MANAGEMENT**

**FOOD AND FEED
CROPS OF THE
UNITED STATES**

**WEED CONTROL
MANUAL**

WCM-E

**FERTILIZER TECHNOLOGY
AND APPLICATION**

Place
First Class
Postage
Here

Meister Publishing Company
Attn: MeisterPro Reference Department
37733 Euclid Avenue
Willoughby OH 44094-5992

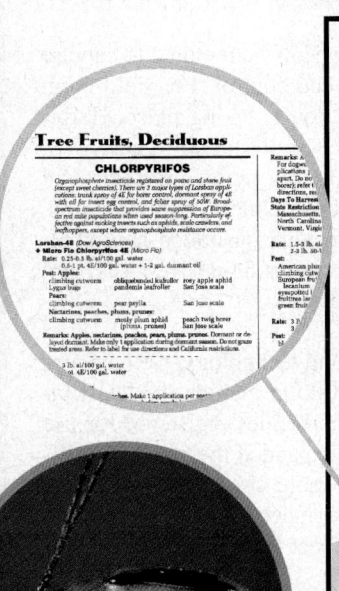

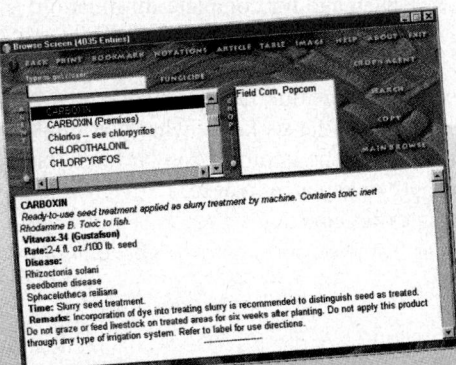

The All Crop, Quick Reference
Weed Control
MANUAL
Weed Control Solutions For The New Millennium

Plus! Complete Worker Protection Info & Comprehensive Indexes!

Volume 32
2000

Cover design
by Susan D'Angelo

Foreword

Welcome to the Weed Control Manual 2000!

With this all-new edition we have attempted to capture the astonishing advances in weed control. For field corn, soybeans, and cotton, a revolution is taking place. Herbicide-resistant seed systems such as Roundup Ready, STS, Liberty Link, and BXN are quickly replacing traditional weed control systems. This new technology solves some tough weed problems, but can also introduce new challenges. Our detailed reports on pages 84-87, 128-131, and 166-167 will help you sort it all out.

In addition to new trends and technology, we have updated Weed Control Manual 2000 to include the latest information – by crop – on all herbicides registered for use in the United States. We have expanded the weed identification section to include even more color photos. And of course, we have revised and expanded all of the great coverage that you have come to expect from the Weed Control Manual:

- Use Reminders, for product comparisons and application tips.
- Weed Efficacy Charts, to help determine which herbicides are the most effective in controlling weeds in the field.
- Our Worker Protection Standard chart, to show you what should be worn in the field when applying herbicides and what notice is required.
- Crop, Product, and Weed indexes – with both common and scientific names – to help you quickly find the control information you need.

Our new WCM-E companion software has been completely redesigned and updated as well. If you have a computer and you didn't purchase the software when you bought this book, we urge you to reconsider. This powerful new package runs on almost all popular Windows® and MacOS® computers, and gives you unprecedented access to the wealth of information in the Weed Control Manual. Please see the WCM-E web site for complete information: **www.meisterpro.com/wcme/**

We're very excited about this new edition, and we hope that you are too. Please let us know what you think about it. Our address and phone numbers can be found on the left side of this page; or zap an e-mail to:
wcm_edit@meisternet.com.
We'd love to hear from you.
– The Editors

Editorial Advisory Board

Dr. Bill Curran

Dr. Curran is Associate Professor of Weed Science at Penn State University, joining the faculty in 1990, after receiving his Ph.D from the University of Illinois. He received his bachelor's degree at Colorado State University and his master's from Washington State University. At Penn State, he has statewide responsibilities for weed science extension and research in agronomic crops. He is also an active member of the American Society of Agronomy, the Weed Science Society of American (WSSA), the North Central Society of Weed Science, and the Northeastern Weed Science Society. He is the Northeastern representative to the WSSA board of directors.

Dr. Rick Foster

Dr. Foster is an associate professor with responsibility for extension and research of insect pests of vegetables and fruit in the Department of Entomology at Purdue University. He received his B.A. from Southern Illinois University, his M.S. from the University of Illinois, and his Ph.D. from Iowa State University. He served on the faculty at the University of Florida for four years before accepting the position at Purdue in 1988. Dr. Foster's research deals with all aspects of pest management, including sampling; development of management decision rules; and cultural, biological, and chemical control. He is actively involved in the development and implementation of IPM programs on vegetables and fruit.

Dr. Robert Holm

Dr. Holm is Executive Director of the IR-4 Project at Rutgers University, taking on that position in 1998. He received his Ph.D in Plant Physiology and Biochemistry from Purdue University. He first worked at Diamond Shamrock Corp. in Ohio before joining Mobil Crop Chemical in New Jersey in 1980 where he was in charge of synthesis, biological evaluation, biochemistry, residue chemistry/environmental fate, formulation, and the research farm. He then went to Rhone Poulenc, moving to Research Triangle Park, N.C. in 1987 to become Director of Field Research and Product Development. In 1991, he moved to California to work with Valent U.S.A. Corp. as vice-president of technology.

Robert H. McCarty

Robert McCarty is Director of the Bureau of Plant Industry, Mississippi Department of Agriculture and Commerce. His duties include supervision of personnel responsible for administering state laws regulating pesticides and pesticide applications. He is responsible for all pesticide regulatory programs and pesticide applicator certification and licensing programs in the state. A former president of the Association of American Pesticide Control Officials, he has served on the States/FIFRA issues Research and Evaluation Group working group on enforcement and certification since 1975. McCarty received his B.S. and M.S. from Mississippi State University.

Dr. John J. Mortvedt

Dr. Mortvedt is a retired soil fertility specialist. Recently he was interim Extension Soil Specialist with Colorado State University. He was formerly with the National Fertilizer and Environmental Research Center (NFERC) of the Tennessee Valley Authority (TVA). With NFERC from 1962-1993, he was involved mainly in research and development of secondary and micronutrient fertilizers, and heavy metal contaminants in phosphate fertilizers and industrial by-products. Dr. Mortvedt just published *Fertilizer Technology and Application*, which is sold through Meister Publishing Co. He is a co-editor of Micronutrients in Agriculture, and a former president and editor-in-chief of the Soil Science Society of America. He received his B.S. and M.S. in soil science from South Dakota State University and his Ph.D. in soil chemistry from the University of Wisconsin.

Table of Contents

Volume 32 ▪ 2000

Exclusive Enhanced Seed Coverage

Field Corn
IMI (Clearfield)	85
Liberty Link	84
Roundup Ready	87
SR	86

Soybeans
Roundup Ready	128
STS	131

Cotton
BXN	166
Roundup Ready	167

Upfront
Weed Identification
Broadleaf Weed Identification Flowcharts	10
Broadleaf Photo Identification Guide	24
Company Profiles	57
Grasses Identification Flowcharts	40
Grasses Photo Identification Guide	46
Quick Glossary	66

Weed Management
Formulation Guide	64
Know Your Nozzles	59

Regulatory Compliance
Quick Guide To Worker Protection Clothing & Equipment	58
WPS Rules Review	70
WPS Chart	72

Herbicide Management
Herbicide Classification	61

1 – Field Corn
Enhanced Seed Coverage	84
Use Reminders	88
Weed Efficacy Charts	96
Herbicide Listings	101

2 – Soybeans
Enhanced Seed Coverage	128
Use Reminders	132
Weed Efficacy Charts	137
Herbicide Listings	143

3 – Cotton
Enhanced Seed Coverage	166
Use Reminders	168
Weed Efficacy Charts	171
Herbicide Listings	173

4 – Small Grains
Weed Efficacy Charts	184

Herbicide Listings
Barley	211
Oats	223
Rye	231
Spring Wheat	199
Winter Wheat	186

5 – Other Field Crops
Weed Efficacy Charts	238

Herbicide Listings
Castor Beans	240
Flax	240
Guar Beans	242
Hops	243
Kenaf	244
Mint	244
Mung Beans	246
Oil Seed Crops	247
Peanuts	248
Rice	253
Safflower	258
Sorghum	259
Sugar Beets	269
Sugarcane	272
Sunflower	279
Tobacco	281

6 – Vegetables
Use Reminders	286
Weed Efficacy Charts	289

Herbicide Listings
Artichokes	292
Asparagus	293

Beans..297
Carrots, Parsley, Parsnips..................301
Celery...303
Cole Crops...305
Cucurbits...307
Eggplant...309
Garbanzos..311
Garlic...312
Greens..314
Herbs & Spices....................................316
Horseradish..316
Lentils..317
Lettuce, Endive....................................318
Okra...320
Onions..320
Peas..324
Peppers...327
Potatoes..329
Radishes...333
Rhubarb..333
Southern Peas.......................................335
Spinach...336
Sweet Corn, Popcorn...........................337
Sweet Potatoes.....................................345
Table Beets...346
Tomatoes..347

7 – Fruits & Nuts

Use Reminders.......................................**352**
Weed Efficacy Charts..........................**354**
Herbicide Listings
    Nuts...384
    Small Fruits...356
    Tree Fruits (citrus)..............................363
    Tree Fruits (deciduous).......................370
    Tree Fruits (subtropical).....................379

8 – Turf, Ornamentals, & Woody Plants

Use Reminders.......................................**394**
Weed Efficacy Charts..........................**396**
Herbicide Listings
    Grasses For Seed Production................411
    Established Lawns And Turf..................399
    Lawn And Turf Seedbeds......................399
    Newly Sprigged/Seeded Turf................399
    Ornamentals And Woody Plants............418
    Turf Grasses For Sod Production...........415

9 – Other Uses

Use Reminders.......................................**430**
Weed Efficacy Charts..........................**432**
Herbicide Listings
    Brush Control......................................436
    Conservation Reserve Program.............442
    Fallow Land...447
    Forage (alfalfa, clover, est. legumes)...455
    Noncropland..467
    Pastures And Rangeland.......................460

10 – Aquatic

Use Reminders.......................................**490**
Weed Efficacy Charts..........................**492**
Herbicide Listings
    Still Water...493
    Moving Water......................................497

Indexes

Crop Index...**502**
Product Index......................................**504**
Weed Index...**520**
Suppliers' Directory...........................**561**

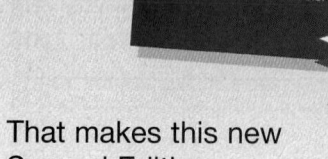

Broadleaf Weeds Photo Index

Weed Flowcharts

Northern broadleaf weeds 10
Western broadleaf weeds 14
Southern broadleaf weeds .18

Bigroot morningglory 24
Buffalobur .24
Bull thistle .24
Burcucumber 25
Canada thistle 25
Common chickweed 25
Common cocklebur 26
Common lambsquarters 26
Common milkweed 26
Common purslane 27
Common ragweed 27
Common sunflower 27
Cutleaf groundcherry 28
Dayflower .28
Eastern black nightshade 28
Field bindweed 28
Field pennycress 29
Giant ragweed 29
Hairy nightshade 29
Hedge bindweed 29
Hemp dogbane 30
Honeyvine milkweed 30
Hophornbeam copperleaf 30
Horseweed 30
Ivyleaf morningglory 30
Jimsonweed 31
Kochia 31
Ladysthumb smartweed 31

Musk thistle 32
Pennsylvania smartweed 32
Prickly lettuce 32
Prickly sida 33
Prostrate pigweed 33
Prostrate spurge 33
Purple loosestrife 33
Redroot pigweed 34
Shepherdspurse 34
Smooth groundcherry 34
Smooth pigweed 35
Swamp smartweed 35
Spiny sowthistle 35
Tall morningglory 35
Tall waterhemp 36
Tansymustard 36
Velvetleaf .36
Venice mallow 36
Wild buckwheat 37
Wild cucumber 37
Wild mustard 37

Comparison photos
Hairy pigweed vs. smooth pigweed . . .38
Pigweed vs. waterhemp 38
Venice mallow vs. velvetleaf 38
Jimsonweed vs. common
    cocklebur 38
Prickly sida vs. Venice mallow 38

Broadleaf Weed Seedlings

Flowchart for Northern Broadleaf Weeds

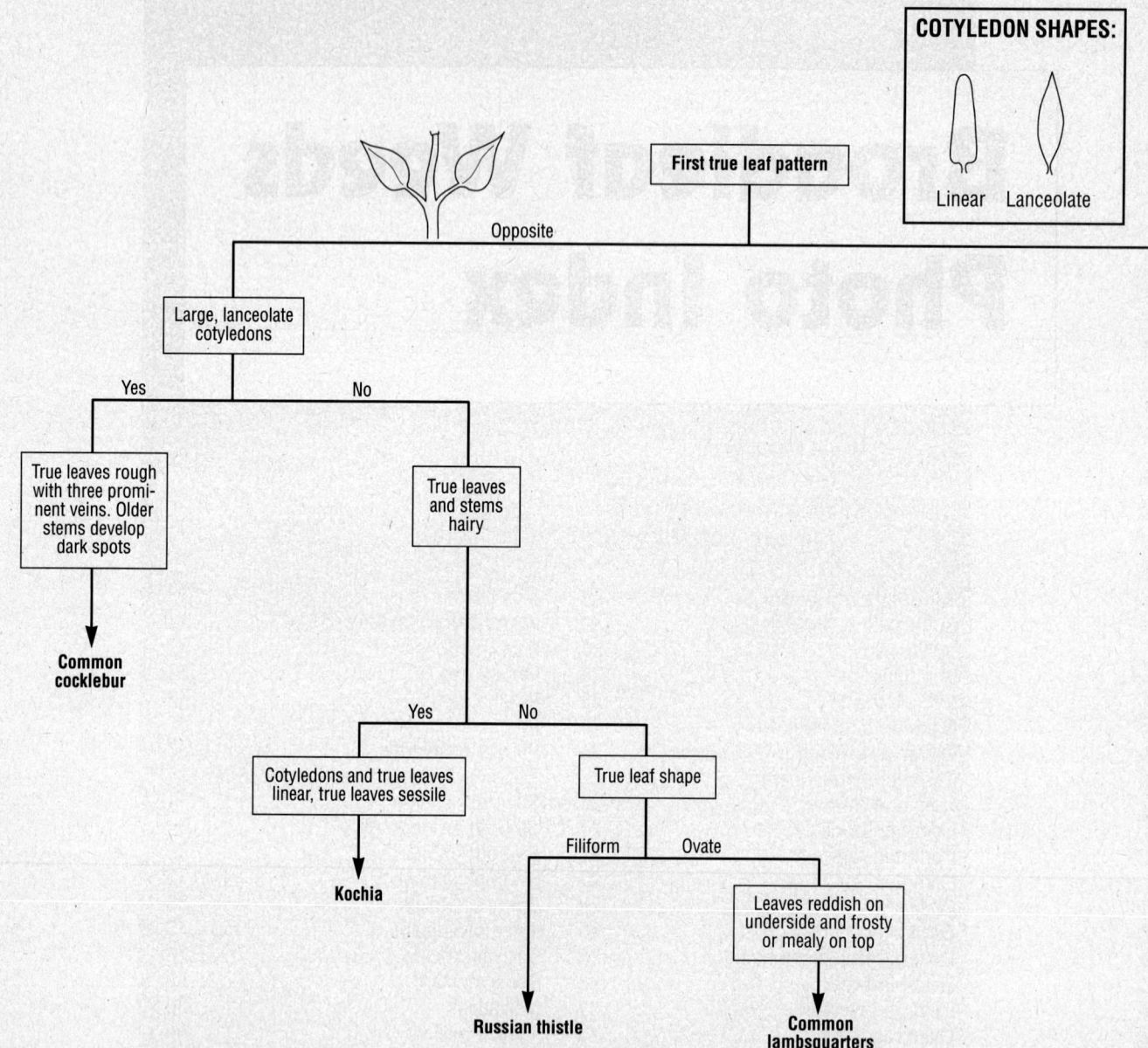

COTYLEDON SHAPES:

Linear   Lanceolate

First true leaf pattern

Opposite

Large, lanceolate cotyledons

Yes — True leaves rough with three prominent veins. Older stems develop dark spots → **Common cocklebur**

No — True leaves and stems hairy

Yes — Cotyledons and true leaves linear, true leaves sessile → **Kochia**

No — True leaf shape

Filiform → **Russian thistle**

Ovate → Leaves reddish on underside and frosty or mealy on top → **Common lambsquarters**

Source: Weed Identification Technical Training Manual, American Cyanamid.

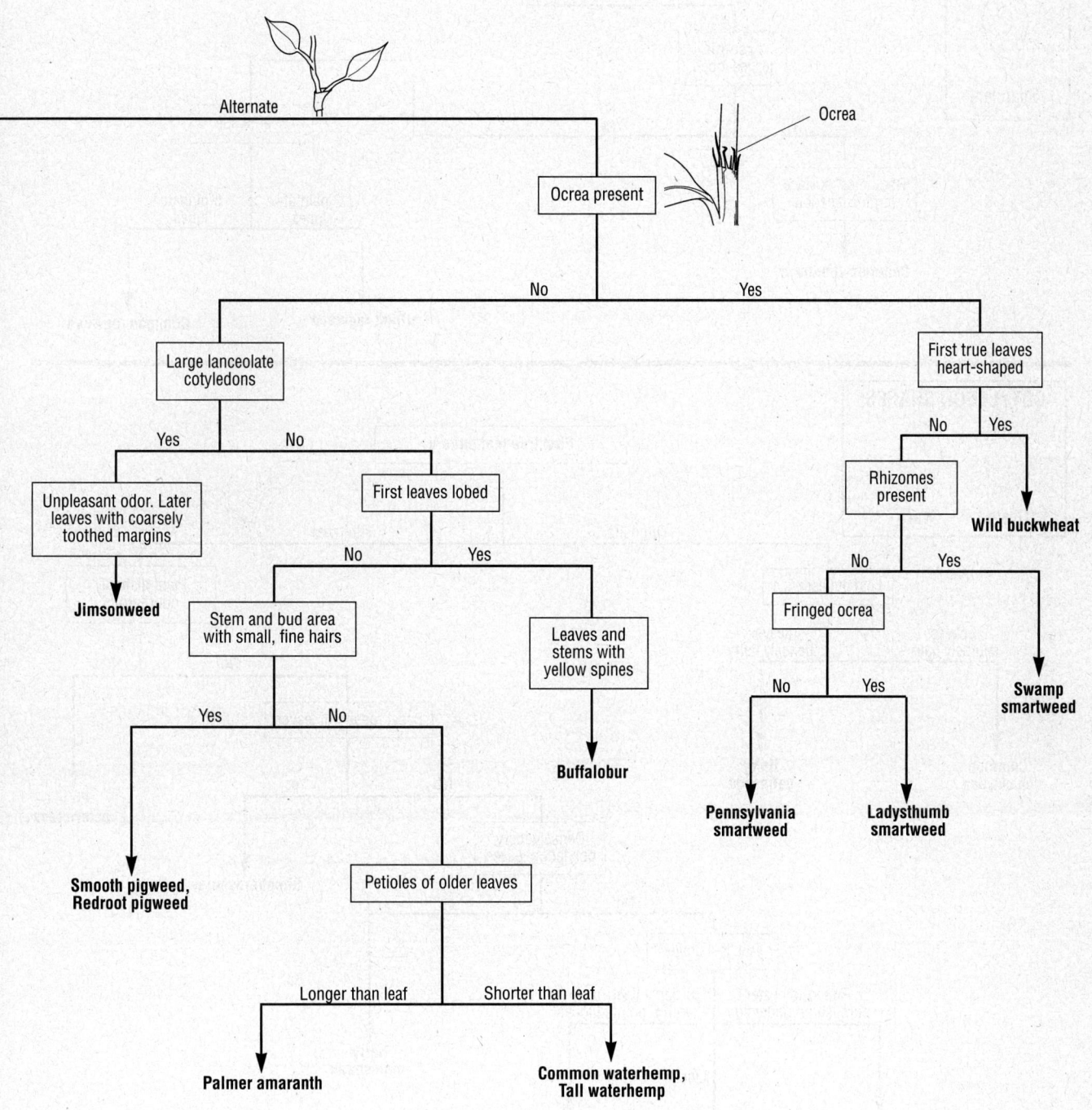

Alternate

Ocrea

Ocrea present

No — Yes

No branch (Alternate, No ocrea):

Large lanceolate cotyledons

Yes — No

Unpleasant odor. Later leaves with coarsely toothed margins

Jimsonweed

First leaves lobed

No — Yes

Stem and bud area with small, fine hairs

Leaves and stems with yellow spines

Buffalobur

Yes — No

Smooth pigweed, Redroot pigweed

Petioles of older leaves

Longer than leaf — Shorter than leaf

Palmer amaranth

Common waterhemp, Tall waterhemp

Yes branch (Ocrea present):

First true leaves heart-shaped

No — Yes

Rhizomes present

Wild buckwheat

No — Yes

Fringed ocrea

Swamp smartweed

No — Yes

Pennsylvania smartweed

Ladysthumb smartweed

Broadleaf Weed Seedlings

Flowchart for Northern Broadleaf Weeds

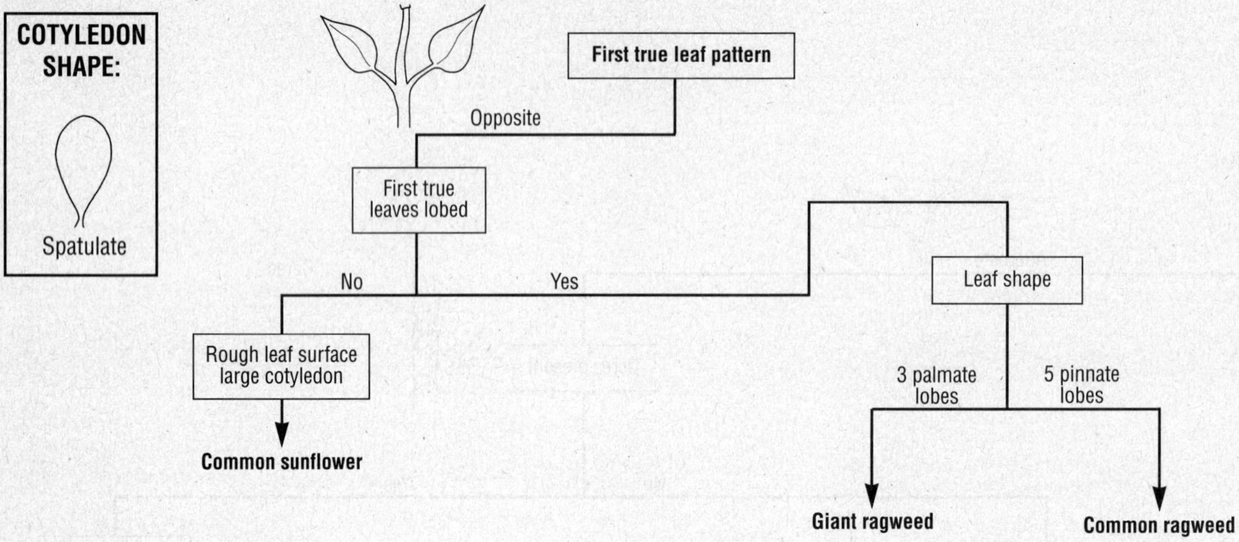

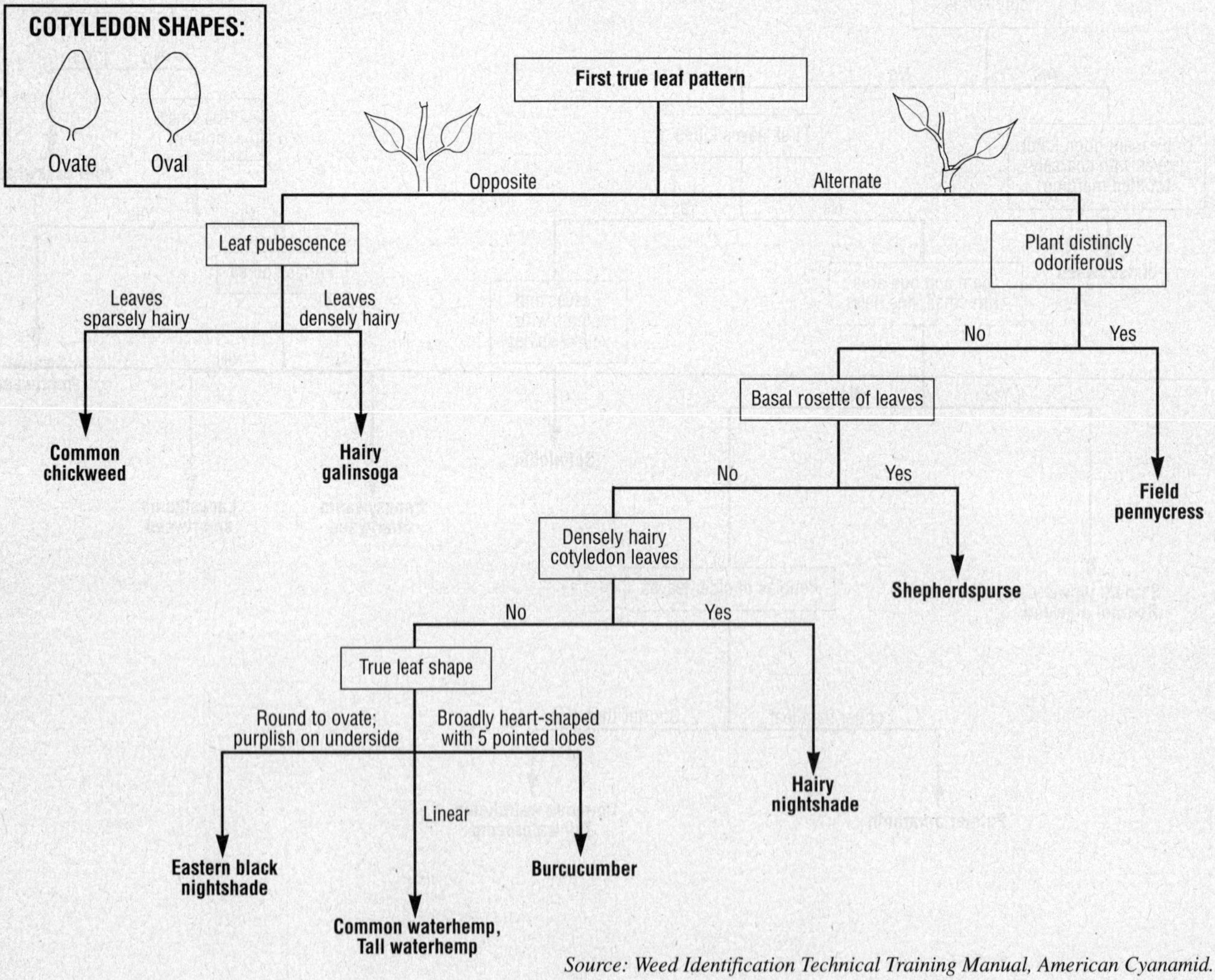

COTYLEDON SHAPE:

Spatulate

First true leaf pattern

Opposite

First true leaves lobed

No → Rough leaf surface large cotyledon → **Common sunflower**

Yes → Leaf shape

3 palmate lobes → **Giant ragweed**

5 pinnate lobes → **Common ragweed**

COTYLEDON SHAPES:

Ovate   Oval

First true leaf pattern

Opposite → Leaf pubescence

Leaves sparsely hairy → **Common chickweed**

Leaves densely hairy → **Hairy galinsoga**

Alternate → Plant distincly odoriferous

No → Basal rosette of leaves

Yes → **Field pennycress**

Basal rosette of leaves:
No → Densely hairy cotyledon leaves

Yes → **Shepherdspurse**

Densely hairy cotyledon leaves:
No → True leaf shape

Yes → **Hairy nightshade**

True leaf shape:
Round to ovate; purplish on underside → **Eastern black nightshade**

Linear → **Common waterhemp, Tall waterhemp**

Broadly heart-shaped with 5 pointed lobes → **Burcucumber**

Source: Weed Identification Technical Training Manual, American Cyanamid.

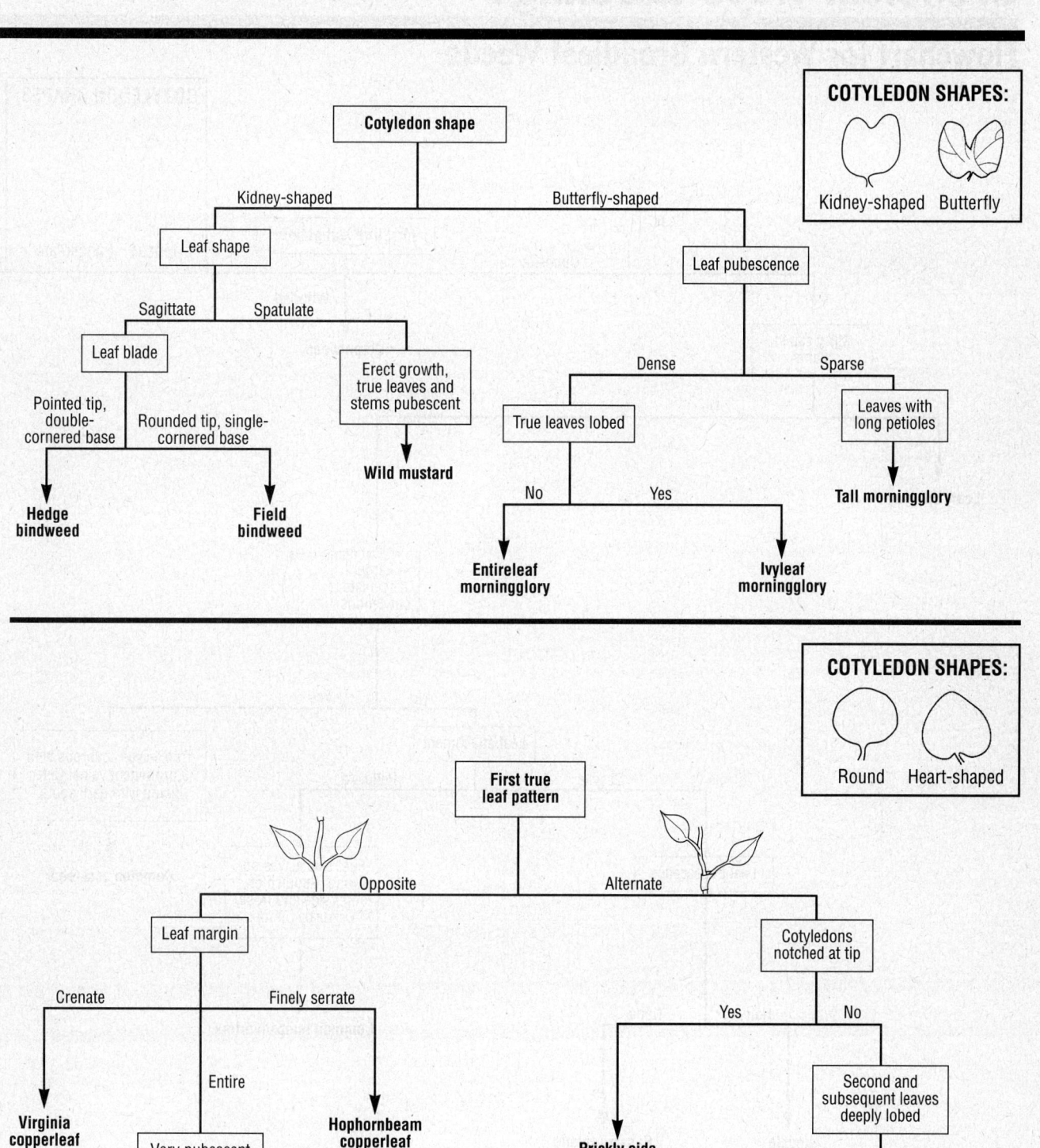

Cotyledon shape

COTYLEDON SHAPES:

Kidney-shaped   Butterfly

Kidney-shaped

Butterfly-shaped

Leaf shape

Leaf pubescence

Sagittate

Spatulate

Leaf blade

Erect growth, true leaves and stems pubescent

Dense

Sparse

Pointed tip, double-cornered base

Rounded tip, single-cornered base

Wild mustard

True leaves lobed

Leaves with long petioles

Hedge bindweed

Field bindweed

No

Yes

Tall morningglory

Entireleaf morningglory

Ivyleaf morningglory

COTYLEDON SHAPES:

Round   Heart-shaped

First true leaf pattern

Opposite

Alternate

Leaf margin

Cotyledons notched at tip

Crenate

Finely serrate

Yes

No

Entire

Virginia copperleaf

Hophornbeam copperleaf

Prickly sida

Second and subsequent leaves deeply lobed

Very pubescent with strong odor

Yes

No

Devilsclaw

Venice mallow

True leaves heart-shaped and densely pubescent

Venice mallow

Velvetleaf

Broadleaf Weed Seedlings

Flowchart for Western Broadleaf Weeds

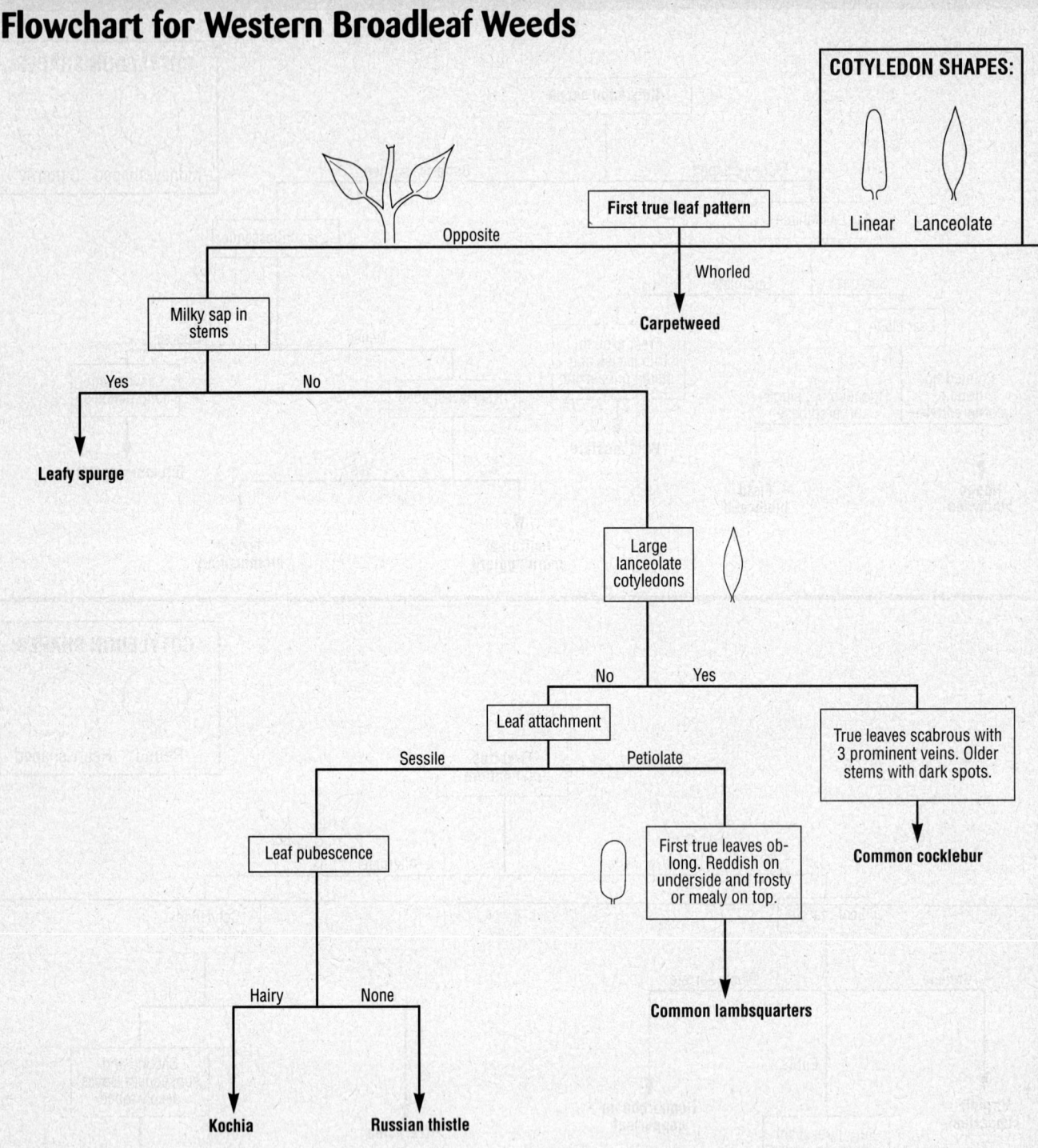

COTYLEDON SHAPES:

Linear   Lanceolate

First true leaf pattern

Opposite

Whorled

Carpetweed

Milky sap in stems

Yes

No

Leafy spurge

Large lanceolate cotyledons

No

Yes

Leaf attachment

True leaves scabrous with 3 prominent veins. Older stems with dark spots.

Sessile

Petiolate

Common cocklebur

Leaf pubescence

First true leaves oblong. Reddish on underside and frosty or mealy on top.

Hairy

None

Common lambsquarters

Kochia

Russian thistle

Source: Weed Identification Technical Training Manual, American Cyanamid.

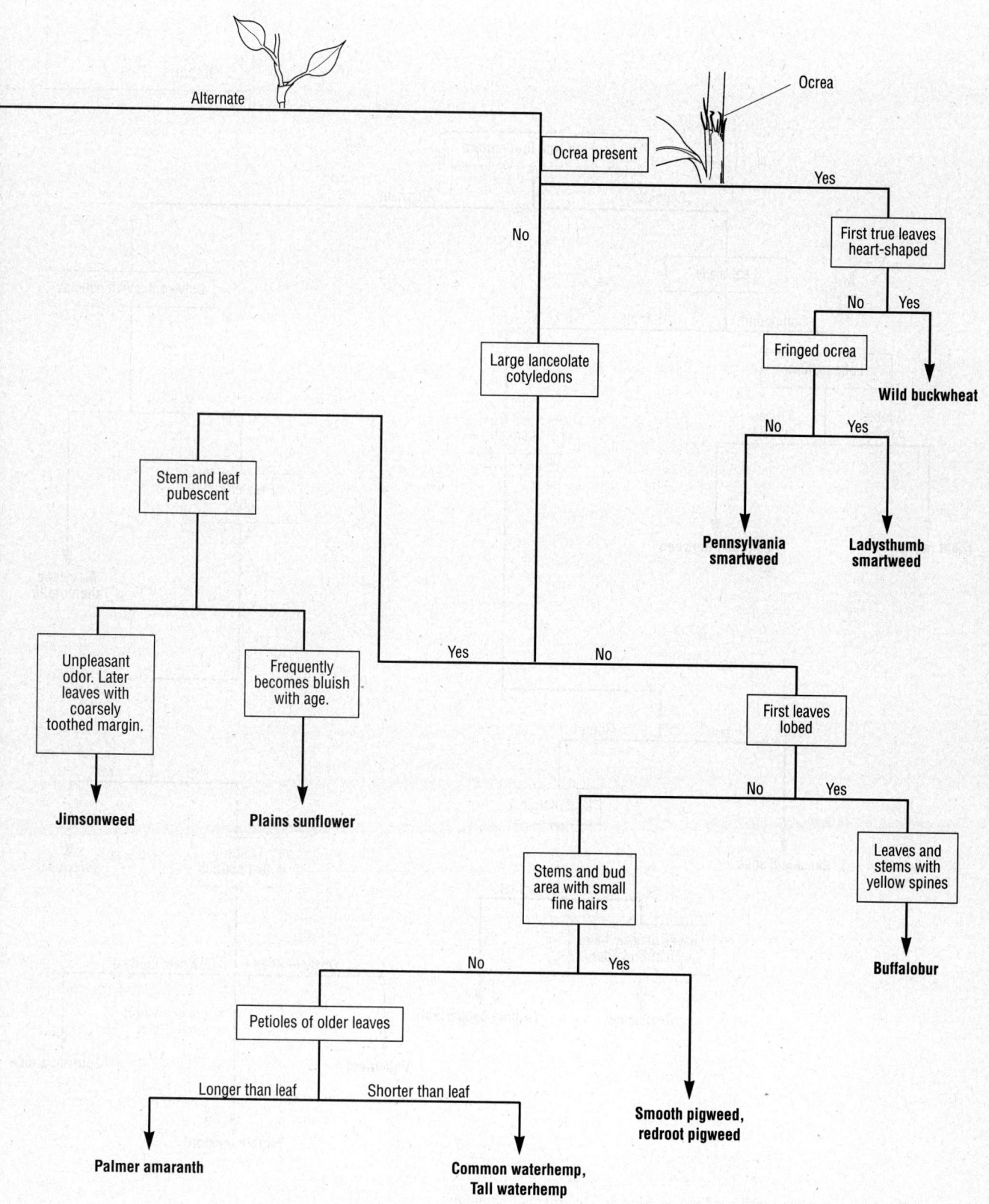

Alternate

Ocrea

Ocrea present

Yes

No

First true leaves heart-shaped

No   Yes

Large lanceolate cotyledons

Fringed ocrea

Wild buckwheat

Stem and leaf pubescent

No   Yes

Pennsylvania smartweed   **Ladysthumb smartweed**

Yes   No

Unpleasant odor. Later leaves with coarsely toothed margin.

Frequently becomes bluish with age.

First leaves lobed

No   Yes

Leaves and stems with yellow spines

Jimsonweed   **Plains sunflower**

Stems and bud area with small fine hairs

No   Yes

Buffalobur

Petioles of older leaves

Longer than leaf   Shorter than leaf

Smooth pigweed, redroot pigweed

Palmer amaranth   **Common waterhemp, Tall waterhemp**

Broadleaf Weed Seedlings

Flowchart for Western Broadleaf Weeds

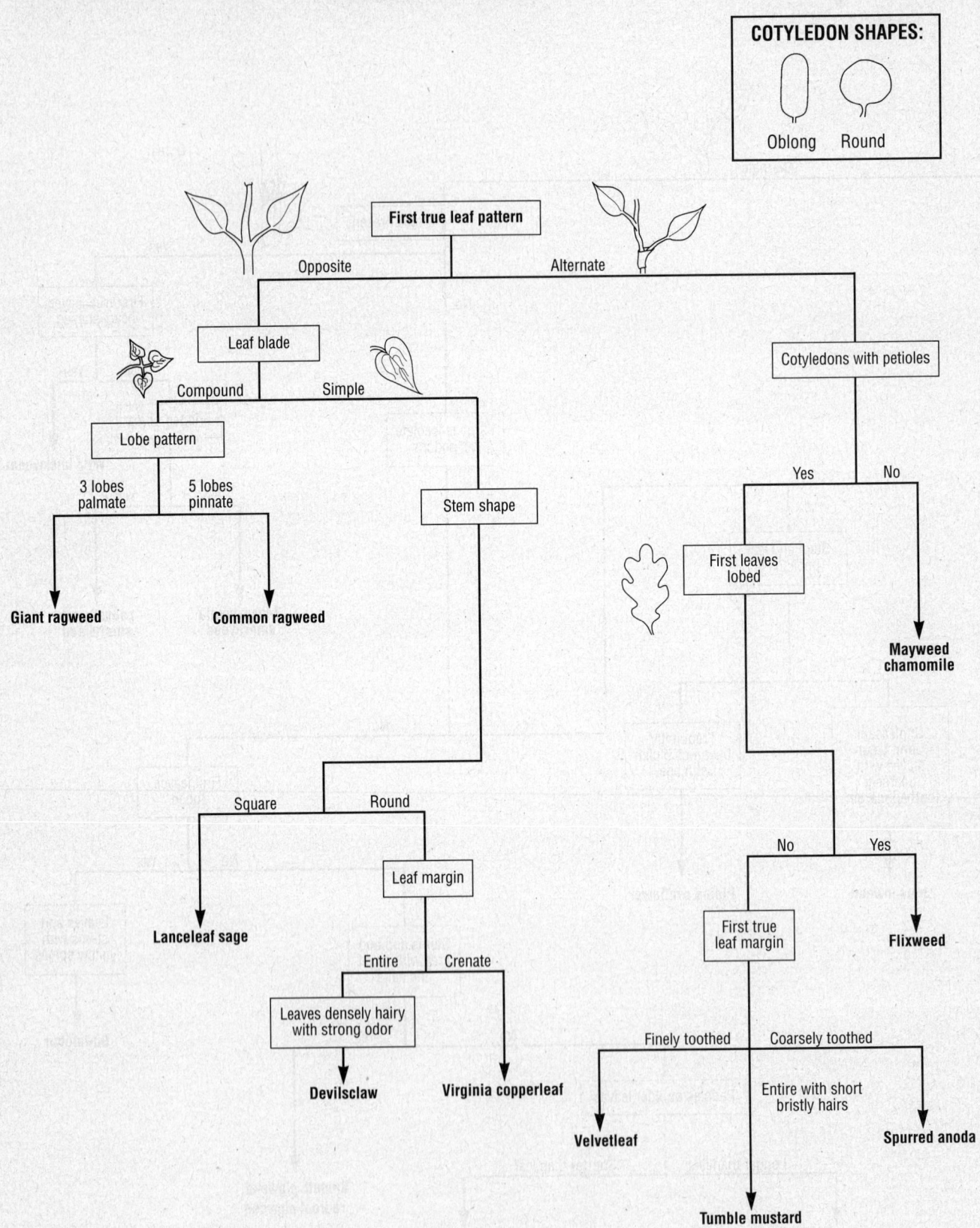

COTYLEDON SHAPES:

Oblong   Round

First true leaf pattern

Opposite — Alternate

Leaf blade

Compound — Simple

Lobe pattern

3 lobes palmate — 5 lobes pinnate

Giant ragweed — **Common ragweed**

Stem shape

Cotyledons with petioles

Yes — No

First leaves lobed

Mayweed chamomile

Square — Round

Lanceleaf sage

Leaf margin

Entire — Crenate

Leaves densely hairy with strong odor

Devilsclaw — **Virginia copperleaf**

No — Yes

First true leaf margin

Flixweed

Finely toothed — Coarsely toothed

Entire with short bristly hairs

Velvetleaf — **Spurred anoda**

Tumble mustard

Source: Weed Identification Technical Training Manual, American Cyanamid.

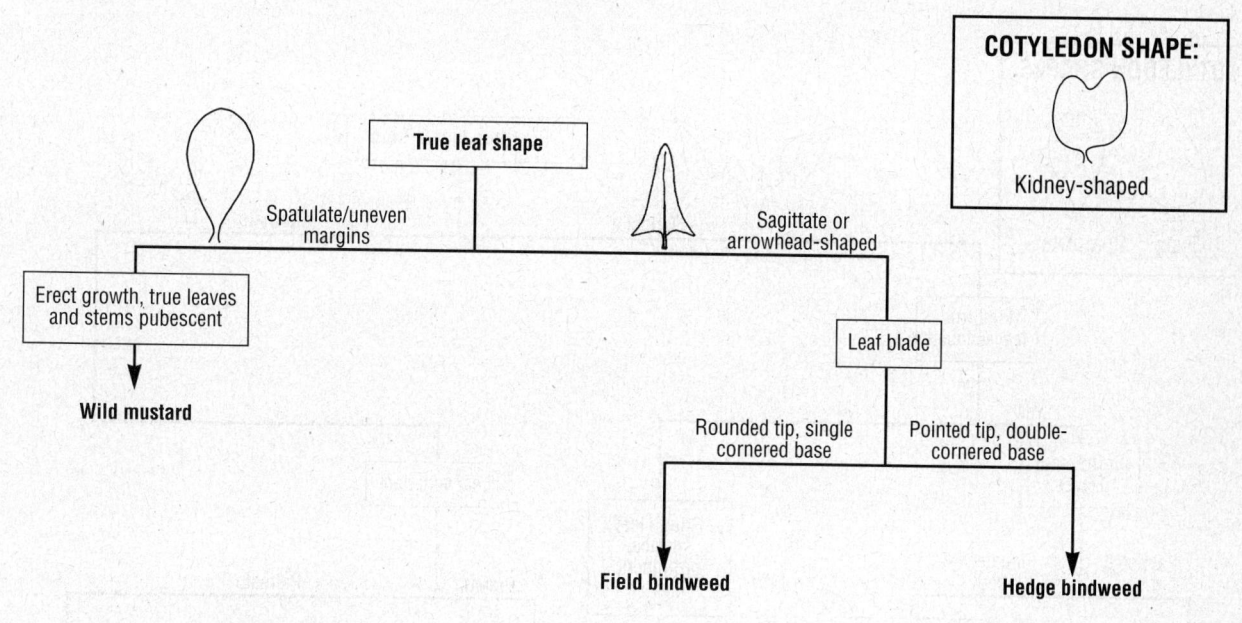

COTYLEDON SHAPE:

Kidney-shaped

True leaf shape

Spatulate/uneven margins

Erect growth, true leaves and stems pubescent

Wild mustard

Sagittate or arrowhead-shaped

Leaf blade

Rounded tip, single cornered base

Pointed tip, double-cornered base

Field bindweed

Hedge bindweed

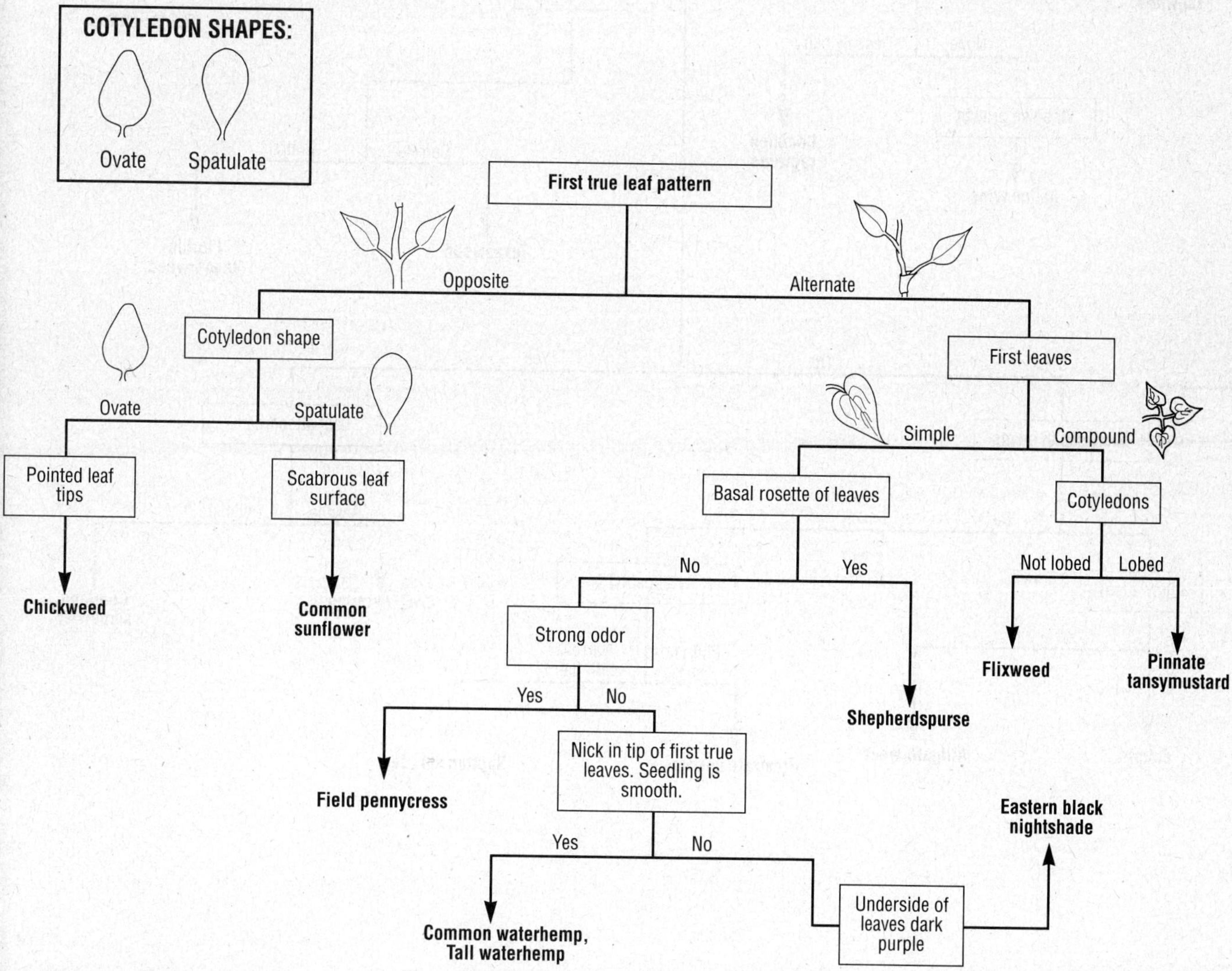

COTYLEDON SHAPES:

Ovate   Spatulate

First true leaf pattern

Opposite

Alternate

Cotyledon shape

First leaves

Ovate

Spatulate

Simple

Compound

Pointed leaf tips

Scabrous leaf surface

Basal rosette of leaves

Cotyledons

Chickweed

Common sunflower

No

Yes

Not lobed

Lobed

Strong odor

Flixweed

Pinnate tansymustard

Yes

No

Shepherdspurse

Nick in tip of first true leaves. Seedling is smooth.

Field pennycress

Eastern black nightshade

Yes

No

Common waterhemp, Tall waterhemp

Underside of leaves dark purple

Broadleaf Weed Seedlings

Flowchart for Southern Broadleaf Weeds

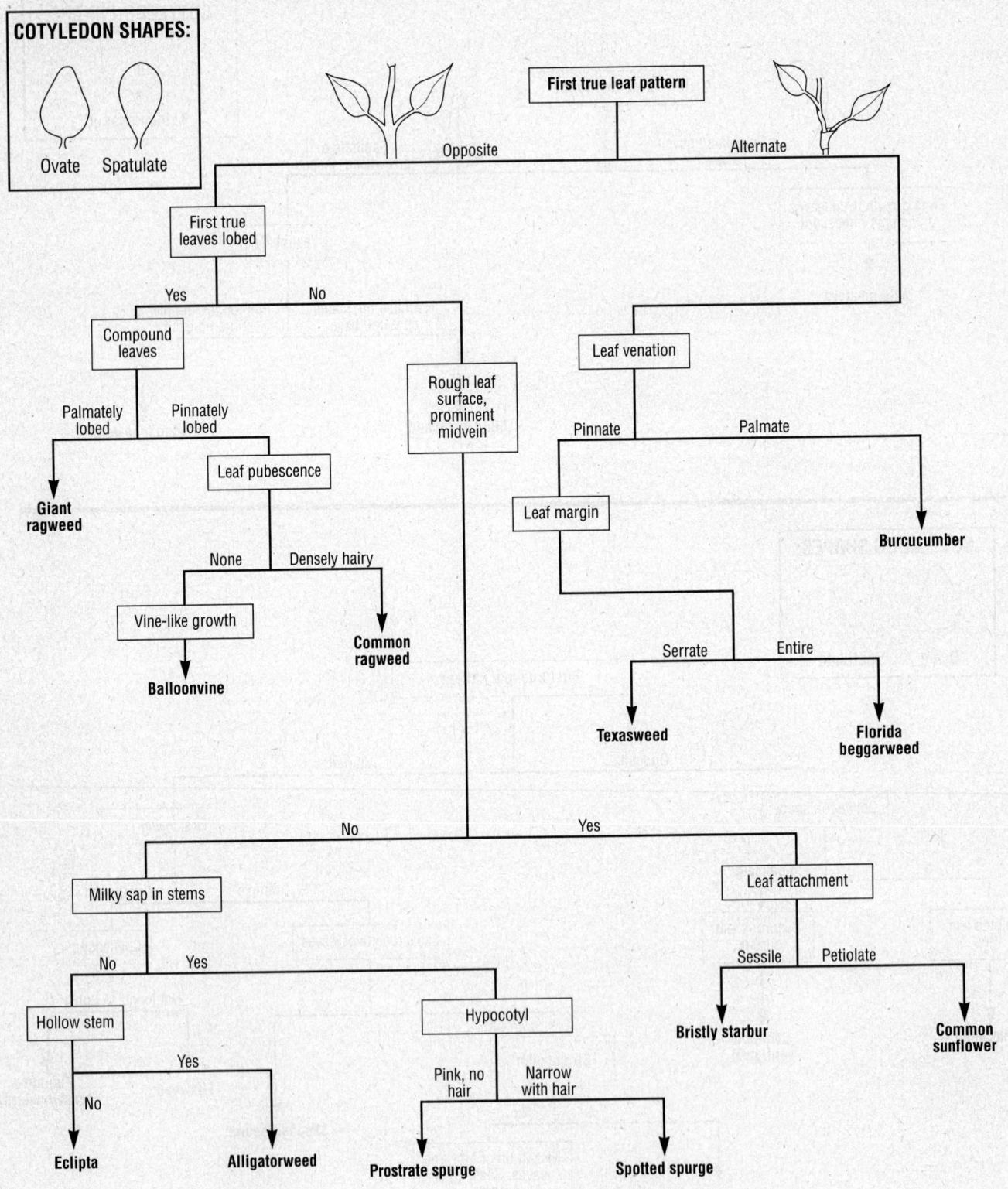

COTYLEDON SHAPES:

Ovate   Spatulate

First true leaf pattern

Opposite   Alternate

First true leaves lobed

Yes   No

Compound leaves

Palmately lobed   Pinnately lobed

Giant ragweed

Leaf pubescence

None   Densely hairy

Vine-like growth

Balloonvine

Common ragweed

Rough leaf surface, prominent midvein

Leaf venation

Pinnate   Palmate

Leaf margin

Burcucumber

Serrate   Entire

Texasweed

Florida beggarweed

No   Yes

Milky sap in stems

No   Yes

Hollow stem

Yes

No

Eclipta

Alligatorweed

Hypocotyl

Pink, no hair   Narrow with hair

Prostrate spurge

Spotted spurge

Leaf attachment

Sessile   Petiolate

Bristly starbur

Common sunflower

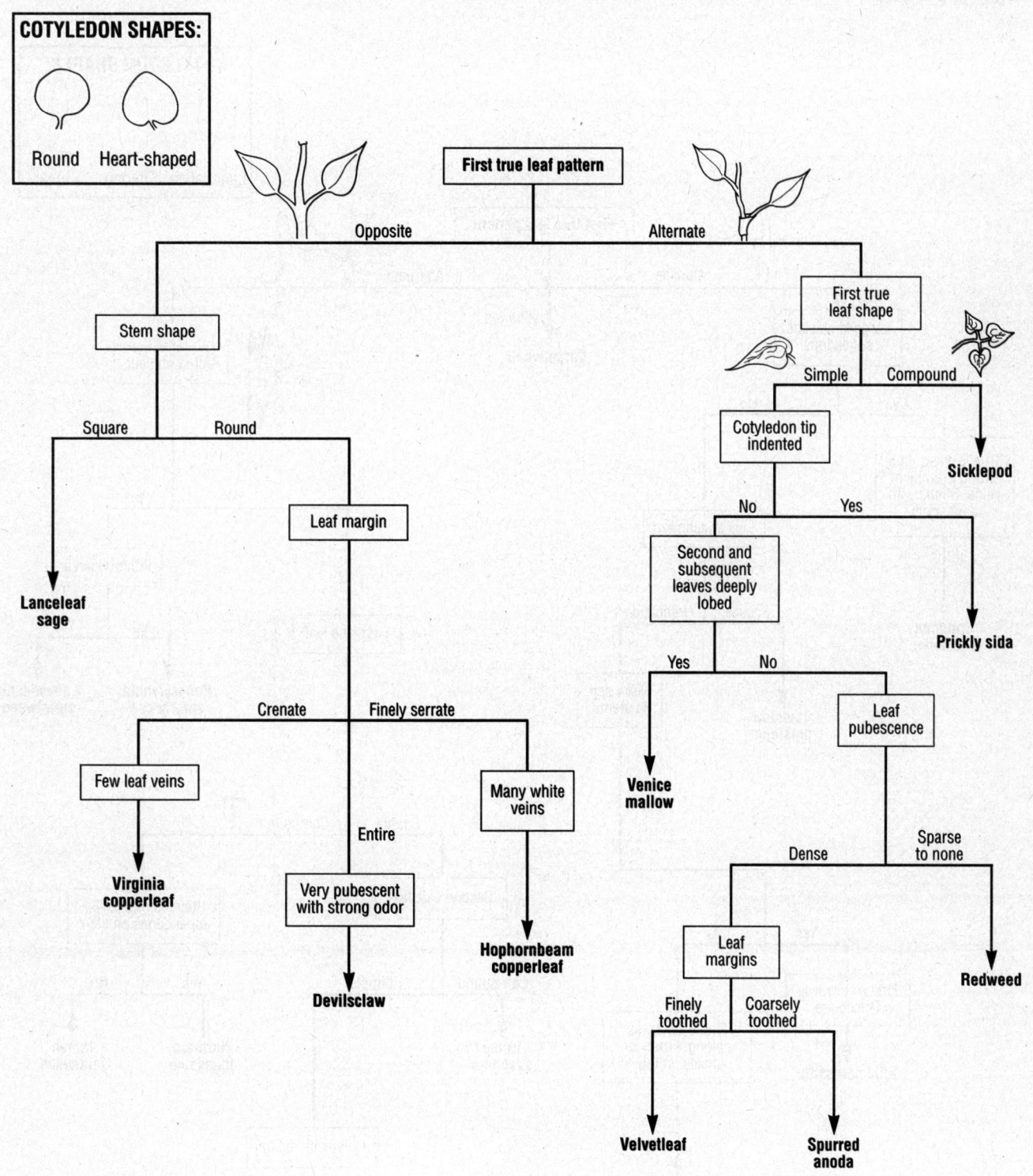

COTYLEDON SHAPES:

Round   Heart-shaped

First true leaf pattern

Opposite

Alternate

Stem shape

First true leaf shape

Simple   Compound

Square   Round

Cotyledon tip indented

Sicklepod

Leaf margin

No   Yes

Lanceleaf sage

Second and subsequent leaves deeply lobed

Prickly sida

Crenate   Finely serrate

Yes   No

Few leaf veins

Many white veins

Venice mallow

Leaf pubescence

Entire

Virginia copperleaf

Dense   Sparse to none

Very pubescent with strong odor

Hophornbeam copperleaf

Leaf margins

Redweed

Devilsclaw

Finely toothed   Coarsely toothed

Velvetleaf   **Spurred anoda**

Source: Weed Identification Technical Training Manual, American Cyanamid.

Broadleaf Weed Seedlings

Flowchart for Southern Broadleaf Weeds

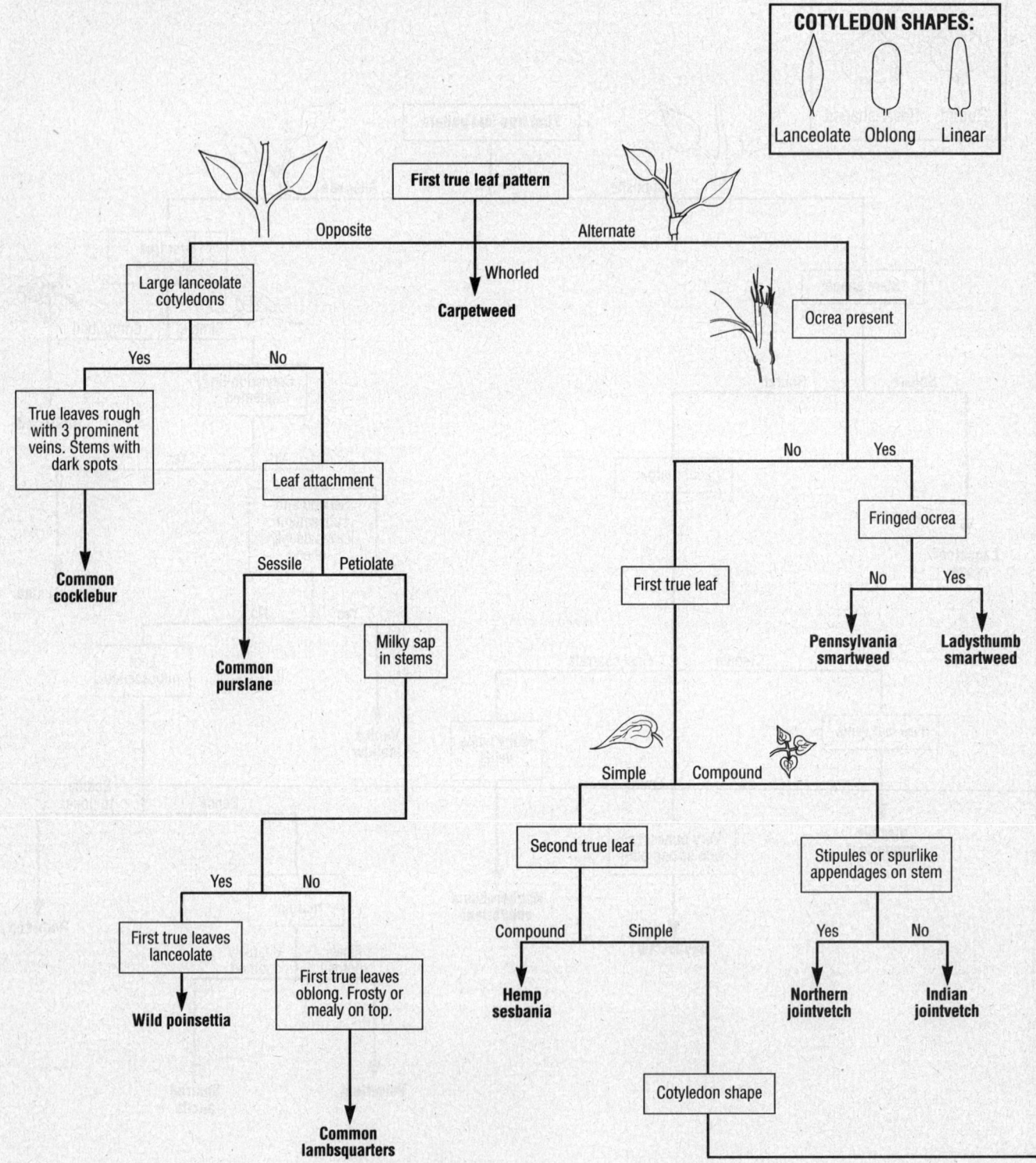

COTYLEDON SHAPES:
Lanceolate Oblong Linear

First true leaf pattern

Opposite — Whorled — Alternate

Whorled → **Carpetweed**

Large lanceolate cotyledons
- Yes → True leaves rough with 3 prominent veins. Stems with dark spots → **Common cocklebur**
- No → Leaf attachment
  - Sessile → **Common purslane**
  - Petiolate → Milky sap in stems
    - Yes → First true leaves lanceolate → **Wild poinsettia**
    - No → First true leaves oblong. Frosty or mealy on top. → **Common lambsquarters**

Ocrea present
- No → First true leaf
  - Simple → Second true leaf
    - Compound → **Hemp sesbania**
    - Simple → Cotyledon shape
  - Compound → Stipules or spurlike appendages on stem
    - Yes → **Northern jointvetch**
    - No → **Indian jointvetch**
- Yes → Fringed ocrea
  - No → **Pennsylvania smartweed**
  - Yes → **Ladysthumb smartweed**

Source: Weed Identification Technical Training Manual, American Cyanamid.

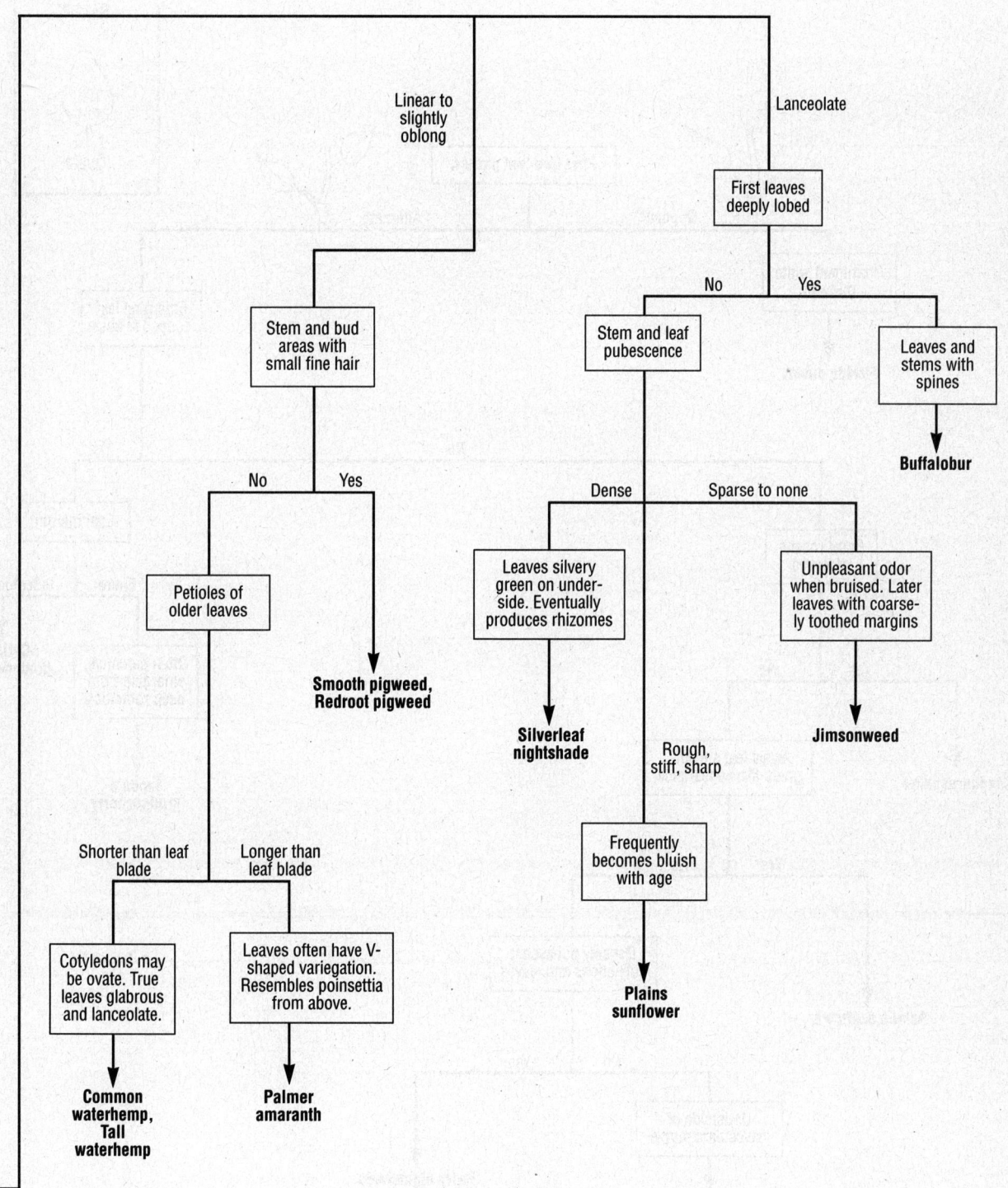

Linear to slightly oblong

Lanceolate

First leaves deeply lobed

No | Yes

Stem and bud areas with small fine hair

Stem and leaf pubescence

Leaves and stems with spines

→ **Buffalobur**

No | Yes

Petioles of older leaves

→ **Smooth pigweed, Redroot pigweed**

Dense | Sparse to none

Leaves silvery green on underside. Eventually produces rhizomes

Unpleasant odor when bruised. Later leaves with coarsely toothed margins

→ **Silverleaf nightshade**

→ **Jimsonweed**

Shorter than leaf blade | Longer than leaf blade

Rough, stiff, sharp

Frequently becomes bluish with age

Cotyledons may be ovate. True leaves glabrous and lanceolate.

Leaves often have V-shaped variegation. Resembles poinsettia from above.

→ **Plains sunflower**

→ **Common waterhemp, Tall waterhemp**

→ **Palmer amaranth**

Broadleaf Weed Seedlings

Flowchart for Southern Broadleaf Weeds

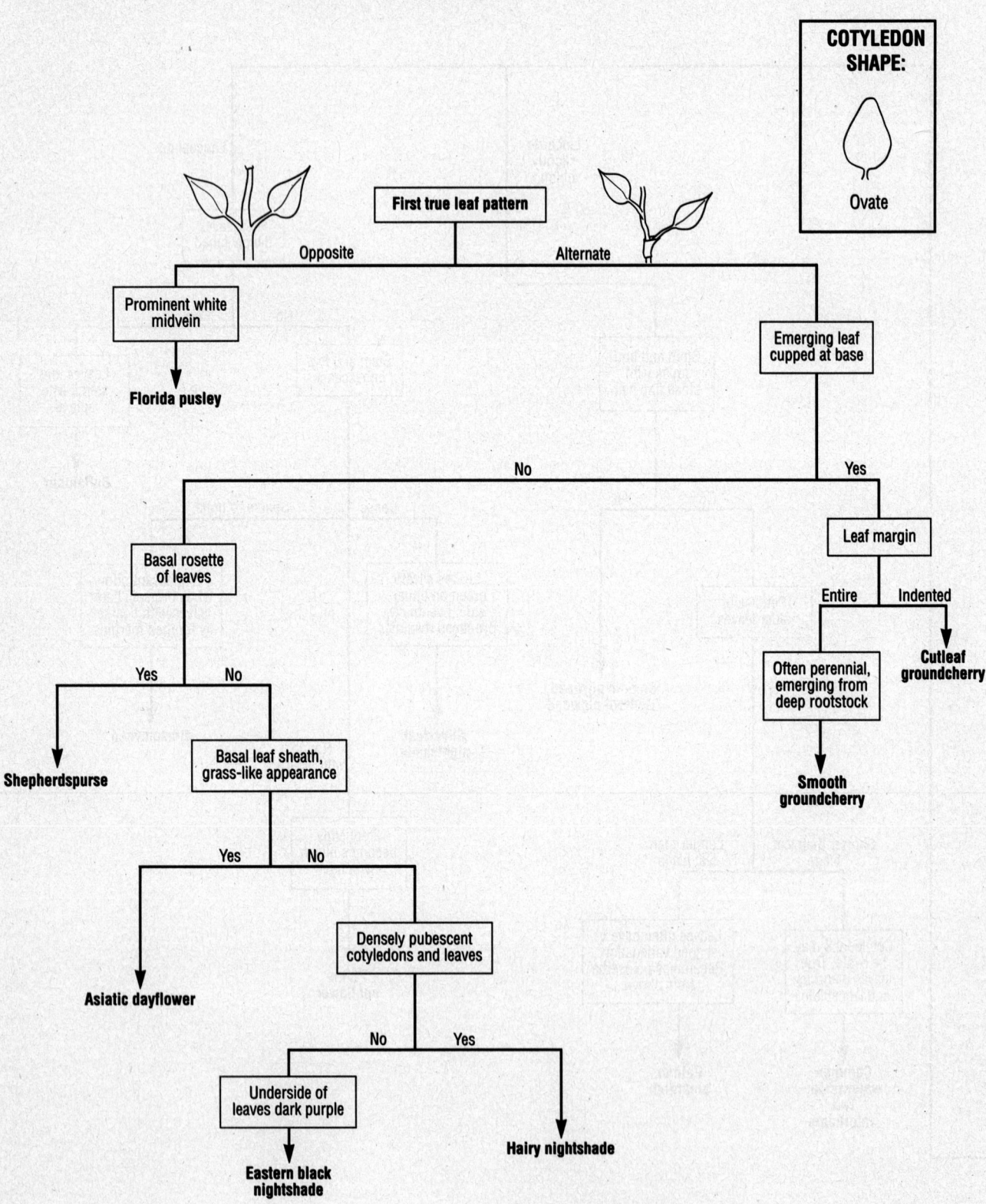

COTYLEDON SHAPE:

Ovate

First true leaf pattern

Opposite — Prominent white midvein → **Florida pusley**

Alternate — Emerging leaf cupped at base

No — Basal rosette of leaves
- Yes → **Shepherdspurse**
- No — Basal leaf sheath, grass-like appearance
  - Yes → **Asiatic dayflower**
  - No — Densely pubescent cotyledons and leaves
    - No — Underside of leaves dark purple → **Eastern black nightshade**
    - Yes → **Hairy nightshade**

Yes — Leaf margin
- Entire — Often perennial, emerging from deep rootstock → **Smooth groundcherry**
- Indented → **Cutleaf groundcherry**

Source: Weed Identification Technical Training Manual, American Cyanamid.

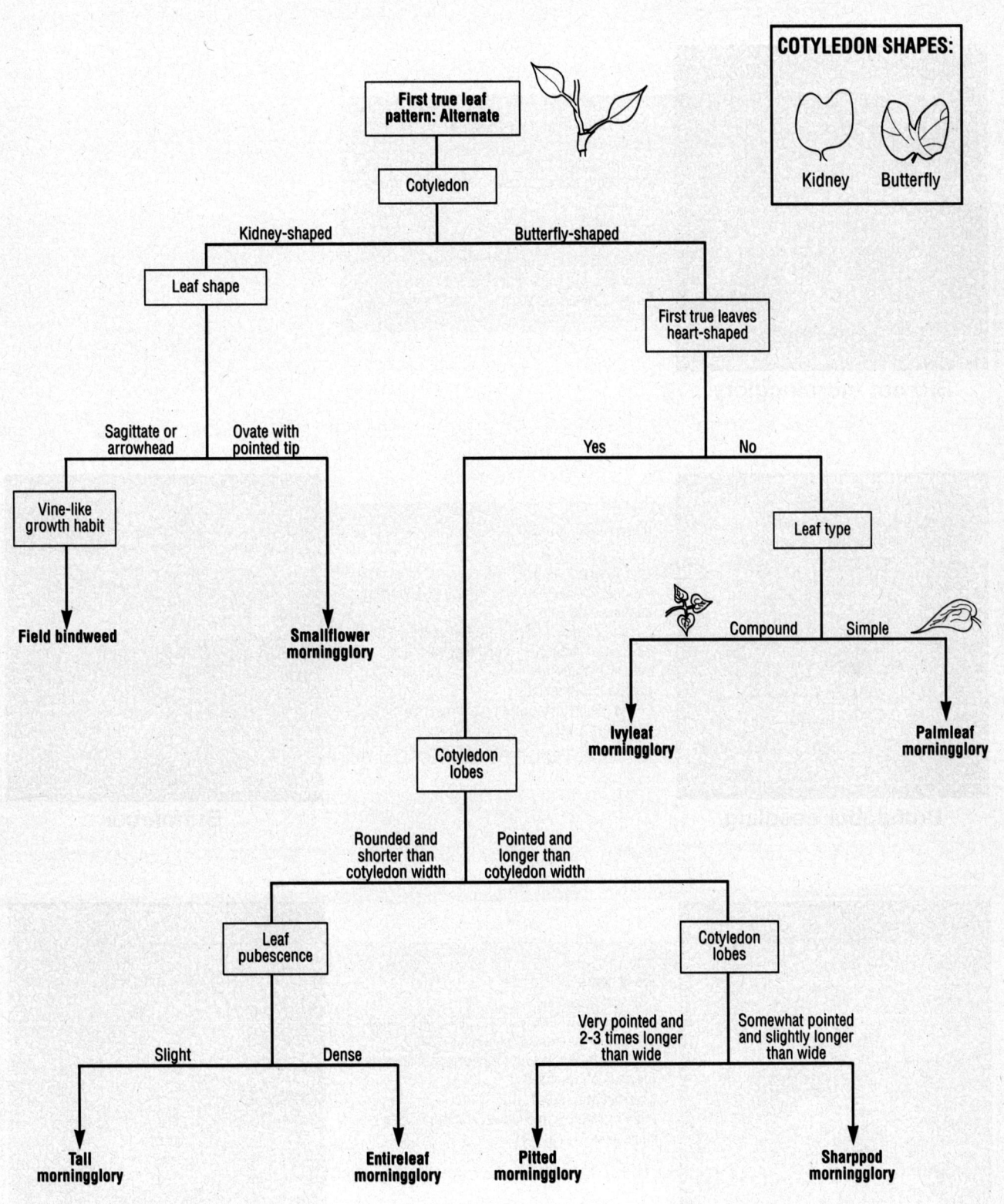

COTYLEDON SHAPES:

Kidney Butterfly

First true leaf pattern: Alternate

Cotyledon

Kidney-shaped | Butterfly-shaped

Leaf shape

First true leaves heart-shaped

Sagittate or arrowhead | Ovate with pointed tip

Yes | No

Vine-like growth habit

Leaf type

Field bindweed

Smallflower morningglory

Compound | Simple

Ivyleaf morningglory

Palmleaf morningglory

Cotyledon lobes

Rounded and shorter than cotyledon width | Pointed and longer than cotyledon width

Leaf pubescence

Cotyledon lobes

Very pointed and 2-3 times longer than wide | Somewhat pointed and slightly longer than wide

Slight | Dense

Tall morningglory

Entireleaf morningglory

Pitted morningglory

Sharppod morningglory

Photo Identification

Broadleaf weeds

Weed name: Bigroot morningglory (wild sweet potato)
Life cycle: perennial
Cotyledon: ovate but seldom seen (emerges underground)
Leaf shape: long-petioled
Leaf arr: alternate
Special charac: large, tuberous root
Growth habit: twining or climbing vine
Found: fields, roadsides, and waste areas

Bigroot morningglory

Weed name: Buffalobur
Life cycle: annual
Leaf shape: long, petioled, densely hairy, veins, midribs, and petioles very prickly (2-5 inches)
Leaf arr: alternate
Special charac: Flowers are yellow with 5 lobes. Seeds are numerous, round flattened, dull brownish-black.
Growth habit: erect
Found: fields, overgrazed pastures, roadsides, and waste areas

Buffalobur seedling

Buffalobur

Weed name: Bull thistle
Life cycle: biennial
Leaf shape: pinnately lobed, hairy, and prickly on upper side and cottony underneath.
Special charac: flower more or less clustered at the ends of branches
Growth habit: erect
Found: pastures, meadows, and other uncultivated land

Bull thistle seedling

Bull thistle

Weed name: Burcucumber
Life cycle: annual
Cotyledon: oblong, thick, green, slightly roughened with spreading hairs on top and bottom
Leaf shape: long petiole, hairy and cordate with 5 pointed lobes
Leaf arr: alternate
Special charac: vine with large 5-lobed leaves with spiny fruit
Growth habit: prostrate vine
Found: moist cultivated fields, lowlands, and fence rows

Burcucumber cotyledon

Burcucumber

Weed name: Canada thistle (creeping thistle)
Life cycle: perennial
Cotyledon: ovate to club-shaped
Leaf shape: oblong, with crinkled edges and spiny margins
Leaf arr: alternate
Special charac: plants establish in patches due to the horizontal creeping of rhizomes
Growth habit: erect thistle
Found: rangelands, pastures, no-till areas

Canada thistle seedling

Canada thistle

Weed name: Common chickweed (starwort, winterweed)
Life cycle: annual
Cotyledon: ovate
Leaf shape: ovate
Leaf arr: alternate
Special charac: stems pubescent in lines
Growth habit: decumbent
Found: roadsides, grassy areas

**Common chickweed
seedling**

Common chickweed

Photo Identification

Broadleaf weeds

Weed name: Common cocklebur
Life cycle: annual
Cotyledon: lanceolate; waxy, thick, dark green upper surface
Leaf shape: lanceolate, irregularly lobed (3-5 inches)
Leaf arr: alternate
Special charac: waxy lanceolate cotyledons, maroon to black stem lesions
Growth habit: erect
Found: cultivated fields and waste areas

Common cocklebur seedling

Common cocklebur

Weed name: Common lambsquarters (green pigweed, white goosefoot)
Life cycle: annual
Cotyledon: oblong to linear, light green with mealy gray cast
Leaf shape: rounded triangular
Leaf arr: simple, alternate
Special charac: leaves with mealy gray-colored underside
Growth habit: erect
Found: cultivated fields, pastures, rangeland, waste areas

Common lambsquarters cotyledon

Common lambsquarters

Weed name: Common milkweed (silkweed, swallow-wort, showy milkweed)
Life cycle: perennial
Cotyledon: linear
Leaf shape: entire, oblong
Leaf arr: opposite
Special charac: perennial herb with milky juice
Growth habit: erect, branched
Found: pastures, undisturbed areas

Common milkweed seedling

Common milkweed

Common purslane seedling

Weed name: Common purslane
Life cycle: annual
Leaf shape: tear-drop shaped, wider at tip
Leaf arr: alternate or clustered
Special charac: stems often reddish; is drought resistant and difficult to kill
Growth habit: prostrate
Found: fields, waste areas; persistent in soils that remain moist

Common purslane

Common ragweed

Weed name: Common ragweed (short ragweed)
Life cycle: annual
Cotyledon: round to oblong with grooved petioles
Leaf shape: pinnately to bi-pinnately lobed
Leaf arr: opposite near base and alternate apically
Special charac: round to oblong cotyledons with underside deep purple, leaves pinnately lobed, fruit resembles queen's crown
Growth habit: erect
Found: cultivated fields, pastures, waste areas

Common sunflower seedling

Weed name: Common sunflower
Life cycle: annual
Leaf shape: simple, rough, hairy, mostly with sawtoothed margins
Leaf arr: alternate
Special charac: flower heads 1-5 inches wide
Growth habit: erect
Found: cultivated land, pastures, and waste places

Common sunflower

Photo Identification

Broadleaf weeds

Weed name: Cutleaf groundcherry (Chinese lantern) **Life cycle:** annual **Cotyledon:** ovate **Leaf shape:** ovate, with margins irregularly indented **Leaf arr:** alternate **Special charac:** plants smooth, berry enclosed in enlarged rounded globe **Growth habit:** erect **Found:** moist cultivated fields and waste areas

Weed name: Dayflower spp. (wandering Jew) **Life cycle:** annual **Cotyledon:** lanceolate **Leaf shape:** ovate **Leaf arr:** alternate **Special charac:** leaves with conspicuous basal sheaths **Growth habit:** creeping, erect, or spreading **Found:** moist fields, wet clearings, open woods

Cutleaf groundcherry

Dayflower

Weed name: Eastern black nightshade
Life cycle: annual
Cotyledon: ovate, short hairs on margins, midribs evident on lower surfaces
Leaf shape: ovate to ovate-lanceolate
Leaf arr: simple, alternate
Special charac: young leaves have red-purple underside, green berries turn purplish-black or dark green at maturity
Growth habit: spreading to erect
Found: cultivated fields, waste areas, pastures

Eastern black nightshade cotyledon

Eastern black nightshade

Weed name: Field bindweed (field morningglory, creeping jenny)
Life cycle: perennial
Cotyledon: kidney-shaped
Leaf shape: ovate
Leaf arr: alternate
Special charac: bracts on flower stalk distant from the flower
Growth habit: climbing or trailing vine
Found: well established in cultivated and noncultivated fields

Field bindweed

Field bindweed

Weed name: Field pennycress (fanweed) **Life cycle:** annual **Leaf shape:** lanceolate **Leaf arr:** alternate **Special charac:** leaves are $1/2$-2 inches long. **Growth habit:** erect **Found:** grain fields, waste areas, roadsides

Weed name: Giant ragweed (kingweed) **Life cycle:** annual **Cotyledon:** spatulate **Leaf shape:** oblanceolate (early leaves), others ovate or elliptic, palmately divided into 3 lobes **Leaf arr:** opposite **Special charac:** large round to oblong cotyledons with grooved petioles **Growth habit:** erect **Found:** cultivated fields, pastures, waste areas

Field pennycress

Giant ragweed seedling

Weed name: Hairy nightshade
Life cycle: annual
Cotyledon: ovate, densely hairy
Leaf shape: ovate, entire margin undulating
Leaf arr: alternate
Special charac: foliage is spreading, hairy, and may feel sticky when handled
Growth habit: spreading, flowers resemble tomato or potato
Found: cultivated fields, waste places

Hairy nightshade

Hairy nightshade

Weed name: Hedge bindweed
Life cycle: perennial
Cotyledon: kidney-shaped, as long as broad
Leaf shape: triangular to oblong
Leaf arr: alternate
Special charac: leaves exhibit an "arrowhead" shape
Growth habit: trailing or climbing, glabrous stems up to 9 feet in length
Found: rangeland, pastures, and no-till areas

Hedge bindweed seedling

Hedge bindweed

Photo Identification

Broadleaf weeds

Weed name: Hemp dogbane (Indian hemp)
Life cycle: perennial **Cotyledon:** ovate **Leaf shape:** oblong, smoothed edges, pubescent beneath petiole **Leaf arr:** opposite **Special charac:** woody base, exuding milky juice when broken **Growth habit:** erect **Found:** pastures, roadsides, wastelands, and cultivated fields

Weed name: Honeyvine milkweed **Life cycle:** perennial **Leaf shape:** heart-shaped, margin serrate **Leaf arr:** alternate **Special charac:** leaf blades heart-shaped at the base **Growth habit:** twining **Found:** cultivated fields and waste places

Hemp dogbane

Honeyvine milkweed

Weed name: Hophornbeam copperleaf **Life cycle:** annual **Cotyledon:** round **Leaf shape:** ovate, margin serrate **Leaf arr:** alternate **Special charac:** leaf blades heart-shaped at the base **Growth habit:** erect **Found:** cultivated fields and waste places

Weed name: Horseweed **Life cycle:** annual **Leaf shape:** upper leaves lanceolate to linear **Leaf arr:** alternate, crowded on stem **Special charac:** lower leaves spatulate **Growth habit:** erect **Found:** low, moist, poorly drained soils

Hophornbeam copperleaf

Horseweed

Weed name: Ivyleaf morningglory (common morningglory)
Life cycle: annual
Cotyledon: butterfly-shaped
Leaf shape: three-lobed
Leaf arr: alternate
Special charac: leaves and stems hairy
Growth habit: twining or climbing vine
Found: moist cultivated fields, waste areas, fence rows

**Ivyleaf morningglory
cotyledon**

Ivyleaf morningglory

Agri-Growth, Inc.

Weed name: Jimsonweed
Life cycle: annual
Cotyledon: linear
Leaf shape: ovate, coarsely toothed
Leaf arr: alternate
Special charac: large flower and leaves, unpleasant odor from disturbed plants
Growth habit: erect
Found: cultivated fields, pastures, waste areas

Weed Science Society of America

Jimsonweed cotyledon

Jimsonweed

Weed Science Society of America

Weed name: Kochia (Mexican fireweed)
Life cycle: annual
Cotyledon: linear
Leaf shape: lanceolate to linear without petioles
Leaf arr: alternate
Special charac: plant often breaks off at ground level and blows in the wind
Growth habit: erect, spreading
Found: rangeland, no-till crops, cultivated fields, and wastelands

Kochia

Weed Science Society of America

Weed name: Ladysthumb smartweed (heart's ease)
Life cycle: annual
Cotyledon: ovate
Leaf shape: oblanceolate, pointed at the tip
Leaf arr: alternate
Special charac: swollen nodes, ocrea with fringe of hair-like bristles
Growth habit: erect to spreading
Found: cultivated fields, waste areas, ditches

Weed Science Society of America

**Ladysthumb smartweed
seedling**

Ladysthumb smartweed

Photo Identification

Broadleaf weeds

Weed name: Musk thistle
Life cycle: biennial
Leaf shape: coarsely toothed, very spiny
Leaf arr: alternate
Special charac: stem has spiny wings 3-6 feet tall, lower portion branched
Growth habit: erect
Found: pastures, meadows, and waste areas

Musk thistle seedling

Musk thistle

Weed name: Pennsylvania smartweed (pinkweed)
Life cycle: annual
Cotyledon: lanceolate
Leaf shape: lanceolate, pointed at tip
Leaf arr: alternate
Special charac: swollen nodes, ocrea, grows 1-4 feet tall; taproot is well developed
Growth habit: erect
Found: moist cultivated fields, waste areas, ditches

Pennsylvania smartweed cotyledon

Pennsylvania smartweed

Weed name: Prickly lettuce
Life cycle: winter annual or biennial
Cotyledon: ovate
Leaf shape: oblong-lanceolate
Leaf arr: alternate
Special charac: prickly leafedges and underside midvein, hollow stem with milky juice
Growth habit: basal rosette
Found: orchards, pastures, roadsides, railroads, and waste areas

Prickly lettuce

Prickly lettuce

Weed name: Prickly sida (teaweed, ironweed, Indian mallow, false-mallow)
Life cycle: annual
Cotyledon: heart-shaped with notch at tip
Leaf shape: lanceolate to oval with serrated margins
Leaf arrangement: alternate
Special charac: heart-shaped cotyledons with notch at tip, leaf margins serrate, long petioles
Growth habit: erect
Found: cultivated fields, pastures, waste areas

Prickly sida cotyledon

Prickly sida

Weed name: Prostrate pigweed
Life cycle: annual
Leaf shape: small, egg-shaped, broadest near tip
Leaf arr: alternate
Special charac: stems are 1-1½ feet long, nearly smooth, reddish, spreading flat over the ground
Growth habit: prostrate
Found: fields, gardens, unused yards

Prostrate pigweed

Prostrate pigweed

Weed name: Prostrate spurge **Life cycle:** annual **Cotyledon:** oval **Leaf shape:** somewhat oval, short, petioled, irregularly toothed **Leaf arr:** opposite **Special charac:** milky sap, pubescent stems and capsule, bitter taste **Growth habit:** prostrate, roots at nodes **Found:** weedy fields, field margins

Weed name: Purple loosestrife **Life cycle:** perennial **Leaf shape:** simple **Leaf arr:** opposite **Special charac:** rose-purple flowers with 5-7 petals arranged in vertical racemes **Growth habit:** grows 6-8 feet tall. **Found:** usually associated with moist or marshy areas

Prostrate spurge

Purple loosestrife

Photo Identification

Broadleaf weeds

Agri-Growth, Inc.

Redroot pigweed cotyledon

Weed name: Redroot pigweed (common amaranth, carelessweed)
Life cycle: annual
Cotyledon: linear
Leaf shape: ovate
Leaf arr: alternate
Special charac: thick spikes in seed head, leaves and young stems hairy, hypocotyl red
Growth habit: erect
Found: cultivated fields, pastures, waste areas

Weed Science Society of America

Redroot pigweed

Weed Science Society of America

Shepherdspurse seedling

Weed name: Shepherdspurse (pepper plant, shepherds bag, case weed, pick-purse)
Life cycle: annual, seed
Cotyledon: broadly ovate to spatulate blades, slightly indented apically
Leaf shape: basal leaves divided into cleft segments or slightly lobed, stem leaves arrow-shaped
Leaf arr: alternate
Special charac: basal rosette of leaves, arrow-shaped stem leaves and triangular fruits
Growth habit: erect
Found: cultivated fields, pastures, waste areas

Weed Science Society of America

Shepherdspurse

Weed Science Society of America

Smooth groundcherry

Weed name: Smooth groundcherry (perennial nightshade)
Life cycle: perennial
Cotyledon: ovate
Leaf shape: ovate or broadly lanceolate, tapering at the apex and the base
Leaf arr: alternate
Special charac: bell-like flowers that are yellowish green, fruit is round and berry-like
Growth habit: erect
Found: wet areas in cultivated fields and non-cultivated fields

Weed Science Society of America

Smooth groundcherry

Weed name: Smooth pigweed (carelessweed) **Life cycle:** annual **Cotyledon:** linear **Leaf shape:** egg-shaped **Leaf arr:** alternate **Special charac:** small spikes in seed head **Growth habit:** erect **Found:** cultivated fields, pastures, waste areas

Weed name: Swamp smartweed (kelp) **Life cycle:** perennial **Leaf shape:** oblong to lanceolate **Leaf arr:** alternate **Special charac:** Stems 1-3 feet in height, enlarged at nodes, usually unbranched. May produce roots at nodes **Growth habit:** erect **Found:** in low, wet places in fields

Smooth pigweed

Swamp smartweed

Weed name: Spiny sowthistle
Life cycle: annual
Leaf shape: entire
Leaf arr: prickly edged, clasping stem with large rounded earlike lobes
Special charac: stem is smooth, erect, 1-6 feet tall
Growth habit: erect
Found: pastures, waste areas, roadsides

Spiny sowthistle

Weed name: Tall morningglory (common morningglory)
Life cycle: annual
Cotyledon: butterfly-shaped; moderately indented with rounded lobes
Leaf shape: heart-shaped, pubescent, with hairs that lie flat on leaf surface
Leaf arr: alternate
Special charac: heart-shaped leaves, hairs that lie flat, sepals short, blunt tip, hairy
Growth habit: trailing or climbing vine
Found: moist cultivated fields, waste areas, fence rows

Tall morningglory seedling

Tall morningglory

Photo Identification

Broadleaf weeds

Weed name: Tall waterhemp (pigweed) **Life cycle:** annual **Cotyledon:** ovate **Leaf shape:** narrowly ovate to lanceolate **Leaf arr:** alternate **Special charac:** separate male and female plants; long petioled, narrow leaves **Growth habit:** erect **Found:** low areas of cultivated fields, waste areas, river flood plains

Weed name: Pinnate tansymustard (green tansymustard) **Life cycle:** winter annual **Cotyledon:** ovate **Leaf shape:** ovate in general **Leaf arr:** alternate **Special charac:** green glandular leaves, sometimes sticky **Growth habit:** erect **Found:** cultivated small grain fields, pastures, rangelands

Tall waterhemp

Tansymustard

Weed name: Velvetleaf (buttonweed, wild cotton, Indian mallow, butterprint)
Life cycle: annual
Cotyledon: ovate to heart-shaped with rounded apexes
Leaf shape: large, heart-shaped with long, tapered ends, velvety, hairy surface
Leaf arr: alternate
Special charac: densely hairy, velvety true leaves, unpleasant odor when crushed
Growth habit: erect, sparingly branched
Found: cultivated fields, waste areas

Velvetleaf cotyledon

Velvetleaf

Weed name: Venice mallow (flower-of-an-hour)
Life cycle: annual
Leaf shape: irregularly shaped with 3-5 coarsely toothed lobes
Leaf arr: alternate
Special charac: grows 10-18 inches tall; stems and petioles are covered with stiff hairs
Growth habit: erect or spreading
Found: waste areas, orchards, cultivated fields

Venice mallow seedling

Venice mallow

Agri-Growth, Inc.

Wild buckwheat cotyledon

Weed name: Wild buckwheat
Life cycle: annual
Cotyledon: lanceolate to oblong
Leaf shape: heart-shaped with tapered point
Leaf arr: alternate
Special charac: has papery leaf sheath; stems trail along ground, often twining about other plants.
Growth habit: creeping vine
Found: cultivated fields, orchards, and non-crop areas

Agri-Growth, Inc.

Wild cucumber cotyledon

Weed name: Wild cucumber
Life cycle: annual
Cotyledon: oval, thick, hairy
Leaf shape: palmate
Leaf arr: alternate
Special charac: leaves hairy, have 5 sharp-angled, pointed, palmate lobes
Growth habit: creeping vine
Found: roadside, fences

Agri-Growth, Inc.

Wild cucumber

Weed name: Wild mustard
Life cycle: annual
Cotyledon: kidney-shaped
Leaf shape: oblong to oval, deeply lobed or toothed, hairy
Leaf arr: alternate
Special charac: stems erect with stiff hairs; flowers yellow with 4 petals
Growth habit: erect
Found: cultivated fields, roadsides, ditchbanks, waste areas

Agri-Growth, Inc.

Wild mustard cotyledon

Photo Identification

Broadleaf weeds comparison photos

Not sure which weed is in your field or orchard? Take a look at these comparison photos of weeds that look a lot alike to help narrow down the choices you might have.

Hairy pigweed leaf (left) vs. smooth pigweed leaf

Hairy pigweed stem (left) vs. smooth pigweed stem

From left to right: Redroot pigweed, Smooth pigweed, Tall waterhemp (female), Tall waterhemp (male)

Venice mallow (left) vs. velvetleaf

Jimsonweed (left) vs. common cocklebur

Prickly sida (left) vs. Venice mallow

Grasses Photo Index

Weed Flowcharts

Northern Grasses 40
Western Grasses 42
Southern Grasses 44

Barnyardgrass 46
Bermudagrass 46
Bristly foxtail 46
Broadleaf signalgrass 46
Cheat 47
Downy brome 47
Fall panicum 47
Fescue 48
Foxtail barley 48
Field sandbur 48
Giant foxtail 48
Green foxtail 49
Johnsongrass 49
Jointed goatgrass 49
Large crabgrass 50
Orchardgrass 50
Purple nutsedge 55
Quackgrass 50
Reed canarygrass 51

Shattercane 51
Smooth brome 51
Smooth crabgrass 52
Sorghum-almum 52
Texas panicum 52
Wild oat 53
Wild proso millet 53
Wirestem muhly 53
Witchgrass 54
Woolly cupgrass 54
Yellow foxtail 54
Yellow nutsedge 55

Comparison photos
Quackgrass vs.
  barnyardgrass 56
Large crabgrass vs. smooth
  crabgrass 56
Fall panicum vs. yellow foxtail 56

Grass & Grasslike Weed Seedlings

Flowchart for Northern Grasses

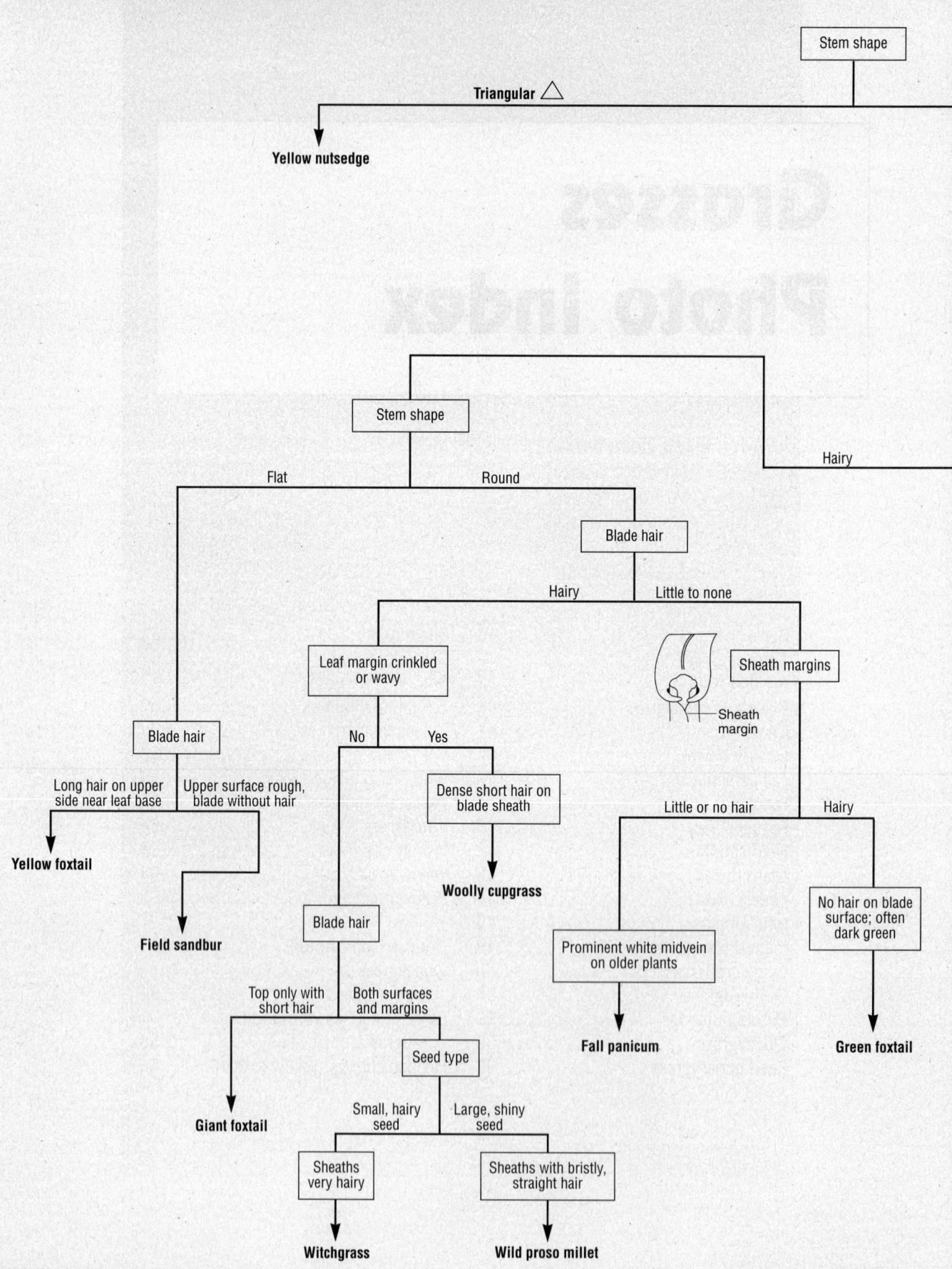

Stem shape

Triangular △

Yellow nutsedge

Stem shape

Hairy

Flat

Round

Blade hair

Hairy

Little to none

Leaf margin crinkled or wavy

Sheath margin

Sheath margins

Blade hair

No

Yes

Long hair on upper side near leaf base

Upper surface rough, blade without hair

Dense short hair on blade sheath

Little or no hair

Hairy

Yellow foxtail

Field sandbur

Woolly cupgrass

Blade hair

No hair on blade surface; often dark green

Top only with short hair

Both surfaces and margins

Prominent white midvein on older plants

Giant foxtail

Seed type

Fall panicum

Green foxtail

Small, hairy seed

Large, shiny seed

Sheaths very hairy

Sheaths with bristly, straight hair

Witchgrass

Wild proso millet

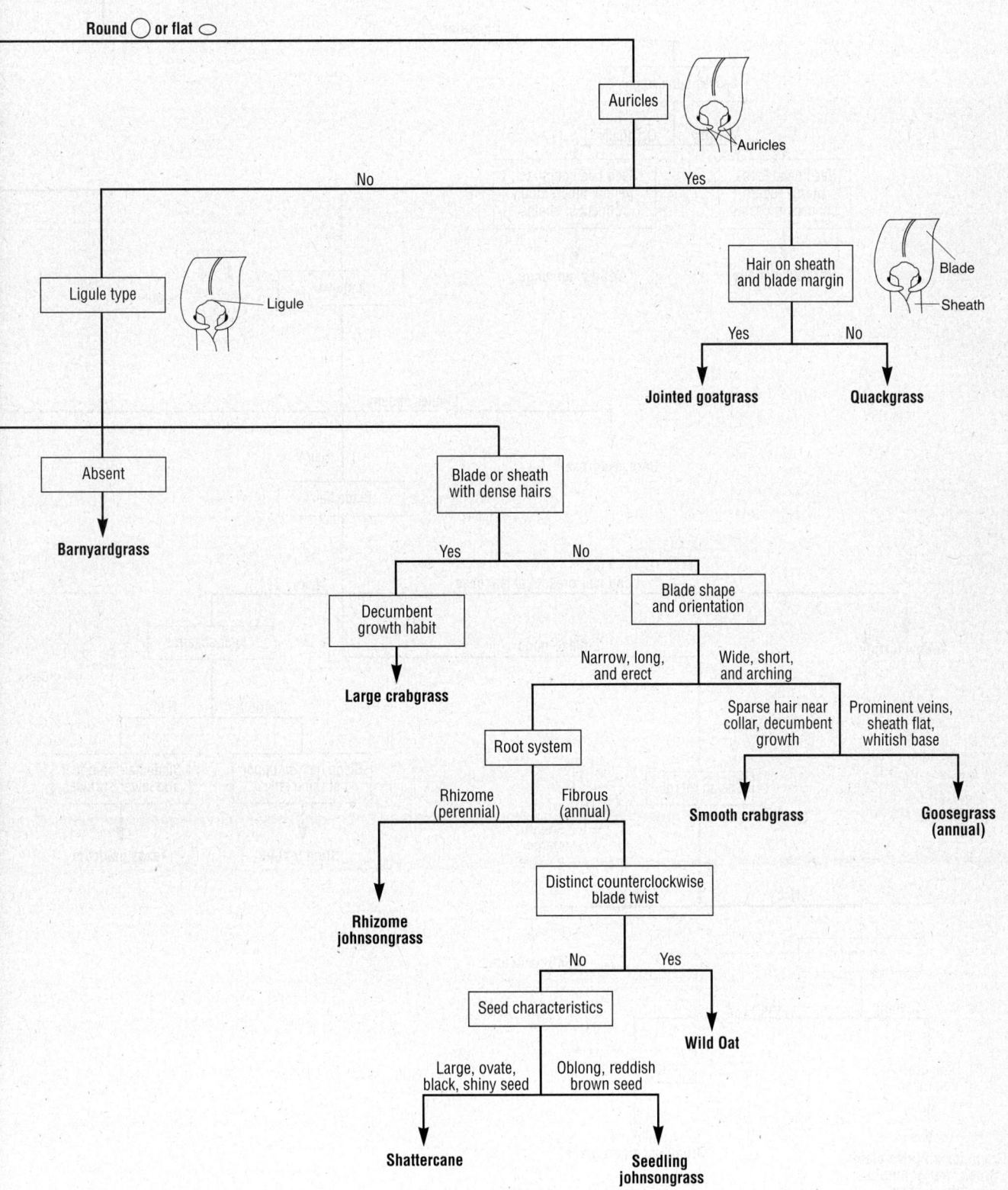

Round ◯ or flat ◯

Auricles

Auricles

No — Yes

Ligule type — Ligule

Hair on sheath and blade margin — Blade — Sheath

Yes — No

Jointed goatgrass — Quackgrass

Absent

Barnyardgrass

Blade or sheath with dense hairs

Yes — No

Decumbent growth habit

Blade shape and orientation

Large crabgrass

Narrow, long, and erect — Wide, short, and arching

Sparse hair near collar, decumbent growth — Prominent veins, sheath flat, whitish base

Root system

Smooth crabgrass — Goosegrass (annual)

Rhizome (perennial) — Fibrous (annual)

Rhizome johnsongrass

Distinct counterclockwise blade twist

No — Yes

Seed characteristics

Wild Oat

Large, ovate, black, shiny seed — Oblong, reddish brown seed

Shattercane — Seedling johnsongrass

Source: Weed Identification Technical Training Manual, American Cyanamid.

Grass & Grasslike Weed Seedlings

Flowchart for Western Grasses

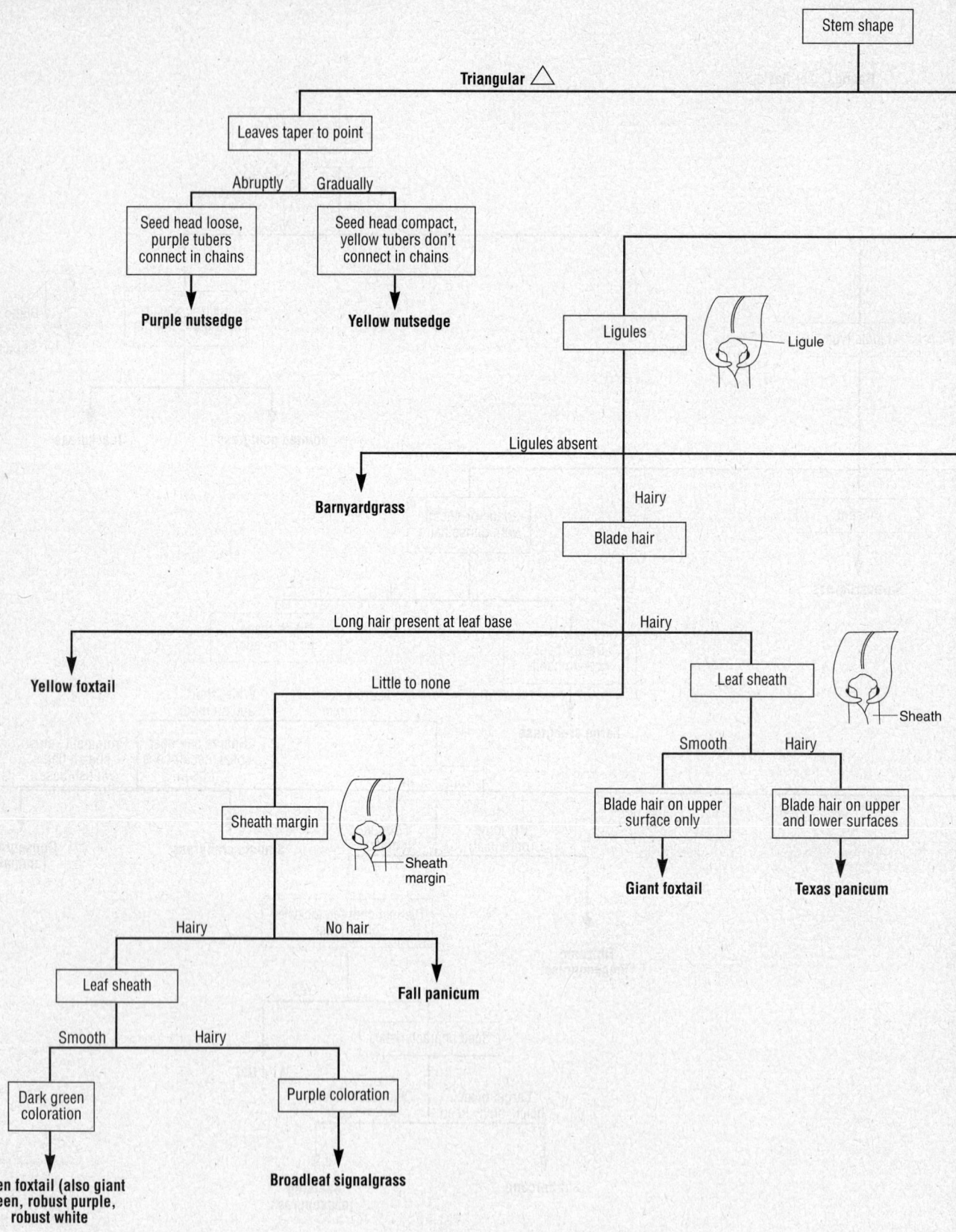

Stem shape

Triangular △

Leaves taper to point

Abruptly — Gradually

Seed head loose, purple tubers connect in chains

Seed head compact, yellow tubers don't connect in chains

Purple nutsedge

Yellow nutsedge

Ligules

Ligule

Ligules absent

Barnyardgrass

Hairy

Blade hair

Long hair present at leaf base

Hairy

Yellow foxtail

Little to none

Leaf sheath

Sheath

Smooth — Hairy

Blade hair on upper surface only

Blade hair on upper and lower surfaces

Giant foxtail

Texas panicum

Sheath margin

Sheath margin

Hairy — No hair

Leaf sheath

Fall panicum

Smooth — Hairy

Dark green coloration

Purple coloration

Green foxtail (also giant green, robust purple, robust white

Broadleaf signalgrass

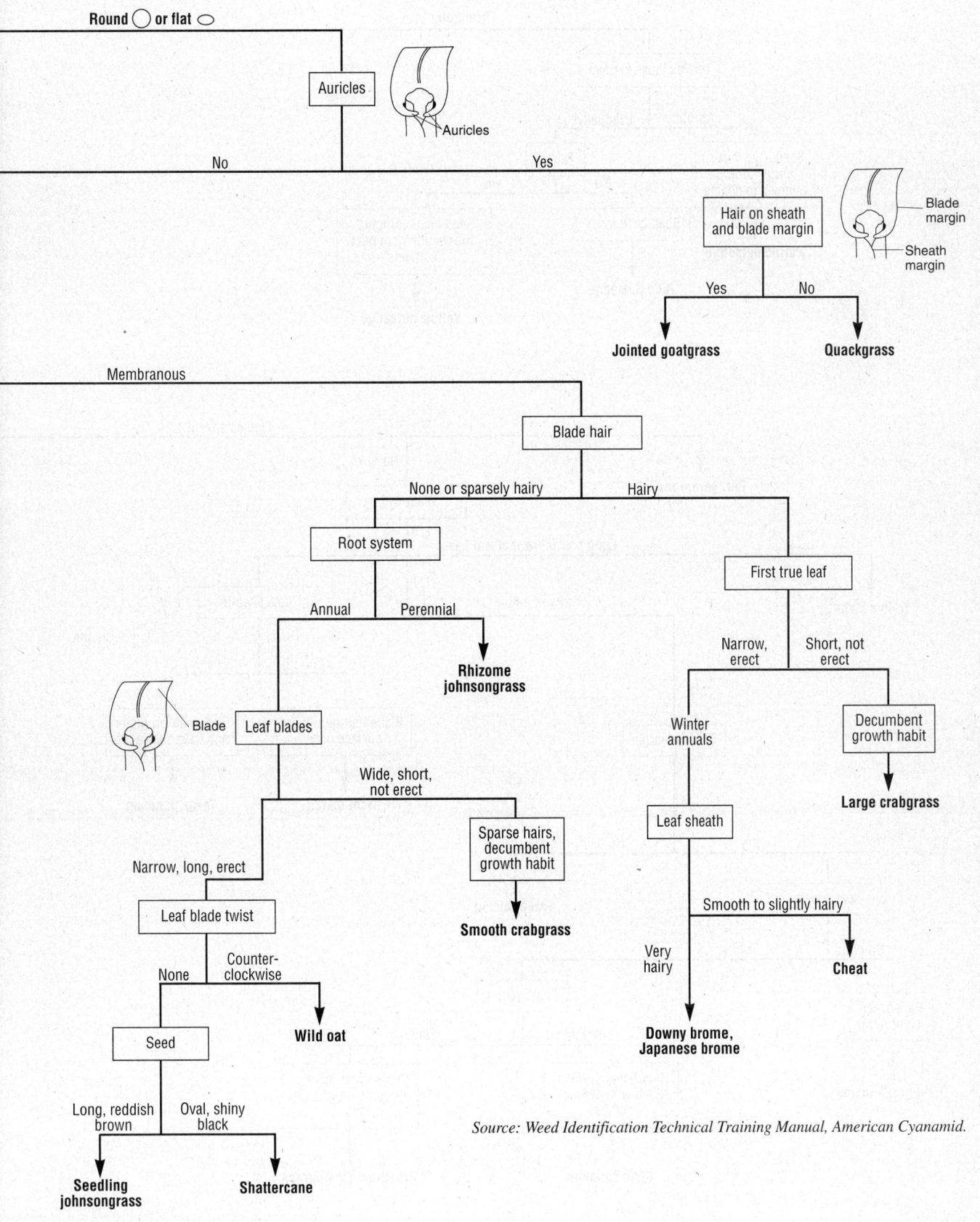

Round ⬭ or flat ⬭

Auricles
└─ Auricles

No | Yes

Hair on sheath and blade margin
└─ Blade margin
└─ Sheath margin

Yes | No

Jointed goatgrass | **Quackgrass**

Membranous

Blade hair

None or sparsely hairy | Hairy

Root system

Annual | Perennial

Rhizome johnsongrass

First true leaf

Narrow, erect | Short, not erect

Winter annuals

Decumbent growth habit

Large crabgrass

Blade
Leaf blades

Wide, short, not erect

Sparse hairs, decumbent growth habit

Smooth crabgrass

Leaf sheath

Narrow, long, erect

Leaf blade twist

Smooth to slightly hairy

None | Counter-clockwise

Very hairy

Cheat

Seed

Wild oat

Downy brome, Japanese brome

Long, reddish brown | Oval, shiny black

Seedling johnsongrass | **Shattercane**

Source: Weed Identification Technical Training Manual, American Cyanamid.

Grass & Grasslike Weed Seedlings

Flowchart for Southern Grasses

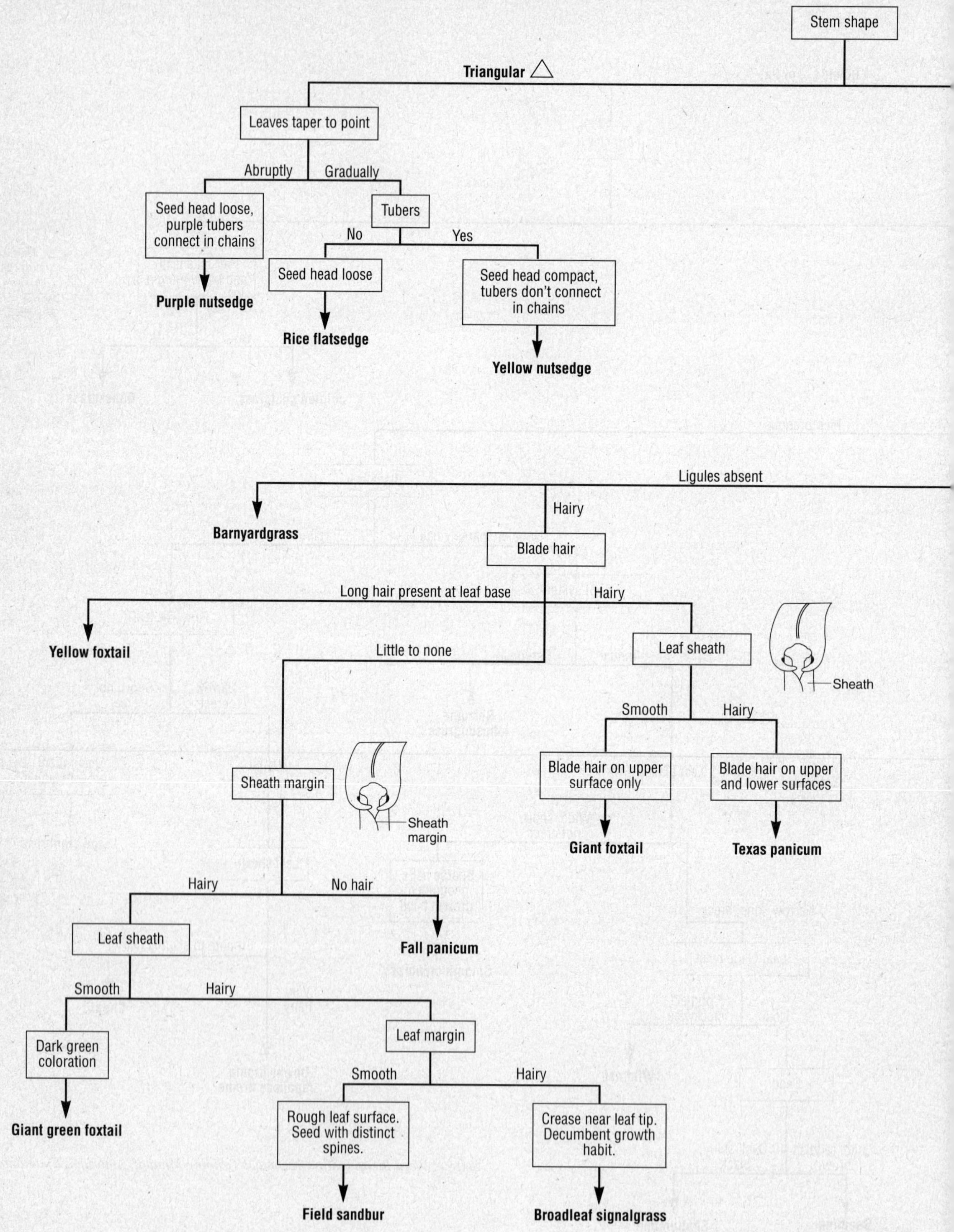

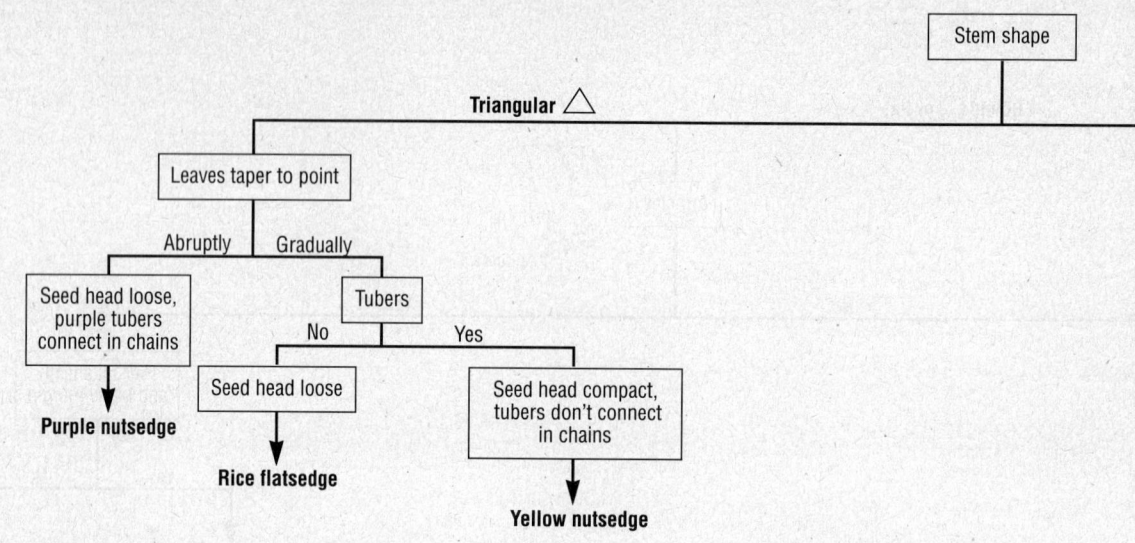

Stem shape

Triangular △

Leaves taper to point

Abruptly — Seed head loose, purple tubers connect in chains → **Purple nutsedge**

Gradually — Tubers
- No → Seed head loose → **Rice flatsedge**
- Yes → Seed head compact, tubers don't connect in chains → **Yellow nutsedge**

Ligules absent

Barnyardgrass

Hairy — Blade hair

Long hair present at leaf base → **Yellow foxtail**

Little to none → Sheath margin
- Hairy → Leaf sheath
  - Smooth → Dark green coloration → **Giant green foxtail**
  - Hairy → Leaf margin
    - Smooth → Rough leaf surface. Seed with distinct spines. → **Field sandbur**
    - Hairy → Crease near leaf tip. Decumbent growth habit. → **Broadleaf signalgrass**
- No hair → **Fall panicum**

Hairy — Leaf sheath (Sheath)
- Smooth → Blade hair on upper surface only → **Giant foxtail**
- Hairy → Blade hair on upper and lower surfaces → **Texas panicum**

Sheath margin

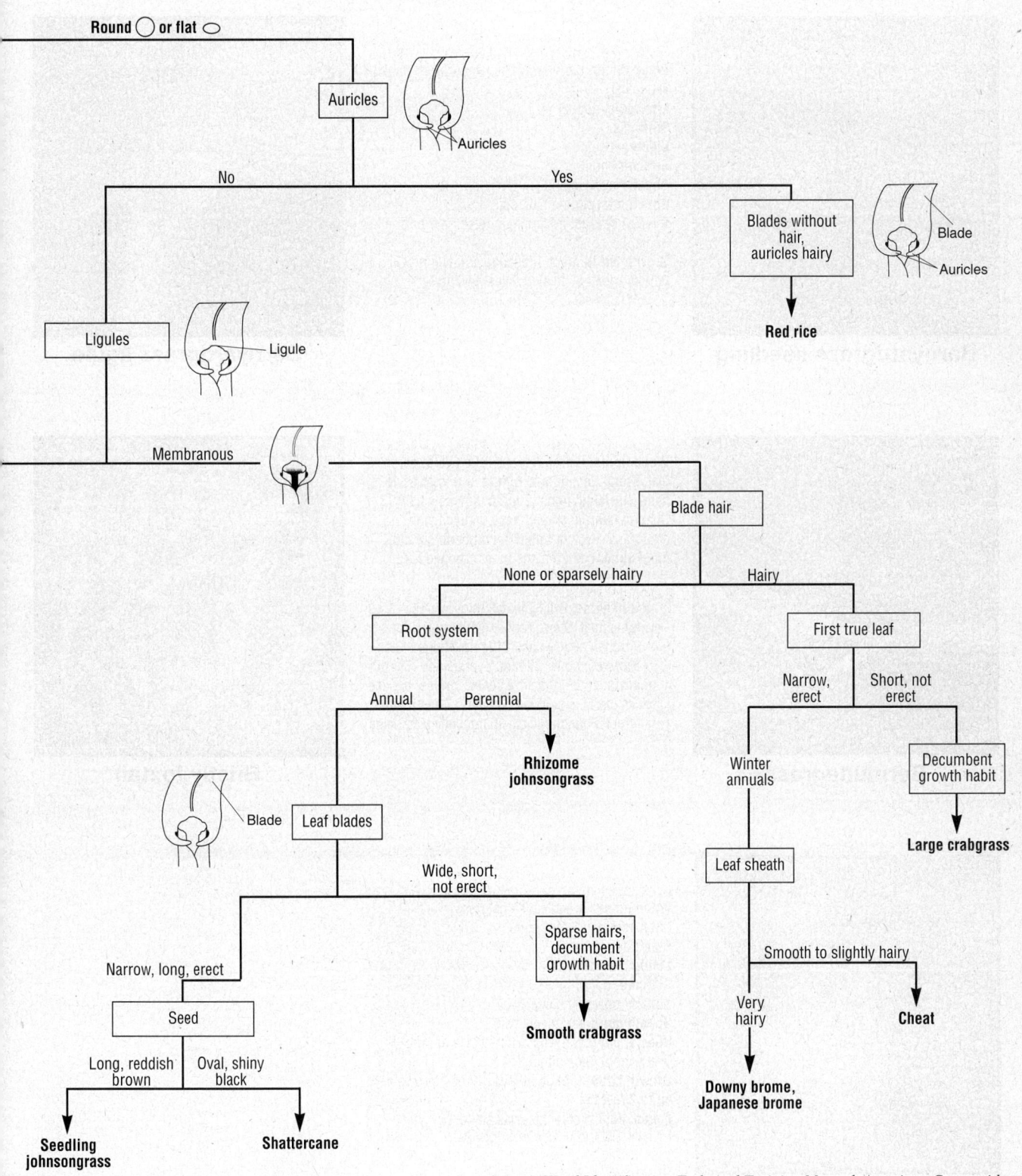

Round ◯ or flat ◯

Auricles
Auricles

No — Ligules
Ligule

Yes — Blades without hair, auricles hairy → **Red rice**
Blade
Auricles

Membranous — Blade hair

None or sparsely hairy — Root system

Hairy — First true leaf

Annual — Leaf blades
Blade

Perennial → **Rhizome johnsongrass**

Narrow, erect — Winter annuals

Short, not erect — Decumbent growth habit → **Large crabgrass**

Leaf sheath

Wide, short, not erect — Sparse hairs, decumbent growth habit → **Smooth crabgrass**

Narrow, long, erect — Seed

Very hairy → **Downy brome, Japanese brome**

Smooth to slightly hairy → **Cheat**

Long, reddish brown → **Seedling johnsongrass**

Oval, shiny black → **Shattercane**

Source: Weed Identification Technical Training Manual, American Cyanamid.

Photo Identification

Grasses

Weed name: Barnyardgrass (watergrass, Japanese millet)
Life cycle: annual
Stem: flat
Ligule: absent
Auricles: none
Sheath: overlapping
Sheath margin: no hair, split
Special charac: no ligule, reddish near bottom of plant
Growth habit: erect, branched at lower nodes
Found: moist cultivated fields, lowlands

Barnyardgrass seedling

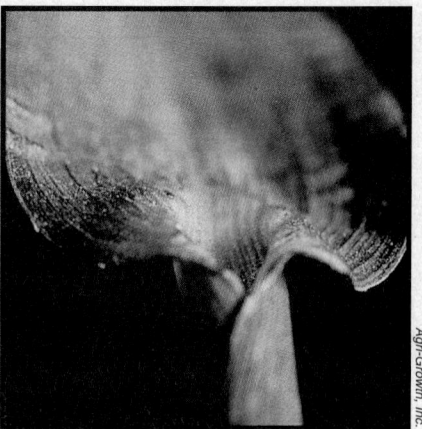

Barnyardgrass ligule

Weed name: Bermudagrass **Life cycle:** perennial **Stem:** decumbent **Ligule:** a ring of white hairs **Auricles:** none **Sheath:** sparsely hairy **Special charac:** sometimes confused with crabgrass **Growth habit:** decumbent, spreading **Found:** pastures and most cropped areas.

Weed name: Bristly foxtail (pigeongrass) **Life cycle:** annual **Stem:** round, erect, more branching than other foxtails **Ligule:** fringe of hairs **Auricles:** none **Sheath:** overlapping **Sheath margin:** smooth, split **Special charac:** panicle sticks easily to clothing, animals **Growth habit:** erect **Found:** cultivated, noncultivated fields

Bermudagrass

Bristly foxtail

Weed name: Broadleaf signalgrass
Life cycle: summer annual
Stem: decumbent
Ligule: row of hairs
Auricles: none
Sheath: sparsely hairy
Sheath margin: densely hairy
Special characteristics: leaf blades are relatively short, wide, smooth
Growth habit: rooting at lower nodes; grows up to 2 feet tall.
Found: cultivated fields, wastelands, ditches

Broadleaf signalgrass

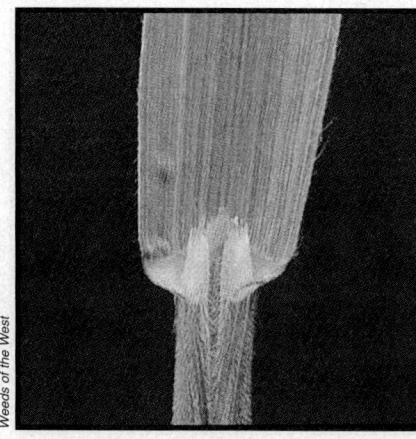

Weeds of the West

Cheat

Weed name: Cheat
Life cycle: annual
Stem: erect
Ligule: hairy
Auricles: tiny
Sheath: smooth or slightly hairy
Sheath margin: smooth or slightly hairy
Special charac: seeds usually germinate in the fall, young plants overwinter, mature by early summer
Growth habit: erect, 12-24 inches tall
Found: grain fields, meadows, waste areas

Weeds of the West

Cheat

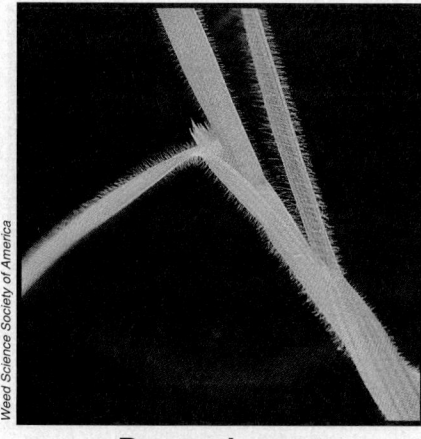

Weed Science Society of America

Downy brome

Weed name: Downy brome (drooping bromegrass)
Life cycle: winter annual
Stem: erect, 24 inches tall, round, pubescent
Ligule: prominent membrane with frayed margin, to 0.08 inches long
Auricles: none
Sheath: pubescent, united
Sheath margin: pubescent
Special charac: stems and leaves pubescent, nodes glabrous
Growth habit: erect, grows 6-24 inches tall
Found: rangelands, pastures, cultivated, no-till winter wheat

Weed Science Society of America

Downy brome

Agri-Growth, Inc.

Fall panicum ligule

Weed name: Fall panicum (smooth witchgrass)
Life cycle: annual
Stem: round, bent at nodes
Ligule: membrane fringed with hairs
Auricles: none
Sheath: compressed, smooth
Sheath margin: split
Special charac: thick compressed sheath
Growth habit: erect to decumbent
Found: cultivated fields, waste areas

Ellery Knake

Fall panicum

Photo Identification

Grasses

Weed name: Tall fescue **Life cycle:** annual
Stem: erect **Ligule:** has glossy appearance
Sheath: smooth **Sheath margin:** smooth
Special charac: leaves numerous, stiff, flat to
somewhat rolled **Growth habit:** grows up to 4
feet tall **Found:** roadsides, dry waste areas

Weed name: Foxtail barley **Life cycle:** perennial
Stem: usually erect **Ligule:** short membrane
Auricles: none **Sheath:** smooth **Sheath margin:**
may be some hairiness at base **Special charac:**
can grow 1-2 feet high **Growth habit:** usually
erect **Found:** pastures, waste areas, roadsides

Fescue

Foxtail barley

Weed name: Field sandbur
Life cycle: annual
Stem: erect or spreading
Ligule: fringe of short hair
Auricles: none
Sheath: loose
Sheath margin: bud leaves folded
Special charac: leaves less than 5 inches long
Growth habit: 6 inches to 2 feet tall
Found: cultivated field, roadsides, fencerows

Field sandbur seedling

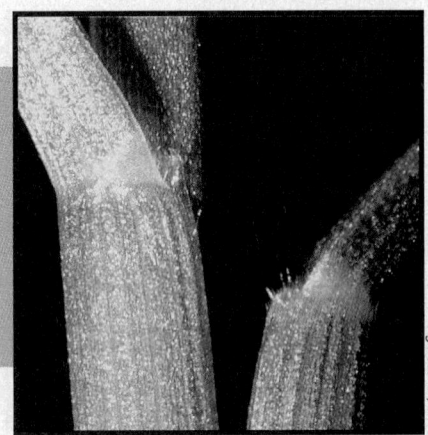

Field sandbur

Weed name: Giant foxtail (Chinese millet)
Life cycle: annual
Stem: round, long, slender, weak, may lodge
Ligule: fringed membranous
Auricles: none
Sheath: glabrous
Sheath margin: split
Special charac: pubescence on leaf margins
Growth habit: 3-7 feet tall
Found: cultivated crops

Giant foxtail

Giant foxtail ligule

Green foxtail ligule

Weed name: Green foxtail (green bristlegrass, pigeongrass)
Several varieties: robust white, robust purple, giant green foxtails (varieties are distinguishable only by genetic testing)
Life cycle: annual
Stem: round, glabrous, bent at nodes
Ligule: membranous, with fringe of hairs
Auricles: none
Sheath: glabrous except at margin
Sheath margin: split, hairy margins
Special characteristics: no hairs on leaf
Growth habit: erect
Found: cultivated fields, pastures, waste areas

Green foxtail

Johnsongrass

Weed name: Johnsongrass
Life cycle: perennial
Stem: round
Ligule: fringed, prominent membranes, some with fringe of hairs around base
Auricles: none
Sheath: glabrous
Sheath margin: split, with hairs at the collar
Special charac: thick scale-like rhizomes, seeds usually black, black fungus spots on leaves
Growth habit: erect
Found: cultivated fields, waste areas, roadsides, ditches

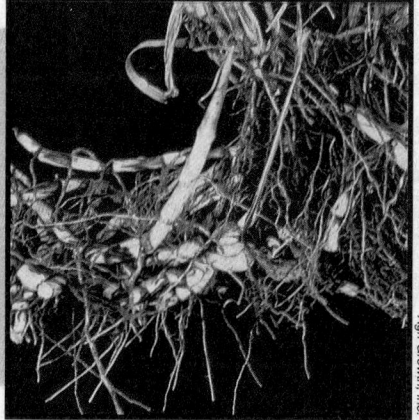

Johnsongrass rhizomes

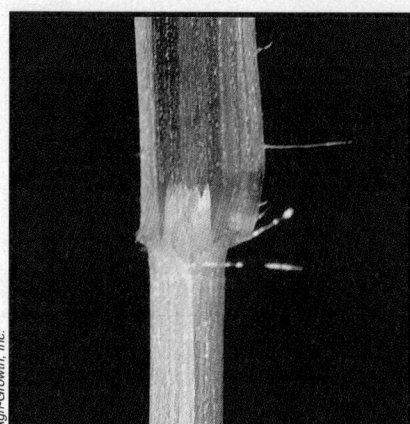

Jointed goatgrass ligule

Weed name: Jointed goatgrass
Life cycle: winter annual
Stem: round
Ligule: membranous
Auricles: present
Sheath: split, overlapping
Sheath margin: hairy, split
Special characteristics: stiff, thick-walled hairs on leaves, distinctive rounded, awned seed head
Growth habit: tufted, erect
Found: wheat fields, waste places

Jointed goatgrass

Photo Identification

Grasses

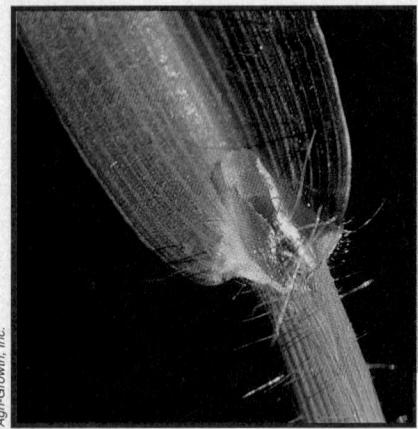

Large crabgrass ligule

Weed name: Large crabgrass
Life cycle: annual
Stem: prostrate at base
Ligule: membranous
Auricles: none
Sheath: hairy, loose
Sheath margin: densely long-haired
Special characteristics: leaves $1/4$-$1/3$ inches wide
Growth habit: stems grow up to 3 feet tall
Found: cultivated fields, waste areas, lawns

Large crabgrass

Orchardgrass ligule

Weed name: Orchardgrass (cock's foot)
Life cycle: perennial
Stem: erect
Ligule: none
Special charac: flowers borne on 1-sided clusters on stiff panicle branches
Growth habit: leaves $1/8$-$1/2$ inches wide
Found: roadsides

Orchardgrass

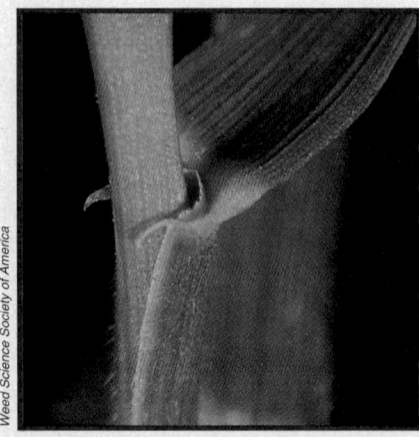

Quackgrass

Weed name: Quackgrass
Life cycle: perennial
Stem: erect, often bent out, up at base
Ligule: membranous, 0.02 inches long
Auricles: yes
Sheath: pubescent to glabrous
Sheath margin: glabrous, split
Special charac: rhizomes, auricles present
Growth habit: erect rhizome-forming plant
Found: waste areas, roadsides, fields

Quackgrass rhizomes

Weed Science Society of America

Weed name: Reed canarygrass
Life cycle: perennial
Stem: erect
Ligule: smooth
Auricles: somewhat blunt
Sheath: smooth
Sheath margin: has waxy coating
Special charac: stout
Growth habit: 2-7 feet tall
Found: wet ground, along streams and marshes

Reed canarygrass

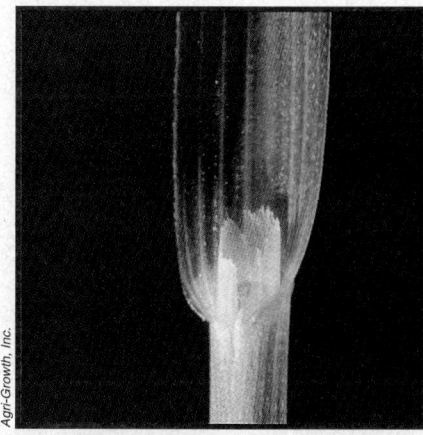

Agri-Growth, Inc.

Weed name: Shattercane
Life cycle: annual
Stem: round, slender to robust
Ligule: membranous with fringe of hairs
Auricles: none
Sheath: glabrous to pubescent
Sheath margin: split
Special charac: seed heads very large and open, ligule $^2/_3$ membranous, $^1/_3$ hair
Growth habit: erect with prop roots
Found: cultivated fields

Shattercane ligule

Weed Science Society of America

Shattercane

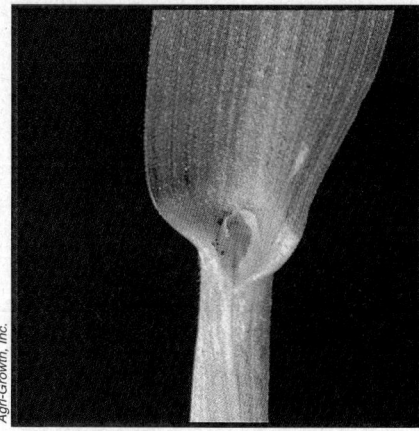

Agri-Growth, Inc.

Weed name: Smooth brome
Life cycle: perennial
Ligule: long ($^1/_3$-inch), membranous, pointed, toothed
Auricles: none
Sheath: pubescent
Special charac: leaf blades smooth, up to 12 inches long and $^1/_2$-inch wide. Flowering stems spreading. Survives periods of drought and temperature extremes.
Growth habit: spreading
Found: cultivated, uncultivated fields

Smooth brome ligule

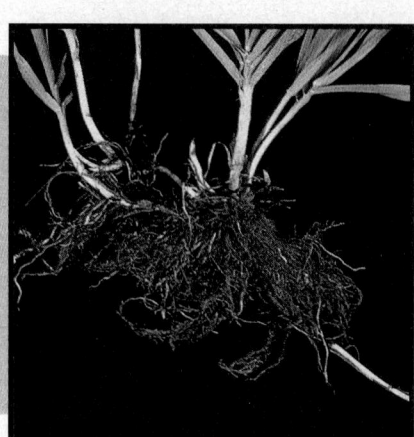

Agri-Growth, Inc.

Smooth brome rhizomes

Photo Identification

Grasses

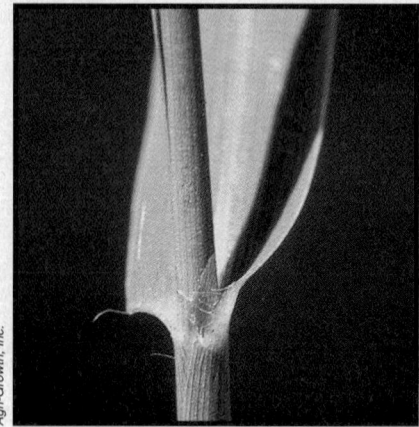

Weed name: Smooth crabgrass (fingergrass, smooth summergrass)
Life cycle: annual
Stem: erect or basally prostrate
Ligule: membranous
Auricles: none
Sheath: smooth
Sheath margin: sparsely hairy
Special charac: roots at lower nodes, stolons often present
Growth habit: grows best in warm conditions
Found: lawns, waste areas, cultivated fields

Smooth crabgrass

Smooth crabgrass

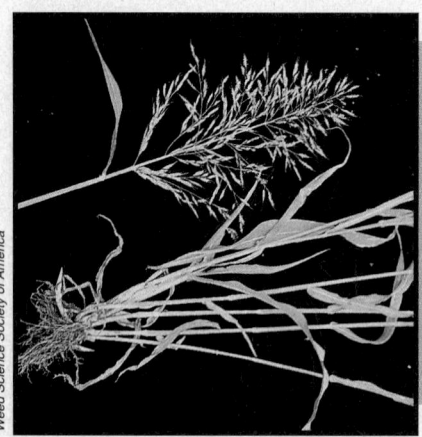

Weed name: Sorghum-almum (Columbusgrass, Desoto grass)
Life cycle: perennial
Stem: erect
Ligule: membranous
Auricles: none
Sheath: glabrous
Sheath margin: glabrous, split
Special charac: rhizomes short in length and not as extensive as rhizomes of Johnsongrass (*Sorghum halepense*); identical to Johnsongrass in the seedling stage of growth
Growth habit: erect rhizominous plant; at maturity twice as tall as Johnsongrass; a cross between shattercane and Johnsongrass
Found: wastelands, roadsides, cultivated and no-till fields

Sorghum-almum

Weed name: Texas panicum (Texas millet, buffalograss, Coloradograss)
Life cycle: annual
Stem: round
Ligule: short, membrane fringed with dense hairs
Auricles: none
Sheath: pubescent
Sheath margin: open
Special charac: soft, velvet-like pubescent leaf
Growth habit: creeping or decumbent
Found: moist cultivated fields, ditches, fence rows

Texas panicum seedling

Texas panicum

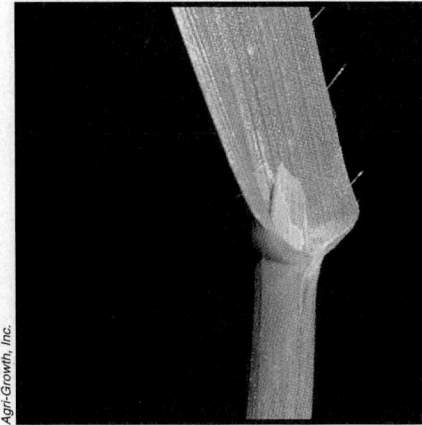

Weed name: Wild oat
Life cycle: annual
Stem: round
Ligule: long membranous
Auricles: none
Sheath: glabrous or pubescent
Sheath margin: split
Special charac: stout stem, long membranous ligule
Growth habit: erect
Found: cultivated fields, waste areas

Wild oat ligule

Wild oat

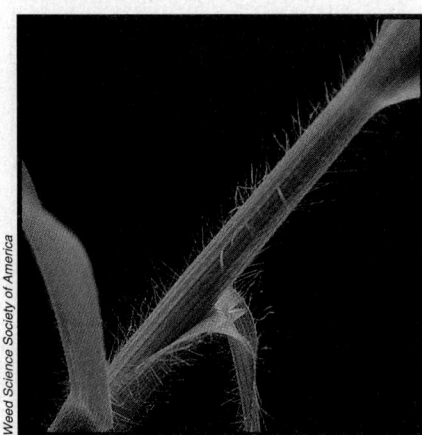

Weed name: Wild proso millet
Life cycle: annual
Stem: erect or spreading
Ligule: fringe of hairs
Auricles: none
Sheath: round, open, coarse hairs
Sheath margin: hairy, split
Special charac: leaves, leaf sheaths covered with dense, stiff hairs
Growth habit: erect and tall, either spreading or branched
Found: cultivated fields

Wild proso millet

Wild proso millet

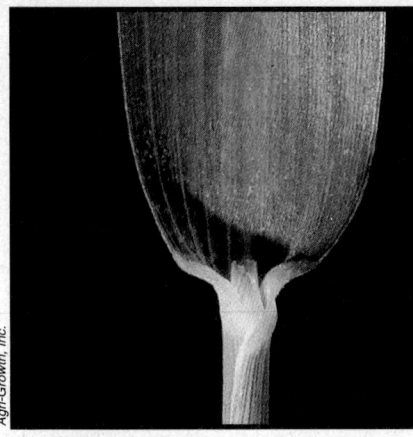

Weed name: Wirestem muhly
Life cycle: perennial
Stem: stout, erect, or prostrate, 24-36 inches tall, smooth below joints, rooting at lower nodes
Ligule: membranous with fine hairs
Auricles: none
Sheath: open and round, no hair
Sheath margin: no hair, split
Special charac: stem difficult to break
Growth habit: erect or prostrate, sprawling in nature with age, 2-3 feet tall
Found: rangelands, roadsides, cultivated fields, no-till fields

Wirestem muhly ligule

Wirestem muhly rhizome

Photo Identification

Grasses

Witchgrass seedling

Weed name: Witchgrass
Life cycle: annual
Stem: round
Ligule: hairy
Auricles: absent
Sheath: hairy
Sheath margin: hairy, split
Special charac: plant very hairy
Growth habit: tufted, erect
Found: grassy areas

Witchgrass

Woolly cupgrass, first leaf

Weed name: Woolly cupgrass
Life cycle: annual
Stem: round
Ligule: hairy membrane
Auricles: absent
Sheath: split, overlapping
Sheath margin: no hair
Special charac: distinct ring or cup below spikelet, pedicel and rachis pubescent; has very large seed
Growth habit: tufted, erect
Found: cultivated fields

Woolly cupgrass

Yellow foxtail ligule

Weed name: Yellow foxtail
Life cycle: annual
Stem: round
Ligule: membranous
Auricles: none
Sheath: overlapping
Sheath margin: split
Special charac: leaf blade is smooth, $^{1}/_{8}$-$^{3}/_{8}$-inch. Plant grows 1-3 feet tall
Growth habit: erect
Found: cultivated fields, roadsides, waste areas

Purple nutsedge

Weed name: Purple nutsedge
Life cycle: perennial
Stem: erect, triangular
Ligule: none
Auricles: none
Sheath: membranous
Sheath margin: tubular, overlapping
Special charac: stem and leaves dark green
Growth habit: two or three leaves emerging from ground simultaneously
Found: in moist conditions in sandy soils, cultivated fields

Yellow nutsedge

Weed name: Yellow nutsedge (chufa, coco, yellow nutgrass)
Life cycle: perennial
Stem: triangular
Leaf shape: linear
Leaf arrangement: three-ranked, mostly basal, blades green
Special charac: tubers not in chains, stem triangular, seed head yellow, leaves tapering to a sharp point
Growth habit: erect, colonial
Found: temperate and tropical regions worldwide

Yellow nutsedge

Photo Identification

Grasses, comparison photos

Not sure which grasses are in your field or orchard? Take a look at these comparison photos of grasses that look a lot alike to help narrow down the choices you might have.

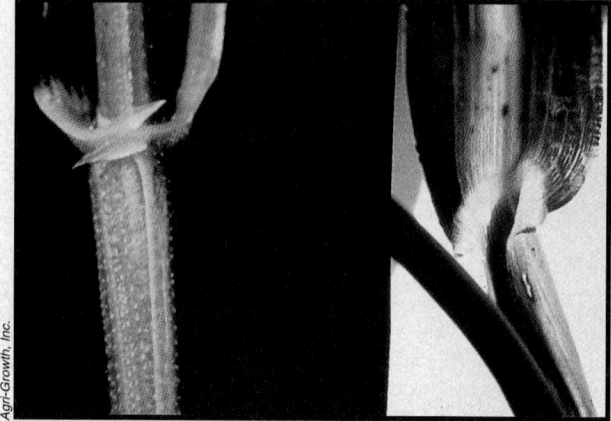

Quackgrass (left) and barnyardgrass

**Large crabgrass (left) and
Smooth crabgrass**

**Fall panicum (left) and
Yellow foxtail**

Agri-Growth Serves Industry

Providing solutions is the key to company services.

Agri-Growth, Inc. is committed to the future of agriculture. The ability to troubleshoot and provide solutions is key to the success of any business. Diagnostic tools range from herbicide injury symptom guides and crop production manuals to weed seedling identification guides (some photos are used in this edition of *Weed Control Manual*). These tools help you supply cost effective answers to today's crop production challenges.

For 20 years, the company's diagnostic materials have provided valuable information for anyone involved in crop production. Detailed disease and herbicide injury guides are organized by mode of action and contain additional photographs of look-alike symptoms. Guides are available for corn, cotton, grain sorghum, small grains, and soybeans. Training manuals, on-screen slide presentations, CD-ROMs, and videos present educational material on topics ranging from seed placement to precision agriculture. Crop production manuals address crop growth and development, plant stress management and other factors affecting productivity and profitability in alfalfa, corn, cotton, peanuts, potatoes, soybeans, sugarbeets, and wheat.

Whether it's programs for Certified Crop Advisers or customized training for agronomists and company representatives, Agri-Growth professional trainers offer a comprehensive hands-on learning experience. Workshops can be individualized to client's specific needs and each

Agri-Growth, Inc.
Route 1, Box 33
Hollandale, MN 56045-9799
507-889-4371, Fax: 507-889-4381
www.agrigrowth.com

offers complete training manuals, as well as live plants. Educational marketing sessions introduce new products to the marketplace or help revitalize interest in existing products.

Laboratory services offer soil testing for soybean cyst and other nematodes. Test results identify population levels and provide management recommendations. In the field, concept research programs look at crop production inputs ranging from seed and tillage to pesticides in commercial size trials using precision farming technology.

Challenge Days offers a day-long in-field program presented by leaders in industry on the newest aspects of increasing profitability in crop production. "The goal is to give industry personnel and producers more ways to increase profits by being on the leading edge of new technology," said Dr. James Ladlie, founder and president of Agri-Growth. □

Weed Science Society of America

The Weed Science Society of America promotes the development of weed science and technology. The organization sponsors an annual meeting where information on weed science is exchanged and technology is transferred.

In addition, the group works to promote high standards of education, research, extension, regulation, and other weed science matters.

The group's web site offers the opportunity to review weed photos (some are used in this edition of *Weed Control Manual*).

It's open to individuals and organizations interested in weed science. To become a member, you must pay annual dues. This allows attendance at the annual meeting as well as copies of Weed Science, Weed Technology, and the WSSA newsletter.

For more information contact:
Weed Science Society of America
P.O. Box 1897, 810 E. 10th St.
Lawrence, KS 66044-8897
800-627-0629, 785-843-1235
Fax: 785-843-1274
www.ext.agn.uiuc.edu/wssa
e-mail: wssa@allenpress.com

QUICK GUIDE TO WORKER PROTECTION CLOTHING & EQUIPMENT

This guide is intended for APPLICATION clothing & equipment, it is **not** intended for EARLY ENTRY or MIXING & LOADING.

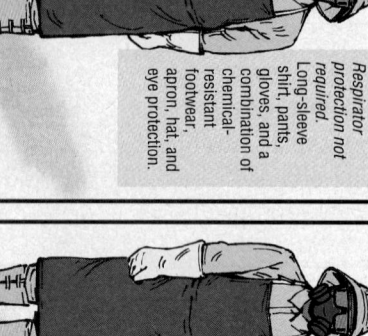

Use chemical-resistant gloves that extend to forearm or farther. Never wear leather, fabric, or fabric-lined gloves.

Minimum personal protective equipment requires long-sleeve shirt, long pants, and shoes with socks. Shirts and pants should be made of sturdy material with the shirt collar fastened to protect neck.

GREEN
These are the minimum requirements – long-sleeve shirt, long pants, shoes with socks, and waterproof or chemical-resistant gloves.

YELLOW
In addition to shirt, pants, and gloves, requires varying combinations of chemical resistant footwear, apron, hat, and eye protection as specified by label. Respirator protection is not required.

PURPLE
Requires coveralls over shirt and pants, chemical-resistant gloves, and varying combinations of chemical-resistant footwear, apron, hat, and eye protection as label specifies. Respirator protection not required.

ORANGE
Respirator protection required, plus coveralls over shirt and pants, chemical-resistant gloves and varying combinations of chemical-resistant footwear, apron, hat, and eye protection as label specifies.

BLUE
Shirt, pants, gloves, and varying combinations of chemical-resistant footwear, apron, hat, eye protection, and respirator as specified by label.

RED
Requires chemical-resistant protective suit, chemical-resistant gloves, chemical-resistant footwear, apron, hat, eye protection, and respirator as label requires.

GREEN
Long-sleeve shirt, long pants, shoes and socks, and waterproof or chemical-resistant gloves.

YELLOW
Respirator protection not required. Long-sleeve shirt, pants, gloves, and a combination of chemical-resistant footwear, apron, hat, and eye protection.

BLUE
Same as yellow, except requires respirator protection.

PURPLE
Respirator protection not required. Coveralls over shirt and pants, and a combination of chemical-resistant gloves, footwear, apron, hat, and eye protection.

ORANGE
Same as purple, except requires respirator protection.

RED
Chemical-resistant protective suit, chemical-resistant gloves, and footwear, apron, hat, eye protection, respirator.

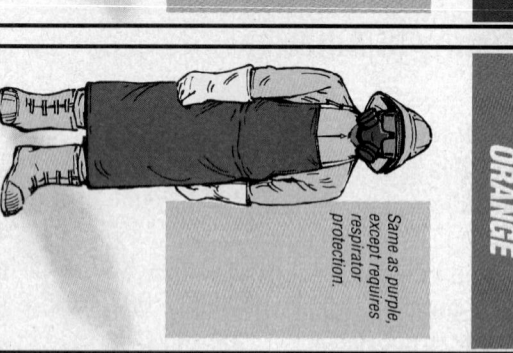

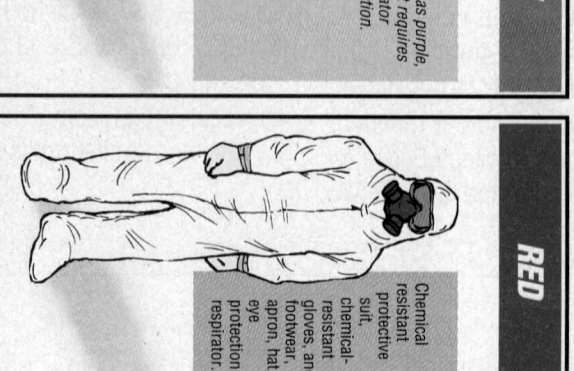

Make The Right Nozzle Selection

Minimize drift, improve droplet size, and make application more efficient with the right nozzle selection.

By Alvin R. Womac, Ph.D.

It's well known that drift can be minimized — and spray efficiency maximized — through selection of the proper sprayer nozzle. Droplet size also comes into play when selecting a nozzle. Typically, the larger the droplet size, the less chance there will be for drift.

But current pesticide labels usually do not recommend specific nozzles for specific pesticides for two reasons:

1. They wouldn't allow applicators any flexibility to best match the nozzle with the spray condition.

2. They wouldn't allow for use of new designs in nozzles without having to change labels as well.

Nonetheless, we know that nozzle type, flow rate, and operating pressure all influence the suitability of a nozzle application relating to droplet size — and that droplet size, in turn, may affect product performance, application efficiency, and drift. We also know that some products require varying levels of application droplet sizes, depending on the situation.

Label Language

Because of these facts, there is a trend toward specifying information for nozzle selection on labels. But, in practical terms, how specific can recommendations be?

The American Society of Agricultural Engineers — working with nozzle manufacturers, regulators, and the Spray Drift Task Force (with EPA and USDA) — has determined that the most practical approach would be to create general droplet size categories (such as very fine, which is the smallest; fine; medium; coarse; very coarse;

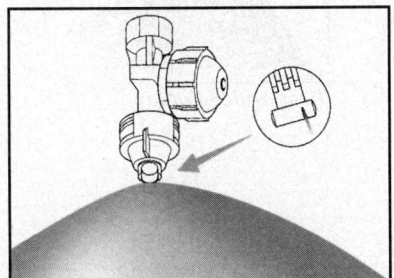
Turbo flat fan front

Flooding flat fan

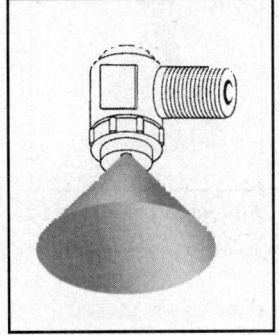
RA-raindrop

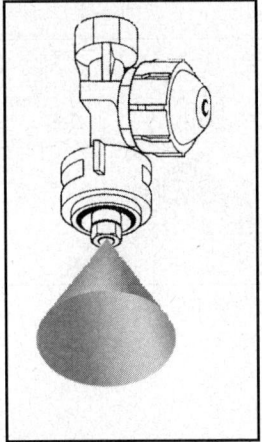
Hollow cone one piece

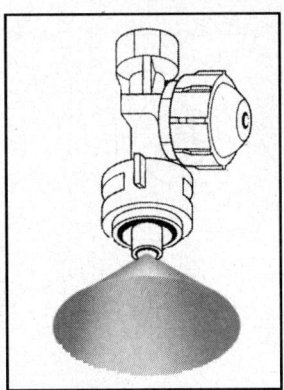
Wide angle full cone

and ultra course, which is the largest), then specify which nozzles would fall into each. This classification system would allow applicators more freedom to select nozzle type, size, and pressure — so long as the combination they selected produces the droplet size that falls within the specified category.

While a system of nozzle classification has not yet been fully developed and is not yet in effect, it likely will be in the next several years. The wise applicator will be well prepared. Here's a sneak preview of how it might work.

More Informed Choices

Currently, selecting a general nozzle type (such as a hollow-cone, flood, flat-fan, etc.) is the main consideration given to droplet size. For instance, cone types and flat-fans are selected for applications needing uniform foliage coverage from small droplets, while flood nozzles are selected for applica-

tions that can use large droplets, such as soil incorporation.

These basic selections will remain unchanged — except that the nozzle user will have more information to see how much the droplets vary in size. Nozzle classification will add a degree of refinement to nozzle selection. The main reason: Nozzle tips at different pressures can be compared for droplet size quality. Therefore, a nozzle can fall into two or more categories because operating pressure affects droplet size.

Other factors to consider when spraying include:

• Sprayer speed. More droplets will not fall on the leaf if the sprayer is going too fast.

• Improper mixing or agitation. If there is not enough herbicide product in the droplets, there won't be adequate control.

• Application timing. According to research, some products work better if applied earlier in the day to allow the plant more time for photosynthesis. ☐

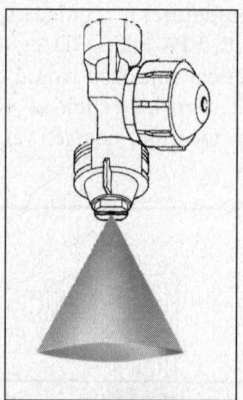
Flat fan extended range

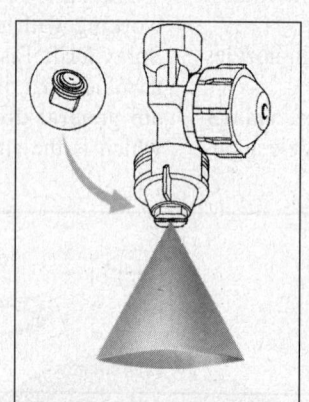
Drift reduction

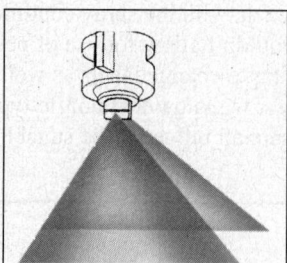
Twin orifice flat fan

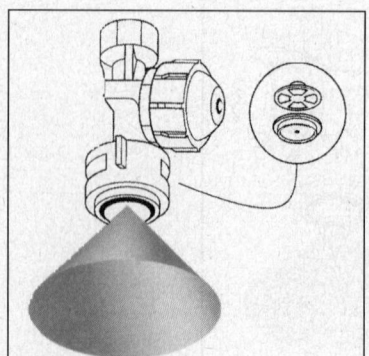
Hollow core disk-core

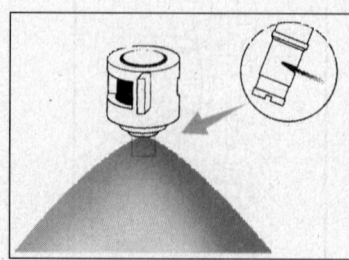
Turbo flood flat fan

Herbicide Classification

The mode of action of herbicides varies, with each acting on a different part of the weed plant. Here's a look at some herbicides and how they work.

Herbicide mode of action can be defined as the primary mechanism of herbicide interference with plant function that leads to death.

Herbicides are often classified according to their mode of action, because as a general rule, herbicides within the same mode of action class will produce similar symptoms on susceptible plants. There are seven major mode of action categories described here. Chemical families, representative herbicides, and some unique characteristics are listed within each category.

Cell Membrane Disruptors

Most of the herbicides listed below are effective only when applied postemergent. Membrane disruption in treated plants causes the foliage to initially have a watersoaked appearance, which is followed by rapid wilting and eventually a "burned" or frost-damaged appearance of the foliage.

Compared with herbicides with other modes of action, symptoms of membrane disruptors develop rapidly after application on susceptible plants, usually within a few hours or up to a couple of days, depending on the specific herbicide. Because these herbicides generally have limited translocation on plant tissues, adequate spray coverage and a proper adjuvant are often required for maximum weed control activity. Activity of these herbicides increases with sunlight, temperature, and humidity. There are four classes:

Bipyridyliums
Gramoxone Extra (paraquat), diquat
Diphenyl ethers
Blazer (acifluorfen), Reflex, Flexstar (fomesafen), Cobra (Lactofen)
N-phenylphthalimides
Resource (flumiclorac-pentyl)
Aryltriazolinones
Authority (sulfentrazone), Aim (carfentrazone-ethyl)

Growth Regulators

Plant growth regulators mimic the activity of hormones occurring naturally in the plant system. However, growth regulators are toxic to many plants because they are much more potent than natural hormones and can cause secondary effects that inhibit normal plant growth. Most herbicides in this family are highly systemic, meaning they translocate internally to other parts of the shoot, the roots, and other underground vegetative organs (rhizomes, creeping roots) if applied to plants at the proper growth stage. They are toxic mainly to broadleaf weeds, but can injure some grasses, including small grains and corn if applied during sensitive stages of growth. Injury symptoms on susceptible plants develop first on the newly developing tissues in the meristematic regions (growing points) of the plant.

Growth regulator herbicides cause growth abnormalities in susceptible plants, and symptoms on breadleaves may include malformed or strapped leaves, parallel leaf veins, twisted stems, and stem splitting or brittleness. Symptoms on grasses include onionleafing, brittle stalks, fused and malformed brace roots, curved stems, and malformed ears or seedheads. There are three classes of growth regulator herbicides:

Benzoic acids
Banvel, Clarity (dicamba)
Phenoxy acids
2,4-D, 2,4-DB, MCPA
Pyridine carboxylic acids
Stinger (clopyralid), Tordon (picloram), Garlon (triclopyr)

Photosynthesis Inhibitors

Photosynthesis inhibitors block the process whereby plants convert sunlight into the chemical energy required for further growth processes. Photosynthesis inhibitors are toxic primarily to broadleaf plants, but some herbicides in this class are toxic to certain grass species at an early growth stage. Some photosynthetic inhibitors are mobile in the plant (triazines, phenylureas, uracils), moving upward from the site of absorption with water and mineral nutrients. For this reason, these herbicides are usually soil-applied so that weeds will absorb the herbicide via the roots, although they also have foliar activity if applied with adjuvants and good spray coverage. Other photosynthetic inhibitors are not mobile in plants and are classified as postemergence contact herbicides (nitriles, benzothiadiazoles).

These herbicides have no soil activity. The most common symptom of mobile photosynthesis inhibitors in susceptible plants is chlorosis (yellowing) of the leaf tissue. In grasses, symptoms first appear on the older leaves near the base of the plant. Leaf tips and margins first show chlorosis and eventually turn necrotic. In broadleaves, the oldest leaves are affected first and show leaf margin and interveinal chlorosis, followed by necrosis. There are several classes of this herbicide:

Mobile Photosynthetic Inhibitors
Triazines

Bladex (atrazine, cyanazine), Sencor (metribuzin), Princep, Caliber 90 (simazine), Pramitol (prometon), Evik (ametryn), Velpar (hexazinone)

Phenylureas

Karmex (diuron), Lorox, linuron, Spike (tebuthiuron)

Uracils

Hyvar (bromacil), Sinbar (terbacil)

Non-mobile Photosynthetic Inhibitors
Benzothiadiazoles

Basagran (bentazon)

Nitriles

Buctril (bromoxynil), Tough (pyridate)

Pigment Inhibitors

In contrast to the photosynthesis inhibitors, pigment inhibitors do not directly block photosynthesis, but inhibit the production of certain plant pigments necessary for photosynthesis. Symptoms include bleaching and chlorosis of the foliar tissue, which sometimes results in plants that appear totally white. Pigment inhibitors are translocated upward and are used primarily as soil-applied treatments.

Isoxazolidinone
Command (clomazone)

Other
Balance (isoxaflutole), Sonar (fluridone), Pyramin (pyrazon)

Seedling Growth Inhibitors

Regions of active cell division (meristems) in plants are located in both the shoots and roots. Seedling growth inhibitors affect some fundamental process in meristematic regions that prevents normal growth and development of young plant tissue. Seedling growth inhibitors must be soil applied because they are taken up by plants after germination until the seedling emerges from the soil. These herbicides are thus effective only on seedling annual or perennial weeds. Plants that emerge from the soil uninjured are likely to remain unaffected, although occasionally root inhibition that occurs early in the plant's development is not noticed until it affects later growth. This broad category can be further subdivided into the following types of herbicides:

1. Shoot meristem inhibitors (chloroacetamides and thiocarbamates)

2. Root meristem inhibitors (dinitroanilines – DNA's)

The exact mode of action of the chloroacetamides and thiocarbamates is not known. The dinitroanilines inhibit a crucial step in the process of cell division. Specific symptoms for each chemical class are listed below.

Shoot Meristem Inhibitors

• Effective primarily on annual grasses and some small-seeded broadleaves.

• Active only as soil-applied treatment.

• Translocated slightly upward.

• Grass injury symptoms include underground leafing out and improper unfurling of new leaves (buggy-whipping).

• Broadleaf injury symptoms are leaf-crinkling and/or drawstring appearance of leaf veins, stunting.

Chloroacetamides
Partner, MicroTech (alachlor), Surpass, TopNotch, Harness (acetochlor), Dual II (*s*-metolachlor), Frontier (dimethenamid), Axiom (flufenacet)

Thiocarbamates
• Effective primarily on annual grasses and some small-seeded broadleaves.

• Active only as soil-applied treatments, must be incorporated due to volatility.

• Grass symptoms include plant malformation and twisting, leaf crinkling, and buggy-whipping.

• Broadleaf symptoms include leaf crinkling, puckering, and bud-seal.

Eptam, Eradicane (EPTC)

Root Meristem Inhibitors

• Effective on annual grasses and some small-seeded broadleaves.

• Active only as soil-applied treatments, some must be incorporated.

• Does not translocate.

• General injury symptoms include stunting and inhibited root development. Affected root systems have a lack of secondary roots and root hairs, and are often short with a club-shaped appearance. Grass shoots may appear purple or reddish, and broadleaves (including soybeans) may have swollen and cracked hypocotyls, crinkled leaves and/or surface callus on stems, and/or brittleness.

Balan (benefin), Treflan (trifluralin), Prowl (pendimethalin), Sonalan (ethalfluralin)

Amino Acid Synthesis Inhibitors

The amino acid synthesis inhibitors act on a specific enzyme to prevent the production of amino acids, which are the building blocks for protein synthesis and, thus, plant growth and development. Sulfonylurea, imidazolinone, and sulfonamide herbicides inhibit the same enzyme, acetolactate synthase (ALS), blocking the production of three essential amino acids.

Glyphosate and sulfosate block the synthesis of three amino acids by inhibiting another enzyme. This category is therefore further subdivided according to the enzyme that is inhibited: ALS inhibitors and EPSP synthase inhibitors. Injury symptoms are slow to develop and include a stunting or slowing of plant growth and eventual death. Symptoms are likely to show in the new plant growth first because movement of these herbicides is to those areas.

ALS Inhibitors

• Translocated in both the apoplast (upward) and symplast (downward).
• Soil and foliar activity.
• Grass symptoms include severe stunting, purpling of new leaves, lateral root pruning with severe injury causing roots to have a "bottle brush" appearance.
• Plant necrosis and death is gradual, usually occurring over several days.

Imidazolinones

Scepter (imazaquin), Pursuit (imazethapyr), Raptor (imazamox), Contain, Arsenal, Lightning (imazapyr)

Sulfonylureas

• Translocated in both the apoplast and symplast.
• Soil and foliar activity.
• Injury symptoms similar to those of imidazolinones.

Classic (chlorimuron), Accent (nicosulfuron), Beacon (primisulfuron), Pinnacle (thifensulfuron), Oust (sulfometuron), Express (tribenuron), Permit (halosulfuron-methyl), Peak (prosulfuron), Basis, Basis Gold (rimsulfuron)

Sulfonamides

• Translocated in both the apoplast and symplast.
• Soil and foliar activity.
• Injury symptoms similar to those of imidazolinones and sulfonylurea herbicides.

Broadstrike, Hornet, Scorpion III (flumetsulam), FirstRate (cloransulam-methyl)

EPSP Synthase Inhibitors

Phosphono Amino Acids

• Non-selective, used for burndown applications or non-crop weed control.
• Translocated in both the apoplast and symplast.
• No soil activity; rapidly inactivated.

• Injury symptoms are relatively slow to develop and include discoloration of the foliage, chlorosis of new leaves often accompanied by red or purplish discoloration of older leaves. Plant decline is gradual, ending with total necrosis.

Roundup Ultra (glyphosate), Touchdown (sulfosate)

Glutamine Synthetase Inhibitors

The enzyme glutamine synthetase allows the plant cell to convert ammonia, a product of various plant processes, into amino acids. Glutamine synthetase inhibitors block the activity of this enzyme. The result is a buildup of phytotoxic ammonia and a lack of essential amino acids, which inhibits photorespiration and photosynthesis and ultimately results in plant death. Glufosinate-ammonium, currently the glutamine synthetase inhibitor, has foliar activity only. Translocation within the plant is limited. Primary symptoms of activity are a rapid necrosis of leaf tissue followed by plant death.

Liberty (glufosinate-ammonium)

ACCase Inhibitors

ACCase or lipid inhibitors prevent the formation of fatty acids, which are essential components for the production of plant lipids. This occurs through the inhibition of a single enzyme involved in fatty acid synthesis. Lipids are vital to the integrity of cell membranes and to new plant growth. Broadleaf plants are unaffected by these herbicides, but most grasses are susceptible.

• Foliar-applied only.
• Selectively toxic only to grasses.
• Translocated in both the apoplast and symplast.
• Some have slight soil activity, relatively short persistance.
• Grass injury symptoms are slow to develop and include chlorosis followed by necrosis of newest leaf tissue emerging from the whorl: the whorl leaves can be easily pulled from the rest of the plant after 4 to 7 days. Plant death occurs within 10 days to 2 weeks.

Aryloxyphenoxypropionates

Fusilade DX, Fusion (fluazifop-P), Assure II (quizalofop-p-ethyl), Option II, Fusion (fenoxaprop)

Cyclohexanediones

Poast, Poast Plus (sethoxydim), Select (clethodim)   □

Source: This article is from *Weed Control Guide for Ohio Field Crops, 1999.*

Formulation Guide

There are many different types of formulations to choose from when making an herbicide decision. Here's a look at what some of the choices are.

The active ingredient (a.i.) is the agent in a formulation which has a specific effect on a pest, weed, or plant. A single active ingredient often is sold in several different kinds of formulations. You must choose the formulation that will be best for each use. In making your choice, consider:

• Application machinery available and best suited for the job;

• Hazard of drift and runoff (nearness to sensitive areas, likelihood of wind or rain);

• Safety to applicator, helpers, other humans, and pets likely to be exposed;

• Habits or growth patterns of the pest (bait vs. broadcast spray, granular vs. foliar spray);

• The plant, animal, or surface to be protected (phytotoxicity, animal absorption, pitting or marring surface);

• Cost; and

• Type of environment in which the application must be made (agricultural, aquatic, forest, urban, etc.).

The amount of active ingredient and the kind of formulation are listed on the label. For instance, a 50 W contains 50% by weight of a.i. and is a wettable powder. If it is a 10 lb. bag, it contains 5 lb. of a.i. and 5 lb. of inert ingredients. Liquid formulations indicate the amount of a.i. in pounds per gallon. For instance, a 4E means 4 lb. per gallon of the a.i. in an emulsifiable concentrate formulation.

Aerosol

1. Ready to use type such as household sprays. Commercial type holds 5 to 10 pounds of formulation and can be refillable.

2. For smoke or fog generators that break the liquid formulation into a fine mist or fog using a rapidly whirling disc or a heated surface.

DF or WDG - Dry Flowables

Dry flowables, also known as water-dispersible granules, are like wettable powders except the active ingredient is formulated on a granule instead of a powder. Requires agitation. Easier to pour and mix than wettable powders because there is less dust.

D - Dusts

Low percentage of a.i. on a very fine dry inert carrier like talc, chalk or clay. Most are ready to use. Danger of drift.

EC or E - Emulsifiable Concentrate

A liquid formulation containing the a.i., one or more solvents, and an emulsifier which allows mixing with water.

Advantages:

• High concentration means price per pound of a.i. is relatively low and product is easy to handle, transport, and store.

• Little agitation required; not abrasive; will not settle out or separate when equipment is running.

• Little visible residue on fresh fruits and vegetables and on finished surfaces.

Disadvantages:

• High concentration makes it easy to overdose or underdose through mixing or calibration errors.

• Phytotoxicity hazard usually greater.

• Easily absorbed through skin of humans or animals.

• Solvents may cause rubber or plastic hoses, gaskets, and pump parts and surfaces to deteriorate.

F or FL - Flowable

A liquid formulation consisting of finely ground active ingredient suspended in liquid. Is mixed with water for application.

Advantages:

• Seldom clog nozzles.

• Easy to handle and apply.

Disadvantages:

• Require moderate agitation.

• May leave a visible residue.

G - Granules

Most often used for soil applications. The a.i. is coated or absorbed onto coarse particles like clay, ground walnut shells, or ground corn cobs.

Advantages:

• Ready to use; no mixing.

• Drift hazard is low because particles settle quickly.

• No spray, little dust mean low hazard to applicator.

• Weight carries formulation through foliage to soil target.

• Simple application equipment, often seeders or fertilizer spreaders.

Disadvantages:
- Won't stick to foliage.
- More expensive than WPs or ECs.
- May need to be incorporated into soil.
- May need moisture to activate pesticidal action.

Invert Emulsion
A water soluble pesticide dispersed in an oil carrier. Forms large droplets which do not drift easily.

Low Concentrate Solution
Small amounts of a.i., 1% or less, used without dilution for structural pests, space sprays in barns, mosquito control, etc.

Microencapsulation
Particles of a pesticide, either liquid or dry, surrounded by a plastic coating. Mixed with water and applied as a spray. Encapsulation makes timed release possible.

SP - Soluble Powder
A dry formulation which, when mixed with water, dissolves readily and forms a true solution. When thoroughly mixed, no agitation necessary. Not many formulations of this type are available because few active ingredients are soluble in water.

S - Solution
For those active ingredients which dissolve readily in water, of which there are relatively few in number. The formulation is a liquid and usually consists of the a.i. and additives. When mixed with water will not settle out or separate.

Water-Soluble Packet
Water-soluble packets are used to reduce the mixing and handling hazards of some highly toxic pesticides. Preweighed amounts of wettable powder or soluble powder formulations are packaged in water-soluble plastic bags. When the bags are dropped into a filled spray tank, they dissolve and release their contents to mix with the water. There are no risks of inhaling or coming into contact with the undiluted pesticide during mixing as long as the packets are not opened.

WP or W - Wettable Powders
Dry, finely ground formulations which look like dusts. The a.i. is combined with a finely ground dry carrier, usually mineral clay, along with other ingredients that enhance the ability of the powder to suspend in water. The powder is mixed with water for application as a spray. Wettable powders are one of the most widely used pesticide formulations.

Advantages:
- Low cost.
- Easy to store, transport, and handle.
- Lower phytotoxicity hazard than ECs and other liquid formulations.
- Easily measured and mixed.
- Less skin and eye absorption than ECs and other liquid formulations.

Disadvantages:
- Inhalation hazard to applicator while pouring, mixing.
- Require good and constant agitation (usually mechanical) in the spray tank.
- Abrasive to many pumps and nozzles.
- Residues may be visible. □

Source: Applying Pesticides Correctly, Ohio State University; Safe & Effective Use of Pesticides, University of California.

Suffixes of Chemical Brand Names

Suffix	Meaning
Formulations:	
AF	Aqueous Flowable
AS	Aqueous Suspension
D	Dust
DF	Dry Flowable, also Water-Dispersible Granule
EC or E	Emulsifiable Concentrate
ES	Emulsifiable Solution
F or FL	Flowable
G	Granular
OL	Oil-Soluble liquid
P or PS	Pelleted
S	Solution
SL	Slurry
SP	Soluble Powder
SG	Sand Granules
ULV	Ultra-Low Volume Concentrate
W or WP	Wettable Powder
WDG	Water-Dispersible Granules, also Dry Flowable
WSB	Water-soluble Bag
WSP	Water-soluble Pak or Packet
How A Pesticide Is Used:	
AG	Agricultural
GS	For Treatment of Grass Seed
LSR	For Leaf Spot and Rust
PM	For Powdery Mildew
RP	For Range and Pasture
RTU	Ready to Use
SD	For Use as a Side Dressing
TC	Termiticide Concentrate
TGF	Turf Grass Fungicide
WK	To Be Used with Weed Killers
Describe Characteristics Of The Formulation:	
BE	The Butyl Ester of 2,4-D
D	An Ester of 2,4-D
K	A Potassium Salt of the Active Ingredient
LO	Low Odor
LV	Low Volatility
MF	Modified Formulation
T	A Triazole
2X	Double Strength

Glossary of Weed Terms

What do all of those weed management terms mean? Find out here.

ACCase inhibitors. Herbicides that inhibit acetyl coenzyme A carboxylase (ACCase), an enzyme necessary for synthesis of fatty acids in a plant.

ACR. Acreage Conservation Reserve. A percentage of each program crop base which must be idled annually to participate in the Acreage Reduction Program. The ACR percentage is set by USDA annually based on supply and demand factors.

Active ingredient (ai). The chemical in a pesticide or herbicide formulation primarily responsible for its phytotoxicity and which is identified as the active ingredient on the product label.

Adjuvant. Any substance in a herbicide formulation or added to the spray tank to modify herbicidal activity or application characteristics.

AHAS inhibitors. Herbicides that inhibit acetohydroxyacid synthase (AHAS), also called acetolactate synthase (ALS), a key enzyme in the biosynthesis of certain amino acids in the plant.

Allelopathy. The adverse effect on the growth of plants or microorganisms caused by the action of chemicals produced by other living or decaying plants.

ALS inhibitors. Herbicides that inhibit acetolactate synthase (ALS), also called acetohydroxyacid synthase (AHAS), a key enzyme in the biosynthesis of certain amino acids in the plant.

Amine formulation. Many chemical structures, 2,4-D for example, can be formulated either as amine salts or ester formulations. Common usage is to treat target weeds with amine formulations in late spring and in the summer when high temperatures and low humidity favor volatilization.

Antagonism. Interaction of two chemicals having an opposing or neutralizing effect on each other, or — given some specific biological effect — a chemical interaction that appears to have an opposing or neutralizing effect over what might otherwise be expected.

Band treatment. Applied to linear restricted strip on or along crop rows rather than being continuous over the field area.

Basal treatment. Applied to encircle the stem of a plant just above the soil surface so that foliage contact is minimal. A term used mostly to describe this particular treatment on woody plants.

Bed. 1. A ridge or elevated strip of soil formed for planting crops above furrows on each side. **2.** An area in which seedlings or nursery stock are grown for later transplanting in the field.

Binding site. Where a herbicide attaches to a site of action.

Boot or Booting. A growth stage of grasses (including cereal crops) when the upper leaf sheath swells due to the growth of the developing spike or panicle.

Broadcast treatment. Application of a herbicide or pesticide over the entire field.

Burndown. A herbicide treatment, most commonly in a conservation tillage situation, designed to kill or stunt a cover crop or weeds in preparation for planting of the next crop.

BXN Cotton. Varieties of cotton developed by Stoneville Seed Co. that are not affected by bromoxynil herbicide when applied over-the-top to the emerged crop.

Compatibility. The characteristic of a substance, especially a pesticide, of being mixable in a formulation or in the spray tank for application in the same carrier without undesirably altering the characteristics or effects of the individual components.

Conservation tillage. Any tillage or planting system that maintains at least 30% coverage of the soil surface by residue after planting. The three broad categories of conservation tillage include no-till, ridge-till, and mulch-till. In no-till, the soil is left undisturbed from harvest to planting except for nutrient injection. This is also true in ridge-till, which differs by having a seedbed prepared on ridges with sweeps, disc openers, coulters, row cleaners, or other equipment. In mulch-till, the soil is disturbed prior to planting.

Contact herbicide. A herbicide that is phytotoxic by contact with plant tissue rather than a result of translocation.

Cotyledons. Seed leaves. They originate from the seed and provide the seedling with energy until the first "true" leaves develop.

Cracking. The time just prior to seedling emergence when the soil cracks and the surface is pushed upward by growth of the emerging seedling.

CRP. Conservation Reserve Program. A voluntary program that offers annual rental payments, incentive payments for certain activities, and assistance to establish approved cover on eligible cropland. It encourages farmers to plant long-term resource-conserving covers to improve soil, water, and wildlife resources. Contract durations range from 10-15 years.

Crust. A surface layer on soils, ranging in thickness from a few millimeters to perhaps as much as 3 cm. This layer is much more compact, hard, and brittle when dry than the material immediately beneath it.

Cultivation. Cultivate shallow to prevent bringing new weed seeds to the surface. Do not cultivate soon after application of most postemergence herbicides unless weeds appear. If weeds appear and dry weather occurs during the 2 weeks following application, rotary hoe or cultivate shallowly. If postemergence herbicide is soil applied, delay cultivation 7 to 10 days to allow chemical to work. Refer to label for instructions.

Days to harvest. The period during which application of a pesticide must not be made because of danger of exceeding the tolerance level. Refer to label for this information.

Defoliant. Any substance or mixture of substances for which the primary use is to cause the leaves or foliage to drop from a plant.

Desiccant. Any substance or mixture of substances used to accelerate the drying of plant tissue.

Directed application. Precise application to a specific area or plant such as to a row or bed or to the leaves or stems of plants.

Early postemergence. A herbicide treatment applied when the weed or crop first emerges.

Emergence. The event in seedling establishment when a shoot becomes visible by pushing through the soil surface.

Enhanced seed. Seed products that have been improved through traditional breeding or genetic engineering to tolerate or resist herbicides, insects, or diseases.

EPP. Early preplant treatment.

Ester formulation. Many chemicals, including 2,4-D, can be formulated as amine salts or esters. Ester formulations can penetrate the plant cuticle more easily than can amine salts. Ester formulations therefore are more suitable to use early in the spring when winter weeds are protected by a thick, waxy cuticle. However, esters tend to be more volatile than amines, which means they can drift when conditions are right — high temperatures and low humidity. At such times, amine salts are more suitable herbicides than ester formulations.

EUP. Experimental Use Permit. Granted to a pesticide for which registration is pending and which is approved for experimental use on certain crops in certain areas.

Foliar application. Application of a herbicide to the leaves or foliage of plants.

Gene stacking. Breeding crops for resistance or tolerance to more than one herbicide, class of herbicides, insects, or diseases.

Glabrous. Hairless, smooth. Used when referring to parts of a plant. Weeds include common and tall waterhemp.

Graminicide. A herbicide for control of grass weeds.

Herbicide resistance. The survival of a crop or weed species after herbicides have been applied to it. Resistance has been bred into some soybean, cotton, field corn, and canola crops.

IMI-Corn. The common term for corn hybrids that are either tolerant or resistant to imidazolinone herbicides. Is now marketed by American Cyanamid as the Clearfield system.

Incorporation. The mixing or blending of a herbicide into the soil with application equipment.

IPM. Integrated Pest Management programs are effective in optimizing inputs in the most efficient way to achieve weed control. IPM involves a combination of tillage practices, crop rotations, and herbicides to achieve most beneficial results. Field monitoring or scouting is an important part of IPM to quantify and identify weed pressures and determine at what population levels control measures should be started before crop yields are adversely affected. The aim is not for "absolutely clean" fields but for "economically" clean fields.

IT-Tolerant. Designation for corn hybrids that are tolerant to imazethapyr, one of the imidazolinone herbicides.

Leaching. Downward movement of a material in solution through soil.

Ligule. A structure on the inside of the collar. It is either membranous, hairy, or absent. Usually don't develop until the third or fourth leaf stage.

LL crops. Varieties developed that are resistant to Liberty (glufosinate-ammonium) herbicide.

Midrib. The central vein running lengthwise along the underside of a leaf or cotyledon; underside of midvein.

Mode of action. Describes the impact of the chemical on key biochemical process(es) responsible for its effect on plant growth, i.e., how the herbicide injures or kills the plant. Some herbicides, for example, inhibit photosynthesis or disrupt cell membranes.

Mulch-till. A form of conservation tillage in which the soil is disturbed prior to planting. Tillage tools such as chisels, field cultivators, discs, openers, coulters, or row cleaners may be used.

Nonselective herbicide. A chemical that is generally toxic to plants without regard to species (may be a function of dosage, methods of application, etc.).

Non-target species. A species affected by a pesticide application but not intentionally targeted.

No-till. A form of conservation tillage in which the soil is left undisturbed from harvest to planting except for nutrient injection.

Noxious weeds. Those weeds regulated by law or those that are so difficult to control that early detection is important. The Noxious Weed Act of 1974 lists more than 90 foreign species tracked by the USDA-ARS. Noxious weeds targeted include witchweed, tropical soda apple, mile-a-minute, hydrilla, salsola, hemp, broomrape, and common crupina. Authority to prevent foreign weeds from the U.S. is provided in the Federal Seed Act of 1939, Federal Pest Act of 1957, and the Noxious Weed Act of 1974. For more information, visit the Noxious Weeds web site: www.aphis.usda.gov:80/ppq/weeds/weedhome.html

Ocrea. Membranous sheaths wrapped around the stem and petiole at the point of attachment. Found in smartweed species.

Over-the-top application. A broadcast or banded application applied over the canopy of crops such as by airplane or a raised spray boom of ground equipment.

Persistant herbicide. A herbicide which, when applied at the recommended rate, will harm susceptible crops planted in normal rotation after harvesting the treated crop or which interferes with regrowth of native vegetation in noncrop sites.

Petiole. Stem or leaf stalk.

Photodegradation. Degradation of a herbicide due to sunlight.

Photosynthesis. Studies indicate photosynthesis helps increase uptake of some herbicides, thus improving weed control.

Poast compatible. Designation for corn hybrids that are resistant to sethoxydim (Poast). Seedbags will contain a tag bearing this logo.

POST. Postemergence. Any herbicide treatment made after a crop emerges from the soil. May be a contact herbicide by burning off above-ground stems and leaves, or a systemic herbicide which is translocated throughout the weed plant. May be soil applied or directed to the weeds.

PP. Preplant. Any treatment of soil, seed, or reproductive vegetable material before the crop is planted. May be surface applied or incorporated.

PPF. Preplant and foliar applied herbicide.

PPI. Preplant incorporated. Some herbicides (Treflan, Eptam, Sutan+, and Eradicane are examples) must be incorporated to prevent loss of volatile active ingredient or to avoid photodegradation. Incorporation will mobilize the herbicide by moving it into moist soil to enhance absorption of the herbicide by the weed seedling soon after germination.

PRE. Preemergence. Any treatment made at planting or after a crop is planted but before it emerges, or before the weeds emerge. Advantage: Planting and herbicide application may be done in one operation.

Premix. Formulated combination of two or more compatible products such as two herbicides or a herbicide with an insecticide.

Rate. For herbicides, the quantity of active ingredient or parent compound equivalent expressed as moles or mass per unit area of treated surface or per unit volume.

Reduced tillage. Reduced tillage systems such as no-till, chisel plow, or ridge-till require carefully planned weed control programs for success. Incorporation of the herbicide is generally not possible without covering much of the residue that is necessary for erosion control and defeating the purpose of minimum-till systems. Generally, weed control in no-till requires:

1. Use of a knockdown herbicide like Bladex, Roundup Ultra, or Gramoxone Extra to control existing vegetation before or at planting or an early application of soil-applied herbicides before weeds emerge, which can reduce need for a knockdown herbicide and reduce costs. A higher labeled rate may be necessary and performance is more dependent on timely rainfall.

2. Use of preemergence herbicides with residual soil activity to control weeds that emerge after planting.

3. Use of postemergence herbicides to control escaped weeds.

Residue. 1. Plants and parts of plants on the soil surface after the crop is harvested. Maintenance of plant residue on the soil surface is one of the most effective means of reducing soil erosion. **2.** The portion of a herbicide or other pesticide which remains in or on the soil, plant parts, animal tissues, whole organisms, and surfaces after pesticide absorption into the target crop and/or photodegradation.

Restricted-entry interval (REI). The time which must elapse after pesticide application before it is safe to enter the treated area without wearing protective clothing and equipment. See the WPS Chart in this book for REI information for herbicide products registered for use in the U.S.

Restricted Use Pesticide (RUP). A pesticide designated by EPA that is available for purchase and use only by certified pesticide applicators or persons under their direct supervision, and only for those uses covered by the Certified Applicator's Certification. This group of pesticides is not available for use by the general public because of the very high toxicities and/or environmental hazards associated with these materials.

Rhizome. An underground stem from which new plants may emerge. It appears to be a root.

Ridge-till. A form of conservation tillage in which the soil is left undisturbed from harvest to planting except for nutrient injection. Planting is completed in a seedbed prepared on ridges with sweeps, disc openers, coulters, row cleaners, or rototillers.

Ropewick spot treatment. For escape weeds taller than the crop where the herbicide can be applied to the weeds while minimizing contact with the crop.

Rosette. A cluster of leaves growing from a common point at the soil surface, without a stem.

Rotary hoe. Iowa State's Bob Hartzler reports that although the rotary hoe is an old tool, it still has a place in today's production systems. Due to the nature of its operation, the effectiveness of the rotary hoe can be more variable than other control strategies. Careful evaluation of field conditions, stage of weed development, and adjustment can help insure successful operation of the rotary hoe. The rotary hoe has several potential uses in a weed management program. The standard role has been as a backup to soil-applied herbicides when rainfall has not occurred within 5-7 days of planting or application. Rotary hoeing in these situations controls any weeds that may have germinated due to the herbicide remaining on the soil surface, helps get the chemical worked into the soil, and can break up a soil crust. This use of the rotary hoe may increase as growers move away from preplant incorporated treatments due to conservation compliance. A potential problem with many postemergence herbicides is the lack of soil residual that may allow late emerging weeds to escape control. An early rotary hoeing may allow the postemergence application to be delayed by one or two weeks, thus reducing the risk of late emerging weeds from becoming a problem. It also provides greater flexibility in timing of the post herbicide.

Roundup-Ready crops. Varieties developed that are tolerant or resistant to Roundup (glyphosate).

Scouting. Early season scouting is important to evaluate effectiveness of weed control programs. When weeds are small they are more easily controlled and appropriate tillage or herbicide measures can be taken. Late season scouting is important for preparing an accurate weed infestation map and developing next year's weed control program.

SEQ. Sequential or Overlay. A treatment of soil or crops made with more than one product applied separately within a time interval. It may be a preplant application of one product followed by a preemergence application or a postemergence of another product. Time of application depends on the products used.

Sessile. Describes a leaf that attaches directly to the stem.

Sheaths. Tubular extensions of a grass leaf that surround the stem. It can be split, overlapping, or united.

Signal word. Indication of the human hazard involved in handling or applying a pesticide, with DANGER being the most hazardous, followed by WARNING and CAUTION.

Site of action. The physical location within the plant where the herbicide acts to exert its phytotoxic mode of action. Herbicides with different modes of action can produce similar injury symptoms at the same site in a plant.

SLN. Special Local Need pesticide. A pesticide which is approved for use only in certain states or areas.

Soil type. Clay and organic matter absorb herbicides, making them less available to kill weeds. Soils with high clay and organic matter require greater herbicide rates. Sandy soils with low organic matter require lower rates to avoid crop injury. Some herbicides (metribuzin) are more available at higher soil pH. Rates must be reduced to avoid crop injury.

SR-resistant. Designation for corn hybrids that are resistant to sethoxydim (Poast).

STS soybeans. Sulfonylurea-tolerant soybeans withstand over-the-top applications of herbicides such as Classic, Concert, Pinnacle, and Reliance STS.

Surfactant. A material which favors or improves the emulsifying, dispersing, spreading, wetting, or other surface-modifying properties of liquids.

Synergism. The joint action of different agents so that the total effect is greater than the sum of the independent effects.

Systemic herbicide. A classification for herbicides that are able to move away from the site of absorption to other parts of the plant.

Tank mix. Two or more pesticides used in a single application.

Temperature. Temperature greatly influences herbicide effectiveness, with the best range being 65° to 80°F. Low temperatures may result in reduced weed control whereas high temperatures may cause crop injury.

Timing. Weeds are easier to control when they are small seedlings and growing rapidly. Early season weed control is very important for corn and soybeans because the crop can usually compete well with weeds that begin growing later.

Toxicity class. Defined as the "quality, state, or degree of being poisonous." A category (I-IV) indicates the level of toxicity a given pesticide possesses. Class I products are most toxic.

Transgenic plant. A plant whose genetic composition has been altered to include selected genes from other plants or species by methods other than those used in traditional plant breeding. These plants can be modified to resist or tolerate herbicides, insects, diseases, or a combination of these.

Tuber. Underground nutlike storage organ located at tips of rhizomes. Yellow nutsedge is an example.

Volatility. The ability to become a vapor; that is, to evaporate or give off fumes.

Weed biotype. A naturally occurring weed or type within a given species that has a slightly different but distinct genetic makeup from other individuals or the general population.

Weeds. Plants that reduce yields and compete with crops for water, nutrients, and sunlight. Some release toxins that inhibit crop growth or encourage insects and viruses. Weeds also foul up the harvest and contaminate the crop with weed seeds. Problem weeds develop from growing the same crop on the same ground year after year. Solutions include crop rotation, tillage methods, and herbicides.

WPS. EPAs Worker Protection Standard was implemented in 1992 to protect agricultural workers from pesticide exposure. Is currently being reviewed by EPA.

Yield drag. Describes a possible reduction in yields associated with herbicide resistant or tolerant crops. ☐

Sources: From state and regional extension publications, including Common Weed Seedlings of Michigan, the Herbicide Handbook of the Weed Science Society of America, the Conservation Technology Information Center's "Tillage Definitions," American Farm Bureau Federation, North Dakota State University Extension Agricultural Economics, Florida Weed Management, and American Cyanamid Co.

WPS Rules Review

Here's a look at some of the rules to follow to comply with EPA's Worker Protection Standard.

In 1992, the EPA revised its Worker Protection Standard (WPS) that protects agricultural workers from pesticide exposure. These regulations apply to "agricultural workers" and "pesticide handlers."

Most pesticide uses involved in the production of agricultural plants on a farm, nursery, forest, or greenhouse are covered by the WPS. If you are using a pesticide product with labeling that refers to the Worker Protection Standard, you must comply with it.

Owners and immediate family who work on the farm are exempt from most regulations under the WPS. But they must comply with requirements for personal protective equipment and restricted-entry intervals.

Protections For Workers

For growers who employ agricultural workers — those who perform tasks related to the cultivation and harvesting of plants on farms or in greenhouses, but who aren't involved in actual pesticide handling or application — the following rules apply:

In a central location at the growing area, the following must be displayed:

• A WPS safety poster (available from EPA or WPS material suppliers) explaining that WPS exists and offering tips on how workers can protect themselves from pesticides' harmful effects.

• Name, address, and phone number of nearest emergency facility.

• Information about each pesticide application from before it begins until 30 days after the restricted-entry interval (REI). Note: An REI is the time following an application when entry into the treated area is prohibited, except in very few cases. REIs are found on pesticide labels.

The posted information must include the pesticide's name, EPA registration number, active ingredient, location and description of treated area, time and date of application, and REI.

Growers must tell workers where this information is posted, allow them access, keep the information updated, and keep it legible. The information must be posted until at least 30 days after the REI expires.

Oral and Posted Warnings

Workers must be orally warned about applications or posted warnings must be placed at entrances to treated areas according to the labeling requirements. Both oral and posted warnings should be used if the labeling requires. If not, workers should be informed which method, oral or posting, is used.

If oral warnings are issued (this need only be done for any workers who will pass within $1/4$ mile of affected area), the following must be provided:

• Location and description of the treated area.

• REI information, including a warning not to enter during this time period.

Affected workers who begin their shifts after application starts must receive the same warnings at the beginning of their shifts.

If 14-inch-by-16-inch, WPS-designed signs are being posted (EPA's compliance manual describes them), they must be placed at all entrances to treated areas including access roads, adjacent labor camp borders, and established walking routes. If no usual entrance points exist, signs must be posted in corners of treated areas or easily seen places. The warning signs should be posted just before application, left up during REI, and removed before workers enter and within 3 days of REI ending.

Training

Workers must be trained in pesticide safety. This must take place before they enter areas where REIs have been in effect within the last 30 days. They must be retrained every 5 years thereafter. Workers must be trained before accumulating 15 days of fieldwork.

Persons eligible to conduct this training include:

• Pesticide applicators in any level of certification.

• Graduates of state or federal "train the trainer" programs.

• Those trained (according to EPA guidelines) as pesticide handlers who work under supervision of certified pesticide applicators.

To verify that workers have been trained, EPA has developed a voluntary program that uses EPA-developed or EPA-approved training materials, issues plastic training verification cards, and keeps rosters of those trained. Trainers issue plastic cards to workers, verifying they have been trained. Even though WPS does not require it, growers who train workers themselves should keep training logs specifying who was trained and when.

Decontamination Sites

Growers must provide decontamination sites for workers in pesticide-treated areas who are performing tasks involving contact with anything which may contain pesticides, be it soil, water, or plant surfaces. These sites must be provided until 30 days after the REI ends or, if no REI was in effect, 30 days after the end of application.

The decontamination sites must be located within $1/4$ of a mile of the work area but must not be in treated areas or areas under REIs.

The sites must contain enough water for routine and emergency whole-body washing and eye flushing, and plenty of soap and single-use towels.

Emergencies

If a worker is poisoned or injured by pesticides, growers must arrange immediate transport to an appropriate medical facility. The victim and medical personnel should be supplied with the following:
• Product name.
• EPA registration number.
• Active ingredient.
• Medical information from label.
• Description of how it was used.
• Information about exposure.

Handlers/Applicators

Any agricultural grower or dealer employing pesticide handlers and applicators — those who mix, load, apply, clean or repair equipment, or act as flaggers, etc. — must comply with the rules for ag workers as well as the following:

Training. Handlers require more extensive training than regular workers and must receive this training before they do any handling tasks.

Information. Before handlers work with any pesticides, they must be informed of all pesticide instructions for safe use. The labeling must be accessible to each handler through the entire handling and application process.

The following information must be displayed at a central location to inform handlers about specific pesticide applications:
• Area treated with both location and description.
• Product name.
• EPA registration number.
• Active ingredient (this would be the common or chemical name).
• Time of application: Must include month/day/time.
• Restricted-entry interval.
• Do not enter until: must include month/day/time.

The grower must ensure that an applicator knows the area to be treated, whether an REI will be in effect while the applicator is on the farm, and restrictions on entering those areas.

Equipment Safety. They must let only properly trained and equipped handlers repair or clean equipment containing pesticides or residues.

Personal Protective Equipment. Pesticide labeling lists what personal protective equipment (PPE) must be worn by handlers coming in contact with the pesticides. This equipment includes coveralls, gloves, goggles, and respirators.

Handlers must be supplied with PPE as required on the label. Handler employers must make sure PPE is:
• Clean and in operating condition.
• Worn and used correctly.
• Inspected each day before use.
• Repaired or replaced as needed.

Handlers must be provided with a pesticide-free area for storing personal clothing, putting PPE on, and taking it off. Handlers cannot take PPE home.

PPE must be stored and washed separately from other laundry. If PPE will be reused, it must be cleaned before each day of reuse. If workers are employed to wash PPE, they must be informed of the following:
• PPE may be contaminated.
• Exposure to pesticides may have harmful effects.
• How they can protect themselves while handling PPE.
• How they can clean PPE correctly by applying instructions from PPE manufacturers.

PPE that are heavily contaminated with undiluted pesticide and the label has Danger or Warning written on it must be discarded in a manner consistent with federal, state, and local laws. □

AgrEvo USA Company

Acclaim* Extra	45639-67	fenoxaprop-ethyl	No	Caution	HE	Oral	24	a g	b e g
Betamix*	45639-87	phenmedipham + desmedipham	No	Warning	HE	Oral	24	c f h k l	c f h l
Betanex*	45639-86	desmedipham	No	Warning	HE	Oral	24	a f g j	b f g j
Cheyenne* FM	45639-189	fenoxaprop-P-ethyl + MCPA	No	Danger	HE	Oral	24	a f g j	b f g j
Dakota*	45639-19	fenoxaprop-P-ethyl + MCPA	No	Warning	HE	Oral	24	a f g j	b f g j
Dropp Ultra*	45639-201	thidiazuron + diuron	No	Caution	DE	Oral	24	a f g	b f g
Dropp* 50WP	45639-89	thidiazuron	No	Caution	DE	Oral	24	a e g	b e g
Finale*	45639-187	glufosinate-ammonium	No	Warning	HE	Oral	12	a f g j	b f g j
Ginstar*	45639-161	thidiazuron + diuron	No	Danger	DE	Oral	24	d f h j	d f h j
Hoelon* 3EC	45639-173	diclofop-methyl	Yes	Danger	HE	Oral	24†	d f h j k l	d f h j
Liberty*	45639-199	glufosinate-ammonium	No	Warning	HE	Oral	12	c f h j k	c f h j
Liberty* ATZ	45639-219	glufosinate-ammonium + atrazine	Yes	Caution	HE	Oral	12	a e g	b e g
Liberty* nc	45639-187	glufosinate-ammonium	No	Warning	HE	Oral	12	a f g j	b f g j
Nortron* SC	45639-8	ethofumesate	No	Caution	HE	Oral	12†	a e g	b e g
Prograss*	45639-68	ethofumesate	No	Danger	HE	Oral	12	a f g j	b f g j
Progress*	45639-159	phenmedipham + desmedipham + ethofumesate	No	Danger	HE	Oral	24	a g j	b e g j
Puma*	45639-212	fenoxaprop-P-ethyl	No	Warning	HE	Oral	24	c f h j	d f h j
Rely*	45639-187	glufosinate-ammonium	No	Warning	HE	Oral	12	a f g j	b f g j
Silverado*	45639-185	fenoxaprop-P-ethyl	Yes	Danger	HE	Oral	24	a f g j	b f g j
Spin-Aid*	45639-76	phenmedipham	No	Warning	HE	Oral	24	a f g	b f g
Tiller*	45639-184	fenoxaprop-P-ethyl + 2,4-D + MCPA	No	Warning	HE	Oral	24	a f g j k	b f g j
Whip* 360	45639-181	fenoxaprop-P-ethyl	No	Caution	HE	Oral	24	a g	b e g
X-TRA*	352-538-45639	thifensulfuron-methyl + tribenuron-methyl	No	Caution	HE	Oral	24	a e g	b f g j

Albaugh Inc.

Amine 4	42750-19	2,4-D	No	Danger	HE	Oral	48	a f g j k l	b f g j l
Butyrac* 175	42750-39	2,4-DB	No	Danger	HE	Oral	48	a e g j	b e g j
Butyrac* 200	42750-38	2,4-DB	No	Danger	HE	Oral	48	a e g j	b e g j
D-638	42750-36	2,4-D	No	Danger	HE	Oral	48	a f g j	b f g j
LV 4 Ester	42750-15	2,4-D	No	Caution	HE	Oral	12	a f g j k	b f g j
LV 6 Ester	42750-20	2,4-D	No	Caution	HE	Oral	12	a e g j k	b e g j
MCPA Amine	42750-14	MCPA	No	Danger	HE	Oral	48	a e g j l	b e g j l
MCPA Ester	42750-23	MCPA	No	Caution	HE	Oral	48	a e g j l	b e g l
Solve* 2,4-D	42750-22	2,4-D	No	Caution	HE	Oral	12	a e g j k	b e g j
Solve* MCPA	42750-25	MCPA	No	Caution	HE	Oral	12	a e g j l	b e g j l
Trifluralin 4EC	42750-32	trifluralin	No	Warning	HE	Oral	12	a f g j	b f g j

American Cyanamid Co.

Arsenal*	241-299	imazapyr	No	Caution	HE	Oral	12	a e g	b e g
Assert*	241-285	imazamethabenz-methyl	No	Danger	HE	Oral	48	a f g j	b f g j
Avenge*	241-266	difenzoquat methyl sulfate	No	Danger	HE	Oral	48	a e g j m	b e g j
Cadre*	241-381	imazapyc	No	Caution	HE	Oral	12	a e g	b e g
Chopper*	241-296	imazapyr	No	Caution	HE	Oral	12	a e g	b e g
Chopper* RTU	241-330	imazapyr	No	Caution	HE	Oral	12	a f g	b f g
Contour*	241-353	atrazine + imazethapyr	Yes	Caution	HE	Oral	12	a f h	b f h
Detail*	241-361	imazaquin + dimethenamid	No	Danger	HE	Oral	12	d f h j k l	d f h j l
Lightning*	241-377	imazethapyr + imazapyr	No	Warning	HE	Oral	12	a e g j	b e g j
Pendulum* 3.3 EC Industrial	241-341	pendimethalin	No	Caution	HE	Oral	12	a f g	b f g
Pendulum* WDG	241-340	pendimethalin	No	Caution	HE	Oral	12	a e g	b e g
Pentagon* DG	241-268	pendimethalin	No	Caution	HE	Oral	12	a e g	b e g
Prowl* 3.3 EC	241-337	pendimethalin	No	Caution	HE	Oral	12	a f g	b f g
Pursuit*	241-310	imazethapyr	No	Caution	HE	Oral	12	a e g	b e g
Pursuit* EcoPak* DG	241-350	imazethapyr	No	Warning	HE	Oral	12	a e g j	b e g j
Pursuit* Plus EC	241-331	imazethapyr + pendimethalin	No	Caution	HE	Oral	12	a f g	b f g
Pursuit* W Eco-Pak*	241-386	imazethapyr	No	Warning	HE	Oral	12	a e g j	b e g j
Resolve* SG	241-359	imazethapyr + dicamba	No	Warning	HE	Oral	12	a e g j	b e g j
Scepter*	241-289	imazaquin	No	Caution	HE	Oral	12	a e g	b e g
Scepter* 70 DG	241-306	imazaquin	No	Caution	HE	Oral	12	a e g	b e g
Scepter* O.T.	241-321	imazaquin + sodium acifluorfen	No	Warning	HE	Oral	48	a e g j	b e g j
Squadron*	241-327	pendimethalin + imazaquin	No	Danger	HE	Oral	12	a f g j	b f g j
Status*	7969-79-241	acifluorfen	No	Danger	HE	Oral	48	a e g j l	b e g j l
Steel*	241-289	imazaquin	No	Caution	HE	Oral	12	a e g	b e g
Tri-4* HF	241-343	trifluralin	No	Warning	HE	Oral	12	c f h j k l	c f h j l
Tri-Scept*	241-307	imazaquin + trifluralin	No	Warning	HE	Oral	12	a f g j	b f g j

Product Name	EPA Number	Active Ingredient(s)	RUP	Signal Word	Action	Notification	REI	PPE	Early Entry PPE
Amvac Chemical Corp.									
Vapam*	5481-466	metam-sodium	No	Danger	FM	Oral, Posted	48	d e h j k l m	d e h j k l m
Vapam* HL	5481-468	metam-sodium	No	Danger	FM/HE	Oral, Posted	48	d e h j k l m	d e h j k l m
BASF Corporation									
Banvel*	7969-131	dicamba	No	Warning	HE	Oral	24	a e g j	b e g j
Banvel SGF*	7969-135	dicamba	No	Warning	HE	Oral	24	a g j	b e g j
Basagran*	7969-45	bentazone	No	Caution	HE	Oral	12	a e g	b e g
Basamid* Granular	7969-99	dazomet	No	Warning	FM/HE	Oral, Posted	24	c e h j m	c e h
Blazer*	7969-79	acifluorfen	No	Danger	HE	Oral	48	a e g j l	b e g j
Celebrity*	7969-166	dicamba + nicosulfuron	No	Warning	HE	Oral	12	a e g j	b e g j
Clarity*	7969-137	dicamba-DGA	No	Caution	HE	Oral, Posted	24	a e g	b e g
Conclude* B	7969-76	bentazone + acifluorfen	No	Danger	HE	Oral	48	a e g j k l	c f h j l
Conclude* G	7969-58	sethoxydim	No	Warning	HE	Oral	48	c f h j k l	c f h j l
Conclude* Ultra	7969-168	bentazone + acifluorfen + sethoxydim	No	Danger	HE	Oral	48	c f h j l	c f h j l
Conclude Xtra* B	7969-76	bentazone + acifluorfen	No	Danger	HE	Oral	48	a e g j k l	c f h j l
Conclude Xtra* G	59639-78-7969	clethodim	No	Warning	HE	Oral	48	c f h j k l	c f h j l
Distinct*	7969-150	dicamba + diflufenzopyr	No	Caution	HE	Oral	12	a e g	b e g
Facet* 75 DF	7969-113	quinclorac	No	Caution	HE	Oral	12	a e g	b e g
Frontier*	7969-147	dimethenamid	No	Warning	HE	Oral	12†	a f g j	b f g j
Galaxy*	7969-77	bentazone + acifluorfen	No	Danger	HE	Oral	48	a e g j	b e g j
Guardsman*	7969-146	dimethenamid + atrazine	Yes	Warning	HE	Oral	12†	a f h j	b f h j
Laddok* S-12	7969-100	bentazone + atrazine	Yes	Danger	HE	Oral	12	a e h j	b e h j
Manifest* B	7969-77	bentazone + acifluorfen	No	Danger	HE	Oral	48	a e g j	b e g j
Manifest* G	7969-58	sethoxydim	No	Warning	HE	Oral	48	c f h j k l	c f h j l
Marksman*	7969-136	dicamba + atrazine	Yes	Caution	HE	Oral	48†	a f h j	b f h
OpTill*	7969-148	dimethenamid + dicamba	No	Danger	HE	Oral	48	a f g j	b f g j
Paramount*	7969-113	quinclorac	No	Caution	HE	Oral	12	a e g	b e g j
Poast*	7969-58	sethoxydim	No	Warning	HE	Oral	12	c f h j k l	c f h j l
Poast Plus*	7969-88	sethoxydim	No	Caution	HE	Oral	12	a f g	b f g
Prompt* 5L	7969-120	bentazone + atrazine	No	Danger	HE	Oral	12	a e h j	b e h j
Pyramin* DF	7969-81	pyrazon	No	Caution	HE	Oral	12†	a e g	b e g
Pyramin* SC	7969-108	pyrazon	No	Caution	HE	Oral	12†	a f g	b f g
Rezult* B	7969-112	bentazone	No	Danger	HE	Oral	12	a e g j	b f g j
Rezult* G	7969-88	sethoxydim	No	Caution	HE	Oral	12	a f g	b f g
Storm*	7969-76	bentazone + acifluorfen	No	Danger	HE	Oral	48	a e g j	b e g j
Torpedo*	7969-88	sethoxydim	No	Caution	HE	Oral	12	a f g	b f g
Vantage*	7969-88	sethoxydim	No	Caution	HE	Oral	12	a f g	b f g
Weedmaster*	7969-133	2,4-D + dicamba	No	Danger	HE	Oral	48	a e g j k	b e g j
Bayer Corporation									
Axiom* DF	3125-488	flufenacet + metribuzin	No	Caution	HE	Oral	12†	a e g	b e g
DEF* 6	3125-282	tribufos	No	Danger	DE	Oral	24	d f h j k l m	d f h j l
Epic* DF	3125-522	flufenacet + isoxaflutole	Yes	Caution	HE	Oral	12†	a e g	b e g
Sencor* 4	3125-314	metribuzin	No	Caution	HE	Oral	12†	a e g	b e g
Sencor* DF	3125-325	metribuzin	No	Caution	HE	Oral	12†	a e g	b e g
Cedar Chemical Corp.									
Butoxone* 175	56077-31	2,4-DB	No	Caution	HE	Oral	48	a e g l	b e g l
Butoxone* 200	56077-26	2,4-DB	No	Danger	HE	Oral	48	a e g j l	b e g j l
Butoxone* 7500	56077-52	2,4-DB	No	Caution	HE	Oral	48	a e g	b e g
Cheminova, Inc.									
Glyfos*	524-445-4787	glyphosate	No	Warning	HE	Oral	12	a g j	b e g j
Glyfos* X-tra	4787-23	glyphosate	No	Warning	HE	Oral	12	a g j	b e g j
Dow AgroSciences LLC									
Broadstrike* + Treflan*	62719-222	trifluralin + flumetsulam	No	Danger	HE	Oral	12†	a f g j	b f g j

---

Action Word Abbreviations

DE = Defoliant
FM = Fumigant
HE = Herbicide

Personal Protective Equipment (PPE) Abbreviations

a....Long-sleeved-shirt and long pants
b....Coveralls
c....Coveralls over short-sleeved shirt and short pants
d ...Coveralls over long-sleeved shirt and long pants
e....Waterproof gloves
f ....Chemical-resistant gloves
g...Shoes plus socks
h....Chemical-resistant footwear plus socks
j....Protective eyewear
k....Chemical-resistant apron when cleaning equipment, mixing, or loading
l....Chemical-resistant headgear for overhead exposure
m...Approved respirator
n....Chemical-resistant protective suit

* = Trade Name/R/TM   † REI may vary; please refer to product label for complete information.
Information presented herein is for preliminary planning only. Exclusive reliance must be placed on information/directions supplied by the manufacturer.

Product Name	EPA Number	Active Ingredient(s)	RUP	Signal Word	Action	Notification	REI	PPE	Early Entry PPE
Curtail*	62719-48	clopyralid + 2,4-D	No	Danger	HE	Oral	48	a e g j	b e g j
Curtail* M	62719-86	clopyralid + MCPA	No	Caution	HE	Oral	48	a f g	b f g
FirstRate*	62719-275	cloransulam-methyl	No	Caution	HE	Oral	12†	a e g	b e g
Frontrow* (Co-Pack)	62719-275/ 62719-277	cloransulam-methyl + flumetsulam	No	Caution	HE	Oral	12	a e g	b e g
Gallery* 75 DF	62719-145	isoxaben	No	Caution	HE	Oral	12	a g j	b e g j
Garlon* 3A	62719-37	triclopyr	No	Danger	HE	Oral	48	a g j	b e g j
Garlon* 4	62719-40	triclopyr	No	Caution	HE	Oral	12	a f g	b f g
Grandstand* CA	62719-215	triclopyr	No	Danger	HE	Oral	48	a e g j	b e g j
Grandstand* R	62719-215	triclopyr	No	Danger	HE	Oral	48	a g j	b e g j
Hornet*	62719-253	flumetsulam + clopyralid	No	Danger	HE	Oral	48†	a e g j	b e g j
Pathfinder* II	62719-176	triclopyr	No	Caution	HE	Oral	12	a f g	b f g
Pathway*	62719-31	picloram + 2,4-D	No	Caution	HE	Oral	48	a f g j	b f g j
Python* WDG	62719-277	flumetsulam	No	Caution	HE	Oral	12†	a e g	b e g
Scorpion* III	62719-264	flumetsulam + clopyralid + 2,4-D	No	Danger	HE	Oral	48	a e g j	b e g j
Snapshot* 2.5 TG	62719-175	trifluralin + isoxaben	No	Caution	HE	Oral	12	a e g j	b e g j
Sonalan* 10G	62719-184	ethalfluralin	No	Danger	HE	Oral	12†	a g j	b g j
Sonalan* HFP	62719-188	ethalfluralin	No	Danger	HE	Oral	24†	d f h j k l	c f h j l
Starane*	62719-286	fluroxypyr	No	Warning	HE	Oral	12	a f g j	b f g j
Starane*+Salvo*	62719-306	fluroxypyr + 2,4-D	No	Caution	HE	Oral	12	a f g j k	b f g j
Starane*+Sword*	62719-307	fluroxypyr + MCPA	No	Caution	HE	Oral	12	a f g	b f g
Stinger*	62719-73	clopyralid	No	Caution	HE	Oral	12	a e g	b e g
Surflan* A.S.	62719-112	oryzalin	No	Caution	HE	Oral	12	a e g j	b e g j
Surflan* A.S. (specialty)	62719-113	oryzalin	No	Caution	HE	Oral	12	a e g j	b e g j
Telone* C-17	62719-12	dichloropropene + chloropicrin	Yes	Danger	FM	Oral	72	c f h j k l m	b f h j m
Telone* II	62719-32	dichloropropene	Yes	Warning	FM	Oral	72	c h j k l m	b f h j m
Tordon* 101	62719-5	picloram + 2,4-D	Yes	Warning	HE	Oral	48	a f g j k	b f g j
Tordon* 22K	62719-6	picloram	Yes	Caution	HE	Oral	12	a e g	b e g
Tordon* K	62719-17	picloram	Yes	Caution	HE	Oral	12	a e g	b e g
Transline*	62719-259	clopyralid	No	Caution	HE	Oral	12	a e g	b e g
Treflan* HFP	62719-250	trifluralin	No	Warning	HE	Oral	12†	a f g j	b f g j
Treflan* TR-10	62719-131	trifluralin	No	Caution	HE	Oral	12†	a e g j	b e g j
Drexel Chemical Co.									
Atra-5*	19713-80	atrazine	Yes	Caution	HE	Oral	12	a e h j	b e h j
Atrazine 90DF	19713-76	atrazine	Yes	Caution	HE	Oral	12	a e h j	b e g j
Atrazine 4L	19713-11	atrazine	Yes	Caution	HE	Oral	12	a e h j	b e h
Calar*	63239-15-19713	CAMA	No	Caution	HE	Oral	12	a e h	b e h
Defol*	19713-12	sodium chlorate	No	Warning	DE	Oral	12	c e h j k l m	c e h j l
Defol* 5	19713-388	sodium chlorate	No	Danger	DE	Oral	12	d e h j k l	d e h j l
Defol* 6	19713-85	sodium chlorate	No	Warning	DE	Oral	12	c e h j k l m	c e h j l
Diuron 80 Herbicide	19713-274	diuron	No	Caution	HE	Oral	12	a e g	b e g
Diuron 4L	19713-36	diuron	No	Caution	HE	Oral	12	a e g	b e g
DSMA Liquid	19713-45	DSMA	No	Caution	HE	Oral	12	a e h j k m	b e h
DSMA Slurry	63239-14-19713	DSMA	No	Caution	HE	Oral	12	a e h j k m	b e h
MSMA 6.6	19713-41	MSMA	No	Caution	HE	Oral	12	a e h j k m	b e h
MSMA 4 Plus	19713-40	MSMA	No	Caution	HE	Oral	12	a e h j k m	b e h
MSMA 6 Plus	19713-42	MSMA	No	Caution	HE	Oral	12	a e h j k m	b e h
Simazat 4L	19713-171	atrazine + simazine	Yes	Caution	HE	Oral	12	a e h j	b e h
Simazine 90DF	19713-252	simazine	No	Caution	HE	Oral	12	a e g	b e g
Simazine 4L	19713-60	simazine	No	Caution	HE	Oral	12	a e g	b e g
Simazine 80W	19713-46	simazine	No	Caution	HE	Oral	12	a e g	b e g
DuPont Agricultural Products									
Accent*	352-560	nicosulfuron	No	Caution	HE	Oral	4	a e g	b e g
Accent* Gold	352-593	clopyralid + flumetsulam + nicosulfuron + rimsulfuron	No	Danger	HE	Oral	48	a e g j	b e g j
Ally*	352-435	metsulfuron-methyl	No	Caution	HE	Oral	4	a g	b g
Assure* II	352-541	quizalofop-P-ethyl	No	Danger	HE	Oral	12	a f g j	b f g j
Authority*	352-590	sulfentrazone	No	Caution	HE	Oral	12	a e g	d e g
Basis*	352-571	rimsulfuron + thifensulfuron-methyl	No	Caution	HE	Oral	12	a e g	b e g
Basis Gold*	352-585	nicosulfuron + rimsulfuron + atrazine	Yes	Caution	HE	Oral	12	a e h j	b e h
Bladex* 90DF	352-495	cyanazine	Yes	Warning	HE	Oral	12	a e h j k	b e g j
Bladex* 4L	352-470	cyanazine	Yes	Warning	HE	Oral	12	a f h j k	b f g j
Canopy*	352-444	chlorimuron-ethyl + metribuzin	No	Caution	HE	Oral	12	a e g	b e g
Canopy* SP	352-596	chlorimuron-ethyl + metribuzin	No	Caution	HE	Oral	12	a e g	b e g
Canopy* XL	352-589	chlorimuron-ethyl + sulfentrazone	No	Caution	HE	Oral	12	a e g	d e g

Product Name	EPA Number	Active Ingredient(s)	RUP	Signal Word	Action	Notification	REI	PPE	Early Entry PPE
Canvas*	352-586	thifensulfuron-methyl + tribenuron-methyl + metsulfuron-methyl	No	Warning	HE	Oral	12	c e g k	b e g
Classic*	352-436	chlorimuron-ethyl	No	Caution	HE	Oral	12	a e g	b e g
Escort*	352-439	metsulfuron-methyl	No	Caution	HE	Oral	4	a g	b g
Express*	352-509	tribenuron-methyl	No	Caution	HE	Oral	12	a e g	b e g
Extrazine* II DF	352-577	cyanazine + atrazine	Yes	Warning	HE	Oral	12	a e h j k	b e h j
Extrazine* II 4L	352-500	cyanazine + atrazine	Yes	Warning	HE	Oral	12	a e h j k	b e h j
Finesse*	352-445	chlorsulfuron + metsulfuron-methyl	No	Caution	HE	Oral	4	a e g	b e g
Glean*	352-522	chlorsulfuron	No	Caution	HE	Oral	4	a e g	b e g
Harmony* Extra	352-538	tribenuron + thifensulfuron-methyl	No	Caution	HE	Oral	12	a e g	b e g
Harmony* GT	352-446	thifensulfuron-methyl	No	Caution	HE	Oral	4	a e g	b e g
Hyvar* X	352-287	bromacil	No	Caution	HE	Oral	12	a e g	b e g
Krovar* I DF	352-505	bromacil + diuron	No	Caution	HE	Oral	12	a e g	b e g
Leadoff*	352-600	dimethenamid + atrazine	Yes	Warning	HE	Oral	12	a f h j	b f h j
Londax*	352-506	bensulfuron-methyl	No	Warning	HE	Oral	24	a e g j	b e g j
Matrix*	352-556	rimsulfuron	No	Caution	HE	Oral	4	a e g	b e g
Oust*	352-401	sulfometuron-methyl	No	Caution	HE	Oral	4	a g	b g
Pinnacle*	352-525	thifensulfuron-methyl	No	Caution	HE	Oral	12	a e g	b e g
Reliance* STS* SP	352-580	thifensulfuron-methyl + chlorimuron-ethyl	No	Caution	HE	Oral	12	a e g	b e g
Shadeout*	352-556	rimsulfuron	No	Caution	HE	Oral	4	a e g	b e g
Sinbar*	352-317	terbacil	No	Caution	HE	Oral	12	a e g	b e g
Staple*	352-576	pyrithiobac	No	Warning	HE	Oral	24	a e g j	b e g j
Synchrony* STS*	352-599	chlorimuron-ethyl + thifensulfuron-methyl	No	Caution	HE	Oral	12	a e g	b e g
Synchrony* STS* DF	352-573	chlorimuron-ethyl + thifensulfuron-methyl	No	Caution	HE	Oral	12	a e g	b e g
Synchrony* STS* SP	352-574	chlorimuron-ethyl + thifensulfuron-methyl	No	Caution	HE	Oral	12	a e g	b e g
UpBeet*	352-569	trisulfuron-methyl	No	Caution	HE	Oral	4	a e g	b e g
Velpar*	352-378	hexazinone	No	Danger	HE	Oral	24	a g j	b e g j
Velpar* DF	352-581	hexazinone	No	Danger	HE	Oral	24	a g j	b e g j
Velpar* L	352-392	hexazinone	No	Danger	HE	Oral	24	a g j	b e g j
Velpar* ULW	352-450	hexazinone	No	Danger	HE	Oral	24	a e g j	b e g j
Velpar* ULW DF	352-582	hexazinone	No	Danger	HE	Oral	24	a g j	b e g j

Elf Atochem North America, Inc.

Product Name	EPA Number	Active Ingredient(s)	RUP	Signal Word	Action	Notification	REI	PPE	Early Entry PPE
Accelerate*	4581-284	endothall	No	Danger	DE	Oral	48	d e h j k l m	d e h j l
Des-I-Cate*	4581-206	endothall	No	Danger	DE	Oral	48	d e h j k l m	d e h j l
Herbicide 273	4581-223	endothall	No	Danger	HE	Oral	48	a e g j m	b e g j

FMC Corp.

Product Name	EPA Number	Active Ingredient(s)	RUP	Signal Word	Action	Notification	REI	PPE	Early Entry PPE
Aim*	279-3194	carfentrazone-ethyl	No	Caution	HE		12	a e g	b e g
Authority Broadleaf*	279-3179	sulfentrazone + chlorimuron-ethyl	No	Caution	HE	Oral	12	a e g	d e g
Command* 4EC	279-3053	clomazone	No	Warning	HE	Oral	12†	a f g j	b f g j
Command* 3ME	279-3158	clomazone	No	Caution	HE	Oral	12†	a f g	b f g
Commence* EC	279-3104	trifluralin + clomazone	No	Caution	HE	Oral	12†	a f g	a f g
Matador*	279-3183	quizalofop-P-ethyl	No	Danger	HE	Oral	12	a f g j	b f g j
Skirmish*	279-3184	chlorimuron-ethyl	No	Caution	HE	Oral	12	a e g	b e g
Spartan*	279-3189	sulfentrazone	No	Caution	HE	Oral	12	a e g	d e g

Gowan Company

Product Name	EPA Number	Active Ingredient(s)	RUP	Signal Word	Action	Notification	REI	PPE	Early Entry PPE
Prefar* 4E	10163-200	bensulide	No	Caution	HE	Oral	12†	a f g	b f g
Prometryne 4L	10163-94	prometryne	No	Caution	HE	Oral	12†	a f g	b f g
Trifluralin 4	10163-101	trifluralin	No	Warning	HE	Oral	12†	a f g j	b f g j
Trifluralin 5	10163-99	trifluralin	No	Warning	HE	Oral	12†	a f g j	b f g j
Trifluralin 10G	10163-120	trifluralin	No	Caution	HE	Oral	12†	a e g j	b e g j
Tupersan* 50WP	10163-213	siduron	No	Caution	HE	Oral	4	a e g	b e g

---

Action Word Abbreviations

DE = Defoliant
FM = Fumigant
HE = Herbicide

Personal Protective Equipment (PPE) Abbreviations

a....Long-sleeved-shirt and long pants
b....Coveralls
c....Coveralls over short-sleeved shirt and short pants
d...Coveralls over long-sleeved shirt and long pants
e....Waterproof gloves
f....Chemical-resistant gloves
g...Shoes plus socks
h....Chemical-resistant footwear plus socks
j....Protective eyewear
k....Chemical-resistant apron when cleaning equipment, mixing, or loading
l....Chemical-resistant headgear for overhead exposure
m....Approved respirator
n....Chemical-resistant protective suit

* = Trade Name/R/TM   † REI may vary; please refer to product label for complete information.
Information presented herein is for preliminary planning only. Exclusive reliance must be placed on information/directions supplied by the manufacturer.

Worker Protection Standard

Product Name	EPA Number	Active Ingredient(s)	RUP	Signal Word	Action	Notification	REI	PPE	Early Entry PPE
Great Lakes Chemical									
Brom-O-Gas*	5785-4	methyl bromide + chloropicrin	Yes	Danger-Poison	FM	Oral, Posted	48†		
Chlor-O-Pic* 100	5785-17	chloropicrin	Yes	Danger-Poison	FM	Oral, Posted	48†		
Terr-O-Gas*	5785-24	methyl bromide + chloropicrin	Yes	Danger-Poison	FM	Oral, Posted	48†		
Griffin L.L.C.									
Cotton-Pro*	1812-274	prometryn	No	Caution	HE	Oral	12	a f g j	b f g j
Cy-Pro* 4L	1812-366	cyanazine	Yes	Warning	HE	Oral	12	a f h j k	b f g j
Direx* 80DF	1812-362	diuron	No	Warning	HE	Oral	12	a e g j	b e g j
Direx* 4L	1812-257	diuron	No	Caution	HE	Oral	12	a e g	b e g
Karmex* DF	352-508	diuron	No	Caution	HE	Oral	12	a e g	b e g
Lorox* DF	352-394	linuron	No	Caution	HE	Oral	24	c e g l	c e g l
Meturon* 80DF	1812-323	fluometuron	No	Caution	HE	Oral	24	a g	b g
Meturon* 4L	1812-285	fluometuron	No	Warning	HE	Oral	24	a f g	b f g
Trilin*	1812-355	trifluralin	No	Warning	HE	Oral	12	a f g j	d f g j
Trilin* 5	1812-353	trifluralin	No	Warning	HE	Oral	12	a f g j	b f g j
Trilin* 10G	1812-328	trifluralin	No	Warning	HE	Oral	12	a e g j	b e g j
Helena Chemical Co.									
Atrazine 4L	5905-470	atrazine	Yes	Caution	HE	Oral	12	a e h j	b e h j
Barrage*	5905-504	2,4-D	No	Caution	HE	Oral	12	a f g j k	b f g j
Barrage* HF	5905-529	2,4-D	No	Caution	HE	Oral	12	a f g j k	b f g j
DSMA 4 LB	42519-15-5905	DSMA	No	Caution	HE	Oral	12	a e g j k m	b e g j
Liquid DSMA	50534-186-38167	DSMA	No	Caution	HE	Oral	12	a e h j k m	b e h j
MSMA	5905-67	MSMA	No	Caution	HE	Oral	12	a e h j k m	b e h
MSMA Plus	5905-66	MSMA	No	Caution	HE	Oral	12	a e g j k m	b e g
MSMA Plus HC	5905-164	MSMA	No	Caution	HE	Oral	12	a e g j k l m	b e g
Opti-Amine*	5905-501	2,4-D	No	Danger	HE	Oral	48	a e g j	a e g j
Rattler*	524-445-5905	glyphosate	No	Warning	HE	Oral	12	a g j	
Trifluralin 4 EC	5905-519	trifluralin	No	Warning	HE	Oral	12†	d f g j	d f g j
Weed Rhap* A-4D	5905-501	2,4-D	No	Danger	HE	Oral	48	a e g j	a e g j
Weed Rhap* LV-6D	5905-508	2,4-D	No	Caution	HE	Oral	12	a e g j	b e g j
XL*2G	62719-136-38167	benefin + oryzalin	No	Caution	HE	Oral	12†	a e g j	b e g j
Luxembourg-Pamol, Inc.									
MAGMA*	42519-12	MSMA	No	Caution	HE	Oral	12	a e h j k m	b e g j l
Target* MSMA 6 Plus	42519-3	MSMA	No	Caution	HE	Oral	12	a e g j k m	b e g j l
Target* MSMA 6.6	42519-1	MSMA	No	Caution	HE	Oral	12	a e g j k m	b e g j l
TurfMate* 6 Plus	42519-3	MSMA	No	Caution	HE	Oral	12	a e g j k m	b e g j l
TurfMate* 6.6	42519-1	MSMA	No	Caution	HE	Oral	12	a e h j k m	b e h j l
Micro Flo Co.									
Bromox + Atrazine	51036-255	bromoxynil + atrazine	Yes	Caution	HE	Oral	12	d f h j k l	d f h j l
Bromox 2E	51036-256	bromoxynil	No	Warning	HE	Oral	12	d f h j k l	d f h j l
Bromox-MCPA 2-2	51036-254	bromoxynil + MCPA	No	Warning	HE	Oral	12	d f h j k l	d f h j l
Flo-Met 80DF	9779-311-51036	fluometuron	No	Warning	HE	Oral	24	a e g j	b e g j
Sutan*+ 6.7-E	51036-248	butylate	No	Caution	HE	Oral	12	a f g j	b f g j
Monsanto Co.									
Accord*	524-326	glyphosate	No	Caution	HE	Oral	4	a g	b e g
Accord Site Prep*	524-475	glyphosate	No	Caution	HE	Oral	4	a g	b e g
Buckle*	524-375	triallate + trifluralin	No	Caution	HE	Oral	12†	a g	b e g
Bullet*	524-418	alachlor + atrazine	Yes	Caution	HE	Oral	12†	a f h j	b f h j
Fallow Master*	524-390	glyphosate + dicamba	No	Danger	HE	Oral	24	a e g j	b e g j
Far-Go*	524-145	triallate	No	Caution	HE	Oral	12†	a f g j	b f g j
Far-Go* Granular	524-292	triallate	No	Caution	HE	Oral	12†	a g	b e g
FieldMaster*	524-497	acetochlor + glyphosate + atrazine	Yes	Caution	HE	Oral	12	a e g	d e h
Freedom*	524-422	alachlor + trifluralin	Yes	Warning	HE	Oral	12†	c f h j k l	c f h j l
Granular Ramrod* 20	524-152	propachlor	No	Danger	HE	Oral	48	a e g j	b e g j
Harness*	524-473	acetochlor	Yes	Warning	HE	Oral	12†	c e h j k l	b e h j l
Harness* 20G	524-487	acetochlor	Yes	Caution	HE	Oral	12	a g	b e g
Harness* Xtra	524-480	acetochlor + atrazine	Yes	Caution	HE	Oral	12†	a e g	b e g
Harness* Xtra 5.6L	524-485	acetochlor + atrazine	Yes	Caution	HE	Oral	12	a e g	d e h
Landmaster* BW	524-351	glyphosate + 2,4-D	No	Danger	HE	Oral	48	a e g j	b e g j
Lariat*	524-329	alachlor + atrazine	Yes	Warning	HE	Oral	12†	c f h j k l	c f h j l
Lasso*	524-314	alachlor	Yes	Danger	HE	Oral	12†	a f h j	b f h j
Lasso* II	524-296	alachlor	Yes	Warning	HE	Oral	12†	a e h j	b e h j
Manage*	524-465	halosulfuron-methyl	No	Caution	HE	Oral	12	a g	b e g
Micro-Tech*	524-344	alachlor	Yes	Caution	HE	Oral	12	a e h j	b e h j

Product Name	EPA Number	Active Ingredient(s)	RUP	Signal Word	Action	Notification	REI	PPE	Early Entry PPE
Partner*	524-403	alachlor	Yes	Caution	HE	Oral	12†	a e h j	b e h j
Permit*	524-465	halosulfuron-methyl	No	Caution	HE	Oral	12	a g	b e g
Ramrod*	524-331	propachlor	No	Danger	HE	Oral	48	d e h j k l	d e h j l
Ramrod*/Atrazine	524-328	propachlor + atrazine	Yes	Warning	HE	Oral	48	a f h j	b e h
Ramrod*/Atrazine DF	524-423	propachlor + atrazine	Yes	Danger	HE	Oral	48	a f h j	b e h j
Rodeo*	524-343	glyphosate	No	Caution	HE	Oral	4	a g	b e g
Roundup* Custom	524-343	glyphosate	No	Caution	HE	Oral	4	a g	b e g
Roundup* Original	524-445	glyphosate	No	Warning	HE	Oral	12	a g j	b e g j
Roundup* Original RT	524-454	glyphosate	No	Warning	HE	Oral	12	a g j	b e g j
Roundup* PRO	524-475	glyphosate	No	Caution	HE	Oral	4	a g	b e g
Roundup* Ultra	524-475	glyphosate	No	Caution	HE	Oral	4	a g	b e g
Roundup* Ultra RT	524-475	glyphosate	No	Caution	HE	Oral	4	a g	b e g

Monterey Chemical Co.

Product Name	EPA Number	Active Ingredient(s)	RUP	Signal Word	Action	Notification	REI	PPE	Early Entry PPE
Cotton-Aide HC*	17545-2	cacodylic acid	No	Caution	FM/HE	Oral	12	a e g	b e g
Montar	17545-3	cacodylic acid	No	Caution	HE	Oral	12	a e g j	b e g j

Mycogen Corp.

Product Name	EPA Number	Active Ingredient(s)	RUP	Signal Word	Action	Notification	REI	PPE	Early Entry PPE
Scythe*	53219-7	pelargonic acid	No	Warning	HE	Oral	24	a f g j	b f g j

Novartis

Product Name	EPA Number	Active Ingredient(s)	RUP	Signal Word	Action	Notification	REI	PPE	Early Entry PPE
AAtrex* 4L	100-497	atrazine	Yes	Caution	HE	Oral	12	a e h j	b e h
AAtrex* Nine-O*	100-585	atrazine	Yes	Caution	HE	Oral	12	a e h j	b e h
Action*	100-806	fluthiacet-methyl	No	Caution	HE	Oral	12	a e g	b e g
Amber* Accu-Pak*	100-701	triasulfuron	No	Caution	HE	Oral	12	a e g	b e g
Amber* CustomPak*	100-768	triasulfuron	No	Caution	HE	Oral	4	a e g	b e g
Barricade* 65WG	100-834	prodiamine	No	Caution	HE	Oral	12	a e g	b e g
Beacon* Accu-Pak*	100-705	primisulfuron-methyl	No	Caution	HE	Oral	12	a e g	b e g
Bicep II MAGNUM*	100-817	atrazine + S-metolachlor	Yes	Caution	HE	Oral	24	a e g	b e g
Bicep Lite II MAGNUM*	100-827	atrazine + S-metolachlor	Yes	Caution	HE	Oral	24	a e g	b e g
Caparol* 4L	100-620	prometryn	No	Caution	HE	Oral	12†	a g	b e g
Cotoran* DF	100-704	fluometuron	No	Warning	HE	Oral	24	a e g j	b e g j
Cotoran* 4L	100-642	fluometuron	No	Caution	HE	Oral	24	a f g	b f g
Dual II MAGNUM*	100-818	S-metolachlor	No	Caution	HE	Oral	24	a f g	b f g
Dual IIG MAGNUM*	100-910	S-metolachlor	No	Caution	HE	Oral	24†	a e g	b e g
Dual MAGNUM*	100-816	S-metolachlor	No	Caution	HE	Oral	24	a f g	b f g
Evik* DF	100-786	ametryn	No	Caution	HE	Oral	12	a g	b e g
Evital* 5G	100-840	norflurazon	No	Caution	HE	Oral	12	a e g	b e g
Exceed* CustomPak*	100-774	prosulfuron + primisulfuron-methyl	No	Caution	HE	Oral	12	a e g	b e g
NorthStar* CustomPak*	100-923	primisulfuron-methyl + dicamba	No	Caution	HE	Oral	12†	a e g j	b e g j
Peak* Accu-Pak*	100-763	prosulfuron	No	Caution	HE	Oral	12	a e g	b e g
Pennant MAGNUM*	100-691	S-metolachlor	No	Caution	HE	Oral	24	c f g	c f g
Princep* Caliber 90*	100-603	simazine	No	Caution	HE	Oral	12	a e g	b e g
Princep* 4L	100-526	simazine	No	Caution	HE	Oral	12	a f g	b f g
Rave*	100-927	dicamba + triasulfuron	No	Caution	HE	Oral	12	a e g	a e g
Solicam* DF	100-849	norflurazon	No	Caution	HE	Oral	12†	a e g	b e g
Spirit* CustomPak*	100-911	prosulfuron + primisulfuron-methyl	No	Caution	HE	Oral	12	a e g	b e g
Tough* 5EC	100-877	pyridate	No	Warning	HE	Oral	12	a f g j	b f g j
Turbo*	3125-366-100	metolachlor + metribuzin	No	Caution	HE	Oral	12†	c e g	d f h
Vanquish*	100-884	dicamba	No	Caution	HE	Oral	24	a e g	b e g
Zorial* 5G	100-840	norflurazon	No	Caution	HE	Oral	12	a e g	b e g
Zorial Rapid 80*	100-848	norflurazon	No	Caution	HE	Oral	12†	a e g	b e g

Nufarm, Inc.

Product Name	EPA Number	Active Ingredient(s)	RUP	Signal Word	Action	Notification	REI	PPE	Early Entry PPE
Credit*	524-445-71368	glyphosate	No	Warning	HE	Oral	12	a g j	b e g j
Thistrol*	71368-5-264	MCPB	No	Caution	HE	Oral	12	a e g	b e g
Weedar* 64	71368-1-264	2,4-D	No	Danger	HE	Oral	48	c e h j k l	c e h j l
Weedone* 638	71368-3-264	2,4-D	No	Danger	HE	Oral	48	a f g j	b f g j

Action Word Abbreviations	Personal Protective Equipment (PPE) Abbreviations
DE = Defoliant FM = Fumigant HE = Herbicide	a....Long-sleeved-shirt and long pants b....Coveralls c....Coveralls over short-sleeved shirt and short pants d ...Coveralls over long-sleeved shirt and long pants e....Waterproof gloves f....Chemical-resistant gloves g ...Shoes plus socks h....Chemical-resistant footwear plus socks j....Protective eyewear k....Chemical-resistant apron when cleaning equipment, mixing, or loading l....Chemical-resistant headgear for overhead exposure m...Approved respirator n....Chemical-resistant protective suit

* = Trade Name/R/TM   † REI may vary; please refer to product label for complete information.
Information presented herein is for preliminary planning only. Exclusive reliance must be placed on information/directions supplied by the manufacturer.

Worker Protection Standard

Product Name	EPA Number	Active Ingredient(s)	RUP	Signal Word	Action	Notification	REI	PPE	Early Entry PPE
Weedone* Lo Vol 6	71368-11-264	2,4-D	No	Caution	HE	Oral	12	a f g j	b f g j
Weedone* LV4 Solventless	71368-14-264	2,4-D	No	Caution	HE	Oral	12	a f g j	b f g j
Nufarm UK Limited									
Chiptox*	11685-20-264	MCPA	No	Danger	HE	Oral	48	c e h j k l	c e h j l
Rhomene*	11685-19-264	MCPA	No	Danger	HE	Oral	48	c e h j k l	c e h j l
Rhonox*	11685-21-264	MCPA	No	Caution	HE	Oral	12	a f g	b f g
PBI/Gordon Corp.									
Barrier*	2217-675	diclobenil	No	Caution	HE	Oral	12	a e g	b e g
Cleanout*	2217-775	2,4-D + 2, 4-DP + dicamba	No	Caution	HE				
Gordon's* Amine 400	2217-2	2,4-D	No	Danger	HE	Oral	48		
Gordon's* LV 400	2217-077	2,4-D	No	Caution	HE	Oral	12	a f g j	b f g j
Gordon's* MPCA Amine 4	2217-362	MPCA	No	Danger	HE	Oral	48	a e g j	b e g j
Hi-Dep*	2217-703	2,4-D	No	Danger	HE	Oral	48	a e g j	b e g j
Orchard Master*	2217-703	2,4-D	No	Danger	HE	Oral	48	a e g j	b e g j
Ornamec* Over-The-Top	2217-728	fluazifop	No	Caution	HE	Oral	4	a f g	b f g
Trimec* 992	2217-656	2,4-D + MCPP + dicamba	No	Danger	HE	Oral	48	c e h j	c e h j
Platte Chemical Co.									
Balan* DF	34704-746	benefin	No	Caution	HE	Oral	12†	a e g	b e g
Broclean*	51036-256-34704	bromoxynil	No	Warning	HE	Oral	12	d f h j k l	d f h j l
Bromac*	51036-254-34704	bromoxynil + MCPA	No	Warning	HE	Oral	12	d f h j k l	d f h j l
Brozine*	51036-255-34704	bromoxynil + atrazine	Yes	Caution	HE	Oral	12	d f h j k l	d f h j l
Clean Crop* Amine 4	34704-120	2,4-D	No	Danger	HE	Oral	48	a e g j	b e g j
Clean Crop* Atrazine 4L	34704-69	atrazine	Yes	Caution	HE	Oral	12†	a e h	b e h
Clean Crop* Atrazine 90 WDG	34704-622	atrazine	Yes	Caution	HE	Oral	12†	a e h	b e h
Clean Crop* DSMA Plus	50534-27-34704	DSMA	No	Caution	HE	Oral	12	a e g j k	b e g j
Clean Crop* Low Vol 4	34704-124	2,4-D	No	Caution	HE	Oral	12	a f g j	b f g j
Clean Crop* Low Vol 6	34704-125	2,4-D	No	Caution	HE	Oral	12	a e g j	b e g j
Clean Crop* MCP Amine 4	34704-130	MCPA	No	Danger	HE	Oral	48	a e g j	b e g j
Clean Crop* MCP 4 Ester	62719-59-34704	MCPA	No	Warning	HE	Oral	24	c f h k l	c f h l
Clean Crop* MCP 2 Sodium	62719-58-34704	MCPA	No	Danger	HE	Oral	48	a e g j	b e g j
Clean Crop* MSMA 6 Plus	34704-115	MSMA	No	Caution	HE	Oral	12	a e h j k m	b e h
Clean Crop* MSMA 6.6	34704-111	MSMA	No	Caution	HE	Oral	12	a e h k m	b e h
Clean Crop* Nemasol* 42%	34704-769	metam-sodium	No	Danger	FM	Oral, Posted	48	d e h j k l m	d e h j m
Clean Crop* Simazine 4L	34704-687	simazine	No	Caution	HE	Oral	12†	a e g	b e g
Clean Crop* Simazine 90 WDG	34704-686	simazine	No	Caution	HE	Oral	12†	a e g	b e g
Clean Crop* Trifluralin HF	34704-792	trifluralin	No	Warning	HE	Oral	12	a f g j	b f g j
Curbit*	34704-610	ethalfluralin	No	Warning	HE	Oral	24	d f g j k	d f g j
Diuron 80 WDG	34704-648	diuron	No	Caution	HE	Oral	12	a e g	b e g
Prometryne 4L	34704-692	prometryne	No	Warning	HE	Oral	12†	a e g m	b e g
Saber*	34704-803	2,4-D	No	Danger	HE	Oral	48	a f g j	b f g j
Salvo*	34704-609	2,4-D	No	Caution	HE	Oral	12	a f g j	b f g j
Savage*	34704-606	2,4-D	No	Danger	HE	Oral	48	a f g j	b f g j
Shotgun*	34704-728	atrazine + 2,4-D	Yes	Danger	HE	Oral	12	a e h j k	b e h
Surefire*	10182-120-34704	paraquat + diuron	Yes	Danger-Poison	HE	Oral, Posted	12	d e g j l m	d e h j l
Sword*	228-267-34704	MCPA	No	Warning	HE	Oral	12	c f h k l	c f h l
Pro-Serve, Inc.									
Pronone 10G or MG	33560-21	hexazinone	No	Caution	HE	Oral	24	a g	b e g
Pronone Power Pellet	33560-41	hexazinone	No	Danger	HE	Oral	24	a e g j	b e g j
Rhone-Poulenc Ag Co.									
Asulox*	264-447	asulam	No	Caution	HE	Oral	12	a e g	b e g
Balance* WDG	264-567	isoxaflutole	Yes	Caution	HE	Oral	12	a e g j k	d e g j
Bronate*	264-438	bromoxynil + MCPA	No	Warning	HE	Oral	12	d f h j k l	d f h j l
Buctril*	264-437	bromoxynil	No	Warning	HE	Oral	12	d f h j k l	d f h j l
Buctril* 4EC	264-540	bromoxynil	No	Warning	HE	Oral	12†	d f h j k l	d f h j l
Buctril* + Atrazine	264-477	bromoxynil + atrazine	Yes	Caution	HE	Oral	12	d f h j k l	d f h j l
Chipco* Ronstar* G	264-445	oxadiazon	No	Warning	HE	Oral	12	c e h j k l	c e h l
Chipco* Ronstar* 50 WSP	264-538	oxadiazon	No	Warning	HE	Oral	12	c e h j k l	c e h j l
Esteron* 99C	62719-9-264	2,4-D	No	Caution	HE	Oral	12	a f g j	b f g j
Folex* 6EC	264-498	tribufos	No	Danger	DE	Oral, Posted	24	d f h j k l m	d f h j l
Formula 40*	62719-1-264	2,4-D	No	Danger	HE	Oral	48	a e g j	b e g j
Sedagri* Trifluralin 480	264-584	trifluralin	No	Warning	HE	Oral	12†	a f g j	b f g j
RiceCo									
Blue Drum*	56077-34	propanil	No	Caution	HE	Oral	24	a f g l	b f g l
Duet*	56077-53	propanil + bensulfuron-methyl	No	Caution	HE	Oral	24	a e g l	b e g l

Product Name	EPA Number	Active Ingredient(s)	RUP	Signal Word	Action	Notification	REI	PPE	Early Entry PPE
Propanil 4	56077-34	propanil	No	Caution	HE	Oral	24	a f g l	b f g l
Propanil 36%	56077-35	propanil	No	Caution	HE	Oral	24	a f g l	b f g l
Super WHAM!*	56077-38	propanil	No	Caution	HE	Oral	24	a e g l	b e g l
Super WHAM!* CA	71085-5	propanil	No	Caution	HE	Oral	24	a e g l	b e g l
WHAM! EZ*	56077-38	propanil	No	Caution	HE	Oral	24	a e g l	b e g l
WHAM! EZ* CA	71085-5	propanil	No	Caution	HE	Oral	24	a e g l	b e g l

Riverdale Chemical Co.

Product Name	EPA Number	Active Ingredient(s)	RUP	Signal Word	Action	Notification	REI	PPE	Early Entry PPE
2,4-D Granules	228-61	2,4-D	No	Caution	HE	Oral	12	a e g	b e g
6 Amine*	228-242	2,4-D	No	Danger	HE	Oral	48	c e h j k l	c e h j l
Dissolve*	228-265	2,4-D + 2,4-DP + MCPP	No	Danger	HE	Oral	48	c e h j k l	c e h j l
DP-4 Ester	228-196	2,4-DP	No	Caution	HE	Oral	12	a f g	b f g
Dri-Clean*	228-260	2,4-D	No	Danger	HE	Oral	48	c e h j l	c e h j l
LV 4	228-139	2,4-D	No	Caution	HE	Oral	12	a f g j	b f g j
LV 6	228-95	2,4-D	No	Caution	HE	Oral	12	a f g j	b f g j
MCPA IOE	229-267	MCPA	No	Warning	HE	Oral	12	c f h k l	c f h l
MCPA LV 4 Ester	229-156	MCPA	No	Warning	HE	Oral	12	c f h k l	c f h l
MCPA-4 Amine	228-143	MCPA	No	Danger	HE	Oral	48	a e g j	b e g j
Patron* 170	228-167	2,4-d + dichlorprop	No	Caution	HE	Oral	12	a f g j	b f g j
Patron* DP-4	228-196	dichlorprop	No	Caution	HE	Oral	12	a f g	b f g
Solution*	228-260	2,4-D	No	Danger	HE	Oral	48	c e h j k l	c e h j l
Turf D + DP	228-167	2,4-d + dichlorprop	No	Caution	HE	Oral	12	a f g j	b f g j
Veteran* CST	228-297	dicamba	No	Caution	HE	Oral	24	a f g	b f g
Weedestroy* AM-40	228-145	2,4-D	No	Danger	HE	Oral	48	c e h j l	c e h j k l

Rohm and Haas Co.

Product Name	EPA Number	Active Ingredient(s)	RUP	Signal Word	Action	Notification	REI	PPE	Early Entry PPE
Goal* 2XL	707-243	oxyfluorfen	No	Warning	HE	Oral	24	c f h j k l	c f h j l
Kerb* 50-W	707-159	pronamide	Yes	Caution	HE	Oral	24	c e h j k l	c e h j l
Kerb* WSP	707-159	pronamide	Yes	Caution	HE	Oral	24	c e h k l	c e h l
Mandate* 2E	707-251	thiazopyr	No	Warning	HE	Oral	12	a f g j	d f g j
Stam* 4E	707-109	propanil	No	Warning	HE	Oral	24	a f g j	b f g j
Stam* 80EDF	707-226	propanil	No	Caution	HE	Oral	24	a e g j	b e g j
Stam* M-4	707-109	propanil	No	Warning	HE	Oral	24	a f g j	b f g j
Stampede* 80EDF	707-226	propanil	No	Caution	HE	Oral	24	a e g j	b e g j
Visor* 2E	707-251	thiazopyr	No	Warning	HE	Oral	12	a f g j	d f g j

The Scotts Company

Product Name	EPA Number	Active Ingredient(s)	RUP	Signal Word	Action	Notification	REI	PPE	Early Entry PPE
Corral*	538-188	pendimethalin	No	Caution	HE	Oral	12	a e g j m	b e g j
OH2*	538-172	oxyfluorfen + pendimethalin	No	Caution	HE	Oral	24	a e g j m	b e g j
ProTurf* Turf Weedgrass Control	538-193	pendimethalin	No	Caution	HE	Oral	12	a e g	b e g
Rout*	58185-27	oxyfluorfen + oryzalin	No	Caution	HE	Oral	24	a e g j m	b e g j

Terra Industries Inc.

Product Name	EPA Number	Active Ingredient(s)	RUP	Signal Word	Action	Notification	REI	PPE	Early Entry PPE
Riverside* 120 Herbicide	9779-96	MSMA	No	Caution	HE	Oral	12	a e h j k m	b e h
Riverside* 912 Herbicide	9779-133	MSMA	No	Caution	HE	Oral	12	a e h j k m	b e h
Riverside* Asulam 3.3	9779-342	asulam	No	Caution	HE	Oral	12	b f g	b f g
Riverside* Atrazine 90DF	9779-253	atrazine	Yes	Caution	HE	Oral	12	a e h j	b e h
Riverside* Atrazine 4L	9779-255	atrazine	Yes	Caution	HE	Oral	12	a e h j	b e h
Riverside* Bison*	51036-254-9779	bromoxynil + MCPA	No	Warning	HE	Oral	12	d f h j k l	d f h j l
Riverside* Brash*	51036-308-9779	2,4-D + dicamba	No	Danger	HE	Oral	48	a e g j	b e g j
Riverside* 2,4-D Amine 4	9779-263	2,4-D	No	Danger	HE	Oral	48	c e h j k l	c e h j l
Riverside* 2,4-D LV4	9779-257	2,4-D	No	Caution	HE	Oral	12	a f g j	b f g j
Riverside* 2,4-D LV6	9779-256	2,4-D	No	Caution	HE	Oral	12	a e g j	b e g j
Riverside* 2,4-DB 1.75	42750-39-9779	2,4-DB	No	Danger	HE	Oral	48	a e g j	b e g j
Riverside* 2,4-DB 200	42750-38-9779	2,4-DB	No	Danger	HE	Oral	48	a e g j	b e g j
Riverside* Diuron 80DF	9779-318	diuron	No	Caution	HE	Oral	12	a e g j k l	b e g
Riverside* Diuron 4L	9779-329	diuron	No	Caution	HE	Oral	12	a e g j	b e g j
Riverside* DSMA 4	50534-158-9779	DSMA	No	Caution	HE	Oral	12	a e g j k m	b e g j

---

Action Word Abbreviations

DE = Defoliant
FM = Fumigant
HE = Herbicide

Personal Protective Equipment (PPE) Abbreviations

a.... Long-sleeved-shirt and long pants
b.... Coveralls
c.... Coveralls over short-sleeved shirt and short pants
d ... Coveralls over long-sleeved shirt and long pants
e.... Waterproof gloves
f.... Chemical-resistant gloves
g ... Shoes plus socks
h.... Chemical-resistant footwear plus socks
j.... Protective eyewear
k.... Chemical-resistant apron when cleaning equipment, mixing, or loading
l.... Chemical-resistant headgear for over-head exposure
m.... Approved respirator
n.... Chemical-resistant protective suit

* = Trade Name/R/TM   † REI may vary; please refer to product label for complete information.
Information presented herein is for preliminary planning only. Exclusive reliance must be placed on information/directions supplied by the manufacturer.

Worker Protection Standard

Product Name	EPA Number	Active Ingredient(s)	RUP	Signal Word	Action	Notification	REI	PPE	Early Entry PPE
Riverside* DSMA Herbicide	50534-27-9779	DSMA	No	Caution	HE	Oral	12	a e g j k m	b e g j
Riverside* Fluometuron 80DF	9779-311	fluometuron	No	Warning	HE	Oral	24	a e g j	b e g j
Riverside* Fluometuron 4L	9779-312	fluometuron	No	Caution	HE	Oral	24	a e g j	b e g j
Riverside* Fluometuron + MSMA	9779-319	fluometuron	No	Caution	HE	Oral	24	a e h j k	b e h j
Riverside* MCPA Amine	9779-262	MCPA	No	Danger	HE	Oral	48	a e g j	b e g j
Riverside* Moxy* + Atrazine	51036-255-9779	bromoxynil + atrazine	Yes	Caution	HE	Oral	12	d f h j k l	d f h j l
Riverside* Moxy* 2E	51036-256-9779	bromoxynil	No	Warning	HE	Oral	12	d f h j k l	d f h j l
Riverside* Phenoxy 088*	42750-36-9779	2,4-D	No	Danger	HE	Oral	48	a f g j	b f g j
Riverside* Prometryne 4L	9779-297	prometryne	No	Caution	HE	Oral	12	a f g k m	d f g
Riverside* Prometryne + MSMA	9779-317	prometryne + MSMA	No	Caution	HE	Oral	12	a e h j k m	d f g
Riverside* Propanil 4E	9779-272	propanil	No	Caution	HE	Oral	24	a f g j	b f g j
Riverside* Propanil 80EDF	707-226-9779	propanil	No	Caution	HE	Oral	24	a e g j	b e g j
Riverside* Simazine 90DF	9779-295	simazine	No	Caution	HE	Oral	12	a e g	b e g
Riverside* Simazine 4L	9779-296	simazine	No	Caution	HE	Oral	12	a e g	b e g
Riverside* Sterling*	51036-289-9779	dicamba	No	Warning	HE	Oral	24	a e g j	b e g j
Riverside* Sterling* Plus	51036-307-9779	atrazine + dicamba	Yes	Caution	HE	Oral	48	a f h j	b f h
Riverside* SWB 2,4-D LV4	42750-22-9779	2,4-D	No	Caution	HE	Oral	12	a e g j	b e g j
Riverside* SWB MCPA Ester	42750-25-9779	MCPA	No	Caution	HE	Oral	12	a e g j l	b e g j l
Riverside* Trific* 60DF	9779-308	trifluralin	No	Danger	HE	Oral	12	a e g j l	b e g j l
Riverside* Trific* 2L	9779-341	trifluralin	No	Caution	HE	Oral	12	a e g	b e g
Riverside* Trifluralin 4EC	9779-303	trifluralin	No	Caution	HE	Oral	12	a f g j	b f g j

UCB Agrochemicals

Product Name	EPA Number	Active Ingredient(s)	RUP	Signal Word	Action	Notification	REI	PPE	Early Entry PPE
Metam CLR*	45728-16	metam-sodium	No	Danger	FM	Oral	48	d e h k j l m	d e h j m

Uniroyal Chemical Co., Inc.

Product Name	EPA Number	Active Ingredient(s)	RUP	Signal Word	Action	Notification	REI	PPE	Early Entry PPE
Alanap*-L	400-49	naptalam-sodium	No	Warning	HE	Oral	48†	a g j	b e g j
Casoron* 4G	400-168	dichlobenil	No	Caution	HE	Oral	12†	a e g	b e g
Harvade*-25F	400-398	dimethipin	No	Danger	PGR/DE	Oral	48	d f h k l	d f h l
Harvade*-5F	400-155	dimethipin	No	Caution	PGR/DE	Oral	48	a f g	b f g

United Phosphorus Inc.

Product Name	EPA Number	Active Ingredient(s)	RUP	Signal Word	Action	Notification	REI	PPE	Early Entry PPE
Devrinol* 50-DF	10182-258-70506	napropamide	No	Caution	HE	Oral	12†	a e g	b e g
Devrinol* 2-E	10182-219-70506	napropamide	No	Danger	HE	Oral	12†	a f g j	b f g j
Devrinol* 10-G	10182-253-70506	napropamide	No	Caution	HE	Oral	12†	a g	b e g

Valent U.S.A. Corp.

Product Name	EPA Number	Active Ingredient(s)	RUP	Signal Word	Action	Notification	REI	PPE	Early Entry PPE
Bolero* 8 EC	59639-79	thiobencarb	No	Caution	HE	Oral	4	a g	b e g
Bolero* 10 G	59639-80	thiobencarb	No	Caution	HE	Oral	12	a g m	b e g
Cobra*	59639-34	lactofen	No	Danger	HE	Oral	12	d f h j k l	d f h j l
Envoy*	59639-78	clethodim	No	Warning	HE	Oral	24	c f h j k l	c f h j l
Prism*	59639-78	clethodim	No	Warning	HE	Oral	24	c f h j k l	c f h j l
Resource* 0.86EC	59639-82	flumiclorac pentyl ester	No	Warning	HE	Oral	12	c f h j	c f h j
Resource* 80WP	59639-100	flumiclorac pentyl ester	No	Caution	HE	Oral	12	a e g	b e g
Select* 2 EC	59639-3	clethodim	No	Warning	HE	Oral	24	a f g j	b f g j
Stellar*	59639-92	flumiclorac pentyl ester + lactofen	No	Danger	HE	Oral	12	a f g j	b f g j

Wilbur-Ellis Co.

Product Name	EPA Number	Active Ingredient(s)	RUP	Signal Word	Action	Notification	REI	PPE	Early Entry PPE
Broadrange*	228-167-2935	2,4-D + 2,4-DP ester	No	Caution	HE	Oral	12	a e g j	b e g j
Deuce*	228-191-2935	2,4-D + MCPP	No	Danger	HE	Oral	†	a e g j	b e g j
Wilbur-Ellis* Amine 4	2935-512	2,4-D	No	Danger	HE	Oral	48	c e h j k l	c e h j l
Wilbur-Ellis* Lo Vol-4 Ester	2935-511	2,4-D	No	Caution	HE	Oral	12	a f g j	b f g j
Wilbur-Ellis* Lo Vol-6 Ester	2935-499	2,4-D	No	Caution	HE	Oral	12	a f g j	b f g j
Wilbur-Ellis* MCPA Amine	228-143-2935	MCPA	No	Danger	HE	Oral	48	a e g j	b e g j
Wilbur-Ellis* MCPA Ester	228-156-2935	MCPA	No	Warning	HE	Oral	12	a f h l	b f h l
Wilbur-Ellis* Sodium Salt of MPCA	228-199-2935	MCPA	No	Danger	HE	Oral	48	a e g j	b e g j
Wilbur-Ellis* Trifluralin 10G	1812-328-652935	trifluralin	No	Warning	HE	Oral	12	a e g j	b e g j

ZENECA Ag Products

Product Name	EPA Number	Active Ingredient(s)	RUP	Signal Word	Action	Notification	REI	PPE	Early Entry PPE
Achieve*	10182-426	tralkoxydim	No	Caution	HE	Oral	12†	a e g	b e g
Ansar* 6.6	50534-16	MSMA	No	Caution	HE	Oral	12	a e g j k m	b e g j
Arrosolo* 3-3E	10182-260	propanil + molinate	No	Warning	HE	Oral	24	d f h k m	b f g j
Bueno* 6	50534-6	MSMA	No	Caution	HE	Oral	12	a e g j k m	b e g j
Cyclone* 2L	10182-111	paraquat	Yes	Danger-Poison	HE	Oral	12/24†	a e g j k	b e g j
Cyclone* 3L	10182-372	paraquat	Yes	Danger-Poison	HE	Oral	12/24	a e g j k	b e g j
Diquat*	10182-353	diquat dibromide	No	Warning	HE	Oral	24	c e h j k l	c e h j l
Doubleplay*	10182-388	EPTC + acetochlor	Yes	Warning	HE	Oral	12	a f g j	b f g j
Eptam* 7E	10182-220	EPTC	No	Caution	HE	Oral	12†	a f g j	b f g j
Eptam* 20-G	10182-199	EPTC	No	Caution	HE	Oral	12†	a e g	b e g

Product Name	EPA Number	Active Ingredient(s)	RUP	Signal Word	Action	Notification	REI	PPE	Early Entry PPE
Eradicane* 6.7-E	10182-223	EPTC	No	Caution	HE	Oral	12†	a f g j	b f g j
Eradicane* 25-G	10182-323	EPTC	No	Caution	HE	Oral	12†	a e g	b e g
Flexstar*	10182-418	fomesafen	No	Warning	HE	Oral	24	c f h k	c f h
FulTime*	10182-419	acetochlor + atrazine	Yes	Caution	HE	Oral	12†	a e g	d e h
Fusilade* DX	10182-367	fluazifop-P-butyl	No	Caution	HE	Oral	12	a f g j k	b f g
Fusilade* II	10182-393	fluazifop-P-butyl	No	Caution	HE	Oral	12	a f g j k	b f g
Fusion*	10182-343	fluazifop-P-butyl + fenoxaprop-P-ethyl	No	Caution	HE	Oral	24	a f g	b f g
Gramoxone* Extra	10182-280	paraquat	Yes	Danger-Poison	HE	Oral	12/24†	a e g j k	b e g j
Ordram* 8E	10182-204	molinate	No	Warning	HE	Oral	12†	d f h k m	b e g
Ordram* 15G	10182-274	molinate	No	Warning	HE	Oral	12	d f h k m	b e g j
Ordram* 15GM	10182-420	molinate	No	Caution	HE	Oral	12	p f h m	b e g j
Reflex*	10182-83	fomesafen	No	Danger	HE	Oral	24	a e g j	b e g j
Reward* or Reward* LS	10182-404	diquat dibromide	No	Warning	HE	Oral	24	c e h j k l	c e h j l
Ro-Neet* 6-E	10182-178	cycloate	No	Caution	HE	Oral	12†	a f g	b f g
Starfire* 1.5L	10182-103	paraquat	Yes	Danger-Poison	HE	Oral	12/24†	a e g j k	b e g j
Starfire* 3L	10182-372	paraquat	Yes	Danger-Poison	HE	Oral	24	a e g j k	b e g j
Surpass* 100	10182-363	acetochlor + atrazine	Yes	Danger	HE	Oral	12†	a e g j k	b e g j
Surpass* EC	10182-325	acetochlor	Yes	Warning	HE	Oral	12†	a e h j k l	b e h j l
Surpass* 20G	10182-407	acetochlor	Yes	Warning	HE	Oral	12†	a e g j	b e g j
Tillam* 6E	10182-158	pebulate	No	Caution	HE	Oral	12†	a f g j	b f g j
TopNotch*	10182-391	acetochlor	Yes	Caution	HE	Oral	12†	a e g	b e g
Tornado*	10182-141	fluazifop-P-butyl + fomesafen	No	Warning	HE	Oral	24	a f g j k	b f g j
Touchdown* 5L	10182-429	sulfosate	No	Caution	HE	Oral	12	a e g	b e g
Touchdown* 6L	10182-324	sulfosate	No	Caution	HE	Oral	4	a e g	b e g
Typhoon*	10182-368	fluazifop-P-butyl + fomesafen	No	Warning	HE	Oral	24	a f g j k	b f g j

---

Action Word Abbreviations

DE = Defoliant
FM = Fumigant
HE = Herbicide

Personal Protective Equipment (PPE) Abbreviations

a....Long-sleeved-shirt and long pants
b....Coveralls
c....Coveralls over short-sleeved shirt and short pants
d....Coveralls over long-sleeved shirt and long pants
e....Waterproof gloves
f....Chemical-resistant gloves
g...Shoes plus socks
h....Chemical-resistant footwear plus socks
j....Protective eyewear
k....Chemical-resistant apron when cleaning equipment, mixing, or loading
l....Chemical-resistant headgear for overhead exposure
m...Approved respirator
n....Chemical-resistant protective suit

* = Trade Name/R/TM   † REI may vary; please refer to product label for complete information.
Information presented herein is for preliminary planning only. Exclusive reliance must be placed on information/directions supplied by the manufacturer.

Notes • Notes • Notes

Section 1
Field Corn

Enhanced Seed Information
Clearfield (IMI) Corn 85
Liberty Link Corn 84
Roundup Ready Corn 87
SR Corn 86

Use Reminders
Corn Herbicide Rotational Restrictions 88
Grass Weed Sizes For Postemergence Corn Herbicides 89
Weed Sizes For Postemergence Corn Herbicides 90
Grazing And Forage Intervals For Herbicide-Treated Corn 91
Characteristics of Preemergence Herbicides 92
Characteristics of "Burndown" And Postemergence Corn Herbicides . .93
Corn "Post" Herbicides: Adjuvant Use Plus Application And Use
    Restrictions 94
Maximum Corn, Weed Sizes for Delayed Preemergence Herbicide
    Application 95

Weed Efficacy Charts
Grass and Nutsedge Herbicide Control Ratings 96
Broadleaf Weed Control Ratings for Corn Herbicides 97
Weed Response To Selected Soil-Applied Field Corn Herbicides 98
Weed Response To Selected Postemergence Field Corn Herbicides . . .99
Weed Response To Burndown Herbicides In No-Till Corn 100

Herbicide Listings 101

Enhanced Seed Systems

Liberty Link Corn

This genetically engineered corn is tolerant of glufosinate-ammonium herbicide.

Compiled by
Tina Grady

LibertyLink (LL) corn is a genetically enhanced seed developed by AgrEvo. This type of corn contains the LL trait, making it resistant to Liberty (glufosinate-ammonium) herbicide. (Glufosinate-ammonium is an amino acid derivative.)

In addition, StarLink Bt, a trait also available from AgrEvo, is stacked with LL. This Bacillus thuringiensis (Bt) enables growers to control insect pests and use Liberty herbicide.

Currently, about 7.1 million acres, out of about 80 million total acres of corn in the U.S., are planted to LL corn.

Liberty is a non-selective, broadspectrum, postemergence herbicide that has a fairly quick contact action on plant foliage by inhibiting photosynthesis. Complete plant death typically occurs in one to two weeks, but chlorosis and wilting usually begin three to five days after application. Moist soil, bright sunlight, and high humidity speeds up the activity of the plant.

The mode of action is inhibition of the glutamine synthetase enzyme that converts glutamate plus ammonia to glutamine in the cell. Since this reaction is inhibited, there is rapid accumulation of ammonia in the plant which destroys cells and directly inhibits photosynthesis reactions.

Licensed Herbicides

A single application of Liberty, when used with LL, can kill more than 100 grass and broadleaf weeds.

A premix of Liberty ATZ on LL or warranted corn also can be used. Liberty ATZ is a combination of Liberty and atrazine, and offering the same benefits as Liberty.

Weeds Controlled

Liberty herbicide is effective on more than 100 grasses and broadleaf weeds and is known to suppress several perennial weeds. Annual weeds that the herbicide works well on include foxtail, cocklebur, velvetleaf, and tall waterhemp. Perennial weeds include bindweed, hemp dogbane, and Canada thistle.

Rate of application will vary by weed size, application timing, and geography. Apply postemergence on corn up to 24 inches tall. When corn is between 24 inches and 36 inches tall, drop nozzle applications of Liberty can be made.

Application Notes

Liberty is considered a flexible herbicide, making it possible for it to fit a variety of corn herbicide programs. The primary methods for application of Liberty include the following:

• A preemergence herbicide such as Dual Magnum, Frontier, Harness/Surpass, or Lasso, followed by Liberty postemergence.

• Total postemergence in which Liberty + AMS + atrazine is applied.

• Postsequential, in which Liberty is applied and then followed by another Liberty treatment. Any herbicide can be used, but Liberty is recommended.

Residuals

When a residual product is used, a reduced rate of a preemergence herbicide should be used with Liberty. Most recommendations for Liberty also include the use of a reduced rate amount of atrazine for added residual control.

Other Comments

AgrEvo does not charge a technology fee for use of the LL seed or use of Liberty herbicide. ☐

Liberty Checklist

1. Start with a clean field...
✔ Use a preemergence such as Dual Magnum, Frontier, Harness/Surpass, or Lasso.
✔ Fits all tillage practices.

2. Good coverage is essential...
✔ Must have a 4-hour rainfall free period after application.
✔ Has effective weed control in 3-7 days.

3. Application notes...
✔ Apply from emergence until corn is 24 inches tall
✔ Add 3 pounds AMS per acre. Don't add any surfactants or crop oils.
✔ Apply broadcast in a minimum of 15 gallons of water per acre.
✔ Wide application window.

4. Rates will vary depending on weed species...
✔ In weed populations with mixed species, apply at highest listed rate.

Enhanced Seed Systems

IMI (Clearfield) Corn

This conventionally-bred seed variety can tolerate imidazolinone herbicides.

Compiled by
Tina Grady

The Clearfield Production System is the new brand name for imidazolinone-tolerant crops including corn, canola, wheat, rice, sugar beets, and sugarcane. The Clearfield Production System for corn is an imidazolinone-tolerant corn developed using enhanced plant breeding methods in conjunction with Pioneer Hi-Bred International; Golden Harvest Seeds; Garst Seeds; and Mycogen Seeds (part of Dow AgroSciences), as well as others.

In 1999, an estimated 6 million acres of Clearfield corn is available with an anticipated 4 million acres planted. In 2000, out of 8 million acres available, an anticipated 5.6 million acres of Clearfield corn will be planted.

Licensed Herbicides

Lightning is the recommended herbicide for use on Clearfield corn. However, any registered herbicide may be used on the imidazolinone-tolerant corn, with the exception of Liberty, Roundup, and Touchdown. Other herbicides specifically designed for use on Clearfield corn include Contour and Resolve.

The Lightening herbicide (imazethapyr [52.5%] and imazapyr [17.5%]) works by inhibiting the ALS enzyme — important for the formation of the three essential amino acids Leucine, Isoleucine, and Valine — in susceptible weed species.

Weeds Controlled

Lightning herbicide is very active on both broadleafs and grasses. The system works particularly well on the annual weeds woolly cupgrass, field sandbur, eastern black nightshade, and velvetleaf. For perennial weeds, it also works well on controlling seedling johnsongrass and suppressing rhizome johnsongrass.

Lightning will not control common ragweed and common waterhemp. An appropriate tank-mix partner must be used on these two weeds.

Application Notes

Lightning must be used in a nonionic surfactant and a nitrogen-based fertilizer. If weeds are present prior to planting, an appropriate burndown herbicide also should be used.

Lightning application should be early postemergence to Clearfield corn before the weeds exceed 1-3 inches in height. This is the optimum weed height for control. Application to large weeds prevents Lightning from reaching the soil surface and providing residual control.

For in-crop application, Lightning may be applied to Clearfield corn up to 20 inches in height. Applications to larger corn may be made if drop nozzles are used. Height restriction will depend on the tank-mix partner that is used.

The application timing for annual and perennial weeds also is early postemergence before the weeds exceed 1-3 inches in height. The rate is the same for all soil types — 1.28 ounces per acre.

Residuals

Lightning has residual effects on both grasses and broadleaf weeds. Other post-application residual products for use on Clearfield corn include Distinct (residual for use on broadleafs only) and atrazine.

Generally speaking, the residual should be used before the non-residuals so good soil coverage can be achieved — a key to using residuals for this corn system.

Other Comments

Soil moisture is the key to maintaining activity so prolonged periods of dry weather may sacrifice some of the residual control Lightning provides. However, the timing doesn't change.

Users of the Clearfield Production System for Clearfield corn should check with their local agricenters and Clearfield production specialists for specific recommendations in their area.

Clearfield Corn Checklist

1. Start with a clean field...
  ✔ Use a burndown herbicide or tillage.

2. Make an early postemergence application of 1.28 ounces Lightning per acre.
  ✔ Apply before weeds exceed 1-3" in height.
  ✔ May be applied to Clearfield corn up to 20" in height; use drop nozzles when applying to corn taller than 20".

3. Use with a nonionic surfactant and a nitrogen-based fertilizer.

Additional tips for best results:

  ✔ Lightning must reach the soil in order to provide residual control.

Enhanced Seed Systems

Poast-Protected Corn

There are more than 300,000 acres planted to this herbicide-resistant corn. This seed was developed through conventional breeding.

Compiled by Tina Grady

SR-corn hybrids are sethoxydim-resistant and also known as Poast-protected. Poast is a non-selective grass herbicide, that works by translocating in grass. Developed by BASF, these hybrids contain a slightly altered gene in the resistant ACC'ase enzyme — essential for plant growth — which is shut down by sethoxydim. The Poast-protected trait is found naturally in certain corn varieties and is put in other varieties, so SR-Corn in not a genetically modified (GM) crop. These types of varieties have a trait that breaks the sethoxydim molecule down before entry into the soybean crop.

More than 300,000 acres are planted to SR-Corn.

Licensed Herbicides

Any licensed herbicide may be used with the SR-corn system. It's mandatory to make sure the Poast-protected trait is in the corn and is compatible with the herbicide used since Poast does kill corn that does not carry the herbicide-resistant trait.

Although any herbicide system is acceptable with SR-corn, it is suggested that a grower start with a strong base program, such as Frontier, preemergence. Use of high-quality, commercially available crop oil concentrates (COCs) is recommended with Poast. It also is suggested that grass is controlled with this system before it competes with the corn — typically when grass reaches 2 inches to 3 inches tall — to get the best yield.

Weeds Controlled

Poast is a non-selective grass herbicide that provides control on most problem grasses — in particular, johnsongrass, shattercane, and woolly cupgrass. However, the system does not control broadleaf weeds or sedges.

On annual weeds, it's best to control the grasses when they are small. With perennial weeds, such as johnsongrass, it is recommended to wait until there is enough chemical on the grass to translocate to the rhizome — even waiting until the grass is up to 6 inches tall is acceptable.

Application Notes

For application on annual grasses, the standard rate is 24 ounces of Poast Plus or 16 ounces of Poast. For perennial grasses, the standard rate of application is 24 ounces for Poast and 36 ounces for Poast Plus. For product information, turn to page 122. turn to page 122.

Residuals

Poast herbicide has limited residual effects. It's often used in combination with a residual herbicide system.

Other Comments

An advantage to use of the Poast-protected system is the wide window of application time. However, as grass gets taller, these weeds may compete for yield so it is recommended to treat grasses when small.

Recordkeeping is important with the Poast-protected system. Although Poast is not a restricted product, it's important to keep track of which fields contain the SR-corn. If Poast is used on a field without the Poast-protected trait, it will kill the crop.

There is no technology fee for using this system. ☐

Poast Checklist

1. Start with a clean field...
  ✔ Use a burndown herbicide to clean the field.
  ✔ Have good seed bed preparation.

2. Apply 16 ounces per acre for general grass control...
  ✔ Annual grass height should be <8 inches.
  ✔ For perennial grasses, delay application until grass height is at least 4-8 inches.
  ✔ Two applications often needed for perennial grass control.

3. Use 10-20 gpa water...
  ✔ Have spray pressure of 40-60 psi.
  ✔ Apply with Dash or crop oil concentrate.

Additional tips for best results:
  ✔ Apply up to onset of pollen shed.
  ✔ Is adaptable to any tillage system.

Enhanced Seed Systems

Roundup Ready Corn

This genetically enhanced seed will tolerate glyphosate herbicides.

Compiled by Tina Grady

Roundup Ready (RR) corn is a genetically enhanced seed developed by Monsanto Co. that is tolerant to Roundup Ultra (glyphosate) herbicide. Roundup Ultra herbicide is a non-selective postemergence, systemic herbicide without any residual soil activity. The glyphosate is absorbed by the plant foliage which then translocates throughout the plant.

In 1999, more than 2 million acres of Roundup Ready corn were planted, up from 900,000 acres in 1998.

Licensed Herbicides

Roundup Ultra and other Roundup brands are the only glyphosate herbicide licensed for over-the-top application of Roundup Ready corn. Roundup Ultra is recommended for postemergence application. In addition to Roundup, Zeneca's Touchdown (sulfosate) has been registered by Monsanto for use over the top of RR corn.

Glyphosate is the isopropylamine salt of the parent whereas sulfosate is the trimethylsulfonium salt of the acid. These herbicides function identically once in the plant.

Weeds Controlled

When using no-till method on RR corn, glyphosate should be applied postemergence. Start with a clean field by using a burndown herbicide. In conventional and conservation tillage systems, tillage should be done prior to planting to eliminate any emerged weeds and to prepare a good seedbed.

Roundup Ultra provides broad spectrum control of annual grasses and broadleaf weeds. The maximum application rate for glyphosate in RR corn is 32 ounces per acre with a maximum of 64 ounces per acre in-crop per season.

On annual weeds, the rate of application for annuals, is before weeds reach 4 inches to reduce weed competition with corn. However, the Roundup Ultra application may be delayed until weeds are 4 to 6 inches if a pre-emergence herbicide is applied at planting. The recommended application timing on perennial weeds depends on the weed species.

With Roundup Ultra, no additional surfactant, etc. are needed or recommended by Monsanto.

Additional Application Notes

In general, dry conditions should not impact performance of Roundup Ultra. However, weeds growing under drought stress conditions may affect control. These conditions may require higher rates of glyphosate and/or the addition of AMS. Fields under stress should be treated earlier to ensure the weeds won't steal moisture from the crop.

Residuals

Three general weed-control programs are recommended with RR corn. They are the following:
• Pre-residual followed by Roundup Ultra post.
• Pre-residual + Roundup Ultra post.
• Roundup Ultra postemergence followed by Roundup Ultra on an as-needed basis.

Some recommended residuals include Harness, Harness Xtra brands, Micro-Tech, and Bullet.

Other Comments

There is a technology fee of $18 per unit of seed for the RR corn system. Finally, careful recordkeeping is a must. When growers plant herbicide-resistant seed, it is important to know which variety is planted on which acreage in order to match herbicide programs. If an herbicide is misapplied, it can result in total crop loss. □

Roundup-Ready Checklist

1. Start with a clean field...
✔ Use a burndown herbicide to clean the field.
✔ Good seed bed preparation in conventional till.

2. Apply 1 quart of glyphosate per acre for general annual weed control...
✔ Annual weed height of 4-6 inches is best timing, but as late as early flower is approved.

3. Use 10-20 gpa water...
✔ Use good spray techniques to manage drift.
✔ Add 8.5 lbs. of AMS for improved effectiveness. For hard to manage perennial weeds, add 17 lbs.

4. A second glyphosate application of up to 2 more qts. per acre may be applied if needed.

Additional tips for best results:
✔ Weeds up to 10" in height will be controlled.

Corn Herbicide Rotational Restrictions

Rotational crops following corn (months after application)[a]

Herbicide	Alfalfa	Barley, winter	Bean, snap	Clover	Corn, field	Corn, sweet	Cucumber	Oats, spring	Peas	Pepper	Potato, white	Pumpkin	Rye, winter	Sorghum, grain	Soybean	Tobacco	Tomato	Wheat, winter
Accent	12	4	10	12	NR	10	10[b]	8	10	10[b]	10[b]	10[b]	4	10	0.5	10[b]	10[b]	4
Aim	1	AH	1	1	1	1	1	AH	1	1	1	1	AH	1	1	1	1	AH
Atrazine	SY	NY	SY	SY	NR	NR	SY	SY	SY	SY	SY	SY	NY	NR	NY	SY	SY	NY
Axiom	NY	NY	NY	NY	NY	NY	NY	NY	NY	1	NY	NY	NY	NR	NY	NY	NY	NY
Banvel	AH	1[d]	AH	AH	NR	AH	AH	1[d]	AH	AH	AH	AH	1[d]	NR	1[c]	NY	AH	1[d]
Basagran	NR	NR	NR	NR	NR	NR	NR	NR	NR	NR	NR	NR	NR	NR	NR	NR	NR	NR
Basis	10	18	8	18	NR	10	18	8	8	18	4	18	18	10	0.5	8	18	4
Basis Gold	18	10	18	18	NR	18	18	18	18	18	18	18	10	10	10	18	18	10
Beacon/NorthStar	8	3	18[p]	18	0.5[i]	8	18	8	8	18	18[l]	18	3	8	8	18	18	3
Bicep products	SY	NY	SY	SY	NR	NY	SY	SY	SY	SY	SY	SY	NY	NR[e]	NY	SY	SY	NY
Bladex	AH	AH	AH	AH	NR	AH	AH	AH	AH	AH	AH	AH	AH	NR[f]	AH	NY	AH	AH
Buctril	1	1	1	1	1	1	1	1	1	1	1	1	1	1	1	1	1	1
Buctril + atrazine	SY	10	SY	SY	NR	NY	SY	10	SY	SY	SY	SY	10	NR	NY	SY	SY	10
Bullet	SY	NY	SY	SY	NR	NY	SY	SY	SY	SY	SY	SY	NY	NR[e]	NY	SY	SY	NY
Clarity	AH	AH	AH	AH	NR	AH	AH	AH	AH	AH	AH	AH	AH	NR	AH	NY	AH	AH
Celebrity	12	4	10	12[m]	NR	10	10[n]	8	10	10[n]	10[n]	10[n]	4	10	1	10[n]	10[n]	4
2,4-D	AH	AH	AH	AH	NR	NR	AH	AH	AH	AH	AH	AH	AH	$\frac{1}{4}$-1[i]	NY	AH	AH
Dual products	4	4.5	NR	9	NR	NR	12	4.5	12	12	NR	12	4.5	NR[e]	NR	NY	6	4.5
Eradicane	AH	AH	AH	AH	NR	NR	AH	AH	AH	AH	AH	AH	NY	AH	NY	AH	AH
Evik	NY	AH	NY	NY	NY	NY	NY	AH	NY	NY	NY	NY	AH	NY	NY	NY	NY	AH
Exceed	18	3	10	18	1[i]	3	18	3	10	18	10	18	3	10	18[k]	10	18	3
Extrazine II	18	15	18	18	NR	NY	18	15	18	18	18	18	15	NR[f]	NY	18	18	15
Field Master	SY	NY	SY	SY	NR	NY	SY	SY	SY	SY	SY	SY	NY	NR[e]	NY	SY	SY	NY
Frontier	NY	4	NY	NY	NY	NY	NY	4	NY	NY	NY	NY	4	NR[e]	NR	NY	NY	4
Gramoxone	NR	NR	NR	NR	NR	NR	NR	NR	NR	NR	NR	NR	NR	NR	NR	NR	NR	NR
Guardsman/Leadoff	SY	NY	SY	SY	NR	NY	SY	SY	SY	SY	SY	SY	NY	NR[e]	NY	SY	SY	NY
Harness	SY	SY	SY	SY	NR	SY	SY	SY	SY	SY	SY	SY	SY	NY	NY	SY	SY	AH
Harness Xtra	SY	SY	SY	SY	NR	SY	SY	SY	SY	SY	SY	SY	SY	NR	NY	SY	SY	NY
Hornet	10.5	4	26[g]	26[g]	NR	18	26[g]	4	18	26[g]	18	26[g]	4	12	10.5	18	26[g]	4
Laddok S-12	SY	NY	SY	SY	NR	SY	SY	SY	SY	SY	SY	SY	NY	NR	SY	SY	SY	NY
Liberty	4	2.5	4	4	NR	4	4	2.5	4	4	4	4	2.5	2.5	NR	4	4	2.5
Lightning	9.5	9.5	9.5	40[g]	8.5[i]	18	40[g]	18	9.5	40[g]	26	40[g]	4	18	9	9.5	40[g]	4
Lorox	4	4	4	4	NR	4	4	4	4	NR	4	4	4	NR	4	4	4
Marksman	SY	10	SY	SY	NR	NR	SY	SY	SY	SY	SY	SY	10	NR	NY	SY	SY	10
Micro-Tech/Partner	AH	AH	NY	AH	NR	NR	NY	AH	NY	NY	NY	NY	AH	NR[e]	NR	NY	NY	AH
Permit	9	2	9	9	1[i]	3	9	2	9	10	9	9	2	2	9	SY	8	2
Poast/Poast Plus	NR	AH	NR	NR	AH	NR	NR	AH	NR	NR	NR	NR	AH	AH	NR	NR	NR	AH
Princep	SY	NY	SY	SY	NR	NY	SY	SY	SY	SY	SY	SY	NY	NY	NY[h]	SY	SY	NY
Prowl/Pentagon	NY	4	NY	NY	NR[o]	NY	NY	NY	NY	NY	NY	NY	4	NY	NR	NR	NY	4
Pursuit	4	9.5	4	40[g]	8.5[i]	18	40[g]	18	4	40[g]	26	40[g]	4	18	9.5	40[g]	4
Python	4	4	26[g]	26[g]	NR	18	26[g]	4	4	26[g]	12	26[g]	4	12	NR	9	26[g]	4
Resource	NR	NR	NR	NR	NR	NR	NR	NR	NR	NR	NR	NR	NR	NR	NR	NR	NR	NR
Roundup Ultra	NR	NR	NR	NR	NR	NR	NR	NR	NR	NR	NR	NR	NR	NR	NR	NR	NR	NR
Scorpion III	10.5	4	26[g]	26[g]	NR	10.5	26[g]	4	18	26[g]	18	26[g]	4	12	10.5	18	26[g]	4
Sencor	4	4	12	12	4	12	12	12	8	12	4	12	12	NR	12	4	4

Corn Herbicide Rotational Restrictions, cont.

Rotational crops following corn (months after application)[a]

Herbicide	Alfalfa	Barley, winter	Bean, snap	Clover	Corn, field	Corn, sweet	Cucumber	Oats, spring	Peas	Pepper	Potato, white	Pumpkin	Rye, winter	Sorghum, grain	Soybean	Tobacco	Tomato	Wheat, winter
Shotgun	SY	NY	SY	SY	NR	NY	SY	SY	SY	SY	SY	SY	NY	NR	NY	SY	SY	NY
Spirit	18	3	10	18	1[i]	8	18	3	10	18	10	18	3	10	10	10	10	3
Surpass/TopNotch/FulTime	SY	SY	SY	SY	NR	SY	SY	SY	SY	SY	SY	SY	NY	NY	NY	SY	SY	4
Surpass 100	SY	SY	SY	SY	NR	SY	SY	SY	SY	SY	SY	SY	NY	NY	NY	SY	SY	15
Sutan+	AH	AH	AH	AH	NR	NR	AH	AH	AH	AH	AH	AH	AH	NY	AH	NY	AH	AH
Tough	AH	AH	AH	AH	NR	NR	AH	AH	AH	AH	AH	AH	AH	NY	NY	NY	AH	AH

[a] AH = after harvest; NY = next year; SY = second year following application; NR = no restrictions.
[b] 18 months with a soil pH $\geq$ 6.5. • [c] 30 days per pint. • [d] 20 days per pint. • [e] Use safener with seed.
[f] Allow 30 days before replanting sorghum. • [g] Plus successful field bioassay.
[h] If no more than 2 lb. ai applied the previous year. • [i] NR for IMI (IR/IT) corn hybrids.
[j] See current 2,4-D label. • [k] 10 months if STS soybeans are planted. • [l] 8 months if 0.38 oz./A Beacon is applied.
[m] Red clover is 12 months, other clovers are 10 months if soil pH $\leq$ 6.5 and 18 months if > 6.5.
[n] 18 months with a soil pH > 6.5. • [o] Plant below herbicide zone. • [p] 8 months for NorthStar.

Source: Penn State Field Crop Weed Control Guide 1999

Grass Weed Sizes For Postemergence Corn Herbicides

Herbicide (rate/A)	Barnyardgrass	Broadleaf signalgrass	Crabgrass	Fall panicum	Field sandbur	Foxtail spp.	Johnsongrass (seedling)	Johnsongrass (rhizome)	Quackgrass	Shattercane	Wirestem muhly	Yellow nutsedge
Accent (0.66 oz)	2-4	2	—	2-4	3	2-4	4-12	8-18	4-10	4-12	8-12*	—
Basis (0.33 oz)	1 2	—	—	1-2	—	1-2	—	—	—	—	—	—
Basis Gold (14 oz)	$\leq$3	2	$\leq$1	$\leq$3	2	$\leq$3[7]	$\leq$8	—	$\leq$4*	$\leq$6	—	$\leq$2*
Beacon (0.76 oz)	—	—	—	<2	4*	1-2	4-12	8-16*	4-8	4-12	—	1-4*
Celebrity (6.67 oz)	2-4	—	—	2-4		2-4	4-12	8-18	4-10	4-12	8-12	—
Liberty[9] (20 fl oz)	$\leq$2*	—	$\leq$2	$\leq$4		$\leq$6[8]	$\leq$4	—	—	$\leq$4	—	—
Liberty[9] (28 fl oz)	$\leq$4	4	$\leq$4	$\leq$4	3	$\leq$10[7]	$\leq$6	—	$\leq$6	$\leq$6	—	—
Lightning (1.28 oz)	1-3	8	1-3	1-3	$\leq$1	1-6[7]	1-8	1-8*	1-3*	1-8	—	1-3*
NorthStar (5 oz)	—	—	—	1-3		1-3*	4-12*	8-16*	4-8*	4-12	—	1-4*
Permit (1.0 oz)	—	—	—	—		—	—	—	—	—	—	4-12
Poast Plus[1] (18 fl oz)[2]	$\leq$4	—	—	$\leq$4		$\leq$4[8]	—	—	—	—	—	—
Poast Plus[1] (24 fl oz)[3]	$\leq$8	8	$\leq$6	$\leq$8	3[11]	$\leq$8	$\leq$8	—	20-25[5]	—	$\leq$18	—
Poast Plus[1] (36 fl oz)[4]	$\leq$12	—	$\leq$8	$\leq$12		$\leq$16	$\leq$16	—	8[5]	—	6[5]	—
Pursuit[6] (1.44 oz)	1-3	—	1-3	—		1-6[7]	1-8	6-12	—	1-8	—	1-3*
Roundup Ultra[10] (32 fl oz)	4-6	—	4-6	4-6		4-6	4-6	4-6	4-6	4-6	4-6	4-6

height range (inches) at application

* Suppression only; additional control measures may be necessary.
[1] For use on SR/Poast Protected corn varieties only. • [2] Special early rate; see label for more details. • [3] Standard rate.
[4] Rescue application rate (or higher rate necessary for quackgrass or wirestem muhly control). Refer to herbicide label for more information.
[5] Sequential application may be necessary. • [6] For use on IMI corn varieties only.
[7] Maximum height at application for yellow foxtail: Basis Gold - 2"; Liberty - 4"; Lightning - 3"; Pursuit - 3".
[8] Yellow foxtail suppression only. • [9] For use on Liberty Link/GR corn hybrids only.
[10] For use on Roundup Ready corn hybrids only. • [11] Requires 30 fl oz.

Sources: Penn State Field Crop Weed Control Guide 1999; Illinois Agronomy Handbook, 1999-2000.

NOTICE The information on these pages is for preliminary planning — not a guide for use. Be sure to follow the manufacturer's directions, notwithstanding information contained here.

Weed Sizes For Postemergence Corn Herbicides

Herbicide (rate/A)	Annual morningglory	Burcucumber	Cocklebur	Common ragweed	Eastern black nightshade	Giant ragweed	Jimsonweed	Lambsquarters	Pigweed	Smartweed	Velvetleaf
				height range (inches) at application							
Accent (0.67 oz)	2	3	—	—	—	—	3	—	4	4	—
Aim (0.33 oz)	2-3 lvs	—	—	—	4	—	—	4	4	—	36
Atrazine[1] (2 qt)	4	4	4	4	4	4	4	6	6	4	2
Banvel/Clarity[1]	4	4	4	4	4	4	4	4	4	6	2
Basagran (2 pt)	—	—	10	3	—	6	10	2*	—	10	5
Basis (0.33 oz)	—	—	—	—	—	—	—	3	3	3	3
Basis Gold (14 oz)	3	—	3	3	2	3	4	3	4	4	3
Beacon (0.38 oz)	—	—	4	6	4	6	4	—	3	2	—
Beacon (0.76 oz)	<1.5*	4	4	9	4	9	4	<1.5*	4	4	4
Beacon + 2,4-D or Banvel	—	3	4	6	4	6	4	3	5	4	4
Buctril (1.5-2 pt)	4	4	10	6	6	6	6	8	2	6	5
Buctril + atrazine (2 pt)	4	4	10	6	6	8	6	10	2-4	6	5
Celebrity (6.67 oz)	3	3	3	3	3	3	3	3	3	3	3
2,4-D[1]	6	—	6	6	2	6	3	4	4	—	2
Exceed (1.0 oz)	4*	8	12	12	4	10	6	4	5	6	8
Exceed + Banvel	6	8	14	12	4	10	6	8	8	8	8
Hornet (2.4 oz)	<2*	—	6	6	<2*	6	6	<2*	<2*	6	6
Laddok S-12 (1.67 pt)	4	—	8	4	1	4	6	5	6	10	5
Liberty[4] (20 fl oz)	4	—	8	6	4	4	4	4	2	8	3
Liberty[4] (28 fl oz)	6	—	12	12	6	8	8	6	4	12	5
Lightning[2] (1.28 oz)	3	—	8	3*	3	3	3	3	8	3	3
Marksman[1]	6	4	6	6	6	6	6	6	6	8	6
NorthStar (5 oz)	3*	4	6	9	6	9	6	4	5	4	4
Permit (0.67 oz)	—	3*	9	9	—	3	—	2*	3	2	9
Permit (1-1.33 oz)	3*	12*	14	12	—	6	—	2*	6	2	12
Pursuit[2] (1.44 oz)	2*	—	8	3*	3	3*	3	2*	8	3	3
Resource[3] (6 oz)	—	—	—	3 lvs	—	—	—	3 lvs	3 lvs	—	6 lvs
Roundup Ultra[5] (32 fl oz)	6	6	6	6	6	6	6	6	6	6	6
Scorpion III (0.25 lb)	6	—	6	6	6	6	6	6	6	6	6
Spirit (1 oz)	4*	6	8	9	5	9	6	3	8	6	6
Tough[3]	—	4 lvs	4 lvs	—	4 lvs	—	4 lvs	4 lvs	4 lvs	—	—

* Suppression only, additional control measures may be necessary.
[1] No sizes given on label, sizes listed above are best estimates.
[2] For use on IMI corn hybrids only.
[3] Resource and Tough labels refer to weed size by number of leaves (lvs).
[4] For use on glufosinate-resistant corn hybrids only.
[5] For use on Roundup Ready corn hybrids only.

Source: Penn State Field Crop Weed Control Guide 1999.

Grazing And Forage Intervals For Herbicide-Treated Corn

Herbicide	Grazing	Forage (silage, etc.)
Accent	30 days	30 days
Accent Gold	85 days	85 days
Aim	none	none
Atrazine	21 days	21 days
Axiom	none	none
Balance	none	none
Banvel/Clarity	Past "milk" stage	Past "milk" stage
Basagran	12 days	None
Basis/Basis Gold	30 days	30 days
Beacon	30 days	45 days
Bladex	None	None
Buctril	30 days	30 days
Celebrity	must reach ensilage stage	must reach ensilage stage
Contour	45 days	45 days
2,4-D	7 days	7 days
Eradicane	None	None
Evik	30 days	30 days
Exceed	30 days	40 days
Extrazine II	None	None
Field Master	8 weeks	8 weeks
Frontier	60 days	60 days
Gramoxone Extra (at planting/post directed)	None/Do not graze	None/Do not feed
Guardsman	40 days	40 days
Harness/Harness Xtra	21 days	21 days
Hornet	85 days	85 days
Laddok S-12	21 days	21 days
Lariat/Bullet	21 days	21 days
Lasso/Micro-Tech/Partner	None	None
Liberty	70 days	60 days
Liberty ATZ	30 days	40 days
Lightning	45 days	45 days
Marksman	Past "milk" stage	Past "milk" stage
NorthStar	30 days	45 days
OpTill	40 days	40 days
Permit	30 days	30 days
Poast/Poast Plus	60 days	45 days
Princep	Do not graze	None
Prowl/Pentagon	None	None
Pursuit	45 days	45 days
Python	85 days	85 days
Resolve	45 days	45 days
Resource	28 days	28 days
Roundup Ultra	50 days[1]	50 days[1]
Scorpion III	85 days	85 days
Sencor	60 days	60 days
Shotgun	Do not graze	Do not graze
Spirit	30 days	40 days
Stinger	40 days	40 days
Surpass/TopNotch	21 days	21 days
Surpass 100/FulTime	21 days	21 days
Touchdown	90 days	90 days

[1]If sequential applications are used, do not graze or feed harvested corn forage or silage.
Source: Penn State Field Crop Weed Control Guide 1999; Weed Control Guide for Ohio Field Crops, 1999 edition.

NOTICE The information on these pages is for preliminary planning — not a guide for use. Be sure to follow the manufacturer's directions, notwithstanding information contained here.

Characteristics Of Preemergence Herbicides

Herbicide	Family	Mode of Action	Site of Action	Injury Symptoms	Weeds Controlled	Residual[1]	Common Causes of Failure/Injury
Aim (carfentrazone-ethyl)	Triazolinone	Cell membrane disruptor (contact)	PPO	Foliar burning	Annual broadleaves	N	Use without a surfactant, poor spray coverage
Atrazine	Triazine	Photosynthesis inhibitor	D-1 quinone Protein	Interveinal yellowing and necrosis of older leaves	Annual broadleaves and certain grasses	L	Triazine-resistant weeds; pH below 6.0; tolerant species such as fall panicum; lack of rain to activate
Axiom (flufenacet + metribuzin)	Oxyacetamide + triazine	Seedling growth inhibitor + photosynthesis inhibitor	Multiple + D-1 quinone protein	Looping of grass leaves at emergence; interveinal yellowing and necrosis of older leaves	Annual grasses and broadleaves	M	Lack of rain to activate emerged weeds at time of application; triazine-resistant weeds; crop injury due to adverse environment
Bladex (cyanazine)	Triazine	Photosynthesis inhibitor	D-1 quinone Protein	Interveinal yellowing and necrosis of older leaves	Annual grasses and certain broadleaves	M	Triazine-resistant weeds; pH below 6.0; lack of rain; tolerant species such as pigweed; crop injury due to not matching rate to soil type
Eradicane (EPTC)	Thiocarbamate	Seedling growth inhibitor (shoot)	Multiple	Looping and knotting of grass leaves at emergence	Annual grasses, shattercane, seedling johnsongrass, nutsedge	M	Poor or delayed incorporation; cool, wet soils; johnsongrass rhizomes not broken up by tillage
Frontier (dimethenamid)	Chloroacetamide	Seedling growth inhibitor (shoot)	Multiple	Looping of grass leaves at emergence	Annual grasses and certain broadleaves	M	Lack of rain to activate surface applications; emerged weeds at time of application, tolerant species
Harness or Surpass/TopNotch (acetochlor)	Chloroacetamide	Seedling growth inhibitor (shoot)	Multiple	Looping of grass leaves at emergence	Annual grasses and certain broadleaves	M	Lack of rain to activate surface applications; emerged weeds at time of application, tolerant species
Lorox (linuron)	Urea	Photosynthesis inhibitor	D-1 quinone protein	Interveinal yellowing and necrosis of older leaves	Annual broadleaves and certain grasses	M	Lack of rain to activate, too much rainfall causes leaching; tolerant species
Micro-Tech (alachlor)	Chloroacetamide	Seedling growth inhibitor (shoot)	Multiple	Looping of grass leaves at emergence	Annual grasses and certain broadleaves	M	Lack of rain to activate surface applications; emerged weeds at time of application; tolerant species
Princep (simazine)	Triazine	Photosynthesis inhibitor	D-1 quinone protein	Interveinal yellowing and necrosis of older leaves	Annual grasses and certain broadleaves	L	Lack of rain to activate; triazine-resistant weeds; pH below 6.0
Prowl (pendimethalin)	Dinitroaniline	Seedling growth inhibitor (root)	Protein Tubulin protein	Stunted shoot growth; P deficiency symptoms; swollen roots	Annual grasses and certain broadleaves	M-L	Poor seed burial resulting in crop injury; lack of rain to activate
Python (flumetsulam)	Sulfonamide	Amino acid biosynthesis inhibitor (protein)	ALS synthase	Prevents true leaf emergence, stunted frowth, chlorosis, or purpling	Annual broadleaves	M-L	Lack of rainfall to activate; pH <5.9 with high organic matter, in-furrow insecticide application, high soil pH (>7.8), and/or sandy-gravelly soils leading to crop injury, tolerant species
Sutan+ (butylate)	Thiocarbamate	Seedling growth inhibitor (shoot)	Multiple	Looping and knotting of grass leaves at emergence	Annual grasses, nutsedge	M	Poor or delayed incorporation

[1]Residual: N = no soil activity; M = one or two months; L = full season, may carry over under certain conditions or if misapplied. Residual activity is dependent upon rate, soil type, and environmental conditions.

Source: Penn State Field Crop Weed Control Guide 1999.

Characteristics Of "Burndown" And Postemergence Corn Herbicides

Herbicide	Family	Mode of Action	Site of Action	Systemic[1]	Injury Symptoms	Weeds Controlled	Residual[2]	Common Causes of Failure/Injury
Accent (nicosulfuron)	Sulfonylurea	Amino acid biosynthesis inhibitor (protein)	ALS synthase	Yes	Quickly stops weed growth, gradually turn yellow and die	Foxtails, shattercane, seedling and rhizome johnsongrass	S-M	Incorrect adjuvant, drought-stressed weeds, tolerant weeds
Atrazine	Triazine	Photosynthesis inhibitor	D-1 quinone protein	No	Foliar burning	Annual broadleaves	M-L	Weeds too large; resistant species
Banvel (dicamba)	Benzoic acid	Growth regulator	Multiple	Yes	Twisting of foliage, leaf cupping	Annual and perennial broadleaves	S-M	Perennials too small, drift onto nontarget plants
Basagran (bentazon)	Benzothiad-iazole	Photosynthesis inhibitor	D-1 quinone protein	No	Foliar burning	Annual broadleaves, yellow nutsedge	N	Weeds too large; tolerant species; droughty weather
Basis (rimsulfuron + thifensulfuron-methyl)	Sulfonylurea	Amino acid biosynthesis inhibitor (protein)	ALS synthase	Yes	Quickly stops weed growth, gradually turn yellow and die	Small annual grasses and broadleaves	S-M	Incorrect adjuvant, drought-stressed weeds plus tolerant weeds; tank-mix for lambsquarters control
Beacon (primisulfuron-methyl)	Sulfonylurea	Amino acid biosynthesis inhibitor (protein)	ALS synthase	Yes	Quickly stops weed growth, gradually turn yellow and die	Annual broadleaves, shattercane, seedling and rhizome johnson-grass	S-M	Incorrect adjuvant, drought-stressed weeds, tolerant weeds
Bladex (cyanazine)	Triazine	Photosynthesis inhibitor	D-1 quinone protein	No	Foliar burning	Annual broadleaves, small grasses	M	Weeds too large; resistant species; crop injury due to cool, wet weather
Buctril (bromoxynil)	Nitrile	Photosynthesis inhibitor	D-1 quinone protein	No	Foliar burning	Annual broadleaves	N	Weeds too large; tolerant species; droughty weather
2,4-D	Phenoxy	Growth regulator	Multiple	Yes	Twisting of foliage, strapped leaves, brittle corn stalks, malformed brace roots	Annual broadleaves and perennials	S	Perennials too small, corn too large, resulting in injury
Exceed (prosulfuron + primisulfuron-methyl)	Sulfonylurea	Amino acid biosynthesis inhibitor (protein)	ALS synthase	Yes	Quickly stops weed growth, gradually turn yellow and die	Annual broadleaves	S-M	Incorrect adjuvant, drought-stressed weeds
Gramoxone Extra (paraquat)	Bipyridilium	Cell membrane disruptor (contact)	Photosystem I	No	Foliar burning	Annual broadleaves and grasses	N	Use without a surfactant, poor coverage
Liberty (glufosinate-ammonium)	Amino acid derivative	Amino acid biosynthesis inhibitor	GS enzyme	Somewhat	Foliar burning and yellowing	Annual broadleaves and some perennials	N	Poor coverage, large weeds, new weed flushes
Permit (halosulfuron-methyl)	Sulfonylurea	Amino acid biosynthesis inhibitor	ALS synthase	Yes	Quickly stops weed growth, gradually turn yellow and die	Annual broadleaves, yellow nutsedge	S-M	Incorrect adjuvant, drought-stressed weeds, tolerant weeds; tank-mix for lambsquarters control
Poast (sethoxydim)	Cyclohex-anedione	Fatty-acid biosynthesis inhibitor	Accase	Yes	Kills growing point, leaves turn purple	Annual and perennial grasses	N	Poor coverage; improper stage of growth; droughty weather; antagonize with tank-mixes
Resource (flumiclorac pentyl)	N-phenyl-phthalimide derivative	Cell membrane disruptor (contact)	PPO	No	Foliar burning	Annual broadleaves	N	Temporary crop injury, poor coverage, droughty weather, weeds too large, tolerant weeds
Roundup (glyphosate)	Amino acid derivative	Amino acid biosynthesis inhibitor (protein)	EPSP synthase	Yes	Quickly stops weed growth, gradually turn yellow and die	Annual and perennial grasses and broadleaves	N	Perennial weed too young, poor spray pattern, high spray volume or application with contact or photo-synthetic inhibitor herbicide
Sencor (metribuzin)	Triazine	Photosynthesis inhibitor	D-1 quinone protein	No	Foliar burning	Annual broadleaves	M	Weeds too large; resistant species
Stinger (clopyralid)	Pyridine	Growth Regulator	Multiple	Yes	Twisting of foliage, leaf cupping	Annual broad-leaves, thistles	S-M	Perennials too small, corn too large, resulting in injury
Touchdown (sulfosate)	Amino acid derivative	Amino acid biosynthesis inhibitor (protein)	EPSP synthase	Yes	Quickly stops weed growth, gradually turn yellow and die	Annual and perennial grasses and broadleaves	N	Perennial weed too young, poor spray pattern, high spray volume or application with contact or photo-synthetic inhibitor herbicide
Tough (pyridate)	Pyridazine	Photosynthesis inhibitor	D-1 quinone protein	No	Chlorosis, foliar burning, stunting	Annual broadleaves, yellow nutsedge	N	Tolerant species, weeds too large

[1]Movement of herbicide from foliage to roots. Important for perennial weed activity.

[2]Residual: N = no soil activity; S = one or two weeks soil activity; M = one or two months; L = full season, may carry over under certain conditions or if misapplied. Residual activity is dependent upon rate, soil type, and environmental conditions.

Source: Penn State Field Crop Weed Control Guide 1999.

NOTICE The information on these pages is for preliminary planning — not a guide for use. Be sure to follow the manufacturer's directions, notwithstanding information contained here.

Corn "Post" Herbicides: Adjuvant Use Plus Application And Use Restrictions

Herbicide	Adjuvant and nitrogen	Rain-free period (hr)	Reentry interval (hr)	PHI days	Apply over the top of corn	Use drop nozzles
Accent	COC or NIS[a] + NH$_4$	4	4	30	20"/V-6	20" to 36"/V-10
Accent Gold	COC + NH$_4$	6	48	85	12"/V-6	
Aim	NIS	1	12	??	8-leaf/V-8	
Atrazine	COC	1-2	12	21	12"	
Banvel	If droughty[b], NIS or NH$_4$	4	24	—	24"[c] to 36"	Reduces drift
Basagran	COC + NH$_4$	6[d]	12	12	Any size?	
Basis	NIS or COC + NH$_4$	4	4	30	6"/V-2	
Basis Gold	COC + NH$_4$	4	12	30	12"/V-6	
Beacon	COC or NIS[a] + NH$_4$	4	12	45	4" to 20"	Splits 20" to tassel
Buctril	COC[e] or NIS[e]	1	12	30	Pretassel	
Buctril + atrazine	COC[e] or NIS[e]	1	12	30	12"	
Celebrity	NIS[a] + UAN (no AMS)	4	12	—	20"/V-6	20" to 36"/V-10
Clarity	UAN + COC[b,f] or NIS[b]	4	12	—	8"; 5" with oil	
Contour[g]	COC or NIS + NH$_4$	1	12	45	12"	
2,4-D amine	None	6-8	48	7	8"	8" to tassel
2,4-D ester	None	1-2	12	7	8"	8" to tassel
Exceed	COC or NIS + NH$_4$	4	12	60/30	4" to 20"	20" to 30"
Hornet	NIS or COC + NH$_4$ if dry	6	48	85	20"/V-6	
Laddok S-12	COC + NH$_4$	6[d]	12	21	12"	
Liberty[h]	AMS only!	4	12	70/60	24"/V-7	24" to 36"
Liberty[h] ATZ	AMS only	4	12	70/60	12"	
Lightning[g]	COC or NIS + NH$_4$	1	12	45	18" ideally	
Marksman	COC[b] or NIS[b] or NH$_4$[b]	4	48	—	5-leaf or 8"	
NorthStar	COC[j] or NIS + NH$_4$	4	12	60/45	4" to 20"/V-6	20" to 36"
Permit	COC or NIS + UAN	4	12	30	Layby (36")	
Poast Plus[i]	COC; NH$_4$ optional	1	12	60/30	Pretassel	Layby sprays
Pursuit[g]	COC or NIS + NH$_4$	1	12	45	See PHI.	
Resolve[g]	NIS + NH$_4$	1	12	45	12"	
Resource	COC + NH$_4$	1	12	28	2- to 10-leaf	
Roundup Ultra[k]	AMS optional	1-2	4	7/50	30"/V-8	
Scorpion III	NIS + NH$_4$[b]	6	48	85	8"	8" to 24"
Sencor	NIS or NH$_4$	—	12	60	Pretassel	See tank-mix partner.
Shotgun	None	4	12	21	8"/4-leaf	8" to 12"
Spirit	COC or NIS + NH$_4$	4	12	60	4" to 20"/V-6	20" to 24"
Stinger	None	6-8	12	40	24"	
Tough	None	1-2	12	68	See PHI.	
Spot treatment only						
Roundup Ultra[l]	AMS optional	1-2	4	56/14	Pretassel	
Touchdown 5[l]	NIS, AMS optional	1-2	4	90/35	See PHI.	

COC = crop oil concentrate, NIS = nonionic surfactant, NH$_4$ = ammonium fertilizer adjuvant (UAN or AMS), UAN = urea-ammonium nitrate (28-0-0), AMS = ammonium sulfate (spray grade 21-0-0), PHI = preharvest interval for grain harvest, shorter for silage.

[a]Use NIS only when Accent or Beacon is mixed with anything except atrazine. • [b]Allowed if arid or droughty conditions exist at application.
[c]Up to 24 inches if nearby soybeans are over 10 inches or are blooming. • [d]Current label: "Rainfall soon after application may decrease the effectiveness."
[e]Adjuvants allowed if injury is acceptable. • [f]Use of oils (penetrants) may cause injury "if corn is > 5 inches tall."
[g]Use only with IMI-designated corn hybrids. • [h]Use only with Liberty Link or GR-designated corn hybrids (glufosinate-resistant).
[i]Use only with PP- or SR (sethoxydim-resistant)-corn hybrids. • [j]COC allowed only up to 12-inch-tall corn.
[k]Use only on Roundup Ready-designated corn hybrids. • [l]Use only as a spot treatment and not as an overall application in corn.

Source: Illinois Agronomy Handbook, 1999-2000.

Maximum Corn And Weed Sizes For Delayed Preemergence Herbicide Application

Herbicide	Maximum corn size	Maximum weed size
Atrazine	12 inches	1.5 inches
Atrazine + Bladex 90 DF or Extrazine II 90 DF	4-leaf	1.5 inches
Banvel or Marksman + Bladex 80W or 90DF	4-leaf	1.5 inch grass
Banvel or Marksman + Frontier	8 inches	1 inch grass
Banvel or Marksman + Lasso EC	3 inches	2-leaf grass
Bicep II MAGNUM, Bicep Lite II MAGNUM	5 inches	2-leaf
Bladex 80W or 90DF	4-leaf	1.5 inches
Bullet or Micro-Tech + atrazine	5 inches	2-leaf
Dual II MAGNUM + Banvel	5 inches	3 inch pigweed
Frontier	8 inches	before emergence or by tank-mix partner
Frontier + Accent[a]	8 inches	3 inches
Frontier + Beacon	8 inches	depends on weed (see Beacon label)
Guardsman, Leadoff	8 inches	1.5 inches
Harness or Harness Xtra[c]	11 inches or by tank-mix partner	before emergence or by tank-mix partner
Marksman + Prowl	2-leaf	1 inch grass
Princep	before emergence	before emergence
Prowl + Accent[b] or Prowl + Accent + Beacon[b]	6-leaf	see herbicide labels
Prowl + atrazine, Prowl + Bladex 90DF, or Prowl + Banvel	4-leaf	1 inch
Prowl + Beacon[b]	6-leaf	depends on weed (see Beacon label)
Prowl + Poast Plus[d]	6-leaf	depends on grass (see Poast Plus label)
Python	2 inches (spike)	before weed emergence
Surpass, Surpass 100, FulTime, or TopNotch[e]	11 inches or by tank-mix partner	before emergence or by tank-mix partner

[a]May use a reduced rate of Frontier and Accent under certain conditions.
[b]Accent rate of $1/3$ to $2/3$ oz/A and Beacon rate of $3/8$ to $3/4$ oz/A. When tank-mixing all three herbicides, Accent rate is 0.33 oz/A and Beacon is 0.38 oz/A.
[c]May be tank-mixed with Accent, atrazine (Harness), Banvel or Clarity, Marksman, Permit, or Pursuit (IMI-corn), Roundup Ultra (Roundup Ready corn).
[d]For use in Poast compatible/SR corn only; Poast Plus rate of 12 to 24 oz/A.
[e]May be tank-mixed with a number of different products including Accent, Banvel or Clarity, Prowl, Pursuit (IMI-corn), etc. See a herbicide label for specific information.

Source: Penn State Field Crop Weed Control Guide 1999.

Grass and Nutsedge Herbicide Control Ratings

Herbicide	Barnyardgrass	Crabgrass	Fall panicum	Giant foxtail	Johnsongrass	Quackgrass	Sandbur	Shattercane	Wirestem muhly	Woolly cupgrass	Yellow foxtail	Yellow nutsedge
Soil-applied												
Atrazine	7	5	3	7	N	6	6	N	5	4	7	6
Axiom	9	9	9	9	N	N	6	5	N	7	9	6
Balance	8	7	8	8	N	N	6	5	N	8	7	N
DoublePlay	9	9	9	9	6	6	8	8	4	8	9	7
Dual II MAGNUM	9	9	9	9	N	N	6	5	N	7	9	8
Eradicane, Sutan+	9	9	9	9	7	6	8+	8	6	8	9	8
Frontier	9	9	9	9	N	N	6	5	N	7	9	7
Harness	9	9	9	9	N	N	7	5	N	8	9	8
Lasso/Micro-Tech	9	9	9	9	N	N	6	5	N	7	9	7
Princep	8	7	7	8	N	N	6	5	4	6	4	8	6
Prowl, Pentagon	8+	8+	8+	8+	N	N	8	7	N	8	9	N
Surpass, TopNotch	9	9	9	9	N	N	7	5	N	8	9	8
Postemergence												
Accent[a] or Celebrity[a]	8	5	8	8+	8+	8	8	9	7	8	8	6
Accent Gold[a]	8+	6	8	8	7	7	7	8	7	6	8	6
Atrazine + oil	7	5	4	7	N	6	6	N	4	6	7	7
Basis[a]	7	6	8	8	4	4	6	8	5	5	8	4
Basis Gold[a]	8+	6	8	8+	7	7	7	8	6	6	8	5
Beacon[a]	4	4	7	6	8	8	6	9	5	N	5	6
Liberty[d]	7	8	7	8+	6	5	7	8	7	8	7	5
Liberty ATZ[d]	7	8	6	9	5	6	7	7	6	8	7	7
Lightning[b]	8	7	8	8+	6	5	7	9	N	8	8	6
Poast Plus[c]	9	9	9	9	7	7	9	8+	7	9	9	N
Resolve[b]	7	7	6	8	5	N	4	8	N	6	6	5
Roundup Ultra[e]	9	9	9	9	9	8+	9	9	8+	8+	9	7

Control ratings: 9 = excellent, 8 = good, 7 = fair, 6 = poor, 5 or 4 = unsatisfactory, N = Nil or None.
[a]Use of IR (imadazilinone-resistant) corn hybrids minimizes insecticide interaction and injury.
[b]Use only with IMI-designated corn hybrids.
[c]Use only with PP- or SR-designated corn hybrids.
[d]Use only with Liberty Link or GR-designated (glufosinate-resistant) corn hybrids.
[e]Use only with Roundup Ready-designated corn hybrids.

Source: 1999 Illinois Agricultural Pest Management Handbook

Broadleaf Weed Control Ratings for Corn Herbicides

Herbicide	Annual morningglories	Burcumber	Cocklebur	Common ragweed	Eastern black nightshade	Giant ragweed	Jimsonweed	Kochia	Lambsquarters	Pigweeds	Prickly sida	Smartweeds	Velvetleaf	Wild sunflower
Soil-applied														
Atrazine[a,b]	8	6	8	9	9	8	9	9a	9a	9a	9	9	7	8
Balance	4	N	4	9	9	6	8	9	9	9	6	8	9	6
Hornet	7	N	8	8	8	8	8	8	8	8	7	8+	8	9
Marksman	8	6	8	9	8	7	8	8	8	9	7	9	7	8
Princep[a,b]	8	6	8	9	9	7	9	9a	9a	9a	9	9	7	8
Python[d]	5	N	7	7	8	5	7	8+	8+	9	7	8	8	8
Postemergence Contact or Triazine[f]														
Aim	7	—	8	6	9	4	6	—	8	8	—	5	9	—
Atrazine[a,b]	9	8	9	9	9	8	9	9a	9a	9a	8+	9	9	8
Buctril	8	7	9	8+	9	8	9	8	9	7	4	9	8	9
Buctril + atrazine	9	8+	9	9	9	9	9	8	9	9	9	9	8+	9
Laddok S-12	8	6	9	9	8	8+	9	8	8+	8	8	9	9	9
Liberty[f]	8	7	9	8+	8+	8	9	8+	8	8	7	8+	8	9
Liberty ATZ	9	7	9	9	9	8+	9	8+	9	9	8	9	8	9
Resource	5	7	7	7	4	6	7	4	7	7	7	7	5	4
Tough	4	5	8	6	9	7	8	9	9	9	5	5	6	7
Plant-growth regulator (PGR)[f]														
Banvel/Clarity	9	7	9	9	8	9	9	8+	9	9	8	9	8	8+
2,4-D	9	N	9	9	7	8+	7	7	9	9	8	6	8	8
Marksman	9	8	9	9	9	9	9	8+	9	9	9	9	8	9
Stinger	N	N	9	9	7	9	8	N	N	N	N	7	N	8+
Acetolactate synthetase (ALS)[g]														
Accent[b,c,i]	7	7	5	4	N	N	8	6	5	8	N	7	5	4
Basis[b,c,i]	4	N	6	5	N	N	4	6	8	8	N	9	8	7
Basis Gold[b,i]	7	7	8	8	7	7	8	6	8	9	7	9	7	8
Beacon[b,c,i]	6	8+	8	9	8	9	8	8	6	8	7	8	7	8+
Exceed[b,c,i]	7	8+	9	9	8	9	8+	8	8	9	8	9	9	9
Lightning[b,c,h]	7	6	9	7	9	7	8	8+	8	9	8	8+	8+	9
Permit[c]	6	5	9	4	8	7	7	4	7	7	7	7	8+	8+
Spirit[b,c,i]	6	8+	8+	9	8	9	8+	8	7	8+	7	8	8+	8+
ALS + PGR[j]														
Accent Gold[b,e]	6	5	8	8+	7	8	7	7	7	8	7	8	8	9
Celebrity[b,h]	8	8	8	8+	6	9	9	8	8	8	6	9	7	7
Hornet	7	5	8+	8+	7	8	7	8	7	8	7	8+	8	9
NorthStar	7	8	8	9	8+	8	8	8	8+	9	7	8	9	9
Resolve SG[b,h]	8	6	8	9	8	9	8+	8	8	9	8	9	8	8
Roundup Ultra[k]	6	7	9	8+	8	8+	9	8	8	9	7	8	8	8+
Scorpion III	8+	6	9	8+	8	8	8	8	8+	9	8	9	8	9

Control ratings: 9 = excellent, 8 = good, 7 = fair, 6 = poor, 5 or 4 = unsatisfactory, N = Nil or None.
[a]These herbicides do not control triazine-resistant biotypes of pigweed, waterhemp, lambsquarters, or kochia.
[b]May also control some grass species.
[c]ALS-resistant waterhemp (pigweed) or kochia is not controlled by these ALS herbicides.
[d]Adjuvant varies with herbicide. • [e]The response rating increases if an NIS or COC is added to the spray mix.
[f]Requires use of Liberty Link corn hybrids. • [g]Use COC or NIS, but NIS only with some tank mixes.
[h]Requires use of IMI-designated corn hybrids.
[i]Use of IR-designated corn hybrids minimizes insecticide interaction and injury potential.
[j]Use an NIS and not COC. • [k]Use Roundup Ready corn hybrids.

Source: 1999 Illinois Agricultural Pest Management Handbook

> **NOTICE** The information on these pages is for preliminary planning — not a guide for use. Be sure to follow the manufacturer's directions, notwithstanding information contained here.

Weed Response To Selected Soil-Applied Field Corn Herbicides

Herbicide	Grasses						Broadleaf Weeds										
	Barnyardgrass	Crabgrass	Fall panicum	Foxtail	Sandbur	Shattercane/Sorghum	Black nightshade	Cocklebur	Kochia	Lambsquarters	Pigweed	Ragweed	Russian thistle	Smartweed	Sunflower	Velvetleaf	Waterhemp
AAtrex/atrazine	6	4	2	7	5	1	9	8	10	10	10	9	9	9	7	7	10
Bicep II MAGNUM	9	9	9	9	6	4	9	7	9	9	9	8	8	8	6	6	9
Bladex/Cy-Pro	7	7	6	8	5	4	8	7	8	9	4	9	9	9	6	6	3
Contour	3	3	9	9	9	8	3	8	5	3	9	9	9	9	8	3	2
DoublePlay	9	9	9	9	7	8	8	2	5	8	8	6	3	1	3	3	8
Eradicane	9	9	9	9	7	8	6	3	5	7	7	5	3	3	2	2	7
Eradicane + atrazine	9	9	9	9	7	8	9	6	9	9	9	7	7	8	7	7	9
Eradicane + Bladex	9	9	9	9	7	8	7	9	9	9	7	7	7	8	5	5	7
Extrazine II/Cy-Pro AT	6	7	2	8	5	4	9	7	8	9	8	9	9	9	7	7	7
Frontier (6.0)	9	9	9	9	4	3	7	2	2	7	7	5	3	2	2	2	7
Guardsman	9	9	9	9	6	4	9	7	9	9	9	8	8	8	6	6	9
Harness	9	9	9	9	6	4	7	2	2	8	8	5	3	2	2	2	8
Harness Xtra	9	9	9	9	6	4	9	7	9	9	9	8	8	8	6	6	9
Lariat/Bullet or Lasso + atrazine	9	9	9	9	6	4	9	7	9	9	9	8	8	8	6	6	9
Lasso/Micro-Tech	9	9	9	9	6	4	7	2	2	8	8	5	3	2	2	2	8
Lasso + Bladex	8	9	9	9	5	4	8	6	9	8	8	8	8	8	6	5	7
Lasso + (atrazine + Bladex) or Extrazine II	9	9	9	8	4	3	9	7	9	9	9	9	7	7	7	7	9
Prowl + atrazine	8	9	9	9	7	3	9	4	9	9	9	7	7	8	6	7	9
Prowl + Bladex	8	9	9	9	7	3	8	4	9	9	7	7	7	8	5	6	7
Surpass	9	9	9	9	6	4	7	2	2	8	8	5	3	2	2	2	8
Surpass 100	9	9	9	9	6	4	9	7	9	9	9	8	8	8	6	6	9
Sutan+	9	9	9	9	8	7	5	2	5	7	5	5	2	2	2	2	5
Sutan+ + atrazine	9	9	9	9	7	7	9	5	9	9	9	7	7	7	6	6	9
Sutan+ + (atrazine + Bladex) or Extrazine II	9	9	9	9	7	7	8	2	9	9	9	7	7	7	6	4	8
Sutan+ + Bladex	9	9	9	9	7	7	7	2	9	9	7	7	7	7	4	4	7
TopNotch	9	9	9	9	6	4	8	3	2	8	8	6	5	3	2	3	8

Response Ratings: Ratings are light to moderate weed populations, favorable conditions and weed growth stage as specified on the product label. High weed populations, adverse conditions, or large weeds will reduce control.
10 — (96-100%), 9 — (90-95%), 8 — (85-89%), 7 — (80-84%), 6 — (70-79%), 5 — (60-69%), 4-2 — less than 60%, 1 — 0%.

Source: Herbicide Use In Nebraska 1997 Guide

Weed Response To Selected Postemergence Field Corn Herbicides

Herbicide	Grasses						Broadleaf Weeds										
	Barnyardgrass	Crabgrass	Fall panicum	Foxtail	Sandbur	Shattercane/Sorghum	Black nightshade	Cocklebur	Kochia	Lambsquarters	Pigweed	Ragweed	Russian thistle	Smartweed	Sunflower	Velvetleaf	Waterhemp
AAtrex/atrazine or Bicep II MAGNUM	5	4	2	6	4	2	9	9	9	9	9	9	4	9	8	8	9
Accent	8	2	8	8	7	10	4	5	6	2	7	1	3	7	2	4	7
Accent + atrazine	8	2	8	8	7	10	9	9	9	9	9	9	4	9	9	8	9
Accent + Banvel	8	2	8	8	7	10	7	9	8	7	7	9	9	9	7	8	7
Accent + Beacon	4	3	7	7	7	10	8	9	8	4	8	9	7	8	9	8	8
Accent + Buctril	8	2	8	8	2	10	9	9	8	7	8	9	9	9	8	7	8
Banvel/Clarity	2	2	2	2	2	2	9	9	8	7	8	8	9	9	7	4	7
Basis	7	7	7	8	7	10	3	9	3	7	9	5	9	8	7	8	8
Basis Gold	8	7	8	8	7	10	9	9	9	9	9	9	4	9	8	8	9
Beacon	2	2	7	4	4	10	8	9	8	4	8	9	4	8	9	7	8
Bladex	4	7	4	7	4	4	9	7	9	9	6	9	4	9	7	7	6
Buctril	2	2	2	2	2	2	9	9	8	7	6	9	7	9	9	7	6
Buctril + atrazine	2	2	2	2	2	2	9	9	9	9	9	9	8	9	9	9	9
Buctril + Banvel	2	2	2	2	2	2	9	9	9	7	8	7	9	9	9	8	8
2,4-D	2	2	2	2	2	2	6	10	5	7	7	7	4	4	7	8	8
Exceed	2	2	3	3	2	9	8	9	8	7	9	9	4	9	8	8	8
Extrazine II	4	7	4	7	4	4	9	9	9	9	6	9	4	9	7	7	6
Laddok S-12	2	2	2	2	2	2	7	9	8	7	8	9	2	9	9	9	8
Liberty	8	8	8	8	8	9	9	8	8	9	9	8	8	8	8	7	9
Marksman	2	2	2	2	2	2	9	9	8	9	9	9	7	9	9	8	9
Peak	1	1	6	6	6	1	3	9	6	5	9	9	—	6	9	9	8
Permit	1	1	1	1	1	1	3	9	6	5	9	9	—	7	9	9	8
Poast[a]	9	9	9	9	9	10	1	1	1	1	1	1	—	1	1	1	1
Pursuit[a]	7	7	—	8	6	9	8	9	8	4	9	7	5	8	9	9	8
Resolve SG[a]	5	6	5	8	6	9	10	9	9	8	9	8	9	8	9	8	9
Resource	1	1	1	1	1	1	3	7	3	7	5	7	3	4	4	10	5
Scorpion III	2	2	2	2	2	1	9	10	8	7	9	8	—	9	9	8	9
Sencor + Banvel	2	2	2	2	2	2	8	9	8	7	8	8	9	9	8	7	8
Sencor + Basagran	2	2	2	2	2	2	7	9	8	7	7	9	2	9	9	9	6
Sencor + 2,4-D	2	2	2	2	2	2	7	10	8	7	7	8	2	7	8	8	7
Tough + atrazine	4	4	2	7	4	2	9	9	9	9	9	9	4	9	9	8	9

Response Ratings: Ratings are light to moderate weed populations, favorable conditions and weed growth stage as specified on the product label. High weed populations, adverse conditions, or large weeds will reduce control.
10 — (96-100%), 9 — (90-95%), 8 — (85-89%), 7 — (80-84%), 6 — (70-79%), 5 — (60-69%), 4-2 — less than 60%, 1 — 0%.

[a]For use in a resistant/tolerant field corn hybrid only.

Source: Herbicide Use In Nebraska 1997 Guide

Weed Response To Burndown Herbicides In No-Till Corn

Herbicide	Alfalfa	Annual bluegrass	Annual smartweed	Barnyardgrass	Chickweed	Dandelion	Downy brome	Evening primrose	Field sandbur	Foxtail	Foxtail barley	Hairy vetch	Henbit	Horseweed (Marestail)	Kochia	Lambsquarters	Pennycress	Prickly lettuce	Purslane speedwell	Russian thistle	Rye	Shepherdspurse	Sunflower	Velvetleaf	Virginia pepperweed	Winter wheat
Atrazine (2 qt)	4	9	10	6	10	4	7	9	6	7	9	6	10	8	10	10	10	9	10	9	6	10	10	10	9	6
Atrazine + Banvel (2 qt + 0.5 pt)	7	10	10	7	10	8	8	10	7	9	10	10	10	10	10	10	10	10	10	9	5	10	10	9	10	5
Atrazine + 2,4-D (2 qt + 1 pt)	5	10	10	7	10	6	8	10	7	8	10	10	10	10	10	10	10	10	10	9	5	10	10	10	10	7
Banvel** (0.5 pt)	9	1	8	1	10	8	1	7	2	1	1	10	9	7	9	7	9	9	4	9	1	7	10	7	7	1
Bladex (2 qt)	3	10	9	7	10	4	7	10	7	8	10	7	10	10	10	10	10	7	10	9	4	10	10	9	10	5
Bladex + 2,4-D (2 qt + 1 pt)	6	10	10	7	10	6	7	9	7	8	10	10	10	9	10	10	10	10	10	9	4	10	10	9	10	6
2,4-D Ester** (1 pt)	5	1	7	1	7	5	1	7	1	1	1	9	5	7	7	9	10	9	7	7	1	10	10	8	8	1
2,4-D Ester + Banvel (0.5 pt + 0.5 pt)	9	1	9	1	10	9	1	8	2	1	1	10	9	8	9	9	10	9	7	9	1	10	10	8	9	1
Extrazine II (4 qt)	3	9	10	7	10	5	7	9	7	8	9	8	10	9	10	10	10	10	10	9	6	10	10	9	9	7
Extrazine II + 2,4-D (4 qt + 1 pt)	5	10	10	8	10	7	8	10	8	8	9	10	10	10	10	10	10	10	10	9	6	10	10	9	10	6
Gramoxone Extra (1.5 pt)	4	9	6	6	10	5	7	7	9	6	7	8	9	7	9	7	10	8	6	6	6	9	10	8	9	6
Gramoxone Extra + atrazine (1.5 pt + 2 qt)	5	10	9	10	10	5	10	10	10	9	10	7	10	9	10	10	10	10	10	9	10	10	10	10	10	10
Gramoxone Extra + Bladex (1.5 pt + 2 qt)	3	10	8	10	10	5	10	10	10	10	8	8	10	9	10	10	10	10	9	10	9	10	10	10	10	10
Gramoxone Extra + Extrazine (1.5 pt + 4 qt)	4	10	10	9	10	6	10	10	10	10	10	7	10	9	10	10	10	10	9	10	9	10	10	10	10	10
Roundup/Touchdown*** (1.0 pt)	4	10	7	10	10	5	10	7	10	9	9	5	7	6	7	7	10	6	10	9	10	9	10	9	7	10
Roundup/Touchdown*** (1.5 pt)	5	10	8	10	10	7	10	8	10	10	9	6	9	8	8	9	10	7	10	9	10	10	9	8	9	10
Roundup/Touchdown + atrazine*** (1 pt + 1.5 pt)	4	10	10	10	10	6	10	10	10	9	8	6	10	10	10	10	10	10	10	10	10	10	10	10	10	10
Roundup/Touchdown + 2,4-D*** (1 pt + 1 pt)	6	10	9	10	10	8	10	9	10	9	9	7	9	9	9	9	10	9	10	9	10	10	10	10	9	10

Response Ratings: 10 — (96-100%), 9 — (90-95%), 8 — (85-90%), 7 — (80-84%), 6 — (70-79%), 5 — (60-69%), 4-2 — less than 60%, 1 — 0%.

* This guide presents burndown information only. It *does not* reflect residual weed control.
** Preplant interval: 2,4-D — 5 days for corn, 7 days for soybean, 10 days for sorghum, 7 days for 2,4-D + Banvel at 1 qt and 0.5 pt, 10 days for corn on sandy soil.
Banvel — 6 months for soybean, 14 days for sorghum. • Postplant interval: 2,4-D — 5 days for corn.
*** Use Touchdown at $^2/_3$ the rate listed for Roundup.

Source: Herbicide Use In Nebraska 1997 Guide

Field Corn, Popcorn

AAtrex — see atrazine

ACCENT

Sulfonylurea herbicide that can provide excellent control of shattercane, johnsongrass, and many annual grass weeds such as giant foxtail.

■ POST

Accent (WDG) (nicosulfuron) (DuPont)

Rate: 0.66 oz. WDG/A (1 packet/4A)

Time: Postemergence. Broadcast applications can be made to corn 20" or less in height (6 collars). Postdirected applications are required for field corn taller than 20" (more than 6 collars). Do not apply to corn taller than 36" or after 10 collar stage, whichever occurs first. Do not apply to popcorn or field corn grown for seed that is taller than 20" or after 6 collar stage, whichever occurs first.

Weeds: Broadleaf weeds:

annual smartweed	jimsonweed	smooth pigweed
burcucumber	pitted morningglory	tall morningglory
ivyleaf morningglory	redroot pigweed	

Annual grasses:

barnyardgrass	green foxtail	sorghum-almum
bristly foxtail	johnsongrass	Texas panicum
broadleaf signalgrass	longspine sandbur	wild proso millet
fall panicum	quackgrass	woolly cupgrass
field sandbur	shattercane	yellow foxtail
giant foxtail		

Remarks: Field, seed corn, popcorn. Always add crop oil concentrate or nonionic surfactant. For corn 20-36" tall, apply with drop nozzles only. Do not apply to popcorn or field corn grown for seed that has been previously treated with Counter insecticide. Do not apply to any white popcorn inbred or white popcorn hybrid (including White Dynamite) unless specifically approved by seed company. Accent may be used on fields previously treated with Counter 15G or 20CR (applied in-furrow, T- or surface-banded) if field has been planted with imidazolinone-resistant hybrid. Do not apply Basagran, 2,4-D, Laddok S-12, Tandem, or organophosphate insecticides to corn that has been treated 7 days before or 3 days after applying Accent. Do not apply by air in California. Do not graze or feed forage or grain from treated areas to livestock within 30 days after application. Refer to label for directions, precautions, and restrictions.

Crop Rotation: Field corn—anytime; rye, winter wheat—4 months; barley, spring wheat—8 months; alfalfa—12 months; cotton, dry beans, oats, popcorn, sorghum, soybeans, sweet corn, and all other rotational crops on soils with 6.5 pH or less—10 months (soils with 6.5 pH or greater—18 months).

Tank Mixes: Atrazine, Buctril + atrazine, Marksman herbicides; Asana or Lannate insecticides. Do not tank mix with Basagran, Bladex, 2,4-D, Laddok S-12, Tandem, or with foliar-applied organophosphate insecticides such as Lorsban, malathion, parathion.

– – – – – – – – – – – – – – – –

Signal Word/Toxicity Class: Caution/III.
REI: 4 hr.

ACCENT GOLD (Premix)

Sulfonylurea herbicide that can provide excellent control of shattercane, johnsongrass, and many annual grass weeds such as foxtail.

■ POST

Accent Gold (WDG) (clopyralid & flumetsulam & nicosulfuron & rimsulfuron) (DuPont)

Rate: 2.9 oz. WDG/A

Time: Postemergence. Apply to corn up to 12" tall. Do not apply to corn taller than 12" or after 10 collar stage, whichever occurs first.

Weeds: Broadleaf weeds:

annual smartweed	jimsonweed	smooth pigweed
burcucumber	pitted morningglory	tall morningglory
ivyleaf morningglory	redroot pigweed	velvetleaf

Annual grasses:

barnyardgrass	green foxtail	volunteer cereals
bristly foxtail	johnsongrass	wild proso millet
fall panicum	(seedling)	woolly cupgrass
field sandbur	quackgrass	yellow foxtail
giant foxtail	shattercane	

Remarks: Field corn. Not for use on field corn grown for seed, popcorn, or sweet corn. For corn 20-36" tall, apply with drop nozzles only. Do not apply to popcorn or field corn grown for seed that has been previously treated with Counter insecticide. Do not apply to any white popcorn inbred or white popcorn hybrid (including White Dynamite) unless specifically approved by seed company. Accent may be used on fields previously treated with Counter 15G or Counter 20CR (applied in-furrow, T- or surface-banded) if field has been planted with imidazolinone-resistant hybrid. Do not apply Basagran, 2,4-D, Laddok S-12, Tandem, or organophosphate insecticides to corn that has been treated 7 days before or 3 days after applying Accent. Do not apply by air in California. Do not graze or feed forage or grain from treated areas to livestock within 30 days after application. Refer to label for directions, precautions, and restrictions.

Days To Harvest: Harvest/grazing/feeding: 85.

Crop Rotation: Field corn—anytime; winter cereals—4 months; spring cereals—8 months; alfalfa, dry beans, soybeans, seed corn, popcorn—10 months (soils with pH greater than 6.5—18 months).

Tank Mixes: Atrazine, Banvel, Buctril + atrazine, Marksman herbicides and Asana or Lannate insecticides. Do not tank mix with Basagran, Bladex, 2,4-D, Laddok S-12, Tandem, or with foliar-applied organophosphate insecticides such as Lorsban, malathion, parathion.

– – – – – – – – – – – – – – – –

Signal Word/Toxicity Class: Danger/I.
REI: 48 hr.

ACETOCHLOR

Surpass EC contains safener dichlormid. TopNotch is micro-encapsulated formulation with safener dichlormid. Restricted Use Pesticide.

■ PP, PPI, PRE, POST

Surpass EC or 20-G (ZENECA)
TopNotch (M-E) (ZENECA)

Rate: 1.2-3 lb. ai/A
1.5-3.75 pt. EC/A
6-15 lb. 20-G/A
1.6-3 lb. ai/A
4-7.5 pt. M-E/A

Time: Early preplant, preplant incorporated, preemergence, early postemergence (up to 11" tall), or lay-by (except TopNotch).

Weeds: Broadleaf weeds:

black nightshade	Florida beggarweed	morningglory
carpetweed	Florida pusley	mustard
cocklebur	galinsoga	pigweed
common	giant ragweed	prickly sida
lambsquarters	groundcherry	sicklepod
common purslane	hairy nightshade	smartweed
common ragweed	jimsonweed	tall waterhemp
common waterhemp	kochia	velvetleaf

Grasses and sedges:

barnyardgrass	goosegrass	southern sandbur
bristly foxtail	green foxtail	southwestern
broadleaf signalgrass	johnsongrass	cupgrass
browntop panicum	(seedling)	Texas panicum
crabgrass	prairie cupgrass	wild proso millet
crowfootgrass	red rice	witchgrass
fall panicum	red sprangletop	woolly cupgrass
field sandbur	robust foxtail	yellow foxtail
foxtail millet	shattercane	yellow nutsedge
giant foxtail		

Remarks: Field corn, production seed corn, silage corn, popcorn. Conventional, reduced, no-till systems, broadcast or band. Do not apply through any type of irrigation system. Refer to label for use directions, restrictions, and precautions.

Crop Rotation: Corn, sorghum, soybeans, or tobacco may be planted the spring following application. Wheat may be planted 4 months after application. Do not rotate to crops other than corn, sorghum, soybeans, tobacco or wheat.

Tank Mixes: Surpass EC: Accent, atrazine, Banvel/Clarity, Basis, Basis Gold, Beacon, Bladex, Buctril, 2,4-D, Eradicane, Extrazine II, Gramoxone Extra, Liberty, Lightning, Lorox, Marksman, Poast, Poast Plus,

Princep, Prowl, Pursuit, Resource, Shotgun, Sutan+, Touchdown, Warrior. **Surpass 20-G:** Atrazine, Banvel, Basagran, Bladex, Buctril, 2,4-D, Doubleplay, Gramoxone Extra, Lorox, Princep, Prowl, Roundup, Surpass 100, TopNotch. **TopNotch:** Accent, atrazine, Banvel, Basis, Basis Gold, Beacon, Bladex, Buctril, Buctril+Atrazine, Clarity, 2,4-D, Exceed, Extrazine II, Gramoxone Extra, Liberty, Lightning, Lorox, Marksman, Peak, Permit, Poast, Poast Plus, Princep, Prowl, Pursuit, Resource, Scorpion III, Sencor, Shotgun, Touchdown, Warrior.

State Restrictions: Fall application in Illinois (north of Rt. 136), Iowa, Minnesota, Nebraska (north of Rt. 20), North Dakota, South Dakota, Wisconsin: Following soybean harvest, apply to soybean stubble after Oct. 15 but before ground freezes. Only corn may be planted the following spring.

– – – – – – – – – – – – – – – –

Signal Word/Toxicity Class: Warning/II (Surpass); Caution (TopNotch).
REI: 12 hr.

AIM

Contact herbicide with little or no residual activity. Rainfast within 1 hr. Very toxic to algae and moderately toxic to fish.

■ POST
◆ Aim (WDG) (carfentrazone-ethyl) *(FMC)*
Rate: 0.33 oz. WDG/A
Time: Apply in all tillage systems to actively growing weeds up to 4" high and rosettes less than 3" across. Do not apply past 8 leaf collar growth stage.
Weeds: Broadleaf weeds:

black nightshade	ivyleaf morningglory	redroot pigweed
common	pitted morningglory	velvetleaf
lambsquarters		

Remarks: Field, seed, silage corn, popcorn. The use of crop oil or crop oil plus either 28% nitrogen or ammonium sulfate with companion herbicides may be recommended under very dry conditions. Do not use with tank additives that alter the pH of the spray solution below pH 5 or above pH 8. Do not apply more than 1.24 oz. WDG/A per season. Refer to label for use directions, restrictions, and precautions.

Crop Rotation: Any crop including wheat—30 days following application; small grains (barley, oats, rye)—12 months after application.

Tank Mixes: Accent, atrazine, Banvel, Basis, Beacon, Clarity, 2,4-D, Exceed, glyphosate, Hornet, Liberty, Lightning, Marksman, NorthStar, Permit, Scorpion III, Shotgun, Spirit, Touchdown.

– – – – – – – – – – – – – – – –

Signal Word/Toxicity Class: Caution.
REI: 12 hr.

ALACHLOR

Preplant or preemergence herbicide, primarily for control of annual grass weeds. Helps control yellow nutsedge. Often combined with atrazine or Bladex for improved broadleaf weed control. Restricted Use Pesticide.

■ PPI, PRE, POST
Lasso (4EC) or Micro-Tech (MT) *(Monsanto)*
Partner (WDG) *(Monsanto)*
Rate: 2-4 lb. ai/A
2-4 qt. 4EC, MT/A
3-6 lb. WDG/A
Time: Early preplant (MT), preplant incorporated, preemergence, early postemergence.
Weeds: Broadleaf weeds:

black nightshade	Florida pusley	prickly sida*
carelessweed	galinsoga	purslane
carpetweed	hairy nightshade	sicklepod*
common ragweed*	lambsquarters*	smartweed*
cutleaf groundcherry	pigweed	teaweed*
Florida beggarweed*		

Grasses and sedges:

barnyardgrass	johnsongrass*	wild proso millet*
broadleaf signalgrass	(seedling)	wildcane*
crabgrass	panicum*	witchgrass
foxtail	sandbur*	woolly cupgrass*
goosegrass	shattercane*	yellow nutsedge

* Suppression

Remarks: Field, seed, silage corn. Can be applied by center pivot irrigation systems. Can be used in fluid fertilizer or impregnated on dry bulk fertilizer. Preplant incorporated for yellow nutsedge control. Refer to labels for specific rates, directions, and precautions.

Tank Mixes: Atrazine, Banvel (Illinois, Iowa, Minnesota, Wisconsin), Bladex, Gramoxone Extra, Roundup Ultra.

– – – – – – – – – – – – – – – –

Signal Word/Toxicity Class:
Danger/I (Lasso); Caution/IV (Micro-Tech, Partner).
REI: 12 hr.

■ PRE
Lasso II (15G) *(Monsanto)*
Rate: 2.4-3.9 lb. ai/A
16-26 lb. 15G/A
Time: Preemergence.
Weeds: Broadleaf weeds:

black nightshade	carpetweed	pigweed
carelessweed	Florida pusley	purslane

Grasses and sedges:

barnyardgrass	giant foxtail	witchgrass
brachiaria	goosegrass	yellow foxtail
crabgrass	green foxtail	yellow nutsedge
fall panicum		

Remarks: Field, seed, silage corn. Refer to label for use directions.

– – – – – – – – – – – – – – – –

Signal Word/Toxicity Class: Warning/II.
REI: 12 hr.

Atra-5 — see atrazine

ATRAZINE

Controls annual broadleaf weeds better than grasses. Incorporation will aid performance if rainfall is limited. Corn tolerance is good but carryover injury to some following crops can occur. Risk of carryover is greater after a cool, dry season and on soils with a pH over 7.3. Same chemical family as Bladex. Restricted Use Pesticide due to ground and surface water concerns.

■ PP, PPI, PRE, POST
AAtrex 4L or AAtrex Nine-0 (WDG) *(Novartis)*
◆ Clean Crop Atrazine 4L or 90 WDG *(Platte)*
Drexel Atrazine 4L, Atra-5 (5L), 90DF *(Drexel)*
Helena Atrazine 4L *(Helena)*
Riverside Atrazine 4L or 90DF *(Terra)*
Rate: Not highly erodible or with at least 30% residue cover (conservation tillage):
2 lb. ai/A
4 pt. 4L/A
3.2 pt. 5L/A
2.2 lb. WDG, 90DF/A
Highly erodible with less than 30% residue cover:
1.6 lb. ai/A
3.2 pt. 4L/A
2.4 pt. 5L/A
1.8 lb. WDG, 90DF/A
Time: Preplant surface-applied: Apply up to 45 days before planting (coarse-textured soils, no more than 2 weeks before planting). Preplant incorporated: Incorporate before, during, or after final seedbed preparation. For best results, apply within 2 weeks prior to planting. Preemergence: Apply during or shortly after planting but before weed emergence. Postemergence (with oil at 2 lb. ai rate): Apply before corn is 12" in height and weeds reach 1¹/₂" in height.
Weeds: Annual broadleaf weeds:

annual morningglory	lambsquarters	purslane
cocklebur	mustard	ragweed
groundcherry	nightshade	sicklepod
jimsonweed	pigweed	velvetleaf
kochia		(buttonweed)

Annual grasses:

barnyardgrass	green foxtail	witchgrass
(watergrass)	wild oat	yellow foxtail
giant foxtail		

Remarks: Field, seed, silage corn, popcorn. Rate varies by soil type and organic matter. Do not apply more than 2.5 lb. ai/A per year. Certain states may have established rate limitations; consult state lead pest control agency. Do not apply through any type of irrigation system. This product may not be mixed/loaded, or used within 50 ft. of wells including abandoned wells, drainage wells, and sink holes. Do not graze treated area or feed treated forage to livestock for 21 days following application.

Crop Rotation: Do not plant to any crop except corn or sorghum until the following year or injury may occur.

Tank Mixes: Alachlor, Dual, Gramoxone Extra, Lasso, Ramrod, Roundup Ultra, simazine, Sutan+. Refer to labels for directions and precautions.

State Restrictions: Preplant surface-applied: Medium- and fine-textured soils with minimum-tillage or no-till systems only in Colorado, Illinois, Indiana, Iowa, Kansas, Kentucky, Minnesota, Missouri, Montana, Nebraska, North Dakota, South Dakota, Wisconsin, Wyoming.

– – – – – – – – – – – – – – – –

IMI-field corn resistant to imidazolinone herbicides • LL-field corn resistant to Liberty herbicide • RR-field corn resistant to Roundup Ultra • SR-field corn resistant to sethoxydim
◆-new product • PP-preplant • PPI-preplant incorporated • PRE-preemergence • POST-postemergence • SEQ-sequential • ae-acid equivalent • ai-active ingredient • DF-dry flowable
E/EC-emulsifiable concentrate • F/FL-flowable • DG/G/WG-dispersable granule • L/LC-liquid • SP/WSP-soluble packet • W/WP-wettable powder • WSB-water soluble bag

102   **Weed Control Manual 2000**

Rate: 1.2 lb. ai/A
2.4 pt. 4L/A
1.9 pt. 5L/A
1.3 lb. WDG, 90DF/A

Time: Postemergence: Apply before corn reaches 12" in height, pigweed and lambsquarters reach 6" in height, and all other weeds reach 4" in height.

Weeds: Broadleaf weeds:

annual morningglory	mustard	smartweed
cocklebur	pigweed	velvetleaf
jimsonweed	ragweed	wild buckwheat
lambsquarters		

Remarks: Field, seed, silage corn, popcorn. Add emulsifiable oil or oil concentrate in water. Do not apply more than 2.5 lb. ai/A per year. Certain states may have established rate limitations; consult state lead pest control agency. Do not apply through any type of irrigation system. This product may not be mixed/loaded, or used within 50 ft. of all wells including abandoned wells, drainage wells, and sink holes. Do not graze treated area or feed treated forage to livestock for 21 days after application.

Crop Rotation: Do not plant to any crop except corn or sorghum until the following year or injury may occur.

- - - - - - - - - - - - - - -

Signal Word/Toxicity Class: Caution/III.
REI: 12 hr.

AXIOM (Premix)

Related to chloroacetamide herbicides.

Axiom (DF) (54.4% flufenacet & 13.6% metribuzin) *(Bayer)*

Rate: Conventional tillage:
13-23 oz. DF/A
Conservation, minimum- or no-till:
14-23 oz. DF/A

Time: Preplant (incorporated, surface), preemergence. For preplant surface, apply up to 45 days before planting; preplant incorporated, apply to upper 1-2" soil surface within 14 days of planting.

Weeds: Broadleaf weeds:

carpetweed	eastern black	Pennsylvania
common	nightshade*	smartweed*
lambsquarters	Florida beggarweed	pigweed
common purslane	Florida pusley	prickly sida*
common ragweed*	galinsoga	spotted spurge
common sunflower*	jimsonweed*	tall waterhemp
common waterhemp	mustard*	velvetleaf*

Grasses:

barnyardgrass	green foxtail	Texas panicum*
broadleaf signalgrass	Indian lovegrass	wild proso millet*
browntop panicum	johnsongrass	witchgrass
fall panicum	(seedling)	woolly cupgrass*
field sandbur*	large crabgrass	yellow foxtail
giant foxtail	shattercane*	yellow nutsedge*
goosegrass	smooth crabgrass	

* **Suppression**

Remarks: Field, silage corn. Not for use on seed corn, popcorn, sweet corn, or white corn. Rates vary by soil texture and organic matter. Do not make second application. Do not apply by air or through any type of irrigation system. Do not use treated crop for food, feed, or forage.

Crop Rotation: Corn, soybeans—anytime; potatoes—1 month; carrots—4 months.

Tank Mixes: Atrazine, Banvel, Bladex, Clarity, 2,4-D LVE, Eradicane, Extrazine II, glyphosate, Gramoxone Extra, Hornet, Marksman, metribuzin, Pentagon, Prowl, Roundup Ultra, Touchdown.

- - - - - - - - - - - - - - -

Signal Word/Toxicity Class: Caution/III.
REI: 12 hr.

BALANCE

Effective in controlling triazine or ALS resistant populations of weed species. May injure phytotoxic susceptible nontarget plants. Restricted Use Pesticide.

■ **PP, PRE**

Balance WDG (isoxaflutole) *(Rhone-Poulenc)*

Rate: Preplant:
1.25-3 oz. WDG/A
Preemergence:
1.25-2.5 oz. WDG/A

Time: Preplant (incorporated, surface), preemergence. May be applied up to 14 days before planting.

Weeds: Broadleaf weeds:

black nightshade	eastern black	prostrate pigweed
broadleaf plantain	nightshade	redroot pigweed
buffalobur	field pennycress	shepherdspurse
burcucumber	galinsoga	smooth pigweed
chamomile	giant ragweed	tall waterhemp
common chickweed	jimsonweed	toothed spurge
common	kochia	velvetleaf
lambsquarters	marestail	Venice mallow
common purslane	Palmer amaranth	wild mustard
common ragweed	Pennsylvania	wild radish
common waterhemp	smartweed	wild sunflower
dandelion		

Grasses:

barnyardgrass	goosegrass	robust purple foxtail
bristly foxtail	green foxtail	robust white foxtail
broadleaf signalgrass	johnsongrass	smooth crabgrass
fall panicum	(seedling)	wild proso millet
field sandbur	large crabgrass	woolly cupgrass
giant foxtail		

Remarks: Conventional, conservation tillage, no-till. Seed corn inbreds vary in their response; consult seed company for advice before using. Rate varies by soil texture and tillage. Do not apply more than 3 oz./A per season. Do not apply by air. Do not apply through any type of irrigation system. Do not forage grain or feed fodder to livestock.

Crop Rotation: Do not plant rotational crops until 6 months after application.

Tank Mixes: Alachlor, atrazine, Bicep, Dual, Extrazine, Frontier, Fultime, Guardsman, Harness, Prowl (preemergence), simazine, Surpass, TopNotch.

State Restriction: For use in Arkansas, Colorado, Illinois, Indiana, Iowa, Kansas, Kentucky, Missouri, Montana, Nebraska, North Dakota, Ohio, Oklahoma. South Dakota, Tennessee, Texas (counties north of or bisected by I-20), and Wyoming. In Colorado, Kansas, and Missouri, check with state regulatory authority for restrictions prior to use.

- - - - - - - - - - - - - - -

Signal Word/Toxicity Class: Caution/III.
REI: 12 hr.

Banvel — see dicamba

Barrage — see 2,4-D

BASAGRAN

Postemergence contact spray for control of many broadleaf weeds and yellow nutsedge. Rainfall within 24 hr. may reduce effectiveness.

■ **POST**

Basagran (bentazon) *(BASF)*

Rate: 0.75-1 lb. ai/A
1.5-2 pt./A

Time: Early postemergence.

Weeds: Broadleaf weeds:

annual morningglory	dayflower	spurred anoda
beggarticks	galinsoga	teaweed
bristly starbur	giant ragweed	tropic croton
Canada thistle	jimsonweed	velvetleaf
cocklebur	ladysthumb	Venice mallow
common	Pennsylvania	wild buckwheat
lambsquarters	smartweed	wild mustard
common ragweed	prickly sida	wild sunflower

Sedges:
yellow nutsedge (except CA)

Remarks: Field, seed, silage corn, popcorn. Rate depends on leaf stage and weed height. For improved control of velvetleaf, add urea ammonium nitrate solution to spray tank in place of oil concentrate. If common ragweed and lambsquarters are present in addition to velvetleaf, then oil concentrate should be used. Seed producers should consult seed company regarding tolerance of seed production inbred lines to Basagran. Do not apply more than 4 pt./A per season. Do not graze treated fields for at least 12 days after last treatment. Refer to label for specific directions.

Tank Mixes: Atrazine.

- - - - - - - - - - - - - - -

Signal Word/Toxicity Class: Caution/III.
REI: 12 hr.

NOTICE The information on these pages is for preliminary planning — not a guide for use. Be sure to follow the manufacturer's directions, notwithstanding information contained here. | For personal protective equipment and EPA registration numbers, please turn to page 70.

BASIS (Premix)

Dispersible granule formulation, premeasured in a water-soluble packet, that provides postemergence weed control.

■ POST

Basis (WDG) (50% rimsulfuron & 25% thifensulfuron-methyl) *(DuPont)*

Rate: 1.33 oz. WDG/4A (1 pack)

Time: Postemergence. Apply to field corn in the spike to 4-leaf (2-collar) stage when weeds are young and actively growing. Do not apply to corn taller than 4-leaf or 6" tall.

Weeds: Broadleaf weeds:

annual smartweed	redroot pigweed	wild mustard
common lambsquarters	velvetleaf	

Grasses:

barnyardgrass	fall panicum	green foxtail
bristly foxtail	giant foxtail	yellow foxtail

Remarks: Field corn. Do not apply to corn grown for seed, popcorn, or sweet corn. Do not apply to corn previously treated with Counter 15G. Application to corn previously treated with Counter 20CR or Thimet may cause unacceptable crop injury, especially on soils of less than 4% organic matter; application to corn previously treated with Dyfonate, Lorsban, or other organophosphate insecticides may result in temporary crop injury. Do not apply to corn that has been treated within 7 days before or 3 days after with foliar-applied organophosphate insecticides such as Lorsban, malathion, parathion, etc., or with herbicides Basagran, Laddok S-12, or 2,4-D. Do not graze or feed forage, grain, or stover from treated areas to livestock within 30 days after application. Do not apply through any type of irrigation system. Refer to label for use directions, precautions, and restrictions.

Crop Rotation: Field corn—anytime; soybeans—15 days; winter wheat, potatoes—4 months; spring cereals (wheat, oats, barley), dry beans, snap beans, peas—8 months; sweet corn, popcorn, alfalfa—10 months; sugar beets—12 months; other crops—18 months.

Tank Mixes: Dicamba.

- - - - - - - - - - - - - - -

Signal Word/Toxicity Class: Caution.
REI: 4 hr.

BASIS GOLD (Premix)

Premix with two different modes of action. Not for use on field corn grown for seed, popcorn, or sweet corn. Rainfast in 4 hr. Restricted use pesticide due to ground and surface water concerns.

■ POST

Basis Gold (WDG) (1.34% nicosulfuron & 1.34% rimsulfuron & 82.44% atrazine) *(DuPont)*

Rate: 14 oz. WDG/A (1 packet/4A)

Time: Postemergence. Apply to corn up to 12" tall. Do not apply to corn taller than 12" or exhibiting 6 collars.

Weeds: Broadleaf weeds:

Canada thistle*	giant ragweed	pokeweed*
common cocklebur	hemp dogbane*	smartweed
common milkweed*	jimsonweed	sunflower
common ragweed	lambsquarters**	velvetleaf
eastern black nightshade	morningglory pigweed	waterhemp**

Grasses:

barnyardgrass	johnsongrass	volunteer cereals
broadleaf signalgrass	(seedling)	wild oat
fall panicum	large crabgrass	wild proso millet
field sandbur	quackgrass	woolly cupgrass
foxtail	shattercane	yellow nutsedge*
Italian ryegrass	Texas panicum	

* Partial control; ** Except triazine resistant

Remarks: Field corn. Apply to hybrids with relative maturity rating of 88 days or more. Add crop oil concentrate and ammonium fertilizer. Before using Basis Gold, ensure compatibility with any other previously applied insecticide. Do not apply any of these materials within 3 days after applying Basis Gold or severe crop injury may result. Do not graze or feed forage, grain, or stover from treated areas to livestock within 30 days after application. Do not apply through any type of irrigation system. Refer to label for use directions, precautions, and restrictions.

Crop Rotation: Field corn—anytime; seed corn, sweet corn, popcorn, speciality corn, soybeans, fall-seeded cereals—10 months; other crops—18 months.

Tank Mixes: Banvel, Clarity, Tough.

- - - - - - - - - - - - - - -

Signal Word/Toxicity Class: Caution/III.
REI: 12 hr.

BEACON

Sulfonylurea herbicide that is more effective than Accent on some broadleaf weeds such as cocklebur and velvetleaf.

■ POST

Beacon (primisulfuron-methyl) *(Novartis)*

Rate: 0.76 oz./A (1 packet/2A)

Weeds: Broadleaf weeds:

alfalfa*	giant ragweed	prickly sida
black nightshade	hairy nightshade	puncturevine
burcucumber	horsenettle*	redroot pigweed
Canada thistle*	Jerusalem artichoke	Russian thistle*
cocklebur	jimsonweed	sesbania
common lambsquarters*	kochia	sicklepod
common ragweed	ladysthumb	smooth pigweed
devilsclaw	marestail*	sunflower
eastern black nightshade	morningglory*	velvetleaf
Florida beggarweed	Pennsylvania smartweed	wild mustard
		wild radish

Grasses and sedges:

annual ryegrass	quackgrass	sorghum-almum
fall panicum	sandbur*	volunteer sorghum
foxtail*	shattercane	yellow nutsedge*
johnsongrass*		

* Partial control

Rate: 0.38 oz./A (1 packet/4A)

Weeds: Broadleaf weeds:

cocklebur	giant ragweed	redroot pigweed
common ragweed	jimsonweed	smooth pigweed
eastern black nightshade	Pennsylvania smartweed	sunflower

Time: Postemergence. Apply over-the-top, directed, or semi-directed when corn is between 4-20".

Remarks: Field, grain, silage corn. May be applied to all field corn hybrids except the few that are classified as potentially susceptible to injury following Beacon application. Consult chemical dealer, seed supplier, or representative of Agricultural Division of Novartis for current listing of corn hybrids classified as potentially susceptible. Some weed species are known to be resistant to ALS-inhibiting herbicides. Where these ALS-resistant biotypes are known to exist, an appropriate registered herbicide with another mode of action should be used alone or in tank mixture with Beacon. Use drop nozzles for directed or semi-directed applications. Do not apply Counter at planting, or before, or within 7 days after applying Beacon. If other organophosphate insecticides such as AAstar, Dyfonate, Lorsban, or Thimet are applied at time of seeding, temporary corn injury may occur following Beacon application. Do not apply by air or through any type of irrigation system. Do not graze or feed forage from treated corn to livestock within 30 days after application, harvest grain within 60 days, or apply more than standard use rate/A. Refer to label for precautions and restrictions.

Crop Rotation: Field corn—14 days; winter wheat, winter barley, rye—3 months; alfalfa, sweet corn, popcorn, cotton, dry beans, peanuts, sorghum, soybeans, sunflowers, spring-seeded small grains—8 months; all other crops—18 months.

Tank Mixes: Accent, atrazine, Banvel/Clarity, Buctril, Buctril + atrazine, 2,4-D, Marksman, Resource. Do not tank mix with cyanazine.

- - - - - - - - - - - - - - -

Signal Word/Toxicity Class: Caution/III.
REI: 12 hr.

BICEP (Premixes)

Combination of AAtrex & Dual offers broad spectrum control of annual broadleaf and grass weeds with considerable flexibility in time and method of application, appropriate length of residual activity, reduced risk of carryover, and relatively good crop tolerance. Contains the safener benoxacor. Restricted Use Pesticide due to ground and surface water concerns.

■ PP, PPI, PRE, POST

Bicep II MAGNUM (3.1 lb./gal. atrazine & 2.4 lb./gal. S-metolachlor) *(Novartis)*
Bicep Lite II MAGNUM (2.67 lb./gal. atrazine & 3.33 lb./gal. S-metolachlor) *(Novartis)*

Rate: 2.9-3.6 lb. ai/A
     2.1-2.6 qt. II/A
     2.25-3.3 lb. ai/A
     1.5-2.2 qt. Lite II/A

Time: Early preplant. Apply up to 45 days before planting. Applications less than 30 days prior to planting may be split or single treatment; use split applications for treatments made 30-45 days before planting.

IMI-field corn resistant to imidazolinone herbicides • LL-field corn resistant to Liberty herbicide • RR-field corn resistant to Roundup Ultra • SR-field corn resistant to sethoxydim
◆-new product • PP-preplant • PPI-preplant incorporated • PRE-preemergence • POST-postemergence • SEQ-sequential • ae-acid equivalent • ai-active ingredient • DF-dry flowable
E/EC-emulsifiable concentrate • F/FL-flowable • DG/G/WG-dispersable granule • L/LC-liquid • SP/WSP-soluble packet • W/WP-wettable powder • WSB-water soluble bag

Rate: 3.6 lb. ai/A
2.6 qt. II/A
1.35-3.3 lb. ai/A
0.9-2.2 qt. Lite II/A
Time: Preplant incorporated, preplant surface, preemergence.
Rate: 1.35-2.85 lb. ai/A
0.9-1.9 qt. Lite II/A
Time: Postemergence-directed.
Weeds: Broadleaf weeds:

carpetweed	giant ragweed*	nightshade
chickweed	henbit	pigweed
cocklebur*	jimsonweed	sicklepod*
common purslane	lambsquarters	smartweed
common ragweed	morningglory*	velvetleaf*
Florida pusley	mustard	waterhemp
galinsoga		

Grasses and sedges:

barnyardgrass	green foxtail	southwestern
crabgrass	johnsongrass	cupgrass
crowfootgrass	(seedling)*	volunteer sorghum*
fall panicum	prairie cupgrass	witchgrass
foxtail millet	sandbur*	woolly cupgrass*
giant foxtail	shattercane*	yellow foxtail
goosegrass	signalgrass*	yellow nutsedge

* Suppression

Rate: 2.2-3.6 lb. ai/A
1.6-2.6 qt. II/A
1.65-2.85 lb. ai/A
1.1-1.9 qt. Lite II/A
Time: Postemergence-broadcast. Apply before grass and broadleaf weeds pass 2-leaf stage and before corn exceeds 5" in height.
Weeds: Broadleaf weeds:

cocklebur	kochia	prickly sida
common ragweed	lambsquarters	purslane
crabgrass	morningglory	smartweed
flixweed	mustard	velvetleaf
jimsonweed	pigweed	waterhemp

Grasses and sedges:

crabgrass	giant foxtail	yellow foxtail
crowfootgrass	green foxtail	yellow nutsedge
fall panicum		(suppression)

Remarks: Rate varies by soil type and organic matter. Certain states may have established rate limitations regarding atrazine; consult state lead pest control agency for additional information. Do not apply through any type of irrigation system. Refer to label for use directions, restrictions, and precautions.
Days To Harvest: Grazing/feeding—30.
Crop Rotation: Corn, cotton, peanuts, sorghum, or soybeans can be planted the spring following treatment. Injury may occur to soybeans planted the year following application on soils having a calcareous surface layer. If applied after June 10, do not rotate with crops other than corn or sorghum the next year. In eastern Dakotas, Kansas, western Minnesota and Nebraska, do not rotate to soybeans for 18 months following application if more than 2 lb. ai atrazine was applied. In High Plains and Intermountain Area of the West where rainfall is sparse and erratic or where irrigation is required, use only when corn or sorghum is to be planted the following year, or a crop of untreated corn or sorghum is to precede other rotational crops. Do not plant sugar beets, tobacco, vegetables, spring-seeded small grains, or small seeded legumes the year following application. All other crops may be planted 15 months after application.
State Restrictions: Do not use in Nassau County or Suffolk County, New York. Bicep—early preplant: Minimum-tillage or no-tillage systems with medium- and fine-textured soils in Colorado, Delaware, Illinois, Iowa, Indiana, Kansas, Kentucky, Maryland, Michigan, Minnesota, Missouri, Montana, Nebraska, North Dakota, New York, Ohio, Pennsylvania, South Dakota, Tennessee, Virginia, West Virginia, Wisconsin, Wyoming.

– – – – – – – – – – – – – – –

Signal Word/Toxicity Class: Caution/III.
REI: 24 hr.

Bladex — see cyanazine

Broclean — see bromoxynil

Bromox — see bromoxynil

Bromox + atrazine — see bromoxynil & atrazine

BROMOXYNIL

Controls some broadleaf weeds better than 2,4-D. Will not vaporize and cause drift problems associated with 2,4-D or Banvel. Toxic to wildlife and fish.

■ **PRE, POST**
◆ **Broclean 2EC** *(Platte)*
◆ **Bromox 2EC** *(Micro Flo)*
Buctril (2EC), Buctril 4EC *(Rhone-Poulenc)*
Moxy 2EC *(Terra)*
Rate: 0.25-0.5 lb. ai/A
1-2 pt. 2EC/A
0.5-1 pt. 4EC/A
Chemigation:
0.5 lb. ai/A
2 pt. 2EC/A
1 pt. 4EC/A
Time: Preemergence, postemergence. Preemergence: Apply before planting until just prior to crop emergence. Postemergence: Apply after emergence but prior to tassel emergence.
Weeds: Broadleaf weeds:

black nightshade	giant ragweed	spiny pigweed
buffalobur	hemp sesbania	sunflower
Canada thistle	ivyleaf morningglory	tall morningglory
(suppression)	jimsonweed	tall waterhemp
common cocklebur	ladysthumb	velvetleaf
common	Pennsylvania	Venice mallow
lambsquarters	smartweed	wild buckwheat
common ragweed	redroot pigweed	wild mustard
eastern black		
nightshade		

Remarks: Field corn, popcorn. Seed corn producers should consult respective seed corn companies regarding tolerance of certain seed production inbred lines. Do not apply to seed corn inbreds or popcorn prior to 3-leaf stage as excessive leaf burn may occur. Refer to label for restrictions and precautions.
Days To Harvest: Harvest/grazing/cutting for feed—30 (45 for Buctril).
Crop Rotation: Do not plant rotational crops until the following season (within 30 days of application for Buctril).
Tank Mixes: Accent, atrazine, Banvel, Beacon, Bladex (except popcorn), Clarity, 2,4-D, Extrazine (except popcorn), Pursuit (only field corn hybrids with resistance to Pursuit), Roundup, Stinger.

– – – – – – – – – – – – – – –

Signal Word/Toxicity Class: Warning/II.
REI: 12 hr.

BROMOXYNIL & ATRAZINE (Premixes)

Good early control of annual broadleaf weeds with reduced risk of carryover, and little risk of movement outside target area. Some residual control of germinating seedlings. A little leafburn may be noted on corn; this is of little significance and not likely to affect yield. Restricted Use Pesticide.

■ **POST**
◆ **Bromox + atrazine (1 lb./gal. bromoxynil & 2 lb./gal. atrazine)** *(Micro Flo)*
◆ **Brozine (1 lb./gal. bromoxynil & 2 lb./gal. atrazine)** *(Platte)*
Buctril + atrazine (1 lb./gal. bromoxynil & 2 lb./gal. atrazine) *(Rhone-Poulenc)*
Moxy + atrazine (1 lb./gal. bromoxynil & 2 lb./gal. atrazine) *(Terra)*
Rate: 0.56-1.125 lb. ai/A
1.5-3 pt./A
Time: Postemergence.
Weeds: Broadleaf weeds:

black nightshade	giant ragweed	purple morningglory
buffalobur	hemp sesbania	redroot pigweed
Canada thistle	ivyleaf morningglory	smooth pigweed
(suppression)	jimsonweed	spiny pigweed
common cocklebur	ladysthumb	sunflower
common	palmleafmorningglory	tall morningglory
lambsquarters	Pennsylvania	tall waterhemp
common ragweed	smartweed	velvetleaf
eastern black	pitted morningglory	Venice mallow
nightshade	prickly sida	wild buckwheat
entireleaf	puncturevine	wild mustard
morningglory		

Remarks: Field corn, popcorn. Seed corn producers should consult respective seed corn companies regarding tolerance of seed production inbred lines. Do not apply through any type of irrigation system. Refer to label for restrictions and precautions.
Days To Harvest: Harvest/feeding/grazing—30 (45 for Buctril + atrazine).

Crop Rotation: Do not rotate to any crop except field corn, popcorn, or grain sorghum until the following year.

Tank Mixes: Accent, Banvel, Clarity (except Bromox + atrazine), 2,4-D, Stinger.

- - - - - - - - - - - - - - -

Signal Word/Toxicity Class: Caution.
REI: 12 hr.

Brozine — see bromoxynil & atrazine

Buctril — see bromoxynil

Buctril + atrazine — see bromoxynil & atrazine

BULLET (Premix)

Combination microtech formulation with atrazine and same active ingredient as Lasso. Restricted Use Pesticide.

■ **PPI, PRE, POST**
Bullet (2.5 lb./gal. alachlor & 1.5 lb./gal. atrazine) *(Monsanto)*
Rate: 2.5-4.5 lb. ai/A
2.5-4.5 qt./A
Time: Preplant incorporated, preemergence, postemergence. Preplant incorporated: Apply within 7 days prior to planting. Preemergence surface: Apply after planting, before crop and weeds emerge and within 5 days after last preplant tillage operation. Postemergence surface (except Texas): Apply before weeds reach 2-leaf stage and crop is no more than 5" tall.

Rate: 3.5-5.3 lb. ai/A
3.5-5.3 qt./A
Time: Early preplant: No-till and other conservation systems in Connecticut, Delaware, Illinois, Indiana, Iowa, Kansas, Kentucky, Maryland, Massachusetts, Michigan, Minnesota, Missouri, Nebraska, New Jersey, New York, North Carolina, Ohio, Pennsylvania, South Dakota, Vermont, Virginia, Wisconsin.
Weeds: Broadleaf weeds:

annual groundcherry	Florida beggarweed	mustard
annual morningglory	Florida pusley	pigweed
black nightshade	galinsoga	prickly sida
buttonweed	hairy nightshade	purslane
carelessweed	jimsonweed	sicklepod*
carpetweed	horseweed	smartweed
common cocklebur	kochia	teaweed
common ragweed	lambsquarters	velvetleaf
cutleaf groundcherry		

Grasses and sedges:

barnyardgrass	grassbur	shattercane*
broadleaf signalgrass	green foxtail	volunteer sorghum*
browntop panicum	johnsongrass*	waterhemp
crabgrass	(seedling)	wildcane*
fall panicum	red rice*	witchgrass
giant foxtail	red sprangletop	yellow foxtail
goosegrass	sandbur	yellow nutsedge

* Reduced competition

Remarks: Field, seed, silage corn. Do not make more than 2 applications per year or exceed 6.4 qt. product/year. Do not apply more than 2.5 lb. atrazine/year; refer to label for restrictions. Do not graze treated area or feed treated forage to livestock for 21 days after application.

Crop Rotation: Plant only corn, peanuts, sorghum (milo), or soybeans the year after treatment. If soybeans are to be planted, there is a possibility of crop injury due to atrazine carryover. Do not plant soybeans where furrow irrigation is practiced.

Tank Mixes: Atrazine, Bladex, Gramoxone Extra, Lasso, linuron, Prowl, and simazine. Refer to labels for use directions and precautions.

- - - - - - - - - - - - - - -

Signal Word/Toxicity Class: Caution/III.
REI: 12 hr.

CELEBRITY (Co-Pack)

Celebrity is comprised of two water-dispersible granule products (Celebrity B is packaged in a foil-lined container and Celebrity G is packaged in water-soluble film packets). The contents must be used completely to treat 8 acres.

■ **POST**
◆ **Celebrity (69.3% dicamba & 7.5% nicosulfuron)** *(BASF)*
Rate: 6 oz. B + 0.67 oz. G/A

Time: Early postemergence Do not apply to popcorn or field corn grown for seed that is taller than 20" or that exhibits 6 collars.
Weeds: Annual broadleaf weeds:

annual clover	common sunflower	rough pigweed
bitterweed	giant ragweed	Russian thistle
black nightshade	green smartweed	sicklepod
buffaloweed	ivyleaf morningglory	smooth pigweed
burcucumber	jimsonweed	spanishneedles
California burclover	knotweed	tall morningglory
carelessweed	kochia	tansy mustard
carpetweed	ladysthumb	teaweed
common chickweed	lanceleaf ragweed	tumble pigweed
common cocklebur	Pennsylvania	velvetleaf
common	smartweed	Venice mallow
lambsquarters	prickly sida	volunteer sunflower
common mallow	prostrate pigweed	waterhemp
common purslane	prostrate spurge	wild buckwheat
common ragweed	puncturevine	wild mustard
common spikeweed	redroot pigweed	yellowtop

Perennial broadleaf weeds:

alfalfa	common dandelion	Jerusalem artichoke
field bindweed	common milkweed	perennial sowthistle
broadleaf dock	curly dock	pokeweed
Canada thistle	hedge bindweed	silverleaf nightshade
Carolina horsenettle	hemp dogbane	swamp smartweed
chicory	honeyvine milkweed	vetch
climbing milkweed	hop clover	

Grasses:

barnyardgrass	green foxtail	shattercane
bristly foxtail	Italian ryegrass	sorghum-almum
broadleaf signalgrass	itchgrass	Texas panicum
browntop panicum	johnsongrass	wild oat
fall panicum	(rhizome, seedling)	wild proso millet
field sandbur	longspine sandbur	woolly cupgrass
giant foxtail	quackgrass	yellow foxtail

Remarks: Field corn (including high lysine, waxy, white, or other food-grade hybrids), corn grown for seed, IT Hybrids, popcorn. Not for use on sweet corn. Include a nonionic surfactant and ammonium nitrogen fertilizer. Do not use ammonium sulfate or any fertilizer that contains ammonium sulfate as a spray adjuvant. Do not make more than 2 applications/A per season. Corn may be harvested or grazed for feed once crop has reached ensilage stage or later in maturity. Do not apply to any white popcorn inbred or white popcorn hybrid unless specifically approved by seed company. Do not apply through any type of irrigation system. Refer to label for restrictions, and precautions.

Crop Rotation: Field corn, seed corn—anytime; soybeans—1 month; winter barley, winter rye, winter wheat—4 months; oats, spring barley, spring wheat—8 months; cotton, dry beans, peas, popcorn, snap beans, sweet corn—10 months; alfalfa, red clover—12 months. For other crops, refer to label for specific restrictions.

Tank Mixes: Accent, atrazine, Banvel, Clarity, Marksman.
State Restrictions: Do not apply by air in California.

- - - - - - - - - - - - - - -

Signal Word/Toxicity Class: Warning/II.
REI: 12 hr.

Clarity — see dicamba

CLOPYRALID

Systemic herbicide absorbed by leaves and roots. Has selective postemergence control of many annual and perennial broadleaf weeds.

■ **POST**
Stinger *(Dow AgroSciences)*
Rate: 0.1-0.25 lb. ae/A
0.25-0.66 pt./A
Time: Postemergence. Apply to actively growing weeds any time after corn emergence through 24" tall corn. For Canada thistle, apply when majority of plants have emerged and thistles are at least 6-8" diameter or up to bud height.
Weeds: Broadleaf weeds:

annual sowthistle	common ragweed	Jerusalem artichoke
Canada thistle	common sunflower	jimsonweed
common cocklebur	giant ragweed	

Remarks: Field corn. Do not apply more than 0.66 pt./A per year. Do not apply through any type of irrigation system. Do not contaminate irrigation ditches or water used for irrigation or domestic purposes.
Days To Harvest: Harvest/grazing—40.
Crop Rotation: Varies by region; refer to label.

- - - - - - - - - - - - - - -

Signal Word/Toxicity Class: Caution/III.
REI: 12 hr.

IMI-field corn resistant to imidazolinone herbicides • LL-field corn resistant to Liberty herbicide • RR-field corn resistant to Roundup Ultra • SR-field corn resistant to sethoxydim
◆-new product • PP-preplant • PPI-preplant incorporated • PRE-preemergence • POST-postemergence • SEQ-sequential • ae-acid equivalent • ai-active ingredient • DF-dry flowable
E/EC-emulsifiable concentrate • F/FL-flowable • DG/G/WG-dispersable granule • L/LC-liquid • SP/WSP-soluble packet • W/WP-wettable powder • WSB-water soluble bag

IMI CONTOUR (Premix)

*Premix containing active ingredients of Pursuit and atrazine. Use postemergence only on IMI-corn hybrids with resistance/ tolerance to imazethapyr (Pursuit) herbicide. If applied postemergence to field corn not designated as IMI-corn, severe crop damage will occur. Restricted Use Pesticide due to ground and surface water concerns. **For more information on IMI-corn, turn to page 85.***

■ **PP, PPI, PRE, POST**

Contour (SC) (0.38 lb./gal. imazethapyr & 3 lb./gal. atrazine) *(American Cyanamid)*

Rate: 0.562 lb. ai/A
1.33 pt. SC/A

Time: Early preplant, preplant incorporated, preemergence, postemergence.

Weeds: Broadleaf weeds:

barnyard sage	galinsoga	prostrate spurge
black nightshade	giant ragweed	puncturevine
bristly starbur	hairy nightshade	redroot pigweed
buffalobur	ivyleaf morningglory	Russian thistle
Canada thistle	Jerusalem artichoke	sicklepod
carpetweed	jimsonweed	smallflower
common cocklebur	kochia	morningglory
common	ladysthumb	smooth pigweed
lambsquarters	marshelder	spiny pigweed
common purslane	mustard	spotted spurge
common ragweed	Palmer pigweed	spurred anoda
eastern black	palmleaf morningglory	sunflower
nightshade	Pennsylvania	tall morningglory
eclipta	smartweed	tall waterhemp
entireleaf	pitted morningglory	velvetleaf
morningglory	prickly sida	Venice mallow
Florida pusley	prostrate pigweed	wild poinsettia

Grasses:

barnyardgrass	giant foxtail	red rice
broadleaf signalgrass	green foxtail	shattercane
crabgrass	johnsongrass	sorghum-almum
fall panicum	(seedling)	yellow foxtail

Remarks: Field corn (IMI-Corn only). Soil insecticides may be used in combination with Contour and Pioneer IMI hybrids. Contour and imidazolinone-tolerant hybrids may be used in combination with banded or in-furrow applications of Counter CR, or banded applications of Counter 15G or Thimet. Do not use Counter 15G in-furrow. If tank mixed, follow label restrictions for all products. In event of crop loss due to weather, IMI-Corn hybrids can be replanted. Refer to label for precautions and use information.

Days To Harvest: Harvest/grazing/feeding—45.

Crop Rotation: IMI-Corn—anytime; field corn, corn grown for seed—8$^{1/2}$ months; barley, edible beans and peas, peanuts, rye, soybeans, tobacco, wheat—9$^{1/2}$ months; alfalfa, cotton, lettuce, oats, popcorn (with restrictions), safflower, sorghum, sunflower, sweet corn (with restrictions)—18 months; potatoes—26 months; all other crops—40 months. Only rotational crops harvested at maturity may be used for feed or food.

State Restrictions: Not for use in North Dakota or north of Hwy 210 in Minnesota.

- - - - - - - - - - - - - - - -

Signal Word/Toxicity Class: Caution/III.
REI: 12 hr.

Credit — see glyphosate

CYANAZINE

Cyanazine registrations are cancelled as of January 1, 2000. Sale and distribution of existing stock may continue through September 30, 2002, and all use is prohibited after December 31, 2002. Restricted Use Pesticide.

■ **PP, PRE**

Bladex 4L or 90DF *(DuPont)*

Cy-Pro 4L *(Griffin)*

Rate: Refer to label for rate limits. Do not apply more than 3 lb. ai/A per year. Enclosed cab required for application.

Time: Preplant incorporated, preemergence. Conservation tillage: (30 days before planting until emergence): Complete any planned early spring tillage prior to application. Do not apply postemergence. Do not apply preemergence on peat or muck soils.

Weeds: Broadleaf weeds:

annual buttercup	curly dock	prickly sida
annual groundcherry	(seedling)	prostrate knotweed
annual morningglory	fiddleneck	prostrate spurge
annual nightshade	Florida purslane	ragweed
annual sedge	Florida pusley	Russian thistle
annual sunflower	hedge mustard	shepherdspurse
black mustard	jimsonweed	smallflower galinsoga
buffalobur	kochia	tarweed cuphea
carpetweed	ladysthumb	teaweed
cocklebur	mayweed	velvetleaf
common chickweed	Pennsylvania	wild buckwheat
common groundsel	smartweed	wild mustard
common mallow	pigweed	wild radish
common purslane	pineappleweed	wild sunflower
common sunflower	plantain	wild turnip
corn spurry	poorjoe	

Grasses:

annual bluegrass	fall panicum	Italian ryegrass
annual fescues	giant foxtail	junglerice
annual ryegrass	goosegrass	stinkgrass
barnyardgrass	green foxtail	witchgrass
bullgrass	Indian lovegrass	yellow foxtail
crabgrass		

Remarks: Field corn (seed), popcorn. Do not use on sands or loamy sands containing less than 1% organic matter. Do not apply by air or through any type of irrigation system. This product may not be mixed, loaded, or used within 50 ft. of all wells including abandoned wells, drainage wells, and sink holes. Certain states may have additional requirements and limitations; consult state lead pest control agency.

Crop Rotation: If crop is lost due to adverse weather, etc., field can be replanted to corn or sorghum. If replanted to sorghum, allow at least 30-day interval between application and planting. Any rotational crop may be planted the fall or spring following treatment.

Tank Mixes: Alachlor, atrazine, Banvel, Dual, Eradicane, Gramoxone Extra, and Sutan+.

- - - - - - - - - - - - - - - -

Signal Word/Toxicity Class: Warning/II.
REI: 12 hr.

CYANAZINE & ATRAZINE (Premix)

Cyanazine registrations are cancelled as of January 1, 2000. Sale and distribution of existing stock may continue through September 30, 2002, and all use is prohibited after December 31, 2002. Restricted Use Pesticide.

■ **PP, PRE, POST**

Extrazine II (4L: 3 lb. cyanazine & 1 lb. atrazine; DF: 67.5% cyanazine & 21.4% atrazine) *(DuPont)*

Rate: Refer to label for rate limits. Do not apply more than 3 lb. ai/A per year. Enclosed cab required for application.

Time: Conservation tillage—preemergence (30 days before planting until emergence): Complete any planned early spring tillage prior to application. Conventional tillage—preplant incorporated, preemergence: Apply just before, at, or after planting but before crop emergence. Postemergence: Apply from crop emergence through 4-leaf stage before corn exceeds 12" in height and weeds exceed 1$^{1/2}$" in height. For best results, apply from crop emergence through 2-leaf stage. Do not apply postemergence on corn grown for seed, popcorn, or sweet corn.

Weeds: Broadleaf weeds:

annual buttercup	curly dock (seedling)	prickly sida
annual groundcherry	fiddleneck	prostrate knotweed
annual morningglory	Florida purslane	prostrate spurge
annual nightshade	Florida pusley	ragweed
annual sedge	hedge mustard	Russian thistle
annual sunflower	jimsonweed	shepherdspurse
black mustard	kochia	smallflower galinsoga
buffalobur	ladysthumb	spiny sida
carpetweed	lambsquarters	tarweed cuphea
cocklebur	mayweed	teaweed
common chickweed	Pennsylvania	velvetleaf
common groundsel	smartweed	wild buckwheat
common mallow	pigweed	wild mustard
common purslane	pineappleweed	wild radish
common sunflower	plantain	wild sunflower
corn spurry	poorjoe	wild turnip

Grasses:

annual bluegrass	fall panicum	Italian ryegrass
annual fescues	giant foxtail	junglerice
annual ryegrass	goosegrass	stinkgrass
barnyardgrass	green foxtail	witchgrass
bullgrass	Indian lovegrass	yellow foxtail
crabgrass		

Plus following weeds if 2,4-D LVE is added in tank mix:

buckwheat	marestail	prickly lettuce
dandelion	pennycress	tansymustard
dock		

NOTICE The information on these pages is for preliminary planning — not a guide for use. Be sure to follow the manufacturer's directions, notwithstanding information contained here. | For personal protective equipment and EPA registration numbers, please turn to page 70.

Remarks: Field corn, field corn grown for seed, popcorn. Do not apply preemergence on peat or muck soils. Do not use on sands or loamy sands containing less than 1% organic matter. Do not apply by air. Do not apply postemergence under cold, wet weather conditions or to weather-stressed or storm-damaged corn. If broadleaf weeds exceed 3" in height, add 2,4-D LVE plus surfactant; if grass weeds exceed 3" in height, add paraquat or Roundup Ultra. May not be mixed, loaded, or used within 50 ft. of all wells including abandoned wells, drainage wells, and sink holes. Certain states may have additional requirements and limitations; consult state lead pest control agency.

Crop Rotation: If crop is lost due to adverse weather, etc., field can be replanted to corn or sorghum. If replanted to sorghum, allow at least 30-day interval between application and planting. Plant only corn, sorghum, or soybeans the year following use of this mixture. If soybeans are to be planted, injury may occur due to atrazine carryover. If applied after June 10, do not rotate with crops other than corn or sorghum the next year or injury may occur. In High Plains and Intermountain Area of the West where rainfall is sparse and erratic or where irrigation is required, use only when corn or sorghum is to be planted the following year, or corn or sorghum not treated with this mixture or atrazine is to precede other rotational crops. Small grains may be planted 15 months after application; all other crops 18 months after application.

Tank Mixes: Alachlor, atrazine, Dual, Eradicane, Frontier, Harness Plus, Surpass, Sutan+.

– – – – – – – – – – – – – – –

Signal Word/Toxicity Class: Warning/II.
REI: 12 hr.

Cy-Pro — see cyanazine

2,4-D - PHENOXY HERBICIDES

2,4-D and 2,4-D-type compounds selectively control broadleaf weeds with little or no control of grasses. Corn is a grass, but can be injured by 2,4-D. Drift can injure adjacent crops either by drift of spray or by volatilization (spray turns into a vapor). Ester formulations are most volatile and amines less volatile. Ester formulations can vaporize and be moved by wind to harm sensitive plants. Vaporization increases as air temperatures rise.

Annual and perennial broadleaf weeds controlled by 2,4-D include:

beggarticks	galinsoga	povertyweed
bindweed	goldenrod	puncturevine
bitterweed	ground ivy	purslane
broomweed	healall	ragweed
bull thistle	hoary cress	Russian thistle
burdock	ironweed	shepherdspurse
Canada thistle	jimsonweed	smartweed
carpetweed	knotweed	sowthistle
catnip	lambsquarters	stinkweed
chickweed	mallow	sumac
chicory	marshelder	sunflower
cocklebur	mexicanweed	sweetclover
coffeeweed	morningglory	velvetleaf
cutleaf	musk thistle	Virginia creeper
eveningprimrose	mustard	wild carrot
creeping jenny	pennywort	wild garlic
croton	pepperweed	wild lettuce
dandelion	pigweed	wild onion
dock	plantain	wild parsnips
dogbane	pokeweed	wild radish

■ **PP, PRE, POST**

Albaugh Amine 4 (2,4-D amine) *(Albaugh)*
◆ **Opti-Amine (4) (2,4-D amine)** *(Helena)*
Riverdale 6 Amine (2,4-D amine) *(Riverdale)*
Weed Rhap A-4D (2,4-D amine) *(Helena)*
Weedestroy AM-40 (2,4-D amine) *(Riverdale)*
Wilbur-Ellis Amine 4 (2,4-D amine) *(Wilbur-Ellis)*
Rate: 0.25-2 lb. ae/A
  0.5-4 pt./A
Time: Preplant, preemergence, emergence, postemergence, preharvest. For preplant, apply 7-14 days before planting. For preemergence, apply after planting but before corn emerges. For emergence, apply just as corn plants are breaking ground. For postemergence, apply when most weeds have germinated; spray before corn is 8" tall. When corn is over 8" or beyond 5-leaf stage, use drop nozzles to keep spray off foliage. For preharvest, apply after hard dough or denting stage. Do not spray corn in tassel to dough stage.

Remarks: Field corn, popcorn. Tolerance to 2,4-D varies; consult seed company, Agricultural Experiment Station, or Extension Service weed specialist.
State Restrictions: Wilbur-Ellis not registered in California.

– – – – – – – – – – – – – – –

Signal Word/Toxicity Class: Danger/I.
REI: 48 hr.

■ **PP, PRE, POST**

Albaugh LV4 or LV6 Ester (2,4-D ester) *(Albaugh)*
Riverdale L.V. 4 or L.V. 6 (2,4-D ester) *(Riverdale)*
Weed Rhap LV-6D (2,4-D ester) *(Helena)*
Weedone LV4 (2,4-D solventless ester) *(Nufarm)*
Wilbur-Ellis Lo Vol-4 or Lo Vol-6 (2,4-D ester) *(Wilbur-Ellis)*
Rate: 0.25-2 lb. ae/A
  0.5-4 pt. 4/A
  0.33-2.33 pt. 6/A
Time: Preplant, preemergence, emergence, postemergence, preharvest. For preplant, apply 7-14 days before planting. For preemergence, apply after planting but before corn emerges. For emergence, apply just as corn plants are breaking ground. For postemergence, apply when most weeds have germinated; spray before corn is 8" tall. When corn is over 8" or beyond 5-leaf stage, use drop nozzles to keep spray off foliage. For preharvest, apply after hard dough or denting stage. Do not spray corn in tassel to dough stage.
Remarks: Field corn, popcorn. Tolerance to 2,4-D varies; consult seed company, Agricultural Experiment Station, or Extension Service weed specialist. Refer to label for use directions and restrictions.
State Restrictions: Weedone not for use on popcorn in California; Wilbur-Ellis not registered in California.

– – – – – – – – – – – – – – –

Signal Word/Toxicity Class: Caution/III.
REI: 12 hr.

■ **PP, PRE, POST**

Albaugh D-638 (2,4-D ester + acid) *(Albaugh)*
Phenoxy 088 (2,4-D ester + acid) *(Terra)*
Weedone 638 (2,4-D ester + acid) *(Nufarm)*
Rate: Field corn:
  Preplant, preharvest:
  0.53-0.88 lb. ae/A
  1.5-2.5 pt./A
  Preemergence:
  0.7-1 lb. ae/A
  2-3 pt./A
  Postemergence:
  0.24-0.35 lb. ae/A
  0.66-1 pt./A
Time: Preplant, preemergence, postemergence, preharvest. Apply when daytime temperatures are below 85°F.

Rate: Popcorn:
  0.5-0.88 lb. ae/A
  1.5-2.5 pt./A
Time: Preharvest. Apply when daytime temperatures are below 85°F.
Remarks: Field corn, popcorn. Do not apply through any type of irrigation system. Do not forage or feed corn fodder for 7 days following application.
State Restrictions: Weedone not for use preemergence or preharvest in California.

– – – – – – – – – – – – – – –

Signal Word/Toxicity Class: Danger/I.
REI: 48 hr.

■ **PP, PRE, POST**

◆ **Barrage or Barrage HF (EC) (2,4-D ester)** *(Helena)*
Rate: 3-26 fl. oz./A
Time: Preplant, preemergence, postemergence, preharvest. For preplant, apply 7-14 days before planting. For preemergence, apply after planting but before corn emerges. For early postemergence, apply up to 8" tall. For late postemergence, apply from 8"-36"; use drop nozzles and direct spray from corn plant. Do not apply from tasseling to dough stage. For preharvest, apply after hard dough or denting stage.
Remarks: Field corn, popcorn. Rate varies by soil type and organic matter. Risk of crop injury is less if lower rates are used. Tolerance to 2,4-D varies, consult local Agricultural Extension Service. Do not forage or feed corn fodder to livestock for 7 days following application. Refer to label for precautions and restrictions.

– – – – – – – – – – – – – – –

Signal Word/Toxicity Class: Caution/III.
REI: 12 hr.

IMI-field corn resistant to imidazolinone herbicides • LL-field corn resistant to Liberty herbicide • RR-field corn resistant to Roundup Ultra • SR-field corn resistant to sethoxydim
◆-new product • PP-preplant • PPI-preplant incorporated • PRE-preemergence • POST-postemergence • SEQ-sequential • ae-acid equivalent • ai-active ingredient • DF-dry flowable
E/EC-emulsifiable concentrate • F/FL-flowable • DG/G/WG-dispersable granule • L/LC-liquid • SP/WSP-soluble packet • W/WP-wettable powder • WSB-water soluble bag

■ **PRE, POST**

◆ **Clean Crop Amine 4 (2,4-D amine)** *(Platte)*

Rate: 0.25-2 lb. ae/A
0.5-4 pt. 4/A

Time: Preemergence, emergence, postemergence. For preemergence, apply after planting but before corn emerges. For emergence, apply just as corn emerges (breaking ground). For postemergence, apply up to 8" tall; if corn is more than 8" tall, use drop nozzles to keep spray off foliage. Do not apply from tasseling to dough stage.

Remarks: Field corn. Do not use on very light, sandy soil. Temporary crop injury may occur under conditions of high soil moisture and high air temperatures; use lower rates. Tolerance to 2,4-D varies, consult seed company or Agricultural Extension Service Weed Specialist. Do not forage or feed corn fodder to livestock for 7 days following application.

Signal Word/Toxicity Class: Danger/I.
REI: 48 hr.

■ **PRE, POST**

◆ **Clean Crop Low Vol 4 or Low Vol 6 (2,4-D ester)** *(Platte)*

Rate: 0.25-2 lb. ae/A
0.5-4 pt. 4/A
0.33-2.66 pt. 6/A

Time: Preemergence, postemergence, preharvest. For preemergence, apply 3-5 days after planting but before corn emerges. For postemergence, apply after emergence up to tasseling. When corn is over 10", use drop nozzles to keep spray off foliage. For preharvest, apply after hard dough or denting stage. Do not spray corn in tassel to dough stage.

Remarks: Field corn, popcorn. Do not apply to light, sandy soils. Tolerance to 2,4-D varies; consult seed company, Agricultural Experiment Station, or Extension Service weed specialist.

Signal Word/Toxicity Class: Caution/III.
REI: 12 hr.

■ **PRE, POST**

Esteron 99C (2,4-D LV ester) *(Rhone-Poulenc)*
Formula 40 (2,4-D mixed amine) *(Rhone-Poulenc)*
Gordon's LV 400 (2,4-D LV ester) *(PBI/Gordon)*
Hi-Dep (2,4-D mixed amine) *(PBI/Gordon)*
Riverside 2,4-D LV4, SWB (2,4-D LV ester) *(Terra)*
Solve 2,4-D (2,4-D LV ester) *(Albaugh)*

Rate: 0.25-2 lb. ae/A
0.5-4 pt./A

Time: Preemergence, emergence, postemergence, preharvest. For preemergence, apply after planting but before corn emerges. Do not use on very light, sandy soil. For emergence, apply just as corn emerges (breaking ground). For postemergence, apply up to 8" tall; use drop nozzles and direct spray from corn plant if more than 8" tall. Do not apply from tasseling to dough stage. For preharvest, apply after hard dough or denting stage.

Remarks: Temporary crop injury may occur under conditions of high soil moisture and high air temperatures; use lower rates. Tolerance to 2,4-D varies, consult seed company or Agricultural Extension Service Weed Specialist. Do not forage or feed corn fodder to livestock for 7 days following application.

Signal Word/Toxicity Class: Danger/I (amine); Caution/III (ester).
REI: Danger—48 hr.; Caution—12 hr.

■ **PRE**

◆ **Riverdale 2,4-D Granules (2,4-D ester)** *(Riverdale)*

Rate: Band/row:
0.7 lb. ae/A
3.5 lb./A
Broadcast:
2 lb. ae/A
10 lb./A

Time: Preemergence. Apply from time of planting up to 2 days before seedlings emerge. Plant corn at least 2" deep.

Remarks: Do not use on light, sandy soils.
State Restrictions: For use in the Midwestern Corn Belt.

Signal Word/Toxicity Class: Caution.
REI: 12 hr.

■ **PP, POST**

Riverside 2,4-D Amine 4 (2,4-D amine) *(Terra)*

Rate: Preplant:
0.5-1 lb. ae/A
1-2 pt./A

Postemergence:
0.25-0.5 lb. ae/A
0.5-1 pt./A

Time: Preplant (burndown), postemergence. For preplant, apply 7-14 days before planting. Do not use on light, sandy soil or where moisture is low. For postemergence, do not spray during this period or after first tassels appear. Use drop nozzles when crop is over 10" high.

Remarks: Field corn. Use lower rate on inbreds. For resistant weeds, use up to 2 pt./A though corn injury may result. Do not cultivate soon after spraying while corn is brittle.

Signal Word/Toxicity Class: Danger/I.
REI: 48 hr.

■ **PP, PRE, POST**

◆ **Saber (2,4-D amine)** *(Platte)*
Savage (WSB) (2,4-D amine) *(Platte)*

Rate: 0.25-0.75 lb. ae/A
0.5-1.5 pt./A
0.24-1.4 lb. ae/A
0.25-1.5 lb. WSB/A

Time: Preplant, preemergence, postemergence, preharvest. For preplant, apply 7-14 days before planting. For preemergence, apply after planting but before corn emerges. For postemergence, apply when corn is less than 8" tall. When corn is over 8", use drop nozzles to keep spray off foliage. Do not apply from 7-10 days before tasseling to dough stage. For preharvest, apply after hard dough or denting stage.

Remarks: Field corn, popcorn. Use lower rate when crop is rapidly growing under high temperature and high soil moisture conditions. Do not cultivate soon after spraying while plants are brittle. Tolerance to 2,4-D varies, consult local Agricultural Extension Service. Do not forage or feed corn fodder for 7 days following application. Refer to label for use directions, restrictions, and precautions.

Signal Word/Toxicity Class: Danger/I.
REI: 48 hr.

■ **PP, PRE, POST**

Salvo (2,4-D LV ester) *(Platte)*

Rate: 0.125-1 lb. ae/A
0.2-1.6 pt./A

Time: Preplant, preemergence, postemergence, preharvest. For preplant, apply 7-14 days before planting. For preemergence, apply 3-5 days after planting but before emergence; do not use on light sandy soils or when moisture is low. Use drop nozzles when crop is 10" tall or higher. For postemergence, apply when crop is small and more resistant to 2,4-D, but when weeds are succulent or in active growth stage. Do not spray after tassels appear. For preharvest, apply after hard dough or denting stage.

Remarks: Field, seed, silage corn. Use lower rate only against succulent, nonresistant annual broadleaf weeds. Keep spray off leaves. Do not forage or feed corn fodder to livestock for 7 days following application.

Signal Word/Toxicity Class: Caution/III.
REI: 12 hr.

■ **PRE, POST**

Solution (WS) (2,4-D amine) *(Riverdale)*

Rate: 1 WS packet in 4-30 gal. water/1.13-2.25 A
Time: Preemergence. Apply after planting but before corn emerges.

Rate: 1 WS packet in 10-100 gal. water/5 A
Time: Emergence. Apply just as corn emerges (breaking ground).

Rate: 1 WS packet in 10-100 gal. water/5-10 A
Time: Postemergence. Apply to corn up to 8" tall. If corn is more than 8" tall, use drop nozzles and keep spray off foliage. Do not apply from tasseling to dough stage.

Rate: 1 WS packet in 5-100 gal. water/2.5-5 A
Time: Preharvest. Apply after hard dough or denting stage.

Remarks: Field corn. Do not use on very light, sandy soil for preemergence application. Temporary crop injury may occur under conditions of high soil moisture and high air temperatures; use lower rates. Tolerance to 2,4-D varies, consult seed company or Agricultural Extension Service Weed Specialist. Do not forage or feed corn fodder to livestock for 7 days following application.

Signal Word/Toxicity Class: Danger/I.
REI: 48 hr.

Field Corn, Popcorn

■ PP, PRE, POST

Weedar 64 (4) (2,4-D amine) *(Nufarm)*

Weedone Lo Vol 6 (2,4-D ester) *(Nufarm)*

Rate: 0.25-1.5 lb. ae/A
0.5-3 pt. 4/A
0.33-2 pt. 6/A

Time: Preplant, preemergence, postemergence. For preplant, apply 7-14 days before planting. For preemergence, apply from 3-5 days after planting but before corn emerges. For postemergence, apply when weeds are small and corn is less than 8" tall. When corn is over 8" tall, use drop nozzles and keep spray off foliage. Treat perennial weeds in bud to bloom stage. Do not spray corn in tassel to dough stage.

Remarks: Field corn. For preemergence application, do not use on light, sandy soils or where moisture is low. Do not forage or feed fodder for 7 days following application.

- - - - - - - - - - - - - - - -

Signal Word/Toxicity Class: Varies by formulation.

REI: Danger—48 hr.; Caution—12 hr.

DICAMBA

From chemical family of benzoics, a growth regulating herbicide similar in action to 2,4-D. Clarity is a diglycolamine salt formulation of dicamba with a little added safety for control of broadleaf weeds. Not labeled for sweet corn.

■ PP, PRE, POST

Banvel (WS) (DMA salt of dicamba) *(BASF)*

Clarity (WS) (dicamba-DGA) *(BASF)*

◆ **Sterling (WS) (DMA salt of dicamba)** *(Terra)*

Rate: 0.25-0.5 lb. ai/A
0.5-1 pt. WS/A

Time: Preplant, preemergence in no-till; preemergence in conventional or reduced tillage; early postemergence in all tillage systems.

Weeds: Annual, biennial, and perennial broadleaf weeds:

annual morningglory	hemp dogbane*	Pennsylvania
Canada thistle*	honeyvine	smartweed
cocklebur	milkweed*	redroot pigweed
common milkweed*	lambsquarters	sunflower
field bindweed*		velvetleaf

* Suppression

Remarks: Field, seed, silage corn, popcorn. Rate varies by soil type. Verify selectivity with seed corn company prior to applying to inbred seed corn lines. Do not apply to coarse-textured soils until after crop emergence. Do not apply when soybeans are growing nearby if corn is more than 24" tall, soybeans are more than 10" tall, or soybeans have begun to bloom. Corn may be harvested or grazed for feed once crop has reached ensilage (milk) stage or later in maturity. Do not apply through any type of irrigation system.

Tank Mixes: Accent, atrazine, Axiom, Beacon, Bladex, Bullet, Celebrity, 2,4-D, DoublePlay, Dual, Eradicane, Exceed, Extrazine II, FieldMaster, Frontier, FulTime, glyphosate, Gramoxone Extra, Guardsman, Harness, Hornet, Laddok S-12, Lasso, Liberty, Marksman, OpTill, Permit, Princep, Prowl, Python, Roundup Ultra, Spirit, Stinger, Surpass, Sutan+, TopNotch, Tough.

- - - - - - - - - - - - - - -

Signal Word/Toxicity Class:
Warning/II (Banvel, Sterling); Caution (Clarity).

REI: 24 hr.

DICAMBA & ATRAZINE (Premixes)

Reduced rate of atrazine reduces risk of carryover. Restricted Use Pesticide due to ground and surface water concerns.

■ PP, PRE, POST

Marksman (FL) (1.1 lb./gal. dicamba & 2.1 lb./gal. atrazine) *(BASF)*

◆ **Sterling Plus (FL) (1.1 lb./gal. dicamba & 2.1 lb./gal. atrazine)** *(Terra)*

Rate: 0.8-1.4 lb. ai/A
2-3.5 pt. FL/A

Time: Preplant, preemergence: no-till. Preemergence: conventional or reduced-tillage. Early postemergence: all tillage systems. Apply before, during, or after planting but before corn exceeds 5-leaf stage or reaches 8" tall.

Weeds: Broadleaf weeds:

alfalfa	field bindweed	redroot pigweed
annual clover	giant ragweed	rough pigweed
black nightshade	green smartweed	Russian thistle
bitterdock	hedge bindweed	sicklepod
broadleaf dock	hemp dogbane	smooth pigweed
buffaloweed	ivyleaf morningglory	spanishneedles
burcucumber	Jerusalem artichoke	swamp smartweed
Canada thistle	jimsonweed	tall morningglory
carelessweed	knotweed	tansymustard
Carolina horsenettle	kochia	teaweed
common chickweed	ladysthumb	tumble pigweed
common cocklebur	lambsquarters*	velvetleaf
common dandelion	lespedeza	Venice mallow
common lambsquarters	Pennsylvania smartweed	vetch
common mallow	perennial clover	volunteer sunflower
common milkweed	pigweed*	wild buckwheat
common purslane	prickly sida	wild cucumber
common ragweed	prostrate pigweed	wild mustard
common sunflower	prostrate spurge	wild sunflower
curly dock	puncturevine	yellowtop mustard

* Triazine resistant weeds

Remarks: Field corn, popcorn, seed corn, silage corn. Rate varies by soil texture and organic matter. Do not apply to seed corn or popcorn without verifying with local seed corn company dicamba selectivity on inbred lines. Preemergence does not require mechanical incorporation to become active. Shallow mechanical incorporation recommended if applications not followed by adequate rainfall or sprinkler irrigation. Use of adjuvants containing oil penetrants after corn emergence may cause injury.

Crop Rotation: If applied after June 10, do not rotate to any crop except corn or sorghum the following spring or injury may occur.

Tank Mixes: Accent, atrazine, Bladex, 2,4-D, Dual, Frontier, Gramoxone Extra, Harness Plus, Lasso, Prowl, Roundup Ultra, Stinger, Surpass.

- - - - - - - - - - - - - - -

Signal Word/Toxicity Class: Caution.

REI: 48 hr.

DIMETHENAMID & ATRAZINE (Premixes)

Restricted Use Pesticide due to ground and surface water concerns.

■ PP, PPI, PRE, POST

Guardsman (2.33 lb./gal. dimethenamid & 2.67 lb./gal. atrazine) *(BASF)*

◆ **Leadoff (2.33 lb./gal. dimethenamid & 2.67 lb./gal. atrazine)** *(DuPont)*

Rate: 1.6-3.2 lb. ai/A
2.5-5 pt./A

Time: Preplant incorporated, preplant surface, preemergence or early postemergence (up to 8" tall).

Weeds: Broadleaf weeds:

annual morningglory	Florida pusley	prostrate pigweed
black nightshade	giant ragweed	redroot pigweed
carpetweed	hairy nightshade	smartweed
cocklebur	jimsonweed	smooth pigweed
common purslane	kochia	spotted spurge
common ragweed	lambsquarters	tall waterhemp
common waterhemp	mustard	tumble pigweed
eastern black nightshade	nodding spurge	velvetleaf
eclipta	Palmer amaranth	wild buckwheat

Grasses and sedges:

barnyardgrass	johnsongrass (seedling)	southwestern cupgrass
broadleaf signalgrass	large crabgrass	wild oat
fall panicum	red rice	witchgrass
giant foxtail	rice flatsedge	yellow nutsedge
green foxtail	smooth crabgrass	

Remarks: Field corn, popcorn, seed corn. Rates vary by soil type. Some weed species may have triazine-resistant biotypes that will not be controlled adequately by this product. If resistant biotypes are suspected, use an alternate program or non-triazine products in combination or sequentially. Do not exceed 5 pt./A in one crop year on any soil. Do not apply through any type of irrigation system.

Days To Harvest: Grazing/feeding—40.

Crop Rotation: In case of crop failure, corn or sorghum can be planted anytime. Corn, cotton, peanuts, sorghum, or soybeans may be planted the year after application. Injury may occur to soybeans planted on soils having a calcareous surface layer. Do not plant dry beans, sugar beets, tobacco, vegetables, spring-seeded small grains, or small-seeded legumes and grasses the year following application.

IMI-field corn resistant to imidazolinone herbicides • LL-field corn resistant to Liberty herbicide • RR-field corn resistant to Roundup Ultra • SR-field corn resistant to sethoxydim
◆-new product • PP-preplant • PPI-preplant incorporated • PRE-preemergence • POST-postemergence • SEQ-sequential • ae-acid equivalent • ai-active ingredient • DF-dry flowable
E/EC-emulsifiable concentrate • F/FL-flowable • DG/G/WG-dispersable granule • L/LC-liquid • SP/WSP-soluble packet • W/WP-wettable powder • WSB-water soluble bag

Tank Mixes: Accent, atrazine, Basagran, Beacon, Bladex, 2,4-D, dicamba, Frontier, Gramoxone Extra, Laddok S-12, Marksman, Princep, Prowl, Pursuit, or Roundup; refer to labels for directions and precautions.

State Restrictions: Not for use in Long Island, New York.

- - - - - - - - - - - - - - - -

Signal Word/Toxicity Class: Warning/II.
REI: 12 hr.

Direx — see diuron

DISTINCT (Premix)

Recommended to be used sequentially or tank mixed with a grass herbicide. Controls weeds by auxin transport inhibition and auxin agonist modes of action. Absorbed by leaves, roots, and shoots, and translocated to growing points of sensitive weeds to provide postemergence control of emerged weeds as well as moderate residual control of germinating weeds. Rainfast in 4 hr.

■ POST

◆ Distinct (WG) (2 lb./gal. diflufenzopyr & 0.5 lb./gal. dicamba) *(BASF)*

Rate: Early postemergence:
6 oz. WG/A
Postemergence:
4 oz. WG/A

Time: Postemergence. For early postemergence, apply when corn is 4"-10" tall; postemergence when corn is 10"-24" tall. Do not apply if corn is more than 24" tall. Allow at least 15 days between sequential applications.

Weeds: Annual broadleaf weeds:

annual sowthistle	Florida beggarweed	prickly sida
black nightshade	giant ragweed	prostrate knotweed
buffalobur	hairy nightshade	prostrate spurge
carpetweed	hemp sesbania	Russian thistle
common cocklebur	jimsonweed	shepherdspurse
common	kochia	sicklepod
lambsquarters	ladysthumb	smellmelon
common purslane	marestail	tall waterhemp
common ragweed	morningglories	tropic croton
common sunflower	palmer amaranth	velvetleaf
common waterhemp	Pennsylvania	Venice mallow
devilsclaw	smartweed	volunteer sunflower
eastern black	pigweed	wild buckwheat
nightshade		

Perennial broadleaf weeds:

alfalfa	common dandelion	pokeweed
bindweed	dock	silverleaf nightshade
broadleaf plantain	hemp dogbane	spotted knapweed
Canada thistle	milkweed	swamp smartweed
Carolina horsenettle	perennial sowthistle	white clover

Annual Grasses:

barnyardgrass	giant foxtail	shattercane
broadleaf signalgrass	green foxtail	yellow foxtail
fall panicum	johnsongrass (seedling)	

* Suppression

Remarks: Field corn grown for grain or silage. Adjuvants must be used. Do not use penetrants such as petroleum-based oils or methylated seed oils. Do not apply through any type of irrigation system.

Days To Harvest: Forage—32; grain/stover—72.

Crop Rotation: In event of crop failure, corn can be replanted 7 or more days after application. Do not plant any crop within 120 days after last application.

- - - - - - - - - - - - - - - -

Signal Word/Toxicity Class: Caution/III.
REI: 12 hr.

DIURON

■ PRE, POST

Direx 4L or 80DF *(Griffin)*
◆ Diuron 80 WDG *(Platte)*
Karmex DF *(Griffin)*
Riverside Diuron 4L or 80DF *(Terra)*

Rate: 0.5-0.8 lb. ai/A
1-1.5 pt. 4L/A
0.66-1 lb. DF, 80DF/A

Time: Preemergence. Apply as broadcast or band treatment after planting but before corn emerges.

Weeds: Broadleaf weeds:

annual groundcherry	gromwell	ragweed
annual morningglory*	knawel	sesbania*
chickweed	lambsquarters	shepherdspurse
cocklebur*	pigweed	sicklepod*
corn spurry	prickly sida*	tansymustard
dogfennel	(teaweed)	wild lettuce
fiddleneck (amsinckia)	purslane	wild mustard

Grasses:

annual bluegrass	barnyardgrass	rattail fescue
annual sweet	crabgrass	red sprangletop
vernalgrass	foxtail	velvetgrass

* Partial Control

Remarks: Field corn. Plant corn at least 1½" deep.

Crop Rotation: Do not replant to crops other than corn or cotton within 4 months after band treatment; 6 months after broadcast treatment.

State Restrictions: For use in Arkansas, Louisiana, Mississippi, Tennessee.

- - - - - - - - - - - - - - - -

Rate: With non-pressure nitrogen solution:
0.5 lb. ai/A
1 pt. 4L/A
0.6 lb. ai/A
0.75 lb. DF, 80DF/A
Without nitrogen solution:
0.8 lb. ai/A
1.5 pt. 4L/A
1 lb. DF, 80DF/A

Time: Postemergence. Apply as directed spray when corn is at least 20" high and weeds are no taller than 3".

Weeds: Same as for preemergence.

Remarks: Field corn. If nitrogen solution is not used, add 1 pt. Surf-Ac 820/25 gal. spray. Do not apply over top of corn.

Crop Rotation: Do not replant to crops within 1 year except cotton, corn, or grain sorghum may be planted the spring after treatment.

- - - - - - - - - - - - - - - -

Signal Word/Toxicity Class: Caution/III.
REI: 12 hr.

DOUBLEPLAY (Premix)

Premix of EPTC and acetochlor. Contains crop safening agent. Toxic to fish. Restricted Use Pesticide.

■ PPI

DoublePlay (5.6 lb./gal. EPTC & 1.4 lb./gal. acetochlor) *(ZENECA)*

Rate: 4-7 lb. ai/A
4.5-8 pt./A

Time: Preplant incorporated. Must be incorporated within 8 hr. after application.

Weeds: Broadleaf weeds:

black nightshade	hairy nightshade	tall waterhemp
common lambsquarters	redroot pigweed	

Grasses:

barnyardgrass	giant foxtail	wild oat
crabgrass	green foxtail	wild proso millet*
fall panicum	volunteer grains	woolly cupgrass*
field sandbur*	(barley, oats, wheat)	yellow foxtail

* Suppression

Remarks: Field corn, popcorn, production seed corn, silage corn. Do not use on seed stock such as Breeders, Foundation or Increase. Do not apply through any type of irrigation system. Refer to label for restrictions.

Crop Rotation: Corn, sorghum, soybeans, or tobacco may be planted the spring following application. Wheat may be planted 4 months after application. Do not rotate to crops other than corn, sorghum, soybeans, tobacco or wheat.

Tank Mixes: Banvel, Basagran, Bladex, Buctril, Extrazine, Laddok S-12.

- - - - - - - - - - - - - - - -

Signal Word/Toxicity Class: Warning/II.
REI: 12 hr.

DPX E-9636 — see rimsulfuron

Dual — see *S*-metolachlor

EPIC (Premix)

Selective herbicide for control of annual grasses and broadleaf weeds. Restricted Use Pesticide.

■ PP, PPI, PRE

EPIC (DF) (48% flufenacet & 10% isoxaflutole) *(Bayer)*

NOTICE The information on these pages is for preliminary planning — not a guide for use. Be sure to follow the manufacturer's directions, notwithstanding information contained here. | For personal protective equipment and EPA registration numbers, please turn to page 70.

Field Corn, Popcorn

Rate: Preplant (0-7 days before planting), preemergence:
8-15 oz. DF/A
Preplant (7-14 days before planting):
10-20 oz. DF/A

Time: Preplant (incorporated, surface), preemergence. For preplant, apply up to 14 days before planting; preemergence apply after planting, but prior to weed or crop emergence.

Weeds: Broadleaf weeds:

annual morningglory*	dandelion (seedling)	Pennsylvania smartweed*
buffalobur	eastern black nightshade	prostrate pigweed
black nightshade	field pennycress	redroot pigweed
carpetweed	Florida beggarweed	shepherdspurse
chamomile	Florida pusley	smooth pigweed
cocklebur*	galinsoga	spotted spurge
common chickweed	giant ragweed	tall waterhemp
common lambsquarters	jimsonweed	velvetleaf
	kochia	Venice mallow
common purslane	marestail	wild mustard
common ragweed	morningglories*	wild radish
common waterhemp	palmer amaranth	wild sunflower

Grasses and sedges:

barnyardgrass	green foxtail	southwestern cupgrass
bristly foxtail	Indian lovegrass	
broadleaf signalgrass	johnsongrass (seedling)	Texas panicum*
browntop panicum	large crabgrass	wild proso millet
fall panicum	robust purple foxtail	witchgrass
field sandbur	robust white foxtail	woolly cupgrass
giant foxtail	shattercane*	yellow foxtail
goosegrass	smooth crabgrass	yellow nutsedge*

* Suppression

Remarks: Field, silage corn. Not for use on popcorn, sweet corn, white corn or corn grown for seed.Do not make more than one application per use season. Rates vary by soil texture and organic matter. For preplant incorporated, apply to upper 1-2" soil surface. Do not use graze or feed forage, hay, or straw to livestock. Do not apply by air or through any type of irrigation system.

Crop Rotation: Corn—anytime; cabbage, carrots, cotton, lettuce, peppers, potatoes, radishes, soybeans, sugar beets, leafy vegetables—6 months; alfalfa, barley, bermudagrass, bluegrass, bromegrass, buckwheat, clover, fescue, millet pearl, millet prose, oats, popcorn, rice, rye, sorghum, triticale, wheat and wild rice—12 months.

Tank Mixes: Atrazine, 2,4-D LVE, dicamba, glyphosate, Hornet, Liberty, Marksman, Roundup Ultra, Touchdown.

State Restrictions: For use in Arkansas, Illinois, Indiana, Iowa, Kansas, Kentucky, Missouri, Montana, Nebraska, North Dakota, Ohio, Oklahoma, South Dakota, Tennessee, Texas (north of I-20), and Wyoming.

Signal Word/Toxicity Class: Caution/III.
REI: 12 hr.

EPTC

Eradicane belongs to thiocarbamate family. Contains crop safening agent. Crop injury is unlikely but may occur when growing conditions are unfavorable or with certain hybrids. Controls annual grasses and at higher rates can control or suppress shattercane and johnsongrass. For best residual control, apply close to planting and incorporate promptly although 4 hr. may be allowed with high rate and dry soil.

■ PPI

Eradicane 6.7-E or 25-G *(ZENECA)*

Rate: 4-6 lb. ai/A
4.75-7.33 pt. 6.7-E/A
16-24 lb. 25-G/A

Time: Preplant incorporated.

Weeds: Broadleaf weeds:

black nightshade	deadnettle (henbit)	redroot pigweed
carpetweed	fiddleneck	shepherdspurse
common chickweed	Florida pusley	sicklepod
common lambsquarters	hairy nightshade	tall morningglory
	prostrate pigweed	teaweed
common purslane	puncturevine	(spiny sida)
corn spurry	(western region)	tumble pigweed

Grasses and sedges:

annual bluegrass	green foxtail	signalgrass (southeast)
annual ryegrass	Italian ryegrass	Texas panicum
barnyardgrass	johnsongrass	volunteer grains
bermudagrass	lovegrass	wild oat
crabgrass	(stinkgrass)	wild proso millet*
fall panicum	nutsedge	(central region)
field sandbur	quackgrass	woolly cupgrass
giant foxtaill	rescuegrass	yellow foxtail

* Suppression

Remarks: Field corn, popcorn, silage corn. Do not use on seed stock (Breeders, Foundation or Increase). May be applied by center pivot sprinkler systems or impregnation on dry bulk fertilizers. Refer to label for regional differences and specific rates for weed suppression/control.

Signal Word/Toxicity Class: Caution.
REI: 12 hr. unless soil injected or soil incorporated.

Eradicane — see EPTC

Esteron 99C — see 2,4-D

EVIK

Postemergence contact spray which must be directed to reduce effect on corn. Penetrates foliage rapidly, minimizing removal from foliage by rain.

■ POST

Evik DF (ametryn) *(Novartis)*

Rate: 0.6-2 lb. ai/A
0.75-2.5 lb. DF/A

Time: Postemergence. Apply as directed spray to weeds after smallest corn plants are at least 12" tall. Do not apply within 3 weeks of tasseling.

Weeds: Broadleaf weeds:

cocklebur	pigweed	velvetleaf
Florida pusley	ragweed	wild mustard
lambsquarters	smartweed	
morningglory		

Grasses and sedges:

barnyardgrass	goosegrass	signalgrass
crabgrass	green foxtail	Texas panicum
fall panicum	nutsedge	wild proso millet
giant foxtail	shattercane	yellow foxtail

Remarks: Add surfactant. Do not spray over top of corn.
Days To Harvest: Harvest/grazing/feeding—30.
Crop Rotation: Do not plant to any rotation crop except small grains until the following year.

Signal Word/Toxicity Class: Caution.
REI: 12 hr.

Exceed — see primisulfuron-methyl & prosulfuron

Extrazine II — see cyanazine & atrazine

FIELD MASTER (Premix)

For use in no-till and minimum tillage systems. Toxic to fish and aquatic invertebrates. Restricted Use Pesticide due to ground and surface water concerns and oncogenicity concerns.

■ PRE

♦ Field Master (2 lb./gal. acetochlor & 1.5 lb./gal. atrazine & 0.75 lb./gal. glyphosate) *(Monsanto)*

Rate: 3.5-5 lb. ai/A
7-10 pt./A

Time: May be applied before, during or after planting, but prior to crop emergence. Do not apply to emerged corn.

Weeds: Annual and perennial broadleaf weeds:

alfalfa*	giant ragweed	redroot pigweed
buttonweed	henbit	Russian thistle
Canada thistle*	horseweed	shepherdspurse
carelessweed	kochia	smallflower
carpetweed	lambsquarters	buttercup
cocklebur	marestail	smartweed
common chickweed	milkweed*	smooth pigweed
common mullein*	mustard	sunflowers
common ragweed	pepperweed	swamp smartweed*
curly dock*	pigweed	tall waterhemp
field pennycress	prickly lettuce	velvetleaf
fleabane	red clover*	white clover*

IMI-field corn resistant to imidazolinone herbicides • LL-field corn resistant to Liberty herbicide • RR-field corn resistant to Roundup Ultra • SR-field corn resistant to sethoxydim
♦-new product • PP-preplant • PPI-preplant incorporated • PRE-preemergence • POST-postemergence • SEQ-sequential • ae-acid equivalent • ai-active ingredient • DF-dry flowable
E/EC-emulsifiable concentrate • F/FL-flowable • DG/G/WG-dispersable granule • L/LC-liquid • SP/WSP-soluble packet • W/WP-wettable powder • WSB-water soluble bag

Annual and perennial grasses:

annual bluegrass	johnsongrass	shattercane*
barnyardgrass	(seedling)*	smooth bromegrass*
broadleaf signalgrass	Kentucky bluegrass*	timothy*
browntop panicum	orchardgrass*	Texas panicum*
crabgrass	perennial ryegrass*	volunteer corn
downy brome	proso millet*	volunteer wheat
fall panicum	quackgrass*	wildcane*
fescue*	red rice	wild oat
field sandbur	red sprangletop	wiresteem muhly*
giant foxtail	robust purple foxtail	witchgrass
goosegrass	robust white foxtail	woolly cupgrass*
green foxtail	sandbur*	yellow foxtail

* Reduced competition

Remarks: Field corn (production seed, silage), popcorn. Rate varies by soil type. Do not apply by air or through any type of irrigation system. Do not feed or graze treated areas within 8 weeks after application. Refer to label for use restrictions and precautions.

Crop Rotation: Corn, sorghum or soybeans may be planted the year after application. Do not plant soybeans year following application on furrow- irrigated corn (possibility of crop injury due to atrazine carryover).

Tank Mixes: Atrazine, Bladex, Harness, Princep, Roundup.

– – – – – – – – – – – – – – – –

Signal Word/Toxicity Class: Caution/III.
REI: 12 hr.

Formula 40 — see 2,4-D

FRONTIER

Chloroacetamide herbicide that controls many annual grasses, several broadleaves, and nutsedge. Corn tolerance appears to be relatively good. Not for use on sweet corn.

■ PP, PPI, PRE, POST

Frontier 6.0 (dimethenamid) *(BASF)*
Rate: 0.94-1.5 lb. ai/A
     20-32 fl. oz. 6.0/A
Time: Preplant (surface or incorporated) in minimum or no-tillage systems; preemergence (surface); early postemergence (corn up to 8" tall); split application.

Weeds: Broadleaf weeds:

carpetweed	nightshade	spurge
common purslane	pigweed	waterhemp
Florida pusley		

Grasses and sedges:

barnyardgrass	green foxtail	smooth crabgrass
broadleaf signalgrass	johnsongrass	southwestern
fall panicum	(seedling)	cupgrass
giant foxtail	large crabgrass	yellow foxtail
goosegrass	rice flatsedge	yellow nutsedge

Remarks: Field, seed, silage corn, popcorn. Rate varies by soil type and organic matter. Check with seed corn or sweet corn company for selectivity prior to use. Do not apply through any type of irrigation system. Corn may be grazed or fed to livestock at 40 days following application.

Crop Rotation: If crop is lost to adverse weather, etc., field may be replanted to any labeled crop immediately. Fall-seeded cereal crops may be planted at 4 or more months after spring application. No restrictions in the spring following previous year's application.

Tank Mixes: Accent, atrazine, Banvel, Basagran, Beacon, Bladex, Celebrity, Clarity, 2,4-D, Eradicane, Extrazine II, Gramoxone Extra, Laddok S-12, Liberty, Marksman, Princep, Prowl, Pursuit, Roundup Ultra, Touchdown.

– – – – – – – – – – – – – – – –

Signal Word/Toxicity Class: Warning/II.
REI: 12 hr.

FULTIME (Premix)

Contains the safener dichlormid. Restricted Use Pesticide.

■ PP, PRE, POST

FulTime (2.4 lb./gal. acetochlor & 1.6 lb./gal. atrazine) *(ZENECA)*
Rate: 2.5-4 lb. ai/A
     2.5-5 qt./A
Time: Conventional tillage: Apply within 14 days before planting. Reduced and no-till: Apply up to 40 days before planting or after planting. Postemergence: Apply up to 11" tall corn.

Weeds: Broadleaf weeds:

black nightshade	galinsoga	Palmer amaranth
carpetweed	giant ragweed	prickly sida
cocklebur	hairy nightshade	redroot pigweed
common purslane	jimsonweed	sicklepod
common ragweed	kochia	smartweed
common waterhemp	lambsquarters	tall waterhemp
Florida beggarweed	morningglory	velvetleaf
Florida pusley		

Grasses and sedges:

barnyardgrass	goosegrass	southwestern
broadleaf signalgrass	green foxtail	cupgrass
browntop panicum	johnsongrass	Texas panicum
crabgrass	(seedling)	wild proso millet
crowfootgrass	red rice	witchgrass
fall panicum	red sprangletop	woolly cupgrass
field sandbur	robust purple foxtail	yellow foxtail
foxtail millet	robust white foxtail	yellow nutsedge
giant foxtail	shattercane	

Remarks: Field corn, popcorn, production seed corn, silage corn. For conventional tillage, rate varies by organic matter; for reduced and no-till, rate varies by planting time. Do not apply after June 10, unless only corn will be planted the following year. Do not apply through any type of irrigation system. Refer to label for use directions, restrictions, and precautions.

Crop Rotation: Corn, sorghum, soybeans, or tobacco may be planted the spring following application. Wheat may be planted 15 months after application. Do not rotate to crops other than corn, sorghum, soybeans, tobacco or wheat.

Tank Mixes: Accent, Banvel, Basis, Basis Gold, Beacon, Bladex, Buctril, Clarity, 2,4-D ester, Extrazine II, Gramoxone Extra, Liberty, Lightning, Lorox, Marksman, Poast HC, Poast Plus, Princep, Prowl, Pursuit, Resource, Shotgun, TopNotch, Touchdown, Warrior.

Signal Word/Toxicity Class: Caution.
REI: 12 hr. unless soil injected or soil incorporated.

LL GLUFOSINATE-AMMONIUM

Use only on seed designated as Liberty Link, resistant to glufosinate-ammonium. If applied to field corn not designated as Liberty Link, severe crop damage will occur. Rainfast within 4 hr. of application. **For more information on Liberty Link, turn to page 84.**

■ POST

Liberty (WS) *(AgrEvo USA)*
Rate: 0.2-0.37 lb. ai/A
     1-1.75 pt. WS/A
Time: Postemergence. Apply from emergence until corn is 24" tall or in the V-7 stage of growth. Applications should be made between dawn and 2 hr. before sunset.

Weeds: Broadleaf weeds:

buckwheat	field bindweed	redroot pigweed
buffalobur	Florida beggarweed	Russian thistle
Canada thistle	giant ragweed	shepherdspurse
carpetweed	hedge bindweed	sicklepod
common chickweed	honeyvine milkweed	smallflower
common cocklebur	ivyleaf morningglory	morningglory
common	jimsonweed	smooth pigweed
lambsquarters	kochia	sowthistle
common milkweed	ladysthumb	spiny pigweed
common ragweed	marestail	tall morningglory
common sunflower	marshelder	tall waterhemp
common waterhemp	Palmer amaranth	tumble pigweed
dandelion	Pennsylvania	velvetleaf
eastern black	smartweed	Venice mallow
nightshade	pitted morningglory	wild buckwheat
entireleaf	prickly sida	wild mustard
morningglory	prostrate pigweed	

Grasses and sedges:

barnyardgrass*	large crabgrass	volunteer sorghum*
broadleaf signalgrass	orchardgrass	wild oat
fall panicum	quackgrass	wild proso millet
field sandbur	shattercane	wiresteem muhly
giant foxtail	smooth crabgrass	woolly cupgrass
green foxtail	Texas panicum	yellow foxtail*
hemp sesbania	volunteer corn*	yellow nutsedge
johnsongrass	volunteer proso millet	

* Suppression

Remarks: Field, silage corn. For corn up to 36" tall, apply with drop nozzles only. Do not apply if crop is stressed or make more than 2 applications to crop. Do not apply through any type of irrigation system. Refer to label for use directions, restrictions, and precautions.

Days To Harvest: Forage—60; grain and fodder—70.
Crop Rotation: Wheat—120 days.

Field Corn, Popcorn

Tank Mixes: Accent, atrazine, Banvel, Basagran, Beacon, Bicep, Buctril, Buctril + Atrazine, Clarity, Curtail, Dual, Frontier, Guardsman, Harness, Harness Xtra, Hornet, Laddok S-12, Marksman, Permit, Prowl, Python, Scorpion III, Shotgun, Spirit, Stinger, Surpass, Surpass 100, TopNotch, Tough.

- - - - - - - - - - - - - - -

Signal Word/Toxicity Class: Warning/II.
REI: 12 hr.

RR Glyfos or Glyfos X-tra — see glyphosate

RR GLYPHOSATE

Roundup Ultra postemergence is for use only on field corn designated as Roundup Ready. If applied on corn not designated as Roundup Ready, severe crop damage will occur. Nonselective herbicide to control existing vegetation before crop emergence. Translocates to roots to give better control of perennials as well as annual weeds. **For more information on Roundup Ready corn, turn to page 87.**

■ POST

Roundup Ultra (4WS) *(Monsanto)*
Rate: 0.75-1 lb. ai/A
1.5-2 pt. 4WS/A
Preplant burndown (no-till, stale seedbed):
0.5-2 lb. ai/A
1-4 pt. 4WS/A
Time: Postemergence. Apply from corn emergence through V8 stage (8 leaves with collars) or until corn is 30" tall.
Weeds: Annual and perennial broadleaf weeds and grasses.
Remarks: For use only on corn hybrids designated as containing the Roundup Ready gene. Rate varies by weed species and height. Refer to label for directions, precautions and restrictions.
Days To Harvest: Grain—7 (4WS); forage—50.
Tank Mixes: Alachlor, Bullet (not for use in Texas), atrazine, Harness, Harness Extra, Permit. Roundup tank mixes not registered in California.
State Restrictions: Roundup Ultra aerial application only in Alabama, Arkansas, Colorado, Florida, Georgia, Kansas, Louisiana, Mississippi, bootheel of Missouri, Nebraska, North Carolina, North Dakota, Oklahoma, South Carolina, South Dakota, Tennessee, Texas, Virginia, and Wyoming.

- - - - - - - - - - - - - - -

Signal Word/Toxicity Class: Caution/III.
REI: 4 hr.

■ PP, PRE

◆ **Credit (4WS)** *(Nufarm)*
◆ **Glyfos or Glyfos X-tra (4WS)** *(Cheminova)*
Rattler (4WS) *(Helena)*
Roundup Custom (5.4WS) *(Monsanto)*
Roundup Original, Original RT, Ultra, Ultra RT (4WS) *(Monsanto)*
Rate: Annual weeds:
0.38-1.5 lb. ai/A
0.56-2.25 pt. 5.4WS/A
0.75-3 pt. 4WS/A
Perennial weeds:
0.5-5 lb. ai/A
0.75-7.5 pt. 5.4WS/A
1-10 pt. 4WS/A
Time: Preplant, preemergence, at-planting, spot treatment, postharvest. For spot treatment, apply prior to silking of corn.
Weeds: Broadleaf weeds:

alfalfa	fanweed	redroot pigweed
alligatorweed	field bindweed	shepherdspurse
barley	field pennycress	sicklepod
blue mustard	filaree	silverleaf nightshade
brackenfern	Florida pusley	smallseed falseflax
buttercup	jagged chickweed	smooth pigweed
Canada thistle	hemp dogbane	spanishneedles
Carolina geranium	horsenettle	swamp smartweed
cocklebur	horseradish	tansymustard
common groundsel	horseweed	teaweed
common	Jerusalem artichoke	Texas blueweed
lambsquarters	knapweed	timothy
common mullein	lantana	tumble mustard
common ragweed	London rocket	velvetleaf
curly dock	marestail	volunteer corn
cutleaf	milkweed	volunteer wheat
eveningprimrose	morningglory	white clover
dandelion	mouseear chickweed	wild mustard
dwarfdandelion	red clover	woollyleaf bursage

Grasses and sedges:

annual bluegrass	fescue	reed canarygrass
bahiagrass	field sandbur	shattercane
barnyardgrass	foxtail	smooth bromegrass
bermudagrass	goosegrass	stinkgrass
broadleaf signalgrass	guineagrass	tall fescue
bulbous bluegrass	Italian ryegrass	Texas panicum
Carolina foxtail	johnsongrass	torpedograss
cheat	napiergrass	vaseygrass
common ryegrass	orchardgrass	western wheatgrass
crabgrass	paragrass	wild oat
dallisgrass	perennial ryegrass	wirestem muhly
downy brome	purple nutsedge	witchgrass
fall panicum	quackgrass	yellow nutsedge

Remarks: Field corn, popcorn, seed corn (except 5.4WS). Rate varies by weed species. Use higher rates for control of large weeds which were growing in crop at harvest. Do not add surfactant to Roundup Ultra or Ultra RT. Do not allow glyphosate to contact desirable plants. Do not apply through any type of irrigation system. Refer to label for directions, precautions, and restrictions.
Days To Harvest: Harvest/feeding—8 weeks.
Tank Mixes: Alachlor, atrazine, Bladex, Bullet, 2,4-D, dicamba (not for use in California), Extrazine II, Guardsman, Lariat, Lorox, Marksman, Princep, Prowl, Surpass, Surpass 100, TopNotch. Roundup tank mixes not registered in California.
State Restrictions: Roundup RT for use in Colorado, Idaho, Montana, North Dakota, South Dakota, Utah, Wyoming and in specific counties only in Kansas, Minnesota, Nebraska, Nevada, Oklahoma, Oregon, and Washington; refer to label for restrictions. Glyfos is not registered for use in California. Glyfos X-tra is not registered for use in mistblowers in California or Arizona.

- - - - - - - - - - - - - - -

Signal Word/Toxicity Class: Varies by formulation.
REI: Warning—12 hr.; Caution—4 hr.

Gramoxone Extra — see paraquat

Guardsman — see dimethenamid & atrazine

IMI HALOSULFURON-METHYL

Can be used postemergence on field corn designated as IMI-corn. Selective herbicide for control of annual broadleaf weeds and nutsedge. **For more information on IMI-corn, turn to page 85.**

■ PP, PRE, POST

Permit *(Monsanto)*
Rate: Soil application:
0.063-0.094 lb. ai/A
1.33-2 oz./A
Time: Preplant (surface, incorporated), preemergence.
Weeds: Broadleaf weeds:

common cocklebur	common ragweed	sunflower
common	pigweed	velvetleaf
lambsquarters	smartweed	

Remarks: Field corn (Pioneer IMI hybrids).
Tank Mixes: Dual, Eradicane, Frontier, Harness, Harness Xtra, MicroTech, Partner, Surpass.

- - - - - - - - - - - - - - -

Rate: 0.032-0.063 lb. ai/A
0.66-1.33 oz./A
Time: Postemergence. Apply from spike through lay-by stage.
Weeds: Broadleaf weeds:

burcucumber*	giant ragweed	pigweed
common cocklebur	kochia*	smartweed
common ragweed	lambsquarters	velvetleaf
common sunflower	morningglory*	Venice mallow

Sedges:

purple nutsedge	yellow nutsedge

* Suppression

Remarks: Field, seed corn. Recommended for use following preemergence application of Bullet, Harness, Harness Xtra, Micro-Tech, or Partner.
Days To Harvest: Harvest/grazing—30.
Crop Rotation: Wheat—3 months; soybeans—10 months. Corn or milo can be replanted same growing season provided maximum rate 0.157 lb. ai/A per season not exceeded.

- - - - - - - - - - - - - - -

Signal Word/Toxicity Class: Caution/III.
REI: 12 hr.

IMI-field corn resistant to imidazolinone herbicides • LL-field corn resistant to Liberty herbicide • RR-field corn resistant to Roundup Ultra • SR-field corn resistant to sethoxydim
◆-new product • PP-preplant • PPI-preplant incorporated • PRE-preemergence • POST-postemergence • SEQ-sequential • ae-acid equivalent • ai-active ingredient • DF-dry flowable
E/EC-emulsifiable concentrate • F/FL-flowable • DG/G/WG-dispersable granule • L/LC-liquid • SP/WSP-soluble packet • W/WP-wettable powder • WSB-water soluble bag

HARNESS

Safening agent added to improve corn tolerance. Toxic to fish.
Restricted Use Pesticide.

■ PP, PRE

Harness (acetochlor) *(Monsanto)*
  Rate: 1.1-3 lb. ai/A
       1.25-3.4 pt./A
  Time: Preplant incorporated, preemergence surface.
  Weeds: Broadleaf weeds:

black nightshade	Florida pusley	lambsquarters
carelessweed	galinsoga	pigweed
carpetweed	hairy nightshade	purslane
common ragweed	henbit	waterhemp

  Grasses and sedges:

barnyardgrass	foxtail	red sprangletop
broadleaf signalgrass	goosegrass	witchgrass
browntop panicum	prairie cupgrass	woolly cupgrass
crabgrass	red rice	yellow nutsedge
fall panicum		

  Remarks: Field, seed, silage corn, popcorn. Rate varies by soil texture. Do not apply through any type of irrigation system.
  Crop Rotation: Do not rotate to crops other than soybeans, corn, milo, wheat or tobacco.
  Tank Mixes: May be tank mixed; refer to label for restrictions.

– – – – – – – – – – – – – –

  Signal Word/Toxicity Class: Warning/II.
  REI: 12 hr.

HARNESS XTRA (Premix)

Premix of acetochlor & atrazine with safener added. Restrict-
ed Use Pesticide due to ground and surface water concerns
and oncogenicity concerns.

■ PP, PRE

Harness Xtra (4.3 lb./gal. acetochlor & 1.7 lb./gal. atrazine)
(Monsanto)
  Rate: 2.7-4.1 lb. ai/A
       1.8-2.7 qt./A
  Time: Preplant incorporated, preemergence surface.
  Weeds: Broadleaf weeds:

annual morningglory	galinsoga	prickly sida
black nightshade	hairy nightshade	(teaweed)
carelessweed	henbit	purslane
carpetweed	kochia	smartweed
common ragweed	lambsquarters	velvetleaf
cutleaf goundcherry	mustard	waterhemp
Florida pusley	pigweed	

  Grasses and sedges:

barnyardgrass	foxtail	volunteer wheat
broadleaf signalgrass	goosegrass	wild oat
browntop panicum	prairie cupgrass	witchgrass
crabgrass	red rice	woolly cupgrass
fall panicum	red sprangletop	yellow nutsedge

  Remarks: Field, seed, silage corn, popcorn. Rate varies by soil texture. Do not apply through any type of irrigation system.
  Crop Rotation: Do not rotate to crops other than soybeans, corn, or milo. If soybeans or other nonlabeled crops are to be planted the following year, there is the possibility of crop injury due to carryover of atrazine. Do not plant soybeans in areas where furrow irrigation is practiced.
  Tank Mixes: May be tank mixed; refer to label for use directions.

– – – – – – – – – – – – – –

  Signal Word/Toxicity Class: Caution/III.
  REI: 12 hr.

Hi-Dep — see 2,4-D

HORNET (Premix)

Selective herbicide for broadleaf weed control. Water dispers-
ible granule formulation. Absorbtion occurs through both fo-
liage and root uptake. Not labeled for popcorn or sweet corn.

■ PPI, PRE, POST

Hornet (62.5% clopyralid & 23.1% flumetsulam) *(Dow AgroSciences)*
  Rate: 3.2-4.8 oz./A
  Time: Preplant incorporated, preplant surface, postplant preemergence, spike stage treatment.

  Rate: 1.6-4 oz./A
  Time: Postemergence.
  Weeds: Broadleaf weeds:

black nightshade	kochia	Russian thistle
Canada thistle	ladysthumb	shepherdspurse
carpetweed	marestail	sicklepod
chickweed	morningglory	smartweed
common cocklebur	nightshade	smooth pigweed
common	nodding spurge	spotted spurge
lambsquarters	Palmer amaranth	spurred anoda
common ragweed	prickly sida	tall waterhemp
common sunflower	prostrate spurge	velvetleaf
Florida beggarweed	puncturevine	Venice mallow
giant ragweed	purslane	wild buckwheat
henbit	red clover	wild mustard
horseweed	redroot pigweed	wild poinsettia
jimsonweed		

  Remarks: Field corn. Not for use on popcorn or sweet corn. Rate varies by soil type. Corn inbred lines grown for hybrid seed production may be injured by Hornet. Do not tank mix with Bladex, Basagran, or Laddok as crop injury may occur. Do not apply by air, use on peat or muck soils, or apply when wind conditions favor drift to nontarget sites. Refer to label for restrictions, precautions, and limitations.
  Days To Harvest: 85.
  Crop Rotation: Barley, oats, rye, wheat—4 months; rice—6 months; seeding of cover crops—9 months; alfalfa, dry beans, soybeans, popcorn, sweet corn (certain varieties with restrictions)—10$1/2$ months; grain sorghum—12 months; cotton, peanuts, peas, potatoes, sunflower, sweet corn, tobacco—18 months; sugar beets, canola, and all other crops—26 months and successful field bioassay.

– – – – – – – – – – – – – –

  Signal Word/Toxicity Class: Danger/I.
  REI: 48 hr. unless soil injected or soil incorporated.

Karmex — see diuron

LADDOK S-12 (Premix)

Very good corn tolerance and control of annual broadleaf
weeds with significant reduction in risk of carryover. Include
another herbicide in program for control of grass weeds. Re-
stricted Use Pesticide due to groundwater concerns.

■ POST

Laddok S-12 (5L) (2.5 lb./gal. bentazon & 2.5 lb./gal. atrazine)
(BASF)
  Rate: 0.83-1.45 lb. ai/A
       1.33-2.33 pt. 5L/A
  Time: Early postemergence.
  Weeds: Broadleaf weeds:

annual morningglory	giant ragweed	smooth pigweed
beggarticks	jimsonweed	spurred anoda
bristly starbur	kochia	tall waterhemp
Canada thistle*	ladysthumb	teaweed
cocklebur	Pennsylvania	velvetleaf
common	smartweed	Venice mallow
lambsquarters	prickly sida	wild buckwheat
common ragweed	redroot pigweed	wild mustard
common waterhemp	smallflower	wild sunflower
dayflower	morningglory	
field bindweed*		

  Sedges:

  yellow nutsedge*

  * Refer to label for special directions

  Remarks: Field corn, seed corn, popcorn. Rate depends on leaf stage and weed height. Urea-ammonium nitrate (UAN) solution may be added in place of oil concentrate for control of above annuals. If UAN solution is not used, oil concentrate should be added to spray tank. Oil concentrate should be used if perennials, yellow nutsedge, Canada thistle, or field bindweed are present. Do not graze treated area or feed treated forage to livestock for 21 days following application.
  Crop Rotation: Do not plant sugar beets or sunflowers the season following application. Do not plant oats the season following application in soils with a calcareous surface layer. Intermountain Area: plant only corn or sorghum the year following application.
  Tank Mixes: Asana XL, atrazine, Banvel, Bladex, Clarity, 2,4-D, dimethoate, Furadan, Lorsban, malathion, Poast, Poast Plus, Pounce, Stinger; refer to labels for use directions.
  State Restrictions: Not for use in California.

– – – – – – – – – – – – – –

  Signal Word/Toxicity Class: Danger/I.
  REI: 48 hr.

NOTICE	The information on these pages is for preliminary planning — not a guide for use. Be sure to follow the manufacturer's directions, notwithstanding information contained here.	For personal protective equipment and EPA registration numbers, please turn to page 70.

LARIAT (Premix)

Good control of annual weeds with reduced carryover risk and good crop tolerance. Restricted Use Pesticide.

■ **PP, PPI, PRE, POST**

Lariat (2.5 lb./gal. alachlor & 1.5 lb./gal. atrazine) *(Monsanto)*

Rate: 2.5-5 lb. ai/A
2.5-5 qt./A

Time: Early preplant, preplant incorporated, preemergence, postemergence.

Weeds: Broadleaf weeds:

annual morningglory	Florida pusley	pigweed
black nightshade	galinsoga	purslane
carpetweed	hairy nightshade	smartweed
cocklebur	jimsonweed	teaweed
common ragweed	kochia	(spiny sida)
cutleaf groundcherry	lambsquarters	velvetleaf
Florida beggarweed	mustard	

Grasses and sedges:

barnyardgrass	goosegrass	sandbur
broadleaf signalgrass	green foxtail	waterhemp
browntop panicum	johnsongrass	witchgrass
crabgrass	(seedling)	yellow foxtail
fall panicum	red rice	yellow nutsedge
giant foxtail	red sprangletop	(PPI)

Remarks: Field, seed, silage corn. Rate depends on soil type or weed species. Can be used in fluid fertilizer or impregnated on dry bulk fertilizer. Do not graze treated areas or feed treated forage to livestock for 21 days following application. Refer to label for specific directions.

Crop Rotation: Plant only corn, peanuts, sorghum (milo), or soybeans the year following use of this mixture. If soybeans are to be planted, there is a possibility of crop injury due to carryover of atrazine.

– – – – – – – – – – – – – – – –

Signal Word/Toxicity Class: Warning/II.
REI: 12 hr.

Lasso — see alachlor

Leadoff — see dimethenamid & atrazine

LL **Liberty — see glufosinate-ammonium**

LL LIBERTY ATZ (Premix)

Foliar-active herbicide with soil-residual activity for use only on field corn designated as Liberty Link or warranted as being tolerant to Liberty ATZ. If applied to field corn not designated as Liberty Link, severe crop damage will occur. Rainfast within 4 hr. after application. Restricted Use Pesticide due to groundwater concerns. **For more information on Liberty Link, turn to page 84.**

■ **POST**

◆ **Liberty ATZ (SC) (3.3 lb./gal. atrazine & 1 lb./gal. glufosinate-ammonium)** *(AgrEvo USA)*

Rate: 2-2.5 pt. SC/A

Time: Postemergence. Apply from emergence until corn is 12" tall. Applications should be made between dawn and 1 hr. before sunset.

Weeds: Broadleaf weeds:

alfalfa	common sunflower	hemp sesbania
annual fleabane	common waterhemp	honeyvine
annual sowthistle	cutleaf geranium	milkweed*
black medic	cutleaf groundcherry	hophornbeam
buffalobur	dandelion	copperleaf
bull thistle	dock	ivyleaf morningglory
burcucumber	eastern black	java bean
burdock	nightshade	Jerusalem artichoke
Canada thistle	eclipta	jimsonweed
carpetweed	entireleaf	kochia
clover	morningglory	ladysthumb
common chickweed	field bindweed	marestail
common cocklebur	Florida beggarweed	marshelder
common	giant ragweed	mouseear chickweed
lambsquarters	gray goldenrod	Palmer amaranth
common mallow	hairy galinsoga	pennycress
common milkweed*	hedge bindweed	Pennsylvania
common ragweed	hemp dogbane*	smartweed

Weeds: Broadleaf weeds, continued:

pokeweed	sicklepod	tall waterhemp
pitted morningglory	smallflower galinsoga	tumble pigweed
prickly sida	smallflower	velvetleaf
prostrate pigweed	morningglory	Venice mallow
puncturevine	smellmelon	volunteer sunflower
redroot pigweed	smooth pigweed	wild buckwheat
Russian thistle	spiny pigweed	wild mustard
shepherdspurse	tall morningglory	wild poinsettia

Grasses and sedges:

annual bluegrass	orchardgrass	timothy
barnyardgrass*	quackgrass	volunteer corn*
broadleaf signalgrass	red rice	volunteer proso millet
fall panicum	shattercane	volunteer sorghum
field sandbur*	smooth bromegrass	witchgrass
foxtail	smooth crabgrass	wild oat
johnsongrass	sprangletop	wild proso millet
Kentucky bluegrass	stinkgrass	wirestem muhly
large crabgrass	Texas panicum	woolly cupgrass

* Suppression

Remarks: Field, seed, silage. Use only on seed designated as Liberty Link or warranted as being tolerant to Liberty ATZ and on corn tolerant to glufosinate-ammonium. Do not apply if crop is stressed. No more than 1 application to crop. Do not add surfactant or crop oil. Must be applied with ammonium sulfate (AMS). Refer to label for restrictions and precautions.

Days To Harvest: Forage—60; grain and fodder—70.

Crop Rotation: Do not rotate to any crop except corn or sorghum until following year. Refer to label for rotation restrictions.

– – – – – – – – – – – – – – – –

Signal Word/Toxicity Class: Caution/III.
REI: 12 hr.

IMI LIGHTNING (Premix)

For use only on field corn designated as IMI-corn. If applied to crops not designated as IMI-corn, severe crop damage will occur. **For more information on IMI corn, turn to page 85.**

■ **POST**

Lightning (WSB) (0.084 lb./gal. imazethapyr + 0.028 lb./gal. imazapyr) *(American Cyanamid)*

Rate: 1.28 oz. WSB/A (1 bag/2A)

Time: Postemergence. For optimal control, apply before weeds exceed 4" tall, and corn 12" tall.

Weeds: Broadleaf weeds:

alligatorweed	giant ragweed	prostrate pigweed
barnyard sage	hairy nightshade	prostrate spurge
black nightshade	honeyvine milkweed	puncturevine
bristly starbur	ivyleaf morningglory	redroot pigweed
buffalobur	Jerusalem artichoke	sicklepod
Canada thistle	jimsonweed	smallflower
carpetweed	knotweed	morningglory
common cocklebur	kochia	smooth pigweed
common	ladysthumb	spiny pigweed
lambsquarters	marshelder	spotted spurge
common purslane	mustard	spurred anoda
common ragweed	Palmer pigweed	sunflower
eastern black	Pennsylvania	tall morningglory
nightshade	smartweed	velvetleaf
entireleaf	pitted morningglory	wild buckwheat
morningglory	prickly sida	wild poinsettia
field bindweed		

Grasses and sedges:

barnyardgrass	johnsongrass	sorghum almum
broadleaf signalgrass	large crabgrass	Texas panicum
fall panicum	red rice	wild proso millet
field sandbur	robust purple foxtail	witchgrass
giant foxtail	robust white foxtail	woolly cupgrass
goosegrass	shattercane	yellow foxtail
green foxtail	smooth crabgrass	yellow nutsedge

Remarks: Field corn (IMI-Corn only). Add surfactant and liquid fertilizer (fertilizer not required in Georgia, Louisiana, bootheel of Missouri, Tennessee, South Carolina). Make only one application per growing season. Soil insecticides (including labeled banded or in-furrow applications) may be used in combination with Lightning and Pioneer IMI hybrids. Do not use Counter 15G when Lightning will be applied to imidazolinone-tolerant corn hybrids. Products containing imazethapyr should not be applied to IMI-Corn the same year as Lightning. Only rotational crops harvested at maturity may be used for feed or food. Refer to label for restrictions and precautions.

Days To Harvest: Harvest/grazing/feeding—45.

Crop Rotation: IMI-Corn—anytime; rye, wheat—4 months; field corn, field corn grown for seed—8 1/2 months; alfalfa, barley, edible beans and peas, peanuts, soybeans, tobacco—9 1/2 months; cotton, lettuce, oats, popcorn, safflower, sorghum, sweet corn—18 months; potatoes—26 months; all other crops—40 months.

IMI-field corn resistant to imidazolinone herbicides • LL-field corn resistant to Liberty herbicide • RR-field corn resistant to Roundup Ultra • SR-field corn resistant to sethoxydim
◆-new product • PP-preplant • PPI-preplant incorporated • PRE-preemergence • POST-postemergence • SEQ-sequential • ae-acid equivalent • ai-active ingredient • DF-dry flowable
E/EC-emulsifiable concentrate • F/FL-flowable • DG/G/WG-dispersable granule • L/LC-liquid • SP/WSP-soluble packet • W/WP-wettable powder • WSB-water soluble bag

Tank Mixes: Atrazine, Basagran, Bicep, Buctril, Buctril + atrazine, dicamba, Dual, Frontier, FulTime, Guardsman, Harness, Harness Extra, Laddok S-12, Lasso, Marksman, Prowl, Shotgun, Surpass, Surpass 100, TopNotch, Tough.

State Restrictions: Not for use in California, New York.

- - - - - - - - - - - - - - -

Signal Word/Toxicity Class: Warning/II.
REI: 12 hr.

LINURON

Postemergence directed spray. Controls annual broadleaf as well as grass weeds.

■ **POST**
Lorox DF (Griffin)
Rate: 0.625-1.5 lb. ai/A
 1.25-3 lb. DF/A
Time: Postemergence. Make single application after corn is 15" high.

Weeds: Broadleaf weeds:

amsinckia	Florida beggarweed	prickly sida
annual morningglory	Florida purslane	purslane
buttonweed	groundsel	sesbania
carpetweed	knawel	sicklepod
cocklebur	lambsquarters	smartweed
common dayflower	mustard	teaweed
dogfennel	nettleleaf goosefoot	velvetleaf
fiddleneck	pigweed	wild buckwheat

Grasses:

annual ryegrass	crabgrass	goosegrass
barnyardgrass	fall panicum	rattail fescue
broadleaf signalgrass	foxtail	teaweed
canarygrass	giant foxtail	Texas panicum

Remarks: Field corn. Add surfactant. Do not spray over top of corn. Apply only when there is sufficient differential between height of corn and weeds. Early cultivation aids in achieving proper differential between height of corn and weeds.

Crop Rotation: Any crop may be planted after 4 months except for cereals where only barley, oats, rye, and wheat may be planted. West of the Rockies: carrots or celery may be planted 4 months after last application. Do not plant any other crop until 1 year after last application.

Tank Mixes: East of the Rockies: Alachlor, atrazine, Ramrod.

- - - - - - - - - - - - - - -

Signal Word/Toxicity Class: Caution.
REI: 24 hr.

Lorox — see linuron

Marksman — see dicamba & atrazine

S-METOLACHLOR

Dual is a cell growth inhibitor. S-metolachlor is a purified isomer of the metolachlor molecule. Primarily for control of annual grasses and helps control yellow nutsedge. Atrazine or Bladex frequently added for improved broadleaf weed control. Same chemical family as Lasso.

■ **PP, PPI, PRE, POST**
Dual MAGNUM or Dual II MAGNUM (EC) (Novartis)
Dual IIG MAGNUM (Novartis)
Rate: 1-2 pt. EC/A
 6-12 lb. IIG/A
Time: Preplant incorporated, preplant surface, preemergence, postemergence or layby (except IIG). For early preplant surface, apply as split application 30-45 days before planting; applications less than 30 days before planting may be either split or single treatment. Fall application in Illinois (north of Rt. 136), Iowa, Minnesota, Nebraska (north of Rt. 20), North Dakota, South Dakota, Wisconsin.

Weeds: Broadleaf weeds:

carpetweed	eclipta*	galinsoga
common purslane*	Florida beggarweed*	hairy nightshade*
common waterhemp	Florida pusley	pigweed
eastern black nightshade		tall waterhemp

Grasses and sedges:

barnyardgrass (watergrass)	green foxtail	southwestern cupgrass
bristly foxtail	johnsongrass (seedling)*	volunteer sorghum*
crabgrass	prairie cupgrass	wild proso millet* **
crowfootgrass	red rice	witchgrass
fall panicum	sandbur*	woolly cupgrass* **
foxtail millet	shattercane*	yellow foxtail
giant foxtail	signalgrass	yellow nutsedge
goosegrass		

*Suppression; ** Preemergence*

Remarks: Field, silage corn, popcorn. Rate varies by soil type and organic matter. Do not use on muck or peat soils. In case of crop failure, any crop on label may be replanted immediately. Do not make second broadcast application. If original application was banded and second crop is planted in untreated row middles, second banded treatment may be applied. Do not graze or feed forage from treated field for 30 days after application. Refer to label for use directions and restrictions.

Crop Rotation: Alfalfa—4 months; barley, oats, rye, wheat—4½ months; tomatoes—6 months; clover—9 months; any labeled crop in addition to barley, buckwheat, cabbage, milo, nuts, oats, peppers, rice, root crops, rye, stone fruits, tobacco, and wheat may be planted in the spring following treatment (including layby or multiple treatments applied previous season); all other rotational crops may be planted 12 months after application.

Tank Mixes: Atrazine, Balance, Banvel, Bladex, Extrazine II, Gramoxone Extra, linuron, Marksman, Prowl, Roundup Ultra, simazine.

State Restrictions: Do not use in Nassau County or Suffolk County, New York. Preplant surface: Medium- and fine-textured soils with minimum- or no-tillage systems in Colorado, Connecticut, Delaware, Illinois, Indiana, Iowa, Kansas, Kentucky, Maine, Maryland, Massachusetts, Michigan, Minnesota, Missouri, Montana, Nebraska, New Hampshire, New York, North Dakota, Ohio, Pennsylvania, Rhode Island, South Dakota, Tennessee, Virginia, West Virginia, Wisconsin, Wyoming.

- - - - - - - - - - - - - - -

Signal Word/Toxicity Class: Caution/III.
REI: 24 hr.

Micro-Tech — see alachlor

Moxy — see bromoxynil

Moxy + atrazine — see bromoxynil & atrazine

NORTHSTAR (Premix)

Premix designed for the Northern Corn Belt with 2 modes of actions for consistent control and to prevent/manage ALS and triazine resistance. Provides up to 3 weeks of residual control.

■ **POST**
◆ **NorthStar (WDG)** (39.9% dicamba & 7.5% primisulfuron-methyl & 28.5% prosulfuron) (Novartis)
Rate: 5 oz. WDG/A
Time: Postemergence. Field corn: Apply single application over-the-top, directed, or semi-directed when corn is between 4-20" tall. Do not apply to corn less than 4" tall. Seed corn and popcorn: Apply only directed or semi-directed to inbred lines and only use drop nozzles when popcorn or inbred lines are between 10-36" tall or 15 days before tassel emergence, whichever comes first. Popcorn and inbred lines should not be sprayed with over-the-top application.

Weeds: Broadleaf weeds:

alfalfa*	field bindweed	Pennsylvania smartweed
black nightshade	Florida beggarweed	pigweed
burcucumber	Florida pusley	poison ivy*
Canada thistle	giant ragweed	prickly sida
carpetweed	hairy nightshade	puncturevine
common cocklebur	hedge bindweed*	Russian thistle*
common lambsquarters	hemp dogbane*	sesbania
common purslane	horsenettle*	sicklepod
common ragweed	horseweed*	sunflower
common waterhemp	Jerusalem artichoke	tall waterhemp
cutleaf eveningprimrose	jimsonweed	velvetleaf
dandelion*	kochia	wild blackberry*
devilsclaw	ladysthumb	wild buckwheat
eastern black nightshade	marestail	wild mustard
	morningglory*	wild radish

NOTICE The information on these pages is for preliminary planning — not a guide for use. Be sure to follow the manufacturer's directions, notwithstanding information contained here. For personal protective equipment and EPA registration numbers, please turn to page 70.

Grasses and sedges:

annual ryegrass	quackgrass	sorghum-almum
fall panicum	sandbur*	volunteer sorghum
foxtail*	shattercane	yellow nutsedge*
johnsongrass		

Partial control

Remarks: Field corn (grain, seed, silage), popcorn. Do not use on sweet corn or ornamental (Indian) corn. Cultivation should be delayed until after corn is growing normally to avoid breakage. Test inbred lines for potential sensitivity before treating large acreages. If normal corn hybrid (not IMI) is planted and an organophosphate insecticide is applied at planting or before applying NorthStar, temporary crop injury may occur. Do not apply if crop was treated with Counter 15G or in-furrow with Counter CR. If IMI corn hybrid is planted, organophosphate insecticides (including Counter), can be applied at any time. Do not make foliar postemergence or soil application with an organophosphate insecticide within 10 days before or 7 days after application. Do not apply to corn under stress or make more than one application during cropping season. If applied on johnsongrass, aphids and other insects may transmit viral diseases to corn; virus-resistant corn hybrids or insect control may be necessary. Do not apply through any type of irrigation system. Certain crops are sensitive to NorthStar; refer to label for restrictions and use precautions.

Days To Harvest: Silage—45; grain—60; grazing/feeding—30.

Crop Rotation: IMI Corn—anytime; field corn—14 days; small grains (rye, winter barley, winter wheat)—3 months; alfalfa, beans (dry, green), cotton, peanuts, peas, popcorn, potatoes, sorghum, soybeans, spring-seeded small grains, sunflower, sweet corn, tobacco—8 months; all other crops—18 months. Refer to label for geographic restrictions and weather precautions.

Tank Mixes: Accent, atrazine, Resource, Tough. Do not tank mix with cyanazine.

- - - - - - - - - - - - - -

Signal Word/Toxicity Class: Caution.
REI: 12 hr.

Opti-Amine — see 2,4-D

OPTILL (Premix)

■ **PP, PPI, PRE, POST**

OpTill (5 lb./gal. dimethenamid & 1 lb./gal. dicamba) *(BASF)*
Rate: 24-38 fl. oz./A
Time: Preplant, preplant incorporated, preemergence, postemergence or split applications.

Weeds: Annual and perennial broadleaf weeds:

alfalfa*	field pennycress	red clover*
annual clover	giant ragweed	redroot pigweed
black nightshade	green smartweed	rough pigweed
buffaloweed	hemp dogbane*	Russian thistle
burcucumber	ivyleaf morningglory	sicklepod
California burclover	jimsonweed	smooth pigweed
carelessweed	knotweed	Spanishneedles
carpetweed	kochia	tall morningglory
common chickweed	ladysthumb	tansymustard
common cocklebur	lanceleaf ragweed	teaweed
common	marestail	tumble pigweed
lambsquarters	(horseweed)	velvetleaf
common mallow	Pennsylvania	Venice mallow
common purslane	smartweed	volunteer sunflower
common ragweed	pigweed	waterhemp
common spikeweed	prickly sida	wild buckwheat
common sunflower	prostrate pigweed	wild mustard
curly dock*	prostrate spurge	wild sunflower
field bindweed*	puncturevine	yellowtop

* *Suppression*

Annual grasses:

barnyardgrass	green foxtail	smooth crabgrass
broadleaf signalgrass	johnsongrass	southwestern
fall panicum	(seedling)	cupgrass
giant foxtail	large crabgrass	witchgrass
goosegrass	red rice	yellow foxtail

Sedges:

rice flatsedge	yellow nutsedge

Remarks: Field Corn. Rate varies by soil type and application timing. Do not apply to sand textured soil with less than 3% organic matter where depth to groundwater is 30 ft. or less. On soil greater than 8% organic matter, use highest rate. Do not exceed 38 fl. oz./A in 1 crop year. Do not apply through any type of irrigation system. Do not graze or feed livestock within 40 days of application. Refer to label for use directions, restrictions, and precautions.

Tank Mixes: Accent, atrazine, Banvel, Beacon, Bladex, Clarity, 2,4-D, Extrazine II, Gramoxone Extra, Marksman, Princep, Prowl, Pursuit, Roundup Ultra, Touchdown, Tough.

- - - - - - - - - - - - - -

Signal Word/Toxicity Class: Danger/I.
REI: 48 hr.

PARAQUAT

To "knock-down" existing foliage before crop emergence. Smartweed, giant ragweed, and fall panicum may not be controlled if more than 4-6" high. Nonselective, fast acting, contact action. Restricted Use Pesticide.

■ **PP, PRE, POST**

Gramoxone Extra (2.5L) *(ZENECA)*
Rate: 0.5-1 lb. ai/A
1.5-3 pt. 2.5L/A
Time: Preplant, preemergence.

Rate: 0.25-0.5 lb. ai/A
0.8-1.5 pt. 2.5L/A
Time: Postemergence-directed. Apply when corn is at least 10" high (plants shorter than 10" may be injured and not recover).
Weeds: Annual broadleaf weeds and grasses; top kill and suppression of perennials.
Remarks: Field corn, seed corn, popcorn. Add nonionic surfactant or crop oil concentrate. Seedbeds should be formed as far ahead of planting and treatment as possible to permit maximum weed and grass emergence. Seeding should be done with a minimum of soil disturbance. Refer to label for use directions, restrictions, and precautions.
Tank Mixes: Atrazine, Bladex, Canopy, Extrazine, Lariat, linuron, metribuzin, Princep.

- - - - - - - - - - - - - -

Rate: 0.5 lb. ai/A
1.5 pt. 2.5L/A
Time: Postemergence-directed. Spray in early July and repeat in early August if regrowth occurs.
Weeds:
witchgrass
Remarks: Field corn (grain, fodder, forage), popcorn. USDA Witchweed Eradication Program.

- - - - - - - - - - - - - -

Signal Word/Toxicity Class: Danger-Poison/I.
REI: 12 hr. (except harvest aid/desiccation 24 hr.).

Partner — see alachlor

PENDIMETHALIN

Member of dinitroaniline family of chemicals to which Treflan also belongs. Not for use on popcorn.

■ **PRE, POST**

Pentagon DG *(American Cyanamid)*
Prowl 3.3 EC *(American Cyanamid)*
Rate: 0.75-2 lb. ai/A
1.8-4.8 pt. 3.3 EC/A
1.25-3.3 lb. DG/A
Time: Preemergence, early postemergence.

Rate: Southern states:
0.5-1.5 lb. ai/A
1.2-3.6 pt. 3.3 EC/A
0.85-2.5 lb. DG/A
Northern states:
0.75-1.5 lb. ai/A
1.8-3.6 pt. 3.3 EC/A
1.25-2.5 lb. DG/A
Time: Postemergence incorporated (Culti-Spray application). Apply when corn is at least 4" tall up to lay-by. Do not apply preplant incorporated.

Weeds: Broadleaf Weeds:

annual spurge	lambsquarters	pigweed
carpetweed	Pennsylvania	purslane
Florida pusley	smartweed	velvetleaf
kochia		

Grasses:

barnyardgrass	goosegrass	signalgrass
crabgrass	green foxtail	Texas panicum
crowfootgrass	johnsongrass	wild proso millet
fall panicum	(seedling)	witchgrass
field sandbur	shattercane	woolly cupgrass
giant foxtail	(Culti-Spray only)	yellow foxtail

IMI-field corn resistant to imidazolinone herbicides • LL-field corn resistant to Liberty herbicide • RR-field corn resistant to Roundup Ultra • SR-field corn resistant to sethoxydim
◆-new product • PP-preplant • PPI-preplant incorporated • PRE-preemergence • POST-postemergence • SEQ-sequential • ae-acid equivalent • ai-active ingredient • DF-dry flowable
E/EC-emulsifiable concentrate • F/FL-flowable • DG/G/WG-dispersable granule • L/LC-liquid • SP/WSP-soluble packet • W/WP-wettable powder • WSB-water soluble bag

Remarks: Field corn. Conventional, minimum, or no-till. Plant corn at least 1¹/₂" deep. Seed must be completely covered with soil. Rate varies by soil type; do not exceed maximum labeled rate for any soil type. Do not use on peat or muck soils. Do not apply in liquid fertilizer for early postemergence application. If crop loss occurs due to weather conditions, corn or any crop registered for preplant incorporated use can be replanted the same year. If corn is replanted, seeding depth must be below retilled area. Do not feed forage or graze livestock for 21 days after Culti-Spray application. Do not feed forage or graze livestock for 75 days after planting wheat or barley in treated land.

Crop Rotation: Winter wheat and winter barley may be planted in the fall 4 months after application or 3 months after Culti-Spray application in irrigated field corn.Treated land may be planted to other crops the following year (see label for beet and spinach restrictions).

Tank Mixes: Accent SP, atrazine, Balance, Beacon, Bladex, Bicep, Bladex, Buctril + atrazine, Bullet, Dual, Frontier, Guardsman, Hornet, Laddok S-12, Lariat, Lasso, Marksman, Python, Surpass, Surpass 100.

State Restrictions: Do not apply no-till in California.

– – – – – – – – – – – – – – –

Signal Word/Toxicity Class: Caution.
REI: 24 hr.

Pentagon — see pendimethalin

Permit — see halosulfuron-methyl

Phenoxy 088 — see 2,4-D

Poast or Poast Plus — see sethoxydim

PRIMISULFURON-METHYL & PROSULFURON (Premixes)

Controls weeds by inhibiting a biochemical process which produces certain essential amino acids necessary for plant growth. The inhibited enzyme system is acetolactate synthase (ALS). Exceed CustomPak is a water-dispersible granule; each bag contains 5 water-soluble packets.

■ **POST**
Exceed (WDG) (28.5% primisulfuron-methyl & 28.5% prosulfuron) *(Novartis)*
◆ **Spirit (WDG) (42.8% primisulfuron-methyl & 14.2% prosulfuron)** *(Novartis)*
Rate: 1 oz. WDG/A
Time: Postemergence (over-the-top or directed). For Exceed, apply to corn between 4-30" in height. For Spirit, apply to corn between 4-24" in height.
Weeds: Broadleaf weeds:

black nightshade	field bindweed*	pitted morningglory*
buffalobur	Florida pusley	prickly sida*
burcucumber	giant ragweed	puncturevine
Canada thistle*	hedge bindweed	redroot pigweed
common cocklebur	hemp sesbania	shattercane
common	horsenettle*	sicklepod
lambsquarters	ivyleaf	smooth pigweed
common mallow*	morningglory*	sorghum-almum*
common pokeweed*	Jerusalem artichoke	spurred anoda
common ragweed	jimsonweed	tall morningglory*
common sunflower	kochia*	tall waterhemp
common waterhemp	marestail	velvetleaf
dandelion	Palmer amaranth	Venice mallow
devilsclaw	Pennsylvania	wild buckwheat
eastern black	smartweed	wild mustard
nightshade		

Grasses:

johnsongrass*	volunteer sorghum*	yellow foxtail*
quackgrass*		

*Partial control

Remarks: Field corn (grain, seed, silage), popcorn. Do not use on sweet corn or ornamental (Indian) corn. Test inbred lines for potential sensitivity before treating large acreages. If normal corn hybrid (not IMI) is planted and an organophosphate insecticide is applied at planting or before applying Exceed or Spirit, temporary crop injury may occur. Some weed species are known to be resistant to ALS-inhibiting herbicides. Where these ALS-resistant biotypes are known to exist, an appropriate registered herbicide with another

mode of action should be used alone or in tank mixture with Spirit or Exceed. Do not apply if crop was treated with Counter 15G or in-furrow with Counter CR. If IMI corn hybrid is planted, organophosphate insecticides (including Counter), can be applied at any time. Do not make foliar postemergence or soil application with an organophosphate insecticide within 10 days before or 7 days after application. Do not apply to corn under stress or make more than one application during cropping season. If applied on johnsongrass, aphids and other insects may transmit viral diseases to corn; virus-resistant corn hybrids or insect control may be necessary. Do not apply through any type of irrigation system. Refer to label for precautions and limitations.

Days To Harvest: Silage—40; grain—60; grazing/feeding—30.
Crop Rotation: Refer to label for rotational crop restrictions.
Tank Mixes: Do not tank mix with cyanazine, Poast, or Poast Plus. May be tank mixed with Accent, atrazine, Banvel/Clarity, Beacon, Buctril, 2,4-D, Marksman, or Tough.
State Restrictions: Do not apply Spirit by air in New York.

– – – – – – – – – – – – – – –

Signal Word/Toxicity Class: Caution.
REI: 12 hr.

Princep or Princep Caliber 90 — see simazine

Prowl — see pendimethalin

⬛ IMI PURSUIT

For use on field corn designated as IMI-resistant if applied postemergence. If applied postemergence to crops not designated as IMI-corn, severe crop damage will occur. For more information on IMI-corn, turn to page 85.

■ **PPI, PRE, POST**
Pursuit or Pursuit W (2AS or DG) (imazethapyr) *(American Cyanamid)*
Rate: 0.063 lb. ae/A
4 oz. 2AS/A
1.44 oz. DG/A (1 packet/2A)
Time: Early preplant, preplant incorporated, preemergence, postemergence. May be applied up to 45 days before planting.
Weeds: Broadleaf weeds:

barnyard sage	Florida pusley	pitted morningglory
black nightshade	galinsoga	prickly sida
Canada thistle	giant ragweed	prostrate spurge
carpetweed	hairy nightshade	puncturevine
cocklebur	ivyleaf morningglory	redroot pigweed
common cocklebur	Jerusalem artichoke	smallflower
common purslane	jimsonweed	morningglory
common ragweed	kochia	smooth pigweed
common sunflower	ladysthumb	spiny pigweed
eastern black	mustard	spotted spurge
nightshade	Palmer pigweed	tall morningglory
entireleaf	Pennsylvania	velvetleaf
morningglory	smartweed	wild poinsettia

Grasses and sedges:

barnyardgrass	green foxtail	shattercane
broadleaf signalgrass	johnsongrass	smooth crabgrass
fall panicum	large crabgrass	Texas panicum
giant foxtail	red rice	woolly cupgrass
giant green foxtail	robust purple foxtail	yellow foxtail
goosegrass	robust white foxtail	yellow nutsedge

Rate: North Dakota, north of Hwy 210 in Minnesota:
0.047 lb. ae/A
3 oz. 2AS/A (except Pursuit W)
1.08 oz. DG/A
Time: Postemergence.
Weeds: Broadleaf weeds:

black nightshade	hairy nightshade	redroot pigweed
eastern black	kochia	wild oat
nightshade	mustard	

Remarks: Field corn (IMI-Corn only). Do not use Counter 15G in-furrow with imidazolinone-resistant (IMI) corn hybrids. Refer to label for restrictions, precautions, and tank mix recommendations.
Days To Harvest: 45.
Crop Rotation: IMI-Corn, lima beans, peanuts, southern peas, soybeans—anytime; alfalfa, edible beans and peas (except lima beans, southern peas), rye, wheat—4 months; field corn, field corn grown for seed—8¹/₂ months (Pursuit W 9¹/₂ months); barley, tobacco—9¹/₂ months; cotton, lettuce, oats, popcorn, safflower, sorghum, sunflower, sweet corn—18 months; flax (Pursuit only), potatoes—26 months; all other crops—40 months after application.

State Restrictions: Pursuit for use in Colorado, New Mexico, North Dakota, Oklahoma, South Dakota, Texas, Wyoming (certain counties), and states east of these states; not for use in New York. Pursuit W for use in Arizona, Idaho, Montana, Nevada, Oregon, Utah, Washington, Wyoming (certain counties); not for use in California.

- - - - - - - - - - - - - - -

Signal Word/Toxicity Class: Warning/II (DG); Caution (2AS).
REI: Warning—12 hr.; Caution—4 hr.

IMI PURSUIT PLUS (Premix)

If applied postemergence, is for use on corn designated as IMI-resistant. If applied postemergence to crop not designated as IMI-corn, severe crop damage will occur. For more information on IMI-corn, turn to page 85.

■ PRE, POST

Pursuit Plus (EC) (0.2 lb./gal. imazethapyr & 2.7 lb./gal. pendimethalin) *(American Cyanamid)*

Rate: 0.9 lb. ae/A
2.5 pt. EC/A
Time: Preemergence, postemergence.
Weeds: Broadleaf weeds:

black nightshade	galinsoga	prickly sida
buffalobur*	giant ragweed*	prostrate spurge
carpetweed	hairy nightshade	puncturevine
common cocklebur	ivyleaf	redroot pigweed
common	morningglory*	smallflower
lambsquarters	jimsonweed	morningglory
common purslane	kochia	smooth pigweed
common ragweed*	ladysthumb	spiny pigweed
common sunflower	mustard	spotted spurge
eastern black	Palmer pigweed	tall morningglory*
nightshade	Pennsylvania	tall waterhemp
entireleaf	smartweed	velvetleaf
morningglory*	pitted morningglory*	Venice mallow*
Florida pusley		

Grasses and sedges:

barnyardgrass	goosegrass	shattercane
broadleaf signalgrass	green foxtail	smooth crabgrass
browntop panicum	itchgrass*	Texas panicum
crowfootgrass	johnsongrass	wild proso millet*
fall panicum	(rhizome*, seedling)	witchgrass
field sandbur	large crabgrass	woolly cupgrass
giant foxtail	robust purple foxtail	yellow foxtail
giant green foxtail	robust white foxtail	yellow nutsedge*

* Reduced competition

Remarks: Field corn (IMI-Corn only). Only rotational crops harvested at maturity may be used for feed or food.
Days To Harvest: Harvest/grazing/feeding—45.
Crop Rotation: Lima beans, peanuts, southern peas, soybeans—anytime; edible beans and peas (except lima beans, southern peas), wheat—4 months; field corn, field corn grown for seed—8 1/2 months; alfalfa, barley, rye, tobacco—9 1/2 months; cotton, lettuce, oats, popcorn, safflower, sorghum, sunflower, sweet corn—18 months; potatoes—26 months; all other crops—40 months after application. Some crops in certain areas have interval exceptions; refer to label.
Tank Mixes: May be tank mixed with other herbicides; refer to label for use directions and precautions.
State Restrictions: Not for use in North Dakota or north of Hwy 210 in Minnesota.

- - - - - - - - - - - - - - -

Signal Word/Toxicity Class: Caution/III.
REI: 12 hr.

PYTHON

Provides residual control of weeds that may emerge after application. May be applied with water, liquid fertilizer, or impregnated on dry bulk fertilizer. Absorption occurs through both shoot and root uptake.

■ POST

Python (WDG) (flumetsulam) *(Dow AgroSciences)*

Rate: 0.8-1.33 oz. WDG/A
Time: Soil application: preplant incorporated, preplant surface, postplant preemergence. Do not apply more than 30 days before planting.
Weeds: Broadleaf weeds:

carpetweed	common ragweed	horseweed
chickweed	Florida beggarweed	jimsonweed
common cocklebur	Florida pusley	ladysthumb
common	giant ragweed	morningglory
lambsquarters	goosefoot	nightshade
common purslane	henbit	nodding spurge

Weeds: Broadleaf weeds, continued:

Pennsylvania	Russian thistle	velvetleaf
smartweed	shepherdspurse	Venice mallow
pigweed	sicklepod	waterhemp
prickly sida	smooth pigweed	wild mustard
puncturevine	spotted spurge	wild poinsettia
redroot pigweed	spurred anoda	wild sunflower

*Suppression

Remarks: Do not apply to popcorn or sweet corn. Rate varies by weed species and soil texture. Not for use on peat or muck soils. Corn must be planted 1 1/2" deep. Do not apply by air or make more than one application per season. Do not graze or feed treated forage, hay, or straw to livestock. Do not apply through any type of chemigation system.
Days To Harvest: 85.
Crop Rotation: Corn, soybeans—0; alfalfa, barley, dry beans, oats, peanuts, rye, sweet potatoes, wheat—4 months; rice—6 months; popcorn, tobacco—9 months; grain sorghum, potatoes—12 months; cotton, sunflower, sweet corn—18 months; canola, sugar beets, all other crops—26 months plus successful field bioassay.
State Restrictions: Not for use in Nassau and Suffolk counties in New York.

- - - - - - - - - - - - - - -

Signal Word/Toxicity Class: Caution/III.
REI: 12 hr. unless soil injected or soil incorporated.

RAMROD

Same family of chemicals as Dual and Lasso. Primarily for control of annual grass weeds.

■ PRE

Ramrod 4L or 20G (propachlor) *(Monsanto)*

Rate: 4-6 lb. ai/A
4-6 qt. 4L/A
20-30 lb. 20G/A
Time: Preemergence.
Weeds: Broadleaf weeds:

carpetweed	ladysthumb	purslane
common ragweed*	lambsquarters*	smartweed*
Florida pusley	pigweed	wild buckwheat*
groundsel*		

Annual grasses:

annual ryegrass	crabgrass	goosegrass
barnyardgrass	fall panicum	green foxtail
broadleaf signalgrass*	giant foxtail	yellow foxtail

* Reduces competition

Remarks: Field, seed, silage corn. Works well in widely diverse climate. More effective in heavier soils. Can be used with nitrogen fertilizer solutions. Can be used with sprayable fluid fertilizers.

- - - - - - - - - - - - - - -

Signal Word/Toxicity Class: Danger/I.
REI: 48 hr.

RAMROD/ATRAZINE (Premix)

Good control of annual broadleaf and grass weeds with reduced carryover risk and good crop tolerance. Restricted Use Pesticide.

■ PRE

Ramrod/Atrazine 4L or DF (3 lb./gal. propachlor & 1 lb./gal. atrazine) *(Monsanto)*

Rate: 3.5-5.5 lb. ai/A
3-5.5 qt. 4L/A
5.5-8.6 lb. DF/A
Time: Preemergence.
Weeds: Broadleaf weeds:

annual	Florida pusley	mustard
morningglory*	groundsel	Pennsylvania
black nightshade	hairy nightshade	smartweed
buttonweed*	jimsonweed*	pigweed
carpetweed	kochia	purslane
cocklebur*	ladysthumb	velvetleaf *
common ragweed	lambsquarters	wild buckwheat

Grasses:

annual ryegrass	crabgrass	goosegrass
barnyardgrass	fall panicum	green foxtail
broadleaf signalgrass*	giant foxtail	yellow foxtail

* Reduces competition

Remarks: Field, seed, silage corn. Can be used with sprayable fluid fertilizers. Do not graze or feed forage, silage, or fodder from treated field to dairy animals.

IMI-field corn resistant to imidazolinone herbicides • LL-field corn resistant to Liberty herbicide • RR-field corn resistant to Roundup Ultra • SR-field corn resistant to sethoxydim
◆-new product • PP-preplant • PPI-preplant incorporated • PRE-preemergence • POST-postemergence • SEQ-sequential • ae-acid equivalent • ai-active ingredient • DF-dry flowable
E/EC-emulsifiable concentrate • F/FL-flowable • DG/G/WG-dispersable granule • L/LC-liquid • SP/WSP-soluble packet • W/WP-wettable powder • WSB-water soluble bag

Crop Rotation: Soybeans, sorghum, or corn can be planted the year following application. If other nonlabeled crops are planted the following year, there is a possibility of crop injury due to carryover of atrazine.

- - - - - - - - - - - - - - -

Signal Word/Toxicity Class: Danger/I (DF); Warning/II (4L).
REI: 48 hr.

Rattler — see glyphosate

IMI RESOLVE (Premix)

For use only on field corn designated as IMI-resistant. If used on corn not designated as IMI-corn, severe crop damage will occur. Resolve SG is a premix containing active ingredients of Pursuit and Banvel. For more information, turn to page 85.

■ POST
Resolve SG (0.158 lb. imazethapyr & 0.467 lb. dicamba)
(American Cyanamid)
Rate: 5.33 oz. SG/A (1 pkg./2.5A)
Time: Postemergence, apply before weeds exceed 3" tall and corn 12" tall.
Weeds: Broadleaf weeds:

alligatorweed	giant ragweed	prostrate spurge
barnyard sage	hairy nightshade	puncturevine
black nightshade	ivyleaf morningglory	redroot pigweed
bristly starbur	Jerusalem artichoke	Russian thistle
buffalobur	jimsonweed	sicklepod
Canada thistle	knotweed	smallflower
carpetweed	kochia	morningglory
common cocklebur	ladysthumb	smooth pigweed
common	marshelder	spiny pigweed
lambsquarters	mustard	spotted spurge
common purslane	Palmer pigweed	spurred anoda
common ragweed	palmleaf	sunflower
eastern black	morningglory	tall morningglory
nightshade	Pennsylvania	tall waterhemp
eclipta	smartweed	velvetleaf
entireleaf	pitted morningglory	Venice mallow
morningglory	prickly sida	wild buckwheat
Florida pusley	prostrate pigweed	wild poinsettia
galinsoga		

Grasses:

barnyardgrass	giant foxtail	red rice
broadleaf signalgrass	green foxtail	shattercane
crabgrass	johnsongrass	sorghum almum
fall panicum	(seedling)	yellow foxtail

Remarks: Field corn (IMI-Corn only). Addition of adjuvant and liquid fertilizer solution required. Soil insecticide may be used in combination with Resolve and Pioneer IMI hybrids. Do not use Counter 15G. Make only one application per growing season.
Days To Harvest: 45.
Crop Rotation: IMI-Corn—anytime; rye, wheat—4 months; field corn, field corn grown for seed—8½ months; alfalfa, barley, edible beans and peas, peanuts, soybeans, tobacco—9½ months; cotton, lettuce, oats, popcorn, safflower, sorghum, sweet corn—18 months; potatoes—26 months; sugar beets, table beets—40 months after application.
Tank Mixes: Accent, Dual, Frontier, Lasso, Prowl.
State Restrictions: Not for use in California, New York, North Dakota, or north of Hwy 210 in Minnesota.

- - - - - - - - - - - - - - -

Signal Word/Toxicity Class: Warning/II.
REI: 12 hr.

RESOURCE

Resource 80WP is packaged in water soluble bags. Because of its outstanding velvetleaf control and mode of action, Resource 80WP fits well with conventional corn or transgenic (HTC) hybrids such as IMI corn, Roundup Ready corn, and Liberty Link corn. Rainfast within 1 hr. Toxic to shrimp.

■ POST
◆ Resource 80WP (WSB) (flumiclorac pentyl) *(Valent)*
Rate: 0.054 lb. ai/A
1.08 oz. 80WP/A (6A/WSB)
Time: Postemergence. Apply from 2-leaf through 10-leaf stage.
Weeds: Broadleaf:
velvetleaf
Remarks: Field corn. Additive such as crop oil concentrate, methylated seed oil, or nonionic surfactant must be added. Do not make more than 2 applications/A per season. Do not graze animals on green forage or use as feed less than 28 days after application. Do not apply through

any type of irrigation system. Refer to label for use directions, restrictions, and precautions.
Tank Mixes: Accent, atrazine, Banvel, Beacon, Buctril, Clarity, 2,4-D, Exceed, glyphosate (use only on varieties designated as Roundup Ready), Hornet, Laddok S-12, Liberty (use only on varieties designated as Liberty Link), Lightning, Pursuit (use only on varieties designated as IMI-Corn), Marksman, NorthStar, Permit, Spirit, Stinger.

- - - - - - - - - - - - - - -

Signal Word/Toxicity Class: Caution.
REI: 12 hr.

■ POST
Resource (0.86EC) (flumiclorac pentyl) *(Valent)*
Rate: 0.027-0.054 lb. ai/A
4-8 fl. oz. 0.86EC/A
Time: Postemergence. Apply from 2-leaf through 10-leaf stage. Determine leaf stage by counting only those leaves with visible leaf collars.
Weeds: Broadleaf:

common lambsquarters	morningglory	prickly sida
common ragweed	Palmer amaranth	spotted spurge
jimsonweed	pigweed	velvetleaf

Remarks: Field corn. Rate varies by weed stage. Add crop oil concentrate at 1 pt./A broadcast; 2 pt./A for drop-nozzle application. Do not apply more than 6 fl. oz./A per application for over-the-top; 8 fl. oz./A per application for directed spray using drop nozzle. Do not apply more than 8 fl. oz./A per growing season. Do not apply under stress conditions or if rainfall is expected in 1 hour. Do not graze animals on green forage or use as feed less than 28 days after application.
Tank Mixes: Accent, atrazine, Banvel, Beacon, Clarity, 2,4-D, Exceed, Spirit, and other broadleaf herbicides.

- - - - - - - - - - - - - - -

Signal Word/Toxicity Class: Warning/II.
REI: 12 hr.

SR REZULT (Co-Pack)

For use only on corn designated as SR-corn. If applied to crop not designated as SR, severe crop damage will occur. Rezult A must be used in combination with Rezult B. Rezult can only be used with the closed Prodigy System in which it comes packaged. The Prodigy System will discharge Result A and Rezult B in a 1:1 ratio; return for cleaning and refilling. For more information on SR corn, turn to page 86.

■ POST
◆ Rezult A (1 lb./gal. sethoxydim) & Rezult B (5 lb./gal. bentazone)
(BASF)
Rate: 3.2 pt. product/A
Time: Postemergence. Apply when weeds are small and actively growing and soybeans are in the 1st to 3rd trifoliate leaf stage.
Weeds: Broadleaf weeds:

balloonvine	giant ragweed	smooth pigweed
beggarticks	jimsonweed	spurred anoda
bristly starbur	ladysthumb	tropic croton
Canada thistle*	marshelder	velvetleaf
cocklebur	Pennsylvania	Venice mallow
common	smartweed	wild buckwheat
lambsquarters	prickly sida	wild mustard
common purslane	(teaweed)	wild sunflower
common ragweed	redweed	wild poinsettia
dayflower	shepherdspurse	

Grasses and sedges:

annual ryegrass	johnsongrass	volunteer corn
barnyardgrass	(rhizome*, seedling)	wild oat
broadleaf signalgrass	junglerice	wild proso millet
browntop panicum	large crabgrass	wirestem muhly*
fall panicum	quackgrass*	witchgrass
giant foxtail	red sprangletop	woolly cupgrass
goosegrass	shattercane	yellow foxtail
green foxtail	smooth crabgrass	yellow nutsedge
	Texas panicum	

* Top growth suppression of perennials

Remarks: SR sethoxydim-resistant field corn. Add 2.5 gal. UAN solution/100 gal. water. Do not graze treated fields or feed treated forage to livestock. Do not apply through any type of irrigation system. Refer to label for use directions, restrictions, and precautions.
Days to Harvest: 75; grazing/cutting for hay—30.
Tank Mixes: Atrazine, Banvel, Clarity, 2,4-D.
State Restrictions: Not for use in California.

- - - - - - - - - - - - - - -

Signal Word/Toxicity Class: Caution/III.
REI: 48 hr.

NOTICE The information on these pages is for preliminary planning — not a guide for use. Be sure to follow the manufacturer's directions, notwithstanding information contained here. For personal protective equipment and EPA registration numbers, please turn to page 70.

RIMSULFURON

■ **PRE**

◆ **DPX-E9636 (25DF)** *(DuPont)*

Rate: 1.5-2 oz. 25DF/A

Time: Preemergence. Apply up to 14 days before planting. Do not apply to emerged or cracking corn.

Weeds: Broadleaf weeds:

lambsquarters*	redroot pigweed*	smooth pigweed*

Annual grasses:

barnyardgrass	green foxtail	yellow foxtail
giant foxtail		

* includes triazine-resistant weeds.

Remarks: Field corn. Not for use on popcorn, seed corn, or sweet corn. Rates vary by soil texture and organic matter. For use only on field corn hybrids of less than 88 day RM (relative maturity). Do not apply by air. Do not apply more than 2 oz./A per season. Do not graze, feed forage, grain or fodder (stover) from treated areas to livestock within 30 days of application. Do not apply through any type of irrigation system. Refer to label for use directions, precautions, and restrictions.

Crop Rotation: Field corn, potatoes—anytime; tomatoes—1 month; winter wheat—4 months; popcorn, dry beans, snap beans, sunflower, sweet corn—10 months; all other crops—18 months.

Tank Mixes: Atrazine. Do not tank mix with products containing cyanazine or flumetsulam.

- - - - - - - - - - - - - - - - - -

Signal Word/Toxicity Class: Caution.
REI: 4 hr.

Roundup — see glyphosate

RR **Roundup Ultra — see glyphosate**

Saber — see 2,4-D

Salvo — see 2,4-D

Savage — see 2,4-D

SCORPION (Premix)

Selective herbicide for broadleaf weed control. Absorption occurs through both foliage and root uptake.

■ **POST**

Scorpion III (25% clopyralid & 9.3% flumetsulam & 50% 2,4-D) *(Dow AgroSciences)*

Rate: 0.25 lb./A

Time: Postemergence. Apply to corn up to 8" tall; weeds at 2-4 true leaf stage.

Weeds: Broadleaf weeds:

black nightshade	jimsonweed	smartweed
chickweed	kochia	smooth pigweed
common cocklebur	morningglory	spotted spurge
common	nodding spurge	spurred anoda
lambsquarters	Palmer amaranth	tall waterhemp
common purslane	prickly sida	velvetleaf
common ragweed	prostrate spurge	Venice mallow
common sunflower	redroot pigweed	wild buckwheat
Florida beggarweed	Russian thistle	wild mustard
giant ragweed	sicklepod	wild poinsettia

Remarks: Field corn. Do not apply to field corn grown for seed, sweet corn, or popcorn. Add surfactant. Refer to label for restrictions and precautions.

Days To Harvest: 85.

Crop Rotation: Barley, oats, rye, wheat—4 months; rice—6 months; alfalfa, dry beans, soybeans, sweet corn, popcorn—10 1/2 months; grain sorghum—12 months; cotton, peanuts, peas, sunflower—18 months; sugar beets, canola, and all other crops—26 months and successful field bioassay.

Tank Mixes: May be tank mixed with registered postemergence herbicides.

- - - - - - - - - - - - - - - - - -

Signal Word/Toxicity Class: Danger/I.
REI: 48 hr.

SCYTHE

◆ **Scythe (pelargonic acid)** *(Mycogen)*

Rate: 4-13 fl. oz./1 gal. spray solution

Time: Apply to actively growing weeds prior to crop emergence.

Weeds: Annual and perennial broadleaf weeds and grasses.

Remarks: Apply in minimum 75 gal. spray solution/A or spray-to-wet. Do not apply by air or through any type of irrigation system. Refer to label for directions and precautions.

Tank Mixes: Glyphosate and other foliar and residual herbicides.

- - - - - - - - - - - - - - - - - -

Signal Word/Toxicity Class: Warning/II.
REI: 24 hr.

SENCOR

Sencor is a photosynthetic inhibitor. Selective herbicide with activity on several broadleaf weeds. Must be tank mixed. Not for use on seed corn, popcorn, white corn, or sweet corn.

■ **POST**

Sencor 4 (FL) or DF (metribuzin) *(Bayer)*

Rate: 1.2-2.25 oz. ai/A
      2.4-4.5 fl. oz. FL/A
      1.6-3 oz. DF/A

Time: Postemergence. Apply after crop emergence until just before tasseling.

Weeds: Broadleaf weeds:

black nightshade	Florida pusley	poorjoe
buffalobur	giant ragweed	prickly lettuce
burcucumber	henbit	prickly sida
carpetweed	horseweed	redroot pigweed
common cocklebur	ivyleaf morningglory	Russian thistle
common	jimsonweed	sicklepod
lambsquarters	knotweed	smooth pigweed
common purslane	kochia	tall morningglory
common ragweed	ladysthumb	tall waterhemp
common sunflower	marestail	tansymustard
eastern black	Palmer amaranth	velvetleaf
nightshade	Pennsylvania	Venice mallow
eclipta	smartweed	wild buckwheat
entireleaf morningglory	pitted morningglory	wild mustard

Remarks: Field corn only. Do not use crop oil concentrate or any adjuvant containing vegetable or petroleum oil. Refer to label for use directions, restrictions, and precautions.

Crop Rotation: Alfalfa, asparagus, barley/wheat (following peas, lentils, soybeans), corn, forage grass, potatoes, sainfoin, soybeans, sugarcane, tomatoes—4 months; barley, cotton, lentils, peas, rice, wheat, peanuts—8 months; all other crops (except root crops)—12 months; onions, sugar beets, and other root crops—18 months. Cover crops for soil building or erosion control may be planted anytime, but do not graze or harvest for food or feed. Stand reductions may occur in some areas.

Tank Mixes: May be tank mixed with certain broadleaf herbicides registered for postemergence use.

- - - - - - - - - - - - - - - - - -

Signal Word/Toxicity Class: Caution/III.
REI: 12 hr.

SR **SETHOXYDIM**

*Postemergence grass herbicide with activity on several annual and certain perennial grasses. Does not control broadleaf weeds. For use on Poast Protected field corn only. Always add spray adjuvant. **For more information on SR-corn, turn to page 86.***

For more information on SR-corn, turn to page 86.

■ **POST**

Poast (1.5EC) or Poast Plus (1EC) *(BASF)*

Rate: 0.09-0.28 lb. ai/A
      0.5-1.5 pt. 1.5EC/A
      0.75-2.25 pt. 1EC/A

Time: Postemergence.

Weeds: Annual and perennial grasses:

annual ryegrass	junglerice	stinkgrass
barnyardgrass	large crabgrass	tall fescue
bermudagrass	lovegrass	Texas panicum
broadleaf signalgrass	orchardgrass	volunteer cereals
browntop panicum	(seedling)	wild oat
fall panicum	perennial ryegrass	wild proso millet
field sandbur	quackgrass	wildcane
giant foxtail	red rice	wirestem muhly
goosegrass	red sprangletop	witchgrass
green foxtail	shattercane	woolly cupgrass
itchgrass	smooth crabgrass	yellow foxtail
johnsongrass	southwestern cupgrass	

IMI-field corn resistant to imidazolinone herbicides • LL-field corn resistant to Liberty herbicide • RR-field corn resistant to Roundup Ultra • SR-field corn resistant to sethoxydim
◆-new product • PP-preplant • PPI-preplant incorporated • PRE-preemergence • POST-postemergence • SEQ-sequential • ae-acid equivalent • ai-active ingredient • DF-dry flowable
E/EC-emulsifiable concentrate • F/FL-flowable • DG/G/WG-dispersable granule • L/LC-liquid • SP/WSP-soluble packet • W/WP-wettable powder • WSB-water soluble bag

Remarks: Field corn (Poast Protected hybrids only). Rate depends on growing region. Add spray adjuvant or oil concentrate. Urea ammonium-nitrate solution (UAN) or ammonium sulfate (AMS) recommended to enhance activity on certain grass species. Do not apply through any type of irrigation system. Refer to label for restrictions and limitations.
Days to Harvest: Grain/fodder—60; forage/silage—45.
Tank Mixes: Poast: Atrazine, Banvel, Basagran, Clarity, 2,4-D, Dual, Frontier, Guardsman, Harness, Laddok S-12, Marksman, Surpass. Poast Plus: Atrazine, Basagran, 2,4-D, Laddok S-12.
State Restrictions: Do not use UAN or AMS in California or Pacific Northwest.

– – – – – – – – – – – – – – – –

Signal Word/Toxicity Class: Warning/II (Poast); Caution/III (Poast Plus).
REI: 12 hr.

SHOTGUN (Premix)

Restricted Use Pesticide due to ground and surface water concerns. Toxic to aquatic invertebrates.

■ PP, PRE, POST
Shotgun (FL) (2.25 lb./gal. atrazine & 1 lb./gal. 2,4-D) *(Platte)*
Rate: 0.563-0.844 lb. ai atrazine/A
0.25-0.375 lb. ae 2,4-D/A
2-3 pt. FL/A
Time: Preplant, preemergence, postemergence. For postemergence, apply from spike to 4-leaf or up to 8" in height; use drop nozzles for later applications up to limit of 12".
Weeds: Broadleaf weeds:

black nightshade	fanweed	sowthistle
buffalobur	giant ragweed	spanishneedles
cocklebur	ivyleaf	sunflower
common	morningglory	tall morningglory
lambsquarters	jimsonweed	velvetleaf
common ragweed	mustard	Venice mallow
common waterhemp	Pennsylvania	vetch
dandelion	smartweed	wild buckwheat
dock	pennycress	wild lettuce
eastern black	redroot pigweed	wild mustard
nightshade		

Grasses (suppression):

downy brome	large crabgrass	witchgrass
green foxtail	wild oat	yellow foxtail
hairy crabgrass		

Remarks: Field corn. Rate varies by soil texture and organic matter (maximum rate 1.6 lb. ai/A applied prior to crop emergence for highly erodible soil with less than 30% plant residue cover). Do not apply more than 2.5 lb. ai/A per year of atrazine. Several states have maximum rates and other limitations that are more restrictive than the product label. Preplant and preemergence applications are surface applications.
Crop Rotation: If applied after June 10 or in the High Plains/Intermountain West, only corn or sorghum can be planted the following year. Do not plant sugar beets, tobacco, vegetables (including dry beans), spring-seeded small grains or small-seeded legumes, soybeans (certain areas of Iowa, Kansas, Minnesota, Nebraska, North Dakota, South Dakota), and grasses the year following application.

– – – – – – – – – – – – – – – –

Signal Word/Toxicity Class: Danger/I.
REI: 12 hr.

SIMAZAT (Premix)

Restricted Use Pesticide.

■ PP, PRE, POST
Simazat 4L (2 lb./gal. simazine & 2 lb./gal. atrazine) *(Drexel)*
Rate: 2-3 lb. ai/A
4-6 pt. 4L/A
Time: Preplant, preemergence, postemergence.
Weeds: Most annual broadleaf weeds and grasses.
Remarks: Field corn. Rate varies by soil type. Do not graze treated area or feed treated forage to livestock for 21 days following application.
Crop Rotation: Do not plant treated areas to any crop except corn and sorghum until following year. Refer to label for additional restrictions.

– – – – – – – – – – – – – – – –

Rate: 1.2 lb. ai/A
2.4 pt. 4L/A
Time: Preplant, preemergence.
Weeds: Broadleaf weeds:

kochia	nightshade	purslane
lambsquarters	pigweed	

Remarks: Field corn. Refer to label for directions and precautions.
Crop Rotation: Same restrictions as above.

State Restrictions: For use in western Kansas and Nebraska, New Mexico, Panhandle of Oklahoma, west Texas, and eastern Wyoming on sands, loamy sands, sandy loams, mild to strongly alkaline soils, and all recently leveled soils.

– – – – – – – – – – – – – – – –

Signal Word/Toxicity Class: Caution.

SIMAZINE

Controls fall panicum and crabgrass better than atrazine, less effective for cocklebur, velvetleaf, and yellow nutsedge. Less soluble and more persistent than atrazine. Belongs to triazine family of chemicals.

■ PP, PRE
◆ **Clean Crop Simazine 4L or 90WDG** *(Platte)*
Drexel Simazine 4L or 90DF *(Drexel)*
Princep 4L or Princep Caliber 90 *(Novartis)*
Riverside Simazine 4L or 90DF *(Terra)*
Rate: 2-4 lb. ai/A
4-8 pt. 4L, 90DF/A
2.2-4.4 lb. 90/A
Quackgrass:
3-4 lb. ai/A
6-8 pt. 4L, 90DF/A
3.3-4.4 lb. 90/A
Time: Preplant, preemergence. For quackgrass, apply in fall.
Weeds: Annual broadleaf weeds:

annual morningglory	flora's paintbrush	ragweed
burclover	Florida pusley	redmaids rockpurslane
carelessweed	German moss	Russian thistle
carpetweed	groundsel	shepherdspurse
common chickweed	henbit	smartweed
common	knawel	spanishneedles
lambsquarters	nightshade	speedwell
common purslane	pepperweed	tansymustard
fiddleneck	pigweed	wild mustard
filaree	pineappleweed	yellowflower
fireweed	prickly lettuce	pepperweed

Grasses:

annual bluegrass	fall panicum	signalgrass
annual ryegrass	foxtail	silver hairgrass
barnyardgrass	goosegrass	watergrass
cheatgrass	junglerice	wild oat
crabgrass	rattail fescue	witchgrass
downy brome		

Remarks: Field, silage corn. Do not graze treated areas.
Crop Rotation: Do not plant any crop except corn in the spring following treatment. Do not plant sugar beets, tobacco, vegetables, spring-seeded small grains, or small-seeded legumes and grasses the year following application.
Tank Mixes: Eradicane, Sutan+.

– – – – – – – – – – – – – – – –

Signal Word/Toxicity Class: Caution/III.
REI: 12 hr.

Solution — see 2,4-D

Solve — see 2,4-D

Spirit — see primisulfuron-methyl & prosulfuron

Sterling — see dicamba

Sterling Plus — see dicamba & atrazine

Stinger — see clopyralid

SUREFIRE (Premix)
Restricted Use Pesticide.

■ PP, PRE
◆ **Surefire (29.4% paraquat & 10.6% diuron)** *(Platte)*

NOTICE	The information on these pages is for preliminary planning — not a guide for use. Be sure to follow the manufacturer's directions, notwithstanding information contained here.	For personal protective equipment and EPA registration numbers, please turn to page 70.

Rate: 0.8-1.6 lb. ai/A
    2-4 pt./A
Time: Apply to young, succulent weeds 1-6" high prior to, during or after planting, but before crop emergence.
Weeds: Annual broadleaf weeds and grasses; top-kill and suppression of perennial weeds.
Remarks: Always use nonionic surfactant. Do not apply through any type of irrigation system. Do not apply to soils lacking clay minerals. Seeding should be done with a minimum amount of soil disturbance. Corn emerged at time of treatment will be killed. Refer to label for directions and precautions.
Tank Mixes: AAtrex, Banvel, Bladex, 2,4-D, Glean, Kerb.

- - - - - - - - - - - - - - - -

Signal Word/Toxicity Class: Danger/I.
REI: 12 hr.

Surpass — see acetochlor

SURPASS 100 (Premix)

Contains safener dichlormid. Restricted Use Pesticide.

■ PP, PPI, PRE, POST
Surpass 100 (3 lb./gal. acetochlor & 2 lb./gal. atrazine) *(ZENECA)*
Rate: 2.5-5 lb. ai/A
    4-8 pt./A
Time: Early preplant, preplant incorporated, preemergence, early post-emergence (up to 11" tall).
Weeds: Broadleaf weeds:

black nightshade	galinsoga	prickly sida
carpetweed	giant ragweed	redroot pigweed
cocklebur	hairy nightshade	sicklepod
common purslane	jimsonweed	smartweed
common ragweed	kochia	tall waterhemp
Florida beggarweed	lambsquarters	velvetleaf
Florida pusley	morningglory	

Grasses and sedges:

barnyardgrass	goosegrass	southwestern
broadleaf signalgrass	green foxtail	cupgrass
browntop panicum	johnsongrass	Texas panicum
crabgrass	(seedling)	wild proso millet
crowfootgrass	red rice	witchgrass
fall panicum	red sprangletop	woolly cupgrass
field sandbur	robust foxtail	yellow foxtail
foxtail millet	shattercane	yellow nutsedge
giant foxtail		

Remarks: Conventional, reduced, or no-till systems. Do not apply after June 10, unless only corn will be planted the following year. Do not apply through any type of irrigation system. Refer to label for use directions, restrictions, and precautions.
Crop Rotation: Corn, sorghum, soybeans, or tobacco may be planted the spring following application. Wheat may be planted 15 months after application. Do not rotate to crops other than corn, sorghum, soybeans, tobacco or wheat.
Tank Mixes: Accent, atrazine, Banvel/Clarity, Basis, Basis Gold, Beacon, Bladex, Buctril, 2,4-D, Eradicane, Extrazine II, Gramoxone Extra, Liberty, Lightning, Lorox, Marksman, Poast, Poast Plus, Princep, Prowl, Pursuit, Resource, Shotgun, Surpass EC, Sutan+, Touchdown, Warrior.

- - - - - - - - - - - - - - - -

Signal Word/Toxicity Class: Danger/I.
REI: 12 hr.

SUTAN+

Commonly used in combination with a triazine herbicide to improve broadleaf weed control. Contains a safening agent.

■ PPI
Sutan+ 6.7-E (butylate) *(Micro Flo)*
Rate: 4-6 lb. ai/A
    4.75-7.33 pt. 6.7E/A
Time: Preplant incorporated.
Weeds: Annual grasses and sedges:

barnyardgrass	fall panicum	purple nutsedge
(watergrass)	field sandbur	shattercane
bermudagrass	giant foxtail	Texas panicum
buffalograss	goosegrass	volunteer sorghum
coloradograss	green foxtail	yellow foxtail
crabgrass	johnsongrass	yellow nutsedge

Remarks: Field, silage, popcorn, production seed corn. Not for use on seed stock, such as Breeders, Foundation, or Increase. For use on mineral soils or those soils containing less than 10% organic matter. Must be mixed into soil thoroughly. In Southeastern U.S. for silage corn, do not plant small-seeded grains until September after corn harvest.

Tank Mixes: Atrazine, Bladex, Princep.
State Restrictions: Not for use in the 10 southernmost California counties except Kern (in Kern county, use only on field and silage corn). In Arizona, use only on field and silage corn at elevation of 2500 ft. or higher.

- - - - - - - - - - - - - - - -

Signal Word/Toxicity Class: Caution/III.
REI: 12 hr.

TopNotch — see acetochlor

RR TOUCHDOWN

Has been licensed for over-the-top postemergence use on Roundup Ready corn. For more information on Roundup Ready corn turn to page 87.

■ PP, PRE, POST
Touchdown (5L or 6L) (sulfosate) *(ZENECA)*
Rate: 0.5-4 lb. ai/A
    0.8-6.4 pt. 5L/A
    0.66-5.33 pt. 6L/A
Time: Preplant, preemergence, postemergence.
Weeds: Broadleaf weeds:

alfalfa	dogfennel	marestail
annual sowthistle	fiddleneck	morningglory
annual spurge	field bindweed	mouseear chickweed
black nightshade	field pennycress	mustard
brackenfern	field sandbur	Pennsylvania
Canada thistle	filaree	smartweed
Carolina geranium	fleabane	prickly lettuce
common chickweed	Florida pusley	red clover
common cocklebur	giant ragweed	redroot pigweed
common groundsel	groundcherry	Russian thistle
common	hemp dogbane	shepherdspurse
lambsquarters	henbit	sicklepod
common milkweed	honeyvine milkweed	smooth pigweed
common ragweed	hophornbeam	spanishneedles
common sunflower	copperleaf	swamp smartweed
curly dock	horsenettle	teaweed
cutleaf	Jerusalem artichoke*	velvetleaf
eveningprimrose	kochia	Virginia creeper
dandelion	little barley	white clover
dayflower*	London rocket	wild buckwheat

Grasses and sedges:

annual bluegrass	goosegrass	smooth bromegrass
bahiagrass	guineagrass	sprangletop
barley	Italian ryegrass	stinkgrass
barnyardgrass	johnsongrass	tall fescue
bermudagrass	(seedling)	Texas panicum
broadleaf signalgrass	Kentucky bluegrass	timothy
bulbous bluegrass	orchardgrass	torpedograss*
cheat	paragrass	vaseygrass
cogongrass*	perennial ryegrass	western wheatgrass
crabgrass	purple nutsedge	wild oat
crowfootgrass	quackgrass	wirestem muhly
downy brome	red rice	witchgrass
fall panicum	reed canarygrass	woolly cupgrass
fescue	shattercane	yellow nutsedge
foxtail		

* Partial control

Remarks: Field corn, seed corn, popcorn. Minimum and no-till systems. Add nonionic surfactant or wetting agent. In addition, ammonium sulfate can be added. Can be applied as spot spray. Do not graze or harvest treated cover crops for feed. Do not apply through any type of irrigation system. Refer to label for use directions, restrictions, and precautions.

Days To Harvest: Grain/fodder—90.

Crop Rotation: Plantback time—35 days.

Tank Mixes: Ambush, atrazine, Banvel, Basis, Bicep, Bladex, Bullet, Clarity, 2,4-D, Dual, Extrazine II, Frontier, FulTime, Guardsman, Harness, Harness Xtra, Hornet, Lariat, Lasso, Lightning, linuron, Marksman, Micro-Tech, Prowl, simazine, Surpass, Surpass 100, TopNotch, Warrior.

State Restrictions: Ammonium sulfate (6L) not for use in California.

- - - - - - - - - - - - - - - -

Signal Word/Toxicity Class: Caution.
REI: 12 hr. (5L); 4 hr. (6L).

IMI-field corn resistant to imidazolinone herbicides • LL-field corn resistant to Liberty herbicide • RR-field corn resistant to Roundup Ultra • SR-field corn resistant to sethoxydim
◆-new product • PP-preplant • PPI-preplant incorporated • PRE-preemergence • POST-postemergence • SEQ-sequential • ae-acid equivalent • ai-active ingredient • DF-dry flowable
E/EC-emulsifiable concentrate • F/FL-flowable • DG/G/WG-dispersable granule • L/LC-liquid • SP/WSP-soluble packet • W/WP-wettable powder • WSB-water soluble bag

TOUGH

For broadleaf weed control, combinations with a triazine may allow reduced triazine rates as well as broadening spectrum of control. Grass weeds can be controlled with earlier soil-applied treatment or approved tank mixes.

■ **POST**

Tough (5EC) (pyridate) *(Novartis)*

Rate: 0.47-0.94 lb. ai/A
12-24 oz. 5EC/A

Time: Postemergence. Apply when weeds are in 2-4 true leaf stage.

Weeds: Broadleaf weeds and sedges:

amaranth	Florida beggarweed	nutsedge
common cocklebur	jimsonweed	(partial control)
common	kochia	pigweed
lambsquarters	nightshade	Russian thistle
eclipta		sunflower

Remarks: Field corn, popcorn, seed corn. Not for use on sweet corn. Will burn back top growth of nutsedge; regrowth may occur. Verify selectivity with seed company prior to applying to inbred line or variety of seed corn. Refer to label for specific instructions.

Days To Harvest: 68.

Tank Mixes: Accent, atrazine, Banvel, Beacon, Clarity, Exceed, North-Star, Spirit.

State Restrictions: Not registered in California.

- - - - - - - - - - - - - - - -

Signal Word/Toxicity Class: Warning/II.
REI: 12 hr.

Treflan — see trifluralin

Trific — see trifluralin

TRIFLURALIN

Postemergence incorporated soil-applied corn herbicide. Will help control late-emerging grasses.

■ **POST**

Albaugh Trifluralin 4EC *(Albaugh)*
◆ **Clean Crop Trifluralin HF (4EC)** *(Platte)*
Gowan Trifluralin 4 or 5 (EC) *(Gowan)*
Helena Trifluralin 4 EC *(Helena)*
Riverside Trifluralin 4EC or Trific 60DF *(Terra)*
◆ **Sedagri Trifluralin 480 (4EC)** *(Rhone-Poulenc)*
Treflan HFP (4EC) or TR-10 (10G) *(Dow AgroSciences)*
Trilin 4 or 5 (EC) or 10G *(Griffin)*
Wilbur-Ellis Trifluralin 10G *(Wilbur-Ellis)*

Rate: 0.375-1 lb. ai/A
0.75-2 pt. 4EC/A
0.6-1.6 pt. 5EC/A
0.625-1.66 lb. 60DF/A
3.75-10 lb. 10G/A

Time: Postemergence. Apply when corn is well established (2 true leaf stage or taller). Do not apply preplant or preemergence. Do not apply after corn is 30" tall.

Weeds: Broadleaf weeds:

carelessweed	knotweed	purslane
carpetweed	kochia	pusley
chickweed	lambsquarters	redroot pigweed
field bindweed	Mexican clover	rough pigweed
fireweed	Mexican fireweed	Russian thistle
Florida purslane	prostrate pigweed	spiny pigweed
Florida pusley	puncturevine	stinging nettle
goosefoot	(western U.S.)	tumbleweed
henbit		

Grasses:

annual bluegrass	fall panicum	sandbur
barnyardgrass	foxtail millet	shattercane
bottlegrass	giant foxtail	smooth crabgrass
brachiaria	green foxtail	sprangletop
bristlegrass	Italian ryegrass	stinkgrass
bromegrass	johnsongrass	Texas panicum
burgrass	(seedling)	watergrass
cheat	junglerice	wildcane
cheatgrass	large crabgrass	woolly cupgrass
chess	pigeongrass	yellow foxtail
downy brome	robust foxtail	

Remarks: Field corn. Do not apply to popcorn or corn grown for seed. Rate depends on soil type. Apply as over-the-top or directed spray.

Days To Harvest: Harvest/forage/fodder/silage—6 weeks.

Crop Rotation: Refer to label.

State Restrictions: For Alabama, Florida, Georgia, North Carolina, South Carolina, Virginia, apply 0.5-0.75 lb. ai/A to control fall panicum and Texas panicum on coarse-textured soils. Trilin 10G and Wilbur-Ellis not for use in California on fodder, forage, or silage corn.

- - - - - - - - - - - - - - - -

Signal Word/Toxicity Class: Varies by formulation.

REI: 12 hr. unless soil injected or soil incorporated.

Trilin — see trifluralin

Weed Rhap — see 2,4-D

Weedar — see 2,4-D

Weedestroy — see 2,4-D

Weedone — see 2,4-D

Notes • Notes • Notes

Section 2
Soybeans

Enhanced Seed Information
Roundup Ready Soybeans 128
STS Soybeans 131

Use Reminders
Weed Sizes For Postemergence Soybean Herbicides (Grasses) 132
Weed Sizes For Postemergence Soybean
    Herbicides (Broadleaf Weeds) 133
Rainfall-Free Periods for Postemergence Herbicides 133
Soybean Herbicide Preplant Or Preemergence Rates Per Acre Based On
    Soil Texture And Organic Matter 134
Compatibility With Fertilizers As Application Carriers 134
Soybean Herbicide Recropping Restrictions, Months 135
Preharvest Application Intervals, Soybeans (PHI) 135
Soybean "Post-Broadleaf" Herbicides: Maximum Weed Sizes And
    Application Rates 136

Weed Efficacy Charts
Weed Response To Selected Postemergence Soybeans Herbicides ..137
Weed Response To Selected Soil Applied Soybeans Herbicides 138
Weed Response To Burndown Herbicides In No-Till Soybeans 139
Grass And Nutsedge Weed Control Ratings 140
Broadleaf Weed Control Ratings 141
Postemergent Herbicides For Partial Control/Suppression Of Perennial
    Weeds 142

Herbicide Listings 143

The information in this Weed Control Manual 2000 is updated to August 15, 1999.

Because manufacturers' product recommendations are constantly being updated and revised as additional product registrations and label changes are approved by EPA, there may be changes after this date. However, every effort has been made to give manufacturers the opportunity to include in the Manual their latest information. This Manual is for preliminary planning – not a use guide. Be sure to follow label directions, notwithstanding information contained herein.

Roundup-Ready Soybeans

This genetically improved seed variety can tolerate glyphosate herbicide. It may also be used with specific glyphosate products from other manufacturers.

Overview

Roundup-Ready soybeans are a family of genetically engineered seed varieties that can tolerate Monsanto's Roundup Ultra herbicide and selected licensed glyphosate products from other manufacturers.

More than 28 million acres of Roundup Ready beans were planted in 1998, and grower satisfaction remains high in both wet and dry conditions. One application of glyphosate when weeds are 4" to 6" high generally provides shoots-to-roots control of annual weeds.

Licensed Herbicides

Under some circumstances, specific glyphosate formulations from other manufacturers may be used; note, though, that not every glyphosate-product has a marketing agreement to be used with Monsanto's Roundup Ready seed. Growers are well advised to thoroughly research the latest information on products when selecting a glyphosate formulation for use with Roundup Ready soybeans, as there may be state or regional variations.

In general, all of the licensed glyphosate products provide the same weed control performance. The manufacturer of Touchdown claims quicker intake into target weeds. Selection criteria include price and the availability of the formulation that is best for use in your environmental conditions and/or with your application equipment.

As of the 1999 season, the following products were licensed for use with Roundup-Ready soybeans:

• Roundup Ultra (glyphosate, Monsanto. See page 152 for product information.)

• Rattler (glyphosate, Helena. See page 152 for product information.)

• Touchdown (sulfosate, Zeneca. See page 162 for product information.)

• Glyfos (glyphosate, Cheminova. See page 152 for product information.)

• Credit (glyphosate, Nufarm. See page 152 for product information.)

Roundup Ultra and Touchdown do not require additional adjuvant while most of the other products do. It is recommended that AMS be added to these products to increase effectiveness.

Glyphosate, Sulfosate

There is a difference between glyphosate and sulfosate. Glyphosate is the isopropylamine salt of the parent whereas sulfosate is the trimethylsulfonium salt of the acid. Once the herbicide is inside the plant, they act the same. Touchdown's manufacturer Zeneca claims a faster action for their product than glyphosate. This claim has not been observed in university trials.

Roundup-Ready Checklist

1. Start with a clean field...
✔ Use a burndown herbicide to clean the field
✔ Good seed bed preparation in conventional till

2. Apply 1 quart of glyphosate per acre for general annual weed control...
✔ Annual weed height of 4-6 inches is best timing, but as late as early flower is approved

3. Use 10-20 gpa water...
✔ Use good spray techniques to manage drift
✔ Add 8.5 lbs. of AMS for improved effectiveness
For hard to manage perennial weeds, add 17 lbs.

4. A second glyphosate application of up to 2 more qts. per acre may be applied if needed to control later weed flushes and/or perennial weeds.

Additional tips for best results:

✔ Weeds up to 10" in height will be controlled. Weeds greater than this height will be suppressed, but may escape complete control.

✔ In wider row soybeans (28 - 30"), a second application may be needed if later weed flushes occur.

Application Notes

First make sure the field is clean before planting. Use a burndown herbicide such as 2,4-D with glyphosate to clean the field.

In the Midwest, make a glyphosate application of 1 quart per acre when annual weeds are 4" to 6" tall. This is typically seven to 10 days later than you would normally apply postemergence products.

For perennial weeds, you can apply a maximum of 2 quarts per acre in any one application in the growing crop. There is a limit of 3 quarts per acre in the season.

Glyphosate is more effective on grasses than broadleaf weeds. Weeds such as common ragweed, eastern black nightshade, and waterhemp may be more difficult to control due to a prolonged period of germination.

Another group of weeds, including dayflower, yellow nutsedge, purple nutsedge, poison ivy, mugwort, bermudagrass, and nightshades have shown some tolerance to glyphosate.

Annual Weeds

Crop canopy growth is the key to successful weed management in soybeans. Time your application close to canopy closure and let your crop serve as a "residual herbicide" for the rest of the season. If a new flush of weeds

---

Supplemental residual herbicides for use on Roundup Ready Soybeans

There are benefits to applying a residual herbicide with a glyphosate program, especially early in the season. Some manufacturers recommend a preemergence application followed by glyphosate. Others recommend tank-mixing with a glyphosate product. All products registered for use on soybeans can be used on Roundup Ready soybeans.

Here's a look at some of the residual products available for use on Roundup Ready soybeans.

Axiom (Bayer)

A premix of flufenacet and metribuzin. Preemergence grass residual herbicide. Use at a reduced rate of up to 13 ounces per acre.

Classic (DuPont)

Postemergence herbicide applied when weeds are young and actively growing. Applications must include a crop oil concentrate or nonionic surfactant. Has good control of ragweed, waterhemp, weeds that may be more difficult to control with glyphosate.

Command 3ME (FMC Corp.)

Used preemergence in a sequential Roundup Ultra program. Provide residual grass and some broadleaf control. Eliminates early grass and broadleaf weed competition.

Dual Magnum (Novartis)

Preplant, preemergence herbicide for grasses and broadleaf weeds. This product has good control of yellow nutsedge and waterhemp, weeds that may be more difficult to control with glyphosate.

FirstRate (Dow AgroSciences)

May be used either soil-applied or postemergent. Tank mixed with Roundup Ultra, it offers residual control and won't compromise crop safety. This product has good control of yellow nutsedge, a weed that might be more difficult to control with glyphosate.

Frontier (BASF)

Apply at 16-24 ounces per acre. Eliminates early season broadleaf and grass weeds. It's the only labeled early post herbicide for soybeans. May be applied up to the 3rd trifoliate. When tank mixed at reduced rates with Roundup Ultra, it provides four to six weeks of residual control on most broadleaf and grass weeds.

Prowl (American Cyanamid)

Use preplant or preemergence at 1.2 to 3.6 pt. per acre. Controls grasses and broadleaf weeds. Do not apply postemergence or serious crop damage can occur. Do not use in California.

Pursuit Plus/Squadron/Steel (American Cyanamid)

Each of these preemergence products may be used at full rate in its own sequential program with Roundup Ultra. Use Pursuit Plus in the North and Squadron and Steel in the South. This product has good control of black nightshade, a weed that might be more difficult to control with glyphosate.

Pursuit Power Mix (American Cyanamid)

A tank mix of Pursuit (imazethapyr) and Roundup Ultra. It is a total postemergence program for Roundup Ready soybeans.

Python (Dow AgroSciences)

For broadleaf weed control. Applied preemergent, it provides a good foundation program for control of waterhemp and black nightshade.

Sencor (Bayer)

Can be used preemergent followed by Roundup postemergent to control small-seeded broadleaf weeds. This product has good control of ragweed, a weed that might be more difficult to control with glyphosate

Treflan (Dow AgroSciences)

Apply 1.5 to 2 pints per acre preplant incorporated before a Roundup Ready program. Controls grasses and small-seeded broadleaf weeds.

Roundup-Ready Soybeans

does emerge, it is usually shaded out and never develops into a competitive problem.

Tillage may bring new weed seeds to the surface and actually increase the chances that you'll need a residual herbicide application. The probability of needing a second application is higher in wide-row beans than in narrow rows.

Perennial Weeds

Use a quart of glyphosate per acre for perennial weed control, timed for optimum control of the annual weeds present in your fields. This rate per acre will suppress perennial weeds. If the aim is to control perennials, it is best to apply when the weed plant is budding. Application at bud to bloom stage or in the fall is generally recommended for best long-term control.

In-crop Applications

Generally, higher temperatures and relative humidity make symptom development and weed burndown faster with in-crop applications than for preplant applications. Grasses will respond much faster than broadleaf weeds, but both weed types typically die within seven to 14 days.

Dry Conditions

In the heat of summer, dry conditions can rapidly lead to drought-stressed weeds and dusty fields. These low-moisture conditions may require higher rates of glyphosate and/or the addition of ammonium sulfate (AMS). Fields under stress due to dry conditions should be treated earlier than those with normal moisture conditions to get better control and ensure that weeds won't steal moisture from the beans.

Residuals

All herbicides registered for use on soybeans may be applied to Roundup Ready soybeans. Some are positioned as a preemergence treatment, while others are positioned to be applied with glyphosate. Weed control early in the season helps reduce total weed pressure throughout the season. The key to the program is to develop a leaf canopy that can then shade out more weed development.

Other Comments

Growers who purchase Roundup Ready seed must sign a grower agreement and pay a $6.50 per bag technology fee. According to the manufacturer, this fee helps fund research and development of other crop technologies.

Finally, careful recordkeeping is a must. When growers plant herbicide-resistant seed, it is important to know which variety is planted on which acreage in order to match herbicide programs. If an herbicide is misapplied, it can result in total crop loss. □

SUPPLEMENTAL RESIDUAL HERBICIDE WEED CONTROL

This chart lists the residual herbicide products that have high efficacy ratings on weeds that glyphosate might not control in soybeans.

Weeds controlled	Axiom	Classic	Commend	Dual Magnum	FirstRate	Frontier	Prowl	Pursuit Plus/Squadron/Steel	Pursuit Plus Power Mix	Python	Sencor
Common ragweed		•			•		•				•
Nightshades			•					•	•	•	
Waterhemp	•									•	
Dayflower				•							
Yellow nutsedge		•		•		•					
Velvetleaf		•	•						•		•

*Purple nutsedge, poison ivy, bermudagras, and poison ivy were not evaluated for efficacy. Treflan did not rate high in efficacy for weeds listed in this table.

Enhanced Seed Systems
STS Soybeans

This genetically improved seed variety can tolerate STS herbicides.

Compiled by
Tina Grady

STS (sulfony-lurea-tolerant soy-beans) soybeans are tolerant to Synchrony STS herbi-cide. A premix of chlorimuron-ethyl and thifensulfuron methyl (a sulfony-lurea herbicide), Synchrony STS works through translocation by inhibiting certain amino acids from being produced in the plant.

STS soybeans provide control of more than 30 broadleaf weeds, and when used with Authority or Canopy XL in a preemergence/postemergence program, give growers full-season control of black nightshade and tall waterhemp.

STS soybeans are developed through traditional breeding techniques and are not a genetically modified (GM) product. Currently, there are about 5 million to 6 million acres of STS soybeans planted.

Licensed Herbicides

Synchrony STS is the only postemergence herbicide licensed for use on STS soybeans. Authority (sulfentra-zone) and Canopy XL (chlorimuron-ethyl) also are recommended as preplant herbicides to give residual season-long control of several broadleaf weeds.

Application Notes

A nonionic surfactant or crop oil concentrate (COC) is required with Synchrony STS. A burndown herbicide may be applied any time prior to planting when using a no-till method. The optimum weed height for control is when the weeds are 3-5 inches tall. However, if planting using a conventional tillage method, no burndown is needed.

Weeds Controlled

Synchrony STS herbicide is for control of broadleaf weeds only, and a grass control material must be applied as part of the planned herbicide program. The STS system with Synchrony STS is weak on black nightshade and tall waterhemp, so a preplant application of Authority or Canopy XL is recommended to control these weeds.

For annual weeds, the application timing for optimum control is 30 days after planting, at a rate of 0.5-0.75 ounces per acre and can work in any tillage system. The STS system controls several annual weeds, in particular cocklebur, lambsquarters, morningglory, nutsedge, and velvetleaf.

Perennial weeds controlled by the STS system include milkweed and Jerusalem artichoke. As with annual weeds, application timing also is 30 days after planting and at a rate of 0.5-0.75 ounces. Weeds are best controlled between 3 inches and 6 inches tall.

In-crop application may be done when the soybeans are in their third to fifth trifoliate.

Residuals

Canopy XL and Authority may be used as residuals in the STS program. Application is best when applied pre-emergence up to 21 days before planting.

Other Comments

When encountering dry conditions with the STS system, follow label recommendations for surfactants or a COC. Generally, COCs perform better in dry conditions.

There are no fees for using the STS soybean system, but it's important – although not required – that growers keep accurate records of all field herbicide applications. If a grower is selling his or her STS soybeans under a non GM-crop contract, there are several procedures which must be followed, including segregation of the crop and accurate field records.

It's also important to keep careful records of where herbicide-resistant seed is planted in order to match herbicide programs. If an herbicide is misapplied, severe crop damage may occur.

STS Checklist

1. Start with a clean field...
  ✔ Use a burndown herbicide.
  ✔ If using a no-till method, no burndown is needed.

2. Apply on 3.4 ounce soluble packet per 4 acres.
  ✔ Include a crop oil concentrate at 8 pints per 100 gallons of spray solution.

  ✔ Ammonium nitrogen fertilizer is recommended at 4-8 qts. per acre for 28-0-0 or 2-4 pts. per acre for 10-34-0.

3. Use in minimum of 10 gallons of water per acre.
  ✔ Increase to 15-25 gallons per acre under heavy weed pressure.
  ✔ Use flat fan nozzles at 25-60 psi.

Weed Sizes For Postemergence Soybean Herbicides

Grasses	Assure II[1] Grass size (in.)	Assure II alone	Assure II w/BH**	Fusilade DX[1,4] Grass size (in.)	Fusilade DX alone	Fusilade DX w/BH**	Fusion[1,4] Grass size (in.)	Fusion alone	Fusion w/BH**	Liberty Grass size (in.)	Liberty Rate/A (fl oz)	Poast Plus[1] Grass size[2] (in.) alone	Poast Plus w/BH**	Poast Plus Rate/A[2] (fl oz) alone	Poast Plus w/BH**	Pursuit DG Grass size (in.)	Pursuit DG Rate/A (oz)	Raptor Grass size (in.)	Raptor Rate/A (fl oz)	Roundup Ultra[7] Grass size (in.)	Roundup Ultra Rate/A (fl oz)	Select[8,9] Grass size (in.)	Select alone	Select w/BH**
Barnyardgrass	2-6	8	S[3]	2-3	12	12	2-4	8	10	≤2* / ≤4	20 / 28	≤4 / ≤8 / ≤12[5]	4 / —	18 / 24 / 36	24	1-3	1.44	2-5	5	4-8	32	1-4 / 2-8	4 / 6	8-10
Broadleaf signalgrass	≤6	≤8[11]					≤4	8-12				≤8 / ≤12[5]		≤24 / ≤36				≤5	5	≤5 / ≤7	≤24 / ≤32	≤4 / ≤6	≤5 / 6-8	
Crabgrass	2-6	8	S[3]	1-2	12	12	1-4	8	10	≤2* / ≤4	20 / 28	≤6 / ≤8[5]	4	24 / 36	24	1-3	1.44	2-4*	5	4-8	32	1-4 / 2-6	4-5 / 6	8-10
Downey brome	—	—					≤6	6-8				—		—						≤6	≤12	≤6	6-8	
Fall panicum	2-6	7	8	2-6	12	12	2-6	8	10	≤4		≤4 / ≤4 / ≤12[5]	≤8	18 / 28 / 36	4	—*	—*	2-6	5	4-8	32	1-4 / 2-8	4 / 6	8-10
Field sandbur	≤6	7-8					≤4	8-10				≤3		≤30						≤12	≤12	≤6	6-8	
Giant foxtail	2-4 / 2-8	5 / 7	5 / 7	2-6	12	12	2-8 / ≤16[5]	7 / 8-14	10 / —	≤6 / ≤10	20 / 28	≤4 / ≤8 / ≤16[5]	6	18 / 24 / 36	24	1-6	1.44	2-6	5	4-8	32	1-4 / 2-12	4 / 6	8-10
Green foxtail	2-4	7	8	2-4	12	12	2-4	8	10	≤6 / ≤10	20 / 28	≤4 / ≤8 / ≤16[5]	6	18 / 24 / 36	24	1-3	1.44	2-6	5	4-8	32	2-8	6	8-10
Johnsongrass (rhizome) 1st application	10-24	10	10	8-18	12	12	8-18	12		—*	—*	20-25		24		6-12	1.44	6-12*	5	≤18	32-64	12-24	8	16
Johnsongrass (rhizome) 2nd application	6-10	7	—	6-12	8	—	6-12	8				6-12		24						≤24	16-32	6-18	6	—
Johnsongrass (seedling)	2-8	5	5	2-8	6	12	2-8	6	8	≤4 / ≤6	20 / 28	≤8 / ≤16[5]	4 / —	24 / 36	24	1-8	1.44	4-8	5	4-8	32	1-6 / 4-10	5 / 6	8-10
Quackgrass 1st application	6-10	10	S[3]	6-10	12	12	6-10	12		—*	—*	6-8		36		—	—	4-8*		6-8	32-64	4-8	8	16
Quackgrass 2nd application	4-8	7	—	<10	8	—	10	8				6-8		36								4-8	8	—
Shattercane	6-12	5	5	6-12	6	12	6-12	6	8	≤4 / ≤6	20 / 28	≤18		24		1-8	1.44	2-8	5	4-8	32	4-10 / 6-18	4 / 6	8-10
Volunteer corn	6-18	5	5	12-24	6	12	12-24	6	8	≤4 / ≤6	20 / 28	≤12 / ≤20	18 / 12	24 / —	24	—	—	2-8[6]		4-8	32	4-12 / 12-24	4 / 6	6-8 / 8-10
Wheat[10], Rye	≤6	7-8					≤6	8-10				≤4		≤36				≤4	5	>18	≤24	≤6	6-8	
Wirestem muhly 1st application	4-8*	8	S[3]	4-12	12	12	4-12	8		—*	—*	≤6		36		—	—			>8	32-64	4-8+	8	16
Wirestem muhly 2nd application	4-8*	7	—	4-12	12	—	4-12	8				≤6		36								4-8	8	—
Woolly cupgrass	≤4	≤9[11]					≤4 / ≤16	8-10 / 12-14[11]				≤8		≤24				4*	5	≤12	≤24	≤8	6-8	
Yellow foxtail	2-4	7	S[3]	2-4	12	12	2-4	8	10	≤2* / ≤4	20 / 28	≤8 / ≤16[5]	6 / —	24 / 36	24	1-3	1.44	2-6	5	4-8	32	2-8	6	8-10

*Suppression only. • **w/BH = with broadleaf herbicide.

[1] May be tank-mixed with certain broadleaf herbicides only; refer to approved tank-mix table or herbicide labels.

[2] Refers to rate per acre of herbicide if applied alone or if tank-mixed with broadleaf herbicides. For Poast Plus, target grass sizes are smaller if tank-mixed with broadleaf herbicides.

[3] Split applications may be necessary. May not provide adequate control of this species if tank-mixed with a broadleaf herbicide.

[4] Special reduced rates may be possible if applied early and under certain conditions; refer to label.

[5] Rescue application only, better control will result if applied alone. (Do not tank-mix Fusion with broadleaf herbicides for rescue treatments).

[6] Except IMI corn hybrids.

[7] For use on Roundup Ready soybean varieties only. Split applications may be necessary if new weed flushes occur. Do not exceed 64 oz/A per year of Roundup for in-crop applications.

[8] Select can be applied at a special high rate of 8 oz/A for annual grasses and 16 oz/A for perennials. These high rates should be used only for heavy grass pressure or when grasses are at maximum height.

[9] Select application rates vary when tank-mixed with certain broadleaf herbicides. Average rate ranges are shown above. Refer to label for additional information.

[10] Volunteer wheat not overwintered, such as in double-cropped soybeans.

[11] For best results, do not tank-mix with a broadleaf herbicide.

Sources: Penn State Field Crop Weed Control Guide 1999; Illinois Agronomy Handbook, 1999-2000.

Soybeans
Use Reminders

Weed Sizes For Postemergence Soybean Herbicides

Broadleaves Herbicide (rate/A)	Annual morningglory	Burcucumber	Cocklebur	Common ragweed	Eastern black nightshade	Giant ragweed	Jimsonweed	Lambsquarters	Pigweed	Smartweed	Velvetleaf
					height range (inches) at application						
Basagran (2 pt)	—	—	≤10	≤3	—	≤6	≤10	≤10*	—	≤10	≤6
Blazer (1.5 pt)	≤2	—	≤2	≤3	≤2	≤3	≤6	≤2	≤4	≤6	—
Classic (1/2 oz)	1-2	—	2-6	—	—	—	2-4	—	1-2	1-2	—
Classic (2/3 oz)	1-3	2-3*	2-8	2-3	—	2-4*	2-5	—	1-3	1-3	2-4
Classic (3/4 oz)	1-4	2-6*	2-12	2-4	—	2-6	2-6	—	1-4	1-4	2-6
Cobra[1] (12.5 oz)	4 lvs	4 lvs	6 lvs	6 lvs	6 lvs	4 lvs	4 lvs	—	6 lvs	4 lvs*	4 lvs
Concert SP (1/2 oz)	1-2*	—	2-4	1-3+	—	—	2-5	2-4	2-12	2-8	2-8
FirstRate (0.3 oz)	≤6	—	≤10	≤10	—	≤10	≤4	—	—	≤6	≤6
Liberty (20 oz)	≤4	—	≤8	≤4	≤4	≤4	≤4	≤4	≤4	≤4	≤4
Liberty (28 oz)	≤6	—	≤12	≤12	≤6	≤8	≤8	≤6	≤4	≤12	≤5
Pinnacle (1/4 oz)	—	—	2-6*	—	—	—	2-4*	2-4	2-8	2-6	2-6
Pursuit DG (1.44 oz)	1-2*	—	1-8	1-3*	1-3	1-3*	1-3	1-2*	1-8	1-3	1-3
Raptor (5 fl oz)	2-4	—	2-8	2-5*	2-5	2-5	2-6	2-5	2-8	2-5	2-8
Reflex[1] (1.25 pt)	2 lvs	—	2 lvs	4 lvs	4 lvs	4 lvs	6 lvs	2 lvs	2-6 lvs	4 lvs	2 lvs
Resource[1] (6 oz)	—	—	—	≤4 lvs	—	—	—	2-3 lvs*	≤3 lvs[4]	—	≤8 lvs
Roundup Ultra[2] (32 oz)	3-6	4-8	4-8	4-8	4-8	4-8	4-8	3-6	4-8	3-6	4-8
Storm (1.5 pt)	≤2	—	≤6	≤3	≤2	≤6	≤6	≤2*	2-3	≤6	≤2*
Synchrony STS[3] (1/2 oz)	1-3*	2-3*	2-8	2-4	—	2-4	2-5	2-4	2-8	2-8	2-8
Stellar[1] (5 fl oz)	≤3 lvs*	—	≤2 lvs	≤4 lvs	≤3 lvs	≤2 lvs	≤4 lvs*	≤2 lvs*	≤3 lvs	—	≤6 lvs

* Suppression only, additional control measures may be necessary.
[1] Labels refer to weed size by number of leaves.
[2] For use on Rounup Ready soybean varieties only.
[3] For use on STS soybean varieties only.
[4] Smooth pigweed control only.

Source: Penn State Field Crop Weed Control Guide 1999.

Rainfall-Free Periods For Postemergence Herbicides

Herbicide	Time Before Rainfall	Herbicide	Time Before Rainfall
Assure II	1 hr	Pursuit	1 hr
Basagran	8 hrs	Reflex, Flexstar, Typhoon	4 hrs
Blazer	6 hrs	Roundup	6 hrs
Classic	4 hrs	Scepter	2 hrs
Cobra	30 min	Scepter O.T.	6 hrs
Fusilade, Fusion	1 hr	Select	1 hr
Gramoxone Extra	30 min	Storm	8 hrs
Liberty	4 hrs	Touchdown	4 hrs
Poast/Poast Plus	1 hr		

Source: Recommended Chemicals for Weed and Brush Control, Arkansas, 1999.

NOTICE The information on these pages is for preliminary planning — not a guide for use. Be sure to follow the manufacturer's directions, notwithstanding information contained here.

Soybean Herbicide Preplant Or Preemergence Rates Per Acre Based On Soil Texture And Organic Matter[a]

Herbicide	Unit	<3% organic matter			≥3% organic matter		Inc. for Conservation tillage
		Coarse	Medium	Fine	Medium	Fine	
Axiom 68DF	oz	13.0	13.0	13.0	13.0	13.0	no
Broadstrike + Treflan 3.65E	pt	1.5	2.0	2.25	2.0	2.25	no
Canopy 75DF[b]	oz	4.0	5.0	6.0	5.0	7.0	no
Canopy XL 56.3DF	oz	5.1	6.4	6.8	6.8	7.9	no
Command 4E	pt	1.0	1.5	2.0	2.0	2.0	no
Command 3ME	pt	1.33	2.0	2.67	2.67	2.67	no
Detail 4.1E	qt	1.0	1.0	1.0	1.0	1.0	no
Dual II MAGNUM 7.62E	pt	1.1	1.33	1.33	1.33	1.67	up to 20%
Dual MAGNUM 7.64E	pt	1.1	1.33	1.33	1.33	1.67	up to 20%
Frontier 6.0E	fl oz	20.0	25.0	28.0	28.0	30.0	add 3-5 oz
Lorox 50DF	lb	0.75	1.3	1.75	1.75	2.0	25%
Micro-Tech 4ME[c]	qt	2.0	2.25	2.5	2.5	2.75	20%
Partner 65WG[c]	lb	3.0	3.5	3.5	3.5	4.0	20%
Pentagon 60DG	lb	1.25	1.7	1.7	1.7	2.1	no
Prowl 3.3E	pt	1.8	2.4	2.4	2.4	3.0	no
Pursuit 2S	fl oz	4.0	4.0	4.0	4.0	4.0	no
Pursuit 70DG	oz	1.44	1.44	1.44	1.44	1.44	no
Pursuit Plus 2.9E	pt	2.5	2.5	2.5	2.5	2.5	no
Python 80WDG	oz	0.8	0.89	1.0	1.14	1.33	no
Scepter 1.5S	pt	0.67	0.67	0.67	0.67	0.67	no
Scepter 70DG	oz	2.8	2.8	2.8	2.8	2.8	no
Sencor	lb	0.33	0.5	0.67	0.67	0.67	
Squadron 2.33E	pt	3.0	3.0	3.0	3.0	3.0	
Steel 2.59E	pt	3.0	3.0	3.0	3.0	3.0	
Treflan 4E	pt	1.0	1.5	2.0	2.0	2.0	
Tri-Scept 3E	pt	2.33	2.33	2.33	2.33	2.33	
Turbo 8E	pt	1.5	2.0	2.75	2.5	3.0	

[a]This table shows application rates for products applied alone. Rates may vary if tank-mixed with other products, if weed infestations are heavy, or if used in conservation tillage situations. See specific product label for additional information.
[b]Reduced rate program. • [c]Reduce rate when tank-mixing. See product label for more information.

Source: Penn State Field Crop Weed Control Guide 1999.

Compatibility With Fertilizers As Application Carriers

Herbicide	Fertilizer Fluid	Dry	Herbicide	Fertilizer Fluid	Dry	Herbicide	Fertilizer Fluid	Dry
Assure II	No	No	Gramoxone Extra	Yes	No	Scepter	Yes	No
Broadstrike + Treflan	Yes	Yes	Lasso	Yes	Yes	Select	No	No
Canopy	Yes	Yes	Liberty	No	No	Sencor	Yes	Yes
Canopy XL	No	No	Prowl	Yes	Yes	Squadron	Yes	No
Command	Yes	Yes	Pursuit	Yes	No	Treflan/Trilin/trifluralin	Yes	Yes
Commence	Yes	Yes	Pursuit Plus	Yes	No	Tri-Scept	No	No
Freedom	Yes	Yes	Roundup	No	No	Turbo	Yes	Yes
Frontier	Yes	Yes						

There are many specific fertilizer incompatibilities and restrictions with most herbicides. Be sure to read the herbicide label for specific mixing or impregnation instructions. Compatibility agents are required for many mixes.

Source: Recommended Chemicals for Weed and Brush Control, Arkansas, 1999.

Soybean Herbicide Recropping Restrictions, Months

Herbicide	Comments	Field corn	Sorghum	Wheat	Oats	Rye	Alfalfa	Clover	Soybeans
Chlorimuron and some of its premixes									
Canopy[a]	w/ metribuzin	10	12	4	30	30	10	12	AT
Classic/Skirmish	high chlorimuron-ethyl	9[b]	9[b]	3	3	3	12[b]	12[b]	AT
Synchrony STS	w/thifensulfuron-methyl	9[b]	9[b]	3	3	3	12[b]	12[b]	AT
Flumetsulam and its premixes; cloransulam-methyl									
Broadstrike + Treflan	w/trifluralin	8	12	4	12	4	4	26[Fba]	AT
FirstRate	cloransulam-methyl	9	9	3	30[Fba]	30[Fba]	9	30[Fba]	AT
Python	flumetsulam	AT	12	4	4	4	4	26[Fba]	AT
Imazaquin and its premixes (full rate = Detail, Squadron, Tri-Scept; Region 3 = north of Peoria)									
Detail—Region 2[c]	w/dimethenamid	9.5[d,e]	11[e]	4[e]	11[e]	18	18	18	AT
Scepter—Region 2[c]	imazaquin	9.5[d,e]	11[e]	3[e]	11[e]	18	18	18	AT
Scepter—Region 3[c]	0.5 rate, post	NY[d]	11	Fall[e]	NY[e]	18	18	18	AT
Scepter—Region 3[c]	imazaquin	18	11	18	18	18	18	18	AT
Squadron—Region 2[c]	w/pendimethalin	9.5[d,e]	11[e]	4[e]	11[e]	18	18	18	AT
Tri-Scept—Region 2[c]	w/trifluralin	9.5[d,e]	11[e]	4[e]	11[e]	18	18	18	AT
Imazethapyr and its premixes (full rate = Pursuit, Pursuit Plus; Steel = Pursuit Plus + 0.5X Scepter)									
Pursuit	imazethapyr	8.5[f]	18	4	18	4	4	40	AT
Pursuit Plus	w/pendimethalin	8.5	18	4	18	9.5	9.5	40	AT
Steel—Region 2[c]	w/ pendimethalin + imazaquin	9.5[d,e]	18	4[e]	18	40	18	40	AT
Sulfentrazone alone or plus chlorimuron									
Authority	Sulfentrazone	10	10	4	30	4	12	18	AT
Canopy XL[a]	w/chlorimuron-ethyl[a]	10	10	4	30	4	12	18	AT
Other active ingredients									
Command 3ME	clomazone	9	9	12	16[g]	16[g]	16[g]	16[g]	AT
Flexstar, Reflex	fomesafen	10	18	4	4	4	10	18	AT
Raptor	imazamox	9	9	3	9	4	9	18	AT
Sencor	metribuzin	4	12	4	12	12	4	12	4
Turbo	metribuzin + metolaclor	8	12	4.5	12	12	12	12	8

Fba = field bioassay needed (see label), NY = next year, 2Y = second year, AT = anytime.
[a]Midwest states' rate, soil pH < 6.8. • [b]Extend 2 months if applied after August 1.
[c]See label for exact area and Region 3 (northern Illinois) full-use rate. • [d]10- to 15-inch annual rainfall is required, or use IMI-corn hybrids.
[e]15 months if Scepter/Scepter O.T. sequence, but 9.5 months or NY for IMI-corn hybrids.
[f]IMI-designated corn hybrids may be planted anytime.
[g]Cover crops may be planted anytime, but stand reductions may occur. Do not graze or harvest for forage for at least 9 months.

Source: Illinois Agronomy Handbook, 1999-2000.

Preharvest Application Intervals, Soybeans (PHI)

Herbicide	PHI	Herbicide	PHI
Assure II	80 days	Liberty	70 days
Basagran	No restrictions	Poast/Poast Plus	90 days
Blazer	50 days	Pursuit	85 days
Classic	60 days	Reflex, Flexstar, Typhoon	1st bloom
Cobra	90 days	Roundup	flowering
2,4-DB	60 days	Scepter	90 days
FirstRate	65 days	Select	60 days
Fusilade DX	1st bloom	Storm	50 days

These intervals are the number of days that must be allowed between herbicide application and harvest. Applications made after these interval restrictions could cause illegal herbicide residues to be present in the harvested grain.

Source: Recommended Chemicals for Weed and Brush Control, Arkansas, 1999.

NOTICE The information on these pages is for preliminary planning — not a guide for use. Be sure to follow the manufacturer's directions, notwithstanding information contained here.

Soybean "Post-Broadleaf" Herbicides: Maximum Weed Sizes and Application Rates

Herbicide	Rate	Annual morningglories (tall and ivyleaf)	Common cocklebur	Common ragweed	Eastern black nightshade	Giant ragweed	Jimsonweed	Lambsquarters[a]	Pigweeds	Prickly sida	Smartweeds	Velvetleaf	Wild Sunflower
ALS translocated[b]	oz/A	— *Label weed height in inches*											
Classic/Skirmish 25DF	0.50	2c	6	—	—	—	4	—	2d	—	2	—	5
Classic/Skirmish 25DF	0.75	4c	12	4	—	6	6	—	4d	—	4	6	8
FirstRate 84WDG	0.30	6	10	10	—	10	4	—	—	—	6	6	12
Pinnacle 25DF	0.25	—	6c	—	—	—	4c	4	8	—	6	6	6c
Pursuit 70DG	1.44e	2	8	3	3	3	3	2c	8	—	3	3	3
Raptor 1S fl oz	4-5	4c	8	5c	5	5	6	5	8	4c	5	8	8
Scepter 70DF	1.40	—	8	—	—	—	—	—	4	—	—	—	4
Scepter O.T. fl oz	16.0	2	6	—	—	—	—	—	4	3c	2	—	4
Synchrony STS	0.50	3c	8	4	—	4c	5	4	8	—	8	8	8
Other Translocated		— *Label weed height in inches*											
Roundup Ultra fl oz	24	2	18	6f-12	12	4	—	8	18	2	6	3f-6	18
Roundup Ultra fl oz	32	4	24	8f-18	12+	6	6	12	24	3	8	4f-12	18+
Contact	pt/A	— *Label weed height in inches*											
Basagran	1.0	—	4	—	—	—	4	1c	—	—	4	2	3
Basagran	2.0	4c	10	3	—	6	10	2c	—	4	10	6	8
Blazer, Status	1.0	2	—	2	<2	<2	4	—	<4	—	4	—	—
Blazer, Status	1.5	4	2c	3	2	3	6	2c	4	—	6	—	—
Galaxy	2.0	2c	6	3	<2	6	6	2c	2	3	6	5	5
Liberty	1.5	2	6	3	2	6	6	2c	3	2	6	2	—
Liberty	1.25	4	8	6	4	6	6	2	2	4	8	3	8
Storm	1.75	6	12	12	6	10	8	4	4	6	12	5	12
Contact	pt/A	— *Label weed height in leaf stage (number)*											
Cobra	0.5	—	4L	6L	4L	4L	4L	—	6L	—	—	—	—
Cobra	0.67	2L	6L	8L	6L	6L	4L	—	6L	4L	4Lc	4L	2L
Flexstar HL	1.25	4L	6L	6L	6L	6L	8L	2Lc	6L	2L	6L	4L	2L
Reflex	1.25	2L	2L	4L	4L	4L	6L	2Lc	4L	—	4L	2L	—
Resource	0.25	—	—	2Lc	—	—	—	—	3Lc	2Lc	—	6L	—
Resource	0.50	—	3Lc	6L	—	—	4L	3Lc	4L	4L	—	10L	—
Stellar	0.31	3Lc	2L	6L	3L	2L	—	2Lc	3L	3Lc	—	6L	—
Stellar	0.44	3Lc	4L	6L	4L	4L	4L	2Lc	4L	3Lc	—	6L	—

[a]Lambsquarters control is erratic with many herbicides.
[b]ALS-resistant waterhemp is not controlled by ALS herbicides.
[c]Suppression or partial control only; may need supplemental control.
[d]Redroot pigweed only; smooth pigweed and waterhemp only suppressed.
[e]Use equivalent rate of other formulations.
[f]Smaller size is used south of Interstate 70 in Illinois.

Source: 1999 Illinois Agricultural Pest Management Handbook

Weed Response To Selected Postemergence Soybeans Herbicides

Herbicide	Grasses						Broadleaf Weeds										
	Barnyardgrass	Crabgrass	Fall panicum	Foxtail	Sandbur	Shattercane/Sorghum	Black nightshade	Cocklebur	Kochia	Lambsquarters	Pigweed	Ragweed	Russian thistle	Smartweed	Sunflower	Velvetleaf	Waterhemp
Broadstrike + Treflan	9	9	9	9	9	9	6	6	9	9	9	7	8	9	9	8	9
Canopy	2	2	2	2	2	3	4	8	7	9	9	9	7	2	3	8	9
Canopy + Lasso	9	9	9	9	4	3	7	8	7	9	9	9	7	4	3	8	9
Canopy + Treflan or Sonalan or Prowl	9	9	9	9	8	7	2	8	9	9	9	9	8	8	7	8	9
Command (3ME)	8	8	8	8	8	8	2	2	9	7	2	4	—	8	8	4	2
Command (3ME) + Canopy	8	8	8	8	8	8	4	9	9	9	9	9	7	8	8	8	9
Command + Treflan or Sonalan or Prowl	9	9	9	9	9	8	3	3	9	9	7	7	7	9	4	10	7
Detail	9	9	8	9	4	5	7	9	7	9	9	9	9	9	9	8	9
Frontier (6.0)	9	9	9	9	4	3	6	2	2	7	8	5	3	2	2	2	7
Lasso/Micro-Tech/Partner	9	9	9	9	4	3	7	2	2	7	8	4	2	2	2	2	7
Lasso + Sencor	9	9	9	9	4	4	7	4	4	9	9	9	7	8	4	6	9
Prowl	9	9	9	9	8	6	2	2	7	7	7	2	7	2	2	4	7
Prowl + Sencor	9	9	9	9	8	7	2	4	7	9	9	9	9	7	4	7	9
Pursuit	2	2	2	2	2	7	4	4	9	4	9	9	—	9	8	8	9
Pursuit Plus	9	9	9	9	7	8	4	4	9	9	9	9	—	9	8	8	9
Scepter + Lasso	9	9	9	9	4	4	7	9	4	9	9	9	—	9	8	7	9
Split Appl.—Treflan/Trifluralin or Prowl + Sencor	9	9	9	9	8	8	2	5	9	9	9	9	9	9	6	8	9
(Squadron) Sonalan or Treflan	9	9	9	9	7	8	4	9	7	9	9	9	—	9	8	7	9
Steel LP	7	7	—	7	—	9	7	9	5	4	9	8	—	9	9	7	9
Treflan	9	9	9	9	8	6	2	2	7	7	7	2	7	2	2	4	7
Treflan + Sencor + Command (3ME)	9	9	9	9	8	8	5	5	9	9	9	9	9	7	5	10	9
Treflan/Trifluralin + Sencor	9	9	9	9	8	7	2	4	7	9	9	9	9	7	4	7	9

Response Ratings: Ratings are light to moderate weed populations, favorable conditions and weed growth stage as specified on the product label. High weed populations, adverse conditions, or large weeds will reduce control.
10 — (96-100%), 9 — (90-95%), 8 — (85-89%), 7 — (80-84%), 6 — (70-79%), 5 — (60-69%), 4-2 — less than 60%, 1 — 0%.

Source: Herbicide Use In Nebraska 1997 Guide

NOTICE	The information on these pages is for preliminary planning — not a guide for use. Be sure to follow the manufacturer's directions, notwithstanding information contained here.

Weed Response To Selected Soil Applied Soybeans Herbicides

Herbicide	Barnyardgrass	Crabgrass	Fall panicum	Foxtail	Sandbur	Shattercane/Sorghum	Black nightshade	Cocklebur	Kochia	Lambsquarters	Pigweed	Ragweed	Russian thistle	Smartweed	Sunflower	Velvetleaf	Waterhemp
	Grasses						Broadleaf Weeds										
Assure II	9	9	9	8	9	10	2	2	2	2	2	2	2	0	2	2	2
Basagran	2	2	2	2	2	2	2	9	7	7	2	7	7	9	8	9	2
Basagran + Blazer or Galaxy	2	2	2	2	8	2	7	9	7	7	8	9	7	9	8	9	8
Basagran + Cobra	2	4	4	4	4	4	7	8	4	4	9	9	7	9	8	8	9
Basagran + Scepter	2	2	2	2	2	2	2	10	7	7	9	7	7	9	9	9	8
Blazer/Status	2	4	4	4	4	4	7	4	4	4	9	9	5	9	2	4	9
Classic	2	2	2	2	2	2	2	10	4	4	8	9	—	9	9	8	—
Cobra	2	4	4	4	4	4	7	7	4	4	9	9	5	9	7	7	9
Fusilade	9	9	9	8	8	10	2	2	2	2	2	2	2	2	2	2	2
Fusion	9	9	9	8	8	10	2	2	2	2	2	2	2	2	2	2	2
Pinnacle + Classic	2	2	2	2	2	2	2	9	4	9	9	9	7	9	9	9	—
Poast Plus	9	9	9	8	9	10	2	2	2	2	2	2	2	2	2	2	2
Poast Plus + Basagran	8	8	8	7	8	9	2	9	7	2	2	7	2	9	8	9	2
Pursuit	7	7	5	8	—	9	8	9	8	4	9	7	—	8	8	8	—
Pursuit + Blazer or Cobra, or Reflex	7	7	4	7	4	9	7	9	5	4	9	9	5	9	7	7	9
Reflex/Flexstar	2	4	4	4	4	4	7	7	4	4	9	9	5	9	7	7	9
Reliance STS[a]	2	2	2	2	2	2	2	10	4	7	9	9	5	9	10	9	—
Resource	1	1	1	1	1	1	2	7	3	7	7	—	1	3	3	10	6
Roundup/Touchdown (1 qt)[a]	9	10	10	10	10	10	9	7	8	8	9	7	7	7	8	8	9
Roundup/Touchdown—ropewicks, wipers, etc.[b]	—	—	—	—	—	10	—	7	2	7	7	7	4	7	4	4	7
Select	9	9	9	8	8	10	2	2	2	2	2	2	2	2	2	2	2
Stellar	2	4	4	4	4	4	7	7	4	7	9	9	5	9	7	10	9
Synchrony STS	2	2	2	2	2	2	2	9	4	9	9	9	7	9	9	9	—

Response Ratings: Ratings are light to moderate weed populations, favorable conditions and weed growth stage as specified on the product label. High weed populations, adverse conditions, or large weeds will reduce control.
10 — (96-100%), 9 — (90-95%), 8 — (85-89%), 7 — (80-84%), 6 — (70-79%), 5 — (60-69%), 4-2 — less than 60%, 1 — 0%.
[a]For use in herbicide tolerant soybean varieties.
[b]Ratings for weeds tall enough for selective treatment.

Source: Herbicide Use In Nebraska 1997 Guide

Weed Response To Burndown Herbicides In No-Till Soybeans

Herbicide	Alfalfa	Annual Bluegrass	Annual Smartweed	Barnyardgrass	Chickweed	Dandelion	Downy Brome	Evening Primrose	Foxtail	Foxtail Barley	Hairy Vetch	Henbit	Horseweed (Marestail)	Kochia	Lambsquarters	Pennycress	Prickly Lettuce	Purslane Speedwell	Russian Thistle	Rye	Sandbur	Shepherdspurse	Sunflower	Sweet Clover	Tall Knotweed	Velvetleaf	Virginia Pepperweed	Winter Wheat
Canopy (6 oz)	4	10	9	4	10	7	3	6	4	7	6	8	8	7	9	10	4	9	3	4	10	8	0	9	8	6	3	
Command (3ME) (1.5 pt)	4	1	7	6	1	3	5	7	6	4	3	1	2	8	6	6	6	5	6	6	6	6	5	3	6	9	6	6
Command (3ME) + Prowl (1.5 pt + 3 pt)	4	2	7	6	1	3	7	7	7	4	3	1	2	9	6	6	6	6	7	6	6	6	6	3	7	9	6	6
2,4-D Ester** (1 pt)	5	1	7	1	4	7	1	7	1	1	7	4	7	6	9	10	9	7	9	1	1	10	10	6	6	8	9	1
Gramoxone Extra (1.5 pt)	4	8	6	7	10	5	7	7	7	8	7	9	7	9	8	10	8	6	9	6	7	9	10	4	9	8	9	6
Gramoxone Extra + Canopy (1.5 pt + 6 oz)	4	9	9	10	10	6	8	8	9	8	8	9	9	9	10	10	10	7	9	6	9	10	10	4	10	9	9	6
Gramoxone Extra + Pursuit (1.5 pt + 4 oz)	4	9	9	9	10	6	8	8	9	9	8	9	8	9	9	9	10	9	7	9	8	9	10	4	10	9	9	6
Gramoxone Extra + Scepter (1.5 pt + 4 oz)	4	9	8	9	10	6	7	8	9	9	8	7	9	10	10	9	6	9	7	9	10	4	10	9	9	6		
Gramoxone Extra + Sencor (1.5 pt + 12 oz)	4	10	8	9	10	6	7	8	9	9	8	9	10	10	10	10	8	10	7	9	10	4	10	10	9	7		
Pursuit (4 oz)	1	5	8	4	8	4	2	5	5	7	2	7	4	6	5	8	7	3	6	1	7	8	8	2	3	9	3	1
Pursuit Plus (2.5 pt)	1	5	8	5	8	4	2	5	6	7	2	7	6	5	8	7	3	6	1	7	8	8	2	3	9	3	1	
Roundup/Touchdown*** (1.0 pt)	4	10	7	10	10	5	10	7	9	9	6	9	6	6	7	10	6	10	9	10	10	10	9	3	9	7	9	10
Roundup/Touchdown*** (1.5 pt)	5	10	8	10	10	7	10	8	10	9	6	9	8	8	9	10	7	10	9	10	10	10	10	4	9	9	9	10
Roundup/Touchdown*** + Canopy (1 pt + 6 oz)	3	10	9	10	10	8	10	7	10	10	7	9	10	10	10	10	10	10	8	10	10	10	10	3	10	9	9	10
Roundup/Touchdown*** + 2,4-D (1 pt + 1 pt)	6	10	9	10	10	8	7	9	9	9	7	9	9	9	10	8	10	9	10	10	10	10	5	9	10	9	10	
Roundup/Touchdown*** + Pursuit (1 pt + 4 oz)	4	10	10	10	10	8	10	8	10	9	7	9	9	9	9	10	9	10	9	10	10	10	3	10	10	9	9	
Roundup/Touchdown*** + Scepter (1 pt + 4 oz)	4	10	9	10	10	7	10	7	10	9	7	9	8	9	10	10	9	10	10	10	10	3	10	9	9			
Roundup/Touchdown*** + Sencor (1 pt + 2-4 oz)	4	10	8	10	10	7	10	7	9	8	7	9	8	8	10	9	10	10	10	10	10	4	10	8	9	10		
Scepter (0.66 pt)	1	5	7	3	9	4	1	5	3	5	3	7	4	7	5	9	6	3	5	1	5	9	8	1	3	7	1	1
Sencor (12 oz)	5	2	7	5	10	5	7	6	5	8	6	8	5	9	5	10	7	2	7	5	6	9	8	5	8	8	6	5

Response Ratings: 10 — (96-100%), 9 — (90-95%), 8 — (85-90%), 7 — (80-84%), 6 — (70-79%), 5 — (60-69%), 4-2 — less than 60%, 1 — 0%.

* This guide presents burndown information only. It *does not* reflect residual weed control.
** Preplant interval: 2,4-D — 7 days for soybean.
*** Use Touchdown at $^2/_3$ the rate listed for Roundup.

Source: Herbicide Use In Nebraska 1997 Guide

NOTICE The information on these pages is for preliminary planning — not a guide for use. Be sure to follow the manufacturer's directions, notwithstanding information contained here.

Grass and Nutsedge Weed Control Ratings

Herbicide	Barnyardgrass	Crabgrass	Fall panicum	Giant foxtail	Johnsongrass	Quackgrass	Sandbur	Shattercane	Wirestem muhly	Woolly cupgrass	Yellow foxtail	Yellow nutsedge
Soil-applied												
Axiom	8	7	8	8	N	N	5	4	N	6	8	5
Command 3ME	9	8	9	9	N	N	8	7	N	7	8+	N
Frontier	9	9	9	9	N	N	5	5	N	7	9	7
Micro-Tech	9	9	9	9	N	N	6	5	N	7	9	7
Prowl, Pentagon	9	9	9	9	N	N	8	7	N	8+	9	N
Sonalan	9	8	9	9	N	N	8	7	N	8	9	N
Trifluralin	9	9	9	9	N	N	8	8	N	8+	9	N
Postemergence												
Assure II	8+	8	9	9	9	8+	9	9	7	8	8	N
Fusilade DX	8	8	8	8	9	8+	8	9	9	8	8	N
Fusion	9	8	9	9	9	8	8	9	7	8	9	N
Liberty	7	8	7	8+	6	5	7	8	7	8	7	5
Matador	8+	8	9	9	9	8+	9	9	7	8	8	N
Poast Plus	9	9	9	9	7	7	9	8	7	9	9	N
Pursuit[a]	7	7	7	8	5	N	7	8+	N	5	7	5
Raptor[a]	8	7	8	8+	6	N	9	9	N	5	8	5
Roundup Ultra[a,b]	9	9	9	9	9	8+		9	8+	8+	9	7
Select	9	9	9	9	9	8	6	9	8	9	9	N

Control ratings: 9 = excellent, 8 = good, 7 = fair, 6 = poor, 5 or 4 = unsatisfactory, N = Nil or None.
[a]These herbicides also control some broadleaf weeds.
[b]Use only with Roundup Ready (glyphosate-resistant) soybean varieties.

Source: 1999 Illinois Agricultural Pest Management Handbook

Broadleaf Weed Control Ratings

Herbicide	Annual morningglories	Burcucumber	Common cocklebur	Common ragweed	Eastern black nightshade	Giant ragweed	Jimsonweed	Kochia	Lambsquarters	Pigweeds	Prickly sida	Smartweeds	Velvetleaf	Wild sunflower
Preemergence														
Authority	8	—	6	6	8	6	8	8	9	8+	8	7	6	6
Axiom	N	N	N	5	6	N	4	N	6	8	N	4	N	N
Canopy	8	7	9	8+	5	8	9	8*	9*	9*	9	9	8	8
Canopy XL	8+	6	8+	8+	8+	8	8+	8+	9	9	8	9	8	8
Command	N	N	6	7	5	5	8	8+	8+	4	8+	8	9	4
Dual II MAGNUM	N	N	N	5	7	N	4	N	6	8	N	N	N	N
FirstRate	8	—	8+	9	5	8	8+	8	8+	8+	7	8	8	9
Frontier	N	N	N	5	7	N	4	N	6	8	N	N	N	N
Lorox	N	N	6	8	5	5	6	7*	9*	9*	6	8	6	5
Micro-Tech	N	N	N	5	7	N	4	N	6	8	N	N	N	N
Prowl/Pentagon	N	N	N	N	N	N	N	8	9	9	N	4	4	N
Pursuit	7	5	7	7	8+	6	7	8	8	9	8	8+	8	8
Python*	5	N	7	8	8	5	7	8	8+	9	7	8	8	8
Scepter	7	7	9	8+	8	8	8	5	9	9	8+	8+	7	9
Sencor	N	N	6	8	N	5	7	8*	9*	9*	8	9	8	6
Sonalan	N	N	N	N	6	N	N	8	8	9	N	4	N	N
Trifluralin	N	N	N	N	N	N	N	8	9	9	N	4	N	N
Postemergence														
Basagran	5	N	9	7	N	7	9	7	7	4	8	9	8+	8+
Blazer	8	7	7	8+	8+	7	9	6	5	9	N	8+	6	6
Classic[ALS]	7	8	9	8	N	7	8+	4[a]	N	8+[a]	N	8	8	9
Cobra	8	7	8	9	8+	8+	9	6	6	9	6	7	7	8
FirstRate[ALS]	8	—	9	9	N	9	9	4[a]	N	5[a]	4	8+	8+	9
Flexstar	8	7	8	8+	8	8+	9	6	6	9	N	8+	7	7
Galaxy	6	5	9	8	6	7	9	7	7	8	7	9	8	8
Liberty	8	7	9	8+	8+	8	9	8+	8	8	7	8+	8	9
Pinnacle[ALS]	4	N	6	5	N	4	5	7[a]	8+	9[a]	N	8+	8	6
Pursuit[ALS]	7	5	8+	7	9	7	8	8[a]	6	9[a]	6	8	8+	9
Raptor[ALS]	7	—	8+	7	9	8	8	8+[a]	8	9[a]	6	8	8+	9
Reflex	7	6	7	8	7	7	9	5	5	9	N	8	6	7
Resource	5	5	7	7	4	6	7	4	7	7	7	5	9	4
Roundup Ultra[c]	7	8	9	8+	8[a]	8+	9	8+	8	9	6	8[a]	8	8+
Scepter[ALS]	N	N	9	5	5	N	4	4[a]	N	9[a]	N	6	N	7
Skirmish[ALS]	7	8	9	8	N	7	8+	4[a]	N	8+[a]	N	8	8	9
Stellar	7	7	8	8+	8	7	8	5	7	9	7	6	9	6
Storm	7	6	8	8+	7	7	9	6	6	9	7	9	7	7
Synchrony STS[ALS,b]	7	8	9	8	N	7	8+	7[a]	8+	9[a]	N	9	8+	9

Control ratings: 9 = excellent, 8 = good, 7 = fair, 6 = poor, 5 or 4 = unsatisfactory, N = Nil or None, — = not on label.

*Control is much less on triazine-resistant biotypes of pigweed, lambsquarters, and kochia.
ALS = acetolactate synthase herbicides
[a]Will not control ALS-resistant waterhemp or kochia.
[b]Use only with STS-designated soybean varieties.
[c]Use only with Roundup Ready-designated soybeans varieties. Control varies with rate and weed size.

Source: 1999 Illinois Agricultural Pest Management Handbook

Postemergent Herbicides For Partial Control/ Suppression Of Perennial Weeds

Postemergent Herbicide	Bigroot morningglory	Bindweed (field or hedge)	Canada thistle	Common milkweed	Curly dock	Hemp dogbane	Honeyvine milkweed (climbing)	Horsenettle	Jerusalem artichoke	Pokeweed	Swamp smartweed	Yellow nutsedge
Basagran[a]	—	5	8	—	—	—	—	5	7	—	—	8
Blazer[b]	5	6	6	6	—	—	—	6	6	—	—	—
Classic/Skirmish[a]	—	7	7	6	6	—	7	5	7	6	—	6
Cobra[c]	6	6	6	6	—	—	—	6	6	—	6	—
Flexstar[d], Reflex	—	6	6	—	—	—	6	6	6	—	—	5
Glyphosate[e] 1-2%	6	8	9	8[i]	7[i]	8	7	8[i]	8[i]	9[i]	8[i]	7
Liberty[f]	—	7	5	6	5	6	6	—	7	—	5	5
Pursuit	—	—	6	—	6	—	—	7	8	—	—	6
Raptor	—	6	7	—	—	—	—	—	8	—	—	6
Roundup Ultra[g] 1 qt	5	7	8	7	6	7	7	7	8	8	7	6
Synchrony STS[h]	—	7	7	7	6	—	7	5	7	6	—	6

Control ratings: 9 = excellent, 8 = good, 7 = fair, 6 = poor, 5 or less = unsatisfactory.
[a]Use either the high rate or a split application for this degree of control.
[b]Label specifies high rate and favorable environmental conditions required for suppression.
[c]Label specifies the use of COC and a maximum of 6-leaf stage for suppression.
[d]Flexstar may provide greater suppression than Reflex.
[e]Spot treatment with 1% Touchdown or 2% Roundup Ultra on a spray-to-wet basis before bloom stage.
[f]Liberty is to be used only on Liberty Link-designated soybean varieties.
[g]Use only with Roundup Ready-designated soybean varieties.
[h]Use only with STS-designated soybean varieties
[i]A ropewick applicator with a mix of 20% Touchdown 5 or 33% Roundup Ultra may also control this weed.

Source: 1999 Illinois Agricultural Pest Management Handbook

Soybeans

ACIFLUORFEN

Diphenyl ether considered to have contact action; frequently combined with other postemergence broadleaf herbicides to give broad spectrum control.

■ POST

Blazer *(BASF)*
Status *(American Cyanamid)*
  Rate: 0.25-0.375 lb. ai/A
       0.5-1.5 pt./A
  Time: Early postemergence. Apply when weeds are small and actively growing.
  Weeds: Broadleaf weeds:

balloonvine	giant ragweed	redvine
black nightshade	hairy galinsoga	showy crotalaria
bristly starbur	hairy indigo	smallflower
buffalobur	heartleaf cocklebur	galinsoga
burgherkin	hedge bindweed	smellmelon
Canada thistle	hemp sesbania	smooth pigweed
carpetweed	hophornbeam	spiny amaranth
citron melon	copperleaf	spotted spurge
climbing milkweed	jimsonweed	tall waterhemp
coffee senna	ladysthumb	Texas gourd
common cocklebur	lambsquarters	tropic croton
common milkweed	lanceleaf	trumpetcreeper
common purslane	groundcherry	velvetleaf
common ragweed	morningglory	Virginia copperleaf
cutleaf	Palmer amaranth	volunteer cowpea
groundcherry	Pennsylvania	wild buckwheat
devilsclaw	smartweed	wild mustard
eastern black	poorjoe	wild poinsettia
nightshade	prostrate pigweed	wild spiny cucumber
field bindweed	prostrate spurge	wild watermelon
Florida pusley	redroot pigweed	woolly croton

  Grasses:

fall panicum	johnsongrass	volunteer small grains
giant foxtail	(seedling)	yellow foxtail
green foxtail	shattercane	

  Remarks: Add 80% nonionic surfactant. Refer to Special Use Directions on label for specific weeds and amounts of surfactant necessary for control. In case of crop failure, only soybeans, peanuts, or rice may be immediately replanted.
  Days To Harvest: 50.
  Crop Rotation: Do not plant root crops such as carrots, turnips, sweet potatoes, etc. in treated fields for 18 months following last application.
  Tank Mixes: Assure II, Basagran, Classic, 2,4-DB, Dual, FirstRate, Frontier, Fusilade, Fusion, Lasso, Matador, Pinnacle, Poast, Poast Plus, Pursuit, Raptor, Reliance STS, Resource, Roundup Ultra, Scepter, Select, Skirmish, Synchrony STS.

  Signal Word/Toxicity Class: Danger/I.
  REI: 48 hr.

ACTION

Selective postemergence herbicide for control of velvetleaf and other broadleaf weeds. Action is a wettable powder packaged in a water-soluble bag.

■ POST

◆ Action (WP) (fluthiacet-methyl) *(Novartis)*
  Rate: 1.5-2.25 oz. WP/A
  Time: Postemergence. Apply from first trifoliate to full flowering stage; velvetleaf up to 36" tall.
  Weeds: Broadleaf weeds:

black nightshade	eastern black	smooth pigweed
burcucumber	nightshade	spurred anoda
common lambsquarters	jimsonweed	tall waterhemp
common waterhemp	redroot pigweed	velvetleaf

  Remarks: Adjuvant required for maximum consistent performance. Do not cultivate 2 days before or after application. Do not apply more than 3 oz./A per cropping season. Do not allow spray to drift to non-target crops. Cotton is very sensitive; contact may cause cotton defoliation. Do not apply by air or through any type of irrigation system. Do not graze or feed treated soybean forage or hay to livestock. Refer to label for directions and precautions.

Days To Harvest: 60.
Crop Rotation: In case of crop failure replant soybeans only; all other crops at normal rotation intervals.
Tank Mixes: Basagran, Blazer, Classic, Cobra, Concert, Flexstar, Galaxy, Manifest, Pinnacle, Pursuit, Raptor, Reflex, Reliance STS, Roundup Original, Roundup Ultra, Scepter O.T., Status, Storm.

Signal Word/Toxicity Class: Caution.
REI: 12 hr.

ALACHLOR

May be tank mixed with several different soil-applied herbicides to provide broad spectrum weed control. Lasso is a cell growth inhibitor. Restricted Use Pesticide.

■ PPI, PRE

Lasso (4EC) or Micro-Tech (MT) *(Monsanto)*
Partner (WDG) *(Monsanto)*
  Rate: 2-3 lb. ai/A
       2-3 qt. 4EC, MT/A
       3-4.5 lb. WDG/A
  Time: Preplant incorporated or preemergence.
  Weeds: Broadleaf weeds:

black nightshade	Florida pusley	prickly sida*
carelessweed	galinsoga	purslane
carpetweed	hairy nightshade	sicklepod*
common ragweed*	lambsquarters*	smartweed*
cutleaf groundcherry	pigweed	teaweed*
Florida beggarweed*		

  Grasses and sedges:

barnyardgrass	johnsongrass*	wild proso millet*
broadleaf signalgrass	(seedling)	wildcane*
crabgrass	panicum	witchgrass
foxtail	sandbur*	woolly cupgrass*
goosegrass	shattercane*	yellow nutsedge

  * *Suppression*
  Remarks: Do not make more than one application per year. Do not feed forage, hay, or straw from treated soybeans. Do not ensile treated soybeans. Refer to label for directions and precautions.
  Tank Mixes: Canopy, Command, Gramoxone Extra, linuron, Lorox Plus, metribuzin, Pursuit, Scepter, trifluralin.

  Signal Word/Toxicity Class:
  Danger/I (Lasso); Caution/IV (Micro-Tech, Partner)
  REI: 12 hr.

■ PRE

Lasso II (15G) *(Monsanto)*
  Rate: 2.4-3.9 lb. ai/A
       16-26 lb. 15G/A
  Time: Preemergence.
  Weeds: Broadleaf weeds:

black nightshade	carpetweed	pigweed
carelessweed	Florida pusley	purslane

  Grasses and sedges:

barnyardgrass	giant foxtail	witchgrass
brachiaria	goosegrass	yellow foxtail
crabgrass	green foxtail	yellow nutsedge
fall panicum		

  Remarks: Do not feed forage, hay, or straw from treated soybeans. Do not ensile treated soybeans. Refer to label for directions, restrictions and precautions.

  Signal Word/Toxicity Class: Warning/II.
  REI: 12 hr.

Assure II — see quizalofop-P-ethyl

STS Authority — see sulfentrazone

NOTICE The information on these pages is for preliminary planning — not a guide for use. Be sure to follow the manufacturer's directions, notwithstanding information contained here.

For personal protective equipment and EPA registration numbers, please turn to page 70.

Authority Broadleaf — see sulfentrazone & chlorimuron-ethyl

AXIOM (Premix)

Related to chloroacetamide herbicides.

■ **PP, PPI, PRE**

Axiom DF (54.4% flufenacet & 13.6% metribuzin) *(Bayer)*

Rate: 7-13 oz. DF/A

Time: Preplant (incorporated, surface), preemergence. For preplant, apply up to 14 days before planting.

Weeds: Broadleaf weeds:

carpetweed	Florida beggarweed*	pigweed*
common	galinsoga	prickly sida*
lambsquarters*	jimsonweed*	spotted spurge
common purslane	mustard*	tall waterhemp*
common ragweed*	Pennsylvania	
common waterhemp*	smartweed*	

Grasses:

barnyardgrass	goosegrass	large crabgrass
broadleaf signalgrass*	green foxtail	shattercane*
browntop panicum*	Indian lovegrass	smooth crabgrass
fall panicum	johnsongrass	witchgrass*
field sandbur*	(seedling)*	yellow foxtail
giant foxtail		

* Suppression

Remarks: Rates varies by soil texture and organic matter. Do not apply by air or through any type of irrigation system. Do not use treated crop for food, feed, or forage.

Crop Rotation: Corn, soybeans—anytime; potatoes—1 month; carrots—4 months.

Tank Mixes: Authority Broadleaf, Canopy, Canopy XL, Command, 2,4-D LVE, FirstRate, glyphosate, Gramoxone Extra, linuron, metribuzin, Pentagon, Prowl, Pursuit, Roundup Ultra, Scepter, Sonalan HFP, Touchdown, trifluralin, Turbo.

– – – – – – – – – – – – – – –

Signal Word/Toxicity Class: Caution/III.
REI: 12 hr.

Barrage — see 2,4-D

BASAGRAN

Postemergence broadleaf herbicide with activity on several broadleaves including velvetleaf, cocklebur, and jimsonweed. Often tank mixed with other postemergent broadleaf or grass herbicides to give broad spectrum control. Effective mainly through contact action.

■ **POST**

Basagran (bentazon) *(BASF)*

Rate: 0.5-1 lb. ai/A
   1-2 pt./A

Time: Early postemergence.

Weeds: Broadleaf weeds and sedges:

annual morningglory	devilsclaw	shepherdspurse
balloonvine	galinsoga	spurred anoda
beggarticks	giant ragweed	teaweed
bristly starbur	jimsonweed	tropic croton
Canada thistle	ladysthumb	velvetleaf
cocklebur	marshelder	Venice mallow
coffee senna	Pennsylvania	wild buckwheat
common lambsquarters	smartweed	wild mustard
common purslane	prickly sida	wild poinsettia
common ragweed	redweed	wild sunflower
dayflower	sesbania	yellow nutsedge

Remarks: Rate varies with weed size and species. For improved control of velvetleaf, add urea ammonium nitrate solution to spray tank in place of oil concentrate. If common ragweed and lambsquarters are present in addition to velvetleaf, then oil concentrate should be used. For morningglory and yellow nutsedge, refer to Special Directions on label. Do not graze or cut treated soybeans fields for forage or hay for at least 30 days after last treatment.

Tank Mixes: Blazer, Classic, 2,4-DB, Pinnacle, Poast, Poast Plus, Pursuit, Reflex, Scepter.

– – – – – – – – – – – – – – –

Signal Word/Toxicity Class: Caution/III.
REI: 12 hr.

Blazer — see acifluorfen

BROADSTRIKE+TREFLAN (Premix)

Selective soil-applied herbicide for preemergence control of annual grass and broadleaf weeds. May be tank mixed or followed by overlay or postemergence treatment with other registered herbicides to broaden spectrum of weeds controlled.

■ **PPI**

Broadstrike+Treflan (0.25 lb./gal. flumetsulam & 3.4 lb./gal. trifluralin) *(Dow AgroSciences)*

Rate: 1.5-2.25 pt./A

Time: Preplant incorporated. Apply prior to bedding, after bedding.

Weeds: Broadleaf weeds:

black nightshade	henbit	prickly sida
carelessweed	jimsonweed	Russian thistle
carpetweed	knotweed	sicklepod
chickweed	kochia	spotted spurge
common cocklebur	ladysthumb	spurred anoda
common	morningglory	stinging nettle
lambsquarters	nodding spurge	tall waterhemp
common purslane	Palmer amaranth	velvetleaf
common ragweed	Pennsylvania	Venice mallow
Florida pusley	smartweed	wild mustard
goosefoot	pigweed	wild sunflower

Grasses:

annual bluegrass	foxtail	signalgrass
annual ryegrass	guineagrass	smooth crabgrass
barnyardgrass	Italian ryegrass	sprangletop
bromegrass	johnsongrass	stinkgrass
burgrass	(seedling)	Texas panicum
cheat	junglerice	watergrass
cheatgrass	large crabgrass	wild oat
chess	lovegrass	wildcane
downy brome	sandbur	woolly cupgrass
fall panicum	shattercane	

Remarks: Rate varies by soil type. Do not apply by air or use on peat or muck soils. Do not graze or feed treated soybean forage, hay, or straw to livestock. Refer to label for restrictions and precautions.

Days To Harvest: 85.

Crop Rotation: Soybeans—4 months; all other crops—interval (4-26 months) varies by area, refer to label.

State Restrictions: Not for use in Pecos County or Reeves County, Texas.

– – – – – – – – – – – – – – –

Signal Word/Toxicity Class: Danger/I.
REI: 12 hr. unless soil injected or soil incorporated.

Butoxone — see 2,4-DB

Butyrac — see 2,4-DB

CANOPY (Premixes)

Premix containing the active ingredients of metribuzin and Classic. Provides selective broad spectrum control of annual broadleaf weeds.

■ **PPI, PRE**

Canopy (DG) (64.3% metribuzin & 10.7% chlorimuron-ethyl) *(DuPont)*
Canopy SP (50% metribuzin & 8.3% chlorimuron-ethyl) *(DuPont)*

Rate: Midwestern states:
   4-7 oz. DG/A
   5.2-9 oz. SP/A
   Southern states:
   6-12 oz. DG/A
   7.7-15.4 oz. SP/A

Time: Preplant incorporated, preemergence. May be applied up to 45 days before planting in Midwestern states, 30 before planting in Southern states. Do not apply after crops have emerged.

Weeds: Broadleaf weeds:

annual morningglory	hophornbeam	smallflower
annual smartweed	copperleaf	morningglory
burcucumber*	ivyleaf morningglory	smooth pigweed
cocklebur	jimsonweed	spiny amaranth
common purslane	lambsquarters	spotted spurge
common ragweed	mexicanweed*	sunflower
entireleaf	Palmer pigweed	tall morningglory
morningglory	pitted morningglory	teaweed
Florida beggarweed	prickly sida	velvetleaf
giant ragweed	redroot pigweed	wild mustard
hemp sesbania	sicklepod	wild poinsettia

RR-soybeans resistant to Roundup Ultra • STS-soybeans resistant to sulfonylurea

◆-new product • PP-preplant • PPI-preplant incorporated • PRE-preemergence • POST-postemergence • SEQ-sequential • ae-acid equivalent • ai-active ingredient • DF-dry flowable
E/EC-emulsifiable concentrate • F/FL-flowable • DG/G/WG-dispersable granule • L/LC-liquid • SP/WSP-soluble packet • W/WP-wettable powder • WSB-water soluble bag

Grasses and sedges:

barnyardgrass*	foxtail*	purple nutsedge*
broadleaf signalgrass*	johnsongrass*	Texas panicum*
crabgrass*	(seedling)	yellow nutsedge*
fall panicum*		

* Partial control

Remarks: Rate varies by soil texture and organic matter. Do not apply to soils with pH greater than 6.8 in Midwestern states, 7.0 in Southern states. Do not graze treated fields, or harvest for forage or hay. Refer to label for use directions, restrictions, and precautions.

Crop Rotation: Recropping depends on soil pH and geographical area. Consult label for complete information.

State Restrictions: For use in Midwestern states: Illinois, Indiana, Iowa, Kansas, Michigan, Missouri (except bootheel), Nebraska, Ohio, Oklahoma, and Pennsylvania. Southern states: Alabama, Arkansas, Delaware, Florida, Georgia, Kentucky, Louisiana, Maryland, Mississippi, Missouri bootheel, New Jersey, North Carolina, South Carolina, Tennessee, Texas, Virginia, and West Virginia.

– – – – – – – – – – – – – –

Signal Word/Toxicity Class: Caution.
REI: 12 hr.

Canopy XL — see sulfentrazone & chlorimuron-ethyl

CHLORIMURON-ETHYL

Postemergence, sulfonylurea herbicide which inhibits production of certain plant amino acids.

■ **POST**

Classic (DG) *(DuPont)*
Skirmish (DG) *(FMC)*

Rate: 0.125-0.1875 oz. ai/A
0.5-0.75 oz. DG/A

Time: Postemergence. Apply to young, actively growing weeds anytime after first soybean trifoliate opens but no later than 60 days before soybean maturity.

Weeds: Broadleaf weeds and sedges:

beggarticks	hemp sesbania	prickly lettuce
bristly starbur	ivyleaf morningglory	purple nutsedge*
burcucumber*	Jerusalem artichoke	sicklepod
Canada thistle*	(above ground)	smallflower
cocklebur	jimsonweed	morningglory
common ragweed	ladysthumb	smooth pigweed*
cowpea	marestail	sunflower
entireleaf	Pennsylvania	tall morningglory
morningglory	smartweed	velvetleaf
Florida beggarweed	pigweed	wild poinsettia
giant ragweed	pitted morningglory	yellow nutsedge

* Suppression

Remarks: Add crop oil concentrate or nonionic surfactant. Do not cultivate within 7 days of application. Do not make more than 2 applications per season. Do not graze treated fields or harvest for forage or hay. Refer to label for precautions.

Days To Harvest: 60.

Crop Rotation: Soybeans—anytime; other crops—rotation intervals vary by soil pH and region. Refer to label for more complete information.

Tank Mixes: Cobra, 2,4-DB, Pinnacle, quizalofop-P-ethyl.

State Restrictions: For use in the eastern U.S.

– – – – – – – – – – – – – –

Signal Word/Toxicity Class: Caution/III.
REI: 12 hr.

Clarity — see dicamba

Classic — see chlorimuron-ethyl

CLETHODIM

Postemergence grass herbicide. Mode of action similar to Poast, Assure, Option II, and Fusilade.

■ **POST**

Prism (0.94EC) or Select (2EC) *(Valent)*

Rate: 0.1-0.25 lb. ai/A
9-34 fl. oz. 0.94EC/A
4-16 fl. oz. 2EC/A

Time: Postemergence. Apply to actively growing grasses.

Weeds: Grasses:

Amazon sprangletop	green foxtail	smooth crabgrass
annual bluegrass	itchgrass	southern crabgrass
barnyardgrass	johnsongrass	Texas panicum
bearded sprangletop	junglerice	volunteer cereals
bermudagrass	large crabgrass	wild oat
broadleaf signalgrass	quackgrass	wild proso millet
crowfootgrass	red rice	wirestem muhly
fall panicum	red sprangletop	witchgrass
giant foxtail	shattercane	woolly cupgrass
goosegrass	southwestern cupgrass	yellow foxtail

Remarks: Rate varies by grass species, stage, and geographical region. Grass crops such as corn, sorghum, wheat, and rice are highly sensitive to clethodim. Do not apply under stress conditions or if rainfall is expected in 1 hour. Do not apply through any type of irrigation system. Do not apply more than 0.5 lb. ai/A (0.25 lb. ai/A on Long Island, NY) per season. Do not graze treated fields or feed treated forage or hay to livestock. Refer to label for restrictions and precautions.

Days To Harvest: 60.

Tank Mixes: Basagran, Blazer, Classic, Cobra, 2,4-D ester (no-till soybeans), Galaxy, Pursuit, Reflex, Resource, Sencor (no-till soybeans), or Storm.

State Restrictions: Not for use on Solano grass in the Vernal Lakes area of Solano County, California; wild rice in Hays County, Texas.

– – – – – – – – – – – – – –

Signal Word/Toxicity Class: Warning/II.
REI: 24 hr.

COBRA

Postemergence, broadleaf herbicide similar to Blazer and Reflex in mode of action. Contact herbicide that has activity on several annual broadleaf weeds and suppresses the growth of certain perennials. Can be tank mixed with certain other postemergent broadleaf herbicides.

■ **PRE, POST**

Cobra (2EC) (lactofen) *(Valent)*

Rate: 0.2 lb. ai/A
12.5 fl. oz. 2EC/A

Time: Preemergence, early postemergence. Apply when weeds are small and actively growing.

Weeds: Broadleaf weeds:

balloonvine	hairy galinsoga	puncturevine
beggarticks	hairy nightshade	redroot pigweed
black nightshade	hemp sesbania	showy crotalaria
bristly starbur	hophornbeam	smallflower
buffalobur	copperleaf	morningglory
burcucumber	ivyleaf morningglory	smellmelon
carpetweed	jimsonweed	smooth pigweed
common cocklebur	lanceleaf	spiny amaranth
common purslane	groundcherry	pigweed
common ragweed	mexicanweed	spotted spurge
cutleaf groundcherry	Palmer amaranth	tall morningglory
cypressvine	pigweed	tall waterhemp
morningglory	palmleaf	tropic croton
devilsclaw	morningglory	velvetleaf
eastern black	pitted morningglory	Venice mallow
nightshade	poorjoe	Virginia copperleaf
eclipta	prickly sida	wild mustard
entireleaf	(teaweed)	wild poinsettia
morningglory	prostrate pigweed	wild sunflower
Florida beggarweed	prostrate spurge	witchweed
Florida pusley	purple moonflower	woolly croton
giant ragweed	morningglory	

Remarks: Rate varies by weed species and size. Do not apply when soybeans or weeds are under stress. Do not graze animals on green foliage or use hay or straw for animal feed or bedding. Refer to label for use directions.

Days To Harvest: 45.

Tank Mixes: Assure, Basagran, Classic, 2,4-DB, Fusilade, Option II, Pinnacle, Pursuit, Reliance STS (STS soybeans), Scepter, Select, or Synchrony STS (STS soybeans).

– – – – – – – – – – – – – –

Signal Word/Toxicity Class: Danger/I.
REI: 12 hr.

COMMAND

Command is a pigment inhibitor and may be utilized as a preemergent soil-applied or soil-incorporated treatment for control of annual grass and broadleaf weeds. Must be applied as soil-incorporated treatment in certain states. Off-site movement of spray drift or vapors can cause foliar whitening or yellowing of some plants.

■ **PP, PPI, PRE**

Command 4EC or 3ME (clomazone) *(FMC)*

NOTICE	The information on these pages is for preliminary planning — not a guide for use. Be sure to follow the manufacturer's directions, notwithstanding information contained here.	For personal protective equipment and EPA registration numbers, please turn to page 70.

Soybeans

Rate: Northern U.S.:
0.5-1 lb. ai/A
1-2 pt. 4EC/A
1.3-2.6 pt. 3ME/A

Time: Preplant incorporated, preemergence (geographical restrictions).

Weeds: Broadleaf weeds:

blackseed plantain	kochia	purslane
cocklebur*	ladysthumb	spurred anoda
common ragweed	lambsquarters	tropic croton
Florida pusley	Pennsylvania	velvetleaf
galinsoga	smartweed	Venice mallow
jimsonweed	prickly sida	

Grasses:

barnyardgrass	goosegrass	smooth crabgrass
bermudagrass*	green foxtail	southwestern
broadleaf signalgrass	johnsongrass	cupgrass
common panicum	(seedling)	Texas panicum
fall panicum	large crabgrass	wild proso millet*
field sandbur	robust foxtail	woolly cupgrass*
giant foxtail	shattercane*	yellow foxtail

* Partial control (rate varies; consult label)

Rate: Southern U.S.:
0.5-1.25 lb. ai/A
1-2.5 pt. 4EC/A
1.3-3.3 pt. 3ME/A

Time: Preplant, preplant incorporated, preemergence.

Weeds: Broadleaf weeds:

balloonvine*	jointvetch*	purslane
black nightshade*	kochia	redvine*
cocklebur	lambsquarters	redweed
common ragweed	Pennsylvania	spurred anoda
curly dock	smartweed	tropic croton
dayflower	pigweed*	velvetleaf
Florida beggarweed	pitted morningglory	Venice mallow
Florida pusley	prickly sida	wild poinsettia
jimsonweed	prostrate spurge	

Grasses:

barnyardgrass	green foxtail	robust foxtail
bermudagrass*	itchgrass (PRE)	shattercane*
broadleaf signalgrass	johnsongrass	smooth crabgrass
common panicum	(seedling)	southwestern cupgrass
fall panicum	junglerice*	Texas panicum
field sandbur	large crabgrass	wild proso millet*
giant foxtail	purple foxtail	woolly cupgrass
goosegrass	red rice*	yellow foxtail

* Partial control (rate varies; consult label)

Remarks: If initial seeding of soybeans fails to produce a stand, soybeans may be replanted in treated fields. Do not retreat with a second application. Do not graze or harvest for food or feed cover crops planted less than 9 months after treatment, allow livestock to graze treated vines, or feed treated vines or vine trash to livestock. Do not apply through any type of irrigation system. Refer to label for directions and precautions.

Crop Rotation: Northern U.S.: all crops—16 months after application. Southern U.S.: all crops—12 months after application. For specific crops at shorter intervals, refer to Rotational Crop Guidelines on label. Cover crops may be planted any time but stand reductions may occur in some areas. Carryover injury to approved rotational crops may result under abnormal conditions.

Tank Mixes: Alachlor, Blazer, Canopy, Dual, linuron, Lorox Plus, metribuzin, Prowl, Scepter, Sonalan, trifluralin.

State Restrictions: Not for use in California.

- - - - - - - - - - - - - - -

Signal Word/Toxicity Class: Warning/II (4EC); Caution/III (3ME).
REI: 12 hr. unless soil injected or soil incorporated.

COMMENCE (Premix)

Premix containing active ingredients of Command and Treflan. Broad spectrum control of grasses and certain broadleaves. Must be incorporated. May be tank mixed with certain soil-applied herbicides. Off-site movement of spray drift or vapors can cause foliar whitening or yellowing of some plants. Toxic to fish.

■ PPI

Commence EC (2.25 lb./gal. clomazone & 3 lb./gal. trifluralin) *(FMC)*

Rate: 1.15-1.73 lb. ai/A
1.75-2.67 pt. EC/A

Time: Preplant incorporated.

Weeds: Broadleaf weeds:

annual morningglory*	common ragweed*	goosefoot
carelessweed	Florida purslane	jimsonweed*
carpetweed	Florida pusley	knotweed
chickweed	(Mexican clover)	kochia

Weeds: Broadleaf weeds, continued:

lambsquarters	purslane	spiny pigweed
Mexican fireweed	redroot pigweed	spurred anoda*
Pennsylvania	redweed*	stinging nettle
smartweed*	rough pigweed	velvetleaf
prickly sida	Russian thistle	(buttonweed)
(teaweed)*	(tumbleweed)	Venice mallow
prostrate pigweed	smallflower galinsoga	

Grasses:

annual bluegrass	cheatgrass	lovegrass
barnyardgrass	downy brome	(sprangletop)
(watergrass)	fall panicum	pigeongrass
bottlegrass	foxtail millet	robust foxtail
brachiaria	giant foxtail	sandbur (burgrass)
(signalgrass)	goosegrass	shattercane
bristlegrass foxtail	green foxtail	smooth crabgrass
bromegrass	johnsongrass	stinkgrass
buffalograss	(seedling)	Texas panicum
(coloradograss)	junglerice	woolly cupgrass
cheat (chess)	large crabgrass	yellow foxtail

* Suppression

Remarks: If initial seeding of soybeans fails to produce a stand, soybeans may be replanted in treated fields. Do not retreat with a second application. Do not graze or harvest cover crops for food or feed, allow livestock to graze treated vines, or feed treated vines or vine trash to livestock. Do not apply by air or through irrigation equipment.

Crop Rotation: Do not rotate to alfalfa, barley, oats, rye, or wheat in the fall of the year of application or in the spring of the following year as crop injury may occur. Beans (dry, snap), corn, cotton, cucurbits, peanuts, peas, peppers, potatoes, rice, soybeans, sweet potatoes, tobacco, and transplanted tomatoes may be planted 9 months after application. Cover crops may be planted anytime but stand reduction may occur. Carryover injury to rotational crops can occur under extremely dry conditions; refer to label for rotational cropping precautions.

Tank Mixes: Acifluorfen, Canopy, Classic, Gemini, metribuzin, Scepter.
State Restrictions: Not for use in California.

- - - - - - - - - - - - - - -

Signal Word/Toxicity Class: Caution/III.
REI: 12 hr. unless soil injected or soil incorporated.

CONCLUDE (Co-Pack)

Conclude B is a premix of bentazon & acifluorfen; Conclude G contains sethoxydim. Conclude B & G are to be tank mixed together. Effective through postemergence contact and systemic activity. One-rate postemergence herbicide allows one-pass control of grasses and broadleaf weeds.

■ POST

Conclude B (2.67 lb./gal. bentazon & 1.33 lb./gal. acifluorfen) & Conclude G (1.5 lb./gal. sethoxydim) *(BASF)*

Rate: 1.5 pt. B/A + 1.5 pt. G/A

Time: Early postemergence. Apply when weeds are small and actively growing and soybeans are in the 2nd to 3rd trifoliate leaf stage.

Weeds: Broadleaf weeds:

black nightshade	crotalaria	redroot pigweed
bristly starbur	giant ragweed	redvine
Canada thistle*	jimsonweed	redweed
carpetweed	ladysthumb	sesbania
cocklebur	morningglory	smooth pigweed
common	Pennsylvania	spurred anoda
lambsquarters	smartweed	tropic croton
common ragweed	prickly sida (teaweed)	velvetleaf

Grasses and sedges:

barnyardgrass	johnsongrass	Texas panicum
broadleaf signalgrass	(rhizome*, seedling)	witchgrass
browntop panicum	junglegrass	woolly croton
fall panicum	large crabgrass	woolly cupgrass
giant foxtail	red sprangletop	yellow foxtail
goosegrass	smooth crabgrass	yellow nutsedge*
green foxtail		

* Top growth suppression

Remarks: Add 1 pt./A crop oil concentrate. Make only one application per season. In case of crop failure, only soybeans or peanuts may be immediately replanted. Do not use treated plants for feed or forage. Do not apply through any type of irrigation system.

Days to Harvest: 75.

Crop Rotation: Root crops (such as carrots, turnips, sweet potatoes) must not be planted in treated fields within 18 months following treatment.

- - - - - - - - - - - - - - -

Signal Word/Toxicity Class: Danger/I (Conclude B); Warning/II (Conclude G).
REI: 48 hr.

RR-soybeans resistant to Roundup Ultra • STS-soybeans resistant to sulfonylurea

◆-new product • PP-preplant • PPI-preplant incorporated • PRE-preemergence • POST-postemergence • SEQ-sequential • ae-acid equivalent • ai-active ingredient • DF-dry flowable
E/EC-emulsifiable concentrate • F/FL-flowable • DG/G/WG-dispersable granule • L/LC-liquid • SP/WSP-soluble packet • W/WP-wettable powder • WSB-water soluble bag

CONCLUDE ULTRA (Co-Pack)

Conclude Ultra B is a premix of bentazone & acifluorfen; Conclude Ultra G contains sethoxydim. Conclude Ultra B & G can only be used with the closed Prodigy System in which it comes packaged. The Prodigy System will discharge Conclude Ultra B and G in a 1:1.7 ratio; return for cleaning and refilling.

■ POST

◆ **Conclude Ultra B (1.69 lb./gal. bentazon & 0.84 lb./gal. acifluorfen) & Conclude Ultra G (1.29 lb./gal. sethoxydim)** *(BASF)*

Rate: 24 oz. Ultra B + 14 oz. Ultra G/A

Time: Early postemergence. Apply when weeds are small and actively growing and soybeans are in the 2nd to 3rd trifoliate leaf stage.

Weeds: Broadleaf weeds:

black nightshade	giant ragweed	redvine
bristly starbur	jimsonweed	redweed
Canada thistle*	ladysthumb	sesbania
carpetweed	morningglory	smooth pigweed
cocklebur	Pennsylvania	spurred anoda
common lambsquarters	smartweed	teaweed
common ragweed	prickly sida	tropic croton
crotalaria	redroot pigweed	velvetleaf

Grasses and sedges:

barnyardgrass	johnsongrass	Texas panicum
broadleaf signalgrass	(rhizome*, seedling)	witchgrass
browntop panicum	junglegrass	woolly croton
fall panicum	large crabgrass	woolly cupgrass
giant foxtail	red sprangletop	yellow foxtail
goosegrass	smooth crabgrass	yellow nutsedge*
green foxtail		

* Top growth suppression

Remarks: Add 1-2 pt./A crop oil concentrate. Make only one application per season. In case of crop failure, only soybeans or peanuts may be immediately replanted. Do not use treated plants for feed or forage. Do not apply through any type of irrigation system.

Days to Harvest: 75.

Crop Rotation: Root crops (such as carrots, turnips, sweet potatoes) must not be planted in treated fields within 18 months following treatment.

– – – – – – – – – – – – – – –

Signal Word/Toxicity Class: Danger/I.
REI: 48 hr.

CONCLUDE XTRA (Co-Pack)

Conclude Xtra B is a premix of bentazon & acifluorfen; Conclude Xtra G contains clethodim. Conclude Xtra B & Xtra G are to be tank mixed together. Effective through postemergence contact and systemic activity. One-rate postemergence herbicide allows one-pass control of grasses and broadleaf weeds.

■ POST

Conclude Xtra B (2.67 lb./gal. bentazon & 1.33 lb./gal. acifluorfen) & Conclude Xtra G (0.94 lb./gal. clethodim) *(BASF)*

Rate: 24 oz. B/A + 17 oz. G/A

Time: Early postemergence. Apply when weeds are small and actively growing and soybeans are in the 2nd to 3rd trifoliate leaf stage.

Weeds: Broadleaf weeds:

black nightshade	crotalaria	redroot pigweed
bristly starbur	giant ragweed	redvine
Canada thistle*	jimsonweed	redweed
carpetweed	ladysthumb	sesbania
cocklebur	morningglory	smooth pigweed
common	Pennsylvania	spurred anoda
lambsquarters	smartweed	tropic croton
common ragweed	prickly sida (teaweed)	velvetleaf

Grasses and sedges:

barnyardgrass	johnsongrass	Texas panicum
broadleaf signalgrass	(rhizome*, seedling)	witchgrass
browntop panicum	junglegrass	woolly croton
fall panicum	large crabgrass	woolly cupgrass
giant foxtail	red sprangletop	yellow foxtail
goosegrass	smooth crabgrass	yellow nutsedge*
green foxtail		

* Top growth suppression

Remarks: Add 1 pt./A crop oil concentrate; add 2 pt./A under excessively dry, wet, or cold conditions. Make only one application per season. In case of crop failure, only soybeans may be immediately replanted. Do not apply to weeds under stress or through any type of irrigation system. Do not use treated plants for feed or forage.

Days to Harvest: 60.

Crop Rotation: Root crops (such as carrots, turnips, sweet potatoes) must not be planted in treated fields within 18 months following treatment.

– – – – – – – – – – – – – – –

Signal Word/Toxicity Class:
Danger/I (Conclude Xtra B); Warning/II (Conclude Xtra G).
REI: 48 hr.

RR Credit — see glyphosate

Cyclone — see paraquat

2,4-D - PHENOXY HERBICIDES

2,4-D and 2,4-D-type compounds selectively control broadleaf weeds with little or no control of grasses. Drift can injure adjacent crops either by spray drift or by volatilization (spray turns into a vapor). Ester formulations are most volatile and amines least volatile. Ester formulations can vaporize at temperatures as low as 70°F and be moved by wind to harm sensitive plants. Vaporization increases as air temperatures rise.

Annual and perennial broadleaf weeds controlled by 2,4-D include:

alfalfa	common purslane	Pennsylvania
annual morningglory	common ragweed	smartweed
annual sowthistle	cutleaf	peppergrass
bindweed	eveningprimrose	prickly lettuce
bittercress	dandelion	red clover
bull thistle	field pennycress	shepherdspurse
bullnettle	giant ragweed	speedwell
Canada thistle	hairy vetch	velvetleaf
Carolina geranium	horseweed	Virginia copperleaf
cinquefoil	ironweed	wild garlic
common cocklebur	marestail	wild mustard
common lambsquarters	mousetail	wild onion

■ PP

Albaugh Amine 4 (2,4-D amine) *(Albaugh)*
Albaugh LV4 or LV6 Ester (2,4-D ester) *(Albaugh)*
◆ **Clean Crop Amine 4 (2,4-D amine)** *(Platte)*
Gordon's LV 400 (2,4-D ester) *(PBI/Gordon)*
Hi-Dep (2,4-D mixed amine) *(PBI/Gordon)*
Riverdale 6 Amine (2,4-D amine) *(Riverdale)*
Riverdale L.V. 4 or L.V. 6 (2,4-D ester) *(Riverdale)*
Riverside 2,4-D Amine 4 (2,4-D amine) *(Terra)*
Solution (WS) (2,4-D amine) *(Riverdale)*
Weedestroy AM-40 (2,4-D amine) *(Riverdale)*
Wilbur-Ellis Amine 4 (2,4-D amine) *(Wilbur-Ellis)*
Wilbur-Ellis Lo Vol-4 or Lo Vol-6 (2,4-D ester) *(Wilbur-Ellis)*

Rate: 0.5-1 lb. ae/A
 1-2 pt. 4/A
 0.66-1.33 pt. 6/A
 1 WS packet/4.5-2.25 A

Time: Preplant. Apply low rate not less than 15 days before planting; high rate not less than 30 days before planting.

Remarks: Crop residue management systems. Do not use any tillage operation between application and planting soybeans. Make only one application per growing season. Do not feed hay, forage, or fodder to livestock. Do not replant treated fields in the same growing season with crops other than those labeled for 2,4-D use.

State Restrictions: Wilbur-Ellis not registered in California.

– – – – – – – – – – – – – – –

Signal Word/Toxicity Class: Danger/I (amine); Caution/III (ester).
REI: Danger—48 hr.; Caution—12 hr.

■ PP

Albaugh D-638 (2,4-D ester + acid) *(Albaugh)*
◆ **Barrage or Barrage HF (EC) (2,4-D ester)** *(Helena)*
Riverside 2,4-D LV4, WSB, or LV6 (2,4-D ester) *(Terra)*
Solve 2,4-D (2,4-D LV ester) *(Albaugh)*
Weed Rhap LV-6D (2,4-D ester) *(Helena)*
Weedar 64 (4) (2,4-D amine) *(Nufarm)*
Weedone 638 (2,4-D ester + acid) *(Nufarm)*
Weedone LV4 (2,4-D solventless ester) *(Nufarm)*
Weedone Lo Vol 6 (2,4-D ester) *(Nufarm)*

Rate: 0.375-1 lb. ae/A
 0.75-2 pt./A
 0.5-1.33 pt. LV6/A
 1-2.66 pt. 638/A

NOTICE	The information on these pages is for preliminary planning — not a guide for use. Be sure to follow the manufacturer's directions, notwithstanding information contained here.	For personal protective equipment and EPA registration numbers, please turn to page 70.

Soybeans

Time: Preplant. Apply low rate not less than 7 days (15 days for Weedar) before planting; high rate not less than 30 days before planting.
Remarks: Make only one application per growing season. Do not feed hay, forage, or fodder to livestock. Refer to label for precautions and restrictions.
State Restrictions: Not for use in California.

- - - - - - - - - - - - - - -

Signal Word/Toxicity Class: Varies by formulation.
REI: Danger—48 hr.; Caution—12 hr.

■ **PP**
◆ **Clean Crop Low Vol 4 or Low Vol 6 (2,4-D ester)** *(Platte)*
Rate: 0.4-1 lb. ae/A
    1-2 pt. 4/A
    0.5-1.33 pt. 6/A
Time: Preplant. Apply low rate not less than 7 days before planting; high rate not less than 30 days before planting.
Remarks: Crop residue management systems. Make only one application per growing season. Do not feed hay, forage, or fodder to livestock. Refer to label for precautions and restrictions.

- - - - - - - - - - - - - - -

Signal Word/Toxicity Class: Caution/III.
REI: 12 hr.

■ **PP**
◆ **Saber (2,4-D amine)** *(Platte)*
Rate: 0.5-1 lb. ae/A
    1-2 pt./A
Time: Preplant. Apply low rate not less than 15 days before planting; high rate not less than 30 days before planting.
Remarks: Crop residue management systems. Make only one application per growing season. Do not feed hay, forage, or fodder to livestock. Refer to label for precautions and restrictions.

- - - - - - - - - - - - - - -

Signal Word/Toxicity Class: Danger/I.
REI: 48 hr.

■ **PP**
Salvo (2,4-D LV ester) *(Platte)*
Rate: 12.8 fl. oz./A
Time: Preplant. Apply not less than 7 days before planting.
Remarks: Crop residue management systems. Make only one application per growing season. Do not feed hay, forage, or fodder to livestock.

- - - - - - - - - - - - - - -

Signal Word/Toxicity Class: Caution/III.
REI: 12 hr.

■ **PP**
Savage (WSB) (2,4-D amine) *(Platte)*
Rate: 0.31-0.95 lb. ae/A
    0.33-1 lb. WSB/A
Time: Preplant. Apply low rate not less than 15 days before planting; high rate not less than 30 days before planting.
Remarks: Crop residue management systems. Make only one application per growing season. Do not feed hay, forage, or fodder to livestock. Do not replant treated fields in same growing season with crops other than those labeled for 2,4-D. Refer to label for use directions and precautions.

- - - - - - - - - - - - - - -

Signal Word/Toxicity Class: Danger/I.
REI: 48 hr.

2,4-DB

Postemergence broadleaf herbicide and growth regulator. Applied alone, use only as directed band application in Midwestern states. Frequently tank mixed with other postemergent broadleaf herbicides to aid in control of morningglories.

■ **POST**
Butoxone 175, 200, or 7500 *(Cedar)*
Rate: Directed:
    0.2-0.38 lb. ae/A
    1-1.75 pt. 175/A
    0.9-1.6 pt. 200/A
    0.3-0.5 lb. 7500/A
    Topical:
    8 pt. 175/8-10 A
    8 pt. 200/9-11 A
    2.33 lb. 7500/8-10 A
Time: Postemergence. For directed application, apply first application to lower 1/3 of plant when soybeans are 8-12" tall and weeds have emerged

and are less than 3" tall; second application no later than mid-bloom stage. For topical application, apply to soybeans from 7-10 days before bloom to mid-bloom when soybeans have turned dark green color. In the Midwest, use only directed application.
Weeds: Broadleaf weeds:

annual morningglory	common	jimsonweed
cocklebur	lambsquarters	sicklepod
(low rate)	common ragweed	velvetleaf

Remarks: Do not apply when soybeans are stressed from lack of moisture or show symptoms of Phytophthora. Do not make more than 2 directed applications per season. Do not feed treated vines and hay to livestock.
Days To Harvest: 60.
Tank Mixes: Roundup Ultra.
State Restrictions: Not for use west of the Rockies.

- - - - - - - - - - - - - - -

Signal Word/Toxicity Class:
    Danger/I (Butoxone 200); Caution/III (Butoxone 175, 7500).
REI: 48 hr.

■ **PP, PRE**
Butyrac 175 or 200 *(Albaugh)*
Riverside 2,4-DB 175 or 200 *(Terra)*
Rate: 0.175-0.2 lb. ae/A
    0.8-1 pt. 175/A
    0.7-0.9 pt. 200/A
Time: Preplant, preemergence, postemergence broadcast (over-the-top). Apply when weeds are small and actively growing and no more than 3" tall. For over-the-top, apply to soybeans grown in Southern states only from 7-10 days before bloom to mid-bloom when soybeans are about knee-high and actively growing and is dark green in color.

Rate: 0.175-0.4 lb. ae/A
    0.8-1.8 pt. 175/A
    0.7-1.6 pt. 200/A
Time: Postemergence directed band. Apply to lower 1/3 of plant when soybeans are at least 8" tall.
Weeds: Broadleaf weeds:

annual morningglory	devilsclaw	prickly sida
(low rate)	field pennycress	sicklepod
cocklebur (low rate)	jimsonweed	velvetleaf
common ragweed	lambsquarters	Virginia copperleaf
croton	pigweed	wild mustard

Remarks: Do not apply on soybeans stressed by drought or Phytophthora. Do not use in or near a greenhouse. Do not apply through any type of irrigation system.
Days To Harvest: 60.
Tank Mixes: Gramoxone Extra, linuron, metribuzin, Prowl, Pursuit Plus, Reflex, Roundup Ultra, Scepter, Squadron; for 200: Basagran, Blazer, Classic, Scepter OT.
State Restrictions: Do not use as preplant or preemergence application in California, or as postemergence broadcast application in Illinois, Indiana, Iowa, Kansas, Kentucky (except Purchase area), Michigan, Minnesota, Missouri (except bootheel), Nebraska, North Dakota, Ohio, South Dakota, Wisconsin.

- - - - - - - - - - - - - - -

Signal Word/Toxicity Class: Danger/I.
REI: 48 hr.

DETAIL (Premix)

Premix containing active ingredients of Scepter and Frontier. Provides broad spectrum control of annual grasses, sedges, and broadleaf weeds.

■ **PP, PPI, PRE**
Detail (EC) (0.5 lb./gal. imazaquin & 3.6 lb./gal. dimethenamid) *(American Cyanamid)*
Rate: 1 lb. ai/A
    2 pt. EC/A
Time: Preplant incorporated, preplant surface, preemergence, or early postemergence. May be applied up to 30 days before, during, or after planting (up to unifoliate stage). For preplant incorporated, apply up to 14 days before planting; incorporate within 7 days after application.
Weeds: Broadleaf weeds:

black nightshade	entireleaf	jimsonweed
bristly starbur	morningglory	ladysthumb
carpetweed	Florida beggarweed	mexicanweed
common cocklebur	Florida pusley	mustard
common	giant ragweed	nodding spurge
lambsquarters	hairy nightshade	Palmer pigweed
common ragweed	ivyleaf	palmleaf
common sunflower	morningglory*	morningglory

RR-soybeans resistant to Roundup Ultra • STS-soybeans resistant to sulfonylurea

◆-new product • PP-preplant • PPI-preplant incorporated • PRE-preemergence • POST-postemergence • SEQ-sequential • ae-acid equivalent • ai-active ingredient • DF-dry flowable
E/EC-emulsifiable concentrate • F/FL-flowable • DG/G/WG-dispersable granule • L/LC-liquid • SP/WSP-soluble packet • W/WP-wettable powder • WSB-water soluble bag

148   **Weed Control Manual 2000**

Weeds: Broadleaf weeds, continued:

Pennsylvania smartweed	redroot pigweed	spotted spurge
pitted morningglory	sicklepod	tall morningglory
prickly sida	smallflower morningglory	tall waterhemp
prostrate pigweed	smooth pigweed	thimble pigweed
puncturevine	spiny pigweed	Venice mallow
purslane		wild poinsettia

Grasses and sedges:

barnyardgrass	giant foxtail	rice flatsedge
broadleaf signalgrass	goosegrass	robust foxtail
crabgrass	green foxtail	Texas panicum
crowfootgrass	johnsongrass	witchgrass
fall panicum	(seedling)	yellow foxtail
field sandbur	red rice	yellow nutsedge

Remarks: Do not apply products containing chlorimuron-ethyl, imazaquin, imazethapyr, or flumetsulam the same year as Detail or injury to follow crops may occur (see label for exceptions). Only rotational crops harvested at maturity may be used for feed or food. Do not graze or feed treated soybean forage, hay, or straw to livestock. Refer to label for restrictions and precautions.

Days To Harvest: 90.

Crop Rotation: Soybeans—anytime; wheat—4 months; field corn—$9^1/_2$ months; rice in the following spring after application; barley, oats, edible beans, grain sorghum, peanuts, tobacco—11 months; beets—40 months; other crops—18 months after application. Some crops in certain areas have interval exceptions; refer to label.

State Restrictions: For use in Alabama, Arkansas, Delaware, Georgia, Illinois, Indiana, Iowa, eastern Kansas, Kentucky, Louisiana, Maryland, Michigan (except Upper Peninsula), southern Minnesota, Mississippi, Missouri including bootheel, Nebraska including southeastern section, New Jersey, North Carolina, Ohio, eastern Oklahoma, Pennsylvania, South Carolina, eastern South Dakota, Tennessee, eastern Texas, Virginia, West Virginia, and southern Wisconsin.

- - - - - - - - - - - - - - -

Signal Word/Toxicity Class: Danger/I.
REI: 12 hr.

DICAMBA

From chemical family of benzoics, a growth regulating herbicide similar in action to 2,4-D. Clarity is a diglycolamine salt formulation of dicamba. Not labeled for sweet corn.

■ PP, POST

Clarity (WS) (dicamba-DGA) *(BASF)*
Rate: 0.125-0.5 lb. ai/A
  0.25-1 pt. WS/A
Time: Preplant. After application and minimum accumulation 1" rainfall or overhead irrigation, there is a 14-day interval for 0.5 pt./A, 28-day interval for 1 pt./A. Do not apply preplant in geographic areas with less than 25" average annual rainfall.

Rate: 0.25-2 lb. ai/A
  0.5-4 pt. WS/A
Time: Preharvest: Apply after soybean pods have reached mature brown color and at least 75% leaf drop has occurred.
Weeds: Broadleaf weeds including:

Canada thistle	field bindweed	pigweed
common lambsquarters	jimsonweed	sunflower
	kochia	velvetleaf

Remarks: Do not feed soybean fodder or hay following preharvest application.
Days To Harvest: Preharvest—14.
Tank Mixes: Preplant—Dual, Frontier, glyphosate. Preharvest—Glyphosate, Gramoxone Extra.

- - - - - - - - - - - - - - -

Signal Word/Toxicity Class: Warning/II.
REI: 24 hr.

DIQUAT DIBROMIDE

◆ **Diquat** *(ZENECA)*
Rate: 0.375-0.5 lb. ai/A
  1.5-2 pt./A
Time: Preharvest desiccation broadcast.
Weeds: Broadleaf weeds and grasses.
Remarks: Seed crop only. Apply by ground or air. Use high rate when weeds are large or dense. Do not use seed from treated plants for food, feed, or oil purposes. Do not apply this product through any type of irrigation system. Do not graze or feed treated forage to livestock. Refer to label for use restrictions and precautions.
Days To Harvest: 1 week.

- - - - - - - - - - - - - - -

Signal Word/Toxicity Class: Warning/II.
REI: 24 hr.

Dual — see *S*-metolachlor

FENOXAPROP-P-ETHYL

Postemergence grass herbicide with activity on several annual and certain perennial grasses. Does not control broadleaf weeds or quackgrass. Mode of action is similar to Poast, Assure, and Fusilade. Restricted Use Pesticide.

■ POST

Option II (EC) *(AgrEvo USA)*
Rate: 6.4-17 fl. oz. EC/A
Time: Postemergence. Apply during periods of rapid growth.
Weeds: Grasses:

barnyardgrass	junglerice	volunteer corn
bristly foxtail	large crabgrass	wild oat
broadleaf signalgrass	purple foxtail	wild proso millet
fall panicum	robust foxtail	wildcane
giant foxtail	smooth crabgrass	wirestem muhly
goosegrass	southwestern cupgrass	witchgrass
green foxtail		woolly cupgrass
itchgrass	sprangletop	yellow foxtail
johnsongrass	Texas panicum	

Remarks: Rate varies by weed height and species. Many grass crops such as sorghum and corn are sensitive to Option II; avoid contact to neighboring fields. Do not spray to runoff. Do not graze treated forage, hay, straw, or vines.
Days To Harvest: 90.
Crop Rotation: Do not plant any rotational crop in treated field for 30 days after application.
Tank Mixes: May be tank mixed; refer to label.
State Restrictions: For use in Colorado, Connecticut, Delaware, Illinois, Indiana, Iowa, Kansas, Maine, Maryland, Massachusetts, Michigan, Minnesota, Missouri (certain counties), Nebraska, New Hampshire, New Jersey, New York, North Dakota, Ohio, Pennsylvania, Rhode Island, South Dakota, Vermont, Virginia, West Virginia, Wisconsin.

- - - - - - - - - - - - - - -

Signal Word/Toxicity Class: Danger/I (eye).
REI: 24 hr.

FIRSTRATE

Selective herbicide for control of broadleaf weeds.

■ PP, PPI, PRE, POST

FirstRate (WSP) (cloransulam-methyl) *(Dow AgroSciences)*
Rate: 0.6-0.75 oz. WSP/A
Time: Soil application: preplant incorporated, preplant surface, postplant preemergence. Do not apply earlier than 4 weeks before planting.
Weeds: Broadleaf weeds.

common cocklebur	common waterhemp	Pennsylvania smartweed
common lambsquarters	giant ragweed	pigweed
common ragweed	horseweed	tall waterhemp
common sunflower	jimsonweed	velvetleaf
	morningglory	

Rate: 0.3 oz. WSP/A
Time: Postemergence. Apply prior to 50% flowering stage of soybeans.
Weeds: Broadleaf weeds.

common cocklebur	horseweed	sicklepod
common ragweed	jimsonweed	velvetleaf
common sunflower	morningglory	Venice mallow
giant ragweed	Pennsylvania smartweed	

Remarks: Rates varies by organic matter. Do not make more than one application per season. Do not apply by air or through any type of irrigation system. Do not harvest for forage or hay for 14 days after application.
Days to Harvest: 65.
Crop Rotation: Soybeans—0; wheat—3 months; alfalfa, corn, cotton, peanuts, rice, sorghum—9 months; sugar beets, sunflower, tobacco, all other crops—30 months plus successful field bioassay.

- - - - - - - - - - - - - - -

Signal Word/Toxicity Class: Caution/III.
REI: 12 hr. unless soil injected or soil incorporated.

Flexstar — see fomesafen

NOTICE The information on these pages is for preliminary planning — not a guide for use. Be sure to follow the manufacturer's directions, notwithstanding information contained here. | For personal protective equipment and EPA registration numbers, please turn to page 70.

FLUAZIFOP-P-BUTYL

Postemergence grass herbicide with activity on several annual and certain perennial grasses. No activity on broadleaf weeds. Mode of action similar to Poast, Assure, and Option.

■ POST

Fusilade DX *(ZENECA)*

Rate: 0.1-0.375 lb. ai/A
0.375-1.5 pt. DX/A

Time: Postemergence. Make last application before soybeans bloom.

Weeds: Annual and perennial grasses:

barnyardgrass	johnsongrass	southern sandbur
bermudagrass	(rhizome, seedling)	Texas panicum
broadleaf signalgrass	junglerice	tropical crabgrass
fall panicum	large crabgrass	volunteer cereals
field sandbur	quackgrass	wild oat
giant foxtail	red rice	wild proso millet
goosegrass	shattercane	wiresterm muhly
green foxtail	smooth crabgrass	witchgrass
Italian ryegrass	sorghum-almum	woolly cupgrass
itchgrass	southern crabgrass	yellow foxtail

Remarks: Rate varies by geographic area and grass species. Add crop oil concentrate or nonionic surfactant. Do not apply more than 2 pt./A per season. Do not graze or harvest for forage or hay. Refer to label for specific directions, restrictions, and precautions.

Crop Rotation: Do not plant rotational grass crops such as corn, sorghum, and cereals within 60 days after last application.

Tank Mixes: Basagran, Blazer, Classic, Pursuit, Reflex.

State Restrictions: Refer to label for geographical regions.

- - - - - - - - - - - - - - - - -

Signal Word/Toxicity Class: Caution.
REI: 12 hr.

FOMESAFEN

Flexstar is a selective postemergence herbicide for control of broadleaf weeds. The high load formulation uses isolink technology to use the more active molecules of fomesafen. Rainfast in 4 hr. Reflex is postemergence broadleaf herbicide with contact/mode of action similar to Blazer and Cobra. Can be tank mixed with other postemergent herbicides for broad spectrum weed control.

■ POST

Flexstar *(ZENECA)*

Rate: 0.188-0.375 lb. ai/A
0.75-1.6 pt./A

Time: Postemergence. Apply to actively growing weeds before soybeans bloom (usually 14-28 days after planting).

Weeds: Broadleaf weeds including:

balloonvine	ladysthumb	Pennsylvania
black nightshade	mexicanweed	smartweed
carpetweed	morningglory	spurred anoda
common cocklebur	pigweed	tall waterhemp
giant ragweed	prickly sida	wild mustard
jimsonweed	ragweed	velvetleaf

Annual grasses and sedges including:

barnyardgrass	fall panicum	johnsongrass (seedling)
broadleaf signalgrass	foxtail	nutsedge
crabgrass	goosegrass	Texas panicum

Remarks: Rate varies by weed species and geographical region. Add nonionic surfactant, crop oil concentrate, or adjuvant. Apply by ground or air. Requires 1 hr. rainfree period for best results. Do not apply through any type of irrigation system. Do not graze treated areas or harvest for forage or hay. Refer to label for use directions, restrictions, and precautions.

Crop Rotation: Barley, rye, wheat—4 months; beans, corn, cotton, peanuts, peas, rice—10 months; alfalfa, sorghum, sugar beets, sunflower—18 months. Use 18 month minimum rotation interval for sweet corn in Connecticut, Maine, Massachusetts, New Hampshire, New York, Rhode Island, Vermont and region five. Sorghum may be replanted after 10 months in region one.

Tank Mixes: Assure II, Basagran, Butyrac, Classic, Convert, Gramoxone Extra, Option II, Pinnacle, Poast, Poast Plus, Pursuit, Raptor, Reliance STS, Resource, Sceptor, Select, Synchrony STS.

State Restrictions: Refer to label for geographical regions.

- - - - - - - - - - - - - - - - -

Signal Word/Toxicity Class: Warning/II.
REI: 24 hr.

■ POST

Reflex (2LC) *(ZENECA)*

Rate: 0.188-0.375 lb. ai/A
0.75-1.5 pt. 2LC/A

Time: Postemergence. Apply when annual broadleaf weeds are in 2- to 6-leaf stage and before soybeans bloom.

Weeds: Annual broadleaf weeds and sedges:

balloonvine	goosegrass	redweed
barnyardgrass	green foxtail	showy crotalaria
black nightshade	hedge binweed	sicklepod
bristly starbur	hemp sesbania	smallflower
broadleaf signalgrass	honeyvine milkweed	morningglory
carpetweed	hophornbeam	smellmelon
climbing milkweed	copperleaf	smooth pigweed
common cocklebur	horsenettle	spiny amaranth
common	ivyleaf morningglory	spotted spurge
lambsquarters	jimsonweed	spurred anoda
common purslane	johnsongrass	tall morningglory
common ragweed	(seedling)	tall waterhemp
common sunflower	ladysthumb	Texas panicum
common waterhemp	mexicanweed	tropic croton
crabgrass	Palmer amaranth	trumpetcreeper
cutleaf groundcherry	palmleaf	velvetleaf
cypressvine	morningglory	Venice mallow
morningglory	Pennsylvania	Virginia copperleaf
eclipta	smartweed	volunteer cucumber
entireleaf	pitted morningglory	wild mustard
morningglory	prickly sida	wild poinsettia
fall panicum	prostrate spurge	wild watermelon
field bindweed	purple moonflower	witchweed
Florida pusley	morningglory	yellow foxtail
giant foxtail	red morningglory	yellow nutsedge
giant ragweed	redroot pigweed	yellow rocket

Remarks: Rate varies by weed species and geographical region. Apply by ground or air. Add crop oil concentrate or nonionic surfactant. Do not apply through any type of irrigation system. Do not graze treated areas or harvest for forage or hay. Refer to label for directions and precautions.

Crop Rotation: Small grains such as barley, rye, wheat—4 months; beans, corn, cotton, peanuts, peas, rice—10 months; alfalfa, sorghum, sugar beets, sunflowers, or any other crop—18 months.

State Restrictions: Refer to label for geographical regions.

- - - - - - - - - - - - - - - - -

Signal Word/Toxicity Class: Danger/I.
REI: 24 hr.

FREEDOM (Premix)

Premix containing active ingredients of Lasso and Treflan. Extremely toxic to freshwater marine, and estuarine fish and aquatic invertebrates including shrimp and oyster. Restricted Use Pesticide.

■ PPI

Freedom (3E) (2.67 lb./gal. alachlor & 0.33 lb./gal. trifluralin)
(Monsanto)

Rate: Preplant incorporated:
2.6-3.38 lb. ai/A
7-9 pt. 3E/A
Preemergence surface:
2.25-3.38 lb. ai/A
6-9 pt. 3E/A

Time: Preplant incorporated, preemergence surface. For preplant, apply any time within 7 days prior to planting. For preemergence, apply before crop and weeds emerge and within 5 days of last preplant tillage operation.

Weeds: Broadleaf weeds:

bristly starbur	Florida pusley	purslane
carelessweed	galinsoga	smallflower
carpetweed	hairy nightshade	morningglory
common ragweed	hemp sesbania	smartweed
cutleaf groundcherry	lambsquarters	tall morningglory
eastern black	pigweed	teaweed
nightshade	prickly sida	waterhemp
Florida beggarweed		

Grasses and sedges:

barnyardgrass	hairy crabgrass	shattercane
broadleaf signalgrass	johnsongrass	(wildcane)
browntop panicum	(seedling)	Texas panicum
fall panicum	red sprangletop	witchgrass
giant foxtail	robust purple foxtail	woolly cupgrass
goosegrass	robust white foxtail	yellow foxtail
green foxtail	sandbur (grassbur)	yellow nutsedge

Remarks: Rate varies by soil texture and organic matter. Do not graze treated area or feed treated forage, hay, or straw to livestock. Do not apply through any type of irrigation system.

Tank Mixes: Canopy, Command, metribuzin, Pursuit, Scepter.

State Restrictions: For use in Alabama, Arkansas, Florida, Georgia, Illinois, Iowa, Kansas, Kentucky, Louisiana, Minnesota, Mississippi, Missouri, Nebraska, South Carolina, South Dakota, Tennessee, Texas, Wisconsin.

- - - - - - - - - - - - - - - - -

Signal Word/Toxicity Class: Warning/II.
REI: 12 hr.

RR-soybeans resistant to Roundup Ultra • STS-soybeans resistant to sulfonylurea

◆-new product • PP-preplant • PPI-preplant incorporated • PRE-preemergence • POST-postemergence • SEQ-sequential • ae-acid equivalent • ai-active ingredient • DF-dry flowable
E/EC-emulsifiable concentrate • F/FL-flowable • DG/G/WG-dispersable granule • L/LC-liquid • SP/WSP-soluble packet • W/WP-wettable powder • WSB-water soluble bag

FRONTIER

Chloroacetamide herbicide that appears to perform in a similar manner as alachlor (Lasso) and S-metolachlor (Dual). However, use rate is lower.

■ PP, PPI, PRE, POST

Frontier 6.0 (dimethenamid) *(BASF)*
Rate: 0.94-1.5 lb. ai/A
  20-32 fl. oz. 6.0/A
Time: Preplant (surface or incorporated); preemergence or early postemergence (up to third trifoliate stage); split application.
Weeds: Broadleaf weeds:

carpetweed	nightshade	spurge
common purslane	pigweed	waterhemp
Florida pusley		

Grasses and sedges:

barnyardgrass	johnsongrass	southwestern
broadleaf signalgrass	(seedling)	cupgrass
fall panicum	large crabgrass	Texas panicum
giant foxtail	rice flatsedge	yellow foxtail
goosegrass	smooth crabgrass	yellow nutsedge
green foxtail		

Remarks: Rate varies by soil type and organic matter. Do not apply through any type of irrigation system. Do not graze or feed forage, hay, or straw to livestock.
Crop Rotation: If crop treated with Frontier is lost to adverse weather (or other reasons), treated area may be replanted to any labeled crop immediately. Fall-seeded crops may be planted at 4 or more months after a spring application. No restrictions in the spring following previous year's application.
Tank Mixes: Assure, Authority, Basagran, Blazer, Canopy, Command, FirstRate, Flexstar, Fusilade, Fusion, Galaxy, Gramoxone Extra, Liberty, linuron, metribuzin, Poast, Poast Plus, Prowl, Pursuit, Python, Raptor, Roundup Ultra, Scepter, Select, Sonalan, Storm, Synchrony STS, Touchdown, trifluralin, or 2,4-D (early preplant only).

– – – – – – – – – – – – – – –

Signal Word/Toxicity Class: Warning/II.
REI: 12 hr.

FRONTROW (Co-Pack)

Co-Pack containing cloransulam-methyl the active ingredient in FirstRate and flumetsulam the active ingredient in Python WDG in separate water-soluble packets and packaged together in a single overpack to be used together. Overpack is not water soluble.

■ POST

Frontrow: FirstRate (cloransulam-methyl) & Python (flumetsulam) *(Dow AgroSciences)*
Rate: One overpack: 1.5 oz. FirstRate + 0.6 oz. Python/5 Acres
Time: Postemergence.
Weeds: Broadleaf weeds.

cocklebur	hemp sesbania*	prickly sida
common ragweed	jimsonweed	sicklepod
common sunflower	morningglory	velvetleaf
giant ragweed	pigweed*	Venice mallow

*Suppression

Remarks: Add either crop oil concentrate, nonionic surfactant, or nonionic surfactant plus urea ammoniun nitrate or ammonium sulfate. Do not apply by air, make more than one application per crop season or apply through any type of irrigation system. Do not graze or feed treated forage, hay, or straw to livestock.
Crop Rotation: Small grains—3 months; corn, cotton, peanuts, sorghum—9 months; sugar beets, sunflower, tobacco, all other crops—26 months plus successful field bioassay.

– – – – – – – – – – – – – – –

Signal Word/Toxicity Class: Caution/III.
REI: 12 hr.

Fusilade — see fluazifop-P-butyl

FUSION (Premix)

Containing active ingredients of Fusilade and Option II. Provides broad spectrum control of several grass species—annuals as well as certain perennials.

■ POST

Fusion (2 lb./gal. fluazifop-P-butyl & 0.56 lb./gal. fenoxaprop-P-ethyl) *(ZENECA)*

Rate: 4-14 fl. oz./A
Time: Postemergence. Make last application before bloom.
Weeds: Annual and perennial grasses:

barnyardgrass	green foxtail	southern sandbur
bermudagrass	Italian ryegrass	Texas panicum
broadleaf signalgrass	itchgrass	volunteer cereals
crabgrass	johnsongrass	wild oat
downy brome	(rhizome, seedling)	wild proso millet
fall panicum	junglerice	wirestem muhly
field sandbur	quackgrass	witchgrass
foxtail	red rice	woolly cupgrass
giant foxtail	shattercane	yellow foxtail
goosegrass	sorghum-almum	

Remarks: Apply by ground or air. Add oil concentrate or nonionic surfactant. Do not apply through any type of irrigation system. Do not graze or harvest for forage or hay. Refer to label for specific directions, restrictions, and precautions.
Crop Rotation: Do not plant rotational crops such as corn, sorghum, and cereals within 60 days of last application.
Tank Mixes: Basagran, Blazer, Canopy, Classic, Cobra, Concert, 2,4-D (LVE), Flexstar, Galaxy, Gramoxone Extra, Pinnacle, Prowl, Pursuit, Reflex, Scepter, Scepter OT, Storm, Synchrony STS, Tornado, Typhoon.
State Restrictions: For use in Alabama, Arkansas, Connecticut, Delaware, Florida, Georgia, Illinois, Indiana, Iowa, Kansas, Kentucky, Louisiana, Maine, Maryland, Massachusetts, Michigan, Minnesota, Mississippi, Missouri, Nebraska, New Hampshire, New Jersey, New York, North Carolina, North Dakota, Ohio, Oklahoma (east of I-35), Pennsylvania, Rhode Island, South Carolina, South Dakota, Tennessee, Texas (east of I-35), Vermont, Virginia, West Virginia, Wisconsin.

– – – – – – – – – – – – – – –

Signal Word/Toxicity Class: Caution.
REI: 24 hr.

GALAXY (Premix)

Premix containing active ingredients of Basagran and Blazer. Provides broad spectrum postemergence control of several broadleaf weeds, including cocklebur and jimsonweed.

■ POST

Galaxy (3 lb./gal. bentazon & 0.67 lb./gal. acifluorfen) *(BASF)*
Rate: 0.92 lb. ai/A
  2 pt./A
Time: Postemergence.
Weeds: Broadleaf weeds and sedges:

beggarticks	galinsoga	smallflower
black nightshade	giant ragweed	morningglory
bristly starbur	ivyleaf morningglory	smooth pigweed
Canada thistle	jimsonweed	spurred anoda
cocklebur	ladysthumb	tall morningglory
common	palmleaf morningglory	tall waterhemp
lambsquarters	Pennsylvania	teaweed
common purslane	smartweed	velvetleaf
common ragweed	pitted morningglory	Venice mallow
cypressvine	prickly sida	wild buckwheat
morningglory	purple moonflower	wild mustard
dayflower	morningglory	wild poinsettia
devilsclaw	redroot pigweed	wild sunflower
entireleaf	redweed	yellow nutsedge
morningglory	shepherdspurse	

Remarks: Add oil concentrate or urea ammonium nitrate solution. Rainfall or overhead irrigation within 8 hr. after application may nullify effectiveness.
Days to Harvest: 50.
Crop Rotation: Do not rotate to root crops such as carrots, turnips, sweet potatoes, etc. into treated fields for 18 months after last application.
Tank Mixes: Assure II, Classic, 2,4-DB, FirstRate, Frontier, Fusilade DX, Fusion, Matador, Pinnacle, Poast, Poast Plus, Pursuit, Raptor, Reliance STS, Resource, Roundup Ultra, Scepter, Select, Skirmish, Synchrony STS.

– – – – – – – – – – – – – – –

Signal Word/Toxicity Class: Danger/I.
REI: 48 hr.

GLUFOSINATE-AMMONIUM

Use only on soybeans designated as Liberty Link. If this product is applied over soybeans not designated as Liberty Link, severe crop damage will occur. Rainfast within 4 hr. of application.

■ POST

Liberty (WS) *(AgrEvo USA)*
Rate: 0.2-0.44 lb. ai/A
  1-2.13 pt. WS/A
Time: Postemergence. Apply to actively growing weeds from crop emergence to bloom. Apply between dawn and 2 hr. before sunset.

Soybeans

Weeds: Broadleaf weeds:

buffalobur
buckwheat
Canada thistle
carpetweed
common chickweed
common cocklebur
common
  lambsquarters
common milkweed
common ragweed
common sunflower
common waterhemp
dandelion
eastern black
  nightshade
entireleaf
  morningglory

field bindweed
Florida beggarweed
giant ragweed
hedge bindweed
honeyvine milkweed
ivyleaf morningglory
jimsonweed
ladysthumb
kochia
marestail
marshelder
Palmer amaranth
Pennsylvania
  smartweed
prickly sida
pitted morningglory
prostrate pigweed

redroot pigweed
Russian thistle
shepherdspurse
sicklepod
smallflower
  morningglory
smooth pigweed
sowthistle
spiny pigweed
tall morningglory
tall waterhemp
tumble pigweed
velvetleaf
Venice mallow
wild buckwheat
wild mustard

Grasses and sedges:

barnyardgrass*
broadleaf signalgrass
fall panicum
field sandbur
giant foxtail
green foxtail
hemp sesbania
johnsongrass

large crabgrass
quackgrass
orchardgrass
shattercane
smooth crabgrass
Texas panicum
volunteer corn*
volunteer proso millet

volunteer sorghum*
wild oat
wild proso millet
wirestem muhly
woolly cupgrass
yellow foxtail*
yellow nutsedge

* Suppression

Remarks: Do not apply if crop is stressed or make more than 2 applications to crop. Do not apply through any type of irrigation system. Do not harvest treated green soybean plants for forage and hay feed.

Days To Harvest: 70.

Crop Rotation: Corn, soybeans—anytime; barley, buckwheat, millet, oats, rye, sorghum, triticale, wheat—70 days; all other crops—120 days.

Tank Mixes: Basagran, Blazer, FirstRate, Flexstar, Frontier, Fusilade DX, Fusion, Galaxy, Manifest, Pinnacle, Poast, Poast Plus, Prism, Pursuit, Raptor, Reflex, Resource, Scepter, Select, Storm, Tornado, Typhoon.

- - - - - - - - - - - - - - - - -

Signal Word/Toxicity Class: Warning/II.
REI: 12 hr.

RR Glyfos or Glyfos X-tra — see glyphosate

RR GLYPHOSATE

Monsanto has agreements with the manufacturers listed below to market these glyphosate products for postemergent application over Roundup Ready soybeans. The products are for use only on seed designated as containing the Roundup Ready gene. If these product are applied over soybeans not designated as Roundup Ready, severe crop damage will occur.
For more information on Roundup Ready soybeans, turn to page 128.

■ POST

◆ **Credit (4WS)** *(Nufarm)*
◆ **Glyfos (4WS)** *(Cheminova)*
Rattler (4WS) *(Helena)*
Roundup Ultra (4WS) *(Monsanto)*

Rate: Annual weeds:
  1-1.5 lb. ai/A
  2-3 pt. 4WS/A
  Perennial weeds:
  1-2 lb. ai/A
  2-4 pt. 4WS/A
  Preplant burndown (no-till, stale seedbed):
  0.5-2 lb. ai/A
  1-4 pt. 4WS/A

Time: Postemergence. Apply from cracking through full flowering stage.

Weeds: Broadleaf weeds:

annual spurge
black nightshade
blue mustard
burcumber
buttercup
Canada thistle
Carolina geranium
cocklebur
common chickweed
common groundsel

common
  lambsquarters
curly dock
cutleaf
  eveningprimrose
dwarfdandelion
fanweed
field bindweed
field pennycress
filaree

Florida pusley
giant ragweed
groundcherry
hemp dogbane
hemp sesbania
henbit
horsenettle
horseweed
jagged chickweed
ladysthumb

Weeds: Broadleaf weeds, continued:

London rocket
marestail
milkweed
morningglory
mouseear chickweed
Pennsylvania
  smartweed
redroot pigweed
redvine

shepherdspurse
sicklepod
smallseed falseflax
smooth pigweed
spanishneedles
spurred anoda
swamp smartweed
tansymustard
teaweed

trumpetcreeper
tumble mustard
umbrella spurry
velvetleaf
volunteer corn
wheat
wild mustard
wild oat

Grasses and sedges:

annual bluegrass
annual ryegrass
barnyardgrass
bermudagrass
broadleaf signalgrass
bulbous bluegrass
Carolina foxtail
cheat
crabgrass
downy brome

fall panicum
field sandbur
foxtail
goosegrass
Italian ryegrass
johnsongrass
  (rhizome)
jointed goatgrass
nutsedge
red rice

quackgrass
shattercane
sprangletop
stinkgrass
Texas panicum
waterhemp
wild proso millet
wirestem muhly
witchgrass
woolly cupgrass

Remarks: For use only on soybean varieties designated as containing the Roundup Ready gene. Rate varies by weed species and height. Do not allow glyphosate to contact desirable plants. Do not apply through any type of irrigation system. Do not feed or graze treated soybean forage. Refer to label for directions, precautions and restrictions.

Days To Harvest: 14.
State Restrictions: Varies by product; refer to label.

- - - - - - - - - - - - - - - - -

Signal Word/Toxicity Class: Varies by formulation.
REI: Warning—12 hr.; Caution—4 hr.

■ PP, PRE

◆ **Credit (4WS)** *(Nufarm)*
◆ **Glyfos or Glyfos X-tra (4WS)** *(Cheminova)*
Rattler (4WS) *(Helena)*
Roundup Custom (5.4WS) *(Monsanto)*
Roundup Original, Original RT, Ultra, Ultra RT (4WS) *(Monsanto)*

Rate: Annual weeds:
  0.38-1.5 lb. ai/A
  0.56-2.25 pt. 5.4WS/A
  0.75-3 pt. 4WS/A
  Perennial weeds:
  0.5-5 lb. ai/A
  0.75-7.5 pt. 5.4WS/A
  1-10 pt. 4WS/A

Time: Preplant, preemergence, at-planting, spot treatment, preharvest. For preharvest, apply after pods have set and lost all green color.

Weeds: Annual and perennial broadleaf weeds and grasses.

Remarks: For preharvest applications, do not apply to soybeans grown for seed. Rate varies by weed species and height. Do not add surfactant to Roundup Ultra or Ultra RT. Refer to label for directions and precautions.

Days To Harvest: 7; grazing/feed—25.

Tank Mixes: Alachlor, Canopy, Command, 2,4-D, Dual, Frontier, Fusion, linuron, metribuzin, Prowl, Pursuit, Pursuit Plus, Scepter, Squadron, Turbo. Roundup tank mixes not registered in California.

State Restrictions: Roundup RT for use in Colorado, Idaho, Montana, North Dakota, South Dakota, Utah, Wyoming, and in specific counties only in Kansas, Minnesota, Nebraska, Nevada, Oklahoma, Oregon, and Washington; refer to label for restrictions. Glyfos is not registered for use in California. Glyfos X-tra is not registered for use in mistblowers in California or Arizona.

- - - - - - - - - - - - - - - - -

Signal Word/Toxicity Class: Varies by formulation.
REI: Warning—12 hr.; Caution—4 hr.

Gramoxone Extra — see paraquat

Lasso — see alachlor

Liberty — see glufosinate-ammonium

LOROX

May be tank mixed with several different soil-applied or "knock-down" herbicides to provide broad spectrum control. Linuron is a photosynthetic inhibitor.

■ PRE, POST

Lorox DF (linuron) *(Griffin)*

RR-soybeans resistant to Roundup Ultra • STS-soybeans resistant to sulfonylurea

◆-new product • PP-preplant • PPI-preplant incorporated • PRE-preemergence • POST-postemergence • SEQ-sequential • ae-acid equivalent • ai-active ingredient • DF-dry flowable
E/EC-emulsifiable concentrate • F/FL-flowable • DG/G/WG-dispersable granule • L/LC-liquid • SP/WSP-soluble packet • W/WP-wettable powder • WSB-water soluble bag

Rate: 0.5-2.5 lb. ai/A
1-5 lb. DF/A
Time: Preemergence.
Weeds: Broadleaf weeds:

annual morningglory*	Florida pusley	purslane
buttonweed*	galinsoga	sicklepod*
carpetweed	lambsquarters	smartweed
chickweed	mustard	teaweed*
cocklebur*	nettleleaf goosefoot	velvetleaf *
common dayflower	pigweed	wild radish
common ragweed	prickly sida*	

Grasses:

barnyardgrass	fall panicum	goosegrass
canarygrass	foxtail	watergrass
crabgrass		

* Partial control

Remarks: Rate varies by soil type. Do not spray over top of emerged soybeans.
Crop Rotation: Do not plant treated areas to any crop not on label within 4 months after treatment.
Tank Mixes: Dual, Lasso, metribuzin, paraquat, Prowl, Roundup Ultra.

- - - - - - - - - - - - - - - -

Rate: 0.5-1 lb. ai/A
1-2 lb. DF/A
Time: Postemergence. Apply when soybeans are at least 12" tall and weeds do not exceed 4"; when soybeans are 8" tall and weeds do not exceed 2".
Weeds: Broadleaf weeds:

amsinckia	fiddleneck	prickly sida
annual morningglory	Florida purslane	purslane
buttonweed	groundsel	sesbania
carpetweed	knawel	sicklepod
cocklebur	lambsquarters	smartweed
common dayflower	mustard	teaweed
dogfennel	nettleleaf goosefoot	velvetleaf
Florida beggarweed	pigweed	wild buckwheat

Grasses:

annual ryegrass	crabgrass	goosegrass
barnyardgrass	fall panicum	rattail fescue
broadleaf signalgrass	foxtail	Texas panicum
canarygrass	giant foxtail	watergrass

Remarks: Apply as directed spray, keeping contact with soybean plants at a minimum. Add surfactant. Do not graze or feed forage from treated areas to livestock.
Days To Harvest: 60.
Crop Rotation: Same restrictions as above.
Tank Mixes: 2,4-DB.

- - - - - - - - - - - - - - - -

Signal Word/Toxicity Class: Caution.
REI: 24 hr.

MANIFEST (Co-Pack)

Combination of Manifest B and Manifest G which is supplied in the closed Prodigy System or Duplex II System. The Prodigy System will discharge Manifest B and Manifest G in a 1:0.75 ratio; return for cleaning and refilling. The Duplex II System contains enough Manifest to treat 5 acres.

■ POST
Manifest B (3 lb./gal. bentazon & 0.67 lb./gal. acifluorfen) &
Manifest G (1.5 lb./gal. sethoxydim) *(BASF)*
Rate: 2 pt. B + 1.5 pt. G/A (3.5 pt. product/A)
Time: Postemergence. Apply when soybeans are in 1st to 3rd trifoliate leaf stage.
Weeds: Broadleaf weeds:

balloonvine	giant ragweed	smooth pigweed
beggarticks	jimsonweed	spurred anoda
bristly starbur	ladysthumb	teaweed
cocklebur	marshelder	tropic croton
common	Pennsylvania	velvetleaf
lambsquarters	smartweed	Venice mallow
Canada thistle	prickly sida	wild mustard
common purslane	redweed	wild poinsettia
common ragweed	shepherdspurse	wild sunflower
dayflower		

Grasses and sedges:

annual ryegrass	junglegrass	wild oat
barnyardgrass	large crabgrass	wild proso millet
broadleaf signalgrass	quackgrass	wirestem muhly
browntop panicum	red sprangletop	witchgrass
fall panicum	shattercane	woolly croton
giant foxtail	smooth crabgrass	woolly cupgrass
goosegrass	Texas panicum	yellow foxtail
green foxtail	volunteer corn	yellow nutsedge
johnsongrass		
(seedling)		

Remarks: Add crop oil concentrate. Do not use treated plants for feed or forage. Refer to label for restrictions, precautions, and limitations.
Days to Harvest: 75.
Crop Rotation: Root crops (such as carrots, turnips, sweet potatoes) must not be planted in treated field for 18 months after application.
Tank Mixes: Blazer, Classic, Pinnacle, Resource.

- - - - - - - - - - - - - - - -

Signal Word/Toxicity Class: Danger/I (Manifest B); Warning/II (Manifest G).
REI: 48 hr.

Matador — see quizalofop-P-ethyl

S-METOLACHLOR

Dual is a cell growth inhibitor. S-metolachlor is a purified isomer of the metolachlor molecule. Dual II MAGNUM contains a safening agent. Preemergence or preplant incorporated grass herbicide with activity on a few annual broadleaves, as well as yellow nutsedge. Often tank mixed with certain soil-applied broadleaf herbicides and used as an early preplant treatment in reduced-tillage systems.

■ PP, PPI, PRE
Dual MAGNUM or Dual II MAGNUM (EC) *(Novartis)*
Dual IIG MAGNUM *(Novartis)*
Rate: 1-2 pt. EC/A
6-12 lb. G/A
Time: Preplant incorporated, preplant surface, preemergence, postemergence, lay-by (except IIG). For early preplant surface, apply as split application 30-45 days before planting; applications less than 30 days before planting may be either split or single treatment. Fall application in Illinois (north of Rt. 136), Iowa, Minnesota, Nebraska (north of Rt. 20), North Dakota, South Dakota, Wisconsin.
Weeds: Broadleaf weeds:

carpetweed	eclipta*	galinsoga
common purslane*	Florida beggarweed*	hairy nightshade*
common waterhemp	Florida pusley	pigweed
eastern black		tall waterhemp
nightshade		

Grasses and sedges:

barnyardgrass	green foxtail	southwestern
(watergrass)	johnsongrass	cupgrass
bristly foxtail	(seedling)*	volunteer sorghum*
crabgrass	prairie cupgrass	wild proso millet* **
crowfootgrass	red rice	witchgrass
fall panicum	sandbur*	woolly cupgrass* **
foxtail millet	shattercane*	yellow foxtail
giant foxtail	signalgrass	yellow nutsedge
goosegrass		

* Suppression; ** Preemergence

Remarks: Rate varies by soil type and organic matter. Do not use on muck or peat soils. In case of crop failure, any crop on label may be replanted immediately. Do not make second broadcast application. If original application was banded and second crop is planted in untreated row middles, second banded treatment may be applied. Do not graze or feed forage from treated field for 30 days after application. Refer to label for use directions and restrictions.
Crop Rotation: Alfalfa—4 months; barley, oats, rye, wheat—4½ months; tomatoes—6 months; clover—9 months; any labeled crop in addition to barley, buckwheat, cabbage, milo, nuts, oats, peppers, rice, root crops, rye, stone fruits, tobacco, and wheat may be planted in the spring following treatment (including layby or multiple treatments applied previous season); all other rotational crops may be planted 12 months after application.
Tank Mixes: Canopy, Command, Lorox, Lorox Plus, metribuzin, Preview, Scepter, Gramoxone Extra, Pursuit, Roundup Ultra, Sonalan, trifluralin.
State Restrictions: Do not use in Nassau County or Suffolk County, New York. Preplant surface: Medium- and fine-textured soils with minimum- or no-tillage systems in Colorado, Connecticut, Delaware, Illinois, Indiana, Iowa, Kansas, Kentucky, Maine, Maryland, Massachusetts, Michigan, Minnesota, Missouri, Montana, Nebraska, New Hampshire, New York, North Dakota, Ohio, Pennsylvania, Rhode Island, South Dakota, Tennessee, Virginia, West Virginia, Wisconsin, Wyoming.

- - - - - - - - - - - - - - - -

Signal Word/Toxicity Class: Caution/III.
REI: 24 hr.

Micro-Tech — see alachlor

2

Soybeans

NORFLURAZON

Dry flowable herbicide for control of grasses and broadleaf weeds.

■ PPI, PRE
Zorial Rapid 80 (DF) *(Novartis)*
Rate: 1-2 lb. ai/A
  1.25-2.5 lb. DF/A
Time: Preplant incorporated, preemergence surface, split application.
Weeds: Broadleaf weeds:

carpetweed	morningglory*	sicklepod*
cocklebur*	Pennsylvania	spotted spurge*
common ragweed*	smartweed*	spurred anoda
Florida pusley	pigweed	tropic croton
hemp sesbania*	prickly sida	velvetleaf
kochia*	purslane	Venice mallow*
lanceleaf sage*	Russian thistle*	

Grasses and sedges:

barnyardgrass	goosegrass	purple nutsedge*
bermudagrass*	johnsongrass	signalgrass
crabgrass	(rhizome*, seedling)	yellow nutsedge*
foxtail	panicum	

* Suppression

Remarks: Rate and timing vary by geography, soil type, and method of application. Do not graze treated fields or feed treated forage to livestock within 90 days of treatment.
Crop Rotation: Rotational crops vary by geography; refer to label.
Tank Mixes: Basagran, Blazer, Canopy, Classic, Dual, Gramoxone Extra, Lasso, Lorox, metribuzin, Prowl, Roundup Ultra, Scepter, Storm, and trifluralin; refer to labels for use instructions.
State Restrictions: For use in Alabama, Arkansas, Florida, Georgia, Kentucky, Louisiana, Mississippi, bootheel of Missouri, North Carolina, Oklahoma, South Carolina, Tennessee, Texas, and Virginia.

– – – – – – – – – – – – – – –

Signal Word/Toxicity Class: Caution.
REI: 12 hr.

Option II — see fenoxaprop-P-ethyl

PARAQUAT

Nonselective, postemergence herbicide used for control of several annual grass and broadleaf weeds. Primarily used as "knock-down" treatment in no-till and minimum tillage systems, but may also be used as harvest aid desiccant. Gramoxone Extra is a contact herbicide and a Restricted Use Pesticide.

■ PP, PRE, POST
Cyclone (2L or 3L), Gramoxone Extra (2.5L), Starfire (1.5L) *(ZENECA)*
Rate: 0.5-1 lb. ai/A
  1.5-3 pt. 2.5L/A
  0.75-2.5 pt. 3L/A
Time: Preplant or preemergence. Apply when weeds and grasses are succulent and growth is from 1-6" tall.
Weeds: Annual broadleaf weeds and grasses; top kill and suppression of perennials.
Remarks: Add nonionic surfactant or crop oil concentrate. Seeding should be done with a minimum amount of soil disturbance. Weeds and grasses emerging after application will not be controlled; crops emerged at time of application will be killed. Refer to label for use directions, restrictions, and precautions.
Tank Mixes: Canopy, 2,4-D ester, 2,4-DB, Dual, Goal, Harmony Extra, Lasso, linuron, metribuzin, Modown, Prowl, Pursuit, Scepter, Surflan, Turbo.

– – – – – – – – – – – – – – –

Rate: 3.5-6 fl. oz. 2.5L/A
  2.7-5.3 fl. oz. 3L/A
Time: Postemergence-directed spray. Do not treat if soybeans are below 8" tall. If needed, make second application 7-14 days later; do not repeat more than twice.
Weeds: Grasses 2-4" tall, weeds 2-3" tall.
Remarks: Add nonionic surfactant or crop oil concentrate. Soybeans treated topically will be killed. Do not graze treated areas or feed treated forage to livestock. Refer to label for restrictions and precautions.
Tank Mixes: Canopy, 2,4-D ester, 2,4-DB, Dual, Goal, Harmony Extra, Lasso, linuron, metribuzin, Modown, Prowl, Pursuit, Scepter, Surflan, Turbo.

– – – – – – – – – – – – – – –

Rate: 0.125-025 lb. ai/A
  11-22 fl. oz. 1.5L/A
  0.5-1 pt. 2L/A
  10.7 fl. oz. 3L/A

Time: Indeterminant varieties: Apply when 65% seed pods have reached mature brown and seed moisture is 30% or less. Determinant varieties: Apply when plants are mature, beans fully developed, 1/2 of leaves have dropped, and remaining leaves are yellowing.
Weeds: Various grasses and weeds.
Remarks: Add nonionic surfactant or crop oil concentrate. Immature soybeans will be injured. Do not graze or harvest for forage or hay. Refer to label for restrictions and precautions.
Days To Harvest: 15.
Tank Mixes: Cyclone (3L): Canopy, 2,4-D ester, 2,4-DB, Dual, Goal, Harmony Extra, Lasso, linuron, metribuzin, Modown, Prowl, Pursuit, Scepter, Surflan, Turbo.

– – – – – – – – – – – – – – –

Signal Word/Toxicity Class: Danger-Poison/I.
REI: 12 hr. (except harvest aid/desiccation 24 hr.).

Partner — see alachlor

PENDIMETHALIN

A dinitroaniline, cell growth inhibitor grass herbicide with activity on a few broadleaves. May be tank mixed with several different soil-applied and nonselective herbicides to provide broad spectrum weed control.

■ PP, PPI, PRE
Pentagon DG *(American Cyanamid)*
Prowl 3.3 EC *(American Cyanamid)*
Rate: Preplant:
  0.5-1.5 lb. ai/A
  1.2-3.6 pt. 3.3 EC/A
  0.85-2.5 lb. DG/A
  Preemergence:
  0.5-1.2 lb. ai/A
  1.2-3 pt. 3.3 EC/A
  0.85-2.1 lb. DG/A
Time: Preplant (incorporated, surface), preemergence. Do not apply preemergence north of I-80. Do not apply postemergence.
Weeds: Broadleaf Weeds:

annual spurge	lambsquarters	pigweed
carpetweed	Pennsylvania	purslane
Florida pusley	smartweed*	velvetleaf*
kochia		

Grasses:

barnyardgrass	giant foxtail	shattercane
crabgrass	goosegrass	signalgrass
crowfootgrass	green foxtail	Texas panicum
fall panicum	johnsongrass	witchgrass
field sandbur	(seedling)	yellow foxtail

Rate: 1-1.5 lb. ai/A
  2.4-3.6 pt. 3.3 EC/A
  1.7-2.5 lb. DG/A
Time: Preplant incorporated.
Weeds: Grasses:

shattercane	woolly cupgrass

Rate: 1-2 lb. ai/A
  2.4-4.8 pt. 3.3 EC/A
  1.7-3.3 lb. DG/A
Time: Preplant incorporated.
Weeds: Grasses:

itchgrass*	johnsongrass	red rice
	(2 yr. program)	

* Reduced competition

Remarks: Conventional, minimum, or no-till. Rate varies by soil type and geographical region. Do not use on peat or muck soils. For rhizome johnsongrass, before application bring rhizomes to surface and chop with disc; incorporate according to label instructions. If crop loss occurs due to weather conditions, soybeans or any crop registered for preplant incorporated use can be replanted the same year. If replanting is necessary, do not rework soil deeper than treated zone. Livestock can graze or be fed forage from treated fields.
Crop Rotation: Winter wheat and winter barley can be planted in the fall 4 months after application. Treated land can be planted to other crops the following year (see label for beet and spinach restrictions).
Tank Mixes: Canopy, Command, Dual, Gramoxone Extra, Lasso, Lorox, metribuzin, Pursuit, Scepter.
State Restrictions: Not for use in California. The 2 yr. program for rhizome johnsongrass not recommended for Arizona and New Mexico.

– – – – – – – – – – – – – – –

Signal Word/Toxicity Class: Caution.
REI: 24 hr.

RR-soybeans resistant to Roundup Ultra • STS-soybeans resistant to sulfonylurea
◆-new product • PP-preplant • PPI-preplant incorporated • PRE-preemergence • POST-postemergence • SEQ-sequential • ae-acid equivalent • ai-active ingredient • DF-dry flowable
E/EC-emulsifiable concentrate • F/FL-flowable • DG/G/WG-dispersable granule • L/LC-liquid • SP/WSP-soluble packet • W/WP-wettable powder • WSB-water soluble bag

154   **Weed Control Manual 2000**

Pentagon — see pendimethalin

Pinnacle — see thifensulfuron-methyl

Poast — see sethoxydim

Prism — see clethodim

Prowl — see pendimethalin

PURSUIT

Imidazolinone herbicide which inhibits the production of certain plant amino acids. May be applied in combination with other registered broadleaf herbicides.

■ PP, PPI, PRE, POST

Pursuit (2AS) (imazethapyr) *(American Cyanamid)*

Rate: 0.063 lb. ae/A
  4 oz. 2AS/A
Time: Early preplant, preplant incorporated, preemergence, and postemergence. May be applied up to 45 days before planting.
Weeds: Broadleaf weeds:

black nightshade	Florida pusley	pitted morningglory
barnyard sage	galinsoga	prickly sida
Canada thistle	giant ragweed	prostrate spurge
carpetweed	hairy nightshade	puncturevine
cocklebur	ivyleaf morningglory	redroot pigweed
common cocklebur	Jerusalem artichoke	smallflower
common purslane	jimsonweed	morningglory
common ragweed	kochia	smooth pigweed
common sunflower	ladysthumb	spiny pigweed
eastern black	mustard	spotted spurge
nightshade	Palmer pigweed	tall morningglory
entireleaf	Pennsylvania	velvetleaf
morningglory	smartweed	wild poinsettia

Grasses and sedges:

barnyardgrass	green foxtail	shattercane
broadleaf signalgrass	johnsongrass	smooth crabgrass
fall panicum	large crabgrass	Texas panicum
giant foxtail	red rice	woolly cupgrass
giant green foxtail	robust purple foxtail	yellow foxtail
goosegrass	robust white foxtail	yellow nutsedge

Remarks: Incorporate within 7 day if adequate rainfall is not received. Do not apply products containing chlorimuron-ethyl or imazaquin same year as Pursuit or injury to follow crops may occur. Do not graze or feed treated soybean forage, hay or straw to livestock.
Days To Harvest: 85.
Crop Rotation: Soybeans, IMI-Corn, lima beans, peanuts, southern peas—anytime; alfalfa, edible beans and peas (except lima beans, southern peas), rye, wheat—4 months; field corn, field corn grown for seed—8^1/$_2$ months; barley, tobacco—9^1/$_2$ months; cotton, lettuce, oats, popcorn, safflower, sorghum, sunflower, sweet corn—18 months; flax, potatoes—26 months; all other crops—40 months after application.
Tank Mixes: Postemergence grass herbicides such as Poast, Fusilade DX, or Assure. Soil-applications with Prowl, trifluralin, Lasso, or Dual when heavy grass pressure is anticipated. Do not tank mix with clomazone.
State Restrictions: For use in Colorado, New Mexico, North Dakota, Oklahoma, South Dakota, Texas, Wyoming (certain counties), and states east of these states.

— — — — — — — — —

Signal Word/Toxicity Class: Caution.
REI: 4 hr.

PURSUIT PLUS (Premix)

Premix containing active ingredients of Prowl and Pursuit.

■ PP, PPI, PRE

Pursuit Plus (EC) (0.2 lb./gal. imazethapyr & 2.7 lb./gal. pendimethalin) *(American Cyanamid)*

Rate: 0.9 lb. ae/A
  2.5 pt. EC/A
Time: Early preplant, preplant incorporated, and preemergence. May be applied up to 45 days before planting.

Weeds: Broadleaf weeds:

black nightshade	galinsoga	prickly sida
buffalobur*	giant ragweed*	prostrate spurge
carpetweed	hairy nightshade	puncturevine
common cocklebur	ivyleaf	redroot pigweed
common	morningglory*	smallflower
lambsquarters	jimsonweed	morningglory
common purslane	kochia	smooth pigweed
common ragweed*	ladysthumb	spiny pigweed
common sunflower	mustard	spotted spurge
eastern black	Palmer pigweed	tall morningglory*
nightshade	Pennsylvania	tall waterhemp
entireleaf	smartweed	velvetleaf
morningglory*	pitted morningglory*	Venice mallow*
Florida pusley		

Grasses and sedges:

barnyardgrass	goosegrass	shattercane
broadleaf signalgrass	green foxtail	smooth crabgrass
browntop panicum	itchgrass*	Texas panicum
crowfootgrass	johnsongrass	wild proso millet*
fall panicum	(rhizome*, seedling)	witchgrass
field sandbur	large crabgrass	woolly cupgrass
giant foxtail	robust purple foxtail	yellow foxtail
giant green foxtail	robust white foxtail	yellow nutsedge*

* Reduced competition

Remarks: Incorporate within 7 days if adequate rainfall is not received. Do not apply products containing chlorimuron-ethyl or imazaquin the same year as Pursuit Plus or injury to follow crops may occur. Do not apply through any type of irrigation system. Do not graze or feed treated soybean forage, hay, or straw to livestock.
Days To Harvest: 85.
Crop Rotation: Lima beans, peanuts, southern peas, soybeans—anytime; edible beans and peas (except lima beans, southern peas), wheat—4 months; field corn, field corn grown for seed—8^1/$_2$ months; alfalfa, barley, rye, tobacco—9^1/$_2$ months; cotton, lettuce, oats, popcorn, safflower, sorghum, sunflower, sweet corn—18 months; potatoes—26 months; all other crops—40 months after application. Some crops in certain areas have interval exceptions; refer to label.
State Restrictions: Not for use in North Dakota or north of Hwy 210 in Minnesota.

— — — — — — — — —

Signal Word/Toxicity Class: Caution/III.
REI: 12 hr.

PYTHON

Selective herbicide in water dispersible granule formulation. Provides residual control of weeds that may emerge after application. May be applied with water, liquid fertilizer, or impregnated on dry bulk fertilizer. Absorption occurs through both shoot and root uptake.

■ POST

Python (WDG) (flumetsulam) *(Dow AgroSciences)*

Rate: 0.8-1.33 oz. WDG/A
Time: Soil application: preplant incorporated, preplant surface, postplant preemergence. Do not apply more than 30 days before planting.
Weeds: Broadleaf weeds.

carpetweed	horseweed	Russian thistle
chickweed	jimsonweed	shepherdspurse
common cocklebur	ladysthumb	sicklepod
common	morningglory	smooth pigweed
lambsquarters	nightshade	spotted spurge
common purslane	nodding spurge	spurred anoda
common ragweed	Pennsylvania	velvetleaf
Florida beggarweed	smartweed	Venice mallow
Florida pusley	pigweed	waterhemp
giant ragweed	prickly sida	wild mustard
goosefoot	puncturevine	wild poinsettia
henbit	redroot pigweed	wild sunflower

*Suppression

Remarks: Rate varies by organic matter. Not for use on peat or muck soils. Do not apply by air or make more than one application per season. Do not graze or feed treated soybean forage, hay, or straw to livestock. Do not apply through any type of chemigation system.
Days To Harvest: 85.
Crop Rotation: Corn, soybeans—0; alfalfa, barley, dry beans, oats, peanuts, rye, sweet potatoes, wheat—4 months; rice—6 months; popcorn, tobacco—9 months; grain sorghum, potatoes—12 months; cotton, sunflower, sweet corn—18 months; canola, sugar beets, all other crops—26 months plus successful field bioassay.
State Restrictions: Not for use in Nassau and Suffolk counties in New York.

— — — — — — — — —

Signal Word/Toxicity Class: Caution/III.
REI: 12 hr. unless soil injected or soil incorporated.

NOTICE	The information on these pages is for preliminary planning — not a guide for use. Be sure to follow the manufacturer's directions, notwithstanding information contained here.	For personal protective equipment and EPA registration numbers, please turn to page 70.

QUIZALOFOP-P-ETHYL

Postemergence grass herbicide with activity on several annual and perennial grasses; does not control broadleaves. Mode of action is similar to Poast, Fusilade, Option II, and Select.

■ POST, SEQ

Assure II (EC) *(DuPont)*
Matador (EC) *(FMC)*

Rate: Annual grasses:
  5-9 oz. EC/A
  Perennial grasses:
  8-10 oz. EC/A

Time: Postemergence, sequential. Apply when weeds are young and actively growing. Do not apply after pod set.

Weeds: Grasses:

barnyardgrass	green foxtail	Texas panicum
bermudagrass	itchgrass	volunteer cereals
bristly foxtail	johnsongrass	volunteer corn
broadleaf signalgrass	junglerice	wild oat
crowfootgrass	large crabgrass	wild proso millet
fall panicum	quackgrass	wirestem muhly
field sandbur	red rice	witchgrass
giant foxtail	shattercane	yellow foxtail
goosegrass	smooth crabgrass	

Remarks: Rate varies by weed species and size and geographic region. Above rates recommended for areas with adequate rainfall; higher rates recommended in arid regions typically supplemented with irrigation. Always include spray adjuvant. Do not cultivate within 7 days of application. Second application may be applied. Do not apply more than 18 oz./A per year. Crops other than soybeans may be injured by spray drift or indirect contact. Do not apply through any type of irrigation system. Do not graze treated fields or harvest for forage or hay.

Days To Harvest: 80.

Crop Rotation: Do not rotate to crops other than soybeans or cotton within 120 days after application.

Tank Mixes: May be tank mixed with postemergence herbicides and insecticides and applied sequentially with postemergence broadleaf herbicides.

- - - - - - - - - - - - - - -

Signal Word/Toxicity Class: Danger/I.
REI: 12 hr.

RAPTOR

Can be applied in a sequential program with Prowl for better control of grasses.

■ POST

Raptor (1E) (imazamox) *(American Cyanamid)*

Rate: 0.04 lb. ai/A
  5 fl. oz. 1E/A

Time: Postemergence. Apply before soybeans bloom when weeds are actively growing and before they exceed 5" in height.

Weeds: Broadleaf weeds:

annual sowthistle*	field bindweed*	pitted morningglory*
black nightshade	giant ragweed	prickly sida*
Canada thistle*	hairy nightshade	prostrate pigweed
carpetweed	hedge bindweed*	redroot pigweed
common chickweed	ivyleaf morningglory	smallflower
common cocklebur	jimsonweed	morningglory
common	Jerusalem artichoke	smooth pigweed
lambsquarters	kochia	spiny pigweed
common purslane	ladysthumb	sunflower
common ragweed	mustard	tall morningglory
eastern black	Palmer amaranth	velvetleaf
nightshade	Pennsylvania	wild radish
entireleaf	smartweed	
morningglory		

Grasses and sedges:

barnyardgrass	johnsongrass	volunteer corn
broadleaf signalgrass	(rhizome*, seedling)	volunteer wheat
browntop panicum	large crabgrass*	yellow foxtail
fall panicum	quackgrass*	wild barley
field sandbur	purple nutsedge*	wild oat
giant foxtail	shattercane	wild proso millet
goosegrass*	smooth crabgrass*	woolly cupgrass*
green foxtail	stinkgrass*	yellow nutsedge*
	Texas panicum	

* Suppression

Remarks: Do not make more than one application per growing season. Do not graze or feed treated soybean forage, hay, or straw to livestock.

Days To Harvest: 85.

Crop Rotation: Soybeans—anytime; wheat—3 months; barley, rye—4 months; alfalfa, broccoli, cabbage, cantaloupe, carrots, corn, cotton, cucumbers, edible beans, grain sorghum, oats, onions, peas, peanuts, peppers, potatoes, pumpkins, rice, squash, sunflower, tobacco, tomatoes, turnips, watermelon—9 months; sugar beets, table beets (pH 6.2 or greater)—18 months, sugar beets, table beets (pH less than 6.2)—26 months.

- - - - - - - - - - - - - - -

Signal Word/Toxicity Class: Caution.
REI: 4 hr.

RR Rattler — see glyphosate

Reflex — see fomesafen

STS RELIANCE (Premix)

For use only on soybeans designated as STS. If applied to soybeans not designated as STS, severe crop damage will occur. Varieties must be purchased from authorized seed supplier. Dispersible granule formulation in water soluble pack. **For more information on STS, turn to page 131.**

■ POST

Reliance STS (SP) (9% thifensulfuron-methyl & 16% chlorimuron-ethyl) *(DuPont)*

Rate: One 2 oz. pack/4A

Time: Postemergence. Apply to small weeds any time after first soybean trifoliate has opened but no later than 60 days before soybean maturity.

Weeds: Broadleaf weeds and sedges:

annual smartweed	lambsquarters	velvetleaf
cocklebur	marestail	wild mustard
common milkweed	morningglories	wild sunflower
common ragweed	(suppression)	yellow nutsedge
jimsonweed	pigweed	(suppression)

Remarks: Add nonionic surfactant or crop oil concentrate and ammonium nitrogen fertilizer. Make only one application per season. Do not apply through any type of irrigation system. Do not graze treated fields or harvest for forage or hay.

Days to Harvest: 60.

Crop Rotation: Soybeans—anytime; cereal grains, pasture grasses—3 months; peanuts—6 months; IMI corn—8 months; alfalfa, beans (dry, kidney, snap), clover, cotton, cucumbers, field corn (grain, silage, seed), peas, popcorn, pumpkins, rice, sorghum, sunflower, sweet corn (processing), transplant tobacco, transplant tomatoes, watermelon—9 months; cabbage, canola, flax, lentils, mustard, sweet corn—18 months; carrots, onions, potatoes, sugar beets, and any crop not listed—26 months.

Tank Mixes: Postemergence grass herbicides such as Assure II.

- - - - - - - - - - - - - - -

Signal Word/Toxicity Class: Caution.
REI: 12 hr.

RESOURCE

Rainfast within 1 hr. Toxic to shrimp.

■ POST

Resource (0.86EC) (flumiclorac pentyl) *(Valent)*

Rate: 0.027-0.080 lb. ai/A
  4-12 fl. oz. 0.86EC/A

Time: Postemergence.

Weeds: Broadleaf:

common	jimsonweed	prickly sida
lambsquarters	Palmer amaranth	spotted spurge
common ragweed	pigweed	velvetleaf

Remarks: Rate varies by weed stage. Add 1 qt./A crop oil concentrate. For late control of tall velvetleaf (up to 30" tall), use 12 fl. oz./A. Do not apply more than 12 fl. oz./A per application, or more than 16 fl. oz./A per growing season. Do not apply under stress conditions. Do not apply by air or through any type of irrigation system.

Days To Harvest: 60.

Tank Mixes: Basagran, Classic, Cobra, Pursuit, Scepter, Select, and other broadleaf herbicides.

- - - - - - - - - - - - - - -

Signal Word/Toxicity Class: Warning/II.
REI: 12 hr.

RR-soybeans resistant to Roundup Ultra • STS-soybeans resistant to sulfonylurea

◆-new product • PP-preplant • PPI-preplant incorporated • PRE-preemergence • POST-postemergence • SEQ-sequential • ae-acid equivalent • ai-active ingredient • DF-dry flowable
E/EC-emulsifiable concentrate • F/FL-flowable • DG/G/WG-dispersible granule • L/LC-liquid • SP/WSP-soluble packet • W/WP-wettable powder • WSB-water soluble bag

REZULT (Co-Pack)

Rezult A must be used in combination with Rezult B. Rezult can only be used with the closed Prodigy System in which it comes packaged. The Prodigy System will discharge Rezult A and Rezult B in a 1:1 ratio; return for cleaning and refilling.

■ POST

Rezult A (1 lb./gal. sethoxydim) & Rezult B (5 lb./gal. bentazone) *(BASF)*

Rate: 3.2 pt. product/A

Time: Postemergence. Apply when weeds are small and actively growing and soybeans are in the 1st to 3rd trifoliate leaf stage.

Weeds: Broadleaf weeds:

balloonvine	giant ragweed	smooth pigweed
beggarticks	jimsonweed	spurred anoda
bristly starbur	ladysthumb	tropic croton
cocklebur	marshelder	velvetleaf
common	Pennsylvania	Venice mallow
lambsquarters	smartweed	wild buckwheat
Canada thistle*	prickly sida	wild mustard
common purslane	(teaweed)	wild sunflower
common ragweed	redweed	wild poinsettia
dayflower	shepherdspurse	

Grasses and sedges:

annual ryegrass	junglerice	wild oat
barnyardgrass	large crabgrass	wild proso millet
broadleaf signalgrass	quackgrass*	wirestem muhly*
browntop panicum	red sprangletop	witchgrass
fall panicum	shattercane	woolly cupgrass
giant foxtail	smooth crabgrass	yellow foxtail
goosegrass	Texas panicum	yellow nutsedge
green foxtail	volunteer corn	
johnsongrass		
(rhizome*, seedling)		

* Top growth suppression of perennials

Remarks: Add 2.5 gal. UAN solution/100 gal. water. Do not graze treated fields or feed treated forage to livestock. Do not apply through any type of irrigation system. Refer to label for directions, restrictions, and precautions.

Days to Harvest: 75; grazing/cutting for hay—30.

Tank Mixes: Blazer, Classic, 2,4-DB, Reflex.

State Restrictions: Not for use in California.

- - - - - - - - - - - - - - - -

Signal Word/Toxicity Class: Caution/III.
REI: 48 hr.

Roundup — see glyphosate

RR Roundup Ultra — see glyphosate

Saber — see 2,4-D

Salvo — see 2,4-D

Savage — see 2,4-D

SCEPTER

Scepter inhibits production of certain plant amino acids and is in the same chemical family as Pursuit. Dispersible granule formulation packaged in Eco-Pak, a water-soluble package.

■ PPI, PRE, POST, SEQ

Scepter (1.5AS or 70DG) (imazaquin) *(American Cyanamid)*

Rate: 0.125 lb. ae/A
0.67 pt. 1.5AS/A
2.8 oz. 70DG/A

Time: Preplant incorporated, preemergence. In Northern U.S., apply before July 1. Preplant incorporated: Up to 45 days before planting (30 days—southern states). Preemergence: Up to 30 days before or after planting. Sequential: Preemergence or preplant incorporated followed by postemergence treatment (recommended states only).

Weeds: Broadleaf weeds:

bristly starbur	ivyleaf	redroot pigweed
burcucumber	morningglory*	redweed
common cocklebur	jimsonweed	sicklepod
common	ladysthumb	smallflower
lambsquarters	mexicanweed*	morningglory
common ragweed	mustard	smooth pigweed
common sunflower	Palmer pigweed	spiny pigweed
eastern black	palmleaf	spotted spurge*
nightshade	morningglory	tall morningglory*
entireleaf	Pennsylvania	tall waterhemp
morningglory*	smartweed	velvetleaf
Florida beggarweed*	pitted morningglory	Venice mallow
Florida pusley	prickly sida	wild poinsettia
giant ragweed	puncturevine	

Grasses and sedges:

barnyardgrass*	johnsongrass	signalgrass*
giant foxtail	(seedling)	yellow foxtail
goosegrass*	shattercane*	yellow nutsedge*
green foxtail		

* Aids in control and reduces competition

Rate: 0.06-0.125 lb. ae/A
0.33-0.67 pt. 1.5AS/A
1.4-2.8 oz. 70DG/A

Time: Postemergence.

Weeds: Broadleaf weeds:

cocklebur	smooth pigweed	tall waterhemp
Palmer pigweed	spiny pigweed	wild poinsettia
redroot pigweed		

Remarks: Do not apply postemergence when soybeans and weeds have been subjected to stress conditions such as temperature and moisture extremes. For postemergence, rate varies by weed height; add approved nonionic surfactant or crop oil concentrate. Do not apply products containing chlorimuron-ethyl, imazaquin, or imazethapyr the same year as Scepter. In the event of crop loss due to weather, soybeans may be replanted. Only rotational crops harvested at maturity may be used for feed or food. Do not graze or feed treated soybean forage, hay, or straw to livestock.

Days To Harvest: 90.

Crop Rotation: Rice—in the spring of the year after application; wheat—4 months; field corn—9½ months; barley, edible beans, grain sorghum, oats, peanuts, tobacco—11 months; sugar beets—26 months (1.5AS); sugar/table beets—40 months (70DG); all other crops may be planted 18 months after application. Some crops in certain areas have interval exceptions; refer to label.

Tank Mixes: Command, 2,4-D, 2,4-DB, Dual, Frontier, glyphosate, Gramoxone Extra, Lasso, metribuzin, Prowl, trifluralin; refer to labels for restrictions and precautions.

State Restrictions: For use in Alabama, Arkansas, Delaware, Florida, Georgia, Iowa, Kentucky, Louisiana, Illinois, Indiana, Maryland, Michigan (except Upper Peninsula), southern Minnesota, Mississippi, Missouri, New Jersey, North Carolina, Ohio, Pennsylvania, South Carolina, eastern South Dakota, Tennessee, Virginia, West Virginia, Wisconsin; eastern parts of Kansas, Nebraska, Oklahoma, and Texas.

- - - - - - - - - - - - - - - -

Signal Word/Toxicity Class: Caution/III.
REI: 12 hr.

SCEPTER O.T. (Premix)

Premix containing active ingredients in Scepter and Blazer for use in soybeans only. Selective postemergence herbicide for control of cocklebur, pigweed, and morningglories.

■ POST

Scepter O.T. (2.5EC) (0.5 lb./gal. imazaquin & 2 lb./gal. acifluorfen) *(American Cyanamid)*

Rate: 0.32 lb. ai/A
1 pt. 2.5EC/A

Time: Postemergence. In Northern U.S., apply before July 1.

Weeds: Broadleaf weeds:

cocklebur	palmleaf	smallflower
hemp sesbania	morningglory	morningglory
entireleaf	pitted morningglory	smooth pigweed
morningglory	redroot pigweed	tall morningglory
ivyleaf morningglory		tall waterhemp

Remarks: Add nonionic surfactant. Additional treatment may be applied in Southern U.S., but do not exceed 2 pt./A per year. Do not apply products containing chlorimuron-ethyl, imazaquin, or imazethapyr the same year as Scepter O.T. or injury to follow crops may occur. Only rotational crops harvested at maturity may be used for feed or food. Do not graze or feed treated soybean forage, hay, or straw to livestock. Do not apply through any type of irrigation system.

Days To Harvest: 90.

NOTICE The information on these pages is for preliminary planning — not a guide for use. Be sure to follow the manufacturer's directions, notwithstanding information contained here.

For personal protective equipment and EPA registration numbers, please turn to page 70.

Crop Rotation: Soybeans—anytime after application; wheat—4 months; rice—in the spring of the year after application; field corn—9½ months; barley, oats, edible beans, grain sorghum, peanuts, tobacco—11 months; sugar/table beets—40 months; all other crops—18 months after application. Some crops in certain areas have interval exceptions; refer to label.

State Restrictions: For use in Northern and Southern U.S.; refer to label. Single postemergence application may be applied following PPI or PRE treatment of Scepter, Squadron, or Tri-Scept in Alabama, Arkansas, Florida, Georgia, Louisiana, Mississippi, North Carolina, Oklahoma, South Carolina, Tennessee, or Texas.

- - - - - - - - - - - - - - -

Signal Word/Toxicity Class: Danger/I.
REI: 48 hr.

SCYTHE

◆ **Scythe (pelargonic acid)** *(Mycogen)*
   Rate: 4-13 fl. oz./1 gal. spray solution
   Time: Apply to actively growing weeds prior to crop emergence.
   Weeds: Annual and perennial broadleaf weeds and grasses.
   Remarks: Apply in minimum 75 gal. spray solution/A or spray-to-wet. Do not apply by air or through any type of irrigation system. Refer to label for directions and precautions.
   Tank Mixes: Glyphosate and other foliar and residual herbicides.

- - - - - - - - - - - - - - -

Signal Word/Toxicity Class: Warning/II.
REI: 24 hr.

Select — see clethodim

SENCOR

Selective herbicide with activity on several broadleaf weeds. May be tank mixed with several soil-applied and certain non-selective herbicides to provide broad spectrum weed control. Sencor is a photosynthetic inhibitor.

■ **PRE, POST**
Sencor 4 (FL) or DF (metribuzin) *(Bayer)*
   Rate: 0.375-1 lb. ai/A
   0.75-2 pt. FL/A
   0.5-1.3 lb. DF/A
   Time: Preemergence.
   Weeds: Broadleaf weeds:

bristly starbur	jimsonweed	sesbania
buffalobur	knotweed	shepherdspurse
carpetweed	kochia	sicklepod
cocklebur	lambsquarters	smartweed
(suppression)	Pennsylvania	spotted spurge
common ragweed	smartweed	spurred anoda
Florida beggarweed	pigweed	sunflower
Florida pusley	prickly sida	teaweed
galinsoga	purslane	velvetleaf
hophornbeam	redweed	Venice mallow
copperleaf	Russian thistle	wild mustard

   Grasses:

barnyardgrass	crabgrass	goosegrass
bluegrass	crowfootgrass	johnsongrass
broadleaf signalgrass	foxtail	(seedling)
browntop millet	(suppression)	junglerice

   Remarks: Do not use on sensitive varieties. Rate varies by soil type and organic matter. On soils having a calcareous surface area or a pH of 7.5 or higher, injury may occur to soybeans following Sencor application. Treated vines may be grazed or fed to livestock 40 days after treatment. Refer to label for directions, limitations, and cautions.
   Crop Rotation: Alfalfa, asparagus, barley/wheat (following peas, lentils, or soybeans), corn, forage grass, potatoes, sainfoin, soybeans, sugarcane, tomatoes—4 months; barley, cotton, lentils, peas, rice, wheat, peanuts—8 months; other crops not listed (except root crops)—12 months; onions, sugar beets, and other root crops—18 months. Cover crops for soil building or erosion control may be planted anytime, but do not graze or harvest for food or feed. Stand reductions may occur in some areas.

- - - - - - - - - - - - - - -

   Rate: 0.25-0.375 lb. ai/A
   0.5-0.75 pt. FL/A
   0.33-0.5 lb. DF/A
   Time: Preemergence.
   Weeds: Same weeds as above.
   Remarks: For use on coarse light soils with organic matter 0.5% or above. Not recommended for use on sand with less than 1% organic matter.
   Crop Rotation: Same restrictions as above.

State Restrictions: For use in Alabama, Arkansas, Florida, Georgia, Louisiana, Mississippi, Missouri, North Carolina, Oklahoma, South Carolina, Tennessee, Texas, Virginia.

- - - - - - - - - - - - - - -

   Rate: 0.25-0.5 lb. ai/A
   0.5-1 pt. FL/A
   0.33-0.67 lb. DF/A
   Time: Postemergence directed spray.
   Weeds: Broadleaf weeds:

carpetweed	dayflower	redroot pigweed
common cocklebur	Florida beggarweed	sesbania
common purslane	mexicanweed	sicklepod
common ragweed	prickly sida	velvetleaf

   Grasses:

large crabgrass	smooth crabgrass

   Remarks: Do not apply directly to soybeans, allow spray to contact more than lower ¼-⅓ of soybean plants, or apply to sensitive varieties. Do not feed or graze green soybean vines.
   Days to Harvest: Harvest/feed or forage of dry vines—70.
   Crop Rotation: Same restrictions as above.
   State Restrictions: For use in Southern and Southeastern states: Alabama, Arkansas, Florida, Georgia, Kentucky, Louisiana, Mississippi, Missouri, North Carolina, Oklahoma, South Carolina, Tennessee, and Texas.

- - - - - - - - - - - - - - -

Signal Word/Toxicity Class: Caution/III.
REI: 12 hr.

SETHOXYDIM

Postemergence grass herbicide with activity on several annual and certain perennial grasses. Does not control broadleaf weeds. Similar in mode of action to that of Assure, Option, and Fusilade. Always add spray adjuvant.

■ **POST**
Poast (1.5EC) or Poast Plus (1EC) *(BASF)*
   Rate: 0.09-0.47 lb. ai/A
   0.5-2.5 pt. 1.5EC/A
   0.75-3.75 pt. 1EC/A
   Time: Postemergence.
   Weeds: Annual and perennial grasses:

annual ryegrass	junglerice	stinkgrass
barnyardgrass	large crabgrass	tall fescue
bermudagrass	lovegrass	Texas panicum
broadleaf signalgrass	orchardgrass	volunteer cereals
browntop panicum	(seedling)	wild oat
fall panicum	perennial ryegrass	wild proso millet
field sandbur	quackgrass	wildcane
giant foxtail	red rice	wirestem muhly
goosegrass	red sprangletop	witchgrass
green foxtail	shattercane	woolly cupgrass
itchgrass	smooth crabgrass	yellow foxtail
johnsongrass	southwestern cupgrass	

   Remarks: Rate depends on growing region. Add spray adjuvant or oil concentrate. Urea ammonium-nitrate solution (UAN) or ammonium sulfate (AMS) recommended to enhance activity on certain grass species. May be tank mixed with Basagran, Blazer, Classic, Cobra, Flexstar, Galaxy, Pursuit, Reflex, Storm, 2,4-D amine (Poast Plus), and 2,4-D LVE (burndown only). Do not apply through any type of irrigation system. Refer to label for restrictions and limitations.
   Days to Harvest: 75.
   Tank Mixes: Poast: Basagran, Blazer, Classic, Cobra, 2,4-D, Flexstar, Frontier, Galaxy, Pursuit, Reflex, Storm. Poast Plus: Basagran, Blazer, Classic, Cobra, 2,4-D, Flexstar, Galaxy, Pursuit, Reflex, Sencor, Storm.
   State Restrictions: Do not use UAN or AMS in California or Pacific Northwest.

- - - - - - - - - - - - - - -

Signal Word/Toxicity Class: Warning/II (Poast); Caution/III (Poast Plus).
REI: 12 hr.

Skirmish — see chlorimuron-ethyl

Solution — see 2,4-D

Solve — see 2,4-D

RR-soybeans resistant to Roundup Ultra • ⁻⁻S-soybeans resistant to sulfonylurea
◆-new product • PP-preplant • PPI-preplant incorporated • PRE-preemergence • POST-postemergence • SEQ-sequential • ae-acid equivalent • ai-active ingredient • DF-dry flowable
E/EC-emulsifiable concentrate • F/FL-flowable • DG/G/WG-dispersable granule • L/LC-liquid • SP/WSP-soluble packet • W/WP-wettable powder • WSB-water soluble bag

SONALAN

Preplant incorporated herbicide with activity on many annual grasses and certain annual broadleaf weeds. May be tank mixed with several different soil-applied herbicides for broad spectrum control. Same chemical family as Prowl and Treflan.

■ PPI

Sonalan HFP or 10G (ethalfluralin) *(Dow AgroSciences)*

Rate: 0.55-1.1 lb. ai/A
1.5-3 pt. HFP/A
5.5-11.5 lb. 10G
Partial control—groundcherry, nightshade from seed:
1.1-1.3 lb. ai/A
3-3.5 pt. HFP/A
11.5-13 lb. 10G

Time: Preplant incorporated. Apply in the spring before planting or in the fall.

Weeds: Broadleaf weeds:

carpetweed	groundcherry	redroot pigweed
common chickweed	henbit	Russian thistle
common	kochia	smooth pigweed
lambsquarters	nightshade	tarweed fiddleneck
common purslane	prostrate pigweed	tumble pigweed
conical catchfly	redmaids	wild buckwheat
Florida pusley	rockpurslane	

Grasses:

annual bluegrass	giant foxtail	shattercane
annual ryegrass	green foxtail	Texas panicum
barnyardgrass	Italian ryegrass	wild oat
broadleaf signalgrass	johnsongrass	wildcane
crabgrass	(seedling)	witchgrass
fall panicum	junglerice	woolly cupgrass
field sandbur	large crabgrass	yellow foxtail
foxtail millet	pigeongrass	

Remarks: Rate varies by soil type. Fall application of Sonalan HFP may be made only with dry bulk fertilizer. Soybeans should be planted no more than 2" deep after early season adverse weather conditions have passed (especially for higher rates). Do not apply to soils which are wet, cloddy, or subject to prolonged periods of flooding. Do not apply through any type of irrigation system. Do not graze or forage crop grown in treated soil or cut for hay or silage.

Crop Rotation: If replanting required, replant only crops listed on label. Do not plant sugar beets or red beets within 13 months after application of 1.1 lb. ai/A or more; for less than 1.1 lb. ai/A, within 8 months after application, provided treated area is moldboard plowed to a depth of at least 12" prior to planting. In Arizona and California, do not plant spinach or oats within 8 months after application of 1.1 lb. ai/A or more. Refer to label for special restrictions for Montana and Wyoming.

Tank Mixes: May be tank mixed with other registered products.

– – – – – – – – – – – – – –

Signal Word/Toxicity Class: Danger/I.
REI: 24 hr. (HFP); 12 hr. (10G) unless soil injected or soil incorporated.

SQUADRON (Premix)

Premix containing active ingredients of Scepter and Prowl. Provides broad spectrum control of annual grass and broadleaf weeds.

■ PPI, PRE

Squadron (2 lb./gal. pendimethalin & 0.33 lb./gal. imazaquin) *(American Cyanamid)*

Rate: 0.875 lb. ai/A
3 pt./A

Time: Preplant incorporated or preemergence. May be applied up to 45 days before planting (30 days—southern states), during, or up to 2 days after planting.

Weeds: Broadleaf weeds:

annual spurge	ivyleaf	purslane
burcucumber**	morningglory*	redroot pigweed
bristly starbur	jimsonweed	redweed**
carpetweed	kochia	shattercane**
common cocklebur	ladysthumb	sicklepod*
common	mexicanweed*	smallflower
lambsquarters	mustard	morningglory
common ragweed	Palmer pigweed	smooth pigweed
common sunflower	palmleaf	spiny pigweed
eastern black	morningglory	spotted spurge
nightshade**	Pennsylvania	tall morningglory*
entireleaf	smartweed	tall waterhemp
morningglory*	pitted morningglory	velvetleaf**
Florida beggarweed*	prickly sida	Venice mallow
Florida pusley	prostrate spurge	wild poinsettia
giant ragweed**	puncturevine	woolly cupgrass**

Grasses and sedges:

barnyardgrass	field sandbur	robust foxtail
broadleaf signalgrass	giant foxtail	Texas panicum
browntop panicum	goosegrass	witchgrass
crabgrass	green foxtail	yellow foxtail
crowfootgrass	johnsongrass	yellow nutsedge*
fall panicum	(seedling)	

* Aids in control and reduces competition; ** PPI only

Remarks: Do not apply products containing chlorimuron-ethyl or imazethapyr the same year as Squadron or injury to follow crops may occur (see label for exceptions). Only rotational crops harvested at maturity may be used for feed or food. Refer to label for directions, restrictions, and precautions.

Days To Harvest: 90.

Crop Rotation: Soybeans—anytime; wheat—4 months; rice—in the spring of the year after application; field corn—9 1/2 months; barley, oats, edible beans, grain sorghum, peanuts, tobacco—11 months; sugar beets—26 months; all other crops—18 months after application. Some crops in certain areas have interval exceptions; refer to label.

Tank Mixes: Command, Prowl.

State Restrictions: For use in Alabama, Arkansas, Delaware, Florida, Georgia, Illinois, Indiana, Iowa, eastern Kansas, eastern South Dakota, Kentucky, Louisiana, Maryland, Michigan (except Upper Peninsula), southern Minnesota, Mississippi, Missouri, eastern Nebraska, New Jersey, North Carolina, Ohio, eastern Oklahoma, Pennsylvania, South Carolina, Tennessee, eastern Texas, Virginia, West Virginia, and southern Wisconsin.

– – – – – – – – – – – – – –

Signal Word/Toxicity Class: Danger/I.
REI: 12 hr.

Starfire — see paraquat

Status — see acifluorfen

STEEL (Premix)

Premix containing the active ingredients imazaquin, imazethapyr, and pendimethalin. Provides broad spectrum control of grass and broadleaf weeds.

■ PPI, PRE

Steel (0.17 lb./gal. imazaquin & 0.17 lb./gal. imazethapyr & 2.25 lb./gal. pendimethalin) *(American Cyanamid)*

Rate: 0.96 lb. ai/A
3 pt./A

Time: Preplant incorporated or preemergence. Do not apply postemergence. Do not apply preemergence in South Dakota.

Weeds: Broadleaf weeds:

barnyard sage*	galinsoga	prostrate spurge
black nightshade	giant ragweed	puncturevine
buffalobur	hairy nightshade	redroot pigweed
burcucumber	ivyleaf	smallflower
carpetweed	morningglory*	morningglory
common cocklebur	jimsonweed	smooth pigweed
common	kochia	spiny pigweed
lambsquarters	ladysthumb	spotted spurge
common purslane	marshelder	spurred anoda
common ragweed	mustard	sunflower
eastern black	Palmer pigweed	tall morningglory*
nightshade	Pennsylvania	texasweed*
entireleaf	smartweed	velvetleaf
morningglory*	pitted morningglory*	Venice mallow
Florida pusley	prickly sida	wild poinsettia

Grasses and sedges:

barnyardgrass	goosegrass*	Texas panicum
broadleaf signalgrass	green foxtail	volunteer corn*
browntop panicum	johnsongrass	witchgrass
crowfootgrass	(seedling)	woolly cupgrass
fall panicum	large crabgrass	yellow foxtail
field sandbur	shattercane*	yellow nutsedge*
giant foxtail	smooth crabgrass	

* Suppression

Remarks: Conventional, minimum, or no-till. Only rotational crops harvested at maturity may be used for feed or food. Do not apply through any type of irrigation system. Do not graze or feed treated forage, hay, or straw to livestock. Refer to label for directions, restrictions, and precautions.

Days To Harvest: 90.

Crop Rotation: Region 2: Soybeans—anytime; wheat—4 months; field corn—9 1/2 months; barley, edible beans, tobacco—11 months; alfalfa, grain sorghum, oats, popcorn, seed corn, sweet corn—18 months; potatoes—26 months; sugar/table beets and all other crops—40 months after application. Region 3: Soybeans—anytime; field corn (IMI)—9 1/2 months; edible beans, tobacco—11 months; alfalfa, barley, field corn (non IMI), grain sorghum, oats, wheat —18 months; popcorn, potatoes, seed corn, sweet corn—26 months; sugar/table beets and all other crops—40 months after application. Some crops in Region 3 have interval exceptions; refer to label.

Tank Mixes: 2,4-D, 2,4-DB, Gramoxone Extra, Prowl, and Roundup Ultra.

State Restrictions: For use in Delaware, Illinois, Indiana, Iowa, eastern Kansas, Kentucky, Maryland, Michigan (except Upper Peninsula), southern Minnesota, Missouri, southeastern Nebraska, New Jersey, Ohio, Pennsylvania, eastern South Dakota, Virginia, West Virginia, and southern Wisconsin.

Signal Word/Toxicity Class: Danger/I.
REI: 12 hr.

STELLAR (Premix)

Premix containing the active ingredients of Cobra and Resource.

■ POST

Stellar (2.4 lb./gal. lactofen & 0.7 lb./gal. flumiclorac pentyl) *(Valent)*

Rate: 5-7 fl. oz./A
Time: Postemergence.
Weeds: Broadleaf weeds:

annual morningglory*	giant ragweed	prickly sida*
common cocklebur	hemp sesbania*	redroot pigweed
common lambsquarters*	hophornbeam copperleaf	smooth pigweed tall waterhemp
common ragweed	jimsonweed*	velvetleaf
common waterhemp	Palmer amaranth	Virginia copperleaf
eastern black nightshade		

* Suppression

Remarks: Do not apply through any type of irrigation system. Do not apply by air. Do not graze treated fields or feed treated forage or hay to livestock.

Days To Harvest: 60.

Tank Mixes: Can be tank mixed with other broadleaf herbicides. For grasses, tank mix with 6-8 fl. oz. Select 2EC/A.

Signal Word/Toxicity Class: Danger/I.
REI: 12 hr.

STORM (Premix)

Premix containing active ingredients of Basagran and Blazer for postemergence control of broadleaf weeds including pigweed, black nightshade, and ragweed.

■ POST

Storm (2.67 lb./gal. bentazon & 1.33 lb./gal. acifluorfen) *(BASF)*

Rate: 0.75 lb. ai/A
    1.5 pt./A
Time: Postemergence.
Weeds: Broadleaf weeds:

black nightshade	hemp sesbania	redweed
bristly starbur	hophornbeam	smooth pigweed
carpetweed	copperleaf	spurred anoda
cocklebur	jimsonweed	tall waterhemp
common ragweed	ladysthumb	teaweed
common waterhemp	lambsquarters	texasweed
crotalaria	morningglory	tropic croton
eastern black nightshade	Pennsylvania smartweed	velvetleaf Venice mallow
eclipta	prickly sida	wild mustard
giant ragweed	redroot pigweed	woolly croton

Remarks: Add oil concentrate, urea ammonium nitrate, or nonionic surfactant. Do not use treated soybean plants for feed or forage. Do not apply through any type of irrigation system.

Days To Harvest: 50.

Crop Rotation: Do not rotate root crops such as carrots, sweet potatoes, turnips, etc. into treated fields for 18 months following last application.

Tank Mixes: Assure II, Basagran, Classic, FirstRate, Frontier, Fusilade DX, Fusion, Matador, Pinnacle, Poast, Pursuit, Raptor, Reliance STS, Resource, Roundup Ultra, Scepter, Select, Skirmish, Synchrony STS.

Signal Word/Toxicity Class: Danger/I.
REI: 48 hr.

SULFENTRAZONE

For use on soybeans preemergence. May be used on Roundup Ready soybeans followed by appropriate Roundup Ultra postemergence application.

■ PPI, PRE, SEQ

Authority (DG) (sulfentrazone) *(DuPont)*

Rate: 4-5.3 oz. DG/A
Time: Preplant incorporated, preplant burndown, or preemergence followed by postemergence application of Classic, Reliance STS, or Synchrony STS. Do not apply after crops have emerged.
Weeds:

nightshade	waterhemp

Sequential with Classic or Reliance:

annual morningglory	entireleaf	redroot pigweed
annual smartweed	morningglory*	smallflower
black nightshade	hairy nightshade*	morningglory*
cocklebur	ivyleaf morningglory*	smooth pigweed
common milkweed	jimsonweed	tall morningglory*
common ragweed	lambsquarters	tall waterhemp
common sunflower	marestail	velvetleaf
common waterhemp	pitted morningglory*	yellow nutsedge*
eastern black nightshade		

Sequential with Classic or Synchrony:

annual morningglory	Florida beggarweed	pitted morningglory
beggarticks	Florida pusley	purple nutsedge*
black nightshade	giant ragweed	redroot pigweed
bristly starbur	hairy nightshade	sicklepod
buffalobur*	hemp sesbania	smallflower
burcucumber	ivyleaf morningglory	morningglory
Canada thistle*	Jerusalem artichoke	smooth pigweed
cocklebur	jimsonweed	spurred anoda*
common milkweed	kochia*	sunflower
common ragweed	ladysthumb	tall morningglory
common waterhemp	lambsquarters	tall waterhemp
cowpea	marestail	velvetleaf
eastern black nightshade	mustard	Venice mallow*
	Pennsylvania smartweed	yellow nutsedge
entireleaf morningglory		wild poinsettia

* Suppression

Remarks: Do not apply more than once per season. Do not apply by air or through any type of irrigation system. Do not feed treated soybean forage or soybean hay to livestock. Refer to label for restrictions, precautions, and geographical use directions.

Crop Rotation: Soybeans—anytime; barley, rye, wheat—4 months; field corn, rice, sorghum—10 months; alfalfa, dry beans—12 months; cabbage, clover, cotton, cucumber, flax, lentils, mustard, pumpkin, sunflower, sweet corn, watermelon—18 months; canola (rapeseed), carrot, onion, potato, sugar beets, and other crops—30 months. Crops other than soybeans may be extremely sensitive to low concentrations remaining in soil the next planting season. Refer to label for geographical restrictions.

Tank Mixes: Early preplant burndown in no-till with Assure II; preplant incorporated with Command 4EC; preemergence with Command 3ME, Dual, Frontier, Lasso, Prowl; following preplant incorporated grass herbicides Sonalan and Treflan. Do not tank mix with organophosphate insecticides.

State Restrictions: For use in Delaware, Illinois, Indiana, Iowa, Kansas, Michigan, Minnesota, Missouri, Nebraska, New Jersey, Ohio, Pennsylvania, South Dakota, Virginia, West Virginia, and Wisconsin. In Kansas and Nebraska, do not apply to land that has been or will be treated with Ally, Glean, or Finesse without observing crop rotation intervals. Check label for specific time and areas for sequential applications.

Signal Word/Toxicity Class: Caution.
REI: 12 hr.

SULFENTRAZONE & CHLORIMURON-ETHYL (Premixes)

Provides selective broad spectrum control of annual broadleaf weeds in soybeans only.

■ PP, PPI, PRE

Authority Broadleaf (DG) (56.3% sulfentrazone & 9.4% chlorimuron-ethyl) *(FMC)*
Canopy XL (DG) (56.3% sulfentrazone & 9.4% chlorimuron-ethyl) *(DuPont)*

Rate: 5.1-7.9 oz. DG/A
Time: Early preplant (no-till, minimum till, stale seedbed), preplant incorporated, preemergence. Do not apply after crops have emerged.

RR-soybeans resistant to Roundup Ultra • STS-soybeans resistant to sulfonylurea

◆-new product • PP-preplant • PPI-preplant incorporated • PRE-preemergence • POST-postemergence • SEQ-sequential • ae-acid equivalent • ai-active ingredient • DF-dry flowable
E/EC-emulsifiable concentrate • F/FL-flowable • DG/G/WG-dispersable granule • L/LC-liquid • SP/WSP-soluble packet • W/WP-wettable powder • WSB-water soluble bag

Weeds: Broadleaf weeds:

annual morningglory	giant ragweed	sicklepod*
annual smartweed	hairy nightshade	smallflower
black nightshade	hemp sesbania*	morningglory
burcucumber*	hophornbeam	smooth pigweed
carpetweed	copperleaf	spiny amaranth
cocklebur	ivyleaf morningglory	spotted spurge
coffee senna	jimsonweed	tall morningglory
common purslane	kochia	tall waterhemp
common ragweed	lambsquarters	velvetleaf
common waterhemp	mexicanweed*	Venice mallow
eastern black	Palmer amaranth	Virginia copperleaf
nightshade	pitted morningglory	wild mustard
entireleaf	prickly sida	wild poinsettia
morningglory	(teaweed)	wild sunflower
Florida beggarweed	redroot pigweed	

Grasses:

barnyardgrass*	foxtail*	purple nutsedge
broadleaf signalgrass*	johnsongrass*	Texas panicum*
crabgrass*	(seedling)	yellow nutsedge
fall panicum*	goosegrass*	

* *Suppression*

Midwestern states—Preplant burndown of annual grasses and following broadleaf weeds:

annual smartweed	lambsquarters	pigweed
chickweed	prickly lettuce	shepherdspurse
common ragweed	marestail	waterhemp
dandelion	nightshade	wild garlic
giant ragweed	pennycress	wild mustard
henbit		

Remarks: Rate varies by soil texture and organic matter. Do not apply to soils with pH greater than 6.8 in Midwestern states; 7 in Southern states. Crops such as sugar beets, cotton, corn, and vegetables may be injured by spray drift or indirect contact. If initial seeding of soybeans fails to produce a stand, only soybeans may be replanted in treated fields; do not retreat with second application. Do not apply by air or through any type of irrigation system. Do not apply more than once per season. Do not feed treated soybean forage or soybean hay to livestock. See label for precautions.

Crop Rotation: Recropping varies by soil pH and geographic region. Soybeans—anytime; wheat—4 months; field corn, rice—10 months; cotton—18 months; canola, sugar beets—30 months; alfalfa, sorghum—42 months; Refer to label for more complete information.

Tank Mixes: Alachlor, Command, Commence, Dual, Frontier, Matador, Prowl, Skirmish, Sonalan, trifluralin. Do not tank mix with organophosphate insecticides.

State Restrictions: For use in Midwestern states: Illinois, Indiana, Iowa, Kansas, Michigan, Missouri (except bootheel), Nebraska, Ohio, Oklahoma, Pennsylvania; Southern states: Alabama, Arkansas, Delaware, Florida, Georgia, Kentucky, Louisiana, Maryland, Mississippi, Missouri bootheel, New Jersey, North Carolina, South Carolina, Tennessee, Texas, Virginia, West Virginia.

- - - - - - - - - - - - - - - -

Signal Word/Toxicity Class: Caution.
REI: 12 hr.

STS SYNCHRONY (Premix)

*For use only on soybean varieties designated as STS. If applied to soybeans not designated as STS, severe crop damage will occur. Dispersible granule formulation provides selective postemergence weed control. **For more information on STS soybeans, turn to page 131.***

■ POST

Synchrony STS (DG: 18.7% chlorimuron-ethyl & 6.3% thifensulfuron-methyl; DF, SP: 31.8% chlorimuron-ethyl & 10.2% thifensulfuron-methyl) *(DuPont)*

Rate: 0.5 oz. DF/A
One 3.4 oz. soluble pack DG/4A
One 2 oz. soluble pack SP/4A

Time: Apply to small weeds any time after first soybean trifoliate has opened but no later than 60 days before soybean maturity.

Weeds: Broadleaf weeds and sedges:

beggarticks	Florida pusley	Pennsylvania
bristly starbur	giant ragweed	smartweed
buffalobur*	hemp sesbania	pigweed
burcucumber*	Jerusalem artichoke	purple nutsedge*
Canada thistle*	jimsonweed	spurred anoda*
cocklebur	kochia*	sunflower
common	ladysthumb	wild poinsettia
milkweed	lambsquarters	velvetleaf
common ragweed	marestail	Venice mallow*
cowpea	morningglory	yellow nutsedge
Florida beggarweed	mustard	

* *Suppression*

Remarks: For use on soybean varieties designated as STS. Add crop oil concentrate and ammonium nitrogen fertilizer. Do not graze treated fields or harvest for forage or hay. Do not apply through any type of irrigation system. Refer to label for restrictions and precautions.

Days To Harvest: 60.

Crop Rotation: Soybeans may be replanted any time after application. Refer to Rotational Crop Guidelines on label.

Tank Mixes: Assure II, Cobra, 2,4-DB.

State Restrictions: For use in Alabama, Arkansas, Delaware, Florida, Georgia, Illinois, Indiana, Iowa, Kansas, Kentucky, Louisiana, Maryland, Michigan, Mississippi, Missouri, Nebraska, North Carolina, Ohio, Oklahoma, Pennsylvania, South Carolina, Tennessee, Texas, Virginia, West Virginia.

- - - - - - - - - - - - - - - -

Signal Word/Toxicity Class: Caution.
REI: 12 hr.

THIFENSULFURON-METHYL

Postemergence herbicide with activity on certain broadleaf weeds, such as lambsquarters, pigweed, smartweed, and velvetleaf. Does not have a soil pH restriction. Pinnacle is a sulfonylurea, same chemical family as Classic.

■ POST

Pinnacle (DF) *(DuPont)*

Rate: 0.0625 oz. ai/A
0.25 oz. DF/A

Time: Postemergence. Apply to small weeds any time after first trifoliate soybean leaf has fully expanded.

Weeds: Broadleaf weeds:

annual smartweed	lambsquarters	wild mustard
cocklebur*	pigweed	wild sunflower*
jimsonweed*	velvetleaf	

* *Suppression*

Remarks: Add surfactant and ammonium nitrogen fertilizer. Prevent spray drift to desirable plants. Do not contaminate any body of water. Refer to label for restrictions and precautions.

Days to Harvest: 60.

Crop Rotation: Any crop may be planted 45 days after application.

Tank Mixes: May be tank mixed with postemergence grass herbicides such as Assure II.

- - - - - - - - - - - - - - - -

Signal Word/Toxicity Class: Caution.
REI: 12 hr.

TORNADO (Premix)

Premix containing active ingredients found in Reflex and Fusilade. May not control heavy infestations of perennial grasses such as johnsongrass from rhizomes.

■ POST

Tornado (0.75 lb./gal. fluazifop-P-butyl & 1 lb./gal. fomesafen) *(ZENECA)*

Rate: 0.44 lb. ai/A
1 qt./A

Time: Postemergence. Apply before soybeans bloom.

Weeds: Annual broadleaf weeds:

black nightshade	ivyleaf morningglory	smallwhite
carpetweed	jimsonweed	morningglory
common	ladysthumb	smooth pigweed
lambsquarters	Pennsylvania	tall morningglory
common purslane	smartweed	Venice mallow
common ragweed	purple moonflower	volunteer cucumber
entireleaf	morningglory	wild mustard
morningglory	redroot pigweed	yellow rocket
giant ragweed	showy crotalaria	

Annual grasses:

barnyardgrass	itchgrass	southern sandbur
broadleaf signalgrass	johnsongrass	Texas panicum
downy brome	(seedling)	tropical crabgrass
fall panicum	junglerice	volunteer cereals
field sandbur	large crabgrass	wild oat
giant foxtail	shattercane	wild proso millet
goosegrass	smooth crabgrass	witchgrass
green foxtail	sorghum-almum	woolly cupgrass
Italian ryegrass	southern crabgrass	yellow foxtail

Remarks: Add nonionic surfactant or crop oil concentrate. In addition, diammonium phosphate (10-34-0) or liquid nitrogen fertilizer 28% can be added. Do not apply through any type of irrigation system. Do not graze treated areas or harvest for forage or hay. Refer to label for use directions, restrictions, and precautions.

NOTICE The information on these pages is for preliminary planning — not a guide for use. Be sure to follow the manufacturer's directions, notwithstanding information contained here. | For personal protective equipment and EPA registration numbers, please turn to page 70.

Soybeans

Crop Rotation: Small grains such as barley, rye, wheat—4 months after application; corn, cotton, peanuts, rice—10 months after application; sorghum, sugar beets, sunflowers, or all other crops—18 months after application.

Tank Mixes: Basagran, Fusilade.

State Restrictions: For Tennessee, make only 1 application per growing season. For Illinois, Indiana, Iowa, Kentucky, Missouri, and Ohio do not apply more than once every 2 years.

- - - - - - - - - - - - - - -

Signal Word/Toxicity Class: Warning/II.
REI: 24 hr.

RR TOUCHDOWN

Has been approved for postemergence use on Roundup Ready soybeans. If applied to soybeans not designated as Roundup Ready, severe crop damage will occur. **For more information on Roundup Ready soybeans, turn to page 128.**

■ PP, PRE, POST

Touchdown (5L or 6L) (sulfosate) *(ZENECA)*

Rate: 1-2 lb. ai/A
1.2-3.2 pt. 5L/A

Time: Postemergence: Apply between cracking and full flower.

Weeds: Broadleaf weeds, annual and perennial grasses, sedges.

Remarks: For use on glyphosate-tolerant soybeans, including Roundup Ready. Rates vary by weed species and size. Nonionic surfactant may be added. Do not graze or harvest treated cover crops for feed. Do not apply through any type of irrigation system. Refer to label for directions.

Tank Mixes: Basagran, Classic, Flexstar, Fusilade, Fusion, Pinnacle, Pursuit, Reflex, Reliance STS, Scepter, Synchrony STS.

- - - - - - - - - - - - - - -

Rate: 0.5-4 lb. ai/A
0.8-6.4 pt. 5L/A
0.66-5.33 pt. 6L/A

Time: Preplant, preemergence: Apply before, during, or after planting, but before crop emergence. Preharvest: Apply to mature soybeans when pods have lost their color.

Weeds: Broadleaf weeds:

alfalfa	field bindweed	Pennsylvania
annual sowthistle	field pennycress	smartweed
annual spurge	field sandbur	prickly lettuce
black nightshade	filaree	red clover
Canada thistle	fleabane	redroot pigweed
Carolina geranium	Florida pusley	redvine*
common chickweed	giant ragweed	Russian thistle
common cocklebur	groundcherry	shepherdspurse
common groundsel	hemp dogbane	sicklepod
common	henbit	smooth pigweed
lambsquarters	honeyvine milkweed	spanishneedles
common milkweed	hophornbeam	spiny amaranth
common mullein	copperleaf	swamp smartweed
common ragweed	Jerusalem artichoke*	teaweed
common sunflower	kochia	trumpetcreeper*
curly dock	little barley	velvetleaf
cutleaf	London rocket	wheat
eveningprimrose	marestail	white clover
dandelion	morningglory	wild buckwheat
dayflower*	mouseear chickweed	
dogfennel	mustard	

Grasses and sedges:

annual bluegrass	goosegrass	shattercane
barnyardgrass	guineagrass	smooth bromegrass
bermudagrass	Italian ryegrass	sprangletop
broadleaf signalgrass	johnsongrass	stinkgrass
bulbous bluegrass	(seedling)	tall fescue
cheat	jointed goatgrass	Texas panicum
cogongrass*	Kentucky bluegrass	timothy
crabgrass	orchardgrass	wild oat
crowfootgrass	perennial ryegrass	wirestem muhly
fall panicum	purple nutsedge	witchgrass
fescue	quackgrass	woolly cupgrass
foxtail	red rice	yellow nutsedge

* Partial control

Remarks: Minimum and no-till systems. Rates vary by weed species and size. Add nonionic surfactant or wetting agent. In addition, ammonium sulfate can be added. Avoid contact with soybean foliage. Do not graze or harvest treated cover crops for feed. Do not apply through any type of irrigation system. Refer to label for use directions and precautions.

Days To Harvest: Wiper/wick application—7 days; spot application—8 weeks.

Crop Rotation: Plantback time—35 days.

Tank Mixes: Authority, Broadstrike, Canopy, Canopy XL, Command, Cover, 2,4-D, Dual, FirstRate, Frontier, Fusilade, Fusion, Karate, Lasso, linuron, metribuzin, Partner, Prowl, Pursuit, Pursuit Plus, Reflex, Scepter, Squadron, Turbo, Warrior.

State Restrictions: Ammonium sulfate (6L) not for use in California.

- - - - - - - - - - - - - - -

Signal Word/Toxicity Class: Caution.
REI: 12 hr. (5L); 4 hr. (6L).

Treflan — see trifluralin

TRI-4 — see trifluralin

Trific — see trifluralin

TRIFLURALIN

Preplant incorporated herbicide with activity on certain annual grasses and broadleaf weeds. Can be tank mixed with several different soil-applied herbicides to provide broad spectrum control. Same chemical family as Sonalan and Prowl.

■ PPI

Albaugh Trifluralin 4EC *(Albaugh)*
◆ Clean Crop Trifluralin HF (4EC) *(Platte)*
Gowan Trifluralin 4 or 5 (EC) or 10G *(Gowan)*
Helena Trifluralin 4 EC *(Helena)*
Riverside Trifluralin 4EC or Trific 60DF *(Terra)*
◆ Sedagri Trifluralin 480 (4EC) *(Rhone-Poulenc)*
Treflan HFP (4EC) or TR-10 (10G) *(Dow AgroSciences)*
TRI-4 HF (4EC) *(American Cyanamid)*
Trilin 4 or 5 (EC) or 10G *(Griffin)*
Wilbur-Ellis Trifluralin 10G *(Wilbur-Ellis)*

Rate: 0.5-1 lb. ai/A
1-2 pt. 4EC/A
0.8-1.6 pt. 5EC/A
0.875-1.66 lb. 60DF/A
5-10 lb. 10G/A

Time: Preplant incorporated. May also be applied in the fall.

Weeds: Broadleaf weeds:

carelessweed	knotweed	purslane
carpetweed	kochia	pusley
chickweed	lambsquarters	redroot pigweed
field bindweed	Mexican clover	rough pigweed
fireweed	Mexican fireweed	Russian thistle
Florida purslane	prostrate pigweed	spiny pigweed
Florida pusley	puncturevine	stinging nettle
goosefoot	(western U.S.)	tumbleweed
henbit		

Grasses:

annual bluegrass	fall panicum	sandbur
barnyardgrass	foxtail millet	shattercane
bottlegrass	giant foxtail	smooth crabgrass
brachiaria	green foxtail	sprangletop
bristlegrass	Italian ryegrass	stinkgrass
bromegrass	johnsongrass	Texas panicum
burgrass	(seedling)	watergrass
cheat	junglerice	wildcane
cheatgrass	large crabgrass	woolly cupgrass
chess	pigeongrass	yellow foxtail
downy brome	robust foxtail	

Remarks: Rate varies by soil type and area. Refer to specific product label for Directions for Use.

Crop Rotation: Refer to label.

State Restrictions: Wilbur-Ellis and Trilin 10G not for use in California. Albaugh, Clean Crop, Helena, Riverside, Sedagri, Treflan, Trific not for use in Pecos or Reeves County, Texas; in Montana, Treflan 60DF not for use, Sedagri and Treflan TR-10 uses limited to supplemental labeling.

- - - - - - - - - - - - - - -

Rate: 1-2 lb. ai/A
2-4 pt. 4EC/A
1.6-3.2 pt. 5EC/A
1.66-3.33 lb. 60DF/A

Time: Preplant—2-yr. program. Spring application: Apply before planting. Fall application: Oct. 15-Dec. 31. Split application: Same rate as spring and fall.

Weeds: Grasses:
johnsongrass (rhizome)

Remarks: Rate varies by soil type and area. Refer to label for directions.

Crop Rotation: Refer to label.

State Restrictions: For use in eastern U.S., Texas (Albaugh, Clean Crop, Helena, Riverside, Sedagri, Treflan, Trific not for use in Pecos or Reeves County).

- - - - - - - - - - - - - - -

Rate: 1-2 lb. ai/A
2-4 pt. 4EC/A
1.6-3.2 pt. 5EC/A
1.66-3.33 lb. 60DF/A

Time: Preplant—2-yr. program.

RR-soybeans resistant to Roundup Ultra • STS-soybeans resistant to sulfonylurea

◆-new product • PP-preplant • PPI-preplant incorporated • PRE-preemergence • POST-postemergence • SEQ-sequential • ae-acid equivalent • ai-active ingredient • DF-dry flowable
E/EC-emulsifiable concentrate • F/FL-flowable • DG/G/WG-dispersable granule • L/LC-liquid • SP/WSP-soluble packet • W/WP-wettable powder • WSB-water soluble bag

Weeds: Grasses:
red rice

Remarks: Apply second application at half rate. Refer to label for directions.
Crop Rotation: Refer to label.
State Restrictions: For use in Arkansas, Louisiana, Mississippi, Texas (Albaugh, Clean Crop, Helena, Riverside, Sedagri, Treflan, Trific not for use in Pecos or Reeves County).

- - - - - - - - - - - - - - -

Signal Word/Toxicity Class: Varies by formulation.
REI: 12 hr. unless soil injected or soil incorporated.

___

Trilin — see trifluralin

___

TRI-SCEPT (Premix)

Premix containing trifluralin and active ingredient found in Scepter. Must be incorporated. Provides broad spectrum control of both annual grasses and broadleaf weeds.

■ **PP**

Tri-Scept (0.43 lb./gal. imazaquin & 2.57 lb./gal. trifluralin)
(American Cyanamid)
Rate: 0.875 lb. ai/A
2.33 pt./A
Time: Preplant incorporated. May be applied immediately before planting or up to 45 days before planting (30 days in southern states).
Weeds: Annual broadleaf weeds:

bristly starbur	ivyleaf morningglory*	purslane
burcucumber	jimsonweed	redroot pigweed
carpetweed	kochia	redwood
common cocklebur	ladysthumb	smallflower
common	mustard	morningglory
lambsquarters	Pennsylvania	smooth pigweed
common ragweed	smartweed	spiny pigweed
common sunflower	Palmer pigweed	spotted spurge*
eastern black	palmleaf	tall morningglory*
nightshade	morningglory	tall waterhemp
entireleaf	pitted morningglory	texasweed*
morningglory*	prickly sida	velvetleaf
Florida pusley	(teaweed)	Venice mallow
giant ragweed	puncturevine	wild poinsettia

Annual grasses and sedges:

barnyardgrass	giant foxtail	shattercane
broadleaf signalgrass	goosegrass	Texas panicum
crabgrass	green foxtail	woolly cupgrass
fall panicum	johnsongrass	yellow foxtail
field sandbur	(seedling)	yellow nutsedge*
	robust foxtail	

* Reduced competition

Remarks: If soybeans are planted on beds, apply and incorporate after bed formation. Soybeans may be replanted in previously treated fields if necessary. Rework soil no deeper than treated zone. Do not apply second treatment. Crops other than soybeans, such as cotton, corn, and vegetables, may be injured by spray drift or other indirect contact with Tri-Scept. Do not apply products containing chlorimuron-ethyl, imazaquin (see label for exceptions), or imazethapyr the same year as Tri-Scept or injury to follow crops may occur. Only rotational crops harvested at maturity may be used for feed or food. Do not graze or feed treated soybean forage, hay, or straw to livestock.
Days To Harvest: 90.
Crop Rotation: Soybeans—anytime; wheat—4 months; rice in the spring of the year after application; barley, oats, field corn, edible beans, grain sorghum, peanuts, tobacco—11 months; beets—40 months. Some crops in certain areas have interval exceptions; refer to label.
Tank Mixes: Command, Prowl, trifluralin.
State Restrictions: For use in Alabama, Arkansas, Delaware, Florida, Georgia, Illinois, Indiana, Iowa, eastern Kansas, Kentucky, Louisiana, Maryland, Michigan (except Upper Peninsula), southern Minnesota, Mississippi, Missouri, eastern Nebraska, New Jersey, North Carolina, Ohio, eastern Oklahoma, Pennsylvania, South Carolina, eastern South Dakota, Tennessee, eastern Texas, Virginia, West Virginia, Wisconsin.

- - - - - - - - - - - - - - -

Signal Word/Toxicity Class: Warning/II.
REI: 12 hr.

___

TURBO (Premix)

Premix containing active ingredients of Dual and Sencor. Can be tank mixed with other soil-applied or nonselective herbicides.

■ **PPI, PRE**

Turbo (EC) (6.55 lb./gal. metolachlor & 1.45 lb./gal. metribuzin)
(Novartis)

Rate: 1.5-3.5 lb. ai/A
1.5-3.5 pt. EC/A
Split shot:
1-2.5 lb. ai/A
1-2.5 pt. EC/A
followed by:
0.75-1 lb. ai/A
0.75-1 pt. EC/A
Time: Preplant, preemergence, split shot (preplant or shallow incorporated application followed by preemergence application).

Rate: Coarse light soils with organic matter 0.5% or above:
1.5-2.5 lb. ai/A
1.5-2.5 pt. EC/A
Time: Preplant incorporated or preemergence application in Alabama, Arkansas, Florida, Georgia, Louisiana, Mississippi, Missouri, North Carolina, Oklahoma, South Carolina, Tennessee, Texas, Virginia.
Weeds: Broadleaf weeds:

black nightshade	hophornbeam	Russian thistle
bristly starbur	copperleaf	sesbania
buffalobur**	jimsonweed	shepherdspurse
carpetweed	knotweed	sicklepod
cocklebur**	kochia	smartweed
common ragweed	lambsquarters	spotted spurge
Florida	pigweed	spurred anoda
beggarweed	prickly sida	sunflower**
Florida pusley	(teaweed)	velvetleaf
galinsoga	purslane	Venice mallow
hairy nightshade*	redweed	wild mustard

Grasses and sedges:

barnyardgrass	goosegrass	shattercane*
bluegrass	johnsongrass*	southwestern
broadleaf signalgrass	(seedling)	cupgrass
crabgrass	junglerice	Texas panicum*
crowfootgrass	prairie cupgrass	volunteer sorghum*
fall panicum	red rice	witchgrass
foxtail	sandbur*	yellow nutsedge

* Suppression; ** Split-shot application

Remarks: For maximum sicklepod control, apply preemergence. Treated vines may be grazed or fed to livestock 40 days after application.
Crop Rotation: Winter barley, winter wheat—4½ months; corn, cotton, peas, potatoes, rice, soybeans, spring barley, spring wheat—8 months; alfalfa, asparagus, forage grasses, lentils, sainfoin, sugarcane, tomatoes, other crops not listed, except root crops—12 months; onions, sugar beets, and other root crops—18 months. Cover crops for soil building or erosion control may be planted anytime, but do not graze or harvest for food or feed. Stand reductions may occur in some areas.
Tank Mixes: Canopy, Command, 2,4-D, Gramoxone Extra, Roundup Ultra, Scepter.
State Restrictions: Not for use in California.

- - - - - - - - - - - - - - -

Signal Word/Toxicity Class: Caution/III.
REI: 12 hr.

___

TYPHOON (Premix)

Premix containing active ingredients found in Reflex and Fusilade. Requires 4 hr. rainfree interval for best results.

■ **POST**

Typhoon (0.47 lb./gal. fluazifop-P-butyl & 0.94 lb./gal. fomesafen)
(ZENECA)
Rate: 0.8 lb. ai/A
1.6 qt./A
Time: Early postemergence. Apply to actively growing weeds 10- to 21-days after emergence before soybeans bloom.
Weeds: Broadleaf weeds:

black nightshade	ladysthumb	smellmelon
bristly starbur	Mexicanweed	smooth pigweed
carpetweed	Palmer amaranth	spiny amaranth
common cocklebur	palmleaf morningglory	spotted spurge*
common	Pennsylvania	spurred anoda
lambsquarters*	smartweed	tall morningglory
common morningglory	pitted morningglory	tall waterhemp
common purslane	prickly sida*	tropic croton
common ragweed	prostrate spurge*	velvetleaf*
cutleaf groundcherry	purple moonflower	Venice mallow
eclipta	morningglory	Virginia copperleaf
entireleaf	redroot pigweed	volunteer cucumber
morningglory	redweed*	wild mustard
Florida pusley	scarlet morningglory	wild poinsettia
giant ragweed	showy crotalaria	wild watermelon
hemp sesbania	sicklepod*	willowleaf
hophornbeam	small white	morningglory
copperleaf	morningglory	witchweed
ivyleaf morningglory	smallflower	yellow nutsedge*
jimsonweed	morningglory	yellow rocket

___

NOTICE The information on these pages is for preliminary planning — not a guide for use. Be sure to follow the manufacturer's directions, notwithstanding information contained here. | For personal protective equipment and EPA registration numbers, please turn to page 70.

Soybeans

Grasses and sedges:

barnyardgrass
broadleaf signalgrass
downy brome
fall panicum
field sandbur
foxtail
giant foxtail
goosegrass
green foxtail

Italian ryegrass
itchgrass
johnsongrass (seedling)
junglerice
large crabgrass
shattercane
smooth crabgrass
sorghum
southern crabgrass

southern sandbur
Texas panicum
tropical crabgrass
volunteer cereals
wild oat
wild proso millet
witchgrass
woolly cupgrass
yellow foxtail

* Suppression

Remarks: Add crop oil concentrate, nonionic surfactant or adjuvant. Apply by ground or air. In event of crop loss due to weather conditions, soybeans can be replanted. Region 1: Apply once per growing season. Region 2: Apply in alternate years by making single application per growing season. Do not apply through any type of irrigation system. Do not graze rotated small grain crops or harvest for livestock forage or straw. Refer to label for use restrictions and precautions.

Crop Rotation: Barley, rye, wheat—4 months after application; alfalfa, beans, corn, cotton, peanuts, peas, rice, sorghum—10 months after application; sugar beets, sunflowers, other crops—18 months after application.

State Restrictions: Region 1: Alabama, Arkansas, Florida, Georgia, Louisiana, Mississippi, Missouri (counties of Butler, Dunklin, Mississippi, New Madrid, Pemiscot, Scott, Stoddard), North Carolina, Oklahoma (east of U.S. Hwy 75 and east of Indian Nation Pkwy), South Carolina, Tennessee, and Texas (counties east of U.S. Hwy 75 and I-35, U.S. Hwy 183 and U.S. Hwy 87, including water all of Calhoun County). Region 2: Delaware, Illinois (south of I-70), Indiana (south of I-70), Kentucky, Maryland, Ohio (south of I-70), Virginia, and West Virginia.

— — — — — — — — — —

Signal Word/Toxicity Class: Warning/II.
REI: 24 hr.

Weed Rhap— see 2,4-D

Weedar — see 2,4-D

Weedestroy — see 2,4-D

Weedone — see 2,4-D

Zorial Rapid 80 — see norflurazon

RR-soybeans resistant to Roundup Ultra • STS-soybeans resistant to sulfonylurea

◆-new product • PP-preplant • PPI-preplant incorporated • PRE-preemergence • POST-postemergence • SEQ-sequential • ae-acid equivalent • ai-active ingredient • DF-dry flowable
E/EC-emulsifiable concentrate • F/FL-flowable • DG/G/WG-dispersable granule • L/LC-liquid • SP/WSP-soluble packet • W/WP-wettable powder • WSB-water soluble bag

164   Weed Control Manual 2000

Weed Control Manual

Section 3
Cotton

Enhanced Seed Information

BXN Cotton 166
Roundup Ready Cotton 167

Use Reminders

Rotational Crop Restrictions 168
Soil-Applied Herbicide Rates For Cotton 169
Compatibility With Fertilizers As Application Carriers 169
Feed, Forage, And Grazing Restrictions For Cotton Herbicides 170
Preharvest Application Intervals, Cotton (PHI) 170

Weed Efficacy Charts

Weed Control Estimated For Cotton Herbicides 171
Weed Response Ratings For Cotton Herbicides 172

Herbicide Listings 173

The information in this Weed Control Manual 2000 is updated to August 15, 1999.
Because manufacturers' product recommendations are constantly being updated and revised as additional product reg-istrations and label changes are approved by EPA, there may be changes after this date. However, every effort has been made to give manufacturers the opportunity to include in the Manual their latest information. This Manual is for pre-liminary planning – not a use guide. Be sure to follow label directions, notwithstanding information contained herein.

Enhanced Seed Systems

BXN Cotton

This genetically engineered cotton is tolerant of Buctril herbicide.

Compiled by Tina Grady

BXN Cotton is grown from a genetically enhanced seed that is resistant to Buctril (bromoxynil) herbicide. The patented BXN gene — oxynitralase — is an enzyme that degrades bromoxynil. BXN cotton differs from Roundup Ready cotton in that the BXN system is metabolic, whereas the Roundup Ready system is an overexpression that provides tolerance to the crop.

Currently, there are about 1.2 million acres planted to BXN cotton. An advantage to planting BXN cotton is being able to have one of the largest windows for over-the-top applications – up to 75 days prior to harvest.

Licensed Herbicides

Buctril 4EC is the only licensed herbicide for use over-the-top of BXN cotton. The herbicide works by shutting down photosynthesis. It is not necessary to supplement the BXN cotton system with adjuvants or surfactants, but use of either is acceptable. Anything that increases coverage will enhance the BXN system, such as commercially available crop oil concentrates (COCs) or non-ionic surfactants.

Weeds Controlled

Buctril controls broadleaf weeds only. The weed height for optimum control is 1 to 6 inches.

Tillage may help, but it's not necessary.

On pigweed, Buctril should be applied at 1 inch in height; morningglory at 2 inches; and velvetleaf between 2 and 4 inches. The BXN system works well on morningglory, cocklebur, velvetleaf, hemp sesbania, wild poinsettia, common lambsquarters, Pennsylvania smartweed, ragweed, devil's claw, nightshade, spurred anoda, Texas blueweed, and lanceleaf sage. It does not control sicklepod and is weak on pigweed.

Perennial weeds are more of a problem in the High Plains and Texas, especially with lanceleaf sage, silverleaf nightshade, Texas blueweed, and woolly leaf bursage. Application should be done when weeds are between 1 and 6 inches in height. Sequential applications work best.

Application Notes

Timing and effectiveness do not change in dry conditions. Buctril 4EC performs in all weather conditions, but works best when weeds are actively growing. Adequate spray coverage is key to weed control programs with Buctril 4EC.

Residuals

Although not necessary, residuals can be used in conjunction with Buctril. Products that have shown to work well with Buctril are Staple and Bladex, both from DuPont Corp., and Caparol and Cotoran, both from Novartis Crop Protection, Inc. The best residual combination is considered the Buctril-Staple tank mix.

A normal weed management program keeps standard residual programs in place.

Other Comments

Stoneville Pedigreed charges a $25 per bag premium.

Finally, maintain careful records. When growers plant herbicide-resistant seed, it is important to know which variety is planted on which acreage in order to match herbicide programs. If an herbicide is misapplied, it can result in total crop loss.

Buctril Checklist

1. Identify fields…

✔ Plant BXN in those fields with broadleaf weeds susceptible to Buctril 4EC.

✔ Morningglory, cocklebur controlled by Buctril 4EC.

2. Application notes…

✔ Clean out sprayer

✔ Do not use Buctril 4EC at a rate higher than 1 pt. per acre per application.

✔ Do not exceed 3 pts. per acre per year.

3. Weed control...

✔ Spray when broadleaf weeds are less than 2 inches tall.

✔ Second application can be made 10-14 days after initial application.

Additional tips

✔ Buctril 4EC is a contact herbicide and thorough coverage is essential.

✔ Don't apply when windy due to drift.

Enhanced Seed Systems

Roundup Ready Cotton

This genetically enhanced seed will tolerate glyphosate herbicides.

*Compiled by
Tina Grady*

Roundup Ready (RR) cotton is a genetically enhanced plant developed by Monsanto Co. that is tolerant to Roundup Ultra (glyphosate) herbicide. Roundup Ultra is a non-selective postemergence, systemic herbicide without residual soil activity. The glyphosate is absorbed by the plant foliage which then translocates throughout the plant. This system is advantageous because it enables the grower to use a reduced tillage system.

In 1999, 40% of total cotton acres had the Roundup Ready gene in it — about 1.9 million acres were planted to RR cotton, with about 1.4 million acres planted to stacked RR/Bt (*Bacillus thuringiensis*) cotton.

Licensed Herbicides

The only licensed herbicide for use over the top of RR cotton is Roundup Ultra (glyphosate). Roundup Ultra has proven tolerance and weed control in Roundup Ready cotton when applied in accordance with the label. Adding other products may impact the herbicide's effectiveness.

A burndown herbicide is required before planting in a no-till or reduced till and stale seed bed systems. Roundup Ultra is the recommended burndown herbicide, but any burndown herbicide product labeled for cotton may be used to eliminate weed competition before planting.

The burndown may be applied from about 14 days prior to planting up to planting. However, in some situations, such as perennial weed infestations, it may be necessary to make sequential burndown applications 21 to 28 days preplant followed by a second treatment 7 days before planting.

Earlier applications of a burndown herbicide also may used to get a head start on developing weed problems and enhance soil exposure to sunlight. This can help warm and dry soil that may remain too wet to plant early.

Weeds Controlled

Roundup Ultra works particularly well on problem weeds such as cocklebur, johnsongrass, and pigweed. Pitted morningglory can be controlled in RR cotton if initial applications are made when the morningglory is small. This should be followed up with a second application 7 to 10 days later.

Yellow nutsedge may be difficult to control with Roundup Ultra under hot, dry weather conditions. Se-quential applications are the key to nutsedge control. Early application is not as critical to nutsedge control as it is with morningglory control.

Application timings on annual weeds will be similar to those for perennial weeds. Annual weeds my be controlled with lower rates and few applications in many cases. This can vary with rainfall patterns.

Application Notes

Sequential applications of Roundup Ultra need to be separated by 10 days and two nodes of growth. Most over-the-top applications are made at the 2-leaf to 4-leaf stages. The rates used are dictated by the particular weed.

A key to RR cotton production is the clearing of troublesome weeds early in the season with over-the-top applications. RR cotton can remain weed free after the 5-leaf stage with post-directed applications of Roundup Ultra.

Roundup Ultra works best when growing conditions are optimum. Effectiveness is reduced in dry, harsh weather conditions.

Residuals

The use of residual herbicides is not generally recommended. However, some producers prefer to use a grass herbicide preemergence. Some producers have successfully used tank mixed residual herbicides with Roundup Ultra as a layby treatment. Good results can be achieved by depending on a total postemergence system using Roundup Ultra alone.

Other comments

There is a technology fee of $9 per acre for use of the Roundup Ready cotton system.

Roundup-Ready Checklist

1. Start with a clean field...
 ✔ Use a burndown herbicide to clean the field
 ✔ In some cases sequential burndown applications may be required.

2. Apply Roundup Ultra postemergence...
 ✔ Application rates vary by weeds controlled.
 ✔ Over-the-top applications are most commonly made at the 2-leaf to 4-leaf stages.

3. Spot applications can be made to control weeds prior to boll opening...
 ✔ Do not spot-treat more than 10% of the field to be harvested.

Additional tips for best results:
 ✔ Dry conditions will reduce effectiveness.

Rotational Crop Restrictions

Herbicides	Rotation interval[1]					
	Corn	Grain Sorghum	Rice	Soybeans	Wheat	Other Grains
Assure II	120 d	120 d	120 d	none	120 d	120 d
Buctril	ns	ns	ns	ns	ns	ns
Cobra	none	none	none	none	none	none
Command	9 m	9 m	9 m	none	12 m[3]	12 m[3]
Cyanazine (Bladex, Cy-Pro)	none	30 d	spring	spring	fall	fall
Diuron (Direx, Karmex)						
band PRE or POE	4 m	4 m	4 m	4 m	4 m	4 m
band PRE + POE	spring	spring	1 y	spring	1 y	1 y
broadcast PRE	spring	spring	1 y	spring	1 y	1 y
broadcast PRE + band POE	spring	spring	1 y	spring	1 y	1 y
broadcast POE	spring	spring	1 y	1 y	1 y	1 y
DSMA	none	none	none	none	none	none
Fluometuron (Cotoran, Meturon, etc.)	6 m	6 m	6 m	6 m	6 m	6 m
Fusilade	60 d	60 d	60 d	60 d	60 d	60 d
Glyphosate	none	none	none	none	none	none
Goal	10 m	10 m	10 m	60 d	10 m	10 m
Gramoxone Extra	none	none	none	none	none	none
Harmony Extra	45 d	45 d	45 d	45 d	none	60 d[4]
MSMA	none	none	none	none	none	none
Poast Plus	none	none	none	none	none	none
Prometryn (Caparol, Cotton-Pro, etc.)	next y	next y	next y	next y	next y[2]	next y[2]
Prowl	none	none	none	none	4 m	NS[5]
Select	none	none	none	none	none	none
Staple	9 m[6]	2 y	9 m	10 m	4 m	10 m[7]
Trifluralin (Treflan, Trilin, TRI-4, etc.)	none	none	none	none	none	none
Zorial	16 m	16 m	16 m	45 d	16 m[8]	16 m[8]

[1] d = days after application, m = months after application, y = years after application, spring = spring following application, fall = fall following application, and ns = next season. PRE = preemergence and POE = postemergence applications.

[2] Wheat or small grain crops may be planted for a cover crop the fall following prometryn application, but may not be harvested for feed or food.

[3] Wheat may be planted for a cover crop at any time, but cannot be harvested for food or feed or grazed if planted less than 9 months after treatment.

[4] Barley or oats may be replanted immediately. Other grains require 60 days before planting.

[5] Do not plant wheat or barley until next season if rhizome johnsongrass or red rice control or itchgrass suppression rates are applied.

[6] This interval can be used only if Staple was applied on a band not to exceed 50% of the row width, and fields are deep tilled prior to corn planting. Otherwise, do not plant corn the season following Staple application.

[7] In addition to the 10-m interval, a successful field bioassay must be conducted. This requires a test strip of the rotational crop be grown to maturity.

[8] Wheat or other small grain may be planted to prevent soil erosion, but cannot be harvested or grazed.

Source: Weed Control Guidelines for Mississippi, 1997.

Soil-Applied Herbicide Rates For Cotton

Herbicide	Soil Texture		
	Coarse (lt.)	Medium	Fine (heavy)
Preplant Herbicides			
Cotoran or Meturon 4L or 80DF	1.6 pt or 1 lb	2.4-3.2 pt or 1.5-2 lb	3.2-4 pt or 2-2.5 lb
Prowl 3.3EC	1.2-1.8 pt	1.8-2.4 pt	2.4-3.6 pt
Prowl 3.3EC or	1.2-1.8 pt	1.8 pt	2.4 pt
Treflan +	1 pt	1.5 pt	2 pt
1/2 x Zorial fb	0.625 lb fb	0.95 lb fb	1.25 lb fb
Treflan 4E	1 pt	1.5 pt	2 pt
Treflan + Cotoran 85DF or 4L	1 pt + 1 lb or 1.6 pt	1.5 pt + 1.25-2 lb or 2-3.2 pt	2 pt + 2-2.4 lb or 3.2-4 pt
Zorial 80DF	1.25 lb	1.9 lb	2.5 lb
Preemergence Herbicides			
Bladex 90DF + Zorial	0.55 lb + 0.8 lb[1]	0.66 to 1.0 lb + 1.3 lb	1.33 lb + 1.6 lb
Bladex 4L + Zorial	0.5 qt + 0.8 lb[1]	0.6-0.9 qt + 1.3 lb	1.2 qt + 1.6 lb
Command 3ME	1.33 pt/A	2 pt/A	2.67 pt/A
Cotoran or Meturon 4L or 80DF	1.6 pt or 1 lb	2.4-3.2 pt or 1.5-2 lb	3.2-4 pt or 2-2.5 lb
Karmex 80DF	0.67 lb	1-1.25 lb	1.25-2 lb
Zorial 80DF	1.25 lb	1.9 lb	2.5 lb

All rates are **broadcast rates**. Reduce rate for appropriate band width.
[1]Do not use on coarse soils with less than 1.0% organic matter.

Source: Recommended Chemicals for Weed and Brush Control, Arkansas, 1999.

Compatibility With Fertilizers As Application Carriers

Herbicide	Fertilizer		Herbicide	Fertilizer	
	Fluid	Dry		Fluid	Dry
Assure II	No	No	Karmex 80WP, 80DF	No	No
Bladex 4L, 80W	Yes (PRE only)	No	MSMA	No	No
Caparol 4L	No	No	Poast Plus	No	No
Cobra 2EC	No	No	Prowl 3.3EC	Yes	Yes
Cotoran 4L, 80W	Yes (PRE only)	No	Select	No	No
DSMA	No	No	Treflan 4EC	Yes	Yes
Fusilade DX	No	No	Zorial	No	No
Goal 2XL	No	No			

PRE = Preemergence
There are many specific fertilizer incompatibilities and restrictions with most herbicides. Be sure to read the herbicide label for specific mixing or impregnation instructions. Compatibility agents are required for many mixes.

Source: Recommended Chemicals for Weed and Brush Control, Arkansas, 1999.

NOTICE The information on these pages is for preliminary planning — not a guide for use. Be sure to follow the manufacturer's directions, notwithstanding information contained here.

Cotton Use Reminders

Feed, Forage, And Grazing Restrictions For Cotton Herbicides

Herbicide	Restrictions
Assure II	Do not graze treated fields or harvest for forage or hay.
Bladex	Do not graze or feed foliage from treated areas to livestock.
Buctril	Do not graze any portion of crop. Do not cut for feed or fodder.
Caparol	Do not feed treated forage to livestock, or graze treated areas or illegal residues may result.
Cobra	Do not graze animals on green forage or stubble. Do not utilize hay or straw for feed or bedding.
Command	Do not allow livestock to graze on treated cotton forage or trash, or feed treated cotton forage or trash to livestock.
Cotoran	Do not feed foliage from treated cotton plants or gin trash to livestock.
DSMA	Do not feed treated foliage to livestock or graze treated areas.
Fusilade DX	Do not graze or harvest for forage or hay.
Goal	Do not use treated plants for feed or forage or allow animals to graze treated areas.
Karmex	Do not allow livestock to graze treated corn.
MSMA	Do not feed treated foliage to livestock or graze treated areas.
Poast Plus	Do not graze treated cotton fields and do not feed treated cotton forage to livestock.
Prowl	Do not feed forage or graze livestock in treated cotton fields.
Select	Do not graze treated fields or feed treated forage or hay to livestock.
Staple	Do not feed treated gin by-products (trash) to livestock.
Treflan	No information on label.
Zorial	Do not graze treated cotton fields with livestock or feed treated cotton forage to livestock. Cover crops planted after harvest should be plowed under and not grazed or harvested.

Restrictions are listed as worded on the labels. Feeding and application restrictions for herbicides are generally based on residue tolerances allowed for animal feeding. The restrictions are generally not due to acute toxicity (poisoning) problems. Livestock that are accidentally fed treated crops earlier than allowed may not be harmed, but may have illegal pesticide residues in their meat or milk. If you have fed livestock treated crops within the restricted period, refer to the label, your dealer, or herbicide company representative for more information.

Source: Recommended Chemicals for Weed and Brush Control, Arkansas, 1999.

Preharvest Application Intervals, Cotton (PHI)

Herbicide	PHI	Herbicide	PHI
Assure II	80 days	Fusilade DX	90 days
Bladex	No restrictions	Goal	75 days
Buctril	60 days	Karmex	No restrictions
Caparol/Cotton-Pro	No restrictions	Lorox	No restrictions
Cobra	70 days	MSMA	1st bloom
Command	65 days	Poast Plus	40 days
Cotoran/Meturon	60 days	Select	60 days
DSMA	1st bloom	Staple	60 days

These intervals are the number of days that must be allowed between herbicide application and harvest. Applications made after these interval restrictions could cause illegal herbicide residues to be present in the harvested seed or fiber.

Source: Recommended Chemicals for Weed and Brush Control, Arkansas, 1999.

Weed Control Estimated For Cotton Herbicides

Herbicides	Annual morningglory	Annual sedge	Barnyardgrass	Bermudagrass	Broadleaf signalgrass	Cocklebur	Crabgrass	Fall panicum	Goosegrass	Hemp sesbania	Honeyvine milkweed	Nodding spurge	Pigweed	Prickly sida	Purple nutsedge	Purslane	Rhizome johnsongrass	Seedling johnsongrass	Sicklepod	Smartweed	Spurred anoda	Velvetleaf	Yellow nutsedge
Preplant[a]																							
Prowl	3	0	9	0	9	0	9	9	9	0	0	1	9	0	0	9	5	9	1	2	0	0	0
Trifluralin	3	0	9	0	9	0	9	9	9	0	0	1	9	0	0	9	6	9	1	2	0	0	0
Zorial (PPI or split)	6	9	9	3	8	4	9	8	8	3	0	7	9	9	5	9	3	8	5	6	8	7	5
Preemergence																							
Command	9	—	9	—	9	5	9	8	9	7		1	9	8	—	8	3	9	0	9	9	10	—
Diuron	7	9	7	0	8	4	8	7	8	4	0	6	9	6	0	9	0	6	5	7	2	7	0
Fluometuron	9	9	8	0	8	6	9	7	8	6	7	3	9	9	0	7	0	6	8	3	3	3	0
Zorial	0	4	1	2	8	9	8	8	9	3	3	6	5	7	2	9	7	7	4	9	8	7	4
Zorial + cyanazine	6	8	7	2	7	4	8	6	7	4	0	8	7	8	3	9	2	6	6	6	7	7	3
Postemergence-directed																							
Cobra	6	2	3	0	3	8	3	3	3	—	5	8	9	8	—	8	2	3	—	7	7	8	2
+ MSMA	9	6	8	0	8	9	8	7	8	7	5	8	9	8	6	9	5	9	5	7	7	8	6
Cyanazine	8	8	8	0	8	9	8	9	8	8	—	1	8	9	8	—	8	2	6	—	7	7	8	2
+ MSMA	9	8	9	0	9	9	9	9	8	8	5	2	9	9	6	9	5	9	7	7	7	7	6
Diuron	7	4	5	0	5	4	6	5	5	4	1	4	7	4	0	5	2	5	8	3	3	3	0
+ MSMA	8	8	8	0	9	9	8	9	8	8	5	2	9	7	6	7	5	9	8	4	4	4	6
DSMA or MSMA	3	6	7	0	8	9	8	7	4	2	1	0	3	2	6	3	5	8	3	1	0	0	6
Fluometuron	—	7	6	5	6	6	6	6	6	5	—	—	—	4	—	6	—	—	6	—	—	—	—
+ MSMA	8	8	8	0	9	9	9	8	8	5	2	4	9	7	6	6	5	8	8	4	3	6	6
Goal	9	2	4	0	4	8	4	4	4	—	2	7	9	8	2	9	2	4	—	9	—	8	2
+ MSMA	9	6	8	0	8	9	8	7	8	7	2	7	9	8	6	9	5	5	9	9	5	8	6
Prometryn	—	8	7	6	7	8	7	7	7	7	—	—	—	—	6	—	—	7	—	—	—	—	—
+ MSMA	8	8	8	0	9	9	9	8	8	5	2	5	9	8	6	5	8	9	8	4	5	7	6
Postemergence-over-the-top																							
Assure II	0	0	8	9	9	0	9	9	8	0	0	0	0	0	0	0	9	9	0	0	0	0	0
Buctril/BXN	7	0	0	0	0	10	0	0	0	9	3	8	6	6	0	0	0	0	0	4	9	9	0
Fusilade	0	0	9	9	9	0	9	9	9	0	0	0	0	0	0	0	9	9	0	0	0	0	0
Poast Plus	0	0	9	8	9	0	9	9	9	0	0	0	0	0	0	0	9	9	0	0	0	0	0
Roundup Ultra/Roundup Ready	8	10	9	6	9	8	9	9	8	6	4	9	9	9	8	9	8	9	8	9	8	7	9	—	7
Select	0	0	9	9	9	0	9	8	9	0	0	0	0	0	0	0	9	9	0	0	0	0	0
Staple	9	—	0	0	0	7	0	0	0	9	—	7	10	7	3	6	3	6	5	9	9	9	5
Layby-preemergence activity																							
Cyanazine	7	0	3	0	3	4	3	3	3	6	0	8	6	7	0	4	0	3	4	4	5	4	0
Diuron	7	0	7	0	7	4	7	7	7	4	0	6	8	6	0	8	2	6	4	7	2	6	0

Rating scale: 9-10 = excellent, 7-8 = good, 4-6 = fair, 0-3 = none to slight. Ratings assume the herbicides are applied in the manner suggested in the guidlines and according to the label under optimum growing conditions.

[a]Overlay (PPI + PRE) Treatment will control a broader spectrum of weeds but effectiveness on any given species will be no better than the highest rating for the best herbicide in the specific combination selected.

Source: Weed Control Guidelines for Mississippi, 1997.

3

Cotton
Weed Efficacy Chart

Weed Response Ratings For Cotton Herbicides

Herbicides	Barnyardgrass	Bermudagrass	Bigroot morningglory	Broadleaf signalgrass	Cocklebur	Crabgrass	Entireleaf morningglory	Fall panicum	Flatsedges	Foxtail	Goosegrass	Honeyvine milkweed	Hophornbeam copperleaf	Jimsonweed	Lambsquarters	Palmer amaranth	Pigweed	Pitted morningglory	Prickly sida (teaweed)	Purslane	Ragweed	Redvine	Rhizome johnsongrass	Seedling johnsongrass	Smartweed	Spotted spurge	Spurred anoda	Velvetleaf (wild cotton)	Yellow nutsedge
Preplant																													
Treflan, Prowl	9	0	0	9	0	9	2	9	3	9	6	0	0	3	8	7	9	2	0	9	3	0	3	9	2	2	0	2	0
Treflan + Cotoran/Meturon	9	0	0	9	7	9	7	9	9	9	9	0	9	7	9	8	9	7	7	9	9	0	3	9	7	3	6	5	0
Zorial	9	0	0	9	5	9	6	9	9	9	9	0	9	7	9	8	9	6	9	9	8	0	0	8	6	7	9	7	4
Preemergence																													
Bladex + Zorial	7	0	0	8	6	8	7	7	9	8	6	0	9	7	9	8	9	7	9	9	9	0	0	7	7	9	9	7	3
Command + Cotoran	8	2	—	9	8	9	8	9	9	9	9	—	9	8	9	7	9	9	9	9	9	4	0	8	8	6	8	9	0
Cotoran/Meturon	7	0	0	8	8	9	8	9	8	9	8	0	9	7	9	8	9	8	9	9	9	0	0	7	7	6	7	6	0
Karmex	7	0	0	8	7	9	8	9	8	8	8	0	6	9	8	9	8	7	9	8	9	0	0	7	7	6	6	5	0
Staple + Cotoran	7	0	0	8	8	9	8	9	8	8	8	0	9	7	9	9	9	9	9	8	9	0	0	7	7	9	8	7	0
Zorial	8	0	0	8	4	8	5	8	9	8	0	0	9	7	9	8	9	5	8	9	8	0	0	7	6	7	9	7	4
Postemergence																													
Assure II o.t.	8	8	0	9	0	9	0	9	0	9	9	0	0	0	0	0	0	0	0	0	0	0	9	9.5	0	0	0	0	0
Bladex + MSMA	9	0	2	9	9	9	9	9	8	9	9	2	9	9	9	9	9	9	8	8	9	0	6	9	7	8	7	7	6
Buctril	0	0	—	0	10	0	9	0	—	0	0	—	8	9	—	0	3	9	4	—	10	—	0	0	9	6	7	7	0
Caparol + MSMA dir.	9	0	2	9	9	9	8	9	8	9	9	2	9	9	9	9	9	8	8	8	8	0	6	9	7	5	7	6	6
Cobra	3	0	0	3	8	3	8	3	2	3	3	5	9	9	—	7	9	8	8	9	9	5	2	3	7	8	7	8	2
Cobra + MSMA	8	0	0	8	9	8	8	8	8	5	5	9	9	—	9	9	8	9	9	9	5	6	8	7	8	7	8	6	6
Cotoran + MSMA dir.	8	0	2	9	9	9	9	8	8	9	7	2	9	9	9	9	9	8	7	6	8	0	6	8	8	5	7	6	6
DSMA or MSMA dir.	8	0	1	8	9	8	3	8	6	8	5	1	3	5	5	3	3	3	2	3	5	0	6	8	2	0	1	1	6
Fusilade DX o.t.	7	9	0	8	0	7	0	9	0	8	9	0	0	0	0	0	0	0	0	0	0	0	9	9	0	0	0	0	0
Karmex + MSMA dir.	9	0	2	9	9	9	8	9	8	9	9	2	9	9	9	9	9	8	8	8	8	0	6	9	7	5	6	6	6
Poast o.t.	8	7	0	9	0	9	0	9.5	0	8.5	0	0	0	0	0	0	0	0	0	0	0	0	8	9	0	0	0	0	0
Roundup Ultra	9	6	7	10	10	10	8	10	8	10	10	4	8	8	9	10	8	8	10	9	6	10	10	7	8	7	8	7	5
Select o.t.	8	8	0	9	0	9	0	9	0	9	9	0	0	0	0	0	0	0	0	0	0	0	9	9.5	0	0	0	0	0
Staple	2	0	—	2	8	2	9	2	—	2	2	—	0	8	0	8	9	8.5	7	—	4	—	4	6	8.5	6	9	9	6

Rating scale: 0 = No control; 10 = 100% control; — = insufficient data.
dir. = directed spray; o.t. = over-the-top.

Source: Recommended Chemicals for Weed and Brush Control, Arkansas, 1999.

Cotton

120 Herbicide — see MSMA

912 Herbicide — see MSMA

Ansar 6.6 — see MSMA

ASSURE

Postemergence grass herbicide with activity on several annual and perennial grasses; does not control broadleaves. Mode of action is similar to Poast, Fusilade, Option II, and Select.

■ POST

Assure II (EC) (quizalofop-P-ethyl) *(DuPont)*

Rate: Annual grasses:
5-9 oz. EC/A
Perennial grasses:
8-10 oz. EC/A

Time: Postemergence.

Weeds: Annual grasses:

barnyardgrass	itchgrass	Texas panicum
broadleaf signalgrass	johnsongrass (seedling)	volunteer cereals
fall panicum	junglerice	volunteer corn
field sandbur	large crabgrass	wild oat
giant foxtail	red rice	wild proso millet
goosegrass	shattercane	witchgrass
green foxtail	smooth crabgrass	yellow foxtail

Perennial grasses:

bermudagrass	johnsongrass (rhizome)	quackgrass

Remarks: Rate varies by weed species and size and geographic region. Above rates recommended for areas with adequate rainfall; higher rates recommended in arid regions typically supplemented with irrigation. Always add nonionic surfactant or petroleum-based oils. Do not use vegetable oils as spray adjuvant. Do not apply through any type of irrigation system. Do not graze treated fields or harvest for forage or hay.

Days To Harvest: 80.

Crop Rotation: Do not rotate to crops other than soybeans or cotton within 120 days after application.

– – – – – – – – – – – – – – –

Signal Word/Toxicity Class: Danger/I.
REI: 12 hr.

Bladex — see cyanazine

BXN BROMOXYNIL

Use only on cotton designated as BXN for postemergent applications. If applied to cotton not designated as BXN, severe crop damage will occur. **For more information on BXN cotton, turn to page 166.**

For more information on BXN cotton, turn to page 166.

■ PRE, POST

Buctril 4EC (bromoxynil) *(Rhone-Poulenc)*

Rate: 0.25-0.5 lb. ai/A
0.5-1 pt. 4EC/A

Time: Preemergence, postemergence. Apply broadcast or over-the-row band application. Apply before planting or cotton emergence, but after weed emergence.

Weeds: Broadleaf weeds:

bristly starbur	Florida pusley	lanceleaf sage
buffalobur	giant ragweed	nightshade
cocklebur	hemp sesbania	Palmer amaranth
coffee senna	ivyleaf morningglory	palmleaf
common ragweed	jimsonweed	morningglory
entireleaf	kochia	Pennsylvania
morningglory	ladysthumb	smartweed
Florida beggarweed	lambsquarters	pitted morningglory

Weeds: Broadleaf weeds, continued:

prickly sida	smallflower	tall waterhemp
purple moonflower	morningglory	tropic croton
morningglory	smooth pigweed	velvetleaf
redroot pigweed	spiny pigweed	venice mallow
Russian thistle	spurred anoda	wild okra
sharppod	sunflower	wild poinsettia
morningglory	tall morningglory	

Remarks: Transgenic BXN cotton. Do not exceed 2 applications before cotton is 12" tall and 1 application after 12" tall. Maximum 3 pt./A per season. Do not graze any portion of crop. Do not cut for feed or fodder.

Days To Harvest: 75.

Crop Rotation: Up to 1 pt./A/season—plant any rotational crop 30 days after last application. More than 1 pt./A/season—only Transgenic BXN cotton may be planted as a rotational crop.

Tank Mixes: MSMA.

State Restrictions: Not for use in Florida, south of Tampa (Florida Rte. 60) or Hawaii (except for test plots or breeding nurseries).

– – – – – – – – – – – – – – –

Signal Word/Toxicity Class: Warning/II.
REI: 96 hr.

BXN Buctril — see bromoxynil

Bueno 6 — see MSMA

Caparol — see prometryn

Clarity — see dicamba

CLETHODIM

Postemergence grass herbicide with activity on several annual and certain perennial grasses. Does not control broadleaf weeds. Mode of action is similar to Poast, Assure, and Fusilade.

■ POST

Prism (0.94EC) or Select (2EC) *(Valent)*

Rate: 0.1-0.25 lb. ai/A
13-34 fl. oz. 0.94EC/A
6-16 fl. oz. 2EC/A

Time: Postemergence. Apply to actively growing grasses.

Weeds: Grasses:

Amazon sprangletop	green foxtail	smooth crabgrass
annual bluegrass	itchgrass	southern crabgrass
barnyardgrass	johnsongrass	Texas panicum
bearded sprangletop	junglerice	volunteer cereals
bermudagrass	large crabgrass	wild oat
broadleaf signalgrass	quackgrass	wild proso millet
crowfootgrass	red rice	wirestem muhly
fall panicum	red sprangletop	witchgrass
giant foxtail	shattercane	woolly cupgrass
goosegrass	southwestern cupgrass	yellow foxtail

Remarks: Rate varies by grass species, stage, and geographical region. Grass crops such as corn, sorghum, wheat, and rice are highly sensitive to clethodim. Do not apply under stress conditions or if rainfall is expected in 1 hour. Do not apply more than 0.5 lb. ai/A (0.25 lb. ai/A on Long Island, NY) per season. Do not graze treated fields or feed treated forage or hay to livestock. Refer to label for restrictions and precautions.

Days To Harvest: 60.

Tank Mixes: Cobra, MSMA.

State Restrictions: Not for use on Solano grass in the Vernal Lakes area of Solano County, California; wild rice in Hays County, Texas.

– – – – – – – – – – – – – – –

Signal Word/Toxicity Class: Warning/II.
REI: 24 hr.

3

Cotton

COBRA

Broad spectrum contact herbicide for postemergent control of broadleaf weeds. Does not move throughout the cotton plant and will not vaporize off soil surface.

■ POST

Cobra (2EC) (lactofen) *(Valent)*

Rate: 0.2 lb. ai/A
  12.5 fl. oz. 2EC/A

Time: Postemergence. Apply post-directed when plant reaches minimum height of 6" and height difference of 3-5" has been established between lower leaves of plant and top of weeds. May also be applied as lay-by application after reaching a height of 12" or more.

Weeds: Broadleaf weeds:

balloonvine	giant ragweed	redroot pigweed
beggarticks	hairy galinsoga	showy crotalaria
black nightshade	hairy nightshade	smallflower
bristly starbur	hemp sesbania	morningglory
buffalobur	hophornbeam	smellmelon
burcucumber	copperleaf	smooth pigweed
carpetweed	ivyleaf morningglory	spiny amaranth
common cocklebur	jimsonweed	spotted spurge
common purslane	lanceleaf groundcherry	tall morningglory
common ragweed	mexicanweed	tall waterhemp
cutleaf groundcherry	Palmer amaranth	tropic croton
cypressvine	palmleaf morningglory	velvetleaf
morningglory	pitted morningglory	Venice mallow
devilsclaw	poorjoe	Virginia copperleaf
eastern black	prickly sida (teaweed)	wild mustard
nightshade	prostrate pigweed	wild poinsettia
eclipta	prostrate spurge	wild sunflower
entireleaf	puncturevine	witchweed
morningglory	purple moonflower	woolly croton
Florida beggarweed	morningglory	
Florida pusley		

Remarks: Rate varies by weed species and size. Do not apply over-the-top or under stress conditions. Do not graze animals on green forage or stubble. Do not utilize hay or straw for animal feed or bedding. Refer to label for use directions.

Days To Harvest: 70.

Tank Mixes: Bladex, Karmex, MSMA.

– – – – – – – – – – – – – – –

Signal Word/Toxicity Class: Danger/I.

REI: 12 hr.

COMMAND

Apply in conventional tillage or conservation tillage systems. Off-site movement of spray drift or vapors can cause foliar whitening or yellowing of some plants.

■ PPI, PRE, SEQ

Command 4EC or 3ME (clomazone) *(FMC)*

Rate: 0.5-1.25 lb. ai/A
  1-2.5 pt. 4EC/A
  1.3-3.3 pt. 3ME/A

Time: Preemergence banded or soil incorporated, sequential.

Weeds: Broadleaf weeds:

balloonvine*	jointvetch*	redroot pigweed*
black nightshade*	kochia	redvine
cocklebur	lambsquarters	redweed
common ragweed	Pennsylvania	smooth pigweed*
curly dock	smartweed	spurred anoda
dayflower	pitted morningglory	tropic croton
Florida beggarweed	prickly sida	velvetleaf
Florida pusley	prostrate spurge	Venice mallow
jimsonweed	purslane	wild poinsettia

Grasses:

barnyardgrass	itchgrass	smooth crabgrass
bermudagrass	johnsongrass	southwestern
broadleaf signalgrass	(seedling)	cupgrass
common panicum	junglerice*	Texas panicum
fall panicum	large crabgrass	velvetgrass
field sandbur	purple foxtail	wild proso millet*
giant foxtail	red rice	woolly cupgrass
goosegrass	robust foxtail	yellow foxtail
green foxtail	shattercane*	

* Partial control

Remarks: Do not apply to cotton unless either disulfoton or phorate organophosphate insecticide is applied in-furrow with seed at planting time at a minimum rate of 0.75 lb. ai/A. Do not reduce rate of organophosphate insecticide when Command is applied as a banded treatment. If initial planting of cotton fails to produce uniform stand, cotton may be replanted in treated fields. Do not retreat with second application. Do not graze or harvest for food or feed cover crops planted less than 9 months after treatment. Do not allow livestock to graze treated cotton forage or trash, or feed treated cotton forage or trash to livestock. Do not apply by air or through irrigation equipment. Refer to label for geographic restrictions and precautions.

Days To Harvest: 65.

Crop Rotation: Cover crops may be planted any time, but stand reductions may occur in some areas. All crops may be planted within 12 months of last application. For specific crops at shorter intervals, refer to Rotational Crop Guidelines.

Tank Mixes: Squadron, Tri-Scept.

State Restrictions: Not for use in California.

– – – – – – – – – – – – – – –

Signal Word/Toxicity Class: Warning/II (4EC); Caution/III (3ME).

REI: 12 hr. unless soil injected or soil incorporated.

Cotoran — see fluometuron

Cotton-Pro — see prometryn

RR Credit — see glyphosate

CYANAZINE

Cyanazine registrations are cancelled as of January 1, 2000. Sale and distribution of existing stock may continue through September 30, 2002, and all use is prohibited after December 31, 2002. Restricted Use Pesticide.

■ PP, PRE, POST

Bladex 4L or 90DF *(DuPont)*

Cy-Pro 4L *(Griffin)*

Rate: Refer to label for rate limits. Do not apply more than 3 lb. ai/A per year. Enclosed cab required for application.

Time: Early preplant: Apply during winter and early spring 30 days before planting before weeds germinate or before weed seedlings are more than 3" tall. Complete any planned tillage prior to application.

Weeds: Broadleaf weeds:

annual henbit	groundsel	pineappleweed
black nightshade	knotweed	prickly lettuce
burclover	lambsquarters	shepherdspurse
cheeseweed	London rocket	sowthistle
chickweed	marestail	wild mustard
fiddleneck	minerslettuce	wild radish

Grasses:

annual bluegrass	rabbitfootgrass	wild oat
annual ryegrass	volunteer small grain	yellow foxtail
barnyardgrass	(suppression)	
bristly foxtail		

State Restrictions: For use in California.

Rate: Refer to label.

Time: Preemergence.

Weeds: Broadleaf weeds:

annual morningglory	prickly sida	spurge
cocklebur	spurge	teaweed

State Restrictions: For use in Alabama, Arkansas, Georgia, Louisiana, Mississippi, Missouri, Tennessee.

Rate: Refer to label.

Time: Postemergence. Apply when cotton is at least 6" high; weeds are more than 2" tall. May be applied directed postemergence or lay-by following preemergence application.

Weeds: Broadleaf weeds:

annual morningglory	small white	spiny pigweed
cocklebur	morningglory	spotted spurge
ivyleaf morningglory	smallflower	tall morningglory
prickly sida	morningglory	teaweed
redroot pigweed		

State Restrictions: For use in all cotton growing states.

Remarks: Failure to wait recommended time interval between application and planting may result in crop injury. Crop injury may also result if used on calcareous soils or caliche soil outcroppings. At least 1" rainfall or equivalent irrigation should precede planting. Do not apply to cotton in irrigation water. Do not apply through any type of irrigation system. This product may not be mixed, loaded, or used within 50 ft. of all wells including abandoned wells, drainage wells, and sink holes. Certain states may have additional requirements and limitations; consult state lead pest control agency.

Days To Harvest: 54.

– – – – – – – – – – – – – – –

BXN-cotton resistant to bromoxynil • RR-cotton resistant to glyphosate

◆-new product • PP-preplant • PPI-preplant incorporated • PRE-preemergence • POST-postemergence • SEQ-sequential • ae-acid equivalent • ai-active ingredient • DF-dry flowable E/EC-emulsifiable concentrate • F/FL-flowable • DG/G/WG-dispersable granule • L/LC-liquid • SP/WSP-soluble packet • W/WP-wettable powder • WSB-water soluble bag

3

Crop Rotation: If crop is lost due to adverse weather, etc., field can be replanted to corn or sorghum. If replanted to sorghum, allow at least 30-day interval between application and planting. Any rotational crop may be planted the fall or spring following treatment.

Tank Mixes: Preplant (California) with Gramoxone Extra; incorporated on fall listed beds with Prowl or Treflan; preemergence with Zorial Rapid 80; postemergence with MSMA (+ surfactant). Refer to all labels for rates, precautions, and restrictions.

Signal Word/Toxicity Class: Warning/II.
REI: 12 hr.

Cyclone — see paraquat

Cy-Pro — see cyanazine

DICAMBA

■ PP, POST

Clarity (WS) (dicamba-DGA) *(BASF)*
Rate: 0.25 lb. ai/A
0.5 pt. WS/A
Time: Preplant. For best results, apply when weeds are in 2-3 leaf stage and rosettes are less than 2" across. Do not apply preplant west of the Rockies or in areas with less than 25" average annual rainfall. After application and minimum accumulation 1" rainfall or overhead irrigation, there is a 21-day interval for 0.5 pt./A or less.
Remarks: Do not apply through any type of irrigation system. Refer to label for directions, restrictions, and precautions.
Tank Mixes: Bladex, Caparol, Gramoxone Extra, Roundup Ultra RT.

Signal Word/Toxicity Class: Warning/II.
REI: 24 hr.

Direx — see diuron

DIURON

Broad spectrum control of annual grass and small-seeded broadleaf weeds.

■ PP, PRE, POST

Direx 4L or 80DF *(Griffin)*
◆ Diuron 80 WDG *(Platte)*
Drexel Diuron 4L or 80 *(Drexel)*
Karmex DF *(Griffin)*
Riverside Diuron 4L or 80DF *(Terra)*
Rate: 0.8-2 lb. ai/A
1.5-4 pt. 4L/A
1-2.5 lb. 80, DF, 80DF/A
Time: Preplant. Apply after beds are formed, pre-irrigated, and final seedbeds prepared. Prior to planting, drag off tops of beds and plant in moist soil not treated with diuron.

Weeds: Broadleaf weeds:

annual groundcherry	gromwell	ragweed
annual morningglory*	knawel	sesbania*
chickweed	lambsquarters	shepherdspurse
cocklebur*	pigweed	sicklepod*
corn spurry	prickly sida*	tansymustard
dogfennel	(teaweed)	wild lettuce
fiddleneck (amsinckia)	purslane	wild mustard

Grasses:

annual bluegrass	barnyardgrass	rattail fescue
annual sweet	crabgrass	red sprangletop
vernalgrass	foxtail	velvetgrass

* Partial control

Remarks: Do not use on sand or graze livestock on treated cotton.
Crop Rotation: Do not plant crops other than cotton, corn, or grain sorghum on treated land for 1 year after application.
State Restrictions: For use in Arizona and California.

Rate: 0.5-1.6 lb. ai/A
1-3.2 pt. 4L/A
0.66-2 lb. 80, 80DF, DF/A
Time: Preemergence. Apply immediately after crop is planted.
Weeds: Same as above.

Remarks: Rate varies by soil type. Use only where cotton is planted on flat or raised seedbeds during one crop season. Do not graze livestock on treated cotton. Refer to label for further use restrictions.
Crop Rotation: Do not plant crops other than cotton, corn, or grain sorghum on treated land in the spring following treatment.
State Restrictions: Not for use in Arizona and California.

Rate: Early-season:
0.4 lb. ai/A
0.8 pt. 4L/A
0.5 lb. 80, DF, 80DF/A
Late-season (lay-by):
0.8-1.2 lb. ai/A
1.5-2.5 pt. 4L/A
1-1.5 lb. 80, DF, 80DF/A
Late-season (lay-by)—AZ, CA:
0.8-1.6 lb. ai/A
1.5-3 pt. 4L/A
1-2 lb. 80, DF, 80DF/A
Time: Postemergence. Early season: Apply as directed spray when cotton is at least 6" tall (12" for western irrigated cotton) and when weeds do not exceed 2". Late season: Apply as directed spray at lay-by when cotton is at least 12" tall (20" for Pima S-2).
Weeds: Same as above.
Remarks: Do not spray over top of cotton. For pigweed (early-season), use 0.2 lb. ai/A rate.
Crop Rotation: Do not plant crops other than cotton, corn, or grain sorghum on treated land for 1 year after application.

Signal Word/Toxicity Class: Caution/III.
REI: 12 hr.

DSMA

Good broad spectrum control of annual grasses and some small-seeded broadleaf weeds. Excellent control of cocklebur and top-kill of nutsedge and small johnsongrass.

■ POST

Drexel DSMA Slurry (WS) (+ surfactant) *(Drexel)*
◆ Dry DSMA 63SG *(Luxembourg-Pamol)*
Rate: Directed:
4 pt. WS/A in 40 gal. water
3.6 lb. 63SG/A in 60 gal. water (topical in 40 gal. water)
Aerial:
3.6 lb. 63SG/A (in 50 gal. water)
Time: Postemergence. For directed application, apply when cotton is 3" high to first bloom; do not apply after first bloom. For aerial and topical application, apply when cotton has 1-2 true leaves to first square formation. Do not make topical application, after first square.

Weeds: Broadleaf weeds:

cocklebur	puncturevine	ragweed

Grasses and sedges:

barnyardgrass	johnsongrass	sandbur
dallisgrass	nutsedge	

Remarks: For Dry DSMA, add surfactant; do not add surfactant to Slurry. Do not graze or feed treated forage to livestock, or apply through any type of irrigation system.

Signal Word/Toxicity Class: Caution/III.
REI: 12 hr.

■ PP, POST

◆ Clean Crop DSMA Plus (3.6L) (+ surfactant) *(Platte)*
Drexel DSMA Liquid (3.6L) (+ surfactant) *(Drexel)*
Drexel DSMA Liquid 4 (4L) *(Drexel)*
DSMA 4 LB (4L) *(Helena)*
Liquid DSMA (3.6L) (+ surfactant) *(Helena)*
Rate: 3.5 lb. ai/A
8 pt. 3.6L/A
7 pt. 4L/A (except Helena)
Time: Preplant, postplant (up to cracking). For preplant, apply single application to prepared seedbeds when planting has been delayed and weeds have emerged. For postplant, apply no later than initial cracking of soil before cotton emergence.

Rate: 1.3-1.8 lb. ai/A
3-4 pt. 3.6L/A
1.5-2 lb. ai/A
3-4 pt. 4L/A
Time: Postemergent (over-the-top). Apply when cotton is 3-6" high or up to early first square stage. Do not apply as over-the-top broadcast after cotton is more than 6" high or after early first square stage.

For personal protective equipment and EPA registration numbers, please turn to page 70.

Rate: 3.5 lb. ai/A
    8 pt. 3.6L/A
    9 lb. ai/A
    18 pt. 4L/A

Time: Postemergence (directed). Apply when cotton is 3" high to first bloom; repeat 1-3 weeks later if needed. Do not apply after first bloom.

Weeds: Broadleaf weeds:

cocklebur	puncturevine	ragweed

Grasses and sedges:

barnyardgrass	johnsongrass	sandbur
dallisgrass	nutsedge	

Remarks: Apply in 40 gal. water (4L postdirected in 100 gal. water) by ground; 5-10 gal. water by air. For Drexel 4L and Helena 4 LB, add surfactant. Do not graze or feed treated forage to livestock, or apply through any type of irrigation system.

- - - - - - - - - - - - - - -

Signal Word/Toxicity Class: Caution/III.
REI: 12 hr.

Dual — see *S*-metolachlor

Eptam — see EPTC

EPTC

◆ **Eptam 7-E** *(ZENECA)*
Rate: 2 lb. ai/A
    2.25 pt. 7-E/A (broadcast)
Time: Apply after stand is established when cotton has 2-4 leaves. Do not apply after first bolls open.

Weeds: Broadleaf weeds:

black nightshade	corn spurry	nettleleaf goosefoot
carpetweed	cutleaf nightshade	prickly sida
common chickweed	deadnettle	prostrate pigweed
common	fiddleneck	redroot pigweed
lambsquarters	Florida pusley	sicklepod
common pigweed	hairy nightshade	tall morningglory
common purslane	henbit	tumble pigweed

Annual grasses:

annual bluegrass	field sandbur	rescuegrass
annual ryegrass	giant foxtail	shattercane
(Italian)	goosegrass	signalgrass
barnyardgrass	green foxtail	Texas panicum
(watergrass)	johnsongrass	volunteer grains
bermudagrass	(seedling)	(barley, oats, wheat)
(seedling)	junglerice	wild oat
crabgrass	lovegrass	witchgrass
fall panicum	(stinkgrass)	yellow foxtail

Remarks: Nonirrigated areas only. Use specially designed injector units or sweeps. If incorporated application is made, use power-driven rotary tillers set to depth of 2-3". Do not apply closer than 4" either side of drill. Refer to label for use restrictions and precautions.
State Restrictions: For use in the Southeast and Southwest.

- - - - - - - - - - - - - - -

Signal Word/Toxicity Class: Caution.
REI: 12 hr. unless soil injected or soil incorporated.

Flo-Met — see fluometuron

FLUOMETURON

Good broad spectrum control of annual grasses and some small-seeded broadleaf weeds. Good to excellent control of prickly sida and morningglory.

■ **PPI, PRE, POST**

Cotoran 4L or DF *(Novartis)*
◆ **Flo-Met 4L or 80DF** *(Micro Flo)*
Meturon 4L or 80DF *(Griffin)*
Riverside Fluometuron 4L or 80DF *(Terra)*
Rate: 1.6 lb. ai/A
    3.2 pt. 4L/A
    1.9 lb. DF/A
    2 lb. 80DF/A
Time: Preplant incorporated (AZ, CA, NM).

Rate: 1-2 lb. ai/A
    2-4 pt. 4L/A
    1.2-2.4 lb. DF/A
    1.25-2.5 lb. 80DF/A
Time: Preemergence, postemergence.

Weeds: Broadleaf weeds:

buttonweed	pigweed	sesbania
cocklebur	prickly sida	sicklepod
Florida pusley	(teaweed)	smartweed
jimsonweed	purslane	tumbleweed
lambsquarters	ragweed	Wright groundcherry
morningglory		

Grasses:

barnyardgrass	fall panicum	ryegrass
crabgrass	foxtail	signalgrass
crowfootgrass	goosegrass	(brachiaria)

Remarks: Rate varies by soil texture. Where dry weather conditions prevail, herbicidal activity may be delayed or reduced. Do not make more than 3 applications per year. Do not feed foliage from treated cotton plants or gin trash to livestock. Do not apply through any type of irrigation system.
Days to Harvest: 60.
Crop Rotation: Do not plant crops other than cotton within 6 months of last application. In Arizona, California, and New Mexico, cotton, corn, and grain sorghum can be planted the next spring; do not plant treated areas to other crops until 1 year after last application.
Tank Mixes: DSMA, MSMA, Prowl, trifluralin.
State Restrictions: In west Texas, do not use on sandy, loamy sand, or fine sandy loam soils, or on cotton planted in furrows. In Arkansas, Louisiana, and Mississippi, use 0.8 lb. ai/A on sandy loam soils low in organic matter.

- - - - - - - - - - - - - - -

Signal Word/Toxicity Class: Varies by formulation.
REI: 24 hr.

FLUOMETURON + MSMA (Premix)

Postemergence herbicide with surfactant. Toxic to wildlife.

■ **POST**

Riverside Fluometuron + MSMA (2 lb. fluometuron & 3.3 lb. MSMA) *(Terra)*
Rate: 0.5 gal./A in 24-40 gal. water
Time: Postemergence. Apply when cotton is 3" high to first bloom.

Weeds: Broadleaf weeds:

buttonweed	lambsquarters	ragweed
cocklebur	morningglory	sesbania
Florida pusley	pigweed	sicklepod
goathead	prickly sida	smartweed
ironweed	puncturevine	teaweed
jimsonweed	purslane	tumbleweed

Grasses:

barnyardgrass	fall panicum	nutgrass
brachiaria	foxtail	ryegrass
crabgrass	goosegrass	sandbur
crowfootgrass	johnsongrass	signalgrass
dallisgrass	nutgrass	

Remarks: Apply direct spray to base of plants avoiding foliage. Do not make more than 2 applications per year. Do not graze treated field or feed plants or gin trash from treated areas to livestock. Do not apply through any type of irrigation system.
Crop Rotation: Do not plant crops other than cotton within 6 months of last application.
State Restrictions: Do not use west of Texas on sand, loamy sand, or fine sandy loam soils.

- - - - - - - - - - - - - - -

Signal Word/Toxicity Class: Caution/III.
REI: 24 hr.

FLUAZIFOP-P-BUTYL

Good to excellent control of most annual grasses, rhizome johnsongrass, and bermudagrass. Rainfast in 1 hour.

■ **POST**

Fusilade DX *(ZENECA)*
Rate: 0.1-0.375 lb. ai/A
    0.375-1.5 pt. DX/A
Time: Postemergence. Make last application before boll set.

BXN-cotton resistant to bromoxynil • RR-cotton resistant to glyphosate

◆-new product • PP-preplant • PPI-preplant incorporated • PRE-preemergence • POST-postemergence • SEQ-sequential • ae-acid equivalent • ai-active ingredient • DF-dry flowable
E/EC-emulsifiable concentrate • F/FL-flowable • DG/G/WG-dispersable granule • L/LC-liquid • SP/WSP-soluble packet • W/WP-wettable powder • WSB-water soluble bag

3

Weeds: Annual and perennial grasses:

barnyardgrass	johnsongrass	southern sandbur
bermudagrass	(rhizome, seedling)	Texas panicum
broadleaf signalgrass	junglerice	tropical crabgrass
fall panicum	large crabgrass	volunteer cereals
field sandbur	quackgrass	wild oat
giant foxtail	red rice	wild proso millet
goosegrass	shattercane	wiregrass muhly
green foxtail	smooth crabgrass	witchgrass
Italian ryegrass	sorghum-almum	woolly cupgrass
itchgrass	southern crabgrass	yellow foxtail

Remarks: Rate varies by geographic area and grass species. Add crop oil concentrate or nonionic surfactant. Do not apply more than 3 pt./A per season. Refer to label for specific restrictions and precautions.
Days To Harvest: 90.
Crop Rotation: Do not plant rotational grass crops such as corn, sorghum, and cereals within 60 days after last application.
Tank Mixes: Ambush, Bidrin, Cygon, Cymbush.
State Restrictions: Refer to label for geographical regions.

- - - - - - - - - - - - - - -

Signal Word/Toxicity Class: Caution.
REI: 12 hr.

Fusilade DX — see fluazifop-P-butyl

FUSION (Premix)

Contains active ingredients of Fusilade and Option II. Provides broad spectrum control of perennial and annual grass weeds.

■ **POST**
Fusion (2 lb./gal. fluazifop-P-butyl & 0.56 lb./gal. fenoxaprop-P-ethyl) *(ZENECA)*
Rate: 4-24 fl. oz./A
Time: Postemergence. Make last application before boll set.
Weeds: Annual and perennial grasses:

barnyardgrass	green foxtail	southern sandbur
bermudagrass	Italian ryegrass	Texas panicum
broadleaf signalgrass	itchgrass	volunteer cereals
crabgrass	johnsongrass	wild oat
downy brome	(rhizome, seedling)	wild proso millet
fall panicum	junglerice	wiregrass muhly
field sandbur	quackgrass	witchgrass
foxtail	red rice	woolly cupgrass
giant foxtail	shattercane	yellow foxtail
goosegrass	sorghum-almum	

Remarks: Apply by ground or air. Add oil concentrate or nonionic surfactant. Do not apply through any type of irrigation system. Do not graze or harvest for forage or hay. Refer to label for specific directions, restrictions, and precautions.
Days To Harvest: 90.
Crop Rotation: Do not plant rotational crops such as corn, sorghum, and cereals within 60 days of last application.
State Restrictions: Region A: For use in Alabama, Arkansas, Florida, Georgia, Louisiana, Mississippi, Missouri, North Carolina, Oklahoma (east of I-35), South Carolina, Tennessee, Texas (east of I-35), Virginia. Region B: For use in New Mexico, Oklahoma (west of I-35), and Texas (west of I-35).

- - - - - - - - - - - - - - -

Signal Word/Toxicity Class: Caution.
REI: 24 hr.

RR **Glyfos or Glyfos X-tra — see glyphosate**

RR GLYPHOSATE

*When used postemergent, apply only to cotton designated as Roundup Ready. If used on cotton not designated as Roundup Ready, severe crop damage will occur. Burndown of most annual and perennial grass and broadleaf weeds. Do not allow glyphosate to contact desirable plants. Do not apply to cotton grown for seed. **For more information on Roundup Ready cotton, turn to page 167.***

■ **PP, PRE**
◆ **Credit (4WS)** *(Nufarm)*
◆ **Glyfos or Glyfos X-tra (4WS)** *(Cheminova)*
Rattler (4WS) *(Helena)*
Roundup Custom (5.4WS) *(Monsanto)*
Roundup Original, Original RT, Ultra, Ultra RT (4WS) *(Monsanto)*

Rate: Annual weeds:
0.38-1.5 lb. ai/A
0.56-2.25 pt. 5.4WS/A
0.75-3 pt. 4WS/A
Perennial weeds:
0.5-5 lb. ai/A
0.75-7.5 pt. 5.4WS/A
1-10 pt. 4WS/A
Time: Preplant, preemergence, at-planting, spot treatment, postharvest. For spot treatment, apply prior to boll opening.
Weeds: Broadleaf weeds:

Canada thistle	hemp dogbane	Pennsylvania
curly dock	milkweed	smartweed
field bindweed		

Grasses:

bermudagrass	johnsongrass	quackgrass
fall panicum	paragrass	wild sweet potato
fescue		

Remarks: For preharvest applications, do not apply to cotton grown for seed. Rate varies by weed species. Do not add surfactant to Roundup Ultra or Ultra RT. For spot treatment, do not treat more than 10% total area to be harvested. Do not apply through any type of irrigation system. Do not feed or graze treated cotton forage after preharvest application. Refer to label for directions, precautions and restrictions.
Days To Harvest: 7.
Tank Mixes: DEF 6, Folex, Prep. Roundup not registered in California.
State Restrictions: Roundup RT for use in Colorado, Idaho, Montana, North Dakota, South Dakota, Utah, Wyoming, and in specific counties only in Kansas, Minnesota, Nevada, Oklahoma, Oregon, and Washington, refer to label for restrictions. Glyfos is not registered for use in California. Glyfos X-tra is not registered for use in mistblowers in California or Arizona.

- - - - - - - - - - - - - - -

Signal Word/Toxicity Class: Varies by formulation.
REI: Warning—12 hr.; Caution—4 hr.

■ **POST**
Roundup Ultra (4WS) *(Monsanto)*
Rate: 0.38-5 lb. ai/A
0.75-10 pt. 4WS/A
Time: Postemergence, directed, preharvest, over-the-top. For postemergence, apply from cracking to 4-leaf stage. For directed, apply through lay-by. Over-the top applications made after 4-leaf stage may result in boll loss, delayed maturity and/or yield loss.
Weeds: Annual and perennial broadleaf weeds and grasses.
Remarks: For use on cotton with Roundup Ready gene. Rate varies by weed species and height. Do not allow glyphosate to contact desirable plants. Do not apply through any type of irrigation system. Refer to label for directions, precautions and restrictions.
State Restrictions: Varies by product; refer to label.

- - - - - - - - - - - - - - -

Signal Word/Toxicity Class: Caution/III.
REI: 4 hr.

GOAL

■ **POST**
Goal 2XL (oxyfluorfen) *(Rohm and Haas)*
Rate: 0.25-0.5 lb. ai/A
1-2 pt. 2XL/A
Time: Postemergence. Apply as post-directed spray to young, actively growing seedling weeds when cotton is minimum 6" in height.
Weeds: Broadleaf weeds:

American black	common purslane	prickly sida
nightshade	cutleaf groundcherry	(teaweed)
annual morningglory	hemp sesbania	redroot pigweed
black nightshade	jimsonweed	velvetleaf
common cocklebur	Pennsylvania	wild poinsettia
common	smartweed	Wright groundcherry
lambsquarters	pigweed	

Remarks: Care must be taken to avoid spray contact with cotton leaves. Do not apply more than 2 pt./A per season (total 4 pt./A for multiple applications on western cotton). Do not apply through any type of irrigation system. Do not feed or graze on treated land.
Days To Harvest: Southern cotton-90; western cotton-75.
Crop Rotation: Refer to label for plantback times for rotation crops.
Tank mixes: Cyanazine, diuron, MSMA.
State Restrictions: Southern cotton: Alabama, Arkansas, Georgia, Louisiana, Mississippi, Missouri, New Mexico, North Carolina, Oklahoma, South Carolina, Tennessee, Texas, and Virginia. Western cotton: Arizona and California.

- - - - - - - - - - - - - - -

Signal Word/Toxicity Class: Warning/II.
REI: 24 hr.

NOTICE	The information on these pages is for preliminary planning — not a guide for use. Be sure to follow the manufacturer's directions, notwithstanding information contained here.	For personal protective equipment and EPA registration numbers, please turn to page 70.

Cotton

Gramoxone Extra — see paraquat

Karmex — see diuron

MAGMA — see MSMA

S-METOLACHLOR

Dual is a cell growth inhibitor. S-metolachlor is a purified isomer of the metolachlor molecule. Dual II MAGNUM contains a safening agent. Good broad spectrum control of annual grasses, small-seeded broadleaf weeds including spurge and yellow nutsedge.

■ PPI, PRE
Dual MAGNUM or Dual II MAGNUM (EC) *(Novartis)*
Rate: 0.5-1.33 pt. EC/A
Time: Preplant incorporated (cotton should be planted below zone of incorporation), preemergence.
Weeds: Broadleaf weeds:

carpetweed	eclipta*	galinsoga
common purslane*	Florida beggarweed*	hairy nightshade*
eastern black nightshade	Florida pusley	pigweed

Grasses and sedges:

barnyardgrass (watergrass)	goosegrass	shattercane*
	green foxtail	signalgrass
crabgrass	johnsongrass	southwestern cupgrass
crowfootgrass	(seedling)*	volunteer sorghum*
fall panicum	prairie cupgrass	witchgrass
foxtail millet	red rice	yellow foxtail
giant foxtail	sandbur*	yellow nutsedge

* Suppression

Remarks: Rate varies by soil type and organic matter. Do not use on muck or peat soils. Do not apply broadcast to furrow planted cotton. Do not apply on Taloka silt loam, on sand or loamy sand soils, or in areas where water is likely to "pond" over the bed or crop injury may occur. In case of crop failure, any crop on label may be replanted immediately. Do not make second broadcast application. If original application was banded and second crop is planted in untreated row middles, second banded treatment may be applied. Do not graze or feed forage or fodder from cotton to livestock.
Crop Rotation: Alfalfa—4 months; barley, oats, rye, wheat—4$\frac{1}{2}$ months; tomatoes—6 months; clover—9 months; any labeled crop in addition to barley, buckwheat, cabbage, milo, nuts, oats, peppers, rice, root crops, rye, stone fruits, tobacco, and wheat may be planted in the spring following treatment (including lay-by or multiple treatments applied previous season); all other rotational crops may be planted 12 months after application.
Tank Mixes: Caparol (NM, OK, TX), Cotoran, Gramoxone Extra, MSMA, Roundup Ultra.
State Restrictions: Do not use in Nassau County or Suffolk County, New York. For use in Arkansas, Louisiana, Mississippi, bootheel of Missouri, New Mexico, Oklahoma, Tennessee, and Texas. Do not use in Gaines county, Texas.

- - - - - - - - - - - - - - - -

Signal Word/Toxicity Class: Caution/III.
REI: 24 hr.

Meturon — see fluometuron

MSMA

Good broad spectrum control of annual grasses and some small-seeded broadleaf weeds. Excellent control of cocklebur and top-kill of nutsedge and johnsongrass.

■ PP, POST
120 Herbicide (6.6) *(Terra)*
912 Herbicide (6) (+ surfactant) *(Terra)*
Rate: 2.5 lb. ai/A
  3 pt. 6, 6.6/A
Time: Preplant or postplant up to cracking. Postemergence: Apply as directed spray when cotton is 3" high to first bloom. Do not spray after first bloom.
Weeds: Broadleaf weeds:

cocklebur	pigweed	ragweed
morningglory	puncturevine	

Grasses and sedges:

bahiagrass	dallisgrass	johnsongrass
barnyardgrass (watergrass)	foxtail	nutsedge
	goosegrass	sandbur
crabgrass		

Remarks: Add surfactant. Apply broadcast 40 gal./A. Keep spray off cotton foliage. Do not graze treated fields or feed treated foliage to livestock.

- - - - - - - - - - - - - - - -

Signal Word/Toxicity Class: Caution/III.
REI: 12 hr.

■ POST
Ansar 6.6 *(ZENECA)*
Bueno 6 (+ surfactant) *(ZENECA)*
Rate: 2.5 lb. ai/A
  3 pt. 6.6/A
  2 lb. ai/A
  2.66 pt. 6/A
Time: Postemergence directed spray. Apply when cotton is 3" high to first bloom. Do not spray after first bloom.
Weeds: Broadleaf weeds:

beggartick	fiddleneck	puncturevine
chickweed	Florida beggarweed	ragweed
cocklebur	jimsonweed	sicklepod
common purslane	morningglory	spurge
dayflower	pigweed	wild mustard

Grasses and sedges:

bahiagrass	foxtail	sandbur
barnyardgrass	goosegrass	smooth crabgrass
brachiaria	johnsongrass	wild oat
dallisgrass	large crabgrass	witchgrass
fall panicum	nutsedge	

Remarks: Add surfactant to Ansar. Keep spray off cotton foliage. Do not apply through any type of irrigation system. Do not graze treated fields or feed treated foliage to livestock. Refer to label for use directions, restrictions, and precautions.
State Restrictions: In Florida, Bueno should be confined to band treatment.

- - - - - - - - - - - - - - - -

Signal Word/Toxicity Class: Caution.
REI: 12 hr.

■ PP, POST
Clean Crop MSMA 6.6 or 6 Plus (+ surfactant) *(Platte)*
Drexel MSMA 6.6 or 6 Plus (+ surfactant) *(Drexel)*
♦ Target MSMA 6 Plus (+ surfactant) *(Luxembourg-Pamol)*
Rate: 2 lb. ai/A
  2.66 pt. 6/A
  2.5 pt. 6.6/A
Time: Preplant, postplant, postemergence. For preplant or postplant, apply up to cracking of soil before cotton emergence. For postemergence, over the top, when cotton is 3-6" high or up to early first square stage, whichever occurs first; postemergence as a directed spray when cotton is 3" high to first bloom. Do not spray after first bloom.
Weeds: Broadleaf weeds:

cocklebur	puncturevine	ragweed

Grasses and sedges:

barnyardgrass (watergrass)	johnsongrass	nutsedge
	large crabgrass	sandbur
dallisgrass	nutgrass	smooth crabgrass
goosegrass		

Remarks: Keep spray off cotton foliage. Do not apply through any type of irrigation system. Do not graze treated fields or feed treated foliage to livestock.
State Restrictions: Applications in Florida should be confined to band treatments.

- - - - - - - - - - - - - - - -

Signal Word/Toxicity Class: Caution/III.
REI: 12 hr.

■ PP, POST
Helena MSMA (6.6) *(Helena)*
Helena MSMA Plus H.C. (6) (+ surfactant) *(Helena)*
Rate: 0.75-2 lb. ai/A
  1-2.66 pt. 6/A
  0.83-2 lb. ai/A
  1-2.5 pt. 6.6/A
Time: Preplant, postplant, postemergence. For preplant or postplant, apply up to cracking of soil before cotton emergence. For postemergence, over the top, when cotton is 3-6" high or up to early first square stage, whichever occurs first; postemergence as a directed spray when cotton is 3" high to first bloom. Do not spray after first bloom.

BXN-cotton resistant to bromoxynil • RR-cotton resistant to glyphosate

♦-new product • PP-preplant • PPI-preplant incorporated • PRE-preemergence • POST-postemergence • SEQ-sequential • ae-acid equivalent • ai-active ingredient • DF-dry flowable
E/EC-emulsifiable concentrate • F/FL-flowable • DG/G/WG-dispersable granule • L/LC-liquid • SP/WSP-soluble packet • W/WP-wettable powder • WSB-water soluble bag

Weeds: Broadleaf weeds:

bullnettle	pigweed	ragweed
chickweed	puncturevine	wood sorrel
cocklebur		

Grasses and sedges:

bahiagrass	green foxtail	sandbur
barnyardgrass	johnsongrass	smooth crabgrass
brachiaria	large crabgrass	watergrass
dallisgrass	morningglory	yellow foxtail
goosegrass	nutsedge	

Remarks: Keep spray off cotton foliage. For 6.6, add surfactant. Do not apply through any type of irrigation system. Do not graze treated fields or feed treated foliage to livestock.

State Restrictions: In Florida, use only band treatments.

– – – – – – – – – – – – – – –

Signal Word/Toxicity Class: Caution/III.
REI: 12 hr.

■ POST

Helena MSMA Plus (4) (+ surfactant) *(Helena)*

Rate: 2 lb. ai/A
4 pt. 4/A

Time: Postemergence as a directed spray when cotton is 3" high to first bloom. Do not spray after first bloom.

Weeds: Broadleaf weeds:

cocklebur

Grasses and sedges:

dallisgrass	johnsongrass	watergrass
goosegrass	nutgrass	

Remarks: Apply at broadcast rate of 40 gal./A. Do not apply through any type of irrigation system. Keep spray off cotton foliage. Do not graze treated fields or feed treated foliage to livestock.

– – – – – – – – – – – – – – –

Signal Word/Toxicity Class: Caution/III.
REI: 12 hr.

■ POST

◆ MAGMA (WSG) *(Luxembourg-Pamol)*

Rate: 1.87 lb. ai/A
3.4 lb. WSG/A (8.5 lb. in 100 gal. water)

Time: Postemergence. Apply as directed spray only when cotton is 3" high to first bloom. Do not spray after first bloom. During humid conditions, retreatment may be needed in 1-3 weeks.

Weeds: Broadleaf weeds:

cocklebur	puncturevine	ragweed

Grasses and sedges:

barnyardgrass	johnsongrass	sandbur
dallisgrass	nutsedge	

Remarks: Keep spray off cotton foliage. Do not apply through any type of irrigation system. Do not graze treated fields or feed treated foliage to livestock. Refer to label for use directions and precautions.

– – – – – – – – – – – – – – –

Signal Word/Toxicity Class: Caution/III.
REI: 12 hr.

NORFLURAZON

Good broad spectrum control of annual grasses, small-seeded broadleaf weeds, prickly sida, purple nutsedge, and spurred anoda. Incorporation ensures activity in dry years.

■ PPI, PRE

Zorial Rapid 80 (DF) *(Novartis)*

Rate: 1-2 lb. ai/A
1.25-2.5 lb. DF/A

Time: Preplant incorporated: Apply from 30 days to just before planting and incorporate not deeper than 2-3" within one week after application. Preemergence surface: Apply at planting, preemergence to weeds. Split application: Preplant incorporated followed by preemergence surface.

Weeds: Broadleaf weeds:

carpetweed	morningglory*	Russian thistle*
cocklebur*	Pennsylvania	sicklepod*
common ragweed*	smartweed*	spotted spurge*
Florida pusley	pigweed	spurred anoda
hemp sesbania*	prickly sida	tropic croton
kochia*	(teaweed)	velvetleaf
lanceleaf sage*	purslane	Venice mallow*

Grasses and sedges:

barnyardgrass	goosegrass	purple nutsedge*
bermudagrass*	johnsongrass	signalgrass
crabgrass	(rhizome*, seedling)	yellow nutsedge*
foxtail	panicum	

* Suppression

Remarks: Rate and timing vary by geography, soil type, and method of application; refer to label.

Crop Rotation: Rotational crops vary by geography; refer to label for specific instructions.

State Restrictions: For use in all cotton producing states except California.

– – – – – – – – – – – – – – –

Signal Word/Toxicity Class: Caution.
REI: 12 hr. (except harvest aid/desiccation 24 hr.).

PARAQUAT

Burndown or top-kill of most annual and perennial grasses and broadleaf weeds. Perennial weeds will regrow. Restricted Use Pesticide.

■ PP, PRE, POST

Cyclone (2L or 3L) or Gramoxone Extra (2.5L) *(ZENECA)*

Rate: 0.6-1 lb. ai/A
2-3 pt. 2.5L/A

Time: Preplant or fallow bed.

Weeds: Annual broadleaf weeds and grasses; top kill and suppression of perennials.

Remarks: Add nonionic surfactant or crop oil concentrate. For fallow bed treatment, beds should be preformed to permit maximum weed and grass emergence prior to treatment. Seeding should be done with minimum amount of soil disturbance. Weeds and grasses emerging after treatment will not be controlled. Refer to label for use directions.

Tank Mixes: Bladex, Caparol, Cotoran, Cotton-Pro, diuron, Goal, Harmony Extra, Meturon, MSMA, Prowl, Zorial Rapid 80.

– – – – – – – – – – – – – – –

Rate: 0.2 lb. ai/A
0.75 pt. 2.5L/A

Time: Preplant.

Weeds:

volunteer barley

Remarks: Add nonionic surfactant or crop oil concentrate. Apply broadcast to preformed seedbeds. Seeding should be done with minimum amount of soil disturbance. Weeds and grasses emerging after application will not be controlled; crops emerged at time of application will be killed. Do not graze treated areas. Refer to label for use directions.

State Restrictions: For use in California.

– – – – – – – – – – – – – – –

Rate: Southern cotton:
4-6 fl. oz. 2L/A
2.1-3.3 fl. oz. 3L/A
Stripper or spindle harvested:
3-11 fl. oz. 2L/A
2.1-7.5 fl. oz. 3L/A
Post defoliation:
1-2 pt. 2L/A
11-21 fl. oz. 3L/A

Time: Apply broadcast. For southern cotton, apply when 60% or more bolls are open and remaining bolls are mature. For post defoliation and stripper or spindle harvested, apply when 75% or more bolls are open and remaining bolls are mature.

Weeds: Emerged broadleaf weeds and grasses.

Remarks: Add nonionic surfactant or crop oil concentrate. Development of immature bolls will be inhibited. Refer to label for use directions.

Tank Mixes: Accelerate, DEF, Dropp, Folex, Harvade, Karate, Prep.

– – – – – – – – – – – – – – –

Signal Word/Toxicity Class: Danger-Poison/I.
REI: 12 hr. (except harvest aid/desiccation 24 hr.).

◆ Starfire (1.5L or 3L) *(ZENECA)*

Rate: Western states early defoliation:
7-11 fl. oz. 1.5L/A
3.7-5.4 fl. oz. 3L/A
Western states mid-to-late defoliation:
11-21 fl. oz. 1/5L/A
5.4-10.7 fl. oz. 3L/A
Southern states early defoliation:
4-6 fl. oz. 1.5L/A
3.7-5.4 fl. oz. 3L/A
Southern states mid-to-late defoliation:
1.5-2.5 pt. 1.5L/A
5.4-10.7 fl. oz. 3L/A

Time: For early defoliation, apply when 60% or more of bolls are open and remaining bolls are mature. For mid-to-late defoliation, apply when 75% or more bolls are open and remaining bolls are mature.

Weeds: Annual broadleaf weeds and grasses; top kill and suppression of perennials.

NOTICE The information on these pages is for preliminary planning — not a guide for use. Be sure to follow the manufacturer's directions, notwithstanding information contained here.	For personal protective equipment and EPA registration numbers, please turn to page 70.

Remarks: Add nonionic surfactant or crop oil concentrate. Development of immature bolls will be inhibited. Do not graze treated fields or feed treated foliage. Refer to label for use directions, restrictions, and precautions.

Days To Harvest: Mid-to-late—3; early—7.

Tank Mixes: Accelerate, DEF, Dropp, Folex, Harvade, Karate, Prep.

Rate: 0.2-0.5 lb. ai/A
 1.5-2.5 pt. 1.5L/A
 0.75-1.25 pt. 3L/A

Time: For late season, apply when 85% bolls are open and remaining bolls are mature. For regrowth, apply after defoliation or desiccation.

Weeds: Annual broadleaf weeds and grasses; top kill and suppression of perennials.

Remarks: Add nonionic surfactant or crop oil concentrate. Refer to label for use directions, restrictions, and precautions.

Days To Harvest: 3.

Tank Mixes: Accelerate, DEF, Dropp, Folex, Harvade, Karate, Prep.

- - - - - - - - - - - - - - -

Signal Word/Toxicity Class: Danger-Poison/I.

REI: 12 hr. (except harvest aid/desiccation 24 hr.).

PENDIMETHALIN

Good broad spectrum control of small-seeded broadleaf weeds and annual grasses. Incorporation increases residual activity.

■ **PP, PPI, PRE, SEQ**

Pentagon DG *(American Cyanamid)*

Prowl 3.3 EC *(American Cyanamid)*

Rate: Conventional, minimum-till:
 0.5-1.5 lb. ai/A
 1.2-3.6 pt. 3.3 EC/A
 0.85-2.5 lb. DG/A
 No-till:
 0.75-2 lb. ai/A
 1.8-4.8 pt. 3.3 EC/A
 1.25-3.3 lb. DG/A
 Fall application:
 0.75-1.5 lb. ai/A
 1.8-3.6 pt. 3.3 EC/A
 1.25-2.5 lb. DG/A

Time: Preplant (surface, incorporated), preemergence, sequential (preplant incorporated followed by preemergence). Preplant surface: Apply up to 15 days before planting. Preplant incorporated: Apply up to 60 days before planting and incorporate within 7 days. Preemergence: Apply at planting or up to 2 days after planting. For fall application, apply after Oct. 15 or up to 140 days before planting.

Weeds: Broadleaf weeds:

annual spurge	lambsquarters	pigweed
carpetweed	Pennsylvania	purslane
Florida pusley	smartweed	velvetleaf
kochia		

Grasses:

barnyardgrass	giant foxtail	signalgrass
crabgrass	goosegrass	Texas panicum
crowfootgrass	green foxtail	volunteer sorghum
fall panicum	johnsongrass	witchgrass
field sandbur	(seedling)	yellow foxtail

Remarks: Conventional, minimum, stale seedbed, no-till. Rate varies by soil type. For sequential application, total rate/A cannot exceed highest labeled rate for any given soil type. Do not use on peat or muck soils. If crop loss occurs due to weather conditions, cotton or any crop registered for preplant incorporated use can be planted the same year. Do not feed forage or graze livestock in treated fields. Refer to label for directions, precautions, and limitations.

Crop Rotation: Winter wheat and winter barley can be planted in the fall 4 months after application (except no-till). Treated land can be planted to other crops the following year (see label for beet and spinach restrictions).

State Restrictions: Not for use in no-till cotton in California. Fall application is for use in Arizona, California, Louisiana, Mississippi, New Mexico, Oklahoma, and Texas.

- - - - - - - - - - - - - - -

Rate: 1-2 lb. ai/A
 2.4-4.8 pt. 3.3 EC/A
 1.7-3.3 lb. DG/A

Time: Preplant incorporated — 2 yr. program.

Weeds: Grasses:

 johnsongrass (rhizome)

Remarks: Rate varies by soil type. Before application, bring rhizomes to surface and chop with disc; incorporate according to label instructions. If crop loss occurs due to adverse weather conditions, cotton or soybeans can be planted the same year. Do not feed forage or graze livestock in treated fields. Refer to label for directions, precautions, and limitations.

Crop Rotation: Do not plant winter wheat or winter barley following increased rate applications for rhizome johnsongrass control.

Tank Mixes: Fluometuron, prometryn, Zorial Rapid 80.

State Restrictions: The 2 yr. program not recommended for Arizona, California, and New Mexico.

- - - - - - - - - - - - - - -

Signal Word/Toxicity Class: Caution.

REI: 24 hr.

Pentagon — see pendimethalin

Poast — see sethoxydim

Prism — see clethodim

PROMETRYN

Good preemergence control of small-seeded weeds. Good broad spectrum control of annual grasses if sprayed before weeds are 3" tall and cotton is 15-24" tall.

■ **PP, PRE, POST**

Caparol 4L *(Novartis)*

Cotton-Pro (4L) *(Griffin)*

Gowan Prometryne 4L *(Gowan)*

♦ **Platte Prometryne 4L** *(Platte)*

Riverside Prometryne 4L *(Terra)*

Rate: 1.2-2.4 lb. ai/A
 2.4-4.8 pt. 4L/A

Time: Preplant incorporated.

Weeds: Broadleaf weeds:

annual morningglory	groundcherry	prickly sida
black nightshade	lambsquarters	purslane
carelessweed	malva	ragweed
cocklebur*	mustard	smartweed
coffeeweed*	pigweed	teaweed
Florida pusley		

Grasses:

barnyardgrass	junglerice	signalgrass
crabgrass	panicum	watergrass
foxtail	sandbur*	wild oat
goosegrass		

 * Shallow-germinating

Remarks: Rate varies by soil type and geographical region. Do not use on glandless cotton varieties. Do not use on sand or loamy sand soils or in newly leveled fields, areas of excess salt, or where flooding over beds may occur. Do not plant in tractor wheel depressions. Do not graze treated areas or feed treated forage to livestock. Do not apply through any type of irrigation system.

Crop Rotation: Root crops—8 months. Following crops may be planted in the fall when prometryn was applied by only one of these methods that year: PPI, PRE, or 1 chemical hoe treatment; cover crops (plowed down and not used for food or feed)—oats, sorghum, winter barley, winter rye, winter wheat; vegetables—cabbage, okra, onions, peas, red beets, sweet corn. Spring-seeded crops in California and Arizona and spring-seeded vegetables in Rio Grande Valley of Texas should not be planted until after April 1.

Tank Mixes: Prowl, trifluralin.

State Restrictions: For use in Arizona and California. In New Mexico, apply PPI or PRE — not both.

- - - - - - - - - - - - - - -

Rate: 0.8-2.8 lb. ai/A
 1.6-5.6 pt. 4L/A

Time: Preemergence.

Weeds: Same weeds as for preplant incorporated.

Remarks: Rate varies by soil type and geographical region. Do not use on glandless cotton varieties. Do not apply broadcast to cotton planted in furrows more than 2" deep. Do not use on sand or loamy sand, on shallow soils with caliche subsoils, or in areas with caliche outcroppings. Cotton may be replanted in previously treated soil, but do not make second preemergence application. Do not graze treated areas or feed treated forage to livestock. Do not apply through any type of irrigation system.

Crop Rotation: Same restrictions as above.

State Restrictions: Not for use in Arizona and California. In New Mexico, apply PPI or PRE — not both.

- - - - - - - - - - - - - - -

Rate: Chemical hoe:
 0.5-0.65 lb. ai/A
 1-1.3 pt. 4L/A
 Layby:
 0.8-1.6 lb. ai/A
 1.6-3.2 pt. 4L/A

BXN-cotton resistant to bromoxynil • RR-cotton resistant to glyphosate

♦-new product • PP-preplant • PPI-preplant incorporated • PRE-preemergence • POST-postemergence • SEQ-sequential • ae-acid equivalent • ai-active ingredient • DF-dry flowable
E/EC-emulsifiable concentrate • F/FL-flowable • DG/G/WG-dispersable granule • L/LC-liquid • SP/WSP-soluble packet • W/WP-wettable powder • WSB-water soluble bag

3

Time: Postemergence-directed. Apply lay-by or chemical hoe (emerged weeds).

Weeds: Same weeds as for preplant incorporated.

Remarks: Do not contact cotton leaves. Do not use on glandless cotton varieties. Do not apply by air. When applying to emerged weeds, add surfactant. Do not graze treated areas or feed treated forage to livestock. Do not apply through any type of irrigation system. Refer to label for directions and precautions.

Crop Rotation: Same restrictions as above. Also, where lay-by or multiple applications have been made, do not plant rotational crops until following year as indicated on label.

Tank Mixes: DSMA, MSMA.

- - - - - - - - - - - - - - -

Rate: 0.6-0.8 lb. ai/A
1.2-1.6 pt. 4L/A

Time: Winter weed control. Apply in fall or winter to land that will be planted to cotton the following spring.

Weeds: Winter weeds such as:

dock (seedling)   henbit

Remarks: Fall bedded cotton land. For postemergence henbit control, add surfactant or emulsifiable oil. Do not use in areas of excess salt or calcareous soil. Refer to labels for precautions and state restrictions.

Crop Rotation: Same restrictions as above.

State Restrictions: Caparol, Gowan, Riverside: For use in Texas Gulf Coast and Blacklands of Texas. Cotton-Pro: For use in Arkansas, Louisiana, Mississippi, and Texas,

- - - - - - - - - - - - - - -

Rate: 1.6-2 lb. ai/A
3.2-4 pt. 4L/A (Caparol only)

Time: Winter weed control. Apply either preemergence or postemergence to weeds less than 2 tall.

Weeds: Winter weeds such as:

annual sowthistle	filaree	pineappleweed
chickweed	London rocket	redmaids rockpurslane
fiddleneck	mustard	shepherdspurse

Remarks: Fall bedded cotton land. Do not use in areas of excess salt or calcareous soil. Refer to label for precautions and restrictions.

Crop Rotation: Same restrictions as above.

State Restrictions: For use in California.

- - - - - - - - - - - - - - -

Signal Word/Toxicity Class: Caution/III.
REI: 12 hr. unless soil injected or soil incorporated.

PROMETRYN + MSMA (premix)

Postemergence herbicide with surfactant. Toxic to wildlife.

■ **POST**

Riverside Prometryne + MSMA (1 lb. prometryn & 4 lb. MSMA) *(Terra)*

Rate: 2.5 lb. ai/A
2 qt./A in 10-40 gal. water

Time: Postemergence. Apply after cotton is 6" tall but before first bloom stage.

Weeds: Broadleaf weeds:

carpetweed	lambsquarters	purslane
cocklebur	malva	ragweed
coffeeweed	morningglory	smartweed
Florida pusley	pigweed	teaweed
groundcherry	prickly sida	velvetleaf

Grasses and sedges:

barnyardgrass	foxtail	nutsedge
crabgrass	goosegrass	sandbur
dallisgrass	johnsongrass	signalgrass
fall panicum	(seedling)	

Remarks: Do not apply to glandless cotton varieties. Do not apply more than 1 gal./A per year. Do not graze treated areas or feed treated foliage to livestock. Do not apply through any type of irrigation system.

Crop Rotation: Root crops—8 months. When single preemergence treatment applied: cover crops (plowed down and not used for food or feed)—oats, sorghum, winter barley, winter rye, winter wheat; vegetables—cabbage, okra, onions, peas, red beets, sweet corn.

State Restrictions: For use on cotton 3-6" tall only in Arkansas, Louisiana, Mississippi, Missouri, Tennessee, Texas. Use extreme care that spray does not contact cotton leaves.

- - - - - - - - - - - - - - -

Signal Word/Toxicity Class: Caution/III.
REI: 12 hr.

Prowl — see pendimethalin

RR Rattler — see glyphosate

Roundup — see glyphosate

RR Roundup Ultra — see glyphosate

SCYTHE

◆ **Scythe (pelargonic acid)** *(Mycogen)*

Rate: 4-13 fl. oz./1 gal. spray solution

Time: Apply to actively growing weeds prior to crop emergence.

Weeds: Annual and perennial broadleaf weeds and grasses.

Remarks: Apply in minimum 75 gal. spray solution/A or spray-to-wet. Do not apply by air or through any type of irrigation system. Refer to label for directions and precautions.

Tank Mixes: Glyphosate and other foliar and residual herbicides.

- - - - - - - - - - - - - - -

Signal Word/Toxicity Class: Warning/II.
REI: 24 hr.

Select — see clethodim

SETHOXYDIM

Good to excellent control of most annual grasses, rhizome johnsongrass, and bermudagrass.

■ **POST**

Poast (1.5EC) or Poast Plus (1EC) *(BASF)*

Rate: 0.09-0.47 lb. ai/A
0.5-2.5 pt. 1.5EC/A
0.75-3.75 pt. 1EC/A

Time: Postemergence.

Weeds: Annual and perennial grasses:

annual ryegrass	junglerice	stinkgrass
barnyardgrass	large crabgrass	tall fescue
bermudagrass	lovegrass	Texas panicum
broadleaf signalgrass	orchardgrass	volunteer cereals
browntop panicum	(seedling)	wild oat
fall panicum	perennial ryegrass	wild proso millet
field sandbur	quackgrass	wildcane
giant foxtail	red rice	wirestem muhly
goosegrass	red sprangletop	witchgrass
green foxtail	shattercane	woolly cupgrass
itchgrass	smooth crabgrass	yellow foxtail
johnsongrass	southwestern cupgrass	

Remarks: Rate depends on growing region. Add spray adjuvant or oil concentrate. Urea ammonium-nitrate solution (UAN) or ammonium sulfate (AMS) recommended to enhance activity on certain grass species. Do not apply through any type of irrigation system. Do not graze treated fields or feed treated forage to livestock. Refer to label for restrictions.

Days To Harvest: 40.

Tank Mixes: Buctril, Staple.

State Restrictions: Do not use UAN or AMS in California or Pacific Northwest.

- - - - - - - - - - - - - - -

Signal Word/Toxicity Class: Warning/II (Poast); Caution/III (Poast Plus).
REI: 12 hr.

STAPLE

■ **POST**

Staple (SP) (pyrithiobac sodium) *(DuPont)*

Rate: 1.2 oz. SP/A

Time: Postemergence. Apply over-the-top or as post-directed spray (at first true leaf stage) to actively growing weeds.

Weeds: Broadleaf weeds and sedges:

black nightshade	hemp sesbania	puncturevine*
bristly starbur	jimsonweed	smellmelon
coffee senna	hairy nightshade	sicklepod*
common cocklebur	lanceleaf sage	spiny spiderflower
common purslane*	morningglories	spurred anoda
common waterhemp	pigweed	sunflower
cowpea	prickly sida	velvetleaf
curly dock	redweed	wild poinsettia
devilsclaw	Pennsylvania	Wright groundcherry
Florida beggarweed	smartweed	yellow nutsedge*

* Suppression

Remarks: Injury can be more severe for Pima cotton varieties than on upland varieties; refer to label for restrictions and precautions. Do not exceed 1.8 oz./A per application or 2.4 oz./A per year. Do not apply through any type of irrigation system. Do not feed gin by-products to livestock.

Days To Harvest: 60.

NOTICE	The information on these pages is for preliminary planning — not a guide for use. Be sure to follow the manufacturer's directions, notwithstanding information contained here.

For personal protective equipment and EPA registration numbers, please turn to page 70.

Cotton

Crop Rotation: Cotton—anytime; wheat—4 months (California—6 months); rice—9 months; peanuts, soybeans, transplant tobacco—10 months; all other crops—after field bioassay. Do not rotate to grain sorghum or field corn in the season following Staple application; refer to label for sorghum and corn restrictions. Arizona: Cantaloupe, grain sorghum, sweet corn, watermelon—10 months; all other crops—after field bioassay. California: tomatoes—8 months.

Tank Mixes: Assure II, DSMA, MSMA, and most insecticides (except those containing malathion).

State Restrictions: For use in Alabama, Arizona, Arkansas, California, Florida, Georgia, Louisiana, Missouri, Mississippi, New Mexico, Oklahoma, South Carolina, Tennessee, Texas, Virginia.

‑ ‑ ‑ ‑ ‑ ‑ ‑ ‑ ‑ ‑ ‑ ‑ ‑ ‑ ‑

Signal Word/Toxicity Class: Warning/II.
REI: 24 hr.

Starfire — see paraquat

Treflan — see trifluralin

TRI-4 — see trifluralin

TRIFLURALIN

Good broad spectrum control of annual grasses and small-seeded broadleaf weeds including pigweed and purslane. Incorporation increases residual activity.

■ **PPI, PRE, POST**

Albaugh Trifluralin 4EC *(Albaugh)*
◆ **Clean Crop Trifluralin HF (4EC)** *(Platte)*
Gowan Trifluralin 4 or 5 (EC) or 10G *(Gowan)*
Helena Trifluralin 4 EC *(Helena)*
Riverside Trifluralin 4EC or Trific 60DF *(Terra)*
◆ **Sedagri Trifluralin 480 (4EC)** *(Rhone-Poulenc)*
Treflan HFP (4EC) or TR-10 (10G) *(Dow AgroSciences)*
TRI-4 HF (4EC) *(American Cyanamid)*
Trilin 4 or 5 (EC) or 10G *(Griffin)*
Wilbur-Ellis Trifluralin 10G *(Wilbur-Ellis)*

Rate: 0.5-1 lb. ai/A
1-2 pt. 4EC/A
0.6-1.6 pt. 5EC/A
0.875-1.66 lb. 60DF/A
5-10 lb. 10G/A

Time: Preplant incorporated, preemergence, lay-by.

Weeds: Broadleaf weeds:

carelessweed	fireweed	henbit
carpetweed	Florida purslane	knotweed
chickweed	Florida pusley	kochia
field bindweed	goosefoot	lambsquarters

Weeds: Broadleaf weeds, continued:

Mexican clover	purslane	Russian thistle
Mexican fireweed	pusley	spiny pigweed
prostrate pigweed	redroot pigweed	stinging nettle
puncturevine (western U.S.)	rough pigweed	tumbleweed

Grasses:

annual bluegrass	fall panicum	sandbur
barnyardgrass	foxtail millet	shattercane
bottlegrass	giant foxtail	smooth crabgrass
brachiaria	green foxtail	sprangletop
bristlegrass	Italian ryegrass	stinkgrass
bromegrass	johnsongrass	Texas panicum
burgrass	(seedling)	watergrass
cheat	junglerice	wildcane
cheatgrass	large crabgrass	woolly cupgrass
chess	pigeongrass	yellow foxtail
downy brome	robust foxtail	

Remarks: Rate varies by soil type. For preplant or preemergence, make first incorporation within 24 hr. after application. A second incorporation is necessary before planting and should be made in a different direction than the first. Incorporate uniformly into top 2-3" of final seedbed. For lay-by application, apply and incorporate any time up to lay-by. Direct applications onto soil between the rows and beneath emerged cotton plants. Refer to specific product label for Directions for Use.

Days To Harvest: 90.
Crop Rotation: Refer to label.
Tank Mixes: Caparol, Cotoran, Karmex.
State Restrictions: Wilbur-Ellis and Trilin 10G not for use in California.

‑ ‑ ‑ ‑ ‑ ‑ ‑ ‑ ‑ ‑ ‑ ‑ ‑ ‑ ‑

Rate: 1-2 lb. ai/A
2-4 pt. 4EC/A
1.6-3.2 pt. 5EC/A
1.66-3.33 lb. 60DF/A
10-20 lb. 10G/A

Time: Preplant—2 yr. program. Spring application: Apply before planting. Fall application: Oct. 15-Dec. 31. Split application: Apply same rate both spring and fall.

Weeds: Grasses:
johnsongrass (rhizome)

Remarks: Rate varies by soil texture and location. Apply double normal spring rate and disk incorporate 4-6" deep. Refer to specific product label for Directions for Use.

Crop Rotation: Refer to label.
State Restrictions: Not for use in Arizona and California.

‑ ‑ ‑ ‑ ‑ ‑ ‑ ‑ ‑ ‑ ‑ ‑ ‑ ‑ ‑

Signal Word/Toxicity Class: Varies by formulation.
REI: 12 hr. unless soil injected or soil incorporated.

Trilin — see trifluralin

Zorial Rapid 80 — see norflurazon

BXN-cotton resistant to bromoxynil • RR-cotton resistant to glyphosate

◆-new product • PP-preplant • PPI-preplant incorporated • PRE-preemergence • POST-postemergence • SEQ-sequential • ae-acid equivalent • ai-active ingredient • DF-dry flowable E/EC-emulsifiable concentrate • F/FL-flowable • DG/G/WG-dispersable granule • L/LC-liquid • SP/WSP-soluble packet • W/WP-wettable powder • WSB-water soluble bag

Section 4

Small Grains

Weed Efficacy Charts

Relative Effectiveness Of Small Grain Herbicides 184
Preplant, Preemergence Herbicides For Grass Control
    In Winter Wheat 184
Weed Response To Postemergence Herbicides 185
Weed Control With Burndown Herbicides 185

Herbicide Listings

Barley 211
Oats 223
Rye 231
Spring Wheat 199
Winter Wheat 186

Relative Effectiveness Of Small Grain Herbicides

	Banvel	Bronate	Buctril	2,4-D	Harmony Extra	Hoelon	MCPA	Peak	Stinger
Winter annuals									
Annual ryegrass	N	N	N	N	N	9	N	N	N
Common chickweed	7	6	6	6	9	N	6	7	N
Field pennycress	7	9	8	9	9	N	9	9	N
Henbit/red deadnettle	7	8	8	6	9	N	6	6	N
Horseweed (marestail)	8	8+	7	8+	7	N	8+	8	9+
Mustard spp.	7	9	9	9	9	N	9	9	N
Shepherdspurse	8	8+	8	9	9	N	8+	8	N
Wild buckwheat	9+	9	9	6	8	N	8	8	9
Wild lettuce	8	9	6	9	8	N	9	8+	9
Summer annuals									
Common lambsquarters	9	9	9	9	9	N	9	7	6
Common ragweed	9	9	8+	9	6	N	9	9	9+
Pennsylvania smartweed	9	9	9	6	9	N	7	6	7
Pigweed spp.	9	9	7	9	9	N	9	8+	6
Perennials									
Canada thistle	8	7	6	7	7	N	7	6+	9
Dandelion	8	8	6	8+	6	N	8	6	8+
Dock spp.	7+	6+	6	6+	8+	N	6+	8	9
White cockle	8+	6	6	7+	—	N	N	—	8+
Wild garlic or onion	6	6	N	7	9	N	6	9	N

Weed control rating: 10 = 95-100%, 9 = 85-95%, 8 = 75-85%, 7 = 65-75%, 6 = 55-65%, N = less than 55% or no control.

Source: Penn State Field Crop Weed Control Guide 1999

Preplant, Preemergence Herbicides For Grass Control In Winter Wheat

Herbicide(s)	Downy brome	Jointed goatgrass
Preplant		
Amber	3	—
Far-Go	5	—
Hoelon	5	—
Treflan	5	3
Preemergence		
Amber	3	—
Finesse	4	—

Response Ratings: Ratings are for light to moderate weed populations, favorable conditions and weed growth stage as specified on the product label. High weed populations, adverse conditions, or large weeds will reduce control. 10 = 96-100%, 9 = 90-95%, 8 = 85-90%, 7 = 80-84%, 6 = 70-79%, 5 = 60-69%, 4-2 = less than 60%, 1 = 0%.

Source: Herbicide Use In Nebraska 1997 Guide

Weed Response to Postemergence Herbicides

Herbicide	Blue mustard	Field pennycress	Horseweed	Knotweed	Kochia	Lambsquarters	Pennsyvania smartweed	Prickly lettuce	Prostrate pigweed	Redroot pigweed	Russian thistle	Shepherdspurse	Sunflower	Tansymustard	Velvetleaf	Wild buckwheat	Wild vetch
Ally	9	9	1	1	6	7	4	8	8	8	6	9	7	9	1	5	1
Ally + Banvel	9	10	6	7	10	10	9	10	10	10	9	10	9	10	6	7	8
Ally + 2,4-D	10	10	6	7	9	10	6	10	10	10	8	10	10	10	8	6	6
Amber	9	9	1	1	7	6	5	8	8	8	6	9	8	9	1	7	1
Amber + Banvel	9	10	6	7	10	10	9	10	10	10	9	10	10	10	6	9	8
Amber + 2,4-D	10	10	6	6	9	10	6	10	10	10	8	10	9	10	8	6	6
Banvel + 2,4-D	6	10	6	8	10	9	10	8	10	10	8	10	10	10	8	7	8
Buctril	7	9	9	8	9	8	8	7	8	8	8	9	9	9	8	8	5
Buctril + 2,4-D	8	10	7	9	10	9	9	9	9	9	9	9	9	9	8	8	7
Curtail	9	10	9	8	9	8	10	10	10	10	9	10	9	10	9	10	9
2,4-D	9	9	5	6	6	9	9	8	9	9	8	9	9	9	9	4	7
Finesse	9	9	1	4	5	8	5	8	8	8	5	9	6	9	1	6	1
Finesse + Banvel	9	10	6	7	10	10	9	10	10	10	9	10	9	10	6	8	8
Finesse + 2,4-D	9	10	6	7	9	10	6	10	10	10	8	10	9	10	8	7	6
Harmony Extra	9	10	7	6	7	9	8	9	9	9	8	10	8	10	8	8	5
MCPA	5	7	4	4	5	7	6	6	6	6	6	8	6	8	6	4	5
Peak	8	9	1	1	5	6	4	8	8	8	6	9	8	9	1	5	1
Peak + Banvel	9	10	6	7	10	10	9	10	10	10	9	10	9	10	6	9	8
Peak + 2,4-D	10	10	6	7	9	10	6	10	10	10	8	10	10	10	8	6	6
Tordon + 2,4-D	8	10	5	6	6	10	8	9	10	10	8	10	9	10	9	9	8

Response Ratings: Ratings are for light to moderate weed populations, favorable conditions and weed growth stage as specified on the product label. High weed populations, adverse conditions, or large weeds will reduce control.
10 = 96-100%, 9 = 90-95%, 8 = 85-90%, 7 = 80-84%, 6 = 70-79%, 5 = 60-69%, 4-2 = less than 60%, 1 = 0%.

Source: Herbicide Use In Nebraska 1997 Guide

Weed Control With Burndown Herbicides

Weed	Herbicide			
	Banvel	Gramoxone Extra	Roundup (fall-applied)	Roundup (spring-applied)
Alfalfa sod	8	N	8+	7
Bromegrass or quackgrass sod	N	6	9	7
Canada thistle	8	6	9	7
Common chickweed	7	8+	9	9
Common lambsquarters	9	8	9	9
Common ragweed	9	8	9	9
Dandelion	8	N	7	6
Foxtail spp.	N	9	9	9
Hairy vetch	9	7	8	6
Hemp dogbane, dewberry, milkweed, etc.	6	6	8+	6
Marestail	8	7	9	9
Mustard spp.	9	8	9	9
Orchardgrass or fescue sod	N	N	9	7
Red clover	9	8	8+	7
Rye cover, volunteer small grains	N	9	10	10
Smartweed	9	7	7	7
Timothy or bluegrass	N	7	10	10

Weed control rating: 10 = 95-100%, 9 = 85-95%, 8 = 75-85%, 7 = 65-75%, 6 = 55-65%, N = less than 55% or no control.

Source: Penn State Field Crop Weed Control Guide 1999

NOTICE The information on these pages is for preliminary planning — not a guide for use. Be sure to follow the manufacturer's directions, notwithstanding information contained here.

Small Grains

Winter Wheat
(fall-seeded)

ACHIEVE

Systemic postemergence herbicide for control of selective grasses. Does not control broadleaf weeds. Rainfast within 1 hr. Comes prepackaged with its own adjuvant.

■ **POST**

◆ **Achieve 40DG (tralkoxydim)** *(ZENECA)*

Rate: 0.18-0.24 lb. ai/A
0.44-0.6 lb. 40DG/A

Time: Postemergence. Apply 1- to 4-leaf stage for ryegrass and Persian darnel; 1- to 5-leaf stage for foxtail; 1- to 6-leaf stage for wild oat.

Weeds: Grasses:

annual ryegrass	Italian ryegrass	wild oat
green foxtail	Persian darnel	yellow foxtail

Remarks: Apply by ground or air. Use high rate when soil is dry, weeds are large, weed population is high, or crop canopy is dense. Maximum seasonal application is 0.25 lb. ai/A. Do not apply to crops or weeds with heavy dew cover. Do not apply through any type of irrigation system. Refer to label for use directions, restrictions, and precautions.

Days To Harvest: 60; grazed or cut for hay—30; straw or grain fed to livestock—45.

Crop Rotation: Cereal grains, leafy crops—30 days after application; all other crops—106 days after application.

Tank Mixes: Buctril, Bronate, Curtail M, Stinger.

— — — — — — — — — — — —

Signal Word/Toxicity Class: Caution.
REI: 12 hr. unless soil injected or soil incorporated.

AIM

Contact herbicide with little or no residual activity. Rainfast within 1 hr. Very toxic to algae and moderately toxic to fish.

■ **POST**

◆ **Aim (WDG) (carfentrazone-ethyl)** *(FMC)*

Rate: 0.33-1.24 oz. WDG/A

Time: Apply in all tillage systems to actively growing weeds up to 4" high and rosettes less than 3" across. Do not apply past jointing stage.

Weeds: Broadleaf weeds:

annual sowthistle	kochia	shepherdspurse
bittercress	lambsquarters	tansymustard
black nightshade	pigweed	tumble mustard
bushy wallflower	redroot pigweed	velvetleaf
catchweed bedstraw	redstem filaree	volunteer rapeseed
field pennycress	Russian thistle	wild buckwheat
flixweed		

Tank mixed with 2,4-D (amine) or MCPA (amine) will also control:

blue mustard	greenflower	smooth pigweed
coast tarweed	pepperweed	sowthistle
common gromwell	ivyleaf speedwell	tall waterhemp
common groundsel	London rocket	tumble pigweed
common	minerslettuce	wild mustard
lambsquarters	prickly lettuce	wild radish
cutleaf	prostrate pigweed	wild sunflower
eveningprimrose	silverleaf nightshade	woolly croton
fiddleneck		

Remarks: The use of crop oil or crop oil plus either 28% nitrogen or ammonium sulfate with companion herbicides may be recommended under very dry conditions. Do not use with tank additives that alter the pH of spray solution below pH 5 or above pH 8. Refer to label for use directions, restrictions, and precautions.

Crop Rotation: Any crop including wheat—30 days following application; small grains (barley, oats, rye)—12 months after application.

Tank Mixes: Ally, Amber, Assert, Banvel, 2,4-D (amine), Express, Finesse, Harmony Extra, MCPA (amine), Peak.

— — — — — — — — — — — —

Signal Word/Toxicity Class: Caution.
REI: 12 hr.

ALLY

Sulfonylurea herbicide with soil residual properties. Especially effective for winter annual mustards like pennycress or tansymustard. Also controls special problem weeds like kochia or wild buckwheat. Consistent performance. Tank mix with low rate of a broadleaf herbicide with a different mode of action. Follow soil pH, use intervals to reduce resistant weed buildup, and crop rotation guidelines for your area.

■ **POST**

Ally (DF) (metsulfuron-methyl) *(DuPont)*

Rate: 0.1 oz. DF/A

Time: Postemergence. For dryland wheat, apply from 2-leaf stage but before boot stage. For irrigated wheat, apply after crop begins tillering but before boot stage. First postemergence irrigations should be delayed for at least 3 days after treatment and should not exceed 1" water. Do not apply during boot stage or early heading stage.

Weeds: Broadleaf weeds:

blue mustard	field pennycress	Russian thistle
bur buttercup	filaree	shepherdspurse
Canada thistle*	flixweed	slimleaf
coast fiddleneck	green smartweed	lambsquarters
common chickweed	henbit	smallseed falseflax
common groundsel	kochia	smooth pigweed
common	jim hill mustard	sowthistle*
lambsquarters	ladysthumb	tansymustard
common purslane	mayweed	tarweed
common sunflower*	minerslettuce	treacle mustard
conical catchfly	pale smartweed	tumble mustard
corn cockle	plains coreopsis	tumble pigweed
corn gromwell*	prickly lettuce	volunteer sunflower
cowcockle	prostrate knotweed*	waterpod
false chamomile	purple mustard	wild buckwheat*
fanweed	redroot pigweed	wild mustard

Grasses:

annual ryegrass*

* Suppression

Remarks: Not underseeded with legumes. Add 1-2 pt. 80% nonionic surfactant/100 gal. spray volume. Do not apply through any type of irrigation system. Refer to label for restrictions and precautions.

Crop Rotation: Determined by crop to be planted and minimum rotation interval. Minimum rotation interval is time from last application to anticipated date of planting. For rotational flexibility, do not use Ally on all your wheat, barley, fallow, pasture, or rangeland at the same time.

Tank Mixes: Banvel, 2,4-D, MCPA.

State Restrictions: For use in Colorado (except Alamosa, Conejos, Costilla, Rio Grande, Saguache counties), Idaho, Kansas, Minnesota, Montana, Nebraska, New Mexico, North Dakota, Oklahoma, Oregon, South Dakota, Texas, Utah, Washington, and Wyoming.

— — — — — — — — — — — —

Signal Word/Toxicity Class: Caution.
REI: 4 hr.

AMBER

Selective sulfonylurea herbicide with extended soil residual activity. Especially effective for pennycress, tansy mustard, and kochia. Follow crop rotational guidelines and rotation intervals based on soil pH for Amber or other herbicides with a similar mode of action.

■ **PP, PPI, PRE, POST**

Amber Accu-Pak or CustomPak (WDG) (triasulfuron) *(Novartis)*

Rate: 0.56 oz. WDG/A

Time: Preplant, preplant shallow incorporated, preemergence. Do not apply preemergence to late fall-seeded winter wheat if environmental conditions that stress wheat are expected within 2 weeks after application.

Weeds: Broadleaf weeds:

henbit

Grasses:

annual ryegrass*	downy brome*	Persian darnel*
cheat*	Japanese brome*	

Rate: 0.28-0.56 oz. WDG/A
Time: Postemergence. Apply when weeds are actively growing.

◆-new product • PP-preplant • PPI-preplant incorporated • PRE-preemergence • POST-postemergence • SEQ-sequential • ae-acid equivalent • ai-active ingredient • DF-dry flowable
E/EC-emulsifiable concentrate • F/FL-flowable • DG/G/WG-dispersable granule • L/LC-liquid • SP/WSP-soluble packet • W/WP-wettable powder • WSB-water soluble bag

Weeds: Broadleaf weeds:

annual fleabane	field pennycress	puncturevine
annual polemonium	flixweed	redroot pigweed
blue mustard (purple)	forget-me-not	rough fleabane
bushy wallflower	giant ragweed	Russian thistle
bur buttercup	hairy vetch	shepherdspurse
buttercup	henbit*	smooth pigweed
Canada thistle*	horseweed	spring whitlowgrass
coast fiddleneck	Indian mustard	tall buttercup
common broomweed	jagged chickweed	tall hedge mustard
common chickweed	jim hill mustard	tansymustard
common cocklebur	kochia	tumble mustard
common mallow	lanceleaf ragweed	Virginia pepperweed
common purslane	London rocket	western ragweed*
common ragweed	marshelder	wild buckwheat
common sunflower	minerslettuce	wild garlic*
common yarrow	morningglory*	wild mustard
corn gromwell	plains coreopsis	wild onion*
cutleaf	prickly lettuce	wild radish
eveningprimrose	prostrate knotweed	woolly croton
fanweed	prostrate pigweed	

* Suppression

Remarks: Do not apply to wheat undersown with legumes or forage grasses. Do not use alone in any field where sulfonylurea-resistant biotypes of any weed species have been identified. Refer to label for further use directions, restrictions, and precautions.

Crop Rotation: Wheat—anytime; proso millet—4 months; barley, oats, rye, bermudagrass—6 months (with conditions); grain sorghum and soybeans—14 months (with conditions). All other crops may be seeded only at completion of successful field bioassay; refer to label.

State Restrictions: For use in Colorado (except San Luis Valley), Idaho, Kansas, Minnesota, Montana, Nebraska, Nevada, New Mexico, North Dakota, Oklahoma, South Dakota, Texas, Utah, Wyoming, and east of the Cascades in Oregon or Washington.

- - - - - - - - - - - - - - -

Signal Word/Toxicity Class: Caution/III.
REI: 12 hr.

ASSERT

Postemergence controls wild oat and wild mustard. Good crop tolerance. Follow crop rotation guidelines.

■ POST

Assert (2.5LC) (imazamethabenz-methyl) *(American Cyanamid)*
Rate: 0.31-0.48 lb. ai/A
1-1.5 pt. 2.5LC/A
Time: Postemergence. Apply when wheat is in 2-5 leaf stage (prior to jointing); wild oat in 1-4 leaf stage. For Avenge tank mix, apply from 2-5 leaf stage of wild oat. Do not apply when wheat flagleaf is exposed.
Weeds: Broadleaf weeds:

catchweed bedstraw	London rocket	wild buckwheat
field pennycress	tansymustard	wild mustard
flixweed	tartary buckwheat	

Grasses:

interrupted windgrass	roughstalk bluegrass	wild oat

Remarks: Rate varies by state; refer to label. Add 2 pt. 80% nonionic surfactant/100 gal. spray solution. When weeds are under moisture or temperature stress, 1.5-2 pt. SUN-IT II spray adjuvant may be used instead of nonionic surfactant. Wheat straw may be fed or used for bedding. Do not apply through any type of irrigation system. Do not graze treated fields or cut treated forage for silage or hay.
Crop Rotation: Barley, canola (IMI-tolerant varieties such as Pioneer 45A71, 46A72; non-IMI tolerant in certain counties in Minnesota and North Dakota), corn, edible beans, safflower, soybeans, sunflower, wheat—anytime; sugar beets—20 months; other crops—15 months after application.
Tank Mixes: Ally, Amber, Avenge (wild oat only), bromoxynil + MCPA ester, Canvas, Curtail M, 2,4-D ester, Express, Finesse, Glean, Harmony, Harmony Extra, MCPA ester, Starane.

- - - - - - - - - - - - - - -

Signal Word/Toxicity Class: Danger/I.
REI: 48 hr.

AVENGE

Some winter wheat varieties are sensitive and should not be treated.

■ POST

Avenge (2ASU) (difenzoquat) *(American Cyanamid)*
Rate: 0.625-1 lb. ai/A
2.5-4 pt. 2ASU/A
Time: Postemergence. Apply when wild oat is in 3-5 leaf stage.

Weeds:
wild oat

Remarks: Refer to label for winter wheat varietal restrictions. Do not apply if rain is predicted within 6 hr., when freezing temperatures are forecast, or when plants are wet with rain or dew. When applied under poor conditions, Avenge can produce yellowing or slight tipburn of wheat; crop recovery is rapid when good growth conditions return.
Crop Rotation: Barley or wheat can be replanted if crop loss occurs. Rotation to other crops can be made the following year.
Tank Mixes: Assert for wild oat only and following broadleaf herbicides: Ally, Amber, bromoxynil, bromoxynil + MCPA, Canvas, Curtail, 2,4-D, Express, Glean, Harmony Extra, MCPA, Peak.

- - - - - - - - - - - - - - -

Signal Word/Toxicity Class: Danger/I.
REI: 48 hr.

Banvel — see dicamba

Barrage — see 2,4-D

Bison — see bromoxynil & MCPA

Brash — see 2,4-D Combinations

Broclean — see bromoxynil

Bromac — see bromoxynil & MCPA

Bromox — see bromoxynil

Bromox-MCPA 2-2 — see bromoxynil & MCPA

BROMOXYNIL

Contact action herbicide. Usually used in combination with 2,4-D, MCPA, or other herbicides to increase consistency and to control additional weed species. Very good crop tolerance.

■ POST

◆ Broclean 2EC *(Platte)*
◆ Bromox 2EC *(Micro Flo)*
Buctril (2EC), Buctril 4EC *(Rhone-Poulenc)*
Moxy 2EC *(Terra)*
Rate: 0.375-0.5 lb. ai/A
1.5-2 pt. 2EC/A
0.75-1 pt. 4EC/A
Underseeded with alfalfa:
0.25-0.375 lb. ai/A
1-1.5 pt. 2EC/A
0.5-0.75 pt. 4EC/A
Time: Postemergence. Apply from emergence to boot stage.
Weeds: Most susceptible broadleaf weeds:

annual pepperweed	common tarweed	Pennsylvania
annual sowthistle	eastern black	smartweed
black nightshade	nightshade	shepherdspurse
blue mustard	field pennycress	silverleaf nightshade
bristly starbur	green smartweed	sunflower
coast fiddleneck	hairy nightshade	tartary buckwheat
common cocklebur	jimsonweed	wild buckwheat
common lambsquarters	ladysthumb	

Susceptible broadleaf weeds:

buffalobur	ivyleaf morningglory	spiny pigweed
burcucumber	knawel	tall morningglory
common groundsel	kochia	tall waterhemp
common ragweed	London rocket	tumble mustard
corn chamomile	mayweed	velvetleaf
corn gromwell	prostrate knotweed	Venice mallow
cowcockle	puncturevine	wild mustard
giant ragweed	redroot pigweed	wild radish
hemp sesbania	Russian thistle	yellow starthistle

NOTICE The information on these pages is for preliminary planning — not a guide for use. Be sure to follow the manufacturer's directions, notwithstanding information contained here. | For personal protective equipment and EPA registration numbers, please turn to page 70.

4

Small Grains

Remarks: Fall-seeded wheat. Apply by ground, air, and sprinkler irrigation equipment. Do not apply when crop canopy covers weeds or when crops are under moisture stress. Do not graze treated fields within 30 days after application (45 days for Buctril). Refer to label for use directions, restrictions and precautions.

Crop Rotation: Do not plant rotational crops until the following season (within 30 days of application for Buctril).

Tank Mixes: Ally, Amber, Avenge (not for use on sensitive varieties), Banvel, Curtail, 2,4-D, diuron (Idaho, Oregon, Washington), Express, Finesse, Glean, Harmony Extra, Hoelon, MCPA, metribuzin (Idaho, Montana, Oregon, Washington).

– – – – – – – – – – – – – – – –

Signal Word/Toxicity Class: Warning/II.
REI: 12 hr.

BROMOXYNIL & MCPA (Premixes)

Premix for several annual broadleaf weeds including winter annual mustards like blue mustard and pennycress and special problem weeds like kochia, sunflower, or wild buckwheat. Weeds should be small and not drought stressed. Very good crop tolerance.

■ **POST**

Bison (EC) (2 lb./gal. bromoxynil & 2 lb./gal. MCPA) *(Terra)*
◆ **Bromac (EC) (2 lb./gal. bromoxynil & 2 lb./gal. MCPA)** *(Platte)*
◆ **Bromox-MCPA 2-2 (EC) (2 lb./gal. bromoxynil & 2 lb./gal. MCPA)** *(Micro Flo)*
Bronate (EC) (2 lb./gal. bromoxynil & 2 lb./gal. MCPA) *(Rhone-Poulenc)*

Rate: 0.5-1 lb. ai/A
1-2 pt. EC/A
Chemigation:
1 lb. ai/A
2 pt. EC/A
Postharvest—MN, MT, ND, SD:
0.38-1 lb. ai/A
0.75-2 pt. EC/A (Bronate)

Time: Postemergence. Apply after 3-leaf stage but before boot stage.

Weeds: Most susceptible broadleaf weeds:

annual sowthistle	field pennycress	Russian thistle
black mustard	green smartweed	shepherdspurse
black nightshade	hairy nightshade	silverleaf nightshade
coast fiddleneck	horned poppy	smooth pigweed
common cocklebur	jimsonweed	spiny pigweed
common lambsquarters	ladysthumb	sunflower
	London rocket	tall waterhemp
common tarweed	marshelder	tartary buckwheat
cowcockle	Pennsylvania smartweed	tumble mustard
cutleaf nightshade		wild buckwheat
eastern black nightshade	pepperweed	wild mustard
	redroot pigweed	yellow rocket

Susceptible broadleaf weeds:

blue mustard	giant ragweed	puncturevine
Canada thistle (suppression)	hemp sesbania	purple mustard
	henbit	tall morningglory
common groundsel	ivyleaf morningglory	tansymustard
common ragweed	knawel	tarweed
corn chamomile	kochia	velvetleaf
corn gromwell	mayweed	wild radish
fumitory	prostrate knotweed	

Remarks: Do not apply when crop canopy covers weeds or when crops are under moisture stress. Do not graze fields within 30 days after application (45 for Bronate).

Tank Mixes: Ally, Amber, Assert, Avenge, Banvel, Curtail, Express, Finesse, Glean, Harmony Extra, MCPA, metribuzin (Idaho, Oregon, Washington).

– – – – – – – – – – – – – – – –

Signal Word/Toxicity Class: Warning/II.
REI: 12 hr.

Bronate — see bromoxynil & MCPA

BUCKLE (Premix)

Granular selective herbicide to control wild oats and foxtail.

■ **PPI**

Buckle (13G) (10% triallate & 3% trifluralin) *(Monsanto)*

Rate: 1.6-1.95 lb. ai/A
12.5-15 lb. 13G/A

Time: Preplant incorporated. Apply in the fall prior to planting within 3 weeks of normal freezeup.

Weeds: Grasses:

downy brome	pigeongrass	wild oat
foxtail		

Remarks: Do not use prior to convention seeding with double-disc press drills. Do not apply on muck soils or soils containing more than 10% organic matter. Do not graze livestock on treated crops. Refer to label for specific rates, directions, and precautions.

Crop Rotation: Certain vegetable crops (refer to Monsanto representative for specific crops)—5 months; sugar beets, red beets, spinach—14 months; sorghum, proso millet, corn, oats—16 months.

State Restrictions: For use in Colorado, Idaho, Kansas, Minnesota, Montana, Nebraska, Nevada, North Dakota, Oregon, South Dakota, Utah, Washington, and Wyoming.

– – – – – – – – – – – – – – – –

Signal Word/Toxicity Class: Caution/III.
REI: 12 hr.

Buctril — see bromoxynil

CANVAS (Premix)

■ **POST**

Canvas (DF) (37.5% thifensulfuron-methyl & 18.75% tribenuron-methyl & 15% metsulfuron-methyl) *(DuPont)*

Rate: 1 soluble pack/5A
MN, MT, ND, SD:
1 soluble pack/10A

Time: Early postemergence. Apply to young, actively growing weeds after wheat is in 2-leaf stage, but before flag leaf is visible.

Weeds: Broadleaf weeds:

annual knawel	cutleaf nightshade*	prostrate pigweed
annual sowthistle*	dogfennel	purple mustard
black mustard	false chamomile	redmaids rockpurslane
blue mustard	fanweed	redroot pigweed
broadleaf dock	field chickweed	Russian thistle
bur buttercup	field pennycress	scentless chamomile
bushy wallflower	filaree	shepherdspurse
Canada thistle	flixweed	smallflower buttercup
Carolina geranium	hairy nightshade*	smallseed falseflax
catchweed bedstraw*	hairy vetch*	smartweed
clasping pepperweed	henbit	smooth pigweed
coast fiddleneck	jim hill mustard	snow speedwell
common buckwheat	kochia	stinking chickweed
common chickweed	lambsquarters	stinking mayweed
common cocklebur	little mallow*	swinecress
common groundsel	London rocket	tall waterhemp*
common mallow	marshelder	tansymustard
common purslane	mayweed chamomile	tarweed
common radish	minerslettuce	treacle mustard
common ragweed	mouseearcress	tumble mustard
common sunflower	narrowleaf lambsquarters	tumble pigweed
common vetch*		volunteer lentils
conical catchfly	nightflowering catchfly	volunteer peas
corn chamomile		volunteer sunflower
corn gromwell	Pennsylvania smartweed	waterpod
corn spurry		wild buckwheat
cowcockle	pineappleweed	wild chamomile
curly dock	plains coreopsis	wild garlic
cutleaf eveningprimrose	prickly lettuce	wild mustard
	prostrate knotweed	wild radish

* Partial control

Remarks: Not underseeded with legumes. Add approved nonionic surfactant. Do not make more than one application per crop season. Do not graze or feed forage or hay from treated areas to livestock (harvested straw may be used for bedding and/or feed).

Days To Harvest: 45.

Crop Rotation: Varies depending on crop and geographic area.

State Restrictions: For use in Colorado (except Alamosa, Conejos, Costilla, Rio Grande, Saguache counties), Idaho, Kansas, Minnesota, Montana, Nebraska, New Mexico, Oklahoma, Oregon, South Dakota, Texas, Utah, Washington, and Wyoming.

– – – – – – – – – – – – – – – –

Signal Word/Toxicity Class: Warning/II.
REI: 12 hr.

CHEYENNE (Co-Pack)

Twin pack product of Cheyenne FM (fenoxaprop & MCPA) & X-TRA (thifensulfuron & tribenuron).

■ **POST**

Cheyenne (3.5 gal. Cheyenne FM & 0.375 lb. X-TRA) *(AgrEvo USA)*

– – – – – – – – – – – – – – – –

◆=new product • PP=preplant • PPI=preplant incorporated • PRE=preemergence • POST=postemergence • SEQ=sequential • ae-acid equivalent • ai-active ingredient • DF-dry flowable
E/EC-emulsifiable concentrate • F/FL-flowable • DG/G/WG-dispersable granule • L/LC-liquid • SP/WSP-soluble packet • W/WP-wettable powder • WSB-water soluble bag

Rate: Cheyenne FM:
0.08 lb. ai/A
1.4 pt./A
+ X-TRA:
0.3 oz./A

Time: Crop: Minimum of 3 tillers. Broadleaf weeds: Up to 4" high or 4" diameter; grasses: wild oat 1-4 leaf, green foxtail 2 leaf-2 tiller.

Weeds: Broadleaf weeds:

common lambsquarters	kochia mustard	redroot pigweed

Grasses:

barnyardgrass foxtail	millet volunteer corn	wild oat

Remarks: Always mix Cheyenne FM with X-TRA Herbicide prior to use to ensure crop safety and adequate control. Do not apply by air.

Days To Harvest: Minnesota, Montana, North Dakota, South Dakota—60; all other states—70.

- - - - - - - - - - - - - -

Signal Word/Toxicity Class:
Danger/I (Cheyenne FM); Caution/III (X-TRA).
REI: 24 hr.

Chiptox — see MCPA

Clarity — see dicamba

CLOPYRALID

Systemic herbicide absorbed by leaves and roots. Has selective postemergence control of many annual and perennial broadleaf weeds. Especially useful for seasonal suppression of Canada thistle. Frequently used in combination with 2,4-D or MCPA to control additional weeds. Note crop rotation limitations.

■ **POST**

Stinger *(Dow AgroSciences)*
Rate: 0.1-0.125 lb. ae/A
0.25-0.33 pt./A

Time: Postemergence. Apply from 3-leaf stage up to early boot stage.

Weeds: Annual and perennial broadleaf weeds:

Canada thistle	jimsonweed	sowthistle
clover	knapweed	spotted knapweed
cocklebur	marshelder	sunflower
diffuse knapweed	Russian knapweed	vetch
Jerusalem artichoke	(suppression)	volunteer soybean

Remarks: Not underseeded with legumes. Do not allow dairy animals or meat animals being finished for slaughter to forage or graze treated fields within 1 week after treatment. Do not harvest hay from treated fields. Do not apply through any type of irrigation system.

Crop Rotation: Varies by region; refer to label.

Tank Mixes: May be tank mixed with other herbicides registered for postemergence application.

- - - - - - - - - - - - - -

Signal Word/Toxicity Class: Caution/III.
REI: 12 hr.

Credit — see glyphosate

CURTAIL OR CURTAIL M (Premixes)

Clopyralid provides good seasonal control of Canada thistle. 2,4-D or MCPA in premix improves control of other broadleaf weeds. Crop tolerance is good. Canada thistle control is best when weeds are treated before they form flower buds.

■ **POST**

Curtail (0.38 lb./gal. clopyralid & 2 lb./gal. 2,4-D) *(Dow AgroSciences)*
Curtail M (0.42 lb./gal. clopyralid & 2.35 lb./gal. MCPA)
(Dow AgroSciences)
Rate: 0.6-0.8 lb. ae/A
2-2.66 pt. Curtail/A
1.75-2.66 pt. Curtail M/A

Time: Postemergence. Apply in spring to actively growing wheat once 4 leaves have unfolded on main stem up to jointing stage. Do not apply after boot stage.

Weeds: Broadleaf weeds:

alfalfa	giant ragweed	red sorrel
annual sowthistle	goatsbeard	redroot pigweed
Canada thistle	hairy nightshade	Russian knapweed*
coffeeweed	horseweed	Russian thistle
common burdock	Jerusalem artichoke	(1-3 leaf)
common cocklebur	jim hill mustard	scentless chamomile
common groundsel	jimsonweed	shepherdspurse
common	kochia* (2-4 leaf)	sicklepod
lambsquarters	ladysthumb	spotted knapweed
common ragweed	mayweed chamomile	sweetclover
common sunflower	meadow salsify	tansymustard
cornflower	musk thistle	tumble mustard
curly dock	narrowleaf	velvetleaf
cutleaf nightshade	hawksbeard	vetch
dandelion	Pennsylvania	volunteer beans
diffuse knapweed	smartweed	volunteer lentils
dogfennel	perennial sowthistle*	volunteer peas
false chamomile	pineappleweed	wild buckwheat
fanweed	plantain	wild mustard
field pennycress	prickly lettuce	wild radish
flixweed*	red clover	yellow starthistle

* Suppression

Remarks: Not underseeded with legumes. Do not harvest hay from treated grain fields. Do not allow lactating dairy animals or meat animals being finished for slaughter to forage or graze treated fields within 1 week after application. Do not apply through any type of irrigation system.

Crop Rotation: Varies by region; refer to label.

Tank Mixes: Ally, Avenge, Banvel, Buctril, 2,4-D, diuron, Express, Harmony Extra, MCPA, metribuzin.

- - - - - - - - - - - - - -

Signal Word/Toxicity Class: Danger/I (Curtail); Caution/III (Curtail M).
REI: 48 hr.

Cyclone — see paraquat

2,4-D - PHENOXY HERBICIDES

Translocated herbicide widely used for general weed control in winter wheat. Frequently tank mixed with several new herbicides. Good choice for seasonal suppression of field bindweed. Ester forms more active during cool weather when treating early winter annual mustards. Risk of crop injury with fall application prior to tillering in northern areas.

Annual and perennial broadleaf weeds controlled by 2,4-D include:

beggarticks	galinsoga	povertyweed
bindweed	goldenrod	puncturevine
bitterweed	ground ivy	purslane
broomweed	healall	ragweed
bull thistle	hoary cress	Russian thistle
burdock	ironweed	shepherdspurse
Canada thistle	jimsonweed	smartweed
carpetweed	knotweed	sowthistle
catnip	lambsquarters	stinkweed
chicory	mallow	sumac
chickweed	marshelder	sunflower
cocklebur	mexicanweed	sweetclover
coffeeweed	morningglory	velvetleaf
cutleaf	musk thistle	Virginia creeper
eveningprimrose	mustard	wild carrot
creeping jenny	pennywort	wild garlic
croton	pepperweed	wild lettuce
dandelion	pigweed	wild onion
dock	plantain	wild parsnips
dogbane	pokeweed	wild radish

■ **POST**

Albaugh Amine 4 (2,4-D amine) *(Albaugh)*
Weedestroy AM-40 (2,4-D amine) *(Riverdale)*
Wilbur-Ellis Amine 4 (2,4-D amine) *(Wilbur-Ellis)*
Rate: 0.25-1 lb. ae/A
0.5-2 pt./A (Riverdale, Wilbur-Ellis)
0.33-0.75 lb. ae/A
0.66-1.5 pt./A (Albaugh)

Time: Postemergence. Apply after tillering (4-8" high) but before boot stage. Do not spray in boot to dough stage.

Remarks: Not underseeded with legumes. For emergency control of perennial broadleaf weeds, up to 3 pt./A may be used when weeds are approaching bud stage. Do not use higher rates unless possible crop injury will be acceptable.

- - - - - - - - - - - - - -

Rate: 0.125-0.25 lb. ae/A
0.25-0.5 pt./A
Time: Postemergence. Apply after grain is 8" tall but before boot stage. Do not spray in boot to dough stage.
Remarks: Underseeded with legumes. Do not spray alfalfa or sweet clover unless infestation is severe and injury to legumes can be tolerated.

Rate: 0.5-1 lb. ae/A
1-2 pt./A
Time: Preharvest. Apply in dough stage.
Remarks: Best results will be obtained when soil moisture is adequate for plant growth and weeds are growing well.
State Restrictions: Wilbur-Ellis not registered in California.

Signal Word/Toxicity Class: Danger/I.
REI: 48 hr.

■ POST

Albaugh LV4 or LV6 Ester (2,4-D ester) *(Albaugh)*
♦ Barrage or Barrage HF (EC) (2,4-D ester) *(Helena)*
♦ Clean Crop Low Vol 4 or Low Vol 6 (2,4-D ester) *(Platte)*
Esteron 99C (2,4-D LV ester) *(Rhone-Poulenc)*
Riverdale 6 Amine (2,4-D amine) *(Riverdale)*
Riverdale L.V. 4 or L.V. 6 (2,4-D ester) *(Riverdale)*
Solve 2,4-D (2,4-D LV ester) *(Albaugh)*
Weed Rhap LV-6D (2,4-D ester) *(Helena)*
Wilbur-Ellis Lo Vol-4 or Lo Vol-6 (2,4-D ester) *(Wilbur-Ellis)*
Rate: 0.25-0.5 lb. ae/A
0.5-1 pt. 4/A
0.33-0.66 pt. 6/A
Perennial weeds, preharvest:
0.5-1 lb. ae/A
1-2 pt. 4/A
0.66-1.33 pt. 6/A
Time: Postemergence, preharvest. Do not spray before tiller or from early boot to dough stage.
Remarks: Not underseeded with legumes. Do not forage or graze treated fields for 2 weeks after application.
State Restrictions: Wilbur-Ellis not registered in California.

Signal Word/Toxicity Class: Danger/I (amine); Caution/III (ester).
REI: Danger—48 hr.; Caution—12 hr.

■ POST

Albaugh D-638 (2,4-D ester + acid) *(Albaugh)*
Phenoxy 088 (2,4-D mixed amine) *(Terra)*
Weedone 638 (2,4-D ester + acid) *(Nufarm)*
Rate: 0.35-0.7 lb. ae/A
1-2 pt./A
Time: Postemergence, preharvest. Apply when weeds are near bud stage. Apply after grain is fully tillered (4-8" high) but not forming joints in stem, and when daytime temperatures are below 85°F. Do not spray in boot to dough stage. Do not apply to grain in seedling stage.
Remarks: Not underseeded with legumes. Do not apply through any type of irrigation system. Do not forage or graze treated fields for 2 weeks after application.
State Restrictions: Weedone not for use preharvest in California.

Signal Word/Toxicity Class: Danger/I.
REI: 48 hr.

■ POST

♦ Clean Crop Amine 4 (2,4-D amine) *(Platte)*
Formula 40 (2,4-D mixed amine) *(Rhone-Poulenc)*
♦ Opti-Amine (4) (2,4-D amine) *(Helena)*
Weed Rhap A-4D (2,4-D amine) *(Helena)*
Rate: 0.33-0.66 lb. ae/A
0.66-1.33 pt./A
Time: Postemergence. Apply in spring. Do not apply before tiller stage or from early boot through milk stage.

Rate: 0.5-1 lb. ae/A
1-2 pt./A
Time: Preharvest. Apply in dough stage.
Remarks: Not underseeded with legumes. Up to 3 pt./A may be used for difficult weed problems such as dry conditions in Western states. Do not allow dairy animals or meat animals being finished for slaughter to forage or graze treated fields within 2 weeks of treatment.

Signal Word/Toxicity Class: Danger/I.
REI: 48 hr.

■ POST

Gordon's LV 400 (2,4-D ester) *(PBI/Gordon)*
Riverside 2,4-D LV4 (2,4-D LV ester) *(Terra)*
Rate: 0.25-0.38 lb. ae/A
0.5-0.75 pt./A
Time: Postemergence. Apply in the spring at full tiller but before early boot stage.
Remarks: Not underseeded with legumes. 1-2 pt./A may be used for difficult weeds problems. Do not use higher rates unless possible crop injury will be acceptable. Do not allow dairy animals or meat animals being finished for slaughter to forage or graze treated fields within 2 weeks of application.

Signal Word/Toxicity Class: Caution/III.
REI: 12 hr.

■ POST

Hi-Dep (2,4-D mixed amine) *(PBI/Gordon)*
Rate: 0.125-0.75 lb. ae/A
0.25-1.5 pt./A
Time: Postemergence. Apply after grain begins tillering and before boot stage (4-8" tall). Do not apply before tiller stage or from early boot through milk stage.

Rate: 0.5-1 lb. ae/A
1-2 pt./A
Time: Preharvest. Apply in dough stage.
Remarks: Not underseeded with legumes. Up to 3 pt./A may be used for difficult weeds problems such as dry conditions in Western states. Do not allow dairy animals or meat animals being finished for slaughter to forage or graze treated fields within 2 weeks of application.

Signal Word/Toxicity Class: Danger/I.
REI: 48 hr.

■ POST

♦ Saber (2,4-D amine) *(Platte)*
Rate: 0.25-0.5 lb. ae/A
0.5-1 pt./A
Time: Postemergence. Apply from onset of tillering to full tillering stage. Do not apply from boot to dough stage.

Rate: Emergency, preharvest:
0.35-1.5 lb. ae/A
0.75-3 pt./A
Time: Preharvest. Apply in hard dough stage. Do not apply before tiller or from boot to dough stage.
Remarks: Not underseeded with legumes. Up to 3 pt./A may be used to control difficult weeds and heavy infestations. Do not forage or graze treated fields for 2 weeks after application. Do not feed treated straw to livestock if emergency and/or preharvest treatment is applied.

Signal Word/Toxicity Class: Danger/I.
REI: 48 hr.

■ POST

Salvo (2,4-D LV ester) *(Platte)*
Rate: 0.25-0.5 lb. ae/A
0.4-0.8 pt./A
Time: Postemergence. Apply in the spring when weeds are small and grain is in full tiller stage (4-8" high) but before boot stage. Do not apply during boot or dough stage.
Remarks: Do not forage or graze treated grain fields within 2 weeks after application. Do not feed treated straw to livestock.

Signal Word/Toxicity Class: Caution/III.
REI: 12 hr.

■ POST

Savage (WSB) (2,4-D amine) *(Platte)*
Rate: 0.24-0.95 lb. ae/A
0.25-1 lb. WSB/A
Time: Postemergence. Apply in spring. Do not apply before tiller stage or from boot to dough stage.

Rate: 0.48-1.43 lb. ae/A
0.5-1.5 lb. WSB/A
Time: Preharvest. Apply in hard dough stage.

♦-new product • PP-preplant • PPI-preplant incorporated • PRE-preemergence • POST-postemergence • SEQ-sequential • ae-acid equivalent • ai-active ingredient • DF-dry flowable
E/EC-emulsifiable concentrate • F/FL-flowable • DG/G/WG-dispersable granule • L/LC-liquid • SP/WSP-soluble packet • W/WP-wettable powder • WSB-water soluble bag

Remarks: Not underseeded with legumes. Do not forage or graze treated fields within 2 weeks after treatment. Do not feed treated straw if preharvest treatment applied. Refer to label for restrictions and precautions.

- - - - - - - - - - - - - - - -

Signal Word/Toxicity Class: Danger/I.
REI: 48 hr.

■ POST
Solution (WS) (2,4-D amine) *(Riverdale)*
  Rate: 1 WS packet/2.5-5 A
  Time: Postemergence. Preharvest application can be applied when grain is in dough stage.
  Remarks: Apply in 5-100 gal. water. Best results will be obtained when soil moisture is adequate for plant growth and weeds are growing well.

- - - - - - - - - - - - - - - -

Signal Word/Toxicity Class: Danger/I.
REI: 48 hr.

■ POST
Weedar 64 (4) (2,4-D amine) *(Nufarm)*
  Rate: 0.25-1 lb. ae/A
    0.5-2 pt./A
  Time: Postemergence. Apply after grain is fully tillered (4-8" high) but not forming joints in stem. Do not spray in boot to dough stage.
  Remarks: Not underseeded with legumes. For emergency control of perennial broadleaf weeds, up to 3 pt./A may be used when weeds are approaching bud stage. Do not use unless possible crop injury will be acceptable.

- - - - - - - - - - - - - - - -

  Rate: 0.125-0.25 lb. ae/A
    0.25-0.5 pt./A
  Time: Postemergence. Apply after grain is 8" tall but before boot stage. Do not spray in boot to dough stage.
  Remarks: Underseeded with legumes. Do not spray alfalfa or sweet clover unless infestation is severe and injury to legumes can be tolerated.

- - - - - - - - - - - - - - - -

Signal Word/Toxicity Class: Danger/I.
REI: 48 hr.

■ POST
Weedone LV4 (2,4-D solventless ester) *(Nufarm)*
Weedone Lo Vol 6 (2,4-D ester) *(Nufarm)*
  Rate: 0.25-1 lb. ae/A
    0.5-2 pt. 4/A
    0.33-1.33 pt. 6/A
  Time: Postemergence. Do not spray in boot to dough stage.
  Remarks: Not underseeded with legumes. For emergency control of perennial broadleaf weeds, up to 2 pt. Lo Vol 6/A may be used when weeds are approaching bud stage. Do not use unless possible crop injury will be acceptable. Refer to label for use directions, restrictions, and precautions.
  Tank Mixes: LV4: Buctril (rate varies by state, refer to label).

- - - - - - - - - - - - - - - -

Signal Word/Toxicity Class: Caution/III.
REI: 12 hr.

2,4-D COMBINATIONS

■ POST
◆ Brash (2.87 lb./gal. 2,4-D & 1 lb./gal. dicamba) *(Terra)*
  Rate: 0.375-0.5 lb. ai/A
    0.75-1 pt./A
  Time: Apply after fully tillered prior to jointing stage. For best results, apply when weeds are in 2-3 leaf stage and rosettes are less than 2" across.
  Weeds: Annual and biennial broadleaf weeds such as:

annual sowthistle	common purslane	Pennsylvania
bittercress	common ragweed	smartweed
black nightshade	cowcockle	redroot pigweed
common chickweed	field pennycress	rough pigweed
common cocklebur	flax	Russian thistle
common	henbit	shepherdspurse
eveningprimrose	knotweed	sunflower
common	kochia	tansymustard
lambsquarters	mustard	velvetleaf
common mallow		wild buckwheat

  Remarks: Not underseeded with legumes. Do not graze or harvest for feed prior to crop maturity.
  Tank Mixes: Bromoxynil, 2,4-D, diuron, MCPA, metribuzin, sulfonylureas. Refer to labels for use directions, restrictions, and precautions.

- - - - - - - - - - - - - - - -

Signal Word/Toxicity Class: Danger/I.
REI: 48 hr.

DAKOTA (Premix)

Commercial twin-pak containing fenoxaprop-ethyl and MCPA ester. Postemergence herbicide for the control of green foxtail and certain broadleaf weeds in spring and winter wheat.

■ POST
Dakota (0.234 lb./gal. fenoxaprop-P-ethyl & 2.84 lb./gal. MCPA) *(AgrEvo USA)*
  Rate: 0.03-0.039 lb. ai/A
    1-1.3 pt./A
  Time: Crop: 3-6 leaf. Broadleaf weeds: not to exceed 4" in height; grasses: 2-leaf 2-tiller.
  Weeds: Broadleaf weeds:

common	field pennycress	tumble mustard
lambsquarters	ragweed	wild mustard

  Grasses:

foxtail millet	green foxtail

  Remarks: Do not make more than one application per season. Do not apply through any type of irrigation system.
  Days To Harvest: 60.
  Tank Mixes: Ally, Amber, Banvel, Buctril/Buctril Gel, Express, Harmony Extra, Stinger, Tordon herbicides; Furadan 4F, Sevin XLR Plus insecticides; mancozeb fungicides.
  State Restrictions: For use in Montana, North Dakota, and South Dakota.

- - - - - - - - - - - - - - - -

Signal Word/Toxicity Class: Warning/II.
REI: 24 hr.

DICAMBA

Controls many broadleaf weeds. Dicamba alone is less effective on winter annual mustards. Must be applied at early crop stages for best crop tolerance. Usually tank mixed with other broadleaf herbicides.

■ PP, PRE, POST
Banvel (WS) (DMA salt of dicamba) *(BASF)*
Banvel SGF (sodium salt of dicamba) *(BASF)*
Clarity (WS) (dicamba-DGA) *(BASF)*
◆ Sterling (WS) (DMA salt of dicamba) *(Terra)*
  Rate: 2-4 fl. oz. WS/A
    4-8 fl. oz. SGF/A
  Time: Preplant, preemergence, postemergence. Apply prior to jointing stage. For best performance, apply when weeds are in 2-3 leaf stage and rosettes are less than 2" across.
  Weeds: Broadleaf weeds:

annual sowthistle	corn cockle	Pennsylvania
black nightshade	cowcockle	smartweed
common cocklebur	field pennycress	redroot pigweed
common	giant ragweed	rough pigweed
lambsquarters	green smartweed	Russian thistle
common mallow	henbit	tumble pigweed
common ragweed	knotweed	velvetleaf
common sunflower	kochia	volunteer sunflower
corn chamomile	ladysthumb	wild buckwheat

  Remarks: Not underseeded with legumes. Do not graze lactating dairy animals within 7 days after application or remove animals for slaughter within 30 days of last application; no waiting period between treatment and grazing for nonlactating animals. Do not apply through any type of irrigation system.
  Days To Harvest: Hay—37.
  Tank Mixes: Ally, Amber, Bronate, Buctril, Curtail, 2,4-D, Dakota, diuron, Express, Finesse, Glean, glyphosate, Harmony Extra, MCPA, metribuzin, Stinger, Tiller.

- - - - - - - - - - - - - - - -

Signal Word/Toxicity Class: Warning/II (Banvel, Sterling); Caution (Clarity).
REI: 24 hr.

Direx — see diuron

DIURON

Controls certain annual broadleaf weeds and some grasses. Applied preemergence or postemergence to winter wheat, depending on area. Controls some important winter annual weeds.

■ PRE, POST
Direx 4L or 80DF *(Griffin)*
◆ Diuron 80 WDG *(Platte)*

4

Small Grains

Drexel Diuron 4L or 80 (Drexel)
Karmex DF (Griffin)
Riverside Diuron 4L or 80DF (Terra)
  Rate: East of Cascades (ID, OR, WA):
    0.8-1.2 lb. ai/A
    1.6-2.5 pt. 4L/A
    1-1.5 lb. 80, DF, 80DF/A
  Time: Preemergence. Fall treatment: Apply 3-6 weeks after planting but before weeds are 3-4" tall. Spring treatment: Apply as soon as wheat starts to grow in the spring.

  Rate: West of Cascades (OR, WA):
    1.2-1.5 lb. ai/A
    2.4-3 pt. 4L/A
    1.5-2 lb. 80, DF, 80DF/A
  Time: Postemergence. Single spring application after wheat resumes growth but before weeds are 3-4" tall. Do not apply after boot stage.

  Rate: KS, OK, TX, Central Plains, Midwest:
    0.8-1.6 lb. ai/A
    1.6-3.2 pt. 4L/A
    1-2 lb. 80, DF, 80DF/A
    Northeast:
    0.8-1.2 lb. ai/A
    1.6-2.4 pt. 4L/A
    1-1.5 lb. 80, DF, 80DF/A
  Time: Preemergence, postemergence. Single application as soon as possible after planting before weeds are 2" tall. Applications later than May 1 may give poor results.
  Weeds: Broadleaf weeds:

amsinckia	fiddleneck	purslane
annual groundcherry	gromwell	ragweed
annual morningglory	groundsel	shepherdspurse
chickweed	knawel	tansymustard
corn spurry	lambsquarters	wild lettuce
dogfennel	pigweed	wild mustard

  Grasses:

annual bluegrass	barnyardgrass	rattail fescue
annual sweet	crabgrass	red sprangletop
vernalgrass	foxtail	velvetgrass

  Remarks: Do not apply to frozen soils, heaved wheat, or soils (sand, loamy sand, gravelly or sandy loam, or exposed subsoils) with less than 1% organic matter. Rate varies by soil type. Refer to label for exact rates and timing for your area.
  Crop Rotation: Do not replant to other crops within 1 year after treatment
  Tank Mixes: Bromoxynil in Oregon, Washington.

- - - - - - - - - - - - - - - -

  Signal Word/Toxicity Class: Caution/III.
  REI: 12 hr.

Esteron 99C — see 2,4-D

EXPRESS

Short residual sulfonylurea herbicide. Active ingredient is one of the components in Harmony Extra. Controls several annual broadleaf weeds. Excellent activity on kochia, mustard, and pigweed. Usually used in tank mix with other herbicides for broadleaf weeds. No crop rotation limitations for the next season.

■ **POST**
Express (DF) (tribenuron-methyl) (DuPont)
  Rate: 0.167-0.33 oz. DF/A
  Time: Early postemergence. Apply after crop is in 2-leaf stage, but before flag leaf is visible (can be treated sequentially with low rates—up to 0.33 oz./A per season).
  Weeds: Broadleaf weeds:

annual sowthistle*	hairy nightshade*	redroot pigweed*
black mustard	henbit*	Russian thistle
blue mustard	jim hill mustard*	shepherdspurse*
bushy wallflower	kochia	slimleaf
Canada thistle*	mayweed chamomile	lambsquarters
coast fiddleneck	minerslettuce	tansymustard*
common chickweed	Pennsylvania	tarweed fiddleneck
common groundsel	smartweed*	tumble mustard*
common	pineappleweed	wild buckwheat*
lambsquarters	prickly lettuce	wild chamomile
common sunflower*	prostrate knotweed*	wild garlic*
corn spurry	purple mustard	wild mustard
false chamomile	redmaids	wild radish*
field pennycress	rockpurslane*	
flixweed		

  * Suppression

Remarks: Not underseeded. Add approved nonionic surfactant. Do not graze or feed forage or hay from treated areas to livestock (dry-harvested straw may be used for bedding and/or feed). Do not apply through any type of irrigation system.
Days To Harvest: 45.
Crop Rotation: Do not plant to any crop other than wheat or barley for 60 days after application.
State Restrictions: Not for use in Alamosa, Conejos, Costilla, Rio Grande and Saguache counties in Colorado.

- - - - - - - - - - - - - - - -

Signal Word/Toxicity Class: Caution.
REI: 12 hr.

FAR-GO

Controls wild oat. Fall application of granules is most consistent in some northern areas.

■ **PPI, PRE**
Far-Go 4E or 10G (triallate) (Monsanto)
  Rate: 1.25-1.5 lb. ai/A
    1.25-1.5 qt. 4E/A
    12.5-15 lb. 10G/A
  Time: Preplant incorporated, preemergence incorporated. Apply in the fall before or after seeding and before wild oats germinate.
  Weeds:
    brome (high rate)   wild oat
  Remarks: Do not graze livestock on treated crops. Refer to label for directions, precautions, and state restrictions.
  Crop Rotation: Domestic oats should not be seeded if Far-Go was used the previous year.
  Tank Mixes: Trifluralin (4E).
  State Restrictions: For use in Colorado, Idaho, Kansas, Minnesota, Montana, Nebraska, Nevada, North Dakota, Oregon, South Dakota, Utah, Washington, and Wyoming. Far-Go 4E for use only in Colorado, Kansas, and Nebraska to control brome. In Colorado, Kansas, Nebraska, and South Dakota, Far-Go 10G may be surface-applied without incorporation when seeding is done with a hoedrill. In Idaho, Montana, Oregon, Utah, Washington, Far-Go 10G may be surface-applied ahead of Yielder type no-till drill.

- - - - - - - - - - - - - - -

Signal Word/Toxicity Class: Caution/III.
REI: 12 hr.

FENOXAPROP-P-ETHYL

Silverado is a Restricted Use Pesticide due to eye irritation.

■ **POST**
◆ **Puma (1EC)** (AgrEvo USA)
  Rate: 0.04-0.08 lb. ai/A
    0.33-0.66 pt. 1EC/A
  Time: Postemergence. Apply to wheat from 2-leaf stage to 6-leaf stage.
  Weeds:

barnyardgrass	hooded canarygrass	wild oat
blackgrass	proso millet	windgrass
foxtail millet	volunteer corn	yellow foxtail
green foxtail		

  Remarks: Do not make more than one application or apply more than 0.66 pt./A per growing season. Do not apply any pesticides other than those listed on label within 5 days of application. Do not apply through any type of irrigation system or when wind conditions favor drift.
  Days To Harvest: 70 days; 60 days in Minnesota, Montana, North Dakota, South Dakota.
  Tank Mixes Ally, Amber, Banvel, Buctril, Bronate, Clarity, Curtail M, Express, Harmony Extra, Harmony GT, MCPA ester, Peak, Stinger, Starane, Tordon herbicides; Furadan 4F, Sevin XLR Plus insecticides; Benlate, Mertect, mancozeb, Tilt fungicides. Do not tank mix with other herbicides unless specifically recommended on label. Do not tank mix with malathion. Refer to label for limitations and state restrictions.

- - - - - - - - - - - - - -

Signal Word/Toxicity Class: Warning/II.
REI: 24 hr.

■ **POST**
Silverado (0.67 EC) (AgrEvo USA)
  Rate: 0.08 lb. ai/A
    1 pt. 0.67EC/A
  Time: Postemergence. Apply to wheat from 3-leaf stage to end of tillering stage; controls wild oat in 2-leaf to 2-tiller stage.
  Weeds:
    wild oat

◆-new product • PP-preplant • PPI-preplant incorporated • PRE-preemergence • POST-postemergence • SEQ-sequential • ae-acid equivalent • ai-active ingredient • DF-dry flowable
E/EC-emulsifiable concentrate • F/FL-flowable • DG/G/WG-dispersable granule • L/LC-liquid • SP/WSP-soluble packet • W/WP-wettable powder • WSB-water soluble bag

Remarks: Do not use on durum wheat, barley, rye, or oats. Complete kill of weeds will take 12-21 days. Do not apply more than 1 pt./A per season. Do not apply through any type of irrigation system.
Days To Harvest: 70 days.
Tank Mixes Do not tank mix with other pesticides or fertilizers.
State Restrictions: For use in Oklahoma, Texas.

- - - - - - - - - - - - - - - -

Signal Word/Toxicity Class: Danger/I.
REI: 24 hr.

FINESSE (Premix)

Premix of sulfonylurea herbicides with same active ingredient as in Glean and Ally. Extended soil residual activity and provides very good to excellent control of many annual broadleaf weeds. Use limited to labeled states.

■ **PP, PRE, POST**
Finesse (DF) (62.5% chlorsulfuron & 12.5% metsulfuron-methyl)
(DuPont)
Rate: Preplant, postemergence:
0.2-0.4 oz. DF/A
Preemergence:
0.2-0.5 oz. DF/A (0.5 oz.—annual ryegrass, bromus)
Preemergence (MN, MT, ND, SD, WY):
0.2-0.3 oz. DF/A
Time: Preplant, preemergence, postemergence. For postemergence, apply after crop is in 1-leaf stage but before boot stage. Do not apply during boot stage or early heading stage. Do not apply preemergence if wheat has germinated and has started to emerge above soil line or on wheat that has been planted into dry soil or on very coarse, uneven soilbeds.
Weeds: Broadleaf weeds:

annual sowthistle	flixweed*	prostrate pigweed
bedstraw*	groundsel	purslane
blue mustard	hempnettle	redroot pigweed
broadleaf dock	henbit	redstem filaree
bur beakchervil	ivyleaf speedwell*	Russian thistle*
bur buttercup	jagged chickweed	shepherdspurse
Canada thistle*	jim hill mustard	smallseed falseflax
Carolina geranium	kochia*	smooth pigweed
coast fiddleneck	ladysthumb	sunflower
common chickweed	lambsquarters	tansymustard*
common speedwell*	mayweed chamomile	tarweed
conical catchfly	minerslettuce	treacle mustard
corn gromwell*	mouseear chickweed	tumble mustard
corn spurry	Pennsylvania	vetch
cowcockle	smartweed*	Virginia pepperweed
curly dock	pineappleweed	white cockle
cutleaf	plains coreopsis	wild buckwheat
eveningprimrose	prickly lettuce	wild carrot
dovefoot geranium	prickly poppy	wild mustard
false chamomile	prostrate knotweed*	wild radish
field pennycress		

Grasses:

annual bluegrass*	cheat	green foxtail*
annual ryegrass*	downy brome	Japanese brome*

* *Suppression*
Remarks: Not underseeded with legumes and grasses. Do not apply within 60 days of crop emergence if organophosphate insecticide has been applied in-furrow. Refer to label for restrictions and precautions.
Crop Rotation: Recropping depends on rate, soil pH, total rainfall, and geographic area. Refer to label for restrictions and pH limitations.
Tank Mixes: Banvel, Bronate, Buctril, Curtail, 2,4-D, Karmex, MCPA. Do not tank mix with malathion, or in Pacific Northwest, with Lorsban.
State Restrictions: Not for use in Alamosa, Conejos, Costilla, Rio Grande, and Saguache counties in Colorado.

- - - - - - - - - - - - - - - -

Signal Word/Toxicity Class: Caution.
REI: 4 hr.

Formula 40 — see 2,4-D

GLEAN

Sulfonylurea herbicide with soil residual activity extending 2 years or more. Recommended for use on land primarily dedicated to long-term production of wheat, barley, or oats. Tank mixing with another herbicide with different mode of action is suggested. Follow soil pH, minimum retreatment intervals, and crop rotation guidelines specified. Use limited to specified areas.

■ **PRE, POST**
Glean FC (DF) (chlorsulfuron) *(DuPont)*

Rate: Northcentral TX, southern OK:
0.5 oz. DF/A
Time: Preemergence.
Weeds: Grasses:
annual ryegrass (suppression)

Rate: Postemergence:
0.167-0.33 oz. DF/A
Time: Postemergence. Apply in fall or spring anytime after wheat is in 2-leaf stage but before boot stage. Apply to small, actively growing weeds that are less than 2" tall or 2" across.
Weeds: Broadleaf weeds:

bedstraw*	flixweed	redstem filaree
blue mustard	hempnettle	Russian thistle*
bur beakchervil	henbit	shepherdspurse
buttercup	jim hill mustard	smooth pigweed
Canada thistle*	kochia*	speedwell*
coast fiddleneck	ladysthumb	sunflower*
common chickweed	lambsquarters	tansymustard*
common groundsel*	mayweed	tarweed
conical catchfly	minerslettuce	treacle mustard
corn gromwell*	mouseear chickweed	tumble mustard
corn spurry	Pennsylvania	white cockle
cowcockle	smartweed*	wild buckwheat*
curly dock	pineappleweed	wild carrot
cutleaf	prickly lettuce	wild mustard
eveningprimrose	prostrate knotweed*	wild radish*
false chamomile	prostrate pigweed	wild turnip
falseflax	purslane	yellow starthistle
field pennycress	redroot pigweed	

Grasses:
annual ryegrass*

Aerial bulblet control:
wild garlic* wild onion*

* *Suppression*
Remarks: Not underseeded with legumes. Glean is mixed in water or directly into liquid nitrogen fertilizer solutions and applied as uniform broadcast spray. Surfactant should be used in spray mix unless otherwise specified.
Crop Rotation: Recropping depends on rate, soil pH, total rainfall, and geographic area. Refer to label for soil pH restrictions and more information.
Tank Mixes: Banvel, Bronate, Buctril, 2,4-D, Karmex, MCPA.
State Restrictions: For use in California, northern Idaho, Kansas, Nebraska, Oklahoma, Oregon, Texas, Washington. For use in central Kansas, Nebraska, Oklahoma, and northcentral Texas for control of kochia and Russian thistle.

- - - - - - - - - - - - - - - -

Signal Word/Toxicity Class: Caution.
REI: 4 hr.

Glyfos or Glyfos X-tra — see glyphosate

GLYPHOSATE

Nonselective, translocated herbicide with no soil residual activity. Used after harvest, during fallow, or prior to planting to control emerged grasses and broadleaf weeds. Ammonium sulfate improves results, especially where water quality is a factor. Do not allow glyphosate to contact desirable plants.

■ **PP, PRE**
◆ **Credit (4WS)** *(Nufarm)*
◆ **Glyfos or Glyfos X-tra (4WS)** *(Cheminova)*
Rattler (4WS) *(Helena)*
Roundup Custom (5.4WS) *(Monsanto)*
Roundup Original, Original RT, Ultra, Ultra RT (4WS) *(Monsanto)*
Rate: Annual weeds:
0.38-1.5 lb. ai/A
0.56-2.25 pt. 5.4WS/A
0.75-3 pt. 4WS/A
Perennial weeds:
0.5-5 lb. ai/A
0.75-7.5 pt. 5.4WS/A
1-10 pt. 4WS/A
Time: Preplant, preemergence, at-planting, spot treatment, wiper applications, preharvest, postharvest. For spot treatment, apply before heading. For preharvest, apply after hard dough stage.
Weeds: Most emerged annual and perennial broadleaf weeds including:

Canada thistle	field bindweed	kochia

Grasses:

downy brome	foxtail	quackgrass

4

Small Grains

Winter Wheat

Remarks: For preharvest applications, do not apply to wheat grown for seed. Do not apply more than 1 lb. ai/A. Wheat stubble may be grazed immediately after harvest. Do not add surfactant to Roundup Ultra or Ultra RT. For spot treatment, do not treat more than 10% total area to be harvested. Do not use roller applicators for wiper application. Do not apply through any type of irrigation system. Refer to label for directions, precautions and restrictions.

Days To Harvest: Preharvest—7 days; wiper application—35 days; post-harvest/feeding—8 weeks.

Tank Mixes: Postharvest: 2,4-D, dicamba. Roundup tank mixes not registered in California by air.

State Restrictions: Roundup RT for use in Colorado, Idaho, Montana, North Dakota, South Dakota, Utah, Wyoming, and in specific counties only in Kansas, Minnesota, Nebraska, Nevada, Oklahoma, Oregon, and Washington; refer to label for restrictions. Glyfos is not registered for use in California. Glyfos X-tra is not registered for use in mistblowers in California or Arizona.

- - - - - - - - - - - - - - - -

Signal Word/Toxicity Class: Varies by formulation.
REI: Warning—12 hr.; Caution—4 hr.

■ PRE
Ranger (WS) *(Monsanto)*

Rate: 0.25-0.5 lb. ai/A
0.75-1.5 pt. WS/A
Time: Preemergence. Apply to vigorously growing weeds.
Weeds: Broadleaf weeds:

blue mustard	field pennycress	shepherdspurse
buttercup	horseweed	smallseed falseflax
cocklebur	London rocket	smooth pigweed
common groundsel	marestail	tansymustard
common lambsquarters	morningglory	tumble mustard
dwarfdandelion	mouseear chickweed	umbrella spurry
fanweed	redroot pigweed	wild mustard

Grasses:

annual bluegrass	downy brome	stinkgrass
barnyardgrass	fall panicum	Texas panicum
bulbous bluegrass	field sandbur	wild oat
cheat	Italian ryegrass	witchgrass
crabgrass	shattercane	

Rate: 1-2 lb. ai/A
3-6 pt. 2EC/A
Time: Preemergence. Apply to vigorously growing weeds.
Weeds: Grasses:

quackgrass	tall fescue	wirestem muhly

Remarks: For quackgrass control in the fall, do not till between harvest and application. For quackgrass control in the spring, do not till in the fall or spring prior to application. Do not apply through any type of irrigation system. Do not feed or forage vegetation from treated areas within 8 weeks after application. Refer to label for directions and restrictions.

- - - - - - - - - - - - - - - -

Signal Word/Toxicity Class: Danger/I.
REI: 12 hr.

Gramoxone Extra — see paraquat

HARMONY EXTRA (Premix)

Sulfonylurea herbicide usually used in combination with other herbicides with different mode of action. No crop rotation limitations for the next season. Gives very good to excellent control of many annual broadleaf weeds. Good crop tolerance.

■ POST
Harmony Extra (DF) (50% thifensulfuron-methyl & 25% tribenuron-methyl) *(DuPont)*

Rate: 0.3-0.6 oz. DF/A
Time: Early postemergence. Apply after wheat is in 2-leaf stage, but before flag leaf is visible.
Weeds: Broadleaf weeds:

annual knawel	clasping pepperweed	common vetch*
annual sowthistle	coast fiddleneck	corn chamomile
black mustard	common chickweed	corn gromwell
blue mustard	common cocklebur*	corn spurry
broadleaf dock	common groundsel	cowcockle
bur buttercup	common lambsquarters	curly dock
bushy wallflower	common mallow*	cutleaf
Canada thistle*	common radish	eveningprimrose*
Carolina geranium*	common ragweed*	dogfennel
catchweed bedstraw*	common sunflower	false chamomile

Weeds: Broadleaf weeds, continued:

field chickweed	nightflowering	smallflower buttercup
field pennycress	catchfly	smallseed falseflax
filaree	Pennsylvania	stinking chickweed
flixweed	smartweed	stinking mayweed
green smartweed	pineappleweed	swinecress
hairy nightshade*	prickly lettuce	tansymustard
henbit	prostrate knotweed	tarweed fiddleneck
jim hill mustard	prostrate pigweed	tumble mustard
kochia	purple mustard	volunteer lentils
ladysthumb	redmaids	volunteer peas
little mallow*	rockpurslane	volunteer sunflower
London rocket	redroot pigweed	wild buckwheat
marshelder	Russian thistle	wild chamomile
minerslettuce	scentless chamomile	wild garlic
mouseearcress	shepherdspurse	wild mustard
narrowleaf	slimleaf lambsquarters	wild radish
lambsquarters		

* Partial control

Remarks: Do not apply to wheat underseeded with another crop. Add approved nonionic surfactant. Do not graze or feed forage or hay from treated areas to livestock (harvested straw may be used for bedding and/or feed).

Days To Harvest: 45.

Crop Rotation: Do not rotate to crops other than wheat, barley, or oats for 60 days after application; after 60 days any crop may be planted.

State Restrictions: Not for use in Alamosa, Conejos, Costilla, Rio Grande, and Saguache counties in Colorado.

- - - - - - - - - - - - - - - -

Signal Word/Toxicity Class: Caution.
REI: 12 hr.

Harmony GT — see thifensulfuron-methyl

Hi-Dep — see 2,4-D

HOELON

Provides selective control of wild oat, foxtail, and certain other annual grasses. Adjust rate according to weed species. Tank mix only according to directions. Restricted Use Pesticide.

■ PPI, PRE, POST
Hoelon 3EC (diclofop) *(AgrEvo USA)*

Rate: 0.75-1 lb. ai/A
2-2.66 pt. 3EC/A
Time: Preplant incorporated. Will not control bromes postemergence.
Weeds: Winter annual bromes:

downy brome	Japanese brome	ripgut

Remarks: Incorporate to a depth of no greater than 2". May be used in conventional and deep furrow planting. Refer to label for directions, precautions, and limitations.

State Restrictions: For use in Colorado, Idaho, Kansas, Montana, Nebraska, Oregon, South Dakota, Utah, Washington.

- - - - - - - - - - - - - - - -

Rate: 0.75-1 lb. ai/A
2-2.66 pt. 3EC/A
Time: Preemergence. Apply at planting.
Weeds: Annual ryegrass.
Remarks: If rainfall does not occur within 7 days after application, reduced control may occur.

- - - - - - - - - - - - - - - -

Rate: Annual ryegrass:
0.5-1 lb. ai/A
1.33-2.66 pt. 3EC/A
Other annual grasses (including wild oat):
0.75-1 lb. ai/A
2-2.66 pt. 3EC/A
Time: Postemergence. Apply when majority of wild oat and annual grasses are in 1- to 4-leaf stage.
Weeds: Grasses:

annual ryegrass	giant foxtail	smallseed canarygrass
barnyardgrass	green foxtail	spring milletgrass
(watergrass)	hooded canarygrass	volunteer corn
broadleaf signalgrass	itchgrass	wild oat
crabgrass	(raoulgrass)	witchgrass
fall panicum	Persian darnel	yellow foxtail

Remarks: Refer to label for directions, precautions, and limitations.
Tank Mixes: Amber, Buctril, Glean, Harmony Extra, MCPA.

- - - - - - - - - - - - - - - -

Signal Word/Toxicity Class: Danger/I.
REI: 24 hr.

◆-new product • PP-preplant • PPI-preplant incorporated • PRE-preemergence • POST-postemergence • SEQ-sequential • ae-acid equivalent • ai-active ingredient • DF-dry flowable
E/EC-emulsifiable concentrate • F/FL-flowable • DG/G/WG-dispersable granule • L/LC-liquid • SP/WSP-soluble packet • W/WP-wettable powder • WSB-water soluble bag

Karmex — see diuron

MCPA

Good crop tolerance at a wide range of crop growth stages. Most effective on mustards and lambsquarters. Frequently used in combination with other herbicides, especially when treatment must be made at early growth stages.

■ POST

Albaugh MCPA Amine 4 *(Albaugh)*
◆ **Clean Crop MCP Amine 4 or Ester** *(Platte)*
◆ **Clean Crop MCP 2 Sodium (sodium salt)** *(Platte)*
Riverdale MCPA-4 Amine *(Riverdale)*
Riverside MCPA Amine *(Terra)*
Wilbur-Ellis MCPA Amine, Ester or ◆ Sodium Salt (2EC) *(Wilbur-Ellis)*

Rate: 0.25-1.5 lb. ae/A
0.5-3 pt./A

Time: Postemergence. Apply low rate for more susceptible weeds after crop has reached 3-4 leaf stage up to boot stage; high rate after crop has tillered and up to early boot stage. Do not spray from boot to dough stage.

Rate: Wheat emergency treatment:
1.5 lb. ae/A
6 pt. 2EC/A

Time: Postemergence. Apply in spring when weeds are approaching bud stage and grain is fully tillered and 8-10" tall. Do not spray from boot to dough stage.

Weeds: Broadleaf weeds:

annual mustard	lambsquarters	sowthistle
buttercup	marshelder	stinging nettle
Canada thistle	pigweed	stinkweed
dandelion	plantain	sunflower
dragonhead mint	puncturevine	vetch
field peppergrass	purslane	whitetop
goatsbeard	ragweed	wild radish
hempnettle	shepherdspurse	yellow rocket
kochia		

Remarks: Not underseeded with legumes. Do not forage or graze animals on treated areas within 7 days of slaughter or treatment.
State Restrictions: Wilbur-Ellis not registered in California.

– – – – – – – – – – – – – – –

Rate: 0.125-0.25 lb. ae/A
0.25-0.5 pt./A

Time: Postemergence. Apply after crop is well tillered in the 4-leaf stage (4-8" tall) when legumes are 2-3" tall. Do not spray from boot to dough stage.

Weeds: Emergency control of:

mustard	yellow rocket

Remarks: Underseeded with legumes (alfalfa, lespedeza, red and white clover). Balance severity of weed problem against possibility of crop damage. Do not forage or graze animals on treated areas within 7 days of slaughter or treatment.
State Restrictions: Wilbur-Ellis not registered in California.

– – – – – – – – – – – – – – –

Signal Word/Toxicity Class: Danger/I (amine); Warning/II (ester).
REI: Danger—48 hr.; Warning—12 hr.

■ POST

Albaugh MCPA Ester 4 *(Albaugh)*
Solve MCPA Ester (4) *(Albaugh)*

Rate: 0.25-1.5 lb. ae/A
0.5-3 pt. 4/A

Time: Postemergence. Apply low rate for more susceptible weeds after crop has reached 3-4 leaf stage up to boot stage; use high rate for less susceptible weeds after crop has tillered and up to early boot stage. Do not spray from boot to dough stage.

Weeds: Broadleaf weeds:

annual mustard	goatsbeard	puncturevine
annual sowthistle	goosefoot	ragweed
beggarticks	hempnettle	shepherdspurse
cocklebur	lambsquarters	stinkweed
dragonhead mint	marshelder	wild radish
fanweed	pennycress	wintercress
field peppergrass	poison hemlock	yellow rocket

Remarks: Do not forage or graze meat animals on treated areas within 7 days of slaughter; dairy animals within 7 days after application.

– – – – – – – – – – – – – – –

Signal Word/Toxicity Class: Caution/III.
REI: 12 hr.

■ POST

Chiptox (sodium salt) *(Nufarm)*

Rate: 0.125-0.25 lb. ae/A
0.5-1 pt./A

Time: Postemergence. Apply when legumes are 2-3" tall, grain is fully tillered but before forming joints in the stem. Do not spray in boot to dough stage.

Weeds: Broadleaf weeds:

annual mustard	lambsquarters	stinging nettle
buttercup	peppergrass	stinkweed
Canada thistle	plantain	vetch
cocklebur	purslane	whitetop
dandelion	ragweed	wild radish
hempnettle	shepherdspurse	wintercress
hoary cress	sowthistle	yellow rocket
kochia		

Remarks: Underseeded with mixed legumes. Use 5-6 gal. water/A; higher volumes may cause injury to legumes. Do not forage or graze treated fields for 2 weeks or feed treated straw to livestock.

– – – – – – – – – – – – – – –

Rate: 0.25-1 lb. ae/A
1-4 pt./A

Time: Postemergence. Apply when grain is fully tillered but before forming joints in the stem. Do not spray in boot to dough stage.

Rate: Emergency treatment:
1.5 lb. ae/A
6 pt./A

Time: Postemergence. Apply when weeds are approaching bud stage. Do not spray from boot to dough stage.
Weeds: Same as above.
Remarks: Not underseeded with legumes. Use 6 pt. rate as emergency treatment for controlling perennial broadleaf weeds; balance severity of weed problem against possible crop injury.

– – – – – – – – – – – – – – –

Signal Word/Toxicity Class: Danger/I.
REI: 48 hr.

■ POST

Gordon's MCPA Amine 4 *(PBI/Gordon)*
Rhomene 4 (amine) *(Nufarm)*

Rate: 0.25-1 lb. ae/A
0.5-2 pt./A

Time: Postemergence. For lower rate, apply after grain is in 4-leaf stage but not forming joints in the stem; for rates over 1 pt., apply after grain is fully tillered. Do not spray in boot to dough stage.

Weeds: Broadleaf weeds:

bull thistle	dandelion	pigweed
common burdock	field pennycress	plantain
common cocklebur	giant ragweed	purslane
common	mustard (except blue)	Russian thistle
lambsquarters	pepperweed	shepherdspurse
common ragweed	(except perennial)	yellow rocket

Remarks: Not underseeded with legumes. For emergency perennial broadleaf weed control, use 3 pt. rate when weeds approach bud stage, balance problem severity against possible crop damage; spot treat scattered perennial weeds.

– – – – – – – – – – – – – – –

Rate: 0.25 lb. ae/A
0.5 pt./A

Time: Postemergence. Apply after crop is well tillered in the 4-leaf stage (4-8" tall) when legumes are 2-3" tall. Do not spray in boot to dough stage.

Weeds: Emergency control of:

mustard	yellow rocket

Remarks: Underseeded with legumes. Do not apply to grain underseeded with vetch or sweet clover. Do not use more than 6 gal. water/A; higher volumes may result in injury to legumes. Do not forage or graze animals on treated areas within 7 days of slaughter or treatment.

– – – – – – – – – – – – – – –

Signal Word/Toxicity Class: Danger/I.
REI: 48 hr.

■ POST

Rhonox (LV ester) *(Nufarm)*

Rate: 0.23-0.69 lb. ae/A
0.5-1.5 pt./A

Time: Postemergence. For lower rate, apply after grain is in 4-leaf stage but not forming joints in the stem; for rates over 1 pt., apply after grain is fully tillered. Do not spray in boot to dough stage.

4

Small Grains

Winter Wheat

Weeds: Broadleaf weeds:

annual sowthistle	pennycress	ragweed
dandelion	peppergrass	shepherdspurse
hempnettle	perennial sowthistle	stinkweed
kochia	pigweed	wild radish
lambsquarters	plantain	yellow rocket
mustard	purslane	

Remarks: Not underseeded to legumes. Do not forage or graze meat animals on treated fields within 7 days of slaughter. Refer to label for further use directions.

‒ ‒ ‒ ‒ ‒ ‒ ‒ ‒ ‒ ‒ ‒ ‒ ‒ ‒ ‒

Signal Word/Toxicity Class: Caution.
REI: 12 hr.

■ **POST**
Riverdale MCPA L.V. 4, IOE (5.2) (ester) *(Riverdale)*
Sword (5.2) (ester) *(Platte)*
Rate: 0.25-1.5 lb. ae/A
0.5-3 pt. L.V. 4/A
0.2-1.3 lb. ae/A
0.33-2 pt. 5.2/A
Time: Postemergence. Apply low rate for more susceptible weeds after crop has reached 3-4 leaf stage up to boot stage; high rate after crop has tillered and up to early boot stage. Do not spray from boot to dough stage.

Rate: Fall-planted:
0.25-0.5 lb. ae/A
0.5-1 pt. L.V. 4/A
0.2-0.4 lb. ae/A
0.33-0.75 pt. 5.2/A
Time: Postemergence. Fall application: Apply when fall-planted small grains are fully tillered and have reached 3-4 leaf stage to boot stage. Spring application: Apply in early spring when annual broadleaf weeds are small and grain is fully tillered, but before grain is in jointed stage.

Weeds: Broadleaf weeds:

annual mustard	lambsquarters	sowthistle
buttercup	marshelder	stinging nettle
Canada thistle	pigweed	stinkweed
dandelion	plantain	sunflower
dragonhead mint	purslane	vetch
field peppergrass	puncturevine	whitetop
goatsbeard	ragweed	wild radish
hempnettle	shepherdspurse	yellow rocket
kochia		

Remarks: Not underseeded with legumes. Do not forage or graze animals on treated areas within 7 days of slaughter or treatment.

‒ ‒ ‒ ‒ ‒ ‒ ‒ ‒ ‒ ‒ ‒ ‒ ‒ ‒ ‒

Rate: 0.125-0.25 lb. ae/A
0.25-0.5 pt. L.V. 4/A
3-6 oz. 5.2/A
Time: Postemergence. Apply after crop is well tillered in the 4-leaf stage (4-8" tall) when legumes are 2-3" tall. Do not spray from boot to dough stage.
Weeds: Emergency control of:
mustard   yellow rocket
Remarks: Underseeded with legumes (alfalfa, lespedeza, red and white clover). Balance severity of weed problem against possibility of crop damage. Do not forage or graze animals on treated areas within 7 days of slaughter or treatment.

‒ ‒ ‒ ‒ ‒ ‒ ‒ ‒ ‒ ‒ ‒ ‒ ‒ ‒ ‒

Signal Word/Toxicity Class: Warning/II.
REI: 12 hr.

Moxy — see bromoxynil

Opti-Amine — see 2,4-D

Paramount — see quinclorac

PARAQUAT

Nonselective herbicide used to control emerged grasses and broadleaf weeds after harvest, during fallow, or prior to planting. No residual weed control. Good spray coverage is important. Toxic to wildlife. Restricted Use Pesticide.

■ **PP, PRE**
Cyclone (2L or 3L) or Gramoxone Extra (2.5L) *(ZENECA)*

Rate: 0.5-1 lb. ai/A
2-4 pt. 2L/A
1.5-3 pt. 2.5L/A
1.25-2.5 pt. 3L/A
Time: Preplant, preemergence. Apply broadcast or band prior to, during, or after planting but before crop emergence.
Weeds: Annual broadleaf weeds and grasses; suppression of perennials.
Remarks: Add nonionic surfactant or crop oil concentrate. Seedbeds should be formed as far ahead of planting and treatment as possible to permit maximum weed and grass emergence. Seeding should be done with minimum amount of soil disturbance. Weeds and grasses emerging after planting will not be controlled; crops emerged at time of application may be killed. Do not apply preplant or preemergence to soils lacking clay minerals. Refer to label for use directions, restrictions, and precautions.
Tank Mixes: Atrazine, Banvel, Bicep, Bladex, Canopy, Command, 2,4-D ester, Extrazine, Lariat, linuron, Marksman, metribuzin, Princep.

‒ ‒ ‒ ‒ ‒ ‒ ‒ ‒ ‒ ‒ ‒ ‒ ‒ ‒ ‒

Signal Word/Toxicity Class: Danger-Poison/I.
REI: 12 hr. (except harvest aid/desiccation 24 hr.).

PEAK

Controls many broadleaf weeds, including triazine-resistant biotypes, by inhibiting a biochemical process which produces certain essential amino acids necessary for plant growth. The inhibited enzyme system is acetolactate synthase (ALS). Peak is a water-dispersible granule; each bag of Peak contains 5 water-soluble packets.

■ **POST**
Peak (WDG) (prosulfuron) *(Novartis)*
Rate: Low rate:
0.38 oz. WDG/A (1 WS packet/8A)
Standard rate:
0.5 oz. WDG/A (1 WS packet/6A)
Time: Postemergence (over-the-top). Apply from 3-leaf stage to before second node is detectable in stem elongation.
Weeds: Broadleaf weeds:

blue mustard	flixweed	prickly sida
buffalobur	Florida pusley	prostrate knotweed*
bur cherval	giant ragweed	puncturevine
bushy wallflower	hairy buttercup	redroot pigweed
Canada thistle*	hedge bindweed*	Russian thistle
coast fiddleneck	hemp sesbania	shepherdspurse
common chickweed*	henbit*	sicklepod
common cocklebur	ivyleaf morningglory	smooth pigweed
common lambsquarters*	jimsonweed	tall morningglory
common mallow*	kochia*	tall waterhemp
common ragweed	mayweed chamomile	tansymustard
common sunflower	minerslettuce	tumble mustard
common waterhemp	mouseear chickweed*	tumble pigweed
corn gromwell*	Palmer amaranth*	velvetleaf
cutleaf eveningprimrose	Pennsylvania smartweed	Venice mallow
devilsclaw	pineappleweed	wild buckwheat
field bindweed*	pitted morningglory	wild garlic
field pennycress	prickly lettuce	wild mustard
		wild radish

* Suppression

Remarks: Rate varies by weed height. Always add crop oil concentrate or nonionic surfactant. Do not apply to crop under stress. Do not make a foliar or soil application with an organophosphate insecticide within 15 days before or 10 days after application. Do not apply through any type of irrigation system.
Days To Harvest: Silage—40; grain—60; grazing/feeding forage to livestock—30.
Crop Rotation: IR/IMR Corn—anytime; normal field corn, grain sorghum—4 weeks; rice, popcorn, sweet corn, small grains (wheat, barley, oats, rye, proso millet, triticale)—2 months; beans (dry, green), cabbage, canola, cotton, flax, forage grasses, peanuts, peas, potatoes, soybeans, tobacco, tomatoes—9 months; alfalfa, clover, lentils—15 months; leeks, onion, sunflower, sugar beets—24 months; all other crops—18 months. Refer to label for geographic restrictions.
Tank Mixes: Low rate: Banvel, Bronate, Buctril, 2,4-D, MCPA; refer to label for use instructions.
State Restrictions: Not for use in San Luis Valley of Colorado, west of the Cascades in Oregon, and certain areas of Washington (abide by all sulfonylurea aerial application rulings by Washington Department of Agriculture).

‒ ‒ ‒ ‒ ‒ ‒ ‒ ‒ ‒ ‒ ‒ ‒ ‒ ‒ ‒

Signal Word/Toxicity Class: Caution.
REI: 12 hr.

Phenoxy 088 — see 2,4-D

◆–new product • PP–preplant • PPI–preplant incorporated • PRE–preemergence • POST–postemergence • SEQ–sequential • ae–acid equivalent • ai–active ingredient • DF–dry flowable
E/EC–emulsifiable concentrate • F/FL–flowable • DG/G/WG–dispersable granule • L/LC–liquid • SP/WSP–soluble packet • W/WP–wettable powder • WSB–water soluble bag

Puma — see fenoxaprop-P-ethyl

QUINCLORAC

■ **PP**

◆ **Paramount (DF)** *(BASF)*
Rate: 3-5.3 oz. DF/A
Time: Preplant. Apply to actively growing weeds. For bindweed, apply after harvest but before first killing frost. For long-term control (3 yr. program), apply 5.3 oz. DF/A the first year and 3-5.3 oz. DF/A in subsequent years.

Weeds: Broadleaf weeds:

bedstraw	dandelion*	morningglory
Canada thistle*	field bindweed	Russian thistle*
clover	giant ragweed*	velvetleaf*
common	hedge bindweed	volunteer flax
lambsquarters*	kochia*	wild sunflower*
common ragweed*		

Grasses:

barnyardgrass	giant foxtail	large crabgrass
broadleaf signalgrass	green foxtail	yellow foxtail

* Suppression

Remarks: Must use additive. Do not apply more than 16 oz. DF/A per calendar year. Do not apply through any type of irrigation system.
Crop Rotation: In case of crop failure, wheat and sorghum may be replanted immediately; other crops—10 months after application; alfalfa, clover, flax, lentils, peas, sugar beets—24 months and successful field bioassy.
Tank Mixes: Clarity, 2,4-D, Fallowmaster, Landmaster, Roundup RT, Roundup Ultra; refer to labels for use directions.
State Restrictions: For use in Colorado, Idaho, Kansas, Montana, Nebraska, North Dakota, Oregon, South Dakota, Utah, Washington, Wyoming.

– – – – – – – – – – – – – – –

Signal Word/Toxicity Class: Caution.
REI: 12 hr.

Ranger — see glyphosate

Rattler — see glyphosate

RAVE (Premix)

Premix with 2 modes of action. One active ingredient inhibits the acetolactate synthase (ALS) enzyme. The other active ingredient disrupts normal plant growth.

■ **POST**

◆ **Rave (WDG) (50% dicamba & 8.8% triasulfuron)** *(Novartis)*
Rate: 4 oz. WDG/A
Time: Postemergence. Apply after emergence up to jointing. Early developing varieties such as TAM 107, Madison, or Wakefield must be treated between early tillering and jointing stage.

Weeds: Broadleaf weeds:

annual morningglory	cutleaf	pepperweed
annual polemonium	eveningprimrose	pigweed
annual sowthistle	fanweed	plains coreopsis
black nightshade	field bindweed	prickly lettuce
blue mustard	field pennycress	prostrate knotweed
bur buttercup	fleabane	prostrate pigweed
bushy wallflower	flixweed	puncturevine
Canada thistle	forget-me-not	ragweed
coast fiddleneck	giant ragweed	redroot pigweed
common broomweed	goldenrod	Russian thistle
common chickweed	hairy vetch	shepherdspurse
common cocklebur	henbit	smooth pigweed
common groundsel	horseweed	tall buttercup
common	houndstongue	tall hedge mustard
lambsquarters	Indian mustard	tansymustard
common mallow	jagged chickweed	tartary buckwheat
common purslane	kochia	tarweed
common ragweed	ladysthumb	tumble mustard
common sunflower	lanceleaf ragweed	tumble pigweed
common yarrow	London rocket	umbrella spurry
corn chamomile	marestail	velvetleaf
corn cockle	marshelder	Virginia pepperweed
corn gromwell	minerslettuce	wild buckwheat
cornflower	musk thistle	wild mustard
creeping buttercup	mustard	wild radish
curly dock	Pennsylvania smartweed	woolly croton

Remarks: Do not apply to wheat undersown with legumes or forage grasses. Do not apply to wheat under stress. Do not apply for at least 60 days after an organophosphate application. Do not apply through any type of irrigation system. Do not graze lactating dairy animals for 7 days after application; for slaughter, 30 days after application.
Days To Harvest: Hay, grain—37.
Crop Rotation: Recropping depends on field bioassay, soil pH, total rainfall, and geographic area. Refer to label for restrictions and more complete information.
Tank Mixes: Bronate, Buctril, 2,4-D, MCPA, Tilt.
State Restrictions: For use in Colorado (except San Luis Valley), Idaho, Kansas, Minnesota, Montana, Nebraska, Nevada, New Mexico, North Dakota, Oklahoma, Oregon, South Dakota, Texas, Utah, Washington, Wyoming. In Washington, abide by all sulfonylurea aerial application rulings by Washington Department of Agriculture.

– – – – – – – – – – – – – – –

Signal Word/Toxicity Class: Caution.
REI: 12 hr.

Rhomene — see MCPA

Rhonox — see MCPA

Roundup — see glyphosate

Saber — see 2,4-D

Salvo — see 2,4-D

Savage — see 2,4-D

SCYTHE

◆ **Scythe (pelargonic acid)** *(Mycogen)*
Rate: 4-13 fl. oz./1 gal. spray solution
Time: Apply to actively growing weeds prior to crop emergence.
Weeds: Annual and perennial broadleaf weeds and grasses.
Remarks: Apply in minimum 75 gal. spray solution/A or spray-to-wet. Do not apply by air or through any type of irrigation system. Refer to label for directions and precautions.
Tank Mixes: Glyphosate and other foliar and residual herbicides.

– – – – – – – – – – – – – – –

Signal Word/Toxicity Class: Warning/II.
REI: 24 hr.

SENCOR

Especially effective for winter annual mustards. Labeling includes suppression of winter annual bromes and other annual grasses. Use limited to certain states and specified varieties.

■ **POST**

Sencor 4 (FL) or DF (metribuzin) *(Bayer)*
Rate: 0.05-0.5 lb. ai/A
1.5-16 fl. oz. FL/A
1-10.66 oz. DF/A
Time: Postemergence. Apply at 21-day intervals if wheat is actively growing; 45-day intervals if wheat is dormant, stressed, or growing in adverse conditions. In Georgia, wheat must be planted before Nov. 15 in Piedmont area and northern part of the state and before Dec. 1 in Coastal Plain area.

Weeds: Broadleaf weeds:

annual polemonium	dogfennel	pineappleweed
bittercress	cutleaf	prostrate knotweed
blue mustard	eveningprimrose	redstem filaree
Carolina geranium	field pennycress	shepherdspurse
catchweed	gromwell	smallseed falseflax
common chickweed	henbit	tarweed fiddleneck
common	ivyleaf speedwell	Virginia pepperweed
lambsquarters	minerslettuce	wild mustard
conical catchfly	mousear chickweed	wild radish
corncockle	pigweed	wild turnip

Remarks: Rate varies by soil texture and organic matter. Certain varieties are sensitive and should not be treated. For dryland winter wheat (non-irrigated), apply highest recommended rate.

4

Small Grains

Winter Wheat

Days To Harvest: Harvest grain—21; grazing—14.
Tank Mixes: May be tank mixed; refer to label for tank mix directions.
State Restrictions: For use in Arkansas, Georgia, Idaho, Illinois, Indiana, Kansas, Kentucky, Louisiana, Mississippi, Missouri, Montana, Nevada, Ohio, Oklahoma, Oregon, Texas, Tennessee, Utah, and Washington.

– – – – – – – – – – – – – –

Signal Word/Toxicity Class: Caution/III.
REI: 12 hr.

Silverado — see fenoxaprop-P-ethyl

Solution — see 2,4-D

Solve — see 2,4-D; MCPA

Sterling — see dicamba

Stinger — see clopyralid

SUREFIRE (Premix)

Restricted Use Pesticide.

■ PP, PRE
◆ Surefire (29.4% paraquat & 10.6% diuron) *(Platte)*
Rate: 0.8-1.6 lb. ai/A
    2-4 pt./A
Time: Apply to young, succulent weeds 1-6" high prior to, during or after planting, but before crop emergence.
Weeds: Annual broadleaf weeds and grasses; top-kill and suppression of perennial weeds.
Remarks: Always use nonionic surfactant. Do not apply through any type of irrigation system. Do not apply to soils lacking clay minerals. Seeding should be done with a minimum amount of soil disturbance. Crops emerged at time of treatment will be killed. Refer to label for directions.
Tank Mixes: AAtrex, Banvel, Bladex, 2,4-D, Glean, Kerb.

– – – – – – – – – – – – – –

Signal Word/Toxicity Class: Danger/I.
REI: 12 hr.

Sword — see MCPA

THIFENSULFURON-METHYL

■ POST
Harmony GT (DF) *(DuPont)*
Rate: 0.3-0.6 oz. DF/A
Time: Postemergence. Apply to young, actively growing weeds after crop is in 2-leaf stage, but before flag leaf is visible.
Weeds: Broadleaf weeds:

annual knawel	dogfennel	redmaids rockpurslane
annual sowthistle	false chamomile	redroot pigweed
black mustard	field pennycress	Russian thistle
bushy wallflower	flixweed	scentless chamomile
Carolina geranium*	green smartweed	shepherdspurse
coast fiddleneck	henbit*	smallflower buttercup
common buckwheat	jim hill mustard	stinking mayweed
common chickweed	kochia	swinecress
common cocklebur*	ladysthumb	tansymustard*
common groundsel	little mallow*	tarweed fiddleneck
common	London rocket	tumble mustard
lambsquarters	marshelder	volunteer lentils
common mallow*	minerslettuce	volunteer peas
common sunflower*	mouseear chickweed	volunteer sunflower
corn chamomile	mouseearcress	wild buckwheat
corn spurry	Pennsylvania	wild chamomile
curly dock	smartweed	wild garlic
cutleaf	prickly lettuce*	wild mustard
eveningprimrose*	prostrate knotweed	wild radish*

* Suppression

Remarks: Not underseeded. Add approved nonionic surfactant. Do not apply through any type of irrigation system. Prevent spray drift to desirable plants. Do not graze or feed forage or hay from treated areas to

---

livestock (harvested straw may be used for bedding and/or feed). Refer to label for restrictions and precautions.
Crop Rotation: Barley, oats, wheat—anytime; all other crops—45 days after application.
Tank Mixes: Assert, Avenge, bromoxynil, 2,4-D, dicamba, Hoelon, MCPA.
State Restrictions: Not for use in Alamosa, Conejos, Costilla, Rio Grande, and Saguache counties in Colorado.

– – – – – – – – – – – – – –

Signal Word/Toxicity Class: Caution.
REI: 4 hr.

TILLER (Premix)

Three-way premix applied postemergence for foxtail, volunteer millet, and wild oat. Crop tolerance is best after tillering.

■ POST
Tiller (EC) (0.375 lb./gal. fenoxaprop-P-ethyl & 0.58 lb./gal. 2,4-D ester & 1.75 lb./gal. MCPA) *(AgrEvo USA)*
Rate: 0.34-0.57 lb. ai/A
    1-1.7 pt. EC/A
Time: Postemergence. Crop: tiller initiation (3-4 leaf) to end of tillering (6 leaf). Broadleaf weeds: up to 4" in height; grass weeds: 2 leaf-2 tiller.
Weeds: Broadleaf weeds:

annual sowthistle	purslane	tumble mustard
common	ragweed	wild mustard
lambsquarters	shepherdspurse	wild radish
field pennycress		

Grasses:

barnyardgrass	green foxtail	wild oat
blackgrass	proso millet	windgrass
foxtail millet	volunteer corn	yellow foxtail

Remarks: Can be used on all winter wheat varieties. Rate varies by weed species. Do not apply through any type of irrigation system. Do not graze or feed treated forage, hay, or straw.
Days To Harvest: Minnesota, Montana, North Dakota, South Dakota—60; all other states—70.
Tank Mixes: Ally, Amber, Banvel, Buctril, Express, Harmony Extra, MCPA ester, Stinger, Tordon herbicides; Furadan 4F, Sevin XLR Plus insecticides.

– – – – – – – – – – – – – –

Signal Word/Toxicity Class: Warning/II.
REI: 12 hr. unless soil injected or soil incorporated.

Treflan — see trifluralin

TRI-4 — see trifluralin

TRIFLURALIN

Controls annual grasses and certain annual broadleaves when applied preplant incorporated prior to planting winter wheat. Limited to specified states.

■ PPI
Albaugh Trifluralin 4EC *(Albaugh)*
◆ Clean Crop Trifluralin HF (4EC) *(Platte)*
Gowan Trifluralin 4 or 5 (EC) or 10G *(Gowan)*
Helena Trifluralin 4 EC *(Helena)*
Riverside Trifluralin 4EC or Trific 60DF *(Terra)*
◆ Sedagri Trifluralin 480 (4EC) *(Rhone-Poulenc)*
Treflan HFP (4EC) or TR-10 (10G) *(Dow AgroSciences)*
TRI-4 HF (4EC) *(American Cyanamid)*
Trilin 4 or 5 (EC) or 10G *(Griffin)*
Wilbur-Ellis Trifluralin 10G *(Wilbur-Ellis)*
Rate: 0.75-1 lb. ai/A
    1.5-2 pt. 4EC/A
    1.2-1.6 pt. 5EC/A
    1.25-1.66 lb. 60DF/A
    7.5-10 lb. 10G/A
Time: Preplant incorporated. Apply up to 3 weeks before planting.
Weeds: Broadleaf weeds:

fiddleneck	henbit	tarweed

Grasses:

annual bluegrass	blackgrass	downy brome
annual ryegrass	cheatgrass	foxtail

◆-new product • PP-preplant • PPI-preplant incorporated • PRE-preemergence • POST-postemergence • SEQ-sequential • ae-acid equivalent • ai-active ingredient • DF-dry flowable
E/EC-emulsifiable concentrate • F/FL-flowable • DG/G/WG-dispersable granule • L/LC-liquid • SP/WSP-soluble packet • W/WP-wettable powder • WSB-water soluble bag

Remarks: Rate varies by soil type. Double incorporate with flextine or diamond harrow 1-2" deep. Make first incorporation within 24 hr. of application; make second incorporation in a different direction prior to planting. Under certain conditions, delayed crop emergence or stand reduction may occur. Refer to label for directions, restrictions, and precautions.
Crop Rotation: Refer to label.
State Restrictions: For use in Colorado, Idaho, Kansas, Montana, Nebraska, Oregon, Washington, and Wyoming; state varies by company.

Signal Word/Toxicity Class: Varies by formulation.
REI: 12 hr. unless soil injected or soil incorporated.

Trilin — see trifluralin

Weed Rhap — see 2,4-D

Weedar — see 2,4-D

Weedestroy — see 2,4-D

Weedone — see 2,4-D

Spring Wheat
(spring-seeded wheat)

ACHIEVE

Systemic postemergence herbicide for control of selective grasses. Does not control broadleaf weeds. Rainfast within 1 hr. Comes prepackaged with its own adjuvant.

■ POST
◆ Achieve 40DG (tralkoxydim) *(ZENECA)*
Rate: 0.18-0.24 lb. ai/A
0.44-0.6 lb. 40DG/A
Time: Postemergence. Apply 1- to 4-leaf stage for ryegrass and Persian darnel; 1- to 5-leaf stage for foxtail; 1- to 6-leaf stage for wild oat.
Weeds: Grasses:

annual ryegrass	Italian ryegrass	wild oat
green foxtail	Persian darnel	yellow foxtail

Remarks: Apply by ground or air. Use high rate when soil is dry, weeds are large, weed population is high, or crop canopy is dense. Maximum seasonal application is 0.25 lb. ai/A. Do not apply to crops or weeds with heavy dew cover. Do not apply through any type of irrigation system. Refer to label for use directions, restrictions, and precautions.
Days To Harvest: 60; grazed or cut for hay—30; straw or grain fed to livestock—45.
Crop Rotation: Cereal grains, leafy crops—30 days after application; all other crops—106 days after application.
Tank Mixes: Buctril, Bronate, Curtail M, Stinger.

Signal Word/Toxicity Class: Caution.
REI: 12 hr. unless soil injected or soil incorporated.

AIM

Contact herbicide with little or no residual activity. Rainfast within 1 hr. Very toxic to algae and moderately toxic to fish.

■ POST
◆ Aim (WDG) (carfentrazone-ethyl) *(FMC)*
Rate: 0.33-1.24 oz. WDG/A
Time: Apply in all tillage systems to actively growing weeds up to 4" high and rosettes less than 3" across. Do not apply past jointing stage.
Weeds: Broadleaf weeds:

annual sowthistle	kochia	shepherdspurse
bittercress	lambsquarters	tansymustard
black nightshade	pigweed	tumble mustard
bushy wallflower	redroot pigweed	velvetleaf
catchweed bedstraw	redstem filaree	volunteer rapeseed
field pennycress	Russian thistle	wild buckwheat
flixweed		

Tank mixed with 2,4-D (amine) or MCPA (amine) will also control:

blue mustard	greenflower	smooth pigweed
coast tarweed	pepperweed	sowthistle
common gromwell	ivyleaf speedwell	tall waterhemp
common groundsel	London rocket	tumble pigweed
common	minerslettuce	wild mustard
lambsquarters	prickly lettuce	wild radish
cutleaf	prostrate pigweed	wild sunflower
eveningprimrose	silverleaf nightshade	woolly croton
fiddleneck		

Remarks: The use of crop oil or crop oil plus either 28% nitrogen or ammonium sulfate with companion herbicides may be recommended under very dry conditions. Do not use with tank additives that alter the pH of spray solution below pH 5 or above pH 8. Refer to label for use directions, restrictions, and precautions.
Crop Rotation: Any crop including wheat—30 days following application; small grains (barley, oats, rye)—12 months after application.
Tank Mixes: Ally, Amber, Assert, Banvel, 2,4-D (amine), Express, Finesse, Harmony Extra, MCPA (amine), Peak.

- - - - - - - - - - - - - - - -

Signal Word/Toxicity Class: Caution.
REI: 12 hr.

ALLY

Sulfonylurea herbicide used for several annual broadleaf weeds. Especially effective for kochia, wild buckwheat, mustard, and pigweed. Not intended for grassy weeds. Consistent performance. Good crop tolerance. Tank mix with low rate of broadleaf herbicide with a different mode of action. Follow soil pH, crop rotation and minimum use interval for your area.

■ POST
Ally (DF) (metsulfuron-methyl) *(DuPont)*
Rate: 0.1 oz. DF/A
Time: Postemergence. Apply from 2-leaf stage but before boot stage. For durum or Wampum variety, apply after crop is tillering but before boot stage. Do not apply during boot stage or early heading.
Weeds: Broadleaf weeds:

blue mustard	field pennycress	Russian thistle
bur buttercup	filaree	shepherdspurse
Canada thistle*	flixweed	slimleaf
coast fiddleneck	green smartweed	lambsquarters
common chickweed	henbit	smallseed falseflax
common groundsel	kochia	smooth pigweed
common	jim hill mustard	sowthistle*
lambsquarters	ladysthumb	tansymustard
common purslane	maywead	tarweed
common sunflower*	minerslettuce	treacle mustard
conical catchfly	pale smartweed	tumble mustard
corn cockle	plains coreopsis	tumble pigweed
corn gromwell*	prickly lettuce	volunteer sunflower
cowcockle	prostrate knotweed*	waterpod
false chamomile	purple mustard	wild buckwheat*
fanweed	redroot pigweed	wild mustard

Grasses:

annual ryegrass*

* **Suppression**

Remarks: Spring, durum wheat. Add 1-2 pt. 80% nonionic surfactant/100 gal. spray volume. Do not apply within 60 days of crop emergence when an organophosphate insecticide has been applied in-furrow. Refer to label for restrictions and precautions. Do not apply through any type of irrigation system.
Crop Rotation: Determined by crop to be planted and minimum rotation interval. Minimum rotation interval is time from last Ally application to anticipated date of planting. For maximum rotational flexibility, do not treat all your wheat, barley, fallow, pasture, or rangeland acres at the same time.
Tank Mixes: Assert, Avenge, Banvel, bromoxynil, 2,4-D, Express, Harmony Extra, MCPA. Do not tank mix with malathion. Follow all restrictions.
State Restrictions: For use in Colorado (except Alamosa, Conejos, Costilla, Rio Grande, Saguache counties), Idaho, Kansas, Minnesota, Montana, Nebraska, New Mexico, North Dakota, Oklahoma, Oregon, South Dakota, Texas, Utah, Washington, and Wyoming.

- - - - - - - - - - - - - - - -

Signal Word/Toxicity Class: Caution/III.
REI: 4 hr.

AMBER

Selective sulfonylurea herbicide with extended soil residual activity. Especially effective for mustard, pigweed, and kochia. Tank mix with low rate of broadleaf herbicide with a different mode of action. Follow crop rotation guidelines and rotational intervals based on soil pH.

4

Small Grains

Spring Wheat

■ PP, PPI, PRE, POST

Amber Accu-Pak or CustomPak (WDG) (triasulfuron) (Novartis)

Rate: 0.56 oz. WDG/A

Time: Preplant, preplant shallow incorporated, preemergence. Do not apply preemergence to late fall-seeded winter wheat if environmental conditions that stress wheat are expected within 2 weeks after application.

Weeds: Broadleaf weeds:

henbit

Grasses:

annual ryegrass*	downy brome*	Persian darnel*
cheat*	Japanese brome*	

Rate: 0.28-0.56 oz. WDG/A

Time: Postemergence. Apply when weeds are actively growing.

Weeds: Broadleaf weeds:

annual fleabane	field pennycress	puncturevine
annual polemonium	flixweed	redroot pigweed
blue mustard (purple)	forget-me-not	rough fleabane
bushy wallflower	giant ragweed	Russian thistle
bur buttercup	hairy vetch	shepherdspurse
buttercup	henbit*	smooth pigweed
Canada thistle*	horseweed	spring whitlowgrass
coast fiddleneck	Indian mustard	tall buttercup
common broomweed	jagged chickweed	tall hedge mustard
common chickweed	jim hill mustard	tansymustard
common cocklebur	kochia	tumble mustard
common mallow	lanceleaf ragweed	Virginia pepperweed
common purslane	London rocket	western ragweed*
common ragweed	marshelder	wild buckwheat
common sunflower	minerslettuce	wild garlic*
common yarrow	morningglory*	wild mustard
corn gromwell	plains coreopsis	wild onion*
cutleaf	prickly lettuce	wild radish
eveningprimrose	prostrate knotweed	woolly croton
fanweed	prostrate pigweed	

* Suppression

Remarks: Do not apply to wheat undersown with legumes or forage grasses. Do not use alone in any field where sulfonylurea-resistant biotypes of any weed species have been identified. Refer to label for further use directions, restrictions, and precautions.

Crop Rotation: Wheat—anytime; proso millet—4 months; barley, oats, rye, bermudagrass—6 months (with conditions); grain sorghum and soybeans—14 months (with conditions). All other crops may be seeded only at completion of successful field bioassay; refer to label.

State Restrictions: For use in Colorado (except San Luis Valley), Idaho, Kansas, Minnesota, Montana, Nebraska, Nevada, New Mexico, North Dakota, Oklahoma, South Dakota, Texas, Utah, Wyoming, and east of the Cascades in Oregon or Washington.

- - - - - - - - - - - - - - - - -

Signal Word/Toxicity Class: Caution/III.

REI: 12 hr.

ASSERT

Postemergence applications control wild oat and wild mustard. Does not control foxtail. Crop tolerance for hard red spring wheat is excellent.

■ POST

Assert (2.5LC) (imazamethabenz methyl) (American Cyanamid)

Rate: 0.31-0.48 lb. ai/A
1-1.5 pt. 2.5LC/A

Time: Postemergence. Apply when wheat is in 2-5 leaf stage (prior to jointing); wild oat in 1-4 leaf stage. For Avenge tank mix, apply from 2-5 leaf stage of wild oat. Do not apply when wheat flagleaf is exposed.

Weeds: Broadleaf weeds:

catchweed bedstraw	London rocket	wild buckwheat
field pennycress	tansymustard	wild mustard
flixweed	tartary buckwheat	

Grasses:

interrupted windgrass   roughstalk bluegrass   wild oat

Remarks: Rate varies by state; refer to label. Add 2 pt. 80% nonionic surfactant/100 gal. spray solution. When weeds are under moisture or temperature stress, 1.5-2 pt. SUN-IT II spray adjuvant may be used instead of nonionic surfactant. Assert may cause slight discoloration and delayed growth of durum wheat if unfavorable growing conditions exist; crop will recover under normal growing conditions and yields will not be affected. Wheat straw may be fed or used for bedding. Do not apply through any type of irrigation system. Do not graze treated fields or cut treated forage for silage or hay.

Crop Rotation: Barley, canola (IMI-tolerant varieties such as Pioneer 45A71, 46A72; non-IMI tolerant in certain counties in Minnesota and North Dakota), corn, edible beans, safflower, soybeans, sunflower, wheat—anytime; sugar beets—20 months; other crops—15 months after application.

Tank Mixes: Ally, Amber, Avenge (wild oat only), bromoxynil + MCPA ester, Canvas, Curtail M, 2,4-D ester, Express, Finesse, Glean, Harmony, Harmony Extra, MCPA ester, Starane.

- - - - - - - - - - - - - - - - -

Signal Word/Toxicity Class: Danger/I.

REI: 48 hr.

AVENGE

Postemergence herbicide for selective wild oat control. Some spring wheat varieties are sensitive; treat only labeled varieties.

■ POST

Avenge (2ASU) (difenzoquat) (American Cyanamid)

Rate: 0.625-1 lb. ai/A
2.5-4 pt. 2ASU/A

Time: Postemergence. Apply when wild oat is in 3-5 leaf stage. Do not apply if wheat flagleaf is exposed.

Weeds:

wild oat

Remarks: Soft-white spring-seeded (all varieties), spring-seeded durum and hard red spring wheat; refer to label for varietal restrictions. Do not apply to hard red spring wheat varieties not listed on label. Do not apply if rain is predicted within 6 hr., when freezing temperatures are forecast, or when plants are wet with rain or dew. When applied under poor conditions for plant growth, Avenge can produce yellowing or slight tipburn of wheat; crop recovery is rapid when good growth conditions return.

Crop Rotation: Barley or wheat can be replanted if loss of crop occurs. Rotation to other crops can be made the following year.

Tank Mixes: Assert for wild oat only; following broadleaf herbicides: Ally, Amber, Assert, bromoxynil, bromoxynil + MCPA, Canvas, Curtail, 2,4-D, Express, Glean, Harmony Extra, MCPA, Peak.

- - - - - - - - - - - - - - - - -

Signal Word/Toxicity Class: Danger/I.

REI: 48 hr.

Banvel — see dicamba

Barrage — see 2,4-D

Bison — see bromoxynil & MCPA

Brash — see 2,4-D Combinations

Broclean — see bromoxynil

Bromac — see bromoxynil & MCPA

Bromox — see bromoxynil

Bromox-MCPA 2-2 — see bromoxynil & MCPA

BROMOXYNIL

Contact action herbicide usually used in combination with MCPA or other labeled herbicides to control more species.

■ POST

◆ **Broclean 2EC** (Platte)

◆ **Bromox 2EC** (Micro Flo)

Buctril (2EC), Buctril 4EC (Rhone-Poulenc)

Moxy 2EC (Terra)

Rate: 0.25-0.5 lb. ai/A
1-2 pt. 2EC/A
0.5-1 pt. 4EC/A
Except CO, ID, OR, MT, WA, WY:
0.375-0.5 lb. ai/A
1.5-2 pt. 2EC/A
0.75-1 pt. 4EC/A

◆-new product • PP-preplant • PPI-preplant incorporated • PRE-preemergence • POST-postemergence • SEQ-sequential • ae-acid equivalent • ai-active ingredient • DF-dry flowable
E/EC-emulsifiable concentrate • F/FL-flowable • DG/G/WG-dispersable granule • L/LC-liquid • SP/WSP-soluble packet • W/WP-wettable powder • WSB-water soluble bag

Underseeded with alfalfa:
0.25-0.375 lb. ai/A
1-1.5 pt. 2EC/A
0.5-0.75 pt. 4EC/A

Time: Postemergence. Apply from emergence to boot stage.
Weeds: Most susceptible broadleaf weeds:

annual pepperweed	common tarweed	Pennsylvania
annual sowthistle	eastern black	smartweed
black nightshade	nightshade	shepherdspurse
blue mustard	field pennycress	silverleaf nightshade
bristly starbur	green smartweed	sunflower
coast fiddleneck	hairy nightshade	tartary buckwheat
common cocklebur	jimsonweed	wild buckwheat
common lambsquarters	ladysthumb	

Susceptible broadleaf weeds:

buffalobur	ivyleaf morningglory	spiny pigweed
burcucumber	knawel	tall morningglory
common groundsel	kochia	tall waterhemp
common ragweed	London rocket	tumble mustard
corn chamomile	mayweed	velvetleaf
corn gromwell	prostrate knotweed	Venice mallow
cowcockle	puncturevine	wild mustard
giant ragweed	redroot pigweed	wild radish
hemp sesbania	Russian thistle	yellow starthistle

Remarks: Spring-seeded wheat. Do not apply when crops are under moisture stress. Do not graze treated fields within 30 days after application (45 days for Buctril). Refer to label for use directions, restrictions and precautions.

Crop Rotation: Do not plant rotational crops until the following season (within 30 days of application for Buctril).

Tank Mixes: Ally, Amber, Avenge (not for use on sensitive varieties), Banvel, Curtail, 2,4-D, Express, Finesse, Glean, Harmony Extra, Hoelon, MCPA, Tiller.

– – – – – – – – – – – – – – – –

Signal Word/Toxicity Class: Warning/II.
REI: 12 hr.

BROMOXYNIL & MCPA (Premixes)

Premix that gives very good to excellent control of several annual broadleaf weeds; including special problems such as kochia and wild buckwheat. Good crop tolerance. Best results when weeds are small and free of drought stress.

■ **POST**

Bison (EC) (2 lb./gal. bromoxynil & 2 lb./gal. MCPA) *(Terra)*
♦ **Bromac (EC) (2 lb./gal. bromoxynil & 2 lb./gal. MCPA)** *(Platte)*
♦ **Bromox-MCPA 2-2 (EC) (2 lb./gal. bromoxynil & 2 lb./gal. MCPA)** *(Micro Flo)*
Bronate (EC) (2 lb./gal. bromoxynil & 2 lb./gal. MCPA) *(Rhone-Poulenc)*

Rate: 0.5-1 lb. ai/A
1-2 pt. EC/A
Chemigation:
1 lb. ai/A
2 pt. EC/A
Postharvest—MN, MT, ND, SD:
0.38-1 lb. ai/A
0.75-2 pt. EC/A (Bronate)

Time: Postemergence. Apply after 3-leaf stage but before boot stage.
Weeds: Most susceptible broadleaf weeds:

annual sowthistle	field pennycress	Russian thistle
black mustard	green smartweed	shepherdspurse
black nightshade	hairy nightshade	silverleaf nightshade
coast fiddleneck	horned poppy	smooth pigweed
common cocklebur	jimsonweed	spiny pigweed
common	ladysthumb	sunflower
lambsquarters	London rocket	tall waterhemp
common tarweed	marshelder	tartary buckwheat
cowcockle	Pennsylvania	tumble mustard
cutleaf nightshade	smartweed	wild buckwheat
eastern black	pepperweed	wild mustard
nightshade	redroot pigweed	yellow rocket

Susceptible broadleaf weeds:

blue mustard	giant ragweed	puncturevine
Canada thistle	hemp sesbania	purple mustard
(suppression)	henbit	tall morningglory
common groundsel	ivyleaf morningglory	tansymustard
common ragweed	knawel	tarweed
corn chamomile	kochia	velvetleaf
corn gromwell	mayweed	wild radish
fumitory	prostrate knotweed	

Remarks: Rates vary by weed species and conditions; refer to label for directions and precautions. Do not apply when crop canopy covers weeds or when crops are under moisture stress. Do not graze fields within 30 days after application (45 for Bronate).

Tank Mixes: Ally, Amber, Assert, Avenge, Banvel, Curtail, Express, Finesse, Glean, Harmony Extra, MCPA.

– – – – – – – – – – – – – – – –

Signal Word/Toxicity Class: Warning/II.
REI: 12 hr.

Bronate — see bromoxynil & MCPA

BUCKLE (Premix)

Granular selective herbicide to control wild oat and foxtail.

■ **PPI**

Buckle (13G) (10% triallate & 3% trifluralin) *(Monsanto)*
Rate: 1.3-1.625 lb. ai/A
10-12.5 lb. 13G/A

Time: Preplant incorporated. In the fall, apply within 3 weeks of normal freezeup.
Weeds:

foxtail	pigeongrass	wild oat

Remarks: Do not apply on muck soils or soils containing more than 10% organic matter. Do not graze livestock on treated fields. Refer to label for directions and precautions.

Crop Rotation: Certain vegetable crops (refer to Monsanto representative for specific crops)—5 months; sugar beets, red beets, spinach—14 months; sorghum, proso millet, corn, oats—16 months. Do not apply prior to durum wheat on soil that has been planted to soybeans or sugar beets and treated with trifluralin the previous year.

State Restrictions: For use in Colorado, Idaho, Kansas, Minnesota, Montana, Nebraska, Nevada, North Dakota, Oregon, South Dakota, Utah, Washington, and Wyoming.

– – – – – – – – – – – – – – – –

Signal Word/Toxicity Class: Caution/III.
REI: 12 hr.

Buctril — see bromoxynil

CANVAS (Premix)

■ **POST**

Canvas (DF) (37.5% thifensulfuron-methyl & 18.75% tribenuron-methyl & 15% metsulfuron-methyl) *(DuPont)*
Rate: 1 soluble pack/5A
MN, MT, ND, SD:
1 soluble pack/10A

Time: Early postemergence. Apply to young actively growing weeds after wheat is in 2-leaf stage, but before flag leaf is visible. For durum and wampam variety, apply after crop is tillering but before boot.
Weeds: Broadleaf weeds:

annual knawel	dogfennel	purple mustard
annual sowthistle*	false chamomile	redmaids
black mustard	fanweed	rockpurslane
blue mustard	field chickweed	redroot pigweed
broadleaf dock	field pennycress	Russian thistle
bur buttercup	filaree	scentless chamomile
bushy wallflower	flixweed	shepherdspurse
Canada thistle	hairy nightshade*	smallflower buttercup
Carolina geranium	hairy vetch*	smallseed falseflax
catchweed bedstraw*	henbit	smartweed
clasping pepperweed	jim hill mustard	smooth pigweed
coast fiddleneck	kochia	snow speedwell
common buckwheat	lambsquarters	stinking chickweed
common chickweed	little mallow*	stinking mayweed
common cocklebur	London rocket	swinecress
common groundsel	marshelder	tall waterhemp*
common mallow	mayweed chamomile	tansymustard
common purslane	minerslettuce	tarweed
common radish	mouseearcress	treacle mustard
common ragweed	narrowleaf	tumble mustard
common sunflower	lambsquarters	tumble pigweed
common vetch*	nightflowering	volunteer lentils
conical catchfly	catchfly	volunteer peas
corn chamomile	Pennsylvania	volunteer sunflower
corn gromwell	smartweed	waterpod
corn spurry	pineappleweed	wild buckwheat
cowcockle	plains coreopsis	wild chamomile
curly dock	prickly lettuce	wild garlic
cutleaf	prostrate knotweed	wild mustard
eveningprimrose	prostrate pigweed	wild radish
cutleaf nightshade*		

* Partial control

4

Small Grains

Spring Wheat

Remarks: Not underseeded with legumes. Add approved nonionic surfactant. Do not make more than one application per crop season. Do not graze or feed forage or hay from treated areas to livestock (harvested straw may be used for bedding and/or feed).

Days To Harvest: 45.

Crop Rotation: Varies depending on crop and geographic area.

Tank Mixes: With 2,4-D for durum or Wampum variety.

State Restrictions: For use in Colorado (except Alamosa, Conejos, Costilla, Rio Grande, Saguache counties), Idaho, Kansas, Minnesota, Montana, Nebraska, New Mexico, Oklahoma, Oregon, South Dakota, Texas, Utah, Washington, and Wyoming.

- - - - - - - - - - - - - - - -

Signal Word/Toxicity Class: Warning/II.

REI: 12 hr.

CHEYENNE (Co-Pack)

Twin pack product of Cheyenne FM premix (fenoxaprop & MCPA) & X-TRA premix (thifensulfuron & tribenuron). Controls several annual grasses and broadleaf weeds.

■ POST

Cheyenne (3.5 gal. Cheyenne FM & 0.375 lb. X-TRA) *(AgrEvo USA)*

Rate: Cheyenne FM:
1.4 pt./A
+ X-TRA:
0.3 oz./A

Time: Crop: Minimum of 3 tillers. Broadleaf weeds: Up to 4" high or 4" diameter; grasses: wild oat 1-4 leaf, green foxtail 2 leaf-2 tiller.

Weeds: Broadleaf weeds:

common lambsquarters	kochia mustard	redroot pigweed

Grasses:

barnyardgrass foxtail	millet volunteer corn	wild oat

Remarks: Always mix Cheyenne FM with X-TRA Herbicide prior to use to ensure crop safety and adequate control. Do not apply by air.

Days To Harvest: Minnesota, Montana, North Dakota, South Dakota—60; all other states—70.

- - - - - - - - - - - - - - - -

Signal Word/Toxicity Class:
Danger/I (Cheyenne FM); Caution/III (X-TRA).

REI: 24 hr.

Chiptox — see MCPA

Clarity — see dicamba

CLOPYRALID

Systemic herbicide absorbed by leaves and roots. Has selective postemergence control of many annual and perennial broadleaf weeds. Especially useful for Canada thistle seasonal suppression. Frequently used in combination with 2,4-D or MCPA. Note crop rotation restrictions.

■ POST

Stinger *(Dow AgroSciences)*

Rate: 0.1-0.125 lb. ae/A
0.25-0.33 pt./A

Time: Postemergence. Apply from 3-leaf stage up to early boot stage.

Weeds: Annual and perennial broadleaf weeds:

Canada thistle	jimsonweed	sowthistle
clover	knapweed	spotted knapweed
cocklebur	marshelder	sunflower
diffuse knapweed	Russian knapweed	vetch
Jerusalem artichoke	(suppression)	volunteer soybean

Remarks: Not underseeded with legumes. Do not allow dairy animals or meat animals being finished for slaughter to forage or graze treated fields within 1 week after treatment. Do not harvest hay from treated fields. Do not apply through any type of irrigation system.

Crop Rotation: Varies by region; refer to label.

Tank Mixes: With other herbicides registered for postemergence application; refer to labels.

- - - - - - - - - - - - - - - -

Signal Word/Toxicity Class: Caution/III.

REI: 12 hr.

Credit — see glyphosate

CURTAIL or CURTAIL M (Premixes)

Clopyralid provides good seasonal control of Canada thistle. 2,4-D or MCPA in premix improves control of other broadleaf weeds. Crop tolerance is good. Canada thistle control is best when weeds are treated before they form flower buds.

■ POST

Curtail (0.38 lb./gal. clopyralid & 2 lb./gal. 2,4-D) *(Dow AgroSciences)*

Curtail M (0.42 lb./gal. clopyralid & 2.35 lb./gal. MCPA) *(Dow AgroSciences)*

Rate: 0.6-0.8 lb. ae/A
2-2.66 pt. Curtail/A
1.75-2.33 pt. Curtail M/A

Time: Postemergence. Apply in spring to actively growing wheat once 4 leaves have unfolded on main stem up to jointing stage. Do not apply after boot stage.

Weeds: Broadleaf weeds:

alfalfa	giant ragweed	red sorrel
annual sowthistle	goatsbeard	redroot pigweed
Canada thistle	hairy nightshade	Russian knapweed*
coffeeweed	horseweed	Russian thistle
common burdock	Jerusalem artichoke	(1-3 leaf)
common cocklebur	jim hill mustard	scentless chamomile
common groundsel	jimsonweed	shepherdspurse
common lambsquarters	kochia* (2-4 leaf) ladysthumb	sicklepod spotted knapweed
common ragweed	mayweed chamomile	sweetclover
common sunflower	meadow salsify	tansymustard
cornflower	musk thistle	tumble mustard
curly dock	narrowleaf	velvetleaf
cutleaf nightshade	hawksbeard	vetch
dandelion	Pennsylvania	volunteer beans
diffuse knapweed	smartweed	volunteer lentils
dogfennel	perennial sowthistle*	volunteer peas
false chamomile	pineappleweed	wild buckwheat
fanweed	plantain	wild mustard
field pennycress	prickly lettuce	wild radish
flixweed*	red clover	yellow starthistle

* Suppression

Remarks: Not underseeded with legumes. Do not harvest hay from treated grain fields. Do not allow lactating dairy or meat animals being finished for slaughter to forage or graze treated fields within 1 week after application. Do not apply through any type of irrigation system.

Crop Rotation: Varies by region; refer to label.

Tank Mixes: Ally, Avenge, Banvel, Buctril, 2,4-D, diuron, Express, Harmony Extra, MCPA, metribuzin.

- - - - - - - - - - - - - - - -

Signal Word/Toxicity Class: Danger/I (Curtail); Caution/III (Curtail M).

REI: 48 hr.

Cyclone — see paraquat

2,4-D - PHENOXY HERBICIDES

Widely used in spring wheat; frequently tank mixed with several new herbicides. Good choice for seasonal suppression of field bindweed. Ester forms are used at slightly lower rate than amines.

Annual and perennial broadleaf weeds controlled by 2,4-D include:

beggarticks	galinsoga	povertyweed
bindweed	goldenrod	puncturevine
bitterweed	ground ivy	purslane
broomweed	healall	ragweed
bull thistle	hoary cress	Russian thistle
burdock	ironweed	shepherdspurse
Canada thistle	jimsonweed	smartweed
carpetweed	knotweed	sowthistle
catnip	lambsquarters	stinkweed
chicory	mallow	sumac
chickweed	marshelder	sunflower
cocklebur	mexicanweed	sweetclover
coffeeweed	morningglory	velvetleaf
cutleaf eveningprimrose	musk thistle	Virginia creeper
creeping jenny	mustard	wild carrot
croton	pennywort	wild garlic
dandelion	pepperweed	wild lettuce
dock	pigweed	wild onion
dogbane	plantain	wild parsnips
	pokeweed	wild radish

◆-new product • PP-preplant • PPI-preplant incorporated • PRE-preemergence • POST-postemergence • SEQ-sequential • ae-acid equivalent • ai-active ingredient • DF-dry flowable E/EC-emulsifiable concentrate • F/FL-flowable • DG/G/WG-dispersable granule • L/LC-liquid • SP/WSP-soluble packet • W/WP-wettable powder • WSB-water soluble bag

■ POST

Albaugh Amine 4 (2,4-D amine) *(Albaugh)*
Weedestroy AM-40 (2,4-D amine) *(Riverdale)*
Wilbur-Ellis Amine 4 (2,4-D amine) *(Wilbur-Ellis)*

Rate: 0.25-0.5 lb. ae/A
  0.5-1 pt./A
Time: Postemergence. Apply after tillering (4-8" high) but before boot stage.
Remarks: Not underseeded with legumes.
State Restrictions: Wilbur-Ellis not registered in California.

- - - - - - - - - - - - - - -

Rate: 0.125-0.25 lb. ae/A
  0.25-0.5 pt./A
Time: Postemergence. Apply in spring, after 8" tall but before boot stage.
Remarks: Underseeded with legumes. Do not spray alfalfa or sweet clover unless infestation is severe and injury to legumes can be tolerated.
State Restrictions: Wilbur-Ellis not registered in California.

- - - - - - - - - - - - - - -

Signal Word/Toxicity Class: Danger/I.
REI: 48 hr.

■ POST

Albaugh LV4 or LV6 Ester (2,4-D ester) *(Albaugh)*
◆ **Barrage or Barrage HF (EC) (2,4-D ester)** *(Helena)*
◆ **Clean Crop Low Vol 4 or Low Vol 6 (2,4-D ester)** *(Platte)*
Esteron 99C (2,4-D LV ester) *(Rhone-Poulenc)*
Riverdale 6 Amine (2,4-D amine) *(Riverdale)*
Riverdale L.V. 4 or L.V. 6 (2,4-D ester) *(Riverdale)*
Solve 2,4-D (2,4-D LV ester) *(Albaugh)*
Weed Rhap LV-6D (2,4-D) *(Helena)*
Wilbur-Ellis Lo Vol-4 or Lo Vol-6 (2,4-D ester) *(Wilbur-Ellis)*

Rate: 0.25-0.5 lb. ae/A
  0.5-1 pt. 4/A
  0.33-0.66 pt. 6/A
  Perennial weeds, preharvest:
  0.5-1 lb. ae/A
  1-2 pt. 4/A
  0.66-1.33 pt. 6/A
Time: Postemergence, preharvest. Do not spray before tiller or from early boot to dough stage.
Remarks: Not underseeded with legumes. Do not forage or graze treated fields for 2 weeks after application.
State Restrictions: Wilbur-Ellis not registered in California.

- - - - - - - - - - - - - - -

Signal Word/Toxicity Class: Danger/I (amine); Caution/III (ester).
REI: Danger—48 hr.; Caution—12 hr.

■ POST

Albaugh D-638 (2,4-D ester + acid) *(Albaugh)*
Phenoxy 088 (2,4-D ester + acid) *(Terra)*
Weedone 638 (2,4-D ester + acid) *(Nufarm)*

Rate: 0.35-0.7 lb. ae/A
  1-2 pt./A
Time: Postemergence, preharvest. Apply when weeds are near bud stage. Apply after grain is fully tillered (4-8" high) but not forming joints in stem, and when daytime temperatures are below 85°F. Do not spray in boot to dough stage. Do not apply to grain in seedling stage.
Remarks: Not underseeded with legumes. Do not apply through any type of irrigation system. Do not forage or graze treated fields for 2 weeks after application.
State Restrictions: Weedone not for use preharvest in California.

- - - - - - - - - - - - - - -

Signal Word/Toxicity Class: Danger/I.
REI: 48 hr.

■ POST

◆ **Clean Crop Amine 4 (2,4-D amine)** *(Platte)*
Formula 40 (2,4-D mixed amine) *(Rhone-Poulenc)*
◆ **Opti-Amine (4) (2,4-D amine)** *(Helena)*
Weed Rhap A-4D (2,4-D amine) *(Helena)*

Rate: 0.33-0.66 lb. ae/A
  0.66-1.33 pt./A
Time: Postemergence. Apply in spring. Do not apply before tiller stage or from early boot through milk stage.

Rate: 0.5-1 lb. ae/A
  1-2 pt./A
Time: Preharvest. Apply in dough stage.

Remarks: Not underseeded with legumes. Up to 3 pt./A may be used for difficult weed problems such as dry conditions in Western states. Do not allow dairy animals or meat animals being finished for slaughter to forage or graze treated fields within 2 weeks of treatment.

- - - - - - - - - - - - - - -

Signal Word/Toxicity Class: Danger/I.
REI: 48 hr.

■ POST

Gordon's LV 400 (2,4-D LV ester) *(PBI/Gordon)*
Riverside 2,4-D LV4 (2,4-D LV ester) *(Terra)*

Rate: 0.25-0.5 lb. ae/A
  0.5-1 pt./A
Time: Postemergence. Apply when grain is in full tiller stage but before early boot stage and when weeds are small. Do not apply before tiller stage or from early boot through milk stage.

Rate: 0.5-1 lb. ae/A
  1-2 pt./A
Time: Preharvest. Apply in dough stage.
Remarks: Not underseeded with legumes. Up to 2 pt./A may be used for difficult weeds problems such as dry conditions in Western states. Do not use higher rates unless possible crop injury will be acceptable.

- - - - - - - - - - - - - - -

Signal Word/Toxicity Class: Caution/III.
REI: 12 hr.

■ POST

Hi-Dep (2,4-D mixed amine) *(PBI/Gordon)*

Rate: 0.125-0.75 lb. ae/A
  0.25-1.5 pt./A
Time: Postemergence. Apply after grain begins tillering and before boot stage (4-8" tall). Do not apply before tiller stage or from early boot through milk stage.

Rate: 0.5-1 lb. ae/A
  1-2 pt./A
Time: Preharvest. Apply in dough stage.
Remarks: Not underseeded with legumes. Up to 3 pt./A may be used for difficult weeds problems such as dry conditions in Western states. Do not allow dairy animals or meat animals being finished for slaughter to forage or graze treated fields within 2 weeks after application.

- - - - - - - - - - - - - - -

Signal Word/Toxicity Class: Danger/I.
REI: 48 hr.

■ POST

◆ **Saber (2,4-D amine)** *(Platte)*

Rate: 0.12-0.75 lb. ae/A
  0.25-1.5 pt./A
Time: Postemergence. Apply from onset of tillering to full tillering stage. Do not apply from boot to dough stage.

Rate: Emergency, preharvest:
  0.35-1.4 lb. ae/A
  0.75-3 pt./A
Time: Preharvest. Apply in hard dough stage. Do not apply before tiller or from boot to dough stage.
Remarks: Not underseeded with legumes. Up to 3 pt./A may be used to control difficult weeds and heavy infestations. Do not forage or graze treated fields for 2 weeks after application. Do not feed treated straw to livestock if emergency and/or preharvest treatment is applied.

- - - - - - - - - - - - - - -

Signal Word/Toxicity Class: Danger/I.
REI: 48 hr.

■ POST

Salvo (2,4-D LV ester) *(Platte)*

Rate: 0.25-0.31 lb. ae/A
  0.4-0.5 pt./A
Time: Postemergence. Apply after plants are fully tillered but before stems begin to joint. Do not apply during boot or dough stage.
Remarks: Do not forage or graze treated grain fields within 2 weeks after treatment. Do not feed treated straw to livestock.

- - - - - - - - - - - - - - -

Signal Word/Toxicity Class: Caution/III.
REI: 12 hr.

4

Small Grains

| NOTICE | The information on these pages is for preliminary planning — not a guide for use. Be sure to follow the manufacturer's directions, notwithstanding information contained here. | For personal protective equipment and EPA registration numbers, please turn to page 70. |

■ POST

Savage (WSB) (2,4-D amine) *(Platte)*

Rate: 0.24-0.95 lb. ae/A
0.25-1 lb. WSB/A

Time: Postemergence. Apply in spring. Do not apply before tiller stage or from boot to dough stage.

Rate: 0.48-1.43 lb. ae/A
0.5-1.5 lb. WSB/A

Time: Preharvest. Apply in hard dough stage.

Remarks: Not underseeded with legumes. For emergency weed control, up to 1.5 lb./A may be used when weeds are approaching bud stage, after grain dough stage. Do not use higher rates unless possible crop injury acceptable. Do not forage or graze treated fields within 2 weeks after treatment. Do not feed treated straw if emergency and/or preharvest treatment is applied. Refer to label for use directions and precautions.

Signal Word/Toxicity Class: Danger/I.
REI: 48 hr.

■ POST

Solution (WS) (2,4-D amine) *(Riverdale)*

Rate: 1 WS packet/3.5-10 A

Time: Postemergence. Apply between full tillering and before boot stage (usually 4-8" tall). Preharvest treatment can be applied when grain is in dough stage.

Remarks: Apply in 5-100 gal. water.

Signal Word/Toxicity Class: Danger/I.
REI: 48 hr.

■ POST

Weedar 64 (4) (2,4-D amine) *(Nufarm)*

Rate: 0.25-1 lb. ae/A
0.5-2 pt./A

Time: Postemergence. Apply after grain is fully tillered (4-8" high) but not forming joints in stem. Do not spray in boot to dough stage.

Remarks: Not underseeded with legumes. For emergency control of perennial broadleaf weeds, up to 3 pt./A may be used when weeds are approaching bud stage. Do not use unless possible crop injury will be acceptable.

Rate: 0.125-0.25 lb. ae/A
0.25-0.5 pt./A

Time: Postemergence. Apply after grain is 8" tall but before boot stage. Do not spray in boot to dough stage.

Remarks: Underseeded with legumes. Do not spray alfalfa or sweet clover unless infestation is severe and injury to legumes can be tolerated.

Signal Word/Toxicity Class: Danger/I.
REI: 48 hr.

■ POST

Weedone LV4 (2,4-D solventless ester) *(Nufarm)*
Weedone Lo Vol 6 (2,4-D ester) *(Nufarm)*

Rate: 0.25-1 lb. ae/A
0.5-2 pt. 4/A
0.33-1.33 pt. 6/A

Time: Postemergence. Do not spray in boot to dough stage.

Remarks: Not underseeded with legumes. For emergency control of perennial broadleaf weeds, up to 2 pt. 6/A may be used when weeds are approaching bud stage. Do not use unless possible crop injury will be acceptable. Refer to label for use directions, restrictions, and precautions.

Tank Mixes: LV4: Buctril (rate varies by state, refer to label).

Signal Word/Toxicity Class: Caution/III.
REI: 12 hr.

2,4-D COMBINATIONS

■ POST

◆ Brash (2.87 lb./gal. 2,4-D & 1 lb./gal. dicamba) *(Terra)*

Rate: 0.375-0.5 lb. ai/A
0.75-1 pt./A

Time: Apply before 5-leaf stage. For best results, apply when weeds are in 2-3 leaf stage and rosettes are less than 2" across.

Weeds: Annual and biennial broadleaf weeds such as:

annual sowthistle	common purslane	Pennsylvania
bittercress	common ragweed	smartweed
black nightshade	cowcockle	redroot pigweed
common chickweed	field pennycress	rough pigweed
common cocklebur	flax	Russian thistle
common	henbit	shepherdspurse
eveningprimrose	knotweed	sunflower
common	kochia	tansymustard
lambsquarters	mustard	velvetleaf
common mallow		wild buckwheat

Remarks: Not underseeded with legumes. Do not graze or harvest for feed prior to crop maturity.

Tank Mixes: Bromoxynil, 2,4-D, diuron, MCPA, metribuzin, sulfonylureas. Refer to labels for use directions, restrictions, and precautions.

Signal Word/Toxicity Class: Danger/I.
REI: 48 hr.

DAKOTA (Premix)

Commercial twin-pak containing fenoxaprop-ethyl and MCPA ester. Postemergence herbicide for the control of green foxtail, foxtail millet, and certain broadleaf weeds in spring and winter wheat.

■ POST

Dakota (0.234 lb./gal. fenoxaprop-P-ethyl & 2.84 lb./gal. MCPA) *(AgrEvo USA)*

Rate: 0.03-0.039 lb. ai/A
1-1.3 pt./A

Time: Crop: 3-6 leaf. Broadleaf weeds: not to exceed 4" in height; grasses: 2 leaf-2 tiller.

Weeds: Broadleaf weeds:

common	field pennycress	tumble mustard
lambsquarters	ragweed	wild mustard

Grasses:

foxtail millet	green foxtail

Remarks: Not for use on durum wheat.
Days To Harvest: 60.
Tank Mixes: Ally, Amber, Banvel, Buctril/Buctril Gel, Express, Harmony Extra, Stinger, Tordon herbicides; Furadan 4F, Sevin XLR Plus insecticides; mancozeb fungicides.
State Restrictions: For use in Montana, North Dakota, and South Dakota.

Signal Word/Toxicity Class: Warning/II.
REI: 24 hr.

DICAMBA

Especially effective for wild buckwheat and kochia. Must be applied at early crop stage for best crop tolerance. Usually used in combination with MCPA, 2,4-D, or other labeled herbicides to provide additional control.

■ PP, PRE, POST

Banvel (WS) (DMA salt of dicamba) *(BASF)*
Banvel SGF (sodium salt of dicamba) *(BASF)*
Clarity (WS) (dicamba-DGA) *(BASF)*
◆ Sterling (WS) (DMA salt of dicamba) *(Terra)*

Rate: 2-4 fl. oz. WS/A
4-8 fl. oz. SGF/A

Time: Preplant, preemergence, postemergence. Apply prior to 6-leaf stage. For best performance, apply when weeds are in 2-3 leaf stage and rosettes are less than 2" across.

Weeds: Broadleaf weeds:

annual sowthistle	corn cockle	Pennsylvania
black nightshade	cowcockle	smartweed
common cocklebur	field pennycress	redroot pigweed
common	giant ragweed	rough pigweed
lambsquarters	green smartweed	Russian thistle
common mallow	henbit	tumble pigweed
common ragweed	knotweed	velvetleaf
common sunflower	kochia	volunteer sunflower
corn chamomile	ladysthumb	wild buckwheat

Remarks: Not underseeded with legumes. Do not graze lactating dairy animals within 7 days after application or remove animals for slaughter within 30 days of last application; no waiting period between treatment and grazing for nonlactating animals. Do not apply through any type of irrigation system.
Days To Harvest: Hay—37.

◆-new product • PP-preplant • PPI-preplant incorporated • PRE-preemergence • POST-postemergence • SEQ-sequential • ae-acid equivalent • ai-active ingredient • DF-dry flowable
E/EC-emulsifiable concentrate • F/FL-flowable • DG/G/WG-dispersable granule • L/LC-liquid • SP/WSP-soluble packet • W/WP-wettable powder • WSB-water soluble bag

Tank Mixes: Ally, Amber, Bronate, Buctril, Curtail, 2,4-D, Dakota, Express, Finesse, Glean, glyphosate, Harmony Extra, MCPA, Stinger, Tiller. Do not tank mix with Dakota or Tiller on durum wheat.

– – – – – – – – – – – – – –

Signal Word/Toxicity Class: Warning/II (Banvel, Sterling); Caution (Clarity).
REI: 24 hr.

Esteron 99C — see 2,4-D

EXPRESS

Short residual sulfonylurea herbicide. Active ingredient is one of the components in Harmony Extra. Controls several annual broadleaf weeds. Excellent activity on kochia, mustard, and pigweed. Usually used in tank mix with other herbicides. No crop rotation limitations for next season.

■ **POST**

Express (DF) (tribenuron-methyl) *(DuPont)*
Rate: 0.167-0.33 oz. DF/A
Time: Early postemergence. Apply after crop is in 2-leaf stage, but before flag leaf is visible (can be treated sequentially with low rates but do not exceed total of 0.33 oz./A per season).
Weeds: Broadleaf weeds:

annual sowthistle*	field pennycress	redmaids
black mustard	flixweed	rockpurslane*
blue mustard (purple)	hairy nightshade*	redroot pigweed*
bushy wallflower	henbit	Russian thistle
Canada thistle*	jim hill mustard*	shepherdspurse*
coast fiddleneck	kochia	slimleaf lambsquarters
common chickweed	mayweed chamomile	tansymustard*
common groundsel	minerslettuce	tarweed fiddleneck
common	Pennsylvania	tumble mustard*
lambsquarters	smartweed*	wild buckwheat*
common sunflower*	pineappleweed	wild chamomile
corn spurry	prickly lettuce	wild garlic*
false chamomile	prostrate knotweed*	wild mustard*
		wild radish*

* *Suppression*

Remarks: Spring, durum wheat. Not underseeded. Add approved non-ionic surfactant. Do not graze or feed forage or hay from treated areas to livestock (dry-harvested straw may be used for bedding and/or feed). Do not apply through any type of irrigation system.
Days To Harvest: 45.
Crop Rotation: Do not plant to any crop other than wheat or barley for 60 days after application.
State Restrictions: Not for use in Alamosa, Conejos, Costilla, Rio Grande, and Saguache counties in Colorado.

– – – – – – – – – – – – – –

Signal Word/Toxicity Class: Caution.
REI: 12 hr.

FAR-GO

Controls wild oat. Fall application of granules is most consistent in some northern areas.

■ **PPI, PRE**

Far-Go 4E or 10G (triallate) *(Monsanto)*
Rate: Fall/spring treatment:
1 lb. ai/A
1 qt. 4E/A
Fall treatment:
1.25-1.5 lb. ai/A
12.5-15 lb. 10G/A
Spring treatment:
1-1.25 lb. ai/A
10-12.5 lb. 10G/A
Time: Preplant incorporated, preemergence incorporated. Fall treatment: Apply within 3 weeks of normal freeze-up. Spring treatment: Apply before or after seeding.
Weeds:
wild oat
Remarks: Spring, durum wheat. Do not graze livestock on treated fields. Refer to label for directions, precautions, and state restrictions.
Crop Rotation: Domestic oats should not be seeded when Far-Go was used the previous year.
State Restrictions: For use in Colorado, Idaho, Kansas, Minnesota, Montana, Nebraska, Nevada, North Dakota, Oregon, South Dakota, Utah, Washington, and Wyoming. In Montana, do not use on fields to be

seeded to hard, red spring wheat with press drills, if field is or will be irrigated in current growing season.

– – – – – – – – – – – – – –

Signal Word/Toxicity Class: Caution/III.
REI: 12 hr.

FENOXAPROP-P-ETHYL

■ **POST**

◆ **Puma (1EC)** *(AgrEvo USA)*
Rate: 0.04-0.08 lb. ai/A
0.33-0.66 pt. 1EC/A
Time: Postemergence. Apply to wheat from 2-leaf stage to 6-leaf stage.
Weeds:

barnyardgrass	hooded canarygrass	wild oat
blackgrass	proso millet	windgrass
foxtail millet	volunteer corn	yellow foxtail
green foxtail		

Remarks: Spring, durum wheat. Do not make more than one application or apply more than 0.66 pt./A per growing season. Do not apply any pesticides other than those listed on label within 5 days of application. Do not apply through any type of irrigation system or when wind conditions favor drift.
Days To Harvest: 70 days; 60 days in Minnesota, Montana, North Dakota, South Dakota.
Tank Mixes Ally, Amber, Banvel, Buctril, Bronate, Clarity, Curtail M, Express, Harmony Extra, Harmony GT, MCPA ester, Peak, Stinger, Starane, Tordon herbicides; Furadan 4F, Sevin XLR Plus insecticides. Benlate, Mertect, mancozeb, Tilt fungicides. Do not tank mix with other herbicides unless specifically recommended on label. Do not tank mix with malathion. Refer to label for limitations and state restrictions.

– – – – – – – – – – – – – –

Signal Word/Toxicity Class: Warning/II.
REI: 24 hr.

FINESSE (Premix)

Premix of sulfonylurea herbicides with same active ingredient as in Glean and Ally. Extended soil residual activity and provides very good to excellent control of many annual broadleaf weeds. Use limited to labeled states.

■ **PP, PRE, POST**

Finesse (DF) (62.5% chlorsulfuron & 12.5% metsulfuron-methyl)
(DuPont)
Rate: Preplant, preemergence, postemergence:
0.2-0.4 oz. DF/A
Preemergence (MN, MT, ND, SD, WY):
0.2-0.3 oz. DF/A
Time: Preplant, preemergence, postemergence. For postemergence, apply after crop is in 1-leaf stage but before boot stage. Do not apply during boot stage or early heading stage. For durum wheat and Wampum variety of spring wheat, apply postemergence only. Do not apply preemergence if wheat has germinated and has started to emerge above soil line or on wheat that has been planted into dry soil or on very coarse, uneven soilbeds.
Weeds: Broadleaf weeds:

annual sowthistle	flixweed*	prostrate pigweed
bedstraw*	groundsel	purslane
blue mustard	hempnettle	redroot pigweed
broadleaf dock	henbit	redstem filaree
bur beakchervil	ivyleaf speedwell*	Russian thistle*
bur buttercup	jagged chickweed	shepherdspurse
Canada thistle*	jim hill mustard	smallseed falseflax
Carolina geranium	kochia*	smooth pigweed
coast fiddleneck	ladysthumb	sunflower
common chickweed	lambsquarters	tansymustard*
common speedwell*	mayweed chamomile	tarweed
conical catchfly	minerslettuce	treacle mustard
corn gromwell*	mouseear chickweed	tumble mustard
corn spurry	Pennsylvania	vetch
cowcockle	smartweed*	Virginia pepperweed
curly dock	pineappleweed	white cockle
cutleaf	plains coreopsis	wild buckwheat
eveningprimrose	prickly lettuce	wild carrot
dovefoot geranium	prickly poppy	wild mustard
false chamomile	prostrate knotweed*	wild radish
field pennycress		

Grasses:

annual bluegrass*	cheat	green foxtail*
annual ryegrass*	downy brome	Japanese brome*

* *Suppression*

4

Small Grains

Remarks: Not underseeded with legumes and grasses. Do not apply less than 0.2 oz./A. Do not apply within 60 days of crop emergence if organophosphate insecticide has been applied in-furrow. Refer to label for restrictions and precautions.

Crop Rotation: Recropping depends on rate, soil pH, total rainfall, and geographic area. Refer to label for restrictions and pH limitations.

Tank Mixes: Banvel, Bronate, Buctril, Curtail, 2,4-D, Karmex. MCPA. Do not tank mix with malathion or, in Pacific Northwest, with Lorsban.

State Restrictions: Not for use in Alamosa, Conejos, Costilla, Rio Grande, and Saguache counties in Colorado.

– – – – – – – – – – – – – – –

Signal Word/Toxicity Class: Caution.
REI: 4 hr.

Formula 40 — see 2,4-D

GLEAN

Sulfonylurea herbicide with soil residual activity that extends 2 years or more. Recommended for use on land primarily dedicated to long-term production of wheat, barley, or oats. Gives very good to excellent control of many annual broadleaf weeds including mustard, kochia and pigweed. Note soil pH, rotation limitations, and minimum retreatment interval.

■ POST
Glean FC (DF) (chlorsulfuron) (DuPont)
Rate: 0.167-0.33 oz. DF/A
Time: Postemergence. Apply in the spring anytime after wheat is in 2-leaf stage but before boot stage (before flag leaf in Pacific Northwest); for Vic durum, apply after early tillering but before boot. Apply to small, actively growing weeds that are less than 2" tall or 2" across.
Weeds: Broadleaf weeds:

bedstraw*	flixweed	redroot pigweed
blue mustard	hempnettle	redstem filaree
bur beakchervil	henbit	Russian thistle*
buttercup	jim hill mustard	shepherdspurse
Canada thistle*	kochia*	smooth pigweed
coast fiddleneck	ladysthumb	speedwell*
common chickweed	lambsquarters	sunflower*
common groundsel*	mayweed	tansymustard*
conical catchfly	minerslettuce	tarweed
corn gromwell*	mouseear	treacle mustard
corn spurry	chickweed	tumble mustard
cowcockle	Pennsylvania	white cockle
curly dock	smartweed*	wild buckwheat*
cutleaf	pineappleweed	wild carrot
eveningprimrose	prickly lettuce*	wild mustard
false chamomile	prostrate knotweed*	wild radish*
falseflax	prostrate pigweed	wild turnip
field pennycress	purslane	yellow starthistle

Grasses:

annual ryegrass*

Aerial bulblet control:

wild garlic*　　　　wild onion*

* *Suppression*

Remarks: Spring, durum wheat. Not underseeded with legumes. Mix in water or directly into liquid nitrogen fertilizer solutions and apply as uniform broadcast spray. Add surfactant unless otherwise specified.
Crop Rotation: Recropping depends on rate, soil pH, total rainfall, and geographic area. Refer to label for soil pH restrictions.
Tank Mixes: Banvel, Bronate, Buctril, 2,4-D, Karmex, MCPA.
State Restrictions: For use in California, northern Idaho, Kansas, Nebraska, Oklahoma, Oregon, Texas, and Washington. Kochia and Russian thistle for central Kansas, Nebraska, Oklahoma, and northcentral Texas.

– – – – – – – – – – – – – – –

Signal Word/Toxicity Class: Caution.
REI: 4 hr.

Glyfos or Glyfos X-tra — see glyphosate

GLYPHOSATE

Very good to excellent control of annual grasses and annual broadleaf weeds prior to planting. Useful for reduced tillage systems. No soil residual activity. Ammonium sulfate at 17 lb./100 gal. improves results, especially where water quality is a factor. Do not allow glyphosate to contact desirable plants.

■ PP, PRE
◆ Credit (4WS) (Nufarm)

◆ **Glyfos or Glyfos X-tra (4WS)** *(Cheminova)*
Rattler (4WS) *(Helena)*
Roundup Custom (5.4WS) *(Monsanto)*
Roundup Original, Original RT, Ultra, Ultra RT (4WS) *(Monsanto)*

Rate: Annual weeds:
0.38-1.5 lb. ai/A
0.56-2.25 pt. 5.4WS/A
0.75-3 pt. 4WS/A
Perennial weeds:
0.5-5 lb. ai/A
0.75-7.5 pt. 5.4WS/A
1-10 pt. 4WS/A

Time: Preplant, preemergence, at-planting, spot treatment, wiper applications, preharvest, postharvest. For spot treatment, apply before heading. For preharvest, apply after hard dough stage.

Weeds: Most emerged annual and perennial broadleaf weeds including:

Canada thistle	field bindweed	kochia

Grasses:

downy brome	foxtail	quackgrass

Remarks: For preharvest application, do not apply to wheat grown for seed. Do not apply more than 1 lb. ai/A. Wheat stubble may be grazed immediately after harvest. Do not add surfactant to Roundup Ultra or Ultra RT. For spot treatment, do not treat more than 10% total area to be harvested. Do not use roller applicators for wiper application. Do not apply through any type of irrigation system. Refer to label for directions, precautions and restrictions.

Days To Harvest: Preharvest—7 days; wiper application—35 days; postharvest/feeding—8 weeks.

Tank Mixes: Postharvest: 2,4-D, dicamba. Roundup tank mixes not registered in California by air.

State Restrictions: Roundup RT for use in Colorado, Idaho, Montana, North Dakota, South Dakota, Utah, Wyoming, and in specific counties only in Kansas, Minnesota, Nebraska, Nevada, Oklahoma, Oregon, and Washington; refer to label for restrictions. Glyfos not registered for use in California. Glyfos X-tra not registered for use in mistblowers in California or Arizona.

– – – – – – – – – – – – – – –

Signal Word/Toxicity Class: Varies by formulation.
REI: Warning—12 hr.; Caution—4 hr.

■ PRE
Ranger (WS) (Monsanto)
Rate: 0.25-0.5 lb. ai/A
0.75-1.5 pt. WS/A broadcast
Time: Preemergence. Apply to vigorously growing weeds.
Weeds: Broadleaf weeds:

blue mustard	field pennycress	shepherdspurse
buttercup	horseweed	smallseed falseflax
cocklebur	London rocket	smooth pigweed
common groundsel	marestail	tansymustard
common lambsquarters	morningglory	tumble mustard
dwarfdandelion	mouseear chickweed	umbrella spurry
fanweed	redroot pigweed	wild mustard

Grasses:

annual bluegrass	downy brome	stinkgrass
barnyardgrass	fall panicum	Texas panicum
bulbous bluegrass	field sandbur	wild oat
cheat	Italian ryegrass	witchgrass
crabgrass	shattercane	

Rate: 1-2 lb. ai/A
3-6 pt. WS/A
Time: Preemergence. Apply to vigorously growing weeds.
Weeds: Grasses:

quackgrass	tall fescue	wirestem muhly

Remarks: For quackgrass control in the fall, do not till between harvest and application; in the spring, do not till in the fall or spring prior to application. Do not apply through any type of irrigation system. Do not feed or forage vegetation from treated areas within 8 weeks after application.

– – – – – – – – – – – – – – –

Signal Word/Toxicity Class: Danger/I.
REI: 12 hr.

Gramoxone Extra — see paraquat

HARMONY EXTRA (Premix)

Premix of sulfonylurea herbicides with no crop rotation limitations for the next season. Very good to excellent control of several annual broadleaf weeds including kochia, pigweed, and mustard. Good crop tolerance. Usually used with low rates of MCPA, 2,4-D, or other labeled broadleaf herbicides.

◆-new product • PP-preplant • PPI-preplant incorporated • PRE-preemergence • POST-postemergence • SEQ-sequential • ae-acid equivalent • ai-active ingredient • DF-dry flowable
E/EC-emulsifiable concentrate • F/FL-flowable • DG/G/WG-dispersable granule • L/LC-liquid • SP/WSP-soluble packet • W/WP-wettable powder • WSB-water soluble bag

■ POST

Harmony Extra (DF) (50% thifensulfuron-methyl & 25% tribenuron-methyl) *(DuPont)*

Rate: 0.3-0.6 oz. DF/A

Time: Early postemergence. Apply after wheat is in 2-leaf stage, but before flag leaf is visible.

Weeds: Broadleaf weeds:

annual knawel	cutleaf	prickly lettuce
annual sowthistle	eveningprimrose*	prostrate knotweed
black mustard	dogfennel	prostrate pigweed
blue mustard	false chamomile	purple mustard
broadleaf dock	field chickweed	redmaids rockpurslane
bur buttercup	field pennycress	redroot pigweed
bushy wallflower	filaree	Russian thistle
Canada thistle*	flixweed	scentless chamomile
Carolina geranium*	green smartweed	shepherdspurse
catchweed bedstraw*	hairy nightshade*	slimleaf lambsquarters
clasping pepperweed	henbit	smallflower buttercup
coast fiddleneck	jim hill mustard	smallseed falseflax
common chickweed	kochia	stinking chickweed
common cocklebur*	ladysthumb	stinking mayweed
common groundsel	little mallow*	swinecress
common lambsquarters	London rocket	tansymustard
common mallow*	marshelder	tarweed fiddleneck
common radish	minerslettuce	tumble mustard
common ragweed*	mouseearcress	volunteer lentils
common sunflower	narrowleaf	volunteer peas
common vetch*	lambsquarters	volunteer sunflower
corn chamomile	nightflowering	wild buckwheat
corn gromwell	catchfly	wild chamomile
corn spurry	Pennsylvania	wild garlic
cowcockle	smartweed	wild mustard
curly dock	pineappleweed	wild radish

* Partial control

Remarks: Spring, durum wheat. Do not apply to wheat underseeded with another crop. Add approved nonionic surfactant. Do not graze or feed forage or hay from treated areas to livestock; harvested straw may be used for bedding and/or feed.

Days To Harvest: 45.

Crop Rotation: Do not rotate to crops other than wheat, barley, or oats for 60 days after application; after 60 days any crop may be planted.

State Restrictions: Not for use in Alamosa, Conejos, Costilla, Rio Grande, and Saguache counties in Colorado.

– – – – – – – – – – – – – – – –

Signal Word/Toxicity Class: Caution.
REI: 12 hr.

Harmony GT — see thifensulfuron-methyl

Hi-Dep — see 2,4-D

HOELON

Provides selective control of wild oat, foxtail, and certain other annual grasses. Adjust rate according to weed species. Tank mix only according to directions. Restricted Use Pesticide.

■ POST

Hoelon 3EC (diclofop) *(AgrEvo USA)*

Rate: 0.75-1 lb. ai/A
2-2.66 pt. 3EC/A

Time: Postemergence. Apply when majority of wild oat and pigeongrass are in 1- to 4-leaf stage.

Weeds: Grasses including:

foxtail	pigeongrass	wild oat

Remarks: Spring, durum wheat. Refer to label for directions, precautions, and limitations.

Tank Mixes: Buctril, MCPA.

– – – – – – – – – – – – – – – –

Signal Word/Toxicity Class: Danger/I.
REI: 24 hr.

MCPA

Good crop tolerance at a wide range of crop growth stages. Most effective on mustards and lambsquarters. Frequently used in combination with other herbicides, especially when treatment must be made at early growth stages.

■ POST

Albaugh MCPA Amine 4 *(Albaugh)*

◆ Clean Crop MCP Amine 4 or Ester *(Platte)*
◆ Clean Crop MCP 2 Sodium (sodium salt) *(Platte)*
Riverdale MCPA-4 Amine *(Riverdale)*
Riverside MCPA Amine *(Terra)*
Wilbur-Ellis MCPA Amine, Ester or ◆ Sodium Salt (2EC) *(Wilbur-Ellis)*

Rate: 0.25-1.5 lb. ae/A
0.5-3 pt./A

Time: Postemergence. Apply low rate for more susceptible weeds after crop has reached 3-4 leaf stage up to boot stage; high rate after crop has tillered and up to early boot stage. Do not spray from boot to dough stage.

Rate: Emergency treatment:
1.5 lb. ae/A
6 pt. 2EC/A

Time: Postemergence. Apply in spring when weeds are approaching bud stage and grain if fully tillered and 8-10" tall. Do not spray from boot to dough stage.

Weeds: Broadleaf weeds:

annual mustard	lambsquarters	sowthistle
buttercup	marshelder	stinging nettle
Canada thistle	pigweed	stinkweed
dandelion	plantain	sunflower
dragonhead mint	puncturevine	vetch
field peppergrass	purslane	whitetop
goatsbeard	ragweed	wild radish
hempnettle	shepherdspurse	yellow rocket
kochia		

Remarks: Not underseeded with legumes. Do not forage or graze animals on treated areas within 7 days of slaughter or treatment.

State Restrictions: Wilbur-Ellis not registered in California.

– – – – – – – – – – – – – – – –

Rate: 0.125-0.25 lb. ae/A
0.25-0.5 pt./A

Time: Postemergence. Apply after crop is well tillered in the 4-leaf stage (4-8" tall) when legumes are 2-3" tall. Do not spray from boot to dough stage.

Weeds: Emergency control of:

mustard	yellow rocket

Remarks: Underseeded with legumes (alfalfa, lespedeza, red and white clover). Balance severity of weed problem against possibility of crop damage. Do not forage or graze animals on treated areas within 7 days of slaughter or treatment.

State Restrictions: Wilbur-Ellis not registered in California.

– – – – – – – – – – – – – – – –

Signal Word/Toxicity Class: Danger/I (amine); Warning/II (ester).
REI: Danger—48 hr.; Warning—12 hr.

■ POST

Albaugh MCPA Ester 4 *(Albaugh)*
Solve MCPA Ester (4) *(Albaugh)*

Rate: 0.25-1.5 lb. ae/A
0.5-3 pt. 4/A

Time: Postemergence. Apply low rate for more susceptible weeds after crop has reached 3-4 leaf stage up to boot stage; use high rate for less susceptible weeds after crop has tillered and up to early boot stage. Do not spray from boot to dough stage.

Weeds: Broadleaf weeds:

annual mustard	goatsbeard	puncturevine
annual sowthistle	goosefoot	ragweed
beggarticks	hempnettle	shepherdspurse
cocklebur	lambsquarters	stinkweed
dragonhead mint	marshelder	wild radish
fanweed	pennycress	wintercress
field peppergrass	poison hemlock	yellow rocket

Remarks: Do not forage or graze meat animals on treated areas within 7 days of slaughter; dairy animals within 7 days after treatment.

– – – – – – – – – – – – – – – –

Signal Word/Toxicity Class: Caution/III.
REI: 12 hr.

■ POST

Chiptox (sodium salt) *(Nufarm)*

Rate: 0.125-0.25 lb. ae/A
0.5-1 pt./A

Time: Postemergence. Apply when legumes are 2-3" tall, grain is fully tillered but before forming joints in stem. Do not spray in boot to dough stage.

Weeds: Broadleaf weeds:

annual mustard	lambsquarters	stinging nettle
buttercup	peppergrass	stinkweed
Canada thistle	plantain	vetch
cocklebur	purslane	whitetop
dandelion	ragweed	wild radish
hempnettle	shepherdspurse	wintercress
hoary cress	sowthistle	yellow rocket
kochia		

4

Small Grains

NOTICE	The information on these pages is for preliminary planning — not a guide for use. Be sure to follow the manufacturer's directions, notwithstanding information contained here.	For personal protective equipment and EPA registration numbers, please turn to page 70.

Remarks: Underseeded with mixed legumes. Use 5-6 gal. water/A; higher volumes may cause injury to legumes. Do not forage or graze treated fields for 2 weeks or feed treated straw to livestock.

Rate: 0.25-1 lb. ae/A
1-4 pt./A

Time: Postemergence. Apply when grain is fully tillered but before forming joints in the stem. Do not spray in boot to dough stage.

Rate: Emergency treatment:
1.5 lb. ae/A
6 pt./A

Time: Postemergence. Apply when weeds are approaching bud stage. Do not spray from boot to dough stage.

Weeds: Same as above.

Remarks: Not underseeded with legumes. Use 6 pt. rate as emergency treatment for controlling perennial broadleaf weeds; balance severity of weed problem against possible crop injury.

Signal Word/Toxicity Class: Danger/I.
REI: 48 hr.

■ POST

Gordon's MCPA Amine 4 *(PBI/Gordon)*
Rhomene 4 (amine) *(Nufarm)*

Rate: 0.25-1 lb. ae/A
0.5-2 pt./A

Time: Postemergence. For lower rate, apply after grain is in 4-leaf stage but not forming joints in the stem; for rates over 1 pt., apply after grain is fully tillered. Do not spray in boot to dough stage.

Weeds: Broadleaf weeds:

bull thistle	dandelion	pigweed
common burdock	field pennycress	plantain
common cocklebur	giant ragweed	purslane
common	mustard (except blue)	Russian thistle
lambsquarters	pepperweed	shepherdspurse
common ragweed	(except perennial)	yellow rocket

Remarks: Not underseeded with legumes. For emergency perennial broadleaf weed control, use 3 pt. rate when weeds approach bud stage, balance severity of weed problem against possible crop damage; spot treat scattered perennial weeds.

Rate: 0.25 lb. ae/A
0.5 pt./A

Time: Postemergence. Apply after crop is well tillered in the 4-leaf stage (4-8" tall) when legumes are 2-3" tall. Do not spray from boot to dough stage.

Weeds: Emergency control of:

mustard	yellow rocket

Remarks: Underseeded with legumes. Do not apply to grain underseeded with vetch or sweet clover. Do not use more than 6 gal. water/A; higher volumes may result in injury to legumes. Do not forage or graze animals on treated areas within 7 days of slaughter or treatment.

Signal Word/Toxicity Class: Danger/I.
REI: 48 hr.

■ POST

Rhonox (LV ester) *(Nufarm)*

Rate: 0.23-0.69 lb. ae/A
0.5-1.5 pt./A

Time: Postemergence. For lower rate, apply after grain is in 4-leaf stage but not forming joints in the stem; for rates over 1 pt., apply after grain is fully tillered. Do not spray in boot to dough stage.

Weeds: Broadleaf weeds:

annual sowthistle	pennycress	ragweed
dandelion	peppergrass	shepherdspurse
hempnettle	perennial sowthistle	stinkweed
kochia	pigweed	wild radish
lambsquarters	plantain	yellow rocket
mustard	purslane	

Remarks: Not underseeded to legumes. Do not forage or graze meat animals on treated fields within 7 days of slaughter. Refer to label for further use directions.

Signal Word/Toxicity Class: Caution.
REI: 12 hr.

■ POST

Riverdale MCPA L.V. 4, IOE (5.2) (ester) *(Riverdale)*
Sword (5.2) (ester) *(Platte)*

Rate: 0.25-1.5 lb. ae/A
0.5-3 pt. L.V. 4/A
0.2-1.3 lb. ae/A
0.33-2 pt. 5.2/A

Time: Postemergence. Apply low rate for more susceptible weeds after crop has reached 3-4 leaf stage up to boot stage; high rate after crop has tillered and up to early boot stage. Do not spray from boot to dough stage.

Weeds: Broadleaf weeds:

annual mustard	lambsquarters	sowthistle
buttercup	marshelder	stinging nettle
Canada thistle	pigweed	stinkweed
dandelion	plantain	sunflower
dragonhead mint	purslane	vetch
field peppergrass	puncturevine	whitetop
goatsbeard	ragweed	wild radish
hempnettle	shepherdspurse	yellow rocket
kochia		

Remarks: Not underseeded with legumes. Do not forage or graze animals on treated areas within 7 days of slaughter or treatment.

Rate: 0.125-0.25 lb. ae/A
0.25-0.5 pt. L.V.4/A
3-6 oz. 5.2/A

Time: Postemergence. Apply after crop is well tillered in the 4-leaf stage (4-8" tall) when legumes are 2-3" tall. Do not spray from boot to dough stage.

Weeds: Emergency control of:

mustard	yellow rocket

Remarks: Underseeded with legumes (alfalfa, lespedeza, red and white clover). Balance severity of weed problem against possibility of crop damage. Do not forage or graze animals on treated areas within 7 days of slaughter or treatment.

Signal Word/Toxicity Class: Warning/II.
REI: 12 hr.

Moxy — see bromoxynil

Opti-Amine — see 2,4-D

Paramount — see quinclorac

PARAQUAT

Nonselective control of emerged weeds prior to planting. Controls grasses and broadleaf weeds. Spray coverage is important. No soil residual activity. Used in no-till systems. Toxic to wildlife. Restricted Use Pesticide.

■ PP, PRE

Cyclone (2L or 3L) or Gramoxone Extra (2.5L) *(ZENECA)*

Rate: 0.5-1 lb. ai/A
2-4 pt. 2L/A
1.5-3 pt. 2.5L/A
1.25-2.5 pt. 3L/A

Time: Preplant, preemergence. Apply broadcast or band prior to, during, or after planting but before crop emergence.

Weeds: Annual broadleaf weeds and grasses; suppression of perennials.

Remarks: Add nonionic surfactant or crop oil concentrate. Seedbeds should be formed as far ahead of planting and treatment as possible to permit maximum weed and grass emergence. Seeding should be done with minimum amount of soil disturbance. Weeds and grasses emerging after planting will not be controlled; crops emerged at time of application may be killed. Do not apply preplant or preemergence to soils lacking clay minerals. Refer to label for use directions, restrictions, and precautions.

Tank Mixes: Atrazine, Banvel, Bicep, Bladex, Canopy, Command, 2,4-D ester, Extrazine, Lariat, linuron, Marksman, metribuzin, Princep.

Signal Word/Toxicity Class: Danger-Poison/I.
REI: 12 hr. (except harvest aid/desiccation 24 hr.).

PEAK

Controls many broadleaf weeds, including triazine-resistant biotypes, by inhibiting a biochemical process which produces certain essential amino acids necessary for plant growth. The inhibited enzyme system is acetolactate synthase (ALS). Peak is a water-dispersible granule; each bag of Peak contains 5 water-soluble packets.

◆-new product • PP-preplant • PPI-preplant incorporated • PRE-preemergence • POST-postemergence • SEQ-sequential • ae-acid equivalent • ai-active ingredient • DF-dry flowable
E/EC-emulsifiable concentrate • F/FL-flowable • DG/G/WG-dispersable granule • L/LC-liquid • SP/WSP-soluble packet • W/WP-wettable powder • WSB-water soluble bag

■ POST
Peak (WDG) (prosulfuron) (Novartis)
Rate: Low rate:
0.38 oz. WDG/A (1 WS packet/8A)
Standard rate:
0.5 oz. WDG/A (1 WS packet/6A)
Time: Postemergence (over-the-top). Apply from 3-leaf stage to before second node is detectable in stem elongation.
Weeds: Broadleaf weeds:

blue mustard	flixweed	prickly sida
buffalobur	Florida pusley	prostrate knotweed*
bur cherval	giant ragweed	puncturevine
bushy wallflower	hairy buttercup	redroot pigweed
Canada thistle*	hedge bindweed*	Russian thistle
coast fiddleneck	hemp sesbania	shepherdspurse
common chickweed*	henbit*	sicklepod
common cocklebur	ivyleaf morningglory	smooth pigweed
common lambsquarters*	jimsonweed	tall morningglory
	kochia*	tall waterhemp
common mallow*	mayweed chamomile	tansymustard
common ragweed	minerslettuce	tumble mustard
common sunflower	mouseear chickweed*	tumble pigweed
common waterhemp	Palmer amaranth*	velvetleaf
corn gromwell*	Pennsylvania smartweed	Venice mallow
cutleaf eveningprimrose	pineappleweed	wild buckwheat
	pitted morningglory	wild garlic
devilsclaw	prickly lettuce	wild mustard
field bindweed*		wild radish
field pennycress		

* *Suppression*

Remarks: Rate varies by weed height. Always add crop oil concentrate or nonionic surfactant. Do not apply to crop under stress. Do not make a foliar or soil application with an organophosphate insecticide within 15 days before or 10 days after application. Do not apply through any type of irrigation system.
Days To Harvest: Silage—40; grain—60; grazing/feeding forage to livestock—30.
Crop Rotation: IR/IMR Corn—anytime; normal field corn, grain sorghum—4 weeks; rice, popcorn, sweet corn, small grains (wheat, barley, oats, rye, proso millet, triticale)—2 months; beans (dry, green), cabbage, canola, cotton, flax, forage grasses, peanuts, peas, potatoes, soybeans, tobacco, tomatoes—9 months; alfalfa, clover, lentils—15 months; leeks, onion, sunflower, sugar beets—24 months; all other crops—18 months.
Tank Mixes: Low rate: Banvel, Bronate, Buctril, 2,4-D, MCPA; refer to label for use instructions.
State Restrictions: Not for use in San Luis Valley of Colorado, west of the Cascades in Oregon, and certain areas of Washington (abide by all sulfonylurea aerial application rulings by Washington Department of Agriculture).

— — — — — — — — — — — — —

Signal Word/Toxicity Class: Caution.
REI: 12 hr.

Phenoxy 088 — see 2,4-D

PROPANIL

Postemergence herbicide that controls green and yellow foxtail, pigweed, wild buckwheat, and wild mustard when tank mixed with MCPA. Control of grasses is reduced if weeds exceed stated growth stage.

■ POST
Stampede 80EDF (Rohm and Haas)
Rate: 1-1.13 lb. ai/A
1.25-1.4 pt. 80EDF/A
Time: Postemergence. Apply 10-17 days after crop emergence when grain is in 3-4 leaf stage; for foxtail, apply at 2-3 leaf stage. Do not apply to hard red spring wheat beyond 5-leaf stage or to durum wheat beyond 4-leaf stage.
Weeds: Broadleaf weeds:

common lambsquarters	prostrate pigweed	wild buckwheat
kochia	redroot pigweed	wild mustard

Grasses:

green foxtail	yellow foxtail

Remarks: Hard red spring wheat, durum wheat. Do not apply to grain crops that have been or will be treated with carbamate or organophosphorus insecticides. Do not apply through any type of irrigation system. Do not graze treated crop or cut for green chop feed.
Tank Mixes: MCPA.
State Restrictions: For use in Minnesota, Montana, North Dakota, and South Dakota.

— — — — — — — — — — — — —

Signal Word/Toxicity Class: Caution.
REI: 24 hr.

Puma — see fenoxaprop-P-ethyl

QUINCLORAC

■ PP
◆ Paramount (DF) (BASF)
Rate: 3-5.3 oz. DF/A
Time: Preplant. Apply to actively growing weeds. For bindweed, apply after harvest but before first killing frost. For long-term control (3 yr. program), apply 5.3 oz. DF/A the first year and 3-5.3 oz. DF/A in subsequent years.
Weeds: Broadleaf weeds:

bedstraw	dandelion*	morningglory
Canada thistle*	field bindweed*	Russian thistle*
clover	giant ragweed*	velvetleaf*
common lambsquarters*	hedge bindweed	volunteer flax
	kochia*	wild sunflower*
common ragweed*		

Grasses:

barnyardgrass	giant foxtail	large crabgrass
broadleaf signalgrass	green foxtail	yellow foxtail

* *Suppression*

Remarks: Must use additive. Do not apply more than 16 oz. DF/A per calendar year. Do not apply through any type of irrigation system.
Crop Rotation: In case of crop failure, wheat and sorghum may be replanted immediately; other crops—10 months after application; alfalfa, clover, flax, lentils, peas, sugar beets—24 months and successful field bioassy.
Tank Mixes: Clarity, 2,4-D, Fallowmaster, Landmaster, Roundup RT, Roundup Ultra; refer to labels for use directions.
State Restrictions: For use in Colorado, Idaho, Kansas, Montana, Nebraska, North Dakota, Oregon, South Dakota, Utah, Washington, Wyoming.

— — — — — — — — — — — — —

Signal Word/Toxicity Class: Caution.
REI: 12 hr.

Ranger — see glyphosate

Rattler — see glyphosate

RAVE (Premix)

Premix with 2 modes of action. One active ingredient inhibits the acetolactate synthase (ALS) enzyme. The other active ingredient disrupts normal plant growth.

■ POST
◆ Rave (WDG) (50% dicamba & 8.8% triasulfuron) (Novartis)
Rate: 4 oz. WDG/A
Time: Postemergence. Apply after emergence up to 6-leaf stage.
Weeds: Broadleaf weeds:

annual morningglory	cutleaf eveningprimrose	pepperweed
annual polemonium		pigweed
annual sowthistle	fanweed	plains coreopsis
black nightshade	field bindweed	prickly lettuce
blue mustard	field pennycress	prostrate knotweed
bur buttercup	fleabane	prostrate pigweed
bushy wallflower	flixweed	puncturevine
Canada thistle	forget-me-not	ragweed
coast fiddleneck	giant ragweed	redroot pigweed
common broomweed	goldenrod	Russian thistle
common chickweed	hairy vetch	shepherdspurse
common cocklebur	henbit	smooth pigweed
common groundsel	horseweed	tall buttercup
common lambsquarters	houndstongue	tall hedge mustard
	Indian mustard	tansymustard
common mallow	jagged chickweed	tartary buckwheat
common purslane	kochia	tarweed
common ragweed	ladysthumb	tumble mustard
common sunflower	lanceleaf ragweed	tumble pigweed
common yarrow	London rocket	umbrella spurry
corn chamomile	marestail	velvetleaf
corn cockle	marshelder	Virginia pepperweed
corn gromwell	minerslettuce	wild buckwheat
cornflower	musk thistle	wild mustard
creeping buttercup	mustard	wild radish
curly dock	Pennsylvania smartweed	woolly croton

Remarks: Do not apply to wheat undersown with legumes or forage grasses. Do not apply to wheat under stress. Do not apply for at least 60 days after an organophosphate application. Do not apply through any type of irrigation system.

Days To Harvest: Hay, grain—37.

Crop Rotation: Recropping depends on field bioassay, soil pH, total rainfall, and geographic area. Refer to label for restrictions and more complete information.

Tank Mixes: Bronate, Buctril, 2,4-D, MCPA, Tilt.

State Restrictions: For use in Colorado (except San Luis Valley), Idaho, Kansas, Minnesota, Montana, Nebraska, Nevada, New Mexico, North Dakota, Oklahoma, Oregon, South Dakota, Texas, Utah, Washington, Wyoming. In Washington, abide by all sulfonylurea aerial application rulings by Washington Department of Agriculture.

- - - - - - - - - - - - - - -

Signal Word/Toxicity Class: Caution.
REI: 12 hr.

Rhomene — see MCPA

Rhonox — see MCPA

Roundup — see glyphosate

Saber — see 2,4-D

Salvo — see 2,4-D

Savage — see 2,4-D

SCYTHE

◆ **Scythe (pelargonic acid)** *(Mycogen)*
Rate: 4-13 fl. oz./1 gal. spray solution
Time: Apply to actively growing weeds prior to crop emergence.
Weeds: Annual and perennial broadleaf weeds and grasses.
Remarks: Apply in minimum 75 gal. spray solution/A or spray-to-wet. Do not apply by air or through any type of irrigation system. Refer to label for directions and precautions.
Tank Mixes: Glyphosate and other foliar and residual herbicides.

- - - - - - - - - - - - - - -

Signal Word/Toxicity Class: Warning/II.
REI: 24 hr.

Solution — see 2,4-D

Solve — see 2,4-D; MCPA

Stampede — see propanil

Sterling — see dicamba

Stinger — see clopyralid

SUREFIRE (Premix)
Restricted Use Pesticide.

■ **PP, PRE**
◆ **Surefire (29.4% paraquat & 10.6% diuron)** *(Platte)*
Rate: 0.8-1.6 lb. ai/A
2-4 pt./A
Time: Apply to young, succulent weeds 1-6" high prior to, during or after planting, but before crop emergence.
Weeds: Annual broadleaf weeds and grasses; top-kill and suppression of perennial weeds.

Remarks: Always use nonionic surfactant. Do not apply through any type of irrigation system. Do not apply to soils lacking clay minerals. Seeding should be done with a minimum amount of soil disturbance. Crop plants emerged at time of treatment will be killed. Refer to label for directions and precautions.
Tank Mixes: AAtrex, Banvel, Bladex, 2,4-D, Glean, Kerb.

- - - - - - - - - - - - - - -

Signal Word/Toxicity Class: Danger/I.
REI: 12 hr.

Sword — see MCPA

THIFENSULFURON-METHYL

■ **POST**
Harmony GT (DF) *(DuPont)*
Rate: 0.3-0.6 oz. DF/A
Time: Postemergence. Apply to young, actively growing weeds after crop is in 2-leaf stage, but before flag leaf is visible.
Weeds: Broadleaf weeds:

annual knawel	dogfennel	redmaids rockpurslane
annual sowthistle	false chamomile	redroot pigweed
black mustard	field pennycress	Russian thistle
bushy wallflower	flixweed	scentless chamomile
Carolina geranium*	green smartweed	shepherdspurse
coast fiddleneck	henbit*	smallflower buttercup
common buckwheat	jim hill mustard	stinking mayweed
common chickweed	kochia	swinecress
common cocklebur*	ladysthumb	tansymustard*
common groundsel	little mallow*	tarweed fiddleneck
common	London rocket	tumble mustard
lambsquarters	marshelder	volunteer lentils
common mallow*	minerslettuce	volunteer peas
common sunflower*	mouseear chickweed	volunteer sunflower
corn chamomile	mouseearcress	wild buckwheat
corn spurry	Pennsylvania	wild chamomile
curly dock	smartweed	wild garlic
cutleaf	prickly lettuce*	wild mustard
eveningprimrose*	prostrate knotweed	wild radish*

* *Suppression*

Remarks: Not underseeded. Add approved nonionic surfactant. Do not apply through any type of irrigation system. Prevent spray drift to desirable plants. Do not graze or feed forage or hay from treated areas to livestock (harvested straw may be used for bedding and/or feed). Refer to label for restrictions and precautions.
Crop Rotation: Barley, oats, wheat—anytime; all other crops—45 days after application.
Tank Mixes: Assert, Avenge, bromoxynil, 2,4-D, dicamba, Hoelon, MCPA.
State Restrictions: Not for use in Alamosa, Conejos, Costilla, Rio Grande, and Saguache counties in Colorado.

- - - - - - - - - - - - - - -

Signal Word/Toxicity Class: Caution.
REI: 4 hr.

TILLER (Premix)

Three-way premix applied postemergence for foxtail, volunteer millet, and wild oat. Rate varies according to weed. Crop tolerance is best after tillering. Performance has been good.

■ **POST**
Tiller (0.375 lb./gal. fenoxaprop-P-ethyl & 0.58 lb./gal. 2,4-D ester & 1.75 lb./gal. MCPA) *(AgrEvo USA)*
Rate: 0.34-0.57 lb. ai/A
1-1.7 pt. EC/A
Time: Postemergence. Crop: tiller initiation (3-4 leaf) to end of tillering (6 leaf). Broadleaf weeds: up to 4" in height; grass weeds: 2 leaf-2 tiller.
Weeds: Broadleaf weeds:

annual sowthistle	purslane	tumble mustard
common	ragweed	wild mustard
lambsquarters	shepherdspurse	wild radish
field pennycress		

Grasses:

barnyardgrass	foxtail millet	wild oat
blackgrass	proso millet	windgrass
green foxtail	volunteer corn	yellow foxtail

Remarks: Can be used on all hard red spring wheat varieties except NK 751 and on soft white spring wheat varieties Centennial, Sprite, Wakanz, and Waverly. Do not apply through any type of irrigation system. Do not graze or feed treated forage, hay or straw.
Days To Harvest: Minnesota, Montana, North Dakota, South Dakota—60; all other states—70.

◆-new product • PP-preplant • PPI-preplant incorporated • PRE-preemergence • POST-postemergence • SEQ-sequential • ae-acid equivalent • ai-active ingredient • DF-dry flowable
E/EC-emulsifiable concentrate • F/FL-flowable • DG/G/WG-dispersable granule • L/LC-liquid • SP/WSP-soluble packet • W/WP-wettable powder • WSB-water soluble bag

210   Weed Control Manual 2000

Tank Mixes: Ally, Amber, Banvel, Buctril, Express, Harmony Extra, MCPA ester, Stinger, Tordon herbicides; Furadan, Sevin XLR insecticides. Tank mix varies depending on grassy weed targeted for control.

– – – – – – – – – – – – – –

Signal Word/Toxicity Class: Warning/II.
REI: 12 hr. unless soil injected or soil incorporated.

TORDON

Not for use on durum wheat or on land planted to sweet sorghum. Restricted Use Pesticide.

Tordon 22K (picloram) *(Dow AgroSciences)*
Rate: 1-1.5 fl. oz. 22K/A
Time: Apply from 3- to 5-leaf stage to early jointing stage of growth.
Weeds: Broadleaf weeds such as:

Canada thistle	pennycress	volunteer sunflower
lambsquarters	pigweed	wild buckwheat
mayweed	Russian thistle	wild mustard

Remarks: Not underseeded with legumes. Not flood or subirrigated. May cause shorter straw on some varieties of cereals but grain yields are usually not affected. Do not apply more than 1.5 fl. oz./A during growing season. Do not graze or feed forage from treated areas for 2 weeks after treatment or harvest hay from treated fields. Do not apply through any type of irrigation system. Refer to label for restrictions and precautions.
Days To Harvest: 50.
Crop Rotation: Use only on land to be planted the following year to grass, barley, oats, wheat, grain sorghum, or fallow. Do no plant grain sorghum within 8 months after application. Do not rotate broadleaf crops.
Tank Mixes: 2,4-D, MCPA.
State Restrictions: For use west of the Mississippi except San Luis Valley of Colorado. Use in Hawaii limited to supplemental labeling.

– – – – – – – – – – – – – –

Signal Word/Toxicity Class: Caution.
REI: 12 hr.

Treflan — see trifluralin

TRI-4 — see trifluralin

TRIFLURALIN

Incorporate preplant or postplant as directed for the particular formulation for your area. Also used in fallow period prior to planting spring wheat the following season. Adjust rate according to time of application and soil type.

■ PRE
Albaugh Trifluralin 4EC *(Albaugh)*
◆ **Clean Crop Trifluralin HF (4EC)** *(Platte)*
Gowan Trifluralin 4 or 5 (EC) or 10G *(Gowan)*
Helena Trifluralin 4 EC *(Helena)*
Riverside Trifluralin 4EC or Trific 60DF *(Terra)*
◆ **Sedagri Trifluralin 480 (4EC)** *(Rhone-Poulenc)*
Treflan HFP (4EC) or TR-10 (10G) *(Dow AgroSciences)*
TRI-4 HF (4EC) *(American Cyanamid)*
Trilin 4 or 5 (EC) or 10G *(Griffin)*
Wilbur-Ellis Trifluralin 10G *(Wilbur-Ellis)*
Rate: 0.5-0.75 lb. ai/A
1-1.5 pt. 4EC/A
0.8-1.2 pt. 5EC/A
0.875-1.25 lb. 60DF/A
5-7.5 lb. 10G/A
Time: Postplant incorporated. Apply after seeding but before crop emergence.
Weeds:

foxtail	pigeongrass

Remarks: Spring, durum wheat. Double incorporate with flextine or diamond harrow 1-1½" deep. Make second incorporation in different direction from the first within 24 hr. of application. Under certain conditions, delayed crop emergence or stand reduction may occur; refer to label for directions, restrictions, and precautions.
Crop Rotation: Refer to label.
State Restrictions: Wilbur-Ellis not registered in California.

– – – – – – – – – – – – – –

Signal Word/Toxicity Class: Varies by formulation.
REI: 12 hr. unless soil injected or soil incorporated.

Trilin — see trifluralin

Weed Rhap — see 2,4-D

Weedar — see 2,4-D

Weedestroy — see 2,4-D

Weedone — see 2,4-D

Barley

ACHIEVE

Systemic postemergence herbicide for control of selective grasses. Does not control broadleaf weeds. Rainfast within 1 hr. Comes prepackaged with its own adjuvant.

■ POST
◆ **Achieve 40DG (tralkoxydim)** *(ZENECA)*
Rate: 0.18-0.24 lb. ai/A
0.44-0.6 lb. 40DG/A
Time: Postemergence. Apply 1- to 4-leaf stage for ryegrass and Persian darnel; 1- to 5-leaf stage for foxtail; 1- to 6-leaf stage for wild oat.
Weeds: Grasses:

annual ryegrass	Italian ryegrass	wild oat
green foxtail	Persian darnel	yellow foxtail

Remarks: Apply by ground or air. Use high rate when soil is dry, weeds are large, weed population is high, or crop canopy is dense. Maximum seasonal application is 0.25 lb. ai/A. Do not apply to crops or weeds with heavy dew cover. Do not apply through any type of irrigation system. Refer to label for use directions, restrictions, and precautions.
Days To Harvest: 60; grazed or cut for hay—30; straw or grain fed to livestock—45.
Crop Rotation: Cereal grains, leafy crops—30 days after application; all other crops—106 days after application.
Tank Mixes: Buctril, Bronate, Curtail M, Stinger.

– – – – – – – – – – – – – –

Signal Word/Toxicity Class: Caution.
REI: 12 hr. unless soil injected or soil incorporated.

ALLY

Early postemergence sulfonylurea herbicide that controls several annual broadleaf weeds. Especially effective for mustards, kochia, and pigweeds. Not intended for grassy weeds. Best results on small weeds; control of larger mustards has been good. A tank mix with another herbicide with a different mode of action is suggested for most situations. Follow soil pH, crop rotation, and minimum use interval guidelines for your area.

■ POST
Ally (DF) (metsulfuron-methyl) *(DuPont)*
Rate: 0.1 oz. DF/A
Time: Postemergence. Apply from 2-leaf stage but before boot stage. Do not apply during boot stage or early heading.
Weeds: Broadleaf weeds:

blue mustard	field pennycress	Russian thistle
bur buttercup	filaree	shepherdspurse
Canada thistle*	flixweed	slimleaf
coast fiddleneck	green smartweed	lambsquarters
common chickweed	henbit	smallseed falseflax
common groundsel	jim hill mustard	smooth pigweed
common	kochia	sowthistle*
lambsquarters	ladysthumb	tansymustard
common purslane	mayweed	tarweed
common sunflower*	minerslettuce	treacle mustard
conical catchfly	pale smartweed	tumble mustard
corn cockle	plains coreopsis	tumble pigweed
corn gromwell*	prickly lettuce	volunteer sunflower
cowcockle	prostrate knotweed*	waterpod
false chamomile	purple mustard	wild buckwheat*
fanweed	redroot pigweed	wild mustard

Grasses:
annual ryegrass*
* *Suppression*

– – – – – – – – – – – – – –

NOTICE	The information on these pages is for preliminary planning — not a guide for use. Be sure to follow the manufacturer's directions, notwithstanding information contained here.	For personal protective equipment and EPA registration numbers, please turn to page 70.

Remarks: Winter, spring barley. Add 1-2 pt. 80% nonionic surfactant/100 gal. spray volume. Refer to label for restrictions and precautions. Do not apply through any type of irrigation system.

Crop Rotation: Determined by crop to be planted and minimum rotation interval. Minimum rotation interval is from last application to anticipated date of planting. For maximum rotational flexibility, do not treat all your barley acres.

Tank Mixes: Banvel, 2,4-D, MCPA.

State Restrictions: Not for use in Alamosa, Conejos, Costilla, Rio Grande, and Saguache counties in Colorado.

- - - - - - - - - - - - - - -

Signal Word/Toxicity Class: Caution/III.
REI: 4 hr.

AMBER

Selective sulfonylurea herbicide with extended soil residual activity. Especially effective for mustard and kochia. Tank mix with a low rate of broadleaf herbicide with a different mode of action. Follow crop rotational guidelines and rotational intervals based on soil pH.

■ **PRE, POST**

Amber Accu-Pak or CustomPak (WDG) (triasulfuron) *(Novartis)*
Rate: 0.28-0.56 oz. WDG/A
Time: Postemergence. Apply when weeds are actively growing.
Weeds: Broadleaf weeds:

annual fleabane	field pennycress	puncturevine
annual polemonium	flixweed	redroot pigweed
blue mustard (purple)	forget-me-not	rough fleabane
bushy wallflower	giant ragweed	Russian thistle
bur buttercup	hairy vetch	shepherdspurse
buttercup	henbit*	smooth pigweed
Canada thistle*	horseweed	spring whitlowgrass
coast fiddleneck	Indian mustard	tall buttercup
common broomweed	jagged chickweed	tall hedge mustard
common chickweed	jim hill mustard	tansymustard
common cocklebur	kochia	tumble mustard
common mallow	lanceleaf ragweed	Virginia pepperweed
common purslane	London rocket	western ragweed*
common ragweed	marshelder	wild buckwheat
common sunflower	minerslettuce	wild garlic*
common yarrow	morningglory*	wild mustard
corn gromwell	plains coreopsis	wild onion*
cutleaf	prickly lettuce	wild radish
eveningprimrose	prostrate knotweed	woolly croton
fanweed	prostrate pigweed	

* Suppression

Remarks: Do not apply to barley undersown with legumes or forage grasses. Do not use alone in any field where sulfonylurea-resistant biotypes of any weed species have been identified. Refer to label for further use directions, restrictions, and precautions.

Crop Rotation: Wheat—anytime; proso millet—4 months; barley, oats, rye, Bermudagrass—6 months (with conditions); grain sorghum and soybeans—14 months (with conditions). All other crops may be seeded only at completion of successful field bioassay; refer to label.

State Restrictions: For use in Colorado (except San Luis Valley), Idaho, Kansas, Minnesota, Montana, Nebraska, Nevada, New Mexico, North Dakota, Oklahoma, South Dakota, Texas, Utah, Wyoming, and east of the Cascades in Oregon or Washington.

- - - - - - - - - - - - - - -

Signal Word/Toxicity Class: Caution/III.
REI: 12 hr.

ASSERT

Postemergence application controls wild oat and wild mustard. Not for foxtail. Control is very good and crop tolerance is excellent. Some crop rotation limitations.

■ **POST**

Assert (2.5LC) (imazamethabenz methyl) *(American Cyanamid)*
Rate: 0.31-0.48 lb. ai/A
1-1.5 pt. 2.5LC/A
Time: Postemergence. Apply when barley is in 2-5 leaf stage (prior to jointing); wild oat in 1-4 leaf stage. For Avenge tank mix, apply from 2-5 leaf stage of wild oat. Do not apply when barley flagleaf is exposed.
Weeds: Broadleaf weeds:

catchweed bedstraw	London rocket	wild buckwheat
field pennycress	tansymustard	wild mustard
flixweed	tartary buckwheat	

Grasses:

interrupted windgrass	roughstalk bluegrass	wild oat

Remarks: Rate varies by state; refer to label. Add 2 pt. 80% nonionic surfactant/100 gal. spray solution. When weeds are under moisture or temperature stress, 1.5-2 pt. SUN-IT II spray adjuvant may be used instead of nonionic surfactant. Wheat straw may be fed or used for bedding. Do not apply through any type of irrigation system. Do not graze treated fields or cut treated forage for silage or hay.

Crop Rotation: Barley, canola (IMI-tolerant varieties such as Pioneer 45A71, 46A72; non-IMI tolerant in certain counties in Minnesota and North Dakota), corn, edible beans, safflower, soybeans, sunflower, wheat—anytime; sugar beets—20 months; other crops—15 months after application.

Tank Mixes: Ally, Amber, Avenge (wild oat only), bromoxynil + MCPA ester, Canvas, Curtail M, 2,4-D ester, Express, Finesse, Glean, Harmony, Harmony Extra, MCPA ester, Starane.

- - - - - - - - - - - - - - -

Signal Word/Toxicity Class: Danger/I.
REI: 48 hr.

AVENGE

Postemergence herbicide for selective wild oat control. Does not control other annual grasses or broadleaf weeds. Crop tolerance is good under most conditions.

■ **POST**

Avenge (2ASU) (difenzoquat) *(American Cyanamid)*
Rate: 0.625-1 lb. ai/A
2.5-4 pt. 2ASU/A
Time: Postemergence. Apply when wild oat is in 3-5 leaf stage. Do not apply if barley flagleaf is exposed.
Weeds:

wild oat

Remarks: Do not apply if rain is predicted within 6 hr., when freezing temperatures are forecast, or when plants are wet with rain or dew. Avenge can produce yellowing or slight tipburn of barley when applied under poor conditions for plant growth; crop recovery is rapid when good growth conditions return.

Crop Rotation: Barley or wheat can be replanted if crop loss occurs. Rotation to other crops can be made the following year.

Tank Mixes: Assert for wild oat only; following broadleaf herbicides: Ally, Amber, bromoxynil, bromoxynil + MCPA, Canvas, Curtail, 2,4-D, Express, Glean, Harmony Extra, MCPA, Peak.

- - - - - - - - - - - - - - -

Signal Word/Toxicity Class: Danger/I.
REI: 48 hr.

Banvel — see dicamba

Barrage — see 2,4-D

Bison — see bromoxynil & MCPA

Broclean — see bromoxynil

Bromac — see bromoxynil & MCPA

Bromox — see bromoxynil

Bromox-MCPA 2-2 — see bromoxynil & MCPA

BROMOXYNIL

Contact herbicide that provides very good to excellent control of broadleaf weeds. Usually used in combination with MCPA or other labeled herbicides to control more species. Very good crop tolerance.

■ **POST**

◆ **Broclean 2EC** *(Platte)*
◆ **Bromox 2EC** *(Micro Flo)*
Buctril (2EC), Buctril 4EC *(Rhone-Poulenc)*
Moxy 2EC *(Terra)*

◆-new product • PP-preplant • PPI-preplant incorporated • PRE-preemergence • POST-postemergence • SEQ-sequential • ae-acid equivalent • ai-active ingredient • DF-dry flowable
E/EC-emulsifiable concentrate • F/FL-flowable • DG/G/WG-dispersable granule • L/LC-liquid • SP/WSP-soluble packet • W/WP-wettable powder • WSB-water soluble bag

Rate: Spring-seeded (except CO, ID, OR, MT, WA, WY):
0.25-0.5 lb. ai/A
1-2 pt. 2EC/A
0.5-1 pt. 4EC/A
Fall-seeded; spring-seeded (CO, ID, OR, MT, WA, WY only):
0.375-0.5 lb. ai/A
1.5-2 pt. 2EC/A
0.75-1 pt. 4EC/A
Underseeded with alfalfa:
0.25-0.375 lb. ai/A
1-1.5 pt. 2EC/A
0.5-0.75 pt. 4EC/A

Time: Postemergence. Apply from emergence to boot stage.

Weeds: Most susceptible broadleaf weeds:

annual pepperweed	common tarweed	Pennsylvania
annual sowthistle	eastern black	smartweed
black nightshade	nightshade	shepherdspurse
blue mustard	field pennycress	silverleaf nightshade
bristly starbur	green smartweed	sunflower
coast fiddleneck	hairy nightshade	tartary buckwheat
common cocklebur	jimsonweed	wild buckwheat
common lambsquarters	ladysthumb	

Susceptible broadleaf weeds:

buffalobur	ivyleaf morningglory	spiny pigweed
burcucumber	knawel	tall morningglory
common groundsel	kochia	tall waterhemp
common ragweed	London rocket	tumble mustard
corn chamomile	mayweed	velvetleaf
corn gromwell	prostrate knotweed	Venice mallow
cowcockle	puncturevine	wild mustard
giant ragweed	redroot pigweed	wild radish
hemp sesbania	Russian thistle	yellow starthistle

Remarks: Do not apply when crops are under moisture stress. Do not graze treated fields within 30 days after application (45 days for Buctril). Refer to label for use directions, restrictions and precautions.

Crop Rotation: Do not plant rotational crops until the following season (within 30 days of application for Buctril).

Tank Mixes: Ally, Amber, Avenge, Curtail, 2,4-D, diuron (winter barley), Express, Finesse, Glean, Harmony Extra, Hoelon (if crop not stressed), MCPA.

– – – – – – – – – – – – – – –

Signal Word/Toxicity Class: Warning/II.
REI: 12 hr.

BROMOXYNIL & MCPA (Premixes)

Provides very good to excellent control of annual broadleaf weeds. Good crop tolerance. Best results when weeds are small and free of drought stress. Good coverage is important.

■ **POST**

Bison (EC) (2 lb./gal. bromoxynil & 2 lb./gal. MCPA) *(Terra)*
◆ **Bromac (EC) (2 lb./gal. bromoxynil & 2 lb./gal. MCPA)** *(Platte)*
◆ **Bromox-MCPA 2-2 (EC) (2 lb./gal. bromoxynil & 2 lb./gal. MCPA)** *(Micro Flo)*
Bronate (EC) (2 lb./gal. bromoxynil & 2 lb./gal. MCPA) *(Rhone-Poulenc)*
   Rate: 0.5-1 lb. ai/A
   1-2 pt. EC/A
   Chemigation:
   1 lb. ai/A
   2 pt. EC/A
   Postharvest—MN, MT, ND, SD:
   0.38-1 lb. ai/A
   0.75-2 pt. EC/A (Bronate)

Time: Postemergence. Apply after 3-leaf stage but before boot stage.

Weeds: Most susceptible broadleaf weeds:

annual sowthistle	field pennycress	Russian thistle
black mustard	green smartweed	shepherdspurse
black nightshade	hairy nightshade	silverleaf nightshade
coast fiddleneck	horned poppy	smooth pigweed
common cocklebur	jimsonweed	spiny pigweed
common lambsquarters	ladysthumb	sunflower
common tarweed	London rocket	tall waterhemp
cowcockle	marshelder	tartary buckwheat
cutleaf nightshade	Pennsylvania	tumble mustard
eastern black nightshade	smartweed	wild buckwheat
	pepperweed	wild mustard
	redroot pigweed	yellow rocket

Susceptible broadleaf weeds:

blue mustard	giant ragweed	puncturevine
Canada thistle (suppression)	hemp sesbania	purple mustard
common groundsel	henbit	tall morningglory
common ragweed	ivyleaf morningglory	tansymustard
corn chamomile	knawel	tarweed
corn gromwell	kochia	velvetleaf
fumitory	mayweed	wild radish
	prostrate knotweed	

– – – – – – – – – – – – – – –

Remarks: Rates vary by weed species and conditions; refer to label for directions and precautions. Do not apply when crop canopy covers weeds or when crops are under moisture stress. Do not graze fields within 30 days after application (45 for Bronate).

Tank Mixes: Ally, Amber, Assert, Avenge, Curtail, Express, Finesse, Glean, Harmony Extra, MCPA.

– – – – – – – – – – – – – – –

Signal Word/Toxicity Class: Warning/II.
REI: 12 hr.

Bronate — see bromoxynil & MCPA

BUCKLE (Premix)

Granular selective herbicide to control wild oat and foxtail.

■ **PPI**

Buckle (13G) (10% triallate & 3% trifluralin) *(Monsanto)*
   Rate: 1.3-1.625 lb. ai/A
   10-12.5 lb. 13G/A

Time: Preplant incorporated. Apply in the spring or fall prior to planting. In the fall, apply within 3 weeks of normal freezeup.

Weeds:

foxtail	pigeongrass	wild oat

Remarks: Do not apply on muck soils or soils containing more than 10% organic matter. Do not graze livestock on treated crops. Refer to label for directions and precautions.

Crop Rotation: Certain vegetable crops (refer to Monsanto representative for specific crops)—5 months; sugar beets, red beets, spinach—14 months; sorghum, proso millet, corn, oats—16 months.

State Restrictions: For use in Colorado, Idaho, Kansas, Minnesota, Montana, Nebraska, Nevada, North Dakota, Oregon, South Dakota, Utah, Washington, and Wyoming.

– – – – – – – – – – – – – – –

Signal Word/Toxicity Class: Caution/III.
REI: 12 hr.

Buctril — see bromoxynil

CANVAS (Premix)

■ **POST**

Canvas (DF) (37.5% thifensulfuron-methyl & 18.75% tribenuron-methyl & 15% metsulfuron-methyl) *(DuPont)*
   Rate: 1 soluble pack/5A
   MN, MT, ND, SD:
   1 soluble pack/10A

Time: Early postemergence. Apply to young actively growing weeds after barley is in 2-leaf stage, but before flag leaf is visible.

Weeds: Broadleaf weeds:

annual knawel	cutleaf nightshade*	prostrate pigweed
annual sowthistle*	dogfennel	purple mustard
black mustard	false chamomile	redmaids rockpurslane
blue mustard	fanweed	redroot pigweed
broadleaf dock	field chickweed	Russian thistle
bur buttercup	field pennycress	scentless chamomile
bushy wallflower	filaree	shepherdspurse
Canada thistle	flixweed	smallflower buttercup
Carolina geranium	hairy nightshade*	smallseed falseflax
catchweed bedstraw*	hairy vetch*	smartweed
clasping pepperweed	henbit	smooth pigweed
coast fiddleneck	jim hill mustard	snow speedwell
common buckwheat	kochia	stinking chickweed
common chickweed	lambsquarters	stinking mayweed
common cocklebur	little mallow*	swinecress
common groundsel	London rocket	tall waterhemp*
common mallow	marshelder	tansymustard
common purslane	mayweed chamomile	tarweed
common radish	minerslettuce	treacle mustard
common ragweed	mouseearcress	tumble mustard
common sunflower	narrowleaf	tumble pigweed
common vetch*	lambsquarters	volunteer lentils
conical catchfly	nightflowering	volunteer peas
corn chamomile	catchfly	volunteer sunflower
corn gromwell	Pennsylvania	waterpod
corn spurry	smartweed	wild buckwheat
cowcockle	pineappleweed	wild chamomile
curly dock	plains coreopsis	wild garlic
cutleaf	prickly lettuce	wild mustard
eveningprimrose	prostrate knotweed	wild radish

* *Partial control*

For personal protective equipment and EPA registration numbers, please turn to page 70.

4

Small Grains

Remarks: Not underseeded with legumes. Add nonionic surfactant. Do not make more than one application per crop season. Do not graze or feed forage or hay from treated areas to livestock (harvested straw may be used for bedding and/or feed).

Days To Harvest: 45.

Crop Rotation: Varies depending on crop and geographic area.

State Restrictions: For use in Colorado (except Alamosa, Conejos, Costilla, Rio Grande, Saguache counties), Idaho, Kansas, Minnesota, Montana, Nebraska, New Mexico, Oklahoma, Oregon, South Dakota, Texas, Utah, Washington, and Wyoming.

Signal Word/Toxicity Class: Warning/II.
REI: 12 hr.

Chiptox — see MCPA

Clarity — see dicamba

CLOPYRALID

Systemic herbicide absorbed by leaves and roots. Has selective postemergence control of many annual and perennial broadleaf weeds. Especially useful for Canada thistle seasonal suppression. Frequently used in combination with 2,4-D or MCPA. Note crop rotation restrictions.

■ POST

Stinger *(Dow AgroSciences)*
Rate: 0.1-0.125 lb. ae/A
0.25-0.33 pt./A
Time: Postemergence. Apply from 3-leaf stage up to early boot stage.
Weeds: Annual and perennial broadleaf weeds:

Canada thistle	jimsonweed	sowthistle
clover	knapweed	spotted knapweed
cocklebur	marshelder	sunflower
diffuse knapweed	Russian knapweed	vetch
Jerusalem artichoke	(suppression)	volunteer soybean

Remarks: Not underseeded with legumes. Do not allow dairy or meat animals being finished for slaughter to forage or graze treated fields within 1 week after treatment. Do not harvest hay from treated fields. Do not apply through any type of irrigation system.

Crop Rotation: Varies by region; refer to label.

Tank Mixes: May be tank mixed with other herbicides registered for postemergence application.

Signal Word/Toxicity Class: Caution/III.
REI: 12 hr.

Credit — see glyphosate

CURTAIL or CURTAIL M (Premixes)

Clopyralid provides good seasonal control of Canada thistle. 2,4-D or MCPA in premix improves control of other broadleaf weeds. Crop tolerance is good. Canada thistle control is best when weeds are treated before they form flower buds.

■ POST

Curtail (0.38 lb./gal. clopyralid & 2 lb./gal. 2,4-D) *(Dow AgroSciences)*
Curtail M (0.42 lb./gal. clopyralid & 2.35 lb./gal. MCPA) *(Dow AgroSciences)*
Rate: 0.6-0.8 lb. ae/A
2-2.66 pt. Curtail/A
1.75-2.33 pt. Curtail M/A
Time: Postemergence. Apply in spring to actively growing barley once 4 leaves have unfolded on main stem up to jointing stage. Do not apply after boot stage.
Weeds: Broadleaf weeds:

alfalfa	cornflower	goatsbeard
annual sowthistle	curly dock	hairy nightshade
Canada thistle	cutleaf nightshade	horseweed
coffeeweed	dandelion	Jerusalem artichoke
common burdock	diffuse knapweed	jim hill mustard
common cocklebur	dogfennel	jimsonweed
common groundsel	false chamomile	kochia* (2-4 leaf)
common lambsquarters	fanweed	ladysthumb
	field pennycress	mayweed chamomile
common ragweed	flixweed*	meadow salsify
common sunflower	giant ragweed	musk thistle

Weeds: Broadleaf weeds, continued:

narrowleaf hawksbeard	redroot pigweed	tumble mustard
	Russian knapweed*	velvetleaf
Pennsylvania smartweed	Russian thistle (1-3 leaf)	vetch
perennial sowthistle*	scentless chamomile	volunteer beans
pineappleweed	shepherdspurse	volunteer lentils
plantain	sicklepod	volunteer peas
prickly lettuce	spotted knapweed	wild buckwheat
red clover	sweetclover	wild mustard
red sorrel	tansymustard	wild radish
		yellow starthistle

* Suppression

Remarks: Not underseeded with legumes. Do not harvest hay from treated fields. Do not allow lactating dairy animals or meat animals being finished for slaughter to forage or graze treated fields within 1 week after application. Do not apply through any type of irrigation system.

Crop Rotation: Varies by region; refer to label.

Tank Mixes: Ally, Avenge, Banvel, Buctril, 2,4-D, diuron, Express, Harmony Extra, MCPA, metribuzin.

Signal Word/Toxicity Class: Danger/I (Curtail); Caution/III (Curtail M).
REI: 48 hr.

Cyclone — see paraquat

2,4-D - PHENOXY HERBICIDES

Common herbicide for annual and perennial broadleaf weeds. Especially useful for perennials like field bindweed. Ester forms are used at slightly lower rates than amines.

Annual and perennial broadleaf weeds controlled by 2,4-D include:

beggarticks	galinsoga	povertyweed
bindweed	goldenrod	puncturevine
bitterweed	ground ivy	purslane
broomweed	healall	ragweed
bull thistle	hoary cress	Russian thistle
burdock	ironweed	shepherdspurse
Canada thistle	jimsonweed	smartweed
carpetweed	knotweed	sowthistle
catnip	lambsquarters	stinkweed
chicory	mallow	sumac
chickweed	marshelder	sunflower
cocklebur	mexicanweed	sweetclover
coffeeweed	morningglory	velvetleaf
cutleaf eveningprimrose	musk thistle	Virginia creeper
	mustard	wild carrot
creeping jenny	pennywort	wild garlic
croton	pepperweed	wild lettuce
dandelion	pigweed	wild onion
dock	plantain	wild parsnips
dogbane	pokeweed	wild radish

■ POST

Albaugh Amine 4 (2,4-D amine) *(Albaugh)*
Weedestroy AM-40 (2,4-D amine) *(Riverdale)*
Wilbur-Ellis Amine 4 (2,4-D amine) *(Wilbur-Ellis)*
Rate: 0.25-1 lb. ae/A
0.5-2 pt./A (Riverdale, Wilbur-Ellis)
0.33-0.75 lb. ae/A
0.66-1.5 pt./A (Albaugh)
Time: Postemergence. Apply to spring grown grains after tillering (4-8" high) but before boot stage. Do not spray in boot to dough stage.
Remarks: Not underseeded with legumes. For emergency control of perennial weeds, up to 3 pt./A may be used when weeds are approaching bud stage. Do not use higher rates unless possible crop injury will be acceptable.

Rate: 0.125-0.25 lb. ae/A
0.25-0.5 pt./A
Time: Postemergence. Apply after grain is 8" tall but before boot stage. Do not spray in boot to dough stage.
Remarks: Underseeded with legumes. Do not spray alfalfa or sweet clover unless infestation is severe and injury to legumes can be tolerated.

Rate: 0.5-1 lb. ae/A
1-2 pt./A
Time: Preharvest. Apply in dough stage.
Remarks: Best results will be obtained when soil moisture is adequate for plant growth and weeds are growing well.
State Restrictions: Wilbur-Ellis not registered in California.

Signal Word/Toxicity Class: Danger/I.
REI: 48 hr.

◆-new product • PP-preplant • PPI-preplant incorporated • PRE-preemergence • POST-postemergence • SEQ-sequential • ae-acid equivalent • ai-active ingredient • DF-dry flowable • E/EC-emulsifiable concentrate • F/FL-flowable • DG/G/WG-dispersable granule • L/LC-liquid • SP/WSP-soluble packet • W/WP-wettable powder • WSB-water soluble bag

4

■ POST

Albaugh LV4 or LV6 Ester (2,4-D ester) *(Albaugh)*
◆ **Barrage or Barrage HF (EC) (2,4-D ester)** *(Helena)*
◆ **Clean Crop Low Vol 4 or Low Vol 6 (2,4-D ester)** *(Platte)*
Esteron 99C (2,4-D LV ester) *(Rhone-Poulenc)*
Riverdale 6 Amine (2,4-D amine) *(Riverdale)*
Riverdale L.V. 4 or L.V. 6 (2,4-D ester) *(Riverdale)*
Solve 2,4-D (2,4-D LV ester) *(Albaugh)*
Weed Rhap LV-6D (2,4-D ester) *(Helena)*
Wilbur-Ellis Lo Vol-4 or Lo Vol-6 (2,4-D ester) *(Wilbur-Ellis)*
  Rate: 0.25-0.5 lb. ae/A
    0.5-1 pt. 4/A
    0.33-0.66 pt. 6/A
    Perennial weeds, preharvest:
    0.5-1 lb. ae/A
    1-2 pt. 4/A
    0.66-1.33 pt. 6/A
  Time: Postemergence, preharvest. Do not spray before tiller or from early boot to dough stage.
  Remarks: Not underseeded with legumes. Do not forage or graze treated fields for 2 weeks after application.
  State Restrictions: Wilbur-Ellis not registered in California.

– – – – – – – – – – – – – – –

  Signal Word/Toxicity Class: Danger/I (amine); Caution/III (ester).
  REI: Danger—48 hr.; Caution—12 hr.

■ POST

Albaugh D-638 (2,4-D ester + acid) *(Albaugh)*
Phenoxy 088 (2,4-D ester + acid) *(Terra)*
Weedone 638 (2,4-D ester + acid) *(Nufarm)*
  Rate: 0.35-0.7 lb. ae/A
    1-2 pt./A
  Time: Postemergence, preharvest. Apply when weeds are near bud stage. Apply after grain is fully tillered (4-8" high) but not forming joints in stem, and when daytime temperatures are below 85°F. Do not spray in boot to dough stage. Do not apply to grain in seedling stage.
  Remarks: Not underseeded with legumes. Do not apply through any type of irrigation system. Do not forage or graze treated fields for 2 weeks after application.
  State Restrictions: Weedone not for use preharvest in California.

– – – – – – – – – – – – – – –

  Signal Word/Toxicity Class: Danger/I.
  REI: 48 hr.

■ POST

◆ **Clean Crop Amine 4 (2,4-D amine)** *(Platte)*
Formula 40 (2,4-D mixed amine) *(Rhone-Poulenc)*
◆ **Opti-Amine (4) (2,4-D amine)** *(Helena)*
Weed Rhap A-4D (2,4-D amine) *(Helena)*
  Rate: 0.33-0.66 lb. ae/A
    0.66-1.33 pt./A
  Time: Postemergence. Apply in spring. Do not apply before tiller stage or from early boot through milk stage.

  Rate: 0.5-1 lb. ae/A
    1-2 pt./A
  Time: Preharvest. Apply in dough stage.
  Remarks: Not underseeded with legumes. Up to 3 pt./A may be used for difficult weeds problems such as dry conditions in Western states. Do not allow dairy animals or meat animals being finished for slaughter to forage or graze treated fields within 2 weeks of treatment.

– – – – – – – – – – – – – – –

  Signal Word/Toxicity Class: Danger/I.
  REI: 48 hr.

■ POST

Gordon's LV 400 (2,4-D LV ester) *(PBI/Gordon)*
Riverside 2,4-D LV4 (2,4-D LV ester) *(Terra)*
  Rate: 0.25-0.5 lb. ae/A
    0.5-1 pt./A
  Time: Postemergence. Apply when grain is in full tiller stage but before early boot stage and when weeds are small. Do not apply before tiller stage or from early boot through milk stage.

  Rate: 0.5-1 lb. ae/A
    1-2 pt./A
  Time: Preharvest. Apply in dough stage.

Remarks: Not underseeded with legumes. Up to 2 pt./A may be used for difficult weeds problems such as dry conditions in Western states. Do not use higher rates unless possible crop injury will be acceptable.

– – – – – – – – – – – – – – –

  Signal Word/Toxicity Class: Caution/III.
  REI: 12 hr.

■ POST

Hi-Dep (2,4-D mixed amine) *(PBI/Gordon)*
  Rate: 0.125-0.75 lb. ae/A
    0.25-1.5 pt./A
  Time: Postemergence. Apply after grain begins tillering and before boot stage (4-8" tall). Do not apply before tiller stage or from early boot through milk stage.

  Rate: 0.5-1 lb. ae/A
    1-2 pt./A
  Time: Preharvest. Apply in dough stage.
  Remarks: Not underseeded with legumes. Up to 3 pt./A may be used for difficult weeds problems such as dry conditions in Western states. Do not allow dairy animals or meat animals being finished for slaughter to forage or graze treated fields within 2 weeks after application.

– – – – – – – – – – – – – – –

  Signal Word/Toxicity Class: Danger/I.
  REI: 48 hr.

■ POST

◆ **Saber (2,4-D amine)** *(Platte)*
  Rate: Spring barley:
    0.12-0.75 lb. ae/A
    0.25-1.5 pt./A
    Winter barley:
    0.25-0.5 lb. ae/A
    0.5-1 pt./A
  Time: Postemergence. Apply from onset of tillering to full tillering stage. Do not apply from boot to dough stage.

  Rate: Emergency, preharvest:
    0.35-1.5 lb. ae/A
    0.75-3 pt./A
  Time: Preharvest. Apply in hard dough stage. Do not apply before tiller or from boot to dough stage.
  Remarks: Not underseeded with legumes. Up to 3 pt./A may be used to control difficult weeds and heavy infestations. Do not forage or graze treated fields for 2 weeks after application. Do not feed treated straw to livestock if emergency and/or preharvest treatment is applied.

– – – – – – – – – – – – – – –

  Signal Word/Toxicity Class: Danger/I.
  REI: 48 hr.

■ POST

Salvo (2,4-D LV ester) *(Platte)*
  Rate: Spring-planted:
    0.25-0.31 lb. ae/A
    0.4-0.5 pt./A
  Time: Postemergence. Apply after plants are fully tillered but before stems begin to joint.

  Rate: Fall-planted:
    0.25-0.5 lb. ae/A
    0.4-0.8 pt./A
  Time: Postemergence. Apply in the spring when weeds are small and barley is in full tiller stage (4-8" high) and before boot stage. Do not apply during boot or dough stage.
  Remarks: Do not forage or graze treated grain fields within 2 weeks after application. Do not feed treated straw to livestock.

– – – – – – – – – – – – – – –

  Signal Word/Toxicity Class: Caution/III.
  REI: 12 hr.

■ POST

Savage (WSB) (2,4-D amine) *(Platte)*
  Rate: 0.24-0.95 lb. ae/A
    0.25-1 lb. WSB/A
  Time: Postemergence. Apply in spring. Do not apply before tiller stage or from boot to dough stage.

  Rate: 0.48-1.43 lb. ae/A
    0.5-1.5 lb. WSB/A
  Time: Preharvest. Apply in hard dough stage.

Remarks: Not underseeded with legumes. For emergency weed control, up to 1.5 lb./A may be used when weeds are approaching bud stage, after grain dough stage. Do not use higher rates unless possible crop injury acceptable. Do not forage or graze treated fields within 2 weeks after treatment. Do not feed treated straw if emergency and/or preharvest treatment is applied. Refer to label for use directions, restrictions, and precautions.

Signal Word/Toxicity Class: Danger/I.
REI: 48 hr.

■ POST

Solution (WS) (2,4-D amine) *(Riverdale)*
Rate: Spring grains:
    1 WS packet/3.5-10 A
    Winter grains:
    1 WS packet/2.5-10 A
Time: Postemergence. For spring grown grains, apply between full tillering and before boot stage (usually 4-8" tall). Preharvest treatment can be applied when grain is in dough stage.
Remarks: Apply in 5-100 gal. water.

Signal Word/Toxicity Class: Danger/I.
REI: 48 hr.

■ POST

Weedar 64 (4) (2,4-D amine) *(Nufarm)*
Rate: 0.25-1 lb. ae/A
    0.5-2 pt./A
Time: Postemergence. Apply after grain is fully tillered (4-8" high) but not forming joints in stem. Do not spray in boot to dough stage.
Remarks: Not underseeded with legumes. Do not use unless possible crop injury will be acceptable.

Rate: 0.125-0.25 lb. ae/A
    0.25-0.5 pt./A
Time: Postemergence. Apply after grain is 8" tall but before boot stage. Do not spray in boot to dough stage.
Remarks: Underseeded with legumes. Do not spray alfalfa or sweet clover unless infestation is severe and injury to legumes can be tolerated.

Signal Word/Toxicity Class: Danger/I.
REI: 48 hr.

■ POST

Weedone LV4 (2,4-D solventless ester) *(Nufarm)*
Weedone Lo Vol 6 (2,4-D ester) *(Nufarm)*
Rate: 0.25-1 lb. ae/A
    0.5-2 pt. 4/A
    0.33-1.33 pt. 6/A
Time: Postemergence. Do not spray in boot to dough stage.
Remarks: Not underseeded with legumes. Refer to label for use directions, restrictions, and precautions.
Tank Mixes: LV4: Buctril (rate varies by state, refer to label).

Signal Word/Toxicity Class: Caution/III.
REI: 12 hr.

DICAMBA

Barley is less tolerant than other small grains; rates are lower. Especially effective for kochia and wild buckwheat. Usually used in combination with MCPA or other labeled herbicides.

■ PP, PRE, POST

Banvel (WS) (DMA salt of dicamba) *(BASF)*
Banvel SGF (sodium salt of dicamba) *(BASF)*
Clarity (WS) (dicamba-DGA) *(BASF)*
◆ Sterling (WS) (DMA salt of dicamba) *(Terra)*
Rate: Fall-seeded:
    2-4 fl. oz. WS/A
    4-8 fl. oz. SGF/A
    Spring-seeded:
    2-3 fl. oz. WS/A
    4-6 fl. oz. SGF/A
Time: Preplant, preemergence, postemergence. For fall-seeded barley, apply prior to jointing stage. For spring-seeded barley, apply prior to 4-leaf stage. For best results, apply when weeds are in 2-3 leaf stage and rosettes are less than 2" across.

Weeds: Broadleaf weeds:

annual sowthistle	corn cockle	Pennsylvania
black nightshade	cowcockle	smartweed
common cocklebur	field pennycress	redroot pigweed
common	giant ragweed	rough pigweed
lambsquarters	green smartweed	Russian thistle
common mallow	henbit	tumble pigweed
common ragweed	knotweed	velvetleaf
common sunflower	kochia	volunteer sunflower
corn chamomile	ladysthumb	wild buckwheat

Remarks: Not underseeded with legumes. For spring barley varieties that are seeded during winter months or later, follow rates and timing for spring-seeded barley. Do not graze lactating dairy animals within 7 days after application or remove animals for slaughter within 30 days of last application; no waiting period between treatment and grazing for non-lactating animals. Do not apply through any type of irrigation system.
Days To Harvest: Hay—37.
Tank Mixes: Ally, Amber, Bronate, Buctril, Canvas, 2,4-D (fall-seeded), Express, Finesse, Glean, Harmony Extra, metribuzin, MCPA.

Signal Word/Toxicity Class: Warning/II (Banvel, Sterling); Caution (Clarity).
REI: 24 hr.

Direx — see diuron

DIURON

Limited to labeled states. Useful for susceptible winter annual mustards in winter barley when applied preemergence.

■ PRE

Direx 4L or 80DF *(Griffin)*
◆ Diuron 80 WDG *(Platte)*
Drexel Diuron 4L or 80 *(Drexel)*
Karmex DF *(Griffin)*
Riverside Diuron 4L or 80DF *(Terra)*
Rate: 1.2-1.5 lb. ai/A
    2.25-3 pt. 4L/A
    1.5-2 lb. 80, DF, 80DF/A
Time: Preemergence. Apply single treatment as soon as possible after planting but before emergence of barley.

Weeds: Broadleaf weeds:

amsinckia	fiddleneck	purslane
annual groundcherry	gromwell	ragweed
annual morningglory	groundsel	shepherdspurse
chickweed	knawel	tansymustard
corn spurry	lambsquarters	wild lettuce
dogfennel	pigweed	wild mustard

Grasses:

annual bluegrass	barnyardgrass	rattail fescue
annual sweet	crabgrass	red sprangletop
vernalgrass	foxtail	velvetgrass

Remarks: Winter barley. Do not apply to cloddy or compacted ground where seed is exposed or improperly planted. Refer to label for soil restrictions.
Crop Rotation: Do not replant to other crops within 1 year after application.
State Restrictions: For use in western Oregon, western Washington.

Signal Word/Toxicity Class: Caution/III.
REI: 12 hr.

Esteron 99C — see 2,4-D

EXPRESS

Sulfonylurea herbicide that gives very good to excellent control of mustard, kochia, and pigweed. No crop rotation restrictions the following season.

■ POST

Express (DF) (tribenuron-methyl) *(DuPont)*
Rate: 0.167-0.33 oz. DF/A
Time: Early postemergence. Apply after crop is in 2-leaf stage, but before flag leaf is visible (can be treated sequentially with low rates but do not exceed total of 0.33 oz./A per season).

◆-new product • PP-preplant • PPI-preplant incorporated • PRE-preemergence • POST-postemergence • SEQ-sequential • ae-acid equivalent • ai-active ingredient • DF-dry flowable
E/EC-emulsifiable concentrate • F/FL-flowable • DG/G/WG-dispersable granule • L/LC-liquid • SP/WSP-soluble packet • W/WP-wettable powder • WSB-water soluble bag

Weeds: Broadleaf weeds:

annual sowthistle*	flixweed*	redroot pigweed*
black mustard	hairy nightshade*	Russian thistle
blue mustard (purple)	henbit*	shepherdspurse*
bushy wallflower	jim hill mustard*	slimleaflambsquarters
Canada thistle*	kochia	tansymustard*
coast fiddleneck	mayweed chamomile	tarweed fiddleneck
common chickweed	minerslettuce	tumble mustard*
common groundsel	Pennsylvania	wild buckwheat*
common	smartweed*	wild chamomile
lambsquarters	pineappleweed	wild garlic*
common sunflower	prickly lettuce	wild mustard
corn spurry	prostrate knotweed*	wild radish*
false chamomile	redmaids	
field pennycress	rockpurslane*	

* Suppression

Remarks: Not underseeded. Add approved nonionic surfactant. Do not graze or feed forage or hay from treated areas to livestock (dry-harvested straw may be used for bedding and/or feed). Do not apply through any type of irrigation system.

Days To Harvest: 45.

Crop Rotation: Do not plant to any crop other than wheat or barley for 60 days after application.

State Restrictions: Not for use in Alamosa, Conejos, Costilla, Rio Grande, and Saguache counties in Colorado.

- - - - - - - - - - - - - - -

Signal Word/Toxicity Class: Caution.

REI: 12 hr.

FAR-GO

Controls wild oat. Fall application of granules is most consistent in some northern areas.

■ PPI, PRE

Far-Go 4E or 10G (triallate) *(Monsanto)*

Rate: 1.25-1.5 lb. ai/A
1.25-1.5 qt. 4E/A
12.5-15 lb. 10G/A

Time: Preplant incorporated, preemergence incorporated. Apply in the fall within 3 weeks of soil freezeup. For winter barley, apply just before or after seeding.

Weeds:

brome (high rate)	wild oat

Remarks: Do not graze livestock on treated crops. Refer to label for directions, precautions, and state restrictions.

Crop Rotation: Domestic oats should not be seeded if Far-Go was used the previous year.

Tank Mixes: Trifluralin (4E).

State Restrictions: For use in Colorado, Idaho, Kansas, Minnesota, Montana, Nebraska, Nevada, North Dakota, Oregon, South Dakota, Utah, Washington, and Wyoming. In Idaho, Montana, Oregon, Utah, and Washington, Far-Go 10G may be surface-applied ahead of Yielder type no-till drill.

- - - - - - - - - - - - - - -

Signal Word/Toxicity Class: Caution/III.

REI: 12 hr.

FENOXAPROP-P-ETHYL

■ POST

◆ **Puma (1EC)** *(AgrEvo USA)*

Rate: 0.04-0.08 lb. ai/A
0.33-0.66 pt. 1EC/A

Time: Postemergence. Apply to barley from 2-leaf stage to 6-leaf stage. Do not apply after jointing begins.

Weeds:

barnyardgrass	hooded canarygrass	wild oat
blackgrass	proso millet	windgrass
foxtail millet	volunteer corn	yellow foxtail
green foxtail		

Remarks: Do not make more than one application or apply more than 0.66 pt./A per growing season. Do not apply any pesticides other than those listed on label within 5 days of application. Do not apply through any type of irrigation system or when wind conditions favor drift.

Days To Harvest: 57.

Tank Mixes: Ally, Amber, Buctril, Bronate, Curtail M, Express, Harmony Extra, Harmony GT, MCPA ester, Peak, Stinger, Starane, Tordon herbicides; Furadan 4F, Sevin XLR Plus insecticides; Benlate, Mertect, mancozeb, Tilt fungicides. Do not tank mix with other herbicides unless

specifically recommended on label. Do not tank mix with malathion. Refer to label for limitations and state restrictions.

- - - - - - - - - - - - - - -

Signal Word/Toxicity Class: Warning/II.

REI: 24 hr.

FINESSE (Premix)

Premix of sulfonylurea herbicides with same active ingredients as in Glean and Ally. Has extended soil residual activity and provides very good to excellent control of many annual broadleaf weeds. Use limited to labeled states.

■ POST

Finesse (DF) (62.5% chlorsulfuron & 12.5% metsulfuron-methyl) *(DuPont)*

Rate: 0.2-0.3 oz. DF/A

Time: Postemergence. Apply after 1-leaf stage but before boot stage.

Weeds: Broadleaf weeds:

annual sowthistle	flixweed*	prostrate pigweed
bedstraw*	groundsel	purslane
blue mustard	hempnettle	redroot pigweed
broadleaf dock	henbit	redstem filaree
bur beakchervil	ivyleaf speedwell*	Russian thistle*
bur buttercup	jagged chickweed	shepherdspurse
Canada thistle*	jim hill mustard	smallseed falseflax
Carolina geranium	kochia*	smooth pigweed
coast fiddleneck	ladysthumb	sunflower
common chickweed	lambsquarters	tansymustard*
common speedwell*	mayweed chamomile	tarweed
conical catchfly	minerslettuce	treacle mustard
corn gromwell*	mouseear chickweed	tumble mustard
corn spurry	Pennsylvania	vetch
cowcockle	smartweed*	Virginia pepperweed
curly dock	pineappleweed	white cockle
cutleaf	plains coreopsis	wild buckwheat
eveningprimrose	prickly lettuce	wild carrot
dovefoot geranium	prickly poppy	wild mustard
false chamomile	prostrate knotweed*	wild radish
field pennycress		

Grasses:

annual bluegrass*	cheat	green foxtail*
annual ryegrass*	downy brome	Japanese brome*

* Suppression

Remarks: Not underseeded with legumes and grasses. Do not apply less than 0.2 oz./A. Do not apply within 60 days of crop emergence if an organophosphate insecticide has been applied in-furrow.

Crop Rotation: Recropping depends on rate, soil pH, total rainfall, and geographic area. Refer to label for restrictions and pH limitations.

Tank Mixes: Banvel, Bronate, Buctril, Curtail, 2,4-D, Karmex, MCPA. Do not tank mix with malathion or, in Pacific Northwest, with Lorsban.

State Restrictions: Not for use in Alamosa, Conejos, Costilla, Rio Grande, and Saguache counties in Colorado.

- - - - - - - - - - - - - - -

Signal Word/Toxicity Class: Caution.

REI: 4 hr.

Formula 40 — see 2,4-D

GLEAN

Sulfonylurea herbicide with soil residual activity extended for 2 seasons or more. Recommended for use on land primarily dedicated to long-term production of wheat, barley, or oats. Especially effective for mustard, kochia, and pigweed. Good crop tolerance. Note crop rotation and maximum use interval for your area.

■ POST

Glean FC (DF) (chlorsulfuron) *(DuPont)*

Rate: 0.167-0.33 oz. DF/A

Time: Postemergence. Winter barley: Apply in 2-leaf stage but before boot stage. Spring barley: Apply in 2-leaf stage but before flag leaf is visible. Apply to small, actively growing weeds that are less than 2" tall or 2" across. Do not apply preemergence.

4

Small Grains

NOTICE The information on these pages is for preliminary planning — not a guide for use. Be sure to follow the manufacturer's directions, notwithstanding information contained here.

For personal protective equipment and EPA registration numbers, please turn to page 70.

Barley

Weeds: Broadleaf weeds:

bedstraw*	flixweed	redroot pigweed
blue mustard	hempnettle	redstem filaree
bur beakchervil	henbit	Russian thistle*
buttercup	jim hill mustard	shepherdspurse
Canada thistle*	kochia*	smooth pigweed
coast fiddleneck	ladysthumb	speedwell*
common chickweed	lambsquarters	sunflower*
common groundsel*	mayweed	tansymustard*
conical catchfly	minerslettuce	tarweed
corn gromwell*	mouseear	treacle mustard
corn spurry	chickweed	tumble mustard
cowcockle	Pennsylvania	white cockle
curly dock	smartweed*	wild buckwheat*
cutleaf	pineappleweed	wild carrot
eveningprimrose	prickly lettuce*	wild mustard
false chamomile	prostrate knotweed*	wild radish*
falseflax	prostrate pigweed	wild turnip
field pennycress	purslane	yellow starthistle

Grasses:
annual ryegrass*

Aerial bulblet control:
wild garlic*   wild onion*

* Suppression

Remarks: Winter, spring barley. Not underseeded with legumes. Glean is mixed in water or directly into liquid nitrogen fertilizer solutions and applied as uniform broadcast spray. Surfactant should be used in spray mix unless otherwise specified.

Crop Rotation: Recropping depends on rate, soil pH, total rainfall, and geographic area. Refer to label for soil pH restrictions and more complete information.

Tank Mixes: Banvel, Bronate, Buctril, 2,4-D, Karmex, MCPA.

State Restrictions: For use in California, northern Idaho, Kansas, Nebraska, Oklahoma, Oregon, Texas, and Washington. Kochia and Russian thistle for central Kansas, Nebraska, Oklahoma, and northcentral Texas.

- - - - - - - - - - - - - - -

Signal Word/Toxicity Class: Caution.
REI: 4 hr.

Glyfos or Glyfos X-tra — see glyphosate

GLYPHOSATE

Gives very good to excellent control of annual grasses and annual broadleaf weeds prior to planting. Useful for reduced-tillage systems. No soil residual activity. Ammonium sulfate at 17 lb./100 gal. improves results, especially where water quality is a factor. Do not allow glyphosate to contact desirable plants.

■ PP, PRE
◆ **Credit (4WS)** *(Nufarm)*
◆ **Glyfos or Glyfos X-tra (4WS)** *(Cheminova)*
Rattler (4WS) *(Helena)*
Roundup Custom (5.4WS) *(Monsanto)*
Roundup Original, Original RT, Ultra, Ultra RT (4WS) *(Monsanto)*

Rate: Annual weeds:
0.38-1.5 lb. ai/A
0.56-2.25 pt. 5.4WS/A
0.75-3 pt. 4WS/A
Perennial weeds:
0.5-5 lb. ai/A
0.75-7.5 pt. 5.4WS/A
1-10 pt. 4WS/A

Time: Preplant, preemergence, at-planting, spot treatment, postharvest. For spot treatment, apply before heading.

Weeds: Most emerged annual and perennial broadleaf weeds including:

Canada thistle	field bindweed	kochia

Grasses:

downy brome	foxtail	quackgrass

Remarks: For preharvest applications, do not apply more than 1 lb. ai/A. Do not add surfactant to Roundup Ultra or Ultra RT. For spot treatment, do not treat more than 10% total area to be harvested. Do not apply through any type of irrigation system. Refer to label for directions, precautions and restrictions.

Days To Harvest: Postharvest: harvest/feeding—8 weeks.

Tank Mixes: Postharvest: 2,4-D, dicamba. Roundup tank mixes not registered in California by air.

State Restrictions: Roundup RT for use in Colorado, Idaho, Montana, North Dakota, South Dakota, Utah, Wyoming, and in specific counties only in Kansas, Minnesota, Nebraska, Nevada, Oklahoma, Oregon, and Washington; refer to label for restrictions. Glyfos is not registered for

use in California. Glyfos X-tra is not registered for use in mistblowers in California or Arizona.

Signal Word/Toxicity Class: Varies by formulation.
REI: Warning—12 hr.; Caution—4 hr.

■ PRE
Ranger (WS) *(Monsanto)*

Rate: 0.25-0.5 lb. ai/A broadcast
0.75-1.5 pt. WS/A

Time: Preemergence. Apply to vigorously growing weeds.

Weeds: Broadleaf weeds:

blue mustard	field pennycress	shepherdspurse
buttercup	horseweed	smallseed falseflax
cocklebur	London rocket	smooth pigweed
common groundsel	marestail	tansymustard
common	morningglory	tumble mustard
lambsquarters	mouseear chickweed	umbrella spurry
dwarfdandelion	redroot pigweed	wild mustard
fanweed		

Grasses:

annual bluegrass	downy brome	stinkgrass
barnyardgrass	fall panicum	Texas panicum
bulbous bluegrass	field sandbur	wild oat
cheat	Italian ryegrass	witchgrass
crabgrass	shattercane	

Rate: 1-2 lb. ai/A
3-6 pt. WS/A

Time: Preemergence. Apply to vigorously growing weeds.

Weeds: Grasses:

quackgrass	tall fescue	wirestem muhly

Remarks: For quackgrass control in the fall, do not till between harvest and application; in the spring, do not till in the fall or spring prior to application. Do not apply through any type of irrigation system. Do not feed or forage vegetation from treated areas within 8 weeks after application.

- - - - - - - - - - - - - - -

Signal Word/Toxicity Class: Danger/I.
REI: 12 hr.

Gramoxone Extra — see paraquat

HARMONY EXTRA (Premix)

Premix of sulfonylurea herbicides with no crop rotation limitations for the next season. Very good to excellent control of several annual broadleaf weeds including kochia, pigweed, and mustard. Good crop tolerance. Usually used with low rates of MCPA, 2,4-D, or other labeled broadleaf herbicides.

■ POST
Harmony Extra (DF) (50% thifensulfuron-methyl & 25% tribenuron-methyl) *(DuPont)*

Rate: 0.3-0.6 oz. DF/A

Time: Early postemergence. Apply after barley is in 2-leaf stage, but before flag leaf is visible.

Weeds: Broadleaf weeds:

annual knawel	cutleaf	prostrate knotweed
annual sowthistle	eveningprimrose*	prostrate pigweed
black mustard	dogfennel	purple mustard
blue mustard	false chamomile	redmaids
broadleaf dock	field chickweed	rockpurslane
bur buttercup	field pennycress	redroot pigweed
bushy wallflower	filaree	Russian thistle
Canada thistle*	flixweed	scentless chamomile
Carolina geranium*	green smartweed	shepherdspurse
catchweed bedstraw*	hairy nightshade*	slimleaf lambsquarters
clasping pepperweed	henbit	smallflower buttercup
coast fiddleneck	jim hill mustard	smallseed falseflax
common chickweed	kochia	stinking chickweed
common cocklebur*	ladysthumb	stinking mayweed
common groundsel	little mallow*	swinecress
common	London rocket	tansymustard
lambsquarters	marshelder	tarweed fiddleneck
common mallow*	minerslettuce	tumble mustard
common radish	mouseearcress	volunteer lentils
common ragweed*	narrowleaf	volunteer peas
common sunflower	lambsquarters	volunteer sunflower
common vetch*	nightflowering	wild buckwheat
corn chamomile	catchfly	wild chamomile
corn gromwell	Pennsylvania	wild garlic
corn spurry	smartweed	wild mustard
cowcockle	pineappleweed	wild radish
curly dock	prickly lettuce	

* Partial control

◆-new product • PP-preplant • PPI-preplant incorporated • PRE-preemergence • POST-postemergence • SEQ-sequential • ae-acid equivalent • ai-active ingredient • DF-dry flowable • E/EC-emulsifiable concentrate • F/FL-flowable • DG/G/WG-dispersable granule • L/LC-liquid • SP/WSP-soluble packet • W/WP-wettable powder • WSB-water soluble bag

218   Weed Control Manual 2000

Remarks: Not underseeded. Add approved nonionic surfactant. Do not graze or feed forage or hay from treated areas to livestock (harvested straw may be used for bedding and/or feed).

Days To Harvest: 45.

Crop Rotation: Do not rotate to crops other than wheat, barley, or oats for 60 days after application; after 60 days any crop may be planted.

State Restrictions: Not for use in Alamosa, Conejos, Costilla, Rio Grande, and Saguache counties in Colorado.

– – – – – – – – – – – – – – –

Signal Word/Toxicity Class: Caution.
REI: 12 hr.

Harmony GT — see thifensulfuron-methyl

Hi-Dep — see 2,4-D

HOELON

Postemergence control of grasses including wild oat and foxtail. Crop tolerance reduced under stress conditions. Variety restrictions for some areas. Antagonistic reaction can reduce grass control if mixed in nonlabeled combinations. Restricted Use Pesticide.

■ POST

Hoelon 3EC (diclofop) *(AgrEvo USA)*

Rate: 0.75-1 lb. ai/A
2-2.66 pt. 3EC/A

Time: Postemergence. Apply when majority of wild oat and annual grasses are in 1-4 leaf stage. Do not apply preemergence.

Weeds: Grasses including:

foxtail	pigeongrass	wild oat

Remarks: Do not tank mix with Glean or crop oil concentrate. Refer to label for variety restrictions, directions, precautions, and limitations.

Days To Harvest: 66.

Tank Mixes: Buctril, MCPA.

State Restrictions: For use in the Southeast and Mid-Atlantic on winter barley. For use in the North Central, Southwest, and Western U.S. (except California) on spring barley.

– – – – – – – – – – – – – – –

Signal Word/Toxicity Class: Danger/I.
REI: 24 hr.

Karmex — see diuron

MCPA

Good crop tolerance at a wide range of crop growth stages. Most effective on mustards and lambsquarters. Frequently used in combination with other herbicides, especially when treatment must be made at early growth stages.

■ POST

Albaugh MCPA Amine 4 *(Albaugh)*
◆ Clean Crop MCP Amine 4 or Ester *(Platte)*
◆ Clean Crop MCP 2 Sodium (sodium salt) *(Platte)*
Riverdale MCPA-4 Amine *(Riverdale)*
Riverside MCPA Amine *(Terra)*
Wilbur-Ellis MCPA Amine, Ester or ◆ Sodium Salt (2EC) *(Wilbur-Ellis)*

Rate: 0.25-1.5 lb. ae/A
0.5-3 pt./A

Time: Postemergence. Apply low rate for more susceptible weeds after crop has reached 3-4 leaf stage up to boot stage; high rate after crop has tillered and up to early boot stage. Do not spray from boot to dough stage.

Weeds: Broadleaf weeds:

annual mustard	lambsquarters	sowthistle
buttercup	marshelder	stinging nettle
Canada thistle	pigweed	stinkweed
dandelion	plantain	sunflower
dragonhead mint	puncturevine	vetch
field peppergrass	purslane	whitetop
goatsbeard	ragweed	wild radish
hempnettle	shepherdspurse	yellow rocket
kochia		

Remarks: Not underseeded with legumes. Do not forage or graze animals on treated areas within 7 days of slaughter or treatment.

State Restrictions: Wilbur-Ellis not registered in California.

– – – – – – – – – – – – – – –

Rate: 0.125-0.25 lb. ae/A
0.25-0.5 pt./A

Time: Postemergence. Apply after crop is well tillered in the 4-leaf stage (4-8" tall) when legumes are 2-3" tall. Do not spray from boot to dough stage.

Weeds: Emergency control of:

mustard	yellow rocket

Remarks: Underseeded with legumes (alfalfa, lespedeza, red and white clover). Balance severity of weed problem against possibility of crop damage. Do not forage or graze animals on treated areas within 7 days of slaughter or treatment.

State Restrictions: Wilbur-Ellis not registered in California.

– – – – – – – – – – – – – – –

Signal Word/Toxicity Class: Danger/I (amine); Warning/II (ester).
REI: Danger—48 hr.; Warning—12 hr.

■ POST

Albaugh MCPA Ester 4 *(Albaugh)*
Solve MCPA Ester (4) *(Albaugh)*

Rate: 0.25-1.5 lb. ae/A
0.5-3 pt. 4/A

Time: Postemergence. Apply low rate for more susceptible weeds after crop has reached 3-4 leaf stage up to boot stage; use high rate for less susceptible weeds after crop has tillered and up to early boot stage. Do not spray from boot to dough stage.

Weeds: Broadleaf weeds:

annual mustard	goatsbeard	puncturevine
annual sowthistle	goosefoot	ragweed
beggarticks	hempnettle	shepherdspurse
cocklebur	lambsquarters	stinkweed
dragonhead mint	marshelder	wild radish
fanweed	pennycress	wintercress
field peppergrass	poison hemlock	yellow rocket

Remarks: Do not forage or graze meat animals on treated areas within 7 days of slaughter; dairy animals within 7 days after treatment.

– – – – – – – – – – – – – – –

Signal Word/Toxicity Class: Caution/III.
REI: 12 hr.

■ POST

Chiptox (sodium salt) *(Nufarm)*

Rate: 0.125-0.25 lb. ae/A
0.5-1 pt./A

Time: Postemergence. Apply when legumes are 2-3" tall, grain is fully tillered but before forming joints in the stem. Do not spray in boot to dough stage.

Weeds: Broadleaf weeds:

annual mustard	lambsquarters	stinging nettle
buttercup	peppergrass	stinkweed
Canada thistle	plantain	vetch
cocklebur	purslane	whitetop
dandelion	ragweed	wild radish
hempnettle	shepherdspurse	wintercress
hoary cress	sowthistle	yellow rocket
kochia		

Remarks: Underseeded with mixed legumes. Use 5-6 gal. water/A; higher volumes may cause injury to legumes. Do not forage or graze treated fields for 2 weeks or feed treated straw to livestock.

– – – – – – – – – – – – – – –

Rate: 0.25-1 lb. ae/A
1-4 pt./A

Time: Postemergence. Apply when grain is fully tillered but before forming joints in the stem. Do not spray in boot to dough stage.

Weeds: Same as above.

Remarks: Not underseeded with legumes. Use 6 pt. rate as emergency treatment for controlling perennial broadleaf weeds; balance severity of weed problem against possible crop injury.

– – – – – – – – – – – – – – –

Signal Word/Toxicity Class: Danger/I.
REI: 48 hr.

■ POST

Gordon's MCPA Amine 4 *(PBI/Gordon)*
Rhomene 4 (amine) *(Nufarm)*

Rate: 0.25-1 lb. ae/A
0.5-2 pt./A

Time: Postemergence. For lower rate, apply after grain is in 4-leaf stage but not forming joints in the stem; for rates over 1 pt., apply after grain is fully tillered. Do not spray in boot to dough stage.

4

Small Grains

NOTICE	The information on these pages is for preliminary planning — not a guide for use. Be sure to follow the manufacturer's directions, notwithstanding information contained here.	For personal protective equipment and EPA registration numbers, please turn to page 70.

Weeds: Broadleaf weeds:

bull thistle	dandelion	pigweed
common burdock	field pennycress	plantain
common cocklebur	giant ragweed	purslane
common	mustard (except blue)	Russian thistle
lambsquarters	pepperweed	shepherdspurse
common ragweed	(except perennial)	yellow rocket

Remarks: Not underseeded with legumes. For emergency perennial broadleaf weed control, use 3 pt. rate when weeds approach bud stage, balance problem severity against possible crop damage; spot treat scattered perennial weeds.

– – – – – – – – – – – – – – –

Rate: 0.25 lb. ae/A
0.5 pt./A

Time: Postemergence. Apply after crop is well tillered in the 4-leaf stage (4-8" tall) when legumes are 2-3" tall. Do not spray from boot to dough stage.

Weeds: Emergency control of:

mustard   yellow rocket

Remarks: Underseeded with legumes. Do not apply to grain underseeded with vetch or sweet clover. Do not use more than 6 gal. water/A; higher volumes may result in injury to legumes. Do not forage or graze animals on treated areas within 7 days of slaughter or treatment.

– – – – – – – – – – – – – – –

Signal Word/Toxicity Class: Danger/I.
REI: 48 hr.

■ POST
Rhonox (LV ester) (Nufarm)
Rate: 0.23-0.69 lb. ae/A
0.5-1.5 pt./A

Time: Postemergence. For lower rate, apply after grain is in 4-leaf stage but not forming joints in the stem; for rates over 1 pt., apply after grain is fully tillered. Do not spray in boot to dough stage.

Weeds: Broadleaf weeds:

annual sowthistle	pennycress	ragweed
dandelion	peppergrass	shepherdspurse
hempnettle	perennial sowthistle	stinkweed
kochia	pigweed	wild radish
lambsquarters	plantain	yellow rocket
mustard	purslane	

Remarks: Not underseeded to legumes. Do not forage or graze meat animals on treated fields within 7 days of slaughter. Refer to label for further use directions.

– – – – – – – – – – – – – – –

Signal Word/Toxicity Class: Caution.
REI: 12 hr.

■ POST
Riverdale MCPA L.V. 4, IOE (5.2) (ester) (Riverdale)
Sword (5.2) (ester) (Platte)
Rate: 0.25-1.5 lb. ae/A
0.5-3 pt. L.V. 4/A
0.2-1.3 lb. ae/A
0.33-2 pt. 5.2/A

Time: Postemergence. Apply low rate for more susceptible weeds after crop has reached 3-4 leaf stage up to boot stage; high rate after crop has tillered and up to early boot stage. Do not spray from boot to dough stage.

Rate: Fall-planted:
0.25-0.5 lb. ae/A
0.5-1 pt. L.V. 4/A
0.2-0.4 lb. ae/A
0.33-0.75 pt. 5.2/A

Time: Postemergence. Fall application: Apply when fall-planted small grains are fully tillered and have reached 3-4 leaf stage to boot stage. Spring application: Apply in early spring when annual broadleaf weeds are small and grain is fully tillered, but before grain is in jointed stage.

Weeds: Broadleaf weeds:

annual mustard	lambsquarters	sowthistle
buttercup	marshelder	stinging nettle
Canada thistle	pigweed	stinkweed
dandelion	plantain	sunflower
dragonhead mint	purslane	vetch
field peppergrass	puncturevine	whitetop
goatsbeard	ragweed	wild radish
hempnettle	shepherdspurse	yellow rocket
kochia		

Remarks: Not underseeded with legumes. Do not forage or graze animals on treated areas within 7 days of slaughter or treatment.

– – – – – – – – – – – – – – –

Rate: 0.125-0.25 lb. ae/A
0.25-0.5 pt. L.V.4/A
3-6 oz. 5.2/A

Time: Postemergence. Apply after crop is well tillered in the 4-leaf stage (4-8" tall) when legumes are 2-3" tall. Do not spray from boot to dough stage.
Weeds: Emergency control of:
mustard   yellow rocket

Remarks: Underseeded with legumes (alfalfa, lespedeza, red and white clover). Balance severity of weed problem against possibility of crop damage. Do not forage or graze animals on treated areas within 7 days of slaughter or treatment.

– – – – – – – – – – – – – – –

Signal Word/Toxicity Class: Warning/II.
REI: 12 hr.

Moxy — see bromoxynil

Opti-Amine — see 2,4-D

PARAQUAT

Nonselective control of emerged weeds prior to planting. Spray coverage is important for good results. No soil residual activity. Used in no-till systems. Restricted Use Pesticide.

■ PP, PRE
Cyclone (2L or 3L) or Gramoxone Extra (2.5L) (ZENECA)
Rate: 0.5-1 lb. ai/A
2-4 pt. 2L/A
1.5-3 pt. 2.5L/A
1.25-2.5 pt. 3L/A

Time: Preplant, preemergence. Apply broadcast or band prior to, during, or after planting but before crop emergence.
Weeds: Annual broadleaf weeds and grasses; suppression of perennials.
Remarks: Add nonionic surfactant or crop oil concentrate. Seedbeds should be formed as far ahead of planting and treatment as possible to permit maximum weed and grass emergence. Seeding should be done with minimum amount of soil disturbance. Weeds and grasses emerging after planting will not be controlled; crops emerged at time of application may be killed. Do not apply preplant or preemergence to soils lacking clay minerals. Refer to label for use directions, restrictions, and precautions.
Tank Mixes: Atrazine, Banvel, Bicep, Bladex, Canopy, Command, 2,4-D ester, Extrazine, Lariat, linuron, Marksman, metribuzin, Princep.

– – – – – – – – – – – – – – –

Signal Word/Toxicity Class: Danger-Poison/I.
REI: 12 hr. (except harvest aid/desiccation 24 hr.).

PEAK

Controls many broadleaf weeds, including triazine-resistant biotypes, by inhibiting a biochemical process which produces certain essential amino acids necessary for plant growth. The inhibited enzyme system is acetolactate synthase (ALS). Each bag of Peak contains 5 water-soluble packets.

■ POST
Peak (WDG) (prosulfuron) (Novartis)
Rate: Low rate:
0.38 oz. WDG/A (1 WS packet/8A)
Standard rate:
0.5 oz. WDG/A (1 WS packet/6A)

Time: Postemergence (over-the-top). Apply from 3-leaf stage to before second node is detectable in stem elongation.
Weeds: Broadleaf weeds:

blue mustard	flixweed	prickly sida
buffalobur	Florida pusley	prostrate knotweed*
bur cherval	giant ragweed	puncturevine
bushy wallflower	hairy buttercup	redroot pigweed
Canada thistle*	hedge bindweed*	Russian thistle
coast fiddleneck	hemp sesbania	shepherdspurse
common chickweed*	henbit*	sicklepod
common cocklebur	ivyleaf morningglory	smooth pigweed
common	jimsonweed	tall morningglory
lambsquarters*	kochia*	tall waterhemp
common mallow*	mayweed chamomile	tansymustard
common ragweed	minerslettuce	tumble mustard
common sunflower	mouseear chickweed*	tumble pigweed
common waterhemp	Palmer amaranth*	velvetleaf
corn gromwell*	Pennsylvania	Venice mallow
cutleaf	smartweed	wild buckwheat
eveningprimrose	pineappleweed	wild garlic
devilsclaw	pitted morningglory	wild mustard
field bindweed*	prickly lettuce	wild radish
field pennycress		

Suppression

◆–new product • PP-preplant • PPI-preplant incorporated • PRE-preemergence • POST-postemergence • SEQ-sequential • ae-acid equivalent • ai-active ingredient • DF-dry flowable
E/EC-emulsifiable concentrate • F/FL-flowable • DG/G/WG-dispersable granule • L/LC-liquid • SP/WSP-soluble packet • W/WP-wettable powder • WSB-water soluble bag

220   Weed Control Manual 2000

Remarks: Rate varies by weed height. Always add crop oil concentrate or nonionic surfactant. Do not apply to crop under stress. Do not make a foliar or soil application with an organophosphate insecticide within 15 days before or 10 days after application. Do not apply through any type of irrigation system.

Days To Harvest: Silage—40; grain—60; grazing/feeding forage to livestock—30.

Crop Rotation: IR/IMR Corn—anytime; normal field corn, grain sorghum—4 weeks; rice, popcorn, sweet corn, small grains (wheat, barley, oats, rye, proso millet, triticale)—2 months; beans (dry, green), cabbage, canola, cotton, flax, forage grasses, peanuts, peas, potatoes, soybeans, tobacco, tomatoes—9 months; alfalfa, clover, lentils—15 months; leeks, onion, sunflower, sugar beets—24 months; all other crops—18 months. Refer to label for geographic restrictions.

Tank Mixes: Low rate: Banvel, Bronate, Buctril, 2,4-D, MCPA; refer to label for use instructions.

State Restrictions: Not for use in San Luis Valley of Colorado, west of the Cascades in Oregon, and certain areas of Washington (abide by all sulfonylurea aerial application rulings by Washington Department of Agriculture).

- - - - - - - - - - - - - - -

Signal Word/Toxicity Class: Caution.
REI: 12 hr.

Phenoxy 088 — see 2,4-D

PROPANIL

Postemergence herbicide that controls green and yellow foxtail, pigweed, wild buckwheat, and wild mustard when tank mixed with MCPA. Control of grasses is reduced if weeds exceed stated growth stage.

■ POST

Stampede 80EDF *(Rohm and Haas)*
Rate: 1-1.13 lb. ai/A
1.25-1.4 pt. 80EDF/A
Time: Postemergence. Apply 10-17 days after crop emergence when grain is in 3-4 leaf stage; for foxtail, apply at 2-3 leaf stage.
Weeds: Broadleaf weeds:

common	prostrate pigweed	wild buckwheat
lambsquarters	redroot pigweed	wild mustard
kochia		

Grasses:

green foxtail	yellow foxtail

Remarks: Spring barley. Do not apply to grain crops that have been or will be treated with carbamate or organophosphorus insecticides. Do not apply through any type of irrigation system. Do not graze treated crop or cut for green chop feed.
Tank Mixes: MCPA.
State Restrictions: For use in Minnesota, Montana, North Dakota, and South Dakota.

- - - - - - - - - - - - - - -

Signal Word/Toxicity Class: Caution.
REI: 24 hr.

Puma — see fenoxaprop-P-ethyl

Ranger — see glyphosate

Rattler — see glyphosate

RAVE (Premix)

Premix with 2 modes of action. One active ingredient inhibits the acetolactate synthase (ALS) enzyme. The other active ingredient disrupts normal plant growth.

■ POST

◆ **Rave (WDG) (50% dicamba & 8.8% triasulfuron)** *(Novartis)*
Rate: Spring barley:
2 oz. WDG/A
Winter barley:
4 oz. WDG/A

Time: Postemergence. For spring barley, apply after emergence up to 4-leaf stage; winter barley, after emergence up to jointing.
Weeds: Broadleaf weeds:

annual morningglory	cutleaf	pepperweed
annual polemonium	eveningprimrose	pigweed
annual sowthistle	fanweed	plains coreopsis
black nightshade	field bindweed	prickly lettuce
blue mustard	field pennycress	prostrate knotweed
bur buttercup	fleabane	prostrate pigweed
bushy wallflower	flixweed	puncturevine
Canada thistle	forget-me-not	ragweed
coast fiddleneck	giant ragweed	redroot pigweed
common broomweed	goldenrod	Russian thistle
common chickweed	hairy vetch	shepherdspurse
common cocklebur	henbit	smooth pigweed
common groundsel	horseweed	tall buttercup
common	houndstongue	tall hedge mustard
lambsquarters	Indian mustard	tansymustard
common mallow	jagged chickweed	tartary buckwheat
common purslane	kochia	tarweed
common ragweed	ladysthumb	tumble mustard
common sunflower	lanceleaf ragweed	tumble pigweed
common yarrow	London rocket	umbrella spurry
corn chamomile	marestail	velvetleaf
corn cockle	marshelder	Virginia pepperweed
corn gromwell	minerslettuce	wild buckwheat
cornflower	musk thistle	wild mustard
creeping buttercup	mustard	wild radish
curly dock	Pennsylvania	woolly croton
	smartweed	

Remarks: Do not apply to wheat undersown with legumes or forage grasses. Do not apply to wheat under stress. Do not apply for at least 60 days after an organophosphate application. Do not apply through any type of irrigation system.

Days To Harvest: Hay, grain—37.

Crop Rotation: Recropping depends on field bioassay, soil pH, total rainfall, and geographic area. Refer to label for restrictions and more complete information.

Tank Mixes: Recommended tank mix partners include Bronate, Buctril, 2,4-D, MCPA, and Tilt fungicide.

State Restrictions: For use in Colorado (except San Luis Valley), Idaho, Kansas, Minnesota, Montana, Nebraska, Nevada, New Mexico, North Dakota, Oklahoma, Oregon, South Dakota, Texas, Utah, Washington, Wyoming. In Washington, abide by all sulfonylurea aerial application rulings by Washington Department of Agriculture.

- - - - - - - - - - - - - - -

Signal Word/Toxicity Class: Caution.
REI: 12 hr.

Rhomene — see MCPA

Rhonox — see MCPA

Roundup — see glyphosate

Saber — see 2,4-D

Salvo — see 2,4-D

Savage — see 2,4-D

SCYTHE

◆ **Scythe (pelargonic acid)** *(Mycogen)*
Rate: 4-13 fl. oz./1 gal. spray solution
Time: Apply to actively growing weeds prior to crop emergence.
Weeds: Annual and perennial broadleaf weeds and grasses.
Remarks: Apply in minimum 75 gal. spray solution/A or spray-to-wet. Do not apply by air or through any type of irrigation system. Refer to label for directions and precautions.
Tank Mixes: Glyphosate and other foliar and residual herbicides.

- - - - - - - - - - - - - - -

Signal Word/Toxicity Class: Warning/II.
REI: 24 hr.

4

Small Grains

NOTICE The information on these pages is for preliminary planning — not a guide for use. Be sure to follow the manufacturer's directions, notwithstanding information contained here. For personal protective equipment and EPA registration numbers, please turn to page 70.

SENCOR

Postemergence herbicide primarily for annual broadleaf weed control; suppresses some grasses. Use limited to labeled states. Most effective on mustards, chickweed, and pigweed.

■ **POST**

Sencor 4 (FL) or DF (metribuzin) *(Bayer)*

Rate: 0.25-0.5 lb. ai/A
0.5-1 pt. FL/A
0.33-0.66 lb. DF/A

Time: Postemergence.

Weeds: Broadleaf weeds:

annual polemonium	dogfennel	pineappleweed
bittercress	cutleaf	prostrate knotweed
blue mustard	eveningprimrose	redstem filaree
Carolina geranium	field pennycress	shepherdspurse
catchweed	gromwell	smallseed falseflax
common chickweed	henbit	tarweed fiddleneck
common	ivyleaf speedwell	Virginia pepperweed
lambsquarters	minerslettuce	wild mustard
conical catchfly	mousear chickweed	wild radish
corncockle	pigweed	wild turnip

Remarks: Spring, winter barley. Rate varies by soil texture and organic matter. Certain varieties are sensitive and should not be treated.

Days To Harvest: Do not graze or harvest before crop maturity.

Crop Rotation: Alfalfa, asparagus, and barley/wheat (following peas, lentils, soybeans), corn, forage grasses, potatoes, sainfoin, soybeans, sugarcane, tomatoes—4 months; barley, cotton, lentils, peas, rice, wheat—8 months; other crops not listed (except root crops)—12 months; onions, sugar beets, and other root crops—18 months.

Tank Mixes: May be tank mixed; refer to label for restrictions and tank mix directions.

State Restrictions: For use east of the Cascades in Idaho, Montana, Oregon, Utah, and Washington.

– – – – – – – – – – – – – –

Signal Word/Toxicity Class: Caution/III.
REI: 12 hr.

Solution — see 2,4-D

Solve — see 2,4-D; MCPA

Stampede — see propanil

Sterling — see dicamba

Stinger — see clopyralid

Sword — see MCPA

THIFENSULFURON-METHYL

■ **POST**

Harmony GT (DF) *(DuPont)*

Rate: 0.3-0.6 oz. DF/A

Time: Postemergence. Apply to young, actively growing weeds after crop is in 2-leaf stage, but before flag leaf is visible.

Weeds: Broadleaf weeds:

annual knawel	corn chamomile	little mallow*
annual sowthistle	corn spurry	London rocket
black mustard	curly dock	marshelder
bushy wallflower	cutleaf	minerslettuce
Carolina geranium*	eveningprimrose*	mouseear chickweed
coast fiddleneck	dogfennel	mouseearcress
common buckwheat	false chamomile	Pennsylvania
common chickweed	field pennycress	smartweed
common cocklebur*	flixweed	prickly lettuce*
common groundsel	green smartweed	prostrate knotweed
common	henbit*	redmaids
lambsquarters	jim hill mustard	rockpurslane
common mallow*	kochia	redroot pigweed
common sunflower*	ladysthumb	Russian thistle

Weeds: Broadleaf weeds, continued:

scentless chamomile	tarweed fiddleneck	wild buckwheat
shepherdspurse	tumble mustard	wild chamomile
smallflower buttercup	volunteer lentils	wild garlic
stinking mayweed	volunteer peas	wild mustard
swinecress	volunteer sunflower	wild radish*
tansymustard*		

*** Suppression**

Remarks: Not underseeded. Add approved nonionic surfactant. Do not apply through any type of irrigation system. Prevent spray drift to desirable plants. Do not graze or feed forage or hay from treated areas to livestock (harvested straw may be used for bedding and/or feed). Refer to label for restrictions and precautions.

Crop Rotation: Barley, oats, wheat—anytime; all other crops—45 days after application.

Tank Mixes: Assert, Avenge, bromoxynil, 2,4-D, dicamba, Hoelon, MCPA.

State Restrictions: Not for use in Alamosa, Conejos, Costilla, Rio Grande, and Saguache counties in Colorado.

– – – – – – – – – – – – – –

Signal Word/Toxicity Class: Caution.
REI: 4 hr.

TORDON

Not for use on winter barley. Restricted Use Pesticide.

Tordon 22K (picloram) *(Dow AgroSciences)*

Rate: 1-1.5 fl. oz. 22K/A

Time: Apply from 3- to 5-leaf stage to early jointing stage of growth.

Weeds: Broadleaf weeds such as:

Canada thistle	pennycress	volunteer sunflower
lambsquarters	pigweed	wild buckwheat
mayweed	Russian thistle	wild mustard

Remarks: Spring barley not underseeded with legumes. Not flood or subirrigated. Not for use on land planted to sweet sorghum. May cause shorter straw on some varieties of cereals but grain yields are usually not affected. Do not apply more than 1.5 fl. oz./A during growing season. Do not graze or feed forage from treated areas for 2 weeks after treatment or harvest hay from treated fields. Do not apply through any type of irrigation system. Refer to label for restrictions and precautions.

Days To Harvest: 50.

Crop Rotation: Use only on land to be planted the following year to grass, barley, oats, wheat, grain sorghum, or fallow. Do not plant grain sorghum within 8 months after application. Do not rotate to broadleaf crops.

Tank Mixes: 2,4-D, MCPA.

State Restrictions: For use west of the Mississippi except San Luis Valley of Colorado. Use in Hawaii limited to supplemental labeling.

– – – – – – – – – – – – – –

Signal Word/Toxicity Class: Caution.
REI: 12 hr.

Treflan — see trifluralin

TRI-4 — see trifluralin

TRIFLURALIN

Useful for annual grasses such as green foxtail. Good crop tolerance if applied properly. Incorporate preemergence applications shallowly to avoid disturbing crop seed.

■ **PRE**

Albaugh Trifluralin 4EC *(Albaugh)*
◆ **Clean Crop Trifluralin HF (4EC)** *(Platte)*
Gowan Trifluralin 4 or 5 (EC) or 10G *(Gowan)*
Helena Trifluralin 4 EC *(Helena)*
Riverside Trifluralin 4EC or Trific 60DF *(Terra)*
◆ **Sedagri Trifluralin 480 (4EC)** *(Rhone-Poulenc)*
Treflan HFP (4EC) or TR-10 (10G) *(Dow AgroSciences)*
TRI-4 HF (4EC) *(American Cyanamid)*
Trilin 4 or 5 (EC) or 10G *(Griffin)*
Wilbur-Ellis Trifluralin 10G *(Wilbur-Ellis)*

Rate: 0.5-0.75 lb. ai/A
1-1.5 pt. 4EC/A
0.8-1.2 pt. 5EC/A
0.875-1.25 lb. 60DF/A
5-7.5 lb. 10G/A

Time: Postplant incorporated. Apply after seeding but before crop emergence.

Weeds:

foxtail	pigeongrass

◆-new product • PP-preplant • PPI-preplant incorporated • PRE-preemergence • POST-postemergence • SEQ-sequential • ae-acid equivalent • ai-active ingredient • DF-dry flowable
E/EC-emulsifiable concentrate • F/FL-flowable • DG/G/WG-dispersable granule • L/LC-liquid • SP/WSP-soluble packet • W/WP-wettable powder • WSB-water soluble bag

222   Weed Control Manual 2000

Remarks: Rate varies by soil type. Double incorporate with flextine or diamond harrow 1-1¹/₂" deep. Make second incorporation in different direction from the first within 24 hr. of application. Under certain conditions, delayed crop emergence or stand reduction may occur; refer to label for directions, restrictions, and precautions.

Crop Rotation: Refer to label.

State Restrictions: Wilbur-Ellis and Trilin 10G not for use in California.

— — — — — — — — — — — —

Signal Word/Toxicity Class: Varies by formulation.

REI: 12 hr. unless soil injected or soil incorporated.

Trilin — see trifluralin

Weed Rhap — see 2,4-D

Weedar — see 2,4-D

Weedestroy — see 2,4-D

Weedone — see 2,4-D

Oats

Banvel — see dicamba

Barrage — see 2,4-D

Bison — see bromoxynil & MCPA

Broclean — see bromoxynil

Bromac — see bromoxynil & MCPA

Bromox — see bromoxynil

Bromox-MCPA 2-2 — see bromoxynil & MCPA

BROMOXYNIL

Provides good to excellent control of labeled annual broadleaf weeds. Frequently used in tank mix with MCPA for broader spectrum control in oats.

■ **POST**

◆ **Broclean 2EC** *(Platte)*

◆ **Bromox 2EC** *(Micro Flo)*

Buctril (2EC), Buctril 4EC *(Rhone-Poulenc)*

Moxy 2EC *(Terra)*

Rate: Spring-seeded (except CO, ID, OR, MT, WA, WY):
 0.25-0.5 lb. ai/A
 1-2 pt. 2EC/A
 0.5-1 pt. 4EC/A
 Fall-seeded; spring-seeded (CO, ID, OR, MT, WA, WY only):
 0.375-0.5 lb. ai/A
 1.5-2 pt. 2EC/A
 0.75-1 pt. 4EC/A
 Underseeded with alfalfa:
 0.25-0.375 lb. ai/A
 1-1.5 pt. 2EC/A
 0.5-0.75 pt. 4EC/A

Time: Postemergence. Apply from crop emergence to boot stage.

Weeds: Most susceptible broadleaf weeds:

annual pepperweed	common tarweed	Pennsylvania
annual sowthistle	eastern black	smartweed
black nightshade	nightshade	shepherdspurse
blue mustard	field pennycress	silverleaf nightshade
bristly starbur	green smartweed	sunflower
coast fiddleneck	hairy nightshade	tartary buckwheat
common cocklebur	jimsonweed	wild buckwheat
common lambsquarters	ladysthumb	

Susceptible broadleaf weeds:

buffalobur	ivyleaf morningglory	spiny pigweed
burcucumber	knawel	tall morningglory
common groundsel	kochia	tall waterhemp
common ragweed	London rocket	tumble mustard
corn chamomile	mayweed	velvetleaf
corn gromwell	prostrate knotweed	Venice mallow
cowcockle	puncturevine	wild mustard
giant ragweed	redroot pigweed	wild radish
hemp sesbania	Russian thistle	yellow starthistle

Remarks: Apply by ground, air, and sprinkler irrigation equipment. Do not apply when crops are under moisture stress. Do not graze treated fields within 30 days after application (45 days for Buctril). Refer to label for use directions, restrictions and precautions.

Crop Rotation: Do not plant rotational crops until the following season (within 30 days of application for Buctril).

Tank Mixes: 2,4-D (high rates will reduce crop tolerance), MCPA.

— — — — — — — — — — — —

Signal Word/Toxicity Class: Warning/II.

REI: 12 hr.

BROMOXYNIL & MCPA (Premixes)

Premix that provides very good to excellent control of several annual broadleaf weeds. Especially effective for weeds such as wild buckwheat and kochia. Good crop tolerance. Drought stress reduces control.

■ **POST**

Bison (EC) (2 lb./gal. bromoxynil & 2 lb./gal. MCPA) *(Terra)*

◆ **Bromac (EC) (2 lb./gal. bromoxynil & 2 lb./gal. MCPA)** *(Platte)*

◆ **Bromox-MCPA 2-2 (EC) (2 lb./gal. bromoxynil & 2 lb./gal. MCPA)** *(Micro Flo)*

Bronate (EC) (2 lb./gal. bromoxynil & 2 lb./gal. MCPA) *(Rhone-Poulenc)*

Rate: 0.5-1 lb. ai/A
 1-2 pt. EC/A
 Chemigation:
 1 lb. ai/A
 2 pt. EC/A
 Postharvest—MN, MT, ND, SD:
 0.38-1 lb. ai/A
 0.75-2 pt. EC/A (Bronate)

Time: Postemergence. Apply after 3-leaf stage but before boot stage.

Weeds: Most susceptible broadleaf weeds:

annual sowthistle	field pennycress	Russian thistle
black mustard	green smartweed	shepherdspurse
black nightshade	hairy nightshade	silverleaf nightshade
coast fiddleneck	horned poppy	smooth pigweed
common cocklebur	jimsonweed	spiny pigweed
common	ladysthumb	sunflower
lambsquarters	London rocket	tall waterhemp
common tarweed	marshelder	tartary buckwheat
cowcockle	Pennsylvania	tumble mustard
cutleaf nightshade	smartweed	wild buckwheat
eastern black	pepperweed	wild mustard
nightshade	redroot pigweed	yellow rocket

Susceptible broadleaf weeds:

blue mustard	giant ragweed	puncturevine
Canada thistle	hemp sesbania	purple mustard
(suppression)	henbit	tall morningglory
common groundsel	ivyleaf morningglory	tansymustard
common ragweed	knawel	tarweed
corn chamomile	kochia	velvetleaf
corn gromwell	mayweed	wild radish
fumitory	prostrate knotweed	

Remarks: Rates vary by weed species and conditions; refer to label for directions and precautions. Do not apply when crop canopy covers weeds or when crops are under moisture stress. Do not graze fields within 30 days after application (45 for Bronate).

Tank Mixes: MCPA.

— — — — — — — — — — — —

Signal Word/Toxicity Class: Warning/II.

REI: 12 hr.

Bronate — see bromoxynil & MCPA

4

Small Grains

Oats

Buctril — see bromoxynil

Chiptox — see MCPA

Clarity — see dicamba

CLOPYRALID

Systemic herbicide absorbed by leaves and roots. Has selective postemergence control of many annual and perennial broadleaf weeds.

■ POST

Stinger *(Dow AgroSciences)*

Rate: 0.1-0.125 lb. ae/A
  0.25-0.33 pt./A

Time: Postemergence. Apply from 3-leaf stage up to early boot stage.

Weeds: Annual and perennial broadleaf weeds:

Canada thistle	jimsonweed	sowthistle
cocklebur	knapweed	spotted knapweed
clover	marshelder	sunflower
diffuse knapweed	Russian knapweed	vetch
Jerusalem artichoke	(suppression)	volunteer soybean

Remarks: Not underseeded with legumes. Do not allow lactating dairy animals or meat animals being finished for slaughter to forage or graze treated fields within 1 week after treatment. Do not harvest hay from treated fields. Do not apply through any type of irrigation system or contaminate irrigation ditches or water used for irrigation or domestic purposes.

Crop Rotation: Varies by region; refer to label.

Tank Mixes: May be tank mixed with other herbicides registered for postemergence application.

- - - - - - - - - - - - - - - -

Signal Word/Toxicity Class: Caution/III.
REI: 12 hr.

Credit — see glyphosate

CURTAIL M (Premix)

Clopyralid provides good seasonal control of Canada thistle. MCPA in premix improves control of other broadleaf weeds. Crop tolerance is good. Canada thistle control is best when weeds are treated before they form flower buds.

■ POST

Curtail M (0.42 lb./gal. clopyralid & 2.35 lb./gal. MCPA)
(Dow AgroSciences)

Rate: 0.6-0.8 lb. ae/A
  1.75-2.66 pt. Curtail M/A

Time: Postemergence. Apply in spring to actively growing oats once 4 leaves have unfolded on main stem up to jointing stage. Do not apply after boot stage.

Weeds: Broadleaf weeds:

alfalfa	giant ragweed	red sorrel
annual sowthistle	goatsbeard	redroot pigweed
Canada thistle	hairy nightshade	Russian knapweed*
coffeeweed	horseweed	Russian thistle
common burdock	Jerusalem artichoke	(1-3 leaf)
common cocklebur	jim hill mustard	scentless chamomile
common groundsel	jimsonweed	shepherdspurse
common	kochia* (2-4 leaf)	sicklepod
lambsquarters	ladysthumb	spotted knapweed
common ragweed	mayweed chamomile	sweetclover
common sunflower	meadow salsify	tansymustard
cornflower	musk thistle	tumble mustard
curly dock	narrowleaf	velvetleaf
cutleaf nightshade	hawksbeard	vetch
dandelion	Pennsylvania	volunteer beans
diffuse knapweed	smartweed	volunteer lentils
dogfennel	perennial sowthistle*	volunteer peas
false chamomile	pineappleweed	wild buckwheat
fanweed	plantain	wild mustard
field pennycress	prickly lettuce	wild radish
flixweed*	red clover	yellow starthistle

* Suppression

Remarks: Not underseeded with legumes. Do not harvest hay from treated grain fields. Do not allow lactating dairy animals or meat animals being finished for slaughter to forage or graze treated fields within 1 week after application. Do not apply through any type of irrigation system.

Crop Rotation: Varies by region; refer to label.

Tank Mixes: Ally, Avenge, Banvel, Buctril, 2,4-D, diuron, Express, Harmony Extra, MCPA, metribuzin.

- - - - - - - - - - - - - - - -

Signal Word/Toxicity Class: Caution/III.
REI: 48 hr.

2,4-D - PHENOXY HERBICIDES

Especially useful for field bindweed and Canada thistle. Amines have greater crop tolerance than ester. Oats are less tolerant to 2,4-D than wheat or barley and more likely to be injured. Some varietal differences have been established.

Annual and perennial broadleaf weeds controlled by 2,4-D include:

beggarticks	galinsoga	povertyweed
bindweed	goldenrod	puncturevine
bitterweed	ground ivy	purslane
broomweed	healall	ragweed
bull thistle	hoary cress	Russian thistle
burdock	ironweed	shepherdspurse
Canada thistle	jimsonweed	smartweed
carpetweed	knotweed	sowthistle
catnip	lambsquarters	stinkweed
chicory	mallow	sumac
chickweed	marshelder	sunflower
cocklebur	mexicanweed	sweetclover
coffeeweed	morningglory	velvetleaf
cutleaf	musk thistle	Virginia creeper
eveningprimrose	mustard	wild carrot
creeping jenny	pennywort	wild garlic
croton	pepperweed	wild lettuce
dandelion	pigweed	wild onion
dock	plantain	wild parsnips
dogbane	pokeweed	wild radish

■ POST

Albaugh Amine 4 (2,4-D amine) *(Albaugh)*
Weedestroy AM-40 (2,4-D amine) *(Riverdale)*
Wilbur-Ellis Amine 4 (2,4-D amine) *(Wilbur-Ellis)*

Rate: Spring postemergence:
  0.25-0.5 lb. ae/A
  0.5-1 pt./A
  Preharvest:
  0.5-1 lb. ae/A
  1-2 pt./A

Time: Postemergence, preharvest. Apply after fully tillered stage, boot to dough stage. For preharvest, apply when grain is in dough stage.

Remarks: Not underseeded with legumes.

State Restrictions: Wilbur-Ellis not registered in California.

- - - - - - - - - - - - - - - -

Rate: 0.125-0.25 lb. ae/A
  0.25-0.5 pt./A

Time: Postemergence. Apply in spring, after 8" tall but before boot stage.

Remarks: Underseeded with legumes.

State Restrictions: Wilbur-Ellis not registered in California.

- - - - - - - - - - - - - - - -

Signal Word/Toxicity Class: Danger/I.
REI: 48 hr.

■ POST

Albaugh LV4 or LV6 Ester (2,4-D ester) *(Albaugh)*
Riverdale 6 Amine (2,4-D amine) *(Riverdale)*
Riverdale L.V. 4 or L.V. 6 (2,4-D ester) *(Riverdale)*
Weed Rhap LV-6D (2,4-D ester) *(Helena)*
Wilbur-Ellis Lo Vol-4 or Lo Vol-6 (2,4-D ester) *(Wilbur-Ellis)*

Rate: Spring:
  0.25 lb. ae/A
  0.5 pt. 4/A
  0.33 pt. 6/A
  Fall:
  0.25-0.38 lb. ae/A
  0.5-0.75 pt. 4/A
  0.33-0.5 pt. 6/A
  Fall (Southern states):
  0.125-0.75 lb. ae/A
  0.25-1.25 pt. 4/A
  0.16-0.83 pt. 6/A

◆-new product • PP-preplant • PPI-preplant incorporated • PRE-preemergence • POST-postemergence • SEQ-sequential • ae-acid equivalent • ai-active ingredient • DF-dry flowable E/EC-emulsifiable concentrate • F/FL-flowable • DG/G/WG-dispersable granule • L/LC-liquid • SP/WSP-soluble packet • W/WP-wettable powder • WSB-water soluble bag

Time: Postemergence. Apply in the spring when grain is fully tillered or stooled but before jointing. Do not spray before tiller stage or from early boot to dough stage. For fall-seeded oats in southern U.S., apply after full tillering but before early bud stage. Do not spray during or immediately following cold weather.

State Restrictions: Wilbur-Ellis not registered in California.

- - - - - - - - - - - - - - - -

Signal Word/Toxicity Class: Danger/I (amine); Caution/III (ester).
REI: Danger—48 hr.; Caution—12 hr.

■ POST
◆ Barrage or Barrage HF (EC) (2,4-D ester) *(Helena)*

Rate: Spring-planted:
6 fl. oz./A

Time: Postemergence. Apply in the full tiller stage. Do not apply before tiller stage or from boot to dough stage.

Rate: Fall-planted:
6-13 fl. oz./A

Time: Postemergence. Apply after full tillering, but prior to jointing. Do not apply until after full tillering or from jointing to dough stage.

Rate: 13-26 fl. oz./A
Time: Preharvest. Apply in hard dough stage.
Remarks: Not underseeded with legumes. Oats are more sensitive to 2,4-D than other grains. Do not forage or graze dairy or meat animals being finished for slaughter within 2 weeks after application.
Crop Rotation: Refer to labels.
Tank Mixes: Bromoxynil, dicamba, diuron, Glean, Harmony Extra, Peak.

Signal Word/Toxicity Class: Caution/III.
REI: 12 hr.

■ POST
◆ Clean Crop Low Vol 4 or Low Vol 6 (2,4-D ester) *(Platte)*
Esteron 99C (2,4-D LV ester) *(Rhone-Poulenc)*
Gordon's LV 400 (2,4-D ester) *(PBI/Gordon)*
Riverside 2,4-D LV4 (2,4-D ester) *(Terra)*

Rate: Spring-seeded:
0.25 lb. ae/A
0.5 pt. 4, 99C/A
0.33 pt. 6/A
Fall-seeded (Southern states):
0.25-0.5 lb. ae/A
0.5-1 pt./A

Time: Postemergence. Apply after full tillering but before early boot stage. Do not spray fall-seeded oats during or immediately following cold weather.

Rate: 0.5-1 lb. ae/A
1-2 pt./A
Time: Preharvest (dough stage).
Remarks: Not underseeded with legumes. Oats are more sensitive to 2,4-D than other grains. Do not feed treated straw to livestock.

- - - - - - - - - - - - - - - -

Signal Word/Toxicity Class: Caution/III.
REI: 12 hr.

■ POST
◆ Clean Crop Amine 4 (2,4-D amine) *(Platte)*
Formula 40 (2,4-D mixed amine) *(Rhone-Poulenc)*
Hi-Dep (2,4-D mixed amine) *(PBI/Gordon)*
◆ Opti-Amine (4) (2,4-D amine) *(Helena)*
Weed Rhap A-4D (2,4-D amine) *(Helena)*

Rate: 0.25-0.5 lb. ae/A
0.5-1 pt./A

Time: Postemergence. Apply after grain begins tillering and before boot stage (4-8" tall). Do not apply before tiller stage or from early boot through milk stage.

Rate: 0.5-1 lb. ae/A
1-2 pt./A
Time: Preharvest (dough stage).
Remarks: Not underseeded with legumes. Up to 3 pt./A may be used for difficult weed problems such as dry conditions in Western states. Do not allow dairy animals or meat animals being finished for slaughter to forage or graze treated fields within 2 weeks of treatment.

- - - - - - - - - - - - - - - -

Signal Word/Toxicity Class: Danger/I.
REI: 48 hr.

■ POST
Riverside 2,4-D Amine 4 (2,4-D amine) *(Terra)*

Rate: 0.25-0.5 lb. ae/A
0.5-1 pt./A

Time: Postemergence. Apply in spring when well established, tillered, and before jointing.

Remarks: Not underseeded with legumes. Oats are more sensitive to 2,4-D than other grains.

- - - - - - - - - - - - - - - -

Signal Word/Toxicity Class: Danger/I.
REI: 48 hr.

■ POST
◆ Saber (2,4-D amine) *(Platte)*

Rate: Spring-seeded:
0.18-1 lb. ae/A
0.375-2 pt./A
Fall-seeded (Southern states):
0.25-0.5 lb. ae/A
0.5-1 pt./A

Time: Postemergence. Apply when crop is in full tiller stage. Do not apply before tiller or from boot to dough stage. Do not spray fall-seeded oats during or immediately following cold weather.

Rate: 0.35-1.5 lb. ae/A
0.75-3 pt./A

Time: Preharvest. Apply in hard dough stage. Do not apply before tiller or from boot to dough stage.

Remarks: Not underseeded with legumes. Oats are more sensitive to 2,4-D than other grains. Emergency applications at 2 pt./A may control difficult weed problems. Do not forage or graze treated fields for 2 weeks after application. Do not feed treated straw to livestock if emergency and/or preharvest treatment is applied.

- - - - - - - - - - - - - - - -

Signal Word/Toxicity Class: Danger/I.
REI: 48 hr.

■ POST
Salvo (2,4-D LV ester) *(Platte)*

Rate: Spring-planted:
0.25-0.31 lb. ae/A
0.4-0.5 pt./A

Time: Postemergence. Apply after plants are fully tillered but before stems begin to joint.

Rate: Fall-planted:
0.25-0.5 lb. ae/A
0.4-0.8 pt./A

Time: Postemergence. Apply in the spring when weeds are small and oats are in full tiller stage (4-8" high) and before boot stage. Do not apply during boot or dough stage.

Remarks: Do not forage or graze treated fields within 2 weeks after application or feed treated straw to livestock.

- - - - - - - - - - - - - - - -

Signal Word/Toxicity Class: Caution/III.
REI: 12 hr.

■ POST
Savage (WSB) (2,4-D amine) *(Platte)*

Rate: 0.24-0.48 lb. ae/A
0.25-0.5 lb. WSB/A

Time: Postemergence. Spring-seeded: Apply in the spring when grain has 3 or more tillers. Flag leaf should not be visible. Do not apply from boot to dough stage. Fall-seeded (Southern states): Apply after full tillering, but prior to joints forming in the stem. Do not apply before tiller or from joint to dough stage.

Rate: 0.48-1.43 lb. ae/A
0.5-1.5 lb. WSB/A
Time: Preharvest. Apply in hard dough stage.
Remarks: Not underseeded with legumes. Oats are more sensitive to 2,4-D than other grains. Do not forage or graze treated fields within 2 weeks after treatment. Do not feed treated straw if a preharvest treatment is applied. Refer to label for use directions, restrictions and precautions.

- - - - - - - - - - - - - - - -

Signal Word/Toxicity Class: Danger/I.
REI: 48 hr.

4

Small Grains

Oats

■ POST

Solve 2,4-D (2,4-D LV ester) *(Albaugh)*

Rate: Spring-planted:
0.25 lb. ae/A
0.5 pt./A

Time: Postemergence. Apply after fully tillered stage, except during boot to dough stage.

Rate: Fall-planted:
0.125-0.75 lb. ae/A
0.25-1.25 pt./A

Time: Postemergence. Apply after full tillering but before early boot stage. Do not spray during or immediately following cold weather.

Remarks: Some difficult weeds may require higher rates (0.75-1.25 pt./A) for maximum control, but crop injury may result. Do not forage or graze treated fields within 2 weeks after application or feed treated straw to livestock.

Signal Word/Toxicity Class: Caution/III.
REI: 12 hr.

■ POST

Solution (WS) (2,4-D amine) *(Riverdale)*

Rate: 1 WS packet/5-10 A

Time: Postemergence. Apply in the spring when oats are well established and tillered and before jointing after crop has reached the dough stage.

Remarks: Apply in 5-100 gal. water.

Signal Word/Toxicity Class: Danger/I.
REI: 48 hr.

■ POST

Weedar 64 (4) (2,4-D amine) *(Nufarm)*

Rate: 0.25-1 lb. ae/A
0.5-2 pt./A

Time: Postemergence. Apply after grain is fully tillered (4-8" high) but not forming joints in stem. Do not spray in boot to dough stage.

Remarks: Not underseeded with legumes. Do not use unless possible crop injury will be acceptable.

Rate: 0.125-0.25 lb. ae/A
0.25-0.5 pt./A

Time: Postemergence. Apply after grain is 8" tall but before boot stage. Do not spray in boot to dough stage.

Remarks: Underseeded with legumes. Do not spray alfalfa or sweet clover unless infestation is severe and injury to legumes can be tolerated.

Signal Word/Toxicity Class: Danger/I.
REI: 48 hr.

DICAMBA

Controls several annual and perennial broadleaf weeds. Consistent control in varied growing conditions. Especially effective on special weeds including kochia, smartweed, and wild buckwheat. Do not apply at crop stages beyond those recommended. Usually tank mixed with MCPA when used in oats.

Banvel (WS) (DMA salt of dicamba) *(BASF)*
Banvel SGF (sodium salt of dicamba) *(BASF)*
Clarity (WS) (dicamba-DGA) *(BASF)*
◆ **Sterling (WS) (DMA salt of dicamba)** *(Terra)*

Rate: 2-4 fl. oz. WS/A
4-8 fl. oz. SGF/A

Time: Preplant, preemergence, postemergence. For fall-seeded oats, apply prior to jointing stage. For spring-seeded oats, apply prior to 5-leaf stage. For best results, apply when weeds are in 2-3 leaf stage and rosettes are less than 2" across.

Weeds: Broadleaf weeds:

annual sowthistle	corn cockle	Pennsylvania
black nightshade	cowcockle	smartweed
common cocklebur	field pennycress	redroot pigweed
common	giant ragweed	rough pigweed
lambsquarters	green smartweed	Russian thistle
common mallow	henbit	tumble pigweed
common ragweed	knotweed	velvetleaf
common sunflower	kochia	volunteer sunflower
corn chamomile	ladysthumb	wild buckwheat

Remarks: Not underseeded with legumes. Do not graze lactating dairy animals within 7 days after application or remove animals for slaughter within 30 days of last application; no waiting period between treatment

and grazing for nonlactating animals. Do not apply through any type of irrigation system.

Days To Harvest: Hay—37.

Tank Mixes: MCPA. Do not tank mix with 2,4-D.

Signal Word/Toxicity Class: Warning/II (Banvel, Sterling); Caution (Clarity).
REI: 24 hr.

Direx — see diuron

DIURON

Controls certain annual broadleaf weeds and some grasses. Applied preemergence or postemergence, depending on area.

■ PRE, POST

Direx 80DF *(Griffin)*
◆ **Diuron 80 WDG** *(Platte)*
Karmex DF *(Griffin)*
Riverside Diuron 4L or 80DF *(Terra)*

Rate: 0.75-1 lb. ai/A
1.5-2 pt. 4L/A
0.8-1.2 lb. ai/A
1-1.5 lb. DF, 80DF/A

Time: Preemergence or postemergence. Apply within 6 weeks of planting either before or after oats emerge and before weeds are 4" tall.

Weeds: Broadleaf weeds:

amsinckia (fiddleneck)	gromwell	sesbania*
annual groundcherry	knawel	shepherdspurse
annual	lambsquarters	sicklepod*
morningglory*	pennycress	tansymustard
chickweed	pigweed	teaweed*
cocklebur*	prickly sida	wild buckwheat
corn spurry	purslane	wild lettuce
dogfennel	ragweed	wild mustard

Grasses:

annual bluegrass	barnyardgrass	rattail fescue
annual sweet	crabgrass	red sprangletop
vernalgrass	foxtail	velvetgrass

* Partial control

Remarks: Spring oats.

Crop Rotation: Do not plant treated area to any other crop within 1 year after application.

State Restrictions: For use in Idaho, eastern Oregon, eastern Washington.

Rate: 1.2-1.5 lb. ai/A
2.25-3 pt. 4L/A
1.5-2 lb. DF, 80DF/A

Time: Preemergence.

Weeds: Broadleaf Weeds:

chickweed	groundsel	shepherdspurse
dogfennel		

Grasses:

annual bluegrass	rattail fescue	sweet vernalgrass
annual ryegrass		

Remarks: For winter oats and mixtures with peas or vetch. Refer to label for restrictions on soil type.

Crop Rotation: Do not replant treated area to any crop within 1 year after last application.

State Restrictions: For use in western Oregon, western Washington.

Signal Word/Toxicity Class: Caution/III.
REI: 12 hr.

Esteron 99C — see 2,4-D

Formula 40 — see 2,4-D

GLEAN

Recommended for use on land primarily dedicated to long-term production of wheat, barley, or oats. Used postemergence in oats to control annual broadleaf weeds. Especially effective for mustard, pigweed, and kochia. Foxtail suppression is noted if applied early. Good crop tolerance. Follow crop rotation limitations in your area.

◆-new product • PP-preplant • PPI-preplant incorporated • PRE-preemergence • POST-postemergence • SEQ-sequential • ae-acid equivalent • ai-active ingredient • DF-dry flowable
E/EC-emulsifiable concentrate • F/FL-flowable • DG/G/WG-dispersable granule • L/LC-liquid • SP/WSP-soluble packet • W/WP-wettable powder • WSB-water soluble bag

■ PRE, POST
Glean FC (DF) (chlorsulfuron) *(DuPont)*
Rate: TX, western OR & WA:
0.33 oz. DF/A
TX—annual ryegrass:
0.33-0.5 oz. DF/A
Time: Preemergence: Apply after planting but before winter oats emerge.

Rate: 0.167-0.33 oz. DF/A
Time: Postemergence: Apply when winter or spring oats are in 2-leaf stage but before boot stage.
Weeds: Broadleaf weeds:

bedstraw*	flixweed	redstem filaree
blue mustard	hempnettle	Russian thistle*
bur beakchervil	henbit	shepherdspurse
buttercup	jim hill mustard	smooth pigweed
Canada thistle*	kochia	speedwell*
coast fiddleneck	ladysthumb	sunflower*
common chickweed	lambsquarters	tansymustard*
common groundsel*	mayweed	tarweed
conical catchfly	minerslettuce	treacle mustard
corn gromwell*	mouseear chickweed	tumble mustard
corn spurry	Pennsylvania	white cockle
cowcockle	smartweed*	wild buckwheat*
curly dock	pineappleweed	wild carrot
cutleaf	prickly lettuce*	wild mustard
eveningprimrose	prostrate knotweed*	wild radish*
false chamomile	prostrate pigweed	wild turnip
falseflax	purslane	yellow starthistle
field pennycress	redroot pigweed	

Grasses:
annual ryegrass*

Aerial bulblet control:
wild garlic*   wild onion*

* *Suppression*

Remarks: Not underseeded with legumes. Glean is mixed in water or directly into liquid nitrogen fertilizer solutions and applied as uniform broadcast spray. Surfactant should be used in spray mix unless otherwise specified.
Crop Rotation: Recropping depends on rate, soil pH, total rainfall, and geographic area. Refer to label for soil pH restrictions and more complete information.
Tank Mixes: Banvel, Bronate, Buctril, 2,4-D, Karmex, or MCPA to expand weed control and assist in controlling naturally occurring weed biotypes that may be resistant to Glean.
State Restrictions: For use in California, northern Idaho, Kansas, Nebraska, Oklahoma, Oregon, Texas, and Washington. Kochia and Russian thistle for central Kansas, Nebraska, Oklahoma, and northcentral Texas.

- - - - - - - - - - - - - - - -

Signal Word/Toxicity Class: Caution.
REI: 4 hr.

Glyfos or Glyfos X-tra — see glyphosate

GLYPHOSATE

Controls emerged weeds before planting in reduced or no-till. Low rates control annual grasses and broadleaves. Ammonium sulfate at 17 lb./100 gal. solution improves results with low rate applications where water quality is a factor. Do not allow glyphosate to contact desirable plants.

■ PP, PRE
◆ **Credit (4WS)** *(Nufarm)*
◆ **Glyfos or Glyfos X-tra (4WS)** *(Cheminova)*
Rattler (4WS) *(Helena)*
Roundup Custom (5.4WS) *(Monsanto)*
Roundup Original, Original RT, Ultra, Ultra RT (4WS) *(Monsanto)*
Rate: Annual weeds:
0.38-1.5 lb. ai/A
0.56-2.25 pt. 5.4WS/A
0.75-3 pt. 4WS/A
Perennial weeds:
0.5-5 lb. ai/A
0.75-7.5 pt. 5.4WS/A
1-10 pt. 4WS/A
Time: Preplant, preemergence, at-planting, spot treatment, postharvest. For spot treatment, apply before heading.
Weeds: Most emerged annual and perennial broadleaf weeds including:

Canada thistle	field bindweed	kochia

Grasses:

downy brome	foxtail	quackgrass

Remarks: For postharvest applications, do not apply more than 1 lb. ai/A. Do not add surfactant to Roundup Ultra or Ultra RT. For spot treatment, do not treat more than 10% total area to be harvested. Do not apply through any type of irrigation system. Refer to label for directions, precautions and restrictions.
Days To Harvest: Postharvest: harvest/feeding—8 weeks.
Tank Mixes: Postharvest: 2,4-D, dicamba. Roundup tank mixes not registered in California by air.
State Restrictions: Roundup RT for use in Colorado, Idaho, Montana, North Dakota, South Dakota, Utah, Wyoming, and in specific counties only in Kansas, Minnesota, Nebraska, Nevada, Oklahoma, Oregon, and Washington; refer to label for restrictions. Glyfos is not registered for use in California. Glyfos X-tra is not registered for use in mistblowers in California or Arizona.

- - - - - - - - - - - - - - - -

Signal Word/Toxicity Class: Varies by formulation.
REI: Warning—12 hr.; Caution—4 hr.

■ PRE
Ranger (WS) *(Monsanto)*
Rate: 0.25-0.5 lb. ai/A
0.75-1.5 pt. WS/A
Time: Preemergence. Apply to vigorously growing weeds.
Weeds: Broadleaf weeds:

blue mustard	field pennycress	shepherdspurse
buttercup	horseweed	smallseed falseflax
cocklebur	London rocket	smooth pigweed
common groundsel	marestail	tansymustard
common	morningglory	tumble mustard
lambsquarters	mouseear chickweed	umbrella spurry
dwarfdandelion	redroot pigweed	wild mustard
fanweed		

Grasses:

annual bluegrass	downy brome	stinkgrass
barnyardgrass	fall panicum	Texas panicum
bulbous bluegrass	field sandbur	wild oat
cheat	Italian ryegrass	witchgrass
crabgrass	shattercane	

Rate: 1-2 lb. ai/A
3-6 pt. WS/A
Time: Preemergence. Apply to vigorously growing weeds.
Weeds: Grasses:

quackgrass	tall fescue	wirestem muhly

Remarks: For quackgrass control in the fall, do not till between harvest and application; in the spring, do not till in the fall or spring prior to application. Do not apply through any type of irrigation system. Do not feed or forage vegetation from treated areas within 8 weeks after application.

- - - - - - - - - - - - - - - -

Signal Word/Toxicity Class: Danger/I.
REI: 12 hr.

HARMONY EXTRA (Premix)

Premix of sulfonylurea herbicides with no crop rotation limitations for the next season. Very good to excellent control of several annual broadleaf weeds including kochia, pigweed, and mustard. Note variety restrictions. Usually used with low rates of MCPA, 2,4-D, or other labeled broadleaf herbicides.

■ POST
Harmony Extra (DF) (50% thifensulfuron-methyl & 25% tribenuron-methyl) *(DuPont)*
Rate: 0.3-0.6 oz. DF/A
Time: Early postemergence. Winter oat: Apply after oat is in 2-leaf stage but before flag leaf is visible. Spring oat: Apply after crop is in 3-leaf stage but before jointing.
Weeds: Broadleaf weeds:

annual knawel	common	false chamomile
annual sowthistle	lambsquarters	field chickweed
black mustard	common mallow*	field pennycress
blue mustard	common radish	filaree
broadleaf dock	common ragweed*	flixweed
bur buttercup	common sunflower	green smartweed
bushy wallflower	common vetch*	hairy nightshade*
Canada thistle*	corn chamomile	henbit
Carolina geranium*	corn gromwell	jim hill mustard
catchweed bedstraw*	corn spurry	kochia
clasping pepperweed	cowcockle	ladysthumb
coast fiddleneck	curly dock	little mallow*
common chickweed	cutleaf	London rocket
common cocklebur*	eveningprimrose*	marshelder
common groundsel	dogfennel	minerslettuce

4
Small Grains

Oats

Weeds: Broadleaf weeds, continued:

mouseeearcress	redmaids	tansymustard
narrowleaf	rockpurslane	tarweed fiddleneck
lambsquarters	redroot pigweed	tumble mustard
nightflowering	Russian thistle	volunteer lentils
catchfly	scentless chamomile	volunteer peas
Pennsylvania	shepherdspurse	volunteer sunflower
smartweed	slimleaf lambsquarters	wild buckwheat
pineappleweed	smallflower buttercup	wild chamomile
prickly lettuce	smallseed falseflax	wild garlic
prostrate knotweed	stinking chickweed	wild mustard
prostrate pigweed	stinking mayweed	wild radish
purple mustard	swinecress	

Partial control

Remarks: Not underseeded. Add approved nonionic surfactant. Do not graze or feed forage or hay from treated areas to livestock (harvested straw may be used for bedding and/or feed).

Days To Harvest: 45.

Crop Rotation: Do not rotate to crops other than wheat, barley, or oats for 60 days after application; after 60 days any crop may be planted.

State Restrictions: Not for use in Alamosa, Conejos, Costilla, Rio Grande, and Saguache counties in Colorado.

- - - - - - - - - - - - -

Signal Word/Toxicity Class: Caution.
REI: 12 hr.

Harmony GT — see thifensulfuron-methyl

Hi-Dep — see 2,4-D

Karmex — see diuron

MCPA

Good crop tolerance at a wide range of crop growth stages. Most effective on mustards and lambsquarters. Frequently used in combination with other herbicides, especially when treatment must be made at early growth stages.

■ POST

Albaugh MCPA Amine 4 *(Albaugh)*
◆ **Clean Crop MCP Amine 4 or Ester** *(Platte)*
◆ **Clean Crop MCP 2 Sodium (sodium salt)** *(Platte)*
Riverdale MCPA-4 Amine *(Riverdale)*
Riverside MCPA Amine *(Terra)*
Wilbur-Ellis MCPA Amine, Ester or ◆ **Sodium Salt (2EC)** *(Wilbur-Ellis)*

Rate: 0.25-1.5 lb. ae/A
  0.5-3 pt./A

Time: Postemergence. Apply low rate for more susceptible weeds after crop has reached 3-4 leaf stage up to boot stage; high rate after crop has tillered and up to early boot stage. Do not spray from boot to dough stage.

Weeds: Broadleaf weeds:

annual mustard	lambsquarters	sowthistle
buttercup	marshelder	stinging nettle
Canada thistle	pigweed	stinkweed
dandelion	plantain	sunflower
dragonhead mint	puncturevine	vetch
field peppergrass	purslane	whitetop
goatsbeard	ragweed	wild radish
hempnettle	shepherdspurse	yellow rocket
kochia		

Do not forage or graze animals on treated areas within 7 days of slaughter or treatment.

State Restrictions: Wilbur-Ellis not registered in California.

- - - - - - - - - - - - -

Rate: 0.125-0.25 lb. ae/A
  0.25-0.5 pt./A

Time: Postemergence. Apply after crop is well tillered in the 4-leaf stage (4-8" tall) when legumes are 2-3" tall. Do not spray from boot to dough stage.

Weeds: Emergency control of:
  mustard   yellow rocket

Remarks: Underseeded with legumes (alfalfa, lespedeza, red and white clover). Balance severity of weed problem against possibility of crop damage. Do not forage or graze animals on treated areas within 7 days of slaughter or treatment.

State Restrictions: Wilbur-Ellis not registered in California.

- - - - - - - - - - - - -

Signal Word/Toxicity Class: Danger/I (amine); Warning/II (ester).
REI: Danger—48 hr.; Warning—12 hr.

■ POST

Albaugh MCPA Ester 4 *(Albaugh)*
Solve MCPA Ester (4) *(Albaugh)*

Rate: 0.25-1.5 lb. ae/A
  0.5-3 pt. 4/A

Time: Postemergence. Apply low rate for more susceptible weeds after crop has reached 3-4 leaf stage up to boot stage; use high rate for less susceptible weeds after crop has tillered and up to early boot stage. Do not spray from boot to dough stage.

Weeds: Broadleaf weeds:

annual mustard	goatsbeard	puncturevine
annual sowthistle	goosefoot	ragweed
beggarticks	hempnettle	shepherdspurse
cocklebur	lambsquarters	stinkweed
dragonhead mint	marshelder	wild radish
fanweed	pennycress	wintercress
field peppergrass	poison hemlock	yellow rocket

Remarks: Do not forage or graze meat animals on treated areas within 7 days of slaughter; dairy animals within 7 days after treatment.

- - - - - - - - - - - - -

Signal Word/Toxicity Class: Caution/III.
REI: 12 hr.

■ POST

Chiptox (sodium salt) *(Nufarm)*

Rate: 0.125-0.25 lb. ae/A
  0.5-1 pt./A

Time: Postemergence. Apply when legumes are 2-3" tall, grain is fully tillered but before forming joints in the stem. Do not spray in boot to dough stage.

Weeds: Broadleaf weeds:

annual mustard	lambsquarters	stinging nettle
buttercup	peppergrass	stinkweed
Canada thistle	plantain	vetch
cocklebur	purslane	whitetop
dandelion	ragweed	wild radish
hempnettle	shepherdspurse	wintercress
hoary cress	sowthistle	yellow rocket
kochia		

Remarks: Underseeded with mixed legumes. Use 5-6 gal. water/A; higher volumes may cause injury to legumes. Do not forage or graze treated fields for 2 weeks or feed treated straw to livestock.

- - - - - - - - - - - - -

Rate: 0.25-1 lb. ae/A
  1-4 pt./A

Time: Postemergence. Apply when grain is fully tillered but before forming joints in the stem. Do not spray in boot to dough stage.

Weeds: Same as above.

Remarks: Not underseeded with legumes. Use 6 pt. rate as emergency treatment for controlling perennial broadleaf weeds; balance severity of weed problem against possible crop injury.

- - - - - - - - - - - - -

Signal Word/Toxicity Class: Danger/I.
REI: 48 hr.

■ POST

Gordon's MCPA Amine 4 *(PBI/Gordon)*
Rhomene 4 (amine) *(Nufarm)*

Rate: 0.25-1 lb. ae/A
  0.5-2 pt./A

Time: Postemergence. For lower rate, apply after grain is in 4-leaf stage but not forming joints in the stem; for rates over 1 pt., apply after grain is fully tillered. Do not spray in boot to dough stage.

Weeds: Broadleaf weeds:

bull thistle	dandelion	pigweed
common burdock	field pennycress	plantain
common cocklebur	giant ragweed	purslane
common	mustard (except blue)	Russian thistle
lambsquarters	pepperweed	shepherdspurse
common ragweed	(except perennial)	yellow rocket

Remarks: Not underseeded with legumes. For emergency perennial broadleaf weed control, use 3 pt. rate when weeds approach bud stage, balance problem severity against possible crop damage; spot treat scattered perennial weeds.

- - - - - - - - - - - - -

Rate: 0.25 lb. ae/A
  0.5 pt./A

Time: Postemergence. Apply after crop is well tillered in the 4-leaf stage (4-8" tall) when legumes are 2-3" tall. Do not spray from boot to dough stage.

Weeds: Emergency control of:
  mustard   yellow rocket

◆-new product • PP-preplant • PPI-preplant incorporated • PRE-preemergence • POST-postemergence • SEQ-sequential • ae-acid equivalent • ai-active ingredient • DF-dry flowable E/EC-emulsifiable concentrate • F/FL-flowable • DG/G/WG-dispersable granule • L/LC-liquid • SP/WSP-soluble packet • W/WP-wettable powder • WSB-water soluble bag

228

Weed Control Manual 2000

Remarks: Underseeded with legumes. Do not apply to grain underseeded with vetch or sweet clover. Do not use more than 6 gal. water/A; higher volumes may result in injury to legumes. Do not forage or graze animals on treated areas within 7 days of slaughter or treatment.

– – – – – – – – – – – – – – –

Signal Word/Toxicity Class: Danger/I.
REI: 48 hr.

■ POST

Rhonox (LV ester) *(Nufarm)*

Rate: 0.23-0.69 lb. ae/A
0.5-1.5 pt./A

Time: Postemergence. For lower rate, apply after grain is in 4-leaf stage but not forming joints in the stem; for rates over 1 pt., apply after grain is fully tillered. Do not spray in boot to dough stage.

Weeds: Broadleaf weeds:

annual sowthistle	pennycress	ragweed
dandelion	peppergrass	shepherdspurse
hempnettle	perennial sowthistle	stinkweed
kochia	pigweed	wild radish
lambsquarters	plantain	yellow rocket
mustard	purslane	

Remarks: Not underseeded to legumes. Do not forage or graze meat animals on treated fields within 7 days of slaughter. Refer to label for further use directions.

– – – – – – – – – – – – – – –

Signal Word/Toxicity Class: Caution.
REI: 12 hr.

■ POST

Riverdale MCPA L.V. 4, IOE (5.2) (ester) *(Riverdale)*
Sword (5.2) (ester) *(Platte)*

Rate: 0.25-1.5 lb. ae/A
0.5-3 pt. L.V. 4/A
0.2-1.3 lb. ae/A
0.33-2 pt. 5.2/A

Time: Postemergence. Apply low rate for more susceptible weeds after crop has reached 3-4 leaf stage up to boot stage; high rate after crop has tillered and up to early boot stage. Do not spray from boot to dough stage.

Rate: Fall-planted:
0.25-0.5 lb. ae/A
0.5-1 pt. L.V. 4/A
0.2-0.4 lb. ae/A
0.33-0.75 pt. 5.2/A

Time: Postemergence. Fall application: Apply when fall-planted small grains are fully tillered and have reached 3-4 leaf stage to boot stage. Spring application: apply in early spring when annual broadleaf weeds are small and grain is fully tillered, but before grain is in jointed stage.

Weeds: Broadleaf weeds:

annual mustard	lambsquarters	sowthistle
buttercup	marshelder	stinging nettle
Canada thistle	pigweed	stinkweed
dandelion	plantain	sunflower
dragonhead mint	purslane	vetch
field peppergrass	puncturevine	whitetop
goatsbeard	ragweed	wild radish
hempnettle	shepherdspurse	yellow rocket
kochia		

Remarks: Not underseeded with legumes. Do not forage or graze animals on treated areas within 7 days of slaughter or treatment.

– – – – – – – – – – – – – – –

Rate: 0.125-0.25 lb. ae/A
0.25-0.5 pt. L.V.4/A
3-6 oz. 5.2/A

Time: Postemergence. Apply after crop is well tillered in the 4-leaf stage (4-8" tall) when legumes are 2-3" tall. Do not spray from boot to dough stage.

Weeds: Emergency control of:

mustard	yellow rocket

Remarks: Underseeded with legumes (alfalfa, lespedeza, red and white clover). Balance severity of weed problem against possibility of crop damage. Do not forage or graze animals on treated areas within 7 days of slaughter or treatment.

– – – – – – – – – – – – – – –

Signal Word/Toxicity Class: Warning/II.
REI: 12 hr.

Moxy — see bromoxynil

Opti-Amine — see 2,4-D

PEAK

Controls many broadleaf weeds, including triazine-resistant biotypes, by inhibiting a biochemical process which produces certain essential amino acids necessary for plant growth. The inhibited enzyme system is acetolactate synthase (ALS). Peak is a water-dispersible granule; each bag of Peak contains 5 water-soluble packets.

■ POST

Peak (WDG) (prosulfuron) *(Novartis)*

Rate: Low rate:
0.38 oz. WDG/A (1 WS packet/8A)
Standard rate:
0.5 oz. WDG/A (1 WS packet/6A)

Time: Postemergence (over-the-top). Apply from 3-leaf stage to before second node is detectable in stem elongation.

Weeds: Broadleaf weeds:

blue mustard	flixweed	prickly sida
buffalobur	Florida pusley	prostrate knotweed*
bur cherval	giant ragweed	puncturevine
bushy wallflower	hairy buttercup	redroot pigweed
Canada thistle*	hedge bindweed*	Russian thistle
coast fiddleneck	hemp sesbania	shepherdspurse
common chickweed*	henbit*	sicklepod
common cocklebur	ivyleaf morningglory	smooth pigweed
common	jimsonweed	tall morningglory
lambsquarters*	kochia*	tall waterhemp
common mallow*	mayweed chamomile	tansymustard
common ragweed	minerslettuce	tumble mustard
common sunflower	mouseear	tumble pigweed
common waterhemp	chickweed*	velvetleaf
corn gromwell*	Palmer amaranth*	Venice mallow
cutleaf	Pennsylvania	wild buckwheat
eveningprimrose	smartweed	wild garlic
devilsclaw	pineappleweed	wild mustard
field bindweed*	pitted morningglory	wild radish
field pennycress	prickly lettuce	

* Suppression

Remarks: Rate varies by weed height. Always add crop oil concentrate or nonionic surfactant. Do not apply to crop under stress. Do not make a foliar or soil application with an organophosphate insecticide within 15 days before or 10 days after application. Do not apply through any type of irrigation system.

Days To Harvest: Silage—40; grain—60; grazing/feeding forage to livestock—30.

Crop Rotation: IR/IMR Corn—anytime; normal field corn, grain sorghum—4 weeks; rice, popcorn, sweet corn, small grains (wheat, barley, oats, rye, proso millet, triticale)—2 months; beans (dry, green), cabbage, canola, cotton, flax, forage grasses, peanuts, peas, potatoes, soybeans, tobacco, tomatoes—9 months; alfalfa, clover, lentils—15 months; leeks, onion, sunflower, sugar beets—24 months; all other crops—18 months. Refer to label for geographic restrictions.

Tank Mixes: Low rate: Banvel, Bronate, Buctril, 2,4-D, MCPA; refer to label for use instructions.

State Restrictions: Not for use in San Luis Valley of Colorado, west of the Cascades in Oregon, and certain areas of Washington (abide by all sulfonylurea aerial application rulings by Washington Department of Agriculture).

– – – – – – – – – – – – – – –

Signal Word/Toxicity Class: Caution.
REI: 12 hr.

PROPANIL

Postemergence herbicide that controls green and yellow foxtail, pigweed, wild buckwheat, and wild mustard when tank mixed with MCPA. Control of grasses is reduced if weeds exceed stated growth stage.

■ POST

Stampede 80EDF *(Rohm and Haas)*

Rate: 1-1.13 lb. ai/A
1.25-1.4 pt. 80EDF/A

Time: Postemergence. Apply 10-17 days after crop emergence when grain is in 3-4 leaf stage; for foxtail, apply at 2-3 leaf stage.

Weeds: Broadleaf weeds:

common	prostrate pigweed	wild buckwheat
lambsquarters	redroot pigweed	wild mustard
kochia		

Grasses:

green foxtail	yellow foxtail

4

Small Grains

| NOTICE | The information on these pages is for preliminary planning — not a guide for use. Be sure to follow the manufacturer's directions, notwithstanding information contained here. | For personal protective equipment and EPA registration numbers, please turn to page 70. |

Weed Control Manual 2000

229

Oats

Remarks: Do not apply to grain crops that have been or will be treated with carbamate or organophosphorus insecticides. Do not apply through any type of irrigation system. Do not graze treated crop or cut for green chop feed.
Tank Mixes: MCPA.
State Restrictions: For use in Minnesota, Montana, North Dakota, and South Dakota.

- - - - - - - - - - - - - - - -

Signal Word/Toxicity Class: Caution.
REI: 24 hr.

Ranger — see glyphosate

Rattler — see glyphosate

Rhomene — see MCPA

Rhonox — see MCPA

Roundup — see glyphosate

Saber — see 2,4-D

Salvo — see 2,4-D

Savage — see 2,4-D

SCYTHE

◆ **Scythe (pelargonic acid)** *(Mycogen)*
Rate: 4-13 fl. oz./1 gal. spray solution
Time: Apply to actively growing weeds prior to crop emergence.
Weeds: Annual and perennial broadleaf weeds and grasses.
Remarks: Apply in minimum 75 gal. spray solution/A or spray-to-wet. Do not apply by air or through any type of irrigation system. Refer to label for directions and precautions.
Tank Mixes: Glyphosate and other foliar and residual herbicides.

- - - - - - - - - - - - - - - -

Signal Word/Toxicity Class: Warning/II.
REI: 24 hr.

Solution — see 2,4-D

Solve — see 2,4-D; MCPA

Stampede — see propanil

Sterling — see dicamba

Stinger — see clopyralid

Sword — see MCPA

THIFENSULFURON-METHYL

■ **POST**
Harmony GT (DF) *(DuPont)*
Rate: 0.3-0.4 oz. DF/A

Time: Postemergence. Apply to young, actively growing weeds after crop is in 2-leaf stage, but before flag leaf is visible (winter oats); 3-leaf stage, but before jointing (spring oats).
Weeds: Broadleaf weeds:

annual knawel	false chamomile	redroot pigweed
annual sowthistle	field pennycress	Russian thistle
black mustard	flixweed	scentless chamomile
bushy wallflower	green smartweed	shepherdspurse
Carolina geranium*	henbit*	smallflower buttercup
coast fiddleneck	jim hill mustard	stinking mayweed
common buckwheat	kochia	swinecress
common chickweed	ladysthumb	tansymustard*
common cocklebur*	little mallow*	tarweed fiddleneck
common groundsel	London rocket	tumble mustard
common	marshelder	volunteer lentils
lambsquarters	minerslettuce	volunteer peas
common mallow*	mouseear chickweed	volunteer sunflower
common sunflower*	mouseearcress	wild buckwheat
corn chamomile	Pennsylvania	wild chamomile
corn spurry	smartweed	wild garlic
curly dock	prickly lettuce*	wild mustard
cutleaf	prostrate knotweed	wild radish*
eveningprimrose*	redmaids	
dogfennel	rockpurslane	

* Suppression

Remarks: Add approved nonionic surfactant. Do not use on Ogle, Porter, or Premier spring oat varieties as injury can occur. Do not apply through any type of irrigation system. Prevent spray drift to desirable plants. Do not make more than 1 application per crop season. Do not graze or feed forage or hay from treated areas to livestock (harvested straw may be used for bedding and/or feed). Refer to label for restrictions and precautions.
Crop Rotation: Barley, oats, wheat—anytime; all other crops—45 days after application.
Tank Mixes: Assert, Avenge, bromoxynil, 2,4-D, dicamba, Hoelon, MCPA.
State Restrictions: Not for use in Alamosa, Conejos, Costilla, Rio Grande, and Saguache counties in Colorado.

- - - - - - - - - - - - - - - -

Signal Word/Toxicity Class: Caution.
REI: 4 hr.

TORDON

Restricted Use Pesticide.

Tordon 22K (picloram) *(Dow AgroSciences)*
Rate: 1-1.5 fl. oz. 22K/A
Time: Apply from 3- to 5-leaf stage to early jointing stage of growth.
Weeds: Broadleaf weeds such as:

Canada thistle	pennycress	volunteer sunflower
lambsquarters	pigweed	wild buckwheat
mayweed	Russian thistle	wild mustard

Remarks: Spring-seeded oats not underseeded with legumes. Not flood or subirrigated. Not for use on land planted to sweet sorghum. May cause shorter straw on some varieties of cereals but grain yields usually not affected. Do not apply more than 1.5 fl. oz./A during growing season. Do not graze or feed forage from treated areas for 2 weeks after treatment or harvest hay from treated fields. Do not apply through any type of irrigation system. Refer to label for restrictions and precautions.
Days To Harvest: 50.
Crop Rotation: Use only on land to be planted the following year to grass, barley, oats, wheat, grain sorghum, or fallow. Do not plant grain sorghum within 8 months after application. Do not rotate to broadleaf crops.
Tank Mixes: MCPA.
State Restrictions: For use west of the Mississippi except San Luis Valley of Colorado. Use in Hawaii limited to supplemental labeling.

- - - - - - - - - - - - - - - -

Signal Word/Toxicity Class: Caution.
REI: 12 hr.

Weed Rhap — see 2,4-D

Weedar — see 2,4-D

Weedestroy — see 2,4-D

◆-new product • PP-preplant • PPI-preplant incorporated • PRE-preemergence • POST-postemergence • SEQ-sequential • ae-acid equivalent • ai-active ingredient • DF-dry flowable
E/EC-emulsifiable concentrate • F/FL-flowable • DG/G/WG-dispersable granule • L/LC-liquid • SP/WSP-soluble packet • W/WP-wettable powder • WSB-water soluble bag

Rye

Barrage — see 2,4-D

Bison — see bromoxynil & MCPA

Broclean — see bromoxynil

Bromac — see bromoxynil & MCPA

Bromox — see bromoxynil

Bromox-MCPA 2-2 — see bromoxynil & MCPA

BROMOXYNIL

Contact herbicide that provides very good to excellent control of broadleaf weeds such as sunflower, cocklebur, kochia, and wild buckwheat. Usually used in combination with MCPA or other labeled herbicides to control more species. Very good crop tolerance.

■ **POST**
◆ **Broclean 2EC** *(Platte)*
◆ **Bromox 2EC** *(Micro Flo)*
Buctril (2EC), Buctril 4EC *(Rhone-Poulenc)*
Moxy 2EC *(Terra)*

Rate: Spring-seeded (except CO, ID, OR, MT, WA, WY):
0.25-0.5 lb. ai/A
1-2 pt. 2EC/A
0.5-1 pt. 4EC/A
Fall-seeded; spring-seeded (CO, ID, OR, MT, WA, WY only):
0.375-0.5 lb. ai/A
1.5-2 pt. 2EC/A
0.75-1 pt. 4EC/A
Underseeded with alfalfa:
0.25-0.375 lb. ai/A
1-1.5 pt. 2EC/A
0.5-0.75 pt. 4EC/A

Time: Postemergence. Apply from crop emergence to boot stage.

Weeds: Most susceptible broadleaf weeds:

annual pepperweed	common tarweed	Pennsylvania
annual sowthistle	eastern black	smartweed
black nightshade	nightshade	shepherdspurse
blue mustard	field pennycress	silverleaf nightshade
bristly starbur	green smartweed	sunflower
coast fiddleneck	hairy nightshade	tartary buckwheat
common cocklebur	jimsonweed	wild buckwheat
common lambsquarters	ladysthumb	

Susceptible broadleaf weeds:

buffalobur	ivyleaf morningglory	spiny pigweed
burcucumber	knawel	tall morningglory
common groundsel	kochia	tall waterhemp
common ragweed	London rocket	tumble mustard
corn chamomile	mayweed	velvetleaf
corn gromwell	prostrate knotweed	Venice mallow
cowcockle	puncturevine	wild mustard
giant ragweed	redroot pigweed	wild radish
hemp sesbania	Russian thistle	yellow starthistle

Remarks: Apply by ground, air, and sprinkler irrigation equipment. Do not apply when crops are under moisture stress. Do not graze treated fields within 30 days after application (45 days for Buctril). Refer to label for use directions, restrictions and precautions.

Crop Rotation: Do not plant rotational crops until the following season (within 30 days of application for Buctril).

Tank Mixes: 2,4-D (high rates will reduce crop tolerance), MCPA.

– – – – – – – – – – – – – –

Signal Word/Toxicity Class: Warning/II.
REI: 12 hr.

BROMOXYNIL & MCPA (Premixes)

Provides very good to excellent control of annual broadleaf weeds, including special problems such as kochia and wild buckwheat. Good crop tolerance. Best results when weeds are small and free of drought stress.

■ **POST**
Bison (EC) (2 lb./gal. bromoxynil & 2 lb./gal. MCPA) *(Terra)*
◆ **Bromac (EC) (2 lb./gal. bromoxynil & 2 lb./gal. MCPA)** *(Platte)*
◆ **Bromox-MCPA 2-2 (EC) (2 lb./gal. bromoxynil & 2 lb./gal. MCPA)** *(Micro Flo)*
Bronate (EC) (2 lb./gal. bromoxynil & 2 lb./gal. MCPA) *(Rhone-Poulenc)*

Rate: 0.5-1 lb. ai/A
1-2 pt. EC/A
Chemigation:
1 lb. ai/A
2 pt. EC/A
Postharvest—MN, MT, ND, SD:
0.38-1 lb. ai/A
0.75-2 pt. EC/A (Bronate)

Time: Postemergence. Apply after 3-leaf stage but before boot stage.

Weeds: Most susceptible broadleaf weeds:

annual sowthistle	field pennycress	Russian thistle
black mustard	green smartweed	shepherdspurse
black nightshade	hairy nightshade	silverleaf nightshade
coast fiddleneck	horned poppy	smooth pigweed
common cocklebur	jimsonweed	spiny pigweed
common	ladysthumb	sunflower
lambsquarters	London rocket	tall waterhemp
common tarweed	marshelder	tartary buckwheat
cowcockle	Pennsylvania	tumble mustard
cutleaf nightshade	smartweed	wild buckwheat
eastern black	pepperweed	wild mustard
nightshade	redroot pigweed	yellow rocket

Susceptible broadleaf weeds:

blue mustard	giant ragweed	puncturevine
Canada thistle	hemp sesbania	purple mustard
(suppression)	henbit	tall morningglory
common groundsel	ivyleaf morningglory	tansymustard
common ragweed	knawel	tarweed
corn chamomile	kochia	velvetleaf
corn gromwell	mayweed	wild radish
fumitory	prostrate knotweed	

Remarks: Rates vary by weed species and conditions; refer to label for directions and precautions. Do not apply when crop canopy covers weeds or when crops are under moisture stress. Do not graze fields within 30 days after application (45 for Bronate).

Tank Mixes: MCPA.

– – – – – – – – – – – – – –

Signal Word/Toxicity Class: Warning/II.
REI: 12 hr.

Bronate — see bromoxynil & MCPA

Buctril — see bromoxynil

Chiptox — see MCPA

Credit — see glyphosate

2,4-D - PHENOXY HERBICIDES

Most effective choice for annual and perennial broadleaf weeds. Ester forms are more effective for early spring application. Amines usually applied at slightly higher rate than esters. Crop tolerance is considered good.

4

Small Grains

Rye

Annual and perennial broadleaf weeds controlled by 2,4-D include:

beggarticks	galinsoga	povertyweed
bindweed	goldenrod	puncturevine
bitterweed	ground ivy	purslane
broomweed	healall	ragweed
bull thistle	hoary cress	Russian thistle
burdock	ironweed	shepherdspurse
Canada thistle	jimsonweed	smartweed
carpetweed	knotweed	sowthistle
catnip	lambsquarters	stinkweed
chicory	mallow	sumac
chickweed	marshelder	sunflower
cocklebur	mexicanweed	sweetclover
coffeeweed	morningglory	velvetleaf
cutleaf	musk thistle	Virginia creeper
eveningprimrose	mustard	wild carrot
creeping jenny	pennywort	wild garlic
croton	pepperweed	wild lettuce
dandelion	pigweed	wild onion
dock	plantain	wild parsnips
dogbane	pokeweed	wild radish

■ POST

Albaugh Amine 4 (2,4-D amine) *(Albaugh)*
Weedestroy AM-40 (2,4-D amine) *(Riverdale)*
Wilbur-Ellis Amine 4 (2,4-D amine) *(Wilbur-Ellis)*

Rate: 0.25-1 lb. ae/A
0.5-2 pt./A (Riverdale, Wilbur-Ellis)
0.33-0.75 lb. ae/A
0.66-1.5 pt./A (Albaugh)

Time: Postemergence. Apply to spring grown grains after tillering (4-8" high) but before boot stage. Do not spray in boot to dough stage.

Remarks: Not underseeded with legumes. For emergency control of perennial broadleaf weeds, up to 3 pt./A may be used when weeds are approaching bud stage. Do not use higher rates unless possible crop injury will be acceptable.

— — — — — — — — — — — — — — — —

Rate: 0.125-0.25 lb. ae/A
0.25-0.5 pt./A

Time: Postemergence. Apply after grain is 8" tall but before boot stage. Do not spray in boot to dough stage.

Remarks: Underseeded with legumes. Do not spray alfalfa or sweet clover unless infestation is severe and injury to legumes can be tolerated.

— — — — — — — — — — — — — — — —

Rate: 0.5-1 lb. ae/A
1-2 pt./A

Time: Preharvest. Apply in dough stage.

Remarks: Best results will be obtained when soil moisture is adequate for plant growth and weeds are growing well.

State Restrictions: Wilbur-Ellis not registered in California.

— — — — — — — — — — — — — — — —

Signal Word/Toxicity Class: Danger/I.
REI: 48 hr.

■ POST

Albaugh LV4 or LV6 Ester (2,4-D ester) *(Albaugh)*
◆ **Barrage or Barrage HF (EC) (2,4-D ester)** *(Helena)*
◆ **Clean Crop Low Vol 4 or Low Vol 6 (2,4-D ester)** *(Platte)*
Esteron 99C (2,4-D LV ester) *(Rhone-Poulenc)*
Riverdale 6 Amine (2,4-D amine) *(Riverdale)*
Riverdale L.V. 4 or L.V. 6 (2,4-D ester) *(Riverdale)*
Solve 2,4-D (2,4-D LV ester) *(Albaugh)*
Weed Rhap LV-6D (2,4-d ester) *(Helena)*
Wilbur-Ellis Lo Vol-4 or Lo Vol-6 (2,4-D ester) *(Wilbur-Ellis)*

Rate: 0.25-0.5 lb. ae/A
0.5-1 pt. 4/A
0.33-0.66 pt. 6/A
Perennial weeds, preharvest:
0.5-1 lb. ae/A
1-2 pt. 4/A
0.66-1.33 pt. 6/A

Time: Postemergence, preharvest. Do not spray before tiller or from early boot to dough stage.

Remarks: Not underseeded with legumes. Do not forage or graze treated fields for 2 weeks after application.

State Restrictions: Wilbur-Ellis not registered in California.

— — — — — — — — — — — — — — — —

Signal Word/Toxicity Class: Danger/I (amine); Caution/III (ester).
REI: Danger—48 hr.; Caution—12 hr.

■ POST

◆ **Clean Crop Amine 4 (2,4-D amine)** *(Platte)*
Formula 40 (2,4-D mixed amine) *(Rhone-Poulenc)*
◆ **Opti-Amine (4) (2,4-D amine)** *(Helena)*
Weed Rhap A-4D (2,4-D amine) *(Helena)*

Rate: 0.33-0.66 lb. ae/A
0.66-1.33 pt./A

Time: Postemergence. Apply in spring. Do not apply before tiller stage or from early boot through milk stage.

Remarks: Not underseeded with legumes. Up to 3 pt./A may be used for difficult weed problems such as dry conditions in Western states. Do not allow dairy animals or meat animals being finished for slaughter to forage or graze treated fields within 2 weeks of treatment.

— — — — — — — — — — — — — — — —

Signal Word/Toxicity Class: Danger/I.
REI: 48 hr.

■ POST

Gordon's LV 400 (2,4-D ester) *(PBI/Gordon)*
Riverside 2,4-D LV4 (2,4-D LV ester) *(Terra)*

Rate: 0.25-0.38 lb. ae/A
0.5-0.75 pt./A

Time: Postemergence. Apply in the spring at full tiller but before early boot stage.

— — — — — — — — — — — — — — — —

Rate: 0.5-1 lb. ae/A
1-2 pt./A

Time: Preharvest. Apply in dough stage.

Remarks: Not underseeded with legumes. Up to 2 pt./A may be used for difficult weeds problems. Do not use higher rates unless possible crop injury will be acceptable. Do not allow dairy animals or meat animals being finished for slaughter to forage or graze treated fields within 2 weeks of application.

— — — — — — — — — — — — — — — —

Signal Word/Toxicity Class: Caution/III.
REI: 12 hr.

■ POST

Hi-Dep (2,4-D mixed amine) *(PBI/Gordon)*

Rate: 0.125-0.75 lb. ae/A
0.25-1.5 pt./A

Time: Postemergence. Apply after grain begins tillering and before boot stage (4-8" tall). Do not apply before tiller stage or from early boot through milk stage.

— — — — — — — — — — — — — — — —

Rate: 0.5-1 lb. ae/A
1-2 pt./A

Time: Preharvest. Apply in dough stage.

Remarks: Not underseeded with legumes. Up to 3 pt./A may be used for difficult weeds problems such as dry conditions in Western states. Do not allow dairy animals or meat animals being finished for slaughter to forage or graze treated fields within 2 weeks of application.

— — — — — — — — — — — — — — — —

Signal Word/Toxicity Class: Danger/I.
REI: 48 hr.

■ POST

◆ **Saber (2,4-D amine)** *(Platte)*

Rate: 0.25-0.5 lb. ae/A
0.5-1 pt./A

Time: Postemergence. Apply from onset of tillering to full tillering stage. Do not apply from boot to dough stage.

— — — — — — — — — — — — — — — —

Rate: Emergency, preharvest:
0.35-1.5 lb. ae/A
0.75-3 pt./A

Time: Preharvest. Apply in hard dough stage. Do not apply before tiller or from boot to dough stage.

Remarks: Not underseeded with legumes. Up to 3 pt./A may be used to control difficult weeds and heavy infestations. Do not forage or graze treated fields for 2 weeks after application. Do not feed treated straw to livestock if emergency and/or preharvest treatment is applied.

— — — — — — — — — — — — — — — —

Signal Word/Toxicity Class: Danger/I.
REI: 48 hr.

◆-new product • PP-preplant • PPI-preplant incorporated • PRE-preemergence • POST-postemergence • SEQ-sequential • ae-acid equivalent • ai-active ingredient • DF-dry flowable
E/EC-emulsifiable concentrate • F/FL-flowable • DG/G/WG-dispersable granule • L/LC-liquid • SP/WSP-soluble packet • W/WP-wettable powder • WSB-water soluble bag

Weed Control Manual 2000

■ POST
Salvo (2,4-D LV ester) *(Platte)*

Rate: Spring:
    0.25-0.31 lb. ae/A
    0.4-0.5 pt./A
Time: Postemergence. Apply after plants are fully tillered but before stems begin to joint.

Rate: Fall:
    0.25-0.5 lb. ae/A
    0.4-0.8 pt./A
Time: Postemergence. Apply in spring when weeds are small and grain is in full tiller stage (4-8" high) and before boot stage.
Remarks: Do not forage or graze treated grain fields within 2 weeks after treatment. Do not feed treated straw to livestock.

- - - - - - - - - - - - - - -

Signal Word/Toxicity Class: Caution/III.
REI: 12 hr.

■ POST
Savage (WSB) (2,4-D amine) *(Platte)*

Rate: 0.24-0.95 lb. ae/A
    0.25-1 lb. WSB/A
Time: Postemergence. Apply in spring. Do not apply before tiller stage or from boot to dough stage.

Rate: 0.48-1.43 lb. ae/A
    0.5-1.5 lb. WSB/A
Time: Preharvest. Apply in hard dough stage.
Remarks: Not underseeded with legumes. For emergency weed control, up to 1.5 lb./A may be used when weeds are approaching bud stage, after grain dough stage. Do not use higher rates unless possible crop injury will be acceptable. Do not forage or graze treated fields within 2 weeks after treatment. Do not feed treated straw if emergency and/or preharvest treatment is applied. Refer to label for use directions, restrictions, and precautions.

- - - - - - - - - - - - - - -

Signal Word/Toxicity Class: Danger/I.
REI: 48 hr.

■ POST
Solution (WS) (2,4-D amine) *(Riverdale)*

Rate: Spring grains:
    1 WS packet/3.5-10 A
    Winter grains:
    1 WS packet/2.5-10 A
Time: Postemergence. For spring grown grains, apply between full tillering and before boot stage (usually 4-8" tall). Preharvest treatment can be applied when grain is in dough stage.
Remarks: Apply in 5-100 gal. water.

- - - - - - - - - - - - - - -

Signal Word/Toxicity Class: Danger/I.
REI: 48 hr.

■ POST
Weedar 64 (4) (2,4-D amine) *(Nufarm)*

Rate: 0.25-1 lb. ae/A
    0.5-2 pt./A
Time: Postemergence. Apply after grain is fully tillered (4-8" high) but not forming joints in stem. Do not spray in boot to dough stage.
Remarks: Not underseeded with legumes.

- - - - - - - - - - - - - - -

Rate: 0.125-0.25 lb. ae/A
    0.25-0.5 pt./A
Time: Postemergence. Apply after grain is 8" tall but before boot stage. Do not spray in boot to dough stage.
Remarks: Underseeded with legumes. Do not spray alfalfa or sweet clover unless infestation is severe and injury to legumes can be tolerated.

- - - - - - - - - - - - - - -

Signal Word/Toxicity Class: Danger/I.
REI: 48 hr.

■ POST
Weedone LV4 (2,4-D solventless ester) *(Nufarm)*
Weedone Lo Vol 6 (2,4-D ester) *(Nufarm)*

Rate: 0.25-1 lb. ae/A
    0.5-2 pt. 4/A
    0.33-1.33 pt. 6/A
Time: Postemergence. Do not spray in boot to dough stage.

Remarks: Not underseeded with legumes. Refer to label for use directions, restrictions, and precautions.
Tank Mixes: LV4: Buctril (rate varies by state, refer to label).

- - - - - - - - - - - - - - -

Signal Word/Toxicity Class: Caution/III.
REI: 12 hr.

Esteron 99C — see 2,4-D

Formula 40 — see 2,4-D

Glyfos or Glyfos X-tra — see glyphosate

GLYPHOSATE

Controls emerged weeds prior to planting in reduced or no-till. Ammonium sulfate at 17 lb./100 gal. solution improves results with low rate applications where water quality is a factor. Do not allow glyphosate to contact desirable plants.

■ PP, PRE
◆ Credit (4WS) *(Nufarm)*
◆ Glyfos or Glyfos X-tra (4WS) *(Cheminova)*
Rattler (4WS) *(Helena)*
Roundup Custom (5.4WS) *(Monsanto)*
Roundup Original, Original RT, Ultra, Ultra RT (4WS) *(Monsanto)*

Rate: Annual weeds:
    0.38-1.5 lb. ai/A
    0.56-2.25 pt. 5.4WS/A
    0.75-3 pt. 4WS/A
    Perennial weeds:
    0.5-5 lb. ai/A
    0.75-7.5 pt. 5.4WS/A
    1-10 pt. 4WS/A
Time: Preplant, preemergence, at-planting, postharvest. For spot treatment, apply before heading.
Weeds: Most emerged annual and perennial broadleaf weeds including:

Canada thistle	field bindweed	kochia

Grasses:

downy brome	foxtail	quackgrass

Remarks: For postharvest applications, do not apply more than 1 lb. ai/A. Do not add surfactant to Roundup Ultra or Ultra RT. For spot treatment, do not treat more than 10% total area to be harvested. Do not apply through any type of irrigation system. Refer to label for directions, precautions and restrictions.
Days To Harvest: Postharvest: harvest/feeding—8 weeks.
Tank Mixes: Postharvest: 2,4-D, dicamba. Roundup tank mixes not registered in California by air.
State Restrictions: Roundup RT for use in Colorado, Idaho, Montana, North Dakota, South Dakota, Utah, Wyoming, and in specific counties only in Kansas, Minnesota, Nebraska, Nevada, Oklahoma, Oregon, and Washington; refer to label for restrictions. Glyfos is not registered for use in California. Glyfos X-tra is not registered for use in mistblowers in California or Arizona.

- - - - - - - - - - - - - - -

Signal Word/Toxicity Class: Varies by formulation.
REI: Warning—12 hr.; Caution—4 hr.

Hi-Dep — see 2,4-D

MCPA

Good crop tolerance at a wide range of crop growth stages. Most effective on mustard and lambsquarters. Frequently used in combination with other herbicides, especially when treatment must be made at early growth stages.

■ POST
Albaugh MCPA Amine 4 *(Albaugh)*
◆ Clean Crop MCP Amine 4 or Ester *(Platte)*
◆ Clean Crop MCP 2 Sodium (sodium salt) *(Platte)*
Riverdale MCPA-4 Amine *(Riverdale)*
Riverside MCPA Amine *(Terra)*
Wilbur-Ellis MCPA Amine, Ester or ◆ Sodium Salt (2EC) *(Wilbur-Ellis)*

Rate: 0.25-1.5 lb. ae/A
    0.5-3 pt./A

NOTICE The information on these pages is for preliminary planning — not a guide for use. Be sure to follow the manufacturer's directions, notwithstanding information contained here.

For personal protective equipment and EPA registration numbers, please turn to page 70.

4

Small Grains

Time: Postemergence. Apply low rate for more susceptible weeds after crop has reached 3-4 leaf stage up to boot stage; high rate after crop has tillered and up to early boot stage. Do not spray from boot to dough stage.

Weeds: Broadleaf weeds:

annual mustard	marshelder	sowthistle
buttercup	marshelder	stinging nettle
Canada thistle	pigweed	stinkweed
dandelion	plantain	sunflower
dragonhead mint	puncturevine	vetch
field peppergrass	purslane	whitetop
goatsbeard	ragweed	wild radish
hempnettle	shepherdspurse	yellow rocket
kochia		

Remarks: Not underseeded with legumes. Do not forage or graze animals on treated areas within 7 days of slaughter or treatment.

State Restrictions: Wilbur-Ellis not registered in California.

Rate: 0.125-0.25 lb. ae/A
    0.25-0.5 pt./A

Time: Postemergence. Apply after crop is well tillered in the 4-leaf stage (4-8" tall) when legumes are 2-3" tall. Do not spray from boot to dough stage.

Weeds: Emergency control of:

mustard	yellow rocket

Remarks: Underseeded with legumes (alfalfa, lespedeza, red and white clover). Balance severity of weed problem against possibility of crop damage. Do not forage or graze animals on treated areas within 7 days of slaughter or treatment.

State Restrictions: Wilbur-Ellis not registered in California.

Signal Word/Toxicity Class: Danger/I (amine); Warning/II (ester).
REI: Danger—48 hr.; Warning—12 hr.

■ POST

Albaugh MCPA Ester 4 *(Albaugh)*
Solve MCPA Ester (4) *(Albaugh)*

Rate: 0.25-1.5 lb. ae/A
    0.5-3 pt./A

Time: Postemergence. Apply low rate for more susceptible weeds after crop has reached 3-4 leaf stage up to boot stage; use high rate for less susceptible weeds after crop has tillered and up to early boot stage. Do not spray from boot to dough stage.

Weeds: Broadleaf weeds:

annual mustard	goatsbeard	puncturevine
annual sowthistle	goosefoot	ragweed
beggarticks	hempnettle	shepherdspurse
cocklebur	lambsquarters	stinkweed
dragonhead mint	marshelder	wild radish
fanweed	pennycress	wintercress
field peppergrass	poison hemlock	yellow rocket

Remarks: Do not forage or graze meat animals on treated areas within 7 days of slaughter; dairy animals within 7 days after treatment.

Signal Word/Toxicity Class: Caution/III.
REI: 12 hr.

■ POST

Chiptox (sodium salt) *(Nufarm)*

Rate: 0.125-0.25 lb. ae/A
    0.5-1 pt./A

Time: Postemergence. Apply when legumes are 2-3" tall, grain is fully tillered but before forming joints in the stem. Do not spray in boot to dough stage.

Weeds: Broadleaf weeds:

annual mustard	lambsquarters	stinging nettle
buttercup	peppergrass	stinkweed
Canada thistle	plantain	vetch
cocklebur	purslane	whitetop
dandelion	ragweed	wild radish
hempnettle	shepherdspurse	wintercress
hoary cress	sowthistle	yellow rocket
kochia		

Remarks: Underseeded with mixed legumes. Use 5-6 gal. water/A; higher volumes may cause injury to legumes. Do not forage or graze treated fields for 2 weeks or feed treated straw to livestock.

Rate: 0.25-1 lb. ae/A
    1-4 pt./A

Time: Postemergence. Apply when grain is fully tillered but before forming joints in the stem. Do not spray in boot to dough stage.

Weeds: Same as above.

Remarks: Not underseeded with legumes. Use 6 pt. rate as emergency treatment for controlling perennial broadleaf weeds; balance severity of weed problem against possible crop injury.

Signal Word/Toxicity Class: Danger/I.
REI: 48 hr.

■ POST

Gordon's MCPA Amine 4 *(PBI/Gordon)*
Rhomene 4 (amine) *(Nufarm)*

Rate: 0.25-1 lb. ae/A
    0.5-2 pt./A

Time: Postemergence. For lower rate, apply after grain is in 4-leaf stage but not forming joints in the stem; for rates over 1 pt., apply after grain is fully tillered. Do not spray in boot to dough stage.

Weeds: Broadleaf weeds:

bull thistle	dandelion	pigweed
common burdock	field pennycress	plantain
common cocklebur	giant ragweed	purslane
common	mustard (except blue)	Russian thistle
lambsquarters	pepperweed	shepherdspurse
common ragweed	(except perennial)	yellow rocket

Remarks: Not underseeded with legumes. For emergency perennial broadleaf weed control, use 3 pt. rate when weeds approach bud stage, balance problem severity against possible crop damage; spot treat scattered perennial weeds.

Rate: 0.25 lb. ae/A
    0.5 pt./A

Time: Postemergence. Apply after crop is well tillered in the 4-leaf stage (4-8" tall) when legumes are 2-3" tall. Do not spray from boot to dough stage.

Weeds: Emergency control of:

mustard	yellow rocket

Remarks: Underseeded with legumes. Do not apply to grain underseeded with vetch or sweet clover. Do not use more than 6 gal. water/A; higher volumes may result in injury to legumes. Do not forage or graze animals on treated areas within 7 days of slaughter or treatment.

Signal Word/Toxicity Class: Danger/I.
REI: 48 hr.

■ POST

Rhonox (LV ester) *(Nufarm)*

Rate: 0.23-0.69 lb. ae/A
    0.5-1.5 pt./A

Time: Postemergence. For lower rate, apply after grain is in 4-leaf stage but not forming joints in the stem; for rates over 1 pt., apply after grain is fully tillered. Do not spray in boot to dough stage.

Weeds: Broadleaf weeds:

annual sowthistle	pennycress	ragweed
dandelion	peppergrass	shepherdspurse
hempnettle	perennial sowthistle	stinkweed
kochia	pigweed	wild radish
lambsquarters	plantain	yellow rocket
mustard	purslane	

Remarks: Not underseeded to legumes. Do not forage or graze meat animals on treated fields within 7 days of slaughter. Refer to label for further use directions.

Signal Word/Toxicity Class: Caution.
REI: 12 hr.

■ POST

Riverdale MCPA L.V. 4, IOE (5.2) (ester) *(Riverdale)*
Sword (5.2) (ester) *(Platte)*

Rate: 0.25-1.5 lb. ae/A
    0.5-3 pt. L.V. 4/A
    0.2-1.3 lb. ae/A
    0.33-2 pt. 5.2/A

Time: Postemergence. Apply low rate for more susceptible weeds after crop has reached 3-4 leaf stage up to boot stage; high rate after crop has tillered and up to early boot stage. Do not spray from boot to dough stage.

Rate: Fall-planted:
    0.25-0.5 lb. ae/A
    0.5-1 pt. L.V. 4/A
    0.2-0.4 lb. ae/A
    0.33-0.75 pt. 5.2/A

◆-new product • PP-preplant • PPI-preplant incorporated • PRE-preemergence • POST-postemergence • SEQ-sequential • ae-acid equivalent • ai-active ingredient • DF-dry flowable • E/EC-emulsifiable concentrate • F/FL-flowable • DG/G/WG-dispersable granule • L/LC-liquid • SP/WSP-soluble packet • W/WP-wettable powder • WSB-water soluble bag

Time: Postemergence. Fall application: Apply when fall-planted small grains are fully tillered and have reached 3-4 leaf stage to boot stage. Spring application: Apply in early spring when annual broadleaf weeds are small and grain is fully tillered, but before grain is in jointed stage.

Weeds: Broadleaf weeds:

annual mustard	lambsquarters	sowthistle
buttercup	marshelder	stinging nettle
Canada thistle	pigweed	stinkweed
dandelion	plantain	sunflower
dragonhead mint	purslane	vetch
field peppergrass	puncturevine	whitetop
goatsbeard	ragweed	wild radish
hempnettle	shepherdspurse	yellow rocket
kochia		

Remarks: Not underseeded with legumes. Do not forage or graze animals on treated areas within 7 days of slaughter or treatment.

– – – – – – – – – – – – – – –

Rate: 0.125-0.25 lb. ae/A
0.25-0.5 pt. L.V.4/A
3-6 oz. 5.2/A

Time: Postemergence. Apply after crop is well tillered in the 4-leaf stage (4-8" tall) when legumes are 2-3" tall. Do not spray from boot to dough stage.

Weeds: Emergency control of:

mustard	yellow rocket

Remarks: Underseeded with legumes (alfalfa, lespedeza, red and white clover). Balance severity of weed problem against possibility of crop damage. Do not forage or graze animals on treated areas within 7 days of slaughter or treatment.

– – – – – – – – – – – – – – –

Signal Word/Toxicity Class: Warning/II.
REI: 12 hr.

Moxy — see bromoxynil

Opti-Amine — see 2,4-D

PEAK

Controls many broadleaf weeds, including triazine-resistant biotypes, by inhibiting a biochemical process which produces certain essential amino acids necessary for plant growth. The inhibited enzyme system is acetolactate synthase (ALS). Peak is a water-dispersible granule; each bag of Peak contains 5 water-soluble packets.

■ POST

Peak (WDG) (prosulfuron) *(Novartis)*
Rate: Low rate:
0.38 oz. WDG/A (1 WS packet/8A)
Standard rate:
0.5 oz. WDG/A (1 WS packet/6A)
Time: Postemergence (over-the-top). Apply from 3-leaf stage to before second node is detectable in stem elongation.

Weeds: Broadleaf weeds:

blue mustard	flixweed	prickly sida
buffalobur	Florida pusley	prostrate knotweed*
bur cherval	giant ragweed	puncturevine
bushy wallflower	hairy buttercup	redroot pigweed
Canada thistle*	hedge bindweed*	Russian thistle
coast fiddleneck	hemp sesbania	shepherdspurse
common chickweed*	henbit*	sicklepod
common cocklebur	ivyleaf morningglory	smooth pigweed
common lambsquarters*	jimsonweed	tall morningglory
	kochia*	tall waterhemp
common mallow*	maymeed chamomile	tansymustard
common ragweed	minerslettuce	tumble mustard
common sunflower	mouseear chickweed*	tumble pigweed
common waterhemp	Palmer amaranth*	velvetleaf
corn gromwell*	Pennsylvania smartweed	Venice mallow
cutleaf eveningprimrose	pineappleweed	wild buckwheat
devilsclaw	pitted morningglory	wild garlic
field bindweed*	prickly lettuce	wild mustard
field pennycress		wild radish

* Suppression

Remarks: Rate varies by weed height. Always add crop oil concentrate or nonionic surfactant. Do not apply to crop under stress. Do not make a foliar or soil application with an organophosphate insecticide within 15 days before or 10 days after application. Do not apply through any type of irrigation system.

Days To Harvest: Silage—40; grain—60; grazing/feeding forage to livestock—30.
Crop Rotation: IR/IMR Corn—anytime; normal field corn, grain sorghum—4 weeks; rice, popcorn, sweet corn, small grains (wheat, barley, oats, rye, proso millet, triticale)—2 months; beans (dry, green), cabbage, canola, cotton, flax, forage grasses, peanuts, peas, potatoes, soybeans, tobacco, tomatoes—9 months; alfalfa, clover, lentils—15 months; leeks, onion, sunflower, sugar beets—24 months; all other crops—18 months. Refer to label for geographic restrictions.
Tank Mixes: Low rate: Banvel, Bronate, Buctril, 2,4-D, MCPA; refer to label for use instructions.
State Restrictions: Not for use in San Luis Valley of Colorado, west of the Cascades in Oregon, and certain areas of Washington (abide by all sulfonylurea aerial application rulings by Washington Department of Agriculture).

– – – – – – – – – – – – – – –

Signal Word/Toxicity Class: Caution.
REI: 12 hr.

Rattler — see glyphosate

Rhomene — see MCPA

Rhonox — see MCPA

Roundup — see glyphosate

Saber — see 2,4-D

Salvo — see 2,4-D

Savage — see 2,4-D

SCYTHE

◆ **Scythe (pelargonic acid)** *(Mycogen)*
Rate: 4-13 fl. oz./1 gal. spray solution
Time: Apply to actively growing weeds prior to crop emergence.
Weeds: Annual and perennial broadleaf weeds and grasses.
Remarks: Apply in minimum 75 gal. spray solution/A or spray-to-wet. Do not apply by air or through any type of irrigation system. Refer to label for directions and precautions.
Tank Mixes: Glyphosate and other foliar and residual herbicides.

– – – – – – – – – – – – – – –

Signal Word/Toxicity Class: Warning/II.
REI: 24 hr.

Solution — see 2,4-D

Solve — see 2,4-D; MCPA

Sword — see MCPA

Weed Rhap — see 2,4-D

Weedar — see 2,4-D

Weedestroy — see 2,4-D

Weedone — see 2,4-D

NOTICE The information on these pages is for preliminary planning — not a guide for use. Be sure to follow the manufacturer's directions, notwithstanding information contained here. | For personal protective equipment and EPA registration numbers, please turn to page 70.

Notes • Notes • Notes

Section 5
Other
Field Crops

Weed Efficacy Charts

Weed Response To Selected Herbicides, Sorghum 238
Weed Response To Burndown Herbicides In
No-Till Grain Sorghum 238
Weed Response Ratings For Rice Herbicides 239

Herbicide Listings

Castor Beans 240
Flax 240
Guar Beans 242
Hops 243
Kenaf 244
Mint 244
Mung Beans 246
Oil Seed Crops 247

Peanuts .248
Rice 253
Safflower 258
Sorghum 259
Sugar Beets 269
Sugarcane 272
Sunflower 279
Tobacco .281

The information in this Weed Control Manual 2000 is updated to August 15, 1999.
Because manufacturers' product recommendations are constantly being updated and revised as additional product registrations and label changes are approved by EPA, there may be changes after this date. However, every effort has been made to give manufacturers the opportunity to include in the Manual their latest information. This Manual is for preliminary planning – not a use guide. Be sure to follow label directions, notwithstanding information contained herein.

Weed Response To Selected Herbicides, Sorghum

Herbicide	Grasses						Broadleaf Weeds										
	Barnyardgrass	Crabgrass	Fall panicum	Foxtail	Sandbur	Shattercane/Sorghum	Black nightshade	Cocklebur	Kochia	Lambsquarters	Pigweed	Ragweed	Russian thistle	Smartweed	Sunflower	Velvetleaf	Waterhemp
Soil Applied																	
AAtrex/atrazine	4	4	2	7	4	2	9	7	9	9	9	9	9	9	7	7	9
Bullet + seed safener	9	7	7	9	4	2	9	5	9	9	9	9	7	7	6	5	9
Lariat + seed safener	9	7	7	9	4	2	9	5	9	9	9	9	7	7	6	5	9
Lasso + seed safener	9	9	9	9	4	2	6	2	2	7	7	4	2	2	2	2	7
Ramrod	7	7	7	9	2	2	2	2	4	7	2	2	4	2	2	2	7
Ramrod + atrazine	7	7	4	9	2	2	8	4	9	9	9	9	7	7	8	6	9
Postemergence																	
AAtrex/atrazine + COC	2	2	2	4	2	2	9	9	9	9	9	9	4	9	9	9	9
Banvel	2	2	2	2	2	2	7	9	8	7	8	7	9	9	8	5	8
Buctril	2	2	2	2	2	2	9	9	6	9	7	6	9	9	9	8	6
Buctril + atrazine	2	2	2	2	2	2	9	9	9	9	9	9	8	9	9	9	9
2,4-D	2	2	2	2	2	3	4	10	4	7	8	7	9	3	7	7	8
Laddok S-12	2	2	2	2	2	2	7	9	8	7	8	8	9	2	9	9	9
Marksman	2	2	2	2	2	2	9	9	9	9	9	9	8	9	9	8	9
Peak	1	1	1	1	1	1	3	9	6	5	8	9	—	1	1	6	9
Permit	1	1	1	1	1	1	3	9	6	5	8	9	—	6	9	9	8
Roundup-ropewicks, wipers, etc.[a]	—	—	—	—	9	7	—	8	6	4	5	7	4	7	7	4	5

Response Ratings: Ratings are for light to moderate weed populations, favorable conditions and weed growth stage as specified on the product label. High weed populations, adverse conditions, or large weeds will reduce control.
10 — (96-100%), 9 — (90-95%), 8 — (85-89%), 7 — (80-84%), 6 — (70-79%), 5 — (60-69%), 4-2 — less than 60%, 1 — 0%.
[a]Ratings for weeds tall enough for selective treatment.

Source: Herbicide Use In Nebraska 1997 Guide

Weed Response To Burndown Herbicides In No-Till Grain Sorghum

Herbicide	Alfalfa	Annual bluegrass	Annual smartweed	Barnyardgrass	Chickweed	Dandelion	Downy brome	Evening primrose	Field sandbur	Foxtail	Foxtail barley	Hairy vetch	Henbit	Horseweed (marestail)	Kochia	Lambsquarters	Pennycress	Prickly lettuce	Purslane speedwell	Russian thistle	Rye	Shepherdspurse	Sunflower	Sweet clover	Tall knotweed	Velvetleaf	Virginia pepperweed	Winter wheat
Atrazine (2 qt)	4	9	10	6	10	4	7	9	6	7	9	6	10	8	10	10	10	9	10	9	6	10	10	3	10	10	9	6
Atrazine + 2,4-D (2 qt + 1 pt)	5	10	10	7	10	6	8	10	7	8	10	10	10	10	10	10	10	10	10	9	5	10	10	8	10	10	10	7
2,4-D Ester (1 pt)**	5	1	7	1	7	5	1	7	1	1	1	9	5	7	7	9	10	9	7	7	1	10	10	7	6	8	8	1
Gramoxone Extra (1.5 pt)	4	9	6	6	10	5	7	7	9	6	7	8	9	7	9	7	10	8	6	6	6	9	10	6	8	8	9	6
Gramoxone Extra + atrazine (1.5 pt + 2 qt)	5	10	9	10	10	5	10	10	10	9	10	7	10	9	10	10	10	10	10	9	7	10	10	7	10	10	10	10
Roundup/Touchdown (1.0 pt)***	4	10	7	10	10	5	10	7	10	9	9	5	7	6	7	7	10	6	10	9	10	10	9	3	9	7	7	10
Roundup/Touchdown (1.5 pt)***	5	10	8	10	10	7	10	8	10	10	9	6	9	8	8	9	10	7	10	9	10	10	9	4	9	9	8	10
Roundup/Touchdown + atrazine (1 pt + 1.5 pt)***	4	10	10	10	10	6	10	10	10	9	6	10	10	10	10	10	10	10	10	10	10	10	10	3	10	10	10	10
Roundup/Touchdown + 2,4-D (1 pt + 1 pt)***	6	10	9	10	10	8	10	9	10	9	7	9	9	9	10	10	9	10	10	9	10	10	10	5	10	10	9	10

Response Ratings: 10 — (96-100%), 9 — (90-95%), 8 — (85-90%), 7 — (80-84%), 6 — (70-79%), 5 — (60-69%), 4-2 — less than 60%, 1 — 0%.

* This guide presents burndown information only. It *does not* reflect residual weed control.
** Preplant interval: 2,4-D—5 days for corn, 7 days for soybean, 10 days for sorghum, 7 days for 2,4-D + Banvel at 1 qt and 0.5 pt, 10 days for corn on sandy soil.
Banvel—6 months for soybean, 14 days for sorghum.
Postplant interval: 2,4-D—5 days for corn.
*** Use Touchdown at 2/3 the rate listed for Roundup.

Source: Herbicide Use In Nebraska 1997 Guide

Weed Response Ratings For Rice Herbicides

Herbicide	Ammania (red stem)	Barnyardgrass	Broadleaf signalgrass	Cocklebur	Crabgrass	Dayflower	Ducksalad	Eclipta	Fall panicum	False pimpernel	Flatsedges	Gooseweed	Groundcherry	Hemp sesbania (coffeebean)	Indian jointvetch	Morningglory	Northern jointvetch	Nutsedge	Palmleaf morningglory	Red rice	Smartweed	Spikerush	Sprangletop (loosehead)	Sprangletop (tighthead)	Waterhyssop
Bolero - Water seeded	3	8	7	0	7	6	6	—	—	5	7	6	—					3		8[a]		5	8	8	5
Ordram ppi - Water seeded	0	7	6	0	7	3	0	2	6	2	8	2	0	2	0	0	0	3	0	8[a]	5	5	5	5	2
Facet pre	3	9	9	—	9	5	3	8	7	3	5	3	0	6	7	7	7	0	7	0	0	—	0	0	6
Bolero delayed pre	7	7	5	4	7	8	7	8	7	8	7	6	0	5	5	5	5	4	5	0	5	7	7	7	7
Facet delayed pre	3	9	9	—	9	5	3	8	9	3	5	3	0	6	7	7	7	0	7	0	0	—	0	0	6
Prowl delayed pre	0	8	6	0	8	0	0	0	7	0	0	0	0	0	0	0	0	0	0	0	0	0	6	6	0
Facet + Bolero delayed pre	6	9	9	—	9	7	7	9	9	7	8	5	0	8	8	8	8	0	8	0	5	7	8	8	6
Facet + Prowl delayed pre	3	9	9	0	9	5	3	8	9	3	5	3	0	7	7	8	7	0	8	0	0	—	7	7	6
Propanil early (weeds less than 2")	6	9	9	5	9	5	7	8	9	7	9	5	0	9	9	9	9	6	9	0	5	4	5	5	8
Propanil + Bolero early	8	9	9[c]	5	9	8	8	9	9	9	9	6	0	9[c]	9[c]	5	9[c]	5	5	0	6	9	9	9	9
Propanil + Prowl early	7	9	9	5	9	5	7	9	9	9	9	6	0	9[c]	9[c]	5	9[c]	5	5	0	6	7	9	9	7
Propanil fb propanil	6	9	9	6	9	6	7	9	9	9	9	5	0	9	9	9	9	6	5	0	8	9	7	8	8
Arrosolo early	6	9	9	5	9	7	7	9	9	9	9	5	0	9	9	4	9	5	4	0	6	9	7	7	9
Facet early post	3	9	9	—	9	3	3	9	6	3	9	3	0	8	8	8	8	0	8	0	0	—	0	0	3
Facet + Bolero early post	6	9	9	—	9	7	7	9	9	7	5	5	0	8	8	8	8	0	8	0	4	7	8	8	6
Facet + propanil early post	6	9	9	—	9	5	6	9	9	7	9	5	0	9	9	8	9	5	8	0	6	9	4	5	8
Propanil + Londax prior to flood	9	9	9	8	9	8	7	9	9	8	9	9	0	9	9	9	9	8	9	0	8	9	4	5	8
Whip 360 (half rate)	0	4	4	0	4	0	0	0	4	0	0	0	0	0	0	0	0	0	0	0	0	0	9	7	0
Ordram 15G early (3-5" barnyardgrass)	0	9	8	0	9	7	0	8	8	0	5	2	0	2	0	0	0	4	0	0	4	7	5	5	2
Londax early post flood	9	0	0	5	0	8	9	9	0	9	8	9	0	6	6	5	6	5	0	6	8	0	0	0	9
Basagran early	8	0	0	9	0	9	6	8	0	7	8	7	0	3	3	3[b]	3	6	8	0	7	8	0	0	8
Blazer + propanil early	6	8	8	5	8	5	7	8	8	7	8	5	8	9	9	9	9	5	8	0	7	8	4	5	8
Basagran + propanil early	9	9	9	9	9	9	7	9	9	8	9	7	4	9	9	5[b]	9	6	8	0	9	8	4	5	9
Grandstand + propanil early	9	9	9	9	9	5	8	9	9	8	8	9	9	9	9	9	9	6	9	0	7	9	4	5	8
Propanil midseason	4	4	4	2	4	0	3	4	4	0	5	0	4	8	0	5	3	3	0	3	7	0	0	0	8
2,4-D midseason	9	0	0	9	0	9	9	9	0	9	8	6	5	9	9	5	9	5	9	0	8	8	0	0	9
MCPA midseason	9	0	0	9	0	9	9	9	0	9	8	6	5	9	9	5	9	5	9	0	8	8	0	0	9
Blazer midseason	0	0	0	0	0	0	0	0	0	0	3	0	3	9	0	3	0	0	0	0	0	0	0	0	0
Propanil + Blazer midseason	5	5	5	6	5	2	4	5	5	5	6	2	5	9	6	8[d]	6	4	7	0	4	7	0	0	8
Grandstand + propanil midseason	9	2	2	9	2	—	6	6	2	8	5	7	3	9	9	9	9	3	9	0	5	8	0	0	8
2,4-D + propanil midseason for levees	9	6	6	9	6	9	8	9	6	9	8	8	5	9	9	8	9	6	8	0	7	8	6	6	9

Rating Scale: 0 = No control, 10 = 100% control

[a]Water seed pin-point flood culture.
[b]8 for palmleaf mornningglory.
[c]Postemergence control only.
[d]Runners less than 1 ft.

Source: Recommended Chemicals for Weed and Brush Control, Arkansas, 1999.

5

Other Field Crops
Weed Efficacy Chart

NOTICE	The information on these pages is for preliminary planning — not a guide for use. Be sure to follow the manufacturer's directions, notwithstanding information contained here.

Other Field Crops

Castor Beans

Eptam — see EPTC

EPTC

■ **PRE**

Eptam 7-E *(ZENECA)*

Rate: 2 lb. ai/A
2.25 pt. 7-E/A

Time: Preemergence. Apply and incorporate immediately after planting.

Weeds: Broadleaf weeds:

black nightshade	corn spurry	nettleleaf goosefoot
carpetweed	cutleaf nightshade	prickly sida
common chickweed	deadnettle	prostrate pigweed
common	fiddleneck	redroot pigweed
lambsquarters	Florida pusley	sicklepod
common pigweed	hairy nightshade	tall morningglory
common purslane	henbit	tumble pigweed

Annual grasses:

annual bluegrass	field sandbur	rescuegrass
annual ryegrass	giant foxtail	shattercane
(Italian)	goosegrass	signalgrass
barnyardgrass	green foxtail	Texas panicum
(watergrass)	johnsongrass	volunteer grains
bermudagrass	(seedling)	(barley, oats, wheat)
(seedling)	junglerice	wild oat
crabgrass	lovegrass	witchgrass
fall panicum	(stinkgrass)	yellow foxtail

Remarks: Use a rotary hoe for incorporation. Refer to label for use directions, restrictions, and precautions.

State Restrictions: For use in Northern states.

- - - - - - - - - - - - - - -

Signal Word/Toxicity Class: Caution.

REI: 12 hr. unless soil injected or soil incorporated.

Treflan — see trifluralin

TRI-4 — see trifluralin

Trific — see trifluralin

TRIFLURALIN

■ **PPI**

Albaugh Trifluralin 4EC *(Albaugh)*

◆ **Clean Crop Trifluralin HF (4EC)** *(Platte)*

Gowan Trifluralin 4 or 5 (EC) or 10G *(Gowan)*

Helena Trifluralin 4 EC *(Helena)*

Riverside Trifluralin 4EC or Trific 60DF *(Terra)*

◆ **Sedagri Trifluralin 480 (4EC)** *(Rhone-Poulenc)*

Treflan HFP (4EC) *(Dow AgroSciences)*

TRI-4 HF (4EC) *(American Cyanamid)*

Trilin 4 or 5 (EC) or 10G *(Griffin)*

Wilbur-Ellis Trifluralin 10G *(Wilbur-Ellis)*

Rate: 0.5-1 lb. ai/A
1-2 pt. 4EC/A
0.8-1.6 pt. 5EC/A
0.875-1.66 lb. 60DF/A
5-10 lb. 10G/A

Time: Preplant incorporated.

Weeds: Broadleaf weeds:

carelessweed	knotweed	purslane
carpetweed	kochia	pusley
chickweed	lambsquarters	redroot pigweed
field bindweed	Mexican clover	rough pigweed
fireweed	Mexican fireweed	Russian thistle
Florida purslane	prostrate pigweed	spiny pigweed
Florida pusley	puncturevine	stinging nettle
goosefoot	(western U.S.)	tumbleweed
henbit		

Grasses:

annual bluegrass	fall panicum	sandbur
barnyardgrass	foxtail millet	shattercane
bottlegrass	giant foxtail	smooth crabgrass
brachiaria	green foxtail	sprangletop
bristlegrass	Italian ryegrass	stinkgrass
bromegrass	johnsongrass	Texas panicum
burgrass	(seedling)	watergrass
cheat	junglerice	wildcane
cheatgrass	large crabgrass	woolly cupgrass
chess	pigeongrass	yellow foxtail
downy brome	robust foxtail	

Remarks: Rate varies by soil type. Refer to label for use directions, restrictions, and precautions.

Crop Rotation: Refer to label.

State Restrictions: Wilbur-Ellis not registered in California.

- - - - - - - - - - - - - - -

Signal Word/Toxicity Class: Varies by formulation.

REI: 12 hr. unless soil injected or soil incorporated.

Trilin — see trifluralin

Flax

Broclean — see bromoxynil

Bromox — see bromoxynil

BROMOXYNIL

■ **POST**

◆ **Broclean 2EC** *(Platte)*

◆ **Bromox 2EC** *(MIcro Flo)*

Buctril (2EC), Buctril 4EC *(Rhone-Poulenc)*

Moxy 2EC *(Terra)*

Rate: 0.25 lb. ai/A
1 pt. 2EC/A
0.5 pt. 4EC/A

Time: Postemergence. Apply when flax is 2-8" tall but before bud stage.

Weeds: Broadleaf weeds:

annual pepperweed	common tarweed	Pennsylvania
annual sowthistle	eastern black	smartweed
black nightshade	nightshade	shepherdspurse
blue mustard	field pennycress	silverleaf nightshade
bristly starbur	green smartweed	sunflower
coast fiddleneck	hairy nightshade	tartary buckwheat
common cocklebur	jimsonweed	wild buckwheat
common lambsquarters	ladysthumb	

Remarks: For use on common flax only. Not for use on ornamental flax. Do not apply if temperature is expected to exceed 85°F. Refer to label for restrictions and precautions.

Tank Mixes: Poast (except California).

- - - - - - - - - - - - - - -

Signal Word/Toxicity Class: Warning/II.

REI: 12 hr.

◆-new product • PP-preplant • PPI-preplant incorporated • PRE-preemergence • POST-postemergence • SEQ-sequential • ae-acid equivalent • ai-active ingredient • DF-dry flowable
E/EC-emulsifiable concentrate • F/FL-flowable • DG/G/WG-dispersable granule • L/LC-liquid • SP/WSP-soluble packet • W/WP-wettable powder • WSB-water soluble bag

BROMOXYNIL & MCPA (Premix)

■ **POST**

Bronate (EC) (2 lb./gal. bromoxynil & 2 lb./gal. MCPA) *(Rhone-Poulenc)*

Rate: 0.45 lb. ai/A
0.9 pt. EC/A

Time: Postemergence. Apply when flax is 2-8" tall but before bud stage.

Weeds: Most susceptible broadleaf weeds:

annual sowthistle	field pennycress	Russian thistle
black mustard	green smartweed	shepherdspurse
black nightshade	hairy nightshade	silverleaf nightshade
coast fiddleneck	horned poppy	smooth pigweed
common cocklebur	jimsonweed	spiny pigweed
common	ladysthumb	sunflower
lambsquarters	London rocket	tall waterhemp
common tarweed	marshelder	tartary buckwheat
cowcockle	Pennsylvania	tumble mustard
cutleaf nightshade	smartweed	wild buckwheat
eastern black	pepperweed	wild mustard
nightshade	redroot pigweed	yellow rocket

Remarks: For use on common flax only. Not for use on ornamental flax. Do not apply if temperature is expected to exceed 85°F. Application under high humidity conditions can injure crop.

– – – – – – – – – – – – – – – –

Signal Word/Toxicity Class: Warning/II.
REI: 12 hr.

Buctril — see bromoxynil

MCPA

■ **POST**

Albaugh MCPA Amine 4 or Ester (4) *(Albaugh)*
◆ **Clean Crop MCP Amine 4** *(Platte)*
Rhonox (LV ester) (4) *(Nufarm)*
Riverdale MCPA-4 Amine, L.V. 4 Ester (4), IOE (5.2) *(Riverdale)*
Riverside MCPA Amine (4) *(Terra)*
Solve MCPA Ester (4) *(Albaugh)*
Sword (5.2) *(Platte)*
Wilbur-Ellis MCPA Amine or Ester (4) *(Wilbur-Ellis)*

Rate: 0.125-0.25 lb. ae/A
0.25-0.5 pt. 4/A
3-6 oz. 5.2/A

Time: Postemergence. Apply when flax is 2-8" tall but before bud stage.

Weeds: Broadleaf weeds including:

Canada thistle	mustard	ragweed
cocklebur	pigweed	stinkweed
lambsquarters		

Remarks: Do not allow livestock to forage or graze treated areas within 7 days of application.

State Restrictions: Wilbur-Ellis not registered in California.

– – – – – – – – – – – – – – –

Signal Word/Toxicity Class: Varies by formulation.
REI: Danger—48 hr.; Warning/Caution—12 hr.

■ **POST**

Gordon's MCPA Amine 4 (amine) *(PBI/Gordon)*
Rhomene 4 (amine) *(Nufarm)*

Rate: 0.17-0.25 lb. ai/A
0.33-0.5 pt./A

Time: Postemergence. Apply when flax is 2-8" tall but before bud stage.

Weeds: Broadleaf weeds including:

cocklebur	mustard	ragweed
lambsquarters	pigweed	stinkweed

Remarks: Avoid spray drift to sensitive crops. Do not allow livestock to forage or graze treated areas within 7 days of application.

– – – – – – – – – – – – – – –

Signal Word/Toxicity Class: Danger/I.
REI: 48 hr.

◆ **Clean Crop MCP 2 Sodium (sodium salt)** *(Platte)*
◆ **Wilbur-Ellis MCPA Sodium Salt** *(Wilbur-Ellis)*

Rate: 0.125-0.25 lb. ae/A
0.5-1 pt./A

Time: Postemergence. Apply when flax is 3-4" tall but before bud stage.

Weeds: Broadleaf weeds including:

Canada thistle	purslane	stinging nettle
cocklebur	ragweed	stinkweed
kochia	Russian thistle	sunflower
lambsquarters	shepherdspurse	wild radish
pigweed	silverleaf nightshade	
puncturevine	sowthistle	

Remarks: Seed flax. For spot spraying, 1.25-1.5 pt./A will prevent seed production by Canada thistle. Do not spray flax underseeded with legumes without first consulting local weed specialists. Do not allow livestock to forage or graze treated areas within 7 days of application.

State Restrictions: Not registered in California.

Signal Word/Toxicity Class: Danger/I.
REI: 48 hr.

Moxy — see bromoxynil

Poast — see sethoxydim

RAMROD

■ **PRE**

Ramrod 4L (propachlor) *(Monsanto)*

Rate: 4 lb. ai/A
4 qt. 4L/A

Time: Preemergence surface treatment.

Weeds: Annual broadleaf weeds:

black nightshade	Florida pusley	prickly sida*
carelessweed	galinsoga	purslane
carpetweed	hairy nightshade	sicklepod*
common ragweed*	lambsquarters*	smartweed*
cutleaf groundcherry	pigweed	teaweed*
Florida beggarweed*		

Annual grasses and sedges:

barnyardgrass	green foxtail	Texas panicum*
broadleaf signalgrass	johnsongrass	wild proso millet*
crabgrass	(seedling)*	wildcane*
fall panicum	robust purple foxtail	witchgrass
giant foxtail	robust white foxtail	woolly cupgrass*
goosegrass	sandbur*	yellow foxtail
grassbur*	shattercane*	yellow nutsedge

* Suppression

Remarks: Apply in at least 15 gal. water or fluid fertilizer.

– – – – – – – – – – – – – – –

Signal Word/Toxicity Class: Danger/I.
REI: 48 hr.

Rhomene — see MCPA

Rhonox — see MCPA

SETHOXYDIM

■ **POST**

Poast (1.5EC) *(BASF)*

Rate: 0.09-0.28 lb. ai/A
0.5-1.5 pt. 1.5EC/A

Time: Postemergence.

Weeds: Annual and perennial grasses:

annual ryegrass	junglerice	stinkgrass
barnyardgrass	large crabgrass	tall fescue
bermudagrass	lovegrass	Texas panicum
broadleaf signalgrass	orchardgrass	volunteer cereals
browntop panicum	(seedling)	wild oat
fall panicum	perennial ryegrass	wild proso millet
field sandbur	quackgrass	wildcane
giant foxtail	red rice	wirestem muhly
goosegrass	red sprangletop	witchgrass
green foxtail	shattercane	woolly cupgrass
itchgrass	smooth crabgrass	yellow foxtail
johnsongrass	southwestern cupgrass	

Remarks: Rate depends on growing region. Add spray adjuvant or oil concentrate. Do not apply through any type of irrigation system. Refer to label for restrictions and limitations.

5

Other Field Crops

NOTICE	The information on these pages is for preliminary planning — not a guide for use. Be sure to follow the manufacturer's directions, notwithstanding information contained here.	For personal protective equipment and EPA registration numbers, please turn to page 70.

Flax

Days To Harvest: 75.
Tank Mixes: Buctril, MCPA.
State Restrictions: Do not use UAN or AMS in California or Pacific Northwest.

- - - - - - - - - - - - - - -

Signal Word/Toxicity Class: Warning/II.
REI: 12 hr.

Solve — see MCPA

Sword — see MCPA

Treflan — see trifluralin

TRIFLURALIN

■ PPI
Albaugh Trifluralin 4EC (Albaugh)
◆ Clean Crop Trifluralin HF (4EC) (Platte)
Gowan Trifluralin 4 or 5 (EC) or 10G (Gowan)
Helena Trifluralin 4 EC (Helena)
◆ Sedagri Trifluralin 480 (4EC) (Rhone-Poulenc)
Treflan HFP (4EC) or TR-10 (10G) (Dow AgroSciences)
Trilin 4 or 5 (EC) or 10G (Griffin)
Wilbur-Ellis Trifluralin 10G (Wilbur-Ellis)

Rate: 0.5-1 lb. ai/A
1-2 pt. 4EC/A
0.8-1.6 pt. 5EC/A
5-10 lb. 10G/A
Time: Preplant incorporated. Fall application.
Weeds: Broadleaf weeds:

carelessweed	knotweed	purslane
carpetweed	kochia	pusley
chickweed	lambsquarters	redroot pigweed
field bindweed	Mexican clover	rough pigweed
fireweed	Mexican fireweed	Russian thistle
Florida purslane	prostrate pigweed	spiny pigweed
Florida pusley	puncturevine	stinging nettle
goosefoot	(western U.S.)	tumbleweed
henbit		

Grasses:

annual bluegrass	fall panicum	sandbur
barnyardgrass	foxtail millet	shattercane
bottlegrass	giant foxtail	smooth crabgrass
brachiaria	green foxtail	sprangletop
bristlegrass	Italian ryegrass	stinkgrass
bromegrass	johnsongrass	Texas panicum
burgrass	(seedling)	watergrass
cheat	junglerice	wildcane
cheatgrass	large crabgrass	woolly cupgrass
chess	pigeongrass	yellow foxtail
downy brome	robust foxtail	

Remarks: Spring-seeded flax. Rate varies by soil type. Do not seed until seedbed has warmed up. Refer to label for directions and precautions.
Crop Rotation: Refer to label.
State Restrictions: Wilbur-Ellis not registered in California. Albaugh, Clean Crop, Helena, Sedagri, Treflan not for use in Pecos or Reeves County, Texas; in Montana, uses limited to supplemental labeling.

- - - - - - - - - - - - - - -

Signal Word/Toxicity Class: Varies by formulation.
REI: 12 hr. unless soil injected or soil incorporated.

Trilin — see trifluralin

Guar Beans

Credit — see glyphosate

Glyfos or Glyfos X-tra — see glyphosate

GLYPHOSATE

■ PRE
◆ Credit (4WS) (Nufarm)
◆ Glyfos or Glyfos X-tra (4WS) (Cheminova)
Rattler (4WS) (Helena)
Roundup Custom (5.4WS) (Monsanto)
Roundup Original, Original RT, Ultra, Ultra RT (4WS) (Monsanto)
Rate: Annual weeds:
0.38-1.5 lb. ai/A
0.56-2.25 pt. 5.4WS/A
0.75-3 pt. 4WS/A
Perennial weeds:
0.5-5 lb. ai/A
0.75-7.5 pt. 5.4WS/A
1-10 pt. 4WS/A
Time: Preemergence: Apply prior to emergence of direct-seeded crop or prior to transplanting.
Weeds: Emerged annual and perennial broadleaf weeds including:

Canada thistle	hemp dogbane	Pennsylvania
curly dock	milkweed	smartweed
field bindweed		

Grasses:

bermudagrass	fescue	paragrass
fall panicum	johnsongrass	quackgrass

Remarks: Prior to transplanting crops into plastic mulch, remove product residue from plastic. Do not add surfactant to Roundup Ultra or Ultra RT. Do not allow glyphosate to contact desirable plants. Do not apply through any type of irrigation system. Refer to label for directions, precautions and restrictions.
State Restrictions: Roundup Ultra RT: For use in Colorado, Idaho, Montana, North Dakota, South Dakota, Utah, and Wyoming. For use in specific counties only in Kansas, Minnesota, Nebraska, Nevada, Oklahoma, Oregon, and Washington, refer to label for restrictions. Glyfos is not registered for use in California. Glyfos X-tra is not registered for use in mistblowers in California or Arizona.

- - - - - - - - - - - - - - -

Signal Word/Toxicity Class: Varies by formulation.
REI: Warning—12 hr.; Caution—4 hr.

Gramoxone Extra — see paraquat

PARAQUAT
Restricted Use Pesticide.

◆ Gramoxone Extra (2.5L) (ZENECA)
Rate: 0.3-0.5 lb. ai/A
1-1.5 pt. 2.5L/A
Time: Apply to mature crop with 80% of pods yellowing and mostly ripe with no more than 40% (bush-type) or 30% (vine-type) leaves still green in color.

Rate: 0.5 lb. ai/A
1.5 pt. 2.5L/A
Time: Preharvest. Apply after pods are fully mature.
Weeds: Annual broadleaf weeds and grasses; top kill and suppression of perennials.
Remarks: Add nonionic surfactant or crop oil concentrate. Seedbeds should be formed as far ahead of planting and treatment as possible to permit maximum weed and grass emergence. Seeding should be done with minimum amount of soil disturbance. Do not graze treated areas or use treated forage for animal feed. Refer to label for use directions.
Days To Harvest: 7; preharvest desiccation—4.

- - - - - - - - - - - - - - -

Signal Word/Toxicity Class: Danger-Poison/I.
REI: 12 hr. (except harvest aid/desiccation 24 hr.).

Rattler — see glyphosate

Roundup — see glyphosate

Treflan — see trifluralin

TRI-4 — see trifluralin

◆-new product • PP-preplant • PPI-preplant incorporated • PRE-preemergence • POST-postemergence • SEQ-sequential • ae-acid equivalent • ai-active ingredient • DF-dry flowable
E/EC-emulsifiable concentrate • F/FL-flowable • DG/G/WG-dispersable granule • L/LC-liquid • SP/WSP-soluble packet • W/WP-wettable powder • WSB-water soluble bag

Trific — see trifluralin

TRIFLURALIN

■ PPI

Albaugh Trifluralin 4EC *(Albaugh)*
◆ **Clean Crop Trifluralin HF (4EC)** *(Platte)*
Gowan Trifluralin 4 or 5 (EC) or 10G *(Gowan)*
Helena Trifluralin 4 EC *(Helena)*
Riverside Trifluralin 4EC or Trific 60DF *(Terra)*
◆ **Sedagri Trifluralin 480 (4EC)** *(Rhone-Poulenc)*
Treflan HFP (4EC) *(Dow AgroSciences)*
TRI-4 HF (4EC) *(America Cyanamid)*
Trilin 4 or 5 (EC) or 10G *(Griffin)*
Wilbur-Ellis Trifluralin 10G *(Wilbur-Ellis)*

Rate: 0.5-0.75 lb. ai/A
1-1.5 pt. 4EC/A
0.8-1.2 pt. 5EC/A
0.875-1.25 lb. 60DF/A
5-7.5 lb. 10G/A

Time: Preplant incorporated.
Weeds: Broadleaf weeds:

carelessweed	knotweed	purslane
carpetweed	kochia	pusley
chickweed	lambsquarters	redroot pigweed
field bindweed	Mexican clover	rough pigweed
fireweed	Mexican fireweed	Russian thistle
Florida purslane	prostrate pigweed	spiny pigweed
Florida pusley	puncturevine	stinging nettle
goosefoot	(western U.S.)	tumbleweed
henbit		

Grasses:

annual bluegrass	fall panicum	sandbur
barnyardgrass	foxtail millet	shattercane
bottlegrass	giant foxtail	smooth crabgrass
brachiaria	green foxtail	sprangletop
bristlegrass	Italian ryegrass	stinkgrass
bromegrass	johnsongrass	Texas panicum
burgrass	(seedling)	watergrass
cheat	junglerice	wildcane
cheatgrass	large crabgrass	woolly cupgrass
chess	pigeongrass	yellow foxtail
downy brome	robust foxtail	

Remarks: Rate varies by soil type. Refer to label for directions, restrictions, and precautions.
Crop Rotation: Refer to label.
State Restrictions: Wilbur-Ellis not registered in California.

- - - - - - - - - - - - - - -

Signal Word/Toxicity Class: Varies by formulation.
REI: 12 hr. unless soil injected or soil incorporated.

Trilin — see trifluralin

Hops

Gramoxone Extra — see paraquat

PARAQUAT

Restricted Use Pesticide.

■ POST

Gramoxone Extra (2.5L) *(ZENECA)*
Rate: 0.5 lb. ai/A
1.5 pt. 2.5L/A
Time: Postemergence. Apply as directed spray.
Weeds: Annual broadleaf weeds and grasses; top kill and suppression of perennials.
Remarks: Add nonionic surfactant or crop oil concentrate. Retreatment or spot treatment may be necessary. Application to hop vines less than 6 ft. tall may cause injury. Vine refuse and silage may be fed to livestock. Do not graze in treated hopyards. Refer to label for use directions.

Days To Harvest: 14.
State Restrictions: For use in Idaho, Oregon, Washington.

- - - - - - - - - - - - - - -

Signal Word/Toxicity Class: Danger-Poison/I.
REI: 12 hr. (except harvest aid/desiccation 24 hr.).

SCYTHE

◆ **Scythe (pelargonic acid)** *(Mycogen)*
Rate: 4-13 fl. oz./1 gal. spray solution.
Time: Apply to actively growing weeds prior to crop emergence.
Weeds: Annual and perennial broadleaf weeds and grasses.
Remarks: Apply in minimum 75 gal. spray solution/A or spray-to-wet. Do not apply by air or through any type of irrigation system. Refer to label for directions and precautions.
Tank Mixes: Glyphosate and other foliar and residual herbicides.

- - - - - - - - - - - - - - -

Signal Word/Toxicity Class: Warning/II.
REI: 24 hr.

Treflan — see trifluralin

Trific — see trifluralin

TRIFLURALIN

■ PRE

Albaugh Trifluralin 4EC *(Albaugh)*
◆ **Clean Crop Trifluralin HF (4EC)** *(Platte)*
Gowan Trifluralin 4 or 5 (EC) *(Gowan)*
Helena Trifluralin 4 EC *(Helena)*
Riverside Trifluralin 4EC or Trific 60DF *(Terra)*
◆ **Sedagri Trifluralin 480 (4EC)** *(Rhone-Poulenc)*
Treflan HFP (4EC) *(Dow AgroSciences)*
Trilin 4 or 5 (EC) or 10G *(Griffin)*
Wilbur-Ellis Trifluralin 10G *(Wilbur-Ellis)*

Rate: 0.5-0.75 lb. ai/A
1-1.5 pt. 4EC/A
0.8-1.2 pt. 5EC/A
0.875-1.25 lb. 60DF/A
5-7.5 lb. 10G/A

Time: Preemergence. Apply and incorporate to established crop during dormancy.
Weeds: Broadleaf weeds:

carelessweed	knotweed	purslane
carpetweed	kochia	pusley
chickweed	lambsquarters	redroot pigweed
field bindweed	Mexican clover	rough pigweed
fireweed	Mexican fireweed	Russian thistle
Florida purslane	prostrate pigweed	tumbleweed
Florida pusley	puncturevine	spiny pigweed
goosefoot	(western U.S.)	stinging nettle
henbit		

Grasses:

annual bluegrass	giant foxtail	sandbur
barnyardgrass	green foxtail	shattercane
bottlegrass	Italian ryegrass	signalgrass
bristlegrass	johnsongrass	smooth crabgrass
bromegrass	(seedling)	sprangletop
burgrass	junglerice	stinkgrass
cheat	large crabgrass	Texas panicum
cheatgrass	lovegrass	watergrass
chess	pigeongrass	wildcane
downy brome	red rice	woolly cupgrass
fall panicum	robust foxtail	yellow foxtail
foxtail millet		

Remarks: Rate varies by soil type. Use incorporation equipment that will ensure thorough soil mixing with minimal damage to crop. Refer to label for directions and precautions.
Crop Rotation: Refer to label.
State Restrictions: Wilbur-Ellis not registered in California.

- - - - - - - - - - - - - - -

Signal Word/Toxicity Class: Varies by formulation.
REI: 12 hr. unless soil injected or soil incorporated.

Trilin — see trifluralin

NOTICE The information on these pages is for preliminary planning — not a guide for use. Be sure to follow the manufacturer's directions, notwithstanding information contained here. | For personal protective equipment and EPA registration numbers, please turn to page 70.

Kenaf

Treflan — see trifluralin

TRIFLURALIN

Preplant incorporated herbicide with activity on certain annual grasses and broadleaf weeds. Same chemical family as Sonalan and Prowl.

■ PPI

Riverside Trifluralin 4EC *(Terra)*
◆ Sedagri Trifluralin 480 (4EC) *(Rhone-Poulenc)*
Treflan HFP (4EC) *(Dow AgroSciences)*
Trilin (4EC) *(Griffin)*
  Rate: 0.5-0.75 lb. ai/A
      1-1.5 pt. 4EC/A (0.75-2 pt. Trilin)
  Time: Preplant incorporated.
  Weeds: Broadleaf weeds:

carelessweed	knotweed	purslane
carpetweed	kochia	pusley
chickweed	lambsquarters	redroot pigweed
field bindweed	Mexican clover	rough pigweed
fireweed	Mexican fireweed	Russian thistle
Florida purslane	prostrate pigweed	spiny pigweed
Florida pusley	puncturevine	stinging nettle
goosefoot	(western U.S.)	tumbleweed
henbit		

  Grasses:

annual bluegrass	fall panicum	sandbur
barnyardgrass	foxtail millet	shattercane
bottlegrass	giant foxtail	smooth crabgrass
brachiaria	green foxtail	sprangletop
bristlegrass	Italian ryegrass	stinkgrass
bromegrass	johnsongrass	Texas panicum
burgrass	(seedling)	watergrass
cheat	junglerice	wildcane
cheatgrass	large crabgrass	woolly cupgrass
chess	pigeongrass	yellow foxtail
downy brome	robust foxtail	

  Remarks: For coarse soils with 2%-5% organic matter, use high rate. Do not graze or harvest treated crop for livestock forage. Refer to label for directions and precautions.

– – – – – – – – – – – – – – –

  Signal Word/Toxicity Class: Varies by formulation.
  REI: 12 hr. unless soil injected or soil incorporated.

Trilin — see trifluralin

Mint

(Peppermint, Spearmint)

BASAGRAN

■ POST

Basagran (bentazon) *(BASF)*
  Rate: 1-2 lb. ai/A
      2-4 pt./A
  Time: Early postemergence.
  Weeds: Broadleaf weeds and sedges:

Canada thistle	common ragweed	Pennsylvania
common groundsel	hairy nightshade	smartweed
common	kochia	wild mustard
lambsquarters	ladysthumb	yellow nutsedge

  Remarks: Peppermint, spearmint. Rate depends on species, leaf stage, and height of weeds to be controlled. For Canada thistle, common groundsel, and yellow nutsedge, refer to Special Directions on label.

– – – – – – – – – – – – – –

  Signal Word/Toxicity Class: Caution/III.
  REI: 12 hr.

Broclean — see bromoxynil

Bromox — see bromoxynil

BROMOXYNIL

■ POST

◆ Broclean 2EC *(Platte)*
◆ Bromox 2EC *(Micro Flo)*
Buctril (2EC), Buctril 4EC *(Rhone-Poulenc)*
Moxy 2EC *(Terra)*
  Rate: 0.25-0.375 lb. ai/A
      1-1.5 pt. 2EC/A
      0.5-0.75 pt. 4EC/A
      Chemigation (except Broclean):
      0.5 lb. ai/A
      2 pt. 2EC/A
      1 pt. 4EC/A
  Time: Postemergence. Do not apply when air temperatures exceed or are expected to exceed 70°F within 5 days after application.
  Weeds: Most susceptible broadleaf weeds:

annual pepperweed	common tarweed	Pennsylvania
annual sowthistle	eastern black	smartweed
black nightshade	nightshade	shepherdspurse
blue mustard	field pennycress	silverleaf nightshade
bristly starbur	green smartweed	sunflower
coast fiddleneck	hairy nightshade	tartary buckwheat
common cocklebur	jimsonweed	wild buckwheat
common lambsquarters	ladysthumb	

  Susceptible broadleaf weeds:

buffalobur	ivyleaf morningglory	spiny pigweed
burcucumber	knawel	tall morningglory
common groundsel	kochia	tall waterhemp
common ragweed	London rocket	tumble mustard
corn chamomile	mayweed	velvetleaf
corn gromwell	prostrate knotweed	Venice mallow
cowcockle	puncturevine	wild mustard
giant ragweed	redroot pigweed	wild radish
hemp sesbania	Russian thistle	yellow starthistle

  Remarks: Peppermint, spearmint. Apply only to established mint. May cause temporary stunting and leaf chlorosis. Do not apply to mint growing under adverse conditions such as insect, nematode, and disease infestations, high soil salt content, drought, excessive moisture, or mint suffering from winter injury.
  Days To Harvest: 70.

– – – – – – – – – – – – – – –

  Signal Word/Toxicity Class: Warning/II.
  REI: 12 hr.

Buctril — see bromoxynil

CLOPYRALID

Systemic herbicide absorbed by leaves and roots. Has selective postemergence control of many annual and perennial broadleaf weeds.

■ POST

Stinger *(Dow AgroSciences)*
  Rate: 0.125-0.25 lb. ae/A
      0.33-0.66 pt./A
  Time: Postemergence. Treat when annual weeds are small and actively growing before they send up a flower stalk; Canada thistle after majority of basal leaves have emerged but prior to bud stage.
  Weeds: Annual and perennial broadleaf weeds:

buffalobur	jimsonweed	sowthistle
Canada thistle	knapweed	sunflower
cocklebur	marshelder	vetch
clover	nightshade	volunteer soybean
dandelion	smartweed	wild buckwheat
Jerusalem artichoke	(suppression)	

  Remarks: Peppermint, spearmint. For distillation (oil extraction) only. Apply as broadcast foliar spray by ground only. Do not apply more than 1 pt./A per growing season. Do not apply through any type of irrigation system. Do not contaminate irrigation ditches or water used for irrigation or domestic purposes. Do not feed spent mint hay slugs to livestock.

– – – – – – – – – – – – – – –

◆-new product • PP-preplant • PPI-preplant incorporated • PRE-preemergence • POST-postemergence • SEQ-sequential • ae-acid equivalent • ai-active ingredient • DF-dry flowable E/EC-emulsifiable concentrate • F/FL-flowable • DG/G/WG-dispersable granule • L/LC-liquid • SP/WSP-soluble packet • W/WP-wettable powder • WSB-water soluble bag

Days To Harvest: 45.
Crop Rotation: Varies by region; refer to label.

- - - - - - - - - - - - - - - -

Signal Word/Toxicity Class: Caution/III.
REI: 12 hr.

DEVRINOL

■ POST

Devrinol 10-G or 50-DF (napropamide) *(United Phosphorus)*

Rate: 4 lb. ai/A
    40 lb. 10-G/A
    8 lb. 50-DF/A

Time: Postemergence. Apply to soil in the fall through early spring prior to weed emergence.

Weeds: Annual broadleaf weeds:

annual sowthistle	common ragweed	pineappleweed
carpetweed	(suppression)	prickly lettuce
coast fiddleneck	horse purslane	prostrate knotweed
common chickweed	lambsquarters	purple cudweed
common groundsel	little mallow	redroot pigweed
common purslane	(from seed)	redstem filaree

Annual grasses:

annual bluegrass	giant foxtail	ripgut brome
annual ryegrass	goosegrass	sandbur
(Italian ryegrass)	green foxtail	smooth crabgrass
barnyardgrass	guineagrass	soft chess
bristly foxtail	hairy crabgrass	southwestern cupgrass
bromegrass	johnsongrass	stinkgrass
canarygrass	(seedling)	Texas panicum
cheatgrass	junglerice	wild barley
downy brome	large crabgrass	wild oat
fall panicum	Mexican sprangletop	witchgrass
foxtail barley	red sprangletop	yellow foxtail

Remarks: Newly planted (50-DF) and established crop. If rainfall does not occur, treatment must be shallowly incorporated or irrigated in following application with sufficient water to wet soil to a depth of 2-4".

Crop Rotation: Do not plant to crops not specified on label until 12 months after last application. Disc plow or moldboard plow at least 10" deep prior to planting succeeding crop.

Tank Mixes: Sinbar (50-DF).

State Restrictions: For use in the Pacific Northwest only.

- - - - - - - - - - - - - - - -

Signal Word/Toxicity Class: Caution.
REI: 12 hr.

Direx — see diuron

DIURON

■ PRE

Direx 4L or 80DF *(Griffin)*
♦ Diuron 80 WDG *(Platte)*
Riverside Diuron 80DF *(Terra)*

Rate: 2.4 lb. ai/A
    2.4 qt. 4L/A
    3 lb. 80DF/A

Time: Preemergence. Apply just after last cultivation in the spring.

Weeds: Broadleaf weeds:

amsinckia	dogfennel	purslane
(fiddleneck)	gromwell	ragweed
annual groundcherry	groundsel	shepherdspurse
annual morningglory	knawel	tansymustard
chickweed	lambsquarters	wild lettuce
corn spurry	pigweed	wild mustard

Grasses:

annual bluegrass	barnyardgrass	rattail fescue
annual sweet	crabgrass	red sprangletop
vernalgrass	foxtail	velvetgrass

Remarks: Peppermint. Do not apply to newly planted (less than 1 year) or emerged peppermint.

Crop Rotation: Do not replant to other crops within 1 year after treatment.

State Restrictions: For use in the Pacific Northwest only.

- - - - - - - - - - - - - - - -

Signal Word/Toxicity Class: Caution/III.
REI: 12 hr.

GOAL

■ PRE

Goal 2XL (oxyfluorfen) *(Rohm and Haas)*

Rate: Peppermint—Willamette Valley (western Oregon):
    0.5-0.75 lb. ai/A
    2-3 pt. 2XL/A
    Peppermint, spearmint—CA, ID, MT, NV, OR, SD, UT, WA:
    1-2 lb. ai/A
    4-8 pt. 2XL/A

Time: Preemergence. Apply prior to emergence of new spring growth. For Willamette Valley, apply from Nov.-Feb. For Oregon and Washington (east of Cascades), California, Montana, Idaho, Nevada, South Dakota and Utah, apply from Dec.-Mar.

Weeds: Broadleaf weeds:

annual sowthistle	flixweed	Russian thistle
blue mustard (purple)	jim hill mustard	shepherdspurse
catchweed bedstraw	prickly lettuce	tansymustard
common groundsel	(China lettuce)	tumble mustard
common	red orach	yellowflower
lambsquarters	redroot pigweed	pepperweed

Grasses:

annual bluegrass	Italian ryegrass	wild oat

Remarks: **Dormant peppermint, spearmint.** Do not apply more than one application per season. Do not apply in Willamette Valley to mint that has been plowed. Do not apply through any type of irrigation system.

Crop Rotation: Refer to label for plantback times for rotation crops.

State Restrictions: For use in California, Idaho, Montana, Nevada, Oregon, South Dakota, Utah, Washington.

- - - - - - - - - - - - - - - -

Signal Word/Toxicity Class: Warning/II.
REI: 24 hr.

Gramoxone Extra — see paraquat

Moxy — see bromoxynil

PARAQUAT

Restricted Use Pesticide.

■ PRE

Gramoxone Extra (2.5L) *(ZENECA)*

Rate: 0.5-0.75 lb. ai/A
    1.5-2.4 pt. 2.5L/A

Time: Preemergence. Apply when dormant and before spring growth begins. Do not apply to weeds greater than 6" tall.

Weeds: Suppression of weeds and grasses such as:

bluegrass	downy brome	Italian ryegrass
chickweed	groundsel	prickly lettuce

Remarks: **Peppermint, spearmint.** Add nonionic surfactant or crop oil concentrate. Do not apply more than 2.4 pt. 2.5L/A per season. Refer to label for use directions, restrictions, and precautions.

Tank Mixes: Sinbar.

- - - - - - - - - - - - - - - -

Signal Word/Toxicity Class: Danger-Poison/I.
REI: 12 hr. (except harvest aid/desiccation 24 hr.).

Poast — see sethoxydim

SCYTHE

♦ Scythe (pelargonic acid) *(Mycogen)*

Rate: 4-13 fl. oz./1 gal. spray solution

Time: Apply to actively growing weeds prior to crop emergence.

Weeds: Annual and perennial broadleaf weeds and grasses.

Remarks: Apply in minimum 75 gal. spray solution/A or spray-to-wet. Do not apply by air or through any type of irrigation system. Refer to label for directions and precautions.

Tank Mixes: Glyphosate and other foliar and residual herbicides.

- - - - - - - - - - - - - - - -

Signal Word/Toxicity Class: Warning/II.
REI: 24 hr.

SETHOXYDIM

■ POST

Poast (1.5EC) (BASF)

Rate: 0.09-0 47 lb. ai/A
0.5-2.5 pt. 1.5EC/A

Time: Postemergence.

Weeds: Annual and perennial grasses:

annual ryegrass	johnsongrass	southwestern cupgrass
barnyardgrass	junglerice	stinkgrass
bermudagrass	large crabgrass	tall fescue
broadleaf signalgrass	lovegrass	Texas panicum
browntop panicum	orchardgrass	volunteer cereals
fall panicum	(seedling)	wild oat
giant foxtail	perennial ryegrass	wild proso millet
goosegrass	red rice	wildcane
green foxtail	red sprangletop	witchgrass
itchgrass	smooth crabgrass	yellow foxtail

Remarks: Rate depends on growing region. Add spray adjuvant or oil concentrate. Urea ammonium-nitrate solution (UAN) or ammonium sulfate (AMS) recommended to enhance activity on certain grass species. Do not apply through any type of irrigation system. Do not graze treated fields or feed treated forage to livestock. Refer to label for restrictions and limitations.

Days To Harvest: 20.

Tank Mixes: Basagran, Buctril.

State Restrictions: Do not use UAN or AMS in California or Pacific Northwest.

_ _ _ _ _ _ _ _ _ _ _ _ _ _ _

Signal Word/Toxicity Class: Warning/II (Poast); Caution/III (Poast Plus).

REI: 12 hr.

SINBAR

■ PRE, POST

Sinbar (WP) (terbacil) (DuPont)

Rate: 0.8-1.6 lb. ai/A
1-2 lb. WP/A

Time: Preemergence. Apply in the spring after last cultivation.

Rate: 0.8-1.2 lb. ai/A
1-1.5 lb. WP/A

Time: Postemergence. Apply before weeds and grasses are 1-2" tall.

Weeds: Broadleaf weeds:

chickweed	nightshade	smartweed
lambsquarters		

Grasses:

barnyardgrass	panicum

Remarks: Moisture needed for activation. Observe use limitations regarding insecticides.

Days To Harvest: 60.

Crop Rotation: Mint may be planted the year after last application; all other crops within 2 years after last application.

State Restrictions: Not for use in California.

_ _ _ _ _ _ _ _ _ _ _ _ _ _ _

Signal Word/Toxicity Class: Caution.

REI: 12 hr.

Stinger — see clopyralid

Mung Beans

Dual — see S-metolachlor

Gramoxone Extra — see paraquat

S-METOLACHLOR

■ PPI, PRE

Dual MAGNUM or Dual II MAGNUM (EC) (Novartis)

Rate: 1-2 pt. EC/A

Time: Preplant incorporated: Incorporate into top 2" soil within 14 days before planting. Preemergence: Apply during or after planting but before weeds emerge.

Weeds: Broadleaf weeds:

carpetweed	eclipta*	galinsoga
common purslane*	Florida beggarweed*	hairy nightshade*
eastern black nightshade	Florida pusley	pigweed

Grasses and sedges:

barnyardgrass (watergrass)	goosegrass	shattercane*
crabgrass	green foxtail	signalgrass
crowfootgrass	johnsongrass	southwestern cupgrass
fall panicum	(seedling)*	volunteer sorghum*
foxtail millet	prairie cupgrass	witchgrass
giant foxtail	red rice	yellow foxtail
	sandbur*	yellow nutsedge

*Suppression

Remarks: Rate varies by soil type and organic matter. In case of crop failure, any crop on label may be replanted immediately. Do not make second broadcast application. If original application was banded and second crop is planted in untreated row middles, second banded treatment may be applied. Do not cut for hay within 120 days after application.

Crop Rotation: Alfalfa—4 months; barley, oats, rye, wheat—4½ months; tomatoes—6 months; clover—9 months; any labeled crop in addition to barley, buckwheat, cabbage, milo, nuts, oats, peppers, rice, root crops, rye, stone fruits, tobacco, and wheat may be planted in the spring following treatment (including lay-by or multiple treatments applied previous season); all other rotational crops may be planted 12 months after application.

State Restrictions: Do not use in Nassau County or Suffolk County, New York.

_ _ _ _ _ _ _ _ _ _ _ _ _ _ _

Signal Word/Toxicity Class: Caution/III.

REI: 24 hr.

PARAQUAT

Restricted Use Pesticide.

Gramoxone Extra (2.5L) (ZENECA)

Rate: 0.3-0.5 lb. ai/A
1-1.5 pt. 2.5L/A

Time: Apply to mature crop with 80% of pods yellowing and mostly ripe with no more than 40% (bush-type) or 30% (vine-type) leaves still green in color.

Weeds: Annual broadleaf weeds and grasses; top kill and suppression of perennials.

Remarks: Add nonionic surfactant or crop oil concentrate. Seedbeds should be formed as far ahead of planting and treatment as possible to permit maximum weed and grass emergence. Seeding should be done with minimum amount of soil disturbance. Refer to label for use directions, restrictions, and precautions.

Days To Harvest: 7.

State Restrictions: Not for use on dry beans in California.

_ _ _ _ _ _ _ _ _ _ _ _ _ _ _

Signal Word/Toxicity Class: Danger-Poison/I.

REI: 12 hr. (except harvest aid/desiccation 24 hr.).

SCYTHE

◆ **Scythe (pelargonic acid)** (Mycogen)

Rate: 4-13 fl. oz./1 gal. spray solution

Time: Apply to actively growing weeds prior to crop emergence.

Weeds: Annual and perennial broadleaf weeds and grasses.

Remarks: Apply in minimum 75 gal. spray solution/A or spray-to-wet. Do not apply by air or through any type of irrigation system. Refer to label for directions and precautions.

Tank Mixes: Glyphosate and other foliar and residual herbicides.

_ _ _ _ _ _ _ _ _ _ _ _ _ _ _

Signal Word/Toxicity Class: Warning/II.

REI: 24 hr.

Treflan — see trifluralin

TRI-4 — see trifluralin

Trific— see trifluralin

◆-new product • PP-preplant • PPI-preplant incorporated • PRE-preemergence • POST-postemergence • SEQ-sequential • ae-acid equivalent • ai-active ingredient • DF-dry flowable
E/EC-emulsifiable concentrate • F/FL-flowable • DG/G/WG-dispersable granule • L/LC-liquid • SP/WSP-soluble packet • W/WP-wettable powder • WSB-water soluble bag

TRIFLURALIN

■ PPI

Albaugh Trifluralin 4EC *(Albaugh)*
◆ **Clean Crop Trifluralin HF (4EC)** *(Platte)*
Gowan Trifluralin 4 or 5 (EC) or 10G *(Gowan)*
Helena Trifluralin 4 EC *(Helena)*
Riverside Trifluralin 4EC or Trific 60DF *(Terra)*
◆ **Sedagri Trifluralin 480 (4EC)** *(Rhone-Poulenc)*
Treflan HFP (4EC) *(Dow AgroSciences)*
TRI-4 HF (4EC) *(American Cyanamid)*
Trilin 4 or 5 (EC) or 10G *(Griffin)*
Wilbur-Ellis Trifluralin 10G *(Wilbur-Ellis)*

Rate: 0.5-0.75 lb. ai/A
1-1.5 pt. 4EC/A
0.8-1.2 pt. 5EC/A
0.875-1.25 lb. 60DF/A
5-7.5 lb. 10G/A
Time: Preplant incorporated.
Weeds: Broadleaf weeds:

carelessweed	knotweed	purslane
carpetweed	kochia	pusley
chickweed	lambsquarters	redroot pigweed
field bindweed	Mexican clover	rough pigweed
fireweed	Mexican fireweed	Russian thistle
Florida purslane	prostrate pigweed	spiny pigweed
Florida pusley	puncturevine	stinging nettle
goosefoot	(western U.S.)	tumbleweed
henbit		

Grasses:

annual bluegrass	fall panicum	sandbur
barnyardgrass	foxtail millet	shattercane
bottlegrass	giant foxtail	smooth crabgrass
brachiaria	green foxtail	sprangletop
bristlegrass	Italian ryegrass	stinkgrass
bromegrass	johnsongrass	Texas panicum
burgrass	(seedling)	watergrass
cheat	junglerice	wildcane
cheatgrass	large crabgrass	woolly cupgrass
chess	pigeongrass	yellow foxtail
downy brome	robust foxtail	

Remarks: Rate varies by soil type. Refer to label for directions and precautions.
Crop Rotation: Refer to label.
State Restrictions: Wilbur-Ellis not registered in California.

- - - - - - - - - - - - - -

Signal Word/Toxicity Class: Varies by formulation.
REI: 12 hr. unless soil injected or soil incorporated.

Trilin — see trifluralin

Oil Seed Crops

DIQUAT DIBROMIDE

◆ **Diquat** *(ZENECA)*
Rate: 0.375-0.5 lb. ai/A
1.5-2 pt./A
Time: Site preparation prior to planting. Repeat as needed.
Weeds: Broadleaf weeds and grasses.
Remarks: Nonbearing jojoba. Apply by ground only. Use high rate when weeds are large or dense. Do not allow spray to contact green stems, foliage, or fruit. Use a shield or wrap plant when spraying around young trees or vines. Do not apply through any type of irrigation system. Do not graze treated areas. Refer to label for restrictions and precautions.
Days To Harvest: 1 year.

- - - - - - - - - - - - - -

Signal Word/Toxicity Class: Warning/II.
REI: 24 hr.

GOAL

■ PRE, POST

Goal 2XL (oxyfluorfen) *(Rohm and Haas)*
Rate: 1-2 lb. ai/A
4-8 pt. 2XL/A

Time: Preemergence, postemergence. Apply lower rate for plants less than 8" tall; higher rate for plants 8-12" tall; repeat as needed. For optimum residual control, apply during fall or winter.
Weeds: Broadleaf weeds:

annual sowthistle	common	prickly lettuce
broadleaf filaree	lambsquarters	prostrate knotweed
burclover	common purslane	redmaids rockpurslane
burning nettle	henbit	redroot pigweed
cheeseweed	little mallow (malva)	redstem filaree
coast fiddleneck	London rocket	shepherdspurse
common groundsel	minerslettuce	whitestem filaree

Remarks: Jojoba. Apply to base of plant. Do not apply more than 8 pt. in a single application. Do not apply through any type of irrigation system.
Crop Rotation: Refer to label for plantback times for rotational crops.

- - - - - - - - - - - - - -

Signal Word/Toxicity Class: Warning/II.
REI: 24 hr.

Poast — see sethoxydim

SCYTHE

◆ **Scythe (pelargonic acid)** *(Mycogen)*
Rate: 4-13 fl. oz./1 gal. spray solution
Time: Apply to actively growing weeds prior to crop emergence.
Weeds: Annual and perennial broadleaf weeds and grasses.
Remarks: Apply in minimum 75 gal. spray solution/A or spray-to-wet. Do not apply by air or through any type of irrigation system. Refer to label for directions and precautions.
Tank Mixes: Glyphosate and other foliar and residual herbicides.

- - - - - - - - - - - - - -

Signal Word/Toxicity Class: Warning/II.
REI: 24 hr.

SETHOXYDIM

■ POST

Poast (1.5EC) *(BASF)*
Rate: 0.09-0.47 lb. ai/A
0.5-2.5 pt. 1.5EC/A
Time: Postemergence.
Weeds: Annual and perennial grasses:

annual ryegrass	johnsongrass	southwestern cupgrass
barnyardgrass	junglerice	stinkgrass
bermudagrass	large crabgrass	tall fescue
broadleaf signalgrass	lovegrass	Texas panicum
browntop panicum	orchardgrass	volunteer grains
fall panicum	(seedling)	wild oat
field sandbur	perennial ryegrass	wild proso millet
giant foxtail	quackgrass	wirestem muhly
goosegrass	red sprangletop	witchgrass
green foxtail	shattercane	woolly cupgrass
itchgrass	smooth crabgrass	yellow foxtail

Remarks: Canola, rapeseed. Rate depends on growing region. Do not apply through any type of irrigation system. Refer to label for restrictions and limitations.
Days To Harvest: 60.
State Restrictions: Do not use UAN or AMS in California or Pacific Northwest.

- - - - - - - - - - - - - -

Signal Word/Toxicity Class: Warning/II.
REI: 12 hr.

Treflan — see trifluralin

TRI-4 — see trifluralin

Trific — see trifluralin

TRIFLURALIN

■ PPI

Albaugh Trifluralin 4EC *(Albaugh)*
◆ **Clean Crop Trifluralin HF (4EC)** *(Platte)*
Gowan Trifluralin 4 or 5 (EC) or 10G *(Gowan)*
Helena Trifluralin 4 EC *(Helena)*
Riverside Trifluralin 4EC or Trific 60DF *(Terra)*

Other Field Crops **5**

Oil Seed Crops

◆ **Sedagri Trifluralin 480 (4EC)** (Rhone-Poulenc)
Treflan HFP (4EC) or TR-10 (10G) (Dow AgroSciences)
TRI-4 HF (4EC) (American Cyanamid)
Trilin 4 or 5 (EC) or 10G (Griffin)
Wilbur-Ellis Trifluralin 10G (Wilbur-Ellis)
 Rate: 0.5-1 lb. ai/A
    1-2 pt. 4EC/A
    0.8-1.6 pt. 5EC/A
    0.875-1.66 lb. 60DF/A
    5-10 lb. 10G/A
 Time: Preplant incorporated. Broadcast in fall or spring.
 Weeds: Broadleaf weeds:

carelessweed	knotweed	purslane
carpetweed	kochia	pusley
chickweed	lambsquarters	redroot pigweed
field bindweed	Mexican clover	rough pigweed
fireweed	Mexican fireweed	Russian thistle
Florida purslane	prostrate pigweed	spiny pigweed
Florida pusley	puncturevine	stinging nettle
goosefoot	(western U.S.)	tumbleweed
henbit		

Grasses:

annual bluegrass	fall panicum	sandbur
barnyardgrass	foxtail millet	shattercane
bottlegrass	giant foxtail	smooth crabgrass
brachiaria	green foxtail	sprangletop
bristlegrass	Italian ryegrass	stinkgrass
bromegrass	johnsongrass	Texas panicum
burgrass	(seedling)	watergrass
cheat	junglerice	wildcane
cheatgrass	large crabgrass	woolly cupgrass
chess	pigeongrass	yellow foxtail
downy brome	robust foxtail	

Remarks: Rapeseed (canola), safflower, soybeans, sunflower. Rate varies by soil type. Refer to label for directions and restrictions.
Crop Rotation: Refer to label.
State Restrictions: Not for use on rapeseed (canola) in Alaska. Wilbur-Ellis not registered in California.

– – – – – – – – – – – – – –

Signal Word/Toxicity Class: Varies by formulation.
REI: 12 hr. unless soil injected or soil incorporated.

Trilin — see trifluralin

Peanuts

ACIFLUORFEN

Postemergence diphenyl-ether herbicide with minimal residual activity.

■ **POST**
Blazer (BASF)
 Rate: 0.125-0.375 lb. ai/A
    0.5-1.5 pt./A
 Time: Postemergence. Apply when weeds are small and actively growing.
 Weeds: Broadleaf weeds:

balloonvine	Florida beggarweed	redvine
black nightshade	Florida pusley	showy crotalaria
buffalobur	giant ragweed	smallflower galinsoga
burgherkin	hairy galinsoga	smellmelon
Canada thistle	hairy indigo	smooth pigweed
carpetweed	heartleaf cocklebur	spiny amaranth
citron melon	hedge bindweed	spotted spurge
climbing milkweed	hemp sesbania	Texas gourd
common cocklebur	jimsonweed	tropic croton
common	lanceleaf groundcherry	trumpetcreeper
lambsquarters	morningglory	Venice mallow
common milkweed	Palmer amaranth	Virginia copperleaf
common purslane	Pennsylvania	volunteer cowpea
common ragweed	smartweed	wild mustard
cutleaf groundcherry	poorjoe	wild poinsettia
eastern black	prostrate pigweed	wild spiny cucumber
nightshade	prostrate spurge	wild watermelon
field bindweed	redroot pigweed	woolly croton

Annual grasses:

fall panicum	johnsongrass	volunteer small
giant foxtail	(seedling)	grains
green foxtail	shattercane	yellow foxtail

Remarks: Do not use treated plants for feed or forage. In case of crop failure, only peanuts, soybeans, or rice may be immediately replanted.

Days To Harvest: 75.
Crop Rotation: Do not plant root crops such as carrots, sweet potatoes, turnips, etc. into treated fields for 18 months following last application.
Tank Mixes: Basagran, Cadre, 2,4-DB, Frontier, Lasso, Poast, Poast HC, Poast Plus.

– – – – – – – – – – – – – –

Signal Word/Toxicity Class: Danger/I.
REI: 48 hr.

ALACHLOR

Residual, chloroacetamide herbicide. Restricted Use Pesticide.

■ **PPI, PRE**
Lasso (4EC) (Monsanto)
 Rate: 3-4 lb. ai/A
    3-4 qt. 4EC/A
 Time: Preplant incorporated, preemergence surface.
 Weeds: Broadleaf weeds:

black nightshade	Florida pusley	prickly sida*
carelessweed	galinsoga	purslane
carpetweed	hairy nightshade	sicklepod*
common ragweed*	lambsquarters*	smartweed*
cutleaf groundcherry	pigweed	teaweed*
Florida beggarweed*		

Grasses and sedges:

barnyardgrass	johnsongrass*	wild proso millet*
broadleaf signalgrass	(seedling)	wildcane*
crabgrass	panicum	witchgrass
foxtail	sandbur*	woolly cupgrass*
goosegrass	shattercane*	yellow nutsedge

 * Suppression
Remarks: Effective under wide range of soil and moisture conditions. Incorporation depth after planting must be kept above seed. Refer to label for proper incorporating instructions.

– – – – – – – – – – – – – –

Signal Word/Toxicity Class: Danger/I.
REI: 12 hr.

■ **PRE**
Lasso II (15G) (Monsanto)
 Rate: 3-3.9 lb. ai/A
    20-26 lb. 15G/A
 Time: Preemergence.
 Weeds: Broadleaf weeds:

black nightshade	carpetweed	pigweed
carelessweed	Florida pusley	purslane

Grasses:

barnyardgrass	fall panicum	green foxtail
brachiaria	giant foxtail	witchgrass
crabgrass	goosegrass	yellow foxtail

Remarks: Effective under wide range of moisture conditions.

– – – – – – – – – – – – – –

Signal Word/Toxicity Class: Warning/II.
REI: 12 hr.

BASAGRAN

Postemergence herbicide with no residual activity. Particularly useful for control of yellow nutsedge.

■ **POST**
Basagran (bentazon) (BASF)
 Rate: 0.5-1 lb. ai/A
    1-2 pt./A
 Time: Early postemergence.
 Weeds: Broadleaf weeds:

annual morningglory	dayflower	prickly sida
balloonvine	devilsclaw	(teaweed)
beggarticks	giant ragweed	spurred anoda
bristly starbur	jimsonweed	tropic croton
cocklebur	ladysthumb	velvetleaf
coffee senna	Pennsylvania	wild sunflower
common ragweed	smartweed	yellow nutsedge

Remarks: Rate depends on weed height and leaf stage. For control of yellow nutsedge, a second application at same rate may be needed. Peanut hay and forage may be fed to livestock. Refer to label for directions.
Tank Mixes: Blazer, 2,4-DB, Poast, Poast Plus, Starfire.
State Restrictions: Certain tank mixes not applicable in California.

– – – – – – – – – – – – – –

Signal Word/Toxicity Class: Caution/III.
REI: 12 hr.

◆-new product • PP-preplant • PPI-preplant incorporated • PRE-preemergence • POST-postemergence • SEQ-sequential • ae-acid equivalent • ai-active ingredient • DF-dry flowable
E/EC-emulsifiable concentrate • F/FL-flowable • DG/G/WG-dispersable granule • L/LC-liquid • SP/WSP-soluble packet • W/WP-wettable powder • WSB-water soluble bag

Blazer — see acifluorfen

Butoxone — see 2,4-DB

Butyrac — see 2,4-DB

CADRE

AHAS/ALS inhibitor. Cadre Eco-Pak is a water-soluble packet formulation.

■ POST

Cadre (DG) (imazapic) *(American Cyanamid)*

Rate: 1.44 oz. DG/A (1 WS packet/2 A)
Time: Early postemergence.
Weeds: Broadleaf weeds:

bristly starbur	entireleaf	prickly sida
burgherkin	morningglory	sicklepod
coffee senna	Florida beggarweed*	smallflower
common cocklebur	Florida pusley	morningglory
common	golden crownbeard	spurred anoda
lambsquarters*	hairy indigo	tall morningglory
common ragweed*	ivyleaf morningglory	wild poinsettia
cypressvine	pigweed	wild radish
morningglory	pitted morningglory	

Grasses:

broadleaf signalgrass	goosegrass*	sandbur
crowfootgrass	johnsongrass	smooth crabgrass
fall panicum	large crabgrass	Texas panicum

Sedges:

purple nutsedge	yellow nutsedge

***Suppression*

Remarks: Add nonionic surfactant or crop oil concentrate. Do not apply products containing imazethapyr or chlorimuron the same year as Cadre or injury to rotational crops may occur. Do not apply by air, if rainfall is threatening, or through any type of irrigation system. Do not graze or feed treated peanut hay to livestock. Refer to label for restrictions and precautions.
Days To Harvest: 90.
Crop Rotation: Peanuts—anytime; bahiagrass, rye, oats—4 months; field corn, snap beans, southern peas, soybeans, tobacco—9 months; barley, cotton (with restrictions), grain sorghum, oats, sweet corn—18 months; all other crops—26 months after application (except canola, potatoes, sugar and table beets—40 months).
Tank Mixes: May be tank mixed; follow the more restrictive label.
State Restrictions: For use only in Alabama, Florida, Georgia, Mississippi, New Mexico, North Carolina, Oklahoma, South Carolina, Texas, Virginia.

- - - - - - - - - - - - - - -

Signal Word/Toxicity Class: Caution.
REI: 12 hr.

Credit — see glyphosate

2,4-DB

Phenoxy herbicide. Beware of drift to sensitive crops such as cotton and vegetables.

■ POST

Butoxone 175, 200, or 7500 *(Cedar)*

Rate: 0.2-0.38 lb. ai/A
     1-1.75 pt. 175/A
     0.9-1.6 pt. 200/A
     0.3-0.5 lb. 7500/A
Time: Postemergence. Second application should be made no later than late bloom stage (about 90-100 days after planting).
Weeds: Broadleaf weeds:

annual morningglory	common	jimsonweed
cocklebur	lambsquarters	sicklepod
(low rate)	common ragweed	velvetleaf

Remarks: Do not apply if peanuts suffer from lack of moisture. Do not make more than 2 applications per season. Do not feed treated vines and hay to livestock.
Days To Harvest: 30.

- - - - - - - - - - - - - - -

Signal Word/Toxicity Class: Danger/I (200); Caution/III (175, 7500).
REI: 48 hr.

■ POST

Butyrac 175 or 200 *(Albaugh)*
Riverside 2,4-DB 175 or 200 *(Terra)*

Rate: 0.2-0.25 lb. ai/A
     0.9-1.1 pt. 175/A
     0.8-1 pt. 200/A
Time: Postplant. Apply 2-12 weeks after planting. Second application may be made for late-germinating cocklebur and morningglory.
Weeds: Broadleaf weeds:

annual morningglory	devilsclaw	prickly sida
cocklebur	field pennycress	teaweed
common ragweed	jimsonweed	velvetleaf
croton	lambsquarters	Virginia copperleaf
devilsclaw	pigweed	wild mustard

Remarks: Do not apply if peanuts are under stress from drought. Do not feed treated vines or hay to livestock.
Days To Harvest: North Carolina, South Carolina, Virginia—45.
State Restrictions: For use in Alabama, Arkansas, Florida, Georgia, Louisiana, Mississippi, North Carolina, South Carolina, Tennessee, Virginia.

- - - - - - - - - - - - - - -

Rate: Cocklebur, morningglory:
     0.2-0.25 lb. ai/A
     0.9-1.1 pt. 175/A
     0.8-1 pt. 200/A
     Broadleaf weeds:
     0.4 lb. ai/A
     1.8 pt. 175/A
     1.6 pt. 200/A
Time: Postplant. Apply 2-12 weeks after planting. Do not apply later than 100 days after planting. For cocklebur and morningglory, apply when actively growing and before they are 3" tall. For sida suppression, repeat in 14 days.
Weeds: Same as above.
Remarks: Do not apply if peanuts are under stress from drought. Do not feed treated vines or hay to livestock.
Days To Harvest: 30.
State Restrictions: For use in New Mexico, Oklahoma, Texas.

- - - - - - - - - - - - - - -

Signal Word/Toxicity Class: Danger/I.
REI: 48 hr.

Dual — see *S*-metolachlor

FRONTIER

Chloroacetamide herbicide that controls many annual grasses, several broadleaf weeds, and nutsedge.

■ PP, PPI, PRE, POST

Frontier 6.0 (dimethenamid) *(BASF)*

Rate: 0.94-1.5 lb. ai/A
     20-32 fl. oz. 6.0/A
Time: Preplant (surface or incorporated), preemergence, or postemergence, single or split application.
Weeds: Broadleaf weeds:

carpetweed	nightshade	spurge
common purslane	pigweed	waterhemp
Florida pusley		

Grasses and sedges:

barnyardgrass	green foxtail	smooth crabgrass
broadleaf signalgrass	johnsongrass	southwestern cupgrass
fall panicum	(seedling)	Texas panicum
giant foxtail	large crabgrass	yellow foxtail
goosegrass	rice flatsedge	yellow nutsedge

Remarks: Rate varies by soil type and organic matter. Do not exceed 2 pt. 6.0/A per crop year. Do not apply through any type of irrigation system. Peanut hay or straw may be grazed or fed to livestock 80 or more days after last application.
Tank Mixes: Balan, Basagran, Blazer, Bugle, Cadre, Classic, 2,4-DB, Lasso, Prowl, Poast, Poast Plus, Pursuit, Sonalan, Starfire, Storm, Tough, Treflan, Vernam, Zorial Rapid 80.
Days To Harvest: 80.

- - - - - - - - - - - - - - -

Signal Word/Toxicity Class: Warning/II.
REI: 12 hr.

Glyfos or Glyfos X-tra — see glyphosate

5

Other Field Crops

GLYPHOSATE

Nonselective herbicide with no residual soil activity.

■ **PP, PRE**
◆ **Credit (4WS)** *(Nufarm)*
◆ **Glyfos or Glyfos X-tra (4WS)** *(Cheminova)*
Rattler (4WS) *(Helena)*
Roundup Custom (5.4WS) *(Monsanto)*
Roundup Original, Original RT, Ultra, Ultra RT (4WS) *(Monsanto)*

Rate: Annual weeds:
0.38-1.5 lb. ai/A
0.56-2.25 pt. 5.4WS/A
0.75-3 pt. 4WS/A
Perennial weeds:
0.5-5 lb. ai/A
0.75-7.5 pt. 5.4WS/A
1-10 pt. 4WS/A
Time: Preplant, preemergence, at-planting.
Weeds: Emerged annual and perennial broadleaf weeds including:

Canada thistle	hemp dogbane	Pennsylvania
curly dock	milkweed	smartweed
field bindweed		

Grasses:

bermudagrass	fescue	paragrass
fall panicum	johnsongrass	quackgrass

Remarks: Do not allow glyphosate to contact desirable plants. Do not add surfactant to Roundup Ultra or Ultra RT. Do not apply through any type of irrigation system. Refer to label for directions and restrictions.
State Restrictions: Roundup RT for use in Colorado, Idaho, Montana, North Dakota, South Dakota, Utah, Wyoming, and in specific counties only in Kansas, Minnesota, Nebraska, Nevada, Oklahoma, Oregon, and Washington; refer to label for restrictions. Glyfos is not registered for use in California. Glyfos X-tra is not registered for use in mistblowers in California or Arizona.
Signal Word/Toxicity Class: Varies by formulation.
REI: Warning—12 hr.; Caution—4 hr.

Lasso, Lasso II — see alachlor

S-METOLACHLOR

Residual, chloroacetamide herbicide that can be applied preplant incorporated, preemergence, at-cracking, lay-by, or through a center pivot system as a preemergence treatment. S-metolachlor is a purified isomer of metolachlor molecule. Dual II MAGNUM contains the safening agent, benoxacor.

■ **PPI, PRE, POST**
Dual MAGNUM or Dual II MAGNUM (EC) *(Novartis)*
Dual IIG MAGNUM *(Novartis)*

Rate: Southeast:
1-1.33 pt. EC/A
6-8 lb. IIG/A
New Mexico, Oklahoma, Texas:
0.8-1.33 pt. EC/A
5-8 lb. IIG/A
Time: Preplant incorporated, postplant incorporated, preemergence, or lay-by. For postplant incorporated, apply and shallowly incorporate into soil after planting, but before peanut germination.
Weeds: Broadleaf weeds:

carpetweed	eclipta*	hairy nightshade*
common purslane*	Florida pusley	pigweed
eastern black nightshade	galinsoga	

Grasses and sedges:

barnyardgrass (watergrass)	goosegrass	shattercane*
crabgrass	green foxtail	signalgrass
crowfootgrass	johnsongrass (seedling)*	southwestern cupgrass
fall panicum	prairie cupgrass	volunteer sorghum*
foxtail millet	red rice	witchgrass
giant foxtail	sandbur*	yellow foxtail
		yellow nutsedge

* Suppression

Rate: Southeast:
1.33-2 pt. EC/A
8-12 lb. IIG/A
Time: Preemergence.
Weeds: Partial control of :
Florida beggarweed

Remarks: Rate varies by soil type and organic matter. In case of crop failure, any crop on label may be replanted immediately. Do not make second broadcast application. If original application was banded and second crop is planted in untreated row middles, second banded treatment may be applied. Do not graze or feed peanut forage or fodder to livestock for 30 days following application.
Days To Harvest: 90.
Crop Rotation: Alfalfa—4 months; barley, oats, rye, wheat—4^{1}/$_{2}$ months; tomatoes—6 months; clover—9 months. Any labeled crop in addition to barley, buckwheat, cabbage, milo, nuts, oats, peppers, rice, root crops, rye, stone fruits, tobacco, and wheat may be planted in the spring following treatment (including layby or multiple treatments applied the previous season); all other rotational crops may be planted 12 months after application.
Tank Mixes: Balan, Prowl, Pursuit, Sonalan.
State Restrictions: Do not use in Nassau County or Suffolk County, New York.

- - - - - - - - - - - - - - - -

Signal Word/Toxicity Class: Caution/III.
REI: 24 hr.

NORFLURAZON

Residual activity greatly enhances control of existing herbicide programs for beggarweed and other grasses and broadleaf weeds.

■ **PRE**
Zorial Rapid 80 (DF) *(Novartis)*

Rate: East of Mississippi river:
1.2-1.4 lb. ai/A
1.5-1.8 lb. DF/A
West of Mississippi river:
0.4 lb. ai/A
0.5 lb. DF/A
Time: Preemergence surface application. If weeds have emerged at planting, a suitable burndown treatment is recommend for best results.
Weeds: Broadleaf weeds and grasses including:
beggarweed
Remarks: Follow label recommendations for soil restrictions and further use directions.
State Restrictions: For use in Alabama, Florida, Georgia, Mississippi, New Mexico, North Carolina, Oklahoma, South Carolina, Texas, and Virginia.

- - - - - - - - - - - - - - - -

Signal Word/Toxicity Class: Caution.
REI: 12 hr.

PARAQUAT

Contact herbicide used to control or suppress a broad spectrum of emerged weeds. Restricted Use Pesticide.

■ **POST**
Starfire (1.5L) *(ZENECA)*

Rate: 11-22 fl. oz. 1.5L/A
Time: Postemergence. Apply from ground crack to 28 days after cracking.
Weeds: Most small (1-6") annual broadleaf weeds and grasses.
Remarks: Do not apply by air. Foliage sprayed will be injured in the form of bronzing and crinkling, but crop will recover and develop normally. Refer to label for use directions, restrictions, and precautions.
Tank Mixes: Basagran, Butoxone, Butyrac.
State Restrictions: Not for use in California.

- - - - - - - - - - - - - - - -

Signal Word/Toxicity Class: Danger-Poison/I.
REI: 12 hr. (except harvest aid/desiccation 24 hr.).

PENDIMETHALIN

Residual dinitroaniline herbicide that should be applied preplant incorporated.

■ **PPI**
Pentagon DG *(American Cyanamid)*
Prowl 3.3 EC *(American Cyanamid)*

Rate: 0.7-1 lb. ai/A
1.8-2.4 pt. 3.3 EC/A
1.25-1.7 lb. DG/A
New Mexico, Oklahoma, Texas:
0.5-1 lb. ai/A
1.2-2.4 pt. 3.3 EC/A
0.85-1.7 lb. DG/A
Time: Preplant incorporated. Apply immediately before planting or up to 60 days prior to planting; incorporate within 7 days after application.

◆-new product • PP-preplant • PPI-preplant incorporated • PRE-preemergence • POST-postemergence • SEQ-sequential • ae-acid equivalent • ai-active ingredient • DF-dry flowable
E/EC-emulsifiable concentrate • F/FL-flowable • DG/G/WG-dispersable granule • L/LC-liquid • SP/WSP-soluble packet • W/WP-wettable powder • WSB-water soluble bag

250   Weed Control Manual 2000

Weeds: Broadleaf weeds:

annual spurge	lambsquarters	pigweed
carpetweed	Pennsylvania	purslane
Florida pusley	smartweed	velvetleaf
kochia		

Grasses:

barnyardgrass	giant foxtail	signalgrass
crabgrass	goosegrass	Texas panicum
crowfootgrass	green foxtail	witchgrass
fall panicum	johnsongrass	yellow foxtail
field sandbur	(seedling)	

Remarks: Rate varies by soil type and location. If crop loss occurs due to weather conditions, peanuts or any crop registered for preplant incorporated use can be replanted the same year into treated soil without adverse effects. If replanting is necessary, do not rework soil deeper than treated zone. Refer to label for directions, precautions, and limitations.

Crop Rotation: Winter wheat and winter barley can be planted in the fall after application in peanuts. Treated land can be planted to other crops the following year (see label for beet and spinach restrictions).

Tank Mixes: Dual, Pursuit, Vernam.

State Restrictions: Not for use in California. In Alabama, Florida, Georgia, up to 1.5 lb. ai/A can be used for heavy weed infestations, especially Texas panicum.

– – – – – – – – – – – – – – – –

Signal Word/Toxicity Class: Caution.
REI: 24 hr.

Pentagon — see pendimethalin

Poast — see sethoxydim

Prowl — see pendimethalin

PURSUIT

Imidazolinone herbicide which inhibits production of certain plant amino acids.

■ **PPI, PRE, POST, SEQ**

Pursuit or Pursuit W (2AS or 70DG) (imazethapyr) *(American Cyanamid)*
Rate: 0.063 lb. ae/A
4 oz. 2AS/A
1.44 oz. 70DG/A
Time: Preplant incorporated, preemergence, ground-cracking, postemergence, sequential.

Weeds: Broadleaf weeds:

black nightshade	galinsoga	prostrate spurge
buffalobur	hairy nightshade	puncturevine
carpetweed	ivyleaf morningglory	redroot pigweed
common cocklebur	jimsonweed	smallflower
common purslane	kochia	morningglory
common sunflower	ladysthumb	smooth pigweed
devilsclaw	marshelder	spiny pigweed
eastern black	mustard	spotted spurge
nightshade	Palmer pigweed	spurred anoda
entireleaf	Pennsylvania	tall morningglory
morningglory	smartweed	velvetleaf
Florida pusley	pitted morningglory	wild poinsettia

Grasses and sedges:

barnyardgrass	green foxtail	shattercane
broadleaf signalgrass	johnsongrass	woolly cupgrass
crabgrass	purple nutsedge	yellow foxtail
giant foxtail	robust purple foxtail	yellow nutsedge
giant green foxtail	robust white foxtail	

Remarks: Sequential application may be made at 2 oz. Pursuit PPI or PRE followed by 2 oz. at ground-crack or POST. Do not apply more than 4 oz. during the growing season. Do not apply preemergence to peanuts in west Texas or New Mexico; crop injury may result. Do not graze wheat or rye forage prior to 60 days after planting. Do not graze or feed peanut forage, vine, hay, or straw to livestock. Do not apply through any type of irrigation system.

Days To Harvest: 85.

Crop Rotation: IMI-Corn, lima beans, peanuts, southern peas, soybeans—anytime; alfalfa, edible beans and peas (except lima beans, southern peas), rye, wheat—4 months; field corn, field corn grown for seed—8 1/2 months (Pursuit W 9 1/2 months); barley, tobacco—9 1/2 months; cotton, lettuce, oats, popcorn, safflower, sorghum, sunflower, sweet corn—18 months; flax (Pursuit only), potatoes—26 months; all other crops—40 months after application.

Tank Mixes: Basagran, Blazer, 2,4-DB, Gramoxone Extra, and Starfire broadleaf herbicides. Do not include Dash when Blazer or Starfire is tank mixed with Pursuit. For PPI or PRE treatments, may be tank mixed with Dual, Lasso, Sonalan, and Vernam.

State Restrictions: Pursuit for use in Colorado, New Mexico, North Dakota, Oklahoma, South Dakota, Texas, Wyoming (certain counties), and states east of these states; not for use in New York. Pursuit W for use in Arizona, Idaho, Montana, Nevada, Oregon, Utah, Washington, Wyoming (certain counties); not for use in California.

– – – – – – – – – – – – – – – –

Signal Word/Toxicity Class: Warning/II (70DG); Caution (2AS).
REI: Warning—12 hr.; Caution—4 hr.

Rattler — see glyphosate

Roundup — see glyphosate

SCYTHE

◆ **Scythe (pelargonic acid)** *(Mycogen)*
Rate: 4-13 fl. oz./1 gal. spray solution
Time: Apply to actively growing weeds prior to crop emergence.
Weeds: Annual and perennial broadleaf weeds and grasses.
Remarks: Apply in minimum 75 gal. spray solution/A or spray-to-wet. Do not apply by air or through any type of irrigation system. Refer to label for directions and precautions.
Tank Mixes: Glyphosate and other foliar and residual herbicides.

– – – – – – – – – – – – – – – –

Signal Word/Toxicity Class: Warning/II.
REI: 24 hr.

SETHOXYDIM

Translocating postemergence herbicide with no activity on broadleaf or nutsedge species.

■ **POST**

Poast (1.5EC) or Poast Plus (1EC) *(BASF)*
Rate: 0.09-0.28 lb. ai/A
0.5-1.5 pt. 1.5EC/A
0.75-2.25 pt. 1EC/A
Time: Postemergence.

Weeds: Annual and perennial grasses:

annual ryegrass	johnsongrass	southwestern cupgrass
barnyardgrass	junglerice	stinkgrass
bermudagrass	large crabgrass	tall fescue
broadleaf signalgrass	lovegrass	Texas panicum
browntop panicum	orchardgrass	volunteer cereals
fall panicum	(seedling)	wild oat
giant foxtail	perennial ryegrass	wild proso millet
goosegrass	red rice	wildcane
green foxtail	red sprangletop	witchgrass
itchgrass	smooth crabgrass	yellow foxtail

Remarks: Rate depends on growing region. Add spray adjuvant or oil concentrate. Urea ammonium-nitrate solution (UAN) or ammonium sulfate (AMS) recommended to enhance activity on certain grass species. Do not apply through any type of irrigation system. Do not graze treated fields or feed treated forage (except processed meal from peanuts) to livestock. Refer to label for restrictions and limitations.

Days To Harvest: 40.

Tank Mixes: Poast: Basagran, Blazer, 2,4-D, 2,4-DB. Poast Plus: Basagran, Blazer, Storm.

State Restrictions: Do not use UAN or AMS in California or Pacific Northwest.

– – – – – – – – – – – – – – – –

Signal Word/Toxicity Class: Warning/II (Poast); Caution/III (Poast Plus).
REI: 12 hr.

SONALAN

Residual dinitroaniline herbicide that should be applied preplant incorporated. Toxic to fish.

■ **PPI**

Sonalan HFP or 10G (ethalfluralin) *(Dow AgroSciences)*
Rate: 0.55-1.1 lb. ai/A
1.5-3 pt. HFP/A
5.5-11.5 lb. 10G/A
Time: Preplant incorporated. Apply in the spring.

Other Field Crops 5

NOTICE The information on these pages is for preliminary planning — not a guide for use. Be sure to follow the manufacturer's directions, notwithstanding information contained here. | For personal protective equipment and EPA registration numbers, please turn to page 70.

Weeds: Broadleaf weeds:

carpetweed	groundcherry	redroot pigweed
common chickweed	henbit	Russian thistle
common	kochia	smooth pigweed
lambsquarters	nightshade	tarweed fiddleneck
common purslane	prostrate pigweed	tumble pigweed
conical catchfly	redmaids	wild buckwheat
Florida pusley	rockpurslane	

Grasses:

annual bluegrass	giant foxtail	shattercane
annual ryegrass	green foxtail	Texas panicum
barnyardgrass	Italian ryegrass	wild oat
broadleaf signalgrass	johnsongrass	wildcane
crabgrass	(seedling)	witchgrass
fall panicum	junglerice	woolly cupgrass
field sandbur	large crabgrass	yellow foxtail
foxtail millet	pigeongrass	

Remarks: Rate varies by soil type. Do not apply to soils which are wet, cloddy, or subject to prolonged periods of flooding. Do not graze or for-age crop grown in treated soil or cut for hay or silage. Do not apply through any type of irrigation system.

Crop Rotation: If replanting is required, replant only crops listed on label. Do not plant sugar beets or red beets within 13 months after application of 1.1 lb. ai/A or more; for less than 1.1 lb. ai/A, within 8 months after application, provided treated area is moldboard plowed to a depth of at least 12" prior to planting. In Arizona and California, do not plant spin-ach or oats within 8 months after application of 1.1 lb. ai/A or more. Re-fer to label for special restrictions for Montana and Wyoming.

Tank Mixes: May be tank mixed with other registered products; refer to labels.

- - - - - - - - - - - - - - -

Signal Word/Toxicity Class: Danger/I.
REI: 24 hr. (HFP); 12 hr. (10G) unless soil injected or soil incorporated.

Starfire — see paraquat

STORM (Premix)

Premix of bentazon and acifluorfen.

■ POST

Storm (2.6 lb./gal. bentazon & 1.33 lb./gal. acifluorfen) *(BASF)*
Rate: 0.75 lb. ai/A
　　　1.5 pt./A
Time: Postemergence.
Weeds: Broadleaf weeds:

black nightshade	hemp sesbania	redweed
bristly starbur	hophornbeam	smooth pigweed
carpetweed	copperleaf	spurred anoda
cocklebur	jimsonweed	tall waterhemp
common ragweed	ladysthumb	teaweed
common waterhemp	lambsquarters	texasweed
crotalaria	morningglory	tropic croton
eastern black	Pennsylvania	velvetleaf
nightshade	smartweed	Venice mallow
eclipta	prickly sida	wild mustard
giant ragweed	redroot pigweed	woolly croton

Remarks: Add oil concentrate, urea-ammonium nitrate (UAN), or non-ionic surfactant. Do not use treated peanut plants for feed or forage. Do not apply through any type of irrigation system.
Days To Harvest: 75.
Crop Rotation: Do not rotate root crops such as carrots, sweet potatoes, turnips, etc. into treated fields for 18 months following last application.
Tank Mixes: 2,4-DB, Frontier, Starfire.

- - - - - - - - - - - - - - -

Signal Word/Toxicity Class: Danger/I.
REI: 48 hr.

TOUGH

Postemergence herbicide with no residual soil activity.

■ POST, SEQ

Tough (5EC) (pyridate) *(Novartis)*
Rate: 0.94-1.41 lb. ai/A
　　　24-36 oz. 5EC/A
Time: Postemergence: Apply when weeds are in 2-4 leaf stage and 2-3" high. Sequential: Apply at cracking or postemergence following pre-plant, preplant incorporated, preemergence, or other at-cracking pro-grams of such herbicides as Balan, Lasso, and Prowl.

Weeds: Broadleaf weeds and sedges:

amaranth	eclipta	nutsedge
common cocklebur	Florida beggarweed	(partial control)
common	jimsonweed	pigweed
lambsquarters	nightshade	

Remarks: May be applied at any crop stage without burning peanuts when applied at labeled rates. Do not graze or feed peanut forage to livestock.
Days To Harvest: 68.
Tank Mixes: 2,4-DB, Dual; refer to label for use instructions.
State Restrictions: Not registered in California.

- - - - - - - - - - - - - - -

Signal Word/Toxicity Class: Warning/II.
REI: 12 hr.

Treflan — see trifluralin

TRI-4 — see trifluralin

Trific — see trifluralin

TRIFLURALIN

Residual dinitroaniline herbicide. Toxic to fish.

■ PPI, PRE

Albaugh Trifluralin 4EC *(Albaugh)*
◆ Clean Crop Trifluralin HF (4EC) *(Platte)*
Gowan Trifluralin 4 or 5 (EC) or 10G *(Gowan)*
Helena Trifluralin 4 EC *(Helena)*
Riverside Trifluralin 4EC or Trific 60DF *(Terra)*
◆ Sedagri Trifluralin 480 (4EC) *(Rhone-Poulenc)*
Treflan HFP (4EC) or TR-10 (10G) *(Dow AgroSciences)*
TRI-4 HF (4EC) *(American Cyanamid)*
Trilin 4 or 5 (EC) or 10G *(Griffin)*
Wilbur-Ellis Trifluralin 10G *(Wilbur-Ellis)*
Rate: 0.5 lb. ai/A
　　　1 pt. 4EC/A
　　　0.8 pt. 5EC/A
　　　0.875 lb. 60DF/A
　　　5 lb. 10G/A
Time: Preplant incorporated, preemergence incorporated. Apply and in-corporate before planting, at planting, or immediately after planting.
Weeds: Broadleaf weeds:

carelessweed	knotweed	purslane
carpetweed	kochia	pusley
chickweed	lambsquarters	redroot pigweed
field bindweed	Mexican clover	rough pigweed
fireweed	Mexican fireweed	Russian thistle
Florida purslane	prostrate pigweed	spiny pigweed
Florida pusley	puncturevine	stinging nettle
goosefoot	(western U.S.)	tumbleweed
henbit		

Grasses:

annual bluegrass	fall panicum	sandbur
barnyardgrass	foxtail millet	shattercane
bottlegrass	giant foxtail	smooth crabgrass
brachiaria	green foxtail	sprangletop
bristlegrass	Italian ryegrass	stinkgrass
bromegrass	johnsongrass	Texas panicum
burgrass	(seedling)	watergrass
cheat	junglerice	wildcane
cheatgrass	large crabgrass	woolly cupgrass
chess	pigeongrass	yellow foxtail
downy brome	robust foxtail	

Remarks: Do not disturb seed when incorporating after planting. Up to 1.5 pt. 4EC/A may be used on medium texture soil. Refer to label for direc-tions, restrictions, and precautions.
Crop Rotation: Refer to label.
State Restrictions: For use in Oklahoma and Texas; New Mexico (Albaugh, Helena, Riverside 4EC, Sedagri, Treflan, Trilin 10G, Wilbur-Ellis).

- - - - - - - - - - - - - - -

Signal Word/Toxicity Class: Varies by formulation.
REI: 12 hr. unless soil injected or soil incorporated.

Trilin — see trifluralin

Zorial Rapid 80 — see norflurazon

◆-new product • PP-preplant • PPI-preplant incorporated • PRE-preemergence • POST-postemergence • SEQ-sequential • ae-acid equivalent • ai-active ingredient • DF-dry flowable
E/EC-emulsifiable concentrate • F/FL-flowable • DG/G/WG-dispersable granule • L/LC-liquid • SP/WSP-soluble packet • W/WP-wettable powder • WSB-water soluble bag

Rice

ACIFLUORFEN

Postemergence herbicide for hemp sesbania.

■ **POST**

Blazer *(BASF)*

Rate: 0.125 lb. ai/A
0.5 pt./A

Time: Postemergence. Apply from late tillering up to early boot stage. Do not apply after boot stage. Apply to actively growing sesbania before flowering stage.

Weeds: Broadleaf weeds:

hemp sesbania

Remarks: Add 2 pt. 80% nonionic surfactant/100 gal. spray mix.

Days To Harvest: 50.

Crop Rotation: Do not plant root crops such as carrots, sweet potatoes, turnips, etc. into treated field for 18 months following last application.

Tank Mixes: Basagran, Facet, Propanil.

State Restrictions: Not for use in California.

- - - - - - - - - - - - - - - -

Signal Word/Toxicity Class: Danger/I.
REI: 48 hr.

ARROSOLO (Premix)

Postemergence contact and residual herbicide. Soil should be sealed by rain or flush. Residual control for up to 1 week.

■ **POST**

Arrosolo 3-3E (3 lb./gal. molinate & 3 lb./gal. propanil) *(ZENECA)*

Rate: 4.5-6 lb. ai/A
3-4 qt. 3-3E/A

Time: Postemergence. Apply to actively growing weeds in 1- to 2-leaf stage.

Weeds: Broadleaf weeds:

barnyardgrass	hoorahgrass	redroot pigweed
broadleaf signalgrass	horned beakrush	redweed
common dayflower	junglerice	spikerush
curly dock	large crabgrass	sprangletop
foxtail	paragrass	Texas millet
goosegrass	Pennsylvania	texasweed
gulf cockspur	smartweed	woolly croton
hemp sesbania		

Remarks: Dry-seeded, water-seeded rice. Apply by ground or air to fields which have been drained of flood water to expose susceptible weeds. Flood field within 5 days after application. Do not apply carbamate or organophosphorus insecticides in combinations with Arrosolo or within 7 days before or after application. Do not apply more than 9 lb. molinate/A per season. Do not apply through any type of irrigation system. Refer to label for use restrictions and precautions.

State Restrictions: For use on rice grown in southern U.S. (Arkansas, Louisiana, Mississippi, bootheel of Missouri, Texas).

- - - - - - - - - - - - - - - -

Signal Word/Toxicity Class: Warning/II.
REI: 24 hr.

BASAGRAN

Postemergence contact herbicide for control of broadleaf and aquatic weeds.

■ **POST**

Basagran (bentazon) *(BASF)*

Rate: 0.75-1 lb. ai/A
1.5-2 pt./A

Time: Postemergence.

Weeds: Broadleaf weeds:

arrowhead	dayflower	redweed
cocklebur	ducksalad	river bulrush
common	gooseweed	smartweed
waterplantain	redstem	spikerush

Sedges:

yellow nutsedge

Remarks: Rate varies by weed growth stage. Do not use on rice fields in which the commercial cultivation of catfish or crayfish is practiced. Rice straw may be fed to livestock. Refer to label for restrictions and limitations.

Tank Mixes: Arrosolo, Facet, Londax, propanil, Storm.

State Restrictions: Not for use in California.

- - - - - - - - - - - - - - - -

Signal Word/Toxicity Class: Caution/III.
REI: 12 hr.

Blazer — see acifluorfen

Blue Drum — see propanil

BOLERO

Use restricted to protect endangered fat pocketbook pearly mussel and its habitat. Toxic to shrimp.

■ **PRE, POST**

Bolero 8EC (thiobencarb) *(Valent)*

Rate: 4 lb. ai/A
4 pt. 8EC/A

Time: Late preemergence. Apply 1-5 days prior to rice emergence. Do not apply preemergence to cracked soil. Split application: Apply 2 pt./A followed by 2 pt./A.

Weeds: Grasses:

barnyardgrass	fall panicum	junglerice
crabgrass	false pimpernel	sprangletop
dayflower		

Time: Early postemergence: Apply when watergrass has developed no further than 2-leaf stage; sprangletop 1/2" or less; other broadleaf weeds are less than 2" tall.

Weeds: Grasses:

barnyardgrass	fall panicum	watergrass
crabgrass	sprangletop	

Remarks: Dry-seeded rice. Do not apply to stressed rice. Soil should be wet at time of application. For water-seeded rice, apply to nonflooded fields only. Do not apply to rice paddies where commercial catfish or crayfish farming is practiced. Do not apply through any type of irrigation system. Refer to label for further use directions and restrictions.

Tank Mixes: Propanil. Do not apply tank mix within 14 days before or after organophosphate or carbamate application.

- - - - - - - - - - - - - - - -

Signal Word/Toxicity Class: Caution.
REI: 4 hr.

■ **POST**

Bolero 10G (thiobencarb) *(Valent)*

Rate: 4 lb. ai/A
40 lb. 10G/A

Time: Postflood. Apply to rice in expanded 2-leaf stage (first open leaf). Smallflower umbrellaplant must be submerged for optimum control.

Weeds: Grasses:

barnyardgrass	smallflower	sprangletop
(watergrass)	umbrellaplant	

Remarks: Do not apply to stressed rice. Variety Cal Pearl may react adversely to some stress conditions more than other varieties. Barnyardgrass beyond 2-leaf stage and smallflower umbrellaplant beyond 3-leaf stage may not be controlled. Do not drain field for minimum of 14 days after application, except where state regulations may allow shorter water holding periods for hydrologically isolated fields (as verified by County Agricultural Commissioner), or for fields associated with systems designated to isolate discharged water from natural bodies of water. Water level in the checks should be maintained at 3-4" with no exposed soil. Do not apply to rice paddies where commercial catfish or crayfish farming is practiced. Do not use adjacent to catfish ponds.

Crop Rotation: Do not plant subsequent crops in treated fields within 6 months of last application.

State Restrictions: For use in California.

- - - - - - - - - - - - - - - -

Rate: 3-4 lb. ai/A
30-40 lb. 10G/A

Time: Postflood. Apply to rice in 2-leaf stage, grass weeds in 2-leaf stage or less, and aquatics less than 1/2" tall.

Weeds: Broadleaf weeds:

ducksalad*	redstem

Grasses:

barnyardgrass	junglerice	sprangletop*

* LA, MS, TX only

Remarks: Do not apply to stressed rice. Weeds larger than those specified will not be controlled and rice smaller than 2-leaf stage will be injured or killed. Water level should be maintained at 3-4" with no soil exposed. Refer to label for directions, restrictions, and worker safety rules.

NOTICE	The information on these pages is for preliminary planning — not a guide for use. Be sure to follow the manufacturer's directions, notwithstanding information contained here.	For personal protective equipment and EPA registration numbers, please turn to page 70.

5

Other Field Crops

Crop Rotation: Do not plant subsequent crops in treated fields within 6 months of last application.
State Restrictions: SLN—Arkansas, Louisiana, Mississippi, Texas.

- - - - - - - - - - - - - - -

Signal Word/Toxicity Class: Caution.
REI: 12 hr.

Credit — see glyphosate

2,4-D - PHENOXY HERBICIDES

Postemergence control of broadleaf weeds. Apply at correct rice growth stage not to exceed 1/2" internode. Do not apply where shellfish are of economic importance or where flood water is used for irrigation of other crops.

■ POST
Albaugh Amine 4 (2,4-D amine) *(Albaugh)*
Formula 40 (2,4-D mixed amine) *(Rhone-Poulenc)*
Hi-Dep (2,4-D mixed amine) *(PBI/Gordon)*
◆ Opti-Amine (4) (2,4-D amine) *(Helena)*
Riverdale 6 Amine (2,4-D amine) *(Riverdale)*
Riverside 2,4-D Amine 4 (2,4-D amine) *(Terra)*
Solution (WS) (2,4-D amine) *(Riverdale)*
Weed Rhap A-4D (2,4-D amine) *(Helena)*
Weedar 64 (4) (2,4-D amine) *(Nufarm)*
Weedestroy AM-40 (2,4-D amine) *(Riverdale)*
Wilbur-Ellis Amine 4 (2,4-D amine) *(Wilbur-Ellis)*
  Rate: 0.5-1.2 lb. ae/A
    1-2.5 pt./A
    0.75-1.25 lb. ae/A
    1.5-2.5 pt./A (Weedestroy, Wilbur-Ellis)
    0.75-1.5 lb. ae/A
    1-2 pt. 6/A (Mississippi—1-1.66 pt.)
    1 WS packet/1.25-1.5 A in 5-50 gal. water
  Time: Postemergence. Apply during late stages of tillering, at first joint development, 6-9 weeks after emergence.
  Weeds: Broadleaf weeds including:
    curly indigo
  Remarks: Some rice varieties can be injured by 2,4-D; consult Extension Specialists for rates and timings of sprays.
  State Restrictions: Weedar and Wilbur-Ellis not registered in California.

- - - - - - - - - - - - - - -

Signal Word/Toxicity Class: Danger/I.
REI: 48 hr.

■ POST
◆ Clean Crop Amine 4 (2,4-D amine) *(Platte)*
◆ Saber (3.8) (2,4-D amine) *(Platte)*
  Rate: 0.70-1.4 lb. ae/A
    1.5-3 pt. 4/A
    0.35-1.4 lb. ae/A
    0.75-3 pt. 3.8/A
  Time: Postemergence. Apply during late stages of tillering, at first joint development, 6-9 weeks after emergence. Do not apply after panicle initiation, after rice internodes exceed 1/2", at early seedling, early panicle, boot, flowering, or early heading growth stages.
  Weeds: Annual, biennial, and perennial broadleaf weeds.
  Remarks: Some rice varieties can be injured by 2,4-D; consult Extension Specialists for rates and timings of sprays.

- - - - - - - - - - - - - - -

Signal Word/Toxicity Class: Danger/I.
REI: 48 hr.

■ PP, POST
Savage (WSB) (2,4-D amine) *(Platte)*
  Rate: 0.48-1.19 lb. ae/A
    0.5-1.25 lb. WSB/A
  Time: Preplant, postemergence. For preplant, apply 4 or more weeks prior to planting. For postemergence, apply when rice is in late stages of tillering, at first joint development. Do not apply after boot or heading stages.
  Weeds: Broadleaf weeds including:
    alligatorweed   ducksalad   hemp sesbania
    dayflower   eclipta   jointvetch
  Remarks: Some rice varieties can be injured by 2,4-D; consult Extension Specialists for rates and timings of sprays.

- - - - - - - - - - - - - - -

Signal Word/Toxicity Class: Danger/I.
REI: 48 hr.

DUET (Premix)

■ POST
Duet (4 lb./gal. propanil & 14 g./gal. bensulfuron-methyl) *(RiceCo)*
  Rate: 3-5 lb. ai/A
    3-5 qt./A
  Time: Postemergence. For best results, apply to actively growing weeds (1-3 leaf stage) in the morning when temperatures are above 75°F.
  Weeds: Broadleaf weeds:
    annual arrowhead   gooseweed   redstem
    blunt spikerush   gulf cockspur   roughseed bulrush
    cocklebur   hemp sesbania   smallflower
    coffeeweed   mexicanweed   umbrellaplant
    croton   morningglory   sour dock
    curly indigo   mud plantain   southern naiad
    dayflower   Pennsylvania   spearhead
    ducksalad   smartweed   Texas millet
    eclipta   pickerelweed   texasweed
    Eisen waterhyssop   pigweed   waterplantain
    false pimpernel   purple ammannia   waterwort
  Grasses and sedges:
    barnyardgrass   foxtail   rice flatsedge
      (watergrass)   goosegrass   yellow nutsedge
    crabgrass   paragrass
  Remarks: Do not apply to any crop except rice. Higher rates should be used under dry conditions, cooler weather, or 4-5 leaf stage. Do not apply more than 8 qt./A per season. In California, apply only where fields are completely drained or minimal amount of water remains. If higher water level is desired, reflood after 12 hr. and within 7 days after treatment. Do not apply through any type of irrigation system.

- - - - - - - - - - - - - - -

Signal Word/Toxicity Class: Caution/III.
REI: 24 hr.

Facet — see quinclorac

FENOXAPROP-P-ETHYL

Selective postemergence annual and perennial grass herbicide. Field should be free of standing water.

■ POST
Whip 360 *(AgrEvo USA)*
  Rate: 0.7-1 pt. 360/A
  Time: Postemergence. Apply when rice is from 4-leaf to panicle initiation stage and annual grassy weeds are in 1-leaf to 2-tiller stage of growth. Do not apply after panicle initiation stage of rice development.
  Weeds: Grasses:
    barnyardgrass   crabgrass   junglerice
      (watergrass)   goosegrass   red rice
    broadleaf signalgrass johnsongrass   sprangletop
  Remarks: Rate varies by weed growth stage. Does not control broadleaf weeds or sedges. Follow water management practices that are recommended on label. Applications to flooded rice may cause significant rice injury.
  Days To Harvest: 65.
  Crop Rotation: Do not plant any rotational crop in treated fields for 30 days after application.
  Tank Mixes: Basagran, Bolero, Prowl.
  State Restrictions: For use in Arkansas, Louisiana, Mississippi, Missouri, Texas.

- - - - - - - - - - - - - - -

Signal Word/Toxicity Class: Caution/III.
REI: 24 hr.

Formula 40 — see 2,4-D

Glyfos or Glyfos X-tra — see glyphosate

GLYPHOSATE

Nonselective postemergence herbicide for preplant vegetation knockdown. Apply 7-10 days before seedbed preparation.

■ PP, PRE
◆ Credit (4WS) *(Nufarm)*

◆-new product • PP-preplant • PPI-preplant incorporated • PRE-preemergence • POST-postemergence • SEQ-sequential • ae-acid equivalent • ai-active ingredient • DF-dry flowable E/EC-emulsifiable concentrate • F/FL-flowable • DG/G/WG-dispersable granule • L/LC-liquid • SP/WSP-soluble packet • W/WP-wettable powder • WSB-water soluble bag

◆ **Glyfos or Glyfos X-tra (4WS)** (Cheminova)
Rattler (4WS) (Helena)
Roundup Custom (5.4WS) (Monsanto)
Roundup Original, Original RT, Ultra, Ultra RT (4WS) (Monsanto)

Rate: Annual weeds:
0.38-1.5 lb. ai/A
0.56-2.25 pt. 5.4WS/A
0.75-3 pt. 4WS/A
Perennial weeds:
0.5-5 lb. ai/A
0.75-7.5 pt. 5.4WS/A
1-10 pt. 4WS/A

Time: Preplant, preemergence, at-planting, postharvest.

Weeds: Emerged annual and perennial broadleaf weeds including:

Canada thistle	field bindweed	kochia

Grasses:

downy brome	foxtail	quackgrass

Remarks: For postharvest applications do not apply more than 1 lb. ai/A. Do not treat rice fields or levees when field contains flood water. Do not allow glyphosate to contact desirable plants. Do not add surfactant to Roundup Ultra or Ultra RT. Do not apply through any type of irrigation system. Refer to label for directions, precautions and restrictions.

Days To Harvest: Postharvest: harvest/feeding—8 weeks.

Tank Mixes: Postharvest: 2,4-D, dicamba. Tank mixes not registered in California by air.

State Restrictions: Roundup RT for use in Colorado, Idaho, Montana, North Dakota, South Dakota, Utah, Wyoming, and in specific counties only in Kansas, Minnesota, Nebraska, Nevada, Oklahoma, Oregon, and Washington; refer to label for restrictions. Glyfos is not registered for use in California. Glyfos X-tra is not registered for use in mistblowers in California or Arizona.

— — — — — — — — — — — — — — —

Signal Word/Toxicity Class: Varies by formulation.
REI: Warning—12 hr.; Caution—4 hr.

Grandstand R — see triclopyr

Gramoxone Extra — see paraquat

Hi-Dep — see 2,4-D

LONDAX

Selective postemergence herbicide for control of many broadleaf and sedge weeds.

■ POST

Londax (60DF) (bensulfuron) (DuPont)

Rate: 1 oz. ai/A
1.6 oz. 60DF/A

Time: Postemergence. Apply to young, emerging, and actively growing weeds (less than 3 leaves) after establishment of permanent flood directly into standing water.

Weeds: Most broadleaf weeds such as:

blunt spikerush	purple ammannia*	smallflower
California arrowhead	redstem*	umbrellaplant
ducksalad	roughseed bulrush*	water plantain
Eisen waterhyssop	southern naiad	waterwort

* Resistant

Remarks: Water-seeded rice. Naturally occurring resistant biotypes of California arrowhead and smallflower umbrellaplant are known to exist in California. Londax will not control these resistant biotypes. Do not apply to wild rice or to rice under stress. Application to standing water and holding for a minimum of 5 days is needed to receive maximum efficacy. May be applied as dry application (without dilution in liquid carrier) by air.

Days To Harvest: Harvest, grazing or feeding treated forage—80.

Crop Rotation: Do not rotate to crops other than rice for 120 days following application.

State Restrictions: For use in California.

— — — — — — — — — — — — — — —

Rate: 0.6-1 oz. ai/A
1-1.6 oz. 60DF/A

Time: Postemergence. Apply to young, emerging, and actively growing weeds (less than 3 leaves) after establishment of permanent flood directly into standing water.

Weeds: Broadleaf weeds:

annual arrowhead	gooseweed	roughseed bulrush
blunt spikerush	mexicanweed	southern naiad
dayflower	mud plantain	texasweed
ducksalad	pickerelweed	water plantain
Eisen waterhyssop	purple ammannia	waterwort
false pimpernel	redstem	

Sedges:

rice flatsedge	yellow nutsedge

Remarks: Water-seeded, dry-seeded rice. Do not apply to wild rice or to rice under stress. Application to standing water and holding for a minimum of 7 days is needed to receive maximum efficacy.

Days To Harvest: Harvest, grazing or feeding treated forage—80.

Crop Rotation: Do not rotate to crops other than rice for 120 days following application.

Tank Mixes: May be applied as tank mix with propanil-containing rice herbicides.

State Restrictions: For use in Arkansas, Louisiana, Missouri, Mississippi, and Texas.

— — — — — — — — — — — — — — —

Signal Word/Toxicity Class: Warning/II.
REI: 24 hr.

MCPA

Broadleaf and aquatic weed control. Apply at correct rice growth stage not to exceed $1/2$" internode.

■ POST

Albaugh MCPA Amine 4 (Albaugh)

Rate: 0.5-0.75 lb. ae/A
1-1.5 pt./A

Time: Postemergence. Apply when rice is in 3-4 leaf stage.

Weeds: Broadleaf weeds and sedges:

annual sedges	curly indigo	mexicanweed
arrowhead	(suppression)	redstem
bulrush	hemp sesbania	waterplantain

Remarks: Do not spray when temperatures are high. Do not apply through any type of irrigation system, or grow crayfish or catfish in treated fields.

State Restrictions: For use in California only.

— — — — — — — — — — — — — — —

Signal Word/Toxicity Class: Danger/I.
REI: 48 hr.

■ POST

◆ **Clean Crop MCP 2 Sodium (sodium salt)** (Platte)
Riverdale MCPA L.V. 4 Ester (Riverdale)
Wilbur-Ellis MCPA Ester or ◆ Sodium Salt (Wilbur-Ellis)

Rate: 0.75-1.25 lb. ae/A
1.5-2.5 pt. ester/A
3-5 pt. sodium salt/A

Time: Postemergence. Apply when rice is well established and 6-8" above water. Do not spray when rice is in boot stage.

Weeds: Broadleaf weeds and sedges:

annual sedges	curly indigo	mexicanweed
arrowhead	(suppression)	redstem
bulrush	hemp sesbania	waterplantain

Remarks: Do not spray when temperatures are over 90°F. Do not apply through any type of irrigation system, or grow crayfish or catfish in treated fields.

State Restrictions: For use in California and other recommended areas. Wilbur-Ellis not registered in California.

— — — — — — — — — — — — — — —

Signal Word/Toxicity Class: Danger/I (sodium salt); Warning/II (ester).
REI: Danger—48hr.; Warning—12 hr.

■ POST

Gordon's MCPA Amine 4 (PBI Gordon)
Riverside MCPA Amine (Terra)

Rate: 0.75-1.25 lb. ae/A
1.5-2.5 pt./A

Time: Postemergence. Apply when rice is 6-8" above water. Do not spray when rice is in boot stage.

Weeds: Broadleaf weeds and sedges:

annual sedges	curly indigo	mexicanweed
arrowhead	(suppression)	redstem
bulrush	hemp sesbania	waterplantain

5

Other Field Crops

Remarks: Do not spray when temperatures are over 90°F. Do not apply through any type of irrigation system, or grow crayfish or catfish in treated fields.
State Restrictions: For use in California only for Riverside.

- - - - - - - - - - - - -

Signal Word/Toxicity Class: Danger/I.
REI: 48 hr.

■ POST
◆ Clean Crop MCP Amine 4 *(Platte)*
Riverdale MCPA-4 Amine *(Riverdale)*
Wilbur-Ellis MCPA Amine *(Wilbur-Ellis)*

Rate: 1-2 lb. ae/A
2-3 pt./A
California:
0.5-0.75 lb. ae/A
1-1.5 pt./A
Time: Postemergence. Apply 7-10 weeks after planting when rice is fully tillered and 6-8" above water. Do not spray when rice is in boot stage. In California, apply when rice is in 3-4 leaf stage.
Weeds: Broadleaf weeds and sedges:

annual sedges	curly indigo	mexicanweed
arrowhead	(suppression)	redstem
bulrush	hemp sesbania	waterplantain

Remarks: Do not spray when temperatures are over 90°F. Do not apply through any type of irrigation system, or grow crayfish or catfish in treated fields.
State Restrictions: Wilbur-Ellis not registered in California.

- - - - - - - - - - - - -

Signal Word/Toxicity Class: Danger/I.
REI: 48 hr.

■ POST
Riverdale MCPA IOE (ester) (5.2) *(Riverdale)*
Sword (ester) (5.2) *(Platte)*

Rate: 0.65-1.1 lb. ae/A
1-1.75 pt. 5.2/A
Time: Postemergence. Apply when rice is well established and 6-8" above water. Do not spray when rice is in boot stage.
Weeds: Broadleaf weeds and sedges:

annual sedges	curly indigo	mexicanweed
arrowhead	(suppression)	redstem
bulrush	hemp sesbania	waterplantain

Remarks: Do not spray when temperatures are over 90°F. Do not apply through any type of irrigation system, or grow crayfish or catfish in treated fields.
State Restrictions: For use in California and other recommended areas.

- - - - - - - - - - - - -

Signal Word/Toxicity Class: Warning/II.
REI: 12 hr.

Opti-Amine — see 2,4-D

ORDRAM

Do not apply in conjunction with other herbicides unless specified on label, or crop injury may result. Toxic to fish.

■ PPI, POST
Ordram 8E (molinate) *(ZENECA)*

Rate: Ground application:
3 lb. ai/A
3 pt. 8E/A
Time: Water-seeded: Preplant incorporated, preflood. Flood field for seeding; hold flood for 4-6 days after seeding.
Weeds:
barnyardgrass   watergrass

Rate: Air application:
3-5 lb. ai/A
3-5 pt. 8E/A
Time: Water-seeded: Postemergence, postflood. Rice should be in seedling stage. Watergrass must be 2-5" tall and at least 2/3 submerged (water level must be maintained until watergrass dies).
Weeds:
barnyardgrass   watergrass
Remarks: For ground application, apply to soil in good tilth; incorporate immediately. For air application, hold flood water a minimum of 4 days after application.

Days To Harvest: 30 days between preflood and postflood treatments; 60 days between last application and harvest.
State Restrictions: For use in California.

- - - - - - - - - - - - -

Rate: Ground application:
3-4 lb. ai/A
3-4 pt. 8E/A
Time: Dry-seeded: Preplant incorporated.
Weeds: Partial control of early-season grasses and sedge:

barnyardgrass	crabgrass	sprangletop
broadleaf signalgrass	nutsedge	

Rate: Air application:
3 lb. ai/A
3 pt. 8E/A
Time: Dry-seeded, water-seeded: Postemergence, postflood. Barnyardgrass must be at least 2-5" tall and at least 2/3 submerged.
Weeds:

barnyardgrass	common dayflower	watergrass
broadleaf signalgrass	sprangletop	

Rate: Flood irrigation:
3 lb. ai/A
3 pt. 8E/A
Time: Dry-seeded: Postemergence at flooding. Rice must be established at time of application. Dayflower must be completely submerged and barnyardgrass 2/3 submerged by flooding.
Weeds:
barnyardgrass   dayflower (under 5" tall)   watergrass
Remarks: For ground application, apply to dry soil surface; incorporate immediately to depth of 1-2". For air application, apply directly to flooded field. For postemergence at flooding, apply through flood (basin) irrigation system.
Days To Harvest: 30 days between preflood and postflood treatments; 60 days between last application and harvest.
State Restrictions: For use in southern regions of Arkansas, Louisiana, MIssissippi, Missouri, Texas.

- - - - - - - - - - - - -

Signal Word/Toxicity Class: Warning/II.
REI: 12 hr. unless soil injected or soil incorporated.

■ PPI, POST
Ordram 15-G or 15-GM (molinate) *(ZENECA)*

Rate: Preplant, preflood, soil incorporated (water-seeded):
3-4 lb. ai/A
20-27 lb. 15-G, 15-GM/A
Postflood, postemergence (water-seeded or dry-seeded):
3-5 lb. ai/A
20-33 lb. 15-G, 15-GM/A
Time: Preplant, preflood soil incorporated; postflood, postemergence.
Weeds: Grasses 15-G:

annual sedge	broadleaf signalgrass	red rice
barnyardgrass	crabgrass	spikerush
(watergrass)	dayflower	sprangletop

Grasses 15-GM:
barnyardgrass (watergrass)

Remarks: Apply by ground or air for preplant, preflood, soil incorporated; by air only for postflood, postemergence. Do not apply more than 4 lb. ai/A preplant; 5 lb. ai/A postflood or postemergence; 9 lb. ai/A per season. Do not feed rice straw if application is made within 40 days of harvest. Refer to label for specific directions, restrictions, and precautions.
Days To Harvest: 30.
State Restrictions: 15-G: For use in Arkansas, Louisiana, Mississippi, bootheel of Missouri, Texas. 15-GM: For use in California.

- - - - - - - - - - - - -

Signal Word/Toxicity Class: Warning/II (15-G); Caution (15-GM).
REI: 12 hr. unless soil injected or soil incorporated.

PARAQUAT

Restricted Use Pesticide.

■ PP, PRE
Gramoxone Extra (2.5L) *(ZENECA)*

Rate: 0.5-1 lb. ai/A
1.5-3 pt. 2.5L/A
Time: Preplant, preemergence. Apply before, during or after planting, but before crop emergence.
Weeds: Annual broadleaf weeds and grasses.
Remarks: Do not flood/flush within 48 hr. of application to ensure complete kill of vegetation. If cool, cloudy and/or wet weather delay speed of kill, do not flood/flush until complete kill is evident. Refer to label for use directions and precautions.

◆-new product • PP-preplant • PPI-preplant incorporated • PRE-preemergence • POST-postemergence • SEQ-sequential • ae-acid equivalent • ai-active ingredient • DF-dry flowable
E/EC-emulsifiable concentrate • F/FL-flowable • DG/G/WG-dispersable granule • L/LC-liquid • SP/WSP-soluble packet • W/WP-wettable powder • WSB-water soluble bag

Tank Mixes: Atrazine, Bladex, Canopy, Extrazine, Lariat, linuron, metribuzin, Princep.

- - - - - - - - - - - - - - - -

Signal Word/Toxicity Class: Danger-Poison/I.
REI: 12 hr. (except harvest aid/desiccation 24 hr.).

PENDIMETHALIN

Pendimethalin alone will not control broadleaf weeds. Toxic to fish and aquatic organisms.

■ PRE
Pentagon DG *(American Cyanamid)*
Prowl 3.3 EC *(American Cyanamid)*
   Rate: 0.75-1 lb. ai/A
      1.8-2.4 pt. 3.3 EC/A
      1.25-1.7 lb. DG/A
   Time: Delayed preemergence, early postemergence in drilled, dry-seeded rice.
   Weeds: Grasses:

barnyardgrass (watergrass)	junglerice	sprangletop

   Remarks: Rate varies by soil type. Do not use on peat or muck soils. For delayed preemergence, do not use on sands, loamy sands. If crop loss occurs due to weather conditions or disease after application alone or in a tank mixture, only drilled dry-seeded rice may be immediately replanted; see label. Do not use on water-seeded rice except as specified on other Cyanamid labeling. Do not apply to rice fields if used for fish production. Do not bale or use rice straw from treated fields for feed or bedding.
   Tank Mixes: Arrosolo, Facet, propanil.
   State Restrictions: Refer to supplemental label for use in California.

- - - - - - - - - - - - - - - -

Signal Word/Toxicity Class: Caution.
REI: 24 hr.

Pentagon — see pendimethalin

PROPANIL

Postemergence weed control for dry or water-seeded rice. Weed foliage must not be covered with water at time of application.

■ POST
Blue Drum or Propanil 4 *(RiceCo)*
Propanil 36% *(RiceCo)*
Riverside Propanil 4E or 80EDF *(Terra)*
Stam 4E/M-4 or 80EDF *(Rohm and Haas)*
   Rate: 3-6 lb. ai/A
      6-12 pt. 4, 4E, M-4, FL/A
      8-16 pt. 36%/A
      3.75-7.5 lb. 80EDF/A
   Time: Postemergence. Applications to rice after 4-leaf stage may cause visible injury under some climatic conditions.
   Weeds: Broadleaf weeds:

croton	mexicanweed	sour dock
curly indigo	pigweed	spearhead
hemp sesbania	redweed	

   Grasses:

barnyardgrass (watergrass)	foxtail	paragrass
broadleaf signalgrass	goosegrass	spikerush
crabgrass	gulf cockspur	Texas panicum
	hoorahgrass	

   Remarks: Do not apply to any crop except rice. Do not apply to fields where commercial catfish farming is practiced or drain water from treated fields into areas where catfish farming is practiced. Do not apply through any type of irrigation system. Refer to labels for further use directions, restrictions, and precautions.
   Tank Mixes: Bolero, Facet, Londax, or pendimethalin to control propanil-resistant barnyardgrass.
   State Restrictions: Stam 80EDF has special restrictions in California, refer to label. Prowl and Facet are not registered for use on rice in California.

- - - - - - - - - - - - - - - -

Signal Word/Toxicity Class: Varies by formulation.
REI: 24 hr.

■ POST
Super Wham! or Wham! EZ *(RiceCo)*
◆ **Super Wham! CA or Wham! EZ CA** *(RiceCo)*
   Rate: 3-6 lb. ai/A
      6-12 pt./A

Time: Postemergence.
Weeds: Broadleaf weeds:

coffeeweed	mexicanweed	spearhead
croton	pigweed	Texas millet
curly indigo	sour dock	

Grasses:

barnyardgrass (watergrass)	foxtail	paragrass
	goosegrass	signalgrass
crabgrass	gulf cockspur	wiregrass

Remarks: Do not apply to any crop except rice. In California, apply only where rice fields are completely drained or a minimal amount of water remains. Does not control arrowhead, bermudagrass, cattail, ducksalad, johnsongrass, nutgrass, red rice, or sprangletop. Do not apply to fields where commercial catfish farming is practiced or drain water from treated fields into areas where catfish farming is practiced. Crop oil concentrate or surfactant may be added. Do not apply through any type of irrigation system. Refer to label for use directions and restrictions.
Tank Mixes: Facet.
State Restrictions: Facet not registered for use in California. Super Wham! CA and Wham! EZ CA for use in California only.

- - - - - - - - - - - - - - - -

Signal Word/Toxicity Class: Caution.
REI: 24 hr.

Prowl — see pendimethalin

QUINCLORAC

Facet is a systemic herbicide absorbed by germinating weed seeds, roots, or leaves, with seed and root uptake activated by water. Rainfall within 7 days after application begins initial herbicidal activity.

■ PRE, POST
Facet 75DF *(BASF)*
   Rate: 0.25-0.5 lb. ai/A
      0.33-0.67 lb. 75DF/A
   Time: Preemergence and delayed preemergence (drill-dry seeded rice only), early postemergence.
   Weeds: Grasses:

barnyardgrass	eclipta	large crabgrass
broadleaf signalgrass	junglerice	sesbania

   Remarks: In case of crop failure, only rice may be immediately replanted.
   Days To Harvest: 80.
   Crop Rotation: Do not plant any crop other than rice for 309 days following application; eggplant and tobacco should not be planted within 12 months; tomatoes and carrots within 2 years.
   Tank Mixes: Basagran, Blazer, Bolero, propanil, Prowl, Storm.
   State Restrictions: Not for use in California.

- - - - - - - - - - - - - - - -

Signal Word/Toxicity Class: Caution/III.
REI: 12 hr.

Rattler — see glyphosate

Roundup — see glyphosate

Saber — see 2,4-D

Savage — see 2,4-D

SCYTHE

◆ **Scythe (pelargonic acid)** *(Mycogen)*
   Rate: 4-13 fl. oz./1 gal. spray solution
   Time: Apply to actively growing weeds prior to crop emergence.
   Weeds: Annual and perennial broadleaf weeds and grasses.
   Remarks: Apply in minimum 75 gal. spray solution/A or spray-to-wet. Do not apply by air or through any type of irrigation system. Refer to label for directions and precautions.
   Tank Mixes: Glyphosate and other foliar and residual herbicides.

- - - - - - - - - - - - - - - -

Signal Word/Toxicity Class: Warning/II.
REI: 24 hr.

5

Other Field Crops

NOTICE	The information on these pages is for preliminary planning — not a guide for use. Be sure to follow the manufacturer's directions, notwithstanding information contained here.	For personal protective equipment and EPA registration numbers, please turn to page 70.

Solution — see 2,4-D

Stam — see propanil

STAMPRO (Premix)

■ POST
◆ Stampro (80.2% propanil & 0.6% bensulfuron-methyl) *(Rohm & Haas)*
 Rate: 3-4 lb. ai/A
  3.8-5 lb./A (1 package/10-13.3A)
 Time: Postemergence. Apply to actively growing weeds up to early 4-leaf stage.
 Weeds: Broadleaf weeds:

cocklebur	hemp sesbania	redstem
croton	mexicanweed	redweed
curly indigo	morningglory	spearhead
curly dock	Pennsylvania	spikerush
eclipta	smartweed	Texas millet
gooseweed	pigweed	texasweed
gulf cockspur		

 Grasses and sedges:

barnyardgrass	goosegrass	rice flatsedge
brachiaria	hoorahgrass	watergrass
crabgrass	paragrass	yellow nutsedge
foxtail		

 Remarks: Not for use on wild rice. Do not use carbamate or organophosphorus insecticides on treated fields. Do not apply where catfish farming is practiced. Do not graze or feed treated forage within 80 days of treatment. Do not apply through any type of irrigation system.
 Crop Rotation: Do not rotate to crops other than rice for 120 days following treatment.
 State Restrictions: For use in Arkansas, Louisiana, Mississippi, Missouri, and Texas.

 - - - - - - - - - - - - - - -

 Signal Word/Toxicity Class: Warning/II.
 REI: 24 hr.

STORM (Premix)

Premix of bentazon and acifluorfen.

■ POST
Storm (2.6 lb./gal. bentazon & 1.33 lb./gal. acifluorfen) *(BASF)*
 Rate: 0.75 lb. ai/A
  1.5 pt./A
 Time: Postemergence. Do not apply after rice reaches early boot stage.
 Weeds: Broadleaf weeds and sedge:

cocklebur	hemp sesbania	smartweed
dayflower	morningglory	spikerush
ducksalad	redstem	yellow nutsedge
gooseweed	redweed	

 Remarks: Add oil concentrate, urea-ammonium nitrate (UAN), or nonionic surfactant. Do not apply through any type of irrigation system.
 Days To Harvest: 50.
 Crop Rotation: Do not rotate root crops such as carrots, sweet potatoes, turnips, etc. into treated fields for 18 months following last application.
 Tank Mixes: Basagran, Facet, Propanil.
 State Restrictions: Not for use in California.

 - - - - - - - - - - - - - - -

 Signal Word/Toxicity Class: Danger/I.
 REI: 48 hr.

Super Wham or Wham! EZ — see propanil

Sword — see MCPA

TRICLOPYR

Systemic postemergence herbicide controls broadleaf weeds through foliar uptake.

■ POST
Grandstand R or CA (WS) *(Dow AgroSciences)*
 Rate: 0.25-0.375 lb. ae/A
  0.67-1 pt. WS/A

 Time: Postemergence. Jointvetch most susceptible from 10" to flowering stage; morningglory when runners are greater than 6".
 Weeds: Broadleaf weeds:

jointvetch	morningglory

 Rate: 0.375 lb. ae/A
  1 pt. WS/A
 Weeds: Broadleaf weeds:

alligatorweed	hemp sesbania	texasweed
common cocklebur	mexicanweed	waterhyssop
eclipta	redstem	

 Time: Postemergence. Do not apply to rice prior to 3-4 leaf stage, after $1/2$" internode elongation stage, or in booting stage.
 Remarks: Not for use on upland rice. Do not apply after Whip herbicide application. Do not apply through any type of irrigation system.
 Days To Harvest: 60.
 Crop Rotation: Do not rotate to crops other than rice for 4 months.
 Tank Mixes: Stam.
 State Restrictions: Not registered in New York. Grandstand CA for use in California.

 - - - - - - - - - - - - - - -

 Signal Word/Toxicity Class: Danger/I.
 REI: 48 hr.

Weed Rhap — see 2,4-D

Weedar — see 2,4-D

Weedestroy — see 2,4-D

Whip — see fenoxaprop-P-ethyl

Safflower

Dual — see *S*-metolachlor

Eptam — see EPTC

EPTC

■ PPI
Eptam 7-E or 20-G *(ZENECA)*
 Rate: 3 lb. ai/A
  3.5 pt. 7-E/A
  15 lb. 20-G/A
 Time: Preplant incorporated. Incorporate immediately after application.
 Weeds: Broadleaf weeds:

black nightshade	corn spurry	nettleleaf goosefoot
carpetweed*	cutleaf nightshade*	prickly sida*
common chickweed	deadnettle	prostrate pigweed
common lambsquarters	fiddleneck*	redroot pigweed
	Florida pusley	sicklepod*
common pigweed	hairy nightshade	tall morningglory*
common purslane	henbit	tumble pigweed

 Annual grasses and sedges:

annual bluegrass	giant foxtail	rescuegrass*
annual ryegrass	goosegrass	shattercane
(Italian)	green foxtail	signalgrass*
barnyardgrass	johnsongrass	Texas panicum*
(watergrass)	(seedling)	volunteer grains
bermudagrass	junglerice	(barley, oats, wheat)
(seedling)	lovegrass	wild oat
crabgrass	(stinkgrass)*	witchgrass*
fall panicum*	purple nutsedge	yellow foxtail
field sandbur	quackgrass	yellow nutsedge

 **7-E only* (*7-E only)
 Remarks: Refer to label for use directions, restrictions, and precautions.
 State Restrictions: 7-E for use in Pacific Northwest.

 - - - - - - - - - - - - - - -

 Signal Word/Toxicity Class: Caution.
 REI: 12 hr. unless soil injected or soil incorporated.

◆-new product • PP-preplant • PPI-preplant incorporated • PRE-preemergence • POST-postemergence • SEQ-sequential • ae-acid equivalent • ai-active ingredient • DF-dry flowable
E/EC-emulsifiable concentrate • F/FL-flowable • DG/G/WG-dispersable granule • L/LC-liquid • SP/WSP-soluble packet • W/WP-wettable powder • WSB-water soluble bag

Gramoxone Extra — see paraquat

Trific — see trifluralin

S-METOLACHLOR

■ **PPI, PRE**

Dual MAGNUM or Dual II MAGNUM (EC) *(Novartis)*

Rate: 1-2 pt. EC/A

Time: Preplant incorporated: Incorporate into top 2" soil within 14 days before planting. Preemergence: Apply during or after planting but before weeds emerge.

Weeds: Broadleaf weeds:

carpetweed	eclipta*	galinsoga
common purslane*	Florida beggarweed*	hairy nightshade*
eastern black nightshade	Florida pusley	pigweed

Grasses and sedges:

barnyardgrass (watergrass)	goosegrass	shattercane*
	green foxtail	signalgrass
crabgrass	johnsongrass	southwestern cupgrass
crowfootgrass	(seedling)*	volunteer sorghum*
fall panicum	prairie cupgrass	witchgrass
foxtail millet	red rice	yellow foxtail
giant foxtail	sandbur*	yellow nutsedge

Suppression

Remarks: Rate varies by soil type and organic matter. In case of crop failure, any crop on label may be replanted immediately. Do not make second broadcast application. If original application was banded and second crop is planted in untreated row middles, second banded treatment may be applied. Do not cut for hay within 120 days after application.

Crop Rotation: Alfalfa—4 months; barley, oats, rye, wheat—4½ months; tomatoes—6 months; clover—9 months; any labeled crop in addition to barley, buckwheat, cabbage, milo, nuts, oats, peppers, rice, root crops, rye, stone fruits, tobacco, and wheat may be planted in the spring following treatment (including lay-by or multiple treatments applied previous season); all other rotational crops may be planted 12 months after application.

State Restrictions: Do not use in Nassau County or Suffolk County, New York.

– – – – – – – – – – – – – – –

Signal Word/Toxicity Class: Caution/III.
REI: 24 hr.

PARAQUAT

Restricted Use Pesticide.

■ **PP, PRE**

Gramoxone Extra (2.5L) *(ZENECA)*

Rate: 0.6-1 lb. ai/A
2-3 pt. 2.5L/A

Time: Preplant, preemergence.

Weeds: Annual broadleaf weeds and grasses; top kill and suppression of perennials.

Remarks: Add nonionic surfactant or crop oil concentrate. Refer to label for use directions, restrictions, and precautions.

State Restrictions: In California, apply 12 fl. oz. 2.5L/A preplant for control of volunteer barley in preformed seedbeds.

– – – – – – – – – – – – – – –

Signal Word/Toxicity Class: Danger-Poison/I.
REI: 12 hr. (except harvest aid/desiccation 24 hr.).

SCYTHE

◆ **Scythe (pelargonic acid)** *(Mycogen)*

Rate: 4-13 fl. oz./1 gal. spray solution

Time: Apply to actively growing weeds prior to crop emergence.

Weeds: Annual and perennial broadleaf weeds and grasses.

Remarks: Apply in minimum 75 gal. spray solution/A or spray-to-wet. Do not apply by air or through any type of irrigation system. Refer to label for directions and precautions.

Tank Mixes: Glyphosate and other foliar and residual herbicides.

– – – – – – – – – – – – – – –

Signal Word/Toxicity Class: Warning/II.
REI: 24 hr.

Treflan — see trifluralin

TRI-4 — see trifluralin

TRIFLURALIN

■ **PPI**

Albaugh Trifluralin 4EC *(Albaugh)*
◆ **Clean Crop Trifluralin HF (4EC)** *(Platte)*
Gowan Trifluralin 4 or 5 (EC) or 10G *(Gowan)*
Helena Trifluralin 4 EC *(Helena)*
Riverside Trifluralin 4EC or Trific 60DF *(Terra)*
◆ **Sedagri Trifluralin 480 (4EC)** *(Rhone-Poulenc)*
Treflan HFP (4EC) or TR-10 (10G) *(Dow AgroSciences)*
TRI-4 HF (4EC) *(American Cyanamid)*
Trilin 4 or 5 (EC) or 10G *(Griffin)*
Wilbur-Ellis Trifluralin 10G *(Wilbur-Ellis)*

Rate: 0.5-1 lb. ai/A
1-2 pt. 4EC/A
0.8-2 pt. 5EC/A
0.875-1.66 lb. 60DF/A
5-10 lb. 10G/A

Time: Preplant incorporated.

Weeds: Broadleaf weeds:

carelessweed	knotweed	purslane
carpetweed	kochia	pusley
chickweed	lambsquarters	redroot pigweed
field bindweed	Mexican clover	rough pigweed
fireweed	Mexican fireweed	Russian thistle
Florida purslane	prostrate pigweed	spiny pigweed
Florida pusley	puncturevine	stinging nettle
goosefoot	(western U.S.)	tumbleweed
henbit		

Grasses:

annual bluegrass	fall panicum	sandbur
barnyardgrass	foxtail millet	shattercane
bottlegrass	giant foxtail	smooth crabgrass
brachiaria	green foxtail	sprangletop
bristlegrass	Italian ryegrass	stinkgrass
bromegrass	johnsongrass	Texas panicum
burgrass	(seedling)	watergrass
cheat	junglerice	wildcane
cheatgrass	large crabgrass	woolly cupgrass
chess	pigeongrass	yellow foxtail
downy brome	robust foxtail	

Remarks: Rate varies by soil type. Up to 2.5 pt. 4EC/A may be used on soils with 5%-10% organic matter. Refer to label for directions, restrictions, and precautions.

Crop Rotation: Refer to label.

State Restrictions: Wilbur-Ellis not registered in California.

– – – – – – – – – – – – – – –

Signal Word/Toxicity Class: Varies by formulation.
REI: 12 hr. unless soil injected or soil incorporated.

Trilin — see trifluralin

Sorghum

(Forage, grain [milo], sweet)

AAtrex — see atrazine

ALACHLOR

Restricted Use Pesticide.

■ **PPI, PRE**

Lasso (4EC) *(Monsanto)*

Rate: 2.5-4 lb. ai/A
2.5-4 qt. 4EC/A

Time: Preplant incorporated: Apply 7 days prior to planting and incorporate in 1-2" soil. Preemergence surface: Apply after planting before crop and weed emergence and within 5 days of last tillage.

5

Other Field Crops

NOTICE	The information on these pages is for preliminary planning — not a guide for use. Be sure to follow the manufacturer's directions, notwithstanding information contained here.	For personal protective equipment and EPA registration numbers, please turn to page 70.

Sorghum

Weeds: Broadleaf weeds:

black nightshade	Florida pusley	prickly sida*
carelessweed	galinsoga	purslane
carpetweed	hairy nightshade	sicklepod*
common ragweed*	lambsquarters*	smartweed*
cutleaf groundcherry	pigweed	teaweed*
Florida beggarweed*		

Grasses and sedges:

barnyardgrass	johnsongrass*	wild proso millet*
broadleaf signalgrass	(seedling)	wildcane*
crabgrass	panicum	witchgrass
foxtail	sandbur*	woolly cupgrass*
goosegrass	shattercane*	yellow nutsedge

* *Suppression*

Remarks: Grain sorghum (milo). Seed must be treated with Screen seed protectant or safener containing active ingredient flurazole.

Days To Harvest: Harvest/grazing—70.

Tank Mixes: Atrazine; Gramoxone Extra, Roundup.

– – – – – – – – – – – – – – – –

Signal Word/Toxicity Class: Danger/I.
REI: 12 hr.

Atra-5 — see atrazine

ATRAZINE

Restricted Use Pesticide due to groundwater concerns.

■ **PP, PPI, PRE, POST**

AAtrex 4L or AAtrex Nine-0 (WDG) *(Novartis)*
◆ **Clean Crop Atrazine 4L, 90 WDG** *(Platte)*
Drexel Atrazine 4L, Atra-5 (5L) or 90DF *(Drexel)*
Helena Atrazine 4L *(Helena)*
Riverside Atrazine 4L or 90DF *(Terra)*

Rate: Not highly erodible or with at least 30% residue cover (conservation tillage):
  2 lb. ai/A
  4 pt. 4L/A
  3.2 pt. 5L/A
  2.2 lb. WDG, 90DF/A
  Highly erodible with less than 30% residue cover:
  1.6 lb. ai/A
  3.2 pt. 4L/A
  2.4 pt. 5L/A
  1.8 lb. WDG, 90DF/A

Time: Preplant surface-applied: Apply up to 45 days prior to planting on medium or fine-textured soils. Preplant incorporated: Broadcast in spring after plowing. Apply to soil and incorporate before, during, or after final seedbed preparation. For best results, apply within 2 weeks prior to planting. Preemergence: Apply during or shortly after planting but before weed emergence. Postemergence (with oil at 4 pt. rate): Apply before sorghum is 12" in height and before weeds reach 1½" in height.

Weeds: Annual broadleaf weeds:

annual morningglory	lambsquarters	ragweed
cocklebur	mustard	sicklepod
groundcherry	nightshade	velvetleaf
jimsonweed	pigweed	(buttonweed)
kochia	purslane	

Annual grasses:

barnyardgrass	green foxtail	witchgrass
(watergrass)	large crabgrass	yellow foxtail
giant foxtail	wild oat	

Remarks: Grain, forage. Rate varies by soil type and organic matter. Do not apply more than 2.5 lb. ai/A per year. Certain states may have additional requirements and limitations; consult state lead pest control agency. Do not apply through any type of irrigation system. This product may not be mixed/loaded, or used within 50 ft. of all wells including abandoned wells, drainage wells, and sink holes. Do not graze treated area or feed treated forage to livestock for 21 days following application.

Crop Rotation: Do not plant any crop except corn or sorghum until the following year or injury may occur.

State Restrictions: Preplant surface-applied: Medium- and fine-textured soils with minimum-tillage or no-tillage systems only in Colorado, Illinois, Indiana, Iowa, Kansas, Kentucky, Minnesota, Missouri, Montana, Nebraska, North Dakota, South Dakota, Wisconsin, Wyoming. Do not apply preplant surface or preplant incorporated in Alabama, Arkansas, Florida, Georgia, Louisiana, Mississippi, North Carolina, New Mexico, Oklahoma, South Carolina, Tennessee, Texas. Do not apply preemergence in New Mexico, northeast Oklahoma, Texas Gulf Coast. Wilbur-Ellis not registered in California.

– – – – – – – – – – – – – – – –

Rate: 1.2 lb. ai/A
  2.4 pt. 4L/A
  1.9 pt. 5L/A
  1.3 lb. WDG, 90DF/A

Time: Postemergence. Apply before sorghum reaches 12" in height, pigweed and lambsquarters reach 6" in height, and all other weeds reach 4" in height.

Weeds: Broadleaf weeds:

annual morningglory	mustards	smartweed
cocklebur	pigweed	velvetleaf
jimsonweed	ragweed	wild buckwheat
lambsquarters		

Remarks: Grain, forage. Add emulsifiable oil or oil concentrate. Certain states may have established rate limitations; consult state lead pest control agency for limitations. Do not apply through any type of irrigation system. This product may not be mixed/loaded, or used within 50 ft. of all wells including abandoned wells, drainage wells, and sink holes. Do not graze treated area or feed treated forage to livestock for 21 days following application.

Crop Rotation: Do not plant to any crop except corn or sorghum until the following year or injury may occur.

State Restrictions: Wilbur-Ellis not registered in California.

– – – – – – – – – – – – – – – –

Signal Word/Toxicity Class: Caution/III.
REI: 12 hr.

Banvel— see dicamba

Barrage— see 2,4-D

BASAGRAN

■ **POST**

Basagran (bentazon) *(BASF)*

Rate: 0.75-1 lb. ai/A
  1.5-2 pt./A

Time: Early postemergence. Do not apply to sorghum that is heading or blooming.

Weeds: Broadleaf weeds:

annual morningglory	dayflower	spurred anoda
beggarticks	galinsoga	teaweed
bristly starbur	giant ragweed	tropic croton
Canada thistle	jimsonweed	velvetleaf
cocklebur	ladysthumb	Venice mallow
common	Pennsylvania	wild buckwheat
lambsquarters	smartweed	wild mustard
common ragweed	prickly sida	wild sunflower

Sedges:

yellow nutsedge (except CA)

Remarks: Forage, grain sorghum. Rate depends on leaf stage and weed height. For improved control of velvetleaf, add urea-ammonium nitrate (UAN) solution to spray tank in place of oil concentrate. If common ragweed and lambsquarters are present in addition to velvetleaf, then oil concentrate should be used. Seed producers should consult seed company regarding tolerance of seed production inbred lines to Basagran. Do not apply more than 2 pt./A per season. Do not graze treated fields for at least 12 days after last treatment. Refer to Special Directions on label.

Tank Mixes: Atrazine.

State Restrictions: Not for use in California on forage sorghum.

– – – – – – – – – – – – – – – –

Signal Word/Toxicity Class: Caution/III.
REI: 12 hr.

BICEP (Premixes)

Contains the safener benoxacor. Restricted Use Pesticide due to ground and surface water concerns.

■ **PP, PPI, PRE**

Bicep II MAGNUM (3.1 lb./gal. atrazine & 2.4 lb./gal. S-metolachlor) *(Novartis)*
Bicep Lite II MAGNUM (2.67 lb./gal. atrazine & 3.33 lb./gal. S-metolachlor) *(Novartis)*

Rate: 3.3-4.1 lb. ai/A
  2.1-2.6 qt. II/A
  2-2.6 lb. ai/A
  1.3-1.9 qt. Lite II/A

◆-new product • PP-preplant • PPI-preplant incorporated • PRE-preemergence • POST-postemergence • SEQ-sequential • ae-acid equivalent • ai-active ingredient • DF-dry flowable
E/EC-emulsifiable concentrate • F/FL-flowable • DG/G/WG-dispersable granule • L/LC-liquid • SP/WSP-soluble packet • W/WP-wettable powder • WSB-water soluble bag

Time: Early preplant. Apply up to 45 days before planting. Applications less than 30 days prior to planting may be split or single treatment; use split applications for treatments made 30-45 days before planting.

Rate: 2.5-3.3 lb. ai/A
1.6-2.1 qt. II/A
1.65-2.25 lb. ai/A
1.1-1.5 qt. Lite/A

Time: Preplant surface: Apply within 14 days before planting. Preplant incorporated: Apply to soil; incorporate into top 2" within 14 days prior to planting (use preplant incorporated if furrow irrigation is used or period of dry weather is expected). Preemergence: Apply at planting (behind planter) or after planting but before weeds or crop emerge.

Weeds: Broadleaf weeds:

carpetweed	galinsoga	mustard
chickweed	giant ragweed*	nightshade
cocklebur*	henbit	pigweed
common purslane	jimsonweed	sicklepod*
common ragweed	lambsquarters	smartweed
Florida pusley	morningglory	velvetleaf*

Grasses and sedges:

barnyardgrass	green foxtail	signalgrass*
browntop panicum	johnsongrass	southwestern
crabgrass	(seedling)*	cupgrass
crowfootgrass	prairie cupgrass	volunteer sorghum*
fall panicum	red rice	witchgrass
foxtail millet	sandbur*	woolly cupgrass*
giant foxtail	shattercane*	yellow foxtail
goosegrass	signalgrass*	yellow nutsedge*

* Suppression

Remarks: Grain, forage sorghum. Must be used with Concep-treated grain sorghum seed. Rate varies by soil type and organic matter. Certain states may have established rate limitations regarding atrazine; consult state lead pest control agency for additional information. Do not apply through any type of irrigation system. Refer to label for use directions.

Crop Rotation: Corn, sorghum, soybeans, cotton or peanuts may be planted the spring following treatment. Injury may occur to soybeans planted the year following application on soils having a calcareous surface layer. If applied after June 10, do not rotate with crops other than corn or sorghum the next year or crop injury may occur. In eastern Dakotas, Kansas, western Minnesota, and Nebraska, do not rotate to soybeans if more than 2 lb. ai atrazine was applied. In high plains and intermountain areas of the west where rainfall is sparse and erratic or where irrigation is required, use only when corn or sorghum is to be planted the following year, or a crop of untreated corn or sorghum is to precede other rotational crops. Do not plant sugar beets, tobacco, vegetables, spring-seeded small grains, or small seeded legumes the year following application. All other crops may be planted 18 months after application.

Tank Mixes: AAtrex, Bladex, Dual, Extrazine II, simazine.

State Restrictions: Do not use in Nassau County or Suffolk County, New York. Early preplant: Minimum-tillage and no-till systems in Illinois, Iowa, eastern Kansas, Missouri, Nebraska, and South Dakota.

– – – – – – – – – – – – – – –

Signal Word/Toxicity Class: Caution/III.
REI: 24 hr.

Brash — see 2,4-D Combinations

Broclean — see bromoxynil

Bromox — see bromoxynil

Bromox + atrazine — see bromoxynil & atrazine

BROMOXYNIL

■ **PRE, POST**
◆ **Broclean 2EC** *(Platte)*
◆ **Bromox 2EC** *(Micro Flo)*
Buctril (2EC), Buctril 4EC *(Rhone-Poulenc)*
Moxy 2EC *(Terra)*
Rate: 0.25-0.375 lb. ai/A
1-1.5 pt. 2EC/A
0.5-0.75 pt. 4EC/A
Chemigation:
0.5 lb. ai/A
2 pt. 2EC/A
1 pt. 4EC/A

Time: Preemergence, postemergence. Preemergence: apply before planting until just prior to crop emergence. Postemergence: apply after emergence but prior to preboot stage.

Weeds: Broadleaf weeds:

black nightshade	giant ragweed	spiny pigweed
buffalobur	hemp sesbania	sunflower
Canada thistle	ivyleaf morningglory	tall morningglory
(suppression)	jimsonweed	tall waterhemp
common cocklebur	ladysthumb	velvetleaf
common lambsquarters	Pennsylvania	Venice mallow
common ragweed	smartweed	wild buckwheat
eastern black	redroot pigweed	wild mustard
nightshade		

Remarks: Grain, forage sorghum. Do not feed or graze treated crop within 30 days (45 for Buctril). Refer to label for restrictions and precautions.

Days To Harvest: 30.

Crop Rotation: Do not plant rotational crops until the following season (within 30 days of application for Buctril).

Tank Mixes: Atrazine, Banvel, Clarity (except Bromox), 2,4-D, Roundup.

– – – – – – – – – – – – – – –

Signal Word/Toxicity Class: Warning/II.
REI: 12 hr.

BROMOXYNIL + ATRAZINE (Premixes)

Restricted Use Pesticide

■ **POST**
◆ **Bromox + atrazine (1 lb./gal. bromoxynil & 2 lb./gal. atrazine)** *(Micro Flo)*
◆ **Brozine (1 lb./gal. bromoxynil & 2 lb./gal. atrazine)** *(Platte)*
Buctril + atrazine (1 lb./gal. bromoxynil & 2 lb./gal. atrazine) *(Rhone-Poulenc)*
Moxy + atrazine (1 lb./gal. bromoxynil & 2 lb./gal. atrazine) *(Terra)*
Rate: 0.56-1.125 lb. ai/A
1.5-3 pt./A

Time: Postemergence. Do not apply to sorghum which has reached boot stage.

Weeds: Broadleaf weeds:

black nightshade	giant ragweed	purple morningglory
buffalobur	hemp sesbania	redroot pigweed
Canada thistle	ivyleaf morningglory	smooth pigweed
(suppression)	jimsonweed	spiny pigweed
common cocklebur	ladysthumb	sunflower
common	palmleaf	tall morningglory
lambsquarters	morningglory	tall waterhemp
common ragweed	Pennsylvania	velvetleaf
eastern black	smartweed	Venice mallow
nightshade	pitted morningglory	wild buckwheat
entireleaf	prickly sida	wild mustard
morningglory	puncturevine	

Remarks: Grain, forage sorghum. Do not use on sorghum grown in sandy or loamy sand soils. Do not apply through any type of irrigation system. Refer to label for restrictions and precautions.

Days To Harvest: Harvest/feeding/grazing—30 (45 for Buctril + atrazine).

Crop Rotation: Do not rotate to any crop except field corn, popcorn, or grain sorghum until the following year.

Tank Mixes: Banvel, Clarity (except Bromox + atrazine), 2,4-D.

– – – – – – – – – – – – – – –

Signal Word/Toxicity Class: Caution.
REI: 12 hr.

Brozine — see bromoxynil + atrazine

Buctril — see bromoxynil

Buctril + atrazine — see bromoxynil + atrazine

BULLET (Premix)

Restricted Use Pesticide

■ **PPI, PRE, POST**
Bullet (2.5 lb./gal. alachlor & 1.5 lb./gal. atrazine) *(Monsanto)*
Rate: 2.5-4 lb. ai/A
2.5-4 qt./A

5
Other Field Crops

Time: Preplant incorporated, preemergence surface. Preplant incorporated: Apply within 7 days prior to planting. Preemergence surface: Apply within 5 days after last preplant tillage operation. Do not apply preplant incorporated in coarse soils.

Weeds: Broadleaf weeds:

annual groundcherry	Florida beggarweed	mustard
annual morningglory	Florida pusley	pigweed
black nightshade	galinsoga	prickly sida
buttonweed	hairy nightshade	purslane
carelessweed	jimsonweed	sicklepod*
carpetweed	horseweed	smartweed
common cocklebur	kochia	teaweed
common ragweed	lambsquarters	velvetleaf
cutleaf groundcherry		

Grasses and sedges:

barnyardgrass	grassbur	shattercane*
broadleaf signalgrass	green foxtail	volunteer sorghum*
browntop panicum	johnsongrass*	waterhemp
crabgrass	(seedling)	wildcane*
fall panicum	red rice*	witchgrass
giant foxtail	red sprangletop	yellow foxtail
goosegrass	sandbur	yellow nutsedge

* Reduced competition

Remarks: Rate varies by soil type. Seed must be treated with Screen seed protectant or safener containing active ingredient flurazole. Do not apply on alkali soils or where cuts, fills, or erosions have exposed calcareous or alkali subsoils. Do not apply more than 2.5 lb. ai atrazine/year; refer to label for restrictions.

Days To Harvest: Harvest forage/grazing—70.

Crop Rotation: Corn, peanuts, milo sorghum (milo), or soybeans can be planted the year after application. If soybeans are to be planted, there is a possibility of crop injury due to carryover of atrazine. Do not plant soybeans where furrow irrigation is practiced.

State Restrictions: In Texas, apply only in Panhandle and fine-textured soils of the Gulf Coast and Blacklands. In Oklahoma Panhandle and Texas Panhandle, apply as preemergence surface application only.

– – – – – – – – – – – – – – –

Signal Word/Toxicity Class: Caution/III.
REI: 12 hr.

Clarity — see dicamba

Credit — see glyphosate

Cyclone — see paraquat

2,4-D - PHENOXY HERBICIDES

2,4-D and 2,4-D-type compounds selectively control broadleaf weeds with little or no control of grasses. 2,4-D drift can injure adjacent crops either by drift of spray or by volatilization (spray turns into a vapor). Ester formulations are most volatile and amines least volatile. Ester formulations can vaporize at temperatures as low as 70°F and move by wind to harm sensitive plants. Vaporization increases as air temperatures rise.

Annual and perennial broadleaf weeds controlled by 2,4-D include:

beggarticks	galinsoga	povertyweed
bindweed	goldenrod	puncturevine
bitterweed	ground ivy	purslane
broomweed	healall	ragweed
bull thistle	hoary cress	Russian thistle
burdock	ironweed	shepherdspurse
Canada thistle	jimsonweed	smartweed
carpetweed	knotweed	sowthistle
catnip	lambsquarters	stinkweed
chicory	mallow	sumac
chickweed	marshelder	sunflower
cocklebur	mexicanweed	sweetclover
coffeeweed	morningglory	velvetleaf
cutleaf	musk thistle	Virginia creeper
eveningprimrose	mustard	wild carrot
creeping jenny	pennywort	wild garlic
croton	pepperweed	wild lettuce
dandelion	pigweed	wild onion
dock	plantain	wild parsnips
dogbane	pokeweed	wild radish

■ POST

Albaugh Amine 4 (2,4-D amine) *(Albaugh)*
◆ **Clean Crop Amine 4 (2,4-D amine)** *(Platte)*
Formula 40 (2,4-D mixed amine) *(Rhone-Poulenc)*
Hi-Dep (2,4-D mixed amine) *(PBI/Gordon)*
◆ **Opti-Amine (4) (2,4-D amine)** *(Helena)*
Solution (WS) (2,4D amine) *(Riverdale)*
Weed Rhap A-4D (2,4-D amine) *(Helena)*
Weedestroy AM-40 (2,4-D amine) *(Riverdale)*
Wilbur-Ellis Amine 4 (2,4-D amine) *(Wilbur-Ellis)*
   Rate: 0.33-0.5 lb. ae/A
      0.66-1 pt./A
      1 WS packet/5-7.5 A in 10-100 gal. water
   Time: Postemergence. Apply when sorghum is 6-15" high. Do not spray in boot, tasseling, or early dough stage.
   Remarks: Milo sorghum. If crop is taller than 8", use drop nozzles to keep spray off foliage. Varieties vary in tolerance to 2,4-D and some hybrids are quite sensitive; spray only tolerant varieties.
   State Restrictions: Wilbur-Ellis not registered in California.

– – – – – – – – – – – – – – –

Signal Word/Toxicity Class: Danger/I.
REI: 48 hr.

■ POST

Albaugh LV4 or LV6 Ester (2,4-D ester) *(Albaugh)*
◆ **Clean Crop Low Vol 4 or Low Vol 6 (2,4-D ester)** *(Platte)*
Esteron 99C (2,4-D LV ester) *(Rhone-Poulenc)*
Gordon's LV 400 (2,4-D ester) *(PBI/Gordon)*
Riverdale 6 Amine (2,4-D amine) *(Riverdale)*
Riverdale L.V. 4 or L.V. 6 (2,4-D ester) *(Riverdale)*
Riverside 2,4-D LV6 (2,4-D ester) *(Terra)*
Solve 2,4-D (2,4-D LV ester) *(Albaugh)*
Weed Rhap LV-6D (2,4-D ester) *(Helena)*
Wilbur-Ellis Lo Vol-4 or Lo Vol-6 (2,4-D ester) *(Wilbur-Ellis)*
   Rate: Average conditions:
      0.25 lb. ae/A
      0.5 pt. 4/A
      0.33 pt. 6/A
      Difficult weeds, dry conditions:
      0.25-0.38 lb. ae/A
      0.5-0.75 pt. 4/A
      0.33-0.5 pt. 6/A
   Time: Postemergence. Apply when sorghum is 5-15" high. Do not spray in boot, flowering, or early dough stage.
   Remarks: Grain sorghum (milo). If crop is taller than 8", use drop nozzles. Do not use with oil. Varieties vary in tolerance to 2,4-D and some hybrids are quite sensitive; spray only tolerant varieties.
   State Restrictions: Wilbur-Ellis not registered in California.

– – – – – – – – – – – – – – –

Signal Word/Toxicity Class: Danger/I (amine); Caution/III (ester).
REI: Danger—48 hr.; Caution—12 hr.

■ POST

Albaugh D-638 (2,4-D ester + acid) *(Albaugh)*
Weedone 638 (2,4-D ester + acid) *(Nufarm)*
   Rate: 0.4-0.5 lb. ae/A
      1-1.5 pt./A
   Time: Postemergence. Apply when crop is 6-15" tall.
   Remarks: Grain sorghum. High rate for perennial broadleaf weeds. Use drop nozzles if sorghum is taller than 8". Do not forage or feed fodder for 7 days following application.

– – – – – – – – – – – – – – –

Signal Word/Toxicity Class: Danger/I.
REI: 48 hr.

■ POST

◆ **Barrage or Barrage HF (EC) (2,4-D ester)** *(Helena)*
Savage (WSB) (2,4-D amine) *(Platte)*
   Rate: Grain sorghum (milo):
      3-10 fl. oz./A
      0.33-1 lb. WSB/A
   Time: Postemergence. Apply when crop is 6-15" tall. Do not spray in boot, flowering, or early dough stage.

   Rate: Forage sorghum:
      6-13 fl. oz./A
      0.25-0.5 lb. WSB/A
   Time: Postemergence. Apply when crop has at least 6 leaves, is well established, and 5-10" tall. Do not treat crop over 10" tall to maturity.

◆-new product • PP-preplant • PPI-preplant incorporated • PRE-preemergence • POST-postemergence • SEQ-sequential • ae-acid equivalent • ai-active ingredient • DF-dry flowable
E/EC-emulsifiable concentrate • F/FL-flowable • DG/G/WG-dispersable granule • L/LC-liquid • SP/WSP-soluble packet • W/WP-wettable powder • WSB-water soluble bag

Remarks: If grain sorghum is taller than 8", use drop nozzles. Tolerance to 2,4-D varies, consult local Agricultural Extension Service. Do not feed fodder or graze livestock and dairy animals 7 days following application. Do not graze meat animals within 3 days of slaughter (forage sorghum).
Crop Rotation: Refer to labels.

- - - - - - - - - - - - - - -

Signal Word/Toxicity Class: Danger/I (Savage); Caution/III (Barrage).
REI: Danger—48 hr.; Caution—12 hr.

■ POST
Riverside 2,4-D Amine 4 (2,4-D amine) *(Terra)*
Weedar 64 (4) (2,4-D amine) *(Nufarm)*
Rate: 0.5 lb. ae/A
1 pt. 4/A
Time: Postemergence. Apply when crop is 6-15" tall. Do not treat during boot, flowering, or dough stage.
Remarks: Grain sorghum (milo). Use drop nozzles to keep spray off crop foliage if sorghum is taller than 8". Do not forage or feed fodder for 7 days following application.

- - - - - - - - - - - - - - -

Signal Word/Toxicity Class: Danger/I.
REI: 48 hr.

■ POST
Riverside 2,4-D LV4 (2,4-D ester) *(Terra)*
Weedone LV4 (2,4-D solventless ester) *(Nufarm)*
Weedone Lo Vol 6 (2,4-D ester) *(Nufarm)*
Rate: 0.25-0.5 lb. ae/A
0.5-1 pt. 4/A
0.5-0.75 pt. 6/A
Time: Postemergence. Apply when crop is 6-15" tall. Do not apply during boot, flowering, or early dough stage.
Remarks: Grain sorghum (milo). If sorghum is over 8" tall, use drop nozzles. Varieties vary in tolerance to 2,4-D and some hybrids are quite sensitive; spray only tolerant varieties. Keep spray drift and vapors away from susceptible crops and ornamentals. Do not forage or feed fodder for 7 days following application. Refer to label for precautions.

- - - - - - - - - - - - - - -

Signal Word/Toxicity Class: Caution/III.
REI: 12 hr.

■ POST
◆ **Saber (2,4-D amine)** *(Platte)*
Rate: Grain sorghum (milo):
0.12-0.5 lb. ae/A
0.25-1 pt./A
Time: Postemergence. Apply after crop is 4-8" tall, but before 15" tall. Do not treat in boot, flowering, or early dough stage.

Rate: Forage sorghum:
0.25-0.5 lb. ae/A
0.5-1 pt./A
Time: Postemergence. Apply when crop has at least 6 leaves, is well established, and 5-10" tall. Do not treat crop over 10" tall to maturity.
Remarks: If grain sorghum is taller than 8", use drop nozzles to keep spray off foliage. Tolerance to 2,4-D varies, consult local Agricultural Extension Service. Do not feed fodder or graze livestock and dairy animals 7 days following application. Do not graze meat animals within 3 days of slaughter (forage sorghum).

- - - - - - - - - - - - - - -

Signal Word/Toxicity Class: Danger/I.
REI: 48 hr.

■ POST
Salvo (2,4-D LV ester) *(Platte)*
Rate: 0.125-0.25 lb. ae/A
0.2-0.4 pt./A
Time: Postemergence.
Remarks: Milo sorghum. Use low rate for succulent, nonresistant annual broadleaf weeds. Use drop nozzles if crop is taller than 10".

- - - - - - - - - - - - - - -

Signal Word/Toxicity Class: Caution/III.
REI: 12 hr.

2,4-D COMBINATIONS

■ POST
◆ **Brash (2.87 lb./gal. 2,4-D & 1 lb./gal. dicamba)** *(Terra)*
Rate: 0.5 lb. ai/A
1 pt./A

Time: Postemergence: Apply between 3-5 leaf stage (4-8" tall).
Weeds: Annual and perennial weeds:

annual sunflower	kochia	silverleaf
Carolina horsenettle*	prostrate pigweed	nightshade*
common cocklebur	redroot pigweed	smooth pigweed
field bindweed*	rough pigweed	tall morningglory
ivyleaf morningglory	Russian thistle	tumble pigweed

* Perennial suppression

Remarks: Grain sorghum (milo). Do not make more than 1 application per growing season. Do not use if potential for injury is not acceptable. Do not graze or feed treated forage or silage prior to mature grain stage.
Tank Mixes: Atrazine; refer to label for restrictions and precautions.

- - - - - - - - - - - - - - -

Signal Word/Toxicity Class: Danger/I.
REI: 48 hr.

DICAMBA

■ PP, POST
Banvel (WS) (DMA salt of dicamba) *(BASF)*
Clarity (4L) (dicamba-DGA) *(BASF)*
◆ **Sterling (WS) (DMA salt of dicamba)** *(Terra)*
Rate: 0.25 lb. ai/A
0.5 pt. WS/A
Time: Preplant: Apply at least 15 days before planting. Postemergence: Apply after spike stage of sorghum but before sorghum is 15" tall. For best results, apply when sorghum is in 3-5 leaf stage and weeds are less than 3" tall. Preharvest: Apply any time after sorghum has reached soft dough stage.
Weeds: Broadleaf weeds:

Canada thistle	kochia	sunflower
field bindweed	pigweed	velvetleaf

Remarks: Grain sorghum (milo). Do not apply to sorghum grow for seed production. Use drop nozzles if sorghum is taller than 8". For preharvest, agriculturally approved surfactant can be added to improve performance. Do not make more than 1 application per growing season. Do not apply through any type of irrigation system Do not graze or feed treated sorghum forage or silage prior to mature grain stage.
Days To Harvest: Preharvest—30.
Tank Mixes: Atrazine, Buctril.
State Restrictions: Preharvest for use in Oklahoma, Texas.

- - - - - - - - - - - - - - -

Signal Word/Toxicity Class: Warning/II (Banvel, Sterling); Caution (Clarity).
REI: 24 hr.

DICAMBA & ATRAZINE (Premixes)

Excellent control of broadleaf weeds plus control of some perennial broadleaf weeds. Reduced rate of atrazine reduces risk of carryover. Restricted Use Pesticide due to ground and surface water concerns.

■ PP, PRE, POST
Marksman (FL) (1.1 lb./gal. dicamba & 2.1 lb./gal. atrazine) *(BASF)*
◆ **Sterling Plus (FL) (1.1 lb./gal. dicamba & 2.1 lb./gal. atrazine)** *(Terra)*
Rate: 0.6-0.8 lb. ai/A
1.5-2 pt. FL/A
Time: Preplant, preemergence: Apply when grain sorghum (milo) is between 2-5 leaf stage (about 2-8" tall). Postemergence: Application must be made before sorghum reaches 8" tall.
Weeds: Broadleaf weeds:

alfalfa	giant ragweed	puncturevine
annual clovers	(buffaloweed)	redroot pigweed
black nightshade	green smartweed	(carelessweed)
broadleaf dock	hedge bindweed	rough pigweed
(bitterdock)	hemp dogbane	Russian thistle
burcucumber	ivyleaf morningglory	sicklepod
Canada thistle	Jerusalem artichoke	smooth pigweed
Carolina horsenettle	jimsonweed	spanishneedles
common chickweed	knotweed	swamp smartweed
common cocklebur	kochia	tall morningglory
common dandelion	ladysthumb	tansymustard
common	lambsquarters*	tumble pigweed
lambsquarters	lespedeza	velvetleaf
common mallow	Pennsylvania	Venice mallow
common milkweed	smartweed	vetch
common purslane	perennial clovers	volunteer sunflower
common ragweed	pigweed*	wild buckwheat
common sunflower	prickly sida	wild cucumber
(wild)	(teaweed)	wild mustard
curly dock	prostrate pigweed	yellowtop mustard
field bindweed	prostrate spurge	

* Triazine resistant weeds

5

Other Field Crops

NOTICE The information on these pages is for preliminary planning — not a guide for use. Be sure to follow the manufacturer's directions, notwithstanding information contained here.   For personal protective equipment and EPA registration numbers, please turn to page 70.

Sorghum

Remarks: Grain sorghum (milo). Do not apply to sorghum grown for seed production. Make only 1 application per growing season. May be harvested or grazed for feed once crop has reached mature grain stage. Do not apply through any type of irrigation system.

Days To Harvest: 30.

Crop Rotation: If applied after June 10, do not rotate to any crop except corn or sorghum until the following year or injury may occur.

Tank Mixes: Atrazine; refer to label for use directions and precautions.

- - - - - - - - - - - - - - -

Signal Word/Toxicity Class: Caution.
REI: 48 hr.

DIMETHENAMID & ATRAZINE (Premixes)

Not for use on sweet or forage sorghum. Restricted Use Pesticide due to ground and surface water concerns.

■ PP, PPI, PRE

Guardsman (2.33 lb./gal. dimethenamid & 2.67 lb./gal. atrazine) *(BASF)*
◆ Leadoff (2.33 lb./gal. dimethenamid & 2.67 lb./gal. atrazine) *(DuPont)*

Rate: 1.8-3.2 lb. ai/A
2.5-5 pt./A

Time: Preplant incorporated, preplant surface, preemergence.

Weeds: Broadleaf weeds:

annual morningglory	Florida pusley	prostrate pigweed
black nightshade	giant ragweed	redroot pigweed
carpetweed	hairy nightshade	smartweed
cocklebur	jimsonweed	smooth pigweed
common purslane	kochia	spotted spurge
common ragweed	lambsquarters	tumble pigweed
eastern black	mustard	velvetleaf
nightshade	nodding spurge	waterhemp
eclipta*	Palmer amaranth	wild buckwheat

Grasses and sedges:

barnyardgrass	large crabgrass	Texas Panicum*
broadleaf signalgrass	red rice	wild oat
fall panicum	rice flatsedge	wild proso millet*
giant foxtail	sandbur*	witchgrass
goosegrass	shattercane*	woolly cupgrass*
green foxtail	smooth crabgrass	yellow foxtail
johnsongrass	southwestern	yellow nutsedge
(seedling)	cupgrass	

* Suppression

Remarks: Grain sorghum. Apply only to seed properly treated with approved chloroacetamide herbicide safener. Rates vary by soil type. For sorghum produced under irrigation, use minimum 3.5 pt./A. Not for use on coarse-textured soils.

Days To Harvest: Grain, fodder—80; forage grazing/feeding—60.

Crop Rotation: In case of crop failure, field can be replanted to corn or sorghum. Corn, cotton, peanuts, sorghum, or soybeans may be planted the year after application. Injury may occur to soybeans planted on soils having a calcareous surface layer. Do not plant dry beans, sugar beets, tobacco, vegetables, spring-seeded small grains, or small-seeded legumes and grasses the year following application.

Tank Mixes: Atrazine, Banvel, Basagran, Buctril, 2,4-D, Fallow Master, glyphosate, Laddok S-12, Landmaster BW, Marksman, Milo-Pro, paraquat; and Weedmaster, refer to labels for directions and precautions.

State Restrictions: Not for use in Long Island, New York.

- - - - - - - - - - - - - - -

Signal Word/Toxicity Class: Warning/II.
REI: 12 hr.

DIQUAT DIBROMIDE

◆ Diquat *(ZENECA)*

Rate: 0.375-0.5 lb. ai/A
1.5-2 pt./A

Time: Preharvest desiccation broadcast. Apply when seeds have no more than 30% moisture.

Weeds: Broadleaf weeds and grasses.

Remarks: Grain sorghum. Seed crop only. Apply by ground or air. Use high rate when weeds are large or dense. Do not use seed from treated plants for food, feed, or oil purposes. Do not apply through any type of irrigation system. Do not graze or feed treated forage to livestock. Refer to label for use restrictions and precautions.

Days To Harvest: 1-2 weeks.

- - - - - - - - - - - - - - -

Signal Word/Toxicity Class: Warning/II.
REI: 24 hr.

Direx — see diuron

DIURON

■ POST

Direx 4L or 80DF *(Griffin)*
◆ Diuron 80 WDG *(Platte)*
Drexel Diuron 4L or 80 *(Drexel)*
Karmex DF *(Griffin)*
Riverside Diuron 80DF *(Terra)*

Rate: 0.2-0.4 lb. ai/A
0.2-0.4 qt. 4L/A
0.25-0.5 lb. 80, DF, 80DF/A

Time: Postemergence. Apply as directed broadcast or band treatment after sorghum is 15" tall and weeds 2-4".

Weeds: Broadleaf weeds:

annual morningglory	pigweed	ragweed
lambsquarters	purslane	

Grasses:

barnyardgrass	crabgrass

Remarks: Grain sorghum. Do not spray over top of sorghum. Add 1 pt. surfactant/25 gal. spray. Do not use on sand as crop injury may result.

Crop Rotation: Do not replant treated areas to crops other than cotton or corn within 4 months following band treatment and 6 months following broadcast treatment as crop injury may result.

State Restrictions: For use in Southwestern states.

- - - - - - - - - - - - - - -

Signal Word/Toxicity Class: Caution/III.
REI: 12 hr.

Dual — see *S*-metolachlor

Esteron 99C — see 2,4-D

Formula 40 — see 2,4-D

FRONTIER

Chloroacetamide herbicide that controls many annual grasses, several broadleaf weeds, and nutsedge. Not registered for use on sweet or forage sorghum.

■ PP, PPI, PRE

Frontier 6.0 (dimethenamid) *(BASF)*

Rate: 0.94-1.5 lb. ai/A
20-32 fl. oz. 6.0/A

Time: Preplant (surface or incorporated), preemergence, single or split application.

Weeds: Broadleaf weeds:

carpetweed	nightshade	spurge
common purslane	pigweed	waterhemp
Florida pusley		

Grasses and sedges:

barnyardgrass	johnsongrass	southwestern
broadleaf signalgrass	(seedling)	cupgrass
fall panicum	large crabgrass	Texas panicum
giant foxtail	rice flatsedge	yellow foxtail
goosegrass	smooth crabgrass	yellow nutsedge
green foxtail		

Remarks: Grain sorghum. Apply only to fields where sorghum seed has been treated with an approved chloroacetamide herbicide safener. Rate varies by soil type and organic matter. Do not apply through any type of irrigation system. Forage may be grazed or fed to livestock 60 or more days after application; grain and fodder may be fed 80 or more days after application.

Days To Harvest: 80.

Tank Mixes: Atrazine, Banvel, Clarity, Cyclone CF, 2,4-D, Fallow Master, Gramoxone Extra, glyphosate, Landmaster BW, Milo-Pro.

- - - - - - - - - - - - - - -

Signal Word/Toxicity Class: Warning/II.
REI: 12 hr.

Glyfos or Glyfos X-tra — see glyphosate

◆-new product • PP-preplant • PPI-preplant incorporated • PRE-preemergence • POST-postemergence • SEQ-sequential • ae-acid equivalent • ai-active ingredient • DF-dry flowable E/EC-emulsifiable concentrate • F/FL-flowable • DG/G/WG-dispersable granule • L/LC-liquid • SP/WSP-soluble packet • W/WP-wettable powder • WSB-water soluble bag

GLYPHOSATE

■ **PP, PRE**

◆ **Credit (4WS)** *(Nufarm)*
◆ **Glyfos or Glyfos X-tra (4WS)** *(Cheminova)*
Rattler (4WS) *(Helena)*
Roundup Custom (5.4WS) *(Monsanto)*
Roundup Original, Original RT, Ultra, Ultra RT (4WS) *(Monsanto)*

Rate: Annual weeds:
0.38-1.5 lb. ai/A
0.56-2.25 pt. 5.4WS/A
0.75-3 pt. 4WS/A
Perennial weeds:
0.5-5 lb. ai/A
0.75-7.5 pt. 5.4WS/A
1-10 pt. 4WS/A

Time: Preplant, preemergence, at-planting, wiper applications, spot treatment, postharvest. For spot treatment, apply before heading.

Weeds: Emerged annual and perennial broadleaf weeds:

Canada thistle	hemp dogbane	Pennsylvania
curly dock	milkweed	smartweed
field bindweed		

Grasses:

bermudagrass	fescues	paragrass
fall panicum	johnsongrass	quackgrass

Remarks: Milo sorghum. Rate varies by weed height and species. Do not add surfactant to Roundup Ultra or Ultra RT. Do not allow glyphosate to contact desirable plants. For spot treatment, do not treat more than 10% total area to be harvested. Do not use roller applicators for wiper application. Do not apply through any type of irrigation system. Do not ensile treated vegetation or feed or graze treated fodder. Refer to label for directions, precautions and restrictions.

Days To Harvest: Wiper application—40 days; postharvest/feeding—8 weeks.

Tank Mixes: Postharvest: 2,4-D, dicamba. Tank mixes not registered in California by air.

State Restrictions: Roundup RT for use in Colorado, Idaho, Montana, North Dakota, South Dakota, Utah, Wyoming, and in specific counties only in Kansas, Minnesota, Nebraska, Nevada, Oklahoma, Oregon, and Washington; refer to label for restrictions. Glyfos is not registered for use in California. Glyfos X-tra is not registered for use in mistblowers in California or Arizona.

– – – – – – – – – – – – – – –

Signal Word/Toxicity Class: Varies by formulation.
REI: Warning—12 hr.; Caution—4 hr.

Gramoxone Extra — see paraquat

Guardsman — see dimethenamid & atrazine

HALOSULFURON-METHYL

Selective herbicide for control of annual broadleaf weeds and nutsedge.

■ **POST**

Permit *(Monsanto)*

Rate: 0.032-0.063 lb. ai/A
0.66-1.33 oz./A

Time: Postemergence. Apply from 2-leaf through lay-by stage (before grain head emergence).

Weeds: Broadleaf weeds:

burcucumber*	giant ragweed	pigweed
common cocklebur	kochia*	smartweed
common ragweed	lambsquarters	velvetleaf
common sunflower	morningglory*	Venice mallow

Sedges:

purple nutsedge	yellow nutsedge

* Suppression

Remarks: Grain sorghum. Recommended for use following a preemergence application of Bullet, Harness, Harness Xtra, Micro-Tech, Partner.

Days To Harvest: Grazing or harvest—30 days.

Crop Rotation: Wheat—3 months after last application; soybeans—10 months after last application. Milo can be replanted same growing season provided maximum rate of 0.157 lb. ai/A per season not exceeded.

– – – – – – – – – – – – – – –

Signal Word/Toxicity Class: Caution/III.
REI: 12 hr.

Hi-Dep — see 2,4-D

Karmex — see diurons

LADDOK S-12 (Premix)

Restricted Use Pesticide due to groundwater concerns.

■ **POST**

Laddok S-12 (5L) (2.5 lb./gal. bentazon & 2.5 lb./gal. atrazine) *(BASF)*

Rate: 0.83-1.45 lb. ai/A
1.33-2.33 pt. 5L/A

Time: Early postemergence.

Weeds: Broadleaf weeds:

annual morningglory	giant ragweed	smooth pigweed
beggarticks	jimsonweed	spurred anoda
bristly starbur	kochia	tall waterhemp
Canada thistle*	ladysthumb	teaweed
cocklebur	Pennsylvania	velvetleaf
common	smartweed	Venice mallow
lambsquarters	prickly sida	wild buckwheat
common ragweed	redroot pigweed	wild mustard
common waterhemp	smallflower	wild sunflower
dayflower	morningglory	
field bindweed*		

Sedges:

yellow nutsedge*

* Refer to label for special directions

Remarks: Rate depends on leaf stage and weed height. Urea-ammonium nitrate (UAN) solution may be added in place of oil concentrate for control of above annuals. If UAN solution is not used, oil concentrate should be added to spray tank. Oil concentrate should be used if perennials, yellow nutsedge, Canada thistle, or field bindweed are present. Do not graze treated area or feed treated forage to livestock for 21 days following application.

Crop Rotation: Do not plant sugar beets or sunflowers the season following application. Do not plant oats the season following application in soils with a calcareous surface layer. Intermountain Area: plant only corn or sorghum the year following application.

Tank Mixes: Atrazine.
State Restrictions: Not for use in California.

– – – – – – – – – – – – – – –

Signal Word/Toxicity Class: Danger/I.
REI: 48 hr.

LARIAT (Premix)

Restricted Use Pesticide.

■ **PPI, PRE**

Lariat (2.5 lb./gal. alachlor & 1.5 lb./gal. atrazine) *(Monsanto)*

Rate: 2.5-5 lb. ai/A
2.5-5 qt./A

Time: Early preplant, preplant incorporated, preemergence.

Weeds: Broadleaf weeds:

annual morningglory	Florida pusley	pigweed
black nightshade	hairy nightshade	purslane
carpetweed	jimsonweed	smartweed
cocklebur	kochia	teaweed
common ragweed	lambsquarters	(spiny sida)
Florida beggarweed	mustard	velvetleaf

Grasses and sedges:

barnyardgrass	goosegrass	red sprangletop
broadleaf signalgrass	green foxtail	sandbur
browntop panicum	johnsongrass	witchgrass
crabgrass	(seedling)	yellow foxtail
fall panicum	red rice	yellow nutsedge
giant foxtail		

Remarks: Milo sorghum. Rate varies by soil type. Apply to sorghum planted with seed that has been properly treated with Screen seed protectant.

Crop Rotation: Plant only corn, peanuts, sorghum (milo), or soybeans the year following the use of this mixture. If soybeans are to be planted, there is a possibility of crop injury due to carryover of atrazine.

– – – – – – – – – – – – – – –

Signal Word/Toxicity Class: Warning/II.
REI: 12 hr.

Lasso — see alachlor

5

Other Field Crops

Sorghum

Leadoff — see dimethenamid & atrazine

LINURON

■ POST

Lorox DF *(Griffin)*
Rate: 0.5-1 lb. ai/A
1-2 lb. DF/A
Time: Postemergence. Apply single application as directed spray.
Weeds: Broadleaf weeds:

buttonweed	pigweed	smartweed
lambsquarters	ragweed	

Grasses:

barnyardgrass	crabgrass	foxtail

Remarks: Rate varies by crop and weed height. Add 1 pt. surfactant/25 gal. spray mixture. Apply only when there is sufficient height differential to allow thorough coverage of weeds without contact to upper leaves or whorl of sorghum. Do not graze or feed plants to livestock within 3 months of treatment. Do not apply through any type of irrigation system.
Crop Rotation: Do not follow treated sorghum with any fall crop, nor with sugar beets, tobacco, vegetables, or potatoes in rotation. Prior to replanting, thorough seedbed preparation including fall or spring plowing is recommended. Sorghum or field corn may be replanted within 4 months; after 4 months any crop may be planted.
Tank Mixes: For preemergence application, may be tank mixed with registered herbicides.

- - - - - - - - - - - - - -

Signal Word/Toxicity Class: Caution.
REI: 24 hr.

Marksman — see dicamba & atrazine

MCPA

■ POST

◆ **Clean Crop MCP 2 Sodium (sodium salt)** *(Platte)*
Rate: 0.75 lb. ae/A
3 pt./A
Time: Postemergence. Apply when sorghum is 6-12" tall but before the boot stage, and weeds are 5" tall or weed branches are 5" long.
Weeds: Broadleaf weeds such as:

lambsquarters	pigweed	shepherdspurse
narrowleaf goosefoot	purslane	

Remarks: Grain sorghum. Hybrids vary in tolerance to MCPA. Consult seed company or your Agricultural Experiment Station or Extension Service Weed Specialist for guidance.

- - - - - - - - - - - - - -

Signal Word/Toxicity Class: Danger/I.
REI: 48 hr.

S-METOLACHLOR

■ PP, PPI, PRE

Dual MAGNUM or Dual II MAGNUM (EC) *(Novartis)*
Rate: Preplant incorporated, preemergence:
1-1.67 pt. EC/A
Preplant surface:
1.33-1.67 pt. EC/A
Time: Preplant incorporated, preplant surface, preemergence. For early preplant surface, apply as split application 30-45 days before planting; applications less than 30 days before planting may be either split or single treatment.
Weeds: Broadleaf weeds:

carpetweed	eclipta*	galinsoga
common purslane*	Florida beggarweed*	hairy nightshade*
eastern black	Florida pusley	pigweed
nightshade		

Grasses and sedges:

barnyardgrass	goosegrass	shattercane*
(watergrass)	green foxtail	signalgrass
crabgrass	johnsongrass	southwestern cupgrass
crowfootgrass	(seedling)*	volunteer sorghum*
fall panicum	prairie cupgrass	witchgrass
foxtail millet	red rice	yellow foxtail
giant foxtail	sandbur*	yellow nutsedge

* Suppression

Remarks: Grain, forage sorghum. Must be used with Concep-treated seed. Rate varies by soil type and organic matter. Do not use on sorghum grown under dry mulch tillage. In case of crop failure, any crop on label may be replanted immediately. Do not make second broadcast application. If original application was banded and second crop is planted in untreated row middles, second banded treatment may be applied.
Crop Rotation: Alfalfa—4 months; barley, oats, rye, wheat—4¹/₂ months; tomatoes—6 months; clover—9 months; any labeled crop in addition to barley, buckwheat, cabbage, milo, nuts, oats, peppers, rice, root crops, rye, stone fruits, tobacco, and wheat may be planted in the spring following treatment (including lay-by or multiple treatments applied previous season); all other rotational crops may be planted 12 months after application.
Tank Mixes: AAtrex, Gramoxone Extra, Landmaster BW, Roundup Ultra.
State Restrictions: Do not use in Nassau County or Suffolk County, New York. Preplant surface: For minimum-tillage or no-till systems only in Colorado, Illinois, Iowa, Kansas, Missouri, Nebraska, South Dakota.

- - - - - - - - - - - - - -

Signal Word/Toxicity Class: Caution/III.
REI: 24 hr.

Moxy — see bromoxynil

Moxy + atrazine — see bromoxynil + atrazine

Opti-amine — see 2,4-D

Paramount — see quinclorac

PARAQUAT

Restricted Use Pesticide. Toxic to wildlife.

■ PP, PRE, POST

Cyclone (2L or 3L) or Gramoxone Extra (2.5L) *(ZENECA)*
Rate: 0.5-1 lb. ai/A
2-4 pt. 2L/A
1.5-3 pt. 2.5L/A
1.25-2.5 pt. 3L/A
Time: Preplant, preemergence.
Weeds: Annual broadleaf weeds and grasses; suppression of perennials.
Remarks: Grain sorghum. Add nonionic surfactant or crop oil concentrate. Seedbeds should be formed as far ahead of planting and treatment as possible to permit maximum weed and grass emergence. Seeding should be done with a minimum amount of soil disturbance. Weeds and grasses emerging after application will not be controlled; crops emerged at time of application will be killed. Refer to label for use directions, restrictions, and precautions.
Tank Mixes: Atrazine, Banvel, Bladex, Canopy, Command, 2,4-D ester, Extrazine, Harmony Extra, Lariat, linuron, Marksman, metribuzin, Princep.

- - - - - - - - - - - - - -

Rate: 0.25-0.5 lb. ai/A
1-2 pt. 2L/A
0.8-1.5 pt. 2.5 L/A
0.6-1.3 pt. 3L/A
Time: Postemergence directed. Apply when sorghum is naturally standing at least 12" tall.
Weeds: Emerged grasses and weeds 3" or less in height.
Remarks: Grain sorghum. Adjust spray so that no more than lower 3" of plant is contacted by spray. Refer to label for use directions, restrictions, and precautions.
Tank Mixes: Atrazine, Banvel, Bladex, Canopy, Command, 2,4-D ester, Extrazine, Harmony Extra, Lariat, linuron, Marksman, metribuzin, Princep.

- - - - - - - - - - - - - -

Signal Word/Toxicity Class: Danger-Poison/I.
REI: 12 hr. (except harvest aid/desiccation 24 hr.).

PEAK

Controls many broadleaf weeds, including triazine-resistant biotypes, by inhibiting a biochemical process which produces certain essential amino acids necessary for plant growth. The inhibited enzyme system is acetolactate synthase (ALS). Peak is a water-dispersible granule; each bag of Peak contains 5 water-soluble packets.

■ PRE, POST

Peak (WDG) (prosulfuron) *(Novartis)*

◆-new product • PP-preplant • PPI-preplant incorporated • PRE-preemergence • POST-postemergence • SEQ-sequential • ae-acid equivalent • ai-active ingredient • DF-dry flowable
E/EC-emulsifiable concentrate • F/FL-flowable • DG/G/WG-dispersable granule • L/LC-liquid • SP/WSP-soluble packet • W/WP-wettable powder • WSB-water soluble bag

Rate: Low rate:
0.5 oz. WDG/A (1 WS packet/6A)
Standard rate:
0.75 oz. WDG/A (1 WS packet/4A)
Enhanced rate:
1 oz. WDG/A (1 WS packet/3A)

Time: Preemergence standard and enhanced rates (Kansas, Nebraska). Postemergence all rates (over-the-top, directed). Apply to actively growing sorghum between 5-30" in height and prior to head emergence; applications after sorghum is 20" should be directed or semi-directed using drop nozzles.

Weeds: Preemergence:

buffalobur	hemp sesbania*	puncturevine
carpetweed	hophornbeam	redroot pigweed
common cocklebur*	copperleaf	sicklepod
common	horse purslane	smallflower
lambsquarters	ivyleaf	morningglory
common purslane	morningglory*	smooth pigweed
common ragweed	kochia	tall morningglory*
common sunflower	Palmer amaranth	tall waterhemp
common waterhemp	Pennsylvania	velvetleaf*
devilsclaw	smartweed	wild mustard
giant ragweed	pitted morningglory*	wild radish
hairy buttercup	prickly sida	

Postemergence:

blue mustard	Florida beggarweed	prickly sida*
buffalobur	Florida pusley	puncturevine
Canada thistle*	giant ragweed	redroot pigweed
coast fiddleneck	hairy buttercup	Russian thistle
common chickweed*	hedge bindweed	shepherdspurse
common cocklebur	hemp sesbania	sicklepod
common	henbit*	smooth pigweed
lambsquarters	horseweed	tall morningglory*
common mallow*	ivyleaf morningglory	tall waterhemp
common ragweed	jimsonweed	tansymustard
common sunflower	kochia	tumble mustard
common waterhemp	ladysthumb	tumble pigweed
cutleaf	mayweed chamomile	velvetleaf
eveningprimrose	Palmer amaranth	Venice mallow
devilsclaw	Pennsylvania	wild buckwheat
field bindweed*	smartweed	wild garlic
field pennycress	pitted morningglory	wild mustard
flixweed	prickly lettuce	wild radish

* Suppression

Remarks: Grain (milo) sorghum. Rate varies by weed height. Always add crop oil concentrate or nonionic surfactant. Do not apply to sorghum under stress. Applications (preemergence or postemergence) to sorghum growing under stress caused by minor element deficiency may result in crop injury; application to fields where iron chlorosis occurs in sorghum may result in enhanced iron chlorosis symptoms. Can be applied to all grain sorghum hybrids except those susceptible to iron chlorosis grown in areas where insufficient iron is available in soil. Do not apply preemergence if an organophosphate insecticide is applied to sorghum at planting time. Do not make a foliar or soil application of any organophosphate insecticide within 15 days before or 10 days after Peak application. If treated crop is lost due to a natural catastrophe, normal field corn or grain sorghum may be replanted at least 4 weeks after application, IR or IMR corn hybrid and small grain cereal crops may be replanted immediately. Do not apply through any type of irrigation system.

Days To Harvest: Silage—40; grain—60; grazing/feeding forage to livestock—30.

Crop Rotation: IR/IMR Corn, small grains (wheat, barley, oats, rye, proso millet, triticale)—anytime; normal field corn, grain sorghum—4 weeks; rice, popcorn, sweet corn—24 months; beans (dry, green), cabbage, canola, cotton, flax, forage grasses, peanuts, peas, potatoes, soybeans, tobacco, tomatoes—10 months; alfalfa, clover, lentils—22 months; leeks, onion, sunflower, sugar beets and all other crops—24 months. Refer to label for geographic restrictions.

State Restrictions: Not for use in San Luis Valley of Colorado. In Washington abide by all sulfonylurea aerial application rulings by Washington Department of Agriculture. Preemergence application for Kansas, Nebraska only.

– – – – – – – – – – – – – –

Signal Word/Toxicity Class: Caution.
REI: 12 hr.

PENDIMETHALIN

■ POST

Pentagon DG *(American Cyanamid)*
Prowl 3.3 EC *(American Cyanamid)*

Rate: 0.5-1.5 lb. ai/A
1.2-3.6 pt. 3.3 EC/A
0.85-2.5 lb. DG/A

Time: Postemergence incorporated (Culti-Spray), early postemergence. Apply from 4" growth stage to as late as last cultivation (lay-by). Do not apply preplant incorporated or preemergence.

Weeds: Broadleaf weeds:

annual spurge	lambsquarters	pigweed
carpetweed	Pennsylvania	purslane
Florida pusley	smartweed	velvetleaf
kochia		

Grasses:

barnyardgrass	goosegrass	signalgrass
crabgrass	green foxtail	wild proso millet*
crowfootgrass	johnsongrass	witchgrass
field sandbur	shattercane*	yellow foxtail
giant foxtail		

*Culti-Spray only

Remarks: Grain sorghum. Rate varies by soil type. Cultivate and destroy all emerged weeds prior to application. Do not apply more than once per season. Do not graze or feed treated forage to livestock for 21 days after application.

Crop Rotation: Winter wheat and winter barley can be planted in the fall 4 months after application or 3 months after Culti-Spray application in irrigated fields. Crop must be grown to maturity and harvested before planting wheat or barley. Treated land can be planted to other crops the following year (see label for beet and spinach restrictions).

Tank Mixes: With atrazine in states east of the Mississippi, Arkansas, east Texas, Louisiana, and bootheel of Missouri.

– – – – – – – – – – – – – –

Signal Word/Toxicity Class: Caution.
REI: 24 hr.

Pentagon — see pendimethalin

Permit — see halosulfuron-methyl

Prowl — see pendimethalin

QUINCLORAC

■ PP, POST

◆ Paramount (DF) *(BASF)*

Rate: Preplant:
3-5.3 oz. DF/A
Postemergence:
3-8 oz. DF/A

Time: Preplant, postemergence. Apply to actively growing weeds. Apply preplant to bindweed after harvesting but before first killing frost. For long-term control (3 yr. program), apply 5.3 oz. DF/A the first year and 3-5.3 oz. DF/A in subsequent years.

Weeds: Broadleaf weeds:

bedstraw	dandelion*	morningglory
Canada thistle*	field bindweed	Russian thistle*
clover	giant ragweed*	velvetleaf*
common	hedge bindweed	volunteer flax
lambsquarters*	kochia*	wild sunflower*
common ragweed*		

Grasses:

barnyardgrass	giant foxtail	large crabgrass
broadleaf signalgrass	green foxtail	yellow foxtail

* Suppression

Remarks: Grain sorghum. Must use additive. Do not apply more than 16 oz. DF/A per calendar year. Do not apply through any type of irrigation system. Refer to label for use directions and restrictions.

Crop Rotation: In case of crop failure, wheat and sorghum may be replanted immediately; other crops—10 months after application; alfalfa, clover, flax, lentils, peas, sugar beets—24 months and successful field bioassay.

Tank Mixes: Atrazine (postemergence grass control), Clarity, 2,4-D, Fallowmaster, Landmaster, Peak, Roundup RT, Roundup Ultra.

State Restrictions: For use in Colorado, Idaho, Kansas, Montana, Nebraska, North Dakota, Oregon, South Dakota, Utah, Washington, Wyoming.

– – – – – – – – – – – – – –

Signal Word/Toxicity Class: Caution.
REI: 12 hr.

5

Other Field Crops

RAMROD

■ PRE

Ramrod 4L or 20G (propachlor) *(Monsanto)*

Rate: 4-5 lb. ai/A
4-5 qt. 4L/A
20-25 lb. 20G/A
Time: Preemergence.
Weeds: Broadleaf weeds:

carpetweed	groundsel	purslane
common ragweed	lambsquarters	smartweed
Florida pusley	pigweed	wild buckwheat

Grasses:

annual ryegrass	crabgrass	goosegrass
barnyardgrass	fall panicum	green foxtail
broadleaf signalgrass	giant foxtail	yellow foxtail

Remarks: Grain sorghum (milo). Do not graze or feed sorghum from treated fields to dairy animals.
Tank Mixes: Atrazine, propazine.

– – – – – – – – – – – – – – –

Signal Word/Toxicity Class: Danger/I.
REI: 48 hr.

RAMROD/ATRAZINE (Premix)

Restricted Use Pesticide.

■ PRE

Ramrod/Atrazine 4L or DF (3 lb./gal. propachlor & 1 lb./gal. atrazine) *(Monsanto)*

Rate: 3.5-5.5 lb. ai/A
3-5.5 qt. 4L/A
5.5-8.6 lb. DF/A
Time: Preemergence.
Weeds: Broadleaf weeds:

annual morningglory*	kochia	purslane
carpetweed	jimsonweed*	ragweed
cocklebur*	lambsquarters	smartweed
Florida pusley	mustard	velvetleaf*
groundsel	nightshade	wild buckwheat
	pigweed	

Grasses:

annual ryegrass	crabgrass	goosegrass
barnyardgrass	fall panicum	green foxtail
broadleaf signalgrass*	giant foxtail	yellow foxtail

Suppression

Remarks: Grain sorghum (milo). Do not graze or feed sorghum (milo) forage or silage from treated fields to dairy animals.
Crop Rotation: Corn, sorghum, or soybeans can be planted the year following application. If soybeans or other nonlabeled crops are planted the following year, there is a possibility of crop injury due to carryover of atrazine.

– – – – – – – – – – – – – – –

Signal Word/Toxicity Class: Danger/I (DF); Warning/II (4L).
REI: 48 hr.

Rattler — see glyphosate

Roundup — see glyphosate

Saber — see 2,4-D

Salvo — see 2,4-D

Savage — see 2,4-D

SCYTHE

◆ **Scythe (pelargonic acid)** *(Mycogen)*
Rate: 4-13 fl. oz./1 gal. spray solution
Time: Apply to actively growing weeds prior to crop emergence.
Weeds: Annual and perennial broadleaf weeds and grasses.

Remarks: Apply in minimum 75 gal. spray solution/A or spray-to-wet. Do not apply by air or through any type of irrigation system. Refer to label for directions and precautions.
Tank Mixes: Glyphosate and other foliar and residual herbicides.

– – – – – – – – – – – – – – –

Signal Word/Toxicity Class: Warning/II.
REI: 24 hr.

SHOTGUN (Premix)

Restricted Use Pesticide due to ground and surface water concerns. Toxic to aquatic invertebrates.

■ POST

Shotgun (FL) (2.25 lb./gal. atrazine & 1 lb./gal. 2,4-D) *(Platte)*

Rate: 0.563 lb. ai atrazine/A
0.25 lb. ae 2,4-D/A
2 pt. FL/A
Time: Postemergence. Apply broadcast from spike to 4-leaf or up to 8"; use drop nozzles for later application up to limit of 12".
Weeds: Broadleaf weeds:

black nightshade	giant ragweed	sowthistle
buffalobur	ivyleaf	spanishneedles
cocklebur	morningglory	sunflower
common lambsquarters	jimsonweed	tall morningglory
	mustard	velvetleaf
common ragweed	Pennsylvania	Venice mallow
common waterhemp	smartweed	vetch
dandelion	pennycress	wild buckwheat
dock	(fanweed)	wild lettuce
eastern black nightshade	redroot pigweed	wild mustard

Grasses (suppression):

downy brome	large crabgrass	witchgrass
green foxtail	wild oat	yellow foxtail
hairy crabgrass		

Remarks: Several states have maximum rates and other limitations that are more restrictive than the product label. Do not make more than 1 application per growing season. Do not graze or feed treated forage for 21 days following application.
Crop Rotation: If applied after June 10 or in High Plains/Intermountain West, only corn or sorghum can be planted the following year. Do not plant sugar beets, tobacco, vegetables (including dry beans), spring-seeded small grains or small-seeded legumes, soybeans (certain areas of IA, KS, MN, ND, NE, SD), and grasses the year following application.

– – – – – – – – – – – – – – –

Signal Word/Toxicity Class: Danger/I.
REI: 12 hr.

Solution — see 2,4-D

Solve — see 2,4-D

Sterling — see dicamba

Sterling Plus — see dicamba & atrazine

Treflan — see trifluralin

TRI-4 — see trifluralin

Trific — see trifluralin

TRIFLURALIN

■ POST

Albaugh Trifluralin 4EC *(Albaugh)*
◆ **Clean Crop Trifluralin HF (4EC)** *(Platte)*
Gowan Trifluralin 4 or 5 (EC) *(Gowan)*
Helena Trifluralin 4 EC *(Helena)*
Riverside Trifluralin 4EC or Trific 60DF *(Terra)*

◆-new product • PP-preplant • PPI-preplant incorporated • PRE-preemergence • POST-postemergence • SEQ-sequential • ae-acid equivalent • ai-active ingredient • DF-dry flowable
E/EC-emulsifiable concentrate • F/FL-flowable • DG/G/WG-dispersable granule • L/LC-liquid • SP/WSP-soluble packet • W/WP-wettable powder • WSB-water soluble bag

◆ **Sedagri Trifluralin 480 (4EC)** *(Rhone-Poulenc)*
Treflan HFP (4EC) *(Dow AgroSciences)*
TRI-4 HF (4EC) *(American Cyanamid)*
Trilin 4 or 5 (EC) or 10G *(Griffin)*
Wilbur-Ellis Trifluralin 10G *(Wilbur-Ellis)*

Rate: 0.375-1 lb. ai/A
0.75-2 pt. 4EC/A
0.6-1.6 pt. 5EC/A
0.625-1.66 lb. 60DF/A
3.75-10 lb. 10G/A

Time: Postemergence incorporated. Apply when milo is 8-24" tall. Do not apply preplant or preemergence.

Weeds: Broadleaf weeds:

carelessweed	knotweed	purslane
carpetweed	kochia	pusley
chickweed	lambsquarters	redroot pigweed
field bindweed	Mexican clover	rough pigweed
fireweed	Mexican fireweed	Russian thistle
Florida purslane	prostrate pigweed	spiny pigweed
Florida pusley	puncturevine	stinging nettle
goosefoot	(western U.S.)	tumbleweed
henbit		

Grasses:

annual bluegrass	fall panicum	sandbur
barnyardgrass	foxtail millet	shattercane
bottlegrass	giant foxtail	smooth crabgrass
brachiaria	green foxtail	sprangletop
bristlegrass	Italian ryegrass	stinkgrass
bromegrass	johnsongrass	Texas panicum
burgrass	(seedling)	watergrass
cheat	junglerice	wildcane
cheatgrass	large crabgrass	woolly cupgrass
chess	pigeongrass	yellow foxtail
downy brome	robust foxtail	

Remarks: Milo sorghum. Rate varies by soil type. Apply over-the-top or directed spray. Over application may result in injury to grain sorghum. Refer to label for directions, restrictions, and precautions.
Crop Rotation: Refer to label.
State Restrictions: Wilbur-Ellis not registered in California.

- - - - - - - - - - - - - - -

Signal Word/Toxicity Class: Varies by formulation.
REI: 12 hr. unless soil injected or soil incorporated.

Trilin — see trifluralin

Weed Rhap — see 2,4-D

Weedar — see 2,4-D

Weedestroy — see 2,4-D

Weedone — see 2,4-D

Sugar Beets

BETAMIX (Premixes) or BETANEX

■ **POST**

Betamix (desmedipham & phenmedipham) *(AgrEvo USA)*
Betanex (desmedipham) *(AgrEvo USA)*

Rate: Conventional:
0.75-1.25 lb. ai/A
4.5-7.5 pt. 1.3EC/A
Repeat application:
0.75-1 lb. ai/A
4.5-6 pt. 1.3EC/A
Multiple low rate application:
0.25-0.5 lb. ai/A
1.5-3 pt. 1.3EC/A

Time: Postemergence. Conventional: Spray when beets are past 2 true leaf stage and weeds are at 2 true leaf stage. Split rate: Spray when beets are cotyledon stage or larger, weeds are cotyledon size, and kochia is in rosette stage (less than 1" in diameter).

Weeds: Broadleaf weeds:

annual sowthistle	common ragweed	prostrate pigweed
black nightshade	groundcherry	purslane
coast fiddleneck	hairy nightshade	redroot pigweed
common chickweed	kochia*	shepherdspurse
common	London rocket	wild buckwheat
lambsquarters	nettleleaf goosefoot	wild mustard

Grasses:

annual bluegrass*	green foxtail	yellow foxtail
canarygrass*		

* Betamix only

Remarks: No split rate applications for Betanex in California.
Days To Harvest: 75.
Tank Mixes: Nortron SC.

- - - - - - - - - - - - - - -

Signal Word/Toxicity Class: Warning/II.

■ **POST**

Betamix Progress (desmedipham & phenmedipham & ethofumesate) *(AgrEvo USA)*

Rate: 0.25-0.74 lb. ai/A
1.13-3.25 pt. 1.8EC/A

Time: Postemergence. Apply at cotyledon stage of weeds.

Weeds: Broadleaf weeds:

annual sowthistle	hairy nightshade	prostrate pigweed
black nightshade	kochia (rosette stage)	purslane
coast fiddleneck	ladysthumb	redroot pigweed
common chickweed	London rocket	shepherdspurse
common	nettleleaf goosefoot	wild buckwheat
lambsquarters	Pennsylvania	wild mustard
common ragweed	smartweed	
groundcherry		

Grasses:

annual bluegrass	green foxtail	yellow foxtail)
canarygrass	pigeongrass	

Remarks: Including beets grown for seed. Do not spray while dew is present.
Days To Harvest: 75.

- - - - - - - - - - - - - - -

Signal Word/Toxicity Class: Danger/I.
REI: 24 hr.

CLETHODIM

Postemergence grass herbicide. Mode of action similar to Poast, Assure, Option II, and Fusilade.

■ **POST**

Prism (0.94EC) or Select (2EC) *(Valent)*

Rate: 0.1-0.25 lb. ai/A
9-34 fl. oz. 0.94EC/A
4-16 fl. oz. 2EC/A

Time: Postemergence. Apply to actively growing grasses.

Weeds: Grasses:

Amazon sprangletop	green foxtail	smooth crabgrass
annual bluegrass	itchgrass	southern crabgrass
barnyardgrass	johnsongrass	Texas panicum
bearded sprangletop	junglerice	volunteer cereals
bermudagrass	large crabgrass	wild oat
broadleaf signalgrass	quackgrass	wild proso millet
crowfootgrass	red rice	wiresten muhly
fall panicum	red sprangletop	witchgrass
giant foxtail	shattercane	woolly cupgrass
goosegrass	southwestern cupgrass	yellow foxtail

Remarks: Rate varies by grass species, stage, and geographical region. Grass crops such as corn, sorghum, wheat, and rice are highly sensitive to clethodim. Do not apply under stress conditions or if rainfall is expected in 1 hour. Do not apply through any type of irrigation system. Do not apply more than 0.5 lb. ai/A (0.25 lb. ai/A on Long Island, NY) per season. Do not graze treated fields or feed treated forage or hay to livestock. Refer to label for restrictions and precautions.
Days To Harvest: 100.
Tank Mixes: Betamix, Betanex, Stinger.
State Restrictions: Not for use on Solano grass in the Vernal Lakes area of Solano County, California; wild rice in Hays County, Texas.

- - - - - - - - - - - - - - -

Signal Word/Toxicity Class: Warning/II.
REI: 24 hr.

5

Other Field Crops

NOTICE The information on these pages is for preliminary planning — not a guide for use. Be sure to follow the manufacturer's directions, notwithstanding information contained here. | For personal protective equipment and EPA registration numbers, please turn to page 70.

Sugar Beets

CLOPYRALID

Systemic herbicide absorbed by leaves and roots. Has selective postemergence control of many annual and perennial broadleaf weeds.

■ POST

Stinger *(Dow AgroSciences)*

Rate: 0.1-0.25 lb. ae/A
0.25-0.66 pt./A

Time: Postemergence. Apply when sugar beets are in cotyledon to 8 leaf stage of growth and weeds are young and actively growing.

Weeds: Annual and perennial broadleaf weeds:

buffalobur	jimsonweed	sowthistle*
Canada thistle	knapweed	spotted knapweed
cocklebur	marshelder	sunflower
clover	nightshade	vetch
diffuse knapweed	Russian knapweed*	volunteer soybean
Jerusalem artichoke	smartweed*	wild buckwheat

* Suppression

Remarks: Do not apply by air. Do not apply more than 0.66 pt./A per year. Do not apply through any type of irrigation system. Do not contaminate irrigation ditches or water used for irrigation or domestic purposes.

Days To Harvest: Beet roots and tops—105.

Crop Rotation: Varies by region; refer to label.

– – – – – – – – – – – – – – –

Signal Word/Toxicity Class: Caution/III.
REI: 12 hr.

Credit — see glyphosate

ENDOTHALL

■ PRE, POST

Herbicide 273 *(ELF Atochem North America)*

Rate: 3-6.6 lb. ae/A broadcast
1-2.2 gal. 273/A

Time: Preemergence.

Weeds: Broadleaf weeds:

blueweed (henbit)	purslane	smartweed
burclover	ragweed	Texas blueweed
carrotweed	redroot pigweed	volunteer barley
kochia	shepherdspurse	wild buckwheat

Grasses:

barnyardgrass	cheatgrass	foxtail
bullgrass		

Remarks: Apply on top of seedbed or incorporate not more than 1½". Use low rate when applying at early growth stage (2-4 true leaves).

– – – – – – – – – – – – – – –

Rate: 0.75-1.5 lb. ae/A broadcast
2-4 pt. 273/A

Time: Postemergence. Do not apply later than 60 days after emergence.

Weeds: Same as above.

Remarks: Use low rate when applying at early growth stage (2-4 true leaves).

Tank Mixes: Betamix, Betanex, Pyramin. Refer to labels for restrictions and precautions.

– – – – – – – – – – – – – – –

Signal Word/Toxicity Class: Danger-Poison/I.
REI: 48 hr.

Eptam — see EPTC

EPTC

■ PPI, POST

Eptam 7-E or 20-G *(ZENECA)*

Rate: 2-3 lb. ai/A
2.25-3.5 pt. 7-E/A
Fall application—MN, ND:
4-4.5 lb. ai/A
4.5-5.25 pt. 7-E/A
20-22.5 lb. 20-G/A

Time: Preplant incorporated. For fall application in Minnesota and North Dakota, apply immediately before ground freezes. Incorporate to 2-3" depth.

Weeds: Broadleaf weeds:

black nightshade	corn spurry	nettleleaf goosefoot
carpetweed*	cutleaf nightshade*	prickly sida*
common chickweed	deadnettle	prostrate pigweed
common	fiddleneck*	redroot pigweed
lambsquarters	Florida pusley	sicklepod*
common pigweed	hairy nightshade	tall morningglory*
common purslane	henbit	tumble pigweed

Annual grasses and sedges:

annual bluegrass	giant foxtail	rescuegrass*
annual ryegrass	goosegrass	shattercane
(Italian)	green foxtail	signalgrass*
barnyardgrass	johnsongrass	Texas panicum*
(watergrass)	(seedling)	volunteer grains
bermudagrass	junglerice	(barley, oats, wheat)
(seedling)	lovegrass	wild oat
crabgrass	(stinkgrass)*	witchgrass*
fall panicum*	purple nutsedge	yellow foxtail
field sandbur	quackgrass	yellow nutsedge

*7-E only

Remarks: Use low rate in coarse-textured soils; high rate in medium- or fine-textured soils. Refer to label for use directions and restrictions.

State Restrictions: Preplant for Iowa, Michigan, Minnesota, eastern Nebraska, North Dakota, and South Dakota.

– – – – – – – – – – – – – – –

Rate: Post-thinning, subsurface injection:
3 lb. ai/A
3.5 pt. 7-E/A
15 lb. 20-G/A
Subsurface injection-band:
1.5 lb. ai/A on 22" row spacing
1.75 pt. 7-E/A
Irrigation water:
2-3 lb. ai/A
2.25-3.5 pt. 7-E/A

Time: Postemergence. For incorporation, apply after thinning and clean cultivation. For irrigation water treatment, apply after last cultivation of season.

Weeds: Same as above.

Remarks: Refer to label for use directions and geographical restrictions.

– – – – – – – – – – – – – – –

Signal Word/Toxicity Class: Caution.
REI: 12 hr. unless soil injected or soil incorporated.

Glyfos or Glyfos X-tra — see glyphosate

GLYPHOSATE

■ PRE

◆ **Credit (4WS)** *(Nufarm)*
◆ **Glyfos or Glyfos X-tra (4WS)** *(Cheminova)*
Rattler (4WS) *(Helena)*
Roundup Custom (5.4WS) *(Monsanto)*
Roundup Original, Original RT, Ultra, Ultra RT (4WS) *(Monsanto)*

Rate: Annual weeds:
0.38-1.5 lb. ai/A
0.56-2.25 pt. 5.4WS/A
0.75-3 pt. 4WS/A
Perennial weeds:
0.5-5 lb. ai/A
0.75-7.5 pt. 5.4WS/A
1-10 pt. 4WS/A

Time: Preemergence. Apply prior to emergence of direct-seeded crop or prior to transplanting.

Weeds: Emerged annual and perennial broadleaf weeds including:

Canada thistle	hemp dogbane	Pennsylvania
curly dock	milkweed	smartweed
field bindweed		

Grasses:

bermudagrass	fescue	paragrass
fall panicum	johnsongrass	quackgrass

Remarks: Prior to transplanting crops into plastic mulch, remove product residue from plastic. Do not add surfactant to Roundup Ultra or Ultra RT. Do not allow glyphosate to contact desirable plants. Do not apply through any type of irrigation system. Refer to label for directions, precautions and restrictions.

State Restrictions: Roundup Ultra RT: For use in Colorado, Idaho, Montana, North Dakota, South Dakota, Utah, and Wyoming. For use in specific counties only in Kansas, Minnesota, Nebraska, Nevada, Oklahoma, Oregon, and Washington, refer to label for restrictions. Glyfos is not registered for use in California. Glyfos X-tra is not registered for use in mistblowers in California or Arizona.

Signal Word/Toxicity Class: Varies by formulation.
REI: Warning—12 hr.; Caution—4 hr.

◆-new product • PP-preplant • PPI-preplant incorporated • PRE-preemergence • POST-postemergence • SEQ-sequential • ae-acid equivalent • ai-active ingredient • DF-dry flowable
E/EC-emulsifiable concentrate • F/FL-flowable • DG/G/WG-dispersable granule • L/LC-liquid • SP/WSP-soluble packet • W/WP-wettable powder • WSB-water soluble bag

Gramoxone Extra — see paraquat

Herbicide 273 — see endothall

NORTRON

■ **PP, PRE**

Nortron (SC) (ethofumesate) *(AgrEvo USA)*
Rate: All areas except MN, ND:
1.125-3.75 lb. ai/A
2.25-7.5 pt. SC/A
MN, ND:
3-3.75 lb. ai/A
6-7.5 pt. SC/A
Time: Preplant incorporated or preemergence.
Weeds: Broadleaf weeds:

annual sowthistle*	common purslane	puncturevine*
black nightshade	kochia	redroot pigweed
common chickweed	ladysthumb	Russian thistle
common	Pennsylvania	shepherdspurse*
lambsquarters	smartweed	wild buckwheat

Grasses and sedges:

annual bluegrass	large crabgrass	wild oat
barnyardgrass	purple nutsedge*	yellow foxtail
canarygrass	volunteer barley	yellow nutsedge
green foxtail	volunteer wheat	

* Reduced competition
Remarks: Do not graze livestock on treated crops.
Crop Rotation: Sugar beets or ryegrass—12 months after application. Thorough tillage, including moldboard plowing, should precede planting of crops other than sugar beets or ryegrass.
Tank Mixes: Betamix, Betanex, Pyramin. Refer to labels for restrictions.

– – – – – – – – – – – – – – –

Signal Word/Toxicity Class: Caution/III.
REI: 12 hr.

PARAQUAT

Restricted Use Pesticide.

■ **PP, PRE**

Gramoxone Extra (2.5L) *(ZENECA)*
Rate: 0.5-1 lb. ai/A
1.5-3 pt. 2.5L/A
Time: Preplant, preemergence. Apply when weeds and grasses are succulent and growth is from 1-6" tall (larger plants less affected).
Weeds: Annual broadleaf weeds and grasses; top kill and suppression of perennials.
Remarks: Add nonionic surfactant or crop oil concentrate. Seedbeds should be formed as far ahead of planting and treatment as possible. Seeding should be done with a minimum of soil disturbance. Crops emerged at time of application will be killed. To prevent injury to germinating crop seedlings, do not apply to soils lacking clay minerals. Refer to label for use directions, restrictions, precautions.

– – – – – – – – – – – – – – –

Rate: 0.2 lb. ai/A
0.75 pt. 2.5L/A
Time: Apply broadcast to preformed seedbeds.
Weeds:
volunteer barley
Remarks: Add nonionic surfactant or crop oil concentrate. Refer to label for use directions, restrictions, precautions.
State Restrictions: For use in California, Idaho, Oregon, Washington.

– – – – – – – – – – – – – – –

Signal Word/Toxicity Class: Danger-Poison/I.
REI: 12 hr. (except harvest aid/desiccation 24 hr.).

Poast — see sethoxydim

Prism — see clethodim

PYRAMIN

■ **PRE, POST, SEQ**

Pyramin FL or DF (chloridazon) *(BASF)*

Rate: 3.2-3.7 lb. ai/A
3-3.5 qt. FL/A
4.6-5.4 lb. DF/A
Time: Preemergence, early postemergence. For early postemergence, apply after beets have 2 true leaves; weeds less than 2-4 leaves.
Weeds: Broadleaf weeds:

fanweed	nettleleaf goosefoot	ragweed
henbit	nightshade	shepherdspurse
lambsquarters	pigweed	smartweed
mustard	purslane	velvetleaf (MI, OH)

Remarks: Higher rates required on heavier soils of the Red River Valley and for velvetleaf control in Michigan and Ohio. Do not apply more than 2 applications in Central and Eastern states or rates more than 7.7 lb. ai/A per season.
Crop Rotation: If beet crop is lost, do not plant crops other than sugar beets on heavy-textured, high organic matter soils in treated band during the same season.
Tank Mixes: Betamix, Betanex, Nortron SC.

– – – – – – – – – – – – – – –

Signal Word/Toxicity Class: Caution/III.
REI: 12 hr.

Rattler — see glyphosate

RO-NEET

■ **PPI**

Ro-Neet 6-E (cycloate) *(ZENECA)*
Rate: 3-4 lb. ai/A
4-5.3 pt. 6-E/A
Time: Preplant incorporated, at planting, immediately postplant, or fall application. For fall application, apply before ground freezes in Idaho, Minnesota, Montana, North Dakota, Oregon, and Wyoming.
Weeds: Annual broadleaf weeds:

black nightshade	lambsquarters	shepherdspurse
common purslane	nettleleaf goosefoot	small stinging nettle
deadnettle	(except CA)	velvetleaf
hairy nightshade	redroot pigweed	(suppression)
henbit		

Annual grasses and sedges:

annual bluegrass	foxtail	watergrass
annual ryegrass	purple nutsedge	wild oat
barnyardgrass	volunteer barley	yellow nutsedge
crabgrass		

Remarks: For use on mineral soils only. Low rate on sandy soils, high rate on heavier soils. Injury may result in highly saline or alkaline soils. Refer to label for use directions, restrictions, and precautions.
Tank Mixes: Eptam for preplant use in Michigan, Minnesota, Ohio, and the Red River Valley area of North Dakota.

– – – – – – – – – – – – – – –

Signal Word/Toxicity Class: Caution.
REI: 12 hr.

Roundup — see glyphosate

Select — see clethodim

SETHOXYDIM

■ **POST**

Poast (1.5EC) *(BASF)*
Rate: 0.09-0.47 lb. ai/A
0.5-2.5 pt. 1.5EC/A
Time: Postemergence.
Weeds: Annual and perennial grasses:

annual ryegrass	johnsongrass	southwestern cupgrass
barnyardgrass	junglerice	stinkgrass
bermudagrass	large crabgrass	tall fescue
broadleaf signalgrass	lovegrass	Texas panicum
browntop panicum	orchardgrass	volunteer grains
fall panicum	(seedling)	wild oat
field sandbur	perennial ryegrass	wild proso millet
giant foxtail	quackgrass	wirestem muhly
goosegrass	red sprangletop	witchgrass
green foxtail	shattercane	woolly cupgrass
itchgrass	smooth crabgrass	yellow foxtail

5

Other Field Crops

Sugar Beets

Remarks: Rate depends on growing region. Add spray adjuvant or oil concentrate. Urea ammonium-nitrate solution (UAN) or ammonium sulfate (AMS) recommended to enhance activity on certain grass species. Do not apply through any type of irrigation system. Refer to label for restrictions and limitations.
Days To Harvest: 60.
Tank Mixes: Betamix.
State Restrictions: Do not use UAN or AMS in California or Pacific Northwest.

Signal Word/Toxicity Class: Warning/II.
REI: 12 hr.

Stinger — see clopyralid

TILLAM

■ PP
Tillam 6-E (pebulate) *(ZENECA)*
Rate: 4-6 lb. ai/A
　　　2.66-4 qt. 6-E/A
Time: Preplant. Apply just prior to planting.
Weeds: Broadleaf weeds:

blackeyedsusan	hairy nightshade	nettleleaf goosefoot
common purslane	(suppression)	prostrate pigweed
deadnettle	henbit	redroot pigweed
Florida pusley	lambsquarters	shepherdspurse

Grasses and sedges:

barnyardgrass	goosegrass	purple nutsedge
bermudagrass	green foxtail	watergrass
(seedling)	millet	wild oat
crabgrass	narrowleaf	yellow foxtail
giant foxtail	signalgrass	yellow nutsedge

Remarks: Use low rate on light-textured soils and soils with less than 10% organic matter; high rate on heavy-textured soils or soils with over 10% organic matter. Refer to label for use directions and precautions.

Signal Word/Toxicity Class: Caution.
REI: 12 hr.

Treflan — see trifluralin

TRI-4 — see trifluralin

Trific — see trifluralin

TRIFLURALIN

■ POST
Albaugh Trifluralin 4EC *(Albaugh)*
◆ **Clean Crop Trifluralin HF (4EC)** *(Platte)*
Gowan Trifluralin 4 or 5 (EC) or 10G *(Gowan)*
Helena Trifluralin 4 EC *(Helena)*
Riverside Trifluralin 4EC or Trific 60DF *(Terra)*
◆ **Sedagri Trifluralin 480 (4EC)** *(Rhone-Poulenc)*
Treflan HFP (4EC) or TR-10 (10G) *(Dow AgroSciences)*
TRI-4 HF (4EC) *(American Cyanamid)*
Trilin 4 or 5 (EC) or 10G *(Griffin)*
Wilbur-Ellis Trifluralin 10G *(Wilbur-Ellis)*
Rate: 0.5-0.75 lb. ai/A
　　　1-1.5 pt. 4EC/A
　　　0.8-1.2 pt. 5EC/A
　　　0.875-1.25 lb. 60DF/A
　　　5-7.5 lb. 10G/A
Time: Postemergence. Apply from when first true leaves have formed until plants are 6" tall.
Weeds: Broadleaf weeds:

carelessweed	knotweed	purslane
carpetweed	kochia	pusley
chickweed	lambsquarters	redroot pigweed
field bindweed	Mexican clover	rough pigweed
fireweed	Mexican fireweed	Russian thistle
Florida purslane	prostrate pigweed	spiny pigweed
Florida pusley	puncturevine	stinging nettle
goosefoot	(western U.S.)	tumbleweed
henbit		

Grasses:

annual bluegrass	fall panicum	sandbur
barnyardgrass	foxtail millet	shattercane
bottlegrass	giant foxtail	smooth crabgrass
brachiaria	green foxtail	sprangletop
bristlegrass	Italian ryegrass	stinkgrass
bromegrass	johnsongrass	Texas panicum
burgrass	(seedling)	watergrass
cheat	junglerice	wildcane
cheatgrass	large crabgrass	woolly cupgrass
chess	pigeongrass	yellow foxtail
downy brome	robust foxtail	

Remarks: Rate varies by soil type. Cover exposed beet roots with soil prior to application. Refer to label for directions and precautions.
Crop Rotation: Refer to label.
State Restrictions: Wilbur-Ellis not registered in California.

Signal Word/Toxicity Class: Varies by formulation.
REI: 12 hr. unless soil injected or soil incorporated.

Trilin — see trifluralin

UPBEET

UpBeet (DF) (triflusulfuron-methyl) *(DuPont)*
Rate: 0.5-1 oz. DF/A
Time: Anytime after planting to small, actively growing weeds.
Weeds: Broadleaf weeds:

annual sowthistle	common ragweed	prostrate pigweed
black mustard	curly dock	redroot pigweed
black nightshade	hairy nightshade	shepherdspurse
California burclover	jimsonweed	silversheath
Canada thistle*	ladysthumb*	knotweed
coast fiddleneck	little mallow	sunflower
common chickweed	London rocket	velvetleaf
common	morningglory	wild buckwheat
lambsquarters	nettleleaf goosefoot	wild mustard
common mallow	Pennsylvania	wild radish
common purslane*	smartweed	Wright groundcherry

Grasses:

green foxtail*	junglerice*	yellow foxtail*

Partial control

Remarks: Apply in minimum 5 gal. water/A. Add nonionic surfactant or crop oil. Use higher rate as weed size/population increases. Do not apply more than 1.5 oz./A. Do not apply through any type of irrigation system.
Days To Harvest: 60.
Crop Rotation: Sugar beets—anytime; corn—21 days; other crops—14 days.
Tank Mixes: Betamix, Betanex, Betamix Progress, Stinger.

Signal Word/Toxicity Class: Caution.
REI: 4 hr.

Sugarcane

AAtrex — see atrazine

ASULAM

■ POST
Asulox (3.34) *(Rhone-Poulenc)*
Riverside Asulam 3.3 *(Terra)*
Rate: 2.5-3.34 lb. ai/A
　　　6-8 pt./A
Time: Postemergence. Apply when weeds are actively growing.
Weeds: Grasses:

alexandergrass	foxtail	johnsongrass
barnyardgrass	goosegrass	paragrass
broadleaf panicum	itchgrass	raoulgrass
crabgrass		

Remarks: Plant cane or stubble cane. When initial weed infestations are heavy, reinfestations from seed occur, or when species germinate at different times per growth season, 2 applications may be required. Cover crops may be planted if plowed under and not grazed. Do not graze or feed sugarcane fodder and forage to livestock. Do not apply through any type of irrigation system.

◆-new product • PP-preplant • PPI-preplant incorporated • PRE-preemergence • POST-postemergence • SEQ-sequential • ae-acid equivalent • ai-active ingredient • DF-dry flowable
E/EC-emulsifiable concentrate • F/FL-flowable • DG/G/WG-dispersable granule • L/LC-liquid • SP/WSP-soluble packet • W/WP-wettable powder • WSB-water soluble bag

Days To Harvest: Hawaii—400; Mainland U.S.—140 (Louisiana—100).

- - - - - - - - - - - - - -

Signal Word/Toxicity Class: Caution.
REI: 12 hr.

Asulox — see asulam

Atra-5 — see atrazine

ATRAZINE

Restricted Use Pesticide due to ground and surface water concerns.

■ PRE, POST
AAtrex 4L or AAtrex Nine-0 (WDG) *(Novartis)*
◆ Clean Crop Atrazine 4L, 90 WDG *(Platte)*
Drexel Atrazine 4L, Atra-5 (5L) or 90DF *(Drexel)*
Helena Atrazine 4L *(Helena)*
Riverside Atrazine 4L or 90DF *(Terra)*
  Rate: 2-4 lb. ai/A
       4-8 pt. 4L/A
       3.2-6.4 pt. 5L/A
       2.2-4.4 lb. WDG, 90DF/A
  Time: Preemergence. Apply at planting or ratooning but before cane emerges (1 additional application may be made over cane as it emerges; 2 additional applications may be applied interline after emergence as directed sprays). Make last application before close-in. In Louisiana, apply during summer fallow period to weed-free beds immediately after bed formation.

Weeds: Broadleaf weeds such as:

amaranth	fireweed	flora's paintbrush

Grasses:

crabgrass	junglerice	wiregrass
foxtail		

Remarks: Rate varies by soil type and organic matter. Do not exceed suggested rate of herbicide for any one crop season. Certain states may have established rate limitations; consult state lead pest control agency. Do not apply through any type of irrigation system. This product may not be mixed/loaded, or used within 50 ft. of all wells including abandoned wells, drainage wells, and sink holes. Do not graze treated area or feed treated forage to livestock for 21 days following application.
State Restrictions: Wilbur-Ellis not registered in California.

- - - - - - - - - - - - - -

  Rate: 4 lb. ai/A
       8 pt. 4L/A
       6.4 pt. 5L/A
       4.4 lb. WDG, 90DF/A
  Time: Split application: Apply 8 pt./A (4 lb. ai/A) rate preemergence; follow with 1-2 postemergence applications at 6 pt./A (3 lb. ai/A) rate to sugarcane and weeds before weeds exceed 1¹/₂" in height. Do not apply after close-in.

Weeds: Broadleaf weeds and grasses:

barnyardgrass	purslane	sunflower
pigweed		

Remarks: Plant, ratoon cane. Apply nonionic surfactant. Do not apply more than 10 lb. ai/A to any one sugarcane crop.
State Restrictions: For use in Texas.

- - - - - - - - - - - - - -

  Rate: 0.4-0.6 lb. ai/A
       0.8-1.2 pt. 4L/A
       0.6-1 pt. 5L/A
       0.4-0.6 lb. WDG, 90DF/A
  Time: Postemergence. Apply postemergence to cane and pellitory weeds before weeds exceed 1¹/₂" in height.

Weeds: Broadleaf weeds:

  pellitory weed (emerged)

Remarks: Apply in at least 40 gal. water as directed spray by ground equipment prior to close-in. Add 4 qt. surfactant/100 gal. spray.
State Restrictions: For use in Florida.

- - - - - - - - - - - - - -

Signal Word/Toxicity Class: Caution/III.
REI: 12 hr.

Banvel — see dicamba

Brash — see 2,4-D Combinations

Clarity — see dicamba

Credit — see glyphosate

2,4-D · PHENOXY HERBICIDES

2,4-D and 2,4-D-type compounds selectively control broadleaf weeds with little or no control of grasses. 2,4-D drift can injure adjacent crops either by drift of spray or by volatilization (spray turns into a vapor). Ester formulations are most volatile and amines least volatile. Ester formulations can vaporize at temperatures as low as 70°F and be moved by wind to harm sensitive plants. Vaporization increases as air temperatures rise.

Annual and perennial broadleaf weeds controlled by 2,4-D include:

beggarticks	galinsoga	povertyweed
bindweed	goldenrod	puncturevine
bitterweed	ground ivy	purslane
broomweed	healall	ragweed
bull thistle	hoary cress	Russian thistle
burdock	ironweed	shepherdspurse
Canada thistle	jimsonweed	smartweed
carpetweed	knotweed	sowthistle
catnip	lambsquarters	stinkweed
chicory	mallow	sumac
chickweed	marshelder	sunflower
cocklebur	mexicanweed	sweetclover
coffeeweed	morningglory	velvetleaf
cutleaf	musk thistle	Virginia creeper
eveningprimrose	mustard	wild carrot
creeping jenny	pennywort	wild garlic
croton	pepperweed	wild lettuce
dandelion	pigweed	wild onion
dock	plantain	wild parsnips
dogbane	pokeweed	wild radish

■ PRE, POST
Albaugh Amine 4 (2,4-D amine) *(Albaugh)*
Weedar 64 (4) (2,4-D amine) *(Nufarm)*
Weedestroy AM-40 (2,4-D amine) *(Riverdale)*
Wilbur-Ellis Amine 4 (2,4-D amine) *(Wilbur-Ellis)*
  Rate: 2 lb. ae/A
       4 pt./A
  Time: Preemergence. Apply as blanket spray through lay-by.

  Rate: 0.75-1 lb. ae/A
       1.5-2 pt./A
  Time: Postemergence. Apply when cane is 1-2" tall.
  Remarks: Aids in control of johnsongrass seedlings. Up to 4 pt./A of Weedar 64 may be used postemergence. Refer to label for restrictions and precautions.
  State Restrictions: Weedar and Wilbur-Ellis not registered in California.

- - - - - - - - - - - - - -

Signal Word/Toxicity Class: Danger/I.
REI: 48 hr.

- - - - - - - - - - - - - -

■ PRE, POST
Albaugh LV4 (2,4-D ester) *(Albaugh)*
Riverdale L.V. 4 or L.V. 6 (2,4-D ester) *(Riverdale)*
Weed Rhap LV-6D (2,4-D ester) *(Helena)*
Wilbur-Ellis Lo Vol-6 (2,4-D ester) *(Wilbur-Ellis)*
  Rate: 1 lb. ae/A
       2 pt. 4/A
       1.33 pt. 6/A
  Time: Preemergence.

  Rate: 2 lb. ae/A
       4 pt. 4/A
       2.66 pt. 6/A
  Time: Postemergence. Apply after cane emerges and through lay-by.
  Remarks: Consult label for restrictions and precautions.
  State Restrictions: Wilbur-Ellis not registered in California.

- - - - - - - - - - - - - -

Signal Word/Toxicity Class: Danger/I (amine); Caution/III (ester).
REI: Danger—48 hr.; Caution—12 hr.

5

Other Field Crops

NOTICE The information on these pages is for preliminary planning — not a guide for use. Be sure to follow the manufacturer's directions, notwithstanding information contained here. | For personal protective equipment and EPA registration numbers, please turn to page 70.

Sugarcane

PRE, POST

Formula 40 (2,4-D mixed amine) *(Rhone-Poulenc)*
Hi-Dep (2,4-D mixed amine) *(PBI/Gordon)*
Rate: Summer:
  1.25 lb. ae/A
  2.5 pt. 4/A
Time: Apply up to 6 weeks before harvest.

Rate: Fall, spring:
  1-2 lb. ae/A
  2-4 pt. 4/A/A
Time: Fall: Apply after harvest or planting. Spring: Apply once or twice before close-in.
Remarks: Up to 4 applications per year may be applied in accordance with state recommendations.
Days To Harvest: 6 weeks.

- - - - - - - - - - - - - - - -

Signal Word/Toxicity Class: Danger/I.
REI: 48 hr.

PRE, POST

◆ **Clean Crop Amine 4 (2,4-D amine)** *(Platte)*
◆ **Opti-amine (4) (2,4-D amine)** *(Helena)*
Weed Rhap A-4D (2,4-D amine) *(Helena)*
Rate: 1-2 lb. ae/A
  2-4 pt./A
Time: Preemergence or postemergence. Apply spray in the spring after cane emerges and through lay-by.
Remarks: Consult label for restrictions and precautions.

- - - - - - - - - - - - - - - -

Signal Word/Toxicity Class: Danger/I.
REI: 48 hr.

PRE, POST

Riverside 2,4-D Amine 4 (2,4-D amine) *(Terra)*
Rate: 1 lb. ae/A
  2 pt. 4/A
Time: Apply as fall and spring drill (or band) spray.

Rate: 2 lb. ae/A
  4 pt. 4/A
Time: Apply as broadcast spray immediately after lay-by.
Remarks: Refer to label for further use directions.

- - - - - - - - - - - - - - - -

Signal Word/Toxicity Class: Danger/I.
REI: 48 hr.

PRE, POST

◆ **Saber (2,4-D amine)** *(Platte)*
Rate: 0.75-2 lb. ae/A
  1.5-4 pt./A
Time: Preemergence, postemergence, postharvest. For preemergence, apply in the spring before cane appears. For postemergence, apply after cane emerges and through lay-by. For postharvest, apply in the fall after harvest or at planting.
Remarks: Do not make more than 4 applications per season. Consult product label for restrictions and precautions.

- - - - - - - - - - - - - - - -

Signal Word/Toxicity Class: Danger/I.
REI: 48 hr.

PRE, POST

Savage (WSB) (2,4-D amine) *(Platte)*
Rate: 0.71-1.9 lb. ae/A
  0.75-2 lb. WSB/A
Time: Preemergence, postemergence. For preemergence, apply before cane appears. For postemergence, apply after cane emerges and through lay-by.
Remarks: Refer to label for further use directions.

- - - - - - - - - - - - - - - -

Rate: 0.48-1.4 lb. ae/A
  0.5-1.5 lb. WSB/A
Time: Apply as needed.
Remarks: Do not exceed 8 lb./A per crop. Refer to label for further use directions.
Days To Harvest: 6 weeks.
State Restrictions: For use in Hawaii.

- - - - - - - - - - - - - - - -

Signal Word/Toxicity Class: Danger/I.
REI: 48 hr.

PRE, POST

Solution (WS) (2,4-D amine) *(Riverdale)*
Rate: 1 WS packet in 10-50 gal. water/1.125 A
Time: Preemergence. Apply as blanket spray through lay-by.

Rate: 1 WS packet in 10-60 gal. water/1.66-2.5 A
Time: Postemergence. Apply when cane is 1-2" tall.
Remarks: Aids in control of johnsongrass seedlings.

- - - - - - - - - - - - - - - -

Signal Word/Toxicity Class: Danger/I.
REI: 48 hr.

PRE, POST

Weedone LV4 (2,4-D solventless ester) *(Nufarm)*
Rate: 1 lb. ae/A
  2 pt. 4/A
Time: Preemergence.

Rate: 1-2 lb. ae/A
  2-4 pt. 4/A
Time: Postemergence. Apply after cane emerges through lay-by.
Remarks: Refer to label for use directions, precautions, and restrictions.
State Restrictions: Not for use postemergence in California.

- - - - - - - - - - - - - - - -

Signal Word/Toxicity Class: Caution/III.
REI: 12 hr.

2,4-D COMBINATIONS

POST

◆ **Brash (2.87 lb./gal. 2,4-D & 1 lb./gal. dicamba)** *(Terra)*
Weedmaster (2.87 lb./gal. 2,4-D & 1 lb./gal. dicamba) *(BASF)*
Rate: Annuals:
  1 lb. ai/A
  2 pt./A
  Perennials:
  1-3 lb. ai/A
  2-6 pt./A
Time: Postemergence. Apply any time after weeds have emerged and are actively growing but prior to close-in stage of sugarcane.
Weeds: Annual and perennial weeds:

annual clover	common ragweed	prickly lettuce
annual fleabane	cressleaf groundsel	prickly sida
annual sowthistle	curly dock	prostrate pigweed
aster	cutleaf	prostrate spurge
buttercup	eveningprimrose	redroot pigweed
California burclover	dogfennel	shepherdspurse
Carolina geranium	field bindweed	smooth pigweed
common chickweed	goldenrod	teaweed
common cocklebur	henbit	Virginia pepperweed
common dandelion	mouseear chickweed	wild garlic
common purslane	perennial sowthistle	wild onion

Remarks: Spray beneath sugarcane canopy when possible to maximize coverage and minimize likelihood of crop injury. Retreatments may be made as needed, but do not exceed 8 qt./A per growing season.
Tank Mixes: Asulox, atrazine, Evik, metribuzin, terbacil.

- - - - - - - - - - - - - - - -

Signal Word/Toxicity Class: Danger/I.
REI: 48 hr.

DICAMBA

POST

Banvel (WS) (DMA salt of dicamba) *(BASF)*
Clarity (WS) (dicamba-DGA) *(BASF)*
◆ **Sterling (WS) (DMA salt of dicamba)** *(Terra)*
Rate: 0.25-2 lb. ai/A
  0.5-4 pt. WS/A
Time: Postemergence. Apply to emerged weeds but before close-in stage of sugarcane. Repeat as needed.
Weeds: Annual broadleaf weeds:

beggarweed	morningglory	prickly sida
cocklebur	pigweed	purslane
lambsquarters		

Biennial broadleaf weeds:

bull thistle	gromwell	spotted knapweed
common burdock	milk thistle	tansy ragwort
diffuse knapweed	musk thistle	white cockle
dwarf mallow	plumeless thistle	yellow starthistle

◆-new product • PP-preplant • PPI-preplant incorporated • PRE-preemergence • POST-postemergence • SEQ-sequential • ae-acid equivalent • ai-active ingredient • DF-dry flowable
E/EC-emulsifiable concentrate • F/FL-flowable • DG/G/WG-dispersable granule • L/LC-liquid • SP/WSP-soluble packet • W/WP-wettable powder • WSB-water soluble bag

Sugarcane

Perennial broadleaf weeds:

black knapweed	dogfennel	perennial sowthistle
Canada goldenrod	field bindweed	pokeweed
common goldenweed	hop clover	Russian knapweed
curly dock	ironweed	spiny aster
dandelion	Missouri goldenrod	white heath aster

Remarks: Rate varies by weed type and stages. Use lower rate on annual weeds; higher rate on perennial weeds. Do not apply more than 4 pt./A during growing season.

Tank Mixes: Asulox, atrazine, 2,4-D, Evik.

- - - - - - - - - - - - - - -

Signal Word/Toxicity Class: Warning/II (Banvel, Sterling); Caution (Clarity).
REI: 24 hr.

Direx — see diuron

DIURON

■ **PRE, POST**

Direx 4L or 80DF *(Griffin)*
◆ **Diuron 80 WDG** *(Platte)*
Drexel Diuron 4L or 80 *(Drexel)*
Karmex DF *(Griffin)*
Riverside Diuron 4L or 80DF *(Terra)*

Rate: 0.4-0.8 lb. ai/A
0.8-1.6 pt. 4L/A
0.5-1 lb. 80, DF, 80DF/A

Time: Postemergence. After cane has emerged but before panicum exceeds 2" in height.

Weeds: Grasses:
panicum

Rate: 1.5-3 lb. ai/A
3-6 pt. 4L/A
2-4 lb. 80, DF, 80DF/A

Time: Preemergence, postemergence. Apply prior to weed emergence after planting or after harvesting plant crop (for ratoon crop).

Weeds: Broadleaf weeds:

amsinckia (fiddleneck)	gromwell	ragweed
annual groundcherry	groundsel	shepherdspurse
annual morningglory	knawel	spanishneedles
chickweed	lambsquarters	tansymustard
corn spurry	pigweed	wild lettuce
dogfennel	purslane	wild mustard

Grasses:

annual bluegrass	barnyardgrass	rattail fescue
annual sweet	crabgrass	red sprangletop
vernalgrass	foxtail	velvetgrass

Remarks: Apply as directed spray. For panicum, add 1 qt. nonionic surfactant/100 gal. spray. Do not make more than 3 applications or apply more than 4.8 lb. ai total/A between planting (or ratooning) and harvest. To prevent injury on new cane varieties, tolerance to diuron should be determined prior to adoption as field practice.
Crop Rotation: Do not replant to other crops within 2 years after treatment as crop injury may result.
State Restrictions: For use in Florida.

- - - - - - - - - - - - - - -

Rate: 3-6 lb. ai/A
6-12 pt. 4L/A
4-8 lb. 80, DF, 80DF/A

Time: Preemergence, postemergence. Apply as broadcast spray prior to weed emergence after planting or after harvesting plant crop (for ratoon crop).
Weeds: Same as above.
Remarks: Second and third application may be made as broadcast spray over emerged cane or by directed spray interrow.
Crop Rotation: Treated areas may be replanted to sugarcane or pineapple 1 year after last application.
State Restrictions: For use in Hawaii, Puerto Rico.

- - - - - - - - - - - - - - -

Rate: 2.5-3 lb. ai /A
5-5.25 pt. 4L/A
3-3.75 lb. 80, DF, 80DF/A

Time: Preemergence. Fall treatment (Aug.-Oct.): treat 2 ft. band over the row after planting cane, but before weeds or cane emerge. Spring treatment (Jan.-Apr.): if shaving and off-barring are practiced, treat 2 ft. band over the row before weeds or cane emerge.
Weeds: Same as above.
Remarks: Single application. Use on plant cane seeded to fallow ground.
Crop Rotation: Do not replant to other crops within 2 years after treatment as crop injury may result.

State Restrictions: For use in Louisiana.

- - - - - - - - - - - - - - -

Signal Word/Toxicity Class: Caution/III.
REI: 12 hr.

EVIK

■ **PRE, POST**

Evik DF (ametryn) *(Novartis)*

Rate: 0.4-1.2 lb. ai/A in a minimum 20 gal. water
0.5-1.5 lb. DF/A

Time: Preemergence, postemergence directed. Apply up to 2 repeat applications at 30-day intervals before close-in.

Weeds: Mixed broadleaf weeds and grasses including:
alexandergrass

Remarks: Avoid wetting sugarcane foliage. For mixed broadleaf weeds and grasses, use 1.5 lb. DF + 0.5 lb. 2,4-D or 0.5% surfactant. Refer to label for further use directions, precautions, and limitations.
Tank Mixes: 2,4-D.
State Restrictions: For use in Florida.

- - - - - - - - - - - - - - -

Rate: 4-8 lb. ai/A
5-10 lb. DF/A

Time: Preemergence, postemergence. Apply up to 9 lb. DF before weeds or sugarcane emerge. Second and third application at up to 3 lb. DF each may be made approximately 30 days prior to close-in and at close-in.

Weeds: Broadleaf weeds:

ageratum	Japanese tea	rattlebox
Amaranthus	kukaipuaa	Richardia spp.
common purslane	morningglory	spanishneedles
fireweed	pualele	wild pea bean
flora's paintbrush	(sowthistle)	

Grasses:

crabgrass species	goosegrass	junglerice
dallisgrass	guineagrass	swollen fingergrass
foxtail		

Remarks: Plant or ratoon sugarcane. Sugarcane growing in areas of exposed subsoil, in rocky areas, or in soils of low adsorptive capacity may show temporary chlorosis following treatment. Injury may occur when sugarcane is under moisture stress. Certain varieties may show temporary chlorosis or stunting as a result of over-the-top application.
Tank Mixes: Karmex.
State Restrictions: For use in Hawaii.

- - - - - - - - - - - - - - -

Rate: 2-2.4 lb. ai/A
2.5-3 lb. DF/A

Time: Preemergence, postemergence. Apply 2.5 lb. DF + 0.5 lb. 2,4-D plus 1 pt. crop oil concentrate or 1 pt. nonionic surfactant in minimum of 20 gal./A. Apply 1-2 additional applications using 3 lb. DF + 0.5 lb. 2,4-D directed to base of cane can be made before close-in. Do not apply over-the-top after April 10 or after cane is 20" tall.

Weeds: Broadleaf weeds:

annual sowthistle	Florida pusley	ragweed
cocklebur	henbit	smartweed
common chickweed	morningglory	swine cress
common	paleseed plantain	velvetleaf
lambsquarters	pigweed	wild mustard

Grasses:

barnyardgrass	crabgrass	goosegrass
brachiaria	fall panicum	itchgrass
browntop panicum	foxtail	Texas panicum

Remarks: Plant, ratoon sugarcane. May not control itchgrass (raoulgrass) germinating after treatment. Temporary yellowing of sugarcane leaves may follow over-the-top application. Refer to label for further use directions, precautions, and limitations.
Tank mixes: 2,4-D.
State Restrictions: For use in Louisiana.

- - - - - - - - - - - - - - -

Rate: 3.2-8 lb. ai/A
4-10 lb. DF/A

Time: Preemergence, postemergence. For plant or ratoon sugarcane, apply before sugarcane or weeds emerge. Apply 1-2 additional applications as needed before close-in, directed to base of sugarcane. For plant sugarcane, apply before sugarcane emerges and before weeds exceed 5" in height. Second application may be made, as needed, over top of sugarcane after sugarcane and weeds emerge, but before close-in. For ratoon sugarcane, apply interline or over top of sugarcane and weeds prior to close-in.

Weeds: Broadleaf weeds:

Amaranthus	pigweed	sowthistle
milkweed	purslane	spanishneedles
morningglory	Richardia spp.	

5

Other Field Crops

NOTICE The information on these pages is for preliminary planning — not a guide for use. Be sure to follow the manufacturer's directions, notwithstanding information contained here.

For personal protective equipment and EPA registration numbers, please turn to page 70.

Sugarcane

Grasses:

crabgrass · itchgrass · purpletop
dallisgrass · junglerice · raoulgrass
foxtail · panicum · sandbur
goosegrass

Remarks: Plant, ratoon sugarcane. Add 1 pt./A nonionic surfactant. Sugarcane growing in areas of exposed subsoil, in rocky areas, or during time of water stress may show temporary chlorosis. Do not apply in combination with other herbicides when making over-the-top application; temporary stunting or chlorosis may occur.

State Restrictions: For use in Puerto Rico.

- - - - - - - - - - - - - -

Rate: 1.2-2 lb. ai/A
1.5-2.5 lb. DF/A
Time: Preemergence, postemergence. Broadcast to sugarcane or weeds.
Weeds: Broadleaf weeds:

cocklebur · morningglory · sunflower
common · pigweed · velvetleaf
  lambsquarters · ragweed · wild mustard
Florida pusley · smartweed

Grasses:

barnyardgrass · fall panicum · Texas panicum
brachiaria

Remarks: Add 2 qt. nonionic surfactant/100 gal. spray mixture; repeat 1-2 applications as needed, prior to close-in. Use higher rate for heavier weed infestations. Temporary yellowing of sugarcane leaves may follow over-the-top application.

State Restrictions: For use in Texas.

- - - - - - - - - - - - - -

Signal Word/Toxicity Class: Caution.
REI: 12 hr.

Formula 40 — see 2,4-D

Glyfos or Glyfos X-tra — see glyphosate

GLYPHOSATE

■ **PP, PRE**
◆ **Credit (4WS)** *(Nufarm)*
◆ **Glyfos or Glyfos X-tra (4WS)** *(Cheminova)*
Rattler (4WS) *(Helena)*
Roundup Custom (5.4WS) *(Monsanto)*
Roundup Original or Ultra (4WS) *(Monsanto)*
Rate: 0.38-5 lb. ai/A
0.75-10 pt. 4WS, 5.4WS/A
Time: Preplant, preemergence, spot treatment. Apply in or around fields or in fields prior to emergence of plant cane.
Weeds: Annual and perennial broadleaf weeds and grasses; volunteer or diseased cane.
Remarks: Use higher rates for perennial weeds. Hooded sprayers, may be used for weed control between rows of sugarcane; do not allow treated weeds to come into contact with crop. Do not apply around ditches, canals, or ponds containing water to be used for irrigation. Do not feed or graze treated foliage after application. Refer to label for directions, precautions and restrictions.

State Restrictions: Glyfos is not registered for use in California. Glyfos X-tra is not registered for use in mistblowers in California or Arizona.

- - - - - - - - - - - - - -

Signal Word/Toxicity Class: Varies by formulation.
REI: Warning—12 hr.; Caution—4 hr.

Gramoxone Extra — see paraquat

HEXAZINONE

■ **PRE, POST**
Velpar (SP) or L *(DuPont)*
Rate: Hawaii:
0.45-3.6 lb. ai/A
0.5-4 lb. SP/A
1.8-14.5 pt. L/A
Louisiana, Texas:
0.45-0.9 lb. ai/A
0.5-1 lb. SP/A
1.8-3.5 pt. L/A
Puerto Rico:
0.9-1.8 lb. ai/A

1-2 lb. SP/A
0.9-1.8 pt. L/A
Time: Preemergence, postemergence. Best results are obtained when weeds are less than 2" in height or diameter.
Weeds: Broadleaf weeds:

castorbean · flora's paintbrush · morningglory
chickweed · henbit · paspalum
crotalaria · lambsquarters

Grasses:

barnyardgrass · goosegrass · junglerice
crabgrass · guineagrass · panicum
fingergrass · johnsongrass · signalgrass
foxtail · (seedling)

Remarks: Rate varies for each state depending on time of application and soil type. Apply single application using a minimum 25 gal. spray/A. Do not use on cane showing poor vigor or on varieties known to be susceptible to weed killers. Do not add surfactant unless otherwise specified or allowed. In Hawaii, surfactant is recommended for all uses; in Texas on dormant cane, surfactant may be added to increase control of emerged weeds. Do not use over top of cane, gravelly or rocky soils, thinly covered subsoils, or coarse-textured soils with less than 1% organic matter. Do not feed forage to livestock.

Days To Harvest: Hawaii-180; Louisiana, Texas-234; Puerto Rico-288.
Crop Rotation: Do not plant any crop other than sugarcane within 18 months of the last application.
State Restrictions: For use in Hawaii, Louisiana, Puerto Rico, Texas. Not for use in Florida.

- - - - - - - - - - - - - -

Signal Word/Toxicity Class: Danger/I.
REI: 24 hr.

Hi-Dep — see 2,4-D

Karmex — see diuron

Opti-Amine — see 2,4-D

PARAQUAT

Restricted Use Pesticide.

■ **POST**
Gramoxone Extra (2.5L) *(ZENECA)*
Rate: 0.5 lb. ai/A
1.5 pt. 2.5L/A
Time: Postemergence: Apply when weeds are 2-6" tall. Make second and final application, if necessary, when new weed growth is 2-6" tall. Florida: For optimum results, apply early in season (Mar.-Apr.) when weeds are small. Do not apply after June 1 as cane growth may be stunted and yields reduced. Hawaii: Do not apply after cane rows have closed-in.
Weeds: Annual broadleaf weeds and grasses; top kill of perennials.
Remarks: Add nonionic surfactant or crop oil concentrate. Apply as shielded or directed spray to avoid contact with cane foliage. Do not graze treated areas or feed treated forage to livestock. Refer to label for use directions, restrictions, precautions.

State Restrictions: For use in Florida, Hawaii.

- - - - - - - - - - - - - -

Rate: 0.3-0.6 lb. ai/A
1-2 pt. 2.5L/A
Time: Postemergence. Make second and final application, if necessary, when new weed growth is 2-6" tall. For tiller control, apply when tillers are less than 18" tall.
Weeds: Same as above plus tiller control.
Remarks: Add nonionic surfactant or crop oil concentrate. Apply as shielded or directed spray to avoid contact with cane foliage. Use higher rate with heavier weed infestations or tiller growth. Do not graze treated areas or feed treated forage to livestock. Refer to label for use directions, restrictions, precautions.

Days To Harvest: 30.
State Restrictions: For use in Louisiana.

- - - - - - - - - - - - - -

Rate: 0.1-0.2 lb. ai/A
0.4-0.75 pt. 2.5L/A
Time: Harvest aid. Apply 3-14 days before burning and harvest.
Weeds: Annual broadleaf weeds and grasses; top kill of perennials.
Remarks: Add nonionic surfactant or crop oil concentrate. Use higher rate under cool, cloudy weather conditions. Do not graze treated areas or feed treated forage to livestock. Refer to label for use directions.

State Restrictions: For use in Florida and Texas.

- - - - - - - - - - - - - -

Signal Word/Toxicity Class: Danger-Poison/I.
REI: 12 hr. (except harvest aid/desiccation 24 hr.).

◆-new product • PP-preplant • PPI-preplant incorporated • PRE-preemergence • POST-postemergence • SEQ-sequential • ae-acid equivalent • ai-active ingredient • DF-dry flowable
E/EC-emulsifiable concentrate • F/FL-flowable • DG/G/WG-dispersable granule • L/LC-liquid • SP/WSP-soluble packet • W/WP-wettable powder • WSB-water soluble bag

PENDIMETHALIN

■ PRE, POST

Pentagon DG (American Cyanamid)
Prowl 3.3 EC (American Cyanamid)

Rate: Except Hawaii:
2-3 lb. ai/A
4.8-7.2 pt. 3.3 EC/A
3.3-5 lb. DG/A
Hawaii:
2-4 lb. ai/A
4.8-9.7 pt. 3.3 EC/A
3.3-6.7 lb. DG/A

Time: Preemergence, postemergence. Apply to newly planted or ratoon sugarcane through lay-by and again in late summer or early fall to newly planted sugarcane. In Hawaii, apply twice per season preemergence through lay-by to plant or ratoon sugarcane. For postemergent application at lay-by, spray must be directed under sugarcane canopy.

Weeds: Broadleaf weeds:

annual spurge	lambsquarters	pigweed
carpetweed	Pennsylvania	purslane
Florida pusley	smartweed	velvetleaf
kochia		

Annual grasses:

barnyardgrass	goosegrass	junglerice
browntop panicum	green foxtail	signalgrass
crabgrass	guineagrass	swollen fingergrass
crowfootgrass	itchgrass	Texas panicum
fall panicum	(high rate)	witchgrass
field sandbur	johnsongrass	yellow foxtail
giant foxtail	(seedling)	

Remarks: Rate varies by soil type. Use high rate for heavy clay soil, if no mechanical incorporation is planned, heavy weed populations are anticipated, or if no shaving is planned. Do not use on peat or muck soils. Do not apply more than 6 lb. ai/A per growing season, apply through irrigation systems, or make aerial applications at close-in. Do not graze treated fields or feed treated forage or fodder to livestock.

Days To Harvest: 90.

Tank Mixes: May be tank mixed with any registered herbicide.

- - - - - - - - - - - - - - -

Signal Word/Toxicity Class: Caution.
REI: 24 hr.

Pentagon — see pendimethalin

Prowl — see pendimethalin

Rattler — see glyphosate

Roundup Ultra — see glyphosate

Saber — see 2,4-D

Savage — see 2,4-D

SCYTHE

◆ **Scythe (pelargonic acid)** (Mycogen)

Rate: 4-13 fl. oz./1 gal. spray solution
Time: Apply to actively growing weeds prior to crop emergence.
Weeds: Annual and perennial broadleaf weeds and grasses.
Remarks: Apply in minimum 75 gal. spray solution/A or spray-to-wet. Do not apply by air or through any type of irrigation system. Refer to label for directions and precautions.
Tank Mixes: Glyphosate and other foliar and residual herbicides.

- - - - - - - - - - - - - - -

Signal Word/Toxicity Class: Warning/II.
REI: 24 hr.

SENCOR

■ PRE, POST

Sencor 4 (FL) or DF (metribuzin) (Bayer)

Rate: Nonirrigated cane:
2-4 lb. ai/A
4-8 pt. FL/A
2.67-5.3 lb. DF/A
Irrigated cane:
4-6 lb. ai/A
8-12 pt. FL/A
5.3-8 lb. DF/A

Time: Preemergence, early postemergence. Preemergence (within 2 weeks after planting). Early postemergence (up to 4-6 weeks after planting).

Rate: 2-4 lb. ai/A
4-8 pt. FL/A
2.67-5.3 lb. DF/A
Spot Treatment:
2.5-5 lb. ai/A in 30-50 gal. finished spray
5-10 pt. FL/A
3.3-6.67 lb. DF/A

Time: Postemergence. Apply when weeds are less than 3" in height as broadcast spray prior to close-in.

Weeds: Broadleaf weeds:

ageratum	graceful spurge	Richardia spp.
common purslane	haloe koa	spiny amaranth
fireweed	hialoa	spleen amaranth
flora's paintbrush	hila hila	tarweed
garden spurge	rattlepod	wild euphorbia

Grasses:

alexandergrass	guineagrass	ricegrass
bristly foxtail	plushgrass	wiregrass
crabgrass		

Remarks: Do not apply more than 8 lb. ai/crop season. Do not use treated foliage for feed or forage.
Days To Harvest: 17 months.
Crop Rotation: Alfalfa, asparagus, barley (following peas, lentils, or soybeans), corn, forage grasses, potatoes, sainfoin, soybeans, sugarcane, tomatoes, wheat (following peas, lentils, or soybeans)—4 months; barley, cotton, lentils, peas, rice, wheat—8 months; other crops not listed, except root crops—12 months; onions, sugar beets, and other root crops—18 months. Cover crops for soil building or erosion control may be planted anytime, but do not graze or harvest for food or feed. Stand reductions may occur in some areas.
State Restrictions: For use in Hawaii.

- - - - - - - - - - - - - - -

Rate: Broadcast:
1.5-3 lb. ai/A
3-6 pt. FL/A
2-4 lb. DF/A
Band:
0.75-1.5 lb. ai/A
1.5-3 pt. FL/A
1-2 lb. DF/A

Time: Preemergence and postemergence. Apply band or broadcast during the fall after planting or to stubble after harvest. Second application may be made in early spring and third application at lay-by, if necessary.

Weeds: Broadleaf weeds:

chickweed	London rocket	sowthistle
field bindweed	marestail	spiny amaranth
henbit	pigweed	wild mustard
lambsquarters	purslane	winter oats

Grasses:

broadleaf	crabgrass	johnsongrass
signalgrass	foxtail	(seedling)

Remarks: Do not use treated foliage for feed or forage. Use higher rate on heavy clay soil and high organic matter soil. Refer to label for directions, limitations, and cautions.
Days To Harvest: 60.
Crop Rotation: Same restrictions as above.
State Restrictions: For use in Louisiana, Texas.

- - - - - - - - - - - - - - -

Rate: 1-2 lb. ai/A
2-4 pt. FL/A
1.3-2.67 lb. DF/A

Time: Postemergence. Apply as directed spray or broadcast/band over top of stubble or plant cane while sugarcane is less than 14" tall. On directed sprays, apply after sugarcane is 14" tall but before row closing.

Weeds: Broadleaf weeds:

broadleaf	butterweed	spiny
panicum	goosegrass	amaranth

5

Other Field Crops

Sugarcane

Remarks: Do not apply more than 2 lb. ai/A per season. Do not use treated foliage for feed or forage.
Days To Harvest: 60.
Crop Rotation: Same restrictions as above.
Tank Mixes: Atrazine.
State Restrictions: For use in Florida.

- - - - - - - - - - - - - - -

Signal Word/Toxicity Class: Caution/III.
REI: 12 hr.

SIMAZAT (Premix)

Restricted Use Pesticide.

■ **PRE**

Simazat 4L (2 lb./gal. simazine & 2 lb./gal. atrazine) *(Drexel)*
Rate: 2-3 lb. ai/A
4-6 pt. 4L/A
Time: At planting or ratooning. Apply before cane emerges (1 additional application may be made over cane as it emerges; 2 additional applications may be made interline after emergence as directed spray).
Weeds: Broadleaf weeds:

amaranth	fireweed	flora's paintbrush

Grasses:

crabgrass	junglerice	wiregrass
foxtail		

Remarks: Do not apply after close-in.

- - - - - - - - - - - - - - -

Signal Word/Toxicity Class: Caution.
REI: 12 hr.

SINBAR

■ **PRE**

Sinbar (WP) (terbacil) *(DuPont)*
Rate: 0.8-2 lb. ai/A
1-2.5 lb. WP/A
Time: Preemergence. In Hawaii, for best results, apply during relatively dry season (Mar.-Oct.).
Weeds: Most annual broadleaf weeds and grasses including:
johnsongrass (seedling)
Remarks: Apply single broadcast application. Do not use on susceptible varieties.
Crop Rotation: Do not replant to any crop other than sugarcane or pineapple within 2 years after last application.
State Restrictions: For use in Hawaii: plant, ratoon cane; Puerto Rico: plant cane.

- - - - - - - - - - - - - - -

Rate: 0.8-1.6 lb. ai/A
1-2 lb. WP/A
Time: Preemergence. Apply broadcast in the fall, repeat application at same rate in early spring.
Weeds: Same as above.
Remarks: Do not use on susceptible varieties.
Crop Rotation: Do not replant to any crop other than sugarcane or pineapple within 2 years after last application.
State Restrictions: For use in Texas on stubble, plant cane.

- - - - - - - - - - - - - - -

Rate: 1.6 lb. ai/A
2 lb. WP/A
Time: Apply broadcast in the fall, repeat at same rate in early spring.
Weeds: Same as above.
Remarks: For fall-planted or stubble cane not treated in the fall, apply broadcast in the spring at 4 lb./A. For lay-by treatment immediately after last cultivation, apply 0.5 lb./A in 30" band as directed spray to row middle. Do not apply over top of cane as crop injury may result. Do not use on susceptible varieties.
Crop Rotation: Do not replant to any other crop other than sugarcane or pineapple within 2 years after last application.
State Restrictions: For use in Louisiana.

- - - - - - - - - - - - - - -

Signal Word/Toxicity Class: Caution.
REI: 12 hr.

Solution — see 2,4-D

Sterling — see dicamba

Treflan — see trifluralin

TRI-4 — see trifluralin

Trific — see trifluralin

TRIFLURALIN

■ **PRE, POST**

Albaugh Trifluralin 4EC *(Albaugh)*
◆ **Clean Crop Trifluralin HF (4EC)** *(Platte)*
Gowan Trifluralin 4 or 5 (EC) *(Gowan)*
Helena Trifluralin 4 EC *(Helena)*
Riverside Trifluralin 4EC or Trific 60DF *(Terra)*
◆ **Sedagri Trifluralin 480 (4EC)** *(Rhone-Poulenc)*
Treflan HFP (4EC) or TR-10 (10G) *(Dow AgroSciences)*
TRI-4 HF (4EC) *(American Cyanamid)*
Trilin 4 or 5 (EC) or 10G *(Griffin)*
Wilbur-Ellis Trifluralin 10G *(Wilbur-Ellis)*
Rate: 1-2 lb. ai/A
2-4 pt. 4EC/A
1.6-3.2 pt. 5EC/A
1.66-3.33 lb. 60DF/A
10-20 lb. 10G/A
Time: Preemergence, postemergence. Apply twice a year. Make first application in the fall immediately after seed pieces are planted; second application in the spring before or shortly after cane emerges.
Weeds: Broadleaf weeds:

carelessweed	knotweed	purslane
carpetweed	kochia	pusley
chickweed	lambsquarters	redroot pigweed
field bindweed	Mexican clover	rough pigweed
fireweed	Mexican fireweed	Russian thistle
Florida purslane	prostrate pigweed	spiny pigweed
Florida pusley	puncturevine	stinging nettle
goosefoot	(western U.S.)	tumbleweed
henbit		

Grasses:

annual bluegrass	fall panicum	sandbur
barnyardgrass	foxtail millet	shattercane
bottlegrass	giant foxtail	smooth crabgrass
brachiaria	green foxtail	sprangletop
bristlegrass	Italian ryegrass	stinkgrass
bromegrass	johnsongrass	Texas panicum
burgrass	(seedling)	watergrass
cheat	junglerice	wildcane
cheatgrass	large crabgrass	woolly cupgrass
chess	pigeongrass	yellow foxtail
downy brome	robust foxtail	

Remarks: Plant cane. Loosen rain-packed beds 2-3" deep before spring application. Take care that incorporation equipment does not damage seed pieces or emerging shoots. Refer to label for directions and precautions.
Crop Rotation: Refer to label.
State Restrictions: Wilbur-Ellis not registered in California.

- - - - - - - - - - - - - - -

Rate: 3-4 lb. ai/A
6-8 pt. 4EC/A
4.8-6.4 pt. 5EC/A
5-6.66 lb. 60DF/A
Time: Postplant. Apply after planting (plant cane) or after harvesting (ratoon cane) before weeds emerge.
Weeds: Annual grasses including:
guineagrass
Remarks: Plant, ratoon cane. Apply just before anticipated rainfall or sprinkle irrigate just after application. Refer to label for directions and precautions.
Days To Harvest: 180.
Crop Rotation: Refer to label.
State Restrictions: For use in Hawaii.

- - - - - - - - - - - - - - -

Rate: 1-2 lb. ai/A
2-4 pt. 4EC/A
1.6-3.2 pt. 5EC/A
1.66-3.33 lb. DF, 60DF/A
10-20 lb. 10G/A
Time: Preemergence, postemergence. Apply in the spring from before or shortly after cane emerges up to lay-by.
Weeds: Same weeds as above plus:
itchgrass (LA-high rate)

◆-new product • PP-preplant • PPI-preplant incorporated • PRE-preemergence • POST-postemergence • SEQ-sequential • ae-acid equivalent • ai-active ingredient • DF-dry flowable
E/EC-emulsifiable concentrate • F/FL-flowable • DG/G/WG-dispersable granule • L/LC-liquid • SP/WSP-soluble packet • W/WP-wettable powder • WSB-water soluble bag

Remarks: Plant, ratoon cane. Loosen rain-packed bed 2-3" deep before application. Take care that incorporation equipment does not damage seed pieces or emerging shoots. Refer to label for directions and precautions.
State Restrictions: For use in Louisiana, Texas.

- - - - - - - - - - - - - -

Signal Word/Toxicity Class: Varies by formulation.
REI: 12 hr. unless soil injected or soil incorporated.

Trilin — see trifluralin

Velpar — see hexazinone

Weed Rhap — see 2,4-D

Weedar — see 2,4-D

Weedestroy — see 2,4-D

Weedmaster — see 2,4-D & dicamba

Weedone — see 2,4-D

Sunflower

ASSERT

■ **POST**
Assert (2.5LC) (imazamethabenz) *(American Cyanamid)*
Rate: 0.19-0.25 lb. ai/A
0.6-0.8 pt. 2.5LC/A
Time: Postemergence. Apply to sunflower in 2- to 8-leaf stage (less than 15" high). For optimum control of wild mustard, apply when majority of plants are in rosette stage and prior to bloom.
Weeds:
wild mustard
Remarks: Do not graze treated fields or cut treated forage for silage or hay.
Days To Harvest: 0.
Crop Rotation: Barley, canola (IMI-tolerant varieties such as Pioneer 45A71, 46A72; non-IMI tolerant in certain counties in Minnesota and North Dakota), corn, edible beans, safflower, soybeans, sunflower, wheat—anytime; sugar beets—20 months; other crops—15 months after application.

- - - - - - - - - - - - - -

Signal Word/Toxicity Class: Danger/I.
REI: 48 hr.

Cyclone — see paraquat

Eptam — see EPTC

EPTC

■ **PPI**
Eptam 7-E or 20-G *(ZENECA)*
Rate: Spring application:
2.18-3 lb. ai/A
2.5-3.5 pt. 7-E/A
Fall application:
4-4.5 lb. ai/A
4.5-5.25 pt. 7-E/A
20-22.5 lb. 20-G/A
Time: Preplant incorporated. Spring application: Apply and incorporate just before planting. Fall application: Apply and incorporate before ground freezes.

Weeds: Broadleaf weeds:

black nightshade	corn spurry	nettleleaf goosefoot
carpetweed*	cutleaf nightshade*	prickly sida*
common chickweed	deadnettle	prostrate pigweed
common	fiddleneck*	redroot pigweed
lambsquarters	Florida pusley	sicklepod*
common pigweed	hairy nightshade	tall morningglory*
common purslane	henbit	tumble pigweed

Annual grasses and sedges:

annual bluegrass	green foxtail	signalgrass*
annual ryegrass	Italian ryegrass	stinkgrass*
barnyardgrass	johnsongrass	Texas panicum*
bermudagrass	(seedling)	volunteer grains
(seedling)	junglerice	(barley, oats, wheat)
crabgrass	lovegrass*	watergrass
fall panicum*	purple nutsedge	wild oat
field sandbur	quackgrass	witchgrass*
giant foxtail	rescuegrass*	yellow foxtail
goosegrass	shattercane	yellow nutsedge

7-E only
Remarks: For spring application, use lower rate on lighter soil. For fall application, use low rate on coarse-textured soils; high rate on medium- and fine-textured soils.
State Restrictions: Spring application: For use in Colorado, Kansas, Minnesota, Nebraska, North Dakota, South Dakota. Fall application: For use in Minnesota, North Dakota.

- - - - - - - - - - - - - -

Signal Word/Toxicity Class: Caution.
REI: 12 hr. unless soil injected or soil incorporated.

Gramoxone Extra — see paraquat

PARAQUAT
Restricted Use Pesticide.

■ **PP, PRE, POST**
Cyclone (2L or 3L) or Gramoxone Extra (2.5L) *(ZENECA)*
Rate: 0.6-1 lb. ai/A
2-3 pt. 2.5L/A
Time: Preplant or preemergence. Apply before, during, or after planting but before crop emergence.

Rate: 0.25-0.5 lb. ai/A
1-2 pt. 2L/A
0.6-1.3 pt. 3L/A
0.3-0.5 lb. ai/A
1-1.5 pt. 2.5L/A
Time: Preharvest, desiccation. Apply when seeds reach maturity or when back of heads are yellow and bracts are turning brown.
Weeds: Annual broadleaf weeds and grasses; top kill and suppression of perennials.
Remarks: Add nonionic surfactant or crop oil concentrate. Seedbeds should be formed as far ahead of planting and treatment as possible to permit maximum weed and grass emergence. Seeding should be done with a minimum amount of soil disturbance. Weeds and grasses emerging after application will not be controlled; crops emerged at time of application will be killed. Do not graze treated areas for feed treated forage to livestock. Refer to label for use directions and precautions.
Days To Harvest: Preharvest, desiccation, broadcast—7.

- - - - - - - - - - - - - -

Signal Word/Toxicity Class: Danger-Poison/I.
REI: 12 hr. (except harvest aid/desiccation 24 hr.).

PENDIMETHALIN

■ **PPI, PRE**
Pentagon DG *(American Cyanamid)*
Prowl 3.3 EC *(American Cyanamid)*
Rate: Spring preplant incorporated:
0.5-1.5 lb. ai/A
1.2-3.6 pt. 3.3 EC/A
0.85-2.5 lb. DG/A
Fall preplant incorporated:
0.9-1.75 lb. ai/A
1.8-4.2 pt. 3.3 EC/A
1.25-2.9 lb. DG/A
Time: Preplant incorporated. For spring application, apply up to 60 days prior to planting and incorporate within 7 days after application. For fall application, incorporate in late fall prior to planting sunflowers the following spring in Minnesota, North Dakota, Oklahoma, South Dakota, Texas. Do not apply when air temperature is below 45°F.

5

Other Field Crops

NOTICE The information on these pages is for preliminary planning — not a guide for use. Be sure to follow the manufacturer's directions, notwithstanding information contained here. | For personal protective equipment and EPA registration numbers, please turn to page 70.

Sunflower

Rate: No-till:
    1.2-1.5 lb. ai/A
    3-3.6 pt. 3.3 EC/A
    2.1-2.5 lb. DG/A

Time: Preplant surface or preemergence application in Colorado, Kansas, Minnesota, Nebraska, North Dakota, and South Dakota.

Weeds: Broadleaf weeds:

annual spurge	lambsquarters	pigweed
carpetweed	Pennsylvania	purslane
Florida pusley	smartweed*	velvetleaf*
kochia		

Annual grasses:

barnyardgrass	giant foxtail	signalgrass
crabgrass	goosegrass	Texas panicum
crowfootgrass	green foxtail	witchgrass
fall panicum	johnsongrass	yellow foxtail
field sandbur	(seedling)	

*Reduced competition

Remarks: Rate varies by soil type. Do not use on peat or muck soils. If loss of crop occurs due to weather conditions, sunflowers or any crop registered for preplant incorporated use can be replanted the same year. If replanting is necessary, do not rework soil deeper than treated zone. Fields treated previous fall should receive at least 1 shallow incorporation in the spring prior to planting sunflowers (incorporation should be made at an angle to last tillage operation). Do not feed forage or graze livestock in treated fields.

Crop Rotation: Winter wheat and winter barley can be planted in the fall after a spring application. Do not plant no-till wheat the fall following a no-till application.Treated land can be planted to other crops the following year (see label for beet and spinach restrictions).

Tank Mixes: Eptam for fall application in Minnesota, North Dakota.

- - - - - - - - - - - - - - -

Signal Word/Toxicity Class: Caution.
REI: 24 hr.

Pentagon — see pendimethalin

Poast — see sethoxydim

Prowl — see pendimethalin

SCYTHE

◆ **Scythe (pelargonic acid)** *(Mycogen)*
Rate: 4-13 fl. oz./1 gal. spray solution
Time: Apply to actively growing weeds prior to crop emergence.
Weeds: Annual and perennial broadleaf weeds and grasses.
Remarks: Apply in minimum 75 gal. spray solution/A or spray-to-wet. Do not apply by air or through any type of irrigation system. Refer to label for directions and precautions.
Tank Mixes: Glyphosate and other foliar and residual herbicides.

- - - - - - - - - - - - - - -

Signal Word/Toxicity Class: Warning/II.
REI: 24 hr.

SETHOXYDIM

■ **POST**

Poast (1.5EC) *(BASF)*
Rate: 0.09-0.47 lb. ai/A
    0.5-2.5 pt. 1.5EC/A
Time: Postemergence.
Weeds: Annual and perennial grasses:

annual ryegrass	johnsongrass	southwestern cupgrass
barnyardgrass	junglerice	stinkgrass
bermudagrass	large crabgrass	tall fescue
broadleaf signalgrass	lovegrass	Texas panicum
browntop panicum	orchardgrass	volunteer grains
fall panicum	(seedling)	wild oat
field sandbur	perennial ryegrass	wild proso millet
giant foxtail	quackgrass	wirestem muhly
goosegrass	red sprangletop	witchgrass
green foxtail	shattercane	woolly cupgrass
itchgrass	smooth crabgrass	yellow foxtail

Remarks: Rate depends on growing region. Add spray adjuvant or oil concentrate. Urea ammonium-nitrate solution (UAN) or ammonium sulfate (AMS) recommended to enhance activity on certain grass species. Do not apply through any type of irrigation system. Refer to label for restrictions and limitations.

Days To Harvest: 70.
State Restrictions: Do not use UAN or AMS in California or Pacific Northwest.

- - - - - - - - - - - - - - -

Signal Word/Toxicity Class: Warning/II.
REI: 12 hr.

SONALAN

■ **PPI**

Sonalan HFP or 10G (ethalfluralin) *(Dow AgroSciences)*
Rate: 0.55-1.1 lb. ai/A
    1.5-3 pt. HFP/A
    5.5-11.5 lb. 10G/A
    Groundcherry, nightshade from seed:
    1.1-1.7 lb. ai/A
    3-4.5 pt. HFP/A
    11.5-17 lb. 10G/A
Time: Preplant incorporated. Apply in the spring before planting or in the fall.
Weeds: Broadleaf weeds:

carpetweed	groundcherry	redroot pigweed
common chickweed	henbit	Russian thistle
common	kochia	smooth pigweed
lambsquarters	nightshade	tarweed fiddleneck
common purslane	prostrate pigweed	tumble pigweed
conical catchfly	redmaids	wild buckwheat
Florida pusley	rockpurslane	

Grasses:

annual bluegrass	giant foxtail	shattercane
annual ryegrass	green foxtail	Texas panicum
barnyardgrass	Italian ryegrass	wild oat
broadleaf signalgrass	johnsongrass	wildcane
crabgrass	(seedling)	witchgrass
fall panicum	junglerice	woolly cupgrass
field sandbur	large crabgrass	yellow foxtail
foxtail millet	pigeongrass	

Remarks: Rate varies by soil type. Fall application of Sonalan HFP may be made only with dry bulk fertilizer. Do not apply to soils which are wet, cloddy, or subject to prolonged periods of flooding. Do not apply through any type of irrigation system. Do not graze or forage crop grown in treated soil or cut for hay or silage.

Crop Rotation: If replanting required, replant only crops listed on label. Do not plant sugar beets or red beets within 13 months after application of 1.1 lb. ai/A or more; for less than 1.1 lb. ai/A, within 8 months after application, provided treated area is moldboard plowed to a depth of at least 12" prior to planting. In Arizona and California, do not plant spinach or oats within 8 months after application of 1.1 lb. ai/A or more. Refer to label for special restrictions for Montana and Wyoming.

Tank Mixes: May be tank mixed with other registered products; refer to labels.

- - - - - - - - - - - - - - -

Signal Word/Toxicity Class: Danger/I.
REI: 24 hr. (HFP); 12 hr. (10G) unless soil injected or soil incorporated.

Treflan — see trifluralin

TRI-4 — see trifluralin

Trific — see trifluralin

TRIFLURALIN

■ **PPI**

Albaugh Trifluralin 4EC *(Albaugh)*
◆ **Clean Crop Trifluralin HF (4EC)** *(Platte)*
Gowan Trifluralin 4 or 5 (EC) or 10G *(Gowan)*
Helena Trifluralin 4 EC *(Helena)*
Riverside Trifluralin 4EC or Trific 60DF *(Terra)*
◆ **Sedagri Trifluralin 480 (4EC)** *(Rhone-Poulenc)*
Treflan HFP (4EC) or TR-10 (10G) *(Dow AgroSciences)*
TRI-4 HF (4EC) *(American Cyanamid)*
Trilin 4 or 5 (EC) or 10G *(Griffin)*
Wilbur-Ellis Trifluralin 10G *(Wilbur-Ellis)*
    Rate: 0.5-1 lb. ai/A
      1-2 pt. 4EC/A
      0.8-1.6 pt. 5EC/A
      0.875-1.66 lb. 60DF/A
      5-10 lb. 10G/A
    Time: Preplant incorporated. Apply in spring or fall (Oct. 15-Dec. 31).

◆-new product • PP-preplant • PPI-preplant incorporated • PRE-preemergence • POST-postemergence • SEQ-sequential • ae-acid equivalent • ai-active ingredient • DF-dry flowable
E/EC-emulsifiable concentrate • F/FL-flowable • DG/G/WG-dispersable granule • L/LC-liquid • SP/WSP-soluble packet • W/WP-wettable powder • WSB-water soluble bag

Weeds: Broadleaf weeds:

carelessweed	knotweed	purslane
carpetweed	kochia	pusley
chickweed	lambsquarters	redroot pigweed
field bindweed	Mexican clover	rough pigweed
fireweed	Mexican fireweed	Russian thistle
Florida purslane	prostrate pigweed	spiny pigweed
Florida pusley	puncturevine	stinging nettle
goosefoot	(western U.S.)	tumbleweed
henbit		

Grasses:

annual bluegrass	fall panicum	sandbur
barnyardgrass	foxtail millet	shattercane
bottlegrass	giant foxtail	smooth crabgrass
brachiaria	green foxtail	sprangletop
bristlegrass	Italian ryegrass	stinkgrass
bromegrass	johnsongrass	Texas panicum
burgrass	(seedling)	watergrass
cheat	junglerice	wildcane
cheatgrass	large crabgrass	woolly cupgrass
chess	pigeongrass	yellow foxtail
downy brome	robust foxtail	

Remarks: Rate varies by soil type. Refer to label for directions, restrictions, and precautions.

Crop Rotation: Refer to label.

State Restrictions: Wilbur-Ellis not registered in California.

- - - - - - - - - - - - - - -

Signal Word/Toxicity Class: Varies by formulation.

REI: 12 hr. unless soil injected or soil incorporated.

Trilin — see trifluralin

Tobacco

BASAMID

■ **PP**

Basamid Granular (dazomet) *(BASF)*

Rate: 13 oz./100 sq. ft.

Time: Preplant.

Weeds: Weed seeds:

henbit mustard	pigweed	purslane

Grasses:

bermudagrass	crabgrass	foxtail

Remarks: Tobacco seedbeds. Seedbed should be well prepared with moisture adequate for good plant growth. Wait 10-30 days before planting. Fall soil treatments recommended if early spring planting is desired (apply when soil is warm). Cover advisable but not required under most conditions.

Crop Rotation: Except as provided on label, do not rotate to food crops for 1 year.

- - - - - - - - - - - - - - -

Signal Word/Toxicity Class: Warning/II.

REI: 24 hr.

COMMAND

Command is a pigment inhibitor and may be utilized as a preemergent soil-applied or soil incorporated treatment for control of annual grass and broadleaf weeds. Must be applied as soil incorporated treatment in certain states. Off-site movement of spray drift or vapors can cause foliar whitening or yellowing of some plants.

■ **PPI, PRE**

Command 4EC or 3ME (clomazone) *(FMC)*

Rate: 0.75-1 lb. ai/A
1.5-2 pt. 4EC/A
2-2.6 pt. 3ME/A

Time: Preplant incorporated, preemergence (prior to transplant, post transplant).

Weeds: Broadleaf weeds:

balloonvine* **	jimsonweed	prickly sida
black nightshade* **	jointvetch* **	prostrate spurge**
blackseed plantain	kochia	purslane
cocklebur	ladysthumb	redvine* **
common ragweed	lambsquarters	redweed**
curly dock**	Pennsylvania	spurred anoda
dayflower	smartweed	tropic croton
Florida beggarweed**	pigweed* **	velvetleaf
Florida pusley	pitted	Venice mallow
galinsoga	morningglory**	wild poinsettia

Grasses:

barnyardgrass	itchgrass	shattercane*
bermudagrass*	(preemergence)**	smooth crabgrass
broadleaf signalgrass	johnsongrass	southwestern
common panicum	(seedling)	cupgrass
fall panicum	junglerice* **	Texas panicum
field sandbur	large crabgrass	wild proso millet*
giant foxtail	purple foxtail**	(Northern U.S.)
goosegrass	red rice* **	woolly cupgrass
green foxtail	robust foxtail	yellow foxtail

* Partial control; ** Southern U.S.

Remarks: Do not use on tobacco seedling beds. Apply single broadcast application in a minimum of 20 gal. water/A. If initial transplanting fails to produce a stand, tobacco may be replanted in treated fields. Do not retreat with a second application. Do not graze or harvest for food or feed cover crops planted less than 9 months after treatment, allow livestock to graze treated vines, or feed treated vines or vine trash to livestock. Do not apply through any type of irrigation system.

Crop Rotation: Northern U.S.: all crops—16 months after application. Southern U.S.: all crops—12 months after application. For specific crops at shorter intervals, refer to Rotational Crop Guidelines on label. Cover crops may be planted any time but stand reductions may occur in some areas. Carryover injury to approved rotational crops may result under abnormal conditions.

State Restrictions: Not for use in California.

- - - - - - - - - - - - - - -

Signal Word/Toxicity Class: Warning/II (4EC); Caution/III (3ME).

REI: 12 hr. unless soil injected or soil incorporated.

DEVRINOL

■ **PRE, POST**

Devrinol 50-DF (napropamide) *(United Phosphorus)*

Rate: 1-2 lb. ai/A
2-4 lb. 50-DF/A

Time: Before transplanting, at transplanting, at lay-by.

Weeds: Annual broadleaf weeds:

carpetweed	Florida pusley	purple cudweed
common purslane	galinsoga (4 lb. rate)	redroot pigweed
common ragweed*	lambsquarters	smooth pigweed

Annual grasses:

barnyardgrass	goosegrass	junglerice
crabgrass	green foxtail	stinkgrass
fall panicum	johnsongrass	witchgrass
giant foxtail	(seedling)	yellow foxtail

* Suppression

Remarks: Before transplanting, apply to weed-free soil and incorporate same day as applied. Application can be made up to 3 weeks before transplanting in Southeast only (except North Carolina and South Carolina). At transplanting, apply to soil surface immediately after transplanting. May be applied over-the-top of transplants. At lay-by, apply as directed spray to row middles after cultivation.

Crop Rotation: Small grains may be seeded in the fall to prevent soil erosion. These small grains may be stunted and cannot be harvested for food or feed production. Do not plant to crops not specified on label until 12 months after last application. Disc plow or moldboard plow at least 10" deep prior to planting succeeding crop.

Tank Mixes: Tillam.

State Restrictions: Do not apply before transplanting in North Carolina or South Carolina. At transplanting and lay-by applications in Kentucky, Maryland, Virginia, and Southeastern region only.

- - - - - - - - - - - - - - -

Signal Word/Toxicity Class: Caution.

REI: 12 hr.

■ **PRE**

Devrinol 2-E (napropamide) *(United Phosphorus)*

Rate: 1-2 lb. ai/A
0.5-1 gal. 2-E/A

Time: Before transplanting.

5

Other Field Crops

NOTICE The information on these pages is for preliminary planning — not a guide for use. Be sure to follow the manufacturer's directions, notwithstanding information contained here. | For personal protective equipment and EPA registration numbers, please turn to page 70.

Tobacco

Weeds: Annual broadleaf weeds:

carpetweed	lambsquarters	redroot pigweed
common purslane		

Annual grasses:

barnyardgrass	fall panicum	johnsongrass
crabgrass	goosegrass	(seedling)

Remarks: Apply to weed-free soil and incorporate same day as applied.

Crop Rotation: Do not plant to crops not specified on label until 12 months after last application. Disc plow or moldboard plow at least 10" deep prior to planting succeeding crop.

Tank Mixes: Tillam.

- - - - - - - - - - - - - -

Signal Word/Toxicity Class: Warning/I.
REI: 12 hr.

___

■ **PRE**

Devrinol 10-G (napropamide) *(United Phosphorus)*

Rate: 1.36 lb. ai/A
13.6 lb. 10-G/A

Time: Preemergence. Apply to weed-free soil immediately after planting.

Weeds:

white clover

Remarks: Direct-seeded plantbeds. Lightly incorporate or sprinkler irrigate within 24 hr. with sufficient water to wet soil to a depth of 2-4".

Crop Rotation: Do not plant to crops not specified on label until 12 months after last application. Disc plow or moldboard plow at least 10" deep prior to planting succeeding crop.

State Restrictions: Indiana, Kentucky, Maryland, Massachusetts, Ohio, Pennsylvania, Tennessee, Virginia, West Virginia.

- - - - - - - - - - - - - -

Signal Word/Toxicity Class: Caution.
REI: 12 hr.

___

PENDIMETHALIN

■ **PPI, PRE, POST**

Pentagon DG *(American Cyanamid)*
Prowl 3.3EC *(American Cyanamid)*

Rate: 0.75-1.5 lb. ai/A
1.8-3.6 pt. 3.3 EC/A
1.25-2.5 lb. DG/A

Time: Preplant incorporated. Apply up to 60 days prior to transplanting tobacco and incorporate within 7 days of application.

Rate: 0.5-1 lb. ai/A
1.2-2.4 pt. 3.3 EC/A
0.85-1.7 lb. DG/A

Time: Layby. Apply following last cultivation.

Weeds: Broadleaf weeds:

annual spurge	lambsquarters	pigweed
carpetweed	Pennsylvania	purslane
Florida pusley	smartweed*	velvetleaf*
kochia		

Grasses:

barnyardgrass	giant foxtail	signalgrass
crabgrass	goosegrass	Texas panicum
crowfootgrass	green foxtail	witchgrass
fall panicum	johnsongrass	yellow foxtail
field sandbur	(seedling)	

* Reduced competition

Remarks: Transplanted tobacco. Emerged weeds must be destroyed prior to application. Do not apply as a broadcast spray over top of tobacco leaf. If crop loss occurs due to weather conditions, transplanted tobacco or any crop registered for preplant incorporated use can be replanted the same year into treated soil. If replanting is necessary, do not rework soil deeper than treated zone.

Crop Rotation: Winter wheat and winter barley can be planted in the fall after a spring application in transplanted tobacco. Treated land can be planted to other crops the following year (see label for beet and spinach restrictions).

State Restrictions: Do not apply more than 1.2 lb. ai/A (PPI) in Florida, Georgia, Maryland, North Carolina, South Carolina, and Virginia.

- - - - - - - - - - - - - -

Signal Word/Toxicity Class: Caution.
REI: 24 hr.

___

Pentagon — see pendimethalin

___

Poast — see sethoxydim

___

Prowl — see pendimethalin

___

SCYTHE

◆ **Scythe (pelargonic acid)** *(Mycogen)*

Rate: 4-13 fl. oz./1 gal. spray solution

Time: Apply to actively growing weeds prior to crop emergence.

Weeds: Annual and perennial broadleaf weeds and grasses.

Remarks: Apply in minimum 75 gal. spray solution/A or spray-to-wet. Do not apply by air or through any type of irrigation system. Refer to label for directions and precautions.

Tank Mixes: Glyphosate and other foliar and residual herbicides.

- - - - - - - - - - - - - -

Signal Word/Toxicity Class: Warning/II.
REI: 24 hr.

___

SETHOXYDIM

■ **POST**

Poast (1.5EC) *(BASF)*

Rate: 0.09-0.25 lb. ai/A
0.5-1 pt. 1.5EC/A

Time: Apply only at seedbed stage of growth.

Weeds: Annual and perennial grasses:

annual ryegrass	junglerice	stinkgrass
barnyardgrass	large crabgrass	tall fescue
bermudagrass	lovegrass	Texas panicum
broadleaf signalgrass	orchardgrass	volunteer cereals
browntop panicum	(seedling)	wild oat
fall panicum	perennial ryegrass	wild proso millet
field sandbur	quackgrass	wildcane
giant foxtail	red rice	wirestem
goosegrass	red sprangletop	muhly witchgrass
green foxtail	shattercane	woolly cupgrass
itchgrass	smooth crabgrass	yellow foxtail
johnsongrass	southwestern cupgrass	

Remarks: Tobacco seedbeds. Do not apply to transplanted tobacco. Add spray adjuvant or oil concentrate. Do not apply through any type of irrigation system. Refer to label for restrictions and limitations.

State Restrictions: Do not use UAN or AMS in California or Pacific Northwest.

- - - - - - - - - - - - - -

Signal Word/Toxicity Class: Warning/II.
REI: 12 hr.

___

SPARTAN

■ **PRE**

Spartan (sulfentrazone) *(FMC)*

Rate: 0.25-0.38 lb. ai/A
5.3-8 oz./A

Time: Apply to soil prior to setting transplants. Do not retreat with second application.

Weeds: Broadleaf weeds:

American daisy	eastern black	Pennsylvania
annual smartweed	nightshade	smartweed
black nightshade	Florida beggarweed	poorjoe
bristly starbur	Florida pusley	prickly sida (teaweed)
carpetweed	giant ragweed	redroot pigweed
clammy groundcherry	hairy galinsoga	silverleaf nightshade
coffee senna	hairy nightshade	smellmelon
common cocklebur	hophornbeam	smooth pigweed
common dayflower	copperleaf	spiny amaranth
common	jimsonweed	spotted spurge
lambsquarters	kochia	spurred anoda
common purslane	ladysthumb	tall waterhemp
common ragweed	mexicanweed	tropic croton
common waterhemp	morningglory	velvetleaf
cutleaf groundcherry	Palmer amaranth	wild mustard

Grasses and sedges:

annual sedge	giant foxtail	orchardgrass
barnyardgrass	goosegrass	purple nutsedge
broadleaf signalgrass	green foxtail	Texas panicum
crabgrass	johnsongrass	yellow foxtail
crowfootgrass	(seedling)	yellow nutsedge
fall panicum		

___

◆-new product • PP-preplant • PPI-preplant incorporated • PRE-preemergence • POST-postemergence • SEQ-sequential • ae-acid equivalent • ai-active ingredient • DF-dry flowable
E/EC-emulsifiable concentrate • F/FL-flowable • DG/G/WG-dispersable granule • L/LC-liquid • SP/WSP-soluble packet • W/WP-wettable powder • WSB-water soluble bag

Remarks: Rates vary by soil texture and organic matter. Do not apply by air or through irrigation system. Do not allow spray drift onto adjacent plants. Tobacco may be replanted in treated fields.

Crop Rotation: Soybeans—anytime; barley, oats, rye, triticale, wheat—4 months; field corn, rice, sorghum—10 months; other cereal grains—12 months; cotton, sweet corn—18 months; canola, sugar beets—24 months after application.

Tank Mixes: Command 3ME.

– – – – – – – – – – – – – – –

Signal Word/Toxicity Class: Caution.

REI: 12 hr.

TILLAM

■ **PP**

Tillam 6-E (pebulate) *(ZENECA)*

Rate: 3-4 lb. ai/A
2-2.66 qt. 6-E/A

Time: Pretransplant. Apply before or after transplanting.

Weeds: Broadleaf weeds:

blackeyedsusan	hairy nightshade	nettleleaf goosefoot
common purslane	(suppression)	prostrate pigweed
deadnettle	henbit	redroot pigweed
Florida pusley	lambsquarters	shepherdspurse

Grasses and sedges:

barnyardgrass	goosegrass	purple nutsedge
bermudagrass	green foxtail	watergrass
(seedling)	millet	wild oat
crabgrass	narrowleaf	yellow foxtail
giant foxtail	signalgrass	yellow nutsedge

Remarks: On flue cured tobacco, use 2 qt. 6-E/A when applying with subsurface sweeps just before transplanting. Do not apply prior to hand transplanting. Refer to label for use directions and precautions.

Tank Mixes: Dasanit, Devrinol, Dyfonate, Mocap, Paarlan.

– – – – – – – – – – – – – – –

Signal Word/Toxicity Class: Caution.

REI: 12 hr.

VAPAM

Water-soluble liquid that when applied to properly prepared soil is converted into a gaseous fumigant. May be applied by sprinkler, soil injection, or chemigation.

Vapam HL (metam-sodium) *(Amvac)*

Rate: Tarp method:
0.5-1 gal. HL in 40 gal. water/100 sq. yd.
Drench method:
2.0 gal. HL in 150-200 gal. water/100 sq. yd.

Time: Fall application. In the south, apply before Nov. 30.

Weeds: Weeds and germinating weed seeds:

carelessweed	henbit	purslane
chickweed	lambsquarters	ragweed
dandelion	pigweed	wild morningglory

Grasses and sedges:

annual bluegrass	johnsongrass	nutsedge
bermudagrass	nutgrass	watergrass

Remarks: Prepare bed 5-7 days before application to ensure best conditions for weed seed germination and fumigant action. Loosen treated soil to a depth of 2" within 7 days after application. Do not seed tobacco earlier than 21 days after application. Do not use in greenhouses, enclosed structures, confined areas, or when fumes may enter nearby houses.

State Restrictions: In California, application must be in compliance with Technical Information Bulletin — California, "Metam Sodium Guidelines for All Application Methods for Metam Sodium in California." Bulletin may be obtained from local pesticide dealer or metam-sodium registrant.

– – – – – – – – – – – – – – –

Signal Word/Toxicity Class: Danger/I.

REI: 48 hr.

5

Other Field Crops

Notes • Notes • Notes

Section 6

Vegetables

Use Reminders

Rotation Guidelines For Vegetable Crops Following Corn
Herbicide Use 286
Rotation Guidelines For Vegetable Crops Following Soybean
Herbicide Use 287
Vegetable Herbicide Registration Chart 288

Weed Efficacy Charts

Herbicide Effectiveness On Weeds In Vegetables 289
Herbicide Effectiveness On Selected Weeds In Florida Vegetables ...290
Weed Response To Selected Herbicides, Sweet Corn 291

Herbicide Listings

Artichokes 292
Asparagus 293
Beans 297
Carrots, Parsley, Parsnips 301
Celery 303
Cole Crops 305
Cucurbits 307
Eggplant 309
Garbanzos 311
Garlic 312
Greens 314
Herbs & Spices 316
Horseradish 316
Lentils 317

Lettuce, Endive 318
Okra 320
Onions 320
Peas 324
Peppers 327
Potatoes 329
Radishes 333
Rhubarb 333
Southern Peas 335
Spinach 336
Sweet Corn 337
Sweet Potatoes 345
Table Beets 346
Tomatoes 347

Rotation Guidelines For Vegetable Crops Following Corn Herbicide Use[1]

Herbicide	Bean, lima	Bean, snap	Cantaloupe	Cole crops[2]	Corn, sweet	Cucumber	Greens[3]	Okra	Onion	Peas, southern	Pepper	Potato, Irish	Potato, sweet	Pumpkin	Squash	Tomato	Watermelon
AAtrex	24 m	24 m	24 m	24 m	none	24 m	24 m	24 m	24 m	24 m	24 m	24 m	24 m	24 m	24 m	24 m	24 m
Accent	10 m[4]	10 m[4]	10 m[4]	10 m[4]	10 m[5]	10 m[4]	10 m[4]	10 m[4]	10 m[4]	10 m[4]	10 m[4]	10 m[4]	10 m[4]	10 m[4]	10 m[4]	10 m[4]	10 m[4]
Banvel	FNH[6]	FNH[6]	FNH[6]	FNH[6]	FNH[6]	FNH[6]	FNH[6]	FNH[6]	FNH[6]	FNH[6]	FNH[6]	FNH[6]	FNH[6]	FNH[6]	FNH[6]	FNH[6]	FNH[6]
Basagran	none	none	none	none	none	none	none	none	none	none	none	none	none	none	none	none	none
Beacon	18 m	18 m	18 m	18 m	18 m	18 m	18 m	18 m	18 m	18 m	18 m	18 m	18 m	18 m	18 m	18 m	18 m
Bladex[7]	NF/S	NF/S	NF/S	NF/S	NF/S	NF/S	NF/S	NF/S	NF/S	NF/S	NF/S	NF/S	NF/S	NF/S	NF/S	NF/S	NF/S
Bullet or Lariat	24 m	24 m	24 m	24 m	24 m	24 m	24 m	24 m	24 m	24 m	24 m	24 m	24 m	24 m	24 m	24 m	24 m
Evik	NS	NS	NS	NS	NS	NS	NS	NS	NS	NS	NS	NS	NS	NS	NS	NS	NS
Exceed	18 m	300 d	18 m	18 m[10]	18 m	18 m	18 m	18 m	24 m	18 m	18 m	300 d	18 m	18 m	18 m[10]	18 m	24 m
Frontier	NS	NS	NS	NS	NS	NS	NS	NS	NS	NS	NS	NS	NS	NS	NS	NS	NS
Guardsman	24 m	24 m	24 m	24 m	24 m	24 m	24 m	24 m	24 m	24 m	24 m	24 m	24 m	24 m	24 m	24 m	24 m
Harness	24 m	24 m	24 m	24 m	24 m	24 m	24 m	24 m	24 m	24 m	24 m	24 m	24 m	24 m	24 m	24 m	24 m
Harness Extra	24 m	24 m	24 m	24 m	24 m	24 m	24 m	24 m	24 m	24 m	24 m	24 m	24 m	24 m	24 m	24 m	24 m
Hornet[8]	26 m	26 m	26 m	26 m	10.5 m	26 m	26 m	26 m	26 m	26 m	26 m	26 m	26 m	26 m	26 m	26 m	26 m
Lasso	none	none	none	none	none	none	none	none	none	none	none	none	none	none	none	none	none
Permit	24 m	24 m	24 m	24 m	24 m	24 m	24 m	24 m	24 m	24 m	24 m	24 m	24 m	24 m	24 m	24 m	24 m
Prowl	NS	NS	NS	NS	NS	NS	NS	NS	NS	NS	NS	NS	NS	NS	NS	NS	NS
Scorpion III[5]	26 m	26 m	26 m	26 m	10.5	26 m	26 m	26 m	26 m	26 m	26 m	26 m	26 m	26 m	26 m	26 m	26 m
Surpass	24 m	24 m	24 m	24 m	24 m	24 m	24 m	24 m	24 m	24 m	24 m	24 m	24 m	24 m	24 m	24 m	24 m
Surpass 100	24 m	24 m	24 m	24 m	24 m	24 m	24 m	24 m	24 m	24 m	24 m	24 m	24 m	24 m	24 m	24 m	24 m

[1] Numbers in the table followed by d or m refer to days and months, respectively.
[2] Cole crops include broccoli, cabbage and cauliflower.
[3] Greens include collard, kale, mustard, and turnips.
[4] Unless soil pH is greater than 6.5, then interval is 18 months.
[5] Except cultivars 'Merit', 'Carnival', and 'Sweet Success', which require 15 months rotation interval.
[6] FNH indicates anytime following normal corn harvest.
[7] NF/S indicates crop can be planted fall or spring following application.
[8] Label requires interval shown plus successful field bioassay; see label for instructions.
[9] Except cabbage which can be planted next season.
[10] Replant interval for cabbage is 300 days. Weed response ratings for vegetable crops herbicides.

Source: Weed Control Guidlines for Mississippi, 1997.

Rotation Guidelines For Vegetable Crops Following Soybean Herbicide Use[1]

Herbicide	Bean, lima	Bean, snap	Cantaloupe	Cole crops[2]	Corn, sweet	Cucumber	Greens[3]	Okra	Onion	Peas, southern	Pepper	Potato, Irish	Potato, sweet	Pumpkin	Squash	Tomato	Watermelon
Assure II	120 d	120 d	120 d	120 d	120 d	120 d	120 d	120 d	120 d	120 d	120 d	120 d	120 d	120 d	120 d	120 d	120 d
Basagran	none	none	none	none	none	none	none	none	none	none	none	none	none	none	none	none	none
Blazer	none	none	none	none	none	none	none[4]	none	none	none	none	18 m	18 m	none	none	none	none
Butyrac	none	none	none	none	none	none	none	none	none	none	none	none	none	none	none	none	none
Canopy pH < 7.0	18 m	18 m	18 m	18 m	18 m	18 m	18 m	18 m	18 m	18 m	18 m	18 m	18 m	18 m	18 m	10 m	18 m
Canopy pH 7.1-7.5	18 m	18 m	18 m	18 m	18 m	18 m	18 m	18 m	18 m	18 m	18 m	18 m	18 m	18 m	18 m	18 m	18 m
Classic	AFB[5]	AFB[5]	AFB[5]	AFB[5]	AFB[5]	AFB[5]	AFB[5]	AFB[5]	AFB[5]	AFB[5]	AFB[5]	AFB[5]	AFB[5]	AFB[5]	AFB[5]	9 m	AFB[5]
Cobra	none	none	none	none	none	none	none	none	none	none	none	none	none	none	none	none	none
Command 1.0 pt/A	12 m	9 m	9 m	12 m	9 m	9 m	12 m	12 m	12 m	12 m	12 m	9 m	9 m	none	12 m	9 m	9 m
Command 1.5-2.0 pt/A	12 m	12 m	12 m	12 m	12 m	12 m	12 m	12 m	12 m	12 m	12 m	12 m	12 m	none	12 m	12 m	12 m
Command 2.5 pt/A	12 m	12 m	12 m	12 m	12 m	12 m	12 m	12 m	12 m	12 m	12 m	12 m	9 m	12 m	12 m	12 m	12 m
Fusilade	none	none	none	none	60d	none	none	none	none	none	none	none	none	none	none	none	none
Lasso	none	none	none	none	none	none	none	none	none	none	none	none	none	none	none	none	none
Lorox	4 m	4 m	4 m	4 m	4 m	4 m	4 m	4 m	4 m	4 m	4 m	4 m	4 m	4 m	4 m	4 m	4 m
Poast Plus	none	none	none	none	none	none	none	none	none	none	none	none	none	none	none	none	none
Prowl	none	none	NS[7]	NS[7]	none	NS[7]	NS[7]	NS[7]	NS[7]	none	NS[7]	NS[7]	NS[7]	NS[7]	NS[7]	NS[7]	NS[7]
Pursuit	none	4 m	26 m	26 m	18 m	26 m	26 m	26 m	26 m	none	26 m	26 m	26 m	26 m	26 m	26 m	26 m
Reflex	18 m	18 m	18 m	18 m	18 m	18 m	18 m	18 m	18 m	18 m	18 m	18 m	18 m	18 m	18 m	18 m	18 m
Scepter	11 m	11 m	18 m	18 m	18 m	18 m	18 m	18 m	18 m	18 m	11 m	18 m	18 m	18 m	18 m	18 m	18 m
Sencor	12 m	12 m	12 m	12 m	12 m	12 m	12 m[4]	12 m	18 m	12 m	12 m	4 m	18 m	12 m	12 m	4 m	12 m
Treflan	none	none	none	none	5 m	none	none	none	5 m	none	none	none	5 m	5 m	5 m	none	none
Zorial	16 m	16 m	16 m	16 m	16 m	16 m	16 m	16 m	16 m	16 m	16 m	16 m	16 m	16 m	16 m	16 m	16 m

[1]Numbers in the table followed by d or m refer to days and months, respectively.
[2]Cole crops include broccoli, cabbage and cauliflower.
[3]Greens include collard, kale, mustard, and turnips.
[4]Product labels restrict root crop production (e.g., turnips grown for root harvest) less than 18 months after application.
[5]AFB = after field bioassay. A successful field bioassay must be conducted prior to crop rotation. See label for bioassay procedure.
[6]NS designates next season.
[7]Except cabbage, which can be planted next year.

Source: Weed Control Guidlines for Mississippi.

Vegetable Herbicide Registration Chart

Herbicide	Asparagus	Beans, dry & lima	Beans, pole & snap	Beets	Broccoli	Cabbage	Carrots	Cauliflower	Celery	Corn, sweet	Cucumbers	Eggplant	Greens	Lettuce	Melons	Okra	Onions, dry bulb	Onions, green	Peas, green	Peas, southern	Peppers	Potatoes, Irish	Potatoes, sweet	Pumpkins	Spinach	Squash	Tomatoes
Alanap-L											R				R												
Atrazine										R																	
Balan														R													
Basagran		R	R							R									R								
Bladex										R																	
Command																			R		R			R			
Curbit											R				R												
2,4-D	R									R																	
Devrinol	R				R	R		R				R									R						R
Eptam		R	R							R												R					
Fusilade DX	R						R										R							R		R	
Goal					R	R		R									R										
Gramoxone Extra	R	R	R		R	R	R	R		R	R	R	R	R	R	R	R	R	R	R	R	R	R	R	R	R	R
Karmex	R																										
Kerb														R													
Lasso										R																	
Lorox	R						R		R	R												R					
Poast	R	R	R		R	R		R	R	R	R				R		R	R	R	R	R	R	R	R	R	R	R
Prefar											R			R										R		R	
Princep	R									R																	
Prowl		R	R																			R					
Pursuit																				R							
Pyramin				R																							
Ro-Neet				R																							
Roundup	R	R	R	R	R	R	R	R	R	R	R	R	R	R	R	R	R	R			R	R	R	R	R	R	
Sencor	R							R														R					R
Sinbar	R																										
Spin-Aid																									R		
Treflan		R	R		R	R	R	R						R		R					R	R	R				R
Turbo																						R					

R = The herbicide is registered on this crop.

Source: Recommended Chemicals for Weed and Brush Control, Arkansas, 1999.

Herbicide Effectiveness On Weeds In Vegetables

Herbicide	Barnyardgrass	Carpetweed	Common cocklebur	Common lambsquarters	Common purslane	Common ragweed	Eastern black nightshade	Fall panicum	Foxtail spp.	Goosegrass	Hairy galinsoga	Jimsonweed	Large crabgrass	Morningglory spp.	Pennsylvania smartweed	Pigweed spp.	Seedling johnsongrass	Shepherdspurse	Velvetleaf	Yellow nutsedge
Preplant or Preplant Incorporated																				
Command	G	N	N/F	G	G	F	—	G	G	G	F	G	G	P	G	N/P	G	F	G	N
Devrinol	G	G	N	F/G	G	P/F	N	G	G	G	F/P	N	G	N	P	F/G	G	—	N	N/P
Eptam	G	G	P	F	G	P	F/G	G	G	G	G	N	P	G	F	P	G	G	—	F/G	G
Goal	P	F/G	—	F	G	F	—	P	P	P	F	—	P	—	—	G	P	G	—	N
Prefar	G	N	N	F/G	F	N	N	G	G	F/G	N	N	G	N	N	F	G	P/F	N	N
Ro-Neet	G	G	N	F	G	N	—	G	G	G	G	N	—	—	G	—	G	F	N/P
Sutan+	G	—	N	P	P	P	F	G	G	G	N	G	F	G	G	P	G	G	—	F	F/G
Tillam	G	—	N	P	P/F	N	F/G	F	G	F	N	F	N	N	—	—	G	—	—	F
Treflan	G	G	N	F/G	G	N	P	G	G	G	N	N	G	P/F	P/F	F	G	N	N	N
Preplant Incorporated or Preemergence																				
Alanap	P	F	P	G	F/G	F	P	P	F	P/F	F	F	P/F	F	P	F/G	—	N	F	N
Atrazine	F	G	F/G	G	G	G	G	P	F	—	G	G	P/F	G	G	G	P	G	F	P/F
Bladex	P	G	F	G	G	F	G	F	P	—	G	P	P	F	—	P	—	G	P	P
Micro-Tech/Partner	G	G	N	P/F	G	N	G	G	G	G	G	P	F/G	N	P	G	G	G	P	F
Prowl	G	G	N	F/G	F/G	N	P	G	G	—	N	N	G	P	F	F/G	G	N	G	N
Pursuit	P/F	G	F	G	G	P	F	P/F	P/F	P/F	P	F	P/F	F	G	G	—	F	G	N
Sencor	F	G	F	G	F	G	P	F	F	F	F	G	F/G	F	F/P	G	F/G	—	G	N
Preemergence																				
Curbit	F	G	N	P/F	F/G	N	P	—	G	N	N	G	P	P	F/G	—	—	—	P	N
Goal	P	G	P	G	G	F	G	P	P	P	G	F	P	F	G	G	P	G	P	P
Karmex	G	G	—	G	G	G	G	G	G	F/G	G	G	F/G	G	G	G	N	G	G	N
Kerb	G	G	N	G	G	P	—	G	G	G	P	N	G	—	—	G	—	—	P	N
Lorox	F	G	P	G	G	F	G	P	F	P/F	G	P/F	P/F	P	G	G	—	F	P	N
Sinbar	F	G	—	G	G	G	G	—	F	F	G	G	F	G	G	G	P	—	G	G
Solicam	G	—	—	F	G	G	—	G	G	—	—	F	G	P	—	G	F	—	F	F
Postemergence																				
Assure II	G	N	N	N	N	N	N	G	G	G	N	N	G	N	N	N	G	N	N	N
Atrazine	F	—	F	G	G	G	G	F	F	F	F	G	G	F	G	G	G	—	G	F/G	G
Banvel	N	G	G	G	G	G	G	N	N	N	N	G	N	G	G	N	G	G	G	P
Basagran	N	N	G	F	F/G	G	P	N	N	N	F	N	P	G	F	N	—	G	F
2,4-D	N	G	F/G	F/G	G	G	G	N	N	N	P	F	N	G	F	N	G	G	P
Fusilade DX	G	N	N	N	N	N	N	G	G	G	N	N	F/G	N	N	G	N	N	N
Gramoxone Extra[1]	F/G	G	G	F/G	F/G	G	—	F/G	G	F/G	G	G	F/G	F/G	P	G	—	—	—	G
Lorox	F	G	P/F	G	G	G	F/G	F	F	F	F/G	P/F	F	—	G	G	F	G	G
Matrix	G	—	F/G	P/F	F/G	P	P	F/G	G	P	F	F	F/G	P/F	—	G	F	F	F
Poast	G	N	N	N	N	N	N	G	G	G	N	N	G	N	N	N	G	N	N	N
Prism	G	N	N	N	N	N	N	G	G	G	N	N	G	N	N	N	G	N	N	N
Pursuit	F/G	G	F	G	G	P/F	—	F/G	F/G	P	G	F	F/G	F	—	G	F/G	P/F	G	—
Reflex	P	G	F/G	P	P/F	F	F	P	P	P	G	G	P	F/G	P/F	G	P	G	F/P	P
Roundup Ultra[1]	G	G	G	G	G	F	G	G	G	G	G	G	G	F	G	G	G	G	G	F
Sencor	F	G	—	G	G	G	P	F	F	F	G	G	F	P	F	G	—	G	P/F	—
Spin-Aid	P	—	P	F	G	F/G	—	P	P	P	G	G	P	G	—	P/F	P	G	N	P

[1]Nonselective G = Good, F = Fair, P = Poor, N = No control, — = Insufficient data

Source: 1998 Commercial Vegetable Production Recommendations, New Jersey

6

Vegetables
Weed Efficacy Chart

NOTICE The information on these pages is for preliminary planning — not a guide for use. Be sure to follow the manufacturer's directions, notwithstanding information contained here.

Vegetables Weed Efficacy Chart

Herbicide Effectiveness On Selected Weeds In Florida Vegetables

Herbicide	Broadleaf Weeds														Grasses							Sedges		
	Amaranthus	Cocklebur	Eclipta alba	Eveningprimrose	Florida beggarweed	Florida pusley	Lambsquarters	Morningglory spp.	Nightshade	Parthenium	Purslane	Ragweed	Sicklepod	Southern sida	Barnyardgrass	Bermudagrass	Broadleaf signalgrass	Crabgrass	Goosegrass	Panicums (fall & Texas)	Sprangletop	Annual sedges	Purple nutsedge	Yellow nutsedge
Preplant Incorporated																								
Command	F-G	P-F	—	G	—	G	G-E	P	—	—	E	F-G	P	—	E	G-E	E	E	E	G-E	—	P	P	P
Devrinol	F-G	P	P	G	P	G-E	G-E	P	P	P	G	—	P	—	E	E	E	E	E	G-E	—	F	P	F
Eptam	G	P	G	G	P	G-E	G	F	P-F	—	G	F	F	G	E	E	G	E	E	G-E	—	E	G-E	G
Prefar	F	P	P	F	P	E	F-G	P	P	—	F	P	P	P	G	G	G	G	G-E	F-G	—	P	P	P
Pursuit	G-E	—	E	E	E	F	E	G-E	G-E	—	E	G	P	G	F	P	F	F	F	P-F	P	E	F-G	G
Sencor	E	G	G	E	G-E	G	E	G-E	P	G	G	G	G	G	F-G	G	G-E	G-E	F-G	—	P	P	P	
Sutan+	G-E	P	G	G-E	P	G-E	G	F-G	—	—	G	F	F-G	G	E	E	G-E	E	E	G	—	E	G	G-E
Treflan	G-E	P	F-G	G	P	E	G-E	P	P	P	E	P	P	P	E	G	G-E	E	E	G	—	P	P	P
Preemergence																								
Alanap	G-E	F	G	G	F	G	E	F	F	—	G	F	P	G	P	P	F	F	P	P	—	P	P	P
Atrazine	E	G-E	G-E	E	G-E	E	E	G	G	E	E	E	F-G	G-E	F	P	F-G	F	F	P	P	P	P	P
Caparol	G-E	—	—	—	F-G	F-G	—	F-G	—	G-E	F-G	—	—	F-G	F-G	F-G	G	F-G	F	—	P	P	P	
Command	F-G	P	—	G	—	G	G	P	—	—	E	F	P	—	E	E	E	E	E	E	—	P	P	P
Curbit	G	P	—	G	P	E	G-E	P	P	P	E	P	P	P	E	G-E	E	E	E	G-E	G	P	P	P
Devrinol	F	P	P	G	P	G	G	P	P	P	G	—	P	—	E	E	E	E	E	G-E	—	F-G	P-F	F
Goal	E	E	E	E	G	G	E	G	G	G	E	G	F	G	F	P	F	F	F	P	—	G	P	F
Kerb	F-G	—	—	G	—	G	E	F-G	G	—	G-E	—	—	—	G-E	P	G	G-E	G-E	F-G	—	P	P	P
Lorox	G	F	—	E	G	E	E	F	—	—	E	G	—	F	F-G	—	G	G	G	F-G	—	F	F	F
Prowl	G-E	P	—	G	P	G	E	P	P	P	G	P	P	—	E	E	E	E	E	G-E	E	P	P	P
Pursuit	G-E	G-E	E	E	P	F	G-E	G-E	G-E	—	G-E	G	P	G	F	P	F	F	F	P-F	P	E	G	G-E
Sencor	G	F	F-G	E	G	G	E	F	P-F	G	G	G	G	G	F-G	F	G	G	G-E	P	P	P	P	P
Postemergence																								
Atrazine	G-E	F	G	E	P	G-E	G	G	F	F-G	F-G	F	F-G	F-G	F-G	F	F	F	F	F	F	P	P	P
Basagran	G	G	G	G	P	F	—	F-G	F-G	—	G	G	P	G	P	P	P	P	P	P	P	G-E	P-F	F-G
Buctril	G	E	E	E	E	G-E	G	G	G	—	G-E	G	—	G	P	P	P	P	P	P	P	P	P	P
*Diquat	E	G	E	E	G-E	G	E	F-G	G	E	G	G	G	G	E-G	G	E	G-E	G-E	G	G	G	F-G	F-G
*Gramoxone Extra	E	G	E	E	G-E	G	E	F-G	F	P	G	G	G	G	E	E	E	E	E	E	G	G	F-G	F-G
Lorox	E	G	—	—	G	G	E	F-G	—	—	E	G	G	G	G	F-G	G	G	G	G	G	F-G	F	F
Poast	N	N	N	N	N	N	N	N	N	N	N	N	N	N	E	G-E	E	E	E	E	E	P	P	P
Pursuit	E	G	G	G	—	F	F-G	G	G	—	P-F	G	P	—	F	P	P-F	P-F	F	P-F	P	G-E	G-E	G-E
Sencor	E	G	F	G	G	G	G	P	P	P	F-G	F-G	F	F	F	P	P	F	F	F	P	P	P	

E = 90-100%, G = 80-90%, F = 60-80%, P = Below 60%, N = No control, — = No data

*Initial burndown with sedges and other perennial weeds can be complete but with regrowth.

Source: Florida Weed Management, 1999

Weed Response To Selected Herbicides, Sweet Corn

Herbicide	Grasses						Broadleaf Weeds										
	Barnyardgrass	Crabgrass	Fall panicum	Foxtail	Sandbur	Shattercane/Sorghum	Black nightshade	Cocklebur	Kochia	Lambsquarters	Pigweed	Ragweed	Russian thistle	Smartweed	Sunflower	Velvetleaf	Waterhemp
Soil-applied																	
AAtrex/atrazine	6	4	2	7	5	1	9	8	10	10	10	9	9	9	7	7	10
Bicep II	9	9	9	9	6	4	9	7	9	9	9	8	8	8	6	6	9
Bladex/Cypro	7	7	6	8	5	4	8	7	8	9	4	9	9	9	6	6	3
Eradicane	9	9	9	9	7	8	6	3	5	7	7	5	3	3	2	2	7
Eradicane + atrazine	9	9	9	9	7	8	9	6	9	9	9	7	7	8	7	7	9
Extrazine II/Cypro AT	6	7	2	8	5	4	7	8	9	8	9	9	9	9	7	7	7
Lariat/Bullet or Lasso + atrazine	9	9	9	9	6	4	9	7	9	9	9	8	8	8	6	6	9
Lasso/Micro-Tech	9	9	9	9	6	4	7	2	2	8	8	5	3	2	2	2	8
Lasso + (atrazine + Bladex) or Extrazine II	9	9	9	8	4	3	9	7	9	9	9	9	9	7	7	7	9
Prowl + atrazine	8	9	9	9	7	3	9	4	9	9	9	9	7	8	6	7	9
Sutan+	9	9	9	9	8	7	5	2	5	7	5	5	2	2	2	2	5
Postemergence																	
AAtrex/atrazine or Bicep II	5	4	2	6	4	2	9	9	9	9	9	9	4	9	8	8	9
Bladex	4	7	4	7	4	4	9	7	9	9	6	9	4	9	7	7	6
2,4-D	2	2	2	2	2	2	6	10	5	7	7	7	4	4	7	8	8
Extrazine II	4	7	4	7	4	4	9	9	9	9	6	9	4	9	7	7	6
Laddok S-12	2	2	2	2	2	2	7	9	8	7	8	9	2	9	9	9	8

Response Ratings: Ratings are light to moderate weed populations, favorable conditions and weed growth stage as specified on the product label. High weed populations, adverse conditions, or large weeds will reduce control.
10 = 96-100%, 9 = 90-95%, 8 = 85-89%, 7 = 80-84%, 6 = 70-79%, 5 = 60-69%, 4-2 = less than 60%, 1 = 0%.

Source: Herbicide Use In Nebraska 1997 Guide

6

Vegetables
Weed Efficacy Chart

Vegetables

Artichokes

Credit — see glyphosate

DEVRINOL

Use in combination with a residual broadleaf herbicide to increase spectrum of weeds controlled.

■ **POST**

Devrinol 50-DF (napropamide) *(United Phosphorus)*

Rate: 4 lb. ai/A
8 lb. 50-DF/A

Time: Postemergence. Apply to weed-free soil in established artichokes.

Weeds: Broadleaf weeds:

annual sowthistle	common ragweed	pineappleweed
carpetweed	(suppression)	prickly lettuce
coast fiddleneck	horse purslane	prostrate knotweed
common chickweed	lambsquarters	purple cudweed
common groundsel	little mallow	redroot pigweed
common purslane	(from seed)	redstem filaree

Grasses:

annual bluegrass	guineagrass	smooth crabgrass
barnyardgrass	hairy crabgrass	soft chess
bristly foxtail	Italian ryegrass	southwestern
canarygrass	johnsongrass	cupgrass
cheatgrass	(seedling)	stinkgrass
downy brome	junglerice	Texas panicum
fall panicum	large crabgrass	wild barley
foxtail barley	Mexican sprangletop	wild oat
giant foxtail	red sprangletop	witchgrass
goosegrass	ripgut brome	yellow foxtail
green foxtail	sandbur	

Remarks: If rainfall does not occur, treatment must be shallowly incorporated or irrigated-in following application with sufficient water to wet soil to a depth of 2-4".

Crop Rotation: Do not plant to crops not specified on label until 12 months after last application. Disc plow or moldboard plow at least 10" deep prior to planting succeeding crop.

State Restrictions: For use in Western Region of U.S. only.

- - - - - - - - - - - - - - -

Signal Word/Toxicity Class: Caution.
REI: 12 hr.

DIQUAT DIBROMIDE

◆ **Diquat** *(ZENECA)*

Rate: 0.375-0.5 lb. ai/A
1.5-2 pt./A

Time: Site preparation prior to planting. Repeat as needed.

Weeds: Broadleaf weeds and grasses.

Remarks: Nonbearing. Apply by ground only. Use high rate when weeds are large or dense. Do not allow spray to contact green stems, foliage, or fruit. Use a shield or wrap plant when spraying around young trees or vines. Do not apply through any type of irrigation system. Do not graze treated areas. Refer to label for use restrictions and precautions.

Days To Harvest: 1 year.

- - - - - - - - - - - - - - -

Signal Word/Toxicity Class: Warning/II.
REI: 24 hr.

Direx — see diuron

DIURON

Use in combination with a residual annual grass herbicide to increase spectrum of weeds controlled. Alternate use of a urea herbicide such as diuron with another residual broadleaf weed herbicide such as simazine.

■ **POST**

Direx 80DF *(Griffin)*
◆ **Diuron 80 WDG** *(Platte)*
Karmex DF *(Griffin)*
Riverside Diuron 4L or 80DF *(Terra)*

Rate: 1.5-3 lb. ai/A
3-6 pt. 4L/A
2-4 lb. DF, 80DF/A

Time: Postemergence. Apply in late fall or early winter after last cultivation.

Weeds: Annual broadleaf weeds:

annual groundcherry	gromwell	shepherdspurse
annual morningglory	knawel	tansymustard
chickweed	mustard	wild buckwheat
corn spurry	pennycress	wild lettuce
crowfoot	pigweed	wild mustard
dogfennel	purslane	wild radish
fiddleneck	redmaids rockpurslane	

Grasses:

annual bluegrass	crabgrass	rattail fescue
annual sweet	foxtail	red sprangletop
vernalgrass	goosegrass	velvetgrass
barnyardgrass		

Remarks: Rate varies by soil type. Use directed spray.

Crop Rotation: Do not replant treated area to any crop within 2 years after last application.

State Restrictions: For use in California.

- - - - - - - - - - - - - - -

Signal Word/Toxicity Class: Caution/III.
REI: 12 hr.

Glyfos or Glyfos X-tra — see glyphosate

GLYPHOSATE

Controls annual and perennial grasses and broadleaf weeds in stale seedbeds and reduced-tillage planting systems.

■ **PRE**

◆ **Credit (4WS)** *(Nufarm)*
◆ **Glyfos or Glyfos X-tra (4WS)** *(Cheminova)*
Rattler (4WS) *(Helena)*
Roundup Custom (5.4WS) *(Monsanto)*
Roundup Original, Original RT, Ultra, Ultra RT (4WS) *(Monsanto)*

Rate: Annual weeds:
0.38-1.5 lb. ai/A
0.56-2.25 pt. 5.4WS/A
0.75-3 pt. 4WS/A
Perennial weeds:
0.5-5 lb. ai/A
0.75-7.5 pt. 5.4WS/A
1-10 pt. 4WS/A

Time: Preemergence: Apply prior to emergence of direct-seeded crop or prior to transplanting.

Weeds: Emerged annual and perennial broadleaf weeds including:

Canada thistle	hemp dogbane	Pennsylvania
curly dock	milkweed	smartweed
field bindweed		

Grasses:

bermudagrass	fescue	paragrass
fall panicum	johnsongrass	quackgrass

Remarks: Prior to transplanting crops into plastic mulch, remove product residue from plastic. Do not add surfactant to Roundup Ultra or Ultra RT. Do not allow glyphosate to contact desirable plants. Do not apply through any type of irrigation system. Refer to label for directions, precautions and restrictions.

State Restrictions: Roundup RT for use in Colorado, Idaho, Montana, North Dakota, South Dakota, Utah, Wyoming, and in specific counties only in Kansas, Minnesota, Nebraska, Nevada, Oklahoma, Oregon, and Washington; refer to label for restrictions. Glyfos not registered for use in California. Glyfos X-tra not registered for use in mistblowers in California or Arizona.

- - - - - - - - - - - - - - -

Signal Word/Toxicity Class: Varies by formulation.
REI: Warning—12 hr.; Caution—4 hr.

◆-new product • PP-preplant • PPI-preplant incorporated • PRE-preemergence • POST-postemergence • SEQ-sequential • ae-acid equivalent • ai-active ingredient • DF-dry flowable
E/EC-emulsifiable concentrate • F/FL-flowable • DG/G/WG-dispersable granule • L/LC-liquid • SP/WSP-soluble packet • W/WP-wettable powder • WSB-water soluble bag

GOAL

Apply as directed spray in the winter for residual and postemergence control on many broadleaf weeds. Combine with residual annual grass herbicide to increase spectrum of weeds controlled.

■ PRE, POST
Goal 2XL (oxyfluorfen) *(Rohm and Haas)*
  Rate: 1-2 lb. ai/A
       4-8 pt. 2XL/A
  Time: Postemergence, preemergence. Initial application should be made to susceptible weed seedlings (up to 8-leaf stage); second application 8-10 weeks later. Do not apply to plantings within 60 days after cutting back or transplanting.
  Weeds: Broadleaf weeds:

annual sowthistle	common groundsel	mustard
Bermuda buttercup	common	oxalis
burning nettle	lambsquarters	shepherdspurse
cheeseweed	malva	

  Remarks: Globe artichokes. Post-directed application. Direct spray toward winter ditch, levees, or flat rows between artichokes. Avoid direct spray or drift contact with artichoke flower or bud as severe injury will occur. Do not apply more than 8 pt./A per season. Do not apply through any type of irrigation system. Refer to label for specific use and timing restrictions.
  Days To Harvest: 5.
  Crop Rotation: Refer to label for plantback times for rotation crops.

  Signal Word/Toxicity Class: Warning/II.
  REI: 24 hr.

Karmex — see diuron

KERB
Restricted Use Pesticide.

■ PRE, POST
Kerb 50-W (pronamide) *(Rohm and Haas)*
  Rate: 2-4 lb. ai/A
       4-8 lb. 50-W/A
  Time: Preemergence, postemergence. Established ratoon artichokes: Apply preemergence to weeds and before new artichoke leaves are greater than 14-16" long. Apply single postemergence application to crop after tillage operations are completed and shoot regrowth has occurred. Transplanted artichoke leaves: Apply single application after transplanting crowns but before new shoots have developed 3-4 new leaves; apply preemergence to weeds.
  Weeds: Broadleaf weeds:

burning nettle	henbit	nettleleaf goosefoot
cheeseweed	little mallow	prostate knotweed
common chickweed	mouseear chickweed	wild mustard
hairy nightshade		

  Annual grasses:

annual bluegrass	volunteer oat	wild oat
Italian ryegrass	volunteer wheat	yellow foxtail
volunteer barley		

  Remarks: Globe artichokes. For both ratoon and transplanted crowns, second application may be directed to soil surface between artichoke rows after ditching operation is completed.
  Days To Harvest: 60.
  Crop Rotation: Refer to label for plantback times for rotation crops.
  State Restrictions: For use in California.

  Signal Word/Toxicity Class: Caution.
  REI: 24 hr.

Poast — see sethoxydim

Rattler — see glyphosate

Roundup — see glyphosate

SCYTHE
◆ **Scythe (pelargonic acid)** *(Mycogen)*
  Rate: 4-13 fl. oz./1 gal. spray solution

  Time: Apply to actively growing weeds prior to crop emergence.
  Weeds: Annual and perennial broadleaf weeds and grasses.
  Remarks: Apply in minimum 75 gal. spray solution/A or spray-to-wet. Do not apply by air or through any type of irrigation system. Refer to label for directions and precautions.
  Tank Mixes: Glyphosate and other foliar and residual herbicides.

  Signal Word/Toxicity Class: Warning/II.
  REI: 24 hr.

SETHOXYDIM

■ POST
Poast (1.5EC) *(BASF)*
  Rate: 0.09-0.47 lb. ai/A
       0.5-2.5 pt. 1.5EC/A
  Time: Postemergence.
  Weeds: Annual and perennial grasses:

annual ryegrass	junglerice	southwestern cupgrass
barnyardgrass	large crabgrass	stinkgrass
bermudagrass	lovegrass	tall fescue
browntop panicum	orchardgrass	volunteer cereals
fall panicum	(seedling)	wild oat
giant foxtail	perennial ryegrass	wildcane
goosegrass	shattercane	witchgrass
green foxtail	smooth crabgrass	yellow foxtail
johnsongrass		

  Remarks: Always add 2 pt./A oil concentrate. Do not apply through any type of irrigation system. Do not graze treated fields or feed treated forage to livestock. Refer to label for restrictions and limitations.
  Days To Harvest: 7.
  State Restrictions: For use in California only.

  Signal Word/Toxicity Class: Warning/II.
  REI: 12 hr.

TOUCHDOWN

◆ **Touchdown (5L or 6L) (sulfosate)** *(ZENECA)*
  Rate: 0.5-4 lb. ai/A
       0.8-6.4 pt. 5L/A
       0.66-5.33 pt. 6L/A
  Time: Apply to actively growing grasses and weeds.
  Weeds: Broadleaf Weeds:

annual sowthistle	fiddleneck	prickly lettuce
common chickweed	Florida pusley	redroot pigweed
common groundsel	groundcherry	Russian thistle
common	henbit	shepherdspurse
lambsquarters	morningglory	spanishneedles
common ragweed	mouseear chickweed	wild buckwheat
dogfennel	mustard	

  Grasses:

annual bluegrass	foxtail	shattercane
barnyardgrass	goosegrass	sprangletop
bermudagrass	guineagrass	stinkgrass
cheat	Italian ryegrass	Texas panicum
crabgrass	johnsongrass	wild oat
downy brome	(seedling)	witchgrass
fall panicum	perennial ryegrass	

  Remarks: Nonionic surfactant or wetting agent required. In addition, ammonium sulfate can be added. Do not apply through any type of irrigation system. Refer to label for use directions, restrictions, and precautions.
  Crop Rotation: Plantback time—35 days.
  Tank Mixes: Devrinol, diuron, Goal, Krovar, Prowl, simazine, Solicam, Surflan.
  State Restrictions: Ammonium sulfate (6L) not for use in California.

  Signal Word/Toxicity Class: Caution.
  REI: 12 hr. (5L); 4 hr. (6L).

Asparagus

Banvel — see dicamba

Clarity — see dicamba

6

Vegetables

NOTICE	The information on these pages is for preliminary planning — not a guide for use. Be sure to follow the manufacturer's directions, notwithstanding information contained here.	For personal protective equipment and EPA registration numbers, please turn to page 70.

CLOPYRALID

Systemic herbicide absorbed by leaves and roots. Has selective postemergence control of many annual and perennial broadleaf weeds.

■ POST

Stinger *(Dow AgroSciences)*

Rate: 0.2-0.25 lb. ae/A
0.5-0.66 pt./A

Time: Postemergence. Apply to asparagus before or during cutting season, or after harvest is complete but prior to fern growth. Treat annual weeds before they send up a flower stalk; Canada thistle after majority of basal leaves have emerged up to bud stage.

Weeds: Broadleaf weeds:

annual sowthistle	common cocklebur	jimsonweed
Canada thistle	common sunflower	ragweed

Remarks: Do not apply during cutting season if crooking of asparagus spears cannot be tolerated; clear-cutting of spears just before application may reduce occurrence. Do not apply more than 0.66 pt./A per year. Do not apply through any type of irrigation system. Do not contaminate irrigation ditches or water used for irrigation or domestic purposes.

Days To Harvest: 12 hr.

Crop Rotation: Varies by region; refer to label.

Signal Word/Toxicity Class: Caution/III.
REI: 12 hr.

Credit — see glyphosate

2,4-D - PHENOXY HERBICIDES

Controls annual broadleaf weeds and suppresses or controls perennial broadleaf weeds. Use in addition to residual grass and broadleaf herbicides. Flavor of sprayed spears may be affected. After harvest, direct spray toward base of plant. Do not use if spray drift may damage sensitive adjacent crops.

■ POST

Formula 40 (2,4-D mixed amine) *(Rhone-Poulenc)*

Rate: 1.5-2 lb. ai/A
3-4 pt./A

Time: Postemergence. Apply on actively growing weeds in spring. If spears are present, apply after cutting.

Weeds: Broadleaf weeds:

dandelion	mustard	ragweed
dock	pigweed	wild morningglory
lambsquarters		

Remarks: Make no more than 2 applications during harvest season at least one month apart. Postharvest spraying should be made with drop nozzles to avoid spraying fern.

Signal Word/Toxicity Class: Danger/I.
REI: 48 hr.

■ POST

Savage (WSB) (2,4-D amine) *(Platte)*

Rate: 1.4-1.9 lb. ae/A
1.5-2 lb. WSB/A

Time: Postemergence. Apply on actively growing weeds in April or May. If spears are present, apply after cutting.

Weeds: Annual broadleaf weeds.

Remarks: Make no more than 2 applications during harvest season at least one month apart. Postharvest spraying should be made with drop nozzles to avoid spraying fern.

Signal Word/Toxicity Class: Danger/I.
REI: 48 hr.

DEVRINOL

■ POST

Devrinol 50-DF (napropamide) *(United Phosphorus)*

Rate: 4 lb. ai/A
8 lb. 50-DF/A

Time: Postemergence. Apply to weed-free soil in established crops.

Weeds: Broadleaf weeds:

annual sowthistle	common ragweed	pineappleweed
carpetweed	(suppression)	prickly lettuce
coast fiddleneck	horse purslane	prostrate knotweed
common chickweed	lambsquarters	purple cudweed
common groundsel	little mallow	redroot pigweed
common purslane	(from seed)	redstem filaree

Grasses:

annual bluegrass	guineagrass	smooth crabgrass
barnyardgrass	hairy crabgrass	soft chess
bristly foxtail	Italian ryegrass	southwestern
canarygrass	johnsongrass	cupgrass
cheatgrass	(seedling)	stinkgrass
downy brome	junglerice	Texas panicum
fall panicum	large crabgrass	wild barley
foxtail barley	Mexican sprangletop	wild oat
giant foxtail	red sprangletop	witchgrass
goosegrass	ripgut brome	yellow foxtail
green foxtail	sandbur	

Remarks: If rainfall does not occur, shallowly incorporate or irrigate-in after application with sufficient water to wet soil to a depth of 2-4".

Crop Rotation: Do not plant to crops not specified on label until 12 months after last application. Disc plow or moldboard plow at least 10" deep prior to planting succeeding crop.

Signal Word/Toxicity Class: Caution.
REI: 12 hr.

DICAMBA

Suppression or control of annual and perennial broadleaf weeds. Use in addition to residual grass and broadleaf herbicides.

■ POST

Banvel (WS) (DMA salt of dicamba) *(BASF)*
Clarity (WS) (dicamba-DGA) *(BASF)*
◆ Sterling (WS) (DMA salt of dicamba) *(Terra)*

Rate: 0.25-0.5 lb. ai/A
0.5-1 pt. WS/A

Time: Apply to emerged and actively growing weeds immediately after cutting the field, but at least 24 hr. before next cutting.

Weeds: Broadleaf weeds:

annual sowthistle	field bindweed	redroot pigweed
black mustard	milk thistle	Russian thistle
Canada thistle	nettleleaf goosefoot	wild radish
common chickweed		

Remarks: If spray contacts emerged spears, crooking or twisting of some spears may result. Multiple applications may be made per growing season. Do not apply more than 1 pt./A per crop year.

Days To Harvest: 24 hr.

Tank Mixes: 2,4-D, Roundup Ultra.

State Restrictions: Not for use in Coachella Valley of California.

Signal Word/Toxicity Class: Warning/II (Banvel, Sterling); Caution (Clarity).
REI: 24 hr.

DIQUAT DIBROMIDE

◆ Diquat *(ZENECA)*

Rate: 0.375-0.5 lb. ai/A
1.5-2 pt./A

Time: Site preparation prior to planting. Repeat as needed.

Weeds: Broadleaf weeds and grasses.

Remarks: Nonbearing. Apply by ground only. Use high rate when weeds are large or dense. Do not allow spray to contact green stems, foliage, or fruit. Use a shield or wrap plant when spraying around young trees or vines. Do not apply through any type of irrigation system. Do not graze treated areas. Refer to label for use restrictions and precautions.

Days To Harvest: 1 year.

Signal Word/Toxicity Class: Warning/II.
REI: 24 hr.

Direx — see diuron

DIURON

Use in combination with a residual annual grass herbicide. Alternate use of a urea herbicide such as diuron with a triazine such as metribuzin or simazine.

◆-new product • PP-preplant • PPI-preplant incorporated • PRE-preemergence • POST-postemergence • SEQ-sequential • ae-acid equivalent • ai-active ingredient • DF-dry flowable
E/EC-emulsifiable concentrate • F/FL-flowable • DG/G/WG-dispersable granule • L/LC-liquid • SP/WSP-soluble packet • W/WP-wettable powder • WSB-water soluble bag

PRE, POST

Direx 4L or 80DF *(Griffin)*
◆ **Diuron 80 WDG** *(Platte)*
Drexel Diuron 4L or 80 *(Drexel)*
Karmex DF *(Griffin)*
Riverside Diuron 4L or 80DF *(Terra)*

Rate: Light sandy soils and soils low in clay or organic matter:
0.75-1.5 lb. ai/A
1.5-3 pt. 4L/A
1-2 lb. 80, DF, 80DF/A
Soils high in clay or organic matter:
1.5-3 lb. ai/A
3-6 pt. 4L/A
2-4 lb. 80, DF, 80DF/A

Time: Preemergence, postemergence. Apply before weeds become established; no earlier than 4 weeks before spear emergence and no later than early cutting period. Second application can be made immediately following harvest if rainfall is expected.

Weeds: Annual broadleaf weeds:

annual groundcherry	lambsquarters	ragweed
annual morningglory	pigweed	wild lettuce
chickweed	purslane	wild mustard
gromwell		

Annual grasses:

annual bluegrass	barnyardgrass	rattail fescue
annual sweet	crabgrass	velvetgrass
vernalgrass	foxtail	

Remarks: Do not apply to newly seeded asparagus, to young plants during first growing season after setting, or on plants with exposed roots.

Signal Word/Toxicity Class: Caution/III.
REI: 12 hr.

FLUAZIFOP-P-BUTYL

Provides selective control of annual and perennial grasses. Use in addition to residual herbicides for season-long control. Do not tank mix with any other herbicides unless specified on label or reduced control may result. Preharvest interval for asparagus listed on label ranges between 1 and 365 days depending on the state.

POST

Fusilade DX *(ZENECA)*

Rate: 0.1-0.375 lb. ai/A
0.375-1.5 pt. DX/A

Time: Postemergence. Apply to actively growing grasses. Do not make sequential applications at less than 14-day intervals; 3-week intervals for California.

Weeds: Annual and perennial grasses:

barnyardgrass	johnsongrass	southern sandbur
bermudagrass	(rhizome, seedling)	Texas panicum
broadleaf signalgrass	junglerice	tropical crabgrass
fall panicum	large crabgrass	volunteer cereals
field sandbur	quackgrass	wild oat
giant foxtail	red rice	wild proso millet
goosegrass	shattercane	wirestem muhly
green foxtail	smooth crabgrass	witchgrass
Italian ryegrass	sorghum-almum	woolly cupgrass
itchgrass	southern crabgrass	yellow foxtail

Remarks: Rate varies by geographic area and grass species. Add crop oil concentrate or nonionic surfactant. Do not apply more than 1.5 pt./A per application. For bearing asparagus, do not apply more than 3 pt./A per season. Refer to label for specific restrictions and precautions.

Days To Harvest: 1.

Crop Rotation: Do not plant rotational grass crops such as corn, sorghum, and cereals within 60 days after last application.

State Restrictions: For use in all states except Arizona and California.

Signal Word/Toxicity Class: Caution.
REI: 12 hr.

Formula 40 — see 2,4-D

Fusilade — see fluazifop-P-butyl

Glyfos or Glyfos X-tra — see glyphosate

GLYPHOSATE

Nonselective, preemergence to crop, postemergence to weed herbicide. Apply when crowns are dormant and brush is dead, brown, and dry, or as spot treatment.

PP, PRE

◆ **Credit (4WS)** *(Nufarm)*
◆ **Glyfos or Glyfos X-tra (4WS)** *(Cheminova)*
Rattler (4WS) *(Helena)*
Roundup Custom (5.4WS) *(Monsanto)*
Roundup Original, Original RT, Ultra, Ultra RT (4WS) *(Monsanto)*

Rate: Annual weeds:
0.38-1.5 lb. ai/A
0.56-2.25 pt. 5.4WS/A
0.75-3 pt. 4WS/A
Perennial weeds:
0.5-5 lb. ai/A
0.75-7.5 pt. 5.4WS/A
1-10 pt. 4WS/A

Time: Preplant, preemergence, spot treatment, postharvest. Preplant, preemergence: Apply prior to emergence of asparagus; do not apply within a week before first spears emerge. Spot treatment: Apply immediately after cutting, but prior to emergence of new spears. Postharvest: Apply after last harvest and all spears have been removed. If spears are allowed to regrow, delay application until ferns have developed.

Weeds: Emerged annual and perennial broadleaf weeds including:

Canada thistle	hemp dogbane	Pennsylvania
curly dock	milkweed	smartweed
field bindweed		

Grasses:

| bermudagrass | fescue | paragrass |
| fall panicum | johnsongrass | quackgrass |

Remarks: Rate varies by weeds species. For spot treatment, do not treat more than 10% total area to be harvested. Do not allow glyphosate to contact asparagus. Do not add surfactant to Roundup Ultra or Ultra RT. Do not apply through any type of irrigation system. Refer to label for directions, precautions and restrictions.

State Restrictions: Roundup RT for use in Colorado, Idaho, Montana, North Dakota, South Dakota, Utah, Wyoming, and in specific counties only in Kansas, Minnesota, Nebraska, Nevada, Oklahoma, Oregon, and Washington; refer to label for restrictions. Glyfos not registered for use in California. Glyfos X-tra not registered for use in mistblowers in California or Arizona.

Signal Word/Toxicity Class: Varies by formulation.
REI: Warning—12 hr.; Caution—4 hr.

Gramoxone Extra — see paraquat

Karmex — see diuron

LINURON

Use in combination with a residual annual grass herbicide. Alternate use of a urea herbicide.

PRE, POST

Lorox DF *(Griffin)*

Rate: Preemergence:
0.5-2 lb. ai/A
1-4 lb. DF/A
Postemergence:
0.5-1 lb. ai/A
1-2 lb. DF/A

Time: Preemergence, postemergence. For postemergence on direct seeded or newly planted crowns apply when ferns are in 6-18" stage; established beds apply before cutting season or weeds exceed 4" in height.

Weeds: Broadleaf seedlings:

| dudaim melon | nightshade | ragweed |
| lambsquarters | pigweed | |

Grass seedlings:

| barnyardgrass | crabgrass | foxtail |

Remarks: Direct-seeded, newly planted crowns, and established beds.

Crop Rotation: Carrots or celery may be planted 4 months after last application. If more than 2 lb. ai is applied per season, do not plant any other crop until 1 year after last application. Refer to label for recommendations.

State Restrictions: For use in California, Michigan, Minnesota, North Carolina, Oregon, and Washington.

Signal Word/Toxicity Class: Caution.
REI: 24 hr.

6
Vegetables

NOTICE The information on these pages is for preliminary planning — not a guide for use. Be sure to follow the manufacturer's directions, notwithstanding information contained here. For personal protective equipment and EPA registration numbers, please turn to page 70.

Lorox — see linuron	**Savage — see 2,4-D**

NORFLURAZON

SCYTHE

■ **PRE**

Solicam DF *(Novartis)*

Rate: 2-4 lb. ai/A
2.5-5 lb. DF/A

Time: Preemergence.

Weeds: Broadleaf weeds:

black mustard	horseweed*	Russian thistle*
chickweed	(marestail)	shepherdspurse
common	little mallow	silverleaf
lambsquarters*	(cheeseweed)	nightshade*
falsedandelion	London rocket	(white horsenettle)
(smooth catsear)	pigweed	tumble mustard
fiddleneck	pineappleweed	Virginia pepperweed
flixweed	puncturevine	whitestem filaree
groundsel*	redstem filaree	

Grasses and sedges:

annual bluegrass	downy brome	sixweeks grama
annual ryegrass	fall panicum	southwestern
(Italian ryegrass)	feather fingergrass	cupgrass
annual sedge	foxtail	tall fescue
barnyardgrass	goosegrass	Texas panicum
bermudagrass*	johnsongrass	wild barley
broadleaf signalgrass	(seedling)	wild onion
cheat	nutsedge	witchgrass
crabgrass	quackgrass*	

*** Suppression**

Remarks: Allow newly planted asparagus to become established one season before application. Do not apply if crop rotation or replacement is expected within 24 months. Improved results may be obtained if crop debris is incorporated or removed prior to application.

Days To Harvest: 14.

Tank Mixes: Banvel, 2,4-D, diuron, Gramoxone Extra, Lorox, metribuzin, Roundup Ultra, simazine, or trifluralin; refer to labels for use directions.

State Restrictions: See label for restrictions on use in Coachella Valley of California.

– – – – – – – – – – – – – –

Signal Word/Toxicity Class: Caution.
REI: 12 hr.

PARAQUAT

Use prior to emergence or immediately following cutting season for nonselective control of seedling weeds. Restricted Use Pesticide.

■ **PP, PRE**

Gramoxone Extra (2.5L) *(ZENECA)*

Rate: 0.6-1 lb. ai/A
2-3 pt. 2.5L/A

Time: Preplant, preemergence. For established plantings at least 2 years old, apply prior to emergence of crop or after last harvest.

Weeds: Annual broadleaf weeds and grasses; top kill and suppression of perennials.

Remarks: Add nonionic surfactant or crop oil concentrate. Crops emerged at time of application will be killed; weeds and grasses emerging after treatment will not be controlled. Seeding or transplanting should be done with a minimum of soil disturbance. Do not apply preplant or preemergence to soils lacking clay minerals. Refer to label for use directions, restrictions, and precautions.

Days To Harvest: Established plantings at least 2 years old—6.

Tank Mixes: Princep.

– – – – – – – – – – – – – –

Signal Word/Toxicity Class: Danger-Poison/I.
REI: 12 hr. (except harvest aid/desiccation 24 hr.).

Poast — see sethoxydim

Rattler — see glyphosate

Roundup — see glyphosate

◆ **Scythe (pelargonic acid)** *(Mycogen)*

Rate: 4-13 fl. oz./1 gal. spray solution

Time: Apply to actively growing weeds prior to crop emergence.

Weeds: Annual and perennial broadleaf weeds and grasses.

Remarks: Apply in minimum 75 gal. spray solution/A or spray-to-wet. Do not apply by air or through any type of irrigation system. Refer to label for directions and precautions.

Tank Mixes: Glyphosate and other foliar and residual herbicides.

– – – – – – – – – – – – – –

Signal Word/Toxicity Class: Warning/II.
REI: 24 hr.

SENCOR

■ **PRE, POST**

Sencor 4 (FL) or DF (metribuzin) *(Bayer)*

Rate: 1-2 lb. ai/A
2-4 pt. FL/A
1.33-2.67 lb. DF/A

Time: Preemergence, postharvest. Preemergence: Apply early spring before spears or ferns emerge. If field is to be disked, apply after disking but before crop emerges. Postharvest: Apply after last harvest of season but prior to emergence.

Weeds: Broadleaf weeds:

common chickweed	lambsquarters	red sorrel
common ragweed	Pennsylvania	redroot pigweed
jimsonweed	smartweed	velvetleaf

Grasses:

crabgrass	giant foxtail	yellow foxtail
field sandbur		

Remarks: Established asparagus. Do not use on newly seeded asparagus or on young plants during first growing season after setting crowns. Do not apply postharvest until after last harvest of spears. Do not apply more than 2 lb. ai/A.

Days To Harvest: 14.

Crop Rotation: Alfalfa, asparagus, barley/wheat (following peas, lentils, or soybeans), corn, forage grass, potatoes, sainfoin, soybeans, sugarcane, tomatoes—4 months; barley, cotton, lentils, peas, rice, wheat—8 months; other crops not listed (except root crops)—12 months; onions, sugar beets, and other root crops—18 months. Cover crops for soil building or erosion control may be planted anytime, but do not graze or harvest for food or feed. Stand reductions may occur in some areas.

– – – – – – – – – – – – – –

Signal Word/Toxicity Class: Caution/III.
REI: 12 hr.

SETHOXYDIM

■ **POST**

Poast (1.5EC) *(BASF)*

Rate: 0.09-0.47 lb. ai/A
0.5-2.5 pt. 1.5EC/A

Time: Postemergence.

Weeds: Annual and perennial grasses:

annual ryegrass	junglerice	southwestern cupgrass
barnyardgrass	large crabgrass	stinkgrass
bermudagrass	lovegrass	tall fescue
browntop panicum	orchardgrass	volunteer cereals
fall panicum	(seedling)	wild oat
giant foxtail	perennial ryegrass	wildcane
goosegrass	shattercane	witchgrass
green foxtail	smooth crabgrass	yellow foxtail
johnsongrass		

Remarks: Always add 2 pt./A oil concentrate. Do not apply through any type of irrigation system. Do not graze treated fields or feed treated forage to livestock. Refer to label for restrictions and limitations.

Days To Harvest: 1.

State Restrictions: Do not use UAN or AMS in California or Pacific Northwest.

– – – – – – – – – – – – – –

Signal Word/Toxicity Class: Warning/II.
REI: 12 hr.

◆-new product • PP-preplant • PPI-preplant incorporated • PRE-preemergence • POST-postemergence • SEQ-sequential • ae-acid equivalent • ai-active ingredient • DF-dry flowable
E/EC-emulsifiable concentrate • F/FL-flowable • DG/G/WG-dispersable granule • L/LC-liquid • SP/WSP-soluble packet • W/WP-wettable powder • WSB-water soluble bag

SINBAR

■ **PRE, POST**
Sinbar (WP) (terbacil) *(DuPont)*
Rate: Direct seeded:
 0.8-1.6 lb. ai/A
 1-2 lb. WP/A
 Established beds:
 1.2-2 lb. ai/A
 1.5-2.5 lb. WP/A
Time: Apply prior to spear and weed emergence or to small weeds.
Weeds: Broadleaf weeds:

chickweed	horseweed	pigweed
dandelion	jimsonweed	prickly lettuce
(seedling)	knotweed	purslane
fiddleneck	lambsquarters	ragweed
flixweed	marestail	red sorrel
Florida pusley	mustard	shepherdspurse
henbit	nightshade	smartweed

Grasses and sedges:

annual sedge	foxtail	panicum
barnyardgrass	guineagrass	quackgrass
cheatgrass	johnsongrass	sandbur
crabgrass	(seedling)	wild barley
downy brome	junglerice	

Remarks: Rate varies depending on soil texture. Do not use on areas where subsoil or roots are exposed. Do not use on plants that are diseased or lacking in vigor. Refer to label for use directions, restrictions, and precautions.
Days To Harvest: 5.
Crop Rotation: Treated areas may be planted to asparagus 1 year after application. Do not replant to any other crop within 2 years after treatment.
State Restrictions: Not for use in California.

— — — — — — — — — — — — — —

Signal Word/Toxicity Class: Caution.
REI: 12 hr.

Solicam — see norflurazon

Sterling — see dicamba

Stinger — see clopyralid

TOUCHDOWN

◆ **Touchdown (5L or 6L) (sulfosate)** *(ZENECA)*
Rate: 0.5-4 lb. ai/A
 0.8-6.4 pt. 5L/A
 0.66-5.33 pt. 6L/A
Time: Apply to actively growing grasses and weeds.
Weeds: Broadleaf Weeds:

annual sowthistle	field bindweed	morningglory
Canada thistle	field sandbur	mustard
common chickweed	Florida pusley	Pennsylvania
common groundsel	groundcherry	smartweed
common lambsquarters	hemp dogbane	prickly lettuce
common ragweed	henbit	redroot pigweed
curly dock	kochia	Russian thistle
dandelion	London rocket	shepherdspurse
fiddleneck	marestail	velvetleaf

Grasses:

annual bluegrass	foxtail	shattercane
barnyardgrass	goosegrass	sprangletop
bermudagrass	guineagrass	stinkgrass
broadleaf signalgrass	Italian ryegrass	tall fescue
cheat	johnsongrass	Texas panicum
crabgrass	(seedling)	wild oat
downy brome	paragrass	wiresteam muhly
fall panicum	quackgrass	witchgrass
fescue	red rice	woolly cupgrass

Remarks: Nonionic surfactant or wetting agent required. In addition, ammonium sulfate can be added. Do not apply through any type of irrigation system. Refer to label for use directions, restrictions, and precautions.
Crop Rotation: Plantback time—35 days.
Tank Mixes: Devrinol, diuron, Goal, Krovar, Prowl, simazine, Solicam, Surflan.
State Restrictions: Ammonium sulfate (6L) not for use in California.

— — — — — — — — — — — — — —

Signal Word/Toxicity Class: Caution.
REI: 12 hr. (5L); 4 hr. (6L).

Treflan — see trifluralin

Trific — see trifluralin

TRIFLURALIN

Use in combination with a triazine such as simazine or metribuzin and a urea such as diuron or linuron. Alternate use of triazines with use of a urea herbicide.

■ **PRE, POST**
Albaugh Trifluralin 4EC *(Albaugh)*
◆ **Clean Crop Trifluralin HF (4EC)** *(Platte)*
Gowan Trifluralin 4 or 5 (EC) or 10G *(Gowan)*
Helena Trifluralin 4 EC *(Helena)*
Riverside Trifluralin 4EC or Trific 60DF *(Terra)*
◆ **Sedagri Trifluralin 480 (4EC)** *(Rhone-Poulenc)*
Treflan HFP (4EC) *(Dow AgroSciences)*
Trilin 4 or 5 (EC) or 10G *(Griffin)*
Wilbur-Ellis Trifluralin 10G *(Wilbur-Ellis)*
Rate: 0.5-2 lb. ai/A
 1-4 pt. 4EC/A
 0.8-3.2 pt. 5EC/A
 0.875-3.33 lb. 60DF/A
 5-20 lb. 10G
Time: Preemergence and/or postharvest incorporated.
Weeds: Broadleaf weeds:

carelessweed	knotweed	purslane
carpetweed	kochia	pusley
chickweed	lambsquarters	redroot pigweed
field bindweed	Mexican clover	rough pigweed
fireweed	Mexican fireweed	Russian thistle
Florida purslane	prostrate pigweed	spiny pigweed
Florida pusley	puncturevine	stinging nettle
goosefoot	(western U.S.)	tumbleweed
henbit		

Grasses:

annual bluegrass	fall panicum	sandbur
barnyardgrass	foxtail millet	shattercane
bottlegrass	giant foxtail	smooth crabgrass
brachiaria	green foxtail	sprangletop
bristlegrass	Italian ryegrass	stinkgrass
bromegrass	johnsongrass	Texas panicum
burgrass	(seedling)	watergrass
cheat	junglerice	wildcane
cheatgrass	large crabgrass	woolly cupgrass
chess	pigeongrass	yellow foxtail
downy brome	robust foxtail	

Remarks: Apply to established asparagus as single or split application. Rate varies by soil type. Refer to label for directions and precautions.
Crop Rotation: Vegetable crops other than those listed on label should not be planted within 5 months following application. Refer to label for other restrictions.
State Restrictions: Wilbur-Ellis not registered in California.

— — — — — — — — — — — — — —

Signal Word/Toxicity Class: Varies by formulation.
REI: 12 hr. unless soil injected or soil incorporated.

Trilin — see trifluralin

Beans

(Dry, Great Northern, Kidney, Lima, Navy, Pink, Pinto, Red, Snap, Wax, White)

ALACHLOR

Control of yellow nutsedge, galinsoga, and nightshade. Use in combination with another herbicide to increase spectrum of broadleaf weeds controlled. Restricted Use Pesticide.

■ **PPI**
Lasso (4EC) or Micro-Tech (MT) *(Monsanto)*
Partner (WDG) *(Monsanto)*

6

Vegetables

NOTICE The information on these pages is for preliminary planning — not a guide for use. Be sure to follow the manufacturer's directions, notwithstanding information contained here. | For personal protective equipment and EPA registration numbers, please turn to page 70.

Beans

Rate: 2.5-3 lb. ai/A
    2.5-3 qt. 4EC, MT/A
    3.8-4.5 lb. WDG/A
Time: Preplant incorporated.
Weeds: Broadleaf weeds:

black nightshade	Florida pusley	prickly sida*
carelessweed	galinsoga	purslane
carpetweed	hairy nightshade	sicklepod*
common ragweed*	lambsquarters*	smartweed*
cutleaf groundcherry	pigweed	teaweed*
Florida beggarweed*		

Grasses and sedges:

barnyardgrass	johnsongrass*	wild proso millet*
broadleaf signalgrass	(seedling)	wildcane*
crabgrass	panicum	witchgrass
foxtail	sandbur*	woolly cupgrass*
goosegrass	shattercane*	yellow nutsedge

* Suppression

Remarks: Dry, lima, red kidney beans. Alachlor may delay maturity and/or reduce yield if cold, wet soil conditions occur after planting. Do not feed forage or hay from treated crop.
Tank Mixes: Dry beans. Eptam: Michigan and west of the Mississippi except California (except Kern County for MT). Treflan: West of the Mississippi except Kern County, California.
State Restrictions: Dry beans: For use in New York (4EC, MT), Minnesota (WDG), and west of the Mississippi except Kern County, California. Lima beans: For use in all states except Kern County, California. Red kidney beans: For use in Illinois, Indiana, Wisconsin.

– – – – – – – – – – – – – – –

Signal Word/Toxicity Class:
Danger/I (Lasso); Caution/IV (Micro-Tech, Partner).
REI: 12 hr.

BASAGRAN

Postemergence to control yellow nutsedge and many broadleaf weeds. May cause bronzing, temporary stunting, and delay maturity on some edible bean types, especially when applied when weather is hot and humid. Delay application until beans have 2 fully expanded trifoliate leaves to minimize risk of delaying maturity.

■ POST

Basagran (bentazon) (BASF)
Rate: 0.5-1 lb. ai/A
    1-2 pt./A
Time: Early postemergence.
Weeds: Broadleaf weeds:

Canada thistle	hairy nightshade	prickly sida
cocklebur	jimsonweed	shepherdspurse
common purslane	ladysthumb	velvetleaf
common ragweed	lambsquarters	Venice mallow
devilsclaw	marshelder	wild mustard
galinsoga	Pennsylvania	wild sunflower
giant ragweed	smartweed	

Sedges:
yellow nutsedge

Remarks: Great northern, kidney, lima, navy, pink, pinto, red, snap, white beans. Rate depends on leaf stage and weed height. For control of yellow nutsedge and Canada thistle, make a second application at same rate if needed; refer to Special Directions on label.
Days To Harvest: Green (succulent) beans—30.

– – – – – – – – – – – – – – –

Signal Word/Toxicity Class: Caution/III.
REI: 12 hr.

Credit — see glyphosate

Dual — see S-metolachlor

Eptam — see EPTC

EPTC

■ PPI, POST
Eptam 7-E or 20-G (ZENECA)

Rate: Fall application:
    4-4.5 lb. ai/A
    4.5-5.25 pt. 7-E/A
    20-22.5 lb. 20-G/A
    At planting or lay-by:
    3-4 lb. ai/A
    3.5-4.5 pt. 7-E/A
    15-20 lb. 20-G/A
Time: Preplant incorporated: Apply before planting. Postemergence lay-by application: Apply at base of plants before bean pods start to form.
Weeds: Broadleaf weeds:

black nightshade	corn spurry	nettleleaf goosefoot
carpetweed*	cutleaf nightshade*	prickly sida*
common chickweed	deadnettle	prostrate pigweed
common	fiddleneck*	redroot pigweed
lambsquarters	Florida pusley	sicklepod*
common pigweed	hairy nightshade	tall morningglory*
common purslane	henbit	tumble pigweed

Annual grasses and sedges:

annual bluegrass	giant foxtail	rescuegrass*
annual ryegrass	goosegrass	shattercane
(Italian)	green foxtail	signalgrass*
barnyardgrass	johnsongrass	Texas panicum*
(watergrass)	(seedling)	volunteer grains
bermudagrass	junglerice	(barley, oats, wheat)
(seedling)	lovegrass	wild oat
crabgrass	(stinkgrass)*	witchgrass*
fall panicum*	purple nutsedge	yellow foxtail
field sandbur	quackgrass	yellow nutsedge

*7-E only

Remarks: Dry, green beans. Do not use on Adzuki, blackeyed peas or beans, soybeans, lima beans or other flat-podded beans, except Romano. Do not feed or pasture areas within 45 days after lay-by application. Consult label for regional application recommendations.
State Restrictions: Dry beans: Fall application for Minnesota, North Dakota.

– – – – – – – – – – – – – – –

Signal Word/Toxicity Class: Caution.
REI: 12 hr. unless soil injected or soil incorporated.

FRONTIER

Chloroacetamide herbicide that controls many annual grasses, several broadleaf weeds, and nutsedge. Not registered for use in succulent beans or cowpeas.

■ PP, PPI, PRE, POST
Frontier 6.0 (dimethenamid) (BASF)
Rate: 0.94-1.5 lb. ai/A
    20-32 fl. oz. 6.0/A
Time: Preplant (surface or incorporated), preemergence, early postemergence (1st to 3rd trifoliate stage), single or split application.
Weeds: Broadleaf weeds:

carpetweed	nightshade	spurge
common purslane	pigweed	waterhemp
Florida pusley		

Grasses and sedges:

barnyardgrass	johnsongrass	southwestern
broadleaf signalgrass	(seedling)	cupgrass
fall panicum	large crabgrass	Texas panicum
giant foxtail	rice flatsedge	yellow foxtail
goosegrass	smooth crabgrass	yellow nutsedge
green foxtail		

Remarks: Dry beans (black turtle soup, cranberry, great northern, navy, pink, pinto, red kidney, red Mexican, small white). Rate varies by soil type and organic matter. Do not apply through any type of irrigation system. Refer to label for limitations and precautions.
Tank Mixes: Basagran, Eptam, Far-Go, glyphosate, paraquat, Poast, Prowl, Pursuit, Sonalan, trifluralin.

– – – – – – – – – – – – – –

Signal Word/Toxicity Class: Warning/II.
REI: 12 hr.

Glyfos or Glyfos X-tra — see glyphosate

GLYPHOSATE

Nonselective control of established annual and perennial grass and broadleaf weeds in stale seedbeds and reduced-tillage planting systems.

■ PRE
◆ Credit (4WS) (Nufarm)
◆ Glyfos or Glyfos X-tra (4WS) (Cheminova)
Rattler (4WS) (Helena)

◆-new product • PP-preplant • PPI-preplant incorporated • PRE-preemergence • POST-postemergence • SEQ-sequential • ae-acid equivalent • ai-active ingredient • DF-dry flowable
E/EC-emulsifiable concentrate • F/FL-flowable • DG/G/WG-dispersable granule • L/LC-liquid • SP/WSP-soluble packet • W/WP-wettable powder • WSB-water soluble bag

Roundup Custom (5.4WS) *(Monsanto)*
Roundup Original, Original RT, Ultra, Ultra RT (4WS) *(Monsanto)*
Rate: Annual weeds:
0.38-1.5 lb. ai/A
0.56-2.25 pt. 5.4WS/A
0.75-3 pt. 4WS/A
Perennial weeds:
0.5-5 lb. ai/A
0.75-7.5 pt. 5.4WS/A
1-10 pt. 4WS/A
Time: Preemergence: Apply prior to emergence of direct-seeded crop or prior to transplanting.
Weeds: Emerged annual and perennial broadleaf weeds including:

Canada thistle	hemp dogbane	Pennsylvania
curly dock	milkweed	smartweed
field bindweed		

Grasses:

| bermudagrass | fescue | paragrass |
| fall panicum | johnsongrass | quackgrass |

Remarks: Prior to transplanting crops into plastic mulch, remove product residue from plastic. Do not add surfactant to Roundup Ultra or Ultra RT. Do not allow glyphosate to contact desirable plants. Do not apply through any type of irrigation system. Refer to label for directions, precautions and restrictions.
State Restrictions: Roundup RT for use in Colorado, Idaho, Montana, North Dakota, South Dakota, Utah, Wyoming, and in specific counties only in Kansas, Minnesota, Nebraska, Nevada, Oklahoma, Oregon, and Washington; refer to label for restrictions. Glyfos not registered for use in California. Glyfos X-tra not registered for use in mistblowers in California or Arizona.

Signal Word/Toxicity Class: Varies by formulation.
REI: Warning—12 hr.; Caution—4 hr.

Gramoxone Extra — see paraquat

Lasso — see alachlor

S-METOLACHLOR

Dual is a cell growth inhibitor. S-metolachlor is a purified isomer of the metolachlor molecule. Dual II MAGNUM contains the safener benoxacor. Use in combination with another herbicide to increase spectrum of broadleaf weeds controlled.

■ PPI, PRE
Dual MAGNUM or Dual II MAGNUM (EC) *(Novartis)*
Rate: 1-2 pt. EC/A
Time: Preplant incorporated: Incorporate into top 2" of soil within 14 days before planting. Preemergence: Apply during or after planting but before weeds emerge.
Weeds: Broadleaf weeds:

carpetweed	eclipta*	galinsoga
common purslane*	Florida beggarweed*	hairy nightshade*
eastern black	Florida pusley	pigweed
nightshade		

Grasses and sedges:

barnyardgrass	goosegrass	shattercane*
(watergrass)	green foxtail	signalgrass
crabgrass	johnsongrass	southwestern cupgrass
crowfootgrass	(seedling)*	volunteer sorghum*
fall panicum	prairie cupgrass	witchgrass
foxtail millet	red rice	yellow foxtail
giant foxtail	sandbur*	yellow nutsedge

*Suppression
Remarks: Great northern, green, kidney, lima, navy, pinto, snap, string, wax beans. In case of crop failure, any crop on label may be replanted immediately. Do not make second broadcast application. If original application was banded and second crop is planted in untreated row middles, second banded treatment may be applied. Do not cut for hay within 120 days after application.
Crop Rotation: Alfalfa—4 months; barley, oats, rye, wheat—4¹⁄₂ months; tomatoes—6 months; clover—9 months; any labeled crop in addition to barley, buckwheat, cabbage, milo, oats, peppers, rice, root crops, rye, stone fruits, tobacco, tree nuts, and wheat may be planted in the spring following treatment (including lay-by or multiple treatments applied previous season); all other rotational crops may be planted 12 months after application.
Tank Mixes: Eptam (dry, green beans), trifluralin (dry, kidney, lima, navy, pinto, snap beans).
State Restrictions: Do not use in Nassau County or Suffolk County, New York.

Signal Word/Toxicity Class: Caution/III.
REI: 24 hr.

Micro-Tech — see alachlor

PARAQUAT

Restricted Use Pesticide.

■ PP, PRE
Gramoxone Extra (2.5L) *(ZENECA)*
Rate: Lima, snap (seeded or transplanted):
0.5-1 lb. ai/A
1.5-3 pt. 2.5L/A
Time: Preplant, preemergence. Apply when weeds and grasses are succulent and growth is from 1-6" tall (larger plants less affected by treatment).
Weeds: Annual broadleaf weeds and grasses; top kill and suppression of perennials.
Remarks: Add nonionic surfactant or crop oil concentrate. Seedbeds or plantbeds should be formed as far ahead of planting and treatment as possible to permit maximum weed and grass emergence. Seeding or transplanting should be done with minimum amount of soil disturbance. Refer to label for use directions, restrictions, and precautions.

Rate: Dry, kidney, lima, navy, pinto, snap, wax, white:
0.3-0.5 lb. ai/A
1-1.5 pt. 2.5L/A
Time: Harvest aid. Apply to mature crop with 80% of pods yellowing and mostly ripe with no more than 40% (bush-type) or 30% (vine-type) leaves still green in color.
Weeds: Same as above.
Remarks: Add nonionic surfactant or crop oil concentrate. Do not make more than 2 applications or exceed a total of 1.5 pt./A. Refer to label for use directions, restrictions, and precautions.
Days To Harvest: 7.
State Restrictions: Not registered for use on dry beans in California.

Signal Word/Toxicity Class: Danger-Poison/I.
REI: 12 hr. (except harvest aid/desiccation 24 hr.).

Partner — see alachlor

PENDIMETHALIN

Use in combination with another herbicide to increase spectrum of broadleaf weeds controlled. Cold, wet soil conditions after planting increase risk of crop injury.

■ PPI
Pentagon DG *(American Cyanamid)*
Prowl 3.3 EC *(American Cyanamid)*
Rate: 0.5-1.5 lb. ai/A
1.2-3.6 pt. 3.3 EC/A
0.5-2.5 lb. DG/A
Time: Preplant incorporated: Apply immediately before planting or up to 60 days prior to planting and incorporate within 7 days. Do not use preemergence.
Weeds: Broadleaf weeds:

annual spurge	lambsquarters	pigweed
carpetweed	Pennsylvania	purslane
Florida pusley	smartweed*	velvetleaf*
kochia		

Grasses:

barnyardgrass	giant foxtail	signalgrass
crabgrass	goosegrass	Texas panicum
crowfootgrass	green foxtail	witchgrass
fall panicum	johnsongrass	yellow foxtail
field sandbur	(seedling)	

* Reduced competition
Remarks: Dry beans (cranberry, great northern, navy, red kidney, small white), lima beans, snap beans. Rate varies by soil type and geographical region. Do not use on peat or muck soils. If crop loss occurs due to weather conditions, beans or any crop registered for preplant incorporated use can be replanted the same year. If replanting is necessary, do not rework soil deeper than treated zone.
Crop Rotation: Winter wheat and winter barley can be planted in the fall 4 months after application. Treated land can be planted to other crops the following year (see label for beet and spinach restrictions).
Tank Mixes: Alachlor for dry beans only west of the Mississippi; not for use in California. Dual for dry, lima, snap beans. Eptam for dry, snap beans only, not for use on Adzuki, lima, or other flat-podded beans.

Signal Word/Toxicity Class: Caution.
REI: 24 hr.

6 Vegetables

NOTICE The information on these pages is for preliminary planning — not a guide for use. Be sure to follow the manufacturer's directions, notwithstanding information contained here. For personal protective equipment and EPA registration numbers, please turn to page 70.

Beans

Pentagon — see pendimethalin

Poast — see sethoxydim

Prowl — see pendimethalin

Rattler — see glyphosate

Roundup — see glyphosate

SCYTHE

◆ **Scythe (pelargonic acid)** *(Mycogen)*
Rate: 4-13 fl. oz./1 gal. spray solution
Time: Apply to actively growing weeds prior to crop emergence.
Weeds: Annual and perennial broadleaf weeds and grasses.
Remarks: Apply in minimum 75 gal. spray solution/A or spray-to-wet. Do not apply by air or through any type of irrigation system. Refer to label for directions and precautions.
Tank Mixes: Glyphosate and other foliar and residual herbicides.

- - - - - - - - - - - - - -

Signal Word/Toxicity Class: Warning/II.
REI: 24 hr.

SETHOXYDIM

Provides selective control of annual and perennial grasses. Rainfast in 1 hr.

■ **POST**

Poast (1.5EC) *(BASF)*
Rate: 0.09-0.47 lb. ai/A
  0.5-2.5 pt. 1.5EC/A
Time: Postemergence.
Weeds: Annual and perennial grasses:

annual ryegrass	johnsongrass	Texas panicum
barnyardgrass	junglerice	volunteer cereals
bermudagrass	large crabgrass	wild oat
broadleaf signalgrass	perennial ryegrass	wild proso millet
browntop panicum	quackgrass	wildcane
fall panicum	red sprangletop	wirestem muhly
field sandbur	shattercane	witchgrass
giant foxtail	smooth crabgrass	woolly cupgrass
goosegrass	southwestern	yellow foxtail
green foxtail	cupgrass	

Remarks: Dry, succulent beans. Rate depends on growing region. Add 2 pt./A oil concentrate. Refer to label for restrictions and limitations.
Days To Harvest: Dry beans—30; succulent beans—15.
Tank Mixes: Basagran, Frontier (dry only).
State Restrictions: Do not use UAN or AMS in California or Pacific Northwest.

- - - - - - - - - - - - - -

Signal Word/Toxicity Class: Warning/II.
REI: 12 hr.

SONALAN

Controls annual grass and broadleaf weeds, including common lambsquarters and pigweed. Use in combination with another herbicide to increase spectrum of broadleaf weeds controlled. Cold, wet soil conditions after planting increase crop injury risk.

■ **PPI**

Sonalan HFP or 10G (ethalfluralin) *(Dow AgroSciences)*
Rate: 0.55-1.1 lb. ai/A
  1.5-3 pt. HFP/A
  5.5-11.5 lb. 10G/A
  Groundcherry, nightshade from seed:
  1.1-1.7 lb. ai/A
  3-4.5 pt. HFP/A
  11.5-17 lb. 10G/A

Time: Preplant incorporated. Apply in the spring before planting or in the fall.
Weeds: Broadleaf weeds:

carpetweed	groundcherry	redroot pigweed
common chickweed	henbit	Russian thistle
common	kochia	smooth pigweed
lambsquarters	nightshade	tarweed fiddleneck
common purslane	prostrate pigweed	tumble pigweed
conical catchfly	redmaids	wild buckwheat
Florida pusley	rockpurslane	

Grasses:

annual bluegrass	giant foxtail	shattercane
annual ryegrass	green foxtail	Texas panicum
barnyardgrass	Italian ryegrass	wild oat
broadleaf signalgrass	johnsongrass	wildcane
crabgrass	(seedling)	witchgrass
fall panicum	junglerice	woolly cupgrass
field sandbur	large crabgrass	yellow foxtail
foxtail millet	pigeongrass	

Remarks: Dry beans. Rate varies by soil type. Fall application of Sonalan HFP may be made only with dry bulk fertilizer. Do not apply to soils which are wet, cloddy, or subject to prolonged periods of flooding. Do not apply through any type of irrigation system. Do not graze or forage crop grown in treated soil or cut for hay or silage.
Crop Rotation: If replanting is required, replant only crops listed on label. Do not plant sugar beets or red beets within 13 months after application of 1.1 lb. ai/A or more; for less than 1.1 lb. ai/A, within 8 months after application, provided treated area is moldboard plowed to a depth of at least 12" prior to planting. In Arizona and California, do not plant spinach or oats within 8 months after application of 1.1 lb. ai/A or more. Refer to label for special restrictions for Montana and Wyoming.
Tank Mixes: May be tank mixed with other registered products; refer to labels.

- - - - - - - - - - - - - -

Signal Word/Toxicity Class: Danger/I.
REI: 24 hr. (HFP); 12 hr. (10G) unless soil injected or soil incorporated.

Treflan — see trifluralin

TRI-4 — see trifluralin

Trific — see trifluralin

TRIFLURALIN

Controls annual grasses and certain broadleaf weeds, including common lambsquarters and pigweed species. Combine with another herbicide to increase spectrum of broadleaf weeds controlled. Cold, wet soil conditions after planting increase risk of crop injury.

■ **PPI**

Albaugh Trifluralin 4EC *(Albaugh)*
◆ **Clean Crop Trifluralin HF (4EC)** *(Platte)*
Gowan Trifluralin 4 or 5 (EC) or 10G *(Gowan)*
Helena Trifluralin 4 EC *(Helena)*
Riverside Trifluralin 4EC or Trific 60DF *(Terra)*
◆ **Sedagri Trifluralin 480 (4EC)** *(Rhone-Poulenc)*
Treflan HFP (4EC) or TR-10 (10G) *(Dow AgroSciences)*
TRI-4 HF (4EC) *(American Cyanamid)*
Trilin 4 or 5 (EC) or 10G *(Griffin)*
Wilbur-Ellis Trifluralin 10G *(Wilbur-Ellis)*
Rate: Dry beans:
  0.5-1 lb. ai/A
  1-2 pt. 4EC/A
  0.8-1.6 pt. 5EC/A
  0.875-1.66 lb. 60DF/A
  5-10 lb. 10G/A
  Lima, snap beans:
  0.5-0.75 lb. ai/A
  1-1.5 pt. 4EC/A
  0.8-1.2 pt. 5EC/A
  0.875-1.33 lb. 60DF/A
  5-7.5 lb. 10G/A
Time: Preplant incorporated.

◆-new product • PP-preplant • PPI-preplant incorporated • PRE-preemergence • POST-postemergence • SEQ-sequential • ae-acid equivalent • ai-active ingredient • DF-dry flowable
E/EC-emulsifiable concentrate • F/FL-flowable • DG/G/WG-dispersable granule • L/LC-liquid • SP/WSP-soluble packet • W/WP-wettable powder • WSB-water soluble bag

Weeds: Broadleaf weeds:

carelessweed	knotweed	purslane
carpetweed	kochia	pusley
chickweed	lambsquarters	redroot pigweed
field bindweed	Mexican clover	rough pigweed
fireweed	Mexican fireweed	Russian thistle
Florida purslane	prostrate pigweed	spiny pigweed
Florida pusley	puncturevine	stinging nettle
goosefoot	(western U.S.)	tumbleweed
henbit		

Grasses:

annual bluegrass	fall panicum	sandbur
barnyardgrass	foxtail millet	shattercane
bottlegrass	giant foxtail	smooth crabgrass
brachiaria	green foxtail	sprangletop
bristlegrass	Italian ryegrass	stinkgrass
bromegrass	johnsongrass	Texas panicum
burgrass	(seedling)	watergrass
cheat	junglerice	wildcane
cheatgrass	large crabgrass	woolly cupgrass
chess	pigeongrass	yellow foxtail
downy brome	robust foxtail	

Remarks: Rate depends on soil type. Refer to label for restrictions, precautions, and limitations.

Crop Rotation: Vegetable crops other than those listed on label should not be planted within 5 months following application. Refer to label for other restrictions.

State Restrictions: Wilbur-Ellis not registered in California.

- - - - - - - - - - - - - - -

Signal Word/Toxicity Class: Varies by formulation.
REI: 12 hr. unless soil injected or soil incorporated.

Trilin — see trifluralin

Carrots

(Parsley, Parsnips)

Credit — see glyphosate

FLUAZIFOP-P-BUTYL

Provides selective control of annual and perennial grasses. Use in addition to residual herbicides for season-long control. Do not tank mix with any other herbicide unless specified on label.

■ **POST**
Fusilade DX *(ZENECA)*
Rate: 0.1-0.375 lb. ai/A
0.375-1.5 pt. DX/A
Time: Early postemergence. Apply to actively growing grasses.
Weeds: Annual and perennial grasses:

barnyardgrass	johnsongrass	southern sandbur
bermudagrass	(rhizome, seedling)	Texas panicum
broadleaf signalgrass	junglerice	tropical crabgrass
fall panicum	large crabgrass	volunteer cereals
field sandbur	quackgrass	wild oat
giant foxtail	red rice	wild proso millet
goosegrass	shattercane	wirestem muhly
green foxtail	smooth crabgrass	witchgrass
Italian ryegrass	sorghum-almum	woolly cupgrass
itchgrass	southern crabgrass	yellow foxtail

Remarks: Includes seed carrots. Rate varies by geographic area and grass species. Add crop oil concentrate or nonionic surfactant. Do not apply more than 3 pt./A per season. Refer to label for use directions.
Days To Harvest: 45.
Crop Rotation: Do not plant rotational grass crops such as corn, sorghum, and cereals within 60 days after last application.
State Restrictions: Refer to label for geographical regions.

- - - - - - - - - - - - - - -

Signal Word/Toxicity Class: Caution.
REI: 12 hr.

Fusilade — see fluazifop-P-butyl

Glyfos or Glyfos X-tra — see glyphosate

GLYPHOSATE

Postemergence control of annual and perennial grasses and broadleaf weeds in stale seedbeds and reduced-tillage planting systems prior to crop emergence.

■ **PRE**
◆ **Credit (4WS)** *(Nufarm)*
◆ **Glyfos or Glyfos X-tra (4WS)** *(Cheminova)*
Rattler (4WS) *(Helena)*
Roundup Custom (5.4WS) *(Monsanto)*
Roundup Original, Original RT, Ultra, Ultra RT (4WS) *(Monsanto)*
Rate: Annual weeds:
0.38-1.5 lb. ai/A
0.56-2.25 pt. 5.4WS/A
0.75-3 pt. 4WS/A
Perennial weeds:
0.5-5 lb. ai/A
0.75-7.5 pt. 5.4WS/A
1-10 pt. 4WS/A
Time: Preemergence: Apply prior to emergence of direct-seeded crop or prior to transplanting.
Weeds: Emerged annual and perennial broadleaf weeds including:

Canada thistle	hemp dogbane	Pennsylvania
curly dock	milkweed	smartweed
field bindweed		

Grasses:

bermudagrass	fescue	paragrass
fall panicum	johnsongrass	quackgrass

Remarks: Prior to transplanting crops into plastic mulch, remove product residue from plastic. Do not add surfactant to Roundup Ultra or Ultra RT. Do not allow glyphosate to contact desirable plants. Do not apply through any type of irrigation system. Refer to label for directions, precautions and restrictions.
State Restrictions: Roundup RT for use in Colorado, Idaho, Montana, North Dakota, South Dakota, Utah, Wyoming, and in specific counties only in Kansas, Minnesota, Nebraska, Nevada, Oklahoma, Oregon, and Washington; refer to label for restrictions. Glyfos not registered for use in California. Glyfos X-tra not registered for use in mistblowers in California or Arizona.

- - - - - - - - - - - - - - -

Signal Word/Toxicity Class: Varies by formulation.
REI: Warning—12 hr.; Caution—4 hr.

Gramoxone Extra — see paraquat

LINURON

Applied postemergence, controls broadleaf weeds and yellow nutsedge. Additional residual broadleaf weed control occurs when applications are made to carrots growing in mineral soils.

■ **PRE, POST**
Lorox DF *(Griffin)*
Rate: Carrots—PRE:
0.5-1.5 lb. ai/A
1-3 lb. DF/A
Carrots—POST, Parsnips—PRE:
0.75-1.5 lb. ai/A
1.5-3 lb. DF/A
Time: Preemergence: Apply once after planting before crop emerges; Postemergence (carrots): Apply after carrots are at least 3" tall.
Weeds: Broadleaf weeds:

annual morningglory*	lambsquarters	purslane
buttonweed*	mustard	sicklepod*
carpetweed	nettleleaf goosefoot	smartweed
cocklebur*	pigweed	teaweed*
Florida pusley	prickly sida*	velvetleaf*

Grasses:

barnyardgrass	crabgrass	foxtail
canarygrass	fall panicum	goosegrass

* Partial control

Remarks: Carrots, parsnips. Plant seed at least 1/2" deep. Do not apply when temperature exceeds 85°F or tank mix with other pesticides.
Crop Rotation: Any crop after 4 months except cereals where only barley, oats, rye, and wheat may be planted. West of the Rockies: carrots or celery may be planted after 4 months. Do not plant any other crop until 1 year after last application.
State Restrictions: Preemergence: Florida, Michigan, Ohio, Wisconsin; postemergence: All states.

- - - - - - - - - - - - - - -

Signal Word/Toxicity Class: Caution.
REI: 24 hr.

6

Vegetables

Lorox — see linuron

PARAQUAT

Restricted Use Pesticide.

■ PP, PRE

Gramoxone Extra (2.5L) *(ZENECA)*
Rate: 0.5-1 lb. ai/A
1.5-3 pt. 2.5L/A
Time: Preplant, preemergence. Apply when weeds and grasses are succulent and growth is from 1-6" tall (larger plants less affected by treatment).
Weeds: Annual broadleaf weeds and grasses; top kill and suppression of perennials.
Remarks: Add nonionic surfactant or crop oil concentrate. Seedbeds should be formed as far ahead of planting and treatment as possible to permit maximum weed and grass emergence. Seeding should be done with minimum amount of soil disturbance. Refer to label for use directions, restrictions, and precautions.

- - - - - - - - - - - - - -

Signal Word/Toxicity Class: Danger-Poison/I.
REI: 12 hr. (except harvest aid/desiccation 24 hr.).

Poast — see sethoxydim

PREFAR

For use on mineral soils only. Registered for use on many vegetable crops in certain states. Use to maintain flexibility in crop rotations. May be used on labeled crops grown through or under plastic. Toxic to fish.

■ PPI, PRE

Prefar 4-E (bensulide) *(Gowan)*
Rate: 5-6 lb. ai/A
5-6 qt. 4E/A
Time: Preplant incorporated, preemergence. Apply preemergence only on carrots to be irrigated up.
Weeds: Broadleaf weeds—AZ, CA, NM, TX:

burning nettle (AZ, CA only)	nettleleaf goosefoot (AZ, CA only)	purslane redroot pigweed
lambsquarters		

Grasses:

barnyardgrass	foxtail	sprangletop
crabgrass	goosegrass	watergrass
fall panicum	junglerice	

Remarks: Carrots (TX), parsley. Do not feed treated carrots to livestock. Rate varies by soil type. Refer to label for use directions, precautions.
Crop Rotation: Carrots, cotton, and labeled crops may be replanted following application without restrictions; all other crops 120 days after application and soil should be tilled to minimum depth 4" prior to planting.
State Restrictions: For use on carrots in Texas only.

- - - - - - - - - - - - - -

Signal Word/Toxicity Class: Caution/III.
REI: 12 hr. unless soil injected or soil incorporated.

PROMETRYN

Residual broadleaf weed control occurs when applications are made to crops growing in mineral soils. Residual activity is minimal on muck and other high organic matter soils.

■ PRE

Gowan Prometryne 4L *(Gowan)*
◆ **Platte Prometryne 4L** *(Platte)*
Rate: 1-2 lb. ai/A
2-4 pt. 4L/A in 20 gal. water
Time: Preemergence. Apply at planting or shortly after planting before parsley emerges.
Weeds: Broadleaf weeds:

annual morningglory	Florida pusley	pigweed
black nightshade	groundcherry	purslane
carelessweed	lambsquarters	ragweed
cocklebur*	malva	smartweed
coffeeweed*	mustard	teaweed (prickly sida)

Grasses:

barnyardgrass (watergrass)	goosegrass junglerice	sandbur* signalgrass
crabgrass	panicum	wild oat
foxtail		

* Shallow-germinating

Remarks: Parsley. Do not apply if parsley is under water stress. Use on sand or loamy sand may cause crop injury. Do not apply preemergence applications with other pesticides, apply only after foliar applications of other pesticides are dry, and do not apply within 2 weeks after a herbicidal oil such as carrot oil.
State Restrictions: For use in California only.

- - - - - - - - - - - - - -

Signal Word/Toxicity Class: Caution/III.
REI: 12 hr. unless soil injected or soil incorporated.

Rattler — see glyphosate

Roundup — see glyphosate

SCYTHE

◆ **Scythe (pelargonic acid)** *(Mycogen)*
Rate: 4-13 fl. oz./1 gal. spray solution
Time: Apply to actively growing weeds prior to crop emergence.
Weeds: Annual and perennial broadleaf weeds and grasses.
Remarks: Carrots, parsley, parsnips. Apply in minimum 75 gal. spray solution/A or spray-to-wet. Do not apply by air or through any type of irrigation system. Refer to label for directions and precautions.
Tank Mixes: Glyphosate and other foliar and residual herbicides.

- - - - - - - - - - - - - -

Signal Word/Toxicity Class: Warning/II.
REI: 24 hr.

SENCOR

Conditions for use developed under direction of IR-4. Varietal differences exist in carrot tolerance to metribuzin. Use caution when treating new varieties.

■ POST

Sencor 4 (FL) or DF (metribuzin) *(Bayer)*
Rate: 0.25 lb. ai/A
0.5 pt. FL/A
0.33 lb. DF/A
Time: Postemergence. Broadcast spray over tops of carrots after 5-6 true leaves but before weeds are 1" in height or diameter. Second application may be made after 3-week interval if needed.
Weeds: Broadleaf weeds:

carpetweed	pineappleweed	shepherdspurse
galinsoga	prickly lettuce	smooth pigweed
horseweed	redroot pigweed	wild mustard
lambsquarters		

Remarks: Carrots. Do not apply to carrots grown for seed. Do not apply within 3 days of any other chemical or within 3 days after periods of cool, wet, or cloudy weather. Refer to label for additional restrictions.
Days To Harvest: 60.
Crop Rotation: Alfalfa, asparagus, barley/wheat (following peas, lentils, or soybeans), corn, forage grass, potatoes, sainfoin, soybeans, sugarcane, tomatoes—4 months; barley, cotton, lentils, peas, rice, wheat—8 months; other crops not listed, except root crops—12 months; onions, sugar beets, and other root crops—18 months. Cover crops for soil building or erosion control may be planted anytime, but do not graze or harvest for food or feed. Stand reductions may occur in some areas.

- - - - - - - - - - - - - -

Signal Word/Toxicity Class: Caution/III.
REI: 12 hr.

SETHOXYDIM

Provides selective control of annual and perennial grasses. Rainfast in 1 hr.

■ POST

Poast (1.5EC) *(BASF)*
Rate: 0.09-0.47 lb. ai/A
0.5-2.5 pt. 1.5EC/A
Time: Postemergence.

◆-new product • PP-preplant • PPI-preplant incorporated • PRE-preemergence • POST-postemergence • SEQ-sequential • ae-acid equivalent • ai-active ingredient • DF-dry flowable
E/EC-emulsifiable concentrate • F/FL-flowable • DG/G/WG-dispersable granule • L/LC-liquid • SP/WSP-soluble packet • W/WP-wettable powder • WSB-water soluble bag

Weeds: Annual and perennial grasses:

annual ryegrass	junglerice	stinkgrass
barnyardgrass	large crabgrass	tall fescue
bermudagrass	lovegrass	Texas panicum
broadleaf signalgrass	orchardgrass	volunteer cereals
browntop panicum	(seedling)	wild oat
fall panicum	perennial ryegrass	wild proso millet
field sandbur	quackgrass	wildcane
giant foxtail	red sprangletop	wirestem muhly
goosegrass	shattercane	witchgrass
green foxtail	smooth crabgrass	woolly cupgrass
johnsongrass	southwestern cupgrass	yellow foxtail

Remarks: Rate depends on growing region. Add 2 pt./A oil concentrate. Do not graze treated fields or feed treated forage to livestock. Refer to label for restrictions and limitations.
Days To Harvest: 30.
State Restrictions: Do not use UAN or AMS in California or Pacific Northwest.

- - - - - - - - - - - - - - -

Signal Word/Toxicity Class: Warning/II.
REI: 12 hr.

Treflan — see trifluralin

Trific — see trifluralin

TRIFLURALIN

Use in combination with another herbicide to increase spectrum of broadleaf weeds controlled. Poor weed control observed when used on muck soils.

■ PPI
Albaugh Trifluralin 4EC *(Albaugh)*
◆ Clean Crop Trifluralin HF (4EC) *(Platte)*
Gowan Trifluralin 4 or 5 (EC) or 10G *(Gowan)*
Helena Trifluralin 4 EC *(Helena)*
Riverside Trifluralin 4EC or Trific 60DF *(Terra)*
◆ Sedagri Trifluralin 480 (4EC) *(Rhone-Poulenc)*
Treflan HFP (4EC) *(Dow AgroSciences)*
Trilin 4 or 5 (EC) or 10G *(Griffin)*
Wilbur-Ellis Trifluralin 10G *(Wilbur-Ellis)*
  Rate: 0.5-1 lb. ai/A
       1-2 pt. 4EC/A
       0.8-1.6 pt. 5EC/A
       0.875-1.66 lb. 60DF/A
       5-10 lb. 10G/A
Time: Preplant incorporated.
Weeds: Broadleaf weeds:

carelessweed	knotweed	purslane
carpetweed	kochia	pusley
chickweed	lambsquarters	redroot pigweed
field bindweed	Mexican clover	rough pigweed
fireweed	Mexican fireweed	Russian thistle
Florida purslane	prostrate pigweed	spiny pigweed
Florida pusley	puncturevine	stinging nettle
goosefoot	(western U.S.)	tumbleweed
henbit		

Grasses:

annual bluegrass	fall panicum	sandbur
barnyardgrass	foxtail millet	shattercane
bottlegrass	giant foxtail	smooth crabgrass
brachiaria	green foxtail	sprangletop
bristlegrass	Italian ryegrass	stinkgrass
bromegrass	johnsongrass	Texas panicum
burgrass	(seedling)	watergrass
cheat	junglerice	wildcane
cheatgrass	large crabgrass	woolly cupgrass
chess	pigeongrass	yellow foxtail
downy brome	robust foxtail	

Remarks: Rate varies by soil type. Refer to label for directions, restrictions, and precautions.
Crop Rotation: Vegetable crops other than those listed on label should not be planted within 5 months following application. Refer to label for other restrictions.
State Restrictions: Wilbur-Ellis not registered in California.

- - - - - - - - - - - - - - -

Signal Word/Toxicity Class: Varies by formulation.
REI: 12 hr. unless soil injected or soil incorporated.

Trilin — see trifluralin

Celery

Caparol — see prometryn

Cotton-Pro — see prometryn

Credit — see glyphosate

Glyfos or Glyfos X-tra — see glyphosate

GLYPHOSATE

Controls annual and perennial grasses and broadleaf weeds in stale seedbeds and reduced-tillage planting systems prior to planting.

■ PRE
◆ Credit (4WS) *(Nufarm)*
◆ Glyfos or Glyfos X-tra (4WS) *(Cheminova)*
Rattler (4WS) *(Helena)*
Roundup Custom (5.4WS) *(Monsanto)*
Roundup Original, Original RT, Ultra, Ultra RT (4WS) *(Monsanto)*
  Rate: Annual weeds:
       0.38-1.5 lb. ai/A
       0.56-2.25 pt. 5.4WS/A
       0.75-3 pt. 4WS/A
       Perennial weeds:
       0.5-5 lb. ai/A
       0.75-7.5 pt. 5.4WS/A
       1-10 pt. 4WS/A
Time: Preemergence: Apply prior to emergence of direct-seeded crop or prior to transplanting.
Weeds: Emerged annual and perennial broadleaf weeds including:

Canada thistle	hemp dogbane	Pennsylvania
curly dock	milkweed	smartweed
field bindweed		

Grasses:

bermudagrass	fescue	paragrass
fall panicum	johnsongrass	quackgrass

Remarks: Prior to transplanting crops into plastic mulch, remove product residue from plastic. Do not add surfactant to Roundup Ultra or Ultra RT. Do not allow glyphosate to contact desirable plants. Do not apply through any type of irrigation system. Refer to label for directions, precautions and restrictions.
State Restrictions: Roundup RT for use in Colorado, Idaho, Montana, North Dakota, South Dakota, Utah, Wyoming, and in specific counties only in Kansas, Minnesota, Nebraska, Nevada, Oklahoma, Oregon, and Washington; refer to label for restrictions. Glyfos not registered for use in California. Glyfos X-tra not registered for use in mistblowers in California or Arizona.

- - - - - - - - - - - - - - -

Signal Word/Toxicity Class: Varies by formulation.
REI: Warning—12 hr.; Caution—4 hr.

LINURON

Residual preemergence broadleaf weed control occurs when applications are made to celery growing in mineral soils. Residual activity is minimal on muck and other high organic matter soils.

■ POST
Lorox DF *(Griffin)*
  Rate: 0.75-1.5 lb. ai/A
       1.5-3 lb. DF/A
Time: Posttransplant. Apply before celery is 8" tall.
Weeds: Broadleaf weeds:

carpetweed	nettleleaf goosefoot	ragweed
lambsquarters	pigweed	smartweed
mustard	purslane	

Grasses:

canarygrass	foxtail	goosegrass
crabgrass	giant foxtail	watergrass

Remarks: Apply single application as nondirected spray. Do not apply when temperature exceeds 85°F.

6

Vegetables

Celery

Crop Rotation: Do not replant to crops other than celery or carrots within 4 months after application.
State Restrictions: For use east of the Rockies.

- - - - - - - - - - - - - - -

Signal Word/Toxicity Class: Caution.
REI: 24 hr.

Lorox — see linuron

Poast — see sethoxydim

PREFAR

For use on mineral soils only. Registered for use on many vegetable crops in certain states. Use to maintain flexibility in crop rotations. May be used on labeled crops grown through or under plastic. Toxic to fish.

■ PPI, PRE
Prefar 4-E (bensulide) *(Gowan)*
Rate: 5-6 lb. ai/A
5-6 qt. 4E/A
Time: Preplant incorporated, preemergence. Apply preemergence only on crops to be irrigated up.
Weeds: Broadleaf weeds—AZ, CA, NM, TX:

burning nettle (AZ, CA only)	nettleleaf goosefoot (AZ, CA only)	purslane redroot pigweed
lambsquarters		

Grasses:

barnyardgrass	foxtail	sprangletop
crabgrass	goosegrass	watergrass
fall panicum	junglerice	

Remarks: Rate varies by soil type. Incorporate to a depth of 1-2" before planting. Apply preemergence only on crops where application is followed by immediate irrigation.
Crop Rotation: Carrots, cotton, and labeled crops may be replanted following application without restrictions; all other crops 120 days after application and soil should be tilled to minimum depth 4" prior to planting.

- - - - - - - - - - - - - - -

Signal Word/Toxicity Class: Caution/III.
REI: 12 hr. unless soil injected or soil incorporated.

PROMETRYN

Residual broadleaf weed control occurs when applications are made to celery growing in mineral soils. Residual activity is minimal on muck and other high organic matter soils.

■ PRE, POST
Caparol 4L *(Novartis)*
◆ Platte Prometryne 4L *(Platte)*
Riverside Prometryne 4L *(Terra)*
Rate: Seedbeds—FL only:
0.6-0.8 lb. ai/A
1.2-1.6 pt. 4L/A
Time: Apply after celery has 2-5 true leaves.

Rate: Direct-seeded celery—CA only:
0.8-1.6 lb. ai/A
1.6-3.2 pt. 4L/A
Time: Preemergence, postemergence. For preemergence, apply at or shortly after planting before celery emerges. For postemergence, apply after celery has 2-5 true leaves and before weeds are 2" tall.

Rate: Transplants (rate varies by state):
0.8-2 lb. ai/A
1.6-6.4 pt. 4L/A
Time: Apply 2-6 weeks after transplanting and before weeds are 2" tall.
Weeds: Broadleaf weeds:

annual morningglory	Florida pusley	pigweed
black nightshade	groundcherry	purslane
carelessweed	lambsquarters	ragweed
cocklebur*	malva	smartweed
coffeeweed*	mustard	teaweed (prickly sida)

Grasses:

barnyardgrass (watergrass)	goosegrass	sandbur*
	junglerice	signalgrass
crabgrass	panicum	wild oat
foxtail		

* Shallow-germinating

Remarks: Application may be made over celery. For seedbeds, apply only once per year and only after seedbed covers have been removed from seedbeds for at least one week.
Crop Rotation: Cabbage, celery, corn, onions, peas, red beets—5 months.
State Restrictions: For use in Arizona, California, Florida, Hawaii, Michigan, Ohio, Texas, Wisconsin.

- - - - - - - - - - - - - - -

Signal Word/Toxicity Class: Caution/III.
REI: 12 hr.

■ POST
Cotton-Pro (4L) *(Griffin)*
Gowan Prometryne 4L *(Gowan)*
Rate: Seedbeds—FL only:
0.6-0.8 lb. ai/A
1.2-1.6 pt. 4L/A
Time: Broadcast after celery has 2-5 true leaves.

Rate: Transplants (rate varies by state):
0.8-3.2 lb. ai/A
1.6-6.4 pt. 4L/A
Time: Apply during 2-6 week period after transplanting before weeds are 2" tall.
Weeds: Broadleaf weeds:

annual morningglory	Florida pusley	pigweed
black nightshade	groundcherry	purslane
carelessweed	lambsquarters	ragweed
cocklebur*	malva	smartweed
coffeeweed*	mustard	teaweed (prickly sida)

Grasses:

barnyardgrass (watergrass)	goosegrass	sandbur*
	junglerice	signalgrass
crabgrass	panicum	wild oat
foxtail		

* Shallow-germinating

Remarks: Application may be made over celery. For seedbeds, apply only once per year and only after covers have been removed from seedbeds for at least one week. Use on sand or loamy sand may cause crop injury. Gowan: Do not apply preemergence applications with other pesticides, apply only after foliar applications of other pesticides are dry, and do not apply within 2 weeks after a herbicidal oil such as carrot oil.
Crop Rotation: Cabbage, celery, corn, onions, peas, red beets—5 months (not more than 4 pt./A).
State Restrictions: For use in Arizona, Florida, Hawaii, Michigan, Ohio, Wisconsin.

- - - - - - - - - - - - - - -

Signal Word/Toxicity Class: Caution/III.
REI: 12 hr. unless soil injected or soil incorporated.

Rattler — see glyphosate

Roundup — see glyphosate

SCYTHE

◆ Scythe (pelargonic acid) *(Mycogen)*
Rate: 4-13 fl. oz./1 gal. spray solution
Time: Apply to actively growing weeds prior to crop emergence.
Weeds: Annual and perennial broadleaf weeds and grasses.
Remarks: Apply in minimum 75 gal. spray solution/A or spray-to-wet. Do not apply by air or through any type of irrigation system. Refer to label for directions and precautions.
Tank Mixes: Glyphosate and other foliar and residual herbicides.

- - - - - - - - - - - - - - -

Signal Word/Toxicity Class: Warning/II.
REI: 24 hr.

SETHOXYDIM

Provides selective control of annual and perennial grasses. Rainfast in 1 hr.

■ POST
Poast (1.5EC) *(BASF)*
Rate: 0.09-0.28 lb. ai/A
0.5-1.5 pt. 1.5EC/A
Time: Postemergence.

◆-new product • PP-preplant • PPI-preplant incorporated • PRE-preemergence • POST-postemergence • SEQ-sequential • ae-acid equivalent • ai-active ingredient • DF-dry flowable
E/EC-emulsifiable concentrate • F/FL-flowable • DG/G/WG-dispersable granule • L/LC-liquid • SP/WSP-soluble packet • W/WP-wettable powder • WSB-water soluble bag

Weeds: Annual and perennial grasses:

annual ryegrass	large crabgrass	stinkgrass
barnyardgrass	lovegrass	tall fescue
bermudagrass	orchardgrass	Texas panicum
broadleaf signalgrass	(seedling)	volunteer cereals
browntop panicum	perennial ryegrass	wild oat
fall panicum	quackgrass	wild proso millet
field sandbur	red sprangletop	wildcane
giant foxtail	shattercane	wiresteam muhly
goosegrass	smooth crabgrass	witchgrass
green foxtail	southwestern	woolly cupgrass
johnsongrass	cupgrass	yellow foxtail
junglerice		

Remarks: Rate depends on growing region. Add 2 pt./A oil concentrate. Do not apply through any type of irrigation system. Do not graze treated fields or feed treated forage to livestock. Refer to label for restrictions and limitations.
Days To Harvest: 30.
State Restrictions: Do not use UAN or AMS in California or Pacific Northwest.

- - - - - - - - - - - - - -

Signal Word/Toxicity Class: Warning/II.
REI: 12 hr.

Treflan — see trifluralin

Trific — see trifluralin

TRIFLURALIN

Use in combination with another herbicide to increase spectrum of broadleaf weeds controlled. Poor weed control observed when used on muck soils.

■ **PPI**
Albaugh Trifluralin 4EC *(Albaugh)*
◆ **Clean Crop Trifluralin HF (4EC)** *(Platte)*
Gowan Trifluralin 4 or 5 (EC) or 10G *(Gowan)*
Helena Trifluralin 4 EC *(Helena)*
Riverside Trifluralin 4EC or Trific 60DF *(Terra)*
◆ **Sedagri Trifluralin 480 (4EC)** *(Rhone-Poulenc)*
Treflan HFP (4EC) *(Dow AgroSciences)*
Trilin 4 or 5 (EC) or 10G *(Griffin)*
Wilbur-Ellis Trifluralin 10G *(Wilbur-Ellis)*
Rate: 0.5-1 lb. ai/A
  1-2 pt. 4EC/A
  0.8-1.6 pt. 5EC/A
  0.875-1.66 lb. 60DF/A
  5-10 lb. 10G/A
Time: Preplant incorporated, preemergence incorporated. Apply and incorporate before planting, at planting, or immediately after planting.

Weeds: Broadleaf weeds:

carelessweed	knotweed	purslane
carpetweed	kochia	pusley
chickweed	lambsquarters	redroot pigweed
field bindweed	Mexican clover	rough pigweed
fireweed	Mexican fireweed	Russian thistle
Florida purslane	prostrate pigweed	spiny pigweed
Florida pusley	puncturevine	stinging nettle
goosefoot	(western U.S.)	tumbleweed
henbit		

Grasses:

annual bluegrass	fall panicum	sandbur
barnyardgrass	foxtail millet	shattercane
bottlegrass	giant foxtail	smooth crabgrass
brachiaria	green foxtail	sprangletop
bristlegrass	Italian ryegrass	stinkgrass
bromegrass	johnsongrass	Texas panicum
burgrass	(seedling)	watergrass
cheat	junglerice	wildcane
cheatgrass	large crabgrass	woolly cupgrass
chess	pigeongrass	yellow foxtail
downy brome	robust foxtail	

Remarks: Direct seeded or transplanted celery. Rate varies by soil type. Refer to label for directions and precautions.
Crop Rotation: Vegetable crops other than those listed on label should not be planted within 5 months following application. Refer to label for other restrictions.
State Restrictions: Wilbur-Ellis not registered in California.

- - - - - - - - - - - - - -

Signal Word/Toxicity Class: Varies by formulation.
REI: 12 hr. unless soil injected or soil incorporated.

Trilin — see trifluralin

Cole Crops

(Broccoli, Brussels Sprouts, Cabbage, Cauliflower, Chinese Cabbage, Turnips)

Credit — see glyphosate

DEVRINOL

Incorporate with irrigation to maximize galinsoga suppression or control. May cause temporary stunting that can result in reduced yield or a delay in maturity when used on coarse-textured soils. Cold, wet weather during seedling emergence or transplant establishment increases risk of injury. Registered for certain cole crops only.

■ **PPI, PRE**
Devrinol 50-DF (napropamide) *(United Phosphorus)*
Rate: 1-2 lb. ai/A
  2-4 lb. 50-DF/A
Time: Preplant incorporated, preemergence. May be applied to direct-seeded and transplanted crop or surface applied after planting.

Weeds: Broadleaf weeds:

carpetweed	Florida pusley	purple cudweed
common purslane	galinsoga (4 lb. rate)	redroot pigweed
common ragweed*	lambsquarters	smooth pigweed

Grasses:

barnyardgrass	goosegrass	junglerice
crabgrass	green foxtail	stinkgrass
fall panicum	johnsongrass	witchgrass
giant foxtail	(seedling)	yellow foxtail

*** Suppression**

Remarks: Broccoli, brussels sprouts, cabbage, cauliflower. Rates vary by region and soil type, refer to label before using. Incorporate to a depth of 1-2" same day as applied or sprinkler irrigate within 24 hr.
Crop Rotation: Do not plant to crops not specified on label until 12 months after last application. Disc plow or moldboard plow at least 10" deep prior to planting succeeding crop.

- - - - - - - - - - - - - -

Signal Word/Toxicity Class: Caution.
REI: 12 hr.

Glyfos or Glyfos X-tra — see glyphosate

GLYPHOSATE

Controls annual and perennial grasses and broadleaf weeds in stale seedbeds and reduced-tillage planting systems.

■ **PRE**
◆ **Credit (4WS)** *(Nufarm)*
◆ **Glyfos or Glyfos X-tra (4WS)** *(Cheminova)*
Rattler (4WS) *(Helena)*
Roundup Custom (5.4WS) *(Monsanto)*
Roundup Original, Original RT, Ultra, Ultra RT (4WS) *(Monsanto)*
Rate: Annual weeds:
  0.38-1.5 lb. ai/A
  0.56-2.25 pt. 5.4WS/A
  0.75-3 pt. 4WS/A
  Perennial weeds:
  0.5-5 lb. ai/A
  0.75-7.5 pt. 5.4WS/A
  1-10 pt. 4WS/A
Time: Preemergence: Apply prior to emergence of direct-seeded crop or prior to transplanting.

Weeds: Emerged annual and perennial broadleaf weeds including:

Canada thistle	hemp dogbane	Pennsylvania
curly dock	milkweed	smartweed
field bindweed		

Grasses:

bermudagrass	fescue	paragrass
fall panicum	johnsongrass	quackgrass

6

Vegetables

NOTICE	The information on these pages is for preliminary planning — not a guide for use. Be sure to follow the manufacturer's directions, notwithstanding information contained here.	For personal protective equipment and EPA registration numbers, please turn to page 70.

Cole Crops

Remarks: Broccoli, Brussels sprouts, cabbage, cauliflower, Chinese cabbage, kohlrabi, rutabagas, turnips. Prior to transplanting crops into plastic mulch, remove product residue from plastic. Do not add surfactant to Roundup Ultra or Ultra RT. Do not allow glyphosate to contact desirable plants. Do not apply through any type of irrigation system. Refer to label for directions, precautions and restrictions.

Days To Harvest: Rutabagas: wiper applications—14 days.

State Restrictions: Roundup RT for use in Colorado, Idaho, Montana, North Dakota, South Dakota, Utah, Wyoming, and in specific counties only in Kansas, Minnesota, Nebraska, Nevada, Oklahoma, Oregon, and Washington; refer to label for restrictions. Glyfos not registered for use in California. Glyfos X-tra not registered for use in mistblowers in California or Arizona.

- - - - - - - - - - - - - - - -

Signal Word/Toxicity Class: Varies by formulation.
REI: Warning—12 hr.; Caution—4 hr.

GOAL

Apply to soil surface before transplanting, and plant through herbicide barrier to control broadleaf weeds. Use in combination with grass herbicides that may cause stunting increases risk of crop injury. Registered for certain cole crops only.

■ PRE

Goal 2XL (oxyfluorfen) *(Rohm and Haas)*
Rate: 0.25-0.5 lb. ai/A
    1-2 pt. 2XL/A
Time: Pretransplanting. Apply after completion of soil preparation but prior to transplanting.
Weeds: Broadleaf weeds:

carpetweed	galinsoga*	redroot pigweed
common	Pennsylvania	wild mustard*
lambsquarters*	smartweed	
common purslane		

* Suppression

Remarks: Broccoli, cabbage, cauliflower (field use only). Transplanting should be completed with minimal soil disturbance. Pretransplant applications may result in temporary initial crop response (leaf cupping or crinkling). Do not apply posttransplant or postemergence (over the top). Do not apply more than 2 pt./A per season. Do not apply through any type of irrigation system.

Crop Rotation: Refer to label for plantback times for rotation crops.

- - - - - - - - - - - - - - - -

Signal Word/Toxicity Class: Warning/II.
REI: 24 hr.

Gramoxone Extra — see paraquat

PARAQUAT

Restricted Use Pesticide.

■ PP, PRE

Gramoxone Extra (2.5L) *(ZENECA)*
Rate: 0.5-1 lb. ai/A
    1.5-3 pt. 2.5L/A
Time: Preplant, preemergence. Apply when weeds and grasses are succulent and growth is from 1-6" tall (larger plants less affected by treatment).
Weeds: Annual broadleaf weeds and grasses; top kill and suppression of perennials.
Remarks: Broccoli, cabbage, Chinese cabbage, cauliflower, turnips. Add nonionic surfactant or crop oil concentrate. Seedbeds should be formed as far ahead of planting and treatment as possible to permit maximum weed and grass emergence. Seeding should be done with minimum amount of soil disturbance. Refer to label for use directions.

- - - - - - - - - - - - - - - -

Signal Word/Toxicity Class: Danger-Poison/I.
REI: 12 hr. (except harvest aid/desiccation 24 hr.).

Poast — see sethoxydim

PREFAR

For use on mineral soils only. Registered for use on many vegetable crops in certain states. Use to maintain flexibility in crop rotations. May be used on labeled crops grown through or under plastic. Toxic to fish.

■ PPI, PRE

Prefar 4-E (bensulide) *(Gowan)*

Rate: 5-6 lb. ai/A
    5-6 qt. 4E/A
Time: Preplant incorporated, preemergence. Apply preemergence only on crops to be irrigated up.
Weeds: Broadleaf weeds—AZ, CA, NM, TX:

burning nettle	nettleleaf goosefoot	purslane
(AZ, CA only)	(AZ, CA only)	redroot pigweed
lambsquarters		

Grasses:

barnyardgrass	foxtail	sprangletop
crabgrass	goosegrass	watergrass
fall panicum	junglerice	

Remarks: Bok choy, broccoli, Brussels sprouts, cabbage, cauliflower, Chinese cabbage. Rate varies by soil type. Incorporate to a depth of 1-2" before planting. Apply preemergence only on crops where application is followed by immediate irrigation.

Crop Rotation: Carrots, cotton, and labeled crops may be replanted following application without restrictions; all other crops 120 days after application and soil should be tilled to minimum depth 4" prior to planting.

- - - - - - - - - - - - - - - -

Signal Word/Toxicity Class: Caution/III.
REI: 12 hr. unless soil injected or soil incorporated.

Rattler — see glyphosate

Roundup — see glyphosate

SCYTHE

◆ Scythe (pelargonic acid) *(Mycogen)*
Rate: 4-13 fl. oz./1 gal. spray solution
Time: Apply to actively growing weeds prior to crop emergence.
Weeds: Annual and perennial broadleaf weeds and grasses.
Remarks: Broccoli, Brussels sprouts, cabbage, cauliflower, kohlrabi, rutabagas, turnips. Apply in minimum 75 gal. spray solution/A or spray-to-wet. Do not apply by air or through any type of irrigation system. Refer to label for directions and precautions.
Tank Mixes: Glyphosate and other foliar and residual herbicides.

- - - - - - - - - - - - - - - -

Signal Word/Toxicity Class: Warning/II.
REI: 24 hr.

SETHOXYDIM

Provides selective control of annual and perennial grasses. Do not tank mix with any other herbicide unless specified on label, or reduced control may result.

■ POST

Poast (1.5EC) *(BASF)*
Rate: 0.09-0.28 lb. ai/A
    0.5-1.5 pt. 1.5EC/A
Time: Postemergence.
Weeds: Annual and perennial grasses:

annual ryegrass	large crabgrass	stinkgrass
barnyardgrass	lovegrass	tall fescue
bermudagrass	orchardgrass	Texas panicum
broadleaf signalgrass	(seedling)	volunteer cereals
browntop panicum	perennial ryegrass	wild oat
fall panicum	quackgrass	wild proso millet
giant foxtail	red sprangletop	wildcane
goosegrass	shattercane	wirestem muhly
green foxtail	smooth crabgrass	witchgrass
johnsongrass	southwestern	woolly cupgrass
junglerice	cupgrass	yellow foxtail

Remarks: Broccoli, Brussels sprouts, cabbage, cauliflower, kohlrabi. Rate depends on growing region. Add 2 pt./A oil concentrate. Refer to label for restrictions and limitations.
Days To Harvest: 30.
State Restrictions: Do not use UAN or AMS in California or Pacific Northwest.

- - - - - - - - - - - - - - - -

Signal Word/Toxicity Class: Warning/II.
REI: 12 hr.

Treflan — see trifluralin

Trific — see trifluralin

◆-new product ● PP-preplant ● PPI-preplant incorporated ● PRE-preemergence ● POST-postemergence ● SEQ-sequential ● ae-acid equivalent ● ai-active ingredient ● DF-dry flowable
E/EC-emulsifiable concentrate ● F/FL-flowable ● DG/G/WG-dispersable granule ● L/LC-liquid ● SP/WSP-soluble packet ● W/WP-wettable powder ● WSB-water soluble bag

TRIFLURALIN

Cold, wet soil conditions after planting in early spring increase risk of crop injury. Poor weed control observed when used on muck soil.

■ PPI

Albaugh Trifluralin 4EC *(Albaugh)*
◆ Clean Crop Trifluralin HF (4EC) *(Platte)*
Gowan Trifluralin 4 or 5 (EC) or 10G *(Gowan)*
Helena Trifluralin 4 EC *(Helena)*
Riverside Trifluralin 4EC or Trific 60DF *(Terra)*
◆ Sedagri Trifluralin 480 (4EC) *(Rhone-Poulenc)*
Treflan HFP (4EC) or TR-10 (10G) *(Dow AgroSciences)*
Trilin 4 or 5 (EC) or 10G *(Griffin)*
Wilbur-Ellis Trifluralin 10G *(Wilbur-Ellis)*

Rate: 0.5-0.75 lb. ai/A
1-1.5 pt. 4EC/A
0.8-1.2 pt. 5EC/A
0.8-1.33 lb. 60DF/A
5-7.5 lb. 10G/A

Time: Preplant incorporated. Apply and incorporate before transplanting or seeding.

Weeds: Broadleaf weeds:

carelessweed	knotweed	purslane
carpetweed	kochia	pusley
chickweed	lambsquarters	redroot pigweed
field bindweed	Mexican clover	rough pigweed
fireweed	Mexican fireweed	Russian thistle
Florida purslane	prostrate pigweed	spiny pigweed
Florida pusley	puncturevine	stinging nettle
goosefoot	(western U.S.)	tumbleweed
henbit		

Grasses:

annual bluegrass	fall panicum	sandbur
barnyardgrass	foxtail millet	shattercane
bottlegrass	giant foxtail	smooth crabgrass
brachiaria	green foxtail	sprangletop
bristlegrass	Italian ryegrass	stinkgrass
bromegrass	johnsongrass	Texas panicum
burgrass	(seedling)	watergrass
cheat	junglerice	wildcane
cheatgrass	large crabgrass	woolly cupgrass
chess	pigeongrass	yellow foxtail
downy brome	robust foxtail	

Remarks: Broccoli, brussels sprouts, cabbage, cauliflower. Rate varies by soil type. Maximum rate for direct-seeded crops is 0.75 lb. ai/A. Direct-seeded cole crops have exhibited marginal tolerance to higher than recommended rates. Refer to label for further use directions.

Crop Rotation: Vegetable crops other than those listed on label should not be planted within 5 months following application. Refer to label for other restrictions.

State Restrictions: Wilbur-Ellis not registered in California.

– – – – – – – – – – – – – –

Signal Word/Toxicity Class: Varies by formulation.
REI: 12 hr. unless soil injected or soil incorporated.

Trilin — see trifluralin

Cucurbits

(Cucumbers, Melons, Pumpkins, Squash)

ALANAP-L

High water solubility results in short-term weed control when rainfall is above average. Heavy rainfall can cause weed control failure on coarse-textured soils low in organic matter. Temporary stunting may occur when cold, wet conditions prevail during crop emergence.

■ PRE, POST

Alanap-L (naptalam) *(Uniroyal)*

Rate: 3-4 lb. ai/A
6-8 qt./A

Time: Preemergence, postemergence. Apply immediately after seeding, or when plants are ready to vine.

Weeds: Broadleaf weeds:

carpetweed	common purslane	hedge bindweed
common chickweed	common ragweed	redroot pigweed
common cocklebur	cutleaf groundcherry	shepherdspurse
common	field bindweed	velvetleaf
lambsquarters	hairy galinsoga	white mustard

Remarks: Cucumbers, melons (cantaloupe, muskmelon, watermelon). Rate varies by soil type. Postemergent applications require weed-free soil. Do not apply through any type of irrigation system. Refer to label for use directions, restrictions, and precautions.

Tank Mixes: Prefar.

– – – – – – – – – – – – – –

Signal Word/Toxicity Class: Warning/II.
REI: 48 hr.

COMMAND

Spray and incorporate shallowly with rolling basket cultivators or a rotary hoe to improve weed control and reduce crop injury. In some states, must be soil incorporated and rates lower than labeled rate may be recommended. Spray or vapor drift may injure sensitive crops and other vegetation up to several hundred yards from point of application. Immediate incorporation will reduce or eliminate vapor drift. Do not apply to fields adjacent to horticultural, fruit, vegetable, other sensitive crops, or neighbors. Registered for use on pumpkins only. Certain states also have additional cucurbit crop labels.

■ PPI, PRE

Command 4EC (clomazone) *(FMC)*

Rate: 0.5-1 lb. ai/A
1-2 pt. 4EC/A

Time: Preplant incorporated, preemergence soil applied.

Weeds: Broadleaf weeds:

balloonvine* **	jimsonweed	prickly sida
black nightshade* **	jointvetch* **	prostrate spurge**
blackseed plantain	kochia	purslane
cocklebur	ladysthumb	redvine* **
common ragweed	lambsquarters	redweed**
curly dock**	Pennsylvania	spurred anoda
dayflower	smartweed	tropic croton
Florida beggarweed**	pigweed* **	velvetleaf
Florida pusley	pitted	Venice mallow
galinsoga	morningglory**	wild poinsettia

Grasses:

barnyardgrass	itchgrass	shattercane*
bermudagrass*	(preemergence)**	smooth crabgrass
broadleaf signalgrass	johnsongrass	southwestern
common panicum	(seedling)	cupgrass
fall panicum	junglerice* **	Texas panicum
field sandbur	large crabgrass	wild proso millet*
giant foxtail	purple foxtail**	(Northern U.S.)
goosegrass	red rice* **	woolly cupgrass
green foxtail	robust foxtail	yellow foxtail

* Partial control; ** Southern U.S.

Remarks: Pumpkins. Do not apply more than 2 pt./A. If initial seeding of pumpkins fails to produce a stand, pumpkins may be replanted in treated fields. Do not retreat fields with second application. Water or liquid fertilizer may be used as a carrier for Command when applied alone, or when tank mixed unless use directions specifically state otherwise. Do not apply through any type of irrigation system. Do not graze or harvest for food or feed cover crops planted less than 9 months after treatment, allow livestock to graze treated vines, or feed treated vines or vine trash to livestock.

Crop Rotation: Northern U.S.: all crops—16 months after application. Southern U.S.: all crops—12 months after application. For specific crops at shorter intervals, refer to Rotational Crop Guidelines on label. Cover crops may be planted any time but stand reductions may occur in some areas. Carryover injury to approved rotational crops may result under abnormal conditions.

Tank Mixes: May be tank mixed with other herbicides registered for pumpkins; observe all rotation guidelines, precautions, and replanting instructions of each label.

State Restrictions: Not for use in California.

– – – – – – – – – – – – – –

Signal Word/Toxicity Class: Warning/II.
REI: 12 hr. unless soil injected or soil incorporated.

Credit — see glyphosate

6

Vegetables

CURBIT

Cold, wet soil conditions after planting in early spring increase risk of crop injury.

■ PRE

Curbit EC (ethalfluralin) *(Platte)*

Rate: 1.125-1.7 lb. ai/A
3-4.5 pt. EC/A

Time: Preemergence. Apply postplant surface-applied prior to weed emergence. Apply to seeded crop prior to its emergence or as banded spray between rows after crop emergence or transplanting. For broadcast application on direct-seeded crop, apply to soil surface at seeding, or no later than 2 days after seeding.

Weeds: Broadleaf weeds:

carpetweed	common purslane	redroot pigweed
common	Florida pusley	smooth pigweed
lambsquarters	prostrate pigweed	spiny pigweed

Grasses:

broadleaf signalgrass	johnsongrass	sandbur
fall panicum	(from seed)	smooth crabgrass
foxtail millet	large crabgrass	Texas panicum
goosegrass		

Remarks: Cucumbers, melons including watermelon, pumpkins, and squash (certain areas). Not for use on soils containing more than 10% organic matter. Do not soil incorporate prior to planting, make broadcast applications to transplants, or plant in a furrow. Do not use under or over row covers, hot caps, plastic mulches, or other plant covers as severe crop injury will occur. Do not graze or forage crop grown in treated soil or cut for hay or silage.

Crop Rotation: Replant only crops listed on this or other ethalfluralin labels. Do not plant sugar beets or red beets within 13 months following application of 3 pt. or more/A. If less than 3 pt./A have been applied and treated soil is moldboard plowed to a depth of at least 12" prior to planting, sugar beets or red beets may be planted 8 months after application. In Arizona, California, and Texas, do not plant spinach or oats within 8 months following an application of 3 pt./A or more.

– – – – – – – – – – – – – – –

Signal Word/Toxicity Class: Warning/II.
REI: 12 hr.

Glyfos or Glyfos X-tra — see glyphosate

GLYPHOSATE

Nonselective control of annual and perennial grasses and broadleaf weeds in stale seedbeds and reduced-tillage planting systems.

■ PRE

◆ **Credit (4WS)** *(Nufarm)*
◆ **Glyfos or Glyfos X-tra (4WS)** *(Cheminova)*
Rattler (4WS) *(Helena)*
Roundup Custom (5.4WS) *(Monsanto)*
Roundup Original, Original RT, Ultra, Ultra RT (4WS) *(Monsanto)*

Rate: Annual weeds:
0.38-1.5 lb. ai/A
0.56-2.25 pt. 5.4WS/A
0.75-3 pt. 4WS/A
Perennial weeds:
0.5-5 lb. ai/A
0.75-7.5 pt. 5.4WS/A
1-10 pt. 4WS/A

Time: Preemergence: Apply prior to emergence of direct-seeded crop or prior to transplanting. Allow at least 3 days between application and planting.

Weeds: Emerged annual and perennial broadleaf weeds including:

Canada thistle	hemp dogbane	Pennsylvania
curly dock	milkweed	smartweed
field bindweed		

Grasses:

bermudagrass	fescue	paragrass
fall panicum	johnsongrass	quackgrass

Remarks: Cucumbers, melons, pumpkins, squash (winter, summer). Prior to transplanting crops into plastic mulch, remove product residue from plastic. Do not add surfactant to Roundup Ultra or Ultra RT. Do not allow glyphosate to contact desirable plants. Do not apply through any type of irrigation system. Refer to labels for directions and restrictions.

State Restrictions: Roundup RT for use in Colorado, Idaho, Montana, North Dakota, South Dakota, Utah, Wyoming, and in specific counties only in Kansas, Minnesota, Nebraska, Nevada, Oklahoma, Oregon, and Washington; refer to label for restrictions. Glyfos not registered for use in California. Glyfos X-tra not registered for use in mistblowers in California or Arizona.

– – – – – – – – – – – – – – –

Signal Word/Toxicity Class: Varies by formulation.
REI: Warning—12 hr.; Caution—4 hr.

Gramoxone Extra — see paraquat

PARAQUAT

Restricted Use Pesticide.

■ PP, PRE

Gramoxone Extra (2.5L) *(ZENECA)*

Rate: 0.5-1 lb. ai/A
1.5-3 pt. 2.5L/A

Time: Preplant, preemergence. Apply when weeds and grasses are succulent and growth is from 1-6" tall (larger plants less affected by treatment).

Weeds: Annual broadleaf weeds and grasses; top kill and suppression of perennials.

Remarks: Melons. Add nonionic surfactant or crop oil concentrate. Seedbeds should be formed as far ahead of planting and treatment as possible to permit maximum weed and grass emergence. Seeding should be done with minimum amount of soil disturbance. Refer to label for use directions, restrictions, and precautions.

Tank Mixes: Goal.

– – – – – – – – – – – – – – –

Rate: 0.2 lb. ai/A
0.75 pt. 2.5L/A

Time: Apply broadcast to preformed seedbeds.

Weeds:
volunteer barley

Remarks: Melons. Add nonionic surfactant or crop oil concentrate. Refer to label for use directions, restrictions, precautions.

State Restrictions: For use in California, Idaho, Oregon, Washington.

– – – – – – – – – – – – – – –

Signal Word/Toxicity Class: Danger-Poison/I.
REI: 12 hr. (except harvest aid/desiccation 24 hr.).

Poast — see sethoxydim

PREFAR

For use on mineral soils only. Registered for use on many vegetable crops in certain states. Use to maintain flexibility in crop rotations. May be used on labeled crops grown through or under plastic. Toxic to fish.

■ PPI, PRE

Prefar 4-E (bensulide) *(Gowan)*

Rate: 5-6 lb. ai/A
5-6 qt. 4E/A

Time: Preplant incorporated, preemergence. Apply preemergence only on crops to be irrigated up.

Weeds: Broadleaf weeds—AZ, CA, NM, TX:

burning nettle	nettleleaf goosefoot	purslane
(AZ, CA only)	(AZ, CA only)	redroot pigweed
lambsquarters		

Grasses:

barnyardgrass	foxtail	sprangletop
crabgrass	goosegrass	watergrass
fall panicum	junglerice	

Remarks: Cucumbers, gherkins, melons (cantaloupe, crenshaw, muskmelon, Persian, watermelon), pumpkins, squash (summer, winter). Flat-planted or bedded crops. Rate varies by soil type. Refer to label for use directions, restrictions, and precautions.

Crop Rotation: Carrots, cotton, and labeled crops may be replanted following application without restrictions; all other crops 120 days after application and soil should be tilled to minimum depth 4" prior to planting.

Tank Mixes: Alanap-L.

– – – – – – – – – – – – – – –

Signal Word/Toxicity Class: Caution/III.
REI: 12 hr. unless soil injected or soil incorporated.

Rattler — see glyphosate

◆-new product • PP-preplant • PPI-preplant incorporated • PRE-preemergence • POST-postemergence • SEQ-sequential • ae-acid equivalent • ai-active ingredient • DF-dry flowable
E/EC-emulsifiable concentrate • F/FL-flowable • DG/G/WG-dispersable granule • L/LC-liquid • SP/WSP-soluble packet • W/WP-wettable powder • WSB-water soluble bag

Roundup — see glyphosate

SCYTHE

◆ **Scythe (pelargonic acid)** *(Mycogen)*
Rate: 4-13 fl. oz./1 gal. spray solution
Time: Apply to actively growing weeds prior to crop emergence.
Weeds: Annual and perennial broadleaf weeds and grasses.
Remarks: Cucumbers, melons (cantaloupe, muskmelon, watermelon), pumpkins, squash. Apply in minimum 75 gal. spray solution/A or spray-to-wet. Do not apply by air or through any type of irrigation system. Refer to label for directions and precautions.
Tank Mixes: Glyphosate and other foliar and residual herbicides.

- - - - - - - - - - - - - - - -

Signal Word/Toxicity Class: Warning/II.
REI: 24 hr.

SETHOXYDIM

Provides selective control of annual and perennial grasses. Do not tank mix with any other herbicide unless specified on label or reduced control may occur.

■ POST
Poast (1.5EC) *(BASF)*
Rate: 0.09-0.28 lb. ai/A
0.5-1.5 pt. 1.5EC/A
Time: Postemergence.
Weeds: Annual and perennial grasses:

annual ryegrass	large crabgrass	stinkgrass
barnyardgrass	lovegrass	tall fescue
bermudagrass	orchardgrass	Texas panicum
broadleaf signalgrass	(seedling)	volunteer cereals
browntop panicum	perennial ryegrass	wild oat
fall panicum	quackgrass	wild proso millet
field sandbur	red sprangletop	wildcane
giant foxtail	shattercane	wirestem muhly
goosegrass	smooth crabgrass	witchgrass
green foxtail	southwestern	woolly cupgrass
johnsongrass	cupgrass	yellow foxtail
junglerice		

Remarks: Cucumbers, melons (cantaloupe, muskmelon, watermelon), pumpkins, squash. Rate depends on growing region. Add 2 pt./A oil concentrate. Do not apply through any type of irrigation system. Do not graze treated fields or feed treated forage to livestock. Refer to label for restrictions and limitations.
Days To Harvest: 14.
State Restrictions: Do not use UAN or AMS in California or Pacific Northwest.

- - - - - - - - - - - - - - - -

Signal Word/Toxicity Class: Warning/II.
REI: 12 hr.

Treflan — see trifluralin

Trific — see trifluralin

TRIFLURALIN

Use in combination with other herbicides for early season control. Hoe emerged weeds in the row prior to spraying trifluralin. Incorporate with a ridging cultivation.

■ POST
Albaugh Trifluralin 4EC *(Albaugh)*
◆ **Clean Crop Trifluralin HF (4EC)** *(Platte)*
Gowan Trifluralin 4 or 5 (EC) or 10G *(Gowan)*
Helena Trifluralin 4 EC *(Helena)*
Riverside Trifluralin 4EC or Trific 60DF *(Terra)*
◆ **Sedagri Trifluralin 480 (4EC)** *(Rhone-Poulenc)*
Treflan HFP (4EC) or TR-10 (10G) *(Dow AgroSciences)*
Trilin 4 or 5 (EC) or 10G *(Griffin)*
Wilbur-Ellis Trifluralin 10G *(Wilbur-Ellis)*
Rate: 0.5-1 lb. ai/A
1-2 pt. 4EC/A
0.8-1.6 pt. 5EC/A
0.8-1.66 lb. 60DF/A
5-10 lb. 10G/A

Time: Postemergence. Apply when plants are in 3- to 4-true-leaf stage.
Weeds: Broadleaf weeds:

carelessweed	knotweed	purslane
carpetweed	kochia	pusley
chickweed	lambsquarters	redroot pigweed
field bindweed	Mexican clover	rough pigweed
fireweed	Mexican fireweed	Russian thistle
Florida purslane	prostrate pigweed	spiny pigweed
Florida pusley	puncturevine	stinging nettle
goosefoot	(western U.S.)	tumbleweed
henbit		

Grasses:

annual bluegrass	fall panicum	sandbur
barnyardgrass	foxtail millet	shattercane
bottlegrass	giant foxtail	smooth crabgrass
brachiaria	green foxtail	sprangletop
bristlegrass	Italian ryegrass	stinkgrass
bromegrass	johnsongrass	Texas panicum
burgrass	(seedling)	watergrass
cheat	junglerice	wildcane
cheatgrass	large crabgrass	woolly cupgrass
chess	pigeongrass	yellow foxtail
downy brome	robust foxtail	

Remarks: Cucumbers, melons (cantaloupe, watermelon). Rate varies by soil type. Apply as directed spray to soil between rows. Set incorporation equipment to move treated soil around base of plants. Avoid foliage contact. Refer to label for further use directions.
Days To Harvest: 30; watermelon-60.
Crop Rotation: Vegetable crops other than those listed on label should not be planted within 5 months following application. Refer to label for other restrictions.
State Restrictions: Wilbur-Ellis not registered in California.

- - - - - - - - - - - - - - - -

Signal Word/Toxicity Class: Varies by formulation.
REI: 12 hr. unless soil injected or soil incorporated.

Trilin — see trifluralin

Eggplant

Credit — see glyphosate

DEVRINOL

Shallow, thorough incorporation improves control of certain weeds, including galinsoga. Apply and incorporate after ridging or bedding to improve drainage so concentrating the herbicide can be avoided. Spray soil strips between rows of plastic after laying the mulch.

■ PPI
Devrinol 50-DF (napropamide) *(United Phosphorus)*
Rate: 1-2 lb. ai/A
2-4 lb. 50-DF/A
Time: Preplant incorporated. Apply to transplanted crop only.
Weeds: Broadleaf weeds:

carpetweed	Florida pusley	purple cudweed
common purslane	galinsoga (4 lb. rate)	redroot pigweed
common ragweed*	lambsquarters	smooth pigweed

Grasses:

barnyardgrass	goosegrass	junglerice
crabgrass	green foxtail	stinkgrass
fall panicum	johnsongrass	witchgrass
giant foxtail	(seedling)	yellow foxtail

* *Suppression*

Remarks: Incorporate same day as applied to a depth of 1-2". Use lower rate on light soil and higher rate on heavy soil.
Crop Rotation: Do not plant to crops not specified on label until 12 months after last application. Disc plow or moldboard plow at least 10" deep prior to planting succeeding crop.

- - - - - - - - - - - - - - - -

Signal Word/Toxicity Class: Caution.
REI: 12 hr.

Glyfos or Glyfos X-tra — see glyphosate

NOTICE The information on these pages is for preliminary planning — not a guide for use. Be sure to follow the manufacturer's directions, notwithstanding information contained here. | For personal protective equipment and EPA registration numbers, please turn to page 70.

6

Vegetables

GLYPHOSATE

Nonselective control of annual and perennial grasses and broad-leaf weeds in stale seedbeds and reduced-tillage planting systems.

■ **PRE**
◆ **Credit (4WS)** *(Nufarm)*
◆ **Glyfos or Glyfos X-tra (4WS)** *(Cheminova)*
Rattler (4WS) *(Helena)*
Roundup Custom (5.4WS) *(Monsanto)*
Roundup Original, Original RT, Ultra, Ultra RT (4WS) *(Monsanto)*

Rate: Annual weeds:
  0.38-1.5 lb. ai/A
  0.56-2.25 pt. 5.4WS/A
  0.75-3 pt. 4WS/A
  Perennial weeds:
  0.5-5 lb. ai/A
  0.75-7.5 pt. 5.4WS/A
  1-10 pt. 4WS/A
Time: Preemergence: Apply prior to emergence of direct-seeded crop or prior to transplanting. Allow at least 3 days between application and planting.
Weeds: Emerged annual and perennial broadleaf weeds including:

Canada thistle	hemp dogbane	Pennsylvania
curly dock	milkweed	smartweed
field bindweed		

Grasses:

bermudagrass	fescue	paragrass
fall panicum	johnsongrass	quackgrass

Remarks: Prior to transplanting crops into plastic mulch, remove product residue from plastic. Do not add surfactant to Roundup Ultra or Ultra RT. Do not allow glyphosate to contact desirable plants. Do not apply through any type of irrigation system. Refer to labels for directions, precautions and restrictions.
State Restrictions: Roundup RT for use in Colorado, Idaho, Montana, North Dakota, South Dakota, Utah, Wyoming, and in specific counties only in Kansas, Minnesota, Nevada, Nebraska, Oklahoma, Oregon, and Washington; refer to label for restrictions. Glyfos not registered for use in California. Glyfos X-tra not registered for use in mistblowers in California or Arizona.

– – – – – – – – – – – – – –

Signal Word/Toxicity Class: Varies by formulation.
REI: Warning—12 hr.; Caution—4 hr.

Gramoxone Extra — see paraquat

PARAQUAT

Restricted Use Pesticide.

■ **PP, PRE, POST**
Gramoxone Extra (2.5L) *(ZENECA)*
Rate: 0.5-1 lb. ai/A
  1.5-3 pt. 2.5L/A
Time: Preplant, preemergence. Apply when weeds and grasses are succulent and growth is from 1-6" tall (larger plants less affected by treatment).
Weeds: Annual broadleaf weeds and grasses; top kill and suppression of perennials.
Remarks: Add nonionic surfactant or crop oil concentrate. Seedbeds should be formed as far ahead of planting and treatment as possible to permit maximum weed and grass emergence. Seeding should be done with minimum amount of soil disturbance. Refer to label for use directions, restrictions, and precautions.
Tank Mixes: Goal.

– – – – – – – – – – – – – –

Rate: 0.5 lb. ai/A
  1.5 pt. 2.5L/A
Time: Postemergence. Apply directed spray after crop emergence or when weeds and grasses are succulent and growth is 1-6" high.
Weeds: Annual broadleaf weeds and grasses; top kill and suppression of perennials between rows.
Remarks: Add nonionic surfactant or crop oil concentrate. Apply using precision-directed spray equipment to prevent contact with crops. Do not allow spray to contact crop. Do not graze treated areas. Refer to label for use directions, restrictions, and precautions.

– – – – – – – – – – – – – –

Signal Word/Toxicity Class: Danger-Poison/I.
REI: 12 hr. (except harvest aid/desiccation 24 hr.).

Poast — see sethoxydim

PREFAR

For use on mineral soils only. Registered for use on many vegetable crops in certain states. Use to maintain flexibility in crop rotations. May be used on labeled crops grown through or under plastic. Toxic to fish.

■ **PPI, PRE**
Prefar 4-E (bensulide) *(Gowan)*
Rate: 5-6 lb. ai/A
  5-6 qt. 4E/A
Time: Preplant incorporated, preemergence. Apply preemergence only on crops to be irrigated up.
Weeds: Broadleaf weeds—AZ, CA, NM, TX:

burning nettle (AZ, CA only)	nettleleaf goosefoot (AZ, CA only)	purslane
lambsquarters		redroot pigweed

Grasses:

barnyardgrass	foxtail	sprangletop
crabgrass	goosegrass	watergrass
fall panicum	junglerice	

Remarks: Rate varies by soil type. Incorporate to a depth of 1-2" before planting. Apply preemergence only on crops where application is followed by immediate irrigation.
Crop Rotation: Carrots, cotton, and labeled crops may be replanted following application without restrictions; all other crops 120 days after application and soil should be tilled to minimum depth 4" prior to planting.

– – – – – – – – – – – – – –

Signal Word/Toxicity Class: Caution/III.
REI: 12 hr. unless soil injected or soil incorporated.

Rattler — see glyphosate

Roundup — see glyphosate

SCYTHE

◆ **Scythe (pelargonic acid)** *(Mycogen)*
Rate: 4-13 fl. oz./1 gal. spray solution
Time: Apply to actively growing weeds prior to crop emergence.
Weeds: Annual and perennial broadleaf weeds and grasses.
Remarks: Apply in minimum 75 gal. spray solution/A or spray-to-wet. Do not apply by air or through any type of irrigation system. Refer to label for directions and precautions.
Tank Mixes: Glyphosate and other foliar and residual herbicides.

– – – – – – – – – – – – – –

Signal Word/Toxicity Class: Warning/II.
REI: 24 hr.

SETHOXYDIM

Selective control of annual and perennial grasses.

■ **POST**
Poast (1.5EC) *(BASF)*
Rate: 0.09-0.28 lb. ai/A
  0.5-1.5 pt. 1.5EC/A
Time: Postemergence.
Weeds: Annual and perennial grasses:

annual ryegrass	large crabgrass	tall fescue
barnyardgrass	lovegrass	Texas panicum
bermudagrass	orchardgrass	volunteer grains
broadleaf signalgrass	(seedling)	wild oat
browntop panicum	perennial ryegrass	wild proso millet
fall panicum	red sprangletop	wildcane
giant foxtail	shattercane	wirestem muhly
goosegrass	smooth crabgrass	witchgrass
green foxtail	southwestern	woolly cupgrass
johnsongrass	cupgrass	yellow foxtail
junglerice	stinkgrass	

Remarks: Rate depends on growing region. Add 2 pt./A oil concentrate. Refer to label for restrictions and limitations.
Days To Harvest: 20.
State Restrictions: Do not use UAN or AMS in California or Pacific Northwest.

– – – – – – – – – – – – – –

Signal Word/Toxicity Class: Warning/II.
REI: 12 hr.

◆-new product • PP-preplant • PPI-preplant incorporated • PRE-preemergence • POST-postemergence • SEQ-sequential • ae-acid equivalent • ai-active ingredient • DF-dry flowable E/EC-emulsifiable concentrate • F/FL-flowable • DG/G/WG-dispersable granule • L/LC-liquid • SP/WSP-soluble packet • W/WP-wettable powder • WSB-water soluble bag

TRIFLURALIN

■ PPI

Trilin 4EC, 5EC, or 10G *(Griffin)*

Rate: 0.5-1 lb. ai/A
1-2 pt. 4EC/A
0.8-1.6 pt. 5EC/A
5-10 lb. 10G/A

Time: Pretransplant. Apply and incorporate before transplanting

Weeds: Broadleaf weeds:

carelessweed	knotweed	purslane
carpetweed	kochia	pusley
chickweed	lambsquarters	redroot pigweed
field bindweed	Mexican clover	rough pigweed
fireweed	Mexican fireweed	Russian thistle
Florida purslane	prostrate pigweed	spiny pigweed
Florida pusley	puncturevine	stinging nettle
goosefoot	(western U.S.)	tumbleweed
henbit		

Grasses:

annual bluegrass	fall panicum	sandbur
barnyardgrass	foxtail millet	shattercane
bottlegrass	giant foxtail	smooth crabgrass
brachiaria	green foxtail	sprangletop
bristlegrass	Italian ryegrass	stinkgrass
bromegrass	johnsongrass	Texas panicum
burgrass	(seedling)	watergrass
cheat	junglerice	wildcane
cheatgrass	large crabgrass	woolly cupgrass
chess	pigeongrass	yellow foxtail
downy brome	robust foxtail	

Remarks: Avoid transplanting until soil temperatures have warmed in late spring. Rate varies by soil type and amount of rainfall. Refer to label for directions and precautions.

Crop Rotation: Vegetable crops other than those listed on label should not be planted within 5 months following application. Refer to label for other restrictions.

State Restrictions: Not for use in California.

Signal Word/Toxicity Class: Varies by formulation.
REI: 12 hr. unless soil injected or soil incorporated.

Trilin — see trifluralin

Garbanzos

(Chickpeas)

Credit — see glyphosate

Dual — see S-metolachlor

FAR-GO

Use in Pacific Northwest and Northern Plains where target weed is prevalent. Primarily absorbed by wild oat shoots from treated layer of oil. Wild oats are usually controlled before they emerge from soil.

■ PPI, PRE

Far-Go 4E or 10G (triallate) *(Monsanto)*

Rate: 1.25 lb. ai/A
1.25 qt. 4E/A
1.25-1.5 lb. ai/A
12.5-15 lb. 10G/A

Time: Preplant incorporated, preemergence incorporated. Apply in the spring up to 3 weeks before seeding or immediately after seeding.

Weeds:
wild oat

Remarks: Do not graze livestock on treated crops. Refer to label for directions, precautions, and state restrictions.

Crop Rotation: Domestic oats should not be seeded if Far-Go was used the previous year.

State Restrictions: For use in Colorado, Idaho, Kansas, Minnesota, Montana, Nebraska, Nevada, North Dakota, Oregon, South Dakota, Utah, Washington, and Wyoming.

– – – – – – – – – – – – – – – –

Signal Word/Toxicity Class: Caution/III.
REI: 12 hr.

Glyfos or Glyfos X-tra — see glyphosate

GLYPHOSATE

Nonselective control of annual and perennial grasses and broadleaf weeds in stale seedbeds and reduced-tillage planting systems.

■ PRE

◆ Credit (4WS) *(Nufarm)*
◆ Glyfos or Glyfos X-tra (4WS) *(Cheminova)*
Rattler (4WS) *(Helena)*
Roundup Custom (5.4WS) *(Monsanto)*
Roundup Original, Original RT, Ultra, Ultra RT (4WS) *(Monsanto)*

Rate: Annual weeds:
0.38-1.5 lb. ai/A
0.56-2.25 pt. 5.4WS/A
0.75-3 pt. 4WS/A
Perennial weeds:
0.5-5 lb. ai/A
0.75-7.5 pt. 5.4WS/A
1-10 pt. 4WS/A

Time: Preemergence: Apply prior to emergence of direct-seeded crop or prior to transplanting.

Weeds: Emerged annual and perennial broadleaf weeds including:

Canada thistle	hemp dogbane	Pennsylvania
curly dock	milkweed	smartweed
field bindweed		

Grasses:

bermudagrass	fescue	paragrass
fall panicum	johnsongrass	quackgrass

Remarks: Prior to transplanting crops into plastic mulch, remove product residue from plastic. Do not add surfactant to Roundup Ultra or Ultra RT. Do not allow glyphosate to contact desirable plants. Do not apply through any type of irrigation system. Refer to label for directions, precautions and restrictions.

State Restrictions: Roundup RT for use in Colorado, Idaho, Montana, North Dakota, South Dakota, Utah, Wyoming, and in specific counties only in Kansas, Minnesota, Nebraska, Nevada, Oklahoma, Oregon, and Washington; refer to label for restrictions. Glyfos not registered for use in California. Glyfos X-tra not registered for use in mistblowers in California or Arizona.

– – – – – – – – – – – – – – – –

Signal Word/Toxicity Class: Varies by formulation.
REI: Warning—12 hr.; Caution—4 hr.

Gramoxone Extra — see paraquat

S-METOLACHLOR

Dual is a cell growth inhibitor. S-metolachlor is a purified isomer of the metolachlor molecule. Dual II MAGNUM contains the safener benoxacor. Use in combination with another herbicide to increase spectrum of broadleaf weeds controlled.

■ PPI, PRE

Dual MAGNUM or Dual II MAGNUM (EC) *(Novartis)*

Rate: 1-2 pt. EC/A

Time: Preplant incorporated: Incorporate into top 2" of soil within 14 days before planting. Preemergence: Apply during or after planting but before weeds emerge.

Weeds: Broadleaf weeds:

carpetweed	eclipta*	galinsoga
common purslane*	Florida beggarweed*	hairy nightshade*
eastern black	Florida pusley	pigweed
nightshade		

Grasses and sedges:

barnyardgrass	goosegrass	shattercane*
(watergrass)	green foxtail	signalgrass
crabgrass	johnsongrass	southwestern cupgrass
crowfootgrass	(seedling)*	volunteer sorghum*
fall panicum	prairie cupgrass	witchgrass
foxtail millet	red rice	yellow foxtail
giant foxtail	sandbur*	yellow nutsedge

***Suppression**

6

Vegetables

Garbanzos

Remarks: Rate varies by soil type and organic matter. In case of crop failure, any crop on label may be replanted immediately. Do not make second broadcast application. If original application was banded and second crop is planted in untreated row middles, second banded treatment may be applied. Do not cut for hay within 120 days after application.

Crop Rotation: Alfalfa—4 months; barley, oats, rye, wheat—4½ months; tomatoes—6 months; clover—9 months; any labeled crop in addition to barley, buckwheat, cabbage, milo, nuts, oats, peppers, rice, root crops, rye, stone fruits, tobacco, and wheat may be planted in the spring following treatment (including lay-by or multiple treatments applied previous season); all other rotational crops may be planted 12 months after application.

- - - - - - - - - - - - - - -

Signal Word/Toxicity Class: Caution/III.
REI: 24 hr.

PARAQUAT

Restricted Use Pesticide.

Gramoxone Extra (2.5L) *(ZENECA)*
Rate: 0.3-0.5 lb. ai/A
   1-1.5 pt. 2.5L/A
Time: Apply to mature crop with 80% of pods yellowing and mostly ripe with no more than 40% (bush-type) or 30% (vine-type) leaves still green in color.
Weeds: Annual broadleaf weeds and grasses; top kill and suppression of perennials.
Remarks: Add nonionic surfactant or crop oil concentrate. Seedbeds should be formed as far ahead of planting and treatment as possible to permit maximum weed and grass emergence. Seeding should be done with minimum amount of soil disturbance. Refer to label for use directions, restrictions, and precautions.
Days To Harvest: 7.
State Restrictions: Not for use on dry beans in California.

- - - - - - - - - - - - - - -

Signal Word/Toxicity Class: Danger-Poison/I.
REI: 12 hr. (except harvest aid/desiccation 24 hr.).

PENDIMETHALIN

Use in combination with another herbicide to increase spectrum of broadleaf weeds controlled. Cold, wet soil conditions after planting increase risk of crop injury.

■ **PPI**
Pentagon DG *(American Cyanamid)*
Prowl 3.3 EC *(American Cyanamid)*
Rate: 0.5-1.5 lb. ai/A
   1.2-3.6 pt. 3.3 EC/A
   0.85-2.5 lb. DG/A
Time: Preplant incorporated: Apply immediately before planting or up to 60 days prior to planting and incorporate within 7 days. Do not use preemergence.
Weeds: Broadleaf weeds:

annual spurge	lambsquarters	pigweed
carpetweed	Pennsylvania	purslane
Florida pusley	smartweed*	velvetleaf*
kochia		

Grasses:

barnyardgrass	giant foxtail	signalgrass
crabgrass	goosegrass	Texas panicum
crowfootgrass	green foxtail	witchgrass
fall panicum	johnsongrass	yellow foxtail
field sandbur	(seedling)	

* Reduced competition

Remarks: Rate varies by soil type and geographical region. Do not use on peat or muck soils. If crop loss occurs due to weather conditions, beans or any crop registered for preplant incorporated use can be replanted the same year. If replanting is necessary, do not rework soil deeper than treated zone.
Crop Rotation: Winter wheat and winter barley can be planted in the fall 4 months after application. Treated land can be planted to other crops the following year (see label for beet and spinach restrictions).

- - - - - - - - - - - - - - -

Signal Word/Toxicity Class: Caution.
REI: 24 hr.

Pentagon — see pendimethalin

Prowl — see pendimethalin

Rattler — see glyphosate

Roundup — see glyphosate

Garlic

Broclean — see bromoxynil

Bromox — see bromoxynil

BROMOXYNIL

High soil moisture, high humidity, cloudy weather, and cool or moderate temperatures the week before treatment increase risk of crop injury. Delay application until several days of bright, sunny, dry weather precede treatment.

■ **POST**
◆ **Broclean 2EC** *(Platte)*
◆ **Bromox 2EC** *(Micro Flo)*
Buctril (2EC), Buctril 4EC *(Rhone-Poulenc)*
Moxy 2EC *(Terra)*
Rate: 0.375-0.5 lb. ai/A
   1.5-2 pt. 2EC/A
   0.75-1 pt. 4EC/A
Time: Postemergence. Apply after emergence but before garlic is 12" tall.
Weeds: Most susceptible broadleaf weeds:

annual pepperweed	common tarweed	Pennsylvania
annual sowthistle	eastern black	smartweed
black nightshade	nightshade	shepherdspurse
blue mustard	field pennycress	silverleaf nightshade
bristly starbur	green smartweed	sunflower
coast fiddleneck	hairy nightshade	tartary buckwheat
common cocklebur	jimsonweed	wild buckwheat
common lambsquarters	ladysthumb	

Susceptible broadleaf weeds:

buffalobur	ivyleaf morningglory	spiny pigweed
burcucumber	knawel	tall morningglory
common groundsel	kochia	tall waterhemp
common ragweed	London rocket	tumble mustard
corn chamomile	mayweed	velvetleaf
corn gromwell	prostrate knotweed	Venice mallow
cowcockle	puncturevine	wild mustard
giant ragweed	redroot pigweed	wild radish
hemp sesbania	Russian thistle	yellow starthistle

Remarks: Can be applied through automated sprinkler irrigation application.
Days To Harvest: 112; 60 if grown in muck soils in northeastern U.S.

- - - - - - - - - - - - - - -

Signal Word/Toxicity Class: Warning/II.
REI: 12 hr.

Buctril — see bromoxynil

CLETHODIM

Postemergence grass herbicide. Mode of action similar to Poast, Assure, Option II, and Fusilade.

■ **POST**
Prism (0.94EC) or Select (2EC) *(Valent)*
Rate: 0.1-0.25 lb. ai/A
   13-34 fl. oz. 0.94EC/A
   6-16 fl. oz. 2EC/A
Time: Postemergence. Apply to actively growing grasses.

◆-new product • PP-preplant • PPI-preplant incorporated • PRE-preemergence • POST-postemergence • SEQ-sequential • ae-acid equivalent • ai-active ingredient • DF-dry flowable
E/EC-emulsifiable concentrate • F/FL-flowable • DG/G/WG-dispersable granule • L/LC-liquid • SP/WSP-soluble packet • W/WP-wettable powder • WSB-water soluble bag

Weeds: Grasses:

Amazon sprangletop	green foxtail	smooth crabgrass
annual bluegrass	itchgrass	southern crabgrass
barnyardgrass	johnsongrass	Texas panicum
bearded sprangletop	junglerice	volunteer cereals
bermudagrass	large crabgrass	wild oat
broadleaf signalgrass	quackgrass	wild proso millet
crowfootgrass	red rice	wiresteam muhly
fall panicum	red sprangletop	witchgrass
giant foxtail	shattercane	woolly cupgrass
goosegrass	southwestern cupgrass	yellow foxtail

Remarks: Rate varies by grass species, stage, and geographical region. Grass crops such as corn, sorghum, wheat, and rice are highly sensitive to clethodim. Do not apply under stress conditions or if rainfall is expected in 1 hour. Do not apply through any type of irrigation system. Do not apply more than 0.5 lb. ai/A (0.25 lb. ai/A on Long Island, NY) per season. Do not graze treated fields or feed treated forage or hay to livestock. Refer to label for restrictions and precautions.

Days To Harvest: 45.

State Restrictions: Not for use on Solano grass in the Vernal Lakes area of Solano County, California; wild rice in Hays County, Texas.

– – – – – – – – – – – – – –

Signal Word/Toxicity Class: Warning/II.
REI: 24 hr.

Credit — see glyphosate

FLUAZIFOP-P-BUTYL

Provides selective control of annual and perennial grasses.

■ **POST**

Fusilade DX *(ZENECA)*

Rate: 0.1-0.375 lb. ai/A
0.375-1.5 pt. DX/A

Time: Early postemergence. Apply to actively growing grasses.

Weeds: Annual and perennial grasses:

barnyardgrass	johnsongrass	southern sandbur
bermudagrass	(rhizome, seedling)	Texas panicum
broadleaf signalgrass	junglerice	tropical crabgrass
fall panicum	large crabgrass	volunteer cereals
field sandbur	quackgrass	wild oat
giant foxtail	red rice	wild proso millet
goosegrass	shattercane	wiresteam muhly
green foxtail	smooth crabgrass	witchgrass
Italian ryegrass	sorghum-almum	woolly cupgrass
itchgrass	southern crabgrass	yellow foxtail

Remarks: Rate varies by geographic area and grass species. Add crop oil concentrate or nonionic surfactant. Do not apply more than 3 pt./A per season. Refer to label for specific directions and precautions.

Days To Harvest: 45.

Crop Rotation: Do not plant rotational grass crops such as corn, sorghum, and cereals within 60 days after last application.

State Restrictions: Refer to label for geographical regions.

– – – – – – – – – – – – – –

Signal Word/Toxicity Class: Caution.
REI: 12 hr.

Fusilade DX — see fluazifop-P-butyl

Glyfos or Glyfos X-tra — see glyphosate

GLYPHOSATE

Controls annual and perennial grasses and broadleaf weeds in stale seedbeds and reduced-tillage planting systems.

■ **PRE**

◆ **Credit (4WS)** *(Nufarm)*
◆ **Glyfos or Glyfos X-tra (4WS)** *(Cheminova)*
Rattler (4WS) *(Helena)*
Roundup Custom (5.4WS) *(Monsanto)*
Roundup Original, Original RT, Ultra, Ultra RT (4WS) *(Monsanto)*

Rate: Annual weeds:
0.38-1.5 lb. ai/A
0.56-2.25 pt. 5.4WS/A
0.75-3 pt. 4WS/A
Perennial weeds:
0.5-5 lb. ai/A
0.75-7.5 pt. 5.4WS/A
1-10 pt. 4WS/A

Time: Preemergence: Apply prior to emergence of direct-seeded crop or prior to transplanting. Allow at least 3 days between application and planting.

Weeds: Emerged annual and perennial broadleaf weeds including:

Canada thistle	hemp dogbane	Pennsylvania
curly dock	milkweed	smartweed
field bindweed		

Grasses:

bermudagrass	fescue	paragrass
fall panicum	johnsongrass	quackgrass

Remarks: Prior to transplanting crops into plastic mulch, remove product residue from plastic. Do not add surfactant to Roundup Ultra or Ultra RT. Do not allow glyphosate to contact desirable plants. Do not apply through any type of irrigation system. Refer to labels for directions, precautions and restrictions.

State Restrictions: Roundup RT for use in Colorado, Idaho, Montana, North Dakota, South Dakota, Utah, Wyoming, and in specific counties only in Kansas, Minnesota, Nebraska, Nevada, Oklahoma, Oregon, and Washington; refer to label for restrictions. Glyfos not registered for use in California. Glyfos X-tra not registered for use in mistblowers in California or Arizona.

Signal Word/Toxicity Class: Varies by formulation.
REI: Warning—12 hr.; Caution—4 hr.

Gramoxone Extra — see paraquat

Moxy — see bromoxynil

PARAQUAT

Restricted Use Pesticide.

■ **PP, PRE**

Gramoxone Extra (2.5L) *(ZENECA)*

Rate: 0.6-1 lb. ai/A
2-3 pt. 2.5L/A

Time: Preplant, preemergence. Apply when weeds and grasses are succulent and growth is from 1-6" tall (larger plants less affected by treatment).

Weeds: Annual broadleaf weeds and grasses; top kill and suppression of perennials.

Remarks: Add nonionic surfactant or crop oil concentrate. Seedbeds should be formed as far ahead of planting and treatment as possible to permit maximum weed and grass emergence. Seeding should be done with minimum amount of soil disturbance. Refer to label for use directions, restrictions, and precautions.

Days To Harvest: 60; California—200.

– – – – – – – – – – – – – –

Signal Word/Toxicity Class: Danger-Poison/I.
REI: 12 hr. (except harvest aid/desiccation 24 hr.).

PENDIMETHALIN

Use in combination with another herbicide to increase spectrum of broadleaf weeds controlled.

■ **PRE, POST**

Pentagon DG *(American Cyanamid)*
Prowl 3.3 EC *(American Cyanamid)*

Rate: 0.5-1.5 lb. ai/A
1.2-3.6 pt. 3.3 EC/A
0.5-2.5 lb. DG/A

Time: Preemergence, postemergence. Preemergence: apply after planting but before crop and weeds emerge. Postemergence: apply to garlic at 1-5 true-leaf growth stage. May be applied as split application, both preemergence and postemergence.

Weeds: Broadleaf weeds:

annual spurge	lambsquarters	pigweed
carpetweed	Pennsylvania	purslane
Florida pusley	smartweed*	velvetleaf*
kochia		

Grasses:

barnyardgrass	giant foxtail	signalgrass
crabgrass	goosegrass	Texas panicum
crowfootgrass	green foxtail	witchgrass
fall panicum	johnsongrass	yellow foxtail
field sandbur	(seedling)	

* *Reduced competition*

Remarks: Do not use on peat or muck soils. Do not feed or graze this crop. If crop loss occurs due to weather conditions, any crop registered for preplant incorporated use can be replanted the same year. If replanting is necessary, do not rework soil deeper than 2".

Days To Harvest: 45; California—60.

6

Vegetables

Garlic

Crop Rotation: Winter wheat and winter barley can be planted in the fall 4 months after application. Treated land can be planted to other crops the following year (see label for beet and spinach restrictions).

- - - - - - - - - - - - - - -

Signal Word/Toxicity Class: Caution.
REI: 24 hr.

Pentagon — see pendimethalin

Poast — see sethoxydim

PREFAR

For use on mineral soils only. Registered for use on many vegetable crops in certain states. Use to maintain flexibility in crop rotations. May be used on labeled crops grown through or under plastic. Toxic to fish.

■ PPI, PRE
Prefar 4-E (bensulide) *(Gowan)*
  Rate: 5-6 lb. ai/A
    5-6 qt. 4E/A
  Time: Preplant incorporated. Fall-applied.
  Weeds: Broadleaf weeds:

  lambsquarters   redroot pigweed

  Remarks: Apply in 10-12" band, bed-up, and leave undisturbed until spring. Prior to planting, drag-off bed tops and plant in center of beds.
  Crop Rotation: Carrots, cotton, and labeled crops may be replanted following application without restrictions; all other crops 120 days after application and soil should be tilled to minimum depth 4" prior to planting.
  State Restrictions: For use in Idaho, Oregon.

- - - - - - - - - - - - - - -

  Rate: 5-6 lb. ai/A
    5-6 qt. 4E/A
  Time: Preplant incorporated, preemergence. Apply preemergence only on crops to be irrigated up.
  Weeds: Broadleaf weeds—AZ, CA, NM, TX:

burning nettle (AZ, CA only)	nettleleaf goosefoot (AZ, CA only)	purslane
lambsquarters		redroot pigweed

  Grasses:

barnyardgrass (watergrass)	fall panicum	junglerice
crabgrass	foxtail	sprangletop
	goosegrass	

  Remarks: Rate varies by soil type. Incorporate to a depth of 1-2" before planting. Apply preemergence only on crops where application is followed by immediate irrigation.
  Crop Rotation: Carrots, cotton, and labeled crops may be replanted following application without restrictions; all other crops 120 days after application and soil should be tilled to minimum depth 4" prior to planting.
  State Restrictions: Not for use in Willamette Valley of Oregon.

- - - - - - - - - - - - - - -

Signal Word/Toxicity Class: Caution/III.
REI: 12 hr. unless soil injected or soil incorporated.

Prism — see clethodim

Prowl — see pendimethalin

Rattler — see glyphosate

Roundup — see glyphosate

SCYTHE

◆ **Scythe (pelargonic acid)** *(Mycogen)*
  Rate: 4-13 fl. oz./1 gal. spray solution
  Time: Apply to actively growing weeds prior to crop emergence.
  Weeds: Annual and perennial broadleaf weeds and grasses.
  Remarks: Apply in minimum 75 gal. spray solution/A or spray-to-wet. Do not apply by air or through any type of irrigation system. Refer to label for directions and precautions.

Tank Mixes: Glyphosate and other foliar and residual herbicides.

- - - - - - - - - - - - - - -

Signal Word/Toxicity Class: Warning/II.
REI: 24 hr.

Select — see clethodim

SETHOXYDIM

■ POST
Poast (1.5EC) *(BASF)*
  Rate: 0.09-0.28 lb. ai/A
    0.5-1.5 pt. 1.5EC/A
  Time: Postemergence.
  Weeds: Annual and perennial grasses:

annual ryegrass	large crabgrass	stinkgrass
barnyardgrass	lovegrass	tall fescue
bermudagrass	orchardgrass	Texas panicum
broadleaf signalgrass	(seedling)	volunteer cereals
browntop panicum	perennial ryegrass	wild oat
fall panicum	quackgrass	wild proso millet
giant foxtail	red sprangletop	wildcane
goosegrass	shattercane	wirestem muhly
green foxtail	smooth crabgrass	witchgrass
johnsongrass	southwestern	woolly cupgrass
junglerice	cupgrass	yellow foxtail

  Remarks: Rate depends on growing region. Add 2 pt./A oil concentrate. Refer to label for restrictions and limitations.
  Days To Harvest: 30.
  State Restrictions: Do not use UAN or AMS in California or Pacific Northwest.

- - - - - - - - - - - - - - -

Signal Word/Toxicity Class: Warning/II.
REI: 12 hr.

Greens

(Collards, Kale, Mustard, Swiss Chard, Turnip Greens)

Credit — see glyphosate

Glyfos or Glyfos X-tra — see glyphosate

GLYPHOSATE

Nonselective control of established annual and perennial grasses and broadleaf weeds in stale seedbeds and reduced-tillage planting systems.

■ PRE
◆ **Credit (4WS)** *(Nufarm)*
◆ **Glyfos or Glyfos X-tra (4WS)** *(Cheminova)*
Rattler (4WS) *(Helena)*
Roundup Custom (5.4WS) *(Monsanto)*
Roundup Original, Original RT, Ultra, Ultra RT (4WS) *(Monsanto)*
  Rate: Annual weeds:
    0.38-1.5 lb. ai/A
    0.56-2.25 pt. 5.4WS/A
    0.75-3 pt. 4WS/A
    Perennial weeds:
    0.5-5 lb. ai/A
    0.75-7.5 pt. 5.4WS/A
    1-10 pt. 4WS/A
  Time: Preemergence: Apply prior to emergence of direct-seeded crop or prior to transplanting.
  Weeds: Emerged annual and perennial broadleaf weeds including:

Canada thistle	hemp dogbane	Pennsylvania
curly dock	milkweed	smartweed
field bindweed		

  Grasses:

bermudagrass	fescue	paragrass
fall panicum	johnsongrass	quackgrass

  Remarks: Collards, kale, mustard greens, swiss chard. Prior to transplanting crops into plastic mulch, remove product residue from plastic. Do not add surfactant to Roundup Ultra or Ultra RT. Do not allow glyphosate to contact desirable plants. Do not apply through any type of irrigation system. Refer to label for directions, precautions and restrictions.

◆-new product • PP-preplant • PPI-preplant incorporated • PRE-preemergence • POST-postemergence • SEQ-sequential • ae-acid equivalent • ai-active ingredient • DF-dry flowable
E/EC-emulsifiable concentrate • F/FL-flowable • DG/G/WG-dispersable granule • L/LC-liquid • SP/WSP-soluble packet • W/WP-wettable powder • WSB-water soluble bag

State Restrictions: Roundup RT for use in Colorado, Idaho, Montana, North Dakota, South Dakota, Utah, Wyoming, and in specific counties only in Kansas, Minnesota, Nebraska, Nevada, Oklahoma, Oregon, and Washington; refer to label for restrictions. Glyfos not registered for use in California. Glyfos X-tra not registered for use in mistblowers in California or Arizona.

– – – – – – – – – – – – – – –

Signal Word/Toxicity Class: Varies by formulation.
REI: Warning—12 hr.; Caution—4 hr.

Gramoxone Extra — see paraquat

PARAQUAT

Restricted Use Pesticide.

■ PP, PRE
Gramoxone Extra (2.5L) *(ZENECA)*
  Rate: 0.5-1 lb. ai/A
      1.5-3 pt. 2.5L/A
  Time: Preplant, preemergence. Apply when weeds and grasses are succulent and growth is from 1-6" tall (larger plants less affected by treatment).
  Weeds: Annual broadleaf weeds and grasses; top kill and suppression of perennials.
  Remarks: Collards. Add nonionic surfactant or crop oil concentrate. Seedbeds should be formed as far ahead of planting and treatment as possible to permit maximum weed and grass emergence. Seeding should be done with minimum amount of soil disturbance. Refer to label for use directions, restrictions, and precautions.

– – – – – – – – – – – – – – –

Signal Word/Toxicity Class: Danger-Poison/I.
REI: 12 hr. (except harvest aid/desiccation 24 hr.).

Poast — see sethoxydim

PREFAR

For use on mineral soils only. Registered for use on many vegetable crops in certain states. Use to maintain flexibility in crop rotations. May be used on labeled crops grown through or under plastic. Toxic to fish.

■ PPI, PRE
Prefar 4-E (bensulide) *(Gowan)*
  Rate: 5-6 lb. ai/A
      5-6 qt. 4E/A
  Time: Preplant incorporated, preemergence. Apply preemergence only on crops to be irrigated up.
  Weeds: Broadleaf weeds—AZ, CA, NM, TX:

burning nettle	nettleleaf goosefoot	purslane
(AZ, CA only)	(AZ, CA only)	redroot pigweed
lambsquarters		

  Grasses:

barnyardgrass	foxtail	sprangletop
crabgrass	goosegrass	watergrass
fall panicum	junglerice	

  Remarks: Collards, kale, mustard greens. Rate varies by soil type. Incorporate to a depth of 1-2" before planting. Apply preemergence only on crops where application is followed by immediate irrigation.
  Crop Rotation: Carrots, cotton, and labeled crops may be replanted following application without restrictions; all other crops 120 days after application and soil should be tilled to minimum depth 4" prior to planting.

– – – – – – – – – – – – – – –

Signal Word/Toxicity Class: Caution/III.
REI: 12 hr. unless soil injected or soil incorporated.

Rattler — see glyphosate

Roundup — see glyphosate

SCYTHE

◆ **Scythe (pelargonic acid)** *(Mycogen)*
  Rate: 4-13 fl. oz./1 gal. spray solution
  Time: Apply to actively growing weeds prior to crop emergence.
  Weeds: Annual and perennial broadleaf weeds and grasses.

Remarks: Collards, kale, mustard greens, Swiss chard, turnip greens. Apply in minimum 75 gal. spray solution/A or spray-to-wet. Do not apply by air or through any type of irrigation system. Refer to label for directions and precautions.
Tank Mixes: Glyphosate and other foliar and residual herbicides.

– – – – – – – – – – – – – – –

Signal Word/Toxicity Class: Warning/II.
REI: 24 hr.

SETHOXYDIM

■ POST
Poast (1.5EC) *(BASF)*
  Rate: 0.09-0.28 lb. ai/A
      0.5-1.5 pt. 1.5EC/A
  Time: Postemergence.
  Weeds: Annual and perennial grasses:

annual ryegrass	large crabgrass	stinkgrass
barnyardgrass	lovegrass	tall fescue
bermudagrass	orchardgrass	Texas panicum
broadleaf signalgrass	(seedling)	volunteer cereals
browntop panicum	perennial ryegrass	wild oat
fall panicum	quackgrass	wild proso millet
giant foxtail	red sprangletop	wildcane
goosegrass	shattercane	wirestem muhly
green foxtail	smooth crabgrass	witchgrass
johnsongrass	southwestern	woolly cupgrass
junglerice	cupgrass	yellow foxtail

  Remarks: Collards, kale, mustard greens. Rate depends on growing region. Add 2 pt./A oil concentrate. Refer to label for restrictions.
  Days To Harvest: 30.
  State Restrictions: Do not use UAN or AMS in California or Pacific Northwest.

– – – – – – – – – – – – – – –

Signal Word/Toxicity Class: Warning/II.
REI: 12 hr.

Treflan — see trifluralin

Trific — see trifluralin

TRIFLURALIN

■ PPI
Albaugh Trifluralin 4EC *(Albaugh)*
◆ **Clean Crop Trifluralin HF (4EC)** *(Platte)*
Gowan Trifluralin 4 or 5 (EC) or 10G *(Gowan)*
Helena Trifluralin 4 EC *(Helena)*
Riverside Trifluralin 4EC or Trific 60DF *(Terra)*
◆ **Sedagri Trifluralin 480 (4EC)** *(Rhone-Poulenc)*
Treflan HFP (4EC) *(Dow AgroSciences)*
Trilin 4 or 5 (EC) or 10G *(Griffin)*
Wilbur-Ellis Trifluralin 10G *(Wilbur-Ellis)*
  Rate: 0.5-0.75 lb. ai/A
      1-1.5 pt. 4EC/A
      0.8-1.2 pt. 5EC/A
      0.8-1.33 lb. 60DF/A
      5-7.5 lb. 10G/A
  Time: Preplant incorporated.
  Weeds: Broadleaf weeds:

carelessweed	knotweed	purslane
carpetweed	kochia	pusley
chickweed	lambsquarters	redroot pigweed
field bindweed	Mexican clover	rough pigweed
fireweed	Mexican fireweed	Russian thistle
Florida purslane	prostrate pigweed	spiny pigweed
Florida pusley	puncturevine	stinging nettle
goosefoot	(western U.S.)	tumbleweed
henbit		

  Grasses:

annual bluegrass	fall panicum	sandbur
barnyardgrass	foxtail millet	shattercane
bottlegrass	giant foxtail	smooth crabgrass
brachiaria	green foxtail	sprangletop
bristlegrass	Italian ryegrass	stinkgrass
bromegrass	johnsongrass	Texas panicum
burgrass	(seedling)	watergrass
cheat	junglerice	wildcane
cheatgrass	large crabgrass	woolly cupgrass
chess	pigeongrass	yellow foxtail
downy brome	robust foxtail	

6

Vegetables

NOTICE	The information on these pages is for preliminary planning — not a guide for use. Be sure to follow the manufacturer's directions, notwithstanding information contained here.	For personal protective equipment and EPA registration numbers, please turn to page 70.

Remarks: Collards, kale, mustard greens, turnip greens (grown for processing). Mustard for seed or processing for food in Minnesota, Montana, North Dakota, and South Dakota. Rate varies by soil type. Refer to label for use directions, restrictions, and precautions.

Crop Rotation: Vegetable crops other than those listed on label should not be planted within 5 months following application. Refer to label for other restrictions.

State Restrictions: Wilbur-Ellis not registered in California.

- - - - - - - - - - - - - -

Signal Word/Toxicity Class: Varies by formulation.
REI: 12 hr. unless soil injected or soil incorporated.

Trilin — see trifluralin

Herbs & Spices

PROMETRYN

Residual broadleaf weed control occurs when applications are made to dill growing in mineral soils. Residual activity is minimal on muck and other high organic matter soils.

■ PRE, POST
◆ Platte Prometryne 4L *(Platte)*
Rate: 1.6 lb. ai/A
3.2 pt. 4L/A in 20 gal. water
Time: Make one application preemergence or one postemergence (not both). For postemergence, apply before weeds are 2" tall.
Weeds: Broadleaf weeds:

annual morningglory	Florida pusley	pigweed
black nightshade	groundcherry	purslane
carelessweed	lambsquarters	ragweed
cocklebur*	malva	smartweed
coffeeweed*	mustard	teaweed (prickly sida)

Grasses:

barnyardgrass	goosegrass	sandbur*
(watergrass)	junglerice	signalgrass
crabgrass	panicum	wild oat
foxtail		

* Shallow-germinating

Remarks: Dill. Do not apply if dill is under water stress. Use on sand or loamy sand may cause crop injury. Do not apply preemergence applications with other pesticides, apply only after foliar applications of other pesticides are dry, and do not apply within 2 weeks after a herbicidal oil such as carrot oil.
Days To Harvest: 48.
Crop Rotation: Cabbage, celery, corn, onions, peas, red beets—5 months (not more than 3.2 pt./A).
State Restrictions: For use in California only.

- - - - - - - - - - - - - -

Signal Word/Toxicity Class: Caution/III.
REI: 12 hr.

SCYTHE
◆ Scythe (pelargonic acid) *(Mycogen)*
Rate: 4-13 fl. oz./1 gal. spray solution
Time: Apply to actively growing weeds prior to crop emergence.
Weeds: Annual and perennial broadleaf weeds and grasses.
Remarks: Anise, basil, chive, dill, fennel, ginger, oregano, rosemary, sage, savory, tarragon, thyme, etc. Apply in minimum 75 gal. spray solution/A or spray-to-wet. Do not apply by air or through any type of irrigation system. Refer to label for directions and precautions.
Tank Mixes: Glyphosate and other foliar and residual herbicides.

- - - - - - - - - - - - - -

Signal Word/Toxicity Class: Warning/II.
REI: 24 hr.

Horseradish

Credit — see glyphosate

Glyfos or Glyfos X-tra — see glyphosate

GLYPHOSATE

Nonselective control of annual and perennial grasses and broadleaf weeds in stale seedbeds and reduced-tillage planting systems.

■ PRE
◆ Credit (4WS) *(Nufarm)*
◆ Glyfos or Glyfos X-tra (4WS) *(Cheminova)*
Rattler (4WS) *(Helena)*
Roundup Custom (5.4WS) *(Monsanto)*
Roundup Original, Original RT, Ultra, Ultra RT (4WS) *(Monsanto)*
Rate: Annual weeds:
0.38-1.5 lb. ai/A
0.56-2.25 pt. 5.4WS/A
0.75-3 pt. 4WS/A
Perennial weeds:
0.5-5 lb. ai/A
0.75-7.5 pt. 5.4WS/A
1-10 pt. 4WS/A
Time: Preemergence: Apply prior to emergence of direct-seeded crop or prior to transplanting.
Weeds: Emerged annual and perennial broadleaf weeds including:

Canada thistle	hemp dogbane	Pennsylvania
curly dock	milkweed	smartweed
field bindweed		

Grasses:

bermudagrass	fescue	paragrass
fall panicum	johnsongrass	quackgrass

Remarks: Prior to transplanting crops into plastic mulch, remove product residue from plastic. Do not add surfactant to Roundup Ultra or Ultra RT. Do not allow glyphosate to contact desirable plants. Do not apply through any type of irrigation system. Refer to label for directions, precautions and restrictions.
State Restrictions: Roundup RT for use in Colorado, Idaho, Montana, North Dakota, South Dakota, Utah, Wyoming, and in specific counties only in Kansas, Minnesota, Nebraska, Nevada, Oklahoma, Oregon, and Washington; refer to label for restrictions. Glyfos not registered for use in California. Glyfos X-tra not registered for use in mistblowers in California or Arizona.

- - - - - - - - - - - - - -

Signal Word/Toxicity Class: Varies by formulation.
REI: Warning—12 hr.; Caution—4 hr.

GOAL

Incorporation or cultivation after application will reduce effectiveness. Do not use on horseradish roots that are weak or under stress due to temperature, disease, fertilizer, insects, drought, or excess moisture. Emerged plants will be injured.

■ PRE
Goal 2XL (oxyfluorfen) *(Rohm and Haas)*
Rate: 0.5 lb. ai/A
2 pt. 2XL/A
Time: Preemergence. Apply after roots have been planted, but before emergence.
Weeds: Broadleaf weeds:

common	Pennsylvania	redroot pigweed
lambsquarters	smartweed	shepherdspurse
common purslane		

Remarks: Do not apply more than 2 pt./A in a single application. Do not apply through any type of irrigation system.

- - - - - - - - - - - - - -

Signal Word/Toxicity Class: Warning/II.
REI: 24 hr.

Rattler — see glyphosate

Roundup — see glyphosate

SCYTHE
◆ Scythe (pelargonic acid) *(Mycogen)*
Rate: 4-13 fl. oz./1 gal. spray solution
Time: Apply to actively growing weeds prior to crop emergence.

◆-new product • PP-preplant • PPI-preplant incorporated • PRE-preemergence • POST-postemergence • SEQ-sequential • ae-acid equivalent • ai-active ingredient • DF-dry flowable
E/EC-emulsifiable concentrate • F/FL-flowable • DG/G/WG-dispersable granule • L/LC-liquid • SP/WSP-soluble packet • W/WP-wettable powder • WSB-water soluble bag

Weeds: Annual and perennial broadleaf weeds and grasses.
Remarks: Apply in minimum 75 gal. spray solution/A or spray-to-wet. Do not apply by air or through any type of irrigation system. Refer to label for directions and precautions.
Tank Mixes: Glyphosate and other foliar and residual herbicides.

- - - - - - - - - - - - - -

Signal Word/Toxicity Class: Warning/II.
REI: 24 hr.

Lentils

Credit — see glyphosate

FAR-GO

Use in Pacific Northwest and Northern Plains where target weed is prevalent. Primarily absorbed by wild oat shoots from treated layer of soil. Wild oats are usually controlled before they emerge from soil.

■ PPI, PRE

Far-Go 4E or 10G (triallate) *(Monsanto)*
Rate: 1.25 lb. ai/A
    1.25 qt. 4E/A
    1.25-1.5 lb. ai/A
    12.5-15 lb. 10G/A
Time: Preplant incorporated, preemergence incorporated. Apply in the spring up to 3 weeks before seeding or immediately after seeding.
Weeds:
    wild oat
Remarks: Do not graze livestock on treated crops. Refer to label for directions, precautions, and state restrictions.
Crop Rotation: Domestic oats should not be seeded if Far-Go was used the previous year.
State Restrictions: For use in Colorado, Idaho, Kansas, Minnesota, Montana, Nebraska, Nevada, North Dakota, Oregon, South Dakota, Utah, Washington, and Wyoming.

- - - - - - - - - - - - - - -

Signal Word/Toxicity Class: Caution/III.
REI: 12 hr.

Glyfos or Glyfos X-tra — see glyphosate

GLYPHOSATE

Nonselective control of annual and perennial grasses and broadleaf weeds in stale seedbeds and reduced-tillage planting systems.

■ PRE
◆ **Credit (4WS)** *(Nufarm)*
◆ **Glyfos or Glyfos X-tra (4WS)** *(Cheminova)*
Rattler (4WS) *(Helena)*
Roundup Custom (5.4WS) *(Monsanto)*
Roundup Original, Original RT, Ultra, Ultra RT (4WS) *(Monsanto)*
Rate: Annual weeds:
    0.38-1.5 lb. ai/A
    0.56-2.25 pt. 5.4WS/A
    0.75-3 pt. 4WS/A
    Perennial weeds:
    0.5-5 lb. ai/A
    0.75-7.5 pt. 5.4WS/A
    1-10 pt. 4WS/A
Time: Preemergence: Apply prior to emergence of direct-seeded crop or prior to transplanting.
Weeds: Emerged annual and perennial broadleaf weeds including:

Canada thistle	hemp dogbane	Pennsylvania
curly dock	milkweed	smartweed
field bindweed		

Grasses:

bermudagrass	fescue	paragrass
fall panicum	johnsongrass	quackgrass

Remarks: Prior to transplanting crops into plastic mulch, remove product residue from plastic. Do not add surfactant to Roundup Ultra or Ultra RT. Do not allow glyphosate to contact desirable plants. Do not apply through any type of irrigation system. Refer to label for directions, precautions and restrictions.

State Restrictions: Roundup RT for use in Colorado, Idaho, Montana, North Dakota, South Dakota, Utah, Wyoming, and in specific counties only in Kansas, Minnesota, Nebraska, Nevada, Oklahoma, Oregon, and Washington; refer to label for restrictions. Glyfos not registered for use in California. Glyfos X-tra not registered for use in mistblowers in California or Arizona.

- - - - - - - - - - - - - - -

Signal Word/Toxicity Class: Varies by formulation.
REI: Warning—12 hr.; Caution—4 hr.

Gramoxone Extra — see paraquat

PARAQUAT

Restricted Use Pesticide.

◆ **Gramoxone Extra (2.5L)** *(ZENECA)*
Rate: 0.3-0.5 lb. ai/A
    1-1.5 pt. 2.5L/A
Time: Apply to mature crop with 80% of pods yellowing and mostly ripe with no more than 30% leaves still green in color.
Weeds: Annual broadleaf weeds and grasses; top kill and suppression of perennials.
Remarks: Add nonionic surfactant or crop oil concentrate. Seedbeds should be formed as far ahead of planting and treatment as possible to permit maximum weed and grass emergence. Seeding should be done with minimum amount of soil disturbance. Refer to label for use directions, restrictions, and precautions.
Days To Harvest: 7.
State Restrictions: Not for use in California.

- - - - - - - - - - - - - - -

Signal Word/Toxicity Class: Danger-Poison/I.
REI: 12 hr. (except harvest aid/desiccation 24 hr.).

Poast — see sethoxydim

Rattler — see glyphosate

Roundup — see glyphosate

SCYTHE

◆ **Scythe (pelargonic acid)** *(Mycogen)*
Rate: 4-13 fl. oz./1 gal. spray solution
Time: Apply to actively growing weeds prior to crop emergence.
Weeds: Broad spectrum of annual and perennial broadleaf and grass weeds.
Remarks: Apply in minimum 75 gal. spray solution/A or spray-to-wet. Do not apply by air or through any type of irrigation system. Refer to label for directions and precautions.
Tank Mixes: Glyphosate and other foliar and residual herbicides.

- - - - - - - - - - - - - - -

Signal Word/Toxicity Class: Warning/II.
REI: 24 hr.

SETHOXYDIM

Selectively controls annual and perennial grasses. Do not tank mix with any other herbicide unless specified on label or reduced control may result.

■ POST
Poast (1.5EC) *(BASF)*
Rate: 0.28-0.47 lb. ai/A
    1.5-2.5 pt. 1.5EC/A
Time: Postemergence.
Weeds: Annual and perennial grasses:

annual ryegrass	junglerice	southwestern
barnyardgrass	large crabgrass	cupgrass
bermudagrass	lovegrass	stinkgrass
browntop panicum	orchardgrass	tall fescue
fall panicum	(seedling)	volunteer cereals
giant foxtail	perennial ryegrass	wild oat
goosegrass	quackgrass	wildcane
green foxtail	shattercane	witchgrass
johnsongrass	smooth crabgrass	yellow foxtail

Remarks: Add 2 pt./A oil concentrate. Do not apply through any type of irrigation system. Do not graze treated fields or feed treated forage to livestock. Refer to label for restrictions and limitations.

NOTICE	The information on these pages is for preliminary planning — not a guide for use. Be sure to follow the manufacturer's directions, notwithstanding information contained here.

For personal protective equipment and EPA registration numbers, please turn to page 70.

6

Vegetables

Lentils

Days To Harvest: 50.
State Restrictions: Do not use UAN or AMS in California or Pacific Northwest.

Signal Word/Toxicity Class: Warning/II.
REI: 12 hr.

Lettuce, Endive

BALAN

Selective preplant incorporated herbicide for the control of many annual grasses and broadleaf weeds throughout the growing season.

■ PPI
Balan DF (benefin) *(Platte)*
Rate: 1.12-1.5 lb. ai/A
2-2.5 lb. DF/A
Time: Preplant incorporated. Apply and incorporate before seeding or transplanting.
Weeds: Broadleaf weeds:

carelessweed	lambsquarters	redmaids
carpetweed	Mexican clover	rockpurslane
chickweed	prostrate pigweed	redroot pigweed
Florida purslane	purslane	rough pigweed
knotweed	pusley	spiny pigweed

Annual grasses:

annual bluegrass	coloradograss	large crabgrass
annual ryegrass	fall panicum	pigeongrass
barnyardgrass	giant foxtail	robust foxtail
(watergrass)	green foxtail	sandbur
bottlegrass	Italian ryegrass	smooth crabgrass
bristlegrass	johnsongrass	spreading panicgrass
broadleaf signalgrass	(seedling)	Texas panicum
buffalograss	junglerice	yellow foxtail
burgrass		

Remarks: Rate varies by soil type. Do not apply through any type of irrigation system. Refer to label for further use directions.
Crop Rotation: Do not plant barley, oats, rye, wheat or other grasses, corn, milo (grain sorghum), onions, red beets, spinach, sugar beets or other root crops for 10 months following application.

- - - - - - - - - - - - - - - -

Signal Word/Toxicity Class: Caution/III.
REI: 12 hr.

Credit — see glyphosate

FLUAZIFOP-P-BUTYL

Controls many annual and perennial grasses. Annual bluegrass and stinkgrass will not be controlled.

■ POST
Fusilade DX *(ZENECA)*
Rate: 0.1-0.375 lb. ai/A
0.375-1.5 pt. DX/A
Time: Early postemergence. Apply to actively growing grasses.
Weeds: Annual and perennial grasses:

barnyardgrass	johnsongrass	southern sandbur
bermudagrass	(rhizome, seedling)	Texas panicum
broadleaf signalgrass	junglerice	tropical crabgrass
fall panicum	large crabgrass	volunteer cereals
field sandbur	quackgrass	wild oat
giant foxtail	red rice	wild proso millet
goosegrass	shattercane	wirestem muhly
green foxtail	smooth crabgrass	witchgrass
Italian ryegrass	sorghum-almum	woolly cupgrass
itchgrass	southern crabgrass	yellow foxtail

Remarks: Endive. Rate varies by geographic area and grass species. Add crop oil concentrate or nonionic surfactant. Do not apply more than 3 pt./A per season. Refer to label for specific directions.
Days To Harvest: 28.
Crop Rotation: Do not plant rotational grass crops such as corn, sorghum, and cereals within 60 days after last application.
State Restrictions: Refer to label for geographical regions.

- - - - - - - - - - - - - - -

Signal Word/Toxicity Class: Caution.
REI: 12 hr.

Fusilade — see fluazifop-P-butyl

Glyfos or Glyfos X-tra — see glyphosate

GLYPHOSATE

Controls annual and perennial grasses and broadleaf weeds in stale seedbeds and reduced-tillage planting systems.

■ PRE
◆ **Credit (4WS)** *(Nufarm)*
◆ **Glyfos or Glyfos X-tra (4WS)** *(Cheminova)*
Rattler (4WS) *(Helena)*
Roundup Custom (5.4WS) *(Monsanto)*
Roundup Original, Original RT, Ultra, Ultra RT (4WS) *(Monsanto)*
Rate: Annual weeds:
0.38-1.5 lb. ai/A
0.56-2.25 pt. 5.4WS/A
0.75-3 pt. 4WS/A
Perennial weeds:
0.5-5 lb. ai/A
0.75-7.5 pt. 5.4WS/A
1-10 pt. 4WS/A
Time: Preemergence: Apply prior to emergence of direct-seeded crop or prior to transplanting.
Weeds: Emerged annual and perennial broadleaf weeds including:

Canada thistle	hemp dogbane	Pennsylvania
curly dock	milkweed	smartweed
field bindweed		

Grasses:

bermudagrass	fescue	paragrass
fall panicum	johnsongrass	quackgrass

Remarks: Chicory, endive, lettuce. Prior to transplanting crops into plastic mulch, remove product residue from plastic. Do not add surfactant to Roundup Ultra or Ultra RT. Do not allow glyphosate to contact desirable plants. Do not apply through any type of irrigation system. Refer to label for directions, precautions and restrictions.
State Restrictions: Roundup RT for use in Colorado, Idaho, Montana, North Dakota, South Dakota, Utah, Wyoming, and in specific counties only in Kansas, Minnesota, Nevada, Oklahoma, Oregon, and Washington; refer to label for restrictions. Glyfos not registered for use in California. Glyfos X-tra not registered for use in mistblowers in California or Arizona.

- - - - - - - - - - - - - - - -

Signal Word/Toxicity Class: Varies by formulation.
REI: Warning—12 hr.; Caution—4 hr.

Gramoxone Extra — see paraquat

KERB

Incorporate shallowly and thoroughly before planting, or apply to newly worked soil immediately after seeding or transplanting and follow with irrigation. Restricted Use Pesticide.

■ PP, PRE, POST
Kerb 50-W (pronamide) *(Rohm and Haas)*
Rate: 1-2 lb. ai/A
2-4 lb. 50-W/A
Time: Preplant, preemergence, postplant, postemergence. For postemergence, apply before or after lettuce thinning but prior to weed germination.
Weeds: Broadleaf weeds:

annual morningglory	common purslane	nettleleaf goosefoot
black nightshade	hairy nightshade	pale smartweed
burning nettle	henbit	shepherdspurse
carpetweed	knotweed	volunteer tomato
common chickweed	London rocket	wild mustard
common lambsquarters		

Grasses:

annual bluegrass	fall panicum	volunteer barley
barnyardgrass	foxtail barley	volunteer oats
canarygrass	goosegrass	volunteer rye
cheatgrass	Italian ryegrass	volunteer wheat
crabgrass	lovegrass	yellow foxtail
downy brome		

Remarks: Endive, escarole, lettuce. Do not apply postemergence to leaf lettuce. Moisture is necessary to activate Kerb.
Days To Harvest: 55.

◆-new product • PP-preplant • PPI-preplant incorporated • PRE-preemergence • POST-postemergence • SEQ-sequential • ae-acid equivalent • ai-active ingredient • DF-dry flowable E/EC-emulsifiable concentrate • F/FL-flowable • DG/G/WG-dispersable granule • L/LC-liquid • SP/WSP-soluble packet • W/WP-wettable powder • WSB-water soluble bag

Crop Rotation: Refer to label for plantback times for rotational crops.

- - - - - - - - - - - - - - - -

Signal Word/Toxicity Class: Caution.
REI: 24 hr.

PARAQUAT

Restricted Use Pesticide.

■ PP, PRE

Gramoxone Extra (2.5L) *(ZENECA)*
Rate: 0.5-1 lb. ai/A
    1.5-3 pt. 2.5L/A
Time: Preplant, preemergence. Apply when weeds and grasses are succulent and growth is from 1-6" tall (larger plants less affected by treatment).
Weeds: Annual broadleaf weeds and grasses; top kill and suppression of perennials.
Remarks: Add nonionic surfactant or crop oil concentrate. Seedbeds should be formed as far ahead of planting and treatment as possible to permit maximum weed and grass emergence. Seeding should be done with minimum amount of soil disturbance. Refer to label for use directions, restrictions, and precautions.
Tank Mixes: Goal.

- - - - - - - - - - - - - - - -

Rate: 0.2 lb. ai/A
    0.75 pt. 2.5L/A
Time: Apply broadcast to preformed seedbeds.
Weeds:
  volunteer barley
Remarks: Add nonionic surfactant or crop oil concentrate. Refer to label for use directions, restrictions, precautions.
State Restrictions: For use in California, Idaho, Oregon, Washington.

- - - - - - - - - - - - - - - -

Signal Word/Toxicity Class: Danger-Poison/I.
REI: 12 hr. (except harvest aid/desiccation 24 hr.).

Poast — see sethoxydim

PREFAR

For use on mineral soils only. Registered for use on many vegetable crops in certain states. Use to maintain flexibility in crop rotations. May be used on labeled crops grown through or under plastic. Toxic to fish.

■ PPI, PRE

Prefar 4-E (bensulide) *(Gowan)*
Rate: 5-6 lb. ai/A
    5-6 qt. 4E/A
Time: Preplant incorporated, preemergence. Apply preemergence only on crops to be irrigated up.
Weeds: Broadleaf weeds—AZ, CA, NM, TX:

burning nettle (AZ, CA only)	nettleleaf goosefoot (AZ, CA only)	purslane
lambsquarters		redroot pigweed

Grasses:

barnyardgrass	foxtail	sprangletop
crabgrass	goosegrass	watergrass
fall panicum	junglerice	

Remarks: Rate varies by soil type. Incorporate to a depth of 1-2" before planting. Apply preemergence only on crops where application is followed by immediate irrigation.
Crop Rotation: Carrots, cotton, and labeled crops may be replanted following application without restrictions; all other crops 120 days after application and soil should be tilled to minimum depth 4" prior to planting.

- - - - - - - - - - - - - - - -

Signal Word/Toxicity Class: Caution/III.
REI: 12 hr. unless soil injected or soil incorporated.

Rattler — see glyphosate

Roundup — see glyphosate

SCYTHE

◆ **Scythe (pelargonic acid)** *(Mycogen)*
Rate: 4-13 fl. oz./1 gal. spray solution

Time: Apply to actively growing weeds prior to crop emergence.
Weeds: Broad spectrum of annual and perennial broadleaf and grass weeds.
Remarks: Lettuce, Endive. Apply in minimum 75 gal. spray solution/A or spray-to-wet. Do not apply by air or through any type of irrigation system. Refer to label for directions and precautions.
Tank Mixes: Glyphosate and other foliar and residual herbicides.

- - - - - - - - - - - - - - - -

Signal Word/Toxicity Class: Warning/II.
REI: 24 hr.

SETHOXYDIM

Selective control of annual and perennial grasses. Do not tank mix with any other herbicide unless specified on label, or reduced control may result.

■ POST

Poast (1.5EC) *(BASF)*
Rate: 0.09-0.28 lb. ai/A
    0.5-1.5 pt. 1.5EC/A
Time: Postemergence.
Weeds: Annual and perennial grasses:

annual ryegrass	junglerice	stinkgrass
barnyardgrass	large crabgrass	tall fescue
bermudagrass	lovegrass	Texas panicum
broadleaf signalgrass	orchardgrass	volunteer cereals
browntop panicum	(seedling)	wild oat
fall panicum	perennial ryegrass	wild proso millet
field sandbur	quackgrass	wildcane
giant foxtail	red sprangletop	wirestem muhly
goosegrass	shattercane	witchgrass
green foxtail	smooth crabgrass	woolly cupgrass
johnsongrass	southwestern cupgrass	yellow foxtail

Remarks: Head, leaf lettuce. Rate depends on growing region. Add 2 pt./A oil concentrate. Refer to label for restrictions and limitations.
Days To Harvest: Head lettuce—30; leaf lettuce—15.
State Restrictions: Do not use UAN or AMS in California or Pacific Northwest.

- - - - - - - - - - - - - - - -

Signal Word/Toxicity Class: Warning/II.
REI: 12 hr.

Treflan — see trifluralin

TRIFLURALIN

Controls annual grasses and certain broadleaf weeds, including common lambsquarters and pigweed species. Cold, wet soil conditions after planting may increase risk of crop injury.

■ PPI

Albaugh Trifluralin 4EC *(Albaugh)*
Helena Trifluralin 4 EC *(Helena)*
Riverside Trifluralin 4EC *(Terra)*
◆ **Sedagri Trifluralin 480 (4EC)** *(Rhone-Poulenc)*
Treflan HFP (4EC) *(Dow AgroSciences)*
Trilin 4EC or 10G *(Griffin)*
Wilbur-Ellis Trifluralin 10G *(Wilbur-Ellis)*
Rate: 0.5-1 lb. ai/A
    1-2 pt. 4EC/A
    5-10 lb. 10G/A
Time: Preplant incorporated.
Weeds: Broadleaf weeds:

carelessweed	knotweed	purslane
carpetweed	kochia	pusley
chickweed	lambsquarters	redroot pigweed
field bindweed	Mexican clover	rough pigweed
fireweed	Mexican fireweed	Russian thistle
Florida purslane	prostrate pigweed	spiny pigweed
Florida pusley	puncturevine	stinging nettle
goosefoot	(western U.S.)	tumbleweed
henbit		

Grasses:

annual bluegrass	fall panicum	sandbur
barnyardgrass	foxtail millet	shattercane
bottlegrass	giant foxtail	smooth crabgrass
brachiaria	green foxtail	sprangletop
bristlegrass	Italian ryegrass	stinkgrass
bromegrass	johnsongrass	Texas panicum
burgrass	(seedling)	watergrass
cheat	junglerice	wildcane
cheatgrass	large crabgrass	woolly cupgrass
chess	pigeongrass	yellow foxtail
downy brome	robust foxtail	

6 **Vegetables**

Remarks: Chicory, endive. Rate varies by soil type. Do not seed until seedbed has warmed up. Refer to label for use directions and precautions.

Crop Rotation: Vegetable crops other than those listed on label should not be planted within 5 months following application. Refer to label for other restrictions.

State Restrictions: Wilbur-Ellis not registered in California.

- - - - - - - - - -

Signal Word/Toxicity Class: Warning/II.
REI: 12 hr. unless soil injected or soil incorporated.

Trilin — see trifluralin

Okra

Credit — see glyphosate

Glyfos or Glyfos X-tra — see glyphosate

GLYPHOSATE

Nonselective control of annual and perennial grasses and broadleaf weeds in stale seedbeds and reduced-tillage planting systems prior to transplanting.

■ **PRE**
◆ **Credit (4WS)** *(Nufarm)*
◆ **Glyfos or Glyfos X-tra (4WS)** *(Cheminova)*
Rattler (4WS) *(Helena)*
Roundup Custom (5.4WS) *(Monsanto)*
Roundup Original, Original RT, Ultra, Ultra RT (4WS) *(Monsanto)*

Rate: Annual weeds:
  0.38-1.5 lb. ai/A
  0.56-2.25 pt. 5.4WS/A
  0.75-3 pt. 4WS/A
  Perennial weeds:
  0.5-5 lb. ai/A
  0.75-7.5 pt. 5.4WS/A
  1-10 pt. 4WS/A

Time: Preemergence: Apply prior to emergence of direct-seeded crop or prior to transplanting.

Weeds: Emerged annual and perennial broadleaf weeds including:

Canada thistle	hemp dogbane	Pennsylvania
curly dock	milkweed	smartweed
field bindweed		

Grasses:

bermudagrass	fescue	paragrass
fall panicum	johnsongrass	quackgrass

Remarks: Prior to transplanting crops into plastic mulch, remove product residue from plastic. Do not add surfactant to Roundup Ultra or Ultra RT. Do not allow glyphosate to contact desirable plants. Do not apply through any type of irrigation system. Refer to label for directions, precautions and restrictions.

State Restrictions: Roundup RT for use in Colorado, Idaho, Montana, North Dakota, South Dakota, Utah, Wyoming, and in specific counties only in Kansas, Minnesota, Nebraska, Nevada, Oklahoma, Oregon, and Washington; refer to label for restrictions. Glyfos not registered for use in California. Glyfos X-tra not registered for use in mistblowers in California or Arizona.

- - - - - - - - - -

Signal Word/Toxicity Class: Varies by formulation.
REI: Warning—12 hr.; Caution—4 hr.

Rattler — see glyphosate

Roundup — see glyphosate

SCYTHE

◆ **Scythe (pelargonic acid)** *(Mycogen)*
Rate: 4-13 fl. oz./1 gal. spray solution
Time: Apply to actively growing weeds prior to crop emergence.
Weeds: Broad spectrum of annual and perennial broadleaf and grass weeds.

Remarks: Apply in minimum 75 gal. spray solution/A or spray-to-wet. Do not apply by air or through any type of irrigation system. Refer to label for directions and precautions.

Tank Mixes: Glyphosate and other foliar and residual herbicides.

- - - - - - - - - -

Signal Word/Toxicity Class: Warning/II.
REI: 24 hr.

Treflan — see trifluralin

Trific — see trifluralin

TRIFLURALIN

Controls annual grasses and certain broadleaf weeds, including common lambsquarters and pigweed species. Cold, wet soil conditions after planting may increase risk of crop injury.

■ **PPI, PRE**
Albaugh Trifluralin 4EC *(Albaugh)*
◆ **Clean Crop Trifluralin HF (4EC)** *(Platte)*
Gowan Trifluralin 4 or 5 (EC) or 10G *(Gowan)*
Helena Trifluralin 4 EC *(Helena)*
Riverside Trifluralin 4EC or Trific 60DF *(Terra)*
◆ **Sedagri Trifluralin 480 (4EC)** *(Rhone-Poulenc)*
Treflan HFP (4EC) or TR-10 (10G) *(Dow AgroSciences)*
Trilin 4 or 5 (EC) or 10G *(Griffin)*
Wilbur-Ellis Trifluralin 10G *(Wilbur-Ellis)*

Rate: 0.5-1 lb. ai/A
  1-2 pt. 4EC/A
  0.8-1.6 pt. 5EC/A
  0.875-1.66 lb. 60DF/A
  5-10 lb. 10G/A

Time: Preplant incorporated, preemergence incorporated. Apply and incorporate before planting or immediately after planting.

Weeds: Broadleaf weeds:

carelessweed	knotweed	purslane
carpetweed	kochia	pusley
chickweed	lambsquarters	redroot pigweed
field bindweed	Mexican clover	rough pigweed
fireweed	Mexican fireweed	Russian thistle
Florida purslane	prostrate pigweed	spiny pigweed
Florida pusley	puncturevine	stinging nettle
goosefoot	(western U.S.)	tumbleweed
henbit		

Grasses:

annual bluegrass	fall panicum	sandbur
barnyardgrass	foxtail millet	shattercane
bottlegrass	giant foxtail	smooth crabgrass
brachiaria	green foxtail	sprangletop
bristlegrass	Italian ryegrass	stinkgrass
bromegrass	johnsongrass	Texas panicum
burgrass	(seedling)	watergrass
cheat	junglerice	wildcane
cheatgrass	large crabgrass	woolly cupgrass
chess	pigeongrass	yellow foxtail
downy brome	robust foxtail	

Remarks: Rate varies by soil type. Incorporate within 24 hr. after application and again any time before planting. Refer to label for further use directions, restrictions, and precautions.

Crop Rotation: Vegetable crops other than those listed on label should not be planted within 5 months following application. Refer to label for other restrictions.

State Restrictions: Wilbur-Ellis not registered in California.

- - - - - - - - - -

Signal Word/Toxicity Class: Varies by formulation.
REI: 12 hr. unless soil injected or soil incorporated.

Trilin — see trifluralin

Onions

Broclean — see bromoxynil

◆—new product • PP-preplant • PPI-preplant incorporated • PRE-preemergence • POST-postemergence • SEQ-sequential • ae-acid equivalent • ai-active ingredient • DF-dry flowable
E/EC-emulsifiable concentrate • F/FL-flowable • DG/G/WG-dispersable granule • L/LC-liquid • SP/WSP-soluble packet • W/WP-wettable powder • WSB-water soluble bag

320   Weed Control Manual 2000

Bromox — see bromoxynil

BROMOXYNIL

Contact herbicide for control of certain broadleaf weeds.

■ **PRE, POST**
◆ **Broclean 2EC** *(Platte)*
◆ **Bromox 2EC** *(MIcro Flo)*
Buctril (2EC), Buctril 4EC *(Rhone-Poulenc)*
Moxy 2EC *(Terra)*
  Rate: 0.25-0.375 lb. ai/A
      1-1.5 pt. 2EC/A
      0.5-0.75 pt. 4EC/A
  Time: Preemergence, postemergence. For preemergence, apply at least 3-4 days prior to emergence. For postemergence, apply only to onions which have 2-5 true leaves.
  Weeds: Most susceptible broadleaf weeds:

annual pepperweed	common tarweed	Pennsylvania
annual sowthistle	eastern black	smartweed
black nightshade	nightshade	shepherdspurse
blue mustard	field pennycress	silverleaf nightshade
bristly starbur	green smartweed	sunflower
coast fiddleneck	hairy nightshade	tartary buckwheat
common cocklebur	jimsonweed	wild buckwheat
common lambsquarters	ladysthumb	

  Susceptible broadleaf weeds:

buffalobur	ivyleaf morningglory	spiny pigweed
burcucumber	knawel	tall morningglory
common groundsel	kochia	tall waterhemp
common ragweed	London rocket	tumble mustard
corn chamomile	mayweed	velvetleaf
corn gromwell	prostrate knotweed	Venice mallow
cowcockle	puncturevine	wild mustard
giant ragweed	redroot pigweed	wild radish
hemp sesbania	Russian thistle	yellow starthistle

  Remarks: Preemergence use restricted to onions grown east of the Mississippi only on muck soils containing greater than 10% organic matter. Rainfall or irrigation within 2 days following preemergence applications or 3 days prior to crop emergence may result in unacceptable injury. For postemergence application, apply by ground equipment or chemigation in at least 50-70 gal. water/A (water volume important); concentrated sprays kill onions. Soil and onion foliage should be dry at time of application; humidity should be low and dew should be off plants. In Oregon, west of the Cascades, do not use on onions grown under low light intensity. Refer to label for precautions and restrictions.

- - - - - - - - - - - - - - -

Signal Word/Toxicity Class: Warning/II.
REI: 12 hr.

Buctril — see bromoxynil

CLETHODIM

Postemergence grass herbicide. Mode of action similar to Poast, Assure, Option II, and Fusilade.

■ **POST**
Prism (0.94EC) or Select (2EC) *(Valent)*
  Rate: 0.1-0.25 lb. ai/A
      13-34 fl. oz. 0.94EC/A
      6-16 fl. oz. 2EC/A
  Time: Postemergence. Apply to actively growing grasses.
  Weeds: Grasses:

Amazon sprangletop	green foxtail	smooth crabgrass
annual bluegrass	itchgrass	southern crabgrass
barnyardgrass	johnsongrass	Texas panicum
bearded sprangletop	junglerice	volunteer cereals
bermudagrass	large crabgrass	wild oat
broadleaf signalgrass	quackgrass	wild proso millet
crowfootgrass	red rice	wirestem muhly
fall panicum	red sprangletop	witchgrass
giant foxtail	shattercane	woolly cupgrass
goosegrass	southwestern cupgrass	yellow foxtail

  Remarks: Dry bulb onions, shallots. Rate varies by grass species, stage, and geographical region. Grass crops such as corn, sorghum, wheat, and rice are highly sensitive to clethodim. Do not apply under stress conditions or if rainfall is expected in 1 hour. Do not apply through any type of irrigation system. Do not apply more than 0.5 lb. ai/A (0.25 lb. ai/A on Long Island, NY) per season. Do not graze treated fields or feed treated forage or hay to livestock. Refer to label for restrictions and precautions.
  Days To Harvest: 45.

State Restrictions: Not for use on Solano grass in the Vernal Lakes area of Solano County, California; wild rice in Hays County, Texas.

- - - - - - - - - - - - - - -

Signal Word/Toxicity Class: Warning/II.
REI: 24 hr.

Credit — see glyphosate

FLUAZIFOP-P-BUTYL

Provides excellent control of annual and perennial grasses. Do not tank mix with any other herbicide unless specified on label or reduced control may result.

■ **POST**
Fusilade DX *(ZENECA)*
  Rate: 0.1-0.375 lb. ai/A
      0.375-1.5 pt. DX/A
  Time: Early postemergence. Apply to actively growing grasses.
  Weeds: Annual and perennial grasses:

barnyardgrass	johnsongrass	southern sandbur
bermudagrass	(rhizome, seedling)	Texas panicum
broadleaf signalgrass	junglerice	tropical crabgrass
fall panicum	large crabgrass	volunteer cereals
field sandbur	quackgrass	wild oat
giant foxtail	red rice	wild proso millet
goosegrass	shattercane	wirestem muhly
green foxtail	smooth crabgrass	witchgrass
Italian ryegrass	sorghum-almum	woolly cupgrass
itchgrass	southern crabgrass	yellow foxtail

  Remarks: Dry bulb onions. Rate varies by geographic area and grass species. Add crop oil concentrate or nonionic surfactant. Do not apply more than 3 pt./A per season. Refer to label for use directions.
  Days To Harvest: 45.
  Crop Rotation: Do not plant rotational grass crops such as corn, sorghum, and cereals within 60 days after last application.
  State Restrictions: Refer to label for geographical regions.

- - - - - - - - - - - - - - -

Signal Word/Toxicity Class: Caution.
REI: 12 hr.

Fusilade — see fluazifop-P-butyl

Glyfos or Glyfos X-tra — see glyphosate

GLYPHOSATE

Nonselective control of annual and perennial grasses and broadleaf weeds in stale seedbeds and reduced-tillage planting systems.

■ **PRE**
◆ **Credit (4WS)** *(Nufarm)*
◆ **Glyfos or Glyfos X-tra (4WS)** *(Cheminova)*
Rattler (4WS) *(Helena)*
Roundup Custom (5.4WS) *(Monsanto)*
Roundup Original, Original RT, Ultra, Ultra RT (4WS) *(Monsanto)*
  Rate: Annual weeds:
      0.38-1.5 lb. ai/A
      0.56-2.25 pt. 5.4WS/A
      0.75-3 pt. 4WS/A
      Perennial weeds:
      0.5-5 lb. ai/A
      0.75-7.5 pt. 5.4WS/A
      1-10 pt. 4WS/A
  Time: Preemergence: Apply prior to emergence of direct-seeded crop or prior to transplanting.
  Weeds: Emerged annual and perennial broadleaf weeds including:

Canada thistle	hemp dogbane	Pennsylvania
curly dock	milkweed	smartweed
field bindweed		

  Grasses:

bermudagrass	fescue	paragrass
fall panicum	johnsongrass	quackgrass

  Remarks: Leeks, onions, shallots. Prior to transplanting crops into plastic mulch, remove product residue from plastic. Do not add surfactant to Roundup Ultra or Ultra RT. Do not allow glyphosate to contact desirable plants. Do not apply through any type of irrigation system. Refer to label for directions, precautions and restrictions.

6

Vegetables

NOTICE	The information on these pages is for preliminary planning — not a guide for use. Be sure to follow the manufacturer's directions, notwithstanding information contained here.

For personal protective equipment and EPA registration numbers, please turn to page 70.

Onions

State Restrictions: Roundup RT for use in Colorado, Idaho, Montana, North Dakota, South Dakota, Utah, Wyoming, and in specific counties only in Kansas, Minnesota, Nebraska, Nevada, Oklahoma, Oregon, and Washington; refer to label for restrictions. Glyfos not registered for use in California. Glyfos X-tra not registered for use in mistblowers in California or Arizona.

Signal Word/Toxicity Class: Varies by formulation.
REI: Warning—12 hr.; Caution—4 hr.

GOAL

Avoid application during extended periods of cloudy, humid weather when soil moisture is plentiful.

■ POST

Goal 2XL (oxyfluorfen) *(Rohm and Haas)*
Rate: 0.12 lb. ai/A
　　　0.5 pt. 2XL/A
　　　Western states—dry bulb:
　　　0.12-0.25 lb. ai/A
　　　0.5-1 pt. 2XL/A
　　　Northeastern states—dry bulb:
　　　0.03-0.06 lb. ai/A
　　　2-4 fl. oz. 2XL/A
　　　Northeastern states—grown for seed:
　　　0.03 lb. ai/A
　　　2 fl. oz. 2XL/A
Time: Postemergence. Do not apply until at least 3 true leaves in northeastern states for dry bulb onions; 2 true leaves in all other states for dry bulb onions, 4 true leaves for onions grown for seed.
Weeds: Broadleaf weeds:

annual sowthistle	lanceleaf sage	prostrate pigweed*
black nightshade	little mallow	puncturevine
common groundsel	(malva)	redroot pigweed*
common purslane*	London rocket	shepherdspurse*
cutleaf		
eveningprimrose		

Grasses:

annual canarygrass

* *Northeastern states*

Remarks: Dry bulb onions, onions grown for seed. Do not use on onions grown for seed except as specified on label. Multiple treatments may be applied. Do not apply through any type of irrigation system. Refer to label for restrictions and use directions.
Days To Harvest: Dry bulb-45; Grown for seed-60.
Crop Rotation: Refer to label for plantback times for rotation crops.
State Restrictions: Northeastern states include: Connecticut, Maine, Massachusetts, New Hampshire, New Jersey, New York, Rhode Island, Vermont. Western states include: Arizona, California, Colorado, Idaho, Nevada, New Mexico, Oregon, Texas, Utah, Washington.

Signal Word/Toxicity Class: Warning/II.
REI: 24 hr.

Gramoxone Extra — see paraquat

Moxy — see bromoxynil

PARAQUAT

Restricted Use Pesticide.

■ PP, PRE

Gramoxone Extra (2.5L) *(ZENECA)*
Rate: 0.6-1 lb. ai/A
　　　2-3 pt. 2.5L/A
Time: Preplant, preemergence. Apply when weeds and grasses are succulent and growth is from 1-6" tall (larger plants less affected by treatment).
Weeds: Annual broadleaf weeds and grasses; top kill and suppression of perennials.
Remarks: Onions (seeded). Add nonionic surfactant or crop oil concentrate. Seedbeds should be formed as far ahead of planting and treatment as possible to permit maximum weed and grass emergence. Seeding should be done with minimum amount of soil disturbance. Refer to label for use directions, restrictions, and precautions.
Days To Harvest: 60; California—200.

Signal Word/Toxicity Class: Danger-Poison/I.
REI: 12 hr. (except harvest aid/desiccation 24 hr.).

PENDIMETHALIN

Label restricts use to certain states.

■ PPI, PRE, POST

Pentagon DG *(American Cyanamid)*
Prowl 3.3 EC *(American Cyanamid)*
Rate: Mineral soils:
　　　0.5-1.5 lb. ai/A
　　　1.2-3.6 pt. 3.3 EC/A
　　　0.85-2.5 lb. DG/A
　　　Dodder control (ID, OR, WA):
　　　1.5-2 lb. ai/A
　　　3.6-4.8 pt. 3.3 EC/A
　　　2.5-3.3 lb. DG/A
Time: Preplant incorporated, preemergence, postemergence, sequential. Postemergence: Apply when onions or shallots have 2-9 true leaves (California: 2-6 true leaves—single application). Sequential—California, Kansas, Nebraska for seeded onions: make first application at loop stage, second application early post (2-9 true-leaf stage). Preplant incorporated—Colorado, Texas High Plains for transplanted onions: shallow incorporate less than 2" deep into preformed beds prior to transplanting. Postemergence—Idaho, Oregon, Washington: Apply banded in the fall or spring to furrow area of land bedded in the fall in preparation for planting seed of dry bulb onions the following spring.
Weeds: Broadleaf weeds:

annual spurge	kochia	pigweed
carpetweed	lambsquarters	purslane
dodder (ID, OR, WA)	Pennsylvania	velvetleaf*
Florida pusley	smartweed*	

Grasses:

barnyardgrass	giant foxtail	signalgrass
crabgrass	goosegrass	Texas panicum
crowfootgrass	green foxtail	witchgrass
fall panicum	johnsongrass	yellow foxtail
field sandbur	(seedling)	

* *Reduced competition*

Remarks: Dry bulb onions (direct-seeded, transplanted), dry bulb shallots. Do not apply to green onions or leeks. Do not apply using chemigation at dodder control rate. Do not feed or graze this crop. If crop loss occurs due to weather conditions, any crop registered for preplant incorporated use can be replanted the same year.
Days To Harvest: 45; California—60.
Crop Rotation: Winter wheat and winter barley can be planted in the fall 4 months after application. Treated land can be planted to other crops the following year (see label for beet and spinach restrictions).
State Restrictions: Not for use on onions in New York, except as specified in other labeling. In Idaho, Oregon, and Washington, apply on medium or fine-textured soils for dodder control.

Rate: Muck soils; mineral soils >10% organic matter (MI):
　　　1-2 lb. ai/A
　　　2.4-4.8 pt. 3.3 EC/A
　　　1.7-3.3 lb. DG/A
Time: Sequential: preemergence, postemergence.
Weeds: Same as above.
Remarks: Do not apply to green onions or leeks. Do not feed or graze this crop. If crop loss occurs due to weather conditions, do not replant any crop other than onions in muck soil during the same crop year; do not rework soil deeper than 2".
Days To Harvest: 45.
Crop Rotation: Do not plant sugar beets, red beets, spinach, winter wheat, or winter barley on muck soils for 12 months after application if more than 1.5 lb. ai/A was applied.
State Restrictions: For use on muck soils in all states except California; mineral soils containing more than 10% organic matter in Michigan.

Signal Word/Toxicity Class: Caution.
REI: 24 hr.

Pentagon — see pendimethalin

Poast — see sethoxydim

PREFAR

For use on mineral soils only. Registered for use on many vegetable crops in certain states. Use to maintain flexibility in crop rotations. May be used on labeled crops grown through or under plastic. Toxic to fish.

◆-new product • PP-preplant • PPI-preplant incorporated • PRE-preemergence • POST-postemergence • SEQ-sequential • ae-acid equivalent • ai-active ingredient • DF-dry flowable
E/EC-emulsifiable concentrate • F/FL-flowable • DG/G/WG-dispersable granule • L/LC-liquid • SP/WSP-soluble packet • W/WP-wettable powder • WSB-water soluble bag

■ PPI, PRE

Prefar 4-E (bensulide) *(Gowan)*
Rate: 5-6 lb. ai/A
5-6 qt. 4E/A
Time: Preplant incorporated. Fall-applied.
Weeds: Broadleaf weeds:

lambsquarters   redroot pigweed

Remarks: Dry bulb onions, shallots. Apply in 10-12" band, bed-up, and leave undisturbed until spring. Prior to planting, drag-off bed tops and plant in center of beds.
Crop Rotation: Carrots, cotton, and labeled crops may be replanted following application without restrictions; all other crops 120 days after application and soil should be tilled to minimum depth 4" prior to planting.
State Restrictions: For use in Idaho, Oregon.

– – – – – – – – – – – – – – –

Rate: 5-6 lb. ai/A
5-6 qt. 4E/A
Time: Preplant incorporated, preemergence. Apply preemergence only on crops to be irrigated up.
Weeds: Broadleaf weeds—AZ, CA, NM, TX:

burning nettle (AZ, CA only)	nettleleaf goosefoot (AZ, CA only)	purslane redroot pigweed
lambsquarters		

Grasses:

barnyardgrass (watergrass)	fall panicum foxtail	junglerice sprangletop
crabgrass	goosegrass	

Remarks: Dry bulb onions, shallots. Rate varies by soil type. Incorporate to a depth of 1-2" before planting. Apply preemergence only on crops where application is followed by immediate irrigation.
Crop Rotation: Carrots, cotton, and labeled crops may be replanted following application without restrictions; all other crops 120 days after application and soil should be tilled to minimum depth 4" prior to planting.
State Restrictions: Not for use in Willamette Valley of Oregon.

– – – – – – – – – – – – – – –

Signal Word/Toxicity Class: Caution/III.
REI: 12 hr. unless soil injected or soil incorporated.

Prism — see clethodim

Prowl — see pendimethalin

Rattler — see glyphosate

Roundup — see glyphosate

SCYTHE

◆ **Scythe (pelargonic acid)** *(Mycogen)*
Rate: 4-13 fl. oz./1 gal. spray solution
Time: Apply to actively growing weeds prior to crop emergence.
Weeds: Broad spectrum of annual and perennial broadleaf and grass weeds.
Remarks: Leeks, onions, shallots. Apply in minimum 75 gal. spray solution/A or spray-to-wet. Do not apply by air or through any type of irrigation system. Refer to label for directions and precautions.
Tank Mixes: Glyphosate and other foliar and residual herbicides.

– – – – – – – – – – – – – – –

Signal Word/Toxicity Class: Warning/II.
REI: 24 hr.

Select — see clethodim

SETHOXYDIM

■ POST

Poast (1.5EC) *(BASF)*
Rate: 0.09-0.28 lb. ai/A
0.5-1.5 pt. 1.5EC/A
Time: Postemergence.

Weeds: Annual and perennial grasses:

annual ryegrass	large crabgrass	stinkgrass
barnyardgrass	lovegrass	tall fescue
bermudagrass	orchardgrass	Texas panicum
broadleaf signalgrass	(seedling)	volunteer cereals
browntop panicum	perennial ryegrass	wild oat
fall panicum	quackgrass	wild proso millet
giant foxtail	red sprangletop	wildcane
goosegrass	shattercane	wiresstem muhly
green foxtail	smooth crabgrass	witchgrass
johnsongrass	southwestern	woolly cupgrass
junglerice	cupgrass	yellow foxtail

Remarks: Leeks, onions (dry bulb, green), shallots. Rate depends on growing region. Add 2 pt./A oil concentrate. Refer to label for restrictions and limitations.
Days To Harvest: 30.
State Restrictions: Do not use UAN or AMS in California or Pacific Northwest.

– – – – – – – – – – – – – – –

Signal Word/Toxicity Class: Warning/II.
REI: 12 hr.

Treflan — see trifluralin

Trific — see trifluralin

TRIFLURALIN

Apply to established onions as a shielded spray. Avoid contacting roots, bulbs, or foliage with spray. Cultivate after application to incorporate the herbicide.

■ POST

Albaugh Trifluralin 4EC *(Albaugh)*
Gowan Trifluralin 4 (EC) *(Gowan)*
Helena Trifluralin 4 EC *(Helena)*
Riverside Trifluralin 4EC or Trific 60DF *(Terra)*
◆ **Sedagri Trifluralin 480 (4EC)** *(Rhone-Poulenc)*
Treflan HFP (4EC), TR-10 (10G) *(Dow AgroSciences)*
Trilin 4EC, 5EC, or 10G *(Griffin)*
Wilbur-Ellis Trifluralin 10G *(Wilbur-Ellis)*
Rate: 0.375-0.625 lb. ai/A
0.75-1.25 pt. 4EC/A
0.6-1 pt. 5EC/A
3.75-6.25 lb. 10G/A
0.4-1 lb. ai/A
0.66-1.75 lb. 60DF/A
Time: Postemergence incorporated. Apply to established onions as a soil incorporated treatment. Do not apply preplant or preemergence.
Weeds: Broadleaf weeds:

carelessweed	knotweed	purslane
carpetweed	kochia	pusley
chickweed	lambsquarters	redroot pigweed
field bindweed	Mexican clover	rough pigweed
fireweed	Mexican fireweed	Russian thistle
Florida purslane	prostrate pigweed	spiny pigweed
Florida pusley	puncturevine	stinging nettle
goosefoot	(western U.S.)	tumbleweed
henbit		

Grasses:

annual bluegrass	fall panicum	sandbur
barnyardgrass	foxtail millet	shattercane
bottlegrass	giant foxtail	smooth crabgrass
brachiaria	green foxtail	sprangletop
bristlegrass	Italian ryegrass	stinkgrass
bromegrass	johnsongrass	Texas panicum
burgrass	(seedling)	watergrass
cheat	junglerice	wildcane
cheatgrass	large crabgrass	woolly cupgrass
chess	pigeongrass	yellow foxtail
downy brome	robust foxtail	

Remarks: Dry bulb onions. Rate varies by soil type. Apply as a directed spray to soil between onion rows. Incorporate once within 24 hr. after application. Avoid covering exposed onion bulbs with treated soil during incorporation. Do not apply to muck soils. Refer to label for further use directions, restrictions, and precautions.
Days To Harvest: 60.
Crop Rotation: Vegetable crops other than those listed on label should not be planted within 5 months following application. Refer to label for other restrictions.

6

Vegetables

Onions

State Restrictions: Wilbur-Ellis not registered in California. Albaugh, Clean Crop, Helena, Riverside, Sedagri, Treflan, Trific not for use in Pecos or Reeves County, Texas; in Montana, uses limited to supplemental labeling.

- - - - - - - - - - - - - -

Signal Word/Toxicity Class: Varies by formulation.
REI: 12 hr. unless soil injected or soil incorporated.

Trilin — see trifluralin

Peas

BASAGRAN

Most effective when weather is hot and humid; least effective when conditions are cold and dry.

■ POST
Basagran (bentazon) *(BASF)*
Rate: 0.75-1 lb. ai/A
    1.5-2 pt./A
Time: Early postemergence.
Weeds: Broadleaf weeds:

Canada thistle	jimsonweed	prickly sida
cocklebur	ladysthumb	shepherdspurse
common purslane	marshelder	Venice mallow
giant ragweed	Pennsylvania	wild mustard
hairy nightshade	smartweed	wild sunflower

Remarks: Rate depends on leaf stage and weed height. Do not add oil. For control of Canada thistle, a second application at same rate is needed; refer to Special Directions on label.
Tank Mixes: MCPA, Thistrol.

- - - - - - - - - - - - - -

Signal Word/Toxicity Class: Caution/III.
REI: 12 hr.

BUCKLE (Premix)

Granular selective herbicide to control wild oat and foxtail.

■ PPI
Buckle (13G) (10% triallate & 3% trifluralin) *(Monsanto)*
Rate: 1.3-1.625 lb. ai/A
    10-12.5 lb. 13G/A
Time: Preplant incorporated. Apply prior to planting in spring or fall. In the fall, apply within 3 weeks of normal freezeup.
Weeds: Grasses:

foxtail	pigeongrass	wild oat

Remarks: Do not apply on muck soils or soils containing more than 10% organic matter. Do not graze livestock on treated crops. Refer to label for directions and precautions.
Crop Rotation: Certain vegetable crops (refer to Monsanto representative for specific crops)—5 months; sugar beets, red beets, spinach—14 months; sorghum, proso millet, corn, oats—16 months.
State Restrictions: For use in Colorado, Idaho, Kansas, Minnesota, Montana, Nebraska, Nevada, North Dakota, Oregon, South Dakota, Utah, Washington, and Wyoming.

- - - - - - - - - - - - - -

Signal Word/Toxicity Class: Caution/III.
REI: 12 hr.

COMMAND

Spray or vapor drift may affect adjacent vegetation. Incorporate immediately to control vapor drift. Temporary crop injury may be observed as white leaves. Must be soil incorporated in some states.

■ PPI, PRE
Command 4EC (clomazone) *(FMC)*
Rate: 0.5 lb. ai/A
    1 pt. 4EC/A
Time: Preplant incorporated, preemergence soil-applied.
Weeds: Broadleaf weeds:

galinsoga*	prickly sida*	velvetleaf
lambsquarters*	spurred anoda	Venice mallow*

Grasses:

barnyardgrass*	goosegrass	large crabgrass
common panicum	green foxtail	robust foxtail
fall panicum	johnsongrass*	smooth crabgrass
field sandbur*	(seedling)	
giant foxtail		

* Partial control

Remarks: Succulent peas. If initial seeding of peas fails to produce a stand, peas may be replanted in treated fields. Do not retreat with a second application. Water or liquid fertilizer may be used as a carrier for Command when applied alone, or when tank mixed unless use directions specifically state otherwise. Do not apply through any type of irrigation system. Do not graze or harvest for food or feed cover crops planted less than 9 months after treatment, allow livestock to graze on treated vines, or feed treated vines or vine trash to livestock.
Crop Rotation: Northern U.S.: all crops—16 months after application. Southern U.S.: all crops—12 months after application. For specific crops at shorter intervals, refer to Rotational Crop Guidelines on label. Cover crops may be planted any time but stand reductions may occur in some areas. Carryover injury to approved rotational crops may result under abnormal conditions.
Tank Mixes: When applying tank mixes, observe all rotation guidelines, precautions, and replanting instructions of each product label.
State Restrictions: Not for use in California.

- - - - - - - - - - - - - -

Signal Word/Toxicity Class: Warning/II.
REI: 12 hr. unless soil injected or soil incorporated.

Credit — see glyphosate

Dual — see S-metolachlor

FAR-GO

Controls wild oat and other annual grasses in the Pacific Northwest and Northern Plains. Leaf crinkling and maturity delay may occur, but risk of crop injury is minor compared to the effect of wild oat and annual ryegrass competition with crop.

■ PPI, PRE
Far-Go 4E or 10G (triallate) *(Monsanto)*
Rate: 1.25 lb. ai/A
    1.25 qt. 4E/A
    1.25-1.5 lb. ai/A
    12.5-15 lb. 10G/A
Time: Preplant incorporated, preemergence incorporated. Apply in the spring just before or immediately after seeding and before wild oats germinate.
Weeds:

wild oat

Remarks: Leaf crinkling and delayed maturity may occur with Far-Go 4E, particularly on clay points in the Northwest. Do not graze livestock on treated crops. Refer to label for directions, precautions, and state restrictions.
Crop Rotation: Domestic oats should not be seeded if Far-Go was used the previous year.
State Restrictions: For use in Colorado, Idaho, Kansas, Minnesota, Montana, Nebraska, Nevada, North Dakota, Oregon, South Dakota, Utah, Washington, and Wyoming.

- - - - - - - - - - - - - -

Signal Word/Toxicity Class: Caution/III.
REI: 12 hr.

Glyfos or Glyfos X-tra — see glyphosate

GLYPHOSATE

Nonselective control of annual and perennial grasses and broadleaf weeds in stale seedbeds and reduced-tillage planting systems.

■ PRE
◆ **Credit (4WS)** *(Nufarm)*
◆ **Glyfos or Glyfos X-tra (4WS)** *(Cheminova)*
Rattler (4WS) *(Helena)*
Roundup Custom (5.4WS) *(Monsanto)*
Roundup Original, Original RT, Ultra, Ultra RT (4WS) *(Monsanto)*

◆-new product • PP-preplant • PPI-preplant incorporated • PRE-preemergence • POST-postemergence • SEQ-sequential • ae-acid equivalent • ai-active ingredient • DF-dry flowable
E/EC-emulsifiable concentrate • F/FL-flowable • DG/G/WG-dispersable granule • L/LC-liquid • SP/WSP-soluble packet • W/WP-wettable powder • WSB-water soluble bag

324

Weed Control Manual 2000

Rate: Annual weeds:
  0.38-1.5 lb. ai/A
  0.56-2.25 pt. 5.4WS/A
  0.75-3 pt. 4WS/A
  Perennial weeds:
  0.5-5 lb. ai/A
  0.75-7.5 pt. 5.4WS/A
  1-10 pt. 4WS/A

Time: Preemergence: Apply prior to emergence of direct-seeded crop or prior to transplanting.

Weeds: Emerged annual and perennial broadleaf weeds including:

Canada thistle	hemp dogbane	Pennsylvania
curly dock	milkweed	smartweed
field bindweed		

Grasses:

bermudagrass	fescue	paragrass
fall panicum	johnsongrass	quackgrass

Remarks: Prior to transplanting crops into plastic mulch, remove product residue from plastic. Do not add surfactant to Roundup Ultra or Ultra RT. Do not allow glyphosate to contact desirable plants. Do not apply through any type of irrigation system. Refer to label for directions, precautions and restrictions.

State Restrictions: Roundup RT for use in Colorado, Idaho, Montana, North Dakota, South Dakota, Utah, Wyoming, and in specific counties only in Kansas, Minnesota, Nebraska, Nevada, Oklahoma, Oregon, and Washington; refer to label for restrictions. Glyfos not registered for use in California. Glyfos X-tra not registered for use in mistblowers in California or Arizona.

Signal Word/Toxicity Class: Varies by formulation.
REI: Warning—12 hr.; Caution—4 hr.

Gramoxone Extra — see paraquat

KERB

Label restricts use to certain states. Restricted Use Pesticide.

■ **PRE, POST**

Kerb 50-W (pronamide) *(Rohm and Haas)*
Rate: 0.75-1.5 lb. ai/A
  1.5-3 lb. 50-W/A
Time: Early postemergence. Mid-fall to early winter (Nov.-Jan.). Peas should be in 2nd node stage of growth (2-3"). Henbit apply preemergence only.

Weeds: Broadleaf weeds:

common chickweed	henbit	mouseear chickweed

Annual grasses:

downy brome	volunteer barley	volunteer wheat
Italian ryegrass	volunteer oat	wild oat

Remarks: Winter peas. Do not feed treated vines to livestock or allow animals to graze on treated areas.
Crop Rotation: Refer to label for plantback time for rotation crops.
State Restrictions: For use in Idaho, Oregon, and Washington.

Signal Word/Toxicity Class: Caution.
REI: 24 hr.

MCPA

Suppression of Canada thistle and prevention of Canada thistle bud formation. May cause temporary crop injury and delay maturity, split the set or spread set, especially if application is made close to or during bloom.

■ **POST**

Albaugh MCPA Amine 4 *(Albaugh)*
◆ **Clean Crop MCP Amine 4** *(Platte)*
◆ **Clean Crop MCP 2 Sodium (sodium salt)** *(Platte)*
Gordon's MCPA Amine 4 *(PBI/Gordon)*
Rhomene (amine) (4) *(Nufarm)*
Riverdale MCPA-4 Amine *(Riverdale)*
Wilbur-Ellis MCPA Amine or ◆ **Sodium Salt** *(Wilbur-Ellis)*
Rate: 0.25-0.38 lb. ae/A
  0.5-0.75 pt./A
  0.125-0.38 lb. ae/A
  0.5-1.5 pt. sodium salt/A
Time: Postemergence. Apply when peas are 4-6" tall. Do not spray while peas are in blossom.

Weeds: Broadleaf weeds:

arrowhead	kochia	redroot pigweed
bulrush	lambsquarters	redstem
Canada thistle	mustard	shepherdspurse
cocklebur	perennial	sowthistle
corn spurry	peppergrass	stinkweed
curly indigo	puncturevine	sunflower
dandelion	purslane	tartary buckwheat
hempnettle	ragweed	waterplantain
hoary cress		

Remarks: Use higher rate before buds form on Canada thistle to prevent from going to seed. Do not apply when peas are stressed from lack of moisture, temperatures are over 90°F. Do not forage or graze treated pea fields or feed treated vines to livestock.
State Restrictions: Albaugh, Chiptox, and Rhomene for use in Pacific Northwest only. Wilbur Ellis not registered in California.

Signal Word/Toxicity Class: Danger/I.
REI: 48 hr.

MCPB

Useful for suppression of Canada thistle and prevention of Canada thistle bud formation. May cause temporary crop injury and delay maturity, split the set or spread set, especially if application is made close to or during bloom.

■ **POST**

Thistrol (2EC) *(Nufarm)*
Rate: 0.5-1.5 lb. ai/A
  2-6 pt. 2EC/A
Time: Postemergence. Apply to annual broadleaf weeds soon after emergence, before 3" tall, and when crop is in 6-12 node stage and before flowering. Do not apply later than 3 nodes before first pea flowering.

Weeds: Broadleaf weeds:

Canada thistle	giant ragweed	shepherdspurse
cocklebur	henbit	smartweed
common	jimsonweed	sowthistle
lambsquarters	marshelder	velvetleaf
common purslane	morningglory	wild mustard
common ragweed	pigweed	wild radish
field pepperweed	prickly sida	wild sunflower

Remarks: Do not spray when peas are stressed from lack of moisture, when temperatures are over 90°F. Do not graze or forage treated pea fields or feed treated vines to livestock.
Tank Mixes: Basagran.

Signal Word/Toxicity Class: Caution.
REI: 12 hr.

S-METOLACHLOR

Dual is a cell growth inhibitor. S-metolachlor is a purified isomer of the metolachlor molecule. Dual II MAGNUM contains the safener benoxacor. Do not use in the Northeast, or crop injury may occur.

■ **PRE**

Dual MAGNUM or Dual II MAGNUM (EC) *(Novartis)*
Rate: 1-2 pt. EC/A
Time: Preemergence: Apply during or after planting but before weed or crop emergence.

Weeds: Broadleaf weeds:

carpetweed	eclipta*	galinsoga
common purslane*	Florida beggarweed*	hairy nightshade*
eastern black nightshade	Florida pusley	pigweed

Grasses and sedges:

barnyardgrass (watergrass)	green foxtail	southwestern cupgrass
crabgrass	johnsongrass (seedling)*	volunteer sorghum*
crowfootgrass	prairie	wild proso millet*
fall panicum	red rice	witchgrass
foxtail millet	sandbur*	woolly cupgrass*
giant foxtail	shattercane*	yellow foxtail
goosegrass	signalgrass	yellow nutsedge

*Suppression

Remarks: English peas. Do not use on English peas in northeastern U.S. Rate varies by soil type and organic matter. If crop treated with Dual fails, any crop on label may be replanted immediately. Do not make second broadcast application. If original application was banded and second crop is planted in untreated row middles, second banded treatment may be applied. Do not cut for hay within 120 days after application.

Peas

Crop Rotation: Alfalfa—4 months; barley, oats, rye, wheat—4¹/₂ months; tomatoes—6 months; clover—9 months; any labeled crop in addition to barley, buckwheat, cabbage, milo, oats, peppers, rice, root crops, rye, stone fruits, tobacco, tree nuts, and wheat may be planted in the spring following treatment (including lay-by or multiple treatments applied previous season); all other rotational crops may be planted 12 months after application.
State Restrictions: Do not use in Nassau County or Suffolk County, New York.

- - - - - - - - - - - - - - -

Signal Word/Toxicity Class: Caution/III.
REI: 24 hr.

PARAQUAT

Restricted Use Pesticide.

■ PP, PRE
Gramoxone Extra (2.5L) *(ZENECA)*
Rate: 0.5-1 lb. ai/A
    1.5-3 pt. 2.5L/A
Time: Preplant, preemergence. Apply when weeds and grasses are succulent and growth is from 1-6" tall (larger plants less affected by treatment).
Weeds: Annual broadleaf weeds and grasses; top kill and suppression of perennials.
Remarks: Add nonionic surfactant or crop oil concentrate. Seedbeds should be formed as far ahead of planting and treatment as possible to permit maximum weed and grass emergence. Seeding should be done with minimum amount of soil disturbance. Refer to label for use directions, restrictions, and precautions.

- - - - - - - - - - - - - - -

Signal Word/Toxicity Class: Danger-Poison/I.
REI: 12 hr. (except harvest aid/desiccation 24 hr.).

Poast — see sethoxydim

Rattler — see glyphosate

Rhomene — see MCPA

Roundup — see glyphosate

SCYTHE

◆ **Scythe (pelargonic acid)** *(Mycogen)*
Rate: 4-13 fl. oz./1 gal. spray solution
Time: Apply to actively growing weeds prior to crop emergence.
Weeds: Annual and perennial broadleaf weeds and grasses.
Remarks: Apply in minimum 75 gal. spray solution/A or spray-to-wet. Do not apply by air or through any type of irrigation system. Refer to label for directions and precautions.
Tank Mixes: Glyphosate and other foliar and residual herbicides.

- - - - - - - - - - - - - - -

Signal Word/Toxicity Class: Warning/II.
REI: 24 hr.

SETHOXYDIM

Selective control of annual and perennial grasses.

■ POST
Poast (1.5EC) *(BASF)*
Rate: 0.09-0.47 lb. ai/A
    0.5-2.5 pt. 1.5EC/A
Time: Postemergence.
Weeds: Annual and perennial grasses:

annual ryegrass	large crabgrass	tall fescue
barnyardgrass	lovegrass	Texas panicum
bermudagrass	orchardgrass	volunteer grains
broadleaf signalgrass	(seedling)	wild oat
browntop panicum	perennial ryegrass	wild proso millet
fall panicum	red sprangletop	wildcane
giant foxtail	shattercane	wirestem muhly
goosegrass	smooth crabgrass	witchgrass
green foxtail	southwestern	woolly cupgrass
johnsongrass	cupgrass	yellow foxtail
junglerice	stinkgrass	

Remarks: Dry, succulent peas. Rate depends on growing region. Add 2 pt./A oil concentrate. Refer to label for restrictions and limitations.
Days To Harvest: Dry—30; succulent—15.
State Restrictions: Do not use UAN or AMS in California or Pacific Northwest.

- - - - - - - - - - - - - - -

Signal Word/Toxicity Class: Warning/II.
REI: 12 hr.

SONALAN

Residual dinitroaniline herbicide that should be applied preplant incorporated.

■ PPI
Sonalan HFP or 10G (ethalfluralin) *(Dow AgroSciences)*
Rate: 0.5-0.75 lb. ai/A
    1.5-2 pt. HFP/A
    5.5-7.5 lb. 10G/A
Time: Preplant incorporated. Apply in the spring before planting or in the fall.
Weeds: Broadleaf weeds:

carpetweed	groundcherry	redroot pigweed
common chickweed	henbit	Russian thistle
common	kochia	smooth pigweed
lambsquarters	nightshade	tarweed fiddleneck
common purslane	prostrate pigweed	tumble pigweed
conical catchfly	redmaids	wild buckwheat
Florida pusley	rockpurslane	

Grasses:

annual bluegrass	giant foxtail	shattercane
annual ryegrass	green foxtail	Texas panicum
barnyardgrass	Italian ryegrass	wild oat
broadleaf signalgrass	johnsongrass	wildcane
crabgrass	(seedling)	witchgrass
fall panicum	junglerice	woolly cupgrass
field sandbur	large crabgrass	yellow foxtail
foxtail millet	pigeongrass	

Remarks: Dry peas. Rate varies by soil type. Do not exceed labeled rates. Consult seed contractor before Sonalan application to determine tolerance of a particular pea variety; application to nontolerant peas may result in crop injury and reduced yields. Do not apply to soils which are wet, cloddy, or subject to prolonged periods of flooding. Do not apply through any type of irrigation system. Do not graze or forage crop grown in treated soil or cut for hay or silage.
Crop Rotation: Replant only crops listed on label. Do not plant sugar beets or red beets within 13 months after application of at least 1.1 lb. ai/A; 8 months after application of less than 1.1 lb. ai/A (provided treated area moldboard plowed to a depth of at least 12" before planting). In Arizona and California, do not plant spinach or oats within 8 months after application of at least 1.1 lb. ai/A. Refer to label for special restrictions for Montana and Wyoming.
State Restrictions: Not for use in California.

- - - - - - - - - - - - - - -

Signal Word/Toxicity Class: Danger/I.
REI: 24 hr. (HFP); 12 hr. (10G) unless soil injected or soil incorporated.

Thistrol — see MCPB

Treflan — see trifluralin

TRI-4 — see trifluralin

Trific — see trifluralin

TRIFLURALIN

Cold, wet soil conditions after planting increase risk of crop injury.

■ PPI
Albaugh Trifluralin 4EC *(Albaugh)*
◆ **Clean Crop Trifluralin HF (4EC)** *(Platte)*
Gowan Trifluralin 4 or 5 (EC) *(Gowan)*
Helena Trifluralin 4 EC *(Helena)*
Riverside Trifluralin 4EC or Trific 60DF *(Terra)*
◆ **Sedagri Trifluralin 480 (4EC)** *(Rhone-Poulenc)*
Treflan HFP (4EC) *(Dow AgroSciences)*
TRI-4 HF (4EC) *(American Cyanamid)*

◆-new product • PP-preplant • PPI-preplant incorporated • PRE-preemergence • POST-postemergence • SEQ-sequential • ae-acid equivalent • ai-active ingredient • DF-dry flowable
E/EC-emulsifiable concentrate • F/FL-flowable • DG/G/WG-dispersable granule • L/LC-liquid • SP/WSP-soluble packet • W/WP-wettable powder • WSB-water soluble bag

Weed Control Manual 2000

Trilin 4 or 5 (EC) or 10G *(Griffin)*
Wilbur-Ellis Trifluralin 10G *(Wilbur-Ellis)*
Rate: 0.5-0.75 lb. ai/A
1-1.5 pt. 4EC/A
0.8-1.2 pt. 5EC/A
0.875-1.33 lb. 60DF/A
5-7.5 lb. 10G/A
Time: Preplant incorporated.
Weeds: Broadleaf weeds:

carelessweed	knotweed	purslane
carpetweed	kochia	pusley
chickweed	lambsquarters	redroot pigweed
field bindweed	Mexican clover	rough pigweed
fireweed	Mexican fireweed	Russian thistle
Florida purslane	prostrate pigweed	spiny pigweed
Florida pusley	puncturevine	stinging nettle
goosefoot	(western U.S.)	tumbleweed
henbit		

Grasses:

annual bluegrass	fall panicum	sandbur
barnyardgrass	foxtail millet	shattercane
bottlegrass	giant foxtail	smooth crabgrass
brachiaria	green foxtail	sprangletop
bristlegrass	Italian ryegrass	stinkgrass
bromegrass	johnsongrass	Texas panicum
burgrass	(seedling)	watergrass
cheat	junglerice	wildcane
cheatgrass	large crabgrass	woolly cupgrass
chess	pigeongrass	yellow foxtail
downy brome	robust foxtail	

Remarks: Dry, English peas. Rate varies by soil type. Incorporate within 24 hr. of application and again before planting. Refer to label for directions and precautions.
Crop Rotation: Refer to label.
State Restrictions: Wilbur-Ellis not registered in California. May be fall-applied in Idaho, Oregon, and Washington.

- - - - - - - - - - - - - - -

Signal Word/Toxicity Class: Varies by formulation.
REI: 12 hr. unless soil injected or soil incorporated.

Trilin — see trifluralin

Peppers

COMMAND

Spray or vapor drift may affect adjacent vegetation. Incorporate immediately to control vapor drift. Temporary crop injury may be observed as white leaves. Must be soil incorporated in some states.

■ **PPI, PRE**
Command 4EC (clomazone) *(FMC)*
Rate: 0.25-1 lb. ai/A
0.5-2 pt. 4EC/A
Time: Preplant incorporated, preemergence soil applied.
Weeds: Broadleaf weeds:

common ragweed*	prickly sida	spurred anoda
galinsoga	purslane	velvetleaf
jimsonweed*	smartweed*	Venice mallow
lambsquarters		

Grasses:

barnyardgrass	goosegrass	large crabgrass
common panicum	green foxtail	robust foxtail
fall panicum	johnsongrass	smooth crabgrass
field sandbur	(seedling)*	yellow foxtail
giant foxtail		

* Partial control

Remarks: Bell, hot, pimento, sweet peppers. Do not use on banana peppers. Rate varies by weed and soil type. If initial seeding or transplants fail to produce a stand, peppers may be replanted in treated fields. Do not retreat with a second application. Water or liquid fertilizer may be used as a carrier for Command when applied alone, or when tank mixed unless use directions specifically state otherwise. Do not apply through any type of irrigation system. Do not graze or harvest for food or feed cover crops planted less than 9 months after treatment, allow livestock to graze on treated vines, or feed treated vines or vine trash to livestock.

Crop Rotation: Northern U.S.: all crops—16 months after application. Southern U.S.: all crops—12 months after application. For specific crops at shorter intervals, refer to Rotational Crop Guidelines on label. Cover crops may be planted any time but stand reductions may occur in some areas. Carryover injury to approved rotational crops may result under abnormal conditions.
Tank Mixes: When applying tank mixes, observe all rotation guidelines, precautions, and replanting instructions of each product label.
State Restrictions: Not for use in California.

- - - - - - - - - - - - - - -

Signal Word/Toxicity Class: Warning/II.
REI: 12 hr. unless soil injected or soil incorporated.

Credit — see glyphosate

DEVRINOL

Shallow, thorough incorporation improves control of certain weeds, including galinsoga. Apply and incorporate afterward, if ridging or bedding, to avoid concentrating herbicide in the row. Spray strips of soil between rows of plastic after laying mulch.

■ **PPI**
Devrinol 2-E or 50-DF (napropamide) *(United Phosphorus)*
Rate: 1-2 lb. ai/A
0.5-1 gal. 2-E/A
2-4 lb. 50-DF/A
Time: Preplant incorporated. May be applied to direct-seeded or transplanted crop.
Weeds: Broadleaf weeds:

carpetweed	Florida pusley	purple cudweed
common purslane	galinsoga	redroot pigweed
common ragweed	(50-DF)	smooth pigweed
(suppression)	lambsquarters	

Grasses:

barnyardgrass	goosegrass	junglerice
crabgrass	green foxtail	stinkgrass
fall panicum	johnsongrass	witchgrass
giant foxtail	(seedling)	yellow foxtail

Remarks: Incorporate same day as applied to a depth of 1-2".
Crop Rotation: Do not plant to crops not specified on label until 12 months after last application. Disc plow or moldboard plow at least 10" deep prior to planting succeeding crop.

- - - - - - - - - - - - - - -

Signal Word/Toxicity Class: Danger/I (2-E); Caution (50-DF).
REI: 12 hr.

FLUAZIFOP-P-BUTYL

Selective control of annual and perennial grasses. Do not tank mix with any other herbicide unless specified on label or reduced control may result.

■ **POST**
Fusilade DX *(ZENECA)*
Rate: 0.094-0.375 lb. ai/A
0.375-1.5 pt. DX/A
Time: Early postemergence. Apply to actively growing grasses.
Weeds: Annual and perennial grasses:

barnyardgrass	johnsongrass	southern sandbur
bermudagrass	(rhizome, seedling)	Texas panicum
broadleaf signalgrass	junglerice	tropical crabgrass
fall panicum	large crabgrass	volunteer cereals
field sandbur	quackgrass	wild oat
giant foxtail	red rice	wild proso millet
goosegrass	shattercane	wirestem muhly
green foxtail	smooth crabgrass	witchgrass
Italian ryegrass	sorghum-almum	woolly cupgrass
itchgrass	southern crabgrass	yellow foxtail

Remarks: Tabasco peppers. Rate varies by geographic area and grass species. Add crop oil concentrate or nonionic surfactant. Do not apply more than 3 pt./A per season. Refer to label for specific directions.
Days To Harvest: 45.
Crop Rotation: Do not plant rotational grass crops such as corn, sorghum, and cereals within 60 days after last application.
State Restrictions: For use in Louisiana only.

- - - - - - - - - - - - - - -

Signal Word/Toxicity Class: Caution.
REI: 12 hr.

Fusilade — see fluazifop-P-butyl

6
Vegetables

Peppers

Glyfos or Glyfos X-tra — see glyphosate

GLYPHOSATE

Nonselective control of annual and perennial grasses and broadleaf weeds in stale seedbeds and reduced-tillage planting systems.

■ **PRE**
◆ **Credit (4WS)** *(Nufarm)*
◆ **Glyfos or Glyfos X-tra (4WS)** *(Cheminova)*
Rattler (4WS) *(Helena)*
Roundup Custom (5.4WS) *(Monsanto)*
Roundup Original, Original RT, Ultra, Ultra RT (4WS) *(Monsanto)*

Rate: Annual weeds:
0.38-1.5 lb. ai/A
0.56-2.25 pt. 5.4WS/A
0.75-3 pt. 4WS/A
Perennial weeds:
0.5-5 lb. ai/A
0.75-7.5 pt. 5.4WS/A
1-10 pt. 4WS/A

Time: Preemergence: Apply prior to emergence of direct-seeded crop or prior to transplanting. Allow at least 3 days between application and planting.

Weeds: Emerged annual and perennial broadleaf weeds including:

Canada thistle	hemp dogbane	Pennsylvania
curly dock	milkweed	smartweed
field bindweed		

Grasses:

bermudagrass	fescue	paragrass
fall panicum	johnsongrass	quackgrass

Remarks: Prior to transplanting crops into plastic mulch, remove product residue from plastic. Do not add surfactant to Roundup Ultra or Ultra RT. Do not allow glyphosate to contact desirable plants. Do not apply through any type of irrigation system. Refer to labels for directions, precautions and restrictions.

State Restrictions: Roundup RT for use in Colorado, Idaho, Montana, North Dakota, South Dakota, Utah, Wyoming, and in specific counties only in Kansas, Minnesota, Nebraska, Nevada, Oklahoma, Oregon, and Washington; refer to label for restrictions. Glyfos not registered for use in California. Glyfos X-tra not registered for use in mistblowers in California or Arizona.

- - - - - - - - - - - - - - -

Signal Word/Toxicity Class: Varies by formulation.
REI: Warning—12 hr.; Caution—4 hr.

Gramoxone Extra — see paraquat

PARAQUAT

Restricted Use Pesticide.

■ **PP, PRE, POST**
Gramoxone Extra (2.5L) *(ZENECA)*

Rate: 0.5-1 lb. ai/A
1.5-3 pt. 2.5L/A
Time: Preplant, preemergence. Apply when weeds and grasses are succulent and growth is from 1-6" tall (larger plants less affected by treatment).
Weeds: Annual broadleaf weeds and grasses; top kill and suppression of perennials.
Remarks: Add nonionic surfactant or crop oil concentrate. Seedbeds should be formed as far ahead of planting and treatment as possible to permit maximum weed and grass emergence. Seeding should be done with minimum amount of soil disturbance. Refer to label for use directions, restrictions, and precautions.
Tank Mixes: Goal.

- - - - - - - - - - - - - - -

Rate: Hot chili peppers:
0.1-0.5 lb. ai/A
0.5-1.5 pt. 2.5L/A
Time: Postemergence. Apply directed spray after crop emergence or when weeds and grasses are succulent and growth is 1-6" tall.
Weeds: Annual broadleaf weeds and grasses; top kill and suppression of perennials between rows.
Remarks: Add nonionic surfactant or crop oil concentrate. Apply using precision-directed spray equipment to prevent contact with crops. Do not allow spray to contact crop. Do not graze treated areas. Refer to label for use directions, restrictions, and precautions.
State Restrictions: Hot chili peppers only for Louisiana, New Mexico, Texas.

- - - - - - - - - - - - - - -

Signal Word/Toxicity Class: Danger-Poison/I.
REI: 12 hr. (except harvest aid/desiccation 24 hr.).

Poast — see sethoxydim

PREFAR

For use on mineral soils only. Registered for use on many vegetable crops in certain states. Use to maintain flexibility in crop rotations. May be used on labeled crops grown through or under plastic. Toxic to fish.

■ **PPI, PRE**
Prefar 4-E (bensulide) *(Gowan)*

Rate: 5-6 lb. ai/A
5-6 qt. 4E/A
Time: Preplant incorporated, preemergence. Apply preemergence only on crops to be irrigated up.
Weeds: Broadleaf weeds—AZ, CA, NM, TX:

burning nettle	nettleleaf goosefoot	purslane
(AZ, CA only)	(AZ, CA only)	redroot pigweed
lambsquarters		

Grasses:

barnyardgrass	foxtail	sprangletop
crabgrass	goosegrass	watergrass
fall panicum	junglerice	

Remarks: Rate varies by soil type. Incorporate to a depth of 1-2" before planting. Apply preemergence only on crops where application is followed by immediate irrigation.
Crop Rotation: Carrots, cotton, and labeled crops—anytime; all other crops 120 days after application (soil should be tilled to minimum depth 4" prior to planting).

- - - - - - - - - - - - - - -

Signal Word/Toxicity Class: Caution/III.
REI: 12 hr. unless soil injected or soil incorporated.

Rattler — see glyphosate

Roundup — see glyphosate

SCYTHE

◆ **Scythe (pelargonic acid)** *(Mycogen)*

Rate: 4-13 fl. oz./1 gal. spray solution
Time: Apply to actively growing weeds prior to crop emergence.
Weeds: Annual and perennial broadleaf weeds and grasses.
Remarks: Apply in minimum 75 gal. spray solution/A or spray-to-wet. Do not apply by air or through any type of irrigation system. Refer to label for directions and precautions.
Tank Mixes: Glyphosate and other foliar and residual herbicides.

- - - - - - - - - - - - - - -

Signal Word/Toxicity Class: Warning/II.
REI: 24 hr.

SETHOXYDIM

■ **POST**
Poast (1.5EC) *(BASF)*

Rate: 0.09-0.28 lb. ai/A
0.5-1.5 pt. 1.5EC/A
Time: Postemergence.
Weeds: Annual and perennial grasses:

annual ryegrass	large crabgrass	tall fescue
barnyardgrass	lovegrass	Texas panicum
bermudagrass	orchardgrass	volunteer grains
broadleaf signalgrass	(seedling)	wild oat
browntop panicum	perennial ryegrass	wild proso millet
fall panicum	red sprangletop	wildcane
giant foxtail	shattercane	wirestem muhly
goosegrass	smooth crabgrass	witchgrass
green foxtail	southwestern	woolly cupgrass
johnsongrass	cupgrass	yellow foxtail
junglerice	stinkgrass	

Remarks: Rate depends on growing region. Add 2 pt./A oil concentrate. Refer to label for restrictions and limitations.
Days To Harvest: 20.
State Restrictions: Do not use UAN or AMS in California or Pacific Northwest.

- - - - - - - - - - - - - - -

Signal Word/Toxicity Class: Warning/II.
REI: 12 hr.

◆-new product • PP-preplant • PPI-preplant incorporated • PRE-preemergence • POST-postemergence • SEQ-sequential • ae-acid equivalent • ai-active ingredient • DF-dry flowable E/EC-emulsifiable concentrate • F/FL-flowable • DG/G/WG-dispersable granule • L/LC-liquid • SP/WSP-soluble packet • W/WP-wettable powder • WSB-water soluble bag

Treflan — see trifluralin

TRI-4 — see trifluralin

Trific — see trifluralin

TRIFLURALIN

Thorough incorporation improves weed control and reduces risk of crop injury. Cold, wet soil conditions after planting increase risk of crop injury. Apply and incorporate after ridging or bedding to improve drainage so concentrating the herbicide can be avoided.

■ **PPI**
Albaugh Trifluralin 4EC *(Albaugh)*
◆ **Clean Crop Trifluralin HF (4EC)** *(Platte)*
Gowan Trifluralin 4 or 5 (EC) or 10G *(Gowan)*
Helena Trifluralin 4 EC *(Helena)*
Riverside Trifluralin 4EC or Trific 60DF *(Terra)*
◆ **Sedagri Trifluralin 480 (4EC)** *(Rhone-Poulenc)*
Treflan HFP (4EC) or TR-10 (10G) *(Dow AgroSciences)*
TRI-4 HF (4EC) *(American Cyanamid)*
Trilin 4 or 5 (EC) or 10G *(Griffin)*
Wilbur-Ellis Trifluralin 10G *(Wilbur-Ellis)*
  Rate: 0.5-1 lb. ai/A
      1-2 pt. 4EC/A
      0.8-1.6 pt. 5EC/A
      0.875-1.66 lb. 60DF/A
      5-10 lb. 10G/A
Time: Pretransplant. Incorporate prior to transplanting.
Weeds: Broadleaf weeds:

carelessweed	knotweed	purslane
carpetweed	kochia	pusley
chickweed	lambsquarters	redroot pigweed
field bindweed	Mexican clover	rough pigweed
fireweed	Mexican fireweed	Russian thistle
Florida purslane	prostrate pigweed	spiny pigweed
Florida pusley	puncturevine	stinging nettle
goosefoot	(western U.S.)	tumbleweed
henbit		

Grasses:

annual bluegrass	fall panicum	sandbur
barnyardgrass	foxtail millet	shattercane
bottlegrass	giant foxtail	smooth crabgrass
brachiaria	green foxtail	sprangletop
bristlegrass	Italian ryegrass	stinkgrass
bromegrass	johnsongrass	Texas panicum
burgrass	(seedling)	watergrass
cheat	junglerice	wildcane
cheatgrass	large crabgrass	woolly cupgrass
chess	pigeongrass	yellow foxtail
downy brome	robust foxtail	

Remarks: Rate varies by soil type. Refer to label for directions, restrictions, and precautions.
Crop Rotation: Refer to label.
State Restrictions: Wilbur-Ellis not registered in California.

Signal Word/Toxicity Class: Varies by formulation.
REI: 12 hr. unless soil injected or soil incorporated.

Trilin — see trifluralin

Potatoes

Credit — see glyphosate

DIQUAT DIBROMIDE

◆ **Diquat** *(ZENECA)*
  Rate: 0.25-0.5 lb. ai/A
      1-2 pt./A

Time: Preharvest desiccation broadcast. Repeat at 5-day intervals if necessary.
Weeds: Broadleaf weeds and grasses.
Remarks: Apply by ground or air. Use high rate when weeds are large or dense. Do not apply to drought-stressed potatoes. Do not exceed total of 4 pt./A. Refer to label for use restrictions and precautions.
Days To Harvest: 7.

Signal Word/Toxicity Class: Warning/II.
REI: 24 hr.

Dual — see *S*-metolachlor

Eptam — see EPTC

EPTC

Incorporation immediately after application prevents herbicide loss by evaporation from soil surface. Use in combination with another herbicide to improve spectrum of broadleaf weeds controlled.

■ **PPI, POST**
Eptam 7-E or 20-G *(ZENECA)*
  Rate: 3-6 lb. ai/A
      3.5-7 pt. 7-E/A
      15-30 lb. 20-G/A
Time: Preplant incorporated, postemergence (drag-off incorporation, lay-by incorporation), or by irrigation (7-E).
Weeds: Broadleaf weeds:

black nightshade	corn spurry	nettleleaf goosefoot
carpetweed*	cutleaf nightshade*	prickly sida*
common chickweed	deadnettle	prostrate pigweed
common	fiddleneck*	redroot pigweed
lambsquarters	Florida pusley	sicklepod*
common pigweed	hairy nightshade	tall morningglory*
common purslane	henbit	tumble pigweed

Annual grasses and sedges:

annual bluegrass	giant foxtail	rescuegrass*
annual ryegrass	goosegrass	shattercane
(Italian)	green foxtail	signalgrass*
barnyardgrass	johnsongrass	Texas panicum*
(watergrass)	(seedling)	volunteer grains
bermudagrass	junglerice	(barley, oats, wheat)
(seedling)	lovegrass	wild oat
crabgrass	(stinkgrass)*	witchgrass*
fall panicum*	purple nutsedge	yellow foxtail
field sandbur	quackgrass	yellow nutsedge

*7-E only

Remarks: Irish potatoes. Superior variety potato is sensitive under stress conditions. Refer to label for regional information on rates and application timing.
Days To Harvest: 45.
State Restrictions: Fall application only for Minnesota and North Dakota.

Signal Word/Toxicity Class: Caution.
REI: 12 hr. unless soil injected or soil incorporated.

Glyfos or Glyfos X-tra — see glyphosate

GLYPHOSATE

Nonselective control of annual and perennial grasses and broadleaf weeds in stale seedbeds and reduced-tillage planting systems.

■ **PRE**
◆ **Credit (4WS)** *(Nufarm)*
◆ **Glyfos or Glyfos X-tra (4WS)** *(Cheminova)*
Rattler (4WS) *(Helena)*
Roundup Custom (5.4WS) *(Monsanto)*
Roundup Original, Original RT, Ultra, Ultra RT (4WS) *(Monsanto)*
  Rate: Annual weeds:
      0.38-1.5 lb. ai/A
      0.56-2.25 pt. 5.4WS/A
      0.75-3 pt. 4WS/A
      Perennial weeds:
      0.5-5 lb. ai/A
      0.75-7.5 pt. 5.4WS/A
      1-10 pt. 4WS/A
Time: Preemergence: Apply prior to emergence of direct-seeded crop or prior to transplanting.

6
Vegetables

Potatoes

Weeds: Emerged annual and perennial broadleaf weeds including:

Canada thistle	hemp dogbane	Pennsylvania
curly dock	milkweed	smartweed
field bindweed		

Grasses:

bermudagrass	fescue	paragrass
fall panicum	johnsongrass	quackgrass

Remarks: Prior to transplanting crops into plastic mulch, remove product residue from plastic. Do not add surfactant to Roundup Ultra or Ultra RT. Do not allow glyphosate to contact desirable plants. Do not apply through any type of irrigation system. Refer to label for directions, precautions and restrictions.

State Restrictions: Roundup RT for use in Colorado, Idaho, Montana, North Dakota, South Dakota, Utah, Wyoming, and in specific counties only in Kansas, Minnesota, Nebraska, Nevada, Oklahoma, Oregon, and Washington; refer to label for restrictions. Glyfos not registered for use in California. Glyfos X-tra not registered for use in mistblowers in California or Arizona.

Signal Word/Toxicity Class: Varies by formulation.
REI: Warning—12 hr.; Caution—4 hr.

Gramoxone Extra — see paraquat

LINURON

Residual weed control may be reduced by deep incorporation or streaked by cultivation. Postemergence applications require 8-hour rain-free period following application, after which rainfall or sprinkler irrigation improves residual weed control.

■ PRE
Lorox DF *(Griffin)*
Rate: East of the Rockies:
0.75-2 lb. ai/A
1.5-4 lb. DF/A
Wisconsin (Central Sands Area):
0.5-1 lb. ai/A
1-2 lb. DF/A
Time: Preemergence. Apply before grasses are 2" tall and before broadleaf weeds are 6" tall.
Weeds: Broadleaf weeds:

annual morningglory*	Florida pusley	purslane
buttonweed*	galinsoga	sicklepod*
carpetweed	lambsquarters	smartweed
chickweed	mustard	teaweed*
cocklebur*	nettleleaf goosefoot	velvetleaf *
common dayflower	pigweed	wild radish
common ragweed	prickly sida*	

Grasses:

barnyardgrass	fall panicum	goosegrass
canarygrass	foxtail	watergrass
crabgrass		

* Partial control

Remarks: Rate varies by soil type. Plant seed at least 2" deep. Do not spray over top of emerged potatoes. If emerged weeds are present, add 1 pt. surfactant/25 gal. spray mixture.

Crop Rotation: Any crop after 4 months except for cereals where only barley, oats, rye, and wheat may be planted. West of the Rockies: carrots or celery may be planted after 4 months. Do not plant any other crop until 1 year after last application.

Signal Word/Toxicity Class: Caution.
REI: 24 hr.

Lorox — see linuron

Matrix — see rimsulfuron

S-METOLACHLOR

Dual is a cell growth inhibitor. S-metolachlor is a purified isomer of the metolachlor molecule. Dual II MAGNUM contains the safener benoxacor. Second layby application may be used to improve late-season weed control.

■ PPI, PRE
Dual MAGNUM or Dual II MAGNUM (EC) *(Novartis)*
Dual IIG MAGNUM *(Novartis)*

Rate: 1-2 pt. EC/A
6-12 lb. IIG/A
Time: Preplant incorporated, preemergence. Do not apply as both preemergence and incorporated treatment.
Weeds: Broadleaf weeds:

carpetweed	eclipta*	galinsoga
common purslane*	Florida beggarweed*	hairy nightshade*
eastern black	Florida pusley	pigweed
nightshade		

Grasses and sedges:

barnyardgrass	green foxtail	signalgrass
crabgrass	johnsongrass	southwestern cupgrass
crowfootgrass	(seedling)*	volunteer sorghum*
fall panicum	prairie	watergrass
foxtail millet	red rice	witchgrass
giant foxtail	sandbur*	yellow foxtail
goosegrass	shattercane*	yellow nutsedge

* Suppression

Remarks: Do not use on sweet potatoes or yams. Do not use on muck or peat soils. If cool, wet soil conditions occur after application, Dual may delay maturity and/or reduce yield of Superior and other early maturing varieties. If crop treated with Dual fails, any crop on label may be replanted immediately. Do not make second broadcast application. If original application was banded and second crop is planted in untreated row middles, second banded treatment may be applied.

Days To Harvest: At planting to drag-off application—60.
Crop Rotation: Alfalfa—4 months; barley, oats, rye, wheat—4½ months; tomatoes—6 months; clover—9 months; any labeled crop in addition to barley, buckwheat, cabbage, milo, oats, peppers, rice, root crops, rye, stone fruits, tobacco, tree nuts, and wheat may be planted in the spring following treatment (including layby or multiple treatments applied previous season); all other rotational crops may be planted 12 months after application.
Tank Mixes: Metribuzin.
State Restrictions: Do not use in Nassau County or Suffolk County, New York.

Signal Word/Toxicity Class: Caution/III.
REI: 24 hr.

PARAQUAT

Restricted Use Pesticide.

■ PP, PRE
Gramoxone Extra (2.5L) *(ZENECA)*
Rate: 0.5 lb. ai/A
1.5 pt. 2.5L/A
Time: Preplant, preemergence. Apply before potatoes have emerged. Do not apply later than ground cracking.
Weeds: Annual broadleaf weeds and grasses; top kill and suppression of perennials.
Remarks: Add nonionic surfactant or crop oil concentrate. Do not apply preplant or preemergence to soils lacking clay minerals. Refer to label for use directions.

Rate: 0.2 lb. ai/A
0.75 pt. 2.5L/A
Time: Preplant.
Weeds:
volunteer barley
Remarks: Add nonionic surfactant or crop oil concentrate. Do not apply preplant to soils lacking clay minerals. Refer to label for use directions and precautions.
State Restrictions: For use in California, Idaho, Oregon, Washington.

Signal Word/Toxicity Class: Danger-Poison/I.
REI: 12 hr. (except harvest aid/desiccation 24 hr.).

PENDIMETHALIN

Combine with another residual herbicide to improve control of velvetleaf and to increase spectrum of weeds controlled.

■ PRE, POST
Pentagon DG *(American Cyanamid)*
Prowl 3.3 EC *(American Cyanamid)*
Rate: 0.75-1.5 lb. ai/A
1.2-3.6 pt. 3.3 EC/A
0.85-2.5 lb. DG/A
Time: Preemergence, preemergence incorporated, early postemergence. Do not apply prior to planting crop. Preemergence: Apply after planting but before potatoes and weeds emerge or after drag-off. Preemergence incorporated: Incorporate into top 1-2" soil within 7 days after application. Early post: Apply from crop emergence to 6" stage of growth.

◆-new product • PP-preplant • PPI-preplant incorporated • PRE-preemergence • POST-postemergence • SEQ-sequential • ae-acid equivalent • ai-active ingredient • DF-dry flowable
E/EC-emulsifiable concentrate • F/FL-flowable • DG/G/WG-dispersable granule • L/LC-liquid • SP/WSP-soluble packet • W/WP-wettable powder • WSB-water soluble bag

Weeds: Broadleaf weeds:

annual spurge	lambsquarters	purslane
carpetweed	Pennsylvania	stinging nettle
Florida pusley	smartweed*	velvetleaf*
kochia	pigweed	

Grasses:

barnyardgrass	giant foxtail	signalgrass
crabgrass	goosegrass	Texas panicum
crowfootgrass	green foxtail	witchgrass
fall panicum	johnsongrass	yellow foxtail
field sandbur	(seedling)	

* Aids in control and reduces competition

Remarks: Not for use on sweet potatoes or yams. Rate varies by soil type. Do not use on peat or muck soils. If crop loss occurs due to weather conditions, any crop registered for preplant incorporated use can be replanted. If replanting is necessary, do not rework soil deeper than treated zone.

Crop Rotation: Winter wheat and winter barley can be planted in the fall 4 months after application. Treated land can be planted to other crops the following year (see label for beet and spinach restrictions).

Tank Mixes: Eptam, Lorox, metribuzin.

– – – – – – – – – – – – – –

Signal Word/Toxicity Class: Caution.
REI: 24 hr.

Pentagon — see pendimethalin

Poast — see sethoxydim

Prowl — see pendimethalin

Rattler — see glyphosate

RIMSULFURON

Dry flowable herbicide that rapidly inhibits growth of susceptible weeds in potatoes.

■ **PRE, POST**

Matrix (DF) *(DuPont)*
Rate: 1-1.5 oz./A
Time: Preemergence: Apply after hilling or drag-off prior to potato emergence and before weeds emerge. Postemergence: Apply to young, actively growing weed after crop emergence.

Weeds: Broadleaf weeds:

birdsrape mustard	false chamomile	prostrate pigweed
black mustard	galinsoga	redroot pigweed
Canada thistle	hairy nightshade	redstem filaree
cocklebur	henbit	Russian thistle
common chickweed	ivyleaf morningglory	shepherdspurse
common	kochia	smooth pigweed
lambsquarters	ladysthumb	velvetleaf
common purslane	mayweed chamomile	wild kale
common ragweed	Pennsylvania	wild mustard
common sunflower	smartweed	wild oat
crabgrass	proso millet	wild radish

Grasses and sedges:

annual bluegrass	johnsongrass (seedling)	volunteer sorghum
barnyardgrass	quackgrass	volunteer wheat
goosegrass	stinkgrass	yellow foxtail
green foxtail	volunteer barley	yellow nutsedge

Remarks: Not for use on sweet potatoes or yams. Naturally occurring biotypes resistant to other sulfonylurea herbicides may also be resistant to Matrix. Do not apply by air. Do not exceed 2.5 oz./A per season.

Days To Harvest: 60.

Crop Rotation: Field corn, potatoes—anytime; tomatoes—1 month; winter wheat, cover crops (erosion control)—4 months; spring barley, spring oats, spring wheat—9 months; dry beans, succulent beans, popcorn, sweet corn, soybeans, sugar beets, sunflower—10 months; crops not listed—12 months.

Tank Mixes: Eptam, metribuzin, Lorox, Prowl.

State Restrictions: Do not use in Alamosa, Conejos, Costilla, Rio Grande, and Saguache counties in Colorado.

– – – – – – – – – – – – – –

Signal Word/Toxicity Class: Caution.
REI: 4 hr.

Roundup — see glyphosate

SCYTHE

◆ **Scythe (pelargonic acid)** *(Mycogen)*
Rate: 4-13 fl. oz./1 gal. spray solution
Time: Apply to actively growing weeds prior to crop emergence.
Weeds: Annual and perennial broadleaf weeds and grasses.
Remarks: Apply in minimum 75 gal. spray solution/A or spray-to-wet. Do not apply by air or through any type of irrigation system. Refer to label for directions and precautions.
Tank Mixes: Glyphosate and other foliar and residual herbicides.

– – – – – – – – – – – – – –

Signal Word/Toxicity Class: Warning/II.
REI: 24 hr.

SENCOR

Residual weed control may be streaked by cultivation. Postemergence applications require 8 hr. rainfree period following application, after which rainfall or sprinkler irrigation improves residual weed control. Postemergence treatments may cause temporary yellowing of crop foliage, or minor burn.

■ **PRE, POST**

Sencor 4 (FL) or DF (metribuzin) *(Bayer)*
Rate: 0.5-1 lb. ai/A
     1-2 pt. FL/A
     0.66-1.33 lb. DF/A
Time: Preemergence. Apply after planting but before crop emerges.

Rate: Russetted, white-skinned not early maturing:
     0.25-0.5 lb. ai/A
     0.5-1 pt. FL/A
     0.33-0.66 lb. DF/A
Time: Postemergence.

Weeds: Broadleaf weeds:

carpetweed	lambsquarters	redroot pigweed
hophornbeam	mustard	shepherdspurse
copperleaf	prostrate pigweed	sicklepod
jimsonweed	ragweed	smartweed

Grasses:

crabgrass	green foxtail	signalgrass
fall panicum	johnsongrass	yellow foxtail
giant foxtail	(seedling)	

Remarks: Not for use on sweet potatoes or yams. Do not apply postemergence on red-skinned potatoes, early maturing smooth-skinned white potatoes, or Atlantic, Shepody, Chipbelle, Bellchip, and Centennial potato varieties. In Idaho, Oregon, and Washington, 2 postemergence sprays can be applied over top of plants if metribuzin has not been applied preemergence. Do not apply within 24 hr. of application of other pesticides.

Days To Harvest: 60.

Crop Rotation: Alfalfa, asparagus, barley/wheat (following peas, lentils, or soybeans), corn, forage grass, potatoes, sainfoin, soybeans, sugarcane, tomatoes—4 months; barley, cotton, lentils, peas, rice, wheat—8 months; other crops not listed (except root crops)—12 months; onions, sugar beets, and other root crops—18 months. Cover crops for soil building or erosion control may be planted anytime, but do not graze or harvest for food or feed.

Tank Mixes: Prowl.

State Restrictions: Not for use in Kern County, California.

– – – – – – – – – – – – – –

Signal Word/Toxicity Class: Caution/III.
REI: 12 hr.

SETHOXYDIM

■ **POST**

Poast (1.5EC) *(BASF)*
Rate: 0.09-0.47 lb. ai/A
     0.5-2.5 pt. 1.5EC/A
Time: Postemergence.

6

Vegetables

NOTICE The information on these pages is for preliminary planning — not a guide for use. Be sure to follow the manufacturer's directions, notwithstanding information contained here. | For personal protective equipment and EPA registration numbers, please turn to page 70.

Potatoes

Weeds: Annual and perennial grasses:

annual ryegrass	large crabgrass	stinkgrass
barnyardgrass	lovegrass	tall fescue
bermudagrass	orchardgrass	Texas panicum
broadleaf signalgrass	(seedling)	volunteer cereals
browntop panicum	perennial ryegrass	wild oat
fall panicum	quackgrass	wild proso millet
giant foxtail	red rice	wildcane
goosegrass	red sprangletop	wiresetem muhly
green foxtail	shattercane	witchgrass
itchgrass	smooth crabgrass	woolly cupgrass
johnsongrass	southwestern	yellow foxtail
junglerice	cupgrass	

Remarks: Rate depends on growing region. Add 2 pt./A oil concentrate. Do not apply through any type of irrigation system. Refer to label for restrictions and limitations.

Days To Harvest: 30.

Tank Mixes: Metribuzin.

State Restrictions: Do not use UAN or AMS in California or Pacific Northwest.

- - - - - - - - - - - - - - -

Signal Word/Toxicity Class: Warning/II.

REI: 12 hr.

Treflan — see trifluralin

TRI-4 — see trifluralin

Trific — see trifluralin

TRIFLURALIN

Effective for control of weeds germinating from seed. Control emerged weeds by cultivation or other herbicides that are effective postemergence. Incorporate within 8 hours after application to prevent herbicide loss from breakdown by sunlight.

■ PRE, POST

Albaugh Trifluralin 4EC *(Albaugh)*
◆ Clean Crop Trifluralin HF (4EC) *(Platte)*
Gowan Trifluralin 4 or 5 (EC) *(Gowan)*
Helena Trifluralin 4 EC *(Helena)*
Riverside Trifluralin 4EC or Trific 60DF *(Terra)*
◆ Sedagri Trifluralin 480 (4EC) *(Rhone-Poulenc)*
Treflan HFP (4EC) *(Dow AgroSciences)*
TRI-4 HF (4EC) *(American Cyanamid)*
Trilin 4 or 5 (EC) or 10G *(Griffin)*
Wilbur-Ellis Trifluralin 10G *(Wilbur-Ellis)*

Rate: 0.5-1 lb. ai/A
1-2 pt. 4EC/A
0.8-1.6 pt. 5EC/A
0.875-1.66 lb. 60DF/A
5-10 lb. 10G/A

Time: Preemergence, postemergence. Apply after planting, before emergence, following drag-off, or after potato plants have fully emerged.

Weeds: Broadleaf weeds:

carelessweed	knotweed	purslane
carpetweed	kochia	pusley
chickweed	lambsquarters	redroot pigweed
field bindweed	Mexican clover	rough pigweed
fireweed	Mexican fireweed	Russian thistle
Florida purslane	prostrate pigweed	spiny pigweed
Florida pusley	puncturevine	stinging nettle
goosefoot	(western U.S.)	tumbleweed
henbit		

Grasses:

annual bluegrass	fall panicum	sandbur
barnyardgrass	foxtail millet	shattercane
bottlegrass	giant foxtail	smooth crabgrass
brachiaria	green foxtail	sprangletop
bristlegrass	Italian ryegrass	stinkgrass
bromegrass	johnsongrass	Texas panicum
burgrass	(seedling)	watergrass
cheat	junglerice	wildcane
cheatgrass	large crabgrass	woolly cupgrass
chess	pigeongrass	yellow foxtail
downy brome	robust foxtail	

Remarks: Rate varies by soil type. Care should be taken that incorporation machinery does not damage seed pieces or elongating sprouts. Refer to label for directions and precautions.

Crop Rotation: Refer to label.

State Restrictions: Not for use in Maine. Wilbur-Ellis not registered in California.

- - - - - - - - - - - - - - -

Signal Word/Toxicity Class: Varies by formulation.

REI: 12 hr. unless soil injected or soil incorporated.

Trilin — see trifluralin

TURBO (Premix)

■ PRE

Turbo (EC) (6.55 lb./gal. metolachlor & 1.45 lb./gal. metribuzin) *(Novartis)*

Rate: 2-4 lb. ai/A
2-4 pt. EC/A

Time: Preemergence.

Weeds: Broadleaf weeds:

black nightshade	Pennsylvania	sicklepod
carpetweed	smartweed	velvetleaf
cocklebur*	pigweed	Venice mallow
common ragweed	prickly sida	volunteer sorghum*
galinsoga	Russian thistle	western hairy
jimsonweed	sesbania	nightshade
kochia*	shepherdspurse	wild mustard
lambsquarters		

Grasses and sedges:

barnyardgrass	goosegrass	southwestern
crabgrass	prairie cupgrass	cupgrass
fall panicum	red rice	witchgrass
foxtail	sandbur*	yellow nutsedge

* Suppression

Remarks: Do not apply to sweet potatoes or yams. Applications to Atlantic, Shepody, Chip Bell, Bell Chip, and Centennial varieties may cause crop injury. Do not apply within 24 hr. of application of other pesticides. Refer to label for restrictions and limitations.

Days To Harvest: 60.

Crop Rotation: Winter barley, winter wheat—4 1/2 months; corn, cotton, peas, potatoes, rice, soybeans, spring barley, spring wheat—8 months; asparagus, forage grasses, lentils, sainfoin, soybeans, sugarcane, tomatoes, other crops not listed (except root crops)—12 months; onions, sugar beets, and other root crops—18 months. Cover crops for soil building or erosion control may be planted anytime, but do not graze or harvest for food or feed. Stand reductions may occur in some areas.

Tank Mixes: Sencor.

State Restrictions: Not for use in California.

- - - - - - - - - - - - - - -

Signal Word/Toxicity Class: Caution/III.

VAPAM

Water-soluble liquid that when applied to properly prepared soil is converted into a gaseous fumigant. May be applied where crop stubble or vegetation exists without prior tillage, provided there is adequate soil penetration of Vapam.

■ PP

Vapam HL (metam-sodium) *(Amvac)*

Rate: Soil injection:
30 gal. HL/A
Sprinkler system preplant:
37.5-75 gal. HL/A

Time: Preplant.

Weeds: Weed seeds.

Remarks: Sprinkler system: Soil temperatures should be in the range of 40-50°F in treatment zone. On very light soil, keep surface area moist by sprinkling periodically for 2-3 days. Apply in a minimum 1 acre/" water. Do not apply to desirable lawns and plants or within 3 ft. of drip line of desirable plants, shrubs, or trees. Do not use in greenhouses, enclosed structures, confined areas, or when fumes may enter nearby houses.

State Restrictions: In California, application must be in compliance with Technical Information Bulletin — California, "Metam-Sodium Guidelines for All Application Methods for Metam-Sodium in California." Bulletin may be obtained from local pesticide dealer or metam-sodium registrant.

- - - - - - - - - - - - - - -

Signal Word/Toxicity Class: Danger/I.

REI: 48 hr.

◆–new product • PP-preplant • PPI-preplant incorporated • PRE-preemergence • POST-postemergence • SEQ-sequential • ae-acid equivalent • ai-active ingredient • DF-dry flowable
E/EC-emulsifiable concentrate • F/FL-flowable • DG/G/WG-dispersable granule • L/LC-liquid • SP/WSP-soluble packet • W/WP-wettable powder • WSB-water soluble bag

Radishes

Credit — see glyphosate

Glyfos or Glyfos X-tra — see glyphosate

GLYPHOSATE

Nonselective control of annual and perennial grasses and broadleaf weeds in stale seedbeds and reduced tillage planting systems.

■ **PRE**
◆ **Credit (4WS)** *(Nufarm)*
◆ **Glyfos or Glyfos X-tra (4WS)** *(Cheminova)*
Rattler (4WS) *(Helena)*
Roundup Custom (5.4WS) *(Monsanto)*
Roundup Original, Original RT, Ultra, Ultra RT (4WS) *(Monsanto)*
  Rate: Annual weeds:
    0.38-1.5 lb. ai/A
    0.56-2.25 pt. 5.4WS/A
    0.75-3 pt. 4WS/A
    Perennial weeds:
    0.5-5 lb. ai/A
    0.75-7.5 pt. 5.4WS/A
    1-10 pt. 4WS/A
  Time: Preemergence: Apply prior to emergence of direct-seeded crop or prior to transplanting.
  Weeds: Emerged annual and perennial broadleaf weeds including:

Canada thistle	hemp dogbane	Pennsylvania
curly dock	milkweed	smartweed
field bindweed		

  Grasses:

bermudagrass	fescue	paragrass
fall panicum	johnsongrass	quackgrass

  Remarks: Prior to transplanting crops into plastic mulch, remove product residue from plastic. Do not add surfactant to Roundup Ultra or Ultra RT. Do not allow glyphosate to contact desirable plants. Do not apply through any type of irrigation system. Refer to label for directions, precautions and restrictions.
  State Restrictions: Roundup RT for use in Colorado, Idaho, Montana, North Dakota, South Dakota, Utah, Wyoming, and in specific counties only in Kansas, Minnesota, Nebraska, Nevada, Oklahoma, Oregon, and Washington; refer to label for restrictions. Glyfos not registered for use in California. Glyfos X-tra not registered for use in mistblowers in California or Arizona.

- - - - - - - - - - - - - - -

  Signal Word/Toxicity Class: Varies by formulation.
  REI: Warning—12 hr.; Caution—4 hr.

Rattler — see glyphosate

Roundup — see glyphosate

SCYTHE

◆ **Scythe (pelargonic acid)** *(Mycogen)*
  Rate: 4-13 fl. oz./1 gal. spray solution
  Time: Apply to actively growing weeds prior to crop emergence.
  Weeds: Annual and perennial broadleaf weeds and grasses.
  Remarks: Apply in minimum 75 gal. spray solution/A or spray-to-wet. Do not apply by air or through any type of irrigation system. Refer to label for directions and precautions.
  Tank Mixes: Glyphosate and other foliar and residual herbicides.

- - - - - - - - - - - - - - -

  Signal Word/Toxicity Class: Warning/II.
  REI: 24 hr.

Treflan — see trifluralin

TRIFLURALIN

■ **PPI**
Albaugh Trifluralin 4EC *(Albaugh)*
◆ **Clean Crop Trifluralin HF (4EC)** *(Platte)*
Helena Trifluralin 4 EC *(Helena)*
◆ **Sedagri Trifluralin 480 (4EC)** *(Rhone-Poulenc)*
Treflan HFP (4EC) *(Dow AgroSciences)*
Trilin 10G *(Griffin)*
Wilbur-Ellis Trifluralin 10G *(Wilbur-Ellis)*
  Rate: 0.5-0.75 lb. ai/A
    1-1.5 pt. 4EC/A
    0.5-1 lb. ai/A
    5-10 lb. 10G/A
  Time: Preplant incorporated.
  Weeds: Broadleaf weeds:

carelessweed	knotweed	purslane
carpetweed	kochia	pusley
chickweed	lambsquarters	redroot pigweed
field bindweed	Mexican clover	rough pigweed
fireweed	Mexican fireweed	Russian thistle
Florida purslane	prostrate pigweed	spiny pigweed
Florida pusley	puncturevine	stinging nettle
goosefoot	(western U.S.)	tumbleweed
henbit		

  Grasses:

annual bluegrass	fall panicum	sandbur
barnyardgrass	foxtail millet	shattercane
bottlegrass	giant foxtail	smooth crabgrass
brachiaria	green foxtail	sprangletop
bristlegrass	Italian ryegrass	stinkgrass
bromegrass	johnsongrass	Texas panicum
burgrass	(seedling)	watergrass
cheat	junglerice	wildcane
cheatgrass	large crabgrass	woolly cupgrass
chess	pigeongrass	yellow foxtail
downy brome	robust foxtail	

  Remarks: Rate varies by soil type.
  Crop Rotation: Refer to label.
  State Restrictions: Wilbur-Ellis not registered in California.

- - - - - - - - - - - - - - -

  Signal Word/Toxicity Class: Varies by formulation.
  REI: 12 hr. unless soil injected or soil incorporated.

Trilin — see trifluralin

Rhubarb

Credit — see glyphosate

DEVRINOL

■ **POST**
Devrinol 50-DF (napropamide) *(United Phosphorus)*
  Rate: 4 lb. ai/A
    8 lb. 50-DF/A
  Time: Postemergence. Apply to a weed-free soil surface in winter when rhubarb is dormant.
  Weeds: Annual broadleaf weeds:

annual sowthistle	common ragweed	pineappleweed
carpetweed	(suppression)	prickly lettuce
coast fiddleneck	horse purslane	prostrate knotweed
common chickweed	lambsquarters	purple cudweed
common groundsel	little mallow	redroot pigweed
common purslane	(from seed)	redstem filaree

  Annual grasses:

annual bluegrass	giant foxtail	ripgut brome
annual ryegrass	goosegrass	sandbur
(Italian ryegrass)	green foxtail	smooth crabgrass
barnyardgrass	guineagrass	soft chess
bristly foxtail	hairy crabgrass	southwestern cupgrass
bromegrass	johnsongrass	stinkgrass
canarygrass	(seedling)	Texas panicum
cheatgrass	junglerice	wild barley
downy brome	large crabgrass	wild oat
fall panicum	Mexican sprangletop	witchgrass
foxtail barley	red sprangletop	yellow foxtail

6

Vegetables

Rhubarb

Remarks: Do not apply to frozen ground. If rainfall does not occur, treatment must be shallowly incorporated or irrigated in following application with sufficient water to wet soil to a depth of 2-4".

Crop Rotation: Do not plant to crops not specified on label until 12 months after last application. Disc plow or moldboard plow at least 10" deep prior to planting succeeding crop.

State Restrictions: For use in the Pacific Northwest only.

- - - - - - - - - - - - - -

Signal Word/Toxicity Class: Caution.
REI: 12 hr.

FLUAZIFOP-P-BUTYL

Provides selective control of annual and perennial grasses. Do not tank mix with any other herbicide unless specified on label or reduced control may result.

■ POST

Fusilade DX *(ZENECA)*
Rate: 0.1-0.375 lb. ai/A
0.375-1.5 pt. DX/A
Time: Early postemergence. Apply to actively growing grasses.
Weeds: Annual and perennial grasses:

barnyardgrass	johnsongrass	southern sandbur
bermudagrass	(rhizome, seedling)	Texas panicum
broadleaf signalgrass	junglerice	tropical crabgrass
fall panicum	large crabgrass	volunteer cereals
field sandbur	quackgrass	wild oat
giant foxtail	red rice	wild proso millet
goosegrass	shattercane	wirestem muhly
green foxtail	smooth crabgrass	witchgrass
Italian ryegrass	sorghum-almum	woolly cupgrass
itchgrass	southern crabgrass	yellow foxtail

Remarks: Rate varies by geographic area and grass species. Add crop oil concentrate or nonionic surfactant. Do not apply more than 2.25 pt./A per season. Refer to label for specific directions and precautions.
Days To Harvest: 14.
Crop Rotation: Do not plant rotational grass crops such as corn, sorghum, and cereals within 60 days after last application.
State Restrictions: For use in Maryland, New Jersey.

- - - - - - - - - - - - - -

Signal Word/Toxicity Class: Caution.
REI: 12 hr.

Fusilade — see fluazifop-P-ethyl

Glyfos or Glyfos X-tra — see glyphosate

GLYPHOSATE

Nonselective control of annual and perennial grasses and broadleaf weeds in stale seedbeds and reduced-tillage planting systems.

■ PRE

◆ Credit (4WS) *(Nufarm)*
◆ Glyfos or Glyfos X-tra (4WS) *(Cheminova)*
Rattler (4WS) *(Helena)*
Roundup Custom (5.4WS) *(Monsanto)*
Roundup Original, Original RT, Ultra, Ultra RT (4WS) *(Monsanto)*
Rate: Annual weeds:
0.38-1.5 lb. ai/A
0.56-2.25 pt. 5.4WS/A
0.75-3 pt. 4WS/A
Perennial weeds:
0.5-5 lb. ai/A
0.75-7.5 pt. 5.4WS/A
1-10 pt. 4WS/A
Time: Preemergence: Apply prior to emergence of direct-seeded crop or prior to transplanting.
Weeds: Emerged annual and perennial broadleaf weeds including:

Canada thistle	hemp dogbane	Pennsylvania
curly dock	milkweed	smartweed
field bindweed		

Grasses:

bermudagrass	fescue	paragrass
fall panicum	johnsongrass	quackgrass

Remarks: Prior to transplanting crops into plastic mulch, remove product residue from plastic. Do not add surfactant to Roundup Ultra or Ultra RT. Do not allow glyphosate to contact desirable plants. Do not apply through any type of irrigation system. Refer to label for directions, precautions and restrictions.

State Restrictions: Roundup RT for use in Colorado, Idaho, Montana, North Dakota, South Dakota, Utah, Wyoming, and in specific counties only in Kansas, Minnesota, Nebraska, Nevada, Oklahoma, Oregon, and Washington; refer to label for restrictions. Glyfos not registered for use in California. Glyfos X-tra not registered for use in mistblowers in California or Arizona.

- - - - - - - - - - - - - -

Signal Word/Toxicity Class: Varies by formulation.
REI: Warning—12 hr.; Caution—4 hr.

Gramoxone Extra — see paraquat

KERB

Established dormant rhubarb plants are tolerant. Apply in late fall or early winter when soil temperatures are between 33-55°F. Registered for use in certain states only. Restricted Use Pesticide.

■ PRE, POST

Kerb 50-W (pronamide) *(Rohm and Haas)*
Rate: 1-2 lb. ai/A
2-4 lb. 50-W/A
Time: Preemergence, postemergence. Apply in fall or winter to established rhubarb plants in a dormant growth condition prior to soil freeze-up and snow cover. Do not apply to newly transplanted rhubarb or when rhubarb is actively growing.
Weeds: Broadleaf weeds:

common chickweed	mouseear chickweed	red sorrel

Grasses:

annual bluegrass	Kentucky bluegrass	tall fescue
bentgrass	orchardgrass	velvetgrass
cheatgrass	perennial ryegrass	wild oat
downy brome	quackgrass	

Remarks: Do not make more than one application.
Days To Harvest: 38.
Crop Rotation: Refer to label for plantback times for rotation crops.
State Restrictions: For use in Oregon and Washington.

- - - - - - - - - - - - - -

Signal Word/Toxicity Class: Caution.
REI: 24 hr.

PARAQUAT

Restricted Use Pesticide.

Gramoxone Extra (2.5L) *(ZENECA)*
Rate: 0.6-1 lb. ai/A
2-3 pt. 2.5L/A
Time: Apply during dormant season before buds in crown begin to grow.
Weeds: Annual broadleaf weeds and grasses; top kill and suppression of emerged perennial weeds in dormant rhubarb.
Remarks: Add nonionic surfactant or crop oil concentrate. Seedbeds should be formed as far ahead of planting and treatment as possible to permit maximum weed and grass emergence. Seeding should be done with minimum amount of soil disturbance. Refer to label for use directions, restrictions, and precautions.

- - - - - - - - - - - - - -

Signal Word/Toxicity Class: Danger-Poison/I.
REI: 12 hr. (except harvest aid/desiccation 24 hr.).

Poast — see sethoxydim

Rattler — see glyphosate

Roundup — see glyphosate

SCYTHE

◆ Scythe (pelargonic acid) *(Mycogen)*
Rate: 4-13 fl. oz./1 gal. spray solution
Time: Apply to actively growing weeds prior to crop emergence.
Weeds: Annual and perennial broadleaf weeds and grasses.
Remarks: Apply in minimum 75 gal. spray solution/A or spray-to-wet. Do not apply by air or through any type of irrigation system. Refer to label for directions and precautions.

◆-new product • PP-preplant • PPI-preplant incorporated • PRE-preemergence • POST-postemergence • SEQ-sequential • ae-acid equivalent • ai-active ingredient • DF-dry flowable
E/EC-emulsifiable concentrate • F/FL-flowable • DG/G/WG-dispersable granule • L/LC-liquid • SP/WSP-soluble packet • W/WP-wettable powder • WSB-water soluble bag

Tank Mixes: Glyphosate and other foliar and residual herbicides.

- - - - - - - - - - - - - - - -

Signal Word/Toxicity Class: Warning/II.
REI: 24 hr.

SETHOXYDIM

■ POST
Poast (1.5EC) *(BASF)*
Rate: 0.01-0.28 lb. ai/A
0.5-1.5 pt. 1.5EC/A
Time: Postemergence.
Weeds: Annual and perennial grasses:

annual ryegrass	large crabgrass	stinkgrass
barnyardgrass	lovegrass	tall fescue
bermudagrass	orchardgrass	Texas panicum
broadleaf signalgrass	(seedling)	volunteer cereals
browntop panicum	perennial ryegrass	wild oat
fall panicum	quackgrass	wild proso millet
field sandbur	red sprangletop	wildcane
giant foxtail	shattercane	wirestem muhly
goosegrass	smooth crabgrass	witchgrass
green foxtail	southwestern	woolly cupgrass
johnsongrass	cupgrass	yellow foxtail
junglerice		

Remarks: Rate varies by growing region. Always add 2 pt./A oil concentrate. Refer to label for restrictions and limitations.
Days To Harvest: 15.
State Restrictions: Do not use UAN or AMS in California or Pacific Northwest.

- - - - - - - - - - - - - - - -

Signal Word/Toxicity Class: Warning/II.
REI: 12 hr.

Southern Peas
(Blackeyed, Crowder, Pinkeyed)

Dual — see *S*-metolachlor

Gramoxone Extra — see paraquat

S-METOLACHLOR

Dual is a cell growth inhibitor. S-metolachlor is a purified isomer of the metolachlor molecule. Dual II MAGNUM contains the safener benoxacor. Do not use in the Northeast, or crop injury may occur.

■ PPI, PRE
Dual MAGNUM or Dual II MAGNUM (EC) *(Novartis)*
Rate: 1-2 pt. EC/A
Time: Preplant incorporated: Incorporate into top 2" of soil within 14 days before planting. Preemergence: Apply during or after planting but before weeds emerge.
Weeds: Broadleaf weeds:

carpetweed	eclipta*	galinsoga
common purslane*	Florida beggarweed*	hairy nightshade*
eastern black	Florida pusley	pigweed
nightshade		

Grasses and sedges:

barnyardgrass	green foxtail	signalgrass
crabgrass	johnsongrass	southwestern cupgrass
crowfootgrass	(seedling)*	volunteer sorghum*
fall panicum	prairie	watergrass
foxtail millet	red rice	witchgrass
giant foxtail	sandbur*	yellow foxtail
goosegrass	shattercane*	yellow nutsedge

*Suppression

Remarks: Rate varies by soil type and organic matter. If crop treated with Dual fails, any crop on label may be replanted immediately. Do not make second broadcast application. If original application was banded and second crop is planted in untreated row middles, second banded treatment may be applied. Do not cut for hay within 120 days after application.

Crop Rotation: Alfalfa—4 months; barley, oats, rye, wheat—4½ months; tomatoes—6 months; clover—9 months; any labeled crop in addition to barley, buckwheat, cabbage, milo, oats, peppers, rice, root crops, rye, stone fruits, tobacco, tree nuts, and wheat may be planted in the spring following treatment (including lay-by or multiple treatments applied previous season); all other rotational crops may be planted 12 months after application.

- - - - - - - - - - - - - - - -

Signal Word/Toxicity Class: Caution/III.
REI: 24 hr.

PARAQUAT

Restricted Use Pesticide.

Gramoxone Extra (2.5L) *(ZENECA)*
Rate: 0.3-0.5 lb. ai/A
1-1.5 pt. 2.5L/A
Time: Apply to mature crop with 80% of pods yellowing and mostly ripe with no more than 40% (bush-type) or 30% (vine-type) leaves still green in color.
Weeds: Annual broadleaf weeds and grasses; top kill and suppression of perennials.
Remarks: Southern peas (blackeyed, crowder). Add nonionic surfactant or crop oil concentrate. Seedbeds should be formed as far ahead of planting and treatment as possible to permit maximum weed and grass emergence. Seeding should be done with minimum amount of soil disturbance. Refer to label for use directions, restrictions, and precautions.
Days To Harvest: 7.
State Restrictions: Not for use on dry beans in California.

- - - - - - - - - - - - - - - -

Signal Word/Toxicity Class: Danger-Poison/I.
REI: 12 hr. (except harvest aid/desiccation 24 hr.).

PENDIMETHALIN

Use in combination with another herbicide to increase spectrum of broadleaf weeds controlled. Cold, wet soil conditions after planting increase risk of crop injury.

■ PPI
Pentagon DG *(American Cyanamid)*
Prowl 3.3 EC *(American Cyanamid)*
Rate: 0.5-1.5 lb. ai/A
1.2-3.6 pt. 3.3 EC/A
0.85-2.5 lb. DG/A
Time: Preplant incorporated: Apply immediately before planting or up to 60 days prior to planting and incorporate within 7 days. Do not use preemergence.
Weeds: Broadleaf weeds:

annual spurge	lambsquarters	pigweed
carpetweed	Pennsylvania	purslane
Florida pusley	smartweed*	velvetleaf*
kochia		

Grasses:

barnyardgrass	giant foxtail	signalgrass
crabgrass	goosegrass	Texas panicum
crowfootgrass	green foxtail	witchgrass
fall panicum	johnsongrass	yellow foxtail
field sandbur	(seedling)	

* Reduced competition

Remarks: Rate varies by soil type and geographical region. Do not use on peat or muck soils.
Crop Rotation: If crop loss occurs due to weather condition, beans or any crop registered for preplant incorporated use can be replanted the same year. If replanting is necessary, do not rework soil deeper than treated zone. Winter wheat and winter barley can be planted in the fall 4 months after application. Treated land can be planted to other crops the following year (see label for beet and spinach restrictions).

- - - - - - - - - - - - - - - -

Signal Word/Toxicity Class: Caution.
REI: 24 hr.

Pentagon — see pendimethalin

Prowl — see pendimethalin

6

Vegetables

Southern Peas

SCYTHE

◆ **Scythe (pelargonic acid)** *(Mycogen)*
Rate: 4-13 fl. oz./1 gal. spray solution
Time: Apply to actively growing weeds prior to crop emergence.
Weeds: Annual and perennial broadleaf weeds and grasses.
Remarks: Apply in minimum 75 gal. spray solution/A or spray-to-wet. Do not apply by air or through any type of irrigation system. Refer to label for directions and precautions.
Tank Mixes: Glyphosate and other foliar and residual herbicides.

Signal Word/Toxicity Class: Warning/II.
REI: 24 hr.

Treflan — see trifluralin

TRI-4 — see trifluralin

Trific — see trifluralin

TRIFLURALIN

Controls annual grasses and certain broadleaf weeds, including common lambsquarters and pigweed species. Combine with another herbicide to increase spectrum of broadleaf weeds controlled. Cold, wet soil conditions after planting increase risk of crop injury.

■ **PPI**
Albaugh Trifluralin 4EC *(Albaugh)*
◆ **Clean Crop Trifluralin HF (4EC)** *(Platte)*
Gowan Trifluralin 4 or 5 (EC) or 10G *(Gowan)*
Helena Trifluralin 4 EC *(Helena)*
Riverside Trifluralin 4EC or Trific 60DF *(Terra)*
◆ **Sedagri Trifluralin 480 (4EC)** *(Rhone-Poulenc)*
Treflan HFP (4EC) or TR-10 (10G) *(Dow AgroSciences)*
TRI-4 HF (4EC) *(American Cyanamid)*
Trilin 4 or 5 (EC) or 10G *(Griffin)*
Wilbur-Ellis Trifluralin 10G *(Wilbur-Ellis)*
Rate: 0.5-1 lb. ai/A
1-2 pt. 4EC/A
0.8-1.6 pt. 5EC/A
0.875-1.66 lb. 60DF/A
5-10 lb. 10G/A
Time: Preplant incorporated.
Weeds: Broadleaf weeds:

caltrop	goosefoot	purslane
carelessweed	henbit	pusley
carpetweed	knotweed	redroot pigweed
chickweed	kochia	rough pigweed
field bindweed	lambsquarters	Russian thistle
fireweed	Mexican clover	spiny pigweed
Florida purslane	Mexican fireweed	stinging nettle
Florida pusley	prostrate pigweed	tumbleweed
goathead	puncturevine	

Grasses:

annual bluegrass	fall panicum	robust foxtail
barnyardgrass	foxtail millet	sandbur
bottlegrass	giant foxtail	smooth crabgrass
brachiaria	green foxtail	sprangletop
bristlegrass	itchgrass	stinkgrass
bromegrass	johnsongrass	Texas panicum
burgrass	(seedling)	watergrass
cheat	junglerice	wildcane
cheatgrass	large crabgrass	woolly cupgrass
chess	pigeongrass	yellow foxtail
downy brome	red rice	

Remarks: Rate varies by soil type. Refer to label for directions and precautions.
Crop Rotation: Vegetable crops other than those listed on label should not be planted within 5 months following application.
State Restrictions: Wilbur-Ellis not registered in California.

Signal Word/Toxicity Class: Varies by formulation.
REI: 12 hr. unless soil injected or soil incorporated.

Trilin — see trifluralin

Spinach

Credit — see glyphosate

Glyfos or Glyfos X-tra — see glyphosate

GLYPHOSATE

Nonselective control of annual and perennial grasses and broadleaf weeds in stale seedbeds and reduced tillage planting systems.

■ **PRE**
◆ **Credit (4WS)** *(Nufarm)*
◆ **Glyfos or Glyfos X-tra (4WS)** *(Cheminova)*
Rattler (4WS) *(Helena)*
Roundup Custom (5.4WS) *(Monsanto)*
Roundup Original, Original RT, Ultra, Ultra RT (4WS) *(Monsanto)*
Rate: Annual weeds:
0.38-1.5 lb. ai/A
0.56-2.25 pt. 5.4WS/A
0.75-3 pt. 4WS/A
Perennial weeds:
0.5-5 lb. ai/A
0.75-7.5 pt. 5.4WS/A
1-10 pt. 4WS/A
Time: Preemergence: Apply prior to emergence of direct-seeded crop or prior to transplanting.
Weeds: Emerged annual and perennial broadleaf weeds including:

Canada thistle	hemp dogbane	Pennsylvania
curly dock	milkweed	smartweed
field bindweed		

Grasses:

bermudagrass	fescue	paragrass
fall panicum	johnsongrass	quackgrass

Remarks: Prior to transplanting crops into plastic mulch, remove product residue from plastic. Do not add surfactant to Roundup Ultra or Ultra RT. Do not allow glyphosate to contact desirable plants. Do not apply through any type of irrigation system. Refer to label for directions, precautions and restrictions.
State Restrictions: Roundup RT for use in Colorado, Idaho, Montana, North Dakota, South Dakota, Utah, Wyoming, and in specific counties only in Kansas, Minnesota, Nebraska, Nevada, Oklahoma, Oregon, and Washington; refer to label for restrictions. Glyfos not registered for use in California. Glyfos X-tra not registered for use in mistblowers in California or Arizona.

Signal Word/Toxicity Class: Varies by formulation.
REI: Warning—12 hr.; Caution—4 hr.

Poast — see sethoxydim

RO-NEET

Incorporate immediately to prevent herbicide loss due to volatilization. Reduce herbicide rate, and/or apply and incorporate 5-7 days before planting to reduce risk of temporary crop injury.

■ **PPI**
Ro-Neet 6-E (cycloate) *(ZENECA)*
Rate: 3 lb. ai/A
4 pt. 6-E/A
California:
4 lb. ai/A
5.3 pt. 6-E/A
Time: Preplant incorporated, at planting, or immediately post planting.
Weeds: Broadleaf weeds:

black nightshade	lambsquarters	shepherdspurse
common purslane	nettleleaf goosefoot	small stinging nettle
hairy nightshade	(except CA)	velvetleaf
henbit (deadnettle)	redroot pigweed	(suppression)

Annual grasses and sedges:

annual bluegrass	crabgrass	volunteer barley
annual ryegrass	foxtail	wild oat
barnyardgrass	purple nutsedge	yellow nutsedge
(watergrass)		

◆-new product • PP-preplant • PPI-preplant incorporated • PRE-preemergence • POST-postemergence • SEQ-sequential • ae-acid equivalent • ai-active ingredient • DF-dry flowable E/EC-emulsifiable concentrate • F/FL-flowable • DG/G/WG-dispersable granule • L/LC-liquid • SP/WSP-soluble packet • W/WP-wettable powder • WSB-water soluble bag

Remarks: Use on sandy mineral soils only. Refer to label for use directions, restrictions, and precautions.
State Restrictions: For use in Arkansas, Colorado, Connecticut, Delaware, Illinois, Maine, Maryland, Massachusetts, Mississippi, New Hampshire, New Jersey, New York, North Carolina, Ohio, Oklahoma, Pennsylvania, South Carolina, western Tennessee, Texas, Vermont, Virginia.

- - - - - - - - - - - - - - -

Signal Word/Toxicity Class: Caution.
REI: 12 hr.

Rattler — see glyphosate

Roundup — see glyphosate

SCYTHE

◆ **Scythe (pelargonic acid)** *(Mycogen)*
   Rate: 4-13 fl. oz./1 gal. spray solution
   Time: Apply to actively growing weeds prior to crop emergence.
   Weeds: Annual and perennial broadleaf weeds and grasses.
   Remarks: Apply in minimum 75 gal. spray solution/A or spray-to-wet. Do not apply by air or through any type of irrigation system. Refer to label for directions and precautions.
   Tank Mixes: Glyphosate and other foliar and residual herbicides.

- - - - - - - - - - - - - - -

Signal Word/Toxicity Class: Warning/II.
REI: 24 hr.

SETHOXYDIM

Selective control of many annual and perennial grasses. Annual bluegrass will not be controlled. Do not tank mix with any other herbicide unless specified on label or reduced control may result.

■ POST
Poast (1.5EC) *(BASF)*
   Rate: 0.01-0.28 lb. ai/A
      0.5-1.5 pt. 1.5EC/A
   Time: Postemergence.
   Weeds: Annual and perennial grasses:

annual ryegrass	large crabgrass	stinkgrass
barnyardgrass	lovegrass	tall fescue
bermudagrass	orchardgrass	Texas panicum
broadleaf signalgrass	(seedling)	volunteer cereals
browntop panicum	perennial ryegrass	wild oat
fall panicum	quackgrass	wild proso millet
field sandbur	red sprangletop	wildcane
giant foxtail	shattercane	wirestem muhly
goosegrass	smooth crabgrass	witchgrass
green foxtail	southwestern	woolly cupgrass
johnsongrass	cupgrass	yellow foxtail
junglerice		

   Remarks: Rate varies by growing region. Always add 2 pt./A oil concentrate. Refer to label for restrictions and limitations.
   Days To Harvest: 15.
   State Restrictions: Do not use UAN or AMS in California or Pacific Northwest.

- - - - - - - - - - - - - - -

Signal Word/Toxicity Class: Warning/II.
REI: 12 hr.

SPIN-AID

Temporary stunting, yellowing, or tip burn may be observed after treatment. Use only when temperature will remain below 75°F for several days, and spray just before sunset, rather than early in the day to reduce the risk of crop injury.

■ POST
Spin-Aid (EC) (phenmedipham) *(AgrEvo USA)*
   Rate: Conventional:
      0.5-1 lb. ai/A
      3-6 pt. EC/A
      Split rate:
      0.4-0.5 lb. ai/A
      2.5-3 pt. EC/A
   Time: Postemergence. Conventional: Apply when spinach is past 4-6 true leaf stage and weeds are at 2-true leaf stage. Split rate: Apply at 2-leaf stage of spinach, repeat 4-6 days later with 3 pt./A.

Weeds: Broadleaf weeds:

annual sowthistle	common ragweed	purslane
coast fiddleneck	groundcherry	shepherdspurse
common chickweed	London rocket	wild mustard
common	nettleleaf goosefoot	
lambsquarters		

Remarks: Do not apply through any type of irrigation system.
Days To Harvest: 40.

- - - - - - - - - - - - - - -

Signal Word/Toxicity Class: Warning/II.
REI: 24 hr.

Sweet Corn

AAtrex — see atrazine

ALACHLOR

Preplant incorporate to improve yellow nutsedge suppression. Cultivate or rotary hoe if rainfall does not occur after preemergence application, unless irrigation is not available to activate herbicide before weeds emerge. Restricted Use Pesticide.

■ PPI, PRE
Lasso (4EC) or Micro-Tech *(Monsanto)*
Partner (WDG) *(Monsanto)*
   Rate: 2-4 lb. ai/A
      2-4 qt. 4EC, MT/A
      3-6 lb. WDG/A
   Time: Preplant incorporated or preemergence.
   Weeds: Broadleaf weeds:

black nightshade	Florida pusley	prickly sida*
carelessweed	galinsoga	purslane
carpetweed	hairy nightshade	sicklepod*
common ragweed*	lambsquarters*	smartweed*
cutleaf groundcherry	pigweed	teaweed*
Florida beggarweed*		

   Grasses and sedges:

barnyardgrass	johnsongrass*	wild proso millet*
broadleaf signalgrass	(seedling)	wildcane*
crabgrass	panicum	witchgrass
foxtail	sandbur*	woolly cupgrass*
goosegrass	shattercane*	yellow nutsedge

   Suppression
   Remarks: Effective under a wide range of soil and moisture conditions. Can be used with sprayable fluid fertilizers.

- - - - - - - - - - - - - - -

Signal Word/Toxicity Class:
Danger/I (Lasso); Caution/IV (Micro-Tech, Partner).
REI: 12 hr.

■ PRE
Lasso II (15G) *(Monsanto)*
   Rate: 2.4-3.9 lb. ai/A
      16-26 lb. 15G/A
   Time: Preemergence.
   Weeds: Broadleaf weeds:

black nightshade	Florida beggarweed	purslane
carelessweed	Florida pusley	smartweed
carpetweed	lambsquarters*	spiny sida
common ragweed	pigweed	teaweed

   Grasses and sedges:

barnyardgrass	goosegrass	sandbur
brachiaria	green foxtail	witchgrass
crabgrass	johnsongrass	yellow foxtail
fall panicum	(seedling)	yellow nutsedge
giant foxtail	red rice	

   Suppression
   Remarks: Effective under a wide range of soil and moisture conditions; can be used with sprayable fluid fertilizers.
   Tank Mixes: Atrazine, Bladex.

- - - - - - - - - - - - - - -

Signal Word/Toxicity Class: Warning/II.
REI: 12 hr.

Atra-5 — see atrazine

6

Vegetables

NOTICE	The information on these pages is for preliminary planning — not a guide for use. Be sure to follow the manufacturer's directions, notwithstanding information contained here.	For personal protective equipment and EPA registration numbers, please turn to page 70.

Sweet Corn

ATRAZINE

Use in combination with annual grass herbicide to increase spectrum of weeds controlled. Herbicide residues may limit crop alternatives after harvest. Soil texture, rainfall, herbicide rate, and other factors affect potential for herbicide carryover. Resistant weeds have been reported in locations where continuous corn has been grown and only atrazine or other triazine herbicides used. Same chemical family as Bladex. Restricted Use Pesticide due to ground and surface water concerns.

■ PP, PPI, PRE, POST

AAtrex 4L or AAtrex Nine-0 (WDG) *(Novartis)*
◆ Clean Crop Atrazine 4L or 90 WDG *(Platte)*
Drexel Atrazine 4L, Atra-5 (5L) or 90DF *(Drexel)*
Helena Atrazine 4L *(Helena)*
Riverside Atrazine 4L or 90DF *(Terra)*

Rate: Not highly erodible or at least 30% residue cover (conservation tillage):
   2 lb. ai/A
   4 pt. 4L/A
   3.2 pt. 5L/A
   2.2 lb. WDG, 90DF/A
Highly erodible with less than 30% residue cover:
   1.6 lb. ai/A
   3.2 pt. 4L/A
   2.4 pt. 5L/A
   1.8 lb. WDG, 90DF/A

Time: Preplant surface-applied: Apply up to 45 days prior to planting (coarse-textured soils, do not apply more than 2 weeks prior to planting). Preplant incorporated: Apply to soil and incorporate before, during, or after final seedbed preparation. For best results, apply within 2 weeks prior to planting. Preemergence: Apply during or shortly after planting but before weed emergence. Postemergence (with oil at 4 pt. rate): Apply before corn is 12" in height and before weeds reach 1¹/₂" in height.

Weeds: Annual broadleaf weeds:

annual morningglory	kochia	purslane
buttonweed	lambsquarters	ragweed
cocklebur	mustard	sicklepod
groundcherry	nightshade	velvetleaf
jimsonweed	pigweed	

Annual grasses:

barnyardgrass	watergrass	witchgrass
giant foxtail	wild oat	yellow foxtail
green foxtail		

Remarks: Rate varies by soil type and organic matter. Do not apply more than 2.5 lb. ai/A per year. Certain states may have established rate limitations; consult state lead pest control agency. Do not apply through any type of irrigation system. This product may not be mixed/loaded, or used within 50 ft. of all wells including abandoned wells, drainage wells, and sink holes. Do not graze treated area or feed treated forage to livestock for 21 days following application. Refer to labels for use directions, restrictions, and precautions.

Crop Rotation: Do not plant to any crop except corn or sorghum until the following year or injury may occur.

Tank Mixes: Alachlor, butylate, Dual, glyphosate, paraquat, simazine.

State Restrictions: Preplant surface-applied: Medium- and fine-textured soils with minimum-tillage or no-tillage systems only in Colorado, Illinois, Indiana, Iowa, Kansas, Kentucky, Minnesota, Missouri, Montana, Nebraska, North Dakota, South Dakota, Wisconsin, Wyoming.

- - - - - - - - - - - - - - -

Rate: 1.2 lb. ai/A
   2.4 pt. 4L/A
   1.9 pt. 5L/A
   1.3 lb. WDG, 90DF/A

Time: Postemergence. Apply before corn reaches 12" in height, before pigweed and lambsquarters reach 6" in height, and before all other weeds reach 4" in height.

Weeds: Broadleaf weeds:

annual morningglory	mustards	smartweed
cocklebur	pigweed	velvetleaf
jimsonweed	ragweed	wild buckwheat
lambsquarters		

Remarks: Add emulsifiable oil or oil concentrate. Do not apply more than 2.5 lb. ai/A per year. Certain states may have established rate limitations; consult state lead pest control agency for limitations. Do not apply through any type of irrigation system. This product may not be mixed/loaded, or used within 50 ft. of all wells including abandoned wells, drainage wells, and sink holes. Do not graze treated area or feed treated forage to livestock for 21 days following application.

Crop Rotation: Do not plant to any crop except corn or sorghum until the following year or injury may occur.

- - - - - - - - - - - - - - -

Signal Word/Toxicity Class: Caution/III.
REI: 12 hr.

Barrage — see 2,4-D

BASAGRAN

Use to control yellow nutsedge and common cocklebur, or when no plant-back restrictions are desirable.

■ POST

Basagran (bentazon) *(BASF)*

Rate: 0.75-1 lb. ai/A
   1.5-2 pt./A

Time: Early postemergence.

Weeds: Broadleaf weeds:

annual morningglory	dayflower	spurred anoda
beggarticks	galinsoga	teaweed
bristly starbur	giant ragweed	tropic croton
Canada thistle	jimsonweed	velvetleaf
cocklebur	ladysthumb	Venice mallow
common lambsquarters	Pennsylvania smartweed	wild buckwheat wild mustard
common ragweed	prickly sida	wild sunflower

Sedges:
yellow nutsedge (except CA)

Remarks: Rate depends on leaf stage and weed height. For improved control of velvetleaf, add urea ammonium nitrate solution to spray tank in place of oil concentrate. If common ragweed and lambsquarters are present in addition to velvetleaf, then oil concentrate should be used. Seed producers should consult seed company regarding tolerance of seed production inbred lines to Basagran. Do not apply more than 4 pt./A per season. Do not graze treated fields for at least 12 days after last treatment. Refer to label for specific directions.

Tank Mixes: Atrazine.

- - - - - - - - - - - - - - -

Signal Word/Toxicity Class: Caution/III.
REI: 12 hr.

BICEP (Premixes)

Combination of AAtrex & Dual offers broad-spectrum control of annual broadleaf and grass weeds with considerable flexibility in time and method of application, appropriate length of residual activity, reduced risk of carryover, and relatively good crop tolerance. Contains the safener benoxacor. Restricted Use Pesticide due to ground and surface water concerns.

■ PP, PPI, PRE, POST

Bicep II MAGNUM (3.1 lb./gal. atrazine & 2.4 lb./gal. S-metolachlor) *(Novartis)*

Bicep Lite II MAGNUM (2.67 lb./gal. atrazine & 3.33 lb./gal. S-metolachlor) *(Novartis)*

Rate: 2.9-3.6 lb. ai/A
   2.1-2.6 qt. II/A
   2.25-3.3 lb. ai/A
   1.5-2.2 qt. Lite II/A

Time: Early preplant. Apply up to 45 days before planting. Applications less than 30 days prior to planting may be split or single treatment; use split applications for treatments made 30-45 days before planting.

Rate: 3.6 lb. ai/A
   2.6 qt. II/A
   1.35-3.3 lb. ai/A
   0.9-2.2 qt. Lite II/A

Time: Preplant incorporated, preplant surface, preemergence.

Rate: 1.35-2.85 lb. ai/A
   0.9-1.9 qt. Lite II/A

Time: Postemergence-directed.

Weeds: Broadleaf weeds:

carpetweed	giant ragweed*	nightshade
chickweed	henbit	pigweed
cocklebur*	jimsonweed	sicklepod*
common purslane	lambsquarters	smartweed
common ragweed	morningglory*	velvetleaf*
Florida pusley	mustard	waterhemp
galinsoga		

◆-new product • PP-preplant • PPI-preplant incorporated • PRE-preemergence • POST-postemergence • SEQ-sequential • ae-acid equivalent • ai-active ingredient • DF-dry flowable
E/EC-emulsifiable concentrate • F/FL-flowable • DG/G/WG-dispersable granule • L/LC-liquid • SP/WSP-soluble packet • W/WP-wettable powder • WSB-water soluble bag

Grasses and sedges:

barnyardgrass	green foxtail	southwestern
crabgrass	johnsongrass	cupgrass
crowfootgrass	(seedling)*	volunteer sorghum*
fall panicum	prairie cupgrass	witchgrass
foxtail millet	sandbur*	woolly cupgrass*
giant foxtail	shattercane*	yellow foxtail
goosegrass	signalgrass*	yellow nutsedge

* Suppression

Rate: 2.2-3.6 lb. ai/A
      1.6-2.6 qt. II/A
      1.65-2.85 lb. ai/A
      1.1-1.9 qt. Lite II/A

Time: Postemergence-broadcast. Apply before grass and broadleaf weeds pass 2-leaf stage and before corn exceeds 5" in height.

Weeds: Broadleaf weeds:

cocklebur	kochia	prickly sida
common ragweed	lambsquarters	purslane
crabgrass	morningglory	smartweed
flixweed	mustard	velvetleaf
jimsonweed	pigweed	waterhemp

Grasses and sedges:

crabgrass	giant foxtail	yellow foxtail
crowfootgrass	green foxtail	yellow nutsedge
fall panicum		(suppression)

Remarks: Rate varies by soil type and organic matter. Certain states may have established rate limitations regarding atrazine; consult state lead pest control agency for additional information. Do not apply through any type of irrigation system. Refer to label for use directions, restrictions, and precautions.

Days To Harvest: Grazing/feeding—30.

Crop Rotation: Corn, cotton, peanuts, sorghum, or soybeans can be planted the spring following treatment. Injury may occur to soybeans planted the year following application on soils having a calcareous surface layer. If applied after June 10, do not rotate with crops other than corn or sorghum the next year. In eastern Dakotas, Kansas, western Minnesota and Nebraska, do not rotate to soybeans for 18 months following application if more than 2 lb. ai atrazine was applied. In High Plains and Intermountain Area of the West where rainfall is sparse and erratic or where irrigation is required, use only when corn or sorghum is to be planted the following year, or a crop of untreated corn or sorghum is to precede other rotational crops. Do not plant sugar beets, tobacco, vegetables, spring-seeded small grains, or small-seeded legumes the year following application. All other crops may be planted 15 months after application.

State Restrictions: Do not use in Nassau County or Suffolk County, New York. Bicep—early preplant: Minimum-tillage or no-tillage systems with medium- and fine-textured soils in Colorado, Delaware, Illinois, Iowa, Indiana, Kansas, Kentucky, Maryland, Michigan, Minnesota, Missouri, Montana, Nebraska, North Dakota, New York, Ohio, Pennsylvania, South Dakota, Tennessee, Virginia, West Virginia, Wisconsin, Wyoming.

- – – – – – – – – – – – – –

Signal Word/Toxicity Class: Caution/III.
REI: 24 hr.

Bladex — see cyanazine

BULLET (Premix)

Combination Micro-Tech formulation with atrazine and same active ingredient as Lasso for broad-spectrum preemergence weed control. Restricted Use Pesticide.

■ PPI, PRE, POST

Bullet (2.5 lb./gal. alachlor & 1.5 lb./gal. atrazine) *(Monsanto)*

Rate: 2.5-4.5 lb. ai/A
      2.5-4.5 qt./A

Time: Preplant incorporated, preemergence, postemergence. Preplant incorporated: Apply within 7 days prior to planting. Preemergence surface: Apply after planting, before crop and weeds emerge within 5 days after last preplant tillage operation. Do not apply postemergence on sweet corn.

Weeds: Broadleaf weeds:

annual groundcherry	Florida beggarweed	mustard
annual morningglory	Florida pusley	pigweed
black nightshade	galinsoga	prickly sida
buttonweed	hairy nightshade	purslane
carelessweed	jimsonweed	sicklepod*
carpetweed	horseweed	smartweed
common cocklebur	kochia	teaweed
common ragweed	lambsquarters	velvetleaf
cutleaf groundcherry		

Grasses and sedges:

barnyardgrass	grassbur	shattercane*
broadleaf signalgrass	green foxtail	volunteer sorghum*
browntop panicum	johnsongrass*	waterhemp
crabgrass	(seedling)	wildcane*
fall panicum	red rice*	witchgrass
giant foxtail	red sprangletop	yellow foxtail
goosegrass	sandbur	yellow nutsedge

* Reduced competition

Remarks: Rate varies by soil type. Do not make more than one application per year or exceed 6.4 qt. product/year. Do not apply more than 2.5 lb. ai atrazine/year; refer to label for atrazine restrictions. Do not graze treated area or feed treated forage to livestock for 21 days after application.

Crop Rotation: Plant only corn, peanuts, sorghum (milo), or soybeans the year after application. If soybeans are to be planted, there is a possibility of crop injury due to carryover of atrazine. Do not plant soybeans where furrow irrigation is practiced.

Tank Mixes: Atrazine, Bladex, Gramoxone Extra, Lasso, linuron, Prowl, and simazine. Refer to labels for use directions and precautions.

- – – – – – – – – – – – – –

Signal Word/Toxicity Class: Caution/III.
REI: 12 hr.

Credit — see glyphosate

CYANAZINE

Cyanazine registrations are cancelled as of January 1, 2000. Sale and distribution of existing stock may continue through September 30, 2002, and all use is prohibited after December 31, 2002. Restricted Use Pesticide.

■ PP, PRE

Bladex 4L or 90DF *(DuPont)*

Cy-Pro 4L *(Griffin)*

Rate: Refer to label for rate limits. Do not apply more than 3 lb. ai/A per year. Enclosed cab required for application.

Time: Preplant incorporated, preemergence. Conservation tillage (30 days before planting until emergence): Complete any planned early spring tillage prior to application. Do not apply postemergence.

Weeds: Broadleaf weeds:

annual buttercup	curly dock (seedling)	prickly sida
annual groundcherry	fiddleneck	prostrate knotweed
annual morningglory	Florida purslane	prostrate spurge
annual nightshade	Florida pusley	ragweed
annual sedge	hedge mustard	Russian thistle
annual sunflower	jimsonweed	shepherdspurse
black mustard	kochia	smallflower galinsoga
buffalobur	ladysthumb	tarweed cuphea
carpetweed	mayweed	teaweed
cocklebur	Pennsylvania	velvetleaf
common chickweed	smartweed	wild buckwheat
common groundsel	pigweed	wild mustard
common mallow	pineappleweed	wild radish
common purslane	plantain	wild sunflower
common sunflower	poorjoe	wild turnip
corn spurry		

Grasses:

annual bluegrass	fall panicum	Italian ryegrass
annual fescues	giant foxtail	junglerice
annual ryegrass	goosegrass	stinkgrass
barnyardgrass	green foxtail	witchgrass
bullgrass	Indian lovegrass	yellow foxtail
crabgrass		

Remarks: Do not apply preemergence on peat or muck soils. Do not use on sands or loamy sands containing less than 1% organic matter. Do not apply by air or through any type of irrigation system. This product may not be mixed, loaded, or used within 50 ft. of all wells including abandoned wells, drainage wells, and sink holes. Certain states may have additional requirements and limitations; consult state lead pest control agency.

Crop Rotation: If crop is lost due to adverse weather, etc., field can be replanted to corn or sorghum. If replanted to sorghum, allow at least 30-day interval between application and planting. Any rotational crop may be planted the fall or spring following treatment.

Tank Mixes: Alachlor, atrazine, Banvel, Eradicane, Gramoxone Extra, and Sutan+.

- – – – – – – – – – – – – –

Signal Word/Toxicity Class: Warning/II.
REI: 12 hr.

6

Vegetables

For personal protective equipment and EPA registration numbers, please turn to page 70.

CYANAZINE & ATRAZINE (Premix)

Cyanazine registrations are cancelled as of January 1, 2000. Sale and distribution of existing stock may continue through September 30, 2002, and all use is prohibited after December 31, 2002. Restricted Use Pesticide.

■ PP, PRE

Extrazine II (4L: 3 lb. cyanazine & 1 lb. atrazine; DF: 67.5% cyanazine & 21.4% atrazine) *(DuPont)*

Rate: Refer to label for rate limits. Do not apply more than 3 lb. ai/A per year. Enclosed cab required for application.

Time: Conservation tillage—preemergence (30 days before planting until emergence): Complete any planned early spring tillage prior to application. Conventional tillage—preplant incorporated, preemergence: Apply just before, at, or after planting but before crop emergence. Do not apply postemergence. Do not apply preemergence on peat or muck soils.

Weeds: Broadleaf weeds:

annual buttercup	curly dock (seedling)	prickly sida
annual groundcherry	fiddleneck	prostrate knotweed
annual morningglory	Florida purslane	prostrate spurge
annual nightshade	Florida pusley	ragweed
annual sedge	hedge mustard	Russian thistle
annual sunflower	jimsonweed	shepherdspurse
black mustard	kochia	smallflower galinsoga
buffalobur	ladysthumb	spiny sida
carpetweed	lambsquarters	tarweed cuphea
cocklebur	mayweed	teaweed
common chickweed	Pennsylvania	velvetleaf
common groundsel	smartweed	wild buckwheat
common mallow	pigweed	wild mustard
common purslane	pineappleweed	wild radish
common sunflower	plantain	wild sunflower
corn spurry	poorjoe	wild turnip

Grasses:

annual bluegrass	fall panicum	Italian ryegrass
annual fescues	giant foxtail	junglerice
annual ryegrass	goosegrass	stinkgrass
barnyardgrass	green foxtail	witchgrass
bullgrass	Indian lovegrass	yellow foxtail
crabgrass		

Plus following weeds if 2,4-D LVE is added in tank mix:

buckwheat	marestail	prickly lettuce
dandelion	pennycress	tansymustard
dock		

Remarks: Do not use on sands or loamy sands containing less than 1% organic matter. Do not apply by air. If broadleaf weeds exceed 3" in height, add 2,4-D LVE plus surfactant; if grass weeds exceed 3" in height, add paraquat or Roundup Ultra. May not be mixed, loaded, or used within 50 ft. of all wells including abandoned wells, drainage wells, and sink holes. Certain states may have additional requirements and limitations; consult state lead pest control agency.

Crop Rotation: If crop is lost due to adverse weather, etc., field can be replanted to corn or sorghum. If replanted to sorghum, allow at least 30-day interval between application and planting. Plant only corn, sorghum, or soybeans the year following use of this mixture. If soybeans are to be planted, injury may occur due to atrazine carryover. If applied after June 10, do not rotate with crops other than corn or sorghum the next year or injury may occur. In the High Plains and Intermountain Areas of the West where rainfall is sparse and erratic or where irrigation is required, use only when corn or sorghum is to be planted the following year, or corn or sorghum not treated with this mixture or atrazine is to precede other rotational crops. Small grains may be planted 15 months after application; all other crops 18 months after application.

Tank Mixes: Alachlor, atrazine, 2,4-D, Eradicane, Frontier, Harness Plus, paraquat, Roundup, Surpass, and Sutan+.

– – – – – – – – – – – – – – –

Signal Word/Toxicity Class: Warning/II.
REI: 12 hr.

Cy-Pro — see cyanazine

2,4-D - PHENOXY HERBICIDES

2,4-D and 2,4-D-type compounds selectively control broadleaf weeds with little or no control of grasses. Corn is a grass, but can be injured by 2,4-D. Sweet corn varieties may differ in tolerance. Use caution when treating new varieties. 2,4-D drift can injure adjacent crops either by spray drift or by volatilization (spray turns into a vapor). Ester formulations are most volatile, amines least volatile. Ester formulations can vaporize at temperatures as low as 70°F and can be moved by wind to harm sensitive plants. Vaporization increases as air temperatures rise.

Annual and perennial broadleaf weeds controlled by 2,4-D include:

beggarticks	galinsoga	povertyweed
bindweed	goldenrod	puncturevine
bitterweed	ground ivy	purslane
broomweed	healall	ragweed
bull thistle	hoary cress	Russian thistle
burdock	ironweed	shepherdspurse
Canada thistle	jimsonweed	smartweed
carpetweed	knotweed	sowthistle
catnip	lambsquarters	stinkweed
chickweed	mallow	sumac
chicory	marshelder	sunflower
cocklebur	mexicanweed	sweetclover
coffeeweed	morningglory	velvetleaf
cutleaf	musk thistle	Virginia creeper
eveningprimrose	mustard	wild carrot
creeping jenny	pennywort	wild garlic
croton	pepperweed	wild lettuce
dandelion	pigweed	wild onion
dock	plantain	wild parsnips
dogbane	pokeweed	wild radish

■ PP, PRE, POST

Albaugh Amine 4 (2,4-D amine) *(Albaugh)*
Albaugh LV4 or LV6 Ester (2,4-D ester) *(Albaugh)*
♦ Opti-Amine (4) (2,4-D amine) *(Helena)*
Riverdale 6 Amine (2,4-D amine) *(Riverdale)*
Riverdale L.V. 4 or L.V. 6 (2,4-D ester) *(Riverdale)*
Weed Rhap A-4D (2,4-D amine) *(Helena)*
Weed Rhap LV-6D (2,4-D ester) *(Helena)*
Weedestroy AM-40 (2,4-D amine) *(Riverdale)*
Wilbur-Ellis Amine 4 (2,4-D amine) *(Wilbur-Ellis)*
Wilbur-Ellis Lo Vol-4 or Lo Vol-6 (2,4-D ester) *(Wilbur-Ellis)*

Rate: 0.25-2 lb. ae/A
0.5-4 pt. 4/A
0.33-2.33 pt. 6/A

Time: Preplant, preemergence, emergence, preharvest, postemergence. For preplant, apply 7-14 days before planting. For preemergence, apply after planting but before corn emerges. For emergence, apply just as corn plants are breaking ground. For preharvest, apply after hard dough or denting stage. For postemergence, apply when most weeds have germinated and before corn is 8" tall. When corn is over 8" or beyond 5-leaf stage, use drop nozzles to keep spray off foliage. Do not spray corn in tassel to dough stage.

Remarks: Sweet corn. Tolerance to 2,4-D varies; consult seed company, Agricultural Experiment Station, or Extension Service weed specialist.

State Restrictions: Wilbur-Ellis not registered in California.

– – – – – – – – – – – – – – –

Signal Word/Toxicity Class: Danger/I (amine); Caution/III (ester).
REI: Danger—48 hr.; Caution—12 hr.

■ PP, PRE, POST

♦ Barrage or Barrage HF (EC) (2,4-D ester) *(Helena)*

Rate: 3-26 fl. oz./A

Time: Preplant, preemergence, postemergence, preharvest. For preplant, apply 7-14 days before planting. For preemergence, apply after planting but before corn emerges. For early postemergence, apply up to 8" tall. For late postemergence, apply from 8-36"; use drop nozzles and direct spray from corn plant. Do not apply from tasseling to dough stage. For preharvest, apply after hard dough or denting stage.

Remarks: Rate varies by soil type and organic matter. Tolerance to 2,4-D varies, consult local Agricultural Extension Service. Do not forage or feed corn fodder to livestock for 7 days following application.

Crop Rotation: Refer to labels.

– – – – – – – – – – – – – – –

Signal Word/Toxicity Class: Caution/III.
REI: 12 hr.

■ PRE, POST

Formula 40 (2,4-D mixed amine) *(Rhone-Poulenc)*

Rate: 0.25-2 lb. ae/A
0.5-4 pt./A

Time: Preemergence, emergence, postemergence, preharvest. For preemergence, apply after planting but before corn emerges. Do not use on very light, sandy soil. For emergence, apply just as corn emerges (breaking ground). For postemergence, apply up to 8" tall; use drop nozzles and direct spray from corn plant if more than 8" tall. Do not apply from tasseling to dough stage. For preharvest, apply after hard dough or denting stage.

– – – – – – – – – – – – – – –

♦-new product • PP-preplant • PPI-preplant incorporated • PRE-preemergence • POST-postemergence • SEQ-sequential • ae-acid equivalent • ai-active ingredient • DF-dry flowable E/EC-emulsifiable concentrate • F/FL-flowable • DG/G/WG-dispersable granule • L/LC-liquid • SP/WSP-soluble packet • W/WP-wettable powder • WSB-water soluble bag

Remarks: Temporary crop injury may occur under conditions of high soil moisture and high air temperatures; use lower rates. Tolerance to 2,4-D varies, consult seed company or Agricultural Extension Service Weed Specialist. Do not forage or feed corn fodder to livestock for 7 days following application.

- - - - - - - - - - - - - - -

Signal Word/Toxicity Class: Danger/I.
REI: 48 hr.

■ PRE
◆ Riverdale 2,4-D Granules (2,4-D ester) *(Riverdale)*
Rate: Band/row:
  0.7 lb. ae/A
  3.5 lb./A
  Broadcast:
  2 lb. ae/A
  10 lb./A
Time: Preemergence. Apply from time of planting up to 2 days before seedlings emerge. Plant corn at least 2" deep.
Remarks: Do not use on light, sandy soils.
State Restrictions: For use in the Midwestern Corn Belt.

- - - - - - - - - - - - - - -

Signal Word/Toxicity Class: Caution.
REI: 12 hr.

■ PP, PRE, POST
◆ Saber (2,4-D amine) *(Platte)*
Rate: 0.25-0.75 lb. ae/A
  0.5-1.5 pt./A
Time: Preplant, preemergence, postemergence, preharvest. For preplant, apply 7-14 days before planting. For preemergence, apply after planting but before corn emerges. For postemergence, apply from spike to 4-leaf stage, or up to 8" tall. When corn is over 8" use drop nozzles to keep spray off foliage. Do not apply from 7-10 days before tasseling to dough stage. For preharvest, apply after hard dough or denting stage.
Remarks: Sweet corn. Tolerance to 2,4-D varies; consult seed company, Agricultural Experiment Station, or Extension Service weed specialist. Do not feed corn fodder for 7 days after treatment.

- - - - - - - - - - - - - - -

Signal Word/Toxicity Class: Danger/I.
REI: 48 hr.

■ PP, PRE, POST
Savage (WSB) (2,4-D amine) *(Platte)*
Rate: 0.24-1.4 lb. ae/A
  0.25-1.5 lb. WSB/A
Time: Preplant, preemergence, postemergence, preharvest. For preplant, apply 7-14 days before planting. For preemergence, apply after planting but before corn emerges. For postemergence, apply when corn is less than 8" tall. When corn is over 8", use drop nozzles to keep spray off foliage. Do not apply from 7-10 days before tasseling to dough stage. For preharvest, apply after hard dough or denting stage.
Remarks: Sweet corn. Use lower rate when crop is rapidly growing under high temperature and high soil moisture conditions. Do not cultivate soon after spraying while plants are brittle. Tolerance to 2,4-D varies, consult local Agricultural Extension Service. Do not forage or feed corn fodder for 7 days following application. Refer to label for use directions, restrictions, and precautions.

- - - - - - - - - - - - - - -

Signal Word/Toxicity Class: Danger/I.
REI: 48 hr.

■ PP, PRE, POST
Weedar 64 (4) (2,4-D amine) *(Nufarm)*
Rate: 0.25-1.5 lb. ae/A
  0.5-3 pt. 4/A
Time: Preplant, preemergence, postemergence. For preplant, apply 7-14 days before planting. For preemergence, apply from 3-5 days after planting but before corn emerges. For postemergence, apply when weeds are small and corn is less than 8" tall. When corn is over 8" tall, use drop nozzles and keep spray off foliage. Treat perennial weeds in bud to bloom stage. Do not spray corn in tassel to bloom stage.
Remarks: For preemergence application, do not use on light, sandy soils or where moisture is low. Do not forage or feed fodder for 7 days following application.

- - - - - - - - - - - - - - -

Signal Word/Toxicity Class: Danger/I.
REI: 48 hr.

DIMETHENAMID & ATRAZINE
(Premixes)

Not for use on sweet corn grown for seed. Restricted Use Pesticide due to ground and surface water concerns.

■ PP, PPI, PRE, POST
Guardsman (2.33 lb./gal. dimethenamid & 2.67 lb./gal. atrazine) *(BASF)*
◆ Leadoff (2.33 lb./gal. dimethenamid & 2.67 lb./gal. atrazine) *(DuPont)*
Rate: 1.6-3.2 lb. ai/A
  2.5-5 pt./A
Time: Preplant incorporated, preplant surface, preemergence or early postemergence (up to 8" tall).
Weeds: Broadleaf weeds:

annual morningglory	Florida pusley	prostrate pigweed
black nightshade	giant ragweed	redroot pigweed
carpetweed	hairy nightshade	smartweed
cocklebur	jimsonweed	smooth pigweed
common purslane	kochia	spotted spurge
common ragweed	lambsquarters	tumble pigweed
eastern black	mustard	velvetleaf
nightshade	nodding spurge	waterhemp
eclipta*	Palmer amaranth	wild buckwheat

Grasses and sedges:

barnyardgrass	large crabgrass	Texas Panicum*
broadleaf signalgrass	red rice	wild oat
fall panicum	rice flatsedge	wild proso millet*
giant foxtail	sandbur*	witchgrass
goosegrass	shattercane*	woolly cupgrass*
green foxtail	smooth crabgrass	yellow foxtail
johnsongrass	southwestern	yellow nutsedge
(seedling)	cupgrass	

* *Suppression*

Remarks: Rates vary by soil type. Some weed species may have triazine-resistant biotypes that will not be controlled adequately by this product. If resistant biotypes are suspected, use an alternate program or use non-triazine products in combination or sequentially. Do not exceed 5 pt./A in one crop year on any soil. Do not apply through any type of irrigation system.
Days To Harvest: Harvest—50; grazing/feeding—40.
Crop Rotation: In case of crop failure, corn or sorghum can be planted anytime. Corn, cotton, peanuts, sorghum, or soybeans may be planted the year after application. Injury may occur to soybeans planted on soils having a calcareous surface layer. Do not plant dry beans, sugar beets, tobacco, vegetables, spring-seeded small grains, or small-seeded legumes and grasses the year following application.
Tank Mixes: Accent, atrazine, Basagran, Beacon, Bladex, Celebrity, 2,4-D, dicamba, Frontier, Gramoxone Extra, Laddok S-12, Marksman, Princep, Prowl, Pursuit, Roundup Ultra; refer to labels for use directions.
State Restrictions: Not for use in Long Island, New York.

- - - - - - - - - - - - - - -

Signal Word/Toxicity Class: Warning/II.
REI: 12 hr.

Dual — see *S*-metolachlor

EPTC

Eradicane belongs to the thiocarbamate family. Contains crop safening agent. Crop injury is unlikely but may occur when growing conditions are unfavorable or with certain hybrids. For residual control, apply close to planting and incorporate immediately to prevent loss by volatilization.

■ PPI
Eradicane 6.7-E or 25-G *(ZENECA)*
Rate: 4-6 lb. ai/A
  4.75-7.33 pt. 6.7-E/A
  16-24 lb. 25-G/A
Time: Preplant incorporated.
Weeds: Broadleaf weeds:

black nightshade*	deadnettle	puncturevine
carpetweed	(henbit)	(western region)
common chickweed	fall morningglory	redroot pigweed
common	fiddleneck	shepherdspurse
lambsquarters	Florida pusley	sicklepod
common purslane	hairy nightshade	teaweed (spiny sida)
corn spurry	prostrate pigweed	tumble pigweed

6
Vegetables

Sweet Corn

Grasses and sedges:

annual bluegrass	Italian ryegrass	Texas panicum
annual ryegrass	johnsongrass	volunteer grains
barnyardgrass	(rhizome*, seedling)	wild oat
bermudagrass	lovegrass (stinkgrass)	wild proso millet*
crabgrass	purple nutsedge	(central region)
fall panicum	quackgrass*	woolly cupgrass
field sandbur	rescuegrass	yellow foxtail
giant foxtail	signalgrass	yellow nutsedge
green foxtail	(southeast)	

*** Suppression**

Remarks: Refer to label for regional differences and specific rates for weed suppression/control.

- - - - - - - - - - - - - - - -

Signal Word/Toxicity Class: Caution.
REI: 12 hr. unless soil injected or soil incorporated.

EVIK

Controls many seedling annual grass and broadleaf weeds up to 2-4" tall postemergence. Use drop nozzles. Do not wet corn foliage or spray into whorl or corn injury will occur.

■ **POST**

Evik DF (ametryn) *(Novartis)*

Rate: 0.6-2 lb. ai/A
0.75-2.5 lb. DF/A

Time: Postemergence. Apply as directed spray to weeds after smallest corn plants are at least 12" tall. Do not apply within 3 weeks of tasseling.

Weeds: Broadleaf weeds:

cocklebur	pigweed	velvetleaf
Florida pusley	ragweed	wild mustard
lambsquarters	smartweed	
morningglory		

Grasses and sedges:

barnyardgrass	goosegrass	signalgrass
crabgrass	green foxtail	Texas panicum
fall panicum	nutsedge	wild proso millet
giant foxtail	shattercane	yellow foxtail

Remarks: Add surfactant. Do not spray over top of corn.
Days To Harvest: Harvest/grazing/feeding—30.
Crop Rotation: Do not plant to any rotation crop except small grains until the following year.

- - - - - - - - - - - - - - -

Signal Word/Toxicity Class: Caution.
REI: 12 hr.

Eradicane — see EPTC

Extrazine II — see cyanazine & atrazine

Formula 40 — see 2,4-D

FRONTIER

■ **PP, PPI, PRE, POST**

Frontier 6.0 (dimethenamid) *(BASF)*

Rate: 0.94-1.5 lb. ai/A
20-32 fl. oz. 6.0/A

Time: Preplant (surface or incorporated) in minimum or no-tillage systems; preemergence (surface); early postemergence (corn up to 8" tall); split application.

Weeds: Broadleaf weeds:

carpetweed	nightshade	spurge
common purslane	pigweed	waterhemp
Florida pusley		

Grasses and sedges:

barnyardgrass	green foxtail	smooth crabgrass
broadleaf signalgrass	johnsongrass	southwestern
fall panicum	(seedling)	cupgrass
giant foxtail	large crabgrass	yellow foxtail
goosegrass	rice flatsedge	yellow nutsedge

Remarks: Rate varies by soil type and organic matter. Check with seed corn or sweet corn company for selectivity prior to use. Do not apply through any type of irrigation system. Corn may be grazed or fed to livestock at 40 days following application.

Crop Rotation: If crop is lost, field may be replanted to any labeled crop immediately. Fall-seeded cereal crop may be planted 4 months after spring application. No restrictions in the spring following previous year's application.

Tank Mixes: Accent, atrazine, Banvel, Basagran, Beacon, Bladex, Celebrity, Clarity, 2,4-D, Eradicane, Extrazine II, Gramoxone Extra, Laddok S-12, Liberty, Marksman, Princep, Prowl, Pursuit, Roundup Ultra, Touchdown.

- - - - - - - - - - - - - - - -

Signal Word/Toxicity Class: Warning/II.
REI: 12 hr.

Glyfos or Glyfos X-tra — see glyphosate

GLYPHOSATE

Nonselective control of annual and perennial grasses and broadleaf weeds in stale seedbeds and reduced-tillage planting systems.

■ **PP, PRE**

◆ **Credit (4WS)** *(Nufarm)*
◆ **Glyfos or Glyfos X-tra (4WS)** *(Cheminova)*
Rattler (4WS) *(Helena)*
Roundup Custom (5.4WS) *(Monsanto)*
Roundup Original, Original RT, Ultra, Ultra RT (4WS) *(Monsanto)*

Rate: Annual weeds:
0.38-1.5 lb. ai/A
0.56-2.25 pt. 5.4WS/A
0.75-3 pt. 4WS/A
Perennial weeds:
0.5-5 lb. ai/A
0.75-7.5 pt. 5.4WS/A
1-10 pt. 4WS/A

Time: Preplant, preemergence, at-planting, spot treatment, postharvest. For spot treatment, apply prior to silking of corn.

Weeds: Broadleaf weeds:

alfalfa	fanweed	redroot pigweed
alligatorweed	field bindweed	shepherdspurse
barley	field pennycress	sicklepod
blue mustard	filaree	silverleaf nightshade
brackenfern	Florida pusley	smallseed falseflax
buttercup	jagged chickweed	smooth pigweed
Canada thistle	hemp dogbane	spanishneedles
Carolina geranium	horsenettle	swamp smartweed
cocklebur	horseradish	tansymustard
common groundsel	horseweed	teaweed
common	Jerusalem artichoke	Texas blueweed
lambsquarters	knapweed	timothy
common mullein	lantana	tumble mustard
common ragweed	London rocket	velvetleaf
curly dock	marestail	volunteer corn
cutleaf	milkweed	volunteer wheat
eveningprimrose	morningglory	white clover
dandelion	mouseear chickweed	wild mustard
dwarfdandelion	red clover	woollyleaf bursage

Grasses and sedges:

annual bluegrass	fescue	reed canarygrass
bahiagrass	field sandbur	shattercane
barnyardgrass	foxtail	smooth bromegrass
bermudagrass	goosegrass	stinkgrass
broadleaf signalgrass	guineagrass	tall fescue
bulbous bluegrass	Italian ryegrass	Texas panicum
Carolina foxtail	johnsongrass	torpedograss
cheat	napiergrass	vaseygrass
common ryegrass	orchardgrass	western wheatgrass
crabgrass	paragrass	wild oat
dallisgrass	perennial ryegrass	wirestem muhly
downy brome	purple nutsedge	witchgrass
fall panicum	quackgrass	yellow nutsedge

Remarks: Sweet corn. Rate varies by weed species. Use higher rate for large weeds which were growing in crop at harvest. Do not add surfactant to Roundup Ultra or Ultra RT. Do not allow glyphosate to contact desirable plants. Do not apply through any type of irrigation system. Refer to label for precautions and restrictions.

Days To Harvest: Harvest/feeding—8 weeks.

Tank Mixes: Alachlor, atrazine, Bladex, Bullet, 2,4-D, dicamba (not for use in California), Extrazine II, Guardsman, Lariat, Lorox, Marksman, Princep, Prowl, Surpass, Surpass 100, TopNotch. Roundup tank mixes not registered in California.

State Restrictions: Roundup RT for use in Colorado, Idaho, Montana, North Dakota, South Dakota, Utah, Wyoming and in specific counties only in Kansas, Minnesota, Nebraska, Nevada, Oklahoma, Oregon, and Washington; refer to label for restrictions. Glyfos not registered for use in California. Glyfos X-tra not registered for use in mistblowers in California or Arizona.

- - - - - - - - - - - - - - -

Signal Word/Toxicity Class: Varies by formulation.
REI: Warning—12 hr.; Caution—4 hr.

◆-new product • PP-preplant • PPI-preplant incorporated • PRE-preemergence • POST-postemergence • SEQ-sequential • ae-acid equivalent • ai-active ingredient • DF-dry flowable
E/EC-emulsifiable concentrate • F/FL-flowable • DG/G/WG-dispersable granule • L/LC-liquid • SP/WSP-soluble packet • W/WP-wettable powder • WSB-water soluble bag

■ PRE
Ranger (WS) *(Monsanto)*
Rate: 0.25-0.5 lb. ai/A
0.75-1.5 pt. WS/A
Time: Preemergence. Apply to vigorously growing weeds.
Weeds: Broadleaf weeds:

blue mustard	field pennycress	shepherdspurse
buttercup	horseweed	smallseed falseflax
cocklebur	London rocket	smooth pigweed
common groundsel	marestail	tansymustard
common	morningglory	tumble mustard
lambsquarters	mouseear chickweed	umbrella spurry
dwarfdandelion	redroot pigweed	wild mustard
fanweed		

Grasses:

annual bluegrass	downy brome	stinkgrass
barnyardgrass	fall panicum	Texas panicum
bulbous bluegrass	field sandbur	wild oat
cheat	Italian ryegrass	witchgrass
crabgrass	shattercane	

Remarks: Do not apply through any type of irrigation system. Do not feed or forage vegetation from treated areas within 8 weeks after application.

- - - - - - - - - - - - - -

Rate: 1-2 lb. ai/A
3-6 pt. WS/A
Time: Preemergence. Apply to vigorously growing weeds.
Weeds: Grasses:

quackgrass	tall fescue	wirestem muhly

Remarks: For quackgrass control in the fall, do not till between harvest and application; in the spring, do not till in the fall or spring prior to application. Tillage operation following application may give improved quackgrass control (allow 3 or more days after application before tillage). Do not apply through any type of irrigation system. Do not feed or forage vegetation from treated areas within 8 weeks after application.

- - - - - - - - - - - - - -

Signal Word/Toxicity Class: Danger/I.
REI: 12 hr.

Gramoxone Extra — see paraquat

Guardsman — see dimethenamid & atrazine

LADDOK S-12 (Premix)

Premix containing bentazon and atrazine. Restricted Use Pesticide due to groundwater concerns.

■ POST
Laddok S-12 (5L) (2.5 lb./gal. bentazon & 2.5 lb./gal. atrazine) *(BASF)*
Rate: 0.83-1.45 lb. ai/A
1.33-2.33 pt. 5L/A
Time: Early postemergence.
Weeds: Broadleaf weeds:

annual morningglory	giant ragweed	smooth pigweed
beggarticks	jimsonweed	spurred anoda
bristly starbur	kochia	tall waterhemp
Canada thistle*	ladysthumb	teaweed
cocklebur	Pennsylvania	velvetleaf
common	smartweed	Venice mallow
lambsquarters	prickly sida	wild buckwheat
common ragweed	redroot pigweed	wild mustard
common waterhemp	smallflower	wild sunflower
dayflower	morningglory	
field bindweed*		

Sedges:

yellow nutsedge*

* Refer to label for special directions

Remarks: Rate depends on leaf stage and weed height. Urea-ammonium nitrate (UAN) solution may be added in place of oil concentrate for control of above annuals. If UAN solution is not used, oil concentrate should be added to spray tank. Oil concentrate should be used if perennials, yellow nutsedge, Canada thistle, or field bindweed are present. Do not graze treated area or feed treated forage to livestock for 21 days following application.

Crop Rotation: Do not plant sugar beets or sunflowers the season following application. Do not plant oats the season following application in soils with a calcareous surface layer. Intermountain Area: plant only corn or sorghum the year following application.

Tank Mixes: Asana XL, atrazine, Banvel, Bladex, Clarity, 2,4-D, dimethoate, Furadan, Lorsban, malathion, Poast, Poast Plus, Pounce, Stinger; refer to labels for use directions.
State Restrictions: Not for use in California.

- - - - - - - - - - - - - -

Signal Word/Toxicity Class: Danger/I.
REI: 48 hr.

Lasso — see alachlor

Leadoff — see dimethenamid & atrazine

LINURON

Do not wet corn foliage or spray into whorl or corn injury will occur. Use drop nozzles and shields to minimize crop damage.

■ POST
Lorox DF *(Griffin)*
Rate: 0.63-1.5 lb. ai/A
1.25-3 lb. DF/A
Time: Postemergence. Make single application after corn is 15" high.
Weeds: Broadleaf weeds:

amsinckia	Florida purslane	purslane
(fiddleneck)	groundsel	sesbania
annual morningglory	knawel	sicklepod
carpetweed	lambsquarters	smartweed
cocklebur	mustard	teaweed
common dayflower	nettleleaf goosefoot	velvetleaf
dogfennel	pigweed	(buttonweed)
Florida beggarweed	prickly sida	wild buckwheat

Grasses:

annual ryegrass	canarygrass	giant foxtail
barnyardgrass	crabgrass	goosegrass
(watergrass)	fall panicum	rattail fescue
broadleaf signalgrass	foxtail	Texas panicum

Remarks: Add 1 pt. surfactant/25 gal. spray mixture. Do not spray over top of corn. Apply only when there is sufficient differential between height of corn and weeds. Early cultivation aids in achieving proper differential between height of corn and weeds.

Crop Rotation: Any crop after 4 months except for cereals where only barley, oats, rye, and wheat may be planted. West of the Rockies: carrots or celery may be planted after 4 months. Do not plant any other crop until 1 year after last application.

- - - - - - - - - - - - - -

Signal Word/Toxicity Class: Caution.
REI: 24 hr.

Lorox — see linuron

S-METOLACHLOR

Dual is a cell growth inhibitor. S-metolachlor is a purified isomer of the metolachlor molecule. Primarily for control of annual grasses and helps control yellow nutsedge. Atrazine or Bladex frequently added for improved broadleaf weed control. Same chemical family as Lasso.

■ PP, PPI, PRE, POST
Dual MAGNUM or Dual II MAGNUM (EC) *(Novartis)*
Dual IIG MAGNUM *(Novartis)*
Rate: 1-2 pt. EC/A
6-12 lb. IIG/A
Time: Preplant incorporated, preplant surface, preemergence, postemergence or layby (except IIG). For early preplant surface, apply as split application 30-45 days before planting; applications less than 30 days before planting may be either split or single treatment. Fall application in Illinois (north of Rt. 136), Iowa, Minnesota, Nebraska (north of Rt. 20), North Dakota, South Dakota, Wisconsin.
Weeds: Broadleaf weeds:

carpetweed	eclipta*	galinsoga
common purslane*	Florida beggarweed*	hairy nightshade*
common waterhemp	Florida pusley	pigweed
eastern black		tall waterhemp
nightshade		

Sweet Corn

Grasses and sedges:

barnyardgrass
  (watergrass)
bristly foxtail
crabgrass
crowfootgrass
fall panicum
foxtail millet
giant foxtail
goosegrass

green foxtail
johnsongrass
  (seedling)*
prairie cupgrass
red rice
sandbur*
shattercane*
signalgrass

southwestern
  cupgrass
volunteer sorghum*
wild proso millet* **
witchgrass
woolly cupgrass* **
yellow foxtail
yellow nutsedge

*Suppression; ** Preemergence*

Remarks: Rate varies by soil type and organic matter. Do not use on muck or peat soils. In case of crop failure, any crop on label may be replanted immediately. Do not make second broadcast application. If original application was banded and second crop is planted in untreated row middles, second banded treatment may be applied. Do not graze or feed forage from treated field for 30 days after application. Refer to label for use directions and restrictions.

Crop Rotation: Alfalfa—4 months; barley, oats, rye, wheat—4$^1/_2$ months; tomatoes—6 months; clover—9 months; any labeled crop in addition to barley, buckwheat, cabbage, milo, nuts, oats, peppers, rice, root crops, rye, stone fruits, tobacco, and wheat may be planted in the spring following treatment (including layby or multiple treatments applied previous season); all other rotational crops may be planted 12 months after application.

Tank Mixes: Atrazine, Balance, Banvel, Bladex, Extrazine II, Gramoxone Extra, linuron, Marksman, Prowl, Roundup Ultra, simazine.

State Restrictions: Do not use in Nassau County or Suffolk County, New York. Preplant surface: Medium- and fine-textured soils with minimum- or no-tillage systems in Colorado, Connecticut, Delaware, Illinois, Indiana, Iowa, Kansas, Kentucky, Maine, Maryland, Massachusetts, Michigan, Minnesota, Missouri, Montana, Nebraska, New Hampshire, New York, North Dakota, Ohio, Pennsylvania, Rhode Island, South Dakota, Tennessee, Virginia, West Virginia, Wisconsin, Wyoming.

- - - - - - - - - - - - - - -

Signal Word/Toxicity Class: Caution/III.
REI: 24 hr.

Micro-Tech — see alachlor

Opti-Amine — see 2,4-D

PARAQUAT

Restricted Use Pesticide.

■ PP, PRE, POST
Gramoxone Extra (2.5L) *(ZENECA)*
Rate: 0.5-1 lb. ai/A
    1.5-3 pt. 2.5L/A
Time: Preplant, preemergence. Apply when weeds and grasses are succulent and growth is from 1-6" tall (larger plants less affected by treatment).

Rate: 0.3-0.5 lb. ai/A
    0.8-1.5 pt. 2.5L/A
Time: Postemergence-directed. Apply when corn is at least 10" tall (plants shorter than 10" tall may be injured and not recover).
Weeds: Annual broadleaf weeds and grasses; top kill and suppression of perennials.
Remarks: Add nonionic surfactant or crop oil concentrate. Seedbeds should be formed as far ahead of planting and treatment as possible to permit maximum weed and grass emergence. Seeding should be done with minimal soil disturbance. Weeds and grasses emerging after application will not be controlled; crops emerged at time of application will be killed. Do not apply to soils lacking clay minerals. Refer to label for use directions.

- - - - - - - - - - - - - - -

Signal Word/Toxicity Class: Danger-Poison/I.
REI: 12 hr. (except harvest aid/desiccation 24 hr.).

Partner — see alachlor

PENDIMETHALIN

Use in combination with broadleaf weed herbicide to increase consistency of velvetleaf control and to improve spectrum of weeds controlled. Cool, wet weather increases the risk of crop injury. Do not incorporate or severe crop injury may occur.

■ PRE, POST
Pentagon DG *(American Cyanamid)*
Prowl 3.3 EC *(American Cyanamid)*
Rate: 0.75-2 lb. ai/A
    1.8-4.8 pt. 3.3 EC/A
    1.25-3.3 lb. DG/A
Time: Preemergence, early postemergence. May be applied preemergence only on all varieties of sweet corn in Arizona, California, Idaho, Montana, Oregon, Texas, and Washington. May be applied preemergence or early postemergence in processing varieties of sweet corn in Illinois, Minnesota, New York, and Wisconsin. Do not apply preplant incorporated or serious corn injury can result; see label for early postemergence restrictions.

Weeds: Broadleaf Weeds:

annual spurge
carpetweed
Florida pusley
kochia

lambsquarters
Pennsylvania
  smartweed

pigweed
purslane
velvetleaf

Grasses:

barnyardgrass
crabgrass
crowfootgrass
fall panicum
field sandbur
giant foxtail

goosegrass
green foxtail
johnsongrassnot reg
  (seedling)
shattercane
signalgrass

Texas panicum
wild proso millet
witchgrass
woolly cupgrass
yellow foxtail

Remarks: Rate varies by soil type. Do not use on peat or muck soils. Plant corn at least 1$^1/_2$" deep. Seed must be completely covered with soil. If crop loss occurs due to weather conditions, corn or any crop registered for preplant incorporated use can be replanted the same year. If corn is replanted, seeding depth must be below retilled area.

Crop Rotation: Winter wheat and winter barley may be planted in the fall 4 months after application. Treated land may be planted to other crops the following year (see label for beet and spinach restrictions).

Tank Mixes: Atrazine, Bicep, Bladex, Bullet, Extrazine II, Lariat, Lasso.

State Restrictions: For postemergence use in Illinois, Minnesota, New York, and Wisconsin. Do not apply postemergence in Arizona, California, Idaho, Montana, Oregon, Texas, and Washington. For early postemergence use with atrazine in Alabama, Florida, and Georgia.

- - - - - - - - - - - - - - -

Signal Word/Toxicity Class: Caution.
REI: 24 hr.

Pentagon — see pendimethalin

Princep or Princep Caliber 90 — see simazine

Prowl — see pendimethalin

Ranger — see glyphosate

Rattler — see glyphosate

Roundup — see glyphosate

Saber — see 2,4-D

Savage — see 2,4-D

SCYTHE

◆ **Scythe (pelargonic acid)** *(Mycogen)*
Rate: 4-13 fl. oz./1 gal. spray solution
Time: Apply to actively growing weeds prior to crop emergence.
Weeds: Annual and perennial broadleaf weeds and grasses.
Remarks: Apply in minimum 75 gal. spray solution/A or spray-to-wet. Do not apply by air or through any type of irrigation system. Refer to label for directions and precautions.
Tank Mixes: Glyphosate and other foliar and residual herbicides.

- - - - - - - - - - - - - - -

Signal Word/Toxicity Class: Warning/II.
REI: 24 hr.

◆-new product • PP-preplant • PPI-preplant incorporated • PRE-preemergence • POST-postemergence • SEQ-sequential • ae-acid equivalent • ai-active ingredient • DF-dry flowable
E/EC-emulsifiable concentrate • F/FL-flowable • DG/G/WG-dispersable granule • L/LC-liquid • SP/WSP-soluble packet • W/WP-wettable powder • WSB-water soluble bag

SIMAZAT (Premix)

Premix containing atrazine and simazine. Herbicide residues may limit crop alternatives after harvest. Soil texture, rainfall, rate, and other factors affect potential for herbicide carryover. Resistant weeds have been reported where continuous corn has been grown and atrazine, simazine, or other triazine herbicides were used. Restricted Use Pesticide due to ground and surface water concerns.

■ PP, PRE, POST

Simazat 4L (2 lb./gal. simazine & 2 lb./gal. atrazine) *(Drexel)*

Rate: 2-3 lb. ai/A
    4-6 pt. 4L/A
Time: Preplant, preemergence, postemergence.
Weeds: Most annual broadleaf weeds and grasses.
Remarks: Rate varies by soil type. Do not graze treated area or feed treated forage to livestock for 21 days following application.
Crop Rotation: Do not plant treated areas to any crop except corn and sorghum until the following year. Refer to label for additional suggestions.

— — — — — — — — — — — — — —

Signal Word/Toxicity Class: Caution.

SIMAZINE

Use in combination with residual annual grass herbicide to increase spectrum of weeds controlled. Herbicide residues may limit crop alternatives after harvest. Soil texture, rainfall, rate, and other factors affect potential for herbicide carryover. Resistant weeds have been reported in locations where continuous corn has been grown and only simazine or other triazine herbicides were used. Use in combination or choose an alternate broadleaf weed herbicide when resistance has been confirmed.

■ PP, PRE

◆ **Clean Crop Simazine 4L or 90WDG** *(Platte)*
Drexel Simazine 4L or 90DF *(Drexel)*
Princep 4L or Princep Caliber 90 *(Novartis)*
Riverside Simazine 4L or 90DF *(Terra)*

Rate: 2-4 lb. ai/A
    4-8 pt. 4L/A
    2.2-4.4 lb. 90, 90DF/A
    Quackgrass:
    3-4 lb. ai/A
    6-8 pt. 4L/A
    3.3-4.4 lb. 90, 90DF/A
Time: Preplant, preemergence. For quackgrass, apply in fall.
Weeds: Annual broadleaf weeds:

annual morningglory	flora's paintbrush	ragweed
burclover	Florida pusley	redmaids rockpurslane
carelessweed	German moss	Russian thistle
carpetweed	groundsel	shepherdspurse
common chickweed	henbit	smartweed
common	knawel	spanishneedles
lambsquarters	nightshade	speedwell
common purslane	pepperweed	tansymustard
fiddleneck	pigweed	wild mustard
filaree	pineappleweed	yellowflower
fireweed	prickly lettuce	pepperweed

Grasses:

annual bluegrass	fall panicum	signalgrass
annual ryegrass	foxtail	silver hairgrass
barnyardgrass	goosegrass	watergrass
cheatgrass	junglerice	wild oat
crabgrass	rattail fescue	witchgrass
downy brome		

Remarks: Do not graze treated areas.
Crop Rotation: Do not plant any crop except corn until following year. If replanting perennial crops or rotating land to crops other than corn, do not apply in year preceding planting these crops. Do not plant dry beans, sugar beets, tobacco, vegetables, spring-seeded small grains, or small-seeded legumes and grasses the year following application.
Tank Mixes: Atrazine, Eradicane, Gramoxone Extra, Sutan+.

— — — — — — — — — — — — — —

Signal Word/Toxicity Class: Caution.
REI: 12 hr.

SUREFIRE (Premix)

Restricted Use Pesticide.

■ PP, PRE

◆ **Surefire (29.4% paraquat & 10.6% diuron)** *(Platte)*

Rate: 0.8-1.6 lb. ai/A
    2-4 pt./A
Time: Apply to young, succulent weeds 1-6" high prior to, during or after planting, but before crop emergence.
Weeds: Annual broadleaf weeds and grasses; top-kill and suppression of perennial weeds.
Remarks: Always use nonionic surfactant. Do not apply through any type of irrigation system. Do not apply to soils lacking clay minerals. Seeding should be done with a minimum amount of soil disturbance. Crop plants emerged at time of treatment will be killed. Refer to label for directions and precautions.
Tank Mixes: AAtrex, Banvel, Bladex, 2,4-D, Glean, Kerb.

— — — — — — — — — — — — — —

Signal Word/Toxicity Class: Danger/I.
REI: 12 hr.

SUTAN+

Commonly used in combination with a triazine herbicide to improve broadleaf weed control. Contains a safening agent.

■ PPI

Sutan+ 6.7-E (butylate) *(Micro Flo)*

Rate: 4 lb. ai/A
    4.75 pt. 6.7E/A
Time: Preplant incorporated.
Weeds: Grasses and sedges:

barnyardgrass	fall panicum	nutsedge
(watergrass)	field sandbur	shattercane
bermudagrass	giant foxtail	Texas panicum
buffalograss	goosegrass	volunteer
coloradograss	green foxtail	sorghum
crabgrass	johnsongrass	yellow foxtail

Remarks: Sweet corn. For use on mineral soils or those soils containing less than 10% organic matter. Must be mixed into soil thoroughly.
Tank Mixes: Atrazine, Bladex, Princep.
State Restrictions: Not for use in Arizona or the 10 southernmost California counties.

— — — — — — — — — — — — — —

Signal Word/Toxicity Class: Caution/III.
REI: 12 hr.

Weed Rhap — see 2,4-D

Weedar — see 2,4-D

Weedestroy — see 2,4-D

Sweet Potatoes

Credit — see glyphosate

DEVRINOL

■ PRE, POST

Devrinol 50-DF (napropamide) *(United Phosphorus)*

Rate: 1-2 lb. ai/A
    2-4 lb. 50-DF/A
Time: Posttransplant surface and plant bed applications. At transplanting (all regions): apply to soil surface immediately after transplanting. Plant beds (North Carolina only): apply to soil surface after sweet potato roots are covered with soil, but prior to soil cracking and emergence of sweet potato plants.
Weeds: Annual broadleaf weeds:

carpetweed	Florida pusley	purple cudweed
common purslane	galinsoga	redroot pigweed
common ragweed	lambsquarters	smooth pigweed

Annual grasses:

barnyardgrass	goosegrass	junglerice
crabgrass	green foxtail	stinkgrass
fall panicum	johnsongrass	witchgrass
giant foxtail	(seedling)	yellow foxtail

6

Vegetables

NOTICE	The information on these pages is for preliminary planning — not a guide for use. Be sure to follow the manufacturer's directions, notwithstanding information contained here.	For personal protective equipment and EPA registration numbers, please turn to page 70.

Weed Control Manual 2000

345

Sweet Potatoes

Remarks: Apply 20-100 gal. spray/A. For best results, treatment must reach zone of weed seed germination. Must be shallowly incorporated or irrigated-in with sufficient overhead irrigation to wet soil to a depth of 2-4" if rainfall does not occur within 24 hr. after application.

Crop Rotation: Do not plant to crops not specified on label until 12 months after last application. Disc plow or moldboard plow at least 10" deep prior to planting succeeding crop.

- - - - - - - - - - - - - - -

Signal Word/Toxicity Class: Caution.
REI: 12 hr.

FLUAZIFOP-P-BUTYL

Provides selective control of annual and perennial grasses. Do not tank mix with any other herbicide unless specified on label, or reduced control may result.

■ **POST**
Fusilade DX *(ZENECA)*
Rate: 0.1-0.375 lb. ai/A
0.375-1.5 pt. DX/A
Time: Early postemergence. Apply to actively growing grasses.
Weeds: Annual and perennial grasses:

barnyardgrass	johnsongrass	southern sandbur
bermudagrass	(rhizome, seedling)	Texas panicum
broadleaf signalgrass	junglerice	tropical crabgrass
fall panicum	large crabgrass	volunteer cereals
field sandbur	quackgrass	wild oat
giant foxtail	red rice	wild proso millet
goosegrass	shattercane	wiregrass muhly
green foxtail	smooth crabgrass	witchgrass
Italian ryegrass	sorghum-almum	woolly cupgrass
itchgrass	southern crabgrass	yellow foxtail

Remarks: Sweet potatoes, yams. Rate varies by geographic area and grass species. Add crop oil concentrate or nonionic surfactant. Do not apply more than 3 pt./A per season. Refer to label for specific directions and precautions.
Days To Harvest: 55.
Crop Rotation: Do not plant rotational grass crops such as corn, sorghum, and cereals within 60 days after last application.
State Restrictions: Refer to label for geographical regions.

- - - - - - - - - - - - - - -

Signal Word/Toxicity Class: Caution.
REI: 12 hr.

Fusilade — see fluazifop-P-butyl

Glyfos or Glyfos X-tra — see glyphosate

GLYPHOSATE

Nonselective control of annual and perennial grasses and broadleaf weeds in stale seedbeds before planting.

■ **PRE**
◆ **Credit (4WS)** *(Nufarm)*
◆ **Glyfos or Glyfos X-tra (4WS)** *(Cheminova)*
Rattler (4WS) *(Helena)*
Roundup Custom (5.4WS) *(Monsanto)*
Roundup Original, Original RT, Ultra, Ultra RT (4WS) *(Monsanto)*
Rate: Annual weeds:
0.38-1.5 lb. ai/A
0.56-2.25 pt. 5.4WS/A
0.75-3 pt. 4WS/A
Perennial weeds:
0.5-5 lb. ai/A
0.75-7.5 pt. 5.4WS/A
1-10 pt. 4WS/A
Time: Preemergence: Apply prior to emergence of direct-seeded crop or prior to transplanting.
Weeds: Emerged annual and perennial broadleaf weeds including:

Canada thistle	hemp dogbane	Pennsylvania
curly dock	milkweed	smartweed
field bindweed		

Grasses:

bermudagrass	fescue	paragrass
fall panicum	johnsongrass	quackgrass

Remarks: Prior to transplanting crops into plastic mulch, remove product residue from plastic. Do not add surfactant to Roundup Ultra or Ultra RT. Do not allow glyphosate to contact desirable plants. Do not apply through any type of irrigation system. Refer to label for directions, precautions and restrictions.

State Restrictions: Roundup RT for use in Colorado, Idaho, Montana, North Dakota, South Dakota, Utah, Wyoming, and in specific counties only in Kansas, Minnesota, Nebraska, Nevada, Oklahoma, Oregon, and Washington; refer to label for restrictions. Glyfos not registered for use in California. Glyfos X-tra not registered for use in mistblowers in California or Arizona.

- - - - - - - - - - - - - - -

Signal Word/Toxicity Class: Varies by formulation.
REI: Warning—12 hr.; Caution—4 hr.

Poast — see sethoxydim

Rattler — see glyphosate

Roundup — see glyphosate

SCYTHE

◆ **Scythe (pelargonic acid)** *(Mycogen)*
Rate: 4-13 fl. oz./1 gal. spray solution
Time: Apply to actively growing weeds prior to crop emergence.
Weeds: Annual and perennial broadleaf weeds and grasses.
Remarks: Apply in minimum 75 gal. spray solution/A or spray-to-wet. Do not apply by air or through any type of irrigation system. Refer to label for directions and precautions.
Tank Mixes: Glyphosate and other foliar and residual herbicides.

- - - - - - - - - - - - - - -

Signal Word/Toxicity Class: Warning/II.
REI: 24 hr.

SETHOXYDIM

Selective control of annual and perennial grasses. Do not tank mix with any other herbicide unless specified on label, or reduced control may result.

■ **POST**
Poast (1.5EC) *(BASF)*
Rate: Eastern U.S.:
0.09-0.18 lb. ai/A
0.5-1 pt. 1.5EC/A
Western U.S.:
0.09-0.18 lb. ai/A
0.5-1.5 pt. 1.5EC/A
Time: Postemergence.
Weeds: Annual and perennial grasses:

annual ryegrass	large crabgrass	stinkgrass
barnyardgrass	lovegrass	tall fescue
bermudagrass	orchardgrass	Texas panicum
broadleaf signalgrass	(seedling)	volunteer cereals
browntop panicum	perennial ryegrass	wild oat
fall panicum	quackgrass	wild proso millet
giant foxtail	red rice	wildcane
goosegrass	red sprangletop	wirestem muhly
green foxtail	shattercane	witchgrass
itchgrass	smooth crabgrass	woolly cupgrass
johnsongrass	southwestern	yellow foxtail
junglerice	cupgrass	

Remarks: Rate depends on growing region. Always add oil concentrate at rate of 2 pt./A. Do not apply through any type of irrigation system. Refer to label for restrictions and precautions.
Days To Harvest: Eastern U.S.—30; western U.S.—60.
Tank Mixes: Metribuzin.
State Restrictions: Do not use UAN or AMS in California or Pacific Northwest.

- - - - - - - - - - - - - - -

Signal Word/Toxicity Class: Warning/II.
REI: 12 hr.

Table Beets
(Red Beets)

Credit — see glyphosate

◆-new product • PP-preplant • PPI-preplant incorporated • PRE-preemergence • POST-postemergence • SEQ-sequential • ae-acid equivalent • ai-active ingredient • DF-dry flowable
E/EC-emulsifiable concentrate • F/FL-flowable • DG/G/WG-dispersable granule • L/LC-liquid • SP/WSP-soluble packet • W/WP-wettable powder • WSB-water soluble bag

Glyfos or Glyfos X-tra — see glyphosate

GLYPHOSATE

Nonselective control of annual and perennial grasses and broadleaf weeds in stale seedbeds and reduced-tillage planting systems.

■ PRE
◆ **Credit (4WS)** *(Nufarm)*
◆ **Glyfos or Glyfos X-tra (4WS)** *(Cheminova)*
Rattler (4WS) *(Helena)*
Roundup Custom (5.4WS) *(Monsanto)*
Roundup Original, Original RT, Ultra, Ultra RT (4WS) *(Monsanto)*
Rate: Annual weeds:
    0.38-1.5 lb. ai/A
    0.56-2.25 pt. 5.4WS/A
    0.75-3 pt. 4WS/A
    Perennial weeds:
    0.5-5 lb. ai/A
    0.75-7.5 pt. 5.4WS/A
    1-10 pt. 4WS/A
Time: Preemergence: Apply prior to emergence of direct-seeded crop or prior to transplanting.
Weeds: Emerged annual and perennial broadleaf weeds including:

Canada thistle	hemp dogbane	Pennsylvania
curly dock	milkweed	smartweed
field bindweed		

Grasses:

bermudagrass	fescue	paragrass
fall panicum	johnsongrass	quackgrass

Remarks: Prior to transplanting crops into plastic mulch, remove product residue from plastic. Do not add surfactant to Roundup Ultra or Ultra RT. Do not allow glyphosate to contact desirable plants. Do not apply through any type of irrigation system. Refer to label for directions, precautions and restrictions.
State Restrictions: Roundup RT for use in Colorado, Idaho, Montana, North Dakota, South Dakota, Utah, Wyoming, and in specific counties only in Kansas, Minnesota, Nebraska, Nevada, Oklahoma, Oregon, and Washington; refer to label for restrictions. Glyfos not registered for use in California. Glyfos X-tra not registered for use in mistblowers in California or Arizona.

Signal Word/Toxicity Class: Varies by formulation.
REI: Warning—12 hr.; Caution—4 hr.

PYRAMIN

May injure crop when applied preemergence to beets planted in coarse-textured soils low in organic matter; consult local Cooperative Extension Service for information.

■ PRE, POST
Pyramin FL or DF (chloridazon) *(BASF)*
Rate: Broadcast:
    3.2-3.7 lb. ai/A
    3-3.5 qt. FL/A
    4.6-5.4 lb. DF/A
Time: Preemergence: Spray after beet seeds are planted but before beets and weeds emerge. If rain does not fall within 5-10 days after treatment, beets should be irrigated to activate Pyramin; if irrigation is not possible, use a shallow cultivation before weeds are 2" tall. Postemergence: Apply after beets have 2 expanded true leaves and before any weeds have more than 2-4 true leaves (usually within 2 weeks after planting); treatment on larger weeds will not be effective.
Weeds: Broadleaf weeds:

fanweed	mustard	ragweed
goosefoot	nightshade	shepherdspurse
henbit	pigweed	smartweed
lambsquarters	purslane	

Remarks: Do not apply more than 2 applications in Central and Eastern states or apply rates more than 7.7 lb. ai/A per season.
Crop Rotation: If beet crop is lost, do not plant crops other than sugar beets on heavy-textured, high organic matter soils in treated band during the same season.

Signal Word/Toxicity Class: Caution/III.
REI: 12 hr.

Rattler — see glyphosate

RO-NEET

Incorporate immediately to prevent loss due to volatilization. Reduce herbicide rate and/or apply and incorporate 5-7 days before planting to reduce the risk of temporary crop injury.

■ PPI
Ro-Neet 6-E (cycloate) *(ZENECA)*
Rate: 3-4 lb. ai/A
    4-5.3 pt. 6-E/A
Time: Preplant incorporated, at planting or immediately post planting.
Weeds: Broadleaf weeds:

black nightshade	lambsquarters	shepherdspurse
common purslane	nettleleaf goosefoot	small stinging nettle
hairy nightshade	(except CA)	velvetleaf
henbit (deadnettle)	redroot pigweed	(suppression)

Grasses and sedges:

annual bluegrass	crabgrass	volunteer barley
annual ryegrass	foxtail	wild oat
barnyardgrass	purple nutsedge	yellow nutsedge
(watergrass)		

Remarks: For use on mineral soils only. Low rate on sandy soils, high rate on heavier soils. Refer to label for use directions, restrictions, and precautions.

Signal Word/Toxicity Class: Caution.
REI: 12 hr.

Roundup — see glyphosate

SCYTHE

◆ **Scythe (pelargonic acid)** *(Mycogen)*
Rate: 4-13 fl. oz./1 gal. spray solution
Time: Apply to actively growing weeds prior to crop emergence.
Weeds: Annual and perennial broadleaf weeds and grasses.
Remarks: Apply in minimum 75 gal. spray solution/A or spray-to-wet. Do not apply by air or through any type of irrigation system. Refer to label for directions and precautions.
Tank Mixes: Glyphosate and other foliar and residual herbicides.

Signal Word/Toxicity Class: Warning/II.
REI: 24 hr.

SPIN-AID

Temporary stunting, yellowing, or tip burn may be observed after treatment. To minimize risk of injury, avoid application during hot humid weather, and spray just before sunset, rather than early in the day.

■ POST
Spin-Aid (EC) (phenmedipham) *(AgrEvo USA)*
Rate: 0.5-1 lb. ai/A
    3-6 pt. EC/A
Time: Postemergence. Apply when beets are past 4-6 true leaf stage and weeds are at 2-true leaf stage.
Weeds: Broadleaf weeds:

annual sowthistle	common ragweed	purslane
coast fiddleneck	groundcherry	shepherdspurse
common chickweed	London rocket	wild mustard
common lambsquarters	nettleleaf goosefoot	

Remarks: Red beets. Rainfall within 6 hours of spraying may reduce weed kill. Refer to label for band rates. Do not apply through any type of irrigation system.
Days To Harvest: 60.

Signal Word/Toxicity Class: Warning/II.
REI: 24 hr.

Tomatoes

Credit — see glyphosate

6
Vegetables

NOTICE The information on these pages is for preliminary planning — not a guide for use. Be sure to follow the manufacturer's directions, notwithstanding information contained here. | For personal protective equipment and EPA registration numbers, please turn to page 70.

DEVRINOL

Shallow, thorough incorporation improves control of certain weeds, including galinsoga. Apply and incorporate afterward, if ridging or bedding, to avoid concentrating herbicide in the row. Spray strips of soil between rows of plastic after laying mulch.

■ PPI

Devrinol 2-E or 50-DF (napropamide) *(United Phosphorus)*

Rate: 1-2 lb. ai/A
    0.5-1 gal. 2-E/A
    2-4 lb. 50-DF/A

Time: Preplant incorporated. May be applied to direct-seeded or transplanted crop.

Weeds: Annual broadleaf weeds:

carpetweed	lambsquarters	redroot pigweed
common purslane		

Annual grasses:

barnyardgrass	fall panicum	johnsongrass
crabgrass	goosegrass	(seedling)

Remarks: Incorporate same day as applied to a depth of 1-2".
Crop Rotation: See label for specific recommendations.
Tank Mixes: Tillam.

– – – – – – – – – – – – – – – –

Signal Word/Toxicity Class: Danger/I (2-E); Caution (50-DF).
REI: 12 hr.

Eptam — see EPTC

EPTC

◆ **Eptam 7-E** *(ZENECA)*
Rate: 3 lb. ai/A
    3.5 pt. 7-E/A
Time: Layby application. Incorporate immediately.
Weeds: Broadleaf weeds:

black nightshade	corn spurry	nettleleaf goosefoot
carpetweed	cutleaf nightshade	prickly sida
common chickweed	deadnettle	prostrate pigweed
common	fiddleneck	redroot pigweed
lambsquarters	Florida pusley	sicklepod
common pigweed	hairy nightshade	tall morningglory
common purslane	henbit	tumble pigweed

Annual grasses:

annual bluegrass	field sandbur	rescuegrass
annual ryegrass	giant foxtail	shattercane
(Italian)	goosegrass	signalgrass
barnyardgrass	green foxtail	Texas panicum
(watergrass)	johnsongrass	volunteer grains
bermudagrass	(seedling)	(barley, oats, wheat)
(seedling)	junglerice	wild oat
crabgrass	lovegrass	witchgrass
fall panicum	(stinkgrass)	yellow foxtail

Remarks: For use on clay and clay loam soils only, not for use on sandy soils. Do not use where grain will be planted within 90 days. Do not irrigate for at least 5 days after application. Refer to label for restrictions.
Days To Harvest: 21.
State Restrictions: For use only in the following counties of Northern California: Butte, Colusa, Contra Costa, Fresno, Glenn, Madera, Merced, Sacramento, San Joaquin, Solano, Stanislaus, Sutter, Yolo, and Yuba.

– – – – – – – – – – – – – – – –

Signal Word/Toxicity Class: Caution.
REI: 12 hr. unless soil injected or soil incorporated.

Glyfos or Glyfos X-tra — see glyphosate

GLYPHOSATE

Nonselective control of annual and perennial grasses and broadleaf weeds in stale seedbeds and reduced-tillage planting systems.

■ PRE

◆ **Credit (4WS)** *(Nufarm)*
◆ **Glyfos or Glyfos X-tra (4WS)** *(Cheminova)*
Rattler (4WS) *(Helena)*
Roundup Custom (5.4WS) *(Monsanto)*
Roundup Original, Original RT, Ultra, Ultra RT (4WS) *(Monsanto)*

Rate: Annual weeds:
    0.38-1.5 lb. ai/A
    0.56-2.25 pt. 5.4WS/A
    0.75-3 pt. 4WS/A
    Perennial weeds:
    0.5-5 lb. ai/A
    0.75-7.5 pt. 5.4WS/A
    1-10 pt. 4WS/A
Time: Preemergence: Apply prior to emergence of direct-seeded crop or prior to transplanting. Allow at least 3 days between application and planting.
Weeds: Emerged annual and perennial broadleaf weeds including:

Canada thistle	hemp dogbane	Pennsylvania
curly dock	milkweed	smartweed
field bindweed		

Grasses:

bermudagrass	fescue	paragrass
fall panicum	johnsongrass	quackgrass

Remarks: Prior to transplanting crops into plastic mulch, remove product residue from plastic. Do not add surfactant to Roundup Ultra or Ultra RT. Do not allow glyphosate to contact desirable plants. Do not apply through any type of irrigation system. Refer to labels for directions, precautions and restrictions.
State Restrictions: Roundup RT for use in Colorado, Idaho, Montana, North Dakota, South Dakota, Utah, Wyoming, and in specific counties only in Kansas, Minnesota, Nebraska, Nevada, Oklahoma, Oregon, and Washington; refer to label for restrictions. Glyfos not registered for use in California. Glyfos X-tra not registered for use in mistblowers in California or Arizona.

– – – – – – – – – – – – – – – –

Signal Word/Toxicity Class: Varies by formulation.
REI: Warning—12 hr.; Caution—4 hr.

Gramoxone Extra — see paraquat

PARAQUAT

Restricted Use Pesticide.

■ PP, PRE, POST

Gramoxone Extra (2.5L) *(ZENECA)*
Rate: 0.5-1 lb. ai/A
    1.5-3 pt. 2.5L/A
Time: Preplant, preemergence. Apply when weeds and grasses are succulent and growth is from 1-6" tall (larger plants less affected by treatment).
Weeds: Annual broadleaf weeds and grasses; top kill and suppression of perennials.
Remarks: Add nonionic surfactant or crop oil concentrate. Seedbeds should be formed as far ahead of planting and treatment as possible to permit maximum weed and grass emergence. Seeding should be done with minimal soil disturbance. Weeds and grasses emerging after application will not be controlled; crops emerged at time of application will be killed. Do not apply to soils lacking clay minerals. Refer to label for use directions.
Tank Mixes: Goal.

– – – – – – – – – – – – – – – –

Rate: 0.5 lb. ai/A
    1.5 pt. 2.5L/A
Time: Postemergence. Apply as directed spray.
Weeds: Annual broadleaf weeds and grasses; top kill and suppression of perennials between rows.
Remarks: Add nonionic surfactant or crop oil concentrate. Apply using precision directed spray equipment to prevent contact with crops. Weeds and grasses emerging after application will not be controlled. Do not allow spray to contact tomato plants. Do not allow livestock to graze on treated areas. Refer to label for use directions and precautions.

– – – – – – – – – – – – – – – –

Rate: 0.2 lb. ai/A
    0.75 pt. 2.5L/A
Time: Apply broadcast to preformed seedbeds.
Weeds:
  volunteer barley
Remarks: Add nonionic surfactant or crop oil concentrate. Refer to label for use directions, restrictions, and precautions.
State Restrictions: For use in California, Idaho, Oregon, Washington.

– – – – – – – – – – – – – – – –

Signal Word/Toxicity Class: Danger-Poison/I.
REI: 12 hr. (except harvest aid/desiccation 24 hr.).

Poast — see sethoxydim

◆-new product • PP-preplant • PPI-preplant incorporated • PRE-preemergence • POST-postemergence • SEQ-sequential • ae-acid equivalent • ai-active ingredient • DF-dry flowable
E/EC-emulsifiable concentrate • F/FL-flowable • DG/G/WG-dispersable granule • L/LC-liquid • SP/WSP-soluble packet • W/WP-wettable powder • WSB-water soluble bag

        Weed Control Manual 2000

PREFAR

For use on mineral soils only. Registered for use on many vegetable crops in certain states. Use to maintain flexibility in crop rotations. May be used on labeled crops grown through or under plastic. Toxic to fish.

■ PPI, PRE

Prefar 4-E (bensulide) *(Gowan)*

Rate: 5-6 lb. ai/A
  5-6 qt. 4E/A

Time: Preplant incorporated, preemergence. Apply preemergence only on crops to be irrigated up.

Weeds: Broadleaf weeds—AZ, CA, NM, TX:

burning nettle (AZ, CA only)	nettleleaf goosefoot (AZ, CA only)	purslane redroot pigweed
lambsquarters		

Grasses:

barnyardgrass	foxtail	sprangletop
crabgrass	goosegrass	watergrass
fall panicum	junglerice	

Remarks: Tomatillos. Rate varies by soil type. Incorporate to a depth of 1-2" before planting. Apply preemergence only on crops where application is followed by immediate irrigation.

Crop Rotation: Carrots, cotton, and labeled crops may be replanted following application without restrictions; all other crops 120 days after application and soil should be tilled to minimum depth 4" prior to planting.

- - - - - - - - - - - - - - - -

Signal Word/Toxicity Class: Caution/III.
REI: 12 hr. unless soil injected or soil incorporated.

Rattler — see glyphosate

RIMSULFURON

■ PRE, POST

◆ Shadeout (DF) *(DuPont)*

Rate: 2 oz. DF/A

Time: Preemergence: Apply after seeding. Postemergence: Apply to young, actively growing weed after crop has reached 2-leaf stage.

Weeds: Broadleaf weeds:

birdsrape mustard	false chamomile	prostrate pigweed
black mustard	galinsoga	redroot pigweed
Canada thistle	hairy nightshade	redstem filaree
cocklebur	henbit	Russian thistle
common chickweed	ivyleaf morningglory	shepherdspurse
common	kochia	smooth pigweed
lambsquarters	ladysthumb	velvetleaf
common purslane	mayweed chamomile	wild kale
common ragweed	Pennsylvania	wild mustard
common sunflower	smartweed	wild radish
crabgrass	proso millet	

Grasses and sedges:

annual bluegrass	johnsongrass	volunteer sorghum
barnyardgrass	(seedling)	volunteer wheat
crabgrass	quackgrass	wild oat
goosegrass	stinkgrass	yellow foxtail
green foxtail	volunteer barley	yellow nutsedge

Remarks: Field tomatoes. Not for use in greenhouses, cold frames, pot cultures, etc. Naturally occurring biotypes resistant to other sulfonylurea herbicides may also be resistant to Shadeout. Do not apply by air or through any type of irrigation system. Do not exceed 4 oz./A per year.

Days To Harvest: 45.

Crop Rotation: Field corn, potatoes, tomatoes—anytime; winter wheat—4 months; dry beans, cotton, soybeans, sweet corn—10 months; crops not listed—12 months.

Tank Mixes: Eptam, metribuzin, Prowl, Lorox. Tank mixing with organophosphate insecticides may result in crop injury.

State Restrictions: Do not use in Alamosa, Conejos, Costilla, Rio Grande, and Saguache counties in Colorado.

- - - - - - - - - - - - - - - -

Signal Word/Toxicity Class: Caution.
REI: 4 hr.

Roundup — see glyphosate

SCYTHE

◆ Scythe (pelargonic acid) *(Mycogen)*

Rate: 4-13 fl. oz./1 gal. spray solution
Time: Apply to actively growing weeds prior to crop emergence.
Weeds: Annual and perennial broadleaf weeds and grasses.
Remarks: Apply in minimum 75 gal. spray solution/A or spray-to-wet. Do not apply by air or through any type of irrigation system. Refer to label for directions and precautions.
Tank Mixes: Glyphosate and other foliar and residual herbicides.

- - - - - - - - - - - - - - - -

Signal Word/Toxicity Class: Warning/II.
REI: 24 hr.

SENCOR

Use repeated postemergence applications to control yellow nutsedge. Do not apply to direct-seeded tomatoes before crop has 5 fully expanded true leaves. Do not apply during extended periods of cloudy, humid weather. Delay postemergence application until after 3 sunny days with low humidity.

■ PPI, POST

Sencor 4 (FL) or DF (metribuzin) *(Bayer)*

Rate: 0.25-0.5 lb. ai/A
  0.5-1 pt. FL/A
  0.33-0.66 lb. DF/A

Time: Preplant incorporated. Apply immediately before transplanting.

Weeds: Broadleaf weeds:

common purslane	lambsquarters	redroot pigweed
galinsoga		

Grasses:

goosegrass

Remarks: Transplanted tomatoes.

Rate: Broadcast spray:
  0.25-0.5 lb. ai/A
  0.5-1 pt. FL/A
  0.33-0.66 lb. DF/A
  Directed spray:
  0.5-1 lb. ai/A
  1-2 pt. FL/A
  0.66-1.33 lb. DF/A

Time: Postemergence. Allow at least 14 days between applications. Do not treat seeded tomatoes until plants have reached 5- to 6- leaf stage.

Weeds: Broadleaf weeds:

carpetweed	ladysthumb	purslane
common ragweed	lambsquarters	toadflax
fumitory	Pennsylvania	velvetleaf
galinsoga	smartweed	wild mustard
jimsonweed	pigweed	

Grasses:

goosegrass	yellow foxtail

Remarks: Established tomatoes. Do not apply until transplants have recovered from transplant shock and new growth is evident. Do not use hot caps on tomatoes within 7 days before or any time after application. Do not apply postemergence within 24 hr. of application of other pesticides. Treat only small area of newly introduced tomato varieties with unknown tolerance to metribuzin.

Days To Harvest: 7.

Crop Rotation: Alfalfa, asparagus, barley/wheat (following peas, lentils, or soybeans), corn, forage grass, potatoes, sainfoin, soybeans, sugarcane, tomatoes—4 months; barley, cotton, lentils, peas, rice, wheat—8 months; other crops not listed (except root crops)—12 months; onions, sugar beets, and other root crops—18 months. Cover crops for soil building or erosion control may be planted anytime, but do not graze or harvest for food or feed. Stand reductions may occur in some areas.

Tank Mixes: Trifluralin.
State Restrictions: Not for use in Kern County, California.

- - - - - - - - - - - - - - - -

Signal Word/Toxicity Class: Caution/III.
REI: 12 hr.

SETHOXYDIM

Selective control of annual and perennial grasses.

■ POST

Poast (1.5EC) *(BASF)*

Rate: 0.09-0.28 lb. ai/A
  0.5-1.5 pt. 1.5EC/A

6

Vegetables

Tomatoes

Time: Postemergence.

Weeds: Annual and perennial grasses:

annual ryegrass	large crabgrass	tall fescue
barnyardgrass	lovegrass	Texas panicum
bermudagrass	orchardgrass	volunteer grains
broadleaf signalgrass	(seedling)	wild oat
browntop panicum	perennial ryegrass	wild proso millet
fall panicum	red sprangletop	wildcane
giant foxtail	shattercane	wirestem muhly
goosegrass	smooth crabgrass	witchgrass
green foxtail	southwestern	woolly cupgrass
johnsongrass	cupgrass	yellow foxtail
junglerice	stinkgrass	

Remarks: Rate depends on growing region. Add 2 pt./A oil concentrate. Refer to label for restrictions and limitations.

Days To Harvest: 20.

Tank Mixes: Metribuzin.

State Restrictions: Do not use UAN or AMS in California or Pacific Northwest.

- - - - - - - - - - - - - - - -

Signal Word/Toxicity Class: Warning/II.

REI: 12 hr.

Shadeout — see rimsulfuron

TILLAM

■ **PP, POST**

Tillam 6-E (pebulate) *(ZENECA)*

Rate: 4-10 lb. ai/A
2.66-6.66 qt. 6-E/A

Time: Preplant, postemergence.

Weeds: Broadleaf weeds:

blackeyedsusan	hairy nightshade	prostrate pigweed
common purslane	(suppression)	redroot pigweed
deadnettle (henbit)	lambsquarters	shepherdspurse
Florida pusley	nettleleaf goosefoot	

Grasses and sedges:

barnyardgrass	giant foxtail	purple nutsedge
(watergrass)	goosegrass	wild oat
bermudagrass	green foxtail	yellow foxtail
(seedling)	millet	yellow nutsedge
crabgrass	narrowleaf signalgrass	

Remarks: Direct-seeded, transplanted tomatoes. Do not apply prior to hand transplanting. Refer to label for use directions and precautions.

Days To Harvest: 8 excluding western region.

Tank Mixes: Devrinol, Dyfonate.

State Restrictions: For transplants in South Carolina, use 2 qt. 6-E/A. Refer to label for California recommendations.

- - - - - - - - - - - - - - - -

Signal Word/Toxicity Class: Caution.

REI: 12 hr.

Treflan — see trifluralin

TRI-4 — see trifluralin

Trific — see trifluralin

TRIFLURALIN

Incorporate after ridging or bedding to improve drainage so concentrating herbicide can be avoided. Cold, wet soil conditions after planting increase risk of crop injury.

■ **PPI**

Albaugh Trifluralin 4EC *(Albaugh)*

◆ **Clean Crop Trifluralin HF (4EC)** *(Platte)*

Gowan Trifluralin 4 or 5 (EC) or 10G *(Gowan)*

Helena Trifluralin 4 EC *(Helena)*

Riverside Trifluralin 4EC or Trific 60DF *(Terra)*

◆ **Sedagri Trifluralin 480 (4EC)** *(Rhone-Poulenc)*

Treflan HFP (4EC) or TR-10 (10G) *(Dow AgroSciences)*

TRI-4 HF (4EC) *(American Cyanamid)*

Trilin 4 or 5 (EC) or 10G *(Griffin)*

Wilbur-Ellis Trifluralin 10G *(Wilbur-Ellis)*

Rate: 0.5-1 lb. ai/A
1-2 pt. 4EC/A
0.8-1.6 pt. 5EC/A
0.875-1.66 lb. 60DF
5-10 lb. 10G/A

Time: Preplant incorporated. Direct-seeded: Apply as directed spray between rows and incorporate at time of blocking or thinning. Transplants: Incorporate before transplanting or apply postplant as directed spray to soil between rows and beneath plant and incorporate.

Weeds: Broadleaf weeds:

carelessweed	knotweed	purslane
carpetweed	kochia	pusley
chickweed	lambsquarters	redroot pigweed
field bindweed	Mexican clover	rough pigweed
fireweed	Mexican fireweed	Russian thistle
Florida purslane	prostrate pigweed	spiny pigweed
Florida pusley	puncturevine	stinging nettle
goosefoot	(western U.S.)	tumbleweed
henbit		

Grasses:

annual bluegrass	fall panicum	sandbur
barnyardgrass	foxtail millet	shattercane
bottlegrass	giant foxtail	smooth crabgrass
brachiaria	green foxtail	sprangletop
bristlegrass	Italian ryegrass	stinkgrass
bromegrass	johnsongrass	Texas panicum
burgrass	(seedling)	watergrass
cheat	junglerice	wildcane
cheatgrass	large crabgrass	woolly cupgrass
chess	pigeongrass	yellow foxtail
downy brome	robust foxtail	

Remarks: Rate varies by soil type. Refer to label for directions and precautions.

Crop Rotation: Refer to label.

State Restrictions: Wilbur-Ellis not registered in California.

- - - - - - - - - - - - - - - -

Signal Word/Toxicity Class: Varies by formulation.

REI: 12 hr. unless soil injected or soil incorporated.

Trilin — see trifluralin

◆-new product • PP-preplant • PPI-preplant incorporated • PRE-preemergence • POST-postemergence • SEQ-sequential • ae-acid equivalent • ai-active ingredient • DF-dry flowable
E/EC-emulsifiable concentrate • F/FL-flowable • DG/G/WG-dispersable granule • L/LC-liquid • SP/WSP-soluble packet • W/WP-wettable powder • WSB-water soluble bag

Section 7

Fruits & Nuts

Use Reminders

Recommended Preemergence Herbicide Rates For Common Tree Fruit
    Soil Types 352
Crop Safety Of Herbicides For Use In Tree Fruits 352
Suggested Uses Of Herbicides On Fruit And Nut Crops 353

Weed Efficacy Charts

Weed Susceptibility For Small Fruit Herbicides 354
Herbicide Effectiveness On Weeds In Tree Fruits 355

Herbicide Listings

Nuts 384
Small Fruits 356
Tree Fruits (Citrus) 363
Tree Fruits (Deciduous) 370
Tree Fruits (Subtropical) 379

Recommended Preemergence Herbicide Rates (In Active Ingredients) For Common Tree Fruit Soil Types

Soil Type	Sand		Loamy Sand		Sandy Loam			Loam		Silt Loam		Clay Loam	
% Organic Matter	0-1	1-2	0-1	1-2	0-1	1-2	2-4	1-2	2-4	1-2	2-4	1-2	2-4
Casoron	4-6	4-6	4-6	4-6	4-6	4-6	4-6	4-6	4-6	4-6	4-6	4-6	4-6
Devrinol[1]	2-4	2-4	2-4	2-4	2-4	2-4	2-4	2-4	2-4	2-4	2-4	2-4	2-4
Goal	2	2	2	2	2	2	2	2	2	2	2	2	2
Karmex[2]	—	—	—	—	—	1½	2	2	2½	2½	3	3	3
Kerb	2	2	2	2	2	2½	2½	3	3	3½	3½	3½	4
Princep[2]	—	—	—	—	—	2	2	2	3	2	3	3	4
Prowl	2-4	2-4	2-4	2-4	2-4	2-4	2-4	2-4	2-4	2-4	2-4	2-4	2-4
Sinbar[2]	—	—	—	—	—	1½	2	2	2½	2½	3	3	3
Solicam	—	—	—	2	—	2	2½	2½	2½	2½	3	3	4
Surflan[1]	2-4	2-4	2-4	2-4	2-4	2-4	2-4	2-4	2-4	2-4	2-4	2-4	2-4

[1]Use the lower recommended rate when tank-mixing with another preemergence herbicide, unless annual grass pressure is severe.
[2]Use one-half the recommended rate when tank-mixing with another preemergence herbicide.
— = Not labeled (do not use).

Source: 1998 New Jersey Commercial Tree Fruit Production Guide.

Crop Safety Of Herbicides For Use In Tree Fruits

	Apples		Peaches		Pears		Plums		Cherries	
	New	Established	New	Established	New	Established	New	Established	New	Established
Incorporated (residual)										
Treflan	—	—	L	L	—	—	L	L	—	—
Preemergence (residual)										
Casoron	L	G	L	G	L	L	L	L	L	L
Devrinol	G	G	G	G	G	G	G	G	G	G
Goal	G	G	G	G	G	G	G	G	G	G
Karmex	—	F/G	—	F/G	—	F/G	—	—	—	—
Princep	—	F/G	—	F/G	—	F/G	—	L	—	L
Prowl	G	—	G	—	G	—	G	—	G	—
Sinbar	—	F/G	—	F	—	—	—	—	—	—
Solicam	G	G	F/G	G	—	L	—	L	—	L
Surflan	G	G	G	G	G	G	G	G	G	G
Postemergence (selective)										
2,4-D[1]	F	G	F	G	F	G	—	—	—	—
Fusilade DX	G	—	G	G	G	—	G	G	G	G
Kerb	—	G	—	G	—	G	—	G	—	G
Poast	G	G	G	—	G	G	G	—	G	—
Postemergence (nonselective)										
Gramoxone Extra[1]	G	G	G	G	G	G	G	G	G	G
Roundup Ultra[1]	G	G	G[2]	G[2]	G	G	G[2]	G[2]	G	G

G = Good • F = Fair (use with care) • P = Poor (not recommended) • L = Labeled (data insufficient or not recommended) • — = Not Labeled for use (DO NOT USE)

[1]Do NOT allow spray to contact young green bark.
[2]Do NOT allow spray to contact any part of tree, including mature bark (labeled for use only in New Jersey and certain other states).

Source: 1998 New Jersey Commercial Tree Fruit Production Guide.

Suggested Uses Of Herbicides On Fruit And Nut Crops

Herbicide	Apple	Blackberry	Blueberry	Grape	Peach	Pecan	Strawberry
2,4-D	Yes[1]	No	No	No	No	No	Yes
Dichlobenil	Yes	Yes[1]	Yes	Yes	Yes	No	No
Diuron	Yes[2]	No	Yes[2]	Yes[3]	Yes[3]	Yes[3]	No
Fluazifop-P-butyl[4]	Yes	Yes	Yes	Yes	Yes	Yes	Yes
Glyphosate	Yes	Yes	Yes	Yes	Yes	Yes	No
Isoxaben[4]	Yes	Yes	Yes	Yes	Yes	Yes	No
Napropamide	Yes	Yes	Yes	Yes	Yes	Yes	Yes
Norflurazon	Yes	Yes	Yes	Yes[6]	Yes[2]	Yes	No
Oryzalin	Yes	Yes	Yes	Yes	Yes	Yes	No
Oxyfluorfen[7]	Yes	No	No	Yes	Yes	Yes	No
Paraquat	Yes	Yes	Yes	Yes	Yes	Yes	Yes
Pronamide	Yes	No	Yes	Yes	Yes	No	No
Sethoxydim	Yes	No	Yes	Yes	Yes[5]	Yes[5]	Yes
Simazine	Yes	Yes[9]	Yes[2]	Yes[3]	Yes	Yes[6]	No
Sulfosate[4]	Yes	Yes	Yes	Yes	Yes	Yes	No
Terbacil	No	Yes[2]	Yes[2]	No	No	Yes[2]	No

[1]Do not apply to bare ground.
[2]Apply to established crops only.
[3]Apply to plants established 3 years or more.
[4]Apply to nonbearing crops only.
[5]Do not apply to crops that will bear harvestable fruit within 12 months.
[6]Do not apply to transplants less than 2 years old.
[7]Apply to dormant crops only.
[8]Consult label for correct application procedure.
[9]Use $1/2$ rate on plantings less than 6 months old.

Source: Weed Control Guidelines for Mississippi.

7

Fruits & Nuts Use Reminders

Fruits & Nuts Weed Efficacy Chart

Weed Susceptibility For Small Fruit Herbicides

Weeds	Clethodim	Dichlobenil	Diuron	Fluazifop	Glyphosate	Napropamide	Norflurazon	Oryzalin	Paraquat	Pronamide	Sethoxydim	Simazine
Broadleaf Weeds												
Annual sowthistle	P		F	P	G	G	F	P	G	P	P	F
Bedstraw	P	G	P	P				F	P	P	P	
Bittercress	P	G	G	P	G	G		P	G	P	P	F
Black nightshade	P	G	G	P	G	P	G	P	G	F	P	G
Bull thistle	P	G	G	P	G			F*	P	P	P	G*
Canada thistle	P	G	P	P	G	P		P	P	P	P	
Chickweed	P	G	G	P	G	G	G	G	G	G	P	G
Clovers	P		P	P	P		P	P	P	P	P	P
Common dandelion	P	G	P	P	G	G*	G*	P	P	P	P	G*
Common groundsel	P	G	F	P	G	G	F	P	G	P	P	P-F
Corn spurry	P	G	G	P	G	G		G	G		P	G
Falsedandelion	P	G	P	P	G	P	G*	P	P	P	P	G*
Field bindweed	P	F-P	P	P	F	P		P	P	P	P	P
Field horsetail	P	G	P	P	P	P	P	P	P	P	P	P
Fireweed	P		G	P	G	P			G		P	
Geranium	P	G	G	P	G	G			G	P	P	
Hedge mustard	P	F-G	F-P	P	G	P		P	F	F	P	G*
Henbit	P	G	G	P	G	P	G	F	G	F	P	G
Knotweed	P	G	F	P	G	F	G	G	P	F	P	G
Ladysthumb	P	G	F	P	G	F	G	F	F	F	P	F
Lambsquarters	P	G	G	P	G	G	G	G	F	F	P	F
Pineappleweed	P		G	P	G	G	G	P	G*	P	P	P
Plantain	P	G	P	P	G			P	G	P	P	G
Prickly lettuce	P		G	P	G	G		P	G	P	P	G
Purslane	P	G	G	P	G	G	F	G	G	F	P	G
Redroot pigweed	P	G	G	P	G	G	F	G	G	P	P	F
Redstem filaree	P	G	F	P	G	G	G	P	F	P	P	P
Shepherdspurse	P		F	P	G	G	F	P	G	P	P	F
Tansy ragwort	P	G	P	P	G	P		P	G*	P	P	
Wild buckwheat	P	G	G	P	G				G		P	G
Wild mustard	P	G	G	P	G	G	G	G	G	F	P	G
Grasses												
Annual bluegrass	G	G	G	P	G	G	G	G	G	G	P	G
Annual ryegrass	G*		G	F	G	G*	G	G	G	G	G	G*
Barnyardgrass	G	G	G	G	G	F	G	G	G	P	G	F
Bentgrass	G*			G	G				P	F	F	G*
Orchardgrass	G			G	G				G*	G	G	P
Quackgrass	G	G	P	G	G	P	P	P	F	G	P	P
Velvetgrass	P		P	F	G	P			F	G	F	P

G = Good (85-100%), F = Fair (70-84%), P = Poor (0-69%)   *seedling stage only

Source: 1997 Pest Management Guide For Commercial Small Fruits, Washington

Herbicide Effectiveness On Weeds In Tree Fruits

Herbicide	Barnyardgrass	Carpetweed	Common cocklebur	Common lambsquarters	Common purslane	Common ragweed	Eastern black nightshade	Fall panicum	Foxtail spp.	Goosegrass	Hairy galinsoga	Jimsonweed	Large crabgrass	Morningglory spp.	Pennsylvania smartweed	Pigweed spp.	Seedling johnsongrass	Shepherdspurse	Velvetleaf	Yellow nutsedge
Preemergence (residual)																				
Casoron	F/G	—	—	G	—	G	—	F/G	F/G	F/G	—	—	F/G	—	—	G	F/G	G	—	—
Devrinol	G	G	N	F/G	F	P/F	N	G	G	G	F/P	N	G	N	P	G	G	—	N	N/P
Goal	F	G	—	G	G	G	G	F	F	—	G	G	F	—	G	G	—	G	G	P
Karmex	G	G	—	G	G	G	G	G	G	F/G	G	G	F/G	G	F	G	N	G	G	N
Princep	F	—	F/G	G	G	G	G	F	G	F/G	G	G	P/F	G	G	F	P	G	—	N
Prowl	G	G	—	F/G	F/G		G	G	G	G	N	N	G	N	—	F/G	G		F	N
Sinbar	G	G	—	G	G	G	G	G	G	G	G	G	G	G	F	G	F	—	G	P
Solicam	G	P	P	F	G	F/G	—	G	G	G	—	F	G	—	—	F	—	—	F	F
Surflan	G	F/G	N	F/G	F/G	N	P	G	G	G	N	N	G	N	P	F/G	G	N	P	N
Postemergence (selective)																				
2,4-D	N	G	F/G	F/G	G		G	N	N	N	F/G	F	N	G	F	G	N	G	G	P
Fusilade DX	G	N	N	N	N	N	N	G	G	G	N	N	F/G	N	N	N	G	N	N	N
Kerb	G	G	N	G	G	P	—	G	G	G	P	N	G	—	—	G	—	G	P	N
Poast	G	N	N	N	N	N	N	G	G	G	N	N	G	N	N	N	G	N	N	N
Postemergence (non-selective)																				
Gramoxone Extra	F/G	—	G	F/G	F/G	G	—	F/G	G	F/G	G	G	F/G	F/G	—	G	—	—	—	G
Roundup Ultra	G	G	G	G	G	F	G	G	G	G	G	G	G	F	G	G	G	G	G	F

G = Good, F = Fair, P = Poor, N = None, — = Insufficient data

Herbicide performance is affected by weather, soil type, herbicide rate, weed pressure, and other factors. These ratings indicate ONLY relative effectiveness in tests conducted by the University of Maryland and Rutgers, The State University of New Jersey, on coarse- to medium-textured soils. Actual performance may be better or worse than indicated in this chart.

Source: 1998 New Jersey Commercial Tree Fruit Production Guide

7

Fruits & Nuts
Weed Efficacy Chart

NOTICE The information on these pages is for preliminary planning — not a guide for use. Be sure to follow the manufacturer's directions, notwithstanding information contained here.

Fruits & Nuts

Small Fruits

(Blueberries, Caneberries, Cranberries, Currants, Gooseberries, Grapes, Strawberries)

120 Herbicide — see MSMA

912 Herbicide — see MSMA

Casoron — see dichlobenil

CLETHODIM

Postemergence grass herbicide. Mode of action similar to Poast, Assure, Option II, and Fusilade.

Envoy or Prism (0.94EC), Select (2EC) *(Valent)*

Rate: 0.1-0.25 lb. ai/A
13-34 fl. oz. 0.94EC/A
6-16 fl. oz. 2EC/A

Time: Postemergence. Apply to actively growing grasses.

Weeds: Grasses:

Amazon sprangletop	green foxtail	smooth crabgrass
annual bluegrass	itchgrass	southern crabgrass
barnyardgrass	johnsongrass	Texas panicum
bearded sprangletop	junglerice	volunteer cereals
bermudagrass	large crabgrass	wild oat
broadleaf signalgrass	quackgrass	wild proso millet
crowfootgrass	red rice	wirestem muhly
fall panicum	red sprangletop	witchgrass
giant foxtail	shattercane	woolly cupgrass
goosegrass	southwestern cupgrass	yellow foxtail

Remarks: Nonbearing berries, grapes, strawberries. Nonbearing are plants that will not bear fruit for at least 1 year after application. Rate varies by grass species, stage, and geographical region. Grass crops such as corn, sorghum, wheat, and rice are highly sensitive to clethodim. Do not apply under stress conditions or if rainfall is expected in 1 hour. Do not apply through any type of irrigation system. Do not apply more than 0.5 lb. ai/A (0.25 lb. ai/A on Long Island, NY) per season. Do not graze treated fields or feed treated forage or hay to livestock. Refer to label for restrictions and precautions.

State Restrictions: Not for use on Solano grass in the Vernal Lakes area of Solano County, California; wild rice in Hays County, Texas.

– – – – – – – – – – – – – – –

Signal Word/Toxicity Class: Warning/II.
REI: 24 hr.

Credit — see glyphosate

2,4-D - PHENOXY HERBICIDES

Dri-Clean (2,4-D amine) *(Riverdale)*

Rate: 5 packets/1.66-2.5 A in 10-100 gal. water

Time: Apply when weeds are in bud to early bloom stage and growing vigorously, after shatter following bloom and before grape shoots reach the ground, or during dormant season.

Weeds: Broadleaf weeds including:

Canada thistle   field bindweed

Remarks: Grapes. Established vineyards (at least 3 years old). Apply using direct application so no contact will be made to leaves and young shoots or stems. Do not apply when temperature exceeds 90°F.

– – – – – – – – – – – – – – –

Signal Word/Toxicity Class: Danger/I.
REI: 48 hr.

Formula 40 (2,4-D mixed amine) *(Rhone-Poulenc)*

Rate: 1-1.5 lb. ai/A
2-3 pt./A

Time: Apply in early spring when strawberries are dormant or immediately after last picking.

Weeds: Broadleaf weeds:

cocklebur	morningglory	ragweed
lambsquarters	pigweed	smartweed

Remarks: Strawberries. Follow advice of horticultural experts.

– – – – – – – – – – – – – – –

Signal Word/Toxicity Class: Danger/I.
REI: 48 hr.

◆ **Riverdale 2,4-D Granules (2,4-D ester)** *(Riverdale)*

Rate: 2-4 lb. ae/A
10-20 lb./A

Time: Preemergence. Apply in the spring after removal of the winter flood from dormant vines. In Wisconsin, granules may be applied on ice over plants prior to spring thaw.

Weeds: Broadleaf weeds including:

annual smartweed	northern St. Johnswort	sticktight
common ragweed	smartweed	tearthumb

Remarks: Cranberries. Do not use on light, sandy soils.

– – – – – – – – – – – – – – –

Signal Word/Toxicity Class: Caution.
REI: 12 hr.

Savage (WSB) (2,4-D amine) *(Platte)*

Rate: 0.95-1.4 lb. ae/A
1-1.5 lb. WSB/A

Time: Apply when weeds are young and actively growing, up to the point of bud break.

Weeds: Broadleaf weeds including:

Canada thistle   field bindweed   morningglory

Remarks: Grapes. Established vineyards (at least 3 years old). Do not allow spray to contact foliage, fruit, vines, stems, or exposed roots. Grapes are extremely sensitive to 2,4-D, consult a local Agricultural Extension Service specialist.

– – – – – – – – – – – – – – –

Signal Word/Toxicity Class: Danger/I.
REI: 48 hr.

DEVRINOL

Devrinol 2-E (napropamide) *(United Phosphorus)*

Rate: 4 lb. ai/A
2 gal. 2-E/A

Time: Apply in fall through early spring, prior to weed emergence. Do not apply from bloom through harvest.

Weeds: Annual broadleaf weeds:

chickweed	common sowthistle	little mallow
common fiddleneck	filaree	pineappleweed
common knotweed	groundsel	prickly lettuce
common purslane	lambsquarters	redroot pigweed

Annual grasses:

annual bluegrass	hairy crabgrass	wild barley
barnyardgrass	ripgut brome	wild oat
bristly foxtail	southwestern cupgrass	

Remarks: Strawberries. Posttransplant and established. Treatments made other than Nov.-Feb. must be irrigated-in within 24 hr. with sufficient water to wet soil to a depth of 2-4". From Nov.-Feb., if no rainfall occurs within one week irrigation or shallow incorporation recommended.

– – – – – – – – – – – – – – –

Signal Word/Toxicity Class: Warning/II.
REI: 12 hr.

Devrinol 10-G or 50-DF (napropamide) *(United Phosphorus)*

Rate: 4 lb. ai/A
40 lb. 10-G/A
8 lb. 50-DF/A

Time: Apply in fall through early spring prior to weed emergence. For strawberries, delay until desired number of daughter plants have been established; do not apply from bloom through harvest.

◆-new product • PP-preplant • PPI-preplant incorporated • PRE-preemergence • POST-postemergence • SEQ-sequential • ae-acid equivalent • ai-active ingredient • DF-dry flowable
E/EC-emulsifiable concentrate • F/FL-flowable • DG/G/WG-dispersable granule • L/LC-liquid • SP/WSP-soluble packet • W/WP-wettable powder • WSB-water soluble bag

Weeds: Annual broadleaf weeds:

annual sowthistle	common ragweed	pineappleweed
carpetweed	(suppression)	prickly lettuce
coast fiddleneck	horse purslane	prostrate knotweed
common chickweed	lambsquarters	purple cudweed
common groundsel	little mallow	redroot pigweed
common purslane	(from seed)	redstem filaree

Annual grasses:

annual bluegrass	green foxtail	sandbur
barnyardgrass	guineagrass	smooth crabgrass
bristly foxtail	hairy crabgrass	soft chess
canarygrass	Italian ryegrass	southwestern cupgrass
cheatgrass	johnsongrass (seedling)	stinkgrass
downy brome	junglerice	Texas panicum
fall panicum	large crabgrass	wild barley
foxtail barley	Mexican sprangletop	wild oat
giant foxtail	red sprangletop	witchgrass
goosegrass	ripgut brome	yellow foxtail

Remarks: Blueberries, caneberries (blackberries, boysenberries, loganberries, raspberries), currants (50-DF), grapes, strawberries. If rainfall does not occur, shallowly incorporate or irrigate-in following application with sufficient water to wet soil to a depth of 2-4". See label for allowable time for Devrinol to remain on soil surface prior to incorporation.

Tank Mixes: 50-DF: Glyphosate, Goal, Gramoxone Extra (except caneberries), Karmex, Simazine. Refer to labels for restrictions and precautions.

- - - - - - - - - - - - - - -

Rate: 3-15 lb. ai/A
30-150 lb. 10G/A

Time: Apply in fall through early spring, prior to weed emergence.

Weeds: Broadleaf weeds:

aster	clover	red sorrel
birdsfoot trefoil	purplestem beggarticks	

Grasses and sedges:

nutsedge	rice cutgrass

Remarks: Cranberries. Rate varies by soil type and region. Do not apply in spring to bogs which do not have sprinkler systems for frost control.

Crop Rotation: Do not plant to crops not specified on label until 12 months after last application.

- - - - - - - - - - - - - - -

Signal Word/Toxicity Class: Caution.
REI: 12 hr.

DICHLOBENIL

Casoron 4G (Uniroyal)

Rate: 4 lb. ai/A
100 lb. 4G/A

Time: Do not apply during new shoot emergence.

Weeds: Broadleaf weeds:

carpetweed	Florida pusley	lambsquarters
chickweed	henbit	purslane
dandelion	horsetail	shepherdspurse

Grasses:

bluegrass	crabgrass	foxtail

Remarks: Blackberries, raspberries. Established plantings. Do not graze treated areas.

Crop Rotation: Do not plant rotational crops on which dichlobenil is not registered within 1 year after application.

- - - - - - - - - - - - - - -

Rate: 4-6 lb. ai/A
100-150 lb. 4G/A

Time: Do not apply until 4 weeks after transplanting.

Weeds: Perennial weeds:

artemisia	leafy spurge	timothy
Canada thistle	orchardgrass	wild artichoke
curly dock	quackgrass	wild aster
falsedandelion	Russian knapweed	wild carrot
(catsear)	smooth brome	yellow rocket
fescue		

Remarks: Blueberries, grapes. Bearing, nonbearing nursery stock. Do not graze treated areas.

Days To Harvest: 1 month.

- - - - - - - - - - - - - - -

Rate: 4 lb. ai/A
100 lb. 4G/A

Time: Prebloom or postharvest: Apply as needed at 3-6 week intervals in early spring while perennial weeds are still dormant and annual weeds have not started to germinate or in late fall after harvest. Do not apply after cranberry plants start to bloom.

Weeds: Broadleaf weeds:

arrowleaved tearthumb	knotweed	ragweed
aster	loosestrife	royal fern
beggarticks	marsh pea	sensitive fern
brackenfern	marsh St. Johnswort	sorrell
buckbean	marshpepper	spotted smartweed
common horsetail	smartweed	swamp smartweed
dodder	Pennsylvania	tideland clover
haircap moss	smartweed	water smartweed
hawkweed	plantain	wild strawberry

Grasses and sedges:

bentgrass	needlegrass	stargrass
bluejointgrass	nutsedge (nutgrass)	summergrass
(western wheatgrass)	oniongrass	velvetgrass
bunchgrass	rattlesnakegrass	water horsetail
cottongrass	(mannagrass)	(pipes)
crabgrass	rice cutgrass	western lilaeopsis
little hairgrass	rush	wideleaf grass
muskrat grass	short wiregrass	woolgrass

Remarks: Cranberries. Do not apply on young or newly sanded beds, or on bogs prior to or immediately after mowing for vines. Do not exceed 100 lb./A per year. Do not graze treated areas.

- - - - - - - - - - - - - - -

Signal Word/Toxicity Class: Caution/III.
REI: 12 hr.

DIQUAT DIBROMIDE

Diquat (ZENECA)

Rate: 0.375-0.5 lb. ai/A
1.5-2 pt./A

Time: Site preparation prior to planting. Repeat as needed.

Weeds: Broadleaf weeds and grasses.

Remarks: Nonbearing blueberries, caneberries (blackberries, boysenberries, dewberries, elderberries, huckleberries, loganberries, raspberries), cranberries, gooseberries, grapes. Apply by ground only. Use high rate when weeds are large or dense. Do not allow spray to contact green stems, foliage, or fruit. Use a shield or wrap plant when spraying around young trees or vines. Do not apply through any type of irrigation system. Do not graze treated areas. Refer to label for use restrictions and precautions.

Days To Harvest: 1 year.

- - - - - - - - - - - - - - -

Signal Word/Toxicity Class: Warning/II.
REI: 24 hr.

Direx — see diuron

DIURON

Direx 4L or 80DF (Griffin)
◆ Diuron 80 WDG (Platte)
Drexel Diuron 4L or 80 (Drexel)
Karmex DF (Griffin)
Riverside Diuron 4L or 80DF (Terra)

Rate: 1.5-4.5 lb. ai/A
1.5-4.5 qt. 4L/A
2-6 lb. 80, DF, 80DF/A

Time: Preemergence. Apply in the spring just prior to germination of annual weeds.

Weeds: Annual broadleaf weeds:

annual morningglory	mustard	ragweed
lambsquarters	pigweed	wild lettuce

Annual grasses:

barnyardgrass	crabgrass	johnsongrass (seedling)

Remarks: Grapes. Apply only to established vineyards (at least 3 years old) as a band to grape row.

State Restrictions: For use east of the Rockies.

- - - - - - - - - - - - - - -

Rate: 2.4-3.2 lb. ai/A
2.4-3.2 qt. 4L/A
3-4 lb. 80, DF, 80DF/A

Time: Apply during winter months when weeds are less than 2" tall.

Weeds: Same as above.

Remarks: Grapes. Apply only to established vineyards (at least 3 years old) as a band to grape row. Do not apply to vines with trunks less than 1½" in diameter.

State Restrictions: For use west of the Rockies.

- - - - - - - - - - - - - - -

7

Fruits & Nuts

NOTICE The information on these pages is for preliminary planning — not a guide for use. Be sure to follow the manufacturer's directions, notwithstanding information contained here. | For personal protective equipment and EPA registration numbers, please turn to page 70.

Small Fruits

Rate: 6.4-9.6 lb. ai/A
6.4-9.6 qt. 4L/A
8-12 lb. 80, DF, 80DF/A
Time: Apply in the spring.
Weeds: Spot control of perennial grasses:

orchardgrass   quackgrass   ryegrass

Remarks: Grapes. Apply only to established vineyards (at least 4 years old) as a band treatment to ridged soil under the trellis. Band width should not exceed 30". Do not apply more than once every 4 years.
State Restrictions: For use in New York and Pennsylvania.

- - - - - - - - - - - - - - -

Rate: 1.2-3 lb. ai/A
1.2-3 qt. 4L/A
1.5-4 lb. 80, DF, 80DF/A
Time: For spring application, apply before germination and growth of annual weeds and grasses.
Weeds: Annual broadleaf weeds:

annual morningglory	mustard	ragweed
lambsquarters	pigweed	wild lettuce

Annual grasses:

barnyardgrass	crabgrass	johnsongrass (seedling)

Remarks: Blueberries, caneberries, gooseberries. Apply to fields which have been established for at least 1 year. Do not apply to berries interplanted with fruit trees or where roots are exposed. Rate varies by type of berry, geographical regions, and restrictions. Do not use on sand, loamy sand, or gravelly soils. Use directed spray, avoiding contact of foliage and fruit.
State Restrictions: Blueberries: Georgia, Indiana, Massachusetts, Michigan, New Jersey, Ohio, western Oregon, western Washington. **Blackberries, boysenberries, dewberries, loganberries:** California. **Caneberries, gooseberries:** Western Oregon, western Washington. **Raspberries:** California, Indiana, Michigan, Ohio.

- - - - - - - - - - - - - - -

Signal Word/Toxicity Class: Caution/III.
REI: 12 hr.

Dri-Clean — see 2,4-D

DSMA

◆ **Clean Crop DSMA Plus (3.6L) (+ surfactant)** *(Platte)*
Liquid DSMA (3.6L) (+ surfactant) *(Helena)*
Rate: 3.2-6.3 lb. ai/A
3.5-7 qt. 3.6L/A
Time: Postemergence (directed spray).
Weeds: Grassy weeds.
Remarks: Nonbearing vineyards. Do not use around trees from which crop will be harvested within 1 year of treatment. Do not allow to contact leaves, stems, or bark of trees. If necessary, use shield for nursery plantings or young trees. For regrowth, up to 3 applications per year may be applied.

- - - - - - - - - - - - - - -

Signal Word/Toxicity Class: Caution/III.
REI: 12 hr.

Envoy — see clethodim

Evital — see norflurazon

FLUAZIFOP-P-BUTYL

Fusilade DX *(ZENECA)*
Rate: 0.25-0.375 lb. ai/A
1-1.5 pt. DX/A
Time: Annual grasses: Apply at 2-8" tall before tillering and/or heading. Perennial grasses: Apply by growth stage dependent on species.
Weeds: Annual and perennial grasses:

barnyardgrass	johnsongrass	southern sandbur
bermudagrass	(rhizome, seedling)	Texas panicum
broadleaf signalgrass	junglerice	tropical crabgrass
fall panicum	large crabgrass	volunteer cereals
field sandbur	quackgrass	wild oat
giant foxtail	red rice	wild proso millet
goosegrass	shattercane	wirestem muhly
green foxtail	smooth crabgrass	witchgrass
Italian ryegrass	sorghum-almum	woolly cupgrass
itchgrass	southern crabgrass	yellow foxtail

Remarks: Nonbearing berries, grapes. Rate varies by geographic area and grass species. Add crop oil concentrate or nonionic surfactant. Do not apply to berries or grapes that may be harvested for food within 1 year after application. Refer to label for specific directions and precautions.
Crop Rotation: Do not plant rotational grass crops such as corn, sorghum, and cereals within 60 days after last application.
State Restrictions: Refer to label for geographical regions.

- - - - - - - - - - - - - - -

Signal Word/Toxicity Class: Caution.
REI: 12 hr.

Formula 40 — see 2,4-D

Fusilade DX — see fluazifop-P-butyl

GALLERY

Gallery 75DF (isoxaben) *(Dow AgroSciences)*
Rate: 0.5-1 lb. ai/A
0.66-1.33 lb. 75DF/A
Time: Preemergence. Apply in late summer to early fall or in early spring, prior to germination of target weeds.
Weeds: Broadleaf weeds:

annual sowthistle	dandelion	prostrate spurge
bittercress	dogfennel	redmaids
black mustard	green tansymustard	rockpurslane
black nightshade	hairy galinsoga	redstem filaree
blackleaved fleabane	henbit	shepherdspurse
bracted plantain	horseweed	sibara
buckhorn plantain	ladysthumb	slender plantain
Carolina geranium	lambsquarters	southern brassbuttons
coast fiddleneck	London rocket	spotted spurge
common chickweed	marestail	thymeleaf speedwell
common groundsel	mouseear chickweed	velvetleaf
common purslane	pennywort	white clover
common ragweed	pigweed	whitestem filaree
common sowthistle	pineappleweed	wild celery
creeping woodsorrel	prickly lettuce	wild mustard
cudweed	prostrate knotweed	yellow woodsorrel

Remarks: Nonbearing: blueberries, caneberries (blackberries, boysenberries, dewberries, elderberries, loganberries, raspberries), currants, gooseberries, grapes. Do not apply through any type of irrigation system. Refer to label for additional use precautions.

- - - - - - - - - - - - - - -

Signal Word/Toxicity Class: Caution/III.
REI: 12 hr.

GLUFOSINATE-AMMONIUM

Provides faster knockdown of most emerged weeds than glyphosate but slower than paraquat. A contact herbicide; not systemic but suppresses perennial broadleaf weeds. Excellent control of suckers or cane without injury to mature vines.

Rely *(AgrEvo USA)*
Rate: Broadcast:
3-5 qt./A
Time: Apply low rate when weeds are less than 6" tall; high rate when weeds are 6" or taller.
Weeds: Broadleaf weeds:

chickweed	jimsonweed	marestail
clover	kochia	purslane
common cocklebur	London rocket	shepherdspurse
filaree	malva	smartweed
horseweed		

Grasses:

barnyardgrass	goosegrass	shattercane
cupgrass	green foxtail	stinkgrass
fall panicum	johnsongrass	windgrass
giant foxtail	lovegrass	yellow foxtail

Rate: Broadcast:
4-6 qt./A
Time: Apply low rate when weeds are less than 8" tall; high rate when weeds are 8" or taller.

◆-new product • PP-preplant • PPI-preplant incorporated • PRE-preemergence • POST-postemergence • SEQ-sequential • ae-acid equivalent • ai-active ingredient • DF-dry flowable
E/EC-emulsifiable concentrate • F/FL-flowable • DG/G/WG-dispersable granule • L/LC-liquid • SP/WSP-soluble packet • W/WP-wettable powder • WSB-water soluble bag

Weeds: Broadleaf weeds:

annual sowthistle	leafy spurge	vervain
bindweed	mugwort	vetch
buffalobur	musk thistle	Virginia copperleaf
burdock	nettle	white clover
Canada thistle	nightshade	white heath aster
curly dock	pennycress	wild buckwheat
dandelion	plantain	wild mustard
dogbane	prickly lettuce	wild onion
field gromwell	ragweed	wild rose
fleabane	redroot pigweed	wild turnip
goldenrod	Russian thistle	woodsorrel
horsetail	tansymustard	yellow rocket
lambsquarters	velvetleaf	

Grasses and sedges:

annual bluegrass	fescue	ryegrass
bahiagrass	guineagrass	sandbur
barley	johnsongrass	smooth bromegrass
bermudagrass	(rhizome)	torpedograss
carpetgrass	Kentucky bluegrass	vaseygrass
crabgrass	nutsedge	wheat
dallisgrass	paragrass	wild oat
downy bromegrass	quackgrass	

Rate: Split application: 4 qt./A
Time: Apply approximately 4 weeks apart. Suckers should not exceed 12" in length.
Weeds: Sucker control.
Remarks: Grapes. Do not apply on desirable foliage, or allow spray to drift on foliage. Avoid contact with foliage or green tissue of desirable vegetation. Do not graze or feed treated orchard cover crops. Do not apply by air or through any type of irrigation system. Refer to label for directions and precautions.
Tank Mixes: Devrinol, Karmex, Sinbar, simazine, Solicam, Surflan.
State Restrictions: Not for use in Nassau and Suffolk counties in New York.

Signal Word/Toxicity Class: Warning/II.
REI: 12 hr.

Glyfos or Glyfos X-tra — see glyphosate

GLYPHOSATE

◆ **Credit (4WS)** *(Nufarm)*
◆ **Glyfos or Glyfos X-tra (4WS)** *(Cheminova)*
Rattler (4WS) *(Helena)*
Roundup Custom (5.4WS) *(Monsanto)*
Roundup Original, Original RT, Ultra, Ultra RT (4WS) *(Monsanto)*
Rate: 0.5-5 lb. ai/A
0.75-7.5 pt. 5.4WS/A
1-10 pt. 4WS/A
Wiper application:
6 pt. 5.4WS/4 gal. water
8 pt. 4WS/4 gal. water
Time: Preplant, preemergence, directed spray (except cranberries), wiper application. For grapes, in the Northeast and Great Lakes area, apply prior to end of bloom stage or apply with shielded sprayers or wiper equipment.
Weeds: Annual and perennial weeds, grasses and ground covers.
Remarks: Blueberries, caneberries (blackberries, boysenberries, dewberries, elderberries, loganberries, olallieberries, raspberries, youngberries), cranberries, currants, gooseberries, grapes, huckleberries. Do not apply when green shoots, canes, or foliage are in spray zone or allow solution to contact desirable vegetation. Do not add surfactant to Roundup Ultra or Ultra RT. Refer to label for directions, restrictions, and precautions.
Days To Harvest: 14; cranberries—30.
State Restrictions: Roundup RT for use in Colorado, Idaho, Montana, North Dakota, South Dakota, Utah, Wyoming, and in specific counties only in Kansas, Minnesota, Nebraska, Nevada, Oklahoma, Oregon, and Washington; refer to label for restrictions. Glyfos not registered for use in California. Glyfos X-tra not registered for use in mistblowers in California or Arizona.

Signal Word/Toxicity Class: Varies by formulation.
REI: Warning—12 hr.; Caution—4 hr.

GOAL

Goal 2XL (oxyfluorfen) *(Rohm and Haas)*
Rate: Preemergence:
1.25-2 lb. ai/A
5-8 pt. 2XL/A
Postemergence:
0.5-2 lb. ai/A
2-8 pt. 2XL/A

Time: Preemergence, postemergence. Dormant application in Arizona and California, apply after final harvest up to Feb. 15 (in Coachella Valley, CA, do not apply after Feb. 1). Do not use should bud swell occur prior to dates listed.
Weeds: Broadleaf weeds—AZ, CA:

annual sowthistle	common	prickly lettuce
broadleaf filaree	lambsquarters	prostrate knotweed
burclover	common purslane	redmaids
burning nettle	henbit	rockpurslane
cheeseweed	London rocket	redroot pigweed
coast fiddleneck	malva	redstem filaree
common groundsel	minerslettuce	shepherdspurse

Broadleaf weeds—All States:

American black nightshade	common purslane	prostrate spurge
annual morningglory	cutleaf	redroot pigweed
annual sowthistle	eveningprimrose	shepherdspurse
balsamapple	cutleaf groundcherry	spotted spurge
black nightshade	hemp sesbania	teaweed
camphorweed	jimsonweed	velvetleaf
common cocklebur	narrowleaf cudweed	Virginia pepperweed
common lambsquarters	Pennsylvania smartweed	wild poinsettia
	prickly sida	Wright groundcherry

Remarks: Grapes. Direct spray toward base of tree or vine, avoiding direct plant contact. Add 2 pt./100 gal. spray nonionic surfactant. Do not apply to grapes less than 3 years old unless vines are on a trellis wire at least 3 ft. above soil surface. Refer to label for complete use directions.
Tank Mixes: Diuron, glyphosate, napropamide, norflurazon, oryzalin, paraquat, pronamide, simazine.

Signal Word/Toxicity Class: Warning/II.
REI: 24 hr.

Gramoxone Extra — see paraquat

HEXAZINONE

Pronone 10G or MG *(Pro-Serve)*
Rate: 0.5-3 lb. ai/A
5-30 lb. 10G, MG/A
Time: Preemergence. Apply to nonbearing fields after frost is out of the ground until tip dieback growth stage.
Weeds: Annual grasses, herbaceous weeds, and woody plants.
Remarks: Blueberries (lowbush). Do not apply to wet foliage, snow covered or frozen soil, or if standing water is in field. Use lower rate on steep slopes or erosion may occur. Refer to label for additional precautions.
State Restrictions: SLN-Maine.

Signal Word/Toxicity Class: Caution.
REI: 24 hr.

Karmex — see diuron

KERB

Restricted Use Pesticide.

Kerb 50-W (pronamide) *(Rohm and Haas)*
Rate: 1-4 lb. ai/A
2-8 lb. 50-W/A
Time: Apply in fall after fruit is harvested, but prior to soil freeze-up.
Weeds: Broadleaf weeds:

chickweed	red sorrel (seedling)

Grasses:

annual bluegrass	Italian ryegrass	quackgrass
annual ryegrass	Kentucky bluegrass	tall fescue
downy brome (cheatgrass)	orchardgrass	volunteer grains
	ryegrass	wild oat

Remarks: Grapes. Do not apply to seedling trees or vines less than 1 year old, fall transplanted stock that has been transplanted less than 1 year, or to spring transplanted stock that has been transplanted less than 6 months. Do not graze treated orchards.

Rate: 1-3 lb. ai/A
2-6 lb. 50-W/A
Time: Apply in fall or winter before ground is frozen.
Weeds: Broadleaf weeds:

chickweed

Grasses:

annual bluegrass	perennial ryegrass	quackgrass

7

Fruits & Nuts

Small Fruits

Remarks: Blackberries, boysenberries, raspberries. Do not apply until roots are well established or to blackberries or raspberries transplanted less than 3 months.
State Restrictions: For use in Oregon, Washington.

- - - - - - - - - - - - - -

Rate: 1-2 lb. ai/A
      2-4 lb. 50-W/A
Time: Apply in fall or early winter prior to soil freeze-up and snow cover.
Weeds: Broadleaf weeds:

chickweed	red sorrel (seedling)

Grasses:

annual bluegrass	Kentucky bluegrass	tall fescue
bentgrass	orchardgrass	velvetgrass
downy brome	perennial ryegrass	wild oat
(cheatgrass)	quackgrass	

Remarks: Blueberries. Do not apply to newly transplanted blueberries until roots are well established. Best activity occurs when applied under cool temperatures (55°F or less) and followed by rainfall or overhead irrigation.

- - - - - - - - - - - - - -

Signal Word/Toxicity Class: Caution.
REI: 24 hr.

MSMA

120 Herbicide (6.6) *(Terra)*
912 Herbicide (6) (+ surfactant) *(Terra)*
Rate: Nonbearing:
      2-3 lb. ai/A
      2.66-4 pt. 6.6/A
      2-4 lb. ai/A
      2.66-5.32 pt. 6/A
Time: Do not exceed 3 applications per year.
Weeds: Grassy weeds.
Remarks: Nonbearing vineyards. Do not use around vines from which crop will be harvested within 1 year after application.

- - - - - - - - - - - - - -

Signal Word/Toxicity Class: Caution/III.
REI: 12 hr.

NORFLURAZON

Evital (5G) *(Novartis)*
Rate: 4-8 lb. ai/A
      80-160 lb. 5G/A
Time: Apply as single early spring application after removal of winter flood and before weed growth resumes or in the fall after harvest at least 2 weeks before winter flood.
Weeds: Grasses and sedges:

barnyardgrass	needlegrass	smokegrass
bog rush	nutsedge	spikerush
broomsedge	redroot	stargrass
fall panicum	redtop grass	summergrass
little bluestem	rice cutgrass	switchgrass
(povertygrass)	(sicklegrass)	woolgrass

Remarks: Cranberries only. Rate varies by weed and bog conditions. Flooding after application may reduce weed control. Injury to cranberry plant may occur where applications overlap or where water stands in low, wet areas of a treated bog. Refer to label for further use directions.
State Restrictions: For use in Massachusetts, New Jersey, Oregon, Washington, Wisconsin.

- - - - - - - - - - - - - -

Signal Word/Toxicity Class: Caution.
REI: 12 hr.

Solicam DF *(Novartis)*
Rate: 1-4 lb. ai/A
      1.25-5 lb. DF/A
Time: Apply from fall to early spring before weeds emerge.
Weeds: Broadleaf weeds:

black mustard	horseweed*	redstem filaree
chickweed	(marestail)	Russian thistle*
common	little mallow	shepherdspurse
lambsquarters*	(cheeseweed)	silverleaf nightshade*
falsedandelion	London rocket	(white horsenettle)
(smooth catsear)	pigweed*	tumble mustard
fiddleneck	pineappleweed	Virginia pepperweed
flixweed	puncturevine	whitestem filaree
groundsel*	redroot pigweed*	

Grasses:

annual bluegrass	downy brome	quackgrass*
annual ryegrass	fall panicum	sixweeks grama
annual sedge	feather fingergrass	southwestern cupgrass
barnyardgrass	foxtail	tall fescue
bermudagrass*	goosegrass	Texas panicum
broadleaf signalgrass	Italian ryegrass	wild barley
cheat	johnsongrass (seedling)	wild onion
crabgrass	nutsedge	witchgrass

* Suppression

Remarks: Blueberries, caneberries (blackberries, raspberries), grapes. Rate varies by soil type. Refer to label.
Tank Mixes: Grapes: Diuron, Goal, Gramoxone, Prowl, Roundup, simazine, Surflan. Blackberries, blueberries, raspberries: Diuron, Gramoxone, simazine, Sinbar, Surflan; refer to label for use instructions.
State Restrictions: Do not apply to wine grapes grown in coarse soils in Washington. See label for use restrictions in Coachella Valley of California.

- - - - - - - - - - - - - -

Signal Word/Toxicity Class: Caution.
REI: 12 hr.

PARAQUAT

Restricted Use Pesticide.

Gramoxone Extra (2.5L) *(ZENECA)*
Rate: 0.6-1 lb. ai/A
      2-3 pt. 2.5L/A
Time: Postemergence directed spray. Apply before emergence of new canes or shoots.
Weeds: Annual broadleaf weeds and grasses; top kill and suppression of perennials in interspaces and around base of bushes or vines.
Remarks: Blueberries, caneberries (blackberries, boysenberries, raspberries), grapes. Add nonionic surfactant or crop oil concentrate. Refer to label for use directions, restrictions, and precautions.

- - - - - - - - - - - - - -

Rate: 0.5 lb. ai/A
      1.5 pt. 2.5L/A
Time: Postemergence directed spray. For best results, apply when weeds and grasses are succulent and weed growth is 1-6" tall.
Weeds: Annual broadleaf weeds and grasses; top kill and suppression of emerged perennial weeds between rows after crop emergence or establishment.
Remarks: Strawberries. Add nonionic surfactant or crop oil concentrate. Apply by directing spray between rows and using shields to prevent spray contact with crop. Weeds and grasses emerging after application will not be controlled. Do not allow spray to contact plants. Do not graze treated areas. Refer to label for use directions and precautions.
Days To Harvest: 21.

- - - - - - - - - - - - - -

Signal Word/Toxicity Class: Danger-Poison/I.
REI: 12 hr. (except harvest aid/desiccation 24 hr.).

PENDIMETHALIN

Pentagon DG *(American Cyanamid)*
Prowl 3.3 EC *(American Cyanamid)*
Rate: 2-4 lb. ai/A
      2.4-4.8 qt. 3.3 EC/A
      3.3-6.6 lb. DG/A
Time: For newly transplanted and 1 year old grapevines. Apply only to dormant grapevines. Do not apply if buds have started to swell.
Weeds: Broadleaf weeds:

annual spurge	knotweed	pigweed
carpetweed	kochia	puncturevine
chickweed	lambsquarters	purslane
fiddleneck	London rocket	shepherdspurse
Florida pusley	Pennsylvania	velvetleaf
henbit	smartweed	

Grasses:

annual bluegrass	giant foxtail	red sprangletop
barnyardgrass	green foxtail	signalgrass
browntop panicum	johnsongrass	Texas panicum
crabgrass	(seedling)	witchgrass
crowfootgrass	junglerice	woolly cupgrass
fall panicum	lovegrass	yellow foxtail
field sandbur	Mexican sprangletop	

Remarks: Nonbearing grapes. Use low rate for short-term control; high rate for long-term. Apply spray directly to ground beneath vines. Do not apply over the top of vines with leaves or buds. Do not apply to newly transplanted vines until ground has settled and no cracks are present. Refer to label for directions, precautions, and limitations.

- - - - - - - - - - - - - -

Signal Word/Toxicity Class: Caution.
REI: 24 hr.

◆-new product • PP-preplant • PPI-preplant incorporated • PRE-preemergence • POST-postemergence • SEQ-sequential • ae-acid equivalent • ai-active ingredient • DF-dry flowable
E/EC-emulsifiable concentrate • F/FL-flowable • DG/G/WG-dispersable granule • L/LC-liquid • SP/WSP-soluble packet • W/WP-wettable powder • WSB-water soluble bag

Pentagon — see pendimethalin

Poast — see sethoxydim

Princep — see simazine

Prism — see clethodim

Pronone — see hexazinone

Prowl — see pendimethalin

Rattler — see glyphosate

Rely — see glufosinate-ammonium

Roundup — see glyphosate

Savage — see 2,4-D

SCYTHE

Nonselective, postemergent herbicide. May be used to control suckers.

◆ **Scythe (pelargonic acid)** *(Mycogen)*
Rate: 4-13 fl. oz./1 gal. spray solution
Time: Apply to actively growing weeds prior to crop emergence.
Weeds: Annual and perennial broadleaf weeds and grasses.
Remarks: Blueberries, caneberries (blackberries, boysenberries, dewberries, loganberries olallieberries, raspberries), cranberries, currants, grapes, strawberries. Apply in minimum 75 gal. spray solution/A or spray-to-wet. Do not apply by air or through any type of irrigation system. Refer to label for directions and precautions.
Tank Mixes: Glyphosate and other foliar and residual herbicides.

— — — — — — — — — — — — —

Signal Word/Toxicity Class: Warning/II.
REI: 24 hr.

Select — see clethodim

SETHOXYDIM

Poast (1.5EC) *(BASF)*
Rate: 0.3-0.5 lb. ai/A
1.5-2.5 pt. 1.5EC/A
Time: Apply to actively growing grasses.
Weeds: Annual and perennial grasses:

annual ryegrass	large crabgrass	southwestern cupgrass
barnyardgrass	lovegrass	stinkgrass
bermudagrass	orchardgrass	tall fescue
broadleaf signalgrass	(seedling)	Texas panicum
browntop panicum	perennial ryegrass	volunteer grains
fall panicum	quackgrass	wild oat
giant foxtail	red rice	wild proso millet
goosegrass	red sprangletop	wirestem muhly
green foxtail	shattercane	witchgrass
itchgrass	(wildcane)	woolly cupgrass
johnsongrass	smooth crabgrass	yellow foxtail
junglerice		

Remarks: Blueberries, cranberries, grapes, raspberries, strawberries; nonbearing blackberries. Rate varies by growing region. Add 2 pt./A crop oil concentrate. Refer to label for restrictions and limitations.
Days To Harvest: Strawberries—7; blueberries—30; raspberries—45; grapes—50; cranberries—60; nonbearing blackberries—1 year.

State Restrictions: Not registered for use in California on blueberries. Do not use UAN or AMS in California or Pacific Northwest.

— — — — — — — — — — — — —

Signal Word/Toxicity Class: Warning/II.
REI: 12 hr.

SIMAZINE

◆ **Clean Crop Simazine 4L or 90WDG** *(Platte)*
Drexel Simazine 4L or 90DF *(Drexel)*
Princep 4L or Caliber 90 *(Novartis)*
Riverside Simazine 4L or 90DF *(Terra)*
Rate: Grapes:
2-4.8 lb. ai/A
2-4.8 qt. 4L/A
2.2-5.3 lb. 90, 90DF, 90WDG/A
Time: Apply any time between harvest and early spring.

Rate: Blueberries, caneberries:
2-4 lb. ai/A in 40 gal. water
2-4 qt. 4L/A
2.2-4.4 lb. 90, 90DF, 90WDG/A
Time: Apply single application in the spring or split applications once in the spring and again in the fall. For quackgrass, apply single application in the fall or split applications once in the fall and again in the spring.

Rate: Cranberries (except MA):
2 lb. ai/A
2 qt. 4L/A
2.2 lb. 90, 90DF, 90WDG/A
Cranberries (MA):
4 lb. ai/A
4 qt. 4L/A
4.4 lb. 90, 90DF, 90WDG/A
Time: Apply in the spring before growth begins. In Massachusetts, apply after fall harvest or before spring growth begins.

Rate: Strawberries (OR,WA):
1 lb. ai/A
1 qt. 4L/A
1.1 lb. 90, 90DF, 90WDG/A
Time: Apply Oct.-Nov. in fields where overhead irrigation is not used. Apply after harvest at time of bed renovation where overhead irrigation is used.
Weeds: Annual broadleaf weeds:

annual morningglory	flora's paintbrush	ragweed
burclover	Florida pusley	redmaids
carelessweed	German moss	rockpurslane
carpetweed	groundsel	Russian thistle
common chickweed	henbit	shepherdspurse
common	knawel	smartweed
lambsquarters	nightshade	spanishneedles
common purslane	pepperweed	speedwell
fiddleneck	pigweed	tansymustard
filaree	pineappleweed	wild mustard
fireweed	prickly lettuce	yellowflower pepperweed

Grasses:

annual bluegrass	fall panicum	signalgrass
annual ryegrass	foxtail	silver hairgrass
barnyardgrass	goosegrass	watergrass
cheatgrass	junglerice	wild oat
crabgrass	quackgrass	witchgrass
downy brome	rattail fescue	

Remarks: Blueberries, caneberries (blackberries, boysenberries, loganberries, raspberries), cranberries, grapes, strawberries. For blueberries and caneberries, do not apply when fruit is present, or illegal residues may result. For grapes, do not use in vineyards established less than 3 years. For plantings less than 6 months old use 1/2 rate. For strawberries, make only 1 application per growing season and do not apply within 4 months after transplanting.
Tank Mixes: Glyphosate, Gramoxone Extra (grapes); Surflan (grapes and caneberries). Refer to labels for restrictions and precautions.

— — — — — — — — — — — — —

Signal Word/Toxicity Class: Caution/III.
REI: 12 hr.

SINBAR

Sinbar (WP) (terbacil) *(DuPont)*
Rate: Caneberries:
0.8-1.6 lb. ai/A
1-2 lb. WP/A
Blueberries:
1.6-3.2 lb. ai/A
2-4 lb. WP/A

7

Fruits & Nuts

Time: Apply before weeds emerge or during early seedling stage of weed growth. For caneberries, apply in spring or after harvest in fall; for blueberries, apply in fall or spring.

Weeds: Broadleaf weeds:

chickweed	lambsquarters	purslane
dogfennel	marestail	ragweed
Florida pusley	mustard	shepherdspurse
groundsel	nightshade	smartweed
henbit	prickly lettuce	tansymustard
knotweed		

Grasses and sedges:

annual bluegrass	foxtail	quackgrass*
barnyardgrass	guineagrass	red sorrel*
crabgrass	junglerice	ryegrass
crowfootgrass	nutsedge	sandbur
downy brome	panicum	

* Partial control

Remarks: Blueberries, caneberries (blackberries, boysenberries, dewberries, loganberries, raspberries, youngberries). Established for 1 year or more. Rate varies by soil texture. Refer to label for limitations and directions.

Days To Harvest: Caneberries—70.

Crop Rotation: Caneberries may be planted to alfalfa, apples, blueberries, mint, peaches, or strawberries 1 year after last treatment; blueberries to blueberries 1 year after last application. Do not replant to other crops within 2 years of last application.

State Restrictions: Not for use in California.

– – – – – – – – – – – – – – –

Signal Word/Toxicity Class: Caution.
REI: 12 hr.

SNAPSHOT (Premix)

Snapshot 2.5TG (2% trifluralin & 0.5% isoxaben) *(Dow AgroSciences)*

Rate: 2.5-5 lb. ai/A
100-200 lb. 2.5TG/A

Time: Apply in late summer to early fall, early spring, or immediately after cultivation.

Weeds: Broadleaf weeds:

annual bursage	eveningprimrose	prickly sida
annual sowthistle	fall panicum	prostrate knotweed
black medic	hairy fleabane	purple cudweed
black nightshade	hairy galinsoga	purslane speedwell
bristly oxtongue	hare barley	rattail fescue
broadleaf plantain	heath aster	redstem filaree
burning nettle	henbit	Russian thistle
California burclover	horseweed	scarlet pimpernel
Carolina geranium	Indian mustard	shepherdspurse
clover	jimsonweed	sibara
coast fiddleneck	kochia	silversheath knotweed
common chickweed	lanceleaf groundcherry	slender aster
common groundsel	little mallow	slender plantain
common lambsquarters	London rocket	spiny sowthistle
common purslane	marestail	spotted spurge
common ragweed	Mexican sprangletop	sunflower
creeping woodsorrel	nettleleaf goosefoot	swinecress
curly dock	panicle willowweed	tall morningglory
dandelion	Pennsylvania smartweed	telegraphplant
datura	petty spurge	turkey mullein
desert rockpurslane	pigweed	velvetleaf
dwarf fleabane	pineappleweed	Virginia pepperweed
dwarf mallow	prickly lettuce	yellow sweetclover
		yellow woodsorrel

Annual grasses:

annual bluegrass	junglerice	wild mustard
barnyardgrass	lovegrass	wild oat
bromegrass	southwestern cupgrass	wild radish
crabgrass	wild carrot	witchgrass
giant foxtail	wild celery	yellow foxtail
Italian ryegrass		

Remarks: Nonbearing grape vineyards. Do not apply to bedding plants, nursery seedbeds, or transplant beds.

State Restrictions: Refer to label for use restrictions in Arizona.

– – – – – – – – – – – – – – –

Signal Word/Toxicity Class: Caution/III.
REI: 12 hr.

Solicam — see norflurazon

SURFLAN

Surflan A.S. (oryzalin) *(Dow AgroSciences)*

Rate: 2-6 lb. ai/A
2-6 qt. A.S./A

Time: Apply before weeds emerge.

Weeds: Broadleaf weeds:

annual morningglory*	field sandbur	puncturevine
annual smartweed*	Florida purslane	red sprangletop
annual sowthistle*	Florida pusley	redmaids rockpurslane
black mustard*	giant ragweed*	redroot pigweed
black nightshade*	henbit	redstem filaree*
carelessweed	ladysthumb*	rough pigweed
carpetweed	lambsquarters	shepherdspurse
chickweed	London rocket*	smooth pigweed
climbing milkweed*	Mexican clover	spiny pigweed
coast fiddleneck	prickly lettuce*	teaweed*
common groundsel*	prickly sida*	tumble pigweed
common mallow*	prostrate knotweed	velvetleaf*
common purslane	prostrate pigweed	whitestem filaree*
common ragweed*	prostrate spurge*	wild mustard*
cudweed		

Grasses:

annual bluegrass	green foxtail	robust foxtail
annual ryegrass	guineagrass	signalgrass
barnyardgrass	Italian ryegrass	smooth crabgrass
bottlegrass	johnsongrass	spreading panicgrass
bristlegrass	(seedling)	southwestern cupgrass
browntop panicum	junglerice	Texas panicum
crowfootgrass	large crabgrass	watergrass
downy brome	little barley	wild oat
fall panicum	Mexican lovegrass	witchgrass
foxtail	Orcutt lovegrass	yellow foxtail
giant foxtail	pigeongrass	

*Suppression

Remarks: Bearing, nonbearing: blueberries, caneberries (blackberries, boysenberries, dewberries, elderberries, loganberries, raspberries), currants, gooseberries, grapes. Rate varies by length of control desired. Surface apply once existing weeds are controlled by tillage or contact herbicide. Single 1/2-1" rain or sprinkler irrigation within 21 days required. Not recommended on soils with organic matter higher than 5%.

Tank Mixes: Gramoxone Extra, Karmex, Princep, Sinbar.

– – – – – – – – – – – – – – –

Signal Word/Toxicity Class: Caution/III.
REI: 12 hr.

TOUCHDOWN

Touchdown (5L or 6L) (sulfosate) *(ZENECA)*

Rate: 0.5-4 lb. ai/A
0.8-6.4 pt. 5L/A
0.66-5.33 pt. 6L/A

Time: Apply to actively growing grasses and weeds.

Weeds: Broadleaf weeds:

annual sowthistle	fiddleneck	marestail
annual spurge	field bindweed	morningglory
black nightshade	field sandbur	mouseear chickweed
brackenfern	filaree	mustard
camphorweed	fleabane	Pennsylvania smartweed
Canada thistle	Florida pusley	prickly lettuce
Carolina geranium	giant ragweed	redroot pigweed
common chickweed	groundcherry	Russian thistle
common cocklebur	hairy fleabane	shepherdspurse
common groundsel	hemp dogbane	sicklepod
common lambsquarters	henbit	smooth pigweed
common ragweed	hophornbeam copperleaf	spanishneedles
curly dock	kochia	velvetleaf
cutleaf eveningprimrose	leafy spurge*	white clover
dandelion	little barley	wild buckwheat
dogfennel	London rocket	

Grasses:

annual bluegrass	fescue	shattercane
bahiagrass	foxtail	smooth bromegrass
barley	goosegrass	sprangletop
barnyardgrass	guineagrass	stinkgrass
bermudagrass	Italian ryegrass	tall fescue
broadleaf signalgrass	johnsongrass (seedling)	Texas panicum
cheat	Kentucky bluegrass	timothy
cogongrass*	orchardgrass	vaseygrass
crabgrass	paragrass	wild oat
crowfootgrass	perennial ryegrass	wirestem muhly
downy brome	quackgrass	witchgrass
fall panicum	red rice	woolly cupgrass

* Partial control

Remarks: Nonbearing blueberries, caneberries (blackberries, boysenberries, dewberries, elderberries, loganberries, raspberries, youngberries, cranberries, currants, gooseberries, grapes. Nonionic surfactant or wetting agent required. In addition, ammonium sulfate can be added. Do not allow spray, spray drift, or mist to contact green foliage or green bark on trunk, suckers, open wounds, or other green parts of trees and vines. Avoid contact with stumps as tree injury may occur from root grafting. Do not graze or harvest treated cover crops for feed. Do not apply through any type of irrigation system. Refer to label for restrictions and precautions.

◆-new product • PP-preplant • PPI-preplant incorporated • PRE-preemergence • POST-postemergence • SEQ-sequential • ae-acid equivalent • ai-active ingredient • DF-dry flowable
E/EC-emulsifiable concentrate • F/FL-flowable • DG/G/WG-dispersable granule • L/LC-liquid • SP/WSP-soluble packet • W/WP-wettable powder • WSB-water soluble bag

Days To Harvest: 1 year.

Tank Mixes: Devrinol, diuron, Goal, Krovar, Prowl, simazine, Solicam, Surflan.

State Restrictions: Ammonium sulfate (6L) not for use in California.

- - - - - - - - - - - - - - - -

Signal Word/Toxicity Class: Caution.
REI: 12 hr. (5L); 4 hr. (6L).

Treflan — see trifluralin

TRI-4 — see trifluralin

Trific — see trifluralin

TRIFLURALIN

Albaugh Trifluralin 4EC *(Albaugh)*
◆ **Clean Crop Trifluralin HF (4EC)** *(Platte)*
Gowan Trifluralin 4 or 5 (EC) or 10G *(Gowan)*
Helena Trifluralin 4 EC *(Helena)*
Riverside Trifluralin 4EC or Trific 60DF *(Terra)*
◆ **Sedagri Trifluralin 480 (4EC)** *(Rhone-Poulenc)*
Treflan HFP (4EC) or TR-10 (10G) *(Dow AgroSciences)*
TRI-4 HF (4EC) *(American Cyanamid)*
Trilin 4EC or 10G *(Griffin)*
Wilbur-Ellis Trifluralin 10G *(Wilbur-Ellis)*

Rate: New plantings:
0.5-2 lb. ai/A
1-4 pt. 4EC/A
0.8-3.2 pt. 5EC/A
0.875-1.66 lb. 60DF/A
5-20 lb. 10G/A
Established plantings:
1-2 lb. ai/A
2-4 pt. 4EC/A
1.6-3.2 pt. 5EC/A
1.66-3.33 lb. 60DF/A
10-20 lb. 10G/A

Time: New plantings: Preplant incorporated. Established plantings: Apply as directed spray to soil.

Weeds: Broadleaf weeds:

carelessweed	knotweed	purslane
carpetweed	kochia	pusley
chickweed	lambsquarters	redroot pigweed
field bindweed	Mexican clover	rough pigweed
fireweed	Mexican fireweed	Russian thistle
Florida purslane	prostrate pigweed	spiny pigweed
Florida pusley	puncturevine	stinging nettle
goosefoot	(western U.S.)	tumbleweed
henbit		

Grasses:

annual bluegrass	fall panicum	sandbur
barnyardgrass	foxtail millet	shattercane
bottlegrass	giant foxtail	smooth crabgrass
brachiaria	green foxtail	sprangletop
bristlegrass	Italian ryegrass	stinkgrass
bromegrass	johnsongrass	Texas panicum
burgrass	(seedling)	watergrass
cheat	junglerice	wildcane
cheatgrass	large crabgrass	woolly cupgrass
chess	pigeongrass	yellow foxtail
downy brome	robust foxtail	

Remarks: Grapes. Rate varies by soil type and amount of rainfall. Do not use more than 1 lb. ai/A on heat-treated grape rootings. Use incorporation methods not injurious to plants. Refer to label for directions and precautions.

Days To Harvest: 60.
State Restrictions: Trilin 10G and Wilbur-Ellis not for use in California.

- - - - - - - - - - - - - - - -

Signal Word/Toxicity Class: Varies by formulation.
REI: 12 hr. unless soil injected or soil incorporated.

Trilin — see trifluralin

XL 2G (Premix)

Selective preemergence herbicide for control of certain annual grasses and broadleaf weeds. Does not control established weeds. Requires rainfall or sprinkler irrigation within 21 days to activate.

XL 2G (1% benefin & 1% oryzalin) *(Helena)*

Rate: 4-6 lb. ai/A
200-300 lb./A
0.09-0.14 lb. ai/sq. ft.
4.6-6.9 lb./1000 sq. ft.

Time: Apply prior to germination of target weeds.

Weeds: Broadleaf weeds:

annual sowthistle*	desert rockpurslane	prostrate spurge
bittercress	Florida pusley	puncturevine
black mustard*	henbit	redstem filaree
black nightshade*	horseweed*	shepherdspurse
carpetweed	ladysthumb*	smartweed*
chickweed	lambsquarters	spotted spurge*
climbing milkweed*	London rocket	teaweed*
coast fiddleneck	morningglory*	velvetleaf*
common groundsel	pigweed	whitestem filaree
common mallow*	prickly lettuce*	wild mustard*
common purslane	prickly sida*	yellow woodsorrel
common ragweed*	prostrate knotweed	

Grasses:

annual bluegrass	foxtail	Orcutt lovegrass
barnyardgrass	goosegrass	red sprangletop
browntop panicum	Italian ryegrass	signalgrass
crabgrass	johnsongrass	Texas panicum
crowfootgrass	(seedling)	volunteer wheat*
cupgrass	junglerice	wild oat
fall panicum	little barley	witchgrass
field sandbur	Mexican lovegrass	

* Suppression

Remarks: Nonbearing berries and grapes. Do not apply to plants that may be harvested for food within 1 year after application. Refer to label for use directions and precautions.

- - - - - - - - - - - - - - - -

Signal Word/Toxicity Class: Caution/III.
REI: 12 hr. unless soil-injected or soil-incorporated.

Tree Fruits
(Citrus)

---

120 Herbicide — see MSMA

---

912 Herbicide — see MSMA

Bueno 6 — see MSMA

CLETHODIM

Postemergence grass herbicide. Mode of action similar to Poast, Assure, Option II, and Fusilade.

Envoy or Prism (0.94EC), Select (2EC) *(Valent)*

Rate: 0.1-0.25 lb. ai/A
13-34 fl. oz. 0.94EC/A
6-16 fl. oz. 2EC/A

Time: Postemergence. Apply to actively growing grasses.

Weeds: Grasses:

Amazon sprangletop	green foxtail	smooth crabgrass
annual bluegrass	itchgrass	southern crabgrass
barnyardgrass	johnsongrass	Texas panicum
bearded sprangletop	junglerice	volunteer cereals
bermudagrass	large crabgrass	wild oat
broadleaf signalgrass	quackgrass	wild proso millet
crowfootgrass	red rice	wirestem muhly
fall panicum	red sprangletop	witchgrass
giant foxtail	shattercane	woolly cupgrass
goosegrass	southwestern cupgrass	yellow foxtail

7

Fruits & Nuts

Remarks: Nonbearing citrus. Nonbearing are plants that will not bear fruit for at least 1 year. Rate varies by grass species, stage, and geographical area. Grass crops such as corn, sorghum, wheat, and rice are highly sensitive to clethodim. Do not apply under stress conditions or if rainfall is expected in 1 hr. Do not apply through any type of irrigation system. Do not apply more than 0.5 lb. ai/A (0.25 lb. ai/A on Long Island, NY) per season. Do not graze treated fields or feed treated forage or hay to livestock. Refer to label for restrictions and precautions.

State Restrictions: Not for use on Solano grass in the Vernal Lakes area of Solano County, California; wild rice in Hays County, Texas.

– – – – – – – – – – – – – – –

Signal Word/Toxicity Class: Warning/II.
REI: 24 hr.

Credit — see glyphosate

DEVRINOL

Devrinol 10-G or 50-DF (napropamide) *(United Phosphorus)*
Rate: 4 lb. ai/A
 40 lb. 10-G/A
 8 lb. 50-DF/A
Time: Apply in fall through early spring, prior to weed emergence.
Weeds: Annual broadleaf weeds:

annual sowthistle	common ragweed	pineappleweed
carpetweed	(suppression)	prickly lettuce
coast fiddleneck	horse purslane	prostrate knotweed
common chickweed	lambsquarters	purple cudweed
common groundsel	little mallow	redroot pigweed
common purslane	(from seed)	redstem filaree

Annual grasses:

annual bluegrass	guineagrass	sandbur
barnyardgrass	hairy crabgrass	smooth crabgrass
bristly foxtail	Italian ryegrass	soft chess
canarygrass	johnsongrass	southwestern cupgrass
cheatgrass	(seedling)	stinkgrass
downy brome	junglerice	Texas panicum
fall panicum	large crabgrass	wild barley
foxtail barley	Mexican sprangletop	wild oat
giant foxtail	red sprangletop	witchgrass
goosegrass	ripgut brome	yellow foxtail
green foxtail		

Remarks: Grapefruit, lemons, oranges, tangelos (50-DF), tangerines. Newly planted and established crop. An additional 8 lb. 50-DF/A may be applied during growing season in the West. See label for allowable time for Devrinol to remain on soil surface prior to incorporation.
Days To Harvest: 35.
Tank Mixes: 50-DF: Glyphosate, Gramoxone Extra, Karmex, Simazine, Sinbar. Refer to labels for restrictions and precautions.

– – – – – – – – – – – – – – –

Signal Word/Toxicity Class: Caution.
REI: 12 hr.

DIQUAT DIBROMIDE

◆ **Diquat** *(ZENECA)*
Rate: 0.375-0.5 lb. ai/A
 1.5-2 pt./A
Time: Site preparation prior to planting. Repeat as needed.
Weeds: Broadleaf weeds and grasses.
Remarks: Nonbearing grapefruit, lemons, limes, oranges, tangelos, tangerines. Apply by ground only. Use high rate when weeds are large or dense. Do not allow spray to contact green stems, foliage, or fruit. Use a shield or wrap plant when spraying around young trees or vines. Do not apply through any type of irrigation system. Do not graze treated areas. Refer to label for use restrictions and precautions.
Days To Harvest: 1 year.

– – – – – – – – – – – – – – –

Signal Word/Toxicity Class: Warning/II.
REI: 24 hr.

Direx — see diuron

DIURON

Direx 4L or 80DF *(Griffin)*
◆ **Diuron 80 WDG** *(Platte)*
Drexel Diuron 4L or 80 *(Drexel)*
Karmex DF *(Griffin)*
Riverside Diuron 4L or 80DF *(Terra)*

Rate: 2.4-3 lb. ai/A
 2.4-3 qt. 4L/A
 3-4 lb. 80, DF, 80DF/A
Time: Apply single application as broadcast spray after grove has been laidup in final form (no-till program) in late fall or early winter.
Weeds: Broadleaf weeds:

amsinckia	fiddleneck	purslane
annual groundcherry	gromwell	ragweed
annual morningglory	groundsel	shepherdspurse
chickweed	knawel	tansymustard
corn spurry	lambsquarters	wild lettuce
dogfennel	pigweed	wild mustard

Grasses:

annual bluegrass	barnyardgrass	rattail fescue
annual sweet	crabgrass	red sprangletop
vernalgrass	foxtail	velvetgrass

Remarks: Apply single directed spray to orchard established at least 1 year. Do not spray fruit or foliage. Refer to label for soil limitations.
Crop Rotation: Do not replant treated areas to any crop within 1 year after application.
State Restrictions: For use in Arizona (except Yuma area), California (except Imperial and Coachella valleys).

– – – – – – – – – – – – – – –

Rate: 3-6 lb. ai/A
 3-6 qt. 4L/A
 4-8 lb. 80, DF, 80DF/A
Time: On nonbearing trees, treat when winter banks are pulled down. On bearing citrus, apply any time when seasonal rains are expected.
Weeds: Broadleaf weeds:

groundsel	primrose-willow	sea myrtle
maidencane		

Grasses:

guineagrass	paragrass

Remarks: In bedded groves, do not treat water furrows between beds as injury to trees may result. Refer to label for soil limitations.
Crop Rotation: Same as above.
State Restrictions: For use in Florida and Puerto Rico.

– – – – – – – – – – – – – – –

Rate: Annual weeds:
 1.5-2 lb. ai/A
 1.5-2 qt. 4L/A
 2-4 lb. 80, DF, 80DF/A
 Johnsongrass (seedling):
 3-4.5 lb. ai/A
 3-4.5 qt./A
 4-6 lb. 80, DF, 80DF/A
Time: Apply in spring.
Weeds: Broadleaf weeds:

amsinckia	fiddleneck	purslane
annual groundcherry	gromwell	ragweed
annual morningglory	groundsel	shepherdspurse
chickweed	knawel	tansymustard
corn spurry	lambsquarters	wild lettuce
dogfennel	pigweed	wild mustard

Grasses:

annual bluegrass	crabgrass	rattail fescue
annual sweet	foxtail	red sprangletop
vernalgrass	johnsongrass	velvetgrass
barnyardgrass	(seedling)	

Remarks: Well-established weeds should be eliminated by cultivation prior to treatment.
Crop Rotation: Same as above.
State Restrictions: For use in Texas.

– – – – – – – – – – – – – – –

Signal Word/Toxicity Class: Caution/III.
REI: 12 hr.

DSMA

◆ **Clean Crop DSMA Plus (3.6L) (+ surfactant)** *(Platte)*
Drexel DSMA Liquid (3.6L) or Slurry (+ surfactant) *(Drexel)*
DSMA 4 LB (4L) *(Helena)*
Rate: 3.6-7.2 lb. ai/A
 1-2 gal. 3.6L/A
 0.5-1 gal. Slurry/A
 3.5-6.5 lb. ai/A
 3.5-6.5 qt. 4L/A
Time: Postemergence (directed spray). Apply when temperature is 70°F or above.
Weeds: Broadleaf weeds, grasses, sedges such as:

cocklebur (seedling)	johnsongrass	nutsedge
	(seedling)	

◆-new product • PP-preplant • PPI-preplant incorporated • PRE-preemergence • POST-postemergence • SEQ-sequential • ae-acid equivalent • ai-active ingredient • DF-dry flowable E/EC-emulsifiable concentrate • F/FL-flowable • DG/G/WG-dispersable granule • L/LC-liquid • SP/WSP-soluble packet • W/WP-wettable powder • WSB-water soluble bag

364

Weed Control Manual 2000

Remarks: Bearing, nonbearing: grapefruit, lemons, limes, oranges, tangerines. Surfactant formulated into product. Do not allow to contact leaves, stems, or bark of trees. Use a shield, if necessary, for nursery plantings or young trees. For control of regrowth, up to 3 applications per year may be applied.
State Restrictions: Not for use in Florida.

Signal Word/Toxicity Class: Caution/III.
REI: 12 hr.

- - - - - - - - - - - - - - - -

Drexel DSMA Liquid 4 (4L) *(Drexel)*
Liquid DSMA (3.6L) (+ surfactant) *(Helena)*
Rate: 3.5-6.5 lb. ai/A
3.5-6.5 qt. 4L/A
3.2-6.3 lb. ai/A
3.5-7 qt. 3.6L/A
Time: Postemergence (directed spray).
Weeds: Broadleaf weeds, grasses, sedges:

cocklebur (seedling)   johnsongrass (seedling)   nutsedge

Remarks: Nonbearing: grapefruit, lemons, limes, oranges, tangerines. For Drexel 4L, mix 3.5 qt. 4L + 1 qt. nonionic surfactant in 50 gal. water. Do not use around trees from which crop will be harvested within 1 year of treatment. Do not allow to contact leaves, stems, or bark of trees. If necessary, use shield for nursery plantings or young trees. For regrowth, up to 3 applications per year may be applied.

- - - - - - - - - - - - - - - -

Signal Word/Toxicity Class: Caution/III.
REI: 12 hr.

Envoy — see clethodim

Eptam — see EPTC

EPTC

Eptam 7-E *(ZENECA)*
Rate: Bearing:
3 lb. ai/A
3.5 pt. 7-E/A
Nonbearing:
3-6 lb. ai/A
3.5-7 pt. 7-E/A
Time: Bearing: Apply by flood or furrow irrigation after cultivation or before weed emergence. Nonbearing: Apply directed spray after lining out.
Weeds: Broadleaf weeds including:

carpetweed	fiddleneck	sicklepod
cutleaf nightshade	prickly sida	tall morningglory

Annual grasses including:

fall panicum	signalgrass	Texas panicum
lovegrass	stinkgrass	witchgrass
rescuegrass		

Remarks: Grapefruit, lemons (Western Region), oranges, tangerines. For bearing, apply no more than 10.5 pt./season in Western Region. For nonbearing, incorporate with cultivation equipment such as tree hoes or rotary hoes. Use lower rate on coarse-textured soils. Refer to label for regional recommendations.
Days To Harvest: Bearing—15.
State Restrictions: For use in the Southeast, Southwest, and the West.

- - - - - - - - - - - - - - - -

Signal Word/Toxicity Class: Caution.
REI: 12 hr. unless soil injected or soil incorporated.

FLUAZIFOP-P-BUTYL

Fusilade DX *(ZENECA)*
Rate: 0.25-0.375 lb. ai/A
1-1.5 pt. DX/A
Time: Annual grasses: Apply at 2-8" tall before tillering and/or heading. Perennial grasses: Apply by growth stage dependent on species.
Weeds: Annual and perennial grasses:

barnyardgrass	johnsongrass	southern sandbur
bermudagrass	(rhizome, seedling)	southwestern
broadleaf signalgrass	junglerice	cupgrass
fall panicum	kikuyugrass	Texas panicum
field sandbur	large crabgrass	tropical crabgrass
giant foxtail	prairie cupgrass	volunteer cereals
goosegrass	quackgrass	wild oat
green foxtail	red rice	wild proso millet
guineagrass	shattercane	wiresrem muhly
(seedling)	smooth crabgrass	witchgrass
Italian ryegrass	sorghum-almum	woolly cupgrass
itchgrass	southern crabgrass	yellow foxtail

Remarks: Nonbearing: grapefruit, lemons, limes, oranges, tangelos, tangerines. Rate varies by geographic area and grass species. Add crop oil concentrate or nonionic surfactant. Apply only to nonbearing fruit trees. Do not apply to tree fruits that may be harvested for food within 1 year after application. Refer to label for specific directions, restrictions, and precautions.
Crop Rotation: Do not plant rotational grass crops such as corn, sorghum, and cereals within 60 days after last application.
State Restrictions: Refer to label for geographical regions.

- - - - - - - - - - - - - - - -

Signal Word/Toxicity Class: Caution.
REI: 12 hr.

Fusilade — see fluazifop-P-butyl

GALLERY

Gallery 75DF (isoxaben) *(Dow AgroSciences)*
Rate: 0.5-1 lb. ai/A
0.66-1.33 lb. 75DF/A
Time: Preemergence. Apply in late summer to early fall or in early spring, prior to germination of target weeds.
Weeds: Broadleaf weeds:

annual sowthistle	dandelion	prostrate spurge
bittercress	dogfennel	redmaids
black mustard	green tansymustard	rockpurslane
black nightshade	hairy galinsoga	redstem filaree
blackleaved fleabane	henbit	shepherdspurse
bracted plantain	horseweed	sibara
buckhorn plantain	ladysthumb	slender plantain
Carolina geranium	lambsquarters	southern brassbuttons
coast fiddleneck	London rocket	spotted spurge
common chickweed	marestail	thymeleaf speedwell
common groundsel	mouseear chickweed	velvetleaf
common purslane	pennywort	white clover
common ragweed	pigweed	whitestem filaree
common sowthistle	pineappleweed	wild celery
creeping woodsorrel	prickly lettuce	wild mustard
cudweed	prostrate knotweed	yellow woodsorrel

Remarks: Nonbearing grapefruit, lemons, oranges. Do not apply through any type of irrigation system. Refer to label for directions and precautions.

- - - - - - - - - - - - - - - -

Signal Word/Toxicity Class: Caution/III.
REI: 12 hr.

Glyfos or Glyfos X-tra — see glyphosate

GLYPHOSATE

◆ **Credit (4WS)** *(Nufarm)*
◆ **Glyfos or Glyfos X-tra (4WS)** *(Cheminova)*
Rattler (4WS) *(Helena)*
Roundup Custom (5.4WS) *(Monsanto)*
Roundup Original, Ultra (4WS) *(Monsanto)*
Rate: 0.5-5 lb. ai/A
0.75-7.5 pt. 5.4WS/A
1-10 pt. 4WS/A
Time: Apply when weeds are actively growing.
Weeds: Annual and perennial weeds, grasses and ground covers.

Rate: Florida, Texas:
1-5 lb. ai/A
1.5-7.5 pt. 5.4WS/A
2-10 pt. 4WS/A in 3-30 gal. water
Time: Apply burndown or when weeds are actively growing.
Weeds: Grasses:

bermudagrass	paragrass	torpedograss
guineagrass		(suppression)

Remarks: Citron, grapefruit, kumquats, lemons, limes, oranges, tangelos, tangerines. General weed control, middles (between rows of trees), strips (in row of trees). For citron, apply as post-directed spray only. Do not allow spray, drift, or mist to contact foliage or green bark of trunk, branches, suckers, fruit, or other parts of trees and vines.
Days To Harvest: 4WS: 1 day; 5.4WS: 14 days.
Tank Mixes: Devrinol, diuron, Goal, Krovar I, Prowl, simazine, Solicam, Surflan. Do not apply these tank mixes in Puerto Rico.

- - - - - - - - - - - - - - - -

Rate: 4-12 fl. oz. 5.4WS/A
6-16 fl. oz. 4WS
Time: For cool-season grasses, apply in spring 3-4 days after mowing.

7

Fruits & Nuts

NOTICE The information on these pages is for preliminary planning — not a guide for use. Be sure to follow the manufacturer's directions, notwithstanding information contained here. | For personal protective equipment and EPA registration numbers, please turn to page 70.

Tree Fruits (Citrus)

Weeds: Perennial grasses:

bahiagrass	Kentucky bluegrass	quackgrass
bermudagrass	orchardgrass	tall fescue
fine fescue		

Remarks: Suppression on orchard floors. Rate varies by grass species and geographic area. For Kentucky bluegrass, do not add ammonium sulfate. Refer to label for use directions, restrictions, and precautions.

Signal Word/Toxicity Class: Varies by formulation.
REI: Warning—12 hr.; Caution—4 hr.

GOAL

Goal 2XL (oxyfluorfen) *(Rohm and Haas)*
Rate: Preemergence—AZ, CA, FL, LA, TX:
    2 lb. ai/A
    8 pt. 2XL/A
    Postemergence—AZ, CA, FL, LA, TX:
    0.5-2 lb. ai/A
    2-8 pt. 2XL/A
Time: Preemergence, postemergence. Apply only after foliage has fully expanded and hardened off. Do not apply during periods of new foliage growth.

Weeds: Broadleaf weeds—AZ, CA:

annual sowthistle	common	prostrate knotweed
broadleaf filaree	lambsquarters	prostrate spurge
burclover	common	redmaids rockpurslane
burning nettle	purslane	redroot pigweed
cheeseweed	henbit	redstem filaree
(malva)	London rocket	shepherdspurse
coast fiddleneck	minerslettuce	spotted spurge
common groundsel	prickly lettuce	whitestem filaree

Broadleaf weeds—FL, LA, TX:

American black	common purslane	prickly sida
nightshade	cutleaf	(teaweed)
annual morningglory	eveningprimrose	prostrate spurge
annual sowthistle	cutleaf groundcherry	redroot pigweed
balsamapple	Florida pusley	spotted spurge
black nightshade	narrowleaf cudweed	Virginia pepperweed
common	Pennsylvania	wild poinsettia
lambsquarters	smartweed	Wright groundcherry

Rate: Preemergence—AZ, CA:
    0.5-2 lb. ai/A
    5-8 pt. 2XL/A
Time: Preemergence. Apply only after foliage has fully expanded and hardened off. Do not apply during periods of new foliage growth.

Weeds: Broadleaf weeds—AZ, CA:

annual sowthistle	common	prostrate spurge
broadleaf filaree	lambsquarters	redmaids rockpurslane
burclover	common purslane	redroot pigweed
cheeseweed	henbit	redstem filaree
(malva)	London rocket	shepherdspurse
coast fiddleneck	prickly lettuce	spotted spurge
common groundsel	prostrate knotweed	whitestem filaree

Remarks: Nonbearing: **calamondin, chironja, citrus citron, grapefruit, kumquat, lemons, limes, mandarin, pummelo, satsuma mandarin, sour orange, sweet orange, tangelo, tangerine, tangor.** Apply only to nonbearing citrus trees. Add 2 pt./100 gal. spray nonionic surfactant. Refer to label for complete use directions.
Tank Mixes: Glyphosate, napropamide, norflurazon, oryzalin, paraquat, simazine.
State Restrictions: For use in permanently established nonbearing groves in Arizona, California, Florida, Louisiana, Texas.

Signal Word/Toxicity Class: Warning/II.
REI: 24 hr.

Gramoxone Extra — see paraquat

HYVAR

Hyvar X (WP) (bromacil) *(DuPont)*
Rate: 1.6-6.4 lb. ai/A
    2-8 lb. WP/A
    Florida:
    1.6-3.2 lb. ai/A
    2-4 lb. WP/A
Time: For annual weed control, apply any time of year, preferably just before or after weeds emerge. For perennial weeds, apply before or shortly after weed growth begins.

Weeds: Grasses and sedges:

bahiagrass	nutgrass	paragrass
bermudagrass	pangolagrass	torpedograss
johnsongrass		

Remarks: Use lower rates on annual grasses; higher rates on perennial grasses. May be planted to citrus trees 1 year after last application. Do not replant to other crops within 2 years after last treatment. Do not apply more than 8 lb./A per year.
State Restrictions: Not for use in Kern County, California.

Signal Word/Toxicity Class: Caution.
REI: 12 hr.

Karmex — see diuron

KROVAR (Premix)

Krovar I (DF) (40% bromacil & 40% diuron) *(DuPont)*
Rate: 1.6-4.8 lb. ai/A
    2-6 lb. DF/A
Time: Apply when rains or overhead irrigation have settled soil and when rain or overhead irrigation can be anticipated in 2 weeks.

Weeds: Broadleaf weeds:

annual nightshade	groundsel	puncturevine
annual sowthistle	horseweed	purslane
balsamapple	lambsquarters	ragweed
chickweed	milkweed vine	shepherdspurse
drymary	(stranglervine)	spanishneedles
filaree	pigweed	wild lettuce
fleabane	pineappleweed	wild mustard
Florida pusley		

Grasses:

barnyardgrass	foxtail	junglerice
(watergrass)	guineagrass	natalgrass (redtop)
bermudagrass	johnsongrass	sandbur
crabgrass	(seedling)	(sandspur)

Remarks: Grapefruit, lemons, oranges. Rate varies by soil type and weed pressure. Higher rates and/or application to younger trees allowed in Florida and Texas. In Central Ridge area of Florida, do not apply more than 4.2 lb. ai/A per year.
Crop Rotation: Do not replant treated areas to any crop within 2 years after application except citrus which may be planted after 1 year.
State Restrictions: For use in Arizona, California, Florida, Louisiana, Texas.

Signal Word/Toxicity Class: Caution.
REI: 12 hr.

MAGMA — see MSMA

Mandate — see thiazopyr

MSMA

120 Herbicide (6.6) *(Terra)*
912 Herbicide (6) (+ surfactant) *(Terra)*
Rate: Nonbearing:
    2-3 lb. ai/A
    2.66-4 pt. 6.6/A
    Bearing, nonbearing:
    2-4 lb. ai/A
    2.66-5.32 pt. 6/A
Time: Do not exceed 3 applications per year.
Weeds: Grassy weeds.
Remarks: Bearing (912 Herbicide), nonbearing: grapefruit, lemons, limes, oranges, tangerines. Do not allow spray to contact leaves, stems, or bark of trees.
State Restrictions: 912 Herbicide: Not for use in Florida.

Signal Word/Toxicity Class: Caution/III.
REI: 12 hr.

Bueno 6 (+ surfactant) *(ZENECA)*
Rate: 2 lb. ai/A
    2.66 pt. 6/A
    SLN—CA:
    2-4 lb. ai/A
    2.66-5.33 pt. 6/A

◆—new product • PP-preplant • PPI-preplant incorporated • PRE-preemergence • POST-postemergence • SEQ-sequential • ae-acid equivalent • ai-active ingredient • DF-dry flowable
E/EC-emulsifiable concentrate • F/FL-flowable • DG/G/WG-dispersable granule • L/LC-liquid • SP/WSP-soluble packet • W/WP-wettable powder • WSB-water soluble bag

Time: Apply as directed spray in warm weather when weeds are small and conditions are favorable for good weed growth.

Weeds: Broadleaf weeds:

chickweed	fiddleneck	puncturevine
cocklebur	jimsonweed	ragweed
common purslane	morningglory	sicklepod
dandelion	pigweed	wild mustard

Grasses and sedges:

bahiagrass	foxtail	nutsedge
barnyardgrass	goosegrass	sandbur
brachiaria	guineagrass	smooth crabgrass
dallisgrass	johnsongrass	wild oat
fall panicum	large crabgrass	witchgrass

Remarks: Nonbearing grapefruit, lemons, limes, oranges, tangerines. SLN—CA: bearing grapefruit, lemons, limes, oranges, tangerines. Do not allow spray to contact leaves, stems, or bark of trees. Do not use around trees from which crops will be harvested within 1 year following application. Up to 3 applications per year may be applied. Do not graze treated areas. Refer to label for use directions and precautions.

State Restrictions: In Florida, use only as spot treatment.

- - - - - - - - - - - - - - - -

Signal Word/Toxicity Class: Caution.
REI: 12 hr.

Drexel MSMA 6 Plus (+ surfactant) *(Drexel)*
Helena MSMA (6.6) *(Helena)*
Helena MSMA Plus H.C. (6) (+ surfactant) *(Helena)*
◆ **MAGMA (WSG)** *(Luxembourg-Pamol)*
◆ **Target MSMA 6 Plus (+ surfactant)** *(Luxembourg-Pamol)*
◆ **TurfMate 6 Plus (+ surfactant)** *(Luxembourg-Pamol)*

Rate: 2 lb. ai/A
2.66 pt. 6/A
2.5 pt. 6.6/A
4.6 lb. ai/A
8.5 lb. WSG/A (100 gal. water—directed; 50 gal. water—spot)

Time: Apply as directed spray during warm weather when weeds are small and conditions are favorable for good weed growth. Up to 3 applications per year may be applied.

Weeds: Broadleaf weeds:

chickweed	pigweed	puncturevine
cocklebur		

Grasses and sedges:

barnyardgrass	dallisgrass	nutsedge
brachiaria	goosegrass	sandbur
crabgrass	johnsongrass	

Remarks: Bearing (Helena), nonbearing: grapefruit, lemons, limes, oranges, tangerines. For 6.6, add suitable surfactant. Do not allow spray to contact leaves, stems, or bark of trees. Do not use around trees from which crop will be harvested within 1 year following application. Do not graze treated areas.

State Restrictions: Use only as a spot treatment in Florida.

- - - - - - - - - - - - - - - -

Signal Word/Toxicity Class: Caution/III.
REI: 12 hr.

NORFLURAZON

Solicam DF *(Novartis)*

Rate: 2-8 lb. ai/A
2.5-10 lb. DF/A

Time: Apply any time during the year according to local practice. In Florida and Texas, sequential applications up to 5 lb. DF/A may be made during any 4-month period. Do not exceed 10 lb./A for each 12-month period. In Florida citrus, a single 10 lb./A ring drench application may be used.

Weeds: Broadleaf weeds:

black mustard	groundsel*	redstem filaree
chickweed	horseweed	Russian thistle*
common	(marestail)*	shepherdspurse
lambsquarters*	little mallow	silverleaf nightshade*
false dandelion	(cheeseweed)	(white horsenettle)
(smooth catsear)	London rocket	tumble pigweed*
fiddleneck	pineappleweed	Virginia pepperweed
flixweed	puncturevine	whitestem filaree
green amaranth	redroot pigweed*	

Grasses and sedges:

annual bluegrass	foxtail	sixweeks grama
barnyardgrass	Italian ryegrass	southwestern
bermudagrass*	nutsedge	cupgrass
crabgrass	quackgrass*	wild barley
downy brome	sandbur	witchgrass
feather fingergrass		

* *Suppression*

Remarks: Rate varies by soil type; refer to label for higher rates on Florida and Texas citrus. Do not use on germinating citrus seedbeds in which citrus seed has or will be planted or where citrus is interplanted with palm trees. May be used in chemigation systems.

Tank Mixes: Diuron, Goal, Gramoxone, Hyvar, Krovar, Prowl, Roundup, simazine, Sinbar, or Surflan; refer to label for use instructions.

State Restrictions: See label for use restrictions in Coachella Valley of California.

- - - - - - - - - - - - - - - -

Signal Word/Toxicity Class: Caution.
REI: 12 hr.

PARAQUAT

Restricted Use Pesticide.

Gramoxone Extra (2.5L) *(ZENECA)*

Rate: 0.6-1 lb. ai/A
2-3 pt. 2.5L/A

Time: Apply as directed spray when weeds and grasses are succulent and new growth is from 1-6" tall.

Weeds: Annual broadleaf weeds and grasses; top kill and suppression of perennials.

Remarks: Add nonionic surfactant or crop oil concentrate. Do not allow spray to contact green stems, fruit, or foliage. Use a shield or wrap when spraying around young trees. For mature woody weeds, green suckers, late germinating weeds, grasses, and perennials, retreatment or spot treatment may be necessary. Do not graze treated areas. Refer to label for use directions, restrictions, and precautions.

Tank Mixes: Devrinol, Goal, Karmex, Krovar, Princep, Sinbar, Solicam, Surflan.

- - - - - - - - - - - - - - - -

Signal Word/Toxicity Class: Danger-Poison/I.
REI: 12 hr. (except harvest aid/desiccation 24 hr.).

PENDIMETHALIN

Pentagon DG *(American Cyanamid)*
Prowl 3.3EC *(American Cyanamid)*

Rate: 2-4 lb. ai/A
2.4-4.8 qt. 3.3 EC/A
3.3-6.6 lb. DG/A

Time: Apply before weeds emerge.

Weeds: Broadleaf weeds:

annual spurge	knotweed	pigweed
carpetweed	kochia	puncturevine
chickweed	lambsquarters	purslane
fiddleneck	London rocket	shepherdspurse
Florida pusley	Pennsylvania	velvetleaf
henbit	smartweed	

Grasses:

annual bluegrass	giant foxtail	red sprangletop
barnyardgrass	green foxtail	signalgrass
browntop panicum	johnsongrass	Texas panicum
crabgrass	(seedling)	witchgrass
crowfootgrass	junglerice	woolly cupgrass
fall panicum	lovegrass	yellow foxtail
field sandbur	Mexican sprangletop	

Remarks: Nonbearing citrus. Use low rate for short-term control; high rate for long-term control. Apply spray directly to ground beneath trees. Refer to label for directions, precautions, and limitations.

- - - - - - - - - - - - - - - -

Signal Word/Toxicity Class: Caution.
REI: 24 hr.

Pentagon — see pendimethalin

Poast — see sethoxydim

Princep — see simazine

Prism — see clethodim

7

Fruits & Nuts

NOTICE The information on these pages is for preliminary planning — not a guide for use. Be sure to follow the manufacturer's directions, notwithstanding information contained here.

For personal protective equipment and EPA registration numbers, please turn to page 70.

Tree Fruits (Citrus)

Prowl — see pendimethalin

Rattler — see glyphosate

Roundup — see glyphosate

SCYTHE

Nonselective, postemergent herbicide. May be used to control suckers. May also be used with other herbicides having systemic or residual activity.

◆ **Scythe (pelargonic acid)** *(Mycogen)*
Rate: 4-13 fl. oz./1 gal. spray solution
Time: Apply to actively growing weeds prior to crop emergence.
Weeds: Annual and perennial broadleaf weeds and grasses.
Remarks: Grapefruit, kumquat, lemons, limes, oranges, tangerines, tangelos. Apply in minimum 75 gal. spray solution/A or spray-to-wet. Do not apply by air or through any type of irrigation system. Refer to label for directions and precautions.
Tank Mixes: Glyphosate and other foliar and residual herbicides.

– – – – – – – – – – – – – – – –

Signal Word/Toxicity Class: Warning/II.
REI: 24 hr.

Select — see clethodim

SETHOXYDIM

Poast (1.5EC) *(BASF)*
Rate: 0.28-0.47 lb. ai/A
1.5-2.5 pt. 1.5EC/A
Time: Postemergence. Apply to actively growing grasses.
Weeds: Grasses:

barnyardgrass	large crabgrass	stinkgrass
bermudagrass	lovegrass	tall fescue
broadleaf signalgrass	orchardgrass	Texas panicum
browntop panicum	(seedling)	wild proso millet
fall panicum	perennial ryegrass	wildcane
giant foxtail	quackgrass	wiresteam muhly
goosegrass	red sprangletop	witchgrass
green foxtail	shattercane	woolly cupgrass
johnsongrass	smooth crabgrass	yellow foxtail
junglerice	southwestern cupgrass	

Remarks: Rate depends on growing region. Add 2 pt./A oil concentrate. Do not apply through any type of irrigation system. Refer to label for restrictions and limitations.
Days To Harvest: 15.
State Restrictions: Do not use UAN or AMS in California or Pacific Northwest.

– – – – – – – – – – – – – – – –

Signal Word/Toxicity Class: Warning/II.
REI: 12 hr.

Torpedo (1EC) *(BASF)*
Rate: 0.28-0.47 lb. ai/A
2.25-3.75 pt. 1EC/A
Time: Postemergence.
Weeds: Grasses:

barnyardgrass	johnsongrass	tall fescue
bermudagrass	junglerice	Texas panicum
broadleaf signalgrass	large crabgrass	torpedograss
fall panicum	lovegrass	wild proso millet
giant foxtail	orchardgrass	wildcane
goosegrass	red sprangletop	witchgrass
green foxtail	shattercane	woolly cupgrass
guineagrass	smooth crabgrass	yellow foxtail

Remarks: Bearing, nonbearing: grapefruit, lemons, limes, oranges, tangerines. Rate depends on growing region. Add 1% crop oil concentrate. Apply by ground only. Do not apply through any type of irrigation system. Refer to label for restrictions and limitations.
Days To Harvest: 15.

– – – – – – – – – – – – – – – –

Signal Word/Toxicity Class: Caution/III.
REI: 12 hr.

SIMAZINE

◆ **Clean Crop Simazine 4L or 90WDG** *(Platte)*
Drexel Simazine 4L, 80W or 90DF *(Drexel)*
Princep 4L or Caliber 90 *(Novartis)*
Riverside Simazine 4L or 90DF *(Terra)*
Rate: AZ-lemons, oranges
1.6 lb. ai/A
1.6 qt. 4L/A
1.75 lb. 90, 90DF, 90WDG/A
CA-grapefruit, lemons, oranges
2-4 lb. ai/A
2-4 qt. 4L/A
2.2-4.4 lb. 90, 90DF, 90WDG/A
FL-grapefruit, oranges
4 lb. ai/A
4 qt. 4L/A
4.4 lb. 90, 90DF, 90WDG/A
TX-grapefruit, oranges
4-4.8 lb. ai/A
4-4.8 qt. 4L/A
4.4-5.3 lb. 90, 90DF, 90 WDG/A
Time: Apply preemergence or after removal of weed growth. Arizona: Split application in spring and fall. California: Single application or as split application in spring and fall. Florida: Apply once in spring and/or fall.
Weeds: Broadleaf weeds:

annual morningglory	Florida pusley	redmaids
burclover	German moss	rockpurslane
carelessweed	groundsel	Russian thistle
carpetweed	henbit	shepherdspurse
common chickweed	knawel	smartweed
common lambsquarters	nightshade	spanishneedles
common purslane	pepperweed	speedwell
fiddleneck	pigweed	tansymustard
filaree	pineappleweed	wild mustard
fireweed	prickly lettuce	yellowflower
flora's paintbrush	ragweed	pepperweed

Grasses:

annual bluegrass	fall panicum	signalgrass
annual ryegrass	foxtail	silver hairgrass
barnyardgrass	goosegrass	watergrass
cheatgrass	junglerice	wild oat
crabgrass	quackgrass	witchgrass
downy brome	rattail fescue	

Remarks: Do not use in nurseries. Do not apply to bedded citrus (except FL grapefruit and oranges) or to trees under stress from freeze damage for one year after freeze. Do not exceed 8 qt./A per year in Florida.
Tank Mixes: Bromacil, glyphosate, Gramoxone Extra, Solicam, Surflan. Refer to labels for specific crop and state restrictions.
State Restrictions: For use in Arizona, California (except Imperial, Coachella, or Palo Verde Valleys), Florida, Texas.

– – – – – – – – – – – – – – – –

Signal Word/Toxicity Class: Caution/III.
REI: 12 hr.

SNAPSHOT (Premix)

Snapshot 2.5TG (2% trifluralin & 0.5% isoxaben) *(Dow AgroSciences)*
Rate: 2.5-5 lb. ai/A
100-200 lb. 2.5/A
Time: Apply late summer-early fall, early spring, or right after cultivation.
Weeds: Broadleaf weeds:

annual bursage	evening primrose	prickly sida
annual sowthistle	fall panicum	prostrate knotweed
black medic	hairy fleabane	purple cudweed
black nightshade	hairy galinsoga	purslane speedwell
bristly oxtongue	hare barley	rattail fescue
broadleaf plantain	heath aster	redstem filaree
burning nettle	henbit	Russian thistle
California burclover	horseweed	scarlet pimpernel
Carolina geranium	Indian mustard	shepherdspurse
clover	jimsonweed	sibara
coast fiddleneck	kochia	silversheath knotweed
common chickweed	lanceleaf groundcherry	slender aster
common groundsel	little mallow	slender plantain
common	London rocket	spiny sowthistle
lambsquarters	marestail	spotted spurge
common purslane	Mexican sprangletop	sunflower
common ragweed	nettleleaf goosefoot	swinecress
creeping woodsorrel	panicle willowweed	tall morningglory
curly dock	Pennsylvania	telegraphplant
dandelion	smartweed	turkey mullein
datura	petty spurge	velvetleaf
desert rockpurslane	pigweed	Virginia pepperweed
dwarf fleabane	pineappleweed	yellow sweetclover
dwarf mallow	prickly lettuce	yellow woodsorrel

◆-new product • PP-preplant • PPI-preplant incorporated • PRE-preemergence • POST-postemergence • SEQ-sequential • ae-acid equivalent • ai-active ingredient • DF-dry flowable
E/EC-emulsifiable concentrate • F/FL-flowable • DG/G/WG-dispersable granule • L/LC-liquid • SP/WSP-soluble packet • W/WP-wettable powder • WSB-water soluble bag

Annual grasses:

annual bluegrass	junglerice	wild mustard
barnyardgrass	lovegrass	wild oat
bromegrass	southwestern	wild radish
crabgrass	cupgrass	witchgrass
giant foxtail	wild carrot	yellow foxtail
Italian ryegrass	wild celery	

Remarks: Nonbearing grapefruit, oranges. Apply to trees that will not bear fruit for at least 1 year. Do not apply to bedding plants, nursery seedbeds, or transplant beds.

State Restrictions: Refer to label for use restrictions in Arizona.

– – – – – – – – – – – – – – –

Signal Word/Toxicity Class: Caution/III.
REI: 12 hr.

Solicam — see norflurazon

SURFLAN

Surflan A.S. (oryzalin) *(Dow AgroSciences)*

Rate: 2-6 lb. ai/A
2-6 qt. A.S./A

Time: Apply before weeds emerge.

Weeds: Broadleaf weeds:

annual morningglory*	cudweed	prostrate spurge*
annual smartweed*	field sandbur	puncturevine
annual sowthistle*	Florida purslane	red sprangletop
black mustard*	Florida pusley	redmaids rockpurslane
black nightshade*	giant ragweed*	redroot pigweed
carelessweed	henbit	redstem filaree*
carpetweed	ladysthumb*	rough pigweed
chickweed	lambsquarters	shepherdspurse
climbing milkweed*	London rocket*	smooth pigweed
coast fiddleneck	Mexican clover	spiny pigweed
common groundsel*	prickly lettuce*	tumble pigweed
common mallow*	prickly sida (teaweed)*	velvetleaf*
common purslane	prostrate knotweed*	whitestem filaree*
common ragweed*	prostrate pigweed	wild mustard*

Grasses:

annual bluegrass	green foxtail	robust foxtail
annual ryegrass	guineagrass	signalgrass
barnyardgrass	Italian ryegrass	smooth crabgrass
bottlegrass	johnsongrass	spreading panicgrass
bristlegrass	(seedling)	southwestern
browntop panicum	junglerice	cupgrass
crowfootgrass	large crabgrass	Texas panicum
downy brome	little barley	watergrass
fall panicum	Mexican lovegrass	wild oat
foxtail	Orcutt lovegrass	witchgrass
giant foxtail	pigeongrass	yellow foxtail

Suppression

Remarks: Bearing, nonbearing: grapefruit, lemons, oranges. Rate depends on length of control desired. Not for use on soils with at least 5% organic matter.

Tank Mixes: Gramoxone Extra, Hyvar, Karmex, Krovar I, Princep, Roundup Ultra, Sinbar, Solicam.

– – – – – – – – – – – – – – –

Signal Word/Toxicity Class: Caution/III.
REI: 12 hr.

Target — see MSMA

THIAZOPYR

Mandate or Visor (2E) (thiazopyr) *(Rohm and Haas)*

Rate: Short term control:
0.25-0.5 lb. ai/A
1-2 pt. 2E/A
Long term control:
0.5-1 lb. ai/A
2-4 pt. 2E/A

Time: Preemergence.

Weeds: Annual broadleaf weeds controlled/suppressed:

annual sowthistle	common	London rocket
annual spurge	lambsquarters	malva
black nightshade	common purslane	mustard
carpetweed	common ragweed	pigweed
chickweed	eclipta	redmaids rockpurslane
common groundsel	Florida beggarweed	shepherdspurse

Annual grasses controlled:

alexandergrass	goosegrass	little barley
barnyardgrass	green foxtail	natalgrass
broadleaf signalgrass	guineagrass	ripgut brome
canarygrass	itchgrass	shattercane
crowfootgrass	junglerice	sprangletop
field sandbur	large crabgrass	yellow foxtail
giant foxtail		

Sedges—suppression:
nutsedge

Remarks: Grapefruit, oranges. Permanent established groves. Do not apply more than 4 pt./A per year. Do not apply through any type of irrigation system. Do not feed or graze treated area. Refer to label for restrictions.

Days To Harvest: 90.

Tank Mixes: Preemergence: Devrinol, diuron, Goal, Hyvar, Krovar, simazine, Solicam. Postemergence: Gramoxone Extra, Roundup Ultra, Touchdown.

State Restrictions: Mandate: For use in Florida, Texas. Visor: For use in all states except Florida and Texas.

– – – – – – – – – – – – – – –

Signal Word/Toxicity Class: Warning/II.
REI: 12 hr.

Torpedo — see sethoxydim

TOUCHDOWN

Touchdown (5L or 6L) (sulfosate) *(ZENECA)*

Rate: 0.5-4 lb. ai/A
0.8-6.4 pt. 5L/A
0.66-5.33 pt. 6L/A

Time: Apply to actively growing weeds.

Weeds: Broadleaf weeds:

annual sowthistle	field bindweed	marestail
annual spurge	field sandbur	morningglory
black nightshade	filaree	mouseear chickweed
Canada thistle	fleabane	mustard
Carolina geranium	Florida pusley	Pennsylvania
common chickweed	giant ragweed	smartweed
common groundsel	groundcherry	prickly lettuce
common lambsquarters	hairy fleabane	redroot pigweed
common ragweed	hemp dogbane	Russian thistle
curly dock	henbit	shepherdspurse
cutleaf	hophornbeam	sicklepod
eveningprimrose	copperleaf	smooth pigweed
dandelion	kochia	spanishneedles
dogfennel	little barley	velvetleaf
fiddleneck	London rocket	white clover

Grasses and sedges:

annual bluegrass	goosegrass	stinkgrass
bahiagrass	guineagrass	tall fescue
barnyardgrass	Italian ryegrass	Texas panicum
bermudagrass	johnsongrass	timothy
broadleaf signalgrass	(seedling)	torpedograss*
cheat	orchardgrass	vaseygrass
cogongrass*	paragrass	wild oat
crabgrass	perennial ryegrass	wirestem muhly
crowfootgrass	quackgrass	witchgrass
downy brome	red rice	woolly cupgrass
fall panicum	shattercane	yellow nutsedge
foxtail	sprangletop	

Partial control

Rate: Florida, Texas:
1-4 lb. ai/A
1.6-6.4 pt. 5L/A
1.33-5.33 pt. 6L/A

Time: Apply burndown or to actively growing weeds.

Weeds: Grasses:

bermudagrass	paragrass	torpedograss
guineagrass		(suppression)

Remarks: Bearing calamondin, chironja, citron, mandarin. Bearing and nonbearing grapefruit, kumquat, lemons, limes, oranges, tangelos, tangerines. General weed control, middles (between rows of trees), strips (in row of trees). Nonionic surfactant or wetting agent required. In addition, ammonium sulfate can be added to nonbearing crops. Do not allow spray, drift, or mist to contact foliage or green bark of trunk, branches, suckers, fruit, or other parts of trees and vines. Do not apply through any type of irrigation system. Refer to label for use directions, restrictions, and precautions.

Days To Harvest: 1 year.

Tank Mixes: 2,4-D, Devrinol, diuron, Goal, Kerb, Krovar, Prowl, simazine, Sinbar, Solicam, Surflan.

State Restrictions: Ammonium sulfate (6L) not for use in California.

– – – – – – – – – – – – – – –

7

Fruits & Nuts

NOTICE The information on these pages is for preliminary planning — not a guide for use. Be sure to follow the manufacturer's directions, notwithstanding information contained here.

For personal protective equipment and EPA registration numbers, please turn to page 70.

Tree Fruits (Citrus)

Rate: 5-12 fl. oz. 5L/A
4-10 fl. oz. 6L/A
Time: Apply after green-up or after 3-4" of regrowth following mowing.
Weeds: Perennial grasses:

bahiagrass	Kentucky bluegrass	quackgrass
bermudagrass	orchardgrass	tall fescue
fine fescue		

Remarks: Suppression on orchard floors. Rate varies by grass species and geographic area. Nonionic surfactant or wetting agent required. In addition, ammonium sulfate can be added (except Kentucky bluegrass). Refer to label for use directions, restrictions, and precautions.

– – – – – – – – – – – – – –

Signal Word/Toxicity Class: Caution.
REI: 12 hr. (5L); 4 hr. (6L).

Treflan — see trifluralin

TRI-4 — see trifluralin

Trific — see trifluralin

TRIFLURALIN

Controls many grasses and some broadleaf weeds but must be incorporated for effective weed control.

Albaugh Trifluralin 4EC (Albaugh)
◆ **Clean Crop Trifluralin HF (4EC)** (Platte)
Gowan Trifluralin 4 or 5 (EC) or 10G (Gowan)
Helena Trifluralin 4 EC (Helena)
Riverside Trifluralin 4EC or Trific 60DF (Terra)
◆ **Sedagri Trifluralin 480 (4EC)** (Rhone-Poulenc)
Treflan HFP (4EC) or TR-10 (10G) (Dow AgroSciences)
TRI-4 HF (4EC) (American Cyanamid)
Trilin 4 or 5 (EC) or 10G (Griffin)
Wilbur-Ellis Trifluralin 10G (Wilbur-Ellis)
Rate: New plantings:
0.5-1 lb. ai/A
1-2 pt. 4EC/A
0.8-1.6 pt. 5EC/A
0.875-1.66 lb. 60DF/A
5-10 lb. 10G/A
Established plantings:
1-2 lb. ai/A
2-4 pt. 4EC/A
1.6-3.2 pt. 5EC/A
1.66-3.33 lb. 60DF/A
10-20 lb. 10G/A
Time: New plantings: Preplant incorporated. Established plantings: Apply as directed spray to soil.
Weeds: Broadleaf weeds:

carelessweed	knotweed	purslane
carpetweed	kochia	pusley
chickweed	lambsquarters	redroot pigweed
field bindweed	Mexican clover	rough pigweed
fireweed	Mexican fireweed	Russian thistle
Florida purslane	prostrate pigweed	spiny pigweed
Florida pusley	puncturevine	stinging nettle
goosefoot	(western U.S.)	tumbleweed
henbit		

Grasses:

annual bluegrass	fall panicum	sandbur
barnyardgrass	foxtail millet	shattercane
bottlegrass	giant foxtail	smooth crabgrass
brachiaria	green foxtail	sprangletop
bristlegrass	Italian ryegrass	stinkgrass
bromegrass	johnsongrass	Texas panicum
burgrass	(seedling)	watergrass
cheat	junglerice	wildcane
cheatgrass	large crabgrass	woolly cupgrass
chess	pigeongrass	yellow foxtail
downy brome	robust foxtail	

Remarks: **Grapefruit, lemons, oranges, tangelos, tangerines.** Use incorporation methods not injurious to plants. Refer to label for directions and precautions.
Days To Harvest: 60.
State Restrictions: Trilin 10G and Wilbur-Ellis not for use in California.

– – – – – – – – – – – – – –

Signal Word/Toxicity Class: Varies by formulation.
REI: 12 hr. unless soil injected or soil incorporated.

Trilin — see trifluralin

TurfMate — see MSMA

Visor — see thiazopyr

XL 2G (Premix)

Selective preemergence herbicide for control of certain annual grasses and broadleaf weeds. Does not control established weeds. Requires rainfall or sprinkler irrigation within 21 days to activate.

XL 2G (1% benefin & 1% oryzalin) (Helena)
Rate: 4-6 lb. ai/A
200-300 lb./A
0.09-0.14 lb. ai/sq. ft.
4.6-6.9 lb./1000 sq. ft.
Time: Apply prior to germination of target weeds.
Weeds: Broadleaf weeds:

annual sowthistle*	desert rockpurslane	prostrate spurge
bittercress	Florida pusley	puncturevine
black mustard*	henbit	redstem filaree
black nightshade*	horseweed*	shepherdspurse
carpetweed	ladysthumb*	smartweed*
chickweed	lambsquarters	spotted spurge*
climbing milkweed*	London rocket	teaweed*
coast fiddleneck	morningglory*	velvetleaf*
common groundsel	pigweed	whitestem filaree
common mallow*	prickly lettuce*	wild mustard*
common purslane	prickly sida*	yellow woodsorrel
common ragweed*	prostrate knotweed	

Grasses:

annual bluegrass	foxtail	Orcutt lovegrass
barnyardgrass	goosegrass	red sprangletop
browntop panicum	Italian ryegrass	signalgrass
crabgrass	johnsongrass	Texas panicum
crowfootgrass	(seedling)	volunteer wheat*
cupgrass	junglerice	wild oat
fall panicum	little barley	witchgrass
field sandbur	Mexican lovegrass	

* Suppression

Remarks: **Nonbearing grapefruit, kumquat, lemon, orange.** Do not apply to trees that may be harvested for food within 1 year after application. Refer to label for use directions and precautions.

– – – – – – – – – – – – – –

Signal Word/Toxicity Class: Caution/III.
REI: 12 hr. unless soil-injected or soil-incorporated.

Tree Fruits
(Deciduous)

---

120 Herbicide — see MSMA

---

912 Herbicide — see MSMA

BASAMID

Basamid Granular (dazomet) (BASF)
Rate: 8 oz./100 sq. ft. (350 lb./A)
Time: Preplant.
Weeds: Weed seeds.
Remarks: **Nonbearing: apples, apricots, cherries, nectarines, peaches, pears, plums, prunes.** Soil treatment prior to propagating or outplanting nonbearing plants. Rates are for incorporation depth of 8"; for annual weeds, incorporate into top 4-6".
Days To Harvest: 1 year.

– – – – – – – – – – – – – –

Signal Word/Toxicity Class: Warning/II.
REI: 24 hr.

◆-new product • PP-preplant • PPI-preplant incorporated • PRE-preemergence • POST-postemergence • SEQ-sequential • ae-acid equivalent • ai-active ingredient • DF-dry flowable
E/EC-emulsifiable concentrate • F/FL-flowable • DG/G/WG-dispersable granule • L/LC-liquid • SP/WSP-soluble packet • W/WP-wettable powder • WSB-water soluble bag

Bueno 6 — see MSMA

Casoron — see dichlobenil

CLETHODIM

Postemergence grass herbicide. Mode of action similar to Poast, Assure, Option II, and Fusilade.

Envoy or Prism (0.94EC), Select (2EC) *(Valent)*
Rate: 0.1-0.25 lb. ai/A
   13-34 fl. oz. 0.94EC/A
   6-16 fl. oz. 2EC/A
Time: Postemergence. Apply to actively growing grasses.
Weeds: Grasses:

Amazon sprangletop	green foxtail	smooth crabgrass
annual bluegrass	itchgrass	southern crabgrass
barnyardgrass	johnsongrass	Texas panicum
bearded sprangletop	junglerice	volunteer cereals
bermudagrass	large crabgrass	wild oat
broadleaf signalgrass	quackgrass	wild proso millet
crowfootgrass	red rice	wiregrass muhly
fall panicum	red sprangletop	witchgrass
giant foxtail	shattercane	woolly cupgrass
goosegrass	southwestern cupgrass	yellow foxtail

Remarks: Nonbearing apples, pears, stone fruits. Nonbearing are plants that will not bear fruit for at least 1 year after application. Rate varies by grass species, stage, and geographical region. Grass crops such as corn, sorghum, wheat, and rice are highly sensitive to clethodim. Do not apply under stress conditions or if rainfall is expected in 1 hour. Do not apply through any type of irrigation system. Do not apply more than 0.5 lb. ai/A (0.25 lb. ai/A on Long Island, NY) per season. Do not graze treated fields or feed treated forage or hay to livestock. Refer to label for restrictions and precautions.
State Restrictions: Not for use on Solano grass in the Vernal Lakes area of Solano County, California; wild rice in Hays County, Texas.

- - - - - - - - - - - - - -

Signal Word/Toxicity Class: Warning/II.
REI: 24 hr.

Credit — see glyphosate

2,4-D - PHENOXY HERBICIDES

Albaugh Amine 4 (2,4-D amine) *(Albaugh)*
◆ **Clean Crop Amine 4 (2,4-D amine)** *(Platte)*
Dri-Clean (SP) (2,4-D amine) *(Riverdale)*
◆ **Saber (2,4-D amine)** *(Platte)*
Savage (WSB) (2,4-D amine) *(Platte)*
Rate: 1.5 lb. ae/A
   3 pt. 4/A
   27 oz. SP/A (5 packets/1.66 A)
   1.5 lb. WSB/A
Time: Apply to point of runoff when weeds are young and actively growing (pre-bud to early bud stage). For apples and pears, minimum retreatment interval is 75 days.
Weeds: Annual broadleaf weeds on orchard floor.
Remarks: Apples, pears, stone fruits. Nonbearing apple and pear trees (1 year or older) and bearing trees (before and after bloom). Maximum 2 applications per season. Do not use on Gala variety apple orchards. Do not graze or feed cover crops from treated orchards. Consult label for restrictions and precautions.
Days To Harvest: Apples, pears—14; stone fruits—40.

- - - - - - - - - - - - - -

Signal Word/Toxicity Class: Danger/I.
REI: 48 hr.

Formula 40 (2,4-D mixed amine) *(Rhone-Poulenc)*
Hi-Dep (2,4-D mixed amine) *(PBI/Gordon)*
◆ **Opti-Amine (4) (2,4-D amine)** *(Helena)*
Riverdale 6 Amine (2,4-D amine) *(Riverdale)*
Weed Rhap A-4D (2,4-D amine) *(Helena)*
Weedestroy AM-40 (2,4-D amine) *(Riverdale)*
Wilbur-Ellis Amine 4 (2,4-D amine) *(Wilbur-Ellis)*
Rate: 1.5 lb. ae/A
   3 pt. 4/A
   2 pt. 6/A

Time: Apply when weeds are small and actively growing.
Weeds: Annual broadleaf weeds on orchard floor.
Remarks: Stone fruits. Trees must be at least 1 year old. Apply using coarse sprays and low pressure in sufficient volume of water to obtain thorough wetting of weeds. Do not use on light, sandy soil. Do not apply more than twice a year. Do not graze or feed cover crops from treated orchards.
Days To Harvest: 40.
State Restrictions: Not for use in California.

- - - - - - - - - - - - - -

Signal Word/Toxicity Class: Danger/I.
REI: 48 hr.

◆ **Orchard Master (2,4-D mixed amine)** *(PBI/Gordon)*
Rate: 1-1.5 lb. ai/A
   2-3 pt. 4/A
Time: Applications in early spring and late fall after harvest preferred. Sequential applications may be needed to control biennial and perennial broadleaf weeds.
Weeds: Annual, biennial, perennial broadleaf weeds on orchard floor.
Remarks: Pome fruits (apples, pears); stone fruits (peaches, plums, prunes, sweet or tart cherries). Trees must be at least 1 year old. Avoid contact with fruit, foliage, stems, lower limbs, tree trunks, and exposed roots. Do not use on shallow or sandy soil, or to dry soil without vegetation. Do not apply more than twice a year. Do not graze or feed cover crops from treated orchards. Do not apply during windy periods or extremely high temperatures. Do not apply through any type of irrigation system. Refer to label for directions, restrictions, and precautions.
Days To Harvest: Pome fruits—14; stone fruits—40.
Tank Mixes: Glyphosate.
State Restrictions: Orchard Master not registered in California. Orchard Master CA registered in California; refer to label.

- - - - - - - - - - - - - -

Signal Word/Toxicity Class: Danger/I.
REI: 48 hr.

Weedar 64 (4) (2,4-D amine) *(Nufarm)*
Rate: 1.5 lb. ae/A
   3 pt. 4/A
Time: Apply when weeds are small and actively growing.
Weeds: Annual broadleaf weeds on orchard floor.
Remarks: Apples, pears, stone fruits. Trees must be at least 1 year old. Apply using coarse sprays and low pressure in sufficient volume of water to obtain thorough wetting of weeds. Do not use on light, sandy soil. Do not apply more than twice a year. Do not graze or feed cover crops from treated orchards.
Days To Harvest: Apples, pears—14; stone fruits—40.
State Restrictions: Not for use in California.

- - - - - - - - - - - - - -

Signal Word/Toxicity Class: Danger/I.
REI: 48 hr.

DEVRINOL

Controls annual grasses and some broadleaf weeds from seed. Does not control established weeds. Chemical is rapidly inactivated by light and should be incorporated into soil by tillage, irrigation or rainfall within 24 hours following application.

Devrinol 10-G or 50-DF (napropamide) *(United Phosphorus)*
Rate: 4 lb. ai/A
   40 lb. 10-G/A
   8 lb. 50-DF/A
Time: Apply in fall through early spring, prior to weed emergence.
Weeds: Annual broadleaf weeds:

annual sowthistle	common ragweed	pineappleweed
carpetweed	(suppression)	prickly lettuce
coast fiddleneck	horse purslane	prostrate knotweed
common chickweed	lambsquarters	purple cudweed
common groundsel	little mallow	redroot pigweed
common purslane	(from seed)	redstem filaree

Annual grasses:

annual bluegrass	guineagrass	sandbur
barnyardgrass	hairy crabgrass	smooth crabgrass
bristly foxtail	Italian ryegrass	soft chess
canarygrass	johnsongrass	southwestern cupgrass
cheatgrass	(seedling)	stinkgrass
downy brome	junglerice	Texas panicum
fall panicum	large crabgrass	wild barley
foxtail barley	Mexican sprangletop	wild oat
giant foxtail	red sprangletop	witchgrass
goosegrass	ripgut brome	yellow foxtail
green foxtail		

7

Fruits & Nuts

Tree Fruits (Deciduous)

Remarks: Apples, apricots, cherries, nectarines, peaches, pears, plums, prunes. Newly planted and established crop. An additional 8 lb. 50-DF/A may be applied during growing season in the West. Allowable time for Devrinol to remain on soil surface is 24 hours (West and Northwest in Nov.-Feb. is 3 weeks). See label for use and irrigation directions and precautions.

Days To Harvest: 35.

Tank Mixes: 50-DF: Glyphosate, Goal, Gramoxone Extra, Karmex, Simazine, Sinbar. Refer to labels for restrictions and precautions.

- - - - - - - - - - - - - - - -

Signal Word/Toxicity Class: Caution.

REI: 12 hr.

DICHLOBENIL

Proper timing of application is critical for obtaining optimum results. Apply in late fall or very early spring. Granular formulation is superior to the wettable powder. Wettable powder requires shallow incorporation.

Casoron 4G *(Uniroyal)*

Rate: Annual weeds:
4-6 lb. ai/A
100-150 lb. 4G/A
Perennial weeds:
6 lb. ai/A
150 lb. 4G/A

Time: Apply early spring. Do not apply until 4 weeks after transplanting.

Weeds: Broadleaf weeds:

artemisia	gisekia	redroot pigweed
camphorweed	goosefoot	rosarypea
Canada thistle	groundsel	Russian knapweed
carpetweed	henbit	Russian thistle
chickweed	horsetail	shepherdspurse
citronmelon	Jerusalem oak	smartweed
coffeeweed	knotweed	spanishneedles
cudweed	lambsquarters	spurge
curly dock	leafy spurge	teaweed
dandelion	maypop	wild artichoke
dogfennel	milkweed vine	wild aster
eveningprimrose	minerslettuce	wild carrot
false dandelion	pineappleweed	wild mustard
(catsear)	plantain	wild radish
fiddleneck	purslane	yellow rocket
Florida purslane	ragweed	yellow woodsorrel
(pusley)	red deadnettle	

Grasses:

annual bluegrass	natalgrass	timothy
crabgrass	old witchgrass	Texas panicum
fescue	orchardgrass	(hurrahgrass)
foxtail	quackgrass	wild barley

Remarks: Bearing, nonbearing: apples, cherries, pears. Shallow incorporation immediately after application is recommended in southern areas. Do not graze treated areas.

Crop Rotation: Do not plant rotational crops on which dichlobenil is not registered within 1 year after application.

- - - - - - - - - - - - - - - -

Signal Word/Toxicity Class: Caution/III.

REI: 12 hr.

DIQUAT DIBROMIDE

◆ **Diquat** *(ZENECA)*

Rate: 0.375-0.5 lb. ai/A
1.5-2 pt./A

Time: Site preparation prior to planting. Repeat as needed.

Weeds: Broadleaf weeds and grasses.

Remarks: Nonbearing apples, apricots, cherries, crabapples, nectarines, peaches, pears, plums, prunes. Apply by ground only. Use high rate when weeds are large or dense. Do not allow spray to contact green stems, foliage, or fruit. Use a shield or wrap plant when spraying around young trees or vines. Do not apply through any type of irrigation system. Do not graze treated areas. Refer to label for use restrictions and precautions.

Days To Harvest: 1 year.

- - - - - - - - - - - - - - - -

Signal Word/Toxicity Class: Warning/II.

REI: 24 hr.

Direx — see diuron

DIURON

Provides season-long control of annual grasses and broadleaf weeds when used as preemergence treatment. Can be utilized with paraquat or glyphosate to obtain season-long control of most weeds.

Direx 4L or 80DF *(Griffin)*

◆ **Diuron 80 WDG** *(Platte)*

Drexel Diuron 4L or 80 *(Drexel)*

Karmex DF *(Griffin)*

Riverside Diuron 4L or 80DF *(Terra)*

Rate: 3 lb. ai/A
6 pt. 4L/A
4 lb. 80, DF, 80DF/A

Time: Apply in spring (Mar.-May) except in the Far West, where application may be made in the winter (Dec.-Feb.) or apply 2 lb. ai postharvest followed by 2 lb. ai in spring.

Weeds: Annual broadleaf weeds:

amsinckia	fiddleneck	purslane
annual groundcherry	gromwell	ragweed
annual morningglory	groundsel	shepherdspurse
chickweed	knawel	tansymustard
corn spurry	lambsquarters	wild lettuce
dogfennel	pigweed	wild mustard

Annual grasses:

annual bluegrass	barnyardgrass	rattail fescue
annual sweet	crabgrass	red sprangletop
vernalgrass	foxtail	velvetgrass

Remarks: Apples, pears. Do not treat dwarf varieties. Avoid contact with foliage or fruit. Do not use on apples where organic matter is less than 1%.

Crop Rotation: Do not replant treated areas to any crop within 1 year after application.

- - - - - - - - - - - - - - - -

Rate: 1.6-4 lb. ai/A
3.2-8 pt. 4L/A
2-5 lb. 80, DF, 80DF/A

Time: Apply in early spring.

Weeds: Broadleaf weeds:

chickweed	mustard	purslane
lambsquarters	pigweed	ragweed

Grasses:

crabgrass	foxtail

Remarks: Peaches. Use only where peach trees have been established for at least 3 years. Apply as directed spray avoiding contact of fruit and foliage with spray. Refer to label for soil limitations.

Days To Harvest: 3 months; Far West—8 months.

Tank Mixes: Sinbar for apples and peaches.

- - - - - - - - - - - - - - - -

Signal Word/Toxicity Class: Caution/III.

REI: 12 hr.

Dri-Clean — see 2,4-D

DSMA

◆ **Clean Crop DSMA Plus (3.6L) (+ surfactant)** *(Platte)*

Liquid DSMA (3.6L) (+ surfactant) *(Helena)*

Rate: 3.2-6.3 lb. ai/A
3.5-7 qt. 3.6L/A

Time: Postemergence (directed spray).

Weeds: Grassy weeds.

Remarks: Nonbearing: apple, apricot, cherry, peach, pear, plum. Do not use around trees from which crop will be harvested within 1 year of treatment. Do not allow to contact leaves, stems, or bark of trees. If necessary, use shield for nursery plantings or young trees. For regrowth, up to 3 applications per year may be applied.

- - - - - - - - - - - - - - - -

Signal Word/Toxicity Class: Caution/III.

REI: 12 hr.

Envoy — see clethodim

◆-new product • PP-preplant • PPI-preplant incorporated • PRE-preemergence • POST-postemergence • SEQ-sequential • ae-acid equivalent • ai-active ingredient • DF-dry flowable
E/EC-emulsifiable concentrate • F/FL-flowable • DG/G/WG-dispersable granule • L/LC-liquid • SP/WSP-soluble packet • W/WP-wettable powder • WSB-water soluble bag

372   Weed Control Manual 2000

FLUAZIFOP-P-BUTYL

Effective only on grasses.

Fusilade DX *(ZENECA)*

Rate: Bearing: apricots, cherries, nectarines, peaches, plums, prunes:
0.1-0.375 lb. ai/A
0.375-1.5 pt. DX/A

Time: Apply by growth stage dependent on species.

Rate: Nonbearing: apples, apricots, cherries, nectarines, peaches, pears, plums, prunes:
0.25-0.375 lb. ai/A
1-1.5 pt. DX/A

Time: Annual grasses: 2-8" tall before tillering and/or seedhead formation. Perennial grasses: apply by growth stage dependent on species.

Weeds: Annual and perennial grasses:

barnyardgrass	johnsongrass	southern sandbur
bermudagrass	(rhizome, seedling)	southwestern
broadleaf signalgrass	junglerice	cupgrass
fall panicum	kikuyugrass	Texas panicum
field sandbur	large crabgrass	tropical crabgrass
giant foxtail	prairie cupgrass	volunteer cereals
goosegrass	quackgrass	wild oat
green foxtail	red rice	wild proso millet
guineagrass	shattercane	wirestem muhly
(seedling)	smooth crabgrass	witchgrass
Italian ryegrass	sorghum-almum	woolly cupgrass
itchgrass	southern crabgrass	yellow foxtail

Remarks: Rate varies by geographic area and grass species. Add crop oil concentrate or nonionic surfactant. Do not apply to tree fruits that may be harvested for food within 1 year after application. Refer to label for specific directions, restrictions, and precautions.

Days To Harvest: Bearing—14.

Crop Rotation: Do not plant rotational grass crops such as corn, sorghum, and cereals within 60 days after last application.

State Restrictions: Refer to label for geographical regions.

- - - - - - - - - - - - - - - - -

Signal Word/Toxicity Class: Caution.
REI: 12 hr.

Formula 40 — see 2,4-D

Fusilade — see fluazifop-P-butyl

GALLERY

Provides control of broadleaf weeds when applied as post-emergence treatment.

Gallery 75DF (isoxaben) *(Dow AgroSciences)*

Rate: 0.5-1 lb. ai/A
0.66-1.33 lb. 75DF/A

Time: Apply late summer to early fall or early spring, prior to germination of target weeds.

Weeds: Broadleaf weeds:

annual sowthistle	dandelion	prostrate spurge
bittercress	dogfennel	redmaids
black mustard	green tansymustard	rockpurslane
black nightshade	hairy galinsoga	redstem filaree
blackleaved fleabane	henbit	shepherdspurse
bracted plantain	horseweed	sibara
buckhorn plantain	ladysthumb	slender plantain
Carolina geranium	lambsquarters	southern brassbuttons
coast fiddleneck	London rocket	spotted spurge
common chickweed	marestail	thymeleaf speedwell
common groundsel	mouseear chickweed	velvetleaf
common purslane	pennywort	white clover
common ragweed	pigweed	whitestem filaree
common sowthistle	pineappleweed	wild celery
creeping woodsorrel	prickly lettuce	wild mustard
cudweed	prostrate knotweed	yellow woodsorrel

Remarks: Nonbearing: apples, apricots, cherries, nectarines, peaches, pears, plums, prunes. Do not apply through any type of irrigation system. Refer to label for directions and precautions.

- - - - - - - - - - - - - - - - -

Signal Word/Toxicity Class: Caution/III.
REI: 12 hr.

GLUFOSINATE-AMMONIUM

Provides faster knockdown of most emerged weeds than glyphosate but slower than paraquat. Contact herbicide; not systemic but suppresses perennial broadleaf weeds. Excellent control of suckers or cane without injury to mature trees or vines.

Rely *(AgrEvo USA)*

Rate: 3-5 qt./A (broadcast)

Weeds: Broadleaf weeds:

chickweed	kochia	purslane
clover	London rocket	shepherdspurse
common cocklebur	malva	smartweed
filaree	marestail	
jimsonweed	(horseweed)	

Grasses:

barnyardgrass	goosegrass	shattercane
cupgrass	green foxtail	stinkgrass
fall panicum	johnsongrass	windgrass
giant foxtail	lovegrass	yellow foxtail

Rate: 4-6 qt./A (broadcast)

Weeds: Broadleaf weeds:

annual sowthistle	leafy spurge	vervain
bindweed	mugwort	vetch
buffalobur	musk thistle	Virginia copperleaf
burdock	nettle	white clover
Canada thistle	nightshade	white heath aster
curly dock	pennycress	wild buckwheat
dandelion	redroot pigweed	wild mustard
dogbane	plantain	wild onion
field gromwell	prickly lettuce	wild rose
fleabane	ragweed	wild turnip
goldenrod	Russian thistle	woodsorrel
horsetail	tansymustard	yellow rocket
lambsquarters	velvetleaf	

Grasses and sedges:

annual bluegrass	fescue	ryegrass
bahiagrass	guineagrass	sandbur
barley	johnsongrass	smooth bromegrass
bermudagrass	(rhizome)	torpedograss
carpetgrass	Kentucky bluegrass	vaseygrass
crabgrass	nutsedge	wheat
dallisgrass	paragrass	wild oat
downy bromegrass	quackgrass	

Time: Apply low rate when weeds are less than 6" tall; high rate when weeds are 6" or taller.

Rate: 4 qt./A
Weeds: Sucker control.
Time: Split application: Apply approximately 4 weeks apart. Suckers should not exceed 12" in length.
Remarks: Apples. Do not use on trees within 1 year of transplanting, apply on desirable foliage, or allow spray to drift on foliage of trees and vines. Avoid contact with green or uncalloused bark on young trees and vines. Do not graze or feed treated orchard cover crops. Do not apply by air or through any type of irrigation system. Refer to label for directions and precautions.
Tank Mixes: Devrinol, Karmex, Sinbar, simazine, Solicam, Surflan; refer to respective labels.

- - - - - - - - - - - - - - - - -

Signal Word/Toxicity Class: Warning/II.
REI: 12 hr.

Glyfos or Glyfos X-tra — see glyphosate

GLYPHOSATE

Systemic herbicide which kills annual and perennial weeds. Absorbed by foliage, usually applied after perennial weeds have large amount of foliage. Timing is critical for control of perennial weeds. Rapidly inactivated by soil and will not prevent emergence of annual weeds.

◆ **Credit (4WS)** *(Nufarm)*
◆ **Glyfos or Glyfos X-tra (4WS)** *(Cheminova)*
Rattler (4WS) *(Helena)*
Roundup Custom (5.4WS) *(Monsanto)*
Roundup Original, Original RT, Ultra, Ultra RT (4WS) *(Monsanto)*

7

Fruits & Nuts

NOTICE	The information on these pages is for preliminary planning — not a guide for use. Be sure to follow the manufacturer's directions, notwithstanding information contained here.

For personal protective equipment and EPA registration numbers, please turn to page 70.

Tree Fruits (Deciduous)

Rate: 0.5-5 lb. ai/A
0.75-7.5 pt. 5.4WS/A
1-10 pt. 4WS/A
Hand-held and high volume equipment:
0.5%-2% solution
Wiper applicator:
33% solution

Time: For peaches, apply no later than first bloom.

Weeds: Annual and perennial weeds and grasses.

Remarks: Apples, apricots, cherries (sweet, sour), crabapples, nectarines, peaches, pears, plums, prunes, quince. General weed control, middles (between rows of trees), strips (in row of trees). Apply only to peach trees planted in orchards for at least 2 years. Refer to label for state restrictions on application equipment and peach restrictions. Do not allow spray, drift, or mist to contact foliage or green bark of trunk, branches, suckers, fruit, or other parts of trees and vines.

Days To Harvest: Apples, crabapples, pears, quince—1 (4WS), 14 (5.4WS); apricots, cherries, nectarines, peaches, plums, prunes—17.

Tank Mixes: Devrinol, diuron, Goal, Krovar I, Prowl, simazine, Solicam, Surflan. Do not use in Puerto Rico.

State Restrictions: Refer to labels for specific geographic instructions and restrictions.

- - - - - - - - - - - - - - - - - -

Rate: 4-12 fl. oz. 5.4WS/A
6-16 fl. oz. 4WS

Time: For cool-season grasses, apply in the spring 3-4 days after mowing.

Weeds: Perennial grasses:

bahiagrass	Kentucky bluegrass	quackgrass
bermudagrass	orchardgrass	tall fescue
fine fescue		

Remarks: Suppression on orchard floors. Rate varies by grass species and geographic area. For Kentucky bluegrass, do not add ammonium sulfate. Refer to label for use directions, restrictions, and precautions.

- - - - - - - - - - - - - - - - - -

Signal Word/Toxicity Class: Varies by formulation.
REI: Warning—12 hr.; Caution—4 hr.

GOAL

Goal 2XL (oxyfluorfen) *(Rohm and Haas)*

Rate: Preemergence:
1.25-2 lb. ai/A
5-8 pt. 2XL/A
Postemergence:
0.5-2 lb. ai/A
2-8 pt. 2XL/A

Time: Preemergence, postemergence. Dormant application in AZ and CA, apply after final harvest or before Feb. 15 (in Coachella Valley, CA, do not apply after Feb. 1). Applications made after calendar dates above, but prior to bud swell may result in significant crop injury.

Weeds: Broadleaf weeds—Arizona, California:

annual sowthistle	common groundsel	prickly lettuce
broadleaf filaree	common lambsquarters	prostrate knotweed
burclover	common purslane	redmaids rockpurslane
burning nettle	henbit	redroot pigweed
cheeseweed	London rocket	redstem filaree
coast fiddleneck	minerslettuce	shepherdspurse

Broadleaf weeds—All other States:

American black	common purslane	prickly sida
nightshade	cutleaf	prostrate spurge
annual morningglory	eveningprimrose	redroot pigweed
annual sowthistle	cutleaf	shepherdspurse
balsamapple	groundcherry	spotted spurge
black nightshade	hemp sesbania	teaweed
camphorweed	jimsonweed	velvetleaf
common cocklebur	narrowleaf cudweed	Virginia pepperweed
common	Pennsylvania	wild poinsettia
lambsquarters	smartweed	Wright groundcherry

Remarks: Apples, apricots, cherries, crabapple, nectarines, peaches, pears, plums, prunes, quince. Direct spray toward base of tree or vine, avoiding direct plant contact. Add 2 pt./100 gal. spray nonionic surfactant.

Tank Mixes: Diuron, glyphosate, napropamide, norflurazon, oryzalin, paraquat, pronamide, simazine.

- - - - - - - - - - - - - - -

Signal Word/Toxicity Class: Warning/II.
REI: 24 hr.

Gramoxone Extra — see paraquat

Hi-Dep — see 2,4-D

Karmex — see diuron

KERB

Absorbed through roots. Should be applied in late fall or cool wet season to kill quackgrass rhizomes and germinating annual weeds. Most effective on grasses, controlling seedlings, and established cool-season grasses. Restricted Use Pesticide.

Kerb 50-W (pronamide) *(Rohm and Haas)*

Rate: 1-4 lb. ai/A
2-8 lb. 50-W/A

Time: Apply in fall after fruit is harvested, but prior to soil freeze-up.

Weeds: Broadleaf weeds:

chickweed	red sorrel (seedling)

Grasses:

annual bluegrass	Italian ryegrass	quackgrass
annual ryegrass	Kentucky bluegrass	tall fescue
downy brome	orchardgrass	volunteer grains
(cheatgrass)	ryegrass	wild oat

Remarks: Apples, cherries, nectarines, peaches, pears, plums, prunes. Do not apply to seedling trees less than 1 year old, fall transplanted stock that has been transplanted less than 1 year, or to spring transplanted stock that has been transplanted less than 6 months. Do not graze treated orchards.

- - - - - - - - - - - - - - -

Signal Word/Toxicity Class: Caution.
REI: 24 hr.

MAGMA — see MSMA

MSMA

Postemergent herbicide primarily for grass control.

120 Herbicide (6.6) *(Terra)*
912 Herbicide (6) (+ surfactant) *(Terra)*

Rate: Nonbearing:
2-3 lb. ai/A
2.66-4 pt. 6.6/A
2-4 lb. ai/A
2.66-5.32 pt. 6/A

Time: Do not exceed 3 applications per year.

Weeds: Grassy weeds.

Remarks: Nonbearing: apples, apricots, cherries, peaches, pears, plums, prunes. Do not allow spray to contact leaves, stems, bark of trees, or use around trees from which crop will be harvested within 1 year after application.

- - - - - - - - - - - - - - -

Signal Word/Toxicity Class: Caution/III.
REI: 12 hr.

Bueno 6 (+ surfactant) *(ZENECA)*

Rate: 2 lb. ai/A
2.66 pt. 6/A

Time: Apply as directed spray in warm weather when weeds are small and conditions are favorable for good weed growth.

Weeds: Broadleaf weeds:

chickweed	jimsonweed	sicklepod
cocklebur	morningglory	spurge
common purslane	pigweed	wild mustard
dandelion	puncturevine	woodsorrel
fiddleneck	ragweed	

Grasses and sedges:

bahiagrass	foxtail	nutsedge
barnyardgrass	goosegrass	sandbur
brachiaria	guineagrass	smooth crabgrass
dallisgrass	johnsongrass	wild oat
fall panicum	large crabgrass	witchgrass

Remarks: Nonbearing apples, cherries, peaches, pears, plums, prunes. Do not allow spray to contact leaves, stems, or bark of trees. Do not use around trees from which crops will be harvested within 1 year following application. Up to 3 applications per year may be applied. Do not graze treated areas. Refer to label for use directions and precautions.

- - - - - - - - - - - - - - -

Signal Word/Toxicity Class: Caution.
REI: 12 hr.

◆-new product • PP-preplant • PPI-preplant incorporated • PRE-preemergence • POST-postemergence • SEQ-sequential • ae-acid equivalent • ai-active ingredient • DF-dry flowable
E/EC-emulsifiable concentrate • F/FL-flowable • DG/G/WG-dispersable granule • L/LC-liquid • SP/WSP-soluble packet • W/WP-wettable powder • WSB-water soluble bag

Drexel MSMA 6 Plus (+ surfactant) *(Drexel)*
Helena MSMA (6.6) *(Helena)*
Helena Plus H.C. (6) (+ surfactant) *(Helena)*
◆ **MAGMA (WSG)** *(Luxembourg-Pamol)*
◆ **Target MSMA 6 Plus (+ surfactant)** *(Luxembourg-Pamol)*
◆ **TurfMate 6 Plus (+ surfactant)** *(Luxembourg-Pamol)*

Rate: 2 lb. ai/A
2.5 pt. 6.6/A
2.66 pt. 6/A
4.6 lb. ai/A
8.5 lb. WSG/A (100 gal. water—directed; 50 gal. water—spot)

Time: Apply as directed spray in warm weather when weeds are small. Up to 3 applications per year may be made for control of regrowth.

Weeds: Broadleaf weeds:

chickweed	pigweed	puncturevine
cocklebur		

Grasses and sedges:

barnyardgrass	dallisgrass	nutsedge
brachiaria	goosegrass	sandbur
crabgrass	johnsongrass	

Remarks: Nonbearing: apples, cherries, peaches, pears, plums, prunes. For 6.6, add suitable surfactant. Do not allow spray to contact leaves, stems, bark of trees, or use around trees from which crop will be harvested within 1 year after application. Do not graze treated areas.

State Restrictions: Use only as a spot treatment in Florida.

- - - - - - - - - - - - - - - -

Signal Word/Toxicity Class: Caution/III.
REI: 12 hr.

NORFLURAZON

More effective on grasses than broadleaf weeds; does not control established weeds. Absorbed by plant roots and kills weeds by inhibiting pigment formation. Apply before weeds emerge or combine with paraquat or glyphosate to kill existing vegetation. Rainfall is necessary to move chemical into weed root zone.

Solicam DF *(Novartis)*

Rate: 2-4 lb. ai/A
2.5-5 lb. DF/A

Time: Apply to soil surface from fall to early spring before weeds emerge, except on crops where otherwise specified.

Weeds: Broadleaf weeds:

annual bursage	green amaranth*	redmaids
black mustard*	groundsel*	rockpurslane
chickweed	horseweed	redroot pigweed*
common	(marestail)*	redstem filaree
lambsquarters*	little mallow	Russian thistle
common purslane	(cheeseweed)	shepherdspurse
falsedandelion	London rocket	silverleaf nightshade*
(smooth catsear)	pineappleweed	(white horsenettle)
fiddleneck	puncturevine	Virginia pepperweed*
flixweed*		whitestem filaree

Grasses and sedges:

annual bluegrass	foxtail	sixweeks grama
barnyardgrass	Italian ryegrass	southwestern
bermudagrass*	purple nutsedge	cupgrass
crabgrass	quackgrass*	wild barley
downy brome	sandbur	witchgrass
feather fingergrass		

* Suppression

Remarks: Apples, apricots, cherries, nectarines, peaches, pears, plums, prunes. Do not use on nursery stock. Rate varies by soil type. Refer to label for length of time trees must be established in the field.

Tank Mixes: Diuron (apples, peaches, pears), Goal, Gramoxone, Prowl, Roundup, simazine (apples, cherries, peaches, pears, plums), Sinbar (apples, peaches), Surflan; refer to label for use instructions.

State Restrictions: Do not use on stone fruits on western slope of Colorado. See label for use restrictions in Coachella Valley of California.

- - - - - - - - - - - - - - - -

Signal Word/Toxicity Class: Caution.
REI: 12 hr.

Opti-Amine — see 2,4-D

Orchard Master — see 2,4-D

PARAQUAT

Effective herbicide for burning-off existing annual and perennial weeds but has no residual action. Applications repeated at 4-6 week intervals provide excellent vegetation suppression. Can be tank mixed with simazine, oryzalin, or norflurazon for control of germinating weeds after existing vegetation has been burned off by paraquat. Restricted Use Pesticide.

Gramoxone Extra (2.5L) *(ZENECA)*

Rate: 0.6-1 lb. ai/A
2-3 pt. 2.5L/A

Time: Apply as directed spray when weeds and grasses are succulent and new growth is from 1-6^h high.

Weeds: Annual broadleaf weeds and grasses; top kill and suppression of perennials.

Remarks: Apples, apricots, cherries, nectarines, peaches, pears, plums, prunes. Add nonionic surfactant or crop oil concentrate. Do not allow spray to contact green stems, fruit, or foliage. Use a shield or wrap when spraying around young trees. For mature woody weeds, green suckers, late germinating weeds, grasses, and perennials, retreatment or spot treatment may be necessary. Do not graze treated areas. Refer to label for use directions, restrictions, and precautions.

Days To Harvest: Plums—28.

Tank Mixes: Devrinol, Goal, Karmex, Krovar, Princep, Sinbar, Surflan, Solicam.

- - - - - - - - - - - - - - - -

Signal Word/Toxicity Class: Danger-Poison/I.
REI: 12 hr. (except harvest aid/desiccation 24 hr.).

◆ **Starfire (1.5L)** *(ZENECA)*

Rate: 0.5-1 lb. ai/A
2.5-5.25 pt. 1.5L/A

Time: Preplant. Apply prior to planting with minimum soil disturbance.

Weeds: Annual broadleaf weeds and grasses; top kill and suppression of perennials.

Remarks: Add nonionic surfactant or crop oil concentrate. Refer to label for use directions, restrictions, and precautions.

- - - - - - - - - - - - - - - -

Signal Word/Toxicity Class: Danger-Poison/I.
REI: 12 hr. (except harvest aid/desiccation 24 hr.).

PENDIMETHALIN

Preemergent control of small-seeded broadleaf weeds and annual grasses. At least $1/2$" of rainfall within one week after application is important for adequate weed control.

Pentagon DG *(American Cyanamid)*
Prowl 3.3 EC *(American Cyanamid)*

Rate: 2-4 lb. ai/A
2.4-4.8 qt. 3.3 EC/A
3.3-6.6 lb. DG/A

Time: Apply before weeds emerge.

Weeds: Broadleaf Weeds:

annual spurge	knotweed	pigweed
carpetweed	kochia	puncturevine
chickweed	lambsquarters	purslane
fiddleneck	London rocket	shepherdspurse
Florida pusley	Pennsylvania	velvetleaf
henbit	smartweed	

Grasses:

annual bluegrass	giant foxtail	red sprangletop
barnyardgrass	green foxtail	signalgrass
browntop panicum	johnsongrass	Texas panicum
crabgrass	(seedling)	witchgrass
crowfootgrass	junglerice	woolly cupgrass
fall panicum	lovegrass	yellow foxtail
field sandbur	Mexican sprangletop	

Remarks: Nonbearing: apples, apricots, cherries, nectarines, peaches, pears, plums, prunes. Use low rate for short-term control; high rate for long-term control. Apply spray directly to ground beneath trees. Refer to label for further use directions and precautions.

- - - - - - - - - - - - - - - -

Signal Word/Toxicity Class: Caution.
REI: 12 hr.

Pentagon — see pendimethalin

7

Fruits & Nuts

Tree Fruits (Deciduous)

Poast — see sethoxydim

Princep — see simazine

Prism — see clethodim

Prowl — see pendimethalin

Rattler — see glyphosate

Rely — see glufosinate-ammonium

Roundup — see glyphosate

Saber — see 2,4-D

Savage — see 2,4-D

SCYTHE

Nonselective, postemergent herbicide. May be used to control suckers. May also be used with other herbicides having systemic or residual activity.

Scythe (pelargonic acid) *(Mycogen)*
Rate: 4-13 fl. oz./1 gal. spray solution
Time: Apply to actively growing weeds prior to crop emergence.
Weeds: Annual and perennial broadleaf weeds and grasses.
Remarks: Apples, crabapples, pears, quince, stone fruit. Apply in minimum 75 gal. spray solution/A or spray-to-wet. Do not apply by air or through any type of irrigation system. Refer to label for directions and precautions.
Tank Mixes: Glyphosate and other foliar and residual herbicides.

– – – – – – – – – – – – – – – – –

Signal Word/Toxicity Class: Warning/II.
REI: 24 hr.

Select — see clethodim

SETHOXYDIM

Postemergent contact spray which controls actively growing grasses.

Poast (1.5EC) *(BASF)*
Rate: 0.3-0.5 lb. ai/A
    1.5-2.5 pt. 1.5EC/A
Time: Postemergence.
Weeds: Annual grasses up to 12" in height and perennial grasses:

barnyardgrass	large crabgrass	stinkgrass
bermudagrass	lovegrass	tall fescue
broadleaf signalgrass	orchardgrass	Texas panicum
browntop panicum	(seedling)	wild proso millet
fall panicum	perennial ryegrass	wildcane
giant foxtail	quackgrass	wiremstem muhly
goosegrass	red sprangletop	witchgrass
green foxtail	shattercane	woolly cupgrass
johnsongrass	smooth crabgrass	yellow foxtail
junglerice	southwestern cupgrass	

Remarks: Apples, apricots, cherries, crabapples, nectarines, peaches, pears, quince; nonbearing plums, prunes. Add 2 pt./A oil concentrate. Refer to label for restrictions and limitations.
Days To Harvest: Apples, apricots, cherries, crabapples, nectarines, peaches, pears, quince—14; plums, prunes—1 year.
State Restrictions: Do not use UAN or AMS in California or Pacific Northwest.

– – – – – – – – – – – – – – – – –

Signal Word/Toxicity Class: Warning/II.
REI: 12 hr.

SIMAZINE

Effective herbicide on germinating annual weeds. Provides quackgrass suppression when applied in combination with paraquat or glyphosate. Rate varies by soil type and injury may occur to stone fruit on sandy soils when rate exceeds 2 lb./A.

◆ **Clean Crop Simazine 4L or 90WDG** *(Platte)*
Rate: Apples, pears, sour cherries:
    2-4 lb. ai/A
    2-4 qt. 4L/A
    2.2-4.4 lb. 90WDG/A
Time: Apply prior to weed emergence.

Rate: Peaches (AR, LA, MO, OK, TX, east of the Mississippi):
    1.5-4 lb. ai/A
    2-4 qt. 4L/A
    1.75-4.4 lb. 90WDG/A
Time: Apply before weeds emerge in late fall to early spring.

Rate: Peaches (CA only):
    1-2 lb. ai/A
    1.1-2.2 lb. 90WDG/A
Time: Apply before weeds emerge in late fall or early winter.

Rate: Plums, sweet cherries (MO, east of the Mississippi except TN):
    1.5-4 lb. ai/A
    2-4 qt. 4L/A
    1.75-4.4 lb. 90WDG/A
Time: Apply before weeds emerge in late fall to early spring.
Weeds: Broadleaf weeds:

annual morningglory	Florida pusley	redmaids
burclover	groundsel	rockpurslane
carelessweed	henbit	Russian thistle
carpetweed	knawel	shepherdspurse
common chickweed	(German moss)	smartweed
common	nightshade	spanishneedles
lambsquarters	pepperweed	speedwell
common purslane	pigweed	tansymustard
fiddleneck	pineappleweed	wild mustard
filaree	prickly lettuce	yellowflower
fireweed	ragweed	pepperweed
flora's paintbrush		

Grasses:

annual bluegrass	fall panicum	signalgrass
annual ryegrass	foxtail	silver hairgrass
barnyardgrass	goosegrass	watergrass
cheatgrass	junglerice	wild oat
crabgrass	rattail fescue	witchgrass
downy brome		

Remarks: Apples, pears, cherries (sour, sweet), peaches, plums. Trees must be established 1 year or more (3 years for peaches in California). Make only one application per year. Refer to label for use directions and precautions.

– – – – – – – – – – – – – – – – –

Signal Word/Toxicity Class: Caution/III.
REI: 12 hr.

Drexel Simazine 4L or 90DF *(Drexel)*
Princep 4L or Caliber 90 *(Novartis)*
Riverside Simazine 4L or 90DF *(Terra)*
Rate: Apples, pears, sour cherries:
    2-4 lb. ai/A
    2-4 qt. 4L/A
    2.2-4.4 lb. 90, 90DF/A
Time: Apply prior to weed emergence.

Rate: Nectarines, peaches:
    1-2 lb. ai/A
    1-2 qt. 4L/A
    1.1-2.2 lb. 90, 90DF/A
Time: Apply before weeds emerge in late fall or early winter.
Weeds: Broadleaf weeds:

annual morningglory	Florida pusley	redmaids
burclover	groundsel	rockpurslane
carelessweed	henbit	Russian thistle
carpetweed	knawel	shepherdspurse
common chickweed	(German moss)	smartweed
common lambsquarters	nightshade	spanishneedles
common purslane	pepperweed	speedwell
fiddleneck	pigweed	tansymustard
filaree	pineappleweed	wild mustard
fireweed	prickly lettuce	yellowflower
flora's paintbrush	ragweed	pepperweed

◆-new product • PP-preplant • PPI-preplant incorporated • PRE-preemergence • POST-postemergence • SEQ-sequential • ae-acid equivalent • ai-active ingredient • DF-dry flowable
E/EC-emulsifiable concentrate • F/FL-flowable • DG/G/WG-dispersable granule • L/LC-liquid • SP/WSP-soluble packet • W/WP-wettable powder • WSB-water soluble bag

Weed Control Manual 2000

Grasses:

annual bluegrass	downy brome	rattail fescue
annual ryegrass	fall panicum	signalgrass
barnyardgrass (watergrass)	foxtail	silver hairgrass
cheatgrass	goosegrass	wild oat
crabgrass	junglerice	witchgrass
	quackgrass	

Remarks: Apples, pears, cherries (sour), nectarines, peaches. Trees must be established 1 year or more for apples, pears, and cherries and at least 3 years for peaches and nectarines. Do not replant peaches or nectarines in treated soil for 12 months after treatment. Refer to label for use directions, restrictions, and precautions.

Tank Mixes: Gramoxone Extra, Roundup Ultra, Surflan.

State Restrictions: For use in California only on nectarines and peaches.

– – – – – – – – – – – – – –

Signal Word/Toxicity Class: Caution/III.
REI: 12 hr.

SINBAR

Controls most annual broadleaf and grassy weeds and will also suppress the growth of some perennial weeds. Do not apply in areas where there is essentially no organic matter in the soil.

Sinbar (WP) (terbacil) *(DuPont)*

Rate: 1.6-3.2 lb. ai/A
2-4 lb. WP/A

Time: Apply in spring before weeds emerge or during early seedling stage.

Weeds: Broadleaf weeds:

American burnweed (fireweed)	fiddleneck	nightshade
chickweed	flora's paintbrush	plantain
China lettuce	Florida pusley	pigweed
clover	henbit	purslane
crotalaria	horseweed	ragweed
dandelion (seedling)	jimsonweed	sheep sorrel
dogfennel	knotweed	smartweed
	lambsquarters	wild geranium
	mustard	

Grasses:

barnyardgrass	foxtail	orchardgrass
bluegrass	guineagrass	panicum
crabgrass	junglerice	sandbur (sandspur)
crowfootgrass	natalgrass	signalgrass

Remarks: Bearing, nonbearing: apples, peaches. Established for at least 3 years. Do not allow drift to come in contact with fruit. Do not graze or feed forage to livestock.

Crop Rotation: Do not replant to any crop within 2 years after treatment.

Tank Mixes: Karmex.

State Restrictions: Not for use in California.

– – – – – – – – – – – – – –

Signal Word/Toxicity Class: Caution.
REI: 12 hr.

SNAPSHOT (Premix)

Combination of isoxaben and trifluralin that provides control of a broader spectrum of weeds than either chemical by itself. Does not control established weeds.

Snapshot 2.5TG (2% trifluralin & 0.5% isoxaben) *(Dow AgroSciences)*

Rate: 2.5-5 lb. ai/A
100-200 lb. 2.5TG/A

Time: Apply in late summer to early fall or early spring or immediately after cultivation.

Weeds: Broadleaf weeds:

annual bursage	creeping woodsorrel	kochia
annual sowthistle	curly dock	lanceleaf groundcherry
black medic	dandelion	little mallow
black nightshade	datura	London rocket
bristly oxtongue	desert rockpurslane	marestail
broadleaf plantain	dwarf fleabane	Mexican sprangletop
burning nettle	dwarf mallow	nettleleaf goosefoot
California burclover	eveningprimrose	panicle willowweed
Carolina geranium	fall panicum	Pennsylvania smartweed
clover	hairy fleabane	
coast fiddleneck	hairy galinsoga	petty spurge
common chickweed	hare barley	pigweed
common groundsel	heath aster	pineappleweed
common lambsquarters	henbit	prickly lettuce
	horseweed	prickly sida
common purslane	Indian mustard	prostrate knotweed
common ragweed	jimsonweed	purple cudweed

Weeds: Broadleaf weeds, continued:

purslane speedwell	silversheath knotweed	tall morningglory
rattail fescue	slender aster	telegraphplant
redstem filaree	slender plantain	turkey mullein
Russian thistle	spiny sowthistle	velvetleaf
scarlet pimpernel	spotted spurge	Virginia pepperweed
shepherdspurse	sunflower	yellow sweetclover
sibara	swinecress	yellow woodsorrel

Annual grasses:

annual bluegrass	junglerice	wild mustard
barnyardgrass	lovegrass	wild oat
bromegrass	southwestern cupgrass	wild radish
crabgrass		witchgrass
giant foxtail	wild carrot	yellow foxtail
Italian ryegrass	wild celery	

Remarks: Nonbearing apples, nectarines, peaches, pears, plums, sweet cherries. Apply to trees that will not bear fruit for at least 1 year. Do not apply to bedding plants, nursery seedbeds, or transplant beds.

State Restrictions: Refer to label for use restrictions in Arizona.

– – – – – – – – – – – – – –

Signal Word/Toxicity Class: Caution/III.
REI: 12 hr.

Solicam — see norflurazon

Starfire — see paraquat

SURFLAN

Preemergence herbicide effective in controlling annual grasses and many broadleaf weeds. Little effect on established weeds and grasses but may be combined with paraquat to kill established weeds and prevent regrowth. May be combined with simazine, diuron, terbacil, or norflurazon for broad-spectrum, season-long control.

Surflan A.S. (oryzalin) *(Dow AgroSciences)*

Rate: 2-6 lb. ai/A
2-6 qt. A.S./A

Time: Apply before weeds emerge.

Weeds: Broadleaf weeds:

annual morningglory*	cudweed	prostrate spurge*
annual smartweed*	field sandbur	puncturevine
annual sowthistle*	Florida purslane	red sprangletop
black mustard*	Florida pusley	redmaids rockpurslane
black nightshade*	giant ragweed*	redroot pigweed
carelessweed	henbit	redstem filaree*
carpetweed	ladysthumb*	rough pigweed
chickweed	lambsquarters	shepherdspurse
climbing milkweed*	London rocket*	smooth pigweed
coast fiddleneck	Mexican clover	spiny pigweed
common groundsel*	prickly lettuce*	tumble pigweed
common mallow*	prickly sida (teaweed)*	velvetleaf*
common purslane	prostrate knotweed	whitestem filaree*
common ragweed*	prostrate pigweed	wild mustard*

Grasses:

annual bluegrass	green foxtail	robust foxtail
annual ryegrass	guineagrass	signalgrass
barnyardgrass	Italian ryegrass	smooth crabgrass
bottlegrass	johnsongrass (seedling)	spreading panicgrass
bristlegrass		southwestern cupgrass
browntop panicum	junglerice	
crowfootgrass	large crabgrass	Texas panicum
downy brome	little barley	watergrass
fall panicum	Mexican lovegrass	wild oat
foxtail	Orcutt lovegrass	witchgrass
giant foxtail	pigeongrass	yellow foxtail

*Suppression

Remarks: Bearing, nonbearing: apples, apricots, cherries, nectarines, peaches, pears, plums, prunes. Rate depends on length of control desired. Surface apply once existing weeds are controlled by tillage or contact herbicide. May be applied through solid set sprinkler irrigation system. Single $1/_2$-1" rain or sprinkler irrigation within 21 days required. Not recommended on soils with organic matter higher than 5%.

Tank Mixes: Goal, Gramoxone Extra, Karmex, Princep, Sinbar, and Solicam.

– – – – – – – – – – – – – –

Signal Word/Toxicity Class: Caution/III.
REI: 12 hr.

7

Fruits & Nuts

Target — see MSMA

Trific — see trifluralin

TOUCHDOWN

Trimethylsulfonium salt of glyphosate that moves into the plant and is translocated more rapidly than glyphosate. Has same mode of action as glyphosate and is similar to Roundup Ultra.

Touchdown (5L or 6L) (sulfosate) *(ZENECA)*

Rate: 0.5-4 lb. ai/A
  0.8-6.4 pt. 5L/A
  0.66-5.33 pt. 6L/A
Time: Apply to actively growing grasses and weeds.
Weeds: Broadleaf weeds:

annual sowthistle	field bindweed	morningglory
annual spurge	field sandbur	mouseear chickweed
black nightshade	filaree	mustard
camphorweed	fleabane	Pennsylvania
Canada thistle	Florida pusley	smartweed
Carolina geranium	giant ragweed	prickly lettuce
common chickweed	grouncherry	redroot pigweed
common cocklebur	hairy fleabane	Russian thistle
common groundsel	hemp dogbane	shepherdspurse
common	henbit	sicklepod
lambsquarters	hophornbeam	smooth pigweed
common ragweed	copperleaf	spanishneedles
curly dock	kochia	teaweed
cutleaf	leafy spurge*	velvetleaf
eveningprimrose	little barley	wheat
dandelion	London rocket	white clover
dogfennel	marestail	wild buckwheat
fiddleneck		

Grasses and sedges:

annual bluegrass	foxtail	smooth bromegrass
bahiagrass	goosegrass	sprangletop
barley	guineagrass	stinkgrass
barnyardgrass	Italian ryegrass	tall fescue
bermudagrass	johnsongrass	Texas panicum
broadleaf signalgrass	(seedling)	timothy
cheat	Kentucky bluegrass	torpedograss*
cogongrass*	orchardgrass	vaseygrass
crabgrass	paragrass	wild oat
crowfootgrass	perennial ryegrass	wirestem muhly
downy brome	quackgrass	witchgrass
fall panicum	red rice	woolly cupgrass
fescue	shattercane	yellow nutsedge

  * Partial control

Remarks: Bearing and nonbearing apricots, cherries, nectarines, peaches, plums, prunes. Nonbearing apples, apricots, cherries, crabapples, nectarines, peaches, pears, plums, prunes, quince. Nonionic surfactant or wetting agent required. In addition, ammonium sulfate can be added to nonbearing crops. Do not allow spray, spray drift, or mist to contact green foliage or green bark on trunk, suckers, open wounds, or other green parts of trees and vines. Avoid contact with stumps as tree injury may occur from root grafting. Do not apply through any type of irrigation system. Refer to label for use directions, restrictions, and precautions.

Days To Harvest: 1 year.
Tank Mixes: 2,4-D, Devrinol, diuron, Goal, Kerb, Krovar, Prowl, simazine, Sinbar, Solicam, Surflan.
State Restrictions: Ammonium sulfate (6L) not for use in California.

– – – – – – – – – – – – – – – –

Rate: 5-12 fl. oz. 5L/A
  4-10 fl. oz. 6L/A
Time: Apply after green-up or after 3-4" of regrowth following mowing.
Weeds: Perennial grasses:

bahiagrass	Kentucky bluegrass	quackgrass
bermudagrass	orchardgrass	tall fescue
fine fescue		

Remarks: Suppression on orchard floors. Rate varies by grass species and geographic area. Nonionic surfactant or wetting agent required. In addition, ammonium sulfate can be added (except Kentucky bluegrass). Refer to label for use directions, restrictions, and precautions.

– – – – – – – – – – – – – – – –

Signal Word/Toxicity Class: Caution.
REI: 12 hr. (5L); 4 hr. (6L).

Treflan — see trifluralin

TRI-4 — see trifluralin

TRIFLURALIN

Controls many grasses and some broadleaf weeds but must be incorporated for effective weed control.

Albaugh Trifluralin 4EC *(Albaugh)*
◆ **Clean Crop Trifluralin HF (4EC)** *(Platte)*
Gowan Trifluralin 4 or 5 (EC) or 10G *(Gowan)*
Helena Trifluralin 4 EC *(Helena)*
Riverside Trifluralin 4EC or Trific 60DF *(Terra)*
◆ **Sedagri Trifluralin 480 (4EC)** *(Rhone-Poulenc)*
Treflan HFP (4EC) or TR-10 (10G) *(Dow AgroSciences)*
TRI-4 HF (4EC) *(American Cyanamid)*
Trilin 4 or 5 (EC) or 10G *(Griffin)*
Wilbur-Ellis Trifluralin 10G *(Wilbur-Ellis)*

Rate: New plantings
  0.5-1 lb. ai/A
  1-2 pt. 4EC/A
  0.8-1.6 pt. 5EC/A
  0.875-1.66 lb. 60DF/A
  5-10 lb. 10G/A
  Established bearing, nonbearing
  1-2 lb. ai/A
  2-4 pt. 4EC/A
  1.6-3.2 pt. 5EC/A
  1.66-3.33 lb. 60DF/A
  10-20 lb. 10G/A
Time: New plantings: Apply and incorporate before planting. Established plantings: Apply as directed spray to soil.
Weeds: Broadleaf weeds:

carelessweed	knotweed	purslane
carpetweed	kochia	pusley
chickweed	lambsquarters	redroot pigweed
field bindweed	Mexican clover	rough pigweed
fireweed	Mexican fireweed	Russian thistle
Florida purslane	prostrate pigweed	spiny pigweed
Florida pusley	puncturevine	stinging nettle
goosefoot	(western U.S.)	tumbleweed
henbit		

Grasses:

annual bluegrass	fall panicum	sandbur
barnyardgrass	foxtail millet	shattercane
bottlegrass	giant foxtail	smooth crabgrass
brachiaria	green foxtail	sprangletop
bristlegrass	Italian ryegrass	stinkgrass
bromegrass	johnsongrass	Texas panicum
burgrass	(seedling)	watergrass
cheat	junglerice	wildcane
cheatgrass	large crabgrass	woolly cupgrass
chess	pigeongrass	yellow foxtail
downy brome	robust foxtail	

Remarks: Apricots, nectarines, peaches, plums, prunes. Rate varies by soil type and amount of rainfall. Use incorporation methods not injurious to crop. Refer to label for directions and precautions.
Days To Harvest: 60.
State Restrictions: Trilin 10G and Wilbur-Ellis not for use in California.

– – – – – – – – – – – – – – – –

Signal Word/Toxicity Class: Varies by formulation.
REI: 12 hr. unless soil injected or soil incorporated.

Trilin — see trifluralin

TurfMate — see MSMA

VAPAM

Water-soluble liquid that when applied to properly prepared soil is converted into a gaseous fumigant. May be applied by sprinkler, soil injection, or chemigation.

Vapam HL (metam-sodium) *(Amvac)*
Rate: 0.75 qt./100 sq. ft.
Time: Tree replant sites in commercial orchards.

◆-new product • PP-preplant • PPI-preplant incorporated • PRE-preemergence • POST-postemergence • SEQ-sequential • ae-acid equivalent • ai-active ingredient • DF-dry flowable
E/EC-emulsifiable concentrate • F/FL-flowable • DG/G/WG-dispersable granule • L/LC-liquid • SP/WSP-soluble packet • W/WP-wettable powder • WSB-water soluble bag

Weeds: Weeds and germinating weed seeds:

carelessweed	henbit	purslane
chickweed	lambsquarters	ragweed
dandelion	pigweed	wild morningglory

Grasses:

annual bluegrass	johnsongrass	watergrass
bermudagrass	nutgrass	

Remarks: Make shallow basin over planting site after removing dead or diseased trees and as much of root system as possible. Add Vapam to stream of water while filling basin. Apply in sufficient water to penetrate at least 6 ft. Tarping of replant sites is required when within 1/2 mile of populated areas. Do not apply to desirable lawns and plants or to within 3 ft. of drip line of desirable plants, shrubs, or trees. Do not use in greenhouses, enclosed structures, confined areas, or when fumes may enter nearby houses.

State Restrictions: In California, application must be in compliance with Technical Information Bulletin — California, "Metam-Sodium Guidelines for All Application Methods for Metam-Sodium in California." Bulletin may be obtained from local pesticide dealer or metam-sodium registrant.

– – – – – – – – – – – – – – –

Signal Word/Toxicity Class: Danger/I.

REI: 48 hr.; if tarps are used for application, entry prohibited while tarps are being removed.

Weed Rhap — see 2,4-D

Weedar — see 2,4-D

Weedestroy — see 2,4-D

XL 2G (Premix)

A selective preemergence herbicide for control of certain annual grasses and broadleaf weeds. Does not control established weeds. Requires rainfall or sprinkler irrigation within 21 days to activate.

XL 2G (1% benefin & 1% oryzalin) *(Helena)*

Rate: 4-6 lb. ai/A
200-300 lb./A
0.09-0.14 lb. ai/sq. ft.
4.6-6.9 lb./1000 sq. ft.

Time: Apply prior to germination of target weeds.

Weeds: Broadleaf weeds:

annual sowthistle*	desert rockpurslane	prostrate spurge
bittercress	Florida pusley	puncturevine
black mustard*	henbit	redstem filaree
black nightshade*	horseweed*	shepherdspurse
carpetweed	ladysthumb*	smartweed*
chickweed	lambsquarters	spotted spurge*
climbing milkweed*	London rocket	teaweed*
coast fiddleneck	morningglory*	velvetleaf*
common groundsel	pigweed	whitestem filaree
common mallow*	prickly lettuce*	wild mustard*
common purslane	prickly sida*	yellow woodsorrel
common ragweed*	prostrate knotweed	

Grasses:

annual bluegrass	foxtail	Orcutt lovegrass
barnyardgrass	goosegrass	red sprangletop
browntop panicum	Italian ryegrass	signalgrass
crabgrass	johnsongrass	Texas panicum
crowfootgrass	(seedling)	volunteer wheat*
cupgrass	junglerice	wild oat
fall panicum	little barley	witchgrass
field sandbur	Mexican lovegrass	

* Suppression

Remarks: Nonbearing apple, pear, stone fruits. Do not apply to trees that may be harvested for food within 1 year after application. Refer to label for use directions and precautions.

– – – – – – – – – – – – – – –

Signal Word/Toxicity Class: Caution/III.

REI: 12 hr. unless soil-injected or soil-incorporated.

Tree Fruits
(Subtropical)

AAtrex — see atrazine

Atra-5 — see atrazine

ATRAZINE

Restricted Use Pesticide.

AAtrex 4L or AAtrex Nine-0 (WDG) *(Novartis)*
◆ **Clean Crop Atrazine 4L or 90 WDG** *(Platte)*
Drexel Atrazine 4L, Atra-5 (5L) or 90DF *(Drexel)*
Helena Atrazine 4L *(Helena)*

Rate: 2-4 lb. ai/A
4-8 pt. 4L/A
3.2-6.4 pt. 5L/A
2.2-4.4 lb. WDG, 90DF/A

Time: Do not apply more frequently than at 4-month intervals.

Weeds: Annual broadleaf weeds and grasses including:

fireweed	scarlet pimpernel	spanishneedles
purslane	sowthistle	

Remarks: Guava. Established plantings at least 18 months old. Apply as directed to weeds; do not allow spray to contact foliage or fruit. Do not apply more than 8 lb. ai/A or apply through any type of irrigation system. Refer to label for precautions and restrictions.

State Restrictions: Wilbur-Ellis not registered in California.

– – – – – – – – – – – – – – –

Signal Word/Toxicity Class: Caution/III.
REI: 12 hr.

CLETHODIM

Postemergence grass herbicide. Mode of action similar to Poast, Assure, Option II, and Fusilade.

Envoy or Prism (0.94EC), Select (2EC) *(Valent)*

Rate: 0.1-0.25 lb. ai/A
13-34 fl. oz. 0.94EC/A
6-16 fl. oz. 2EC/A

Time: Postemergence. Apply to actively growing grasses.

Weeds: Grasses:

Amazon sprangletop	green foxtail	smooth crabgrass
annual bluegrass	itchgrass	southern crabgrass
barnyardgrass	johnsongrass	Texas panicum
bearded sprangletop	junglerice	volunteer cereals
bermudagrass	large crabgrass	wild oat
broadleaf signalgrass	quackgrass	wild proso millet
crowfootgrass	red rice	wirestem muhly
fall panicum	red sprangletop	witchgrass
giant foxtail	shattercane	woolly cupgrass
goosegrass	southwestern cupgrass	yellow foxtail

Remarks: Nonbearing olives. Nonbearing are plants that will not bear fruit for at least 1 year after application. Rate varies by grass species, stage, and geographical region. Grass crops such as corn, sorghum, wheat, and rice are highly sensitive to clethodim. Do not apply under stress conditions or if rainfall is expected in 1 hour. Do not apply through any type of irrigation system. Do not apply more than 0.5 lb. ai/A (0.25 lb. ai/A on Long Island, NY) per season. Do not graze treated fields or feed treated forage or hay to livestock. Refer to label for restrictions and precautions.

State Restrictions: Not for use on Solano grass in the Vernal Lakes area of Solano County, California; wild rice in Hays County, Texas.

– – – – – – – – – – – – – – –

Signal Word/Toxicity Class: Warning/II.
REI: 24 hr.

Credit — see glyphosate

7

Fruits & Nuts

DEVRINOL

Devrinol 50-DF (napropamide) *(United Phosphorus)*
Rate: 4 lb. ai/A
8 lb. 50-DF/A
Time: Apply in fall through early spring, prior to weed emergence.
Weeds: Annual broadleaf weeds:

annual sowthistle	common ragweed	pineappleweed
carpetweed	(suppression)	prickly lettuce
coast fiddleneck	horse purslane	prostrate knotweed
common chickweed	lambsquarters	purple cudweed
common groundsel	little mallow	redroot pigweed
common purslane	(from seed)	redstem filaree

Annual grasses:

annual bluegrass	guineagrass	sandbur
barnyardgrass	hairy crabgrass	smooth crabgrass
bristly foxtail	Italian ryegrass	soft chess
canarygrass	johnsongrass	southwestern cupgrass
cheatgrass	(seedling)	stinkgrass
downy brome	junglerice	Texas panicum
fall panicum	large crabgrass	wild barley
foxtail barley	Mexican sprangletop	wild oat
giant foxtail	red sprangletop	witchgrass
goosegrass	ripgut brome	yellow foxtail
green foxtail		

Remarks: Figs (newly planted, established); **Western Region: avocados** (established), **kiwifruit** (newly planted, established), **olives** (newly planted, established), **persimmons** (established), **pomegranates** (established). Rainfall or irrigation necessary for activation. Refer to label for directions and precautions.
Days To Harvest: 35; pomegranates—6 months.
Tank Mixes: Goal for use on figs.

— — — — — — — — — — — — — —

Signal Word/Toxicity Class: Caution.
REI: 12 hr.

DIQUAT DIBROMIDE

◆ **Diquat** *(ZENECA)*
Rate: 0.375-0.5 lb. ai/A
1.5-2 pt./A
Time: Site preparation prior to planting. Repeat as needed.
Weeds: Broadleaf weeds and grasses.
Remarks: Nonbearing avocados, bananas, coffee, dates, figs, guava, kiwifruit, mangos, olives, papayas, passion fruit, persimmons, plantains, pomegranates. Apply by ground only. Use high rate when weeds are large or dense. Do not allow spray to contact green stems, foliage, or fruit. Use a shield or wrap plant when spraying around young trees or vines. Do not apply through any type of irrigation system. Do not graze treated areas. Refer to label for use restrictions and precautions.
Days To Harvest: 1 year.

— — — — — — — — — — — — — —

Signal Word/Toxicity Class: Warning/II.
REI: 24 hr.

Direx — see diuron

DIURON

Direx 4L or 80DF *(Griffin)*
◆ **Diuron 80 WDG** *(Platte)*
Karmex DF *(Griffin)*
Riverside Diuron 4L or 80DF *(Terra)*
Rate: New plantings:
1.2.-2.4 lb. ai/A
1.2-2.4 qt. 4L/A
1.5-3 lb. DF, 80DF/A
Established plantings:
2.4-4.8 lb. ai/A
2.4-4.8 qt. 4L/A
3-6 lb. DF, 80DF/A
Time: For new plantings, apply after planting but before plants emerge.
Weeds: New plantings:
guineagrass
Established plantings:

bermudagrass	birdseedgrass

Remarks: Bananas, plantains. For established plantings, add 1 pt. surfactant/25 gal. spray. Do not apply to loose soil directly over the planting material.

Crop Rotation: Treated areas may be planted to sugarcane and pineapple 1 year after last application.

— — — — — — — — — — — — — —

Rate: 1.5 lb. ai/A
1.5 qt. 4L/A (Terra)
2 lb. DF, 80DF/A
Time: Apply after grove is laid-up in late Oct.-Nov.; repeat at same rate in Mar.-Apr.
Weeds: Broadleaf weeds:

chickweed	pigweed	ragweed
lambsquarters	purslane	wild mustard

Grasses:

barnyardgrass	crabgrass	foxtail

Remarks: Olives. Use only under trees established in grove for at least 1 year. Keep spray or drift off foliage. Remove weed growth before treatment.
State Restrictions: For use in California.

— — — — — — — — — — — — — —

Rate: 2-4 lb. ai/A
2-4 qt. 4L/A
2.5-5 lb. DF, 80DF/A
Time: Apply before weeds emerge.
Weeds: Controls most annual and seedling perennial weeds.
Remarks: Papayas. Use only under trees established in orchard for at least 1 year. If weeds have emerged, add surfactant.

— — — — — — — — — — — — — —

Rate: Hawaii, Florida:
3.2-5 lb. ai/A
3.2-5 qt. 4L/A
3.2-6.4 lb. ai/A
4-8 lb. DF, 80DF/A
Puerto Rico:
3-5 lb. ai/A
3-5 qt. 4L/A
3.75-6.25 lb. DF, 80DF/A
Time: Apply as broadcast spray just before or immediately after planting but prior to weed emergence.
Weeds: Controls most annual and seedling perennial weeds.
Remarks: Pineapple. For ratoon crop, use low rate after harvesting.
Crop Rotation: Treated areas may be planted to pineapple or sugarcane 1 year after last application.
State Restrictions: For use in Florida, Hawaii, Puerto Rico.

— — — — — — — — — — — — — —

Signal Word/Toxicity Class: Caution/III.
REI: 12 hr.

Envoy — see clethodim

EVIK

Evik DF (ametryn) *(Novartis)*
Rate: Hawaii
4-8 lb. ai/A
5-10 lb. DF/A
Puerto Rico
3.2-4.8 lb. ai/A
4-6 lb. DF/A
Time: Apply as directed basal spray immediately after setting plants or any time thereafter. Apply before weeds emerge or to emerged, growing weeds. Repeat as needed at 3-4 month intervals.
Weeds: Broadleaf and grass weeds—Hawaii:

Amaranthus	foxtail	pualele
common purslane	goosegrass	rattlebox
crabgrass	Japanese tea	Richardia
dallisgrass	junglerice	sowthistle
fireweed	kukaipuaa	spanishneedles
flora's paintbrush	panicum	wild pea bean

Broadleaf and grass weeds—Puerto Rico:

Anoxopus compressus	foxtail	Paspalum
crabgrass	panicum	spreading dayflower

Remarks: Bananas, plantains. Use higher rates for more residual control and for hard-to-kill weeds. Not to exceed 30 lb. DF/yr. in Hawaii (16 lb. DF/yr. Puerto Rico).
State Restrictions: For use in Hawaii, Puerto Rico.

— — — — — — — — — — — — — —

Rate: 7.2 lb. ai/A
9 lb. DF/A
Time: Apply as blanket spray immediately after planting or after plant crop harvest is completed and before weeds emerge.

◆-new product • PP-preplant • PPI-preplant incorporated • PRE-preemergence • POST-postemergence • SEQ-sequential • ae-acid equivalent • ai-active ingredient • DF-dry flowable
E/EC-emulsifiable concentrate • F/FL-flowable • DG/G/WG-dispersable granule • L/LC-liquid • SP/WSP-soluble packet • W/WP-wettable powder • WSB-water soluble bag

Weeds: Broadleaf weeds including:

Amaranthus	Japanese tea	Richardia
common purslane	kukaipuaa	sowthistle
fireweed	pualele	spanishneedles
flora's paintbrush	rattlebox	wild pea bean

Grasses:

crabgrass	foxtail	junglerice
dallisgrass	goosegrass	panicum

Remarks: Pineapple. Do not apply more than 9 lb. DF/A per crop cycle.
Days To Harvest: 160.

– – – – – – – – – – – – – – –

Signal Word/Toxicity Class: Caution.
REI: 12 hr.

FLUAZIFOP-P-BUTYL

Fusilade DX *(ZENECA)*
Rate: 0.25-0.375 lb. ai/A
    1-1.5 pt. DX/A
Time: Annual grasses: 2-8" tall before tillering and/or seedhead formation. Perennial grasses: apply by growth stage dependent on species.
Weeds: Annual and perennial grasses:

barnyardgrass	johnsongrass	southern sandbur
bermudagrass	(rhizome, seedling)	southwestern
broadleaf signalgrass	junglerice	cupgrass
fall panicum	kikuyugrass	Texas panicum
field sandbur	large crabgrass	tropical crabgrass
giant foxtail	prairie cupgrass	volunteer cereals
goosegrass	quackgrass	wild oat
green foxtail	red rice	wild proso millet
guineagrass	shattercane	wiresteam muhly
(seedling)	smooth crabgrass	witchgrass
Italian ryegrass	sorghum-almum	woolly cupgrass
itchgrass	southern crabgrass	yellow foxtail

Remarks: Nonbearing: avocados, coffee, dates, figs, guava, kiwifruit, mangos, olives, pomegranates. Rate varies by geographic area and grass species. Add crop oil concentrate or nonionic surfactant. Do not apply to tree fruits that may be harvested for food within 1 year after application.
Crop Rotation: Do not plant rotational grass crops such as corn, sorghum, and cereals within 60 days after last application.
State Restrictions: Coffee for use in Hawaii only; for other crops refer to label for geographical regions.

– – – – – – – – – – – – – – –

Signal Word/Toxicity Class: Caution.
REI: 12 hr.

Fusilade — see fluazifop-P-butyl

GALLERY

Gallery 75DF (isoxaben) *(Dow AgroSciences)*
Rate: 0.5-1 lb. ai/A
    0.66-1.33 lb. 75DF/A
Time: Preemergence. Apply in late summer to early fall or in early spring, prior to germination of target weeds.
Weeds: Broadleaf weeds:

annual sowthistle	dandelion	prostrate spurge
bittercress	dogfennel	redmaids
black mustard	green tansymustard	rockpurslane
black nightshade	hairy galinsoga	redstem filaree
blackleaved fleabane	henbit	shepherdspurse
bracted plantain	horseweed	sibara
buckhorn plantain	ladysthumb	slender plantain
Carolina geranium	lambsquarters	southern brassbuttons
coast fiddleneck	London rocket	spotted spurge
common chickweed	marestail	thymeleaf speedwell
common groundsel	mouseear chickweed	velvetleaf
common purslane	pennywort	white clover
common ragweed	pigweed	whitestem filaree
common sowthistle	pineappleweed	wild celery
creeping woodsorrel	prickly lettuce	wild mustard
cudweed	prostrate knotweed	yellow woodsorrel

Grasses (suppression):

annual bluegrass	crabgrass	goosegrass
annual ryegrass	dandelion (from seed)	Italian ryegrass
barnyardgrass	foxtail	mallow

Remarks: Nonbearing: avocados, figs, kiwifruit, olives, pomegranates. Refer to label for directions and precautions. Do not apply through any type of irrigation system.

– – – – – – – – – – – – – – –

Signal Word/Toxicity Class: Caution/III.
REI: 12 hr.

Glyfos or Glyfos X-tra — see glyphosate

GLYPHOSATE

◆ **Credit (4WS)** *(Nufarm)*
◆ **Glyfos or Glyfos X-tra (4WS)** *(Cheminova)*
Rattler (4WS) *(Helena)*
Roundup Custom (5.4WS) *(Monsanto)*
Roundup Original, Original RT, Ultra (4WS) *(Monsanto)*
Rate: 0.5-5 lb. ai/A
    0.75-7.5 pt. 5.4WS/A
    1-10 pt. 4WS/A
Time: For coffee or bananas, do not apply until 3 months after transplanting to allow new plants to become established.
Weeds: General weed control or site preparation prior to transplanting.
Remarks: Avocados, bananas, coconut, coffee, dates, figs, guava, kiwifruit, loquat, mangos, olives, papaya, passion fruit, persimmon, pineapple, plantain, pomegranate, tea. For olives, apply as post-directed spray only. Do not feed or graze treated pineapple forage after application.
Days To Harvest: Varies by product; refer to individual labels.
Tank Mixes: Devrinol, diuron, Goal, Krovar I, Prowl, simazine, Solicam, Surflan. Do not apply these tank mixes in Puerto Rico.

– – – – – – – – – – – – – – –

Rate: 4-12 fl. oz. 5.4WS/A
    6-16 fl. oz. 4WS
Time: For cool-season grasses, apply in the spring 3-4 days after mowing.
Weeds: Perennial grasses:

bahiagrass	Kentucky bluegrass	quackgrass
bermudagrass	orchardgrass	tall fescue
fine fescue		

Remarks: Suppression on orchard floors. Rate varies by grass species and geographic area. For Kentucky bluegrass, do not add ammonium sulfate. Refer to label for use directions, restrictions, and precautions.

– – – – – – – – – – – – – – –

Signal Word/Toxicity Class: Varies by formulation.
REI: Warning—12 hr.; Caution—4 hr.

GOAL

Goal 2XL (oxyfluorfen) *(Rohm and Haas)*
Rate: Preemergence:
    1.25-2 lb. ai/A
    5-8 pt. 2XL/A
    Postemergence:
    0.5-2 lb. ai/A
    2-8 pt. 2XL/A
Time: Preemergence, postemergence. Dormant application in Arizona and California, apply after final harvest or before Feb. 15 (in Coachella Valley, California, do not apply after Feb. 1). Applications made after calendar dates above, but prior to bud swell may result in significant crop injury.
Weeds: Broadleaf weeds—AZ, CA:

annual sowthistle	common groundsel	prickly lettuce
broadleaf filaree	common	prostrate knotweed
burclover	lambsquarters	redmaids
burning nettle	common purslane	rockpurslane
cheeseweed	henbit	redroot pigweed
(malva)	London rocket	redstem filaree
coast fiddleneck	minerslettuce	shepherdspurse

Broadleaf weeds—All States:

American black	common purslane	prickly sida
nightshade	cutleaf	(teaweed)
annual morningglory	eveningprimrose	prostrate spurge
annual sowthistle	cutleaf	redroot pigweed
balsamapple	groundcherry	shepherdspurse
black nightshade	hemp sesbania	spotted spurge
camphorweed	jimsonweed	velvetleaf
common cocklebur	narrowleaf cudweed	Virginia pepperweed
common	Pennsylvania	wild poinsettia
lambsquarters	smartweed	Wright groundcherry

Remarks: Avocados, dates, figs, kiwifruit, loquat, olives, persimmons, pomegranates. Direct spray toward base of tree or vine, avoiding direct plant contact. Do not apply to kiwi less than 3 years old unless vines are on a trellis wire at least 3 ft. above soil surface. Refer to label for restrictions and precautions.
Tank Mixes: Diuron, glyphosate, napropamide, norflurazon, oryzalin, paraquat, pronamide, simazine.

– – – – – – – – – – – – – – –

Rate: Cacao, coffee:
    0.5-2 lb. ai/A
    2-8 pt. 2XL/A
    Guava—preemergence:
    1.25-2 lb. ai/A
    5-8 pt. 2XL/A

7

Fruits & Nuts

Tree Fruits (Subtropical)

Time: Preemergence, postemergence. Cacao: apply to established, pre-transplanted, or recently transplanted plants. Coffee: apply postemergence to dormant transplants; do not apply after buds start to swell or preplant or preemergence to direct-seeded coffee. Guava: apply to healthy trees after new foliage has hardened off.

Weeds: Broadleaf weeds:

Ageratum	common purslane	garden spurge
buttonweed	crotalaria	

Remarks: Cacao, coffee, guava. Do not apply to direct-seeded cacao. Care must be taken to prevent direct spray from contacting plants. Refer to label for restrictions and precautions.

Days To Harvest: 1.

Tank Mixes: Diuron, glyphosate, napropamide, norflurazon, oryzalin, paraquat, pronamide, simazine.

State Restrictions: For use in Hawaii only on coffee, and guava.

- - - - - - - - - - - - - - -

Rate: **Papaya:**
1 lb. ai/A
4 pt. 2XL/A
Taro:
Broadcast:
0.5 lb. ai/A
2 pt. 2XL/A
Post-directed:
0.25 lb. ai/A
1 pt. 2XL/A

Time: Preemergence, postemergence. Papaya: apply after plant has reached minimum height of 4 ft. Taro: apply within 1 week of transplanting and prior to emergence.

Weeds: Broadleaf weeds:

common purslane	garden spurge	spiny amaranth

Remarks: Papaya, taro (dryland only). Care must be taken to prevent direct spray from contacting taro plants, or green bark, stems, fruit, or foliage of papaya. Refer to label for restrictions and precautions.

Days To Harvest: Papaya-1 day; taro-6 months (after taro corms, leaves).

Tank Mixes: Diuron, glyphosate, napropamide, norflurazon, oryzalin, paraquat, pronamide, simazine.

State Restrictions: For use in Hawaii only.

- - - - - - - - - - - - - - -

Signal Word/Toxicity Class: Warning/II.
REI: 24 hr.

Gramoxone Extra — see paraquat

HEXAZINONE

Velpar (SP) or L (DuPont)
Rate: 0.22-1.8 lb. ai/A
0.25-2 lb. SP/A
0.9-7 pt. L/A
Spot treatment:
0.9-1.8 lb. ai/100 gal. water
1-2 lb. SP/100 gal. water
3.5-7 pt. L/100 gal. water

Time: Intercrop period, postmulch, preplant, postplant, directed postemergence interspace application.

Weeds: Broadleaf weeds:

ageratum	kao haole*	oxalis
balsamapple	mauna loa*	popolo
castor bean	morningglory	richardsonium
crotalaria		

Grasses:

crabgrass	guineagrass	vaseygrass
dallisgrass	junglerice	

* Suppression

Remarks: Pineapple. Add surfactant. Use lower rates on coarse-textured soils or in areas where rainfall exceeds 65" per year; higher rates on fine-textured soils or areas where rainfall is less than 65" per year. Do not exceed 3.6 lb. ai/year.

Days To Harvest: 181.

- - - - - - - - - - - - - - -

Signal Word/Toxicity Class: Danger/I.
REI: 24 hr.

HYVAR

Hyvar X (WP) (bromacil) (DuPont)
Rate: 1.6-4.8 lb. ai/A
2-6 lb. WP/A
Ratoon crop:
0.8-3.2 lb. ai/A
1-4 lb. WP/A

Time: Apply before planting material begins to grow. For ratoon crop, apply after harvesting plant but before differentiation.

Weeds: Seedling weeds and grasses:

Amaranthus spp.	crabgrass	goosegrass
balsamapple	flora's paintbrush	(wiregrass)
chloris	foxtail	Hialoa

Remarks: Pineapple. Do not apply through any type of irrigation system.

Crop Rotation: Do not replant to any crop other than pineapple within 2 years after last application as injury to subsequent crops may result.

State Restrictions: For use in Florida, Hawaii.

- - - - - - - - - - - - - - -

Rate: 1.6-3.2 lb. ai/A
2-4 lb. WP/A

Time: Apply after planting and before planting material begins to grow.

Weeds: Seedling weeds and grasses such as:

crabgrass	pigweed	purslane
junglerice		

Remarks: Pineapple. Do not apply through any type of irrigation system.

Crop Rotation: Do not replant to any crop other than pineapple within 2 years after last application as injury to subsequent crops may result.

State Restrictions: For use in Puerto Rico.

- - - - - - - - - - - - - - -

Signal Word/Toxicity Class: Caution.
REI: 12 hr.

Karmex — see diuron

NORFLURAZON

Solicam DF (Novartis)
Rate: 2-4 lb. ai/A
2.5-5 lb. DF/A

Time: Apply to soil surface from fall to early spring before weeds emerge, except on crops where otherwise specified.

Weeds: Broadleaf weeds:

annual bursage	green amaranth*	redmaids
black mustard*	groundsel*	rockpurslane
chickweed	horseweed*	redroot pigweed*
common	(marestail)	redstem filaree
lambsquarters*	little mallow	Russian thistle
common purslane	(cheeseweed)	shepherdspurse
falsedandelion	London rocket	silverleaf nightshade*
(smooth catsear)	pineappleweed	(white horsenettle)
fiddleneck	puncturevine	Virginia pepperweed*
flixweed*		whitestem filaree

Grasses and sedges:

annual bluegrass	foxtail	sixweeks grama
barnyardgrass	Italian ryegrass	southwestern
bermudagrass*	purple nutsedge	cupgrass
crabgrass	quackgrass*	wild barley
downy brome	sandbur	witchgrass
feather fingergrass		

* Suppression

Remarks: Avocados. Do not use on nursery stock. Rate varies by soil type.

Tank Mixes: Goal, Gramoxone, Roundup, simazine, Surflan; refer to label for use instructions.

State Restrictions: Do not use on western slope of Colorado. See label for use restrictions in Coachella Valley of California.

- - - - - - - - - - - - - - -

Signal Word/Toxicity Class: Caution.
REI: 12 hr.

PARAQUAT

Restricted Use Pesticide.

Gramoxone Extra (2.5L) (ZENECA)
Rate: **Avocados, bananas, coffee, figs, kiwifruit, olives, papaya:**
0.6-1 lb. ai/A
2-3 pt. 2.5L/A
Guava, passion fruit:
1 lb. ai/A
3 pt. 2.5L/A
Pineapple:
0.47-1 lb. ai/A
1.5-3 pt. 2.5L/A
Cacao:
0.5-1 lb. ai/A
1.6-3 pt. 2.5L/A

Time: Apply as directed spray when weeds and grasses are succulent and new growth is from 1-6" tall.

Weeds: Annual broadleaf weeds and grasses; top kill and suppression of perennials.

◆-new product • PP-preplant • PPI-preplant incorporated • PRE-preemergence • POST-postemergence • SEQ-sequential • ae-acid equivalent • ai-active ingredient • DF-dry flowable
E/EC-emulsifiable concentrate • F/FL-flowable • DG/G/WG-dispersable granule • L/LC-liquid • SP/WSP-soluble packet • W/WP-wettable powder • WSB-water soluble bag

Remarks: Add nonionic surfactant or crop oil concentrate. Do not allow spray to contact green stems, fruit, or foliage. Use a shield or wrap when spraying around young trees. For mature woody weeds, green suckers, late germinating weeds, grasses, and perennials, retreatment or spot treatment may be necessary. Do not graze treated areas. Refer to label for use directions, restrictions, and precautions.

Days To Harvest: Cacao—1; figs, olives—13; kiwifruit—14; pineapple—20.

Tank Mixes: Devrinol, Goal, Karmex, Krovar, Princep, Sinbar, Solicam, Surflan.

State Restrictions: Not for use on Cacao in California.

- - - - - - - - - - - - - - -

Signal Word/Toxicity Class: Danger-Poison/I.
REI: 12 hr. (except harvest aid/desiccation 24 hr.).

Poast — see sethoxydim

Princep — see simazine

Prism — see clethodim

Rattler — see glyphosate

Roundup — see glyphosate

SCYTHE

Nonselective, postemergent herbicide. May be used to control suckers. May also be used with other herbicides having systemic or residual activity.

◆ **Scythe (pelargonic acid)** *(Mycogen)*
Rate: 4-13 fl. oz./1 gal. spray solution
Time: Apply to actively growing weeds prior to crop emergence.
Weeds: Annual and perennial broadleaf weeds and grasses.
Remarks: Avocados, bananas, coconut, dates, figs, guava, kiwifruit, mangos, olives, persimmons, papayas, pineapple. Apply in minimum 75 gal. spray solution/A or spray-to-wet. Do not apply by air or through any type of irrigation system. Refer to label for directions, restrictions, and precautions.
Tank Mixes: Glyphosate and other foliar and residual herbicides.

- - - - - - - - - - - - - - -

Signal Word/Toxicity Class: Warning/II.
REI: 24 hr.

Select — see clethodim

SETHOXYDIM

Poast (1.5EC) *(BASF)*
Rate: 0.28-0.47 lb. ai/A
1.5-2.5 pt. 1.5EC/A
Time: Postemergence. Apply to actively growing grasses.
Weeds: Annual grasses up to 12" height and perennial grasses:

barnyardgrass	large crabgrass	stinkgrass
bermudagrass	lovegrass	tall fescue
broadleaf signalgrass	orchardgrass	Texas panicum
browntop panicum	(seedling)	wild proso millet
fall panicum	perennial ryegrass	wildcane
giant foxtail	quackgrass	wiresten muhly
goosegrass	red sprangletop	witchgrass
green foxtail	shattercane	woolly cupgrass
johnsongrass	smooth crabgrass	yellow foxtail
junglerice	southwestern cupgrass	

Remarks: Nonbearing: avocados, dates, figs, olives, pomegranates. Add 2 pt./A oil concentrate. Refer to label for directions, restrictions, and limitations.
Days To Harvest: 1 year.
State Restrictions: Do not use UAN or AMS in California or Pacific Northwest.

- - - - - - - - - - - - - - -

Signal Word/Toxicity Class: Warning/II.
REI: 12 hr.

SIMAZINE

◆ **Clean Crop Simazine 4L or 90WDG** *(Platte)*
Drexel Simazine 4L or 90DF *(Drexel)*
Princep 4L or Caliber 90 *(Novartis)*
Riverside Simazine 4L or 90DF *(Terra)*
Rate: 2-4 lb. ai/A
2-4 qt. 4L/A
2.2-4.4 lb. 90, 90DF, 90WDG/A
Time: Avocados: Apply after final preparation of grove. Olives: Apply following grove preparation in the fall; repeat annually in midwinter.
Weeds: Annual broadleaf weeds:

annual morningglory	Florida pusley	redmaids
burclover	German moss	rockpurslane
carelessweed	groundsel	Russian thistle
carpetweed	henbit	shepherdspurse
common chickweed	knawel	smartweed
common lambsquarters	nightshade	spanishneedles
common purslane	pepperweed	speedwell
fiddleneck	pigweed	tansymustard
filaree	pineappleweed	wild mustard
fireweed	prickly lettuce	yellowflower
flora's paintbrush	ragweed	pepperweed

Grasses:

annual bluegrass	fall panicum	signalgrass
annual ryegrass	foxtail	silver hairgrass
barnyardgrass	goosegrass	watergrass
cheatgrass	junglerice	wild oat
crabgrass	quackgrass	witchgrass
downy brome	rattail fescue	

Remarks: Avocados, olives. Make only 1 application per year. Refer to label for use directions, restrictions, and precautions.
Tank Mixes: Avocados, olives—Gramoxone Extra, avocados—Surflan.
State Restrictions: For use in California, Florida on avocados.

- - - - - - - - - - - - - - -

Signal Word/Toxicity Class: Caution/III.
REI: 12 hr.

SNAPSHOT (Premix)

Snapshot 2.5TG (2% trifluralin & 0.5% isoxaben) *(Dow AgroSciences)*
Rate: 2.5-5 lb. ai/A
100-200 lb. 2.5TG/A
Time: Apply in late summer to early fall or in early spring or immediately after cultivation.
Weeds: Broadleaf weeds:

annual bursage	eveningprimrose	prostrate knotweed
annual sowthistle	fall panicum	purple cudweed
black medic	hairy fleabane	purslane speedwell
black nightshade	hairy galinsoga	rattail fescue
bristly oxtongue	hare barley	redstem filaree
broadleaf plantain	heath aster	Russian thistle
burning nettle	henbit	scarlet pimpernel
California burclover	horseweed	shepherdspurse
Carolina geranium	Indian mustard	sibara
clover	jimsonweed	silversheath knotweed
coast fiddleneck	kochia	slender aster
common chickweed	lanceleaf groundcherry	slender plantain
common groundsel	little mallow	spiny sowthistle
common	London rocket	spotted spurge
lambsquarters	marestail	sunflower
common purslane	Mexican sprangletop	swinecress
common ragweed	nettleaf goosefoot	tall morningglory
creeping woodsorrel	panicle willowweed	telegraphplant
curly dock	Pennsylvania	turkey mullein
dandelion	smartweed	velvetleaf
datura	petty spurge	Virginia pepperweed
desert rockpurslane	pigweed	yellow sweetclover
dwarf fleabane	pineappleweed	yellow woodsorrel
dwarf mallow	prickly lettuce	

Annual grasses:

annual bluegrass	junglerice	wild mustard
barnyardgrass	lovegrass	wild oat
bromegrass	southwestern	wild radish
crabgrass	cupgrass	witchgrass
giant foxtail	wild carrot	yellow foxtail
Italian ryegrass	wild celery	

Remarks: Nonbearing olives, pomegranates. Apply to trees that will not bear fruit for at least 1 year. Do not apply to bedding plants, nursery seedbeds, or transplant beds.
State Restrictions: Refer to label for use restrictions in Arizona.

- - - - - - - - - - - - - - -

Signal Word/Toxicity Class: Caution/III.
REI: 12 hr.

Fruits & Nuts

7

NOTICE The information on these pages is for preliminary planning — not a guide for use. Be sure to follow the manufacturer's directions, notwithstanding information contained here.

For personal protective equipment and EPA registration numbers, please turn to page 70.

Solicam — see norflurazon

SURFLAN

Surflan A.S. (oryzalin) *(Dow AgroSciences)*
Rate: 2-6 lb. ai/A
2-6 qt. A.S./A
Time: Apply before weeds emerge.
Weeds: Broadleaf weeds:

annual morningglory*	cudweed	puncturevine
annual smartweed*	field sandbur	red sprangletop
annual sowthistle*	Florida purslane	redmaids
black mustard*	Florida pusley	rockpurslane
black nightshade*	giant ragweed*	redroot pigweed
carelessweed	henbit	redstem filaree*
carpetweed	ladysthumb*	rough pigweed
chickweed	lambsquarters	shepherdspurse
climbing milkweed*	London rocket*	smooth pigweed
coast fiddleneck	Mexican clover	spiny pigweed
common groundsel*	prickly lettuce*	teaweed*
common mallow*	prickly sida*	tumble pigweed
common purslane	prostrate knotweed	velvetleaf*
common ragweed*	prostrate pigweed	whitestem filaree*
	prostrate spurge*	wild mustard*

Grasses:

annual bluegrass	green foxtail	pigeongrass
annual ryegrass	guineagrass	robust foxtail
barnyardgrass	Italian ryegrass	signalgrass
bottlegrass	johnsongrass	smooth crabgrass
bristlegrass	(seedling)	spreading panicgrass
browntop panicum	junglerice	southwestern cupgrass
crowfootgrass	large crabgrass	Texas panicum
downy brome	little barley	watergrass
fall panicum	lovegrass	wild oat
foxtail	Mexican lovegrass	witchgrass
giant foxtail	Orcutt lovegrass	yellow foxtail

Suppression

Remarks: Bearing, nonbearing: avocados, figs, kiwifruit, olives, pomegranates. Rate depends on length of control desired. Surface apply once existing weeds are controlled by tillage or contact herbicide. May be applied through solid set sprinkler irrigation system; single 1/2-1" rain or sprinkler irrigation within 21 days is required. Not for use on soils with at least 5% organic matter.
Tank Mixes: Gramoxone Extra, Princep.

Signal Word/Toxicity Class: Caution/III.
REI: 12 hr.

TOUCHDOWN

Touchdown (5L or 6L) (sulfosate) *(ZENECA)*
Rate: 0.5-4 lb. ai/A
0.8-6.4 pt. 5L/A
0.66-5.33 pt. 6L/A
Time: Apply to actively growing grasses and weeds.
Weeds: Broadleaf weeds:

annual sowthistle	fiddleneck	marestail
black nightshade	field bindweed	morningglory
camphorweed	field sandbur	mouseear chickweed
Canada thistle	filaree	mustard
Carolina geranium	fleabane	Pennsylvania
common chickweed	Florida pusley	smartweed
common cocklebur	giant ragweed	prickly lettuce
common groundsel	groundcherry	redroot pigweed
common lambsquarters	hairy fleabane	Russian thistle
	hemp dogbane	shepherdspurse
common ragweed	henbit	sicklepod
curly dock	hophornbeam	smooth pigweed
cutleaf eveningprimrose	copperleaf	spanishneedles
	kochia	velvetleaf
dandelion	little barley	white clover
dogfennel	London rocket	

Grasses and sedges:

annual bluegrass	foxtail	sprangletop
bahiagrass	goosegrass	stinkgrass
barnyardgrass	guineagrass	tall fescue
bermudagrass	Italian ryegrass	Texas panicum
broadleaf signalgrass	johnsongrass	timothy
cheat	(seedling)	vaseygrass
cogongrass (suppression)	orchardgrass	wild oat
	perennial ryegrass	wirestem muhly
crabgrass	quackgrass	witchgrass
crowfootgrass	red rice	woolly cupgrass
downy brome	shattercane	yellow nutsedge
fall panicum		

Remarks: Nonbearing avocados, bananas, coffee, dates, figs, guava, kiwifruit, loquat, mangos, olives, papayas, passion fruit, persimmons, pineapple, plantains, pomegranates, tea. Nonionic surfactant or wetting agent required. In addition, ammonium sulfate can be added. Do not allow spray, spray drift, or mist to contact green foliage or green bark on trunk, suckers, open wounds, or other green parts of trees and vines. Avoid contact with stumps as tree injury may occur from root grafting. Do not apply through any type of irrigation system. Refer to label for directions and precautions.
Days To Harvest: 1 year.
Tank Mixes: 2,4-D, Devrinol, diuron, Goal, Kerb, Krovar, Prowl, simazine, Sinbar, Solicam, Surflan.
State Restrictions: Ammonium sulfate (6L) not for use in California.

Rate: 5-12 fl. oz. 5L/A
4-10 fl. oz. 6L/A
Time: Apply after green-up or after 3-4" of regrowth following mowing.
Weeds: Perennial grasses:

bahiagrass	Kentucky bluegrass	quackgrass
bermudagrass	orchardgrass	tall fescue
fine fescue		

Remarks: Suppression on orchard floors. Rate varies by grass species and geographic area. Nonionic surfactant or wetting agent required. In addition, ammonium sulfate can be added (except Kentucky bluegrass). Refer to label for directions and precautions.

Signal Word/Toxicity Class: Caution.
REI: 12 hr. (5L); 4 hr. (6L).

Velpar — see hexazinone

XL 2G (Premix)

Selective preemergence herbicide for control of certain annual grasses and broadleaf weeds. Does not control established weeds. Requires rainfall or sprinkler irrigation within 21 days to activate.

XL 2G (1% benefin & 1% oryzalin) *(Helena)*
Rate: 4-6 lb. ai/A
200-300 lb./A
0.09-0.14 lb. ai/sq. ft.
4.6-6.9 lb./1000 sq. ft.
Time: Apply prior to germination of target weeds.
Weeds: Broadleaf weeds:

annual sowthistle*	desert rockpurslane	prostrate spurge
bittercress	Florida pusley	puncturevine
black mustard*	henbit	redstem filaree
black nightshade*	horseweed*	shepherdspurse
carpetweed	ladysthumb*	smartweed*
chickweed	lambsquarters	spotted spurge*
climbing milkweed*	London rocket	teaweed*
coast fiddleneck	morningglory*	velvetleaf*
common groundsel	pigweed	whitestem filaree
common mallow*	prickly lettuce*	wild mustard*
common purslane	prickly sida*	yellow woodsorrel
common ragweed*	prostrate knotweed	

Grasses:

annual bluegrass	foxtail	Orcutt lovegrass
barnyardgrass	goosegrass	red sprangletop
browntop panicum	Italian ryegrass	signalgrass
crabgrass	johnsongrass	Texas panicum
crowfootgrass	(seedling)	volunteer wheat*
cupgrass	junglerice	wild oat
fall panicum	little barley	witchgrass
field sandbur	Mexican lovegrass	

Suppression

Remarks: Nonbearing avocado, fig, kiwi, olive, pomegranate. Do not apply to trees that may be harvested for food within 1 year after application. Refer to label for use directions and precautions.

Signal Word/Toxicity Class: Caution/III.
REI: 12 hr. unless soil-injected or soil-incorporated.

Nuts

120 Herbicide — see MSMA

912 Herbicide — see MSMA

◆-new product • PP-preplant • PPI-preplant incorporated • PRE-preemergence • POST-postemergence • SEQ-sequential • ae-acid equivalent • ai-active ingredient • DF-dry flowable
E/EC-emulsifiable concentrate • F/FL-flowable • DG/G/WG-dispersable granule • L/LC-liquid • SP/WSP-soluble packet • W/WP-wettable powder • WSB-water soluble bag

AAtrex — see atrazine

Atra-5 — see atrazine

ATRAZINE
Restricted Use Pesticide.

AAtrex 4L or AAtrex Nine-0 (WDG) (Novartis)
◆ **Clean Crop Atrazine 4L or 90 WDG** (Platte)
Drexel Atrazine 4L, Atra-5 (5L) or 90DF (Drexel)
Helena Atrazine 4L (Helena)
Riverside Atrazine 4L or 90DF (Terra)

Rate: 2-4 lb. ai/A
4-8 pt. 4L/A
3.2-6.4 5L/A
2.2-4.4 lb. WDG, 90DF/A

Time: Before harvest and prior to weed emergence; repeat as necessary.
Weeds: Many broadleaf weeds such as:

crabgrass	flora's paintbrush	spanishneedles
fireweed		

Grasses:

foxtail	wiregrass

Remarks: Macadamias. Do not apply by air or spray when nuts are on the ground during harvest period.
State Restrictions: Wilbur-Ellis not registered in California.

- - - - - - - - - - - - - -

Signal Word/Toxicity Class: Caution/III.
REI: 12 hr.

BASAMID

Basamid Granular (dazomet) (BASF)

Rate: 255-535 lb./A
Time: Apply prior to planting or interplanting and incorporate 8".
Weeds: Weed seeds.
Remarks: Nonbearing: filberts, walnuts. Soil must be well prepared with adequate moisture. Plant 10-30 days after treatment.
Days To Harvest: 1 year.
Crop Rotation: No limitations after 1 year.
State Restrictions: SLN-Oregon, SLN-Washington.

- - - - - - - - - - - - - -

Signal Word/Toxicity Class: Warning/II.
REI: 24 hr.

Bueno 6 — see MSMA

Casoran — see dichlobenil

CLETHODIM
Postemergence grass herbicide. Mode of action similar to Poast, Assure, Option II, and Fusilade.

Envoy or Prism (0.94EC), Select (2EC) (Valent)

Rate: 0.1-0.25 lb. ai/A
13-34 fl. oz. 0.94EC/A
6-16 fl. oz. 2EC/A

Time: Postemergence. Apply to actively growing grasses.
Weeds: Grasses:

Amazon sprangletop	green foxtail	smooth crabgrass
annual bluegrass	itchgrass	southern crabgrass
barnyardgrass	johnsongrass	Texas panicum
bearded sprangletop	junglerice	volunteer cereals
bermudagrass	large crabgrass	wild oat
broadleaf signalgrass	quackgrass	wild proso millet
crowfootgrass	red rice	wirestem muhly
fall panicum	red sprangletop	witchgrass
giant foxtail	shattercane	woolly cupgrass
goosegrass	southwestern cupgrass	yellow foxtail

Remarks: Nonbearing nut crops. Nonbearing are plants that will not bear fruit for at least 1 year after application. Rate varies by grass species, stage, and geographical region. Grass crops such as corn, sorghum, wheat, and rice are highly sensitive to clethodim. Do not apply under stress conditions or if rainfall is expected in 1 hour. Do not apply through any type of irrigation system. Do not apply more than 0.5 lb. ai/A (0.25 lb. ai/A on Long Island, NY) per season. Do not graze treated fields or feed treated forage or hay to livestock. Refer to label for restrictions and precautions.
State Restrictions: Not for use on Solano grass in the Vernal Lakes area of Solano County, California; wild rice in Hays County, Texas.

- - - - - - - - - - - - - -

Signal Word/Toxicity Class: Warning/II.
REI: 24 hr.

Credit — see glyphosate

2,4-D - PHENOXY HERBICIDES
Albaugh Amine 4 (2,4-D amine) (Albaugh)
◆ **Clean Crop Amine 4 (2,4-D amine)** (Platte)
Formula 40 (2,4-D mixed amine) (Rhone-Poulenc)
◆ **Opti-Amine (4) (2,4-D amine)** (Helena)
Riverdale 6 Amine (2,4-D amine) (Riverdale)
Weed Rhap A-4D (2,4-D amine) (Helena)
Weedar 64 (4) (2,4-D amine) (Nufarm)
Weedestroy AM-40 (2,4-D amine) (Riverdale)
Wilbur-Ellis Amine 4 (2,4-D amine) (Wilbur-Ellis)

Rate: 1.5 lb. ae/A
3 pt. 4/A
2 pt. 6/A

Time: Apply when weeds are small and actively growing.
Weeds: Annual broadleaf weeds on orchard floor.
Remarks: Trees must be at least 1 year old. Apply using coarse sprays and low pressure in sufficient volume of water to obtain thorough wetting of weeds. Do not use on light, sandy soil. Do not apply more than twice a year. Do not graze or feed cover crops from treated orchards.
Days To Harvest: 60.
State Restrictions: Not for use in California.

- - - - - - - - - - - - - -

Signal Word/Toxicity Class: Danger/I.
REI: 48 hr.

Dri-Clean (2,4-D amine) (Riverdale)

Rate: 18-28 oz./A (5 packets/1.66 A)
Time: Apply to point of runoff when weeds are young and actively growing (pre-bud to early bud stage).
Weeds: Annual broadleaf weeds on orchard floor.
Remarks: Pistachios, nut orchards. Nonbearing trees (1 year or older), and bearing trees (before and after bloom). Apply up to 2 applications through dormant or growing season as needed. Do not apply when temperature exceeds 90°F. Do not graze or feed cover crops from treated orchards.
Days To Harvest: 60.

- - - - - - - - - - - - - -

Signal Word/Toxicity Class: Danger/I.
REI: 48 hr.

Hi-Dep (2,4-D mixed amine) (PBI/Gordon)

Rate: 1 lb. ai/A
2 pt. 4/A

Time: Sucker control. Spray when suckers are 6-9" tall.
Weeds: Annual broadleaf weeds on orchard floor.
Remarks: Filberts. Apply in 100 gal. water plus surfactant. Do not apply more than 4 times per season. Do not graze or feed cover crops from treated orchards.

- - - - - - - - - - - - - -

Rate: 1.5 lb. ai/A
3 pt. 4/A

Time: Apply when weeds are young and actively growing.
Weeds: Annual broadleaf weeds on orchard floor.
Remarks: Pistachios. Apply as a directed spray to point of runoff. Do not use on light, sandy soil. Do not apply more than twice a year. Do not graze or feed cover crops from treated orchards.
Days To Harvest: Filberts—45; pistachios—60.

- - - - - - - - - - - - - -

Signal Word/Toxicity Class: Danger/I.
REI: 48 hr.

7

Fruits & Nuts

NOTICE	The information on these pages is for preliminary planning — not a guide for use. Be sure to follow the manufacturer's directions, notwithstanding information contained here.	For personal protective equipment and EPA registration numbers, please turn to page 70.

◆ **Orchard Master (2,4-D mixed amine)** *(PBI/Gordon)*
Rate: 1-1.5 lb. ai/A
    2-3 pt. 4/A
Time: Applications in early spring and late fall after harvest are preferred. Sequential applications may be needed to control biennial and perennial broadleaf weeds.
Weeds: Annual, biennial, perennial broadleaf weeds on orchard floor.
Remarks: Almonds, filberts, hazelnuts, pecans, pistachios, walnuts (black, English). Trees must be at least 1 year old. Avoid contact with fruit, foliage, stems, lower limbs, tree trunks, and exposed roots. Do not use on shallow or sandy soil, or to dry soil without vegetation. Do not apply more than twice a year. Do not graze or feed cover crops from treated orchards. Do not apply during windy periods or extremely high temperatures. Do not apply through any type of irrigation system. Refer to label for directions, restrictions, and precautions.
Days To Harvest: 60.
Tank Mixes: Glyphosate.

– – – – – – – – – – – – – – –

Rate: 1 lb. ai/A
    2 pt. 4/A in 100 gal. water
Time: Sucker control. Spray when suckers are 6-9" tall.
Weeds: Annual, biennial, perennial broadleaf weeds on orchard floor.
Remarks: Filberts. Add suractant. Do not apply more than 4 times per season. Do not graze or feed cover crops from treated orchards. Do not apply during windy periods or extremely high temperatures. Do not apply through any type of irrigation system. Refer to label for directions, restrictions, and precautions.
Days To Harvest: 45.
Tank Mixes: Glyphosate.
State Restrictions: Orchard Master not registered in California. Orchard Master CA registered in California; refer to label.

– – – – – – – – – – – – – – –

Signal Word/Toxicity Class: Danger/I.
REI: 48 hr.

◆ **Saber (2,4-D amine)** *(Platte)*
Rate: 0.75-1 lb. ae/A
    1.5-2 pt./A in 100 gal. water
Time: Sucker control. Spray to runoff when suckers are 6-9" tall.
Weeds: Annual broadleaf weeds on orchard floor.
Remarks: Filberts. Add surfactant. Do not apply more than 4 times per season. Do not graze or feed cover crops from treated orchards.

– – – – – – – – – – – – – – –

Rate: 1-1.5 lb. ae/A
    2-3 pt./A
Time: Apply when weeds are young and actively growing.
Weeds: Annual broadleaf weeds on orchard floor.
Remarks: Pistachios, nut orchards. Apply as a directed spray to point of runoff. Do not use on light, sandy soil. Do not apply more than twice a year. Do not graze or feed cover crops from treated orchards.
Days To Harvest: Filberts—45; pistachios—60.

– – – – – – – – – – – – – – –

Signal Word/Toxicity Class: Danger/I.
REI: 48 hr.

Savage (WSB) (2,4-D amine) *(Platte)*
Rate: 1.4 lb. ae/A
    1.5 lb. WSB/A
Time: Apply when weeds are young and actively growing.
Weeds: Annual broadleaf weeds on orchard floor.
Remarks: Pistachios, nut orchards. Apply using coarse spray and low pressure in sufficient water for thorough wetting of weeds. Do not graze or feed cover crops from treated orchards. Consult label for restrictions and precautions.
Days To Harvest: 60.

– – – – – – – – – – – – – – –

Signal Word/Toxicity Class: Danger/I.
REI: 48 hr.

DEVRINOL

Devrinol 10-G or 50-DF (napropamide) *(United Phosphorus)*
Rate: 4 lb. ai/A
    40 lb. 10-G/A
    8 lb. 50-DF/A
Time: Apply in fall through early spring.
Weeds: Annual broadleaf weeds:

annual sowthistle	common ragweed	pineappleweed
carpetweed	(suppression)	prickly lettuce
coast fiddleneck	horse purslane	prostrate knotweed
common chickweed	lambsquarters	purple cudweed
common groundsel	little mallow	redroot pigweed
common purslane	(from seed)	redstem filaree

Annual grasses:

annual bluegrass	green foxtail	sandbur
barnyardgrass	guineagrass	smooth crabgrass
bristly foxtail	hairy crabgrass	soft chess
canarygrass	Italian ryegrass	southwestern cupgrass
cheatgrass	johnsongrass	stinkgrass
downy brome	(seedling)	Texas panicum
fall panicum	junglerice	wild barley
foxtail barley	large crabgrass	wild oat
giant foxtail	Mexican sprangletop	witchgrass
goosegrass	red sprangletop	yellow foxtail
	ripgut brome	

Remarks: Almonds (50-DF), filberts, pecans, pistachios (50-DF), walnuts. Newly planted and established crop. An additional 8 lb. 50-DF/A may be applied during growing season in the West (except pistachios). See label for allowable time for Devrinol to remain on soil surface prior to incorporation.
Days To Harvest: 35.
Tank Mixes: 50-DF: Glyphosate, Goal, Gramoxone Extra, Karmex, simazine. Refer to labels for restrictions and precautions.

– – – – – – – – – – – – – – –

Signal Word/Toxicity Class: Caution.
REI: 12 hr.

DICHLOBENIL

Casoron 4G *(Uniroyal)*
Rate: Annual weeds:
    4-6 lb. ai/A
    100-150 lb. 4G/A
    Perennial weeds:
    6 lb. ai/A
    150 lb. 4G/A
Time: Apply early spring. Do not apply until 4 weeks after transplanting.
Weeds: Broadleaf weeds:

artemisia	gisekia	redroot pigweed
camphorweed	goosefoot	rosarypea
Canada thistle	groundsel	Russian knapweed
carpetweed	henbit	Russian thistle
chickweed	horsetail	shepherdspurse
citronmelon	Jerusalem oak	smartweed
coffeeweed	knotweed	spanishneedles
cudweed	lambsquarters	spurge
curly dock	leafy spurge	teaweed
dandelion	maypop	wild artichoke
dogfennel	milkweed vine	wild aster
eveningprimrose	minerslettuce	wild carrot
false dandelion	pineappleweed	wild mustard
(catsear)	plantain	wild radish
fiddleneck	purslane	yellow rocket
Florida purslane	ragweed	yellow woodsorrel
(pusley)	red deadnettle	

Grasses:

annual bluegrass	natalgrass	timothy
crabgrass	old witchgrass	Texas panicum
fescue	orchardgrass	(hurrahgrass)
foxtail	quackgrass	wild barley

Remarks: Bearing, nonbearing: filberts. Shallow incorporation immediately after application is recommended in southern areas. Do not graze livestock on treated areas.
Crop Rotation: Do not plant rotational crops on which dichlobenil is not registered within 1 year after application.

– – – – – – – – – – – – – – –

Signal Word/Toxicity Class: Caution/III.
REI: 12 hr.

DIQUAT DIBROMIDE

◆ **Diquat** *(ZENECA)*
Rate: 0.375-0.5 lb. ai/A
    1.5-2 pt./A
Time: Site preparation prior to planting. Repeat as needed.
Weeds: Broadleaf weeds and grasses.
Remarks: Nonbearing almonds, filberts, macadamia, pecans, pistachios, walnuts. Apply by ground only. Use high rate when weeds are large or dense. Do not allow spray to contact green stems, foliage, or fruit. Use a shield or wrap plant when spraying around young trees or vines. Do not apply through any type of irrigation system. Do not graze treated areas. Refer to label for use restrictions and precautions.
Days To Harvest: 1 year. – – – – – – – – – –

Signal Word/Toxicity Class: Warning/II.
REI: 24 hr.

Direx — see diuron

◆-new product • PP-preplant • PPI-preplant incorporated • PRE-preemergence • POST-postemergence • SEQ-sequential • ae-acid equivalent • ai-active ingredient • DF-dry flowable
E/EC-emulsifiable concentrate • F/FL-flowable • DG/G/WG-dispersable granule • L/LC-liquid • SP/WSP-soluble packet • W/WP-wettable powder • WSB-water soluble bag

DIURON

Direx 4L or 80DF (Griffin)
◆ **Diuron 80 WDG** (Platte)
Drexel Diuron 4L or 80 (Drexel)
Karmex DF (Griffin)
Riverside Diuron 4L or 80DF (Terra)

Rate: 1.5-4.5 lb. ai/A
3-9 pt. 4L/A
2-6 lb. 80, DF, 80DF/A

Time: Apply immediately after harvest, preferably before weeds emerge; retreat as needed.

Weeds: Controls most annual and seedling perennial weeds.

Remarks: Macadamias. Trees established at least 1 year. Apply as directed spray avoiding contact of foliage with spray or drift. If weeds have emerged, add 1-2 pt. surfactant/25 gal. spray. Do not graze livestock.

State Restrictions: For use in Hawaii.

- - - - - - - - - - - - - - -

Rate: 1.5-3 lb. ai/A
3-6 pt. 4L/A
2-4 lb. 80, DF, 80DF/A

Time: Apply in spring or early summer before weeds emerge or during early seedling stage of growth.

Weeds: Barnyardgrass and the following broadleaf weeds:

annual morningglory	pigweed	ragweed
lambsquarters		

Remarks: Pecans.
Tank Mixes: Sinbar.

- - - - - - - - - - - - - - -

Rate: 2.5-3.75 lb. ai/A
3-5 lb. 80, DF, 80DF/A

Time: Apply as initial treatment after orchard has been laid up in final form in late fall or early winter.

Weeds: Broadleaf weeds:

annual morningglory	pigweed	ragweed
lambsquarters		

Grasses:

barnyardgrass	johnsongrass (seedling)

Remarks: English walnuts. Trees established at least 1 year. Apply as directed spray avoiding contact of foliage with spray or drift.

State Restrictions: For use in California.

- - - - - - - - - - - - - - -

Signal Word/Toxicity Class: Caution/III.
REI: 12 hr.

Dri-Clean — see 2,4-D

DSMA

◆ **Clean Crop DSMA Plus (3.6L) (+ surfactant)** (Platte)
Liquid DSMA (3.6L) (+ surfactant) (Helena)

Rate: 3.2-6.3 lb. ai/A
3.5-7 qt. 3.6L/A

Time: Postemergence (directed spray).
Weeds: Grassy weeds.

Remarks: Nonbearing nut orchards. Do not use around trees from which crop will be harvested within 1 year of treatment. Do not allow to contact leaves, stems, or bark of trees. If necessary, use shield for nursery plantings or young trees. For regrowth, up to 3 applications per year may be applied.

- - - - - - - - - - - - - - -

Signal Word/Toxicity Class: Caution/III.
REI: 12 hr.

Envoy — see clethodim

Eptam — see EPTC

EPTC

Eptam 7-E (ZENECA)

Rate: Almonds—Western Region:
2.18-3 lb. ai/A
2.5-3.5 pt. 7-E/A
Walnuts—Pacific Northwest, Western Region:
3 lb. ai/A
3.5 pt. 7-E/A

Time: Apply after cultivation in irrigation water.

Weeds: Broadleaf weeds:

black nightshade	corn spurry	nettleleaf goosefoot
carpetweed	cutleaf nightshade	prickly sida
common chickweed	deadnettle	prostrate pigweed
common	fiddleneck	redroot pigweed
lambsquarters	Florida pusley	sicklepod
common pigweed	hairy nightshade	tall morningglory
common purslane	henbit	tumble pigweed

Annual grasses:

annual bluegrass	goosegrass	signalgrass
annual ryegrass	green foxtail	stinkgrass
barnyardgrass	Italian ryegrass	Texas panicum
bermudagrass	johnsongrass	volunteer grains
(seedling)	(seedling)	(barley, oats, wheat)
crabgrass	junglerice	watergrass
fall panicum	lovegrass	wild oat
field sandbur	rescuegrass	witchgrass
giant foxtail	shattercane	yellow foxtail

Remarks: Almonds, walnuts. For almonds, do not apply more than 2 applications; walnuts, apply 1 application only.
Days To Harvest: Almonds—16.

- - - - - - - - - - - - - - -

Signal Word/Toxicity Class: Caution.
REI: 12 hr. unless soil injected or soil incorporated.

FLUAZIFOP-P-BUTYL

Fusilade DX (ZENECA)

Rate: Bearing: pecans:
0.1-0.375 lb. ai/A
0.375-1.5 pt. DX/A

Time: Apply by growth stage dependent on species.

Rate: Nonbearing: almonds, filberts, macadamias, pecans, pistachios, walnuts:
0.25-0.375 lb. ai/A
1-1.5 pt. DX/A

Time: Annual grasses: 2-8" tall before tillering and/or seedhead formation. Perennial grasses: Apply by growth stage dependent on species.

Weeds: Annual and perennial grasses:

barnyardgrass	johnsongrass	southern sandbur
bermudagrass	(rhizome, seedling)	southwestern
broadleaf	junglerice	cupgrass
signalgrass	kikuyugrass	Texas panicum
fall panicum	large crabgrass	tropical crabgrass
field sandbur	prairie cupgrass	volunteer cereals
giant foxtail	quackgrass	wild oat
goosegrass	red rice	wild proso millet
green foxtail	shattercane	wirestem muhly
guineagrass	smooth crabgrass	witchgrass
(seedling)	sorghum-almum	woolly cupgrass
Italian ryegrass	southern crabgrass	yellow foxtail
itchgrass		

Remarks: Rate varies by geographic area and grass species. Add crop oil concentrate or nonionic surfactant. Do not apply to tree fruits that may be harvested for food within 1 year after application. Refer to label for specific directions, restrictions, and precautions.

Days To Harvest: Bearing—30.

Crop Rotation: Do not plant rotational grass crops such as corn, sorghum, and cereals within 60 days after last application.

State Restrictions: Refer to label for geographical regions.

- - - - - - - - - - - - - - -

Signal Word/Toxicity Class: Caution.
REI: 12 hr.

Formula 40 — see 2,4-D

Fusilade — see fluazifop-P-butyl

GALLERY

Gallery 75DF (isoxaben) (Dow AgroSciences)

Rate: 0.5-1 lb. ai/A
0.66-1.33 lb. DF/A

Time: Preemergence. Apply late summer to early fall or early spring, prior to germination of target weeds.

7

Fruits & Nuts

NOTICE The information on these pages is for preliminary planning — not a guide for use. Be sure to follow the manufacturer's directions, notwithstanding information contained here. For personal protective equipment and EPA registration numbers, please turn to page 70.

Weeds: Broadleaf weeds:

annual sowthistle	dandelion	prostrate spurge
bittercress	dogfennel	redmaids
black mustard	green tansymustard	rockpurslane
black nightshade	hairy galinsoga	redstem filaree
blackleaved fleabane	henbit	shepherdspurse
bracted plantain	horseweed	sibara
buckhorn plantain	ladysthumb	slender plantain
Carolina geranium	lambsquarters	southern brassbuttons
coast fiddleneck	London rocket	spotted spurge
common chickweed	marestail	thymeleaf speedwell
common groundsel	mouseear chickweed	velvetleaf
common purslane	pennywort	white clover
common ragweed	pigweed	whitestem filaree
common sowthistle	pineappleweed	wild celery
creeping woodsorrel	prickly lettuce	wild mustard
cudweed	prostrate knotweed	yellow woodsorrel

Remarks: Nonbearing: almonds, filberts, macadamias, pecans, pistachios, walnuts. Do not apply through any type of irrigation system. Refer to label for directions and precautions.

– – – – – – – – – – – – – –

Signal Word/Toxicity Class: Caution/III.
REI: 12 hr.

GLUFOSINATE-AMMONIUM

Provides faster knockdown of most emerged weeds than glyphosate but slower than paraquat. A contact herbicide; not systemic but suppresses perennial broadleaf weeds. Excellent control of suckers or cane without injury to mature trees or vines.

Rely *(AgrEvo USA)*
Rate: 3-5 qt./A (broadcast)
Weeds: Broadleaf weeds:

chickweed	kochia	purslane
clover	London rocket	shepherdspurse
common cocklebur	malva	smartweed
filaree	marestail	
jimsonweed	(horseweed)	

Grasses:

barnyardgrass	goosegrass	shattercane
cupgrass	green foxtail	stinkgrass
fall panicum	johnsongrass	windgrass
giant foxtail	lovegrass	yellow foxtail

Rate: 4-6 qt./A (broadcast)
Weeds: Broadleaf weeds:

annual sowthistle	leafy spurge	vervain
bindweed	mugwort	vetch
buffalobur	musk thistle	Virginia
burdock	nettle	copperleaf
Canada thistle	nightshade	white clover
curly dock	pennycress	white heath aster
dandelion	redroot pigweed	wild buckwheat
dogbane	plantain	wild mustard
field gromwell	prickly lettuce	wild onion
fleabane	ragweed	wild rose
goldenrod	Russian thistle	wild turnip
horsetail	tansymustard	woodsorrel
lambsquarters	velvetleaf	yellow rocket

Grasses and sedges:

annual bluegrass	fescue	ryegrass
bahiagrass	guineagrass	sandbur
barley	johnsongrass	smooth bromegrass
bermudagrass	(rhizome)	torpedograss
carpetgrass	Kentucky bluegrass	vaseygrass
crabgrass	nutsedge	wheat
dallisgrass	paragrass	wild oat
downy bromegrass	quackgrass	

Time: Apply low rate when weeds are less than 6" tall; high rate when weeds are 6" or taller.

Rate: 4 qt./A
Weeds: Sucker control.
Time: Split application: Apply approximately 4 weeks apart. Suckers should not exceed 12" in length.
Remarks: Filberts, hickory, macadamias, pecans, walnuts. Do not use on trees within 1 year of transplanting, apply on desirable foliage, or allow spray to drift on foliage of trees and vines. Avoid contact with green or uncalloused bark on young trees and vines.
Tank Mixes: Devrinol, Karmex, Sinbar, simazine, Solicam, Surflan; refer to respective labels.

– – – – – – – – – – – – – –

Signal Word/Toxicity Class: Warning/II.
REI: 12 hr.

Glyfos or Glyfos X-tra — see glyphosate

GLYPHOSATE

◆ **Credit (4WS)** *(Nufarm)*
◆ **Glyfos or Glyfos X-tra (4WS)** *(Cheminova)*
Rattler (4WS) *(Helena)*
Roundup Custom (5.4WS) *(Monsanto)*
Roundup Original, Ultra (4WS) *(Monsanto)*
Rate: 0.5-5 lb. ai/A
   0.75-7.5 pt. 5.4WS/A
   1-10 pt. 4WS/A
Time: Apply when weeds are actively growing.
Weeds: Broadleaf weeds:

Canada thistle	field bindweed	smartweed

Grasses:

guineagrass	johnsongrass

Remarks: Almonds, beechnut, Brazil, butternut, cashew, chestnut, chinquapin, filberts, hickory, macadamias, pecans, pistachios, walnuts (black, English). General weed control, middles (between rows of trees), strips (in row of trees). Do not allow spray, drift, or mist to contact foliage or green bark of trunk, branches, suckers, fruit, or other parts of trees and vines.
Days To Harvest: 3; pistachios—21.
Tank Mixes: Devrinol, diuron, Goal, Krovar I, Prowl, simazine, Solicam, Surflan. Do not use in Puerto Rico.

– – – – – – – – – – – – – –

Rate: 4-12 fl. oz. 5.4WS/A
   6-16 fl. oz. 4WS
Time: For cool-season grasses, apply in the spring 3-4 days after mowing.
Weeds: Perennial grasses:

bahiagrass	Kentucky bluegrass	quackgrass
bermudagrass	orchardgrass	tall fescue
fine fescue		

Remarks: Suppression on orchard floors. Rate varies by grass species and geographic area. For Kentucky bluegrass, do not add ammonium sulfate. Refer to label for use directions, restrictions, and precautions.

– – – – – – – – – – – – – –

Signal Word/Toxicity Class: Varies by formulation.
REI: Warning—12 hr.; Caution—4 hr.

GOAL

Goal 2XL (oxyfluorfen) *(Rohm and Haas)*
Rate: Preemergence:
   1.25-2 lb. ai/A
   5-8 pt. 2XL/A
   Postemergence:
   0.5-2 lb. ai/A
   2-8 pt. 2XL/A
Time: Preemergence, postemergence. Dormant application in Arizona and California: Apply after final harvest or before Feb. 15 (in Coachella Valley, CA, do not apply after Feb. 1). Applications made after calendar dates above, but prior to bud swell may result in significant crop injury.
Weeds: Broadleaf weeds—AZ, CA:

annual sowthistle	common	prickly lettuce
broadleaf filaree	lambsquarters	prostrate knotweed
burclover	common purslane	redmaids
burning nettle	henbit	rockpurslane
cheeseweed	London rocket	redroot pigweed
coast fiddleneck	malva	redstem filaree
common groundsel	minerslettuce	shepherdspurse

Broadleaf weeds—All States:

American black	common purslane	prostrate spurge
nightshade	cutleaf	redroot pigweed
annual morningglory	eveningprimrose	shepherdspurse
annual sowthistle	cutleaf groundcherry	spotted spurge
balsamapple	hemp sesbania	teaweed
black nightshade	jimsonweed	velvetleaf
camphorweed	narrowleaf cudweed	Virginia pepperweed
common cocklebur	Pennsylvania	wild poinsettia
common	smartweed	Wright groundcherry
lambsquarters	prickly sida	

Remarks: Almonds, beechnuts, Brazil nuts, butternuts, cashews, chestnuts, chinquapins, filberts, hickory, macadamias, pecans, pistachios, walnuts. Direct spray toward base of tree or vine, avoiding direct plant contact. Add 2 pt./100 gal. spray nonionic surfactant. Refer to label for restrictions and precautions.
Tank Mixes: Diuron, glyphosate, napropamide, norflurazon, oryzalin, paraquat, pronamide, simazine.

– – – – – – – – – – – – – –

Signal Word/Toxicity Class: Warning/II.
REI: 24 hr.

◆–new product • PP–preplant • PPI–preplant incorporated • PRE–preemergence • POST–postemergence • SEQ–sequential • ae–acid equivalent • ai–active ingredient • DF–dry flowable
E/EC–emulsifiable concentrate • F/FL–flowable • DG/G/WG–dispersable granule • L/LC–liquid • SP/WSP–soluble packet • W/WP–wettable powder • WSB–water soluble bag

Gramoxone Extra — see paraquat

Hi-Dep — see 2,4-D

Karmex — see diuron

MAGMA — see MSMA

MSMA

120 Herbicide (6.6) *(Terra)*
912 Herbicide (6) (+ surfactant) *(Terra)*
Rate: Nonbearing:
2-3 lb. ai/A
2.66-4 pt. 6.6/A
2-4 lb. ai/A
2.66-5.32 pt. 6/A
Time: Do not exceed 3 applications per year.
Weeds: Grassy weeds.
Remarks: Nonbearing almonds. Do not allow spray to contact leaves, stems, bark of trees, or use around trees from which crop will be harvested within 1 year after application.

– – – – – – – – – – – – – –

Signal Word/Toxicity Class: Caution/III.
REI: 12 hr.

Bueno 6 (+ surfactant) *(ZENECA)*
Rate: 2 lb. ai/A
2.66 pt. 6/A
Time: Apply as directed spray in warm weather when weeds are small and conditions are favorable for good weed growth.
Weeds: Broadleaf weeds:

chickweed	jimsonweed	sicklepod
cocklebur	morningglory	wild mustard
common purslane	pigweed	woodsorrel
dandelion	puncturevine	
fiddleneck	ragweed	

Grasses and sedges:

bahiagrass	foxtail	nutsedge
barnyardgrass	goosegrass	sandbur
brachiaria	guineagrass	smooth crabgrass
dallisgrass	johnsongrass	wild oat
fall panicum	large crabgrass	witchgrass

SLN—GA: Sedge:
nutsedge
Remarks: Nonbearing almonds, walnuts. SLN—GA: Nonbearing pecan orchards and nurseries. Apply after pecan trees are established, producing new growth, and at least 12" tall. Do not allow spray to contact leaves, stems, or bark of trees. Do not use around trees from which crop will be harvested within 1 year following application. Up to 3 applications per year may be applied. Do not graze treated areas. Refer to label for use directions, restrictions, and precautions.
State Restrictions: In Florida, use only as spot treatment.

– – – – – – – – – – – – – –

Signal Word/Toxicity Class: Caution.
REI: 12 hr.

Drexel MSMA 6 Plus (+ surfactant) *(Drexel)*
Helena MSMA (6.6) *(Helena)*
Helena MSMA Plus H.C. (6) (+ surfactant) *(Helena)*
◆ **MAGMA (WSG)** *(Luxembourg-Pamol)*
◆ **Target MSMA 6 Plus (+ surfactant)** *(Luxembourg-Pamol)*
◆ **TurfMate 6 Plus (+ surfactant)** *(Luxembourg-Pamol)*
Rate: 2 lb. ai/A
2.5 pt. 6.6/A
2.66 pt. 6/A
4.6 lb. ai/A
8.5 lb. WSG/A (100 gal. water—directed; 50 gal. water—spot)
Time: Apply in nonbearing orchards when weeds are small and temperature is 80°F or above.
Weeds: Broadleaf weeds:

chickweed	pigweed	puncturevine
cocklebur		

Grasses and sedges:

barnyardgrass	dallisgrass	nutsedge
brachiaria	goosegrass	sandbur
crabgrass	johnsongrass	

Remarks: Nonbearing: almonds, walnuts. For 6.6, add suitable surfactant. Do not allow spray to contact leaves, stems, or bark of trees. Do not use around trees from which crop will be harvested within 1 year following application. Up to 3 applications per year may be made for control of regrowth. Do not graze treated areas.
State Restrictions: Use only as a spot treatment in Florida.

– – – – – – – – – – – – – –

Signal Word/Toxicity Class: Caution/III.
REI: 12 hr.

NORFLURAZON

Solicam DF *(Novartis)*
Rate: 1-4 lb. ai/A
1.25-5 lb. DF/A
Time: Apply from fall to early spring before weeds emerge. Almonds: May be soil-applied preemergence treatment prior to harvest.
Weeds: Broadleaf weeds:

black mustard	groundsel*	redstem filaree
chickweed	horseweed*	Russian thistle
common	(marestail)	shepherdspurse
lambsquarters*	little mallow	silverleaf nightshade*
common purslane	(cheeseweed)	sowthistle
falsedandelion	London rocket	tumble mustard
(smooth catsear)	pineappleweed	tumble pigweed*
fiddleneck	puncturevine	Virginia pepperweed
flixweed	quackgrass*	whitestem filaree
green amaranth*	redroot pigweed*	

Grasses and sedges:

annual bluegrass	feather fingergrass	sixweeks grama
barnyardgrass	foxtail	southwestern
bermudagrass*	Italian ryegrass	cupgrass
crabgrass	nutsedge	wild barley
downy brome	sandbur	witchgrass

* Suppression:
Remarks: Almonds, filberts, pecans, walnuts. Do not use on nursery stock. Incorporate with 1/2" irrigation water prior to weed germination and shaking or nut drop. Rainfall or irrigation is required within 4 weeks of application.
Tank Mixes: Diuron (pecans, walnuts), Goal, Gramoxone, Prowl (almonds, walnuts), roundup, simazine, Sinbar (pecans), Surflan; refer to label for use instructions.
State Restrictions: See label for use restrictions in Coachella Valley of California.

– – – – – – – – – – – – – –

Signal Word/Toxicity Class: Caution.
REI: 12 hr.

Opti-Amine — see 2,4-D

Orchard Master — see 2,4-D

PARAQUAT

Restricted Use Pesticide.

Gramoxone Extra (2.5L) *(ZENECA)*
Rate: 0.6-1 lb. ai/A
2-3 pt. 2.5L/A
Time: Apply as directed spray when weeds and grasses are succulent and new growth is from 1-6" tall.
Weeds: Annual broadleaf weeds and grasses; top kill and suppression of perennials.
Remarks: Almonds, beechnuts, Brazil nuts, butternuts, cashews, chestnuts, chinquapins, filberts, hickory, macadamias, pecans, pistachios, walnuts. Add nonionic surfactant or crop oil concentrate. Do not allow spray to contact green stems, fruit, or foliage. Use a shield or wrap when spraying around young trees. For mature woody weeds, green suckers, late germinating weeds, grasses, and perennials, retreatment or spot treatment may be necessary. Do not graze treated areas. Refer to label for use directions, restrictions, and precautions.
Days To Harvest: Pistachios—7.
Tank Mixes: Devrinol, Goal, Karmex, Krovar, Princep, Sinbar, Solicam, Surflan.

– – – – – – – – – – – – – –

Signal Word/Toxicity Class: Danger-Poison/I.
REI: 12 hr. (except harvest aid/desiccation 24 hr.).

7

Fruits & Nuts

NOTICE	The information on these pages is for preliminary planning — not a guide for use. Be sure to follow the manufacturer's directions, notwithstanding information contained here.	For personal protective equipment and EPA registration numbers, please turn to page 70.

PENDIMETHALIN

◆ **Pentagon DG** (American Cyanamid)
Prowl 3.3 EC (American Cyanamid)
Rate: 2-4 lb. ai/A
2.4-4.8 qt. 3.3 EC/A
3.3-6.6 lb. DG/A
Time: Apply before weeds emerge.
Weeds: Broadleaf Weeds:

annual spurge	knotweed	pigweed
carpetweed	kochia	puncturevine
chickweed	lambsquarters	purslane
fiddleneck	London rocket	shepherdspurse
Florida pusley	Pennsylvania	velvetleaf
henbit	smartweed	

Grasses:

annual bluegrass	giant foxtail	red sprangletop
barnyardgrass	green foxtail	signalgrass
browntop panicum	johnsongrass	Texas panicum
crabgrass	(seedling)	witchgrass
crowfootgrass	junglerice	woolly cupgrass
fall panicum	lovegrass	yellow foxtail
field sandbur	Mexican sprangletop	

Remarks: Nonbearing: almonds, pistachios, English walnuts. Use low rate for short-term control; high rate for long-term control. Apply spray directly to ground beneath trees. Refer to label for further use directions and precautions.

Signal Word/Toxicity Class: Caution.
REI: 12 hr.

Pentagon — see pendimethalin

Poast — see sethoxydim

Princep — see simazine

Prism — see clethodim

Prowl — see pendimethalin

Rattler — see glyphosate

Rely — see glufosinate-ammonium

Roundup — see glyphosate

Saber — see 2,4-D

Savage — see 2,4-D

SCYTHE

Nonselective, postemergent herbicide. May be used to control suckers. May also be used with other herbicides having systemic or residual activity.

◆ **Scythe (pelargonic acid)** (Mycogen)
Rate: 4-13 fl. oz./1 gal. spray solution
Time: Apply to actively growing weeds prior to crop emergence.
Weeds: Annual and perennial broadleaf weeds and grasses.
Remarks: Almonds, Brazil nuts, chestnuts, filberts, macadamias, pecans, pistachios, walnuts. Apply in minimum 75 gal. spray solution/A or spray-to-wet. Do not apply by air or through any type of irrigation system. Refer to label for directions and precautions.

Tank Mixes: Glyphosate and other foliar and residual herbicides.

Signal Word/Toxicity Class: Warning/II.
REI: 24 hr.

Select — see clethodim

SETHOXYDIM

Poast (1.5EC) (BASF)
Rate: 0.28-0.47 lb. ai/A
1.5-2.5 pt. 1.5EC/A
Time: Postemergence. Apply to actively growing grasses.
Weeds: Annual grasses up to 12" in height and perennial grasses:

barnyardgrass	junglerice	tall fescue
bermudagrass	large crabgrass	Texas panicum
broadleaf signalgrass	lovegrass	wild proso millet
fall panicum	orchardgrass	wildcane
giant foxtail	quackgrass	wirestem muhly
goosegrass	red sprangletop	witchgrass
green foxtail	shattercane	woolly cupgrass
johnsongrass	smooth crabgrass	yellow foxtail

Remarks: Nonbearing. Add 2 pt./A oil concentrate. Almond hulls may be fed to animals. Refer to label for restrictions and limitations.
Days To Harvest: 15; pistachios—1 year.
State Restrictions: Do not use UAN or AMS in California or Pacific Northwest.

Signal Word/Toxicity Class: Warning/II.
REI: 12 hr.

SIMAZINE

◆ **Clean Crop Simazine 4L or 90WDG** (Platte)
Drexel Simazine 4L or 90DF (Drexel)
Princep 4L or Caliber 90 (Novartis)
Riverside Simazine 4L or 90DF (Terra)
Rate: 1-2 lb. ai/A
2-4 pt. 4L/A
1.1-2.2 lb. 90, 90DF, 90WDG/A
Time: Apply before weeds emerge in late fall or early winter.
Weeds: Broadleaf weeds:

burclover	shepherdspurse	wild mustard
common chickweed		

Remarks: Almonds. Apply in 2-4 ft. band on each side of tree. Do not treat trees established in grove less than 3 years, apply to almond trees propagated on plum rootstocks, treat Mission (Texas) variety of almonds, or replant almonds in treated soil for 12 months after treatment. Do not apply to soil with less than 1% organic matter or treat areas where water will accumulate.
Tank Mixes: Roundup Ultra, Starfire, Surflan.
State Restrictions: For use in California.

Rate: 2-4 lb. ai/A
2-4 qt. 4L/A
2.2-4.4 lb. 90, 90DF, 90WDG/A
Time: Apply in fall or split application fall and spring.
Weeds: Broadleaf weeds:

annual bluegrass	carelessweed	purslane
annual morningglory	henbit	ragweed
burclover	mustard	

Grasses:

barnyardgrass	fall panicum	foxtail

Remarks: Filberts. Do not use on sandy soils. Do not contact foliage or spray while nuts are on the ground during harvest season.
Tank Mixes: Roundup Ultra, Surflan.
State Restrictions: For use in Oregon and Washington.

Rate: 2-4 lb. ai/A
2-4 qt. 4L/A
2.2-4.4 lb. 90, 90DF, 90WDG/A
Time: For macadamias, apply before harvest and prior to weed emergence; repeat as necessary.
Weeds: Same as above.
Tank Mixes: Macadamias—Roundup Ultra, walnuts—Surflan.
Remarks: Macadamias, walnuts. Do not use on orchards less than 1 year old. Do not apply to foliage or spray when nuts are on the ground.

Rate: 2-4 lb. ai/A
2-4 qt. 4L/A
2.2-4.4 lb. 90, 90DF, 90WDG/A

◆—new product • PP-preplant • PPI-preplant incorporated • PRE-preemergence • POST-postemergence • SEQ-sequential • ae-acid equivalent • ai-active ingredient • DF-dry flowable
E/EC-emulsifiable concentrate • F/FL-flowable • DG/G/WG-dispersable granule • L/LC-liquid • SP/WSP-soluble packet • W/WP-wettable powder • WSB-water soluble bag

Time: Apply before weeds emerge in spring.

Weeds: Same as above.

Remarks: Pecans. Do not apply to transplanted trees established less than 2 years in grove or when nuts are on the ground. Do not graze treated areas.

Tank Mixes: Roundup Ultra, Surflan.

State Restrictions: Not for use west of the Pecos River in Texas or in Arizona, California, New Mexico.

– – – – – – – – – – – – – – –

Signal Word/Toxicity Class: Caution/III.

REI: 12 hr.

SINBAR

Sinbar (terbacil) *(DuPont)*

Rate: 1.6-2.4 lb. ai/A
2-3 lb. 80W/A

Time: Apply prior to weed emergence or during early weed growth in spring.

Weeds: Broadleaf weeds:

American burnweed	flora's paintbrush	nightshade
(fireweed)	Florida pusley	pigweed
chickweed	groundsel*	plantain
China lettuce	henbit	purslane
clover	horsenettle*	ragweed
crotalaria	horseweed	red sorrel*
dandelion	jimsonweed	sheep sorrel
(seedling)	knotweed	smartweed
dogfennel	lambsquarters	wild geranium
fiddleneck	mustard	

Grasses and sedges:

barnyardgrass	guineagrass	quackgrass*
bluegrass	junglerice	sandbur
crabgrass	natalgrass	(sandspur)
crowfootgrass	orchardgrass	signalgrass
foxtail	panicum	yellow nutsedge*

* *Partial control*

Remarks: Pecans. Trees established at least 1 year. Rate varies depending on soil texture. Avoid contact of foliage. Do not use on eroded area where subsoil or roots are exposed or on trees planted in furrow irrigation channels. Do not graze or feed forage from treated areas to livestock.

Crop Rotation: Do not replant to any crop within 2 years after treatment.

– – – – – – – – – – – – – – –

Signal Word/Toxicity Class: Caution.

REI: 12 hr.

SNAPSHOT (Premix)

Snapshot 2.5TG (2% trifluralin & 0.5% isoxaben) *(Dow AgroSciences)*

Rate: 2.5-5 lb. ai/A
100-200 lb. 2.5TG/A

Time: Apply in late summer to early fall or in early spring or immediately after cultivation.

Weeds: Broadleaf weeds:

annual bursage	eveningprimrose	prickly sida
annual sowthistle	fall panicum	prostrate knotweed
black medic	hairy fleabane	purple cudweed
black nightshade	hairy galinsoga	purslane speedwell
bristly oxtongue	hare barley	rattail fescue
broadleaf plantain	heath aster	redstem filaree
burning nettle	henbit	Russian thistle
California burclover	horseweed	scarlet pimpernel
Carolina geranium	Indian mustard	shepherdspurse
clover	jimsonweed	sibara
coast fiddleneck	kochia	silversheath knotweed
common chickweed	lanceleaf groundcherry	slender aster
common groundsel	little mallow	slender plantain
common	London rocket	spiny sowthistle
lambsquarters	marestail	spotted spurge
common purslane	Mexican sprangletop	sunflower
common ragweed	nettleleaf goosefoot	swinecress
creeping woodsorrel	panicle willowweed	tall morningglory
curly dock	Pennsylvania	telegraphplant
dandelion	smartweed	turkey mullein
datura	petty spurge	velvetleaf
desert rockpurslane	pigweed	Virginia pepperweed
dwarf fleabane	pineappleweed	yellow sweetclover
dwarf mallow	prickly lettuce	yellow woodsorrel

Annual grasses:

annual bluegrass	junglerice	wild mustard
barnyardgrass	lovegrass	wild oat
bromegrass	southwestern	wild radish
crabgrass	cupgrass	witchgrass
giant foxtail	wild carrot	yellow foxtail
Italian ryegrass	wild celery	

Remarks: Nonbearing orchards. Apply to trees that will not bear fruit for at least 1 year. Do not apply to bedding plants, nursery seedbeds, or transplant beds.

State Restrictions: Refer to label for use restrictions in Arizona.

– – – – – – – – – – – – – – –

Signal Word/Toxicity Class: Caution/III.

REI: 12 hr.

Solicam — see norflurazon

SURFLAN

Surflan A.S. (oryzalin) *(Dow AgroSciences)*

Rate: 2-6 lb. ai/A
2-6 qt. A.S./A

Time: Apply before weeds emerge.

Weeds: Broadleaf weeds:

annual morningglory*	field sandbur	puncturevine
annual smartweed*	Florida purslane	red sprangletop
annual sowthistle*	Florida purslane	redmaids rockpurslane
black mustard*	giant ragweed*	redroot pigweed
black nightshade*	henbit	redstem filaree*
carelessweed	ladysthumb*	rough pigweed
carpetweed	lambsquarters	shepherdspurse
chickweed	London rocket*	smooth pigweed
climbing milkweed*	Mexican clover	spiny pigweed
coast fiddleneck	prickly lettuce*	teaweed*
common groundsel*	prickly sida*	tumble pigweed
common mallow*	prostrate knotweed	velvetleaf*
common purslane	prostrate pigweed	whitestem filaree*
common ragweed*	prostrate spurge*	wild mustard*
cudweed		

Grasses:

annual bluegrass	green foxtail	pigeongrass
annual ryegrass	guineagrass	robust foxtail
barnyardgrass	Italian ryegrass	signalgrass
bottlegrass	johnsongrass	smooth crabgrass
bristlegrass	(seedling)	spreading panicgrass
browntop panicum	junglerice	southwestern cupgrass
crowfootgrass	large crabgrass	Texas panicum
downy brome	little barley	watergrass
fall panicum	lovegrass	wild oat
foxtail	Mexican lovegrass	witchgrass
giant foxtail	Orcutt lovegrass	yellow foxtail

**Suppression*

Remarks: Bearing, nonbearing: almonds, filberts, macadamias, pecans, pistachios, English walnuts. Not for use on soils with at lesat 5% organic matter. May be applied through solid set sprinkler irrigation system. Surface apply once existing weeds are controlled by tillage or contact herbicide; single $^1/_2$-1" rain or sprinkler irrigation within 21 days required.

Tank Mixes: Goal, Gramoxone Extra, Princep, Roundup Ultra and Solicam.

– – – – – – – – – – – – – – –

Signal Word/Toxicity Class: Caution/III.

REI: 12 hr.

Target — see MSMA

TOUCHDOWN

Touchdown (5L or 6L) (sulfosate) *(ZENECA)*

Rate: 0.5-4 lb. ai/A
0.8-6.4 pt. 5L/A
0.66-5.33 pt. 6L/A

Time: Apply to actively growing grasses and weeds.

Weeds: Broadleaf weeds:

annual sowthistle	dogfennel	kochia
annual spurge	fiddleneck	leafy spurge*
black nightshade	field bindweed	little barley
camphorweed	field sandbur	London rocket
Canada thistle	filaree	marestail
Carolina geranium	fleabane	morningglory
common chickweed	Florida pusley	mouseear chickweed
common cocklebur	giant ragweed	mustard
common groundsel	groundcherry	Pennsylvania
common lambsquarters	hairy fleabane	smartweed
common ragweed	hemp dogbane	prickly lettuce
curly dock	henbit	redroot pigweed
cutleaf	hophornbeam	Russian thistle
eveningprimrose	copperleaf	shepherdspurse
dandelion	horsenettle	sicklepod
smooth pigweed	velvetleaf	white clover
spanishneedles	wheat	wild buckwheat

7

Fruits & Nuts

– – – – – – – – – – – – – – –

Nuts

Grasses and sedges:

annual bluegrass	foxtail	smooth bromegrass
bahiagrass	goosegrass	sprangletop
barley	guineagrass	stinkgrass
barnyardgrass	Italian ryegrass	tall fescue
bermudagrass	johnsongrass	Texas panicum
broadleaf signalgrass	(seedling)	timothy
cheat	Kentucky bluegrass	torpedograss*
cogongrass*	orchardgrass	vaseygrass
crabgrass	paragrass	wild oat
crowfootgrass	perennial ryegrass	wirestem muhly
downy brome	quackgrass	witchgrass
fall panicum	red rice	woolly cupgrass
fescue	shattercane	yellow nutsedge

* Partial control

Remarks: Bearing and nonbearing: almonds, filberts, macadamias, pecans, pistachios, walnuts (black, English). Bearing only: beechnuts, Brazil nuts, butternuts, cashews, chestnuts, chinquapin, hickory. Add nonionic surfactant or wetting agent. In addition, ammonium sulfate can be added to nonbearing nuts. Do not allow spray, spray drift, or mist to contact green foliage or green bark on trunk, suckers, open wounds, or other green parts of trees and vines. Contact with any tree or vine part other than mature brown woody bark may cause crop injury. Do not graze or harvest treated cover crops for feed. Do not apply through any type of irrigation system. Refer to label for directions, restrictions, and precautions.

Days To Harvest: 1 year.

Tank Mixes: Devrinol, diuron, Goal, Krovar, Prowl, simazine, Solicam, Surflan.

State Restrictions: Ammonium sulfate (6L) not for use in California.

- - - - - - - - - - - - - - -

Signal Word/Toxicity Class: Caution.
REI: 12 hr. (5L); 4 hr. (6L).

Treflan — see trifluralin

Trific — see trifluralin

TRIFLURALIN

Albaugh Trifluralin 4EC *(Albaugh)*
◆ **Clean Crop Trifluralin HF (4EC)** *(Platte)*
Gowan Trifluralin 4 or 5 (EC) or 10G *(Gowan)*
Helena Trifluralin 4 EC *(Helena)*
Riverside Trifluralin 4EC or Trific 60DF *(Terra)*
◆ **Sedagri Trifluralin 480 (4EC)** *(Rhone-Poulenc)*
Treflan HFP (4EC) or TR-10 (10G) *(Dow AgroSciences)*
Trilin 4 or 5 (EC) or 10G *(Griffin)*
Wilbur-Ellis Trifluralin 10G *(Wilbur-Ellis)*

Rate: New plantings:
0.5-1 lb. ai/A
1-2 pt. 4EC/A
0.8-1.6 pt. 5EC/A
0.875-1.66 lb. 60DF/A
5-10 lb. 10G/A
Established plantings:
1-2 lb. ai/A
2-4 pt. 4EC/A
1.6-3.2 pt. 5EC/A
1.66-3.33 lb. 60DF/A
10-20 lb. 10G/A

Time: New plantings: Apply and incorporate prior to planting. Established plantings: Apply as directed spray to soil.

Weeds: Broadleaf weeds:

carelessweed	knotweed	purslane
carpetweed	kochia	pusley
chickweed	lambsquarters	redroot pigweed
field bindweed	Mexican clover	rough pigweed
fireweed	Mexican fireweed	Russian thistle
Florida purslane	prostrate pigweed	spiny pigweed
Florida pusley	puncturevine	stinging nettle
goosefoot	(western U.S.)	tumbleweed
henbit		

Grasses:

annual bluegrass	fall panicum	sandbur
barnyardgrass	foxtail millet	shattercane
bottlegrass	giant foxtail	smooth crabgrass
bristlegrass	green foxtail	sprangletop
bromegrass	Italian ryegrass	stinkgrass
burgrass	johnsongrass (seedling)	Texas panicum
cheat	junglerice	watergrass
cheatgrass	large crabgrass	wildcane
chess	pigeongrass	woolly cupgrass
downy brome	robust foxtail	yellow foxtail

Remarks: Almonds, pecans, walnuts. Rate varies by soil type and amount of rainfall. Refer to label for use directions, restrictions, and precautions.
Days To Harvest: 60.
State Restrictions: Trilin 10G and Wilbur-Ellis not for use in California.

- - - - - - - - - - - - - - -

Signal Word/Toxicity Class: Varies by formulation.
REI: 12 hr. unless soil injected or soil incorporated.

Trilin — see trifluralin

TurfMate — see MSMA

Weed Rhap — see 2,4-D

Weedar — see 2,4-D

Weedestroy — see 2,4-D

XL 2G (Premix)

A selective preemergence herbicide for control of certain annual grasses and broadleaf weeds. Does not control established weeds. Requires rainfall or sprinkler irrigation within 21 days to activate.

XL 2G (1% benefin & 1% oryzalin) *(Helena)*
Rate: 4-6 lb. ai/A
200-300 lb./A
0.09-0.14 lb. ai/sq. ft.
4.6-6.9 lb./1000 sq. ft.
Time: Apply prior to germination of target weeds.
Weeds: Broadleaf weeds:

annual sowthistle*	desert rockpurslane	prostrate spurge
bittercress	Florida pusley	puncturevine
black mustard*	henbit	redstem filaree
black nightshade*	horseweed*	shepherdspurse
carpetweed	ladysthumb*	smartweed*
chickweed	lambsquarters	spotted spurge*
climbing milkweed*	London rocket	teaweed*
coast fiddleneck	morningglory*	velvetleaf*
common groundsel	pigweed	whitestem filaree
common mallow*	prickly lettuce*	wild mustard*
common purslane	prickly sida*	yellow woodsorrel
common ragweed*	prostrate knotweed	

Grasses:

annual bluegrass	foxtail	Orcutt lovegrass
barnyardgrass	goosegrass	red sprangletop
browntop panicum	Italian ryegrass	signalgrass
crabgrass	johnsongrass	Texas panicum
crowfootgrass	(seedling)	volunteer wheat*
cupgrass	junglerice	wild oat
fall panicum	little barley	witchgrass
field sandbur	Mexican lovegrass	

* Suppression

Remarks: Nonbearing almonds, filberts, macadamias, pecans, pistachios, walnuts. Do not apply to trees that may be harvested for food within 1 year after application. Refer to label for use directions and precautions.

- - - - - - - - - - - - - - -

Signal Word/Toxicity Class: Caution/III.
REI: 12 hr. unless soil-injected or soil-incorporated.

◆-new product • PP-preplant • PPI-preplant incorporated • PRE-preemergence • POST-postemergence • SEQ-sequential • ae-acid equivalent • ai-active ingredient • DF-dry flowable
E/EC-emulsifiable concentrate • F/FL-flowable • DG/G/WG-dispersable granule • L/LC-liquid • SP/WSP-soluble packet • W/WP-wettable powder • WSB-water soluble bag

392   Weed Control Manual 2000

Section 8

Turf, Ornamentals & Woody Plants

Use Reminders

Chemical Weed Control In Greenhouses 394
Turfgrass Tolerance Of Preemergence Herbicides 394
Turfgrass Tolerance Of Postemergence Herbicides 395

Weed Efficacy Chart

Broadleaf Weed Control In Turf 396
Ornamental Herbicide Weed Response Ratings 397
Turf Preemergence Herbicide Efficacy Ratings 398

Herbicide Listings

Lawn & Turf Seedbeds 399
Newly Sprigged/Seeded Turf 399
Established Lawns & Turf 399
Grasses For Seed Production 411
Turf Grasses For Sod Production 415
Ornamentals & Woody Plants 418

Chemical Weed Control In Greenhouses

Herbicide	Active ingredient(s)	Type	Labelled Uses
Surflan	oryzalin	Preemergent	Under benches; along walkways
Weeds Controlled: Many annual grasses including crabgrasses, foxtails, goosegrass, and lovegrass; some broadleaf weeds including bittercress, common chickweed, prostrate spurge, and yellow woodsorrel.			
Diquat	diquat dibromide	Postemergent - nonselective; contact	Under benches; along walkways
Weeds Controlled: General weed killer; apply to young weeds. Grasses and established weeds may require more than one treatment.			
Finale	glufosinate-ammonium	Postemergent - nonselective; translocated	Inside greenhouse; around greenhouse
Weeds Controlled: Many annual and perennial grasses and broadleaf weeds; some woody plants.			
Fusilade II	fluazifop-P-butyl	Postemergent - selective; translocated	Commercial greenhouses only; inside greenhouse; around greenhouse
Weeds Controlled: Many annual and perennial grasses.			
Roundup	glyphosate	Postemergent - nonselective; translocated	Inside greenhouse - desirable vegetation must not be present during application
Weeds Controlled: Many annual and perennial grasses and broadleaf weeds; some woody plants.			
Scythe	pelargonic acid + related fatty acids	Postemergent - nonselective; contact	Inside greenhouse; around greenhouse
Weeds Controlled: Controls both annual broadleaf and grass weeds that are less than 6 inches in height.			

Source: 1999 Florida Weed Management.

Turfgrass Tolerance Of Preemergence Herbicides

Herbicide	Bahiagrass	Bermudagrass	Centipede-grass	Overseed Ryegrass	St. Augustine-grass	Tall Fescue	Zoysiagrass
atrazine (AAtrex)	NR	S	S	D	S	NR	I-S
benefin (Balan)	S	S	S	NR	S	S	S
benefin + oryzalin (XL 2G)	S	S	S	NR	S	S	S
benefin + trifluralin (Team)	S	S	S	NR	S	S	S
bensulide (Pre-San)	S	S	S	I-S	S	S	S
bensulide + oxadiazon (ProTurf Goosegrass/Crabgrass)	NR	S	NR	NR	NR	NR	S
dithiopyr (Dimension)	S	S	S	I	S	S	S
ethofumesate[1] (Prograss)	NR	S (D)	NR	S (D)	I	S	NR
isoxaben (Gallery)	S	S	S	NR	S	S	S
S-metolachlor (Pennant MAGNUM)	S	S	S	D	S	S	S
napropamide (Devrinol)	S	S	S	NR	S	S	NR
oryzalin (Surflan)	S	S	S	NR	S	S	S
oxadiazon (Chipco Ronstar G)	NR	S	NR	I	S	S	S
pendimethalin (Pendulum)	S	S	S	NR	S	S	S
prodiamine (Barricade)	S	S	S	I	S	S	S
pronamide (Kerb)	NR	S	NR	D	NR	NR	NR
simazine (Princep)	NR	I	S	D	S	NR	S

S = Safe at labeled rates on mature, healthy turf. I = Intermediate safety — may cause minor damage to mature, healthy turf. Lower rates recommended when turf is under stress. NR = Not registered for use on this species.

[1]Ethofumesate is labeled only for Dormant (D) bemudagrass overseeded with perennial ryegrass.

Sources: 1999 Florida Weed Management; Recommended Chemicals for Weed and Brush Control, Arkansas, 1999.

Turfgrass Tolerance Of Postemergence Herbicides

Herbicide	Bermudagrass	Centipedegrass	St. Augustinegrass	Tall Fescue	Zoysiagrass
atrazine (AAtrex)	S-I	S-I	S-I	NR	S-I
bentazon (Basagran)	S	S	S	S	S
bromoxynil (Buctril)	S	S	S	S	S
2,4-D	S	I	I	S	S
2,4-D + dicamba	S	I	I	S	S
2,4-D + dichlorprop (2,4-DP)	S	I	I	S	S
2,4-D + mecoprop	S	I	I	S	S
2,4-D + mecoprop + dichlorprop	S	I	I	S	S
2,4-D + mecoprop + dicamba	S	I	I	S	S
dicamba (Banvel)	S	I	I	S	S
diclofop (Illoxan)	S	NR	NR	NR	NR
fenoxaprop-P-ethyl (Acclaim Extra)	NR	NR	NR	S	S
fluazifop-P-butyl (Fusilade II)	NR	NR	NR	S-I	S-I
imazaquin (Image)	I	NR	S	NR	S
MCPA + MCPP + dichlorprop	S	I	I	S	S
mecoprop (MCPP)	S	I	I	S	S
metribuzin (Sencor)	S-I	NR	NR	NR	NR
MSMA, DSMA	S	NR	NR	I	I
pronamide (Kerb)	S	NR	NR	NR	NR
sethoxydim (Vantage)	NR	S	NR	NR	NR
triclopyr + clopyralid (Confront)	I	NR	NR	S	I

S = Safe at labeled rates, I = Intermediate safety, use at reduced rates, NR = Not registered for use on this turfgrass, do not use.

Source: Recommended Chemicals for Weed and Brush Control, Arkansas, 1999.

8

Turf, Ornamentals
Use Reminders

NOTICE The information on these pages is for preliminary planning — not a guide for use. Be sure to follow the manufacturer's directions, notwithstanding information contained here.

Turf, Ornamentals Weed Efficacy Chart

Broadleaf Weed Control In Turf

Weed	Atrazine/Simazine	2,4-D	2,4-D + 2,4-DP	2,4-D + MCPP	2,4-D + MCPP, Dicamba	2,4-D + Triclopyr	Dicamba	Mecoprop (or MCPP)	Metsulfuron-methyl	Triclopyr + Clopyralid
Black medic	—	P	E	F	E	—	E	F	—	E
Burclover	—	F-P	E	E-F	E	—	E	E	—	—
Buttercup	F	E-F	E	E	E	—	F-P	F	—	E
Carolina geranium	—	E	E	E	E	—	E	E-F	E-F	—
Carpetweed	E	E	E	E	E	—	E	F	—	—
Catsear	—	E-F	E	E	E	—	E	F	—	E
Chicory	—	E	E	E	E	—	E	E	E	—
Common chickweed	E	P	E	E	E	E	E	E-F	E	E
Common cinquefoil	—	E-F	E-F	E-F	E-F	—	E-F	E-F	—	—
Common lambsquarters	—	E	E	E	E	—	E	E	E-F	—
Common purslane	F	F	F	F	E-F	—	E	P	F	—
Crimson clover	—	E	E	E	E	—	E	E	—	—
Dandelion	E-F	E	E	E	E	F-E	E	E	E	—
Dichondra	E-F	E	E	E	E	—	E-F	F	—	E
Dock (broadleaf & curly)	F	F	F	F	E-F	F	E	F-P	F	E
English daisy	—	P	F	F	E	—	E	E	—	—
Field bindweed	—	E-F	E	E-F	E	—	E	F	—	—
Ground ivy	—	F-P	F-E	F	E-F	—	E-F	F	—	—
Hairy bittercress	—	E	E	E	E	—	E	E	—	—
Hawkweed	—	E-F	E-F	E-F	E-F	—	E-F	P	—	—
Healall	—	E	E	E	E	—	E-F	P	—	E
Henbit	E	F-P	E-F	F	E	E	E	F	E-F	—
Hop clover	E	F	E	E	E	E	E	E	—	E
Knawel	—	P	E-F	E-F	E	—	E	F	—	—
Lawn burweed	E-F	F	F	E-F	E	E	E	E-F	—	E
Lespedeza	E	F-P	F	E-F	E	—	E	E	—	E
Mallow	—	F-P	E-F	E-F	E-F	—	E-F	F	—	—
Mouseear chickweed	F	F-P	E	E	E	E-F	E	E-F	—	E
Mugwort	—	F	F	F	F	—	E-F	F-P	—	—
Oxeye daisy	—	F	F	F	E-F	—	F	F	—	—
Pennywort (dollarweed)	E	E-F	E-F	E-F	E-F	—	E-F	E-F	—	—
Pigweed	—	E	E	E	E	—	E	E	E-F	—
Plantain	F-P	E	E	E	E	F-P	P	F-P	F	E
Prostrate knotweed	E	P	E-F	E-F	E	—	E	F	—	—
Prostrate spurge	E-F	F	E-F	F	E-F	E-F	E	F	—	E-F
Red sorrel	—	P	F	E-F	E	—	E	E	—	E
Shepherdspurse	—	E	E-F	E-F	E	—	E	E-F	—	—
Spotted spurge	E	F-P	E-F	E-F	E	E-F	E-F	E-F	—	E-F
Spreading dayflower	F-E	F	F	F	F	F	F	F	P	—
Thistle	—	E-F	E-F	E-F	E	—	E	F	F	—
Virginia pepperweed	—	E	E	E-F	E	—	E	E-F	—	—
Wild carrot	—	F	E-F	F	E	—	E	F	E	—
White clover	E	F	E	E	E	E-F	E	E	E	E
Wild garlic	—	E-F	E-F	E-F	E-F	—	E-F	P	E-F	—
Wild mustard	E	E	E-F	E	E	—	E	F	F	—
Wild onion	—	F	F	F	E	—	E-F	P	E-F	—
Wild violet	—	F-P	F	F-P	F-P	F-P	E-F	F-P	—	E-F
Yarrow	—	F	F	F-P	E-F	—	E	F-P	E-F	—
Yellow rocket	—	E-F	E-F	E-F	E	—	E-F	F	—	—
Yellow woodsorrel	F	P	F-P	F-P	F-P	—	F	P	E-F	E-F

E = Excellent (>89%) control; F = Fair to good (70-89%), good control sometimes with high rates, however a repeat treatment 1-3 weeks later each at the standard or reduced rate is usually more effective; P = Poor (<70%) control in most cases. Not all weeds have been tested for susceptibility to each herbicide listed.

Source: Florida Weed Management, 1999

Ornamental Herbicide Weed Response Ratings

	Annual Weeds												Perennial Weeds								
	Annual bluegrass	Carolina geranium	Carpetweed	Chickweed	Crabgrass	Dodder	Hairy bittercress	Henbit	Morningglory	Pepperweed	Prostrate spurge	Shepherspurse	Bermudagrass	Greenbriar (sawbriar)	Johnsongrass	Poison ivy	Purple nutsedge	Trumpetcreeper	White clover	Woodsorrel (oxalis)	Yellow nutsedge
Postemergence Herbicides																					
AcclaimExtra (fenoxaprop-P-ethyl)	—	—	—	—	G	—	—	—	—	—	—	—	F	—	F	—	P	P	—	—	P
Basagran (bentazon)	—	—	—	G	—	—	—	—	F	F	G	—	—	—	—	—	P	P	—	G	G
Finale (glufosinate-ammonium)	—	—	—	—	—	—	—	—	—	—	—	—	G	—	—	—	—	—	E	—	—
Fusilade (fluazifop-P-butyl)	G	—	—	—	G	—	—	—	—	—	—	—	E	—	E	—	P	P	—	—	P
Goal (oxyfluorfen)	—	E	E	—	—	—	E	—	E	E	E	E	—	—	—	—	P	P	E	E	P
Gramoxone Extra (paraquat)	E	E	E	E	E	—	E	E	G	G	G	E	F	P	F	F	F	F	G	G	F
Image (imazaquin)	—	G	—	G	—	—	G	G	—	—	—	—	—	—	—	—	G	—	G	—	G
Roundup (glyphosate)	E	G	E	E	E	—	E	F	F	G	G	E	E	F	E	E	G	E	F	G	G
Vantage (sethoxydim)	E	—	—	—	—	—	—	—	—	—	—	—	E	—	E	—	P	P	—	—	P
Preemergence Herbicides																					
Barricade (prodiamine)	E	—	E	G	E	—	—	G	P	—	G	G	—	—	—	—	P	—	—	—	P
Casoron (dichlobenil)	E	E	E	E	G	G	E	G	E	E	G	G	—	—	—	—	—	—	E	G	G
Chipco Ronstar (oxadiazon)	F	—	E	P	G	—	—	—	P	E	F	—	—	—	—	—	P	—	—	G	P
Devrinol (napropamide)	E	P	E	G	G	G	—	—	E	P	—	—	P	—	P	—	—	—	—	—	P
Dimension (dithiopyr)	E	G	—	G	E	—	G	G	—	—	—	G	P	P	P	P	P	P	P	P	P
Eptam (EPTC)	E	—	E	—	G	—	—	G	F	—	—	—	—	—	—	—	P	—	—	—	P
Gallery (isoxaben)	F	G	E	E	F	—	E	E	P	E	G	G	—	—	—	—	P	—	G	G	P
OH2 (pendimethalin + oxyfluorfen)	E	—	E	—	E	—	G	—	P	G	G	G	—	—	—	—	P	—	G	G	P
Pendulum (pendimethalin)	E	—	E	—	E	—	—	G	P	G	—	—	—	—	—	—	P	—	—	G	P
Pennant MAGNUM (S-metolachlor)	E	—	E	F	G	—	P	—	P	—	F	—	—	—	—	—	P	—	—	P	F
Predict (norflurazon)	E	G	E	G	G	—	—	—	—	—	G	G	—	—	—	—	P	—	—	—	P
Princep (simazine)	E	—	E	E	F	—	E	E	E	E	E	F	—	—	—	—	P	—	G	F	P
Rout (oxyfluorfen + oryzalin)	E	—	E	—	E	—	—	—	P	G	G	G	—	—	—	—	P	—	F	E	P
Snapshot (isoxaben + trifluralin)	E	—	E	E	E	—	E	G	F	E	G	G	—	—	—	—	P	—	G	G	P
Surflan (oryzalin)	E	—	E	—	E	P	F	G	P	E	G	—	—	—	—	—	P	—	P	G	P
Treflan (trifluralin)	E	—	E	—	E	—	—	—	P	—	—	—	—	—	—	—	P	—	—	—	P
XL 2G (benefin + oryzalin)	E	—	E	—	E	—	—	G	P	E	G	—	—	—	—	—	P	—	P	G	P

E = Excellent, G = Good, F = Fair, P = Poor, — = No data.

Source: Recommended Chemicals for Weed and Brush Control, Arkansas, 1999

NOTICE The information on these pages is for preliminary planning — not a guide for use. Be sure to follow the manufacturer's directions, notwithstanding information contained here.

Turf, Ornamentals Weed Efficacy Chart

Turf Preemergence Herbicide Efficacy Ratings

Herbicide	Annual bluegrass	Common chickweed	Corn speedwell	Crabgrass	Goosegrass	Henbit	Lawn burweed
Atrazine (AAtrex)	E	E	E	F	P	E	E
Benefin (Balan)	G-E	G	E	G-E	F	G	P
Benefin + oryzalin (XL 2G)	E	L	—	E	G	L	—
Benefin + trifluralin (Team)	E	L	—	E	G	L	—
Bensulide (Pre-San)	F	P	P	G-E	F	P	P
Bensulide + oxadiazon (ProTurf Goosegrass/Crabgrass Control)	—	—	—	E	G-E	—	—
Dithiopyr (Dimension)	G-E	G	—	E	G-E	—	—
Isoxaben (Gallery)	F	E	—	F	P	L	—
S-metolachlor (Pennant MAGNUM)	—	—	—	G	F	—	—
Napropamide (Devrinol)	G	E	E	G-E	G	P	E
Oryzalin (Surflan)	E	L	P	E	G-E	L	—
Oxadiazon (Chipco Ronstar)	G	P	G	G	E	P	P
Pendimethalin (Pendulum)	G-E	E	E	E	G-E	L	—
Prodiamine (Barricade)	G	G	G	E	G-E	G	G
Pronamide (Kerb)	G-E	E	E	F	P	P	P
Simazine (Princep)	E	E	E	F	P	E	E

E = Excellent, >89% control; G = Good, 80-89% control; F = Fair, 70-79% control; P = Poor, <70% control; L = Listed on the label but has not yet been tested fully at the University of Florida; — = Data not available.

Source: Florida Weed Management, 1999

Turf, Ornamentals & Woody Plants

Lawn & Turf Seedbeds
(Prior to Establishment)

BASAMID

Granular soil fumigant that kills weed seeds in soil prior to planting. Toxic to fish.

Basamid Granular (dazomet) *(BASF)*
Rate: 6.5-13 oz./100 sq. ft.
Time: Preplant. Fall soil treatments are recommended if early spring planting is desired. Do not use if soil temperature below 43°F.
Weeds: Broadleaf weeds:

henbit	pigweed	purslane
mustard		

Grasses:

bermudagrass	crabgrass	foxtail

Remarks: Apply 15 gal. water/100 sq. ft. to prepared soil surface immediately after application.

– – – – – – – – – – – – – – –

Signal Word/Toxicity Class: Warning/II.
REI: 24 hr.

Newly Sprigged/ Seeded Turf

TUPERSAN

Use only on cool-season turfgrasses and zoysiagrass.

Tupersan (50WP) (siduron) *(Gowan)*
Rate: 2-6 lb. ai/A
4-12 lb. 50WP/A
Time: Apply at any stage of development, including new seedlings.
Weeds: Annual grasses:

barnyardgrass	hairy crabgrass	smooth crabgrass
foxtail	large crabgrass	

Remarks: New spring plantings. Not for use on golf course greens. Do not apply to bermudagrass. Water within 3 days after treatment if there has been no rain. Do not apply through any type of irrigation system.
Tank Mixes: May be tank mixed; refer to label.

– – – – – – – – – – – – – – –

Signal Word/Toxicity Class: Caution.
REI: 4 hr.

Est. Lawns & Turf

3 Plus 3 — see 2,4-D Combinations

120 Herbicide — see MSMA

912 Herbicide — see MSMA

2D + 2 MCPP — see 2,4-D Combinations

AAtrex — see atrazine

Acclaim Extra — see fenoxaprop-P-ethyl

Ansar 6.6 — see MSMA

ASULAM

Riverside Asulam 3.3 *(Terra)*
Rate: 2 lb. ai/A
5 pt./A
Time: Apply when weeds are actively growing.
Weeds: Grasses:

bullgrass	goosegrass	sandbur
crabgrass		

Remarks: For use on Tifway 419 bermudagrass and St. Augustinegrass. Do not use surfactant or apply to turf which is under stress or newly mowed.

– – – – – – – – – – – – – – –

Signal Word/Toxicity Class: Caution.

Atra-5 — see atrazine

ATRAZINE

Controls wide range of winter annual weeds in non-overseeded warm-season turfgrass. Restricted Use Pesticide due to ground and surface water concerns.

AAtrex 4L or AAtrex Nine-0 (WDG) *(Novartis)*
◆ **Clean Crop Atrazine 4L or 90 WDG** *(Platte)*
Drexel Atrazine 4L, Atra-5 (5L) or 90DF *(Drexel)*
Helena Atrazine 4L *(Helena)*
Riverside Atrazine 4L or 90DF *(Terra)*
Rate: 1-2 lb. ai/A
2-4 pt. 4L/A
3.2-6.4 pt. 5L/A
1.1-2.2 lb. WDG, 90DF/A
Time: Preemergence.
Weeds: Annual broadleaf weeds and grasses such as:

annual bluegrass	chickweed	hop clover
burclover	corn speedwell	spurweed
carpet burweed	henbit	

Remarks: Bermudagrass, centipedegrass, St. Augustinegrass, and zoysiagrass for fairways, lawns and similar areas. Do not apply through any type of irrigation system. Refer to label for precautions and restrictions.
State Restrictions: Wilbur-Ellis not registered in California.

– – – – – – – – – – – – – – –

Signal Word/Toxicity Class: Caution/III.

Banvel — see dicamba

Barrage — see 2,4-D

BARRICADE

Selective preemergence herbicide that provides residual control of many grass and broadleaf weeds in turf grasses and landscapes. Controls susceptible weeds during the seed germination process.

Barricade (65WG) (prodiamine) *(Novartis)*
Rate: 0.38-1.5 lb. ai/A
0.5-2.3 lb. 65WG/A per year

8

Turf, Ornamentals & Woody Plants

Time: Apply single application or as a sequential to control weeds germinating throughout the year. Apply prior to germination of target weeds.

Weeds: Annual broadleaf weeds:

carpetweed	Florida pusley	pigweed
common chickweed	henbit	prostrate spurge
common	knotweed	shepherdspurse
lambsquarters	kochia	yellow woodsorrel
common purslane	mouseear chickweed	

Grasses:

annual bluegrass	goosegrass	rescuegrass
annual foxtail	itchgrass	(suppression)
barnyardgrass	johnsongrass	smooth crabgrass
broadleaf signalgrass	(seedling)	Texas panicum
browntop panicum	junglerice	witchgrass
crowfootgrass	large crabgrass	woolly cupgrass
fall panicum	lovegrass	yellow foxtail

Remarks: For use on bermudagrass (lower rate for newly sprigged or plugged), centipedegrass, creeping bentgrass, creeping red fescue, perennial bluegrass and ryegrass, St. Augustinegrass, seashore paspalum, tall fescue, and zoysiagrass. Do not apply to golf course putting greens, or to areas where dichondra, colonial bentgrass, velvet bentgrass, or annual bluegrass (*Poa annua*) are desirable species. Do not apply to fall-seeded turf treated the following spring until after second mowing. Do not apply to spring-seeded turf or newly set sod until following year. Do not graze or feed livestock forage cut from areas treated with Barricade. Do not apply through any type of irrigation system. Refer to label for use directions, restrictions, and precautions.

Tank Mixes: May be tank mixed with other registered turf herbicides in states where product and application site are registered.

Signal Word/Toxicity Class: Caution.
REI: 12 hr. unless soil injected or soil incorporated.

BASAGRAN

Provides postemergence control of yellow nutsedge and annual sedges. Does not control grasses.

Basagran T/O (bentazon) *(BASF)*
Rate: 1 lb. ai/A
     2 pt./A
Time: Apply when weeds are actively growing. For yellow nutsedge, second application 10-14 days later may be needed.

Weeds: Broadleaf weeds:

common groundsel	dayflower	wild mustard
common purslane		

Sedges:

annual sedge	yellow nutsedge

Remarks: Established bahiagrass, bentgrass, bermudagrass, bluegrass, centipedegrass, fescue, ryegrass, St. Augustinegrass, and zoysiagrass. Do not apply to golf course greens or collars or to any newly seeded or newly sprigged turf until seedlings or sprigs are well established. Do not apply to lakes, ponds, streams, or wetlands. Refer to label for specific directions and restrictions.

Tank Mixes: Atrazine, 2,4-D, 2,4-DP, Image, MCPP, MSMA, Prompt, Turflon, Vantage.

Signal Word/Toxicity Class: Caution/III.

BENSULIDE

Effectively controls crabgrass.

Bensumec 4LF *(PBI/Gordon)*
◆ **Pre-San 7G or 12.5G** *(PBI/Gordon)*
Rate: Crabgrass:
     5.6-7.3 fl. oz. 4LF/1000 sq. ft.
     2.4-3.2 lb. 7G/1000 sq. ft.
     1.8 lb. 12.5G/1000 sq. ft.
     Annual bluegrass & other annual weeds:
     9.4 fl. oz. 4LF/1000 sq. ft.
     4.1 lb. 7G/1000 sq. ft.
     2.3 lb. 12.5G/1000 sq. ft.
Time: Apply before weeds emerge from soil. Sequential or repeated applications may be required.

Weeds: Broadleaf weeds:

deadnettle	lambsquarters	shepherdspurse
henbit	redroot pigweed	

Grasses:

annual bluegrass	foxtail	large crabgrass
barnyardgrass	goosegrass	smooth crabgrass
fall panicum	hairy crabgrass	

Remarks: Apply only to well-established grass lawns. Do not reseed within 120 days after application. Irrigate immediately following application. Refer to label for use directions, restrictions, and precautions.

Signal Word/Toxicity Class: Warning/II—Pre-San; Caution/III—Bensumec.

ProTurf Weedgrass Preventer *(Scotts)*
Rate: 37 lb./11,000 sq. ft.
Time: Apply in fall, winter, or spring before germination. For annual bluegrass, apply in late summer or early fall before germination.

Weeds: Grasses:

annual bluegrass	barnyardgrass	green foxtail
(*Poa annua*)	crabgrass	yellow foxtail

Remarks: Do not use on putting greens composed of about 50% or more of *Poa annua*. Refer to label for use directions and precautions.

Signal Word/Toxicity Class: Caution.

Bensumec — see bensulide

Broadrange — see 2,4-D Combinations

Broclean — see bromoxynil

Bromox — see bromoxynil

BROMOXYNIL

Contact broadleaf control herbicide that can be used on seedling grasses and newly sprigged zoysiagrass.

◆ **Broclean 2EC** *(Platte)*
◆ **Bromox 2EC** *(MIcro Flo)*
Buctril (2EC), Buctril 4EC *(Rhone-Poulenc)*
Moxy 2EC *(Terra)*
Rate: 0.25-0.5 lb. ai/A
     1-2 pt. 2EC/A
     0.5-1 pt. 4EC/A
Time: Postemergence. Apply before boot stage.

Weeds: Broadleaf weeds:

buffalobur	knawel	Russian thistle
burcucumber	knotweed	spiny pigweed
common groundsel	kochia	tall morningglory
common ragweed	London rocket	tall waterhemp
corn chamomile	mayweed	tumble mustard
corn gromwell	prostrate knotweed	velvetleaf
cowcockle	plantain	Venice mallow
dandelion	puncturevine	wild mustard
giant ragweed	red sorrel	wild radish
hemp sesbania	redroot pigweed	yellow starthistle
ivyleaf morningglory		

Remarks: Established: bentgrass, bermudagrass, fescues, Kentucky bluegrass, ryegrass, St. Augustine, and zoysiagrass. Seedling grasses: Delta, Merion, Park or common Kentucky bluegrass, Pennlawn, Chewings, Illahee or Alta fescues, orchardgrass, Highland, Seaside or Astoria bentgrass, perennial ryegrass, bahiagrass, and zoysiagrass. Not for residential use. Do not allow livestock to graze or feed in treated areas.

Signal Word/Toxicity Class: Warning/II.

Brushmaster — see 2,4-D Combinations

Buctril — see bromoxynil

Bueno 6 — see MSMA

◆-new product • PP-preplant • PPI-preplant incorporated • PRE-preemergence • POST-postemergence • SEQ-sequential • ae-acid equivalent • ai-active ingredient • DF-dry flowable E/EC-emulsifiable concentrate • F/FL-flowable • DG/G/WG-dispersable granule • L/LC-liquid • SP/WSP-soluble packet • W/WP-wettable powder • WSB-water soluble bag

CHIPCO RONSTAR

Effective control of most annual grass weeds.

Chipco Ronstar G (oxadiazon) *(Rhone-Poulenc)*
Rate: 2-4 lb. ai/A
100-200 lb. G/A
Time: Preemergence to weeds.
Weeds: Broadleaf weeds:

Florida pusley	pigweed	stinging nettle
oxalis		

Grasses:

annual bluegrass	crabgrass	goosegrass
carpetgrass	field sandbur	

Remarks: For use on established bermudagrass, buffalograss, perennial bluegrass, perennial ryegrass, St. Augustinegrass, tall fescue, zoysiagrass. Do not apply to newly seeded areas or use on putting greens or tees. Do not seed for 4 months after application.

Signal Word/Toxicity Class: Warning/II.

Chipco Ronstar 50WSP (oxadiazon) *(Rhone-Poulenc)*
Rate: 2-3 lb. ai/A
4-6 lb. 50WSP/A
Time: Preemergence to weeds. Apply at least 2-3 weeks prior to greenup.
Weeds: Broadleaf weeds:

Virginia buttonweed

Grasses and sedges:

annual sedge	crabgrass	goosegrass
annual bluegrass		

Remarks: For use in dormant, established bermudagrass, St. Augustinegrass, zoysiagrass. Do not apply to newly seeded areas. Do not seed for 4 months after application or use on putting greens or tees.
State Restrictions: Do not use on St. Augustinegrass or zoysiagrass in California.

Signal Word/Toxicity Class: Warning/II.

Cleanout — see 2,4-D Combinations

CONFRONT (Premix)

Broad spectrum nonphenoxy herbicide for control of many broadleaf weeds. Repeat if necessary for wild violet and creeping woodsorrel control.

Confront (2.25 lb./gal. triclopyr & 0.75 lb./gal. clopyralid) *(Dow AgroSciences)*
Rate: 0.37-0.55 fl. oz./1000 sq. ft.
Time: Apply to actively growing weeds.
Weeds: Broadleaf weeds:

black medic	false dandelion	red clover
common chickweed	hawkweed	roundleaf mallow
common cocklebur	henbit	sheep sorrel
common vetch	hop clover	spotted catsear
creeping beggarweed	matchweed	spurweed
dwarf beggarweed	mouseear chickweed	white clover

Remarks: For use on cool-season grasses such as Kentucky bluegrass, ryegrass, turfgrass, and fescues (chewing, red, sheep and tall). Do not use on golf course putting greens or tees. Do not apply to exposed roots of shallow rooted trees and shrubs. Do not apply directly to or permit contact with cotton, grapes, tobacco, vegetable crops, flowers, fruit or ornamental trees, or desirable broadleaf weeds. Do not reseed for 3 weeks after application. Do not use grass clippings from treated turf for mulch. Newly seeded turf should be mowed 2-3 times before being treated. Do not water for 6 hrs. after application.

Signal Word/Toxicity Class: Danger/I.

COOL POWER (Premix)

■ **POST**

Cool Power (3.0 lb./gal. MCPA & 0.3 lb./gal. triclopyr & 0.3 lb./gal. dicamba) *(Riverdale)*
Rate: 1.125-1.575 lb. ae/A
2.5-3.5 pt./A (in 20-240 gal. water)
Time: Postemergence. Do not apply when temperature exceeds 85°F.

Weeds: Broadleaf weeds including:

chickweed	oxalis	spurge
dandelion	plantain	

Remarks: For use on lawns, golf courses (except greens), parks, and cemeteries. Do not use on dichondra, hybrids of Bermuda and St. Augustine, or lawns or turf where desirable clovers are present. Do not use on bahia, bent, bermuda, centipede, St. Augustine, or zoysia grasses unless turf injury can be tolerated. Do not apply immediately before rainfall, water within 24 hr. after application, mow for 1-2 days before or after application, or reseed for 3-4 weeks after application. Do not apply through any type of irrigation system. Refer to label for restrictions and precautions.

Signal Word/Toxicity Class: Caution.

Corral — see pendimethalin

Credit — see glyphosate

2,4-D - PHENOXY HERBICIDES

2,4-D and 2,4-D-type compounds selectively control broadleaf weeds with little or no control of grasses. Established cool-season turfgrasses, bermudagrass, and zoysiagrass have good tolerance for 2,4-D. Centipedegrass and St. Augustinegrass are prone to injury from 2,4-D. Ester formulations are most volatile and amines least volatile.

Annual and perennial broadleaf weeds controlled by 2,4-D include:

beggarticks	dogbane	plantain
bindweed	goldenrod	pokeweed
bitterweed	ground ivy	povertyweed
broomweed	healall	puncturevine
bull thistle	hemp	purslane
burdock	hoary cress	ragweed
carpetweed	ironweed	rush
chickweed	jimsonweed	Russian thistle
chicory	lambsquarters	shepherdspurse
cocklebur	locoweed	sowthistle
coffeeweed	mallow	stinkweed
common	marshelder	sumac
eveningprimrose	mexicanweed	sunflower
creeping jenny	morningglory	velvetleaf
croton	musk thistle	Virginia creeper
curly indigo	mustard	wild lettuce
dandelion	pennywort	wild parsnips
dock	pigweed	wild radish

Albaugh Amine 4 (2,4-D amine) *(Albaugh)*
Esteron 99C (2,4-D LV ester) *(Rhone-Poulenc)*
Formula 40 (2,4-D mixed amine) *(Rhone-Poulenc)*
Hi-Dep (2,4-D mixed amine) *(PBI/Gordon)*
Riverdale 6 Amine (2,4-D amine) *(Riverdale)*
Weedar 64 (4) (2,4-D amine) *(Nufarm)*
Weedar IVM 44 (4) (2,4-D amine) *(Nufarm)*
Weedone 638 (2,4-D ester + acid) *(Nufarm)*
Weedone LV4 (2,4-D solventless ester *(Nufarm)*
Wilbur-Ellis Amine 4 (2,4-D amine) *(Wilbur-Ellis)*
Rate: 1-2 lb. ae/A
2-4 pt. 4/A
1.3-4.5 pt. 6/A
2.5-5 pt. 638/A
Time: Apply when weeds are young and actively growing. Perennial weeds should be near bud stage but not flowering at application.
Remarks: For use on lawns, golf courses, cemeteries, and parks. Do not use on susceptible southern grasses such as St. Augustine. May cause injury to bentgrass, clover, legumes, and dichondra. Do not apply to newly seeded areas until grass is well established.
State Restrictions: Wilbur-Ellis not registered in California.

Signal Word/Toxicity Class: Danger/I (amine); Caution/III (ester).

Albaugh LV4 or LV6 Ester (2,4-D ester) *(Albaugh)*
Solve 2,4-D (2,4-D LV ester) *(Albaugh)*
Rate: 0.5-1.5 lb. ae/A
1-3 pt. 4/A
0.6-2 pt. 6/A
Time: Treat when weeds are young and growing well.

8

Turf, Ornamentals & Woody Plants

Remarks: Established stands of perennial grasses. Do not use on creeping grasses such as bent except for spot treating. Newly seeded areas should not be treated.

– – – – – – – – – – – – – – – – –

Signal Word/Toxicity Class: Caution/III.

◆ Barrage or Barrage HF (EC) (2,4-D ester) *(Helena)*
Rate: 13-19 fl. oz./A
Time: Apply when small weeds are emerged and actively growing.
Remarks: For use on lawns, golf courses, parks and cemeteries. Do not use on centipede, carpetgrass, St. Augustine, bentgrass, dichondra or desirable clovers. Do not mow 1-2 days before or after treatment, or water within one hour after application. Maximum 2 applications per year.

– – – – – – – – – – – – – – – – –

Signal Word/Toxicity Class: Caution/III.

◆ Clean Crop Low Vol 4 or Low Vol 6 (2,4-D ester) *(Platte)*
Rate: 1-2 lb. ae/A
2-4 pt. 4/A
1.33-2.66 pt. 6/A
Time: Apply when weeds are young and growing well.
Remarks: Lawns, golf courses, cemeteries, and parks. Do not use on creeping grasses such as bent and St. Augustine except for spot treating. Do not apply to newly seeded areas until grass is well established. Do not make more than 2 applications per year.

– – – – – – – – – – – – – – – – –

Signal Word/Toxicity Class: Caution/III.

Dri-Clean (2,4-D amine) *(Riverdale)*
Solution (WS) (2,4-D amine) *(Riverdale)*
Rate: 5 packets, 9 oz. each/1.13 A (per application per site)
1 WS packet/1.13 A in 15-50 gal. water
Time: Apply when weeds are young and actively growing. With spring application, reseed in fall; with fall application, reseed in spring.
Remarks: Lawns, golf courses, lawns, parks, and cemeteries. Do not use on dichondra or other herbaceous ground covers, creeping grasses such as bent (except for spot treatment), or on freshly seeded turf until grass is well established. Reseeding of lawns should be delayed following treatment. Do not apply when temperature exceeds 90°F. Legumes are usually damaged or killed.

– – – – – – – – – – – – – – – – –

Signal Word/Toxicity Class: Danger/I.

◆ Opti-Amine or Weed Rhap A-4D (2,4-D amine) *(Helena)*
Weed Rhap LV-6D (2,4-D ester) *(Helena)*
Rate: 0.5-2 lb. ae/A
1-4 pt. 4/A
0.5-1.5 lb. ae/A
0.6-2 pt. 6/A
Time: Perennial weeds should be near bud stage but not flowering at application.
Remarks: Established stands of perennial grasses. Do not use on creeping grasses such as bent except for spot treating. Newly seeded areas should not be treated. Maximum 2 applications per year.

– – – – – – – – – – – – – – – – –

Signal Word/Toxicity Class: Danger/I (amine); Caution/III (ester).

◆ Riverdale 2,4-D Granules (2,4-D ester) *(Riverdale)*
Rate: 2.1 lb. ae/A
10.5 lb./A
Time: Apply in early spring when shoots are young and actively growing. Repeat application after one month to control skipped spots.
Remarks: Do not use on bentgrass, carpetgrass, dichondra, and St. Augustine. Do not use on newly plugged or seeded turf. Repeat application after one month to control skipped spots.

– – – – – – – – – – – – – – – – –

Signal Word/Toxicity Class: Caution.

Riverdale L.V. 4 or L.V. 6 (2,4-D ester) *(Riverdale)*
Wilbur-Ellis Lo Vol-4 or Lo Vol-6 (2,4-D ester) *(Wilbur-Ellis)*
Rate: 1-3 lb. ae/A
2-4 pt. 4/A (Wilbur-Ellis)
2-6 pt. 4/A (Riverdale)
1.3-4.5 pt. 6/A
Time: Treat when weeds are young and growing well.
Remarks: Lawns, golf courses (except greens), cemeteries, and parks. Do not use on dichondra or other broadleaf herbaceous ground covers. Do not use on creeping grasses such as bent and St. Augustine except for spot treating. Do not apply to newly seeded areas until grass is well established.
State Restrictions: Wilbur-Ellis not registered in California.

– – – – – – – – – – – – – – – – –

Signal Word/Toxicity Class: Caution/III.

Riverside 2,4-D Amine 4 (2,4-D amine) *(Terra)*
Rate: 1-1.5 lb. ae/A
2-3 pt./A
Time: Fall or spring best time to treat.
Remarks: May cause injury to bentgrass, buffalo, carpetgrass, dichondra, and St. Augustine.

– – – – – – – – – – – – – – – – –

Signal Word/Toxicity Class: Danger/I.

Riverside 2,4-D LV4 or LV6 (2,4-D LV ester) *(Terra)*
Rate: 2 lb. ae/A
4 pt. 4/A
2.6 pt. 6/A
Time: Apply when weeds are young and growing well.
Remarks: Lawns, golf courses (except greens), cemeteries, parks. Do not use on dichondra or other broadleaf herbaceous ground covers. Do not use on creeping grasses such as bent and St. Augustine except for spot treating. Do not apply to newly seeded areas until grass is well established.

– – – – – – – – – – – – – – – – –

Signal Word/Toxicity Class: Danger/I.

◆ Saber (2,4-D amine) *(Platte)*
Rate: 0.5-2 lb. ae/A
1-4 pt./A
Time: Apply when weeds are young and actively growing.
Remarks: Lawns, golf courses, cemeteries, and parks. For use on cool season grasses such as tall fescue and bluegrass. Do not use on centipede, carpetgrass, St. Augustine, bentgrass, dichondra or desirable clovers. Do not apply to newly seeded areas until grass is well established and has been mowed several times. Do not make more than 2 applications per year.

– – – – – – – – – – – – – – – – –

Signal Word/Toxicity Class: Danger/I.

Salvo (2,4-D LV ester) *(Platte)*
Rate: 0.94 lb. ae/A
1.5 pt./A
Time: Spray 3-5 days after mowing.
Remarks: Retreatment of perennial weed areas may be necessary. Protect ornamentals from spray drift. May cause injury to bentgrass, carpetgrass, dichondra, St. Augustine, and clovers.

– – – – – – – – – – – – – – – – –

Signal Word/Toxicity Class: Caution/III.

Savage (WSB) (2,4-D amine) *(Platte)*
Rate: 0.95-1.9 lb. ae/A
1-2 lb. WSB/A
Time: Apply when weeds are young and actively growing.
Remarks: Golf courses, cemeteries, parks, and lawns. Do not apply to newly seeded areas until grass is well established. Do not apply more than 2 broadcast applications per year. Refer to label for further use directions.

– – – – – – – – – – – – – – – – –

Signal Word/Toxicity Class: Danger/I.

2,4-D COMBINATIONS

Combinations of 2,4-D with MCPP, 2,4-DP, or dicamba generally control a wider range of weed species than each herbicide applied alone.

3 Plus 3 (2.82 lb./gal. 2,4-D & 2.82 lb./gal. MCPP) *(Riverdale)*
2D + 2 MCPP (1.9 lb./gal. 2,4-D & 1.8 lb./gal. MCPP) *(Riverdale)*
Rate: 2-3 qt. 2D + 2 MCPP/A
1.66-2 qt. 3 Plus 3/A
Time: Postemergence. Apply spring or fall when weeds are actively growing.
Weeds: Broadleaf weeds:

buckhorn	lambsquarters	red clover
clover	mallow	red sorrel
common chickweed	morningglory	speedwell
curly dock	mouseear chickweed	stitchwort
dandelion	pigweed	white clover
English daisy	plantain	wild garlic
ground ivy	purslane	wild onion
knotweed	ragweed	yarrow

Remarks: For use on turf grasses such as bluegrasses, fescues, bermudagrass, and ryegrass. Do not apply when turf is suffering from drought conditions or during very hot weather. Do not mow for several days before or after application. Refer to label.

– – – – – – – – – – – – – – – – –

Signal Word/Toxicity Class: Danger/I (2D + 2); Caution (3 Plus 3).

◆-new product • PP-preplant • PPI-preplant incorporated • PRE-preemergence • POST-postemergence • SEQ-sequential • ae-acid equivalent • ai-active ingredient • DF-dry flowable
E/EC-emulsifiable concentrate • F/FL-flowable • DG/G/WG-dispersable granule • L/LC-liquid • SP/WSP-soluble packet • W/WP-wettable powder • WSB-water soluble bag

Broadrange (2,4-D & 2,4-DP) *(Wilbur-Ellis)*
◆ **Patron 170 (2,4-D & 2,4-DP)** *(Riverdale)*
Riverdale Turf D + DP (2,4-D & 2,4-DP) *(Riverdale)*
Rate: 1 pt. product/10,000 sq. ft.
Time: Apply when weeds are growing actively. Clovers, dandelion, plantain, and woodsorrel are best treated in the fall or in the spring before flower heads develop. Winter weeds such as chickweed and henbit should be treated in early spring; summer weeds such as knotweed, oxalis, and spurge should be sprayed when small.

Weeds:

chickweed	henbit	plantain
clover	knotweed	spurge
dandelion	oxalis	woodsorrel

Remarks: Golf courses, athletic fields, parks, etc. May injure bentgrass, carpetgrass, centipedegrass, St. Augustinegrass, and newly seeded lawns. Do not use on dichondra, lippia, bentgrass greens and tees, or where desirable clovers are present.
State Restrictions: Wilbur-Ellis not registered in California.

- - - - - - - - - - - - - - -

Signal Word/Toxicity Class: Danger/I (amine); Caution (ester).

Brushmaster (2.3S) (2,4-D & 2,4-DP & dicamba) *(PBI/Gordon)*
Cleanout (1.1S) (2,4-D & 2,4-DP & dicamba) *(PBI/Gordon)*
Rate: 1.1-1.7 lb. ai/A
4-6 pt. 2.3S/A
8-12 pt. 1.1S/A
Time: Do not apply to newly seeded grasses until well established. Apply from spring or early fall when weeds have emerged and are actively growing. Do not spray when air temperature exceeds 85°F. Seed can be sown 3-4 weeks after application.

Weeds: Broadleaf weeds including:

chickweed	henbit	plantain
clover	knotweed	spurge
dandelion		

Remarks: Cool-season grasses. Not for use on bentgrass, carpetgrass, dichondra, St. Augustine, or lawns/turf where desirable clovers are present. Apply in 20-260 gal. water. Hose-end sprayers not recommended for small area applications. Do not apply through any type of irrigation system.

- - - - - - - - - - - - - - -

Signal Word/Toxicity Class: Caution.

Deuce (2,4-D & MCPP) *(Wilbur-Ellis)*
Rate: 2.3-2.8 lb. ai/A
2.5-3 qt./A
Time: Apply spring or fall when weeds are actively growing. Knotweed is controlled more easily in spring or early summer when weeds are young.

Weeds:

buckhorn	lambsquarters	red clover
clover	mallow	red sorrel
common chickweed	morningglory	speedwell
curly dock	mouseear chickweed	stitchwort
dandelion	pigweed	white clover
English daisy	plantain	wild garlic
ground ivy	purslane	wild onion
knotweed	ragweed	yarrow

Remarks: May be used on Bermudagrass, Kentucky bluegrass, Merion, fescues, and rye grasses. Refer to label for directions and precautions.
State Restrictions: Not registered in California.

- - - - - - - - - - - - - - -

Signal Word/Toxicity Class: Danger/I.

Dissolve (WS) (2,4-D & 2,4-DP & MCPP) *(Riverdale)*
PAR-3 (2,4-D & 2,4-DP & MCPP) *(Riverdale)*
Triamine (2,4-D & 2,4-DP & MCPP) *(Riverdale)*
Tri-Ester (2,4-D & 2,4-DP & MCPP) *(Riverdale)*
Rate: Cool-season grasses (bluegrass, fescue, rye):
2.5 lb. WS packet/1-1.33 A
1.5-2 lb. ae/A
3-4 pt. amine/A
1.2-1.9 lb. ae/A
2-3 pt. ester/A
Warm-season grasses (bahia, common Bermuda, centipede, St. Augustine, zoysia):
2.5 lb. WS packet/1.33-2 A
1-1.5 lb. ae/A
2-3 pt. amine/A
0.9-1.2 lb. ae/A
1.5-2 pt. ester/A
Closely mowed bentgrass (except greens & tees):
2.5 lb. WS packet/1.33-2 A
1 oz./1500 sq. ft.

Time: Apply spring or early fall when weeds are actively growing. For bentgrass, apply in May or mid-Aug. through Sept. when weeds are actively growing.
Remarks: Apply to newly seeded lawns or turf after grasses are well established. Some hybrid bermudagrasses are sensitive to this product; consult local extension service weed control specialist.

- - - - - - - - - - - - - - -

Signal Word/Toxicity Class: Danger/I (amine); Caution/III (ester).

Threesome (C) (2,4-D & MCPP & dicamba) *(Riverdale)*
Triplet or Tri-Plex (L, WS) (2,4-D & MCPP & dicamba) *(Riverdale)*
Rate: Cool-season grasses (bluegrass, fescue, rye):
1.36-2 lb. ai/A
2.5-3.66 pt. C/A
1.5-2 lb. ae/A
3-4 pt. L/A
or 2.5 lb. WS packet/0.9-1.25 A
Warm-season grasses (bahia, common Bermuda, centipede, St. Augustine, zoysia):
0.9-1.23 lb. ai/A
1.66-2.25 pt. C/A
1-1.25 lb. ae/A
2-2.5 pt. L/A
or 2.5 lb. WS packet/1.5-1.9 A
Closely mowed bentgrass (except greens & tees):
1 oz. L/1500 sq. ft.
0.75 oz. C, WS/1500 sq. ft.
Time: For warm-season grasses, exercise care when applying from dormancy to greenup and from greenup to dormancy. Do not apply to newly seeded grasses until well established.
Remarks: Lawns, turf, golf courses (fairways, tees, roughs), parks, cemeteries. Not for use on turf being grown for sale, sod, or commercial seed production. Do not spray on carpetgrass, dichondra, or on lawns/turf where desirable clovers are present. Some hybrid bermudagrasses are sensitive to this product; consult extension service weed control specialist.
State Restrictions: Threesome not registered in California.

- - - - - - - - - - - - - - -

Signal Word/Toxicity Class: Danger/I.

Deuce — see 2,4-D Combinations

DICAMBA

Avoid application over root zone of desirable trees and shrubs.

Banvel (WS) (DMA salt of dicamba) *(BASF)*
◆ **Sterling (WS) (DMA salt of dicamba)** *(Terra)*
Rate: 0.25-1 lb. ai/A
0.5-2 pt. WS/A
Time: Apply when weeds are emerged and actively growing.
Weeds: Annual, biennial, and perennial broadleaf weeds:

carpetweed	field bindweed	prostrate spurge
clover	henbit	purslane
common chickweed	knotweed	red sorrel
curly dock	mouseear chickweed	sweetclover
English daisy	pepperweed	spurry

Remarks: Repeat as needed, but do not exceed 2 pt./A per growing season. In areas where roots of sensitive plants extend, do not apply more than 0.25 pt./A on coarse-textured soils or 0.5 pt./A in fine-textured soils. Do not repeat application in these areas for 30 days. Rates greater than 1 pt./A may cause noticeable stunting or discoloration of sensitive grasses such as bentgrass, buffalograss, carpetgrass, and St. Augustinegrass. Refer to label for precautions and restrictions.
Tank Mixes: Bromoxynil, 2,4-D, MCPA, MCPP.

- - - - - - - - - - - - - - -

Signal Word/Toxicity Class: Warning/II.

ProTurf K-O-G Weed Control (dicamba) *(Scotts)*
Rate: 35.5 lb./5500 sq. ft.
Weeds: Broadleaf weeds:

Canada thistle	ground ivy	wild onion
cudweed	horseweed	yarrow
curly dock	wild garlic	

Rate: 35.5 lb./11,000 sq. ft.
Weeds: Broadleaf weeds:

black medic	common chickweed	mouseear chickweed
clover (22,000 sq. ft.)	knotweed	sheep sorrel

Rate: 35.5 lb./44,000 sq. ft.
Weeds: Bentgrass putting greens:

chickweed	clover

NOTICE The information on these pages is for preliminary planning — not a guide for use. Be sure to follow the manufacturer's directions, notwithstanding information contained here. | For personal protective equipment and EPA registration numbers, please turn to page 70.

Weed Control Manual 2000 403

8

Turf, Ornamentals & Woody Plants

Time: Apply when weeds are actively growing; repeat in 3 weeks if needed. For yarrow, wild garlic, and wild onion, apply either spring or fall; repeat at 6-month intervals for a total of 2-3 applications as needed.

Remarks: Not for use on St. Augustinegrass or dichondra. Avoid application to garden plants, flowers, and rootzone areas. Do not apply when ground is frozen. Refer to label for use directions and precautions.

- - - - - - - - - - - - - - - -

Signal Word/Toxicity Class: Warning/II.

Vanquish (dicamba-DGA) (Novartis)
Rate: 0.25-1 lb. ai/A
0.5-2 pt./A
Time: Apply when weeds are emerged and actively growing.
Weeds: Annual, biennial, and perennial broadleaf weeds found in turf.
Remarks: Golf courses (fairways, aprons, tees, rough), parks, recreational areas. Do not treat irrigation ditches, water used for crop irrigation or domestic uses, or apply through any type of irrigation system.
Tank Mixes: Bromoxynil, Confront, 2,4-D, MCPA, MCPP. Refer to labels for use directions and precautions.

- - - - - - - - - - - - - - - -

Signal Word/Toxicity Class: Caution.

DIMENSION

Selective herbicide for preemergence control of crabgrass, and other susceptible annual broadleaf weeds and grasses and postemergence control of crabgrass in established lawns and ornamental turf.

Dimension (dithiopyr) (Rohm and Haas)
Rate: 0.25-0.5 lb. ai/A
2-4 pt./A
Time: Preemergence, postemergence. May be applied as a single application, split application, or as a sequential application for crabgrass control in the spring, summer, or fall. Do not apply in the fall before covering greens for winter protection.

Weeds: Broadleaf weeds:

bittercress	corn speedwell	pineappleweed
buttercup oxalis	creeping woodsorrel	prostrate spurge
Carolina geranium	henbit	shepherdspurse
chickweed	lespedeza	spotted spurge
common purslane	parsley-piert	yellow woodsorrel

Grasses:

annual bluegrass	crowfootgrass	kikuyugrass
barnyardgrass	goosegrass	smutgrass
crabgrass	green foxtail	yellow foxtail

Remarks: Cool-season grasses: creeping bentgrass, Kentucky bluegrass, fine fescue, perennial ryegrass, tall fescue. Warm-season grasses: bahiagrass bermudagrass, buffalograss, carpetgrass, centipedegrass, kikuyugrass, St. Augustinegrass, zoysiagrass. Use on certain varieties of creeping bentgrass and fine fescue may result in undesirable turf injury. Do not apply to Colonial bentgrass. Do not apply to desirable flowers, vegetables, shrubs, trees, or pastures. Do not apply through any type of irrigation system.

- - - - - - - - - - - - - - - -

Signal Word/Toxicity Class: Warning/II.
REI: 12 hr.

DIQUAT DIBROMIDE

◆ Reward or Reward LS (ZENECA)
Rate: 0.25-0.5 lb. ai/A
1-2 pt./A
Time: For turf renovation, apply to dry turf only. For little barley, apply prior to mid-boot stage. For bermudagrass, zoysiagrass, apply dormant.

Weeds: Broadleaf weeds and grasses:

annual bluegrass	henbit	rescuegrass
buttercup	little barley	sixweeks fescue
Carolina geranium		

Remarks: Lawns, parks, and golf courses. Add nonionic surfactant. Avoid spray contact with desirable foliage. Do not apply through any type of irrigation system. Do not graze livestock on treated turf or feed treated thatch to livestock. Refer to label for directions and restrictions.
Tank Mixes: May be tank mixed with preemergent herbicides.

- - - - - - - - - - - - - - - -

Signal Word/Toxicity Class: Warning/II.
REI: 24 hr.

Dissolve — see 2,4-D Combinations

Dri-Clean — see 2,4-D

DSMA

◆ **Clean Crop DSMA Plus (3.6L) (+ surfactant)** *(Platte)*
Drexel DSMA Liquid (3.6L) or Slurry (WS) (+ surfactant) *(Drexel)*
◆ **Dry DSMA 63SG** *(Luxembourg-Pamol)*
DSMA 4 LB (4L) or Liquid DSMA (3.6L) (+ surfactant) *(Helena)*
Rate: 4-5 oz. 63SG/1000 sq. ft.
2 fl. oz. WS/1000 sq. ft.
3 fl. oz. 4L, Helena 3.6L/1000 sq. ft.
4 fl. oz. Drexel 3.6L/1000 sq. ft.
Time: Postemergence. Apply during warm weather. Repeat applications, 10-14 days apart, may be needed for good control.
Weeds: Broadleaf weeds, grasses and sedges including:

bahiagrass	dallisgrass	sandbur
chickweed	nutsedge	woodsorrel
crabgrass		

Remarks: Do not add surfactant except for Helena 4L and 63SG. Do not use on centipedegrass or St. Augustinegrass. Bent and fescue grasses may be temporarily discolored. Mow lawns to 1-1½" high before treatment. Do not apply with hose-end applicators.

- - - - - - - - - - - - - - - -

Signal Word/Toxicity Class: Caution/III.

Methar 30 (DSMA) (Cleary)
Rate: 1 pt./3000 sq. ft.
Weeds: Grasses:
crabgrass

Rate: 2 pt./3000 sq. ft.
Weeds: Grasses:
dallisgrass

Rate: Bentgrass and fescue turf:
1 pt./5000 sq. ft.
Weeds: Grasses:

crabgrass	dallisgrass

Time: Postemergence. 2-3 applications are necessary at 7-day intervals.
Remarks: Bermudagrass, Kentucky bluegrass, fescue, Merion bluegrass, Zoysiagrass. Do not use on carpetgrass, centipedegrass, dichondra, or St. Augustinegrass.

- - - - - - - - - - - - - - - -

Signal Word/Toxicity Class: Caution/III.

Esteron 99C — see 2,4-D

FENOXAPROP-P-ETHYL

Provides postemergence control of annual grass weeds and suppresses common bermudagrass. Will not control broadleaf weeds, nutsedges, or rushes.

Acclaim Extra (0.57E) (AgrEvo USA)
Rate: Annual grasses:
3.5-39 fl. oz. 0.57E/A
Perennial grasses:
20 fl. oz. 0.57E/A
Time: Apply when annual grassy weeds are in the 1-leaf to 5-tiller stage. Repeat at 28- to 35-day intervals to suppress perennial grasses.
Weeds: Annual grasses:

barnyardgrass	johnsongrass	silver crabgrass
foxtail	(seedling)	smooth crabgrass
goosegrass	panicum	sprangletop
hairy crabgrass	sandbur	

Perennial grasses (suppression):

common bermudagrass	johnsongrass (rhizome)

Remarks: Established annual bluegrass, creeping bentgrass (special recommendations for bentgrass), fescues (fine, tall), Kentucky bluegrass, perennial ryegrass, zoysiagrass. Do not apply to bentgrass putting greens. Do not mow treated area for at least 24 hr. after application.
Tank Mixes: May be tank mixed with other labeled pesticides or fertilizers.

- - - - - - - - - - - - - - - -

Signal Word/Toxicity Class: Caution/III.

◆-new product • PP-preplant • PPI-preplant incorporated • PRE-preemergence • POST-postemergence • SEQ-sequential • ae-acid equivalent • ai-active ingredient • DF-dry flowable E/EC-emulsifiable concentrate • F/FL-flowable • DG/G/WG-dispersable granule • L/LC-liquid • SP/WSP-soluble packet • W/WP-wettable powder • WSB-water soluble bag

FLUAZIFOP-P-BUTYL

◆ **Fusilade II** *(ZENECA)*
Rate: 3-6 oz. II/A
Time: For tall fescue, apply early spring (Apr./May); repeat in fall (Sept./Oct.). For zoysia, apply late spring (around June 1); repeat at 28- to 30-day intervals.
Weeds: Grasses:

tall fescue zoysia

Remarks: Rate varies by grass species. Add nonionic surfactant. Do not apply through any type of irrigation system. Do not graze treated areas. Refer to label for specific directions, restrictions, and precautions.
State Restrictions: Refer to label for geographical regions.

- - - - - - - - - - - - - -

Signal Word/Toxicity Class: Caution.
REI: 12 hr.

Formula 40 — see 2,4-D

Fusilade — see fluazifop-P-butyl

GALLERY

Gallery 75DF (isoxaben) *(Dow AgroSciences)*
Rate: 0.5-1 lb. ai/A
0.66-1.33 lb. 75DF/A
Time: Apply in late summer to early fall, or in early spring, prior to germination of target weeds.
Weeds: Broadleaf weeds:

annual sowthistle	dogfennel	redstem filaree
bittercress	green tansymustard	redmaids
black mustard	hairy galinsoga	rockpurslane
black nightshade	henbit	shepherdspurse
blackleaved fleabane	horseweed	sibara
bracted plantain	ladysthumb	slender plantain
buckhorn plantain	lambsquarters	southern
Carolina geranium	London rocket	brassbuttons
coast fiddleneck	marestail	spotted spurge
common chickweed	mouseear chickweed	thymeleaf speedwell
common groundsel	pennywort	velvetleaf
common purslane	pigweed	white clover
common ragweed	pineappleweed	wild celery
common sowthistle	prickly lettuce	wild mustard
creeping woodsorrel	prostrate knotweed	whitestem filaree
cudweed	prostrate spurge	yellow woodsorrel
dandelion		

Remarks: Established warm- and cool-season turf grasses. Do not use on golf course putting greens or grass grown for seed. Do not apply through any type of irrigation system.
Tank Mixes: May be tank mixed with other herbicides registered for use on established turfgrass; refer to labels.

- - - - - - - - - - - - - -

Signal Word/Toxicity Class: Caution/III.
REI: 12 hr.

Glyfos or Glyfos X-tra — see glyphosate

GLYPHOSATE

Broad spectrum, nonselective postemergence herbicide.

◆ **Credit (4WS)** *(Nufarm)*
◆ **Glyfos or Glyfos X-tra (4WS)** *(Cheminova)*
Rattler (4WS) *(Helena)*
Rate: Annual weeds:
0.38-1.5 lb. ai/A
0.75-3 pt. 4WS/A
Perennial weeds:
0.5-5 lb. ai/A
1-10 pt. 4WS/A
Time: Preplant or renovation. Apply when weeds are actively growing and at proper growth stage.
Weeds: Annual and perennial weeds and grasses.
Remarks: Do not disturb soil or underground plant parts prior to treatment. Tillage or renovation techniques should be delayed for at least 7 days after application. Where vegetation is growing under mowed turfgrass management, omit at least one regular mowing before treatment.

State Restrictions: Glyfos not registered for use in California. Glyfos X-tra not registered for use in mistblowers in California or Arizona.

- - - - - - - - - - - - - -

Signal Word/Toxicity Class: Warning/II.
REI: 12 hr.

Roundup PRO (4WS) *(Monsanto)*
Rate: Dormant:
0.25-2 lb. ai/A
0.5-4 pt. 4WS/A
Actively growing:
0.5 lb. ai/A
1 pt. 4WS/A
Time: For dormant application, apply prior to spring greenup.
Weeds: Winter annual weeds including:

tall fescue

Remarks: Bermudagrass. Do not apply more than 1 pt./A in highly maintained areas. For dormant turfgrass, rate greater than 1 pt./A may result in injury or delayed greenup in highly maintained areas, such as golf courses and lawns.

- - - - - - - - - - - - - -

Signal Word/Toxicity Class: Caution/III.

HALOSULFURON-METHYL

Manage *(Monsanto)*
Rate: 0.031-0.063 lb. ai/A
0.66-1.33 oz./A
Time: Postemergence. Apply after nutsedge has reached 3-8 leaf stage. A sequential treatment may be required 6-10 weeks after initial treatment.
Weeds: Grasses and sedges:

green kyllinga	purple nutsedge	yellow nutsedge

Remarks: Do not mow turf for 2 days before or after application. Do not apply to golf course putting greens or through any type of irrigation system. Do not use clippings from treated turf for mulching around vegetables or ornamentals.

- - - - - - - - - - - - - -

Signal Word/Toxicity Class: Caution/III.

Hi-Dep — see 2,4-D

HORSEPOWER (Premix)

Horsepower (3.80 lb./gal. MCPA & 0.38 lb./gal. triclopyr & 0.38 lb./gal. dicamba) *(Riverdale)*
Rate: 1.14-1.70 lb. ae/A
2-3 pt./A (in 20-240 gal. water)
Time: Postemergence. Do not apply when temperature exceeds 90°F.
Weeds: Broadleaf weeds including:

black medic	cocklebur	oxalis
chickweed	dandelion	plantain
clover	knotweed	thistle

Remarks: Bahiagrass, bentgrass, bermudagrass, bluegrass, fescues, ryegrass, and zoysiagrass for lawns, golf courses, fairways, aprons, tees, roughs, parks, and cemeteries. Do not use on Bermuda and St. Augustine hybrids, dichondra, and lawns/turf where desirable clovers are present, unless turf injury can be tolerated. Do not apply immediately before rainfall or water within 24 hr. after application. Do not mow for 1-2 days before or after application or reseed for 3-4 weeks after application. Do not apply through any type of irrigation system. Refer to label for restrictions and precautions.

- - - - - - - - - - - - - -

Signal Word/Toxicity Class: Danger/I.

ILLOXAN

Provides excellent postemergence control of small, emerged goosegrass. Restricted Use Pesticide.

Illoxan (3EC) (diclofop) *(AgrEvo USA)*
Rate: 0.75-1 lb. ai/A
32.6-43.5 fl. oz. 3EC/A
Time: Apply to established bermudagrass turf (stolon 4" long).
Weeds: Grasses:

goosegrass silver crabgrass

Remarks: Do not apply through any type of irrigation system.
State Restrictions: For use on golf course turf in Alabama, Arkansas, Florida, Georgia, Louisiana, Mississippi, North Carolina, Oklahoma, South Carolina, and Texas under FIFRA Section 24 (c).

- - - - - - - - - - - - - -

Signal Word/Toxicity Class: Danger/I.

8

Turf, Ornamentals & Woody Plants

NOTICE The information on these pages is for preliminary planning — not a guide for use. Be sure to follow the manufacturer's directions, notwithstanding information contained here.

For personal protective equipment and EPA registration numbers, please turn to page 70.

IMAGE

Image 1.5 LC (imazaquin) *(American Cyanamid)*
Rate: 0.375-0.5 lb. ai/A
1-1.33 qt. 1.5 LC/A (0.75-1 fl. oz./1000 sq. ft.)
Time: Postemergence. Do not apply just prior to or during spring transition.
Weeds: Broadleaf weeds:

black medic	dovetail geranium	parsley-piert
buttercup	hairy bittercress	purple deadnettle
Carolina geranium	henbit	red sorrel
common chickweed	knawel	white clover
cutleaf	lawn burweed	wild garlic
eveningprimrose	mouseear chickweed	wild onion

Grasses and sedges:

field sandbur	perennial ryegrass	rice flatsedge
globe sedge	(overseeded)	yellow nutsedge
green kyllinga	purple nutsedge	

Remarks: Established bermudagrass, centipedegrass, St. Augustinegrass, and zoysiagrass. Add 2 pt./100 gal. spray (0.25% v/v) nonionic surfactant. Use only on well-established nonstressed turfgrass with a dense and uniform stand. Do not apply to newly planted or sprigged lawns or use on unlabeled turfgrass species including tall fescue or mixed stands of tall fescue and bermudagrass. Do not mow St. Augustinegrass until 48 hr. after application.

Signal Word/Toxicity Class: Caution.

KERB

Provides excellent preemergence or postemergence control of annual bluegrass. Restricted Use Pesticide.

Kerb WSP (pronamide) *(Rohm and Haas)*
Rate: Preemergence:
0.5-1 lb. ai/A
1-2 lb. WSP/A
Early postemergence:
0.75-1.5 lb. ai/A
1.5-3 lb. WSP/A
Time: Preemergence, early postemergence.
Weeds: Broadleaf weeds:

chickweed	red sorrel*	shepherdspurse*
London rocket*	(seedling)	wild mustard*

Grasses:

annual bluegrass	Italian ryegrass	perennial ryegrass
downy brome	Kentucky bluegrass	quackgrass
(cheatgrass)	orchardgrass	volunteer grain
foxtail barley		

* Preemergence only

Remarks: Ornamental bermudagrass. Annual and perennial ryegrass, bentgrass, bluegrass, dichondra, and fescues are injured by pre- and postemergence application. Avoid spraying areas that drain onto bentgrass greens or that have been overseeded with cool-season grass or that will be overseeded with cool-season grasses within 90 days of treatment. Do not apply through any type of irrigation system.
Crop Rotation: Refer to label for specific times for rotation crops.

Signal word/Toxicity Class: Caution.
REI: 24 hr.

MAGMA — see MSMA

Manage — see halosulfuron-methyl

MCPA

◆ **Clean Crop MCP Amine 4** *(Platte)*
◆ **Clean Crop MCP 2 Sodium (sodium salt)** *(Platte)*
Rhonox (LV ester) (4) *(Nufarm)*
Riverdale MCPA-4 Amine, L.V. 4 Ester (4), IOE (5.2) *(Riverdale)*
Sword (5.2) *(Platte)*
Wilbur-Ellis MCPA Amine, Ester (4) or ◆ Sodium Salt *(Wilbur-Ellis)*
Rate: 0.5-1.5 lb. ae/A
1-3 pt. 4/A
2-6 pt. sodium salt/A
0.48-1.3 lb. ae/A
0.75-2 pt. 5.2/A

Time: Postemergence. Spring and fall best times to apply.
Weeds: Including:

Canada thistle	dandelion	whitetop

Remarks: Established lawns, golf courses. Do not use on creeping grasses, such as bent (except for spot spraying), or on newly seeded turf until grass is well established. Do not mow turf for 1-2 days before or after application.
State Restrictions: Wilbur-Ellis not registered in California.

Signal Word/Toxicity Class: Varies by formulation.

MCPP (MECOPROP)

◆ **Mecomec 2.5** *(PBI/Gordon)*
Rate: Established greens:
1.25 lb. ai/A
4 pt. /A
Fairways, lawns:
1.25-1.88 lb. ai/A
4-6 pt. /A
Time: Apply while weeds are actively growing. Do not apply to bentgrasses during heat of summer.
Weeds: Broadleaf weeds:

black medic	clover	plantain
chickweed	knotweed	

Remarks: Do not mow for several days before or after treatment. Do not water for 1 day following treatment. Do not allow mist, vapors, or spray to contact susceptible crops. Refer to label for further use directions.

Signal Word/Toxicity Class: Caution/III.

Mecomec 4 *(PBI/Gordon)*
Rate: Established greens:
1-1.35 lb. ai/A
2-2.75 pt./A
Fairways, lawns:
1.66-2 lb. ai/A
3.33-4 pt./A
Time: Apply on a warm day when weeds are growing vigorously.
Weeds: Broadleaf weeds:

black medic	lambsquarters	ragweed
common chickweed	morningglory	red clover
ground ivy	mouseear chickweed	white clover
knotweed	plantain	

Remarks: Not recommended for centipedegrass and St. Augustinegrass. Do not cut or mow grass 2-3 days before or after treatment. Do not water turfgrass for at least 24 hr. after application. For established greens, see label for use directions. Do not allow mist, vapors, or spray to contact susceptible crops.

Signal Word/Toxicity Class: Caution/III.

Riverdale MCPP-2 Amine *(Riverdale)*
Weedestroy MCPP-4 Amine *(Riverdale)*
Rate: Established greens:
1.25 lb. ai/A
5 pt. MCPP-2/A
2.5 pt. MCPP-4/A
Fairways, lawns:
2 lb. ai/A
8 pt. MCPP-2/A
4 pt. MCPP-4/A
Time: Apply on a warm day when weeds are growing vigorously.
Weeds: More susceptible weeds:

bindweed	dandelion	plantain
buttercup	ground ivy	ragweed
cinquefoil	lambsquarters	spotted spurge
clover	mouseear chickweed	thistle
common chickweed	pigweed	

Less susceptible weeds:

black medic	knotweed	purslane
dock	morningglory	speedwell
henbit	pennywort	yarrow

Remarks: Not recommended for centipedegrass and St. Augustinegrass. Do not cut or mow grass 2-3 days before or after treatment. Do not water turfgrass for at least 24 hr. after application. For established greens, see label for use directions. Do not allow mist, vapors, or spray to contact susceptible crops.

Signal Word/Toxicity Class: Danger/I (MCPP-4); Caution (MCPP-2).

◆-new product • PP-preplant • PPI-preplant incorporated • PRE-preemergence • POST-postemergence • SEQ-sequential • ae-acid equivalent • ai-active ingredient • DF-dry flowable
E/EC-emulsifiable concentrate • F/FL-flowable • DG/G/WG-dispersable granule • L/LC-liquid • SP/WSP-soluble packet • W/WP-wettable powder • WSB-water soluble bag

Riverdale MCPP L.V. 4 Ester *(Riverdale)*
Rate: Established greens, fine turf:
1-1.25 lb. ai/A
2-2.5 pt. L.V. 4/A
Fairways, other turf:
1.5-1.75 lb. ai/A
3-3.5 pt. L.V. 4/A
Time: Apply in spring or fall when weeds are growing actively. For knot-weed, apply in spring or early summer when weeds are young.
Weeds: Weeds controlled:

common chickweed	mouseear chickweed	stitchwort
ground ivy	red clover	white clover
knotweed		

Remarks: Not recommended for dichondra or St. Augustinegrass. Do not mow grass for 24 hr. after application. For established greens, see label for use directions. Do not allow mist, vapors, or spray to contact susceptible crops.

– – – – – – – – – – – – –

Signal Word/Toxicity Class: Caution.

Mecomec — see MCPP

Methar 30 — see DSMA

S-METOLACHLOR

Pennant MAGNUM (7.62L) *(Novartis)*
Rate: 1.2-2.5 lb. ai/A
1.3-2.6 pt. 7.62L/A
Time: Apply before weeds emerge.
Weeds: Grasses and sedges:

annual bluegrass	large crabgrass	smooth crabgrass
annual sedge	Mexican sprangletop	yellow nutsedge
bearded sprangletop		

Remarks: Golf course fairways, commercial lawns (warm-season grasses such as bermudagrass, centipedegrass, St. Augustinegrass, bahiagrass and zoysiagrass), cemeteries. Do not use on golf greens, tees, or aprons. Irrigate with $^1/_2$" water if rainfall does not occur within 7 days after treatment. Do not apply more than 4.2 pt. 7.62L/A per year or more than once every 6 weeks. Do not graze or feed turf clippings to animals.
State Restrictions: Do not use on turfgrass in New York.

– – – – – – – – – – – – –

Signal Word/Toxicity Class: Caution.

MONTAR

Montar (cacodylic acid) *(Monterey)*
Rate: 7.44 lb. ai/A
3 gal./A
Time: Spray to runoff on a warm, sunny day. Reapply 5 days later if green areas remain.
Weeds: Lawn renovation — kills existing lawn and weeds.
Remarks: Mow lawn weeds to 1" height before application. Do not use in vegetable gardens or around crops grown for food or feed. Do not contaminate irrigation or domestic water supplies. Do not apply through any type of irrigation system.

– – – – – – – – – – – – –

Signal Word/Toxicity Class: Caution/III.

Moxy — see bromoxynil

MSMA

120 Herbicide (6.6) *(Terra)*
912 Herbicide (6) (+ surfactant) *(Terra)*
Drexel MSMA 6.6 *(Drexel)*
Helena MSMA 6.6 *(Helena)*
Helena MSMA Plus H.C. (+ surfactant) *(Helena)*
◆ **MAGMA (WSG)** *(Luxembourg-Pamol)*
◆ **Target MSMA 6.6 or TurfMate 6.6** *(Luxembourg-Pamol)*
◆ **Target MSMA 6 Plus (+ surfactant)** *(Luxembourg-Pamol)*
◆ **TurfMate 6 Plus (+ surfactant)** *(Luxembourg-Pamol)*
Rate: 1 fl. oz./1000 sq. ft.
1.5 oz. WSG/1000 sq. ft.
Time: Repeat at 10- to 14-day intervals if needed.

Weeds: Broadleaf weeds:

chickweed	woodsorrel

Grasses and sedges:

bahiagrass	crabgrass	nutsedge
barnyardgrass	dallisgrass	sandbur

Remarks: Golf courses, ornamental turfgrass. Bluegrass, bermudagrass, and zoysiagrass are quite tolerant. Do not apply to carpetgrass, centipedegrass, dichondra, or St. Augustinegrass. For 6.6, add suitable surfactant. Mow lawn 1-1½" high before treatment. On new lawns, do not treat until after 3 mowings. Do not apply with hose-end applicators.

– – – – – – – – – – – – –

Signal Word/Toxicity Class: Caution/III.

Ansar 6.6 *(ZENECA)*
Bueno 6 (+ surfactant) *(ZENECA)*
Rate: 1 fl. oz. 6.6, 6/1000 sq. ft.
Time: Apply during warm weather; repeat at 14-day intervals if needed.
Weeds: Broadleaf weeds:

beggartick	dayflower	puncturevine
chickweed	fiddleneck	ragweed
cocklebur	jimsonweed	spurge
common purslane	morningglory	wild mustard
dandelion	pigweed	woodsorrel

Grasses and sedges:

bahiagrass	fall panicum	large crabgrass
barnyardgrass	foxtail	nutsedge
broomsedge	goosegrass	sandbur
dallisgrass	johnsongrass	smooth crabgrass

Remarks: Ornamental turfgrass. Bermudagrass, bluegrass, and zoysiagrass are quite tolerant. Do not apply to carpetgrass, centipedegrass, dichondra or St. Augustinegrass. For 6.6, add suitable surfactant. Mow lawn 1-1½" high before treatment. Do not reseed until 2 weeks after last application. Do not apply with hose-end applicators. Do not apply through any type of irrigation system. Do not graze treated fields or feed treated foliage to livestock. Refer to label for directions and restrictions.

– – – – – – – – – – – – –

Signal Word/Toxicity Class: Caution.
REI: 12 hr.

Drexar 530 or MSMA 4 Plus (+ surfactant) *(Drexel)*
Drexel MSMA 6 Plus (+ surfactant) *(Drexel)*
Rate: 2-3 lb. ai/A
4-6 pt. 4/A
2.66-4 pt. 6/A
Time: Postemergence to weeds. Repeat at 10- to 14-day intervals if needed.
Weeds: Grasses and sedges:

bahiagrass	dallisgrass	sandbur
crabgrass	nutsedge	woodsorrel

Remarks: Do not use on centipedegrass or St. Augustinegrass. Mow lawn 1-1½" high before treatment.

– – – – – – – – – – – – –

Signal Word/Toxicity Class: Caution/III.

Opti-Amine — see 2,4-D

PAR-3 — see 2,4-D Combinations

Patron 170 — see 2,4-D Combinations

PENDIMETHALIN

Provides effective residual weed control in established turf-grasses. Will not control established weeds.

Corral (2.68G) *(Scotts)*
ProTurf Turf Weedgrass Control (1.71%) *(Scotts)*
Rate: Cool-season grasses:
1.5-2 lb. ai/A
56-76 lb. 2.68G/A
88-118 lb. 1.71%/A
Warm-season grasses:
1.5-3 lb. ai/A
76-114 lb. 2.68G/A
88-177 lb. 1.71%/A
Bentgrass, *Poa annua:*
1.5 lb. ai/A
57 lb. 2.68G/A
88 lb. 1.71%/A

8

Turf, Ornamentals & Woody Plants

Time: Preemergence.
Weeds: Broadleaf weeds:

chickweed	henbit	oxalis
cudweed	hop clover	prostrate spurge
eveningprimrose	knotweed	purslane

Grasses:

annual bluegrass	crabgrass	foxtail
barnyardgrass	fall panicum	goosegrass

Remarks: For use on bentgrass, *Poa annua* (except putting greens and tees); cool-season grasses: Kentucky bluegrass, fescue (fine, tall), perennial ryegrass; warm-season grasses: bahiagrass, bermudagrass, centipedegrass, St. Augustinegrass, zoysiagrass. Not for use on dichondra. Refer to label for use directions and precautions.

Signal Word/Toxicity Class: Caution.

Pendulum (3.3EC or WDG) *(American Cyanamid)*
Rate: 1.5-3 lb. ai/A
    3.6-7.2 pt. 3.3EC/A
    2.5-5 lb. WDG/A
Time: Preemergence. Apply in spring before weeds germinate. For annual bluegrass, chickweed, and henbit, apply in late summer to early fall before weeds germinate. Repeat at 2.5-3.6 pt. 3.3EC in 5-8 weeks, 1.7-2.5 lb. WDG in 6-8 weeks if necessary.
Weeds: Broadleaf weeds:

common chickweed	henbit	prostrate spurge
cudweed	mouseear chickweed	purslane

Grasses:

annual bluegrass	crabgrass	foxtail
barnyardgrass	fall panicum	goosegrass

Remarks: Northern grasses: fescues (fine, tall), Kentucky bluegrass, perennial ryegrass. Southern grasses: bahiagrass, bermudagrass, centipedegrass, St. Augustinegrass, tall fescue, zoysiagrass. For control of established weeds, use with herbicides registered for postemergence use; refer to labels for rates, precautions, and restrictions. Do not use on newly seeded or sprigged turfgrass, or on bentgrass, *Poa annua* (putting greens and tees), or dichondra maintained as desirable turf. Do not apply through any type of irrigation system.

Signal Word/Toxicity Class: Caution.

Pendulum — see pendimethalin

Pennant MAGNUM — see *S*-metolachlor

Pre-San — see bensulide

PROGRASS

Prograss (EC) (ethofumesate) *(AgrEvo USA)*
Rate: 0.5-2 lb. ai/A
    0.33-1.33 gal. EC/A
Time: Preemergence or early postemergence. Do not apply after Feb. 1.
Weeds: Annual broadleaf weeds:

common chickweed	common purslane	redroot pigweed

Annual grasses and sedges:

annual bluegrass	crabgrass	purple nutsedge*
barnyardgrass	green foxtail	yellow foxtail
canarygrass	large crabgrass	yellow nutsedge

* *Reduces competition*
Remarks: Newly established or mature perennial ryegrass, Kentucky bluegrass, fairway height bentgrass, or dormant bermudagrass overseeded with perennial ryegrass. Refer to label for rates, timing, and precautions.

Signal Word/Toxicity Class: Danger/I.

PROMPT (Premix)

Restricted Use Pesticide due to groundwater concerns.

Prompt (5L) (2.5 lb./gal. bentazon & 2.5 lb./gal. atrazine) *(BASF)*
Rate: 1.1-1.5 lb. ai/A
    1.8-2.4 pt. 5L/A
Time: Early postemergence. Apply when weeds are actively growing. Additional applications at 7- to 10-day intervals may be necessary for yellow nutsedge.

Weeds: Annual broadleaf weeds:

alyce clover*	dayflower	redweed
annual morningglory	dollarweed	Venice mallow
annual sedge	giant ragweed	smallflower
beggarticks	hop clover	morningglory
bristly starbur	(small)	smooth pigweed
common	ladysthumb	spurred anoda
lambsquarters	oldfield toadflax	tall waterhemp
common purslane	oxalis	teaweed
common ragweed	partridgepea*	white clover
corn speedwell	Pennsylvania	(Florida only)
cudweed	smartweed	wild buckwheat
cutleaf	prickly sida	wild mustard
eveningprimrose	redroot pigweed	wild sunflower

Perennial weeds and sedge:

field bindweed	Canada thistle	yellow nutsedge

**Suppression*
Remarks: Established bermudagrass, St. Augustinegrass, centipedegrass, and zoysiagrass. Do not graze treated area or feed treated forage to livestock. Do not apply through any type of irrigation system.
Tank Mixes: Atrazine, Basagran, Basagran T/O, 2,4-D, 2,4-DP, Image, MCPP, MSMA, Turflon, Vantage; refer to label for use directions.
State Restrictions: Not for use in California.

Signal Word/Toxicity Class: Danger/I.

PROTURF GOOSEGRASS/ CRABGRASS CONTROL (Premix)

ProTurf Goosegrass/Crabgrass Control (5.25% bensulide & 1.31% oxadiazon) *(Scotts)*
Rate: Ready To Use: one bag/11,000 sq. ft.
Time: Preemergence. For established bermudagrass and zoysiagrass, apply early spring (Jan.-early Apr.) before turf greenup and weed germination. For perennial bluegrass, ryegrass, bentgrass, and tall fescue, apply spring (Mar.-early May) prior to germination.
Weeds: Grasses:

crabgrass	goosegrass

Remarks: For use on fairways, tees, bermudagrass and bentgrass greens. Do not use on dichondra, annual ryegrass, fine fescue, or where *Poa annua* is a desired turf. Not for use on turf being grown for sale, other commercial use as sod, for commercial seed production, or for research purposes. Refer to label for use directions and precautions.

Signal Word/Toxicity Class: Warning/II.

ProTurf K-O-G Weed Control — see dicamba

ProTurf Turf Weedgrass Control — see pendimethalin

ProTurf Weedgrass Preventer — see bensulide

Rattler — see glyphosate

Reward — see diquat dibromide

Rhonox — see MCPA

Riverdale Turf D + DP — see 2,4-D Combinations

Roundup PRO — see glyphosate

Saber — see 2,4-D

Salvo — see 2,4-D

◆-new product • PP-preplant • PPI-preplant incorporated • PRE-preemergence • POST-postemergence • SEQ-sequential • ae-acid equivalent • ai-active ingredient • DF-dry flowable E/EC-emulsifiable concentrate • F/FL-flowable • DG/G/WG-dispersable granule • L/LC-liquid • SP/WSP-soluble packet • W/WP-wettable powder • WSB-water soluble bag

Savage — see 2,4-D

SCYTHE

Nonselective, postemergent herbicide.

Scythe (pelargonic acid) *(Mycogen)*
Rate: 4-13 fl. oz./1 gal. spray solution
Time: May be applied to dormant turf prior to spring greenup.
Weeds: Annual broadleaf weeds and grasses; top-kill of perennial weeds.
Remarks: Apply prior to establishment of turfgrass, or for trimming and edging in established turf. Apply in minimum 75 gal. spray solution/A or spray-to-wet. Do not apply by air or through any type of irrigation system. Refer to label for directions and precautions.
Tank Mixes: Glyphosate and other foliar and residual herbicides.

Signal Word/Toxicity Class: Warning/II.
REI: 24 hr.

SETHOXYDIM

For postemergence control of annual grass weeds and bahiagrass. Will not control broadleaf weeds, nutsedges, or rushes.

Vantage (1EC) *(BASF)*
Rate: 0.19-0.28 lb. ai/A
1.5-2.25 pt. 1EC/A
Time: Apply to actively growing weeds. On centipedegrass, apply no earlier than 3 weeks after spring greenup. To control bahiagrass, 2 applications at 10-14 day intervals will be necessary.
Weeds: Grasses:

bahiagrass	large crabgrass	smooth crabgrass
goosegrass		

Remarks: For use on centipedegrass and fine fescues (seedling or established) such as chewings, creeping red, and hard fescue. Do not use on tall fescue or other turfgrass species. May be applied to established or newly planted centipedegrass that has 3" new stolon growth.

Signal Word/Toxicity Class: Caution/III.

SIMAZINE

Riverside Simazine 90DF *(Terra)*
Rate: 1-2 lb. ai/A
1.1-2.2 lb. 90DF/A
Time: Apply after Sept. 1 (Oct. 1 for annual bluegrass) before emergence of winter annual weeds. For control of summer annual weeds, apply in late winter before weeds emerge.
Weeds: Annual broadleaf weeds:

burclover	henbit	mouseear chickweed
common chickweed	hop clover	parsley-piert
corn speedwell	lawn burweed	spurweed

Grasses:
annual bluegrass

Remarks: Bermudagrass, centipedegrass, St. Augustinegrass, and zoysiagrass. Irrigate with 1/2" of water if rainfall does not occur within 10 days after treatment. Before June 1, additional 1.1 lb. may be applied at least 30 days after first application to control summer annuals. Refer to label for precautions and restrictions concerning species and areas of use.
State Restrictions: Not for use in Florida.

Signal Word/Toxicity Class: Caution/III.

Solution — see 2,4-D

Solve — see 2,4-D

Sterling — see dicamba

Super Trimec — see Trimec Complexes

SURFLAN

Orange color serves as marker dye.

Surflan A.S. (oryzalin) *(Dow AgroSciences)*
Rate: 2 lb. ai/A
2 qt. A.S./A
Time: Spray at least 2 weeks prior to germination of annual grasses.
Weeds: Early- and late- germinating annual grasses such as:

annual bluegrass	crabgrass	goosegrass
barnyardgrass	foxtail	

Remarks: Established bahiagrass, bermudagrass, centipedegrass, St. Augustinegrass, tall fescue, and zoysiagrass. Delay reseeding for 90-120 days.

Signal Word/Toxicity Class: Caution/III.
REI: 12 hr.

Sword — see MCPA

Threesome — see 2,4-D Combinations

Triamine — see 2,4-D Combinations

TRIAMINE II (Premix)

Postemergent selective broadleaf herbicide containing the amines of 2,4-DP, MCPA, and MCPP.

Triamine II (2,4-DP & MCPA & MCPP) *(Riverdale)*
Rate: Cool-season grasses (bluegrass, fescue, rye:)
1.5-2 lb. ai/A
3-4 pt. II/ A
Warm-season grasses (bahia, common Bermuda, centipede, St. Augustine, zoysia):
1-1.5 lb. ai/A
2-3 pt. II/A
Bentgrass (except golf course greens and tees):
1.75 pt. II/A (0.66 oz./1000 sq. ft. in 3 gal. water)
Time: Apply spring or early fall when weeds are actively growing. Apply to newly seeded lawns or turf after grasses are well established.
Weeds: Grasses:

bahiagrass	centipedegrass	fescue
bentgrass	common	rye
bluegrass	bermudagrass	

Remarks: Lawns, turf, golf courses (fairways, aprons, tees, roughs), and parks. Do not use on carpetgrass, dichondra, or on grasses where desirable clovers are present. Some hybrid bermudagrasses are sensitive to this product; consult extension service weed control specialist.

Signal Word/Toxicity Class: Danger/I.

Tri-Ester — see 2,4-D Combinations

TRI-ESTER II (Premix)

Postemergent selective broadleaf herbicide containing the esters of 2,4-DP MCPA, and MCPP for use in cool weather.

Tri-Ester II (2,4-DP & MCPA & MCPP) *(Riverdale)*
Rate: Cool-season grasses (bluegrass, fescue, rye):
1-2 lb. ae/A
2-4 pt. II/A
Warm-season grasses (bahia, common Bermuda, centipede, St. Augustine, zoysia):
1-1.5 lb. ae/A
2-3 pt. II/A
Bentgrass (except golf course greens and tees):
1.75 pt. II/A (0.66 oz./1000 sq. ft. in 3 gal. water)
Time: Apply when temperature is between 50°-85°. For bentgrass, apply in May or mid-Aug. through Sept. when weeds are actively growing.
Weeds: Grasses:

bahiagrass	centipedegrass	fescue
bentgrass	common	rye
bluegrass	bermudagrass	

8
Turf, Ornamentals & Woody Plants

Remarks: Some hybrid bermudagrasses are sensitive to this product; consult extension service weed control specialist.

– – – – – – – – – – – – – – –

Signal Word/Toxicity Class: Warning/II.

TRIMEC (Complexes)

Super Trimec or ◆ Trimec Turf Ester (2,4-D & 2,4-DP & dicamba) (PBI/Gordon)

◆ Trimec 992 or Trimec Classic (2,4-D & MCPP & dicamba) (PBI/Gordon)

Rate: 1.8-6 pt./A

Time: Apply when weeds are actively growing.

Weeds: Broadleaf weeds:

bedstraw	knotweed	purslane
bindweed**	kochia**	ragweed
black medic	lambsquarters	redweed*
buckhorn	lawn burweed*	sheep sorrel
burdock	lespedeza	shepherdspurse
chickweed	mallow	smartweed**
chicory	morningglory	speedwell
clover	mustard**	spurge
cocklebur**	nettle**	sunflower**
corn speedwell*	old world diamond flower*	thistle**
dandelion	oxalis**	trumpetcreeper**
dock	peppergrass	velvetleaf**
ground ivy	pigweed	wild carrot
healall	plantain	wild garlic
henbit	poison ivy	wild lettuce
Innocence*	poison oak	wild onion
jimsonweed**	purple cudweed*	yarrow

* Classic only; ** Super and Turf Ester only.

Remarks: Rates vary by product and grass species. Do not use on "Florafam" St. Augustine, carpetgrass, dichondra, or on lawns where desirable clovers are present. Do not make more than 2 applications per year. Seed can be sown 3-4 weeks after application. Avoid spray or drift onto vegetables, flowers, ornamental plants, shrubs, trees, and other desirable plants. Do not apply through any type of irrigation system. Refer to label for directions, precautions, and restrictions.

– – – – – – – – – – – – – – –

Signal Word/Toxicity Class: Varies by formulation.

Trimec Encore (MCPA & MCPP & dicamba) (PBI/Gordon)

Rate: 3-4.25 pt./A

Time: Apply in spring or early fall when weeds are actively growing.

Weeds: Broadleaf weeds including:

bedstraw	healall	poison oak
black medic	henbit	purslane
buckhorn	knotweed	ragweed
burdock	lambsquarters	sheep sorrel
chickweed	lespedeza	shepherdspurse
chicory	mallow	spurge
clover	morningglory	wild carrot
dandelion	peppergrass	wild garlic
dock	pigweed	wild onion
ground ivy	poison ivy	yarrow

Remarks: Do not use on carpetgrass, dichondra, or on lawns where desirable clovers are present. Do not apply to newly seeded grasses until well established. Avoid spray or drift onto vegetables, flowers, ornamental plants, shrubs, trees, and other desirable plants. Refer to label for bentgrass use directions, precautions, and restrictions.

– – – – – – – – – – – – – – –

Signal Word/Toxicity Class: Danger/I.

Trimec Plus (MSMA & 2,4-D & MCPP & dicamba) (PBI/Gordon)

Rate: Est. bermudagrass, zoysiagrass:
1-1.66 gal./A (in 50-100 gal. water)
Est. Kentucky bluegrass, tall fescue, turf-type tall fescues:
1 gal./A (in 50-100 gal. water)

Time: Postemergence. Do not spray while grass is emerging from dormancy. Refer to label for temperature precautions.

Weeds: Broadleaf weeds:

bedstraw	henbit	purslane
black medic	knotweed	ragweed
buckhorn	lambsquarters	sheep sorrel
burdock	lespedeza	shepherdspurse
chickweed	mallow	speedwell
chicory	morningglory	spurge
clover	peppergrass	wild carrot
dandelion	pigweed	wild garlic
dock	plantain	wild onion
ground ivy	poison ivy	yarrow
healall	poison oak	

Grasses:

crabgrass	goosegrass	sandbur
dallisgrass		

Remarks: Do not use on carpetgrass, centipedegrass, dichondra, red fescue, St. Augustine. Do not use on lawns or turf where desirable clovers are present. Refer to label for directions, precautions, and restrictions.

– – – – – – – – – – – – – – –

Signal Word/Toxicity Class: Warning/II.

Trimec Southern (MCPP & 2,4-D & dicamba) (PBI/Gordon)

Rate: Bermuda, bentgrass:
2 pt./A
Bluegrass, fescue, zoysiagrass:
2-3 pt./A
Centipede, St. Augustinegrass:
1-1.5 pt./A

Time: Apply when weeds are young and actively growing. Avoid applications during long, excessively dry or hot periods. Do not spray while grass is in or emerging from dormancy.

Weeds: Broadleaf weeds:

bedstraw	henbit	poison oak
black medic	knotweed	purslane
buckhorn	lambsquarters	ragweed
burdock	lespedeza	sheep sorrel
chickweed	mallow	shepherdspurse
chicory	morningglory	speedwell
clover	peppergrass	spurge
dandelion	pigweed	wild carrot
dock	plantain	wild garlic
ground ivy	poison ivy	wild onion
healall		yarrow

Remarks: On centipedegrass and St. Augustinegrass, do not overdose. Do not use on "Florafam" St. Augustine. Do not use more than recommended rate. Use reduced rates when grasses are under stress. Do not apply to newly seeded turf until after first mowing. Avoid spray drift onto vegetables, flowers, ornamental plants, shrubs, trees, and other desirable plants. Refer to label for directions, precautions, and restrictions.

– – – – – – – – – – – – – – –

Signal Word/Toxicity Class: Danger/I.

Triplet — see 2,4-D Combinations

Tri-Plex — see 2,4-D Combinations

TRI-POWER (Premix)

Tri-Power (L) or Tri-Power Dry (MCPA & MCPP & dicamba) (Riverdale)

Rate: Cool-season grasses (Kentucky bluegrass, perennial ryegrass, tall or fine fescue):
2.5-3.5 pt. L/A in 20-250 gal. water
Two 1.33 lb. packets Dry/A in 20-250 gal. water
Warm-season grasses (bermudagrass, zoysiagrass):
2-3 pt. L/A in 20-240 gal. water
One 1.3 lb. packet Dry/A in 20-240 gal. water

Time: Apply spring or early fall when weeds are actively growing.

Weeds: Broadleaf weeds including:

black medic	cocklebur	oxalis
chickweed	dandelion	plantains
clover	knotweed	thistles

Remarks: Lawns, turf, golf courses (fairways, aprons, tees, and roughs), and parks. Applications to bahiagrass, buffalograss, centipedegrass, carpetgrass, kikuyugrass, or St. Augustinegrass should be avoided unless injury can be tolerated. Do not apply to bentgrass maintained as desired turfgrass. Where bentgrass or other sensitive grasses are predominant, use lower rate. Do not use Tri-Power liquid on dichondra or on lawns or turf where desirable clovers are present.

– – – – – – – – – – – – – – –

Signal Word/Toxicity Class: Danger/I.

TUPERSAN

Tupersan (50WP) (siduron) (Gowan)

Rate: 8-12 lb. ai/A
16-24 lb. 50WP/A

Time: Apply in spring just before emergence of annual weed grasses.

Weeds: Grasses:

barnyardgrass	hairy crabgrass	smooth crabgrass
foxtail	large crabgrass	

◆-new product • PP-preplant • PPI-preplant incorporated • PRE-preemergence • POST-postemergence • SEQ-sequential • ae-acid equivalent • ai-active ingredient • DF-dry flowable
E/EC-emulsifiable concentrate • F/FL-flowable • DG/G/WG-dispersable granule • L/LC-liquid • SP/WSP-soluble packet • W/WP-wettable powder • WSB-water soluble bag

410   **Weed Control Manual 2000**

Remarks: Bentgrass (except certain strains—see label), bluegrass, fescue, orchardgrass, perennial ryegrass, redtop, smooth brome, zoysiagrass. Not for use on bermudagrass or golf course greens. Does not control *Poa annua*, clover, or most broadleaf weeds. Water within 3 days after treatment if there has been no rain. Do not apply through any type of irrigation system.
Tank Mixes: May be tank mixed; refer to label.

- - - - - - - - - - - - - - - -

Signal Word/Toxicity Class: Caution.
REI: 4 hr.

TurfMate — see MSMA

Vanquish — see dicamba

Vantage — see sethoxydim

Weed Rhap — see 2,4-D

Weedar — see 2,4-D

Weedestroy — see MCPP

Weedone — see 2,4-D

XL 2G (Premix)

Selective preemergence herbicide for control of certain annual grasses and broadleaf weeds. Does not control established weeds. Requires rainfall or sprinkler irrigation within 21 days to activate.

XL 2G (1% benefin + 1% oryzalin) *(Helena)*
Rate: 2-3 lb. ai/A
100-150 lb./A
0.05-0.07 lb. ai/sq. ft.
2.3-3.4 lb./1000 sq. ft.
Time: Single application: Apply high rate in late fall or early spring. Split application: Apply low rate well in advance of weed germination; repeat 10 weeks later. In Florida, apply 150 lb. 3 times per year or every 90-100 days in the fall, early spring, and early summer.
Weeds: Broadleaf weeds:

carpetweed	dwarf fleabane*	prostrate spurge*
chickweed	henbit	wild carrot*
common groundsel	Indian mustard*	yellow woodsorrel*
common purslane	prostrate knotweed	

Grasses:

annual bluegrass	field sandbur	Italian ryegrass
barnyardgrass	field sandbur	johnsongrass
crabgrass	foxtail	(seedling)
crowfootgrass	goosegrass	

* Partial control

Remarks: Warm-season turf: bahiagrass, bermudagrass, buffalograss, centipedegrass, St. Augustinegrass, zoysiagrass and tall fescue. Do not apply to cool-season turf other than tall fescue. Do not apply to golf course putting greens or tees. Do not apply more than 150 lb./A in a single application, or over 900 lb./A per year. Refer to label for directions and precautions.

- - - - - - - - - - - - - - - -

Signal Word/Toxicity Class: Caution/III.

Grasses For Seed Production

Banvel — see dicamba

Barrage — see 2,4-D

Bison — see bromoxynil & MCPA

Broclean — see bromoxynil

Bromac — see bromoxynil & MCPA

Bromox — see bromoxynil

Bromox-MCPA 2-2 — see bromoxynil & MCPA

BROMOXYNIL

◆ **Broclean 2EC** *(Platte)*
◆ **Bromox 2EC** *(MIcro Flo)*
Buctril (2EC), Buctril 4EC *(Rhone-Poulenc)*
Moxy 2EC *(Terra)*
Rate: 0.25-0.5 lb. ai/A
1-2 pt. 2EC/A
0.5-1 pt. 4EC/A
Time: Postemergence. Apply before boot stage.
Weeds: Broadleaf weeds:

buffalobur	ivyleaf morningglory	spiny pigweed
burcucumber	knawel	tall morningglory
common groundsel	kochia	tall waterhemp
common ragweed	London rocket	tumble mustard
corn chamomile	mayweed	velvetleaf
corn gromwell	prostrate knotweed	Venice mallow
cowcockle	puncturevine	wild mustard
giant ragweed	redroot pigweed	wild radish
hemp sesbania	Russian thistle	yellow starthistle

Remarks: Bentgrass, bermudagrass, Kentucky bluegrass, fescues, ryegrass, St. Augustine, and zoysiagrass. Do not apply with backpack or hand-held equipment. Refer to label for restrictions and precautions.

- - - - - - - - - - - - - - - -

Signal Word/Toxicity Class: Warning/II.

BROMOXYNIL & MCPA (Premixes)

Bison (EC) (2 lb./gal. bromoxynil & 2 lb./gal. MCPA) *(Terra)*
◆ **Bromac (EC) (2 lb./gal. bromoxynil & 2 lb./gal. MCPA)** *(Platte)*
◆ **Bromox-MCPA 2-2 (EC) (2 lb./gal. bromoxynil & 2 lb./gal. MCPA)** *(Micro Flo)*
Bronate (EC) (2 lb./gal. bromoxynil & 2 lb./gal. MCPA) *(Rhone-Poulenc)*
Rate: 0.5-1 lb./A
1-2 pt. EC/A
Chemigation (Bronate only):
1 lb. ai/A
2 pt. EC/A
Time: Apply before boot stage.
Weeds: Broadleaf weeds:

blue mustard	giant ragweed	puncturevine
Canada thistle	hemp sesbania	purple mustard
(suppression)	henbit	tall morningglory
common groundsel	ivyleaf morningglory	tansymustard
common ragweed	knawel	tarweed
corn chamomile	kochia	velvetleaf
corn gromwell	mayweed	wild radish
fumitory	prostrate knotweed	

Remarks: Bentgrass, bermudagrass, Kentucky bluegrass, fescues, ryegrass, St. Augustine, and zoysiagrass. May also be used on seedling grasses such as Delta, Merion, Park or common Kentucky bluegrass, Pennlawn, Chewings, Illahee or Alta fescues, orchardgrass, Highland, Seaside or Astoria bentgrasses, perennial ryegrass, bahiagrass, and zoysiagrass. Do not apply with backpack or hand-held application equipment.

- - - - - - - - - - - - - - - -

Signal Word/Toxicity Class: Warning/II.

Bronate — see bromoxynil & MCPA

Buctril — see bromoxynil

8

Turf, Ornamentals & Woody Plants

NOTICE The information on these pages is for preliminary planning — not a guide for use. Be sure to follow the manufacturer's directions, notwithstanding information contained here. | For personal protective equipment and EPA registration numbers, please turn to page 70.

CLOPYRALID

Systemic herbicide absorbed by leaves and roots.

Stinger *(Dow AgroSciences)*
Rate: 0.1-0.25 lb. ae/A
0.25-0.66 pt./A
Time: Apply to established grasses before boot stage. For late emerging Canada thistle, preharvest treatment may be made after grass seed is fully developed; treatment at bud stage or later may result in less consistent control. Postharvest fall treatments may be made to actively growing Canada thistle after majority of basal leaves have emerged.
Weeds: Annual and perennial broadleaf weeds:

Canada thistle	jimsonweed	sowthistle
cocklebur	knapweed	spotted knapweed
clover	marshelder	sunflower
diffuse knapweed	Russian knapweed	vetch
Jerusalem artichoke	(suppression)	volunteer soybean

Remarks: Do not apply to bentgrass unless injury can be tolerated. Do not apply more than 0.66 pt./A per season. Do not apply through any type of irrigation system. Do not contaminate irrigation ditches or water used for irrigation or domestic purposes.

Signal Word/Toxicity Class: Caution/III.
REI: 12 hr.

Credit — see glyphosate

CURTAIL OR CURTAIL M (Premixes)

Curtail (0.38 lb./gal. clopyralid & 2 lb./gal. 2,4-D) *(Dow AgroSciences)*
Curtail M (0.42 lb./gal. clopyralid & 2.35 lb./gal. MCPA)
(Dow AgroSciences)
Rate: 0.6-1.2 lb. ae/A
2-4 pt. Curtail/A
1.75-3.5 pt. Curtail M/A
Time: Apply to established grasses before boot stage. For late emerging Canada thistle, preharvest treatment may be made after grass seed is fully developed; treatment at bud stage or later may result in less consistent control. Postharvest fall treatments may be made to actively growing Canada thistle after majority of basal leaves have emerged.
Weeds: Annual broadleaf weeds plus:
Canada thistle
Remarks: Do not use unless injury risk acceptable. Do not exceed 4 pt./A per season.
Tank Mixes: May be tank mixed; refer to label.

Signal Word/Toxicity Class: Danger/I (Curtail); Caution/III (Curtail M).
REI: 48 hr.

2,4-D - PHENOXY HERBICIDES

Established cool-season turfgrasses, bermudagrass, and zoysiagrass have good tolerance to 2,4-D. Centipedegrass, St. Augustinegrass, and bentgrass are prone to injury from 2,4-D. 2,4-D and 2,4-D-type compounds selectively control broadleaf weeds with little or no control of grasses. Ester formulations are most volatile and the amines least volatile.

Annual and perennial broadleaf weeds controlled by 2,4-D include:

beggarticks	ground ivy	primrose
bindweed	healall	puncturevine
bitterweed	hemp	purslane
broomweed	hoary cress	ragweed
bull thistle	ironweed	rush
burdock	jimsonweed	Russian thistle
Canada thistle	knotweed	shepherdspurse
carpetweed	lambsquarters	smartweed
catnip	locoweed	sowthistle
chickweed	mallow	stinkweed
chicory	marshelder	sumac
cocklebur	mexicanweed	sunflower
coffeeweed	morningglory	sweetclover
creeping jenny	musk thistle	velvetleaf
croton	mustard	Virginia creeper
curly indigo	pennywort	wild carrot
dandelion	pepperweed	wild garlic
dock	pigweed	wild lettuce
dogbane	plantain	wild onion
galinsoga	pokeweed	wild parsnips
goldenrod	povertyweed	wild radish

Albaugh Amine 4 (2,4-D amine) *(Albaugh)*
Albaugh LV4 or LV6 Ester (2,4-D ester) *(Albaugh)*
◆ **Clean Crop Amine 4 (2,4-D amine)** *(Platte)*
Esteron 99C (2,4-D LV ester) *(Rhone-Poulenc)*
Formula 40 (2,4-D mixed amine) *(Rhone-Poulenc)*
Hi-Dep (2,4-D amine) *(PBI/Gordon)*
◆ **Opti-Amine (4) (2,4-D amine)** *(Helena)*
Riverdale 6 Amine (2,4-D amine) *(Riverdale)*
Riverdale L.V. 4 or L.V. 6 (2,4-D ester) *(Riverdale)*
Solve 2,4-D (2,4-D LV ester) *(Albaugh)*
Weed Rhap A-4D (2,4-D amine) *(Helena)*
Weed Rhap LV-6D (2,4-D ester) *(Helena)*
Weedestroy AM-40 (2,4-D amine) *(Riverdale)*
Wilbur-Ellis Amine 4 (2,4-D amine) *(Wilbur-Ellis)*
Wilbur-Ellis Lo Vol-4 or Lo Vol-6 (2,4-D ester) *(Wilbur-Ellis)*
Rate: 0.5-2 lb. ae/A
1-4 pt./A
0.66-2.66 pt. 6/A
Seedling grass:
0.37-5 lb. ae/A
0.75-1 pt./A
0.5-0.66 pt. 6/A
Time: Apply in the spring or fall. Do not apply from early boot to milk stage.
Remarks: Spray seedling grass only after 5-leaf stage. After grass is well established, higher rates up to 2 lb. ai can be used to control hard-to-kill or perennial weeds. Do not use on bentgrass unless grass injury can be tolerated. Refer to label for precautions and restrictions.
State Restrictions: Wilbur-Ellis not registered in California.

Signal Word/Toxicity Class: Danger/I (amine); Caution/III (ester).

◆ **Barrage or Barrage HF (EC) (2,4-D ester)** *(Helena)*
Rate: 6-26 fl. oz./A
Time: Apply in the spring or fall. Do not apply from early boot to milk stage or after heading begins.
Remarks: Spray seedling grass only after 5-leaf stage. For use on established grasses such as bluegrass, fine fescue, tall fescues, orchard grass, annual ryegrass, and perennial ryegrass. Do not use on bentgrass unless injury can be tolerated. Refer to label for precautions and restrictions.

Signal Word/Toxicity Class: Caution/III.

◆ **Clean Crop Low Vol 4 or Low Vol 6 (2,4-D ester)** *(Platte)*
Gordon's LV 400 (2,4-D ester) *(PBI/Gordon)*
Riverside 2,4-D LV4 (2,4-D ester) *(Terra)*
Rate: 0.5-0.75 lb. ae/A
1-1.5 pt. 4, 400/A
0.66-1 pt. 6/A
Time: Apply to established stands in spring from tiller to early boot stage. Do not spray in boot stage. Perennial weed regrowth may be treated in the fall.
Remarks: New spring seedlings may be treated with lower rate after seedlings have at least 5 leaves. Do not graze meat animals on treated areas later than 3 days prior to slaughter; dairy animals within 7 days after treatment. Do not cut treated grass for hay within 30 days of treatment.

Signal Word/Toxicity Class: Caution/III.

Riverside 2,4-D Amine 4 (2,4-D amine) *(Terra)*
Rate: 0.5-1 lb. ae/A
1-2 pt./A
Time: Apply in the spring before head comes into boot.

Rate: New seedlings:
0.5-1.5 pt./A
Time: Treat after grass has tillered.
Remarks: Use higher rate for hard-to-kill weeds and where grass stands are heavy.

Signal Word/Toxicity Class: Danger/I.

◆ **Saber (2,4-D amine)** *(Platte)*
Rate: 0.35-2 lb. ae/A
0.75-4 pt./A
Seedling grass:
0.25-0.5 lb. ae/A
0.5-1 pt./A
Time: Apply in the spring or fall. Do not apply from early boot to milk stage.
Remarks: Spray seedling grass only after 5-leaf stage. On established stands that have had seed crop removed, up to 4 pt./A may be used on perennial regrowth in the fall. Do not use on bentgrass unless grass injury can be tolerated.

Signal Word/Toxicity Class: Danger/I.

◆-new product • PP-preplant • PPI-preplant incorporated • PRE-preemergence • POST-postemergence • SEQ-sequential • ae-acid equivalent • ai-active ingredient • DF-dry flowable
E/EC-emulsifiable concentrate • F/FL-flowable • DG/G/WG-dispersable granule • L/LC-liquid • SP/WSP-soluble packet • W/WP-wettable powder • WSB-water soluble bag

Savage (WSB) (2,4-D amine) *(Platte)*
Rate: 0.95-1.9 lb. ae/A
    1-2 lb. WSB/A
Time: Apply in the spring or fall. Do not apply in boot stage.
Remarks: Spray seedling grass only after 5-leaf stage using lower rate. After grass is well established, up to 2 lb./A may be used on hard-to-kill annual or perennial weeds. Do not graze dairy animals or cut forage for hay within 7 days of treatment.

- - - - - - - - - - - - - - - -

Signal Word/Toxicity Class: Danger/I.

Solution (WS) (2,4-D amine) *(Riverdale)*
Rate: 2 lb. 13 oz. WS/5-100 gal. water (1 packet/1.125-4.5 A)
Time: Spring or fall application. Do not apply from early boot to milk stage. Spray seedling grass only after 5-leaf stage.
Remarks: Use 1 packet/4.5 A rate for small seedling weeds. After grass is well established, higher rates of 1 packet/1.125 A can be used to control hard-to-kill annual or perennial weeds. Do not use on bentgrass unless grass injury can be tolerated.

- - - - - - - - - - - - - - - -

Signal Word/Toxicity Class: Danger/I.

Weedar 64 (4) (2,4-D amine) *(Nufarm)*
Weedone 638 (2,4-D ester + acid) *(Nufarm)*
Weedone LV4 (2,4-D solventless ester) *(Nufarm)*
Weedone Lo Vol 6 (2,4-D ester) *(Nufarm)*
Rate: 1-2 lb. ae/A
    2-4 pt. 64/A
    0.4-1.2 lb. ae/A
    1-3 pt. 638/A
    0.5-1.5 lb. ae/A
    1-3 pt. LV4/A
    0.66-2 pt. LV6/A
Time: Apply to established stands in spring from tiller to early boot stage. Do not spray in boot stage. Perennial weed regrowth may be treated in the fall.
Remarks: New spring seedlings may be treated with lower rate after seedlings have at least 5 leaves.
State Restrictions: Not for use in California.

- - - - - - - - - - - - - - - -

Signal Word/Toxicity Class: Danger/I (amine); Caution/III (ester).

DICAMBA

Banvel (WS) (DMA salt of dicamba) *(BASF)*
◆ **Sterling (WS) (DMA salt of dicamba)** *(Terra)*
Rate: Seedling grasses after crop reaches 3-5 leaf:
    0.25-0.5 lb. ai/A
    0.5-1 pt. WS/A
    Well-established perennial grasses:
    0.25-1 lb. ai/A
    0.5-2 pt. WS/A
Time: Do not apply after grass seed crop begins to joint.
Weeds: Broadleaf weeds including:

alfalfa	curly dock	nightflowering catchfly
Canada thistle*	field bindweed*	red sorrel
clover	knotweed	Russian knapweed*
common chickweed	little starwort	sheep sorrel
corn chamomile	mouseear chickweed	white cockle

    * Top growth control

Rate: 0.25-2 lb. ai/A
    0.5-4 pt. WS/A
Time: Apply in fall or late summer after harvest and burning of established grass seed crops. Apply immediately following first irrigation when soil is moist and before weeds have more than 2 leaves.
Weeds: Annual grass weeds such as:

downy brome	rattail fescue	ripgut brome

Remarks: Grasses such as Bermudagrass, bluegrass, fescue, and ryegrass. Do not use on bentgrass unless possible crop injury can be tolerated. Refer to label for grazing and feeding restrictions.

- - - - - - - - - - - - - - - -

Signal Word/Toxicity Class: Warning/II.

Direx — see diuron

DIURON

Direx 4L or 80DF *(Griffin)*
◆ **Diuron 80 WDG** *(Platte)*
Drexel Diuron 4L or 80 *(Drexel)*
Karmex DF *(Griffin)*
Riverside Diuron 4L or 80DF *(Terra)*
Rate: 1.5-2.25 lb. ai/A
    3-4.5 pt. 4L/A
    1.6-2.4 lb. ai/A
    2-3 lb. 80, DF, 80DF/A
Time: Apply during dormant period before seedlings emerge.
Weeds: Broadleaf weeds:

ageratum	dogfennel	Mexican clover
amsinckia	gromwell	pineappleweed
(fiddleneck)	groundsel	pokeweed
annual smartweed	hawksbeard	rabbit tobacco
annual sowthistle	horseweed	shepherdspurse
buttonweed	knawel	spanishneedles
chickweed	kochia	speedwell
corn spurry	kyllinga	wild radish

  Grasses:

annual ryegrass	johnsongrass	red sprangletop
annual sweet	(seedling)	ricegrass
vernalgrass	orchardgrass	sandbur
bluegrass	peppergrass	velvetgrass
foxtail	rattail fescue	

Remarks: Switchgrass, sideoats grama, and sand bluestem. Perennial plantings. Do not apply after crop begins growth in spring as crop injury may result.
State Restrictions: For use in Colorado, Kansas, New Mexico, Oklahoma.

- - - - - - - - - - - - - - - -

Rate: 1.5-3 lb. ai/A
    4.5-6 pt. 4L/A
    1.6-3.2 lb. ai/A
    2-4 lb. 80, DF, 80DF/A
Time: Apply between Oct. 1-Nov. 15 after fall rains start.
Weeds: Same as above.
Remarks: Alta fescue, astoria bentgrass, highland bentgrass, Kentucky bluegrass, merion bluegrass, orchardgrass. Perennial plantings. Weeds beyond 2-4 leaf stage should be removed prior to treatment.
State Restrictions: For use in western Oregon.

- - - - - - - - - - - - - - - -

Signal Word/Toxicity Class: Caution/III.

Esteron 99C — see 2,4-D

Formula 40 — see 2,4-D

Glyfos or Glyfos X-tra — see glyphosate

GLYPHOSATE

◆ **Credit (4WS)** *(Nufarm)*
◆ **Glyfos or Glyfos X-tra (4WS)** *(Cheminova)*
Rattler (4WS) *(Helena)*
Rate: Annual weeds:
    0.38-1.5 lb. ai/A
    0.75-3 pt. 4WS/A
    Perennial weeds:
    0.5-5 lb. ai/A
    1-10 pt. 4WS/A
Time: Preplant or renovation. Apply when weeds are actively growing and at proper growth stage.
Weeds: Annual and perennial weeds and grasses.
Remarks: Do not disturb soil or underground plant parts prior to treatment. Tillage or renovation techniques should be delayed for at least 7 days after application. Where vegetation is growing under mowed turfgrass management, omit at least 1 regular mowing before treatment.
State Restrictions: Glyfos is not registered for use in California. Glyfos X-tra is not registered for use in mistblowers in California or Arizona.

- - - - - - - - - - - - - - - -

Signal Word/Toxicity Class: Varies by formulation.
REI: Warning—12 hr.; Caution—4 hr.

8

Turf, Ornamentals & Woody Plants

NOTICE	The information on these pages is for preliminary planning — not a guide for use. Be sure to follow the manufacturer's directions, notwithstanding information contained here.	For personal protective equipment and EPA registration numbers, please turn to page 70.

Roundup PRO (4WS) (Monsanto)
Rate: Annual weeds:
0.25-1.5 lb. ai/A
0.5-3 pt. 4WS/A
Perennial weeds:
2-5 lb. ai/A
4-10 pt. 4WS/A
Time: Apply when weeds are actively growing and at proper growth stage.
Weeds: Many broadleaf weeds and the following grasses:

annual bluegrass	crabgrass	johnsongrass
bermudagrass	fescue	quackgrass

Remarks: Do not disturb soil or underground plant parts prior to treatment. Tillage or renovation techniques should be delayed for at least 7 days after application.

– – – – – – – – – – – – – – –

Signal Word/Toxicity Class: Caution/III.

Gramoxone Extra — see paraquat

Hi-Dep — see 2,4-D

HORIZON

Horizon (1EC) (fenoxaprop-ethyl) (AgrEvo USA)
Rate: 0.15-0.25 lb. ai/A
1.2-2 pt. 1EC/A
Time: Apply when annual grassy weeds are young and actively growing and grass crops are between the 4-5 leaf stage and 1 node (jointing) stage.
Weeds: Annual and perennial grasses:

barnyardgrass	johnsongrass	smooth crabgrass
blackgrass	panicum	sprangletop
foxtail	roughstalk bluegrass	tame oat
goosegrass	sandbur	wild oat
hairy crabgrass	silver crabgrass	

Remarks: Can be applied to cool season grasses such as perennial ryegrass, fine fescue, or tall fescue. Do not apply to Kentucky bluegrass seed production fields. Do not apply within 2 weeks following fertilizer application. Do not apply through any type of irrigation system. Do not cut treated turfgrass for hay or forage. Refer to label for directions.
Tank Mixes: May be tank mixed with other pesticides or fertilizers.
State Restrictions: SLN-Oregon.

– – – – – – – – – – – – – – –

Signal Word/Toxicity Class: Warning/II.

Karmex — see diuron

KERB

Restricted Use Pesticide.

Kerb WSP (pronamide) (Rohm and Haas)
Rate: Preemergence:
0.5-1 lb. ai/A
1-2 lb. WSP/A
Early postemergence:
0.75-1.5 lb. ai/A
1.5-3 lb. WSP/A
Time: Preemergence, early postemergence.
Weeds: Broadleaf weeds:

chickweed	red sorrel*	shepherdspurse*
London rocket*	(seedling)	wild mustard*

Grasses:

annual bluegrass	Italian ryegrass	perennial ryegrass
downy brome	Kentucky bluegrass	quackgrass
(cheatgrass)	orchardgrass	volunteer grain
foxtail barley		

* Controls preemergence only

Remarks: Bermudagrass. Annual and perennial ryegrass, bentgrass, bluegrass, dichondra, and fescues are injured by pre- and postemergence application. Not for use on golf greens. Do not apply through any type of irrigation system.
Crop Rotation: Refer to label for specific times for rotation crops.

– – – – – – – – – – – – – – –

Signal word/Toxicity Class: Caution.
REI: 24 hr.

MCPA

Albaugh MCPA Amine or Ester (4) (Albaugh)
◆ **Clean Crop MCP Amine 4 or Ester** (Platte)
◆ **Clean Crop MCP 2 Sodium (sodium salt)** (Platte)
Rhonox (LV ester) (4) (Nufarm)
Riverdale MCPA-4 Amine, L.V. 4 Ester (4), IOE (5.2) (Riverdale)
Solve MCPA Ester (4) (Albaugh)
Sword (5.2) (Platte)
Wilbur-Ellis MCPA Amine, Ester (4) or ◆ Sodium Salt (Wilbur-Ellis)
Rate: 0.5-1 lb. ae/A
1-2 pt. 4/A
0.75-1.5 pt. 5.2/A
2-4 pt. sodium salt/A
Time: Apply on established grasses in the spring before head comes in to boot and on seedling grass after grass has tillered.
Weeds: Broadleaf weeds including:

annual mustard	hempnettle	ragweed
buttercup	kochia	shepherdspurse
Canada thistle	lambsquarters	sowthistle
cocklebur	marshelder	stinging nettle
dandelion	pigweed	stinkweed
dragonhead mint	plantain	whitetop
field peppergrass	puncturevine	wild radish
goatsbeard	purslane	yellow rocket

Remarks: In some areas, bent, buffalo, carpet, and St. Augustinegrass may be injured by treatment. May be combined with liquid nitrogen fertilizer suitable for foliar application in one operation, but do not apply in cold weather.
State Restrictions: Wilbur-Ellis not registered in California.

– – – – – – – – – – – – – – –

Signal Word/Toxicity Class: Varies by formulation.

Rhomene (amine) (4) (Nufarm)
Rate: 0.5-1.5 lb. ae/A
1-3 pt. 4/A
Time: Apply on established grasses in the spring before head comes in to boot and on seedling grass after grass has tillered.
Weeds: Broadleaf weeds including:

bull thistle	dandelion	pigweed
common burdock	field pennycress	plantain
common cocklebur	giant ragweed	purslane
common	mustard	Russian thistle
lambsquarters	pepperweed (except	shepherdspurse
common ragweed	perennial)	yellow rocket

Remarks: Do not apply through any type of irrigation system. Do not graze dairy animals or cut forage for hay within 21 days of application.
State Restrictions: Not for use in California.

– – – – – – – – – – – – – – –

Signal Word/Toxicity Class: Danger/I.

Moxy — see bromoxynil

MSMA

Helena MSMA (6.6) (Helena)
Helena MSMA Plus H.C. (6) (+ surfactant) (Helena)
Rate: 4.5-6 lb. ai/A
5.5-7.25 pt. 6.6/A
6-8 pt. 6/A
Time: After weed emergence, before boot stage. Do not apply after boot stage.
Weeds: Wild oats and other broadleaf and grassy weeds.
Remarks: Bluegrass, fescue and ryegrass grown for seed. For 6.6, add suitable surfactant. Do not make more than 1 application per year. Do not graze or allow hay, seeds or seed screenings from treated crop to be used for food or feed.
State Restrictions: For use in the Pacific Northwest.

– – – – – – – – – – – – – – –

Signal Word/Toxicity Class: Caution/III.

NORTRON

Nortron SC (ethofumesate) (AgrEvo USA)
Rate: 0.625-1.875 lb. ai/A
1.5-3.75 pt. SC/A
Time: Preemergence, postemergence. Apply in fall to moist soil. Apply preemergence to new seedlings of annual ryegrass or postemergence to established stands of perennial ryegrass, tall fescue, or bentgrass.

◆-new product • PP-preplant • PPI-preplant incorporated • PRE-preemergence • POST-postemergence • SEQ-sequential • ae-acid equivalent • ai-active ingredient • DF-dry flowable
E/EC-emulsifiable concentrate • F/FL-flowable • DG/G/WG-dispersable granule • L/LC-liquid • SP/WSP-soluble packet • W/WP-wettable powder • WSB-water soluble bag

Weeds: Weeds and annual grasses:

annual bluegrass	downy brome	volunteer barley
common chickweed	mannagrass	volunteer wheat
common velvetgrass	rattail fescue	wild oat
common vetch	soft chess	

Remarks: For use in ryegrass, tall fescue, and established bentgrass in grass seed crops. All existing vegetable matter should be thoroughly worked into soil before treatment. Do not graze livestock on treated crop.

Crop Rotation: Do not rotate with any other crop except ryegrass or sugar beets for 12 months following application.

– – – – – – – – – – – – – –

Signal Word/Toxicity Class: Caution/III.

Opti-Amine — see 2,4-D

PARAQUAT

Restricted Use Pesticide.

Gramoxone Extra (2.5L) *(ZENECA)*
Rate: 0.5-1 lb. ai/A
1.5-3 pt. 2.5L/A
Time: Preplant, at planting, or preemergence. Allow weed seeds to germinate. Apply when broadleaf weeds and grasses are in 3- to 5-leaf stage. Repeated as necessary prior to grass emergence.
Weeds: Grasses and broadleaf weeds.
Remarks: Add nonionic surfactant or crop oil concentrate. Do not graze treated areas or use seed or straw from treated areas for animal feed or bedding. Refer to label for use directions and precautions.

– – – – – – – – – – – – – –

Signal Word/Toxicity Class: Danger-Poison/I.
REI: 12 hr. (except harvest aid/desiccation 24 hr.).

Rattler — see glyphosate

Rhomene — see MCPA

Rhonox — see MCPA

Roundup PRO — see glyphosate

Saber — see 2,4-D

Savage — see 2,4-D

SCYTHE

Nonselective, postemergent herbicide.

◆ **Scythe (pelargonic acid)** *(Mycogen)*
Rate: 4-13 fl. oz./1 gal. spray solution
Time: May be applied to dormant turf prior to spring greenup.
Weeds: Annual broadleaf weeds and grasses; top-kill of perennial weeds.
Remarks: Apply prior to establishment of turfgrass, or for trimming and edging in established turf. Apply in minimum 75 gal. spray solution/A or spray-to-wet. Do not apply by air or through any type of irrigation system. Refer to label for directions and precautions.
Tank Mixes: Glyphosate and other foliar and residual herbicides.

– – – – – – – – – – – – – –

Signal Word/Toxicity Class: Warning/II.
REI: 24 hr.

Solution — see 2,4-D

Solve — see 2,4-D; MCPA

Sterling — see dicamba

Stinger — see clopyralid

Sword — see MCPA

Weed Rhap — see 2,4-D

Weedar — see 2,4-D

Weedestroy — see 2,4-D

Weedone — see 2,4-D

Turf Grasses For Sod Production

AAtrex — see atrazine

Acclaim Extra — see fenoxaprop-P-ethyl

ASULAM

Asulox (3.34) *(Rhone-Poulenc)*
Rate: 2 lb. ai/A
5 pt./A
Time: Apply when weeds are actively growing.
Weeds: Grasses:

bullgrass	goosegrass	sandbur
crabgrass		

Remarks: For use on St. Augustinegrass and Tifway 419 bermudagrass. Do not use surfactant or apply to turf which is under stress or newly mowed.

– – – – – – – – – – – – – –

Signal Word/Toxicity Class: Caution.

Asulox — see asulam

Atra-5 — see atrazine

ATRAZINE

Particularly effective for control of winter annual weeds. Restricted Use Pesticide due to ground and surface water concerns.

AAtrex 4L or AAtrex Nine-0 (WDG) *(Novartis)*
◆ **Clean Crop Atrazine 4L or 90 WDG** *(Platte)*
Drexel Atrazine 4L, Atra-5 (5L) or 90DF *(Drexel)*
Helena Atrazine 4L *(Helena)*
Riverside Atrazine 4L or 90DF *(Terra)*
Rate: Except Florida:
1-2 lb. ai/A
2-4 pt. 4L/A
1.6-3.2 pt. 5L/A
1.1-2.2 lb. WDG, 90DF/A
Florida:
1-2 lb. ai/A
4-8 pt. 4L/A
3.2-6.4 pt. 5L/A
2.2-4.4 lb. WDG, 90DF/A
Time: Preemergence.

8

Turf, Ornamentals & Woody Plants

Weeds: Most annual broadleaf weeds:

annual	kochia	purslane
morningglory	lambsquarters	ragweed
cocklebur	mustard	sicklepod
groundcherry	nightshade	velvetleaf
jimsonweed	pigweed	(buttonweed)

Grasses:

annual bluegrass	giant foxtail	witchgrass
barnyardgrass	green foxtail	yellow foxtail
(watergrass)	wild oat	

Remarks: Bermudagrass (except FL), centipedegrass, St. Augustinegrass, and zoysiagrass for sod production. Do not graze or feed turf clippings to animals or illegal residues may result. Do not apply through any type of irrigation system. Refer to label for precautions and restrictions.

State Restrictions: Wilbur-Ellis not registered in California.

– – – – – – – – – – – – – –

Signal Word/Toxicity Class: Caution/III.

Barrage — see 2,4-D

Bison — see bromoxynil & MCPA

Broclean — see bromoxynil

Bromac — see bromoxynil & MCPA

Bromox — see bromoxynil

Bromox-MCPA 2-2 — see bromoxynil & MCPA

BROMOXYNIL

Contact broadleaf control herbicide that can be used on seedling grasses and newly sprigged zoysiagrass.

◆ **Broclean 2EC** *(Platte)*
◆ **Bromox 2EC** *(MIcro Flo)*
Buctril (2EC), Buctril 4EC *(Rhone-Poulenc)*
Moxy 2EC *(Terra)*
Rate: 0.25-0.5 lb. ai/A
  1-2 pt. 2EC/A
  0.5-1 pt. 4EC/A
Time: Postemergence. Apply before boot stage.
Weeds: Broadleaf weeds:

buffalobur	ivyleaf morningglory	spiny pigweed
burcucumber	knawel	tall morningglory
common groundsel	kochia	tall waterhemp
common ragweed	London rocket	tumble mustard
corn chamomile	mayweed	velvetleaf
corn gromwell	prostrate knotweed	Venice mallow
cowcockle	puncturevine	wild mustard
giant ragweed	redroot pigweed	wild radish
hemp sesbania	Russian thistle	yellow starthistle

Remarks: Bentgrass, bermudagrass, Kentucky bluegrass, fescues, ryegrass, St. Augustine, and zoysiagrass. Do not apply with backpack or hand-held equipment. Do not allow livestock to graze or feed in treated areas. Refer to label for restrictions and precautions.

– – – – – – – – – – – – – –

Signal Word/Toxicity Class: Warning/II.

BROMOXYNIL & MCPA (Premixes)

Bison (EC) (2 lb./gal. bromoxynil & 2 lb./gal. MCPA) *(Terra)*
◆ **Bromac (EC) (2 lb./gal. bromoxynil & 2 lb./gal. MCPA)** *(Platte)*
◆ **Bromox-MCPA 2-2 (EC) (2 lb./gal. bromoxynil & 2 lb./gal. MCPA)** *(Micro Flo)*
Bronate (EC) (2 lb./gal. bromoxynil & 2 lb./gal. MCPA) *(Rhone-Poulenc)*
Rate: 0.5-1 lb. ai/A
  1-2 pt. EC/A
  Chemigation (Bronate only):
  1 lb. ai/A
  2 pt. EC/A
Time: Apply before boot stage.

Weeds: Broadleaf weeds:

blue mustard	giant ragweed	puncturevine
Canada thistle	hemp sesbania	purple mustard
(suppression)	henbit	tall morningglory
common groundsel	ivyleaf morningglory	tansymustard
common ragweed	knawel	tarweed
corn chamomile	kochia	velvetleaf
corn gromwell	mayweed	wild radish
fumitory	prostrate knotweed	

Remarks: Bentgrass, bermudagrass, Kentucky bluegrass, fescues, ryegrass, St. Augustine, and zoysiagrass. May also be used on seedling grasses such as Delta, Merion, Park or common Kentucky bluegrass, Pennlawn, Chewings, Illahee or Alta fescues, orchardgrass, Highland, Seaside or Astoria bentgrass, perennial ryegrass, bahiagrass, and zoysiagrass. Do not graze treated areas or feed treated grasses to livestock.

– – – – – – – – – – – – – –

Signal Word/Toxicity Class: Warning/II.

Bronate — see bromoxynil & MCPA

Buctril — see bromoxynil

2,4-D - PHENOXY HERBICIDES

◆ **Barrage or Barrage HF (EC) (2,4-D ester)** *(Helena)*
Rate: 6-19 fl. oz./A
Time: Apply when weeds are small and actively growing.
Weeds: Broadleaf weeds controlled by 2,4-D include:

bindweed	ironweed	shepherdspurse
bull thistle	lambsquarters	smartweed
Canada thistle	morningglory	sowthistle
cocklebur	plantain	velvetleaf
cutleaf	purslane	wild garlic
eveningprimrose	ragweed	wild onion
dandelion		

Remarks: Apply to well established grasses such as tall fescue, bluegrass or perennial ryegrass. Do not use on centipede, carpetgrass, St. Augustine, bentgrass, dichondra or desirable clovers. Do not mow 1-2 days before or after treatment, or water until the day after application. Refer to label for precautions and restrictions.

– – – – – – – – – – – – – –

Signal Word/Toxicity Class: Caution/III.

Formula 40 (2,4-D mixed amine) *(Rhone-Poulenc)*
Rate: 1-3 lb. ae/A
  2-6 pt./A
Time: Apply when weeds are young and growing well.
Weeds: Broadleaf weeds.
Remarks: Do not apply to newly seeded turf until grass is well established. Do not use on dichondra or other herbaceous ground covers or on creeping grasses such as bent (except spot treatment). Reseeding should be delayed following treatment: spring treatment, reseed in fall; fall treatment, reseed in spring. Refer to label for precautions and restrictions.

– – – – – – – – – – – – – –

Signal Word/Toxicity Class: Danger/I.

◆ **Saber (2,4-D amine)** *(Platte)*
Rate: 0.25-0.75 lb. ae/A
  0.5-1.5 pt./A
Time: Apply when weeds are small and actively growing under good moisture conditions.
Weeds: Broadleaf weeds.
Remarks: For use on cool-season grasses such as tall fescue and bluegrass. Do not use on centipede, carpetgrass, St. Augustine, bentgrass, dichondra or desirable clovers. Delay mowing 1-2 days before and after application. Watering should be delayed until day after treatment. Do not apply to newly seeded areas until grass is well established and has been mowed several times. Treated areas may be reseeded 30 days after application.

– – – – – – – – – – – – – –

Signal Word/Toxicity Class: Danger/I.

DICAMBA

Controls wide range of broadleaf weeds. Avoid applications over root zone of desirable trees and shrubs.

◆ **Vanquish (dicamba-DGA)** *(Novartis)*
Rate: 0.25-1 lb. ai/A
  0.5-2 pt./A

◆-new product • PP-preplant • PPI-preplant incorporated • PRE-preemergence • POST-postemergence • SEQ-sequential • ae-acid equivalent • ai-active ingredient • DF-dry flowable
E/EC-emulsifiable concentrate • F/FL-flowable • DG/G/WG-dispersable granule • L/LC-liquid • SP/WSP-soluble packet • W/WP-wettable powder • WSB-water soluble bag

Time: Apply when weeds are emerged and actively growing.

Weeds: Annual, biennial, and perennial broadleaf weeds found in turf.

Remarks: Sod farms. Do not treat irrigation ditches, water used for crop irrigation or domestic uses, or apply through any type of irrigation system.

Tank Mixes: Bromoxynil, Confront, 2,4-D, MCPA, MCPP. Refer to label of all products for use directions and precautions.

- - - - - - - - - - - - - - -

Signal Word/Toxicity Class: Caution.

FENOXAPROP-P-ETHYL

Acclaim Extra (0.57E) *(AgrEvo USA)*

Rate: Annual grasses:
3.5-39 fl. oz. 0.57E/A
Perennial grasses:
20 fl. oz. 0.57E/A

Time: Apply when annual grassy weeds are in the 1-leaf to 5-tiller stage. Repeat every 28-35 days to suppress perennial grasses.

Weeds: Annual grasses:

barnyardgrass	johnsongrass	silver crabgrass
foxtail	(seedling)	smooth crabgrass
goosegrass	panicum	sprangletop
hairy crabgrass	sandbur	

Perennial grasses (suppression):

common bermudagrass   johnsongrass (rhizome)

Remarks: Established annual bluegrass, creeping bentgrass (special recommendations for bentgrass), fescues (fine, tall), Kentucky bluegrass, perennial ryegrass, zoysiagrass. Do not apply to sod within 4 weeks before cutting for transplanting or 4 weeks after transplanting. Do not mow treated area for at least 24 hr. after application.

Tank Mixes: May be tank mixed with other labeled pesticides or fertilizers.

- - - - - - - - - - - - - - -

Signal Word/Toxicity Class: Caution/III.

GLYPHOSATE

Use prior to seeding, sprigging, or sodding for nonselective weed control. Does not provide residual weed control.

Roundup PRO (4WS) *(Monsanto)*

Rate: Annual weeds:
0.25-1.5 lb. ai/A
0.5-3 pt. 4WS/A
Perennial weeds:
2-5 lb. ai/A
4-10 pt. 4WS/A

Time: Apply when weeds are actively growing and at proper growth stage.

Weeds: Many broadleaf weeds and the following grasses:

annual bluegrass	crabgrass	johnsongrass
bermudagrass	fescue	quackgrass

Remarks: Do not disturb soil or underground plant parts prior to treatment. Tillage or renovation techniques should be delayed for at least 7 days after application.

- - - - - - - - - - - - - - -

Signal Word/Toxicity Class: Caution/III.

S-METOLACHLOR

Pennant MAGNUM (7.62L) *(Novartis)*

Rate: 1.2-2.5 lb. ai/A
1.3-2.6 pt. 7.62L/A

Time: Apply before weeds emerge.

Weeds: Grasses and sedges:

annual bluegrass	large crabgrass	smooth crabgrass
annual sedge	Mexican sprangletop	yellow nutsedge
bearded sprangletop		

Remarks: Commercial St. Augustinegrass sod production. Irrigate with ¹/₂" water if rainfall does not occur within 7 days after treatment. Do not apply more than 4.2 pt. 7.62L/A per year or more than once every 6 weeks. Do not graze or feed turf clippings to animals.

- - - - - - - - - - - - - - -

Signal Word/Toxicity Class: Caution.

Moxy — see bromoxynil

NORTRON

Nortron SC (ethofumesate) *(AgrEvo USA)*

Rate: 1.125-1.5 lb. ai/A
2.25-3 pt. SC/A

Time: Preemergence, postemergence. Apply in fall to moist soil. Apply preemergence to new seedings of annual ryegrass or postemergence to established stands of perennial ryegrass, tall fescue, or bentgrass.

Weeds: Broadleaf weeds and annual grasses:

annual bluegrass	downy brome	soft chess
barnyardgrass	green foxtail	volunteer barley
canarygrass	large crabgrass	volunteer wheat
common chickweed	mannagrass	wild oat
common velvetgrass	rattail fescue	yellow foxtail
common vetch		

Remarks: For use in ryegrass, tall fescue, and established bentgrass in commercial sod. All existing vegetable matter should be thoroughly worked into soil before treatment. Do not graze livestock on treated crop.

Crop Rotation: Do not rotate with any other crop except ryegrass or sugar beets for 12 months following application.

- - - - - - - - - - - - - - -

Signal Word/Toxicity Class: Caution/III.

Pennant MAGNUM — see *S*-metolachlor

Princep — see simazine

Roundup PRO — see glyphosate

Saber — see 2,4-D

SCYTHE

Nonselective, postemergent herbicide.

◆ **Scythe (pelargonic acid)** *(Mycogen)*

Rate: 4-13 fl. oz./1 gal. spray solution

Time: May be applied to dormant turf prior to spring greenup.

Weeds: Annual broadleaf weeds and grasses; top-kill of perennial weeds.

Remarks: Apply prior to establishment of turfgrass, or for trimming and edging in established turf. Apply in minimum 75 gal. spray solution/A or spray-to-wet. Do not apply by air or through any type of irrigation system. Refer to label for directions and precautions.

Tank Mixes: Glyphosate and other foliar and residual herbicides.

- - - - - - - - - - - - - - -

Signal Word/Toxicity Class: Warning/II.
REI: 24 hr.

SIMAZINE

◆ **Clean Crop Simazine 4L** *(Platte)*
Drexel Simazine 4L or 90DF *(Drexel)*
Princep 4L *(Novartis)*
Riverside Simazine 4L or 90DF *(Terra)*

Rate: 2-4 lb. ai/A
2-4 qt. 4L/A
2.2-4.4 lb. 90DF/A

Time: Preemergence.

Weeds: Broadleaf weeds:

annual	carelessweed	purslane
morningglory	henbit	ragweed
burclover	mustard	

Grasses:

annual bluegrass	fall panicum	foxtail
barnyardgrass		

Remarks: Centipedegrass, St. Augustinegrass, and zoysiagrass being grown for sod production. Rate depends on age of beds and soil type. Do not apply within 30 days of cutting or lifting.

State Restrictions: Do not use north of North Carolina.

- - - - - - - - - - - - - - -

Signal Word/Toxicity Class: Caution/III.

8

Turf, Ornamentals & Woody Plants

TRIMEC (Complexes)

Trimec S.I. or ◆ Trimec 992 (2,4-D & MCPP & dicamba) *(PBI/Gordon)*
Rate: Cool season:
2.2-4 pt. S.I./A
3-4 pt. 992/A
Warm season:
2.2-3 pt. S.I./A
2-2.5 pt. 992/A
Creeping bentgrass:
2.3 pt. S.I./A
1.8 pt. 992/A
Time: Apply to actively growing weeds.
Remarks: Delay mowing 1-2 days before and after application. Do not apply immediately before rainfall or irrigation. Do not irrigate or water within 24 hr. after application. Treated areas may be reseeded 3-4 weeks after application. Do not apply through any type of irrigation system.

Signal Word/Toxicity Class: Danger/I.
REI: 48 hr.

Vanquish — see dicamba

Ornamentals & Woody Plants

(Christmas Trees, Flowers, Forest Plantings, Nurseries, Shelterbelts)

AAtrex — see atrazine

Acclaim Extra — see fenoxaprop-P-ethyl

Accord — see glyphosate

ALACHLOR

Preemergence for effective control of annual grasses, sedges, and certain broadleaf weeds. Sprayable forms injure certain plants whereas the granular formulation is more broadly selective in woody ornamentals. Combine or follow with a preemergence broadleaf herbicide for broad spectrum weed control. Micro-Tech formulation usually provides longer weed control than 4EC. Restricted Use Pesticide.

Lasso (4EC), Lasso II (15G), or Micro-Tech (MT) *(Monsanto)*
Rate: 4 lb. ai/A
4 qt. 4EC, MT/A
27 lb. 15G/A
Time: Apply before weeds emerge or after existing weeds have been removed.
Weeds: Broadleaf weeds:

black nightshade*	Florida pusley	purslane
carpetweed	galinsoga	smartweed*
common ragweed*	lambsquarters*	teaweed*
Florida beggarweed*	pigweed	

Grasses and sedges:

barnyardgrass	goosegrass	robust white foxtail
broadleaf signalgrass	green foxtail	witchgrass
crabgrass	red rice	yellow foxtail
fall panicum	robust purple foxtail	yellow nutsedge
giant foxtail		

* *Reduces competition*

Remarks: 4EC or MT: Field grown junipers, yews. Lasso 15G: Field and liner grown cotoneaster, crabapple, dogwood, euonymus, holly, junipers, yews; container grown juniper and holly. Not for use in greenhouses or other enclosed structures, in seedbeds, unrooted cuttings, or prior to transplanting.

Signal Word/Toxicity Class:
Danger/I (Lasso); Warning/II (Lasso II); Caution/IV (Micro-Tech).
REI: 12 hr.

ALANAP-L

Provides 6-8 weeks of preemergence control of several broadleaf weeds, but does not control grasses.

Alanap-L (naptalam) *(Uniroyal)*
Rate: 6 lb. ai/A
12 qt./A
Time: Apply prior to transplanting or as directed spray after transplanting.
Weeds: Broadleaf weeds:

carpetweed	common purslane	hedge bindweed
common chickweed	common ragweed	redroot pigweed
common cocklebur	cutleaf groundcherry	shepherdspurse
common	field bindweed	velvetleaf
lambsquarters	hairy galinsoga	white mustard

Remarks: Woody ornamentals and shelterbelts. For established woody plants such as elm, holly, lilac, plum, pine, etc., direct spray to strike no higher than 2-3" from soil line. Refer to label for use directions.

Signal Word/Toxicity Class: Warning/II.
REI: 48 hr.

ASULAM

Provides systemic control of brackenfern, horseweed, and other broadleaves and annual grasses; suppresses Canada thistle. No residual control. Growth of weeds is stopped soon after spraying but kill may take 3-4 weeks or longer.

Asulox (3.34) *(Rhone-Poulenc)*
Riverside Asulam 3.3 *(Terra)*
Rate: 3.34 lb. ai/A
8 pt./A
Time: Apply after bud break and hardening of new tree growth. Bracken should be in full frond.
Weeds:
western bracken
Remarks: Christmas tree plantings: Douglas fir, Grand fir, Nobel fir, Scotch pine. Do not use a wetting agent.

Rate: 3.34 lb. ai/A
9 pt./A
Time: Apply when weeds are between stage of early seeding and early seed head formation.
Weeds: Grasses:

barnyardgrass	fall panicum	goosegrass
crabgrass	foxtail	horseweed (marestail)

Remarks: Junipers, yews. Do not use a surfactant.

Signal Word/Toxicity Class: Caution.
REI: 12 hr.

Asulox — see asulam

Atra-5 — see atrazine

ATRAZINE

Triazine herbicide similar to simazine but more soluble and more effective on emerged weeds. As little as 1 lb. ai atrazine/A substituted for 1 lb. ai simazine/A used in Christmas tree plantations can provide improved control of emerged annuals. Resistant annuals of several species have proliferated where atrazine has been used continuously for many years. Restricted Use Pesticide due to ground and surface water concerns.

AAtrex 4L or AAtrex Nine-0 (WDG) *(Novartis)*
◆ Clean Crop Atrazine 4L or 90 WDG *(Platte)*
Drexel Atrazine 4L, Atra-5 (5L) or 90DF *(Drexel)*
Helena Atrazine 4L *(Helena)*
Riverside Atrazine 4L or 90DF *(Terra)*
Rate: 2-4 lb. ai/A
4-8 pt. 4L/A
3.2-6.4 pt. 5L/A
2.2-4.4 lb. WDG, 90DF/A
Time: Apply to established trees between fall to early spring while trees are dormant.

◆-new product • PP-preplant • PPI-preplant incorporated • PRE-preemergence • POST-postemergence • SEQ-sequential • ae-acid equivalent • ai-active ingredient • DF-dry flowable
E/EC-emulsifiable concentrate • F/FL-flowable • DG/G/WG-dispersable granule • L/LC-liquid • SP/WSP-soluble packet • W/WP-wettable powder • WSB-water soluble bag

Weeds: Annual broadleaf weeds:

annual morningglory	kochia	purslane
cocklebur	lambsquarters	ragweed
groundcherry	mustard	velvetleaf
jimsonweed	nightshade	(buttonweed)
	pigweed	

Annual grasses:

barnyardgrass (watergrass)	green foxtail	witchgrass
giant foxtail	quackgrass (high rate)	yellow foxtail

Remarks: Conifers: Douglas fir, grand fir, noble fir, white fir, Austrian pine, bishop pine, Jeffrey pine, knobcone pine, loblolly pine, lodgepole pine (shore pine), Monterey pine, ponderosa pine, Scotch pine, slash pine, blue spruce, Sitka spruce. Do not apply to seedbeds. Do not apply through any type of irrigation system. Refer to label for directions.

State Restrictions: Wilbur-Ellis not registered in California.

Signal Word/Toxicity Class: Caution/III.
REI: 12 hr.

Barrage — see 2,4-D

BASAGRAN

Postemergence contact herbicide that controls yellow nutsedge and certain annual and perennial broadleaf weeds including Canada thistle. Repeat application may be required. Directed sprays are necessary to avoid injury to most ornamentals, but certain ground covers may be sprayed over the top.

Basagran T/O (bentazon) *(BASF)*
Rate: 0.75-1 lb. ai/A
　　1.5-2 pt./A
Time: Apply when weeds are actively growing. For thistle and yellow nutsedge, 2 applications may be needed.
Weeds: Broadleaf weeds:

balloonvine	dayflower	redweed
Canada thistle	devilsclaw	sesbania
coffee senna	galinsoga	shepherdspurse
cocklebur	giant ragweed	spurred anoda
common groundsel	lawn burweed	teaweed
common lambsquarters	musk thistle	wild buckwheat
	Pennsylvania	wild poinsettia
common purslane	smartweed	wild sunflower
common ragweed	prickly sida	wild mustard

Sedges:

annual sedge	yellow nutsedge

Remarks: Add oil concentrate. Apply as directed spray, away from foliage of desired plants, unless otherwise directed. Do not apply to lakes, ponds, streams, or wetlands. Refer to label for directions and restrictions.
Tank Mixes: Pennant, Vantage.

Signal Word/Toxicity Class: Caution/III.
REI: 12 hr.

BASAMID

Fumigant that kills weed seeds in soil ahead of planting.

Basamid Granular (dazomet) *(BASF)*
Rate: 6.5-13 oz./100 sq. ft.
Time: Preplant. Fall soil treatments recommended if early spring planting desired. Do not use at soil temperature below 43°F.
Weeds: Broadleaf weeds:

henbit mustard	pigweed	purslane

Grasses:

bermudagrass	crabgrass	foxtail

Remarks: Ornamental production fields, landscape beds, conifer seed beds. Drench immediately with 15-20 gal. water/100 sq. ft. Plastic cover required.

Signal Word/Toxicity Class: Warning/II.
REI: 24 hr.

Casoron — see dichlobenil

CHIPCO RONSTAR

Selective preemergent herbicide for the control of annual grasses and broadleaf weeds in woody ornamental shrubs, vines, and trees.

Chipco Ronstar G or 50WSP (oxadiazon) *(Rhone-Poulenc)*
Rate: 2-4 lb. ai/A
　　100-200 lb. G/A
　　4-8 lb. 50WSP/A
Time: Ronstar G: Apply to actively growing or dormant ornamentals any time during the year prior to weed seed germination. Ronstar 50WSP: Apply prior to weed seed germination, as directed spray to soil surface or as an over the top spray only on labeled ornamentals. Do not apply during bud break or during the 4 weeks after bud break.
Weeds: Broadleaf weeds:

bittercress	golden ragwort	prostrate spurge
carpetweed	lambsquarters	speedwell
common groundsel	liverwort	spotted catsear
common purslane	Pennsylvania	swinecress
eveningprimrose	smartweed	yellow woodsorrel
galinsoga	petty spurge	

Grasses:

annual bluegrass	crabgrass	goosegrass
barnyardgrass	fall panicum	green foxtail

Remarks: Ronstar G: Apply to both newly transplanted and established ornamentals. Do not apply to wet foliage or under conditions in which granules will collect on leaves. Ronstar 50WSP: Irrigate immediately after application. Do not mix into soil or cultivate. Refer to label for restrictions and precautions.
Tank Mixes: Ronstar 50WSP: Roundup.

Signal Word/Toxicity Class: Warning/II.

CLETHODIM

Envoy (0.94EC) *(Valent)*
Rate: 0.1-0.25 lb. ai/A
　　13-34 fl. oz. 0.94EC/A
Time: Postemergence. Apply to actively growing grasses.
Weeds: Annual grasses:

Amazon sprangletop	green foxtail	smooth crabgrass
annual bluegrass	itchgrass	southern crabgrass
barnyardgrass	johnsongrass	Texas panicum
bearded sprangletop	junglerice	volunteer cereals
bermudagrass	large crabgrass	wild oat
broadleaf signalgrass	quackgrass	wild proso millet
crowfootgrass	red rice	wiresteem muhly
fall panicum	red sprangletop	witchgrass
giant foxtail	shattercane	woolly cupgrass
goosegrass	southwestern cupgrass	yellow foxtail

Remarks: Woody ornamentals, Christmas trees. Rate varies by grass species, stage, and geographical region. Grass crops such as corn, sorghum, wheat, and rice are highly sensitive to clethodim. Do not apply under stress conditions or if rainfall is expected in 1 hour. Do not apply through any type of irrigation system. Do not apply more than 0.5 lb. ai/A (0.25 lb. ai/A on Long Island, NY) per season. Do not graze treated fields or feed treated forage or hay to livestock. Refer to label for restrictions and precautions.
State Restrictions: Not for use on Solano grass in the Vernal Lakes area of Solano County, California; wild rice in Hays County, Texas.

Signal Word/Toxicity Class: Warning/II.
REI: 24 hr.

CLOPYRALID

Selective systemic postemergence broadleaf herbicide that controls many weeds in legume, aster, and smartweed families, but not brush, grasses, or sedges. Provides excellent control of perennials such as Canada thistle, bird vetch, volunteer alfalfa, dock, and red sorrel without injury to labeled Christmas tree species during active growth.

Stinger *(Dow AgroSciences)*
Rate: 0.1-0.25 lb. ae/A
　　0.25-0.66 pt./A
Time: Apply to actively growing weeds. For annual weeds, apply up to 5-leaf stage. For Canada thistle and knapweed, apply after majority of basal leaves have emerged up to bud stage.

8
Turf, Ornamentals & Woody Plants

Weeds: Annual and perennial broadleaf weeds:

buffalobur
Canada thistle
cocklebur
clover
diffuse knapweed
Jerusalem artichoke

jimsonweed
knapweed
marshelder
nightshade
Russian knapweed*
smartweed*

sowthistle*
spotted knapweed
sunflower
vetch
volunteer soybean
wild buckwheat

* *Suppression*

Remarks: Christmas tree plantations: balsam fir, blue spruce, Douglas fir, Fraser fir, grand fir, lodgepole pine, noble fir, ponderosa pine, Scotch pine, white pine. Apply only to trees transplanted 1 year. In the Pacific Northwest, do not apply in the first year of transplanting. Do not apply through any type of irrigation system.

- - - - - - - - - - - - - - - -

Signal Word/Toxicity Class: Caution.
REI: 12 hr.

Corral — pendimethalin

Credit — glyphosate

2,4-D - PHENOXY HERBICIDES

◆ **Barrage or Barrage HF (EC) (2,4-D ester)** *(Helena)*
Rate: Directed/spot spray:
2 lb. ae/100 gal. water
3.2 pt./100 gal. water
Time: Apply in spring to emerged weeds.

Rate: Over-the-top:
1 lb. ae/A
1.6 pt./A (in minimum 10 gal. spray mix)
Time: Apply in spring prior to budbreak or in late summer after complete bud set and hardening.
Weeds: Broadleaf weeds.
Remarks: Christmas tree plantations. Spot treatment: Do not contact foliage with spray.
Days To Harvest: 1 year.

- - - - - - - - - - - - - - - -

Signal Word/Toxicity Class: Caution/III.
REI: 12 hr.

Riverdale L.V. 4 (2,4-D ester) *(Riverdale)*
Wilbur-Ellis Lo Vol-4 (2,4-D ester) *(Wilbur-Ellis)*
Rate: 0.5-1 lb. ae/A
1-2 pt. 4/A
Time: Apply when trees are dormant, prior to bud break.
Weeds: Broadleaf weeds.
Remarks: Christmas tree plantations. Apply over top of Douglas fir. Do not spray over top of pine or true firs. Directed spray may be made to all conifer species but spray must not contact tree foliage. Do not apply to weakened, diseased, or stressed seedlings.
Tank Mixes: May be tank mixed with atrazine; refer to both labels.
State Restrictions: Wilbur-Ellis not registered in California.

- - - - - - - - - - - - - - - -

Signal Word/Toxicity Class: Caution/III.

Wilbur-Ellis Amine 4 (2,4-D amine) *(Wilbur-Ellis)*
Rate: 0.25-1.5 lb. ae/A
0.5-3 pt. 4/A
Time: Apply before or after planting.
Weeds: Broadleaf weeds.
Remarks: Poplar, cottonwood trees grown for pulp. Apply through wick applicators or conventional ground sprayers (except irrigation systems). Do not contact leaves of tree.
State Restrictions: Wilbur-Ellis not registered in California.

- - - - - - - - - - - - - - - -

Signal Word/Toxicity Class: Danger/I.

DICHLOBENIL

Controls many established annual and perennial weeds by root inhibition. Highly volatile and must be applied in cool seasons or covered by mulch. Nov.-Mar. applications just before rain, snow, or irrigation are most effective. Summer preemergence herbicide may be required to extend season-long control.

Casoron 4G *(Uniroyal)*
Dyclomec 4G *(PBI/Gordon)*

Rate: Annual weeds:
4-6 lb. ai/A
100-150 lb. 4G/A
Perennial weeds:
6-8 lb. ai/A
150-200 lb. 4G/A
Time: Apply as soil surface treatment in late fall through early winter.
Weeds: Broadleaf weeds:

bull thistle
camphorweed
carpetweed
chickweed
citronmelon
coffeeweed
cudweed
dandelion
dogfennel
eveningprimrose
fiddleneck
Florida purslane
Florida pusley
gisekia

goosefoot
groundsel
henbit
horsetail
Jerusalem oak
knotweed
lambsquarters
maypop
milkweed vine
minerslettuce
pineappleweed
plantain
purslane
ragweed

red deadnettle
redroot pigweed
rosarypea
Russian thistle
shepherdspurse
smartweed
spanishneedles
spurge
teaweed
wild artichoke
wild aster
wild carrot
yellow woodsorrel

Perennial weeds:

artemisia
Canada thistle
curly dock

false dandelion
horsetail
leafy spurge

Russian knapweed
wild artichoke
yellow rocket

Grasses:

annual bluegrass
crabgrass
foxtail

natalgrass
old witchgrass

Texas panicum
wild barley

Perennial grasses:

fescue

orchardgrass

quackgrass

Remarks: Woody ornamentals (established and nursery stock). Do not use in greenhouses. Do not graze treated areas. Refer to label for precautions and restrictions.

- - - - - - - - - - - - - - - -

Signal Word/Toxicity Class: Caution/III.
REI: 12 hr.

DIQUAT DIBROMIDE

Diquat *(ZENECA)*
Rate: 0.375-0.5 lb. ai/A
1.5-2 pt./A
Time: Site preparation prior to planting. Repeat as needed.
Weeds: Broadleaf weeds and grasses.
Remarks: Nonbearing conifers. Apply by ground only. Use high rate when weeds are large or dense. Do not allow spray to contact green stems, foliage, or fruit. Use a shield or wrap plant when spraying around young trees or vines. Do not apply through any type of irrigation system. Do not graze treated areas. Refer to label for directions, restrictions, and precautions.
Days To Harvest: 1 year.

- - - - - - - - - - - - - - - -

Signal Word/Toxicity Class: Warning/II.
REI: 24 hr.

◆ **Reward or Reward LS** *(ZENECA)*
Rate: Broadcast:
0.25-0.5 lb. ai/A
1-2 pt./A
Spot spray:
0.5-1 lb. ai/100 gal. water
2-4 pt./100 gal. water
Time: Preplant, postplant preemergence, directed spray, or preemergence in ornamental seed crops. For seed crops, repeat at 5-day intervals for up to 3 applications.
Weeds: For control of undesirable broadleaf and grassy weeds.
Remarks: Commercial greenhouses, nurseries, and ornamental seed crops. Add nonionic surfactant. Avoid spray contact with desirable foliage of ornamental plants. Do not apply through any type of irrigation system. Do not use on food or feed crops. Refer to label for directions, restrictions, and precautions.
Tank Mixes: May be tank mixed with preemergent herbicides.
State Restrictions: Not for use in California.

- - - - - - - - - - - - - - - -

Signal Word/Toxicity Class: Warning/II.
REI: 24 hr.

Direx — see diuron

◆-new product • PP-preplant • PPI-preplant incorporated • PRE-preemergence • POST-postemergence • SEQ-sequential • ae-acid equivalent • ai-active ingredient • DF-dry flowable
E/EC-emulsifiable concentrate • F/FL-flowable • DG/G/WG-dispersable granule • L/LC-liquid • SP/WSP-soluble packet • W/WP-wettable powder • WSB-water soluble bag

DIURON

Photosynthetic inhibitor that provides postemergence control of many weed seedlings and long residual preemergence control of annual weeds. Safety margin in ornamental plants is less in areas of high rainfall.

◆ **Diuron 80 WDG** *(Platte)*
Drexel Diuron 4L or 80 *(Drexel)*
Riverside Diuron 80DF *(Terra)*
Rate: 2-4 lb. ai/A
    2.5-5 lb. 4L, 80, 80DF/A
Time: Apply early spring before weeds emerge and before trees leaf out.
Weeds: Broadleaf weeds:

pigweed	ragweed	Russian thistle

Grasses:

cheatgrass	foxtail

Remarks: Established plantings: American elm, casagana, cottonwood, Douglas fir, green ash, honeysuckle, ponderosa pine, red cedar, Russian olive, and Siberian elm. Do not apply to foliage of trees. Refer to label for soil limitations.
State Restrictions: For use in Colorado, Montana, Nebraska, North Dakota, South Dakota, Wyoming.

– – – – – – – – – – – – – – –

Rate: 3.2 lb. ai/A
    4 lb. 80, DF, 80DF/A
Time: Apply after planting but no later than 4 weeks prior to bulb emergence.
Weeds: Broadleaf weeds and grasses:

annual ryegrass	lambsquarters	wild mustard
chickweed	shepherdspurse	

Remarks: Bulbous iris, narcissus. Rate varies by soil type. Do not use on very light soils.
Crop Rotation: Do not replant areas to any crop within 1 year after last application as crop injury may result.
State Restrictions: For use in western Washington.

– – – – – – – – – – – – – – –

Rate: 2.4 lb. ai/A
    3 lb. 80, DF, 80DF/A
Time: Hand-weed and mow fern; make single application within 3-5 days.
Weeds: Broadleaf weeds:

Mexican clover	pokeweed	sowthistle
nightshade	rabbit tobacco	spanishneedles

Grasses:

crabgrass	peppergrass

Remarks: Plumosus fern. Treat only established stands. Do not cultivate or disturb soil after applications.
State Restrictions: For use in Florida.

– – – – – – – – – – – – – – –

Signal Word/Toxicity Class: Caution/III.
REI: 12 hr.

Direx 4L or 80DF *(Griffin)*
Karmex DF *(Griffin)*
Rate: 2-4 lb. ai/A
    2-4 qt. 4L/A
    2.5-5 lb. DF, 80DF/A
Time: Apply early spring before weeds emerge and before trees leaf out.
Weeds: Broadleaf weeds:

pigweed	ragweed	Russian thistle

Grasses:

cheatgrass	foxtail

Remarks: Tree plantings: American elm, caragana, cottonwood, Douglas fir, green ash, honeysuckle, ponderosa pine, red cedar, Russian olive, and Siberian elm. Do not apply to foliage of trees.
State Restrictions: For use in Colorado, Montana, Nebraska, North Dakota, South Dakota, Wyoming.

– – – – – – – – – – – – – – –

Signal Word/Toxicity Class:
Warning/II (Direx 80DF); Caution/III (Direx 4L, Karmex).
REI: 12 hr.

Dyclomec — see dichlobenil

Envoy — see clethodim

Eptam — see EPTC

EPTC

◆ **Eptam 7-E or 20-G** *(ZENECA)*
Rate: 6 lb. ai/A
    7 pt. 7-E/A
    3-6 lb. ai/A
    15-30 lb. 20-G/A
Time: Apply and incorporate 14 days prior to seeding.
Weeds: Broadleaf weeds:

black nightshade	corn spurry	nettleleaf goosefoot
carpetweed*	cutleaf nightshade*	prickly sida*
common chickweed	deadnettle	prostrate pigweed
common	fiddleneck*	redroot pigweed
lambsquarters	Florida pusley	sicklepod*
common pigweed	hairy nightshade	tall morningglory*
common purslane	henbit	tumble pigweed

Annual grasses and sedges:

annual bluegrass	green foxtail	signalgrass*
annual ryegrass	Italian ryegrass	stinkgrass*
barnyardgrass	johnsongrass	Texas panicum*
bermudagrass	(seedling)	volunteer grains
(seedling)	junglerice	(barley, oats, wheat)
crabgrass	lovegrass*	watergrass
fall panicum*	purple nutsedge	wild oat
field sandbur	quackgrass	witchgrass*
giant foxtail	rescuegrass*	yellow foxtail
goosegrass	shattercane	yellow nutsedge

*7-E only

Remarks: 7-E: Pine seedlings (loblolly, slash, longleaf, shortleaf). 20-G: 2-year old lining out stock of Austrian pine, eastern hemlock, Norway pine, red pine, scotch pine, and white pine. Refer to label for directions, incorporation recommendations, use restrictions and precautions.
State Restrictions: 7-E for use in the Southeast and Southwest.

– – – – – – – – – – – – – – –

Signal Word/Toxicity Class: Caution.
REI: 12 hr. unless soil injected or soil incorporated.

FENOXAPROP-P-ETHYL

Provides postemergence control of annual grass weeds and suppresses common bermudagrass. Will not control broadleaf weeds, nutsedges, or rushes.

Acclaim Extra (0.57E) *(AgrEvo USA)*
Rate: Annual grasses:
    13-39 fl. oz. 0.57E/A
    Perennial grasses:
    20 fl. oz. 0.57E/A
Time: Apply when annual grassy weeds are in the 1-leaf to 5-tiller stage. Repeat every 28-35 days to suppress perennial grasses.
Weeds: Annual grasses:

barnyardgrass	johnsongrass	silver crabgrass
foxtail	(seedling)	smooth crabgrass
goosegrass	panicum	sprangletop
hairy crabgrass	sandbur	

Perennial grasses (suppression):
common bermudagrass johnsongrass (rhizome)

Remarks: Deciduous and evergreen trees and shrubs, herbaceous and flowering plants. Do not apply through any type of irrigation system.
Tank Mixes: May be tank mixed with other labeled pesticides or fertilizers.

– – – – – – – – – – – – – – –

Signal Word/Toxicity Class: Caution.
REI: 24 hr.

Finale — see glufosinate-ammonium

FLUAZIFOP-P-BUTYL

Systemic postemergence grass herbicide for use on nonbearing ornamentals. Does not control broadleaf weeds or sedges. Rainfast in 1 hour. Toxic to fish.

Fusilade II *(ZENECA)*
Ornamec Over-The-Top (0.5E) *(PBI/Gordon)*
Rate: 0.25-0.375 lb. ai/A
    11-1.5 pt. II/A
    4-6 pt. 0.5E/A
Time: Apply to actively growing grasses before they exceed recommended growth stages.

8

Turf, Ornamentals & Woody Plants

NOTICE	The information on these pages is for preliminary planning — not a guide for use. Be sure to follow the manufacturer's directions, notwithstanding information contained here.	For personal protective equipment and EPA registration numbers, please turn to page 70.

Ornamentals & Woody Plants

Weeds: Annual grasses:

barnyardgrass
broadleaf signalgrass
fall panicum
field sandbur
giant foxtail
goosegrass
green foxtail
guineagrass
itchgrass

johnsongrass
  (seedling)
junglerice
large crabgrass
prairie cupgrass
red rice
shattercane
smooth crabgrass
southern sandbur

southwestern
  cupgrass
Texas panicum
volunteer cereals
wild oat
wild proso millet
witchgrass
woolly cupgrass
yellow foxtail

Perennial Grasses:

bermudagrass
guineagrass
Italian ryegrass

johnsongrass (rhizome)
quackgrass
sorghum-almum

southern crabgrass
torpedograss
wirestem muhly

Remarks: Newly transplanted and established nongrassy ornamentals, trees, shrubs, and ground covers. Add nonionic surfactant; do not use crop oil concentrate. Do not apply to grasses which are stressed due to moisture, temperature, low soil fertility, mechanical or chemical injury, or to grasses which have tillered, formed seed heads, or exceeded recommended growth stages. Do not apply to ornamentals that may be harvested for food within 1 year after application.

– – – – – – – – – – – – – – – –

Signal Word/Toxicity Class: Caution/III.
REI: 12 hr. (Fusilade II); 4 hr. (Ornamec).

Fusilade — see fluazifop-P-butyl

GALLERY

Long residual preemergence herbicide with no foliar activity on weeds or ornamental plants. Annual grass control is short but combinations with preemergence grass herbicides such as Surflan or Devrinol provide broad spectrum control. Possible alternative to simazine in many ornamentals.

Gallery 75DF (isoxaben) *(Dow AgroSciences)*
Rate: 0.5-1 lb. ai/A
0.66-1.33 lb. 75DF/A
Time: Apply in late summer to early fall, or in early spring, prior to germination of target weeds.

Weeds: Broadleaf weeds:

bittercress
black mustard
black nightshade
blackleaved fleabane
bracted plantain
buckhorn plantain
Carolina geranium
coast fiddleneck
common chickweed
common groundsel
common purslane
common ragweed
common sowthistle
creeping woodsorrel
cudweed
dandelion

dogfennel
green tansymustard
hairy galinsoga
henbit
horseweed
ladysthumb
lambsquarters
London rocket
marestail
mouseear chickweed
pennywort
pigweed
pineappleweed
prickly lettuce
prostrate knotweed
prostrate spurge

redmaids
  rockpurslane
redstem filaree
shepherdspurse
sibara
slender plantain
southern brassbuttons
spotted spurge
thymeleaf speedwell
velvetleaf
white clover
whitestem filaree
wild celery
wild mustard
yellow woodsorrel

Remarks: For use on over 400 ornamental species; refer to label for species treated and use precautions.

– – – – – – – – – – – – – – –

Signal Word/Toxicity Class: Caution/III.
REI: 12 hr.

Garlon — see triclopyr

GLUFOSINATE-AMMONIUM

Partially systemic, nonselective postemergence herbicide with no residual effects in soil. Controls many perennial as well as annual weeds. Fully directed low pressure sprays are required to avoid drift injury to ornamentals. Combinations with preemergence herbicides can provide long lasting control.

Finale *(AgrEvo USA)*
Rate: 0.73-1.46 lb. ai/A
3-6 qt./A
Time: Postemergence.

Weeds: Broadleaf weeds (up to 12"):

annual sowthistle
bindweed
buffalobur
burdock
Canada thistle
chickweed
clover
common cocklebur
curly dock
dandelion
field gromwell
filaree
fleabane
goldenrod
horsetail
jimsonweed

kochia
lambsquarters
leafy spurge
little mallow
London rocket
malva
marestail
musk thistle
nettle
nightshade
pennycress
plantain
prickly lettuce
purslane
ragweed
redroot pigweed

Russian thistle
shepherdspurse
smartweed
tansymustard
velvetleaf
vervain
Virginia copperleaf
white heath aster
wild buckwheat
wild mustard
wild onion
wild rose
wild turnip
woodsorrel
yellow rocket

Grasses:

annual bluegrass
bahiagrass
barley
barnyardgrass
bermudagrass
carpetgrass
crabgrass
cupgrass
dallisgrass
downy bromegrass
fall panicum
fescue

giant foxtail
goosegrass
green foxtail
guineagrass
johnsongrass
  (rhizome)
Kentucky bluegrass
lovegrass
nutsedge
paragrass
quackgrass

ryegrass
sandbur
shattercane
smooth bromegrass
stinkgrass
torpedograss
vaseygrass
wheatgrass
wild oat
windgrass
yellow foxtail

Remarks: Flower beds, greenhouses, mulch beds, nurseries, shade trees, shrubs. Avoid direct spray of drift contact with desirable vegetation and green tissue including turfgrass, trees, shrubs, and flowers. Do not apply as an over-the-top broadcast spray. Do not apply by air or through any type of irrigation system. Refer to label for use directions and precautions.

– – – – – – – – – – – – – – –

Signal Word/Toxicity Class: Warning/II.
REI: 12 hr.

Liberty nc (WS) *(AgrEvo USA)*
Rate: Broadcast:
0.25-0.75 lb. ai/A
2-6 qt. WS/A
Spot or directed application:
1.5-4 fl. oz. WS/gal. water

Weeds: Nonselective general broadleaf weed control:

annual sowthistle
bindweed
buffalobur
burdock
Canada thistle
chickweed
clover
common cocklebur
curly dock
dandelion
dogbane (hemp)
field gromwell
filaree
fleabane
goldenrod
horsetail

jimsonweed
kochia
lambsquarters
leafy spurge
London rocket
malva
marestail
mugwort
musk thistle
nettle
nightshade
pennycress
plantain
prickly lettuce
purslane
ragweed

redroot pigweed
Russian thistle
shepherdspurse
smartweed
tansymustard
velvetleaf
vervain
Virginia copperleaf
white heath aster
wild buckwheat
wild mustard
wild onion
wild rose
wild turnip
woodsorrel
yellow rocket

Grasses and sedges:

barnyardgrass
bermudagrass
cupgrass
crabgrass
dallisgrass
fall panicum
giant foxtail

goosegrass
green foxtail
johnsongrass
  (rhizome)
lovegrass
nutsedge

sandbur
shattercane
stinkgrass
wild oat
windgrass
yellow foxtail

Remarks: Ornamentals and Christmas trees. Site preparation prior to planting, around and within shade and greenhouses, and as a post-directed spray around containers and field-grown established ornamentals and Christmas trees. Avoid direct spray or drift contact with foliage and green bark. Do not apply as over-the-top broadcast spray in ornamentals and shade or Christmas trees. In greenhouses and shadehouses, apply as directed spray; air circulation fans must be turned off during application. Do not use in greenhouses or shadehouses with edible crops. Do not apply by air or through any type of irrigation system.

– – – – – – – – – – – – – – –

Signal Word/Toxicity Class: Warning/II.
REI: 12 hr.

◆–new product • PP-preplant • PPI-preplant incorporated • PRE-preemergence • POST-postemergence • SEQ-sequential • ae-acid equivalent • ai-active ingredient • DF-dry flowable E/EC-emulsifiable concentrate • F/FL-flowable • DG/G/WG-dispersable granule • L/LC-liquid • SP/WSP-soluble packet • W/WP-wettable powder • WSB-water soluble bag

GLYPHOSATE

Systemic, nonselective postemergence herbicide with broad spectrum activity for preplant, fully directed or semi-directed use (certain dormant conifers), and conifer site release. In most established ornamentals, applications must be fully directed at low pressure to avoid plant injury. Excellent tool for nursery, landscape, and Christmas tree maintenance. No residual preemergence activity in mineral soils but may persist in peat or highly organic soils.

Accord (4WS) *(Monsanto)*
Rate: Broadcast:
2-10 lb. ai/A
2-10 qt. 4WS/A in 10-60 gal. water
Directed spray—woody brush & trees:
2% spray solution
Directed spray—herbaceous weeds:
1-2% spray solution
Time: After formation of final conifer resting buds in the fall or prior to initial bud swelling in the spring.
Weeds: Herbaceous and woody plants.
Remarks: Release of forestry conifer and hardwood sites including Christmas tree plantations and silvicultural nurseries. For conifers established for more than 1 year. Avoid contact with foliage, green bark, or nonwoody roots of desirable species.

- - - - - - - - - - - - - - -

Rate: Conifers outside Southeastern states:
1-2 lb. ai/A
1-2 qt. 4WS/A
Conifers in Southeastern states:
1.5-2.5 lb. ai/A
1.5-2.5 qt. 4WS/A
Time: For conifer species in Southeastern states, apply during late summer or early fall after conifers have hardened off.
Weeds: Herbaceous and woody plants.
Remarks: Conifers outside of Southeastern states: Douglas fir, hemlock, pines (with exceptions), California redwood, spruce. Conifers in Southeastern states: Eastern white, loblolly, longleaf, shortleaf, slash, Virginia pine. In Maine, up to 6 pt./A may be used for control of difficult species. Surfactant not recommended for hemlock or California redwood. Avoid contact with foliage, green bark, or nonwoody roots of desirable species.

- - - - - - - - - - - - - - -

Signal Word/Toxicity Class: Caution/III.
REI: 4 hr.

- - - - - - - - - - - - - - -

◆ **Credit (4WS)** *(Nufarm)*
◆ **Glyfos or Glyfos X-tra (4WS)** *(Cheminova)*
Rattler (4WS) *(Helena)*
Roundup PRO (4WS) *(Monsanto)*
Rate: Annual weeds:
0.38-1.5 lb. ai/A
0.75-3 pt. 4WS/A
Perennial weeds:
0.5-5 lb. ai/A
1-10 pt. 4WS/A
Time: Apply prior to planting ornamentals, nursery, or Christmas tree species or as post-directed or spot treatment around established woody ornamentals.
Weeds: Many annual and perennial grasses and broadleaf weeds.
Remarks: Christmas trees, greenhouse/shadehouse, ornamentals (arborvitae, azalea, boxwood, crabapple, euonymus, fir, Douglas fir, holly, lilac, magnolia, maple, oak, pine, privet, spruce, yew). Not for use as over-the-top broadcast spray. Avoid contact of spray, drift, or mist with foliage or green bark of established ornamentals. For greenhouses and shadehouses, desirable vegetation must be present during application and air circulation fans must be turned off.

- - - - - - - - - - - - - - -

Signal Word/Toxicity Class: Varies by formulation.
REI: Warning—12 hr.; Caution—4 hr.

Roundup Custom (5.4WS) or Ultra (4WS) *(Monsanto)*
Rate: Annual weeds:
0.38-1.5 lb. ai/A
0.56-2.25 pt. 5.4WS/A
0.75-3 pt. 4WS/A
Perennial weeds:
0.5-5 lb. ai/A
0.75-7.5 pt. 5.4WS/A
1-10 pt. 4WS/A
Time: Apply prior to planting trees or as post-directed or spot treatment around established trees.
Weeds: Many annual and perennial grasses and broadleaf weeds.
Remarks: Christmas trees. Not for use as over-the-top broadcast spray. Protect nontarget plants during site preparation applications.

- - - - - - - - - - - - - - -

Signal Word/Toxicity Class: Caution/III.
REI: 4 hr.

GOAL

Useful in conifer seedbeds, transplant beds, and plantations. Many conifers tolerate over-the-top sprays except during flush periods but deciduous plants in leafy and herbaceous annuals and perennials are injured.

Goal 2XL (oxyfluorfen) *(Rohm and Haas)*
Rate: Conifer seedbeds:
0.25-1 lb. ai/A
1-4 pt. 2XL/A
Time: Preemergence. Apply after seeding but before conifer emergence.

Rate: Conifer seedbeds:
0.25-0.5 lb. ai/A
1-2 pt. 2XL/A
Time: Postemergence. Apply no sooner than 5 weeks after emergence of conifer seedlings and seedling weeds less than 4" tall.

Rate: Conifer transplants:
1-2 lb. ai/A
4-8 pt. 2XL/A
Time: Preemergence, postemergence. For preemergence, apply immediately after transplanting seedlings; postemergence, apply to seedling weeds less than 4" tall.
Weeds: Broadleaf weeds:

annual sowthistle	hairy nightshade	red sorrel (from seed)
birdseye speedwell	henbit	redmaids
black nightshade	ivyleaf morningglory	rockpurslane
blue mustard	jimsonweed	redroot pigweed
broadleaf filaree	ladysthumb	redstem filaree
bull thistle	little bittercress	Russian thistle
burclover	little mallow	scarlet pimpernel
burning nettle	London rocket	shepherdspurse
carpetweed	mayweed	spotted spurge
catchweed bedstraw	minerslettuce	tall morningglory
coast fiddleneck	Pennsylvania	tansymustard
common cocklebur	smartweed	tumble mustard
common groundsel	prickly lettuce	velvetleaf
common	prickly sida	white clover
lambsquarters	prostrate knotweed	wild buckwheat
common purslane	prostrate pigweed	wild mustard
corn spurry	prostrate spurge	Wright groundcherry
cutleaf groundcherry	red clover	yellow woodsorrel
fireweed (from seed)	red orach	yellowflower
flixweed	red sandspurry	pepperweed

Grasses:

annual bluegrass	goosegrass	wild oat
barnyardgrass	large crabgrass	witchgrass
giant foxtail		

Remarks: Conifer seedbeds and transplants. Not for conifer release in forest management programs or for forest regeneration applications. Refer to label for restrictions and use directions.
Tank Mixes: Glyphosate, napropamide, oryzalin, pendimethalin, prodiamine, pronamide, sethoxydim.

- - - - - - - - - - - - - - -

Rate: 0.5-2 lb. ai/A
2-8 pt. 2XL/A
Time: Preemergence, postemergence. Apply prior to bud swell in spring or after trees have initiated dormancy in fall.
Weeds: Same as above.
Remarks: Field-grown deciduous trees. Use higher rate where heavy weed pressure anticipated or where medium and fine soil textures exist and high organic matter soils are present. Do not allow spray drift or mist to contact foliage or green bark of trees. Add 2 pt./100 gal. spray nonionic surfactant.

- - - - - - - - - - - - - - -

Rate: 1-2 lb. ai/A
4-8 pt. 2XL/A
Time: Preemergence, postemergence. Apply dormant or before bud break.
Weeds: Cottonwood:

common groundsel	hedge mustard	prostrate knotweed
common	Pennsylvania	shepherdspurse
lambsquarters	smartweed	

Eucalyptus:

annual sowthistle	hedge mustard	prostrate knotweed
broadleaf filaree	henbit	prostrate spurge
burning nettle	little mallow	redmaids rockpurslane
coast fiddleneck	London rocket	redroot pigweed
cheeseweed	minerslettuce	redstem filaree
common groundsel	Pennsylvania	shepherdspurse
common lambsquarters	smartweed	spotted spurge
common purslane	prickly lettuce	whitestem filaree

Remarks: Cottonwood, eucalyptus. Add nonionic surfactant.

- - - - - - - - - - - - - - -

Signal Word/Toxicity Class: Warning/II.
REI: 24 hr.

8

NOTICE The information on these pages is for preliminary planning — not a guide for use. Be sure to follow the manufacturer's directions, notwithstanding information contained here. | For personal protective equipment and EPA registration numbers, please turn to page 70.

Gramoxone Extra — see paraquat

HEXAZINONE

Triazine herbicide absorbed through foliage and roots with postemergence and preemergence activity. Controls certain deciduous woody plants in addition to many annual and perennial broadleaves and grasses. Not considered safe on Douglas firs, True firs (Abies spp.), or spruce in the eastern U.S.

Velpar (SP) or Velpar L *(DuPont)*

Rate: 0.9-1.8 lb. ai/A
1-2 lb. SP/A
4-8 pt. L/A

Time: Apply in the spring prior to conifer budbreak to seedling weeds that are actively growing. If applied after budbreak, use directional sprays to prevent contact with conifer foliage.

Weeds: Broadleaf weeds:

catsear	false dandelion	Pennsylvania
common groundsel	fleabane	smartweed
common ragweed	goldenrod*	wild carrot
curly dock*	horseweed*	fireweed*
dandelion*	oxeye daisy	

Grasses:

annual bluegrass	bromegrass	orchardgrass*
barnyardgrass	fescue*	ryegrass*
bentgrass	foxtail	velvetgrass

* Partial control

Remarks: Field grown established Christmas trees: Austrian pine, Douglas fir, Grand fir, loblolly pine, Noble fir, ponderosa pine, scotch pine, and Sitka spruce. Apply only to transplant stock that is at least 2 years old (1 year for loblolly pine). Do not use in nurseries, seedbeds, or ornamental plantings. Use higher rates on established plantations and lower rates on first year plantations.

State Restrictions: Do not use in certain states east of the Rockies (see label).

– – – – – – – – – – – – – – –

Signal Word/Toxicity Class: Danger/I.
REI: 24 hr.

IMAGE

For use on well-established, nonstressed landscape ornamentals.

Image 1.5 LC *(American Cyanamid)*

Rate: 0.375-0.5 lb. ai/A
1-1.3 qt. 1.5 LC/A

Time: Preemergence or postemergence.

Weeds: Broadleaf weeds:

black medic	dovetail geranium	parsley-piert
buttercup	hairy bittercress	purple deadnettle
Carolina geranium	henbit	red sorrel
common chickweed	knawel	white clover
cutleaf	lawn burweed	wild garlic
evening primrose	mouseear chickweed	wild onion

Grasses and sedges:

field sandbur	perennial ryegrass	rice flatsedge
globe sedge	(overseeded)	yellow nutsedge
green kyllinga	purple nutsedge	

Remarks: Established landscape plantings: shrubs, trees, ground covers, perennials. Abelia, Azalea, Ligustrum, Pieris, and Viburnum are known to be severely injured by Image; consult label for specific tolerant species. Temporary growth suppression may be observed on some treated plants. Add 2 pt./100 gal. nonionic surfactant. Do not apply to unlabeled or container grown ornamentals or annual bedding plants. Do not apply to rooting area of unlabeled ornamentals or annual bedding plants or to soil where annual bedding plants may be planted the following year.

– – – – – – – – – – – – – – –

Signal Word/Toxicity Class: Caution.

Karmex — see diuron

KERB

Controls certain perennial and winter-annual grasses and broadleaves with late fall, winter, and early spring applications. To provide season-long control, other preemergence herbicides may be required in the spring. Restricted Use Pesticide.

Kerb 50-W or WSP (pronamide) *(Rohm and Haas)*

Rate: 1-2 lb. ai/A
2-4 lb. 50-W, WSP/A

Time: Preemergence or early postemergence for fall applications prior to leaf drop and soil freeze-up.

Weeds: Broadleaf weeds:

chickweed	red sorrel	shepherdspurse
London rocket	(seedling)	wild mustard

Grasses:

annual bluegrass	Italian ryegrass	perennial ryegrass
cheatgrass	Kentucky bluegrass	quackgrass
downy brome	orchardgrass	volunteer grain
foxtail barley		

Remarks: Woody ornamentals, nursery stock, Christmas trees. Most groundcovers are sensitive to Kerb; refer to label for tolerant species. Avoid contact with these plants from direct application, spray drift, or from applications to areas that may drain onto established ornamental groundcovers. Not recommended for use on seedling trees or shrubs less than 1 year old or to fall transplanted stock less than 1 year or to spring transplanted stock less than 6 months. Do not soil incorporate. Do not apply through any type of irrigation system.

Crop Rotation: Refer to label for specific times for rotation crops.

– – – – – – – – – – – – – – –

Signal Word/Toxicity Class: Caution.
REI: 24 hr.

Lasso — see alachlor

Liberty nc — see glufosinate-ammonium

LINURON

Lorox DF *(Griffin)*

Rate: 1 lb. ai/A
2 lb. DF/A

Time: Apply before emergence of plants.

Weeds: Broadleaf weeds:

annual morningglory*	galinsoga	purslane
carpetweed	lambsquarters	sicklepod*
chickweed	mustard	smartweed
cocklebur*	nettleleaf goosefoot	velvetleaf*
common dayflower	pigweed	(buttonweed)
common ragweed	prickly sida*	wild radish
Florida pusley	(teaweed)	

Grasses:

barnyardgrass	crabgrass	giant foxtail
canarygrass	fall panicum	goosegrass

* Partial Control

Remarks: Calla lily, daffodil, Dutch iris, tulip bulbs. Treat only during growing season.

State Restrictions: For use in California.

– – – – – – – – – – – – – – –

Rate: 1-2 lb. ai/A
2-4 lb. DF/A

Time: Apply before bud break in the spring; after bud break, apply as directed spray. For best results, treat at seedling stage.

Weeds: Same as above.

Remarks: Hybrid poplar. Spray should be directed to weed growth and avoid contact with plant. Do not spray over top. More than 1 treatment may be made; no more than 8 lb. DF/A should be applied per year.

State Restrictions: For use in the Midwest.

– – – – – – – – – – – – – – –

Signal Word/Toxicity Class: Caution.
REI: 24 hr.

Lorox — see linuron

S-METOLACHLOR

Pennant MAGNUM (7.62L) *(Novartis)*

Rate: 1.2-2.5 lb. ai/A
1.3-2.6 pt. 7.62L/A

Time: Apply before weeds emerge or after existing weeds have been removed.

Weeds: Broadleaf weeds:

black nightshade	Florida pusley	hairy nightshade*
carpetweed	galinsoga	pigweed
common purslane*	groundsel*	

◆-new product • PP-preplant • PPI-preplant incorporated • PRE-preemergence • POST-postemergence • SEQ-sequential • ae-acid equivalent • ai-active ingredient • DF-dry flowable
E/EC-emulsifiable concentrate • F/FL-flowable • DG/G/WG-dispersable granule • L/LC-liquid • SP/WSP-soluble packet • W/WP-wettable powder • WSB-water soluble bag

Annual grasses and sedges:

annual bluegrass	green foxtail	southwestern
barnyardgrass	johnsongrass*	cupgrass
crabgrass	(seedling)	volunteer sorghum*
crowfootgrass	prairie cupgrass	watergrass
fall panicum	red rice	witchgrass
foxtail millet	sandbur*	yellow foxtail
giant foxtail	shattercane*	yellow nutsedge
goosegrass	signalgrass	

* Partial control

Remarks: Nurseries and landscape plantings including container-grown and field-grown ornamentals, nonbearing nursery stock. Do not use in greenhouses or other enclosed structures. Rate varies by soil type and organic matter. Do not apply to seedbeds, cutting beds, or unrooted cuttings before transplanting or to plants until soil has firmly settled around roots. When applied broadcast over-the-top of foliage, follow with sufficient overhead irrigation to wash Pennant from foliage. Do not apply more than 4.2 pt./A per year or more than once every 6 weeks.

- - - - - - - - - - - - - -

Signal Word/Toxicity Class: Caution.

Micro-Tech — see alachlor

Ornamec — see fluazifop-P-butyl

OH2 (Premix)

OH2 (2% oxyfluorfen & 1% pendimethalin) *(Scotts)*
Rate: 2.3 lb./1000 sq. ft.
Time: Preemergence. For field grown ornamentals, apply immediately after planting or prior to weed seed germination following complete weed removal. For season-long weed control, repeat at 3-month intervals during growing season.
Weeds: Broadleaf weeds:

bittercress	fleabane	pepperweed
common chickweed	garden spurge	pigweed
cudweed	groundsel	prostrate spurge
dandelion	marestail	shepherdspurse
eclipta	oxalis	sowthistle
fireweed	pearlwort	spotted spurge

Grasses:

annual bluegrass	crabgrass	sprangletop
barnyardgrass		

Remarks: Container and field grown ornamentals. Do not apply in enclosed greenhouses or polyhouse structures. Apply to dry foliage only. Refer to label for directions, restrictions, and precautions.

- - - - - - - - - - - - - -

Signal Word/Toxicity Class: Caution.
REI: 24 hr.

PARAQUAT

◆ **Gramoxone Extra (2.5L)** *(ZENECA)*
Rate: 0.6-1 lb. ai/A
2-3 pt. 2.5L/A
Time: Apply as directed spray when weeds and grasses are succulent and new growth is from 1-6" tall. Apply preemergence for Easter lilies.
Weeds: Annual broadleaf weeds and grasses; top kill and suppression of perennials.
Remarks: Field grown Easter lilies, shade and ornamental trees. Add nonionic surfactant or crop oil concentrate. Do not allow spray to contact green stems, fruit, or foliage. For mature woody weeds, green suckers, late germinating weeds, grasses, and perennials, retreatment or spot treatment may be necessary. Refer to label for restrictions and precautions.
Tank Mixes: Devrinol, Goal, Karmex, Krovar, Princep, Sinbar, Solicam, Surflan.

- - - - - - - - - - - - - -

Signal Word/Toxicity Class: Danger-Poison/I.
REI: 12 hr. (except harvest aid/desiccation 24 hr.).

◆ **Starfire (1.5L)** *(ZENECA)*
Rate: 0.5-1 lb. ai/A
2.5-5.25 pt. 1.5L/A
Time: Preplant. Apply prior to planting with minimum soil disturbance.
Weeds: Annual broadleaf weeds and grasses; top kill and suppression of perennials.
Remarks: Tree plantation establishment for conifers. Add nonionic surfactant or crop oil concentrate. Refer to label for restrictions and precautions.

- - - - - - - - - - - - - -

Signal Word/Toxicity Class: Danger-Poison/I.
REI: 12 hr. (except harvest aid/desiccation 24 hr.).

PENDIMETHALIN

Preemergence root inhibitor chemically related to Treflan and Surflan; primarily effective in controlling annual grasses and certain annual broadleaves. Provides effective residual weed control which may affect new turfgrass seedling or sprigs. Will not control established weeds.

Corral (2.68G) *(Scotts)*
Rate: 1.5-3 lb. ai/A
76-114 lb. 2.68G/A
Time: Preemergence.
Weeds: Broadleaf weeds:

chickweed	hop clover	prostrate spurge
cudweed	knotweed	puncturevine
eveningprimrose	kochia	purslane
fall panicum	lambsquarters	shepherdspurse
fiddleneck	London rocket	smartweed
filaree	oxalis	sprangleweed
Florida pusley	pearlwort	velvetleaf
henbit	pigweed	

Grasses:

annual bluegrass	field sandbur	junglerice
barnyardgrass	foxtail	lovegrass
carpetgrass	goosegrass	signalgrass
crabgrass	itchgrass	witchgrass
crowfootgrass	johnsongrass (seedling)	woolly cupgrass

Remarks: Container and field grown ornamentals, groundcovers, perennials, ornamental grasses. Do not use on fruit trees that will bear fruit within 1 year of application. Apply to dry foliage only, either prior to weed seed germination or following complete weed removal. Repeat using low rate in 3-5 months to extend control or for weeds that germinate in the fall. Water immediately ($1/2$-1") to remove granules from plant foliage and activate the herbicide. Refer to label for directions.

- - - - - - - - - - - - - -

Signal Word/Toxicity Class: Caution.

Pendulum (3.3EC or WDG) *(American Cyanamid)*
Rate: Short term control (2-4 months):
2 lb. ai/A
2.4 qt. 3. EC/A
3.3 lb. WDG/A (one 1.2 oz. soluble bag/1000 sq. ft.)
Long-term control (6-8 months):
4 lb. ai/A
4.8 qt. 3.3EC/A
6.6 lb. WDG/A (two 1.2 oz. soluble bag/1000 sq. ft.)
Time: Preemergence. Apply prior to germination of weed seeds. Most effective when adequate rainfall is received within 30 days after application.
Weeds: Broadleaf weeds:

carpetweed	knotweed	pigweed
common chickweed	kochia	prostrate knotweed
common mouseear	lambsquarters	puncturevine
cudweed	lawn burweed	purslane
fiddleneck	London rocket	shepherdspurse
filaree	mouseear chickweed	spurge
Florida pusley	Pennsylvania	yellow woodsorrel
henbit	smartweed	velvetleaf
hop clover		

Grasses:

annual bluegrass	green foxtail	Mexican sprangletop
barnyardgrass	goosegrass	red sprangletop
browntop panicum	itchgrass	signalgrass
crabgrass	johnsongrass (seedling)	Texas panicum
crowfootgrass	junglerice	witchgrass
fall panicum	lovegrass	woolly cupgrass
field sandbur		yellow foxtail
giant foxtail		

Remarks: Established field grown and container ornamentals, plants, trees, shrubs, groundcovers, perennials, ornamental grasses, and selected annual bedding plants.
Tank Mixes: For established weeds, use registered postemergence herbicides.

- - - - - - - - - - - - - -

Signal Word/Toxicity Class: Caution.
REI: 12 hr.

Pendulum — pendimethalin

Pennant MAGNUM — S-metolachlor

Princep or Princep Caliber 90 — see simazine

NOTICE The information on these pages is for preliminary planning — not a guide for use. Be sure to follow the manufacturer's directions, notwithstanding information contained here.	For personal protective equipment and EPA registration numbers, please turn to page 70.

8

Turf, Ornamentals & Woody Plants

Ornamentals & Woody Plants

Rattler — see glyphosate

Reward — see diquat dibromide

Roundup — see glyphosate

ROUT (Premix)

Granular premix of Goal plus Surflan that provides broad spectrum preemergence weed control.

Rout (2% oxyfluorfen & 1% oryzalin) *(Scotts)*
Rate: 100 lb. product/A
Time: Preemergence. Apply prior to weed seed germination or following weed removal. In container production, repeat at 3-month intervals during growing season.
Weeds: Broadleaf weeds:

ageratum	fireweed	pearlwort
artilleryweed	garden spurge	pigweed
bittercress	groundsel	primrose
buttonweed	hairy spurge	prostrate spurge
castor bean	lambsquarters	purslane
common chickweed	marestail	shepherdspurse
common sowthistle	medic	sowthistle
cutleaf	moss	spotted spurge
eveningprimrose	oxalis	white clover
dandelion		

Grasses:

annual bluegrass	fall panicum	kikuyugrass
barnyardgrass	goosegrass	yellow foxtail
crabgrass	green foxtail	

Remarks: Christmas trees, cut flowers, foliage crops, field and container grown ornamentals. Apply to dry foliage. After planting and prior to chemical application, irrigate with approximately 1/2" water. Do not apply in enclosed greenhouses or apply other labeled herbicides to treated areas within 2 months following treatment. Refer to label for directions and precautions.

– – – – – – – – – – – – – –

Signal Word/Toxicity Class: Caution.
REI: 24 hr.

SCYTHE

Nonselective, postemergent foliar herbicide. May be used to control mosses, lichens, and other cryptogens.

Scythe (pelargonic acid) *(Mycogen)*
Rate: 4-13 fl. oz./1 gal. spray solution
Time: Apply to young, succulent weeds; repeat as needed. May be used prior to emergence of desirable ornamentals.
Weeds: Annual broadleaf weeds and grasses; top-kill of perennial weeds.
Remarks: Flowers, bedding and landscape plants, trees, shrubs. Apply broadcast or directed spray in minimum 75 gal. spray solution/A or spray-to-wet. In established ornamentals, direct spray to base of woody stems and onto target weeds; do not use over-the-top broadcast spray. Do not apply by air or through any type of irrigation system. Refer to label for directions and precautions.
Tank Mixes: Glyphosate and other foliar and residual herbicides.

– – – – – – – – – – – – – –

Signal Word/Toxicity Class: Warning/II.
REI: 24 hr.

SETHOXYDIM

Systemic postemergence annual and perennial grass herbicide; no residual weed control. Safe on wide range of ornamental plants. Perennials may require repeat application. Grasses may take 2 to 4 weeks to die. Immature grasses most sensitive.

Vantage (1EC) *(BASF)*
Rate: 0.28-0.47 lb. ai/A
2.25-3.75 pt. 1EC/A
Time: Apply when weeds are actively growing.
Weeds: Annual and perennial grasses.
Remarks: Christmas trees, ornamental nursery plantings. Refer to label for restrictions and limitations.

– – – – – – – – – – – – – –

Signal Word/Toxicity Class: Caution/III.
REI: 12 hr.

SIMAZAT (Premix)

Restricted Use Pesticide due to groundwater concerns.

Simazat 4L (2 lb./gal. atrazine & 2 lb./gal. simazine) *(Drexel)*
Rate: 2-4 lb. ai/A
4-8 pt. 4L/A
Time: Apply between fall and early spring while trees are dormant or soon after transplanting and before weeds are 1 1/2" high.
Weeds: Annual broadleaf and grass control.
Remarks: Christmas trees: Douglas fir, grand fir, noble fir, white fir, Scotch pine. Do not apply to seedbeds. Do not graze treated areas or apply through any type of irrigation system.
State Restrictions: For use in the Pacific Northwest, west of the Cascades.

– – – – – – – – – – – – – – –

Signal Word/Toxicity Class: Caution.

SIMAZINE

Triazine herbicide that is root absorbed and kills weeds in their early stages of germination and growth by inhibiting photosynthesis. Triazine resistant annuals may proliferate in areas treated with simazine for several years. Combinations of lower rates of simazine with standard rates of preemergence grass herbicides provide long residual broad spectrum control and are widely used in woody ornamentals and Christmas tree plantings.

◆ **Clean Crop Simazine 4L or 90WDG** *(Platte)*
Drexel Simazine 4L or 90DF *(Drexel)*
Princep 4L or Princep Caliber 90 *(Novartis)*
Riverside Simazine 4L or 90DF *(Terra)*
Rate: Nurseries:
2-3 lb. ai/A
2-3 qt. 4L/A
2.2-3.4 lb. 90, 90DF, 90WDG/A
Christmas tree plantings and shelterbelts:
2-4 lb. ai/A
2-4 qt. 4L/A
2.2-4.4 lb. 90, 90DF, 90WDG/A
Time: Apply in fall or spring before weeds emerge. For quackgrass, apply in fall or as split application, using 1/2 rate in fall and 1/2 in early spring after growth begins.
Weeds: Broadleaf weeds:

annual morningglory	Florida pusley	redmaids
burclover	German moss	rockpurslane
carelessweed	groundsel	Russian thistle
carpetweed	henbit	shepherdspurse
common chickweed	knawel	smartweed
common lambsquarters	nightshade	spanishneedles
common purslane	pepperweed	speedwell
fiddleneck	pigweed	tansymustard
filaree	pineappleweed	wild mustard
fireweed	prickly lettuce	yellowflower
flora's paintbrush	ragweed	pepperweed

Grasses:

annual bluegrass	fall panicum	rattail fescue
annual ryegrass	foxtail	signalgrass
barnyardgrass	goosegrass	silver hairgrass
cheatgrass	junglerice	watergrass
crabgrass	quackgrass	wild oat
downy brome	(high rate)	witchgrass

Remarks: Refer to label for rates and tolerant species. For nurseries, do not apply for at least 1 year after transplanting. For Christmas tree plantings or shelterbelts, do not use in seedbeds or cutting beds. In California, Oregon, and Washington, do not apply to Christmas trees or shelterbelts sooner than 1 year after transplanting; other areas, 2 years of age.
Tank Mixes: Surflan (field grown Christmas trees).

– – – – – – – – – – – – – – –

Signal Word/Toxicity Class: Caution/III.
REI: 12 hr.

SNAPSHOT (Premix)

Combination of Gallery and Treflan for preemergence weed control. Does not control established weeds.

Snapshot 2.5TG (2% trifluralin & 0.5% isoxaben) *(Dow AgroSciences)*
Rate: 2-5 lb. ai/A
100-200 lb. 2.5TG/A
Time: Apply in late summer to early fall or in early spring or immediately after cultivation.

◆-new product • PP-preplant • PPI-preplant incorporated • PRE-preemergence • POST-postemergence • SEQ-sequential • ae-acid equivalent • ai-active ingredient • DF-dry flowable
E/EC-emulsifiable concentrate • F/FL-flowable • DG/G/WG-dispersable granule • L/LC-liquid • SP/WSP-soluble packet • W/WP-wettable powder • WSB-water soluble bag

Weeds: Broadleaf weeds:

annual bursage	hairy galinsoga	prostrate knotweed
black medic	hare barley	purple cudweed
black nightshade	heath aster	purslane speedwell
bristly oxtongue	henbit	rattail fescue
burning nettle	horseweed	redstem filaree
California burclover	Indian mustard	Russian thistle
Carolina geranium	jimsonweed	scarlet pimpernel
clover	kochia	shepherdspurse
coast fiddleneck	lanceleaf groundcherry	sibara
common chickweed	London rocket	silversheath knotweed
common groundsel	mallow	slender aster
common lambsquarters	marestail	sowthistle
common purslane	Mexican sprangletop	spurge
common ragweed	nettleleaf goosefoot	sunflower
creeping woodsorrel	panicle willowweed	swinecress
curly dock	Pennsylvania	tall morningglory
dandelion	smartweed	telegraphplant
datura	pigweed	turkey mullein
desert rockpurslane	pineappleweed	velvetleaf
dwarf fleabane	plantain	Virginia pepperweed
eveningprimrose	prickly lettuce	yellow sweetclover
fall panicum	prickly sida	yellow woodsorrel
hairy fleabane		

Annual grasses:

annual bluegrass	Italian ryegrass	wild celery
barnyardgrass	junglerice	wild mustard
bromegrass	lovegrass	wild oat
crabgrass	southwestern cupgrass	wild radish
foxtail	wild carrot	witchgrass

Remarks: Landscape and container grown ornamentals, groundcovers, and nursery stock. Do not apply to bedding plants, nursery seedbeds, or transplant beds. Certain ornamental species sensitive to Snapshot; refer to label.
State Restrictions: Refer to label for use restrictions in Arizona.

– – – – – – – – – – – – – – –

Signal Word/Toxicity Class: Caution/III.
REI: 12 hr.

Starfire — see paraquat

Stinger — see clopyralid

SURFLAN

Preemergence root inhibitor effective in controlling most annual grasses and certain annual broadleaves. No foliar activity on weeds or tolerant ornamental plants. Seedlings of certain conifers less than 3 to 4 years old are also susceptible to injury.

Surflan A.S. (oryzalin) *(Dow AgroSciences)*
Rate: 2-4 lb. ai/A
    2-4 qt. A.S./A
Time: Apply before weeds emerge.
Weeds: Broadleaf weeds:

annual morningglory*	common ragweed*	mustard*
annual smartweed*	cudweed	pigweed
annual sowthistle*	field sandbur	prickly lettuce*
black nightshade*	filaree*	prickly sida *
carelessweed	Florida purslane	prostrate knotweed
carpetweed	Florida pusley	prostrate spurge*
chickweed	giant ragweed*	puncturevine
climbing milkweed*	henbit	red sprangletop
coast fiddleneck	ladysthumb*	redmaids rockpurslane
common groundsel*	lambsquarters	shepherdspurse
common mallow*	London rocket*	teaweed*
common purslane	Mexican clover	velvetleaf*

Grasses:

annual bluegrass	foxtail	panicum
annual ryegrass	goosegrass	pigeongrass
bristlegrass	guineagrass	signalgrass
crabgrass	johnsongrass (seedling)	watergrass
crowfootgrass	junglerice	wild oat
cupgrass	little barley	wiregrass
downy brome	lovegrasszs	witchgrass

* Suppression

Remarks: Apply only to established plants as directed or over-the-top spray on field grown roses and field and container grown ornamentals such as begonias, chrysanthemums, gardenias, impatiens, petunias, zinnias. Not for use in seedbeds. Rate depends on length of control desired.
Tank Mixes: Roundup Ultra.

– – – – – – – – – – – – – – –

Signal Word/Toxicity Class: Caution/III.
REI: 12 hr.

TRICLOPYR

Garlon 3A *(Dow AgroSciences)*
Rate: 0.75-1.88 lb. ae/A
    2-5 pt. 3A/A
Time: Apply when woody plants and weeds are actively growing.
Weeds: Broadleaf weeds and woody plants:

arrowwood	dandelion	poplar
aspen	elderberry	ragweed
beech	field bindweed	sassafras
birch	fireweed	smartweed
blackberry	ground ivy	sumac
Canada thistle	lambsquarters	sycamore
chicory	lespedeza	vetch
chinquapin	mulberry	Virginia creeper
clover	oxalis	wild grape
cottonwood	plantain	wild lettuce
curly dock	poison ivy	wild violet

Remarks: Established Christmas tree plantations. Apply only to trees established 1 yr. Do not reseed treated Christmas tree areas for at least 3 weeks after application. Direct sprays to minimize contact with foliage. Blue spruce, white spruce, balsam fir and Frazier fir less susceptible to injury than white pine and Douglas fir.
State Restrictions: Not for use in Arizona on plants grown for commercial production, specifically, forests grown for commercial timber production.

– – – – – – – – – – – – – – –

Signal Word/Toxicity Class: Danger/I.
REI: 48 hr.

Vantage — see sethoxydim

Velpar — see hexazinone

XL 2G (Premix)

Selective preemergence herbicide for control of certain annual grasses and broadleaf weeds. Does not control established weeds. Requires rainfall or sprinkler irrigation within 21 days to activate.

XL 2G (1% benefin + 1% oryzalin) *(Helena)*
Rate: 4-6 lb. ai/A
    200-300 lb./A
    4.6-6.9 lb./1000 sq. ft.
    Ornamental bulbs:
    1.5-3 lb. ai/A
    75-150 lb./A
    1.7-3.4 lb./1000 sq. ft.
Time: Apply prior to germination of target weeds or immediately after cultivation. Repeat at 60 day intervals.
Weeds: Broadleaf weeds:

annual sowthistle*	desert rockpurslane	prostrate spurge
bittercress	Florida pusley	puncturevine
black mustard*	henbit	redstem filaree
black nightshade*	horseweed*	shepherdspurse
carpetweed	ladysthumb*	smartweed*
chickweed	lambsquarters	spotted spurge*
climbing milkweed*	London rocket	teaweed*
coast fiddleneck	morningglory*	velvetleaf*
common groundsel	pigweed	whitestem filaree
common mallow*	prickly lettuce*	wild mustard*
common purslane	prickly sida*	yellow woodsorrel
common ragweed*	prostrate knotweed	

Grasses:

annual bluegrass	goosegrass	Orcutt lovegrass
barnyardgrass	Italian ryegrass	panicum
crabgrass	johnsongrass	red sprangletop
crowfootgrass	(seedling)	signalgrass
cupgrass	junglerice	volunteer wheat*
field sandbur	little barley	wild oat
foxtail	Mexican lovegrass	witchgrass

* Partial control

Remarks: Container grown ornamentals, landscape ornamentals, nursery stock, groundcovers, established flowers, ornamental bulbs, Christmas trees; refer to label for plant species. Apply only to established plantings. Do not apply to seedbeds or seedling transplant beds. Do not apply over 900 lb./A per year. Refer to label for use directions and precautions.

– – – – – – – – – – – – – – –

Signal Word/Toxicity Class: Caution/III.
REI: 12 hr. unless soil-injected or soil-incorporated.

8

Turf, Ornamentals & Woody Plants

NOTICE The information on these pages is for preliminary planning — not a guide for use. Be sure to follow the manufacturer's directions, notwithstanding information contained here.

For personal protective equipment and EPA registration numbers, please turn to page 70.

Notes • Notes • Notes

Weed Control Manual

Section 9

Other Uses

Use Reminders

Foliar Herbicide Treatment: Susceptibility Of Common
    Brush Species 430
Spray Applications For Long-Term Weed Control 431

Weed Efficacy Charts

Weed Response Ratings For Forage Herbicides 432
Relative Effectiveness of Grass Pasture Herbicides 433
Pasture Brush Weed Control Ratings 434
Susceptibility Of Common Brush Species To Foliar Herbicides 435

Herbicide Listings

Brush Control 436
Conservation Reserve Program 442
Fallow Land 447
Forage 455
Pastures & Rangeland 460
Noncropland 467

Foliar Herbicide Treatment: Susceptibility Of Common Brush Species

Herbicide	Arsenal	Banvel	Brushmaster	Crossbow	2,4-D	Escort	Garlon/Remedy	Hyvar	Krenite S	Roundup	Tordon 101	Weedmaster
Ash, white	G	F	F	F	P	G	F	F	F	F	P	P
Birch	P	G	G	F	F	P	F	F	G	F	F	F
Boxelder	F	—	G	F	F	P	P	G	FP	F	G	F
Brambles	P	F	F	G	P	G	G	F	G	F	F	F
Cedar, eastern red	P	F	P	P	P	F	P	F	P	P	F	P
Cherry, black and choke	G	G	F	FG	FP	G	FG	G	F	G	FG	G
Cottonwood, eastern	G	G	G	FG	FG	F	G	G	FG	F	G	G
Crabapple	—	G	G	FG	F	—	FG	—	—	G	G	G
Elderberry	G	G	G	FG	FG	P	G	G	FG	G	G	G
Elm, American and slippery	P	F	F	F	F	G	F	F	F	F	F	F
Grapes, wild	G	F	FG	G	FG	F	G	—	FG	G	FG	F
Greenbriar	G	F	F	P	P	P	P	P	P	P	F	F
Hackberry	P	F	F	G	FP	P	G	F	FP	F	FG	F
Hawthorn	G	F	F	F	FP	G	F	F	P	F	F	F
Honeylocust	G	F	F	F	P	P	F	F	F	P	G	P
Honeysuckle	G	F	F	P	F	F	P	F	F	F	G	F
Locust, black	P	G	G	G	F	F	G	P	G	F	F	G
Maple, red	G	FP	P	F	P	F	FG	F	F	F	FP	P
Maple, silver or sugar	G	F	F	G	P	G	G	F	F	F	F	F
Mulberry, red or white	G	FP	F	P	P	P	F	F	F	P	F	P
Oak	G	F	F	F	P	FG	FG	F	G	FG	P	F
Olive, Russian	G	F	—	F	F	P	FG	—	F	F	G	F
Osage orange (hedge)	P	FP	P	F	P	F	P	F	F	P	F	P
Persimmon, eastern	F	FG	F	F	F	P	F	P	F	F	FG	FP
Plum, wild	G	FG	FG	F	FG	P	FG	—	FG	G	G	F
Poison ivy	G	FG	F	G	F	P	G	F	P	F	F	F
Rose, multiflora	G	G	G	G	F	F	FG	F	F	G	G	G
Sassafras	G	F	F	F	F	P	F	P	F	F	G	F
Sumac	G	G	G	G	P	P	G	F	G	F	FG	G
Tree-of-heaven	FP	P	F	FG	F	P	G	—	FG	F	FG	P
Trumpetcreeper	G	FG	FP	P	P	P	P	P	F	F	P	F
Virginia creeper	G	FP	G	F	FG	P	F	P	P	F	F	F
Willow	G	FG	G	G	G	G	FG	F	F	F	G	G

G = Good • F = Fair • P = Poor • FG = Fair to Good • FP = Fair to Poor • — = no information available.
Data are adapted from Response of Selected Woody Plants in the United States to Herbicides, Agricultural Handbook No. 493, USDA and from herbicide companies.

Source: 1999 Illinois Agricultural Pest Management Handbook.

Spray Applications For Long-Term Weed Control

Herbicide	Formulations	Rate of formulation per acre		
		Annuals	Shallow perennials	Deep perennials
Arsenal	2S	2 to 4 pt	1 to 6 pt	4 to 6 pt
Hyvar X	80W	3 to 6 lb	7 to 15 lb	7 to 15 lb
Hyvar X-L	2L	1.5 to 3 gal	3 to 6 gal	6 to 12 gal
Karmex	80DF	5 to 15 lb	5 to 15 lb	5 to 15 lb
Krovar	80DF	4 to 6 lb	7 to 18 lb	19 to 30 lb
Oust	75WDG[a]	3 to 5 oz	6 to 8 oz	6 to 8 oz
Pramitol 25E	2S	5 to 7.5 gal	7.5 to 10 gal	10 gal
Spike	80W	5 to 7.5 lb	2.5 to 5 lb	3.75 to 7.5 lb
Velpar	75DF	2.5 to 6.5 lb	6 to 10 lb	—
Velpar L	2L	1 to 2.5 gal	3 to 6 gal	—

— = not labeled for this formulation.
[a]Note that the rate of this product is in ounces per acre.

Source: 1999 Illinois Agricultural Pest Management Handbook.

9

Other Uses
Use Reminders

Weed Response Ratings For Forage Herbicides

Herbicides	Bahiagrass	Bitterweed	Bull thistle	Buttercup	Cheat	Chickweed	Common ragweed	Coreopsis	Crabgrass	Curly dock	Dogfennel	Foxtail	Goldenrod	Groundsel	Henbit	Horsenettle	Horseweed	Lanceleaf ragweed	Little barley	Mullein	Pricklypear cactus	Red sorrel	Smartweed	Smooth pigweed	Tall fescue	Wild garlic	Woolly croton
Preplant Incorporated																											
Balan	N	N	N	N	R	H	R	N	H	N	N	H	N	N	R	N	N	N	R	N	N	N	R	H	N	N	N
Eptam	N	N	N	N	H	H	H	N	H	N	N	H	N	N	H	N	N	N	H	N	N	N	N	H	N	N	N
Preemergence																											
Kerb	N	N	N	R	R	N	N	N	R	N	N	R	N	N	N	N	N	N	N	N	R	N	N	N	N	N	N
Sinbar	N	N	N	N	H	H	N	N	H	N	N	H	N	N	H	N	N	N	H	N	N	N	N	N	N	N	N
Postemergence																											
Ally	H	H	R	H	N	H	N	N	N	H	R	N	N	H	H	R	R	N	H	N	H	N	H	R	H	N	H	H
Banvel	N	H	H	H	N	H	H	R	N	H	H	N	H	N	H	R	H	R	N	N	N	H	H	H	H	N	R	H
Buctril	N	N	N	R	N	R	N	N	N	N	N	N	N	N	N	N	N	N	N	N	N	R	R	N	N	N	N
Crossbow	N	H	H	H	N	R	H	R	N	R	N	H	N	H	N	R	R	H	R	N	H	N	H	H	N	R	H
2,4-D amine	N	H	H	H	N	R	H	N	N	R	R	N	R	R	N	R	H	R	N	N	N	R	N	R	N	R	H
2,4-D ester	N	H	H	H	N	H	H	N	N	R	R	N	N	H	N	R	H	R	N	N	N	R	N	R	N	R	H
2,4-DB	N	R	R	R	N	H	H	N	N	R	N	N	R	N	N	N	N	N	N	N	N	R	N	N	N	N	R
Gramoxone Extra	N	N	N	H	N	H	H	R	N	N	N	H	N	N	N	N	N	H	N	N	N	N	N	N	H	N	R
Grazon P + D	N	H	H	H	N	R	R	N	N	H	H	N	H	R	R	H	H	R	N	R	N	R	H	H	N	N	H
Karmex	N	N	N	N	R	N	N	N	R	N	N	R	N	N	N	N	N	N	R	N	N	N	N	N	N	N	R
Poast/Poast Plus	N	N	N	N	R	N	N	N	R	R	N	R	R	N	N	N	N	N	R	N	N	N	N	N	R	N	N
Pursuit	N	N	N	N	R	R	R	N	N	N	N	N	N	N	N	N	N	N	N	N	N	N	R	N	R	N	N
Roundup Ultra	H	R	N	R	R	R	R	R	R	R	R	R	R	N	N	N	N	R	N	R	N	R	R	R	H	H	H
Select	N	N	N	N	R	N	N	N	H	N	N	N	N	N	N	N	N	N	N	N	N	N	N	R	N	N	N
Sencor	N	N	N	R	R	R	N	N	N	N	N	N	N	N	N	N	N	R	N	N	N	R	N	N	R	N	N
Tordon 22K	N	N	H	N	N	N	N	N	R	N	N	R	R	N	R	H	R	R	N	N	R	H	R	R	N	N	N
Velpar	N	N	N	N	R	N	N	N	N	N	N	N	N	N	N	N	N	R	N	N	N	R	N	N	N	N	N
Weedmaster	N	H	H	H	N	H	H	R	N	H	H	N	H	N	H	R	H	H	N	R	N	R	H	H	N	R	H
Zorial	N	N	N	N	R	R	N	N	R	N	N	R	N	N	R	N	N	N	R	N	N	N	N	N	R	N	N

H = Highly recommended, R = Recommended, N = Not recommended

Source: Recommended Chemicals for Weed and Brush Control, Arkansas, 1999

Relative Effectiveness Of Grass Pasture Herbicides

Species	Ally 0.1-0.3 oz/A	Banvel[1] 1 pt	Crossbow 2-4 qt	2,4-D[1] 2-3 pt	2,4-D + Banvel[1] 1 + 1 pt	Roundup 1-2 qt	Stinger 0.66-1.33 pt
Winter annuals							
Common chickweed	10	7	9	7	8	10	6
Corn cockle	—	10	8+	8	10	10	N
Cowcockle	—	10	8+	8	10	10	N
Field pennycress	9	8	9+	9	10	10	7
Horseweed (marestail)	9	9	10	9	9	9+	9+
Mayweed chamomile	10	8+	8	7	10	9	9
Mustard spp.	10	8	10	9	10	10	7
Pepperweed spp.	10	8	9+	9	10	10	7
Shepherdspurse	10	8	9	8+	10	10	7
Summer annuals							
Black nightshade	8	8+	8+	7+	8+	9	7
Common cocklebur	10	10	10	9	10	9	9
Common lambsquarters	10	10	10	10	10	9	6
Common ragweed	7	9	10	9	10	10	9+
Giant ragweed	—	9	10	8+	10	10	9+
Jimsonweed	10	10	9	8	10	9	7
Pigweed spp.	10	9	9	9	10	9	6
Velvetleaf	9	10	9	8+	10	9	6
Biennials							
Bull thistle	10	9	9+	8+	10	9	9+
Common burdock	9	8	9	9	10	9	9
Common evening primrose	—	8	9+	9	10	10	—
Musk thistle	10	9	9+	9	10	9	9+
Plumeless thistle	10	9	9+	8+	10	9	9+
Poison hemlock	—	8	9	7+	9	9	N
Wild lettuce	10	8+	9	9	10	9	9
Wild parsnip	9	9	10	9	10	9	N
Yellow rocket	10	9	10	9	10	9	6
Herbaceous perennials							
Aster spp.	7	8+	9	9	10	9	9+
Bedstraw spp.	N	N	9+	7	7	9	7+
Brackenfern	—	N	7+	7	7	—	—
Buttercup spp.	10	8	10	8+	9	9	—
Canada thistle	8+	8	8+	8	8+	8	9+
Chicory	10	8	9	7	10	9	9
Clover spp.	10	8+	8+	7	8+	10	9
Common milkweed	N	8	7+	7	8+	8+	7
Common yarrow	—	9	—	7	9	9	8
Daisy spp.	10	8+	9+	9	10	8+	9+
Dandelion	10	8	9+	9+	10	8	9
Dock spp.	9	8	9	8	10	9	8+
Field bindweed	N	8+	8+	8	8+	8	N
Fleabane spp.	9	9	9+	9	10	8+	9
Goldenrod spp.	7+	7+	9	9	9	9	8
Groundcherry spp.	—	7	8	7	7+	8	N
Hawkweed spp.	7	7+	9	9	9	9	8
Hedge bindweed	N	9	9	9	10	9	N
Hemp dogbane	8	8	7	7	8+	8	6
Horsenettle	9+	8	8+	7	9	8	N
Ironweed	—	8+	9	8	9	9	7
Mouseear chickweed	10	7+	8+	7	8	9	6
Mugwort	7	7	8	6	7	7	8+

> **NOTICE** The information on these pages is for preliminary planning — not a guide for use. Be sure to follow the manufacturer's directions, notwithstanding information contained here.

Relative Effectiveness Of Grass Pasture Herbicides, cont.

Species	Ally 0.1-0.3 oz/A	Banvel[1] 1 pt	Crossbow 2-4 qt	2,4-D[1] 2-3 pt	2,4-D + Banvel[1] 1 + 1 pt	Roundup 1-2 qt	Stinger 0.66-1.33 pt
Perennial sowthistle	—	8	8+	7	9	9	8
Plantain spp.	7	8	9	9	10	9	7
Red sorrel	10	8+	—	7	10	9	8
Spotted knapweed	—	8	8+	8	9	9	9
Stinging nettle	—	8	9	8	9	9	—
White cockle	—	8+	9	7	9	9+	9
Wild carrot	10	8	9+	9	10	9	6
Wild garlic or onion	10	7	8	8	8+	9	N
Yellow woodsorrel	10	7	8	7	7+	9	8
Woody perennials[1]							
Autumn olive	—	7+	8	7	8	8	N
Black locust	7	8	8	7	8+	8	N
Blackberry spp.	9	6	8	7	7+	8	7
Dewberry spp.	9	6	8	7	7+	7	7
Honeysuckle spp.	10	N	8+	7	7+	8	N
Multiflora rose	8+	6	8+	6	7+	8	N
Poison ivy or oak	6	7+	8+	7	8+	8	N
Sumac spp.	N	7+	8+	7	7+	8	7
Trumpetcreeper	N	7	8	7	7+	8	N
Virginia creeper	7	8	8+	7	9	8	N
Wild grape	8	8	9	8	9	8	N

[1]Higher rates may be more effective on some species.

Weed Control Rating: 10 = 95-100%, 9 = 85-95%, 8 = 75-85%, 7 = 65-75%, 6 = 55-65%, N = Less than 55% or no control, — = Unknown. Consult label for use rates and precautions.

Source: Penn State Field Crop Weed Control Guide 1999

Pasture Brush Weed Control Ratings

Herbicides	Black locust	Blackberry	Buckbrush	Cedar	Cherry	Elm	Greenbriar	Hawthorn	Honey locust	Honeysuckle	Kudzu	Oaks	Osage orange	Persimmon	Pine	Poison ivy	Sassafrass	Sumac	Sweetgum	Wild rose	Willow
Ally	N	R	R	N	R	R	N	R	N	R	H	N	R	N	N	N	N	N	N	R	R
Banvel, Vanquish	N	R	N	N	N	N	N	N	N	N	H	N	N	R[4]	N	N	N	N	N	R	N
Crossbow	R	R	R	N	R	R	N	R	R	R	R	R	R	N	R	N	R	N	R	N	R
2,4-D	H	N	H	N	N	N	N	H	N	N	R	N	R	N	N	N	N	H	N	N	H
Grazon P+D	R	R	R	N	R	R	R[3]	R	H	R	R	R	N	R	N	R	N	R	R	R	R
Remedy	R	H	R	N	R	R	R[3]	R	R	R	R	R	H	N	R	N	R	N	R	H	N
Roundup Ultra	R	H[2]	N	N	R	N	R	N	R	H[2]	R	N	N	N	H[2]	N	R	N	R	H	R
Spike	R	R	R	R[1]	R	H	N	R	R	R	H	R	R	N	R	N	R	N	R	R	R
Tordon 22K	N	R	N	R	N	N	N	H	N	N	N	N	N	R[4]	N	R	N	R	N	R	N
Velpar	R	R	R	R[1]	N	R	N	R	H	H	R	R	N	N	R	N	R	N	R	H	R
Weedmaster	N	R	R	R	N	R	N	R	R	R	R	R	N	N	R	N	N	R	N	R	R

[1]Small red cedar   [2]September application   [3]Suppression only   [4]Soil application

H = Highly recommended, has been shown to be effective if used properly.
R = Recommended, intermediately susceptible or listed by the manufacturer on the label.
N = Not recommended, has not performed in research or is not listed on the label.

Source: Recommended Chemicals for Weed and Brush Control, Arkansas, 1999

Other Uses Weed Efficacy Chart

Susceptibility Of Common Brush Species To Foliar Herbicides

	Arsenal	Banvel	Brushmaster	Crossbow	2,4-D	Escort	Garlon/Remedy	Hyvar	Krenite	Roundup	Tordon 101	Weedmaster
Birch	P	G	G	F	F	P	F	F	G	F	F	F
Black locust	P	G	G	G	F	F	G	P	G	F	F	G
Boxelder	F	—	G	F	F	P	P	G	FP	F	G	F
Brambles (blackberry, etc.)	P	F	F	G	P	G	G	F	G	F	F	F
Cherry (black & choke)	G	G	F	FG	FP	G	FG	G	F	G	FG	G
Crabapple	—	G	G	FG	F	—	FG	—	—	G	G	G
Eastern cottonwood	G	G	G	FG	FG	F	G	G	FG	F	G	G
Eastern persimmon	F	FG	F	F	F	P	F	P	F	F	FG	FP
Eastern red cedar	P	F	P	P	P	P	P	F	P	P	F	P
Elderberry	G	G	G	FG	FG	P	G	G	FG	G	G	G
Elm (American & slippery)	P	F	F	F	F	G	F	F	F	F	F	F
Greenbriar	G	F	F	P	P	P	P	P	P	P	F	F
Hackberry	P	F	F	G	FP	F	G	F	FP	F	FG	F
Hawthorn	G	F	F	F	FP	G	F	F	P	F	F	F
Honeylocust	G	F	F	F	P	F	F	F	F	P	G	P
Honeysuckle	G	F	F	P	F	F	P	F	F	F	G	F
Maple (silver or sugar)	G	F	F	G	P	G	G	F	F	F	F	F
Mulberry (red or white)	G	FP	F	P	P	P	F	F	F	P	F	P
Multiflora rose	G	G	G	G	F	F	FG	F	G	G	G	G
Oak	G	F	F	F	P	FG	FG	F	G	FG	P	F
Osageorange (hedge)	P	FP	P	F	P	F	P	F	F	P	F	P
Poison ivy	G	FG	F	G	F	F	G	P	F	F	F	F
Red maple	G	FP	P	F	P	F	FG	F	F	F	FP	P
Russian olive	G	F	—	F	F	P	FG	—	F	F	G	F
Sassafras	G	F	F	F	P	P	F	P	F	F	G	F
Sumac	G	G	G	G	F	P	G	F	G	F	FG	G
Tree-of-heaven	FP	P	F	FG	F	P	G	—	FG	F	FG	P
Trumpetcreeper	G	FG	FP	P	P	P	P	P	F	F	F	F
Virginia creeper	G	FP	G	F	FG	P	F	P	P	F	F	F
White ash	G	F	F	F	P	G	F	F	F	F	P	P
Wild grapes	G	F	FG	G	FG	F	G	—	FG	G	FG	F
Wild plum	G	FG	FG	F	FG	P	FG	—	FG	G	G	F
Willow	G	FG	G	G	G	G	FG	F	F	F	G	G

G = Good; F = Fair; P = Poor; FG = Fair to good; FP = Fair to poor; — = No information available.
Data are adapted from *Response of Selected Woody Plants in the United States to Herbicides*, Agricultural Handbook No. 493, U.S. Department of Agriculture, and from herbicide companies.

Source: 1999 Illinois Agricultural Pest Management Handbook

9

Other Uses
Weed Efficacy Chart

Other Uses

Brush Control

Accord — see glyphosate

Banvel — see dicamba

Barrage — see 2,4-D

Brash — see 2,4-D Combinations

Broadrange — see 2,4-D Combinations

Brushmaster — see 2,4-D Combinations

Chopper — see imazapyr

Cleanout — see 2,4-D Combinations

Credit — see glyphosate

2,4-D - PHENOXY HERBICIDES

2,4-D and 2,4-D-type compounds selectively control broadleaf weeds with little or no control of grasses. Drift can injure adjacent crops either by spray drift or by volatilization (spray turns into a vapor). Ester formulations most volatile and amines least volatile. Ester formulations can vaporize at temperatures as low as 70°F and can be moved by wind to harm sensitive plants.

Albaugh Amine 4 (2,4-D amine) *(Albaugh)*
Albaugh LV4 or LV6 Ester (2,4-D ester) *(Albaugh)*
◆ **Opti-Amine (4) (2,4-D amine)** *(Helena)*
Riverdale 4 Amine IVM or 6 Amine (2,4-D amine) *(Riverdale)*
Riverdale L.V. 4 or L.V. 6 (2,4-D ester) *(Riverdale)*
Weed Rhap A-4D (2,4-D amine) *(Helena)*
Weed Rhap LV-6D (2,4-D ester) *(Helena)*
Weedestroy AM-40 (2,4-D amine) *(Riverdale)*
Wilbur-Ellis Amine 4 (2,4-D amine) *(Wilbur-Ellis)*
Wilbur-Ellis Lo Vol-4 or Lo Vol-6 (2,4-D ester) *(Wilbur-Ellis)*
 Rate: 1 lb. ae/A
      2 pt. 4/A
      1.5 pt. 6/A
 Time: For sagebrush, apply when foliage is fully expanded and brush is actively growing. For sand shinnery oak, apply between May 15-June 15.
 Weeds:
  sagebrush   sand shinnery oak

 Rate: 2-3 lb. ae/A
      4-6 pt. 4/A
      2.66-4 pt. 6/A
 Time: Apply up to 3 weeks before frost as long as soil moisture is sufficient for active growth of brush. Hard-to control species may require retreatment next season.
 Weeds: Woody plants such as:

alder	elderberry	willow
buckbrush	sumac	

Rate: Pine release:
    1 ml undiluted product (4)/injection
    7 ml undiluted product (6)/injection
Time: Treatments can be made at any season. For best results, apply during growing season, May 15-Oct.15.
Weeds: Unwanted hardwoods such as:

ash	hawthorn	pecan
beech	hickory	sumac
dogwood	maple	sweetgum
elm	oak	

Remarks: For pine release, space injections 2" apart (1-1¹⁄₂" for hard-to-kill species), edge to edge, completely around tree and close to base.
Tank Mixes: Wilbur-Ellis Amine: Accord.
State Restrictions: Wilbur-Ellis not registered in California.
— — — — — — — — — — — — — — —
Signal Word/Toxicity Class: Danger/I (amine); Caution/III (ester).
REI: Danger—48 hr.; Caution—12 hr.

◆ **Barrage or Barrage HF (EC) (2,4-D ester)** *(Helena)*
 Rate: 3.2-6 pt./A (in minimum 10 gal. spray mixture)
 Time: Bud break spray: Apply after alder buds break, but before foliage is ¹⁄₄ size. Foliage spray: Apply after alder has reached full size. Conifer release: Apply in the spring when ³⁄₄ brush foliage has full size leaves and before conifer reaches 2" in length.
 Weeds: Controls broadleaf weeds and woody plants such as:

alder	ceanothus	manzanita
canyon live oak	madrone	tanoak

 Remarks: Oil or oil concentrate may be added to the spray mixture. Refer to label for use directions and precautions.
— — — — — — — — — — — — — — —
 Signal Word/Toxicity Class: Caution/III.
 REI: 12 hr.

◆ **Clean Crop Amine 4 (2,4-D amine)** *(Platte)*
Riverside 2,4-D Amine 4 (2,4-D amine) *(Terra)*
 Rate: 0.75 ml undiluted product/injection
 Time: Treatments can be made at any season.
 Weeds: Unwanted hardwoods such as:

elm	maple	pecan
hawthorn	oak	sumac
hickory		

 Remarks: Use on Southern pine stands.
— — — — — — — — — — — — — — —
 Signal Word/Toxicity Class: Danger/I.
 REI: 48 hr.

◆ **Clean Crop Low Vol 4 or Low Vol 6 (2,4-D ester)** *(Platte)*
Riverside 2,4-D LV4 (2,4-D ester) *(Terra)*
 Rate: 1 lb. ae/A
    2 pt. 4/A
    1.33pt. 6/A
 Time: For sagebrush, apply when foliage is fully expanded and brush is actively growing. For sand shinnery oak, apply between May 15-June 15.
 Weeds:
  sagebrush   sand shinnery oak

 Rate: 2 lb. ae/A
    4 pt. 4/A
    2.66 pt. 6/A
 Time: Apply when brush is leafed out and actively growing.
 Weeds:
  rabbitbrush   sagebrush
 Remarks: Do not graze meat animals on treated areas later than 3 days prior to slaughter, dairy animals within 7 days after treatment.
— — — — — — — — — — — — — — —
 Signal Word/Toxicity Class: Caution/III.
 REI: 12 hr.

Formula 40 (2,4-D mixed amine) *(Rhone-Poulenc)*
 Rate: Elm, hickory, oak, sweetgum:
    1 ml undiluted product/injection site
    Ash, maples, dogwood:
    2 ml undiluted product/injection site
 Time: Treatments can be made at any season.

◆-new product • PP-preplant • PPI-preplant incorporated • PRE-preemergence • POST-postemergence • SEQ-sequential • ae-acid equivalent • ai-active ingredient • DF-dry flowable
E/EC-emulsifiable concentrate • F/FL-flowable • DG/G/WG-dispersable granule • L/LC-liquid • SP/WSP-soluble packet • W/WP-wettable powder • WSB-water soluble bag

Weeds: Unwanted hardwood in forest and other noncrop areas:

dogwood	hickory	oak
elm	maple	sweetgum

Remarks: Continuous cuts around trunk often provide improved control. Cuts nearer ground level may be more effective than at higher levels. Effectiveness may be less when treated during winter months.

- - - - - - - - - - - - - - -

Signal Word/Toxicity Class: Danger/I.
REI: 48 hr.

◆ Saber (2,4-D amine) *(Platte)*
Rate: 1-2 ml undiluted product/injection
Time: Treatments can be made at any season. For best results, apply during growing season, May 15-Oct.1.
Weeds: Unwanted hardwood trees.
Remarks: Make injections as near root collar as possible using 1 injection/" trunk diameter at breast height (DBH). Continuous cuts around trunk often provide improved control. Maples should not be treated during spring sap flow.

- - - - - - - - - - - - - - -

Signal Word/Toxicity Class: Danger/I.
REI: 48 hr.

Savage (WSB) (2,4-D amine) *(Platte)*
Rate: 4 lb. WSB in 1 gal. water
    1-2 ml/injection site
Time: For best results, apply during growing season, May 15-Oct.15.
Weeds: Unwanted hardwoods such as:

alder	blackgum	oak
aspen	cherry	sweetgum
birch	hickory	tulip poplar

Remarks: Make injections or cuts around tree or stem, using 1 injection/" trunk diameter (DBH). For resistant species such as hickory, injection cuts should touch. For forestry site preparation, mix 2-4 lb./A in 5-25 gal. water.

- - - - - - - - - - - - - - -

Signal Word/Toxicity Class: Danger/I.
REI: 48 hr.

Solution (WS) (2,4-D amine) *(Riverdale)*
Rate: 1 WS packet (2 lb. 13 oz.) in 1.5 gal. water
    0.75 ml/injection site
Time: Treatments can be made at any season. For best results, apply during growing season, May 15-Oct.15.
Weeds: Unwanted hardwoods such as:

ash	hawthorn	pecan
beech	hickory	sumac
dogwood	maple	sweetgum
elm	oak	

Remarks: Space injections 2" apart (1-1½" hard-to-kill species), edge to edge, completely around tree and close to base. Maximum rate for forestry site preparation is 2 packets/1.13 A per application per site.

- - - - - - - - - - - - - - -

Signal Word/Toxicity Class: Danger/I.

Solve 2,4-D (2,4-D LV ester) *(Albaugh)*
Rate: 2-3 lb. ae/A
    4-6 pt. 4/A
Time: Apply to actively growing plants. Do not apply during time of severe drought or in early fall when leaves lose their green color. Hard-to control species may require re-treatment next season.
Weeds: Woody plants such as:

alder	elderberry	willow
buckbrush	sumac	

Rate: Pine release:
    1 ml undiluted product/injection
Time: Treatments can be made at any season. For best results, apply during growing season, May 15-Oct.15.
Weeds: Unwanted hardwoods such as:

dogwood	hickory	pecan
elm	maple	sumac
hawthorn	oak	sweetgum

Remarks: For pine release, space injections 2" apart (1-1½" for hard-to-kill species), edge to edge.

- - - - - - - - - - - - - - -

Signal Word/Toxicity Class: Caution/III.
REI: 12 hr.

Weedar 64 (4) (2,4-D amine) *(Nufarm)*
Rate: Dilute injection:
    1 gal/19 gal. water
    Concentrate injection:
    1-2 ml undiluted product/injection
Time: For best results, apply during growing season, May 15-Oct.15.
Weeds: Unwanted hardwoods such as:

alder	blackgum	oak
aspen	cherry	sweetgum
birch	hickory	tulip poplar

Remarks: Make injections as near root collar as possible using 1 injection/" trunk diameter at breast height (DBH). For resistant species such as hickory, injections should overlap.

- - - - - - - - - - - - - - -

Signal Word/Toxicity Class: Danger/I.
REI: 48 hr.

Weedone LV4 (2,4-D solventless ester) *(Nufarm)*
Weedone Lo Vol 6 (2,4-D ester) *(Nufarm)*
Rate: 2 lb. ae/A
    4 pt. LV4/A
    0.5-2 lb. ae/A
    0.66-2.75 pt. LV6/A
Time: Consult state or local specialists for timing of spray applications.
Weeds:

sagebrush	sand sage	shinnery oak

Remarks: Do not graze treated areas within 7 days after treatment.

- - - - - - - - - - - - - - -

Rate: 1.5-4 lb. ae/A
    3-8 pt. LV4/A (in 6-25 gal. water)
    1-4.5 lb. ae/A
    1.33-6 pt. LV6/A (in 6-25 gal. water)
Time: Bud break spray: Apply after alder buds break, but before foliage is ¼ size. Foliage spray: Apply after alder has reached full size. Conifer release: Apply in the spring when ¾ brush foliage has full size leaves and before conifer reaches 2" in length.
Weeds: Controls broadleaf weeds and woody plants such as:

alder	ceanothus	manzanita
canyon live oak	madrone	tanoak

Remarks: Fuel oil may be added to spray mixture. Refer to label for use directions and precautions.
State Restrictions: Lo Vol 6 not registered for use in California.

- - - - - - - - - - - - - - -

Signal Word/Toxicity Class: Caution/III.
REI: 12 hr.

2,4-D COMBINATIONS

BK 800/SuperBrush (4.5S) (2,4-D & 2,4-DP & dicamba) *(PBI/Gordon)*
Brushmaster (2.3S) (2,4-D & 2,4-DP & dicamba) *(PBI/Gordon)*
Cleanout (1.1S) (2,4-D & 2,4-DP & dicamba) *(PBI/Gordon)*
Rate: High Volume:
    0.5-1 gal. 4.5S/100 gal. water
    1-2 gal. 2.3S/100 gal. water at
    2-4 gal. 1.1S/100 gal. water at
    Basal, cut surface, frill:
    10 fl. oz. 2.3S/1 gal.oil
    20 fl. oz. 1.1S/1 gal.oil
    4.5S: Rate depends on method used and number of stems.
Time: Apply when brush is young and actively growing, from full leaf to leaf drop for mixed brush during warm weather throughout growing season. Basal bark, cut stump, frill: Apply during dormant period before bud growth or any signs of active growth. Basal bark treatment may be applied any time of year except when water or snow prevents spraying to ground line; cut stump treatment can be applied throughout year except when snow, ice, or water prevents thorough spray coverage.
Weeds: Brush:

ash	cottonwood	multiflora rose
aspen	dogwood	oak
birch	elm	pine
black cherry	gooseberry	spruce
black locust	honeylocust	sumac
brambles	honeysuckle	sycamore
buckbrush	kudzu	wild plum
cedar	maple	willow

Remarks: Foliar application: Apply in 100-300 gal. spray/A as full cover spray, wetting all leaves, stems, and root collars of woody plants. Basal bark: Apply coarse spray as drench treatment to base of stems and trunks up to a height of 18-24". Total coverage essential. Cut surface (stump treatment): Apply on stumps with diameters larger than 3-4". Frill treatment recommended for culling trees with trunk diameters greater than 5".

- - - - - - - - - - - - - - -

Signal Word/Toxicity Class: Caution (1.1S, 2.3S); Warning (4.5S).

9

Other Uses

NOTICE The information on these pages is for preliminary planning — not a guide for use. Be sure to follow the manufacturer's directions, notwithstanding information contained here.

For personal protective equipment and EPA registration numbers, please turn to page 70.

◆ Brash (2.87 lb./gal. 2,4-D & 1 lb./gal. dicamba) *(Terra)*
Weedmaster (2.87 lb./gal. 2,4-D & 1 lb./gal. dicamba) *(BASF)*
Rate: Apply undiluted.
Trees and vines such as:

alder	hawthorn	poison oak
ash	hemlock	poplar
aspen	hickory	rabbitbrush
basswood	honeylocust	Russian olive
beech	honeysuckle	sagebrush
black locust	hornbeam	sassafras
blackberry	huisache	spruce
blackgum	kudzu	sumac
cedar	maple	sweetgum
cherry	mesquite	sycamore
cottonwood	multiflora rose	tarbush
creosotebush	oak	willow
dewberry	persimmon	witchhazel
dogwood	pine	yaupon
elm	poison ivy	yucca
greenbriar		

Remarks: For frill or girdle treatments, make continuous cut or series of overlapping cuts using axe to girdle tree trunk and then spray or paint cut surface. For stump treatment, spray or paint cut surface, thoroughly wetting cambium layer (area adjacent to bark). Treat stumps within 6 hr. after cutting.

– – – – – – – – – – – – – –

Signal Word/Toxicity Class: Danger/I.
REI: 48 hr.

Broadrange (2,4-D & 2,4-DP) *(Wilbur-Ellis)*
Rate: 1-2 pt./A in 1 gal. oil + 3 gal. water
Weeds:
sand shinnery oak

Rate: 0.66 gal./A in 1 gal. oil + 5 gal. water
Weeds:

blackjack oak	post oak	winged elm

Time: Apply in spring after hardwoods have developed full sized leaves. Apply from early May/mid-June in Texas and California; early May/early July in Oklahoma and northern states.
Remarks: For maximum control, use higher rate and repeat spray the second year using 2 pt./A.

– – – – – – – – – – – – – –

Rate: Basal bark, frill, cut surface treatment—stumps:
3-4 gal./A in 100 gal. oil
Weeds: Woody plants and brush including:

alder	fir	poplar
ash	gooseberry	raspberry
aspen	greenbriar	red elder
birch	gum	salmonberry
black cherry	hemlock	sand sagebrush
black locust	honeysuckle	sassafras
blackberry	kudzu	serviceberry
box elder	locust	snowberry
brambles	manzanita	spicebrush
buckbrush	maple	spruce
Ceanothus	multiflora rose	sumac
chamise	oak	sweetgum
coffeeberry	osageorange	sycamore
currant	palmetto	Virginia creeper
dewberry	persimmon	wild cherry
dogwood	pine	wild grape
elderberry	poison ivy	wild oak
elm	poison oak	willow

Time: Apply any time of year.
Remarks: For cut surface treatments, spray entire stump as quickly as possible after trees are cut.
Tank Mixes: Banvel.
State Restrictions: Not registered in California.

– – – – – – – – – – – – – –

Signal Word/Toxicity Class: Caution.

◆ Clean Crop DPD Ester Brush Killer (2,4-D & 2,4-DP ester) *(Platte)*
Rate: High volume spray:
1-1.5 gal./100 gal. water
Basal, cut surface, frill treatment:
3-4 gal./100 gal. oil
Time: High volume spray may be applied any time of year when plants are well leafed and actively growing. Basal bark and cut stump treatments may be applied throughout the year except when snow, ice, or water prevent thorough coverage.

Weeds: Woody plants including:

alder	elderberry	poison oak
aspen	elm	poplar
birch	hawthorn	sagebrush
boxelder	hickory	sassafras
buckbrush	honeysuckle	sumac
cherokee rose	locust	sweetgum
chokecherry	mulberry	wild cherry
cottonwood	oak	wild grape
elder	osageorange	wild plum

Remarks: High volume spray: Apply 200-600 gal. spray/A as full cover spray; thoroughly wet foliage and bark. Basal treatment: Apply to bark around trunk and stems to a height of 12-15". Spray thoroughly to point of runoff at the soil line. Stump treatment: Thoroughly wet both side and top of freshly cut stumps. Frill treatment: Apply to overlapping cuts made in the bark around tree trunk as close to the ground as possible. Repeat as needed.

– – – – – – – – – – – – – –

Signal Word/Toxicity Class: Caution

◆ Patron 170 (2,4-D & 2,4-DP) *(Riverdale)*
Rate: High volume:
1-1.5 gal./100 gal. water (200-600 gal. spray/A)
Basal, cut surface, frill:
3-4 gal./100 gal. oil
Time: Apply to matured stems and foliage before plants start to go dormant. Basal bark, cut stump, frill: Treatments may be applied any time of the year.
Weeds: Woody plants and brush including:

alder	fir	poplar
ash	gooseberry	raspberry
aspen	greenbriar	red elder
birch	gum	salmonberry
black cherry	hemlock	sand sagebrush
black locust	honeysuckle	sassafras
blackberry	kudzuvine	serviceberry
box elder	locust	snowberry
brambles	manzanita	spicebrush
buckbrush	maple	spruce
Ceanothus	multiflora rose	sumac
chamise	oak	sweetgum
coffeeberry	osageorange	sycamore
currant	palmetto	Virginia creeper
dewberry	persimmon	wild cherry
dogwood	pine	wild grape
elderberry	poison ivy	wild rose
elm	poison oak	willow

Remarks: Foliar application: Apply to stems and foliage, wetting all leaves, stems and suckers to ground line. Basal bark: Apply coarse spray to base and root collar of all stems until spray accumulates at ground line. Rate depends on species, season, and volume of spray used. Cut surface (stump treatment): Apply on stumps with diameters larger than 3-4". Frill treatment recommended for trees with trunk diameters greater than 5".

– – – – – – – – – – – – – –

Rate: Pine release:
2-4 lb. ae/A
2-4 qt./A in 10 gal. water
Time: Apply midsummer after pine height growth is complete and conifer buds are set.
Weeds: Woody plants and brush including:

alder	cherry	pine
aspen	hazel	spruce
birch		

Remarks: Apply as broadcast spray. Do not apply through any type of irrigation system. Avoid spray drift that might injure desirable plants.
Tank Mixes: Banvel to control mixed brush.

– – – – – – – – – – – – – –

Signal Word/Toxicity Class: Caution.

DICAMBA

Banvel (WS) (DMA salt of dicamba) *(BASF)*
◆ Sterling (WS) (DMA salt of dicamba) *(Terra)*
Rate: 1 fl. oz. WS/10 ft. canopy diameter.
Time: Dormant application.
Weeds:
multiflora rose

Remarks: Apply when plants are dormant as undiluted spot concentrate directly to soil or as low-oil basal bark treatment using oil-water emulsion solution. Do not exceed 4 pt./A per year.

– – – – – – – – – – – – – –

Signal Word/Toxicity Class: Warning/II.
REI: 24 hr.

◆-new product • PP-preplant • PPI-preplant incorporated • PRE-preemergence • POST-postemergence • SEQ-sequential • ae-acid equivalent • ai-active ingredient • DF-dry flowable
E/EC-emulsifiable concentrate • F/FL-flowable • DG/G/WG-dispersable granule • L/LC-liquid • SP/WSP-soluble packet • W/WP-wettable powder • WSB-water soluble bag

◆ **Vanquish (dicamba-DGA)** *(Novartis)*
Rate: 2 lb. ai/A
    4 pt./A in 15 gal. water
Time: Do not spray under windy or gusty conditions.
Weeds: Broadleaf weeds, undesirable conifers, brambles, hardwood brush and trees.
Remarks: Forest site preparation. Apply by ground or air as broadcast or foliar spray.
Tank Mixes: Accord, Arsenal, Garlon, etc. Refer to labels for directions and precautions.

- - - - - - - - - - - - - - -

Rate: 1 part product/1-3 part water
Time: Apply within 30 minutes of cutting.
Weeds: Unwanted trees and prevention of sprouts of cut trees.
Remarks: Cut surface treatment. For frill or girdle treatment, make continuous cut or series of overlapping cuts using axe to girdle tree trunk; spray or paint cut surface with mix. For stump treatment, spray or paint freshly cut surface with water mix; area adjacent to bark should be thoroughly wet.

- - - - - - - - - - - - - - -

Rate: Spot concentrate:
    1 fl. oz./10 ft. canopy diameter
    Lo oil basal bark:
    2 gal. spray solution/A
Time: Dormant. For spot concentrate, do not apply when snow or water prevents application directly to soil. For basal bark, do not apply after bud break, when plants are showing signs of active growth, or when snow or water prevent application to ground line.
Weeds:
    multiflora rose
Remarks: For spot concentrate, apply undiluted directly to soil as close as possible to root crown but within 6-8" of crown. For basal bark, apply to basal stem region from ground line up to 12-18" tall; spray to runoff.

- - - - - - - - - - - - - - -

Signal Word/Toxicity Class: Caution.

2,4-DP (DICHLORPROP)

◆ **Patron DP-4 Ester or Riverdale DP-4 Ester** *(Riverdale)*
Rate: 0.5-2 lb. ai/A
    1-4 pt. 4/A
Time: Apply when plants have just developed full-sized leaves, soil moisture is sufficient for good growing conditions, humidity is high, and wind velocities are less than 5 mph.
Weeds: Woody plants and brush:

alder	pine	sandsage
black cherry	post oak	spruce
blackjack oak	red oak	white oak
elm	sand shinnery oak	willow
fir		

Remarks: Complete coverage required. For post and blackjack oak, retreat second year with 2 pt./A; sand shinnery oak 1 pt./A. Refer to label for use directions and precautions.

- - - - - - - - - - - - - - -

Rate: 4 lb. ai/A
    1 gal./A in 24 gal. water
Time: Apply when hardwoods are in full leaf, actively growing, and soil moisture is high.
Weeds: Woody plants and brush:

boxelder	hickory	sumac
cherry	oak	sweetgum
chinquapin	sassafras	waxmyrtle

Remarks: Pine plantations. Apply 5-10 gal. spray mixture/A to 1-3 yr. old plantations with 2-4 ft. brush of average density. Avoid spraying planted pines, some needle damage may result. Refer to label for directions.

- - - - - - - - - - - - - - -

Signal Word/Toxicity Class: Caution.
REI: 12 hr.

ESCORT

Escort (DF) (metsulfuron-methyl) *(DuPont)*
Rate: Low volume:
    1-3 oz. DF/A
Weeds: Woody brush:

ash	blackberry	mulberry
aspen	cherry	red oak
black locust	elm	tulip tree

Rate: High volume:
    0.5-2 oz. DF/100 gal. water
Time: Foliar applications should be made after brush is fully leafed until beginning of fall leaf coloration.

Weeds: Woody brush and vines:

ash	elder	red maple
aspen	elm	salmonberry
blackberry	multiflora rose	thimbleberry
cherry	oak	willow
cottonwood	oceanspray	

Rate: Spotgun basal soil treatment:
    1 oz. DF/gal. water
Time: Apply from early spring to summer when ground is not frozen.
Weeds:
    multiflora rose
Remarks: Complete coverage of all foliage and stems required.

- - - - - - - - - - - - - - -

Signal Word/Toxicity Class: Caution.
REI: 4 hr.

Formula 40 — see 2,4-D

GLYPHOSATE

Accord or Accord Site Prep (4WS) *(Monsanto)*
Rate: Broadcast:
    2-10 lb. ai/A
    2-10 qt. 4WS/A
    Low volume directed spray:
    0.5-10% solution
    Spray-to-wet:
    0.75-2% solution
Time: Apply to actively growing woody brush and trees after full leaf expansion and before fall color and leaf drop.
Weeds: Woody brush, trees, and herbaceous weeds.
Remarks: Add nonionic surfactant to Accord; Accord Site Prep already has surfactant included. Refer to label for use directions and restrictions.

- - - - - - - - - - - - - - -

Rate: Injection or frill application:
    1 ml 4WS/2-3" trunk diameter (DBH)
Time: Apply during periods of active growth and full leaf expansion.
Weeds: Woody brush and trees:

black gum	oak	sweetgum
dogwood	poplar	sycamore
hickory	red maple	

Remarks: Apply 50-100% solution either to continuous frill around tree or as cuts evenly spaced around tree below all branches.

- - - - - - - - - - - - - - -

Rate: Cut stump:
    50-100% solution
Time: Apply to freshly cut surface immediately after cutting.
Woody brush and trees:

alder	hickory	saltcedar
coyotebrush	madrone	sweetgum
dogwood	maple	sycamore
eucalyptus	oak	tan oak
giant reed	poplar	willow

Remarks: Refer to label for use directions, restrictions, and precautions.

- - - - - - - - - - - - - - -

Signal Word/Toxicity Class: Caution.
REI: 4 hr.

◆ **Credit (4WS)** *(Nufarm)*
◆ **Glyfos or Glyfos X-tra (4WS)** *(Cheminova)*
Rattler (4WS) *(Helena)*
Roundup Custom (5.4WS)
Roundup PRO, Original, or Ultra (4WS) *(Monsanto)*
Rate: 2-5 lb. ai/A
    3-7.5 pt. 5.4WS
    4-10 pt. 4WS/A
    Hand-held:
    0.75-1.5 5.4WS solution
    1-2% 4WS solution
Time: Apply after full leaf expansion.
Woody brush and trees:

alder	California sagebrush	elderberry
ash*	cascara*	elm*
bearclover	catsclaw*	eucalyptus
bearmat	Ceanothus	Florida holly
birch	chamise	French broom
black locust*	cherry	hasardia
blackberry	Chinese tallowtree	hawthorn
bluegum	dewberry	hazel
Brazilian peppertree	dogwood	hickory
California buckwheat	eastern redbud	honeysuckle

9

Other Uses

Brush Control

Woody brush and trees, continued:

kudzu	sage	sumac
manzanita	salmonberry	sweetgum
multiflora rose	saltbush	swordfern
oak	saltcedar*	thimbleberry
persimmon*	sassafras	tree tobacco
poison ivy	Scotch broom	trumpetcreeper
poison oak	sea myrtle	Virginia creeper*
quaking aspen	sourwood*	willow
Russian olive	southern waxmyrtle	yellow poplar*

Partial control

Remarks: Allow 7 or more days after application before tillage, mowing, or removal.

- - - - - - - - - - - - - - -

Rate: Cut stump:
50-100% solution

Time: Apply to freshly cut surface immediately after cutting. For best results, apply during periods of active growth and full leaf expansion.

Woody brush and trees:

alder	madrone	sweetgum
eucalyptus	oak	tan oak
giant reed	saltcedar	willow

Remarks: Do not make cut stump application when roots of desirable woody brush or trees may to grafted to root of cut stump.

- - - - - - - - - - - - - - -

Signal Word/Toxicity Class: Varies by formulation.
REI: Warning—12 hr.; Caution—4 hr.

Roundup PRO (4WS) *(Monsanto)*

Rate: Injection or frill application:
1 ml 4WS/2-3" trunk diameter (DBH)

Time: Apply during periods of active growth and full leaf expansion.

Weeds: Woody brush and trees:

black gum	oak	sweetgum
dogwood	poplar	sycamore
hickory	red maple	

Remarks: Apply 50-100% solution either to continuous frill around tree or as cuts evenly spaced around tree below all branches.

Signal Word/Toxicity Class: Caution/III.
REI: 4 hr.

HEXAZINONE

Pronone 10G/MG or Power Pellet *(Pro-Serve)*

Rate: 4-5 lb. ai/A
40-50 lb. 10G, MG/A
1-2 pellets/1" stem diameter

Time: Apply between late winter and early summer.

Weeds: Brush:

aspen	huisache	red cedar
black cherry	junipers	small soapweed
blackgum	lotebush	snowbrush
catclaw acacia	manzanita	sumac
deerbrush	mesquite	sweet gum
dogwood	multiflora rose	tallow
elm	myrtle	whitebrush
green ash	oak (except line oak)	whitehorn
hackberry	osageorange	wild cherry
hawthorn	persimmon	willow
hickory		

Remarks: For individual stem treatment, apply pellets to soil within 3 ft. of root collar. For larger stems, apply on opposite side of stem. Do not apply to brush standing in water or near desirable trees or shrubs.

- - - - - - - - - - - - - - -

Signal Word/Toxicity Class: Caution/III.
REI: 24 hr.

Velpar (SP) or L *(DuPont)*

Rate: 3.6-7.2 lb. ai/A
4-8 lb. SP/A
2-4 gal. L/A

Time: Apply between late winter and early summer.

Weeds: Brush:

aspen	huisache	red cedar
black cherry	junipers	small soapweed
blackgum	lotebush	snowbrush
catclaw acacia	manzanita	sumac
deerbrush	mesquite	sweet gum
dogwood	multiflora rose	tallow
elm	myrtle	whitebrush
green ash	oak (except line oak)	whitehorn
hackberry	osageorange	wild cherry
hawthorn	persimmon	willow
hickory		

Remarks: Do not apply to brush standing in water, use water from treated ditches for irrigation, or use near desirable trees or shrubs.

- - - - - - - - - - - - - - -

Signal Word/Toxicity Class: Danger/I.
REI: 24 hr.

IMAZAPYR

Chopper or Stalker (2EC) *(American Cyanamid)*

Rate: 8-12 fl. oz. 2EC/1 gal. solution

Time: For Chopper, apply as cut stump, tree injection, frill or girdle, or as low volume basal bark treatment. For Stalker, apply as cut stump, cut stubble, thinline, or as low volume basal bark treatment.

Weeds: Trees and vines such as:

ash	hickory	red alder
beech	madrone	red maple
bigleaf maple	maple	Russian olive
blackgum	mulberry	sassafras
boxelder	multiflora rose	sourwood
cherry	oak	sumac
chinaberry	persimmon	sweetgum
Chinese tallowtree	poplar	willow
dogwood	prickly wild rose	yellow poplar
hawthorn	privet	

Remarks: Apply in 1 gal. water, diesel oil, or penetrating oil (use water only when temperatures are sufficient to prevent freezing). Do not use on food or feed crops. Do not apply on ditches used to transport irrigation water. Do not use on lawns, driveways, tennis courts, etc.

State Restrictions: Not for use in California.

- - - - - - - - - - - - - - -

Signal Word/Toxicity Class: Caution.
REI: 12 hr.

MCPA

Sword (5.2) *(Platte)*
Wilbur-Ellis MCPA Amine or Ester (4) *(Wilbur-Ellis)*

Rate: 1.25 lb. ae/A
2.5 pt. 4/A
2 pt. 5.2/A

Time: Apply in spring or fall under good moisture condition, full leaf, and before blossoms begin to fall.

Weeds:
whitebrush

Remarks: Add 1 gal. diesel oil to mixture with enough water to make 8 gal. solution/A.

State Restrictions: Wilbur-Ellis not registered in California.

- - - - - - - - - - - - - - -

Signal Word/Toxicity Class: Danger/I (amine); Warning/II (ester).
REI: 12 hr.

MSMA

Helena MSMA (6.6) *(Helena)*
Helena MSMA Plus H.C. (+ surfactant) *(Helena)*

Rate: 1-2 ml/cut

Time: Apply during dormant or growing season.

Weeds: Undesirable trees such as:

big leaf maple	Jack pine	red pine
cedar	lodgepole pine	silver pine
Douglas fir	ponderosa pine	western hemlock
grand fir		

Remarks: Crown kill through injection or frill application. For trees under 8" diameter, space injections 2" apart; over 8" diameter, 1" apart. Refer to label for additional directions and recommendations.

- - - - - - - - - - - - - - -

Signal Word/Toxicity Class: Caution/III.
REI: 12 hr.

Opti-Amine — see 2,4-D

Patron 170— see 2,4-D Combinations

Patron DP-4 — see 2,4-DP

◆-new product • PP-preplant • PPI-preplant incorporated • PRE-preemergence • POST-postemergence • SEQ-sequential • ae-acid equivalent • ai-active ingredient • DF-dry flowable
E/EC-emulsifiable concentrate • F/FL-flowable • DG/G/WG-dispersable granule • L/LC-liquid • SP/WSP-soluble packet • W/WP-wettable powder • WSB-water soluble bag

Pronone — see hexazinone

Rattler — see glyphosate

Roundup — see glyphosate

Saber — see 2,4-D

Savage — see 2,4-D

Solution — see 2,4-D

Solve — see 2,4-D

SPIKE

Spike 20P (tebuthiuron) *(Dow AgroSciences)*
Rate: Low volume:
0.75-6 lb. ai/A
3.75-30 lb. 20P/A
Time: Apply when more than 10% grass cover is present and grass is dormant.
Weeds: Over 40 species of woody brush including:

blackbrush acacia	post oak	whitebrush
blackjack oak	sand shinnery oak	

Remarks: Rate varies by weed species. Grazing allowed in areas treated with 20 lb./A or less.

– – – – – – – – – – – – –

Signal Word/Toxicity Class: Caution/III.

Stalker — see imazapyr

Sterling — see dicamba

SuperBrush — see 2,4-D Combinations

Sword — see MCPA

Vanquish — see dicamba

Velpar — see hexazinone

VENGEANCE (Premix)

◆ **Vengeance (2.5 lb./gal. MCPA & 1.25 lb./gal. dicamba)** *(Wilbur-Ellis)*
Rate: 1-2.33 gal./A
Weeds: Annual, biennial, perennial, woody brush and vines such as:

alder	gum	Russian olive
ash	hawthorn	sagebrush
aspen	hemlock	sassafras
basswood	honeysuckle	schinus
beech	kudzu	serviceberry
birch	locust	snowberry
blackberry	maple	spruce
Brazil peppertree	multiflora rose	sumac
cherry	oak	sycamore
christmas-berry	persimmon	trumpetcreeper
cucumbertree	pine	Virginia creeper
dogwood	poison ivy	waxmyrtle
eastern redcedar	poplar	wild plum
elderberry	puncturevine	willow
elm	raspberry	witchhazel
Florida holly	redvine	yaupon

Time: Apply to actively growing weeds, vines, and brush.
Remarks: Spray all foliage, stems, and root collars to wet. Surfactant or drift control agent may be added. Refer to label for directions, restrictions, and precautions.
Tank Mixes: Asulam, bromacil, chlorsulfuron, 2,4-D, 2,4-DP, diuron, fosamine ammonium, glyphosate, hexazinone, imazapyr, MSMA, picloram, simazine, sulfometuron-methyl, tebuthiuron, triclopyr.
State Restrictions: Not registered in California.

– – – – – – – – – – – – –

Signal Word/Toxicity Class: Danger/I.

VETERAN (Premixes)

◆ **Veteran 720 (WS) (1.9 lb./gal. 2,4-D & 1 lb./gal. dicamba)** *(Riverdale)*
Rate: 0.725-2.9 lb. ai/A
1-4 qt. WS/A
Time: Apply when weeds and brush are actively growing. Repeat as needed.
Weeds: Annual broadleaf weeds:

carpetweed	knawel	purslane
chickweed	lambsquarters	ragweed
clover	morningglory	smartweed
cocklebur	mustard	velvetleaf
English daisy	pigweed	wild buckwheat
henbit		

Biennial weeds:

musk thistle	tansy ragwort

Perennial weeds:

Canada thistle	field bindweed	Russian knapweed
curly dock	leafy spurge	sheep sorrel
dalmation toadflax	milkweed	wild carrot
dogfennel	Queen Anne's lace	

Rate: 2.9-5.8 lb. ai/A
1-2 gal. WS/A
Time: Apply when weeds and brush are actively growing. Repeat as needed.
Weeds: Woody brush and vines:

alder	Florida holly	redvine
ash	gum	Russian olive
aspen	hawthorn*	sagebrush
basswood	hemlock	sassafras
beech	honeysuckle	serviceberry
birch	kudzu	snowberry
blackberry*	locust	spruce
Brazil peppertree	maple	sumac
cherry	multiflora rose*	sycamore
Christmasberry	oak	trumpetcreeper
creosotebush*	persimmon	Virginia creeper
cucumbertree	pine	waxmyrtle
dogwood*	poison ivy	wild plum*
eastern red cedar*	poplar	willow
elderberry	puncturevine	witchazel
elm	raspberry	yaupon*

*Suppression

Remarks: Do not apply more than 2 gal./A per season. Do not apply through any type of irrigation system. Do not graze dairy animals within 21 days of applying 1 gal. WS; 40 days for 2 gal. WS. Remove livestock from treated areas 30 days before slaughter.
Days To Harvest: 1 gal.—51; 2 gal.—70.
Tank Mixes: Amitrol, asulam, atratol, bromacil, clorflurecol, chlorsulfuron, 2,4-D, 2,4-DP, dicamba, diquat, diuron, fosamine ammonium, glyphosate, hexazinone, imazapyr, maleic hydrazide, mefluidide, metsulfuron, MSMA, paraquat, picloram, simazine, sulfometuron methyl, tebuthiuron, triclopyr.

– – – – – – – – – – – – –

Signal Word/Toxicity Class: Caution.

Veteran 2010 (2.5 lb./gal. MCPA & 1.25 lb./gal. dicamba) *(Riverdale)*
Rate: 1-2.33 gal./A
Time: Apply when weeds and brush are actively growing.
Weeds: Broadleaf weeds such as:

buckwheat	field bindweed	pigweed
Canada thistle	henbit	purslane
carpetweed	knawel	ragweed
chickweed	lambsquarters	Russian knapweed
clover	leafy spurge	sheep sorrel
cocklebur	milkweed	smartweed
curly dock	morningglory	tansy ragwort
dalmation toadflax	musk thistle	velvetleaf
dogfennel	mustard	wild carrot
English daisy	perennial ragweed	

9

Other Uses

Brush Control

Woody brush and vines such as:

alder	Florida holly	redvine
ash	gum	Russian olive
aspen	hawthorn	sagebrush
basswood	hemlock	sassafras
beech	honeysuckle	serviceberry
birch	kudzu	snowberry
blackberry	locust	spruce
Brazil peppertree	maple	sumac
cherry	multiflora rose	sycamore
Christmas-berry	oak	trumpetcreeper
creosotebush	persimmon	Virginia creeper
(suppression)	pine	waxmyrtle
cucumbertree	poison ivy	wild plum
dogwood	poplar	willow
eastern red cedar	puncturevine	witchhazel
elderberry	raspberry	yaupon
elm		

Remarks: Forest brush. Refer to label for use directions and precautions.

Tank Mixes: May be tank mixed.

- - - - - - - - - - - - - - -

Signal Word/Toxicity Class: Danger/I.

Weed Rhap — see 2,4-D

Weedar — see 2,4-D

Weedestroy — see 2,4-D

Weedmaster — see 2,4-D Combinations

Weedone — see 2,4-D

Conservation Reserve Program

AAtrex — see atrazine

AMBER

◆ **Amber Accu-Pak or CustomPak (WDG) (triasulfuron)** (Novartis)

Rate: Standard:
0.28 oz. WDG/A
Enhanced:
0.56 oz. WDG/A

Time: Postemergence. Apply when weeds are actively growing.

Weeds: Broadleaf weeds:

annual fleabane	downy brome*	prostrate pigweed
annual morningglory	fanweed	puncturevine
annual ryegrass*	field pennycress	purple mustard
blue mustard	flixweed	redroot pigweed
Canada thistle*	giant ragweed	Russian thistle*
cheat*	goldenrod*	shepherdspurse
coast fiddleneck	henbit	smooth pigweed
common cocklebur	horseweed	tansymustard
common mallow	jim hill mustard	tarweed
common purslane	kochia*	tumble mustard
common ragweed	London rocket	wild buckwheat
common sunflower	marestail	wild garlic*
corn gromwell	marshelder	wild mustard
curly dock*	musk thistle*	wild radish
cutleaf	prickly lettuce	yellow starthistle
eveningprimrose		

Established grasses:

bermudagrass	crested wheatgrass	sheep fescue
big bluestem	intermediate	sideoats grama
blue grama	wheatgrass	smooth brome
bluebunch wheatgass	little bluestem	redtop
buffalograss	pubescent wheatgrass	timothy

* *Suppression*

Remarks: Add nonionic surfactant. Do not use alone in any field where ALS-resistant biotypes of any weed species have been identified. Do not apply for at least 60 days after in-furrow application of organophosphate insecticide. Do not cut for hay for 30 days following application. No grazing restrictions. Do not apply through any type of irrigation system. Refer to label for directions and precautions.

Tank Mixes: Banvel, Crossbow, 2,4-D, Grazon, Stinger, Weedone LV6, Weedmaster.

State Restrictions: For use in Colorado (except San Luis Valley), Idaho, Kansas, Minnesota, Montana, Nebraska, Nevada, New Mexico, North Dakota, Oklahoma, South Dakota, Texas, Utah, Wyoming, and east of the Cascades in Oregon or Washington.

- - - - - - - - - - - - - - -

Signal Word/Toxicity Class: Caution.

REI: 12 hr.

ATRAZINE

◆ **AAtrex 4L or Nine-0 (WDG)** (Novartis)

◆ **Helena Atrazine 4L** (Helena)

Rate: 0.5-2 lb. ai/A
1-4 pt. 4L/A
0.6-2.2 lb. WDG/A

Time: Preplant incorporated or preemergence at time of seeding and prior to emergence of weeds.

Weeds: Annual broadleaf weeds:

annual ragweeds	kochia	pigweed
black nightshade	lambsquarters	prickly lettuce
cocklebur	little barley	sunflower
field pennycress	marestail	

Annual grasses:

barnyardgrass	fall panicum	Kentucky bluegrass
(watergrass)	giant foxtail	smooth brome
cheat	Japanese brome	yellow foxtail
downy brome		

Remarks: Rate varies by soil type and organic matter. Make only 1 application per year. Do not apply through any type of irrigation system. This product may not be mixed/loaded, or used within 50 ft. of wells including abandoned wells, drainage wells, and sink holes. Do not cut or feed grass hay to livestock or graze treated area. Refer to label for precautions and restrictions.

State Restrictions: For use in Nebraska, Oklahoma, Oregon, Texas

- - - - - - - - - - - - - - -

Signal Word/Toxicity Class: Caution/III.

REI: 12 hr.

Banvel — see dicamba

Barrage — see 2,4-D

Bison — see bromoxynil & MCPA

Broclean — see bromoxynil

Bromac — see bromoxynil & MCPA

Bromox — see bromoxynil

Bromox-MCPA 2-2 — see bromoxynil & MCPA

BROMOXYNIL

◆ **Broclean 2EC** (Platte)

◆ **Bromox 2EC** (Micro Flo)

Buctril (2EC), Buctril 4EC (Rhone-Poulenc)

Moxy 2EC (Terra)

Rate: 0.25-0.5 lb. ai/A
1-2 pt. 2EC/A
0.5-1 pt. 4EC/A

◆-new product • PP-preplant • PPI-preplant incorporated • PRE-preemergence • POST-postemergence • SEQ-sequential • ae-acid equivalent • ai-active ingredient • DF-dry flowable • E/EC-emulsifiable concentrate • F/FL-flowable • DG/G/WG-dispersable granule • L/LC-liquid • SP/WSP-soluble packet • W/WP-wettable powder • WSB-water soluble bag

Time: Apply to grasses after emergence. If alfalfa is planted, apply after 4 trifoliate leaf stage.

Weeds: Most susceptible broadleaf weeds:

annual pepperweed	common tarweed	Pennsylvania
annual sowthistle	eastern black	smartweed
black nightshade	nightshade	shepherdspurse
blue mustard	field pennycress	silverleaf nightshade
bristly starbur	green smartweed	sunflower
coast fiddleneck	hairy nightshade	tartary buckwheat
common cocklebur	jimsonweed	wild buckwheat
common lambsquarters	ladysthumb	

Susceptible broadleaf weeds:

buffalobur	ivyleaf morningglory	spiny pigweed
burcucumber	knawel	tall morningglory
common groundsel	kochia	tall waterhemp
common ragweed	London rocket	tumble mustard
corn chamomile	mayweed	velvetleaf
corn gromwell	prostrate knotweed	Venice mallow
cowcockle	puncturevine	wild mustard
giant ragweed	redroot pigweed	wild radish
hemp sesbania	Russian thistle	yellow starthistle

Remarks: Do not apply to CRP areas planted with alfalfa if temperatures are expected to exceed 80°F. If legumes other than alfalfa have been planted, severe crop injury may occur at any temperature. Do not allow livestock to graze or feed treated areas. Refer to label for restrictions and precautions.

– – – – – – – – – – – – – –

Signal Word/Toxicity Class: Warning/II.
REI: 12 hr.

BROMOXYNIL & MCPA (Premixes)

Bison (EC) (2 lb./gal. bromoxynil & 2 lb./gal. MCPA) *(Terra)*
◆ **Bromac (EC) (2 lb./gal. bromoxynil & 2 lb./gal. MCPA)** *(Platte)*
◆ **Bromox-MCPA 2-2 (EC) (2 lb./gal. bromoxynil & 2 lb./gal. MCPA)** *(Micro Flo)*
Bronate (EC) (2 lb./gal. bromoxynil & 2 lb./gal. MCPA) *(Rhone-Poulenc)*

Rate: 0.5-1 lb. ai/A
1-2 pt. EC/A

Time: Apply to grasses after 3-leaf stage. Apply lower rate to most susceptible weeds; higher rate to susceptible weeds up to 8 leaf stage, 4" in height, or 2" in diameter, whichever comes first.

Weeds: Most susceptible broadleaf weeds:

annual sowthistle	field pennycress	Russian thistle
black mustard	green smartweed	shepherdspurse
black nightshade	hairy nightshade	silverleaf nightshade
coast fiddleneck	horned poppy	smooth pigweed
common cocklebur	jimsonweed	spiny pigweed
common	ladysthumb	sunflower
lambsquarters	London rocket	tall waterhemp
common tarweed	marshelder	tartary buckwheat
cowcockle	Pennsylvania	tumble mustard
cutleaf nightshade	smartweed	wild buckwheat
eastern black	pepperweed	wild mustard
nightshade	redroot pigweed	yellow rocket

Susceptible broadleaf weeds:

blue mustard (purple)	giant ragweed	prostrate knotweed
Canada thistle	hemp sesbania	puncturevine
(suppression)	henbit	tall morningglory
common groundsel	ivyleaf morningglory	tansymustard
common ragweed	knawel	tarweed
corn chamomile	kochia	velvetleaf
corn gromwell	mayweed	wild radish
fumitory		

Remarks: If legumes are included in area planting, severe injury may occur to treated legumes. Do not allow livestock to graze treated fields or feed treated grasses to livestock.

– – – – – – – – – – – – – –

Signal Word/Toxicity Class: Warning/II.
REI: 12 hr.

Bronate — see bromoxynil & MCPA

Buctril — see bromoxynil

Butyrac — see 2,4-DB

CLOPYRALID

Systemic herbicide absorbed by leaves and roots. Has selective postemergence control of many annual and perennial broadleaf weeds.

Stinger *(Dow AgroSciences)*
Rate: 0.25-0.5 lb. ae/A
0.66-1.33 pt./A

Time: Apply when perennial grasses are well established. For actively growing knapweed and thistle, apply after majority of basal leaves have emerged up to bud stage.

Weeds: Annual and perennial broadleaf weeds:

Canada thistle	musk thistle	volunteer sunflower
diffuse knapweed	spotted knapweed	wild buckwheat

Remarks: For seeding to permanent grasses only. Do not use if legumes or bentgrass are desired cover. Do not use on newly seeded areas until grass is established. Do not apply through any type of irrigation system or contaminate irrigation ditches or water used for irrigation or domestic purposes.

Crop Rotation: Do not plant broadleaf crops in treated areas until adequately sensitive bioassay shows that clopyralid is not longer detected in soil.

State Restrictions: In California, do not apply more that 0.66 pt./A per growing season.

– – – – – – – – – – – – – –

Signal Word/Toxicity Class: Caution/III.
REI: 12 hr.

CURTAIL OR CURTAIL M (Premixes)

Curtail (0.38 lb./gal. clopyralid & 2 lb./gal. 2,4-D) *(Dow AgroSciences)*
Curtail M (0.42 lb./gal. clopyralid & 2.35 lb./gal. MCPA) *(Dow AgroSciences)*

Rate: 1.2-2.4 lb. ae/A
2-4 qt. Curtail/A
1.2-3.3 lb. ae/A
1.75-4.75 qt. Curtail M/A

Time: Apply when perennial grasses are well established. For actively growing knapweed and thistle, apply after majority of basal leaves have emerged up to bud stage.

Weeds: Broadleaf weeds:

alfalfa	giant ragweed	redroot pigweed
annual sowthistle	goatsbeard	Russian knapweed*
Canada thistle	hairy nightshade	Russian thistle
coffeeweed	horseweed	(1-3 leaf)
common burdock	Jerusalem artichoke	scentless chamomile
common cocklebur	jim hill mustard	shepherdspurse
common groundsel	jimsonweed	sicklepod
common	kochia* (2-4 leaf)	spotted knapweed
lambsquarters	ladysthumb	sweetclover
common ragweed	meadow salsify	tansymustard
common sunflower	musk thistle	tumble mustard
cornflower	narrowleaf hawksbeard	velvetleaf
curly dock	Pennsylvania	vetch
cutleaf nightshade	smartweed	volunteer beans
dandelion	perennial sowthistle*	volunteer lentils
diffuse knapweed	pineappleweed	volunteer peas
false chamomile	plantain	wild buckwheat
fanweed	prickly lettuce	wild mustard
field pennycress	red clover	wild radish
flixweed*	red sorrel	yellow starthistle

* Suppression

Remarks: For seeding to permanent grasses only. Do not use if legumes or bentgrass are a desired cover crop during CRP. Do not use on newly seeded areas until grass is established. Wait at least 30 days after application before seeding grasses. Apply only once per crop cycle. Do not apply through any type of irrigation system.

Crop Rotation: Varies by region; refer to label.

– – – – – – – – – – – – – –

Signal Word/Toxicity Class: Danger/I (Curtail); Caution/III (Curtail M).
REI: 48 hr.

Cyclone — see paraquat

Credit — see glyphosate

9

Other Uses

NOTICE	The information on these pages is for preliminary planning — not a guide for use. Be sure to follow the manufacturer's directions, notwithstanding information contained here.	For personal protective equipment and EPA registration numbers, please turn to page 70.

2,4-D - PHENOXY HERBICIDES

2,4-D and 2,4-D-type compounds selectively control broadleaf weeds with little or no control of grasses. 2,4-D drift can injure adjacent crops either by drift of spray or by volatilization (spray turns into a vapor). Ester formulations most volatile and amines least volatile. Ester formulations can vaporize at temperatures as low as 70°F and can be moved by wind to harm sensitive plants.

Albaugh Amine 4 (2,4-D amine) *(Albaugh)*
Albaugh D-638 (2,4-D ester + acid) *(Albaugh)*
Albaugh LV4 or LV6 Ester (2,4-D ester) *(Albaugh)*
◆ **Opti-Amine (4) (2,4-D amine)** *(Helena)*
Riverdale 6 Amine (2,4-D amine) *(Riverdale)*
◆ **Riverdale 4 Amine IVM (2,4-D amine)** *(Riverdale)*
Riverdale L.V. 6 (2,4-D ester) *(Riverdale)*
Weed Rhap A-4D (2,4-D amine) *(Helena)*
Weedar 64 (4) (2,4-D amine) *(Nufarm)*
Weedestroy AM-40 (2,4-D amine) *(Riverdale)*
Weedone 638 (2,4-D ester + acid) *(Nufarm)*
Wilbur-Ellis Amine 4 (2,4-D amine) *(Wilbur-Ellis)*
Wilbur-Ellis Lo Vol-6 (2,4-D ester) *(Wilbur-Ellis)*
  Rate: 0.25-2 lb. ai/A
    0.5-4 pt. /A
    0.66-5.33 pt. 638/A
    0.33-2.66 pt. Lo Vol-6/A
  Time: Annual weeds: apply when actively growing. Biennial weeds: apply in seedling to rosette stage before flower stalks become apparent. Perennial weeds: apply to actively growing weeds in bud to bloom stage. Do not apply to grasses in boot to dough stage if grass seed production is desired.
  Weeds: Annual, biennial, and perennial weeds.
  Remarks: Do not harvest or graze treated CRP areas.
  State Restrictions: Wilbur-Ellis not registered in California.

  - - - - - - - - - - - - - - -

  Signal Word/Toxicity Class: Varies by formulation.
  REI: Danger—48 hr.; Caution—12 hr.

◆ **Barrage or Barrage HF (EC) (2,4-D ester)** *(Helena)*
  Rate: 0.22-1.88 lb. ae/A
    0.375-3.2 pt./A
  Time: Preseeding: Apply at least 30 days prior to seeding. New stands: Apply when weeds are small and actively growing; seedling grass should be treated only after 5-leaf stage. Established stands: Weeds must be actively growing; biennial weeds in seedling to rosette stage before flower stalks become apparent; perennial weeds in bud to bloom stage. Do not apply to grasses in boot to dough stage if grass seed production is desired.
  Weeds: Annual, biennial, perennial broadleaf weeds, and brush species.
  Remarks: Do not graze dairy animals on treated areas within 7 days or meat animals within 3 days of slaughter. Do not cut treated grass for hay within 30 days of application.

  - - - - - - - - - - - - - - -

  Signal Word/Toxicity Class: Caution/III.
  REI: 12 hr.

Esteron 99C (2,4-D LV ester) *(Rhone-Poulenc)*
Formula 40 (2,4-D mixed amine) *(Rhone-Poulenc)*
  Rate: 1-2 lb. ai/A
    2-4 pt./A
  Time: Apply when weeds are actively growing prior to bud stage. Do not use from early boot to milk stage where grass seed production is desired.
  Weeds: Broadleaf weeds, herbaceous perennials, and woody plants.
  Remarks: Do not harvest grass cut for hay within 30 days, or graze dairy animals within 7 days of treatment. Withdraw meat animals from treated forage at least 3 days before slaughter.

  - - - - - - - - - - - - - - -

  Signal Word/Toxicity Class: Danger/I (amine); Caution/III (ester).
  REI: Danger—48 hr.; Caution—12 hr.

◆ **Saber (2,4-D amine)** *(Platte)*
  Rate: 0.25-2 lb. ae/A
    0.5-4 pt./A
  Time: Apply when weeds are actively growing. For biennial weeds, apply in seedling to rosette stage before flower stalks become apparent. For perennial weeds, apply in bud to bloom stage. Do not apply to grasses in boot to dough stage if grass seed production is desired.
  Weeds: Annual, biennial, and perennial weeds.
  Remarks: Do not graze dairy cattle in treated areas for 7 days after application; meat animals 3 days before slaughter. Do not cut treated grass hay within 30 days after application.

  - - - - - - - - - - - - - - -

  Signal Word/Toxicity Class: Danger/I.
  REI: 48 hr.

Savage (WSB) (2,4-D amine) *(Platte)*
  Rate: 0.95-1.9 lb. ae/A
    1-2 lb. WSB/A
  Time: Apply when weeds are small and actively growing prior to bud stage. Do not apply to grasses in early boot to milk stage if grass seed production is desired.
  Weeds: Annual, biennial, and perennial weeds.
  Remarks: Do not apply to newly seeded areas until grass is well established. Bentgrass and legumes may be injured by this treatment. Do not graze dairy cattle in treated areas for 7 days after application; meat animals 3 days before slaughter. Do not cut forage for hay within 30 days after application.

  - - - - - - - - - - - - - - -

  Signal Word/Toxicity Class: Danger/I.
  REI: 48 hr.

2,4-DB

Butyrac 200 *(Albaugh)*
Riverside 2,4-DB 200 *(Terra)*
  Rate: 0.5-1.5 lb. ai/A
    1-3 qt. 200/A
  Time: Postemergence.
  Weeds: Broadleaf weeds:

annual morningglory	common ragweed	Russian thistle
cocklebur	curly dock	smartweed
common lambsquarters	field pennycress	wild mustard
	redroot pigweed	yellow rocket

  Remarks: Grasses and forage legumes (seedling or established alfalfa, seedling alsike, birdsfoot trefoil, ladino, red clover). Do not use on sweet clover, peas, other legumes. Do not add wetting agents or detergents to spray solution. Rainfall within 10 days after treatment can cause injury to legumes. Do not graze or harvest treated CRP acres.

  - - - - - - - - - - - - - - -

  Signal Word/Toxicity Class: Danger/I.
  REI: 48 hr.

DICAMBA

Banvel (WS) (DMA salt of dicamba) *(BASF)*
Banvel SGF (sodium salt of dicamba) *(BASF)*
◆ **Sterling (WS) (DMA salt of dicamba)** *(Terra)*
  Rate: 0.125-2 lb. ai/A
    0.25-4 pt. WS/A
    0.5-8 pt. SGF/A
  Time: Annual weeds are actively growing; biennial weeds are in rosette stage; top growth control or suppression of perennial weeds. Do not apply to seedling grasses until grasses exceed 3-leaf growth stage.
  Weeds: Annual broadleaf weeds:

annual sowthistle	corn cockle	Pennsylvania smartweed
black nightshade	cowcockle	
common cocklebur	field pennycress	redroot pigweed
common lambsquarters	giant ragweed	rough pigweed
	green smartweed	Russian thistle
common mallow	henbit	tumble pigweed
common ragweed	knotweed	velvetleaf
common sunflower	kochia	volunteer sunflower
corn chamomile	ladysthumb	wild buckwheat

  Biennial weeds:

bull thistle	plumeless thistle	sweetclover
diffuse knapweed	spotted knapweed	yellow starthistle
musk thistle		

  Perennial weeds:

bur ragweed	hedge bindweed	silverleaf nightshade
bursage	hemp dogbane	swamp smartweed
Canada thistle	Jerusalem artichoke	Texas blueweed
Carolina horsenettle	leafy spurge	trumpetcreeper
common dandelion	perennial sowthistle	volunteer alfalfa
curly dock	redvine	wild garlic
field bindweed	Russian knapweed	

  Remarks: Newly seeded and established grasses. Will injure or may kill alfalfa, clover, lespedeza, wild winter peas, vetch, and other legumes. Surfactant may be added. Do not use adjuvants containing penetrants such as petroleum-based oils after grass emergence on newly seeded grasses.
  Tank Mixes: Ally, Amber, atrazine, Bladex, Curtail, Cyclone, 2,4-D, Fallow Master, Finesse, Gramoxone Extra, Kerb, Landmaster, Roundup Ultra, Sencor, Tordon.

  - - - - - - - - - - - - - - -

  Signal Word/Toxicity Class: Warning/II.
  REI: 24 hr.

◆-new product • PP-preplant • PPI-preplant incorporated • PRE-preemergence • POST-postemergence • SEQ-sequential • ae-acid equivalent • ai-active ingredient • DF-dry flowable
E/EC-emulsifiable concentrate • F/FL-flowable • DG/G/WG-dispersable granule • L/LC-liquid • SP/WSP-soluble packet • W/WP-wettable powder • WSB-water soluble bag

Esteron 99C — see 2,4-D

FENOXAPROP-P-ETHYL
Restricted Use Pesticide.

Option II (EC) *(AgrEvo USA)*
Rate: 12-16 fl. oz./A
Time: Postemergence. Apply during periods of rapid growth.
Weeds: Annual grassy weeds.
Remarks: Acreage often seeded to following cover crops: alfalfa, bromegrass, clover, ryegrass (timothy and orchardgrass sensitive to Option II), and tall fescue. Do not apply to cover crops such as oats, sorghum, sudangrass, and timothy. Do not graze treated forage, hay, straw, or vines.
Days To Harvest: 90.
Crop Rotation: Do not plant any rotational crop in treated field for 30 days after application.
Tank Mixes: May be tank mixed; refer to label.
State Restrictions: For use in Colorado, Connecticut, Delaware, Illinois, Indiana, Iowa, Kansas, Maine, Maryland, Massachusetts, Michigan, Minnesota, Missouri (certain counties), Nebraska, New Hampshire, New Jersey, New York, North Dakota, Ohio, Pennsylvania, Rhode Island, South Dakota, Vermont, Virginia, West Virginia, Wisconsin.

— — — — — — — — — — — — — —

Signal Word/Toxicity Class: Danger/I.
REI: 24 hr.

Formula 40 — see 2,4-D

GLYPHOSATE

◆ **Credit (4WS)** *(Nufarm)*
◆ **Glyfos or Glyfos X-tra (4WS)** *(Cheminova)*
Rattler (4WS) *(Helena)*
Roundup Custom (5.4WS) *(Monsanto)*
Roundup Original, Original RT, Ultra, Ultra RT (4WS) *(Monsanto)*
Rate: 0.38-0.5 lb. ai/A
0.56-0.75 pt. 5.4WS/A
0.75-1 pt. 4WS/A
Time: Apply in early spring before desirable CRP grasses break dormancy and initiate green growth. Late fall application can be made after desirable perennial grasses have reached dormancy.
Weeds: Suppress competitive growth and seed production of undesirable vegetation in CRP acres.
Remarks: Some stunting of CRP perennial grasses will occur if broadcast applications are made when plants are not dormant.
State Restrictions: Roundup Ultra tank mixes not registered in California. Roundup RT: For use in Colorado, Idaho, Montana, North Dakota, South Dakota, Utah, and Wyoming. For use in specific counties only in Kansas, Minnesota, Nebraska, Nevada, Oklahoma, Oregon, and Washington, refer to label for restrictions. Glyfos not registered for use in California. Glyfos X-tra not registered for use in mistblowers in California or Arizona.

— — — — — — — — — — — — — —

Signal Word/Toxicity Class: Varies by formulation.
REI: Warning—12 hr.; Caution—4 hr.

Gramoxone Extra — see paraquat

KERB
Restricted Use Pesticide.

Kerb 50-W (pronamide) *(Rohm and Haas)*
Rate: Established grass stands:
0.19 lb. ai/A
0.38 lb. 50-W/A
Grasses:

bulbous bluegrass	downy brome	jointed goatgrass
cereal rye		

Rate: Fallow land:
0.25-0.5 lb. ai/A
0.5-1 lb. 50-W/A
Grasses:

bulbous bluegrass	jointed goatgrass	volunteer rye
cheatgrass	volunteer barley	volunteer wheat
downy brome		

Time: Preemergence, postemergence. Apply prior to soil freeze-up (mid-Oct./mid-Dec.). Applications outside these dates could result in poor weed control.
Remarks: Established grass stands, fallow land. Established grass stands restricted to those CRP acres that have an acceptable stand of grass (creeping foxtail, crested wheatgrass, intermediate wheatgrass, orchard grass, slender wheatgrass, tall fescue, tall wheatgrass, western wheatgrass). In accordance with CRP provisions, any CRP acres cannot be grazed or cut for feed. Fallow land restricted to summer fallow land which will be planted back the following year to grass cover crops for soil erosion or other conservation purposes. Do not use any tillage in the fall prior to or after application.
Crop Rotation: Refer to the label for plantback time for rotation crops.
State Restrictions: For use in Idaho, Oregon, and Washington.

— — — — — — — — — — — — — —

Signal Word/Toxicity Class: Caution.
REI: 24 hr.

Moxy — see bromoxynil

Opti-Amine — see 2,4-D

Option II — see fenoxaprop-P-ethyl

PARAQUAT
Restricted Use Pesticide.

Cyclone (2L or 3L) or Gramoxone Extra (2.5L) *(ZENECA)*
Rate: 0.5-1 lb. ai/A
2-4 pt. 2L/A
1.3-2.7 pt. 3L/A
0.6-1 lb. ai/A
2-3 pt. 2.5L/A
Time: Apply broadcast.
Weeds: Controls existing cover crops, broadleaf weeds and grasses.
Remarks: Add nonionic surfactant or crop oil concentrate. Refer to labels for directions and precautions.
Tank Mixes: Atrazine, Banvel, Bladex, Canopy, Command, 2,4-D ester, Extrazine, Harmony Extra, Lariat, linuron, Marksman, metribuzin, Princep.

— — — — — — — — — — — — — —

Signal Word/Toxicity Class: Danger-Poison/I.
REI: 12 hr. (except harvest aid/desiccation 24 hr.).

PENDIMETHALIN

Pentagon DG *(American Cyanamid)*
Prowl 3.3EC *(American Cyanamid)*
Rate: 0.5-1.2 lb. ai/A
1.2-3 pt. 3.3 EC/A
0.85-2.1 lb. DG/A
Time: Preplant incorporated, preemergence.
Weeds: Broadleaf Weeds:

annual spurge	lambsquarters	pigweed
carpetweed	Pennsylvania	purslane
Florida pusley	smartweed	velvetleaf
kochia		

Grasses:

barnyardgrass	giant foxtail	signalgrass
crabgrass	goosegrass	Texas panicum
crowfootgrass	green foxtail	witchgrass
fall panicum	johnsongrass	yellow foxtail
field sandbur		

Remarks: Legume cover crops. Do not feed or graze legume cover crops established following application; refer to label.
Crop Rotation: If crop loss occurs due to weather conditions, any crop registered for preplant incorporated use can be replanted the same year in treated soil.

— — — — — — — — — — — — — —

Signal Word/Toxicity Class: Caution.
REI: 12 hr.

Pentagon — see pendimethalin

9

Other Uses

NOTICE	The information on these pages is for preliminary planning — not a guide for use. Be sure to follow the manufacturer's directions, notwithstanding information contained here.	For personal protective equipment and EPA registration numbers, please turn to page 70.

PLATEAU

Plateau (AS) (imazapic) *(American Cyanamid)*
Rate: 4 fl. oz. AS/A
Time: Either preemergence or postemergence to weeds (postemergence preferred method).
Weeds: Broadleaf weeds:

bristly starbur	Florida beggarweed	sicklepod
common cocklebur	morningglory	velvetleaf
common	pigweed	wild radish
lambsquarters	prickly sida	

Grasses and sedges:

crabgrass	goosegrass	sedge
fall panicum	johnsongrass (seedling)	shattercane
giant foxtail	purple nutsedge	yellow nutsedge

Remarks: Establishment or release of big bluestem, blue grama, Indiangrass, little bluestem, and sideoats. For postemergence application, add surfactant. Do not exceed 4 fl.oz./A per year. Do not use on areas to be grazed or cut for hay. Do not apply though any type of irrigation system.
Crop Rotation: Bahiagrass, rye, wheat—4 months; field corn, snap beans, southern peas, soybeans, tobacco—9 months; barley, cotton (with restrictions), grain sorghum, oats, sweet corn—18 months; canola, potatoes, sugar beets, table beets—40 months; all other crops—26 months.

- - - - - - - - - - - - - - - -

Signal Word/Toxicity Class: Caution.

Prowl — see pendimethalin

Rattler — see glyphosate

RAVE (Premix)

Premix with 2 modes of action. One active ingredient inhibits the acetolactate synthase (ALS) enzyme. The other active ingredient disrupts normal plant growth.

◆ **Rave (WDG) (50% dicamba & 8.8% triasulfuron)** *(Novartis)*
Rate: 2-4 oz. WDG/A
Heavy infestations:
5 oz. WDG/A
Time: Postemergence. Apply to actively growing weeds at least 60 days after emergence of desirable grasses or sprigged-bermudagrass.
Weeds: Broadleaf weeds:

annual morningglory	cutleaf	pepperweed
annual polemonium	eveningprimrose	pigweed
annual sowthistle	fanweed	plains coreopsis
black nightshade	field bindweed	prickly lettuce
blue mustard	field pennycress	prostrate knotweed
bur buttercup	fleabane	prostrate pigweed
bushy wallflower	flixweed	puncturevine
Canada thistle	forget-me-not	ragweed
coast fiddleneck	giant ragweed	redroot pigweed
common broomweed	goldenrod	Russian thistle
common chickweed	hairy vetch	shepherdspurse
common cocklebur	henbit	smooth pigweed
common groundsel	horseweed	tall buttercup
common	houndstongue	tall hedge mustard
lambsquarters	Indian mustard	tansymustard
common mallow	jagged chickweed	tartary buckwheat
common purslane	kochia	tarweed
common ragweed	ladysthumb	tumble mustard
common sunflower	lanceleaf ragweed	tumble pigweed
common yarrow	London rocket	umbrella spurry
corn chamomile	marestail	velvetleaf
corn cockle	marshelder	Virginia pepperweed
corn gromwell	minerslettuce	wild buckwheat
cornflower	musk thistle	wild mustard
creeping buttercup	mustard	wild radish
curly dock	Pennsylvania smartweed	woolly croton

Remarks: Bermudagrass, big bluestem, little bluestem, buffalograss, sheep fescue, smooth brome, blue grama, sideoats grama, redtop, timothy, wheatgrass (bluebunch, crested, intermediate, pubescent). Desirable broadleaves, such as clover and alfalfa may be severely injured by Rave. Add nonionic surfactant or crop oil concentrate. Do not apply for at least 60 days after organophosphate application. Do not apply through any type of irrigation system.
Crop Rotation: Recropping depends on field bioassay, soil pH, total rainfall, and geographic area. Refer to label for restrictions and more complete information.
Tank Mixes: Crossbow, 2,4-D, Grazon P+D, Remedy, Stinger, Tordon 22K, and Weedmaster.

State Restrictions: For use in Colorado (except San Luis Valley), Idaho, Kansas, Minnesota, Montana, Nebraska, Nevada, New Mexico, North Dakota, Oklahoma, Oregon, South Dakota, Texas, Utah, Washington, Wyoming. In Washington, abide by all sulfonylurea aerial application rulings by Washington Department of Agriculture.

- - - - - - - - - - - - - - - -

Signal Word/Toxicity Class: Caution.
REI: 12 hr.

Roundup — see glyphosate

Saber — see 2,4-D

Savage — see 2,4-D

Solution — see 2,4-D

Sterling — see dicamba

Stinger — see clopyralid

TORDON

Restricted Use Pesticide.

Tordon 22K (picloram) *(Dow AgroSciences)*
Rate: Annual weeds:
0.06-0.125 lb. ae/A
0.25-0.5 pt. 22K/A
Perennial weeds:
0.5 lb. ae/A
2 pt. 22K/A
Time: Apply after perennial grasses are well established.
Weeds: Annual, biennial, and perennial broadleaf weeds such as:

annual broomweed	henbane	Russian thistle
bitter sneezeweed	horsenettle	silverleaf nightshade
bitterweed	horseweed	smartweed
broom snakeweed	knapweed	sowthistle
buffalobur	ironweed	St. Johnswort
bullnettle	leafy spurge	starthistle
burroweed	larkspur	sunflower
bursage	locoweed	tansy ragwort
camphorweed	lupine	thistle
cinquefoil	marshelder	toadflax
cocklebur	mayweed	upright prairie
croton	milkweed	coneflower
curly dock	oxeye daisy	western bitterweed
field bindweed	perennial sowthistle	wild buckwheat
goldaster	plains pricklypear	wild carrot
goldenweed	prickly lettuce	wild licorice
gorse	ragweed	yankeeweed
groundsel	rush skeletonweed	yellow toadflax

Woody plants such as:

absinth wormwood	fringed sagebrush	Macartney rose
acacia	granjeno	mesquite
aspen	guajillo	multiflora rose
camelthorn	huisache	pinyon pine
cedar	(suppression)	pricklypear
chaparral	juniper	Scotch broom
Chinese tallowtree	locust	tasajillo

Remarks: Do not use if legumes are desired cover during CRP or on land planted to sweet sorghum. To reduce possible damage to subsequent small grain crops, use lower rate or discontinue at least 2 years prior to seeding. Do not allow spray to contact desirable broadleaf plants. Do not graze treated areas until poisonous plants are dry and no longer palatable to livestock. Do not apply through any type of irrigation system.
Crop Rotation: Do not rotate to grain sorghum if more than 1 pt./A has been applied or plant sorghum within 8 months after application. Do not rotate to food or plant broadleaf crops until adequately sensitive bioassay shows no detectable picloram present in soil.
Tank Mixes: 2,4-D.
State Restrictions: For use west of the Mississippi except San Luis Valley of Colorado. Use in Hawaii limited to supplemental labeling.

- - - - - - - - - - - - - - - -

Signal Word/Toxicity Class: Caution.
REI: 12 hr.

◆-new product • PP-preplant • PPI-preplant incorporated • PRE-preemergence • POST-postemergence • SEQ-sequential • ae-acid equivalent • ai-active ingredient • DF-dry flowable
E/EC-emulsifiable concentrate • F/FL-flowable • DG/G/WG-dispersable granule • L/LC-liquid • SP/WSP-soluble packet • W/WP-wettable powder • WSB-water soluble bag

TOUCHDOWN

Touchdown (5L or 6L) (sulfosate) *(ZENECA)*

Rate: 0.5-4 lb. ai/A
0.8-6.4 pt. 5L/A
0.66-5.33 pt. 6L/A

Time: Apply to actively growing grasses and weeds. Repeat as necessary.

Weeds: Broadleaf weeds:

annual fleabane	field pennycress	mouseear chickweed
annual sowthistle	field sandbur	mustard
annual spurge	Florida pusley	Pennsylvania
black nightshade	hemp dogbane	smartweed
Canada thistle	henbit	pigweed
common cocklebur	hophornbeam	prickly lettuce
common groundsel	copperleaf	ragweed
common lambsquarters	horsenettle	red clover
common sunflower	Jerusalem artichoke*	redvine
curly dock	kochia	Russian thistle
cutleaf	leafy spurge	shepherdspurse
eveningprimrose	little barley	sicklepod
dandelion	London rocket	trumpetcreeper
dogfennel	marestail	velvetleaf
field bindweed	morningglory	wild buckwheat

Grasses and sedges:

annual bluegrass	foxtail	stinkgrass
barnyardgrass	goosegrass	tall fescue
bermudagrass	johnsongrass	Texas panicum
cheat	(seedling)	timothy
cogongrass*	jointed goatgrass	wild oat
crabgrass	perennial ryegrass	witchgrass
crowfootgrass	quackgrass	woolly cupgrass
downy brome	red rice	yellow nutsedge
fall panicum	sprangletop	

* Partial control

Remarks: Nonionic surfactant or wetting agent required. In addition, ammonium sulfate can be added. Do not apply through any type of irrigation system. Refer to label for directions, restrictions, and precautions.

Crop Rotation: Plantback time—35 days.

Tank Mixes: Devrinol, diuron, Goal, Krovar, Prowl, simazine, Solicam, Surflan.

State Restrictions: Ammonium sulfate (6L) not for use in California.

– – – – – – – – – – – – – – –

Signal Word/Toxicity Class: Caution.
REI: 12 hr. (5L); 4 hr. (6L).

Treflan — see trifluralin

TRIFLURALIN

Albaugh Trifluralin 4EC *(Albaugh)*
Helena Trifluralin 4 EC *(Helena)*
Riverside Trifluralin 4EC or Trific 60DF *(Terra)*
◆ **Sedagri Trifluralin 480 (4EC)** *(Rhone-Poulenc)*
Treflan HFP (4EC), TR-10 (10G) *(Dow AgroSciences)*
Trilin 10G *(Griffin)*
Wilbur-Ellis Trifluralin 10G *(Wilbur-Ellis)*

Rate: 0.5-0.75 lb. ai/A
1-1.5 pt. 4EC/A
0.8-1.2 pt. 5EC/A
0.875-1.33 lb. 60DF/A
5-7.5 lb. 10G/A

Time: Apply preplant incorporated for preemergence control of grasses and broadleaf weeds in direct-seeded forage legumes.

Weeds: Broadleaf weeds:

carelessweed	henbit	puncturevine
carpetweed	knotweed	(western U.S.)
chickweed	kochia	purslane
field bindweed	lambsquarters	pusley
fireweed	Mexican clover	Russian thistle
Florida purslane	Mexican fireweed	stinging nettle
Florida pusley	pigweed	tumbleweed
goosefoot		

Grasses:

annual bluegrass	foxtail millet	sandbur
barnyardgrass	giant foxtail	shattercane
bottlegrass	green foxtail	smooth crabgrass
bristlegrass	Italian ryegrass	sprangletop
bromegrass	johnsongrass	stinkgrass
burgrass	(seedling)	Texas panicum
cheat	junglerice	watergrass
cheatgrass	large crabgrass	wildcane
chess	pigeongrass	woolly cupgrass
downy brome	robust foxtail	yellow foxtail
fall panicum		

Remarks: Rate varies by soil type. Some stand reduction may occur, however, excellent weed control will allow time for establishment of a quality stand. Follow the most severe grazing restrictions imposed by either label or USDA Conservation Use Program, whichever is longest. Consult local ASCS committee or other state agency for grazing restrictions.

State Restrictions: For use on barley in Minnesota, North Dakota, South Dakota.

– – – – – – – – – – – – – – –

Signal Word/Toxicity Class: Varies by formulation.
REI: 12 hr. unless soil injected or soil incorporated.

Trilin — see trifluralin

Weed Rhap — see 2,4-D

Weedar — see 2,4-D

Weedestroy — see 2,4-D

Weedone — see 2,4-D

Fallow Land

AAtrex — see atrazine

ALLY

Ally (DF) (metsulfuron-methyl) *(DuPont)*

Rate: 0.1-0.3 oz. DF/A

Time: Postemergence. Apply in early spring when weeds are small and actively growing. For bahiagrass, apply after greenup in the spring but before seedhead formation.

Weeds: Broadleaf weeds:

annual marshelder	dandelion	purple mustard
bitter sneezeweed	dogfennel	purple scabious
blackeyed susan	false chamomile	redroot pigweed
blue mustard	fanweed	Russian thistle
buckbrush	field pennycress	sercia lespedeza
bur buttercup	filaree	shepherdspurse
burclover	flixweed	slimleaf
buttercup	green smartweed	lambsquarters
Canada thistle*	henbit	smallseed falseflax
Carolina geranium	horsemint	smooth pigweed
coast fiddleneck	kochia	sowthistle*
common broomweed	jim hill mustard	tansymustard
common chickweed	ladysthumb	tarweed
common groundsel	marestail	treacle mustard
common	mayweed	tumble mustard
lambsquarters	minerslettuce	tumble pigweed
common mullein	musk thistle	volunteer sunflower
common purslane	pale smartweed	waterpod
common sunflower*	Pensacola	western snowberry
common yarrow	bahiagrass	wild buckwheat*
conical catchfly	plains coreopsis	wild carrot
corn cockle	plantain	wild garlic
corn gromwell*	prickly lettuce	wild mustard
cowcockle	prostrate knotweed*	woolly croton
curly dock		

Brush:

blackberry	dewberry	multiflora rose

*Suppression

Remarks: For control of Pensacola bahiagrass in established bermudagrass pastures.

Tank Mixes: Banvel, 2,4-D, Tordon, Weedmaster in states where labeled.

State Restrictions: For use in all states except California.

– – – – – – – – – – – – – – –

Signal Word/Toxicity Class: Caution/III.
REI: 4 hr.

9

Other Uses

NOTICE The information on these pages is for preliminary planning — not a guide for use. Be sure to follow the manufacturer's directions, notwithstanding information contained here. | For personal protective equipment and EPA registration numbers, please turn to page 70.

AMBER

◆ **Amber Accu-Pak or CustomPak (WDG) (triasulfuron)** *(Novartis)*

Rate: 0.28-0.56 oz. WDG/A

Time: Postemergence. Apply when weeds are actively growing.

Weeds: Broadleaf weeds:

annual polemonium	field pennycress	Russian thistle
blue mustard (purple)	flixweed	shepherdspurse
bushy wallflower	forget-me-not	smooth pigweed
buttercup	hairy vetch	spring whitlowgrass
Canada thistle*	jagged chickweed	tall hedge mustard
coast fiddleneck	jim hill mustard	tansymustard
common chickweed	kochia	tumble mustard
common mallow	London rocket	Virginia pepperweed
common purslane	marshelder	western ragweed*
common ragweed	minerslettuce	wild buckwheat
common sunflower	morningglory*	wild garlic*
corn gromwell	plains coreopsis	wild mustard
cutleaf	prickly lettuce	wild onion*
evening primrose	prostrate knotweed	wild radish
fanweed	redroot pigweed	yellow starthistle

* Suppression

Remarks: Do not use alone in any field where ALS-resistant biotypes of any weed species have been identified. Do not plant durum wheat less than 8 months after application. Refer to label for directions and precautions.

Crop Rotation: Wheat—anytime; proso millet—4 months; barley, oats, rye, bermudagrass—6 months (with conditions); grain sorghum and soybeans—14 months (with conditions). All other crops may be seeded only after completion of successful field bioassay; refer to label.

State Restrictions: For use in Colorado (except San Luis Valley), Idaho, Kansas, Minnesota, Montana, Nebraska, Nevada, New Mexico, North Dakota, Oklahoma, South Dakota, Texas, Utah, Wyoming, and east of the Cascades in Oregon or Washington.

- - - - - - - - - - - - - - - -

Signal Word/Toxicity Class: Caution.

REI: 12 hr.

Atra-5 — see atrazine

ATRAZINE

Restricted Use Pesticide.

AAtrex 4L or AAtrex Nine-0 (WDG) *(Novartis)*
◆ **Clean Crop Atrazine 4L or 90 WDG** *(Platte)*
Drexel Atrazine 4L, Atra-5 (5L) or 90DF *(Drexel)*
Helena Atrazine 4L *(Helena)*
Riverside Atrazine 4L or 90DF *(Terra)*

Rate: 0.5-1 lb. ai/A
    1-2 pt. 4L/A
    0.8-1.6 pt. 5L/A
    1.1 lb. WDG, 90DF/A

Time: Wheat-fallow-wheat. Apply only once during same fallow period.

Weeds: Broadleaf weeds:

common	kochia	Russian thistle
lambsquarters	mustard	wild lettuce
field pennycress	pigweed	wild sunflower

Grasses:

cheatgrass	volunteer wheat (suppression)

Remarks: Apply to stubble ground.

State Restrictions: For use in Colorado, Kansas, Montana (AAtrex, Riverside 90DF), Nebraska, North Dakota, South Dakota, Wyoming.

- - - - - - - - - - - - - - - -

Rate: 3 lb. ai/A
    6 pt. 4L/A
    4.9 pt. 5L/A
    3.3 lb. WDG, 90DF/A

Time: Wheat-sorghum-fallow, wheat-corn-fallow.

Weeds: Same weeds as above.

Remarks: Apply to wheat stubble after harvest. For wheat-corn-fallow, broadcast by ground only. Plant sorghum or corn into wheat stubble with minimum disturbance to soil. Use only on silt loam or heavier soil. Do not graze treated area or feed treated forage to livestock.

Crop Rotation: Do not plant treated area to any crop other than those on label within 18 months following treatment.

State Restrictions: Wheat-corn-fallow: For use in Kansas, Nebraska; Helena, Novartis also Colorado, North Dakota, South Dakota, Wyoming. Refer to label for pH restrictions in North Dakota and South Dakota.

- - - - - - - - - - - - - - - -

Signal Word/Toxicity Class: Caution/III.

REI: 12 hr.

Banvel — see dicamba

Barrage — see 2,4-D

Brash — see 2,4-D Combinations

CANVAS (Premix)

Canvas (DF) (37.5% thifensulfuron-methyl & 18.75% tribenuron-methyl & 15% metsulfuron-methyl) *(DuPont)*

Rate: 1 soluble package/5A
    MN, MT, ND, SD:
    1 soluble package/10A

Time: Apply in spring or fall when majority of weeds have emerged and are actively growing.

Weeds: Broadleaf weeds:

annual knawel	dogfennel	purple mustard
annual sowthistle*	false chamomile	redmaids
black mustard	fanweed	rockpurslane
blue mustard	field chickweed	redroot pigweed
broadleaf dock	field pennycress	Russian thistle
bur buttercup	filaree	scentless chamomile
bushy wallflower	flixweed	shepherdspurse
Canada thistle	hairy nightshade*	smallflower buttercup
Carolina geranium	hairy vetch*	smallseed falseflax
catchweed bedstraw*	henbit	smartweed
clasping pepperweed	jim hill mustard	smooth pigweed
coast fiddleneck	kochia	snow speedwell
common buckwheat	lambsquarters	stinking chickweed
common chickweed	little mallow*	stinking mayweed
common cocklebur	London rocket	swinecress
common groundsel	marshelder	tall waterhemp*
common mallow	mayweed chamomile	tansymustard
common purslane	minerslettuce	tarweed
common radish	mouseearcress	treacle mustard
common ragweed	narrowleaf	tumble mustard
common sunflower	lambsquarters	tumble pigweed
common vetch*	nightflowering	volunteer lentils
conical catchfly	catchfly	volunteer peas
corn chamomile	Pennsylvania	volunteer sunflower
corn gromwell	smartweed	waterpod
corn spurry	pineappleweed	wild buckwheat
cowcockle	plains coreopsis	wild chamomile
curly dock	prickly lettuce	wild garlic
cutleaf	prostrate knotweed	wild mustard
evening primrose	prostrate pigweed	wild radish
cutleaf nightshade*		

* Partial control

Remarks: Add approved nonionic surfactant. Do not make more than one application per crop season. Do not graze or feed forage or hay from treated areas to livestock; harvested straw may be used for bedding and/or feed.

Days To Harvest: 45.

Crop Rotation: Varies depending on location and crop.

State Restrictions: For use in Colorado (except Alamosa, Conejos, Costilla, Rio Grande, Saguache counties), Idaho, Kansas, Minnesota, Montana, Nebraska, New Mexico, Oklahoma, Oregon, South Dakota, Texas, Utah, Washington, Wyoming.

- - - - - - - - - - - - - - - -

Signal Word/Toxicity Class: Warning/II.

REI: 12 hr.

CLETHODIM

Prism (0.94EC) or Select (2EC) *(Valent)*

Rate: 0.1-0.25 lb. ai/A
    13-34 fl. oz. 0.94EC/A
    6-16 fl. oz. 2EC/A

Time: Postemergence. Apply to actively growing grasses.

Weeds: Grasses:

Amazon sprangletop	green foxtail	smooth crabgrass
annual bluegrass	itchgrass	southern crabgrass
barnyardgrass	johnsongrass	Texas panicum
bearded sprangletop	junglerice	volunteer cereals
bermudagrass	large crabgrass	wild oat
broadleaf signalgrass	quackgrass	wild proso millet
crowfootgrass	red rice	wirestem muhly
fall panicum	red sprangletop	witchgrass
giant foxtail	shattercane	woolly cupgrass
goosegrass	southwestern cupgrass	yellow foxtail

◆-new product • PP-preplant • PPI-preplant incorporated • PRE-preemergence • POST-postemergence • SEQ-sequential • ae-acid equivalent • ai-active ingredient • DF-dry flowable
E/EC-emulsifiable concentrate • F/FL-flowable • DG/G/WG-dispersable granule • L/LC-liquid • SP/WSP-soluble packet • W/WP-wettable powder • WSB-water soluble bag

Remarks: Rate varies by grass species, stage and geographical region. Grass crops such as corn, sorghum, wheat, and rice are highly sensitive to clethodim. Do not apply under stress conditions or if rainfall is expected in 1 hr. Do not apply through any type of irrigation system. Do not apply more than 0.5 lb. ai/A per season (0.25 lb. ai/A on Long Island, New York). Do not graze treated fields or feed treated forage or hay to livestock. Refer to label for directions, restrictions, and precautions.

Crop Rotation: Do not plant any crop for 30 days after application unless clethodim is registered for use in that crop.

Tank Mixes: Banvel SGF, 2,4-D ester.

State Restrictions: Not for use on Solano grass in the Vernal Lakes area of Solano County, California; wild rice in Hays County, Texas.

Signal Word/Toxicity Class: Warning/II.
REI: 24 hr.

CLOPYRALID

Stinger (Dow AgroSciences)
Rate: 0.1-0.25 lb. ae/A
0.25-0.66 pt./A
Time: Apply either postharvest, in the spring/summer (during fallow period), or to set-aside acres. For perennial weeds such as Canada thistle, apply after majority of basal leaves have emerged up to bud stage.
Weeds: Annual and perennial broadleaf weeds:

Canada thistle	jimsonweed	spotted knapweed
cocklebur	marshelder	sunflower
clover	Russian knapweed	vetch
diffuse knapweed	(suppression)	volunteer soybean
Jerusalem artichoke	sowthistle*	

Remarks: Application to fallow cropland preceding or following application to dryland small grains is allowed; not allowed preceding or following application to irrigated small grains. Use high rate on perennial weeds or when condition of weeds at time of treatment may prevent optimum control. Do not apply by air or through any type of irrigation system.
Crop Rotation: Varies by region; refer to label.
Tank Mixes: 2,4-D.
State Restrictions: In California, do not apply more that 0.66 pt./A per growing season.

Signal Word/Toxicity Class: Caution/III.
REI: 12 hr.

COMMAND

Command 4EC (clomazone) (FMC)
Rate: 0.75-1 lb. ai/A
1.5-2 pt. 4EC/A
Time: Preemergence surface applied. Winter wheat-fallow-winter wheat: apply after wheat harvest (Aug. 15-Oct. 31).
Weeds: Broadleaf weeds:

common lambsquarters	kochia	tumble mustard
common purslane	prickly lettuce	wild buckwheat
	tansymustard	

Grasses:

cheatgrass	jointed goatgrass	volunteer rye
downy bromegrass	volunteer barley	volunteer wheat

Remarks: Non-target spray drift should be avoided to prevent whitening of desirable vegetation. Do not apply within 500 ft. of emerged winter wheat or within 1000 ft. of towns, subdivisions, commercial vegetable and fruit production (except sweet corn), commercial nurseries, and greenhouses. Do not apply through any type of irrigation system. Do not graze livestock on treated fields.
Crop Rotation: Do not plant wheat sooner than 9 months after late summer or fall application. For specific crops at shorter intervals, refer to Rotational Crop Guidelines on label. Cover crops may be planted any time but stand reductions may occur in some areas. Carryover injury to approved rotational crops may result under abnormal conditions.
Tank Mixes: May be tank mixed with other herbicides registered for fallow cropland use; observe all rotation guidelines, precautions, and replanting instructions of each product label.
State Restrictions: Not for use in California.

Signal Word/Toxicity Class: Warning/II.
REI: 12 hr. unless soil injected or soil incorporated.

Credit — see glyphosate

CURTAIL (Premix)

Curtail (0.38 lb./gal. clopyralid & 2 lb./gal. 2,4-D) (Dow AgroSciences)
Rate: 0.6-1.2 lb. ae/A
2-4 pt./A
Time: Apply either postharvest, in the spring/summer (fallow period), or to set-aside acres to control.
Weeds: Broadleaf weeds:

alfalfa	giant ragweed	redroot pigweed
annual sowthistle	goatsbeard	Russian knapweed*
Canada thistle	hairy nightshade	Russian thistle
coffeeweed	horseweed	(1-3 leaf)
common burdock	Jerusalem artichoke	scentless chamomile
common cocklebur	jim hill mustard	shepherdspurse
common groundsel	jimsonweed	sicklepod
common lambsquarters	kochia* (2-4 leaf)	spotted knapweed
common ragweed	ladysthumb	sweetclover
common sunflower	meadow salsify	tansymustard
cornflower	musk thistle	tumble mustard
curly dock	narrowleaf hawksbeard	velvetleaf
cutleaf nightshade	Pennsylvania	vetch
dandelion	smartweed	volunteer beans
diffuse knapweed	perennial sowthistle*	volunteer lentils
false chamomile	pineappleweed	volunteer peas
fanweed	plantain	wild buckwheat
field bindweed	prickly lettuce	wild mustard
field pennycress	red clover	wild radish
flixweed*	red sorrel	yellow starthistle

* Suppression

Remarks: Allow at least 30 days after application before seeding to wheat, barley, or grasses.
Crop Rotation: Varies by region; refer to label.
Tank Mixes: 2,4-D.

Signal Word/Toxicity Class: Danger/I.
REI: 48 hr.

2,4-D - PHENOXY HERBICIDES

Albaugh Amine 4 (2,4-D amine) (Albaugh)
Albaugh LV4 or LV6 (2,4-D ester) (Albaugh)
Albaugh D-638 (6) (2,4-D ester) (Albaugh)
Esteron 99C (4) (2,4-D LV ester) (Rhone-Poulenc)
Formula 40 (4) (2,4-D mixed amine) (Rhone-Poulenc)
Hi-Dep (4) (2,4-D amine) (PBI/Gordon)
♦ **Opti-Amine (4) (2,4-D amine)** (Helena)
Weed Rhap A-4D (2,4-D amine) (Helena)
Weed Rhap LV-6D (2,4-D ester) (Helena)
Weedar 64 (4) (2,4-D amine) (Nufarm)
Weedone 638 (6) (2,4-D ester + acid) (Nufarm)
Weedone LV4 (2,4-D solventless ester) (Nufarm)
Weedone Lo Vol 6 (2,4-D ester) (Nufarm)
Wilbur-Ellis Amine 4 (2,4-D amine) (Wilbur-Ellis)
Wilbur-Ellis Lo Vol-4 or Lo Vol-6 (2,4-D ester) (Wilbur-Ellis)
Rate: 1-6 pt. 4/A
0.66-4 pt. Lo Vol 6/A
1.33-4 pt. Lo Vol-6, LV-6D/A
1.33-8 pt. 638, LV6/A
Time: Apply to actively growing weeds. Do not apply within 90 days of planting or until chemical has disappeared from soil.
Weeds: Broadleaf weeds and crop stubble including:

Canada thistle	musk thistle	wild onion
field bindweed	wild garlic	

Remarks: Rate varies by company; refer to labels. Do not graze dairy animals within 7 days of treatment (14 days for Wilbur-Ellis).
State Restrictions: Wilbur-Ellis not registered in California.

Signal Word/Toxicity Class: Varies by formulation.
REI: Danger—48 hr.; Caution—12 hr.

♦ **Barrage or Barrage HF (EC) (2,4-D ester)** (Helena)
Rate: 6-26 fl. oz./A
Time: Apply to actively growing weeds.
Weeds: Annual, biennial, and perennial broadleaf weeds.
Remarks: Apply higher rates for older plants, drought stressed, or hard-to-kill species. May be used to kill fall alfalfa stands in preparation for spring planting of row crops under conservation tillage. Treated alfalfa cannot be grazed, fed to livestock or cut for hay.

Signal Word/Toxicity Class: Caution/III.
REI: 12 hr.

9

Other Uses

Fallow Land

◆ **Clean Crop Amine 4 (2,4-D amine)** *(Platte)*
Solve 2,4-D LV4 (2,4-D LV ester) *(Albaugh)*
Rate: Annual weeds:
    1-2 lb. ae/A
    2-4 pt./A
    Perennial weeds such as Canada thistle, field bindweed:
    up to 3 lb. ae/A
    up to 6 pt./A
Time: Apply to actively growing weeds.
Weeds: Annual and perennial broadleaf weeds.
Remarks: Do not plant any crops for 3 months after treatment or until chemical has disappeared from soil.

– – – – – – – – – – – – – –

Signal Word/Toxicity Class: Danger/I (amine); Caution/III (ester).
REI: Danger—48 hr.; Caution—12 hr.

◆ **Riverdale 6 Amine (2,4-D amine)** *(Riverdale)*
Rate: 1-3 lb. ae/A
    1.33-4 pt. 6/A
Time: Apply lower rate in spring during rosette stage, higher rate in fall or after flower stalks have developed.
Remarks: Do not disturb for at least 2 weeks after treatment, or until weed tops are dead.

– – – – – – – – – – – – – –

Signal Word/Toxicity Class: Danger/I.
REI: 48 hr.

◆ **Riverdale L.V. 4 or L.V. 6 (2,4-D ester)** *(Riverdale)*
Weedestroy AM-40 (2,4-D amine) *(Riverdale)*
Rate: 0.5-2 lb. ae/A
    1-4 pt./A
    0.66-2.66 pt. 6/A
    Seedling grass:
    0.37-5 lb. ae/A
    0.75-1 pt./A
    0.5-0.66 pt. 6/A
Time: Apply in the spring or fall. Do not apply from early boot to milk stage.
Remarks: Spray seedling grass only after 5-leaf stage. After grass is well established, higher rates up to 2 lb. ai can be used to control hard-to-kill weeds. Do not use on bentgrass unless injury can be tolerated.

– – – – – – – – – – – – – –

Signal Word/Toxicity Class: Danger/I (amine); Caution/III (ester).
REI: Danger—48 hr.; Caution—12 hr.

◆ **Saber (2,4-D amine)** *(Platte)*
Rate: Annual weeds:
    0.75-2 lb. ae/A
    1.5-4 pt./A
    Perennial and biennial weeds:
    1.5-3 lb. ae/A
    3-6 pt./A
Time: Apply to actively growing weeds.
Weeds: Annual, perennial, and biennial broadleaf weeds.
Remarks: Use higher rate on hard-to-kill species such as Canada thistle and field bindweed. Do not use on bentgrass, alfalfa, clover, or other legumes unless risk of injury acceptable. Do not use on newly seeded areas until grass is well established.
Days To Harvest: 30 days—prior to cutting grass for hay; 7 days—pregrazing interval for dairy cattle; 3 days—preslaughter interval for meat animals.

– – – – – – – – – – – – – –

Signal Word/Toxicity Class: Danger/I.
REI: 48 hr.

Savage (WSB) (2,4-D amine) *(Platte)*
Rate: 0.48-2.85 lb. ae/A
    0.5-3 lb. WSB/A
Time: Apply to actively growing weeds.
Weeds: Annual and perennial broadleaf weeds and crop stubble.
Remarks: Apply at lower rates on annual weeds; up to 3 lb./A on established perennial weeds. Refer to label for restrictions and precautions.
Days To Harvest: 30 days—prior to cutting grass for hay; 7 days—pregrazing interval for dairy cattle; 3 days—preslaughter interval for meat animals.

– – – – – – – – – – – – – –

Signal Word/Toxicity Class: Danger/I.
REI: 48 hr.

Solution (WS) (2,4 amine) *(Riverdale)*
Rate: Annual broadleaf weeds:
    1 WS packet (2 lb. 13 oz.)/1.25-1.5 A
    Perennial weeds such as Canada thistle, field bindweed:
    1 WS packet (2 lb. 13 oz.)/A

Time: Apply to actively growing weeds.
Weeds: Annual and perennial broadleaf weeds.
Remarks: Do not make application within 90 days of planting or until chemical has disappeared from soil.

– – – – – – – – – – – – – –

Signal Word/Toxicity Class: Danger/I.
REI: 48 hr.

2,4-D COMBINATIONS

◆ **Brash (2.87 lb./gal. 2,4-D & 1 lb./gal. dicamba)** *(Terra)*
Weedmaster (2.87 lb./gal. 2,4-D & 1 lb./gal. dicamba) *(BASF)*
Rate: 0.5-4 lb. ai/A
    1-8 pt./A
Time: Apply when weeds are actively growing; retreat as needed.
Weeds: Annual broadleaf weeds:

annual sowthistle	common purslane	redroot pigweed
black nightshade	common ragweed	rough pigweed
cowcockle	knotweed	Russian thistle
common cocklebur	kochia	sunflower
common	mustard	tansymustard
lambsquarters	Pennsylvania	velvetleaf
common mallow	smartweed	wild buckwheat

Biennial weeds:

bull thistle	plumeless thistle	wild carrot
musk thistle	tansy ragwort	yellow starthistle

Perennial weeds:

Canada thistle	curly dock	field bindweed

Remarks: Land rotated to wheat. Do not exceed total of 8 pt./A.
Tank Mixes: Atrazine, chlorsulfuron, cyanazine, glyphosate, metribuzin, or paraquat. Refer to labels for use directions, precautions, and geographic restrictions.

– – – – – – – – – – – – – –

Signal Word/Toxicity Class: Danger/I.
REI: 48 hr.

DICAMBA

Banvel (WS) (DMA salt of dicamba) *(BASF)*
Banvel SGF (sodium salt of dicamba) *(BASF)*
◆ **Sterling (WS) (DMA salt of dicamba)** *(Terra)*
Rate: Annual weeds (less than 6" tall):
    0.25-0.5 lb. ai/A
    0.5-1 pt. WS/A
    1-2 pt. SGF/A
    Biennial weeds (rosette stage):
    0.5-1 lb. ai/A
    1-2 pt. WS/A
    2-4 pt. SGF/A
    Perennial weeds:
    0.5-2 lb. ai/A
    1-4 pt. WS/A
    2-8 pt. SGF/A
Time: Apply when weeds are actively growing after crop harvest and before a killing frost or in fallow cropland the following spring or summer.
Weeds: Annual broadleaf weeds plus the following biennial and perennial broadleaf weeds:

alfalfa	field bindweed	silverleaf nightshade
bursage	hedge bindweed	swamp smartweed
Canada thistle	hemp dogbane	Texas blueweed
Carolina horsenettle	Jerusalem artichoke	trumpetcreeper
common dandelion	perennial sowthistle	wild garlic
curly dock	redvine	

Remarks: Broadcast or spot treatment. Spray additives may be used. Avoid disturbing treated areas for at least 7 days following treatment.
Tank Mixes: Ally, Amber, atrazine, Bladex, Curtail, Cyclone, 2,4-D, Fallow Master, Finesse, Gramoxone Extra, Kerb, Landmaster, paraquat, Roundup Ultra/Ultra RT, Sencor, Tordon.

– – – – – – – – – – – – – –

Signal Word/Toxicity Class: Warning/II.
REI: 24 hr.

DICAMBA & ATRAZINE (Premixes)

Restricted Use Pesticide due to ground and surface water concerns.

Marksman (FL) (1.1 lb./gal. dicamba & 2.1 lb./gal. atrazine) *(BASF)*
◆ **Sterling Plus (FL) (1.1 lb./gal. dicamba & 2.1 lb./gal. atrazine)** *(Terra)*

◆-new product • PP-preplant • PPI-preplant incorporated • PRE-preemergence • POST-postemergence • SEQ-sequential • ae-acid equivalent • ai-active ingredient • DF-dry flowable E/EC-emulsifiable concentrate • F/FL-flowable • DG/G/WG-dispersable granule • L/LC-liquid • SP/WSP-soluble packet • W/WP-wettable powder • WSB-water soluble bag

Rate: Wheat/fallow/wheat:
   0.8-1.4 lb. ai/A
   2-3.5 pt. FL/A
   Wheat/corn or sorghum/fallow:
   0.8-4.4 lb. ai/A
   2-11 pt. FL/A

Time: Postharvest. May be applied from summer to fall after wheat harvest to fallow ground in wheat/fallow/wheat or wheat/corn or sorghum/fallow (Eco-Fallow).

Weeds: Broadleaf weeds:

alfalfa	giant ragweed	puncturevine
annual clover	(buffaloweed)	redroot pigweed
bitterdock	green smartweed	(carelessweed)
black nightshade	hedge bindweed	rough pigweed
broadleaf dock	hemp dogbane	Russian thistle
burcucumber	ivyleaf morningglory	sicklepod
Canada thistle	Jerusalem artichoke	smooth pigweed
Carolina horsenettle	jimsonweed	spanishneedles
common chickweed	knotweed	swamp smartweed
common cocklebur	kochia	tall morningglory
common dandelion	ladysthumb	tansymustard
common	lambsquarters*	tumble pigweed
lambsquarters	lespedeza	velvetleaf
common mallow	Pennsylvania	Venice mallow
common milkweed	smartweed	vetch
common purslane	perennial clover	volunteer sunflower
common ragweed	pigweed*	wild buckwheat
common sunflower	prickly sida (teaweed)	wild cucumber
curly dock	prostrate pigweed	wild mustard
field bindweed	prostrate spurge	yellowtop mustard

* Triazine resistant weeds

Remarks: Do not graze or feed forage from treated areas to livestock.

Crop Rotation: If applied after June 10, rotation with crops other than corn or sorghum the following spring may result in crop injury.

Tank Mixes: Atrazine, Banvel, Command, 2,4-D, Fallow Master, Landmaster, paraquat, Roundup Ultra, sulfonylureas.

State Restrictions: Wheat/fallow/wheat in Colorado, Kansas, Nebraska, Oklahoma, South Dakota, Texas, and Wyoming. Wheat/corn or sorghum/fallow (Eco-Fallow) in Colorado, Kansas, Nebraska, Oklahoma, and Texas.

- - - - - - - - - - - - - - -

Signal Word/Toxicity Class: Caution.
REI: 48 hr.

Esteron 99C — see 2,4-D

FALLOW MASTER (Premix)

Fallow Master (1.5 lb./gal. glyphosate & 0.6 lb./gal. dicamba) *(Monsanto)*

Rate: 22-52 oz./A

Time: Postemergence. Apply 15 days prior to planting of wheat, barley, oats, or sorghum.

Weeds: Broadleaf weeds:

barley	kochia	Russian thistle
blue mustard	lambsquarters	tansymustard
buffalobur	prickly lettuce	tumble mustard
field sandbur	pigweed	

Grasses:

barnyardgrass	goatgrass	wheat
downy brome	green foxtail	wild oat
fall panicum	stinkgrass	witchgrass

Remarks: Do not feed or forage treated vegetation within 8 weeks after application. Refer to label for precautions.

Crop Rotation: Do not plant any crop other than wheat, barley, corn, oats, rye, or sorghum for 3 months after treatment or until product has disappeared from soil.

State Restrictions: For use in Colorado, Idaho, Montana, Nevada, North Dakota, Oregon, Utah, Washington, and Wyoming and in specific counties only in Kansas, Nebraska, New Mexico, Oklahoma, South Dakota, and Texas; refer to label for restrictions.

- - - - - - - - - - - - - - -

Signal Word/Toxicity Class: Danger/I.
REI: 24 hr.

FINESSE (Premix)

Finesse (DF) (62.5% chlorsulfuron & 12.5% metsulfuron-methyl) *(DuPont)*

Rate: 0.2-0.3 oz. DF/A
Time: Wheat/fallow/wheat.

Weeds: Broadleaf weeds:

annual sowthistle	false chamomile	pineappleweed
bedstraw*	field pennycress	prickly lettuce
blue mustard	flixweed*	prickly poppy
broadleaf dock	hempnettle	prostrate knotweed
bur beakchervil	henbit	prostrate pigweed
bur buttercup	ivyleaf speedwell*	redroot pigweed
Canada thistle*	jacob's ladder	redstem filaree
coast fiddleneck	jagged chickweed	shepherdspurse
common chickweed	jim hill mustard	smooth pigweed
common groundsel	ladysthumb	tansymustard*
common purslane	lambsquarters	tarweed
common speedwell*	little bittercress	vetch
conical catchfly	mayweed	white cockle
corn gromwell*	minerslettuce	wild buckwheat
corn spurry	mouseear chickweed	wild carrot
cowcockle	Pennsylvania	wild mustard
dovefoot geranium	smartweed	wild radish

Grasses:

annual bluegrass*	annual ryegrass*	green foxtail*

* Suppression

Remarks: Wheat/fallow wheat or where interval between application and planting of corn or sorghum is at least 24 months. Do not use long residual herbicide having the same mode of action as Finesse on these fields during this 24 month period. Do not let weed escapes go to seed. No grazing restrictions.

State Restrictions: For use in all states (except Alamosa, Conejos, Costilla, Rio Grande, Saguache counties of Colorado).

- - - - - - - - - - - - - - -

Signal Word/Toxicity Class: Caution.
REI: 4 hr.

FLUAZIFOP-P-BUTYL

◆ **Fusilade DX or II** *(ZENECA)*

Rate: 0.25-0.375 lb. ai/A
   1-1.5 pt. DX, II/A

Time: Annual grasses: 2-8" tall before tillering and/or heading. Perennial grasses: apply by growth stage dependent on species.

Weeds: Annual and perennial grasses including:

barnyardgrass	johnsongrass	southern sandbur
bermudagrass	(rhizome, seedling)	southwestern
broadleaf signalgrass	junglerice	cupgrass
fall panicum	kikuyugrass	Texas panicum
field sandbur	large crabgrass	tropical crabgrass
giant foxtail	prairie cupgrass	volunteer cereals
goosegrass	quackgrass	wild oat
green foxtail	red rice	wild proso millet
guineagrass	shattercane	wiremuhly
(seedling)	smooth crabgrass	witchgrass
Italian ryegrass	sorghum-almum	woolly cupgrass
itchgrass	southern crabgrass	yellow foxtail

Remarks: Rate varies by geographic area and grass species. Add crop oil concentrate or nonionic surfactant. Do not apply through any type of irrigation system. Do not graze treated areas. Refer to label for specific directions, restrictions, and precautions.

Crop Rotation: Do not plant rotational grass crops such as corn, sorghum, or cereals within 60 days of last application.

State Restrictions: Refer to label for geographical regions.

- - - - - - - - - - - - - - -

Signal Word/Toxicity Class: Caution.
REI: 12 hr.

Formula 40 — see 2,4-D

Fusilade — see fluazifop-P-butyl

GLYPHOSATE

◆ **Credit (4WS)** *(Nufarm)*
◆ **Glyfos or Glyfos X-tra (4WS)** *(Cheminova)*
Rattler (4WS) *(Helena)*
Roundup Custom (5.4WS) *(Monsanto)*
Roundup Original, Original RT, Ultra, Ultra RT (4WS) *(Monsanto)*

Rate: Annual weeds:
   0.38-1.5 lb. ai/A
   0.56-2.25 pt. 5.4WS/A
   0.75-3 pt. 4WS/A
   Perennial weeds:
   0.5-5 lb. ai/A
   0.75-7.5 pt. 5.4WS/A
   1-10 pt. 4WS/A

Other Uses — 9

NOTICE	The information on these pages is for preliminary planning — not a guide for use. Be sure to follow the manufacturer's directions, notwithstanding information contained here.

For personal protective equipment and EPA registration numbers, please turn to page 70.

Fallow Land

Time: Apply during fallow period prior to planting or crop emergence.
Weeds: Broadleaf weeds, grasses, and woody brush including:

cheat	foxtail	volunteer wheat
downy brome	tansymustard	

Remarks: May be applied by ground or air. Refer to label for directions, restrictions, and precautions.
Tank Mixes: Banvel, 2,4-D, Goal. Refer to labels for precautions and crop rotation restrictions. Roundup Ultra tank mixes not registered in California. Do not apply Banvel or 2,4-D by air in California.
State Restrictions: Roundup RT: For use in Colorado, Idaho, Montana, North Dakota, South Dakota, Utah, and Wyoming. For use in specific counties only in Kansas, Minnesota, Nebraska, Nevada, Oklahoma, Oregon, and Washington, refer to label for restrictions. Glyfos not registered for use in California. Glyfos X-tra not registered for use in mistblowers in California or Arizona.

- - - - - - - - - - - - - - - - -

Signal Word/Toxicity Class: Varies by formulation.
REI: Warning—12 hr.; Caution—4 hr.

GOAL

Goal 2XL (oxyfluorfen) *(Rohm and Haas)*
Rate: 0.25-0.5 lb. ai/A
   1-2 pt. 2XL/A
Time: Time of application depends on crop to be planted following fallow bed treatment; refer to label for minimum treatment-planting intervals.
Weeds: Broadleaf weeds:

annual sowthistle	common groundsel	redmaids
broadleaf filaree	henbit	rockpurslane
burning nettle	London rocket	redstem filaree
cheeseweed (malva)	minerslettuce	shepherdspurse
coast fiddleneck	mustard	

Remarks: Direct seeded and transplanted crops (except cotton/soybeans).
Tank Mixes: Glyphosate.

- - - - - - - - - - - - - - - -

Rate: 0.25-0.5 lb. ai/A
   1-2 pt. 2XL/A
Time: Do not apply within 7 days of planting.
Weeds: Broadleaf weeds:

annual sowthistle	cutleaf	prickly sida
broadleaf filaree	eveningprimrose	redmaids rockpurslane
burning nettle	henbit	redroot pigweed
Carolina geranium	ladysthumb	redstem filaree
cheeseweed (malva)	London rocket	shepherdspurse
coast fiddleneck	minerslettuce	smallflower buttercup
common groundsel	mustard	velvetleaf
common purslane	oxalis	

Remarks: Cotton/soybeans.
Crop Rotation: Refer to label for plantback times for rotation crops.
Tank Mixes: Glyphosate, paraquat.
State Restrictions: Not for use on fallow beds to be planted to soybeans in California.

- - - - - - - - - - - - - - - -

Signal Word/Toxicity Class: Warning/II.
REI: 24 hr.

Gramoxone Extra — see paraquat

Harmony GT — see thifensulfuron-methyl

Hi-Dep — see 2,4-D

KERB

Restricted Use Pesticide.

■ **PRE, POST**
Kerb 50-W (pronamide) *(Rohm and Haas)*
Rate: 0.25-0.5 lb. ai/A
   0.5-1 lb. 50-W/A
Time: Preemergence, postemergence. Apply prior to soil freeze-up (mid-Oct./mid-Dec.).
Weeds: Grasses:

bulbous bluegrass	jointed goatgrass	volunteer rye
cheatgrass	volunteer barley	volunteer wheat
downy brome		

Remarks: Restricted to summer fallow land that will be planted back the following year to winter wheat, barley or oats. Do not use any tillage in the fall prior to or after application. Refer to label for use directions and precautions.
Crop Rotation: Do not plant winter wheat, barley or oats within 9 months following treatment.
Tank Mixes: Glean.
State Restrictions: For use in Idaho, Oregon, Washington.

- - - - - - - - - - - - - - - -

Signal Word/Toxicity Class: Caution.
REI: 24 hr.

LANDMASTER (Premix)

Landmaster BW (1.2 lb./gal. glyphosate & 1.9 lb./gal. 2,4-D)
(Monsanto)
Rate: 1.3-1.6 lb. ai/A
   44-64 oz./A
Time: Apply to actively growing weeds 2-12" tall in fallow and reduced-tillage systems prior to planting or emergence of wheat, barley, corn, rye, oats, and sorghum. Allow 1 day after treatment before tillage.
Weeds: Broadleaf weeds:

barley	field bindweed	puncturevine
blue mustard	kochia	redroot pigweed
buffalobur	lambsquarters	Russian thistle
cocklebur	leafy spurge	tansymustard
common purslane	prickly lettuce	tumble mustard

Grasses:

barnyardgrass	goatgrass	wheat
downy brome	rye	wild oat
fall panicum	stinkgrass	witchgrass
foxtail		

Remarks: Do not feed or forage treated vegetation within 8 weeks after application. Do not apply in vicinity of 2,4-D sensitive crops such as cotton, grapes, tomatoes, and other desirable vegetation. Refer to label for directions, restrictions, and precautions.
Crop Rotation: Do not plant any crop other than wheat, barley, corn, oats, rye, or sorghum for 3 months after treatment, or until product has disappeared from soil.

- - - - - - - - - - - - - - - -

Signal Word/Toxicity Class: Danger/I.
REI: 48 hr.

Marksman — see dicamba & atrazine

Opti-Amine — see 2,4-D

Paramount — see quinclorac

PARAQUAT

Restricted Use Pesticide.

Gramoxone Extra (2.5L) *(ZENECA)*
Rate: 0.4-0.84 lb. ai/A
   1.3-2.7 pt. 2.5L/A
Time: Apply during fallow period of wheat-fallow, wheat-annual crop, and continuous wheat cropping systems.

Rate: 0.5-1 lb. ai/A
   1.5-3 pt. 2.5L/A
Time: Apply from immediately after harvest up to emergence of newly seeded crop as broadcast or band treatment.
Weeds: Annual broadleaf weeds and grasses; suppression of many perennial weeds.
Remarks: Add nonionic surfactant or crop oil concentrate. Refer to label for use directions, restrictions, and precautions.

- - - - - - - - - - - - - - - -

Signal Word/Toxicity Class: Danger-Poison/I.
REI: 12 hr. (except harvest aid/desiccation 24 hr.).

Prism — see clethodim

◆-new product • PP-preplant • PPI-preplant incorporated • PRE-preemergence • POST-postemergence • SEQ-sequential • ae-acid equivalent • ai-active ingredient • DF-dry flowable E/EC-emulsifiable concentrate • F/FL-flowable • DG/G/WG-dispersable granule • L/LC-liquid • SP/WSP-soluble packet • W/WP-wettable powder • WSB-water soluble bag

QUINCLORAC

◆ **Paramount (DF)** *(BASF)*
Rate: 3-5.3 oz. DF/A
Time: Preplant. Apply to actively growing weeds. For bindweed, apply after harvesting but before first killing frost. For long-term control, use in a 3 yr. program, applying 5.3 oz. DF/A the first year and 3-5.3 oz. DF/A in subsequent years.
Weeds: Broadleaf weeds:

bedstraw	dandelion*	morningglory
Canada thistle*	field bindweed	Russian thistle*
clover	giant ragweed*	velvetleaf*
common	hedge bindweed	volunteer flax
lambsquarters*	kochia*	wild sunflower*
common ragweed*		

Grasses:

barnyardgrass	giant foxtail	large crabgrass
broadleaf signalgrass	green foxtail	yellow foxtail

* Suppression

Remarks: Must use additive. Do not apply more than 16 oz. DF/A per calendar year. Do not apply through any type of irrigation system.
Crop Rotation: In case of crop failure, wheat and sorghum may be replanted immediately; other crops—10 months after application; alfalfa, clover, flax, lentils, peas, sugar beets—24 months and successful field bioassy.
Tank Mixes: Clarity, 2,4-D, Fallow Master, Landmaster, Roundup RT, Roundup Ultra; refer to labels for use directions.
State Restrictions: For use in Colorado, Idaho, Kansas, Montana, Nebraska, North Dakota, Oregon, South Dakota, Utah, Washington, Wyoming.

- - - - - - - - - - - - - - -

Signal Word/Toxicity Class: Caution.
REI: 12 hr.

Rattler — see glyphosate

Roundup — see glyphosate

Saber — see 2,4-D

Savage — see 2,4-D

SCYTHE

◆ **Scythe (pelargonic acid)** *(Mycogen)*
Rate: 4-13 fl. oz./1 gal. spray solution
Time: Apply to young succulent weeds.
Weeds: Annual broadleaf weeds and grasses; top-kill of perennial weeds.
Remarks: Apply in minimum 75 gal. spray solution/A or spray-to-wet. Do not apply by air or through any type of irrigation system. Refer to label for directions and precautions.
Tank Mixes: Glyphosate and other foliar and residual herbicides.

- - - - - - - - - - - - - - -

Signal Word/Toxicity Class: Warning/II.
REI: 24 hr.

Select — see clethodim

SENCOR

Sencor 4 (FL) or DF (metribuzin) *(Bayer)*
Rate: Fall fallow:
0.5-0.625 lb. ai/A
1-1.25 pt. FL/A
0.67-1 lb. DF/A
Summer fallow:
0.375-0.5 lb. ai/A
0.75-1 pt. FL/A
0.5-0.67 lb. DF/A
Time: Fall fallow: Apply after wheat harvest before weeds emerge. Summer fallow: Apply in spring before winter wheat is planted and weeds emerge.

Weeds: Broadleaf weeds:

blue mustard	kochia	tansymustard
common chickweed	lambsquarters	treacle mustard
field pennycress	pigweed	wild mustard
henbit	purple mustard	wild sunflower
jim hill mustard	Russian thistle	

Grasses:

cheatgrass	downy brome	volunteer wheat

Remarks: If Sencor was applied in the fall, do not apply in the spring. Do not graze treated fields.
Crop Rotation: Wheat or barley can be seeded 4 months after spring application. Do not plant crops in treated areas for at least 10 months following fall application. Do not plant spring-seeded cereals following fall fallow application.
Tank Mixes: With Gramoxone Extra or other contact herbicide if weed growth is present at application.
State Restrictions: For use in Idaho, Oregon, Utah, Washington.

- - - - - - - - - - - - - - -

Rate: Fall fallow:
0.625-0.75 lb. ai/A
1.25-1.5 pt. FL/A
0.83-1 lb. DF/A
Summer fallow:
0.375-0.5 lb. ai/A
0.75-1 pt. FL/A
0.5-0.67 lb. DF/A
Time: Apply to stubble after harvest in the fall or in the spring.
Weeds, Remarks, Crop Rotation: Same as above.
State Restrictions: For use in Colorado, Kansas, Montana, Nebraska, North Dakota, South Dakota, Texas, Wyoming.

- - - - - - - - - - - - - - -

Signal Word/Toxicity Class: Caution/III.
REI: 12 hr.

SETHOXYDIM

Vantage (1EC) *(BASF)*
Rate: 0.28-0.47 lb. ai/A
2.25-3.75 pt. 1EC/A
Time: Apply when weeds are actively growing.
Weeds: Grasses:

barnyardgrass	johnsongrass	tall fescue (seedling)
bermudagrass	junglerice	Texas panicum
broadleaf signalgrass	large crabgrass	torpedograss
browntop panicum	lovegrass	volunteer grains
fall panicum	orchardgrass	wild proso millet
giant foxtail	(seedling)	wildcane
goosegrass	quackgrass	wirestem muhly
green foxtail	red sprangletop	witchgrass
guineagrass	shattercane	woolly cupgrass
	smooth crabgrass	yellow foxtail

Remarks: Refer to label for restrictions and limitations.

- - - - - - - - - - - - - - -

Signal Word/Toxicity Class: Caution/III.
REI: 12 hr.

SHOTGUN (Premix)

Restricted Use Pesticide due to ground and surface water concerns.

Shotgun (FL) (2.25 lb./gal. atrazine & 1 lb./gal. 2,4-D) *(Platte)*
Rate: 1.75-10.5 pt. FL/A
Time: Postharvest wheat stubble. Wheat/fallow/wheat or wheat/corn or sorghum/fallow.
Weeds: Broadleaf weeds:

black nightshade	giant ragweed	sowthistle
buffalobur	ivyleaf	spanishneedles
cocklebur	morningglory	sunflower
common	jimsonweed	tall morningglory
lambsquarters	mustard	velvetleaf
common ragweed	Pennsylvania	Venice mallow
common waterhemp	smartweed	vetch
dandelion	pennycress	wild buckwheat
dock	(fanweed)	wild lettuce
eastern black	redroot pigweed	wild mustard
nightshade		

Grasses (suppression):

downy brome	large crabgrass	witchgrass
green foxtail	wild oat	yellow foxtail
hairy crabgrass		

Remarks: Certain states may have maximum rates and other limitations more restrictive than product label. Do not graze or feed treated forage.

NOTICE The information on these pages is for preliminary planning — not a guide for use. Be sure to follow the manufacturer's directions, notwithstanding information contained here. | For personal protective equipment and EPA registration numbers, please turn to page 70.

9

Other Uses

Fallow Land

State Restrictions: Wheat/fallow/wheat in Colorado, Kansas, Montana, Nebraska, Oklahoma, South Dakota, Texas, and Wyoming. Wheat/corn or sorghum/fallow (Eco-Fallow) in Colorado, Kansas, Nebraska, Oklahoma, and Texas.

Signal Word/Toxicity Class: Danger/I.
REI: 12 hr.

Solution — see 2,4-D

Solve — see 2,4-D

Sterling — see dicamba

Sterling Plus — see dicamba & atrazine

Stinger — see clopyralid

SUREFIRE (Premix)

Restricted Use Pesticide.

◆ **Surefire (29.4% paraquat & 10.6% diuron)** *(Platte)*
Rate: 0.6-1.6 lb. ai./A
1.5-2 pt./A
Time: Apply to weeds 1-6" tall.
Weeds: Annual broadleaf weeds and grasses.
Remarks: Wheat/barley and milo/corn fallow rotation systems. Always use nonionic surfactant. Do not apply through any type of irrigation system. Refer to label for directions and precautions.
Tank Mixes: AAtrex, Banvel, Bladex, 2,4-D, Glean, Kerb.

Signal Word/Toxicity Class: Danger/I.
REI: 12 hr.

THIFENSULFURON-METHYL

Harmony GT (DF) *(DuPont)*
Rate: 0.3-0.6 oz. DF/A
Time: Apply in spring or fall when majority of weeds have emerged and are actively growing.
Weeds: Broadleaf weeds:

annual knawel	false chamomile	redroot pigweed
annual sowthistle	field pennycress	Russian thistle
black mustard	flixweed	scentless chamomile
bushy wallflower	green smartweed	shepherdspurse
Carolina geranium*	henbit*	smallflower buttercup
coast fiddleneck	jim hill mustard	stinking mayweed
common buckwheat	kochia	swinecress
common chickweed	ladysthumb	tansymustard*
common cocklebur*	little mallow*	tarweed fiddleneck
common groundsel	London rocket	tumble mustard
common	marshelder	volunteer lentils
lambsquarters	minerslettuce	volunteer peas
common mallow*	mouseear chickweed	volunteer sunflower
common sunflower*	mouseearcress	wild buckwheat
corn chamomile	Pennsylvania	wild chamomile
corn spurry	smartweed	wild garlic
curly dock	prickly lettuce*	wild mustard
cutleaf	prostrate knotweed	wild radish*
eveningprimrose*	redmaids	
dogfennel	rockpurslane	

  * Suppression

Remarks: Add approved nonionic surfactant. Do not apply through any type of irrigation system. Do not graze or feed forage or hay from treated areas to livestock (harvested straw may be used for bedding and/or feed). Refer to label for restrictions and precautions.
Crop Rotation: Any crop may be planted 45 days after application.
Tank Mixes: 2,4-D, dicamba, glyphosate.
State Restrictions: Not for use in Alamosa, Conejos, Costilla, Rio Grande, and Saguache counties in Colorado.

Signal Word/Toxicity Class: Caution.
REI: 4 hr.

TORDON

Restricted Use Pesticide.

Tordon 22K (picloram) *(Dow AgroSciences)*
Rate: Annual weeds:
0.06-0.125 lb. ae/A
0.25-0.5 pt. 22K/A
Canada thistle:
0.25 lb. ae/A
1 pt. 22K/A
Field bindweed:
0.125-0.25 lb. ae/A
0.5-1 pt. 22K/A
Time: Apply as postharvest or fallow treatment in continuous grain or during fallow period when weeds are actively growing or when majority of thistle plants are emerged but prior to bud stage. Preplant interval prior to planting small grains recommended; minimum interval (with soil temperatures above 40°F) is 45 days for up to 0.5 pt./A, 60 days for 0.5-1 pt./A (except 90 days for Idaho, Montana, Nebraska, North Dakota, Oregon, South Dakota, Washington, Wyoming).
Weeds: Broadleaf weeds such as:

Canada thistle	Russian thistle	wild buckwheat
field bindweed		

Remarks: Do not use on land planted to sweet sorghum. To reduce possible damage to subsequent small grain crops, use lower rate or discontinue at least 2 years prior to seeding. Do not allow spray to contact desirable broadleaf plants. Do not graze treated areas until poisonous plants are dry and no longer palatable to livestock. Do not apply through any type of irrigation system. Refer to label for restrictions and precautions.
Crop Rotation: Use only on land to be planted the following year to grass, barley, oats, wheat, grain sorghum, or fallow. Do not plant grain sorghum within 8 months after application. Do not rotate to broadleaf crops. Do not plant sensitive broadleaf crops for 36 months after treatment or until soil residues have declined to safe level following sensitive bioassay.
Tank Mixes: 2,4-D.
State Restrictions: For use west of the Mississippi except San Luis Valley of Colorado. Use in Hawaii limited to supplemental labeling.

Signal Word/Toxicity Class: Caution.
REI: 12 hr.

TOUCHDOWN

◆ **Touchdown (5L or 6L) (sulfosate)** *(ZENECA)*
Rate: 0.5-4 lb. ai/A
0.8-6.4 pt. 5L/A
0.66-5.33 pt. 6L/A
Time: Apply to actively growing grasses and weeds. Repeat as necessary.
Weeds: Broadleaf weeds:

annual sowthistle	field bindweed	mustard
black nightshade	field pennycress	Pennsylvania
Canada thistle	field sandbur	smartweed
common chickweed	Florida pusley	prickly lettuce
common cocklebur	giant ragweed	red clover
common groundsel	hemp dogbane	redroot pigweed
common	henbit	redvine
lambsquarters	Jerusalem artichoke	Russian thistle
common ragweed	(partial control)	shepherdspurse
common sunflower	kochia	sicklepod
curly dock	leafy spurge	smooth pigweed
cutleaf	London rocket	trumpetcreeper
eveningprimrose	morningglory	velvetleaf
dandelion	mouseear chickweed	wild buckwheat
dogfennel		

Grasses and sedges:

annual bluegrass	foxtail	shattercane
barnyardgrass	goosegrass	sprangletop
bermudagrass	johnsongrass	stinkgrass
cheat	(seedling)	Texas panicum
crabgrass	jointed goatgrass	wild oat
downy brome	quackgrass	witchgrass
fall panicum	red rice	woolly cupgrass

Remarks: Nonionic surfactant or wetting agent required. In addition, ammonium sulfate can be added. Do not apply through any type of irrigation system. Refer to label for directions, restrictions, and precautions.
Crop Rotation: Plantback time—35 days.
Tank Mixes: Devrinol, diuron, Goal, Krovar, Prowl, simazine, Solicam, Surflan.
State Restrictions: Ammonium sulfate (6L) not for use in California.

Signal Word/Toxicity Class: Caution.
REI: 12 hr. (5L); 4 hr. (6L).

◆-new product • PP-preplant • PPI-preplant incorporated • PRE-preemergence • POST-postemergence • SEQ-sequential • ae-acid equivalent • ai-active ingredient • DF-dry flowable
E/EC-emulsifiable concentrate • F/FL-flowable • DG/G/WG-dispersable granule • L/LC-liquid • SP/WSP-soluble packet • W/WP-wettable powder • WSB-water soluble bag

Treflan — see trifluralin

TRIFLURALIN

Albaugh Trifluralin 4EC *(Albaugh)*
◆ **Clean Crop Trifluralin HF (4EC)** *(Platte)*
Gowan Trifluralin 4 (EC) or 10G *(Gowan)*
Helena Trifluralin 4 EC *(Helena)*
Riverside Trifluralin 4EC *(Terra)*
◆ **Sedagri Trifluralin 480 (4EC)** *(Rhone-Poulenc)*
Treflan HFP (4EC), TR-10 (10G) *(Dow AgroSciences)*
Trilin 4EC or 10G *(Griffin)*
Wilbur-Ellis Trifluralin 10G *(Wilbur-Ellis)*

Rate: 0.5-1 lb. ai/A
   5-10 lb. 10G/A
Time: Summer fallow (Apr. 15-Aug. 31) followed by spring-seeded wheat, durum, or barley.
Weeds: Broadleaf weeds:

carpetweed	Florida pusley	pigweed
common chickweed	goosefoot	puncturevine
common	henbit	(western U.S.)
lambsquarters	knotweed	purslane
common purslane	lambsquarters	stinging nettle

Grasses:

annual bluegrass	crabgrass	pigeongrass
annual ryegrass	downy brome	sandbur
barnyardgrass	foxtail	shattercane
broadleaf signalgrass	johnsongrass	sprangletop
bromegrass	(seedling)	stinkgrass
cheatgrass	junglerice	woolly cupgrass

Remarks: Pigeongrass is controlled in wheat, durum, and barley seeded the following spring. Refer to label for incorporation procedures.
State Restrictions: Wilbur-Ellis not registered zin California. Treflan TR-10 not for use in Pecos or Reeves County, Texas; in Montana, uses limited to supplemental labeling.

- - - - - - - - - - - - - - -

Rate: 0.75-1 lb. ai/A
   1.5-2 pt. 4EC/A
   7.5-10 lb. 10G/A
Time: Apply any time from May-Sept. prior to fall planting of winter wheat.
Weeds: Annual grasses and broadleaf weeds including
   cheatgrass
Remarks: Winter wheat. Shallowly incorporate into fallow soil up to 4 months ahead of planting.
State Restrictions: For use in Colorado, Idaho, Kansas, Montana, Nebraska, Oregon, Washington, Wyoming; state varies by company, refer to label.

- - - - - - - - - - - - - - -

Signal Word/Toxicity Class: Varies by formulation.
REI: 12 hr. unless soil injected or soil incorporated.

Vantage — see sethoxydim

Weed Rhap — see 2,4-D

Weedestroy — see 2,4-D

Weedmaster — see 2,4-D Combinations

Weedone — see 2,4-D

Forage
(Alfalfa, Clover, Est. Legumes)

BALAN

Balan DF (benefin) *(Platte)*
Rate: 1.12-1.5 lb. ai/A
   2-2.5 lb. DF/A

Time: Preplant incorporated. Apply and incorporate before seeding.
Weeds: Broadleaf weeds:

carelessweed	lambsquarters	redmaids
carpetweed	Mexican clover	rockpurslane
chickweed	prostrate pigweed	redroot pigweed
Florida purslane	purslane	rough pigweed
knotweed	pusley	spiny pigweed

Annual grasses:

annual bluegrass	fall panicum	pigeongrass
annual ryegrass	giant foxtail	robust foxtail
barnyardgrass	green foxtail	sandbur
bottlegrass	Italian ryegrass	smooth crabgrass
bristlegrass	johnsongrass	spreading panicgrass
broadleaf signalgrass	(seedling)	Texas panicum
buffalograss	junglerice	watergrass
burgrass	large crabgrass	yellow foxtail
coloradograss		

Remarks: Alfalfa, birdsfoot trefoil, clover. Rate varies by soil type. Do not apply through any type of irrigation system. Refer to label for further use directions.
Crop Rotation: Do not plant barley, oats, rye, wheat or other grasses, corn, milo (grain sorghum), onions, red beets, spinach, sugar beets or other root crops for 10 months following application.

- - - - - - - - - - - - - - -

Signal Word/Toxicity Class: Caution/III.
REI: 12 hr.

Broclean — see bromoxynil

Bromox — see bromoxynil

BROMOXYNIL

◆ **Broclean 2EC** *(Platte)*
◆ **Bromox 2EC** *(Micro Flo)*
Buctril (2EC), Buctril 4EC *(Rhone-Poulenc)*
Moxy 2EC *(Terra)*

Rate: 0.25-0.375 lb. ai/A
   1-1.5 pt. 2EC/A
   0.5-0.75 pt. 4EC/A
   Chemigation:
   0.5 lb. ai/A
   2 pt. 2EC/A
   1 pt. 4EC/A
Time: Apply in the fall or spring to seedling alfalfa when majority of field has minimum of 4 trifoliate leaves except Arizona, California, Colorado, Idaho, Montana, Nevada, New Mexico, Utah, Washington, Wyoming and western Kansas, Nebraska, North Dakota, South Dakota, when majority of field has minimum of 2 trifoliates.
Weeds: Most susceptible broadleaf weeds:

annual pepperweed	common tarweed	Pennsylvania
annual sowthistle	eastern black	smartweed
black nightshade	nightshade	shepherdspurse
blue mustard	field pennycress	silverleaf nightshade
bristly starbur	green smartweed	sunflower
coast fiddleneck	hairy nightshade	tartary buckwheat
common cocklebur	jimsonweed	wild buckwheat
common lambsquarters	ladysthumb	

Susceptible broadleaf weeds:

buffalobur	ivyleaf morningglory	spiny pigweed
burcucumber	knawel	tall morningglory
common groundsel	kochia	tall waterhemp
common ragweed	London rocket	tumble mustard
corn chamomile	mayweed	velvetleaf
corn gromwell	prostrate knotweed	Venice mallow
cowcockle	puncturevine	wild mustard
giant ragweed	redroot pigweed	wild radish
hemp sesbania	Russian thistle	yellow starthistle

Remarks: Seedling alfalfa. Do not cut for feed or graze spring-treated alfalfa within 30 days following treatment; winter-treated alfalfa within 60 days. Refer to label for restrictions and precautions.
Tank Mixes: 2,4-DB, Pursuit + nonionic surfactant.

- - - - - - - - - - - - - - -

Signal Word/Toxicity Class: Warning/II.
REI: 12 hr.

Buctril — see bromoxynil

Butoxone — see 2,4-DB

9

Other Uses

NOTICE	The information on these pages is for preliminary planning — not a guide for use. Be sure to follow the manufacturer's directions, notwithstanding information contained here.	For personal protective equipment and EPA registration numbers, please turn to page 70.

Forage

Butyrac — see 2,4-DB

Credit — see glyphosate

2,4-DB

Butoxone 175, 200, or 7500 *(Cedar)*
Rate: 1 lb. ai/A
   4.33 pt. 175/A
   4 pt. 200/A
   1.33 lb. 7500/A

Weeds: Broadleaf weeds:

annual morningglory	jimsonweed	velvetleaf
cocklebur	kochia	wild turnip
common lambsquarters	pigweed	

Rate: 1.5 lb. ai/A
   6.5 pt. 175/A
   6 pt. 200/A
   2 lb. 7500/A

Weeds: Broadleaf weeds:

black mustard	field pennycress	shepherdspurse
buckhorn plantain	hedge smartweed	sweetclover
common ragweed	ladysthumb	wild beet
curly dock	prickly lettuce	wild mustard

Time: Apply to crop at 1-2 trifoliate leaf stage; weeds at 2-5 leaf stage. For established alfalfa, make late fall or early winter application.

Remarks: Alfalfa. Do not spray if daytime temperature is expected to exceed 90°F within next 2-3 days or is expected to fall below 40°F. Do not graze or feed straw or hay from established alfalfa to livestock within 30 days after application; seedling alfalfa within 60 days after application.

– – – – – – – – – – – – – –

Signal Word/Toxicity Class:
Danger/I (Butoxone 200); Caution/III (Butoxone 175, 7500).
REI: 48 hr.

Butyrac 200 *(Albaugh)*
Riverside 2,4-DB 200 *(Terra)*
Rate: 0.5-1.5 lb. ai/A
   2-6 pt. 200/A

Time: Apply in spring or fall when seedling legumes have 2-4 trifoliate leaves and weeds are less than 3" high. Certain fall-emerged weeds in established alfalfa are controlled best by late fall or early winter treatment (follow state recommendations for timing and rate).

Weeds: Broadleaf weeds:

annual morningglory	common ragweed	Russian thistle
cocklebur	curly dock	smartweed
common lambsquarters	field pennycress	wild mustard
	redroot pigweed	yellow rocket

Remarks: Alfalfa, birdsfoot trefoil, clovers (alsike, ladino, red). Do not use on sweet clover, peas, or other legumes. Use high rate for seedling weeds 1-3" high. Rainfall within 7-10 days after treatment can cause injury to legumes. Do not graze established crops within 30 days or seedling legumes within 60 days after application.

Tank Mixes: Buctril for seedling alfalfa. Poast for seedling and established alfalfa.

– – – – – – – – – – – – – –

Signal Word/Toxicity Class: Danger/I.
REI: 48 hr.

DIQUAT DIBROMIDE

◆ **Diquat**
Rate: 0.375-0.5 lb. ai/A
   1.5-2 pt./A

Time: Preharvest desiccation broadcast.
Weeds: Broadleaf weeds and grasses.
Remarks: Alfalfa, clover. Seed crop only. On thin stands of seed alfalfa use 1 pt./A. Apply by ground or air. Use high rate when weeds are large or dense. Do not use seed from treated plants for food, feed, or oil purposes. Do not apply through any type of irrigation system. Do not graze or feed treated forage to livestock. Refer to label for use restrictions and precautions.
Days To Harvest: 3.

– – – – – – – – – – – –

Signal Word/Toxicity Class: Warning/II.
REI: 24 hr.

Direx — see diuron

DIURON

Direx 4L or 80DF *(Griffin)*
◆ **Diuron 80 WDG** *(Platte)*
Drexel Diuron 4L or 80 *(Drexel)*
Karmex DF *(Griffin)*
Riverside Diuron 4L or 80DF *(Terra)*
Rate: 1.2-2.4 lb. ai/A
   1.2-2.4 qt. 4L/A
   1.5-3 lb. 80, DF, 80DF/A

Time: Idaho, Oregon, Washington: After dormancy to mid-Dec.; Arizona, Nevada: After dormancy but no later than Jan.; fall or winter after alfalfa becomes dormant or semi-dormant, but before spring growth.

Rate: 1.2-1.6 lb. ai/A
   1.2-1.6 qt. 4L/A
   1.5-2 lb. 80, DF, 80DF/A

Time: East of Appalachian Mountains: Mar.-Apr. but before spring growth.

Weeds: Seedling annual broadleaf weeds including:

amsinckia (fiddleneck)	corn spurry	shepherdspurse
annual groundcherry	dogfennel	tansymustard
annual morningglory	gromwell	wild lettuce
chickweed	knawel	wild mustard

Grasses:

annual bluegrass	foxtail	red sprangletop
annual ryegrass	peppergrass	velvetgrass
annual sweet vernalgrass	rattail fescue	

Rate: 0.8 lb. ai/A
   0.8 qt. 4L/A
   1 lb. 80, DF, 80DF/A

Time: Eastern Colorado, Kansas: Apply in fall or winter after emergence of mustard.

Weeds: Broadleaf weeds:
tansymustard

Remarks: Established alfalfa. Do not apply to seedling alfalfa or alfalfa-grass mixtures. Use 2 lb. ai if weeds are 2-4" in height.

Crop Rotation: Do not replant treated areas to any crop within 1 yr. after application.

– – – – – – – – – – – – –

Rate: 1.6 lb. ai/A
   1.6 qt. 4L/A
   2 lb. 80, DF, 80DF/A

Time: Western Oregon: Apply when dormant (Oct. 15-Dec. 15).
Weeds: Annual broadleaf weeds and grasses including:

annual bluegrass	chickweed	rattail fescue
annual ryegrass	hawksbeard	velvetgrass

Remarks: Birdsfoot trefoil, clover (red). Stands established at least 1 year. Do not apply to seedling as injury may result.
Crop Rotation: Same restrictions as above.

– – – – – – – – – – – – –

Signal Word/Toxicity Class: Caution/III.
REI: 12 hr.

Eptam — see EPTC

EPTC

Eptam 7-E or 20-G *(ZENECA)*
Rate: Northern Region:
   3-4 lb. ai/A
   3.5-4.5 pt. 7-E/A
   4 lb. ai/A
   20 lb. 20-G/A
   Southeastern, Southwestern Region:
   3 lb. ai/A
   3.5 pt. 7-E/A
   Pacific Northwest, Western Region:
   2-4 lb. ai/A
   2.25-4.5 pt. 7-E/A
   4 lb. ai/A
   20 lb. 20-G/A
Time: Apply preplant.

◆-new product • PP-preplant • PPI-preplant incorporated • PRE-preemergence • POST-postemergence • SEQ-sequential • ae-acid equivalent • ai-active ingredient • DF-dry flowable
E/EC-emulsifiable concentrate • F/FL-flowable • DG/G/WG-dispersable granule • L/LC-liquid • SP/WSP-soluble packet • W/WP-wettable powder • WSB-water soluble bag

456   **Weed Control Manual 2000**

Weeds: Broadleaf weeds:

black nightshade	corn spurry	henbit
carpetweed*	cutleaf nightshade*	nettleleaf goosefoot
common chickweed	deadnettle	pigweed
common	fiddleneck*	prickly sida*
lambsquarters	Florida pusley	sicklepod*
common purslane	hairy nightshade	tall morningglory*

Annual grasses and sedges:

annual bluegrass	goosegrass	shattercane
annual ryegrass	green foxtail	signalgrass*
barnyardgrass	johnsongrass	Texas panicum*
bermudagrass	(seedling)	volunteer grains
(seedling)	junglerice	(barley, oats, wheat)
crabgrass	lovegrass*	wild oat
fall panicum*	purple nutsedge	witchgrass*
field sandbur	quackgrass	yellow foxtail
giant foxtail	rescuegrass*	yellow nutsedge

*7-E only

Remarks: Alfalfa, birdsfoot trefoil, clovers, lespedeza. Refer to label for application and incorporation recommendations.

– – – – – – – – – – – – – – –

Signal Word/Toxicity Class: Caution.
REI: 12 hr. unless soil injected or soil incorporated.

GLYPHOSATE

◆ **Credit (4WS)** *(Nufarm)*
◆ **Glyfos or Glyfos X-tra (4WS)** *(Cheminova)*
Rattler (4WS) *(Helena)*
Roundup Custom (5.4WS) *(Monsanto)*
Roundup Original, Original RT, Ultra, Ultra RT (4WS) *(Monsanto)*
Rate: Annual weeds:
  0.38-1.5 lb. ai/A
  0.56-2.25 pt. 5.4WS/A
  0.75-3 pt. 4WS/A
  Perennial weeds:
  0.5-5 lb. ai/A
  0.75-7.5 pt. 5.4WS/A
  1-10 pt. 4WS/A
Time: Preplant, preemergence, at planting, spot treatment, preharvest (alfalfa). Apply before, during, or after planting, but prior to crop emergence. Preharvest application for declining alfalfa stands or any stand of alfalfa where crop destruction is acceptable.
Weeds: Broadleaf weeds:

Canada thistle	hemp dogbane	Pennsylvania
curly dock	milkweed	smartweed
field bindweed		

Grasses:

bermudagrass	fescues	paragrass
fall panicum	johnsongrass	quackgrass

Remarks: Alfalfa, clover. Remove livestock before application. For preharvest, make only 1 application per year to existing stand; do not use for alfalfa grown for seed. For spot treatment, apply in areas where movement of livestock can be controlled; do not treat more than 1/10 acre at one time. Refer to label for directions, restrictions, and precautions.
Days To Harvest: Harvest/grazing—8 weeks; spot treatment—14 days; preharvest for alfalfa—36 hr.
State Restrictions: Roundup Ultra tank mixes not registered in California. Roundup Ultra RT: For use in Colorado, Idaho, Montana, North Dakota, South Dakota, Utah, and Wyoming. For use in specific counties only in Kansas, Minnesota, Nebraska, Nevada, Oklahoma, Oregon, and Washington; refer to label. Glyfos not registered for use in California. Glyfos X-tra not registered for use in mistblowers in California or Arizona.

– – – – – – – – – – – – – – –

Signal Word/Toxicity Class: Varies by formulation.
REI: Warning—12 hr.; Caution—4 hr.

Gramoxone Extra — see paraquat

Karmex — see diuron

KERB

Restricted Use Pesticide.

■ **PRE, POST**
Kerb 50-W (pronamide) *(Rohm and Haas)*
Rate: 0.5-2 lb. ai/A
  1-4 lb. 50-W/A
Time: Preemergence, postemergence. Apply during fall or winter months before soil freeze-up.

Weeds: Broadleaf weeds:

chickweed	red sorrel (seedling)	wild mustard
London rocket	shepherdspurse	wild radish

Grasses:

annual bluegrass	Italian ryegrass	quackgrass
cheatgrass	Kentucky bluegrass	volunteer grains
downy brome	orchardgrass	wild oat
foxtail barley	perennial ryegrass	

Remarks: Established legumes grown for forage and seed: alfalfa, clover, birdsfoot trefoil, crownvetch, sainfoin. Rate varies by available moisture and weed problem; refer to label for further use directions.
Days To Harvest: Alfalfa (east of the Mississippi), birdsfoot trefoil, clover, crownvetch, sainfoin: up to 4 lb.—120; alfalfa (west of the Mississippi): under 3 lb.—25, 3-4 lb.—45.
Crop Rotation: Refer to label for plantback times for rotational crops.

– – – – – – – – – – – – – – –

Rate: Furrow irrigation:
  1.5-2 lb. ai/A
  3-4 lb. 50-W/A
  Overhead sprinkler or flood irrigation:
  1.5 lb. ai/A
  3 lb. 50-W/A
Time: Apply in spring before dodder germinates.
Weeds:
  dodder

Remarks: Established legumes grown for seed: alfalfa seed crops. Furrow irrigation: Incorporate lightly and irrigate within 7 days before dodder germinates. Overhead sprinkler or flood irrigation: Irrigate with $1/2$-1" water within 1-3 days after application before dodder germinates. If irrigation of treated field must be delayed, light mechanical incorporation should follow application and field irrigated within 2 weeks.
Crop Rotation: Refer to label for specific times for rotation crops.
State Restrictions: For use in California, Idaho, Nevada, Oregon, Utah, Washington.

– – – – – – – – – – – – – – –

Signal Word/Toxicity Class: Caution.
REI: 24 hr.

MCPA

◆ **Clean Crop MCP Amine 4** *(Platte)*
Riverdale MCPA-4 Amine *(Riverdale)*
Wilbur-Ellis MCPA Amine *(Wilbur-Ellis)*
Rate: 0.5 lb. ae/A
  1 pt./A
Time: Apply in late fall following frosts when legumes are dormant or in the spring before new growth starts. Temperature should be above 40°F.
Weeds: Broadleaf weeds:

fanweed	pennycress	yellow rocket

Remarks: Established alfalfa, red clover.
State Restrictions: Wilbur-Ellis not registered in California.

– – – – – – – – – – – – – – –

Signal Word/Toxicity Class: Danger/I.
REI: 48 hr.

Moxy — see bromoxynil

NORFLURAZON

Zorial (5G) or Zorial Rapid 80 (DF) *(Novartis)*
Rate: 1-2 lb. ai/A
  20-40 lb. 5G/A
  1.25-2.5 lb. DF/A
Time: Preemergence.
Weeds: 5G: Broadleaf weeds and grasses:

annual bluegrass	downy brome	sandbur*
cheat	henbit*	shepherdspurse
chickweed	Italian ryegrass	

DF: Broadleaf weeds, grasses, and sedges:

barnyardgrass	johnsongrass	purslane
bermudagrass*	(rhizome*, seedling)	Russian thistle*
carpetweed	kochia*	sicklepod*
cocklebur*	lanceleaf sage*	signalgrass
common ragweed*	morningglory*	spotted spurge*
crabgrass	panicum	spurred anoda
Florida pusley	Pennsylvania	teaweed
foxtail	smartweed	tropic croton
goosegrass	pigweed	velvetleaf
hemp sesbania*	prickly sida*	Venice mallow*
	purple nutsedge*	yellow nutsedge*

* Suppression

9

Other Uses

Remarks: Apply to established alfalfa which has been actively growing for at least 5 months. Do not apply through any type of irrigation system.

Days To Harvest: 28.

Tank Mixes: (DF): 2,4-DB, diuron, EPTC, Gramoxone, metribuzin, Poast, pronamide, Pursuit, Sinbar, trifluralin, Velpar.

State Restrictions: For use in Alabama, Arizona, Arkansas, California, Florida, Georgia, Idaho, Louisiana, Mississippi, Nevada, New Mexico, North Carolina, Oklahoma, Oregon, South Carolina, Tennessee, Texas, Washington, and portions of Colorado, Kansas, and Missouri south of I-70.

- - - - - - - - - - - - - -

Signal Word/Toxicity Class: Caution.
REI: 12 hr.

PARAQUAT

Restricted Use Pesticide.

Gramoxone Extra (2.5L) *(ZENECA)*
Rate: 0.6-1 lb. ai/A
2-3 pt. 2.5L/A
Time: Preplant, preemergence. Apply prior to emergence of crop.
Weeds: Annual broadleaf weeds and grasses; top kill and suppression of perennials.
Remarks: Alfalfa. No-till or conventional planting. Add nonionic surfactant or crop oil concentrate. Crops emerged at time of application will be killed. Seedbeds should be done with minimum amount of soil disturbance. To prevent injury to germinating crop seedlings, do not apply preplant or preemergence to soils lacking clay minerals. Do not graze treated area. Refer to label for directions, restrictions, and precautions.

- - - - - - - - - - - - - -

Rate: 0.13-0.5 lb. ai/A
6.5-24 fl. oz. 2.5L/A
Time: Apply during late winter or early spring.
Weeds: Broadleaf weeds and grasses:

annual bluegrass	redmaids rockpurslane	spikeweed
chickweed	(6" tall or less)	(4" tall or less)
fiddleneck	shepherdspurse	volunteer small grain
(6" tall or less)	(suppression only)	(8" tall or less)

Remarks: Alfalfa (new seedlings). Not for seedling alfalfa grown for seed. Add nonionic surfactant or crop oil concentrate. Foliage present at time of application will be burned. Seedling alfalfa stands will be reduced and replanting may be necessary. Do not pasture animals in treated fields prior to first cutting. Refer to label for directions, restrictions, and precautions.
Days To Harvest: Harvest, grazing, or cutting—70.
State Restrictions: For use in California only.

- - - - - - - - - - - - - -

Rate: 0.25 lb. ai/A
0.8 pt. 2.5L/A
Time: Between cuttings. Apply immediately after alfalfa has been removed for hay or silage. Make 1-3 applications, as needed, during growing season. Do not treat more than 5 days after cutting. May be applied in addition to a dormant application.
Weeds: Small annual grasses and broadleaf weeds.
Remarks: Established alfalfa. Weeds beyond seedling stage and stubble of weeds cut off during harvest will be less affected by treatment. First-year alfalfa stands and yields may be reduced if alfalfa is allowed to regrow more than 2". Foliage present at time of application will be burned. For first-year alfalfa, do not apply more than twice during first growing season. Refer to label for directions and precautions.
Days To Harvest: 30.
State Restrictions: For use east of the Rockies.

- - - - - - - - - - - - - -

Signal Word/Toxicity Class: Danger-Poison/I.
REI: 12 hr. (except harvest aid/desiccation 24 hr.).

PURSUIT

Pursuit (2AS), Eco-Pak or W Eco-Pak (DG) (imazethapyr)
(American Cyanamid)
Rate: 3-6 oz. 2AS/A
1.08-2.16 oz. DG/A
Time: Early preplant, preplant incorporated, preemergence, postemergence (apply only postemergence when alfalfa has at least 2 trifoliate leaves). May be applied up to 45 days prior to planting.
Weeds: Broadleaf weeds:

barnyard sage	common purslane	galinsoga
bedstraw	common ragweed	giant ragweed
black nightshade	common sunflower	hairy nightshade
burning nettle	eastern black	henbit
Canada thistle	nightshade	ivyleaf morningglory
carpetweed	entireleaf	Jerusalem artichoke
catchweed	morningglory	jimsonweed
cocklebur	field pennycress	knotweed
common cocklebur	filaree	kochia
common mallow	Florida pusley	ladysthumb

Weeds: Broadleaf weeds, continued:

London rocket	puncturevine	spiny pigweed
mustard	redmaids	spotted spurge
Palmer pigweed	rockpurslane	tall morningglory
Pennsylvania	redroot pigweed	tansymustard
smartweed	shepherdspurse	velvetleaf
pitted morningglory	smallflower	wild beet
prickly sida	morningglory	wild buckwheat
prostrate spurge	smooth pigweed	wild poinsettia

Grasses and sedges:

barnyardgrass	green foxtail	shattercane
broadleaf	johnsongrass	smooth crabgrass
signalgrass	large crabgrass	Texas panicum
fall panicum	red rice	woolly cupgrass
giant foxtail	robust purple	(emerged)
giant green foxtail	foxtail	yellow foxtail
goosegrass	robust white foxtail	yellow nutsedge

Remarks: Alfalfa. Do not use on crops other than alfalfa, IMI-Corn, soybeans, edible beans, or peas.
Days To Harvest: 30.
Crop Rotation: IMI-Corn, lima beans, peanuts, southern peas, soybeans—anytime; alfalfa, edible beans and peas (except lima beans, southern peas), rye, wheat—4 months; field corn, field corn grown for seed—$8^{1}/_{2}$ months (Pursuit W $9^{1}/_{2}$ months); barley, tobacco—$9^{1}/_{2}$ months; cotton, lettuce, oats, popcorn, safflower, sorghum, sunflower, sweet corn—18 months; flax (Pursuit only), potatoes—26 months; all other crops—40 months after application.
Tank Mixes: Buctril, 2,4-DB, or Poast Plus.
State Restrictions: Pursuit for use in Colorado, New Mexico, North Dakota, Oklahoma, South Dakota, Texas, Wyoming (certain counties), and states east of these states; not for use in New York. Pursuit W for use in Arizona, Idaho, Montana, Nevada, Oregon, Utah, Washington, Wyoming (certain counties); not for use in California.

- - - - - - - - - - - - - -

Signal Word/Toxicity Class: Warning/II (DG); Caution (2AS).
REI: Warning—12 hr.; Caution—4 hr.

Rattler — see glyphosate

Roundup — see glyphosate

SCYTHE

◆ **Scythe (pelargonic acid)** *(Mycogen)*
Rate: 4-13 fl. oz./1 gal. spray solution
Time: Apply to young succulent weeds.
Weeds: Annual broadleaf weeds and grasses; top-kill of perennial weeds.
Remarks: Apply in minimum 75 gal. spray solution/A or spray-to-wet. Do not apply by air or through any type of irrigation system. Refer to label for directions and precautions.
Tank Mixes: Glyphosate and other foliar and residual herbicides.

- - - - - - - - - - - - - -

Signal Word/Toxicity Class: Warning/II.
REI: 24 hr.

SENCOR

Sencor 4 (FL) or DF (metribuzin) *(Bayer)*
Rate: 0.25-1 lb. ai/A
0.5-2 pt. FL/A
0.33-1.3 lb. DF/A
Time: Apply when weeds are less than 2" tall or before weed foliage is 2" in diameter. Do not apply after spring growth begins or before growth ceases in the fall.
Weeds: Broadleaf weeds:

blue mustard	henbit	pigweed
common chickweed	jim hill mustard	prickly lettuce
curly dock	knapweed	ragweed
(suppression)	kochia	shepherdspurse
dandelion	lambsquarters	tansymustard
field pennycress	marestail	white cockle
fleabane	meadow salsify	wild buckwheat
flixweed	pepperweed	yellow rocket

Grasses:

barnyardgrass	foxtail barley	rescuegrass
bluegrass	green foxtail	smooth brome
cheat	Japanese brome	wild oat
downy brome	little barley	

Remarks: Established alfalfa, sainfoin. On loamy sand soils in Oregon and Washington, do not apply more than 0.5 lb. ai/A.
Days To Harvest: Harvest or grazing—28.

◆-new product • PP-preplant • PPI-preplant incorporated • PRE-preemergence • POST-postemergence • SEQ-sequential • ae-acid equivalent • ai-active ingredient • DF-dry flowable
E/EC-emulsifiable concentrate • F/FL-flowable • DG/G/WG-dispersable granule • L/LC-liquid • SP/WSP-soluble packet • W/WP-wettable powder • WSB-water soluble bag

Crop Rotation: Alfalfa, asparagus, barley/wheat (following peas, lentils, or soybeans), corn, forage grass, potatoes, sainfoin, soybeans, sugarcane, tomatoes—4 months; barley, cotton, lentils, peas, rice, wheat—8 months; other crops not listed (except root crops)—12 months; onions, sugar beets, and other root crops—18 months. Cover crops for soil building or erosion control may be planted anytime, but do not graze or harvest for food or feed. Stand reductions may occur in some areas.
State Restrictions: Not for use in California.

- - - - - - - - - - - - - - -

Rate: 0.375-1 lb. ai/A
     0.75-2 pt. FL/A
     0.5-1.3 lb. DF/A
Time: Do not apply after spring growth begins or before growth ceases in the fall. Do not apply during first growing season after seeding.
Weeds: Broadleaf weeds:

blue mustard	foxtail barley	shepherdspurse
common chickweed	henbit	tansymustard
curly dock	kochia	white cockle
(suppression)	meadow salsify	wild buckwheat
dandelion	pepperweed	yellow rocket
flixweed		

Grasses:

barnyardgrass	downy brome	wild oat
bluegrass	smooth brome	

Remarks: Dormant established alfalfa, sainfoin.
Days To Harvest, Crop Rotation: Same as above.
State Restrictions: For use in California.

- - - - - - - - - - - - - - -

Rate: 0.5-0.75 lb. ai/A
     1-1.5 pt. FL/A
     0.33-1.3 lb. DF/A
Weeds: Partial reduction of forage grass stands.
Remarks: Mixed stands of alfalfa and grasses. Refer to label for restrictions, precautions, and limitations.
Days To Harvest, Crop Rotation: Same as above.

- - - - - - - - - - - - - - -

Signal Word/Toxicity Class: Caution/III.
REI: 12 hr.

SETHOXYDIM

Poast (1.5EC) or Poast Plus (1EC) (BASF)
Rate: 0.09-0.47 lb. ai/A
     0.5-2.5 pt. 1.5EC/A
     0.75-3.75 pt. 1EC/A
Time: Postemergence.
Weeds: Annual and perennial grasses:

annual ryegrass	large crabgrass	stinkgrass
barnyardgrass	lovegrass	tall fescue
bermudagrass	orchardgrass	Texas panicum
broadleaf signalgrass	(seedling)	volunteer cereals
browntop panicum	perennial ryegrass	wild oat
fall panicum	quackgrass	wild proso millet
field sandbur	red rice	wildcane
giant foxtail	red sprangletop	wiresteam muhly
goosegrass	shattercane	witchgrass
green foxtail	smooth crabgrass	woolly cupgrass
itchgrass	southwestern	yellow foxtail
johnsongrass	cupgrass	
junglerice		

Remarks: Alfalfa, birdsfoot trefoil, clover, sanfoin. May be applied to seedling or established alfalfa or clover grown for hay, silage, green chop, direct grazing, or seed.
Days To Harvest: Grazing, feeding, or harvesting undried forage—7; feeding or harvesting dry hay—14.
Tank Mixes: 2,4-DB; refer to label for use directions.
State Restrictions: Do not use UAN or AMS in California or Pacific Northwest.

- - - - - - - - - - - - - - -

Signal Word/Toxicity Class: Warning/II (Poast); Caution/III (Poast Plus).
REI: 12 hr.

SINBAR

Sinbar (WP) (terbacil) (DuPont)
Rate: 0.4-1.2 lb. ai/A broadcast
     0.5-1.5 lb. WP/A
Time: Apply single application to established alfalfa in the fall after plants become dormant or in spring before new growth starts. For semidormant and nondormant varieties, apply in fall or winter after last cutting.
Weeds: Broadleaf weeds:

chickweed	mustard	snow weed
henbit	prickly lettuce	tansymustard
lambsquarters	shepherdspurse	yellow rocket
marestail		

Grasses:

cheatgrass	foxtail	ryegrass
crabgrass	peppergrass	wild barley
downy brome		

Remarks: Established alfalfa. Do not use on seedling alfalfa, alfalfa grass mixtures, or other mixed stands. Use low rates on coarse-textured soils (sandy loams, loams); high rates on fine-textured soils (clay loams, clays).
Crop Rotation: Do not replant to any crop within 2 years after last application as injury to subsequent crops may result.
State Restrictions: Not for use in California.

- - - - - - - - - - - - - - -

Signal Word/Toxicity Class: Caution.
REI: 12 hr.

Treflan — see trifluralin

TRI-4 — see trifluralin

TRIFLURALIN

Albaugh Trifluralin 4EC (Albaugh)
◆ **Clean Crop Trifluralin HF (4EC)** (Platte)
Gowan Trifluralin 4 or 5 (EC) or 10G (Gowan)
Helena Trifluralin 4 EC (Helena)
Riverside Trifluralin 4EC or Trific 60DF (Terra)
◆ **Sedagri Trifluralin 480 (4EC)** (Rhone-Poulenc)
Treflan HFP (4EC), TR-10 (10G) (Dow AgroSciences)
TRI-4 HF (4EC) (American Cyanamid)
Trilin 4EC, 5EC or 10G (Griffin)
Wilbur-Ellis Trifluralin 10G (Wilbur-Ellis)
Rate: 0.75-1 lb. ai/A
     1.5-2 pt. 4EC/A
     1.2-1.6 pt. 5EC/A
     1.4-1.66 lb. 60DF/A
     2 lb. ai/A
     20 lb. 10G/A
Time: Preemergence.
Weeds: Grasses:

annual bluegrass	chess	junglerice
bromegrass	crabgrass	sandbur
canarygrass	downy brome	wild barley
cheat	foxtail	woolly cupgrass
cheatgrass		

Remarks: Established alfalfa. Must be incorporated. Single rainfall or overhead sprinkle irrigation of 0.5" or more can be used to incorporate (within 48 hr.) instead of mechanical equipment. Use incorporation equipment to ensure thorough soil mixing with minimal damage to established alfalfa. Refer to label for Directions for Use.
Days To Harvest: 21.
State Restrictions: Wilbur-Ellis not registered in California.

- - - - - - - - - - - - - - -

Signal Word/Toxicity Class: Varies by formulation.
REI: 12 hr. unless soil injected or soil incorporated.

Trilin — see trifluralin

VELPAR

Velpar (SP) or Velpar L (hexazinone) (DuPont)
Rate: 0.45-1.35 lb. ai/A
     0.5-1.5 lb. SP/A
     2-6 pt. L/A
     Tansymustard:
     0.225-0.45 lb. ai/A
     0.25-0.5 lb. SP/A
     1-3 pt. L/A
Time: Nondormant and semidormant: apply during winter months when alfalfa is in least active stage of growth. Dormant: apply after alfalfa becomes dormant and before new growth begins in the spring.
Weeds: Broadleaf weeds:

blue mustard	filaree	purslane speedwell
common chickweed	flixweed	salsify
common groundsel	henbit	shepherdspurse
dogfennel (mayweed)	ivyleaf speedwell	spurry
English catchfly	jim hill mustard	tansymustard
fiddleneck (tarweed)	London rocket	wild radish
field pennycress	minerslettuce	yellow rocket

9

Other Uses

NOTICE	The information on these pages is for preliminary planning — not a guide for use. Be sure to follow the manufacturer's directions, notwithstanding information contained here.	For personal protective equipment and EPA registration numbers, please turn to page 70.

Forage

Grasses:

annual bluegrass	cheatgrass	foxtail
annual ryegrass	(downy brome)	

Northeastern, Midwestern States:

common	fleabane	jimsonweed
lambsquarters	foxtail	redroot pigweed
crabgrass		

Remarks: Alfalfa. Do not use on gravelly or rock soils, exposed subsoil, hardpan sand, poorly drained, or alkali soils. Do not graze or feed treated forage or hay to livestock within 30 days following application.

Crop Rotation: Corn may be planted 12 months after last treatment, except in areas of low rainfall (20" or less) where corn may be planted 12 months after last treatment provided rate did not exceed 0.675 lb. ai/A. Do not plant treated areas to any other crop within 2 years after treatment.

State Restrictions: Not for use in Montana, North Dakota, South Dakota, and Wyoming. California only for seed alfalfa.

– – – – – – – – – – – – – – –

Signal Word/Toxicity Class: Danger/I.
REI: 24 hr.

Zorial — see norflurazon

Zorial Rapid 80 — see norflurazon

Pastures & Rangeland

GENERAL CAUTION: Do not use phenoxy compounds on newly seeded pastures or rangeland. If poisonous weeds or woody plants are known to occur in pastures or on rangeland, remove livestock from area for at least 30 days after treatments. Several herbicides, including 2,4-D, are known to produce marked changes in the chemical composition of treated plants. There is also evidence that some herbicides affect the palatability of certain plants, and that livestock will eat some treated species that they normally would not eat. Do not contaminate water for irrigation, spraying, or domestic purposes. Single application of foliage sprays will often control big sagebrush, mosquito, and sand sage. Repeated treatments, however, are frequently needed. For satisfactory control of mixed stands of oak species and buckbrush, repeated annual applications for two or more consecutive years are normally required. When native grasses are present, deferred grazing during the growing season for one or two years is often desirable.

ALLY

Ally (DF) (metsulfuron-methyl) *(DuPont)*
Rate: 0.1 oz. DF/A
Time: Wheat/fallow/wheat and ecofallow rotations.
Weeds: Broadleaf weeds:

blue mustard	field pennycress	Russian thistle
bur buttercup	filaree	shepherdspurse
Canada thistle*	flixweed	slimleaf
coast fiddleneck	green smartweed	lambsquarters
common chickweed	henbit	smallseed falseflax
common groundsel	kochia	smooth pigweed
common	jim hill mustard	sowthistle*
lambsquarters	ladysthumb	tansymustard
common purslane	mayweed	tarweed
common sunflower*	minerslettuce	treacle mustard
conical catchfly	pale smartweed	tumble mustard
corn cockle	plains coreopsis	tumble pigweed
corn gromwell*	prickly lettuce	volunteer sunflower
cowcockle	prostrate knotweed*	waterpod
false chamomile	purple mustard	wild buckwheat*
fanweed	redroot pigweed	wild mustard

*Suppression

Remarks: To control escaped weeds when using Ally in these types of rotations, use either tillage, tank mixes, or sequential herbicide applications with a different mode of action than Ally.

State Restrictions: For use in Colorado (except Alamosa, Conejos, Costilla, Rio Grande, Saguache counties), Idaho, Kansas, Minnesota, Montana, Nebraska, New Mexico, North Dakota, Oklahoma, Oregon, South Dakota, Texas, Utah, Washington, and Wyoming.

– – – – – – – – – – – – – – –

Signal Word/Toxicity Class: Caution/III.
REI: 4 hr.

AMBER

◆ **Amber Accu-Pak or CustomPak (WDG) (triasulfuron)** *(Novartis)*
Rate: Standard:
0.28 oz. WDG/A
Enhanced:
0.56 oz. WDG/A
Time: Postemergence. Apply when weeds are actively growing.
Weeds: Broadleaf weeds:

annual fleabane	field pennycress	redroot pigweed
bur buttercup	goldenrod*	Russian thistle*
Canada thistle*	henbit	shepherdspurse
coast fiddleneck	hoary cress	tall buttercup
cocklebur	horseweed	Virginia pepperweed
common chickweed*	kochia*	whitetop
common cocklebur	marestail	wild buckwheat
common ragweed	marshelder	wild garlic*
common sunflower	musk thistle*	wild mustard
creeping buttercup	plains coreopsis	wild onion*
curly dock*	poison hemlock	wild radish
cutleaf	puncturevine	woolly croton
eveningprimrose		

Established grasses:

bermudagrass	crested wheatgrass	sheep fescue
big bluestem	intermediate	sideoats grama
blue grama	wheatgrass	smooth brome
bluebunch wheatgass	little bluestem	redtop
buffalograss	pubescent wheatgrass	timothy

* Suppression

Remarks: Add nonionic surfactant. Do not use alone in any field where ALS-resistant biotypes of any weed species have been identified. Do not apply for at least 60 days after in-furrow application of organophosphate insecticide. Do not cut for hay for 30 days following application. Grazing may occur immediately following application. Do not apply through any type of irrigation system. Refer to label for use directions, restrictions, and precautions.

Tank Mixes: Banvel, Crossbow, 2,4-D, Grazon, Stinger, Weedone LV6, Weedmaster.

State Restrictions: For use in Colorado (except San Luis Valley), Idaho, Kansas, Minnesota, Montana, Nebraska, Nevada, New Mexico, North Dakota, Oklahoma, South Dakota, Texas, Utah, Wyoming, and east of the Cascades in Oregon or Washington.

– – – – – – – – – – – – – – –

Signal Word/Toxicity Class: Caution.
REI: 12 hr.

Banvel — see dicamba

Barrage — see 2,4-D

Brash — see 2,4-D Combinations

CLOPYRALID

Systemic herbicide absorbed by leaves and roots. Has selective postemergence control of many annual and perennial broadleaf weeds.

Reclaim *(Dow AgroSciences)*
Rate: 0.5 lb. ae/A
1.33 pt./A
Time: Apply in spring or early summer (40-90 days after first green growth appears) and when soil moisture is adequate for good growth.
Weeds: Brush and weed species such as:

acacia	mesquite

Remarks: Do not treat more than once per year. Do not spray pastures containing desirable forbs, especially legumes, unless injury can be tolerated. Stand and growth of established perennial grasses usually improved after spraying, especially when rainfall is adequate and grazing is deferred. Do not apply through any type of irrigation system.

State Restrictions: For use in New Mexico, Oklahoma, and Texas.

– – – – – – – – – – – – – – –

Signal Word/Toxicity Class: Caution/III.

Stinger *(Dow AgroSciences)*
Rate: 0.2 -0.5 lb. ae/A
0.6-1.33 pt./A
Time: Apply when weeds are young and actively growing.

◆-new product • PP-preplant • PPI-preplant incorporated • PRE-preemergence • POST-postemergence • SEQ-sequential • ae-acid equivalent • ai-active ingredient • DF-dry flowable
E/EC-emulsifiable concentrate • F/FL-flowable • DG/G/WG-dispersable granule • L/LC-liquid • SP/WSP-soluble packet • W/WP-wettable powder • WSB-water soluble bag

Weeds: Annual and perennial broadleaf weeds:

Canada thistle	jimsonweed	spotted knapweed
cocklebur	marshelder	sunflower
clover	Russian knapweed	vetch
diffuse knapweed	(suppression)	volunteer soybean
Jerusalem artichoke	sowthistle*	

Remarks: Do not spray pastures containing desirable broadleaf plants, especially legumes, unless injury can be tolerated. Stand and growth of established perennial grasses usually improved after spraying, especially when rainfall is adequate and grazing is deferred. Do not use hay or straw from treated areas for composting or mulching on susceptible broadleaf crops. Do not apply through any type of irrigation system.

Days To Harvest: No grazing or harvest restrictions.

Crop Rotation: Do not plant broadleaf crops in treated areas until adequately sensitive bioassay shows that clopyralid no longer detected in soil.

State Restrictions: In California, do not apply more that 0.66 pt./A per growing season.

– – – – – – – – – – – – – – –

Signal Word/Toxicity Class: Caution/III.
REI: 12 hr.

Credit — see glyphosate

CROSSBOW (Premix)

Crossbow (1 lb./gal. triclopyr & 2 lb./gal. 2,4-D) *(Dow AgroSciences)*

Rate: 2-4 qt. product/A

Time: Apply during warm weather when brush or weeds are actively growing.

Weeds: Broadleaf weeds:

annual buttercup	goatsbeard	redroot pigweed
annual fleabane	goldenrod	Russian thistle
annual sowthistle	ground ivy	shepherdspurse
bedstraw	hairy galinsoga	spiny amaranth
bitter sneezeweed	hemp dogbane	sunflower
blueweed	hemp sesbania	sweetclover
broadleaf plantain	henbit	tall buttercup
bull thistle	horsenettle	tall ironweed
burclover	horseweed	tansy ragwort
burdock	kochia	tansymustard
Canada thistle	leafy spurge	thymeleaf spurge
chicory*	lespedeza	vetch
cinquefoil	marestail	western ironweed
cocklebur	marshelder	white clover
common lambsquarters	milkweed*	wild carrot
common ragweed	mouseear chickweed	wild lettuce
curly dock	musk thistle	wild mustard
dandelion	narrowleaf plantain	wild radish
dogfennel*	oxalis	wild violet
field bindweed	pepperweed	woolly croton
field pennycress	perennial sowthistle	yarrow
field pepperweed	pokeweed	yellow rocket
	purslane	

Woody plants:

alder	elderberry	sassafras
ash	elm	Scotch broom
aspen	hazel	sumac
birch	honeysuckle	sweetgum
black locust	maple	sycamore
blackberry	multiflora rose	tamarack
boneset	pine	tanoak
buckbrush*	poison ivy	white oak
Ceanothus	poison oak	willow
cherry (except black)	Russian olive	

* Suppression

Remarks: Do not reseed pastures for at least 3 weeks after treatment. Do not spray pastures containing desirable forbs like clover unless injury or loss can be tolerated. Withdraw livestock from treated forage at least 3 days before slaughter during year of treatment; refer to label for grazing or harvesting restrictions. Do not apply through any type of irrigation system.

State Restrictions: Refer to label for use restrictions in Arizona.

– – – – – – – – – – – – – – –

Signal Word/Toxicity Class: Caution/III.

CURTAIL (Premix)

Curtail (0.38 lb./gal. clopyralid & 2 lb./gal. 2,4-D)
(Dow AgroSciences)

Rate: 1.2-2.4 lb. ae/A
2-4 qt./A

Time: Apply when weeds are actively growing.

Weeds: Broadleaf weeds:

alfalfa	giant ragweed	redroot pigweed
annual sowthistle	goatsbeard	Russian knapweed*
Canada thistle	hairy nightshade	Russian thistle
coffeeweed	horseweed	(1-3 leaf)
common burdock	Jerusalem artichoke	scentless chamomile
common cocklebur	jim hill mustard	shepherdspurse
common groundsel	jimsonweed	sicklepod
common	kochia* (2-4 leaf)	spotted knapweed
lambsquarters	ladysthumb	sweetclover
common ragweed	meadow salsify	tansymustard
common sunflower	musk thistle	tumble mustard
cornflower	narrowleaf hawksbeard	velvetleaf
curly dock	Pennsylvania	vetch
cutleaf nightshade	smartweed	volunteer beans
dandelion	perennial sowthistle*	volunteer lentils
diffuse knapweed	pineappleweed	volunteer peas
false chamomile	plantain	wild buckwheat
fanweed	prickly lettuce	wild mustard
field pennycress	red clover	wild radish
flixweed*	red sorrel	yellow starthistle

* Suppression

Remarks: Do not transfer livestock from treated grazing areas to sensitive broadleaf crop areas without first allowing 7 days of grazing on untreated pastures. Do not graze lactating dairy cattle in treated areas for 14 days after application. Remove meat animals from freshly treated areas 7 days before slaughter. Withdrawal not needed if 2 weeks or more have elapsed since application. Do not cut treated grass for hay within 30 days after application.

Crop Rotation: Do not plant broadleaf crops in treated areas until adequately sensitive bioassay shows no detectable clopyralid present in soil.

– – – – – – – – – – – – – – –

Signal Word/Toxicity Class: Danger/I.
REI: 48 hr.

2,4-D - PHENOXY HERBICIDES

Annual and perennial broadleaf weeds controlled by 2,4-D include:

beggarticks	galinsoga	povertyweed
bindweed	goldenrod	puncturevine
bitterweed	ground ivy	purslane
broomweed	healall	ragweed
bull thistle	hoary cress	Russian thistle
burdock	ironweed	shepherdspurse
Canada thistle	jimsonweed	smartweed
carpetweed	knotweed	sowthistle
catnip	lambsquarters	stinkweed
chicory	mallow	sumac
chickweed	marshelder	sunflower
cocklebur	mexicanweed	sweetclover
coffeeweed	morningglory	velvetleaf
cutleaf	musk thistle	Virginia creeper
eveningprimrose	mustard	wild carrot
creeping jenny	pennywort	wild garlic
croton	pepperweed	wild lettuce
dandelion	pigweed	wild onion
dock	plantain	wild parsnips
dogbane	pokeweed	wild radish

Albaugh Amine 4 (2,4-D amine) *(Albaugh)*
Albaugh LV4 or LV6 Ester (2,4-D ester) *(Albaugh)*
◆ **Opti-Amine (4) (2,4-D amine)** *(Helena)*
Riverdale 6 Amine (2,4-D amine) *(Riverdale)*
◆ **Riverdale 4 Amine IVM (2,4-D amine)** *(Riverdale)*
Riverdale L.V. 4 or L.V. 6 (2,4-D ester) *(Riverdale)*
Solution (WS) (2,4-D amine) *(Riverdale)*
Solve 2,4-D (2,4-D LV ester) *(Albaugh)*
Weed Rhap A-4D (2,4-D amine) *(Helena)*
Weed Rhap LV-6D (2,4-D ester) *(Helena)*
Weedestroy AM-40 (2,4-D amine) *(Riverdale)*
Wilbur-Ellis Lo Vol-4 or Lo Vol-6 (2,4-D ester) *(Wilbur-Ellis)*

Rate: 0.5-2 lb. ae/A
1-4 pt. 4/A
0.66-2.66 pt. 6/A
2 lb. 13 oz. WS packet/1.125-2.25 A

Time: Apply when weeds are small and growing actively before bud stage. Fall or spring best time to treat.

Remarks: Established stands of perennial grasses. Use low rate on more easily injured grasses. Treatments will kill or injure alfalfa, sweet clover, and other legumes. For southern wild rose, use maximum 4 pt. 4/A, 2.9 pt. 6/A, or 1 WS packet/1.13 A per application per site.

Days To Harvest: 30 days—prior to cutting grass for hay; 7 days—pregrazing interval for dairy cattle; 3 days—preslaughter interval for meat animals.

State Restrictions: Wilbur-Ellis not registered in California.

– – – – – – – – – – – – – – –

Signal Word/Toxicity Class: Danger/I (amine); Caution/III (ester).
REI: Danger—48 hr.; Caution—12 hr.

9

Other Uses

NOTICE	The information on these pages is for preliminary planning — not a guide for use. Be sure to follow the manufacturer's directions, notwithstanding information contained here.	For personal protective equipment and EPA registration numbers, please turn to page 70.

◆ **Barrage or Barrage HF (EC) (2,4-D ester)** *(Helena)*
Rate: 6-26 fl. oz./A
Time: Apply when weeds are small and actively growing. Early spring or fall is the best time to treat. Do not apply to grasses in boot to milk stage or after heading begins if grass seed production is desired.
Remarks: Do not apply to newly seeded areas until grass is well established. Do not graze dairy animals on treated areas within 7 days or meat animals within 3 days of slaughter. Do not cut treated grass for hay within 30 days of application.

- - - - - - - - - - - - - -

Signal Word/Toxicity Class: Caution/III.
REI: 12 hr.

◆ **Clean Crop Amine 4 (2,4-D amine)** *(Platte)*
◆ **Clean Crop Low Vol 4 or Low Vol 6 (2,4-D ester)** *(Platte)*
Gordon's LV 400 (2,4-D ester) *(PBI/Gordon)*
Riverside 2,4-D LV4 (2,4-D LV ester) *(Terra)*
Weedar 64 (4) (2,4-D amine) *(Nufarm)*
Weedone LV4 (2,4-D solventless ester) *(Nufarm)*
Wilbur-Ellis Amine 4 (2,4-D amine) *(Wilbur-Ellis)*
Rate: 1-2 lb. ae/A
2-4 pt./A
1.33-2.66 pt. LV6/A
Time: Apply when weeds are young and growing actively before bud stage. Deep-rooted perennial weeds may require repeated treatments in the same year or in subsequent years. Do not use from early boot to milk stage where grass seed production is desired.
Remarks: Do not use on bentgrass, alfalfa, clover, or other legumes. Do not use on newly seeded areas until grass is well established.
Days To Harvest: 30 days—prior to cutting grass for hay; 7 days—pregrazing interval for dairy cattle; 3 days—preslaughter interval for meat animals.
State Restrictions: Wilbur-Ellis not registered in California.

- - - - - - - - - - - - - -

Signal Word/Toxicity Class: Varies by formulation.
REI: Danger—48 hr.; Caution—12 hr.

Esteron 99C (2,4-D LV ester) *(Rhone-Poulenc)*
Weedone 638 (2,4-D ester + acid) *(Nufarm)*
Weedone Lo Vol 6 (2,4-D ester) *(Nufarm)*
Rate: 1-3 lb. ae/A
2-6 pt./A
1-2 lb. ae/A
1.3-2.75 pt. LV6/A
2.5-5 pt. 638/A
Time: Apply when weeds are actively growing prior to bud stage. Do not use from early boot to milk stage where grass seed production is desired.
Remarks: Established grass pastures.
Days To Harvest: 30 days—prior to cutting grass for hay; 7 days—pregrazing interval for dairy cattle; 3 days—preslaughter interval for meat animals.

- - - - - - - - - - - - - -

Signal Word/Toxicity Class: Varies by formulation.
REI: Danger—48 hr.; Caution—12 hr.

Formula 40 (2,4-D amine) *(Rhone-Poulenc)*
Hi-Dep (2,4-D amine) *(PBI/Gordon)*
◆ **Orchard Master (2,4-D mixed amine)** *(PBI/Gordon)*
Rate: Formula 40, Hi-Dep:
1-4 lb. ae/A
2-8 pt./A
Orchard Master:
1-2 lb. ae/A
2-4 pt./A
Time: Apply when weeds are actively growing. Do not use from early boot to milk stage where grass seed production is desired.
Weeds: Broadleaf weeds.
Remarks: Established grass pastures. Do not use on bentgrass, alfalfa, clover, or other legumes. Do not use on newly seeded areas until grass is well established.
Days To Harvest: 30 days—prior to cutting grass for hay; 7 days—pregrazing interval for dairy cattle; 3 days—preslaughter interval for meat animals.

- - - - - - - - - - - - - -

Signal Word/Toxicity Class: Danger/I.
REI: 48 hr.

Riverside 2,4-D Amine 4 (2,4-D amine) *(Terra)*
Rate: 0.75 lb. ai/A
1.5 pt./A
Time: Apply when weeds are actively growing in spring or fall; perennials near bud stage. Do not apply when grass is in boot to milk stage.
Remarks: Do not apply to seedling grasses or after heading begins.

Days To Harvest: 30 days—prior to cutting grass for hay; 7 days—pregrazing interval for dairy cattle; 3 days—preslaughter interval for meat animals.

- - - - - - - - - - - - - -

Signal Word/Toxicity Class: Danger/I.
REI: 48 hr.

◆ **Saber (2,4-D amine)** *(Platte)*
Rate: 0.75-2 lb. ae/A
1.5-4 pt./A
Time: Apply in early spring when weeds are small and actively growing.
Remarks: Do not use on bentgrass, alfalfa, clover, or other legumes unless risk of injury is acceptable. Do not use on newly seeded areas until grass is well established.
Days To Harvest: 30 days—prior to cutting grass for hay; 7 days—pregrazing interval for dairy cattle; 3 days—preslaughter interval for meat animals.

- - - - - - - - - - - - - -

Signal Word/Toxicity Class: Danger/I.
REI: 48 hr.

Salvo (2,4-D LV ester) *(Platte)*
Rate: 0.5 lb. ai/A
0.8 pt./A
Time: Apply in early spring when sufficient weeds have emerged and are actively growing and not too mature. Do not apply when grass is in boot to milk stage.
Remarks: Injury may result to bentgrass and clover. Usually clover will recover from early spring application. Do not apply to newly seeded areas or after heading begins.
Days To Harvest: 30 days—prior to cutting grass for hay; 7 days—pregrazing interval for dairy cattle; 3 days—preslaughter interval for meat animals.

- - - - - - - - - - - - - -

Signal Word/Toxicity Class: Caution/III.
REI: 12 hr.

Savage (WSB) (2,4-D amine) *(Platte)*
Rate: 0.95-1.9 lb. ae/A
1-2 lb. WSB/A
Time: Apply when weeds are small and actively growing prior to bud stage. Do not apply to grasses in early boot to milk stage if grass seed production is desired.
Weeds: Annual, biennial, and perennial weeds.
Remarks: Do not apply to newly seeded areas until grass is well established.
Days To Harvest: 30 days—prior to cutting grass for hay; 7 days—pregrazing interval for dairy cattle; 3 days—preslaughter interval for meat animals.

- - - - - - - - - - - - - -

Signal Word/Toxicity Class: Danger/I.
REI: 48 hr.

2,4-D COMBINATIONS

◆ **Brash (2.87 lb./gal. 2,4-D & 1 lb./gal. dicamba)** *(Terra)*
Weedmaster (2.87 lb./gal. 2,4-D & 1 lb./gal. dicamba) *(BASF)*
Rate: 0.25-2 lb. ai/A
0.5-4 pt./A
Time: Apply when weeds are actively growing. For pasture renovation, wait 3 weeks for each qt./A used before interseeding or injury may occur.
Weeds: Annual and perennial broadleaf weeds and woody plants:

annual fleabane	curly dock	poison ivy
annual mustard	dogfennel	poorjoe
bitterweed	eastern persimmon	prickly lettuce
black knapweed*	elderberry*	red sorrel
broomweed	field bindweed	redroot pigweed
buckeye	field pennycress	redvine*
buffalobur	hairy honeysuckle	Russian knapweed*
bull thistle	hairy vetch	silverleaf nightshade
burclover	henbit	southern dewberry
burdock	knotweed	spotted beebalm
buttercup	kochia	spotted knapweed
Canada thistle*	late eupatorium	sunflower
Carolina horsenettle	leafy spurge*	tall morningglory
chicory	mesquite	tansy ragwort
common chickweed	Missouri goldenrod	Texas groundsel
common cocklebur	musk thistle	velvetleaf
common dandelion	Pennsylvania	Virginia pepperweed
common goldenweed	smartweed	woolly croton
common	perennial sowthistle*	yankeeweed
lambsquarters	plains coreopsis	yellow starthistle

* Suppression

Remarks: Do not use on bentgrass, susceptible grass pastures, lespedeza, wild winter peas, vetch, clover, or alfalfa pastures. Agriculturally approved adjuvants or other spray additives may be used for wetting, penetration, or drift control; follow all recommendations and label precautions.

- - - - - - - - - - - - - -

Signal Word/Toxicity Class: Danger/I.
REI: 48 hr.

◆-new product • PP-preplant • PPI-preplant incorporated • PRE-preemergence • POST-postemergence • SEQ-sequential • ae-acid equivalent • ai-active ingredient • DF-dry flowable E/EC-emulsifiable concentrate • F/FL-flowable • DG/G/WG-dispersable granule • L/LC-liquid • SP/WSP-soluble packet • W/WP-wettable powder • WSB-water soluble bag

DICAMBA

Banvel (WS) (DMA salt of dicamba) *(BASF)*
◆ **Sterling (WS) (DMA salt of dicamba)** *(Terra)*
Rate: Annuals:
0.25-0.75 lb. ai/A
0.5-1.5 pt. WS/A
Biennials:
0.25-1.5 lb. ai/A
0.5-3 pt. WS/A
Perennials:
0.5-2 lb. ai/A
1-4 pt. WS/A
Time: Apply when weeds are actively growing.
Weeds: Broadleaf weeds including:

burdock	kochia	Russian thistle
Canada thistle	leafy spurge	tansy ragwort
field bindweed	pigweeds	

Many woody brush and vine species including:

ash	fringed sagebrush	multiflora rose
aspen	honeysuckle	sumac
blackberry	huisache	tarbush
blackgum	kudzu	trumpetcreeper
creosotebush	Macartney rose	willow
dewberry	mesquite	yaupon
eastern persimmon		

Remarks: Do not apply more than 1 lb. ai/A. Rates above 2 lb. ai/A for spot treatment. Do not remove animals from treated areas for slaughter prior to 30 days after last application. Do not graze lactating dairy within 7 days after application for 1 pt./A, 21 days for 2 pt./A, 40 days for 4 pt./A. No waiting period between treatment and grazing for nonlactating animals.
Days To Harvest: Up to 1 pt./A—37; 2 pt./A—51; 4 pt./A—70.
Tank Mixes: Ally, 2,4-D, Garlon, paraquat, Tordon.

Signal Word/Toxicity Class: Warning/II.
REI: 24 hr.

◆ **Veteran 10G (dicamba)** *(Riverdale)*
Rate: 0.05-0.2 lb. ai/1000 sq. ft.
0.5-2 lb. 10G/1000 sq. ft.
Time: Apply in the spring before or during active growth.
Weeds: Biennial and perennial broadleaf weeds:

artichoke thistle	lakeweed	skeletonleaf bursage
brackenfern	leafy spurge	tansy ragwort
bull thistle	perennial sowthistle	Texas blueweed
bur ragweed	povertyweed	woollyleaf bursage
Canada thistle	Russian knapweed	yellow starthistle
field bindweed	silverleaf nightshade	

Woody brush and vine species including:

autumn olive	kudzu	Siberian elm
creosotebush	saltcedar	sumac
eastern persimmon	sand plum	tarbush

Remarks: Rate varies by species. Sufficient moisture needed to activate product. Soil must not be frozen. Do not apply more than 20 lb./A per yr. Do not graze or harvest grasses for lactating dairy animals within 60 days of treatment. Remove meat animals from treated areas 30 days before slaughter.

Signal Word/Toxicity Class: Warning.

Direx — see diuron

DIURON

Direx 4L or 80DF *(Griffin)*
◆ **Diuron 80 WDG** *(Platte)*
Drexel Diuron 4L or 80 *(Drexel)*
Karmex DF *(Griffin)*
Riverside Diuron 4L or 80DF *(Terra)*
Rate: 0.8-2.4 lb. ai/A
0.8-2.4 qt. 4L/A
1-3 lb. 80, DF, 80DF/A
Time: Preemergence or postemergence.
Weeds: Broadleaf weeds and grasses:

barnyardgrass	crabgrass	pigweed
coloradograss	lambsquarters	ragweed

Remarks: Newly sprigged bermudagrass pastures. Do not graze treated fields or feed forage from treated areas to livestock within 70 days after application or replant treated areas to any crop within 2 yr. after application.

Signal Word/Toxicity Class: Caution/III.
REI: 12 hr.

ESCORT

Escort (DF) (metsulfuron methyl) *(DuPont)*
Rate: 0.1-0.75 oz. DF/A
Time: Apply preemergence or early postemergence to seedling weeds. For broom snakeweed, apply fall through spring.
Weeds: Broadleaf weeds and new seedlings including:

blackberry	curly dock	multiflora rose
broom snakeweed	dyer's woad	prostrate knotweed
buckhorn plantain	hoary cress	sunflower
Canada thistle		

Remarks: Native grasses: bermudagrass, crested wheatgrass, hairy grama, hooded windmill, sideoats grama, smooth brome, purple threeawn, switchgrass, western wheatgrass. Do not use on bahiagrass pasture or on grasses grown for seed. Add surfactant for emerged weeds.

Signal Word/Toxicity Class: Caution.
REI: 4 hr.

Esteron 99C — see 2,4-D

Formula 40 — see 2,4-D

GLYPHOSATE

◆ **Credit (4WS)** *(Nufarm)*
◆ **Glyfos or Glyfos X-tra (4WS)** *(Cheminova)*
Rattler (4WS) *(Helena)*
Roundup Custom (5.4WS) *(Monsanto)*
Roundup Original, Original RT, Ultra, Ultra RT (4WS) *(Monsanto)*
Rate: Annual weeds:
0.38-1.5 lb. ai/A
0.56-2.25 pt. 5.4WS/A
0.75-3 pt. 4WS/A
Perennial weeds:
0.5-5 lb. ai/A
0.75-7.5 pt. 5.4WS/A
1-10 pt. 4WS/A
Time: Preplant, preemergence, spot treatment, wiper application, pasture renovation.
Weeds: Annual and perennial broadleaf weeds and grasses.
Remarks: Bahiagrass, bermudagrass, bluegrass, brome, clover, fescue, orchardgrass, ryegrass, timothy, wheatgrass. Refer to label for restrictions.
State Restrictions: Roundup Ultra tank mixes not registered in California. Roundup Ultra RT: For use in Colorado, Idaho, Montana, North Dakota, South Dakota, Utah, and Wyoming. For use in specific counties only in Kansas, Minnesota, Nebraska, Nevada, Oklahoma, Oregon, and Washington, refer to label for restrictions. Glyfos not registered for use in California. Glyfos X-tra not registered for use in mistblowers in California or Arizona.

Signal Word/Toxicity Class: Varies by formulation.
REI: Warning—12 hr.; Caution—4 hr.

Gramoxone Extra — see paraquat

GRAZON P+D (Premix)

Restricted Use Pesticide.

Grazon P+D (WS) (0.54 lb./gal. picloram & 2 lb./gal. 2,4-D)
(Dow AgroSciences)
Rate: Broadcast:
0.3-2.5 lb. ae/A
1-8 pt./A
High volume foliar:
2.5-5 lb. ae/100 gal. spray
1-2 gal./100 gal. spray
Time: Apply at indicated growth stage on label.
Weeds: Broadleaf weeds and woody plants including:

annual broomweed	Carolina horsenettle	groundsel
bitter sneezeweed	Chinese tallowtree	honeylocust
bitterweed	cocklebur	(foliar)
blackberry	common goldenweed	horseweed
buffalobur	common ragweed	lambsquarters
bull thistle	croton	Macartney rose
bullnettle	curly dock	marshelder
bursage	dogfennel	mesquite
camphorweed	garbancillo	multiflora rose

9

Other Uses

Weeds: Broadleaf weeds and woody plants including, continued:

musk thistle	smartweed	western horsenettle
narrowleaf goldaster	sunflower	western ragweed
oak (sprouts)	tasajillo	wild carrot
pigweed	tropical soda apple	woolly loco
prickly lettuce	upright prairie	yankeeweed
pricklypear cactus	coneflower	
silverleaf nightshade	vervain	

Rate: CO, ID, MT, NE, ND, OR, SD, UT, WA, WY:
  0.6-1.2 lb. ae/A
  2-4 pt./A

Time: Apply at indicated growth stage on label.

Weeds: Broadleaf weeds and woody plants including:

absinth wormwood	geyer larkspur	plains pricklypear
broom snakeweed	goldenrod	thistle
common ragweed	hairy goldenaster	western ironweed
curly dock	locoweed	western ragweed
curlycup gumweed	oxeye daisy	yarrow
fringed sagebrush		

Remarks: Permanent grass pastures and rangeland. Do not spray pastures unless injury to existing forage legumes can be tolerated. For early season control, use lower rate; mid- to late season, use higher rate. For poisonous plants such as groundsel, garbancillo, and woolly loco, do not graze treated areas until toxic plants have dried up and lost their palatability. Do not allow lactating dairy animals to graze treated areas within 7 days after application; withdraw livestock from treated forage at least 3 days before slaughter. Do not transfer livestock from treated grazing areas onto broadleaf crop areas with first allowing 7 days of grazing on untreated grass pasture. Do not apply through any type of irrigation system.

Days To Harvest: Grass cut for hay—30.

Crop Rotation: Do not rotate to crops intended for food or feed use other than range or pasture grasses, or wheat, barley, and oats not underseeded with legumes.

State Restrictions: For use in Alabama, Georgia, Louisiana, Mississippi, South Carolina, and states west of the Mississippi.

– – – – – – – – – – – – – –

Signal Word/Toxicity Class: Warning/II.

HEXAZINONE

Pronone Power Pellet (Pro-Serve)
Rate: 1-2 pellets/1" stem diameter
Time: Apply late winter to mid-spring.
Weeds: Brush:

aspen	huisache	red cedar
black cherry	junipers	small soapweed
blackgum	lotebush	snowbrush
catclaw acacia	manzanita	sumac
deerbrush	mesquite	sweet gum
dogwood	multiflora rose	tallow
elm	myrtle	whitebrush
green ash	oak	whitehorn
hackberry	(except line oak)	wild cherry
hawthorn	osageorange	willow
hickory	persimmon	

Remarks: Apply to soil within 3 ft. of root collar. For larger stems using more than 1 pellet, apply on opposite side of stem. For effective brush control and prevention of damage to desirable vegetation, do not apply to brush standing in water or near desirable trees or shrubs. Do not treat more than 300 1" stem equivalents/A per season. Refer to label for use directions and precautions.

– – – – – – – – – – – – – –

Signal Word/Toxicity Class: Danger/I.
REI: 24 hr.

Hi-Dep — see 2,4-D

Karmex — see diuron

MCPA

Albaugh MCPA Amine (4) (Albaugh)
◆ **Clean Crop MCP 4 Ester** (Platte)
◆ **Clean Crop MCP 2 Sodium (sodium salt)** (Platte)
Riverdale MCPA-4 Amine, L.V. 4 Ester (4), IOE (5.2) (Riverdale)
Solve MCPA Ester (4) (Albaugh)
Sword (5.2) (Platte)
Wilbur-Ellis MCPA Amine, Ester (4) or ◆ Sodium Salt (Wilbur-Ellis)

Rate: 0.5-1.5 lb. ae/A
  1-3 pt. 4/A
  0.75-2 pt. 5.2/A
  2-6 pt. sodium salt/A

Time: Apply on perennials in early bud to full bloom stage and regrowth in the fall; other weeds in spring or fall.

Weeds: Broadleaf weeds including:

annual mustard	kochia	shepherdspurse
buttercup	lambsquarters	silverleaf nightshade
Canada thistle	marshelder	sowthistle
cocklebur	pigweed	stinging nettle
dandelion	plantain	stinkweed
dragonhead mint	puncturevine	vetch
field peppergrass	purslane	whitetop
goatsbeard	ragweed	wild radish
hempnettle	Russian thistle	yellow rocket

Remarks: Established grassland and pastures. Do not forage or graze meat animals on treated areas within 7 days of slaughter.
State Restrictions: Wilbur-Ellis not registered in California.

– – – – – – – – – – – – – –

Rate: 1.25 lb. ae/A
  2.5 pt. 4/A
  2 pt. 5.2/A

Time: Apply in spring or fall under good moisture conditions, full leaf, before blossoms begin to fall.

Weeds: Broadleaf weeds:

  whitebrush

Remarks: Rangeland and timber grasses. Apply in 1 gal. diesel oil and sufficient water to make 8 gal. solution/A. Do not forage or graze meat animals on treated areas within 7 days of slaughter.
State Restrictions: Wilbur-Ellis not registered in California.

– – – – – – – – – – – – – –

Signal Word/Toxicity Class: Varies by formulation.
REI: Danger—48 hr.; Warning/Caution—12 hr.

– – – – – – – – – – – – – –

◆ **Clean Crop MCP Amine 4** (Platte)
Rate: 1-2 lb. ae/A
  2-4 pt. 4/A

Time: Apply when weeds are small and actively growing. Do not apply from early boot to milk stage where grass seed production is desired.

Weeds: Broadleaf weeds including:

buttercup	lambsquarters	shepherdspurse
Canada thistle	marshelder	stinkweed
cocklebur	pigweed	whitetop
dandelion	plantain	wild radish
goatsbeard	ragweed	yellow rocket
hempnettle		

Remarks: Established grassland and pastures. Do not use where legumes, especially alfalfa, are present and desirable. Do not forage or graze meat animals on treated areas within 7 days of slaughter.

– – – – – – – – – – – – – –

Rate: 1.5 lb. ae/A
  3 pt. 4/A

Time: Apply in spring or fall when plant is well developed and actively growing. Spraying during bloom is recommended but not immediately after shedding of blossoms.

Weeds: Broadleaf weeds:

  whitebrush

Remarks: Rangeland. Apply in 1 gal. diesel oil and sufficient water to make 6-10 gal. solution/A. Do not forage or graze meat animals on treated areas within 7 days of slaughter.

– – – – – – – – – – – – – –

Signal Word/Toxicity Class: Danger/I.
REI: 48 hr.

– – – – – – – – – – – – – –

Rhonox (LV ester) (4) (Nufarm)
Rate: 0.5-1.5 lb. ae/A
  1-3 pt. 4/A

Time: Apply when weeds are small and actively growing before bud stage. Do not apply in boot to milk stage if grass seed production is desired.

Weeds: Broadleaf weeds including:

bull thistle	dandelion	pigweed
common burdock	field pennycress	plantain
common cocklebur	giant ragweed	purslane
common	mustard	Russian thistle
lambsquarters	pepperweed (except	shepherdspurse
common ragweed	perennial)	yellow rocket

Remarks: Established grassland and pastures. Do not apply to newly seeded areas. Bentgrass and legumes may be damaged by this treatment. Do not graze animals on treated areas within 7 days of application.

– – – – – – – – – – – – – –

Signal Word/Toxicity Class: Caution.
REI: 12 hr.

◆–new product • PP–preplant • PPI–preplant incorporated • PRE–preemergence • POST–postemergence • SEQ–sequential • ae–acid equivalent • ai–active ingredient • DF–dry flowable
E/EC–emulsifiable concentrate • F/FL–flowable • DG/G/WG–dispersable granule • L/LC–liquid • SP/WSP–soluble packet • W/WP–wettable powder • WSB–water soluble bag

Opti-Amine — see 2,4-D

Orchard Master — see 2,4-D

PARAQUAT

Restricted Use Pesticide.

Gramoxone Extra (2.5L) *(ZENECA)*
  Rate: 0.28-0.5 lb. ai/A
       0.8-1.5 pt. 2.5L/A
  Time: West of Cascades and Sierra Nevadas: Apply Oct.-Dec. after first fall rains, and weeds have emerged and sod has started new growth. East of the Rockies: Apply prior to or at time of seeding grasses or forage legumes. Apply only to grazed or mowed pastures which are not more than 2-3" in height at time of treatment. For bermudagrass or bahiagrass sod, apply late summer or early fall not exceeding 3" in height. For bermudagrass and coastal bermudagrass pastures, apply dormant.
  Weeds: Suppression of existing sod and undesirable emerged broadleaf weeds and grasses to permit pasture and range reseeding.
  Remarks: Add nonionic surfactant or crop oil concentrate. West of Cascades and Sierra Nevadas: Do not use in areas with heavy sod and weed growth. East of the Rockies: Use high rate to suppress vigorous and coarse sod species. Do not pasture or mow for hay until 40 days after treatment. Refer to label for directions, restrictions, and precautions.

  Signal Word/Toxicity Class: Danger-Poison/I.
  REI: 12 hr. (except harvest aid/desiccation 24 hr.).

Pronone — see hexazinone

Rattler — see glyphosate

RAVE (Premix)

Premix with 2 modes of action. One active ingredient inhibits the acetolactate synthase (ALS) enzyme. The other active ingredient disrupts normal plant growth.

◆ **Rave (WDG) (50% dicamba & 8.8% triasulfuron)** *(Novartis)*
  Rate: 2-4 oz. WDG/A
       Heavy infestations:
       5 oz. WDG/A
  Time: Postemergence. Apply to actively growing weeds at least 60 days after emergence of desirable grasses or sprigged-bermudagrass.
  Weeds: Broadleaf weeds:

annual morningglory	cutleaf	pepperweed
annual polemonium	eveningprimrose	pigweed
annual sowthistle	fanweed	plains coreopsis
black nightshade	field bindweed	prickly lettuce
blue mustard	field pennycress	prostrate knotweed
bur buttercup	fleabane	prostrate pigweed
bushy wallflower	flixweed	puncturevine
Canada thistle	forget-me-not	ragweed
coast fiddleneck	giant ragweed	redroot pigweed
common broomweed	goldenrod	Russian thistle
common chickweed	hairy vetch	shepherdspurse
common cocklebur	henbit	smooth pigweed
common groundsel	horseweed	tall buttercup
common	houndstongue	tall hedge mustard
lambsquarters	Indian mustard	tansymustard
common mallow	jagged chickweed	tartary buckwheat
common purslane	kochia	tarweed
common ragweed	ladysthumb	tumble mustard
common sunflower	lanceleaf ragweed	tumble pigweed
common yarrow	London rocket	umbrella spurry
corn chamomile	marestail	velvetleaf
corn cockle	marshelder	Virginia pepperweed
corn gromwell	minerslettuce	wild buckwheat
cornflower	musk thistle	wild mustard
creeping buttercup	mustard	wild radish
curly dock	Pennsylvania	woolly croton
	smartweed	

  Remarks: Bermudagrass, big bluestem, little bluestem, buffalograss, sheep fescue, smooth brome, blue grama, sideoats grama, redtop, timothy, wheatgrass (bluebunch, crested, intermediate, pubescent). Desirable broadleaves, such as clover and alfalfa may be severely injured. Add nonionic surfactant or crop oil concentrate. Do not apply for at least 60 days after organophosphate application. Do not apply through any type of irrigation system.

Crop Rotation: Recropping depends on field bioassay, soil pH, total rainfall, and geographic area. Refer to label for restrictions and more complete information.
Tank Mixes: Crossbow, 2,4-D, Grazon P+D, Remedy, Stinger, Tordon 22K, and Weedmaster.
State Restrictions: For use in Colorado (except San Luis Valley), Idaho, Kansas, Minnesota, Montana, Nebraska, Nevada, New Mexico, North Dakota, Oklahoma, Oregon, South Dakota, Texas, Utah, Washington, Wyoming. In Washington, abide by all sulfonylurea aerial application rulings by Washington Department of Agriculture.

Signal Word/Toxicity Class: Caution.
REI: 12 hr.

Reclaim — see clopyralid

Remedy — see triclopyr

Rhonox — see MCPA

Roundup — see glyphosate

Saber — see 2,4-D

Salvo — see 2,4-D

Savage — see 2,4-D

SCYTHE

◆ **Scythe (pelargonic acid)** *(Mycogen)*
  Rate: 4-13 fl. oz./1 gal. spray solution
  Time: Apply to young succulent weeds.
  Weeds: Annual broadleaf weeds and grasses; top-kill of perennial weeds.
  Remarks: Apply in minimum 75 gal. spray solution/A or spray-to-wet. Do not apply by air or through any type of irrigation system. Refer to label for directions and precautions.
  Tank Mixes: Glyphosate and other foliar and residual herbicides.

  Signal Word/Toxicity Class: Warning/II.
  REI: 24 hr.

Solution — see 2,4-D

Solve — see 2,4-D; MCPA

SPIKE

Spike 20P (tebuthiuron) *(Dow AgroSciences)*
  Rate: 0.75-4 lb. ai/A
       3.75-20 lb. 20P/A
  Time: Dormant season application recommended to minimize herbicidal effects on desirable forage grasses.
  Weeds: Over 125 grass and weed species and 110 woody species including hard-to-control species such as:

maple	white ash	willow
oak		

  Remarks: Rate varies by weed species. Grazing allowed in areas treated with no more than 20 lb./A. In areas treated with 20 lb./A or less, grass may be cut for hay 1 year after application.

  Signal Word/Toxicity Class: Caution/III.

Sterling — see dicamba

9

Other Uses

NOTICE The information on these pages is for preliminary planning — not a guide for use. Be sure to follow the manufacturer's directions, notwithstanding information contained here. | For personal protective equipment and EPA registration numbers, please turn to page 70.

Stinger — see clopyralid

Sword — see MCPA

TORDON

Restricted Use Pesticide.

Tordon 22K (picloram) *(Dow AgroSciences)*
Rate: 0.125-0.5 lb. ae/A
   0.5-2 pt. 22K/A
   Noxious weeds:
   1 lb. ae/A
   4 pt. 22K/A
Time: Apply when weeds are small and actively growing in the spring before full bloom.
Weeds: Annual, biennial, and perennial broadleaf weeds such as:

absinth wormwood	groundsel	ragweed
annual broomweed	henbane	rush skeletonweed
bindweed	horsenettle	silverleaf nightshade
bitter sneezeweed	horseweed	smartweed
broom snakeweed	knapweed	sowthistle
buffalobur	ironweed	St. Johnswort
bullnettle	leafy spurge	starthistle
burroweed	larkspur	sunflower
bursage	locoweed	tansy ragwort
camphorweed	lupine	thistle
cinquefoil	marshelder	toadflax
cocklebur	mayweed	upright prairie
croton	milkweed	coneflower
curly dock	oxeye daisy	western bitterweed
goldaster	perennial sowthistle	wild licorice
goldenweed	plains pricklypear	yankeeweed
gorse	prickly lettuce	yellow toadflax

Rate: 2 lb. ae/100 gal spray
   8 pt. 22K/100 gal spray
Time: Apply when plants are actively growing.
Weeds: Woody plants such as:

acacia	huisache	multiflora rose
Chinese tallowtree	(suppression)	pinyon pine
fringed sagebrush	juniper	pricklypear
granjeno	Macartney rose	tasajillo
guajillo	mesquite	

Remarks: Permanent pastures and rangelands. Do not allow spray to contact desirable broadleaf plants. Do not graze treated areas until poisonous plants are dry and no longer palatable to livestock. Do not graze lactating dairy animals on treated areas within 2 weeks after treatment; livestock grazing up to 2 weeks after treatment should be removed within 3 days prior to slaughter. Do not cut grass for feed within 2 weeks after treatment. Do not apply through any type of irrigation system. Refer to label for restrictions and precautions.
Tank Mixes: 2,4-D.
State Restrictions: For use west of the Mississippi except San Luis Valley of Colorado. Use in Hawaii limited to supplemental labeling. Refer to label for specific use directions for New Mexico, Oklahoma, and Texas

Signal Word/Toxicity Class: Caution.
REI: 12 hr.

TRICLOPYR

Remedy *(Dow AgroSciences)*
Rate: Foliar-broadcast:
   1 lb. ae/A
   2 pt./A
   High-volume leaf stem treatment:
   1-3 lb. ae/A
   2-6 pt./A
   Oklahoma, New Mexico, Texas: Mesquite:
   0.5 lb. ae/A
   1 pt./A
   Oklahoma, New Mexico, Texas: Sand shinnery oak suppression:
   0.25-1 lb. ae/A
   0.5-2 pt./A
Time: Apply when plants are actively growing.
Weeds: Annual and perennial broadleaf weeds:

black medic	curly dock	plantain
burdock	dandelion	vetch
chicory	lambsquarters	wild carrot
cinquefoil	lespedeza	wild violet
clover	mustard	yarrow

Woody plants such as:

alder	elderberry	poison ivy
ash	elm	poison oak
aspen	(except winged)	poplar
beech	granjeno	saltbush
birch	guajillo	sand shinnery oak
blackberry	hawthorn	sassafras
blackbrush	huisache	sumac
cascara	locust	tropical soda apple
Ceanothus	maple (except bigleaf	trumpet creeper
cherry	and vine)	twisted acacia
cottonwood	mesquite	waxmyrtle
dogfennel	milkweed vine	wild roses
dogwood	oak	willow
eastern persimmon	peppervine	willow primrose

Remarks: Do not spray pastures containing desirable forbs, especially legumes such as clover, unless injury or loss of plants can be tolerated. Stand and growth of established grasses usually improved after spraying, especially when rainfall is adequate and grazing is deferred. Do not reseed treated areas for at least 3 weeks after treatment. Withdraw livestock from treated forage at least 3 days before slaughter. Refer to label for further use directions and precautions. Do not apply through any type of irrigation system.
Days To Harvest: Grazing lactating dairy animals or harvesting grass for hay—1 year.
Tank Mixes: 2,4-D.

Signal Word/Toxicity Class: Caution.

Veteran 10G — see dicamba

VETERAN 720 (Premix)

♦ **Veteran 720 (WS) (1.9 lb./gal. 2,4-D & 1 lb./gal. dicamba)** *(Riverdale)*
Rate: 0.725-2.9 lb. ai/A
   1-4 qt. WS/A
Weeds: Annual broadleaf weeds:

carpetweed	knawel	purslane
chickweed	lambsquarters	ragweed
clover	morningglory	smartweed
cocklebur	mustard	velvetleaf
English daisy	pigweed	wild buckwheat
henbit		

Biennial weeds:

musk thistle	tansy ragwort

Perennial weeds:

Canada thistle	field bindweed	Russian knapweed
curly dock	leafy spurge	sheep sorrel
dalmation toadflax	milkweed	wild carrot
dogfennel	Queen Anne's lace	

Rate: 2.9-5.8 lb. ai/A
   1-2 gal. WS/A
Weeds: Woody brush and vines:

alder	Florida holly	redvine
ash	gum	Russian olive
aspen	hawthorn*	sagebrush
basswood	hemlock	sassafras
beech	honeysuckle	serviceberry
birch	kudzu	snowberry
blackberry*	locust	spruce
Brazil peppertree	maple	sumac
cherry	multiflora rose*	sycamore
Christmasberry	oak	trumpetcreeper
creosotebush*	persimmon	Virginia creeper
cucumbertree	pine	waxmyrtle
dogwood*	poison ivy	wild plum*
eastern red cedar*	poplar	willow
elderberry	puncturevine	witchazel
elm	raspberry	yaupon*

***Suppression**

Remarks: Apply when weeds and brush are actively growing; repeat as needed. Do not apply more than 2 gal. WS/A per season. Do not apply through any type of irrigation system. Do not graze dairy animals within 21 days of applying 1 gal. WS; 40 days for 2 gal. WS. Remove meat animals from treated areas 30 days before slaughter. Do not cut grass for hay within 51 days of applying 1 gal. WS; 70 days for 2 gal. WS.
Tank Mixes: Amitrol, asulam, bromacil, clorflurecol, chlorsulfuron, 2,4-D, 2,4-DP, dicamba, diquat, diuron, fosamine-ammonium, glyphosate, hexazinone, imazapyr, maleic hydrazide, mefluidide, metsulfuron, MSMA, paraquat, picloram, simazine, sulfometuron-methyl, tebuthiuron, triclopyr.

Signal Word/Toxicity Class: Caution.

♦-new product • PP-preplant • PPI-preplant incorporated • PRE-preemergence • POST-postemergence • SEQ-sequential • ae-acid equivalent • ai-active ingredient • DF-dry flowable
E/EC-emulsifiable concentrate • F/FL-flowable • DG/G/WG-dispersable granule • L/LC-liquid • SP/WSP-soluble packet • W/WP-wettable powder • WSB-water soluble bag

Weed Rhap — see 2,4-D

Weedar — see 2,4-D

Weedestroy — see 2,4-D

Weedmaster — see 2,4-D Combinations

Weedone — see 2,4-D

Noncropland

875 Brushkiller — see 2,4-D Combinations

120 Herbicide — see MSMA

912 Herbicide — see MSMA

AAtrex — see atrazine

Accord — see glyphosate

Ansar 6.6 — see MSMA

Arsenal — see imazapyr

ASULAM

Asulox (3.34) (Rhone-Poulenc)
Riverside Asulam 3.3 (Terra)
Rate: 2.9-3.34 lb. ai/A
7-8 pt./A
Weeds: Grasses:

| crabgrass | paragrass | western bracken |
| johnsongrass | | |

Remarks: Apply postemergence.
Areas Of Application: Boundary fences; ditchbanks; fence rows; highway, pipeline, roadside, railroad, and utility rights-of-way; lumberyards; storage areas; industrial plant sites; warehouse lots.

Signal Word/Toxicity Class: Caution.
REI: 12 hr.

Asulox — see asulam

ATRAZINE

♦ **AAtrex 4L or AAtrex Nine-0 (WDG)** (Novartis)
♦ **Clean Crop Atrazine 4L or 90 WDG** (Platte)
Helena Atrazine 4L (Helena)
Rate: 2 lb. ai/A
4 pt. 4L/A
1.1 lb. WDG/A
Time: In the fall before ground freezes, or in the spring after thawing, but before established grasses greenup and weeds emerge.

Weeds: Broadleaf weeds:

| broomweed | sagewort | tumble mustard |
| little barley | | |

Grasses:

| cheat (chess) | downy brome | medusahead |

Remarks: Apply only once a year. Temporary discoloration or other injury to desirable grasses may occur. Do not cut or feed roadside grass hay, or allow livestock to graze treated areas.
Areas Of Application: Roadsides.
State Restrictions: For use in Colorado, Kansas, Montana, Nebraska, North Dakota, South Dakota, Wyoming.

Signal Word/Toxicity Class: Caution/III.
REI: 12 hr.

Banvel — see dicamba

BAREGROUND/TOTAL (Premixes)

Bareground BD (2% bromacil & 2% diuron & 40% sodium chlorate & 50% sodium metaborate) (Pro-Serve)
Total (2% bromacil & 2% diuron & 40% sodium chlorate & 50% sodium metaborate) (Terra)
Rate: Annual:
0.5-1 lb./100 sq. ft.
Perennial:
1-2 lb./100 sq. ft.
Weeds: Annual and perennial broadleaf weeds and grasses.
Remarks: Apply before or after plant growth begins. Use higher rates for long growing season, high rainfall, or deep-rooted perennials. Sodium metaborate for fire retardation. Keep animals off treated areas. Refer to label for directions and precautions.
Areas Of Application: Around farm buildings, fence lines, industrial sites, lumberyards, petroleum tank farms, rights-of-way, and other non-crop areas.

Signal Word/Toxicity Class: Danger/I.

BARESPOT (Premixes)

♦ **BareSpot Monobor-Chlorate (68% sodium metaborate & 30% sodium chlorate)** (Pro-Serve)
♦ **BareSpot Ureabor (66.5% sodium metaborate & 30% sodium chlorate & 1.5% bromacil)** (Pro-Serve)
♦ **BareSpot Weed & Grass (66.5% sodium metaborate & 30% sodium chlorate & 1.25% diuron)** (Pro-Serve)
Rate: 0.5-4 lb./100 sq. ft.
Weeds: Annual and perennial broadleaf weeds and grasses.
Remarks: Rate varies by location, weather, soil composition, and type of vegetation; refer to label. Apply anytime during growing season. Do not use near lawns, trees, shrubs or other desirable plants.
Areas Of Application: Around bleachers, bridge abutments, buildings, bunkers, buried cable closures, catwalks, cemeteries, compressor stations, cooling towers, cross connect boxes, ditchbanks, electrical generators, fence lines, fire hydrants, plugs or walls, fuel tanks, generating plants, guardrails, helo pads, highway & street markers, loading stations, lumberyards, microwave towers, pipelines, oil refineries, parking lots, pump decks, railroad lines & sidings, runway lights, runways, sign posts, storage & equipment yards, utility poles & substations, vacant lots, valves & manifolds, waste lagoons. BareSpot Monobor-Chlorate and BareSpot Weed & Grass can also be used under asphalt, concrete, gravel driveways, sidewalks or walkways.

Signal Word/Toxicity Class: Danger/I.

Barrage — see 2,4-D

BK 800 — see 2,4-D Combinations

Brash — see 2,4-D Combinations

Broadrange — see 2,4-D Combinations

9

Other Uses

NOTICE The information on these pages is for preliminary planning — not a guide for use. Be sure to follow the manufacturer's directions, notwithstanding information contained here. | For personal protective equipment and EPA registration numbers, please turn to page 70.

Broclean — see bromoxynil

Bromox — see bromoxynil

BROMOXYNIL

◆ **Broclean 2EC** *(Platte)*
◆ **Bromox 2EC** *(Micro Flo)*
Buctril (2EC), Buctril 4EC *(Rhone-Poulenc)*
Moxy 2EC *(Terra)*
Rate: 0.25-0.5 lb. ai/A
　　　 1-2 pt. 2EC/A
　　　 0.5-1 pt. 4EC/A
Weeds: Broadleaf weeds:

buffalobur	ivyleaf morningglory	spiny pigweed
burcucumber	knawel	tall morningglory
common groundsel	kochia	tall waterhemp
common ragweed	London rocket	tumble mustard
corn chamomile	mayweed	velvetleaf
corn gromwell	prostrate knotweed	Venice mallow
cowcockle	puncturevine	wild mustard
giant ragweed	redroot pigweed	wild radish
hemp sesbania	Russian thistle	yellow starthistle

Remarks: Do not apply through backpack or hand-held application equipment. Do not allow livestock to graze treated areas or feed treated plant material to livestock.
Areas Of Application: Noncropland and industrial sites.

- - - - - - - - - - - - - - -

Signal Word/Toxicity Class: Warning/II.
REI: 12 hr.

Brushmaster — see 2,4-D Combinations

Buctril — see bromoxynil

Bueno 6 — see MSMA

CAMPAIGN (Premix)

Campaign (1.2 lb./gal. glyphosate & 1.9 lb./gal. 2,4-D) *(Monsanto)*
Rate: 0.5-1.5 lb. ai/A
　　　 1.5-4 pt./A
Time: Apply when weeds have emerged and are vigorously growing.
Weeds: Annual, biennial and perennial broadleaf weeds such as:

bedstraw	crimson clover	partridgepea
buckhorn plantain	curly dock	spotted spurge
Carolina geranium	field bindweed*	trumpetcreeper*
common chickweed	henbit	vetch
common ragweed	hop clover	wild carrot
corn speedwell	horsenettle*	

Annual and perennial grasses:

annual bluegrass*	ryegrass	ryegrass*
bahiagrass	johnsongrass	tall fescue*
crabgrass	little barley	vaseygrass
foxtail		

Perennial woody plants and vine species:

greenbriar*	peppervine	raspberry*
honeysuckle		

Suppression

Remarks: Do not apply near 2,4-D sensitive crops such as cotton, grapes, tomatoes, and other desirable vegetation. Refer to label for use directions and precautions.
Tank Mixes: Oust.
Areas Of Application: Airports, dry canals, roadsides, highway rights-of-way, ditchbanks, dry ditches, parking areas, parks, etc.

- - - - - - - - - - - - - - -

Signal Word/Toxicity Class: Danger/I.

Chopper — see imazapyr

Cleanout — see 2,4-D Combinations

CLETHODIM

Envoy or Prism (0.94EC), Select (2EC) *(Valent)*
Rate: 0.1-0.25 lb. ai/A
　　　 13-34 fl. oz. 0.94EC/A
　　　 6-16 fl. oz. 2EC/A
Time: Postemergence. Apply to actively growing grasses.
Weeds: Grasses:

Amazon sprangletop	green foxtail	smooth crabgrass
annual bluegrass	itchgrass	southern crabgrass
barnyardgrass	johnsongrass	Texas panicum
bearded sprangletop	junglerice	volunteer cereals
bermudagrass	large crabgrass	wild oat
broadleaf signalgrass	quackgrass	wild proso millet
crowfootgrass	red rice	wirestem muhly
fall panicum	red sprangletop	witchgrass
giant foxtail	shattercane	woolly cupgrass
goosegrass	southwestern cupgrass	yellow foxtail

Remarks: Rate varies by grass species, stage, and geographical region. Grass crops such as corn, sorghum, wheat, and rice are highly sensitive to clethodim. Do not apply under stress conditions or if rainfall is expected in 1 hr. Do not apply more than 0.5 lb. ai/A (0.25 lb. ai/A on Long Island, NY) per season. Do not apply through any type of irrigation system. Do not graze treated fields or feed treated forage or hay to livestock. Refer to label for restrictions and precautions.
Areas Of Application: Rights-of-way including railroads, highways, roads, dividers, medians, pipelines, public utility lines, pumping stations, transformer stations, and substations. Around airports, electric utilities, commercial buildings, manufacturing plants, storage yards, rail yards, fence lines, and parkways.
State Restrictions: Not for use on Solano grass in the Vernal Lakes area of Solano County, California; wild rice in Hays County, Texas.

- - - - - - - - - - - - - - -

Signal Word/Toxicity Class: Warning/II.
REI: 24 hr.

CLOPYRALID

Stinger *(Dow AgroSciences)*
Rate: 0.1-0.5 lb. ae/A
　　　 0.25-1.33 pt./A
Weeds: Annual and perennial broadleaf weeds:

Canada thistle	jimsonweed	spotted knapweed
cocklebur	marshelder	sunflower
clover	Russian knapweed	vetch
diffuse knapweed	(suppression)	volunteer soybean
Jerusalem artichoke	sowthistle	

Remarks: Do not apply by air or through any type of irrigation system. Do not contaminate irrigation ditches or water used for irrigation or domestic purposes.
Tank Mixes: 2,4-D.
Areas Of Application: Noncrop areas including fence rows, around farm buildings, and equipment pathways.
State Restrictions: In California, do not apply more that 0.66 pt./A per growing season.

- - - - - - - - - - - - - - -

Signal Word/Toxicity Class: Caution/III.
REI: 12 hr.

Transline *(Dow AgroSciences)*
Rate: 0.1-0.5 lb. ae/A
　　　 0.25-1.33 pt./A
Weeds: Annual and perennial broadleaf weeds such as:

buckwheat	knapweed	sunflower
chamomile	ragweed	thistle
clover	smartweed	vetch

Remarks: Apply broadcast or as spot treatment to actively growing weeds. Do not apply by air. Do not apply in drought situations, to soils having rapid to very rapid permeability, where a shallow aquifer exists, or to soils containing sinkholes over limestone bedrock or fractured surfaces.
Areas Of Application: Rights-of-way, industrial sites, and noncrop areas.

- - - - - - - - - - - - - - -

Signal Word/Toxicity Class: Caution/III.
REI: 12 hr.

COTTON-AIDE HC

Cotton-Aide HC (cacodylic acid) *(Monterey)*
Rate: 8.125 lb. ai/A
　　　 2.5 gal./A
Weeds: Nonselective general weed control.

◆-new product • PP-preplant • PPI-preplant incorporated • PRE-preemergence • POST-postemergence • SEQ-sequential • ae-acid equivalent • ai-active ingredient • DF-dry flowable • E/EC-emulsifiable concentrate • F/FL-flowable • DG/G/WG-dispersable granule • L/LC-liquid • SP/WSP-soluble packet • W/WP-wettable powder • WSB-water soluble bag

Remarks: Do not use on crops grown for food or feed. Do not contaminate irrigation or domestic water supplies. Do not apply through any type of irrigation system.

Areas Of Application: Around buildings, storage yards, industrial sites, vacant lots, rights-of-way, fence rows, and drainage ditchbanks.

— — — — — — — — — — — — — —

Signal Word/Toxicity Class: Caution/III.

Credit — see glyphosate

CROSSBOW (Premix)

Crossbow (1 lb./gal. triclopyr & 2 lb./gal. 2,4-D) *(Dow AgroSciences)*

Rate: HV foliar through handguns:
1-1.5 gal./100 gal. total spray
Foliar broadcast (ground or helicopter):
1.5-4 gal./10-30 gal. total spray/A

Weeds: Woody plants:

alder	cherry (except black)	Russian olive
ash	elderberry	sassafras
aspen	elm	Scotch broom
birch	hazel	sumac
black locust	honeysuckle	sweetgum
blackberry	maple	sycamore
boneset	multiflora rose	tamarack
buckbrush	pine	tanoak
(suppression)	poison ivy	white oak
Ceanothus	poison oak	willow

Rate: Broadcast (ground or helicopter):
1.5 gal./10-30 gal. total spray/A

Weeds: Broadleaf weeds:

annual buttercup	goatsbeard	redroot pigweed
annual fleabane	goldenrod	Russian thistle
annual sowthistle	ground ivy	shepherdspurse
bedstraw	hairy galinsoga	spiny amaranth
bitter sneezeweed	hemp dogbane	sunflower
blueweed	hemp sesbania	sweetclover
broadleaf plantain	henbit	tall buttercup
bull thistle	horsenettle	tall ironweed
burclover	horseweed	tansy ragwort
burdock	kochia	tansymustard
Canada thistle	leafy spurge	thymeleaf spurge
chicory*	lespedeza	vetch
cinquefoil	marestail	western ironweed
cocklebur	marshelder	white clover
common	milkweed*	wild carrot
lambsquarters	mouseear chickweed	wild lettuce
common ragweed	musk thistle	wild mustard
curly dock	narrowleaf plantain	wild radish
dandelion	oxalis	wild violet
dogfennel*	pepperweed	woolly croton
field bindweed	perennial sowthistle	yarrow
field pennycress	pokeweed	yellow rocket
field pepperweed	purslane	

* Suppression

Remarks: Do not apply through any type of irrigation system.

Areas Of Application: Fence rows, nonirrigation ditchbanks, roadsides, industrial sites, and other noncrop areas.

State Restrictions: Refer to label for use restrictions in Arizona.

— — — — — — — — — — — — — —

Signal Word/Toxicity Class: Caution/III.

2,4-D - PHENOXY HERBICIDES

Annual and perennial broadleaf weeds controlled by 2,4-D include:

alder	dock	plantain
arrowhead	elderberry	pokeweed
bindweed	goldenrod	povertyweed
bitter wintercress	ground ivy	puncturevine
boxelder	hemp	purslane
buckbrush	hoary cress	rush
buckhorn	honeysuckle	Russian thistle
bull thistle	ironweed	shepherdspurse
bulrush	jimsonweed	sowthistle
burdock	lambsquarters	stinkweed
buttercup	locoweed	sumac
catnip	mallow	sunflower
chickweed	marshelder	vetch
chicory	mexicanweed	Virginia creeper
cocklebur	morningglory	wild garlic
coffeebean	mustard	wild lettuce
creeping jenny	parrotfeather	wild onion
curly indigo	pennywort	wild radish
dandelion	pigweed	willow

Albaugh Amine 4 (2,4-D amine) *(Albaugh)*
◆ **Riverdale 4 Amine IVM (2,4-D amine)** *(Riverdale)*
Riverside 2,4-D Amine 4 (2,4-D amine) *(Terra)*
Solution (WS) (2,4-D amine) *(Riverdale)*
Weedestroy AM-40 (2,4-D amine) *(Riverdale)*
Wilbur-Ellis Amine 4 (2,4-D amine) *(Wilbur-Ellis)*

Rate: 2-4 lb. ae/A
4-8 pt./A
1-2 WS packets (2 lb. 13 oz./packet)/A

Remarks: Apply on vigorous spring growth to early bloom stage. Noxious 2,4-D resistant perennials will require repeat treatments. For southern wild rose on roadsides and fence rows, use 8 pt. 4/100 gal. water + 4-8 oz. surfactant or 2 WS packets. Spray as soon as foliage is well developed (2 or more treatments may be required). For small areas of woody plants susceptible to 2,4-D, apply in 100 gal. water; thoroughly wet plants when in full leaf. For large areas of woody plants, brushkiller products suggested. Refer to label for directions, restrictions, and precautions.

Areas Of Application: Roadsides, vacant lots, drainage ditchbanks, fence rows, rights-of-way, and other noncrop areas.

State Restrictions: Wilbur-Ellis not registered in California.

— — — — — — — — — — — — — —

Signal Word/Toxicity Class: Danger/I.
REI: 48 hr.

Albaugh LV4 or LV6 Ester (2,4-D ester) *(Albaugh)*
Riverdale 6 Amine (2,4-D amine) *(Riverdale)*
Riverdale L.V. 4 or L.V. 6 (2,4-D ester) *(Riverdale)*
Wilbur-Ellis Lo Vol-4 or Lo Vol-6 (2,4-D ester) *(Wilbur-Ellis)*

Rate: 1-3 lb. ae/A
2-6 pt. 4/A
1.33-4 pt. 6/A
Wild onion, wild garlic:
2 lb. ae/100 gal. water
4 pt. 4 in 2 qt. kerosene or diesel oil/100 gal. water
2.66 pt. 6 in 2 qt. kerosene or diesel oil/100 gal. water

Remarks: Apply when annual broadleaf weeds are still young and growing vigorously; perennial and biennial weeds are actively growing and near bud stage but before flowering. For tansy ragwort and musk thistle, treat in rosette stage before bolting. For wild onion or garlic, apply 200-500 gal. spray/A in early spring and in the fall when young and actively growing. For southern wild rose on roadsides and fence rows, use 8 pt. 4 or 6 pt. 6/100 gal. water + 4-8 oz. surfactant and spray as soon as foliage is well developed; 2 or more treatments may be required. Refer to label for directions, restrictions, and precautions.

Areas Of Application: Roadsides, vacant lots, drainage ditchbanks, fence rows, rights-of-way, and other noncrop areas.

State Restrictions: Wilbur-Ellis not registered in California.

— — — — — — — — — — — — — —

Signal Word/Toxicity Class: Danger/I (amine); Caution/III (ester).
REI: Danger—48 hr.; Caution—12 hr.

Albaugh D-638 (2,4-D ester) *(Albaugh)*
Hi-Dep (2,4-D mixed amine) *(PBI/Gordon)*
◆ **Opti-Amine (4) (2,4-D amine)** *(Helena)*
Solve 2,4-D (2,4-D LV ester) *(Albaugh)*
Weed Rhap A-4D (2,4-D amine) *(Helena)*
Weed Rhap LV-6D (2,4-D ester) *(Helena)*
Weedar 64 (4) (2,4-D amine) *(Nufarm)*
Weedar IVM 44 (4) (2,4-D amine) *(Nufarm)*
Weedone 638 (2,4-D ester + acid) *(Nufarm)*
Weedone LV4 (2,4-D solventless ester) *(Nufarm)*
Weedone Lo Vol 6 (2,4-D ester) *(Nufarm)*

Rate: 1-4 lb. ae/A
2-8 pt. 4/A
1-3 lb. ae/A
2.66-8 pt. 638/A
1-6 lb. ae/A
1.33-8 pt. 6/A

Remarks: Apply when annuals are young and growing vigorously. Refer to label for further use directions and precautions.

Tank Mixes: Hi-Dep: Banvel, Tordon for control of leafy spurge in CO, ID, MT, MN, ND, NE, SD, WA, WY. Weedone LV4 and Lo Vol 6: Banvel, Garlon 3A, Garlon 4.

Areas Of Application: Airfields, roadsides, vacant lots, drainage ditchbanks, fence rows, industrial sites, golf courses, lawns, and other noncrop areas.

— — — — — — — — — — — — — —

Signal Word/Toxicity Class: Varies by formulation.
REI: Danger—48 hr.; Caution—12 hr.

9

Other Uses

NOTICE The information on these pages is for preliminary planning — not a guide for use. Be sure to follow the manufacturer's directions, notwithstanding information contained here. | For personal protective equipment and EPA registration numbers, please turn to page 70.

◆ **Barrage or Barrage HF (EC) (2,4-D ester)** (Helena)
Rate: 0.5-1.88 lb. ae/A
　0.8-3.2 pt./A
Remarks: Apply when weeds are small and actively growing.
Areas Of Application: Roadsides, medians, rights-of-way, vacant lots, utility installations, storage areas, fences, guardrails, lumber yards, industrial sites, airports, tank farms, and similar noncrop areas.

Signal Word/Toxicity Class: Caution/III.
REI: 12 hr.

◆ **Clean Crop Amine 4 (2,4-D amine)** (Platte)
Formula 40 (2,4-D mixed amine) (Rhone-Poulenc)
Rate: 1-2 lb. ae/A
　2-4 pt. /A
Remarks: Apply when weeds are young and actively growing. Deeprooted perennial weeds may require repeat application. For southern wild rose on roadsides and fence rows, use 8 pt./100 gal. water + 4-8 oz. surfactant; spray as soon as foliage is well developed (2 or more treatments may be required). Do not exceed 2 treatments per year on turf sites.
Areas Of Application: Cemeteries, golf courses, parks, airfields, roadsides, vacant lots, drainage ditchbanks.

Signal Word/Toxicity Class: Danger/I
REI: 48 hr.

◆ **Clean Crop Low Vol 4 or Low Vol 6 (2,4-D ester)** (Platte)
Rate: 1-2 lb. ae/A
　2-4 pt. 4/A
　1.33-2.66 pt. 6/A
　Wild onion, wild garlic:
　2 lb. ae/A
　4 pt. 4/A
　2.66 pt. 6/A
Remarks: Thoroughly wet all foliage to runoff. For wild onion or garlic. make 3 applications (fall-spring-fall or spring-fall-spring) starting in late fall or early spring.
Areas Of Application: Fencerows, roadsides, industrial sites, farm buildings and similar areas.

Signal Word/Toxicity Class: Caution/III.
REI: 12 hr.

Drl-Clean (2,4-D amine) (Riverdale)
Rate: 18-28 oz./A (5-10 9 oz. packets/1.13 A in 100 gal. water)
Weeds: Annual broadleaf weeds including:

alder	Virginia creeper	willow
honeysuckle		

Remarks: Retreat as necessary for control of regrowth and seedlings. Cut tall woody growth and spray suckers when 2-4 ft. high. Do not apply when temperature exceeds 90°F.
Areas Of Application: Airfields, drainage ditchbanks, fence rows, rights-of-way, roadsides, vacant lots, and other noncrop areas.

Signal Word/Toxicity Class: Danger/I.
REI: 48 hr.

Gordon's LV 400 (2,4-D ester) (PBI/Gordon)
Riverside 2,4-D LV4 (2,4-D ester) (Terra)
Rate: 3-4 lb. ae/A
　6-8 pt./A
Remarks: Spray brush up to 5-8 ft. high after spring foliage is well developed, wetting all parts of brush. Effective any time up to 3 weeks before frost as long as soil moisture is sufficient for active brush growth; less effective in midsummer. Oil or wetting agent may be added to spray.
Areas Of Application: Roadsides, vacant lots, drainage ditchbanks, fence rows, rights-of-way, and other noncrop areas.

Signal Word/Toxicity Class: Caution/III.
REI: 12 hr.

◆ **Saber (2,4-D amine)** (Platte)
Rate: 0.75-4 lb. ae/A
　1.5-8 pt./A
Remarks: Apply when weeds are young and actively growing. Use lower rates for small broadleaf weeds; higher rates for woody plants and dense stands of brush.
Areas Of Application: Drainage ditchbanks, rights-of-way, vacant lots, storage areas, fences, industrial sites, airports and similar noncropland areas.

Signal Word/Toxicity Class: Caution/III.
REI: 12 hr.

Savage (WSB) (2,4-D amine) (Platte)
Rate: Annual broadleaf weeds:
　0.95-1.9 lb. ae/A
　1-2 lb. WSB/A
　Perennial and biennial weeds:
　1.9-3.8 lb. ae/A
　2-4 lb. WSB/A
Remarks: Apply when weeds are young and actively growing. Do not apply to newly seeded area until grass is well established. Bentgrass, clover, legumes and dichondra may be injured.
Areas Of Application: Fencerows, hedgerows, roadsides, drainage ditches, rights-of-way, utility power lines, railroads, and other noncrop areas.

Signal Word/Toxicity Class: Danger/I.
REI: 48 hr.

2,4-D Combinations

875 Brushkiller (4.2S) (2,4-D & 2,4-DP & dicamba) (PBI/Gordon)
BK 800/SuperBrush (4.5S) (2,4-D & 2,4-DP & dicamba) (PBI/Gordon)
Brushmaster (2.3S) (2,4-D & 2,4-DP & dicamba) (PBI/Gordon)
Cleanout (1.1S) (2,4-D & 2,4-DP & dicamba) (PBI/Gordon)
Rate: 0.5-1 gal. 4.2S, 4.5S/100 gal. water
　1-2 gal. 2.3S/100 gal. water
　2-4 gal. 1.1S/100 gal. water
Weeds: Broadleaf weeds:

bedstraw	kochia	ragweed
bindweed	lambsquarters	sheep sorrel
black medic	leafy spurge	shepherdspurse
buckhorn	lespedeza	smartweed
burdock	mallow	speedwell
chickweed	morningglory	spurge
chicory	mustard	sunflower
clover	nettles	thistle
cocklebur	oxalis	trumpetvine
dandelion	peppergrass	velvetleaf
dock	pigweed	wild carrot
ground ivy	plantain	wild garlic
healall	poison ivy	wild lettuce
henbit	poison oak	wild onion
jimsonweed	purslane	yarrow
knotweed		

Brush:

ash	cottonwood	multiflora rose
aspen	dogwood	oak
birch	elm	pine
black cherry	gooseberry	spruce
black locust	honeylocust	sumac
brambles	honeysuckle	sycamore
buckbrush	kudzu	wild plum
cedar	maple	willow

Remarks: Foliar application: Apply high-volume full-cover spray at 100-300 gal./A, wetting all leaves, stems, and root collars of woody plants.
Areas Of Application: Airports, fairgrounds, roadsides, rights-of-way, field storage areas, industrial sites, drainage ditchbanks, firebreaks, fence rows.

Signal Word/Toxicity Class: Varies by formulation.

◆ **Brash (2.87 lb./gal. 2,4-D & 1 lb./gal. dicamba)** (Terra)
Weedmaster (2.87 lb./gal. 2,4-D & 1 lb./gal. dicamba) (BASF)
Rate: 0.25-2 lb. ai/A
　0.5-4 pt./A
Weeds: Annual and perennial broadleaf weeds and woody plants:

annual fleabane	curly dock	poison ivy
annual mustard	dogfennel	poorjoe
bitterweed	eastern persimmon	prickly lettuce
black knapweed*	elderberry*	red sorrel
broomweed	field bindweed	redroot pigweed
buckeye	field pennycress	redvine*
buffalobur	hairy honeysuckle	Russian knapweed*
bull thistle	hairy vetch	silverleaf nightshade
burclover	henbit	southern dewberry
burdock	knotweed	spotted beebalm
buttercup	kochia	spotted knapweed
Canada thistle*	late eupatorium	sunflower
Carolina horsenettle	leafy spurge*	tall morningglory
chicory	mesquite	tansy ragwort
common chickweed	Missouri goldenrod	Texas groundsel
common cocklebur	musk thistle	velvetleaf
common dandelion	Pennsylvania	Virginia pepperweed
common goldenweed	smartweed	woolly croton
common	perennial sowthistle*	yankeeweed
lambsquarters	plains coreopsis	yellow starthistle

　* *Suppression*

◆-new product • PP-preplant • PPI-preplant incorporated • PRE-preemergence • POST-postemergence • SEQ-sequential • ae-acid equivalent • ai-active ingredient • DF-dry flowable
E/EC-emulsifiable concentrate • F/FL-flowable • DG/G/WG-dispersable granule • L/LC-liquid • SP/WSP-soluble packet • W/WP-wettable powder • WSB-water soluble bag

Remarks: Apply when weeds are actively growing. Add adjuvant or other spray additives. Refer to label for restrictions and precautions.
Areas Of Application: Fence rows and around farm buildings.

Signal Word/Toxicity Class: Danger/I.
REI: 48 hr.

Broadrange (2,4-D & 2,4-DP ester) (Wilbur-Ellis)
Rate: Foliage stem treatment:
1-1.5 gal./100 gal. water
Basal, cut surface, frill:
3-4 gal./100 gal. oil
Weeds: Woody plants and brush including:

alder	fir	raspberry
ash	gooseberry	red elder
aspen	greenbriar	salmonberry
birch	gum	sand sagebrush
black cherry	hemlock	sassafras
black locust	honeysuckle	serviceberry
blackberry	kudzu	shinnery oak
blackjack oak	locust	snowberry
boxelder	manzanita	spicebrush
brambles	maple	spruce
buckbrush	multiflora rose	sumac
Ceanothus	oak	sweetgum
chamise	osageorange	sycamore
coffeeberry	palmetto	Virginia creeper
currant	persimmon	wild cherry
dewberry	pine	wild grape
dogwood	poison ivy	wild oak
elderberry	poison oak	willow
elm	poplar	winged elm

Remarks: For foliage stem treatment, apply 200-600 gal. spray/A to stems and foliage from time foliage is completely matured until plants start to go dormant. For basal bark, frill, or cut surface, apply any time of year.
Areas Of Application: Fence rows, highways, utility and railroad rights-of-way, and drainage ditchbanks.

Rate: Aerial spray:
2-4 qt./A in 100 gal. water
Weeds: Solid stands of mixed brush.
Remarks: Apply 3-12 gal. volume/A; 1-4 qt. fuel oil may be added.
Areas Of Application: Utility rights-of-way.
State Restrictions: Wilbur-Ellis not registered in California.

Signal Word/Toxicity Class: Caution.
REI: 12 hr.

◆ Clean Crop DPD Ester Brush Killer (2,4-D & 2,4-DP ester) (Platte)
Rate: High volume spray:
1-1.5 gal./100 gal. water
Basal, cut surface, frill treatment:
3-4 gal./100 gal. oil
Weeds: Broadleaf weeds and woody plants including:

alder	elderberry	poison oak
aspen	elm	poplar
birch	hawthorn	sagebrush
boxelder	hickory	sassafras
buckbrush	honeysuckle	sumac
cherokee rose	locust	sweetgum
chokecherry	mulberry	wild cherry
cottonwood	oak	wild grape
elder	osageorange	wild plum

Remarks: High volume spray: Apply 200-600 gal. spray/A any time of year as full cover spray; thoroughly wet foliage and bark. Basal treatment: Apply to bark around trunk and stems to a height of 12-15"; spray thoroughly to point of runoff at soil line. Stump treatment: Thoroughly wet both side and top of freshly cut stumps. Frill treatment: Apply to overlapping cuts made in bark around tree trunk as close to the ground as possible. Repeat as needed.
Areas Of Application: Fence rows, highway, utility, pipeline or railroad rights-of-way.

Signal Word/Toxicity Class: Caution

Dissolve (WS) (2,4-D amine & 2,4-DP & MCPP) (Riverdale)
PAR-3 (2,4-D amine & 2,4-DP & MCPP) (Riverdale)
Triamine (2,4-D amine & 2,4-DP & MCPP) (Riverdale)
Tri-Ester (2,4-D ester & 2,4-DP & MCPP) (Riverdale)
Rate: Broadleaf weeds:
2.5 lb. WS packet/50-300 gal. water
0.33-1 gal. amine/50-300 gal. water
0.5-1 gal. ester/100-300 gal. water
Woody plants:
2 or 3-2.5 lb. WS packets/100 gal. water
1-1.5 gal./100 gal. water

Weeds: Broadleaf weeds and woody plants including:

alder	dogfennel	purslane
bindweed	elderberry	ragweed
black medic	Florida pusley	smartweed
broomweed	kochia	sorrel
bull thistle	lambsquarters	sowthistle
burdock	mustard	spurge
buttercup	nettle	sunflower
Canada thistle	oxalis	sweet clover
carpetweed	pepperweed	wild carrot
chickweed	pigweed	wild lettuce
clover	plantains	wild radish
cocklebur	poison hemlock	woollyleaf bursage
daisy fleabane	pokeweed	yarrow
dandelion	primrose	yellow rocket
dock		

Remarks: For broadleaf weeds, apply when plants come into full leaf to when plants start to go dormant. For woody plants, apply to stems and foliage from time foliage is completely matured until plants start to go dormant.
Areas Of Application: Roadsides (including aprons and guardrails), rights-of-way, and other similar noncrop areas.

Signal Word/Toxicity Class: Varies by formulation.

◆ Patron 170 (2,4-D & 2,4-DP) (Riverdale)
Rate: High volume:
1-1.5 gal./100 gal. water
Spot treatment:
8 oz./5 gal. water
Weeds: Woody plants and brush including:

alder	fir	poplar
ash	gooseberry	raspberry
aspen	greenbriar	red elder
birch	gum	salmonberry
black cherry	hemlock	sand sagebrush
black locust	honeysuckle	sassafras
blackberry	kudzuvine	serviceberry
box elder	locust	snowberry
brambles	manzanita	spicebrush
buckbrush	maple	spruce
Ceanothus	multiflora rose	sumac
chamise	oak	sweetgum
coffeeberry	osageorange	sycamore
currant	palmetto	Virginia creeper
dewberry	persimmon	wild cherry
dogwood	pine	wild grape
elderberry	poison ivy	wild rose
elm	poison oak	willow

Remarks: Wet brush, stems, and foliage thoroughly. Do not apply through any type of irrigation system. Avoid drift that might injure desirable plants.
Tank Mixes: Banvel to control mixed brush.
Areas Of Application: Utility rights-of-way, highways, drainage ditchbanks, fence rows, golf courses, athletic fields, parks and similar noncrop areas.

Signal Word/Toxicity Class: Caution.

DIBRO 2 + 2 (Premix)
◆ DiBro 2 + 2 (2% bromacil & 2% diuron) (Riverdale)
Rate: 8-16 lb. ai./A
200-400 lb./A
Weeds: Annual and perennial weeds and grasses.
Remarks: Apply to ground by spreader. Do not apply on or near valuable woody or herbaceous plants. Do not use on cropland or land to be used for subsequent cropping.
Areas Of Application: Rights-of-way for pipeline, utility, highway and railroad; industrial areas such as airports, petroleum tank farms, lumberyards and plant sites.

Signal Word/Toxicity Class: Caution.

DICAMBA
Banvel (WS) (DMA salt of dicamba) (BASF)
◆ Sterling (WS) (DMA salt of dicamba) (Terra)
Rate: Annuals:
0.25-0.75 lb. ai/A
0.5-1.5 pt. WS/A
Biennials:
0.25-1.5 lb. ai/A
0.5-3 pt. WS/A
Perennials, woody brush and vines:
0.5-2 lb. ai/A
1-4 pt. WS/A

9

Other Uses

NOTICE The information on these pages is for preliminary planning — not a guide for use. Be sure to follow the manufacturer's directions, notwithstanding information contained here. | For personal protective equipment and EPA registration numbers, please turn to page 70.

Weeds: Annual, biennial, and perennial broadleaf weeds:

burdock	kochia	Russian thistle
Canada thistle	leafy spurge	tansy ragwort
field bindweed	pigweed	

Woody brush and vine species including:

ash	fringed sagebrush	multiflora rose
aspen	honeysuckle	sumac
blackberry	huisache	tarbush
blackgum	kudzu	trumpetcreeper
creosotebush	Macartney rose	willow
dewberry	mesquite	yaupon
eastern persimmon		

Remarks: Apply when weeds are actively growing. Retreat as needed, but do not exceed 4 pt./A during growing season.

Areas Of Application: Noncrop areas such as fence rows, roadways, wasteland, and rights-of-way.

– – – – – – – – – – – – – –

Rate: Cut surface treatment:
1 part product/1-3 parts water

Weeds: Woody brush and trees such as:

ash	cedar	serviceberry
aspen	elm	sycamore
basswood	hickory	

Remarks: Use lower dilution for hard-to-control species. Frill or girdle treatments should be made on a series of overlapping or continuous cuts using an axe. Stump treatment should be made by painting or spraying freshly cut surface with water mix. Adjacent bark should be thoroughly wet.

Tank Mixes: 2,4-D for more rapid foliar effects.

Areas Of Application: Noncrop areas such as fence rows and rights-of-way.

– – – – – – – – – – – – – –

Signal Word/Toxicity Class: Warning./II.
REI: 24 hr.

– – – – – – – – – – – – – –

◆ Vanquish (dicamba-DGA) *(Novartis)*

Rate: 0.25-2 lb. ai/A
0.5-4 pt./A

Weeds: Annual, biennial, and perennial broadleaf weeds, and woody brush and vine species.

Remarks: Do not treat irrigation ditches, water used for crop irrigation or domestic uses, or apply through any type of irrigation system.

Tank Mixes: Bromoxynil, 2,4-D, MCPA, MCPP. Refer to all labels for use directions and precautions.

Areas Of Application: Industrial areas, public utility facilities, rights-of-way.

– – – – – – – – – – – – – –

Signal Word/Toxicity Class: Caution.

Veteran CST (dicamba) *(Riverdale)*

Rate: Requires no dilution or mixing

Weeds: Woody brush and trees such as:

ash	cedar	hickory
aspen	dogwood	serviceberry
basswood	elm	sycamore

Remarks: Apply to freshly cut surface. For frill, girdle, or stump treatments, spray or paint freshly cut surface until wet. Frill or girdle treatments should be overlapping or continuous.

Areas Of Application: Noncrop areas such as fence rows, drainage ditchbanks, and rights-of-way.

– – – – – – – – – – – – – –

Signal Word/Toxicity Class: Caution/III.
REI: 24 hr.

– – – – – – – – – – – – – –

◆ Veteran 10G (dicamba) *(Riverdale)*

Rate: 0.05-0.2 lb. ai/1000 sq. ft.
0.5-2 lb. 10G/1000 sq. ft.

Weeds: Biennial and perennial broadleaf weeds:

artichoke thistle	lakeweed	skeletonleaf bursage
brackenfern	leafy spurge	tansy ragwort
bull thistle	perennial sowthistle	Texas blueweed
bur ragweed	povertyweed	woollyleaf bursage
Canada thistle	Russian knapweed	yellow starthistle
field bindweed	silverleaf nightshade	

Woody brush and vine species including:

autumn olive	kudzu	Siberian elm
creosotebush	saltcedar	sumac
eastern persimmon	sand plum	tarbush

Remarks: Rates varies by species. Apply in the spring before or during active growth. Sufficient moisture needed to activate product. Soil must not be frozen. Do not apply more than 20 lb./A per year.

Areas Of Application: Fence rows, roadways, wasteland, general farmstead, and similar noncrop areas.

– – – – – – – – – – – – – –

Signal Word/Toxicity Class: Warning.

DICHLOBENIL

Casoron 4G *(Uniroyal)*
Dyclomec 4G *(PBI/Gordon)*

Rate: Annual:
4-6 lb. ai/A
100-150 lb. 4G/A
Perennial:
6-8 lb. ai/A
150-200 lb. 4G/A
Nutsedge:
10-20 lb. ai/A
250-500 lb. 4G/A

Weeds: Broadleaf weeds:

artemisia	Florida purslane	redroot pigweed
aster	gisekia	rosarypea
bindweed	goosefoot	Russian knapweed
camphorweed	groundsel	Russian thistle
Canada thistle	henbit	sheep sorrel
carpetweed	horsetail	shepherdspurse
catsear	Jerusalem oak	smartweed
chickweed	knotweed	spanishneedles
citronmelon	lambsquarters	spurge
coffeeweed	leafy spurge	teaweed
cudweed	maypop	wild artichoke
curly dock	milkweed vine	wild aster
dandelion	minerslettuce	wild carrot
dogfennel	pineappleweed	wild mustard
eveningprimrose	plantain	wild radish
false dandelion	purslane	yellow rocket
fiddleneck	ragweed	yellow woodsorrel
Florida betony	red deadnettle	

Grasses and nutsedge:

annual bluegrass	natalgrass	Texas panicum
crabgrass	nutsedge	timothy
fescue	old witchgrass	wild barley
foxtail	orchardgrass	

Remarks: Apply late fall through early spring. Applications in the Northeast and upper Midwest should be made in early spring after ground has thawed. Do not apply if air temperatures are expected to exceed 70°F within the following week. Nonselective in action and may destroy all types of vegetation. Apply only where complete plant control is desired. Treated area may be totally or partially nonproductive for one or more years.

Areas Of Application: Electric substations (equipment sales and storage areas), lumberyards (above-ground pipes and tanks), nonsurface roadways (railroad and highway rights-of-way), petroleum installations (around buildings, along fence rows), fuel storage tanks, and under asphalt.

– – – – – – – – – – – – – –

Signal Word/Toxicity Class: Caution/III.
REI: 12 hr.

2,4-DP (DICHLORPROP)

◆ Patron DP-4 Ester *(Riverdale)*
Riverdale DP-4 Ester *(Riverdale)*

Rate: Foliar:
4 lb. ai/A
1 gal./A in 99 gal. water
Aerial utility rights-of-way:
8-12 lb. ai/A
2-3 gal./A in 12-30 gal. water (+ 1 gal. fuel oil—optional)
Railroad on-track:
12 lb. ai/A
3 gal./A in 25-50 gal. water

Weeds: Mixed woody brush including:

alder	oak	sandsage
black cherry	persimmon	sassafras
black locust	pine	spruce
blackjack oak	post oak	sumac
conifers	red maple	white oak
elm	red oak	willow
fir	sand shinnery oak	

Remarks: Apply to foliage and stems from time foliage is fully developed until plants begin to go dormant. Must be thoroughly wet to ground line. Refer to label for use directions and precautions.

Tank Mixes: May be tank mixed.

Areas Of Application: Rights-of-way, including railroad, drainage ditchbanks, firebreaks.

– – – – – – – – – – – – – –

Signal Word/Toxicity Class: Caution.
REI: 12 hr.

◆-new product • PP-preplant • PPI-preplant incorporated • PRE-preemergence • POST-postemergence • SEQ-sequential • ae-acid equivalent • ai-active ingredient • DF-dry flowable
E/EC-emulsifiable concentrate • F/FL-flowable • DG/G/WG-dispersable granule • L/LC-liquid • SP/WSP-soluble packet • W/WP-wettable powder • WSB-water soluble bag

DIQUAT DIBROMIDE

Diquat *(ZENECA)*
Rate: 0.5-1 lb. ai/100 gal.
2-4 pt./100 gal.
Weeds: Broadleaf weeds and grasses.
Remarks: Broadcast or spot treatment. Apply as needed. Use high rate when weeds are large or dense. Avoid contact with foliage of food crops, ornamental plants, or desirable vegetation. Do not apply through any type of irrigation system. Refer to label for restrictions and precautions.
Areas Of Application: Fence lines, farmyards, farm buildings, fuel storage areas, barrier strips, equipment areas, nonflooded portions of ponds, lakes, and drainage ditches on farms.

– – – – – – – – – – – – – – – –

Signal Word/Toxicity Class: Warning/II.
REI: 24 hr.

◆ **Reward or Reward LS** *(ZENECA)*
Rate: Broadcast:
0.25-0.5 lb. ai/A
1-2 pt./A
Spot spray:
0.5-1 lb. ai/100 gal. water
2-4 pt./100 gal. water
Weeds: For control of undesirable broadleaf and grassy weeds.
Remarks: Apply to young weeds since control decreases as weeds mature. Do not use on food or feed crops. Do not apply through any type of irrigation system. Refer to label for directions and precautions.
Tank Mixes: May be tank mixed with preemergent herbicides.
Areas Of Application: Rights-of-way, including railroad, highways, roads, dividers and medians, pipelines, public utility lines, including pumping stations, transformer stations and substations. Around electric utilities, commercial buildings, manufacturing plants, storage yards, railyards, fence lines and parkways, edges and nonflooded portions of ponds, lakes and ditches. Also around ornamental gardens, walkways, patios, beneath greenhouse benches, along driveways, and around golf courses.

– – – – – – – – – – – – – – – –

Signal Word/Toxicity Class: Warning/II.
REI: 24 hr.

Direx — see diuron

Dissolve — see 2,4-D Combinations

DIURON

Direx 4L or 80DF *(Griffin)*
Karmex DF *(Griffin)*
Rate: 4-12 lb. ai/A
4-12 qt. 4L/A (1-3.75 gal.)
5-15 lb. DF, 80DF/A
Weeds: Annual weeds.
Remarks: Add 1 qt. surfactant/100 gal. spray mixture for established weeds. Refer to label for detailed use in irrigation ditches. Higher rates for use on perennial grass and herbaceous weeds. Deep-rooted perennials may require retreatment.
Areas Of Application: Railroad, highway, utility, and pipeline rights-of-way, petroleum tank farms, lumberyards, storage areas, industrial plant sites, around farm buildings.

– – – – – – – – – – – – – – – –

Signal Word/Toxicity Class:
Warning/II (Direx DF); Caution/III (Direx 4L, Karmex).
REI: 12 hr.

◆ **Diuron 80 WDG** *(Platte)*
Drexel Diuron 4L or 80 *(Drexel)*
Riverside Diuron 4L or 80DF *(Terra)*
Rate: Annual weeds:
4-16 lb. ai/A
1-3.75 gal. 4L/A
5-20 lb. 80, 80DF/A
Perennial weeds:
16-48 lb. ai/A
4-11.25 gal. 4L/A
20-60 lb. 80, 80DF/A
Weeds: Broadleaf weeds:

horsenettle	ragweed	thistle
morningglory		

Grasses:

guineagrass	pangolagrass	quackgrass
johnsongrass		

Remarks: Refer to label for detailed use in irrigation ditches. Deep-rooted perennials may require retreatment. Do not use in the presence of valuable plants. Use only where bare ground is not objectionable.
Areas Of Application: Utility, highway, pipeline, and railroad rights-of-way, irrigation and drainage ditches, lumberyards, petroleum tank farms, storage areas, industrial plant sites, and around farm buildings.

– – – – – – – – – – – – – – – –

Signal Word/Toxicity Class: Caution/III.
REI: 12 hr.

Drexar 530 — see MSMA

Dri-Clean — see 2,4-D

DSMA

◆ **Clean Crop DSMA Plus (3.6L) (+ surfactant)** *(Platte)*
Drexel DSMA Liquid (3.6L) or Slurry (WS) (+ surfactant) *(Drexel)*
◆ **Dry DSMA 63SG** *(Luxembourg-Pamol)*
DSMA 4 LB (4L) or Liquid DSMA (3.6L) (+ surfactant) *(Helena)*
Rate: 5 lb. 63SG/50 gal. water
1-2 gal. 3.6L/100 gal. water
0.5-1 gal. WS/100 gal. water
1 gal. 4L/40 gal water
Weeds: Broadleaf weeds, grasses and sedges:

cocklebur	nutsedge	ragweed
dallisgrass	puncturevine	sandbur
johnsongrass		

Remarks: Add surfactant for Helena 4L and 63SG. Spray unwanted vegetation thoroughly to just short of runoff. If regrowth occurs, reapply as required.
Areas Of Application: Drainage ditchbanks, rights-of-way, storage yards, and similar noncrop areas.

– – – – – – – – – – – – – – – –

Signal Word/Toxicity Class: Caution/III.
REI: 12 hr.

Dyclomec — see dichlobenil

Envoy — see clethodim

ESCORT

Escort (DF) (metsulfuron methyl) *(DuPont)*
Rate: 0.3-2 oz. DF/A
Weeds: Broadleaf weeds:

aster	common yarrow	plantain
bahiagrass	crown vetch	Russian thistle
bitter sneezeweed	curly dock	scouringrush
blackberry	dandelion	sweet clover
blackeyed susan	dogfennel	tansymustard
broom snakeweed	field bindweed*	treacle mustard
broomweed	flixweed	tumble mustard
buckhorn plantain	goldenrod	white clover
bull thistle	gumweed	wild carrot
Canada thistle*	henbit	wild lettuce
chicory	kudzu (3-4 oz.)	woodsorrel
common chickweed	marestail	yankeeweed
common mullein	multiflora rose	

* Suppression

Remarks: Nonselective control. Not for use on bahiagrass. May be used at low rates to selectively control annual broadleaf weeds in rough turf and native perennial rangeland grasses. Kochia, Russian thistle, and prickly lettuce may be resistant (biotypes). Apply any time except when ground is frozen. No grazing restrictions for up to 0.75 oz. 60DF/A.
Tank Mixes: Tank mix combinations or sequential treatments of other registered herbicides are recommended; refer to label for restrictions.
Areas Of Application: Airports, highways, roadsides, utility, pipeline, and railroad rights-of-way, petroleum tank farms, plant sites, and other noncrop areas.
State Restrictions: Use restricted to railroad rights-of-way in Montana, North Dakota, and South Dakota. Not for use in California and Alamosa, Costilla, Conejos, Rio Grande and Saguache counties in Colorado.

– – – – – – – – – – – – – – – –

Signal Word/Toxicity Class: Caution.
REI: 4 hr.

9

Other Uses

EVIK

Evik DF (ametryn) *(Novartis)*
Rate: 1-2 lb. ai/A
1.25-2.5 lb. DF/A
Weeds: Broadleaf weeds:

annual sowthistle	lambsquarters	smartweed
cocklebur	morningglory	swinecress
common chickweed	paleseed plantain	velvetleaf
Florida pusley	pigweed	wild mustard
henbit	ragweed	

Grasses and sedges:

barnyardgrass	goosegrass	shattercane
crabgrass	green foxtail	signalgrass
fall panicum	itchgrass	Texas panicum
giant foxtail	nutsedge	yellow foxtail

Remarks: Apply to emerged actively growing weeds. Add surfactant. Do not exceed 7.5 lb. DF/A per year. Do not plant desirable plants in treated area for one year.
Areas Of Application: Industrial sites, railroad rights-of-way, lumberyards, petroleum tank farms, etc.

— — — — — — — — — —

Signal Word/Toxicity Class: Caution.
REI: 12 hr.

FLUAZIFOP-P-BUTYL

Fusilade DX or II *(ZENECA)*
Rate: 0.25-0.375 lb. ai/A
1-1.5 pt. DX, II/A
Weeds: Annual and perennial grasses including:

barnyardgrass	johnsongrass	southern sandbur
bermudagrass	(rhizome, seedling)	southwestern
broadleaf signalgrass	junglerice	cupgrass
fall panicum	kikuyugrass	Texas panicum
field sandbur	large crabgrass	tropical crabgrass
giant foxtail	prairie cupgrass	volunteer cereals
goosegrass	quackgrass	wild oat
green foxtail	red rice	wild proso millet
guineagrass	shattercane	wirestem muhly
(seedling)	smooth crabgrass	witchgrass
Italian ryegrass	sorghum-almum	woolly cupgrass
itchgrass	southern crabgrass	yellow foxtail

Remarks: Rate varies by geographic area and grass species. Add crop oil concentrate or nonionic surfactant. Do not apply through any type of irrigation system. Do not graze treated areas. Refer to label for specific directions, restrictions, and precautions.
Areas Of Application: Nonfood areas.
State Restrictions: Refer to label for geographical regions.

— — — — — — — — — —

Signal Word/Toxicity Class: Caution.
REI: 12 hr.

Fusilade — see fluazifop-P-butyl

FUSION (Premix)

◆ **Fusion (2 lb./gal. fluazifop-P-butyl & 0.56 lb./gal. fenoxaprop-P-ethyl)**
(ZENECA)
Rate: 7-9 fl. oz./A
Weeds: Annual and perennial grasses:

barnyardgrass	junglerice	southwestern
bermudagrass	large crabgrass	cupgrass
broadleaf signalgrass	perennial ryegrass	tall fescue
downy brome	quackgrass	Texas panicum
fall panicum	red rice	tropical crabgrass
fescue	roughstalk bluegrass	volunteer cereals
field sandbur	shattercane	wild oat
giant foxtail	smooth brome	wild proso millet
goosegrass	smooth crabgrass	wirestem muhly
green foxtail	sorghum-almum	witchgrass
itchgrass	southern crabgrass	woolly cupgrass
johnsongrass	southern sandbur	yellow foxtail
(rhizome, seedling)		

Remarks: Add crop oil concentrate or nonionic surfactant. Refer to label for specific directions, restrictions, and precautions.
Tank Mixes: 2,4-D, Escort, Garlon, Telar.
Areas Of Application: Highway and roadside rights-of-way.

— — — — — — — — — —

Signal Word/Toxicity Class: Caution.
REI: 24 hr.

GALLERY

Gallery 75DF (isoxaben) *(Dow AgroSciences)*
Rate: 0.5-1 lb. ai/A
0.66-1.33 lb. 75DF/A
Weeds: Broadleaf weeds:

annual sowthistle	cudweed	prostrate spurge
bittercress	dogfennel	redmaids rockpurslane
black mustard	green tansymustard	redstem filaree
black nightshade	hairy galinsoga	shepherdspurse
blackleaved fleabane	henbit	sibara
bracted plantain	horseweed (marestail)	slender plantain
buckhorn plantain	ladysthumb	southern brassbuttons
Carolina geranium	lambsquarters	spotted spurge
coast fiddleneck	London rocket	thymeleaf speedwell
common chickweed	mouseear chickweed	velvetleaf
common groundsel	pennywort	white clover
common purslane	pigweed	whitestem filaree
common ragweed	pineappleweed	wild celery
common sowthistle	prickly lettuce	wild mustard
creeping woodsorrel	prostrate knotweed	yellow woodsorrel

Remarks: Apply in late summer to early fall, or in early spring before weeds germinate. Do not apply through any type of irrigation system.
Areas Of Application: Industrial sites, utility substations, highway guard rails, sign posts, and delineators.

— — — — — — — — — —

Signal Word/Toxicity Class: Caution/III.
REI: 12 hr.

Garlon — see triclopyr

GLUFOSINATE-AMMONIUM

Liberty nc (WS) *(AgrEvo USA)*
Rate: 0.5-1.5 lb. ai/A
2-6 qt. WS/A
Spot or directed application:
1.5-4 fl. oz. WS/gal. water
Weeds: Nonselective general broadleaf weed control:

annual sowthistle	jimsonweed	redroot pigweed
bindweed	kochia	Russian thistle
buffalobur	lambsquarters	shepherdspurse
burdock	leafy spurge	smartweed
Canada thistle	London rocket	tansymustard
chickweed	malva	velvetleaf
clover	marestail	vervain
common cocklebur	mugwort	Virginia copperleaf
curly dock	musk thistle	white heath aster
dandelion	nettle	wild buckwheat
dogbane (hemp)	nightshade	wild mustard
field gromwell	pennycress	wild onion
filaree	plantain	wild rose
fleabane	prickly lettuce	wild turnip
goldenrod	purslane	woodsorrel
horsetail	ragweed	yellow rocket

Grasses and sedges:

barnyardgrass	giant foxtail	sandbur
bermudagrass	goosegrass	shattercane
cupgrass	green foxtail	stinkgrass
crabgrass	johnsongrass (rhizome)	wild oat
dallisgrass	lovegrass	windgrass
fall panicum	nutsedge	yellow foxtail

Remarks: Rainfall within 4 hr. may necessitate retreatment. Avoid direct spray or drift with green tissue of desirable vegetation. Do not apply by air or through any type of irrigation system.
Tank Mixes: Arsenal, Barricade, Gallery, Pendulum, Surflan, Vanquish.
Areas Of Application: Ditchbanks, fence lines, highways, parking lots, tank farms, utility rights-of-way, and other public and industrial areas.

— — — — — — — — — —

Signal Word/Toxicity Class: Warning/II.

GLYPHOSATE

Accord (4WS) *(Monsanto)*
Rate: Broadcast:
2-10 lb. ai/A
2-10 qt. 4WS/A
Low volume directed spray:
5-10% solution/A
Spray-to-wet:
0.75-2% solution/A

◆-new product • PP-preplant • PPI-preplant incorporated • PRE-preemergence • POST-postemergence • SEQ-sequential • ae-acid equivalent • ai-active ingredient • DF-dry flowable
E/EC-emulsifiable concentrate • F/FL-flowable • DG/G/WG-dispersable granule • L/LC-liquid • SP/WSP-soluble packet • W/WP-wettable powder • WSB-water soluble bag

Weeds: Woody brush, trees, and herbaceous weeds.
Remarks: Add nonionic surfactant.
Areas Of Application: Utility rights-of-way.

- - - - - - - - - - - - - - -

Signal Word/Toxicity Class: Caution/III.
REI: 4 hr.

◆ **Credit (4WS)** *(Nufarm)*
◆ **Glyfos or Glyfos X-tra (4WS)** *(Cheminova)*
Rattler (4WS) *(Helena)*
Roundup Custom (5.4WS) *(Monsanto)*
Roundup Original, Original RT, Ultra, Ultra RT (4WS) *(Monsanto)*
Rate: Annual weeds:
  0.38-1.5 lb. ai/A
  0.56-2.25 pt. 5.4WS/A
  0.75-3 pt. 4WS/A
  Perennial weeds:
  0.5-5 lb. ai/A
  0.75-7.5 pt. 5.4WS/A
  1-10 pt. 4WS/A
Weeds: Annual and perennial weeds and woody brush found in any part of the farmstead.
Remarks: Apply to actively growing weeds and grasses at recommended growth stage. Not a residual herbicide; follow with label-approved program for effective annual and perennial seedling weed control. Do not mix with other herbicides, allow spray or spray drift to contact desirable plants, or mow or till prior to treatment. Refer to label for directions, restrictions, and precautions.
Areas Of Application: Around building foundations, along and in fences, dry ditches and canals, along ditchbanks, shelterbelts, etc.

- - - - - - - - - - - - - - -

Signal Word/Toxicity Class: Varies by formulation.
REI: Warning—12 hr.; Caution—4 hr.

Rodeo (5.4WS) *(Monsanto)*
Rate: Boom equipment:
  1-5 lb. ai/A
  1.5-7.5 pt. 5.4WS/A
  Hand-held equipment:
  0.75%-1.5% solution
Weeds: Annual and perennial weeds and woody brush and trees.
Remarks: Rate varies by weed species. Do not exceed 7.5 pt./A in a single application. Always use nonionic surfactant. Does not control plants which are completely submerged or have most of their foliage under water. Do not apply within 1/2-mile of potable water intakes.
Areas Of Application: Terrestrial noncrop sites and/or aquatic sites within airports, golf courses, highways, roadsides, industrial plant sites, parking lots, parks, railroads, schools and similar sites.

- - - - - - - - - - - - - - -

Signal Word/Toxicity Class: Caution/IV.

Roundup PRO (4WS) *(Monsanto)*
Rate: Annual weeds:
  0.25-1.5 lb. ai/A
  0.5-3 pt. 4WS/A
  Perennial weeds:
  2-5 lb. ai/A
  4-10 pt. 4WS/A
Weeds: Annual and perennial weeds and woody brush and trees.
Remarks: May be used to trim and edge around objects and as spot treatment of unwanted vegetation. Repeat application to maintain bare ground.
Tank Mixes: Arsenal, Banvel, Barricade, 2,4-D, diuron, Escort, Karmex, Krovar I, Oust, Pendulum, Plateau, simazine, Surflan, Telar, Vanquish; refer to labels for restrictions. Banvel, 2,4-D, and Oust, may not be applied by air in California.
Areas Of Application: General noncrop areas such as airports, ditchbanks, dry canals, dry ditches, fencerows, golf courses, industrial sites, lumberyards, manufacturing sites, parking areas, parks, petroleum tank farms, pumping installations, railroads, recreational areas, roadsides, storage areas, utility substations, warehouse areas, and other public areas

- - - - - - - - - - - - - - -

Rate: Broadcast:
  4-10 lb. ai/A
  8-20 pt. 4WS/A (80 gal. spray solution/A)
  High volume spray-to-wet:
  0.75-2% solution/A
  Low volume spot treatment:
  5-10% solution/A
Weeds: Woody brush and trees.
Remarks: For broadcast, apply using boom-type or boomless nozzles.
Tank Mixes: Arsenal, Escort, Garlon 3A, Garlon 4, Tordon K.
Areas Of Application: Railroad rights-of-way.

- - - - - - - - - - - - - - -

Signal Word/Toxicity Class: Caution/III.
REI: 4 hr.

Gramoxone Extra — see paraquat

HEXAZINONE

Pronone 10G or MG *(Pro-Serve)*
Rate: Short-term control (up to 3 months):
  3-5 lb. ai/A
  30-50 lb. 10G, MG/A
  Season-long control:
  6-12 lb. ai/A
  60-120 lb. 10G, MG/A
Weeds: Broadleaf weeds:

camphorweed	heath aster	prickly lettuce
Canada thistle	honeysuckle	ragweed
chickweed	lantana	Spanish needle
clover	marestail	wild blackberry
dewberry	plantain	wild carrot
dogfennel		

Grasses and sedges:

bahiagrass	fescue	natalgrass
bermudagrass	fingergrass	smutgrass
bluegrass	foxtail	vaseygrass
broomsedge	guineagrass	

Rate: Short-term control (up to 3 months):
  3-5 lb. ai/A
  30-50 lb. 10G, MG/A
Weeds: Broadleaf weeds:

bindweed	filaree	pigweed
bouncingbet	fleabane	purslane
burdock	goatsbeard	smartweed
cocklebur	goldenrod	spurge
crown vetch	lespedeza	trumpetcreeper
curly dock	milkweed	wild oat
dandelion	mustard	wild parsnip
dogbane	oxalis	wild starthistle
fiddleneck		

Grasses and sedges:

barnyardgrass	crabgrass	paragrass
bromegrass	nutsedge	quackgrass
buffalograss	orchardgrass	ryegrass

Remarks: Apply between late winter and mid-spring. Do not apply to brush standing in water or near desirable trees or shrubs. Do not apply to inside of ditchbanks or inside of banks along waterways. Refer to label for use directions and precautions.
Areas Of Application: Railroad, highway, utility, and pipeline rights-of-way, petroleum tank farms, storage areas, industrial plant sites, drainage ditchbanks, and similar areas.

- - - - - - - - - - - - - - -

Signal Word/Toxicity Class: Caution.
REI: 24 hr.

Pronone Power Pellet *(Pro-Serve)*
Rate: 1-2 pellets/1" stem diameter
Time: Apply late winter to mid-spring.
Weeds: Brush:

aspen	huisache	red cedar
black cherry	junipers	small soapweed
blackgum	lotebush	snubbers
catclaw acacia	manzanita	sumac
deerbrush	mesquite	sweet gum
dogwood	multiflora rose	tallow
elm	myrtle	whitebrush
green ash	oak (except line oak)	whitehorn
hackberry	osageorange	wild cherry
hawthorn	persimmon	willow
hickory		

Remarks: Apply to soil within 3 ft. of root collar. For larger stems using more than 1 pellet, apply on opposite side of stem. For effective brush control and prevention of damage to desirable vegetation, do not apply to brush standing in water or near desirable trees or shrubs. Do not treat more than 300 1" stem equivalents/A per season. Refer to label for use directions and precautions.

- - - - - - - - - - - - - - -

Signal Word/Toxicity Class: Danger/I.
REI: 24 hr.

Velpar (SP) or L *(DuPont)*
Rate: Short term control—up to 3 months:
  1.8-4.5 lb. ai/A
  2-5 lb. SP/A
  2-5 lb. ai/A
  1-2.5 gal. L/A

9

Other Uses

Weeds: Broadleaf weeds:

bindweed	fiddleneck	oxalis
bouncingbet*	filaree	pigweed
burdock	fleabane	purslane
cocklebur	goatsbeard vine	smartweed
crown vetch	goldenrod	trumpet creeper*
curly dock*	lespedeza	wild oat*
dandelion	milkweed*	wild parsnip
dogbane*	mustard	wild starthistle

Grasses and sedges:

barnyardgrass	crabgrass	paragrass
bromegrass	nutsedge	quackgrass
buffalograss*	orchardgrass*	ryegrass

Rate: Season long control:
5.4-10.8 lb. ai/A
6-12 lb. SP/A
6-12 lb. ai/A
3-6 gal. L/A

Weeds: Broadleaf weeds

camphorweed	heath aster	prickly lettuce
Canada thistle*	honeysuckle	ragweed
chickweed	lantana	spanishneedles
clover	marestail	wild blackberry*
dewberry	plantain	wild carrot
dogfennel*		

Grasses and sedges:

bahiagrass*	fescue*	natalgrass
bermudagrass*	fingergrass	smutgrass
bluegrass	foxtail	vaseygrass
broomsedge	guineagrass	

* Suppression

Remarks: Apply as postemergent spray during active growth.

Areas Of Application: Railroad, highway, utility, and pipeline rights-of-way; petroleum tank farms, storage areas, industrial plant sites, drainage ditchbanks, and similar areas.

– – – – – – – – – – – – – – – –

Signal Word/Toxicity Class: Danger/I.
REI: 24 hr.

Hi-Dep — see 2,4-D

HYVAR

Hyvar X (WP) (bromacil) *(DuPont)*
Rate: 2.4-4.8 lb. ai/A
3-6 lb. WP/A

Weeds: Annual broadleaf weeds:

lambsquarters	ragweed	turkey mullein
puncturevine		

Annual grasses:

cheat	downy brome	ryegrass
crabgrass	foxtail	wild oat

Rate: 5.6-9.6 lb. ai/A
7-15 lb. WP/A

Weeds: Perennial broadleaf weeds:

dandelion	goldenrod	purpletop
dogfennel	plantain	wild carrot

Perennial grasses and sedges:

bahiagrass	broomsedge	nutsedge
bermudagrass	johnsongrass	quackgrass
bluegrass	natalgrass (redtop)	smooth brome

Remarks: Refer to label for registered tank mixes.

Areas Of Application: Railroad, highway, and pipeline rights-of-way; petroleum tank farms, lumberyards, storage areas, and industrial plant sites.

– – – – – – – – – – – – – – – –

Signal Word/Toxicity Class: Caution.
REI: 12 hr.

Hyvar X-L (WS) (bromacil) *(DuPont)*
Rate: 3-6 lb. ai/A
1.5-3 gal. WS/A

Weeds: Broadleaf weeds:

lambsquarters	ragweed	turkey mullein
puncturevine		

Grasses:

bromegrass	foxtail	ryegrass
cheatgrass	orchardgrass	wild oat
crabgrass		

Rate: 6-12 lb. ai/A
3-6 gal. WS/A

Weeds: Broadleaf weeds:

aster	goldenrod	purpletop
dandelion	plantain	wild carrot
dogfennel		

Grasses:

bahiagrass	broomsedge	redtop
bluegrass	quackgrass	smooth brome

Rate: 12-24 lb. ai/A
6-12 gal. WS/A

Weeds: Broadleaf weeds:

bouncingbet	dogbane	horsetail
brackenfern		

Grasses and sedges:

bermudagrass	dallisgrass	saltgrass
broomsedge	johnsongrass	vaseygrass

Rate: 4.5-10 lb. ai/A
2.25-5 gal. WS/A

Weeds: Brush:

oak	sweetgum	willow
pine		

Rate: 12-24 lb. ai/A
6-12 gal. WS/A

Weeds: Brush:

American elm	hackberry	winged elm
cottonwood	sumac	

Remarks: For brush control, use higher rate on absorptive soils. For drainage ditches, apply as basal (soil) treatment; applying undiluted with exact delivery handgun at 5-10 ml/stem 2-4" basal diameter. Direct spot treatment at base of brush (root collar area). When treating large stems and more than one delivery of solution is needed per stem, apply on opposite side of stem. For diluted spot treatment, mix 1 gal./A in 5 gal. water and apply 1-2 fl. oz./stem 2-4" basal diameter; wet base of stem to runoff.

Areas Of Application: Railroad, highway, pipeline rights-of-way; petroleum tank farms, lumberyards, storage areas, and industrial plant sites.

– – – – – – – – – – – – – – – –

Signal Word/Toxicity Class: Warning/II.

IMAZAPYR

Arsenal (AS) or 0.5 Granule *(American Cyanamid)*
Rate: 0.5-1.5 lb. ae/A
2-6 pt. AS/A
1-1.5 lb. ae/A
200-300 lb. 0.5G/A

Weeds: Broadleaf weeds:

broom snakeweed	Indian mustard	Russian knapweed
burdock	Japanese bamboo	saltbush
camphorweed	kochia	silverleaf nightshade
Carolina geranium	lambsquarters	smartweed
carpetweed	lespedeza	sorrel
clover	little mallow	sowthistle
cocklebur	milkweed	stinging nettle
common chickweed	minerslettuce	sunflower
common ragweed	mullein	sweet clover
dandelion	nettleleaf goosefoot	tansymustard
desert camelthorn	oxeye daisy	thistle
diffuse knapweed	pepperweed	western ragweed
dock	pigweed	wild carrot
dogfennel	plantain	wild lettuce
filaree	pokeweed	wild parsnip
fleabane	primrose	wild turnip
giant ragweed	puncturevine	woollyleaf bursage
goldenrod	purple loosestrife	yellow starthistle
hoary vervain	purslane	yellow woodsorrel
horseweed	rush skeletonweed	

Grasses:

annual bluegrass	feathertop	quackgrass
bahiagrass	fescue	reed canarygrass
beardgrass	foxtail	saltgrass
bermudagrass	goosegrass	sand dropseed
big bluestem	guineagrass	sandbur
broadleaf signalgrass	Italian ryegrass	smooth brome
Canada bluegrass	johnsongrass	timothy
cattail	Kentucky bluegrass	torpedograss
cheat	lovegrass	vaseygrass
cogongrass	orchardgrass	Virginia creeper
crabgrass	paragrass	wild barley
dallisgrass	phragmites	wild oat
downy brome	prairie cordgrass	wiregrass muhly
fall panicum	prairie threeawn	witchgrass

– – – – – – – – – – – – – – – –

◆-new product • PP-preplant • PPI-preplant incorporated • PRE-preemergence • POST-postemergence • SEQ-sequential • ae-acid equivalent • ai-active ingredient • DF-dry flowable E/EC-emulsifiable concentrate • F/FL-flowable • DG/G/WG-dispersable granule • L/LC-liquid • SP/WSP-soluble packet • W/WP-wettable powder • WSB-water soluble bag

Vines and brambles:

blackberry	kudzu	trumpetcreeper
dewberry	Macartney rose	Virginia creeper
field bindweed	morningglory	wild buckwheat
greenbriar	multiflora rose	wild grape
hedge bindweed	poison ivy	wild rose
honeysuckle	redvine	

Woody brush and trees:

American beech	hawthorn	rubber rabbitbrush
ash	hickory	Russian olive
baldcypress	maple	saltcedar
bigleaf maple	mulberry	sassafras
blackgum	oak	sourwood
boxelder	persimmon	sumac
cherry	poplar	sweetgum
chinaberry	privet	willow
Chinese tallow-tree	red alder	yellow poplar
dogwood	red maple	

Remarks: Biotypes of kochia have been identified that are not adequately controlled by Arsenal; use with other registered herbicides that have different mode of action. Control of kudzu requires minimum 75 gal./A total solution and may require repeat applications.

Areas Of Application: Railroad, utility, and pipeline rights-of-way; utility plant sites; petroleum tank farms; pumping installations; nonirrigation ditchbanks; fence rows; and storage areas.

- - - - - - - - - - - - - - -

Signal Word/Toxicity Class: Caution.

Arsenal Applicators Concentrate (AS) *(American Cyanamid)*
Rate: 0.375-1.25 lb. ai/A
0.75-2.5 pt. AS/A
Weeds: Same as for Arsenal.
Remarks: Rate varies by conifer species and purpose of application (site preparation, herbaceous weed control, conifer release). Apply during growing season after leaves have attained full flush up to color change in late summer or early fall. Some minor growth inhibition may be observed when release treatments are made during periods of active conifer growth. Degree of control on blackberries is species dependent. Kudzu control requires at least 75 gal./A total solution and may need repeat applications.
Areas Of Application: Forest roads, forestry site preparation, conifer release from woody and herbaceous competition, non-irrigation ditchbanks and the establishment and maintenance of wildlife openings.

- - - - - - - - - - - - - - -

Signal Word/Toxicity Class: Caution.

Chopper or Stalker (2EC) *(American Cyanamid)*
Rate: 0.125-0.188 lb. ae/1 gal. solution
8-12 fl. oz. 2EC/1 gal. solution
Weeds: Trees and vines such as:

ash	hickory	red alder
beech	madrone	red maple
bigleaf maple	maple	Russian olive
blackgum	mulberry	sassafras
boxelder	multiflora rose	sourwood
cherry	oak	sumac
chinaberry	persimmon	sweetgum
Chinese tallowtree	poplar	willow
dogwood	prickly wild rose	yellow poplar
hawthorn	privet	

Remarks: Apply in 1 gal. water, diesel oil, or penetrating oil (use water only when temperatures sufficient to prevent freezing). For Chopper, apply as cut stump, tree injection, frill or girdle, or as low volume basal bark treatment. For Stalker, apply as cut stump, cut stubble, thinline, or low volume basal bark treatment. Do not use on food or feed crops. Do not apply on ditches used to transport irrigation water. Do not use on lawns, driveways, tennis courts, etc.
Areas Of Application: Railroad, utility, highway, and pipeline rights-of-way, utility plant sites, petroleum tank farms, pumping installations, fence rows, storage areas, non-irrigation ditchbanks.

- - - - - - - - - - - - - - -

Signal Word/Toxicity Class: Caution.
REI: 12 hr.

◆ **Truce (0.5G)** *(Riverdale)*
Rate: 1-1.5 lb. ae/A
200-300 lb. 0.5G/A
Weeds: Broadleaf weeds such as:

bull thistle	common chickweed	giant ragweed
burdock	common ragweed	hoary vervain
camphorweed	dandelion	horseweed
Canada thistle	dock	Indian mustard
carpetweed	dogfennel	lambsquarters
clover	filaree	little mallow
cocklebur	fleabane	milkweed

Weeds: Broadleaf weeds: continued:

minerslettuce	purslane	western ragweed
mullein	silverleaf nightshade	wild carrot
nettleleaf goosefoot	smartweed	wild lettuce
oxeye daisy	sorrel	wild parsnip
pepperweed	sowthistle	wild turnip
pigweed	sunflower	woollyleaf bursage
plantain	sweet clover	yellow starthistle
pokeweed	tansymustard	yellow woodsorrel
primrose	Texas thistle	

Grasses such as:

annual bluegrass	fall panicum	prairie threeawn
bahiagrass	fescue	quackgrass
beardgrass	foxtail	sand dropseed
bermudagrass	goosegrass	sandbur
big bluestem	guineagrass	smooth brome
broadleaf signalgrass	Italian ryegrass	timothy
Canada bluegrass	johnsongrass	torpedograss
cattail	Kentucky bluegrass	vaseygrass
cheat	lovegrass	wild barley
crabgrass	orchardgrass	wild oat
dallisgrass	paragrass	wirestem muhly
downy brome	prairie cordgrass	

Remarks: Apply anytime during the year prior to weed emergence. Do not use on food or feed crops. Do not use on lawns, walks, driveways, tennis courts, or similar areas.
Areas Of Application: Railroad, utility, pipeline and highway rights-of-way, petroleum tank farms, pumping installations, fence rows, storage areas, and similar areas.
State Restrictions: Not for use in California.

- - - - - - - - - - - - - - -

Signal Word/Toxicity Class: Caution.

Karmex — see diuron

KRENITE S

Krenite S (fosamine) *(DuPont)*
Rate: 6-24 lb. ai/A
1.5-6 gal./A
Weeds: Brush/herbaceous plants:

American elder	hickory*	sweetgum
basswood*	leafy spurge*	sycamore
bigleaf maple*	loblolly pine	thimbleberry
birch	multiflora rose	tree-of-heaven
black cherry*	persimmon*	tuliptree*
black locust	pin cherry	(yellow poplar)
blackberry	quaking aspen	vine maple
blackgum*	red alder	Virginia pine
brackenfern	red maple*	water oak
chokecherry*	red oak	white ash*
eastern cottonwood	salmonberry	white oak
eastern white pine	sassafras*	wild grape
elm*	slippery elm	wild plum
field bindweed*	sourwood*	willow*
hawthorn*	sumac	winged elm*

* Suppression

Remarks: Applied to brush in summer or early fall. Susceptible treated plants fail to refoliate the following spring. For control of only a portion of plant, as in trimming, direct spray to thoroughly cover only section of plant to be killed. For field bindweed, apply after plants begin to bloom. Do not apply through any type of irrigation system.
Areas Of Application: Railroads, pipeline, utility and highway rights-of-way; reforestation areas, drainage ditchbanks, storage areas, industrial plant sites, and similar areas.
State Restrictions: Not for sale or use in Arizona or California.

- - - - - - - - - - - - - - -

Signal Word/Toxicity Class: Caution/III.

KROVAR (Premix)

Krovar I (DF) (40% bromacil & 40% diuron) *(DuPont)*
Rate: Annuals:
3.2-4.8 lb. ai/A
4-6 lb. DF/A
Perennials:
6.6-14.4 lb. ai/A
7-18 lb. DF/A
Hard-to-kill perennials:
15.2-24 lb. ai/A
19-30 lb. DF/A

9

Other Uses

Weeds: Broadleaf weeds:

annual nightshade	fleabane	purslane
annual sowthistle	Florida pusley	ragweed
bouncingbet	groundsel	sandspur
(hard-to-kill)	horseweed	shepherdspurse
chickweed	lambsquarters	spanishneedles
dogbane	pigweed	wild lettuce
(hard-to-kill)	pineappleweed	wild mustard
filaree	puncturevine	

Grasses (hard-to-kill):

barnyardgrass	johnsongrass	natalgrass
bermudagrass	(seedling)	nutsedge
crabgrass	junglerice	saltgrass
foxtail		

Remarks: Apply preemergence or in early stages of weed growth. Refer to label for directions, restrictions, and precautions.

Tank Mixes: May be tank mixed; refer to label.

Areas Of Application: Railroad, highway, and pipeline rights-of-way; tank farms, lumberyards, industrial sites, storage areas.

Signal Word/Toxicity Class: Caution.

REI: 12 hr.

Liberty nc — see glufosinate-ammonium

LINURON

Lorox DF *(Griffin)*

Rate: 1-3 lb. ai/A
2-6 lb. DF/A

Weeds: Broadleaf weeds:

carpetweed	galinsoga	pigweed
chickweed	lambsquarters	purslane
common ragweed	mustard	smartweed
Florida pusley	nettleleaf goosefoot	wild radish

Grasses:

barnyardgrass	crabgrass	foxtail
canarygrass	fall panicum	goosegrass

Remarks: For established weeds, add surfactant and apply as thorough coverage spray when daily temperatures exceed 70°F and before weed growth exceeds 8" in height. Refer to label for directions, restrictions, and precautions.

Areas Of Application: Roadsides and fence rows.

Signal Word/Toxicity Class: Caution.

REI: 24 hr.

Lorox — see linuron

MAGMA — see MSMA

MCPA

Albaugh MCPA Amine or Ester (4) *(Albaugh)*
◆ **Clean Crop MCP Amine 4 or Ester** *(Platte)*
◆ **Clean Crop MCP 2 Sodium (sodium salt)** *(Platte)*
Riverdale MCPA-4 Amine, L.V. 4 Ester (4), IOE (5.2) *(Riverdale)*
Solve MCPA Ester (4) *(Albaugh)*
Sword (5.2) *(Platte)*
Wilbur-Ellis MCPA Amine, Ester (4) or ◆ Sodium Salt *(Wilbur-Ellis)*

Rate: 0.75 gal. 4/A
0.5 gal. 5.2/A
1.5 gal. sodium salt/A

Weeds: Broadleaf weeds:

Canada thistle	meadow buttercup	whitetop
field bindweed (salt)	morningglory (salt)	

Remarks: Spray to wet weeds thoroughly when in bud to early bloom and again on fall regrowth. Refer to label for directions, restrictions, and precautions.

Areas Of Application: Fence rows, rights-of-way, roadsides.

State Restrictions: Wilbur-Ellis not registered in California.

Signal Word/Toxicity Class: Varies by formulation.

REI: Danger—48 hr.; Warning/Caution—12 hr.

Rhonox (LV ester) (4) *(Nufarm)*

Rate: 3 lb. ae/A
6 pt. 4/A

Weeds: Broadleaf weeds including:

bull thistle	dandelion	pigweed
common burdock	field pennycress	plantain
common cocklebur	giant ragweed	purslane
common	mustard	Russian thistle
lambsquarters	pepperweed	shepherdspurse
common ragweed	(except perennial)	yellow rocket

Remarks: Apply when annual weeds are young and actively growing and perennial and biennial weeds are actively growing and near bud stage but before flowering. Repeat if needed.

Areas Of Application: Fence rows, rights-of-way, roadsides, vacant lots, and similar areas.

Signal Word/Toxicity Class: Caution.

REI: 12 hr.

MONCIDE (Premix)

Moncide (3 lb./gal. MSMA & 1.25 lb./gal. cacodylic acid) *(Monterey)*

Rate: 4.25-8.5 lb. ai/A
1-2 gal./A

Weeds: Nonselective general broadleaf weed control:

chickweed	common ragweed	purslane
cocklebur	puncturevine	

Grasses and sedges:

barnyardgrass	goosegrass	nutsedge
crabgrass	green foxtail	sandbur
dallisgrass	johnsongrass	yellow foxtail

Remarks: If regrowth occurs, retreat as needed at 5-day intervals. Best results obtained on young, actively growing weeds at temperatures above 70°F. Avoid contact with desirable plants or fruit and food crops. Do not apply through any type of irrigation system.

Areas Of Application: Around buildings, industrial sites, storage yards, vacant lots, rights-of-way, roadways, fence rows and drainage ditchbanks.

Signal Word/Toxicity Class: Caution/III.

MONTAR

Montar (cacodylic acid) *(Monterey)*

Rate: 7.44 lb. ai/A
3 gal./A

Weeds: Nonselective general weed control.

Remarks: Do not use in vegetable gardens or around crops grown for food or feed. Do not contaminate irrigation or domestic water supplies. Do not apply through any type of irrigation system.

Areas Of Application: Around buildings, industrial sites, storage yards, vacant lots, rights-of-way, roadways, fence rows and drainage ditchbanks.

Signal Word/Toxicity Class: Caution/III.

Moxy — see bromoxynil

MSMA

120 Herbicide (6.6) *(Terra)*
912 Herbicide (6) (+ surfactant) *(Terra)*

Rate: 2 lb. ai/50 gal. water
4 pt./50 gal. water

Weeds: Broadleaf weeds:

cocklebur	pigweed	ragweed
morningglory		

Grasses and sedge:

crabgrass	goosegrass	nutsedge
dallisgrass	johnsongrass	watergrass

Remarks: Add 1 qt. surfactant to 120 Herbicide. Spray unwanted vegetation thoroughly to point of runoff. If regrowth occurs, reapply as necessary.

Areas Of Application: Drainage ditchbanks, rights-of-way, storage yards, and similar noncrop areas.

Signal Word/Toxicity Class: Caution/III.

REI: 12 hr.

◆-new product • PP-preplant • PPI-preplant incorporated • PRE-preemergence • POST-postemergence • SEQ-sequential • ae-acid equivalent • ai-active ingredient • DF-dry flowable E/EC-emulsifiable concentrate • F/FL-flowable • DG/G/WG-dispersable granule • L/LC-liquid • SP/WSP-soluble packet • W/WP-wettable powder • WSB-water soluble bag

Ansar 6.6 *(ZENECA)*
Bueno 6 (+ surfactant) *(ZENECA)*
  Rate: 2.5 lb. ai/50 gal. water
         3 pt. 6.6/50 gal. water
         1.875-2 lb. ai/40 gal. water
         2.5-2.66 pt./6/40 gal. water
  Weeds: Broadleaf weeds:

chickweed	Florida beggarweed	ragweed
cocklebur	jimsonweed	sicklepod
common purslane	morningglory	spurge
dandelion	pigweed	wild mustard
dayflower	puncturevine	woodsorrel
fiddleneck		

  Grasses and sedges:

bahiagrass	foxtail	nutsedge
barnyardgrass	goosegrass	sandbur
brachiaria	guineagrass	smooth crabgrass
broomsedge	johnsongrass	wild oat
dallisgrass	large crabgrass	witchgrass
fall panicum		

  Remarks: Spray to point of runoff. Adequate coverage and complete wetting of foliage important for effective control. If regrowth occurs, repeat as necessary. Do not apply through any type of irrigation system. Do not graze treated fields or feed treated foliage to livestock.
  Areas Of Application: Drainage ditchbanks, fence rows, rights-of-way, storage yards, and similar noncrop areas.

  Signal Word/Toxicity Class: Caution.
  REI: 12 hr.

Drexar 530 or MSMA 4 Plus (+ surfactant) *(Drexel)*
Drexel MSMA 6 Plus (+ surfactant) *(Drexel)*
  Rate: 2-5 lb. ai/100 gal. water
         4-10 pt. 4 Plus/100 gal. water
         6-12 pt. 6 Plus/100 gal. water
  Weeds: Broadleaf weeds, grasses and sedges including:

johnsongrass	nutsedge

  Remarks: Spray unwanted vegetation thoroughly to just short of runoff. If regrowth occurs, reapply as necessary.
  Areas Of Application: Noncrop areas such as drainage ditchbanks, rights-of-way, fence rows, storage yards.

  Signal Word/Toxicity Class: Caution/III.
  REI: 12 hr.

Drexel MSMA 6.6 *(Drexel)*
◆ **MAGMA (WSG)** *(Luxembourg-Pamol)*
◆ **Target MSMA 6.6 or TurfMate 6.6** *(Luxembourg-Pamol)*
  Rate: 2.5-5 lb. ai/100 gal. water
         3-6 pt. 6.6/100 gal. water
         2.34-4.68 lb. ai/100 gal. water
         4.25-8.5 lb./100 gal. water
  Weeds: Grasses and sedges:

barnyardgrass	johnsongrass	nutsedge

  Remarks: Add surfactant. Spray unwanted vegetation thoroughly to just short of runoff. If regrowth occurs, reapply as necessary.
  Areas Of Application: Noncrop areas such as drainage ditchbanks, rights-of-way, fence rows, storage yards.

  Signal Word/Toxicity Class: Caution/III.
  REI: 12 hr.

Helena MSMA (6.6) *(Helena)*
Helena MSMA Plus H.C. (6) (+ surfactant) *(Helena)*
  Rate: 2.5-6 pt./A (in 40-50 gal. water)
         1-2 fl. oz./1000 sq. ft. (in 5 gal. water)
  Weeds: Broadleaf weeds:

bullnettle	pigweed	ragweed
chickweed	puncturevine	wood sorrel
cocklebur		

  Grasses and sedges:

bahiagrass	green foxtail	sandbur
barnyardgrass	johnsongrass	smooth crabgrass
brachiaria	large crabgrass	watergrass
dallisgrass	morningglory	yellow foxtail
goosegrass	nutsedge	

  Remarks: For 6.6, add surfactant. Spray unwanted vegetation thoroughly to just short of runoff. If regrowth occurs, reapply as needed.
  State Restrictions: Use only as spot treatment in Florida.
  Areas of application: Drainage ditchbanks, rights-of-way, fence rows, golf course sand traps, storage yards, and similar areas.

  Signal Word/Toxicity Class: Caution/III.
  REI: 12 hr.

Helena MSMA Plus (4) (+ surfactant) *(Helena)*
  Rate: 2 lb. ai/40 gal. water
         4 pt./40 gal. water
  Weeds: Broadleaf weeds:

    cocklebur

  Grasses:

dallisgrass	johnsongrass	watergrass
goosegrass	nutgrass	

  Remarks: Spray unwanted vegetation thoroughly to just short of runoff. If regrowth occurs, reapply as needed.
  Areas of application: Drainage ditchbanks, rights-of-way, fence rows, storage yards, and similar noncrop areas.

  Signal Word/Toxicity Class: Caution/III.
  REI: 12 hr.

◆ **Target MSMA 6 Plus (+ surfactant)** *(Luxembourg-Pamol)*
◆ **TurfMate 6 Plus (+ surfactant)** *(Luxembourg-Pamol)*
  Rate: 1.875-2 lb. ai/40 gal. water
         2.5-2.66 pt./40 gal. water
  Weeds: Broadleaf weeds:

chickweed	pigweed	puncturevine
cocklebur		

  Grasses and sedges:

barnyardgrass	dallisgrass	nutsedge
brachiaria	goosegrass	sandbur
crabgrass	johnsongrass	

  Remarks: Apply when weeds are small and conditions favor active weed growth. Spray to point of runoff. If regrowth occurs, repeat if necessary.
  Areas Of Application: Drainage ditchbanks, fence rows, rights-of-way, storage yards, and similar noncrop areas.

  Signal Word/Toxicity Class: Caution/III.
  REI: 12 hr.

NORFLURAZON

Solicam DF *(Novartis)*
  Rate: 2-4 lb. ai/A
         2.5-5 lb. DF/A
  Weeds: Broadleaf weeds:

annual sowthistle*	flixweed	prostrate spurge
black mustard	Florida pusley*	puncturevine
camphorweed	goldenrod	purple cudweed
Carolina geranium	groundsel*	redmaids rockpurslane
common chickweed	hairy fleabane*	Russian thistle*
common	henbit*	shepherdspurse
lambsquarters*	horseweed*	silverleaf nightshade*
common mallow*	little mallow	spreading dayflower
common purslane*	London rocket	stinging nettle
common ragweed	marestail*	tumble mustard
dogfennel	pigweed*	velvetleaf
falsedandelion	pineappleweed	Virginia pepperweed
fiddleneck	plantain*	wild buckwheat
filaree	poorjoe*	

  Grasses and sedges:

annual bluegrass	feather fingergrass	quackgrass*
annual sedge	foxtail	sandbur
bahiagrass (seedling)	goosegrass	sixweeks grama
barnyardgrass	guineagrass	southwestern
bearded sprangletop	(seedling)	cupgrass
bermudagrass*	Italian ryegrass	tall fescue
broadleaf signalgrass	johnsongrass	Texas panicum
cheat	(rhizome*, seedling)	torpedograss*
crabgrass	natalgrass (seedling)	vaseygrass
crowfootgrass	nutsedge*	wild barley
(seedling)	orchardgrass*	wild onion
downy brome	pangolagrass	wirestem muhly*
fall panicum	(seedling)	witchgrass

  * Suppression

  Remarks: Apply before weeds germinate. Refer to label for use directions.
  Areas Of Application: Above high water lines, ditchbanks, driveways, equipment lots, fence lines, on-farm roads, turn rows.
  Tank Mixes: Arsenal, atrazine, Banvel, 2,4-D, diuron, Garlon, Gramoxone, Hyvar, Krovar, Oust; refer to label for use directions.
  State Restrictions: See label for use restrictions in Coachella Valley of California.

  Signal Word/Toxicity Class: Caution.
  REI: 12 hr.

9

Other Uses

NOTICE The information on these pages is for preliminary planning — not a guide for use. Be sure to follow the manufacturer's directions, notwithstanding information contained here.

For personal protective equipment and EPA registration numbers, please turn to page 70.

Noncropland

Opti-Amine — see 2,4-D

OUST

Oust (sulfometuron-methyl) *(DuPont)*

Rate: Arid areas:
1-1.5 oz. ai/A
1.33-2 oz./A

Weeds: Broadleaf weeds:

annual sowthistle	common speedwell	seaside heliotrope
black mustard	common yarrow	spreading orach
buckhorn plantain	curly dock	sunflower
burclover	prickly coontail	western ragweed
chickweed	prickly lettuce	whitestem filaree
common mallow		

Grasses:

annual bluegrass	Italian ryegrass	ripgut brome
barnyardgrass	jointed goatgrass	seashore saltgrass
cheat	red brome	signalgrass
foxtail barley	reed canarygrass	yellow foxtail
foxtail fescue		

Rate: 2.25-3.8 oz. ai/A
3-5 oz./A

Weeds: Broadleaf weeds:

annual sowthistle	hoary cress	Russian thistle
bouncingbet	kochia	sunflower
burclover	little mallow	sweet clover
Carolina geranium	mustard	tansy ragwort
common chickweed	oxeye daisy	tansymustard
common dandelion	pepperweed	tumble mustard
common speedwell	pigweed	vetch
common yarrow	prickly lettuce	wild carrot
crimson clover	purple starthistle	wild oat
dogfennel	ragweed	yellow rocket

Grasses (up to 6-12" in height):

alta fescue	fescue	red fescue
annual bluegrass	foxtail	reed canarygrass
annual ryegrass	(except green)	ripgut brome
annual sprangletop	Indiangrass	ryegrass
bahiagrass	Italian ryegrass	smooth brome
barley	Kentucky bluegrass	sprangletop
barnyardgrass	little barley	volunteer wheat
downy brome	red brome	

Rate: 4.5-9 oz. ai/A
6-12 oz./A

Weeds: Broadleaf weeds:

bedstraw	groundsel	musk thistle
Canada thistle	hemlock	poison ivy
curly dock	honeysuckle	redstem filaree
dewberry	horsetail	spanishneedles
fiddleneck	Jerusalem artichoke	turkey mullein
fleabane	kudzu	Virginia pepperweed
goldenrod	mayweed	wild blackberry

Grasses and sedges:

johnsongrass	yellow nutsedge

Remarks: Best results obtained if applied before or during early stages of weed growth. Requires extreme care in use near crops. Refer to label for application restrictions.

Areas Of Application: Noncrop areas such as railroad, roadsides, utility, and pipeline rights-of-way, utility plant sites, petroleum tank farms, pumping installations, fence rows, storage areas, airports, lumberyards, and similar noncrop areas.

- - - - - - - - - - - - - - -

Signal Word/Toxicity Class: Caution.
REI: 12 hr.

OUTRIDER

◆ **Outrider (WDG) (sulfosulfuron)** *(Monsanto)*

Rate: 0.75-1.33 oz. WDG/A

Weeds: Broadleaf weeds:

buttercup	flixweed	sand vetch
catchweed bedstraw	horseweed	shepherdspurse
common chickweed	ladysthumb	tarweed fiddleneck
common ragweed	mayweed chamomile	tumble mustard
common sunflower	pinnate	volunteer barley
field pennycress	tansymustard	wild mustard

Grasses and sedges:

bulbous bluegrass	johnsongrass	ripgut brome
cheat	purple nutsedge	roughstalk bluegrass
downy brome	quackgrass	yellow nutsedge
hairy chess		

Remarks: Best results obtained when weeds are in early stage of growth and are not disturbed 12 days before or after application.
Tank Mixes: Banvel, Campaign, 2,4-D, diuron, Escort, Garlon 3A, Karmex, MSMA, Oust, Plateau, Roundup Pro, Telar, Transline, Vanquish.
Areas Of Application: Roadsides, utility rights-of-way, airports, ditch-banks, dry ditches, dry canals, fencerows, industrial sites, lumberyards, petroleum tank farms, railroads, storage areas, and similar noncrop sites.

- - - - - - - - - - - - - - -

Signal Word/Toxicity Class: Caution.

PAR-3 — see 2,4-D Combinations

PARAQUAT

Restricted Use Pesticide.

Gramoxone Extra (2.5L) *(ZENECA)*

Rate: 0.6-1 lb. ai/A
2-3 pt. 2.5L/A

Weeds: Annual broadleaf weeds and grasses; suppression of many perennial weeds.

Remarks: Add nonionic surfactant or crop oil concentrate; repeat as necessary. Avoid contact with foliage of ornamentals or desired plants. Do not use around home gardens, schools, recreation parks, or playgrounds. Refer to label for use directions and precautions.

Areas Of Application: Public airports, electric transformer stations, pipeline pumping stations, around commercial buildings, storage yards and other installations, fence lines, and similar noncrop areas.

- - - - - - - - - - - - - - -

Signal Word/Toxicity Class: Danger-Poison/I.
REI: 12 hr. (except harvest aid/desiccation 24 hr.).

Pathfinder II — see triclopyr

PATHWAY (Premix)

Pathway (3% picloram & 11.2% 2,4-D) *(Dow AgroSciences)*

Rate: Ready-to-use

Weeds: Woody plants:

ailanthus	dogwood	maple
alder	Douglas-fir	oak
aspen	elm	pecan
balsam fir	green ash	persimmon
birch	gum	serviceberry
cedar	hickory	sourwood
cherry	hornbeam	sweetbay

Remarks: Apply undiluted to injector wounds, frills, or girdles, or freshly cut stumps or stubs of individual stems. Apply to cut surface of woody plants.

Areas Of Application: Forests and noncrop areas such as fence rows, rights-of-way, and industrial sites.

- - - - - - - - - - - - - - -

Signal Word/Toxicity Class: Caution.
REI: 48 hr.

Patron 170 — see 2,4-D Combinations

Patron DP-4 — see 2,4-DP

PENDIMETHALIN

Pendulum 3.3 EC Industrial or WDG Industrial *(American Cyanamid)*

Rate: Short-term control (2-4 months):
2 lb. ai/A
2.4 qt. 3.3 EC/A
3.3 lb. WDG/A
Long-term control (6-8 months):
4 lb. ai/A
4.8 qt. 3.3 EC/A
6.6 lb. WDG/A

◆-new product • PP-preplant • PPI-preplant incorporated • PRE-preemergence • POST-postemergence • SEQ-sequential • ae-acid equivalent • ai-active ingredient • DF-dry flowable
E/EC-emulsifiable concentrate • F/FL-flowable • DG/G/WG-dispersable granule • L/LC-liquid • SP/WSP-soluble packet • W/WP-wettable powder • WSB-water soluble bag

Weeds: Broadleaf weeds:

annual spurge	henbit	prostrate knotweed
carpetweed	hop clover	prostrate spurge
common chickweed	kochia	puncturevine
corn speedwell	lambsquarters	purslane
cudweed	lawn burweed	shepherdspurse
fiddleneck	London rocket	velvetleaf
filaree	mouseear chickweed	yellow woodsorrel
Florida pusley	pigweed	

Grasses:

annual bluegrass	giant foxtail	Mexican sprangletop
barnyardgrass	goosegrass	red sprangletop
browntop panicum	green foxtail	signalgrass
crabgrass	johnsongrass	Texas panicum
crowfootgrass	(seedling)	witchgrass
fall panicum	junglerice	woolly cupgrass
field sandbur	lovegrass	yellow foxtail

Remarks: Will not control established weeds.

Tank Mixes: Arsenal (except California) for postemergence control or use in conjunction with herbicides registered for postemergence use. Refer to labels for rates, precautions, and restrictions.

Areas Of Application: Railroad, utility, and pipeline rights-of-way, highway guardrails, delineators, and sign posts, utility substations, petroleum tank farms, pumping installations, fence rows, storage areas, windbreaks, and shelterbelts.

– – – – – – – – – – – – – – –

Signal Word/Toxicity Class: Caution.
REI: 12 hr.

Pendulum — see pendimethalin

PLATEAU

Plateau (AS) (imazapic) *(American Cyanamid)*

Rate: 2-12 fl. oz. AS/A

Weeds: Broadleaf weeds:

annual fleabane	field bindweed	Russian knapweed
bristly houndstongue	Florida beggarweed	sicklepod
bristly starbur	Florida pusley	silverleaf nightshade
buffalobur	golden crownbeard	smartweed
burclover	groundcherry	spurge
Carolina geranium	hairy indigo	spurred anoda
catchweed bedstraw	henbit	sunflower
coffee senna	hoary cress	tansymustard
common chickweed	jimsonweed	thistle
common cocklebur	kochia	velvetleaf
common cornsalad	morningglory	vervain
common	narrowleaf plantain	whitetop
lambsquarters	perennial pepperweed	wild mustard
common purslane	pigweed	wild poinsettia
common teasel	poison hemlock	wild radish
cranesbill geranium	prickly sida	willowherb
curly dock	prostrate knotweed	yellow rocket
dandelion	puncturevine	yellow starthistle
fiddleneck	Queen Anne's lace	yellow woodsorrel
field bindweed	ragweed	

Grasses:

annual ryegrass	foxtail	smutgrass
annual stinkgrass	goosegrass	squirreltail barley
bahiagrass	itchgrass	stinkgrass
barnyardgrass	Japanese stiltgrass	tall dropseed
broadleaf signalgrass	johnsongrass	tall fescue
cheat	little barley	Texas panicum
crabgrass	perennial ryegrass	torpedograss
crowfootgrass	sandbur	vaseygrass
dallisgrass	shattercane	wild garlic
downy brome	signalgrass	wild oat
fall panicum		

Sedges:

purple nutsedge	sedge	yellow nutsedge
rush		

Remarks: For postemergence application, add surfactant. Do not exceed 12 oz./A per year. Do not use on areas to be grazed or cut for hay. Do not apply though any type of irrigation system. Refer to label for directions, restrictions, and precautions.

Tank Mixes: Accord, Arsenal, Campaign, diuron, Escort, Finale, Garlon 3A, glyphosate, MSMA, Oust, Pendulum, Vanquish.

Areas Of Application: Railroad, utility, and pipeline rights-of-way, utility plant sites, petroleum tank farms, pumping installations, fence rows, storage areas, nonirrigation ditchbanks, and other similar areas.

– – – – – – – – – – – – – – –

Signal Word/Toxicity Class: Caution.

PRAMITOL

Pramitol 25E (prometon) *(Makhteshim-Agan)*

Rate: 8-12.25 lb. ai/A
4-6.125 gal. 25E/A

Weeds: Annual and susceptible perennial weeds and grasses such as:

downy brome	oatgrass	puncturevine
goldenrod	plantain	quackgrass
goosegrass		

Rate: 15-20 lb. ai/A
7.5-10 gal. 25E/A

Weeds: Hard-to-kill perennial weeds and grasses such as:

bindweed	johnsongrass	wild carrot

Remarks: Apply before weeds emerge or up to 3 months after emergence. Apply to ground before laying asphalt, or may be mixed with cutback asphalts. Use only in areas where complete control of all vegetation is desired and not on land to be cropped, or near adjacent desirable trees, shrubs, or plants because injury may occur. Refer to label for directions, restrictions, and precautions.

Areas Of Application: Noncrop areas such as industrial sites, rights-of-way, lumberyards, petroleum tank farms, around farm buildings, along fence lines, and similar areas.

– – – – – – – – – – – – – – –

Signal Word/Toxicity Class: Danger/I.

PRAMITOL 5PS (Premix)

Pramitol 5PS (5% prometon & 0.76% simazine & 90% chlorate-borate) *(Makhteshim-Agan)*

Rate: 152-400 lb. 5PS/A

Weeds: Most annual and perennial broadleaf weeds and grasses.

Remarks: High rate should be used in areas having long growing season or high rainfall and will also provide longer residual control. Do not use on land to be cropped. Refer to label for directions, restrictions, and precautions.

Areas Of Application: Noncrop areas such as industrial sites, rights-of-way, lumberyards, petroleum tank farms, around farm buildings, along fence lines, and similar areas.

– – – – – – – – – – – – – – –

Signal Word/Toxicity Class: Danger/I.

Prism — see clethodim

Pronone — see hexazinone

Rattler — see glyphosate

Remedy — see triclopyr

Reward — see diquat dibromide

Rhonox — see MCPA

Rodeo — see glyphosate

Roundup — see glyphosate

Saber — see 2,4-D

9

Other Uses

NOTICE The information on these pages is for preliminary planning — not a guide for use. Be sure to follow the manufacturer's directions, notwithstanding information contained here. | For personal protective equipment and EPA registration numbers, please turn to page 70.

SAHARA (Premix)

Sahara DG (7.78%. imazapyr & 62.22% diuron) (American Cyanamid)

Rate: 5-19 lb. DG/A

Weeds: Broadleaf weeds:

ageratum	horsenettle	rush skeletonweed
arrowwood	horseweed	Russian knapweed
broom snakeweed	Indian mustard	Russian thistle
bull thistle	Japanese bamboo	saltbush
burdock	knawel	sesbania
camphorweed	kochia	sicklepod
Canada thistle	lambsquarters	silverleaf nightshade
Carolina geranium	lespedeza	shepherdspurse
carpetweed	little mallow	smartweed
clover	marigold	sorrel
cocklebur	milkweed	sowthistle
common chickweed	minerslettuce	speedwell
common ragweed	morningglory	stinging nettle
corn spurry	mullein	sunflower
dandelion	nettleleaf goosefoot	sweet clover
dayflower	oxeye daisy	tansymustard
desert camelthorn	pennycress	Texas thistle
diffuse knapweed	pepperweed	velvetleaf
dock	pigweed	western ragweed
dogfennel	pineappleweed	wild buckwheat
filaree	plantain	wild carrot
fleabane	pokeweed	wild lettuce
giant ragweed	prickly sida	wild parsnip
goldenrod	primrose	wild radish
gray rabbitbrush	puncturevine	wild turnip
gromwell	purple loosestrife	woollyleaf bursage
groundcherry	purslane	yellow starthistle
hawksbeard	ragweed	yellow woodsorrel
hoary vervain		

Grasses:

annual bluegrass	fall panicum	quackgrass
annual ryegrass	feathertop	rattail fescue
annual sweet	fescue	reed canarygrass
vernalgrass	foxtail	ricegrass
bahiagrass	goosegrass	saltgrass
barnyardgrass	guineagrass	sand dropseed
beardgrass	Italian ryegrass	sandbur
bermudagrass	johnsongrass	smooth brome
big bluestem	Kentucky bluegrass	sprangletop
broadleaf signalgrass	kyllinga	timothy
Canada bluegrass	lovegrass	torpedograss
cattail	maidencane	vaseygrass
cheat	orchardgrass	velvetgrass
cogongrass	paragrass	western muhly
crabgrass	phragmites	wild barley
dallisgrass	prairie cordgrass	wild oat
downy brome	prairie threeawn	witchgrass

Vines and Brambles:

blackberry	honeysuckle	trumpetcreeper
dewberry	kudzu	Virginia creeper
field bindweed	morningglory	wild buckwheat
greenbriar	poison ivy	wild grape
hedge bindweed	redvine	wild rose

Remarks: Apply postemergence or as spot treatment. Postemergence applications require an adjuvant. Rates vary depending on average annual rainfall. Do not apply to food or feed.

Tank Mixes: Arsenal, Banvel, Finale, Garlon, glyphosate, Karmex, MSMA, Oust, Pendulum, Vanquish.

Areas Of Application: Railroad, utility, and pipeline rights-of-way, utility plant sites, petroleum tank farms, pumping installations, farmyards and around farm buildings, fence rows, storage areas, nonirrigation ditchbanks, and other similar areas.

State Restrictions: Not for use in California.

– – – – – – – – – – – – – –

Signal Word/Toxicity Class: Caution.

Savage — see 2,4-D

SCYTHE

Scythe (pelargonic acid) (Mycogen)

Rate: 4-13 fl. oz./gal. spray solution

Weeds: Annual broadleaf weeds and grasses; top-kill of perennial weeds.

Remarks: Apply in minimum 75 gal. spray solution/A or spray-to-wet. May also be used to control mosses, lichens, and other cryptogens. For dry aquatic sites, apply within 72 hr. prior to reflooding. Do not apply by air or through any type of irrigation system. Refer to label for directions and precautions.

Tank Mixes: May be tank mixed.

Areas Of Application: Dry aquatic sites, dry ditches, ditchbanks, storage areas, schools, paved areas, road, railroad and utility rights-of-way, parking lots, recreation areas, campgrounds, golf courses, walks, and industrial areas.

– – – – – – – – – – – – – –

Signal Word/Toxicity Class: Warning/II.

REI: 24 hr.

Select — see clethodim

SETHOXYDIM

Vantage (1EC) (BASF)

Rate: 0.28-0.47 lb. ai/A
2.25-3.75 pt. 1EC/A

Time: Apply when weeds are actively growing.

Weeds: Grasses:

barnyardgrass	johnsongrass	tall fescue (seedling)
bermudagrass	junglerice	Texas panicum
broadleaf signalgrass	large crabgrass	torpedograss
browntop panicum	lovegrass	volunteer grains
fall panicum	orchardgrass	wild proso millet
field sandbur	(seedling)	wildcane
giant foxtail	quackgrass	wiresteim muhly
goosegrass	red sprangletop	witchgrass
green foxtail	shattercane	woolly cupgrass
guineagrass	smooth crabgrass	yellow foxtail

Remarks: Refer to label for restrictions and limitations.

– – – – – – – – – – – – – –

Signal Word/Toxicity Class: Caution/III.

REI: 12 hr.

SIMAZINE

◆ **Clean Crop Simazine 4L or 90WDG** (Platte)

Rate: 0.8-4.8 lb. ai/A
0.8-4.8 qt. 4L/A
0.9-5.3 lb. 90/A

Weeds: Annual broadleaf weeds and grasses.

Remarks: Apply before weeds emerge. Do not use near adjacent desirable trees, shrubs or plants. Do not use in areas accessible to livestock or allow livestock to graze treated foliage.

Areas Of Application: Industrial sites, highway medians and shoulders, railroad rights-of-way, lumber yards, petroleum tank farms, farm buildings, along fences, roadsides and lanes, and similar noncrop areas.

– – – – – – – – – – – – – –

Signal Word/Toxicity Class: Caution/III.

REI: 12 hr.

SNAPSHOT (Premix)

Snapshot 2.5TG (2% trifluralin & 0.5% isoxaben) (Dow AgroSciences)

Rate: 2.5-5 lb. ai/A
100-200 lb. 2.5TG/A

Weeds: Broadleaf weeds:

annual bursage	eveningprimrose	prickly sida
annual sowthistle	fall panicum	prostrate knotweed
black medic	hairy fleabane	purple cudweed
black nightshade	hairy galinsoga	purslane speedwell
bristly oxtongue	hare barley	rattail fescue
broadleaf plantain	heath aster	redstem filaree
burning nettle	henbit	Russian thistle
California burclover	horseweed	scarlet pimpernel
Carolina geranium	Indian mustard	shepherdspurse
clover	jimsonweed	sibara
coast fiddleneck	kochia	silversheath knotweed
common chickweed	lanceleaf groundcherry	slender aster
common groundsel	little mallow	slender plantain
common	London rocket	spiny sowthistle
lambsquarters	marestail	spotted spurge
common purslane	Mexican sprangletop	sunflower
common ragweed	nettleleaf goosefoot	swinecress
creeping woodsorrel	panicle willowweed	tall morningglory
curly dock	Pennsylvania	telegraphplant
dandelion	smartweed	turkey mullein
datura	petty spurge	velvetleaf
desert rockpurslane	pigweed	Virginia pepperweed
dwarf fleabane	pineappleweed	yellow sweetclover
dwarf mallow	prickly lettuce	yellow woodsorrel

◆-new product • PP-preplant • PPI-preplant incorporated • PRE-preemergence • POST-postemergence • SEQ-sequential • ae-acid equivalent • ai-active ingredient • DF-dry flowable
E/EC-emulsifiable concentrate • F/FL-flowable • DG/G/WG-dispersable granule • L/LC-liquid • SP/WSP-soluble packet • W/WP-wettable powder • WSB-water soluble bag

482

Weed Control Manual 2000

Annual grasses:

annual bluegrass	Italian ryegrass	wild celery
annual ryegrass	junglerice	wild mustard
barnyardgrass	lovegrass	wild oat
bromegrass	southwestern	wild radish
crabgrass	cupgrass	witchgrass
giant foxtail	wild carrot	yellow foxtail

Remarks: Does not control established weeds. Refer to label for directions, restrictions, and precautions.

Areas Of Application: Industrial sites, utility substations, highway guardrails, sign posts, and delineators.

State Restrictions: Refer to label for use restrictions in Arizona.

- - - - - - - - - - - - - - - -

Signal Word/Toxicity Class: Caution/III.
REI: 12 hr.

Solicam — see norflurazon

Solution — see 2,4-D

Solve — see 2,4-D; MCPA

SPIKE

Spike 20P or 80W (tebuthiuron) *(Dow AgroSciences)*
Rate: 1-6 lb. ai/A
5-30 lb. 20P/A
1.25-7.5 lb. 80W/A

Weeds: Over 125 grass and weed species and 110 woody species including hard-to-control species such as:

maple	white ash	willow
oak		

Remarks: Rate varies by weed species, treatment, and geographic area. Degree and duration of control may vary with rate applied, soil type, and other conditions. Will injure or control other herbaceous vegetation in treated area, therefore, do not apply where injury cannot be tolerated. Do not apply on field crops, near desirable trees or other plants, on areas where their roots may extend, or in locations where chemical may be washed into contact with their roots. Refer to label for directions, restrictions, and precautions.

Areas Of Application: Noncrop areas such as railroad and utility rights-of-way, wildlife openings, industrial sites, pipelines, fence rows, firebreaks, ditchbanks, and along highways.

- - - - - - - - - - - - - - - -

Signal Word/Toxicity Class: Caution/III.

STAA-FREE (Premix)

Staa-Free 2+2 (4G) (2% bromacil & 2% diuron) *(Pro-Serve)*
Rate: 0.02-0.04 lb. ai/sq. ft.
0.5-1 lb. 4G/100 sq. ft.

Weeds: Annual and perennial broadleaf weeds and grasses.

Remarks: For best results, apply early in season. Repeat spot treatment for deep-rooted perennials. Keep animals off treated areas. Refer to label for directions and precautions.

Areas Of Application: Industrial sites and railroad rights-of-way.

- - - - - - - - - - - - - - - -

Signal Word/Toxicity Class: Caution.

Stalker — see imazapyr

Sterling — see dicamba

Stinger — see clopyralid

SuperBrush — see 2,4-D Combinations

SUREFIRE (Premix)

Restricted Use Pesticide.

◆ **Surefire (29.4% paraquat & 10.6% diuron)** *(Platte)*
Rate: 0.8 lb. ai/A
2 pt./A

Weeds: Broadleaf weeds such as:

burclover	mustard	ragweed
carelessweed	nettle	red clover
chickweed	pigweed	shepherdspurse
filaree	plantain	thistle
groundsel	puncturevine	wild oat
henbit	purslane	wild radish
morningglory*		

Grasses such as:

barnyardgrass	cheatgrass	foxtail
bermudagrass*	crabgrass	johnsongrass*
bluegrass	fall panicum	

*Suppression

Remarks: Apply to young, succulent weeds and grasses. Repeat as needed. Always use nonionic surfactant. Do not apply through any type of irrigation system. Refer to label for directions and precautions.

Areas Of Application: Airports, electric transformer stations, pipeline pumping stations, commercial buildings, storage yards, fence lines, and similar noncrop areas.

- - - - - - - - - - - - - - - -

Signal Word/Toxicity Class: Danger/I.
REI: 12 hr.

Sword — see MCPA

Target — see MSMA

TELAR

Telar (DF) (chlorsulfuron) *(DuPont)*
Rate: 0.25-3 oz. DF/A
Unimproved industrial turf:
0.25-1 oz. DF/A

Weeds:

annual ryegrass	corn spurry	prostrate pigweed
annual sowthistle	cowcockle	puncturevine
aster	curly dock	red clover
bedstraw	dandelion	redroot pigweed
black mustard	dyers woad	Russian knapweed
blue mustard	fiddleneck	Scotch thistle
bouncingbet	(tarweed)	scouringrush
bull thistle	field pennycress	shepherdspurse
bur beakchervil	filaree	smooth pigweed
burclover	flixweed	sweetclover
buttercup	foxtail	tansymustard
Canada thistle	goldenrod	treacle mustard
common chickweed	groundsel	tumble mustard
common cinquefoil	hempnettle	(jim hill)
common	henbit	turkey mullein
lambsquarters	horsetail	white clover
common mallow	London rocket	whitetop
common mullein	mayweed	(hoary cress)
common ragweed	minerslettuce	wild carrot
common sunflower	musk thistle	wild garlic
common speedwell	pepperweed	wild onion
common tansy	pineappleweed	wild mustard
common yarrow	poison hemlock	wild parsnip
conical catchfly	prostrate knotweed*	yellow starthistle

Remarks: Apply when weeds are actively growing. Do not use on food or feed crops. Do not apply through any type of irrigation system. Refer to label for directions and precautions.

Tank Mixes: 2,4-D, dicamba, glyphosate, Karmex, Krovar I. Do not tank mix with Hyvar XL, or with Embark on bahiagrass turf or turf under stress.

Areas Of Application: Airports, highways, roadsides, utility, pipeline, and railroad rights-of-way, petroleum tank farms, plant sites, etc.

State Restrictions: Not for use in Alamosa, Costilla, Conejos, Rio Grande, and Saguache counties in Colorado.

- - - - - - - - - - - - - - - -

Signal Word/Toxicity Class: Caution.

9

Other Uses

NOTICE	The information on these pages is for preliminary planning — not a guide for use. Be sure to follow the manufacturer's directions, notwithstanding information contained here.	For personal protective equipment and EPA registration numbers, please turn to page 70.

TOPSITE (Premixes)

◆ **Riverdale Topsite 2.5G (0.5% imazapyr & 2% diuron)** *(Riverdale)*

Topsite 2.5G (0.5% imazapyr & 2% diuron) *(American Cyanamid)*

Rate: 5-7.5 lb. ai/A
200-300 lb. 2.5G/A

Weeds: Broadleaf weed:

bigleaf aster	Florida pusley	prostrate knotweed
blue mustard	giant ragweed	purslane
bull thistle	hoary vervain	silverleaf
burdock	horseweed	nightshade
buttercup	Indian mustard	smartweed
camphorweed	kochia	sorrel
Canada thistle	lambsquarters	sowthistle
Carolina geranium	lespedeza	sunflower
carpetweed	little mallow	sweet clover
clover	milkweed	tansymustard
cocklebur	minerslettuce	Texas thistle
common chickweed	mullein	western ragweed
common ragweed	nettleleaf goosefoot	white heat aster
dandelion	oxeye daisy	wild carrot
dock	pepperweed	wild lettuce
dogfennel	pigweed	wild parsnip
eclipta	plantain	wild turnip
filaree	poison hemlock	woollyleaf bursage
fleabane	pokeweed	yellow starthistle
Florida beggarweed	primrose	yellow woodsorrel

Grasses:

annual bluegrass	downy brome	prairie threeawn
bahiagrass	fall panicum	quackgrass
beardgrass	fescue	sand dropseed
bermudagrass	foxtail	sandbur
big bluestem	goosegrass	smooth brome
broadleaf signalgrass	guineagrass	timothy
browntop millet	Italian ryegrass	torpedograss
Canada bluegrass	johnsongrass	vaseygrass
cattail	Kentucky bluegrass	wild barley
centipedegrass	lovegrass	wild iris
cheat	orchardgrass	wild oat
crabgrass	paragrass	wiresteam muhly
dallisgrass	prairie cordgrass	witchgrass

Remarks: Do not use on food or feed crops, lawns, walks, driveways, or tennis courts. Apply any time throughout the year but prior to weed emergence and expected rainfall.

Areas Of Application: Railroad, utility, pipeline, and highway rights-of-way, petroleum tank farms, pumping installations, fence rows, and storage areas.

State Restrictions: Not for use in California.

– – – – – – – – – – – – – – –

Signal Word/Toxicity Class: Caution/III.

TORDON

Restricted Use Pesticide.

Tordon K (picloram) *(Dow AgroSciences)*

Rate: 0.125-1 lb. ae/A
0.5-4 pt./A

Weeds: Broadleaf annual and perennial weeds and woody vines:

bindweed	horsenettle	oxeye daisy
broom snakeweed	knapweed	poison oak
buffalobur	larkspur	rush skeletonweed
burroweed	leafy spurge	thistle
cactus	locoweed	yellow starthistle
henbane	lupine	

Rate: 0.25-1 lb. ae/A
1-4 pt./A

Weeds: Woody plants such as:

catclaw acacia	juniper	poison oak
cedar	mesquite	poplar
chaparral	oak	rabbitbrush
Douglas fir	pinyon pine	willow
gorse		

Remarks: Do not exceed 4 pt./A per growing season on rights-of-way and other noncrop areas. Do not allow spray to contact desirable broadleaf plants. Refer to label for restrictions and precautions.

Areas Of Application: Forest planting sites, wildlife openings in forest, and noncrop areas including rights-of-way such as electrical power lines, communication lines, pipelines, roadsides, and railroads.

– – – – – – – – – – – – – – –

Signal Word/Toxicity Class: Caution.
REI: 12 hr.

TORDON 101 (Premix)

Restricted Use Pesticide.

Tordon 101 Mixture (0.54 lb./gal. picloram & 2 lb./gal. 2,4-D) *(Dow AgroSciences)*

Rate: Broadleaf Weeds:
1.25-5 lb. ae/A
2-8 qt./A
Woody plants and vines:
2.5-5 lb. ae/A
4-8 qt./A

Weeds: Annual and perennial broadleaf weeds:

bouncingbet	horsenettle	sowthistle
chicory	knapweed	tansy ragwort
clover	leafy spurge	thistle
dandelion	milkweed	toadflax
dock	plantain	vetch
field bindweed	prickly lettuce	wild carrot
fleabane	ragweed	yellow starthistle
goldenrod	rush skeletonweed	

Woody plants and vines such as:

ailanthus	elm	persimmon
alder	gorse	pine
aspen	gum	poison oak
balsam fir	hemlock	sassafras
birch	hickory	sourwood
blackberry	honeysuckle	spruce
brackenfern	kudzu	sumac
buttonbush	locust	tulip poplar
cherry	maple	wild rose
Douglas fir	oak	willow

Remarks: Avoid injury to newly planted conifers. Do not allow spray to contact desirable broadleaf plants. Refer to label for restrictions and precautions.

Areas Of Application: Forest planting sites, wildlife openings in forest and noncrop areas including rights-of-way such as electrical power lines, communication lines, pipelines, roadsides, and railroads.

– – – – – – – – – – – – – – –

Signal Word/Toxicity Class: Warning/II.
REI: 48 hr.

– – – – – – – – – – – – – – –

Total — see Bareground/Total

TOUCHDOWN

Touchdown (5L or 6L) (sulfosate) *(ZENECA)*

Rate: 0.5-4 lb. ai/A
0.8-6.4 pt. 5L/A
0.66-5.33 pt. 6L/A

Weeds: Broadleaf weeds:

annual fleabane	dogfennel	marestail
annual sowthistle	fiddleneck	morningglory
annual spurge	field bindweed	mouseear chickweed
black nightshade	field pennycress	mustard
brackenfern	field sandbur	Pennsylvania
camphorweed	filaree	smartweed
Canada thistle	fleabane	prickly lettuce
Carolina geranium	Florida pusley	red clover
common chickweed	giant ragweed	redroot pigweed
common cocklebur	groundcherry	redvine
common groundsel	hairy fleabane	Russian thistle
common	hemp dogbane	shepherdspurse
lambsquarters	henbit	sicklepod
common mullein	hophornbeam	smooth pigweed
common ragweed	copperleaf	spanishneedles
common sunflower	horsenettle	teaweed
curly dock	Jerusalem artichoke*	trumpetcreeper
cutleaf	kochia	velvetleaf
eveningprimrose	leafy spurge	Virginia creeper
dandelion	little barley	white clover
dayflower*	London rocket	wild buckwheat

Grasses and sedges:

annual bluegrass	crabgrass	johnsongrass
bahiagrass	crowfootgrass	(seedling)
barley	downy brome	jointed goatgrass
barnyardgrass	fall panicum	Kentucky bluegrass
bermudagrass	fescue	orchardgrass
broadleaf signalgrass	foxtail	paragrass
cattail	goosegrass	perennial ryegrass
cheat	guineagrass	purple nutsedge
cogongrass*	Italian ryegrass	quackgrass

◆-new product • PP-preplant • PPI-preplant incorporated • PRE-preemergence • POST-postemergence • SEQ-sequential • ae-acid equivalent • ai-active ingredient • DF-dry flowable
E/EC-emulsifiable concentrate • F/FL-flowable • DG/G/WG-dispersable granule • L/LC-liquid • SP/WSP-soluble packet • W/WP-wettable powder • WSB-water soluble bag

Grasses and sedges, continued:

red rice	tall fescue	wild oat
reed canarygrass	Texas panicum	wirestem muhly
shattercane	torpedograss*	witchgrass
smooth bromegrass	timothy	woolly cupgrass
sprangletop	vaseygrass	yellow nutsedge
stinkgrass		

* Partial control

Remarks: Nonionic surfactant or wetting agent required; ammonium sulfate can be added. Avoid contact with foliage of ornamentals or other desirable plants. Repeat as necessary. Do not apply through any type of irrigation system. Refer to label for directions, restrictions, and precautions.

Tank Mixes: Devrinol, diuron, Goal, Krovar, Prowl, simazine, Solicam, Surflan.

Areas Of Application: Barrier strips, equipment areas, farm buildings and yards, fence rows, fuel storage areas, rights-of-way, soil bank land.

State Restrictions: Ammonium sulfate (6L) not for use in California.

Signal Word/Toxicity Class: Caution.
REI: 12 hr. (5L); 4 hr. (6L).

Transline — see clopyralid

Triamine — see 2,4-D Combinations

TRIAMINE II (Premix)

Triamine II (2,4-DP & MCPA & MCPP) *(Riverdale)*
Rate: 0.33-1 gal. II/50-300 gal. water (43,500 sq. ft.)
Weeds: Broadleaf weeds including:

dandelion	oxalis	
chickweed	plantain	spurge

Remarks: For broadleaf weeds, apply when plants come into full leaf until plants start to go dormant. For woody plants, apply to stems and foliage from time foliage is completely matured until plants start to go dormant.

Areas Of Application: Roadsides (including aprons and guardrails), rights-of-way, and other similar noncrop areas.

Signal Word/Toxicity Class: Danger/I.

TRICLOPYR

Garlon 3A *(Dow AgroSciences)*
Rate: 1-9 lb. ae/A
1.33-12 qt. 3A/A
Weeds: Annual and perennial broadleaf weeds:

bindweed	dandelion	smartweed
burdock	field bindweed	tansy ragwort
Canada thistle	lambsquarters	vetch
chicory	plantain	wild lettuce
curly dock	ragweed	

Woody plants:

alder	Douglas-fir	poplar
arrowwood	elderberry	red maple
ash	elm	sassafras
aspen	hawthorn	Scotch broom
beech	hazel	sumac
birch	hornbeam	sweetbay magnolia
blackberry	locust	sweetgum
blackgum	madrone	sycamore
Brazilian pepper	mulberry	tanoak
cascara	oaks	thimbleberry
chinquapin	persimmon	tulip poplar
chokecherry	pin cherry	waxmyrtle
cottonwood	pine	western hemlock
dogwood	poison oak	willow

Remarks: Foliar spray: Apply when weeds and brush are actively growing. Use lower rates for weed control; higher rates for hard-to-control brush and applications made in late summer or during drought conditions (refer to label for application directions). Cut surface treatment: Apply either undiluted or diluted in 1:1 ratio with water using tree injector method with frill or girdle method, or as cut stump treatment. Apply at any season except during period of heavy sap flow of certain species such as maples.

Areas Of Application: Forest management applications, on noncrop sites including industrial manufacturing and storage sites, rights-of-way, fence rows, nonirrigation ditchbanks, wildlife openings, and around farm buildings.

Signal Word/Toxicity Class: Danger/I.
REI: 48 hr.

Garlon 4 *(Dow AgroSciences)*
Rate: 1-8 lb. ae/A
1-8 qt./A
Weeds: Same as Garlon 3A plus:

black medic	ground ivy	wild carrot
clover	mustard	wild violet
goldenrod	oxalis	

Remarks: Foliar spray same as Garlon 3A. Basal bark treatment: Apply to stems less than 6" basal diameter at any time, including winter months, except when snow or ice prevent spraying to ground line. Conventional basal bark treatment: Mix 1-5 gal. product in enough oil to make 100 gal. spray and spray basal parts of brush and tree trunks until thoroughly wet and runoff at ground is noticeable. Low volume basal bark treatment: Mix 20-30 gal. product in enough oil to make 100 gal. spray and spray basal parts of brush and tree trunk in a manner which thoroughly wets lower stems and root collar area, but not to runoff. Thinline basal bark treatment: Apply undiluted in thin stream to form a narrow band which completely encircles lower stem of brush and tree species.

Areas Of Application: Same as for Garlon 3A.

Signal Word/Toxicity Class: Caution.
REI: 12 hr.

Pathfinder II *(Dow AgroSciences)*
Rate: Apply undiluted
Weeds: Over 80 woody plant species including:

alder	Douglas-fir	poplar
arrowwood	elderberry	red maple
ash	elm	sassafras
aspen	hawthorn	Scotch broom
beech	hazel	sumac
birch	hornbeam	sweetbay magnolia
blackberry	locust	sweetgum
blackgum	madrone	sycamore
Brazilian pepper	mulberry	tanoak
cascara	oaks	thimbleberry
chinquapin	persimmon	tulip poplar
chokecherry	pin cherry	waxmyrtle
cottonwood	pine	western hemlock
dogwood	poison oak	willow

Remarks: Ready-to-use product. Apply to woody plant stems less than 6". Low volume basal treatment: Spray to runoff around entire circumference of lower 12-15". Cut stump treatment: Wet area adjacent to the cambium and bark around the entire circumference and sides of freshly cut stumps.

Areas Of Application: Rights-of-way, forests, industrial sites, nonirrigation ditchbanks, wildlife openings.

Signal Word/Toxicity Class: Caution.

Remedy *(Dow AgroSciences)*
Rate: Foliar-broadcast:
1 lb. ae/A
2 pt./A
High-volume leaf stem treatment:
1-3 lb. ae/A
2-6 pt./A
Weeds: Annual and perennial broadleaf weeds:

black medic	curly dock	plantain
burdock	dandelion	vetch
chicory	lambsquarters	wild carrot
cinquefoil	lespedeza	wild violet
clover	mustard	yarrow

Mesquite and woody plants such as:

alder	cherry	mulberry
ash	cottonwood	oak
aspen	dogwood	poison oak
beech	elderberry	poplar
birch	elm (except winged)	sassafras
blackberry	hawthorn	sumac
blackbrush	locust	waxmyrtle
cascara	maple	wild roses
Ceanothus	(except bigleaf, vine)	willow

Remarks: Do not apply through any type of irrigation system. Refer to label for directions and precautions.
Tank Mixes: 2,4-D.
Areas Of Application: Roadsides, fence rows, non-irrigation ditchbanks.

Signal Word/Toxicity Class: Caution.

Tri-Ester — see 2,4-D Combinations

9

Other Uses

NOTICE The information on these pages is for preliminary planning — not a guide for use. Be sure to follow the manufacturer's directions, notwithstanding information contained here.

For personal protective equipment and EPA registration numbers, please turn to page 70.

TRI-ESTER II (Premix)

Tri-Ester II (2,4-DP & MCPA & MCPP) *(Riverdale)*
Rate: 0.33-1 gal. II/50-300 gal. water (43,500 sq. ft.)
Weeds: Broadleaf weeds and woody plants.
Remarks: For broadleaf weeds, apply when plants come into full leaf to when plants start to go dormant. For woody plants, apply to stems and foliage from time foliage is completely matured until plants start to go dormant.
Areas Of Application: Roadsides (including aprons and guardrails), rights-of-way, and other similar noncrop areas.

– – – – – – – – – – – – – – –

Signal Word/Toxicity Class: Warning/II.

Truce — see imazapyr

TurfMate — see MSMA

Vanquish — see dicamba

Vantage — see sethoxydim

VEGEMEC (Premix)

Vegemec Vegetation Killer (3.6% prometon & 1% 2,4-D) *(PBI/Gordon)*
Rate: 1 pt. product/100 sq. ft.
Weeds: Broadleaf weeds and grasses such as:

Canada thistle	johnsongrass	milkweed

Remarks: Nonselective. Not for use on lawns.
Areas Of Application: Along fence lines, gravel drives, patio blocks, and around buildings where no grass is desired.

– – – – – – – – – – – – – –

Signal Word/Toxicity Class: Danger/I.

Velpar — see hexazinone

VENGEANCE (Premix)

◆ **Vengeance (2.5 lb./gal. MCPA & 1.25 lb./gal. dicamba)** *(Wilbur-Ellis)*
Rate: 1.5-3 lb. ai/A
3.2-6.4 pt./A
Weeds: Top growth control of:

Canada thistle	leafy spurge	Russian knapweed
field bindweed	perennial sowthistle	

Remarks: Apply as foliar spray to actively growing plants.
Tank Mixes: Asulam, bromacil, chlorsulfuron, 2,4-D, 2,4-DP, diuron, fosamine ammonium, glyphosate, hexazinone, imazapyr, MSMA, picloram, simazine, sulfometuron-methyl, tebuthiuron, triclopyr.
Areas Of Application: Fence rows, roadsides, similar areas.
State Restrictions: Not registered in California.

– – – – – – – – – – – – – –

Signal Word/Toxicity Class: Danger/I.

VETERAN (Premixes)

◆ **Veteran 720 (WS) (1.9 lb./gal. 2,4-D & 1 lb./gal. dicamba)** *(Riverdale)*
Rate: 0.725-2.9 lb. ai/A
1-4 qt. WS/A
Weeds: Annual broadleaf weeds:

carpetweed	knawel	purslane
chickweed	lambsquarters	ragweed
clover	morningglory	smartweed
cocklebur	mustard	velvetleaf
English daisy	pigweed	wild buckwheat
henbit		

Biennial weeds:

musk thistle	tansy ragwort

Perennial weeds:

Canada thistle	field bindweed	Russian knapweed
curly dock	leafy spurge	sheep sorrel
dalmation toadflax	milkweed	wild carrot
dogfennel	Queen Anne's lace	

Rate: 2.9-5.8 lb. ai/A
1-2 gal. WS/A
Weeds: Woody brush and vines:

alder	Florida holly	redvine
ash	gum	Russian olive
aspen	hawthorn*	sagebrush
basswood	hemlock	sassafras
beech	honeysuckle	serviceberry
birch	kudzu	snowberry
blackberry*	locust	spruce
Brazil peppertree	maple	sumac
cherry	multiflora rose*	sycamore
Christmasberry	oak	trumpetcreeper
creosotebush*	persimmon	Virginia creeper
cucumbertree	pine	waxmyrtle
dogwood*	poison ivy	wild plum*
eastern red cedar*	poplar	willow
elderberry	puncturevine	witchazel
elm	raspberry	yaupon*

*Suppression

Remarks: Apply when weeds and brush are actively growing; repeat as needed. Do not apply more than 2 gal. WS/A per season. Do not apply through any type of irrigation system. Do not graze dairy animals within 21 days of applying 1 gal. WS; 40 days for 2 gal. WS. Remove meat animals from treated areas 30 days before slaughter.
Tank Mixes: Amitrol, asulam, bromacil, clorflurecol, chlorsulfuron, 2,4-D, 2,4-DP, dicamba, diquat, diuron, fosamine-ammonium, glyphosate, hexazinone, imazapyr, maleic hydrazide, mefluidide, metsulfuron, MSMA, paraquat, picloram, simazine, sulfometuron-methyl, tebuthiuron, triclopyr. Refer to labels for directions and precautions.
Areas Of Application: Rights-of-way, fence rows, non-irrigation ditchbanks, wasteland, general farmstead, and similar noncrop areas.

– – – – – – – – – – – – – – –

Signal Word/Toxicity Class: Caution.

Veteran 2010 (2.5 lb./gal. MCPA & 1.25 lb./gal. dicamba) *(Riverdale)*
Rate: 3.2-6.4 pt./A
Weeds: Top growth control of:

field bindweed	leafy spurge	Russian knapweed
Canada thistle	perennial sowthistle	

Remarks: Apply when weeds are actively growing. May be tank mixed; refer to label for use directions and precautions.
Areas Of Application: Fence rows, roadsides, and rights-of-way.

– – – – – – – – – – – – – – –

Signal Word/Toxicity Class: Danger/I.
REI: 24 hr.

Veteran CST or 10G — see dicamba

Weed Blast (Premix)

Weed Blast (4% bromacil & 4% diuron) *(Platte)*
Rate: Short-term control:
3.2-4.8 lb. ai/A
40-60 lb./A
Extended control:
8-16 lb. ai/A
100-200 lb./A
Remarks: Apply before weed emergence or in early stages of weed growth. Use lower rate for retreatment.Spot treatment may be required for deep-rooted perennial weeds. Use higher rate on absorptive soils. Refer to label for further use directions.
Areas Of Application: Industrial areas, railroad rights-of-way.

– – – – – – – – – – – – – – –

Signal Word/Toxicity Class: Caution.

Weed Rhap — see 2,4-D

Weedar — see 2,4-D

Weedestroy — see 2,4-D

Weedmaster — see 2,4-D Combinations

Weedone — see 2,4-D

◆-new product • PP-preplant • PPI-preplant incorporated • PRE-preemergence • POST-postemergence • SEQ-sequential • ae-acid equivalent • ai-active ingredient • DF-dry flowable
E/EC-emulsifiable concentrate • F/FL-flowable • DG/G/WG-dispersable granule • L/LC-liquid • SP/WSP-soluble packet • W/WP-wettable powder • WSB-water soluble bag

XL 2G (Premix)

XL 2G (1% benefin + 1% oryzalin) *(Helena)*

Rate: 4-6 lb. ai/A
  200-300 lb./A (4.6-6.9 lb./1000 sq. ft.)

Time: Apply prior to germination of target weeds.

Weeds: Broadleaf weeds:

annual sowthistle*	desert rockpurslane	prostrate spurge
bittercress	Florida pusley	puncturevine
black mustard*	henbit	redstem filaree
black nightshade*	horseweed*	shepherdspurse
carpetweed	ladysthumb*	smartweed*
chickweed	lambsquarters	spotted spurge*
climbing milkweed*	London rocket	teaweed*
coast fiddleneck	morningglory*	velvetleaf*
common groundsel	pigweed	whitestem filaree
common mallow*	prickly lettuce*	wild mustard*
common purslane	prickly sida*	yellow woodsorrel
common ragweed*	prostrate knotweed	

Grasses:

annual bluegrass	foxtail	Orcutt lovegrass
barnyardgrass	goosegrass	red sprangletop
browntop panicum	Italian ryegrass	signalgrass
crabgrass	johnsongrass	Texas panicum
crowfootgrass	(seedling)	volunteer wheat*
cupgrass	junglerice	wild oat
fall panicum	little barley	witchgrass
field sandbur	Mexican lovegrass	

*** Suppression**

Remarks: Do not apply more than 900 lb./A per year. Requires rainfall or sprinkler irrigation within 21 days to activate. Refer to label for directions and precautions.

Areas Of Application: Industrial sites, utility substations, highway guardrails, sign posts and delineators.

– – – – – – – – – – – – – – –

Signal Word/Toxicity Class: Caution/III.

REI: 12 hr. unless soil-injected or soil-incorporated.

9

Other Uses

Notes • Notes • Notes

Section 10

Aquatic

Use Reminders

Control Of Some Common Aquatic Weeds With Herbicides 490
Herbicides Labeled For Aquatic Weed Control 491

Weed Efficacy Charts

Herbicide Effectiveness For Aquatic Weed Control 492

Herbicide Listings

Still Water 493
Moving Water 497

Control Of Some Common Aquatic Weeds With Herbicides

	Aquathol (granular) / Aquathol-K (liquid)	Copper Complexes / Copper Sulfate[1]	2,4-D	Hydrothol 191	Reward	Rodeo	Sonar
Algae							
Plankton (single cell)		•					
Filamentous and water net		•		•	•		
Chara and Nitella		•		•			
Floating Weeds (not attached to bottom)							
Duckweed					•		•
Watermeal					•		
Waterhyacinth			•		•	•	
Emersed Weeds (attached to bottom)							
American lotus			•				•
Watershield			•				
White waterlily			•				•
Frogbit			•				
Water pennywort					•		
Submersed Weeds (not attached to bottom)							
Bladderwort	•				•		•
Submersed Weeds (attached to bottom)							
Coontail	•				•		•
Parrottfeather	•		•		•		•
Eurasian watermilfoil	•		•		•		•
Fanwort							•
Pondweed (Najas, Potamogeton)	•				•		•
Hydrilla and elodea	•				•		•
Spikerush			•				•
Marginal Weeds							
Alligatorweed						•	•
Creeping waterprimrose			•				•
Smartweed			•			•	•
Arrowhead			•				•
Willow			•			•	
Cattail and cutgrass					•	•	•
Bulrush			•				
Burweed			•				

NOTE: It is not intended that any suggested usage in this table be in violation with existing regulations or manufacturer's label.

[1] Use products containing copper with caution because its toxicity to fish and its effectiveness in controlling aquatic weeds depend on total alkalinity of the water.

Source: Weed Control Guidelines for Mississippi, 1997.

Herbicides Labeled For Aquatic Weed Control

Aquatic Weed Common Name	Scientific Name	Aquathol	Coppers	2,4-D	Diquat Dibromide	Glyphosate	Hydrothol	Sonar
ALGAE								
Filamentous algae	many	NL	L	NL	L	NL	L	NL
Microscopic algae	many	NL	L	NL	NL	NL	NL	NL
Chara	Chara	NL	L	NL	NL	NL	L	NL
FLOWERING PLANTS								
Submerged								
American elodea	Elodea canadensis	NL	NL	NL	L	NL	L	L
Bladderwort	Utricularia vulgaris	NL	NL	C	L	NL	NL	L
Brittle naiad	Najas minor	L	NL	NL	L	NL	L	L
Buttercup	Ranunculus spp.	NL	NL	C	NL	L	NL	NL
Clasping-leaf pondweed	Potamogeton richardsonii	NL	NL	NL	L	NL	L	L
Coontail	Ceratophyllum demersum	L	NL	C	L	NL	L	L
Curly-leaf pondweed	Potamogeton crispus	L	NL	NL	L	NL	L	L
Eel grass	Vallisneria americana	NL	NL	NL	NL	NL	L	NL
Flat-stemmed pondweed	Potamogeton zosteriformis	L	NL	NL	L	NL	L	L
Horned pondweed	Zannichellia palustris	L	NL	NL	NL	NL	L	NL
Leafy pondweed	Potamogeton foliosus	NL	NL	NL	L	NL	L	L
Sago pondweed	Potamogeton pectinatus	L	NL	NL	L	NL	L	L
Small pondweed	Potamogeton pusillus	L	NL	NL	L	NL	L	L
Southern naiad	Najas guadalupensis	L	NL	NL	L	NL	L	L
Water milfoil	Myriophyllum spp.	L	NL	C	L	NL	L	L
Waterstargrass	Heteranthera dubia	L	NL	C	NL	NL	NL	NL
Free-floating								
Common duckweed	Lemna minor	NL	NL	L	L	NL	NL	L
Star duckweed	Lemna trisulca	NL	NL	L	L	NL	NL	NL
Water pennywort	Hydrocotyle spp.	NL	NL	C	L	L	NL	NL
Watermeal	Wolffia spp.	NL	NL	NL	NL	NL	NL	L
Rooted floating								
American lotus	Nelumbo lutea	NL	NL	C	NL	C	NL	C
American pondweed	Potamogeton nodosus	L	NL	NL	L	NL	L	L
Floating pondweed	Potamogeton natans	L	NL	NL	L	NL	L	L
Illinois pondweed	Potamogeton illinoensis	NL	NL	NL	L	NL	C	NL
Largeleaf pondweed	Potamogeton amplifolius	L	NL	NL	L	NL	L	L
Spatterdock	Nuphar advena	NL	NL	C	NL	L	NL	C
Water lily	Nymphaea spp.	NL	NL	C	NL	L	NL	C
Waterpurslane	Ludwigia palustris	NL	NL	NL	NL	NL	NL	C
Watershield	Brasenia schreberi	NL	NL	C	NL	NL	NL	C
Waterthread pondweed	Potamogeton diversifolius	L	NL	NL	L	NL	L	L
Emergent								
Arrowhead	Sagittaria spp.	NL	NL	C	NL	NL	NL	NL
Bulrush	Scirpus spp.	NL	NL	C	NL	L	NL	NL
Bur reed	Sparganium spp.	L	NL	C	NL	NL	NL	NL
Cattail	Typha spp.	NL	NL	C	L	L	NL	C
Creeping water primrose	Jussiaea repens	NL	NL	C	NL	L	NL	C
Pickerelweed	Pontederia spp.	NL	NL	C	NL	NL	NL	NL
Purple loosestrife	Lythrum salicaria	NL	NL	NL	NL	L	NL	NL
Spikerush	Eleocharis spp.	NL	NL	NL	NL	NL	NL	C
Water smartweed	Polygonum spp.	NL	NL	C	NL	L	NL	C
Willow	Salix spp.	NL	NL	C	NL	L	NL	NL

NL = not labeled for control of this species • L = labeled for control of this species • C = check labels for specific species listed (each 2,4-D and Sonar product is different).
SOURCE: Information has been collected from chemical manufacturers' labels. Although some products could control more species, only the species listed on the label are included.

Source: 1999 Illinois Agricultural Pest Management Handbook.

10

Aquatic
Use Reminders

NOTICE	The information on these pages is for preliminary planning — not a guide for use. Be sure to follow the manufacturer's directions, notwithstanding information contained here.

Herbicide Effectiveness For Aquatic Weed Control

| | Copper Compounds | 2,4-D | Diquat Dibromide | Endothall | | Fluridone | Glyphosate |
				Aquathol	Hydrothol		
Floating Plants							
Alligatorweed *(Altemanthera philoxeroides)*	*	F	*	*	*	F	G
Duckweed *(Lemna spp.)*	*	F	G	*	*	E	*
Watermeal *(Wolffia spp.)*	*	*	*	*	*	G	*
Filamentous Algae	G	*	G	*	G	*	*
Submersed Plants							
Bladderwort *(Utricularia spp.)*	*	F	G	F	F	G	*
Brazilian elodea *(Egeria densa)*	F	*	E	*	*	G	*
Coontail *(Ceratophyllum spp.)*	*	F	E	E	E	E	*
Hydrilla *(Hydrilla verticillata)*	F	*	E	E	E	E	*
Parrotsfeather *(Myriophyllum aquaticum)*	*	E	G	E	E	F	*
Pondweed *(Potamogeton spp.)*	*	*	G	E	E	F	*
Slender naiad *(Najas minor)*	*	*	E	E	E	E	*
Southern naiad *(Najas quadalupensis)*	*	*	E	G	G	G	*
Spikerush *(Eleocharis baldwinii)*	*	*	*	*	*	G	*
Variable leaf milfoil *(Myriophyllum heterophyllum)*	*	E	G	G	G	G	*
Emersed Plants							
American lotus *(Nelumbo lutea)*	*	G	*	*	*	G	G
Cattail *(Typha spp.)*	*	F	G	*	*	F	E
Fragrant waterlily *(Nymphea odorata)*	*	G	*	*	*	G	E
Rush *(Juncus spp.)*	*	F	*	*	*	*	G
Spadderdock *(Nuphar spp.)*	*	F	*	*	*	G	E
Waterpennywort *(Hydrocotyle spp.)*	*	G	F	*	*	*	E

* = not recommended; G = Good; F = Fair; E = Excellent

Source: Florida Weed Management, 1999.

Aquatic

Still Water
(Ponds & Lakes, Marshes, Spot Treatment of Shorelines)

Algae Pro — see copper complexes

Aqua-Kleen — see 2,4-D

AQUASHADE

Aquatic plant growth regulator that filters light penetration into body of water to suppress submersed weeds and algae. Should only be used in bodies of water with little to no outflow in order to maintain dye concentration and should be applied before weeds reach the surface.

Aquashade (blue & yellow dye) *(Applied Biochemists)*
Rate: 1 gal./A water (4 ft. depth)
Calculated Concentration In Water: 1 ppm copper.
Condition Of Application: Apply near shoreline into water before growing season starts or when growth is on the bottom.
Weeds: Aquatic weeds and algae.
Remarks: Colors water aqua-blue. Nontoxic to fish, wildlife, livestock, humans, and turf. Safe for swimming after complete dispersal. Do not apply to water that will be used for human consumption.

– – – – – – – – – – – – – – –

Signal Word/Toxicity Class: Caution.

Aquathol — see endothall

Aquatrine — see copper complexes

Captain — see copper complexes

COPPER COMPLEXES

Copper sulfate and various chelated copper compounds that are used primarily for algae control. Some chelates can also be used for Hydrilla and southern naiad control. Copper sulfate is widely used but may not be effective in hard water; chelates are formulated to provide longer lasting effect in hard water. Copper sulfate and chelates are the only compounds for which there are no restrictions on water use after treatment, except that they should not be used in trout-bearing waters. When used for filamentous algae, good distribution and contact with the mats essential for optimal control.

Algae Pro (copper-triethanolamine) *(SePRO)*
Rate: 0.7-1.7 gal./A ft.
Calculated Concentration In Water: 0.2-0.5 ppm copper.
Weeds: Free floating algae:
planktonic

Rate: 1.7-3.4 gal./A ft.
Calculated Concentration In Water: 0.5-1 ppm copper.
Weeds: Mat forming algae:

Chara	filamentous	Phormidium

Conditions of Application: Apply early in the day when conditions are calm and water temperatures are above 60°F when algae first appear.
Remarks: Use in irrigation water storage and supply systems; potable water reservoirs; farm, fish, and fire ponds; lake and fish hatcheries. Use lower rate in soft water; higher rate in hard water. Treat $1/3$-$1/2$ water area in single operation; wait 10-14 days between treatments. Begin treatment along shoreline and proceed outwards in bands to allow fish

to move into untreated areas. Consult Sate Fish and Game Agency before applying to public water.

Signal Word/Toxicity Class: Caution.

Aquatrine (mixed copper-ethanolamine) *(Applied Biochemists)*
Rate: 0.27-2.72 lb. ai/A ft.
    0.3-3 gal./A ft.
Calculated Concentration In Water: 0.1-1 ppm copper.
Weeds: Algae:

Chara	filamentous	planktonic

Remarks: For use in fish and shrimp aqua-culture facilities. No waiting period for harvesting following use. Refer to label for specific use instructions for ponds, tanks, and raceways.

– – – – – – – – – – – – – – –

Signal Word/Toxicity Class: Danger/I.

Captain (mixed copper-ethanolamine) *(SePRO)*
Cutrine-Plus (mixed copper-ethanolamine) *(Applied Biochemists)*
Rate: 0.6-1.2 gal./A ft.
Calculated Concentration In Water: 0.2-0.4 ppm copper.
Weeds: Algae:

Chara	Nitella	planktonic
filamentous		

Rate: 1.2-3 gal./A ft.
Calculated Concentration In Water: 0.4-1 ppm copper.
Weeds:
Hydrilla verticillata
Condition Of Application: Apply early in the day under calm, sunny conditions when water temperatures are at least 60°F. Do not use in water having less than 50 ppm carbonate hardness.
Remarks: Treated water may be used for drinking, swimming, fishing, and irrigation. Repeat at 1- to 2-day intervals as needed. Some states may require permits for application to public water; check with local authorities.
Tank Mixes: Diquat for hydrilla control. Refer to label for directions.

– – – – – – – – – – – – – – –

Signal Word/Toxicity Class: Danger/I.

Clearigate (mixed copper-ethanolamine) *(Applied Biochemists)*
Rate: 0.27-2.72 lb. ai/A ft.
    0.9-8.7 gal./A ft.
Calculated Concentration In Water: 0.1-1 ppm copper.
Condition Of Application: Apply early in the day under bright or sunny conditions when water temperatures are at least 60°F.
Weeds: Algae:

Chara	filamentous	planktonic

Submersed weeds:

Brazilian elodea	*Hydrilla verticillata*	pondweed
Elodea canadensis	naiad	(Potamogeton)
		water milfoil

Floating weeds:

duckweed	waterhyacinth

Remarks: Treated water can be used for swimming, fishing, or irrigation immediately after treatment. Can be used for spot treatment where localized infestations exist. Heavy infestations should be treated in sections to avoid fish suffocation.

– – – – – – – – – – – – – – –

Signal Word/Toxicity Class: Danger/I.

◆ **Copper-Z 4/4 (Liquid) or 6/2 (Granular) (copper sulfate)** *(Helena)*
Rate: 1.6-12.8 qt. Liquid/A ft.
    2.8-22.5 lb. Granular/A ft.
Calculated Concentration In Water: 0.25-2 ppm copper.
Condition Of Application: Apply when not over 5-10% of water surface is covered with algae.
Weeds: Algae:

filamentous	planktonic

Remarks: Treat $1/3$-$1/2$ of water area in single operation; wait 10-14 days between treatments. May be toxic to fish. Refer to label for directions.

– – – – – – – – – – – – – – –

Signal Word/Toxicity Class: Danger/I.

10

Aquatic

NOTICE The information on these pages is for preliminary planning — not a guide for use. Be sure to follow the manufacturer's directions, notwithstanding information contained here. | For personal protective equipment and EPA registration numbers, please turn to page 70.

Cutrine-Plus Granular (mixed copper-ethanolamine)
(Applied Biochemists)
Rate: 2.22 lb. ai G/surface A
    60 lb./surface A
Condition Of Application: Apply when algae first appears; repeat as needed.
Weeds: Bottom growing-algae such as:
Chara   Nitella
Remarks: Treated water can be used for swimming, fishing, or irrigation immediately after treatment. Heavy infestations should be treated in sections to avoid fish suffocation. Begin treatment along shore and proceed outwards in bands to allow fish to move into untreated areas. Can be used for spot treatment. Consult state fish and game agency before applying to public water.

– – – – – – – – – – – – – – – –

Signal Word/Toxicity Class: Caution.

Komeen (copper-ethylenediamine) *(Griffin)*
Rate: 4.8-12.8 lb. ai/surface A
    6-16 gal./surface A
Calculated Concentrations in Water: 0.03-0.04 ppm copper.
Conditions of Application: Apply when weeds are actively growing and in a manner which will deposit herbicide on leaf surfaces.
Weeds: Aquatic weeds:
Brazilian elodea   *Hydrilla verticillata*   southern naiad
Remarks: Low fish toxicity. Use in potable water reservoirs; recreation lakes; golf courses; ornamental, fish, and fire ponds; and industrial ponds. Safe for swimming.

– – – – – – – – – – – – – – – –

Signal Word/Toxicity Class: Caution.

K-Tea (copper-triethanolamine) *(Griffin)*
Rate: 0.54-8.16 lb. ai/surface A
    0.68-10.2 gal./surface A
Calculated Concentration In Water: 0.2-1 ppm copper.
Conditions of Application: Apply when first signs of algae appear. If Hydrilla is present, apply in bright sunlight.
Weeds: Free floating algae:
filamentous   planktonic
Remarks: Treat 1/3-1/2 water area in single operation; wait 10-14 days between treatments. Refer to label for precautions.

– – – – – – – – – – – – – – – –

Signal Word/Toxicity Class: Caution.

Nautique (mixed copper-ethylenediamine/triethanolamine) *(SePRO)*
Rate: 5-10 gal./surface A
Weeds: Free floating algae:
Brazilian elodea   horned pondweed   wedgeon grass
egeria   southern naiad

Rate: 7-14 gal./surface A
Weeds: Free floating algae:
Hydrilla verticillata
Conditions of Application: Apply when plants and weeds are actively growing.
Remarks: Treat 1/3-1/2 water area in single operation; wait 10-12 days before treating remaining area. Begin treatment along shore and proceed outwards in bands to allow fish to move into untreated areas. Water may be used immediately after treatment for swimming or fishing. Some states may require permits for application to public waters; check with local authorities

– – – – – – – – – – – – – – – –

Signal Word/Toxicity Class: Danger/I.

Stocktrine II (mixed copper-ethanolamine) *(Applied Biochemists)*
Rate: 1 fl. oz. II/250 gal. tank capacity
Calculated Concentration In Water: 0.4 ppm copper.
Condition Of Application: Apply at first visible signs of algae growth.
Weeds: Algae:
Chara   filamentous   planktonic
Remarks: Can be used in stock watering troughs and ponds. Livestock may drink treated water immediately after application. Follow label directions.

– – – – – – – – – – – – – – – –

Signal Word/Toxicity Class: Danger/I.

Triangle Brand Copper Sulfate Crystal (copper sulfate) *(Phelps Dodge)*
Rate: 0.67-5.32 lb./A ft.
Calculated Concentration In Water: 0.25-2 ppm copper.
Weeds: Algae.

Remarks: Treat 1/3-1/2 of water area in a single operation; wait 10-14 days between treatments. Begin treatment along shore and proceed outwards in bands to allow fish to move into untreated areas. May be toxic to fish. Do not exceed 4 ppm in potable water.

– – – – – – – – – – – – – – – –

Signal Word/Toxicity Class: Danger/I.

Clearigate — see copper complexes

Copper-Z — see copper complexes

Cutrine-Plus — see copper complexes

Cutrine-Plus Granular — see copper complexes

2,4-D - PHENOXY HERBICIDES

Granular ester formulations are labeled for use on submersed weeds and are particularly effective on Eurasian watermilfoil. Liquid amine formulations are effective for water hyacinth control. Caution should be used when applying liquid ester formulations because they can cause a fish kill.

Albaugh Amine 4 (2,4-D amine) *(Albaugh)*
Albaugh LV4 or LV6 (2,4-D ester) *(Albaugh)*
◆ **Opti-Amine (4) (2,4-D amine)** *(Helena)*
Riverdale 6 Amine (2,4-D amine) *(Riverdale)*
Riverdale 4 Amine IVM (2,4-D amine) *(Riverdale)*
Riverdale L.V. 4 or L.V. 6 (2,4-D ester) *(Riverdale)*
Solution (WS) 4 (2,4-D amine) *(Riverdale)*
Solve 2,4-D (2,4-D LV ester) *(Albaugh)*
Weed Rhap A-4D (2,4-D amine) *(Helena)*
Weedestroy AM-40 (2,4-D amine) *(Riverdale)*
Rate: Boat application:
    1.25-2.25 lb. ae/A
    2.5-4.5 pt. 4/A
    1.66-3 pt. 6/A
    2.38 lb. ae/A
    4.75 pt. AM-40/A
    2 lb. 13 oz. WS/A (1 packet)
Condition Of Application: Apply when leaves are fully developed above water line and plants are actively growing.
Weeds: Aquatic weeds.
Remarks: For boat application, apply in 50-100 gal. water. For aerial application, apply in 5-15 gal. water/surface A. Consult State Game and Fish Department or Water Control Agency prior to application. Do not apply to more than 1/3-1/2 of a lake or pond in any one month because excessive decaying vegetation may deplete oxygen content of water and kill fish.

– – – – – – – – – – – – – – – –

Signal Word/Toxicity Class: Danger/I (amine); Caution/III (ester).

Aqua-Kleen (20G) (2,4-D butoxyethyl ester) *(Rhone-Poulenc)*
Navigate (20G) (2,4-D butoxyethyl ester) *(Applied Biochemists)*
Rate: 20-40 lb. ae/A
    100-200 lb. 20G/A
Condition Of Application: Apply in spring or early summer when weeds are starting to grow.
Weeds: Aquatic weeds:

bladderwort	watermilfoil	white waterlily
coontail	watershield	yellow waterlily
waterchestnut	waterstargrass	(spatterdock)

Remarks: Do not apply to water used for irrigation, agricultural sprays, watering dairy animals, or domestic water supplies. Use higher rate for dense weeds, where water volume is more than 8 ft. deep, and where there is a large volume turnover. Refer to label for precautions and directions.

– – – – – – – – – – – – – – – –

Signal Word/Toxicity Class: Caution.

Gordon's Amine 400 (2,4-D amine) *(PBI/Gordon)*
Riverside 2,4-D Amine 4 (2,4-D amine) *(Terra)*
Weedar 64 (4) (2,4-D amine) *(Nufarm)*
Weedar IVM 44 (4) (2,4-D amine) *(Nufarm)*
Rate: 2-4 lb. ae/A
    4-8 pt./A

◆-new product • PP-preplant • PPI-preplant incorporated • PRE-preemergence • POST-postemergence • SEQ-sequential • ae-acid equivalent • ai-active ingredient • DF-dry flowable
E/EC-emulsifiable concentrate • F/FL-flowable • DG/G/WG-dispersable granule • L/LC-liquid • SP/WSP-soluble packet • W/WP-wettable powder • WSB-water soluble bag

Still Water

Condition Of Application: Spray only when weed mass is dense or water-hyacinths are actively growing.

Weeds: Waterhyacinth.

Remarks: Consult State Game and Fish Department or Water Control Agency prior to application.

Signal Word/Toxicity Class: Danger/I.

◆ Riverdale 2,4-D Granules (2,4-D ester) *(Riverdale)*
Rate: 20-40 lb. ae/A
100-200 lb./A

Weeds: Aquatic:

arrowhead	hornwort	watermilfoil
bladderwort	naiad	watershield
bulrush	pickerelweed	waterstargrass
burreed	pondweed	waterweed
coontail	spatterdock	white waterlily
creeping	water smartweed	yellow waterlily
waterprimrose	waterchestnut	

Condition Of Application: Apply in spring and early summer when weeds start to grow.

Remarks: Two treatments may be necessary. Half-treatment of large areas recommended to avoid excessive weed decomposition harmful to fish. Consult State Agricultural Experiment Station or Extension Service for existing regulations.

Signal Word/Toxicity Class: Caution.

Savage (WSB) (2,4-D amine) *(Platte)*
Rate: 1.9-3.8 lb. ae/A
2-4 lb. WSB/A

Condition Of Application: Spray weed mass only. Use higher rate when plants are matured or when mass is dense. Apply when weeds are actively growing; repeat when necessary.

Weeds: Aquatic weeds including:
waterhyacinth

Remarks: For surface application, apply in 100-400 gal. water. For aerial application, apply in 5 gal. water/surface A. Consult state and local authorities prior to application. To avoid fish kill from decaying plant material, do not apply to more than 1/2 of a lake or pond at one time.

Signal Word/Toxicity Class: Danger/I.

◆ Wilbur-Ellis Amine 4 (2,4-D amine) *(Wilbur-Ellis)*
Rate: 2-4 lb. ae/A
4-8 pt./A

Condition Of Application: Apply when plants are actively growing; repeat when necessary.

Weeds:
water hyacinth

Rate: 10-40 lb. ae/A
2.5-10 gal./A

Condition Of Application: Apply in spring or early summer when milfoil starts to grow.

Weeds:
water milfoil

Remarks: Subsurface, surface, air applications. For Eurasian water milfoil in programs conducted by the Tennessee Valley Authority in dams and reservoirs of the TVA system.

State Restrictions: Not registered in California.

Signal Word/Toxicity Class: Danger/I.

◆ Wilbur-Ellis Lo Vol-4 or Lo Vol-6 (2,4-D ester) *(Wilbur-Ellis)*
Rate: Boat application:
2.25 lb. ae/A in 50-100 gal. water
4.5 pt. 4/A in 50-100 gal. water
3 pt. 6/A in 50-100 gal. water

Condition Of Application: Apply when leaves are fully developed above water line and plants are actively growing. Avoid submerging plants after treatment. Uniform coverage is essential.

Weeds: Aquatic weeds.

Remarks: Consult State Game and Fish Department or Water Control Agency prior to application.

State Restrictions: Not registered in California.

Signal Word/Toxicity Class: Caution/III.

DIQUAT DIBROMIDE

Primarily used as contact herbicide for submersed and free-floating aquatic weeds. Provides short-term top kill on emergent plants such as cattails. Surfactant or spreader should be added to solution when treating free-floating or emergent weeds. Chemical binds to suspended soil particles; therefore, do not use in or dilute in muddy water. Do not apply in areas where commercial fish processing, resulting in production of fish protein concentrate or fish meal, is practiced.

Reward *(ZENECA)*
Rate: 2-4 lb. ai/surface A
1-2 gal./surface A

Condition Of Application: Apply before weed growth reaches water surface. For *P. robbinsii*, apply when plants are in early stages of growth, such as in spring or early summer.

Weeds: Submersed or bottom placement weeds and algae:

bladderwort	hydrilla	pondweed*
coontail	naiad	Spirogyra
elodea	Pithophora	watermilfoil

* Except P. richardsonii

Rate: 1-4 lb. ai/surface A
0.5-2 gal./surface A

Condition Of Application: For cattails, apply before flowering and repeat as necessary to control regrowth.

Weeds: Surface weeds and algae:

bladderwort	hydrilla	Spirogyra
cattails	naiad	waterhyacinth
coontail	pennywort	waterlettuce
duckweed	Pithophora	watermilfoil
elodea	pondweed	
frog's bit (except CA)	salvinia	

Remarks: For use in drainage ditches, lakes, ponds where there is little or no outflow of water and which are totally under control of user. In mixed populations, use high rate. Do not apply through any type of irrigation system. Refer to label for use directions, restrictions, and precautions.

State Restrictions: SLN— Florida, SLN— New York, SLN— South Carolina.

Signal Word/Toxicity Class: Warning/II.
REI: 24 hr.

Weedtrine-D (diquat dibromide) *(Applied Biochemists)*
Rate: 1-4 lb. ai/surface A
2.5-10 gal./surface A

Condition Of Application: Apply when weeds are actively growing but before weed growth has reached water surface.

Weeds: Aquatic weeds:

bladderwort	elodea	salvinia
cattail	naiad	waterhyacinth
coontail	pennywort	waterlettuce
duckweed	pondweed	

Remarks: Refer to label for specific rates to control weeds listed. Do not use treated water for animal consumption, drinking, spraying, irrigation, or domestic purposes for 1-3 days.

Signal Word/Toxicity Class: Warning/II.

ENDOTHALL

Contact herbicide used for submersed weeds (Aquathol) or algae and submersed weeds (Hydrothol). Fish are particularly sensitive to liquid formulation of Hydrothol, and open water should be left untreated to provide an escape for them. Aquathol is safe for fish, and liquid formulation is often tank mixed with copper chelates to provide both algae and submersed weed control. Water use restrictions vary from 3-25 days depending on use and dosage applied.

Aquathol (G) or Aquathol K *(ELF Atochem North America)*
Rate: 1-9.7 lb. ae/A ft.
13-135 lb. G/A ft.
0.3-3.2 gal. K/A ft.

Calculated Concentration In Water: 0.5-5 ppm dipotassium salt.
Condition Of Application: Apply after weeds are actively growing.

Weeds: Aquatic Weeds:

bassweed	hydrilla	pondweed
burreed	milfoil	(Potamogeton)
coontail	naiad	waterstargrass

NOTICE The information on these pages is for preliminary planning — not a guide for use. Be sure to follow the manufacturer's directions, notwithstanding information contained here.

For personal protective equipment and EPA registration numbers, please turn to page 70.

Still Water

Remarks: Do not use treated water for irrigation, agricultural sprays, livestock, or domestic purposes for at least 7 days for Aquathol G and 7-25 days for Aquathol K. Fish may be used for food or feed 3 days after treatment.

- - - - - - - - - - - - - - -

Signal Word/Toxicity Class:
Danger-Poison/I (Aquathol K); Danger/I (Aquathol).

Hydrothol 191 (Liquid) or Granular *(ELF Atochem North America)*
Rate: 0.16-14 lb. ae/A ft.
  0.08-7 gal. Liquid/A ft.
  0.15-13.5 lb. ae/A ft.
  3-270 lb. Granular/A ft.

Calculated Concentration In Water: 0.05-2.5 ppm.

Condition Of Application: Apply in late spring or early summer when weeds are actively growing or algae first appear.

Weeds: Aquatic weeds and algae:

Chara	milfoil	pondweed
Cladophora	naiad	(Potamogeton)
coontail	Pithophora	Spirogyra
elodea		

Remarks: Do not use treated water for irrigation, agricultural sprays, livestock, or domestic purposes for at least 7-25 days after treatment. Do not treat more than $1/10$ area at one time with doses in excess of 1 ppm. If growth is heavy, treat in strips. Fish may be used for food or feed 3 days after treatment. Fish may be killed by rates in excess of 0.3 ppm.

- - - - - - - - - - - - - - -

Signal Word/Toxicity Class:
Danger-Poison/I (191 Liquid); Danger/I (191 Granular).

GLYPHOSATE

Used strictly for emergent and floating plant control. Surfactant must be added to Rodeo to ensure foliage penetration. Broad spectrum activity. Only restriction is within $1/2$ -mile of potable water intakes.

Rodeo (5.4WS) *(Monsanto)*
Rate: Boom equipment:
  2-5 lb. ai/A
  3-7.5 pt. 5.4WS/A
  Hand-held equipment:
  0.75%-1.5% solution

Condition Of Application: Apply to foliage of emerged weeds at early growth stages of annual weeds and when perennial weeds are approaching maturity.

Weeds: Aquatic weeds:

alligatorweed	paragrass	torpedograss
American lotus	Phragmites	waterhyacinth
cattail	reed canarygrass	waterlettuce
giant cutgrass	spatterdock	waterprimrose
maidencane		

Remarks: Rate varies by weed species. Do not exceed 7.5 pt./A in a single application. Always use nonionic surfactant. Effective on emerged and floating plants as well as ditchbanks or shoreline aquatic weeds. Does not control plants which are completely submerged or have most of their foliage under water. Can be used in and around all bodies of water which may be flowing, nonflowing, or transient.

- - - - - - - - - - - - - - -

Signal Word/Toxicity Class: Caution/IV.

Hydrothol 191 — see endothall

Komeen — see copper complexes

K-Tea — see copper complexes

Nautique — see copper complexes

Navigate — see 2,4-D

Opti-Amine — see 2,4-D

Reward — see diquat dibromide

Rodeo — see glyphosate

Savage — see 2,4-D

Solution — see 2,4-D

Solve — see 2,4-D

SONAR

Primarily used for submersed flowering plant control. Slow-acting; however, in some cases, treatment will provide more than one year's control. Must be used as a whole pond treatment.

Sonar A.S. or SRP (fluridone) *(SePRO)*
Rate: Ponds:
  0.16-1.25 qt. A.S./surface A
  3.2-25 lb. SRP/surface A
  Lakes and reservoirs:
  0.2-4 qt. A.S./surface A
  4-80 lb. SRP/surface A

Calculated Concentration In Water: Ponds: 0.06-0.09 ppm; lakes and reservoirs: 0.075-0.15 ppm.

Condition Of Application: Apply prior to initiation of weed growth or when weeds are actively growing. Under optimum conditions, 30-90 days required before desired level of weed management is achieved.

Weeds: Floating weeds:
common duckweed (A.S. only)

Emersed weeds:

spatterdock	waterlily

Submersed weeds:

bladderwort	common elodea	naiad
Brazilian elodea	fanwort	pondweed
common coontail	hydrilla	watermilfoil

Shoreline grasses:
paragrass

Vascular aquatic weeds (partial control):

alligatorweed	giant cutgrass	southern watergrass
American lotus	Illinois pondweed	spikerush
cattail	parrotfeather	torpedograss
common watermeal	reed canarygrass	waterpurslane
creeping	smartweed	watershield
waterprimrose		

Rate: Whole lakes and reservoirs:
  0.027-0.54 qt. A.S./surface A

Calculated Concentration In Water: 0.01-0.02 ppm.

Condition Of Application: Apply early in growing season.

Weeds: Submersed weeds:
Eurasian watermilfoil

Remarks: For treating lakes or reservoirs where little dilution with treated water is expected to occur. May be applied to entire surface area of pond. In lakes and reservoirs, apply to areas greater than 5 acres. Treatment of narrow strips such as boat lanes or shorelines may not produce satisfactory results due to dilution with untreated water. In reservoirs, do not apply within $1/4$ mile (1320 ft.) of any potable water intake. Trees and shrubs growing in treated water may be injured. Do not apply in tidewater or brackish water. Do not apply through any type of irrigation system.

- - - - - - - - - - - - - - -

Signal Word/Toxicity Class: Caution.

Stocktrine II — see copper complexes

Triangle Brand — see copper complexes

Weed Rhap — see 2,4-D

◆-new product • PP-preplant • PPI-preplant incorporated • PRE-preemergence • POST-postemergence • SEQ-sequential • ae-acid equivalent • ai-active ingredient • DF-dry flowable E/EC-emulsifiable concentrate • F/FL-flowable • DG/G/WG-dispersable granule • L/LC-liquid • SP/WSP-soluble packet • W/WP-wettable powder • WSB-water soluble bag

Weedar — see 2,4-D

Weedestroy AM-40 — see 2,4-D

Weedtrine-D — see diquat

Moving Water
(Bayous, Ditchbanks, Drainage Canals, Irrigation)

Algae Pro — see copper complexes

Aquathol K — see endothall

Captain — see copper complexes

COPPER COMPLEXES

Copper sulfate and various chelated copper compounds that are used primarily for algae control. Some chelates can also be used for hydrilla and southern naiad control. Copper sulfate is widely used but may not be effective in hard water; chelates are formulated to provide longer lasting effect in hard water. Copper sulfate and chelates are the only compounds for which there are no restrictions on water use after treatment, with the exception that they should not be used in trout-bearing waters. When used for filamentous algae, good distribution and contact with the mats is essential for optimal control.

Algae Pro (copper-triethanolamine) *(SePRO)*
Rate: 1.25-6.25 qt./cfs water flow/hr. for 3 hr.
Calculated Concentration In Water: 1 ppm copper.
Conditions of Application: Apply in anticipation of algae that may interfere with normal flow or delivery of water.
Weeds: Mat forming algae:

Chara	filamentous	Phormidium

Remarks: Irrigation conveyance systems. Repeat application at a point 3 hr. downstream from previous treatment station; repeat as necessary.

- - - - - - - - - - - - - - -

Signal Word/Toxicity Class: Caution.

Clearigate (mixed copper-ethanolamine) *(Applied Biochemists)*
Rate: 0.3-2.8 qt./cfs water flow/hr. for 3 hr.
Calculated Concentration In Water: 0.1-1 ppm copper.
Weeds: Submerged weeds and the following algae:

Chara	Nitella	planktonic
filamentous		

Remarks: Effective aquatic plant control in flowing water is dependent upon maintaining suitable contact time with sufficient chemical concentrations. Accurately determine water flow rates prior to treatment.

- - - - - - - - - - - - - - -

Signal Word/Toxicity Class: Danger/I.

◆ Copper-Z 4/4 (Liquid) or 6/2 (Granular) (copper sulfate) *(Helena)*
Triangle Brand Copper Sulfate Crystal (copper sulfate) *(Phelps Dodge)*
Rate: Continuous application:
7.9-15.8 fl. oz. Liquid/cfs water flow/during each 24 hr.
0.4-0.9 lb. Granular/cfs water flow/during each 24 hr.
0.1-0.2 lb. Crystal/cfs water flow/12 of each 24 hr.
Slug application:
1.4-9.6 pt. Liquid/cfs water flow/treatment
1.2-8.4 lb. Granular/cfs water flow/treatment
0.5-2 lb. Crystal/cfs water flow/treatment
Condition Of Application: Apply as growth develops. For slug application, treat every 5-30 miles of length; repeat in 2 weeks.
Weeds:

filamentous algae	flagellates	diatoms

Remarks: Irrigation systems. May be toxic to fish. Do not exceed 4 ppm in potable water.

- - - - - - - - - - - - - - -

Signal Word/Toxicity Class: Danger/I.

Captain (mixed copper-ethanolamine) *(SePRO)*
Cutrine-Plus (mixed copper-ethanolamine) *(Applied Biochemists)*
Rate: 1 qt./cfs water flow/hr. for 3 hr.
Calculated Concentration In Water: 1 ppm copper.
Condition Of Application: Apply early in the day under calm, sunny conditions when water temperatures are at least 60°F. Treat as soon as algae or hydrilla begins to interfere with normal delivery of water.
Weeds: Algae:

Chara	hydrilla	Nitella
filamentous		

Remarks: Accurately determine water flow rates prior to treatment. Treat when there is sufficient water flow to allow dispersion of product. Product should be introduced at points of turbulence-creating structures such as weirs. Cleared for use in potable water up to 1 ppm copper. Follow all label directions.

- - - - - - - - - - - - - - -

Signal Word/Toxicity Class: Danger/I.

Clearigate — see copper complexes

Copper-Z — see copper complexes

Cutrine-Plus — see copper complexes

2,4-D - PHENOXY HERBICIDES

Granular ester formulations are labeled for use on submersed weeds and are particularly effective on Eurasian watermilfoil. Liquid amine formulations are effective for water hyacinth control. Caution should be used when applying liquid ester formulations because they can cause fish kill. Note restrictions on water use.

Albaugh Amine 4 (2,4-D amine) *(Albaugh)*
◆ Opti-Amine (4) (2,4-D amine) *(Helena)*
Riverdale 6 Amine (2,4-D amine) *(Riverdale)*
Riverdale 4 Amine IVM (2,4-D amine) *(Riverdale)*
Solution (WS) 4 (2,4-D amine) *(Riverdale)*
Weed Rhap A-4D (2,4-D amine) *(Helena)*
Weedestroy AM-40 (2,4-D amine) *(Riverdale)*
Rate: Boat application:
1.25-2.25 lb. ae/A
2.5-4.5 pt. 4/A
1.66-3 pt. 6/A
2.38 lb. ae/A
4.75 pt. AM-40/A
2 lb. 13 oz. WS/A (1 packet)
Condition Of Application: Apply when leaves are fully developed above water line and plants are actively growing.
Weeds: Aquatic weeds.
Remarks: For boat application, apply in 50-100 gal. water. For aerial application, apply in 5-15 gal. water/surface A. Consult State Game and Fish Department or Water Control Agency prior to application. Do not apply to more than $1/3$-$1/2$ of a lake or pond in any one month because excessive decaying vegetation may deplete oxygen content of water and kill fish.

- - - - - - - - - - - - - - -

Rate: 1-2 lb. ae/A
2-4 pt./A
2 lb. 13 oz. WS/1.5-3 A (1 packet)
Condition Of Application: Apply when weeds are young and growing vigorously before bud or early bloom stage.
Weeds: Weeds and brush.
Remarks: Apply no more than 2 treatments per season.
State Restrictions: For use on irrigation canal ditchbanks in Arizona, California, Colorado, Idaho, Kansas, Montana, Nebraska, Nevada, New Mexico, North Dakota, Oklahoma, Oregon, South Dakota, Texas, Utah, Washington, Wyoming.

- - - - - - - - - - - - - - -

Signal Word/Toxicity Class: Danger/I.

10

Aquatic

NOTICE The information on these pages is for preliminary planning — not a guide for use. Be sure to follow the manufacturer's directions, notwithstanding information contained here.

For personal protective equipment and EPA registration numbers, please turn to page 70.

Albaugh LV4 or LV6 (2,4-D ester) *(Albaugh)*
Riverdale L.V. 4 or L.V. 6 (2,4-D ester) *(Riverdale)*
Solve 2,4-D (2,4-D LV ester) *(Albaugh)*
Rate: Boat application:
1.25-2.25 lb. ae/A
2.5-4.5 pt. 4/A
1.66-3 pt. 6/A
Condition Of Application: Apply when leaves are fully developed above water line and plants are actively growing.
Weeds: Aquatic weeds.
Remarks: For boat application, apply in 50-100 gal. water. For aerial application, apply in 5-15 gal. water/surface A. Consult State Game and Fish Department or Water Control Agency prior to application. Do not apply to more than 1/3-1/2 of a lake or pond in any one month because excessive decaying vegetation may deplete oxygen content of water and kill fish.

- - - - - - - - - - - - - - -

Signal Word/Toxicity Class: Caution/III.

Riverside 2,4-D Amine 4 (2,4-D amine) *(Terra)*
Weedar 64 (4) (2,4-D amine) *(Nufarm)*
Weedar IVM 44 (4) (2,4-D amine) *(Nufarm)*
Rate: 1-2 lb. ae/A
2-4 pt./A
Condition Of Application: Apply when weeds are young and growing vigorously.
Weeds: Annual and perennial broadleaf weeds and woody brush.
Remarks: Apply no more than 2 treatments per season.
State Restrictions: For use on irrigation canal ditchbanks in Arizona, California, Colorado, Idaho, Kansas, Montana, Nebraska, New Mexico, Nevada, North Dakota, Oklahoma, Oregon, South Dakota, Texas, Utah, Washington, Wyoming.

- - - - - - - - - - - - - - -

Signal Word/Toxicity Class: Danger/I.

Savage (WSB) (2,4-D amine) *(Platte)*
Rate: 1.9-3.8 lb. ae/A
2-4 lb. WSB/A
Condition Of Application: Spray weed mass only. Use higher rate when plants are matured or when mass is dense. Apply when weeds are actively growing; repeat when necessary.
Weeds: Aquatic weeds including:
waterhyacinth
Remarks: For surface application, apply in 100-400 gal. water. For aerial application, apply in 5 gal. water/surface A. Consult state and local authorities prior to application. To avoid fish kill from decaying plant material, do not apply to more than 1/2 of a lake or pond at one time.

- - - - - - - - - - - - - - -

Rate: 0.95-3.8 lb. ae/A
1-4 lb. WSB/A
Condition Of Application: Apply when weeds are young and actively growing before bud or early bloom stage.
Weeds: Weeds and brush.
Remarks: Apply no more than 2 treatments per season. Refer to label for use directions, precautions, and restrictions.
State Restrictions: For use on irrigation canal ditchbanks in Arizona, California, Colorado, Idaho, Kansas, Montana, Nebraska, Nevada, New Mexico, North Dakota, Oklahoma, Oregon, South Dakota, Texas, Utah, Washington, Wyoming.

- - - - - - - - - - - - - - -

Signal Word/Toxicity Class: Danger/I.

◆ **Wilbur-Ellis Amine 4 (2,4-D amine)** *(Wilbur-Ellis)*
Rate: 1-2 lb. ae/A in 20-100 gal. water
2-4 pt./A in 20-100 gal. water
Condition Of Application: Apply when weeds are young and growing vigorously before bud or early bloom stage.
Weeds: Weeds and brush.
Remarks: Apply no more than 2 treatments per season.
State Restrictions: For use on irrigation canal ditchbanks in Arizona, Colorado, Idaho, Kansas, Montana, Nebraska, Nevada, New Mexico, North Dakota, Oklahoma, Oregon, South Dakota, Texas, Utah, Washington, Wyoming. Not registered in California.

- - - - - - - - - - - - - - -

Signal Word/Toxicity Class: Danger/I.

◆ **Wilbur-Ellis Lo Vol-4 or Lo Vol-6 (2,4-D ester)** *(Wilbur-Ellis)*
Rate: Boat application:
2.25 lb. ae/A in 50-100 gal. water
4.5 pt. 4/A in 50-100 gal. water
3 pt. 6/A in 50-100 gal. water

Condition Of Application: Apply when leaves are fully developed above water line and plants are actively growing. Avoid submerging plants after treatment. Uniform coverage is essential.
Weeds: Aquatic weeds.
Remarks: Consult State Game and Fish Department or Water Control Agency prior to application.
State Restrictions: Not registered in California.

- - - - - - - - - - - - - - -

Signal Word/Toxicity Class: Caution/III.

DIQUAT DIBROMIDE

Primarily used as contact herbicide for submersed and free-floating aquatic weeds. Only provides short-term top kill on emergent plants such as cattails. Surfactant or spreader should be added to diquat solution when treating free-floating or emergent weeds. Chemical binds to suspended soil particles; therefore, do not use in or dilute in muddy water. Do not apply in areas where commercial fish processing, resulting in production of fish protein concentrate or fish meal, is practiced.

Reward *(ZENECA)*
Rate: 2-4 lb. ai/surface A
1-2 gal./surface A
Condition Of Application: Apply before weed growth reaches water surface. For *P. robbinsii*, apply when plants are in early stages of growth, such as in spring or early summer.
Weeds: Submersed or bottom placement weeds and algae:

bladderwort	hydrilla	pondweed*
coontail	naiad	Spirogyra
elodea	Pithophora	watermilfoil

* Except P. richardsonii

Rate: 1-4 lb. ai/surface A
0.5-2 gal./surface A
Condition Of Application: For cattails, apply before flowering and repeat as necessary to control regrowth.
Weeds: Surface weeds and algae:

bladderwort	hydrilla	Spirogyra
cattails	naiad	waterhyacinth
coontail	pennywort	waterlettuce
duckweed	Pithophora	watermilfoil
elodea	pondweed	
frog's bit (except CA)	salvinia	

Remarks: For use in bayous, canals, drainage ditches, lakes, marshes, ponds, reservoirs, rivers, streams. In mixed populations, use high rate. Do not apply through any type of irrigation system. Refer to label for use directions, restrictions, and precautions.
State Restrictions: SLN— Florida, SLN— New York, SLN— South Carolina.

- - - - - - - - - - - - - - -

Signal Word/Toxicity Class: Warning/II.
REI: 24 hr.

Weedtrine-D (diquat) *(Applied Biochemists)*
Rate: 0.5-2 lb. ai/surface A
1.25-5 gal./surface A
Condition Of Application: Apply before flowering and repeat as necessary to control regrowth.
Weeds: Aquatic weeds:
cattail
Remarks: Drainage ditches. Dilute with sufficient water and add nonionic surfactant to spray solution prior to application. Wet foliage thoroughly and avoid drift onto desirable plants.

- - - - - - - - - - - - - - -

Signal Word/Toxicity Class: Warning/II.

ENDOTHALL

Contact herbicide used for submersed weeds (Aquathol) or algae and submersed weeds (Hydrothol). Fish are particularly sensitive to liquid formulation of Hydrothol, and open water should be left untreated to provide an escape for them. Aquathol is safe for fish, and liquid formulation is often tank mixed with copper chelates to provide both algae and submersed weed control. Water use restrictions vary from 3-25 days depending on use and dosage applied.

Aquathol K *(ELF Atochem North America)*
Rate: 2-9.7 lb. ae/A ft.
0.6-3.2 gal. K/A ft.
Calculated Concentration In Water: 1-5 ppm dipotassium salt.
Condition Of Application: Apply after water has warmed and weed growth is visible.

◆-new product • PP-preplant • PPI-preplant incorporated • PRE-preemergence • POST-postemergence • SEQ-sequential • ae-acid equivalent • ai-active ingredient • DF-dry flowable
E/EC-emulsifiable concentrate • F/FL-flowable • DG/G/WG-dispersable granule • L/LC-liquid • SP/WSP-soluble packet • W/WP-wettable powder • WSB-water soluble bag

Weeds: Aquatic weeds:

bassweed	hydrilla	pondweed
burreed	milfoil	(Potamogeton)
coontail	naiad	waterstargrass

Remarks: Do not use treated water for irrigation, agricultural sprays, livestock, or domestic purposes for at least 7-25 days after treatment. Fish may be used for food or feed 3 days after treatment.

- - - - - - - - - - - - - - -

Signal Word/Toxicity Class: Danger-Poison/I.

Hydrothol 191 (Liquid) or 191 Granular *(ELF Atochem North America)*
Rate: 2.8-13.5 lb. ae/A ft.
     1.4-6.75 gal. Liquid/A ft.
     55-270 lb. Granular/A ft.
Calculated Concentration In Water: 1-5 ppm.
Condition Of Application: Refer To Label.
Weeds: Aquatic weeds and algae:

Chara	milfoil	pondweed
Cladophora	naiad	(Potamogeton)
coontail	Pithophora	Spirogyra
elodea		

Remarks: Do not use treated water for irrigation, agricultural sprays, livestock, or domestic purposes for at least 7-25 days after treatment. Do not treat more than $1/10$ area at one time with doses in excess of 1 ppm. Fish may be used for food or feed 3 days after treatment. If growth is heavy, treat in strips. Fish may be killed by rates in excess of 0.3 ppm.

- - - - - - - - - - - - - - -

Signal Word/Toxicity Class:
Danger-Poison/I (191 Liquid); Danger/I (191 Granular).

GLYPHOSATE

Used strictly for emergent and floating plant control. Broad spectrum activity. Only restriction is within $1/2$ mile of potable water intakes.

Rodeo (5.4WS) *(Monsanto)*
Rate: Boom equipment:
    2-5 lb. ai/A
    3-7.5 pt. 5.4WS/A
    Hand-held equipment:
    0.75%-1.5% solution
Condition Of Application: Apply to foliage of emerged weeds at early growth stages of annual weeds and when perennial weeds are approaching maturity.
Weeds: Aquatic weeds:

alligatorweed	paragrass	torpedograss
American lotus	Phragmites	waterhyacinth
cattail	reed canarygrass	waterlettuce
giant cutgrass	spatterdock	waterprimrose
maidencane		

Remarks: Rate varies by weed species. Do not exceed 7.5 pt./A in a single application. Always use nonionic surfactant. Effective on emerged and floating plants as well as ditchbanks or shoreline aquatic weeds. Does not control plants which are completely submerged or have most of their foliage under water. Can be used in and around all bodies of water which may be flowing, nonflowing, or transient.

- - - - - - - - - - - - - - -

Signal Word/Toxicity Class: Caution/IV.

Hydrothol 191 — see endothall

Opti-Amine — see 2,4-D

Reward — see diquat dibromide

Rodeo — see glyphosate

Savage — see 2,4-D

Solution — see 2,4-D

Solve — see 2,4-D

SONAR

Primarily used for submersed flowering plant control. Can be applied before or soon after weeds emerge. Slow-acting; however, in some cases, treatment will provide more than one year's control. Must be used as a whole pond treatment.

Sonar A.S. or SRP (fluridone) *(SePRO)*
Rate: 2 qt. A.S./surface A
    40 lb. SRP/surface A
Condition Of Application: Apply prior to initiation of weed growth or when weeds are actively growing. Under optimum conditions, 30-90 days required before desired level of weed management is achieved.
Weeds: Floating weeds:
common duckweed (A.S. only)

Emersed weeds:

spatterdock	waterlily

Submersed weeds:

bladderwort	egeria	naiad
Brazilian elodea	fanwort	pondweed
common coontail	hydrilla	watermilfoil
common elodea		

Shoreline grasses:
paragrass

Vascular aquatic weeds-suppression:

alligatorweed	giant cutgrass	southern watergrass
American lotus	Illinois pondweed	spikerush
cattail	parrotfeather	torpedograss
common watermeal	reed canarygrass	waterpurslane
creeping	smartweed	watershield
waterprimrose		

Remarks: Drainage canals, irrigation canals, rivers. To achieve satisfactory control, water flow must be restricted for minimum of 7 days to prevent dilution of Sonar. Use application pattern that will provide uniform distribution and avoid concentration of herbicide. Trees and shrubs growing in treated water may be injured. Do not apply in tidewater or brackish water. Do not apply through any type of irrigation system.

- - - - - - - - - - - - - - -

Signal Word/Toxicity Class: Caution.

Triangle Brand — see copper complexes

Weed Rhap — see 2,4-D

Weedar — see 2,4-D

Weedestroy AM-40 — see 2,4-D

Weedtrine-D — see diquat

10

Aquatic

NOTICE The information on these pages is for preliminary planning — not a guide for use. Be sure to follow the manufacturer's directions, notwithstanding information contained here.	For personal protective equipment and EPA registration numbers, please turn to page 70.

Notes • Notes • Notes

Weed Control Manual

Indexes

Crop Index 502
Product Index 504
Weed Index 520
Suppliers Directory 561

The information in *WEED CONTROL MANUAL 2000* is updated to August 15, 1999.

Because manufacturers' product recommendations are constantly being updated and revised as additional product registrations and label changes are approved by EPA, there may be changes after this date. However, every effort has been made to give manufacturers the opportunity to include in the Manual their latest information. This Manual is for preliminary planning – not a use guide. Be sure to follow label directions, notwithstanding information contained herein.

Crop Index

A

Alfalfa (Forage) 455-460
Almonds (Nuts).. 386-392
Alsike (Forage) 456
Anise (Herbs & Spices) 316
Apples (Tree Fruits, Deciduous)............... 370-379
Apricots (Tree Fruits, Deciduous) 370,372-378
Aquatic.. 493-499
Artichokes..292,293
Asparagus 293-297
Avocados (Tree Fruits, Subtropical)............. 380-384

B

Bananas (Tree Fruits, Subtropical)............... 380-384
Barley... 211-222
Basil (Herbs & Spices)..316
Beans 297-300
Beans, Guar 242,243
Beans, Mung..246,247
Beechnuts (Nuts) 388,389,392
Beets, Sugar.. 269-272
Beets, Table 346,347
Bell peppers (Peppers)..327
Birdsfoot trefoil (Forage)...................... 455-457,459
Black turtle soup (Beans) 298
Black walnuts (Nuts) 386,388,392
Blackberries (Small Fruits)......................... 357-362
Blackeyed peas (Southern Peas).......................335
Blueberries (Small Fruits) 356-362
Bok choy (Cole Crops) 306
Boysenberries (Small Fruits)..................... 357-362
Brazil nuts (Nuts) 388-390,392
Broccoli (Cole Crops)................................... 305-307
Brush Control... 436-442
Brussels sprouts (Cole Crops) 305-307
Bulb onions (Onions)................................... 321-323
Butternuts (Nuts) 388,390,392

C

Cabbage (Cole Crops) 305-307
Cacao (Tree Fruits, Subtropical)....................381,382
Calamondin (Tree Fruits, Citrus)....................366,369
Caneberries (Small Fruits) 357-362
Canola (Oil Seed Crops)................................247,248
Cantaloupe (Cucurbits) 307-309
Carrots 301-303
Cashews (Nuts)......................................388,389,392
Castor Beans..240
Cauliflower (Cole Crops) 305-307
Celery... 303-305
Cherries (Tree Fruits, Deciduous) 370-378
Chestnuts (Nuts)....................................388-390,392
Chickpeas (Garbanzos) 311,312
Chicory (Lettuce, Endive)............................318,320
Chili peppers (Peppers) 327,328

Chinese cabbage (Cole Crops)....................305,306
Chinquapins (Nuts)..............................388,389,392
Chironja (Tree Fruits, Citrus) 366,369
Chive (Herbs & Spices) 316
Citron (Tree Fruits, Citrus)....................365,366,369
Citrus (Tree Fruits) 363-370
Citrus citron (Tree Fruits, Citrus) 366
Clover (Forage)..455-457,459
Coconut (Tree Fruits, Subtropical)...............381,383
Coffee (Tree Fruits, Subtropical)............380-382,384
Cole Crops 305-307
Collards (Greens).. 314-316
Conservation Reserve Program 442-447
Corn, Field 101-125
Corn, Sweet..337-345
Cotton..173-182
Crabapples (Tree Fruits, Deciduous) 372,374,376
Cranberries (Small Fruits) 356,357,359-362
Cranberry beans (Beans) 298,299
Crenshaw melons (Cucurbits) 308
Crowder peas (Southern Peas)..........................335
Crownvetch (Forage) 457
Cucumbers (Cucurbits) 307-309
Cucurbits 307-309
Currants (Small Fruits) 357-359,361,362

D

Dates (Tree Fruits, Subtropical)...... 380,381,383,384
Deciduous (Tree Fruits) 370-379
Dewberries (Small Fruits)...............357-359,361,362
Dill (Herbs & Spices)..316
Dry beans (Beans)..297-300
Dry bulb onions (Onions) 321-323
Dry peas (Peas)..326,327
Durum wheat (Spring Wheat)...................199-202,
....205-207,209,211

E

Eggplant 309-311
Elderberries (Small Fruits)...............357-359,362
Endive...318-320
English peas (Peas)..325,327
English walnuts (Nuts) 386-388,390-392
Escarole (Lettuce, Endive)................................. 318
Established Lawns and Turf.......................399-411
Established legumes (Forage) 457

F

Fallow Land 447-455
Fennel (Herbs & Spices).................................... 316
Field Corn 101-125
Figs (Tree Fruits, Subtropical) 380-384
Filberts (Nuts)...385-392
Flax 240-242
Forage 455-460

Forage sorghum (Sorghum) 259-263,266

G

Garbanzos 311,312
Garlic..312-314
Gherkin (Cucurbits) 308
Ginger (Herbs & Spices) 316
Gooseberries (Small Fruits) 357-359,362
Grain corn (Field Corn).................... 104,111,119
Grain sorghum (Sorghum) 259-268
Grapefruit (Tree Fruits, Citrus) 364-370
Grapes (Small Fruits) 356-363
Grasses for Seed Production.......................411-415
Great northern beans (Beans) 297-299
Green beans (Beans) 298,299
Greens..314-316
Guar Beans..242,243
Guava (Tree Fruits, Subtropical)...................379-384

H

Hazelnuts (Nuts) 386
Head lettuce (Lettuce, Endive).................... 319
Herbs & Spices 316
Hickory (Nuts)..388,389,392
Hops 243
Horseradish.. 316
Huckleberries (Small Fruits)...................... 357,359

I

Irish potatoes (Potatoes)................................... 329

J

Jojoba (Oil Seed Crops) 247

K

Kale (Greens) 314-316
Kenaf 244
Kidney beans (Beans) 297-299
Kiwifruit (Tree Fruits, Subtropical) 380-384
Kohlrabi (Cole Crops) 306
Kumquats (Tree Fruits, Citrus) 365,366,368-370

L

Ladino clover (Forage) 456
Lawn and Turf Seedbeds............................... 399
Lawns and Turf, Established 399-411
Leaf lettuce (Lettuce, Endive)...................... 319
Leeks (Onions) 321,323
Lemons (Tree Fruits, Citrus) 364-370
Lentils 317
Lespedeza (Forage) 457
Lettuce 318,319

Lima beans (Beans) 297-300
Limes (Tree Fruits, Citrus) 364-369
Loganberries (Small Fruits) 357-359,361,362
Loquat (Tree Fruits, Subtropical) 381,384

M

Macadamias (Nuts)................................. 385-392
Mandarins (Tree Fruits, Citrus)..................366,369
Mangos (Tree Fruits, Subtropical)....380,381,383,384
Melons (Cucurbits) 307-309
Milo (Sorghum) 259-268
Mint 244-246
Moving Water 497-499
Mung Beans 246,247
Muskmelon (Cucurbits) 307-309
Mustard (Greens) 314-316

N

Navy beans (Beans) 297-299
Nectarines (Tree Fruits, Deciduous)...... 370,372-378
Newly Sprigged or Seeded Turf 399
Noncropland 467-487
Nuts 384-392

O

Oats 223-230
Oil Seed Crops 247,248
Okra 320
Olives (Tree Fruits, Subtropical).................. 379-384
Olallieberries (Small Fruits)........................359,361
Onions 320-323
Oranges (Tree Fruits, Citrus)..................... 364-370
Oregano (Herbs & Spices) 316
Ornamentals & Woody Plants.................... 418-427

P

Papayas (Tree Fruits, Subtropical) 380-384
Parsley (Carrots).......................................301,302
Parsnips (Carrots)......................................301,302
Passion fruit (Tree Fruits, Subtropical) ... 380-382,384
Pastures & Rangeland 460-467
Peaches (Tree Fruits, Deciduous) 370-378
Peanuts.. 248-252
Pears (Tree Fruits, Deciduous) 370-379
Peas.. 324-327
Peas, Southern...335,336
Pecans (Nuts) 386-392
Peppermint (Mint)......................................244,245
Peppers...327-329
Persian melons (Cucurbits) 308
Persimmons (Tree Fruits, Subtropical) 380,381,
....383,384
Pimento (Peppers)...327
Pineapple (Tree Fruits, Subtropical)............. 380-384
Pink beans (Beans) 297,298
Pinkeyed peas (Southern Peas) 335

Pinto beans (Beans) 297-299
Pistachio (Nuts)...385-392
Plantains (Tree Fruits, Subtropical) 380-382,384
Plums (Tree Fruits, Deciduous) 370-378
Pome fruits (Tree Fruits, Deciduous)....................371
Pomegranates (Tree Fruits, Subtropical) 380,381,
....383,384
Popcorn............ 101-103,105-115,117-119,124,125
Potatoes...329-332
Potatoes, Sweet 345,346
Prunes (Tree Fruits, Deciduous)..................370-378
Pummelo (Tree Fruits, Citrus) 366
Pumpkins (Cucurbits)................................307-309

Q

Quince (Tree Fruits, Deciduous) 374,376,378

R

Radishes...333
Rangeland, Pastures & 460-467
Rapeseed (Oil Seed Crops).........................247,248
Raspberries (Small Fruits) 357-362
Red beans (Beans) 297-299
Red Beets (Table Beets) 347
Red clover (Forage) 456
Red Mexican beans (Beans) 298
Rhubarb..333-335
Rice 253-258
Rosemary (Herbs & Spices) 316
Rutabaga (Cole Crops) 306
Rye 231-235

S

Safflower 248,258,259
Sage (Herbs & Spices) 316
Sainfoin (Forage) 457-459
Satsuma mandarin (Tree Fruits, Citrus)............366
Savory (Herbs & Spices) 316
Seed corn (Field Corn)............... 101-103,106-111,
...............................113-116,118-120,124,125
Shallots (Onions).......................................321-323
Silage corn (Field Corn).....................101-104,106,
...............................109-113,115-120,123,124
Small Fruits...356-363
Small Grains 186-235
Snap beans (Beans)...................................297-300
Sorghum..259-269
Sour cherries (Tree Fruits, Deciduous)..374,376,377
Sour orange (Tree Fruits, Citrus)......................366
Southern Peas 335,336
Soybeans...143-164,248
Spearmint (Mint) 244,245
Spinach 336,337
Spring Wheat...199-211
Squash (Cucurbits)...................................307-309
Still Water..493-497
Stone fruits (Tree Fruits, Deciduous).....371,376,379

Strawberries (Small Fruits) 356,357,361
String beans (Beans)...................................... 299
Subtropical (Tree Fruits) 379-384
Succulent beans (Beans) 300
Succulent peas (Peas) 324,326
Sugar Beets.. 269-272
Sugarcane 272-279
Summer squash (Cucurbits) 308
Sunflower...248,279-281
Sweet cherries (Tree Fruits, Deciduous) 371,374,
....376,377
Sweet Corn.. 337-345
Sweet orange (Tree Fruits, Citrus)..................... 366
Sweet peppers (Peppers) 327
Sweet Potatoes 345,346
Swiss Chard (Greens) 314,315

T

Tabasco peppers (Peppers) 327
Table Beets... 346,347
Tangelos (Tree Fruits, Citrus)........364-366,368-370
Tangerines (Tree Fruits, Citrus)................... 364-370
Tangor (Tree Fruits, Citrus) 366
Tarragon (Herbs & Spices) 316
Taro (Tree Fruits, Subtropical) 382
Tea (Tree Fruits, Subtropical)........................381,384
Thyme (Herbs & Spices) 316
Tobacco 281-283
Tomatillo (Tomatoes) 349
Tomatoes 347-350
Tree Fruits (Citrus) 363-370
Tree Fruits (Deciduous).............................. 370-379
Tree Fruits (Subtropical) 379-384
Turf, Newly Sprigged or Seeded...................... 399
Turf Grasses for Sod Production 415-418
Turnip greens (Greens) 315,316
Turnips (Cole Crops)...................................305,306

V

Vegetables.. 292-350

W

Walnuts (Nuts)......................................385-390,392
Watermelon (Cucurbits).............................. 307-309
Wax beans (Beans) 297,299
Wheat, Spring 199-211
Wheat, Winter 186-198
White beans (Beans) 297-299
Winter peas (Peas)... 325
Winter squash (Cucurbits) 308
Winter Wheat 186-198
Woody Plants, Ornamentals & 418-427

Y

Yams (Sweet Potatoes)................................... 346
Youngberries (Small Fruits) 359,362

Product Index

3 Plus 3 (2,4-D & MCPP)...................Riverdale
- est. lawns/turf...... 402

120 Herbicide (MSMA) .... Terra
- WPS chart...... 79
- cotton...... 178
- est. lawns/turf...... 407
- noncropland...... 478
- nuts...... 389
- small fruits...... 360
- tree fruits, citrus...... 366
- tree fruits, deciduous...... 374

875 Brushkiller (2,4-D & 2,4-DP & dicamba) ....PBI/Gordon
- noncropland...... 470

912 Herbicide (MSMA) .... Terra
- WPS chart...... 79
- cotton...... 178
- est. lawns/turf...... 407
- noncropland...... 478
- nuts...... 389
- small fruits...... 360
- tree fruits, citrus...... 366
- tree fruits, deciduous...... 374

2D + 2 MCPP (2,4-D & MCPP).............Riverdale
- est. lawns/turf...... 402

A

AAtrex (atrazine) .... Novartis
- WPS chart...... 77
- conservation reserve program...... 442
- est. lawns/turf...... 399
- fallow land...... 448
- field corn, popcorn...... 102
- noncropland...... 467
- nuts...... 385
- ornamentals/woody plants...... 418
- sorghum...... 260
- sugarcane...... 273
- sweet corn...... 338
- tree fruits, subtropical...... 379
- turf grasses for sod...... 415

Accent (nicosulfuron) ....DuPont
- WPS chart...... 74
- field corn, popcorn...... 101

Accent Gold (clopyralid & flumetsulam & nicosulfuron & rimsulfuron) ....DuPont
- WPS chart...... 74
- field corn, popcorn...... 101

Acclaim Extra (fenoxaprop-P-ethyl) .... AgrEvo USA
- WPS chart...... 72
- est. lawns/turf...... 404
- ornamentals/woody plants...... 421
- turf grasses for sod...... 417

Accord (glyphosate)...................... Monsanto
- WPS chart...... 76
- brush control...... 439
- noncropland...... 474
- ornamentals/woody plants...... 423

Accord Site Prep (glyphosate)........... Monsanto
- WPS chart...... 76
- brush control...... 439

acetochlor (see Harness, Surpass, TopNotch)

acetochlor & atrazine (see FulTime, Harness Xtra, Surpass 100)

acetochlor & atrazine & glyphosate (see Field Master)

Achieve (tralkoxydim) ....ZENECA
- WPS chart...... 80
- barley...... 211
- spring wheat...... 199
- winter wheat...... 186

acifluorfen (see Blazer, Status)

Action (fluthiacet-methyl).................. Novartis
- WPS chart...... 77
- soybeans...... 143

Aim (carfentrazone-ethyl)...................... FMC
- WPS chart...... 75
- field corn, popcorn...... 102
- spring wheat...... 199
- winter wheat...... 186

alachlor (see Lasso, Lasso II, Micro-Tech, Partner)

alachlor & atrazine (see Bullet, Lariat)

alachlor & trifluralin (see Freedom)

Alanap-L (naptalam)...................... Uniroyal
- WPS chart...... 80
- cucurbits...... 307
- ornamentals/woody plants...... 418

Albaugh Amine 4 (2,4-D amine) .... Albaugh
- WPS chart...... 72
- barley...... 214
- brush control...... 436
- conservation reserve program...... 444
- est. lawns/turf...... 401
- fallow land...... 449
- field corn, popcorn...... 108
- grasses for seed production...... 412
- moving water...... 497
- noncropland...... 469
- nuts...... 385
- oats...... 224
- pastures/rangeland...... 461
- rice...... 254
- rye...... 232
- sorghum...... 262
- soybeans...... 147
- spring wheat...... 203
- still water...... 494
- sugarcane...... 273
- sweet corn...... 340
- tree fruit, deciduous...... 371
- winter wheat...... 186

Albaugh D-638 (2,4-D ester + acid) .... Albaugh
- WPS chart...... 72
- barley...... 215
- conservation reserve program...... 444
- fallow land...... 449
- field corn, popcorn...... 108
- noncropland...... 469
- sorghum...... 262
- soybeans...... 147
- spring wheat...... 203
- winter wheat...... 190

Albaugh LV4 or LV6 (2,4-D ester).......... Albaugh
- WPS chart...... 72
- barley...... 215
- brush control...... 436
- conservation reserve program...... 444
- est. lawns/turf...... 401
- fallow land...... 449
- field corn, popcorn...... 108
- grasses for seed production...... 412
- moving water...... 498
- noncropland...... 169
- oats...... 224
- pastures/rangeland...... 461
- rye...... 232
- sorghum...... 262
- soybeans...... 147
- spring wheat...... 203
- still water...... 494
- sugarcane...... 273
- sweet corn...... 340
- winter wheat...... 190

Albaugh MCPA (MCPA) .... Albaugh
- WPS chart...... 72
- barley...... 219
- flax...... 241
- grasses for seed production...... 414
- noncropland...... 478
- oats...... 228
- pastures/rangeland...... 464
- peas...... 325
- rice...... 255
- rye...... 233,234
- spring wheat...... 207
- winter wheat...... 195

Albaugh Trifluralin (trifluralin)............. Albaugh
- WPS chart...... 72
- asparagus...... 297
- barley...... 222
- beans...... 300
- carrots...... 303
- castor beans...... 240
- celery...... 305
- cole crops...... 307
- conservation reserve program...... 447
- cotton...... 182
- cucurbits...... 309
- fallow land...... 455
- field corn, popcorn...... 125
- flax...... 242
- forage...... 459
- greens...... 315
- guar beans...... 243
- hops...... 243
- lettuce, endive...... 319
- mung beans...... 247
- nuts...... 392
- oil seed crops...... 247
- okra...... 320
- onions...... 323
- peanuts...... 252
- peas...... 326
- peppers...... 329
- potatoes...... 332
- radishes...... 333
- safflower...... 259
- small fruits...... 363
- sorghum...... 268
- southern peas...... 336
- soybeans...... 162
- spring wheat...... 211
- sugar beets...... 272
- sugarcane...... 278
- sunflower...... 280
- tomatoes...... 350
- tree fruits, citrus...... 370
- tree fruits, deciduous...... 378
- winter wheat...... 198

Algae Pro (copper complex) ....SePRO
- moving water...... 497
- still water...... 493

Ally (metsulfuron-methyl).................. DuPont
- WPS chart...... 74
- barley...... 211
- fallow land...... 447
- pastures/rangeland...... 460
- spring wheat...... 199
- winter wheat...... 186

Amber (triasulfuron) .... Novartis
- WPS chart...... 77
- barley...... 212
- conservation reserve program...... 442
- fallow land...... 448
- pastures/rangeland...... 460
- spring wheat...... 199
- winter wheat...... 186

ametryn (see Evik)

Ansar 6.6 (MSMA)...........................ZENECA
- WPS chart...... 80
- cotton...... 178
- est. lawns/turf...... 407
- noncropland...... 479

Aqua-Kleen (2,4-D ester)............Rhone-Poulenc
- still water...... 494

Aquashade (dye)............... Applied Biochemists
- still water...... 493

Aquathol (endothall) .... Elf Atochem
- moving water...... 498
- still water...... 495

Aquatrine (mixed copper complex) .... Applied Biochemists
still water 493
Arrosolo (molinate & propanil) ..... ZENECA
WPS chart 80
rice 253
Arsenal (imazapyr) ..... American Cyanamid
WPS chart 72
noncropland 476,477
Assert (imazamethabenz) ..... American Cyanamid
WPS chart 72
barley 212
spring wheat 200
sunflower 279
winter wheat 187
Assure II (quizalofop-P-ethyl) ..... DuPont
WPS chart 74
cotton 173
soybeans 156
asulam (see Asulox, Riverside)
Asulox (asulam) ..... Rhone-Poulenc
WPS chart 78
noncropland 467
ornamentals/woody plants 418
sugarcane 272
turf grasses for sod 415
Atra-5 (atrazine) ..... Drexel
WPS chart 74
est. lawns/turf 399
fallow land 448
field corn, popcorn 102
nuts 385
ornamentals/woody plants 418
sorghum 260
sugarcane 273
sweet corn 338
tree fruits, subtropical 379
turf grasses for sod 415
atrazine (see AAtrex, Clean Crop, Drexel, Helena, Riverside, Wilbur-Ellis)
atrazine & 2,4-D (see Shotgun)
Authority (sulfentrazone) ..... DuPont
WPS chart 74
soybeans 160
Authority Broadleaf (sulfentrazone & chlorimuron-ethyl) ..... FMC
WPS chart 75
soybeans 160
Avenge (difenzoquat) ..... American Cyanamid
WPS chart 72
barley 212
spring wheat 200
winter wheat 187
Axiom (flufenacet & metribuzin) ..... Bayer
WPS chart 73
field corn, popcorn 103
soybeans 144

B

Balan (benefin) ..... Platte
WPS chart 78
forage 455
lettuce, endive 318
Balance WDG (isoxaflutole) ..... Rhone-Poulenc
WPS chart 78
field corn, popcorn 103
Banvel (dicamba) ..... BASF
WPS chart 73
asparagus 294
barley 216
brush control 438
conservation reserve program 444
est. lawns/turf 403
fallow land 450
field corn, popcorn 110
grasses for seed production 413
noncropland 471
oats 226
pastures/rangeland 463
sorghum 263
spring wheat 204
sugarcane 274
winter wheat 191
Bareground (bromacil & diuron & sodium chlorate & sodium metaborate) ..... Pro-Serve
noncropland 467
BareSpot Monobor-Chlorate (sodium metaborate & sodium chlorate) ..... Pro-Serve
noncropland 467
BareSpot Ureabor (sodium metaborate & sodium chlorate & bromacil) ..... Pro-Serve
noncropland 467
BareSpot Weed & Grass (sodium metaborate & sodium chlorate & diuron) ..... Pro-Serve
noncropland 467
Barrage or Barrage HF (2,4-D ester) ..... Helena
WPS chart 76
barley 215
brush control 436
conservation reserve program 444
est. lawns/turf 402
fallow land 449
field corn, popcorn 108
grasses for seed production 412
noncropland 470
oats 225
ornamentals/woody plants 420
pastures/rangeland 462
rye 232
sorghum 262
soybeans 147
spring wheat 203
sweet corn 340
turf grasses for sod 416
winter wheat 190
Barricade (prodiamine) ..... Novartis
WPS chart 77
est. lawns/turf 399
Basagran (bentazon) ..... BASF
WPS chart 73
beans 298
est. lawns/turf 400
field corn, popcorn 103
mint 244
ornamentals/woody plants 419
peanuts 248
peas 324
rice 253
sorghum 260
soybeans 144
sweet corn 338
Basamid Granular (dazomet) ..... BASF
WPS chart 73
lawns/turf seedbeds 399
nuts 385
ornamentals/woody plants 419
tobacco 281
tree fruits, deciduous 370
Basis (rimsulfuron & thifensulfuron-methyl) ... DuPont
WPS chart 74
field corn, popcorn 104
Basis Gold (nicosulfuron & rimsulfuron & atrazine) ..... DuPont
WPS chart 74
field corn, popcorn 104
Beacon (primisulfuron-methyl) ..... Novartis
WPS chart 77
field corn, popcorn 104
benefin (see Balan)
benefin & oryzalin (see XL 2G)
bensulfuron (see Londax)
bensulide (see Bensumec, Prefar, Pre-San, ProTurf Weedgrass Preventer)
bensulide & oxadiazon (see ProTurf Goosegrass/ Crabgrass Control)
Bensumec (bensulide) ..... PBI/Gordon
est. lawns/turf 400
bentazon (see Basagran, Rezult)
bentazon & acifluorfen (see Conclude, Conclude Ultra, Conclude Xtra, Galaxy, Manifest, Storm)
bentazon & atrazine (see Laddok S-12, Prompt)
Betamix (phenmedipham & desmedipham) ..... AgrEvo USA
WPS chart 72
sugar beets 269
Betanex (desmedipham) ..... AgrEvo USA
WPS chart 72
sugar beets 269
Bicep II MAGNUM (*S*-metolachlor & atrazine) ..... Novartis
WPS chart 77
field corn, popcorn 104
sorghum 260
sweet corn 338
Bicep Lite II MAGNUM (*S*-metolachlor & atrazine) ..... Novartis
WPS chart 77
field corn, popcorn 104
sorghum 260
sweet corn 338
Bison (bromoxynil & MCPA) ..... Terra
WPS chart 79
barley 213
conservation reserve program 443
grasses for seed production 411
oats 223
rye 231
spring wheat 201
turf grasses for sod 416
winter wheat 188
BK 800 (2,4-D & 2,4-DP & dicamba) ... PBI/Gordon
brush control 437
noncropland 470
Bladex (cyanazine) ..... DuPont
WPS chart 74
cotton 174
field corn, popcorn 107
sweet corn 339
Blazer (acifluorfen) ..... BASF
WPS chart 73
peanuts 248
rice 253
soybeans 143
Blue Drum (propanil) ..... RiceCo
WPS chart 78
rice 257
Bolero (thiobencarb) ..... Valent
WPS chart 80
rice 253
Brash (2,4-D & dicamba) ..... Terra
WPS chart 79
brush control 438
fallow land 450
noncropland 470
pastures/rangeland 462
sorghum 263
spring wheat 204
sugarcane 274
winter wheat 191
Broadrange (2,4-D & 2,4-DP) ..... Wilbur-Ellis
WPS chart 80
brush control 438
est. lawns/turf 403
noncropland 471
Broadstrike+Treflan (flumetsulam & trifluralin) ..... Dow AgroSciences
WPS chart 73
soybeans 144
Broclean (bromoxynil) ..... Platte
WPS chart 78
barley 212
conservation reserve program 442
est. lawns/turf 400
field corn, popcorn 105
flax 240
forage 455
garlic 312
grasses for seed production 411
mint 244
noncropland 468
oats 223
onions 321
rye 231
sorghum 261
spring wheat 200
turf grasses for sod 416
winter wheat 187
Bromac (bromoxynil & MCPA) ..... Platte
WPS chart 78
barley 213
conservation reserve program 443
grasses for seed production 411
oats 223
rye 231
spring wheat 201

turf grasses for sod ... 416
winter wheat ... 188
bromacil (see Hyvar)
bromacil & diuron (see DiBro 2 + 2, Krovar, Weed Blast)
bromacil & diuron & sodium chlorate & sodium metaborate (see Bareground, Total)
Bromox (bromoxynil) ... Micro Flo
WPS chart ... 76
barley ... 212
conservation reserve program ... 442
est. lawns/turf ... 400
field corn, popcorn ... 105
flax ... 240
forage ... 455
garlic ... 312
grasses for seed production ... 411
mint ... 244
noncropland ... 468
oats ... 223
onions ... 321
rye ... 231
sorghum ... 261
spring wheat ... 200
turf grasses for sod ... 416
winter wheat ... 187
Bromox + atrazine (bromoxynil & atrazine) ... Micro Flo
WPS chart ... 76
field corn, popcorn ... 105
sorghum ... 261
Bromox-MCPA 2-2 (bromoxynil & MCPA) ... Micro Flo
WPS chart ... 76
barley ... 213
conservation reserve program ... 443
grasses for seed production ... 411
oats ... 223
rye ... 231
spring wheat ... 201
turf grasses for sod ... 416
winter wheat ... 188
bromoxynil (see Broclean, Bromox, Buctril, Moxy)
bromoxynil & atrazine (see Bromox + atrazine, Brozine, Buctril + atrazine, Moxy + atrazine)
bromoxynil & MCPA (see Bison, Bromac, Bromox-MCPA 2-2, Bronate)
Bronate (bromoxynil & MCPA) ... Rhone-Poulenc
WPS chart ... 78
barley ... 213
conservation reserve program ... 443
flax ... 241
grasses for seed production ... 411
oats ... 223
rye ... 231
spring wheat ... 201
turf grasses for sod ... 416
winter wheat ... 188
Brozine (bromoxynil & atrazine) ... Platte
WPS chart ... 78
field corn, popcorn ... 105
sorghum ... 261
Brushmaster (2,4-D & 2,4-DP & dicamba) ... PBI/Gordon
brush control ... 437
est. lawns/turf ... 403
noncropland ... 470
Buckle (triallate & trifluralin) ... Monsanto
WPS chart ... 76
barley ... 213
peas ... 324
spring wheat ... 201
winter wheat ... 188
Buctril (bromoxynil) ... Rhone-Poulenc
WPS chart ... 78
barley ... 212
conservation reserve program ... 442
cotton ... 166,173
est. lawns/turf ... 400
field corn, popcorn ... 105
flax ... 240
forage ... 455
garlic ... 312
grasses for seed production ... 411
mint ... 244
noncropland ... 468
oats ... 223
onions ... 321
rye ... 231
sorghum ... 261
spring wheat ... 200
turf grasses for sod ... 416
winter wheat ... 187
Buctril + atrazine (bromoxynil & atrazine) ... Rhone-Poulenc
WPS chart ... 78
field corn, popcorn ... 105
sorghum ... 261
Bueno (MSMA) ... ZENECA
WPS chart ... 80
cotton ... 178
est. lawns/turf ... 407
noncropland ... 479
nuts ... 389
tree fruits, citrus ... 366
tree fruits, deciduous ... 374
Bullet (alachlor & atrazine) ... Monsanto
WPS chart ... 76
field corn, popcorn ... 106
sorghum ... 261
sweet corn ... 339
Butoxone (2,4-DB) ... Cedar
WPS chart ... 73
forage ... 456
peanuts ... 249
soybeans ... 148
butylate (see Sutan+)
Butyrac (2,4-DB) ... Albaugh
WPS chart ... 72
conservation reserve program ... 444
forage ... 456
peanuts ... 249
soybeans ... 148

C

cacodylic acid (see Montar)
cacodylic acid & MSMA (see Moncide)
Cadre (imazapyc) ... American Cyanamid
WPS chart ... 72
peanuts ... 249
Campaign (glyphosate & 2,4-D) ... DuPont
noncropland ... 468
Canopy (metribuzin & chlorimuron-ethyl) ... DuPont
WPS chart ... 74
soybeans ... 144
Canopy XL (sulfentrazone & chlorimuron-ethyl) ... DuPont
WPS chart ... 74
soybeans ... 160
Canvas (thifensulfuron-methyl & tribenuron-methyl & metsulfuron-methyl) ... DuPont
WPS chart ... 75
barley ... 213
fallow land ... 448
spring wheat ... 201
winter wheat ... 188
Caparol (prometryn) ... Novartis
WPS chart ... 77
celery ... 304
cotton ... 180
Captain (mixed copper complex) ... SePRO
moving water ... 497
still water ... 493
carfentrazone-ethyl (see Aim)
Casoron (dichlobenil) ... Uniroyal
WPS chart ... 80
noncropland ... 472
nuts ... 386
ornamentals/woody plants ... 420
small fruits ... 357
tree fruits, deciduous ... 372
Celebrity (dicamba & nicosulfuron) ... BASF
WPS chart ... 73
field corn, popcorn ... 106
Cheyenne [Cheyenne FM (fenoxaprop-P-ethyl & MCPA) + X-TRA (thifensulfuron-methyl & tribenuron-methyl)] ... AgrEvo USA
WPS chart ... 72
spring wheat ... 202
winter wheat ... 188
Chipco Ronstar (oxadiazon) ... Rhone-Poulenc
WPS chart ... 78
est. lawns/turf ... 401
ornamentals/woody plants ... 419
Chiptox (MCPA sodium salt) ... Nufarm
WPS chart ... 78
barley ... 219
oats ... 228
rye ... 234
spring wheat ... 207
winter wheat ... 195
chloridazon (see Pyramin)
chlorimuron-ethyl (see Classic, Skirmish)
chlorimuron-ethyl & thifensulfuron-methyl (see Reliance STS, Synchrony STS)
chlorsulfuron (see Glean, Telar)
chlorsulfuron & metsulfuron-methyl (see Finesse)
Chopper (imazapyr) ... American Cyanamid
WPS chart ... 72
brush control ... 440
noncropland ... 477
Clarity (dicamba-DGA) ... BASF
WPS chart ... 73
asparagus ... 294
barley ... 216
cotton ... 175
field corn, popcorn ... 110
oats ... 226
sorghum ... 263
soybeans ... 149
spring wheat ... 204
sugarcane ... 274
winter wheat ... 191
Classic (chlorimuron-ethyl) ... DuPont
WPS chart ... 75
soybeans ... 145
Clean Crop Amine 4 (2,4-D amine) ... Platte
WPS chart ... 78
barley ... 215
brush control ... 436
fallow land ... 450
field corn, popcorn ... 109
grasses for seed production ... 412
noncropland ... 470
nuts ... 385
oats ... 225
pastures/rangeland ... 462
rice ... 254
rye ... 232
sorghum ... 262
soybeans ... 147
spring wheat ... 203
sugarcane ... 274
tree fruits, deciduous ... 371
winter wheat ... 190
Clean Crop Atrazine (atrazine) ... Platte
WPS chart ... 78
est. lawns/turf ... 399
fallow land ... 448
field corn, popcorn ... 102
noncropland ... 467
nuts ... 385
ornamentals/woody plants ... 418
sorghum ... 260
sugarcane ... 273
sweet corn ... 338
tree fruits, subtropical ... 379
turf grasses for sod ... 415
Clean Crop DPD Ester Brush Killer (2,4-D & 2,4-DP ester) ... Platte
brush control ... 438
noncropland ... 471
Clean Crop DSMA Plus (DSMA) ... Platte
WPS chart ... 78
cotton ... 175
est. lawns/turf ... 404
noncropland ... 473
nuts ... 387
small fruits ... 358
tree fruits, citrus ... 364
tree fruits, deciduous ... 372
Clean Crop Low Vol 4 or 6 (2,4-D ester) ... Platte
WPS chart ... 78
barley ... 215
brush control ... 436
est. lawns/turf ... 402
field corn, popcorn ... 109
grasses for seed production ... 412
noncropland ... 470
oats ... 225
pastures/rangeland ... 462
rye ... 232
sorghum ... 262
soybeans ... 148

spring wheat ... 203
winter wheat ... 190
Clean Crop MCP (MCPA) ... Platte
WPS chart ... 78
barley ... 219
est. lawns/turf ... 406
flax ... 241
forage ... 457
grasses for seed production ... 414
noncropland ... 478
oats ... 228
pastures/rangeland ... 464
peas ... 325
rice ... 255,256
rye ... 233
sorghum ... 266
spring wheat ... 207
winter wheat ... 195
Clean Crop MSMA (MSMA) ... Platte
WPS chart ... 78
cotton ... 178
Clean Crop Simazine (simazine) ... Platte
WPS chart ... 78
field corn, popcorn ... 123
noncropland ... 482
nuts ... 390
ornamentals/woody plants ... 426
small fruits ... 361
sweet corn ... 345
tree fruits, citrus ... 368
tree fruits, deciduous ... 376
tree fruits, subtropical ... 383
turf grasses for sod ... 417
Clean Crop Trifluralin HF (trifluralin) ... Platte
WPS chart ... 78
asparagus ... 297
barley ... 222
beans ... 300
carrots ... 303
castor beans ... 240
celery ... 305
cole crops ... 307
cotton ... 182
cucurbits ... 309
fallow land ... 455
field corn, popcorn ... 125
flax ... 242
forage ... 459
greens ... 315
guar beans ... 243
hops ... 243
mung beans ... 247
nuts ... 392
oil seed crops ... 247
okra ... 320
peanuts ... 252
peas ... 326
peppers ... 329
potatoes ... 332
radishes ... 333
safflower ... 259
small fruits ... 363
sorghum ... 268
southern peas ... 336
soybeans ... 162
spring wheat ... 211
sugar beets ... 272
sugarcane ... 278
sunflower ... 280
tomatoes ... 350
tree fruits, citrus ... 370
tree fruits, deciduous ... 378
winter wheat ... 198
Cleanout (2,4-D & 2,4-DP & dicamba) ... PBI/Gordon
WPS chart ... 78
brush control ... 437
est. lawns/turf ... 403
noncropland ... 470
Clearigate (mixed copper complex) ... Applied Biochemists
moving water ... 497
still water ... 493
clethodim (see Conclude Xtra, Envoy, Prism, Select)
clomazone (see Command)
clomazone & trifluralin (see Commence)
clopyralid (see Reclaim, Stinger, Transline)
clopyralid & 2,4-D (see Curtail)
clopyralid & flumetsulam (see Hornet)
clopyralid & flumetsulam & 2,4-D (see Scorpion III)
clopyralid & flumetsulam & nicosulfuron & rimsulfuron (see Accent Gold)
clopyralid & MCPA (see Curtail M)
cloransulam-methyl (see FirstRate)
cloransulam-methyl & flumetsulam (see Frontrow)
Cobra (lactofen) ... Valent
WPS chart ... 80
cotton ... 174
soybeans ... 145
Command (clomazone) ... FMC
WPS chart ... 75
cotton ... 174
cucurbits ... 307
fallow land ... 449
peas ... 324
peppers ... 327
soybeans ... 145
tobacco ... 281
Commence (clomazone & trifluralin) ... FMC
WPS chart ... 75
soybeans ... 146
Conclude [Conclude B (bentazon & acifluorfen) + Conclude G (sethoxydim)] ... BASF
WPS chart ... 73
soybeans ... 146
Conclude Ultra [Conclude Ultra B (bentazon & acifluorfen) + Conclude Ultra G (sethoxydim)] ... BASF
WPS chart ... 73
soybeans ... 147
Conclude Xtra [Conclude Xtra B (bentazon & acifluorfen) + Conclude Xtra G (clethodim)] ... BASF
WPS chart ... 73
soybeans ... 147
Confront (triclopyr & clopyralid) ... Dow AgroSciences
est. lawns/turf ... 401
Contour (imazethapyr & atrazine) ... American Cyanamid
WPS chart ... 72
field corn, popcorn ... 85,107
Cool Power (MCPA & triclopyr & dicamba) ... Riverdale
est. lawns/turf ... 401
copper complex (see Algae Pro, Komeen, K-Tea, Nautique, Stocktrine II)
copper sulfate (see Copper-Z, Triangle Brand Copper Sulfate)
Copper-Z (copper sulfate) ... Helena
moving water ... 497
still water ... 493
Corral (pendimethalin) ... Scotts
WPS chart ... 79
est. lawns/turf ... 407
ornamentals/woody plants ... 425
Cotoran (fluometuron) ... Novartis
WPS chart ... 77
cotton ... 176
Cotton-Aide (cacodylic acid) ... Monterey
WPS chart ... 77
noncropland ... 468
Cotton-Pro (prometryn) ... Griffin
WPS chart ... 76
celery ... 304
cotton ... 180
Credit (glyphosate) ... Nufarm
WPS chart ... 77
artichokes ... 292
asparagus ... 295
barley ... 218
beans ... 298
brush control ... 439
carrots ... 301
celery ... 303
cole crops ... 305
conservation reserve program ... 445
cotton ... 167,177
cucurbits ... 308
eggplant ... 310
est. lawns/turf ... 405
fallow land ... 451
field corn, popcorn ... 114
forage ... 457
garbanzos ... 311
garlic ... 313
grasses for seed production ... 413
greens ... 314
guar beans ... 242
horseradish ... 316
lentils ... 317
lettuce, endive ... 318
noncropland ... 475
nuts ... 388
oats ... 227
okra ... 320
onions ... 321
ornamentals/woody plants ... 423
pastures/rangeland ... 463
peanuts ... 250
peas ... 324
peppers ... 328
potatoes ... 329
radishes ... 333
rhubarb ... 334
rice ... 254
rye ... 233
small fruits ... 359
sorghum ... 265
soybeans ... 128,152
spinach ... 336
spring wheat ... 206
sugar beets ... 270
sugarcane ... 276
sweet corn ... 342
sweet potatoes ... 346
table beets ... 347
tomatoes ... 348
tree fruits, citrus ... 365
tree fruits, deciduous ... 373
tree fruits, subtropical ... 381
winter wheat ... 193
Crossbow (triclopyr & 2,4-D) ... Dow AgroSciences
noncropland ... 469
pastures/rangeland ... 461
Curbit (ethalfluralin) ... Platte
WPS chart ... 78
cucurbits ... 308
Curtail (clopyralid & 2,4-D) ... Dow AgroSciences
WPS chart ... 74
barley ... 214
conservation reserve program ... 443
fallow land ... 449
grasses for seed production ... 412
pastures/rangeland ... 461
spring wheat ... 202
winter wheat ... 189
Curtail M (clopyralid & MCPA) ... Dow AgroSciences
WPS chart ... 74
barley ... 214
conservation reserve program ... 443
grasses for seed production ... 412
oats ... 224
spring wheat ... 202
winter wheat ... 189
Cutrine-Plus (mixed copper complex) ... Applied Biochemists
moving water ... 497
still water ... 493
Cutrine-Plus Granular (mixed copper complex) ... Applied Biochemists
still water ... 494
cyanazine (see Bladex, Cy-Pro)
cyanazine & atrazine (see Extrazine II)
cycloate (see Ro-Neet)
Cyclone (paraquat) ... ZENECA
WPS chart ... 80
barley ... 220
conservation reserve program ... 445
cotton ... 179
sorghum ... 266
soybeans ... 154
spring wheat ... 208
sunflower ... 279
winter wheat ... 196
Cy-Pro (cyanazine) ... Griffin
WPS chart ... 76
cotton ... 174
field corn, popcorn ... 107
sweet corn ... 339

D

2,4-D (see Albaugh, Aqua-Kleen, Barrage, Clean Crop, Dri-Clean, Esteron 99C, Formula 40, Hi-Dep, Navigate, Opti-Amine, Orchard Master, Phenoxy 088, Riverdale, Riverside, Saber, Salvo, Savage, Solve 2,4-D, Solution, Weed Rhap, Weedar, Weedestroy AM-40, Weedone 638, Wilbur-Ellis)
2,4-D & dicamba (see Brash, Veteran 720, Weedmaster)
2,4-D & 2,4-DP (see Broadrange, Clean Crop DPD Ester, Patron 170, Riverdale Turf D + DP)
2,4-D & 2,4-DP & dicamba (see 875 Brushkiller, BK 800, Brushmaster, Cleanout, Super Trimec, SuperBrush, Trimec Turf Ester)
2,4-D & 2,4-DP & MCPP (see Dissolve, PAR-3, Triamine, Tri-Ester)
2,4-D & MCPP (see Deuce)
2,4-D & MCPP & dicamba (see Threesome, Trimec 992, Trimec Classic, Triplet, Tri-Plex)
2,4-DB (see Butoxone, Butyrac, Riverside 2,4-DB)
2,4-DP (see Patron DP-4, Riverdale DP-4)
2,4-DP & MCPA & MCPP (see Triamine II, Tri-Ester II)

Dakota (fenoxaprop-P-ethyl & MCPA) ... AgrEvo USA
- WPS chart 72
- spring wheat 204
- winter wheat 191

dazomet (DMTT) (see Basamid Granular)
desmedipham (see Betanex)

Detail (imazaquin & dimethenamid) ..... American Cyanamid
- WPS chart 72
- soybeans 148

Deuce (2,4-D & MCPP) ..... Wilbur-Ellis
- WPS chart 80
- est. lawns/turf 403

Devrinol (napropamide) ..... United Phosphorus
- WPS chart 80
- artichokes 292
- asparagus 294
- cole crops 305
- eggplant 309
- mint 245
- nuts 386
- peppers 327
- rhubarb 333
- small fruits 356
- sweet potatoes 345
- tobacco 281
- tomatoes 348
- tree fruits, citrus 364
- tree fruits, deciduous 371
- tree fruits, subtropical 380

DiBro 2 + 2 (bromacil & diuron) ..... Riverdale
- noncropland 471

dicamba (see Banvel, ProTurf K-O-G Weed Control, Veteran CST or 10G)
dicamba & atrazine (see Marksman, Sterling Plus)
dicamba-DGA (see Clarity, Vanquish)
dicamba & MCPA (see Vengeance, Veteran 2010)
dicamba & nicosulfuron (see Celebrity)
dicamba & primisulfuron-methyl & prosulfuron (see NorthStar)
dicamba & triasulfuron (see Rave)
dichlobenil (see Casoron, Dyclomec)
diclofop (see Hoelon, Illoxan)
dichlorprop (see 2,4-DP)
difenzoquat (see Avenge)
diflufenzopyr & dicamba (see Distinct)

Dimension (dithiopyr) ..... Rohm and Haas
- est. lawns/turf 404

dimethenamid (see Frontier)
dimethenamid & atrazine (see Guardsman, Leadoff)
dimethenamid & dicamba (see OpTill)
diquat dibromide (see Diquat, Reward, Weedtrine-D)

Diquat (diquat dibromide) ..... ZENECA
- WPS chart 80
- artichokes 292
- asparagus 294
- forage 456
- noncropland 473
- nuts 386
- oil seed crops 247
- ornamentals/woody plants 420
- potatoes 329
- small fruits 357
- sorghum 264
- soybeans 149
- tree fruits, citrus 364
- tree fruits, deciduous 372
- tree fruits, subtropical 380

Direx (diuron) ..... Griffin
- WPS chart 76
- artichokes 292
- asparagus 295
- barley 216
- cotton 175
- field corn, popcorn 111
- forage 456
- grasses for seed production 413
- mint 245
- noncropland 473
- nuts 387
- oats 226
- ornamentals/woody plants 421
- pastures/rangeland 463
- small fruits 357
- sorghum 264
- sugarcane 275
- tree fruits, citrus 364
- tree fruits, deciduous 372
- tree fruit, subtropical 380
- winter wheat 191

disodium methanearsonate (see DSMA)

Dissolve (2,4-D & 2,4-DP & MCPP) ..... Riverdale
- WPS chart 79
- est. lawns/turf 403
- noncropland 471

Distinct (diflufenzopyr & dicamba) ..... BASF
- WPS chart 73
- field corn, popcorn 111

dithiopyr (see Dimension)
diuron (see Direx, Diuron 80, Drexel, Karmex, Riverside, Wilbur-Ellis)

Diuron 80 (diuron) ..... Platte
- WPS chart 78
- artichokes 292
- asparagus 295
- barley 216
- cotton 175
- field corn, popcorn 111
- forage 456
- grasses for seed production 413
- mint 245
- noncropland 473
- nuts 387
- oats 226
- ornamentals/woody plants 421
- pastures/rangeland 463
- small fruits 357
- sorghum 264
- sugarcane 275
- tree fruits, citrus 364
- tree fruits, deciduous 372
- tree fruits, subtropical 380
- winter wheat 191

DMTT (see dazomet)

DoublePlay (EPTC & acetochlor) ..... ZENECA
- WPS chart 80
- field corn, popcorn 111

DPX-E9636 (rimsulfuron) ..... DuPont
- field corn, popcorn 122

Drexar 530 (MSMA) ..... Drexel
- est. lawns/turf 407
- noncropland 479

Drexel Atrazine (atrazine) ..... Drexel
- WPS chart 74
- est. lawns/turf 399
- fallow land 448
- field corn, popcorn 102
- nuts 385
- ornamentals/woody plants 418
- sorghum 260
- sugarcane 273
- sweet corn 338
- tree fruits, subtropical 379
- turf grasses for sod 415

Drexel Diuron (diuron) ..... Drexel
- WPS chart 74
- asparagus 295
- barley 216
- cotton 175
- forage 456
- grasses for seed production 413
- noncropland 473
- nuts 387
- ornamentals/woody plants 421
- pastures/rangeland 463
- small fruits 357
- sorghum 264
- sugarcane 275
- tree fruits, citrus 364
- tree fruits, deciduous 372
- winter wheat 192

Drexel DSMA (DSMA) ..... Drexel
- WPS chart 74
- cotton 175
- est. lawns/turf 404
- noncropland 473
- tree fruits, citrus 364,365

Drexel MSMA (MSMA) ..... Drexel
- WPS chart 74
- cotton 178
- est. lawns/turf 407
- noncropland 479
- nuts 389
- tree fruits, citrus 367
- tree fruits, deciduous 375

Drexel Simazine (simazine) ..... Drexel
- WPS chart 74
- field corn, popcorn 123
- nuts 390
- ornamentals/woody plants 426
- small fruits 361
- sweet corn 345
- tree fruits, citrus 368
- tree fruits, deciduous 376
- tree fruits, subtropical 383
- turf grasses for sod 417

Dri-Clean (2,4-D amine) ..... Riverdale
- WPS chart 79
- est. lawns/turf 402
- noncropland 470
- nuts 385
- small fruits 356
- tree fruits, deciduous 371

Dry DSMA 63SG (DSMA) ..... Luxembourg-Pamol
- cotton 175
- est. lawns/turf 404
- noncropland 473

DSMA (see Clean Crop, Drexel, Dry DSMA 63SG, DSMA 4 LB, Liquid DSMA, Methar)

DSMA 4 LB (DSMA) ..... Helena
- WPS chart 76
- cotton 175
- est. lawns/turf 404
- noncropland 473
- tree fruits, citrus 364

Dual II MAGNUM (*S*-metolachlor) ..... Novartis
- WPS chart 77
- beans 299
- cotton 178
- field corn, popcorn 117
- garbanzos 311
- mung beans 246
- peanuts 250
- peas 325
- potatoes 330
- safflower 259
- sorghum 266
- southern peas 335
- soybeans 153
- sweet corn 343

Dual MAGNUM (*S*-metolachlor) ..... Novartis
- WPS chart 77
- beans 299
- cotton 178
- field corn, popcorn 117
- garbanzos 311
- mung beans 247
- peanuts 250
- peas 325
- potatoes 330
- safflower 259
- sorghum 266
- southern peas 335
- soybeans 153
- sweet corn 343

Duet (propanil & bensulfuron-methyl) ..... RiceCo
- WPS chart 78
- rice 254

Dyclomec (dichlobenil) ..... PBI/Gordon
- noncropland 472
- ornamentals/woody plants 420

E

endothall (see Aquathol, Herbicide 273, Hydrothal)
endothall & copper ethanolamine (see Weedtrine-Plus)
Envoy (clethodim) .... Valent
  WPS chart 80
  noncropland 468
  nuts 385
  ornamentals/woody plants 419
  small fruits 356
  tree fruits, citrus 363
  tree fruits, deciduous 371
  tree fruits, subtropical 379
Epic (flufenacet & isoxaflutole) .... Bayer
  WPS chart 73
  field corn, popcorn 111
Eptam (EPTC) .... ZENECA
  WPS chart 80
  beans 298
  castor beans 240
  cotton 176
  forage 456
  nuts 387
  ornamentals/woody plants 421
  potatoes 329
  safflower 258
  sugar beets 270
  sunflower 279
  tomatoes 348
  tree fruits, citrus 365
EPTC (see Eptam, Eradicane)
EPTC & acetochlor (see DoublePlay)
Eradicane (EPTC) .... ZENECA
  WPS chart 81
  field corn, popcorn 112
  sweet corn 341
Escort (metsulfuron-methyl) .... DuPont
  WPS chart 75
  brush control 439
  noncropland 473
  pastures/rangeland 463
Esteron 99C (2,4-D LV ester) .... Rhone-Poulenc
  WPS chart 78
  barley 215
  conservation reserve program 444
  est. lawns/turf 401
  fallow land 449
  field corn, popcorn 109
  grasses for seed production 412
  oats 225
  pastures/rangeland 462
  rye 232
  sorghum 262
  spring wheat 203
  winter wheat 190
ethalfluralin (see Curbit, Sonalan)
ethofumesate (see Nortron, Prograss)
Evik (ametryn) .... Novartis
  WPS chart 77
  field corn, popcorn 112
  noncropland 474
  sugarcane 275
  sweet corn 342
  tree fruits, subtropical 380
Evital (norflurazon) .... Novartis
  WPS chart 77
  small fruits 360
Exceed (primisulfuron-methyl & prosulfuron)
  .... Novartis
  WPS chart 77
  field corn, popcorn 119
Express (tribenuron-methyl) .... DuPont
  WPS chart 75
  barley 216
  spring wheat 205
  winter wheat 192
Extrazine II (cyanazine & atrazine) .... DuPont
  WPS chart 75
  field corn, popcorn 107
  sweet corn 340

F

Facet (quinclorac) ....BASF
  WPS chart 73
  rice 257

Fallow Master (glyphosate & dicamba) ... Monsanto
  WPS chart 76
  fallow land 451
Far-Go (triallate) .... Monsanto
  WPS chart 76
  barley 217
  garbanzos 311
  lentils 317
  peas 324
  spring wheat 205
  winter wheat 192
fenoxaprop-ethyl (see Horizon)
fenoxaprop-P-ethyl (see Acclaim Extra, Option II,
  Puma, Silverado, Whip)
fenoxaprop-P-ethyl & 2,4-D & MCPA (see Tiller)
fenoxaprop-P-ethyl & MCPA (see Dakota)
fenoxaprop-P-ethyl & MCPA + thifensulfuron-methyl &
  tribenuron-methyl (see Cheyenne)
Field Master (acetochlor & atrazine & glyphosate)
  .... Monsanto
  WPS chart 76
  field corn, popcorn 112
Finale (glufosinate-ammonium).........AgrEvo USA
  WPS chart 72
  ornamentals/woody plants 422
Finesse (chlorsulfuron & metsulfuron-methyl)
  .... DuPont
  WPS chart 75
  barley 217
  fallow land 451
  spring wheat 205
  winter wheat 193
FirstRate (cloransulam-methyl)... Dow AgroSciences
  WPS chart 74
  soybeans 149
Flexstar (fomesafen) .... ZENECA
  WPS chart 81
  soybeans 150
Flo-Met (fluometuron) .... Micro Flo
  WPS chart 76
  cotton 176
fluazifop-P-butyl (see Fusilade DX, Fusilade II, Ornamec)
fluazifop-P-butyl & fenoxaprop-P-ethyl (see Fusion)
fluazifop-P-butyl & fomesafen (see Tornado, Typhoon)
flufenacet & isoxaflutole (see Epic)
flufenacet & metribuzin (see Axiom)
flumetsulam (see Python)
flumiclorac pentyl (see Resource)
fluometuron (see Cotoran, Flo-Met, Meturon, Riverside)
fluometuron & MSMA (see Riverside Fluometuron + MSMA)
fluridone (see Sonar)
fluthiacet-methyl (see Action)
fomesafen (see Flexstar, Reflex)
Formula 40 (2,4-D mixed amine) ....Rhone-Poulenc
  WPS chart 78
  asparagus 294
  barley 215
  brush control 436
  conservation reserve program 444
  est. lawns/turf 401
  fallow land 449
  field corn, popcorn 109
  grasses for seed production 412
  noncropland 470
  nuts 385
  oats 225
  pastures/rangeland 462
  rice 254
  rye 232
  small fruits 356
  sorghum 262
  spring wheat 203
  sugarcane 274
  sweet corn 340
  tree fruits, deciduous 371
  turf grasses for sod 416
  winter wheat 190
fosamine (see Krenite)
Freedom (alachlor & trifluralin) .... Monsanto
  WPS chart 76
  soybeans 150
Frontier (dimethenamid) .... BASF
  WPS chart 73
  beans 298
  field corn, popcorn 113
  peanuts 249
  sorghum 264

  soybeans 151
  sweet corn 342
Frontrow [FirstRate (cloransulam-methyl) +
  Python (flumetsulam)] .... Dow AgroSciences
  WPS chart 74
  soybeans 151
FulTime (acetochlor & atrazine)............. ZENECA
  WPS chart 81
  field corn, popcorn 113
Fusilade DX (fluazifop-P-butyl) .... ZENECA
  WPS chart 81
  asparagus 295
  carrots 301
  cotton 176
  fallow land 451
  garlic 313
  lettuce, endive 318
  noncropland 474
  nuts 387
  onions 321
  peppers 327
  rhubarb 334
  small fruits 358
  soybeans 150
  sweet potatoes 346
  tree fruits, citrus 365
  tree fruits, deciduous 373
  tree fruits, subtropical 381
Fusilade II (fluazifop-P-butyl) .... ZENECA
  WPS chart 81
  est. lawns/turf 405
  fallow land 451
  noncropland 474
  ornamentals/woody plants 421
Fusion (fluazifop-P-butyl & fenoxaprop-P-ethyl)
  .... ZENECA
  WPS chart 81
  cotton 177
  noncropland 474
  soybeans 151

G

Galaxy (bentazon & acifluorfen) .... BASF
  WPS chart 73
  soybeans 151
Gallery (isoxaben) .... Dow AgroSciences
  WPS chart 74
  est. lawns/turf 405
  noncropland 474
  nuts 387
  ornamentals/woody plants 422
  small fruits 358
  tree fruits, citrus 365
  tree fruits, deciduous 373
  tree fruits, subtropical 381
Garlon (triclopyr)................. Dow AgroSciences
  WPS chart 74
  ornamentals/woody plants 427
  noncropland 485
Glean (chlorsulfuron) .... DuPont
  WPS chart 75
  barley 217
  oats 226
  spring wheat 206
  winter wheat 193
glufosinate-ammonium (see Finale, Liberty, Rely)
glufosinate-ammonium & atrazine (see Liberty ATZ)
Glyfos or Glyfos X-tra (glyphosate) ..... Cheminova
  WPS chart 73
  artichokes 292
  asparagus 295
  barley 218
  beans 298
  brush control 439
  carrots 301
  celery 303
  cole crops 305
  conservation reserve program 445
  cotton 167,177
  cucurbits 308
  eggplant 310
  est. lawns/turf 405
  fallow land 451
  field corn, popcorn 114
  forage 457
  garbanzos 311
  garlic 313

grasses for seed production 413
greens 314
guar beans 242
horseradish 316
lentils 317
lettuce, endive 318
noncropland 475
nuts 388
oats 227
okra 320
onions 321
ornamentals/woody plants 423
pastures/rangeland 463
peanuts 250
peas 324
peppers 328
potatoes 329
radishes 333
rhubarb 334
rice 255
rye 233
small fruits 359
sorghum 265
soybeans 128,152
spinach 336
spring wheat 206
sugar beets 270
sugarcane 276
sweet corn 342
sweet potatoes 346
table beets 347
tomatoes 348
tree fruits, citrus 365
tree fruits, deciduous 373
tree fruits, subtropical 381
winter wheat 193

glyphosate (see Accord, Accord Site Prep, Credit, Glyfos, Glyfos X-tra, Rattler, Rodeo, Roundup)
glyphosate & 2,4-D (see Campaign, Landmaster)
glyphosate & dicamba (see Fallow Master)

Goal (oxyfluorfen) .... Rohm and Haas
WPS chart 79
artichokes 293
cole crops 306
cotton 177
fallow land 452
horseradish 316
mint 245
nuts 388
oil seed crops 247
onions 322
ornamentals/woody plants 423
small fruits 359
tree fruits, citrus 366
tree fruits, deciduous 374
tree fruits, subtropical 381

Gordon's Amine 400 (2,4-D LV amine).... PBI/Gordon
still water 494

Gordon's LV 400 (2,4-D LV ester) .... PBI/Gordon
WPS chart 78
barley 215
field corn, popcorn 109
grasses for seed production 412
noncropland 470
oats 225
pastures/rangeland 462
rye 232
sorghum 262
soybeans 147
spring wheat 203
winter wheat 190

Gordon's MCPA Amine 4 (MCPA) .... PBI/Gordon
WPS chart 78
barley 219
flax 241
oats 228
peas 325
rice 255
rye 234
spring wheat 208
winter wheat 195

Gowan Prometryne (prometryn) .... Gowan
WPS chart 75
carrots 302
celery 304
cotton 180

Gowan Trifluralin (trifluralin) .... Gowan
WPS chart 75
asparagus 297
barley 222
beans 300
carrots 303
castor beans 240
celery 305
cole crops 307
cotton 182
cucurbits 309
fallow land 455
field corn, popcorn 125
flax 242
forage 459
greens 315
guar beans 243
hops 243
mung beans 247
nuts 392
oil seed crops 247
okra 320
onions 323
peanuts 252
peas 326
peppers 329
potatoes 332
safflower 259
small fruits 363
sorghum 268
southern peas 336
soybeans 162
spring wheat 211
sugar beets 272
sugarcane 278
sunflower 280
tomatoes 350
tree fruits, citrus 370
tree fruits, deciduous 378
winter wheat 198

Gramoxone Extra (paraquat) .... ZENECA
WPS chart 81
asparagus 296
barley 220
beans 299
carrots 302
cole crops 306
conservation reserve program 445
cotton 179
cucurbits 308
eggplant 310
fallow land 452
field corn, popcorn 118
forage 458
garbanzos 312
garlic 313
grasses for seed production 415
greens 315
guar beans 242
hops 243
lentils 317
lettuce, endive 319
mint 245
mung beans 246
noncropland 480
nuts 389
onions 322
ornamentals/woody plants 425
pastures/rangeland 465
peas 326
peppers 328
potatoes 330
rhubarb 334
rice 256
safflower 259
small fruits 360
sorghum 266
southern peas 335
soybeans 154
spring wheat 208
sugar beets 271
sugarcane 276
sunflower 279
sweet corn 344
tomatoes 348
tree fruits, citrus 367
tree fruits, deciduous 375
tree fruits, subtropical 382
winter wheat 196

Grandstand (triclopyr) .... Dow AgroSciences
WPS chart 74
rice 258

Grazon P+D (picloram + 2,4-D) ... Dow AgroSciences
WPS chart 74
pastures/rangeland 463

Guardsman (dimethenamid & atrazine) .... BASF
WPS chart 73
field corn, popcorn 110
sorghum 264
sweet corn 341

H

halosulfuron-methyl (see Manage, Permit)

Harmony Extra (thifensulfuron-methyl & tribenuron-methyl) .... DuPont
WPS chart 75
barley 218
oats 227
spring wheat 206
winter wheat 194

Harmony GT (thifensulfuron-methyl) .... DuPont
WPS chart 75
barley 222
fallow land 454
oats 230
spring wheat 210
winter wheat 198

Harness (acetochlor) .... Monsanto
WPS chart 76
field corn, popcorn 115

Harness Xtra (acetochlor & atrazine)..... Monsanto
WPS chart 76
field corn, popcorn 115

Helena Atrazine (atrazine) .... Helena
WPS chart 76
conservation reserve program 442
est. lawns/turf 399
fallow land 448
field corn, popcorn 102
noncropland 467
nuts 385
ornamentals/woody plants 418
sorghum 260
sugarcane 273
sweet corn 338
tree fruits, subtropical 379
turf grasses for sod 415

Helena MSMA (MSMA) .... Helena
WPS chart 76
brush control 440
cotton 178
est. lawns/turf 407
grasses for seed production 414
noncropland 479
nuts 389
tree fruits, citrus 367
tree fruits, deciduous 375

Helena MSMA Plus (MSMA) .... Helena
WPS chart 76
brush control 440
cotton 178,179
est. lawns/turf 407
grasses for seed production 414
noncropland 479
nuts 389
tree fruits, citrus 367
tree fruits, deciduous 375

Helena Trifluralin (trifluralin) .... Helena
WPS chart 76
asparagus 297
barley 222
beans 300
carrots 303
castor beans 240
celery 305
cole crops 307
conservation reserve program 447
cotton 182
cucurbits 309
fallow land 455
field corn, popcorn 125
flax 242
forage 459
greens 315
guar beans 243
hops 243
lettuce, endive 319
mung beans 247
nuts 392
oil seed crops 247
okra 320
onions 323
peanuts 252

peas 326
peppers 329
potatoes 332
radishes 333
safflower 259
small fruits 363
sorghum 268
southern peas 336
soybeans 162
spring wheat 211
sugar beets 272
sugarcane 278
sunflower 280
tomatoes 350
tree fruits, citrus 370
tree fruits, deciduous 378
winter wheat 198

Herbicide 273 (endothall) .... Elf Atochem
WPS chart 75
sugar beets 270

hexazinone (see Pronone, Velpar)

Hi-Dep (2,4-D mixed amine) .... PBI/Gordon
WPS chart 78
barley 215
est. lawns/turf 401
fallow land 449
field corn, popcorn 109
grasses for seed production 412
noncropland 469
nuts 385
oats 225
pastures/rangeland 462
rice 254
rye 232
sorghum 262
soybeans 147
spring wheat 203
sugarcane 274
tree fruits, deciduous 371
winter wheat 190

Hoelon (diclofop) .... AgrEvo USA
WPS chart 72
barley 219
spring wheat 207
winter wheat 194

Horizon (fenoxaprop-ethyl) .... AgrEvo USA
grasses for seed production 414

Hornet (clopyralid & flumetsulam) .... Dow AgroSciences
WPS chart 74
field corn, popcorn 115

Horsepower (MCPA & triclopyr & dicamba) .... Riverdale
est. lawns/turf 405

Hydrothol 191 (endothall) .... Elf Atochem
moving water 499
still water 496

Hyvar (bromacil) .... DuPont
WPS chart 75
noncropland 476
tree fruits, citrus 366
tree fruits, subtropical 382

I

Illoxan (diclofop) .... AgrEvo USA
est. lawns/turf 405

Image (imazaquin) .... American Cyanamid
est. lawns/turf 406
ornamentals/woody plants 424

imazamethabenz (see Assert)
imazamox (see Raptor)
imazapic (see Cadre, Plateau)
imazapyr (see Arsenal, Chopper, Stalker, Truce)
imazapyr & diuron (see Sahara, Topsite)
imazaquin (see Image, Scepter)
imazaquin & acifluorfen (see Scepter O.T.)
imazaquin & dimethenamid (see Detail)
imazethapyr (see Pursuit)
imazethapyr & atrazine (see Contour)
imazethapyr & dicamba (see Resolve SG)
imazethapyr & imazapyr (see Lightning)
imazethapyr & pendimethalin (see Pursuit Plus)
isoxaben (see Gallery)
isoxaben & trifluralin (see Snapshot)
isoxaflutole (see Balance)

K

Karmex (diuron) .... Griffin
WPS chart 76
artichokes 292
asparagus 295
barley 216
cotton 175
field corn, popcorn 111
forage 456
grasses for seed production 413
noncropland 473
nuts 387
oats 226
ornamentals/woody plants 421
pastures/rangeland 463
small fruits 357
sorghum 264
sugarcane 275
tree fruits, citrus 364
tree fruits, deciduous 372
tree fruits, subtropical 380
winter wheat 192

Kerb (pronamide) .... Rohm and Haas
WPS chart 79
artichokes 293
conservation reserve program 445
est. lawns/turf 406
fallow land 452
forage 457
grasses for seed production 414
lettuce, endive 318
ornamentals/woody plants 424
peas 325
rhubarb 334
small fruits 359
tree fruits, deciduous 374

Komeen (copper complex) .... Griffin
still water 494

Krenite S (fosamine) .... DuPont
noncropland 477

Krovar (bromacil & diuron) .... DuPont
WPS chart 75
noncropland 477
tree fruits, citrus 366

K-Tea (copper complex) .... Griffin
still water 494

L

lactofen (see Cobra)
lactofen & flumiclorac pentyl (see Stellar)

Laddok S-12 (bentazon & atrazine) .... BASF
WPS chart 73
field corn, popcorn 115
sorghum 265
sweet corn 343

Landmaster BW (glyphosate & 2,4-D) .... Monsanto
WPS chart 76
fallow land 452

Lariat (alachlor & atrazine) .... Monsanto
WPS chart 76
field corn, popcorn 116
sorghum 265

Lasso (alachlor) .... Monsanto
WPS chart 76
beans 297
field corn, popcorn 102
ornamentals/woody plants 418
peanuts 248
sorghum 259
soybeans 143
sweet corn 337

Lasso II (alachlor) .... Monsanto
WPS chart 76
field corn, popcorn 102
ornamentals/woody plants 418
peanuts 248
soybeans 143
sweet corn 337

Leadoff (dimethenamid & atrazine) .... DuPont
WPS chart 75
field corn, popcorn 110
sorghum 264
sweet corn 341

Liberty (glufosinate-ammonium) .... AgrEvo USA
WPS chart 72
field corn, popcorn 84,113
noncropland 474
ornamentals/woody plants 422
soybeans 151

Liberty ATZ (glufosinate-ammonium & atrazine) .... AgrEvo USA
WPS chart 72
field corn, popcorn 84,116

Lightning (imazethapyr & imazapyr) .... American Cyanamid
WPS chart 72
field corn, popcorn 85,116

linuron (see Lorox)

Liquid DSMA (DSMA) .... Helena
WPS chart 76
cotton 175
est. lawns/turf 404
noncropland 473
nuts 387
small fruits 358
tree fruits, citrus 365
tree fruits, deciduous 372

Londax (bensulfuron) .... DuPont
WPS chart 75
rice 255

Lorox (linuron) .... Griffin
WPS chart 76
asparagus 295
carrots 301
celery 303
field corn, popcorn 117
noncropland 478
ornamentals/woody plants 424
potatoes 330
sorghum 266
soybeans 152
sweet corn 343

M

MAGMA (MSMA) .... Luxembourg-Pamol
WPS chart 76
cotton 179
est. lawns/turf 407
noncropland 479
nuts 389
tree fruits, citrus 367
tree fruits, deciduous 375

Manage (halosulfuron-methyl) .... Monsanto
WPS chart 76
est. lawns/turf 405

Mandate (thiazopyr) .... Rohm and Haas
WPS chart 79
tree fruits, citrus 369

Manifest [Manifest B (bentazon & acifluorfen) + Manifest G (sethoxydim)] .... BASF
WPS chart 73
soybeans 153

Marksman (dicamba & atrazine) .... BASF
WPS chart 73
fallow land 450
field corn, popcorn 110
sorghum 263

Matador (quizalofop-P-ethyl) .... FMC
WPS chart 75
soybeans 156

Matrix (rimsulfuron) .... DuPont
WPS chart 75
potatoes 331

MCPA (see Albaugh, Chiptox, Clean Crop MCP, Gordon's, Rhomene, Rhonox, Riverdale, Riverside, Solve MCPA, Sword, Wilbur-Ellis)
MCPA & MCPP & dicamba (see Trimec Encore, Tri-Power)
MCPA & triclopyr & dicamba (see Cool Power, Horsepower)
MCPB (see Thistrol)
MCPP (see Mecomec, Riverdale, Riverdale MCPP-2, Weedestroy MCPP-4)
MCPP & 2,4-D (see 3 Plus 3, 2D + 2 MCPP, Deuce)

Mecomec (MCPP) .... PBI/Gordon
est. lawns/turf 406

mecoprop (see MCPP)
metam-sodium (see Vapam HL)

Methar 30 (DSMA) .... Cleary
est. lawns/turf 404
S-metolachlor (see Dual II MAGNUM, Dual MAGNUM, Pennant MAGNUM)
S-metolachlor & atrazine (see Bicep II MAGNUM, Bicep Lite II MAGNUM)
metolachlor & metribuzin (see Turbo)
metribuzin (see Sencor)
metribuzin & chlorimuron-ethyl (see Canopy)
metsulfuron-methyl (see Ally, Escort)
Meturon (fluometuron) .... Griffin
WPS chart 76
cotton 176
Micro-Tech (alachlor) .... Monsanto
WPS chart 76
beans 297
field corn, popcorn 102
ornamentals/woody plants 418
soybeans 143
sweet corn 337
mixed copper complex (see Aquatrine, Captain, Clearigate, Cutrine Plus, Stocktrine II)
molinate (see Ordram)
molinate & propanil (see Arrosolo)
Moncide (MSMA & cacodylic acid) .... Monterey
noncropland 478
monosodium acid methanearsonate (see MSMA)
Montar (cacodylic acid) .... Monterey
WPS chart 77
est. lawns/turf 407
noncropland 478
Moxy (bromoxynil) .... Terra
WPS chart 80
barley 212
conservation reserve program 442
est. lawns/turf 400
field corn, popcorn 105
flax 240
forage 455
garlic 312
grasses for seed production 411
mint 244
noncropland 468
oats 223
onions 321
rye 231
sorghum 261
spring wheat 200
turf grasses for sod 416
winter wheat 187
Moxy + atrazine (bromoxynil & atrazine) ...... Terra
WPS chart 80
field corn, popcorn 105
sorghum 261
MSMA (see 120 Herbicide, 912 Herbicide, Ansar, Bueno, Drexar 530, Drexel, Helena, Helena MSMA Plus, MAGMA, Target, TurfMate)
MSMA & 2,4-D & MCPP & dicamba (see Trimec Plus)

N

napropamide (see Devrinol)
naptalam (see Alanap)
Nautique (mixed copper complex) .... SePRO
still water 494
Navigate (2,4-D ester) .... Applied Biochemists
still water 494
nicosulfuron (see Accent)
nicosulfuron & rimsulfuron & atrazine (see Basis Gold)
norflurazon (see Evital, Solicam, Zorial)
NorthStar (dicamba & primisulfuron-methyl & prosulfuron) .... Novartis
WPS chart 77
field corn, popcorn 117
Nortron (ethofumesate) .... AgrEvo USA
WPS chart 72
grasses for seed production 414
sugar beets 271
turf grasses for sod 417

O

OH2 (oxyfluorfen & pendimethalin) .... Scotts
WPS chart 79
ornamentals/woody plants 425
Opti-Amine (2,4-D amine) .... Helena
WPS chart 76
barley 215
brush control 436
conservation reserve program 444
est. lawns/turf 402
fallow land 449
field corn, popcorn 108
grasses for seed production 412
moving water 497
noncropland 469
nuts 385
oats 225
pastures/rangeland 461
rice 254
rye 232
sorghum 262
spring wheat 203
still water 494
sugarcane 274
sweet corn 340
tree fruits, deciduous 371
winter wheat 190
OpTill (dimethenamid & dicamba) .... BASF
WPS chart 73
field corn, popcorn 118
Option II (fenoxaprop-P-ethyl) .... AgrEvo USA
WPS chart 72
conservation reserve program 445
soybeans 149
Orchard Master (2,4-D) .... PBI/Gordon
WPS chart 78
nuts 386
pastures/rangeland 462
tree fruits, deciduous 371
Ordram (molinate) .... ZENECA
WPS chart 81
rice 256
Ornamec (fluazifop-P-butyl) .... PBI/Gordon
WPS chart 78
ornamentals/woody plants 421
oryzalin (see Surflan)
Oust (sulfometuron-methyl) .... DuPont
WPS chart 75
noncropland 480
Outrider (sulfosulfuron) .... Monsanto
noncropland 480
oxadiazon (see Chipco Ronstar G)
oxyfluorfen (see Goal)
oxyfluorfen & oryzalin (see Rout)
oxyfluorfen & pendimethalin (see OH2)

P

Paramount (quinclorac) .... BASF
WPS chart 73
fallow land 453
sorghum 267
spring wheat 209
winter wheat 197
paraquat (see Cyclone, Gramoxone Extra, Starfire)
paraquat & diuron (see Surefire)
PAR-3 (2,4-D & 2,4-DP & MCPP) .... Riverdale
est. lawns/turf 403
noncropland 471
Partner (alachlor) .... Monsanto
WPS chart 77
beans 297
field corn, popcorn 102
soybeans 143
sweet corn 337
Pathfinder II (triclopyr) .... Dow AgroSciences
WPS chart 74
noncropland 485
Pathway (picloram & 2,4-D) ..... Dow AgroSciences
WPS chart 74
noncropland 480
Patron 170 (2,4-D & 2,4-DP) .... Riverdale
WPS chart 79
brush control 438
est. lawns/turf 403
noncropland 471
Patron DP-4 (2,4-DP) .... Riverdale
WPS chart 79
brush control 439
noncropland 472
Peak (prosulfuron) .... Novartis
WPS chart 77
barley 220
oats 229
rye 235
sorghum 266
spring wheat 208
winter wheat 196
pebulate (PEBC) (see Tillam)
pelargonic acid (see Scythe)
pendimethalin (see Corral, Pendulum, Pentagon, ProTurf Turf Weedgrass Control, Prowl)
pendimethalin & imazaquin (see Squadron)
pendimethalin & imazaquin & imazethapyr (see Steel)
Pendulum (pendimethalin) .... American Cyanamid
WPS chart 72
est. lawns/turf 408
noncropland 480
ornamentals/woody plants 425
Pennant MAGNUM (*S*-metolachlor) .... Novartis
WPS chart 77
est. lawns/turf 407
ornamentals/woody plants 424
turf grasses for sod 417
Pentagon (pendimethalin) ..... American Cyanamid
WPS chart 72
beans 299
conservation reserve program 445
cotton 180
field corn, popcorn 118
garbanzos 312
garlic 313
nuts 390
onions 322
peanuts 250
potatoes 330
rice 257
small fruits 360
sorghum 267
southern peas 335
soybeans 154
sugarcane 277
sunflower 279
sweet corn 344
tobacco 282
tree fruits, citrus 367
tree fruits, deciduous 375
Permit (halosulfuron-methyl) .... Monsanto
WPS chart 77
field corn, popcorn 85,114
sorghum 265
phenmedipham (see Spin-Aid)
phenmedipham & desmedipham (see Betamix)
phenmedipham & desmedipham & ethofumesate (see Progress)
Phenoxy 088 (2,4-D ester + acid) .... Terra
WPS chart 80
barley 215
field corn, popcorn 108
spring wheat 203
winter wheat 190
picloram (see Tordon K)
picloram & 2,4-D (see Grazon P+D, Pathway, Tordon 101)
Pinnacle (thifensulfuron-methyl) .... DuPont
WPS chart 75
soybeans 161
Plateau (imazapic) .... American Cyanamid
conservation reserve program 446
noncropland 481
Platte Prometryne (prometryn) .... Platte
WPS chart 78
carrots 302
celery 304
cotton 180
herbs & spices 316
Poast (sethoxydim) .... BASF
WPS chart 73
artichokes 293
asparagus 296
beans 300
carrots 302
celery 304
cole crops 306
cotton 181
cucurbits 309
eggplant 310
field corn, popcorn 122
flax 241
forage 459

garlic 314
greens 315
lentils 217
lettuce, endive 319
mint 246
nuts 390
oil seed crops 247
onions 323
peanuts 251
peas 326
peppers 328
potatoes 331
rhubarb 335
small fruits 361
soybeans 158
spinach 337
sugar beets 271
sunflower 280
sweet potatoes 346
tobacco 282
tomatoes 349
tree fruits, citrus 368
tree fruits, deciduous 376
tree fruits, subtropical 383

Poast Plus (sethoxydim) ... BASF
WPS chart 73
cotton 181
forage 459
peanuts 251
soybeans 158

Pramitol (prometon) ... Makhteshim-Agan
noncropland 481

Pramitol 5PS (prometon & simazine & chlorate-borate) ... Makhteshim-Agan
noncropland 481

Prefar (bensulide) ... Gowan
WPS chart 75
carrots 302
celery 304
cole crops 306
cucurbits 308
eggplant 310
garlic 314
greens 315
lettuce, endive 319
onions 322
peppers 328
tomatoes 349

Pre-San (bensulide) ... PBI/Gordon
est. lawns/turf 400

primisulfuron-methyl (see Beacon)
primisulfuron-methyl & prosulfuron (see Exceed, Spirit)

Princep (simazine) ... Novartis
WPS chart 77
field corn, popcorn 123
nuts 390
ornamentals/woody plants 426
small fruits 361
sweet corn 345
tree fruits, citrus 368
tree fruits, deciduous 376
tree fruits, subtropical 383
turf grasses for sod 417

Prism (clethodim) ... Valent
WPS chart 80
cotton 173
fallow land 448
garlic 312
noncropland 468
nuts 385
onions 321
small fruits 356
soybeans 145
sugar beets 269
tree fruits, citrus 363
tree fruits, deciduous 371
tree fruits, subtropical 379

prodiamine (see Barricade)

Prograss (ethofumesate) ... AgrEvo USA
WPS chart 72
est. lawns/turf 408

Progress (phenmedipham & desmedipham & ethofumesate) ... AgrEvo USA
WPS chart 72
sugar beets 269

prometon (see Pramitol)
prometon & 2,4-D (see Vegemec)
prometon & simazine & chlorate-borate (see Pramitol 5PS)
prometryn (see Caparol, Cotton-Pro, Gowan, Platte, Riverside)
prometryn & MSMA (see Riverside Prometryne + MSMA)

Prompt (bentazon & atrazine) ... BASF
WPS chart 73
est. lawns/turf 408

pronamide (see Kerb)

Pronone (hexazinone) ... Pro-Serve
WPS chart 78
brush control 440
noncropland 475
pastures & rangeland 464
small fruits 359

propachlor (see Ramrod)
propachlor & atrazine (see Ramrod/Atrazine)
propanil (see Blue Drum, Propanil 4, Propanil 36%, Riverside, Stam, Stampede, SuperWHAM!, Wham! EZ)
propanil & bensulfuron-methyl (see Duet, Stampro)

Propanil 4 (propanil) ... RiceCo
WPS chart 79
rice 257

Propanil 36% (propanil) ... RiceCo
WPS chart 79
rice 257

ProTurf Goosegrass/Crabgrass Control (bensulide & oxadiazon) ... Scotts
est. lawns/turf 408

ProTurf K-O-G Weed Control (dicamba) ... Scotts
est. lawns/turf 403

ProTurf Turf Weedgrass Control (pendimethalin) ... Scotts
WPS chart 79
est. lawns/turf 407

ProTurf Weedgrass Preventer (bensulide) ... Scotts
est. lawns/turf 400

Prowl (pendimethalin) ... American Cyanamid
WPS chart 72
beans 299
conservation reserve program 445
cotton 180
field corn, popcorn 118
garbanzos 312
garlic 313
nuts 390
onions 322
peanuts 250
potatoes 330
rice 257
small fruits 360
sorghum 267
southern peas 335
soybeans 154
sugarcane 277
sunflower 279
sweet corn 344
tobacco 282
tree fruits, citrus 367
tree fruits, deciduous 375

Puma (fenoxaprop-P-ethyl) ... AgrEvo USA
WPS chart 72
barley 217
spring wheat 205
winter wheat 192

Pursuit (imazethapyr) ... American Cyanamid
WPS chart 72
field corn, popcorn 85,119
forage 458
peanuts 250
soybeans 155

Pursuit Plus (imazethapyr & pendimethalin) ... American Cyanamid
WPS chart 72
field corn, popcorn 85,119
soybeans 155

Pyramin (chloridazon) ... BASF
WPS chart 73
sugar beets 271
table beets 347

pyridate (see Tough)
pyrithiobac sodium (see Staple)

Python (flumetsulam) ... Dow AgroSciences
WPS chart 74
field corn, popcorn 120
soybeans 155

Q

quinclorac (see Facet, Paramount)
quizalofop-P-ethyl (see Assure II, Matador)

R

Ramrod (propachlor) ... Monsanto
WPS chart 77
field corn, popcorn 120
sorghum 268

Ramrod/Atrazine (propachlor & atrazine) ... Monsanto
WPS chart 77
field corn, popcorn 120
flax 241
sorghum 268

Ranger (glyphosate) ... Monsanto
barley 218
oats 227
spring wheat 206
sweet corn 343
winter wheat 194

Raptor (imazamox) ... American Cyanamid
soybeans 156

Rattler (glyphosate) ... Helena
WPS chart 76
artichokes 292
asparagus 295
barley 218
beans 298
brush control 439
carrots 301
celery 303
cole crops 305
conservation reserve program 445
cotton 167,177
cucurbits 308
eggplant 310
est. lawns/turf 405
fallow land 451
field corn, popcorn 114
forage 457
garbanzos 311
garlic 313
grasses for seed production 413
greens 314
guar beans 242
horseradish 316
lentils 317
lettuce, endive 318
noncropland 475
nuts 388
oats 227
okra 320
onions 321
ornamentals/woody plants 423
pastures/rangeland 463
peanuts 250
peas 324
peppers 328
potatoes 329
radishes 333
rhubarb 334
rice 255
rye 233
small fruits 359
sorghum 265
soybeans 128,152
spinach 336
spring wheat 206
sugar beets 270
sugarcane 276
sweet corn 342
sweet potatoes 346
table beets 347
tomatoes 348
tree fruits, citrus 365
tree fruits, deciduous 373
tree fruits, subtropical 381
winter wheat 193

Rave (dicamba & triasulfuron) ... Novartis
WPS chart 77
barley 221
conservation reserve program 446
pastures/rangeland 465
spring wheat 209
winter wheat 197

Reclaim (clopyralid)..............Dow AgroSciences
pastures/rangeland............460
Reflex (fomesafen)..............ZENECA
WPS chart............81
soybeans............150
Reliance STS (chlorimuron-ethyl & thifensulfuron-methyl)..............DuPont
WPS chart............75
soybeans............131,156
Rely (glufosinate-ammonium)..........AgrEvo USA
WPS chart............72
nuts............388
small fruits............358
tree fruits, deciduous............373
Remedy (triclopyr)..............Dow AgroSciences
noncropland............485
pastures/rangeland............466
Resolve SG (imazethapyr & dicamba)..............American Cyanamid
WPS chart............72
field corn, popcorn............85,121
Resource (flumiclorac pentyl)..............Valent
WPS chart............80
field corn, popcorn............121
soybeans............156
Reward (diquat dibromide)..............ZENECA
WPS chart............81
est. lawns/turf............404
moving water............498
noncropland............473
ornamentals/woody plants............420
still water............495
Rezult [Rezult A (bentazon) + Rezult B (sethoxydim)]..............BASF
WPS chart............73
field corn, popcorn............86,121
soybeans............157
Rhomene (MCPA)..............Nufarm
WPS chart............78
barley............219
flax............241
grasses for seed production............414
oats............228
peas............325
rye............234
spring wheat............208
winter wheat............195
Rhonox (MCPA)..............Nufarm
WPS chart............78
barley............220
est. lawns/turf............406
flax............241
grasses for seed production............414
noncropland............478
oats............229
pastures/rangeland............464
rye............234
spring wheat............208
winter wheat............195
rimsulfuron (see DPX-E9636, Matrix, Shadeout)
rimsulfuron & thifensulfuron-methyl (see Basis)
Riverdale 4 Amine IVM (2,4-D amine)....Riverdale
brush control............436
conservation reserve program............444
moving water............498
noncropland............469
pastures/rangeland............461
still water............494
Riverdale 6 Amine (2,4-D amine)..........Riverdale
WPS chart............79
barley............215
brush control............436
conservation reserve program............444
est. lawns/turf............401
fallow land............450
field corn, popcorn............108
grasses for seed production............412
moving water............497
noncropland............469
nuts............385
oats............224
pastures/rangeland............461
rice............254
rye............232
sorghum............262
soybeans............147
spring wheat............203
still water............494
sweet corn............340
tree fruits, deciduous............371
winter wheat............190
Riverdale 2,4-D Granules (2,4-D ester)....Riverdale
WPS chart............79
est. lawns/turf............402
field corn, popcorn............109
small fruits............356
still water............495
sweet corn............341
Riverdale DP-4 (2,4-DP)..............Riverdale
WPS chart............79
brush control............439
noncropland............472
Riverdale IOE (MCPA)..............Riverdale
WPS chart............79
barley............220
est. lawns/turf............406
flax............241
grasses for seed production............414
noncropland............478
oats............229
pastures/rangeland............464
rice............256
rye............224
spring wheat............208
winter wheat............196
Riverdale L.V. 4 or L.V. 6 (2,4-D ester)...Riverdale
WPS chart............79
barley............215
brush control............436
conservation reserve program............444
est. lawns/turf............402
fallow land............450
field corn, popcorn............108
grasses for seed production............412
moving water............498
noncropland............469
oats............224
ornamentals/woody plants............420
pastures/rangeland............461
rye............232
sorghum............262
soybeans............147
spring wheat............203
still water............494
sugarcane............273
sweet corn............340
winter wheat............190
Riverdale MCPA (MCPA)..............Riverdale
WPS chart............79
barley............219,220
est. lawns/turf............406
flax............241
forage............457
grasses for seed production............414
noncropland............478
oats............228,229
pastures/rangeland............464
peas............325
rice............255,256
rye............223,224
spring wheat............207,208
winter wheat............195,196
Riverdale MCPP (MCPP)..............Riverdale
est. lawns/turf............406,407
Riverdale Topsite (imazapyr & diuron)....Riverdale
noncropland............484
Riverdale Turf D + DP (2,4-D & 2,4-DP)...Riverdale
est. lawns/turf............403
Riverside Asulam (asulam)..............Terra
WPS chart............79
est. lawns/turf............399
noncropland............467
ornamentals/woody plants............418
sugarcane............272
Riverside Atrazine (atrazine)..............Terra
WPS chart............79
est. lawns/turf............399
fallow land............448
field corn, popcorn............102
nuts............385
ornamentals/woody plants............418
sorghum............260
sugarcane............273
sweet corn............338
turf grasses for sod............415
Riverside 2,4-D Amine 4 (2,4-D amine).......Terra
WPS chart............79
brush control............436
est. lawns/turf............402
field corn, popcorn............109
grasses for seed production............412
moving water............498
noncropland............469
oats............225
pastures/rangeland............462
rice............254
sorghum............263
soybeans............147
still water............494
sugarcane............274
Riverside 2,4-D LV4 (2,4-D LV ester)..........Terra
WPS chart............79
barley............215
brush control............436
est. lawns/turf............402
field corn, popcorn............109
grasses for seed production............412
noncropland............470
oats............225
pastures/rangeland............462
rye............232
sorghum............263
soybeans............147
spring wheat............203
winter wheat............190
Riverside 2,4-DB (2,4-DB)..............Terra
WPS chart............79
conservation reserve program............444
forage............456
peanuts............249
soybeans............148
Riverside Diuron (diuron)..............Terra
WPS chart............79
artichokes............292
asparagus............295
barley............216
cotton............175
field corn, popcorn............111
forage............456
grasses for seed production............413
mint............245
noncropland............473
nuts............387
oats............226
ornamentals/woody plants............421
pastures/rangeland............463
small fruits............357
sorghum............264
sugarcane............275
tree fruits, citrus............364
tree fruits, deciduous............372
tree fruits, subtropical............380
winter wheat............192
Riverside Fluometuron (fluometuron)..........Terra
WPS chart............80
cotton............176
Riverside Fluometuron + MSMA (fluometuron & MSMA)..............Terra
WPS chart............80
cotton............176
Riverside MCPA (MCPA)..............Terra
WPS chart............80
barley............219
flax............241
oats............228
rice............255
rye............233
spring wheat............207
winter wheat............195
Riverside Prometryne (prometryn)..............Terra
WPS chart............80
celery............304
cotton............180
Riverside Prometryne + MSMA (prometryn & MSMA)..............Terra
WPS chart............80
cotton............181
Riverside Propanil (propanil)..............Terra
WPS chart............80
rice............257
Riverside Simazine (simazine)..............Terra
WPS chart............80
est. lawns/turf............409
field corn, popcorn............123
nuts............390
ornamentals/woody plants............426
small fruits............361
sweet corn............345

tree fruits, citrus 368
tree fruits, deciduous 376
tree fruits, subtropical 383
turf grasses for sod 417

Riverside Trifluralin (trifluralin) .... Terra
WPS chart 80
asparagus 297
barley 222
beans 300
carrots 303
castor beans 240
celery 305
cole crops 307
conservation reserve program 447
cotton 182
cucurbits 309
fallow land 455
field corn, popcorn 125
forage 459
greens 315
guar beans 243
hops 243
kenaf 244
lettuce, endive 319
mung beans 247
nuts 392
oil seed crops 247
okra 320
onions 323
peanuts 252
peas 326
peppers 329
potatoes 332
safflower 259
small fruits 363
sorghum 268
southern peas 336
soybeans 162
spring wheat 211
sugar beets 272
sugarcane 278
sunflower 280
tomatoes 350
tree fruits, citrus 370
tree fruits, deciduous 378
winter wheat 198

Rodeo (glyphosate) .... Monsanto
WPS chart 77
moving water 499
noncropland 475
still water 496

Ro-Neet (cycloate) .... ZENECA
WPS chart 81
spinach 336
sugar beets 271
table beets 347

Roundup (glyphosate) .... Monsanto
WPS chart 77
artichokes 292
asparagus 295
barley 218
beans 299
brush control 439,440
carrots 301
celery 303
cole crops 305
conservation reserve program 445
cotton 167,177
cucurbits 308
eggplant 310
est. lawns/turf 405
fallow land 451
field corn, popcorn 87,114
forage 457
garbanzos 311
garlic 313
grasses for seed production 414
greens 314
guar beans 242
horseradish 316
lentils 317
lettuce, endive 318
noncropland 475
nuts 388
oats 227
okra 320
onions 321
ornamentals/woody plants 423
pastures/rangeland 463
peanuts 250
peas 324
peppers 328

potatoes 329
radishes 333
rhubarb 334
rice 255
rye 233
small fruits 359
sorghum 265
soybeans 128,152
spinach 336
spring wheat 206
sugar beets 270
sugarcane 276
sweet corn 342
sweet potatoes 346
table beets 347
tomatoes 348
tree fruits, citrus 365
tree fruits, deciduous 373
tree fruits, subtropical 381
turf grasses for sod 417
winter wheat 193

Rout (oxyfluorfen & oryzalin) .... Scotts
WPS chart 79
ornamentals/woody plants 426

S

Saber (2,4-D amine) .... Platte
WPS chart 78
barley 215
brush control 437
conservation reserve program 444
est. lawns/turf 402
fallow land 450
field corn, popcorn 109
grasses for seed production 412
noncropland 470
nuts 386
oats 225
pastures/rangeland 462
rice 254
rye 232
sorghum 263
soybeans 148
spring wheat 203
sugarcane 274
sweet corn 341
tree fruits, deciduous 371
turf grasses for sod 416
winter wheat 190

Sahara (imazapyr & diuron) ... American Cyanamid
noncropland 482

Salvo (2,4-D LV ester) .... Platte
WPS chart 78
barley 215
est. lawns/turf 402
field corn, popcorn 109
oats 225
pastures/rangeland 462
rye 233
sorghum 263
soybeans 148
spring wheat 203
winter wheat 190

Savage (2,4-D amine) .... Platte
WPS chart 78
asparagus 294
barley 215
brush control 437
conservation reserve program 444
est. lawns/turf 402
fallow land 450
field corn, popcorn 109
grasses for seed production 413
moving water 498
noncropland 470
nuts 386
oats 225
pastures/rangeland 462
rice 254
rye 233
small fruits 356
sorghum 262
soybeans 148
spring wheat 204
still water 495
sugarcane 274
sweet corn 341
tree fruits, deciduous 371
winter wheat 190

Scepter (imazaquin) .... American Cyanamid
WPS chart 72
soybeans 157

Scepter O.T. (imazaquin & acifluorfen)
.... American Cyanamid
WPS chart 72
soybeans 157

Scorpion III (clopyralid & flumetsulam & 2,4-D)
.... Dow AgroSciences
WPS chart 74
field corn, popcorn 122

Scythe (pelargonic acid) .... Mycogen
WPS chart 77
artichokes 293
asparagus 296
barley 221
beans 300
carrots 302
celery 304
cole crops 306
cotton 181
cucurbits 309
eggplant 310
est. lawns/turf 409
fallow land 453
field corn, popcorn 122
forage 458
garlic 314
grasses for seed production 415
greens 315
herbs & spices 316
hops 243
horseradish 316
lentils 317
lettuce, endive 319
mint 245
mung beans 246
noncropland 482
nuts 390
oats 230
okra 320
oil seed crops 247
onions 323
ornamentals/woody plants 426
pastures/rangeland 465
peanuts 251
peas 326
peppers 328
potatoes 331
radishes 333
rhubarb 334
rice 257
rye 235
safflower 259
small fruits 361
sorghum 268
southern peas 336
soybeans 158
spinach 337
spring wheat 210
sugarcane 277
sunflower 280
sweet corn 344
sweet potatoes 346
table beets 347
tobacco 282
tomatoes 349
tree fruits, citrus 368
tree fruits, deciduous 376
tree fruits, subtropical 383
turf grasses for sod 417
winter wheat 197

Sedagri Trifluralin (trifluralin) ...... Rhone-Poulenc
WPS chart 78
asparagus 297
barley 222
beans 300
carrots 303
castor beans 240
celery 305
cole crops 307
conservation reserve program 447
cotton 182
cucurbits 309
fallow land 455
field corn, popcorn 125
flax 242
forage 459
greens 315
guar beans 243
hops 243

kenaf ... 244
lettuce, endive ... 319
mung beans ... 247
nuts ... 392
oil seed crops ... 248
okra ... 320
onions ... 323
peanuts ... 252
peas ... 326
peppers ... 329
potatoes ... 332
radishes ... 333
safflower ... 259
small fruits ... 363
sorghum ... 269
southern peas ... 336
soybeans ... 162
spring wheat ... 211
sugar beets ... 272
sugarcane ... 278
sunflower ... 280
tomatoes ... 350
tree fruits, citrus ... 370
tree fruits, deciduous ... 378
winter wheat ... 198

Select (clethodim) ... Valent
WPS chart ... 80
cotton ... 173
fallow land ... 448
garlic ... 312
noncropland ... 468
nuts ... 385
onions ... 321
small fruits ... 356
soybeans ... 145
sugar beets ... 269
tree fruits, citrus ... 363
tree fruits, deciduous ... 371
tree fruits, subtropical ... 379

Sencor (metribuzin) ... Bayer
WPS chart ... 73
asparagus ... 296
barley ... 222
carrots ... 302
fallow land ... 453
field corn, popcorn ... 122
forage ... 458
potatoes ... 331
soybeans ... 158
sugarcane ... 277
tomatoes ... 349
winter wheat ... 197

sethoxydim (see Conclude, Conclude Ultra, Manifest, Poast, Rezult, Torpedo, Vantage)

Shadeout (rimsulfuron) ... DuPont
WPS chart ... 75
tomatoes ... 349

Shotgun (atrazine & 2,4-D) ... Platte
WPS chart ... 78
fallow land ... 453
field corn, popcorn ... 123
sorghum ... 268

siduron (see Tupersan)

Silverado (fenoxaprop-P-ethyl) ... AgrEvo USA
WPS chart ... 72
winter wheat ... 192

Simazat (simazine & atrazine) ... Drexel
WPS chart ... 74
field corn, popcorn ... 123
ornamentals/woody plants ... 426
sugarcane ... 278
sweet corn ... 345

simazine (see Clean Crop, Drexel, Princep, Riverside)
simazine & atrazine (see Simazat)

Sinbar (terbacil) ... DuPont
WPS chart ... 75
asparagus ... 297
forage ... 459
mint ... 246
nuts ... 391
small fruits ... 361
sugarcane ... 278
tree fruits, deciduous ... 377

Skirmish (chlorimuron-ethyl) ... FMC
WPS chart ... 75
soybeans ... 145

Snapshot (isoxaben & trifluralin) ... Dow AgroSciences
WPS chart ... 74
noncropland ... 482
nuts ... 391
ornamentals/woody plants ... 426
small fruits ... 362
tree fruits, citrus ... 368
tree fruits, deciduous ... 377
tree fruits, subtropical ... 383

sodium metaborate & sodium chlorate (see BareSpot Monobor-Chlorate)
sodium metaborate & sodium chlorate & bromacil (see BareSpot Ureabor)
sodium metaborate & sodium chlorate & diuron (see BareSpot Weed & Grass)

Solicam (norflurazon) ... Novartis
WPS chart ... 77
asparagus ... 296
noncropland ... 479
nuts ... 389
small fruits ... 360
tree fruits, citrus ... 367
tree fruits, deciduous ... 375
tree fruits, subtropical ... 382

Solution (2,4-D amine) ... Riverdale
WPS chart ... 79
barley ... 216
brush control ... 437
est. lawns/turf ... 402
fallow land ... 450
field corn, popcorn ... 109
grasses for seed production ... 413
moving water ... 497
noncropland ... 469
oats ... 226
pastures/rangeland ... 461
rice ... 254
rye ... 233
sorghum ... 262
soybeans ... 147
spring wheat ... 204
still water ... 494
sugarcane ... 274
winter wheat ... 191

Solve 2,4-D (2,4-D LV ester) ... Albaugh
WPS chart ... 72
barley ... 215
brush control ... 437
est. lawns/turf ... 401
fallow land ... 450
field corn, popcorn ... 109
grasses for seed production ... 412
moving water ... 498
noncropland ... 469
oats ... 226
pastures/rangeland ... 461
rye ... 232
sorghum ... 262
soybeans ... 147
spring wheat ... 203
still water ... 494
winter wheat ... 190

Solve MCPA (MCPA) ... Albaugh
WPS chart ... 72
barley ... 219
flax ... 241
grasses for seed production ... 414
noncropland ... 478
oats ... 228
pastures/rangeland ... 464
rye ... 234
spring wheat ... 207
winter wheat ... 195

Sonalan (ethalfluralin) ... Dow AgroSciences
WPS chart ... 74
beans ... 300
peanuts ... 251
peas ... 326
soybeans ... 159
sunflower ... 280

Sonar (fluridone) ... SePRO
moving water ... 499
still water ... 496

Spartan (sulfentrazone) ... FMC
WPS chart ... 75
tobacco ... 282

Spike (tebuthiuron) ... Dow AgroSciences
brush control ... 441
noncropland ... 483
pastures/rangeland ... 465

Spin-Aid (phenmedipham) ... AgrEvo USA
WPS chart ... 72
spinach ... 337
table beets ... 347

Spirit (primisulfuron-methyl & prosulfuron) .. Novartis
WPS chart ... 77
field corn, popcorn ... 119

Squadron (pendimethalin & imazaquin) ... American Cyanamid
WPS chart ... 72
soybeans ... 159

Staa-Free (bromacil & diuron) ... Pro-Serve
noncropland ... 483

Stalker (imazapyr) ... American Cyanamid
brush control ... 440
noncropland ... 477

Stam (propanil) ... Rohm and Haas
WPS chart ... 79
rice ... 257

Stampede (propanil) ... Rohm and Haas
WPS chart ... 79
barley ... 221
oats ... 229
spring wheat ... 209

Stampro (propanil & bensulfuron-methyl) ... Rohm and Haas
rice ... 257

Staple (pyrithiobac sodium) ... DuPont
WPS chart ... 75
cotton ... 181

Starfire (paraquat) ... ZENECA
WPS chart ... 81
cotton ... 179
ornamentals/woody plants ... 425
peanuts ... 250
soybeans ... 154
tree fruits, deciduous ... 375

Status (acifluorfen) ... American Cyanamid
WPS chart ... 72
soybeans ... 143

Steel (pendimethalin & imazaquin & imazethapyr) ... American Cyanamid
WPS chart ... 72
soybeans ... 159

Stellar (lactofen & flumiclorac pentyl) ... Valent
WPS chart ... 80
soybeans ... 160

Sterling (dicamba) ... Terra
WPS chart ... 80
asparagus ... 294
barley ... 216
brush control ... 438
conservation reserve program ... 444
est. lawns/turf ... 403
fallow land ... 450
field corn, popcorn ... 110
grasses for seed production ... 413
noncropland ... 471
oats ... 226
pastures/rangeland ... 463
sorghum ... 263
spring wheat ... 204
sugarcane ... 274
winter wheat ... 191

Sterling Plus (dicamba & atrazine) ... Terra
WPS chart ... 80
fallow land ... 450
field corn, popcorn ... 110
sorghum ... 263

Stinger (clopyralid) ... Dow AgroSciences
WPS chart ... 74
asparagus ... 294
barley ... 214
conservation reserve program ... 443
fallow land ... 449
field corn, popcorn ... 106
grasses for seed production ... 412
mint ... 244
noncropland ... 468
oats ... 224
ornamentals/woody plants ... 419
pastures/rangeland ... 460
spring wheat ... 202
sugar beets ... 270
winter wheat ... 189

Stocktrine II (mixed copper complex) ... Applied Biochemists
still water ... 494

Storm (bentazon & acifluorfen) ... BASF
WPS chart ... 73
peanuts ... 252

rice 258
soybeans 160
sulfentrazone (see Authority, Spartan)
sulfentrazone & chlorimuron-ethyl (see Authority Broadleaf, Canopy XL)
sulfometuron-methyl (see Oust)
sulfosate (see Touchdown)
sulfosulfuron (see Outrider)
Super Trimec (2,4-D & 2,4-DP & dicamba) .... PBI/Gordon
est. lawns/turf 410
Super WHAM! (propanil) .... RiceCo
WPS chart 79
rice 257
SuperBrush (2,4-D & 2,4-DP & dicamba) ... PBI/Gordon
brush control 437
noncropland 470
Surefire (paraquat & diuron) .... Platte
WPS chart 78
fallow land 454
field corn, popcorn 123
noncropland 483
spring wheat 210
sweet corn 345
winter wheat 198
Surflan (oryzalin) .... Dow AgroSciences
WPS chart 74
est. lawns/turf 409
nuts 391
ornamentals/woody plants 427
small fruits 362
tree fruits, citrus 369
tree fruits, deciduous 377
tree fruits, subtropical 384
Surpass (acetochlor) .... ZENECA
WPS chart 81
field corn, popcorn 101
Surpass 100 (acetochlor & atrazine) .... ZENECA
WPS chart 81
field corn, popcorn 124
Sutan+ (butylate) .... Micro Flo
WPS chart 76
field corn, popcorn 124
sweet corn 345
Sword (MCPA) .... Platte
WPS chart 78
barley 220
brush control 440
est. lawns/turf 406
flax 241
grasses for seed production 414
noncropland 478
oats 229
pastures/rangeland 464
rice 256
rye 234
spring wheat 208
winter wheat 196
Synchrony STS (chlorimuron-ethyl & thifensulfuron-methyl) .... DuPont
WPS chart 75
soybeans 131,161

T

Target (MSMA) .... Luxembourg-Pamol
WPS chart 76
cotton 178
est. lawns/turf 407
noncropland 479
nuts 389
tree fruits, citrus 367
tree fruits, deciduous 375
tebuthiuron (see Spike)
Telar (chlorsulfuron) .... DuPont
noncropland 483
terbacil (see Sinbar)
thiazopyr (see Mandate, Visor)
thifensulfuron-methyl (see Harmony GT, Pinnacle)
thifensulfuron-methyl & tribenuron-methyl (see Harmony Extra)
thifensulfuron-methyl & tribenuron-methyl + fenoxaprop-P-ethyl & MCPA (see Cheyenne)
thifensulfuron-methyl & tribenuron-methyl & metsulfuron-methyl (see Canvas)
thiobencarb (see Bolero)
Thistrol (MCPB) .... Nufarm
WPS chart 77
peas 325
Threesome (2,4-D & MCPP & dicamba) ... Riverdale
est. lawns/turf 403
Tillam (pebulate) .... ZENECA
WPS chart 81
sugar beets 272
tobacco 283
tomatoes 350
Tiller (fenoxaprop-P-ethyl & 2,4-D & MCPA) .... AgrEvo USA
WPS chart 72
spring wheat 210
winter wheat 198
TopNotch (acetochlor) .... ZENECA
WPS chart 81
field corn, popcorn 101
Topsite (imazapyr & diuron) ... American Cyanamid
noncropland 484
Tordon 101 (picloram & 2,4-D) ... Dow AgroSciences
WPS chart 74
noncropland 484
Tordon K (picloram) .... Dow AgroSciences
WPS chart 74
noncropland 484
Tordon 22K (picloram) .... Dow AgroSciences
WPS chart 74
barley 222
conservation reserve program 446
fallow land 454
oats 230
pastures/rangeland 466
spring wheat 211
Tornado (fluazifop-P-butyl & fomesafen) ... ZENECA
WPS chart 81
soybeans 161
Torpedo (sethoxydim) .... BASF
WPS chart 73
tree fruits, citrus 368
Total (bromacil & diuron & sodium chlorate & sodium metaborate) .... Terra
noncropland 467
Touchdown (sulfosate) .... ZENECA
WPS chart 81
artichokes 293
asparagus 297
conservation reserve program 447
fallow land 454
field corn, popcorn 87,124
noncropland 484
nuts 391
small fruits 362
soybeans 128,162
tree fruits, citrus 369
tree fruits, deciduous 378
tree fruits, subtropical 384
Tough (pyridate) .... Novartis
WPS chart 77
field corn, popcorn 125
peanuts 252
tralkoxydim (see Achieve)
Transline (clopyralid) .... Dow AgroSciences
WPS chart 74
noncropland 468
Treflan (trifluralin) .... Dow AgroSciences
WPS chart 74
asparagus 297
barley 222
beans 300
carrots 303
castor beans 240
celery 305
cole crops 307
conservation reserve program 447
cotton 182
cucurbits 309
fallow land 455
field corn, popcorn 125
flax 242
forage 459
greens 315
guar beans 243
hops 243
kenaf 244
lettuce, endive 319
mung beans 247
nuts 392
oil seed crops 248
okra 320
onions 323
peanuts 252
peas 326
peppers 329
potatoes 332
radishes 333
safflower 259
small fruits 363
sorghum 269
southern peas 336
soybeans 162
spring wheat 211
sugar beets 272
sugarcane 278
sunflower 280
tomatoes 350
tree fruits, citrus 370
tree fruits, deciduous 378
winter wheat 198
TRI-4 (trifluralin) .... American Cyanamid
WPS chart 72
barley 222
beans 300
castor beans 240
cotton 182
forage 459
guar beans 243
mung beans 247
oil seed crops 248
peanuts 252
peas 326
peppers 329
potatoes 332
safflower 259
small fruits 363
sorghum 269
southern peas 336
soybeans 162
spring wheat 211
sugar beets 272
sugarcane 278
sunflower 280
tomatoes 350
tree fruits, citrus 370
tree fruits, deciduous 378
winter wheat 198
triallate (see Far-Go)
triallate & trifluralin (see Buckle)
Triamine (2,4-D & 2,4-DP & MCPP) .... Riverdale
est. lawns/turf 403
noncropland 471
Triamine II (2,4-DP & MCPA & MCPP) ... Riverdale
est. lawns/turf 409
noncropland 485
Triangle Brand Copper Sulfate (copper sulfate) .... Phelps Dodge
moving water 497
still water 494
triasulfuron (see Amber)
tribenuron-methyl (see Express)
triclopyr (see Garlon, Grandstand, Pathfinder, Remedy)
triclopyr & 2,4-D (see Crossbow)
Tri-Ester (2,4-D & 2,4-DP & MCPP) .... Riverdale
est. lawns/turf 403
noncropland 471
Tri-Ester II (2,4-DP & MCPA & MCPP) .... Riverdale
est. lawns/turf 409
noncropland 486
Trific (trifluralin) .... Terra
WPS chart 80
asparagus 297
barley 222
beans 300
carrots 303
castor beans 240
celery 305
cole crops 307
conservation reserve program 447
cotton 182
cucurbits 309
field corn, popcorn 125
forage 459
greens 315
guar beans 243
hops 243
mung beans 247
nuts 392
oil seed crops 247

okra ... 320
onions ... 323
peanuts ... 252
peas ... 326
peppers ... 329
potatoes ... 332
safflower ... 259
small fruits ... 363
sorghum ... 268
southern peas ... 336
soybeans ... 162
spring wheat ... 211
sugar beets ... 272
sugarcane ... 278
sunflower ... 280
tomatoes ... 350
tree fruits, citrus ... 370
tree fruits, deciduous ... 378
winter wheat ... 198

trifluralin (see Albaugh, Clean Crop, Gowan, Helena, Riverside, Sedagri, Treflan, TRI-4, Trific, Trilin, Wilbur-Ellis)

trifluralin & flumetsulam (see Broadstrike+Treflan)

triflusulfuron-methyl (see UpBeet)

Trilin (trifluralin) ... Griffin
WPS chart ... 76
asparagus ... 297
barley ... 222
beans ... 300
carrots ... 303
castor beans ... 240
celery ... 305
cole crops ... 307
conservation reserve program ... 447
cotton ... 182
cucurbits ... 309
eggplant ... 311
fallow land ... 455
field corn, popcorn ... 125
flax ... 242
forage ... 459
greens ... 315
guar beans ... 243
hops ... 243
kenaf ... 244
lettuce, endive ... 319
mung beans ... 247
nuts ... 392
oil seed crops ... 248
okra ... 320
onions ... 323
peanuts ... 252
peas ... 327
peppers ... 329
potatoes ... 332
radishes ... 333
safflower ... 259
small fruits ... 363
sorghum ... 269
southern peas ... 336
soybeans ... 162
spring wheat ... 211
sugar beets ... 272
sugarcane ... 278
sunflower ... 280
tomatoes ... 350
tree fruits, citrus ... 370
tree fruits, deciduous ... 378
winter wheat ... 198

Trimec 992 (2,4-D & MCPP & dicamba) ... PBI/Gordon
WPS chart ... 78
est. lawns/turf ... 410
turf grasses for sod ... 418

Trimec Classic (2,4-D & mecoprop & dicamba) ... PBI/Gordon
est. lawns/turf ... 410

Trimec Encore (MCPA & MCPP & dicamba) ... PBI/Gordon
est. lawns/turf ... 410

Trimec Plus (MSMA & 2,4-D & MCPP & dicamba) ... PBI/Gordon
est. lawns/turf ... 410

Trimec S.I. (2,4-D & MCPP & dicamba) ... PBI/Gordon
turf grasses for sod ... 418

Trimec Southern (2,4-D & mecoprop & dicamba) ... PBI/Gordon
est. lawns/turf ... 410

Trimec Turf Ester (2,4-D & 2,4-DP & dicamba) ... PBI/Gordon
est. lawns/turf ... 410

Triplet (2,4-D & MCPP & dicamba) ... Riverdale
est. lawns/turf ... 403

Tri-Plex (2,4-D & MCPP & dicamba) ... Riverdale
est. lawns/turf ... 403

Tri-Power (MCPA & MCPP & dicamba) ... Riverdale
est. lawns/turf ... 410

Tri-Scept (imazaquin & trifluralin) ... American Cyanamid
WPS chart ... 72
soybeans ... 163

Truce (imazapyr) ... Riverdale
noncropland ... 477

Tupersan (siduron) ... Gowan
WPS chart ... 75
est. lawn/turf ... 410
newly sprigged/seeded turf ... 399

Turbo (metolachlor & metribuzin) ... Novartis
WPS chart ... 77
potatoes ... 332
soybeans ... 163

TurfMate (MSMA) ... Luxembourg-Pamol
WPS chart ... 76
est. lawns/turf ... 407
noncropland ... 479
nuts ... 389
tree fruits, citrus ... 367
tree fruits, deciduous ... 375

Typhoon (fluazifop-P-butyl & fomesafen) ... ZENECA
WPS chart ... 81
soybeans ... 163

U

UpBeet (triflusulfuron-methyl) ... DuPont
WPS chart ... 75
sugar beets ... 272

V

Vanquish (dicamba-DGA) ... Novartis
WPS chart ... 77
brush control ... 439
est. lawns/turf ... 404
noncropland ... 472
turf grasses for sod ... 416

Vantage (sethoxydim) ... BASF
WPS chart ... 73
est. lawns/turf ... 409
fallow land ... 453
noncropland ... 482
ornamentals/woody plants ... 426

Vapam HL (metam-sodium) ... Amvac
WPS chart ... 73
potatoes ... 332
tobacco ... 283
tree fruits, deciduous ... 378

Vegemec (prometon & 2,4-D) ... PBI/Gordon
noncropland ... 486

Velpar (hexazinone) ... DuPont
WPS chart ... 75
brush control ... 440
forage ... 459
noncropland ... 475
ornamentals/woody plants ... 424
sugarcane ... 276
tree fruits, subtropical ... 382

Vengeance (dicamba & MCPA) ... Wilbur-Ellis
brush control ... 441
noncropland ... 486

Veteran 720 (2,4-D & dicamba) ... Riverdale
brush control ... 441
noncropland ... 486
pastures/rangeland ... 466

Veteran 2010 (dicamba & MCPA) ... Riverdale
brush control ... 441
noncropland ... 486

Veteran CST or 10G (dicamba) ... Riverdale
WPS chart ... 79
noncropland ... 472
pastures/rangeland ... 463

Visor (thiazopyr) ... Rohm and Haas
WPS chart ... 79
tree fruits, citrus ... 369

W

Weed Blast (bromacil & diuron) ... Platte
noncropland ... 486

Weed Rhap A-4D (2,4-D amine) ... Helena
WPS chart ... 76
barley ... 215
brush control ... 436
conservation reserve program ... 444
fallow land ... 449
field corn, popcorn ... 108
grasses for seed production ... 412
moving water ... 497
noncropland ... 469
nuts ... 385
oats ... 225
pastures/rangeland ... 461
rice ... 254
rye ... 232
sorghum ... 262
spring wheat ... 203
still water ... 494
sugarcane ... 274
sweet corn ... 340
tree fruits, deciduous ... 371
winter wheat ... 190

Weed Rhap LV-6D (2,4-D ester) ... Helena
WPS chart ... 76
barley ... 215
brush control ... 436
est. lawns/turf ... 402
fallow land ... 449
field corn, popcorn ... 108
grasses for seed production ... 412
noncropland ... 469
oats ... 224
pastures/rangeland ... 461
rye ... 232
sorghum ... 262
soybeans ... 147
spring wheat ... 203
sugarcane ... 273
sweet corn ... 340
winter wheat ... 190

Weedar (2,4-D amine) ... Nufarm
WPS chart ... 77
barley ... 216
brush control ... 437
conservation reserve program ... 444
est. lawns/turf ... 401
fallow land ... 449
field corn, popcorn ... 110
grasses for seed production ... 413
moving water ... 498
noncropland ... 469
nuts ... 385
oats ... 226
pastures/rangeland ... 462
rice ... 254
rye ... 233
sorghum ... 263
soybeans ... 147
spring wheat ... 204
still water ... 494
sugarcane ... 273
sweet corn ... 341
tree fruits, deciduous ... 371
winter wheat ... 191

Weedestroy AM-40 (2,4-D amine) ... Riverdale
WPS chart ... 79
barley ... 214
brush control ... 436
conservation reserve program ... 444
fallow land ... 450
field corn, popcorn ... 108
grasses for seed production ... 412
moving water ... 497
noncropland ... 469
nuts ... 385
oats ... 224
pastures/rangeland ... 461
rice ... 254
rye ... 232
sorghum ... 262
soybeans ... 147
spring wheat ... 203

still water 494
sugarcane 273
sweet corn 340
tree fruits, deciduous 371
winter wheat 189
Weedestroy MCPP-4 Amine (MCPP)...... Riverdale
est. lawns/turf 406
Weedmaster (2,4-D & dicamba) ....BASF
WPS chart 73
brush control 438
fallow land 450
noncropland 470
pastures/rangeland 462
sugarcane 274
Weedone 638 (2,4-D ester + acid) .... Nufarm
WPS chart 77
barley 215
conservation reserve program 444
est. lawns/turf 401
fallow land 449
field corn, popcorn 108
grasses for seed production 413
noncropland 469
pastures/rangeland 462
sorghum 262
soybeans 147
spring wheat 203
winter wheat 190
Weedone LV4 or LV6 (2,4-D ester) .... Nufarm
WPS chart 78
barley 216
brush control 437
est. lawns/turf 401
fallow land 449
field corn, popcorn 108,110
grasses for seed production 413
noncropland 469
pastures/rangeland 462
rye 233
sorghum 263
soybeans 147
spring wheat 204
sugarcane 274
winter wheat 191
Weedtrine-D (diquat dibromide).. Applied Biochemists
moving water 498
still water 495
Wham! EZ (propanil) .... RiceCo
WPS chart 79
rice 257
Whip (fenoxaprop-P-ethyl) ....AgrEvo USA
WPS chart 72
rice 254
Wilbur-Ellis Amine 4 (2,4-D amine) ....Wilbur-Ellis
WPS chart 80
barley 214
brush control 436
conservation reserve program 444
est. lawns/turf 401
fallow land 449
field corn, popcorn 108
grasses for seed production 412
moving water 498

noncropland 469
nuts 385
oats 224
ornamentals/woody plants 420
pastures/rangeland 462
rice 254
rye 232
sorghum 262
soybeans 147
spring wheat 203
still water 495
sugarcane 273
sweet corn 340
tree fruit, deciduous 371
winter wheat 189
Wilbur-Ellis Lo Vol (2,4-D ester) .... Wilbur-Ellis
WPS chart 80
barley 215
brush control 436
conservation reserve program 444
est. lawns/turf 402
fallow land 449
field corn, popcorn 108
grasses for seed production 412
moving water 498
noncropland 469
oats 224
ornamentals/woody plants 420
pastures/rangeland 461
rye 232
sorghum 262
soybeans 147
spring wheat 203
still water 495
sugarcane 273
sweet corn 340
winter wheat 190
Wilbur-Ellis MCPA (MCPA) .... Wilbur-Ellis
WPS chart 80
barley 219
brush control 440
est. lawns/turf 406
flax 241
forage 457
grasses for seed production 414
noncropland 478
oats 228
pastures/rangeland 464
peas 325
rice 255,256
rye 233
spring wheat 207
winter wheat 195
Wilbur-Ellis Trifluralin (trifluralin) ..... Wilbur-Ellis
WPS chart 80
asparagus 297
barley 222
beans 300
carrots 303
castor beans 240
celery 305
cole crops 307
conservation reserve program 447
cotton 182

cucurbits 309
fallow land 455
field corn, popcorn 125
flax 242
forage 459
greens 315
guar beans 243
hops 243
lettuce, endive 319
mung beans 247
nuts 392
oil seed crops 248
okra 320
onions 323
peanuts 252
peas 327
peppers 329
potatoes 332
radishes 333
safflower 259
small fruits 363
sorghum 269
southern peas 336
soybeans 162
spring wheat 211
sugar beets 272
sugarcane 278
sunflower 280
tomatoes 350
tree fruits, citrus 370
tree fruits, deciduous 378
winter wheat 198

X

XL 2G (benefin & oryzalin) .... Helena
WPS chart 76
est lawns/turf 411
noncropland 487
nuts 392
ornamentals/woody plants 427
small fruits 363
tree fruits, citrus 370
tree fruits, deciduous 379
tree fruits, subtropical 384
X-TRA — see Cheyenne

Z

Zorial (norflurazon) ....Novartis
WPS chart 77
forage 457
Zorial Rapid 80 (norflurazon) ....Novartis
WPS chart 77
cotton 179
forage 457
peanuts 250
soybeans 154

Weed Index

A

Abies balsamea — balsam fir
Abies grandis — grand fir
Abrus precatorius — precatory bean (rosarypea)
Absinth wormwood Artemisia absinthium:
  conservation reserve program ... 446
  pastures/rangeland ... 464,466
Abutilon theophrasti — velvetleaf
Acacia *Acacia* spp.:
  conservation reserve program ... 446
  pastures/rangeland ... 460,466
Acacia farnesiana — huisache
Acacia greggii — catclaw acacia
Acacia rigidula — blackbrush acacia
Acacia spp. — acacia
Acacia tortuosa — twisted acacia
Acalypha rhomboidea — rhombic copperleaf
Acalypha ostryaefolia — hophornbeam copperleaf
Acalypha virginica — Virginia copperleaf
Acanthospermum hispidum — bristly starbur
Acer circinatum — vine maple
Acer macrophyllum — bigleaf maple
Acer pensylvanicum — striped maple
Acer rubrum — red maple
Acer saccharum — sugar maple
Acer spicatum — mountain maple
Acer spp. — maple
Achillea millefolium — common yarrow (milfoil)
Achillea spp. — yarrow
Adenostoma fasciculatum — chamise
Aegilops cylindrica — jointed goatgrass
Aeschynomene virginica — northern jointvetch (curly indigo)
Aesculus spp.— buckeye
Ageratum *Ageratum* spp.:
  grasses for seed production ... 413
  noncropland ... 482
  ornamentals/woody plants ... 426
  sugarcane ... 275,277
  tree fruits, subtropical ... 382
Ageratum spp. — ageratum
Agropyron cristatum — crested wheatgrass
Agropyron intermedium — intermediate wheatgrass
Agropyron smithii — western wheatgrass (bluejointgrass)
Agropyron spicatum — bluebunch wheatgrass
Agropyron spp. — wheatgrass
Agropyron tricophorum — pubescent wheatgrass
Agrostemma githago — corn cockle
Agrostis alba — redtop
Agrostis gigantea — redtop
Agrostis scabra — rough bentgrass
Agrostis spp. — bentgrass
Ailanthus *Ailanthus* spp.:
  noncropland ... 480,484
Ailanthus spp. — ailanthus
Ailanthus altissima — tree-of-heaven
Aira caryophyllea — silver hairgrass
Alchemilla arvensis — parsley-piert
Alder *Alnus* spp.:
  brush control ... 436-442
  noncropland ... 469-472,480,484-486
  pastures/rangeland ... 461,466
Alexandergrass *Brachiaria plantaginea:*
  sugarcane ... 272,275,277
  tree fruits, citrus ... 369
Alfalfa *Medicago sativa:*
  barley ... 214
  conservation reserve program ... 443
  fallow land ... 449-451
  field corn, popcorn ... 104,106,110-112,114, ... 116-118,124
  grasses for seed production ... 413
  oats ... 224
  pastures/rangeland ... 461
  sorghum ... 263
  soybeans ... 147,162
  spring wheat ... 202
  sweet corn ... 342
  winter wheat ... 189
Alisma plantago-aquatica — common waterplantain
Alisma spp. — waterplantain
Alligatorweed *Alternanthera philoxeroides:*
  field corn, popcorn ... 114,116,121
  moving water ... 499
  rice ... 254,258
  still water ... 496
  sweet corn ... 342
Allium canadense — wild onion
Allium vineale — wild garlic
Alnus rubra — red alder
Alnus spp. — alder
Alopecurus carolinianus — Carolina foxtail
Alopecurus saccatus — Pacific meadow foxtail
Aloysia gratissima — Texas whitebrush (whitebrush)
Alta fescue *Festuca arundinacea* (tall fescue):
  noncropland ... 480
Alternanthera philoxeroides — alligatorweed
Alysicarpus vaginalis — alyceclover
Alyce clover *Alysicarpus vaginalis:*
  est. lawns/turf ... 408
Amaranth *Amaranthus* spp.:
  field corn, popcorn ... 125
  peanuts ... 252
  sugarcane ... 273,278
Amaranthus:
  sugarcane ... 275
  tree fruits, subtropical ... 380-382
Amaranthus albus — tumble pigweed (tumbleweed)
Amaranthus blitoides — prostrate pigweed
Amaranthus fimbriatus — fringed pigweed
Amaranthus hybridus — smooth pigweed
Amaranthus palmeri — Palmer amaranth
Amaranthus powellii — Powell amaranth
Amaranthus retroflexus — redroot pigweed (carelessweed, green amaranth)
Amaranthus rudis — common waterhemp
Amaranthus spinosus — spiny amaranth (spiny pigweed)
Amaranthus spp. — amaranth (waterhemp)
Amaranthus tricolor — spleen amaranth
Amaranthus tuberculatus — tall waterhemp
Amazon sprangletop *Leptochloa panicoides:*
  cotton ... 173
  fallow land ... 448
  garlic ... 313
  noncropland ... 468
  nuts ... 385
  onions ... 321
  ornamentals/woody plants ... 419
  small fruits ... 356
  soybeans ... 145
  sugar beets ... 269
  tree fruits, citrus ... 363
  tree fruits, deciduous ... 371
  tree fruits, subtropical ... 379
Ambrosia acanthicarpa — annual bursage
Ambrosia artemisiifolia — common ragweed (carrotweed)
Ambrosia bidentata — lanceleaf ragweed
Ambrosia tomentosa — skeletonleaf bursage
Ambrosia grayi — woollyleaf bursage
Ambrosia psilostachya — western ragweed
Ambrosia spp. — annual ragweed, bursage, ragweed
Ambrosia trifida — giant ragweed
Amelanchier spp. — serviceberry
American beech *Fagus grandifolia:*
  noncropland ... 477
American black nightshade *Solanum americanum:*
  cotton ... 177
  nuts ... 388
  small fruits ... 359
  tree fruits, citrus ... 366
  tree fruits, deciduous ... 374
  tree fruits, subtropical ... 381
American burnweed *Erechtites hieraciifolia:*
  nuts ... 391
  tree fruits, deciduous ... 377
American daisy:
  tobacco ... 282
American elder *Sambucus canadensis:*
  noncropland ... 477
American elm *Ulmus americana:*
  noncropland ... 476
American lotus *Nelumbo lutea:*
  moving water ... 499
  still water ... 496
Ammannia auriculata — redstem
Ammannia coccinea — purple ammannia
Ampelamus albidus — honeyvine milkweed
Ampelopsis arborea — peppervine
Amsinckia:
  barley ... 216
  field corn, popcorn ... 117
  forage ... 456
  grasses for seed production ... 413
  mint ... 245
  oats ... 226
  soybeans ... 153
  sugarcane ... 275
  tree fruits, citrus ... 364
  tree fruits, deciduous ... 372
  winter wheat ... 192
Amsinckia intermedia — coast fiddleneck
Amsinckia lycopsoides — tarweed fiddleneck
Amsinckia spp. — fiddleneck
Anagallis arvensis — scarlet pimpernel
Andropogon gerardii — big bluestem
Andropogon scorparius — little bluestem
Andropogon spp. — beardgrass
Andropogon virginicus — broomsedge
Annual arrowhead:
  rice ... 254,255
Annual bluegrass *Poa annua:*
  artichokes ... 292,293
  asparagus ... 294-297
  barley ... 216-218
  beans ... 298,300,301
  carrots ... 303
  castor beans ... 240
  celery ... 305
  cole crops ... 307
  conservation reserve program ... 447
  cotton ... 173-176,182
  cucurbits ... 309
  eggplant ... 311
  est. lawns/turf ... 399-401,404,406-409,411
  fallow land ... 448,451,454,455
  field corn, popcorn ... 107,111-114,116,123-125
  flax ... 240,242
  forage ... 455-460
  garlic ... 313
  grasses for seed production ... 414,415
  greens ... 315
  guar beans ... 243
  hops ... 243
  kenaf ... 244
  lettuce, endive ... 318,319
  mint ... 245
  mung beans ... 247
  noncropland ... 468,472,476,477,479-484,487
  nuts ... 385-392
  oats ... 226,227
  oil seed crops ... 248
  okra ... 320
  onions ... 321,323
  ornamentals/woody plants ... 419-427
  peanuts ... 252
  peas ... 326
  peppers ... 327
  potatoes ... 329,331,332
  rhubarb ... 333,334
  safflower ... 258,259
  small fruits ... 356,357,359-363
  sorghum ... 269
  southern peas ... 336
  soybeans ... 144-146,152,159,162
  spinach ... 336
  spring wheat ... 205,206
  sugar beets ... 269-272
  sugarcane ... 275,278
  sunflower ... 279-281
  sweet corn ... 339,340,342,343,345
  tobacco ... 283
  tomatoes ... 347-350
  tree fruits, citrus ... 363,364,367-370
  tree fruits, deciduous ... 371-379
  tree fruits, subtropical ... 379-384
  turf grasses for sod ... 416,417
  winter wheat ... 192-194,198
Annual broomweed:
  conservation reserve program ... 446
  pastures/rangeland ... 463,466
Annual bursage *Ambrosia acanthicarpa:*
  noncropland ... 482
  nuts ... 391
  ornamentals/woody plants ... 427
  small fruits ... 362
  tree fruits, citrus ... 368
  tree fruits, deciduous ... 375,377
  tree fruits, subtropical ... 382,383
Annual buttercup:
  field corn, popcorn ... 107
  noncropland ... 469
  pastures/rangeland ... 461
  sweet corn ... 339,340
Annual canarygrass:
  onions ... 322
Annual clover:
  fallow land ... 451
  field corn, popcorn ... 106,110,118
  sorghum ... 263
  sugarcane ... 274
Annual fescue *Festuca* spp.:
  field corn, popcorn ... 107
  sweet corn ... 339,340
Annual fleabane *Erigeron annuus:*
  barley ... 212
  conservation reserve program ... 442,447
  field corn, popcorn ... 116
  noncropland ... 469,470,481,484
  pastures/rangeland ... 460-462
  spring wheat ... 200
  sugarcane ... 274
  winter wheat ... 187

Annual foxtail:
est. lawns/turf 400
Annual groundcherry:
artichokes 292
asparagus 295
barley 216
cotton 175
field corn, popcorn 106,107,111
forage 456
mint 245
oats 226
sorghum 262
sugarcane 275
sweet corn 339,340
tree fruits, citrus 364
tree fruits, deciduous 372
winter wheat 192
Annual henbit:
cotton 174
Annual knavel:
barley 213,218,222
fallow land 448,454
oats 227,230
spring wheat 201,207,210
winter wheat 188,194,198
Annual marshelder:
fallow land 447
Annual morningglory *Ipomoea purpurea* (tall morningglory):
artichokes 292
asparagus 295
barley 216,221
carrots 301,302
celery 304
conservation reserve program 442,444,446
cotton 174,175,177,180
est. lawns/turf 408
field corn, popcorn 102,103,106,107,110-112,
..... 115-117,120,123
forage 456
herbs/spices 316
lettuce, endive 318
mint 245
nuts 387,388,390,391
oats 226
ornamentals/woody plants 419,424,426,427
pastures/rangeland 465
peanuts 248,249
potatoes 330
small fruits 357,359,361,362
sorghum 260,262,264,265,268
soybeans 144,146-148,153,160,161
spring wheat 209
sugarcane 275
sweet corn 338-341,343,345
tree fruits, citrus 364,366,368,369
tree fruits, deciduous 372,374,376,377
tree fruits, subtropical 381,383,384
turf grasses for sod 416,417
winter wheat 192,197
Annual mustard:
barley 219,220
grasses for seed production 414
noncropland 470
oats 228,229
pastures/rangeland 462,464
rye 234,235
spring wheat 207,208
winter wheat 195,196
Annual nightshade *Solanum* spp. (nightshade):
field corn, popcorn 107
noncropland 478
sweet corn 339,340
tree fruits, citrus 366
Annual pepperweed:
barley 213
conservation reserve program 443
flax 240
forage 455
garlic 312
mint 244
oats 223
onions 321
rye 231
spring wheat 201
winter wheat 187
Annual polemonium *Polemonium micranthum:*
barley 212,221,222
conservation reserve program 446
fallow land 448
pastures/rangeland 465
spring wheat 200,209
winter wheat 187,197
Annual ragweed:
conservation reserve program 442
Annual ryegrass *Lolium multiflorum* (Italian):
artichokes 293
asparagus 296
barley 211,217,218
beans 298,300
carrots 303
castor beans 240
celery 305
cole crops 306
conservation reserve program 442
cotton 174,176,181
cucurbits 309
eggplant 310
fallow land 451,455
field corn, popcorn 104,107,112,117,118,120-123
flax 241
forage 455-457,459,460
garlic 314
grasses for seed production 413
greens 315
lentils 317
lettuce, endive 318,319
mint 245,246
noncropland 480-483
nuts 387,391
oats 226,227
oil seed crops 247
onions 323
ornamentals/woody plants 421,426,427
peanuts 251,252
peas 326
peppers 328
potatoes 329,332
radishes 333
safflower 258
small fruits 359-362
sorghum 268
southern peas 335
soybeans 144,152,153,157-159
spinach 336,337
spring wheat 199,200,205,206
sugar beets 270,271
sunflower 279,280
sweet corn 339,340,342,343,345
table beets 346
tobacco 282
tomatoes 347,348,350
tree fruits, citrus 368,369
tree fruits, deciduous 374,376,377
tree fruits, subtropical 381,383,384
winter wheat 186,193,194,198
Annual sedge *Cyperus compressus:*
asparagus 296,297
est. lawns/turf 400,401,407,408
field corn, popcorn 107
noncropland 479
ornamentals/woody plants 419
rice 255,256
small fruits 360
sweet corn 339,340
tobacco 282
turf grasses for sod 417
Annual smartweed *Polygonum pensylvanicum* (Pennsylvania smartweed):
field corn, popcorn 101,104
grasses for seed production 413
nuts 391
ornamentals/woody plants 427
small fruits 356,362
soybeans 144,156,160,161
tobacco 282
tree fruits, citrus 369
tree fruits, deciduous 377
tree fruits, subtropical 384
Annual sowthistle *Sonchus oleraceus:*
artichokes 292,293
asparagus 294,297
barley 213,214,216-222
conservation reserve program 443,444,446,447
cotton 181
est. lawns/turf 405
fallow land 448-452,454
field corn, popcorn 106,111,116,124
flax 240,241
forage 455
garlic 312
grasses for seed production 413
mint 244,245
noncropland 469,474,478-480,482-484,487
nuts 386,388,391,392
oats 223,224,226-230
oil seed crops 247
onions 321,322
ornamentals/woody plants 422,423,427
pastures/rangeland 461,465
radishes 333
rye 231,234
small fruits 357-359,362,363
soybeans 147,156,162
spring wheat 199,201,202,204,205,207-210
sugar beets 269,271,272
sugarcane 274,275
sweet corn 337
tomatoes 347
tree fruits, citrus 364-366,368-370
tree fruits, deciduous 371,373,374,377-379
tree fruits, subtropical 380,381,383,384
winter wheat 186-189,191-198
Annual sprangletop:
noncropland 480
Annual spurge *Euphorbia maculata* (spotted spurge):
beans 299
conservation reserve program 445,447
cotton 180
field corn, popcorn 118,124
garbanzos 312
garlic 313
noncropland 481,484
nuts 390,391
onions 322
peanuts 251
potatoes 331
small fruits 360,362
sorghum 267
southern peas 335
soybeans 152,154,159,162
sugarcane 277
sunflower 280
sweet corn 344
tobacco 282
tree fruits, citrus 367,369
tree fruits, deciduous 375,378
Annual stinkgrass:
noncropland 481
Annual sunflower *Helianthus annuus* (common sunflower):
field corn, popcorn 107
sorghum 263
sweet corn 339,340
Annual sweet vernalgrass:
artichokes 292
asparagus 295
barley 216
cotton 175
field corn, popcorn 111
forage 456
grasses for seed production 413
mint 245
noncropland 482
oats 226
sugarcane 275
tree fruits, citrus 364
tree fruits, deciduous 372
winter wheat 192
Anoda cristata — spurred anoda
Anoxopus compressus:
tree fruits, subtropical 380
Anthemis arvensis — corn chamomile
Anthemis cotula — mayweed chamomile
Anthoxanthum odoratum — sweet vernalgrass
Anthriscus caucalis — bur chervil (bur beakchervil)
Anthriscus cerefolium — chervil
Apera spica-venti — windgrass
Apocynum cannabinum — hemp dogbane
Apocynum spp. — dogbane
Arbutus spp. — madrone
Arctium minus — common burdock
Arctium spp. — burdock
Arctostaphylos spp. — manzanita
Argemone spp. — pricklepoppy
Aristida oligantha — prairie threeawn
Aristida spp. — threeawn (triple awn)
Armoracia rusticana — horseradish
Arrhenatherum spp. — oatgrass
Arrowhead *Sagittaria sagittifolia:*
noncropland 469
peas 325
rice 253,255,256
still water 495
Arrowleaved tearthumb *Polygonum sagittatum:*
small fruits 357
Arrowwood *Pluchea sericea:*
noncropland 482,485
ornamentals/woody plants 427
Artemisia:
noncropland 472
nuts 386
ornamentals/woody plants 420
small fruits 357
tree fruits, deciduous 372
Artemisia absinthium — absinth wormwood
Artemisia filifolia — sand sagebrush (sand sage)
Artemisia frigida — fringed sagebrush
Artemisia spp. — sagewort
Artemisia californica — California sagebrush
Artemisia tridentata — big sagebrush
Artemisia vulgaris — mugwort
Artichoke thistle *Cynara cardunculus:*
noncropland 472
pastures/rangeland 463
Artilleryweed *Pilea microphylla:*
ornamentals/woody plants 426
Arundo donax — giant reed
Asclepias syriaca — common milkweed
Ash *Fraxinus* spp.:
brush control 436-442
noncropland 469-472,477,485,486
pastures/rangeland 461,463,466
Aspen *Populus* spp.:
brush control 437-442
conservation reserve program 446
noncropland 469-472,475,480,484-486
ornamentals/woody plants 427
pastures/rangeland 461,463,464,466
Asperugo procumbens — catchweed
Aster:
noncropland 472,473,476,483
small fruits 357
sugarcane 274
Aster exilis — slender aster
Aster pilosus — white heather aster
Aster spinosus — spiny aster
Astragalus rosa — red orach
Astragalus spp. — loco, milkvetch
Astragalus mollissimus — woolly loco
Atriplex patula — spreading orach
Atriplex spp. — saltbush
Autumn olive *Elaeagnus umbellata:*
noncropland 472
pastures/rangeland 463
Avena fatua — wild oat
Axonopus affinis — carpetgrass
Axyris amaranthoides — Russian pigweed

B

Baccharis halimifolia — groundsel baccharis (sea myrtle)
Bacillariophyceae — diatoms
Bacopa eisenii — Eisen waterhyssop

Weed Index

Bacopa spp. — waterhyssop

Bahiagrass *Paspalum notatum:*
- cotton ... 178,179
- est. lawns/turf ... 404,407,409
- field corn, popcorn ... 114,124
- noncropland ... 468,473,475-477,479-482,484
- nuts ... 388,389,392
- ornamentals/woody plants ... 422
- small fruits ... 359,362
- sweet corn ... 342
- tree fruits, citrus ... 366,367,369,370
- tree fruits, deciduous ... 373,374,378
- tree fruits, subtropical ... 381,384

Baldcypress *Taxodium distichum:*
- noncropland ... 477

Balloonvine *Cardiospermum halicacabum:*
- cotton ... 174
- cucurbits ... 307
- field corn, popcorn ... 121
- ornamentals/woody plants ... 419
- peanuts ... 248
- soybeans ... 144-146,150,153,157
- tobacco ... 281

Balsam fir *Abies balsamea:*
- noncropland ... 480,484

Balsamapple *Momordica charantia:*
- nuts ... 388
- small fruits ... 359
- tree fruits, citrus ... 366
- tree fruits, deciduous ... 374
- tree fruits, subtropical ... 381,382

Barbarea spp. — wintercress

Barbarea vulgaris — yellow rocket

Barley *Hordeum vulgare:*
- fallow land ... 451,452
- field corn, popcorn ... 114,124
- noncropland ... 480,484
- nuts ... 388,392
- ornamentals/woody plants ... 422
- small fruits ... 359,362
- sweet corn ... 342
- tree fruits, deciduous ... 373,378

Barnyard sage:
- field corn, popcorn ... 107,116,119,121
- forage ... 458
- soybeans ... 155,159

Barnyardgrass *Echinochloa crus-galli:*
- artichokes ... 292,293
- asparagus ... 294-297
- barley ... 216-218
- beans ... 298-301
- carrots ... 301-303
- castor beans ... 240
- celery ... 304,305
- cole crops ... 305-307
- conservation reserve program ... 442,445,447
- cotton ... 173-182
- cucurbits ... 307-309
- eggplant ... 309-311
- est. lawns/turf ... 400,404,407-411
- fallow land ... 448,451-455
- field corn, popcorn ... 101-107,110-125
- flax ... 240-242
- forage ... 455,457-459
- garbanzos ... 311,312
- garlic ... 313,314
- grasses for seed production ... 414
- greens ... 315
- guar beans ... 243
- herbs/spices ... 316
- hops ... 243
- kenaf ... 244
- lentils ... 317
- lettuce, endive ... 318,319
- mint ... 245,246
- mung beans ... 246,247
- newly sprigged/seeded turf ... 399
- noncropland ... 468,474-476,478-484,487
- nuts ... 385-392
- oats ... 226,227
- oil seed crops ... 247,248
- okra ... 320
- onions ... 321-323
- ornamentals/woody plants ... 418,419,421-427
- pastures/rangeland ... 463
- peanuts ... 248-252
- peas ... 324-326
- peppers ... 327,328
- potatoes ... 329-332
- rhubarb ... 333,334
- rice ... 253,254,256-258
- safflower ... 258,259
- small fruits ... 356-358,360-363
- sorghum ... 260-262,264-269
- southern peas ... 335,336
- soybeans ... 143-147,149-159,161-164
- spinach ... 336,337
- spring wheat ... 202,205,206,209,210
- sugar beets ... 269-272
- sugarcane ... 272,273,275-278
- sunflower ... 279-281
- sweet corn ... 337-345
- sweet potatoes ... 345,346
- table beets ... 346
- tobacco ... 281-283
- tomatoes ... 347-350
- tree fruits, citrus ... 363-370
- tree fruits, deciduous ... 371-379
- tree fruits, subtropical ... 379-384
- turf grasses for sod ... 416,417
- winter wheat ... 189,192,194,197,198

Bassia spp. — smotherweed

Bassweed *Potamogeton amplifolius* (largeleaf pondweed):
- moving water ... 499
- still water ... 495

Basswood *Tilia* spp.:
- brush control ... 438,441,442
- noncropland ... 472,477,486
- pastures/rangeland ... 466

Bearclover:
- noncropland ... 439

Bearded sprangletop *Leptochloa fascicularis:*
- cotton ... 173
- est. lawns/turf ... 407
- fallow land ... 448
- garlic ... 313
- noncropland ... 468,479
- nuts ... 385
- onions ... 321
- ornamentals/woody plants ... 419
- small fruits ... 356
- soybeans ... 145
- sugar beets ... 269
- tree fruits, citrus ... 363
- tree fruits, deciduous ... 371
- tree fruits, subtropical ... 379
- turf grasses for sod ... 417

Beardgrass *Andropogon* spp.:
- noncropland ... 476,477,482,484

Bearmat *Chamaebatia foliolosa:*
- noncropland ... 439

Bedstraw *Galium* spp.:
- barley ... 217,218
- est. lawns/turf ... 410
- fallow land ... 451,453
- forage ... 458
- noncropland ... 468-470,480,483
- oats ... 227
- pastures/rangeland ... 461
- sorghum ... 267
- spring wheat ... 205,206,209
- winter wheat ... 193,197

Beech *Fagus* spp.
- brush control ... 436-438,440-442
- noncropland ... 477,485,486
- ornamentals/woody plants ... 427
- pastures/rangeland ... 466

Beggarticks *Bidens* spp.:
- barley ... 214,219
- cotton ... 174,178
- est. lawns/turf ... 401,407,408
- field corn, popcorn ... 103,108,115,121
- grasses for seed production ... 412
- oats ... 224,228
- pastures/rangeland ... 461
- peanuts ... 248
- rye ... 232,234
- small fruits ... 357
- sorghum ... 260,262,265
- soybeans ... 144,145,151,153,157,160,161
- spring wheat ... 202,207
- sugarcane ... 273
- sweet corn ... 338,340,343
- winter wheat ... 189,195

Beggarweed *Desmodium* spp.:
- peanuts ... 250
- sugarcane ... 274

Bellis perennis — English daisy

Bentgrass *Agrostis* spp.:
- est. lawns/turf ... 409
- ornamentals/woody plants ... 424
- rhubarb ... 334
- small fruits ... 357,360

Bermuda buttercup:
- artichokes ... 293

Bermudagrass *Cynodon dactylon:*
- artichokes ... 292,293
- asparagus ... 295-297
- beans ... 298-300
- carrots ... 301,303
- castor beans ... 240
- celery ... 303,305
- cole crops ... 305,306
- conservation reserve program ... 442,447
- cotton ... 173,174,176,177,179,181
- cucurbits ... 307-309
- eggplant ... 310
- fallow land ... 448,451,453,454
- field corn, popcorn ... 112,114,122,124
- flax ... 241
- forage ... 457,459
- garbanzos ... 311
- garlic ... 313,314
- grasses for seed production ... 414
- greens ... 314,315
- guar beans ... 242
- horseradish ... 316
- lawn/turf seedbeds ... 399
- lentils ... 317
- lettuce, endive ... 318,319
- mint ... 246
- noncropland ... 468,474-479,482-484
- nuts ... 385,387-390,392
- oil seed crops ... 247
- okra ... 320
- onions ... 321,323
- ornamentals/woody plants ... 419,421,422
- pastures/rangeland ... 460
- peanuts ... 250,251
- peas ... 325,326
- peppers ... 327,328
- potatoes ... 329,330,332
- radishes ... 333
- rhubarb ... 334
- safflower ... 258
- small fruits ... 356,358-362
- sorghum ... 265
- southern peas ... 335
- soybeans ... 145,146,150-152,154,156,158,162
- spinach ... 336,337
- sugar beets ... 269-272
- sunflower ... 279,280
- sweet corn ... 342
- sweet potatoes ... 345,346
- table beets ... 346,347
- tobacco ... 281-283
- tomatoes ... 348,350
- tree fruits, citrus ... 363,365-370
- tree fruits, deciduous ... 371,373-376,378,379
- tree fruits, subtropical ... 379-384
- turf grasses for sod ... 417

Betula spp. — birch

Bidens bipinnata — spanishneedles

Bidens connata — connate beggarticks (purplestem beggarticks)

Bidens spp. — beggarticks

Big bluestem *Andropogon gerardii:*
- conservation reserve program ... 442
- noncropland ... 476,477,482,484
- pastures/rangeland ... 460

Bigleaf aster:
- noncropland ... 484

Bigleaf maple *Acer macrophyllum:*
- brush control ... 440
- noncropland ... 477

Bindweed *Convolvulus* spp.:
- barley ... 214
- est. lawns/turf ... 401,406,410
- field corn, popcorn ... 108,111
- grasses for seed production ... 412
- noncropland ... 469-472,474-476,481,484,485
- nuts ... 388
- oats ... 224
- ornamentals/woody plants ... 422
- pastures/rangeland ... 461,466
- rye ... 232
- small fruits ... 359
- sorghum ... 262
- soybeans ... 147
- spring wheat ... 202
- sugarcane ... 273
- sweet corn ... 340
- tree fruits, deciduous ... 373
- turf grasses for sod ... 416
- winter wheat ... 189

Birch *Betula* spp.:
- brush control ... 437-439,441,442
- noncropland ... 469-471,477,480,484-486
- ornamentals/woody plants ... 427
- pastures/rangeland ... 461,466

Birdseedgrass *Phalaris canariensis* (canarygrass):
- tree fruits, subtropical ... 380

Birdseye speedwell:
- ornamentals/woody plants ... 423

Birdsfoot trefoil *Lotus corniculatus:*
- small fruits ... 357

Birdsrape mustard *Brassica rapa:*
- potatoes ... 331
- tomatoes ... 349

Bitter sneezeweed *Helenium amarum:*
- conservation reserve program ... 446
- fallow land ... 447
- noncropland ... 469,473
- pastures/rangeland ... 461,463,466

Bitter wintercress:
- noncropland ... 469

Bittercress *Cardamine* spp.:
- barley ... 222
- est. lawns/turf ... 404,405
- noncropland ... 474,487
- nuts ... 388,392
- ornamentals/woody plants ... 419,422,425-427
- small fruits ... 358,363
- soybeans ... 147
- spring wheat ... 199,204
- tree fruits, citrus ... 365,370
- tree fruits, deciduous ... 373,379
- tree fruits, subtropical ... 381,384
- winter wheat ... 186,191,197

Bitterdock *Rumex obtusifolius* (broadleaf dock):
- fallow land ... 451
- field corn, popcorn ... 110

Bitterweed:
- barley ... 214
- conservation reserve program ... 446
- est. lawns/turf ... 401
- field corn, popcorn ... 106,108
- grasses for seed production ... 412
- noncropland ... 470
- oats ... 224
- pastures/rangeland ... 461-463
- rye ... 232
- sorghum ... 262
- spring wheat ... 202
- sugarcane ... 273
- sweet corn ... 340
- winter wheat ... 189

Black cherry *Prunus serotina:*
- brush control ... 437-440
- noncropland ... 470-472,475,477
- pastures/rangeland ... 464

Black gum:
brush control ... 439,440
Black knapweed *Centaurea nigra:*
noncropland ... 470
pastures/rangeland ... 462
sugarcane ... 275
Black locust *Robinia pseudoacacia:*
brush control ... 437-439
noncropland ... 469-472,477
pastures/rangeland ... 461
Black medic *Medicago lupulina:*
est. lawns/turf ... 401,403,405,406,410
field corn, popcorn ... 116
noncropland ... 470,471,482,485
nuts ... 391
ornamentals/woody plants ... 424,427
pastures/rangeland ... 466
small fruits ... 362
tree fruits, citrus ... 368
tree fruits, deciduous ... 377
tree fruits, subtropical ... 383
Black mustard *Brassica nigra:*
asparagus ... 294,296
barley ... 213,217,218,222
conservation reserve program ... 443
est. lawns/turf ... 405
fallow land ... 448,454
field corn, popcorn ... 107
flax ... 241
forage ... 456
noncropland ... 474,479,480,483,487
nuts ... 388,389,391,392
oats ... 223,227,230
ornamentals/woody plants ... 422,427
potatoes ... 331
rye ... 231
small fruits ... 358,360,362,363
spring wheat ... 201,205,207,210
sugar beets ... 272
sweet corn ... 339,340
tomatoes ... 349
tree fruits, citrus ... 365,367,369,370
tree fruits, deciduous ... 373,375,377,379
tree fruits, subtropical ... 381,382,384
winter wheat ... 188,192,194,198
Black nightshade *Solanum nigrum:*
barley ... 213,216,221
beans ... 298
carrots ... 302
castor beans ... 240
celery ... 304
conservation reserve program ... 442-444,446,447
cotton ... 174,176,177,180,181
cucurbits ... 307
est. lawns/turf ... 405
fallow land ... 450,451,453,454
field corn, popcorn ... 101-107,110-113,115-124
flax ... 240,241
forage ... 455,457,458
garlic ... 312
herbs/spices ... 316
lettuce, endive ... 318
mint ... 244
noncropland ... 474,482,484,487
nuts ... 387,388,391,392
oats ... 223,226
onions ... 321,322
ornamentals/woody plants ... 418,421-424,427
pastures/rangeland ... 465
peanuts ... 248,251,252
potatoes ... 329,332
rye ... 231
safflower ... 258
small fruits ... 358,359,362,363
sorghum ... 260-265,268
soybeans ... 143-148,150-152,155,156,159-163
spinach ... 336
spring wheat ... 199,201,204,209
sugar beets ... 269-272
sunflower ... 279
sweet corn ... 337,339,341
tobacco ... 281,282
tomatoes ... 347,348
tree fruits, citrus ... 365,366,368-370
tree fruits, deciduous ... 373,374,377-379
tree fruits, subtropical ... 381,383,384
winter wheat ... 186-188,191,197
Blackberry *Rubus* spp.:
brush control ... 438,439,441,442
fallow land ... 447
noncropland ... 469,471-473,477,482,484-486
ornamentals/woody plants ... 427
pastures/rangeland ... 461,463,466
Blackbrush:
noncropland ... 485
pastures/rangeland ... 486
Blackbrush acacia *Acacia rigidula:*
brush control ... 441
Blackeyedsusan *Rudbeckia hirta:*
fallow land ... 447
noncropland ... 473
sugar beets ... 272
tobacco ... 283
tomatoes ... 350
Blackgrass:
barley ... 217
grasses for seed production ... 414
spring wheat ... 205,210
winter wheat ... 192,198
Blackgum *Nyssa sylvatica:*
brush control ... 437,438,440
noncropland ... 472,475,477,485
pastures/rangeland ... 463,464
Blackjack oak *Quercus marilandica:*
brush control ... 438,439,441
noncropland ... 471,472
Blackleaved fleabane:
est. lawns/turf ... 405
noncropland ... 474
nuts ... 388
ornamentals/woody plants ... 422
small fruits ... 358
tree fruits, citrus ... 365
tree fruits, deciduous ... 373
tree fruits, subtropical ... 381
Blackseed plantain *Plantago rugelii:*
cucurbits ... 307
soybeans ... 146
tobacco ... 281
Bladderwort *Utricularia* spp.:
moving water ... 498,499
still water ... 494-496
Blue grama *Bouteloua gracilis:*
conservation reserve program ... 442
pastures/rangeland ... 460
Blue mustard *Chlorispora tenella:*
barley ... 211-213,217,218,220-222
conservation reserve program ... 442,443,446
fallow land ... 447,448,451-453
field corn, popcorn ... 114
flax ... 240
forage ... 455,458,459
garlic ... 312
grasses for seed production ... 411
mint ... 244,245
noncropland ... 483,484
oats ... 223,227,229
onions ... 321
ornamentals/woody plants ... 423
pastures/rangeland ... 460,465
rye ... 231,235
sorghum ... 267
soybeans ... 152
spring wheat ... 199-201,205-207,209
sweet corn ... 342,343
turf grasses for sod ... 416
winter wheat ... 186-188,192-194,196,197
Bluebunch wheatgrass *Agropyron spicatum:*
conservation reserve program ... 442
pastures/rangeland ... 460
Bluegrass *Poa* spp.:
est. lawns/turf ... 409
forage ... 458,459
grasses for seed production ... 413
mint ... 245
noncropland ... 475,476,483
nuts ... 391
small fruits ... 357
soybeans ... 158,163
tree fruits, deciduous ... 377
Bluegum:
brush control ... 439
Bluejointgrass *Agropyron smithii* (western wheatgrass):
small fruits ... 357
Blueweed *Echium vulgare:*
noncropland ... 469
pastures/rangeland ... 461
sugar beets ... 270
Blunt spikerush *Eleocharis obtusa:*
rice ... 254,255
Bog rush *Juncus elliottii:*
small fruits ... 360
Boneset *Eupatorium perfoliatum:*
noncropland ... 469
pastures/rangeland ... 461
Bottlegrass *Setaria viridis* (green foxtail):
asparagus ... 297
beans ... 301
carrots ... 303
celery ... 305
cole crops ... 307
conservation reserve program ... 447
cotton ... 182
cucurbits ... 309
eggplant ... 311
field corn, popcorn ... 125
flax ... 240,242
forage ... 455
greens ... 315
guar beans ... 243
hops ... 243
kenaf ... 244
lettuce, endive ... 318,319
mung beans ... 247
nuts ... 391,392
oil seed crops ... 248
okra ... 320
onions ... 323
peanuts ... 252
peppers ... 327
potatoes ... 329,332
radishes ... 333
safflower ... 259
small fruits ... 362,363
sorghum ... 269
southern peas ... 336
soybeans ... 146,162
sugar beets ... 272
sugarcane ... 278
sunflower ... 281
tomatoes ... 350
tree fruits, citrus ... 369,370
tree fruits, deciduous ... 377,378
tree fruits, subtropical ... 384
Bouncingbet *Saponaria officinalis:*
noncropland ... 475,476,478,480,483,484
Bouteloua barbata — sixweeks grama
Bouteloua curtipendula — sideoats grama
Bouteloua gracilis — blue grama
Boxelder *Acer negundo:*
brush control ... 438-440
noncropland ... 469,471,477
Brachiaria:
asparagus ... 297
beans ... 301
carrots ... 303
celery ... 305
cole crops ... 307
cotton ... 176,178,179,182
cucurbits ... 309
eggplant ... 311
field corn, popcorn ... 102,125
flax ... 240,242
greens ... 315
guar beans ... 243
kenaf ... 244
lettuce, endive ... 319
mung beans ... 247
noncropland ... 479
nuts ... 389
oil seed crops ... 248
okra ... 320
onions ... 323
peanuts ... 248,252
peppers ... 327
potatoes ... 329,332
radishes ... 333
rice ... 258
safflower ... 259
small fruits ... 363
sorghum ... 269
southern peas ... 336
soybeans ... 143,146,162
sugar beets ... 272
sugarcane ... 275,276,278
sunflower ... 281
sweet corn ... 337
tomatoes ... 350
tree fruits, citrus ... 367,370
tree fruits, deciduous ... 374,375,378
Brachiaria mutica — paragrass
Brachiaria peligera — narrowleaf signalgrass
Brachiaria plantaginea — alexandergrass
Brachiaria platyphylla — broadleaf signalgrass
Brachiaria ramosa — browntop millet
Brachiaria spp. — signalgrass
Brackenfern *Pteridium aquilinum:*
field corn, popcorn ... 114,124
noncropland ... 472,476,477,484
pastures/rangeland ... 463
small fruits ... 357,362
sweet corn ... 342
Bracted plantain *Plantago aristata:*
est. lawns/turf ... 405
noncropland ... 474
nuts ... 388
ornamentals/woody plants ... 422
small fruits ... 358
tree fruits, citrus ... 365
tree fruits, deciduous ... 373
tree fruits, subtropical ... 381
Brambles *Rubus* spp.:
brush control ... 437,438
noncropland ... 470,471
Brasenia schreberi — watershield
Brassica juncea — Indian mustard
Brassica kaber — wild mustard
Brassica nigra — black mustard
Brassica rapa — birdsrape mustard (wild turnip)
Brazil (Brazilian) peppertree *Schinus terebinthifolius*:
brush control ... 439,441,442
noncropland ... 486
pastures/rangeland ... 466
Brazilian elodea *Egeria densa:*
moving water ... 499
still water ... 493,494,496
Brazilian pepper:
noncropland ... 485
Bristlegrass *Setaria* spp. (foxtail):
asparagus ... 297
beans ... 301
carrots ... 303
celery ... 305
cole crops ... 307
conservation reserve program ... 447
cotton ... 182
cucurbits ... 309
eggplant ... 311
field corn, popcorn ... 125
flax ... 240,242
forage ... 455
greens ... 315
guar beans ... 243
hops ... 243
kenaf ... 244
lettuce, endive ... 318,319
mung beans ... 247
nuts ... 391,392
oil seed crops ... 248
okra ... 320
onions ... 323

ornamentals/woody plants ... 427
peanuts ... 252
peppers ... 327
potatoes ... 329,332
radishes ... 333
safflower ... 259
small fruits ... 362,363
sorghum ... 269
southern peas ... 336
soybeans ... 162
sugar beets ... 272
sugarcane ... 278
sunflower ... 281
tomatoes ... 350
tree fruits, citrus ... 369,370
tree fruits, deciduous ... 377,378
tree fruits, subtropical ... 384

Bristlegrass foxtail:
soybeans ... 146

Bristly foxtail *Setaria verticillata:*
artichokes ... 292
asparagus ... 294
cotton ... 174
field corn, popcorn ... 101,103,104,106,112,117
mint ... 245
nuts ... 386
radishes ... 333
small fruits ... 356,357
soybeans ... 149,153,156
sugarcane ... 277
sweet corn ... 344
tree fruits, citrus ... 364
tree fruits, deciduous ... 371
tree fruits, subtropical ... 380

Bristly houndstongue:
noncropland ... 481

Bristly oxtongue *Picris echioides:*
noncropland ... 482
nuts ... 391
ornamentals/woody plants ... 427
small fruits ... 362
tree fruits, citrus ... 368
tree fruits, deciduous ... 377
tree fruits, subtropical ... 383

Bristly starbur *Acanthospermum hispidum:*
barley ... 213
conservation reserve program ... 443,446
cotton ... 173,174,181
est. lawns/turf ... 408
field corn, popcorn ... 103,107,115,116,121
flax ... 240
forage ... 455
garlic ... 312
mint ... 244
noncropland ... 481
oats ... 223
onions ... 321
peanuts ... 248,249,252
rye ... 231
sorghum ... 260,265
soybeans ... 143-148,150,151,153,157-161,163
spring wheat ... 201
sweet corn ... 338,343
tobacco ... 282
winter wheat ... 187

Broadleaf dock *Rumex obtusifolius:*
barley ... 213,217,218
fallow land ... 448,451
field corn, popcorn ... 106,110
oats ... 227
sorghum ... 263
spring wheat ... 201,205,207
winter wheat ... 188,193,194

Broadleaf filaree *Erodium botrys:*
fallow land ... 452
nuts ... 388
oil seed crops ... 247
ornamentals/woody plants ... 423
small fruits ... 359
tree fruits, citrus ... 366
tree fruits, deciduous ... 374
tree fruits, subtropical ... 381

Broadleaf panicum *Panicum adspersum:*
sugarcane ... 272,277

Broadleaf plantain *Plantago major:*
field corn ... 103,111
noncropland ... 469,482
nuts ... 391
pastures/rangeland ... 461
small fruits ... 362
tree fruits, citrus ... 368
tree fruits, deciduous ... 377
tree fruits, subtropical ... 383

Broadleaf signalgrass *Brachiaria platyphylla:*
asparagus ... 295-297
beans ... 298,300
carrots ... 301,303
celery ... 305
cole crops ... 306
cotton ... 173,174,177,181
cucurbits ... 307-309
eggplant ... 310
est. lawns/turf ... 400
fallow land ... 448,451,453,455
field corn, popcorn ... 101-104,106,107,110-122,124
flax ... 241
forage ... 455,458,459
garlic ... 313,314
greens ... 315
lettuce, endive ... 318,319
mint ... 246
noncropland ... 468,474,476,477,479,481,482,484
nuts ... 385,387,390,392
oil seed crops ... 247
onions ... 321,323
ornamentals/woody plants ... 418,419,422
peanuts ... 248,249,251,252
peas ... 326
peppers ... 327,328
potatoes ... 332
rhubarb ... 334
rice ... 253,254,256,257
small fruits ... 356,358,360-362
sorghum ... 260,262,264,265,267,268
southern peas ... 335
soybeans ... 143-147,149-153,155-159,161-164
spinach ... 337
spring wheat ... 209
sugar beets ... 269,271
sugarcane ... 277
sunflower ... 280
sweet corn ... 337,339,341-343
sweet potatoes ... 346
table beets ... 346
tobacco ... 281,282
tomatoes ... 350
tree fruits, citrus ... 363,365,368,369
tree fruits, deciduous ... 371,373,376,378
tree fruits, subtropical ... 379,381,383,384
winter wheat ... 194,197

Brome (bromegrass) *Bromus* spp.:
barley ... 217
asparagus ... 297
beans ... 301
carrots ... 303
celery ... 305
cole crops ... 307
conservation reserve program ... 447
cotton ... 182
cucurbits ... 309
eggplant ... 311
fallow land ... 455
field corn, popcorn ... 125
flax ... 240,242
forage ... 459
greens ... 315
guar beans ... 243
hops ... 243
kenaf ... 244
lettuce, endive ... 319
mint ... 245
mung beans ... 247
noncropland ... 475,476,483
nuts ... 391,392
oil seed crops ... 248
okra ... 320
onions ... 323
ornamentals/woody plants ... 424,427
peanuts ... 252
peppers ... 327
potatoes ... 329,332
radishes ... 333
safflower ... 259
small fruits ... 362,363
sorghum ... 269
southern peas ... 336
soybeans ... 144,146,162
sugar beets ... 272
sugarcane ... 278
sunflower ... 281
tomatoes ... 350
tree fruits, citrus ... 369,370
tree fruits, deciduous ... 377,378
tree fruits, subtropical ... 383
winter wheat ... 192

Bromus catharticus — rescuegrass
Bromus commutatus — hairy chess
Bromus diandrus — ripgut brome (ripgutgrass)
Bromus inermis — smooth brome
Bromus japonicus — Japanese brome
Bromus mollis — soft chess
Bromus rubens — foxtail brome (red brome)
Bromus secalinus — cheat (cheatgrass)
Bromus spp. — brome (bromegrass), chess
Bromus tectorum — downy brome

Broom snakeweed *Gutierrezia sarothrae:*
conservation reserve program ... 446
noncropland ... 473,476,482,484
pastures/rangeland ... 463,464,466

Broomsedge *Andropogon virginicus:*
est. lawns/turf ... 407
noncropland ... 475,476,479
small fruits ... 360

Broomweed *Gutierrezia* spp.:
barley ... 214
est. lawns/turf ... 401
field corn, popcorn ... 108
grasses for seed production ... 412
noncropland ... 467,470,471,473
oats ... 224
pastures/rangeland ... 461,462
rye ... 232
sorghum ... 262
spring wheat ... 202
sugarcane ... 273
sweet corn ... 340
winter wheat ... 189

Browntop millet *Brachiaria ramosa:*
noncropland ... 484
soybeans ... 158

Browntop panicum *Panicum fasciculatum:*
artichokes ... 293
asparagus ... 296
beans ... 300
carrots ... 303
celery ... 305
cole crops ... 306
cotton ... 181
cucurbits ... 309
eggplant ... 310
est. lawns/turf ... 400
fallow land ... 453
field corn, popcorn ... 101,103,106,112,113,115,116, 120-122,124
flax ... 241
forage ... 459
garlic ... 314
greens ... 315
lentils ... 317
lettuce, endive ... 319
mint ... 246
noncropland ... 481,482,487
nuts ... 390-392
oil seed crops ... 247
onions ... 323
ornamentals/woody plants ... 425
peanuts ... 251
peas ... 326
peppers ... 328
potatoes ... 332
small fruits ... 360-363
sorghum ... 261,262,265
southern peas ... 335
soybeans ... 144,146,147,150,153,155-159
spinach ... 337
sugar beets ... 271
sugarcane ... 275,277
sunflower ... 280
sweet corn ... 339
table beets ... 346
tobacco ... 282
tomatoes ... 350
tree fruits, citrus ... 367-370
tree fruits, deciduous ... 375-377,379
tree fruits, subtropical ... 383,384

Bryophyta — moss
Buchloe dactyloides — buffalograss

Buckbean *Menyanthes trifoliata* (common bogbean):
small fruits ... 357

Buckbrush *Symphoricarpos orbiculatus:*
brush control ... 436-438
fallow land ... 447
noncropland ... 469-471
pastures/rangeland ... 461

Buckeye *Aesculus* spp.:
noncropland ... 470
pastures/rangeland ... 462

Buckhorn:
est. lawns/turf ... 402,403,410
noncropland ... 469,470

Buckhorn plantain *Plantago lanceolata:*
est. lawns/turf ... 405
forage ... 456
noncropland ... 468,473,474,480
nuts ... 388
ornamentals/woody plants ... 422
pastures/rangeland ... 463
small fruits ... 358
tree fruits, citrus ... 365
tree fruits, deciduous ... 373
tree fruits, subtropical ... 381

Buckwheat:
brush control ... 441
field corn, popcorn ... 107,113
noncropland ... 468
soybeans ... 152
sweet corn ... 340

Buffalobur *Solanum rostratum:*
barley ... 213,220
conservation reserve program ... 443,446
cotton ... 173,174
est. lawns/turf ... 400
fallow land ... 451-453
field corn, popcorn ... 103,105,107,111-113, 116,119-123
forage ... 455
garlic ... 312
grasses for seed production ... 411
mint ... 244
noncropland ... 468,470,474,481,484
nuts ... 388
oats ... 223,229
onions ... 321
ornamentals/woody plants ... 420,422
pastures/rangeland ... 462,463,466
peanuts ... 248,251
rye ... 231,235
small fruits ... 359
sorghum ... 261,267,268
soybeans ... 143,145,152,155,158-161,163
spring wheat ... 201,209
sugar beets ... 270
sweet corn ... 339,340
tree fruits, deciduous ... 373
turf grasses for sod ... 416
winter wheat ... 187,196

Buffalograss *Buchloe dactyloides:*
conservation reserve program ... 442
field corn, popcorn ... 124
forage ... 455
lettuce, endive ... 318
noncropland ... 475,476
pastures/rangeland ... 460

- soybeans 146
- sweet potatoes 345

Buffaloweed:
- field corn, popcorn 106,110,118

Bulbous bluegrass *Poa bulbosa:*
- barley 218
- conservation reserve program 445
- fallow land 452
- field corn, popcorn 114,124
- noncropland 480
- oats 227
- soybeans 152,162
- spring wheat 206
- sweet corn 342,343
- winter wheat 194

Bull thistle *Cirsium vulgare:*
- barley 241,220
- conservation reserve program 444
- est. lawns/turf 401
- fallow land 450
- field corn, popcorn 108,116
- grasses for seed production 412,414
- noncropland 469-473,477,478,482-484
- oats 224,228
- ornamentals/woody plants 420,423
- pastures/rangeland 461-464
- rye 232,234
- sorghum 262
- soybeans 147
- spring wheat 202,208
- sugarcane 273,274
- sweet corn 340
- turf grasses for sod 416
- winter wheat 189,195

Bullgrass *Paspalum boscianum* (bull paspalum):
- est. lawns/turf 399
- field corn, popcorn 107
- sugar beets 270
- sweet corn 339,340
- turf grasses for sod 415

Bullnettle *Cnidoscolus stimulosus* :
- conservation reserve program 446
- cotton 179
- noncropland 479
- pastures/rangeland 463,466
- soybeans 147

Bulrush *Scirpus* spp.:
- noncropland 469
- peas 325
- rice 255,256
- still water 495

Bunchgrass:
- small fruits 357

Bur beakchervil *Anthriscus caucalis* (bur chervil):
- barley 217,218
- fallow 451
- noncropland 483
- oats 227
- spring wheat 205,206
- winter wheat 193

Bur buttercup *Ranunculus testiculatus:*
- barley 211-213,217,218,221
- conservation reserve program 446
- fallow land 447,448,451
- oats 227
- pastures/rangeland 460,465
- spring wheat 199-201,205,207,209
- winter wheat 186-188,193,194,197

Bur cherval:
- barley 220
- oats 229
- rye 235
- spring wheat 209
- winter wheat 196

Bur ragweed *Ambrosia* spp. (bursage):
- conservation reserve program 444
- noncropland 472
- pastures/rangeland 463

Burclover *Medicago* spp.:
- cotton 174
- est. lawns/turf 399,409
- fallow land 447
- field corn, popcorn 123
- noncropland 469,470,480,481,483
- nuts 388,390
- oil seed crops 247
- ornamentals/woody plants 423,426
- pastures/rangeland 461,462
- small fruits 359,361
- sugar beets 270
- sweet corn 345
- tree fruits, citrus 366,368
- tree fruits, deciduous 374,376
- tree fruits, subtropical 381,383
- turf grasses for sod 417

Burcucumber *Sicyos angulatus:*
- barley 213
- conservation reserve program 443
- cotton 174
- est. lawns/turf 400
- fallow land 451
- field corn, popcorn 101,103,104,106,110, 114,116-119,122
- forage 455
- garlic 312
- grasses for seed production 411
- mint 244
- noncropland 468
- oats 223
- onions 321
- rye 231
- sorghum 263,265
- soybeans 143-145,152,157,159-161,163
- spring wheat 201
- turf grasses for sod 416
- winter wheat 187

Burdock *Arctium* spp.:
- barley 214
- est. lawns/turf 401,410
- field corn, popcorn 108,116
- grasses for seed production 412
- noncropland 469-472,474-477,482,484,485
- nuts 388
- oats 224
- ornamentals/woody plants 422
- pastures/rangeland 461-463,466
- rye 232
- small fruits 359
- sorghum 262
- spring wheat 202
- sugarcane 273
- sweet corn 340
- tree fruits, deciduous 373
- winter wheat 189

Burgherkin *Cucumis anguria:*
- peanuts 248,249
- soybeans 143

Burgrass *Cenchrus* spp. (sandbur):
- asparagus 297
- beans 301
- carrots 303
- celery 305
- cole crops 307
- conservation reserve program 447
- cotton 182
- cucurbits 309
- eggplant 311
- field corn, popcorn 125
- flax 240,242
- forage 455
- greens 315
- guar beans 243
- hops 243
- kenaf 244
- lettuce, endive 318,319
- mung beans 247
- nuts 392
- oil seed crops 248
- okra 320
- onions 323
- peanuts 252
- peppers 327
- potatoes 329,332
- radishes 333
- safflower 259
- small fruits 363
- sorghum 269
- southern peas 336
- soybeans 144,162
- sugar beets 272
- sugarcane 278
- sunflower 281
- tomatoes 350
- tree fruits, citrus 370
- tree fruits, deciduous 378

Burning nettle *Urtica urens:*
- artichokes 293
- carrots 302
- celery 304
- cole crops 306
- cucurbits 308
- eggplant 310
- fallow land 452
- forage 458
- garlic 314
- greens 315
- lettuce, endive 318,319
- noncropland 482
- nuts 388,391
- oil seed crops 247
- onions 323
- ornamentals/woody plants 423,427
- peppers 328
- small fruits 359,362
- tree fruits, citrus 366,368
- tree fruits, deciduous 374,377
- tree fruits, subtropical 381,383

Burreed *Sparganium* spp.:
- moving water 499
- still water 495

Burroweed:
- conservation reserve program 446
- noncropland 484
- pastures/rangeland 466

Bursage *Ambrosia* spp.:
- conservation reserve program 444,446
- fallow land 450
- pastures/rangeland 463,466

Bushy wallflower *Erysimum repandum:*
- barley 212,213,217,218,220-222
- conservation reserve program 446
- fallow land 448,454
- oats 227,229,230
- pastures/rangeland 465
- rye 235
- spring wheat 199-201,205,207,209,210
- winter wheat 186-188,192,194,196-198

Buttercup *Ranunculus* spp.:
- barley 212,218-220
- est. lawns/turf 404,406
- fallow land 447,448
- field corn, popcorn 114
- grasses for seed production 414
- noncropland 469-471,480,483,484
- oats 227-229
- ornamentals/woody plants 424
- pastures/rangeland 462,464
- rye 234,235
- soybeans 152
- spring wheat 200,206-208
- sugarcane 274
- sweet corn 342,343
- winter wheat 187,193-196

Buttercup oxalis:
- est. lawns/turf 404

Butterweed *Abutilon theophrasti* (velvetleaf):
- sugarcane 277

Buttonbush:
- noncropland 484

Buttonweed:
- carrots 301
- cotton 176
- field corn, popcorn 106,112,117,120
- grasses for seed production 413
- ornamentals/woody plants 426
- potatoes 330
- sorghum 262,266
- soybeans 153
- sweet corn 338,339
- tree fruits, subtropical 382

C

Cactus:
- noncropland 484

Calandrinia ciliata — desert rockpurslane (redmaids rockpurslane)

California arrowhead *Sagittaria montevidensis:*
- rice 255

California buckwheat:
- brush control 439

California burclover *Medicago polymorpha:*
- field corn, popcorn 106,118
- noncropland 482
- nuts 391
- ornamentals/woody plants 427
- small fruits 362
- sugar beets 272
- sugarcane 274
- tree fruits, citrus 368
- tree fruits, deciduous 377
- tree fruits, subtropical 383

California sagebrush *Artemisia californica:*
- brush control 439

Caltrop:
- southern peas 336

Calystegia sepium — hedge bindweed

Camelina microcarpa — smallseed falseflax

Camelina spp. — falseflax

Camelthorn:
- conservation reserve program 446

Camphorweed *Heterotheca subaxillaris:*
- conservation reserve program 446
- noncropland 472,475-477,479,482,484
- nuts 386,388,391
- ornamentals/woody plants 420
- pastures/rangeland 463,466
- small fruits 359,362
- tree fruits, deciduous 372,374,378
- tree fruits, subtropical 381,384

Campsis radicans — trumpetcreeper (trumpetvine)

Canada bluegrass *Poa compressa:*
- noncropland 476,477,482,484

Canada goldenrod *Solidago canadensis:*
- sugarcane 275

Canada thistle *Cirsium arvense:*
- artichokes 292
- asparagus 294,295,297
- barley 211-214,217-222
- beans 298,299
- brush control 441
- carrots 301
- celery 303
- cole crops 305
- conservation reserve program 442-444,446,447
- cotton 177
- cucurbits 308
- eggplant 310
- est. lawns/turf 403,406,408
- fallow land 447-451,453,454
- field corn, popcorn 103-108,110-117,119,121,124
- flax 241
- forage 457,458
- garbanzos 311
- garlic 313
- grasses for seed production 411-414
- greens 314
- guar beans 242
- horseradish 316
- lentils 317
- lettuce, endive 318
- mint 244
- noncropland 468-478,480,482-486
- nuts 386,388,391
- oats 223,224,227-230
- okra 320
- onions 321
- ornamentals/woody plants 419,420,422,427
- pastures/rangeland 460-466
- peanuts 248,250
- peas 324,325
- peppers 328

potatoes 330,331
radishes 333
rhubarb 334
rice 255
rye 231-235
small fruits 356,357,359,362
sorghum 260-263,265,267
soybeans 143-147,149,151-153,155-157,160-162
spinach 336
spring wheat 199-202,205-209,211
sugar beets 270,272
sugarcane 273
sweet corn 338,340,342,343
sweet potatoes 346
table beets 347
tomatoes 348,349
tree fruits, citrus 369
tree fruits, deciduous 372,373,378
tree fruits, subtropical 384
turf grasses for sod 416
winter wheat 186-189,192-197

Canarygrass *Phalaris canariensis:*
artichokes 292
asparagus 294
carrots 301
celery 303
est. lawns/turf 408
field corn, popcorn 117
forage 459
lettuce, endive 318
mint 245
noncropland 478
nuts 386
ornamentals/woody plants 424
potatoes 330
radishes 333
small fruits 357
soybeans 153
sugar beets 269,271
sweet corn 343
tree fruits, citrus 364,369
tree fruits, deciduous 371
tree fruits, subtropical 380
turf grasses for sod 417

Candalia obtusifolia — lotebush

Canyon live oak *Quercus chrysolepis:*
brush control 436,437

Caperonia castaniifolia — mexicanweed

Capsella bursa-pastoris — shepherdspurse

Cardamine spp. — bittercress

Cardamine hirsuta — hairy bittercress

Cardaria draba — hoary cress

Cardaria spp. — whitetop

Cardiospermum halicacabum — balloonvine

Carduus acanthoides — plumeless thistle

Carduus nutans — musk thistle (nodding thistle)

Carduus pycnocephalus — Italian thistle

Carduus spp. — thistles

Carelessweed *Amaranthus retroflexus* (redroot pigweed):
asparagus 297
beans 298,301
carrots 302,303
celery 304,305
cole crops 307
conservation reserve program 447
cotton 180,182
cucurbits 309
eggplant 311
field corn, popcorn 102,106,110,112,115, 118,123,125
flax 240-242
forage 455
greens 315
guar beans 243
herbs/spices 316
hops 243
kenaf 244
lettuce, endive 318,319
mung beans 247
noncropland 483
nuts 390-392
oil seed crops 248
okra 320
onions 323
ornamentals/woody plants 426,427
peanuts 248,252
peppers 327
potatoes 329,332
radishes 333
safflower 259
small fruits 361-363
sorghum 260,262,269
southern peas 336
soybeans 143,144,146,150,162
sugar beets 272
sugarcane 278
sunflower 281
sweet corn 337,339,345
tobacco 283
tomatoes 350
tree fruits, citrus 368-370
tree fruits, deciduous 376-379
tree fruits, subtropical 383,384
turf grasses for sod 417

Carex aquatilis — water sedge

Carex spp. — sedge

Carolina foxtail *Alopecurus carolinianus:*
field corn, popcorn 114
soybeans 152
sweet corn 342

Carolina geranium *Geranium carolinianum:*
barley 213,217,218,222
est. lawns/turf 404-406
fallow land 447,448,452,454
field corn, popcorn 114,124
noncropland 468,474,476,479-482,484
nuts 388,391
oats 227,230
ornamentals/woody plants 422,424,427
small fruits 358,362
soybeans 147,152,162
spring wheat 201,205,207,210
sugarcane 274
sweet corn 342
tree fruits, citrus 365,368,369
tree fruits, deciduous 373,377,378
tree fruits, subtropical 381,383,384
winter wheat 188,193,194,197,198

Carolina horsenettle *Solanum carolinense* (horsenettle):
conservation reserve program 444
fallow land 450,451
field corn, popcorn 106,110,111
noncropland 470
pastures/rangeland 462,463
sorghum 263

Carpet burweed:
est. lawns/turf 399

Carpetgrass *Axonopus affinis:*
est. lawns/turf 401
nuts 388
ornamentals/woody plants 422,425
small fruits 359
tree fruits, deciduous 373

Carpetweed *Mollugo verticillata:*
artichokes 292
asparagus 294,297
barley 214
beans 298-301
brush control 441
carrots 301-303
castor beans 240
celery 303,305
cole crops 305-307
conservation reserve program 445,447
cotton 174,176,178-182
cucurbits 307-309
eggplant 309,311
est. lawns/turf 400,401,403,411
fallow land 455
field corn, popcorn 101-103,105-108,110-113, 115-125
flax 240-242
forage 455,457,458
garbanzos 311,312
garlic 313
grasses for seed production 412
greens 315
guar beans 243
hops 243
kenaf 244
lettuce, endive 318,319
mint 245
mung beans 246,247
noncropland 471,472,476-478,481,482, 484,486,487
nuts 386,387,390-392
oats 224
oil seed crops 248
okra 320
onions 322,323
ornamentals/woody plants 418-421,423-427
pastures/rangeland 461,466
peanuts 248-252
peas 325,326
peppers 327
potatoes 329-332
radishes 333
rye 232
safflower 258,259
small fruits 357,360-363
sorghum 260-262,264-269
southern peas 335,336
soybeans 143-148,150-156,158-163
spring wheat 202
sugar beets 270,272
sugarcane 273,277,278
sunflower 279-281
sweet corn 337-345
sweet potatoes 345
tobacco 281,282
tomatoes 348-350
tree fruits, citrus 364,365,367-370
tree fruits, deciduous 371,372,375-379
tree fruits, subtropical 380,383,384
winter wheat 189

Carpinus spp. — hornbeam

Carrotweed *Ambrosia artemisiifolia* (common ragweed):
sugar beets 270

Carya illinoinensis — pecan

Carya spp. — hickory

Caryophyllaceae spergularia rubra — red sandspurry

Cascara:
brush control 439
noncropland 485
pastures/rangeland 466

Cassia fasciulata — partridgepea

Cassia mimosoides — Japanese tea

Cassia obtusifolia — sicklepod

Cassia occidentalis — coffee senna

Castanea spp. — chinquapin

Castorbean *Ricinus communis:*
ornamentals/woody plants 426
sugarcane 276
tree fruits, subtropical 382

Catchweed *Asperugo procumbens:*
barley 222
forage 458
winter wheat 197

Catchweed bedstraw *Galium aparine:*
barley 212,213,218
fallow land 448
mint 245
noncropland 480,481
oats 227
ornamentals/woody plants 423
spring wheat 199-201,207
winter wheat 186-188,194

Catclaw acacia *Acacia greggii:*
brush control 439,440
noncropland 475,484
pastures/rangeland 464

Catnip *Nepeta cataria:*
barley 214
field corn, popcorn 108
grasses for seed production 412
noncropland 469
oats 224
pastures/rangeland 461
rye 232
sorghum 262
spring wheat 202
sugarcane 273
sweet corn 340
winter wheat 189

Catsear *Hypochaeris* spp.:
noncropland 472
ornamentals/woody plants 424

Cattail *Typha* spp.:
moving water 498,499
noncropland 476,477,482,484
still water 495,496

Ceanothus integerrimus — deerbrush

Ceanothus:
brush control 436-439
noncropland 469,471,485
pastures/rangeland 461,466

Cedar:
brush control 437,438,440
conservation reserve program 446
noncropland 470,472,480,484

Celtis pallida — granjeno

Celtis spp. — hackberry

Cenchrus echinatus — southern sandbur

Cenchrus incertus — field sandbur

Cenchrus spp. — sandbur

Centaurea calcitrapa — purple starthistle

Centaurea cyanus — cornflower

Centaurea diffusa — diffuse knapweed

Centaurea maculosa — spotted knapweed

Centaurea nigra — black knapweed

Centaurea repens — Russian knapweed

Centaurea solstitialis — yellow starthistle

Centaurea spp. — knapweed

Centaurea triumfetti — squarrose knapweed

Centipedegrass *Eremochloa ophiuroides:*
est. lawns/turf 409
noncropland 484

Cerastium vulgatum — mouseear chickweed

Ceratophyllum demersum — coontail (hornwort, prickly coontail)

Cercis spp. — redbud

Cercis canadensis — eastern redbud

Cereal rye:
conservation reserve program 445

Chamaebatia foliolosa — bearmat

Chamise *Adenostoma fasciculatum:*
brush control 438,439
noncropland 471

Chamomile *Matricaria* spp.:
field corn, popcorn 103,112
noncropland 468

Chaparral:
conservation reserve program 446
noncropland 484

Chara:
moving water 497,499
still water 493,494,496

Cheat (cheatgrass) *Bromus secalinus:*
artichokes 292,293
asparagus 294,296,297
barley 217,218
beans 301
carrots 303
celery 305
cole crops 307
conservation reserve program 442,445,447
cotton 182
cucurbits 309
eggplant 311
fallow land 448,449,452-455
field corn, popcorn 114,123-125
flax 240,242
forage 457-460
greens 315
guar beans 243
hops 243
kenaf 244
lettuce, endive 318,319
mint 245
mung beans 247

noncropland 467,476,477,479-484
nuts 386,392
oats 227
oil seed crops 248
okra 320
onions 323
ornamentals/woody plants 421,424,426
peanuts 252
peppers 327
potatoes 329,332
rhubarb 333,334
safflower 259
small fruits 357,360-363
sorghum 269
southern peas 336
soybeans 144,146,152,162
spring wheat 200,205,206
sugar beets 270,272
sugarcane 278
sunflower 281
sweet corn 342,343,345
tomatoes 350
tree fruits, citrus 364,368-370
tree fruits, deciduous 371,376-378
tree fruits, subtropical 380,383,384
winter wheat 186,193,194,198

Cheeseweed *Malva* spp. (mallow):
artichokes 293
cotton 174
fallow land 452
nuts 388
oil seed crops 247
ornamentals/woody plants 423
small fruits 359
tree fruits, citrus 366
tree fruits, deciduous 374
tree fruits, subtropical 381

Chenopodium album — common lambsquarters (fat hen)
Chenopodium botrys — jerusalemoak goosefoot (jerusalem oak)
Chenopodium leptophyllum — slimleaf lambsquarters
Chenopodium murale — nettleleaf goosefoot
Chenopodium spp. — goosefoot, lambsquarters

Cherokee rose:
brush control 438
noncropland 471

Cherry *Prunus* spp.:
brush control 437-442
noncropland 469,477,480,484-486
pastures/rangeland 461,466

Chess *Bromus* spp.:
asparagus 297
beans 301
carrots 303
celery 305
cole crops 307
conservation reserve program 447
cotton 182
cucurbits 309
eggplant 311
field corn, popcorn 125
flax 240,242
forage 459
greens 315
guar beans 243
hops 243
kenaf 244
lettuce, endive 319
mung beans 247
nuts 392
oil seed crops 248
okra 320
onions 323
peanuts 252
peppers 327
potatoes 329,332
radishes 333
safflower 259
small fruits 363
sorghum 269
southern peas 336
soybeans 144,162
sugar beets 272
sugarcane 278
sunflower 281
tomatoes 350
tree fruits, citrus 370
tree fruits, deciduous 378

Chickweed:
artichokes 292
asparagus 295-297
barley 214,216
beans 301
brush control 441
carrots 303
celery 305
cole crops 307
conservation reserve program 447
cotton 174,175,178,179,181,182
cucurbits 309
eggplant 311
est. lawns/turf 399,401,403-408,410,411
field corn, popcorn ...105,108,111,115,120,122,125
flax 240,242
forage 455-459
grasses for seed production 412-414
greens 315
guar beans 243
hops 243
kenaf 244
lettuce, endive 318,319
mint 245,246

mung beans 247
noncropland 469-472,474-476,478-480,
                   483,485-487
nuts 386,388-392
oats 224,226
oil seed crops 248
okra 320
onions 323
ornamentals/woody plants 420-422,424,425,427
pastures/rangeland 461,466
peanuts 252
peppers 327
potatoes 329,330,332
radishes 333
rye 232
safflower 259
small fruits 356-360,362,363
sorghum 261,262,269
southern peas 336
soybeans 144,146,153,155,161,162
spring wheat 202
sugar beets 272
sugarcane 273,275-278
sunflower 281
sweet corn 338,340
tobacco 283
tomatoes 350
tree fruits, citrus 364,366,367,369,370
tree fruits, deciduous 372-375,377-379
tree fruits, subtropical 380,382,384
winter wheat 189,192

Chicory *Cichorium intybus:*
barley 214
est. lawns/turf 401,410
field corn, popcorn 106,108
grasses for seed production 412
noncropland 469,470,473,484,485
oats 224
ornamentals/woody plants 427
pastures/rangeland 461,462,466
rye 232
sorghum 262
spring wheat 202
sugarcane 273
sweet corn 340
winter wheat 189

China lettuce *Lactuca serriola* (prickly lettuce):
nuts 391
tree fruits, deciduous 377

Chinaberry *Melia azedarach:*
brush control 440
noncropland 477

Chinese tallowtree *Sapium sebiferum:*
brush control 439,440
conservation reserve program 446
noncropland 477
pastures/rangeland 463,466

Chinquapin *Castanea* spp.:
brush control 439
noncropland 485
ornamentals/woody plants 427

Chloris:
tree fruits, subtropical 382
Chloris barbata — swollen fingergrass
Chloris radiata — radiate fingergrass (plushgrass)
Chloris spp. — fingergrass, stargrass
Chloris virgata — feather fingergrass

Chokecherry *Prunus* spp.:
brush control 438
noncropland 471,477,485
Chondrilla juncea — rush skeletonweed
Chorispora tenella — blue mustard (purple mustard)

Christmasberry *Heteromeles arbutifolia* :
brush control 441,442
noncropland 486
pastures/rangeland 466

Chrysanthemum leucanthemum — oxeye daisy
Chrysopsis spp. — goldaster
Chrysothamnus nauseosus — gray rabbitbrush
Chrysothamnus spp. — rabbitbrush
Cichorium intybus — chicory

Cinquefoil *Potentilla* spp.:
conservation reserve program 446
est. lawns/turf 406
noncropland 469,485
pastures/rangeland 461,466
soybeans 147

Cirsium arvense — Canada thistle
Cirsium spp. — thistles
Cirsium texanum — Texas thistle
Cirsium vulgare — bull thistle

Citron *Citrullus lanatus* (citronmelon):
soybeans 143

Citronmelon *Citrullus lanatus:*
noncropland 472
nuts 386
ornamentals/woody plants 420
peanuts 248
soybeans 143
tree fruits, deciduous 372

Citrullus lanatas — citronmelon (citron), wild watermelon

Cladophora:
moving water 499
still water 496

Clammy groundcherry *Physalis heterophylla:*
tobacco 282

Clasping pepperweed *Lepidum perfoliatum:*
barley 213,218
fallow land 448
oats 227

spring wheat 201,207
winter wheat 188,194
Cleome hassleriana — spiderflower (spiny spiderflower)
Climbing milkweed *Sarcostemma cyanchoides:*
field corn 106
noncropland 487
nuts 391,392
ornamentals/woody plants 427
peanuts 248
small fruits 362,363
soybeans 143,150
tree fruits, citrus 369,370
tree fruits, deciduous 377,379
tree fruits, subtropical 384

Clover *Trifolium* spp.:
barley 214
brush control 441
est. lawns/turf 402,403,405,406,410
fallow land 449,453
field corn, popcorn 116
grasses for seed production 412,413
mint 244
noncropland 468,470,471,474-477,482,484-486
nuts 388,391
oats 224
ornamentals/woody plants 420,422,427
pastures/rangeland 461,466
small fruits 357,358,362
sorghum 267
spring wheat 202,209
sugar beets 270
tree fruits, citrus 368
tree fruits, deciduous 373,377
tree fruits, subtropical 383
winter wheat 189,197

Cnidoscolus stimulosus — bullnettle
Coast fiddleneck *Amsinckia intermedia:*
artichokes 292
asparagus 294
barley 211-213,217,218,220-222
conservation reserve program 442,443,446
est. lawns/turf 405
fallow land 447,448,451,452,454
flax 240,241
forage 455
garlic 312
mint 244,245
noncropland 474,482,487
nuts 386,388,391,392
oats 223,227,229,230
oil seed crops 247
onions 321
ornamentals/woody plants 422,423,427
pastures/rangeland 460,465
radishes 333
rye 231,235
small fruits 357-359,362,363
sorghum 267
spring wheat 199-201,205-207,209,210
sugar beets 269,272
sweet corn 337
tomatoes 347
tree fruits, citrus 364-366,368-370
tree fruits, deciduous 371,373,374,377,379
tree fruits, subtropical 380,381,383,384
winter wheat 186-188,192-194,196-198

Coast tarweed:
spring wheat 199
winter wheat 186

Cocklebur *Xanthium* spp.:
barley 214,218,219
beans 298
brush control 441
carrots 301,302
celery 304
conservation reserve program 442,444,446
cotton 173-176,178-181
cucurbits 307
est. lawns/turf 401,405,407,410
fallow land 449,452,453
field corn, popcorn 101-105,107,108,110-117,
                       119-121,123,124
flax 241
forage 456-458
grasses for seed production 412,414
herbs/spices 316
mint 244
noncropland 468-471,473-479,482,484,486
nuts 389
oats 224,226-228
ornamentals/woody plants 419,420,424
pastures/rangeland 460,461,463,464,466
peanuts 248,249,252
peas 324,325
potatoes 330-332
rice 253,254,258
rye 232,234
small fruits 356
sorghum 260-262,264,265,268
soybeans 144-148,151-158,160,161,163
spring wheat 202,206,207
sugar beets 270
sugarcane 273-276
sweet corn 338-343
tobacco 281
tomatoes 349
tree fruits, citrus 364,365,367
tree fruits, deciduous 374,375
turf grasses for sod 416
winter wheat 189,194,195

Coffee senna *Cassia occidentalis:*
- cotton ... 173,181
- noncropland ... 481
- ornamentals/woody plants ... 419
- peanuts ... 248,249
- soybeans ... 143,144,161
- tobacco ... 282

Coffeebean *Sesbania exaltata* (hemp sesbania):
- noncropland ... 469

Coffeeberry *Rhamnus* spp.:
- brush control ... 438
- noncropland ... 471

Coffeeweed *Daubentonia texana:*
- barley ... 214
- carrots ... 302
- celery ... 304
- conservation reserve program ... 443
- cotton ... 180,181
- est. lawns/turf ... 401
- fallow land ... 449
- field corn, popcorn ... 108
- grasses for seed production ... 412
- herbs/spices ... 316
- noncropland ... 472
- nuts ... 386
- oats ... 224
- ornamentals/woody plants ... 420
- pastures/rangeland ... 461
- rice ... 254,257
- rye ... 232
- sorghum ... 262
- spring wheat ... 202
- sugarcane ... 273
- sweet corn ... 340
- tree fruits, deciduous ... 372
- winter wheat ... 189

Cogongrass *Imperata cylindrica* :
- conservation reserve program ... 447
- field corn, popcorn ... 124
- noncropland ... 476,482,484
- nuts ... 392
- small fruits ... 362
- soybeans ... 162
- tree fruits, citrus ... 369
- tree fruits, deciduous ... 378
- tree fruits, subtropical ... 384

Coloradograss *Panicum texanum* (Texas panicum):
- field corn, popcorn ... 124
- forage ... 455
- lettuce, endive ... 318
- pastures/rangeland ... 463

Commelina communis — Asiatic dayflower (common dayflower)

Commelina diffusa — spreading dayflower

Commelina spp. — dayflower

Common bermudagrass:
- est. lawns/turf ... 404,409
- ornamentals/woody plants ... 421
- turf grasses for sod ... 417

Common broomweed *Gutierrezia dracunculoides:*
- barley ... 212,221
- conservation reserve program ... 446
- fallow land ... 447
- pastures/rangeland ... 465
- spring wheat ... 200,209
- winter wheat ... 187,197

Common buckwheat:
- barley ... 212,222
- fallow land ... 448,454
- oats ... 230
- spring wheat ... 201,210
- winter wheat ... 188,198

Common burdock *Arctium minus:*
- barley ... 214,220
- conservation reserve program ... 443
- fallow land ... 449
- grasses for seed production ... 414
- noncropland ... 478
- oats ... 224,228
- pastures/rangeland ... 461,464
- rye ... 234
- spring wheat ... 202,208
- sugarcane ... 274
- winter wheat ... 189,195

Common chickweed *Stellaria media:*
- artichokes ... 292,293
- asparagus ... 294,296,297
- barley ... 211-213,217,218,220-222
- beans ... 298,300
- castor beans ... 240
- conservation reserve program ... 446
- cotton ... 176
- cucurbits ... 307
- est. lawns/turf ... 400-403,405-409
- fallow land ... 447,448,451,453-455
- field corn, popcorn ... 103,106,107,110,112,113,116, 118,123,124
- forage ... 457-459
- grasses for seed production ... 413,415
- lettuce, endive ... 318
- mint ... 245
- noncropland ... 468,470,473,474,476,477,479-484
- nuts ... 386-388,390,391
- oats ... 227,229,230
- ornamentals/woody plants ... 418,421,422,424-427
- pastures/rangeland ... 460,462,465
- peanuts ... 252
- peas ... 325,326
- potatoes ... 329,331
- rhubarb ... 333,334
- rye ... 235
- safflower ... 258
- small fruits ... 357,358,361,362
- sorghum ... 263,267
- soybeans ... 152,156,159,162
- spring wheat ... 199-201,204-207,209,210
- sugar beets ... 269-272
- sugarcane ... 274,275
- sunflower ... 279,280
- sweet corn ... 337,339-341,345
- tomatoes ... 347-349
- tree fruits, citrus ... 364,365,368,369
- tree fruits, deciduous ... 371,373,376-378
- tree fruits, subtropical ... 380,381,383,384
- turf grasses for sod ... 417
- winter wheat ... 186-188,191-194,196-198

Common cinquefoil *Potentilla canadensis:*
- noncropland ... 483

Common cocklebur *Xanthium strumarium:*
- asparagus ... 294
- barley ... 212-214,216,218,220-222
- conservation reserve program ... 442-444,446,447
- cotton ... 174,177,181
- cucurbits ... 307
- est. lawns/turf ... 401
- fallow land ... 448-451,454
- field corn, popcorn ... 104-107,110,111,113-122, 124,125
- flax ... 240,241
- forage ... 455,458
- garlic ... 312
- grasses for seed production ... 414
- mint ... 244
- noncropland ... 470,474,478,481,484
- nuts ... 388,391
- oats ... 223,224,226-230
- onions ... 321
- ornamentals/woody plants ... 418,422,423
- pastures/rangeland ... 460-462,464,465
- peanuts ... 248,249,251,252
- rice ... 258
- rye ... 231,234,235
- small fruits ... 358,359,362
- sorghum ... 261-263,265,267
- soybeans ... 143-145,147-150,152,155-160,162,163
- spring wheat ... 200-202,204,207-210
- sugarcane ... 274
- sweet corn ... 339
- tobacco ... 282
- tree fruits, deciduous ... 373,374,378
- tree fruits, subtropical ... 381,384
- winter wheat ... 187-189,191,194-198

Common coontail *Ceratophyllum demersum* (coontail):
- moving water ... 499
- still water ... 496

Common cornsalad *Valerianella locusta:*
- noncropland ... 481

Common dandelion *Taraxacum officinale* (dandelion):
- conservation reserve program ... 444
- fallow land ... 450,451
- field corn, popcorn ... 106,110,111
- noncropland ... 470,480
- pastures/rangeland ... 462
- sorghum ... 263
- sugarcane ... 274

Common dayflower *Commelina communis* (Asiatic dayflower):
- field corn, popcorn ... 117
- ornamentals/woody plants ... 424
- potatoes ... 330
- rice ... 253,256
- soybeans ... 153
- tobacco ... 282

Common duckweed *Lemna minor:*
- moving water ... 499
- still water ... 496

Common elodea *Elodea canadensis:*
- moving water ... 499
- still water ... 496

Common eveningprimrose *Oenothera biennis:*
- est. lawns/turf ... 401
- spring wheat ... 204
- winter wheat ... 191

Common fiddleneck::
- small fruits ... 356

Common goldenweed *Isocoma coronopifolia:*
- noncropland ... 470
- pastures/rangeland ... 462,463
- sugarcane ... 275

Common gromwell:
- spring wheat ... 199
- winter wheat ... 186

Common groundsel *Senecio vulgaris:*
- artichokes ... 292,293
- asparagus ... 294,297
- barley ... 211,213,214,217,218,221,222
- conservation reserve program ... 443,446,447
- est. lawns/turf ... 400,405,411
- fallow land ... 447-449,451,452,454
- field corn, popcorn ... 107,114,124
- forage ... 455,459
- garlic ... 312
- grasses for seed production ... 411
- mint ... 244,245
- noncropland ... 468,474,482,484,487
- nuts ... 386,388,391,392
- oats ... 223,224,227,230
- oil seed crops ... 247
- onions ... 321,322
- ornamentals/woody plants ... 419,422-424,427
- pastures/rangeland ... 460,461,465
- radishes ... 333
- rye ... 231
- small fruits ... 357-359,362,363
- soybeans ... 152,162
- spring wheat ... 199,201,202,205-207,209,210
- sweet corn ... 339,340,342,343
- tree fruits, citrus ... 364-366,368-370
- tree fruits, deciduous ... 371,373,374,377-379
- tree fruits, subtropical ... 380,381,383,384
- turf grasses for sod ... 416
- winter wheat ... 186-189,192-194,197,198

Common horsetail *Equiseteum arvense* (field horsetail):
- small fruits ... 357

Common knotweed:
- small fruits ... 356

Common lambsquarters *Chenopodium album:*
- artichokes ... 293
- asparagus ... 296,297
- barley ... 211,213,214,216-218,220-222
- beans ... 298,300
- castor beans ... 240
- cole crops ... 306
- conservation reserve program ... 443,444,446,447
- cotton ... 176,177
- cucurbits ... 307,308
- est. lawns/turf ... 400,408
- fallow land ... 447-451,453-455
- field corn, popcorn ... 101-107,110-125
- flax ... 240,241
- forage ... 455-457,460
- garlic ... 312
- grasses for seed production ... 414
- horseradish ... 316
- lettuce, endive ... 318
- mint ... 244,245
- noncropland ... 469,470,478,479,481-484
- nuts ... 387-389,391
- oats ... 223,224,226-230
- oil seed crops ... 247
- onions ... 321
- ornamentals/woody plants ... 418,419,421,423, 426,427
- pastures/rangeland ... 460-462,464,465
- peanuts ... 248,249,252
- peas ... 325,326
- potatoes ... 329,331
- rye ... 231,234,235
- safflower ... 258
- small fruits ... 359-362
- sorghum ... 260,261,263,265,267,268
- soybeans ... 143,144,146-153,155-157,159-163
- spring wheat ... 199,201,202,204-210
- sugar beets ... 269-272
- sugarcane ... 275,276
- sunflower ... 279,280
- sweet corn ... 337,338,341-343,345
- tobacco ... 282
- tomatoes ... 347-349
- tree fruits, citrus ... 366-369
- tree fruits, deciduous ... 374-378
- tree fruits, subtropical ... 381-384
- winter wheat ... 186-189,191,192,194-198

Common mallow *Malva neglecta:*
- barley ... 212,213,216,218,220-222
- conservation reserve program ... 442,444,446
- fallow land ... 448,450,451,454
- field corn, popcorn ... 106,107,110,116,118,119
- forage ... 458
- noncropland ... 479,480,483,487
- nuts ... 391,392
- oats ... 226,227,229,230
- ornamentals/woody plants ... 427
- pastures/rangeland ... 465
- rye ... 235
- small fruits ... 362,363
- sorghum ... 263,267
- spring wheat ... 200,201,204,207,209,210
- sugar beets ... 272
- sweet corn ... 339,340
- tree fruits, citrus ... 369,370
- tree fruits, deciduous ... 377,379
- tree fruits, subtropical ... 384
- winter wheat ... 187,188,191,194,196-198

Common milkweed *Asclepias syriaca:*
- fallow land ... 451
- field corn, popcorn ... 104,106,110,113,116,124
- peanuts ... 248
- sorghum ... 263
- soybeans ... 143,152,156,160-162

Common morningglory *Ipomoea purpurea* (tall morningglory):
- soybeans ... 163

Common mouseear:
- ornamentals/woody plants ... 425

Common mullein *Verbascum thapsus:*
- fallow land ... 447
- field corn, popcorn ... 112,114
- noncropland ... 473,483,484
- soybeans ... 162
- sweet corn ... 342

Common panicum:
- cotton ... 174
- cucurbits ... 307
- peas ... 324
- peppers ... 327
- soybeans ... 146
- tobacco ... 281

Common pigweed:
- beans ... 298
- castor beans ... 240
- cotton ... 176
- nuts ... 387

- ornamentals/woody plants ... 421
- potatoes ... 329
- safflower ... 258
- sugar beets ... 270
- sunflower ... 279
- tomatoes ... 348

Common pokeweed:
- field corn, popcorn ... 119

Common purslane *Portulaca oleracea:*
- artichokes ... 292
- asparagus ... 294
- barley ... 211-213,221
- beans ... 298-300
- castor beans ... 240
- cole crops ... 305,306
- conservation reserve program ... 442,446
- cotton ... 174,176-178,181
- cucurbits ... 307,308
- eggplant ... 309
- est. lawns/turf ... 400,404,405,407,408,411
- fallow land ... 447-452,455
- field corn, popcorn ... 101,103,105-107,110-113, ... 116-124
- forage ... 457,458
- garbanzos ... 311
- horseradish ... 316
- lettuce, endive ... 318
- mint ... 245
- mung beans ... 246
- noncropland ... 474,479,481,482,487
- nuts ... 386-389,391,392
- oil seed crops ... 247
- onions ... 322
- ornamentals/woody plants ... 418,419,421-424, ... 426,427
- pastures/rangeland ... 460,465
- peanuts ... 248-252
- peas ... 324-326
- peppers ... 327
- potatoes ... 329-331
- radishes ... 333
- safflower ... 258,259
- small fruits ... 356-359,361-363
- sorghum ... 261,263,264,266,267
- southern peas ... 335
- soybeans ... 143-145,147,150,151,153, ... 155-159,161,163
- spinach ... 336
- spring wheat ... 199-201,204,209
- sugar beets ... 270-272
- sugarcane ... 274,275,277
- sunflower ... 279,280
- sweet corn ... 338-343,345
- sweet potatoes ... 345
- tobacco ... 281-283
- tomatoes ... 347-350
- tree fruits, citrus ... 364-370
- tree fruits, deciduous ... 371,373-377,379
- tree fruits, subtropical ... 380-384
- winter wheat ... 186-188,191,197

Common radish:
- barley ... 213,218
- fallow land ... 448
- oats ... 227
- spring wheat ... 201,207
- winter wheat ... 188,194

Common ragweed *Ambrosia artemisiifolia:*
- artichokes ... 292,293
- asparagus ... 294,296,297
- barley ... 212-214,216,218,220,221
- beans ... 298
- cole crops ... 305
- conservation reserve program ... 442-444,446
- cotton ... 173,174,179
- cucurbits ... 307
- eggplant ... 309
- est. lawns/turf ... 400,405,408
- fallow land ... 448-451,453,454
- field corn, popcorn ... 101-107,110-124
- flax ... 241
- forage ... 455-458
- garlic ... 312
- grasses for seed production ... 411,414
- mint ... 244,245
- noncropland ... 468,469,474,476-480,482-484,487
- nuts ... 386,388,391,392
- oats ... 223,224,226-229
- onions ... 321
- ornamentals/woody plants ... 418,419,422,424,427
- pastures/rangeland ... 460,461,463-465
- peanuts ... 248,249,252
- peas ... 325
- peppers ... 327
- potatoes ... 330-332
- radishes ... 333
- rye ... 231,234,235
- small fruits ... 356-358,362,363
- sorghum ... 260-265,267,268
- soybeans ... 143-163
- spring wheat ... 200-202,204,207-209
- sugar beets ... 269,272
- sugarcane ... 274
- sweet corn ... 337-339,341-343
- sweet potatoes ... 345
- tobacco ... 281,282
- tomatoes ... 347,349
- tree fruits, citrus ... 364,365,368-370
- tree fruits, deciduous ... 371,373,377-379
- tree fruits, subtropical ... 380,381,383,384
- turf grasses for sod ... 416
- winter wheat ... 187-189,191,194-197

Common ryegrass:
- field corn ... 114
- sweet corn ... 342

Common sowthistle *Sonchus oleraceus* (annual sowthistle):
- est. lawns/turf ... 405
- noncropland ... 474
- nuts ... 388
- ornamentals/woody plants ... 422,426
- small fruits ... 356,358
- tree fruits, citrus ... 365
- tree fruits, deciduous ... 373
- tree fruits, subtropical ... 381

Common speedwell *Veronica officinalis:*
- barley ... 217
- fallow land ... 451
- noncropland ... 480,483
- spring wheat ... 205
- winter wheat ... 193

Common spikeweed *Hemizonia pungens* (spikeweed):
- field corn, popcorn ... 106,118

Common sunflower *Helianthus annuus:*
- asparagus ... 294
- barley ... 211-214,216-218,220-222
- conservation reserve program ... 442-444,446,447
- fallow land ... 447-449,451,454
- field corn, popcorn ... 103,106,107,110,111,113-116, ... 118-120,122,124
- forage ... 458
- noncropland ... 480,483,484
- oats ... 224,226,227,229,230
- pastures/rangeland ... 460,461,465
- peanuts ... 251
- potatoes ... 331
- rye ... 235
- sorghum ... 263,265,267
- soybeans ... 148-152,155,157,159,160,162,163
- spring wheat ... 199-202,204,205,207,209,210
- sweet corn ... 339,340
- tomatoes ... 349
- winter wheat ... 186-189,191,192,194,196-198

Common tansy *Tanacetum vulgare:*
- noncropland ... 483

Common tarweed *Hemizonia congesta* (hayfield tarweed):
- barley ... 213
- conservation reserve program ... 443
- flax ... 240,241
- forage ... 455
- garlic ... 312
- mint ... 244
- oats ... 223
- onions ... 321
- rye ... 231
- spring wheat ... 201
- winter wheat ... 187,188

Common teasel:
- noncropland ... 481

Common velvetgrass *Holcus lanatus:*
- grasses for seed production ... 415
- turf grasses for sod ... 417

Common vetch *Vicia sativa:*
- barley ... 213,218
- est. lawns/turf ... 401
- fallow land ... 448
- grasses for seed production ... 415
- oats ... 227
- spring wheat ... 201,207
- turf grasses for sod ... 417
- winter wheat ... 188,194

Common waterhemp *Amaranthus rudis:*
- barley ... 220
- cotton ... 181
- fallow land ... 453
- field corn, popcorn ... 101,103,110-113,115-117, ... 119,123
- oats ... 229
- peanuts ... 252
- rye ... 235
- sorghum ... 265,267,268
- soybeans ... 143,144,149,150,152,153,160,161
- spring wheat ... 209
- sweet corn ... 343
- tobacco ... 282
- winter wheat ... 196

Common watermeal *Wolffia columbiana:*
- moving water ... 499
- still water ... 496

Common waterplantain *Alisma plantago-aquatica:*
- rice ... 253

Common yarrow *Achillea millefolium:*
- barley ... 212,221
- conservation reserve program ... 446
- fallow land ... 447
- noncropland ... 473,480,483
- pastures/rangeland ... 465
- spring wheat ... 200,209
- winter wheat ... 187,197

Conical catchfly *Silene conica* (sand catchfly):
- barley ... 211,213,217,218,222
- beans ... 300
- fallow land ... 447,448,451
- noncropland ... 483
- oats ... 227
- pastures/rangeland ... 460
- peanuts ... 252
- peas ... 326
- soybeans ... 159
- spring wheat ... 199,201,205,206
- sunflower ... 280
- winter wheat ... 186,188,193,197

Conifers *Coniferales:*
- noncropland ... 472

Conium maculatum — poison hemlock

Convolvulus arvensis — field bindweed

Convolvulus spp. — bindweed

Conyza bonariensis — hairy fleabane

Conyza canadensis — horseweed

Conyza ramosissima — dwarf fleabane

Coontail *Ceratophyllum demersum:*
- moving water ... 498,499
- still water ... 494-496

Coreopsis tinctoria — plains coreopsis

Corn chamomile *Anthemis arvensis:*
- barley ... 213,216,218,221,222
- conservation reserve program ... 443,444,446
- est. lawns/turf ... 400
- fallow land ... 448,454
- forage ... 455
- garlic ... 312
- grasses for seed production ... 411,413
- mint ... 244
- noncropland ... 468
- oats ... 223,226,227,230
- onions ... 321
- pastures/rangeland ... 465
- rye ... 231
- spring wheat ... 201,204,207,209,210
- turf grasses for sod ... 416
- winter wheat ... 187,188,191,194,197,198

Corn cockle *Agrostemma githago:*
- barley ... 211,216,221
- conservation reserve program ... 444,446
- fallow land ... 447
- oats ... 226
- pastures/rangeland ... 460,465
- spring wheat ... 199,204,209
- winter wheat ... 186,191,197

Corn gromwell *Lithospermum arvense:*
- barley ... 211-213,217,218,220,221
- conservation reserve program ... 442,443,446
- est. lawns/turf ... 400
- fallow land ... 447,448,451
- forage ... 455
- garlic ... 312
- grasses for seed production ... 411
- mint ... 244
- noncropland ... 468
- oats ... 223,227,229
- onions ... 321
- pastures/rangeland ... 460,465
- rye ... 231,235
- spring wheat ... 199-201,205-207,209
- turf grasses for sod ... 416
- winter wheat ... 186-188,193,194,196,197

Corn speedwell *Veronica arvensis:*
- est. lawns/turf ... 399,404,408-410
- noncropland ... 468,481

Corn spurry *Spergula arvensis:*
- artichokes ... 292
- barley ... 213,216-218,222
- beans ... 298
- castor beans ... 240
- cotton ... 175,176
- fallow land ... 448,451,454
- field corn, popcorn ... 107,111,112
- forage ... 456,457
- grasses for seed production ... 413
- mint ... 245
- noncropland ... 482,483
- nuts ... 387
- oats ... 226,227,230
- ornamentals/woody plants ... 421,423
- peas ... 325
- potatoes ... 329
- safflower ... 258
- spring wheat ... 201,205-207,210
- sugar beets ... 270
- sugarcane ... 275
- sunflower ... 279
- sweet corn ... 339-341
- tomatoes ... 348
- tree fruits, citrus ... 364
- tree fruits, deciduous ... 372
- winter wheat ... 188,192-194,198

Corncockle:
- barley ... 222
- winter wheat ... 197

Cornflower *Centaurea cyanus:*
- barley ... 214,221
- conservation reserve program ... 443,446
- fallow land ... 449
- oats ... 224
- pastures/rangeland ... 461,465
- spring wheat ... 202,209
- winter wheat ... 189,197

Cornus florida — flowering dogwood

Cornus spp. — dogwood

Coronilla varia — trailing crownvetch (crownvetch)

Coronopus didymus — swinecress

Corylus spp. — hazel

Cottongrass *Eriophorum* spp.:
- small fruits ... 357

Cottonwood *Populus* spp.:
- brush control ... 437-439
- noncropland ... 470,471,476,485
- ornamentals/woody plants ... 427
- pastures/rangeland ... 466

Cotula australis — southern brassbuttons

Weed Index

- **Cowcockle** *Vaccaria pyramidata:*
  - barley....211,213,216-218
  - conservation reserve program....443,444
  - est. lawns/turf....400
  - fallow land....447,448,450,451
  - flax....241
  - forage....455
  - garlic....312
  - grasses for seed production....411
  - mint....244
  - noncropland....468,483
  - oats....223,226,227
  - onions....321
  - pastures/rangeland....460
  - rye....231
  - spring wheat....199,201,204-207
  - turf grasses for sod....416
  - winter wheat....186-188,191,193,194
- **Cowpea** *Vigna unguiculata:*
  - cotton....181
  - soybeans....145,160,161
- **Coyotebrush:**
  - brush control....439
- **Crabgrass** *Digitaria* spp.:
  - artichokes....292,293
  - asparagus....294-297
  - barley....216,218
  - beans....298-301
  - carrots....301-303
  - castor beans....240
  - celery....303-305
  - cole crops....305-307
  - conservation reserve program....445-447
  - cotton....173-182
  - cucurbits....307-309
  - eggplant....309-311
  - est. lawns/turf....399-401,404,407-411
  - fallow land....448,451,453-455
  - field corn, popcorn....101-107,110-125
  - flax....240-242
  - forage....457-460
  - garbanzos....311,312
  - garlic....313,314
  - grasses for seed production....414
  - greens....315
  - guar beans....243
  - herbs/spices....316
  - hops....243
  - kenaf....244
  - lawns/turf seedbeds....399
  - lentils....317
  - lettuce, endive....318,319
  - mint....245,246
  - mung beans....246,247
  - newly sprigged/seeded turf....399
  - noncropland....467,468,472,474-479,481-484,487
  - nuts....385-392
  - oats....226,227
  - oil seed crops....247,248
  - okra....320
  - onions....321-323
  - ornamentals/woody plants....418-427
  - pastures/rangeland....463
  - peanuts....248-252
  - peas....324-326
  - peppers....327,328
  - potatoes....329-332
  - rice....253,254,256-258
  - rhubarb....333,334
  - safflower....258,259
  - small fruits....356-363
  - sorghum....260-262,264-269
  - southern peas....335,336
  - soybeans....143-147,149-159,161-164
  - spinach....336,337
  - spring wheat....206
  - sugar beets....269-272
  - sugarcane....272,273,275-278
  - sunflower....279-281
  - sweet corn....337,339,340-345
  - sweet potatoes....345,346
  - table beets....346
  - tobacco....281-283
  - tomatoes....347-350
  - tree fruits, citrus....363-370
  - tree fruits, deciduous....371-379
  - tree fruits, subtropical....379-384
  - turf grasses for sod....415,417
  - winter wheat....192,194,197
- **Cranesbill geranium:**
  - noncropland....481
- ***Crataegus*** spp. — hawthorn
- **Creeping beggarweed:**
  - est. lawns/turf....401
- **Creeping buttercup** *Ranunculus repens:*
  - barley....221
  - conservation reserve program....446
  - pastures/rangeland....460,465
  - spring wheat....209
  - winter wheat....197
- **Creeping jenny:**
  - barley....214
  - est. lawns/turf....401
  - field corn, popcorn....108
  - grasses for seed production....412
  - noncropland....469
  - oats....224
  - pastures/rangeland....461
  - rye....232
  - sorghum....262
  - spring wheat....202
  - sugarcane....273
  - sweet corn....340
  - winter wheat....189
- **Creeping waterprimrose** *Ludwigia peploides:*
  - moving water....499
  - still water....495,496
- **Creeping woodsorrel** *Oxalis corniculata:*
  - est. lawns/turf....404,405
  - noncropland....474,482
  - nuts....388,391
  - ornamentals/woody plants....422,427
  - small fruits....358,362
  - tree fruits, citrus....365,368
  - tree fruits, deciduous....373,377
  - tree fruits, subtropical....381,383
- **Creosotebush** *Larrea tridentata:*
  - brush control....438,441,442
  - noncropland....472,486
  - pastures/rangeland....463,466
- **Cressleaf groundsel** *Senecio glabellus:*
  - sugarcane....274
- **Crested wheatgrass** *Agropyron cristatum:*
  - conservation reserve program....442
  - pastures/rangeland....460
- **Crimson clover** *Trifolium incarnatum:*
  - noncropland....468,480
- **Crotalaria:**
  - nuts....391
  - peanuts....252
  - soybeans....146,147,160
  - sugarcane....276
  - tree fruits, deciduous....377
  - tree fruits, subtropical....382
- ***Crotalaria sagittalis*** — rattlebox (rattlepod)
- ***Crotalaria spectabilis*** — showy crotalaria
- **Croton:**
  - barley....214
  - conservation reserve program....446
  - est. lawns/turf....401
  - field corn, popcorn....108
  - grasses for seed production....412
  - oats....224
  - pastures/rangeland....461,463,466
  - peanuts....249
  - rice....254,257,258
  - rye....232
  - sorghum....262
  - soybeans....148
  - spring wheat....202
  - sugarcane....273
  - sweet corn....340
  - winter wheat....189
- ***Croton capitatus*** — woolly croton
- ***Croton glandulosus*** — tropic croton
- **Crowfoot** *Ranunculus* spp. (buttercup):
  - artichokes....292
- **Crowfootgrass** *Dactyloctenium aegyptium:*
  - beans....299
  - conservation reserve program....445,447
  - cotton....173,176,178,180
  - est. lawns/turf....400,404,411
  - fallow land....448
  - field corn, popcorn....101,105,113,117,118,120,124
  - garbanzos....311,312
  - garlic....313
  - mung beans....246
  - noncropland....468,479,481,484,487
  - nuts....385,390-392
  - onions....321,322
  - ornamentals/woody plants....419,425,427
  - peanuts....249-251
  - peas....325
  - potatoes....330,331
  - safflower....259
  - small fruits....356,360,362,363
  - sorghum....261,266,267
  - southern peas....335
  - soybeans....145,149,153-156,158,159,162,163
  - sugar beets....269
  - sugarcane....277
  - sunflower....280
  - sweet corn....339,344
  - tobacco....282
  - tree fruits, citrus....363,367,369,370
  - tree fruits, deciduous....371,375,377-379
  - tree fruits, subtropical....379,384
- **Crownvetch** *Coronilla varia* (trailing crownvetch):
  - noncropland....473,475,476
- **Cucumbertree** *Magnolia acuminata* :
  - brush control....441,442
  - noncropland....486
  - pastures/rangeland....466
- ***Cucumis anguria*** — burgherkin
- ***Cucumis dipsaceus*** — wild spiny gourd (wild spiny cucumber)
- ***Cucumis melo*** — smellmelon (dudaim melon)
- ***Cucurbita texana*** —Texas gourd
- **Cudweed** *Gnaphalium* spp.:
  - est. lawns/turf....403,405,408
  - noncropland....472,474,481
  - nuts....386,388,391
  - ornamentals/woody plants....420,422,425,427
  - small fruits....358,362
  - tree fruits, citrus....365,369
  - tree fruits, deciduous....372,373,377
  - tree fruits, subtropical....381,384
- **Cupgrass** *Eriochloa* spp.:
  - noncropland....474,487
  - nuts....388,392
  - ornamentals/woody plants....422,427
  - small fruits....358,363
  - tree fruits, citrus....370
  - tree fruits, deciduous....373,379
  - tree fruits, subtropical....384
- ***Cuphea carthagenesis*** — tarweed cuphea
- **Curly dock** *Rumex crispus:*
  - artichokes....292
  - asparagus....295,297
  - barley....213,214,217,218,221,222
  - beans....299
  - brush control....441
  - carrots....301
  - celery....303
  - cole crops....305
  - conservation reserve program....442-444,446,447
  - cotton....174,177,181
  - cucurbits....307,308
  - eggplant....310
  - est. lawns/turf....402,403
  - fallow land....447-451,454
  - field corn, popcorn....106,107,110,112,114,118,124
  - forage....456-459
  - garbanzos....311
  - garlic....313
  - grasses for seed production....413
  - greens....314
  - guar beans....242
  - horseradish....316
  - lentils....317
  - lettuce, endive....318
  - noncropland....468-470,472-476,480-486
  - nuts....386,388,391
  - oats....224,227,230
  - okra....320
  - onions....321
  - ornamentals/woody plants....420,422,424,427
  - pastures/rangeland....460-466
  - peanuts....250
  - peas....325
  - peppers....328
  - potatoes....330
  - radishes....333
  - rhubarb....334
  - rice....253,258
  - small fruits....357,359,362
  - sorghum....263,265
  - soybeans....146,152,162
  - spinach....336
  - spring wheat....201,202,205-207,209,210
  - sugar beets....270,272
  - sugarcane....274,275
  - sweet corn....339,340,342
  - sweet potatoes....346
  - table beets....347
  - tobacco....281
  - tomatoes....348
  - tree fruits, citrus....368,369
  - tree fruits, deciduous....372,373,377,378
  - tree fruits, subtropical....383,384
  - winter wheat....188,189,193,194,197,198
- **Curly indigo** *Aeschynomene virginica* (northern jointvetch):
  - est. lawns/turf....401
  - grasses for seed production....412
  - noncropland....469
  - peas....325
  - rice....254-258
- **Curlycup gumweed** *Grindelia squarrosa:*
  - pastures/rangeland....464
- ***Cuscuta*** spp. — dodder
- **Currant** *Ribes* spp.:
  - brush control....438
  - noncropland....471
- **Cutleaf eveningprimrose** *Oenothera laciniata:*
  - barley....212-214,217,218,220-222
  - conservation reserve program....442,446,447
  - est. lawns/turf....406,408
  - fallow land....448,452,454
  - field corn, popcorn....108,114,117,124
  - noncropland....484
  - nuts....388,391
  - oats....224,227,229,230
  - onions....322
  - ornamentals/woody plants....424,426
  - pastures/rangeland....460,461,465
  - rye....232,235
  - small fruits....359,362
  - sorghum....262,267
  - soybeans....147,152,162
  - spring wheat....199-202,205-207,209,210
  - sugarcane....273,274
  - sweet corn....340,342
  - tree fruits, citrus....366,369
  - tree fruits, deciduous....374,378
  - tree fruits, subtropical....381,384
  - turf grasses for sod....416
  - winter wheat....186-189,193,194,196-198
- **Cutleaf geranium:**
  - field corn, popcorn....116
- **Cutleaf groundcherry** *Physalis angulata:*
  - beans....298
  - cotton....174,177
  - cucurbits....307
  - field corn, popcorn....102,106,115,116
  - flax....241
  - nuts....388
  - ornamentals/woody plants....418,423
  - peanuts....248
  - small fruits....359
  - sorghum....260,262
  - soybeans....143,145,150,163
  - sweet corn....337,339

tobacco 282
tree fruits, citrus 366
tree fruits, deciduous 374
tree fruits, subtropical 381
Cutleaf nightshade *Solanum triflorum:*
barley 213,214
beans 298
castor beans 240
conservation reserve program 443
cotton 176
fallow land 448,449
flax 241
forage 457
nuts 387
oats 223,224
ornamentals/woody plants 421
pastures/rangeland 461
potatoes 329
rye 231
safflower 258
spring wheat 201,202
sugar beets 270
sunflower 279
tomatoes 348
tree fruits, citrus 365
winter wheat 188,189
Cynara cardunculus — artichoke thistle
Cynodon dactylon — bermudagrass
Cynoglossum officanale — houndstongue
Cyperus compressus — annual sedge
Cyperus difformis — smallflower umbrella sedge/plant
Cyperus esculentus — yellow nutsedge
Cyperus globolosus — globe sedge
Cyperus iria — rice flatsedge
Cyperus odoratus — flatsedge
Cyperus spp. — nutsedge (nutgrass)
Cypressvine morningglory *Ipomoea quamoclit:*
cotton 174
peanuts 249
soybeans 145,150,151
Cytisus monspessulanus — French broom
Cytisus scoparius — Scotch broom

D

Dactylis glomerata — orchardgrass
Dactyloctenium aegyptium — crowfootgrass
Daisy fleabane:
noncropland 471
Dallisgrass *Paspalum dilatatum:*
cotton 175,176,178,179,181
est. lawns/turf 404,407,410
field corn, popcorn 114
noncropland 473,474,476-479,481,482,484
nuts 388,389
ornamentals/woody plants 422
small fruits 359
sugarcane 275,276
sweet corn 342
tree fruits, citrus 367
tree fruits, deciduous 373-375
tree fruits, subtropical 380-382
Dalmation toadflax *Linaria genistifolia:*
brush control 441
noncropland 486
pastures/rangeland 466
Dandelion *Taraxacum officinale:*
asparagus 294,297
barley 214,219,220
conservation reserve program 443,447
est. lawns/turf 400-403,405-407,410
fallow land 447,449,453,454
field corn, popcorn 103,107,108,112-114, 116,117,119,123,124
forage 458,459
grasses for seed production 412,414
mint 244
noncropland 469-479,481-485
nuts 386,388,389,391
oats 224,228,229
ornamentals/woody plants 420,422,424-427
pastures/rangeland 461,464,466
peas 325
rye 232,234,235
small fruits 357-359,362
sorghum 262,267,268
soybeans 147,152,161,162
spring wheat 202,207-209
sugarcane 273,275
sweet corn 340,342
tobacco 283
tree fruits, citrus 365-369
tree fruits, deciduous 372-374,377-379
tree fruits, subtropical 381,383,384
turf grasses for sod 416
winter wheat 189,195-197
Datura:
noncropland 482
nuts 391
ornamentals/woody plants 427
small fruits 362
tree fruits, citrus 368
tree fruits, deciduous 377
tree fruits, subtropical 383
Datura stramonium — jimsonweed
Daubentonia texana — coffeeweed
Daucus carota — wild carrot (Queen Anne's lace)
Dayflower *Commelina* spp.:
cotton 174,178
cucurbits 307
est. lawns/turf 400,407,408
field corn, popcorn 103,115,121,124
noncropland 479,482,484
ornamentals/woody plants 419
peanuts 248
rice 253-256,258
sorghum 260,265
soybeans 144,146,151,153,157,158,162
sweet corn 338,343
tobacco 281
Deadnettle *Lamium* spp.:
beans 298
castor beans 240
cotton 176
est. lawns/turf 400
field corn, popcorn 112
forage 457
nuts 387
ornamentals/woody plants 421
potatoes 329
safflower 258
sugar beets 270-272
sunflower 279
sweet corn 341
tobacco 283
tomatoes 348,350
Deerbrush *Ceanothus integerrimus:*
brush control 440
noncropland 475
pastures/rangeland 464
Delphinium spp. — larkspur
Descurainia pinnata — green tansymustard
Descurainia sophia — flixweed
Desert camelthorn:
noncropland 476,482
Desert rockpurslane *Calandrinia ciliata:*
noncropland 482,487
nuts 391,392
ornamentals/woody plants 427
small fruits 362,363
tree fruits, citrus 368,370
tree fruits, deciduous 377,379
tree fruits, subtropical 383,384
Desmodium spp. — beggarweed
Desmodium tortuosum — Florida beggarweed
Devilsclaw *Proboscidea louisianica:*
barley 220
beans 298
cotton 174,181
field corn, popcorn 104,111,117,119
oats 229
ornamentals/woody plants 419
peanuts 248,249,251
rye 235
sorghum 267
soybeans 143-145,148,151
spring wheat 209
winter wheat 196
Dewberry *Rubus* spp.:
brush control 438,439
fallow land 447
noncropland 471,472,475-477,480,482
pastures/rangeland 463
Diatoms *Bacillariophyceae:*
moving water 497
Diffuse knapweed *Centaurea diffusa:*
barley 214
conservation reserve program 443,444
fallow land 449
grasses for seed production 412
noncropland 468,476,482
oats 224
ornamentals/woody plants 420
pastures/rangeland 461
spring wheat 202
sugar beets 270
sugarcane 274
winter wheat 189
Digitaria bicornis — tropical crabgrass
Digitaria ciliaris — southern crabgrass
Digitaria decumbens — pangolagrass
Digitaria ischaemum — smooth crabgrass
Digitaria microbachne — kukaipuaa
Digitaria sanguinalis — large crabgrass (hairy crabgrass)
Digitaria spp. — crabgrass
Diodia teres — poorjoe
Diodia virginiana — Virginia buttonweed
Diospyros spp. — persimmon
Diospyros virginiana — eastern persimmon
Distichlis spicata — saltgrass (seashore saltgrass)
Dock *Rumex:*
asparagus 294
barley 214
cotton 181
est. lawns/turf 401,406,410
fallow land 453
field corn, popcorn 107,108,111,116,123
grasses for seed production 412
noncropland 469-471,476,477,482,484
oats 224
pastures/rangeland 461
rye 232
sorghum 262,268
sugarcane 273
sweet corn 340
winter wheat 189
Dodder *Cuscuta* spp.:
forage 457
onions 322
small fruits 357
Dogbane *Apocynum* spp.:
barley 214
est. lawns/turf 401
field corn, popcorn 108
grasses for seed production 412
noncropland 474-478
nuts 388
oats 224
ornamentals/woody plants 422
pastures/rangeland 461
rye 232
small fruits 359
sorghum 262
spring wheat 202
sugarcane 273
sweet corn 340
tree fruits, deciduous 373
winter wheat 189
Dogfennel *Eupatorium capillifolium:*
artichokes 292,293
barley 213,214,216,218,222
brush control 441
conservation reserve program 447
cotton 175
est. lawns/turf 405
fallow land 447,448,454
field corn, popcorn 111,117,124
forage 456,459
grasses for seed production 413
mint 245
noncropland 469-477,479,480,482,484,486
nuts 386,388,391
oats 224,226,227,230
ornamentals/woody plants 420,422
pastures/rangeland 461-463,466
small fruits 358,362
soybeans 153,162
spring wheat 201,202,207,210
sugarcane 274,275
sweet corn 343
tree fruits, citrus 364,365,369
tree fruits, deciduous 372,373,377,378
tree fruits, subtropical 381,384
winter wheat 188,189,192,194,197,198
Dogwood *Cornus* spp.:
brush control 436-442
noncropland 470-472,475,477,480,485,486
pastures/rangeland 464,466
Dollarweed *Sida hederacea:*
est. lawns/turf 408
Douglas-fir *Pseudotsuga menziesii:*
brush control 440
noncropland 480,484,485
Dovefoot geranium *Geranium molle:*
barley 217
fallow land 451
spring wheat 205
winter wheat 193
Dovetail geranium:
est. lawns & turf 406
ornamentals/woody plants 424
Downy brome (bromegrass) *Bromus tectorum:*
artichokes 292,293
asparagus 294,296,297
barley 217,218
beans 301
carrots 303
celery 305
cole crops 307
conservation reserve program 442,445,447
cotton 177,182
curcurbits 309
eggplant 311
est. lawns & turf 406
fallow land 449,451-455
field corn, popcorn 113,114,123-125
flax 240,242
forage 457-459
grasses for seed production 413-415
greens 315
guar beans 243
hops 243
kenaf 244
lettuce, endive 318,319
mint 245
mung beans 247
noncropland 467,476,477,479-482,484
nuts 386,388,389,391,392
oats 227
oil seed crops 248
okra 320
onions 323
ornamentals/woody plants 422,424,426,427
peanuts 252
peas 325
peppers 327
potatoes 329,332
radishes 333
rhubarb 333,334
rice 255
rye 233
safflower 259
small fruits 357,359-363
sorghum 268,269
southern peas 336
soybeans 144,146,151,152,161,162,164
spring wheat 200,205,206
sugar beets 272
sugarcane 278
sunflower 281
sweet corn 342,343,345

tomatoes 350
tree fruits, citrus 364,367-370
tree fruits, deciduous 371,373-378
tree fruits, subtropical 380,382-384
turf grasses for sod 417
winter wheat 186,188,193,194,198

Draba verna — spring whitlowgrass, vernal whitlowgrass

Dracocephalum spp. — dragonhead (dragonhead mint)

Dragonhead mint *Dracocephalum* spp. (dragonhead):
barley 219,220
grasses for seed production 414
oats 228,229
pastures/rangeland 464
rye 234,235
spring wheat 207,208
winter wheat 195,196

Drymary *Drymaria:*
tree fruits, citrus 366

Ducksalad *Heteranthera limosa:*
rice 253-255,258

Duckweed *Lemna* spp.:
moving water 498
still water 493,495

Dudaim melon *Cucumis melo* (smellmelon):
asparagus 295

Descurainia pinnata — pinnate tansymustard

Dwarf beggarweed:
est. lawns/turf 401

Dwarf fleabane *Conyza ramosissima:*
est. lawns/turf 411
noncropland 482
nuts 391
ornamentals/woody plants 427
small fruits 362
tree fruits, citrus 368
tree fruits, deciduous 377
tree fruits, subtropical 383

Dwarf mallow *Malva pusilla:*
noncropland 482
nuts 391
small fruits 362
sugarcane 274
tree fruits, citrus 368
tree fruits, deciduous 377
tree fruits, subtropical 383

Dwarfdandelion *Krigia* spp.:
barley 218
field corn, popcorn 114
oats 227
soybeans 152
spring wheat 206
sweet corn 342,343
winter wheat 194

Dyers woad *Isatis tinctoria:*
noncropland 483
pastures/rangeland 463

E

Eastern black nightshade *Solanum ptycanthum:*
barley 213
beans 299
conservation reserve program 443
cotton 174,178
fallow land 453
field corn, popcorn 103-105,107,110-113,
.... 116,117,119-123
flax 240,241
forage 455,458
garbanzos 311
garlic 312
mint 244
mung beans 246
oats 223
onions 321
peanuts 248,250-252
peas 325
potatoes 330
rye 231
safflower 259
sorghum 261,264,266,268
southern peas 335
soybeans 143,145,150,152,153-157,159-161,163
spring wheat 201
sweet corn 341,343
tobacco 282
winter wheat 187,188

Eastern cottonwood *Populus deltoides:*
noncropland 477

Eastern persimmon *Diospyros virginiana* (common persimmon):
noncropland 470,472
pastures/rangeland 462,463,466

Eastern red cedar *Juniperus virginiana:*
brush control 441,442
noncropland 486
pastures/rangeland 466

Eastern redbud *Cercis canadensis:*
noncropland 439

Eastern white pine *Pinus strobus:*
noncropland 477

Echinochloa colona — junglerice

Echinochloa crus-galli — barnyardgrass (watergrass)

Echinochloa crus-pavonis — gulf cockspur

Echinocystis lobata — wild cucumber

Echium vulgare — blueweed

Eclipta *Eclipa prostrata:*
beans 299
cotton 174,178
field corn, popcorn 107,110,116,117,121,122,125
garbanzos 311
mung beans 246
noncropland 484
ornamentals/woody plants 425
peanuts 250,252
peas 325
potatoes 330
rice 254,257,258
safflower 259
sorghum 264,266
southern peas 335
soybeans 145,150,153,160,163
sweet corn 341,343
tree fruits, citrus 369

Egeria:
moving water 499
still water 494

Egeria densa — Brazilian elodea

Eichornia crassipes — waterhyacinth

Eisen waterhyssop *Bacopa eisenii:*
rice 254,255

Elaeagnus angustifolia — Russian olive

Elaeagnus umbellata — autumn olive

Elatine triandra — waterwort

Elder *Sambucus* spp.:
brush control 438,439
noncropland 471

Elderberry *Sambucus* spp. (elder):
brush control 436-439,441,442
noncropland 469-471,485,486
ornamentals/woody plants 427
pastures/rangeland 461,462,466

Eleocharis obtusa — blunt spikerush

Eleocharis spp. — spikerush

Eleusine indica — goosegrass (silver crabgrass)

Ellisia nyctelea — waterpod

Elm *Ulmus* spp.:
brush control 436-442
noncropland 469-472,475,477,480,484-486
pastures/rangeland 461,464,466

Elodea:
moving water 498,499
still water 493,495,496

Elodea canadensis — common elodea

Elytrigia repens — quackgrass

Emilia sonchifolia — red tasselflower (flora's paintbrush)

English catchfly *Silene gallica:*
forage 459

English daisy *Bellis perennis:*
brush control 441
est. lawns/turf 402,403
noncropland 486
pastures/rangeland 466

Entireleaf morningglory *Ipomoea hederacea:*
cotton 173,174
field corn, popcorn 105,107,113,116,119-122
forage 458
peanuts 249,251
sorghum 261
soybeans 144,145,148,150-152,
.... 155-157,159-161,163

Epilobium angustifolium — fireweed

Epilobium paniculatum — panicle willowweed

Epilobium spp. — willowweed (willowherb)

Equisetum arvense — field horsetail (common horsetail)

Equisetum fluviatile — water horsetail

Equisetum hyemale — scouringrush

Equisetum spp. — horsetail

Eragrostis barrelieri — Mediterranean lovegrass

Eragrostis cilianensis — stinkgrass

Eragrostis mexicana — Mexican lovegrass

Eragrostis orcuttiana — Orcutt lovegrass

Eragrostis pilosa — India lovegrass

Eragrostis spp. — lovegrass

Erechtites hieraciifolia — American burnweed

Eremocarpus setigerus — turkey mullein

Eremochloa ophiuroides — centipedegrass

Erigeron annuus — annual fleabane

Erigeron spp. — fleabane

Erigeron strigosus — rough fleabane

Eriochloa contracta — prairie cupgrass

Eriochloa gracilis — southwestern cupgrass

Eriochloa spp. — cupgrass

Eriochloa villosa — woolly cupgrass

Eriophorum spp. — cottongrass

Erodium botyrs — broadleaf filaree

Erodium cicutarium — redstem filaree

Erodium moschatum — whitestem filaree

Erodium spp. — filaree

Erysimum repandum — bushy wallflower

Erysimum spp. — wallflower (treacle mustard)

Eucalyptus:
brush control 439,440

Eupatorium capillifolium — dogfennel

Eupatorium compositifolium — yankeeweed

Eupatorium perfoliatum — boneset

Euphorbia dentata — toothed spurge

Euphorbia esula — leafy spurge

Euphorbia glomerifera — graceful spurge

Euphorbia heterophylla — wild poinsettia

Euphorbia hirta — garden spurge

Euphorbia humistrata — prostrate spurge

Euphorbia maculata — spotted spurge (annual spurge)

Euphorbia nutans — nodding spurge

Euphorbia peplus — petty spurge

Euphorbia spp. — spurge

Euphorbia thymifolia — thymeleaf spurge

Euphorbia vermiculata — hairy spurge

Eurasian watermilfoil *Myriophyllum spicatum:*
still water 496

Eveningprimrose *Oenothera* spp.:
est. lawns/turf 408
noncropland 472,482
nuts 386,391
ornamentals/woody plants 419,420,425,427
small fruits 362
tree fruits, citrus 368
tree fruits, deciduous 372,377
tree fruits, subtropical 383

F

Fagopyrum tataricum — tartary buckwheat

Fagus grandifolia — American beech

Fagus spp. — beech

Fall panicum *Panicum dichotomiflorum* (fall panicgrass):
artichokes 292,293
asparagus 294-297
barley 218
beans 298-301
carrots 301-303
castor beans 240
celery 303-305
cole crops 305-307
conservation reserve program 442,445-447
cotton 173,174,176-178,180-182
cucurbits 307-309
eggplant 309-311
est. lawns/turf 400,407,408
fallow land 448,451-454
field corn, popcorn 101-107,110-125
flax 240-242
forage 455,457-459
garbanzos 311,312
garlic 313,314
greens 314,315
guar beans 242,243
hops 243
horseradish 316
kenaf 244
lentils 317
lettuce, endive 318,319
mint 245,246
mung beans 246,247
noncropland 468,474,476-479,481-484,487
nuts 385-392
oats 227
oil seed crops 247,248
okra 320
onions 321-323
ornamentals/woody plants ... 418,419,421,422,424-427
peanuts 248-252
peas 324-326
peppers 327,328
potatoes 329-332
radishes 333
rhubarb 333,334
rice 253
safflower 258,259
small fruits 356-358,360-363
sorghum 261,262,264-266,268,269
southern peas 335,336
soybeans 143-147,149-159,161-164
spinach 336,337
spring wheat 206
sugar beets 269-272
sugarcane 275-278
sunflower 279-281
sweet corn 337,339-345
sweet potatoes 345,346
table beets 346,347
tobacco 281,282
tomatoes 348-350
tree fruits, citrus 363-370
tree fruits, deciduous 371,373-379
tree fruits, subtropical 379-381,383,384
turf grasses for sod 417
winter wheat 194

False chamomile *Matricaria maritima:*
barley 211,213,214,217,218,222
conservation reserve program 443
fallow land 447-449,451,454
oats 224,227,230
pastures/rangeland 460,461
potatoes 331
spring wheat 199,201,202,205-207,210
tomatoes 349
winter wheat 186,188,189,192-194,198

Falsedandelion *Pyrrhopappus* spp.:
asparagus 296
est. lawns/turf 401
noncropland 472,479
nuts 386,389
ornamentals/woody plants 420,424
small fruits 357,360
tree fruits, citrus 367
tree fruits, deciduous 372,375
tree fruits, subtropical 382

Falseflax *Camelina* spp.:
barley 218
oats 227
spring wheat 206
winter wheat 193

Falsepimpernel *Lindernia anagallidea:*
rice 253-255

Fanweed *Thlaspi arvense* (field pennycress):
barley 211-214,218,219,221
conservation reserve program 442,443,446
fallow land 447-449
field corn, popcorn 114,123
forage 457

oats 224,227,228
pastures/rangeland 460,461,465
rye 234
soybeans 152
spring wheat 199-202,206,207,209
sugar beets 271
sweet corn 342,343
table beets 347
winter wheat 186-189,194,195,197

Fanwort *Cabomba* spp. (cabomba):
moving water 499
still water 496

Feather fingergrass *Chloris virgata:*
asparagus 296
noncropland 479
nuts 389
tree fruits, citrus 367
tree fruits, deciduous 375
tree fruits, subtropical 382

Feathertop:
noncropland 476,482

Fescue:
artichokes 292
asparagus 295,297
beans 299
carrots 301
celery 303
cole crops 305
cotton 177
cucurbits 308
eggplant 310
est. lawns/turf 409
field corn, popcorn 113,114,124
forage 457
garbanzos 311
garlic 313
grasses for seed production 414
greens 314
guar beans 242
horseradish 316
lentils 317
lettuce, endive 318
noncropland 472,474-477,480,482,484
nuts 386,388,392
okra 320
onions 321
ornamentals/woody plants 420,422,424
peanuts 250
peas 325
peppers 328
potatoes 330
radishes 333
rhubarb 334
small fruits 357,359,362
sorghum 265
soybeans 162
spinach 336
sugar beets 270
sweet corn 342
sweet potatoes 346
table beets 347
tomatoes 348
tree fruits, deciduous 372,373,378
turf grasses for sod 417

Festuca arundinacea — tall fescue (alta fescue)
Festuca ovina — sheep fescue
Festuca rubra — red fescue
Festuca spp. — annual fescue, fescue

Fiddleneck *Amsinckia* spp.:
artichokes 292,293
asparagus 296,297
barley 216
beans 298
castor beans 240
cotton 174-176,178,181
est. lawns/turf 407
field corn, popcorn 107,111,112,117,123,124
forage 457-459
noncropland 472,475,476,479-481,483,484
nuts 386,387,389-391
ornamentals/woody plants 420.421,425,426
potatoes 329
safflower 258
small fruits 360-362
soybeans 153
spring wheat 199
sugar beets 270
sunflower 279
sweet corn 339-341,345
tomatoes 348
tree fruits, citrus 364,365,367-369
tree fruits, deciduous 372,374-378
tree fruits, subtropical 382-384
winter wheat 186,192,198

Field bindweed *Convolvulus arvensis:*
artichokes 292
asparagus 294,295,297
barley 218,220,221
beans 299,301
brush control 441
carrots 301,303
celery 303,305
cole crops 305,307
conservation reserve program 444,446,447
cotton 172,182
cucurbits 307-309
eggplant 310,311
est. lawns/turf 403,408
fallow land 449-454
field corn, popcorn 106,110,113-119,124,125
flax 240,242
forage 457
garbanzos 311
garlic 313
grasses for seed production 413
greens 314,315
guar beans 242,243
hops 243
horseradish 316
kenaf 244
lentils 317
lettuce, endive 318,319
mung beans 247
noncropland 468-470,472,473,477,
.... 478,481,482,484-486
nuts 388,391,392
oats 227,229
oil seed crops 248
okra 320
onions 321,323
ornamentals/woody plants 418,427
pastures/rangelands 461-463,465,466
peanuts 248,250,252
peas 325
peppers 327,328
potatoes 329,330,332
radishes 333
rhubarb 334
rice 255
rye 233,235
safflower 259
small fruits 356,362,363
sorghum 263,265,267,269
southern peas 336
soybeans 143,149,150,152,156,162
spinach 336
spring wheat 206,209
sugar beets 270,272
sugarcane 274,275,277,278
sunflower 281
sweet corn 342,343
sweet potatoes 346
table beets 347
tomatoes 347
tree fruits, citrus 348,350
tree fruits, deciduous 369,370
tree fruits, subtropical 378
winter wheat 193,196,197

Field chickweed *Cerastium arvense:*
barley 213,218
fallow land 448
oats 227
spring wheat 201,207
winter wheat 188,194

Field gromwell *Lithospermum arvense* (corn gromwell):
noncropland 474
nuts 388
ornamentals/woody plants 422
small fruits 359
tree fruits, deciduous 373

Field pennycress *Thlaspi arvense:*
barley 211-214,216-218,220-222
conservation reserve program 442-444,446,447
fallow land 447-449,451,453,454
field corn, popcorn 103,112,114,118,124
flax 240,241
forage 455,456,458,459
garlic 312
grasses for seed production 414
mint 244
noncropland 469,470,478,480,483,484
oats 223,224,226-230
onions 321
pastures/rangeland 460-462,464,465
peanuts 249
rye 231,234,235
sorghum 267
soybeans 147,148,152,162
spring wheat 199-202,204-210
sweet corn 342,343
winter wheat 186-189,191-198

Field peppergrass *Lepidium campestre* (field pepperweed):
barley 219,220
grasses for seed production 414
oats 228,229
pastures/rangeland 464
rye 234,235
spring wheat 207,208
winter wheat 195,196

Field pepperweed *Lepidium campestre:*
noncropland 469
pastures/rangeland 461
peas 325

Field sandbur *Cenchrus incertus:*
asparagus 295-297
barley 218
beans 298-300
carrots 301,303
castor beans 240
celery 305
conservation reserve program 445,447
cotton 173,174,176,177,180,181
cucurbits 307,309
est. lawns/turf 401,406,411
fallow land 451,453,454
field corn, popcorn 101,103,104,106,111-114,
.... 116,118,120,122,124
flax 241
forage 457,459
garbanzos 312
garlic 313
lettuce, endive 318,319
noncropland 474,481,482,484,487
nuts 387,390-392
oats 227
oil seed crops 247
onions 321,322
ornamentals/woody plants 421,422,424,425,427
peanuts 251,252
peas 324,326
peppers 327
potatoes 329,331
rhubarb 334
safflower 258
small fruits 358,362,363
sorghum 267
southern peas 335
soybeans 144,146,149-152,
.... 154-156,158,159,161-164
spinach 337
spring wheat 206
sugar beets 270,271
sugarcane 277
sunflower 279,280
sweet corn 342-344
sweet potatoes 345,346
tobacco 281,282
tree fruits, citrus 365,367,369,370
tree fruits, deciduous 373,375,377-379
tree fruits, subtropical 381,384
winter wheat 194

Filamentous algae *algae:*
moving water 497
still water 493,494

Filaree *Erodium* spp.:
barley 211,213,218
cotton 181
fallow land 447,448
field corn, popcorn 114,123,124
forage 458,459
noncropland 474-479,481-484
nuts 388,391
oats 227
ornamentals/woody plants 422,425-427
pastures/rangeland 460
small fruits 356,358,361,362
soybeans 152,162
spring wheat 199,201,207
sweet corn 342,345
tree fruits, citrus 366,368,369
tree fruits, deciduous 373,376,378
tree fruits, subtropical 383,384
winter wheat 186,188,194

Filicinae — ferns

Fine fescue
nuts 388
tree fruits, citrus 366,370
tree fruits, deciduous 374,378
tree fruits, subtropical 381,384

Fingergrass *Chloris* spp.:
noncropland 475,476
sugarcane 276

Fir*: Albies*spp.
brush control 438,439
noncropland 471,472

Fireweed *Epilobium angustifolium:*
asparagus 297
beans 301
carrots 303
celery 305
cole crops 307
conservation reserve program 447
cotton 182
cucurbits 309
eggplant 311
field corn, popcorn 123,125
flax 240,242
greens 315
guar beans 243
hops 243
kenaf 244
lettuce, endive 319
mung beans 247
nuts 385,392
oil seed crops 248
okra 320
onions 323
ornamentals/woody plants 423-427
peanuts 252
peppers 327
potatoes 329,332
radishes 333
safflower 259
small fruits 361,363
sorghum 269
southern peas 336
soybeans 162
sugar beets 272
sugarcane 273,275,277,278
sunflower 281
sweet corn 345
tomatoes 350
tree fruits, citrus 368,370
tree fruits, deciduous 376,378
tree fruits, subtropical 379-381,383

Flagellates:
moving water 497

Flax *Linum* spp.:
spring wheat 204
winter wheat 191

Fleabane *Erigeron* spp.:
barley 221
conservation reserve program 446

- field corn, popcorn 112,124
- forage 458,460
- noncropland 474-478,480,482,484
- nuts 388,391
- ornamentals/woody plants 422,424,425
- pastures/rangeland 465
- small fruits 359,362
- soybeans 162
- spring wheat 209
- tree fruits, citrus 366,369
- tree fruits, deciduous 373,378
- tree fruits, subtropical 384
- winter wheat 197

Flixweed *Descurainia sophia:*
- asparagus 296,297
- barley 211-214,217,218,220-222
- conservation reserve program 442,443,446
- fallow land 447-449,451,454
- field corn, popcorn 105
- forage 458,459
- mint 245
- noncropland 473,479,480,483
- nuts 389
- oats 224,227,229,230
- ornamentals/woody plants 423
- pastures/rangeland 460,461,465
- rye 235
- small fruits 360
- sorghum 267
- spring wheat 199-202,205-207,209,210
- sweet corn 339
- tree fruits, citrus 367
- tree fruits, deciduous 375
- tree fruits, subtropical 382
- winter wheat 186-189,192-194,196-198

Flora's paintbrush *Emilia sonchifolia* (red tasselflower):
- field corn, popcorn 123
- nuts 385,391
- ornamentals/woody plants 426
- small fruits 361
- sugarcane 273,275-278
- sweet corn 345
- tree fruits, citrus 368
- tree fruits, deciduous 376,377
- tree fruits, subtropical 380-383

Florida beggarweed *Desmodium tortuosum:*
- beans 298,299
- conservation reserve program 446
- cotton 173,174,178,181
- cucurbits 307
- field corn, popcorn 101-104,106,111-113, 115-117,120,122,124,125
- flax 241
- garbanzos 311
- mung beans 246
- noncropland 479,481,484
- ornamentals/woody plants 418
- peanuts 248-250,252
- peas 325
- potatoes 330
- safflower 259
- sorghum 260,262,265-267
- soybeans 143-146,148,150,152, 153,155,157-161,163
- sweet corn 337,339,343
- tobacco 281,282
- tree fruits, citrus 369

Florida betony *Stachys floridana:*
- noncropland 472

Florida holly:
- brush control 439,441,442
- noncropland 486
- pastures/rangeland 466

Florida purslane *Richardia scabra:*
- asparagus 297
- beans 301
- carrots 303
- celery 305
- cole crops 307
- conservation reserve program 447
- cotton 182
- cucurbits 309
- eggplant 311
- field corn, popcorn 107,117,125
- flax 240,242
- forage 455
- greens 315
- guar beans 243
- hops 243
- kenaf 244
- lettuce, endive 318,319
- mung beans 247
- noncropland 472
- nuts 386,391,392
- oli seed crops 248
- okra 320
- onions 323
- ornamentals/woody plants 420,427
- peanuts 252
- peppers 327
- potatoes 329,332
- radishes 333
- safflower 259
- small fruits 362,363
- sorghum 269
- southern peas 336
- soybeans 146,153,162
- sugar beets 272
- sugarcane 278
- sunflower 281
- sweet corn 339,340,343
- tomatoes 350
- tree fruits, citrus 369,370
- tree fruits, deciduous 372,377,378
- tree fruits, subtropical 384

Florida pusley *Richardia scabra* (Florida purslane):
- artichokes 293
- asparagus 297
- barley 220
- beans 298-301
- carrots 301-303
- castor beans 240
- celery 304,305
- cole crops 305,307
- conservation reserve program 445,447
- cotton 173,174,176,178-182
- cucurbits 307-309
- eggplant 309,311
- est. lawns/turf 400,411
- fallow land 454,455
- field corn, popcorn 101-103,105-107,110,112-125
- flax 240-242
- forage 457,458
- garbanzos 311,312
- garlic 313
- greens 315
- guar beans 243
- herbs & spices 316
- hops 243
- kenaf 244
- lettuce, endive 319
- mung beans 246,247
- noncropland 471,474,478,479,481,484,487
- nuts 387,390-392
- oats 229
- oil seed crops 248
- okra 320
- onions 322,323
- ornamentals/woody plants 418,420,421,424-427
- peanuts 248-252
- peas 325,326
- peppers 327
- potatoes 329-332
- radishes 333
- rye 235
- safflower 258,259
- small fruits 357,360-363
- sorghum 260-262,264-269
- southern peas 335,336
- soybeans 143-146,148,150-155,157-163
- spring wheat 209
- sugar beets 270,272
- sugarcane 275-278
- sunflower 279-281
- sweet corn 337-345
- sweet potatoes 345
- tobacco 281-283
- tomatoes 348,350
- tree fruits, citrus 366-370
- tree fruits, deciduous 375-379
- tree fruits, subtropical 383,384
- winter wheat 196

Flourensia cernua — tarbush

Forget-me-not:
- barley 212,221
- conservation reserve program 446
- fallow land 448
- spring wheat 200,209
- winter wheat 187,197

Foxtail *Setaria* spp.:
- artichokes 292,293
- asparagus 294-297
- barley 211,213,216-219,221,222
- beans 298-301
- carrots 301-303
- castor beans 240
- celery 303-305
- cole crops 305-307
- conservation reserve program 442,445-447
- cotton 173-182
- cucurbits 307-309
- eggplant 309-311
- est. lawns/turf 400,404,407-411
- fallow land 448,451-455
- field corn, popcorn 101-107,110-125
- flax 240-242
- forage 455-460
- garbanzos 311,312
- garlic 313,314
- grasses for seed production 413,414
- greens 315
- guar beans 243
- herbs & spices 316
- hops 243
- kenaf 244
- lawn/turf seedbeds 399
- lentils 317
- lettuce, endive 318,319
- mint 245,246
- mung beans 246,247
- newly sprigged/seeded turf 399
- noncropland 468,472,474-484,487
- nuts 385-388,390-392
- oats 226,227
- oil seed crops 247,248
- okra 320
- onions 321-323
- ornamentals/woody plants 418-427
- peanuts 248-252
- peas 324-326
- peppers 327,328
- potatoes 329-332
- rhubarb 333,334
- rice 253-255,257,258
- rye 233
- safflower 258,259
- small fruits 356-358,360-363
- sorghum 260-262,264-269
- southern peas 335,336
- soybeans 143-147,149-159,161-164
- spinach 336,337
- spring wheat 199,201,202,204-207,209-211
- sugar beets 269-272
- sugarcane 272,273,275-278
- sunflower 279-281
- sweet corn 337-345
- sweet potatoes 345,346
- table beets 346
- tobacco 281-283
- tomatoes 347-350
- tree fruits, citrus 363-370
- tree fruits, deciduous 371-379
- tree fruits, subtropical 379-384
- turf grass for sod 416,417
- winter wheat 186,188,189,191-194,197,198

Foxtail barley *Hordeum jubatum:*
- artichokes 292
- asparagus 294
- est. lawns/turf 406
- forage 457-459
- grasses for seed production 414
- lettuce, endive 318
- mint 245
- noncropland 480
- nuts 386
- ornamentals/woody plants 424
- rhubarb 333
- small fruits 357
- tree fruits, citrus 364
- tree fruits, deciduous 371
- tree fruits, subtropical 380

Foxtail fescue *Vulpia myuros:*
- noncropland 480

Foxtail millet *Setaria italica:*
- asparagus 297
- barley 217
- beans 299-301
- carrots 303
- celery 305
- cole crops 307
- conservation reserve program 447
- cotton 178,182
- cucurbits 308,309
- eggplant 311
- field corn, popcorn 101,105,113,117,124,125
- flax 240,242
- garbanzos 311
- greens 315
- guar beans 243
- hops 243
- kenaf 244
- lettuce, endive 319
- mung beans 246,247
- nuts 392
- oil seed crops 248
- okra 320
- onions 323
- ornamentals/woody plants 425
- peanuts 250,252
- peas 325,326
- peppers 327
- potatoes 329,330,332
- radishes 333
- safflower 259
- small fruits 363
- sorghum 261,266,269
- southern peas 335,336
- soybeans 146,153,159,162
- spring wheat 204,205,210
- sugar beets 272
- sugarcane 278
- sunflower 280,281
- sweet corn 339,344
- tomatoes 350
- tree fruits, citrus 370
- tree fruits, deciduous 378
- winter wheat 191,192,198

Fragaria virginiana — Virginia strawberry (wild strawberry)

Fraxinus americana — white ash

Fraxinus pennsylvanica — green ash

Fraxinus spp. — ash

French broom *Cytisus monspessulanus:*
- brush control 439

Fringed sagebrush *Artemisia frigida:*
- conservation reserve program 446
- noncropland 472
- pastures/rangeland 463,464,466

Frog's bit:
- moving water 498
- still water 495

Fumaria officinalis — fumitory

Fumitory *Fumaria officinalis:*
- barley 213
- conservation reserve program 443
- grasses for seed production 411
- oats 223
- rye 231
- spring wheat 201
- tomatoes 349
- turf grasses for sod 416
- winter wheat 188

G

Galinsoga:
barley ... 214
beans ... 298,299
carrots ... 302
cole crops ... 305,306
cotton ... 178
cucurbits ... 307
eggplant ... 309
field corn, popcorn ... 101-103,105-108,112, 113,115-117,119-121,124
flax ... 241
forage ... 458
garbanzos ... 311
grasses for seed production ... 412
mung beans ... 246
noncropland ... 478
oats ... 224
ornamentals/woody plants ... 418,419,424
pastures/rangeland ... 461
peanuts ... 248,250,251
peas ... 324,325
peppers ... 327
potatoes ... 330-332
rye ... 232
safflower ... 259
sorghum ... 260-262,266
southern peas ... 335
soybeans ... 143-146,150,151,153,155,158,159,163
spring wheat ... 202
sugarcane ... 273
sweet corn ... 337-340,343
sweet potatoes ... 345
tobacco ... 281
winter wheat ... 189
Galinsoga ciliata — hairy galinsoga
Galinsoga parviflora — smallflower galinsoga
Galinsoga spp. — galinsoga
Galium spp. — bedstraw
Garbancillo:
pastures/rangeland ... 463
Garden spurge *Euphorbia hirta:*
ornamentals/woody plants ... 425,426
sugarcane ... 277
tree fruits, subtropical ... 382
Geranium carolinianum — Carolina geranium
Geranium molle — dovefoot geranium
Geranium spp. — geranium (wild geranium)
German moss *Scleranthus annuus* (knawel):
field corn, popcorn ... 123
ornamentals/woody plants ... 426
small fruits ... 361
sweet corn ... 345
tree fruits, citrus ... 368
tree fruits, subtropical ... 383
Geyer larkspur Delphimium geyeri:
pastures/rangeland ... 464
Giant cutgrass *Zizaniopsis miliacea:*
moving water ... 499
still water ... 496
Giant foxtail *Setaria faberi:*
artichokes ... 292,293
asparagus ... 294-297
beans ... 298-301
carrots ... 301,303
castor beans ... 240
celery ... 303,305
cole crops ... 305-307
conservation reserve program ... 442,445-447
cotton ... 173,174,176-178,180-182
cucurbits ... 307,309
eggplant ... 309-311
fallow land ... 448,451,453
field corn, popcorn ... 101-107,110-113, 116-122,124,125
flax ... 240-242
forage ... 455,457-459
garbanzos ... 311,312
garlic ... 313,314
greens ... 315
guar beans ... 243
hops ... 243
kenaf ... 244
lentils ... 317
lettuce, endive ... 318,319
mint ... 245,246
mung beans ... 246,247
noncropland ... 468,474,481-483
nuts ... 385-392
oil seed crops ... 247,248
okra ... 320
onions ... 321-323
ornamentals/woody plants ... 418,419,421-425
peanuts ... 248-252
peas ... 324-326
peppers ... 327,328
potatoes ... 329-332
radishes ... 333
rhubarb ... 333,334
safflower ... 258,259
small fruits ... 356-358,360-363
sorghum ... 260-262,264-269
southern peas ... 335,336
soybeans ... 143-147,149-159,161-164
spinach ... 337
spring wheat ... 209
sugar beets ... 269-272
sugarcane ... 277,278
sunflower ... 279-281
sweet corn ... 337-344
sweet potatoes ... 345,346
table beets ... 346
tobacco ... 281-283
tomatoes ... 348-350
tree fruits, citrus ... 363-370
tree fruits, deciduous ... 371,373,375-378
tree fruits, subtropical ... 379-381,383,384
turf grasses for sod ... 416
winter wheat ... 194,197
Giant green foxtail *Setaria viridis:*
field corn, popcorn ... 119,120
forage ... 458
peanuts ... 251
soybeans ... 155
Giant ragweed *Ambrosia trifida:*
barley ... 212-214,216,220,221
beans ... 298
conservation reserve program ... 442-444,446
cotton ... 173,174
est. lawns/turf ... 400,408
fallow land ... 449,451,453,454
field corn, popcorn ... 101,103-107,110-124
forage ... 455,458
garlic ... 312
grasses for seed production ... 411,414
mint ... 244
noncropland ... 468,476-478,482,484
nuts ... 391
oats ... 223,224,226,228,229
onions ... 321
ornamentals/woody plants ... 419,427
pastures/rangeland ... 461,464,465
peanuts ... 248,252
peas ... 324,325
rye ... 231,234,235
small fruits ... 362
sorghum ... 260,261,263-265,267,268
soybeans ... 143-153,155-157,159-163
spring wheat ... 200-202,204,208,209
sweet corn ... 338,341,343
tobacco ... 282
tree fruits, citrus ... 369
tree fruits, deciduous ... 377,378
tree fruits, subtropical ... 384
turf grasses for sod ... 416
winter wheat ... 187-189,191,195-197
Giant reed *Arundo donax:*
brush control ... 439,440
Gisekia:
noncropland ... 472
nuts ... 386
ornamentals/woody plants ... 420
tree fruits, deciduous ... 372
Globe sedge *Cyperus globolosus:*
est. lawns/turf ... 406
ornamentals/woody plants ... 424
Glechoma hederacea — ground ivy
Gleditsia triacanthos — honeylocust
Glyceria canadensis — rattlesnakegrass
Glyceria spp. — mannagrass
Gnaphalium obtusifolium — fragrant cudweed (rabbit tobacco)
Gnaphalium purpureum — narrowleaf cudweed, purple cudweed
Gnaphalium spp. — cudweed
Goatgrass:
fallow land ... 451,452
Goathead *Tribulus terrestris* (puncturevine):
cotton ... 176
southern peas ... 336
Goatsbeard *Tragopogon pratensis* (meadow salsify):
barley ... 214,219,220
conservation reserve program ... 443
fallow land ... 449
grasses for seed production ... 414
noncropland ... 469,475,476
oats ... 224,228,229
pastures/rangeland ... 461,464
rye ... 234,235
spring wheat ... 202,207,208
winter wheat ... 189,195,196
Goldaster *Chrysopsis* spp.:
conservation reserve program ... 446
pastures/rangeland ... 466
Golden crownbeard:
noncropland ... 481
peanuts ... 249
Golden ragwort *Senecio aureus:*
ornamentals/woody plants ... 419
Goldenrod *Solidago* spp.:
barley ... 214,221
conservation reserve program ... 442,446
est. lawns/turf ... 401
field corn, popcorn ... 108
grasses for seed production ... 412
noncropland ... 469,473-476,479-486
nuts ... 388
oats ... 224
ornamentals/woody plants ... 422,424
pastures/rangeland ... 460,461,464,465
rye ... 232
small fruits ... 359
sorghum ... 262
spring wheat ... 202,209
sugarcane ... 273,274
sweet corn ... 340
tree fruits, deciduous ... 373
winter wheat ... 189,197
Goldenweed
conservation reserve program ... 446
pastures/rangeland ... 466
Gooseberry *Ribes* spp.:
brush control ... 437,438
noncropland ... 470,471
Goosefoot *Chenopodium* spp.:
asparagus ... 297
barley ... 219
beans ... 301
carrots ... 303
celery ... 305
cole crops ... 307
conservation reserve program ... 447
cotton ... 182
cucurbits ... 309
eggplant ... 311
fallow land ... 455
field corn, popcorn ... 120,125
flax ... 240,242
greens ... 315
guar beans ... 243
hops ... 243
kenaf ... 244
lettuce, endive ... 319
mung beans ... 247
noncropland ... 472
nuts ... 386,392
oats ... 228
oil seed crops ... 248
okra ... 320
onions ... 323
ornamentals/woody plants ... 420
peanuts ... 252
peppers ... 327
potatoes ... 329,332
radishes ... 333
rye ... 234
safflower ... 259
small fruits ... 363
sorghum ... 269
southern peas ... 336
soybeans ... 144,146,155,162
spring wheat ... 207
sugar beets ... 272
sugarcane ... 278
sunflower ... 281
table beets ... 347
tomatoes ... 350
tree fruits, citrus ... 370
tree fruits, deciduous ... 372,378
winter wheat ... 195
Goosegrass *Eleusine indica:*
artichokes ... 292,293
asparagus ... 294-297
beans ... 298-300
carrots ... 301-303
castor beans ... 240
celery ... 303-305
cole crops ... 305,306
conservation reserve program ... 445-447
cotton ... 173,174,176-181
cucurbits ... 307-309
eggplant ... 309,310
est. lawns/turf ... 399-401,404,405,407-411
fallow land ... 448,451,453,454
field corn, popcorn ... 101-103,105-107,112-124
flax ... 241
forage ... 457-459
garbanzos ... 311,312
garlic ... 313,314
grasses for seed production ... 414
greens ... 315
herbs & spices ... 316
lentils ... 317
lettuce, endive ... 318,319
mint ... 245,246
mung beans ... 246
noncropland ... 468,474,476-479,481,482,484,487
nuts ... 385-390,392
oil seed crops ... 247
onions ... 321-323
ornamentals/woody plants ... 418,419,421-427
peanuts ... 248-251
peas ... 324-326
peppers ... 327,328
potatoes ... 329-332
radishes ... 333
rhubarb ... 334
rice ... 253,254,257,258
safflower ... 258,259
small fruits ... 356-358,361-363
sorghum ... 260-262,264-268
southern peas ... 335
soybeans ... 143-147,149-159,161-164
spinach ... 337
sugar beets ... 269-272
sugarcane ... 272,275-277
sunflower ... 279,280
sweet corn ... 337,339-345
sweet potatoes ... 345,346
table beets ... 346
tobacco ... 281-283
tomatoes ... 348-350
tree fruits, citrus ... 363-370
tree fruits, deciduous ... 371,373-379
tree fruits, subtropical ... 379-384
turf grasses for sod ... 415,417
Gooseweed *Sphenoclea zeylanica:*
rice ... 253-255,258
Gorse *Ulex europaeus:*
conservation reserve program ... 446
noncropland ... 484
pastures/rangeland ... 466

Graceful spurge *Euphorbia glomerifera:*
sugarcane ... 277
Gramineae — longspine sandbur
Grand fir *Abies grandis:*
brush control ... 440
Granjeno *Celtis pallida:*
conservation reserve program ... 446
pastures/rangeland ... 466
Grassbur *Cenchrus* spp. (sandbur):
field corn, popcorn ... 106
flax ... 241
sorghum ... 262
sweet corn ... 339
Gray goldenrod *Solidago nemoralis:*
field corn, popcorn ... 116
Gray rabbitbrush *Chrysothamnus nauseosus:*
noncropland ... 482
Green amaranth *Amaranthus retroflexus* (redroot pigweed):
nuts ... 389
tree fruits, citrus ... 367
tree fruits, deciduous ... 375
tree fruits, subtropical ... 382
Green ash *Fraxinus pennsylvanica:*
brush control ... 440
noncropland ... 475,480
pastures/rangeland ... 464
Green foxtail *Setaria viridis:*
artichokes ... 292,293
asparagus ... 294-297
barley ... 217,221
beans ... 298-301
carrots ... 301,303
castor beans ... 240
celery ... 305
cole crops ... 305-307
conservation reserve program ... 445,447
cotton ... 173,174,176-182
cucurbits ... 307,309
eggplant ... 309-311
est. lawns/turf ... 400,404,408
fallow land ... 448,451,453
field corn, popcorn ... 101-107,110-113,116-125
flax ... 240-242
forage ... 455,457-459
garbanzos ... 311,312
garlic ... 313,314
greens ... 315
guar beans ... 243
hops ... 243
kenaf ... 244
lentils ... 317
lettuce, endive ... 318,319
mint ... 245,246
mung beans ... 246,247
noncropland ... 468,474,478,479,481,482
nuts ... 385-388,390-392
oats ... 229
oil seed crops ... 247,248
okra ... 320
onions ... 321-323
ornamentals/woody plants ... 418,419,421,422,425,426
peanuts ... 248-252
peas ... 324-326
peppers ... 327,328
potatoes ... 329-332
radishes ... 333
rhubarb ... 334
safflower ... 258,259
small fruits ... 356-358,360-363
sorghum ... 260-262,264-269
southern peas ... 335,336
soybeans ... 143-147,149-159,161-164
spinach ... 337
spring wheat ... 199,204,205,209,210
sugar beets ... 269-272
sugarcane ... 277,278
sunflower ... 279-281
sweet corn ... 337-342,344
sweet potatoes ... 345,346
table beets ... 346
tobacco ... 281-283
tomatoes ... 348-350
tree fruits, citrus ... 363-365,367-370
tree fruits, deciduous ... 371,373,375-378
tree fruits, subtropical ... 379-381,383,384
turf grasses for sod ... 416,417
winter wheat ... 191-194,197,198
Green kyllinga *Kyllinga brevifolia:*
est. lawns/turf ... 405,406
ornamentals/woody plants ... 424
Green smartweed *Polygonum lapathifolium* (pale smartweed):
barley ... 211,213,216,218,222
conservation reserve program ... 443,444
fallow land ... 447,451,454
field corn, popcorn ... 106,110,118
flax ... 240,241
forage ... 455
garlic ... 312
mint ... 244
oats ... 223,226,227,230
onions ... 321
pastures/rangeland ... 460
rye ... 231
sorghum ... 263
spring wheat ... 199,201,204,207,210
winter wheat ... 186-188,191,194,198
Green tansymustard *Descurainia pinnata:*
est. lawns/turf ... 405
noncropland ... 474
nuts ... 388
ornamentals/woody plants ... 422
small fruits ... 358
tree fruits, citrus ... 365
tree fruits, deciduous ... 373
tree fruits, subtropical ... 381
Greenbriar *Smilax* spp.:
brush control ... 438
noncropland ... 468,471,477,482
Greenflower pepperweed *Lepidium densiflorum:*
spring wheat ... 199
winter wheat ... 186
Grindelia squarrosa — curlycup gumweed (gumweed)
Gromwell *Lithospermum* spp.:
artichokes ... 292
asparagus ... 295
barley ... 216,222
cotton ... 175
field corn, popcorn ... 111
forage ... 456
grasses for seed production ... 413
mint ... 245
noncropland ... 482
oats ... 226
sugarcane ... 274,275
tree fruits, citrus ... 364
tree fruits, deciduous ... 372
winter wheat ... 192,197
Ground ivy *Glechoma hederacea:*
barley ... 214
est. lawns/turf ... 401-403,406,407,410
field corn, popcorn ... 108
grasses for seed production ... 412
noncropland ... 469,470,485
oats ... 224
ornamentals/woody plants ... 427
pastures/rangeland ... 461
rye ... 232
sorghum ... 262
spring wheat ... 202
sugarcane ... 273
sweet corn ... 340
winter wheat ... 189
Groundcherry:
artichokes ... 293
asparagus ... 297
beans ... 300
carrots ... 302
celery ... 304
cotton ... 180,181
field corn, popcorn ... 101,102,104
herbs & spices ... 316
noncropland ... 481,482,484
nuts ... 391
ornamentals/woody plants ... 419
peanuts ... 252
peas ... 326
small fruits ... 362
sorghum ... 260
soybeans ... 152,159,162
sugar beets ... 269
sunflower ... 280
sweet corn ... 337,338
tomatoes ... 347
tree fruits, citrus ... 369
tree fruits, deciduous ... 378
tree fruits, subtropical ... 384
turf grasses for sod ... 416
Groundsel *Senecio* spp.:
asparagus ... 296
barley ... 216,217
conservation reserve program ... 446
cotton ... 174
field corn, popcorn ... 117,120,123
grasses for seed production ... 413
mint ... 245
noncropland ... 472,478-480,483
nuts ... 386,389,391
oats ... 226
ornamentals/woody plants ... 420,424-426
pastures/rangeland ... 463,466
small fruits ... 356,360-362
sorghum ... 268
soybeans ... 153
spring wheat ... 205
sugarcane ... 275
sweet corn ... 343,345
tree fruits, citrus ... 364,366-368
tree fruits, deciduous ... 372,375,376
tree fruits, subtropical ... 382,383
winter wheat ... 192,193
Guajillo *Acacia berlandieri:*
conservation reserve program ... 446
pastures/rangeland ... 466
Guineagrass *Panicum maximum:*
artichokes ... 292,293
asparagus ... 294,297
fallow land ... 451,453
field corn, popcorn ... 114,124
mint ... 245
noncropland ... 473-477,479,482,484
nuts ... 386-389,391,392
ornamentals/woody plants ... 422,427
rhubarb ... 333
small fruits ... 357,359,362
soybeans ... 144,162
sugarcane ... 275-278
sweet corn ... 342
tree fruits, citrus ... 364-369
tree fruits, deciduous ... 371,373,374,377,378
tree fruits, subtropical ... 380-382,384
Gulf cockspur *Echinochloa crus-pavonis:*
rice ... 253,254,257,258
Gum:
brush control ... 438,441,442
noncropland ... 471,480,484,486
pastures/rangeland ... 466
Gumweed *Grindelia squarrosa* (curlycup gumweed):
noncropland ... 473
Gutierrezia dracunculoides — common broomweed
Gutierrezia spp. — broomweed, perennial broomweed
Gylceria spp. — mannagrass

H

Hackberry *Celtis* spp.:
brush control ... 440
noncropland ... 475,476
pastures/rangeland ... 464
Haircap moss *Polytrichum* spp.:
small fruits ... 357
Hairy bittercress *Cardamine hirsuta:*
est. lawns/turf ... 406
ornamentals/woody plants ... 424
Hairy buttercup *Ranunculus sardous:*
barley ... 220
oats ... 229
rye ... 235
sorghum ... 267
spring wheat ... 209
winter wheat ... 196
Hairy chess *Bromus commutatus:*
noncropland ... 480
Hairy crabgrass *Digitaria sanguinalis* (large crabgrass):
artichokes ... 292
asparagus ... 294
est. lawns/turf ... 400,404,410
fallow land ... 453
field corn, popcorn ... 123
grasses for seed production ... 414
mint ... 245
newly sprigged/seeded turf ... 399
nuts ... 386
ornamentals/woody plants ... 421
rhubarb ... 333
small fruits ... 356,357
sorghum ... 268
soybeans ... 150
tree fruits, citrus ... 364
tree fruits, deciduous ... 371
tree fruits, subtropical ... 380
turf grasses for sod ... 417
Hairy fleabane *Conyza bonariensis:*
noncropland ... 479,482,484
nuts ... 391
ornamentals/woody plants ... 427
small fruits ... 362
tree fruits, citrus ... 368,369
tree fruits, deciduous ... 377,378
tree fruits, subtropical ... 383,384
Hairy galinsoga *Galinsoga ciliata:*
cotton ... 174
cucurbits ... 307
est. lawns/turf ... 405
field corn, popcorn ... 116
noncropland ... 469,474,482
nuts ... 388,391
ornamentals/woody plants ... 418,422,427
pastures/rangeland ... 461
peanuts ... 248
small fruits ... 358,362
soybeans ... 143,145
tobacco ... 282
tree fruits, citrus ... 365,368
tree fruits, deciduous ... 373,377
tree fruits, subtropical ... 381,383
Hairy goldenaster:
pastures/rangeland ... 464
Hairy honeysuckle *Lonicera hirsuta:*
noncropland ... 470
pastures/rangeland ... 462
Hairy indigo *Indigofera hirsuta:*
noncropland ... 481
peanuts ... 248,249
soybeans ... 143
Hairy nightshade *Solanum sarrachoides:*
artichokes ... 293
barley ... 213,214,217,218
beans ... 298,299
castor beans ... 240
conservation reserve program ... 443
cotton ... 174,176,178,181
fallow land ... 448,449
field corn, popcorn ... 101,102,104,106,107, 110-113,115-117,119-121,124
flax ... 240,241
forage ... 455,457,458
garbanzos ... 311
garlic ... 312
lettuce, endive ... 318
mint ... 244
mung beans ... 246
nuts ... 387
oats ... 223,224,227
onions ... 321
ornamentals/woody plants ... 421,423,424
pastures/rangeland ... 461
peanuts ... 248,250,251
peas ... 324,325
potatoes ... 329-331
rye ... 231
safflower ... 258,259

sorghum ... 260,262,264-266
southern peas ... 335
soybeans ... 143,145,148,150,153, 155,156,159-161,163
spinach ... 336
spring wheat ... 201,202,205,207
sugar beets ... 269-272
sunflower ... 279
sweet corn ... 337,339,341,343
tobacco ... 282,283
tomatoes ... 347-350
winter wheat ... 187-189,192,194
Hairy spurge *Euphorbia vermiculata:*
ornamentals/woody plants ... 426
Hairy vetch *Vicia villosa:*
barley ... 212,213,221
conservation reserve program ... 446
fallow land ... 448
noncropland ... 470
pastures/rangeland ... 462,465
soybeans ... 147
spring wheat ... 200,201,209
winter wheat ... 187,188,197
Hamamelis spp. — witchhazel
Haloe koa *Leucaena glauca:*
sugarcane ... 277
Hare barley *Hordeum leporinum:*
noncropland ... 482
nuts ... 391
ornamentals/woody plants ... 427
small fruits ... 362
tree fruits, citrus ... 368
tree fruits, deciduous ... 377
tree fruits, subtropical ... 383
Hasardia:
brush control ... 439
Hawksbeard:
forage ... 456
grasses for seed production ... 413
noncropland ... 482
Hawkweed *Hieracium* spp.:
est. lawns/turf ... 401
small fruits ... 357
Hawthorn *Crataegus* spp.:
brush control ... 436-442
noncropland ... 471,475,477,485,486
pastures/rangeland ... 464,466
Hazel *Corylus* spp.:
brush control ... 438,439
noncropland ... 469,485
pastures/rangeland ... 461
Healall *Prunella vulgaris:*
barley ... 214
est. lawns/turf ... 401,410
field corn, popcorn ... 108
grasses for seed production ... 412
noncropland ... 470
oats ... 224
pastures/rangeland ... 461
rye ... 232
sorghum ... 262
spring wheat ... 202
sugarcane ... 273
sweet corn ... 340
winter wheat ... 189
Heartleaf cocklebur *Xanthium strumarium* (common cocklebur):
peanuts ... 248
soybeans ... 143
Heath aster *Aster ericoides:*
noncropland ... 475,476,482
nuts ... 391
ornamentals/woody plants ... 427
small fruits ... 362
tree fruits, citrus ... 368
tree fruits, deciduous ... 377
tree fruits, subtropical ... 383
Hedge bindweed *Calystegia sepium:*
barley ... 220
conservation reserve program ... 444
cucurbits ... 307
fallow land ... 450,451,453
field corn, popcorn ... 106,110,113,116,117,119
noncropland ... 477,482
oats ... 229
ornamentals/woody plants ... 418
peanuts ... 248
rye ... 235
sorghum ... 263,267
soybeans ... 143,150,152,156
spring wheat ... 209
winter wheat ... 196,197
Hedge mustard *Sisymbrium officinale:*
field corn, popcorn ... 107
ornamentals/woody plants ... 423
sweet corn ... 339,340
Hedge smartweed *Polygonum scandens:*
forage ... 456
Hedyotis corymbosa — old world diamond flower
Helenium amarum — bitter sneezeweed
Helianthus annuus — common sunflower (annual sunflower, wild artichoke)
Helianthus ciliaris — Texas blueweed
Helianthus spp. — sunflower (wild sunflower)
Helianthus tuberosus — jerusalem artichoke
Heliotropium curassavicum — seaside heliotrope
Hemizonia congesta — hayfield tarweed (common tarweed)
Hemizonia pungens — spikeweed (common spikeweed)
Hemlock *Tsuga* spp.:
brush control ... 438,441,442

noncropland ... 471,480,484,486
pastures/rangeland ... 466
Hemp *Cannabis sativa* (marijuana):
est. lawns/turf ... 401
grasses for seed production ... 412
noncropland ... 469
Hemp dogbane *Apocynum cannabinum:*
artichokes ... 292
asparagus ... 295,297
beans ... 299
carrots ... 301
celery ... 303
cole crops ... 305
conservation reserve program ... 444,447
cotton ... 177
cucurbits ... 308
eggplant ... 310
fallow land ... 450,451,454
field corn, popcorn ... 104,106,110,111, 114,116-118,124
forage ... 457
garbanzos ... 311
garlic ... 313
greens ... 314
guar beans ... 242
horseradish ... 316
lentils ... 317
lettuce, endive ... 318
noncropland ... 469,484
nuts ... 391
okra ... 320
onions ... 321
pastures/rangeland ... 461
peanuts ... 250
peas ... 325
peppers ... 328
potatoes ... 330
radishes ... 333
rhubarb ... 334
small fruits ... 362
sorghum ... 263,265
soybeans ... 152,162
spinach ... 336
sugar beets ... 270
sweet corn ... 342
sweet potatoes ... 346
table beets ... 347
tomatoes ... 348
tree fruits, citrus ... 369
tree fruits, deciduous ... 378
tree fruits, subtropical ... 384
Hemp sesbania *Sesbania exaltata:*
barley ... 213,220
conservation reserve program ... 443
cotton ... 173,174,177,179,181
est. lawns/turf ... 400
field corn, popcorn ... 105,111,113,116,119
forage ... 455,457
garlic ... 312
grasses for seed production ... 411
mint ... 244
noncropland ... 468,469
nuts ... 388
oats ... 223,229
onions ... 321
pastures/rangeland ... 461
peanuts ... 248,252
rice ... 253-258
rye ... 231,235
small fruits ... 359
sorghum ... 261,267
soybeans ... 143-145,150-152,154,157,160,161,163
spring wheat ... 201,209
tree fruits, deciduous ... 374
tree fruits, subtropical ... 381
turf grasses for sod ... 416
winter wheat ... 187,188,196
Hempnettle:
barley ... 217-220
fallow land ... 451
grasses for seed production ... 414
noncropland ... 483
oats ... 227-229
pastures/rangeland ... 464
peas ... 325
rye ... 234,235
spring wheat ... 205-208
winter wheat ... 193,195,196
Henbane *Hyoscyamus* spp:
conservation reserve program ... 446
noncropland ... 484
pastures/rangeland ... 466
Henbit *Lamium amplexicaule:*
artichokes ... 293
asparagus ... 297
barley ... 211-213,216-218,220-222
beans ... 298,300,301
brush control ... 441
carrots ... 303
castor beans ... 240
celery ... 305
cole crops ... 307
conservation reserve program ... 442-444,446,447
cotton ... 176,181,182
cucurbits ... 309
eggplant ... 311
est. lawns/turf ... 309-401,403-406,408-411
fallow land ... 447,448,451-455
field corn, popcorn ... 105,112,115,120,122-125
flax ... 240,242
forage ... 457-459

grasses for seed production ... 411
greens ... 315
guar beans ... 243
hops ... 243
kenaf ... 244
lawn/turf seedbeds ... 399
lettuce, endive ... 318,319
mung beans ... 247
noncropland ... 468-470,472-474,479,481-484,486,487
nuts ... 386-388,390-392
oats ... 223,226,227,229,230
oil seed crops ... 247,248
okra ... 320
onions ... 323
ornamentals/woody plants ... 419-427
pastures/rangeland ... 460-462,465,466
peanuts ... 252
peas ... 325,326
peppers ... 327
potatoes ... 329,331,332
radishes ... 333
rye ... 231,235
safflower ... 258,259
small fruits ... 357-363
sorghum ... 261,267,269
southern peas ... 336
soybeans ... 144,152,155,159,161,162
spinach ... 336
spring wheat ... 199-201,204-207,209,210
sugar beets ... 270-272
sugarcane ... 274-278
sunflower ... 279-281
sweet corn ... 338,345
table beets ... 347
tobacco ... 281,283
tomatoes ... 347-350
tree fruits, citrus ... 365-370
tree fruits, deciduous ... 372-379
tree fruits, subtropical ... 381,383,384
turf grasses for sod ... 416,417
winter wheat ... 186-188,191-194,196-198
Heteranthera dubia — waterstargrass
Heteranthera limosa — ducksalad
Heteromeles arbutifolia — christmasberry
Heterotheca subaxillaris — camphorweed
Hialoa *Waltheria indica* (Indian waltheria):
sugarcane ... 277
tree fruits, subtropical ... 382
Hibiscus moscheutos — wild cotton
Hickory *Carya* spp.:
brush control ... 436-440
noncropland ... 471,472,475,477,480,484
pastures/rangeland ... 464
Hieracium spp. — hawkweed
Hila hila *Mimosa pudica* (sensitiveplant):
sugarcane ... 277
Hippuris vulgaris — marestail
Hoary cress *Cardaria draba:*
barley ... 214,219
est. lawns/turf ... 401
field corn, popcorn ... 108
grasses for seed production ... 412
noncropland ... 469,480,481
oats ... 224,228
pastures/rangeland ... 460,461,463
peas ... 325
rye ... 232,234
sorghum ... 262
spring wheat ... 202,207
sugarcane ... 273
sweet corn ... 340
winter wheat ... 189,195
Hoary vervain *Verbena stricta:*
noncropland ... 476,477,482,484
Holcus lanatus — common velvetgrass (velvetgrass)
Holodiscus discolor — oceanspray
Holosteum umbellatum — umbrella spurry (jagged chickweed)
Honeylocust *Gleditsia triacanthos:*
brush control ... 437,438
noncropland ... 470
pastures/rangeland ... 463
Honeysuckle *Lonicera* spp.:
brush control ... 437-439,441,442
noncropland ... 468-472,475-477,480,482,484,486
pastures/rangeland ... 461,463,466
Honeyvine milkweed *Ampelamus albidus:*
field corn, popcorn ... 106,110,113,116,124
soybeans ... 150,152,162
Hood canarygrass *Phalaris paradoxa:*
barley ... 217
spring wheat ... 205
winter wheat ... 19,194
Hoorahgrass:
rice ... 253,257,258
Hop clover *Trifolium aureum:*
est. lawns/turf ... 399,401,408,409
field corn, popcorn ... 106
noncropland ... 468,481
ornamentals/woody plants ... 425
sugarcane ... 275
Hophornbeam copperleaf *Acalypha ostryaefolia:*
conservation reserve program ... 447
cotton ... 174
field corn, popcorn ... 116,124
noncropland ... 484
nuts ... 391
peanuts ... 252
potatoes ... 331
small fruits ... 362
sorghum ... 267

soybeans 143-145,150,158,160-163
tobacco 282
tree fruits, citrus 369
tree fruits, deciduous 378
tree fruits, subtropical 384
Hordeum glaucum — wall barley (mouse barley)
Hordeum jubatum — foxtail barley
Hordeum leporinum — hare barley (wild barley)
Hordeum pusilium — little barley
Hornbeam *Carpinus* spp.:
brush control 438
noncropland 480,485
Horned beakrush *Rhynchospora corniculata:*
rice 253
Horned poppy:
barley 213
conservation reserve program 443
flax 241
oats 223
rye 231
spring wheat 201
winter wheat 188
Hornwort *Ceratophyllum demersum* (coontail):
still water 495
Horse mint *Mentha longifolia:*
fallow land 447
Horse purslane *Trianthema portulacastrum:*
artichokes 292
asparagus 294
mint 245
nuts 386
rhubarb 333
small fruits 357
sorghum 267
tree fruits, citrus 364
tree fruits, deciduous 371
tree fruits, subtropical 380
Horsenettle *Solanum carolinense:*
conservation reserve program 446,447
field corn, popcorn 104,114,117,119,124
noncropland 468,469,473,482,484
nuts 391
pastures/rangeland 461,466
soybeans 150,152
sweet corn 342
Horseradish *Armoracia rusticana:*
field corn, popcorn 114
sweet corn 342
Horsetail *Equisetum* spp.:
noncropland 472,474,476,480,483
nuts 386,388
ornamentals/woody plants 420,422
small fruits 357,359
tree fruits, deciduous 372,373
Horseweed *Conyza canadensis:*
asparagus 296,297
barley 212,214,218,221
carrots 302
conservation reserve program 442,443,446
est. lawns/turf 403,405
fallow land 449
field corn, popcorn 106,112,114,115,117,120,122
grasses for seed production 413
noncropland 469,474,476-480,482,484,487
nuts 388,389,391,392
oats 224,227
ornamentals/woody plants 418,422,424,427
pastures/rangeland 460,461,463,465,466
small fruits 358,360,362,363
sorghum 262,267
soybeans 147,149,152,155
spring wheat 200,202,206,209
sweet corn 339,342,343
tree fruits, citrus 365-368,370
tree fruits, deciduous 373,375,377,379
tree fruits, subtropical 381-384
winter wheat 187,189,194,197
Horsetail *Equisetum* spp.:
noncropland 472,474,476,480,483
nuts 386,388
ornamentals/woody plants 420,422
small fruits 357,359
tree fruits, deciduous 372,373
Houndstongue *Cynoglossum officanale:*
barley 221
conservation reserve program 446
pastures/rangeland 465
spring wheat 209
winter wheat 197
Hydrilla *Hydrilla verticillata:*
moving water 497-499
still water 493-496
Hydrilla verticullata — hydrilla
Hydrocotyle spp. — pennywort
Hyoscyamus spp. — henbane
Hypericum boreale — northern St. Johnswort
Hypericum virginicum — marsh St. Johnswort
Hypochaeris glabra — smooth catsear
Hypochaeris radicata — catsear dandelion (spotted catsear)
Hypochaeris spp. — catsear

I

Ilex vomitoria — yaupon
Illinois pondweed *Potamogeton illinoensis:*
moving water 499
still water 496
Impatiens spp. — snapweed
Imperata ciylindrica spp. — cogongrass
Indian lovegrass:
field corn, popcorn 103,107,112
soybeans 144
sweet corn 339,340
Indian mustard *Brassica juncea:*
barley 212,221
conservation reserve program 446
est. lawns/turf 411
noncropland 476,477,482,484
nuts 391
ornamentals/woody plants 427
pastures/rangeland 465
small fruits 362
spring wheat 200,209
tree fruits, citrus 368
tree fruits, deciduous 377
tree fruits, subtropical 383
winter wheat 187,197
Indiangrass *Sorghastrum nutans:*
noncropland 480
Indigofera hirsuta — hairy indigo
Indigofera spp. — indigo
Innocence:
est. lawns/turf 410
Intermediate wheatgrass *Agropyron intermedium:*
conservation reserve program 442
pastures/rangeland 460
Interrupted windgrass:
barley 212
spring wheat 200
winter wheat 187
Ipomoea coccinea — red morningglory (scarlet morningglory)
Ipomoea hederacea — entireleaf morningglory, ivyleaf morningglory
Ipomoea lacunosa — pitted morningglory
Ipomoea obscura — small white morningglory
Ipomoea pandurata — wild sweet potato
Ipomoea purpurea — tall morningglory (annual morningglory, common morningglory)
Ipomoea quamoclit — cypressvine morningglory
Ipomoea trichocarpa — sharppod morningglory
Ipomoea turbinata — purple moonflower (purple morningglory)
Ipomoea wrightii — palmleaf morningglory (willowleaf morningglory)
Ironweed *Vernonia* spp.:
barley 214
conservation reserve program 446
cotton 176
est. lawns/turf 401
field corn, popcorn 108
grasses for seed production 412
noncropland 469
oats 224
pastures/rangeland 461,466
rye 232
sorghum 262
soybeans 147
spring wheat 202
sugarcane 273,275
sweet corn 340
turf grasses for sod 416
winter wheat 189
Isatis tinctoria — dyers woad
Isocoma coronopifolia — common goldenweed
Italian ryegrass *Lolium multiflorum:*
artichokes 292,293
asparagus 294,295,297
barley 211,218
beans 300,301
carrots 301,303
celery 305
cole crops 307
conservation reserve program 447
cotton 177,182
cucurbits 309
eggplant 311
est. lawns/turf 406,411
fallow land 451
field corn, popcorn 104,106,107,112,114,124,125
forage 455,457
garlic 313
grasses for seed production 414
greens 315
guar beans 243
hops 243
kenaf 244
lettuce, endive 318,319
mint 245
mung beans 247
noncropland 474,476,477,479,480,482-484,487
nuts 386,387,389,391,392
oats 227
oil seed crops 248
okra 320
onions 321,333
ornamentals/woody plants 421,422,424,427
peanuts 252
peas 325,326
peppers 327
potatoes 329,332
radishes 333
rhubarb 333,334
safflower 259
small fruits 357-359,362,363
sorghum 269
soybeans 144,150-152,159,161,162,164
spring wheat 199,206
sugar beets 272
sugarcane 278
sunflower 279-281
sweet corn 339,340,342,343
sweet potatoes 346
tomatoes 350
tree fruits, citrus 364-367,369,370
tree fruits, deciduous 371,373-375,377-379
tree fruits, subtropical 380-384
winter wheat 194
Itchgrass *Rottboellia cochinchinensis* (raoulgrass):
asparagus 295
carrots 301
cotton 173,174,177,181
cucurbits 307
est. lawns/turf 400
fallow land 448,451
field corn, popcorn 106,120,122
flax 241
forage 459
garlic 313
lettuce, endive 318
mint 246
noncropland 468,474,481
nuts 385,387
oil seed crops 247
onions 321
ornamentals/woody plants 419,422,425
peanuts 251
peppers 327
potatoes 332
rhubarb 334
small fruits 356,358,361
southern peas 336
soybeans 145,146,149-151,154-156,158,161,164
sugar beets 269,271
sugarcane 272,275-278
sunflower 280
sweet potatoes 346
table beets 346
tobacco 281,282
tree fruits, citrus 363,365,369
tree fruits, deciduous 371,373
tree fruits, subtropical 379,381
winter wheat 194
Iva axillaris — poverty sumpweed (povertyweed)
Iva xanthifolia — marshelder
Ivyleaf morningglory *Ipomoea hederacea:*
barley 213,220
conservation reserve program 443
cotton 173,174
est. lawns/turf 400
fallow land 451,453
field corn, popcorn 101,102,105-107, 110,113,116,118-123
forage 455,458
garlic 312
grasses for seed production 411
mint 244
noncropland 468
oats 223,229
onions 321
ornamentals/woody plants 423
peanuts 249,251
potatoes 331
rye 231,235
sorghum 261,263,267,268
soybeans 144,145,148,150-152,155-157,159-161,163
spring wheat 201,209
tomatoes 349
turf grasses for sod 416
winter wheat 187,188,196
Ivyleaf speedwell *Veronica hederifolia:*
barley 217,222
fallow land 451
forage 459
spring wheat 199,205
winter wheat 186,193,197

J

Jack pine *Pinus banksiana:*
brush control 440
Jacob's ladder:
fallow land 451
Jacquemontia tamnifolia — smallflower morningglory
Jagged chickweed *Holosteum umbellatum* (umbrella spurry):
barley 212,217,221
conservation reserve program 446
fallow land 448,451
field corn, popcorn 114
pastures/rangeland 465
soybeans 152
spring wheat 200,205,209
winter wheat 187,193,197
Japanese bamboo:
noncropland 476,482
Japanese brome *Bromus japonicus:*
barley 217
conservation reserve program 442
forage 458
spring wheat 200,205
winter wheat 186,193,194
Japanese stiltgrass:
noncropland 481
Japanese tea *Cassia mimosoides:*
sugarcane 275
tree fruits, subtropical 380,381
Java bean:
field corn, popcorn 116
Jerusalem artichoke *Helianthus tuberosus:*
barley 214
conservation reserve program 443,444,447
fallow land 449-451,454

field corn, popcorn 104,106,107,110,114, 116,117,119,121,124
forage 458
grasses for seed production 412
mint 244
noncropland 468,480,484
oats 224
ornamentals/woody plants 420
pastures/rangeland 461
sorghum 263
soybeans 145,155,156,160-162
spring wheat 202
sugar beets 270
sweet corn 342
winter wheat 189

Jerusalem oak *Chenopodium botrys* (jerusalemoak goosefoot):
noncropland 472
nuts 386
ornamentals/woody plants 420
tree fruits, deciduous 372

Jim hill mustard *Sisymbrium altissimum* (tumble mustard):
barley 211-214,217,218,222
conservation reserve program 442,443
fallow land 447-449,451,453,454
forage 458,459
mint 245
oats 224,227,230
pastures/rangeland 460,461
spring wheat 199-202,205-207,210
winter wheat 186-189,192-194,198

Jimsonweed *Datura stramonium:*
asparagus 294,296,297
barley 213,214,220
beans 298
conservation reserve program 443
cotton 173,174,176-178,181
cucurbits 307
est. lawns/turf 401,404,410
fallow land 449,451,453
field corn, popcorn 101-108,110-113,115-125
flax 240,241
forage 455,456,458,460
garlic 312
grasses for seed production 412
mint 244
noncropland 468-470,474,479,481,482
nuts 388,389,391
oats 223,224,229
onions 321
ornamentals/woody plants 419,420,423,427
pastures/rangeland 461
peanuts 248,249,251,252
peas 324,325
peppers 327
potatoes 331,332
rye 231,232,235
small fruits 358,359,362
sorghum 260-265,267,268
soybeans 143-153,155-161,163
spring wheat 201,202,209
sugar beets 270,272
sugarcane 273
sweet corn 338-341,343
tobacco 281,282
tomatoes 349
tree fruits, citrus 367,368
tree fruits, deciduous 373,374,377
tree fruits, subtropical 381,383
turf grasses for sod 416
winter wheat 187-189,196

Johnsongrass *Sorghum halepense:*
artichokes 292,293
asparagus 294-297
beans 298-301
carrots 301,303
castor beans 240
celery 303,305
cole crops 305-307
conservation reserve program 445-447
cotton 173-182
cucurbits 307-309
eggplant 309-311
est. lawns/turf 400,404,407,411
fallow land 448,451,453-455
field corn, popcorn 101-107,110-114, 116-122,124,125
flax 240-242
forage 455,457-459
garbanzos 311,312
garlic 313,314
grasses for seed production 413,414
greens 314,315
guar beans 242,243
hops 243
horseradish 316
kenaf 244
lentils 317
lettuce, endive 318,319
mint 245,246
mung beans 246,247
noncropland 467,468,473,474,476-484,486,487
nuts 385-392
oil seed crops 247,248
okra 320
onions 321-323
ornamentals/woody plants 419,421,422,425,427
peanuts 248-252
peas 324-326
peppers 327,328
potatoes 329-332
radishes 333
rhubarb 333,334
rice 254
safflower 258,259
small fruits 356-363
sorghum 260-262,264-267,269
southern peas 335,336
soybeans 143-147,149-159,161-164
spinach 337
sugar beets 269-272
sugarcane 272,276-278
sunflower 279-281
sweet corn 337,339,341,342,344
sweet potatoes 345,346
table beets 346,347
tobacco 281-283
tomatoes 348-350
tree fruits, citrus 363-370
tree fruits, deciduous 371,373-379
tree fruits, subtropical 379-381,383,384
turf grasses for sod 417

Jointed goatgrass *Aegilops cylindrica:*
conservation reserve program 445,447
fallow land 449,452,454
noncropland 480,484
soybeans 152,162

Jointvetch:
cotton 174
cucurbits 307
rice 254,258
soybeans 146
tobacco 281

Juncus elliottii — bog rush
Juncus spp. — rush

Junglegrass *Koeleria cristata:*
soybeans 146,147,153

Junglerice *Echinochloa colona:*
artichokes 292,293
asparagus 294-297
beans 298,300,301
carrots 301-303
castor beans 240
celery 304,305
cole crops 305-307
conservation reserve program 447
cotton 173,174,176,177,180-182
cucurbits 307-309
eggplant 309-311
est. lawns/turf 400
fallow land 448,451,453,455
field corn, popcorn 107,121-123,125
flax 240-242
forage 455,457,459
garlic 313,314
greens 315
guar beans 243
hops 243
kenaf 244
lentils 317
lettuce, endive 318,319
mint 245,246
mung beans 247
noncropland 448,474,478,481-484,487
nuts 385-387,390-392
oil seed crops 247,248
okra 320
onions 321,323
ornamentals/woody plants 419,421,422,425-427
peanuts 251,252
peas 326
peppers 327,328
potatoes 329,332
radishes 333
rhubarb 333,334
rice 253,254,257
safflower 258,259
small fruits 356-358,360-363
sorghum 269
southern peas 335,336
soybeans 144-146,149-151,156-159,161-164
spinach 337
sugar beets 269-272
sugarcane 273,275-278
sunflower 279-281
sweet corn 339,340,345
sweet potatoes 345,346
table beets 346
tobacco 281,282
tomatoes 348-350
tree fruits, citrus 363-370
tree fruits, deciduous 371,373,375-379
tree fruits, subtropical 379-384

Juniper *Juniperus* spp.:
brush control 440
conservation reserve program 446
noncropland 475,484
pastures/rangeland 464,466

Juniperus spp. — juniper
Juniperus virginiana — eastern red cedar

K

Kao haole:
tree fruits, subtropical 382

Kentucky bluegrass *Poa pratensis:*
conservation reserve program 442
est. lawns/turf 406
field corn, popcorn 113,116,124
forage 457
grasses for seed production 414
noncropland 476,477,480,482,484
nuts 388,392
ornamentals/woody plants 422,424
rhubarb 334
small fruits 359,360,362
soybeans 162
tree fruits, citrus 366,370
tree fruits, deciduous 373,374,378
tree fruits, subtropical 381,384

Kikuyugrass *Pennisetum clandestinum:*
est. lawns/turf 404
fallow land 451
noncropland 474
nuts 387
ornamentals/woody plants 426
tree fruits, citrus 365
tree fruits, deciduous 373
tree fruits, subtropical 381

Knapweed *Centaurea* spp.:
barley 214
conservation reserve program 446
field corn, popcorn 114
forage 458
grasses for seed production 412
mint 244
noncropland 468,484
oats 224
ornamentals/woody plants 420
pastures/rangeland 466
spring wheat 202
sugar beets 270
sweet corn 342
winter wheat 189

Knawel *Scleranthus annuus:*
artichokes 292
barley 213,216
brush control 441
conservation reserve program 443
cotton 175
est. lawns/turf 400,406
field corn, popcorn 111,117,123
forage 455,456
garlic 312
grasses for seed production 411,413
mint 244,245
noncropland 468,482,486
oats 223,226
onions 321
ornamentals/woody plants 424,426
rye 231
small fruits 361
soybeans 153
spring wheat 201
sugarcane 275
sweet corn 343,345
tree fruits, citrus 364,368
tree fruits, deciduous 372,376
tree fruits, subtropical 383
turf grasses for sod 416
winter wheat 187,188,192

Knotweed *Polygonum* spp.:
asparagus 297
barley 214,216
beans 301
carrots 303
celery 305
cole crops 307
conservation reserve program 444,447
cotton 174,182
cucurbits 309
eggplant 311
est. lawns/turf 400,402,403,405-408,410
fallow land 450,451,455
field corn, popcorn... 106-108,110,116,118,121,122,125
flax 240,242
forage 455,458
grasses for seed production 412,413
greens 315
guar beans 243
hops 243
kenaf 244
lettuce, endive 318,319
mung beans 247
noncropland 470,472
nuts 386,390-392
oats 224,226
oil seed crops 248
okra 320
onions 323
ornamentals/woody plants 420,425
pastures/rangeland 461,462
peanuts 252
peppers 327
potatoes 329,332
radishes 333
rye 232
safflower 259
small fruits 357,360,362,363
sorghum 262,263,269
southern peas 336
soybeans 144,146,158,162,163
spring wheat 202,204
sugar beets 272
sugarcane 273,278
sunflower 281
sweet corn 340
tomatoes 350
tree fruits, citrus 367,370
tree fruits, deciduous 372,375,377,378
winter wheat 189,191

Kochia *Kochia scoparia:*
asparagus ... 297
barley ... 211-214,216-222
beans ... 299-301
carrots ... 303
celery ... 305
cole crops ... 307
conservation reserve program ... 442-447
cotton ... 173,174,179,180,182
cucurbits ... 307,309
eggplant ... 311
est. lawns/turf ... 400,410
fallow land ... 447-454
field corn, popcorn ... 101-107,110-125
flax ... 240-242
forage ... 455-459
garbanzos ... 312
garlic ... 312,313
grasses for seed production ... 411,413,414
greens ... 315
guar beans ... 243
hops ... 243
kenaf ... 244
lettuce, endive ... 319
mint ... 244
mung beans ... 247
noncropland ... 468-472,474,476,480-482,484
nuts ... 388-392
oats ... 223,224,226-230
oil seed crops ... 248
okra ... 320
onions ... 321-323
ornamentals/woody plants ... 419,422,425,427
pastures/rangeland ... 460-465
peanuts ... 251,252
peas ... 325,326
peppers ... 327
potatoes ... 329,331,332
radishes ... 333
rice ... 255
rye ... 231,233-235
safflower ... 259
small fruits ... 358,360,362,363
sorghum ... 260,262-265,267-269
southern peas ... 335,336
soybeans ... 144,146,149,152,154-156,158-163
spring wheat ... 199-202,204-210
sugar beets ... 269-272
sugarcane ... 277,278
sunflower ... 280,281
sweet corn ... 338-341,343,344
tobacco ... 281,282
tomatoes ... 349,350
tree fruits, citrus ... 367-370
tree fruits, deciduous ... 373,375,377,378
tree fruits, subtropical ... 383,384
turf grasses for sod ... 416
winter wheat ... 186-189,191-198
Kochia scoparia — kochia (Mexican fireweed)
Koeleria cristata — junglegrass
Krigia spp. — dwarfdandelion
Kudzu *Pueraria lobata:*
brush control ... 437,438,440-442
noncropland ... 470-473,477,480,482,484,486
pastures/rangeland ... 463,466
Kukaipuaa *Digitaria microbachne:*
sugarcane ... 275
tree fruits, subtropical ... 380,381
Kyllinga:
grasses for seed production ... 413
noncropland ... 482
Kyllings brevifolia — green kyllingia

L

Lachanathes caroliana — redroot
Lactuca canadensis — tall lettuce (wild lettuce)
Lactuca serriola — prickly lettuce (china lettuce)
Ladysthumb *Polygonum persicaria:*
barley ... 211,213,214,216-218,221,222
beans ... 298
conservation reserve program ... 443,444,446
cotton ... 173
cucurbits ... 307
est. lawns/turf ... 405,408
fallow land ... 447,449,451,452,454
field corn, popcorn ... 103-107,110,111,113,115-122
flax ... 240,241
forage ... 455,456,458
garlic ... 312
mint ... 244
noncropland ... 474,480,487
nuts ... 388,391,392
oats ... 223,224,226,227,230
onions ... 321
ornamentals/woody plants ... 422,423,427
pastures/rangeland ... 460,461,465
peanuts ... 248,251,252
peas ... 324
potatoes ... 331
rye ... 231
small fruits ... 358,362,363
sorghum ... 260,261,263,265,267
soybeans ... 143-148,150-153,155-157,159-161,163
spring wheat ... 199,201,202,204-107,209,210
sugar beets ... 269,271,272
sweet corn ... 338-340,343
tobacco ... 281,282
tomatoes ... 349
tree fruits, citrus ... 365-370
tree fruits, deciduous ... 373,377,379
tree fruits, subtropical ... 381,384
winter wheat ... 186-189,191,193,194,197,198
Lakeweed:
noncropland ... 472
pastures/rangeland ... 463
Lambsquarters *Chenopodium* spp.:
artichokes ... 292,293
asparagus ... 294-297
barley ... 211,213,214,216-222
beans ... 298-301
brush control ... 441
carrots ... 301-303
castor beans ... 240
celery ... 303-305
cole crops ... 305-307
conservation reserve program ... 442-447
cotton ... 173-177,180-182
cucurbits ... 307-309
eggplant ... 309-311
est. lawns/turf ... 400-403,405,406,408,410
fallow land ... 447-455
field corn, popcorn ... 101-108,110-125
flax ... 240-242
forage ... 455-460
garbanzos ... 312
garlic ... 312-314
grasses for seed production ... 412,414
greens ... 315
guar beans ... 243
herbs & spices ... 316
hops ... 243
horseradish ... 316
kenaf ... 244
lettuce, endive ... 318,319
mint ... 244-246
mung beans ... 247
noncropland ... 469-472,474,476-479,481-487
nuts ... 386-392
oats ... 223,224,226-230
oil seed crops ... 247,248
okra ... 320
onions ... 321-323
ornamentals/woody plants ... 418-427
pastures/rangeland ... 460-466
peanuts ... 248,249,251,252
peas ... 324-326
peppers ... 327,328
potatoes ... 329-332
radishes ... 333
rye ... 231-235
safflower ... 258,259
small fruits ... 356-363
sorghum ... 260-269
southern peas ... 335,336
soybeans ... 143,144,146-163
spinach ... 336
spring wheat ... 199,201,202,204-211
sugar beets ... 269-272
sugarcane ... 273-278
sunflower ... 279-281
sweet corn ... 337-344
sweet potatoes ... 345
table beets ... 347
tobacco ... 281-283
tomatoes ... 347-350
tree fruits, citrus ... 364-370
tree fruits, deciduous ... 371-379
tree fruits, subtropical ... 380-384
turf grasses for sod ... 416
winter wheat ... 186-189,191-196
Lamium amplexicaule — henbit
Lamium maculatum — spotted deadnettle
Lamium purpureum — purple deadnettle (red deadnettle)
Lamium spp. — deadnettle
Lanceleaf groundcherry *Physalis lanceifolia:*
cotton ... 174
noncropland ... 482
nuts ... 391
ornamentals/woody plants ... 427
peanuts ... 248
small fruits ... 362
soybeans ... 143,145
tree fruits, citrus ... 368
tree fruits, deciduous ... 377
tree fruits, subtropical ... 383
Lanceleaf ragweed *Ambrosia bidentata:*
barley ... 212,221
conservation reserve program ... 446
field corn ... 106,118
pastures/rangeland ... 465
spring wheat ... 200,209
winter wheat ... 187,197
Lanceleaf sage *Salvia reflexa:*
cotton ... 173,179,181
forage ... 457
onions ... 322
soybeans ... 154
Lantana:
field corn, popcorn ... 114
noncropland ... 475,476
sweet corn ... 342
Large crabgrass *Digitaria sanguinalis:*
artichokes ... 292,293
asparagus ... 294-297
beans ... 298.300,301
carrots ... 301,303
celery ... 305
cole crops ... 306,307
conservation reserve program ... 447
cotton ... 173,174,177-179,181,182
cucurbits ... 307-309
eggplant ... 310,311
est. lawns/turf ... 400,407-410
fallow land ... 448,451,453
field corn, popcorn ... 103,104,110,112, 113,116,118-123,125
flax ... 240-242
forage ... 455,458,459
garlic ... 313,314
greens ... 315
guar beans ... 243
hops ... 243
kenaf ... 244
lentils ... 317
lettuce, endive ... 318,319
mint ... 245,246
mung beans ... 247
newly sprigged/seeded turf ... 399
noncropland ... 468,474,479,482
nuts ... 385-387,389,392
oil seed crops ... 247,248
okra ... 320
onions ... 321,323
ornamentals/woody plants ... 419,422,423
peanuts ... 249,251,252
peas ... 324,328
peppers ... 327,328
potatoes ... 329,332
radishes ... 333
rhubarb ... 334
rice ... 253,257
safflower ... 259
small fruits ... 356-358,361,363
sorghum ... 260,264,267-269
southern peas ... 335,336
soybeans ... 144-147,149-153,155-159,161,162,164
spinach ... 337
spring wheat ... 209
sugar beets ... 269,271,272
sugarcane ... 278
sunflower ... 280,281
sweet corn ... 341,342
sweet potatoes ... 346
table beets ... 346
tobacco ... 281,282
tomatoes ... 350
tree fruits, citrus ... 363-365,367-370
tree fruits, deciduous ... 371,373,374,376,378
tree fruits, subtropical ... 379-381,383
turf grasses for sod ... 417
winter wheat ... 197
Larix laricina — tamarack
Larkspur *Delphinium* spp.:
conservation reserve program ... 446
noncropland ... 484
pastures/rangeland ... 466
Larrea tridentata — creosotebush
Late eupatorium:
noncropland ... 470
pastures/rangeland ... 462
Lawn burweed *Soliva pterosperma:*
est. lawns/turf ... 406,409,410
noncropland ... 481
ornamentals/woody plants ... 419,424,425
Leafy spurge *Euphorbia esula:*
brush control ... 441
conservation reserve program ... 444,446,447
fallow land ... 452,454
noncropland ... 469,470,472,474,477,484,486
nuts ... 386,388,391
ornamentals/woody plants ... 420,421
pastures/rangeland ... 461-463,466
small fruits ... 357,359,362
tree fruits, deciduous ... 372,373,378
Leersia oryzoides — rice cutgrass
Lemna minor — common duckweed
Lemna spp. — duckweed
Lepidium campestre — field pepperweed (field peppergrass)
Lepidium densiflorum — greenflower pepperweed
Lepidium perfoliatum — clasping pepperweed (shieldcress, yellowflower pepperweed)
Lepidium spp. — pepperweed (peppergrass)
Lepidium virginicum — Virginia pepperweed
Leptochloa fascicularis — bearded sprangletop
Leptochloa filiformis — red sprangletop
Leptochloa panicoides — Amazon sprangletop
Leptochloa spp. — sprangletop
Leptochloa uninervia — Mexican sprangletop
Lespedeza:
est. lawns/turf ... 404,410
fallow land ... 451
field corn, popcorn ... 110
noncropland ... 469,470,475,476,482,484,485
ornamentals/woody plants ... 427
pastures/rangeland ... 461,466
sorghum ... 263
Leucaena glauca — haloe koa
Linaria canadensis — oldfield toadflax
Linaria genistifolia — dalmatian toadflax
Linaria spp. — toadflax
Lindernia anagallidea — falsepimpernel
Linum spp. — flax
Liquidambar styraciflua — sweetgum
Liriodendron tulipifera — tuliptree (tulip poplar, yellow poplar)
Lithocarpus densiflorus — tanoak
Lithospermum arvense — corn gromwell
Lithospermum spp. — gromwell
Little barley *Hordeum pusilium:*
conservation reserve program ... 442,447
est. lawns/turf ... 404
field corn, popcorn ... 124

forage ... 458
noncropland ... 467,468,480,481,484,487
nuts ... 391,392
ornamentals/woody plants ... 427
small fruits ... 362,363
soybeans ... 162
tree fruits, citrus ... 369,370
tree fruits, deciduous ... 378,379
tree fruits, subtropical ... 384

Little bittercress:
fallow land ... 451
ornamentals/woody plants ... 423

Little bluestem *Andropogon scoparius:*
conservation reserve program ... 442
pastures/rangeland ... 460
small fruits ... 360

Little hairgrass:
small fruits ... 357

Little mallow *Malva parviflora:*
artichokes ... 292,293
asparagus ... 294,296
barley ... 213,218,222
fallow land ... 448,454
mint ... 245
noncropland ... 476,477,479,480,482,484
nuts ... 386,389,391
oats ... 227,230
oil seed crops ... 247
onions ... 322
ornamentals/woody plants ... 422,423
rhubarb ... 333
small fruits ... 356,357,360,362
spring wheat ... 201,207,210
sugar beets ... 272
tree fruits, citrus ... 364,367,368
tree fruits, deciduous ... 371,375,377
tree fruits, subtropical ... 380,382,383
winter wheat ... 188,194,198

Little starwort *Stellaria graminea:*
grasses for seed production ... 413

Liverwort:
ornamentals/woody plants ... 419

Loblolly pine *Pinus taeda:*
noncropland ... 477

Locoweed *Astragalus* spp.:
conservation reserve program ... 446
est. lawns/turf ... 401
grasses for seed production ... 412
noncropland ... 469,484
pastures/rangeland ... 464,466

Locust *Robinia* spp.:
brush control ... 438,441,442
conservation reserve program ... 446
noncropland ... 471,484-486
pastures/rangeland ... 466

Lodgepole pine *Pinus contorta:*
brush control ... 440

Lolium multiflorum — Italian ryegrass (annual ryegrass)
Lolium perenne — perennial ryegrass
Lolium persicum — Persian darnel
Lolium spp. — ryegrass

London rocket *Sisymbrium irio:*
asparagus ... 296,297
barley ... 212,213,218,221,222
conservation reserve program ... 442,443,446,447
cotton ... 174,181
est. lawns/turf ... 400,405,406
fallow land ... 448,452,454
field corn, popcorn ... 114,124
flax ... 241
forage ... 455,457-459
garlic ... 312
grasses for seed production ... 411,414
lettuce, endive ... 318
mint ... 244
noncropland ... 468,474,479,481-484,487
nuts ... 388-392
oats ... 223,227,230
oil seed crops ... 247
onions ... 321,322
ornamentals/woody plants ... 422-425,427
pastures/rangeland ... 465
rye ... 231
small fruits ... 358-360,362,363
soybeans ... 152,162
spring wheat ... 199-201,206,207,209,210
sugar beets ... 269,272
sugarcane ... 277
sweet corn ... 337,342,343
tomatoes ... 347
tree fruits, citrus ... 365-370
tree fruits, deciduous ... 373-375,377-379
tree fruits, subtropical ... 381-384
turf grasses for sod ... 416
winter wheat ... 186-188,194,197,198

Longspine sandbur *Gramineae:*
field corn, popcorn ... 101,106

Lonicera hirsuta — hairy honeysuckle
Lonicera spp. — honeysuckle

Loosestrife *Lythrum* spp.:
small fruits ... 357

Lotebush *Condalia obtusifolia:*
brush control ... 440
noncropland ... 475
pastures/rangeland ... 464

Lotus corniculatus — birdsfoot trefoil

Lovegrass *Eragrostis* spp.:
artichokes ... 293
asparagus ... 296
beans ... 298
carrots ... 303
castor beans ... 305
celery ... 305
cole crops ... 306
cotton ... 176,181
cucurbits ... 309
eggplant ... 310
est. lawns/turf ... 400
fallow land ... 453
field corn, popcorn ... 112,122
flax ... 241
forage ... 457,459
garlic ... 314
greens ... 315
hops ... 243
lentils ... 317
lettuce, endive ... 318,319
mint ... 246
noncropland ... 474,476,477,481-484
nuts ... 387,388,390,391
oil seed crops ... 247
onions ... 323
ornamentals/woody plants ... 421,422,425,427
peanuts ... 251
peas ... 326
peppers ... 328
potatoes ... 329,332
safflower ... 258
small fruits ... 360-362
southern peas ... 335
soybeans ... 144,146,158
spinach ... 337
sugar beets ... 270,271
sunflower ... 279,280
sweet corn ... 342
table beets ... 346
tobacco ... 282
tomatoes ... 348,350
tree fruits, citrus ... 365,367,368,369
tree fruits, deciduous ... 373,375-377
tree fruits, subtropical ... 383

Ludwigia palustris — waterpurslane
Ludwigia peploides — creeping waterprimrose
Ludwigia peruviana — primrose-willow

Lupine *Lupinus* spp.:
conservation reserve program ... 446
noncropland ... 484
pastures/rangeland ... 466

Lupinus spp. — lupine
Luziola fluitans— southern watergrass
Lythrum salicaria — purple loosestrife
Lythrum spp. — loosestrife

M

Macartney rose *Rosa bracteata:*
conservation reserve program ... 446
noncropland ... 472,477
pastures/rangeland ... 463,466

Maclura pomifera — osageorange

Madrone *Arbutus* spp.:
brush control ... 436,437,439,440
noncropland ... 477,485

Magnolia acuminata — cucumbertree
Magnolia virginiana — sweetbay magnolia

Maidencane *Panicum hemitomon:*
moving water ... 499
noncropland ... 482
still water ... 496
tree fruits, citrus ... 364

Mallow *Malva* spp.:
barley ... 214
est. lawns/turf ... 401-403,410
field corn, popcorn ... 108
grasses for seed production ... 412
noncropland ... 469,470
oats ... 224
ornamentals/woody plants ... 427
pastures/rangeland ... 461
rye ... 232
sorghum ... 262
spring wheat ... 202
sugarcane ... 273
sweet corn. popcorn ... 340
tree fruits, subtropical ... 381
winter wheat ... 189

Malva (mallow):
artichokes ... 293
carrots ... 302
celery ... 304
cotton ... 180,181
herbs/spices ... 316
noncropland ... 474
nuts ... 388
ornamentals/woody plants ... 422
small fruits ... 358,359
tree fruits, citrus ... 369
tree fruits, deciduous ... 373

Malva neglecta — common mallow
Malva parviflora — little mallow
Malva pusilla — dwarf mallow
Malva spp. — mallow

Mannagrass *Glyceria* spp.:
grasses for seed production ... 415
turf grasses for sod ... 417

Manzanita *Arctostaphylos* spp.:
brush control ... 436-438,440
noncropland ... 471,475
pastures/rangeland ... 464

Maple *Acer* spp.:
brush control ... 436-442
noncropland ... 469-471,477,480,483-486
pastures/rangeland ... 461,465,466

Marestail *Hippuris vulgaris:*
asparagus ... 297
barley ... 218,221
conservation reserve program ... 442,446,447
cotton ... 174
est. lawns/turf ... 405
fallow land ... 447
field corn, popcorn ... 103,104,107,111-119,122,124
forage ... 458,459
noncropland ... 469,473-476,479,482,484
nuts ... 388,391
oats ... 227
ornamentals/woody plants ... 422,425-427
pastures/rangeland ... 460,461,465
small fruits ... 358,362
soybeans ... 145,147,152,156,160-162
spring wheat ... 206,209
sugarcane ... 277
sweet corn ... 340,342,343
tree fruits, citrus ... 365,368,369
tree fruits, deciduous ... 373,377,378
tree fruits, subtropical ... 381,383,384
winter wheat ... 194,197

Marigold:
noncropland ... 482

Marsh pea:
small fruits ... 357

Marsh St. Johnswort *Hypericum virginicum:*
small fruits ... 357

Marshelder *Iva xanthifolia:*
barley ... 212-214,218-222
beans ... 298
conservation reserve program ... 442,443,446
est. lawns/turf ... 401
fallow land ... 448,449,454
field corn, popcorn ... 107,108,113,116,121
flax ... 241
grasses for seed production ... 412,414
mint ... 244
noncropland ... 468,469
oats ... 223,224,227-230
ornamentals/woody plants ... 420
pastures/rangeland ... 460,461,463-466
peanuts ... 251
peas ... 324,325
rye ... 231,232,234,235
sorghum ... 262
soybeans ... 144,152,153,157,159
spring wheat ... 200-202,207-210
sugar beets ... 270
sugarcane ... 273
sweet corn ... 340
winter wheat ... 187-189,194-198

Marshpepper smartweed *Polygonum hydropiper:*
small fruits ... 357

Matchweed:
est. lawns/turf ... 401

Matricaria spp.— chamomile
Matricaria maritima — false chamomile
Matricaria matricarioides — pineappleweed
Matricaria perforata — scentless chamomile

Mauna loa:
tree fruits, subtropical ... 382

Maypop *Passiflora incarnata* (maypop passionflower):
noncropland ... 472
nuts ... 386
ornamentals/woody plants ... 420
tree fruits, deciduous ... 372

Mayweed:
barley ... 211,213,218,222
conservation reserve program ... 443,446
est. lawns/turf ... 400
fallow land ... 447,451
field corn, popcorn ... 107
forage ... 455
garlic ... 312
grasses for seed production ... 411
mint ... 244
noncropland ... 468,480,483
oats ... 223,227,230
onions ... 321
ornamentals/woody plants ... 423
pastures/rangeland ... 460,466
rye ... 231
spring wheat ... 199,201,206,211
sweet corn ... 339,340
turf grasses for sod ... 416
winter wheat ... 186-188,193

Mayweed chamomile *Anthemis cotula:*
barley ... 213,214,217,220
fallow land ... 448
noncropland ... 480
oats ... 224,229
potatoes ... 331
rye ... 235
sorghum ... 267
spring wheat ... 201,202,205,209
tomatoes ... 349
winter wheat ... 188,189,192,193,196

Meadow buttercup *Ranunculus acris* (tall buttercup):
noncropland ... 478

Meadow salsify *Tragopogon pratensis:*
barley ... 214
conservation reserve program ... 443
fallow land ... 449
forage ... 458,459

oats ... 224
pastures/rangeland ... 461
spring wheat ... 202
winter wheat ... 189
Medic *Medicago trunculata:*
ornamentals/woody plants ... 426
Medicago lupulina — black medic
Medicago polymorpha — California burclover
Medicago sativa — alfalfa
Medicago spp. — burclover
Medicago trunculata — medic
Medusahead *Taeniatherum caput-medusae:*
noncropland ... 467
Melia azedarach — chinaberry
Melica bulbosa — oniongrass
Melilotus indica — annual yellow sweetclover (Indian sweetclover)
Melilotus officinalis — yellow sweetclover
Melilotus spp. — sweetclover
Melochia corchorifolia — redweed
Mentha longifolia — horse mint
Menyanthes trifoliata — common bogbean (buckbean)
Mesquite *Prosopis juliflora:*
brush control ... 438,440
conservation reserve program ... 446
noncropland ... 470,472,475,484
pastures/rangeland ... 460,462-464,466
Mexican clover *Richardia* spp.:
asparagus ... 297
beans ... 301
carrots ... 303
celery ... 305
cole crops ... 307
conservation reserve program ... 447
cotton ... 182
cucurbits ... 309
eggplant ... 311
field corn, popcorn ... 125
flax ... 240,242
forage ... 455
grasses for seed production ... 413
greens ... 315
guar beans ... 243
hops ... 243
kenaf ... 244
lettuce, endive ... 318,319
mung beans ... 247
nuts ... 391,392
oil seed crops ... 248
okra ... 320
onions ... 323
ornamentals/woody plants ... 421,427
peanuts ... 252
peppers ... 327
potatoes ... 329,332
radishes ... 333
safflower ... 259
small fruits ... 362,363
sorghum ... 269
southern peas ... 336
soybeans ... 162
sugar beets ... 272
sugarcane ... 275,277,278
sunflower ... 281
tomatoes ... 350
tree fruits, citrus ... 369,370
tree fruits, deciduous ... 377,378
tree fruits, subtropical ... 380,381,384
Mexican fireweed *Kochia scoparia* (kochia):
asparagus ... 297
beans ... 301
carrots ... 303
celery ... 305
cole crops ... 307
conservation reserve program ... 447
cotton ... 182
cucurbits ... 309
eggplant ... 311
field corn, popcorn ... 125
flax ... 240,242
greens ... 315
guar beans ... 243
hops ... 243
kenaf ... 244
lettuce, endive ... 319
mung beans ... 247
nuts ... 392
oil seed crops ... 248
okra ... 320
onions ... 323
peanuts ... 252
peppers ... 327
potatoes ... 329,332
radishes ... 333
safflower ... 259
small fruits ... 363
sorghum ... 269
southern peas ... 336
soybeans ... 146,162
sugar beets ... 272
sugarcane ... 278
sunflower ... 281
tomatoes ... 350
tree fruits, citrus ... 370
tree fruits, deciduous ... 378
Mexican lovegrass *Eragrostis mexicana:*
noncropland ... 487
nuts ... 392
ornamentals/woody plants ... 427
small fruits ... 363
tree fruits, citrus ... 370
tree fruits, deciduous ... 379
tree fruits, subtropical ... 384
Mexican sprangletop *Leptochloa uninervia:*
artichokes ... 292
asparagus ... 294
est. lawns/turf ... 407
mint ... 245
noncropland ... 481,482
nuts ... 386,390,391
ornamentals/woody plants ... 425,427
radishes ... 333
small fruits ... 357,360,362
tree fruits, citrus ... 364,367,368
tree fruits, deciduous ... 371,375,377
tree fruits, subtropical ... 380,383
turf grasses for sod ... 417
Mexicanweed *Caperonia castaniifolia:*
barley ... 214
cotton ... 174
est. lawns/turf ... 401
field corn, popcorn ... 108
grasses for seed production ... 412
noncropland ... 469
oats ... 224
pastures/rangeland ... 461
rice ... 254-258
rye ... 232
sorghum ... 262
soybeans ... 144,145,148,150,157-159,161,163
spring wheat ... 202
sugarcane ... 273
sweet corn ... 340
tobacco ... 282
winter wheat ... 189
Milfoil *Achillea millefolium* (common yarrow):
moving water ... 499
still water ... 495,496
Milium scabrum — spring milletgrass
Milk thistle:
asparagus ... 294
sugarcane ... 274
Milkweed:
artichokes ... 292
asparagus ... 295
beans ... 299
brush control ... 441
carrots ... 301
celery ... 303
cole crops ... 305
conservation reserve program ... 446
cotton ... 177
cucurbits ... 308
eggplant ... 310
field corn, popcorn ... 111,112,114
forage ... 457
garbanzos ... 311
garlic ... 313
greens ... 314
guar beans ... 242
horseradish ... 316
lentils ... 317
lettuce, endive ... 318
noncropland ... 469,475-477,482,484,486
okra ... 320
onions ... 321
pastures/rangeland ... 461,466
peanuts ... 250
peas ... 325
peppers ... 328
potatoes ... 330
radishes ... 333
rhubarb ... 334
sorghum ... 265
soybeans ... 152
spinach ... 336
sugar beets ... 270
sugarcane ... 275
sweet corn ... 342
sweet potatoes ... 346
table beets ... 347
tomatoes ... 348
Milkweed vine *Morrenia odorata:*
noncropland ... 472
nuts ... 386
ornamentals/woody plants ... 420
pastures/rangeland ... 466
tree fruits, citrus ... 366
tree fruits, deciduous ... 372
Millet:
spring wheat ... 202
sugar beets ... 272
tobacco ... 283
tomatoes ... 350
winter wheat ... 189
Mimosa pudica — sensitiveplant (hila hila)
Minerslettuce *Montia perfoliata:*
barley ... 211-213,217,218,220-222
conservation reserve program ... 446
cotton ... 174
fallow land ... 447,448,451,452,454
forage ... 459
noncropland ... 472,476,477,482-484
nuts ... 386,388
oats ... 227,229,230
oil seed crops ... 247
ornamentals/woody plants ... 420,423
pastures/rangeland ... 460,465
rye ... 235
small fruits ... 359
spring wheat ... 199-201,205-207,209,210
tree fruits, citrus ... 366
tree fruits, deciduous ... 372,374
tree fruits, subtropical ... 381
winter wheat ... 186-188,192-194,196-198
Missouri goldenrod *Solidago missouriensis:*
noncropland ... 470
pastures/rangeland ... 462
sugarcane ... 275
Mollugo verticillata — carpetweed
Momordica charantia — balsamapple
Monarda punctata — spotted beebalm
Montia perfoliata — minerslettuce, endive
Morningglory:
artichokes ... 292,293
asparagus ... 294,295,297
barley ... 212-214,216,218,220,221
beans ... 298
brush control ... 441
carrots ... 301,302
castor beans ... 240
celery ... 304
conservation reserve program ... 442-444,446,447
cotton ... 173-181
cucurbits ... 307
est. lawns/turf ... 400-403,406-408,410
fallow land ... 448,451,453,454
field corn, popcorn ... 101-108,110-124
forage ... 455-458
garlic ... 312
grasses for seed production ... 411,412
herbs/spices ... 316
lettuce, endive ... 318
mint ... 244,245
noncropland ... 468-470,473,474,477-479, 481-484,486,487
nuts ... 387-392
oats ... 223,224,226,227,229
onions ... 321
ornamentals/woody plants .. 419,421,423,424,426,427
pastures/rangeland ... 461,462,465,466
peanuts ... 248,249,251,252
peas ... 325
potatoes ... 329-331
rice ... 254,258
rye ... 231,232,235
safflower ... 258
small fruits ... 356,357,359,361-363
sorghum ... 260-265,267,268
soybeans ... 143-157,159-163
spring wheat ... 200-202,206,209
sugar beets ... 270,272
sugarcane ... 273-276
sunflower ... 279
sweet corn ... 338-343,345
tobacco ... 281-283
tomatoes ... 348
tree fruits, citrus ... 364-370
tree fruits, deciduous ... 372,374,376-379
tree fruits, subtropical ... 381-384
turf grasses for sod ... 416,417
winter wheat ... 187-189,192,194,196,197
Morrenia odorata — stranglervine (milkweed vine)
Morus spp. — mulberry
Moss *Bryophyta:*
ornamentals/woody plants ... 426
Mouseear chickweed *Cerastium vulgatum:*
artichokes ... 293
barley ... 217,218,220,222
conservation reserve program ... 447
est. lawns/turf ... 400-403,405-409
fallow lands ... 451,454
field corn, popcorn ... 114,116,124
grasses for seed production ... 413
noncropland ... 469,474,481,484
nuts ... 388,391
oats ... 227,229,230
ornamentals/woody plants ... 422,424,425
pastures/rangeland ... 461
peas ... 325
rhubarb ... 334
rye ... 235
small fruits ... 358,362
soybeans ... 152,162
spring wheat ... 205,206,209,210
sugarcane ... 274
sweet corn ... 342,343
tree fruits, citrus ... 365,369
tree fruits, deciduous ... 373,378
tree fruits, subtropical ... 381,384
winter wheat ... 193,194,196-198
Mouseearcress *Arabidopsis thaliana:*
barley ... 213,218,222
fallow land ... 448,454
oats ... 228,230
spring wheat ... 201,207,210
winter wheat ... 188,194,198
Mousetail *Myosurus minimus:*
soybeans ... 147
Mud plantain:
rice ... 254,255
Mugwort *Artemisia vulgaris:*
noncropland ... 474
nuts ... 388
ornamentals/woody plants ... 422
small fruits ... 359
tree fruits, deciduous ... 373
Muhlenbergia frondosa — wirestem muhly
Muhlenbergia uniflora — smokegrass
Muhly witchgrass:
tobacco ... 282

Mulberry *Morus* spp.:
- brush control 438-440
- noncropland 471,477,485
- ornamentals/woody plants 427

Mullein:
- noncropland 476,477,482,484

Multiflora rose *Rosa multiflora:*
- brush control 437-442
- conservation reserve program 446
- fallow land 447
- noncropland 469-473,475,477,486
- pastures/rangeland 461,463,464,466

Musk thistle *Carduus nutans:*
- barley 214,221
- brush control 441
- conservation reserve program 442-444,446
- est. lawns/turf 401
- fallow land 447,449,450
- field corn, popcorn 108
- grasses for seed production 412
- noncropland 469,470,474,480,483,486
- nuts 388
- oats 224
- ornamentals/woody plants 419,422
- pastures/rangeland 460-462,464-466
- rye 232
- small fruits 359
- sorghum 262
- spring wheat 202,209
- sugarcane 273,274
- sweet corn 340
- tree fruits, deciduous 373
- winter wheat 189,197

Muskrat grass:
- small fruits 357

Mustard:
- artichokes 292,293
- asparagus 294,297
- barley 214,219-221
- brush control 441
- carrots 301,302
- celery 303,304
- conservation reserve program 446,447
- cotton 180,181
- est. lawns/turf 401,410
- fallow land 448,450,452-454
- field corn, popcorn 101-103,105-108,110,112, 115-117,119-121,123,124
- flax 241
- forage 458,459
- grasses for seed production 412,414
- herbs/spices 316
- lawn/turf seedbeds 399
- noncropland 469-471,475,476,478,480,483-486
- nuts 390,391
- oats 224,228,229
- ornamentals/woody plants 419,424,427
- pastures/rangeland 461,464-466
- peanuts 251
- peas 325
- potatoes 330,331
- rye 232,234,235
- small fruits 357,358,362
- sorghum 260-262,264,265,268
- soybeans 144,148,153,155-157,159-163
- spring wheat 202,204,207-209
- sugar beets 271
- sugarcane 273
- sweet corn 338-341,343
- table beets 347
- tobacco 281
- tree fruits, citrus 369
- tree fruits, deciduous 372,377,378
- tree fruits, subtropical 384
- turf grasses for sod 416,417
- winter wheat 189,191,195-197

Myosurus minimus — mousetail
Myrica spp. — waxmyrtle
Myrica cerifera — southern waxmyrtle
Myriophyllum aquaticum — parrotfeather
Myriophyllum spicatum — Eurasian watermilfoil
Myriophyllum spp. — watermilfoil

Myrtle:
- brush control 440
- noncropland 475
- patsures/rangland 464

N

Naiad *Najas* spp.:
- moving water 498,499
- still water 493,495,496

Najas guadalupensis — southern naiad

Napiergrass *Pennisetum purpureum:*
- field corn, popcorn 114
- sweet corn 342

Narrowleaf cudweed *Gnaphalium purpureum:*
- nuts 388
- small fruits 359
- tree fruits, citrus 366
- tree fruits, deciduous 374
- tree fruits, subtropical 381

Narrowleaf goldaster:
- pastures/rangeland 464

Narrowleaf goosefoot:
- sorghum 266

Narrowleaf hawksbeard *Crepis tectorum:*
- barley 214
- conservation reserve program 443
- fallow land 449
- oats 224
- pastures/rangeland 461
- spring wheat 202
- winter wheat 189

Narrowleaf lambsquarters:
- barley 213,218
- fallow land 448
- oats 228
- spring wheat 201,207
- winter wheat 188,194

Narrowleaf plantain:
- noncropland 469,481
- pastures/rangeland 461

Narrowleaf signalgrass *Brachiaria peligera:*
- sugar beets 272
- tobacco 283
- tomatoes 350

Natalgrass *Rhynchelytrum repens:*
- noncropland 472,475,476,478,479
- nuts 386,391
- ornamentals/woody plants 420
- tree fruits, citrus 366,369
- tree fruits, deciduous 372,377

Needlegrass *Stipa* spp.:
- small fruits 357,360

Nelumbo lutea — American lotus
Nepeta cataria — catnip
Nephrolepis spp. — sword fern

Nettle *Urtica* spp.:
- est. lawns/turf 410
- noncropland 470,471,474,483
- nuts 388
- ornamentals/woody plants 422
- small fruits 359
- tree fruits, deciduous 373

Nettleleaf goosefoot *Chenopodium murale:*
- artichokes 293
- asparagus 294
- beans 298
- carrots 301,302
- castor beans 240
- celery 303,304
- cole crops 306
- cotton 176
- cucurbits 308
- eggplant 310
- field corn, popcorn 117
- forage 457
- garlic 314
- greens 315
- lettuce, endive 318,319
- noncropland 476-478,482,484
- nuts 387,391
- onions 323
- ornamentals/woody plants 421,424,427
- peppers 328
- potatoes 329,330
- safflower 258
- small fruits 362
- soybeans 153
- spinach 336
- sugar beets 269-272
- sunflower 279
- sweet corn 337,343
- tobacco 283
- tomatoes 347-350
- tree fruits, citrus 368
- tree fruits, deciduous 377
- tree fruits, subtropical 383

Nicotiana glauca — tree tobacco

Nightflowering catchfly *Silene noctiflora:*
- barley 213,218
- fallow land 448
- grasses for seed production 413
- oats 228
- spring wheat 201,207
- winter wheat 188,194

Nightshade *Solanum* spp.:
- asparagus 295,297
- beans 298,300
- cotton 173
- field corn, popcorn 102,105,113,115,120,123,125
- mint 244,246
- noncropland 474
- nuts 388,391
- ornamentals/woody plants 419-422,426
- peanuts 249,252
- peas 326
- small fruits 359,361,362
- sorghum 260,261,264,268
- soybeans 151,155,159-161
- sugar beets 270,271
- sunflower 280
- sweet corn 338,342,345
- table beets 347
- tree fruits, citrus 368
- tree fruits, deciduous 373,376,377
- tree fruits, subtropical 383
- turf grasses for sod 416

Nitella:
- moving water 497
- stll water 493,494

Nodding spurge *Euphorbia nutans:*
- field corn, popcorn 110,115,120,122
- sorghum 264
- soybeans 144,148,155
- sweet corn 341

Nuphar luteum — spatterdock, yellow waterlily

Northern St. Johnswort *Hypericum boreale:*
- small fruits 356

Nutgrass *Cyperus* spp. (nutsedge):
- cotton 176,178,179
- noncropland 479
- tobacco 283
- tree fruits, citrus 366
- tree fruits, deciduous 379

Nutsedge *Cyperus* spp.:
- asparagus 296
- cotton 175,176,178,179,181
- est. lawns/turf 404,407
- field corn, popcorn 112,125
- noncropland 472-476,478,479
- nuts 388,389
- ornamentals/woody plants 422
- peanuts 252
- rice 256
- small fruits 357,360,362
- soybeans 150,152
- sweet corn 342
- sweet potatoes 345
- tobacco 283
- tree fruits, citrus 364,365,367,369
- tree fruits, deciduous 373-375

Nymphaea spp. — waterlily
Nymphaea tuberosa — magnolia waterlily (white waterlily)
Nyssa sylvatica — blackgum

O

Oak *Quercus* spp.:
- brush control 436-442
- noncropland 470-472,475-477,480,483-486
- pastures/rangeland 464-466

Oatgrass *Arrhenatherum* spp.:
- noncropland 481

Oceanspray *Holodiscus discolor:*
- brush control 439

Oenothera biennis — common eveningprimrose
Oenothera lacinata — cutleaf eveningprimrose
Oenothera spp. — eveningprimrose

Old witchgrass *Panicum capillare* (witchgrass):
- noncropland 472
- nuts 386
- ornamentals/woody plants 420
- tree fruits, deciduous 372

Old world diamond flower *Hedyotis corymbosa:*
- est. lawns/turf 410

Oldfield toadflax *Linaria canadensis:*
- est. lawns/turf 408

Oniongrass *Melica bulbosa:*
- small fruits 357

Onoclea sensibilis — sensitive fern
Onopordum acanthium — Scotch thistle
Opuntia leptocaulis — tasajillo
Opuntia polycantha — plains pricklypear

Orchardgrass *Dactylis glomerata:*
- artichokes 293
- asparagus 296
- carrots 303
- celery 305
- cole crops 306
- cotton 181
- cucurbits 309
- eggplant 310
- est. lawns/turf 406
- fallow land 453
- field corn, popcorn 113,114,116,122,124
- flax 241
- forage 457,459
- garlic 314
- grasses for seed production 413,414
- greens 315
- lentils 317
- lettuce, endive 319
- mint 246
- noncropland 472,475-477,479,482,484
- nuts 386,388,390-392
- oil seed crops 247
- onions 323
- ornamentals/woody plants 420,424
- peanuts 251
- peas 326
- peppers 328
- potatoes 332
- rhubarb 334
- small fruits 357-362
- southern peas 335
- soybeans 152,158,162
- spinach 337
- sugar beets 271
- sunflower 280
- sweet corn 342
- table beets 346
- tobacco 282
- tomatoes 350
- tree fruits, citrus 366,368-370
- tree fruits, deciduous 372,374,376-378
- tree fruits, subtropical 381,383,384

Orcutt lovegrass *Eragrostis orcuttiana:*
- noncropland 487
- nuts 392
- ornamentals/woody plants 427
- small fruits 363
- tree fruits, citrus 370
- tree fruits, deciduous 379
- tree fruits, subtropical 384

Oryza sativa — rice (red rice)
Oryzopsis spp. — ricegrass

Osageorange *Maclura pomifera:*
- brush control 438,440

noncropland 471,475
pastures/rangeland 464
Osmunda regalis — royal fern
Oxalis (woodsorrel):
artichokes 293
est. lawns/turf 401,403,405,408,410
fallow land 452
noncropland 469-471,475,476,485
ornamentals/woody plants 425-427
pastures/rangeland 461
tree fruits, subtropical 382
Oxalis corniculata — creeping woodsorrel
Oxalis pes-caprae — buttercup oxalis
Oxalis spp. — woodsorrel
Oxalis stricta — yellow woodsorrel
Oxeye daisy *Chrysanthemum leucanthemum:*
conservation reserve program 446
noncropland 476,477,480,482,484
ornamentals/woody plants 424
pastures/rangeland 464,466
Oxydendrum arboreum — sourwood

P

Pale smartweed *Polygonum lapathifolium*
barley 211
fallow land 447
lettuce, endive 318
pastures/rangeland 460
spring wheat 199
winter wheat 186
Paleseed plantain *Plantago virginica:*
noncropland 474
sugarcane 275
Palmer amaranth *Amaranthus palmeri:*
barley 220
cotton 173,174
field corn, popcorn 103,110-113,115,116, 119,121,122
oats 229
peanuts 248
rye 235
sorghum 264,267
soybeans 143-145,150,152,156,160,161,163
spring wheat 209
sweet corn 341
tobacco 282
winter wheat 196
Palmer pigweed:
field corn, popcorn 107,116,119,120,121
forage 458
peanuts 251
soybeans 144,148,155,157,159,163
Palmetto:
brush control 438
noncropland 471
Palmleaf morningglory *Ipomoea wrightii:*
cotton 173,174
field corn, popcorn 105,107,121
sorghum 261
soybeans 145,148,150,151,157,159,163
Pangolagrass *Digitaria decumbens:*
noncropland 473,479
tree fruits, citrus 366
Panicle willowweed *Epilobium paniculatum:*
noncropland 482
nuts 391
ornamentals/woody plants 427
small fruits 362
tree fruits, citrus 368
tree fruits, deciduous 377
tree fruits, subtropical 383
Panicum:
asparagus 297
beans 298
carrots 302
celery 304
cotton 179,180
est. lawns/turf 404
field corn, popcorn 102
forage 457
grasses for seed production 414
herbs/spices 316
mint 246
nuts 391
ornamentals/woody plants 421,427
peanuts 248
small fruits 362
sorghum 260
soybeans 143,154
sugarcane 275,276
sweet corn 337
tree fruits, deciduous 377
tree fruits, subtropical 380,381
turf grasses for sod 417
Panicum adspersum — broadleaf panicum
Panicum capillare — witchgrass
Panicum dichotomiflorum — fall panicum (fall panicgrass, spreading panicum)
Panicum fasciculatum — browntop panicum
Panicum hemitomon — maidencane
Panicum maximum — guineagrass
Panicum miliaceum — wild proso millet (proso millet)
Panicum repens — torpedograss
Panicum spp. — panicum
Panicum texanum — Texas panicum (coloradograss, Texas millet)
Panicum virgatum — switchgrass
Paragrass *Brachiaria mutica:*
artichokes 292
asparagus 295,297
beans 299
carrots 301
celery 303
cole crops 305
cotton 177
cucurbits 308
eggplant 310
field corn, popcorn 114,124
forage 457
garbanzos 311
garlic 313
greens 314
guar beans 242
horseradish 316
lentils 317
lettuce, endive 318
moving water 499
noncropland 467,475-477,482,484
nuts 388,392
okra 320
onions 321
ornamentals/woody plants 422
peanuts 250
peas 325
peppers 328
potatoes 330
radishes 333
rhubarb 334
rice 253,254,257,258
small fruits 362
sorghum 265
spinach 336
still water 496
sugar beets 270
sugarcane 272
sweet corn 342
sweet potatoes 346
table beets 347
tomatoes 348
tree fruits, citrus 365,366,369
tree fruits, deciduous 373,378
Parietaria spp.— pellitory weed
Parrotfeather *Myriophyllum aquaticum:*
moving water 499
noncropland 469
still water 496
Parsley-piert *Alchemilla arvensis:*
est. lawns/turf 404,406,409
ornamentals/woody plants 424
Parthenocissus quinquefolia — Virginia creeper
Partridgepea *Cassia fasciculata:*
est. lawns/turf 408
noncropland 468
Paspalum:
sugarcane 276
tree fruits, subtropical 380
Paspalum boscianum — bull paspalum (bullgrass)
Paspalum conjugatum — sour paspalum (hilograss)
Paspalum dilatatum — dallisgrass
Paspalum notatum — bahiagrass
Paspalum spp. — paspalum
Paspalum urvillei — vaseygrass
Passiflora incarnata — maypop passionflower (maypop)
Pastinaca sativa — wild parsnip
Pastinaca spp. — parsnip
Pearlwort *Sagina* spp.:
ornamentals/woody plants 425,426
Pecan *Carya illinoinensis:*
brush control 436,437
noncropland 480
Pellitory weed:
sugarcane 273
Pennisetum clandestinum — kikuyugrass
Pennisetum purpureum — napiergrass
Pennsylvania smartweed *Polygonum pensylvanicum:*
artichokes 292
asparagus 295-297
barley 213,214,216-218,220-222
beans 298,299
carrots 301
celery 303
cole crops 305,306
conservation reserve program 443-447
cotton 173,174,177,179-181
cucurbits 307,308
eggplant 310
est. lawns/turf 408
fallow land 448-451,453,454
field corn, popcorn 103-107,110-113,115-124
flax 240,241
forage 455,457,458
garbanzos 311,312
garlic 312,313
greens 314
guar beans 242
horseradish 316
lentils 317
lettuce, endive 318
mint 244
noncropland 470,482,484
nuts 388,390,391
oats 223,224,226-230
okra 320
onions 321,322
ornamentals/woody plants 419,423-425,427
pastures/rangeland 461,462,465
peanuts 248,250-252
peas 324,325
peppers 328
potatoes 330-332
radishes 333
rhubarb 334
rice 253,254,258
rye 231,235
small fruits 357,359,360,362
sorghum 260,261,263,265,267,268
southern peas 335
soybeans 143-147,149-163
spinach 336
spring wheat 201,202,204-207,209,210
sugar beets 269-272
sugarcane 277
sunflower 280
sweet corn 338-340,343,344
sweet potatoes 346
table beets 347
tobacco 281,282
tomatoes 348,349
tree fruits, citrus 366-369
tree fruits, deciduous 374,375,377,378
tree fruits, subtropical 381,383,384
winter wheat 187-189,191-194,196-198
Pennycress *Thlaspi* spp.:
artichokes 292
barley 219-222
fallow land 453
field corn, popcorn 107,116,123
forage 457
noncropland 474,482
nuts 388
oats 226,228-230
ornamentals/woody plants 422
rye 234
small fruits 359
sorghum 268
soybeans 161
spring wheat 207,208,211
sweet corn 340
tree fruits, deciduous 373
winter wheat 195,196
Pennywort *Hydrocotyle* spp.:
barley 214
est. lawns/turf 401,405,406
field corn, popcorn 108
grasses for seed production 412
moving water 498
noncropland 469,474
nuts 388
oats 224
ornamentals/woody plants 422
pastures/rangeland 461
rye 232
small fruits 358
sorghum 262
spring wheat 202
still water 495
sugarcane 273
sweet corn 340
tree fruits, citrus 365
tree fruits, deciduous 373
tree fruits, subtropical 381
winter wheat 189
Pensacola bahiagrass:
fallow land 447
Peppergrass *Lepidium* spp. (pepperweed):
barley 219,220
est. lawns/turf 410
forage 456,459
grasses for seed production 413
noncropland 470
oats 228,229
ornamentals/woody plants 421
rye 234
soybeans 147
spring wheat 207,208
winter wheat 195,196
Peppervine *Ampelopsis arborea:*
noncropland 468
pastures/rangeland 466
Pepperweed *Lepidium* spp.:
barley 213,214,220,221
conservation reserve program 443,446
est. lawns/turf 403
field corn, popcorn 108,112,123
flax 241
forage 458,459
grasses for seed production 412,414
noncropland 469,471,476-478,480,482-484
oats 223,224,228
ornamentals/woody plants 425,426
pastures/rangeland 461,464,465
rye 231,232,234
small fruits 361
sorghum 262
spring wheat 201,202,208,209
sugarcane 273
sweet corn 340,345
tree fruits, citrus 368
tree fruits, deciduous 376
tree fruits, subtropical 383
winter wheat 188,189,195,197
Perennial clover:
fallow land 451
field corn, popcorn 110
sorghum 263
Perennial peppergrass:
peas 325
Perennial pepperweed:
noncropland 481
Perennial ragweed:
brush control 441

Perennial ryegrass *Lolium perenne:*
artichokes....293
asparagus....296
beans....300
carrots....303
celery....305
cole crops....306
conservation reserve program....447
cotton....181
cucurbits....309
eggplant....310
est. lawns/turf....406
field corn, popcorn....113,114,122,124
flax....241
forage....457,459
garlic....314
grasses for seed production....414
greens....315
lentils....317
lettuce, endive....319
mint....246
noncropland....474,481,484
nuts....392
oil seed crops....247
onions....323
ornamentals/woody plants....424
peanuts....251
peas....326
peppers....328
potatoes....332
rhubarb....334
small fruits....359-362
southern peas....335
soybeans....158,162
spinach....337
sugar beets....271
sunflower....280
sweet corn....342
table beets....346
tobacco....282
tomatoes....350
tree fruits, citrus....368,369
tree fruits, deciduous....376,378
tree fruits, subtropical....383,384
Perennial sowthistle *Sonchus arvensis:*
barley....214,220
conservation reserve program....443,444,446
fallow land....449,450
field corn, popcorn....106,111
noncropland....469,470,472,486
oats....224,229
pastures/rangeland....461-463,466
rye....234
spring wheat....202,208
sugarcane....274,275
winter wheat....189,196
Persian darnel *Lolium persicum:*
barley....211
spring wheat....199,200
winter wheat....186,194
Persimmon *Diospyros* spp.:
brush control....438,440-442
noncropland....471,472,475,477,480,484-486
pastures/rangeland....464,466
Petty spurge *Euphorbia peplus:*
noncropland....482
nuts....391
ornamentals/woody plants....419
small fruits....362
tree fruits, citrus....368
tree fruits, deciduous....377
tree fruits, subtropical....383
Phalaris arundinacea — reed canarygrass
Phalaris canariensis — canarygrass (birdseedgrass)
Phalaris paradoxa — hood canarygrass
Phaseolus lathyroides — wild pea bean
Phleum pratense — timothy
Phormidium:
moving water....497
still water....493
Phragmites *Phragmites* spp.:
moving water....499
noncropland....476,482
still water....496
Phragmites spp. — phragmites
Physalis angulata — cutleaf groundcherry
Physalis heterophylla — clammy groundcherry
Physalis lanceifolia — lanceleaf groundcherry
Physalis wrightii — Wright groundcherry
Phytolacca spp. — pokeweed
Picea spp. — spruce
Pickerelweed *Pontederia cordata:*
rice....254,255
still water....495
Picris echioides — bristly oxtongue
Pigeongrass *Setaria glauca* (yellow foxtail):
asparagus....297
barley....213,219,222
beans....300,301
carrots....303
celery....305
cole crops....307
conservation reserve program....447
cotton....182
cucurbits....309
eggplant....311
fallow land....455
field corn, popcorn....125
flax....240,242
forage....455
greens....315
guar beans....243
hops....243
kenaf....244
lettuce, endive....318,319
mung beans....247
nuts....391,392
oil seed crops....248
okra....320
onions....323
ornamentals/woody plants....427
peanuts....252
peas....324,326
peppers....327
potatoes....329,332
rhubarb....333
safflower....259
small fruits....363
sorghum....269
southern peas....336
soybeans....146,159,162
spring wheat....201,207,211
sugar beets....269,272
sugarcane....278
sunflower....280,281
tomatoes....350
tree fruits, citrus....370
tree fruits, deciduous....378
tree fruits, subtropical....384
winter wheat....188
Pigweed:
artichokes....292,293
asparagus....294-297
barley....214,216,219-222
beans....298-301
brush control....441
carrots....301-303
castor beans....240
celery....303-305
cole crops....305-307
conservation reserve program....442,444-447
cotton....173-182
cucurbits....307-309
eggplant....309-311
est. lawns/turf....400-403,405-408,410
fallow land....447-455
field corn, popcorn....101-108,110-125
flax....240-242
forage....455-458,460
garbanzos....311,312
garlic....312-314
grasses for seed production....411,412,414
greens....315
guar beans....243
herbs/spices....316
hops....243
horseradish....316
kenaf....244
lawn/turf seedbeds....399
lettuce, endive....318,319
mint....244,245
mung beans....246,247
noncropland....468-472,474-484,486,487
nuts....386-392
oats....223,224,226-230
oil seed crops....247,248
okra....320
onions....321-323
ornamentals/woody plants....418,419-427
pastures/rangeland....460-466
peanuts....248-252
peas....325,326
peppers....327,328
potatoes....329-332
radishes....333
rice....253,254,257,258
rye....231,232,234,235
safflower....258,259
small fruits....356-363
sorghum....260-269
southern peas....335,336
soybeans....143-163
spinach....336
spring wheat....199-202,204-211
sugar beets....269-272
sugarcane....273-278
sunflower....279-281
sweet corn....337-345
sweet potatoes....345
table beets....347
tobacco....281-283
tomatoes....348-350
tree fruits, citrus....364-370
tree fruits, deciduous....371-379
tree fruits, subtropical....380-384
turf grasses for sod....416
winter wheat....186-189,191-198
Pilea microphylla — artilleryweed
Pin cherry *Prunus pensylvanica:*
noncropland....477,485
Pine *Pinus* spp.:
brush control....437-439,441,442
noncropland....469-472,476,484-486
pastures/rangeland....461,466
Pineappleweed *Matricaria matricarioides:*
artichokes....292
asparagus....294,296
barley....213,214,217,218,220,222
carrots....302
conservation reserve program....443
cotton....174,181
est. lawns/turf....404,405
fallow land....448,449,451
field corn, popcorn....107,123
grasses for seed production....413
mint....245
noncropland....472,474,478,479,482,483
nuts....386,388,389,391
oats....224,227-229
ornamentals/woody plants....420,422,426,427
pastures/rangeland....461
rhubarb....333
rye....235
small fruits....356-358,360-362
spring wheat....201,202,205-207,209
sweet corn....339,340,345
tree fruits, citrus....364-368
tree fruits, deciduous....371-373,375-377
tree fruits, subtropical....380-383
winter wheat....188,189,192-194,196,197
Pinnate tansymustard *Descurainia pinnata:*
noncropland....480
Pinus contorta — lodgepole pine
Pinus banksiana — jack pine
Pinus spp. — pine
Pinus strobus — eastern white pine
Pinus taeda — loblolly pine
Pinus virginiana — Virginia pine
Pinyon pine:
conservation reserve program....446
noncropland....484
pastures/rangeland....466
Pistia stratiotes — waterlettuce, endive
Pithophora:
moving water....498,499
still water....495,496
Pitted morningglory *Ipomoea lacunosa:*
barley....220
cotton....173,174
cucurbits....307
field corn, popcorn....101,102,105,107,113,
....116,119-122
forage....458
oats....229
peanuts....249,251
rye....235
sorghum....261,267
soybeans....144-146,149-152,155-157,159-161,163
spring wheat....209
tobacco....281
winter wheat....196
Plains coreopsis *Coreopsis tinctoria:*
barley....211-213,217,221
conservation reserve program....446
fallow land....447,448
noncropland....470
pastures/rangeland....460,462,465
spring wheat....199-201,205,209
winter wheat....186-188,193,197
Plains pricklypear Opuntia polycantha:
conservation reserve program....446
pastures/rangeland....464,466
Planktonic algae:
moving water....497
still water....493,494
Plagiobothrys spp. — popcornflower
Plantago aristata — bracted plantain
Plantago lanceolata — buckhorn plantain
Plantago major — broadleaf plantain
Plantago rugelii — blackseed plantain
Plantago spp. — plantain
Plantago virginica — paleseed plantain
Plantain *Plantago* spp.:
barley....214,219,220
conservation reserve program....443
est. lawns/turf....400-403,405,406,410
fallow land....447,449
field corn, popcorn....107,108
grasses for seed production....412,414
noncropland....469,470-479,481-485
nuts....386,388,391
oats....224,228,229
ornamentals/woody plants....420,422,427
pastures/rangeland....461,464,466
rye....232,234,235
small fruits....357,359
sorghum....262
spring wheat....202,207,208
sugarcane....273
sweet corn....339,340
tree fruits, deciduous....372,373,377
turf grasses for sod....416
winter wheat....189,195,196
Platanus spp. — sycamore
Pluchea camphorata — stinkweed
Pluchea sericea — arrowwood
Plumeless thistle *Carduus acanthoides:*
conservation reserve program....444
fallow land....450
sugarcane....274
Plushgrass *Chloris radiata* (radiate fingergrass):
sugarcane....277
Poa annua — annual bluegrass
Poa bulbosa — bulbous bluegrass
Poa compressa — Canada bluegrass
Poa pratensis — Kentucky bluegrass
Poa spp. — bluegrass
Poa trivialis — roughstalk bluegrass
Poison hemlock *Conium maculatum:*
barley....219
noncropland....471,481,483,484

Weed Index

- oats ... 228
- pastures/rangeland ... 460
- rye ... 234
- spring wheat ... 207
- winter wheat ... 195

Poison ivy *Toxicodrendron radicans:*
- brush control ... 438,440-442
- est. lawns/turf ... 410
- field corn, popcorn ... 117
- noncropland ... 469-471,477,480,482,486
- ornamentals/woody plants ... 427
- pastures/rangeland ... 461,462,466

Poison oak *Toxicodendron pubescens:*
- brush control ... 438,440
- est. lawns/turf ... 410
- noncropland ... 469-471,484,485
- pastures/rangeland ... 461,466

Pokeweed *Phytolacca* spp.:
- barley ... 214
- est. lawns/turf ... 401
- field corn, popcorn ... 104,106,108,111,116
- grasses for seed production ... 412,413
- noncropland ... 469,471,476,477,482,484
- oats ... 224
- ornamentals/woody plants ... 421
- pastures/rangeland ... 461
- rye ... 232
- sorghum ... 262
- spring wheat ... 202
- sugarcane ... 273,275
- sweet corn ... 340
- winter wheat ... 189

Polemonium micranthum — annual polemonium

Polygonum amphibium — water smartweed

Polygonum argyrocoleon — silversheath knotweed

Polygonum aviculare — prostrate knotweed

Polygonum coccineum — swamp smartweed

Polygonum convolvulus — wild buckwheat

Polygonum hydropiper — marshpepper smartweed

Polygonum lapathifolium — pale smartweed (green smartweed)

Polygonum pensylvanicum — Pennsylvania smartweed (annual smartweed)

Polygonum persicaria — ladysthumb (spotted smartweed)

Polygonum sagittatum — arrowleaved tearthumb

Polygonum scandens — hedge smartweed

Polygonum spp. — knotweed, smartweed, tearthumb

Polypogon monspeliensis — rabbitfoot polypogon (rabbitfootgrass)

Polytrichum spp. — haircap moss

Ponderosa pine:
- brush control ... 440

Pondweed:
- moving water ... 498,499
- still water ... 493,495,496

Pontederia cordata — pickerelweed

Poorjoe *Diodia teres:*
- cotton ... 174
- field corn, popcorn ... 107,122
- noncropland ... 470,479
- pastures/rangeland ... 462
- peanuts ... 248
- soybeans ... 143,145
- sweet corn ... 339,340
- tobacco ... 282

Poplar *Populus* spp.:
- brush control ... 438-442
- noncropland ... 471,477,484-486
- ornamentals/woody plants ... 427
- pastures/rangeland ... 466

Popolo *Solanum americanum* (American black nightshade):
- tree fruits, subtropical ... 382

Populus deltoides — eastern cottonwood

Populus spp. — aspen, cottonwood, poplar

Populus tremuloides — quaking aspen

Portulaca oleracea — common purslane

Post oak *Quercus stellata:*
- brush control ... 438,439,441
- noncropland ... 472

Potamogeton amplifolius — largeleaf pondweed (bassweed)

Potamogeton crispus — curlyleaf pondweed

Potamogeton foliosus — leafy pondweed

Potamogeton illinoensis — Illinois pondweed

Potamogeton nodosus — American pondweed

Potamogeton pectinatus — sago pondweed

Potamogeton strictifolius — narrowleaf pondweed

Potentilla anserina — silverweed cinquefoil

Potentilla canadensis — common cinquefoil

Potentilla spp. — cinquefoil

Povertyweed:
- barley ... 214
- est. lawns/turf ... 401
- field corn, popcorn ... 108
- grasses for seed production ... 412
- noncropland ... 469,472
- oats ... 224
- pastures/rangeland ... 461,463
- rye ... 232
- sorghum ... 262
- spring wheat ... 202
- sugarcane ... 273
- sweet corn ... 340
- winter wheat ... 189

Prairie cordgrass *Spartina pectinata:*
- noncropland ... 476,477,482,484

Prairie cupgrass *Eriochloa contracta:*
- beans ... 299
- cotton ... 178
- fallow land ... 451
- field corn, popcorn ... 101,105,115,117
- garbanzos ... 311
- mung beans ... 246
- noncropland ... 474
- nuts ... 387
- ornamentals/woody plants ... 422,425
- peanuts ... 250
- potatoes ... 332
- safflower ... 259
- sorghum ... 261,266
- soybeans ... 153,163
- sweet corn ... 339,344
- tree fruits, citrus ... 365
- tree fruits, deciduous ... 373
- tree fruits, subtropical ... 381

Prairie threeawn *Aristida oligantha:*
- noncropland ... 476,477,482,484

Prickly coontail *Ceratophyllum dermersum* (coontail):
- noncropland ... 480

Prickly lettuce *Lactuca serriola:*
- artichokes ... 292,293
- asparagus ... 294,297
- barley ... 211-214,217,218,220-222
- carrots ... 302
- conservation reserve program ... 442,443,446,447
- cotton ... 174
- est. lawns/turf ... 405
- fallow land ... 447-449,451,452,454
- field corn, popcorn ... 107,112,122-124
- forage ... 456,458,459
- mint ... 245
- noncropland ... 470,474-476,480,482,484,487
- nuts ... 386,388,391,392
- oats ... 224,227-230
- oil seed crops ... 247
- ornamentals/woody plants ... 422,423,426,427
- pastures/rangeland ... 460-462,464-466
- rhubarb ... 333
- rye ... 235
- small fruits ... 356-359,361-363
- sorghum ... 267
- soybeans ... 145,147,161,162
- spring wheat ... 199-202,205-207,209,210
- sugarcane ... 274
- sweet corn ... 340,345
- tree fruits, citrus ... 364-366,368-370
- tree fruits, deciduous ... 371,373,374,376-379
- tree fruits, subtropical ... 380,381,383,384
- winter wheat ... 186-189,192-194,196-198

Prickly poppy *Argemone* spp.:
- barley ... 217
- fallow land ... 451
- spring wheat ... 205
- winter wheat ... 193

Prickly sida *Sida spinosa:*
- barley ... 220
- beans ... 298
- carrots ... 301
- castor beans ... 240
- conservation reserve program ... 446
- cotton ... 173-177,179-181
- cucurbits ... 307
- est. lawns/turf ... 408
- fallow land ... 451,452
- field corn, popcorn ... 101-107,110,111,113, 115-122,124
- flax ... 241
- forage ... 457,458
- noncropland ... 481,482,487
- nuts ... 387,388,391,392
- oats ... 226,229
- ornamentals/woody plants ... 419,421,423,424,427
- peanuts ... 248,249,252
- peas ... 324,325
- peppers ... 327
- potatoes ... 329,330,332
- rye ... 235
- safflower ... 258
- small fruits ... 259,362,363
- sorghum ... 260-263,265,267
- soybeans ... 143-161,163
- spring wheat ... 209
- sugar beets ... 270
- sugarcane ... 274
- sunflower ... 279
- sweet corn ... 337-340,343
- tobacco ... 281,282
- tomatoes ... 348
- tree fruits, citrus ... 365,366,368-370
- tree fruits, deciduous ... 374,377,379
- tree fruits, subtropical ... 381,384
- winter wheat ... 196

Prickly wild rose:
- brush control ... 440
- noncropland ... 477

Pricklypear cactus:
- conservation reserve program ... 446
- pastures/rangeland ... 464,466

Primrose *Primula* spp.:
- grasses for seed production ... 412
- noncropland ... 471,476,477,482,484
- ornamentals/woody plants ... 426

Primrose-willow *Ludwigia peruviana:*
- tree fruits, citrus ... 364

Primula spp. — primrose

Privet:
- brush control ... 440
- noncropland ... 477

Proboscidea louisianica — devilsclaw

Proso millet *Panicum miliaceum* (wild proso millet):
- barley ... 217
- field corn, popcorn ... 113
- potatoes ... 331
- spring wheat ... 205,210
- tomatoes ... 349
- winter wheat ... 192,198

Prosopis juliflora — mesquite

Prostrate knotweed *Polygonum aviculare:*
- artichokes ... 293
- asparagus ... 294
- barley ... 211-213,217,218,220-222
- conservation reserve program ... 443,446
- est. lawns/turf ... 400,405,411
- fallow land ... 447,448,451,454
- field corn, popcorn ... 107,111
- forage ... 455
- garlic ... 312
- grasses for seed production ... 411
- mint ... 244,245
- noncropland ... 468,474,481-484,487
- nuts ... 386,388,391,392
- oats ... 223,227-230
- oil seed crops ... 247
- onions ... 321
- ornamentals/woody plants ... 422,423,425,427
- pastures/rangeland ... 460,463,465
- rhubarb ... 333
- rye ... 231,235
- small fruits ... 357-359,362,363
- spring wheat ... 199-201,205-207,209,210
- sweet corn ... 339,340
- tree fruits, citrus ... 364-366,368-370
- tree fruits, deciduous ... 371,373,374,377,379
- tree fruits, subtropical ... 380,381,383,384
- turf grasses for sod ... 416
- winter wheat ... 186-188,192-194,196-198

Prostrate pigweed *Amaranthus blitoides:*
- asparagus ... 297
- barley ... 212,213,217,218,221
- beans ... 298,300,301
- carrots ... 303
- castor beans ... 240
- celery ... 305
- cole crops ... 307
- conservation reserve program ... 442,446
- cotton ... 174,176,182
- cucurbits ... 308,309
- eggplant ... 311
- fallow land ... 448,451
- field corn, popcorn ... 103,106,107,110,112,113,116, 118,121,125
- flax ... 240,242
- forage ... 455
- greens ... 315
- guar beans ... 243
- hops ... 243
- kenaf ... 244
- lettuce, endive ... 318,319
- mung beans ... 247
- noncropland ... 483
- nuts ... 387,391,392
- oats ... 227-229
- oil seed crops ... 248
- okra ... 320
- onions ... 322,323
- ornamentals/woody plants ... 421,423
- pastures/rangeland ... 465
- peanuts ... 248,252
- peas ... 326
- peppers ... 327
- potatoes ... 329,331,332
- radishes ... 333
- safflower ... 258,259
- small fruits ... 362,363
- sorghum ... 263,264,269
- southern peas ... 336
- soybeans ... 143,145,146,149,152,156,159,162
- spring wheat ... 199-201,205-207,209
- sugar beets ... 269,270,272
- sugarcane ... 274,278
- sunflower ... 279-281
- sweet corn ... 341
- tobacco ... 283
- tomatoes ... 348-350
- tree fruits, citrus ... 369,370
- tree fruits, deciduous ... 377,378
- tree fruits, subtropical ... 384
- winter wheat ... 186-188,193,194,197

Prostrate spurge *Euphorbia humistrata:*
- cotton ... 174
- cucurbits ... 307
- est. lawns/turf ... 400,403-405,408,411
- fallow land ... 451
- field corn, popcorn ... 106,107,110,111,115, 116,118-122
- forage ... 458
- noncropland ... 474,479,481,487
- nuts ... 388,391,392
- ornamentals/woody plants ... 419,422,423,425-427
- peanuts ... 248,251
- small fruits ... 358,359,362,363
- sorghum ... 263
- soybeans ... 143,145,146,150,155,159,163
- sugarcane ... 274
- sweet corn ... 339,340
- tobacco ... 281
- tree fruits, citrus ... 365,366,369,370
- tree fruits, deciduous ... 373,374,377,379
- tree fruits, subtropical ... 381,384

Prunella vulgaris — healall

Prunus americana — American plum (wild plum)
Prunus angustifolia — sand plum
Prunus pensylvanica — pin cherry
Prunus serotina — black cherry
Prunus spp. — cherry (wild cherry)
Pseudotsuga menziesii — Douglas-fir
Pteridium aquilinum — brackenfern, western brackenfern
Pualele *Sonchus oleraceus* (annual sowthistle):
- sugarcane ... 275
- tree fruits, subtropical ... 380,381

Pubescent wheatgrass *Agropyron tricophorum:*
- conservation reserve program ... 442
- pastures/rangeland ... 460

Pueraria lobata — kudzu
Puncturevine *Tribulus terrestris:*
- asparagus ... 296,297
- barley ... 212,213,214,219-221
- beans ... 301
- brush control ... 441,442
- carrots ... 303
- celery ... 305
- cole crops ... 307
- conservation reserve program ... 442,443,446,447
- cotton ... 174-176,178,179,181,182
- cucurbits ... 309
- eggplant ... 311
- est. lawns/turf ... 400,401,407
- fallow land ... 451,452,455
- field corn, popcorn .. 104-108,110,1125,115-121,125
- flax ... 240-242
- forage ... 455,458
- garlic ... 312
- grasses for seed production ... 411,412,414
- greens ... 315
- guar beans ... 243
- hops ... 243
- kenaf ... 244
- lettuce, endive ... 319
- mint ... 244
- mung beans ... 247
- noncropland ... 468,469,473,476,478,479, ... 481-483,486,487
- nuts ... 389-392
- oats ... 223,224,228,229
- oil seed crops ... 248
- okra ... 320
- onions ... 321-323
- ornamentals/woody plants ... 425,427
- pastures/rangeland ... 460,461,464-466
- peanuts ... 251,252
- peas ... 325
- peppers ... 327
- potatoes ... 332
- rye ... 231,232,234,235
- safflower ... 259
- small fruits ... 360,362,363
- sorghum ... 261-263,267,269
- southern peas ... 336
- soybeans ... 145,149,155,157,159,162,163
- spring wheat ... 200-202,207-209
- sugar beets ... 271,272
- sugarcane ... 273,278
- sunflower ... 281
- sweet corn ... 340,341
- tomatoes ... 350
- tree fruits, citrus ... 366,367,369,370
- tree fruits, deciduous ... 374,375,377-379
- tree fruits, subtropical ... 382,384
- turf grasses for sod ... 416
- winter wheat ... 187-189,195-197

Purple ammannia *Ammannia coccinea:*
- rice ... 254,255

Purple cudweed *Gnaphalium purpureum:*
- artichokes ... 292
- asparagus ... 294
- cole crops ... 305
- eggplant ... 309
- est. lawns/turf ... 410
- mint ... 245
- noncropland ... 479,482
- nuts ... 386,391
- ornamentals/woody plants ... 427
- peppers ... 327
- rhubarb ... 333
- small fruits ... 357,362
- sweet potatoes ... 345
- tobacco ... 281
- tree fruits, citrus ... 364,368
- tree fruits, deciduous ... 371,377
- tree fruits, subtropical ... 380,383

Purple deadnettle *Lamium purpureum:*
- est. lawns/turf ... 406
- ornamentals/woody plants ... 424

Purple foxtail:
- cotton ... 174
- cucurbits ... 307
- soybeans ... 146,149
- tobacco ... 281

Purple loosestrife *lythrum salicaria:*
- noncropland ... 476,482

Purple moonflower morningglory *Ipomoea turbinata:*
- cotton ... 173,174
- soybeans ... 145,150,151,161,163

Purple morningglory *Ipomoea turbinata* (purple moonflower):
- field corn, popcorn ... 105
- sorghum ... 261

Purple mustard *Chorispora tenella* (blue mustard):
- barley ... 211,213,218
- conservation reserve program ... 442
- fallow land ... 447,448,453
- grasses for seed production ... 411
- oats ... 223,228
- pastures/rangeland ... 460
- rye ... 231
- spring wheat ... 199,201,207
- turf grasses for sod ... 416
- winter wheat ... 186,188,192,194

Purple nutsedge *Cyperus rotundus:*
- beans ... 298
- conservation reserve program ... 446
- cotton ... 179
- est. lawns/turf ... 405,406,408
- field corn, popcorn ... 114,124
- forage ... 457
- noncropland ... 480,481,484
- ornamentals/woody plants ... 421,424
- peanuts ... 249,251
- potatoes ... 329
- safflower ... 258
- sorghum ... 265
- soybeans ... 145,154,156,160-162
- spinach ... 336
- sugar beets ... 270-272
- sunflower ... 279
- sweet corn ... 342
- tobacco ... 282,283
- tomatoes ... 347,350
- tree fruits, deciduous ... 375
- tree fruits, subtropical ... 382

Purple scabious:
- fallow land ... 447

Purple starthistle *Centaurea calcitrapa:*
- noncropland ... 480

Purplestem beggarticks *Bidens connata* (connate beggarticks):
- small fruits ... 357

Purpletop *Tridens flavus:*
- noncropland ... 476
- sugarcane ... 276

Purslane:
- artichokes ... 292
- asparagus ... 295,297
- barley ... 214,216-220
- beans ... 298,299,301
- brush control ... 441
- carrots ... 301-303
- celery ... 303-305
- cole crops ... 306,307
- conservation reserve program ... 445,447
- cotton ... 174-176,179-182
- cucurbits ... 307-309
- eggplant ... 310,311
- est. lawns/turf ... 401-403,406,408,410
- fallow land ... 455
- field corn, popcorn ... 101-103,105-108, ... 110-113,115-125
- flax ... 240-242
- forage ... 455,457
- garbanzos ... 312
- garlic ... 313,314
- grasses for seed production ... 412,414
- greens ... 315
- guar beans ... 243
- herbs/spices ... 316
- hops ... 243
- kenaf ... 244
- lawn/turf seedbeds ... 399
- lettuce, endive ... 318,319
- mint ... 245
- mung beans ... 247
- noncropland ... 469-472,474-478,481-484,486
- nuts ... 386,388,390-392
- oats ... 224,226-229
- oil seed crops ... 248
- okra ... 320
- onions ... 322,323
- ornamentals/woody plants ... 418-420,422,424-426
- pastures/rangeland ... 461,464,466
- peanuts ... 248,251,252
- peas ... 325
- peppers ... 327,328
- potatoes ... 329-332
- radishes ... 333
- rye ... 232,234,235
- safflower ... 259
- small fruits ... 357,358,360,362,363
- sorghum ... 260,262,264-269
- southern peas ... 335,336
- soybeans ... 143-147,149-151,153-159,161-163
- spring wheat ... 202,205-208,210
- sugar beets ... 269-272
- sugarcane ... 273-275,277,278
- sunflower ... 280,281
- sweet corn ... 337-340,343,344
- table beets ... 347
- tobacco ... 281-283
- tomatoes ... 347,349,350
- tree fruits, citrus ... 364,366,367,370
- tree fruits, deciduous ... 372,373,375,377-379
- tree fruits, subtropical ... 379,380,382
- turf grasses for sod ... 416,417
- winter wheat ... 189,192,193,195,196,198

Purslane speedwell *Veronica peregrina:*
- forage ... 459
- noncropland ... 482
- nuts ... 391
- ornamentals/woody plants ... 427
- small fruits ... 362
- tree fruits, citrus ... 368
- tree fruits, deciduous ... 377
- tree fruits, subtropical ... 383

Pusley:
- asparagus ... 297
- beans ... 301
- carrots ... 303
- celery ... 305
- cole crops ... 307
- conservation reserve program ... 447
- cotton ... 182
- cucurbits ... 309
- eggplant ... 311
- field corn, popcorn ... 125
- flax ... 240,242
- forage ... 455
- greens ... 315
- guar beans ... 243
- hops ... 243
- kenaf ... 244
- lettuce, endive ... 318,319
- mung beans ... 247
- nuts ... 392
- oil seed crops ... 248
- okra ... 320
- onions ... 323
- peanuts ... 252
- peppers ... 327
- potatoes ... 329,332
- radishes ... 333
- safflower ... 259
- small fruits ... 363
- sorghum ... 269
- southern peas ... 336
- soybeans ... 162
- sugar beets ... 272
- sugarcane ... 278
- sunflower ... 281
- tomatoes ... 350
- tree fruits, citrus ... 370
- tree fruits, deciduous ... 378

Pyrrhopappus spp. — falsedandelion

Q

Quackgrass *Elytrigia repens:*
- artichokes ... 292
- asparagus ... 295-297
- barley ... 218
- beans ... 298-300
- carrots ... 301,303
- celery ... 303,305
- cole crops ... 305,306
- conservation reserve program ... 447
- cotton ... 173,177,181
- cucurbits ... 308,309
- eggplant ... 310
- est. lawns/turf ... 406
- fallow land ... 448,451,453,454
- field corn, popcorn ... 101,104,106,112-114, ... 116,118,119,121,122,124
- flax ... 241
- forage ... 457,459
- garbanzos ... 311
- garlic ... 313,314
- grasses for seed production ... 414
- greens ... 314,315
- guar beans ... 242
- horseradish ... 316
- lentils ... 317
- lettuce, endive ... 318,319
- noncropland ... 468,473-477,479-482,484
- nuts ... 385-392
- oats ... 227
- oil seed crops ... 247
- okra ... 320
- onions ... 321,323
- ornamentals/woody plants ... 419,421,422,424,426
- peanuts ... 250
- peas ... 325
- peppers ... 327,328
- potatoes ... 329-332
- radishes ... 333
- rhubarb ... 334
- rice ... 255
- rye ... 233
- safflower ... 258
- small fruits ... 356-362
- sorghum ... 265
- southern peas ... 335
- soybeans ... 145,150-153,156-158,162
- spinach ... 336,337
- spring wheat ... 206
- sugar beets ... 269-271
- sunflower ... 279,280
- sweet corn ... 342,343
- sweet potatoes ... 346
- table beets ... 346,347
- tobacco ... 282
- tomatoes ... 348,349
- tree fruits, citrus ... 363,365-370
- tree fruits, deciduous ... 371-376,378
- tree fruits, subtropical ... 379,381-384
- turf grasses for sod ... 417
- winter wheat ... 193,194

Quaking aspen *Populus tremuloides* (trembling aspen):
- brush control ... 440
- noncropland ... 477

Queen Anne's lace *Daucus carota* (wild carrot):
- brush control ... 441
- noncropland ... 481,486
- pastures/rangeland ... 466

Quercus alba — white oak
Quercus chrysolepis — canyon live oak

Weed Index

Quercus havardii — shinnery oak (sand shinnery oak)
Quercus laevis — turkey oak
Quercus marilandica — blackjack oak
Quercus nigra — water oak
Quercus rubra — northern red oak (red oak)
Quercus spp. — oak
Quercus stellata — post oak
Quercus velutina — beach oak

R

Rabbit tobacco *Gnaphalium obtusifolium* (fragrant cudweed):
grasses for seed production ... 413
ornamentals/woody plants ... 421
Rabbitbrush *Chrysothamnus* spp.:
brush control ... 436,438
noncropland ... 484
Rabbitfootgrass *Polypogon monspeliensis:*
(rabbitfoot polypogon):
cotton ... 174
Ragweed *Ambrosia* spp.:
asparagus ... 294,295,297
barley ... 214,216,219-221
brush control ... 441
carrots ... 302
celery ... 303,304
conservation reserve program ... 446,447
cotton ... 175,176,178-181
est. lawns/turf ... 401-403,406,407,410
field corn, popcorn ... 102,103,107,108,111,112,123
flax ... 241
forage ... 458
grasses for seed production ... 412,414
herbs/spices ... 316
mint ... 245
noncropland ... 468,470-476,478-486
nuts ... 386-391
oats ... 224,226,228,229
ornamentals/woody plants ... 419-422,426,427
pastures/rangeland ... 461,463-466
peas ... 325
potatoes ... 331
rye ... 232,234,235
small fruits ... 356-359,361,362
sorghum ... 260,262,264,266,268
soybeans ... 150
spring wheat ... 202,204,207-210
sugar beets ... 270,271
sugarcane ... 273,275,276
sweet corn ... 338-340,342,345
table beets ... 347
tobacco ... 283
tree fruits, citrus ... 364,366-368
tree fruits, deciduous ... 372-374,376,377,379
tree fruits, subtropical ... 380,383
turf grasses for sod ... 416,417
winter wheat ... 189,191,192,195-198
Ranunculus abortivus — smallflower buttercup
Ranunculus acris — tall buttercup
Ranunculus muricatus — roughseed buttercup (spinyfruited crowfoot)
Ranunculus repens — creeping buttercup
Ranunculus sardous — hairy buttercup
Ranunculus spp. — buttercup
Ranunculus testiculatus — bur buttercup
Raoulgrass *Rottboellia cochinchineosis* (itchgrass):
sugarcane ... 272,276
Raphanus raphanistrum — wild radish
Raphanus sativus — radish
Raspberry *Rubus* spp.:
brush control ... 438,441,442
noncropland ... 468,471,486
pastures/rangeland ... 466
Ratibida columnifera — upright prairie coneflower
Rattail fescue *Vulpia myuros:*
artichokes ... 292
asparagus ... 295
barley ... 216
cotton ... 175
field corn, popcorn ... 111,117,123
forage ... 456
grasses for seed production ... 413,415
mint ... 245
noncropland ... 482
nuts ... 391
oats ... 226
ornamentals/woody plants ... 426,427
small fruits ... 362
soybeans ... 153
sugarcane ... 275
sweet corn ... 343,345
tree fruits, citrus ... 368
tree fruits, deciduous ... 372,377
tree fruits, subtropical ... 383
turf grasses for sod ... 417
winter wheat ... 192
Rattlebox *Crotalaria sagittalis:*
sugarcane ... 275
tree fruits, subtropical ... 380,381
Rattlepod *Crotalaria sagittalis* (rattlebox):
sugarcane ... 277
Rattlesnakegrass *Glyceria canadensis:*
small fruits ... 357
Red alder *Alnus rubra:*
brush control ... 440
noncropland ... 477
Red brome *Bromus rubens* (foxtail brome):
noncropland ... 480
Red cedar:
brush control ... 440
noncropland ... 475
pastures/rangeland ... 464
Red clover *Trifolium pratense:*
barley ... 214
conservation reserve program ... 443,447
est. lawns/turf ... 401-403,406,407
fallow land ... 449,454
field corn, popcorn ... 112,114,115,118,124
noncropland ... 483,484
oats ... 224
ornamentals/woody plants ... 423
pastures/rangeland ... 461
soybeans ... 147,162
spring wheat ... 202
sweet corn ... 342
winter wheat ... 189
Red deadnettle *Lamium purpureum* (purple deadnettle):
noncropland ... 472
nuts ... 386
ornamentals/woody plants ... 420
tree fruits, deciduous ... 372
Red elder *Sambucus pubens michx* (redberried elder):
brush control ... 438
noncropland ... 471
Red fescue *Festuca rubra:*
noncropland ... 480
Red maple *Acer rubrum:*
brush control ... 439,440
noncropland ... 472,477,485
Red morningglory *Ipomoea coccinea:*
soybeans ... 150
Red oak *Quercus rubra* (northern red oak):
brush control ... 439
noncropland ... 472,477
Red orach *Atriplex rosea:*
mint ... 245
ornamentals/woody plants ... 423
Red pine:
brush control ... 440
Red rice *Oryza sativa* (rice):
asparagus ... 295,297
beans ... 299
carrots ... 301
conservation reserve program ... 447
cotton ... 173,174,177,178,181
cucurbits ... 307
fallow land ... 448,451,454
field corn, popcorn ... 101,106,107,110,113, 115-119,121,122,124
flax ... 241
forage ... 458,459
garbanzos ... 311
garlic ... 313
hops ... 243
lettuce, endive ... 318
mint ... 246
mung beans ... 246
noncropland ... 468,474,485
nuts ... 385,387,392
onions ... 321
ornamentals/woody plants ... 418,419,422,425
peanuts ... 250,251
peas ... 325
peppers ... 327
potatoes ... 330,332
rhubarb ... 334
rice ... 254,256
safflower ... 259
small fruits ... 356,358,361,362
sorghum ... 261,262,264-266
southern peas ... 335,336
soybeans ... 145,146,149-156,158,162,163
sugar beets ... 269
sweet corn ... 337,339,341,344
sweet potatoes ... 346
table beets ... 346
tobacco ... 281,282
tree fruits, citrus ... 363,365,369
tree fruits, deciduous ... 371,373,378
tree fruits, subtropical ... 379,381,384
Red sandspurry *Caryophyllaceae spergularia rubra:*
ornamentals/woody plants ... 423
Red sorrel *Rumex acetosella:*
asparagus ... 296,297
barley ... 214
conservation reserve program ... 443
est. lawns/turf ... 400,402,403,406
fallow land ... 449
forage ... 457
grasses for seed production ... 413,414
noncropland ... 470
nuts ... 391
oats ... 224
ornamentals/woody plants ... 423,424
pastures/rangeland ... 461,462
rhubarb ... 334
small fruits ... 357,359,360
spring wheat ... 202
tree fruits, deciduous ... 374
winter wheat ... 189
Red sprangletop *Leptochloa filiformis:*
artichokes ... 292
asparagus ... 294
barley ... 216
beans ... 300
carrots ... 303
celery ... 305
cole crops ... 306
cotton ... 173,175,181
cucurbits ... 309
eggplant ... 310
fallow land ... 448,453
field corn, popcorn ... 101,106,111,113, 115,116,121,122,124
flax ... 241
forage ... 456,459
garlic ... 313,314
grasses for seed production ... 413
greens ... 315
lettuce, endive ... 319
mint ... 245,246
noncropland ... 468,481,482,487
nuts ... 385,386,390-392
oats ... 226
oil seed crops ... 247
onions ... 321,323
ornamentals/woody plants ... 419,425,427
peanuts ... 251
peas ... 326
peppers ... 328
potatoes ... 332
rhubarb ... 333
small fruits ... 356,357,361-363
sorghum ... 262,265
southern peas ... 335
soybeans ... 145-147,150,153,157,158
spinach ... 337
sugar beets ... 269,271
sugarcane ... 275
sunflower ... 280
sweet corn ... 339
table beets ... 346
tobacco ... 282
tomatoes ... 350
tree fruits, citrus ... 363,364,367-370
tree fruits, deciduous ... 371,372,375-377,379
tree fruits, subtropical ... 379,380,383,384
winter wheat ... 192
Redmaids rockpurslane *Calandrinia ciliata* (desert rockpurslane):
artichokes ... 292
barley ... 213,217,218,222
beans ... 300
cotton ... 181
est. lawns/turf ... 405
fallow land ... 448,452,454
field corn, popcorn ... 123
forage ... 455,458
lettuce, endive ... 318
noncropland ... 474,479
nuts ... 388,391
oats ... 228,230
oil seed crops ... 247
ornamentals/woody plants ... 422,423,426,427
peanuts ... 252
peas ... 326
small fruits ... 358,359,361,362
soybeans ... 159
spring wheat ... 201,205,207,210
sunflower ... 280
sweet corn ... 345
tree fruits, citrus ... 365,366,368,369
tree fruits, deciduous ... 373-377
tree fruits, subtropical ... 381-384
winter wheat ... 188,192,194,198
Redroot pigweed *Amaranthus retroflexus:*
artichokes ... 292,293
asparagus ... 294,296,297
barley ... 211-214,216-218,220-222
beans ... 298,300,301
carrots ... 302,303
castor beans ... 240
celery ... 304,305
cole crops ... 305-307
conservation reserve program ... 442-444,446
cotton ... 173,174,176,177,182
cucurbits ... 307-309
eggplant ... 309-311
est. lawns/turf ... 400,408
fallow land ... 447-454
field corn, popcorn ... 101-107,110-116,118-125
flax ... 240-242
forage ... 455,456,458,460
garlic ... 312,314
grasses for seed production ... 411
greens ... 315
guar beans ... 243
hops ... 243
horseradish ... 316
kenaf ... 244
lettuce, endive ... 318,319
mint ... 244,245
mung beans ... 247
noncropland ... 468-470,472,474,483,484
nuts ... 386-389,391,392
oats ... 223,224,226-230
oil seed crops ... 247,248
okra ... 320
onions ... 321-323
ornamentals/woody plants ... 418,420-423
pastures/rangeland ... 460,461,462,465
peanuts ... 248,251,252
peas ... 325,326
peppers ... 327,328
potatoes ... 329,331,332
radishes ... 333
rice ... 253
rye ... 231,235
safflower ... 258,259
small fruits ... 356,357,359,360,362,363
sorghum ... 261,263-265,267-269
southern peas ... 336
soybeans ... 143-147,149-152,155-163

spinach 336
spring wheat 199-202,204-207,209,210
sugar beets 269-272
sugarcane 274,278
sunflower 279-281
sweet corn 341-343
sweet potatoes 345
tobacco 281-283
tomatoes 348-350
tree fruits, citrus 364,366,367,369,370
tree fruits, deciduous 371-375,377,378
tree fruits, subtropical 380-382,384
turf grasses for sod 416
winter wheat 186-189,191-194,196-198
Redstem *Ammannia auriculata:*
peas 325
rice 253-256,258
Redstem filaree *Erodium cicutarium:*
artichokes 292
asparagus 294,296
barley 217,218,222
est. lawns/turf 405
fallow land 451,452
mint 245
noncropland 474,480,482,487
nuts 386,388,389,391,392
oats 227
oil seed crops 247
ornamentals/woody plants 422,423,427
potatoes 331
radishes 333
small fruits 357-360,362,363
spring wheat 199,205,206
tomatoes 349
tree fruits, citrus 364-370
tree fruits, deciduous 371,373-375,377,379
tree fruits, subtropical 380-384
winter wheat 186,193,197
Redtop *Agrostis alba:*
conservation reserve program 442
pastures/rangeland 460
Redtop *Agrostis gigantea:*
noncropland 476
Redtop grass:
small fruits 360
Redvine *Brunnichia ovata:*
brush control 441,442
conservation reserve program 444,447
cotton 174
cucurbits 307
fallow land 450,454
noncropland 470,477,482,484,486
pastures/rangeland 462,466
peanuts 248
soybeans 143,146,147,152,162
tobacco 281
Redweed *Melochia corchorifolia:*
cotton 174,181
cucurbits 307
est. lawns/turf 408,410
field corn, popcorn 121
ornamentals/woody plants 419
peanuts 252
rice 253,257,258
soybeans 144,146,147,150,151,153,157-160,163
tobacco 281
Reed canarygrass *Phalaris arundinacea:*
field corn, popcorn 114,124
moving water 499
noncropland 476,480,482,485
still water 496
sweet corn 342
Rescuegrass *Bromus catharticus:*
beans 298
castor beans 240
cotton 176
est. lawns/turf 400,404
field corn, popcorn 112
forage 457,458
nuts 387
ornamentals/woody plants 421
potatoes 329
safflower 258
sugar beets 270
sunflower 279
sweet corn 342
tomatoes 348
tree fruits, citrus 365
Rhamnus spp. — coffeeberry
Rhus spp. — sumac
Rhynchelytrum repens — natalgrass
Rhynchospora corniculata — horned beakrush (spearhead)
Ribes spp. — gooseberry (currant)
Rice cutgrass *Leersia oryzoides:*
small fruits 357,360
Rice flatsedge *Cyperus iria:*
beans 298
est. lawns/turf 406
field corn, popcorn 110,113,118
ornamentals/woody plants 424
peanuts 249
rice 254,255,258
sorghum 264
soybeans 149,151
sweet corn 341,342
Ricegrass *Oryzopsis* spp.:
grasses for seed production 413
noncropland 482
sugarcane 277
Richardia scabra — Florida pusley (Florida purslane)
Richardia spp. — Mexican clover
Richardsonium:
tree fruits, subtropical 382
Ricinus communis — castorbean
Ripgut brome *Bromus diandrus:*
artichokes 292
asparagus 294
grasses for seed production 413
mint 245
noncropland 480
nuts 386
rhubarb 333
small fruits 356,357
tree fruits, citrus 364,369
tree fruits, deciduous 371
tree fruits, subtropical 380
winter wheat 194
River bulrush *Scirpus fluviatilis:*
rice 253
Robinia pseudoacacia — black locust
Robinia spp. — locust
Robust foxtail *Setaria viridis:*
asparagus 297
beans 301
carrots 303
celery 305
cole crops 307
conservation reserve program 447
cotton 174,182
cucurbits 307,309
eggplant 311
field corn, popcorn 101,124,125
flax 240,242
forage 455
greens 315
guar beans 243
hops 243
kenaf 244
lettuce, endive 318,319
mung beans 247
nuts 391,392
oil seed crops 248
okra 320
onions 323
peanuts 252
peas 324
peppers 327
potatoes 329,332
radishes 333
safflower 259
small fruits 362,363
sorghum 269
southern peas 336
soybeans 146,149,159,162,163
sugar beets 272
sugarcane 278
sunflower 281
tobacco 281
tomatoes 350
tree fruits, citrus 369,370
tree fruits, deciduous 377,378
tree fruits, subtropical 384
Robust purple foxtail *Setaria viridis v. robusta-purpurea:*
field corn, popcorn 103,112,113,116,119,120
flax 241
forage 458
ornamentals/woody plants 418
peanuts 251
soybeans 150,155
Robust white foxtail *Setaria viridis v. robusta-alba:*
field corn, popcorn 103,112,113,116,119,120
flax 241
forage 458
ornamentals/woody plants 418
peanuts 251
soybeans 150,155
Rosa bracteata — Macartney rose
Rosa laevigata — Cherokee rose
Rosa multiflora — multiflora rose
Rosa spp.— rose (wild rose)
Rosarypea *Abrus precatorius* (precatory bean):
noncropland 472
nuts 386
ornamentals/woody plants 420
tree fruits, deciduous 372
Rottboellia cochinchinensis — itchgrass (raoulgrass)
Rough fleabane *erigeron strigosus:*
barley 212
spring wheat 200
winter wheat 187
Rough pigweed:
asparagus 297
barley 216
beans 301
carrots 303
celery 305
cole crops 307
conservation reserve program 444
cotton 182
cucurbits 309
eggplant 311
fallow land 450,451
field corn, popcorn 106,110,118,125
flax 240,242
forage 455
greens 315
guar beans 243
hops 243
kenaf 244
lettuce, endive 318,319
mung beans 247
nuts 391,392
oats 226
oil seed crops 248
okra 320
onions 323
peanuts 252
peppers 327
potatoes 329,332
radishes 333
safflower 259
small fruits 362,363
sorghum 263,269
southern peas 336
soybeans 146,162
spring wheat 204
sugar beets 272
sugarcane 278
sunflower 281
tomatoes 350
tree fruits, citrus 369,370
tree fruits, deciduous 377,378
tree fruits, subtropical 384
winter wheat 191
Roughseed bulrush *Scirpus mucronatus* (ricefield bulrush):
rice 254,255
Roughstalk bluegrass *Poa trivialis:*
barley 212
grasses for seed production 414
noncropland 474,480
spring wheat 200
winter wheat 187
Roundleaf mallow:
est. lawns/turf 401
Royal fern *Osmunda regalis:*
small fruits 357
Rubber rabbitbrush:
noncropland 477
Rubus spectabilis — salmonberry
Rubus spp. — blackberry (wild blackberry), brambles, dewberry, raspberry, thimbleberry
Rubus trivialis — southern dewberry
Rudbeckia hirta v. pulcherrima — blackeyedsusan
Rumex acetosa — green sorrel (sorrel)
Rumex acetosella — red sorrel
Rumex crispus — curly dock
Rumex obtusifolius — broadleaf dock (bitterdock)
Rumex spp. — dock, sour dock
Rush *Juncus* spp.:
est. lawns/turf 401
grasses for seed production 412
noncropland 469,481
small fruits 357
Rush skeletonweed *Chondrilla juncea:*
conservation reserve program 446
noncropland 476,482,484
pastures/rangeland 466
Russian knapweed *Centaurea repens:*
barley 214
brush control 441
conservation reserve program 443,444
fallow land 449
grasses for seed production 412,413
noncropland 468,470,472,476,481-483,486
nuts 386
oats 224
ornamentals/woody plants 420
pastures/rangeland 461-463,466
small fruits 357
spring wheat 202
sugar beets 270
sugarcane 275
tree fruits, deciduous 372
winter wheat 189
Russian olive *Elaeagnus angustifolia:*
brush control 438,440-442
noncropland 469,477,486
pastures/rangeland 461,466
Russian thistle *Salsola iberica:*
artichokes 293
asparagus 294,296,297
barley 211-214,216-218,220-222
beans 300,301
carrots 303
celery 305
cole crops 307
conservation reserve program 442-444,446,447
cotton 173,179,182
cucurbits 309
eggplant 311
est. lawns/turf 400,401
fallow land 447-454
field corn, popcorn 104,106-108,110-113, 115-118,120-125
flax 240-242
forage 455-457
garlic 312
grasses for seed production 411,412,414
greens 315
guar beans 243
hops 243
kenaf 244
lettuce, endive 319
mint 244,245
mung beans 247
noncropland 468,469,472-474,478-480,482,484
nuts 386,388,389,391,392
oats 223,224,226-230
oil seed crops 248
okra 320

onions ... 321,323
ornamentals/woody plants ... 420-423,426,427
pastures/rangeland ... 460,461,463-465
peanuts ... 252
peas ... 326
peppers ... 327
potatoes ... 329,331,332
radishes ... 333
rye ... 231,232,234,235
safflower ... 259
small fruits ... 359-363
sorghum ... 262,263,267,269
southern peas ... 336
soybeans ... 144,146,152,154,155,158,159,162,163

S

Sagattaria sagittifolia — arrowhead
Sage:
noncropland ... 440
Sagebrush *Artemisia* spp.:
brush control ... 436-438,441,442
noncropland ... 471,486
pastures/rangeland ... 466
Sagewort *Artemisia* spp.:
noncropland ... 467
Sagina spp. — pearlwort
Salix spp. — willow
Salmonberry *Rubus spectabilis:*
brush control ... 438-440
noncropland ... 471,477
Salsify *Tragopogon* spp.:
forage ... 459
Salsola iberica — Russian thistle
Saltbush *Atriplex* spp.:
brush control ... 440
noncropland ... 476,482
pastures/rangeland ... 466
Saltcedar *Tamarix ramosissima:*
brush control ... 439,440
noncropland ... 472,477
pastures/rangeland ... 463
Saltgrass *Distichlis spicata:*
noncropland ... 476,478,482
Salvia aethiopis — Mediterranean sage
Salvia reflexa — lanceleaf sage
Salvinia:
moving water ... 498
still water ... 495
Sambucus canadensis — American elder
Sambucus pubens — redberried elder (red elder)
Sambucus spp. — elder (elderberry)
Sand dropseed *Sporobolus cryptandrus:*
noncropland ... 476,477,482,484
Sand plum *Prunus angustifolia:*
noncropland ... 472
pastures/rangeland ... 463
Sand sage *Artemisia filifolia* (sand sagebrush):
brush control ... 437,439
noncropland ... 472
Sand sagebrush:
brush control ... 438
noncropland ... 471
Sand shinnery oak *Quercus havardii* (shinnery oak):
brush control ... 436,438,439,441
noncropland ... 472
pastures/rangeland ... 466
Sand vetch *Vicia acutifolia:*
noncropland ... 480
Sandbur *Cenchrus* spp.:
artichokes ... 292
asparagus ... 294,297
beans ... 298,299,301
carrots ... 302,303
celery ... 304,305
cole crops ... 307
conservation reserve program ... 447
cotton ... 175,176,178-182
cucurbits ... 308,309
eggplant ... 311
est. lawns/turf ... 399,404,407,410
fallow land ... 455
field corn, popcorn ... 102,104-106,113,116-118,125
flax ... 240-242
forage ... 455,457,459
garbanzos ... 311
grasses for seed production ... 413,414
greens ... 315
guar beans ... 243
herbs/spices ... 316
hops ... 243
kenaf ... 244
lettuce, endive ... 318,319
mint ... 245
mung beans ... 246,247
noncropland ... 473,474,476-479,481,482,484
nuts ... 386,388,389,391,392
oil seed crops ... 248
okra ... 320
onions ... 323
ornamentals/woody plants ... 421,422,425
peanuts ... 248-250,252
peas ... 325
peppers ... 327
potatoes ... 329,330,332
radishes ... 333
safflower ... 259
small fruits ... 357,363
sorghum ... 260-262,264-266,269
southern peas ... 335,336
soybeans ... 143,144,146,150,153,162,163
sugar beets ... 272
sugarcane ... 276,278
sunflower ... 281
sweet corn ... 337,339,341,344
tomatoes ... 350
tree fruits, citrus ... 364,366,367,370
tree fruits, deciduous ... 371,373-375,377,378
tree fruits, subtropical ... 380,382
turf grasses for sod ... 415,417
Sandspur *Cenchrus* spp. (sandbur):
noncropland ... 478
Sapium sebiferum — Chinese tallowtree
Saponaria officinalis — bouncingbet
Sarcostemma cyanchoides — climbing milkweed
Sassafras *Sassafras albidum:*
brush control ... 438-442
noncropland ... 469,471,472,477,484,485,486
ornamentals/woody plants ... 427
pastures/rangeland ... 461,466
Sassafras albidum — sassafras
Scarlet morningglory *Ipomoea coccinea:*
soybeans ... 163
Scarlet pimpernel *Anagallis arvensis:*
noncropland ... 482
nuts ... 391
ornamentals/woody plants ... 423,427
small fruits ... 362
tree fruits, citrus ... 368
tree fruits, deciduous ... 377
tree fruits, subtropical ... 379,383
Scentless chamomile *Matricaria perforata:*
barley ... 213,214,218,222
conservation reserve program ... 443
fallow land ... 448,449,454
oats ... 224,228,230
pastures/rangeland ... 461
spring wheat ... 201,202,207,210
winter wheat ... 188,189,194,198
Schinus:
brush control ... 441
Schinus terebinthifolius — Brazilian peppertree (Brazil peppertree)
Scirpus cyperinus — woolgrass bulrush (woolgrass)
Scirpus fluviatilis — river bulrush
Scirpus mucronatus — ricefield bulrush (roughseed bulrush)
Scirpus spp. — bulrush, tules
Scleranthus annuus — knawel (German moss)
Scotch broom *Cytisus scoparius:*
brush control ... 440
conservation reserve program ... 446
noncropland ... 469,485
pastures/rangeland ... 461
Scotch thistle *Onopordum acanthium:*
noncropland ... 483
Scouringrush *Equisetum hyemale:*
noncropland ... 473,483
Sea myrtle *Baccharis halimifolia* (groundsel baccharis):
brush control ... 440
tree fruits, citrus ... 364
Seashore saltgrass *Distichlis spicata:*
noncropland ... 480
Seaside heliotrope *Heliotropium curassavicum:*
noncropland ... 480
Secale cereale — common rye
Secale spp. — rye
Sedge *Carex* spp.:
conservation reserve program ... 446
noncropland ... 481
Senecio aureus — golden ragwort
Senecio glabellus — cressleaf groundsel
Senecio jacobaea — tansy ragwort, yellowtop mustard
Senecio spp. — groundsel
Senecio vulgaris — common groundsel
Sensitive fern *Onoclea sensibilis:*
small fruits ... 357
Sercia lespedeza:
fallow land ... 447
Serviceberry *Amelanchier* spp.:
brush control ... 438,441,442
noncropland ... 471,472,480,486
pastures/rangeland ... 466
Sesbania:
cotton ... 175,176
field corn, popcorn ... 104,111,117
noncropland ... 482
oats ... 226
ornamentals/woody plants ... 419
potatoes ... 332
rice ... 257
soybeans ... 144,146,147,153,158,163
sweet corn ... 343
Sesbania exaltata — hemp sesbania (coffeebean)
Setaria faberi — giant foxtail
Setaria glauca — yellow foxtail (pigeongrass)
Setaria italica — foxtail millet (German millet)
Setaria spp. — foxtail (bristlegrass)
Setaria verticillata — bristly foxtail
Setaria viridis — green foxtail (bottlegrass foxtail, giant green foxtail, robust foxtail, robust purple foxtail, robust white foxtail)
Setaria viridis v. robusta-alba — robust white foxtail
Setaria viridis v. robusta-purpurea — robust purple foxtail
Sharppod morningglory *Ipomoea trichocarpa:*
cotton ... 173
Shattercane *Sorghum bicolor:*
artichokes ... 293
asparagus ... 295-297
barley ... 218
beans ... 298-301
carrots ... 301,303
castor beans ... 240
celery ... 305
cole crops ... 306,307
conservation reserve program ... 446,447
cotton ... 173,174,176-178,181,182
cucurbits ... 307,309
eggplant ... 310,311
fallow land ... 448,451,453-455
field corn, popcorn ... 101-107,111-114,116-125
flax ... 240-242
forage ... 457-459
garbanzos ... 311
garlic ... 313,314
greens ... 315
guar beans ... 243
hops ... 243
kenaf ... 244
lentils ... 317
lettuce, endive ... 318,319
mung beans ... 246,247
noncropland ... 468,474,481,482,485
nuts ... 385,387,388,390,392
oats ... 227
oil seed crops ... 247,248
okra ... 320
onions ... 321,323
ornamentals/woody plants ... 419,421,422,425
peanuts ... 248,250-252
peas ... 325,326
peppers ... 327,328
potatoes ... 329,330,332
rhubarb ... 333,334
safflower ... 258,259
small fruits ... 356,358,361-363
sorghum ... 260-262,264,266,267,269
southern peas ... 335
soybeans ... 143-146,150-159,161-164
spinach ... 337
spring wheat ... 206
sugar beets ... 269-272
sugarcane ... 278
sunflower ... 279-281
sweet corn ... 337,339,341-344
sweet potatoes ... 345,346
table beets ... 346
tobacco ... 281,282
tomatoes ... 348,350
tree fruits, citrus ... 363,365,368-370
tree fruits, deciduous ... 371,373,376,378
tree fruits, subtropical ... 379,381,383,384
winter wheat ... 194
Sheep fescue *Festuca ovina:*
conservation reserve program ... 442
pastures/rangeland ... 460
Sheep sorrel *Rumex acetosella* (red sorrel):
brush control ... 441
est. lawns/turf ... 401,403,410
grasses for seed production ... 413
noncropland ... 470,472,486
nuts ... 391
pastures/rangeland ... 466
tree fruits, deciduous ... 377
Shepherdspurse *Capsella bursa-pastoris:*
artichokes ... 292,293
asparagus ... 296,297
barley ... 211-214,216-222
beans ... 298
carrots ... 302
conservation reserve program ... 442,443,446,447
cotton ... 174,175,181
cucurbits ... 307
est. lawns/turf ... 400,401,404-406,410
fallow land ... 447-449,451,452,454
field corn, popcorn ... 103,107,108,111-116, 120,121,123,124
flax ... 240,241
forage ... 455-459
garlic ... 312
grasses for seed production ... 412-414
horseradish ... 316
lettuce, endive ... 318
mint ... 244,245
noncropland ... 469,470,472,474,478-484,487
nuts ... 386,388-392
oats ... 223,224,226-230
oil seed crops ... 247
onions ... 321,322
ornamentals/woody plants ... 418-427
pastures/rangeland ... 460,461,464,465
peas ... 324,325
potatoes ... 331,332
rye ... 231,232,234,235
small fruits ... 357-363
sorghum ... 262,266,267
soybeans ... 144,147,151-153,155,157,158,161-163
spinach ... 336
spring wheat ... 199-202,204-210
sugar beets ... 269-272
sugarcane ... 273-275
sweet corn ... 337,339-343,345
table beets ... 347
tobacco ... 283
tomatoes ... 347,349,350
tree fruits, citrus ... 364-370
tree fruits, deciduous ... 372-379
tree fruits, subtropical ... 381-384
turf grasses for sod ... 416
winter wheat ... 186-189,191-198

Shinnery oak *Quercus havardii:*
brush control ... 437
noncropland ... 471
Short wiregrass:
small fruits ... 357
Showy crotalaria *Crotalaria spectabilis:*
cotton ... 174
peanuts ... 248
soybeans ... 143,145,150,161,163
Sibara *Sibara virginica:*
est. lawns/turf ... 405
noncropland ... 474,482
nuts ... 388,391
ornamentals/woody plants ... 422,427
small fruits ... 358,362
tree fruits, citrus ... 365,368
tree fruits, deciduous ... 373,377
tree fruits, subtropical ... 381,383
Sibara virginica — sibara
Siberian elm *Ulmus pumila:*
noncropland ... 472
pastures/rangeland ... 463
Sicklepod *Cassia obtusifolia:*
barley ... 214,220
beans ... 298
carrots ... 301
castor beans ... 240
conservation reserve program ... 443,446,447
cotton ... 175,176,178,179,181
fallow land ... 449,451,454
field corn, popcorn ... 101,102,104-107,110-122,124
flax ... 241
forage ... 457
noncropland ... 479,481,482,484
nuts ... 387,389,391
oats ... 224,226,229
ornamentals/woody plants ... 421,424
pastures/rangeland ... 461
peanuts ... 248,249
potatoes ... 329-332
rye ... 235
safflower ... 258
small fruits ... 362
sorghum ... 260-263,267
soybeans ... 143-145,148-155,157-163
spring wheat ... 202,209
sugar beets ... 270
sunflower ... 279
sweet corn ... 337-339,341-343
tomatoes ... 348
tree fruits, citrus ... 365,367,369
tree fruits, deciduous ... 374,378
tree fruits, subtropical ... 384
turf grasses for sod ... 416
winter wheat ... 189,196
Sicyos angulatus — burcucumber
Sida hederacea — dollarweed
Sida spinosa — prickly sida (spiny sida)
Sideoats grama *Bouteloua curtipendula*:
conservation reserve program ... 442
pastures/rangeland ... 460
Signalgrass *Brachiaria* spp.:
beans ... 298,299
carrots ... 302
castor beans ... 240
celery ... 304
conservation reserve program ... 445
cotton ... 176,178-181
field corn, popcorn ... 105,112,117,118,123
forage ... 457
garbanzos ... 311,312
garlic ... 313
herbs/spices ... 316
hops ... 243
mung beans ... 246
noncropland ... 474,480,481,487
nuts ... 387,390-392
onions ... 322
ornamentals/woody plants ... 421,425-427
peanuts ... 250,251
peas ... 325
potatoes ... 329-331
rice ... 257
safflower ... 258,259
small fruits ... 362,363
sorghum ... 261,266,267
southern peas ... 335
soybeans ... 144,153,154,157
sugar beets ... 270
sugarcane ... 276,277
sunflower ... 279,280
sweet corn ... 339,342,344,345
tobacco ... 282
tomatoes ... 348
tree fruits, citrus ... 365,367,369,370
tree fruits, deciduous ... 375,377,379
tree fruits, subtropical ... 384
Silene alba — white campion (white cockle)
Silene conica — sand catchfly (conical catchfly)
Silene gallica — English catchfly
Silene noctiflora — nightflowering catchfly
Silver crabgrass *Eleusine indica* (goosegrass):
est. lawns/turf ... 404,405
grasses for seed production ... 414
ornamentals/woody plants ... 421
turf grasses for sod ... 417
Silver hairgrass *Aira caryophyllea:*
field corn, popcorn ... 123
ornamentals/woody plants ... 426
sweet corn ... 345
Silver pine:
brush control ... 440
Silverleaf nightshade *Solanum elaeagnifolium:*
asparagus ... 296
barley ... 213
conservation reserve program ... 443,444,446
fallow land ... 450
field corn, popcorn ... 106,111,114
flax ... 240,241
forage ... 455
garlic ... 312
mint ... 244
noncropland ... 470,472,476,477,479,481,482,484
nuts ... 389
oats ... 223
onions ... 321
pastures/rangeland ... 462-464,466
rye ... 231
small fruits ... 360
sorghum ... 263
spring wheat ... 199,201
sweet corn ... 342
tobacco ... 282
tree fruits, citrus ... 367
tree fruits, deciduous ... 375
tree fruits, subtropical ... 382
winter wheat ... 186-188
Silversheath knotweed *Polygonum argyrocoleon:*
noncropland ... 482
nuts ... 391
ornamentals/woody plants ... 427
small fruits ... 362
sugar beets ... 272
tree fruits, citrus ... 368
tree fruits, deciduous ... 377
tree fruits, subtropical ... 383
Sinapis alba — white mustard
Sisymbrium altissimum — tumble mustard (jim hill mustard)
Sisymbrium irio — London rocket
Sisymbrium loeselii — tall hedge mustard
Sisymbrium officinale — hedge mustard
Sixweeks fescue *Vulpia octoflora:*
est. lawns/turf ... 404
Sixweeks grama *Bouteloua barbata:*
asparagus ... 296
noncropland ... 479
nuts ... 389
tree fruits, citrus ... 367
tree fruits, deciduous ... 375
tree fruits, subtropical ... 382
Skeletonleaf bursage *Ambrosia tomentosa:*
noncropland ... 472
pastures/rangeland ... 463
Slender aster *Aster exilis:*
noncropland ... 482
nuts ... 391
ornamentals/woody plants ... 427
small fruits ... 362
tree fruits, citrus ... 368
tree fruits, deciduous ... 377
tree fruits, subtropical ... 383
Slender plantain *Plantago elongata:*
est. lawns/turf ... 405
noncropland ... 474,482
nuts ... 388,391
ornamentals/woody plants ... 422
small fruits ... 358,362
tree fruits, citrus ... 365,368
tree fruits, deciduous ... 373,377
tree fruits, subtropical ... 381,383
Slimleaf lambsquarters *Chenopodium leptophyllum:*
barley ... 211,217,218
fallow land ... 447
oats ... 228
pastures/rangeland ... 460
spring wheat ... 199,205,207
winter wheat ... 186,192,194
Slippery elm *Ulmus rubra:*
noncropland ... 477
Small soapweed *Yucca glauca* (Great Plains yucca):
brush control ... 440
noncropland ... 475
pastures/rangeland ... 464
Small stinging nettle *Urtica urens* (burning nettle):
spinach ... 336
sugar beets ... 271
tomatoes ... 347
Small white morningglory *Ipomoea obscura:*
cotton ... 174
soybeans ... 161,163
Smallflower buttercup *Ranunculus abortivus:*
barley ... 213,218,222
fallow land ... 448,452,454
field corn, popcorn ... 112
oats ... 228,230
spring wheat ... 201,207,210
winter wheat ... 188,194,198
Smallflower galinsoga *Galinsoga parviflora:*
field corn, popcorn ... 107,116
peanuts ... 248
soybeans ... 143,146
sweet corn ... 339,340
Smallflower morningglory *Jacquemontia tamnifolia:*
cotton ... 173,174
est. lawns/turf ... 408
field corn, popcorn ... 107,113,115,116,119-121
forage ... 458
peanuts ... 249,251
sorghum ... 265,267
soybeans ... 144,145,149-152,155-157,159-161,163
sweet corn ... 343
Smallflower umbrellaplant *Cyperus difformis*:
rice ... 253-255
Smallseed canarygrass:
winter wheat ... 194
Smallseed falseflax *Camelina microcarpa:*
barley ... 211,213,217,218,222
fallow land ... 447,448
field corn, popcorn ... 114
oats ... 227,228
pastures/rangeland ... 460
soybeans ... 152
spring wheat ... 199,201,205-207
sweet corn ... 342,343
winter wheat ... 186,188,196,194,197
Smartweed *Polygonum* spp.:
asparagus ... 297
barley ... 213,214
beans ... 298
brush control ... 441
carrots ... 301,302
celery ... 303,304
conservation reserve program ... 444,446
cotton ... 176,180,181
est. lawns/turf ... 410
fallow land ... 448
field corn, popcorn ... 101-106,108,110,112-117, 120,122-124
flax ... 241
forage ... 456
grasses for seed production ... 412
herbs/spices ... 316
mint ... 244,246
moving water ... 499
noncropland ... 468,470-472,474-478,481, 482,484-487
nuts ... 386,388,391,392
oats ... 224
ornamentals/woody plants ... 418,420,422,424-427
pastures/rangeland ... 461,464,466
peanuts ... 248
peas ... 325
peppers ... 327
potatoes ... 330,331
rice ... 253,258
rye ... 232
small fruits ... 356,358,361-363
sorghum ... 260-262,264-266,268
soybeans ... 143,150,153,158,163
spring wheat ... 201,202
still water ... 496
sugar beets ... 270,271
sugarcane ... 273,275,276
sweet corn ... 337-343,345
table beets ... 347
tree fruits, citrus ... 368,370
tree fruits, deciduous ... 372,373,376,377,379
tree fruits, subtropical ... 383,384
turf grasses for sod ... 416
winter wheat ... 188,189
Smellmelon *Cucumis melo:*
cotton ... 174,181
field corn ... 111,116
peanuts ... 248
soybeans ... 143,145,150,163
tobacco ... 282
Smilax spp. — greenbriar
Smooth brome (bromegrass) *Bromus inermis:*
conservation reserve program ... 442
field corn, popcorn ... 113,114,116,124
forage ... 458,459
noncropland ... 474,476,477,480,482,484,485
nuts ... 388,392
ornamentals/woody plants ... 422
pastures/rangeland ... 460
small fruits ... 357,362
soybeans ... 162
sweet corn ... 342
tree fruits, deciduous ... 373,378
Smooth crabgrass *Digitaria ischaemum:*
artichokes ... 292,293
asparagus ... 294-297
beans ... 298,300,301
carrots ... 301,303
celery ... 305
cole crops ... 306,307
conservation reserve program ... 447
cotton ... 173,174,177-179,181,182
cucurbits ... 307-309
eggplant ... 310,311
est. lawns/turf ... 400,404,407,409,410
fallow land ... 448,451,453
field corn, popcorn ... 103,110,112,113,116, 118-122,125
flax ... 240-242
forage ... 455,458,459
garlic ... 313,314
grasses for seed production ... 414
greens ... 315
guar beans ... 243
hops ... 243
kenaf ... 244
lentils ... 317
lettuce, endive ... 318,319
mint ... 245,246
mung beans ... 247
newly sprigged/seeded turf ... 399
noncropland ... 468,474,479,482
nuts ... 385-387,389-392
oil seed crops ... 247,248

okra 320
onions 321,323
ornamentals/woody plants 419,421,422
peanuts 249,251,252
peas 324,326
peppers 327,328
potatoes 329,332
rhubarb 333,334
safflower 259
small fruits 356-358,361-363
sorghum 264,269
southern peas 335,336
soybeans 144-147,149-153,155-159,161,162,164
spinach 337
sugar beets 269,271,272
sugarcane 278
sunflower 280,281
sweet corn 341,342
sweet potatoes 346
table beets 346
tobacco 281,282
tomatoes 350
tree fruits, citrus 363-365,367-370
tree fruits, deciduous 371,373,374,376-378
tree fruits, subtropical 379-381,383,384
turf grasses for sod 417

Smooth pigweed *Amaranthus hybridus:*
barley 211-213,217,218,220,221
beans 300
carrots 302
cole crops 305
conservation reserve program 442,443,446
cotton 173,174
cucurbits 308
eggplant 309
est. lawns/turf 408
fallow land 447,448,451,454
field corn, popcorn 101,103-107,110,112-116, 118-122,124
flax 241
forage 458
noncropland 483,484
nuts 391
oats 223,227,229
pastures/rangeland 460,465
peanuts 248,251,252
peas 326
peppers 327
potatoes 331
rye 231,235
small fruits 362
sorghum 261,263-265,267
soybeans 143-147,149-153,155-157,159-163
spring wheat 199-201,205,206,209
sugarcane 274
sunflower 280
sweet corn 341-343
sweet potatoes 345
tobacco 281,282
tomatoes 349
tree fruits, citrus 369
tree fruits, deciduous 377,378
tree fruits, subtropical 384
winter wheat 186-188,193,194,196,197

Smutgrass *Sporobolus indicus:*
est. lawns/turf 404
noncropland 475,476,481

Snow speedwell:
barley 213
fallow land 448
spring wheat 201
winter wheat 188

Snow weed:
forage 459

Snowberry *Symphoricarpos* spp.:
brush control 438,441,442
noncropland 471,486
pastures/rangeland 466

Snowbrush:
brush control 440
pastures/rangeland 464

Snubbers:
noncropland 475

Soft chess *Bromus mollis* (soft brome):
artichokes 292
asparagus 294
grasses for seed production 415
mint 245
nuts 386
rhubarb 333
small fruits 357
tree fruits, citrus 364
tree fruits, deciduous 371
tree fruits, subtropical 380
turf grasses for sod 417

Solanum americanum — American black nightshade (popolo)
Solanum carolinense — horsenettle (Carolina horsenettle)
Solanum elaeagnifolium — silverleaf nightshade
Solanum nigrum — black nightshade
Solanum ptycanthum — eastern black nightshade
Solanum rostratum — buffalobur
Solanum sarrachoides — hairy nightshade
Solanum spp. — annual nightshade, nightshade
Solanum triflorum — cutleaf nightshade
Solidago canadensis — Canada goldenrod
Solidago missouriensis — Missouri goldenrod
Solidago nemoralis — gray goldenrod
Solidago spp. — goldenrod
Soliva pterosperma — lawn burweed
Sonchus arvensis — perennial sowthistle
Sonchus asper — spiny sowthistle
Sonchus oleraceus — annual sowthistle
Sonchus spp. — sowthistle
Sorghastrum nutans — indiangrass

Sorghum:
sorghum 259
soybeans 164

Sorghum almum — sorghum-almum
Sorghum bicolor — shattercane (black ambercane, wildcane)
Sorghum halepense — johnsongrass

Sorghum-almum *Sorghum almum:*
asparagus 295
carrots 301
cotton 177
fallow land 451
field corn, popcorn 101,104,106,107,116,118, 119,121
garlic 313
lettuce, endive 318
noncropland 474
nuts 387
onions 321
ornamentals/woody plants 422
peppers 327
rhubarb 334
small fruits 358
soybeans 150,151,161
sweet potatoes 346
tree fruits, citrus 365
tree fruits, deciduous 373
tree fruits, subtropical 381

Sorrel *Rumex acetosa* (green sorrel):
noncropland 471,476,477,482,484
small fruits 357

Sour dock *Rumex* spp.:
rice 254,257

Sourwood *Oxydendrum arboreum:*
brush control 440
noncropland 477,480,484

Southern brassbuttons *Cotula australis:*
est. lawns/turf 405
noncropland 474
nuts 388
ornamentals/woody plants 422
small fruits 358
tree fruits, citrus 365
tree fruits, deciduous 373
tree fruits, subtropical 381

Southern crabgrass *Digitaria ciliaris:*
asparagus 295
carrots 301
cotton 173,177
fallow land 448,451
garlic 313
lettuce, endive 318
noncropland 468,474
nuts 385,387
onions 321
ornamentals/woody plants 419,422
peppers 327
rhubarb 334
small fruits 356,358
soybeans 145,150,161,164
sugar beets 269
sweet potatoes 346
tree fruits, citrus 363,365
tree fruits, deciduous 371,373
tree fruits, subtropical 379,381

Southern dewberry *Rubus trivialis:*
noncropland 470
pastures/rangeland 462

Southern naiad *Najas guadalupensis:*
rice 254,255
still water 494

Southern sandbur *Cenchrus echinatus:*
asparagus 295
carrots 301
cotton 177
fallow land 451
field corn, popcorn 101
garlic 313
lettuce, endive 318
noncropland 474
nuts 387
onions 321
ornamentals/woody plants 422
peppers 327
rhubarb 334
small fruits 358
soybeans 150,151,161,164
sweet potatoes 346
tree fruits, citrus 365
tree fruits, deciduous 373
tree fruits, subtropical 381

Southern watergrass *Luziola fluitans:*
moving water 499
still water 496

Southern waxmyrtle *Myrica cerifera:*
noncropland 440

Southwestern cupgrass *Eriochloa gracilis:*
artichokes 292,293
asparagus 294,296
beans 298-300
carrots 303
celery 305
cole crops 306
cotton 173,174,178,181
cucurbits 307,309
eggplant 310
fallow land 448,451
field corn, popcorn 101,105,110,112,113,117, 118,122,124
flax 241
forage 459
garbanzos 311
garlic 313,314
greens 315
lentils 317
lettuce, endive 319
mint 245,246
mung beans 246
noncropland 468,474,479,483
nuts 385-387,389,391
oil seed crops 247
onions 321,323
ornamentals/woody plants 419,422,425,427
peanuts 243-251
peas 325,326
peppers 328
potatoes 330,332
radishes 333
safflower 259
small fruits 356,357,360-362
sorghum 261,264,265
southern peas 335
soybeans 145,146,149,151,153,158,163
spinach 337
sugar beets 269,271
sunflower 280
sweet corn 339,341,342,344
table beets 346
tobacco 281,282
tomatoes 350
tree fruits, citrus 363-365,367-369
tree fruits, deciduous 371,373,375-377
tree fruits, subtropical 379-384

Sowthistle *Sonchus* spp.:
barley 211,214,219,220
conservation reserve program 446
cotton 174
est. lawns/turf 401
fallow land 447,449,453
field corn, popcorn 108,113,123
flax 241
grasses for seed production 412,414
mint 244
noncropland 468,469,471,476,477,482,484
nuts 389
oats 224,228,229
ornamentals/woody plants 420,421,425-427
pastures/rangeland 460,461,464,466
peas 325
rye 232,234,235
sorghum 262,268
soybeans 152
spring wheat 199,202,207,208
sugar beets 270
sugarcane 273,275,277
sweet corn 340
tree fruits, subtropical 379-381
turf grasses for sod 416
winter wheat 186,189,195,196

Spanishneedles *Bidens bipinnata:*
artichokes 293
fallow land 451,453
field corn, popcorn 106,110,114,118,123,124
grasses for seed production 413
noncropland 472,475,476,478,480,484
nuts 385,386,391
ornamentals/woody plants 420,421,426
small fruits 361,362
sorghum 263,268
soybeans 152,162
sugarcane 275
sweet corn 342,345
tree fruits, citrus 366,368,369
tree fruits, deciduous 372,376,378
tree fruits, subtropical 379-381,383,384

Sparganium spp. — burreed
Spartina pectinata — prairie cordgrass

Spatterdock *Nuphar luteum:*
moving water 499
still water 495,496

Spearhead *Rhynchospora corniculata* (horned beakrush):
rice 254,257,258

Speedwell *Veronica* spp.:
barley 218
est. lawns/turf 402,403,406,410
field corn, popcorn 123
grasses for seed production 413
noncropland 470,482
oats 227
ornamentals/woody plants 419,426
small fruits 361
soybeans 147
spring wheat 206
sweet corn 345
tree fruits, citrus 368
tree fruits, deciduous 376
tree fruits, subtropical 383
winter wheat 193

Spergula arvensis — corn spurry
Spergula spp. — spurry
Spergularia rubra — red sandspurry
Sphenoclea zeylanica — gooseweed

Spicebrush:
brush control 438
noncropland 471

Spikerush *Eleocharis* spp.:
- moving water ... 499
- rice ... 253,256-258
- still water ... 496

Spikeweed *Hemizonia pungens:*
- forage ... 458

Spiny amaranth *Amaranthus spinosus:*
- cotton ... 174
- noncropland ... 469
- pastures/rangeland ... 461
- peanuts ... 248
- soybeans ... 143-145,150,161-163
- sugarcane ... 277
- tobacco ... 282
- tree fruits, subtropical ... 382

Spiny aster *Aster spinosus:*
- sugarcane ... 275

Spiny pigweed *Amaranthus spinosus* (spiny amaranth):
- asparagus ... 297
- barley ... 213
- beans ... 301
- carrots ... 303
- celery ... 305
- cole crops ... 307
- conservation reserve program ... 443
- cotton ... 173,174,182
- cucurbits ... 308,309
- eggplant ... 311
- est. lawns/turf ... 400
- field corn, popcorn ... 105,107,113,116,119-121,125
- flax ... 240-242
- forage ... 455,458
- garlic ... 312
- grasses for seed production ... 411
- greens ... 315
- guar beans ... 243
- hops ... 243
- kenaf ... 244
- lettuce, endive ... 318,319
- mint ... 244
- mung beans ... 247
- noncropland ... 468
- nuts ... 391,392
- oats ... 223
- oil seed crops ... 248
- okra ... 320
- onions ... 321,323
- peanuts ... 251,252
- peppers ... 327
- potatoes ... 329,332
- radishes ... 333
- rye ... 231
- safflower ... 259
- small fruits ... 362,363
- sorghum ... 261,269
- southern peas ... 336
- soybeans ... 146,149,152,155-157,159,162,163
- spring wheat ... 201
- sugar beets ... 272
- sugarcane ... 278
- sunflower ... 281
- tomatoes ... 350
- tree fruits, citrus ... 369,370
- tree fruits, deciduous ... 377,378
- tree fruits, subtropical ... 384
- turf grasses for sod ... 416
- winter wheat ... 187,188

Spiny sida *Sida spinosa* (prickly sida):
- field corn, popcorn ... 107
- sweet corn ... 337,340

Spiny sowthistle *Sonchus asper:*
- noncropland ... 482
- nuts ... 391
- small fruits ... 362
- tree fruits, citrus ... 368
- tree fruits, deciduous ... 377
- tree fruits, subtropical ... 383

Spiny spiderflower *Cleome hassleriana* (spiderflower):
- cotton ... 181

Spirogyra:
- moving water ... 498,499
- still water ... 495,496

Spleen amaranth *Amaranthus tricolor:*
- sugarcane ... 277

Sporobolus cryptandrus — sand dropseed

Sporobolus indicus — smutgrass

Spotted beebalm *Monarda punctata:*
- noncropland ... 470
- pastures/rangeland ... 462

Spotted catsear *Hypochaeris radicata* (catsear dandelion):
- est. lawns/turf ... 401
- ornamentals/woody plants ... 419

Spotted knapweed *Centaurea maculosa:*
- barley ... 214
- conservation reserve program ... 443,444
- fallow land ... 449
- field corn ... 111
- grasses for seed production ... 412
- noncropland ... 468,470
- oats ... 224
- ornamentals/woody plants ... 420
- pastures/rangeland ... 461,462
- spring wheat ... 202
- sugar beets ... 270
- sugarcane ... 274
- winter wheat ... 189

Spotted smartweed *Polygonum persicaria* (ladysthumb):
- small fruits ... 357

Spotted spurge *Euphorbia maculata:*
- cotton ... 174,179
- est. lawns/turf ... 404-406
- field corn, popcorn ... 103,107,110,112,115, 116,119-122
- forage ... 457,458
- noncropland ... 468,474,482,487
- nuts ... 388,391,392
- ornamentals/woody plants ... 422,423,425-427
- peanuts ... 248,251
- small fruits ... 358,359,362,363
- sorghum ... 264
- soybeans ... 143-145,149,150,154-159,161,163
- sweet corn ... 341
- tobacco ... 282
- tree fruits, citrus ... 365,366,368,370
- tree fruits, deciduous ... 373,374,377,379
- tree fruits, subtropical ... 381,383,384

Sprangletop *Leptochloa* spp.:
- artichokes ... 293
- asparagus ... 297
- beans ... 301
- carrots ... 302,303
- celery ... 304,305
- cole crops ... 306,307
- conservation reserve program ... 447
- cotton ... 182
- cucurbits ... 308,309
- eggplant ... 310,311
- est. lawns/turf ... 404
- fallow land ... 454,455
- field corn, popcorn ... 116,124,125
- flax ... 240,242
- garlic ... 314
- grasses for seed production ... 414
- greens ... 315
- guar beans ... 243
- hops ... 243
- kenaf ... 244
- lettuce, endive ... 319
- mung beans ... 247
- noncropland ... 480,482,485
- nuts ... 392
- oil seed crops ... 248
- okra ... 320
- onions ... 323
- ornamentals/woody plants ... 421,425
- peanuts ... 252
- peppers ... 327,328
- potatoes ... 329,332
- radishes ... 333
- rice ... 253,254,256,257
- safflower ... 259
- small fruits ... 362,363
- sorghum ... 269
- southern peas ... 336
- soybeans ... 144,149,152,162
- sugar beets ... 272
- sugarcane ... 278
- sunflower ... 281
- tomatoes ... 349,350
- tree fruits, citrus ... 369,370
- tree fruits, deciduous ... 378
- tree fruits, subtropical ... 384
- turf grasses for sod ... 417

Sprangleweed:
- ornamentals/woody plants ... 425

Spreading dayflower *Commelina diffusa:*
- noncropland ... 479
- tree fruits, subtropical ... 380

Spreading orach *Atriplex patula:*
- noncropland ... 480

Spreading panicgrass *Panicum dichotomiflorum* (fall panicum)
- forage ... 455
- lettuce, endive ... 318
- nuts ... 391
- small fruits ... 362
- tree fruits, citrus ... 369
- tree fruits, deciduous ... 377
- tree fruits, subtropical ... 384

Spring milletgrass *Milium scabrum:*
- winter wheat ... 194

Spring whitlowgrass *Draba verna:*
- barley ... 212
- fallow land ... 448
- spring wheat ... 200
- winter wheat ... 187

Spruce *Picea* spp.:
- brush control ... 437-439,441,442
- noncropland ... 470-472,484,486
- pastures/rangeland ... 466

Spurge *Euphorbia* spp.:
- beans ... 298
- cotton ... 174,178
- est. lawns/turf ... 401,403,407,410
- field corn, popcorn ... 113
- noncropland ... 470-472,475,479,481,485
- nuts ... 386
- ornamentals/woody plants ... 420,425,427
- peanuts ... 249
- sorghum ... 264
- soybeans ... 151
- sweet corn ... 342
- tree fruits, deciduous ... 372,374

Spurred anoda *Anoda cristata:*
- cotton ... 173,174,179,181
- cucurbits ... 307
- est. lawns/turf ... 408
- field corn, popcorn ... 103,107,115,116,119-122
- forage ... 457
- noncropland ... 481
- ornamentals/woody plants ... 419
- peanuts ... 248,249,251,252
- peas ... 324
- peppers ... 327
- sorghum ... 260,265
- soybeans ... 143,144,146,147,150-155,157-161,163
- sweet corn ... 338,343
- tobacco ... 281,282

Spurry *Spergula* spp.:
- est. lawns/turf ... 403
- forage ... 459

Spurweed:
- est. lawns/turf ... 399,401,409

Squirreltail barley:
- noncropland ... 481

St. Johnswort:
- conservation reserve program ... 446
- pastures/rangeland ... 466

Stachys floridana — Florida betony

Stargrass *Chloris* spp.:
- small fruits ... 357

Starthistle:
- conservation reserve program ... 446
- pastures/rangeland ... 466

Stellaria graminea — little starwort

Stellaria media — common chickweed

Sticktight:
- small fruits ... 356

Stinging nettle *Urtica dioica:*
- asparagus ... 297
- barley ... 219,220
- beans ... 301
- carrots ... 303
- celery ... 305
- cole crops ... 307
- conservation reserve program ... 447
- cotton ... 182
- cucurbits ... 309
- eggplant ... 311
- est. lawns/turf ... 401
- fallow land ... 455
- field corn, popcorn ... 125
- flax ... 240-242
- grasses for seed production ... 414
- greens ... 315
- guar beans ... 243
- hops ... 243
- kenaf ... 244
- lettuce, endive ... 319
- mung beans ... 247
- noncropland ... 476,479,482
- nuts ... 392
- oats ... 228,229
- oil seed crops ... 248
- okra ... 320
- onions ... 323
- pastures/rangeland ... 464
- peanuts ... 252
- peppers ... 327
- potatoes ... 329,331,332
- radishes ... 333
- rye ... 234,235
- safflower ... 259
- small fruits ... 363
- sorghum ... 269
- southern peas ... 336
- soybeans ... 144,146,162
- spring wheat ... 207,208
- sugar beets ... 272
- sugarcane ... 278
- sunflower ... 281
- tomatoes ... 350
- tree fruits, citrus ... 370
- tree fruits, deciduous ... 378
- winter wheat ... 195,196

Stinkgrass *Eragrostis cilianensis:*
- artichokes ... 292,293
- asparagus ... 294,296,297
- barley ... 218
- beans ... 301
- carrots ... 303
- celery ... 305
- cole crops ... 305-307
- conservation reserve program ... 447
- cotton ... 181,182
- cucurbits ... 309
- eggplant ... 309-311
- fallow land ... 451,452,454,455
- field corn, popcorn ... 107,114,116,122,124,125
- flax ... 240-242
- forage ... 459
- garlic ... 314
- greens ... 315
- guar beans ... 243
- hops ... 243
- kenaf ... 244
- lentils ... 317
- lettuce, endive ... 319
- mint ... 245,246
- mung beans ... 247
- noncropland ... 474,481,485
- nuts ... 386-388,392
- oats ... 227
- oil seed crops ... 247,248
- okra ... 320
- onions ... 323
- ornamentals/woody plants ... 421,422
- peanuts ... 251,252
- peas ... 326
- peppers ... 327,328
- potatoes ... 329,331,332
- radishes ... 333

Weed Index

safflower 259
small fruits 357,361-363
sorghum 269
southern peas 335,336
soybeans 144,146,152,156,158,162
spinach 337
spring wheat 206
sugar beets 271,272
sugarcane 278
sunflower 279-281
sweet corn 339,340,342,343
sweet potatoes 345
table beets 346
tobacco 281,282
tomatoes 349,350
tree fruits, citrus 364,365,368-370
tree fruits, deciduous 371,373,376,378
tree fruits, subtropical 380,383,384
winter wheat 194

Stinking chickweed:
barley 213,218
fallow land 448
oats 228
spring wheat 201,207
winter wheat 188,194

Stinking mayweed:
barley 213,218,222
fallow land 448,454
oats 228,230
spring wheat 201,207,210
winter wheat 188,194,198

Stinkweed *Pluchea camphorata:*
barley 214,219,220
est. lawns/turf 401
field corn, popcorn 108
flax 241
grasses for seed production 412,414
noncropland 469
oats 224,228,229
pastures/rangeland 461,464
peas 325
rye 232,234,235
sorghum 262
spring wheat 202,207,208
sugarcane 273
sweet corn 340
winter wheat 189,195,196

***Stipa* spp.** — needlegrass

Stitchwort *Stellaria graminea* (little starwort):
est. lawns/turf 402,403,407

Striga asiatica — witchweed

Sumac *Rhus* spp.:
barley 214
brush control 436-442
est. lawns/turf 401
field corn, popcorn 108
grasses for seed production 412
noncropland 469-472,475-477,484-486
oats 224
ornamentals/woody plants 427
pastures/rangeland 461,463,464,466
rye 232
sorghum 262
spring wheat 202
sugarcane 273
sweet corn 340
winter wheat 189

Sunflower *Helianthus* spp.:
barley 213,214,217-220
conservation reserve program 442,443,446
cotton 173,181
est. lawns/turf 401,410
fallow land 449,450,453
field corn, popcorn 104,105,107,108,110,112,114, 116,117,121,123,125
flax 240,241
forage 455
garlic 312
grasses for seed production 412
mint 244
noncropland 468-471,476,477,480-482,484
nuts 391
oats 223,224,227-229
onions 321
ornamentals/woody plants 420,427
pastures/rangeland 461-464,466
peas 325
rye 231,232,234,235
small fruits 362
sorghum 261-263,268
soybeans 144,145,149,156,158-161,163
spring wheat 201,202,204-208
sugar beets 270,272
sugarcane 273,276
sunflower 279
sweet corn 340
tree fruits, citrus 368
tree fruits, deciduous 377
tree fruits, subtropical 383
winter wheat 187-189,191,193,195,196

Swamp smartweed *Polygonum coccineum:*
conservation reserve program 444
fallow land 450,451
field corn, popcorn 106,110-112,114,124
small fruits 357
sorghum 263
soybeans 152,162
sweet corn 342

Sweet vernalgrass *Anthoxanthum odoratum:*
oats 226

Sweetrbay:
noncropland 480

Sweetbay magnolia *Magnolia virginiana:*
noncropland 485

Sweetclover *Melilotus* spp.:
barley 214
conservation reserve program 443,444
est. lawns/turf 403
fallow land 449
field corn, popcorn 108
forage 456
grasses for seed production 412
noncropland 469,471,473,476,477,480,482-484
oats 224
pastures/rangeland 461
rye 232
sorghum 262
spring wheat 202
sugarcane 273
sweet corn 340
winter wheat 189

Sweetgum *Liquidambar styraciflua:*
brush control 436-440
noncropland 469,471,475-477,485
pastures/rangeland 461,464

Swinecress *Coronopus didymus:*
barley 213,218,222
fallow land 448,454
noncropland 474,482
nuts 391
oats 228,230
ornamentals/woody plants 419,427
small fruits 362
spring wheat 201,207,210
sugarcane 275
tree fruits, citrus 368
tree fruits, deciduous 377
tree fruits, subtropical 383
winter wheat 188,194,198

Swollen fingergrass *Chloris barbata:*
sugarcane 275,277

Sword fern *Nephrolepis* spp.:
brush control 440

Sycamore *Platanus* spp.:
brush control 437-442
noncropland 469-472,477,485,486
ornamentals/woody plants 427
pastures/rangeland 461,466

Symphoricarpos orbiculatus — buckbrush

***Symphoricarpos* spp.** — snowberry

T

Taeniatherum caput-medusae — medusahead

Tall buttercup *Ranunculus acris:*
barley 212,221
conservation reserve program 446
noncropland 469
pastures/rangeland 460,461,465
spring wheat 200,209
winter wheat 187,197

Tall dropseed:
noncropland 481

Tall fescue *Festuca arundinacea:*
artichokes 293
asparagus 296,297
barley 218
carrots 303
celery 305
cole crops 306
conservation reserve program 447
cotton 181
cucurbits 309
eggplant 310
est. lawns/turf 405
fallow land 453
field corn, popcorn 114,122,124
flax 241
forage 459
garlic 314
greens 315
lentils 317
lettuce, endive 319
mint 246
noncropland 468,474,479,481,482,485
nuts 388,390,392
oats 227
oil seed crops 247
onions 323
peanuts 251
peas 326
peppers 328
potatoes 332
rhubarb 334
small fruits 359,361,362
southern peas 335
soybeans 158,162
spinach 337
spring wheat 206
sugar beets 271
sunflower 280
sweet corn 342,343
table beets 346
tobacco 282
tomatoes 350
tree fruits, citrus 366,368-370
tree fruits, deciduous 374,376,378
tree fruits, subtropical 381,383,384
winter wheat 194

Tall hedge mustard *Sisymbrium loeselii:*
barley 212,221
conservation reserve program 446
fallow land 448
pastures/rangeland 465
spring wheat 200,209
winter wheat 187,197

Tall ironweed *Vernonia altissima:*
noncropland 469
pastures/rangeland 461

Tall morningglory *Ipomoea purpurea:*
barley 213,220
beans 298
castor beans 240
conservation reserve program 443
cotton 173,174,176
est. lawns/turf 400
fallow land 451,453
field corn, popcorn 101,105-107,110,112, 113,116,118-123
forage 455,457,458
garlic 312
grasses for seed production 411
mint 244
noncropland 468,470,482
nuts 387,391
oats 223,229
onions 321
ornamentals/woody plants 421,423,427
pastures/rangeland 462
peanuts 249,251
potatoes 329
rye 231,235
safflower 258
small fruits 362
sorghum 261,263,267,268
soybeans 144,145,149-152,155-157,159-161,163
spring wheat 201,209
sugar beets 270
sunflower 279
tomatoes 348
tree fruits, citrus 365,368
tree fruits, deciduous 377
tree fruits, subtropical 383
turf grasses for sod 416
winter wheat 187,188,196

Tall waterhemp *Amaranthus tuberculatus:*
barley 213,220
conservation reserve program 443
cotton 173,174
est. lawns/turf 400,408
fallow land 448
field corn, popcorn 101,103,105,107,110-113, 115-117,119-122,124
flax 241
forage 455
garlic 312
grasses for seed production 411
mint 244
noncropland 468
oats 223,229
onions 321
peanuts 252
rye 231,235
sorghum 261,265,267
soybeans 143-145,149-153,155,157,159-161,163
spring wheat 199,201,209
sweet corn 343
tobacco 282
turf grasses for sod 416
winter wheat 186-188,196

Tallow:
brush control 440
noncropland 475
pastures/rangeland 464

Tamarack *Larix laricina:*
noncropland 469
pastures/rangeland 461

Tamarix ramosissima — saltcedar:

Tame oat:
grasses for seed production 414

Tanacetum vulgare — common tansy:

Tanoak *Lithocarpus densiflorus:*
brush control 436,437,439,440
noncropland 469,485
pastures/rangeland 461

Tansy ragwort *Senecio jacobaea:*
brush control 441
conservation reserve program 446
fallow land 450
noncropland 469,470,472,480,484-486
pastures/rangeland 461-463,466
sugarcane 274

Tansymustard:
artichokes 292
barley 211-214,216-218,220-222
conservation reserve program 442,443,446
cotton 175
fallow land 447-454
field corn, popcorn 106,107,110,111,114,118, 122,123
forage 456,458,459
grasses for seed production 411
mint 245
noncropland 469,473,474,476,477,480-484
nuts 388
oats 223,224,226-230
ornamentals/woody plants 422,423,426
pastures/rangeland 460,461,465
rye 231,235
small fruits 359,361,362
sorghum 263,267
soybeans 152

spring wheat.....199-202,204-207,209,210
sugarcane.....275
sweet corn.....340,342,343,345
tree fruits, citrus.....364,368
tree fruits, deciduous.....372,373,376
tree fruits, subtropical.....383
turf grasses for sod.....416
winter wheat.....186-189,191-194,196-198
Taraxacum officinale — dandelion (common dandelion)
Tarbush *Flourensia cernua:*
brush control.....438
noncropland.....472
pastures/rangeland.....463
Tartary buckwheat *Fagopyrum tataricum:*
barley.....212,213,221
conservation reserve program.....443,446
flax.....240,241
forage.....455
garlic.....312
mint.....244
oats.....223
onions.....321
pastures/rangeland.....465
peas.....325
rye.....231
spring wheat.....200,201,209
winter wheat.....187,188,197
Tarweed *Sida spinosa* (prickly sida):
barley.....211,213,217,218,221
conservation reserve program.....442,443,446
fallow land.....447,448,451
grasses for seed production.....411
oats.....223,227
pastures/rangeland.....460,465
rye.....231
spring wheat.....199,201,205,206,209
sugarcane.....277
turf grasses for sod.....416
winter wheat.....186,188,193,197,198
Tarweed cuphea *Cuphea carthagenesis:*
field corn, popcorn.....107
sweet corn.....339,340
Tarweed fiddleneck *Amsinckia lycopsoides:*
barley.....217,218,222
beans.....300
fallow land.....454
noncropland.....480
oats.....228,230
peanuts.....252
peas.....326
soybeans.....159
spring wheat.....205,207,210
sunflower.....280
winter wheat.....192,194,197,198
Tasajillo *Opuntia leptocaulis:*
conservation reserve program.....446
pastures/rangeland.....464,466
Taxodium distichum — baldcypress
Tearthumb *Polygonum* spp.:
small fruits.....356
Teaweed:
beans.....298
carrots.....301,302
celery.....304
cotton.....174,176,180,181
est. lawns/turf.....408
field corn, popcorn.....102,103,106,107,110,112,
.....114-118,124
flax.....241
forage.....457
herbs/spices.....316
noncropland.....472,484,487
nuts.....386,388,391,392
oats.....226
ornamentals/woody plants.....418-420,427
peanuts.....248,249,252
potatoes.....330
small fruits.....359,362,363
sorghum.....260,262,265
soybeans.....143,144,147,150-153,158,160,162
sugarcane.....274
sweet corn.....337-343
tree fruits, citrus.....370
tree fruits, deciduous.....372,374,378,379
tree fruits, subtropical.....384
Telegraphplant *Heterotheca grandiflora:*
noncropland.....482
nuts.....391
ornamentals/woody plants.....427
small fruits.....362
tree fruits, citrus.....368
tree fruits, deciduous.....377
tree fruits, subtropical.....383
Texas blueweed *Helianthus ciliaris:*
conservation reserve program.....444
fallow land.....450
field corn, popcorn.....114
noncropland.....472
pastures/rangeland.....463
sugar beets.....270
sweet corn.....342
Texas gourd *Cucurbita texana:*
peanuts.....248
soybeans.....143
Texas groundsel:
noncropland.....470
pastures/rangeland.....462
Texas millet *Panicum texanum* (Texas panicum):
rice.....253,254,257,258
Texas panicum *Panicum texanum:*
artichokes.....292,293
asparagus.....294-297
barley.....218
beans.....298-301
carrots.....301,303
castor beans.....240
celery.....305
cole crops.....306,307
conservation reserve program.....445,447
cotton.....173,174,176,177,180-182
cucurbits.....307-309
eggplant.....310,311
est. lawns/turf.....400
fallow land.....448,451,453,454
field corn, popcorn.....101,103,104,106,112-114,
.....116-122,124,125
flax.....240-242
forage.....455,457-459
garbanzos.....312
garlic.....313,314
greens.....315
guar beans.....243
hops.....243
kenaf.....244
lettuce, endive.....318,319
mint.....245,246
mung beans.....247
noncropland.....468,472,474,479,481,482,485,487
nuts.....385-387,390-392
oats.....227
oil seed crops.....247,248
okra.....320
onions.....321-323
ornamentals/woody plants.....419,421,422,425
peanuts.....249,251,252
peas.....326
peppers.....327,328
potatoes.....329,331,332
radishes.....333
rhubarb.....334
rice.....257
safflower.....258,259
small fruits.....356-358,361-363
sorghum.....264,269
southern peas.....335,336
soybeans.....144-147,149-159,161-164
spinach.....337
spring wheat.....206
sugar beets.....269-272
sugarcane.....275-278
sunflower.....279-281
sweet corn.....341-344
sweet potatoes.....345,346
table beets.....346
tobacco.....281,282
tomatoes.....348,350
tree fruits, citrus.....363-365,367-370
tree fruits, deciduous.....371-373,375-379
tree fruits, subtropical.....379-381,383,384
winter wheat.....194
Texas thistle *Cirsium texanum:*
noncropland.....477,482,484
Texasweed *Caperonia palustris:*
peanuts.....252
rice.....253-255,258
soybeans.....159,160,163
Thimble pigweed:
soybeans.....149
Thimbleberry *Rubus* spp.:
brush control.....439,440
noncropland.....477,485
Thistles *Carduus* spp., *Cirsium* spp.:
conservation reserve program.....446
est. lawns/turf.....405,406,410
noncropland.....468,470,473,476,481,483,484
pastures/rangeland.....464,466
Thlaspi arvense — field pennycress (fanweed, frenchweed)
Thlaspi spp. — pennycress
Thymeleaf speedwell *Veronica serphyllifolia:*
est. lawns/turf.....405
noncropland.....474
nuts.....388
ornamentals/woody plants.....422
small fruits.....358
tree fruits, citrus.....365
tree fruits, deciduous.....373
tree fruits, subtropical.....381
Thymeleaf spurge *Euphorbia thymifolia:*
noncropland.....469
pastures/rangeland.....461
Tideland clover:
small fruits.....357
Tilia spp. — basswood
Timothy *Phleum pratense:*
conservation reserve program.....442,447
field corn, popcorn.....113,114,116,124
noncropland.....472,476,477,482,484,485
nuts.....386,392
pastures/rangeland.....460
small fruits.....357,362
soybeans.....162
sweet corn.....342
tree fruits, citrus.....369
tree fruits, deciduous.....372,378
tree fruits, subtropical.....384
Toadflax *Linaria* spp.:
conservation reserve program.....446
noncropland.....484
pastures/rangeland.....466
tomatoes.....349
Toothed spurge *Euphorbia dentata:*
field corn, popcorn.....103
Torpedograss *Panicum repens:*
fallow land.....453
field corn, popcorn.....114,124
moving water.....499
noncropland.....476,477,479,481,482,484,485
nuts.....388,392
ornamentals/woody plants.....422
still water.....496
sweet corn.....342
tree fruits, citrus.....365,366,368,369
tree fruits, deciduous.....373,378
Toxicodendron pubescens — poison oak
Toxicodendron radicans — poison ivy
Tragopogon pratensis — meadow salsify
Tragopogon spp. — salsify
Trapa natans — waterchestnut
Treacle mustard *Erysimum* spp. (wallflower):
barley.....211,213,217,218
fallow land.....447,448,453
noncropland.....473,483
oats.....227
pastures/rangeland.....460
spring wheat.....199,201,205,206
winter wheat.....186,188,193
Tree-of-heaven *Ailanthus altissima:*
noncropland.....477
Tree tobacco *Nicotiana glauca:*
brush control.....440
Trianthema portulacastrum — horse purslane
Tribulus terrestris — puncturevine
Tridens flavus — purpletop
Trifolium aureum — hop clover
Trifolium incarnatum — crimson clover
Trifolium pratense — red clover
Trifolium repens — white clover
Trifolium spp. — clover
Tropic croton *Croton glandulosus:*
cotton.....173,174,179
cucurbits.....307
field corn, popcorn.....103,111,121
forage.....457
peanuts.....248,252
sorghum.....260
soybeans.....143-147,150,153,154,157,160,163
sweet corn.....338
tobacco.....281,282
Tropical crabgrass *Digitaria bicornis:*
asparagus.....295
carrots.....301
cotton.....177
fallow land.....451
garlic.....313
lettuce, endive.....318
noncropland.....474
nuts.....387
onions.....321
peppers.....327
rhubarb.....334
small fruits.....358
soybeans.....150,161,164
sweet potatoes.....346
tree fruits, citrus.....365
tree fruits, deciduous.....373
tree fruits, subtropical.....381
Tropical soda apple:
pastures/rangeland.....464,466
Trumpetcreeper *Campsis radicans:*
brush control.....440-442
conservation reserve program.....444,447
est. lawns/turf.....410
fallow land.....450,454
noncropland.....468,472,475-477,482,484,486
pastures/rangeland.....463,466
peanuts.....248
soybeans.....143,150,152,162
Trumpetvine *Campsis radicans* (trumpetcreeper):
noncropland.....470
Tsuga heterophylla — western hemlock
Tsuga spp. — hemlock
Tulip poplar *Liriodendron tulipifera* (tuliptree):
brush control.....437
noncropland.....484,485
Tuliptree *Liriodendron tulipifera:*
brush control.....439
noncropland.....477
Tumble mustard *Sisymbrium altissimum:*
asparagus.....296
barley.....211-214,217,218,220-222
conservation reserve program.....442,443,446
est. lawns/turf.....400
fallow land.....447-449,451,452,454
field corn, popcorn.....114
flax.....241
forage.....455
garlic.....312
grasses for seed production.....411
mint.....244,245
noncropland.....467,468,473,479,480,483
nuts.....389
oats.....223,224,227-230
onions.....321
ornamentals/woody plants.....423
pastures/rangeland.....460,461,465
rye.....231,235
small fruits.....360
sorghum.....267
soybeans.....152
spring wheat.....199-202,204-207,209,210

sweet corn ... 342,343
turf grasses for sod ... 416
winter wheat ... 186-189,191-194,196-198

Tumble pigweed *Amaranthus albus:*
barley ... 211,213,216,220,221
beans ... 298,300
castor beans ... 240
conservation reserve program ... 444,446
cotton ... 176
fallow land ... 447,448,451
field corn, popcorn ... 106,110,112,113,116,118
nuts ... 387,389,391
oats ... 226,229
ornamentals/woody plants ... 421
pastures/rangeland ... 460,465
peanuts ... 252
peas ... 326
potatoes ... 329
rye ... 235
safflower ... 258
small fruits ... 362
sorghum ... 263,264,267
soybeans ... 152,159
spring wheat ... 199,201,204,209
sugar beets ... 270
sunflower ... 279,280
sweet corn ... 341
tomatoes ... 348
tree fruits, citrus ... 367,369
tree fruits, deciduous ... 377
tree fruits, subtropical ... 384
winter wheat ... 186,188,191,196,197

Tumbleweed:
asparagus ... 297
beans ... 301
carrots ... 303
celery ... 305
cole crops ... 307
conservation reserve program ... 447
cotton ... 176,182
cucurbits ... 309
eggplant ... 311
field corn, popcorn ... 125
flax ... 240,242
greens ... 315
guar beans ... 243
hops ... 243
kenaf ... 244
lettuce, endive ... 319
mung beans ... 247
nuts ... 392
oil seed crops ... 248
okra ... 320
onions ... 323
peanuts ... 252
peppers ... 327
potatoes ... 329,332
radishes ... 333
safflower ... 259
small fruits ... 363
sorghum ... 269
southern peas ... 336
soybeans ... 162
sugar beets ... 272
sugarcane ... 278
sunflower ... 281
tomatoes ... 350
tree fruits, citrus ... 370
tree fruits, deciduous ... 378

Turkey mullein *Eremocarpus setigerus:*
noncropland ... 476,480,482,483
nuts ... 391
ornamentals/woody plants ... 427
small fruits ... 362
tree fruits, citrus ... 368
tree fruits, deciduous ... 377
tree fruits, subtropical ... 383

Twisted acacia *Acacia tortuosa:*
pastures/rangeland ... 466

Typha spp. — cattail

U,V

Ulex europaeus — gorse
Ulmus alata — winged elm
Ulmus americana — American elm
Ulmus pumila — Siberian elm
Ulmus rubra — slippery elm
Ulmus spp. — elm

Umbrella spurry *Holosteum umbellatum:*
barley ... 218,221
conservation reserve program ... 446
oats ... 227
pastures/rangeland ... 465
soybeans ... 152
spring wheat ... 206,209
sweet corn ... 343
winter wheat ... 194,197

Upright prairie coneflower *Ratibida columnifera:*
conservation reserve program ... 446
pastures/rangeland ... 464,466

Urtica dioica — stinging nettle
Urtica spp. — nettle
Urtica urens — burning nettle
Utricularia spp. — bladderwort
Vaccaria pyramidata — cowcockle
Valerianella locusta — common cornsalad

Vaseygrass *Paspalum urvillei:*
field corn, popcorn ... 114,124
noncropland ... 468,475-477,479,481,482,484,485
nuts ... 388,392
ornamentals/woody plants ... 422
small fruits ... 362
sweet corn ... 342
tree fruits, citrus ... 369
tree fruits, deciduous ... 373,378
tree fruits, subtropical ... 382,384

Velvetgrass *Holcus lanatus* (common velvetgrass):
artichokes ... 292
asparagus ... 295
barley ... 216
cotton ... 174,175
field corn, popcorn ... 111
forage ... 456
grasses for seed production ... 413
mint ... 245
noncropland ... 482
oats ... 226
ornamentals/woody plants ... 424
rhubarb ... 334
sugarcane ... 275
tree fruits, deciduous ... 372
winter wheat ... 192

Velvetleaf *Abutilon theophrasti:*
asparagus ... 296,297
barley ... 213,214,216,220,221
beans ... 298,299
brush control ... 441
carrots ... 301
conservation reserve program ... 443-447
cotton ... 173,174,177,179-181
cucurbits ... 307
est. lawns/turf ... 400,401,405,410
fallow land ... 449-454
field corn, popcorn ... 101-108,110-124
forage ... 455-458
garbanzos ... 312
garlic ... 312,313
grasses for seed production ... 411,412
mint ... 244
noncropland ... 468,470,474,479,481,482, ... 484,486,487
nuts ... 388,390,391,392
oats ... 223,224,226,229
onions ... 321,322
ornamentals/woody plants ... 418,419,422-425,427
pastures/rangeland ... 461,462,465,466
peanuts ... 248,249,251,252
peas ... 324,325
peppers ... 327
potatoes ... 330-332
rye ... 231,232,235
small fruits ... 358-360,362,363
sorghum ... 260-265,267,268
southern peas ... 335
soybeans ... 143-163
spinach ... 336
spring wheat ... 199,201,202,204,209
sugar beets ... 271,272
sugarcane ... 273,275,276,277
sunflower ... 280
sweet corn ... 338-344
tobacco ... 281,282
tomatoes ... 347,349
tree fruits, citrus ... 365,367-370
tree fruits, deciduous ... 373-375,377-379
tree fruits, subtropical ... 381,383,384
turf grasses for sod ... 416
winter wheat ... 186-189,191,196,197

Venice mallow *Hibiscus trionum:*
barley ... 213,220
beans ... 298
conservation reserve program ... 443
cotton ... 173,174,179
cucurbits ... 307
est. lawns/turf ... 400,408
fallow land ... 451,453
field corn, popcorn ... 103,105-107,110,116,118-123
forage ... 455,457
garlic ... 312
grasses for seed production ... 411
mint ... 244
noncropland ... 468
oats ... 223,229
onions ... 321
peanuts ... 248,252
peas ... 324
peppers ... 327
potatoes ... 332
rye ... 231,235
sorghum ... 260,261,263,265,267,268
soybeans ... 144-146,149-155,157-161,163
spring wheat ... 201,209
sweet corn ... 338,343
tobacco ... 281
turf grasses for sod ... 416
winter wheat ... 187,196

Verbascum thapsus — common mullein
Verbena spp. — vervain
Verbena stricta — hoary vervain
Vernonia altissima — tall ironweed
Vernonia spp. — ironweed
Veronica arvensis — corn speedwell
Veronica baldwinii — western ironweed
Veronica hederifolia — ivyleaf speedwell
Veronica officinalis — common speedwell
Veronica peregrina — purslane speedwell
Veronica persica — persian speedwell
Veronica serphyllifolia — thymeleaf speedwell
Veronica spp. — speedwell

Vervain *Verbena* spp.:
noncropland ... 474,481
nuts ... 388
ornamentals/woody plants ... 422
pastures/rangeland ... 464
small fruits ... 359
tree fruits, deciduous ... 373

Vetch *Vicia* spp.:
barley ... 214,217,219,220
conservation reserve program ... 443
fallow land ... 449,451,453
field corn, popcorn ... 106,110,123
grasses for seed production ... 412
mint ... 244
noncropland ... 468,469,480,484,485
nuts ... 388
oats ... 224,228,229
ornamentals/woody plants ... 420,427
pastures/rangeland ... 461,464,466
rye ... 234,235
small fruits ... 359
sorghum ... 263,268
spring wheat ... 202,205,207,208
sugar beets ... 270
tree fruits, deciduous ... 373
winter wheat ... 189,193,195,196

Vicia acutifolia — sand vetch
Vicia sativa — common vetch
Vicia spp. — vetch
Vicia villosa — hairy vetch
Vicia vollosa — winter vetch
Vigna unguiculata — cowpea

Vine maple *Acer circinatum:*
noncropland ... 477

Viola tricolor — wild violet (pansy)

Virginia buttonweed *Diodia virginiana:*
est. lawns/turf ... 401

Virginia copperleaf *Acalypha virginica:*
cotton ... 174
noncropland ... 474
nuts ... 388
ornamentals/woody plants ... 422
peanuts ... 248,249
small fruits ... 359
soybeans ... 143,145,147,148,150,160,161,163
tree fruits, deciduous ... 373

Virginia creeper *Parthenocissus quinquefolia:*
barley ... 214
brush control ... 438,440-442
est. lawns/turf ... 401
field corn, popcorn ... 108,124
grasses for seed production ... 412
noncropland ... 469-471,476,477,482,484,486
oats ... 224
ornamentals/woody plants ... 427
pastures/rangeland ... 461,466
rye ... 232
sorghum ... 262
spring wheat ... 202
sugarcane ... 273
sweet corn ... 340
winter wheat ... 189

Virginia pepperweed *Lepidium virginicum:*
asparagus ... 296
barley ... 212,217,221,222
conservation reserve program ... 446
fallow land ... 448
noncropland ... 470,479,480,482
nuts ... 388,389,391
ornamentals/woody plants ... 427
pastures/rangeland ... 460,462,465
small fruits ... 359,360,362
spring wheat ... 200,205,209
sugarcane ... 274
tree fruits, citrus ... 366-368
tree fruits, deciduous ... 374,375,377
tree fruits, subtropical ... 381-383
winter wheat ... 187,193,197

Virginia pine *Pinus virginiana:*
noncropland ... 477

Vitis spp. — grape (wild grape)

Volunteer alfalfa:
conservation reserve program ... 444

Volunteer barley:
artichokes ... 293
conservation reserve program ... 445
cotton ... 179
cucurbits ... 308
fallow land ... 449,452
grasses for seed production ... 415
lettuce, endive ... 318,319
noncropland ... 480
peas ... 325
potatoes ... 330,331
spinach ... 336
sugar beets ... 270,271
tomatoes ... 347-349
turf grasses for sod ... 417

Volunteer beans:
barley ... 214
conservation reserve program ... 443
fallow land ... 449
oats ... 224
pastures/rangeland ... 461
spring wheat ... 202
winter wheat ... 189

Volunteer corn:
barley ... 217
coton ... 173
field corn, popcorn ... 113,114,116,121
soybeans ... 149,152,153,156,157,159
spring wheat ... 202,205,210

sweet corn 342
winter wheat 189,192,194,198
Volunteer cowpeas:
peanuts 248
soybeans 143
Volunteer cucumber:
soybeans 150,161,163
Volunteer flax:
fallow land 453
sorghum 267
spring wheat 209
winter wheat 197
Volunteer (grains) (cereals):
artichokes 293
asparagus 295,296
barley 298
beans 300
carrots 301,303
castor beans 240
celery 305
cole crops 306
cotton 173,176,177,181
cucurbits 309
eggplant 310
est. lawns/turf 406
fallow land 448,451,453
field corn, popcorn 101,104,112,122
flax 241
forage 457,459
garlic 313,314
grasses for seed production 414
greens 315
lentils 317
lettuce, endive 318,319
mint 246
noncropland 468,474,482
nuts 385,387
oil seed crops 247
onions 321,323
ornamentals/woody plants 419,421,422,424
peanuts 251
peas 326
peppers 327,328
potatoes 329,332
rhubarb 334
safflower 258
small fruits 356,358,359,361
southern peas 335
soybeans 145,150,151,156,158,161,164
spinach 337
sugar beets 269-271
sunflower 279,280
sweet corn 342
sweet potatoes 346
table beets 346
tobacco 282
tomatoes 348,350
tree fruits, citrus 363,365
tree fruits, deciduous 371,373,374
tree fruits, subtropical 379,381
Volunteer lentils:
barley 213,214,218,222
conservation reserve program 443
fallow land 448,449,454
oats 224,228,230
pastures/rangeland 461
spring wheat 201,202,207,210
winter wheat 188,189,194,198
Volunteer oat:
artichokes 293
lettuce, endive 318
peas 325
Volunteer peas:
barley 213,214,218,222
conservation reserve program 443
fallow land 448,449,454
oats 224,228,230
pastures/rangeland 461
spring wheat 201,202,207,210
winter wheat 188,189,194,198
Volunteer proso millet:
field corn, popcorn 113,116
soybeans 152
Volunteer rapeseed:
spring wheat 199
winter wheat 186
Volunteer rye:
conservation reserve program 445
fallow land 449,452
lettuce, endive 318
Volunteer small grains:
cotton 174
forage 458
peanuts 248
soybeans 143
Volunteer sorghum:
beans 299
cotton 178,180
field corn, popcorn 104-106,113,116-119,124
garbanzos 311
mung beans 246
ornamentals/woody plants 425
peanuts 250
peas 325
potatoes 330-332
safflower 259
sorghum 261,262,266
southern peas 335
soybeans 152,153,163
sweet corn 339,344
sweet potatoes 345
tomatoes 349
Volunteer soybeans:
barley 214
fallow land 449
grasses for seed production 412
mint 244
noncropland 468
oats 224
ornamentals/woody plants 420
pastures/rangeland 461
spring wheat 202
sugar beets 270
winter wheat 189
Volunteer sunflower:
barley 211,213,216,218,222
conservation reserve program 443,444
fallow land 447,448,451,454
field corn, popcorn 106,110,111,116,118
oats 226,228,230
pastures/rangeland 460
sorghum 263
spring wheat 199,201,204,207,210,211
winter wheat 186,188,191,194,198
Volunteer tomato:
lettuce, endive 318
Volunteer wheat:
artichokes 293
conservation reserve program 445
fallow land 448,449,452,453
field corn, popcorn 113-115
grasses for seed production 415
lettuce, endive 318
noncropland 480-487
nuts 392
ornamentals/woody plants 427
peas 325
potatoes 331
small fruits 363
soybeans 156
sugar beets 271
sweet corn 342
tomatoes 349
tree fruits, citrus 370
tree fruits, deciduous 379
tree fruits, subtropical 384
turf grasses for sod 417
Vulpia myuros — foxtail fescue, rattail fescue
Vulpia octoflora — sixweeks fescue

W

Waltheria indica — Indian waltheria (hialoa)
Water horsetail *Equisetum fluviatile:*
small fruits 357
Water oak *Quercus nigra:*
noncropland 477
Water smartweed *Polygonum amphibium:*
small fruits 357
still water 495
Waterchestnut *Trapa natans:*
still water 494,495
Watergrass *Echinochloa crus-galli* (barnyardgrass):
asparagus 297
beans 301
carrots 302,303
celery 303-305
cole crops 306,307
conservation reserve program 447
cotton 179,180,182
cucurbits 308,309
eggplant 310,311
field corn, popcorn 123,125
flax 240,242
forage 455
greens 315
guar beans 243
hops 243
kenaf 244
lettuce, endive 319
mung beans 247
noncropland 478,479
nuts 387,391,392
oil seed crops 248
okra 320
onions 323
ornamentals/woody plants 421,425-427
peanuts 252
peppers 327,328
potatoes 329,330,332
rhubarb 333
rice 253,256,258
safflower 259
small fruits 362,363
sorghum 269
southern peas 335,336
soybeans 144,153,162
sugar beets 271,272
sugarcane 278
sunflower 279,281
sweet corn 338,345
tobacco 283
tomatoes 349,350
tree fruits, citrus 369,370
tree fruits, deciduous 377-379
tree fruits, subtropical 384
Waterhemp *Amaranthus* spp.:
beans 298
field corn, popcorn 104-106,113,115,116,118,120
peanuts 249
sorghum 262,264
soybeans 150-152,155,160,161
sweet corn 338,339,341,342
Waterhyacinth *Eichornia crassipes:*
moving water 498,499
still water 493,495,496
Waterhyssop *Bacopa* spp.:
rice 258
Waterlettuce *Pistia stratiotes:*
moving water 498,499
still water 495,496
Waterlily *Nymphaea* spp.:
moving water 499
still water 496
Watermilfoil *Myriophyllum* spp.:
moving water 498,499
still water 493-496
Waterplantain *Alisma* spp.:
peas 325
rice 254-256
Waterpod *Ellisia nyctelea:*
barley 211,213
fallow land 447,448
pasture/rangeland 460
spring wheat 199,201
winter wheat 186,188
Waterprimrose:
moving water 499
still water 496
Waterpurslane *Ludwigia palustris:*
moving water 499
still water 496
Watershield *Brasenia schreberi:*
moving water 499
still water 494-496
Waterstargrass *Heteranthera dubia:*
moving water 499
still water 494,495
Waterweed:
still water 495
Waterwort *Elatine triandra:*
rice 254,255
Waxmyrtle *Myrica* spp.:
brush control 439,441,442
noncropland 485,486
pastures/rangeland 466
Wedgeon grass:
still water 494
Western bitterweed:
conservation reserve program 446
pastures/rangeland 466
Western bracken *Pteridium aquilinum* (western brackenfern):
noncropland 467
ornamentals/woody plants 418
Western hairy nightshade:
potatoes 332
Western hemlock *Tsuga heterophylla:*
brush control 440
noncropland 485
Western horsenettle:
pastures/rangeland 464
Western ironweed *Vernonia baldwinii:*
noncropland 469
pastures/rangeland 461,464
Western muhly:
noncropland 482
Western ragweed *Ambrosia psilostachya:*
barley 212
fallow land 448
noncropland 476,477,480,482,484
pastures/rangeland 464
spring wheat 200
winter wheat 187
Western snowberry:
fallow land 447
Western wheatgrass *Agropyron smithii:*
field corn, popcorn 114,124
sweet corn 342
Wheat *Triticum aestivum:*
fallow land 451,452
nuts 388,391
soybeans 152,162
tree fruits, deciduous 373,378
Wheatgrass *Agropyron* spp.:
ornamentals/woody plants 422
White ash *Fraxinus americana:*
noncropland 477,483
pastures/rangeland 465
White clover *Trifolium repens:*
est. lawns/turf 401-403,405-408
field corn, popcorn 111,112,114,124
noncropland 469,473,474,483,484
nuts 388,391
ornamentals/woody plants 422-424,426
pastures/rangeland 461
small fruits 358,359,362
soybeans 162
sweet corn 342
tobacco 282
tree fruits, citrus 365,369
tree fruits, deciduous 373,378
tree fruits, subtropical 381,384
White cockle *Silene alba:*
barley 217,218
fallow land 451
forage 458,459
grasses for seed production 413
oats 227
spring wheat 205,206

- sugarcane 274
- winter wheat 193

White heath aster *Aster pilosus:*
- noncropland 474,484
- nuts 388
- ornamentals/woody plants 422
- small fruits 359
- sugarcane 275
- tree fruits, deciduous 373

White mustard *Brassica kaber:*
- cucurbits 307
- ornamentals/woody plants 418

White oak *Quercus alba:*
- brush control 439
- noncropland 469,472,477
- pastures/rangeland 461

White waterlily *Nymphaea tuberosa* (magnolia waterlily):
- still water 494,495

Whitebrush *Aloysia gratissima* (Texas whitebrush):
- brush control 440,441
- noncropland 475
- pastures/rangeland 464

Whitehorn:
- brush control 440
- noncropland 475
- pastures/rangeland 464

Whitestem filaree *Erodium moschatum:*
- asparagus 296
- est. lawns/turf 405
- noncropland 474,480,487
- nuts 388,389,391,392
- oil seed crops 247
- ornamentals/woody plants 422,423,427
- small fruits 358,360,362,363
- tree fruits, citrus 365-367,369,370
- tree fruits, deciduous 373,375,377,379
- tree fruits, subtropical 381,382,384

Whitetop *Cardaria* spp.:
- barley 219,220
- est. lawns/turf 406
- grasses for seed production 414
- noncropland 478,481,483
- oats 228,229
- pastures/rangeland 460,464
- rye 234,235
- spring wheat 207,208
- winter wheat 195,196

Wild artichoke *Helianthus annuus* (common sunflower):
- noncropland 472
- nuts 386
- ornamentals/woody plants 420
- small fruits 357
- tree fruits, deciduous 372

Wild aster:
- noncropland 472
- nuts 386
- ornamentals/woody plants 420
- small fruits 357
- tree fruits, deciduous 372

Wild barley *Hordeum leporinum* (hare barley):
- artichokes 292
- asparagus 294,296,297
- forage 459
- mint 245
- noncropland 472,476,477,479,482,484
- nuts 386,389
- rhubarb 333
- small fruits 356,357
- soybeans 156
- tree fruits, citrus 364,367
- tree fruits, deciduous 371,372,375
- tree fruits, subtropical 380,382

Wild beet *Amaranthus hybridus* (smooth pigweed):
- forage 456,458

Wild blackberry *Rubus* spp. (blackberry):
- field corn, popcorn 117
- noncropland 475,476,480

Wild buckwheat *Polygonum convolvulus:*
- artichokes 292,293
- barley 211-214,216-218,220-222
- beans 300
- brush control 441
- conservation reserve program 442-444,446,447
- est. lawns/turf 408
- fallow land 447-451,453,454
- field corn, popcorn 103,105-107,110,111, 113,115-124
- flax 240,241
- forage 455,458,459
- garlic 312
- mint 244
- noncropland 474,477,479,482,484,486
- nuts 388,391
- oats 223,224,226-230
- onions 321
- ornamentals/woody plants 419,420,422,423
- pastures/rangeland 460,461,465,466
- peanuts 252
- peas 326
- rye 231,235
- small fruits 359,362
- sorghum 260,261,263-265,267,268
- soybeans 143,144,151-153,157,159,162
- spring wheat 199-202,204-207,209-211
- sugar beets 269-272
- sunflower 280
- sweet corn 338-341,343
- tree fruits, deciduous 373,378
- winter wheat 186-189,191-194,196-198

Wild carrot *Daucus carota:*
- barley 214,217,218
- brush control 441
- conservation reserve program 446
- est. lawns/turf 410,411
- fallow land 447,450,451
- field corn, popcorn 108
- grasses for seed production 412
- noncropland 468-473,475-477,480-486
- nuts 386,391
- oats 224,227
- ornamentals/woody plants 420,424,427
- pastures/rangeland 461,464,466
- rye 232
- small fruits 357
- sorghum 262
- spring wheat 202,205,206
- sugarcane 273
- sweet corn 340
- tree fruits, citrus 369
- tree fruits, deciduous 372,377
- tree fruits, subtropical 383
- winter wheat 189,193

Wild celery *Apium leptophyllum:*
- est. lawns/turf 405
- noncropland 474,483
- nuts 388,391
- ornamentals/woody plants 422,427
- small fruits 358
- tree fruits, citrus 365,369
- tree fruits, deciduous 373,377
- tree fruits, subtropical 381,383

Wild chamomile *Matricaria chamomilla:*
- barley 213,217,218,222
- fallow land 448,454
- oats 228,230
- spring wheat 201,205,207,210
- winter wheat 188,192,194,198

Wild cherry *Prunus* spp. (cherry)
- brush control 438,440
- noncropland 471,475
- pastures/rangeland 464

Wild cucumber *Echinocystis lobata:*
- fallow land 451
- field corn, popcorn 110
- sorghum 263

Wild euphorbia:
- sugarcane 277

Wild garlic *Allium vineale:*
- barley 212-214,217,218,220,222
- conservation reserve program 442,444
- est. lawns/turf 402,403,406,410
- fallow land 447-450,454
- field corn, popcorn 108
- grasses for seed production 412
- noncropland 469,470,481,483
- oats 224,227-230
- ornamentals/woody plants 424
- pastures/rangeland 460,461
- rye 232,235
- sorghum 262,267
- soybeans 147,161
- spring wheat 200-202,205-207,209,210
- sugarcane 273,274
- sweet corn 340
- turf grasses for sod 416
- winter wheat 187-189,192-194,196,198

Wild geranium *Geranium* spp. (geranium):
- nuts 391
- tree fruits, deciduous 377

Wild grape *Vitis* spp. (grape):
- brush control 438
- noncropland 471,477,482
- ornamentals/woody plants 427

Wild iris:
- noncropland 484

Wild kale:
- potatoes 331
- tomatoes 349

Wild lettuce *Lactuca canadensis* (tall lettuce):
- artichokes 292
- asparagus 295
- barley 214,216
- cotton 175
- est. lawns/turf 401,410
- fallow land 448,453
- field corn, popcorn 108,111,123
- forage 456
- grasses for seed production 412
- mint 245
- noncropland 469-471,473,476-478,482,484,485
- oats 224,226
- ornamentals/woody plants 427
- pastures/rangeland 461
- rye 232
- small fruits 357,358
- sorghum 262,268
- spring wheat 202
- sugarcane 273,275
- sweet corn 340
- tree fruits, citrus 364,366
- tree fruits, deciduous 372
- winter wheat 189,192

Wild licorice:
- conservation reserve program 446
- pastures/rangeland 466

Wild morningglory *Calystegia sepium* (hedge bindweed):
- asparagus 294
- tobacco 283
- tree fruits, deciduous 379

Wild mustard *Brassica kaber:*
- artichokes 292,293
- asparagus 295
- barley 211-214,216-218,220-222
- beans 298
- carrots 302
- cole crops 306
- conservation reserve program 442-444,446
- cotton 174,175,178
- est. lawns/turf 400,405-408
- fallow land 447-449,451,453,454
- field corn, popcorn 103-107,110-123
- flax 241
- forage 455-457
- garlic 312
- grasses for seed production 411,414
- lettuce, endive 318
- mint 244,245
- noncropland 468,469,472,474,478-481,483,487
- nuts 386,388-392
- oats 223,224,226-230
- onions 321
- ornamentals/woody plants 419,421-424,426,427
- pastures/rangeland 460,461,465
- peanuts 248,249,252
- peas 324,325
- potatoes 331,332
- rye 231,235
- small fruits 358,359,361-363
- sorghum 260,261,263,265,267,268
- soybeans 143-145,147,148,150-153,155-158, 160,161,163
- spring wheat 199-202,204-207,209-211
- sugar beets 269,272
- sugarcane 275-277
- sunflower 279
- sweet corn 337-340,342,343,345
- tobacco 282
- tomatoes 347,349
- tree fruits, citrus 364-370
- tree fruits, deciduous 372-374,376,377,379
- tree fruits, subtropical 380,381,383,384
- turf grasses for sod 416
- winter wheat 186-189,191-194,196-198

Wild oak:
- brush control 438
- noncropland 471

Wild oat *Avena fatua:*
- artichokes 292,293
- asparagus 294-297
- barley 211-213,217-219
- beans 298,300
- carrots 301-303
- castor beans 240
- celery 304,305
- cole crops 306
- conservation reserve program 447
- cotton 173,174,176-178,180,181
- cucurbits 309
- eggplant 310
- fallow land 448,451-454
- field corn, popcorn 102,104,106,110-116, 119,121-124
- flax 241
- forage 457-459
- garbanzos 311
- garlic 313,314
- grasses for seed production 414,415
- greens 315
- herbs/spices 316
- lentils 317
- lettuce, endive 318,319
- mint 245,246
- noncropland 468,474-477,479-485,487
- nuts 385-389,391,392
- oats 227
- oil seed crops 247
- onions 321,323
- ornamentals/woody plants 419,421-423,426,427
- peanuts 251,252
- peas 324-326
- peppers 327,328
- potatoes 329,331,332
- rhubarb 333,334
- safflower 258
- small fruits 356-359,361-363
- sorghum 260,264,268
- southern peas 335
- soybeans 144,145,149-153,156-159,161,162,164
- spinach 336,337
- spring wheat 199-202,205-207,210
- sugar beets 269-272
- sunflower 279,280
- sweet corn 338,341-343,345
- sweet potatoes 346
- table beets 346
- tobacco 282,283
- tomatoes 347-350
- tree fruits, citrus 363-365,367,369,370
- tree fruits, deciduous 371,373,374,377-379
- tree fruits, subtropical 379-381,383,384
- turf grasses for sod 416,417
- winter wheat 186-189,192,194,198

Wild okra:
- cotton 173

Wild onion *Allium canadense:*
- asparagus 296
- barley 212,214,218
- est. lawns/turf 402,403,406,410
- fallow land 448,449
- field corn, popcorn 108
- grasses for seed production 412
- noncropland 469,470,474,479,483
- nuts 388

- oats 224,227
- ornamentals/woody plants 422,424
- pastures/rangeland 460,461
- rye 232
- small fruits 359
- sorghum 262
- soybeans 147
- spring wheat 200,202,206
- sugarcane 273,274
- sweet corn 340
- tree fruits, deciduous 373
- turf grasses for sod 416
- winter wheat 187,189,193

Wild parsnip *Pastinaca sativa:*
- barley 214
- est. lawns/turf 401
- field corn, popcorn 108
- grasses for seed production 412
- noncropland 475-477,482-484
- oats 224
- pastures/rangeland 461
- rye 232
- sorghum 262
- spring wheat 202
- sugarcane 273
- sweet corn 340
- winter wheat 189

Wild pea bean *Phaseolus lathyroides:*
- sugarcane 275
- tree fruits, subtropical 380,381

Wild plum *Prunus americana* (American plum):
- brush control 437,438,441,442
- noncropland 470,471,477,486
- pastures/rangeland 466

Wild poinsettia *Euphorbia heterophylla:*
- cotton 173,174,177,181
- cucurbits 307
- field corn, popcorn 107,115,116,119-122
- forage 458
- noncropland 481
- nuts 388
- ornamentals/woody plants 419
- peanuts 248,249,251
- small fruits 359
- soybeans 143-146,149-151,153, 155,157,159-161,163
- tobacco 281
- tree fruits, citrus 366
- tree fruits, deciduous 374
- tree fruits, subtropical 381

Wild proso millet *Panicum miliaceum:*
- asparagus 295
- beans 298,300
- carrots 301,303
- celery 305
- cole crops 306
- cotton 173,174,177,181
- cucurbits 307,309
- eggplant 310
- fallow land 448,451,453
- field corn, popcorn 101-104,106,111-113, 116-118,120-122,124
- flax 241
- forage 459
- garlic 313,314
- greens 315
- lettuce, endive 318,319
- mint 246
- noncropland 468,474,482
- nuts 385,387,390
- oil seed crops 247
- onions 321,323
- ornamentals/woody plants 419,422
- peanuts 248,251
- peas 325,326
- peppers 327,328
- potatoes 332
- rhubarb 334
- small fruits 356,358,361
- sorghum 260,264,267
- southern peas 335
- soybeans 143,145,146,149-153,155-158,161,164
- spinach 337
- sugar beets 269,271
- sunflower 280
- sweet corn 337,341,342,344
- sweet potatoes 346
- table beets 346
- tobacco 281,282
- tomatoes 350
- tree fruits, citrus 363,365,368
- tree fruits, deciduous 371,373,376
- tree fruits, subtropical 379,381,383

Wild radish *Raphanus raphanistrum:*
- artichokes 292
- asparagus 294
- barley 212-214,217-222
- conservation reserve program 442,443,446
- cotton 174
- est. lawns/turf 400,401
- fallow land 448,449,451,454
- field corn, popcorn 103,104,107,108,112,117
- flax 241
- forage 455,457,459
- garlic 312
- grasses for seed production 411-414
- mint 244
- noncropland 468,469,471,472,478,481-483
- nuts 386,391
- oats 223,224,227-230
- onions 321
- ornamentals/woody plants 424,427
- pastures/rangeland 460,461,464,465
- peanuts 249
- peas 325
- potatoes 330,331
- rye 231,232,234,235
- sorghum 262,267
- soybeans 153,156
- spring wheat 199-202,205-210
- sugar beets 272
- sugarcane 273
- sweet corn 339,340
- tomatoes 349
- tree fruits, citrus 369
- tree fruits, deciduous 372,377
- tree fruits, subtropical 383
- turf grasses for sod 416
- winter wheat 186-189,192-198

Wild rose *Rosa* spp. (rose):
- brush control 438
- noncropland 471,474,477,482,484,485
- nuts 388
- ornamentals/woody plants 422
- pastures/rangeland 466
- small fruits 359
- tree fruits, deciduous 373

Wild spiny cucumber *Cucumis dipsaceus* (wild spiny gourd):
- peanuts 248
- soybeans 143

Wild starthistle:
- noncropland 475,476

Wild strawberry *Fragaria virginiana* (Virginia strawberry):
- small fruits 357

Wild sunflower *Helianthus* spp. (sunflower):
- beans 298
- cotton 174
- est. lawns/turf 408
- fallow land 448,453
- field corn, popcorn 103,107,110,112,115, 118,120,121
- ornamentals/woody plants 419
- peanuts 248
- peas 324,325
- sorghum 260,265,267
- soybeans 144,145,151,153,155-157,161
- spring wheat 199,209
- sweet corn 338-340,343
- winter wheat 186,197

Wild sweet potato *Ipomoea pandurata:*
- cotton 177

Wild turnip *Brassica rapa* (birdsrape mustard):
- barley 218,222
- field corn, popcorn 107
- forage 456
- noncropland 474,476,477,482,484
- nuts 388
- oats 227
- ornamentals/woody plants 422
- small fruits 359
- spring wheat 206
- sweet corn 339,340
- tree fruits, deciduous 373
- winter wheat 193,197

Wild violet *Viola tricolor* (pansy):
- noncropland 469,485
- ornamentals/woody plants 427
- pastures/rangeland 461,466

Wild watermelon *Citrullus lanatus* (citronmelon):
- peanuts 248
- soybeans 143,150,163

Wildcane *Sorghum bicolor* (shattercane):
- artichokes 293
- asparagus 296,297
- beans 298,300,301
- carrots 303
- celery 305
- cole crops 306,307
- conservation reserve program 447
- cotton 181,182
- cucurbits 309
- eggplant 310,311
- fallow land 453
- field corn, popcorn 102,106,113,122,125
- flax 240-242
- forage 459
- garlic 314
- greens 315
- guar beans 243
- hops 243
- kenaf 244
- lentils 317
- lettuce, endive 319
- mint 246
- mung beans 247
- noncropland 482
- nuts 390,392
- oil seed crops 248
- okra 320
- onions 323
- peanuts 248,251,252
- peas 326
- peppers 327,328
- potatoes 329,332
- radishes 333
- safflower 259
- small fruits 363
- sorghum 260,262,269
- southern peas 335,336
- soybeans 143,144,149,158,159,162
- spinach 337
- sugar beets 272
- sugarcane 278
- sunflower 280,281
- sweet corn 337,339
- table beets 346
- tobacco 282
- tomatoes 350
- tree fruits, citrus 368,370
- tree fruits, deciduous 376,378
- tree fruits, subtropical 383

Willow *Salix* spp.:
- brush control 436-442
- noncropland 469-472,475-477,483-486
- pastures/rangeland 461,463-466

Willow primrose:
- pastures/rangeland 466

Willowherb *Epilobium* spp. (willowweed):
- noncropland 481

Willowleaf morningglory *Ipomoea wrightii* (palmleaf morningglory):
- soybeans 163

Windgrass *Apera spica-venti:*
- barley 217
- noncropland 474
- nuts 388
- ornamentals/woody plants 422
- spring wheat 205,210
- tree fruits, deciduous 373
- winter wheat 192,198

Winged elm *Ulmus alata:*
- brush control 438
- noncropland 471,476,477

Winter oats:
- sugarcane 277

Wintercress *Barbarea* spp.:
- barley 219
- oats 228
- rye 234
- spring wheat 207
- winter wheat 195

Wiregrass:
- nuts 385
- ornamentals/woody plants 427
- rice 257
- sugarcane 273,277,278

Wirestem muhly *Muhlenbergia frondosa:*
- asparagus 295,297
- barley 218
- beans 300
- carrots 301,303
- celery 305
- cole crops 306
- cotton 173,177,181
- cucurbits 309
- eggplant 310
- fallow land 448,451,453
- field corn, popcorn 113,114,116,121,122,124
- flax 241
- forage 459
- garlic 313,314
- greens 315
- lettuce, endive 318,319
- noncropland 468,474,476,477,479,482,484,485
- nuts 385,387,390,392
- oats 227
- oil seed crops 247
- onions 321,323
- ornamentals/woody plants 419,422
- peas 326
- peppers 327,328
- potatoes 332
- rhubarb 334
- small fruits 356,358,361,362
- southern peas 335
- soybeans 145,149-153,156-158,162
- spinach 337
- spring wheat 206
- sugar beets 269,271
- sunflower 280
- sweet corn 342,343
- sweet potatoes 346
- table beets 346
- tobacco 282
- tomatoes 350
- tree fruits, citrus 363,365,368,369
- tree fruits, deciduous 371,373,376,378
- tree fruits, subtropical 379,381,383,384
- winter wheat 194

Witchgrass *Panicum capillare:*
- artichokes 292,293
- asparagus 294-297
- barley 218
- beans 298-300
- carrots 301,303
- castor beans 240
- celery 305
- cole crops 305,306
- conservation reserve program 445,447
- cotton 173,176-178,180,181
- cucurbits 309
- eggplant 309,310
- est. lawns/turf 400
- fallow land 448,451-454
- field corn, popcorn 101-103,105-107,110, 112-118,120-124
- flax 241
- forage 457,459
- garbanzos 311,312
- garlic 313,314
- greens 315
- lentils 317
- lettuce, endive 318,319

mint 245,246
mung beans 246
noncropland 468,474,476,479,481-485,487
nuts 385-387,389-392
oats 227
oil seed crops 247
onions 321-323
ornamentals/woody plants 418,419,421-423, 425-427
peanuts 248,250-252
peas 325,326
peppers 327,328
potatoes 329-332
radishes 333
rhubarb 334
safflower 258,259
small fruits 356-358,361-363
sorghum 260-262,264-268
southern peas 335
soybeans 143-147,149-159,161-164
spinach 337
spring wheat 206
sugar beets 269-271
sugarcane 277
sunflower 279,280
sweet corn 337-345
sweet potatoes 345,346
table beets 346
tobacco 281,282
tomatoes 348,350
tree fruits, citrus 363-365,367-370
tree fruits, deciduous 371,373-379
tree fruits, subtropical 379-384
turf grasses for sod 416
winter wheat 194

Witchhazel *Hamamelis* spp.:
brush control 438,441,442
noncropland 486
pastures/rangeland 466

Witchweed *Striga asiatica:*
cotton 174
field corn, popcorn 118
soybeans 145,150,163

Wolffia columbiana — common watermeal

Woodsorrel *Oxalis* spp.:
cotton 179
est. lawns/turf 403,404,407
noncropland 473,474,479
nuts 388,389
ornamentals/woody plants 422
small fruits 359
tree fruits, deciduous 373,374

Woolly croton *Croton capitatus:*
barley 212,221
conservation reserve program 446
cotton 174
fallow land 447
noncropland 469,470
pastures/rangeland 460-462,465
peanuts 248,252
rice 253
soybeans 143,145-147,153,160
spring wheat 199,200,209
winter wheat 186,187,197

Woolly cupgrass *Eriochloa villosa:*
asparagus 295,297
beans 298,300,301
carrots 301,303
celery 305
cole crops 306,307
conservation reserve program 447
cotton 173,174,177,181,182
cucurbits 307,309
eggplant 310,311
est. lawns/turf 400
fallow land 448,451,453-455
field corn, popcorn 101-106,111-113, 115-122,124,125
flax 240-242
forage 458,459
garlic 313,314
greens 315
guar beans 243
hops 243
kenaf 244
lettuce, endive 318,319
mung beans 247
noncropland 468,474,481,482,485
nuts 385,387,390,392
oil seed crops 247,248
okra 320
onions 321,323
ornamentals/woody plants 419,422,425
peanuts 248,251,252
peas 325,326
peppers 327,328
potatoes 329,332
radishes 333
rhubarb 334
safflower 259
small fruits 356,358,361-363
sorghum 260,261,264,269
southern peas 336
soybeans 143-147,149-159,161-164
spinach 337
sugar beets 269,271,272
sugarcane 278
sunflower 280,281
sweet corn 337,339,341,342,344
sweet potatoes 346
table beets 346
tobacco 281,282
tomatoes 350
tree fruits, citrus 363,365,367-370
tree fruits, deciduous 371,373,375,376,378
tree fruits, subtropical 379,381,383,384

Woolly loco *Astragalus mollissimus:*
pastures/rangeland 464

Woollyleaf bursage *Ambrosia grayi:*
field corn, popcorn 114
noncropland 471,472,476,477,482,484
pastures/rangeland 463
sweet corn 342

Wright groundcherry *Physalis wrightii:*
cotton 176,177,181
nuts 388
ornamentals/woody plants 423
small fruits 359
sugar beets 272
tree fruits, citrus 366
tree fruits, deciduous 374
tree fruits, subtropical 381

X,Y,Z

Xanthium spp. — cocklebur
Xanthium strumarium — common cocklebur (heartleaf cocklebur)

Yankeeweed *Eupatorium compositifolium:*
conservation reserve program 446
noncropland 470,473
pastures/rangeland 462,464,466

Yarrow *Achillea* spp.:
est. lawns/turf 402,403,406,410
noncropland 469-471,485
pastures/rangeland 461,464,466

Yaupon *Ilex vomitoria:*
brush control 438,441,442
noncropland 472,486
pastures/rangeland 463,466

Yellow foxtail *Setaria glauca:*
artichokes 292,293
asparagus 294-297
barley 211,217
beans 298-301
carrots 301,303
castor beans 240
celery 305
cole crops 305-307
conservation reserve program 442,445,447
cotton 176,174,176-182
cucurbits 307,309
eggplant 309-311
est. lawns/turf 400,404,408
fallow land 448,451,453
field corn, popcorn 101-107,111-113,116-125
flax 240-242
forage 455,457-459
garbanzos 311,312
garlic 313,314
greens 315
guar beans 243
hops 243
kenaf 244
lentils 317
lettuce, endive 318,319
mint 245,246
mung beans 246,247
noncropland 468,474,478-483
nuts 385-388,390-392
oil seed crops 247,248
okra 320
onions 321-323
ornamentals/woody plants 418,419,421,422, 425,426
peanuts 248-252
peas 325,326
peppers 327,328
potatoes 329-332
radishes 333
rhubarb 334
safflower 258,259
small fruits 356-358,361-363
sorghum 260-262,264-269
southern peas 335,336
soybeans 143-147,149-159,161-164
spinach 337
spring wheat 199,205,209,210
sugar beets 269-272
sugarcane 277,278
sunflower 279-281
sweet corn 337-342,344
sweet potatoes 345,346
table beets 346
tobacco 281-283
tomatoes 348-350
tree fruits, citrus 363-365,367-370
tree fruits, deciduous 371,373,375-378
tree fruits, subtropical 379-381,383,384
turf grasses for sod 416,417
winter wheat 186,192,194,197,198

Yellow nutsedge *Cyperus esculentus:*
beans 298,299
conservation reserve program 446,447
cotton 178,179,181
est. lawns/turf 400,405-408
field corn, popcorn 101-106,110,112-121,124
flax 241
forage 457,458
garbanzos 311
mint 244
mung beans 246
noncropland 480,481,485
nuts 391,392
ornamentals/woody plants 418,419,421,424,425
peanuts 248-251
peas 325
potatoes 329-332
rice 253-255,258
safflower 258,259
sorghum 260-262,264-266
southern peas 335
soybeans 143-147,149-157,159-163
spinach 336
sugar beets 270-272
sunflower 279
sweet corn 337-339,347-344
tobacco 282,283
tomatoes 347,349,350
tree fruits, citrus 369
tree fruits, deciduous 378
tree fruits, subtropical 384
turf grasses for sod 417

Yellow poplar *Liriodendron tulipifera* (tuliptree):
brush control 440
noncropland 477

Yellow rocket *Barbarea vulgaris:*
barley 213,219,220
conservation reserve program 443,444
flax 241
forage 456-459
grasses for seed production 414
noncropland 469,471,472,474,478,480,481
nuts 386,388
oats 223,228,229
ornamentals/woody plants 422
pastures/rangeland 461,464
rye 231,234,235
small fruits 357,359
soybeans 150,161,163
spring wheat 201,207,208
tree fruits, deciduous 372,373
winter wheat 188,195,196

Yellow starthistle *Centaurea solstitialis:*
barley 213,214,218
conservation reserve program 442-444
est. lawns/turf 400
fallow land 448-450
forage 455
garlic 312
grasses for seed production 411
mint 244
noncropland 468,470,472,476,477,481-484
oats 223,224,227
onions 321
pastures/rangeland 461-463
rye 231
spring wheat 201,202,206
sugarcane 274
turf grasses for sod 416
winter wheat 187,189,193

Yellow sweetclover *Melilotus officinalis:*
noncropland 482
nuts 391
ornamentals/woody plants 427
small fruits 362
tree fruits, citrus 368
tree fruits, deciduous 377
tree fruits, subtropical 383

Yellow toadflax:
conservation reserve program 446
pastures/rangeland 466

Yellow waterlily *Nuphar luteum:*
still water 494,495

Yellow woodsorrel *Oxalis stricta:*
est. lawns/turf 400,404,405,411
noncropland 472,474,476,477,481,482,484,487
nuts 386,388,391,392
ornamentals/woody plants 419,420,422,423, 425,427
small fruits 358,362,363
tree fruits, citrus 365,368,370
tree fruits, deciduous 372,373,377,379
tree fruits, subtropical 381,383,384

Yellowflower pepperweed *Lepidium perfoliatum* (clasping pepperweed):
field corn, popcorn 123
mint 245
ornamentals/woody plants 423,426
small fruits 361
sweet corn 345
tree fruits, citrus 368
tree fruits, deciduous 376
tree fruits, subtropical 383

Yellowtop (mustard) *Senecio jacobaea* (tansy ragwort):
fallow land 451
field corn, popcorn 106,110,118
sorghum 263

Yucca:
brush control 438

Yucca glauca — Great Plains yucca (small soapweed)
Zizaniopsis miliacea — giant cutgrass

Suppliers Directory

AgrEvo USA Company
Little Falls Centre One
2711 Centerville Rd.
Wilmington DE 19808
Telephone: 302-892-3000
Fax: 302-892-3013
Website: www.na.agrevo.com

Albaugh Inc.
121 NE 18th St.
Ankeny IA 50021
Telephone: 515-964-9444
Fax: 515-964-7813
Toll Free: 800-247-8013

American Cyanamid Co.
One Campus Dr.
Parsippany NJ 07054-4492
Telephone: 973-683-2000
Fax: 973-683-4001
Toll Free: 800-327-4645

Amvac Chemical Corp.
4100 E. Washington Blvd.
Los Angeles CA 90023
Telephone: 323-264-3910
Fax: 323-887-9221

Applied Biochemists
Div. of Laporte Water Technologies & Biochem
W175 N11163 Stonewood Dr.
Suite 234
Germantown WI 53022
Telephone: 414-255-4449
Fax: 414-255-4268
Toll Free: 800-558-5106
E-Mail: info@appliedbiochemists.com
Website: www.appliedbiochemists.com

BASF Corp.
26 Davis Dr.
P.O. Box 13528
Research Triangle Park NC 27709-3528
Fax: 919-547-2419
Toll Free: 800-962-7830

Bayer Corp.
8400 Hawthorn Rd.
P.O. Box 4913
Kansas City MO 64210-0013
Telephone: 816-242-2000
Fax: 816-242-2738
Toll Free: 800-842-8020

Cedar Chemical Corp.
5100 Poplar Ave.
Suite 2414
Memphis TN 38137
Telephone: 901-685-5348
Fax: 901-684-5398/5391
Toll Free: 800-423-8629

Cheminova, Inc.
Oak Hill Park
1700 Rt. 23
Suite 210
Wayne NJ 07470
Telephone: 973-305-6600
Fax: 973-305-1382
Toll Free: 800-548-6113

Cleary Chemical Corp.
178 Ridge Rd.
Suite A
Dayton NJ 08810-1501
Telephone: 732-329-8399
Fax: 732-274-0894
Toll Free: 800-524-1662

Dow AgroSciences LLC
9330 Zionsville Rd.
Indianapolis IN 46268-1054
Fax: 800-905-7326
Toll Free: 800-258-3033
E-Mail: info@dowagro.com
Website: www.dowagro.com

Drexel Chemical Co.
1700 Channel Ave.
Memphis TN 38106-1412
Telephone: 901-774-4370
Fax: 901-774-4666

DuPont Agricultural Products
Walker's Mill, Barley Mill Plaza
WM3-116
P.O. Box 80038
Wilmington DE 19880-0038
Fax: 302-992-2276
Toll Free: 888-638-7668

Elf Atochem North America, Inc.
Three Parkway
2000 Market St., 21st. Fl.
Philadelphia PA 19103-3222
Telephone: 215-587-7409
Fax: 215-419-5012

FMC Corp.
1735 Market St.
Philadelphia PA 19103
Telephone: 215-299-6661
Fax: 215-299-6256
Toll Free: 800-321-1362

Gowan Co.
P.O. Box 5569
Yuma AZ 85366-5569
Telephone: 520-783-8844
Fax: 520-343-9255
E-Mail: gowan@primenet.com
Website: www.gowanco.com

Griffin L.L.C.
Rocky Ford Rd.
P.O. Box 1847
Valdosta GA 31601-1847
Telephone: 912-242-8635
Fax: 912-244-5813

Helena Chemical Co.
6075 Poplar Ave.
Suite 500
Memphis TN 38119
Telephone: 901-752-4420
Fax: 901-756-9947

Luxembourg-Pamol, Inc.
5100 Poplar Ave.
Suite 2700
Memphis TN 38137
Telephone: 901-761-9475
Fax: 901-761-9477
E-Mail: luxpam@netten.net

Makhteshim-Agan North America Inc.
551 5th Ave.
Suite 1100
New York NY 10176
Telephone: 212-661-9800
Fax: 212-661-9043

Micro Flo Co.
P.O. Box 5948
Lakeland FL 33807
Telephone: 941-647-3608
Fax: 941-647-3412
Toll Free: 800-451-8461

Monsanto Co.
800 N. Lindbergh Blvd.
Suite C3-NH
St. Louis MO 63167
Telephone: 314-694-1000
Toll Free: 800-332-3111

Monterey Chemical Co.
3654 S. Willow Ave.
P.O. Box 35000
Fresno CA 93745
Telephone: 559-499-2100
Fax: 559-499-1015
Website: www.montereychemical.com

Mycogen Corp. — see Dow AgroSciences LLC

Novartis Crop Protection
P.O. Box 18300
Greensboro NC 27419-8300
Telephone: 336-632-6000
Fax: 336-632-2861
Toll Free: 800-334-9481

Suppliers Directory

Nufarm, Inc.
1009-D West St. Maartens Dr.
St. Joseph MO 64506
Telephone: 816-279-1500
Fax: 816-279-1883
Toll Free: 800-852-5234

PBI/Gordon Corp.
1217 W. 12th St.
Kansas City MO 64101
Telephone: 816-421-4070
Fax: 816-474-0462
Toll Free: 800-821-7925
E-Mail: gcustis@pbigordon.com
Website: www.trimec.com

Phelps Dodge Refining Corp.
Specialty Metal & Chemical Sales
6999 N. Loop & Trowbridge Rd.
P.O. Box 20001
El Paso TX 79998
Telephone: 915-775-8826
Fax: 915-775-8350
Toll Free: 800-223-8567

Platte Chemical Co.
419 18th St.
Greeley CO 80632-5852
Telephone: 970-356-4400
Fax: 970-356-4418

Pro-Serve, Inc.
400 E. Brooks Rd.
Memphis TN 38109
Telephone: 901-332-7052
Fax: 901-346-7157
E-Mail: Proserve@headgap.com
Website: www.pro-serveinc.com

Rhone-Poulenc Ag Co.
2 T.W. Alexander Dr.
P.O. Box 12014
Research Triangle Park NC 27709
Telephone: 919-549-2000
Fax: 919-549-3900
Toll Free: 800-334-9745

RiceCo
5100 Poplar Ave.
Suite 2428
Memphis TN 38137
Telephone: 901-818-9161
Fax: 901-684-5391
Toll Free: 800-423-8629

Riverdale Chemical Co.
425 W. 194th Street
Glenwood IL 60425-1584
Telephone: 708-754-3330
Fax: 708-754-0314
Toll Free: 800-345-3330
Website: www.riverdalecc.com

Rohm and Haas Co.
100 Independence Mall West
Philadelphia PA 19106
Telephone: 215-592-3000
Fax: 215-592-2797
Toll Free: 800-523-0762
Website: www.rohmhaas.com

The Scotts Co.Professional Business Group
14111 Scottslawn Rd.
Marysville OH 43041
Telephone: 937-644-0011
Fax: 937-644-7679
Toll Free: 800-543-0006
Website: www.scottscompany.com

SePRO Corp.
11550 N. Meridian St.
Suite 600
Carmel IN 46032
Telephone: 317-580-8299
Fax: 317-580-8290
Toll Free: 800-419-7779
E-Mail: sepro@worldnet.att.net
Website: www.sepro.com

Terra Industries Inc.
Terra Centre
600 Fourth St.
P.O. Box 6000
Sioux City IA 51102-6000
Telephone: 712-277-1340
Fax: 712-233-3648
Toll Free: 800-831-1002
Website: www.terraindustries.com

Uniroyal Chemical Co., Inc.
Benson Rd.
Middlebury CT 06749
Telephone: 203-573-2000
Fax: 203-573-3394
Toll Free: 800-243-2850
Website: www.uniroyalchemical.com

United Phosphorus, Inc.
740 Springdale Dr
Suite 204
P.O. Box 570
Exton PA 19341
Telephone: 610-524-4120
Fax: 610-524-4184
Toll Free: 800-395-8965
E-Mail: upipa@aol.com

Valent USA Corp.
1333 N. California Blvd
Suite 600
P.O. Box 8025
Walnut Creek CA 94596
Telephone: 925-256-2700
Fax: 925-256-2776
Toll Free: 800-682-5368
E-Mail: Valent@valent.com

Wilbur-Ellis Co.
191 W. Shaw Ave.
Suite 107
Fresno CA 93704-2876
Telephone: 559-226-1934
Fax: 559-226-7630
Website: www.wilburellis.com

ZENECA Ag Products
1800 Concord Pike
Wilmington DE 19850-5458
Fax: 302-886-1660
Toll Free: 800-759-4500